ALCATRAS

WEBSTER'S
New Explorer
Spanish-English
Dictionary

NEW EDITION

WEBSTER'S
New Explorer
Spanish-English
Dictionary

NEW EDITION

Created in Cooperation with the Editors of
Merriam-Webster

**FEDERAL
STREET
PRESS**

A Division of Merriam-Webster, Incorporated
Springfield, Massachusetts

This edition published by
Federal Street Press,
A division of Merriam-Webster, Incorporated
P.O. Box 281
Springfield, MA 01102

Federal Street Press books are available for bulk purchase
for sales promotion and premium use.
For details write the manager of special sales,
Federal Street Press, P.O. Box 281, Springfield, MA 01102

ISBN 13   978-1-59695-000-9
ISBN 10   1-59695-000-5

Printed in the United States of America

07   08   09   10   5   4   3

Contents

Preface

The volume you are holding is a new edition of a dictionary designed to meet the needs of English and Spanish speakers in a time of ever-expanding communication among the countries of the Western Hemisphere. It is intended for language learners, teachers, office workers, tourists, business travelers—anyone who needs to communicate effectively in the Spanish and English languages as they are spoken and written in the Americas. This new dictionary provides accurate and up-to-date coverage of current vocabulary in both languages, as well as abundant examples of words used in context to illustrate idiomatic usage. The selection of Spanish words and idioms was based on evidence drawn from a wide variety of modern Latin-American sources and interpreted by trained Merriam-Webster bilingual lexicographers. The English entries were chosen by Merriam-Webster editors from the most recent Merriam-Webster dictionaries, and they represent the current basic vocabulary of American English.

All of this material is presented in a format which is based firmly upon and, in many important ways, is similar to the traditional styling found in the Merriam-Webster monolingual dictionaries. The reader who is familiar with Merriam-Webster dictionaries will immediately recognize this style, with its emphasis on convenience and ease of use, clarity and conciseness of the information presented, precise discrimination of senses, and frequent inclusion of example phrases showing words in actual use. Other features include pronunciations (in the International Phonetic Alphabet) for all English words, full coverage of irregular verbs in both languages, a section on basic Spanish grammar, tables of the most common Spanish and English abbreviations, and a detailed Explanatory Notes section which answers any questions the reader might have concerning the use of this book.

This dictionary represents the combined efforts of many members of the Merriam-Webster Editorial Department, along with advice and assistance from consultants outside the company. The primary defining work was done by Charlene M. Chateauneuf, Seán O'Mannion-Espejo, James L. Rader, Donna L. Rickerby, Adrienne M. Scholz, Amy West, Karen L. Wilkinson, and Linda Picard Wood. Brian M. Sietsema, Ph.D., provided the pronunciations. Cross-reference services were provided by Donna L. Rickerby. Karen L. Levister assisted in inputting revisions. Carol Fugiel contributed many hours of clerical assistance and other valuable support. The editorial work relating to typesetting and production was begun b

Preface

Jennifer S. Goss and continued by Susan L. Brady, who also offered helpful suggestions regarding format. Madeline L. Novak provided guidance on typographic matters. John M. Morse was responsible for the conception of this book as well as for numerous ideas and continued support along the way.

Eileen M. Haraty
Editor

Explanatory Notes

Entries

1. Main Entries

A boldface letter, word, or phrase appearing flush with the left-hand margin of each column of type is a main entry or entry word. The main entry may consist of letters set solid, of letters joined by a hyphen, or of letters separated by a space:

cafetalero[1], **-ra** *adj* . . .

eye–opener . . . *n* . . .

walk out *vi* . . .

The main entry, together with the material that follows it on the same line and succeeding indented lines, constitutes a dictionary entry.

2. Order of Main Entries

Alphabetical order throughout the book follows the order of the English alphabet, with one exception: words beginning with the Spanish letter *ñ* follow all entries for the letter *n*. The main entries follow one another alphabetically letter by letter without regard to intervening spaces or hyphens; for example, *shake-up* follows *shaker*.

Homographs (words with the same spelling) having different parts of speech are usually given separate dictionary entries. These entries are distinguished by superscript numerals following the entry word:

hail[1] . . . *vt* . . .

hail[2] *n* . . .

hail[3] *interj* . . .

madrileño[1], **-ña** *adj* . . .

madrileño[2], **-ña** *n* . . .

Numbered homograph entries are listed in the following order: verb, adverb, adjective, noun, conjunction, preposition, pronoun, interjection, article.

Homographs having the same part of speech are normally included at the same dictionary entry, without regard to their different semantic origins. On the English-to-Spanish side, however, separate entries are made if the homographs have distinct inflected forms or if they have distinct pronunciations.

3. Guide Words

A pair of guide words is printed at the top of each page, indicating the first and last main entries that appear on that page:

factura • faringe

4. Variants

When a main entry is followed by the word *or* and another spelling, the two spellings are variants. Both are standard, and either one may be used according to personal inclination:

jailer *or* **jailor** . . . *n* . . .

quizá *or* **quizás** *adv* . . .

Occasionally, a variant spelling is used only for a particular sense of a word. In these cases, the variant spelling is listed after the sense number of the sense to which it pertains:

electric . . . *adj* **1** *or* **electrical** . . .

Sometimes the entry word is used interchangeably with a longer phrase containing the entry word. For the purposes of this dictionary, such phrases are considered variants of the headword:

bunk² *n* **1** *or* **bunk bed** . . .

angina *nf* **1** *or* **angina de pecho** : angina . . .

Variant wordings of boldface phrases may also be shown:

> **madera** *nf* . . . **3 madera dura** *or* **madera noble** . . .

> **atención**[1] *nf* . . . **2 poner atención** *or* **prestar atención** . . .

5. Run-On Entries

A main entry may be followed by one or more derivatives or by a homograph with a different functional label. These are run-on entries. Each is introduced by a boldface dash and each has a functional label. They are not defined, however, since their equivalents can be readily derived by adding the corresponding foreign-language suffix to the terms used to define the entry word or, in the case of homographs, simply substituting the appropriate part of speech:

> **illegal** . . . *adj* : ilegal — **illegally** *adv* (the Spanish adverb is *ilegalmente*)

> **transferir** . . . *vt* trasladar : to transfer — **transferible** *adj* (the English adjective is **transferable**)

> **Bosnian** *n* : bosnio *m*, -nia *f* — **Bosnian** *adj* (the Spanish adjective is *bosnio, -nia*)

On the Spanish side of the book, reflexive verbs are sometimes run on undefined:

> **enrollar** *vt* : to roll up, to coil — **enrollarse** *vr*

The absence of a definition means that *enrollarse* has the simple reflexive meaning "to become rolled up or coiled," "to roll itself up."

6. Bold Notes

A main entry may be followed by one or more phrases containing the entry word or an inflected form of the entry word. These are bold notes. Each bold note is defined at its own numbered sense:

> **álamo** *nm* **1** : poplar **2 álamo temblón**
> : aspen

> **hold**[1] . . . *vi* . . . **4 to hold to** : . . . **5 to**
> **hold with** : . . .

If the bold note consists only of the entry word and a single preposition, the entry word is represented by a boldface swung dash ∼.

> **pegar** . . . *vi* . . . **3** ∼ **con** : to match, to
> go with . . .

The same bold note phrase may appear at two or more senses if it has more than one distinct meaning:

> **wear**[1] . . . *vt* . . . **3 to wear out** : gastar
> ⟨he wore out his shoes . . . ⟩ **4 to wear**
> **out** EXHAUST : agotar, fatigar ⟨to wear
> oneself out . . . ⟩ . . .

> **estar** . . . *vi* . . . **15** ∼ **por** : to be in favor
> of **16** ∼ **por** : to be about to ⟨está por
> cerrar . . . ⟩ . . .

If the use of the entry word is commonly restricted to one particular phrase, then a bold note may be given as the entry word's only sense:

> **ward**[1] . . . *vt* **to ward off** : . . .

Pronunciation

1. Pronunciation of English Entry Words

The matter between a pair of brackets [ ] following the entry word of an English-to-Spanish entry indicates the pronunciation. The symbols used are explained in the International Phonetic Alphabet chart on page 58a.

The presence of variant pronunciations indicates that not all educated speakers pronounce words the same way. A second-place variant is not to be regarded as less acceptable than the pronunciation that is given first. It may, in fact, be used by as many

educated speakers as the first variant, but the requirements of
the printed page are such that one must precede the other:

> **tomato** [təˈmeɪt̬o, -ˈmɑ-] . . .

When a compound word has less than a full pronunciation, the
missing part is to be supplied from the pronunciation at the entry
for the unpronounced element of the compound:

> **gamma ray** [ˈgæmə] . . .
>
> **ray** [ˈreɪ] . . .
>
> **smoke¹** [ˈsmoːk] . . .
>
> **smoke detector** [dɪˈtɛktər] . . .

In general, no pronunciation is given for open compounds consisting of two or more English words that are main entries at their
own alphabetical place:

> **water lily** *n* : nenúfar *m*

Only the first entry in a series of numbered homographs is giv-
en a pronunciation if their pronunciations are the same:

> **dab¹** [ˈdæb] *vt* . . .
>
> **dab²** *n* . . .

No pronunciation is shown for principal parts of verbs that are
formed by regular suffixation, nor for other derivative words
formed by common suffixes.

2. Pronunciation of Spanish Entry Words

Spanish pronunciation is highly regular, so no pronunciations
are given for most Spanish-to-English entries. Exceptions have
been made for certain words (such as foreign borrowings) whose
Spanish pronunciations are not evident from their spellings:

> **pizza** [ˈpitsa, ˈpisa] . . .
>
> **footing** [ˈfu̱ˌtɪŋ] . . .

Functional Labels

An italic label indicating a part of speech or some other functional classification follows the pronunciation or, if no pronunciation is given, the main entry. The eight traditional parts of speech, adjective, adverb, conjunction, interjection, noun, preposition, pronoun, and verb, are indicated as follows:

> **daily**[2] *adj* . . .
>
> **vagamente** *adv* . . .
>
> **and** . . . *conj* . . .
>
> **huy** *interj* . . .
>
> **jackal** . . . *n* . . .
>
> **para** *prep* . . .
>
> **neither**[3] *pron* . . .
>
> **leer** . . . *v* . . .

Verbs that are intransitive are labeled *vi,* and verbs that are transitive are labeled *vt.* Entries for verbs that are both transitive and intransitive are labeled *v;* if such an entry includes irregular verb inflections, it is labeled *v* immediately after the main entry, with the labels *vi* and *vt* serving to introduce transitive and intransitive subdivisions when both are present:

> **deliberar** *vi* : to deliberate
>
> **necessitate** . . . *vt* -tated; -tating : necesitar, requerir
>
> **satisfy** . . . *v* -fied; -fying *vt* . . . — *vi* . . .

Two other labels are used to indicate functional classifications of verbs: *v aux* (auxiliary verb) and *v impers* (impersonal verb).

> **may** . . . *v aux, past* **might** . . .
>
> **haber**[1] . . . *v aux* **1** : have . . . — *v impers*
> **1 hay** : there is, there are . . .

Gender Labels

In Spanish-to-English noun entries, the gender of the entry word is indicated by an italic *m* (masculine), *f* (feminine), or *mf* (masculine or feminine), immediately following the functional label:

> **magnesio** *nm* . . .
>
> **galaxia** *nf* . . .
>
> **turista** *nmf* . . .

If both the masculine and feminine forms are shown for a noun referring to a person, the label is simply *n:*

> **director, -tora** *n* . . .

Spanish noun equivalents of English entry words are also labeled for gender:

> **amnesia** . . . *n* : amnesia *f*
>
> **earache** . . . *n* : dolor *m* de oído
>
> **gamekeeper** . . . *n* : guardabosque *mf*

Inflected Forms

1. Nouns

The plurals of nouns are shown in this dictionary when they are irregular, when plural suffixation brings about a change in accentuation or in the spelling of the root word, when an English noun ends in a consonant plus *-o* or in *-ey*, when an English noun ends in *-oo*, when an English noun is a compound that pluralizes any element but the last, when a noun has variant plurals, or whenever the dictionary user might have reasonable doubts regarding the spelling of a plural:

> **tooth** . . . *n, pl* **teeth** . . .
>
> **garrafón** *nm, pl* **-fones** . . .
>
> **potato** . . . *n, pl* **-toes** . . .

abbey . . . *n, pl* -beys . . .

cuckoo[2] *n, pl* -oos . . .

brother–in–law . . . *n, pl*
  brothers–in–law . . .

quail[2] *n, pl* quail *or* quails . . .

hábitat *nm, pl* -tats . . .

tahúr *nm, pl* tahúres . . .

Cutback inflected forms are used for most nouns on the English-to-Spanish side, regardless of the number of syllables. On the Spanish-to-English side, cutback inflections are given for nouns that have three or more syllables; plurals for shorter words are written out in full:

shampoo[2] *n, pl* -poos . . .

calamity . . . *n, pl* -ties . . .

mouse . . . *n, pl* mice . . .

sartén *nmf, pl* sartenes . . .

hámster *nm, pl* hámsters . . .

federación *nf, pl* -ciones . . .

If only one gender form has a plural which is irregular, that plural form will be given with the appropriate label:

campeón, -ona *n, mpl* -ones : champion

The plurals of nouns are usually not shown when the base word is unchanged by the addition of the regular plural suffix or when the noun is unlikely to occur in the plural:

apple . . . *n* : manzana *f*

inglés[3] *nm* : English (language)

Nouns that are plural in form and that regularly occur in plural constructions are labeled as *npl* (for English nouns), *nmpl* (for Spanish masculine nouns), or *nfpl* (for Spanish feminine nouns):

knickers . . . *npl* . . .

enseres *nmpl* . . .

mancuernas *nfpl* . . .

Explanatory Notes 16a

Entry words that are unchanged in the plural are labeled *ns &
pl* (for English nouns), *nms & pl* (for Spanish masculine nouns),
nfs & pl (for Spanish feminine nouns), and *nmfs & pl* (for Spanish
gender-variable nouns):

> **deer** . . . *ns & pl* . . .
>
> **lavaplatos** *nms & pl* . . .
>
> **tesis** *nfs & pl* . . .
>
> **rompehuelgas** *nmfs & pl* . . .

2. Verbs

ENGLISH VERBS

The principal parts of verbs are shown in English-to-Spanish
entries when they are irregular, when suffixation brings about a
change in spelling of the root word, when the verb ends in *-ey,*
when there are variant inflected forms, or whenever it is believed
that the dictionary user might have reasonable doubts about the
spelling of an inflected form:

> **break**[1] . . . *v* **broke** . . . ; **broken** . . . ;
>   **breaking** . . .
>
> **drag**[1] . . . *v* **dragged; dragging** . . .
>
> **monkey**[1] . . . *vi* **-keyed; -keying** . . .
>
> **label**[1] . . . *vt* **-beled** *or* **-belled; -beling**
>   *or* **-belling** . . .
>
> **imagine** . . . *vt* **-ined; -ining** . . .

Cutback inflected forms are usually used when the verb has
two or more syllables:

> **multiply** . . . *v* **-plied; -plying** . . .
>
> **bevel**[1] . . . *v* **-eled** *or* **-elled; -eling** *or*
>   **-elling** . . .
>
> **forgo** *or* **forego** . . . *vt* **-went; -gone;
>   -going** . . .
>
> **commit** . . . *vt* **-mitted; -mitting** . . .

The principal parts of an English verb are not shown when the
base word is unchanged by suffixation:

delay¹ . . . *vt*

pitch¹ . . . *vt*

SPANISH VERBS

Entries for irregular Spanish verbs are cross-referenced by number to the model conjugations appearing in the Conjugation of Spanish Verbs section:

abnegarse {49} *vr* . . .

volver {89} *vi* . . .

Entries for Spanish verbs with regular conjugations are not cross-referenced; however, model conjugations for regular Spanish verbs are included in the Conjugation of Spanish Verbs section beginning on page 38a.

Adverbs and Adjectives

The comparative and superlative forms of English adjective and adverb main entries are shown when suffixation brings about a change in spelling of the root word, when the inflection is irregular, and when there are variant inflected forms:

wet² *adj* **wetter; wettest** . . .

good² *adj* **better** . . . ; **best** . . .

evil¹ . . . *adj* **eviler** *or* **eviller; evilest** *or* **evillest** . . .

The superlative forms of adjectives and adverbs of two or more syllables are usually cut back; the superlative is shown in full, however, when it is desirable to indicate the pronunciation of the inflected form:

early¹ . . . *adv* **earlier; -est** . . .

gaudy . . . *adj* **gaudier; -est** . . .

secure² *adj* **-curer; -est** . . .

but

young¹ . . . *adj* **younger** ['jʌŋgər]; **youngest** [-gəst] . . .

At a few entries only the superlative form is shown:

mere *adj, superlative* **merest** . . .

The absence of the comparative form indicates that there is no evidence of its use.

The comparative and superlative forms of adjectives and adverbs are usually not shown when the base word is unchanged by suffixation:

quiet³ *adj* **1** . . .

Usage

1. Usage Labels

Two types of usage labels are used in this dictionary—regional and stylistic. Spanish words that are limited in use to a specific area or areas of Latin America, or to Spain, are given labels indicating the countries in which they are most commonly used:

guarachear *vi Cuba, PRi fam* . . .

bucket . . . *n* : . . . cubeta *f Mex*

The following regional labels are used in this book: *Arg* (Argentina), *Bol* (Bolivia), *CA* (Central America), *Car* (Caribbean), *Chile* (Chile), *Col* (Colombia), *CoRi* (Costa Rica), *Cuba* (Cuba), *DomRep* (Dominican Republic), *Ecua* (Ecuador), *Sal* (El Salvador), *Guat* (Guatemala), *Hond* (Honduras), *Mex* (Mexico), *Nic* (Nicaragua), *Pan* (Panama), *Par* (Paraguay), *Peru* (Peru), *PRi* (Puerto Rico), *Spain* (Spain), *Uru* (Uruguay), *Ven* (Venezuela).

Since this book focuses on the Spanish spoken in Latin America, only the most common regionalisms from Spain have been included in order to allow for more thorough coverage of Latin-American forms.

A number of Spanish words are given a *fam* (familiar) label as well, indicating that these words are suitable for informal contexts but would not normally be used in formal writing or speaking. The stylistic label *usu considered vulgar* is added for a word which is usually considered vulgar or offensive but whose widespread use justifies its inclusion in this book. The label is intended to warn the reader that the word in question may be inappropriate in polite conversation.

2. Usage Notes

Definitions are sometimes preceded by parenthetical usage notes that give supplementary semantic information:

> **not** . . . *adv* **1** (*used to form a negative*)
> : no . . .
>
> **within**[2] *prep* . . . **2** (*in expressions of distance*) : . . . **3** (*in expressions of time*)
> : . . .
>
> **e**[2] *conj* (*used instead of* **y** *before words beginning with i or hi*) : . . .
>
> **poder**[1] . . . *v aux* . . . **2** (*expressing possibility*) : . . . **3** (*expressing permission*)
> : . . .

Additional semantic orientation is also sometimes given in the form of parenthetical notes appearing within the definition:

> **calibrate** . . . *vt* . . . : calibrar (armas),
> graduar (termómetros)
>
> **palco** *nm* : box (in a theater or stadium)

Occasionally a usage note is used in place of a definition. This is usually done when the entry word has no single foreign-language equivalent. This type of usage note will be accompanied by examples of common use:

> **shall** . . . *v aux* . . . **1** (*used to express a command*) ⟨you shall do as I say
> : harás lo que te digo⟩ . . .

3. Illustrations of Usage

Definitions are sometimes followed by verbal illustrations that show a typical use of the word in context or a common idiomatic usage. These verbal illustrations include a translation and are enclosed in angle brackets:

> **lejos** *adv* **1** : far away, distant ⟨a lo lejos
> : in the distance, far off⟩ ...
>
> **make**[1] ... **9** ... : ganar ⟨to make a liv-
> ing : ganarse la vida⟩ ...

Sense Division

A boldface colon is used to introduce a definition:

> **fable** ... *n* : fábula *f*

Boldface Arabic numerals separate the senses of a word that has more than one sense:

> **laguna** *nf* **1** : lagoon **2** : lacuna, gap

Whenever some information (such as a synonym, a boldface word or phrase, a usage note, a cross-reference, or a label) follows a sense number, it applies only to that specific numbered sense and not to any other boldface numbered senses:

> **abanico** *nm* ... **2** GAMA : ...
>
> **tonic**[2] *n* ... **2** *or* **tonic water** : ...
>
> **grillo** *nm* ... **2 grillos** *nmpl* : ...
>
> **fairy** ... *n, pl* **fairies** ... **2 fairy tale** : ...
>
> **myself** ... *pron* **1** (*used reflexively*) : ...
>
> **pike** ... *n* ... **3** → **turnpike**
>
> **atado**[2] *nm* ... **2** *Arg* : ...

Cross-References

Three different kinds of cross-references are used in this dictionary: synonymous, cognate, and inflectional. In each instance the cross-reference is readily recognized by the boldface arrow following the entry word.

Synonymous and cognate cross-references indicate that a definition at the entry cross-referred to can be substituted for the entry word:

> **scapula . . . → shoulder blade**
>
> **amuck . . . → amok**

An inflectional cross-reference is used to identify the entry word as an inflected form of another word (as a noun or verb):

> **fue, etc. → ir, ser**
>
> **mice → mouse**

Synonyms

At many entries or senses in this book, a synonym in small capital letters is provided before the boldface colon and the following defining text. These synonyms are all main entries or bold notes elsewhere in the book. They serve as a helpful guide to the meaning of the entry or sense and also give the reader an additional term that might be substituted in a similar context. On the English-to-Spanish side synonyms are particularly abundant, since special care has been taken to guide the English speaker—by means of synonyms, verbal illustrations, or usage notes—to the meaning of the Spanish terms at each sense of a multisense entry.

Spanish Grammar

Accentuation

Spanish word stress is generally determined according to the following rules:

- Words ending in a vowel, or in *-n* or *-s,* are stressed on the penultimate syllable (*zapato*, *llaman*).

- Words ending in a consonant other than *-n* or *-s* are stressed on the last syllable (*perdiz, curiosidad*).

Exceptions to these rules have a written accent mark over the stressed vowel (*fácil, hablará, último*). There are also a few words which take accent marks in order to distinguish them from homonyms (*si, sí*; *que, qué*; *el, él*; etc.).

Adverbs ending in *-mente* have two stressed syllables since they retain both the stress of the root word and of the *-mente* suffix (*lentamente, difícilmente*). Many compounds also have two stressed syllables (*limpiaparabrisas*).

Punctuation and Capitalization

Questions and exclamations in Spanish are preceded by an inverted question mark ¿ and an inverted exclamation mark ¡, respectively:

¿Cuándo llamó Ana?
Y tú, ¿qué piensas?

¡No hagas eso!
Pero, ¡qué lástima!

In Spanish, unlike English, the following words are not capitalized:

- Names of days, months, and languages (*jueves, octubre, español*).

- Spanish adjectives or nouns derived from proper nouns (*los nicaragüenses, una teoría marxista*).

Articles

1. Definite Article

Spanish has five forms of the definite article: *el* (masculine singular), *la* (feminine singular), *los* (masculine plural), *las* (feminine plural), and *lo* (neuter). The first four agree in gender and number with the nouns they limit (*el carro,* the car; *las tijeras,* the scissors), although the form *el* is used with feminine singular nouns beginning with a stressed *a-* or *ha-* (*el águila, el hambre*).

The neuter article *lo* is used with the masculine singular form of an adjective to express an abstract concept (*lo mejor de este método,* the best thing about this method; *lo meticuloso de su trabajo,* the meticulousness of her work; *lo mismo para mí,* the same for me).

Whenever the masculine article *el* immediately follows the words *de* or *a,* it combines with them to form the contractions *del* and *al,* respectively (*viene **del** campo, vi **al** hermano de Roberto*).

The use of *el, la, los,* and *las* in Spanish corresponds largely to the use of *the* in English; some exceptions are noted below.

The definite article is used:

- When referring to something as a class (*los gatos son ágiles,* cats are agile; *me gusta el café,* I like coffee).

- In references to meals and in most expressions of time (*¿comiste el almuerzo?,* did you eat lunch?; *vino el año pasado,* he came last year; *son las dos,* it's two o'clock; *prefiero el verano,* I prefer summer; *la reunión es el lunes,* the meeting is on Monday; but: *hoy es lunes,* today is Monday).

- Before titles (except *don, doña, san, santo, santa, fray,* and *sor*) in third-person references to people (*la señora Rivera llamó,* Mrs. Rivera called; but: *hola, señora Rivera,* hello, Mrs. Rivera).

- In references to body parts and personal possessions (*me duele la cabeza,* my head hurts; *dejó el sombrero,* he left his hat).

- To mean "the one" or "the ones" when the subject is already understood (*la de madera,* the wooden one; *los que vi ayer,* the ones I saw yesterday).

The definite article is omitted:

- Before a noun in apposition, if the noun is not modified (*Caracas, capital de Venezuela;* but: *Pico Bolívar, la montaña más alta de Venezuela*).

- Before a number in a royal title (*Carlos Quinto,* Charles the Fifth).

2. Indefinite Article

The forms of the indefinite article in Spanish are *un* (masculine singular), *una* (feminine singular), *unos* (masculine plural), and *unas* (feminine plural). They agree in number and gender with the nouns they limit (*una mesa,* a table; *unos platos,* some plates), although the form *un* is used with feminine singular nouns beginning with a stressed *a-* or *ha-* (*un ala, un hacha*).

The use of *un, una, unos,* and *unas* in Spanish corresponds largely to the use of *a, an,* and *some* in English, with some exceptions:

- Indefinite articles are generally omitted before nouns identifying someone or something as a member of a class or category (*Paco es profesor/católico,* Paco is a professor/Catholic; *se llama páncreas,* it's called a pancreas).

- They are also often omitted in instances where quantity is understood from context (*vine sin chaqueta,* I came without a jacket; *no tengo carro,* I don't have a car).

Nouns

1. Gender

Nouns in Spanish are either masculine or feminine. A noun's gender can often be determined according to the following guidelines:

- Nouns ending in *-aje, -o,* or *-or* are usually masculine (*el traje, el libro, el sabor*), with some exceptions (*la mano, la foto, la labor,* etc.).

- Nouns ending in *-a, -dad, -ión, -tud,* or *-umbre* are usually feminine (*la alfombra, la capacidad, la excepción, la juventud, la certidumbre*). Exceptions include: *el día, el mapa,* and many learned borrowings ending in *-ma* (*el idioma, el tema*).

Most nouns referring to people or animals agree in gender with the subject (*el hombre, la mujer; el hermano, la hermana; el perro, la perra*). However, some nouns referring to people, including those ending in *-ista,* use the same form for both sexes (*el artista, la artista; el modelo, la modelo;* etc.).

A few names of animals exist in only one gender form (*la jirafa, el sapo,* etc.). In these instances, the adjectives *macho* and *hembra* are sometimes used to distinguish males and females (*una jirafa macho,* a male giraffe).

2. Pluralization

Plurals of Spanish nouns are formed as follows:

- Nouns ending in an unstressed vowel or an accented *-é* are pluralized by adding *-s* (*la vaca, las vacas; el café, los cafés*).

- Nouns ending in a consonant other than *-s,* or in a stressed vowel other than *-é,* are generally pluralized by adding *-es* (*el papel, los papeles; el rubí, los rubíes*). Exceptions include *papá* (*papás*) and *mamá* (*mamás*).

- Nouns with an unstressed final syllable ending in *-s* usually have a zero plural (*la crisis, las crisis; el jueves, los jueves*). Other nouns ending in *-s* add *-es* to form the plural (*el mes, los meses; el país, los países*).

- Nouns ending in *-z* are pluralized by changing the *-z* to *-c* and adding *-es* (*el lápiz, los lápices; la vez, las veces*).

- Many compound nouns have a zero plural (*el paraguas, los paraguas; el aguafiestas, los aguafiestas*).

- The plurals of *cualquiera* and *quienquiera* are *cualesquiera* and *quienesquiera,* respectively.

Adjectives

1. Gender and Number

Most adjectives agree in gender and number with the nouns they modify (un chico *alto*, una chica *alta*, unos chicos *altos*, unas chicas *altas*). Some adjectives, including those ending in *-e* and *-ista* (*fuerte, altruista*) and comparative adjectives ending in *-or* (*mayor, mejor*), vary only for number.

Adjectives whose masculine singular forms end in *-o* generally change the *-o* to *-a* to form the feminine (*pequeño → pequeña*). Masculine adjectives ending in *-án, -ón,* or *-dor,* and masculine adjectives of nationality which end in a consonant, usually add *-a* to form the feminine (*holgazán → holgazana; llorón → llorona; trabajador → trabajadora; irlandés → irlandesa*).

Adjectives are pluralized in much the same manner as nouns:

- The plurals of adjectives ending in an unstressed vowel or an accented *-é* are formed by adding an *-s* (un postre *rico*, unos postres *ricos;* una camisa *café*, unas camisas *cafés*).

- Adjectives ending in a consonant, or in a stressed vowel other than *-é*, are generally pluralized by adding *-es* (un niño *cortés*, unos niños *corteses;* una persona *iraní*, unas personas *iraníes*).

- Adjectives ending in *-z* are pluralized by changing the *-z* to *-c* and adding *-es* (una respuesta *sagaz*, unas respuestas *sagaces*).

2. Shortening

- The following masculine singular adjectives drop their final *-o* when they occur before a masculine singular noun: *bueno* (*buen*), *malo* (*mal*), *uno* (*un*), *alguno* (*algún*), *ninguno* (*ningún*), *primero* (*primer*), *tercero* (*tercer*).

- *Grande* shortens to *gran* before any singular noun.

- *Ciento* shortens to *cien* before any noun.

- The title *Santo* shortens to *San* before all masculine names except those beginning with *To-* or *Do-* (*San Juan, Santo Tomás*).

3. Position

Descriptive adjectives generally follow the nouns they modify (*una cosa útil, un actor famoso*). However, adjectives that express an inherent quality often precede the noun (*la blanca nieve*).

Some adjectives change meaning depending on whether they occur before or after the noun: *un pobre niño,* a poor (pitiable) child; *un niño pobre,* a poor (not rich) child; *un gran hombre,* a great man; *un hombre grande,* a big man; *el único libro,* the only book; *el libro único,* the unique book, etc.

4. Comparative and Superlative Forms

The comparative of Spanish adjectives is generally rendered as *más . . . que* (more . . . than) or *menos . . . que* (less . . . than): *soy más alta que él,* I'm taller than he; *son menos inteligentes que tú,* they're less intelligent than you.

The superlative of Spanish adjectives usually follows the formula *definite article + (noun +) más/menos + adjective: ella es la estudiante más trabajadora,* she is the hardest-working student; *él es el menos conocido,* he's the least known.

A few Spanish adjectives have irregular comparative and superlative forms:

Adjective	Comparative/Superlative
bueno (good)	**mejor** (better, best)
malo (bad)	**peor** (worse, worst)
grande[1] (big, great), **viejo** (old)	**mayor** (greater, older; greatest, oldest)
pequeño[1] (little), **joven** (young)	**menor** (lesser, younger; least, youngest)
mucho (much), **muchos** (many)	**más** (more, most)
poco (little), **pocos** (few)	**menos** (less, least)

[1] These words have regular comparative and superlative forms when used in reference to physical size: *él es más grande que yo; nuestra casa es la más pequeña.*

ABSOLUTE SUPERLATIVE

The absolute superlative is formed by placing *muy* before the adjective, or by adding the suffix *-ísimo* (*ella es muy simpática* or *ella es simpatiquísima*, she is very nice). The absolute superlative using *-ísimo* is formed according to the following rules:

- Adjectives ending in a consonant other than *-z* simply add the *-ísimo* ending (*fácil → facilísimo*).

- Adjectives ending in *-z* change this consonant to *-c* and add *-ísimo* (*feliz → felicísimo*).

- Adjectives ending in a vowel or diphthong drop the vowel or diphthong and add *-ísimo* (*claro → clarísimo; amplio → amplísimo*).

- Adjectives ending in *-co* or *-go* change these endings to *qu* and *gu*, respectively, and add *-ísimo* (*rico → riquísimo; largo → larguísimo*).

- Adjectives ending in *-ble* change this ending to *-bil* and add *-ísimo* (*notable → notabilísimo*).

- Adjectives containing the stressed diphthong *ie* or *ue* will sometimes change these to *e* and *o*, respectively (*ferviente → fervientísimo* or *ferventísimo; bueno → buenísimo* or *bonísimo*).

Adverbs

Adverbs can be formed by adding the adverbial suffix *-mente* to virtually any adjective (*fácil → fácilmente*). If the adjective varies for gender, the feminine form is used as the basis for forming the adverb (*rápido → rápidamente*).

Pronouns

1. Personal Pronouns

The personal pronouns in Spanish are:

Person		Singular	Plural	
FIRST	yo	I	nosotros, nosotras	we
SECOND	tú	you (familiar)	vosotros[2], vosotras[2]	you, all of you
	vos[1]	you		
	usted	you (formal)	ustedes[3]	you, all of you
THIRD	él	he	ellos, ellas	they
	ella	she		
	ello	it (neuter)		

[1] Familiar form used in addition to *tú* in South and Central America.

[2] Familiar form used in Spain.

[3] Formal form used in Spain; familiar and formal form used in Latin America.

FAMILIAR VS. FORMAL

The second person personal pronouns exist in both familiar and formal forms. The familiar forms are generally used when addressing relatives, friends, and children, although usage varies considerably from region to region; the formal forms are used in other contexts to show courtesy, respect, or emotional distance.

In Spain and in the Caribbean, *tú* is used exclusively as the familiar singular "you." In South and Central America, however, *vos* either competes with *tú* to varying degrees or replaces it entirely. (For a more detailed explanation of *vos* and its corresponding verb forms, refer to the Conjugation of Spanish Verbs section.)

The plural familiar form *vosotros, -as* is used only in Spain, where *ustedes* is reserved for formal contexts. In Latin America, *vosotros, -as* is not used, and *ustedes* serves as the all-purpose plural "you."

It should be noted that while *usted* and *ustedes* are regarded as second person pronouns, they take the third person form of the verb.

USAGE

In Spanish, personal pronouns are generally omitted (*voy al cine,* I'm going to the movies; *¿llamaron?,* did they call?), although they are sometimes used for purposes of emphasis or clarity (*se* *lo diré yo,* I will tell them; *vino ella, pero él se quedó,* she came, but he stayed behind). The forms *usted* and *ustedes* are usually included out of courtesy (*¿cómo está usted?,* how are you?).

Personal pronouns are not generally used in reference to inanimate objects or living creatures other than humans; in these instances, the pronoun is most often omitted (*¿es nuevo? no, es viejo,* is it new? no, it's old).

The neuter third person pronoun *ello* is reserved for indefinite subjects (as abstract concepts): *todo ello implica* . . . , all of this implies . . . ; *por si ello fuera poco* . . . , as if that weren't enough . . . . It most commonly appears in formal writing and speech. In less formal contexts, *ello* is often either omitted or replaced with *esto, eso,* or *aquello.*

2. Prepositional Pronouns

Prepositional pronouns are used as the objects of prepositions (*¿es para mí?,* is it for me?; *se lo dio a ellos,* he gave it to them).

The prepositional pronouns in Spanish are:

Singular		**Plural**	
mí	me	**nosotros, nosotras**	us
ti	you	**vosotros[1], vosotras[1]**	you
usted	you (formal)	**ustedes**	you
él	him	**ellos, ellas**	them
ella	her		
ello	it (neuter)		
sí	yourself, himself, herself, itself, oneself	**sí**	yourselves, themselves

[1] Used primarily in Spain.

When the preposition *con* is followed by *mí, ti,* or *sí,* both words are replaced by *conmigo, contigo,* and *consigo,* respectively (*¿vienes conmigo?,* are you coming with me?; *habló contigo,* he spoke with you; *no lo trajo consigo,* she didn't bring it with her).

3. Object Pronouns

DIRECT OBJECT PRONOUNS

Direct object pronouns represent the primary goal or result of the action of a verb. The direct object pronouns in Spanish are:

Singular		Plural	
me	me	**nos**	us
te	you	**os**[1]	you
le[2]	you, him	**les**[2]	you, them
lo	you, him, it	**los**	you, them
la	you, her, it	**las**	you, them

[1] Used only in Spain.
[2] Used mainly in Spain.

Agreement

The third person forms agree in both gender and number with the nouns they replace or the people they refer to (*pintó las paredes,* she painted the walls → *las pintó,* she painted them; *visitaron al señor Juárez*, they visited Mr. Juárez → *lo visitaron*, they visited him). The remaining forms vary only for number.

Position

Direct object pronouns are normally affixed to the end of an affirmative command, a simple infinitive, or a present participle (*¡hazlo!,* do it!; *es difícil hacerlo,* it's difficult to do it; *haciéndolo, aprenderás,* you'll learn by doing it). With constructions involving an auxiliary verb and an infinitive or present participle, the pronoun may occur either immediately before the construction or suffixed to it (*lo voy a hacer* or *voy a hacerlo*, I'm going to do it; *estoy haciéndolo* or *lo estoy haciendo*, I'm doing it). In all other cases, the pronoun immediately precedes the conjugated verb (*no lo haré,* I won't do it).

Regional Variation

In Spain and in a few areas of Latin America, *le* and *les* are used in place of *lo* and *los* when referring to or addressing people (*le vieron,* they saw him; *les vistió,* she dressed them). In most parts of Latin America, however, *los* and *las* are used for the second person plural in both formal and familiar contexts.

The second person plural familiar form *os* is restricted to Spain.

INDIRECT OBJECT PRONOUNS

Indirect object pronouns represent the secondary goal of the action of a verb (*me dio el regalo,* he gave me the gift; *les dije que no,* I told them no). The indirect object pronouns in Spanish are:

Singular		**Plural**	
me	(to, for, from) me	**nos**	(to, for, from) us
te	(to, for, from) you	**os**[1]	(to, for, from) you
le	(to, for, from) you, him, her, it	**les**	(to, for, from) you, them
se[2]		**se**[2]	

[1]Used only in Spain.
[2]See explanation below.

Position

Indirect object pronouns follow the same rules as direct object pronouns with regard to their position in relation to verbs. When they occur with direct object pronouns, the indirect object pronoun always precedes (*nos lo dio,* she gave it to us; *estoy trayéndotela,* I'm bringing it to you).

Use of *Se*

When the indirect object pronouns *le* or *les* occur before any direct object pronoun beginning with an *l-,* the indirect object pronouns *le* and *les* convert to *se* (*les mandé la carta,* I sent them the letter → *se la mandé,* I sent it to them; *vamos a comprarle los aretes,* let's buy her the earrings → *vamos a comprárselos,* let's buy them for her).

4. Reflexive Pronouns

Reflexive pronouns are used to refer back to the subject of the verb (*me hice daño,* I hurt myself; *se vistieron,* they got dressed, they dressed themselves; *nos lo compramos,* we bought it for ourselves).

The reflexive pronouns in Spanish are:

Singular	Plural
me myself	**nos** ourselves
te yourself	**os**[1] yourselves
se yourself, himself,	**se** yourselves,
herself, itself	themselves

[1]Used only in Spain.

Reflexive pronouns are also used:

• When the verb describes an action performed to one's own body, clothing, etc. (*me quité los zapatos,* I took off my shoes; *se arregló el pelo,* he fixed his hair).

• In the plural, to indicate reciprocal action (*se hablan con frecuencia,* they speak with each other frequently).

• In the third person singular and plural, as an indefinite subject reference (*se dice que es verdad,* they say it's true; *nunca se sabe,* one never knows; *se escribieron miles de páginas,* thousands of pages were written).

It should be noted that many verbs which take reflexive pronouns in Spanish have intransitive equivalents in English (*ducharse,* to shower; *quejarse,* to complain; etc.).

5. Relative Pronouns

Relative pronouns introduce subordinate clauses acting as nouns or modifiers (*el libro que escribió* . . . , the book that he wrote . . . ; *las chicas a quienes conociste* . . . , the girls whom you met . . .). In Spanish, the relative pronouns are:

que (that, which, who, whom)

quien, quienes (who, whom, that, whoever, whomever)

el cual, la cual, los cuales, las cuales (which, who)

el que, la que, los que, las que (which, who, whoever)

lo cual (which)

lo que (what, which, whatever)

cuanto, cuanta, cuantos, cuantas (all those that, all that, whatever, whoever, as much as, as many as)

Relative pronouns are not omitted in Spanish as they often are in English: *el carro que vi ayer,* the car (that) I saw yesterday. When relative pronouns are used with prepositions, the preposition precedes the clause (*la película sobre la cual le hablé,* the film I spoke to you about).

The relative pronoun *que* can be used in reference to both people and things. Unlike other relative pronouns, *que* does not take the personal *a* when used as a direct object referring to a person (*el hombre que llamé,* the man that I called; but: *el hombre a quien llamé,* the man whom I called).

Quien is used only in reference to people. It varies in number with the explicit or implied antecedent (*las mujeres con quienes charlamos . . . ,* the women we chatted with; *quien lo hizo pagará,* whoever did it will pay).

El cual and *el que* vary for both number and gender, and are therefore often used in situations where *que* or *quien(es)* might create ambiguity: *nos contó algunas cosas sobre los libros, las cuales eran interesantes,* he told us some things about the books which (the things) were interesting.

Lo cual and *lo que* are used to refer back to a whole clause, or to something indefinite (*dijo que iría, lo cual me alegró,* he said he would go, which made me happy; *pide lo que quieras,* ask for whatever you want).

Cuanto varies for both number and gender with the implied antecedent: *conté a cuantas (personas) pude,* I counted as many (people) as I could. If an indefinite mass quantity is referred to, the masculine singular form is used (*anoté cuanto decía,* I jotted down whatever he said).

Possessives

1. Possessive Adjectives

UNSTRESSED FORMS

Singular		Plural	
mi(s)	my	nuestro(s), nuestra(s)	our
tu(s)	your	vuestro(s)[1], vuestra(s)[1]	your
su(s)	your, his, her, its	su(s)	your, their

[1] Used only in Spain.

STRESSED FORMS

Singular		**Plural**	
mío(s), **mía(s)**	my, mine, of mine	**nuestro(s),** **nuestra(s)**	our, ours, of ours
tuyo(s), **tuya(s)**	your, yours, of yours	**vuestro(s)[1]** **vuestra(s)[1]**	your, yours, of yours
suyo(s), **suya(s)**	your, yours, of yours; his, of his; her, hers, of hers; its, of its	**suyo(s),** **suya(s)**	your, yours, of yours; their, theirs, of theirs

[1]Used only in Spain.

The unstressed forms of possessive adjectives precede the nouns they modify (*mis zapatos,* my shoes; *nuestra escuela,* our school).

The stressed forms occur after the noun and are often used for purposes of emphasis (*el carro tuyo,* your car; *la pluma es mía,* the pen is mine; *unos amigos nuestros,* some friends of ours).

All possessive adjectives agree with the noun in number. The stressed forms, as well as the unstressed forms *nuestro* and *vuestro,* also vary for gender.

2. Possessive Pronouns

The possessive pronouns have the same forms as the stressed possessive adjectives (see table above). They are always preceded by the definite article, and they agree in number and gender with the nouns they replace (*las llaves mías,* my keys → *las mías,* mine; *los guantes nuestros,* our gloves → *los nuestros,* ours).

Demonstratives

1. Demonstrative Adjectives

The demonstrative adjectives in Spanish are:

Singular		Plural	
este, esta	this	**estos, estas**	these
ese, esa	that	**esos, esas**	those
aquel, aquella	that	**aquellos, aquellas**	those

Demonstrative adjectives agree with the nouns they modify in gender and number (*esta chica, aquellos árboles*). They normally precede the noun, but may occasionally occur after for purposes of emphasis or to express contempt: *en la época aquella de cambio,* in that era of change; *el perro ese ha ladrado toda la noche,* that (awful, annoying, etc.) dog barked all night long.

The forms *aquel, aquella, aquellos,* and *aquellas* are generally used in reference to people and things that are relatively distant from the speaker in space or time: *ese libro,* that book (a few feet away); *aquel libro,* that book (way over there).

2. Demonstrative Pronouns

The demonstrative pronouns in Spanish are orthographically identical to the demonstrative adjectives except that they take an accent mark over the stressed vowel (*éste, ése, aquél,* etc.). In addition, there are three neuter forms—*esto, eso,* and *aquello*—which are used when referring to abstract ideas or unidentified things (*¿te dijo eso?,* he said that to you?; *¿qué es esto?,* what is this?; *tráeme todo aquello,* bring me all that stuff).

Except for the neuter forms, demonstrative pronouns agree in gender and number with the nouns they replace (*esta silla,* this chair → *ésta,* this one; *aquellos vasos,* those glasses → *aquéllos,* those ones).

Abbreviations in This Work

adj	adjective	*nm*	masculine noun
adv	adverb	*nmf*	masculine or feminine noun
Arg	Argentina	*nmfpl*	plural noun invariable for gender
Bol	Bolivia		
Brit	British		
CA	Central America	*nmfs & pl*	noun invariable for both gender and number
Car	Caribbean region		
Col	Colombia	*nmpl*	masculine plural noun
conj	conjunction		
CoRi	Costa Rica	*nms & pl*	invariable singular or plural masculine noun
DomRep	Dominican Republic		
Ecua	Ecuador	*npl*	plural noun
esp	especially	*ns & pl*	noun invariable for plural
f	feminine		
fam	familiar or colloquial	*Pan*	Panama
		Par	Paraguay
fpl	feminine plural	*pl*	plural
Guat	Guatemala	*pp*	past participle
Hond	Honduras	*prep*	preposition
interj	interjection	*PRi*	Puerto Rico
m	masculine	*pron*	pronoun
Mex	Mexico	*s*	singular
mf	masculine or feminine	*Sal*	El Salvador
		Uru	Uruguay
mfpl	masculine or feminine plural	*usu*	usually
mpl	masculine plural	*v*	verb (transitive and intransitive)
n	noun		
nf	feminine noun	*v aux*	auxiliary verb
nfpl	feminine plural noun	*Ven*	Venezuela
		vi	intransitive verb
nfs & pl	invariable singular or plural feminine noun	*v impers*	impersonal verb
		vr	reflexive verb
Nic	Nicaragua	*vt*	transitive verb

Conjugation of Spanish Verbs

Simple Tenses

Tense	Regular Verbs Ending in -AR hablar	
PRESENT INDICATIVE	hablo	hablamos
	hablas	habláis
	habla	hablan
PRESENT SUBJUNCTIVE	hable	hablemos
	hables	habléis
	hable	hablen
PRETERIT INDICATIVE	hablé	hablamos
	hablaste	hablasteis
	habló	hablaron
IMPERFECT INDICATIVE	hablaba	hablábamos
	hablabas	hablabais
	hablaba	hablaban
IMPERFECT SUBJUNCTIVE	hablara	habláramos
	hablaras	hablarais
	hablara	hablaran
	or	
	hablase	hablásemos
	hablases	hablaseis
	hablase	hablasen
FUTURE INDICATIVE	hablaré	hablaremos
	hablarás	hablaréis
	hablará	hablarán
FUTURE SUBJUNCTIVE	hablare	habláremos
	hablares	hablareis
	hablare	hablaren
CONDITIONAL	hablaría	hablaríamos
	hablarías	hablaríais
	hablaría	hablarían
IMPERATIVE		hablemos
	habla	hablad
	hable	hablen
PRESENT PARTICIPLE (GERUND)	hablando	
PAST PARTICIPLE	hablado	

Regular Verbs Ending in -ER		Regular Verbs Ending in -IR	
comer		vivir	
como	comemos	vivo	vivimos
comes	coméis	vives	vivís
come	comen	vive	viven
coma	comamos	viva	vivamos
comas	comáis	vivas	viváis
coma	coman	viva	vivan
comí	comimos	viví	vivimos
comiste	comisteis	viviste	vivisteis
comió	comieron	vivió	vivieron
comía	comíamos	vivía	vivíamos
comías	comíais	vivías	vivíais
comía	comían	vivía	vivían
comiera	comiéramos	viviera	viviéramos
comieras	comierais	vivieras	vivierais
comiera	comieran	viviera	vivieran
or		*or*	
comiese	comiésemos	viviese	viviésemos
comieses	comieseis	vivieses	vivieseis
comiese	comiesen	viviese	viviesen
comeré	comeremos	viviré	viviremos
comerás	comeréis	vivirás	viviréis
comerá	comerán	vivirá	vivirán
comiere	comiéremos	viviere	viviéremos
comieres	comiereis	vivieres	viviereis
comiere	comieren	viviere	vivieren
comería	comeríamos	viviría	viviríamos
comerías	comeríais	vivirías	viviríais
comería	comerían	viviría	vivirían
	comamos		vivamos
come	comed	vive	vivid
coma	coman	viva	vivan
comiendo		viviendo	
comido		vivido	

Compound Tenses

1. Perfect Tenses

The perfect tenses are formed with *haber* and the past participle:

PRESENT PERFECT

he hablado, etc. (*indicative*);
haya hablado, etc. (*subjunctive*)

PAST PERFECT

había hablado, etc. (*indicative*);
hubiera hablado, etc. (*subjunctive*)
or
hubiese hablado, etc. (*subjunctive*)

PRETERIT PERFECT

hube hablado, etc. (*indicative*)

FUTURE PERFECT

habré hablado, etc. (*indicative*)

CONDITIONAL PERFECT

habría hablado, etc. (*indicative*)

2. Progressive Tenses

The progressive tenses are formed with *estar* and the present participle:

PRESENT PROGRESSIVE

estoy llamando, etc. (*indicative*);
esté llamando, etc. (*subjunctive*)

IMPERFECT PROGRESSIVE

estaba llamando, etc. (*indicative*);
estuviera llamando, etc. (*subjunctive*)
or
estuviese llamando, etc. (*subjunctive*)

PRETERIT PROGRESSIVE

    estuve llamando, etc. (*indicative*)

FUTURE PROGRESSIVE

    estaré llamando, etc. (*indicative*)

CONDITIONAL PROGRESSIVE

    estaría llamando, etc. (*indicative*)

PRESENT PERFECT PROGRESSIVE

    he estado llamando, etc. (*indicative*);
    haya estado llamando, etc. (*subjunctive*)

PAST PERFECT PROGRESSIVE

    había estado llamando, etc. (*indicative*);
    hubiera estado llamando, etc. (*subjunctive*)
    or
    hubiese estado llamando, etc. (*subjunctive*)

Use of *Vos*

In parts of South and Central America, *vos* often replaces or competes with *tú* as the second person familiar personal pronoun. It is particularly well established in the Río de la Plata region and much of Central America.

The pronoun *vos* often takes a distinct set of verb forms, usually in the present tense and the imperative. These vary widely from region to region; examples of the most common forms are shown below.

INFINITIVE FORM	hablar	comer	vivir
PRESENT INDICATIVE	vos hablás	vos comés	vos vivís
PRESENT SUBJUNCTIVE	vos hablés	vos comás	vos vivás
IMPERATIVE	hablá	comé	viví

In some areas, *vos* may take the *tú* or *vosotros* forms of the verb, while in others (as Uruguay), *tú* is combined with the *vos* verb forms.

Irregular Verbs

The *imperfect subjunctive*, the *future subjunctive*, the *conditional*, and most forms of the *imperative* are not included in the model conjugations list, but can be derived as follows:

The *imperfect subjunctive* and the *future subjunctive* are formed from the third person plural form of the preterit tense by removing the last syllable (*-ron*) and adding the appropriate suffix:

PRETERIT INDICATIVE, THIRD PERSON PLURAL (querer)	quisieron
IMPERFECT SUBJUNCTIVE (querer)	quisiera, quisieras, etc. *or* quisiese, quisieses, etc.
FUTURE SUBJUNCTIVE (querer)	quisiere, quisieres, etc.

The conditional uses the same stem as the future indicative:

FUTURE INDICATIVE (poner)	pondré, pondrás, etc.
CONDITIONAL (poner)	pondría, pondrías, etc.

The third person singular, first person plural, and third person plural forms of the *imperative* are the same as the corresponding forms of the present subjunctive.

The second person plural (*vosotros*) form of the *imperative* is formed by removing the final *-r* of the infinitive form and adding a *-d* (ex.: *oír → oíd*).

Model Conjugations of Irregular Verbs

The model conjugations below include the following simple tenses: the *present indicative* (IND), the *present subjunctive* (SUBJ), the *preterit indicative* (PRET), the *imperfect indicative* (IMPF), the *future indicative* (FUT), the second person singular form of the *imperative* (IMPER), the *present participle* or *gerund* (PRP), and the *past participle* (PP). Each set of conjugations is preceded by the corresponding infinitive form of the verb, shown in bold type. Only tenses containing irregularities are listed, and the irregular verb forms within each tense are displayed in bold type.

Each irregular verb entry in the Spanish-English section of this dictionary is cross-referred by number to one of the following model conjugations. These cross-reference numbers are shown in curly braces { } immediately following the entry's functional label.

1 **abolir** *(defective verb)* : IND abolimos, abolís *(other forms not used);* SUBJ *(not used);* IMPER *(only second person plural is used)*

2 **abrir** : PP abierto

3 **actuar** : IND **actúo, actúas, actúa**, actuamos, actuáis, **actúan**; SUBJ **actúe, actúes, actúe**, actuemos, actuéis, **actúen**; IMPER **actúa**

4 **adquirir** : IND **adquiero, adquieres, adquiere**, adquirimos, adquirís, **adquieren**; SUBJ **adquiera, adquieras, adquiera**, adquiramos, adquiráis, **adquieran**; IMPER **adquiere**

5 **airar** : IND **aíro, aíras, aíra**, airamos, airáis, **aíran**; SUBJ **aíre, aíres, aíre**, airemos, airéis, **aíren**; IMPER **aíra**

6 **andar** : PRET **anduve, anduviste, anduvo, anduvimos, anduvisteis, anduvieron**

7 **asir** : IND **asgo**, ases, ase, asimos, asís, asen; SUBJ **asga, asgas, asga, asgamos, asgáis, asgan**

8 **aunar** : IND **aúno, aúnas, aúna**, aunamos, aunáis, **aúnan**; SUBJ **aúne, aúnes, aúne**, aunemos, aunéis, **aúnen**; IMPER **aúna**

9 **avergonzar** : IND **avergüenzo, avergüenzas, avergüenza**, avergonzamos, avergonzáis, **avergüenzan**; SUBJ **avergüence, avergüences, avergüence, avergoncemos, avergoncéis, avergüencen**; PRET **avergoncé**; IMPER **avergüenza**

10 **averiguar** : SUBJ **averigüe, averigües, averigüe, averigüemos, averigüéis, averigüen**; PRET **averigüé**, averiguaste, averiguó, averiguamos, averiguasteis, averiguaron

11 **bendecir** : *IND* **bendigo, bendices, bendice,** bendecimos, ben-decís, **bendicen;** *SUBJ* **bendiga, bendigas, bendiga, bendig-amos, bendigáis, bendigan;** *PRET* **bendije, bendijiste, bendijo, bendijimos, bendijisteis, bendijeron;** *IMPER* **bendice**

12 **caber** : *IND* **quepo,** cabes, cabe, cabemos, cabéis, caben; *SUBJ* **quepa, quepas, quepa, quepamos, quepáis, quepan;** *PRET* **cupe, cupiste, cupo, cupimos, cupisteis, cupieron;** *FUT* **cabré, cabrás, cabrá, cabremos, cabréis, cabrán**

13 **caer** : *IND* **caigo,** caes, cae, caemos, caéis, caen; *SUBJ* **caiga, caigas, caiga, caigamos, caigáis, caigan;** *PRET* caí, **caíste,** cayó, caímos, caísteis, cayeron; *PRP* **cayendo;** *PP* **caído**

14 **cocer** : *IND* **cuezo, cueces, cuece,** cocemos, cocéis, **cuecen;** *SUBJ* **cueza, cuezas, cueza, cozamos, cozáis, cuezan;** *IMPER* **cuece**

15 **coger** : *IND* **cojo,** coges, coge, cogemos, cogéis, cogen; *SUBJ* **coja, cojas, coja, cojamos, cojáis, cojan**

16 **colgar** : *IND* **cuelgo, cuelgas, cuelga,** colgamos, colgáis, **cuel-gan;** *SUBJ* **cuelgue, cuelgues, cuelgue, colguemos, colguéis, cuelguen;** *PRET* **colgué,** colgaste, colgó, colgamos, colgasteis, colgaron; *IMPER* **cuelga**

17 **concernir** *(defective verb; used only in the third person singular and plural of the present indicative, present subjunctive, and imperfect subjunctive)* see 25 **discernir**

18 **conocer** : *IND* **conozco,** conoces, conoce, conocemos, cono-céis, conocen; *SUBJ* **conozca, conozcas, conozca, conoz-camos, conozcáis, conozcan**

19 **contar** : *IND* **cuento, cuentas, cuenta,** contamos, contáis, **cuen-tan;** *SUBJ* **cuente, cuentes, cuente,** contemos, contéis, **cuenten;** *IMPER* **cuenta**

20 **creer** : *PRET* creí, **creíste, creyó, creímos, creísteis, creyeron;** *PRP* **creyendo;** *PP* **creído**

21 **cruzar** : *SUBJ* **cruce, cruces, cruce, crucemos, crucéis, crucen;** *PRET* **crucé,** cruzaste, cruzó, cruzamos, cruzasteis, cruzaron

22 **dar** : *IND* **doy,** das, da, damos, **dais,** dan; *SUBJ* **dé,** des, **dé,** demos, **deis,** den; *PRET* **di,** diste, dio, **dimos,** disteis, **dieron**

23 **decir** : *IND* **digo, dices, dice**, decimos, decís, **dicen**; *SUBJ* **diga, digas, diga, digamos, digáis, digan**; *PRET* **dije, dijiste, dijo, dijimos, dijisteis, dijeron**; *FUT* **diré, dirás, dirá, diremos, diréis, dirán**; *IMPER* **di**; *PRP* **diciendo**; *PP* **dicho**

24 **delinquir** : *IND* **delinco**, delinques, delinque, delinquimos, delinquís, delinquen; *SUBJ* **delinca, delincas, delinca, delincamos, delincáis, delincan**

25 **discernir** : *IND* **discierno, disciernes, discierne**, discernimos, discernís, **disciernen**; *SUBJ* **discierna, disciernas, discierna**, discernamos, discernáis, **disciernan**; *IMPER* **discierne**

26 **distinguir** : *IND* **distingo**, distingues, distingue, distinguimos, distinguís, distinguen; *SUBJ* **distinga, distingas, distinga, distingamos, distingáis, distingan**

27 **dormir** : *IND* **duermo, duermes, duerme**, dormimos, dormís, **duermen**; *SUBJ* **duerma, duermas, duerma, durmamos, durmáis, duerman**; *PRET* dormí, dormiste, **durmió**, dormimos, dormisteis, **durmieron**; *IMPER* **duerme**; *PRP* **durmiendo**

28 **elegir** : *IND* **elijo**, eliges, elige, elegimos, elegís, **eligen**; *SUBJ* **elija, elijas, elija, elijamos, elijáis, elijan**; *PRET* elegí, elegiste, **eligió**, elegimos, elegisteis, **eligieron**; *IMPER* **elige**; *PRP* **eligiendo**

29 **empezar** : *IND* **empiezo, empiezas, empieza**, empezamos, empezáis, **empiezan**; *SUBJ* **empiece, empieces, empiece, empecemos, empecéis, empiecen**; *PRET* **empecé**, empezaste, empezó, empezamos, empezasteis, empezaron; *IMPER* **empieza**

30 **enraizar** : *IND* **enraízo, enraízas, enraíza**, enraizamos, enraizáis, **enraízan**; *SUBJ* **enraíce, enraíces, enraíce, enraicemos, enraicéis, enraícen**; *PRET* **enraicé**, enraizaste, enraizó, enraizamos, enraizasteis, enraizaron; *IMPER* **enraíza**

31 **erguir** : *IND* **irgo** *or* **yergo, irgues** *or* **yergues, irgue** *or* **yergue**, erguimos, erguís, **irguen** *or* **yerguen**; *SUBJ* **irga** *or* **yerga, irgas** *or* **yergas, irga** *or* **yerga, irgamos, irgáis, irgan** *or* **yergan**; *PRET* erguí, erguiste, **irguió**, erguimos, erguisteis, **irguieron**; *IMPER* **irgue** *or* **yergue**; *PRP* **irguiendo**

32 **errar** : *IND* **yerro, yerras, yerra,** erramos, erráis, **yerran;** *SUBJ* **yerre, yerres, yerre,** erremos, erréis, **yerren;** *IMPER* **yerra**

33 **escribir** : *PP* **escrito**

34 **estar** : *IND* **estoy, estás, está,** estamos, estáis, **están;** *SUBJ* **esté, estés, esté,** estemos, estéis, **estén;** *PRET* **estuve, estuviste, estuvo, estuvimos, estuvisteis, estuvieron;** *IMPER* **está**

35 **exigir** : *IND* **exijo,** exiges, exige, exigimos, exigís, exigen; *SUBJ* **exija, exijas, exija, exijamos, exijáis, exijan**

36 **forzar** : *IND* **fuerzo, fuerzas, fuerza,** forzamos, forzáis, **fuerzan;** *SUBJ* **fuerce, fuerces, fuerce, forcemos, forcéis, fuercen;** *PRET* **forcé,** forzaste, forzó, forzamos, forzasteis, forzaron; *IMPER* **fuerza**

37 **freír** : *IND* **frío, fríes, fríe, freímos,** freís, **fríen;** *SUBJ* **fría, frías, fría,** friamos, friáis, **frían;** *PRET* freí, **freíste, frió, freímos, freísteis, frieron;** *IMPER* **fríe;** *PRP* **friendo;** *PP* **frito**

38 **gruñir** : *PRET* gruñí, gruñiste, **gruñó,** gruñimos, gruñisteis, **gruñeron;** *PRP* **gruñendo**

39 **haber** : *IND* **he, has, ha, hemos,** habéis, **han;** *SUBJ* **haya, hayas, haya, hayamos, hayáis, hayan;** *PRET* **hube, hubiste, hubo, hubimos, hubisteis, hubieron;** *FUT* **habré, habrás, habrá, habremos, habréis, habrán;** *IMPER* **he**

40 **hacer** : *IND* **hago,** haces, hace, hacemos, hacéis, hacen; *SUBJ* **haga, hagas, haga, hagamos, hagáis, hagan;** *PRET* **hice, hiciste, hizo, hicimos, hicisteis, hicieron;** *FUT* **haré, harás, hará, haremos, haréis, harán;** *IMPER* **haz;** *PP* **hecho**

41 **huir** : *IND* **huyo, huyes, huye,** huimos, huís, **huyen;** *SUBJ* **huya, huyas, huya, huyamos, huyáis, huyan;** *PRET* huí, huiste, **huyó,** huimos, huisteis, **huyeron;** *IMPER* **huye;** *PRP* **huyendo**

42 **imprimir** : *PP* **impreso**

43 **ir** : *IND* **voy, vas, va, vamos, vais, van;** *SUBJ* **vaya, vayas, vaya, vayamos, vayáis, vayan;** *PRET* **fui, fuiste, fue, fuimos, fuis-teis, fueron;** *IMPF* **iba, ibas, iba, íbamos, ibais, iban;** *IMPER* **ve;** *PRP* **yendo;** *PP* **ido**

44 **jugar** : *IND* **juego, juegas, juega,** jugamos, jugáis, **juegan;** *SUBJ* **juegue, juegues, juegue, juguemos, juguéis, jueguen;** *PRET*

jugué, jugaste, jugó, jugamos, jugasteis, jugaron; *IMPER* **juega**

45 **lucir** : *IND* **luzco**, luces, luce, lucimos, lucís, lucen; *SUBJ* **luzca, luzcas, luzca, luzcamos, luzcáis, luzcan**

46 **morir** : *IND* **muero, mueres, muere**, morimos, morís, **mueren**; *SUBJ* **muera, mueras, muera, muramos, muráis, mueran**; *PRET* morí, moriste, **murió**, morimos, moristeis, **murieron**; *IMPER* **muere**; *PRP* **muriendo**; *PP* **muerto**

47 **mover** : *IND* **muevo, mueves, mueve**, movemos, movéis, **mueven**; *SUBJ* **mueva, muevas, mueva**, movamos, mováis, **muevan**; *IMPER* **mueve**

48 **nacer** : *IND* **nazco**, naces, nace, nacemos, nacéis, nacen; *SUBJ* **nazca, nazcas, nazca, nazcamos, nazcáis, nazcan**

49 **negar** : *IND* **niego, niegas, niega**, negamos, negáis, **niegan**; *SUBJ* **niegue, niegues, niegue, neguemos, neguéis, nieguen**; *PRET* **negué**, negaste, negó, negamos, negasteis, negaron; *IMPER* **niega**

50 **oír** : *IND* **oigo, oyes, oye, oímos**, oís, **oyen**; *SUBJ* **oiga, oigas, oiga, oigamos, oigáis, oigan**; *PRET* **oí, oíste, oyó, oímos, oísteis, oyeron**; *IMPER* **oye**; *PRP* **oyendo**; *PP* **oído**

51 **oler** : *IND* **huelo, hueles, huele**, olemos, oléis, **huelen**; *SUBJ* **huela, huelas, huela**, olamos, oláis, **huelan**; *IMPER* **huele**

52 **pagar** : *SUBJ* **pague, pagues, pague, paguemos, paguéis, paguen**; *PRET* **pagué**, pagaste, pagó, pagamos, pagasteis, pagaron

53 **parecer** : *IND* **parezco**, pareces, parece, parecemos, parecéis, parecen; *SUBJ* **parezca, parezcas, parezca, parezcamos, parezcáis, parezcan**

54 **pedir** : *IND* **pido, pides, pide**, pedimos, pedís, **piden**; *SUBJ* **pida, pidas, pida, pidamos, pidáis, pidan**; *PRET* pedí, pediste, **pidió**, pedimos, pedisteis, **pidieron**; *IMPER* **pide**; *PRP* **pidiendo**

55 **pensar** : *IND* **pienso, piensas, piensa**, pensamos, pensáis, **piensan**; *SUBJ* **piense, pienses, piense**, pensemos, penséis, **piensen**; *IMPER* **piensa**

56 **perder** : *IND* **pierdo, pierdes, pierde,** perdemos, perdéis, **pierden**; *SUBJ* **pierda, pierdas, pierda,** perdamos, perdáis, **pierdan**; *IMPER* **pierde**

57 **placer** : *IND* **plazco,** places, place, placemos, placéis, placen; *SUBJ* **plazca, plazcas, plazca, plazcamos, plazcáis, plazcan**; *PRET* plací, placiste, plació *or* **plugo,** placimos, placisteis, placieron *or* **pluguieron**

58 **poder** : *IND* **puedo, puedes, puede,** podemos, podéis, **pueden**; *SUBJ* **pueda, puedas, pueda,** podamos, podáis, **puedan**; *PRET* **pude, pudiste, pudo, pudimos, pudisteis, pudieron**; *FUT* **podré, podrás, podrá, podremos, podréis, podrán**; *IMPER* **puede**; *PRP* **pudiendo**

59 **podrir** *or* **pudrir** : *PP* **podrido** *(all other forms based on* pudrir*)*

60 **poner** : *IND* **pongo,** pones, pone, ponemos, ponéis, ponen; *SUBJ* **ponga, pongas, ponga, pongamos, pongáis, pongan**; *PRET* **puse, pusiste, puso, pusimos, pusisteis, pusieron**; *FUT* **pondré, pondrás, pondrá, pondremos, pondréis, pondrán**; *IMPER* **pon**; *PP* **puesto**

61 **producir** : *IND* **produzco,** produces, produce, producimos, producís, producen; *SUBJ* **produzca, produzcas, produzca, produzcamos, produzcáis, produzcan**; *PRET* **produje, produjiste, produjo, produjimos, produjisteis, produjeron**

62 **prohibir** : *IND* **prohíbo, prohíbes, prohíbe,** prohibimos, prohibís, **prohíben**; *SUBJ* **prohíba, prohíbas, prohíba,** prohibamos, prohibáis, **prohíban**; *IMPER* **prohíbe**

63 **proveer** : *PRET* proveí, **proveíste, proveyó, proveímos, proveísteis, proveyeron**; *PRP* **proveyendo**; *PP* **provisto**

64 **querer** : *IND* **quiero, quieres, quiere,** queremos, queréis, **quieren**; *SUBJ* **quiera, quieras, quiera,** queramos, queráis, **quieran**; *PRET* **quise, quisiste, quiso, quisimos, quisisteis, quisieron**; *FUT* **querré, querrás, querrá, querremos, querréis, querrán**; *IMPER* **quiere**

65 **raer** : *IND* rao *or* **raigo** *or* **rayo,** raes, rae, raemos, raéis, raen; *SUBJ* **raiga** *or* **raya, raigas** *or* **rayas, raiga** *or* **raya, raigamos** *or* **rayamos, raigáis** *or* **rayáis, raigan** *or* **rayan**; *PRET* **raí, raíste, rayó, raímos, raísteis, rayeron**; *PRP* **rayendo**; *PP* **raído**

66 **reír** : *IND* **río, ríes, ríe, reímos,** reís, **ríen;** *SUBJ* **ría, rías, ría, riamos, riáis, rían;** *PRET* reí, **reíste, rió, reímos, reísteis, rieron;** *IMPER* **ríe;** *PRP* **riendo;** *PP* **reído**

67 **reñir** : *IND* **riño, riñes, riñe,** reñimos, reñís, **riñen;** *SUBJ* **riña, riñas, riña, riñamos, riñáis, riñan;** *PRET* reñí, reñiste, **riñó,** reñimos, reñisteis, **riñeron;** *IMPER* riñe; *PRP* riñendo

68 **reunir** : *IND* **reúno, reúnes, reúne,** reunimos, reunís, **reúnen;** *SUBJ* **reúna, reúnas, reúna,** reunamos, reunáis, **reúnan;** *IMPER* **reúne**

69 **roer** : *IND* roo *or* **roigo** *or* **royo,** roes, roe, roemos, roéis, roen; *SUBJ* roa *or* **roiga** *or* **roya,** roas *or* **roigas** *or* **royas,** roa *or* **roiga** *or* **roya,** roamos *or* **roigamos** *or* **royamos,** roáis *or* **roigáis** *or* **royáis,** roan *or* **roigan** *or* **royan;** *PRET* roí, **roíste, royó, roímos, roísteis, royeron;** *PRP* **royendo;** *PP* **roído**

70 **romper** : *PP* **roto**

71 **saber** : *IND* **sé,** sabes, sabe, sabemos, sabéis, saben; *SUBJ* **sepa, sepas, sepa, sepamos, sepáis, sepan;** *PRET* **supe, supiste, supo, supimos, supisteis, supieron;** *FUT* **sabré, sabrás, sabrá, sabremos, sabréis, sabrán**

72 **sacar** : *SUBJ* **saque, saques, saque, saquemos, saquéis, saquen;** *PRET* **saqué,** sacaste, sacó, sacamos, sacasteis, sacaron

73 **salir** : *IND* **salgo,** sales, sale, salimos, salís, salen; *SUBJ* **salga, salgas, salga, salgamos, salgáis, salgan;** *FUT* **saldré, saldrás, saldrá, saldremos, saldréis, saldrán;** *IMPER* **sal**

74 **satisfacer** : *IND* **satisfago,** satisfaces, satisface, satisfacemos, satisfacéis, satisfacen; *SUBJ* **satisfaga, satisfagas, satisfaga, satisfagamos, satisfagáis, satisfagan;** *PRET* **satisfice, satisficiste, satisfizo, satisficimos, satisficisteis, satisficieron;** *FUT* **satisfaré, satisfarás, satisfará, satisfaremos, satisfaréis, satisfarán;** *IMPER* **satisfaz** *or* satisface; *PP* **satisfecho**

75 **seguir** : *IND* **sigo, sigues, sigue,** seguimos, seguís, **siguen;** *SUBJ* **siga, sigas, siga, sigamos, sigáis, sigan;** *PRET* seguí, seguiste, **siguió,** seguimos, seguisteis, **siguieron;** *IMPER* **sigue;** *PRP* **siguiendo**

76 **sentir** : *IND* **siento, sientes, siente,** sentimos, sentís, **sienten;** *SUBJ* **sienta, sientas, sienta, sintamos, sintáis, sientan;** *PRET*

sentí, sentiste, **sintió**, sentimos, sentisteis, **sintieron**; *IMPER* **siente**; *PRP* **sintiendo**

77 **ser** : *IND* **soy, eres, es, somos, sois, son;** *SUBJ* **sea, seas, sea, seamos, seáis, sean;** *PRET* **fui, fuiste, fue, fuimos, fuisteis, fueron;** *IMPF* **era, eras, era, éramos, erais, eran;** *IMPER* **sé;** *PRP* **siendo;** *PP* **sido**

78 **soler** (*defective verb; used only in the present, preterit, and imperfect indicative, and the present and imperfect subjunctive*) *see* 47 **mover**

79 **tañer** : *PRET* **tañí**, tañiste, **tañó**, tañimos, tañisteis, **tañeron**; *PRP* **tañendo**

80 **tener** : *IND* **tengo, tienes, tiene**, tenemos, tenéis, **tienen;** *SUBJ* **tenga, tengas, tenga, tengamos, tengáis, tengan;** *PRET* **tuve, tuviste, tuvo, tuvimos, tuvisteis, tuvieron;** *FUT* **tendré, tendrás, tendrá, tendremos, tendréis, tendrán;** *IMPER* **ten**

81 **traer** : *IND* **traigo,** traes, trae, traemos, traéis, traen; *SUBJ* **traiga, traigas, traiga, traigamos, traigáis, traigan;** *PRET* **traje, trajiste, trajo, trajimos, trajisteis, trajeron;** *PRP* **trayendo;** *PP* **traído**

82 **trocar** : *IND* **trueco, truecas, trueca**, trocamos, trocáis, **truecan;** *SUBJ* **trueque, trueques, trueque, troquemos, troquéis, truequen;** *PRET* **troqué**, trocaste, trocó, trocamos, trocasteis, trocaron; *IMPER* **trueca**

83 **uncir** : *IND* **unzo,** unces, unce, uncimos, uncís, uncen; *SUBJ* **unza, unzas, unza, unzamos, unzáis, unzan**

84 **valer** : *IND* **valgo,** vales, vale, valemos, valéis, valen; *SUBJ* **valga, valgas, valga, valgamos, valgáis, valgan;** *FUT* **valdré, valdrás, valdrá, valdremos, valdréis, valdrán**

85 **variar** : *IND* **varío, varías, varía**, variamos, variáis, **varían;** *SUBJ* **varíe, varíes, varíe**, variemos, variéis, **varíen;** *IMPER* **varía**

86 **vencer** : *IND* **venzo,** vences, vence, vencemos, vencéis, vencen; *SUBJ* **venza, venzas, venza, venzamos, venzáis, venzan**

87 **venir** : *IND* **vengo, vienes, viene**, venimos, venís, **vienen;** *SUBJ* **venga, vengas, venga, vengamos, vengáis, vengan;** *PRET* **vine, viniste, vino, vinimos, vinisteis, vinieron;** *FUT* **vendré,**

vendrás, vendrá, vendremos, vendréis, vendrán; *IMPER* ven; *PRP* viniendo

88 ver : *IND* veo, ves, ve, vemos, veis, ven; *PRET* vi, viste, vio, vimos, visteis, vieron; *IMPER* ve; *PRP* viendo; *PP* visto

89 volver : *IND* vuelvo, vuelves, vuelve, volvemos, volvéis, vuelven; *SUBJ* vuelva, vuelvas, vuelva, volvamos, volváis, vuelvan; *IMPER* vuelve; *PP* vuelto

90 yacer : *IND* yazco *or* yazgo *or* yago, yaces, yace, yacemos, yacéis, yacen; *SUBJ* yazca *or* yazga *or* yaga, yazcas *or* yazgas *or* yagas, yazca *or* yazga *or* yaga, yazcamos *or* yazgamos *or* yagamos, yazcáis *or* yazgáis *or* yagáis, yazcan *or* yazgan *or* yagan; *IMPER* yace *or* yaz

Irregular English Verbs

INFINITIVE	PAST	PAST PARTICIPLE
arise	arose	arisen
awake	awoke	awoken *or* awaked
be	was, were	been
bear	bore	borne
beat	beat	beaten *or* beat
become	became	become
befall	befell	befallen
begin	began	begun
behold	beheld	beheld
bend	bent	bent
beseech	beseeched *or* besought	beseeched *or* besought
beset	beset	beset
bet	bet	bet
bid	bade *or* bid	bidden *or* bid
bind	bound	bound
bite	bit	bitten
bleed	bled	bled
blow	blew	blown
break	broke	broken
breed	bred	bred
bring	brought	brought
build	built	built
burn	burned *or* burnt	burned *or* burnt
burst	burst	burst
buy	bought	bought
can	could	—
cast	cast	cast
catch	caught	caught
choose	chose	chosen
cling	clung	clung
come	came	come
cost	cost	cost
creep	crept	crept
cut	cut	cut
deal	dealt	dealt
dig	dug	dug
do	did	done
draw	drew	drawn
dream	dreamed *or* dreamt	dreamed *or* dreamt
drink	drank	drunk *or* drank
drive	drove	driven
dwell	dwelled *or* dwelt	dwelled *or* dwelt

INFINITIVE	PAST	PAST PARTICIPLE
eat	ate	eaten
fall	fell	fallen
feed	fed	fed
feel	felt	felt
fight	fought	fought
find	found	found
flee	fled	fled
fling	flung	flung
fly	flew	flown
forbid	forbade	forbidden
forecast	forecast	forecast
forego	forewent	foregone
foresee	foresaw	foreseen
foretell	foretold	foretold
forget	forgot	forgotten *or* forgot
forgive	forgave	forgiven
forsake	forsook	forsaken
freeze	froze	frozen
get	got	got *or* gotten
give	gave	given
go	went	gone
grind	ground	ground
grow	grew	grown
hang	hung	hung
have	had	had
hear	heard	heard
hide	hid	hidden *or* hid
hit	hit	hit
hold	held	held
hurt	hurt	hurt
keep	kept	kept
kneel	knelt *or* kneeled	knelt *or* kneeled
know	knew	known
lay	laid	laid
lead	led	led
lean	leaned	leaned
leap	leaped *or* leapt	leaped *or* leapt
learn	learned	learned
leave	left	left
lend	lent	lent
let	let	let
lie	lay	lain
light	lit *or* lighted	lit *or* lighted
lose	lost	lost
make	made	made
may	might	—

INFINITIVE	PAST	PAST PARTICIPLE
mean	meant	meant
meet	met	met
mow	mowed	mowed *or* mown
pay	paid	paid
put	put	put
quit	quit	quit
read	read	read
rend	rent	rent
rid	rid	rid
ride	rode	ridden
ring	rang	rung
rise	rose	risen
run	ran	run
saw	sawed	sawed *or* sawn
say	said	said
see	saw	seen
seek	sought	sought
sell	sold	sold
send	sent	sent
set	set	set
shake	shook	shaken
shall	should	—
shear	sheared	sheared *or* shorn
shed	shed	shed
shine	shone *or* shined	shone *or* shined
shoot	shot	shot
show	showed	shown *or* showed
shrink	shrank *or* shrunk	shrunk *or* shrunken
shut	shut	shut
sing	sang *or* sung	sung
sink	sank *or* sunk	sunk
sit	sat	sat
slay	slew	slain
sleep	slept	slept
slide	slid	slid
sling	slung	slung
smell	smelled *or* smelt	smelled *or* smelt
sow	sowed	sown *or* sowed
speak	spoke	spoken
speed	sped *or* speeded	sped *or* speeded
spell	spelled	spelled
spend	spent	spent
spill	spilled	spilled
spin	spun	spun
spit	spit *or* spat	spit *or* spat
split	split	split

INFINITIVE	PAST	PAST PARTICIPLE
spoil	spoiled	spoiled
spread	spread	spread
spring	sprang *or* sprung	sprung
stand	stood	stood
steal	stole	stolen
stick	stuck	stuck
sting	stung	stung
stink	stank *or* stunk	stunk
stride	strode	stridden
strike	struck	struck
swear	swore	sworn
sweep	swept	swept
swell	swelled	swelled *or* swollen
swim	swam	swum
swing	swung	swung
take	took	taken
teach	taught	taught
tear	tore	torn
tell	told	told
think	thought	thought
throw	threw	thrown
thrust	thrust	thrust
tread	trod	trodden *or* trod
wake	woke	woken *or* waked
waylay	waylaid	waylaid
wear	wore	worn
weave	wove *or* weaved	woven *or* weaved
wed	wedded	wedded
weep	wept	wept
will	would	—
win	won	won
wind	wound	wound
withdraw	withdrew	withdrawn
withhold	withheld	withheld
withstand	withstood	withstood
wring	wrung	wrung
write	wrote	written

Spelling-to-Sound Correspondences in Spanish

For example words for the phonetic symbols below, see
Pronunciation Symbols on page 58a.

VOWELS

a   [a]

e   [e] in open syllables
(syllables ending with
a vowel); [ɛ] in closed
syllables (syllables
ending with a conso-
nant)

i   [i]; before another vowel
in the same syllable
pronounced as [j] ([ʒ] or
[ʃ] in Argentina and
Uruguay; [ʤ] when at
the beginning of a word
in the Caribbean)

o   [o] in open syllables
(syllables ending with
a vowel); [ɔ] in closed
syllables (syllables
ending with a conso-
nant)

u   [u]; before another vowel
in the same syllable
pronounced as [w]

y   [i]; before another vowel
in the same syllable
pronounced as [j] ([ʒ] or
[ʃ] in Argentina and
Uruguay; [ʤ] when at
the beginning of a word
in the Caribbean)

CONSONANTS

b   [b] at the beginning of a
word or after *m* or *n*; [β]
elsewhere

c   [s] before *i* or *e* in Latin
America and parts of
southern Spain, [θ] in
northern Spain; [k]
elsewhere

ch [ʧ]; frequently [ʃ] in Chile
and Panama; sometimes
[ts] in Chile

d   [d] at the beginning of a
word or after *n* or *l*; [ð]
elsewhere, frequently
silent between vowels

f   [f]; [Φ] in Honduras (no
English equivalent for
this sound; like [f] but
made with both lips)

g   [x] before *i* or *e* ([h] in the
Caribbean and Central
America); [g] at the
beginning of a word or
after *n* and not before *i*
or *e*; [ɣ] elsewhere,
frequently silent
between vowels

gu [gw] at the beginning of a
word before *a, o;* [ɣw]
elsewhere before *a, o*;
frequently just [w]
between vowels; [g] at
the beginning of a word
before *i, e*; [ɣ] elsewhere
before *i, e*; frequently
silent between vowels

gü [gw] at the beginning of a
word, [ɣw] elsewhere;
frequently just [w]
between vowels

h   silent

j   [x] ([h] in the Caribbean
and Central America)

k   [k]

l   [l]

ll [j]; [ʒ] or [ʃ] in Argentina
and Uruguay; [ʤ] when
at the beginning of a
word in the Caribbean;

[lʲ] in Bolivia, Paraguay, Peru, and parts of northern Spain (no English equivalent; like "lli" in *million*)

m [m]

n [n]; frequently [ŋ] at the end of a word when next word begins with a vowel

ñ [ɲ]

p [p]

qu [k]

r [r] (no English equivalent; a trilled sound) at the beginning of words; [t̺]/[ɾ] elsewhere

rr [r] (no English equivalent; a trilled sound)

s [s]; frequently [z] before

b, *d*, *g*, *m*, *n*, *l*, *r*; at the end of a word [h] or silent in many parts of Latin America and some parts of Spain

t [t]

v [b] at the beginning of a word or after *m* or *n*; [β] elsewhere

x [ks] or [gz] between vowels; [s] before consonants

z [s] in Latin America and parts of southern Spain, [θ] in northern Spain; at the end of a word [h] or silent in many parts of Latin America and some parts of Spain

Pronunciation Symbols

VOWELS

æ	ask, bat, glad
ɑ	cot, bomb
a	*New England* aunt, *British* ask, glass, *Spanish* casa
e	*Spanish* peso, jefe
ɛ	egg, bet, fed
ə	about, javelin, Alabama
ə	when italicized as in *ə*l, *ə*m, *ə*n, indicates a syllabic pronunciation of the consonant as in bottle, prism, button
i	very, any, thirty, *Spanish* piña
i:	eat, bead, bee
ɪ	id, bid, pit
o	Ohio, yellower, potato, *Spanish* óvalo
o:	oats, own, zone, blow
ɔ	awl, maul, caught, paw
ʊ	sure, should, could
u	*Spanish* uva, culpa
u:	boot, few, coo
ʌ	under, putt, bud
eɪ	eight, wade, bay
aɪ	ice, bite, tie
aʊ	out, gown, plow
ɔɪ	oyster, coil, boy
ər	further, stir
ɒ	*British* bond, god
:	indicates that the preceding vowel is long. Long vowels are almost always diphthongs in English, but not in Spanish.

CONSONANTS

b	baby, labor, cab
β	*Spanish* cabo, óvalo
d	day, ready, kid
ʤ	just, badger, fudge
ð	then, either, bathe
f	foe, tough, buff
g	go, bigger, bag
ɣ	*Spanish* tragar, daga
h	hot, aha
j	yes, vineyard
k	cat, keep, lacquer, flock
l	law, hollow, boil
m	mat, hemp, hammer, rim
n	new, tent, tenor, run
ŋ	rung, hang, swinger
ɲ	*Spanish* cabaña, piña
p	pay, lapse, top
r	rope, burn, tar
s	sad, mist, kiss
ʃ	shoe, mission, slush
t	toe, button, mat
t̬	indicates that some speakers of English pronounce this as a voiced alveolar flap [ɾ], as in later, catty, battle
ʧ	choose, batch
θ	thin, ether, bath
v	vat, never, cave
w	wet, software
x	*German* Bach, *Scots* loch, *Spanish* gente, jefe
z	zoo, easy, buzz
ʒ	jaborandi, azure, beige
h, k, p, t	when italicized indicate sounds which are present in the pronunciation of some speakers of English but absent in that of others, so that *whence* [*h*wɛnts] can be pronounced as ['wɛns], ['hwɛns], ['wɛnts], or ['hwɛnts]

STRESS MARKS

ˈ high stress	penmanship
ˌ low stress	penmanship

Spanish–English
Dictionary

A

a¹ *nf* : first letter of the Spanish alphabet

a² *prep* **1** : to ⟨nos vamos a México : we're going to Mexico⟩ **2** (*used before direct or indirect objects referring to persons*) ⟨¿llamaste a tu papá? : did you call your dad?⟩ ⟨como a usted le guste : as you wish⟩ **3** : in the manner of ⟨papas a la francesa : french fries⟩ **4** : on, by means of ⟨a pie : on foot⟩ **5** : per, each ⟨tres pastillas al día : three pills per day⟩ **6** : at ⟨a las dos : at two o'clock⟩ ⟨al principio : at first⟩ **7** (*with infinitive*) ⟨enséñales a leer : teach them to read⟩ ⟨problemas a resolver : problems to be solved⟩

ábaco *nm* : abacus

abad *nm* : abbot

abadesa *nf* : abbess

abadía *nf* : abbey

abajo *adv* **1** : down ⟨póngalo más abajo : put it further down⟩ ⟨arriba y abajo : up and down⟩ **2** : downstairs **3** : under, beneath ⟨el abajo firmante : the undersigned⟩ **4** : down with ⟨¡abajo la inflación! : down with inflation!⟩ **5** ~ **de** : under, beneath **6 de** ~ : bottom ⟨el cajón de abajo : the bottom drawer⟩ **7 hacia** ~ *or* **para** ~ : downwards **8 cuesta abajo** : downhill **9 río abajo** : downstream

abalanzarse {21} *vr* : to hurl oneself, to rush

abanderado, -da *n* : standard-bearer

abandonado, -da *adj* **1** : abandoned, deserted **2** : neglected **3** : slovenly, unkempt

abandonar *vt* **1** DEJAR : to abandon, to leave **2** : to give up, to quit ⟨abandonaron la búsqueda : they gave up the search⟩ — **abandonarse** *vr* **1** : to neglect oneself **2** ~ **a** : to succumb to, to give oneself over to

abandono *nm* **1** : abandonment **2** : neglect **3** : withdrawal ⟨ganar por abandono : to win by default⟩

abanicar {72} *vt* : to fan — **abanicarse** *vr*

abanico *nm* **1** : fan **2** GAMA : range, gamut

abaratamiento *nm* : price reduction

abaratar *vt* : to lower the price of — **abaratarse** *vr* : to go down in price

abarcar {72} *vt* **1** : to cover, to include, to embrace **2** : to undertake **3** : to monopolize

abaritonado, -da *adj* : baritone

abarrotado, -da *adj* : packed, crammed

abarrotar *vt* : to fill up, to pack

abarrotería *nf* CA, Mex : grocery store

abarrotero, -ra *n* Col, Mex : grocer

abarrotes *nmpl* **1** : groceries, supplies **2 tienda de abarrotes** : general store, grocery store

abastecedor, -dora *n* : supplier

abastecer {53} *vt* : to supply, to stock — **abastecerse** *vr* : to stock up

abastecimiento → **abasto**

abasto *nm* : supply, supplying ⟨no da abasto : there isn't enough for all⟩

abatido, -da *adj* : dejected, depressed

abatimiento *nm* **1** : drop, reduction **2** : dejection, depression

abatir *vt* **1** DERRIBAR : to demolish, to knock down **2** : to shoot down **3** DEPRIMIR : to depress, to bring low — **abatirse** *vr* **1** DEPRIMIRSE : to get depressed **2** ~ **sobre** : to swoop down on

abdicación *nf, pl* **-ciones** : abdication

abdicar {72} *vt* : to relinquish, to abdicate

abdomen *nm, pl* **-dómenes** : abdomen

abdominal *adj* : abdominal

abecé *nm* : ABC's *pl*

abecedario *nm* ALFABETO : alphabet

abedul *nm* : birch (tree)

abeja *nf* : bee

abejorro *nm* : bumblebee

aberración *nf, pl* **-ciones** : aberration

aberrante *adj* : aberrant, perverse

abertura *nf* **1** : aperture, opening **2** AGUJERO : hole **3** : slit (in a skirt, etc.) **4** GRIETA : crack

abeto *nm* : fir (tree)

abierto¹ *pp* → **abrir**

abierto², -ta *adj* **1** : open **2** : candid, frank **3** : generous — **abiertamente** *adv*

abigarrado, -da *adj* : multicolored, variegated

abigeato *nm* : rustling (of livestock)

abismal *adj* : abysmal, vast

abismo *nm* : abyss, chasm ⟨al borde del abismo : on the brink of ruin⟩

abjurar *vi* ~ **de** : to abjure — **abjuración** *nf*

ablandamiento *nm* : softening, moderation

ablandar *vt* **1** SUAVIZAR : to soften **2** CALMAR : to soothe, to appease — *vi* : to moderate, to get milder — **ablandarse** *vr* **1** : to become soft, to soften **2** CEDER : to yield, to relent

ablución *nf, pl* **-ciones** : ablution

abnegación *nf, pl* **-ciones** : abnegation, self-denial

abnegado, -da *adj* : self-sacrificing, selfless

abnegarse {49} *vr* : to deny oneself

abobado, -da *adj* **1** : silly, stupid **2** : bewildered

abocarse {72} *vr* **1** DIRIGIRSE : to head, to direct oneself **2** DEDICARSE : to dedicate oneself

abochornar *vt* AVERGONZAR : to embarrass, to shame — **abochornarse** *vr*

abofetear *vt* : to slap

abogacía *nf* : law, legal profession

abogado, -da *n* : lawyer, attorney

abogar {52} *vi* ~ **por** : to plead for, to defend, to advocate

abolengo *nm* LINAJE : lineage, ancestry
abolición *nf, pl* **-ciones** : abolition
abolir {1} *vt* DEROGAR : to abolish, to repeal
abolladura *nf* : dent
abollar *vt* : to dent
abombar *vt* : to warp, to cause to bulge — **abombarse** *vr* : to decompose, to go bad
abominable *adj* ABORRECIBLE : abominable
abominación *nf, pl* **-ciones** : abomination
abominar *vt* ABORRECER : to abominate, to abhor
abonado, -da *n* : subscriber
abonar *vt* **1** : to pay **2** FERTILIZAR : to fertilize — **abonarse** *vr* : to subscribe
abono *nm* **1** : payment, installment **2** FERTILIZANTE : fertilizer **3** : season ticket
abordaje *nm* : boarding
abordar *vt* **1** : to address, to broach **2** : to accost, to waylay **3** : to come on board
aborigen[1] *adj, pl* **-rígenes** : aboriginal, native
aborigen[2] *nmf, pl* **-rígenes** : aborigine, indigenous inhabitant
aborrecer {53} *vt* ABOMINAR, ODIAR : to abhor, to detest, to hate
aborrecible *adj* ABOMINABLE, ODIOSO : abominable, detestable
aborrecimiento *nm* : abhorrence, loathing
abortar *vi* : to have an abortion — *vt* **1** : to abort **2** : to quash, to suppress
abortista *nmf* : abortionist
abortivo, -va *adj* : abortive
aborto *nm* **1** : abortion **2** : miscarriage
abotonar *vt* : to button — **abotonarse** *vr* : to button up
abovedado, -da *adj* : vaulted
abrasador, -dora *adj* : burning, scorching
abrasar *vt* QUEMAR : to burn, to sear, to scorch
abrasivo[1]**, -va** *adj* : abrasive
abrasivo[2] *nm* : abrasive
abrazadera *nf* : clamp, brace
abrazar {21} *vt* : to hug, to embrace — **abrazarse** *vr*
abrazo *nm* : hug, embrace
abrebotellas *nms & pl* : bottle opener
abrelatas *nms & pl* : can opener
abrevadero *nm* BEBEDERO : watering trough
abreviación *nf, pl* **-ciones** : abbreviation
abreviar *vt* **1** : to abbreviate **2** : to shorten, to cut short
abreviatura → **abreviación**
abridor *nm* : bottle opener, can opener
abrigadero *nm* : shelter, windbreak
abrigado, -da *adj* **1** : sheltered **2** : warm, wrapped up (with clothing)
abrigar {52} *vt* **1** : to shelter, to protect **2** : to keep warm, to dress warmly **3** : to cherish, to harbor ⟨abrigar esperanzas : to cherish hopes⟩ — **abrigarse** *vr* : to dress warmly
abrigo *nm* **1** : coat, overcoat **2** : shelter, refuge
abril *nm* : April
abrillantador *nm* : polish
abrillantar *vt* : to polish, to shine
abrir {2} *vt* **1** : to open **2** : to unlock, to undo **3** : to turn on (a tap or faucet) — *vi* : to open, to open up — **abrirse** *vr* **1** : to open up **2** : to clear (of the skies)
abrochar *vt* : to button, to fasten — **abrocharse** *vr* : to fasten, to hook up
abrogación *nf, pl* **-ciones** : abrogation, annulment, repeal
abrogar {52} *vt* : to abrogate, to annul, to repeal
abrojo *nm* : bur (of a plant)
abrumador, -dora *adj* : crushing, overwhelming
abrumar *vt* **1** AGOBIAR : to overwhelm **2** OPRIMIR : to oppress, to burden
abrupto, -ta *adj* **1** : abrupt **2** ESCARPADO : steep — **abruptamente** *adv*
absceso *nm* : abscess
absolución *nf, pl* **-ciones** **1** : absolution **2** : acquittal
absolutismo *nm* : absolutism
absoluto, -ta *adj* **1** : absolute, unconditional **2 en ~** : not at all ⟨no me gustó en absoluto : I did not like it at all⟩ — **absolutamente** *adv*
absolver {89} *vt* **1** : to absolve **2** : to acquit
absorbente *adj* **1** : absorbent **2** : absorbing, engrossing
absorber *vt* **1** : to absorb, to soak up **2** : to occupy, to take up, to engross
absorción *nf, pl* **-ciones** : absorption
absorto, -ta *adj* : absorbed, engrossed
abstemio[1]**, -mia** *adj* : abstemious, teetotal
abstemio[2]**, -mia** *n* : teetotaler
abstención *nf, pl* **-ciones** : abstention
abstenerse {80} *vr* : to abstain, to refrain
abstinencia *nf* : abstinence
abstracción *nf, pl* **-ciones** : abstraction
abstracto, -ta *adj* : abstract
abstraer {81} *vt* : to abstract — **abstraerse** *vr* : to lose oneself in thought
abstraído, -da *adj* : preoccupied, withdrawn
abstruso, -sa *adj* : abstruse
abstuvo, etc. → **abstenerse**
absuelto *pp* → **absolver**
absurdo[1]**, -da** *adj* DISPARATADO, RIDÍCULO : absurd, ridiculous — **absurdamente** *adv*
absurdo[2] *nm* : absurdity
abuchear *vt* : to boo, to jeer
abucheo *nm* : booing, jeering
abuela *nf* **1** : grandmother **2** : old woman **3 ¡tu abuela!** *fam* : no way!, forget about it!
abuelo *nm* **1** : grandfather **2** : old man **3 abuelos** *nmpl* : grandparents, ancestors

abulia *nf* : apathy, lethargy

abúlico, -ca *adj* : lethargic, apathetic

abultado, -da *adj* : bulging, bulky

abultar *vi* : to bulge — *vt* : to enlarge, to expand

abundancia *nf* : abundance

abundante *adj* : abundant, plentiful — **abundantemente** *adv*

abundar *vi* **1** : to abound, to be plentiful **2** ~ **en** : to be in agreement with

aburrido, -da *adj* **1** : bored, tired, fed up **2** TEDIOSO : boring, tedious

aburrimiento *nm* : boredom, weariness

aburrir *vt* : to bore, to tire — **aburrirse** *vr* : to get bored

abusado, -da *adj Mex fam* : sharp, on the ball

abusador, -dora *n* : abuser

abusar *vi* **1** : to go too far, to do something to excess **2** ~ **de** : to abuse (as drugs) **3** ~ **de** : to take unfair advantage of

abusivo, -va *adj* **1** : abusive **2** : outrageous, excessive

abuso *nm* **1** : abuse **2** : injustice, outrage

abyecto, -ta *adj* : despicable, contemptible

acá *adv* AQUÍ : here, over here ⟨ven acá! : come here!⟩

acabado¹, -da *adj* **1** : finished, done, completed **2** : old, worn-out

acabado² *nm* : finish ⟨un acabado brillante : a glossy finish⟩

acabar *vi* **1** TERMINAR : to finish, to end **2** ~ **de** : to have just (done something) ⟨acabo de ver a tu hermano : I just saw your brother⟩ **3** ~ **con** : to put an end to, to stamp out — *vt* TERMINAR : to finish — **acabarse** *vr* TERMINARSE : to come to an end, to run out ⟨se me acabó el dinero : I ran out of money⟩

acacia *nf* : acacia

academia *nf* : academy

académico¹, -ca *adj* : academic, scholastic — **académicamente** *adv*

académico², -ca *n* : academic, academician

acaecer {53} *vt (3rd person only)* : to happen, to take place

acalambrarse *vr* : to cramp up, to get a cramp

acallar *vt* : to quiet, to silence

acalorado, -da *adj* : emotional, heated

acaloramiento *nm* **1** : heat **2** : ardor, passion

acalorar *vt* : to heat up, to inflame — **acalorarse** *vr* : to get upset, to get worked up

acampada *nf* : camp, camping ⟨ir de acampada : to go camping⟩

acampar *vi* : to camp

acanalar *vt* **1** : to groove, to furrow **2** : to corrugate

acantilado *nm* : cliff

acanto *nm* : acanthus

acantonar *vt* : to station, to quarter

acaparador, -dora *adj* : greedy, selfish

acaparar *vt* **1** : to stockpile, to hoard **2** : to monopolize

acápite *nm* : paragraph

acariciar *vt* : to caress, to stroke, to pet

ácaro *nm* : mite

acarrear *vt* **1** : to haul, to carry **2** : to bring, to give rise to ⟨los problemas que acarrea : the problems that come along with it⟩

acarreo *nm* : transport, haulage

acartonarse *vr* **1** : to stiffen **2** : to become wizened

acaso *adv* **1** : perhaps, by any chance **2 por si acaso** : just in case

acatamiento *nm* : compliance, observance

acatar *vt* : to comply with, to respect

acaudalado, -da *adj* RICO : wealthy, rich

acaudillar *vt* : to lead, to command

acceder *vi* ~ **a 1** : to accede to, to agree to **2** : to assume (a position) **3** : to gain access to

accesar *vt* : to access (on a computer)

accesibilidad *nf* : accessibility

accesible *adj* ASEQUIBLE : accessible, attainable

acceso *nm* **1** : access **2** : admittance, entrance

accesorio¹, -ria *adj* **1** : accessory **2** : incidental

accesorio² *nm* **1** : accessory **2** : prop (in the theater)

accidentado¹, -da *adj* **1** : eventful, turbulent **2** : rough, uneven **3** : injured

accidentado², -da *n* : accident victim

accidental *adj* : accidental, unintentional — **accidentalmente** *adv*

accidentarse *vr* : to have an accident

accidente *nm* **1** : accident **2** : unevenness **3 accidente geográfico** : geographical feature

acción *nf, pl* **acciones 1** : action **2** ACTO : act, deed **3** : share, stock

accionamiento *nm* : activation

accionar *vt* : to put into motion, to activate — *vi* : to gesticulate

accionario, -ria *adj* : stock ⟨mercado accionario : stock market⟩

accionista *nmf* : stockholder, shareholder

acebo *nm* : holly

acechar *vt* **1** : to watch, to spy on **2** : to stalk, to lie in wait for

acecho *nm* **al acecho** : lying in wait

acedera *nf* : sorrel (herb)

acéfalo, -la *adj* : leaderless

aceitar *vt* : to oil

aceite *nm* **1** : oil **2 aceite de ricino** : castor oil **3 aceite de oliva** : olive oil

aceitera *nf* **1** : cruet (for oil) **2** : oilcan **3** *Mex* : oil refinery

aceitoso, -sa *adj* : oily

aceituna *nf* OLIVA : olive

aceituno *nm* OLIVO : olive tree

aceleración *nf, pl* **-ciones** : acceleration, speeding up

acelerado, -da *adj* : accelerated, speedy

acelerador *nm* : accelerator

aceleramiento *nm* → **aceleración**

acelerar *vt* **1** : to accelerate, to speed up **2** AGILIZAR : to expedite — *vi* : to accelerate (of an automobile) — **acelerarse** *vr* : to hasten, to hurry up

acelga *nf* : chard, Swiss chard

acendrado, -da *adj* : pure, unblemished

acendrar *vt* : to purify, to refine

acento *nm* **1** : accent **2** : stress, emphasis

acentuación *nf, pl* **-ciones** : accentuation

acentuado, -da *adj* : marked, pronounced

acentuar {3} *vt* **1** : to accent **2** : to emphasize, to stress — **acentuarse** *vr* : to become more pronounced

acepción *nf, pl* **-ciones** SIGNIFICADO : sense, meaning

aceptabilidad *nf* : acceptability

aceptable *adj* : acceptable

aceptación *nf, pl* **-ciones** **1** : acceptance **2** APROBACIÓN : approval

aceptar *vt* **1** : to accept **2** : to approve

acequia *nf* **1** : irrigation ditch **2** *Mex* : sewer

acera *nf* : sidewalk

acerado, -da *adj* **1** : made of steel **2** : steely, tough

acerbo, -ba *adj* **1** : harsh, cutting ⟨comentarios acerbos : cutting remarks⟩ **2** : bitter — **acerbamente** *adv*

acerca *prep* ~ **de** : about, concerning

acercamiento *nm* : rapprochement, reconciliation

acercar {72} *vt* APROXIMAR, ARRIMAR : to bring near, to bring closer — **acercarse** *vr* APROXIMARSE, ARRIMARSE : to approach, to draw near

acería *nf* : steel mill

acerico *nm* : pincushion

acero *nm* : steel ⟨acero inoxidable : stainless steel⟩

acérrimo, -ma *adj* **1** : staunch, steadfast **2** : bitter ⟨un acérrimo enemigo : a bitter enemy⟩

acertado, -da *adj* CORRECTO : accurate, correct, on target — **acertadamente** *adv*

acertante[1] *adj* : winning

acertante[2] *nmf* : winner

acertar {55} *vt* : to guess correctly — *vi* **1** ATINAR : to be correct, to be on target **2** ~ **a** : to manage to

acertijo *nm* ADIVINANZA : riddle

acervo *nm* **1** : pile, heap **2** : wealth, heritage ⟨el acervo artístico del instituto : the artistic treasures of the institute⟩

acetato *nm* : acetate

acético, -ca *adj* : acetic ⟨ácido acético : acetic acid⟩

acetileno *nm* : acetylene

acetona *nf* **1** : acetone **2** : nail-polish remover

achacar {72} *vt* : to attribute, to impute ⟨te achaca todos sus problemas : he blames all his problems on you⟩

achacoso, -sa *adj* : frail, sickly

achaparrado, -da *adj* : stunted, scrubby ⟨árboles achaparrados : scrubby trees⟩

achaques *nmpl* : aches and pains

achatar *vt* : to flatten

achicar {72} *vt* **1** REDUCIR : to make smaller, to reduce **2** : to intimidate **3** : to bail out (water) — **achicarse** *vr* : to become intimidated

achicharrar *vt* : to scorch, to burn to a crisp

achicoria *nf* : chicory

achispado, -da *adj fam* : tipsy

achote *or* **achiote** *nm* : annatto seed

achuchón *nm, pl* **-chones** **1** : push, shove **2** *fam* : squeeze, hug **3** *fam* : mild illness

aciago, -ga *adj* : fateful, unlucky

acicalar *vt* **1** PULIR : to polish **2** : to dress up, to adorn — **acicalarse** *vr* : to get dressed up

acicate *nm* **1** : spur **2** INCENTIVO : incentive, stimulus

acidez *nf, pl* **-deces** **1** : acidity **2** : sourness **3** **acidez estomacal** : heartburn

acidificar {72} *vt* : to acidify

ácido[1]**, -da** *adj* AGRIO : acid, sour

ácido[2] *nm* : acid

acierto *nm* **1** : correct answer, right choice **2** : accuracy, skill, deftness

acimut *nm* : azimuth

acitronar *vt Mex* : to fry until crisp

aclamación *nf, pl* **-ciones** : acclaim, acclamation

aclamar *vt* : to acclaim, to cheer, to applaud

aclaración *nf, pl* **-ciones** CLARIFICACIÓN : clarification, explanation

aclarar *vt* **1** CLARIFICAR : to clarify, to explain, to resolve **2** : to lighten **3 aclarar la voz** : to clear one's throat — *vi* **1** : to get light, to dawn **2** : to clear up — **aclararse** *vr* : to become clear

aclaratorio, -ria *adj* : explanatory

aclimatar *vt* : to acclimatize — **aclimatarse** *vr* ~ **a** : to get used to — **aclimatación** *nf*

acné *nm* : acne

acobardar *vt* INTIMIDAR : to frighten, to intimidate — **acobardarse** *vr* : to be frightened, to cower

acodarse *vr* ~ **en** : to lean (one's elbows) on

acogedor, -dora *adj* : cozy, warm, friendly

acoger {15} *vt* **1** REFUGIAR : to take in, to shelter **2** : to receive, to welcome — **acogerse** *vr* **1** REFUGIARSE : to take refuge **2** ~ **a** : to resort to, to avail oneself of

acogida *nf* **1** AMPARO, REFUGIO : refuge, protection **2** RECIBIMIENTO : reception, welcome

acolchar *vt* **1** : to pad (a wall, etc.) **2** : to quilt

acólito *nm* **1** MONAGUILLO : altar boy **2** : follower, helper, acolyte

acomedido, -da *adj* : helpful, obliging

7

acometer *vt* **1** ATACAR : to attack, to assail **2** EMPRENDER : to undertake, to begin — *vi* ~ **contra** : to rush against
acometida *nf* ATAQUE : attack, assault
acomodado, -da *adj* **1** : suitable, appropriate **2** : well-to-do, prosperous
acomodador, -dora *n* : usher, usherette *f*
acomodar *vt* **1** : to accommodate, to make room for **2** : to adjust, to adapt — **acomodarse** *vr* **1** : to settle in **2** ~ **a** : to adapt to
acomodaticio, -cia *adj* : accommodating, obliging
acomodo *nm* **1** : job, position **2** : arrangement, placement **3** : accommodation, lodging
acompañamiento *nm* : accompaniment
acompañante *nmf* **1** COMPAÑERO : companion **2** : accompanist
acompañar *vt* : to accompany, to go with
acompasado, -da *adj* : rhythmic, regular, measured
acomplejado, -da *adj* : full of complexes, neurotic
acondicionado, -da *adj* **1** : equipped, fitted-out **2 bien acondicionado** : in good shape, in a fit state
acondicionador *nm* **1** : conditioner **2 acondicionador de aire** : air conditioner
acondicionar *vt* **1** : to condition **2** : to fit out, to furnish
acongojado, -da *adj* : distressed, upset
acongojarse *vr* : to grieve, to become distressed
aconsejable *adj* : advisable
aconsejar *vt* : to advise, to counsel
acontecer {53} *vt* (*3rd person only*) : to occur, to happen
acontecimiento *nm* SUCESO : event
acopiar *vt* : to gather, to collect, to stockpile
acopio *nm* : collection, stock
acoplamiento *nm* : connection, coupling
acoplar *vt* : to couple, to connect — **acoplarse** *vr* : to fit together
acoquinar *vt* : to intimidate
acorazado¹, -da *adj* BLINDADO : armored
acorazado² *nm* : battleship
acordado, -da *adj* : agreed upon
acordar {19} *vt* **1** : to agree on **2** OTORGAR : to award, to bestow — **acordarse** *vr* RECORDAR : to remember, to recall
acorde¹ *adj* **1** : in agreement, in accordance **2** ~ **con** : in keeping with
acorde² *nm* : chord
acordeón *nm*, *pl* **-deones** : accordion — **acordeonista** *nmf*
acordonar *vt* **1** : to cordon off **2** : to lace up **3** : to mill (coins)
acorralar *vt* ARRINCONAR : to corner, to hem in, to corral
acortar *vt* : to shorten, to cut short — **acortarse** *vr* **1** : to become shorter **2** : to end early

acosar *vt* PERSEGUIR : to pursue, to hound, to harass
acoso *nm* ASEDIO : harassment ⟨acoso sexual : sexual harassment⟩
acostar {19} *vt* **1** : to lay (something) down **2** : to put to bed — **acostarse** *vr* **1** : to lie down **2** : to go to bed
acostumbrado, -da *adj* **1** HABITUADO : accustomed **2** HABITUAL : usual, customary
acostumbrar *vt* : to accustom — *vi* : to be accustomed, to be in the habit — **acostumbrarse** *vr*
acotación *nf*, *pl* **-ciones** **1** : marginal note **2** : stage direction
acotado, -da *adj* : enclosed
acotamiento *nm Mex* : shoulder (of a road)
acotar *vt* **1** ANOTAR : to note, to annotate **2** DELIMITAR : to mark off (land), to demarcate
acre¹ *adj* **1** : acrid, pungent **2** MORDAZ : caustic, biting
acre² *nm* : acre
acrecentamiento *nm* : growth, increase
acrecentar {55} *vt* AUMENTAR : to increase, to augment
acreditación *nf*, *pl* **-ciones** : accreditation
acreditado, -da *adj* **1** : accredited, authorized **2** : reputable
acreditar *vt* **1** : to accredit, to authorize **2** : to credit **3** : to prove, to verify — **acreditarse** *vr* : to gain a reputation
acreedor¹, -dora *adj* : deserving, worthy
acreedor², -dora *n* : creditor
acribillar *vt* **1** : to riddle, to pepper (with bullets, etc.) **2** : to hound, to harass
acrílico *nm* : acrylic
acrimonia *nf* **1** : pungency **2** : acrimony
acrimonioso, -sa *adj* : acrimonious
acriollarse *vr* : to adopt local customs, to go native
acritud *nf* **1** : pungency, bitterness **2** : intensity, sharpness **3** : harshness, asperity
acrobacia *nf* : acrobatics
acróbata *nmf* : acrobat
acrobático, -ca *adj* : acrobatic
acrónimo *nm* : acronym
acta *nf* **1** : document, certificate ⟨acta de nacimiento : birth certificate⟩ **2 actas** *nfpl* : minutes (of a meeting)
actitud *nf* **1** : attitude **2** : posture, position
activación *nf*, *pl* **-ciones** **1** : activation, stimulation **2** ACELERACIÓN : acceleration, speeding up
activar *vt* **1** : to activate **2** : to stimulate, to energize **3** : to speed up
actividad *nf* : activity
activista *nmf* : activist
activo¹, -va *adj* : active — **activamente** *adv*
activo² *nm* : assets *pl* ⟨activo y pasivo : assets and liabilities⟩

acto *nm* **1** ACCIÓN : act, deed **2** : act (in a play) **3 el acto sexual** : sexual intercourse **4 en el acto** : right away, on the spot **5 acto seguido** : immediately after

actor *nm* ARTISTA : actor

actriz *nf, pl* **actrices** ARTISTA : actress

actuación *nf, pl* **-ciones 1** : performance **2 actuaciones** *nfpl* DILIGENCIAS : proceedings

actual *adj* PRESENTE : present, current

actualidad *nf* **1** : present time ⟨en la actualidad : at present⟩ **2 actualidades** *nfpl* : current affairs

actualización *nf, pl* **-ciones** : updating, modernization

actualizar {21} *vt* : to modernize, to bring up to date

actualmente *adv* : at present, nowadays

actuar {3} *vi* : to act, to perform

actuarial *adj* : actuarial

actuario, -ria *n* : actuary

acuarela *nf* : watercolor

acuario *nm* : aquarium

Acuario *nmf* : Aquarius, Aquarian

acuartelar *vt* : to quarter (troops)

acuático, -ca *adj* : aquatic, water

acuchillar *vt* APUÑALAR : to knife, to stab

acuciante *adj* : pressing, urgent

acucioso, -sa → acuciante

acudir *vi* **1** : to go, to come (someplace for a specific purpose) ⟨acudió a la puerta : he went to the door⟩ ⟨acudimos en su ayuda : we came to her aid⟩ **2** : to be present, to show up ⟨acudí a la cita : I showed up for the appointment⟩ **3 ~ a** : to turn to, to have recourse to ⟨hay que acudir al médico : you must consult the doctor⟩

acueducto *nm* : aqueduct

acuerdo *nm* **1** : agreement **2 estar de acuerdo** : to agree **3 de acuerdo con** : in accordance with **4 de ~** : OK, all right

acuicultura *nf* : aquaculture

acullá *adv* : yonder, over there

acumulación *nf, pl* **-ciones** : accumulation

acumulador *nm* : storage battery

acumular *vt* : to accumulate, to amass — **acumularse** *vr* : to build up, to pile up

acumulativo, -va *adj* : cumulative — **acumulativamente** *adv*

acunar *vt* : to rock, to cradle

acuñar *vt* : to coin, to mint

acuoso, -sa *adj* : aqueous, watery

acupuntura *nf* : acupuncture

acurrucarse {72} *vr* : to cuddle, to nestle, to curl up

acusación *nf, pl* **-ciones 1** : accusation, charge **2 la acusación** : the prosecution

acusado¹, -da *adj* : prominent, marked

acusado², -da *n* : defendant

acusador, -dora *n* **1** : accuser **2** FISCAL : prosecutor

acusar *vt* **1** : to accuse, to charge **2** : to reveal, to betray ⟨sus ojos acusaban la desconfianza : his eyes revealed distrust⟩ — **acusarse** *vr* : to confess

acusativo *nm* : objective (in grammar)

acusatorio, -ria *adj* : accusatory

acuse *nm* **acuse de recibo** : acknowledgment of receipt

acústica *nf* : acoustics

acústico, -ca *adj* : acoustic

adagio *nm* **1** REFRÁN : adage, proverb **2** : adagio

adalid *nm* : leader, champion

adaptable *adj* : adaptable — **adaptabilidad** *nf*

adaptación *nf, pl* **-ciones** : adaptation, adjustment

adaptado, -da *adj* : suited, adapted

adaptador *nm* : adapter (in electricity)

adaptar *vt* **1** MODIFICAR : to adapt **2** : to adjust, to fit — **adaptarse** *vr* : to adapt oneself, to conform

adecentar *vt* : to tidy up

adecuación *nf, pl* **-ciones** ADAPTACIÓN : adaptation

adecuadamente *adv* : adequately

adecuado, -da *adj* **1** IDÓNEO : suitable, appropriate **2** : adequate

adecuar {8} *vt* : to adapt, to make suitable — **adecuarse** *vr* **~ a** : to be appropriate for, to fit in with

adefesio *nm* : eyesore, monstrosity

adelantado, -da *adj* **1** : advanced, ahead **2** : fast (of a clock or watch) **3 por ~** : in advance

adelantamiento *nm* **1** : advancement **2** : speeding up

adelantar *vt* **1** : to advance, to move forward **2** : to overtake, to pass **3** : to reveal (information) in advance **4** : to advance, to lend (money) — **adelantarse** *vr* **1** : to advance, to get in front **2 ~ a** : to forestall, to preempt

adelante *adv* **1** : ahead, in front, forward **2 más adelante** : further on, later on **3 ¡adelante!** : come in!

adelanto *nm* **1** : advance, progress **2** : advance payment **3** : earliness ⟨llevamos una hora de adelanto : we're running an hour ahead of time⟩

adelfa *nf* : oleander

adelgazar {21} *vt* : to thin, to reduce — *vi* : to lose weight

ademán *nm, pl* **-manes 1** GESTO : gesture **2 ademanes** *nmpl* : manners

además *adv* **1** : besides, furthermore **2 ~ de** : in addition to, as well as

adenoides *nfpl* : adenoids

adentrarse *vr* **~ en** : to go into, to penetrate

adentro *adv* : inside, within

adentros *nmpl* **decirse para sus adentros** : to say to oneself ⟨me dije para mis adentros que nunca regresaría : I told myself that I'd never go back⟩

adepto¹, -ta *adj* : supportive ⟨ser adepto a : to be a follower of⟩

adepto², -ta *n* PARTIDARIO : follower, supporter

aderezar {21} *vt* **1** SAZONAR : to season, to dress (salad) **2** : to embellish, to adorn

aderezo *nm* **1** : dressing, seasoning **2** : adornment, embellishment

adeudar *vt* **1** : to debit **2** DEBER : to owe

adeudo *nm* **1** DÉBITO : debit **2** *Mex* : debt, indebtedness

adherencia *nf* **1** : adherence, adhesiveness **2** : appendage, accretion

adherente *adj* : adhesive, sticky

adherirse {76} *vr* : to adhere, to stick

adhesión *nf, pl* **-siones 1** : adhesion **2** : attachment, commitment (to a cause, etc.)

adhesivo[1], **-va** *adj* : adhesive

adhesivo[2] *nm* : adhesive

adicción *nf, pl* **-ciones** : addiction

adición *nf, pl* **-ciones** : addition

adicional *adj* : additional — **adicionalmente** *adv*

adicionar *vt* : to add

adictivo, -va *adj* : addictive

adicto[1], **-ta** *adj* **1** : addicted **2** : devoted, dedicated

adicto[2], **-ta** *n* **1** : addict **2** PARTIDARIO : supporter, advocate

adiestrador, -dora *n* : trainer

adiestramiento *nm* : training

adiestrar *vt* : to train

adinerado, -da *adj* : moneyed, wealthy

adiós *nm, pl* **adioses 1** DESPEDIDA : farewell, good-bye **2** ¡adiós! : good-bye!

aditamento *nm* : attachment, accessory

aditivo *nm* : additive

adivinación *nf, pl* **-ciones 1** : guess **2** : divination, prediction

adivinanza *nf* ACERTIJO : riddle

adivinar *vt* **1** : to guess **2** : to foretell, to predict

adivino, -na *n* : fortune-teller

adjetivo[1], **-va** *adj* : adjectival

adjetivo[2] *nm* : adjective

adjudicación *nf, pl* **-ciones 1** : adjudication **2** : allocation, awarding, granting

adjudicar {72} *vt* **1** : to adjudge, to adjudicate **2** : to assign, to allocate ⟨adjudicar la culpa : to assign the blame⟩ **3** : to award, to grant

adjuntar *vt* : to enclose, to attach

adjunto[1], **-ta** *adj* : enclosed, attached

adjunto[2], **-ta** *n* : deputy, assistant

adjunto[3] *nm* : adjunct

administración *nf, pl* **-ciones 1** : administration, management **2 administración de empresas** : business administration

administrador, -dora *n* : administrator, manager

administrar *vt* : to administer, to manage, to run

administrativo, -va *adj* : administrative

admirable *adj* : admirable, impressive — **admirablemente** *adv*

admiración *nf, pl* **-ciones** : admiration

admirador, -dora *n* : admirer

admirar *vt* **1** : to admire **2** : to amaze, to astonish — **admirarse** *vr* : to be amazed

admirativo, -va *adj* : admiring

admisibilidad *nf* : admissibility

admisible *adj* : admissible, allowable

admisión *nf, pl* **-siones 1** : admission, admittance

admitir *vt* **1** : to admit, to let in **2** : to acknowledge, to concede **3** : to allow, to make room for ⟨la ley no admite cambios : the law doesn't allow for changes⟩

admonición *nf, pl* **-ciones** : admonition, warning

admonitorio, -ria *adj* : admonitory

ADN *nm* (*ácido desoxirribonucleico*) : DNA

adobar *vt* : to marinate

adobe *nm* : adobe

adobo *nm* **1** : marinade, seasoning **2** *Mex* : spicy marinade used for cooking pork

adoctrinamiento *nm* : indoctrination

adoctrinar *vt* : to indoctrinate

adolecer {53} *vi* PADECER : to suffer ⟨adolece de timidez : he suffers from shyness⟩

adolescencia *nf* : adolescence

adolescente[1] *adj* : adolescent, teenage

adolescente[2] *nmf* : adolescent, teenager

adonde *conj* : where ⟨el lugar adonde vamos es bello : the place where we're going is beautiful⟩

adónde *adv* : where ⟨¿adónde vamos? : where are we going?⟩

adondequiera *adv* : wherever, anywhere ⟨adondequiera que vayas : anywhere you go⟩

adopción *nf, pl* **-ciones** : adoption

adoptar *vt* **1** : to adopt (a measure), to take (a decision) **2** : to adopt (children)

adoptivo, -va *adj* **1** : adopted (children, country) **2** : adoptive (parents)

adoquín *nm, pl* **-quines** : paving stone, cobblestone

adorable *adj* : adorable, lovable

adoración *nf, pl* **-ciones** : adoration, worship

adorador[1], **-dora** *adj* : adoring, worshipping

adorador[2], **-dora** *n* : worshipper

adorar *vt* : to adore, to worship

adormecer {53} *vt* **1** : to make sleepy, to lull to sleep **2** : to numb — **adormecerse** *vr* **1** : to doze off **2** : to go numb

adormecimiento *nm* **1** SUEÑO : drowsiness, sleepiness **2** INSENSIBILIDAD : numbness

adormilarse *vr* : to doze, to drowse

adornar *vt* DECORAR : to decorate, to adorn

adorno *nm* : ornament, decoration

adquirido, -da *adj* **1** : acquired **2 mal adquirido** : ill-gotten

adquirir {4} *vt* **1** : to acquire, to gain **2** COMPRAR : to purchase

adquisición · afiliación

10

adquisición *nf, pl* **-ciones** 1 : acquisition 2 COMPRA : purchase
adquisitivo, -va *adj* **poder adquisitivo** : purchasing power
adrede *adv* : intentionally, on purpose
adrenalina *nf* : adrenaline
adscribir {33} *vt* : to assign, to appoint — adscribirse *vr* ~ a : to become a member of
adscripción *nf, pl* **-ciones** : assignment, appointment
adscrito *pp* → adscribir
aduana *nf* : customs, customs office
aduanero[1], -ra *adj* : customs
aduanero[2], -ra *n* : customs officer
aducir {61} *vt* : to adduce, to offer as proof
adueñarse *vr* ~ de : to take possession of, to take over
adulación *nf, pl* **-ciones** : adulation, flattery
adulador[1], -dora *adj* : flattering
adulador[2], -dora *n* : flatterer, toady
adular *vt* LISONJEAR : to flatter
adulteración *nf, pl* **-ciones** : adulteration
adulterar *vt* : to adulterate
adulterio *nm* : adultery
adúltero[1], -ra *adj* : adulterous
adúltero[2], -ra *n* : adulterer
adultez *nf* : adulthood
adulto, -ta *adj & n* : adult
adusto, -ta *adj* : harsh, severe
advenedizo, -za *n* 1 : upstart, parvenu 2 : newcomer
advenimiento *nm* : advent
adverbio *nm* : adverb — adverbial *adj*
adversario[1], -ria *adj* : opposing, contrary
adversario[2], -ria *n* OPOSITOR : adversary, opponent
adversidad *nf* : adversity
adverso, -sa *adj* DESFAVORABLE : adverse, unfavorable — adversamente *adv*
advertencia *nf* AVISO : warning
advertir {76} *vt* 1 AVISAR : to warn 2 : to notice, to tell ⟨no advertí que estuviera enojada : I couldn't tell she was angry⟩
Adviento *nm* : Advent
adyacente *adj* : adjacent
aéreo, -rea *adj* 1 : aerial, air 2 **correo aéreo** : airmail
aeróbic *nm* : aerobics
aeróbico, -ca *adj* : aerobic
aerobio, -bia *adj* : aerobic
aerodinámica *nf* : aerodynamics
aerodinámico, -ca *adj* : aerodynamic, streamlined
aeródromo *nm* : airfield
aeroespacial *adj* : aerospace
aerolínea *nf* : airline
aeromozo, -za *n* : flight attendant, steward *m*, stewardess *f*
aeronáutica *nf* : aeronautics
aeronáutico, -ca *adj* : aeronautical
aeronave *nf* : aircraft

aeropostal *adj* : airmail
aeropuerto *nm* : airport
aerosol *nm* : aerosol, aerosol spray
aeróstata *nmf* : balloonist
aerotransportado, -da *adj* : airborne
aerotransportar *vt* : to airlift
afabilidad *nf* : affability
afable *adj* : affable — afablemente *adv*
afamado, -da *adj* : well-known, famous
afán *nm, pl* **afanes** 1 ANHELO : eagerness, desire 2 EMPEÑO : effort, determination
afanador, -dora *n Mex* : cleaning person, cleaner
afanarse *vr* : to toil, to strive
afanosamente *adv* : zealously, industriously, busily
afanoso, -sa *adj* 1 : eager, industrious 2 : arduous, hard
afear *vt* : to make ugly, to disfigure
afección *nf, pl* **-ciones** 1 : fondness, affection 2 : illness, complaint
afectación *nf, pl* **-ciones** : affectation
afectado, -da *adj* 1 : affected, mannered 2 : influenced 3 : afflicted 4 : feigned
afectar *vt* 1 : to affect 2 : to upset 3 : to feign, to pretend
afectísimo, -ma *adj* **suyo afectísimo** : yours truly
afectivo, -va *adj* : emotional
afecto[1], -ta *adj* 1 : affected, afflicted 2 : fond, affectionate
afecto[2] *nm* CARIÑO : affection
afectuoso, -sa *adj* CARIÑOSO : affectionate, caring
afeitadora *nf* : shaver, electric razor
afeitar *vt* RASURAR : to shave — afeitarse *vr*
afelpado, -da *adj* : plush
afeminado, -da *adj* : effeminate
aferrado, -da *adj* : obstinate, stubborn
aferrarse {55} *vr* : to cling, to hold on
affidávit *nm, pl* **-dávits** : affidavit
afgano, -na *adj & n* : Afghan
AFI *nm* (Alfabeto Fonético Internacional) : IPA
afianzar {21} *vt* 1 : to secure, to strengthen 2 : to guarantee, to vouch for — afianzarse *vr* ESTABLECERSE : to establish oneself
afiche *nm* : poster
afición *nf, pl* **-ciones** 1 : enthusiasm, penchant, fondness ⟨afición al deporte : love of sports⟩ 2 PASATIEMPO : hobby
aficionado[1], -da *adj* ENTUSIASTA : enthusiastic, keen
aficionado[2], -da *n* 1 ENTUSIASTA : enthusiast, fan 2 : amateur
áfido *nm* : aphid
afiebrado, -da *adj* : feverish
afilado, -da *adj* 1 : sharp 2 : long, pointed ⟨una nariz afilada : a sharp nose⟩
afilador *nm* : sharpener
afilalápices *nms & pl* : pencil sharpener
afilar *vt* : to sharpen
afiliación *nf, pl* **-ciones** : affiliation

afiliado¹, -da *adj* : affiliated
afiliado², -da *n* : member
afiliarse *vr* : to become a member, to join, to affiliate
afín *adj, pl* **afines 1** PARECIDO : related, similar ⟨la biología y disciplinas afines : biology and related disciplines⟩ **2** PRÓXIMO : adjacent, nearby
afinación *nf, pl* **-ciones 1** : tune-up **2** : tuning (of an instrument)
afinador, -dora *n* : tuner (of musical instruments)
afinar *vt* **1** : to perfect, to refine **2** : to tune (an instrument) — *vi* : to sing or play in tune
afincarse {72} *vr* : to establish oneself, to settle in
afinidad *nf* : affinity, similarity
afirmación *nf, pl* **-ciones 1** : statement **2** : affirmation
afirmar *vt* **1** : to state, to affirm **2** REFORZAR : to make firm, to strengthen
afirmativo, -va *adj* : affirmative — **afirmativamente** *adv*
aflicción *nf, pl* **-ciones** DESCONSUELO, PESAR : grief, sorrow
afligido, -da *adj* : grief-stricken, sorrowful
afligir {35} *vt* **1** : to distress, to upset **2** : to afflict — **afligirse** *vr* : to grieve
aflojar *vt* **1** : to loosen, to slacken **2** *fam* : to pay up, to fork over — *vi* : to slacken, to ease up — **aflojarse** *vr* : to become loose, to slacken
afloramiento *nm* : outcropping, emergence
aflorar *vi* : to come to the surface, to emerge
afluencia *nf* **1** : flow, influx **2** : abundance, plenty
afluente *nm* : tributary
afluir {41} *vi* **1** : to flock ⟨la gente afluía a la frontera : people were flocking to the border⟩ **2** : to flow
aforismo *nm* : aphorism
aforo *nm* **1** : appraisal, assessment **2** : maximum capacity (of a theater, highway, etc.)
afortunado, -da *adj* : fortunate, lucky — **afortunadamente** *adv*
afrecho *nm* : bran, mash
afrenta *nf* : affront, insult
afrentar *vt* : to affront, to dishonor, to insult
africano, -na *adj & n* : African
afroamericano, -na *adj & n* : Afro-American
afrodisiaco *or* **afrodisíaco** *nm* : aphrodisiac
afrontamiento *nm* : confrontation
afrontar *vt* : to confront, to face up to
afrutado, -da *adj* : fruity
afuera *adv* **1** : out ⟨¡afuera! : get out!⟩ **2** : outside, outdoors
afueras *nfpl* ALEDAÑOS : outskirts
agachadiza *nf* : snipe (bird)
agachar *vt* : to lower (a part of the body) ⟨agachar la cabeza : to bow one's head⟩

— **agacharse** *vr* : to crouch, to stoop, to bend down
agalla *nf* **1** BRANQUIA : gill **2 tener agallas** *fam* : to have guts, to have courage
agarradera *nf* ASA, ASIDERO : handle, grip
agarrado, -da *adj fam* : cheap, stingy
agarrar *vt* **1** : to grab, to grasp **2** : to catch, to take — *vi* **agarrar y** *fam* : to do (something) abruptly ⟨el día siguiente agarró y se fue : the next day he up and left⟩ — **agarrarse** *vr* **1** : to hold on, to cling **2** *fam* : to get into a fight ⟨se agarraron a golpes : they came to blows⟩
agarre *nm* : grip, grasp
agarrotarse *vr* **1** : to stiffen up **2** : to seize up
agasajar *vt* : to fête, to wine and dine
agasajo *nm* : lavish attention
ágata *nf* : agate
agave *nm* : agave
agazaparse *vr* **1** AGACHARSE : to crouch **2** : to hide
agencia *nf* : agency, office
agenciar *vt* : to obtain, to procure — **agenciarse** *vr* : to manage, to get by
agenda *nf* **1** : agenda **2** : appointment book
agente *nmf* **1** : agent **2 agente de viajes** : travel agent **3 agente de bolsa** : stockbroker **4 agente de tráfico** : traffic officer
agigantado, -da *adj* GIGANTESCO : gigantic
agigantar *vt* **1** : to increase greatly, to enlarge **2** : to exaggerate
ágil *adj* **1** : agile, nimble **2** : sharp, lively (of a response, etc.) — **ágilmente** *adv*
agilidad *nf* : agility, nimbleness
agilizar {21} *vt* ACELERAR : to expedite, to speed up
agitación *nf, pl* **-ciones 1** : agitation **2** NERVIOSISMO : nervousness
agitado, -da *adj* **1** : agitated, excited **2** : choppy, rough, turbulent
agitador, -dora *n* PROVOCADOR : agitator
agitar *vt* **1** : to agitate, to shake **2** : to wave, to flap **3** : to stir up — **agitarse** *vr* **1** : to toss about, to flap around **2** : to get upset
aglomeración *nf, pl* **-ciones 1** : conglomeration, mass **2** GENTÍO : crowd
aglomerar *vt* : to cluster, to amass — **aglomerarse** *vr* : to crowd together
aglutinar *vt* : to bring together, to bind
agnóstico, -ca *adj & n* : agnostic
agobiado, -da *adj* : weary, worn-out, weighted-down
agobiante *adj* **1** : exhausting, overwhelming **2** : stifling, oppressive
agobiar *vt* **1** OPRIMIR : to oppress, to burden **2** ABRUMAR : to overwhelm **3** : to wear out, to exhaust
agonía *nf* : agony, death throes
agonizante *adj* : dying

agonizar {21} *vi* **1** : to be dying **2** : to be in agony **3** : to dim, to fade

agorero, -ra *adj* : ominous

agostar *vt* **1** : to parch **2** : to wither — **agostarse** *vr*

agosto *nm* **1** : August **2 hacer uno su agosto** : to make a fortune, to make a killing

agotado, -da *adj* **1** : exhausted, used up **2** : sold out **3** FATIGADO : worn-out, tired

agotador, -dora *adj* : exhausting

agotamiento *nm* FATIGA : exhaustion

agotar *vt* **1** : to exhaust, to use up **2** : to weary, to wear out — **agotarse** *vr*

agraciado¹, -da *adj* **1** : attractive **2** : fortunate

agraciado², -da *n* : winner

agradable *adj* GRATO, PLACENTERO : pleasant, agreeable — **agradablemente** *adv*

agradar *vi* : to be pleasing ⟨nos agradó mucho el resultado : we were very pleased with the result⟩

agradecer {53} *vt* **1** : to be grateful for **2** : to thank

agradecido, -da *adj* : grateful, thankful

agradecimiento *nm* : gratitude, thankfulness

agrado *nm* **1** GUSTO : taste, liking ⟨no es de su agrado : it's not to his liking⟩ **2** : graciousness, agreeableness **3 con ~** : with pleasure, willingly ⟨lo haré con agrado : I will be happy to do it⟩

agrandar *vt* **1** : to exaggerate **2** : to enlarge — **agrandarse** *vr*

agrario, -ria *adj* : agrarian, agricultural

agravación *nf, pl* **-ciones** : aggravation, worsening

agravante *adj* : aggravating

agravar *vt* **1** : to increase (weight), to make heavier **2** EMPEORAR : to aggravate, to worsen — **agravarse** *vr*

agraviar *vt* INJURIAR, OFENDER : to offend, to insult

agravio *nm* INJURIA : affront, offense, insult

agredir {1} *vt* : to assail, to attack

agregado¹, -da *n* **1** : attaché **2** : assistant professor

agregado² ** *nm* **1 : aggregate **2** AÑADIDURA : addition, something added

agregar {52} *vt* **1** AÑADIR : to add, to attach **2** : to appoint — **agregarse** *vr* : to join

agresión *nf, pl* **-siones** **1** : aggression **2** ATAQUE : attack

agresividad *nf* : aggressiveness, aggression

agresivo, -va *adj* : aggressive — **agresivamente** *adv*

agresor¹, -sora *adj* : hostile, attacking

agresor², -sora *n* **1** : aggressor **2** : assailant, attacker

agreste *adj* **1** CAMPESTRE : rural **2** : wild, untamed

agriar *vt* **1** : to sour, to make sour **2** : to embitter — **agriarse** *vr* : to turn sour

agrícola *adj* : agricultural

agricultor, -tora *n* : farmer, grower

agricultura *nf* : agriculture, farming

agridulce *adj* **1** : bittersweet **2** : sweet-and-sour

agrietar *vt* : to crack — **agrietarse** *vr* **1** : to crack **2** : to chap

agrimensor, -sora *n* : surveyor

agrimensura *nf* : surveying

agrio, agria *adj* **1** ÁCIDO : sour **2** : caustic, acrimonious

agriparse *vr* : to catch the flu

agroindustria *nf* : agribusiness

agronomía *nf* : agronomy

agropecuario, -ria *adj* : pertaining to livestock and agriculture

agrupación *nf, pl* **-ciones** GRUPO : group, association

agrupamiento *nm* : grouping, concentration

agrupar *vt* : to group together

agua *nf* **1** : water **2 agua oxigenada** : hydrogen peroxide **3 aguas negras** *or* **aguas residuales** : sewage **4 como agua para chocolate** *Mex fam* : furious **5 echar aguas** *Mex fam* : to keep an eye out, to be on the lookout

aguacate *nm* : avocado

aguacero *nm* : shower, downpour

aguado, -da *adj* **1** DILUIDO : watered-down, diluted **2** *CA, Col, Mex fam* : soft, flabby **3** *Mex, Peru fam* : dull, boring

aguafiestas *nmfs & pl* : killjoy, stick-in-the-mud, spoilsport

aguafuerte *nm* : etching

aguamanil *nm* : ewer, pitcher

aguanieve *nf* : sleet ⟨caer aguanieve : to be sleeting⟩

aguantar *vt* **1** SOPORTAR : to bear, to tolerate, to withstand **2** : to hold **3 aguantar las ganas** : to resist an urge ⟨no pude aguantar las ganas de reír : I couldn't keep myself from laughing⟩ — *vi* : to hold out, to last — **aguantarse** *vr* **1** : to resign oneself **2** : to restrain oneself

aguante *nm* **1** TOLERANCIA : tolerance, patience **2** RESISTENCIA : endurance, strength

aguar {10} *vt* **1** : to water down, to dilute **2 aguar la fiesta** *fam* : to spoil the party

aguardar *vt* ESPERAR : to wait for, to await — *vi* : to be in store

aguardiente *nm* : clear brandy

aguarrás *nm* : turpentine

agudeza *nf* **1** : keenness, sharpness **2** : shrillness **3** : witticism

agudizar {21} *vt* : to intensify, to heighten

agudo, -da *adj* **1** : acute, sharp **2** : shrill, high-pitched **3** PERSPICAZ : clever, shrewd

agüero *nm* AUGURIO, PRESAGIO : augury, omen

aguijón *nm, pl* **-jones** **1** : stinger (of a bee, etc.) **2** : goad

aguijonear *vt* : to goad
águila *nf* **1** : eagle **2 águila o sol** *Mex* : heads or tails
aguileño, -ña *adj* : aquiline
aguilera *nf* : aerie, eagle's nest
aguilón *nm, pl* **-lones** : gable
aguinaldo *nm* **1** : Christmas bonus, year-end bonus **2** *PRi, Ven* : Christmas carol
agüitarse *vr Mex fam* : to have the blues, to feel discouraged
aguja *nf* **1** : needle **2** : steeple, spire
agujerear *vt* : to make a hole in, to pierce
agujero *nm* **1** : hole **2 agujero negro** : black hole (in astronomy)
agujeta *nf* **1** *Mex* : shoelace **2 agujetas** *nfpl* : muscular soreness or stiffness
agusanado, -da *adj* : worm-eaten
aguzar {21} *vt* **1** : to sharpen ⟨aguzar el ingenio : to sharpen one's wits⟩ **2 aguzar el oído** : to prick up one's ears
ah *interj* : oh!
ahí *adv* **1** : there ⟨ahí está : there it is⟩ **2 por ~** : somewhere, thereabouts **3 de ahí que** : with the result that, so that
ahijado, -da *n* : godchild, godson *m*, goddaughter *f*
ahijar {5} *vt* : to adopt (a child)
ahínco *nm* : eagerness, zeal
ahogar {52} *vt* **1** : to drown **2** : to smother **3** : to choke back, to stifle — **ahogarse** *vr*
ahogo *nm* : breathlessness, suffocation
ahondar *vt* : to deepen — *vi* : to elaborate, to go into detail
ahora *adv* **1** : now **2 ahora mismo** : right now **3 hasta ~** : so far **4 por ~** : for the time being
ahorcar {72} *vt* : to hang, to kill by hanging — **ahorcarse** *vr*
ahorita *adv fam* : right now, right away
ahorquillado, -da *adj* : forked
ahorrador, -dora *adj* : thrifty
ahorrar *vt* **1** : to save (money) **2** : to spare, to conserve — *vi* : to save up — **ahorrarse** *vr* : to spare oneself
ahorrativo, -va *adj* : thrifty, frugal
ahorro *nm* : saving ⟨cuenta de ahorros : savings account⟩
ahuecar {72} *vt* **1** : to hollow out **2** : to cup (one's hands) **3** : to plump up, to fluff up
ahuizote *nm Mex fam* : annoying person, pain in the neck
ahumar {8} *vt* : to smoke, to cure
ahuyentar *vt* **1** : to scare away, to chase away **2** : to banish, to dispel ⟨ahuyentar las dudas : to dispel doubts⟩
airado, -da *adj* FURIOSO : angry, irate
airar {5} *vt* : to make angry, to anger
aire *nm* **1** : air **2 aire acondicionado** : air-conditioning **3 darse aires** : to give oneself airs
airear *vt* : to air, to air out — **airearse** *vr* : to get some fresh air
airoso, -sa *adj* **1** : elegant, graceful **2 salir airoso** : to come out winning
aislacionismo *nm* : isolationism

aislacionista *adj & nmf* : isolationist
aislado, -da *adj* : isolated, alone
aislador *nm* : insulator (part)
aislamiento *nm* **1** : isolation **2** : insulation
aislante *nm* : insulator, nonconductor
aislar {5} *vt* **1** : to isolate **2** : to insulate
ajado, -da *adj* **1** : worn, shabby **2** : wrinkled, crumpled
ajar *vt* : to wear out, to spoil
ajardinado, -da *adj* : landscaped
ajedrecista *nmf* : chess player
ajedrez *nm, pl* **-dreces 1** : chess **2** : chess set
ajeno, -na *adj* **1** : alien **2** : of another, of others ⟨propiedad ajena : somebody else's property⟩ **3 ~ a** : foreign to **4 ~ de** : devoid of, free from
ajetreado, -da *adj* : hectic, busy
ajetrearse *vr* : to bustle about, to rush around
ajetreo *nm* : hustle and bustle, fuss
ají *nm, pl* **ajíes** : chili pepper
ajo *nm* : garlic
ajonjolí *nm, pl* **-líes** : sesame
ajuar *nm* : trousseau
ajustable *adj* : adjustable
ajustado, -da *adj* **1** CEÑIDO : tight, tight-fitting **2** : close, tight ⟨una ajustada victoria : a close victory⟩
ajustar *vt* **1** : to adjust, to adapt **2** : to take in (clothing) **3** : to settle, to resolve — **ajustarse** *vr* : to fit, to conform
ajuste *nm* **1** : adjustment **2** : tightening
ajusticiar *vt* EJECUTAR : to execute, to put to death
al *prep* (contraction of a and el) → **a²**
ala *nf* **1** : wing **2** : brim (of a hat)
Alá *nm* : Allah
alabanza *nf* ELOGIO : praise
alabar *vt* : to praise — **alabarse** *vr* : to boast
alabastro *nm* : alabaster
alabear *vt* : to warp — **alabearse** *vr*
alabeo *nm* : warp, warping
alacena *nf* : cupboard, larder
alacrán *nm, pl* **-cranes** ESCORPIÓN : scorpion
alado, -da *adj* : winged
alambique *nm* : still (to distill alcohol)
alambre *nm* **1** : wire **2 alambre de púas** : barbed wire
alameda *nf* **1** : poplar grove **2** : tree-lined avenue
álamo *nm* **1** : poplar **2 álamo temblón** : aspen
alar *nm* : eaves *pl*
alarde *nm* **1** : show, display **2 hacer alarde de** : to make show of, to boast about
alardear *vi* PRESUMIR : to boast, to brag
alargado, -da *adj* : elongated, slender
alargamiento *nm* : lengthening, extension, elongation
alargar {52} *vt* **1** : to extend, to lengthen **2** PROLONGAR : to prolong — **alargarse** *vr*

alarido *nm* : howl, shriek
alarma *nf* : alarm
alarmante *adj* : alarming — alarmante-
mente *adv*
alarmar *vt* : to alarm
alazán *nm*, *pl* -zanes : sorrel (color or
animal)
alba *nf* AMANECER : dawn, daybreak
albacea *nmf* TESTAMENTARIO : executor, executrix *f*
albahaca *nf* : basil
albanés, -nesa *adj & n*, *mpl* -neses : Albanian
albañil *nmf* : bricklayer, mason
albañilería *nf* : bricklaying, masonry
albaricoque *nm* : apricot
albatros *nm* : albatross
albedrío *nm* : will ⟨libre albedrío : free
will⟩
alberca *nf* 1 : reservoir, tank 2 *Mex*
: swimming pool
albergar {52} *vt* ALOJAR : to house, to
lodge, to shelter
albergue *nm* 1 : shelter, refuge 2 : hostel
albino, -na *adj & n* : albino — albinis-
mo *nm*
albóndiga *nf* : meatball
albor *nm* 1 : dawning, beginning 2
BLANCURA : whiteness
alborada *nf* : dawn
alborear *v impers* : to dawn
alborotado, -da *adj* 1 : excited, agitated 2 : rowdy, unruly
alborotador¹, -dora *adj* 1 : noisy, boisterous 2 : rowdy, unruly
alborotador², -dora *n* : agitator, troublemaker, rioter
alborotar *vt* 1 : to excite, to agitate 2
: to incite, to stir up — alborotarse *vr*
1 : to get excited 2 : to riot
alboroto *nm* 1 : disturbance, ruckus 2
MOTÍN : riot
alborozado, -da *adj* : jubilant
alborozar {21} *vt* : to gladden, to cheer
alborozo *nm* : joy, elation
álbum *nm* : album ⟨álbum de recortes
: scrapbook⟩
albúmina *nf* : albumin
albur *nm* 1 : chance, risk 2 *Mex* : pun
alca *nf* : auk
alcachofa *nf* : artichoke
alcahuete, -ta *n* CHISMOSO : gossip
alcaide *nm* : warden (in a prison)
alcalde, -desa *n* : mayor
alcaldía *nf* 1 : mayoralty 2 AYUN-
TAMIENTO : city hall
álcali *nm* : alkali
alcalino, -na *adj* : alkaline — alcalin-
idad *nf*
alcance *nm* 1 : reach 2 : range, scope
alcancía *nf* 1 : piggy bank, money box
2 : collection box (for alms, etc.)
alcanfor *nm* : camphor
alcantarilla *nf* CLOACA : sewer, drain
alcanzar {21} *vt* 1 : to reach 2 : to catch
up with 3 LOGRAR : to achieve, to at-

tain — *vi* 1 DAR : to suffice, to be
enough 2 ~ a : to manage to
alcaparra *nf* : caper
alcapurria *nf PRi* : stuffed fritter made
with taro and green banana
alcaravea *nf* : caraway
alcatraz *nm*, *pl* -traces : gannet
alcázar *nm* : fortress, castle
alce¹, etc. → alzar
alce² *nm* : moose, European elk
alcoba *nf* : bedroom
alcohol *nm* : alcohol
alcohólico, -ca *adj & n* : alcoholic
alcoholismo *nm* : alcoholism
alcoholizarse {21} *vr* : to become an alcoholic
alcornoque *nm* 1 : cork oak 2 *fam* : idiot, fool
alcurnia *nf* : ancestry, lineage
aldaba *nf* : door knocker
aldea *nf* : village
aldeano¹, -na *adj* : village, rustic
aldeano², -na *n* : villager
aleación *nf*, *pl* -ciones : alloy
alear *vt* : to alloy
aleatorio, -ria *adj* : random, fortuitous
— aleatoriamente *adv*
alebrestar *vt* : to excite, to make nervous — alebrestarse *vr*
aledaño, -ña *adj* : bordering, neighboring
aledaños *nmpl* AFUERAS : outskirts,
surrounding area
alegar {52} *vt* : to assert, to allege — *vi*
DISCUTIR : to argue
alegato *nm* 1 : allegation, claim 2 *Mex*
: argument, summation (in law) 3 : argument, dispute
alegoría *nf* : allegory
alegórico, -ca *adj* : allegorical
alegrar *vt* : to make happy, to cheer up
— alegrarse *vr* : to be glad, to rejoice
alegre *adj* 1 : glad, cheerful 2 : colorful, bright 3 *fam* : tipsy
alegremente *adv* : happily, cheerfully
alegría *nf* : joy, cheer, happiness
alejado, -da *adj* : remote
alejamiento *nm* 1 : removal, separation
2 : estrangement
alejar *vt* 1 : to remove, to move away 2
: to estrange, to alienate — alejarse *vr*
1 : to move away, to stray 2 : to drift
apart
alelado, -da *adj* 1 : bewildered, stupe-
fied 2 : foolish, stupid
aleluya *interj* : hallelujah!, alleluia!
alemán¹, -mana *adj & n*, *mpl* -manes
: German
alemán² *nm* : German (language)
alentador, -dora *adj* : encouraging
alentar {55} *vt* : to encourage, to inspire
— *vi* : to breathe
alerce *nm* : larch
alérgeno *nm* : allergen
alergia *nf* : allergy
alérgico, -ca *adj* : allergic
alero *nm* 1 : eaves *pl* 2 : forward (in
basketball)

15

alerón *nm, pl* **-rones** : aileron
alerta¹ *adv* : on the alert
alerta² *adj & nf* : alert
alertar *vt* : to alert
aleta *nf* **1** : fin **2** : flipper **3** : small wing
aletargado, -da *adj* : lethargic, sluggish, torpid
aletargarse {52} *vr* : to feel drowsy, to become lethargic
aletear *vi* : to flutter, to flap one's wings
aleteo *nm* : flapping, flutter
alevín *nm, pl* **-vines 1** : fry, young fish **2** PRINCIPIANTE : beginner
alevosía *nf* **1** : treachery **2** : premeditation
alevoso, -sa *adj* : treacherous
alfabético, -ca *adj* : alphabetical — **alfabéticamente** *adv*
alfabetismo *nm* : literacy
alfabetizado, -da *adj* : literate
alfabetizar {21} *vt* : to alphabetize
alfabeto *nm* : alphabet
alfalfa *nf* : alfalfa
alfanje *nm* : cutlass, scimitar
alfarería *nf* : pottery
alfarero, -ra *n* : potter
alféizar *nm* : sill, windowsill
alfeñique *nm fam* : wimp, weakling
alférez *nmf, pl* **-reces 1** : second lieutenant **2** : ensign
alfil *nm* : bishop (in chess)
alfiler *nm* **1** : pin **2** BROCHE : brooch
alfiletero *nm* : pincushion
alfombra *nf* : carpet, rug
alfombrado *nm* : carpeting
alfombrar *vt* : to carpet
alfombrilla *nf* : small rug, mat
alforfón *nm, pl* **-fones** : buckwheat
alforja *nf* : saddlebag
alforza *nf* : pleat, tuck
alga *nf* **1** : aquatic plant, alga **2** : seaweed
algarabía *nf* **1** : gibberish, babble **2** : hubbub, uproar
álgebra *nf* : algebra
algebraico, -ca *adj* : algebraic
álgido, -da *adj* **1** : critical, decisive **2** : icy cold
algo¹ *adv* : somewhat, rather ⟨es simpático, pero algo tacaño : he's nice but rather stingy⟩
algo² *pron* **1** : something **2** ~ **de** : some, a little ⟨tengo algo de dinero : I've got some money⟩
algodón *nm, pl* **-dones** : cotton
algoritmo *nm* : algorithm
alguacil *nm* : constable
alguien *pron* : somebody, someone
alguno¹, -na *adj* (**algún** *before masculine singular nouns*) **1** : some, any ⟨algún día : someday, one day⟩ **2** (*in negative constructions*) : not any, not at all ⟨no tengo noticia alguna : I have no news at all⟩ **3 algunas veces** : sometimes
alguno², -na *pron* **1** : one, someone, somebody ⟨alguno de ellos : one of them⟩ **2 algunos, -nas** *pron pl* : some,

a few ⟨algunos quieren trabajar : some want to work⟩
alhaja *nf* : jewel, gem
alhajar *vt* : to adorn with jewels
alharaca *nf* : fuss
alhelí *nm* : wallflower
aliado¹, -da *adj* : allied
aliado², -da *n* : ally
alianza *nf* : alliance
aliarse {85} *vr* : to form an alliance, to ally oneself
alias *adv & nm* : alias
alicaído, -da *adj* : depressed, discouraged
alicates *nmpl* PINZAS : pliers
aliciente *nm* **1** INCENTIVO : incentive **2** ATRACCIÓN : attraction
alienación *nf, pl* **-ciones** : alienation, derangement
alienar *vt* ENAJENAR : to alienate
aliento *nm* **1** : breath **2** : courage, strength **3 dar aliento a** : to encourage
aligerar *vt* **1** : to lighten **2** ACELERAR : to hasten, to quicken
alijo *nm* : cache, consignment (of contraband)
alimaña *nf* : pest, vermin
alimentación *nf, pl* **-ciones** NUTRICIÓN : nutrition, nourishment
alimentar *vt* **1** NUTRIR : to feed, to nourish **2** MANTENER : to support (a family) **3** FOMENTAR : to nurture, to foster — **alimentarse** *vr* ~ **con** : to live on
alimentario, -ria → **alimenticio**
alimenticio, -cia *adj* **1** : nutritional, food, dietary **2** : nutritious, nourishing
alimento *nm* : food, nourishment
aliñar *vt* **1** : to dress (salad) **2** CONDIMENTAR : to season
alineación *nf, pl* **-ciones 1** : alignment **2** : lineup (in sports)
alineamiento *nm* : alignment
alinear *vt* **1** : to align **2** : to line up — **alinearse** *vr* **1** : to fall in, to line up **2** ~ **con** : to align oneself with
aliño *nm* : seasoning, dressing
alipús *nm, pl* **-puses** *Mex fam* : booze, drink
alisar *vt* : to smooth
aliso *nm* : alder
alistamiento *nm* : enlistment, recruitment
alistar *vt* **1** : to recruit **2** : to make ready — **alistarse** *vr* : to join up, to enlist
aliteración *nf, pl* **-ciones** : alliteration
aliviar *vt* MITIGAR : to relieve, to alleviate, to soothe — **aliviarse** *vr* : to recover, to get better
alivio *nm* : relief
aljaba *nf* : quiver (for arrows)
aljibe *nm* : cistern, well
allá *adv* **1** : there, over there **2 más allá** : farther away **3 más allá de** : beyond **4 allá tú** : that's up to you

allanamiento *nm* **1** : (police) raid **2 allanamiento de morada** : breaking and entering

allanar *vt* **1** : to raid, to search **2** : to resolve, to solve **3** : to smooth, to level out

allegado¹, -da *adj* : close, intimate

allegado², -da *n* **1** : close friend, relation ⟨parientes y allegados : friends and relations⟩

allegar {52} *vt* : to gather, to collect

allende¹ *adv* : beyond, on the other side

allende² *prep* : beyond ⟨allende las montañas : beyond the mountains⟩

allí *adv* : there, over there ⟨allí mismo : right there⟩ ⟨hasta allí : up to that point⟩

alma *nf* **1** : soul **2** : person, human being **3 no tener alma** : to be pitiless **4 tener el alma en un hilo** : to have one's heart in one's mouth

almacén *nm, pl* **-cenes 1** BODEGA : warehouse, storehouse **2** TIENDA : shop, store **3 gran almacén** *Spain* : department store

almacenaje → **almacenamiento**

almacenamiento *nm* : storage ⟨almacenamiento de datos : data storage⟩

almacenar *vt* : to store, to put in storage

almacenero, -ra *n* : shopkeeper

almacenista *nm* MAYORISTA : wholesaler

almádena *nf* : sledgehammer

almanaque *nm* : almanac

almeja *nf* : clam

almendra *nf* **1** : almond **2** : kernel

almendro *nm* : almond tree

almiar *nm* : haystack

almíbar *nm* : syrup

almidón *nm, pl* **-dones** : starch

almidonar *vt* : to starch

alminar *nm* MINARETE : minaret

almirante *nm* : admiral

almizcle *nm* : musk

almohada *nf* : pillow

almohadilla *nf* **1** : small pillow, cushion **2** : bag, base (in baseball)

almohadón *nm, pl* **-dones** : bolster, cushion

almohazar {21} *vt* : to curry (a horse)

almoneda *nf* SUBASTA : auction

almorranas *nfpl* HEMORROIDES : hemorrhoids, piles

almorzar {36} *vi* : to have lunch — *vt* : to have for lunch

almuerzo *nm* : lunch

alocado, -da *adj* **1** : crazy **2** : wild, reckless **3** : silly, scatterbrained

alocución *nf, pl* **-ciones** : speech, address

áloe *or* **aloe** *nm* : aloe

alojamiento *nm* : lodging, accommodations *pl*

alojar *vt* ALBERGAR : to house, to lodge — **alojarse** *vr* : to lodge, to room

alondra *nf* : lark, skylark

alpaca *nf* : alpaca

alpinismo *nm* : mountain climbing, mountaineering

alpinista *nmf* : mountain climber

alpino, -na *adj* : Alpine, alpine

alpiste *nm* : birdseed

alquilar *vt* ARRENDAR : to rent, to lease

alquiler *nm* ARRENDAMIENTO : rent, rental

alquimia *nf* : alchemy

alquimista *nmf* : alchemist

alquitrán *nm, pl* **-tranes** BREA : tar

alquitranar *vt* : to tar, to cover with tar

alrededor¹ *adv* **1** : around, about ⟨todo temblaba alrededor : all around things were shaking⟩ **2 ~ de** : around, approximately ⟨alrededor de quince personas : around fifteen people⟩

alrededor² *prep* **~ de** : around, about ⟨corrió alrededor de la casa : she ran around the house⟩ ⟨llegaré alrededor de diciembre : I will get there around December⟩

alrededores *nmpl* ALEDAÑOS : surroundings, outskirts

alta *nf* **1** : admission, entry, enrollment **2 dar de alta** : to release, to discharge (a patient)

altanería *nf* ALTIVEZ, ARROGANCIA : arrogance, haughtiness

altanero, -ra *adj* ALTIVO, ARROGANTE : arrogant, haughty — **altaneramente** *adv*

altar *nm* : altar

altavoz *nm, pl* **-voces** ALTOPARLANTE : loudspeaker

alteración *nf, pl* **-ciones 1** MODIFICACIÓN : alteration, modification **2** PERTURBACIÓN : disturbance, disruption

alterado, -da *adj* : upset

alterar *vt* **1** MODIFICAR : to alter, to modify **2** PERTURBAR : to disturb, to disrupt — **alterarse** *vr* : to get upset, to get worked up

altercado *nm* DISCUSIÓN, DISPUTA : altercation, argument, dispute

alternador *nm* : alternator

alternancia *nf* : alternation, rotation

alternar *vi* **1** : to alternate **2** : to mix, to socialize — *vt* : to alternate — **alternarse** *vr* : to take turns

alternativa *nf* OPCIÓN : alternative, option

alternativo, -va *adj* **1** : alternating **2** : alternative — **alternativamente** *adv*

alterno, -na *adj* : alternate ⟨corriente alterna : alternating current⟩

alteza *nf* **1** : loftiness, lofty height **2 Alteza** : Highness

altibajos *nmpl* **1** : unevenness (of terrain) **2** : ups and downs

altímetro *nm* : altimeter

altiplanicie *nf* → **altiplano**

altiplano *nm* : high plateau, upland

altisonante *adj* **1** : pompous, affected (of language) **2** *Mex* : rude, obscene (of language)

altitud *nf* : altitude

altivez *nf, pl* **-veces** ALTANERÍA, ARROGANCIA : arrogance, haughtiness

altivo, -va *adj* ALTANERO, ARROGANTE : arrogant, haughty

alto¹ *adv* **1** : high **2** : loud, loudly

alto², -ta *adj* **1** : tall, high **2** : loud ⟨en voz alta : aloud, out loud⟩

alto³ *nm* **1** ALTURA : height, elevation **2** : stop, halt **3 altos** *nmpl* : upper floors

alto⁴ *interj* : halt!, stop!

altoparlante *nm* ALTAVOZ : loudspeaker

altozano *nm* : hillock

altruismo *nm* : altruism

altruista¹ *adj* : altruistic

altruista² *nmf* : altruist

altura *nf* **1** : height **2** : altitude **3** : loftiness, nobleness **4 a la altura de** : near, up by ⟨en la avenida San Antonio a la altura de la Calle Tres : on San Antonio Avenue up near Third Street⟩ **5 a estas alturas** : at this point, at this stage of the game

alubia *nf* : kidney bean

alucinación *nf, pl* **-ciones** : hallucination

alucinante *adj* : hallucinatory

alucinar *vi* : to hallucinate

alucinógeno¹, -na *adj* : hallucinogenic

alucinógeno² *nm* : hallucinogen

alud *nm* AVALANCHA : avalanche, landslide

aludido, -da *n* **1** : person in question ⟨el aludido : the aforesaid⟩ **2 darse por aludido** : to take it personally

aludir *vi* : to allude, to refer

alumbrado *nm* ILUMINACIÓN : lighting

alumbramiento *nm* **1** : lighting **2** : childbirth

alumbrar *vt* **1** ILUMINAR : to light, to illuminate **2** : to give birth to

alumbre *nm* : alum

aluminio *nm* : aluminum

alumnado *nm* : student body

alumno, -na *n* **1** : pupil, student **2 ex–alumno, -na** : alumnus, alumna *f* **3 ex–alumnos, -nas** *npl* : alumni, alumnae *f*

alusión *nf, pl* **-siones** : allusion, reference

alusivo, -va *adj* **1** : allusive **2 ∼ a** : in reference to, regarding

aluvión *nm, pl* **-viones** : flood, barrage

alza *nf* SUBIDA : rise ⟨precios en alza : rising prices⟩

alzamiento *nm* LEVANTAMIENTO : uprising, insurrection

alzar {21} *vt* **1** ELEVAR, LEVANTAR : to lift, to raise **2** : to erect — **alzarse** *vr* LEVANTARSE : to rise up

ama *nf* → **amo**

amabilidad *nf* : kindness

amable *adj* : kind, nice — **amablemente** *adv*

amado¹, -da *adj* : beloved, darling

amado², -da *n* : sweetheart, loved one

amaestrar *vt* : to train (animals)

amafiarse *vr Mex fam* : to conspire, to be in cahoots

amagar {52} *vt* **1** : to show signs of (an illness, etc.) **2** : to threaten — *vi* **1** : to be imminent, to threaten **2** : to feint, to dissemble

amago *nm* **1** AMENAZA : threat **2** : sign, hint

amainar *vi* : to abate, to ease up, to die down

amalgama *nf* : amalgam

amalgamar *vt* : to amalgamate, to unite

amamantar *v* : to breast-feed, to nurse, to suckle

amanecer¹ {53} *v impers* **1** : to dawn **2** : to begin to show, to appear **3** : to wake up (in the morning)

amanecer² *nm* ALBA : dawn, daybreak

amanerado, -da *adj* : affected, mannered

amansar *vt* **1** : to tame **2** : to soothe, to calm down — **amansarse** *vr*

amante¹ *adj* : loving, fond

amante² *nmf* : lover

amañar *vt* : to rig, to fix, to tamper with — **amañarse** *vr* **amañárselas** : to manage

amaño *nm* **1** : skill, dexterity **2** : trick, ruse

amapola *nf* : poppy

amar *vt* : to love — **amarse** *vr*

amargado, -da *adj* : embittered, bitter

amargar {52} *vt* : to make bitter, to embitter — *vi* : to taste bitter

amargo¹, -ga *adj* : bitter — **amargamente** *adv*

amargo² *nm* : bitterness, tartness

amargura *nf* **1** : bitterness **2** : grief, sorrow

amarilis *nf* : amaryllis

amarillear *vi* : to yellow, to turn yellow

amarillento, -ta *adj* : yellowish

amarillismo *nm* : yellow journalism, sensationalism

amarillo¹, -lla *adj* : yellow

amarillo² *nm* : yellow

amarra *nf* **1** : mooring, mooring line **2 soltar las amarras de** : to loosen one's grip on

amarrar *vt* **1** : to moor (a boat) **2** ATAR : to fasten, to tie up, to tie down

amartillar *vt* : to cock (a gun)

amasar *vt* **1** : to amass **2** : to knead **3** : to mix, to prepare

amasijo *nm* : jumble, hodgepodge

amasio, -sia *n* : lover, paramour

amateur *adj & nmf* : amateur — **amateurismo** *nm*

amatista *nf* : amethyst

amatorio, -ria *adj* : amatory, sexual ⟨poesía amatoria : love poems⟩

amazona *nf* **1** : Amazon (in mythology) **2** : horsewoman

amazónico, -ca *adj* : amazonian

ambages *nmpl* **sin ∼** : without hesitation, straight to the point

ámbar *nm* **1** : amber **2 ámbar gris** : ambergris

ambición *nf, pl* **-ciones** : ambition

ambicionar *vt* : to aspire to, to seek

ambicioso, -sa *adj* : ambitious — **ambiciosamente** *adv*

ambidextro, -tra *adj* : ambidextrous

ambientación *nf, pl* -ciones : setting, atmosphere

ambiental *adj* : environmental — **ambientalmente** *adv*

ambientalista *nmf* : environmentalist

ambientar *vt* : to give atmosphere to, to set (in literature and drama) — **ambientarse** *vr* : to adjust, to get one's bearings

ambiente *nm* 1 : atmosphere 2 : environment 3 : surroundings *pl*

ambigüedad *nf* : ambiguity

ambiguo, -gua *adj* : ambiguous

ámbito *nm* : domain, field, area

ambivalencia *nf* : ambivalence

ambivalente *adj* : ambivalent

ambos, -bas *adj & pron* : both

ambulancia *nf* : ambulance

ambulante *adj* 1 : traveling, itinerant 2 vendedor ambulante : street vendor

ameba *nf* : amoeba

amedrentar *vt* : to frighten, to intimidate — **amedrentarse** *vr*

amén *nm* 1 : amen 2 ~ de : in addition to, besides 3 en un decir amén : in an instant

amenaza *nf* : threat, menace

amenazador, -dora *adj* : threatening, menacing

amenazante → **amenazador**

amenazar {21} *v* : to threaten

amenguar {10} *vt* 1 : to diminish 2 : to belittle, to dishonor

amenidad *nf* : pleasantness, amenity

amenizar {21} *vt* 1 : to make pleasant 2 : to brighten up, to add life to

ameno, -na *adj* : agreeable, pleasant

amento *nm* : catkin

americano, -na *adj & n* : American

amerindio, -dia *adj & n* : Amerindian

ameritar *vt* MERECER : to deserve

ametralladora *nf* : machine gun

amianto *nm* : asbestos

amiba → **ameba**

amigable *adj* : friendly, amicable — **amigablemente** *adv*

amígdala *nf* : tonsil

amigdalitis *nf* : tonsilitis

amigo[1], -ga *adj* : friendly, close

amigo[2], -ga *n* : friend

amigote *nm* : crony, pal

amilanar *vt* 1 : to frighten 2 : to daunt, to discourage — **amilanarse** *vr* : to lose heart

aminoácido *nm* : amino acid

aminorar *vt* : to reduce, to lessen — *vi* : to diminish

amistad *nf* : friendship

amistoso, -sa *adj* : friendly — **amistosamente** *adv*

amnesia *nf* : amnesia

amnésico, -ca *adj & n* : amnesiac, amnesic

amnistía *nf* : amnesty

amnistiar {85} *vt* : to grant amnesty to

amo, ama *n* 1 : master *m*, mistress *f* 2 : owner, keeper (of an animal) 3 ama de casa : housewife 4 ama de llaves : housekeeper

amodorrado, -da *adj* : drowsy

amolar {19} *vt* 1 : to grind, to sharpen 2 : to pester, to annoy

amoldable *adj* : adaptable

amoldar *vt* 1 : to mold 2 : to adapt, to adjust — **amoldarse** *vr*

amonestación *nf, pl* -ciones 1 APERCIBIMIENTO : admonition, warning 2 amonestaciones *nfpl* : banns

amonestar *vt* APERCIBIR : to admonish, to warn

amoníaco *or* amoniaco *nm* : ammonia

amontonamiento *nm* : accumulation, piling up

amontonar *vt* 1 APILAR : to pile up, to heap up 2 : to collect, to gather 3 : to hoard — **amontonarse** *vr*

amor *nm* 1 : love 2 : loved one, beloved 3 amor propio : self-esteem 4 hacer el amor : to make love

amoral *adj* : amoral

amoratado, -da *adj* : black-and-blue, bruised, livid

amordazar {21} *vt* 1 : to gag, to muzzle 2 : to silence

amorfo, -fa *adj* : shapeless, amorphous

amorío *nm* : love affair, fling

amoroso, -sa *adj* 1 : loving, affectionate 2 : amorous ⟨una mirada amorosa : an amorous glance⟩ 3 : charming, cute — **amorosamente** *adv*

amortiguación *nf* : cushioning, absorption

amortiguador *nm* : shock absorber

amortiguar {10} *vt* : to soften (an impact)

amortizar {21} *vt* : to amortize, to pay off — **amortización** *nf*

amotinado[1], -da *adj* : rebellious, insurgent, mutinous

amotinado[2], -da *n* : rebel, insurgent, mutineer

amotinamiento *nm* : uprising, rebellion

amotinar *vt* : to incite (to riot), to agitate — **amotinarse** *vr* 1 : to riot, to rebel 2 : to mutiny

amparar *vt* : to safeguard, to protect — **ampararse** *vr* 1 ~ de : to take shelter from 2 ~ en : to have recourse to

amparo *nm* ACOGIDA, REFUGIO : protection, refuge

amperímetro *nm* : ammeter

amperio *nm* : ampere

ampliable *adj* : expandable, enlargeable, extendible

ampliación *nf, pl* -ciones : expansion, extension

ampliar {85} *vt* 1 : to expand, to extend 2 : to widen 3 : to enlarge (photographs) 4 : to elaborate on, to develop (ideas)

amplificador *nm* : amplifier

amplificar {72} *vt* : to amplify — **amplificación** *nf*

19

amplio, -plia *adj* : broad, wide, ample — **ampliamente** *adj*

amplitud *nf* **1** : breadth, extent **2** : spaciousness

ampolla *nf* **1** : blister **2** : vial, ampoule

ampollar *vt* : to blister — **ampollarse** *vr*

ampolleta *nf* **1** : small vial **2** : hourglass **3** *Chile* : light bulb

ampulosidad *nf* : pompousness, bombast

ampuloso, -sa *adj* GRANDILOCUENTE : pompous, bombastic — **ampulosamente** *adv*

amputar *vt* : to amputate — **amputación** *nf*

amueblar *vt* : to furnish

amuleto *nm* TALISMÁN : amulet, charm

amurallar *vt* : to wall in, to fortify

anacardo *nm* : cashew nut

anaconda *nf* : anaconda

anacrónico, -ca *adj* : anachronistic

anacronismo *nm* : anachronism

ánade *nmf* **1** : duck **2 ánade real** : mallard

anagrama *nm* : anagram

anal *adj* : anal

anales *nmpl* : annals

analfabetismo *nm* : illiteracy

analfabeto, -ta *adj & n* : illiterate

analgésico[1], -ca *adj* : analgesic, painkilling

analgésico[2] *nm* : painkiller, analgesic

análisis *nm* : analysis

analista *nmf* **1** : analyst **2** : annalist

analítico, -ca *adj* : analytical, analytic — **analíticamente** *adv*

analizar {21} *vt* : to analyze

analogía *nf* : analogy

analógico, -ca *adj* **1** : analogical **2** : analog ⟨computadora analógica : analog computer⟩

análogo, -ga *adj* : analogous, similar

ananá *or* **ananás** *nm, pl* **-nás** : pineapple

anaquel *nm* REPISA : shelf

anaranjado[1], -da *adj* NARANJA : orange-colored

anaranjado[2] *nm* NARANJA : orange (color)

anarquía *nf* : anarchy

anárquico, -ca *adj* : anarchic

anarquismo *nm* : anarchism

anarquista *adj & nmf* : anarchist

anatema *nm* : anathema

anatomía *nf* : anatomy — **anatomista** *nmf*

anatómico, -ca *adj* : anatomical — **anatómicamente** *adv*

anca *nf* **1** : haunch, hindquarter **2 ancas de rana** : frogs' legs

ancestral *adj* **1** : ancient, traditional **2** : ancestral

ancestro *nm* ASCENDIENTE : ancestor, forefather *m*

ancho[1], -cha *adj* **1** : wide, broad **2** : ample, loose-fitting

ancho[2] *nm* : width, breadth

anchoa *nf* : anchovy

anchura *nf* : width, breadth

ancianidad *nf* SENECTUD : old age

anciano[1], -na *adj* : aged, old, elderly

anciano[2], -na *n* : elderly person

ancla *nf* : anchor

ancladero → **anclaje**

anclaje *nm* : anchorage

anclar *v* FONDEAR : to anchor

andadas *nfpl* **1** : tracks **2 volver a las andadas** : to go back to one's old ways, to backslide

andador[1] *nm* **1** : walker, baby walker **2** *Mex* : walkway

andador[2], -dora *n* : walker, one who walks

andadura *nf* : course, journey ⟨su agotadora andadura al campeonato : his exhausting journey to the championship⟩

andaluz, -luza *adj & n, mpl* **-luces** : Andalusian

andamiaje *nm* **1** : scaffolding **2** ESTRUCTURA : structure, framework

andamio *nm* : scaffold

andanada *nf* **1** : volley, broadside **2 soltar una andanada a** : to reprimand

andanzas *nfpl* : adventures

andar[1] {6} *vi* **1** CAMINAR : to walk **2** IR : to go, to travel **3** FUNCIONAR : to run, to function ⟨el auto anda bien : the car runs well⟩ **4** : to ride ⟨andar a caballo : to ride on horseback⟩ **5** : to be ⟨anda sin dinero : he's broke⟩ — *vt* : to walk, to travel

andar[2] *nm* : walk, gait

andas *nfpl* : stand (for a coffin), bier

andén *nm, pl* **andenes 1** : (train) platform **2** *CA, Col* : sidewalk

andino, -na *adj* : Andean

andorrano, -na *adj & n* : Andorran

andrajos *nmpl* : rags, tatters

andrajoso, -sa *adj* : ragged, tattered

andrógino, -na *adj* : androgynous

andurriales *nmpl* : remote place

anea *nf* : cattail

anduvo, etc. → **andar**

anécdota *nf* : anecdote

anecdótico, -ca *adj* : anecdotal

anegar {52} *vt* **1** INUNDAR : to flood **2** AHOGAR : to drown **3** : to overwhelm — **anegarse** *vr* : to be flooded

anejo *nm* → **anexo[2]**

anemia *nf* : anemia

anémico, -ca *adj* : anemic

anémona *nf* : anemone

anestesia *nf* : anesthesia

anestesiar *vt* : to anesthetize

anestésico[1], -ca *adj* : anesthetic

anestésico[2] *nm* : anesthetic

anestesista *nmf* : anesthetist

aneurisma *nmf* : aneurysm

anexar *vt* : to annex, to attach

anexión *nf, pl* **-xiones** : annexation

anexo[1], -xa *adj* : attached, joined, annexed

anexo[2] *nm* **1** : annex **2** : supplement (to a book), appendix

anfetamina *nf* : amphetamine

anfibio[1], -bia *adj* : amphibious
anfibio[2] *nm* : amphibian
anfiteatro *nm* **1** : amphitheater **2** : lecture hall
anfitrión, -triona *n, mpl* **-triones** : host, hostess *f*
ánfora *nf* **1** : amphora **2** *Mex, Peru* : ballot box
ángel *nm* : angel
angelical *adj* : angelic, angelical
angélico, -ca *adj* → **angelical**
angina *nf* **1** *or* **angina de pecho** : angina **2** *Mex* : tonsil
anglicano, -na *adj & n* : Anglican
angloparlante[1] *adj* : English-speaking
angloparlante[2] *nmf* : English speaker
anglosajón, -jona *adj & n, mpl* **-jones** : Anglo-Saxon
angoleño, -ña *adj & n* : Angolan
angora *nf* : angora
angostar *vt* : to narrow — **angostarse** *vr*
angosto, -ta *adj* : narrow
angostura *nf* : narrowness
anguila *nf* : eel
angular *adj* : angular — **angularidad** *nf*
ángulo *nm* **1** : angle **2** : corner **3 ángulo muerto** : blind spot
anguloso, -sa *adj* : angular, sharp ⟨una cara angulosa : an angular face⟩ — **angulosidad** *nf*
angustia *nf* **1** CONGOJA : anguish, distress **2** : anxiety, worry
angustiar *vt* **1** : to anguish, to distress **2** : to worry — **angustiarse** *vr*
angustioso, -sa *adj* **1** : anguished, distressed **2** : distressing, worrisome
anhelante *adj* : yearning, longing
anhelar *vt* : to yearn for, to crave
anhelo *nm* : longing, yearning
anidar *vi* **1** : to nest **2** : to make one's home, to dwell — *vt* : to shelter
anillo *nm* SORTIJA : ring
ánima *n* ALMA : soul
animación *nf, pl* **-ciones 1** : animation **2** VIVEZA : liveliness
animado, -da *adj* **1** : animated, lively **2** : cheerful — **animadamente** *adv*
animador, -dora *n* **1** : (television) host **2** : cheerleader
animadversión *nf, pl* **-siones** ANIMOSIDAD : animosity, antagonism
animal[1] *adj* **1** : animal **2** ESTÚPIDO : stupid, idiotic **3** : rough, brutish
animal[2] *nm* : animal
animal[3] *nmf* **1** IDIOTA : idiot, fool **2** : brute, beastly person
animar *vt* **1** ALENTAR : to encourage, to inspire **2** : to animate, to enliven **3** : to brighten up, to cheer up — **animarse** *vr*
anímico, -ca *adj* : mental ⟨estado anímico : state of mind⟩
ánimo *nm* **1** ALMA : spirit, soul **2** : mood, spirits *pl* **3** : encouragement **4** PROPÓSITO : intention, purpose ⟨sociedad sin ánimo de lucro : nonprofit organization⟩ **5** : energy, vitality

animosidad *nf* ANIMADVERSIÓN : animosity, ill will
animoso, -sa *adj* : brave, spirited
aniñado, -da *adj* : childlike
aniquilación *nf* → **aniquilamiento**
aniquilamiento *nm* : annihilation, extermination
aniquilar *vt* **1** : to annihilate, to wipe out **2** : to overwhelm, to bring to one's knees — **aniquilarse** *vr*
anís *nm* **1** : anise **2 semilla de anís** : aniseed
aniversario *nm* : anniversary
ano *nm* : anus
anoche *adv* : last night
anochecer[1] {53} *v impers* : to get dark
anochecer[2] *nm* : dusk, nightfall
anodino, -na *adj* : insipid, dull
ánodo *nm* : anode
anomalía *nf* : anomaly
anómalo, -la *adj* : anomalous
anonadado, -da *adj* : dumbfounded, speechless
anonadar *vt* : to dumbfound, to stun
anonimato *nm* : anonymity
anónimo, -ma *adj* : anonymous — **anónimamente** *adv*
anorexia *nf* : anorexia
anoréxico, -ca *adj* : anorexic
anormal *adj* : abnormal — **anormalmente** *adv*
anormalidad *nf* : abnormality
anotación *nf, pl* **-ciones 1** : annotation, note **2** : scoring (in sports) ⟨lograron una anotación : they managed to score a goal⟩
anotar *vt* **1** : to annotate **2** APUNTAR, ESCRIBIR : to write down, to jot down **3** : to score (in sports) — *vi* : to score
anquilosado, -da *adj* **1** : stiff-jointed **2** : stagnated, stale
anquilosamiento *nm* **1** : stiffness (of joints) **2** : stagnation, paralysis
anquilosarse *vr* **1** : to stagnate **2** : to become stiff or paralyzed
anquilostoma *nm* : hookworm
ánsar *nm* : goose
ansarino *nm* : gosling
ansia *nf* **1** INQUIETUD : apprehensiveness, uneasiness **2** ANGUSTIA : anguish, distress **3** ANHELO : longing, yearning
ansiar {85} *vt* : to long for, to yearn for
ansiedad *nf* : anxiety
ansioso, -sa *adj* **1** : anxious, worried **2** : eager — **ansiosamente** *adv*
antagónico, -ca *adj* : conflicting, opposing
antagonismo *nm* : antagonism
antagonista[1] *adj* : antagonistic
antagonista[2] *nmf* : antagonist, opponent
antagonizar {21} *vt* : to antagonize
antaño *adv* : yesteryear, long ago
antártico, -ca *adj* **1** : antarctic **2 círculo antártico** : antarctic circle
ante[1] *nm* **1** : elk, moose **2** : suede
ante[2] *prep* **1** : before, in front of **2** : considering, in view of **3 ante todo** : first and foremost, above all

21

anteanoche *adv* : the night before last
anteayer *adv* : the day before yesterday
antebrazo *nm* : forearm
antecedente[1] *adj* : previous, prior
antecedente[2] *nm* **1** : precedent **2 antecedentes** *nmpl* : record, background
anteceder *v* : to precede
antecesor, -sora *n* **1** ANTEPASADO : ancestor **2** PREDECESOR : predecessor
antedicho, -cha *adj* : aforesaid, above
antelación *nf, pl* **-ciones 1** : advance notice **2 con ~** : in advance, beforehand
antemano *adv* **de ~** : in advance ⟨se lo agradezco de antemano : I thank you in advance⟩
antena *nf* : antenna
antenoche → anteanoche
anteojera *nf* **1** : eyeglass case **2 anteojeras** *nfpl* : blinders
anteojos *nmpl* GAFAS : glasses, eyeglasses
antepasado[1], **-da** *adj* : before last ⟨el domingo antepasado : the Sunday before last⟩
antepasado[2], **-da** *n* ANTECESOR : ancestor
antepecho *nm* **1** : guardrail **2** : ledge, sill
antepenúltimo, -ma *adj* : third from last
anteponer {60} *vt* **1** : to place before ⟨anteponer al interés de la nación el interés de la comunidad : to place the interests of the community before national interest⟩ **2** : to prefer
anteproyecto *nm* **1** : draft, proposal **2 anteproyecto de ley** : bill
antera *nf* : anther
anterior *adj* **1** : previous **2** : earlier ⟨tiempos anteriores : earlier times⟩ **3** : anterior, forward, front
anterioridad *nf* **1** : priority **2 con ~** : beforehand, in advance
anteriormente *adv* : previously, beforehand
antes *adv* **1** : before, earlier **2** : formerly, previously **3** : rather, sooner ⟨antes prefiero morir : I'd rather die⟩ **4 ~ de** : before, previous to ⟨antes de hoy : before today⟩ **5 antes que** : before ⟨antes que llegue Luis : before Luis arrives⟩ **6 cuanto antes** : as soon as possible **7 antes bien** : on the contrary
antesala *nf* **1** : anteroom, waiting room, lobby **2** : prelude, prologue
antiaborto, -ta *adj* : antiabortion
antiácido *nm* : antacid
antiadherente *adj* : nonstick
antiaéreo, -rea *adj* : antiaircraft
antiamericano, -na *adj* : anti-American
antibalas *adj* : bulletproof
antibiótico[1], **-ca** *adj* : antibiotic
antibiótico[2] *nm* : antibiotic
antichoque *adj* : shockproof
anticipación *nf, pl* **-ciones 1** : expectation, anticipation **2 con ~** : in advance

anticipado, -da *adj* **1** : advance, early **2 por ~** : in advance
anticipar *vt* **1** : to anticipate, to forestall, to deal with in advance **2** : to pay in advance — **anticiparse** *vr* **1** : to be early **2** ADELANTARSE : to get ahead
anticipo *nm* **1** : advance (payment) **2** : foretaste, preview
anticlerical *adj* : anticlerical
anticlimático, -ca : anticlimactic
anticlímax *nm* : anticlimax
anticomunismo *nm* : anticommunism
anticomunista *adj & nmf* : anticommunist
anticoncepción *nf, pl* **-ciones** : birth control, contraception
anticonceptivo *nm* : contraceptive
anticongelante *nm* : antifreeze
anticuado, -da *adj* : antiquated, outdated
anticuario[1], **-ria** *adj* : antique, antiquarian
anticuario[2], **-ria** *n* : antiquarian, antiquary
anticuario[3] *nm* : antique shop
anticuerpo *nm* : antibody
antidemocrático, -ca *adj* : antidemocratic
antideportivo, -va *adj* : unsportsmanlike
antidepresivo *nm* : antidepressant
antídoto *nm* : antidote
antidrogas *adj* : antidrug
antier → anteayer
antiestético, -ca *adj* : unsightly, unattractive
antifascista *adj & nmf* : antifascist
antifaz *nm, pl* **-faces** : mask
antifeminista *adj & nmf* : antifeminist
antífona *nf* : anthem
antígeno *nm* : antigen
antigualla *nf* **1** : antique **2** : relic, old thing
antiguamente *adv* **1** : formerly, once **2** : long ago
antigüedad *nf* **1** : antiquity **2** : seniority **3** : age ⟨con siglos de antigüedad : centuries-old⟩ **4 antigüedades** *nfpl* : antiques
antiguo, -gua *adj* **1** : ancient, old **2** : former **3** : old-fashioned ⟨a la antigua : in the old-fashioned way⟩ **4 Antiguo Testamento** : Old Testament
antihigiénico, -ca *adj* INSALUBRE : unhygienic, unsanitary
antihistamínico *nm* : antihistamine
antiimperialismo *nm* : anti-imperialism
antiimperialista *adj & nmf* : anti-imperialist
antiinflacionario, -ria *adj* : anti-inflationary
antiinflamatorio, -ria *adj* : anti-inflammatory
antillano[1], **-na** *adj* CARIBEÑO : Caribbean, West Indian
antillano[2], **-na** *n* : West Indian
antílope *nm* : antelope
antimilitarismo *nm* : antimilitarism

antimilitarista *adj & nmf* : antimilitarist
antimonio *nm* : antimony
antimonopolista *adj* : antimonopoly, antitrust
antinatural *adj* : unnatural, perverse
antipatía *nf* : aversion, dislike
antipático, -ca *adj* : obnoxious, unpleasant
antipatriótico, -ca *adj* : unpatriotic
antirrábico, -ca *adj* : antirabies ⟨vacuna antirrábica : rabies vaccine⟩
antirreglamentario, -ria *adj* **1** : unlawful, illegal **2** : foul (in sports)
antirrevolucionario, -ria *adj & n* : antirevolutionary
antirrobo, -ba *adj* : antitheft
antisemita *adj* : anti-Semitic
antisemitismo *nm* : anti-Semitism
antiséptico¹, -ca *adj* : antiseptic
antiséptico² *nm* : antiseptic
antisocial *adj* : antisocial
antitabaco *adj* : antismoking
antiterrorista *adj* : antiterrorist
antítesis *nf* : antithesis
antitoxina *nf* : antitoxin
antitranspirante *nm* : antiperspirant
antojadizo, -za *adj* CAPRICHOSO : capricious
antojarse *vr* **1** APETECER : to be appealing, to be desirable ⟨se me antoja un helado : I feel like having ice cream⟩ **2** : to seem, to appear ⟨los árboles se antojaban fantasmas : the trees seemed like ghosts⟩
antojitos *nmpl Mex* : traditional Mexican snack foods
antojo *nm* **1** CAPRICHO : whim **2** : craving
antología *nf* **1** : anthology **2 de ~** *fam* : fantastic, incredible
antónimo *nm* : antonym
antonomasia *nf* **por ~** : par excellence
antorcha *nf* : torch
antracita *nf* : anthracite
antro *nm* **1** : cave, den **2** : dive, seedy nightclub
antropofagia *nf* CANIBALISMO : cannibalism
antropófago¹, -ga *adj* : cannibalistic
antropófago², -ga *n* CANÍBAL : cannibal
antropoide *adj & nmf* : anthropoid
antropología *nf* : anthropology
antropológico, -ca *adj* : anthropological
antropólogo, -ga *n* : anthropologist
anual *adj* : annual, yearly — **anualmente** *adv*
anualidad *nf* : annuity
anuario *nm* : yearbook, annual
anudar *vt* : to knot, to tie in a knot — **anudarse** *vr*
anuencia *nf* : consent
anulación *nf, pl* **-ciones** : annulment, nullification
anular *vt* : to annul, to cancel
anunciador, -dora *n* → **anunciante**
anunciante *nmf* : advertiser
anunciar *vt* **1** : to announce **2** : to advertise

anuncio *nm* **1** : announcement **2** : advertisement, commercial
anzuelo *nm* **1** : fishhook **2 morder el anzuelo** : to take the bait
añadido *nm* : addition
añadidura *nf* **1** : additive, addition **2 por ~** : in addition, furthermore
añadir *vt* **1** AGREGAR : to add **2** AUMENTAR : to increase
añejar *vt* : to age, to ripen
añejo, -ja *adj* **1** : aged, vintage **2** : age-old, musty, stale
añicos *nmpl* : smithereens, bits ⟨hacer(se) añicos : to shatter⟩
añil *nm* **1** : indigo **2** : bluing
año *nm* **1** : year ⟨en el año 1990 : in (the year) 1990⟩ ⟨tiene diez años : she is ten years old⟩ **2** : grade ⟨cuarto año : fourth grade⟩ **3 año bisiesto** : leap year **4 año luz** : light-year **5 Año Nuevo** : New Year
añoranza *nf* : longing, yearning
añorar *vt* **1** DESEAR : to long for **2** : to grieve for, to miss — *vi* : to mourn, to grieve
añoso, -sa *adj* : aged, old
aorta *nf* : aorta
apabullante *adj* : overwhelming, crushing
apabullar *vt* : to overwhelm
apacentar {55} *vt* : to pasture, to put to pasture
apache *adj & nmf* : Apache
apachurrado, -da *adj fam* : depressed, down
apachurrar *vt* : to crush, to squash
apacible *adj* : gentle, mild, calm — **apaciblemente** *adv*
apaciguador, -dora *adj* : calming
apaciguamiento *nm* : appeasement
apaciguar {10} *vt* APLACAR : to appease, to pacify — **apaciguarse** *vr* : to calm down
apadrinar *vt* **1** : to be a godparent to **2** : to sponsor, to support
apagado, -da *adj* **1** : off, out ⟨la luz está apagada : the light is off⟩ **2** : dull, subdued
apagador *nm Mex* : switch
apagar {52} *vt* **1** : to turn off, to shut off **2** : to extinguish, to put out — **apagarse** *vr* **1** : to go out, to fade **2** : to wane, to die down
apagón *nm, pl* **-gones** : blackout (of power)
apalancamiento *nm* : leverage
apalancar {72} *vt* **1** : to jack up **2** : to pry open
apalear *vt* : to beat up, to thrash
apantallar *vt Mex* : to dazzle, to impress
apañar *vt* **1** : to seize, to grasp **2** : to repair, to mend — **apañarse** *vr* : to manage, to get along
apaño *nm fam* **1** : patch **2** HABILIDAD : skill, knack
apapachar *vt Mex fam* : to cuddle, to caress — **apapacharse** *vr*

aparador *nm* **1** : sideboard, cupboard **2** ESCAPARATE, VITRINA : shop window
aparato *nm* **1** : machine, appliance, apparatus ⟨aparato auditivo : hearing aid⟩ ⟨aparato de televisión : television set⟩ **2** : system ⟨aparato digestivo : digestive system⟩ **3** : display, ostentation ⟨sin aparato : without ceremony⟩ **4 aparatos** *nmpl* : braces (for the teeth)
aparatoso, -sa *adj* **1** : ostentatious **2** : spectacular
aparcamiento *nm Spain* **1** : parking **2** : parking lot
aparcar {72} *v Spain* : to park
aparcero, -ra *n* : sharecropper
aparear *vt* **1** : to mate (animals) **2** : to match up — **aparearse** *vr* : to mate
aparecer {53} *vi* **1** : to appear **2** PRESENTARSE : to show up **3** : to turn up, to be found — **aparecerse** *vr* : to appear
aparejado, -da *adj* **1 ir aparejado con** : to go hand in hand with **2 llevar aparejado** : to entail
aparejar *vt* **1** PREPARAR : to prepare, to make ready **2** : to harness (a horse) **3** : to fit out (a ship)
aparejo *nm* **1** : equipment, gear **2** : harness, saddle **3** : rig, rigging (of a ship)
aparentar *vt* **1** : to seem, to appear ⟨no aparentas tu edad : you don't look your age⟩ **2** FINGIR : to feign, to pretend
aparente *adj* **1** : apparent **2** : showy, striking — **aparentemente** *adv*
aparición *nf, pl* -**ciones 1** : appearance **2** PUBLICACIÓN : publication, release **3** FANTASMA : apparition, vision
apariencia *nf* **1** ASPECTO : appearance, look **2 en ~** : seemingly, apparently
apartado *nm* **1** : section, paragraph **2 apartado postal** : post office box
apartamento *nm* DEPARTAMENTO : apartment
apartar *vt* **1** ALEJAR : to move away, to put at a distance **2** : to put aside, to set aside, to separate — **apartarse** *vr* **1** : to step aside, to move away **2** DESVIARSE : to stray
aparte[1] *adv* **1** : apart, aside ⟨modestia aparte : if I say so myself⟩ **2** : separately **3 ~ de** : apart from, besides
aparte[2] *adj* : separate, special
aparte[3] *nm* : aside (in theater)
apartheid *nm* : apartheid
apasionado, -da *adj* : passionate, enthusiastic — **apasionadamente** *adv*
apasionante *adj* : fascinating, exciting
apasionar *vt* : to enthuse, to excite — **apasionarse** *vr*
apatía *nf* : apathy
apático, -ca *adj* : apathetic
apearse *vr* **1** DESMONTAR : to dismount **2** : to get out of or off (a vehicle)
apedrear *vt* : to stone, to throw stones at
apegado, -da *adj* : attached, close, devoted ⟨es muy apegado a su familia : he is very devoted to his family⟩

apegarse {52} *vr* **~ a** : to become attached to, to grow fond of
apego *nm* AFICIÓN : attachment, fondness, inclination
apelación *nf, pl* -**ciones** : appeal (in court)
apelar *vi* **1** : to appeal **2 ~ a** : to resort to
apelativo *nm* APELLIDO : last name, surname
apellidarse *vr* : to have for a last name ⟨¿cómo se apellida? : what is your last name?⟩
apellido *nm* : last name, surname
apelotonar *vt* : to roll into a ball, to bundle up
apenar *vt* : to aggrieve, to sadden — **apenarse** *vr* **1** : to be saddened **2** : to become embarrassed
apenas[1] *adv* : hardly, scarcely
apenas[2] *conj* : as soon as
apéndice *nm* **1** : appendix **2** : appendage
apendicectomía *nf* : appendectomy
apendicitis *nf* : appendicitis
apercibimiento *nm* **1** : preparation **2** AMONESTACIÓN : warning
apercibir *vt* **1** DISPONER : to prepare, to make ready **2** AMONESTAR : to warn **3** OBSERVAR : to observe, to perceive — **apercibirse** *vr* **1** : to get ready **2 ~ de** : to notice
aperitivo *nm* **1** : appetizer **2** : aperitif
apero *nm* : tool, implement
apertura *nf* **1** : opening, aperture **2** : commencement, beginning **3** : openness
apesadumbrar *vt* : to distress, to sadden — **apesadumbrarse** *vr* : to be weighed down
apestar *vt* **1** : to infect with the plague **2** : to corrupt — *vi* : to stink
apestoso, -sa *adj* : stinking, foul
apetecer {53} *vt* **1** : to crave, to long for ⟨apeteció la fama : he longed for fame⟩ **2** : to appeal to ⟨me apetece un bistec : I feel like having a steak⟩ ⟨¿cuándo te apetece ir? : when do you want to go?⟩ — *vi* : to be appealing
apetecible *adj* : appetizing, appealing
apetito *nm* : appetite
apetitoso, -sa *adj* : appetizing
apiario *nm* : apiary
ápice *nm* **1** : apex, summit **2** PIZCA : bit, smidgen
apicultor, -tora *n* : beekeeper
apicultura *nf* : beekeeping
apilar *vt* AMONTONAR : to heap up, to pile up — **apilarse** *vr*
apiñado, -da *adj* : jammed, crowded
apiñar *vt* : to pack, to cram — **apiñarse** *vr* : to crowd together, to huddle
apio *nm* : celery
apisonadora *nf* : steamroller
apisonar *vt* : to pack down, to tamp
aplacamiento *nm* : appeasement
aplacar {72} *vt* APACIGUAR : to appease, to placate — **aplacarse** *vr* : to calm down

aplanadora *nf* : steamroller

aplanar *vt* : to flatten, to level

aplastante *adj* : crushing, overwhelming

aplastar *vt* : to crush, to squash

aplaudir *v* : to applaud

aplauso *nm* **1** : applause, clapping **2** : praise, acclaim

aplazamiento *nm* : postponement

aplazar {21} *vt* : to postpone, to defer

aplicable *adj* : applicable — **aplicabilidad** *nf*

aplicación *nf, pl* **-ciones 1** : application **2** : diligence, dedication

aplicado, -da *adj* : diligent, industrious

aplicador *nm* : applicator

aplicar {72} *vt* : to apply — **aplicarse** *vr* : to apply oneself

aplique *or* **apliqué** *nm* : appliqué

aplomar *vt* : to plumb, to make vertical

aplomo *nm* : aplomb, composure

apocado, -da *adj* : timid

apocalipsis *nms & pl* : apocalypse ⟨el Libro del Apocalipsis : the Book of Revelation⟩

apocalíptico, -ca *adj* : apocalyptic

apocamiento *nm* : timidity

apocarse {72} *vr* **1** : to shy away, to be intimidated **2** : to humble oneself, to sell oneself short

apócrifo, -fa *adj* : apocryphal

apodar *vt* : to nickname, to call — **apodarse** *vr*

apoderado, -da *n* : proxy, agent

apoderar *vt* : to authorize, to empower — **apoderarse** *vr* ∼ **de** : to seize, to take over

apodo *nm* SOBRENOMBRE : nickname

apogeo *nm* : acme, peak, zenith

apología *nf* : defense, apology

apoplejía *nf* : apoplexy, stroke

apoplético, -ca *adj* : apoplectic

aporrear *vt* : to bang on, to beat, to bludgeon

aportación *nf, pl* **-ciones** : contribution

aportar *vt* CONTRIBUIR : to contribute, to provide

aporte *nm* → **aportación**

apostador, -dora *n* : bettor, better

apostar {19} *v* : to bet, to wager ⟨apuesto que no viene : I bet he's not coming⟩

apostasía *nf* : apostasy

apóstata *nmf* : apostate

apostilla *nf* : note

apostillar *vt* : to annotate

apóstol *nm* : apostle

apostólico, -ca *adj* : apostolic

apóstrofe *nmf* : apostrophe

apostura *nf* : elegance, gracefulness

apoyacabezas *nms & pl* : headrest

apoyapiés *nms & pl* : footrest

apoyar *vt* **1** : to support, to back **2** : to lean, to rest — **apoyarse** *vr* **1** ∼ **en** : to lean on **2** ∼ **en** : to be based on, to rest on

apoyo *nm* : support, backing

apreciable *adj* : appreciable, substantial, considerable

apreciación *nf, pl* **-ciones 1** : appreciation **2** : appraisal, evaluation

apreciar *vt* **1** ESTIMAR : to appreciate, to value **2** EVALUAR : to appraise, to assess — **apreciarse** *vr* : to appreciate, to increase in value

aprecio *nm* **1** ESTIMO : esteem, appreciation **2** EVALUACIÓN : appraisal, assessment

aprehender *vt* **1** : to apprehend, to capture **2** : to conceive of, to grasp

aprehensión *nf, pl* **-siones** : apprehension, capture, arrest

apremiante *adj* : pressing, urgent

apremiar *vt* INSTAR : to pressure, to urge — *vi* URGIR : to be urgent ⟨el tiempo apremia : time is of the essence⟩

apremio *nm* : pressure, urgency

aprender *v* : to learn — **aprenderse** *vr*

aprendiz, -diza *n, mpl* **-dices** : apprentice, trainee

aprendizaje *nm* : apprenticeship

aprensión *nf, pl* **-siones** : apprehension, dread

aprensivo, -va *adj* : apprehensive, worried

apresamiento *nm* : seizure, capture

apresar *vt* : to capture, to seize

aprestar *vt* : to make ready, to prepare — **aprestarse** *vr* : to get ready

apresuradamente *adv* **1** : hurriedly **2** : hastily, too fast

apresurado, -da *adj* : hurried, in a rush

apresuramiento *nm* : hurry, haste

apresurar *vt* : to quicken, to speed up — **apresurarse** *vr* : to hurry up, to make haste

apretado, -da *adj* **1** : tight **2** *fam* : cheap, tightfisted — **apretadamente** *adv*

apretar {55} *vt* **1** : to press, to push (a button) **2** : to tighten **3** : to squeeze — *vi* **1** : to press, to push **2** : to fit tightly, to be too tight ⟨los zapatos me aprietan : my shoes are tight⟩

apretón *nm, pl* **-tones 1** : squeeze **2 apretón de manos** : handshake

apretujar *vt* : to squash, to squeeze — **apretujarse** *vr*

aprieto *nm* APURO : predicament, difficulty ⟨estar en un aprieto : to be in a fix⟩

aprisa *adv* : quickly, hurriedly

aprisionar *vt* **1** : to imprison **2** : to trap, to box in

aprobación *nf, pl* **-ciones** : approval, endorsement

aprobar {19} *vt* **1** : to approve of **2** : to pass (a law, an exam) — *vi* : to pass (in school)

aprobatorio, -ria *adj* : approving

apropiación *nf, pl* **-ciones** : appropriation

apropiado, -da *adj* : appropriate, proper, suitable — **apropiadamente** *adv*

apropiarse *vr* ∼ **de** : to take possession of, to appropriate

aprovechable *adj* : usable

aprovechado¹, -da *adj* **1** : diligent, hardworking **2** : pushy, opportunistic
aprovechado², -da *n* : pushy person, opportunist
aprovechamiento *nm* : use, exploitation
aprovechar *vt* : to take advantage of, to make good use of — *vi* **1** : to be of use **2** : to progress, to improve — **aprovecharse** *vr* ~ **de** : to take advantage of, to exploit
aprovisionamiento *nm* : provisions *pl*, supplies *pl*
aprovisionar *vt* : to provide, to supply (with provisions)
aproximación *nf, pl* **-ciones 1** : approximation, estimate **2** : rapprochement
aproximado, -da *adj* : approximate, estimated — **aproximadamente** *adv*
aproximar *vt* ACERCAR, ARRIMAR : to approximate, to bring closer — **aproximarse** *vr* ACERCARSE, ARRIMARSE : to approach, to move closer
aptitud *nf* : aptitude, capability
apto, -ta *adj* **1** : suitable, suited, fit **2** HÁBIL : capable, competent
apuesta *nf* : bet, wager
apuesto, -ta *adj* : elegant, good-looking
apuntador, -dora *n* : prompter
apuntalar *vt* : to prop up, to shore up
apuntar *vt* **1** : to aim, to point **2** ANOTAR : to write down, to jot down **3** INDICAR, SEÑALAR : to point to, to point out **4** : to prompt (in the theater) — *vi* **1** : to take aim **2** : to become evident — **apuntarse** *vr* **1** : to sign up, to enroll **2** : to score
apunte *nm* : note
apuñalar *vt* : to stab
apuradamente *adv* **1** : with difficulty **2** : hurriedly, hastily
apurado, -da *adj* **1** APRESURADO : rushed, pressured **2** : poor, needy **3** : difficult, awkward **4** : embarrassed
apurar *vt* **1** APRESURAR : to hurry, to rush **2** : to use up, to exhaust **3** : to trouble — **apurarse** *vr* **1** APRESURARSE : to hurry up **2** PREOCUPARSE : to worry
apuro *nm* **1** APRIETO : predicament, jam **2** : rush, hurry **3** : embarrassment
aquejar *vt* : to afflict
aquel, aquella *adj, mpl* **aquellos** : that, those
aquél, aquélla *pron, mpl* **aquéllos 1** : that (one), those (ones) **2** : the former
aquello *pron (neuter)* : that, that matter, that business ⟨aquello fue algo serio : that was something serious⟩
aquí *adv* **1** : here **2** : now ⟨de aquí en adelante : from now on⟩ **3 por** ~ : around here, hereabouts
aquiescencia *nf* : acquiescence, approval
aquietar *vt* : to allay, to calm — **aquietarse** *vr* : to calm down
aquilatar *vt* **1** : to assay **2** : to assess, to size up

ara *nf* **1** : altar **2 en aras de** : in the interests of, for the sake of
árabe¹ *adj & nmf* : Arab, Arabian
árabe² *nm* : Arabic (language)
arabesco *nm* : arabesque — **arabesco, -ca** *adj*
arábigo, -ga *adj* **1** : Arabic, Arabian **2 número arábigo** : Arabic numeral
arable *adj* : arable
arado *nm* : plow
aragonés, -nesa *adj & n, mpl* **-neses** : Aragonese
arancel *nm* : tariff, duty
arándano *nm* : blueberry
arandela *nf* : washer (for a faucet, etc.)
araña *nf* **1** : spider **2** : chandelier
arañar *v* : to scratch, to claw
arañazo *nm* : scratch
arar *v* : to plow
arbitraje *nm* **1** : arbitration **2** : refereeing (in sports)
arbitrar *v* **1** : to arbitrate **2** : to referee, to umpire
arbitrariedad *nf* **1** : arbitrariness **2** INJUSTICIA : injustice, wrong
arbitrario, -ria *adj* **1** : arbitrary **2** : unfair, unjust — **arbitrariamente** *adv*
arbitrio *nm* **1** ALBEDRÍO : will **2** JUICIO : judgment
árbitro, -tra *n* **1** : arbitrator, arbiter **2** : referee, umpire
árbol *nm* **1** : tree **2 árbol genealógico** : family tree
arbolado¹, -da *adj* : wooded
arbolado² *nm* : woodland
arboleda *nf* : grove, wood
arbóreo, -rea *adj* : arboreal
arbusto *nm* : shrub, bush, hedge
arca *nf* **1** : ark **2** : coffer, chest
arcada *nf* **1** : arcade, series of arches **2 arcadas** *nfpl* : retching ⟨hacer arcadas : to retch⟩
arcaico, -ca *adj* : archaic
arcángel *nm* : archangel
arcano, -na *adj* : arcane
arce *nm* : maple tree
arcén *nm, pl* **arcenes** : hard shoulder, berm
archidiócesis *nfs & pl* : archdiocese
archipiélago *nm* : archipelago
archivador *nm* : filing cabinet
archivar *vt* **1** : to file **2** : to archive
archivero, -ra *n* : archivist
archivista *nmf* : archivist
archivo *nm* **1** : file **2** : archive, archives *pl*
arcilla *nf* : clay
arco *nm* **1** : arch, archway **2** : bow (in archery) **3** : arc **4** : wicket (in croquet) **5** PORTERÍA : goal, goalposts *pl* **6 arco iris** : rainbow
arder *vi* **1** : to burn ⟨el bosque está ardiendo : the forest is in flames⟩ ⟨arder de ira : to burn with anger, to be seething⟩ **2** : to smart, to sting, to burn ⟨le ardía el estómago : he had heartburn⟩
ardid *nm* : scheme, ruse

ardiente *adj* **1** : burning **2** : ardent, passionate — **ardientemente** *adv*
ardilla *nf* **1** : squirrel **2** *or* **ardilla listada** : chipmunk
ardor *nm* **1** : heat **2** : passion, ardor
ardoroso, -sa *adj* : heated, impassioned
arduo, -dua *adj* : arduous, grueling — **arduamente** *adv*
área *nf* : area
arena *nf* **1** : sand ⟨arena movediza : quicksand⟩ **2** : arena
arenga *nf* : harangue, lecture
arengar {52} *vt* : to harangue, to lecture
arenilla *nf* **1** : fine sand **2 arenillas** *nfpl* : kidney stones
arenisca *nf* : sandstone
arenoso, -sa *adj* : sandy, gritty
arenque *nm* : herring
arepa *nf* : cornmeal bread
arete *nm* : earring
argamasa *nf* : mortar (cement)
argelino, -na *adj & n* : Algerian
argentino, -na *adj & n* : Argentinian, Argentine
argolla *nf* : hoop, ring
argón *nm* : argon
argot *nm* : slang
argucia *nf* : sophistry, subtlety
argüir {41} *vi* : to argue — *vt* **1** ARGUMENTAR : to contend, to argue **2** INFERIR : to deduce **3** PROBAR : to prove
argumentación *nf, pl* **-ciones** : line of reasoning, argument
argumentar *vt* : to argue, to contend
argumento *nm* **1** : argument, reasoning **2** : plot, story line
aria *nf* : aria
aridez *nf, pl* **-deces** : aridity, dryness
árido, -da *adj* : arid, dry
Aries *nmf* : Aries
ariete *nm* : battering ram
arisco, -ca *adj* : surly, sullen, unsociable
arista *nf* **1** : ridge, edge **2** : beard (of a plant) **3 aristas** *nfpl* : rough edges, complications, problems
aristocracia *nf* : aristocracy
aristócrata *nmf* : aristocrat
aristocrático, -ca *adj* : aristocratic
aritmética *nf* : arithmetic
aritmético, -ca *adj* : arithmetic, arithmetical — **aritméticamente** *adv*
arlequín *nm, pl* **-quines** : harlequin
arma *nf* **1** : weapon **2 armas** *nfpl* : armed forces **3 arma de fuego** : firearm
armada *nf* : navy, fleet
armadillo *nm* : armadillo
armado, -da *adj* **1** : armed **2** : assembled, put together **3** *PRi* : obstinate, stubborn
armador, -dora *n* : shipowner
armadura *nf* **1** : armor **2** ARMAZÓN : skeleton, framework
armamento *nm* : armament, arms *pl*, weaponry
armar *vt* **1** : to assemble, to put together **2** : to create, to cause ⟨armar un es-

cándalo : to cause a scene⟩ **3** : to arm — **armarse** *vr* **armarse de valor** : to steel oneself
armario *nm* **1** CLÓSET, ROPERO : closet **2** ALACENA : cupboard
armatoste *nm fam* : monstrosity, contraption
armazón *nmf, pl* **-zones** **1** ESQUELETO : framework, skeleton ⟨armazón de acero : steel framework⟩ **2** : frames *pl* (of eyeglasses)
armenio, -nia *adj & n* : Armenian
armería *nf* **1** : armory **2** : arms museum **3** : gunsmith's shop **4** : gunsmith's craft
armiño *nm* : ermine
armisticio *nm* : armistice
armonía *nf* : harmony
armónica *nf* : harmonica
armónico, -ca *adj* **1** : harmonic **2** : harmonious — **armónicamente** *adv*
armonioso, -sa *adj* : harmonious — **armoniosamente** *adv*
armonizar {21} *vt* **1** : to harmonize **2** : to reconcile — *vi* : to harmonize, to blend together
arnés *nm, pl* **arneses** : harness
aro *nm* **1** : hoop **2** : napkin ring **3** *Arg, Chile, Uru* : earring
aroma *nm* : aroma, scent
aromático, -ca *adj* : aromatic
arpa *nf* : harp
arpegio *nm* : arpeggio
arpía *nf* : shrew, harpy
arpillera *nf* : burlap
arpista *nmf* : harpist
arpón *nm, pl* **arpones** : harpoon — **arponear** *vt*
arquear *vt* : to arch, to bend — **arquearse** *vr* : to bend, to bow
arqueología *nf* : archaeology
arqueológico, -ca *adj* : archaeological
arqueólogo, -ga *n* : archaeologist
arquero, -ra *n* **1** : archer **2** PORTERO : goalkeeper, goalie
arquetípico, -ca *adj* : archetypal
arquetipo *nm* : archetype
arquitecto, -ta *n* : architect
arquitectónico, -ca *adj* : architectural — **aquitectónicamente** *adv*
arquitectura *nf* : architecture
arrabal *nm* **1** : slum **2 arrabales** *nmpl* : outskirts, outlying area
arracada *nf* : hoop earring
arracimarse *vr* : to cluster together
arraigado, -da *adj* : deep-seated, ingrained
arraigar {52} *vi* : to take root, to become established — **arraigarse** *vr*
arraigo *nm* — roots *pl* ⟨con mucho arraigo : deep-rooted⟩
arrancar {72} *vt* **1** : to pull out, to tear out **2** : to pick, to pluck (a flower) **3** : to start (an engine) **4** : to boot (a computer) — *vi* **1** : to start an engine **2** : to get going — **arrancarse** *vr* : to pull out, to pull off

arrancón *nm, pl* **-cones** *Mex* **1** : sudden loud start (of a car) **2 carrera de arrancones** : drag race

arranque *nm* **1** : starter (of a car) **2** ARREBATO : outburst, fit **3 punto de arranque** : beginning, starting point

arrasar *vt* **1** : to level, to smooth **2** : to devastate, to destroy **3** : to fill to the brim

arrastrar *vt* **1** : to drag, to tow **2** : to draw, to attract — *vi* : to hang down, to trail — **arrastrarse** *vr* **1** : to crawl **2** : to grovel

arrastre *nm* **1** : dragging **2** : pull, attraction **3 red de arrastre** : dragnet, trawling net

arrayán *nm, pl* **-yanes** **1** MIRTO : myrtle **2 arrayán brabántico** : bayberry, wax myrtle

arrear *vt* : to urge on, to drive — *vi* : to hurry along

arrebatado, -da *adj* **1** PRECIPITADO : impetuous, hotheaded, rash **2** : flushed, blushing

arrebatar *vt* **1** : to snatch, to seize **2** CAUTIVAR : to captivate — **arrebatarse** *vr* : to get carried away (with anger, etc.)

arrebato *nm* ARRANQUE : fit, outburst

arreciar *vi* : to intensify, to worsen

arrecife *nm* : reef

arreglado, -da *adj* **1** : fixed, repaired **2** : settled, sorted out **3** : neat, tidy **4** : smart, dressed-up

arreglar *vt* **1** COMPONER : to repair, to fix **2** : to tidy up ⟨arregla tu cuarto : pick up your room⟩ **3** : to solve, to work out ⟨quiero arreglar este asunto : I want to settle this matter⟩ — **arreglarse** *vr* **1** : to get dressed (up) ⟨arreglarse el pelo : to get one's hair done⟩ **2 arreglárselas** *fam* : to get by, to manage

arreglo *nm* **1** : repair **2** : arrangement **3** : agreement, understanding

arrellanarse *vr* : to settle (in a chair)

arremangarse {52} *vr* : to roll up one's sleeves

arremeter *vi* EMBESTIR : to attack, to charge

arremetida *nf* EMBESTIDA : attack, onslaught

arremolinarse *vr* **1** : to crowd around, to mill about **2** : to swirl (about)

arrendador, -dora *n* **1** : landlord, landlady *f* **2** : tenant, lessee

arrendajo *nm* : jay

arrendamiento *nm* **1** ALQUILER : rental, leasing **2 contrato de arrendamiento** : lease

arrendar {55} *vt* ALQUILAR : to rent, to lease

arrendatario, -ria *n* : tenant, lessee, renter

arreos *nmpl* GUARNICIONES : tack, harness, trappings

arrepentido, -da *adj* : repentant, remorseful

arrepentimiento *nm* : regret, remorse, repentance

arrepentirse {76} *vr* **1** : to regret, to be sorry **2** : to repent

arrestar *vt* DETENER : to arrest, to detain

arresto *nm* **1** DETENCIÓN : arrest **2 arrestos** *nmpl* : boldness, daring

arriar {85} *vt* **1** : to lower (a flag, etc.) **2** : to slacken (a rope, etc.)

arriate *nm Mex, Spain* : bed (for plants), border

arriba *adv* **1** : up, upwards **2** : above, overhead **3** : upstairs **4 ～ de** : more than **5 de arriba abajo** : from top to bottom, from head to foot

arribar *vi* **1** : to arrive **2** : to dock, to put into port

arribista *nmf* : parvenu, upstart

arribo *nm* : arrival

arriendo *nm* ARRENDAMIENTO : rent, rental

arriero, -ra *n* : mule driver, muleteer

arriesgado, -da *adj* **1** : risky **2** : bold, daring

arriesgar {52} *vt* : to risk, to venture — **arriesgarse** *vr* : to take a chance

arrimado, -da *n Mex fam* : sponger, freeloader

arrimar *vt* ACERCAR, APROXIMAR : to bring closer, to draw near — **arrimarse** *vr* ACERCARSE, APROXIMARSE : to approach, to get close

arrinconar *vt* **1** ACORRALAR : to corner, to box in **2** : to push aside, to abandon

arroba *nf* : arroba (Spanish unit of measurement)

arrobamiento *nm* : rapture, ecstasy

arrobar *vt* : to enrapture, to enchant — **arrobarse** *vr*

arrocero¹, -ra *adj* : rice

arrocero², -ra *n* : rice grower

arrodillarse *vr* : to kneel (down)

arrogancia *nf* ALTANERÍA, ALTIVEZ : arrogance, haughtiness

arrogante *adj* ALTANERO, ALTIVO : arrogant, haughty

arrogarse {52} *vr* : to usurp, to arrogate

arrojado, -da *adj* : daring, fearless

arrojar *vt* **1** : to hurl, to cast, to throw **2** : to give off, to spew out **3** : to yield, to produce **4** *fam* : to vomit — **arrojarse** *vr* PRECIPITARSE : to throw oneself, to leap

arrojo *nm* : boldness, fearlessness

arrollador, -dora *adj* : sweeping, overwhelming

arrollar *vt* **1** : to sweep away, to carry away **2** : to crush, to overwhelm **3** : to run over (with a vehicle)

arropar *vt* : to clothe, to cover (up) — **arroparse** *vr*

arrostrar *vt* : to confront, to face (up to)

arroyo *nm* **1** RIACHUELO : brook, creek, stream **2** : gutter

arroz *nm, pl* **arroces** : rice

arrozal *nm* : rice field, rice paddy

arruga *nf* : wrinkle, fold, crease

arrugado, -da *adj* : wrinkled, creased, lined

arrugar {52} *vt* : to wrinkle, to crease, to pucker — **arrugarse** *vr*

arruinar *vt* : to ruin, to wreck — **arruinarse** *vr* **1** : to be ruined **2** : to fall into ruin, to go bankrupt

arrullar *vt* : to lull to sleep — *vi* : to coo

arrullo *nm* **1** : lullaby **2** : coo (of a dove)

arrumaco *nm fam* : kissing, cuddling

arrumbar *vt* **1** : to lay aside, to put away **2** : to floor, to leave speechless

arsenal *nm* : arsenal

arsénico *nm* : arsenic

arte *nmf (usually m in singular, f in plural)* **1** : art ⟨artes y oficios : arts and crafts⟩ ⟨bellas artes : fine arts⟩ **2** HABILIDAD : skill **3** : cunning, cleverness

artefacto *nm* **1** : artifact **2** DISPOSITIVO : device

artemisa *nf* : sagebrush

arteria *nf* : artery — **arterial** *adj*

arteriosclerosis *nf* : arteriosclerosis, hardening of the arteries

artero, -ra *adj* : wily, crafty

artesanal *adj* : pertaining to crafts or craftsmanship, handmade

artesanía *nf* **1** : craftsmanship **2** : handicrafts *pl*

artesano, -na *n* : artisan, craftsman *m*, craftsperson

artesiano, -na *adj* : artesian ⟨pozo artesiano : artesian well⟩

ártico, -ca *adj* : arctic

articulación *nf, pl* **-ciones** **1** : articulation, pronunciation **2** COYUNTURA : joint

articular *vt* **1** : to articulate, to utter **2** : to connect with a joint **3** : to coordinate, to orchestrate

articulista *nmf* : columnist

artículo *nm* **1** : article, thing **2** : item, feature, report **3 artículo de comercio** : commodity **4 artículos de primera necesidad** : essentials **5 artículos de tocador** : toiletries

artífice *nmf* **1** ARTESANO : artisan **2** : mastermind, architect

artificial *adj* **1** : artificial, man-made **2** : feigned, false — **artificialmente** *adv*

artificio *nm* **1** HABILIDAD : skill **2** APARATO : device, appliance **3** ARDID : artifice, ruse

artificioso, -sa *adj* **1** : skillful **2** : cunning, deceptive

artillería *nf* : artillery

artillero, -ra *n* : artilleryman *m*, gunner

artilugio *nm* : gadget, contraption

artimaña *nf* : ruse, trick

artista *nmf* **1** : artist **2** ACTOR, ACTRIZ : actor, actress *f*

artístico, -ca *adj* : artistic — **artísticamente** *adv*

artrítico, -ca *adj* : arthritic

artritis *nfs & pl* : arthritis

artrópodo *nm* : arthropod

arveja *nf* GUISANTE : pea

arzobispado *nm* : archbishopric

arzobispo *nm* : archbishop

as *nm* : ace

asa *nf* AGARRADERA, ASIDERO : handle, grip

asado¹, -da *adj* : roasted, grilled, broiled

asado² *nm* **1** : roast **2** : barbecued meat **3** : barbecue, cookout

asador *nm* : spit, rotisserie

asaduras *nfpl* : entrails, offal

asalariado¹, -da *adj* : wage-earning, salaried

asalariado², -da *n* : wage earner

asaltante *nmf* **1** : mugger, robber **2** : assailant

asaltar *vt* **1** : to assault **2** : to mug, to rob **3 asaltar al poder** : to seize power

asalto *nm* **1** : assault **2** : mugging, robbery **3** : round (in boxing) **4 asalto al poder** : coup d'etat

asamblea *nf* : assembly, meeting

asambleísta *nmf* : assemblyman *m*, assemblywoman *f*

asar *vt* : to roast, to grill — **asarse** *vr fam* : to roast, to be dying from heat

asbesto *nm* : asbestos

ascendencia *nf* **1** : ancestry, descent **2** ~ **sobre** : influence over

ascendente *adj* : ascending, upward ⟨un curso ascendente : an upward trend⟩

ascender {56} *vt* **1** : to ascend, to rise up **2** : to be promoted ⟨ascendió a gerente : she was promoted to manager⟩ **3** ~ **a** : to amount to, to reach ⟨las deudas ascienden a 20 millones de pesos : the debt amounts to 20 million pesos⟩ — *vt* : to promote

ascendiente¹ *nmf* ANCESTRO : ancestor

ascendiente² *nm* INFLUENCIA : influence, ascendancy

ascensión *nf, pl* **-siones** **1** : ascent, rise **2 Fiesta de la Ascensión** : Ascension Day

ascenso *nm* **1** : ascent, rise **2** : promotion

ascensor *nm* ELEVADOR : elevator

asceta *nmf* : ascetic

ascético, -ca *adj* : ascetic

ascetismo *nm* : asceticism

asco *nm* **1** : disgust ⟨¡qué asco! : that's disgusting!, how revolting!⟩ **2 darle asco (a alguien)** : to sicken, to revolt **3 estar hecho un asco** : to be filthy **4 hacerle ascos a** : to turn up one's nose at

ascua *nf* **1** BRASA : ember **2 estar en ascuas** *fam* : to be on edge

asear *vt* **1** : to wash, to clean **2** : to tidy up — **asearse** *vr*

asechanza *nf* : snare, trap

asechar *vt* : to set a trap for

asediar *vt* **1** SITIAR : to besiege **2** ACOSAR : to harass

asedio *nm* **1** : siege **2** ACOSO : harassment

asegurador¹, -dora *adj* **1** : insuring, assuring **2** : pertaining to insurance

asegurador², -dora *n* : insurer, underwriter

aseguradora *nf* : insurance company

asegurar *vt* **1** : to assure **2** : to secure **3** : to insure — **asegurarse** *vr* **1** CERCIORARSE : to make sure **2** : to take out insurance, to insure oneself

asemejar *vt* **1** : to make similar ⟨ese bigote te asemeja a tu abuelo : that mustache makes you look like your grandfather⟩ **2** *Mex* : to be similar to, to resemble — **asemejarse** *vr* ~ **a** : to look like, to resemble

asentaderas *nfpl fam* : bottom, buttocks *pl*

asentado, -da *adj* : settled, established

asentamiento *nm* : settlement

asentar {55} *vt* **1** : to lay down, to set down, to place **2** : to settle, to establish **3** *Mex* : to state, to affirm — **asentarse** *vr* **1** : to settle **2** ESTABLECERSE : to settle down, to establish oneself

asentimiento *nm* : assent, consent

asentir {76} *vt* : to consent, to agree

aseo *nm* : cleanliness

aséptico, -ca *adj* : aseptic, germ-free

asequible *adj* ACCESIBLE : accessible, attainable

aserción *nf* → **aserto**

aserradero *nm* : sawmill

aserrar {55} *vt* : to saw

aserrín *nm, pl* -**rrines** : sawdust

aserto *nm* : assertion, affirmation

asesinar *vt* **1** : to murder **2** : to assassinate

asesinato *nm* **1** : murder **2** : assassination

asesino¹, -na *adj* : murderous, homicidal

asesino², -na *n* **1** : murderer, killer **2** : assassin

asesor, -sora *n* : advisor, consultant

asesoramiento *nm* : advice, counsel

asesorar *vt* : to advise, to counsel — **asesorarse** *vr* ~ **de** : to consult

asesoría *nf* **1** : consulting, advising **2** : consultant's office

asestar {55} *vt* **1** : to aim, to point (a weapon) **2** : to deliver, to deal (a blow)

aseveración *nf, pl* -**ciones** : assertion, statement

aseverar *vt* : to assert, to state

asexual *adj* : asexual — **asexualmente** *adv*

asfaltado¹, -da *adj* : asphalted, paved

asfaltado² *nm* PAVIMENTO : pavement, asphalt

asfaltar *vt* : to pave, to blacktop

asfalto *nm* : asphalt

asfixia *nf* : asphyxia, asphyxiation, suffocation

asfixiar *vt* : to asphyxiate, to suffocate, to smother — **asfixiarse** *vr*

asga, etc. → **asir**

así¹ *adv* **1** : like this, like that **2** : so, thus ⟨así sea : so be it⟩ **3** ~ **de** : so, about so ⟨una caja así de grande : a box about so big⟩ **4 así que** : so, therefore

5 ~ **como** : as well as **6 así así** : so-so, fair

así² *adj* : such, such a ⟨un talento así es inestimable : a talent like that is priceless⟩

así³ *conj* AUNQUE : even if, even though ⟨no irá, así le paguen : he won't go, even if they pay him⟩

asiático¹, -ca *adj* : Asian, Asiatic

asiático², -ca *n* : Asian

asidero *nm* **1** AGARRADERA, ASA : grip, handle **2** AGARRE : grip, hold

asiduamente *adv* : regularly, frequently

asiduidad *nf* **1** : assiduousness **2** : regularity, frequency

asiduo, -dua *adj* **1** : assiduous **2** : frequent, regular

asiento *nm* **1** : seat, chair ⟨asiento trasero : back seat⟩ **2** : location, site

asignación *nf, pl* -**ciones** **1** : allocation **2** : appointment, designation **3** : allowance, pay **4** *PRi* : homework, assignment

asignar *vt* **1** : to assign, to allocate **2** : to appoint

asignatura *nf* MATERIA : subject, course

asilado, -da *n* : exile, refugee

asilo *nm* : asylum, refuge, shelter

asimetría *nf* : asymmetry

asimétrico, -ca *adj* : asymmetrical, asymmetric

asimilación *nf, pl* -**ciones** : assimilation

asimilar *vt* : to assimilate — **asimilarse** *vr* ~ **a** : to be similar to, to resemble

asimismo *adv* **1** IGUALMENTE : similarly, likewise **2** TAMBIÉN : as well, also

asir {7} *vt* : to seize, to grasp — **asirse** *vr* ~ **a** : to cling to

asistencia *nf* **1** : attendance **2** : assistance **3** : assist (in sports)

asistente¹ *adj* : attending, in attendance

asistente² *nmf* **1** : assistant **2 los asistentes** : those present, those in attendance

asistir *vi* : to attend, to be present ⟨asistir a clase : to attend class⟩ — *vt* : to aid, to assist

asma *nf* : asthma

asmático, -ca *adj* : asthmatic

asno *nm* BURRO : ass, donkey

asociación *nf, pl* -**ciones** **1** : association, relationship **2** : society, group, association

asociado¹, -da *adj* : associate, associated

asociado², -da *n* : associate, partner

asociar *vt* **1** : to associate, to connect **2** : to pool (resources) **3** : to take into partnership — **asociarse** *vr* **1** : to become partners **2** ~ **a** : to join, to become a member of

asolar {19} *vt* : to devastate, to destroy

asoleado, -da *adj* : sunny

asolear *vt* : to put in the sun — **asolearse** *vr* : to sunbathe

asomar *vt* : to show, to stick out — *vi* : to appear, to become visible — **aso-**

marse *vr* **1** : to show, to appear **2** : to lean out, to look out ⟨se asomó por la ventana : he leaned out the window⟩

asombrar *vt* MARAVILLAR : to amaze, to astonish — **asombrarse** *vr* : to marvel, to be amazed

asombro *nm* : amazement, astonishment

asombroso, -sa *adj* : amazing, astonishing — **asombrosamente** *adv*

asomo *nm* **1** : hint, trace **2 ni por asomo** : by no means

aspa *nf* : blade (of a fan or propeller)

aspaviento *nm* : exaggerated movement, fuss, flounce

aspecto *nm* **1** : aspect **2** APARIENCIA : appearance, look

aspereza *nf* RUDEZA : roughness, coarseness

áspero, -ra *adj* : rough, coarse, abrasive — **ásperamente** *adv*

aspersión *nf, pl* **-siones** : sprinkling

aspersor *nm* : sprinkler

aspiración *nf, pl* **-ciones** **1** : inhalation, breathing in **2** ANHELO : aspiration, desire

aspiradora *nf* : vacuum cleaner

aspirante *nmf* : applicant, candidate

aspirar *vi* ∼ **a** : to aspire to — *vt* : to inhale, to breathe in

aspirina *nf* : aspirin

asquear *vt* : to sicken, to disgust

asquerosidad *nf* : filth, foulness

asqueroso, -sa *adj* : disgusting, sickening, repulsive — **asquerosamente** *adv*

asta *nf* **1** : flagpole ⟨a media asta : at half-mast⟩ **2** : horn, antler **3** : shaft (of a weapon)

ástaco *nm* : crayfish

astado, -da *adj* : horned

aster *nm* : aster

asterisco *nm* : asterisk

asteroide *nm* : asteroid

astigmatismo *nm* : astigmatism

astil *nm* : shaft (of an arrow or feather)

astilla *nf* **1** : splinter, chip **2 de tal palo, tal astilla** : like father, like son

astillar *vt* : to splinter — **astillarse** *vr*

astillero *nm* : dry dock, shipyard

astral *adj* : astral

astringente *adj & nm* : astringent — **astringencia** *nf*

astro *nm* **1** : heavenly body **2** : star

astrología *nf* : astrology

astrológico, -ca *adj* : astrological

astrólogo, -ga *n* : astrologer

astronauta *nmf* : astronaut

astronáutica *nf* : astronautics

astronáutico, -ca *adj* : astronautic, astronautical

astronave *nf* : spaceship

astronomía *nf* : astronomy

astronómico, -ca *adj* : astronomical — **astronómicamente** *adv*

astrónomo, -ma *n* : astronomer

astroso, -sa *adj* DESALIÑADO : slovenly, untidy

astucia *nf* **1** : astuteness, shrewdness **2** : cunning, guile

astuto, -ta *adj* **1** : astute, shrewd **2** : crafty, tricky — **astutamente** *adv*

asueto *nm* : time off, break

asumir *vt* **1** : to assume, to take on ⟨asumir el cargo : to take office⟩ **2** SUPONER : to assume, to suppose

asunción *nf, pl* **-ciones** : assumption

asunto *nm* **1** CUESTIÓN, TEMA : affair, matter, subject **2 asuntos** *nmpl* : affairs, business

asustadizo, -za *adj* : nervous, jumpy, skittish

asustado, -da *adj* : frightened, afraid

asustar *vt* ESPANTAR : to scare, to frighten — **asustarse** *vr*

atacante *nmf* : assailant, attacker

atacar {72} *v* : to attack

atado¹, -da *adj* : shy, inhibited

atado² ** *nm* **1 : bundle, bunch **2** *Arg* : pack (of cigarettes)

atadura *nf* LIGADURA : tie, bond

atajar *vt* **1** IMPEDIR : to block, to stop **2** INTERRUMPIR : to interrupt, to cut off **3** CONTENER : to hold back, to restrain — *vi* ∼ **por** : to take a shortcut through

atajo *nm* : shortcut

atalaya *nf* **1** : watchtower **2** : vantage point

atañer {79} *vt* ∼ **a** (*3rd person only*) : to concern, to have to do with ⟨eso no me atañe : that does not concern me⟩

ataque *nm* **1** : attack, assault **2** : fit ⟨ataque de risa : fit of laughter⟩ **3 ataque de nervios** : nervous breakdown **4 ataque cardíaco** *or* **ataque al corazón** : heart attack

atar *vt* AMARRAR : to tie, to tie up, to tie down — **atarse** *vr*

atarantado, -da *adj fam* **1** : restless **2** : dazed, stunned

atarantar *vt fam* : to daze, to stun

atarazana *nf* : shipyard

atardecer¹ {53} *v impers* : to get dark

atardecer² *nm* : late afternoon, dusk

atareado, -da *adj* : busy, overworked

atascar {72} *vt* **1** ATORAR : to block, to clog, to stop up **2** : to hinder — **atascarse** *vr* **1** : to become obstructed **2** : to get bogged down **3** PARARSE : to stall

atasco *nm* **1** : blockage **2** EMBOTELLAMIENTO : traffic jam

ataúd *nm* : coffin, casket

ataviar {85} *vt* : to dress, to clothe — **ataviarse** *vr* : to dress up

atavío *nm* ATUENDO : dress, attire

ateísmo *nm* : atheism

atemorizar {21} *vt* : to frighten, to intimidate — **atemorizarse** *vr*

atemperar *vt* : to temper, to moderate

atención¹ *nf, pl* **-ciones** **1** : attention **2 poner atención** *or* **prestar atención** : to pay attention **3 llamar la atención** : to attract attention **4 en atención a** : in view of

atención² *interj* **1** : attention! **2** : watch out!

atender {56} *vt* **1** : to help, to wait on **2** : to look after, to take care of **3** : to heed, to listen to — *vi* : to pay attention

atenerse {80} *vr* : to abide ⟨tendrás que atenerte a las reglas : you will have to abide by the rules⟩

atentado *nm* : attack, assault

atentamente *adv* **1** : attentively, carefully **2** (*used in correspondence*) : sincerely, sincerely yours

atentar {55} *vi* ~ **contra** : to make an attempt on, to threaten ⟨atentaron contra su vida : they made an attempt on his life⟩

atento, -ta *adj* **1** : attentive, mindful **2** CORTÉS : courteous

atenuación *nf, pl* **-ciones 1** : lessening **2** : understatement

atenuante[1] *adj* : extenuating, mitigating

atenuante[2] *nmf* : extenuating circumstance, excuse

atenuar {3} *vt* **1** MITIGAR : to extenuate, to mitigate **2** : to dim (light), to tone down (colors) **3** : to minimize, to lessen

ateo[1], **atea** *adj* : atheistic

ateo[2], **atea** *n* : atheist

aterciopelado, -da *adj* : velvety, downy

aterido, -da *adj* : freezing, frozen

aterrador, -dora *adj* : terrifying

aterrar {55} *vt* : to terrify, to frighten

aterrizaje *nm* : landing (of a plane)

aterrizar {21} *vt* : to land, to touch down

aterrorizar {21} *vt* **1** : to terrify **2** : to terrorize — **aterrorizarse** *vr* : to be terrified

atesorar *vt* : to hoard, to amass

atestado, -da *adj* : crowded, packed

atestar {55} *vt* **1** ATIBORRAR : to crowd, to pack **2** : to witness, to testify to — *vi* : to testify

atestiguar {10} *vt* : to testify to, to bear witness to — *vi* DECLARAR : to testify

atiborrar *vt* : to pack, to crowd — **atiborrarse** *vr* : to stuff oneself

ático *nm* **1** : penthouse **2** BUHARDILLA, DESVÁN : attic

atigrado, -da *adj* : tabby (of cats), striped (of fur)

atildado, -da *adj* : smart, neat, dapper

atildar *vt* **1** : to put a tilde over **2** : to clean up, to smarten up — **atildarse** *vr* : to get spruced up

atinar *vi* ACERTAR : to be accurate, to be on target

atingencia *nf* : bearing, relevance

atípico, -ca *adj* : atypical

atiplado, -da *adj* : shrill, high-pitched

atirantar *vt* : to make taut, to tighten

atisbar *vt* **1** : to spy on, to watch **2** : to catch a glimpse of, to make out

atisbo *nm* : glimpse, sign, hint

atizador *nm* : poker (for a fire)

atizar {21} *vt* **1** : to poke, to stir, to stoke (a fire) **2** : to stir up, to rouse **3** *fam* : to give, to land (a blow)

atlántico, -ca *adj* : Atlantic

atlas *nm* : atlas

atleta *nmf* : athlete

atlético, -ca *adj* : athletic

atletismo *nm* : athletics

atmósfera *nf* : atmosphere

atmosférico, -ca *adj* : atmospheric

atole *nm Mex* **1** : thick hot beverage prepared with corn flour **2 darle atole con el dedo (a alguien)** : to string (someone) along

atollarse *vr* : to get stuck, to get bogged down

atolón *nm, pl* **-lones** : atoll

atolondrado, -da *adj* **1** ATURDIDO : bewildered, dazed **2** DESPISTADO : scatterbrained, absentminded

atómico, -ca *adj* : atomic

atomizador *nm* : atomizer

atomizar {21} *vt* FRAGMENTAR : to fragment, to break into bits

átomo *nm* : atom

atónito, -ta *adj* : astonished, amazed

atontar *vt* **1** : to stupefy **2** : to bewilder, to confuse

atorar *vt* ATASCAR : to block, to clog — **atorarse** *vr* **1** ATASCARSE : to get stuck **2** ATRAGANTARSE : to choke

atormentador, -dora *n* : tormenter

atormentar *vt* : to torment, to torture — **atormentarse** *vr* : to torment oneself, to agonize

atornillar *vt* : to screw (in, on, down)

atorrante *nmf Arg* : bum, loafer

atosigar {52} *vt* : to harass, to annoy

atracadero *nm* : dock, pier

atracador, -dora *n* : robber, mugger

atracar {72} *vt* **1** : to dock, to land — *vt* : to hold up, to rob, to mug — **atracarse** *vr fam* ~ **de** : to gorge oneself with

atracción *nf, pl* **-ciones** : attraction

atraco *nm* : holdup, robbery

atractivo[1], **-va** *adj* : attractive

atractivo[2] *nm* : attraction, appeal, charm

atraer {81} *vt* : to attract — **atraerse** *vr* **1** : to attract (each other) **2** GANARSE : to gain, to win

atragantarse *vr* : to choke (on food)

atrancar {72} *vt* : to block, to bar — **atrancarse** *vr*

atrapada *nf* : catch

atrapar *vt* : to trap, to capture

atrás *adv* **1** DETRÁS : back, behind ⟨se quedó atrás : he stayed behind⟩ **2** ANTES : ago ⟨mucho tiempo atrás : long ago⟩ **3 para** ~ *or* **hacia** ~ : backwards, toward the rear **4** ~ **de** : in back of, behind

atrasado, -da *adj* **1** : late, overdue **2** : backward **3** : old-fashioned **4** : slow (of a clock or watch)

atrasar *vt* : to delay, to put off — *vi* : to lose time — **atrasarse** *vr* : to fall behind

atraso *nm* **1** RETRASO : lateness, delay ⟨llegó con 20 minutos de atraso : he was 20 minutes late⟩ **2** : backwardness **3 atrasos** *nmpl* : arrears

atravesar {55} vt **1** CRUZAR : to cross, to go across **2** : to pierce **3** : to lay across **4** : to go through (a situation or crisis) — **atravesarse** vr **1** : to be in the way ⟨se me atravesó : it blocked my path⟩ **2** : to interfere, to meddle
atrayente adj : attractive
atreverse vr **1** : to dare **2** : to be insolent
atrevido, -da adj **1** : bold, daring **2** : insolent
atrevimiento nm **1** : daring, boldness **2** : insolence
atribución nf, pl **-ciones** : attribution
atribuible adj IMPUTABLE : attributable, ascribable
atribuir {41} vt **1** : to attribute, to ascribe **2** : to grant, to confer — **atribuirse** vr : to take credit for
atribular vt : to afflict, to trouble — **atribularse** vr
atributo nm : attribute
atril nm : lectern, stand
atrincherar vt : to entrench — **atrincherarse** vr **1** : to dig in, to entrench oneself **2** ~ **en** : to hide behind
atrio nm **1** : atrium **2** : portico
atrocidad nf : atrocity
atrofia nf : atrophy
atrofiar v : to atrophy
atronador, -dora adj : thunderous, deafening
atropellado, -da adj **1** : rash, hasty **2** : brusque, abrupt
atropellamiento → **atropello**
atropellar vt **1** : to knock down, to run over **2** : to violate, to abuse — **atropellarse** vr : to rush through (a task), to trip over one's words
atropello nm : abuse, violation, outrage
atroz adj, pl **atroces** : atrocious, appalling — **atrozmente** adv
atuendo nm ATAVÍO : attire, costume
atufar vt : to vex, to irritate — **atufarse** vr **1** : to get angry **2** : to smell bad, to stink
atún nm, pl **atunes** : tuna fish, tuna
aturdimiento nm : bewilderment, confusion
aturdir vt **1** : to stun, to shock **2** : to bewilder, to confuse, to stupefy
atuvo, etc. → **atenerse**
audacia nf OSADÍA : boldness, audacity
audaz adj, pl **audaces** : bold, audacious, daring — **audazmente** adv
audible adj : audible
audición nf, pl **-ciones** **1** : hearing **2** : audition
audiencia nf : audience
audífono nm **1** : hearing aid **2** **audífonos** nmpl : headphones, earphones
audio nm : audio
audiovisual adj : audiovisual
auditar vt : to audit
auditivo, -va adj : auditory, hearing, aural ⟨aparato auditivo : hearing aid⟩
auditor, -tora n : auditor
auditoría nf : audit

auditorio nm **1** : auditorium **2** : audience
auge nm **1** : peak, height **2** : boom, upturn
augur nm : augur
augurar vt : to predict, to foretell
augurio nm AGÜERO, PRESAGIO : augury, omen
augusto, -ta adj : august
aula nf : classroom
aullar {8} vt : to howl, to wail
aullido nm : howl, wail
aumentar vt ACRECENTAR : to increase, to raise — vi : to rise, to increase, to grow
aumento nm INCREMENTO : increase, rise
aun adv **1** : even ⟨ni aun en coche llegaría a tiempo : I wouldn't arrive on time even if I drove⟩ **2 aun así** : even so **3 aun más** : even more
aún adv **1** TODAVÍA : still, yet ⟨¿aún no ha llegado el correo? : the mail still hasn't come?⟩ **2 más aún** : furthermore
aunar {8} vt : to join, to combine — **aunarse** vr : to unite
aunque conj **1** : though, although, even if, even though **2 aunque sea** : at least
aura nf **1** : aura **2** : turkey buzzard
áureo, -rea adj : golden
aureola nf **1** : halo **2** : aura (of power, fame, etc.)
aurícula nf : auricle
auricular nm : telephone receiver
aurora nf **1** : dawn **2 aurora boreal** : aurora borealis
ausencia nf : absence
ausentarse vr **1** : to leave, to go away **2** ~ **de** : to stay away from
ausente[1] adj : absent, missing
ausente[2] nmf **1** : absentee **2** : missing person
auspiciar vt **1** PATROCINAR : to sponsor **2** FOMENTAR : to foster, to promote
auspicios nmpl : sponsorship, auspices
austeridad nf : austerity
austero, -ra adj : austere
austral[1] adj : southern
austral[2] nm : former monetary unit of Argentina
australiano, -na adj & n : Australian
austriaco or **austríaco, -ca** adj & n : Austrian
autenticar {72} vt : to authenticate — **autenticación** nf
autenticidad nf : authenticity
auténtico, -ca adj : authentic — **auténticamente** adv
autentificar {72} vt : to authenticate — **autentificación** nf
autismo nm : autism
autista adj : autistic
auto nm : auto, car
autoayuda nf : self-help
autobiografía nf : autobiography
autobiográfico, -ca adj : autobiographical
autobús nm, pl **-buses** : bus

autocompasión *nf* : self-pity
autocontrol *nm* : self-control
autocracia *nf* : autocracy
autócrata *nmf* : autocrat
autocrático, -ca *adj* : autocratic
autóctono, -na *adj* : indigenous, native ⟨arte autóctono : indigenous art⟩
autodefensa *nf* : self-defense
autodestrucción *nf* : self-destruction — **autodestructivo, -va** *adj*
autodeterminación *nf* : self-determination
autodidacta[1] *adj* : self-taught
autodidacta[2] *nmf* : self-taught person, autodidact
autodidacto[1], -ta *adj* → **autodidacta[1]**
autodidacto[2], -ta *n* → **autodidacta[2]**
autodisciplina *nf* : self-discipline
autoestima *nf* : self-esteem
autogobierno *nm* : self-government
autografiar *vt* : to autograph
autógrafo *nm* : autograph
autoinfligido, -da *adj* : self-inflicted
automación → **automatización**
autómata *nm* : automaton
automático, -ca *adj* : automatic — **automáticamente** *adv*
automatización *nf* : automation
automatizar {21} *vt* : to automate
automotor, -tora *adj* **1** : self-propelled **2** : automotive, car
automotriz[1] *adj, pl* **-trices** : automotive, car
automotriz[2] *nf, pl* **-trices** : automaker
automóvil *nm* : automobile
automovilista *nmf* : motorist
automovilístico, -ca *adj* : automobile, car ⟨accidente automovilístico : automobile accident⟩
autonombrado, -da *adj* : self-appointed
autonomía *nf* : autonomy
autónomo, -ma *adj* : autonomous — **autónomamente** *adv*
autopista *nf* : expressway, highway
autoproclamado, -da *adj* : self-proclaimed, self-appointed
autopropulsado, -da *adj* : self-propelled
autopsia *nf* : autopsy
autor, -tora *n* **1** : author **2** : perpetrator
autoría *nf* : authorship
autoridad *nf* : authority
autoritario, -ria *adj* : authoritarian
autorización *nf, pl* **-ciones** : authorization
autorizado, -da *adj* **1** : authorized **2** : authoritative
autorizar {21} *vt* : to authorize, to approve
autorretrato *nm* : self-portrait
autoservicio *nm* **1** : self-service restaurant **2** SUPERMERCADO : supermarket
autostop *nm* **1** : hitchhiking **2 hacer autostop** : to hitchhike
autostopista *nmf* : hitchhiker
autosuficiencia *nf* : self-sufficiency — **autosuficiente** *adj*
auxiliar[1] *vt* : to aid, to assist

auxiliar[2] *adj* : assistant, auxiliary
auxiliar[3] *nmf* **1** : assistant, helper **2 auxiliar de vuelo** : flight attendant
auxilio *nm* **1** : aid, assistance **2 primeros auxilios** : first aid
aval *nm* : guarantee, endorsement
avalancha *nf* ALUD : avalanche
avalar *vt* : to guarantee, to endorse
avaluar {3} *vt* : to evaluate, to appraise
avalúo *nm* : appraisal, evaluation
avance *nm* ADELANTO : advance
avanzado, -da *adj* **1** : advanced **2** : progressive
avanzar {21} *v* : to advance, to move forward
avaricia *nf* CODICIA : greed, avarice
avaricioso, -sa *adj* : avaricious, greedy
avaro[1], -ra *adj* : miserly, greedy
avaro[2], -ra *n* : miser
avasallador, -dora *adj* : overwhelming
avasallamiento *nm* : subjugation, domination
avasallar *vt* : to overpower, to subjugate
ave *nf* **1** : bird **2 aves de corral** : poultry **3 ave rapaz** *or* **ave de presa** : bird of prey
avecinarse *vr* : to approach, to come near
avecindarse *vr* : to settle, to take up residence
avellana *nf* : hazelnut, filbert
avellano *nm* : hazel
avena *nf* **1** : oat, oats *pl* **2** : oatmeal
avenencia *nf* : agreement, pact
avenida *nf* : avenue
avenir {87} *vt* : to reconcile, to harmonize — **avenirse** *vr* **1** : to agree, to come to terms **2** : to get along
aventajado, -da *adj* : outstanding
aventajar *vt* **1** : to be ahead of, to lead **2** : to surpass, to outdo
aventar {55} *vt* **1** : to fan **2** : to winnow **3** *Col, Mex* : to throw, to toss — **aventarse** *vr* **1** *Col, Mex* : to hurl oneself **2** *Mex fam* : to dare, to take a chance
aventón *nm, pl* **-tones** *Col, Mex fam* : ride, lift
aventura *nf* **1** : adventure **2** RIESGO : venture, risk **3** : love affair
aventurado, -da *adj* : hazardous, risky
aventurar *vt* : to venture, to risk — **aventurarse** *vr* : to take a risk
aventurero[1], -ra *adj* : adventurous
aventurero[2], -ra *n* : adventurer
avergonzado, -da *adj* **1** : ashamed **2** : embarrassed
avergonzar {9} *vt* APENAR : to shame, to embarrass — **avergonzarse** *vr* APENARSE : to be ashamed, to be embarrassed
avería *nf* **1** : damage **2** : breakdown, malfunction
averiado, -da *adj* **1** : damaged, faulty **2** : broken down
averiar {85} *vt* : to damage — **averiarse** *vr* : to break down
averiguación *nf, pl* **-ciones** : investigation, inquiry

averiguar {10} vt 1 : to find out, to ascertain 2 : to investigate

aversión nf, pl -siones : aversion, dislike

avestruz nm, pl -truces : ostrich

avezado, -da adj : seasoned, experienced

aviación nf, pl -ciones : aviation

aviador, -dora n : aviator, flyer

aviar {85} vt 1 : to prepare, to make ready 2 : to tidy up 3 : to equip, to supply

avicultor, -tora n : poultry farmer

avicultura nf : poultry farming

avidez nf, pl -deces : eagerness

ávido, -da adj : eager, avid — ávidamente adv

avieso, -sa adj 1 : twisted, distorted 2 : wicked, depraved

avinagrado, -da adj : vinegary, sour

avío nm 1 : preparation, provision 2 : loan (for agriculture or mining) 3 avíos nmpl : gear, equipment

avión nm, pl aviones : airplane

avioneta nf : light airplane

avisar vt 1 : to notify, to inform 2 : to advise, to warn

aviso nm 1 : notice 2 : advertisement, ad 3 ADVERTENCIA : warning 4 estar sobre aviso : to be on the alert

avispa nf : wasp

avispado, -da adj fam : clever, sharp

avispero nm : wasps' nest

avispón nm, pl -pones : hornet

avistar vt : to sight, to catch sight of

avituallar vt : to suppy with food, to provision

avivar vt 1 : to enliven, to brighten 2 : to strengthen, to intensify

avizorar vt 1 ACECHAR : to spy on, to watch 2 : to observe, to perceive ⟨se avizoran dificultades : difficulties are expected⟩

axila nf : underarm, armpit

axioma nm : axiom

axiomático, -ca adj : axiomatic

ay interj 1 : oh! 2 : ouch!, ow!

ayer[1] adv : yesterday

ayer[2] nm ANTAÑO : yesteryear, days gone by

ayote nm CA, Mex : squash, pumpkin

ayuda nf 1 : help, assistance 2 ayuda de cámara : valet

ayudante nmf : helper, assistant

ayudar vt : to help, to assist — ayudarse vr ~ de : to make use of

ayunar vi : to fast

ayunas nfpl en ~ : fasting ⟨este medicamento ha de tomarse en ayunas : this medication should be taken on an empty stomach⟩

ayuno nm : fast

ayuntamiento nm 1 : town hall, city hall 2 : town or city council

azabache nm : jet ⟨negro azabache : jet black⟩

azada nf : hoe

azafata nf 1 : stewardess f 2 : hostess f (on a TV show)

azafrán nm, pl -franes 1 : saffron 2 : crocus

azahar nm : orange blossom

azalea nf : azalea

azar nm 1 : chance ⟨juegos de azar : games of chance⟩ 2 : accident, misfortune 3 al azar : at random, randomly

azaroso, -sa adj 1 : perilous, hazardous 2 : turbulent, eventful

azimut nm : azimuth

azogue nm : mercury, quicksilver

azorar vt 1 : to alarm, to startle 2 : to fluster, to embarrass — azorarse vr : to get embarrassed

azotar vt 1 : to whip, to flog 2 : to lash, to batter 3 : to devastate, to afflict

azote nm 1 LÁTIGO : whip, lash 2 fam : spanking, licking 3 : calamity, scourge

azotea nf : flat roof, terraced roof

azteca adj & nmf : Aztec

azúcar nmf : sugar — azucarar vt

azucarado, -da adj : sweetened, sugary

azucarera nf : sugar bowl

azucarero, -ra adj : sugar ⟨industria azucarera : sugar industry⟩

azucena nf : white lily

azuela nf : adze

azufre nm : sulphur — azufroso, -sa adj

azul adj & nm : blue

azulado, -da adj : bluish

azulejo nm : ceramic tile, floor tile

azuloso, -sa adj : bluish

azulete nm : bluing

azur[1] adj CELESTE : azure

azur[2] n CELESTE : azure, sky blue

azuzar {21} vt : to incite, to egg on

B

b nf : second letter of the Spanish alphabet

baba nf 1 : spittle, saliva 2 : dribble, drool (of a baby) 3 : slime, ooze

babear vi 1 : to drool, to slobber 2 : to ooze

babel nmf : babel, chaos, bedlam

babero nm : bib

babor nm : port, port side

babosa nf : slug (mollusk)

babosada nf CA, Mex : silly act or remark

baboso, -sa adj 1 : drooling, slobbering 2 : slimy 3 CA, Mex fam : silly, dumb

babucha nf : slipper

babuino nm : baboon

bacalao nm : cod (fish)

bache *nm* **1** : pothole **2** *PRi* : deep puddle **3** : bad period, rough time ⟨bache económico : economic slump⟩
bachiller *nmf* : high school graduate
bachillerato *nm* : high school diploma
bacilo *nm* : bacillus
bacon *nm Spain* : bacon
bacteria *nf* : bacterium
bacteriano, -na *adj* : bacterial
bacteriología *nf* : bacteriology
bacteriológico, -ca *adj* : bacteriologic, bacteriological
bacteriólogo, -ga *n* : bacteriologist
báculo *nm* **1** : staff, stick **2** : comfort, support
badajo *nm* : clapper (of a bell)
badén *nm, pl* **badenes 1** : (paved) ford, channel **2** : dip, ditch (in a road) **3** : speed bump
bádminton *nm* : badminton
bafle *or* **baffle** *nm* **1** : baffle **2** : speaker, loudspeaker
bagaje *nm* **1** EQUIPAJE : baggage, luggage **2** : background ⟨bagaje cultural : cultural baggage⟩
bagatela *nf* : trifle, trinket
bagre *nm* : catfish
bahía *nf* : bay
bailar *vt* : to dance — *vi* **1** : to dance **2** : to spin **3** : to be loose, to be too big
bailarín[1], -rina *adj, mpl* **-rines 1** : dancing **2** : fond of dancing
bailarín[2], -rina *n, mpl* **-rines 1** : dancer **2** : ballet dancer, ballerina *f*
baile *nm* **1** : dance **2** : dance party, ball **3 llevarse al baile a** *Mex fam* : to take for a ride, to take advantage of
baja *nf* **1** DESCENSO : fall, drop **2** : slump, recession **3** : loss, casualty **4 dar de baja** : to discharge, to dismiss **5 darse de baja** : to withdraw, to drop out
bajada *nf* **1** : descent **2** : dip, slope **3** : decrease, drop
bajar *vt* **1** DESCENDER : to lower, to let down, to take down **2** REDUCIR : to reduce (prices) **3** INCLINAR : to lower, to bow (the head) **4** : to go down, to descend **5 bajar de categoría** : to downgrade — *vi* **1** : to drop, to fall **2** : to come down, to go down **3** : to ebb (of tides) — **bajarse** *vr* ~ **de** : to get off, to get out of (a vehicle)
bajeza *nf* **1** : low or despicable act **2** : baseness
bajío *nm* **1** : lowland **2** : shoal, sandbank, shallows
bajista *nmf* : bass player, bassist
bajo[1] *adv* **1** : down, low **2** : softly, quietly ⟨habla más bajo : speak more softly⟩
bajo[2], -ja *adj* **1** : low **2** : short (of stature) **3** : soft, faint, deep (of sounds) **4** : lower ⟨el bajo Amazonas : the lower Amazon⟩ **5** : lowered ⟨con la mirada baja : with lowered eyes⟩ **6** : base, vile **7 los bajos fondos** : the underworld

bajo[3] *nm* **1** : bass (musical instrument) **2** : first floor, ground floor **3** : hemline
bajo[4] *prep* : under, beneath, below
bajón *nm, pl* **bajones** : sharp drop, slump
bajorrelieve *nm* : bas-relief
bala *nf* **1** : bullet **2** : bale
balacera *nf* TIROTEO : shoot-out, gunfight
balada *nf* : ballad
balance *nm* **1** : balance **2** : balance sheet
balancear *vt* **1** : to balance **2** : to swing (one's arms, etc.) **3** : to rock (a boat) — **balancearse** *vr* **1** OSCILAR : to swing, to sway, to rock **2** VACILAR : to hesitate, to vacillate
balanceo *nm* **1** : swaying, rocking **2** : vacillation
balancín *nm, pl* **-cines 1** : rocking chair **2** SUBIBAJA : seesaw
balandra *nf* : sloop
balanza *nf* BÁSCULA : scales *pl*, balance
balar *vi* : to bleat
balaustrada *nf* : balustrade
balaustre *nm* : baluster
balazo *nm* **1** TIRO : shot, gunshot **2** : bullet wound
balboa *nf* : balboa (monetary unit of Panama)
balbucear *vi* **1** : to mutter, to stammer **2** : to prattle, to babble ⟨los niños están balbuceando : the children are prattling away⟩
balbuceo *nm* : mumbling, stammering
balbucir → **balbucear**
balcánico, -ca *adj* : Balkan
balcón *nm, pl* **balcones** : balcony
balde *nm* **1** CUBO : bucket, pail **2 en** ~ : in vain, to no avail
baldío[1], -día *adj* **1** : fallow, uncultivated **2** : useless, vain
baldío[2] *nm* **1** : wasteland **2** *Mex* : vacant lot
baldosa *nf* LOSETA : floor tile
balear *vt* : to shoot, to shoot at
balero *nm* **1** *Mex* : ball bearing **2** *Mex, PRi* : cup-and-ball toy
balido *nm* : bleat
balín *nm, pl* **balines** : pellet
balística *nf* : ballistics
balístico, -ca *adj* : ballistic
baliza *nf* **1** : buoy **2** : beacon (for aircraft)
ballena *nf* : whale
ballenero[1], -ra *adj* : whaling
ballenero[2], -ra *n* : whaler
ballenero[3] *nm* : whaleboat, whaler
ballesta *nf* **1** : crossbow **2** : spring (of an automobile)
ballet *nm* : ballet
balneario *nm* : spa, bathing resort
balompié *nm* FUTBOL : soccer
balón *nm, pl* **balones** : ball
baloncesto *nm* BASQUETBOL : basketball
balsa *nf* **1** : raft **2** : balsa **3** : pond, pool
balsámico, -ca *adj* : soothing

bálsamo *nm* : balsam, balm
báltico, -ca *adj* : Baltic
baluarte *nm* BASTIÓN : bulwark, bastion
bambolear *vi* **1** : to sway, to swing **2** : to wobble — **bambolearse** *vr*
bamboleo *nm* **1** : swaying, swinging **2** : wobbling
bambú *nm*, *pl* **bambúes** *or* **bambús** : bamboo
banal *adj* : banal, trivial
banalidad *nf* : banality
banana *nf* : banana
bananero[1], -ra *adj* : banana
bananero[2] *nm* : banana tree
banano *nm* **1** : banana tree **2** *CA, Col* : banana
banca *nf* **1** : banking **2** BANCO : bench
bancada *nf* **1** : group, faction **2** : workbench
bancal *nm* **1** : terrace (in agriculture) **2** : plot (of land)
bancario, -ria *adj* : bank, banking
bancarrota *nf* QUIEBRA : bankruptcy
banco *nm* **1** : bank ⟨banco central : central bank⟩ ⟨banco de datos : data bank⟩ ⟨banco de arena : sandbank⟩ ⟨banco de sangre : blood bank⟩ **2** BANCA : stool, bench **3** : pew **4** : school (of fish)
banda *nf* **1** : band, strip **2** *Mex* : belt ⟨banda transportadora : conveyor belt⟩ **3** : band (of musicians) **4** : gang (of persons), flock (of birds) **5 banda de rodadura** : tread (of a tire, etc.) **6 banda sonora** *or* **banda de sonido** : sound track
bandada *nf* : flock (of birds), school (of fish)
bandazo *nm* : swerving, lurch
bandearse *vr* : to look after oneself, to cope
bandeja *nf* : tray, platter
bandera *nf* : flag, banner
banderazo *nm* : starting signal (in sports)
banderilla *nf* : banderilla, dart (in bullfighting)
banderín *nm*, *pl* **-rines** : pennant, small flag
bandidaje *nm* : banditry
bandido, -da *n* BANDOLERO : bandit, outlaw
bando *nm* **1** FACCIÓN : faction, side **2** EDICTO : proclamation
bandolerismo *nm* : banditry
bandolero, -ra *n* BANDIDO : bandit, outlaw
bangladesí *adj & nmf* : Bangladeshi
banjo *nm* : banjo
banquero, -ra *n* : banker
banqueta *nf* **1** : footstool, stool, bench **2** *Mex* : sidewalk
banquete *nm* : banquet
banquetear *v* : to feast
banquillo *nm* **1** : bench (in sports) **2** : dock, defendant's seat
bañadera *nf* → **bañera**

bañar *vt* **1** : to bathe, to wash **2** : to immerse, to dip **3** : to coat, to cover ⟨bañado en lágrimas : bathed in tears⟩ — **bañarse** *vr* **1** : to take a bath, to bathe **2** : to go for a swim
bañera *nf* TINA : bathtub
bañista *nmf* : bather
baño *nm* **1** : bath **2** : swim, dip **3** : bathroom **4 baño María** : double boiler
baquerta *nf* **1** : ramrod **2 baquetas** *nfpl* : drumsticks
bar *nm* : bar, tavern
baraja *nf* : deck of cards
barajar *vt* **1** : to shuffle (cards) **2** : to consider, to toy with
baranda *nf* : rail, railing
barandal *nm* **1** : rail, railing **2** : bannister, handrail
barandilla *nf Spain* : bannister, handrail, railing
barata *nf* **1** *Mex* : sale, bargain **2** *Chile* : cockroach
baratija *nf* : bauble, trinket
baratillo *nm* : rummage sale, flea market
barato[1] *adv* : cheap, cheaply ⟨te lo vendo barato : I'll sell it to you cheap⟩
barato[2], -ta *adj* : cheap, inexpensive
baratura *nf* **1** : cheapness **2** : cheap thing
barba *nf* **1** : beard, stubble **2** : chin
barbacoa *nf* : barbecue
bárbaramente *adv* : barbarously
barbaridad *nf* **1** : barbarity, atrocity **2** ¡qué barbaridad! : that's outrageous!
barbarie *nf* : barbarism, savagery
bárbaro[1] *adv fam* : wildly ⟨anoche lo pasamos bárbaro : we had a wild time last night⟩
bárbaro[2], -ra *adj* **1** : barbarous, wild, uncivilized **2** *fam* : great, fantastic
bárbaro[3], -ra *n* : barbarian
barbecho *nm* : fallow land ⟨dejar en barbecho : to leave fallow⟩
barbero, -ra *n* : barber
barbilla *nf* MENTÓN : chin
barbitúrico *nm* : barbiturate
barbudo[1], -da *adj* : bearded
barbudo[2] *nm* : bearded man
barca *nf* **1** : boat **2 barca de pasaje** : ferryboat
barcaza *nf* : barge
barcia *nf* : chaff
barco *nm* **1** BARCA : boat **2** BUQUE, NAVE : ship
bardo *nm* : bard
bario *nm* : barium
barítono *nm* : baritone
barlovento *nm* : windward
barman *nm* : bartender
barniz *nm*, *pl* **barnices** **1** LACA : varnish, lacquer **2** : glaze (on ceramics, etc.)
barnizar {21} *vt* **1** : to varnish **2** : to glaze
barométrico, -ca *adj* : barometric
barómetro *nm* : barometer
barón *nm*, *pl* **barones** : baron

baronesa *nf* : baroness
baronet *nm* : baronet
barquero, -ra : boatman *m*, boatwoman *f*
barquillo *nm* : wafer, thin cookie or cracker
barra *nf* : bar
barraca *nf* **1** CABAÑA, CHOZA : hut, cabin **2** : booth, stall
barracuda *nf* : barracuda
barranca *nf* **1** : hillside, slope **2** → **barranco**
barranco *nm* : ravine, gorge
barredora *nf* : street sweeper (machine)
barrena *nf* **1** TALADRO : drill, auger, gimlet **2** : tailspin
barrenar *vt* **1** : to drill **2** : to undermine
barrendero, -ra *n* : sweeper, street cleaner
barrer *v* : to sweep — **barrerse** *vr* : to slide (in sports)
barrera *nf* OBSTÁCULO : barrier, obstacle ⟨barrera de sonido : sound barrier⟩
barreta *nf* : crowbar
barriada *nf* **1** : district, quarter **2** : slums *pl*
barrica *nf* BARRIL, TONEL : barrel, cask, keg
barricada *nf* : barricade
barrida *nf* **1** : sweep **2** : slide (in sports)
barrido *nm* : sweeping
barriga *nf* PANZA : belly, paunch
barrigón, -gona *adj, mpl* **-gones** *fam* : potbellied, paunchy
barril *nm* **1** BARRICA : barrel, keg **2 cerveza de barril** : draft beer
barrio *nm* **1** : neighborhood, district **2 barrios bajos** : slums *pl*
barro *nm* **1** LODO : mud **2** ARCILLA : clay **3** ESPINILLA, GRANO : pimple, blackhead
barroco, -ca *adj* : baroque
barroso, -sa *adj* ENLODADO : muddy
barrote *nm* : bar (on a window)
barrunto *nm* **1** SOSPECHA : suspicion **2** INDICIO : sign, indication, hint
bártulos *nmpl* : things, belongings ⟨liar los bártulos : to pack one's things⟩
barullo *nm* BULLA : racket, ruckus
basa *nf* : base, pedestal
basalto *nm* : basalt
basar *vt* FUNDAR : to base — **basarse** *vr* FUNDARSE ∼ **en** : to be based on
báscula *nf* BALANZA : balance, scales *pl*
base *nf* **1** : base, bottom **2** : base (in baseball) **3** FUNDAMENTO : basis, foundation **4 base de datos** : database **5 a base de** : based on, by means of **6 en base a** : based on, on the basis of
básico, -ca *adj* FUNDAMENTAL : basic — **básicamente** *adv*
basílica *nf* : basilica
basquetbol *or* **básquetbol** *nm* BALONCESTO : basketball
basset *nm* : basset hound
bastante¹ *adv* **1** : enough, sufficiently ⟨he trabajado bastante : I have worked enough⟩ **2** : fairly, rather, quite ⟨lle-

garon bastante temprano : they arrived quite early⟩
bastante² *adj* : enough, sufficient
bastante³ *pron* : enough ⟨hemos visto bastante : we have seen enough⟩
bastar *vi* : to be enough, to suffice
bastardilla *nf* CURSIVA : italic type, italics *pl*
bastardo, -da *adj & n* : bastard
bastidor *nm* **1** : framework, frame **2** : wing (in theater) ⟨entre bastidores : backstage, behind the scenes⟩
bastilla *nf* : hem
bastión *nf, pl* **bastiones** BALUARTE ; bastion, bulwark
basto, -ta *adj* : coarse, rough
bastón *nm, pl* **bastones** **1** : cane, walking stick **2** : baton **3 bastón de mando** : staff (of authority)
basura *nf* DESECHOS : garbage, waste, refuse
basurero¹, -ra *n* : garbage collector
basurero² *nm Mex* : garbage can
bata *nf* **1** : bathrobe, housecoat **2** : smock, coverall, lab coat
batalla *nf* **1** : battle **2** : fight, struggle **3 de** ∼ : ordinary, everyday ⟨mis zapatos de batalla : my everyday shoes⟩
batallar *vi* LIDIAR, LUCHAR : to battle, to fight
batallón *nm, pl* **-llones** : battalion
batata *nf* : yam, sweet potato
batazo *nm* HIT : hit (in baseball)
bate *nm* : baseball bat
batea *nf* **1** : tray, pan **2** : flat-bottomed boat, punt
bateador, -dora *n* : batter, hitter
batear *vi* : to bat — *vt* : to hit
bateo *nm* : batting (in baseball)
batería *nf* **1** PILA : battery **2** : drum kit, drums *pl* **3 batería de cocina** : kitchen utensils *pl*
baterista *nmf* : drummer
batido *nm* LICUADO : milk shake
batidor *nm* : eggbeater, whisk, mixer
batidora *nf* : (electric) mixer
batir *vt* **1** GOLPEAR : to beat, to hit **2** VENCER : to defeat **3** REVOLVER : to mix, to beat **4** : to break (a record) — **batirse** *vr* : to fight
batista *nf* : batiste, cambric
batuta *nf* **1** : baton **2 llevar la batuta** : to be the leader, to call the tune
baúl *nm* : trunk, chest
bautismal *adj* : baptismal
bautismo *nm* : baptism, christening
bautista *adj & nmf* : Baptist
bautizar {21} *vt* : to baptize, to christen
bautizo → **bautismo**
bávaro, -ra *adj & n* : Bavarian
baya *nf* **1** : berry **2 baya de saúco** : elderberry
bayeta *nf* : cleaning cloth
bayoneta *nf* : bayonet
baza *nf* **1** : trick (in card games) **2 meter baza en** : to butt in on
bazar *nm* : bazaar
bazo *nm* : spleen

bazofia *nf* 1 : table scraps *pl* 2 : slop, swill 3 : hogwash, rubbish
bazuca *nf* : bazooka
beagle *nm* : beagle
beatificar {72} *vt* : to beatify — beatificación *nf*
beatífico, -ca *adj* : beatific
beatitud *nf* : beatitude
beato, -ta *adj* 1 : blessed 2 : pious, devout 3 : sanctimonious, overly devout
bebé *nm* : baby
bebedero *nm* 1 ABREVADERO : watering trough 2 *Mex* : drinking fountain
bebedor, -dora *n* : drinker
beber *v* TOMAR : to drink
bebida *nf* : drink, beverage
beca *nf* : grant, scholarship
becado, -da *n* : scholar, scholarship holder
becerro, -rra *n* : calf
begonia *nf* : begonia
beige *adj & nm* : beige
beisbol *or* béisbol *nm* : baseball
beisbolista *nmf* : baseball player
beldad *nf* BELLEZA, HERMOSURA : beauty
belén *nf, pl* belenes NACIMIENTO : Nativity scene
belga *adj & nmf* : Belgian
beliceño, -ña *adj & n* : Belizean
belicista[1] *adj* : militaristic
belicista[2] *nmf* : warmonger
bélico, -ca *adj* GUERRERO : war, fighting ⟨esfuerzos bélicos : war efforts⟩
belicosidad *nf* : bellicosity
belicoso, -sa *adj* 1 : warlike, martial 2 : aggressive, belligerent
beligerancia *nf* : belligerence
beligerante *adj & nmf* : belligerent
bellaco[1], -ca *adj* : sly, cunning
bellaco[2], -ca *n* : rogue, scoundrel
belleza *nf* BELDAD, HERMOSURA : beauty
bello, -lla *adj* 1 HERMOSO : beautiful 2 bellas artes : fine arts
bellota *nf* : acorn
bemol *nm* : flat (in music) — bemol *adj*
benceno *nm* : benzene
bendecir {11} *vt* 1 CONSAGRAR : to bless, to consecrate 2 ALABAR : to praise, to extol 3 bendecir la mesa : to say grace
bendición *nf, pl* -ciones : benediction, blessing
bendiga, bendijo etc. → bendecir
bendito, -ta *adj* 1 : blessed, holy 2 : fortunate 3 : silly, simple-minded
benedictino, -na *adj & n* : Benedictine
benefactor[1], -tora *adj* : beneficent
benefactor[2], -tora *n* : benefactor, benefactress *f*
beneficencia *nf* : beneficence, charity
beneficiar *vt* : to benefit, to be of assistance to — beneficiarse *vr* : to benefit, to profit
beneficiario, -ria *n* : beneficiary
beneficio *nm* 1 GANANCIA, PROVECHO : gain, profit 2 : benefit

beneficioso, -sa *adj* PROVECHOSO : beneficial
benéfico, -ca *adj* : charitable, beneficent
benemérito, -ta *adj* : meritorious, worthy
beneplácito *nm* : approval, consent
benevolencia *nf* BONDAD : benevolence, kindness
benévolo, -la *adj* BONDADOSO : benevolent, kind, good
bengala *nf* luz de bengala 1 : flare (signal) 2 : sparkler
bengalí[1] *adj & nmf* : Bengali
bengalí[2] *nm* : Bengali (language)
benignidad *nf* : mildness, kindness
benigno, -na *adj* : benign, mild
beninés, -nesa *adj & n* : Beninese
benjamín, -mina *n, mpl* -mines : youngest child
beodo[1], -da *adj* : drunk, inebriated
beodo[2], -da *n* : drunkard
berberecho *nm* : cockle
berbiquí *nm* : brace (in carpentry)
berenjena *nf* : eggplant
bergantín *nm, pl* -tines : brig (ship)
berilo *nm* : beryl
bermudas *nfpl* : Bermuda shorts
berrear *vi* 1 : to bellow, to low 2 : to bawl, to howl
berrido *nm* 1 : bellowing 2 : howl, scream
berrinche *nm fam* : tantrum, conniption
berro *nm* : watercress
berza *nf* : cabbage
besar *vt* : to kiss
beso *nm* : kiss
bestia[1] *adj* 1 : ignorant, stupid 2 : boorish, rude
bestia[2] *nf* : beast, animal
bestia[3] *nmf* 1 IGNORANTE : ignoramus 2 : brute
bestial *adj* 1 : bestial, beastly 2 *fam* : huge, enormous ⟨hace un frío bestial : it's terribly cold⟩ 3 *fam* : great, fantastic
besuquear *vt fam* : to cover with kisses — besuquearse *vr fam* : to neck, to smooch
betabel *nm Mex* : beet
betún *nm, pl* betunes 1 : shoe polish 2 *Mex* : icing
bianual *adj* : biannual
biatlón *nm, pl* -lones : biathlon
biberón *nm, pl* -rones : baby's bottle
biblia *nf* 1 : bible 2 la Biblia : the Bible
bíblico, -ca *adj* : biblical
bibliografía *nf* : bibliography
bibliográfico, -ca *adj* : bibliographic, bibliographical
bibliógrafo, -fa *n* : bibliographer
biblioteca *nf* : library
bibliotecario, -ria *n* : librarian
bicameral *adj* : bicameral
bicarbonato *nm* 1 : bicarbonate 2 bicarbonato de soda : sodium bicarbonate, baking soda
bicentenario *nm* : bicentennial

bíceps *nms & pl* : biceps
bicho *nm* : small animal, bug, insect
bici *nf fam* : bike
bicicleta *nf* : bicycle
bicolor *adj* : two-tone
bicúspide *adj* : bicuspid
bidón *nm, pl* **bidones** : large can, (oil) drum
bien[1] *adv* **1** : well ⟨¿dormiste bien? : did you sleep well?⟩ **2** CORRECTAMENTE : correctly, properly, right ⟨hay que hacerlo bien : it must be done correctly⟩ **3** : very, quite ⟨el libro era bien divertido : the book was very amusing⟩ **4** : easily ⟨bien puede acabarlo en un día : he can easily finish it in a day⟩ **5** : willingly, readily ⟨bien lo aceptaré : I'll gladly accept it⟩ **6 bien que** : although **7 más bien** : rather
bien[2] *adj* **1** : well, OK, all right ⟨¿te sientes bien? : are you feeling all right?⟩ **2** : pleasant, agreeable ⟨las flores huelen bien : the flowers smell very nice⟩ **3** : satisfactory **4** : correct, right
bien[3] *nm* **1** : good ⟨el bien y el mal : good and evil⟩ **2 bienes** *nmpl* : property, goods, possessions
bienal *adj & nf* : biennial — **bienalmente** *adv*
bienaventurado, -da *adj* **1** : blessed **2** : fortunate, happy
bienaventuranzas *nfpl* : Beatitudes
bienestar *nm* **1** : welfare, well-being **2** CONFORT : comfort
bienhechor[1]**, -chora** *adj* : beneficent, benevolent
bienhechor[2]**, -chora** *n* : benefactor, benefactress *f*
bienintencionado, -da *adj* : well-meaning
bienvenida *nf* **1** : welcome **2 dar la bienvenida a** : to welcome
bienvenido, -da *adj* : welcome
bies *nm* : bias (in sewing)
bife *nm Arg, Chile, Uru* : steak
bífido, -da *adj* : forked
bifocal *adj* : bifocal
bifocales *nmpl* : bifocals
bifurcación *nf, pl* **-ciones** : fork (in a river or road)
bifurcarse {72} *vr* : to fork
bigamia *nf* : bigamy
bígamo, -ma *n* : bigamist
bigote *nm* **1** : mustache **2** : whisker (of an animal)
bigotudo, -da *adj* : mustached, having a big mustache
bikini *nm* : bikini
bilateral *adj* : bilateral — **bilateralmente** *adv*
bilingüe *adj* : bilingual
bilioso, -sa *adj* **1** : bilious **2** : irritable
bilis *nf* : bile
billar *nm* : pool, billiards
billete *nm* **1** : bill ⟨un billete de cinco dólares : a five-dollar bill⟩ **2** BOLETO : ticket ⟨billete de ida y vuelta : round-trip ticket⟩

billetera *nf* : billfold, wallet
billón *nm, pl* **billones 1** : billion (Great Britain) **2** : trillion (U.S.A.)
bimestral *adj* : bimonthly — **bimestralmente** *adv*
bimotor *adj* : twin-engined
binacional *adj* : binational
binario, -ria *adj* : binary
bingo *nm* : bingo
binocular *adj* : binocular
binoculares *nmpl* : binoculars
binomio *nm* **1** : binomial **2** PAREJA : pair, duo
biodegradable *adj* : biodegradable
biodegradarse *vr* : to biodegrade
biodiversidad *nf* : biodiversity
biofísica *nf* : biophysics
biofísico[1]**, -ca** *adj* : biophysical
biofísico[2]**, -ca** *n* : biophysicist
biografía *nf* : biography
biográfico, -ca *adj* : biographical
biógrafo, -fa *n* : biographer
biología *nf* : biology
biológico, -ca *adj* : biological, biologic — **biológicamente** *adv*
biólogo, -ga *n* : biologist
biombo *nm* MAMPARA : folding screen, room divider
biomecánica *nf* : biomechanics
biopsia *nf* : biopsy
bioquímica *nf* : biochemistry
bioquímico[1]**, -ca** *adj* : biochemical
bioquímico[2]**, -ca** *n* : biochemist
biosfera *or* **biósfera** *nf* : biosphere
biotecnología *nf* : biotechnology
biótico, -ca *adj* : biotic
bipartidismo *nm* : two-party system
bipartidista *adj* : bipartisan
bípedo *nm* : biped
birlar *vt fam* : to swipe, to pinch
birmano, -na *adj & n* : Burmese
bis[1] *adv* **1** : twice, again (in music) **2** : a, A ⟨artículo 47 bis : Article 47A⟩ ⟨calle Bolívar, número 70 bis : Bolívar Street, number 70A⟩
bis[2] *nm* : encore
bisabuelo, -la *n* : great-grandfather *m*, great-grandmother *f*, great-grandparent
bisagra *nf* : hinge
bisecar {72} *vt* : bisect — **bisección** *nf*
bisel *nm* : bevel
biselar *vt* : to bevel
bisexual *adj* : bisexual
bisiesto *adj* **año bisiesto** : leap year
bismuto *nm* : bismuth
bisnieto, -ta *n* : great-grandson *m*, great-granddaughter *f*, great-grandchild
bisonte *nm* : bison, buffalo
bisoñé *nm* : hairpiece, toupee
bisoño[1]**, -ña** *adj* : inexperienced, green
bisoño[2]**, -ña** *n* : rookie, greenhorn
bistec *nm* : steak, beefsteak
bisturí *nm* ESCALPELO : scalpel
bisutería *nf* : costume jewelry
bit *nm* : bit (unit of information)
bivalvo *nm* : bivalve
bizarría *nf* **1** : courage, gallantry **2** : generosity

bizarro, -rra *adj* **1** VALIENTE : courageous, valiant **2** GENEROSO : generous

bizco, -ca *adj* : cross-eyed

bizcocho *nm* **1** : sponge cake **2** : biscuit **3** *Mex* : breadstick

bizquera *nf* : crossed eyes, squint

blanco¹, -ca *adj* : white

blanco², -ca *n* : white person

blanco³ *nm* **1** : white **2** : target, bull's-eye ⟨dar en el blanco : to hit the target, to hit the nail on the head⟩ **3** : blank space, blank ⟨un cheque en blanco : a blank check⟩

blancura *nf* : whiteness

blancuzco, -ca *adj* **1** : whitish, off-white **2** PÁLIDO : pale

blandir {1} *vt* : to wave, to brandish

blando, -da *adj* **1** SUAVE : soft, tender **2** : weak (in character) **3** : lenient

blandura *nf* **1** : softness, tenderness **2** : leniency

blanqueador *nm* : bleach, whitener

blanquear *vt* **1** : to whiten, to bleach **2** : to shut out (in sports) **3** : to launder (money) — *vi* : to turn white

blanquillo *nm CA, Mex* : egg

blasfemar *vi* : to blaspheme

blasfemia *nf* : blasphemy

blasfemo, -ma *adj* : blasphemous

blazer *nm* : blazer

bledo *nm* **no me importa un bledo** *fam* : I couldn't care less, I don't give a damn

blindado, -da *adj* ACORAZADO : armored

blindaje *nm* **1** : armor, armor plating **2** : shield (for cables, machinery, etc.)

bloc *nm, pl* **blocs** : writing pad, pad of paper

blof *nm Col, Mex* : bluff

blofear *vi Col, Mex* : to bluff

blondo, -da *adj* : blond, flaxen

bloque *nm* **1** : block **2** GRUPO : bloc ⟨el bloque comunista : the Communist bloc⟩

bloquear *vt* **1** OBSTRUIR : to block, to obstruct **2** : to blockade

bloqueo *nm* **1** OBSTRUCCIÓN : blockage, obstruction **2** : blockade

blusa *nf* : blouse

blusón *nm, pl* **blusones** : loose shirt, smock

boa *nf* : boa

boato *nm* : ostentation, show

bobada *nf* **1** : stupid remark or action **2 decir bobadas** : to talk nonsense

bobalicón, -cona *adj, mpl* **-cones** *fam* : silly, stupid

bobina *nf* CARRETE : bobbin, reel

bobo¹, -ba *adj* : silly, stupid

bobo², -ba *n* : fool, simpleton

boca *nf* **1** : mouth **2 boca arriba** : face up, on one's back **3 boca abajo** : face down, prone **4 boca de riego** : hydrant **5 en boca de** : according to

bocacalle *nf* : entrance to a street ⟨gire a la última bocacalle : take the last turning⟩

bocadillo *nm Spain* : sandwich

bocado *nm* **1** : bite, mouthful **2** FRENO : bit (of a bridle)

bocajarro *nm* **a ~** : point-blank, directly

bocallave *nf* : keyhole

bocanada *nf* **1** : swig, swallow **2** : puff, mouthful (of smoke) **3** : gust (of air) **4** : stream (of people)

boceto *nm* : sketch, outline

bochinche *nm fam* : ruckus, uproar

bochorno *nm* **1** VERGÜENZA : embarrassment **2** : hot and humid weather **3** : hot flash

bochornoso, -sa *adj* **1** EMBARAZOSO : embarrassing **2** : hot and muggy

bocina *nf* **1** : horn, trumpet **2** : automobile horn **3** : mouthpiece (of a telephone) **4** *Mex* : loudspeaker

bocinazo *nm* : honk (of a horn)

bocio *nm* : goiter

bocón, -cona *n, mpl* **bocones** *fam* : blabbermouth, loudmouth

boda *nf* : wedding

bodega *nf* **1** : wine cellar **2** *Chile, Col, Mex* : storeroom, warehouse **3** (*in various countries*) : grocery store

bofetada *nf* CACHETADA : slap on the face

bofetear *vt* CACHETEAR : to slap

bofetón *nm* → **bofetada**

bofo, -fa *adj* : flabby

boga *nf* : fashion, vogue ⟨estar en boga : to be in style⟩

bogotano¹, -na *adj* : of or from Bogotá

bogotano², -na *n* : person from Bogotá

bohemio, -mia *adj & n* : bohemian, Bohemian

boicot *nm, pl* **boicots** : boycott

boicotear *vt* : to boycott

boina *nf* : beret

boiserie *nf* : wood paneling, wainscoting

boj *nm, pl* **bojes** : box (plant), boxwood

bola *nf* **1** : ball ⟨bola de nieve : snowball⟩ **2** *fam* : lie, fib **3** *Mex fam* : bunch, group ⟨una bola de rateros : a bunch of thieves⟩ **4** *Mex* : uproar, tumult

bolear *vt Mex* : to polish (shoes)

bolera *nf* : bowling alley

bolero *nm* : bolero

boleta *nf* **1** : ballot **2** : ticket **3** : receipt

boletería *nf* TAQUILLA : box office, ticket office

boletín *nm, pl* **-tines** **1** : bulletin **2** : journal, review **3 boletín de prensa** : press release

boleto *nm* BILLETE : ticket

boliche *nm* **1** BOLOS : bowling **2** *Arg* : bar, tavern

bólido *nm* **1** : race car **2** METEORO : meteor

bolígrafo *nm* : ballpoint pen

bolillo *nm* **1** : bobbin **2** *Mex* : roll, bun

bolívar *nm* : bolivar (monetary unit of Venezuela)

boliviano¹, -na *adj & n* : Bolivian

boliviano² *nm* : boliviano (monetary unit of Bolivia)

bollo *nm* : bun, sweet roll
bolo *nm* : bowling pin, tenpin
bolos *nmpl* BOLICHE : bowling
bolsa *nf* **1** : bag, sack **2** *Mex* : pocket-book, purse **3** *Mex* : pocket **4 la Bolsa** : the stock market, the stock exchange **5 bolsa de trabajo** : employment agency
bolsear *vi Mex* : to pick pockets
bolsillo *nm* **1** : pocket **2 dinero de bolsillo** : pocket change, loose change
bolso *nm* : pocketbook, handbag
bomba *nf* **1** : bomb **2** : bubble **3** : pump ⟨bomba de gasolina : gas pump⟩
bombachos *nmpl* : baggy pants, bloomers
bombardear *vt* **1** : to bomb **2** : to bombard
bombardeo *nm* **1** : bombing, shelling **2** : bombardment
bombardero *nm* : bomber (airplane)
bombástico, -ca *adj* : bombastic
bombear *vt* : to pump
bombero, -ra *n* : firefighter, fireman *m*
bombilla *nf* : lightbulb
bombillo *nm CA, Col, Ven* : lightbulb
bombo *nm* **1** : bass drum **2** *fam* : exaggerated praise, hype ⟨con bombos y platillos : with great fanfare⟩
bombón *nm*, *pl* **bombones 1** : bonbon, chocolate **2** *Mex* : marshmallow
bonachón¹, -chona *adj*, *mpl* **-chones** *fam* : good-natured, kindhearted
bonachón², -chona *n*, *mpl* **-chones** *fam* BUENAZO : kindhearted person
bonaerense¹ *adj* : of or from Buenos Aires
bonaerense² *nmf* : person from Buenos Aires
bonanza *nf* **1** PROSPERIDAD : prosperity ⟨bonanza económica : economic boom⟩ **2** : calm weather **3** : rich ore deposit, bonanza
bondad *nf* BENEVOLENCIA : goodness, kindness ⟨tener la bondad de hacer algo : to be kind enough to do something⟩
bondadoso, -sa *adj* BENÉVOLO : kind, kindly, good — **bondadosamente** *adv*
bonete *nm* : cap, mortarboard
boniato *nm* : sweet potato
bonificación *nf*, *pl* **-ciones 1** : discount **2** : bonus, extra
bonito¹ *adv* : nicely, well ⟨¡qué bonito canta tu hermana! : your sister sings wonderfully!⟩
bonito², -ta *adj* LINDO : pretty, lovely ⟨tiene un apartamento bonito : she has a nice apartment⟩
bonito³ *nm* : bonito (tuna)
bono *nm* **1** : bond ⟨bono bancario : bank bond⟩ **2** : voucher
boqueada *nf* : gasp ⟨dar la última boqueada : to give one's last gasp⟩
boquear *vi* **1** : to gasp **2** : to be dying
boquete *nm* : gap, opening, breach
boquiabierto, -ta *adj* : open-mouthed, speechless, agape

boquilla *nf* : mouthpiece (of a musical instrument)
borbollar *vi* : to bubble
borbotar *or* **borbotear** *vi* : to boil, to bubble, to gurgle
borboteo *nm* : bubbling, gurgling
borda *nf* : gunwale
bordado *nm* : embroidery, needlework
bordar *v* : to embroider
borde *nm* **1** : border, edge **2 al borde de** : on the verge of ⟨estoy al borde de la locura : I'm about to go crazy⟩
bordear *vt* **1** : to border, to skirt ⟨el Río Este bordea Manhattan : the East River borders Manhattan⟩ **2** : to border on ⟨bordea la irrealidad : it borders on unreality⟩ **3** : to line ⟨una calle bordeada de árboles : a street lined with trees⟩
bordillo *nm* : curb
bordo *nm* **a ~** : aboard, on board
boreal *adj* : northern
borgoña *nf* : burgundy
bórico, -ca *adj* : boric ⟨ácido bórico : boric acid⟩
boricua *adj & nmf fam* : Puerto Rican
borinqueño, -ña → boricua
borla *nf* **1** : pom-pom, tassel **2** : powder puff
boro *nm* : boron
borrachera *nf* : drunkenness ⟨agarró una borrachera : he got drunk⟩
borrachín, -china *n*, *mpl* **-chines** *fam* : lush, drunk
borracho¹, -cha *adj* EBRIO : drunk, intoxicated
borracho², -cha *n* : drunk, drunkard
borrador *nm* **1** : rough copy, first draft ⟨en borrador : in the rough⟩ **2** : eraser
borrar *vt* : to erase, to blot out — **borrarse** *vr* **1** : to fade, to fade away **2** : to resign, to drop out **3** *Mex fam* : to split, to leave ⟨me borro : I'm out of here⟩
borrascoso, -sa *adj* : gusty, blustery
borrego, -ga *n* **1** : lamb, sheep **2** : simpleton, fool
borrico → burro
borrón *nm*, *pl* **borrones** : smudge, blot ⟨borrón y cuenta nueva : let's start on a clean slate, let's start over again⟩
borronear *vt* : to smudge, to blot
borroso, -sa *adj* **1** : blurry, smudgy **2** CONFUSO : unclear, confused
boscoso, -sa *adj* : wooded
bosnio, -nia *adj & n* : Bosnian
bosque *nm* : woods, forest
bosquecillo *nm* : grove, copse, thicket
bosquejar *vt* ESBOZAR : to outline, to sketch
bosquejo *nm* **1** TRAZADO : outline, sketch **2** : draft
bostezar {21} *vi* : to yawn
bostezo *nm* : yawn
bota *nf* **1** : boot **2** : wineskin
botana *nf Mex* : snack, appetizer
botanear *vi Mex* : to have a snack
botánica *nf* : botany

botánico[1], **-ca** *adj* : botanical
botánico[2], **-ca** *n* : botanist
botar *vt* **1** ARROJAR : to throw, to fling, to hurl **2** TIRAR : to throw out, to throw away **3** : to launch (a ship)
bote *nm* **1** : small boat ⟨bote de remos : rowboat⟩ **2** : can, jar **3** : jump, bounce **4** *Mex fam* : jail
botella *nf* : bottle
botica *nf* FARMACIA : drugstore, pharmacy
boticario, -ria *n* FARMACÉUTICO : pharmacist, druggist
botín *nm*, *pl* **botines 1** : baby's bootee **2** : ankle boot **3** : booty, plunder
botiquín *nm*, *pl* **-quines 1** : medicine cabinet **2** : first-aid kit
botón *nm*, *pl* **botones 1** : button **2** : bud **3** INSIGNIA : badge
botones *nmfs & pl* : bellhop
botulismo *nm* : botulism
boulevard [‚bule'var] → **bulevar**
bouquet *nm* **1** : fragrance, bouquet (of wine) **2** RAMILLETE : bouquet (of flowers)
boutique *nf* : boutique
bóveda *nf* **1** : vault, dome **2** CRIPTA : crypt
bovino, -na *adj* : bovine
box *nm*, *pl* **boxes 1** : pit (in auto racing) **2** *Mex* : boxing
boxeador, -dora *n* : boxer
boxear *vi* : to box
boxeo *nm* : boxing
boya *nf* : buoy
boyante *adj* **1** : buoyant **2** : prosperous, thriving
bozal *nm* **1** : muzzle **2** : halter (for a horse)
bracear *vi* **1** : to wave one's arms **2** : to make strokes (in swimming)
bracero, -ra *n* : migrant worker, day laborer
braguero *nm* : truss (in medicine)
bragueta *nf* : fly, pants zipper
braille *adj & nm* : braille
bramante *nm* : twine, string
bramar *vi* **1** RUGIR : to roar, to bellow **2** : to howl (of the wind)
bramido *nm* : bellowing, roar
brandy *nm* : brandy
branquia *nf* AGALLA : gill
brasa *nf* ASCUA : ember, live coal
brasero *nm* : brazier
brasier *nm Col, Mex* : brassiere, bra
brasileño, -ña *adj & n* : Brazilian
bravata *nf* **1** JACTANCIA : boast, bravado **2** AMENAZA : threat
bravo, -va *adj* **1** FEROZ : ferocious, fierce ⟨un perro bravo : a ferocious dog⟩ **2** EXCELENTE : excellent, great ⟨¡bravo! : bravo!, well done!⟩ **3** : rough, rugged, wild **4** : annoyed, angry
bravucón, -cona *n*, *mpl* **-cones** : bully
bravuconadas *nfpl* : bravado
bravura *nf* **1** FEROCIDAD : fierceness, ferocity **2** VALENTÍA : bravery

braza *nf* **1** : breaststroke **2** : fathom (unit of length)
brazada *nf* : stroke (in swimming)
brazalete *nm* PULSERA : bracelet, bangle
brazo *nm* **1** : arm **2 brazo derecho** : right-hand man **3 brazos** *nmpl* : hands, laborers
brea *nf* ALQUITRÁN : tar, pitch
brebaje *nm* : potion, brew
brecha *nf* **1** : gap, breach ⟨estar siempre en la brecha : to be always there when needed, to stay in the thick of things⟩ **2** : gash
brécol *nm* : broccoli
brega *nf* **1** LUCHA : struggle, fight **2** : hard work
bregar {52} *vi* **1** LUCHAR : to struggle **2** : to toil, to work hard **3** ~ **con** : to deal with
brete *nm* : jam, tight spot
breve *adj* **1** CORTO : brief, short **2 en** ~ : shortly, in short — **brevemente** *adv*
brevedad *nf* : brevity, shortness
breviario *nm* : breviary
brezal *nm* : heath, moor
brezo *nm* : heather
bribón, -bona *n*, *mpl* **bribones** : rascal, scamp
bricolaje *or* **bricolage** *nm* : do-it-yourself
brida *nf* : bridle
brigada *nf* **1** : brigade **2** : gang, team, squad
brigadier *nm* : brigadier
brillante[1] *adj* : brilliant, bright — **brillantemente** *adv*
brillante[2] *nm* DIAMANTE : diamond
brillantez *nf* : brilliance, brightness
brillar *vi* : to shine, to sparkle
brillo *nm* **1** LUSTRE : luster, shine **2** : brilliance
brilloso, -sa *adj* LUSTROSO : lustrous, shiny
brincar {72} *vi* **1** SALTAR : to jump around, to leap about **2** : to frolic, to gambol
brinco *nm* **1** SALTO : jump, leap, skip **2 pegar un brinco** : to give a start, to jump
brindar *vi* : to drink a toast ⟨brindó por los vencedores : he toasted the victors⟩ — *vt* OFRECER, PROPORCIONAR : to offer, to provide — **brindarse** *vr* : to offer one's assistance, to volunteer
brindis *nm* : toast, drink ⟨hacer un brindis : to drink a toast⟩
brinque, etc. → **brincar**
brío *nm* **1** : force, determination **2** : spirit, verve
brioso, -sa *adj* : spirited, lively
briqueta *nf* : briquette
brisa *nf* : breeze
británico[1], **-ca** *adj* : British
británico[2], **-ca** *n* **1** : British person **2 los británicos** : the British
brizna *nf* **1** : strand, thread **2** : blade (of grass)

broca *nf* : drill bit
brocado *nm* : brocade
brocha *nf* : paintbrush
broche *nm* **1** ALFILER : brooch **2** : fastener, clasp **3 broche de oro** : finishing touch
brocheta *nf* : skewer
brócoli *nm* : broccoli
broma *nf* **1** CHISTE : joke, prank **2** : fun, merriment **3 en ~** : in jest, jokingly
bromear *vi* : to joke, to fool around ⟨sólo estaba bromeando : I was only kidding⟩
bromista[1] *adj* : fun-loving, joking
bromista[2] *nmf* : joker, prankster
bromo *nm* : bromine
bronca *nf fam* : fight, quarrel, fuss
bronce *nm* : bronze
bronceado[1], **-da** *adj* **1** : tanned, suntanned **2** : bronze
bronceado[2] *nm* **1** : suntan, tan **2** : bronzing
broncearse *vr* : to get a suntan
bronco, -ca *adj* **1** : harsh, rough **2** : untamed, wild
bronquial *adj* : bronchial
bronquio *nm* : bronchial tube, bronchus
bronquitis *nf* : bronchitis
broqueta *nf* : skewer
brotar *vi* **1** : to bud, to sprout **2** : to spring up, to stream, to gush forth **3** : to break out, to appear
brote *nm* **1** : outbreak **2** : sprout, bud, shoot
broza *nf* **1** : brushwood **2** MALEZA : scrub, undergrowth
brujería *nf* HECHICERÍA : witchcraft, sorcery
brujo[1], **-ja** *adj* : bewitching
brujo[2], **-ja** *n* : warlock *m*, witch *f*, sorcerer
brújula *nf* : compass
bruma *nf* : haze, mist
brumoso, -sa *adj* : hazy, misty
bruñir {38} *vt* : to burnish, to polish (metals)
brusco, -ca *adj* **1** SÚBITO : sudden, abrupt **2** : curt, brusque — **bruscamente** *adv*
brusquedad *nf* **1** : abruptness, suddenness **2** : brusqueness
brutal *adj* **1** : brutal **2** *fam* : incredible, terrific — **brutalmente** *adv*
brutalidad *nf* CRUELDAD : brutality
brutalizar {21} *vt* : to brutalize, to maltreat
bruto[1], **-ta** *adj* **1** : gross ⟨peso bruto : gross weight⟩ ⟨ingresos brutos : gross income⟩ **2** : unrefined ⟨petróleo bruto : crude oil⟩ **3** : brutish, stupid
bruto[2], **-ta** *n* **1** : brute **2** : dunce, blockhead
bubónico, -ca *adj* : bubonic
bucal *adj* : oral
bucanero *nm* : buccaneer, pirate
buccino *nm* : whelk
buceador, -dora *n* : diver, scuba diver

bucear *vi* **1** : to dive, to swim underwater **2** : to explore, to delve
buceo *nm* **1** : diving, scuba diving **2** : exploration, searching
buche *nm* **1** : crop (of a bird) **2** *fam* : belly, gut **3** : mouthful ⟨hacer buches : to rinse one's mouth⟩
bucle *nm* **1** : curl, ringlet **2** : loop
bucólico, -ca *adj* : bucolic
budín *nm*, *pl* **budines** : pudding
budismo *nm* : Buddhism
budista *adj* & *nmf* : Buddhist
buen *adj* → **bueno**[1]
buenamente *adv* **1** : easily **2** : willingly
buenaventura *nf* **1** : good luck **2** : fortune, future ⟨le dijo la buenaventura : she told his fortune⟩
buenazo, -za *n fam* BONACHÓN : kindhearted person
bueno[1], **-na** *adj* (**buen** before masculine singular nouns) **1** : good ⟨una buena idea : a good idea⟩ **2** BONDADOSO : nice, kind **3** APROPIADO : proper, appropriate **4** SANO : well, healthy **5** : considerable, goodly ⟨una buena cantidad : a lot⟩ **6 buenos días** : hello, good day **7 buenas tardes** : good afternoon **8 buenas noches** : good evening, good night
bueno[2] *interj* **1** : OK!, all right! **2** *Mex* : hello! (on the telephone)
buey *nm* : ox, steer
búfalo *nm* **1** : buffalo **2 búfalo de agua** : water buffalo
bufanda *nf* : scarf, muffler
bufar *vi* : to snort
bufet *or* **bufé** *nm* : buffet-style meal
bufete *nm* **1** : law firm, law office **2** : writing desk
bufido *nm* : snort
bufo, -fa *adj* : comic
bufón, -fona *n*, *mpl* **bufones** : clown, buffoon, jester
bufonada *nf* **1** : jest, buffoonery **2** : sarcasm
buhardilla *nf* **1** ÁTICO, DESVÁN : attic **2** : dormer window
búho *nm* **1** : owl **2** *fam* : hermit, recluse
buhonero, -ra *n* MERCACHIFLE : peddler
buitre *nm* : vulture
bujía *nf* : spark plug
bula *nf* : papal bull
bulbo *nm* : bulb
bulboso, -sa *adj* : bulbous
bulevar *nm* : boulevard
búlgaro, -ra *adj* & *n* : Bulgarian
bulla *nf* BARULLO : racket, rowdiness
bullicio *nm* **1** : ruckus, uproar **2** : hustle and bustle
bullicioso, -sa *adj* : noisy, busy, turbulent
bullir {38} *vi* **1** HERVIR : to boil **2** MOVERSE : to stir, to bustle about
bulto *nm* **1** : package, bundle **2** : piece of luggage, bag **3** : size, bulk, volume **4** : form, shape **5** : lump (on the body), swelling, bulge

bumerán *nm, pl* **-ranes** : boomerang
búnker *nm, pl* **búnkers** : bunker
búnquer → **búnker**
buñuelo *nm* : fried pastry
buque *nm* BARCO : ship, vessel
burbuja *nf* : bubble, blister (on a surface)
burbujear *vi* 1 : to bubble 2 : to fizz
burbujeo *nm* : bubbling
burdel *nm* : brothel, whorehouse
burdo, -da *adj* 1 : coarse, rough 2 : crude, clumsy ⟨una burda mentira : a clumsy lie⟩ — **burdamente** *adj*
burgués, -guesa *adj & n, mpl* **burgueses** : bourgeois
burguesía *nf* : bourgeoisie, middle class
burla *nf* 1 : mockery, ridicule 2 : joke, trick 3 **hacer burla de** : to make fun of, to mock
burlar *vt* ENGAÑAR : to trick, to deceive — **burlarse** *vr* ~ **de** : to make fun of, to ridicule
burlesco, -ca *adj* : burlesque, comic
burlón¹, -lona *adj, mpl* **burlones** : joking, mocking
burlón², -lona *n, mpl* **burlones** : joker
burocracia *nf* : bureaucracy
burócrata *nmf* : bureaucrat
burocrático, -ca *adj* : bureaucratic
burrada *nf fam* : stupid act, nonsense
burrito *nm* : burrito
burro¹, -rra *adj fam* : dumb, stupid

burro², -rra *n* 1 ASNO : donkey, ass 2 *fam* : dunce, poor student
burro³ *nm* 1 : sawhorse 2 *Mex* : ironing board 3 *Mex* : stepladder
bursátil *adj* : stock-market
bursitis *nf* : bursitis
burundés, -desa *adj & n* : Burundian
bus *nm* : bus
busca *nf* : search
buscador, -dora *n* : hunter (for treasure, etc.), prospector
buscapersonas *nms & pl* : beeper, pager
buscapleitos *nmfs & pl* : troublemaker
buscar {72} *vt* 1 : to look for, to seek 2 : to pick up, to collect 3 : to provoke — *vi* : to look, to search ⟨buscó en los bolsillos : he searched through his pockets⟩
buscavidas *nmf & pl* 1 : busybody 2 : go-getter
busque, etc. → **buscar**
búsqueda *nf* : search
busto *nm* : bust
butaca *nf* 1 SILLÓN : armchair 2 : seat (in a theatre) 3 *Mex* : pupil's desk
butano *nm* : butane
buzo¹, -za *adj Mex fam* : smart, astute ⟨¡ponte buzo! : get with it!, get on the ball!⟩
buzo² *nm* : diver, scuba diver
buzón *nm, pl* **buzones** : mailbox
byte *nm* : byte

C

c *nf* : third letter of the Spanish alphabet
cabal *adj* 1 : exact, correct 2 : complete 3 : upright, honest
cabales *nmpl* **no estar en sus cabales** : not to be in one's right mind
cabalgar {52} *vi* : to ride (on horseback)
cabalgata *nf* : cavalcade, procession
cabalidad *nf* **a** ~ : thoroughly, conscientiously
caballa *nf* : mackerel
caballada *nf* 1 : herd of horses 2 *fam* : nonsense, stupidity, outrageousness
caballar *adj* EQUINO : horse, equine
caballeresco, -ca *adj* : gallant, chivalrous
caballería *nf* 1 : cavalry 2 : horse, mount 3 : knighthood, chivalry
caballeriza *nf* : stable
caballero¹ → **caballeroso**
caballero² *nm* 1 : gentleman 2 : knight
caballerosidad *nf* : chivalry, gallantry
caballeroso, -sa *adj* : gentlemanly, chivalrous
caballete *nm* 1 : ridge 2 : easel 3 : trestle (for a table, etc.) 4 : bridge (of the nose) 5 : sawhorse
caballista *nmf* : horseman *m*, horsewoman *f*
caballito *nm* 1 : rocking horse 2 **caballito de mar** : seahorse 3 **caballitos** *nmpl* : merry-go-round

caballo *nm* 1 : horse 2 : knight (in chess) 3 **caballo de fuerza** *or* **caballo de vapor** : horsepower
cabalmente *adv* : fully, exactly
cabaña *nf* CHOZA : cabin, hut
cabaret *nm, pl* **-rets** : nightclub, cabaret
cabecear *vt* : to nod (in soccer) — *vi* 1 : to nod one's head 2 : to lurch, to pitch
cabecera *nf* 1 : headboard 2 : head ⟨cabecera de la mesa : head of the table⟩ 3 : heading, headline 4 : headwaters *pl* 5 **médico de cabecera** : family doctor 6 **cabecera municipal** *CA, Mex* : downtown area
cabecilla *nmf* : ringleader, kingpin
cabellera *nf* : head of hair, mane
cabello *nm* : hair
cabelludo, -da *adj* 1 : hairy 2 **cuero cabelludo** : scalp
caber {12} *vi* 1 : to fit, to go ⟨no sé si cabremos todos en el coche : I don't know if we'll all fit in the car⟩ 2 : to be possible ⟨no cabe duda alguna : there's no doubt about it⟩ ⟨cabe que llegue mañana : he may come tomorrow⟩
cabestrillo *nm* : sling ⟨llevo el brazo en cabestrillo : my arm is in a sling⟩
cabestro *nm* : halter (for an animal)
cabeza *nf* 1 : head 2 **cabeza hueca** : scatterbrain 3 **de** ~ : head first 4 **dolor de cabeza** : headache

cabezada *nf* **1** : butt, blow with the head **2** : nod ⟨echar una cabezada : to take a nap, to doze off⟩
cabezal *nm* : bolster
cabezazo *nm* : butt, blow with the head
cabezón, -zona *adj, mpl* **-zones** *fam* **1** : having a big head **2** : pigheaded, stubborn
cabida *nf* **1** : room, space, capacity **2 dar cabida a** : to accommodate, to hold
cabildear *vi* : to lobby
cabildeo *nm* : lobbying
cabildero, -ra *n* : lobbyist
cabildo *nm* AYUNTAMIENTO **1** : town or city hall **2** : town or city council
cabina *nf* **1** : cabin **2** : booth **3** : cab (of a truck), cockpit (of an airplane)
cabizbajo, -ja *adj* : dejected, downcast
cable *nm* : cable
cableado *nm* : wiring
cabo *nm* **1** : end ⟨al cabo de dos semanas : at the end of two weeks⟩ **2** : stub, end piece **3** : corporal **4** : cape, headland ⟨el Cabo Cañaveral : Cape Canaveral⟩ **5 al fin y al cabo** : after all, in the end **6 llevar a cabo** : to carry out, to do
caboverdiano, -na *adj & n* : Cape Verdean
cabrá, etc. → **caber**
cabra *nf* : goat
cabrestante *nm* : windlass
cabrío, -ría *adj* : goat, caprine
cabriola *nf* **1** : skip, jump **2 hacer cabriolas** : to prance
cabriolar *vi* : to prance
cabrito *nm* : kid, baby goat
cabús *nm, pl* **cabuses** *Mex* : caboose
cacahuate *or* **cacahuete** *nm* : peanut
cacalote *nm Mex* : crow
cacao *nm* : cacao, cocoa bean
cacarear *vi* : to crow, to cackle, to cluck — *vt fam* : to boast about, to crow about ⟨cacarear un huevo : to brag about an accomplishment⟩
cacareo *nm* **1** : clucking (of a hen), crowing (of a rooster) **2** : boasting
cacatúa *nf* : cockatoo
cace, etc. → **cazar**
cacería *nf* **1** CAZA : hunt, hunting **2** : hunting party
cacerola *nf* : pan, saucepan
cacha *nf* : butt (of a gun)
cachar *vt fam* : to catch
cacharro *nm* **1** *fam* : thing, piece of junk **2** *fam* : jalopy **3 cacharros** *nmpl* : pots and pans
cache *nm* : cache, cache memory
caché *nm* : cachet
cachear *vt* : to search, to frisk
cachemir *nm* : cashmere
cachetada *nf* BOFETADA : slap on the face
cachete *nm* : cheek
cachetear *vt* BOFETEAR : to slap
cachiporra *nf* : bludgeon, club, blackjack
cachirul *nm Mex fam* : cheating ⟨hacer cachirul : to cheat⟩

cachivache *nm fam* : thing ⟨mete tus cachivaches en el maletero : put your stuff in the trunk⟩
cacho *nm fam* : piece, bit
cachorro, -rra *n* **1** : cub **2** PERRITO : puppy
cachucha *nf Mex* : cap, baseball cap
cacique *nm* **1** : chief (of a tribe) **2** : boss (in politics)
cacofonía *nf* : cacophony
cacofónico, -ca *adj* : cacophonous
cacto *nm* : cactus
cactus → **cacto**
cada *adj* **1** : each ⟨cuestan diez pesos cada una : they cost ten pesos each⟩ **2** : every ⟨cada vez : every time⟩ **3** : such, some ⟨sales con cada historia : you come up with such crazy stories⟩ **4 cada vez más** : more and more, increasingly **5 cada vez menos** : less and less
cadalso *nm* : scaffold, gallows
cadáver *nm* : corpse, cadaver
cadavérico, -ca *adj* **1** : cadaverous **2** PÁLIDO : deathly pale
caddie *or* **caddy** *nmf, pl* **caddies** : caddy
cadena *nf* **1** : chain **2** : network, channel **3 cadena de montaje** : assembly line **4 cadena perpetua** : life sentence
cadencia *nf* : cadence, rhythm
cadencioso, -sa *adj* : rhythmic, rhythmical
cadera *nf* : hip
cadete *nmf* : cadet
cadmio *nm* : cadmium
caducar {72} *vi* : to expire
caducidad *nf* : expiration
caduco, -ca *adj* **1** : outdated, obsolete **2** : deciduous
caer {13} *vi* **1** : to fall, to drop **2** : to collapse **3** : to hang (down) **4 caer bien** *fam* : to be pleasant, to be likeable ⟨me caes bien : I like you⟩ **5 caer mal** *or* **caer gordo** *fam* : to be unpleasant, to be unlikeable — **caerse** *vr* : to fall down
café¹ *adj* : brown ⟨ojos cafés : brown eyes⟩
café² *nm* **1** : coffee **2** : café
cafeína *nf* : caffeine
cafetal *nm* : coffee plantation
cafetalero¹, -ra *adj* : coffee ⟨cosecha cafetalera : coffee harvest⟩
cafetalero², -ra *n* : coffee grower
cafetera *nf* : coffeepot, coffeemaker
cafetería *nf* **1** : coffee shop, café **2** : lunchroom, cafeteria
cafetero¹, -ra *adj* : coffee-producing
cafetero², -ra *n* : coffee grower
cafeticultura *nf Mex* : coffee industry
caguama *nf* **1** : large Caribbean turtle **2** *Mex* : large bottle of beer
caída *nf* **1** BAJA, DESCENSO : fall, drop **2** : collapse, downfall
caiga, etc. → **caer**
caimán *nm, pl* **caimanes** : alligator, caiman

caimito *nm* : star apple
caja *nf* 1 : box, case 2 : cash register, checkout counter 3 : bed (of a truck) 4 *fam* : coffin 5 **caja fuerte** *or* **caja de caudales** : safe 6 **caja de seguridad** : safe-deposit box 7 **caja torácica** : rib cage
cajero, -ra *n* 1 : cashier 2 : teller 3 **cajero automático** : automated teller machine, ATM
cajeta *nf Mex* : a sweet caramel-flavored spread
cajetilla *nf* : pack (of cigarettes)
cajón *nm, pl* **cajones** 1 : drawer, till 2 : crate, case 3 **cajón de estacionamiento** *Mex* : parking space
cajuela *nf Mex* : trunk (of a car)
cal *nf* : lime, quicklime
cala *nf* : cove, inlet
calabacín *nm, pl* **-cines** : zucchini
calabacita *nf Mex* : zucchini
calabaza *nf* 1 : pumpkin, squash 2 : gourd 3 **dar calabazas a** : to give the brush-off to, to jilt
calabozo *nm* 1 : prison 2 : jail cell
calado¹, -da *adj* 1 : drenched 2 : openworked
calado² *nm* 1 : draft (of a ship) 2 : openwork
calafatear *vt* : to caulk
calamar *nm* 1 : squid 2 **calamares** *nmpl* : calamari
calambre *nm* 1 ESPASMO : cramp 2 : electric shock, jolt
calamidad *nf* DESASTRE : calamity, disaster
calamina *nf* : calamine
calamitoso, -sa *adj* : calamitous, disastrous
calaña *nf* : ilk, kind, sort ⟨una persona de mala calaña : a bad sort⟩
calar *vt* 1 : to soak through 2 : to pierce, to penetrate — *vi* : to catch on — **calarse** *vr* : to get drenched
calavera¹ *nf* 1 : skull 2 *Mex* : taillight
calavera² *nm* : rake, rogue
calcar {72} *vt* 1 : to trace 2 : to copy, to imitate
calce, etc. → **calzar**
calceta *nf* : knee-high stocking
calcetería *nf* : hosiery
calcetín *nm, pl* **-tines** : sock
calcificar {72} *v* : to calcify — **calcificarse** *vr*
calcinar *vt* : to char, to burn
calcio *nm* : calcium
calco *nm* 1 : transfer, tracing 2 : copy, image
calcomanía *nf* : decal, transfer
calculador, -dora *adj* : calculating
calculadora *nf* : calculator
calcular *vt* 1 : to calculate, to estimate 2 : to plan, to scheme
cálculo *nm* 1 : calculation, estimation 2 : calculus 3 : plan, scheme 4 **cálculo biliar** : gallstone 5 **hoja de cálculo** : spreadsheet
caldas *nfpl* : hot springs

caldear *vt* : to heat, to warm — **caldearse** *vr* 1 : to heat up 2 : to become heated, to get tense
caldera *nf* 1 : cauldron 2 : boiler
caldo *nm* 1 CONSOMÉ : broth, stock 2 **caldo de cultivo** : culture medium, breeding ground
caldoso, -sa *adj* : watery
calefacción *nf, pl* **-ciones** : heating, heat
calefactor *nm* : heater
caleidoscopio → **calidoscopio**
calendario *nm* 1 : calendar 2 : timetable, schedule
caléndula *nf* : marigold
calentador *nm* : heater
calentamiento *nm* 1 : heating, warming 2 : warm-up (in sports)
calentar {55} *vt* 1 : to heat, to warm 2 *fam* : to annoy, to anger 3 *fam* : to excite, to turn on — **calentarse** *vr* 1 : to get warm, to heat up 2 : to warm up (in sports) 3 *fam* : to become sexually aroused 4 *fam* : to get mad
calentura *nf* 1 FIEBRE : temperature, fever 2 : cold sore
calibrador *nm* : gauge, calipers *pl*
calibrar *vt* : to calibrate — **calibración** *nf*
calibre *nm* 1 : caliber, gauge 2 : importance, excellence 3 : kind, sort ⟨un problema de grueso calibre : a serious problem⟩
calidad *nf* 1 : quality, grade 2 : position, status 3 **en calidad de** : as, in the capacity of
cálido, -da *adj* 1 : hot ⟨un clima cálido : a hot climate⟩ 2 : warm ⟨una cálida bienvenida : a warm welcome⟩
calidoscopio *nm* : kaleidoscope
caliente *adj* 1 : hot, warm ⟨mantenerse caliente : to stay warm⟩ 2 : heated, fiery ⟨una disputa caliente : a heated argument⟩ 3 *fam* : sexually excited, horny
califa *nm* : caliph
calificación *nf, pl* **-ciones** 1 NOTA : grade (for a course) 2 : rating, score 3 CLASIFICACIÓN : qualification, qualifying ⟨ronda de calificación : qualifying round⟩
calificar {72} *vt* 1 : to grade 2 : to describe, to rate ⟨la calificaron de buena alumna : they described her as a good student⟩ 3 : to qualify, to modify (in grammar)
calificativo¹, -va *adj* : qualifying
calificativo² *nm* : qualifier, epithet
caligrafía *nf* 1 ESCRITURA : handwriting 2 : calligraphy
calipso *nm* : calypso
calistenia *nf* : calisthenics
cáliz *nm, pl* **cálices** 1 : chalice, goblet 2 : calyx
caliza *nf* : limestone
callado, -da *adj* : quiet, silent — **calladamente** *adv*
callar *vi* : to keep quiet, to be silent — *vt* 1 : to silence, to hush ⟨¡calla a los

niños! : keep the children quiet!⟩ **2** : to keep secret — **callarse** *vr* : to remain silent ⟨¡cállate! : be quiet!, shut up!⟩
calle *nf* : street, road
callejear *vi* : to wander about the streets, to hang out
callejero, -ra *adj* : street ⟨perro callejero : stray dog⟩
callejón *nm, pl* **-jones 1** : alley **2 callejón sin salida** : dead-end street
callo *nm* **1** : callus, corn **2 callos** *nmpl* : tripe
calloso, -sa *adj* : callous
calma *nf* : calm, quiet
calmante[1] *adj* : calming, soothing
calmante[2] *nm* : tranquilizer, sedative
calmar *vt* TRANQUILIZAR : to calm, to soothe — **calmarse** *vr* : to calm down
calmo, -ma *adj* TRANQUILO : calm, tranquil
calmoso, -sa *adj* **1** TRANQUILO : calm, quiet **2** LENTO : slow, sluggish
calor *nm* **1** : heat ⟨hace calor : it's hot outside⟩ ⟨tener calor : to feel hot⟩ **2** : warmth, affection **3** : ardor, passion
caloría *nf* : calorie
calórico, -ca *adj* : caloric
calorífico, -ca *adj* : caloric
calque, etc. → **calcar**
calumnia *nf* : slander, libel — **calumnioso, -sa** *adj*
calumniar *vt* : to slander, to libel
caluroso, -sa *adj* **1** : hot **2** : warm, enthusiastic
calva *nf* : bald spot, bald head
calvario *nm* **1** : Calvary **2** : Stations of the Cross *pl* **3 vivir un calvario** : to suffer great adversity
calvicie *nf* : baldness
calvo[1]**, -va** *adj* : bald
calvo[2]**, -va** *n* : bald person
calza *nf* : block, wedge
calzada *nf* : roadway, avenue
calzado *nm* : footwear
calzador *nm* : shoehorn
calzar {21} *vt* **1** : to wear (shoes) ⟨¿de cuál calza? : what is your shoe size?⟩ ⟨siempre calzaban tenis : they always wore sneakers⟩ **2** : to provide with shoes
calzo *nm* : chock, wedge
calzoncillos *nmpl* : underpants, briefs
calzones *nmpl* : underpants, panties
cama *nf* **1** : bed **2 cama elástica** : trampoline
camada *nf* : litter, brood
camafeo *nm* : cameo
camaleón *nm, pl* **-leones** : chameleon
cámara *nf* **1** : camera **2** : chamber, room **3** : house (in government) **4** : inner tube
camarada *nmf* **1** : comrade, companion **2** : colleague
camaradería *nf* : camaraderie
camarero, -ra *n* **1** MESERO : waiter, waitress *f* **2** : bellhop *m*, chambermaid *f* (in a hotel) **3** : steward *m*, stewardess *f* (on a ship, etc.)

camarilla *nf* : political clique
camarógrafo, -fa *n* : cameraman *m*, camerawoman *f*
camarón *nm, pl* **-rones 1** : shrimp **2** : prawn
camarote *nm* : cabin, stateroom
camastro *nm* : small hard bed, pallet
cambalache *nm fam* : swap
cambiante *adj* **1** : changing **2** VARIABLE : changeable, variable
cambiar *vt* **1** ALTERAR, MODIFICAR : to change **2** : to exchange, to trade — *vi* **1** : to change **2 cambiar de velocidad** : to shift gears — **cambiarse** *vr* **1** : to change (clothing) **2** MUDARSE : to move (to a new address)
cambio *nm* **1** : change, alteration **2** : exchange **3** : change (money) **4 en cambio** : instead **5 en cambio** : however, on the other hand
cambista *nmf* : exchange broker
camboyano, -na *adj & n* : Cambodian
cambur *nm Ven* : banana
camelia *nf* : camellia
camello *nm* : camel
camellón *nm, pl* **-llones** *Mex* : traffic island
camerino *nm* : dressing room
camerunés, -nesa *adj, mpl* **-neses** : Cameroonian
camilla *nf* : stretcher
camillero, -ra *n* : orderly (in a hospital)
caminante *nmf* : wayfarer, walker
caminar *vi* ANDAR : to walk, to move — *vt* : to walk, to cover (a distance)
caminata *nf* : hike, long walk
camino *nm* **1** : path, road **2** : journey ⟨ponerse en camino : to set off⟩ **3** : way ⟨a medio camino : halfway there⟩
camión *nm, pl* **camiones 1** : truck **2** *Mex* : bus
camionero, -ra *n* **1** : truck driver **2** *Mex* : bus driver
camioneta *nf* : light truck, van
camisa *nf* **1** : shirt **2 camisa de fuerza** : straitjacket
camiseta *nf* **1** : T-shirt **2** : undershirt
camisón *nm, pl* **-sones** : nightshirt, nightgown
camorra *nf fam* : fight, trouble ⟨buscar camorra : to pick a fight⟩
camote *nm* **1** : root vegetable similar to the sweet potato **2 hacerse camote** *Mex fam* : to get mixed up
campal *adj* : pitched, fierce ⟨batalla campal : pitched battle⟩
campamento *nm* : camp
campana *nf* : bell
campanada *nf* TAÑIDO : stroke (of a bell), peal
campanario *nm* : bell tower, belfry
campanilla *nf* **1** : small bell, handbell **2** : uvula
campante *adj* : nonchalant, smug ⟨seguir tan campante : to go on as if nothing had happened⟩

campaña *nf* **1** CAMPO : countryside, country **2** : campaign **3 tienda de campaña** : tent
campañol *nm* : vole
campechana *nf Mex* : puff pastry
campechanía *nf* : geniality
campechano, -na *adj* : open, cordial, friendly
campeón, -peona *n, mpl* **-peones** : champion
campeonato *nm* : championship
cámper *nm* : camper (vehicle)
campero, -ra *adj* : country, rural
campesino, -na *n* : peasant, farm laborer
campestre *adj* : rural, rustic
camping *nm* **1** : camping **2** : campsite
campiña *nf* CAMPO : countryside, country
campista *nmf* : camper
campo *nm* **1** CAMPAÑA : countryside, country **2** : field ⟨campo de aviación : airfield⟩ ⟨su campo de responsabilidad : her field of responsibility⟩
camposanto *nm* : graveyard, cemetery
campus *nms & pl* : campus
camuflaje *nm* : camouflage
camuflajear *vt* : to camouflage
camuflar → **camuflajear**
can *nm* : hound, dog
cana *nf* **1** : gray hair **2 salirle canas** : to go gray, to get gray hair **3 echar una cana al aire** : to let one's hair down
canadiense *adj & nmf* : Canadian
canal[1] *nm* **1** : canal **2** : channel
canal[2] *nmf* : gutter, groove
canalé *nm* : rib, ribbing (in fabric)
canaleta *nf* : gutter
canalete *nm* : paddle
canalizar {21} *vt* : to channel
canalla[1] *adj fam* : low, rotten
canalla[2] *nmf fam* : bastard, swine
canapé *nm* **1** : hors d'oeuvre, canapé **2** SOFÁ : couch, sofa
canario[1], **-ria** *adj* : of or from the Canary Islands
canario[2], **-ria** *n* : Canarian, Canary Islander
canario[3] *nm* : canary
canasta *nf* **1** : basket **2** : canasta (card game)
cancel *nm* **1** : sliding door **2** : partition
cancelación *nf, pl* **-ciones 1** : cancellation **2** : payment in full
cancelar *vt* **1** : to cancel **2** : to pay off, to settle
cáncer *nm* : cancer
Cáncer *nmf* : Cancer
cancerígeno[1], **-na** *adj* : carcinogenic
cancerígeno[2] *nm* : carcinogen
canceroso, -sa *adj* : cancerous
cancha *nf* : court, field (for sports)
canciller *nm* : chancellor
cancillería *nf* : chancellery, ministry
canción *nf, pl* **canciones 1** : song **2 canción de cuna** : lullaby
cancionero[1] *nm* : songbook
cancionero[2], **-ra** *n Mex* : songster, songstress *f*

candado *nm* : padlock
candela *nf* **1** : flame, fire **2** : candle
candelabro *nm* : candelabra
candelero *nm* **1** : candlestick **2 estar en el candelero** : to be the center of attention
candente *adj* : red-hot
candidato, -ta *n* : candidate, applicant
candidatura *nf* : candidacy
candidez *nf* **1** : simplicity **2** INGENUIDAD : naïveté, ingenuousness
cándido, -da *adj* **1** : simple, unassuming **2** INGENUO : naive, ingenuous
candil *nm* : oil lamp
candilejas *nfpl* : footlights
candor *nm* : naïveté, innocence
candoroso, -sa *adj* : naive, innocent
canela *nf* : cinnamon
canesú *nm* : yoke (of clothing)
cangrejo *nm* JAIBA : crab
canguro *nm* **1** : kangaroo **2 hacer de canguro** *Spain* : to baby-sit
caníbal[1] *adj* : cannibalistic
caníbal[2] *nmf* ANTROPÓFAGO : cannibal
canibalismo *nm* ANTROPOFAGIA : cannibalism
canibalizar {21} *vt* : to cannibalize
canica *nf* : marble ⟨jugar a las canicas : to play marbles⟩
caniche *nm* : poodle
canijo, -ja *adj* **1** *fam* : puny, weak **2** *Mex fam* : tough, hard ⟨un examen muy canijo : a very tough exam⟩
canilla *nf* **1** : shin, shinbone **2** *Arg, Uru* : faucet
canino[1], **-na** *adj* : canine
canino[2] *nm* **1** COLMILLO : canine (tooth) **2** : dog, canine
canje *nm* INTERCAMBIO : exchange, trade
canjear *vt* INTERCAMBIAR : to exchange, to trade
cannabis *nm* : cannabis
cano, -na *adj* : gray ⟨un hombre de pelo cano : a gray-haired man⟩
canoa *nf* : canoe
canon *nm, pl* **cánones** : canon
canónico, -ca *adj* **1** : canonical **2 derecho canónico** : canon law
canónigo *nm* : canon (of a church)
canonizar {21} *vt* : to canonize — **canonización** *nf*
canoso, -sa → **cano**
cansado, -da *adj* **1** : tired ⟨estar cansado : to be tired⟩ **2** : tiresome, wearying ⟨ser cansado : to be tiring⟩
cansancio *nm* FATIGA : fatigue, weariness
cansar *vt* FATIGAR : to wear out, to tire — *vi* : to be tiresome — **cansarse** *vr* **1** : to wear oneself out **2** : to get bored
cansino, -na *adj* : slow, weary, lethargic
cantaleta *nf fam* : nagging ⟨la misma cantaleta : the same old story⟩
cantalupo *nm* : cantaloupe
cantante *nmf* : singer
cantar[1] *v* : to sing

cantar[2] *nm* : song, ballad
cántaro *nm* **1** : pitcher, jug **2 llover a cántaros** *fam* : to rain cats and dogs
cantata *nf* : cantata
cantera *nf* : quarry ⟨cantera de piedra : stone quarry⟩
cántico *nm* : canticle, chant
cantidad[1] *adv fam* : really ⟨ese carro me costó cantidad : that car cost me plenty⟩
cantidad[2] *nf* **1** : quantity **2** : sum, amount (of money) **3** *fam* : a lot, a great many ⟨había cantidad de niños en el parque : there were tons of kids in the park⟩
cantimplora *nf* : canteen, water bottle
cantina *nf* **1** : tavern, bar **2** : canteen, mess, dining quarters *pl*
cantinero, -ra *n* : bartender
canto *nm* **1** : singing **2** : chant ⟨canto gregoriano : Gregorian chant⟩ **3** : song (of a bird) **4** : edge, end ⟨de canto : on end, sideways⟩ **5 canto rodado** : boulder
cantón *nm, pl* **cantones 1** : canton **2** *Mex fam* : place, home
cantonés[1], **-nesa** *adj & n, mpl* **-neses** : Cantonese
cantonés[2] *nm, pl* **-neses** : Cantonese (language)
cantor[1], **-tora** *adj* **1** : singing **2 pájaro cantor** : songbird
cantor[2], **-tora** *n* **1** : singer **2** : cantor
caña *nf* **1** : cane ⟨caña de azúcar : sugarcane⟩ **2** : reed **3 caña de pescar** : fishing rod **4 caña del timón** : tiller (of a boat)
cañada *nf* : ravine, gully
cáñamo *nm* : hemp
cañaveral *nm* : sugarcane field
cañería *nf* TUBERÍA : pipes *pl*, piping
caño *nm* **1** : pipe **2** : spout **3** : channel (for navigation)
cañón *nm, pl* **cañones 1** : cannon **2** : barrel (of a gun) **3** : canyon
cañonear *vt* : to shell, to bombard
cañoneo *nm* : shelling, bombardment
cañonero *nm* : gunboat
caoba *nf* : mahogany
caolín *nm* : kaolin
caos *nm* : chaos
caótico, -ca *adj* : chaotic
capa *nf* **1** : cape, cloak **2** : coating **3** : layer, stratum **4** : (social) class, stratum
capacidad *nf* **1** : capacity **2** : capability, ability
capacitación *nf, pl* **-ciones** : training
capacitar *vt* : to train, to qualify
caparazón *nm, pl* **-zones** : shell, carapace
capataz *nmf, pl* **-taces** : foreman *m*, forewoman *f*
capaz *adj, pl* **capaces 1** APTO : capable, able **2** COMPETENTE : competent **3** : spacious ⟨capaz para : with room for⟩
capcioso, -sa *adj* : cunning, deceptive ⟨pregunta capciosa : trick question⟩

capea *nf* : amateur bullfight
capear *vt* **1** : to make a pass with the cape (in bullfighting) **2** : to dodge, to weather ⟨capear el temporal : to ride out the storm⟩
capellán *nm, pl* **-llanes** : chaplain
capilar *nm* : capillary — **capilar** *adj*
capilla *nf* : chapel
capirotada *nf Mex* : traditional bread pudding
capirotazo *nm* : flip, flick
capital[1] *adj* **1** : capital **2** : chief, principal
capital[2] *nm* : capital ⟨capital de riesgo : venture capital⟩
capital[3] *nf* : capital, capital city
capitalino[1], **-na** *adj* : of or from a capital city
capitalino[2], **-na** *n* : inhabitant of a capital city
capitalismo *nm* : capitalism
capitalista *adj & nmf* : capitalist
capitalizar {21} *vt* : to capitalize — **capitalización** *nf*
capitán, -tana *n, mpl* **-tanes** : captain
capitanear *vt* : to captain, to command
capitanía *nf* : captaincy
capitel *nm* : capital (of a column)
capitolio *nm* : capitol
capitulación *nf, pl* **-ciones** : capitulation
capitular *vi* : to capitulate, to surrender
capítulo *nm* **1** : chapter, section **2** : matter, subject
capó *nm* : hood (of a car)
capón *nm, pl* **capones** : capon
caporal *nm* **1** : chief, leader **2** : foreman (on a ranch)
capota *nf* : top (of a convertible)
capote *nm* **1** : cloak, overcoat **2** : bullfighter's cape **3** *Mex* COFRE : hood (of a car)
capricho *nm* ANTOJO : whim, caprice
caprichoso, -sa *adj* ANTOJADIZO : capricious, fickle
Capricornio *nmf* : Capricorn
cápsula *nf* : capsule
captar *vt* **1** : to catch, to grasp **2** : to gain, to attract **3** : to harness, to collect (waters)
captor, -tora *n* : captor
captura *nf* : capture, seizure
capturar *vt* : to capture, to seize
capucha *nf* : hood, cowl
capuchina *nf* : nasturtium
capuchino *nm* **1** : Capuchin (monk) **2** : capuchin (monkey) **3** : cappuccino
capullo *nm* **1** : cocoon **2** : bud (of a flower)
caqui *adj & nm* : khaki
cara *nf* **1** : face **2** ASPECTO : look, appearance ⟨¡qué buena cara tiene ese pastel! : that cake looks delicious!⟩ **3** *fam* : nerve, gall **4 ~ a** *or* **de cara a** : facing **5 de cara a** : in view of, in the light of
carabina *nf* : carbine
caracol *nm* **1** : snail **2** CONCHA : conch, seashell **3** : cochlea **4** : ringlet

caracola *nf* : conch
carácter *nm, pl* caracteres 1 ÍNDOLE : character, kind, nature 2 TEMPERAMENTO : disposition, temperament 3 : letter, symbol ⟨caracteres chinos : Chinese characters⟩
característica *nf* RASGO : trait, feature, characteristic
característico, -ca *adj* : characteristic — característicamente *adv*
caracterizar {21} *vt* : to characterize — caracterización *nf*
caramba *interj* 1 (*expressing annoyance*) : darn!, heck! 2 (*expressing disgust or surprise*) : jeez!
carámbano *nm* : icicle
carambola *nf* 1 : carom 2 : ruse, trick ⟨por carambola : by a lucky chance⟩
caramelo *nm* 1 : caramel 2 DULCE : candy
caramillo *nm* 1 : pipe, small flute 2 : heap, pile
caraqueño[1], -ña *adj* : of or from Caracas
caraqueño[2], -ña *n* : person from Caracas
carátula *nf* 1 : title page 2 : cover, dust jacket 3 CARETA : mask 4 *Mex* : face, dial (of a clock or watch)
caravana *nf* 1 : caravan 2 : convoy, motorcade 3 REMOLQUE : trailer
caray → caramba
carbohidrato *nm* : carbohydrate
carbón *nm, pl* carbones 1 : coal 2 : charcoal
carbonatado, -da *adj* : carbonated
carbonato *nm* : carbonate
carboncillo *nm* : charcoal
carbonera *nf* : coal cellar, coal bunker (on a ship)
carbonero, -ra *adj* : coal
carbonizar {21} *vt* : to carbonize, to char
carbono *nm* : carbon
carbunco *or* carbunclo *nm* : carbuncle
carburador *nm* : carburetor
carburante *nm* : fuel
carca *nmf fam* : old fogy
carcacha *nf fam* : jalopy, wreck
carcaj *nm* : quiver (for arrows)
carcajada *nf* : loud laugh, guffaw ⟨reírse a carcajadas : to roar with laughter⟩
carcajearse *vr* : to roar with laughter, to be in stitches
cárcel *nf* PRISIÓN : jail, prison
carcelero, -ra *n* : jailer
carcinogénico, -ca *adj* : carcinogenic
carcinógeno *nm* CANCERÍGENO : carcinogen
carcinoma *nm* : carcinoma
carcomer *vt* : to eat away at, to consume
carcomido, -da *adj* 1 : worm-eaten 2 : decayed, rotten
cardán *nm, pl* cardanes : universal joint
cardar *vt* : to card, to comb
cardenal *nm* 1 : cardinal (in religion) 2 : bruise
cardíaco *or* cardiaco, -ca *adj* : cardiac, heart

cárdigan *nm, pl* -gans : cardigan
cardinal *adj* : cardinal
cardiología *nf* : cardiology
cardiólogo, -ga *n* : cardiologist
cardiovascular *adj* : cardiovascular
cardo *nm* : thistle
cardumen *nm* : school of fish
carear *vt* : to bring face-to-face
carecer {53} *vi* ~ de : to lack ⟨el cheque carecía de fondos : the check lacked funds⟩
carencia *nf* 1 FALTA : lack 2 ESCASEZ : shortage 3 DEFICIENCIA : deficiency
carente *adj* ~ de : lacking (in)
carero, -ra *adj fam* : pricey
carestía *nf* 1 : rise in cost ⟨la carestía de la vida : the high cost of living⟩ 2 : dearth, scarcity
careta *nf* MÁSCARA : mask
carey *nm* 1 : hawksbill turtle, sea turtle 2 : tortoiseshell
carga *nf* 1 : loading 2 : freight, load, cargo 3 : burden, responsibility 4 : charge ⟨carga eléctrica : electrical charge⟩ 5 : attack, charge
cargado, -da *adj* 1 : loaded 2 : bogged down, weighted down 3 : close, stuffy 4 : charged ⟨cargado de tensión : charged with tension⟩ 5 FUERTE : strong ⟨café cargado : strong coffee⟩ 6 cargado de hombros : stoop-shouldered
cargador[1], -dora *n* : longshoreman *m*, longshorewoman *f*
cargador[2] *nm* 1 : magazine (for a firearm) 2 : charger (for batteries)
cargamento *nm* : cargo, load
cargar {52} *vt* 1 : to carry 2 : to load, to fill 3 : to charge — *vi* 1 : to load 2 : to rest (in architecture) 3 ~ sobre : to fall upon
cargo *nm* 1 : burden, load 2 : charge ⟨a cargo de : in charge of⟩ 3 : position, office
cargue, etc. → cargar
carguero[1], -ra *adj* : freight, cargo ⟨tren carguero : freight train⟩
carguero[2] *nm* : freighter, cargo ship
cariarse *vr* : to decay (of teeth)
caribe *adj* : Caribbean ⟨el mar Caribe : the Caribbean Sea⟩
caribeño, -ña *adj* : Caribbean
caribú *nm* : caribou
caricatura *nf* 1 : caricature 2 : cartoon
caricaturista *nmf* : caricaturist, cartoonist
caricaturizar {21} *vt* : to caricature
caricia *nf* 1 : caress 2 hacer caricias : to pet, to stroke
caridad *nf* 1 : charity 2 LIMOSNA : alms *pl*
caries *nfs & pl* : cavity (in a tooth)
carillón *nm, pl* -llones 1 : carillon 2 : glockenspiel
cariño *nm* AFECTO : affection, love
cariñoso, -sa *adj* AFECTUOSO : affectionate, loving — cariñosamente *adv*
carioca[1] *adj* : of or from Rio de Janeiro

carioca² *nmf* : person from Rio de Janeiro
carisma *nf* : charisma
carismático, -ca *adj* : charismatic
carita *adj Mex fam* : cute (said of a man) ⟨tu primo se cree muy carita : your cousin thinks he's gorgeous⟩
caritativo, -va *adj* : charitable
cariz *nm, pl* **carices** : appearance, aspect
carmesí *adj & nm* : crimson
carmín *nm, pl* **carmines 1** : carmine **2 carmín de labios** : lipstick
carnada *nf* CEBO : bait
carnal *adj* **1** : carnal **2 primo carnal** : first cousin
carnaval *nm* : carnival
carnaza *nf* : bait
carne *nf* **1** : meat ⟨carne molida : ground beef⟩ **2** : flesh ⟨carne de gallina : goose bumps⟩
carné → **carnet**
carnero *nm* **1** : ram, sheep **2** : mutton
carnet *nm* **1** : identification card, ID **2** : membership card **3 carnet de conducir** *Spain* : driver's license
carnicería *nf* **1** : butcher shop **2** MATANZA : slaughter, carnage
carnicero, -ra *n* : butcher
carnívoro¹, -ra *adj* : carnivorous
carnívoro² *nm* : carnivore
carnoso, -sa *adj* : fleshy, meaty
caro¹ *adv* : dearly, a lot ⟨pagué caro : I paid a high price⟩
caro², -ra *adj* **1** : expensive, dear **2** QUERIDO : dear, beloved
carpa *nf* **1** : carp **2** : big top (of a circus) **3** : tent
carpelo *nm* : carpel
carpeta *nf* : folder, binder, portfolio (of drawings, etc.)
carpetazo *nm* **dar carpetazo a** : to shelve, to defer
carpintería *nf* **1** : carpentry **2** : carpenter's workshop
carpintero, -ra *n* : carpenter
carraspear *vi* : to clear one's throat
carraspera *nf* : hoarseness ⟨tener carraspera : to have a frog in one's throat⟩
carrera *nf* **1** : run, running ⟨a la carrera : at full speed⟩ ⟨de carrera : hastily⟩ **2** : race **3** : course of study **4** : career, profession **5** : run (in baseball)
carreta *nf* : cart, wagon
carrete *nm* **1** BOBINA : reel, spool **2** : roll of film
carretel → **carrete**
carretera *nf* : highway, road ⟨carretera de peaje : turnpike⟩
carretero, -ra *adj* : highway ⟨el sistema carretero nacional : the national highway system⟩
carretilla *nf* **1** : wheelbarrow **2 carretilla elevadora** : forklift
carril *nm* **1** : lane ⟨carretera de doble carril : two-lane highway⟩ **2** : rail (on a railroad track)
carrillo *nm* : cheek, jowl

carrito *nm* : cart ⟨carrito de compras : shopping cart⟩
carrizo *nm* JUNCO : reed
carro *nm* **1** COCHE : car **2** : cart **3** *Chile, Mex* : coach (of a train) **4 carro alegórico** : float (in a parade)
carrocería *nf* : bodywork, body (of a vehicle)
carroña *nf* : carrion
carroñero, -ra *n* : scavenger (animal)
carroza *nf* **1** : carriage **2** : float (in a parade)
carruaje *nm* : carriage
carrusel *nm* **1** : merry-go-round **2** : carousel ⟨carrusel de equipaje : luggage carousel⟩
carta *nf* **1** : letter **2** NAIPE : playing card **3** : charter, constitution **4** MENÚ : menu **5** : map, chart **6 tomar cartas en** : to intervene in
cártamo *nm* : safflower
cartearse *vr* ESCRIBIRSE : to write to one another, to correspond
cartel *nm* : sign, poster
cártel *or* **cartel** *nm* : cartel
cartelera *nf* **1** : billboard **2** : marquee
cartera *nf* **1** BILLETERA : wallet, billfold **2** BOLSO : pocketbook, purse **3** : portfolio ⟨cartera de acciones : stock portfolio⟩
carterista *nmf* : pickpocket
cartero, -ra *n* : letter carrier, mailman *m*
cartilaginoso, -sa *adj* : cartilaginous, gristly
cartílago *nm* : cartilage
cartilla *nf* **1** : primer, reader **2** : booklet ⟨cartilla de ahorros : bankbook⟩
cartografía *nf* : cartography
cartógrafo, -fa *n* : cartographer
cartón *nm, pl* **cartones 1** : cardboard ⟨cartón madera : fiberboard⟩ **2** : carton
cartucho *nm* : cartridge
cartulina *nf* : poster board, cardboard
carúncula *nf* : wattle (of a bird)
casa *nf* **1** : house, building **2** HOGAR : home **3** : household, family **4** : company, firm **5 echar la casa por la ventana** : to spare no expense
casaca *nf* : jacket
casado¹, -da *adj* : married
casado², -da *n* : married person
casamentero, -ra *n* : matchmaker
casamiento *nm* **1** : marriage **2** BODA : wedding
casar *vt* : to marry — *vi* : to go together, to match up — **casarse** *vr* **1** : to get married **2 ~ con** : to marry
casateniente *nmf Mex* : landlord, landlady *f*
cascabel¹ *nm* : small bell
cascabel² *nf* : rattlesnake
cascada *nf* CATARATA, SALTO : waterfall, cascade
cascajo *nm* **1** : pebble, rock fragment **2** *fam* : piece of junk
cascanueces *nms & pl* : nutcracker

cascar {72} *vt* : to crack (a shell) — **cascarse** *vr* : to crack, to chip

cáscara *nf* 1 : skin, peel, rind, husk 2 : shell (of a nut or egg)

cascarón *nm, pl* **-rones** 1 : eggshell 2 *Mex* : shell filled with confetti

cascarrabias *nmfs & pl fam* : grouch, crab

casco *nm* 1 : helmet 2 : hull 3 : hoof 4 : fragment, shard 5 : center (of a town) 6 *Mex* : empty bottle 7 **cascos** *nmpl* : headphones

caserío *nm* 1 : country house 2 : hamlet

casero¹, -ra *adj* 1 : domestic, household 2 : homemade

casero², -ra *n* DUEÑO : landlord *m*, landlady *f*

caseta *nf* : booth, stand, stall ⟨caseta telefónica : telephone booth⟩

casete → **cassette**

casi *adv* 1 : almost, nearly, virtually 2 (*in negative phrases*) : hardly ⟨casi nunca : hardly ever⟩

casilla *nf* 1 : booth 2 : pigeonhole 3 : box (on a form)

casino *nm* 1 : casino 2 : (social) club

caso *nm* 1 : case 2 **en caso de** : in case of, in the event of 3 **hacer caso de** : to pay attention to, to notice 4 **hacer caso omiso de** : to ignore, to take no notice of 5 **no venir al caso** : to be beside the point

caspa *nf* : dandruff

casque, etc. → **cascar**

casquete *nm* 1 : skullcap 2 **casquete glaciar** : ice cap 3 **casquete corto** *Mex* : crew cut

casquillo *nm* : case, casing (of a bullet)

cassette *nmf* : cassette

casta *nf* 1 : caste 2 : lineage, stock ⟨de casta : thoroughbred, purebred⟩ 3 **sacar la casta** *Mex* : to come out ahead

castaña *nf* : chestnut

castañetear *vi* : to chatter (of teeth)

castaño¹, -ña *adj* : chestnut, brown

castaño² *nm* 1 : chestnut tree 2 : chestnut, brown

castañuela *nf* : castanet

castellano¹, -na *adj & n* : Castilian

castellano² *nm* ESPAÑOL : Spanish, Castilian (language)

castidad *nf* : chastity

castigar {52} *vt* : to punish

castigo *nm* : punishment

castillo *nm* 1 : castle 2 **castillo de proa** : forecastle

casto, -ta *adj* : chaste, pure — **castamente** *adv*

castor *nm* : beaver

castración *nf, pl* **-ciones** : castration

castrar *vt* 1 : to castrate, to spay, to neuter, to geld 2 DEBILITAR : to weaken, to debilitate

castrense *adj* : military

casual *adj* 1 FORTUITO : fortuitous, accidental 2 *Mex* : casual (of clothing)

casualidad *nf* 1 : chance 2 **por** ~ *or* **de** ~ : by chance, by any chance

casualmente *adv* : accidentally, by chance

casucha *or* **casuca** *nf* : shanty, hovel

cataclismo *nm* : cataclysm

catacumbas *nfpl* : catacombs

catador, -dora *n* : wine taster

catalán¹, -lana *adj & n, mpl* **-lanes** : Catalan

catalán² *nm* : Catalan (language)

catálisis *nf* : catalysis

catalítico, -ca *adj* : catalytic

catalizador *nm* 1 : catalyst 2 : catalytic converter

catalogar {52} *vt* : to catalog, to classify

catálogo *nm* : catalog

catamarán *nm, pl* **-ranes** : catamaran

cataplasma *nf* : poultice

catapulta *nf* : catapult

catapultar *vt* : to catapult

catar *vt* 1 : to taste, to sample 2 : to look at, to examine

catarata *nf* 1 CASCADA, SALTO : waterfall 2 : cataract

catarro *nm* RESFRIADO : cold, catarrh

catarsis *nf* : catharsis

catártico, -ca *adj* : cathartic

catástrofe *nf* DESASTRE : catastrophe, disaster

catastrófico, -ca *adj* DESASTROSO : catastrophic, disastrous

catcher *nmf* : catcher (in baseball)

catecismo *nm* : catechism

cátedra *nf* 1 : chair, professorship 2 : subject, class 3 **libertad de cátedra** : academic freedom

catedral *nf* : cathedral

catedrático, -ca *n* PROFESOR : professor

categoría *nf* 1 CLASE : category 2 RANGO : rank, standing 3 **categoría gramatical** : part of speech 4 **de** ~ : first-rate, outstanding

categórico, -ca *adj* : categorical, unequivocal — **categóricamente** *adv*

catéter *nm* : catheter

cátodo *nm* : cathode

catolicismo *nm* : Catholicism

católico, -ca *adj & n* : Catholic

catorce *adj & nm* : fourteen

catorceavo *nm* : fourteenth

catre *nm* : cot

catsup *nm* : ketchup

caucásico, -ca *adj & n* : Caucasian

cauce *nm* 1 LECHO : riverbed 2 : means *pl*, channel

caucho *nm* 1 GOMA : rubber 2 : rubber tree 3 *Ven* : tire

caución *nf, pl* **cauciones** FIANZA : bail, security

caudal *nm* 1 : volume of water 2 RIQUEZA : capital, wealth 3 ABUNDANCIA : abundance

caudillaje *nm* : leadership

caudillo *nm* : leader, commander

causa *nf* **1** MOTIVO : cause, reason, motive ⟨a causa de : because of⟩ **2** IDEAL : cause ⟨morir por una causa : to die for a cause⟩ **3** : lawsuit
causal[1] *adj* : causal
causal[2] *nm* : cause, grounds *pl*
causalidad[1] *nf* : causality
causante[1] *adj* ~ **de** : causing, responsible for
causante[2] *nmf Mex* : taxpayer
causar *vt* **1** : to cause **2** : to provoke, to arouse ⟨eso me causa gracia : that strikes me as being funny⟩
cáustico, -ca *adj* : caustic
cautela *nf* : caution, prudence
cautelar *adj* : precautionary, preventive
cauteloso, -sa *adj* : cautious, prudent — **cautelosamente** *adv*
cauterizar {21} *vt* : to cauterize
cautivador, -dora *adj* : captivating
cautivar *vt* HECHIZAR : to captivate, to charm
cautiverio *nm* : captivity
cautivo, -va *adj & n* : captive
cauto, -ta *adj* : cautious, careful
cavar *vt* : to dig — *vi* ~ **en** : to delve into, to probe
caverna *nf* : cavern, cave
cavernoso, -sa *adj* **1** : cavernous **2** : deep, resounding
caviar *nm* : caviar
cavidad *nf* : cavity
cavilar *vi* : to ponder, to deliberate
cayado *nm* : crook, staff, crosier
cayena *nf* : cayenne pepper
cayó, etc. → **caer**
caza[1] *nf* **1** CACERÍA : hunt, hunting **2** : game
caza[2] *nm* : fighter plane
cazador, -dora *n* **1** : hunter **2 cazador furtivo** : poacher
cazar {21} *vt* **1** : to hunt **2** : to catch, to bag **3** *fam* : to land (a job, a spouse) — *vi* : to go hunting
cazatalentos *nmfs & pl* : talent scout
cazo *nm* **1** : saucepan, pot **2** CUCHARÓN : ladle
cazuela *nf* **1** : pan, saucepan **2** : casserole
cazurro, -ra *adj* : sullen, surly
CD *nm* : CD, compact disk
cebada *nf* : barley
cebar *vt* **1** : to bait **2** : to feed, to fatten **3** : to prime (a pump, etc.) — **cebarse** *vr* ~ **en** : to take it out on
cebo *nm* **1** CARNADA : bait **2** : feed **3** : primer (for firearms)
cebolla *nf* : onion
cebolleta *nf* : scallion, green onion
cebollino *nm* **1** : chive **2** : scallion
cebra *nf* : zebra
cebú *nm, pl* **cebús** *or* **cebúes** : zebu (cattle)
cecear *vi* : to lisp
ceceo *nm* : lisp
cecina *nf* : dried beef, beef jerky
cedazo *nm* : sieve

ceder *vi* **1** : to yield, to give way **2** : to diminish, to abate **3** : to give in, to relent — *vt* : to cede, to hand over
cedro *nm* : cedar
cédula *nf* : document, certificate
céfiro *nm* : zephyr
cegador, -dora *adj* : blinding
cegar {49} *vt* **1** : to blind **2** : to block, to stop up — *vi* : to be blinded, to go blind
cegatón, -tona *adj, mpl* **-tones** *fam* : blind as a bat
ceguera *nf* : blindness
ceiba *nf* : ceiba, silk-cotton tree
ceja *nf* **1** : eyebrow ⟨fruncir las cejas : to knit one's brows⟩ **2** : flange, rim
cejar *vi* : to give in, to back down
celada *nf* : trap, ambush
celador, -dora *n* GUARDIA : guard, warden
celda *nf* : cell (of a jail)
celebración *nf, pl* **-ciones** : celebration
celebrado, -da *adj* CÉLEBRE, FAMOSO : famous, celebrated
celebrante *nmf* OFICIANTE : celebrant
celebrar *vt* **1** FESTEJAR : to celebrate **2** : to hold (a meeting) **3** : to say (Mass) **4** : to welcome, to be happy about — *vi* : to be glad — **celebrarse** *vr* **1** : to be celebrated, to fall **2** : to be held, to take place
célebre *adj* CELEBRADO, FAMOSO : celebrated, famous
celebridad *nf* **1** : celebrity **2** FAMA : fame, renown
celeridad *nf* : celerity, swiftness
celeste[1] *adj* **1** : celestial **2** : sky blue, azure
celeste[2] *nm* : sky blue
celestial *adj* : heavenly, celestial
celibato *nm* : celibacy
célibe *adj & nmf* : celibate
cello *nm* : cello
celo *nm* **1** : zeal, fervor **2** : heat (of females), rut (of males) **3 celos** *nmpl* : jealousy ⟨tenerle celos a alguien : to be jealous of someone⟩
celofán *nm, pl* **-fanes** : cellophane
celosía *nf* **1** : lattice window **2** : latticework, trellis
celoso, -sa *adj* **1** : jealous **2** : zealous — **celosamente** *adv*
celta[1] *adj* : Celtic
celta[2] *nmf* : Celt
célula *nf* : cell
celular *adj* : cellular
celuloide *nm* **1** : celluloid **2** : film, cinema
celulosa *nf* : cellulose
cementar *vt* : to cement
cementerio *nm* : cemetery
cemento *nm* : cement
cena *nf* : supper, dinner
cenador *nm* : arbor
cenagal *nm* : bog, quagmire
cenagoso, -sa *adj* : swampy
cenar *vi* : to have dinner, to have supper — *vt* : to have for dinner or supper

⟨anoche cenamos tamales : we had tamales for supper last night⟩

cencerro *nm* : cowbell

cenicero *nm* : ashtray

ceniciento, -ta *adj* : ashen

cenit *nm* : zenith, peak

ceniza *nf* **1** : ash **2 cenizas** *nfpl* : ashes (of a deceased person)

cenizo, -za *n* : jinx

cenote *nm Mex* : natural deposit of spring water

censar *vt* : to take a census of

censo *nm* : census

censor, -sora *n* : censor, critic

censura *nf* **1** : censorship **2** : censure, criticism

censurable *adj* : reprehensible, blameworthy

censurar *vt* **1** : to censor **2** : to censure, to criticize

centauro *nm* : centaur

centavo *nm* **1** : cent (in English-speaking countries) **2** : unit of currency in various Latin-American countries

centella *nf* **1** : lightning flash **2** : spark

centellear *vi* **1** : to twinkle **2** : to gleam, to sparkle

centelleo *nm* : twinkling, sparkle

centenar *nm* **1** : hundred **2 a centenares** : by the hundreds

centenario¹, -ria *adj & n* : centenarian

centenario² *nm* : centennial

centeno *nm* : rye

centésimo¹, -ma *adj* : hundredth

centésimo² *nm* : hundredth

centígrado *adj* : centigrade, Celsius

centigramo *nm* : centigram

centímetro *nm* : centimeter

centinela *nmf* : sentinel, sentry

central¹ *adj* **1** : central **2** PRINCIPAL : main, principal

central² *nf* **1** : main office, headquarters **2 central camionera** *Mex* : bus terminal

centralita *nf* : switchboard

centralizar {21} *vt* : to centralize — **centralización** *nf*

centrar *vt* **1** : to center **2** : to focus — **centrarse** *vr* ~ **en** : to focus on, to concentrate on

céntrico, -ca *adj* : central

centrífugo, -ga *adj* : centrifugal

centrípeto, -ta *adj* : centripetal

centro¹ *nmf* : center (in sports)

centro² *nm* **1** MEDIO : center ⟨centro de atención : center of attention⟩ ⟨centro de gravedad : center of gravity⟩ **2** : downtown **3 centro de mesa** : centerpiece

centroamericano, -na *adj & n* : Central American

ceñido, -da *adj* AJUSTADO : tight, tight-fitting

ceñir {67} *vt* **1** : to encircle, to surround **2** : to hug, to cling to ⟨me ciñe demasiado : it's too tight on me⟩ — **ceñirse** *vr* ~ **a** : to restrict oneself to, to stick to

ceño *nm* **1** : frown, scowl **2 fruncir el ceño** : to frown, to knit one's brows

cepa *nf* **1** : stump (of a tree) **2** : stock (of a vine) **3** LINAJE : ancestry, stock

cepillar *vt* **1** : to brush **2** : to plane (wood) — **cepillarse** *vr*

cepillo *nm* **1** : brush ⟨cepillo de dientes : toothbrush⟩ **2** : plane (for woodworking)

cepo *nm* : trap (for animals)

cera *nf* **1** : wax ⟨cera de abejas : beeswax⟩ **2** : polish

cerámica *nf* **1** : ceramics *pl* **2** : pottery

cerámico, -ca *adj* : ceramic

ceramista *nmf* ALFARERO : potter

cerca¹ *adv* **1** : close, near, nearby **2** ~ **de** : nearly, almost

cerca² *nf* **1** : fence **2** : (stone) wall

cercado *nm* : enclosure

cercanía *nf* **1** PROXIMIDAD : proximity, closeness **2 cercanías** *nfpl* : outskirts, suburbs

cercano, -na *adj* : near, close

cercar {72} *vt* **1** : to fence in, to enclose **2** : to surround

cercenar *vt* **1** : to cut off, to amputate **2** : to diminish, to curtail

cerceta *nf* : teal (duck)

cerciorarse *vr* ASEGURARSE ~ **de** : to make sure of, to verify

cerco *nm* **1** : siege **2** : cordon, circle **3** : fence

cerda *nf* **1** : bristle **2** : sow

cerdo *nm* **1** : pig, hog **2 carne de cerdo** : pork

cereal *nm* : cereal — **cereal** *adj*

cerebelo *nm* : cerebellum

cerebral *adj* : cerebral

cerebro *nm* : brain

ceremonia *nf* : ceremony — **ceremonial** *adj*

ceremonioso, -sa *adj* : ceremonious

cereza *nf* : cherry

cerezo *nm* : cherry tree

cerilla *nf* **1** : match **2** : earwax

cerillo *nm* (*in various countries*) : match

cerner {56} *vt* : to sift — **cernerse** *vr* **1** : to hover **2** ~ **sobre** : to loom over, to threaten

cernidor *nm* : sieve

cernir → **cerner**

cero *nm* : zero

ceroso, -sa *adj* : waxy

cerque, etc. → **cercar**

cerquita *adv fam* : very close, very near

cerrado, -da *adj* **1** : closed, shut **2** : thick, broad ⟨tiene un acento cerrado : she has a thick accent⟩ **3** : cloudy, overcast **4** : quiet, reserved **5** : dense, stupid

cerradura *nf* : lock

cerrajería *nf* : locksmith's shop

cerrajero, -ra *n* : locksmith

cerrar {55} *vt* **1** : to close, to shut **2** : to turn off **3** : to bring to an end — *vi* **1** : to close up, to lock up **2** : to close down — **cerrarse** *vr* **1** : to close **2** : to fasten, to button up **3** : to conclude, to end

cerrazón *nf, pl* **-zones** : obstinacy, stubbornness

cerro *nm* COLINA, LOMA : hill

cerrojo *nm* PESTILLO : bolt, latch

certamen *nm, pl* **-támenes** : competition, contest

certero, -ra *adj* : accurate, precise — **certeramente** *adv*

certeza *nf* : certainty

certidumbre *nf* : certainty

certificable *adj* : certifiable

certificación *nf, pl* **-ciones** : certification

certificado¹, -da *adj* 1 : certified 2 : registered (of mail)

certificado² *nm* 1 : certificate 2 : registered letter

certificar {72} *vt* 1 : to certify 2 : to register (mail)

cervato *nm* : fawn

cervecera *nf* : brewery

cervecería *nf* 1 : brewery 2 : beer hall, bar

cerveza *nf* : beer ⟨cerveza de barril : draft beer⟩

cervical *adj* : cervical

cerviz *nf, pl* **cervices** : nape of the neck, cervix

cesación *nf, pl* **-ciones** : cessation, suspension

cesante *adj* : laid off, unemployed

cesantía *nf* : unemployment

cesar *vi* : to cease, to stop — *vt* : to dismiss, to lay off

cesárea *nf* : cesarean, C-section

cese *nm* 1 : cessation, stop ⟨cese del fuego : cease-fire⟩ 2 : dismissal

cesio *nm* : cesium

cesión *nf, pl* **cesiones** : transfer, assignment ⟨cesión de bienes : transfer of property⟩

césped *nm* : lawn, grass

cesta *nf* 1 : basket 2 : jai alai racket

cesto *nm* 1 : hamper 2 : basket (in basketball) 3 **cesto de (la) basura** : wastebasket

cetrería *nf* : falconry

cetrino, -na *adj* : sallow

cetro *nm* : scepter

chabacano¹, -na *adj* : tacky, tasteless

chabacano² *nm Mex* : apricot

chacal *nm* : jackal

cháchara *nf fam* 1 : small talk, chatter 2 **chácharas** *nfpl* : trinkets, junk

chacharear *vi fam* : to chatter, to gab

chacra *nf Arg, Chile, Peru* : small farm

chadiano, -na *adj & n* : Chadian

chal *nm* MANTÓN : shawl

chalado¹, -da *adj fam* : crazy, nuts

chalado², -da *n* : nut, crazy person

chalán *nm, pl* **chalanes** *Mex* : barge

chalé → **chalet**

chaleco *nm* : vest

chalet *nm Spain* : house

chalupa *nf* 1 : small boat 2 *Mex* : small stuffed tortilla

chamaco, -ca *n Mex fam* : kid, boy *m*, girl *f*

chamarra *nf* 1 : sheepskin jacket 2 : poncho, blanket

chamba *nf Mex, Peru fam* : job, work

chambear *vi Mex, Peru fam* : to work

chamo, -ma *n Ven fam* 1 : kid, boy *m*, girl *f* 2 : buddy, pal

champaña *or* **champán** *nm* : champagne

champiñón *nm, pl* **-ñones** : mushroom

champú *nm, pl* **-pus** *or* **-púes** : shampoo

champurrado *nm Mex* : hot chocolate thickened with cornstarch

chamuco *nm Mex fam* : devil

chamuscar {72} *vt* : to singe, to scorch — **chamuscarse** *vr*

chamusquina *nf* : scorch

chance *nm* OPORTUNIDAD : chance, opportunity

chancho¹, -cha *adj fam* : dirty, filthy, gross

chancho², -cha *n* 1 : pig, hog 2 *fam* : slob

chanchullero, -ra *adj fam* : shady, crooked

chanchullo *nm fam* : shady deal, scam

chancla *nf* 1 : thong sandal, slipper 2 : old shoe

chancleta → **chancla**

chanclo *nm* 1 : clog 2 **chanclos** *nmpl* : overshoes, galoshes, rubbers

chancro *nm* : chancre

changarro *nm Mex* : small shop, stall

chango, -ga *n Mex* : monkey

chantaje *nm* : blackmail

chantajear *vt* : to blackmail

chantajista *nmf* : blackmailer

chanza *nf* 1 : joke, jest 2 *Mex fam* : chance, opportunity

chapa *nf* 1 : sheet, panel, veneer 2 : lock 3 : badge

chapado, -da *adj* 1 : plated 2 **chapado a la antigua** : old-fashioned

chapar *vt* 1 : to veneer 2 : to plate (metals)

chaparrón *nm, pl* **-rrones** 1 : downpour 2 : great quantity, torrent

chapeado, -da *adj Col, Mex* : flushed

chapopote *nm Mex* : tar, blacktop

chapotear *vi* : to splash about

chapucero¹, -ra *adj* 1 : crude, shoddy 2 *Mex fam* : dishonest

chapucero², -ra *n* 1 : sloppy worker, bungler 2 *Mex fam* : cheat, swindler

chapulín *nm, pl* **-lines** *CA, Mex* : grasshopper, locust

chapuza *nf* 1 : botched job 2 *Mex fam* : fraud, trick ⟨hacer chapuzas : to cheat⟩

chapuzón *nm, pl* **-zones** : dip, swim ⟨darse un chapuzón : to go for a quick dip⟩

chaqueta *nf* : jacket

charada *nf* : charades (game)

charango *nm* : traditional Andean stringed instrument

charca *nf* : pond, pool

charco *nm* : puddle, pool

charcutería *nf* : delicatessen

charla *nf* : chat, talk

charlar *vi* : to chat, to talk

charlatán[1], -tana *adj* : talkative, chatty

charlatán[2], -tana *n, mpl* -tanes 1 : chatterbox 2 FARSANTE : charlatan, phony

charlatanear *vi* : to chatter away

charol *nm* 1 : lacquer, varnish 2 : patent leather 3 : tray

charola *nf Bol, Mex, Peru* : tray

charreada *nf Mex* : charro show, rodeo

charretera *nf* : epaulet

charro[1], -rra *adj* 1 : gaudy, tacky 2 *Mex* : pertaining to charros

charro[2], -rra *n Mex* : charro (Mexican cowboy or cowgirl)

chascarrillo *nm fam* : joke, funny story

chasco *nm* 1 BROMA : trick, joke 2 DECEPCIÓN, DESILUSIÓN : disillusionment, disappointment

chasis *or* chasís *nm* : chassis

chasquear *vt* 1 : to click (the tongue, fingers, etc.) 2 : to snap (a whip)

chasquido *nm* 1 : click (of the tongue or fingers) 2 : snap, crack

chatarra *nf* : scrap metal

chato, -ta *adj* 1 : pug-nosed 2 : flat

chauvinismo *nm* : chauvinism

chauvinista[1] *adj* : chauvinistic

chauvinista[2] *nmf* : chauvinist

chaval, -vala *n fam* : kid, boy *m,* girl *f*

chavo[1], -va *adj Mex fam* : young

chavo[2], -va *n Mex fam* : kid, boy *m,* girl *f*

chavo[3] *nm fam* : cent, buck ⟨no tengo un chavo : I'm broke⟩

chayote *nm* : chayote (plant, fruit)

checar {72} *vt Mex* : to check, to verify

checo[1], -ca *adj & n* : Czech

checo[2] *nm* : Czech (language)

checoslovaco, -ca *adj & n* : Czechoslovakian

chef *nm* : chef

chelín *nm, pl* chelines : shilling

cheque[1], etc. → checar

cheque[2] *nm* 1 : check 2 cheque de viajero : traveler's check

chequear *vt* 1 : to check, to verify 2 : to check in (baggage)

chequeo *nm* 1 INSPECCIÓN : check, inspection 2 : checkup, examination

chequera *nf* : checkbook

chévere *adj fam* : great, fantastic

chic *adj & nm* : chic

chica → chico

chicano, -na *adj & n* : Chicano *m,* Chicana *f*

chicha *nf* : fermented alcoholic beverage made from corn

chícharo *nm* : pea

chicharra *nf* 1 CIGARRA : cicada 2 : buzzer

chicharrón *nm, pl* -rrones 1 : pork rind 2 darle chicharrón a *Mex fam* : to get rid of

chichón *nm, pl* chichones : bump, swelling

chicle *nm* : chewing gum

chicloso *nm Mex* : taffy

chico[1], -ca *adj* 1 : little, small 2 : young

chico[2], -ca *n* 1 : child, boy *m,* girl *f* 2 : young man *m,* young woman *f*

chicote *nm* LÁTIGO : whip, lash

chiffon → chifón

chiflado[1], -da *adj fam* : nuts, crazy

chiflado[2], -da *n fam* : crazy person, lunatic

chiflar *vi* : to whistle — *vt* : to whistle at, to boo — chiflarse *vr fam* ∼ por : to be crazy about

chiflido *nm* : whistle, whistling

chiflón *nm, pl* chiflones : draft (of air)

chifón *nm, pl* chifones : chiffon

chilango[1], -ga *adj Mex fam* : of or from Mexico City

chilango[2], -ga *n Mex fam* : person from Mexico City

chilaquiles *nmpl Mex* : shredded tortillas in sauce

chile *nm* : chili pepper

chileno, -na *adj & n* : Chilean

chillar *vi* 1 : to squeal, to screech 2 : to scream, to yell 3 : to be gaudy, to clash

chillido *nm* 1 : scream, shout 2 : squeal, screech, cry (of an animal)

chillo *nm PRi* : red snapper

chillón, -llona *adj, mpl* chillones 1 : piercing, shrill 2 : loud, gaudy

chilpayate *nmf Mex fam* : child, little kid

chimenea *nf* 1 : chimney 2 : fireplace

chimichurri *nm Arg* : traditional hot sauce

chimpancé *nm* : chimpanzee

china *nf* 1 : pebble, small stone 2 *PRi* : orange

chinchar *vt fam* : to annoy, to pester — chincharse *vr fam* : to put up with something, to grin and bear it

chinchayote *nm Mex* : chayote root

chinche[1] *nf* 1 : bedbug 2 *Ven* : ladybug 3 : thumbtack

chinche[2] *nmf fam* : nuisance, pain in the neck

chinchilla *nf* : chinchilla

chino[1], -na *adj* 1 : Chinese 2 *Mex* : curly, kinky

chino[2], -na *n* : Chinese person

chino[3] *nm* : Chinese (language)

chip *nm, pl* chips : chip ⟨chip de memoria : memory chip⟩

chipote *nm Mex fam* : bump (on the head)

chipotle *nm Mex* : type of chili pepper

chipriota *adj & nmf* : Cypriot

chiquear *vt Mex* : to spoil, to indulge

chiquero *nm* POCILGA : pigpen, pigsty

chiquillada *nf* : childish prank

chiquillo[1], -lla *adj* : very young, little

chiquillo[2], -lla *n* : kid, youngster

chiquito[1], -ta *adj* : tiny

chiquito[2], -ta *n* : little one, baby

chiribita *nf* 1 : spark 2 chiribitas *nfpl* : spots before the eyes

chiribitil *nm* 1 DESVÁN : attic, garret 2 : cubbyhole

chirigota *nf fam* : joke
chirimía *nf* : traditional reed pipe
chirimoya *nf* : cherimoya, custard apple
chiripa *nf* **1** : fluke **2 de ~** : by sheer luck
chirivía *nf* : parsnip
chirona *nf fam* : slammer, jail
chirriar {85} *vi* **1** : to squeak, to creak **2** : to screech — **chirriante** *adj*
chirrido *nm* **1** : squeak, squeaking **2** : screech, screeching
chirrión *nm, pl* **chirriones** *Mex* : whip, lash
chisme *nm* **1** : gossip, tale **2** *Spain fam* : gadget, thingamajig
chismear *vi* : to gossip
chismoso[1], **-sa** *adj* : gossipy, gossiping
chismoso[2], **-sa** *n* **1** : gossiper, gossip **2** *Mex fam* : tattletale
chispa[1] *adj* **1** *Mex fam* : lively, vivacious ⟨un perrito chispa : a frisky puppy⟩ **2** *Spain fam* : tipsy
chispa[2] *nf* **1** : spark **2 echar chispas** : to be furious
chispeante *adj* : sparkling, scintillating
chispear *vi* **1** : to give off sparks **2** : to sparkle
chisporrotear *vi* : to crackle, to sizzle
chiste *nm* **1** : joke, funny story **2 tener chiste** : to be funny **3 tener su chiste** *Mex* : to be tricky
chistoso[1], **-sa** *adj* **1** : funny, humorous **2** : witty
chistoso[2], **-sa** *n* : wit, joker
chivas *nfpl Mex fam* : stuff, odds and ends
chivo[1], **-va** *n* **1** : kid, young goat **2 chivo expiatorio** : scapegoat
chivo[2] *nm* **1** : billy goat **2** : fit of anger
chocante *adj* **1** : shocking **2** : unpleasant, rude
chocar {72} *vi* **1** : to crash, to collide **2** : to clash, to conflict **3** : to be shocking ⟨le chocó : he was shocked⟩ **4** *Mex, Ven fam* : to be unpleasant or obnoxious ⟨me choca tu jefe : I can't stand your boss⟩ — *vt* **1** : to shake (hands) **2** : to clink glasses
chochear *vi* **1** : to be senile **2 ~ por** : to dote on, to be soft on
chochín *nm, pl* **-chines** : wren
chocho, -cha *adj* **1** : senile **2** : doting
choclo *nm* **1** : ear of corn, corncob **2** : corn **3 meter el choclo** *Mex fam* : to make a mistake
chocolate *nm* **1** : chocolate **2** : hot chocolate, cocoa
chofer *or* **chófer** *nm* **1** : chauffeur **2** : driver
choke *nm* : choke (of an automobile)
chole *interj Mex fam* **¡ya chole!** : enough!, cut it out!
cholo, -la *adj & n* : mestizo
cholla *nf fam* : head
chollo *nm Spain fam* : bargain
chongo *nm* **1** *Mex* : bun (chignon) **2 chongos** *nmpl Mex* : dessert made with fried bread

choque[1], **etc.** → **chocar**
choque[2] *nm* **1** : crash, collision **2** : clash, conflict **3** : shock
chorizo *nm* : chorizo, sausage
chorrear *vi* **1** : to drip **2** : to pour out, to gush out
chorrito *nm* : squirt, splash
chorro *nm* **1** : flow, stream, jet **2** *Mex fam* : heap, ton
choteado, -da *adj Mex fam* : worn-out, stale ⟨esa canción está bien choteada : that song's been played to death⟩
chotear *vt* : to make fun of
choteo *nm* : joking around, kidding
chovinismo, chovinista → **chauvinismo, chauvinista**
choza *nf* BARRACA, CABAÑA : hut, shack
chubasco *nm* : downpour, storm
chuchería *nf* : knickknack, trinket
chueco, -ca *adj* **1** : crooked, bent **2** *Chile, Mex fam* : dishonest, shady
chulada *nf Mex, Spain fam* : cute or pretty thing ⟨¡qué chulada de vestido! : what a lovely dress!⟩
chulear *vt Mex fam* : to compliment
chuleta *nf* : cutlet, chop
chulo[1], **-la** *adj* **1** *fam* : cute, pretty **2** *Spain fam* : cocky, arrogant
chulo[2] *nm Spain* : pimp
chupada *nf* **1** : suck, sucking **2** : puff, drag (on a cigarette)
chupado, -da *adj* **1** : gaunt, skinny **2** : plastered, drunk
chupaflor *nm* COLIBRÍ : hummingbird
chupamirto *nm Mex* : hummingbird
chupar *vt* **1** : to suck **2** : to absorb **3** : to puff on **4** *fam* : to drink, to guzzle — *vi* : to suckle — **chuparse** *vr* **1** : to waste away ⟨fam⟩ : to put up with **3 ¡chúpate esa!** *fam* : take that!
chupete *nm* **1** : pacifier **2** *Chile, Peru* : lollipop
chupetear *vt* : to suck (at)
chupón *nm, pl* **chupones** **1** : sucker (of a plant) **2** : baby bottle, pacifier
churrasco *nm* **1** : steak **2** : barbecued meat
churro *nm* **1** : fried dough **2** *fam* : botch, mess **3** *fam* : attractive person, looker
chusco, -ca *adj* : funny, amusing
chusma *nf* GENTUZA : riffraff, rabble
chutar *vi* : to shoot (in soccer)
chute *nm* : shot (in soccer)
cianuro *nm* : cyanide
cibernética *nf* : cybernetics
cicatriz *nf, pl* **-trices** : scar
cicatrizarse {21} *vr* : to form a scar, to heal
cíclico, -ca *adj* : cyclical
ciclismo *nm* : bicycling
ciclista *nmf* : bicyclist
ciclo *nm* : cycle
ciclomotor *nm* : moped
ciclón *nm, pl* **ciclones** : cyclone
cicuta *nf* : hemlock
cidra *nf* : citron (fruit)
ciega, ciegue etc. → **cegar**

ciego · circunstancial

ciego¹, -ga *adj* **1** INVIDENTE : blind **2 a ciegas** : blindly **3 quedarse ciego** : to go blind — **ciegamente** *adv*

ciego², -ga *n* INVIDENTE : blind person

cielo *nm* **1** : sky **2** : heaven **3** : ceiling

ciempiés *nms & pl* : centipede

cien¹ *adj* **1** : a hundred, hundred ⟨las primeras cien páginas : the first hundred pages⟩ **2 cien por cien** *or* **cien por ciento** : a hundred percent, through and through, wholeheartedly

cien² *nm* : one hundred

ciénaga *nf* : swamp, bog

ciencia *nf* **1** : science **2** : learning, knowledge **3 a ciencia cierta** : for a fact, for certain

cieno *nm* : mire, mud, silt

científico¹, -ca *adj* : scientific — **científicamente** *adv*

científico², -ca *n* : scientist

ciento¹ *adj* (*used in compound numbers*) : one hundred ⟨ciento uno : one hundred and one⟩

ciento² *nm* **1** : hundred, group of a hundred **2 por ~** : percent

cierne, etc. → **cerner**

cierra, etc. → **cerrar**

cierre *nm* **1** : closing, closure **2** : fastener, clasp, zipper

cierto, -ta *adj* **1** : true, certain, definite ⟨lo cierto es que ... : the fact is that ... ⟩ **2** : certain, one ⟨cierto día de verano : one summer day⟩ ⟨bajo ciertas circunstancias : under certain circumstances⟩ **3 por ~** : in fact, as a matter of fact — **ciertamente** *adv*

ciervo, -va *n* : deer, stag *m*, hind *f*

cifra *nf* **1** : figure, number **2** : quantity, amount **3** CLAVE : code, cipher

cifrar *vt* **1** : to write in code **2** : to place, to pin ⟨cifró su esperanza en la lotería : he pinned his hopes on the lottery⟩ — **cifrarse** *vr* : to amount ⟨la multa se cifra en millares : the fine amounts to thousands⟩

cigarra *nf* CHICHARRA : cicada

cigarrera *nf* : cigarette case

cigarrillo *nm* : cigarette

cigarro *nm* **1** : cigarette **2** PURO : cigar

cigoto *nm* : zygote

cigüeña *nf* : stork

cilantro *nm* : cilantro, coriander

cilíndrico, -ca *adj* : cylindrical

cilindro *nm* : cylinder

cima *nf* CUMBRE : peak, summit, top

cimarrón, -rrona *adj, mpl* **-rrones** : untamed, wild

címbalo *nm* : cymbal

cimbel *nm* : decoy

cimbrar *vt* : to shake, to rock — **cimbrarse** *vr* : to sway, to swing

cimentar {55} *vt* **1** : to lay the foundation of, to establish **2** : to strengthen, to cement

cimientos *nmpl* : base, foundation(s)

cinc *nm* : zinc

cincel *nm* : chisel

cincelar *vt* **1** : to chisel **2** : to engrave

cincha *nf* : cinch, girth

cinchar *vt* : to cinch (a horse)

cinco *adj & nm* : five

cincuenta *adj & nm* : fifty

cincuentavo¹, -va *adj* : fiftieth

cincuentavo² *nm* : fiftieth (fraction)

cine *nm* **1** : cinema, movies *pl* **2** : movie theater

cineasta *nmf* : filmmaker

cinematográfico, -ca *adj* : movie, film, cinematic ⟨la industria cinematográfica : the film industry⟩

cingalés¹, -lesa *adj & n* : Sinhalese

cingalés² *nm* : Sinhalese (language)

cínico¹, -ca *adj* **1** : cynical **2** : shameless, brazen — **cínicamente** *adv*

cínico², -ca *n* : cynic

cinismo *nm* : cynicism

cinta *nf* **1** : ribbon **2** : tape ⟨cinta métrica : tape measure⟩ **3** : strap, belt ⟨cinta transportadora : conveyor belt⟩

cinto *nm* : strap, belt

cintura *nf* **1** : waist, waistline **2 meter en cintura** *fam* : to bring into line, to discipline

cinturón *nm, pl* **-rones 1** : belt **2 cinturón de seguridad** : seat belt

ciñe, etc. → **ceñir**

ciprés *nm, pl* **cipreses** : cypress

circo *nm* : circus

circón *nm, pl* **circones** : zircon

circonio *nm* : zirconium

circuitería *nf* : circuitry

circuito *nm* : circuit

circulación *nf, pl* **-ciones 1** : circulation **2** : movement **3** : traffic

circular¹ *vi* **1** : to circulate **2** : to move along **3** : to drive

circular² *adj* : circular

circular³ *nf* : circular, flier

circulatorio, -ria *adj* : circulatory

círculo *nm* **1** : circle **2** : club, group

circuncidar *vt* : to circumcise

circuncisión *nf, pl* **-siones** : circumcision

circundar *vt* : to surround — **circundante** *adj*

circunferencia *nf* : circumference

circunflejo, -ja *adj* **acento circunflejo** : circumflex

circunlocución *nf, pl* **-ciones** : circumlocution

circunloquio *nm* → **circunlocución**

circunnavegar {52} *vt* : to circumnavigate — **circunnavegación** *nf*

circunscribir {33} *vt* : to circumscribe, to constrict, to limit — **circunscribirse** *vr*

circunscripción *nf, pl* **-ciones 1** : limitation, restriction **2** : constituency

circunscrito *pp* → **circunscribir**

circunspección *nf, pl* **-ciones** : circumspection, prudence

circunspecto, -ta *adj* : circumspect, prudent

circunstancia *nf* : circumstance

circunstancial *adj* : circumstantial, incidental

circunstante *nmf* **1** : onlooker, bystander **2 los circunstantes** : those present
circunvalación *nf, pl* **-ciones** : surrounding, encircling ⟨carretera de circunvalación : bypass, beltway⟩
circunvecino, -na *adj* : surrounding, neighboring
cirio *nm* : large candle
cirro *nm* : cirrus (cloud)
cirrosis *nf* : cirrhosis
ciruela *nf* **1** : plum **2 ciruela pasa** : prune
cirugía *nf* : surgery
cirujano, -na *n* : surgeon
cisma *nm* : schism, rift
cisne *nm* : swan
cisterna *nf* : cistern, tank
cita *nf* **1** : quote, quotation **2** : appointment, date
citable *adj* : quotable
citación *nf, pl* **-ciones** EMPLAZAMIENTO : summons, subpoena
citadino¹, -na *adj* : of the city, urban
citadino², -na *n* : city dweller
citado, -da *adj* : said, aforementioned
citar *vt* **1** : to quote, to cite **2** : to make an appointment with **3** : to summon (to court), to subpoena — **citarse** *vr* ∼ **con** : to arrange to meet (someone)
cítara *nf* : zither
citatorio *nm* : subpoena
citoplasma *nm* : cytoplasm
cítrico¹, -ca *adj* : citric
cítrico² *nm* : citrus fruit
ciudad *nf* **1** : city, town **2 ciudad universitaria** : college or university campus **3 ciudad perdida** *Mex* : shantytown
ciudadanía *nf* **1** : citizenship **2** : citizenry, citizens *pl*
ciudadano¹, -na *adj* : civic, city
ciudadano², -na *n* **1** NACIONAL : citizen **2** HABITANTE : resident, city dweller
ciudadela *nf* : citadel, fortress
cívico, -ca *adj* **1** : civic **2** : public-spirited
civil¹ *adj* **1** : civil **2** : civilian
civil² *nmf* : civilian
civilidad *nf* : civility, courtesy
civilización *nf, pl* **-ciones** : civilization
civilizar {21} *vt* : to civilize
civismo *nm* : community spirit, civic-mindedness, civics
cizaña *nf* : discord, rift
clamar *vi* : to clamor, to raise a protest — *vt* : to cry out for
clamor *nm* : clamor, outcry
clamoroso, -sa *adj* : clamorous, resounding, thunderous
clan *nm* : clan
clandestinidad *nf* : secrecy ⟨en la clandestinidad : underground⟩
clandestino, -na *adj* : clandestine, secret
clara *nf* : egg white
claraboya *nf* : skylight
claramente *adv* : clearly

clarear *v impers* **1** : to clear, to clear up **2** : to get light, to dawn — *vi* : to go gray, to turn white
claridad *nf* **1** NITIDEZ : clarity, clearness **2** : brightness, light
clarificación *nf, pl* **-ciones** ACLARACIÓN : clarification, explanation
clarificar {72} *vt* ACLARAR : to clarify, to explain
clarín *nm, pl* **clarines** : bugle
clarinete *nm* : clarinet
clarividencia *nf* **1** : clairvoyance **2** : perspicacity, discernment
clarividente¹ *adj* **1** : clairvoyant **2** : perspicacious, discerning
clarividente² *nmf* : clairvoyant
claro¹ *adv* **1** : clearly ⟨habla más claro : speak more clearly⟩ **2** : of course, surely ⟨¡claro!, ¡claro que sí! : absolutely!, of course!⟩ ⟨claro que entendió : of course she understood⟩
claro², -ra *adj* **1** : bright, clear **2** : pale, fair, light **3** : clear, evident
claro³ *nm* **1** : clearing **2 claro de luna** : moonlight
clase *nf* **1** : class **2** ÍNDOLE, TIPO : sort, kind, type
clasicismo *nm* : classicism
clásico¹, -ca *adj* **1** : classic **2** : classical
clásico² *nm* : classic
clasificación *nf, pl* **-ciones** **1** : classification, sorting out **2** : rating **3** CALIFICACIÓN : qualification (in competitions)
clasificado, -da *adj* : classified ⟨aviso clasificado : classified ad⟩
clasificar {72} *vt* **1** : to classify, to sort out **2** : to rate, to rank — *vi* CALIFICAR : to qualify (in competitions) — **clasificarse** *vr*
claudicación *nf, pl* **-ciones** : surrender, abandonment of one's principles
claudicar {72} *vi* : to back down, to abandon one's principles
claustro *nm* : cloister
claustrofobia *nf* : claustrophobia
claustrofóbico, -ca *adj* : claustrophobic
cláusula *nf* : clause
clausura *nf* **1** : closure, closing **2** : closing ceremony **3** : cloister
clausurar *vt* **1** : to close, to bring to a close **2** : to close down
clavadista *nmf* : diver
clavado¹, -da *adj* **1** : nailed, fixed, stuck **2** *fam* : punctual, on the dot **3** *fam* : identical ⟨es clavado a su padre : he's the image of his father⟩
clavado² *nm* : dive
clavar *vt* **1** : to nail, to hammer **2** HINCAR : to plunge, to stick **3** : to fix (one's eyes) on — **clavarse** *vr* : to stick oneself (with a sharp object)
clave¹ *adj* : key, essential
clave² *nf* **1** CIFRA : code **2** : key ⟨la clave del misterio : the key to the mystery⟩ **3** : clef **4** : keystone
clavel *nm* : carnation
clavelito *nm* : pink (flower)

clavicémbalo *nm* : harpsichord
clavícula *nf* : collarbone
clavija *nf* 1 : plug 2 : peg, pin
clavo *nm* 1 : nail ⟨clavo grande : spike⟩ 2 : clove 3 dar en el clavo : to hit the nail on the head
claxon *nm, pl* cláxones : horn (of an automobile)
clemencia *nf* : clemency, mercy
clemente *adj* : merciful
cleptomanía *nf* : kleptomania
cleptómano, -na *n* : kleptomaniac
clerecía *nf* : ministry, ministers *pl*
clerical *adj* : clerical
clérigo, -ga *n* : cleric, member of the clergy
clero *nm* : clergy
cliché *nm* 1 : cliché 2 : stencil 3 : negative (of a photograph)
cliente, -ta *n* : customer, client
clientela *nf* : clientele, customers *pl*
clima *nm* 1 : climate 2 AMBIENTE : atmosphere, ambience
climático, -ca *adj* : climatic
climatización *nf, pl* -ciones : air-conditioning
climatizar {21} *vt* : to air-condition — climatizado, -da *adj*
clímax *nm* : climax
clínica *nf* : clinic
clínico, -ca *adj* : clinical — clínicamente *adv*
clip *nm, pl* clips 1 : clip 2 : paper clip
clítoris *nms & pl* : clitoris
cloaca *nf* ALCANTARILLA : sewer
clocar {82} *vi* : to cluck
cloche *nm* CA, Car, Col, Ven : clutch (of an automobile)
clon *nm* : clone
cloqué, etc. → clocar
cloquear *vi* : to cluck
clorar *vt* : to chlorinate — cloración *nf*
cloro *nm* : chlorine
clorofila *nf* : chlorophyll
cloroformo *nm* : chloroform
cloruro *nm* : chloride
clóset *nm, pl* clósets 1 : closet 2 : cupboard
club *nm* : club
clueca, clueque etc. → clocar
coa *nf Mex* : hoe
coacción *nf, pl* -ciones : coercion, duress
coaccionar *vt* : to coerce
coactivo, -va *adj* : coercive
coagular *v* : to clot, to coagulate — coagulación *nf*
coágulo *nm* : clot
coalición *nf, pl* -ciones : coalition
coartada *nf* : alibi
coartar *vt* : to restrict, to limit
cobalto *nm* : cobalt
cobarde[1] *adj* : cowardly
cobarde[2] *nmf* : coward
cobardía *nf* : cowardice
cobaya *nf* : guinea pig
cobertizo *nm* : shed, shelter
cobertor *nm* COLCHA : bedspread, quilt

cobertura *nf* 1 : coverage 2 : cover, collateral
cobija *nf* FRAZADA, MANTA : blanket
cobijar *vt* : to shelter — cobijarse *vr* : to take shelter
cobra *nf* : cobra
cobrador, -dora *n* 1 : collector 2 : conductor (of a bus or train)
cobrar *vt* 1 : to charge 2 : to collect, to draw, to earn 3 : to acquire, to gain 4 : to recover, to retrieve 5 : to cash (a check) 6 : to claim, to take (a life) 7 : to shoot (game), to bag — *vi* 1 : to be paid 2 llamar por cobrar *Mex* : to call collect
cobre *nm* : copper
cobrizo, -za *adj* : coppery
cobro *nm* : collection (of money), cashing (of a check)
coca *nf* 1 : coca 2 *fam* : coke, cocaine
cocaína *nf* : cocaine
cocal *nm* : coca plantation
cocción *nf, pl* cocciones : cooking
cocear *vi* : to kick (of an animal)
cocer {14} *vt* 1 COCINAR : to cook 2 HERVIR : to boil
cochambre *nmf fam* : filth, grime
cochambroso, -sa *adj* : filthy, grimy
coche *nm* 1 : car, automobile 2 : coach, carriage 3 coche cama : sleeping car 4 coche fúnebre : hearse
cochecito *nm* : baby carriage, stroller
cochera *nf* : garage, carport
cochinada *nf fam* 1 : filthy language 2 : disgusting behavior 3 : dirty trick
cochinillo *nm* : suckling pig, piglet
cochino[1], -na *adj* 1 : dirty, filthy, disgusting 2 *fam* : rotten, lousy
cochino[2], -na *n* : pig, hog
cocido[1], -da *adj* 1 : boiled, cooked 2 bien cocido : well-done
cocido[2] *nm* ESTOFADO, GUISADO : stew
cociente *nm* : quotient
cocimiento *nm* : cooking, baking
cocina *nf* 1 : kitchen 2 : stove 3 : cuisine, cooking
cocinar *v* : to cook
cocinero, -ra *n* : cook, chef
cocineta *nf Mex* : kitchenette
coco *nm* 1 : coconut 2 *fam* : head 3 *fam* : bogeyman
cocoa *nf* : cocoa, hot chocolate
cocodrilo *nm* : crocodile
cocotero *nm* : coconut palm
coctel *or* cóctel *nm* 1 : cocktail 2 : cocktail party
coctelera *nf* : cocktail shaker
codazo *nm* 1 darle un codazo a : to elbow, to nudge 2 abrirse paso a codazos : to elbow one's way through
codearse *vr* : to rub elbows, to hobnob
códice *nm* : codex, manuscript
codicia *nf* AVARICIA : avarice, covetousness
codiciar *vt* : to covet
codicilo *nm* : codicil
codicioso, -sa *adj* : avaricious, covetous

codificación *nf, pl* **-ciones** **1** : codification **2** : coding, encoding

codificar {72} *vt* **1** : to codify **2** : to code, to encode

código *nm* **1** : code **2 código postal** : zip code **3 código morse** : Morse code

codo¹, -da *adj Mex* : cheap, stingy

codo², -da *n Mex* : tightwad, cheapskate

codo³ *nm* : elbow

codorniz *nf, pl* **-nices** : quail

coeficiente *nm* **1** : coefficient **2 coeficiente intelectual** : IQ, intelligence quotient

coexistir *vi* : to coexist — **coexistencia** *nf*

cofa *nf* : crow's nest

cofre *nm* **1** BAÚL : trunk, chest **2** *Mex* CAPOTE : hood (of a car)

coger {15} *vt* **1** : to seize, to take hold of **2** : to catch **3** : to pick up **4** : to gather, to pick **5** : to gore — **cogerse** *vr* AGARRARSE : to hold on

cogida *nf* **1** : gathering, harvest **2** : goring

cognición *nf, pl* **-ciones** : cognition

cognitivo, -va *adj* : cognitive

cogollo *nm* **1** : heart (of a vegetable) **2** : bud, bulb **3** : core, crux ⟨el cogollo de la cuestión : the heart of the matter⟩

cogote *nm* : scruff, nape

cohabitar *vi* : to cohabit — **cohabitación** *nf*

cohechar *vt* SOBORNAR : to bribe

cohecho *nm* SOBORNO : bribe, bribery

coherencia *nf* : coherence — **coherente** *adj*

cohesión *nf, pl* **-siones** : cohesion

cohesivo, -va *adj* : cohesive

cohete *nm* : rocket

cohibición *nf, pl* **-ciones** **1** : (legal) restraint **2** INHIBICIÓN : inhibition

cohibido, -da *adj* : inhibited, shy

cohibir {62} *vt* : to inhibit, to make self-conscious — **cohibirse** *vr* : to feel shy or embarrassed

cohorte *nf* : cohort

coima *nf Arg, Chile, Peru* : bribe

coimear *vt Arg, Chile, Peru* : to bribe

coincidencia *nf* : coincidence

coincidente *adj* **1** : coincident **2** ACORDE : coinciding

coincidir *vi* **1** : to coincide **2** : to agree

coito *nm* : sexual intercourse, coitus

coja, etc. → **coger**

cojear *vi* **1** : to limp **2** : to wobble, to rock **3 cojear del mismo pie** : to be two of a kind

cojera *nf* : limp

cojín *nm, pl* **cojines** : cushion, throw pillow

cojinete *nm* **1** : bearing, bushing **2 cojinete de bola** : ball bearing

cojo¹, -ja *adj* **1** : limping, lame **2** : wobbly **3** : weak, ineffectual

cojo², -ja *n* : lame person

cojones *nmpl usu considered vulgar* **1** : testicles *pl* **2** : guts *pl*, courage

col *nf* **1** REPOLLO : cabbage **2 col de Bruselas** : Brussels sprout **3 col rizada** : kale

cola *nf* **1** RABO : tail ⟨cola de caballo : ponytail⟩ **2** FILA : line (of people) ⟨hacer cola : to wait in line⟩ **3** : cola, drink **4** : train (of a dress) **5** : tails *pl* (of a tuxedo) **6** PEGAMENTO : glue **7** *fam* : buttocks *pl*, rear end

colaboracionista *nmf* : collaborator, traitor

colaborador, -dora *n* **1** : contributor (to a periodical) **2** : collaborator

colaborar *vi* : to collaborate — **colaboración** *nf*

colación *nf, pl* **-ciones** **1** : light meal **2** : comparison, collation ⟨sacar a colación : to bring up, to broach⟩ **3** : conferral (of a degree)

colador *nm* **1** : colander, strainer **2** *PRi* : small coffeepot

colapso *nm* **1** : collapse **2** : standstill

colar {19} *vt* : to strain, to filter — **colarse** *vr* **1** : to sneak in, to cut in line, to gate-crash **2** : to slip up, to make a mistake

colateral¹ *adj* : collateral — **colateralmente** *adv*

colateral² *nm* : collateral

colcha *nf* COBERTOR : bedspread, quilt

colchón *nm, pl* **colchones** **1** : mattress **2** : cushion, padding, buffer

colchoneta *nf* : mat (for gymnastic sports)

colear *vi* **1** : to wag its tail **2 vivito y coleando** *fam* : alive and kicking

colección *nf, pl* **-ciones** : collection

coleccionar *vt* : to collect, to keep a collection of

coleccionista *nmf* : collector

colecta *nf* : collection (of donations)

colectar *vt* : to collect

colectividad *nf* : community, group

colectivo¹, -va *adj* : collective — **colectivamente** *adv*

colectivo² *nm* **1** : collective **2** *Arg, Bol, Peru* : city bus

colector¹, -tora *n* : collector ⟨colector de impuestos : tax collector⟩

colector² *nm* **1** : sewer **2** : manifold (of an engine)

colega *nmf* **1** : colleague **2** HOMÓLOGO : counterpart **3** *fam* : buddy

colegiado¹, -da *adj* : collegiate

colegiado², -da *n* **1** ÁRBITRO : referee **2** : member (of a professional association)

colegial¹, -giala *adj* **1** : school, collegiate **2** *Mex fam* : green, inexperienced

colegial², -giala *n* : schoolboy *m*, schoolgirl *f*

colegiatura *nf Mex* : tuition

colegio *nm* **1** : school **2** : college ⟨colegio electoral : electoral college⟩ **3** : professional association

colegir {28} *vt* **1** JUNTAR : to collect, to gather **2** INFERIR : to infer, to deduce
cólera[1] *nm* : cholera
cólera[2] *nf* FURIA, IRA : anger, rage
colérico, -ca *adj* **1** FURIOSO : angry **2** IRRITABLE : irritable
colesterol *nm* : cholesterol
coleta *nf* **1** : ponytail **2** : pigtail
coletazo *nm* : lash, flick (of a tail)
colgado, -da *adj* **1** : hanging, hanged **2** : pending **3 dejar colgado a** : to disappoint, to let down
colgante[1] *adj* : hanging, dangling
colgante[2] *nm* : pendant, charm (on a bracelet)
colgar {16} *vt* **1** : to hang (up), to put up **2** AHORCAR : to hang (someone) **3** : to hang up (a telephone) **4** *fam* : to fail (an exam) — **colgarse** *vr* **1** : to hang, to be suspended **2** AHORCARSE : to hang oneself **3** : to hang up a telephone
colibrí *nm* CHUPAFLOR : hummingbird
cólico *nm* : colic
coliflor *nf* : cauliflower
colilla *nf* : butt (of a cigarette)
colina *nf* CERRO, LOMA : hill
colindante *adj* CONTIGUO : adjacent, neighboring
colindar *vi* : to adjoin, to be adjacent
coliseo *nm* : coliseum
colisión *nf, pl* **-siones** : collision
colisionar *vi* : to collide
collage *nm* : collage
collar *nm* **1** : collar (for an animal) **2** : necklace ⟨collar de perlas : string of pearls⟩
colmado, -da *adj* : heaping
colmar *vt* **1** : to fill to the brim **2** : to fulfill, to satisfy **3** : to heap, to shower ⟨me colmaron de regalos : they showered me with gifts⟩
colmena *nf* : beehive
colmenar *nm* APIARIO : apiary
colmillo *nm* **1** CANINO : canine (tooth), fang **2** : tusk
colmilludo, -da *adj Mex, PRi* : astute, shrewd, crafty
colmo *nm* : height, extreme, limit ⟨el colmo de la locura : the height of folly⟩ ⟨¡eso es el colmo! : that's the last straw!⟩
colocación *nf, pl* **-ciones** **1** : placement, placing **2** : position, job **3** : investment
colocar {72} *vt* **1** PONER : to place, to put **2** : to find a job for **3** : to invest — **colocarse** *vr* **1** SITUARSE : to position oneself **2** : to get a job
colofón *nm, pl* **-fones** **1** : ending, finale **2** : colophon
colofonia *nf* : rosin
colombiano, -na *adj & n* : Colombian
colon *nm* : (intestinal) colon
colón *nm, pl* **colones** : Costa Rican and Salvadoran unit of currency
colonia *nf* **1** : colony **2** : cologne **3** *Mex* : residential area, neighborhood
colonial *adj* : colonial

colonización *nf, pl* **-ciones** : colonization
colonizador[1], **-dora** *adj* : colonizing
colonizador[2], **-dora** *n* : colonizer, colonist
colonizar {21} *vt* : to colonize, to settle
colono, -na *n* **1** : settler, colonist **2** : tenant farmer
coloquial *adj* : colloquial
coloquio *nm* **1** : discussion, talk **2** : conference, symposium
color *nm* **1** : color **2** : paint, dye **3 colores** *nmpl* : colored pencils
coloración *nf, pl* **-ciones** : coloring, coloration
colorado[1], **-da** *adj* **1** ROJO : red **2 ponerse colorado** : to blush **3 chiste colorado** *Mex* : off-color joke
colorado[2] *nm* ROJO : red
colorante *nm* : coloring ⟨colorante de alimentos : food coloring⟩
colorear *vt* : to color — *vi* **1** : to redden **2** : to ripen
colorete *nm* : rouge, blusher
colorido *nm* : color, coloring
colorín *nm, pl* **-rines** **1** : bright color **2** : goldfinch
colosal *adj* : colossal
coloso *nm* : colossus
coludir *vi* : to be in collusion, to conspire
columna *nf* **1** : column **2 columna vertebral** : spine, backbone
columnata *nf* : colonnade
columnista *nmf* : columnist
columpiar *vt* : to push (on a swing) — **columpiarse** *vr* : to swing
columpio *nm* : swing
colusión *nf, pl* **-siones** : collusion
colza *nf* : rape (plant)
coma[1] *nm* : coma
coma[2] *nf* : comma
comadre *nf* **1** : godmother of one's child **2** : mother of one's godchild **3** *fam* : neighbor, female friend **4** *fam* : gossip
comadrear *vi fam* : to gossip
comadreja *nf* : weasel
comadrona *nf* : midwife
comanche *nmf* : Comanche
comandancia *nf* **1** : command headquarters **2** : command
comandante *nmf* **1** : commander, commanding officer **2** : major
comandar *vt* : to command, to lead
comando *nm* **1** : commando **2** : command (for computers)
comarca *nf* REGIÓN : region
comarcal *adj* REGIONAL : regional, local
comatoso, -sa *adj* : comatose
combar *vt* : to bend, to curve — **combarse** *vr* **1** : to bend, to buckle **2** : to warp, to bulge, to sag
combate *nm* **1** : combat **2** : fight, boxing match
combatiente *nmf* : combatant, fighter
combatir *vt* : to combat, to fight against — *vi* : to fight

combatividad *nf* : fighting spirit
combativo, -va *adj* : combative, spirited
combinación *nf, pl* **-ciones 1** : combination **2** : connection (in travel)
combinar *vt* **1** UNIR : to combine, to mix together **2** : to match, to put together — **combinarse** *vr* : to get together, to conspire
combo *nm* **1** : (musical) band **2** *Chile, Peru* : sledgehammer **3** *Chile, Peru* : punch
combustible[1] *adj* : combustible
combustible[2] *nm* : fuel
combustión *nf, pl* **-tiones** : combustion
comedero *nm* : trough, feeder
comedia *nf* : comedy
comediante *nmf* : actor, actress *f*
comedido, -da *adj* MESURADO : moderate, restrained
comediógrafo, -fa *n* : playwright
comedor *nm* : dining room
comején *nm, pl* **-jenes** : termite
comelón[1], **-lona** *adj, mpl* **-lones** *fam* : gluttonous
comelón[2], **-lona** *n, pl* **-lones** *fam* : big eater, glutton
comensal *nmf* : dinner guest
comentador, -dora *n* → **comentarista**
comentar *vt* **1** : to comment on, to discuss **2** : to mention, to remark
comentario *nm* **1** : comment, remark ⟨sin comentarios : no comment⟩ **2** : commentary
comentarista *nmf* : commentator
comenzar {29} *v* EMPEZAR : to begin, to start
comer[1] *vt* **1** : to eat **2** : to consume, to eat up, to eat into — *vi* **1** : to eat **2** CENAR : to have a meal **3 dar de comer** : to feed — **comerse** *vr* : to eat up
comer[2] *nm* : eating, dining
comercial *adj & nm* : commercial — **comercialmente** *adv*
comercializar {21} *vt* **1** : to commercialize **2** : to market
comerciante *nmf* : merchant, dealer
comerciar *vi* : to do business, to trade
comercio *nm* **1** : commerce, trade **2** NEGOCIO : business, place of business
comestible *adj* : edible
comestibles *nmpl* VÍVERES : groceries, food
cometa[1] *nm* : comet
cometa[2] *nf* : kite
cometer *vt* **1** : to commit **2 cometer un error** : to make a mistake
cometido *nm* : assignment, task
comezón *nf, pl* **-zones** PICAZÓN : itchiness, itching
comible *adj fam* : eatable, edible
comic *or* **cómic** *nm* : comic strip, comic book
comicastro, -tra *n* : second-rate actor, ham
comicidad *nf* HUMOR : humor, wit
comicios *nmpl* : elections, voting
cómico[1], **-ca** *adj* : comic, comical

cómico[2], **-ca** *n* HUMORISTA : comic, comedian, comedienne *f*
comida *nf* **1** : food **2** : meal **3** : dinner **4 comida basura** : junk food **5 comida rápida** : fast food
comidilla *nf* : talk, gossip
comienzo *nm* **1** : start, beginning **2 al comienzo** : at first **3 dar comienzo** : to begin
comillas *nfpl* : quotation marks ⟨entre comillas : in quotes⟩
comilón, -lona → **comelón, -lona**
comilona *nf fam* : feast
comino *nm* **1** : cumin **2 me vale un comino** *fam* : not to matter to someone ⟨no me importa un comino : I couldn't care less⟩
comisaría *nf* : police station
comisario, -ria *n* : commissioner
comisión *nf, pl* **-siones 1** : commission, committing **2** : committee **3** : percentage, commission ⟨comisión sobre las ventas : sales commission⟩
comisionado[1], **-da** *adj* : commissioned, entrusted
comisionado[2], **-da** *n* → **comisario**
comisionar *vt* : to commission
comité *nm* : committee
comitiva *nf* : retinue, entourage
como[1] *adv* **1** : around, about ⟨cuesta como 500 pesos : it costs around 500 pesos⟩ **2** : kind of, like ⟨tengo como mareos : I'm kind of dizzy⟩
como[2] *conj* **1** : how, as ⟨hazlo como dijiste que lo harías : do it the way you said you would⟩ **2** : since, given that ⟨como estaba lloviendo, no salí : since it was raining, I didn't go out⟩ **3** : if ⟨como lo vuelva a hacer lo arrestarán : if he does that again he'll be arrested⟩ **4 como quiera** : in any way
como[3] *prep* **1** : like, as ⟨ligero como una pluma : light as a feather⟩ **2 así como** : as well as
cómo *adv* : how ⟨¿cómo estás? : how are you?⟩ ⟨¿a cómo están las manzanas? : how much are the apples?⟩ ⟨¿cómo? : excuse me?, what was that?⟩ ⟨¿se puede? ¡cómo no! : may I? please do!⟩
cómoda *nf* : bureau, chest of drawers
comodidad *nf* **1** : comfort **2** : convenience
comodín *nm, pl* **-dines 1** : joker, wild card **2** : all-purpose word or thing **3** : pretext, excuse
cómodo, -da *adj* **1** CONFORTABLE : comfortable **2** : convenient — **cómodamente** *adv*
comodoro *nm* : commodore
comoquiera *adv* **1** : in any way **2 comoquiera que** : in whatever way, however ⟨comoquiera que sea eso : however that may be⟩
compa *nm fam* : buddy, pal
compactar *vt* : to compact, to compress
compacto, -ta *adj* : compact

compadecer {53} *vt* : to sympathize with, to feel sorry for — **compadecerse** *vr* **1** ~ **de** : to take pity on, to commiserate with **2** ~ **con** : to fit, to accord (with)

compadre *nm* **1** : godfather of one's child **2** : father of one's godchild **3** *fam* : buddy, pal

compaginar *vt* **1** COORDINAR : to combine, to coordinate **2** : to collate

compañerismo *nm* : comradeship, camaraderie

compañero, -ra *n* : companion, mate, partner

compañía *nf* **1** : company ⟨llegó en compañía de su madre : he arrived with his mother⟩ **2** EMPRESA, FIRMA : firm, company

comparable *adj* : comparable

comparación *nf, pl* **-ciones** : comparison

comparado, -da *adj* : comparative ⟨literatura comparada : comparative literature⟩

comparar *vt* : to compare

comparativo¹, -va *adj* : comparative, relative — **comparativamente** *adv*

comparativo² *nm* : comparative degree or form

comparecencia *nf* **1** : appearance (in court) **2 orden de comparecencia** : subpoena, summons

comparecer {53} *vi* : to appear (in court)

compartimiento *or* **compartimento** *nm* : compartment

compartir *vt* : to share

compás *nm, pl* **-pases 1** : beat, rhythm, time **2** : compass

compasión *nf, pl* **-siones** : compassion, pity

compasivo, -va *adj* : compassionate, sympathetic

compatibilidad *nf* : compatibility

compatible *adj* : compatible

compatriota *nmf* PAISANO : compatriot, fellow countryman

compeler *vt* : to compel

compendiar *vt* : to summarize, to condense

compendio *nm* : summary

compenetración *nf, pl* **-ciones** : rapport, mutual understanding

compenetrarse *vr* **1** : to understand each other **2** ~ **con** : to identify oneself with

compensación *nf, pl* **-ciones** : compensation

compensar *vt* : to compensate for, to make up for — *vi* : to be worth one's while

compensatorio, -ria *adj* : compensatory

competencia *nf* **1** : competition, rivalry **2** : competence

competente *adj* : competent, able — **competentemente** *adv*

competición *nf, pl* **-ciones** : competition

competidor¹, -dora *adj* RIVAL : competing, rival

competidor², -dora *n* RIVAL : competitor, rival

competir {54} *vi* : to compete

competitividad *nf* : competitiveness

competitivo, -va *adj* : competitive — **competitivamente** *adv*

compilar *vt* : to compile — **compilación** *nf*

compinche *nmf fam* **1** : buddy, pal **2** : partner in crime, accomplice

complacencia *nf* : pleasure, satisfaction

complacer {57} *vt* : to please — **complacerse** *vr* ~ **en** : to take pleasure in

complaciente *adj* : obliging, eager to please

complejidad *nf* : complexity

complejo¹, -ja *adj* : complex

complejo² *nm* : complex

complementar *vt* : to complement, to supplement — **complementarse** *vr*

complementario, -ria *adj* : complementary

complemento *nm* **1** : complement, supplement **2** : supplementary pay, allowance

completamente *adv* : completely, totally

completar *vt* TERMINAR : to complete, to finish

completo, -ta *adj* **1** : complete **2** : perfect, absolute **3** : full, detailed

complexión *nf, pl* **-xiones** : (physical) constitution

complicación *nf, pl* **-ciones** : complication

complicado, -da *adj* : complicated

complicar {72} *vt* **1** : to complicate **2** : to involve — **complicarse** *vr*

cómplice *nmf* : accomplice

complicidad *nf* : complicity

complot *nm, pl* **complots** CONFABULACIÓN, CONSPIRACIÓN : conspiracy, plot

componenda *nf* : shady deal, scam

componente *adj & nm* : component, constituent

componer {60} *vt* **1** ARREGLAR : to fix, to repair **2** CONSTITUIR : to make up, to compose **3** : to compose, to write **4** : to set (a bone) — **componerse** *vr* **1** : to improve, to get better **2** ~ **de** : to consist of

comportamiento *nm* CONDUCTA : behavior, conduct

comportarse *vr* : to behave, to conduct oneself

composición *nf, pl* **-ciones 1** OBRA : composition, work **2** : makeup, arrangement

compositor, -tora *n* : composer, songwriter

compostura *nf* **1** : composure **2** : mending, repair

compra *nf* **1** : purchase **2 ir de compras** : to go shopping **3 orden de compra** : purchase order

comprador, -dora *n* : buyer, shopper
comprar *vt* : to buy, to purchase
compraventa *nf* : buying and selling
comprender *vt* **1** ENTENDER : to comprehend, to understand **2** ABARCAR : to cover, to include — *vi* : to understand ⟨¡ya comprendo! : now I understand!⟩
comprensible *adj* : understandable — **comprensiblemente** *adv*
comprensión *nf, pl* **-siones 1** : comprehension, understanding, grasp **2** : understanding, sympathy
comprensivo, -va *adj* : understanding
compresa *nf* **1** : compress **2** *or* **compresa higiénica** : sanitary napkin
compresión *nf, pl* **-siones** : compression
compresor *nm* : compressor
comprimido *nm* PÍLDORA, TABLETA : pill, tablet
comprimir *vt* : to compress
comprobable *adj* : verifiable, provable
comprobación *nf, pl* **-ciones** : verification, confirmation
comprobante *nm* **1** : proof ⟨comprobante de identidad : proof of identity⟩ **2** : voucher, receipt ⟨comprobante de ventas : sales slip⟩
comprobar {19} *vt* **1** : to verify, to check **2** : to prove
comprometedor, -dora *adj* : compromising
comprometer *vt* **1** : to compromise **2** : to jeopardize **3** : to commit, to put under obligation — **comprometerse** *vr* **1** : to commit oneself **2** ~ **con** : to get engaged to
comprometido, -da *adj* **1** : compromising, awkward **2** : committed, obliged **3** : engaged (to be married)
compromiso *nm* **1** : obligation, commitment **2** : engagement ⟨anillo de compromiso : engagement ring⟩ **3** : agreement **4** : awkward situation, fix
compuerta *nf* : floodgate
compuesto[1] *pp* → **componer**
compuesto[2]**, -ta** *adj* **1** : fixed, repaired **2** : compound, composite **3** : decked out, spruced up **4** ~ **de** : made up of, consisting of
compuesto[3] *nm* : compound
compulsión *nf, pl* **-siones** : compulsion
compulsivo, -va *adj* **1** : compelling, urgent **2** : compulsive — **compulsivamente** *adv*
compungido, -da *adj* : contrite, remorseful
compungirse {35} *vr* : to feel remorse
compuso, etc. → **componer**
computable *adj* : countable ⟨años computables : years accrued⟩ ⟨ingresos computables : qualifying income⟩
computación *nf, pl* **-ciones** : computing, computers *pl*
computador *nm* → **computadora**
computadora *nf* **1** : computer **2 computadora portátil** : laptop computer

computar *vt* : to compute, to calculate
computarizar {21} *vt* : to computerize
cómputo *nm* : computation, calculation
comulgar {52} *vi* : to receive Communion
común *adj, pl* **comunes 1** : common **2 común y corriente** : ordinary, regular **3 por lo común** : generally, as a rule
comuna *nf* : commune
comunal *adj* : communal
comunicación *nf, pl* **-ciones 1** : communication **2** : access, link **3** : message, report
comunicado *nm* **1** : communiqué **2 comunicado de prensa** : press release
comunicar {72} *vt* **1** : to communicate, to convey **2** : to notify — **comunicarse** *vr* ~ **con 1** : to contact, to get in touch with **2** : to be connected to
comunicativo, -va *adj* : communicative, talkative
comunidad *nf* : community
comunión *nf, pl* **-niones 1** : communion, sharing **2** : Communion
comunismo *nm* : communism, Communism
comunista *adj & nmf* : communist
comúnmente *adv* : commonly
con *prep* **1** : with ⟨vengo con mi padre : I'm going with my father⟩ ⟨¿con quién hablas? : who are you speaking to?⟩ **2** : in spite of ⟨con todo : in spite of it all⟩ **3** : to, towards ⟨ella es amable con los niños : she is kind to the children⟩ **4** : by ⟨con llegar temprano : by arriving early⟩ **5 con (tal) que** : as long as, so long as
conato *nm* : attempt, effort ⟨conato de robo : attempted robbery⟩
cóncavo, -va *adj* : concave
concebible *adj* : conceivable
concebir {54} *vt* **1** : to conceive **2** : to conceive of, to imagine — *vi* : to conceive, to become pregnant
conceder *vt* **1** : to grant, to bestow **2** : to concede, to admit
concejal, -jala *n* : councilman *m*, councilwoman *f*, alderman *m*, alderwoman *f*
concejo *nm* : council ⟨concejo municipal : town council⟩
concentración *nf, pl* **-ciones** : concentration
concentrado *nm* : concentrate
concentrar *vt* : to concentrate — **concentrarse** *vr*
concéntrico, -ca *adj* : concentric
concepción *nf, pl* **-ciones** : conception
concepto *nm* NOCIÓN : concept, idea, opinion
conceptuar {3} *vt* : to regard, to judge
concernir {17} *vi* : to be of concern
concertar {55} *vt* **1** : to arrange, to set up **2** : to agree on, to settle **3** : to harmonize — *vi* : to be in harmony
concesión *nf, pl* **-siones 1** : concession **2** : awarding, granting
concha *nf* : conch, seashell

conciencia *nf* **1** : conscience **2** : consciousness, awareness
concientizar {21} *vt* : to make aware — **concientizarse** *vr* ~ **de** : to realize, to become aware of
concienzudo, -da *adj* : conscientious
concierto *nm* **1** : concert **2** : agreement **3** : concerto
conciliador[1], -dora *adj* : conciliatory
conciliador[2], -dora *n* : arbitrator, peacemaker
conciliar *vt* : to conciliate, to reconcile — **conciliación** *nf*
conciliatorio, -ria *adj* → **conciliador[1]**
concilio *nm* : (church) council
conciso, -sa *adj* : concise — **concisión** *nf*
conciudadano, -na *n* : fellow citizen
cónclave *nm* : conclave, private meeting
concluir {41} *vt* **1** TERMINAR : to conclude, to finish **2** DEDUCIR : to deduce, to infer — *vi* : to end, to conclude
conclusión *nf, pl* **-siones** : conclusion
concluyente *adj* : conclusive
concomitante *adj* : concomitant
concordancia *nf* : agreement, accordance
concordar {19} *vi* : to agree, to coincide — *vt* : to reconcile
concordia *nf* : concord, harmony
concretar *vt* **1** : to pinpoint, to specify **2** : to fulfill, to realize — **concretarse** *vr* : to become real, to take shape
concretizar → **concretar**
concreto[1], -ta *adj* **1** : concrete, actual **2** : definite, specific ⟨en concreto : specifically⟩ — **concretamente** *adv*
concreto[2] *nm* HORMIGÓN : concrete
concubina *nf* : concubine
concurrencia *nf* **1** : audience, turnout **2** : concurrence
concurrente *adj* : concurrent — **concurrentemente** *adv*
concurrido, -da *adj* : busy, crowded
concurrir *vi* **1** : to converge, to come together **2** : to concur, to agree **3** : to take part, to participate **4** : to attend, to be present ⟨concurrir a una reunión : to attend a meeting⟩ **5** ~ **a** : to contribute to
concursante *nmf* : contestant, competitor
concursar *vt* : to compete in — *vi* : to compete, to participate
concurso *nm* **1** : contest, competition **2** : concurrence, coincidence **3** : crowd, gathering **4** : cooperation, assistance
condado *nm* **1** : county **2** : earldom
conde, -desa *n* : count *m*, earl *m*, countess *f*
condecoración *nf, pl* **-ciones** : decoration, medal
condecorar *vt* : to decorate, to award (a medal)
condena *nf* **1** REPROBACIÓN : disapproval, condemnation **2** SENTENCIA : sentence, conviction

condenable *adj* : reprehensible
condenación *nf, pl* **-ciones** **1** : condemnation **2** : damnation
condenado[1], -da *adj* **1** : fated, doomed **2** : convicted, sentenced **3** *fam* : darn, damned
condenado[2], -da *n* : convict
condenar *vt* **1** : to condemn **2** : to sentence **3** : to board up, to wall up — **condenarse** *vr* : to be damned
condensación *nf, pl* **-ciones** : condensation
condensar *vt* : to condense
condesa *nf* → **conde**
condescendencia *nf* : condescension
condescender {56} *vi* **1** : to condescend **2** : to agree, to acquiesce
condición *nf, pl* **-ciones** **1** : condition, state **2** : capacity, position **3 condiciones** *nfpl* : conditions, circumstances ⟨condiciones de vida : living conditions⟩
condicional *adj* : conditional — **condicionalmente** *adv*
condicionamiento *nm* : conditioning
condicionar *vt* **1** : to condition, to determine **2** ~ **a** : to be contingent on, to depend on
condimentar *vt* SAZONAR : to season, to spice
condimento *nm* : condiment, seasoning, spice
condiscípulo, -la *n* : classmate
condolencia *nf* : condolence, sympathy
condolerse {47} *vr* : to sympathize
condominio *nm* : condominium, condo
condón *nm, pl* **condones** : condom
cóndor *nm* : condor
conducción *nf, pl* **-ciones** **1** : conduction (of electricity, etc.) **2** DIRECCIÓN : management, direction
conducir {61} *vt* **1** DIRIGIR, GUIAR : to direct, to lead **2** MANEJAR : to drive (a vehicle) — *vi* **1** : to drive a vehicle **2** ~ **a** : to lead to — **conducirse** *vr* PORTARSE : to behave, to conduct oneself
conducta *nf* COMPORTAMIENTO : conduct, behavior
conducto *nm* : conduit, channel, duct
conductor[1], -tora *adj* : conducting, leading
conductor[2], -tora *n* : driver
conductor[3] *nm* : conductor (of electricity, etc.)
conectar *vt* : to connect — *vi* ~ **con** : to link up with, to communicate with
conector *nm* : connector
conejera *nf* : rabbit hutch
conejillo *nm* **conejillo de Indias** : guinea pig
conejo, -ja *n* : rabbit
conexión *nf, pl* **-xiones** : connection
confabulación *nf, pl* **-ciones** COMPLOT, CONSPIRACIÓN : plot, conspiracy
confabularse *vr* : to plot, to conspire
confección *nf, pl* **-ciones** **1** : preparation **2** : tailoring, dressmaking
confeccionar *vt* : to make, to produce, to prepare

confederación *nf, pl* **-ciones** : confederation

confederarse *vr* : to confederate, to form a confederation

conferencia *nf* **1** REUNIÓN : conference, meeting **2** : lecture

conferenciante *nmf* : lecturer

conferencista → **conferenciante**

conferir {76} *vt* : to confer, to bestow

confesar {55} *v* : to confess — **confesarse** *vr* : to go to confession

confesión *nf, pl* **-siones 1** : confession **2** : creed, denomination

confesionario *nm* : confessional

confesor *nm* : confessor

confeti *nm* : confetti

confiable *adj* : trustworthy, reliable

confiado, -da *adj* **1** : confident, self-confident **2** : trusting — **confiadamente** *adv*

confianza *nf* **1** : trust ⟨de poca confianza : untrustworthy⟩ **2** : confidence, self-confidence

confianzudo, -da *adj* : forward, presumptuous

confiar {85} *vi* : to have trust, to be trusting — *vt* **1** : to confide **2** : to entrust — **confiarse** *vr* **1** : to be overconfident **2** ~ **a** : to confide in

confidencia *nf* : confidence, secret

confidencial *adj* : confidential — **confidencialmente** *adv*

confidencialidad *nf* : confidentiality

confidente *nmf* **1** : confidant, confidante *f* **2** : informer

configuración *nf, pl* **-ciones** : configuration, shape

configurar *vt* : to shape, to form

confín *nm, pl* **confines** : boundary, limit

confinamiento *nm* : confinement

confinar *vt* **1** : to confine, to limit **2** : to exile — *vi* ~ **con** : to border on

confirmación *nf, pl* **-ciones** : confirmation

confirmar *vt* : to confirm, to substantiate

confiscación *nf, pl* **-ciones** : confiscation

confiscar {72} *vt* DECOMISAR : to confiscate, to seize

confitado, -da *adj* : candied

confite *nm* : comfit, candy

confitería *nf* **1** DULCERÍA : candy store, confectionery **2** : tearoom, café

confitero, -ra *n* : confectioner

confitura *nf* : preserves, jam

conflagración *nf, pl* **-ciones 1** : conflagration, fire **2** : war

conflictivo, -va *adj* **1** : troubled **2** : controversial

conflicto *nm* : conflict

confluencia *nf* : junction, confluence

confluir {41} *vi* **1** : to converge, to join **2** : to gather, to assemble

conformar *vt* **1** : to form, to create **2** : to constitute, to make up — **conformarse** *vr* **1** RESIGNARSE : to resign oneself **2** : to comply, to conform **3** ~ **con** : to content oneself with, to be satisfied with

conforme[1] *adj* **1** : content, satisfied **2** ~ **a** : in accordance with

conforme[2] *conj* : as ⟨entreguen sus tareas conforme vayan saliendo : hand in your homework as you leave⟩

conformidad *nf* **1** : agreement, consent **2** : resignation

confort *nm* : comfort

confortable *adj* CÓMODO : comfortable

confortar *vt* CONSOLAR : to comfort, to console

confraternidad *nf* : brotherhood, fraternity

confraternización *nf, pl* **-ciones** : fraternization

confraternizar *vi* : to fraternize

confrontación *nf, pl* **-ciones** : confrontation

confrontar *vt* **1** ENCARAR : to confront **2** : to compare **3** : to bring face-to-face — *vi* : to border — **confrontarse** *vr* ~ **con** : to face up to

confundir *vt* : to confuse, to mix up — **confundirse** *vr* : to make a mistake, to be confused ⟨confundirse de número : to get the wrong number⟩

confusión *nf, pl* **-siones** : confusion

confuso, -sa *adj* **1** : confused, mixed-up **2** : obscure, indistinct

congelación *nf, pl* **-ciones 1** : freezing **2** : frostbite

congelado, -da *adj* HELADO : frozen

congelador *nm* HELADORA : freezer

congelamiento *nm* → **congelación**

congelar *vt* : to freeze — **congelarse** *vr*

congeniar *vi* : to get along (with someone)

congénito, -ta *adj* : congenital

congestión *nf, pl* **-tiones** : congestion

congestionado, -da *adj* : congested

congestionamiento *nm* → **congestión**

congestionarse *vr* **1** : to become flushed **2** : to become congested

conglomerado[1]**, -da** *adj* : conglomerate, mixed

conglomerado[2] *nm* : conglomerate, conglomeration

congoja *nf* ANGUSTIA : anguish, grief

congoleño, -ña *adj & n* : Congolese

congraciarse *vr* : to ingratiate oneself

congratular *vt* FELICITAR : to congratulate

congregación *nf, pl* **-ciones** : congregation, gathering

congregar {52} *vt* : to bring together — **congregarse** *vr* : to congregate, to assemble

congresista *nmf* : congressman *m*, congresswoman *f*

congreso *nm* : congress, conference

congruencia *nf* **1** : congruence **2** COHERENCIA : coherence — **congruente** *adj*

cónico, -ca *adj* : conical, conic

conífera *nf* : conifer

conífero, -ra *adj* : coniferous
conjetura *nf* : conjecture, guess
conjeturar *vt* : to guess, to conjecture
conjugación *nf, pl* **-ciones** : conjugation
conjugar {52} *vt* **1** : to conjugate **2** : to combine
conjunción *nf, pl* **-ciones** : conjunction
conjuntivo, -va *adj* : connective ⟨tejido conjuntivo : connective tissue⟩
conjunto¹, -ta *adj* : joint
conjunto² ** *nm* **1 : collection, group **2** : ensemble, outfit ⟨conjunto musical : musical ensemble⟩ **3** : whole, entirety ⟨en conjunto : as a whole, altogether⟩
conjurar *vt* **1** : to exorcise **2** : to avert, to ward off — *vi* CONSPIRAR : to conspire, to plot
conjuro *nm* **1** : exorcism **2** : spell
conllevar *vt* **1** : to bear, to suffer **2** IMPLICAR : to entail, to involve
conmemorar *vt* : to commemorate — **conmemoración** *nf*
conmemorativo, -va *adj* : commemorative, memorial
conmigo *pron* : with me ⟨habló conmigo : he talked with me⟩
conminar *vt* AMENAZAR : to threaten, to warn
conmiseración *nf, pl* **-ciones** : pity, commiseration
conmoción *nf, pl* **-ciones** **1** : shock, upheaval **2** *or* **conmoción cerebral** : concussion
conmocionar *vt* : to shake, to shock
conmovedor, -dora *adj* EMOCIONANTE : moving, touching
conmover {47} *vt* **1** EMOCIONAR : to move, to touch **2** : to shake up — **conmoverse** *vr*
conmutador *nm* **1** : switch **2** : switchboard
conmutar *vt* **1** : to commute (a sentence) **2** : to switch, to exchange
connivencia *nf* : connivance
connotación *nf, pl* **-ciones** : connotation
connotar *vt* : to connote, to imply
cono *nm* : cone
conocedor¹, -dora *adj* : knowledgeable
conocedor², -dora *n* : connoisseur, expert
conocer {18} *vt* **1** : to know, to be acquainted with ⟨ya lo conocí : I've already met him⟩ **2** : to meet **3** RECONOCER : to recognize — **conocerse** *vr* **1** : to know each other **2** : to meet **3** : to know oneself
conocido¹, -da *adj* **1** : familiar **2** : well-known, famous
conocido², -da *n* : acquaintance
conocimiento *nm* **1** : knowledge **2** SENTIDO : consciousness
conque *conj* : so, so then, and so ⟨¡ah, conque esas tenemos! : oh, so that's what's going on!⟩
conquista *nf* : conquest
conquistador¹, -dora *adj* : conquering

conquistador², -dora *n* : conqueror
conquistar *vt* : to conquer
consabido, -da *adj* : usual, typical
consagración *nf, pl* **-ciones** : consecration
consagrar *vt* **1** : to consecrate **2** DEDICAR : to dedicate, to devote
consciencia → **conciencia**
consciente *adj* : conscious, aware — **conscientemente** *adv*
conscripción *nf, pl* **-ciones** : conscription, draft
conscripto, -ta *n* : conscript, inductee
consecución *nf, pl* **-ciones** : attainment
consecuencia *nf* **1** : consequence, result ⟨a consecuencia de : as a result of⟩ **2 en ∼** : accordingly
consecuente *adj* : consistent — **consecuentemente** *adv*
consecutivo, -va *adj* : consecutive, successive — **consecutivamente** *adv*
conseguir {75} *vt* **1** : to get, to obtain **2** : to achieve, to attain **3** : to manage to ⟨consiguió acabar el trabajo : she managed to finish the job⟩
consejero, -ra *n* : adviser, counselor
consejo *nm* **1** : advice, counsel **2** : council ⟨consejo de guerra : court-martial⟩
consenso *nm* : consensus
consentido, -da *adj* : spoiled, pampered
consentimiento *nm* : consent, permission
consentir {76} *vt* **1** PERMITIR : to consent to, to allow **2** MIMAR : to pamper, to spoil — *vi* **∼ en** : to agree to, to approve of
conserje *nmf* : custodian, janitor, caretaker
conserva *nf* **1** : preserve(s), jam **2 conservas** *nfpl* : canned goods
conservación *nf, pl* **-ciones** : conservation, preservation
conservacionista *nmf* : conservationist
conservador¹, -dora *adj & n* : conservative
conservador² *nm* : preservative
conservadurismo *nf* : conservatism
conservante *nm* : preservative
conservar *vt* **1** : to preserve **2** GUARDAR : to keep, to conserve
conservatorio *nm* : conservatory
considerable *adj* : considerable — **considerablemente** *adv*
consideración *nf, pl* **-ciones** **1** : consideration **2** : respect **3 de ∼** : considerable, important
considerado, -da *adj* **1** : considerate, thoughtful **2** : respected
considerar *vt* **1** : to consider, to think over **2** : to judge, to deem **3** : to treat with respect
consigna *nf* **1** ESLOGAN : slogan **2** : assignment, orders *pl* **3** : checkroom
consignación *nf, pl* **-ciones** **1** : consignment **2** ASIGNACIÓN : allocation
consignar *vt* **1** : to consign **2** : to record, to write down **3** : to assign, to allocate

consigo *pron* : with her, with him, with you, with oneself ⟨se llevó las llaves consigo : she took the keys with her⟩

consiguiente *adj* **1** : resulting, consequent **2 por ～** : consequently, as a result

consistencia *nf* : consistency

consistente *adj* **1** : firm, strong, sound **2** : consistent — **consistentemente** *adv*

consistir *vi* **1 ～ en** : to consist of **2 ～ en** : to lie in, to consist in

consola *nf* : console

consolación *nf, pl* **-ciones** : consolation ⟨premio de consolación : consolation prize⟩

consolar {19} *vt* CONFORTAR : to console, to comfort

consolidar *vt* : to consolidate — **consolidación** *nf*

consomé *nm* CALDO : consommé, clear soup

consonancia *nf* **1** : consonance, harmony **2 en consonancia con** : in accordance with

consonante[1] *adj* : consonant, harmonious

consonante[2] *nf* : consonant

consorcio *nm* : consortium

consorte *nmf* : consort, spouse

conspicuo, -cua *adj* : eminent, famous

conspiración *nf, pl* **-ciones** COMPLOT, CONFABULACIÓN : conspiracy, plot

conspirador, -dora *n* : conspirator

conspirar *vi* CONJURAR : to conspire, to plot

constancia *nf* **1** PRUEBA : proof, certainty **2** : record, evidence ⟨que quede constancia : for the record⟩ **3** : perseverance, constancy

constante[1] *adj* : constant — **constantemente** *adv*

constante[2] *nf* : constant

constar *vi* **1** : to be evident, to be on record ⟨que conste : believe me, have no doubt⟩ **2 ～ de** : to consist of

constatación *nf, pl* **-ciones** : confirmation, proof

constatar *vt* **1** : to verify **2** : to state

constelación *nf, pl* **-ciones** : constellation

consternación *nf, pl* **-ciones** : consternation, dismay

consternar *vt* : to dismay, to appall

constipación *nf, pl* **-ciones** : constipation

constipado[1], **-da** *adj* **estar constipado** : to have a cold

constipado[2] *nm* RESFRIADO : cold

constiparse *vr* : to catch a cold

constitución *nf, pl* **-ciones** : constitution — **constitucional** *adj* — **constitucionalmente** *adv*

constitucionalidad *nf* : constitutionality

constituir {41} *vt* **1** FORMAR : to constitute, to make up, to form **2** FUNDAR : to establish, to set up — **constituirse**

vr **～ en** : to set oneself up as, to become

constitutivo, -va *adj* : constituent, component

constituyente *adj & nmf* : constituent

constreñir {67} *vt* **1** FORZAR, OBLIGAR : to constrain, to oblige **2** LIMITAR : to restrict, to limit

construcción *nf, pl* **-ciones** : construction, building

constructivo, -va *adj* : constructive — **constructivamente** *adv*

constructor, -tora *n* : builder

constructora *nf* : construction company

construir {41} *vt* : to build, to construct

consuelo *nm* : consolation, comfort

consuetudinario, -ria *adj* **1** : customary, habitual **2 derecho consuetudinario** : common law

cónsul *nmf* : consul — **consular** *adj*

consulado *nm* : consulate

consulta *nf* **1** : consultation **2** : inquiry

consultar *vt* : to consult

consultor[1], **-tora** *adj* : consulting ⟨firma consultora : consulting firm⟩

consultor[2], **-tora** *n* : consultant

consultorio *nm* : office (of a doctor or dentist)

consumación *nf, pl* **-ciones** : consummation

consumado, -da *adj* : consummate, perfect

consumar *vt* **1** : to consummate, to complete **2** : to commit, to carry out

consumible *adj* : consumable

consumición *nf, pl* **-ciones** **1** : consumption **2** : drink (in a restaurant)

consumido, -da *adj* : thin, emaciated

consumidor, -dora *n* : consumer

consumir *vt* : to consume — **consumirse** *vr* : to waste away

consumo *nm* : consumption

contabilidad *nf* **1** : accounting, bookkeeping **2** : accountancy

contabilizar {21} *vt* : to enter, to record (in accounting)

contable[1] *adj* : countable

contable[2] *nmf Spain* : accountant, bookkeeper

contactar *vt* : to contact — *vi* **～ con** : to get in touch with, to contact

contacto *nm* : contact

contado[1], **-da** *adj* **1** : counted ⟨tenía los días contados : his days were numbered⟩ **2** : rare, scarce ⟨en contadas ocasiones : on rare occasions⟩

contado[2] *nm* **al contado** : cash ⟨pagar al contado : to pay in cash⟩

contador[1], **-dora** *n* : accountant

contador[2] *nm* : meter ⟨contador de agua : water meter⟩

contaduría *nf* **1** : accounting office **2** CONTABILIDAD : accountancy

contagiar *vt* **1** : to infect **2** : to transmit (a disease) — **contagiarse** *vr* **1** : to be contagious **2** : to become infected

contagio *nm* : contagion, infection

contagioso, -sa *adj* : contagious, catching

contaminación *nf, pl* **-ciones** : contamination, pollution

contaminante *nm* : pollutant, contaminant

contaminar *vt* : to contaminate, to pollute

contar {19} *vt* **1** : to count **2** : to tell **3** : to include — *vi* **1** : to count (up) **2** : to matter, to be of concern ⟨eso no cuenta : that doesn't matter⟩ **3** ~ **con** : to rely on, to count on — **contarse** *vr* ~ **entre** : to be numbered among

contemplación *nf, pl* **-ciones** : contemplation — **contemplativo, -va** *adj*

contemplar *vt* **1** : to contemplate, to ponder **2** : to gaze at, to look at

contemporáneo, -nea *adj & n* : contemporary

contención *nf, pl* **-ciones** : containment, holding

contencioso, -sa *adj* : contentious

contender {56} *vi* **1** : to contend, to compete **2** : to fight

contendiente *nmf* : contender

contenedor *nm* **1** : container, receptacle **2** : Dumpster™

contener {80} *vt* **1** : to contain, to hold **2** ATAJAR : to restrain, to hold back — **contenerse** *vr* : to restrain oneself

contenido¹, -da *adj* : restrained, reserved

contenido² *nm* : contents *pl*, content

contentar *vt* : to please, to make happy — **contentarse** *vr* : to be satisfied, to be pleased

contento¹, -ta *adj* : contented, glad, happy

contento² *nm* : joy, happiness

contestación *nf, pl* **-ciones 1** : answer, reply **2** : protest

contestar *vt* RESPONDER : to answer — *vi* **1** RESPONDER : to answer, to reply **2** REPLICAR : to answer back

contexto *nm* : context

contienda *nf* **1** : dispute, conflict **2** : contest, competition

contigo *pron* : with you ⟨voy contigo : I'm going with you⟩

contiguo, -gua *adj* COLINDANTE : contiguous, adjacent

continencia *nf* : continence

continente *nm* : continent — **continental** *adj*

contingencia *nf* : contingency, eventuality

contingente *adj & nm* : contingent

continuación *nf, pl* **-ciones 1** : continuation **2 a** ~ : next ⟨lo demás sigue a continuación : the rest follows⟩ **3 a continuación de** : after, following

continuar {3} *v* : to continue

continuidad *nf* : continuity

continuo, -nua *adj* : continuous, steady, constant — **continuamente** *adv*

contonearse *vr* : to sway one's hips

contoneo *nm* : swaying, wiggling (of the hips)

contorno *nm* **1** : outline **2 contornos** *nmpl* : outskirts

contorsión *nf, pl* **-siones** : contortion

contra¹ *nf* **1** *fam* : difficulty, snag **2 llevar la contra a** : to oppose, to contradict

contra² *nm* : con ⟨los pros y los contras : the pros and cons⟩

contra³ *prep* : against

contraalmirante *nm* : rear admiral

contraatacar {72} *v* : to counterattack — **contraataque** *nm*

contrabajo *nm* : double bass

contrabalancear *vt* : to counterbalance — **contrabalanza** *nf*

contrabandear *v* : to smuggle

contrabandista *nmf* : smuggler, black marketeer

contrabando *nm* **1** : smuggling **2** : contraband

contracción *nf, pl* **-ciones** : contraction

contracepción *nf, pl* **-ciones** : contraception

contraceptivo *nm* ANTICONCEPTIVO : contraceptive

contrachapado *nm* : plywood

contracorriente *nf* **1** : crosscurrent **2 ir a contracorriente** : to go against the tide

contractual *adj* : contractual

contradecir {11} *vt* DESMENTIR : to contradict — **contradecirse** *vr* DESDECIRSE : to contradict oneself

contradicción *nf, pl* **-ciones** : contradiction

contradictorio, -ria *adj* : contradictory

contraer {81} *vt* **1** : to contract (a disease) **2** : to establish by contract ⟨contraer matrimonio : to get married⟩ **3** : to tighten, to contract — **contraerse** *vr* : to contract, to tighten up

contrafuerte *nm* : buttress

contragolpe *nm* **1** : counterblow **2** : backlash

contrahecho, -cha *adj* : deformed, hunchbacked

contraindicado, -da *adj* : contraindicated — **contraindicación** *nf*

contralor, -lora *n* : comptroller

contralto *nmf* : contralto

contramaestre *nm* **1** : boatswain **2** : foreman

contramandar *vt* : to countermand

contramano *nm* **a** ~ : the wrong way (on a street)

contramedida *nf* : countermeasure

contraorden *nf* : countermand

contraparte *nf* **1** : counterpart **2 en** ~ : on the other hand

contrapartida *nf* : compensation

contrapelo *nm* **a** ~ : in the wrong direction, against the grain

contrapeso *nm* : counterbalance

contraponer {60} *vt* **1** : to counter, to oppose **2** : to contrast, to compare

contraposición *nf, pl* **-ciones** : comparison

contraproducente *adj* : counterproductive

contrapunto *nm* : counterpoint
contrariar {85} *vt* **1** : to contradict, to oppose **2** : to vex, to annoy
contrariedad *nf* **1** : setback, obstacle **2** : vexation, annoyance
contrario, -ria *adj* **1** : contrary, opposite ⟨al contrario : on the contrary⟩ **2** : conflicting, opposed
contrarrestar *vt* : to counteract
contrarrevolución *nf, pl* **-ciones** : counterrevolution — **contrarrevolucionario, -ria** *adj & n*
contrasentido *nm* : contradiction
contraseña *nf* : password
contrastante *adj* : contrasting
contrastar *vt* **1** : to resist **2** : to check, to confirm — *vi* : to contrast
contraste *nm* : contrast
contratar *vt* **1** : to contract for **2** : to hire, to engage
contratiempo *nm* **1** PERCANCE : mishap, accident **2** DIFICULTAD : setback, difficulty
contratista *nmf* : contractor
contrato *nm* : contract
contravenir {87} *vt* : to contravene, to infringe
contraventana *nf* : shutter
contribución *nf, pl* **-ciones** : contribution
contribuidor, -dora *n* : contributor
contribuir {41} *vt* **1** APORTAR : to contribute **2** : to pay (in taxes) — *vi* **1** : contribute, to help out **2** : to pay taxes
contribuyente[1] *adj* : contributing
contribuyente[2] *nmf* : taxpayer
contrición *nf, pl* **-ciones** : contrition
contrincante *nmf* : rival, opponent
contrito, -ta *adj* : contrite, repentant
control *nm* **1** : control **2** : inspection, check **3** : checkpoint, roadblock
controlador, -dora *n* : controller ⟨controlador aéreo : air traffic controller⟩
controlar *vt* **1** : to control **2** : to monitor, to check
controversia *nf* : controversy
controversial → **controvertido**
controvertido, -da *adj* : controversial
controvertir {76} *vt* : to dispute, to argue about — *vi* : to argue, to debate
contubernio *nm* : conspiracy
contumacia *nf* : obstinacy, stubbornness
contumaz *adj, pl* **-maces** : obstinate, stubbornly disobedient
contundencia *nf* **1** : forcefulness, weight **2** : severity
contundente *adj* **1** : blunt ⟨un objeto contundente : a blunt instrument⟩ **2** : forceful, convincing — **contundentemente** *adv*
contusión *nf, pl* **-siones** : bruise, contusion
contuvo, etc. → **contener**
convalecencia *nf* : convalescence
convalecer {53} *vi* : to convalesce, to recover

convaleciente *adj & nmf* : convalescent
convección *nf, pl* **-ciones** : convection
convencer {86} *vt* : to convince, to persuade — **convencerse** *vr*
convencimiento *nm* : belief, conviction
convención *nf, pl* **-ciones** **1** : convention, conference **2** : pact, agreement **3** : convention, custom
convencional *adj* : conventional — **convencionalmente** *adv*
convencionalismo *nm* : conventionality
conveniencia *nf* **1** : convenience **2** : fitness, suitability, advisability
conveniente *adj* **1** : convenient **2** : suitable, advisable
convenio *nm* PACTO : agreement, pact
convenir {87} *vi* **1** : to be suitable, to be advisable **2** : to agree
convento *nm* **1** : convent **2** : monastery
convergencia *nf* : convergence
convergente *adj* : convergent, converging
converger {15} *vi* **1** : to converge **2** ~ **en** : to concur on
conversación *nf, pl* **-ciones** : conversation
conversador, -dora *n* : conversationalist, talker
conversar *vi* : to converse, to talk
conversión *nf, pl* **-siones** : conversion
converso, -sa *n* : convert
convertible *adj & nm* : convertible
convertidor *nm* : converter
convertir {76} *vt* **1** : to convert **2** : to transform, to change **3** : to exchange (money) — **convertirse** *vr* ~ **en** : to turn into
convexo, -xa *adj* : convex
convicción *nf, pl* **-ciones** : conviction
convicto[1]**, -ta** *adj* : convicted
convicto[2]**, -ta** *n* : convict, prisoner
convidado, -da *n* : guest
convidar *vt* **1** INVITAR : to invite **2** : to offer
convincente *adj* : convincing — **convincentemente** *adv*
convivencia *nf* **1** : coexistence **2** : cohabitation
convivir *vi* **1** : to coexist **2** : to live together
convocación *nf, pl* **-ciones** : convocation
convocar {72} *vt* : to convoke, to call together
convocatoria *nf* : summons, call
convoy *nm* : convoy
convulsión *nf, pl* **-siones** **1** : convulsion **2** : agitation, upheaval
convulsionar *vt* : to shake, to convulse — **convulsionarse** *vr*
convulsivo, -va *adj* : convulsive
conyugal *adj* : conjugal
cónyuge *nmf* : spouse, partner
coñac *nm* : cognac, brandy
cooperación *nf, pl* **-ciones** : cooperation
cooperador, -dora *adj* : cooperative

cooperar *vi* : to cooperate
cooperativa *nf* : cooperative, co-op
cooperativo, -va *adj* : cooperative
cooptar *vt* : to co-opt
coordenada *nf* : coordinate
coordinación *nf, pl* **-ciones** : coordination
coordinador, -dora *n* : coordinator
coordinar *vt* COMPAGINAR : to coordinate, to combine
copa *nf* **1** : wineglass, goblet **2** : drink ⟨irse de copas : to go out drinking⟩ **3** : cup, trophy
copar *vt* **1** : to take ⟨ya está copado el puesto : the job is already taken⟩ **2** : to fill, to crowd
copartícipe *nmf* : joint partner
copete *nm* **1** : tuft (of hair) **2 estar hasta el copete** : to be completely fed up
copia *nf* **1** : copy **2** : imitation, replica
copiadora *nf* : photocopier
copiar *vt* : to copy
copiloto *nmf* : copilot
copioso, -sa *adj* : copious, abundant
copla *nf* **1** : popular song or ballad **2** : couplet, stanza
copo *nm* **1** : snowflake **2 copos de avena** : rolled oats **3 copos de maíz** : cornflakes
copra *nf* : copra
cópula *nf* : copulation
copular *vi* : to copulate
coque *nm* : coke (fuel)
coqueta *nf* : dressing table
coquetear *vi* : to flirt
coqueteo *nm* : flirting, coquetry
coqueto[1], -ta *adj* : flirtatious, coquettish
coqueto[2], -ta *n* : flirt
coraje *nm* **1** VALOR : valor, courage **2** IRA : anger ⟨darle coraje a alguien : to make someone angry⟩
corajudo, -da *adj* : brave
coral[1] *nm* **1** : coral **2** : chorale
coral[2] *nf* : choir
Corán *nm* **el Corán** : the Koran
coraza *nf* **1** : armor, armor plating **2** : shell (of an animal)
corazón *nm, pl* **-zones 1** : heart ⟨de todo corazón : wholeheartedly⟩ ⟨de buen corazón : kindhearted⟩ **2** : core **3** : darling, sweetheart
corazonada *nf* : hunch, impulse
corbata *nf* : tie, necktie
corcel *nm* : steed, charger
corchete *nm* **1** : hook and eye, clasp **2** : square bracket
corcho *nm* : cork
corcholata *nf Mex* : cap, bottle top
corcovear *vi* : to buck
cordel *nm* : cord, string
cordero *nm* : lamb
cordial[1] *adj* : cordial, affable — **cordialmente** *adv*
cordial[2] *nm* : cordial (liqueur)
cordialidad *nf* : cordiality, warmth
cordillera *nf* : mountain range
córdoba *nf* : Nicaraguan unit of currency

cordón *nm, pl* **cordones 1** : cord ⟨cordón umbilical : umbilical cord⟩ **2** : cordon
cordura *nf* **1** : sanity **2** : prudence, good judgment
coreano[1], -na *adj & n* : Korean
coreano[2] *nm* : Korean (language)
corear *vt* : to chant, to chorus
coreografía *nf* : choreography
coreografiar {85} *vt* : to choreograph
coreográfico, -ca *adj* : choreographic
coreógrafo, -fa *n* : choreographer
corista *nmf* **1** : chorister **2** : chorus girl *f*
cormorán *nm, pl* **-ranes** : cormorant
cornada *nf* : goring, butt (with the horns)
córnea *nf* : cornea
cornear *vt* : to gore
cornejo *nm* : dogwood (tree)
corneta *nf* : bugle, horn, cornet
cornisa *nf* : cornice
cornudo, -da *adj* : horned
coro *nm* **1** : choir **2** : chorus
corola *nf* : corolla
corolario *nm* : corollary
corona *nf* **1** : crown **2** : wreath, garland **3** : corona (in astronomy)
coronación *nf, pl* **-ciones** : coronation
coronar *vt* **1** : to crown **2** : to reach the top of, to culminate
coronario, -ria *adj* : coronary
coronel, -nela *n* : colonel
coronilla *nf* **1** : crown (of the head) **2 estar hasta la coronilla** : to be completely fed up
corpiño *nm* **1** : bodice **2 Arg** : brassiere, bra
corporación *nf, pl* **-ciones** : corporation
corporal *adj* : corporal, bodily
corporativo, -va *adj* : corporate
corpóreo, -rea *adj* : corporeal, physical
corpulencia *nf* : corpulence, stoutness, sturdiness
corpulento, -ta *adj* ROBUSTO : robust, stout, sturdy
corpúsculo *nm* : corpuscle
corral *nm* **1** : farmyard **2** : corral, pen, stockyard **3** *or* **corralito** : playpen
correa *nf* : strap, belt
correcaminos *nms & pl* : roadrunner
corrección *nf, pl* **-ciones 1** : correction **2** : correctness, propriety **3** : rebuke, reprimand **4 corrección de pruebas** : proofreading
correccional *nm* REFORMATORIO : reformatory
correctivo, -va *adj* : corrective ⟨lentes correctivos : corrective lenses⟩
correcto, -ta *adj* **1** : correct, right **2** : courteous, polite — **correctamente** *adv*
corrector, -tora *n* : proofreader
corredizo, -za *adj* : sliding ⟨puerta corrediza : sliding door⟩
corredor[1], -dora *n* **1** : runner, racer **2** : agent, broker ⟨corredor de bolsa : stockbroker⟩
corredor[2] *nm* PASILLO : corridor, hallway

correduría *nf* → **corretaje**
corregir {28} *vt* **1** ENMENDAR : to correct, to emend **2** : to reprimand **3 corregir pruebas** : to proofread — **corregirse** *vr* : to reform, to mend one's ways
correlación *nf, pl* **-ciones** : correlation
correo *nm* **1** : mail ⟨correo aéreo : airmail⟩ **2** : post office
correoso, -sa *adj* : leathery, rough
correr *vi* **1** : to run, to race **2** : to rush **3** : to flow — *vt* **1** : to travel over, to cover **2** : to move, to slide, to roll, to draw (curtains) **3 correr un riesgo** : to run a risk — **correrse** *vr* **1** : to move along **2** : to run, to spill over
correspondencia *nf* **1** : correspondence, mail **2** : equivalence **3** : connection, interchange
corresponder *vi* **1** : to correspond **2** : to pertain, to belong **3** : to be appropriate, to fit **4** : to reciprocate — **corresponderse** *vr* : to write to each other
correspondiente *adj* : corresponding, respective
corresponsal *nmf* : correspondent
corretaje *nm* : brokerage
corretear *vi* **1** VAGAR : to loiter, to wander about **2** : to run around, to scamper about — *vt* : to pursue, to chase
corrida *nf* **1** : run, dash **2** : bullfight
corrido[1], -da *adj* **1** : straight, continuous **2** : worldly, experienced
corrido[2] *nm* : Mexican narrative folk song
corriente[1] *adj* **1** : common, everyday **2** : current, present **3** *Mex* : cheap, trashy **4 perro corriente** *Mex* : mutt
corriente[2] *nf* **1** : current ⟨corriente alterna : alternating current⟩ ⟨direct current : corriente continua⟩ **2** : draft **3** TENDENCIA : tendency, trend
corrillo *nm* : small group, clique
corro *nm* : ring, circle (of people)
corroboración *nf, pl* **-ciones** : corroboration
corroborar *vt* : to corroborate
corroer {69} *vt* **1** : to corrode **2** : to erode, to wear away
corromper *vt* **1** : to corrupt **2** : to rot — **corromperse** *vr*
corrompido, -da *adj* CORRUPTO : corrupt, rotten
corrosión *nf, pl* **-siones** : corrosion
corrosivo, -va *adj* : corrosive
corrugar {52} *vt* : to corrugate — **corrugación** *nf*
corrupción *nf, pl* **-ciones** **1** : decay **2** : corruption
corruptela *nf* : corruption, abuse of power
corrupto, -ta *adj* CORROMPIDO : corrupt
corsario *nm* : privateer
corsé *nm* : corset
cortada *nf* : cut, gash
cortador, -dora *n* : cutter
cortadora *nf* : cutter, slicer
cortadura *nf* : cut, slash
cortafuegos *nms & pl* **1** : firebreak **2** : firewall (program)

cortante *adj* : cutting, sharp
cortar *vt* **1** : to cut, to slice, to trim **2** : to cut out, to omit **3** : to cut off, to interrupt **4** : to block, to close off **5** : to curdle (milk) — *vi* **1** : to cut **2** : to break up **3** : to hang up (the telephone) — **cortarse** *vr* **1** : to cut oneself ⟨cortarse el pelo : to cut one's hair⟩ **2** : to be cut off **3** : to sour (of milk)
cortauñas *nms & pl* : nail clippers
corte[1] *nm* **1** : cut, cutting ⟨corte de pelo : haircut⟩ **2** : style, fit
corte[2] *nf* **1** : court ⟨corte suprema : supreme court⟩ **2 hacer la corte a** : to court, to woo
cortejar *vt* GALANTEAR : to court, to woo
cortejo *nm* **1** GALANTEO : courtship **2** : retinue, entourage
cortés *adj* : courteous, polite — **cortésmente** *adv*
cortesano[1], -na *adj* : courtly
cortesano[2], -na *n* : courtier
cortesía *nf* **1** : courtesy, politeness **2 de ~** : complimentary, free
corteza *nf* **1** : bark **2** : crust **3** : peel, rind **4** : cortex ⟨corteza cerebral : cerebral cortex⟩
cortijo *nm* : farmhouse
cortina *nf* : curtain
cortisona *nf* : cortisone
corto, -ta *adj* **1** : short (in length or duration) **2** : scarce **3** : timid, shy **4 corto de vista** : nearsighted
cortocircuito *nm* : short circuit
corvejón *nm, pl* **-jones** JARRETE : hock
corvo, -va *adj* : curved, bent
cosa *nf* **1** : thing, object **2** : matter, affair **3 otra cosa** : anything else, something else
cosecha *nf* : harvest, crop
cosechador, -dora *n* : harvester, reaper
cosechadora *nf* : harvester (machine)
cosechar *vt* **1** : to harvest, to reap **2** : to win, to earn, to garner — *vi* : to harvest
coser *vt* **1** : to sew **2** : to stitch up — *vi* : to sew
cosmético[1], -ca *adj* : cosmetic
cosmético[2] *nm* : cosmetic
cósmico, -ca *adj* : cosmic
cosmonauta *nmf* : cosmonaut
cosmopolita *adj & nmf* : cosmopolitan
cosmos *nm* : cosmos
cosquillas *nfpl* **1** : tickling **2 hacer cosquillas** : to tickle
cosquilleo *nm* : tickling sensation, tingle
cosquilloso, -sa *adj* : ticklish
costa *nf* **1** : coast, shore **2** : cost ⟨a toda costa : at all costs⟩
costado *nm* **1** : side **2 al costado** : alongside
costar {19} *v* : to cost ⟨¿cuánto cuesta? : how much does it cost?⟩
costarricense *adj & nmf* : Costa Rican
costarriqueño, -ña → **costarricense**
coste → **costo**
costear *vt* : to pay for, to finance

costero, -ra *adj* : coastal, coast
costilla *nf* **1** : rib **2** : chop, cutlet **3** *fam* : better half, wife
costo *nm* **1** : cost, price **2 costo de vida** : cost of living
costoso, -sa *adj* : costly, expensive
costra *nf* **1** : crust **2** POSTILLA : scab
costumbre *nf* **1** : custom **2** HÁBITO : habit
costura *nf* **1** : seam **2** : sewing, dressmaking **3 alta costura** : haute couture
costurera *nf* : seamstress *f*
cotejar *vt* : to compare, to collate
cotejo *nm* : comparison, collation
cotidiano, -na *adj* : daily, everyday ⟨la vida cotidiana : daily life⟩
cotización *nf, pl* **-ciones 1** : market price **2** : quote, estimate
cotizado, -da *adj* : in demand, sought after
cotizar {21} *vt* : to quote, to value — **cotizarse** *vr* : to be worth
coto *nm* **1** : enclosure, reserve **2 poner coto a** : to put a stop to
cotorra *nf* **1** : small parrot **2** *fam* : chatterbox, windbag
cotorrear *vi fam* : to chatter, to gab, to blab
cotorreo *nm fam* : chatter, prattle
coyote *nm* **1** : coyote **2** *Mex fam* : smuggler (of illegal immigrants)
coyuntura *nf* **1** ARTICULACIÓN : joint **2** : occasion, moment
coz *nf, pl* **coces** : kick (of an animal)
crac *nm, pl* **cracs** : crash (of the stock market)
cozamos, etc. → **cocer**
craneal *adj* : cranial
cráneo *nf* : cranium, skull — **craneano, -na** *adj*
cráter *nm* : crater
crayón *nm, pl* **-yones** : crayon
creación *nf, pl* **-ciones** : creation
creador[1], -dora *adj* : creative, creating
creador[2], -dora *n* : creator
crear *vt* **1** : to create, to cause **2** : to originate
creatividad *nf* : creativity
creativo, -va *adj* : creative
crecer {53} *vi* **1** : to grow **2** : to increase
crecida *nf* : flooding, floodwater
crecido, -da *adj* **1** : grown, grown-up **2** : large (of numbers)
creciente *adj* **1** : growing, increasing **2 luna creciente** : waxing moon
crecientemente *adv* : increasingly
crecimiento *nm* **1** : growth **2** : increase
credencial *adj* **cartas credenciales** : credentials
credenciales *nfpl* : documents, documentation, credentials
credibilidad *nf* : credibility
crédito *nm* : credit
credo *nm* : creed, credo
credulidad *nf* : credulity
crédulo, -la *adj* : credulous, gullible
creencia *nf* : belief
creer {20} *v* **1** : to believe **2** : to suppose, to think ⟨creo que sí : I think so⟩

— creerse *vr* **1** : to believe, to think **2** : to regard oneself as ⟨se cree guapísimo : he thinks he's so handsome⟩
creíble *adj* : believable, credible
creído, -da *adj* **1** *fam* : conceited **2** : confident, sure
crema *nf* **1** : cream **2 la crema y nata** : the pick of the crop
cremación *nf, pl* **-ciones** : cremation
cremallera *nf* : zipper
cremar *vt* : to cremate
cremoso, -sa *adj* : creamy
crepa *nf Mex* : crepe (pancake)
crepe *or* **crep** *nmf* : crepe (pancake)
crepé *nm* **1** → **crespón 2 papel crepé** : crepe paper
crepitar *vi* : to crackle
crepúsculo *nm* : twilight
crescendo *nm* : crescendo
crespo, -pa *adj* : curly, frizzy
crespón *nm, pl* **crespones** : crepe (fabric)
cresta *nf* **1** : crest **2** : comb (of a rooster)
creta *nf* : chalk (mineral)
cretino, -na *n* : cretin
creyente *nmf* : believer
creyó, etc. → **creer**
crezca, etc. → **crecer**
cría *nf* **1** : breeding, rearing **2** : young **3** : litter
criadero *nm* : hatchery
criado[1], -da *adj* **1** : raised, brought up **2 bien criado** : well-bred
criado[2], -da *n* : servant, maid *f*
criador, -dora *n* : breeder
crianza *nf* : upbringing, rearing
criar {85} *vt* **1** : to breed **2** : to bring up, to raise
criatura *nf* **1** : baby, child **2** : creature
criba *nf* : sieve, screen
cribar *vt* : to sift
cric *nm, pl* **crics** : jack
crimen *nm, pl* **crímenes** : crime
criminal *adj & nmf* : criminal
crin *nf* **1** : mane **2** : horsehair
criollo[1], -lla *adj* **1** : Creole **2** : native, national ⟨comida criolla : native cuisine⟩
criollo[2], -lla *n* : Creole
criollo[3] *nm* : Creole (language)
cripta *nf* : crypt
críptico, -ca *adj* **1** : cryptic, coded **2** : enigmatic, cryptic
criptón *nm* : krypton
críquet *nm* : cricket (game)
crisálida *nf* : chrysalis, pupa
crisantemo *nm* : chrysanthemum
crisis *nf* **1** : crisis **2 crisis nerviosa** : nervous breakdown
crisma *nf fam* : head ⟨romperle la crisma a alguien : to knock someone's block off⟩
crisol *nm* **1** : crucible **2** : melting pot
crispar *vt* **1** : to cause to contract **2** : to irritate, to set on edge ⟨eso me crispa : that gets on my nerves⟩ — **crisparse** *vr* : to tense up

cristal *nm* **1** VIDRIO : glass, piece of glass **2** : crystal
cristalería *nf* **1** : glassware shop ⟨como chivo en cristalería : like a bull in a china shop⟩ **2** : glassware, crystal
cristalino[1], -na *adj* : crystalline, clear
cristalino[2] *nm* : lens (of the eye)
cristalizar {21} *vi* : to crystallize — **cristalización** *nf*
cristiandad *nf* : Christendom
cristianismo *nm* : Christianity
cristiano, -na *adj & n* : Christian
Cristo *nm* : Christ
criterio *nm* **1** : criterion **2** : judgment, sense
crítica *nf* **1** : criticism **2** : review, critique
criticar {72} *vt* : to criticize
crítico[1], -ca *adj* : critical — **críticamente** *adv*
crítico[2], -ca *n* : critic
criticón[1], -cona *adj, mpl* **-cones** *fam* : hypercritical, captious
criticón[2], -cona *n, mpl* **-cones** *fam* : faultfinder, critic
croar *vi* : to croak
croata *adj & nmf* : Croatian
crocante *adj* : crunchy
croché *or* **crochet** *nm* : crochet
cromático, -ca *adj* : chromatic
cromo *nm* **1** : chromium, chrome **2** : picture card, sports card
cromosoma *nm* : chromosome
crónica *nf* **1** : news report **2** : chronicle, history
crónico, -ca *adj* : chronic
cronista *nmf* **1** : reporter, newscaster **2** HISTORIADOR : chronicler, historian
cronología *nf* : chronology
cronológico, -ca *adj* : chronological — **cronológicamente** *adv*
cronometrador, -dora *n* : timekeeper
cronometrar *vt* : to time, to clock
cronómetro *nm* : chronometer
croquet *nm* : croquet
croqueta *nf* : croquette
croquis *nm* : rough sketch
cruce[1], etc. → **cruzar**
cruce[2] *nm* **1** : crossing, cross **2** : crossroads, intersection ⟨cruce peatonal : crosswalk⟩
crucero *nm* **1** : cruise **2** : cruiser, warship **3** *Mex* : intersection
crucial *adj* : crucial — **crucialmente** *adv*
crucificar {72} *vt* : to crucify
crucifijo *nm* : crucifix
crucifixión *nf, pl* **-fixiones** : crucifixion
crucigrama *nm* : crossword puzzle
crudo[1], -da *adj* **1** : raw **2** : crude, harsh
crudo[2] *nm* : crude oil
cruel *adj* : cruel — **cruelmente** *adv*
crueldad *nf* : cruelty
cruento, -ta *adj* : bloody
crujido *nm* **1** : rustling **2** : creaking **3** : crackling (of a fire) **4** : crunching
crujiente *adj* : crunchy, crisp
crujir *vi* **1** : to rustle **2** : to creak, to crack **3** : to crunch

crup *nm* : croup
crustáceo *nm* : crustacean
crutón *nm, pl* **crutones** : crouton
cruz *nf, pl* **cruces** : cross
cruza *nf* : cross (hybrid)
cruzada *nf* : crusade
cruzado[1], -da *adj* : crossed ⟨espadas cruzadas : crossed swords⟩
cruzado[2] *nm* **1** : crusader **2** : Brazilian unit of currency
cruzar {21} *vt* **1** : to cross **2** : to exchange (words, greetings) **3** : to cross, to interbreed — **cruzarse** *vr* **1** : to intersect **2** : to meet, to pass each other
cuaderno *nm* LIBRETA : notebook
cuadra *nf* **1** : city block **2** : stable
cuadrado[1], -da *adj* : square
cuadrado[2] *nm* : square ⟨elevar al cuadrado : to square (a number)⟩
cuadragésimo[1] *adj* : fortieth, forty-
cuadragésimo[2], -ma *n* : fortieth, forty- (in a series)
cuadrante *nm* **1** : quadrant **2** : dial
cuadrar *vi* : to conform, to agree — *vt* : to square — **cuadrarse** *vr* : to stand at attention
cuadriculado *nm* : grid (on a map, etc.)
cuadrilátero *nm* **1** : quadrilateral **2** : ring (in sports)
cuadrilla *nf* : gang, team, group
cuadro *nm* **1** : square ⟨una blusa a cuadros : a checkered blouse⟩ **2** : painting, picture **3** : baseball diamond, infield **4** : panel, board, cadre
cuadrúpedo *nm* : quadruped
cuadruple *adj* : quadruple
cuadruplicar {72} *vt* : to quadruple — **cuadruplicarse** *vr*
cuajada *nf* : curd
cuajar *vi* **1** : to curdle **2** COAGULAR : to clot, to coagulate **3** : to set, to jell **4** : to be accepted ⟨su idea no cuajó : his idea didn't catch on⟩ — *vt* **1** : to curdle **2** ∼ **de** : to fill with
cual[1] *prep* : like, as
cual[2] *pron* **1 el cual, la cual, los cuales, las cuales** : who, whom, which ⟨la razón por la cual lo dije : the reason I said it⟩ **2 lo cual** : which ⟨se rió, lo cual me dio rabia : he laughed, which made me mad⟩ **3 cada cual** : everyone, everybody
cuál[1] *adj* : which, what ⟨¿cuáles libros? : which books?⟩
cuál[2] *pron* **1** (*in questions*) : which (one), what (one) ⟨¿cuál es el mejor? : which one is the best?⟩ ⟨¿cuál es tu apellido? : what is your last name?⟩ **2 cuál más, cuál menos** : some more, some less
cualidad *nf* : quality, trait
cualitativo, -va *adj* : qualitative — **cualitativamente** *adv*
cualquier *adj* → **cualquiera[1]**
cualquiera[1] (**cualquier** *before nouns*) *adj, pl* **cualesquiera 1** : any, whichever ⟨cualquier persona : any person⟩ **2** : everyday, ordinary ⟨un hombre cualquiera : an ordinary man⟩

cualquiera² *pron, pl* **cualesquiera** 1 : anyone, anybody, whoever 2 : whatever, whichever

cuán *adv* : how ⟨¡cuán risible fue todo eso! : how funny it all was!⟩

cuando¹ *conj* 1 : when ⟨cuando llegó : when he arrived⟩ 2 : since, if ⟨cuando lo dices : if you say so⟩ 3 **cuando más** : at the most 4 **de vez en cuando** : from time to time

cuando² *prep* : during, at the time of ⟨cuando la guerra : during the war⟩

cuándo *adv & conj* 1 : when ⟨¿cuándo llegará? : when will she arrive?⟩ ⟨no sabemos cuándo será : we don't know when it will be⟩ 2 **¿de cuándo acá?** : since when?, how come?

cuantía *nf* 1 : quantity, extent 2 : significance, import

cuántico, -ca *adj* : quantum ⟨teoría cuántica : quantum theory⟩

cuantioso, -sa *adj* 1 : abundant, considerable 2 : heavy, grave ⟨cuantiosos daños : heavy damage⟩

cuantitativo, -va *adj* : quantitative — **cuantitativamente** *adv*

cuanto¹ *adv* 1 : as much as ⟨come cuanto puedas : eat as much as you can⟩ 2 **cuanto antes** : as soon as possible 3 **en ~** : as soon as 4 **en cuanto a** : as for, as regards

cuanto², -ta *adj* : as many, whatever ⟨llévate cuantas flores quieras : take as many flowers as you wish⟩

cuanto³, -ta *pron* 1 : as much as, all that, everything ⟨tengo cuanto deseo : I have all that I want⟩ 2 **unos cuantos, unas cuantas** : a few

cuánto¹ *adv* : how much, how many ⟨¿a cuánto están las manzanas? : how much are the apples?⟩ ⟨no sé cuánto desean : I don't know how much they want⟩

cuánto², -ta *adj* : how much, how many ⟨¿cuántos niños tiene? : how many children do you have?⟩

cuánto³ *pron* : how much, how many ⟨¿cuántos quieren participar? : how many want to take part?⟩ ⟨¿cuánto cuesta? : how much does it cost?⟩

cuarenta *adj & nm* : forty

cuarentavo¹, -va *adj* : fortieth

cuarentavo² *nm* : fortieth (fraction)

cuarentena *nf* 1 : group of forty 2 : quarantine

Cuaresma *nf* : Lent

cuartear *vt* 1 : to quarter 2 : to divide up — **cuartearse** *vr* AGRIETARSE : to crack, to split

cuartel *nm* 1 : barracks, headquarters 2 : mercy ⟨una guerra sin cuartel : a merciless war⟩

cuartelazo *nm* : coup d'état

cuarteto *nm* : quartet

cuartilla *nf* : sheet (of paper)

cuarto¹, -ta *adj* : fourth

cuarto², -ta *n* : fourth (in a series)

cuarto³ *nm* 1 : quarter, fourth ⟨cuarto de galón : quart⟩ 2 HABITACIÓN : room

cuarzo *nm* : quartz

cuate, -ta *n Mex* 1 : twin 2 *fam* : buddy, pal

cuatrero, -ra *n* : rustler

cuatrillizo, -za *n* : quadruplet

cuatro *adj & nm* : four

cuatrocientos¹, -tas *adj* : four hundred

cuatrocientos² *nms & pl* : four hundred

cuba *nf* BARRIL : cask, barrel

cubano, -na *adj & n* : Cuban

cubertería *nf* : flatware, silverware

cubeta *nf* 1 : keg, cask 2 : bulb (of a thermometer) 3 *Mex* : bucket, pail

cúbico, -ca *adj* : cubic, cubed

cubículo *nm* : cubicle

cubierta *nf* 1 : covering 2 FORRO : cover, jacket (of a book) 3 : deck

cubierto¹ *pp* → **cubrir**

cubierto² *nm* 1 : cover, shelter ⟨bajo cubierto : under cover⟩ 2 : table setting 3 : utensil, piece of silverware

cubil *nm* : den, lair

cúbito *nm* : ulna

cubo *nm* 1 : cube 2 BALDE : pail, bucket, can ⟨cubo de basura : garbage can⟩ 3 : hub (of a wheel)

cubrecama *nm* COLCHA : bedspread

cubrir {2} *vt* : to cover — **cubrirse** *vr*

cucaracha *nf* : cockroach, roach

cuchara *nf* : spoon

cucharada *nf* : spoonful

cucharilla *or* **cucharita** *nf* : teaspoon

cucharón *nm, pl* **-rones** : ladle

cuchichear *vi* : to whisper

cuchicheo *nm* : whisper

cuchilla *nf* 1 : kitchen knife, cleaver 2 : blade ⟨cuchilla de afeitar : razor blade⟩ 3 : crest, ridge

cuchillada *nf* : stab, knife wound

cuchillo *nm* : knife

cuclillas *nfpl* **en ~** : squatting, crouching

cuco¹, -ca *adj fam* : pretty, cute

cuco² *nm* : cuckoo

cucurucho *nm* : ice-cream cone

cuece, cueza etc. → **cocer**

cuela, etc. → **colar**

cuelga, cuelgue etc. → **colgar**

cuello *nm* 1 : neck 2 : collar (of a shirt) 3 **cuello del útero** : cervix

cuenca *nf* 1 : river basin 2 : eye socket

cuenco *nm* : bowl, basin

cuenta¹, etc. → **contar**

cuenta² *nf* 1 : calculation, count 2 : account 3 : check, bill 4 **darse cuenta** : to realize 5 **tener en cuenta** : to bear in mind

cuentagotas *nfs & pl* 1 : dropper 2 **con ~** : little by little

cuentista *nmf* 1 : short story writer 2 *fam* : liar, fibber

cuento *nm* 1 : story, tale 2 **cuento de hadas** : fairy tale 3 **sin ~** : countless

cuerda *nf* 1 : cord, rope, string 2 **cuerdas vocales** : vocal cords 3 **darle cuerda a** : to wind up (a clock, a toy, etc.)

cuerdo, -da *adj* : sane, sensible
cuerno *nm* **1** : horn, antler **2** : cusp (of the moon) **3** : horn (musical instrument)
cuero *nm* **1** : leather, hide **2 cuero cabelludo** : scalp
cuerpo *nm* **1** : body **2** : corps
cuervo *nm* : crow, raven
cuesta¹, etc. → **costar**
cuesta² *nf* **1** : slope ⟨cuesta arriba : uphill⟩ **2 a cuestas** : on one's back
cuestión *nf, pl* **-tiones** ASUNTO, TEMA : matter, affair
cuestionable *adj* : questionable, dubious
cuestionar *vt* : to question
cuestionario *nm* **1** : questionnaire **2** : quiz
cueva *nf* : cave
cuidado *nm* **1** : care **2** : worry, concern **3 tener cuidado** : to be careful **4 ¡cuidado!** : watch out!, be careful!
cuidador, -dora *n* : caretaker
cuidadoso, -sa *adj* : careful, attentive — **cuidadosamente** *adv*
cuidar *vt* **1** : to take care of, to look after **2** : to pay attention to — *vi* **1** ∼ **de** : to look after **2 cuidar de que** : to make sure that — **cuidarse** *vr* : to take care of oneself
culata *nf* : butt (of a gun)
culatazo *nf* : kick, recoil
culebra *nf* SERPIENTE : snake
culi *nmf* : coolie
culinario, -ria *adj* : culinary
culminante *adj* **punto culminante** : peak, high point, climax
culminar *vi* : to culminate — **culminación** *nf*
culo *nm* **1** *fam* : backside, behind **2** : bottom (of a glass)
culpa *nf* **1** : fault, blame ⟨echarle la culpa a alguien : to blame someone⟩ **2** : sin
culpabilidad *nf* : guilt
culpable¹ *adj* : guilty
culpable² *nmf* : culprit, guilty party
culpar *vt* : to blame
cultivado, -da *adj* **1** : cultivated, farmed **2** : cultured
cultivador, -dora *n* : cultivator
cultivar *vt* **1** : to cultivate **2** : to foster
cultivo *nm* **1** : cultivation, farming **2** : crop
culto¹, -ta *adj* : cultured, educated
culto² *nm* **1** : worship **2** : cult
cultura *nf* : culture
cultural *adj* : cultural — **culturalmente** *adv*
cumbre *nf* CIMA : top, peak, summit
cumpleaños *nms & pl* : birthday
cumplido¹, -da *adj* **1** : complete, full **2** : courteous, correct
cumplido² *nm* : compliment, courtesy ⟨por cumplido : out of courtesy⟩ ⟨andarse con cumplidos : to stand on ceremony, to be formal⟩
cumplimentar *vt* **1** : to congratulate **2** : to carry out, to perform

cumplimiento *nm* **1** : completion, fulfillment **2** : performance
cumplir *vt* **1** : to accomplish, to carry out **2** : to comply with, to fulfill **3** : to attain, to reach ⟨su hermana cumple los 21 el viernes : her sister will be 21 on Friday⟩ — *vi* **1** : to expire, to fall due **2** : to fulfill one's obligations ⟨cumplir con el deber : to do one's duty⟩ ⟨cumplir con la palabra : to keep one's word⟩ — **cumplirse** *vr* **1** : to come true, to be fulfilled ⟨se cumplieron sus sueños : her dreams came true⟩ **2** : to run out, to expire
cúmulo *nm* **1** MONTÓN : heap, pile **2** : cumulus
cuna *nf* **1** : cradle **2** : birthplace ⟨Puerto Rico es la cuna de la música salsa : Puerto Rico is the birthplace of salsa music⟩
cundir *vi* **1** : to propagate, to spread ⟨cundió el pánico en el vecindario : panic spread throughout the neighborhood⟩ **2** : to progress, to make headway
cuneta *nf* : ditch (in a road), gutter
cuña *nf* : wedge
cuñado, -da *n* : brother-in-law *m*, sister-in-law *f*
cuño *nm* : die (for stamping)
cuota *nf* **1** : fee, dues **2** : quota, share **3** : installment, payment
cupé *nm* : coupe
cupo¹, etc. → **caber**
cupo² *nm* **1** : quota, share **2** : capacity, room
cupón *nm, pl* **cupones 1** : coupon, voucher **2 cupón federal** : food stamp
cúpula *nf* : dome, cupola
cura¹ *nm* : priest
cura² *nf* **1** CURACIÓN, TRATAMIENTO : cure, treatment **2** : dressing, bandage
curación *nf, pl* **-ciones** CURA, TRATAMIENTO : cure, treatment
curandero, -ra *nm* **1** : witch doctor **2** : quack, charlatan
curar *vt* **1** : to cure, to heal **2** : to treat, to dress **3** CURTIR : to tan **4** : to cure (meat) — *vi* : to get well, to recover — **curarse** *vr*
curativo, -va *adj* : curative, healing
curiosear *vi* **1** : to snoop, to pry **2** : to browse — *vt* : to look over, to check
curiosidad *nf* **1** : curiosity **2** : curio
curioso, -sa *adj* **1** : curious, inquisitive **2** : strange, unusual, odd — **curiosamente** *adv*
currículo → **currículum**
currículum *nm, pl* **-lums 1** : résumé, curriculum vitae **2** : curriculum, course of study
curry [ˈkurri] *nm, pl* **-rries 1** : curry powder **2** : curry (dish)
cursar *vt* **1** : to attend (school), to take (a course) **2** : to dispatch, to pass on
cursi *adj fam* : affected, pretentious
cursilería *nf* **1** : vulgarity, poor taste **2** : pretentiousness

cursiva *nf* BASTARDILLA : italic type, italics *pl*
curso *nm* **1** : course, direction **2** : school year **3** : course, subject (in school)
cursor *nm* : cursor
curtido, -da *adj* : weather-beaten, leathery (of skin)
curtidor, -dora *n* : tanner
curtiduría *nf* : tannery
curtir *vt* **1** : to tan **2** : to harden, to weather — **curtirse** *vr*
curva *nf* : curve, bend
curvar *vt* : to bend

curvatura *nf* : curvature
curvilíneo, -nea *adj* : curvaceous, shapely
curvo, -va *adj* : curved, bent
cúspide *nf* : zenith, apex, peak
custodia *nf* : custody
custodiar *vt* : to guard, to look after
custodio, -dia *n* : keeper, guardian
cúter *nm* : cutter (boat)
cutícula *nf* : cuticle
cutis *nms & pl* : skin, complexion
cuyo, -ya *adj* **1** : whose, of whom, of which **2 en cuyo caso** : in which case

D

d *nf* : fourth letter of the Spanish alphabet
dable *adj* : feasible, possible
dactilar *adj* **huellas dactilares** : fingerprints
dádiva *nf* : gift, handout
dadivoso, -sa *adj* : generous
dado, -da *adj* **1** : given **2 dado que** : given that, since
dador, -dora *n* : giver, donor
dados *nmpl* : dice
daga *nf* : dagger
dalia *nf* : dahlia
dálmata *nm* : dalmatian
daltónico, -ca *adj* : color-blind
daltonismo *nm* : color blindness
dama *nf* **1** : lady **2 damas** *nfpl* : checkers
damasco *nm* : damask
damisela *nf* : damsel
damnificado, -da *n* : victim (of a disaster)
damnificar {72} *vt* : to damage, to injure
dance, etc. → **danzar**
dandi *nm* : dandy, fop
danés¹, -nesa *adj* : Danish
danés², -nesa *n, mpl* **daneses** : Dane, Danish person
danza *nf* : dance, dancing ⟨danza folklórica : folk dance⟩
danzante, -ta *n* BAILARÍN : dancer
danzar {21} *v* BAILAR : to dance
dañar *vt* **1** : to damage, to spoil **2** : to harm, to hurt — **dañarse** *vr*
dañino, -na *adj* : harmful
daño *nm* **1** : damage **2** : harm, injury **3 hacer daño a** : to harm, to damage **4 daños y perjuicios** : damages
dar {22} *vt* **1** : to give **2** ENTREGAR : to deliver, to hand over **3** : to hit, to strike **4** : to yield, to produce **5** : to perform **6** : to give off, to emit **7 ~ como** *or* **~ por** : to regard as, to consider — *vi* **1** ALCANZAR : to suffice, to be enough ⟨no me da para dos pasajes : I don't have enough for two fares⟩ **2 ~ a** *or* **~ sobre** : to overlook, to look out on **3 ~ con** : to run into **4 ~ con** : to hit upon (an idea) **5 dar de sí** : to give, to stretch — **darse** *vr* **1** : to give in, to

surrender **2** : to occur, to arise **3** : to grow, to come up **4 ~ con** *or* **~ contra** : to hit oneself against **5 dárselas de** : to boast about ⟨se las da de muy listo : he thinks he's very smart⟩
dardo *nm* : dart
datar *vt* : to date — *vi* **~ de** : to date from, to date back to
dátil *nm* : date (fruit)
dato *nm* **1** : fact, piece of information **2 datos** *nmpl* : data, information
dé → **dar**
de *prep* **1** : of ⟨la casa de Pepe : Pepe's house⟩ ⟨un niño de tres años : a three-year-old boy⟩ **2** : from ⟨es de Managua : she's from Managua⟩ ⟨salió del edificio : he left the building⟩ **3** : in, at ⟨a las tres de la mañana : at three in the morning⟩ ⟨salen de noche : they go out at night⟩ **4** : than ⟨más de tres : more than three⟩
deambular *vi* : to wander, to roam
debacle *nf* : debacle
debajo *adv* **1** : underneath, below, on the bottom **2 ~ de** : under, underneath **3 por ~** : below, beneath
debate *nm* : debate
debatir *vt* : to debate, to discuss — **debatirse** *vr* : to struggle
debe *nm* : debit column, debit
deber¹ *vt* : to owe — *v aux* **1** : must, have to ⟨debo ir a la oficina : I must go to the office⟩ **2** : should, ought to ⟨deberías buscar trabajo : you ought to look for work⟩ **3** (*expressing probability*) : must ⟨debe ser mexicano : he must be Mexican⟩ — **deberse** *vr* **~ a** : to be due to
deber² *nm* **1** OBLIGACIÓN : duty, obligation **2 deberes** *nmpl, Spain* : homework
debidamente *adv* : properly, duly
debido, -da *adj* **1** : right, proper, due **2 ~ a** : due to, owing to
débil *adj* : weak, feeble — **débilmente** *adv*
debilidad *nf* : weakness, debility, feebleness
debilitamiento *nm* : debilitation, weakening

debilitar *vt* : to debilitate, to weaken — **debilitarse** *vr*
debilucho[1], **-cha** *adj* : weak, frail
debilucho[2], **-cha** *n* : weakling
debitar *vt* : to debit
débito *nm* 1 DEUDA : debt 2 : debit
debut [de'but] *nm, pl* **debuts** : debut
debutante[1] *nmf* : beginner, newcomer
debutante[2] *nf* : debutante *f*
debutar *vi* : to debut, to make a debut
década *nf* DECENIO : decade
decadencia *nf* 1 : decadence 2 : decline
decadente *adj* 1 : decadent 2 : declining
decaer {13} *vi* 1 : to decline, to decay, to deteriorate 2 FLAQUEAR : to weaken, to flag
decaiga, etc. → **decaer**
decano, -na *n* 1 : dean 2 : senior member
decantar *vt* : to decant
decapitar *vt* : to decapitate, to behead
decayó, etc. → **decaer**
decena *nf* : group of ten
decencia *nf* : decency
decenio *nm* DÉCADA : decade
decente *adj* : decent — **decentemente** *adv*
decepción *nf, pl* **-ciones** : disappointment, letdown
decepcionante *adj* : disappointing
decepcionar *vt* : to disappoint, to let down — **decepcionarse** *vr*
deceso *nm* DEFUNCIÓN : death, passing
dechado *nm* 1 : sampler (of embroidery) 2 : model, paragon
decibelio *or* **decibel** *nm* : decibel
decidido, -da *adj* : decisive, determined, resolute — **decididamente** *adv*
decidir *vt* 1 : to decide, to determine ⟨no he decidido nada : I haven't made a decision⟩ 2 : to persuade, to decide ⟨su padre lo decidió a estudiar : his father persuaded him to study⟩ — *vi* : to decide — **decidirse** *vr* : to make up one's mind
decimal *adj* : decimal
décimo, -ma *adj* : tenth — **décimo, -ma** *n*
decimoctavo[1], **-va** *adj* : eighteenth
decimoctavo[2], **-va** *n* : eighteenth (in a series)
decimocuarto[1], **-ta** *adj* : fourteenth
decimocuarto[2], **-ta** *n* : fourteenth (in a series)
decimonoveno[1], **-na** *or* **decimonono, -na** *adj* : nineteenth
decimonoveno[2], **-na** *or* **decimonono, -na** *n* : nineteenth (in a series)
decimoquinto[1], **-ta** *adj* : fifteenth
decimoquinto[2], **-ta** *n* : fifteenth (in a series)
decimoséptimo[1], **-ma** *adj* : seventeenth
decimoséptimo[2], **-ma** *n* : seventeenth (in a series)
decimosexto[1], **-ta** *adj* : sixteenth
decimosexto[2], **-ta** *n* : sixteenth (in a series)

decimotercero[1], **-ra** *adj* : thirteenth
decimotercero[2], **-ra** *n* : thirteenth (in a series)
decir[1] {23} *vt* 1 : to say ⟨dice que no quiere ir : she says she doesn't want to go⟩ 2 : to tell ⟨dime lo que estás pensando : tell me what you're thinking⟩ 3 : to speak, to talk ⟨no digas tonterías : don't talk nonsense⟩ 4 : to call ⟨me dicen Rosy : they call me Rosy⟩ 5 es **decir** : that is to say 6 **querer decir** : to mean — **decirse** *vr* 1 : to say to oneself 2 : to be said ⟨¿cómo se dice "lápiz" en francés? : how do you say "pencil" in French?⟩
decir[2] *nm* DICHO : saying, expression
decisión *nf, pl* **-siones** : decision, choice
decisivo, -va *adj* : decisive, conclusive — **decisivamente** *adv*
declamar *vi* : to declaim — *vt* : to recite
declaración *nf, pl* **-ciones** 1 : declaration, statement 2 TESTIMONIO : deposition, testimony 3 **declaración de derechos** : bill of rights 4 **declaración jurada** : affidavit
declarado, -da *adj* : professed, open — **declaradamente** *adv*
declarar *vt* : to declare, to state — *vi* ATESTIGUAR : to testify — **declararse** *vr* 1 : to declare oneself, to make a statement 2 : to confess one's love 3 : to plead (in court) ⟨declararse inocente : to plead not guilty⟩
declinación *nf, pl* **-ciones** 1 : drop, downward trend 2 : declination 3 : declension (in grammar)
declinar *vt* : to decline, to turn down — *vi* 1 : to draw to a close 2 : to diminish, to decline
declive *nm* 1 DECADENCIA : decline 2 : slope, incline
decodificador *nm* : decoder
decolar *vi Chile, Col, Ecua* : to take off (of an airplane)
decolorar *vt* : to bleach — **decolorarse** *vr* : to fade
decomisar *vt* CONFISCAR : to seize, to confiscate
decomiso *nm* : seizure, confiscation
decoración *nf, pl* **-ciones** 1 : decoration 2 : decor 3 : stage set, scenery
decorado *nm* : stage set, scenery
decorador, -dora *n* : decorator
decorar *vt* ADORNAR : to decorate, to adorn
decorativo, -va *adj* : decorative, ornamental
decoro *nm* : decorum, propriety
decoroso, -sa *adj* : decent, proper, respectable
decrecer {53} *vi* : to decrease, to wane, to diminish — **decreciente** *adj*
decrecimiento *nm* : decrease, decline
decrépito, -ta *adj* : decrepit
decretar *vt* : to decree, to order
decreto *nm* : decree
decúbito *nm* : horizontal position ⟨en decúbito prono : prone⟩ ⟨en decúbito supino : supine⟩

dedal *nm* : thimble
dedalera *nf* DIGITAL : foxglove
dedicación *nf, pl* **-ciones** : dedication, devotion
dedicar {72} *vt* CONSAGRAR : to dedicate, to devote — **dedicarse** *vr* ~ **a** : to devote oneself to, to engage in
dedicatoria *nf* : dedication (of a book, song, etc.)
dedo *nm* **1** : finger ⟨dedo meñique : little finger⟩ **2 dedo del pie** : toe
deducción *nf, pl* **-ciones** : deduction
deducible *adj* **1** : deducible, inferable **2** : deductible
deducir {61} *vt* **1** INFERIR : to deduce **2** DESCONTAR : to deduct
defecar {72} *vi* : to defecate — **defecación** *nf*
defecto *nm* **1** : defect, flaw, shortcoming **2 en su defecto** : lacking that, in the absence of that
defectuoso, -sa *adj* : defective, faulty
defender {56} *vt* : to defend, to protect — **defenderse** *vr* **1** : to defend oneself **2** : to get by, to know the basics ⟨su inglés no es perfecto pero se defiende : his English isn't perfect but he gets by⟩
defendible *adj* : defensible, tenable
defensa[1] *nf* : defense
defensa[2] *nmf* : defender, back (in sports)
defensiva *nf* : defensive, defense
defensivo, -va *adj* : defensive — **defensivamente** *adv*
defensor[1], **-sora** *adj* : defending, defense
defensor[2], **-sora** *n* **1** : defender, advocate **2** : defense counsel
defeño, -ña *n* : person from the Federal District (Mexico City)
deferencia *nf* : deference
deficiencia *nf* : deficiency, flaw
deficiente *adj* : deficient
déficit *nm, pl* **-cits 1** : deficit **2** : shortage, lack
definición *nf, pl* **-ciones** : definition
definido, -da *adj* : definite, well-defined
definir *vt* **1** : to define **2** : to determine
definitivamente *adv* **1** : finally **2** : permanently, for good **3** : definitely, absolutely
definitivo, -va *adj* **1** : definitive, conclusive **2 en definitiva** : all in all, on the whole **3 en definitiva** *Mex* : permanently, for good
deflación *nf, pl* **-ciones** : deflation
deforestación *nf, pl* **-ciones** : deforestation
deformación *nf, pl* **-ciones 1** : deformation **2** : distortion
deformar *vt* **1** : to deform, to disfigure **2** : to distort — **deformarse** *vr*
deforme *adj* : deformed, misshapen
deformidad *nf* : deformity
defraudación *nf, pl* **-ciones** : fraud
defraudar *vt* **1** ESTAFAR : to defraud, to cheat **2** : to disappoint
defunción *nf, pl* **-ciones** DECESO : death, passing

degeneración *nf, pl* **-ciones 1** : degeneration **2** : degeneracy, depravity
degenerado, -da *adj* DEPRAVADO : degenerate
degenerar *vi* : to degenerate
degenerativo, -va *adj* : degenerative
degollar {19} *vt* **1** : to slit the throat of, to slaughter **2** DECAPITAR : to behead **3** : to ruin, to destroy
degradación *nf, pl* **-ciones 1** : degradation **2** : demotion
degradar *vt* **1** : to degrade, to debase **2** : to demote
degustación *nf, pl* **-ciones** : tasting, sampling
degustar *vt* : to taste
deidad *nf* : deity
deificar {72} *vt* : to idolize, to deify
dejado, -da *adj* **1** : slovenly **2** : careless, lazy
dejar *vt* **1** : to leave **2** ABANDONAR : to abandon, to forsake **3** : to let be, to let go **4** PERMITIR : to allow, to permit — *vi* ~ **de** : to stop, to quit ⟨dejar de fumar : to quit smoking⟩ — **dejarse** *vr* **1** : to let oneself be ⟨se deja insultar : he lets himself be insulted⟩ **2** : to forget, to leave ⟨me dejé las llaves en el carro : I left the keys in the car⟩ **3** : to neglect oneself, to let oneself go **4** : to grow ⟨nos estamos dejando el pelo largo : we're growing our hair long⟩
dejo *nm* **1** : aftertaste **2** : touch, hint **3** : (regional) accent
del (*contraction of* **de** *and* **el**) → **de**
delación *nf, pl* **-ciones** : denunciation, betrayal
delantal *nm* **1** : apron **2** : pinafore
delante *adv* **1** ENFRENTE : ahead, in front **2** ~ **de** : before, in front of
delantera *nf* **1** : front, front part, front row ⟨tomar la delantera : to take the lead⟩ **2** : forward line (in sports)
delantero[1], **-ra** *adj* **1** : front, forward **2 tracción delantera** : front-wheel drive
delantero[2], **-ra** *n* : forward (in sports)
delatar *vt* **1** : to betray, to reveal **2** : to denounce, to inform against
delegación *nf, pl* **-ciones** : delegation
delegado, -da *n* : delegate, representative
delegar {52} *vt* : to delegate
deleitar *vt* : to delight, to please — **deleitarse** *vr*
deleite *nm* : delight, pleasure
deletrear *vi* : to spell ⟨¿como se deletrea? : how do you spell it?⟩
deleznable *adj* **1** : brittle, crumbly **2** : slippery **3** : weak, fragile ⟨una excusa deleznable : a weak excuse⟩
delfín *nm, pl* **delfines 1** : dolphin **2** : dauphin, heir apparent
delgadez *nf* : thinness, skinniness
delgado, -da *adj* **1** FLACO : thin, skinny **2** ESBELTO : slender, slim **3** DELICADO : delicate, fine **4** AGUDO : sharp, clever
deliberación *nf, pl* **-ciones** : deliberation

deliberado, -da *adj* : deliberate, intentional — **deliberadamente** *adv*
deliberar *vi* : to deliberate
deliberativo, -va *adj* : deliberative
delicadeza *nf* **1** : delicacy, fineness **2** : gentleness, softness **3** : tact, discretion, consideration
delicado, -da *adj* **1** : delicate, fine **2** : sensitive, frail **3** : difficult, tricky **4** : fussy, hard to please **5** : tactful, considerate
delicia *nf* : delight
delicioso, -sa *adj* **1** RICO : delicious **2** : delightful
delictivo, -va *adj* : criminal
delictuoso, -sa → **delictivo**
delimitación *nf, pl* **-ciones** **1** : demarcation **2** : defining, specifying
delimitar *vt* **1** : to demarcate **2** : to define, to specify
delincuencia *nf* : delinquency, crime
delincuente[1] *adj* : delinquent
delincuente[2] *nmf* CRIMINAL : delinquent, criminal
delinear *vt* **1** : to delineate, to outline **2** : to draft, to draw up
delinquir {24} *vi* : to break the law
delirante *adj* : delirious
delirar *vi* **1** DESVARIAR : to be delirious **2** : to rave, to talk nonsense
delirio *nm* **1** DESVARÍO : delirium **2** DISPARATE : nonsense, ravings *pl* ⟨delirios de grandeza : delusions of grandeur⟩ **3** FRENESÍ : mania, frenzy ⟨¡fue el delirio! : it was wild!⟩
delito *nm* : crime, offense
delta *nm* : delta
demacrado, -da *adj* : emaciated, gaunt
demagogia *nf* : demagogy
demagógico, -ca *adj* : demagogic, demagogical
demagogo, -ga *n* : demagogue
demanda *nf* **1** : demand ⟨la oferta y la demanda : supply and demand⟩ **2** : petition, request **3** : lawsuit
demandado, -da *n* : defendant
demandante *nmf* : plaintiff
demandar *vt* **1** : to demand **2** REQUERIR : to call for, to require **3** : to sue, to file a lawsuit against
demarcar {72} *vt* : to demarcate — **demarcación** *nf*
demás[1] *adj* : remaining ⟨acabó las demás tareas : she finished the rest of the chores⟩
demás[2] *pron* **1** lo (la, los, las) demás : the rest, everyone else, everything else ⟨Pepe, Rosa, y los demás : Pepe, Rosa, and everybody else⟩ **2** estar por demás : to be of no use, to be pointless ⟨no estaría por demás : it couldn't hurt, it's worth a try⟩ **3** por demás : extremely **4** por lo demás : otherwise **5** y demás : and so on, et cetera
demasía *nf* en ~ : excessively, in excess
demasiado[1] *adv* **1** : too ⟨vas demasiado aprisa : you're going too fast⟩ **2** : too

much ⟨estoy comiendo demasiado : I'm eating too much⟩
demasiado[2], **-da** *adj* : too much, too many, excessive
demencia *nf* **1** : dementia **2** LOCURA : madness, insanity
demente[1] *adj* : insane, mad
demente[2] *nmf* : insane person
demeritar *vt* **1** : to detract from **2** : to discredit
demérito *nm* **1** : fault **2** : discredit, disrepute
democracia *nf* : democracy
demócrata[1] *adj* : democratic
demócrata[2] *nmf* : democrat
democrático, -ca *adj* : democratic — **democráticamente** *adv*
democratizar {21} *vt* : to democratize, to make democratic
demografía *nf* : demography
demográfico, -ca *adj* : demographic
demoledor, -dora *adj* : devastating
demoler {47} *vt* DERRIBAR, DERRUMBAR : to demolish, to destroy
demolición *nf, pl* **-ciones** : demolition
demonio *nm* DIABLO : devil, demon
demora *nf* : delay
demorar *vt* **1** RETRASAR : to delay **2** TARDAR : to take, to last ⟨la reparación demorará varios días : the repair will take several days⟩ — *vi* : to delay, to linger — **demorarse** *vr* **1** : to be slow, to take a long time **2** : to take too long
demostración *nf, pl* **-ciones** : demonstration
demostrar {19} *vt* : to demonstrate, to show
demostrativo, -va *adj* : demonstrative
demudar *vt* : to change, to alter — **demudarse** *vr* : to change one's expression
denegación *nf, pl* **-ciones** : denial, refusal
denegar {49} *vt* : to deny, to turn down
denigrante *adj* : degrading, humiliating
denigrar *vt* **1** DIFAMAR : to denigrate, to disparage **2** : to degrade, to humiliate
denodado, -da *adj* : bold, dauntless
denominación *nf, pl* **-ciones** **1** : name, designation **2** : denomination (of money)
denominador *nm* : denominator
denominar *vt* : to designate, to name
denostar {19} *vt* : to revile
denotar *vt* : to denote, to show
densidad *nf* : density, thickness
denso, -sa *adj* : dense, thick — **densamente** *adv*
dentado, -da *adj* SERRADO : serrated, jagged
dentadura *nf* **1** : teeth *pl* **2** dentadura postiza : dentures *pl*
dental *adj* : dental
dentellada *nf* **1** : bite **2** : tooth mark
dentera *nf* **1** : envy, jealousy **2** dar dentera : to set one's teeth on edge
dentición *nf, pl* **-ciones** **1** : teething **2** : dentition, set of teeth

dentífrico *nm* : toothpaste
dentista *nmf* : dentist
dentro *adv* 1 : in, inside 2 : indoors 3 ~ **de** : within, inside, in 4 **dentro de poco** : soon, shortly 5 **dentro de todo** : all in all, all things considered 6 **por** ~ : inwardly, inside
denuedo *nm* : valor, courage
denuesto *nm* : insult
denuncia *nf* 1 : denunciation, condemnation 2 : police report
denunciante *nmf* : accuser (of a crime)
denunciar *vt* 1 : to denounce, to condemn 2 : to report (to the authorities)
deparar *vt* : to have in store for, to provide with ⟨no sabemos lo que nos depara el destino : we don't know what fate has in store for us⟩
departamental *adj* 1 : departmental 2 **tienda departamental** *Mex* : department store
departamento *nm* 1 : department 2 APARTAMENTO : apartment
departir *vi* : to converse
dependencia *nf* 1 : dependence, dependency ⟨dependencia emocional : emotional dependence⟩ ⟨dependencia del alcohol : dependence on alcohol⟩ 2 : agency, branch office
depender *vi* 1 : to depend 2 ~ **de** : to depend on 3 ~ **de** : to be subordinate to
dependiente[1] *adj* : dependent
dependiente[2], **-ta** *n* : clerk, salesperson
deplorable *adj* : deplorable
deplorar *vt* 1 : to deplore 2 LAMENTAR : to regret
deponer {60} *vt* 1 : to depose, to overthrow 2 : to abandon (an attitude or stance) 3 **deponer las armas** : to lay down one's arms — *vi* 1 TESTIFICAR : to testify, to make a statement 2 EVACUAR : to defecate
deportación *nf, pl* **-ciones** : deportation
deportar *vt* : to deport
deporte *nm* : sport, sports *pl* ⟨hacer deporte : to engage in sports⟩
deportista[1] *adj* 1 : fond of sports 2 : sporty
deportista[2] *nmf* 1 : sports fan 2 : athlete, sportsman *m*, sportswoman *f*
deportividad *nf Spain* : sportsmanship
deportivo, -va *adj* 1 : sports, sporting ⟨artículos deportivos : sporting goods⟩ 2 : sporty
deposición *nf, pl* **-ciones** 1 : statement, testimony 2 : removal from office
depositante *nmf* : depositor
depositar *vt* 1 : to deposit, to place 2 : to store — **depositarse** *vr* : to settle
depósito *nm* 1 : deposit 2 : warehouse, storehouse
depravación *nf, pl* **-ciones** : depravity
depravado, -da *adj* DEGENERADO : depraved, degenerate
depravar *vt* : to deprave, to corrupt
depreciación *nf, pl* **-ciones** : depreciation

depreciar *vt* : to depreciate, to reduce the value of — **depreciarse** *vr* : to lose value
depredación *nf* SAQUEO : depredation, plunder
depredador[1], **-dora** *adj* : predatory
depredador[2] *nm* 1 : predator 2 SAQUEADOR : plunderer
depresión *nf, pl* **-siones** 1 : depression 2 : hollow, recess 3 : drop, fall 4 : slump, recession
depresivo[1], **-va** *adj* 1 : depressive 2 : depressant
depresivo[2] *nm* : depressant
deprimente *adj* : depressing
deprimir *vt* 1 : to depress 2 : to lower — **deprimirse** *vr* ABATIRSE : to get depressed
depuesto *pp* → **deponer**
depuración *nf, pl* **-ciones** 1 PURIFICACIÓN : purification 2 PURGA : purge 3 : refinement, polish
depurar *vt* 1 PURIFICAR : to purify 2 PURGAR : to purge
depuso, etc. → **deponer**
derecha *nf* 1 : right 2 : right hand, right side 3 : right wing, right (in politics)
derechazo *nm* 1 : pass with the cape on the right hand (in bullfighting) 2 : right (in boxing) 3 : forehand (in tennis)
derechista[1] *adj* : rightist, right-wing
derechista[2] *nmf* : right-winger
derecho[1] *adv* 1 : straight 2 : upright 3 : directly
derecho[2], **-cha** *adj* 1 : right 2 : right-hand 3 RECTO : straight, upright, erect
derecho[3] *nm* 1 : right ⟨derechos humanos : human rights⟩ 2 : law ⟨derecho civil : civil law⟩ 3 : right side (of cloth or clothing)
deriva *nf* 1 : drift 2 **a la deriva** : adrift
derivación *nf, pl* **-ciones** 1 : derivation 2 RAMIFICACIÓN : ramification, consequence
derivar *vi* 1 : to drift 2 ~ **de** : to come from, to derive from 3 ~ **en** : to result in — *vt* : to steer, to direct ⟨derivó la discusión hacia la política : he steered the discussion over to politics⟩ — **derivarse** *vr* : to be derived from, to arise from
dermatología *nf* : dermatology
dermatológico, -ca *adj* : dermatological
dermatólogo, -ga *n* : dermatologist
derogación *nf, pl* **-ciones** : abolition, repeal
derogar {52} *vt* ABOLIR : to abolish, to repeal
derramamiento *nm* 1 : spilling, overflowing 2 **derramamiento de sangre** : bloodshed
derramar *vt* 1 : to spill 2 : to shed (tears, blood) — **derramarse** *vr* 1 : to spill over 2 : to scatter
derrame *nm* 1 : spilling, shedding 2 : leakage, overflow 3 : discharge, hemorrhage
derrapar *vi* : to skid

derrape *nm* : skid
derredor *nm* **al derredor** *or* **en derredor** : around, round about
derrengado, -da *adj* **1** : bent, twisted **2** : exhausted
derretir {54} *vt* : to melt, to thaw — **derretirse** *vr* **1** : to melt, to thaw **2** ~ **por** *fam* : to be crazy about
derribar *vt* **1** DEMOLER, DERRUMBAR : to demolish, to knock down **2** : to shoot down, to bring down (an airplane) **3** DERROCAR : to overthrow
derribo *nm* **1** : demolition, razing **2** : shooting down **3** : overthrow
derrocamiento *nm* : overthrow
derrocar {72} *vt* DERRIBAR : to overthrow, to topple
derrochador[1], **-dora** *adj* : extravagant, wasteful
derrochador[2], **-dora** *n* : spendthrift
derrochar *vt* : to waste, to squander
derroche *nm* : extravagance, waste
derrota *nf* **1** : defeat, rout **2** : course (at sea)
derrotar *vt* : to defeat
derrotero *nm* RUTA : course
derrotista *adj & nmf* : defeatist
derruir {41} *vt* : to demolish, to tear down
derrumbamiento *nm* : collapse
derrumbar *vt* **1** DEMOLER, DERRIBAR : to demolish, to knock down **2** DESPEÑAR : to cast down, to topple — **derrumbarse** *vr* DESPLOMARSE : to collapse, to break down
derrumbe *nm* **1** DESPLOME : collapse, fall ⟨el derrumbe del comunismo : the fall of Communism⟩ **2** : landslide
desabastecimiento *nm* : shortage, scarcity
desabasto *nm Mex* : shortage, scarcity
desabrido, -da *adj* : tasteless, bland
desabrigar {52} *vt* **1** : to undress **2** : to uncover **3** : to deprive of shelter
desabrochar *vt* : to unbutton, to undo — **desabrocharse** *vr* : to come undone
desacatar *vt* **1** DESAFIAR : to defy **2** DESOBEDECER : to disobey
desacato *nm* **1** : disrespect **2** : contempt (of court)
desacelerar *vi* : to decelerate, to slow down
desacertado, -da *adj* **1** : mistaken **2** : unwise
desacertar {55} *vi* ERRAR : to err, to be mistaken
desacierto *nm* ERROR : error, mistake
desaconsejable *adj* : inadvisable
desaconsejado, -da *adj* : ill-advised, unwise
desacorde *adj* **1** : conflicting **2** : discordant
desacostumbrado, -da *adj* : unaccustomed, unusual
desacreditar *vt* DESPRESTIGIAR : to discredit, to disgrace
desactivar *vt* : to deactivate, to defuse
desacuerdo *nm* : disagreement
desafiante *adj* : defiant

desafiar {85} *vt* RETAR : to defy, to challenge
desafilado, -da *adj* : blunt
desafinado, -da *adj* : out-of-tune, off-key
desafinarse *vr* : to go out of tune
desafío *nm* **1** RETO : challenge **2** RESISTENCIA : defiance
desafortunado, -da *adj* : unfortunate, unlucky — **desafortunadamente** *adv*
desafuero *nm* ABUSO : injustice, outrage
desagradable *adj* : unpleasant, disagreeable — **desagradablemente** *adv*
desagradar *vi* : to be unpleasant, to be disagreeable
desagradecido, -da *adj* : ungrateful
desagrado *nm* **1** : displeasure **2** **con** ~ : reluctantly
desagravio *nm* **1** : apology **2** : amends, reparation
desagregarse {52} *vr* : to break up, to disintegrate
desaguar {10} *vi* : to drain, to empty
desagüe *nm* **1** : drain **2** : drainage
desahogado, -da *adj* **1** : well-off, comfortable **2** : spacious, roomy
desahogar {52} *vt* **1** : to relieve, to ease **2** : to give vent to — **desahogarse** *vr* **1** : to recover, to feel better **2** : to unburden oneself, to let off steam
desahogo *nm* **1** : relief, outlet **2** **con** ~ : comfortably
desahuciar *vt* **1** : to deprive of hope **2** : to evict — **desahuciarse** *vr* : to lose all hope
desahucio *nm* : eviction
desairar {5} *vt* : to snub, to rebuff
desaire *nm* : rebuff, snub, slight
desajustar *vt* **1** : to disarrange, to put out of order **2** : to upset (plans)
desajuste *nm* **1** : maladjustment **2** : imbalance **3** : upset, disruption
desalentador, -dora *adj* : discouraging, disheartening
desalentar {55} *vt* DESANIMAR : to discourage, to dishearten — **desalentarse** *vr*
desaliento *nm* : discouragement
desaliñado, -da *adj* : slovenly, untidy
desalmado, -da *adj* : heartless, callous
desalojar *vt* **1** : to remove, to clear **2** EVACUAR : to evacuate, to vacate **3** : to evict
desalojo *nm* **1** : removal, expulsion **2** : evacuation **3** : eviction
desamor *nm* **1** FRIALDAD : indifference **2** ENEMISTAD : dislike, enmity
desamparado, -da *adj* DESVALIDO : helpless, destitute
desamparar *vt* : to abandon, to forsake
desamparo *nm* **1** : abandonment, neglect **2** : helplessness
desamueblado, -da *adj* : unfurnished
desandar {6} *vt* : to go back, to return to the starting point
desangelado, -da *adj* : dull, lifeless
desangrar *vt* : to bleed, to bleed dry — **desangrarse** *vr* **1** : to be bleeding **2** : to bleed to death

desanimar *vt* DESALENTAR : to discourage, to dishearten — **desanimarse** *vr*

desánimo *nm* DESALIENTO : discouragement, dejection

desanudar *vt* : to untie, to disentangle

desapacible *adj* : unpleasant, disagreeable

desaparecer {53} *vt* : to cause to disappear — *vi* : to disappear, to vanish

desaparecido[1], **-da** *adj* **1** : late, deceased **2** : missing

desaparecido[2], **-da** *n* : missing person

desaparición *nf, pl* **-ciones** : disappearance

desapasionado, -da *adj* : dispassionate, impartial — **desapasionadamente** *adv*

desapego *nm* : coolness, indifference

desapercibido, -da *adj* **1** : unnoticed **2** DESPREVENIDO : unprepared, off guard

desaprobación *nf, pl* **-ciones** : disapproval

desaprobar {19} *vt* REPROBAR : to disapprove of

desaprovechar *vt* MALGASTAR : to waste, to misuse — *vi* : to lose ground, to slip back

desarmador *nm Mex* : screwdriver

desarmar *vt* **1** : to disarm **2** DESMONTAR : to disassemble, to take apart

desarme *nm* : disarmament

desarraigado, -da *adj* : rootless

desarraigar {52} *vt* : to uproot, to root out

desarreglado, -da *adj* : untidy, disorganized

desarreglar *vt* **1** : to mess up **2** : to upset, to disrupt

desarreglo *nm* **1** : untidiness **2** : disorder, confusion

desarrollar *vt* : to develop — **desarrollarse** *vr* : to take place

desarrollo *nm* : development

desarticulación *nf, pl* **-ciones** **1** : dislocation **2** : breaking up, dismantling

desarticular *vt* **1** DISLOCAR : to dislocate **2** : to break up, to dismantle

desaseado, -da *adj* **1** : dirty **2** : messy, untidy

desastre *nm* CATÁSTROFE : disaster

desastroso, -sa *adj* : disastrous, catastrophic

desatar *vt* **1** : to undo, to untie **2** : to unleash **3** : to trigger, to precipitate — **desatarse** *vr* : to break out, to erupt

desatascar {72} *vt* : to unblock, to clear

desatención *nf, pl* **-ciones** **1** : absentmindedness, distraction **2** : discourtesy

desatender {56} *vt* **1** : to disregard **2** : to neglect

desatento, -ta *adj* **1** DISTRAÍDO : absentminded **2** GROSERO : discourteous, rude

desatinado, -da *adj* : foolish, silly

desatino *nm* : folly, mistake

desautorizar {21} *vt* : to deprive of authority, to discredit

desavenencia *nf* DISCORDANCIA : disagreement, dispute

desayunar *vi* : to have breakfast — *vt* : to have for breakfast

desayuno *nm* : breakfast

desazón *nf, pl* **-zones** INQUIETUD : uneasiness, anxiety

desbalance *nm* : imbalance

desbancar {72} *vt* : to displace, to oust

desbandada *nf* : scattering, dispersal

desbarajuste *nm* DESORDEN : disarray, disorder, mess

desbaratar *vt* **1** ARRUINAR : to destroy, to ruin **2** DESCOMPONER : to break, to break down — **desbaratarse** *vr* : to fall apart

desbloquear *vt* **1** : to open up, to clear, to break through **2** : to free, to release

desbocado, -da *adj* : unbridled, rampant

desbocarse {72} *vr* : to run away, to bolt

desbordamiento *nm* : overflowing

desbordante *adj* : overflowing, bursting ⟨desbordante de energía : bursting with energy⟩

desbordar *vt* **1** : to overflow, to spill over **2** : to surpass, to exceed — **desbordarse** *vr*

descabellado, -da *adj* : outlandish, ridiculous

descafeinado, -da *adj* : decaffeinated

descalabrar *vt* : to hit on the head — **descalabrarse** *vr*

descalabro *nm* : setback, misfortune, loss

descalificación *nf, pl* **-ciones** **1** : disqualification **2** : disparaging remark

descalificar {72} *vt* **1** : to disqualify **2** DESACREDITAR : to discredit — **descalificarse** *vr*

descalzarse {21} *vr* : take off one's shoes

descalzo, -za *adj* : barefoot

descansado, -da *adj* **1** : rested, refreshed **2** : restful, peaceful

descansar *vi* **1** : to rest, to relax — *vt* : to rest ⟨descansar la vista : to rest one's eyes⟩

descansillo *nm* : landing (of a staircase)

descanso *nm* **1** : rest, relaxation **2** : break **3** : landing (of a staircase) **4** : intermission

descapotable *adj & nm* : convertible

descarado, -da *adj* : brazen, impudent — **descaradamente** *adv*

descarga *nf* **1** : discharge **2** : unloading

descargar {52} *vt* **1** : to discharge **2** : to unload **3** : to release, to free **4** : to take out, to vent (anger, etc.) — **descargarse** *vr* **1** : to unburden oneself **2** : to quit **3** : to lose power

descargo *nm* **1** : unloading **2** : defense ⟨testigo de descargo : witness for the defense⟩

descarnado, -da *adj* : scrawny, gaunt

descaro *nm* : audacity, nerve

descarriado, -da *adj* : lost, gone astray
descarrilar *vi* : to derail — **descarrilarse** *vr*
descartar *vt* : to rule out, to reject — **descartarse** *vr* : to discard
descascarar *vt* : to peel, to shell, to husk — **descascararse** *vr* : to peel off, to chip
descendencia *nf* 1 : descendants *pl* 2 LINAJE : descent, lineage
descendente *adj* : downward, descending
descender {56} *vt* 1 : to descend, to go down 2 BAJAR : to lower, to take down, to let down — *vi* 1 : to descend, to come down 2 : to drop, to fall 3 ~ de : to be a descendant of
descendiente *adj & nm* : descendant
descenso *nm* 1 : descent 2 BAJA, CAÍDA : drop, fall
descentralizar {21} *vt* : to decentralize — **descentralizarse** *vr* — **descentralización** *nf*
descifrable *adj* : decipherable
descifrar *vt* : to decipher, to decode
descodificar {72} *vt* : to decode
descolgar {16} *vt* 1 : to take down, to let down 2 : to pick up, to answer (the telephone)
descollar {19} *vi* SOBRESALIR : to stand out, to be outstanding, to excel
descolorarse *vr* : to fade
descolorido, -da *adj* : discolored, faded
descomponer {60} *vt* 1 : to rot, to decompose 2 DESBARATAR : to break, to break down — **descomponerse** *vr* 1 : to break down 2 : to decompose
descomposición *nf, pl* **-ciones** 1 : breakdown, decomposition 2 : decay
descompresión *nf* : decompression
descompuesto¹ *pp* → **descomponer**
descompuesto², -ta *adj* 1 : broken down, out of order 2 : rotten, decomposed
descomunal *adj* 1 ENORME : enormous, huge 2 EXTRAORDINARIO : extraordinary
desconcertante *adj* : disconcerting
desconcertar {55} *vt* : to disconcert — **desconcertarse** *vr*
desconchar *vt* : to chip — **desconcharse** *vr* : to chip off, to peel
desconcierto *nm* : uncertainty, confusion
desconectar *vt* 1 : to disconnect, to switch off 2 : to unplug
desconfiado, -da *adj* : distrustful, suspicious
desconfianza *nf* RECELO : distrust, suspicion
desconfiar {85} *vi* ~ de : to distrust, to be suspicious of
descongelar *vt* 1 : to thaw 2 : to defrost 3 : to unfreeze (assets — **descongelarse** *vr*
descongestionante *adj & nm* : decongestant

desconocer {18} *vt* 1 IGNORAR : to be unaware of 2 : to fail to recognize
desconocido¹, -da *adj* : unknown, unfamiliar
desconocido², -da *n* EXTRAÑO : stranger
desconocimiento *nm* : ignorance
desconsiderado, -da *adj* : inconsiderate, thoughtless — **desconsideradamente** *adj*
desconsolado, -da *adj* : disconsolate, heartbroken
desconsuelo *nm* AFLICCIÓN : grief, distress, despair
descontaminar *vt* : to decontaminate — **descontaminación** *nf*
descontar {19} *vt* 1 : to discount, to deduct 2 EXCEPTUAR : to except, to exclude
descontento¹, -ta *adj* : discontented, dissatisfied
descontento² *nm* : discontent, dissatisfaction
descontrol *nm* : lack of control, disorder, chaos
descontrolarse *vr* : to get out of control, to be out of hand
descorazonado, -da *adj* : disheartened, discouraged
descorazonador, -dora *adj* : disheartening, discouraging
descorrer *vt* : to draw back
descortés *adj, pl* **-teses** : discourteous, rude
descortesía *nf* : discourtesy, rudeness
descrédito *nm* DESPRESTIGIO : discredit
descremado, -da *adj* : nonfat, skim
describir {33} *vt* : to describe
descripción *nf, pl* **-ciones** : description
descriptivo, -va *adj* : descriptive
descrito *pp* → **describir**
descuartizar {21} *vt* 1 : to cut up, to quarter 2 : to tear to pieces
descubierto¹ *pp* → **descubrir**
descubierto², -ta *adj* 1 : exposed, revealed 2 al descubierto : out in the open
descubridor, -dora *n* : discoverer, explorer
descubrimiento *nm* : discovery
descubrir {2} *vt* 1 HALLAR : to discover, to find out 2 REVELAR : to uncover, to reveal — **descubrirse** *vr*
descuento *nm* REBAJA : discount
descuidado, -da *adj* 1 : neglectful, careless 2 : neglected, unkempt
descuidar *vt* : to neglect, to overlook — *vi* : to be careless — **descuidarse** *vr* 1 : to be careless, to drop one's guard 2 : to let oneself go
descuido *nm* 1 : carelessness, negligence 2 : slip, oversight
desde *prep* 1 : from 2 : since 3 **desde ahora** : from now on 4 **desde entonces** : since then 5 **desde hace** : for, since (a time) ⟨ha estado nevando desde hace dos días : it's been snowing for

two days〉 **6 desde luego** : of course **7 desde que** : since, ever since **8 desde ya** : right now, immediately
desdecir {11} *vi* **1** ~ **de** : to be unworthy of **2** ~ **de** : to clash with — **desdecirse** *vr* **1** CONTRADECIRSE : to contradict oneself **2** RETRACTARSE : to go back on one's word
desdén *nm, pl* **desdenes** DESPRECIO : disdain, scorn
desdentado, -da *adj* : toothless
desdeñar *vt* DESPRECIAR : to disdain, to scorn, to despise
desdeñoso, -sa *adj* : disdainful, scornful — **desdeñosamente** *adv*
desdibujar *vt* : to blur — **desdibujarse** *vr*
desdicha *nf* **1** : misery **2** : misfortune
desdichado¹, -da *adj* **1** : unfortunate **2** : miserable, unhappy
desdichado², -da *n* : wretch
desdicho *pp* → desdecir
desdiga, desdijo etc. → desdecir
desdoblar *vt* DESPLEGAR : to unfold
deseable *adj* : desirable
desear *vt* **1** : to wish 〈te deseo buena suerte : I wish you good luck〉 **2** QUERER : to want, to desire
desecar {72} *vt* : to dry (flowers, etc.)
desechable *adj* : disposable
desechar *vt* **1** : to discard, to throw away **2** RECHAZAR : to reject
desecho *nm* **1** : reject **2 desechos** *nmpl* RESIDUOS : rubbish, waste
desembarazarse {21} *vr* ~ **de** : to get rid of
desembarcadero *nm* : jetty, landing pier
desembarcar {72} *vi* : to disembark — *vt* : to unload
desembarco *nm* **1** : landing, arrival **2** : unloading
desembarque → desembarco
desembocadura *nf* **1** : mouth (of a river) **2** : opening, end (of a street)
desembocar {72} *vi* ~ **en** *or* ~ **a 1** : to flow into, to join **2** : to lead to, to result in
desembolsar *vt* PAGAR : to disburse, to pay out
desembolso *nm* PAGO : disbursement, payment
desempacar {72} *v* : to unpack
desempate *nm* : tiebreaker, play-off
desempeñar *vt* **1** : to play (a role) **2** : to fulfill, to carry out **3** : to redeem (from a pawnshop) — **desempeñarse** *vr* : to function, to act
desempeño *nm* **1** : fulfillment, carrying out **2** : performance
desempleado¹, -da *adj* : unemployed
desempleado², -da *n* : unemployed person
desempleo *nm* : unemployment
desempolvar *vt* **1** : to dust off **2** : to resurrect, to revive
desencadenar *vt* **1** : to unchain **2** : to trigger, to unleash — **desencadenarse** *vr*

desencajar *vt* **1** : to dislocate **2** : to disconnect, to disengage
desencantar *vt* : to disenchant, to disillusion — **desencantarse** *vr*
desencanto *nm* : disenchantment, disillusionment
desenchufar *vt* : to disconnect, to unplug
desenfadado, -da *adj* **1** : uninhibited, carefree **2** : confident, self-assured
desenfado *nm* **1** DESENVOLTURA : self-assurance, confidence **2** : naturalness, ease
desenfrenadamente *adv* : wildly, with abandon
desenfrenado, -da *adj* : unbridled, unrestrained
desenfreno *nm* : abandon, unrestraint
desenganchar *vt* : to unhitch, to uncouple
desengañar *vt* : to disillusion, to disenchant — **desengañarse** *vr*
desengaño *nm* : disenchantment, disillusionment
desenlace *nm* : ending, outcome
desenlazar {21} *vt* **1** : to untie **2** : to clear up, to resolve
desenmarañar *vt* : to disentangle, to unravel
desenmascarar *vt* : to unmask, to expose
desenredar *vt* : to untangle, to disentangle
desenrollar *vt* : to unroll, to unwind
desentenderse {56} *vr* **1** ~ **de** : to want nothing to do with, to be uninterested in **2** ~ **de** : to pretend ignorance of
desenterrar {55} *vt* **1** EXHUMAR : to exhume **2** : to unearth, to dig up
desentonar *vi* **1** : to clash, to conflict **2** : to be out of tune, to sing off-key
desentrañar *vt* : to get to the bottom of, to unravel
desenvainar *vt* : to draw, to unsheathe (a sword)
desenvoltura *nf* **1** DESENFADO : confidence, self-assurance **2** ELOCUENCIA : eloquence, fluency
desenvolver {89} *vt* : to unwrap, to open — **desenvolverse** *vr* **1** : to unfold, to develop **2** : to manage, to cope
desenvuelto¹ *pp* → desenvolver
desenvuelto², -ta *adj* : confident, relaxed, self-assured
deseo *nm* : wish, desire
deseoso, -sa *adj* : eager, anxious
desequilibrar *vt* : to unbalance, to throw off balance — **desequilibrarse** *vr*
desequilibrio *nm* : imbalance
deserción *nf, pl* **-ciones** : desertion, defection
desertar *vi* **1** : to desert, to defect **2** ~ **de** : to abandon, to neglect
desertor, -tora *n* : deserter, defector
desesperación *nf, pl* **-ciones** : desperation, despair

desesperado, -da *adj* : desperate, despairing, hopeless — **desesperadamente** *adv*

desesperanza *nf* : despair, hopelessness

desesperar *vi* : to exasperate — *vi* : to despair, to lose hope — **desesperarse** *vr* : to become exasperated

desestimar *vt* **1** : to reject, to disallow **2** : to have a low opinion of

desfachatez *nf, pl* **-teces** : audacity, nerve, cheek

desfalcador, -dora *n* : embezzler

desfalcar {72} *vt* : to embezzle

desfalco *nm* : embezzlement

desfallecer {53} *vi* **1** : to weaken **2** : to faint

desfallecimiento *nm* **1** : weakness **2** : fainting

desfasado, -da *adj* **1** : out of sync **2** : out of step, behind the times

desfase *nm* : gap, lag ⟨desfase horario : jet lag⟩

desfavorable *adj* : unfavorable, adverse — **desfavorablemente** *adv*

desfavorecido, -da *adj* : underprivileged

desfigurar *vt* **1** : to disfigure, to mar **2** : to distort, to misrepresent

desfiladero *nm* : narrow gorge, defile

desfilar *vi* : to parade, to march

desfile *nm* : parade, procession

desfogar {52} *vt* **1** : to vent **2** *Mex* : to unclog, to unblock — **desfogarse** *vr* : to vent one's feelings, to let off steam

desforestación *nf, pl* **-ciones** : deforestation

desgajar *vt* **1** : to tear off **2** : to break apart — **desgajarse** *vr* : to come apart

desgana *nf* **1** INAPETENCIA : lack of appetite **2** APATÍA : apathy, unwillingness, reluctance

desgano *nm* → **desgana**

desgarbado, -da *adj* : ungainly

desgarrador, -dora *adj* : heartrending, heartbreaking

desgarradura *nf* : tear, rip

desgarrar *vt* **1** : to tear, to rip **2** : to break (one's heart) — **desgarrarse** *vr*

desgarre → **desgarro**

desgarro *nm* : tear

desgarrón *nm, pl* **-rrones** : rip, tear

desgastar *vt* **1** : to use up **2** : to wear away, to wear down

desgaste *nm* : deterioration, wear and tear

desglosar *vt* : to break down, to itemize

desglose *nm* : breakdown, itemization

desgobierno *nm* : anarchy, disorder

desgracia *nf* **1** : misfortune **2** : disgrace **3** por ~ : unfortunately

desgraciadamente *adv* : unfortunately

desgraciado¹, -da *adj* **1** : unfortunate, unlucky **2** : vile, wretched

desgraciado², -da *n* : unfortunate person, wretch

desgranar *vt* : to shuck, to shell

deshabitado, -da *adj* : unoccupied, uninhabited

deshacer {40} *vt* **1** : to destroy, to ruin **2** DESATAR : to undo, to untie **3** : to break apart, to crumble **4** : to dissolve, to melt **5** : to break, to cancel — **deshacerse** *vr* **1** : to fall apart, to come undone **2** ~ **de** : to get rid of

deshecho¹ *pp* → **deshacer**

deshecho², -cha *adj* **1** : destroyed, ruined **2** : devastated, shattered **3** : undone, untied

desheredado, -da *adj* MARGINADO : dispossessed, destitute

desheredar *vt* : to disinherit

deshicieron, etc. → **deshacer**

deshidratar *vt* : to dehydrate — **deshidratación** *nf*

deshielo *nm* : thaw, thawing

deshilachar *vt* : to fray — **deshilacharse** *vr*

deshizo → **deshacer**

deshonestidad *nf* : dishonesty

deshonesto, -ta *adj* : dishonest

deshonra *nf* : dishonor, disgrace

deshonrar *vt* : to dishonor, to disgrace

deshonroso, -sa *adj* : dishonorable, disgraceful

deshuesar *vt* **1** : to pit (a fruit, etc.) **2** : to bone, to debone

deshumanizar {21} *vt* : to dehumanize — **deshumanización** *nf*

desidia *nf* **1** APATÍA : apathy, indolence **2** NEGLIGENCIA : negligence, sloppiness

desierto¹, -ta *adj* : deserted, uninhabited

desierto² *nm* : desert

designación *nf, pl* **-ciones** NOMBRAMIENTO : appointment, naming (to an office, etc.)

designar *vt* NOMBRAR : to designate, to appoint, to name

designio *nm* : plan

desigual *adj* **1** : unequal **2** DISPAREJO : uneven

desigualdad *nf* **1** : inequality **2** : unevenness

desilusión *nf, pl* **-siones** DESENCANTO, DESENGAÑO : disillusionment, disenchantment

desilusionar *vt* DESENCANTAR, DESENGAÑAR : to disillusion, to disenchant — **desilusionarse** *vr*

desinfectante *adj* & *nm* : disinfectant

desinfectar *vt* : to disinfect — **desinfección** *nf*

desinflar *vt* : to deflate — **desinflarse** *vr*

desinhibido, -da *adj* : uninhibited, unrestrained

desintegración *nf, pl* **-ciones** : disintegration

desintegrar *vt* : to disintegrate, to break up — **desintegrarse** *vr*

desinterés *nm* **1** : lack of interest, indifference **2** : unselfishness

desinteresado, -da *adj* GENEROSO : unselfish

desintoxicar {72} *vt* : to detoxify, to detox

desistir *vi* **1** : to desist, to stop **2** ~ **de** : to give up, to relinquish
deslave *nm Mex* : landslide
desleal *adj* INFIEL : disloyal — **deslealmente** *adv*
deslealtad *nf* : disloyalty
desleír {66} *vt* : to dilute, to dissolve
desligar {52} *vt* **1** : to separate, to undo **2** : to free (from an obligation) — **desligarse** *vr* ~ **de** : to extricate oneself from
deslindar *vt* **1** : to mark the limits of, to demarcate **2** : to define, to clarify
deslinde *nm* : demarcation
desliz *nm, pl* **deslices** : error, mistake, slip ⟨desliz de la lengua : slip of the tongue⟩
deslizar {21} *vt* **1** : to slide, to slip **2** : to slip in — **deslizarse** *vr* **1** : to slide, to glide **2** : to slip away
deslucido, -da *adj* **1** : unimpressive, dull **2** : faded, dingy, tarnished
deslucir {45} *vt* **1** : to spoil **2** : to fade, to dull, to tarnish **3** : to discredit
deslumbrar *vt* : to dazzle — **deslumbrante** *adj*
deslustrado, -da *adj* : dull, lusterless
deslustrar *vt* : to tarnish, to dull
deslustre *nm* : tarnish
desmán *nm, pl* **desmanes** **1** : outrage, abuse **2** : misfortune
desmandarse *vr* : to behave badly, to get out of hand
desmantelar *vt* DESMONTAR : to dismantle
desmañado, -da *adj* : clumsy, awkward
desmayado, -da *adj* **1** : fainting, weak **2** : dull, pale
desmayar *vi* : to lose heart, to falter — **desmayarse** *vr* DESVANECERSE : to faint, to swoon
desmayo *nm* **1** : faint, fainting **2 sufrir un desmayo** : to faint
desmedido, -da *adj* DESMESURADO : excessive, undue
desmejorar *vt* : to weaken, to make worse — *vi* : to decline (in health), to get worse
desmembramiento *nm* : dismemberment
desmembrar {55} *vt* **1** : to dismember **2** : to break up
desmemoriado, -da *adj* : absentminded, forgetful
desmentido *nm* : denial
desmentir {76} *vt* **1** NEGAR : to deny, to refute **2** CONTRADECIR : to contradict
desmenuzar {21} *vt* **1** : to break down, to scrutinize **2** : to crumble, to shred — **desmenuzarse** *vr*
desmerecer {53} *vt* : to be unworthy of — *vi* **1** : to decline in value **2** ~ **de** : to compare unfavorably with
desmesurado, -da *adj* DESMEDIDO : excessive, inordinate — **desmesuradamente** *adv*
desmigajar *vt* : to crumble — **desmigajarse** *vr*

desmilitarizado, -da *adj* : demilitarized
desmontar *vt* **1** : to clear, to level off **2** DESMANTELAR : to dismantle, to take apart — *vi* : to dismount
desmonte *nm* : clearing, leveling
desmoralizador, -dora *adj* : demoralizing
desmoralizar {21} *vt* DESALENTAR : to demoralize, to discourage
desmoronamiento *nm* : crumbling, falling apart
desmoronar *vt* : to wear away, to erode — **desmoronarse** *vr* : to crumble, to deteriorate, to fall apart
desmotadora *nf* : gin, cotton gin
desmovilizar {21} *vt* : to demobilize — **desmovilización** *nf*
desnaturalizar {21} *vt* **1** : to denature **2** : to distort, to alter
desnivel *nm* **1** : disparity, difference **2** : unevenness (of a surface)
desnivelado, -da *adj* **1** : uneven **2** : unbalanced
desnudar *vt* **1** : to undress **2** : to strip, to lay bare — **desnudarse** *vr* : to undress, to strip off one's clothing
desnudez *nf, pl* **-deces** : nudity, nakedness
desnudismo → nudismo
desnudista → nudista
desnudo[1], -da *adj* : nude, naked, bare
desnudo[2] *nm* : nude
desnutrición *nf, pl* **-ciones** MALNUTRICIÓN : malnutrition, undernourishment
desnutrido, -da *adj* MALNUTRIDO : malnourished, undernourished
desobedecer {53} *v* : to disobey
desobediencia *nf* : disobedience — **desobediente** *adj*
desocupación *nf, pl* **-ciones** : unemployment
desocupado, -da *adj* **1** : vacant, empty **2** : free, unoccupied **3** : unemployed
desocupar *vt* **1** : to empty **2** : to vacate, to move out of — **desocuparse** *vr* : to leave, to quit (a job)
desodorante *adj & nm* : deodorant
desolación *nf, pl* **-ciones** : desolation
desolado, -da *adj* **1** : desolate **2** : devastated, distressed
desolador, -dora *adj* **1** : devastating **2** : bleak, desolate
desollar *vt* : to skin, to flay
desorbitado, -da *adj* **1** : excessive, exorbitant **2 con los ojos desorbitados** : with eyes popping out of one's head
desorden *nm, pl* **desórdenes** **1** DESBARAJUSTE : disorder, mess **2** : disorder, disturbance, upset
desordenado, -da *adj* **1** : untidy, messy **2** : disorderly, unruly
desordenar *vt* : to mess up — **desordenarse** *vr* : to get messed up
desorganización *nf, pl* **-ciones** : disorganization
desorganizar {21} *vt* : to disrupt, to disorganize

desorientación *nf, pl* **-ciones** : disorientation, confusion

desorientar *vt* : to disorient, to mislead, to confuse — **desorientarse** *vr* : to become disoriented, to lose one's way

desovar *vi* : to spawn

despachar *vt* **1** : to complete, to conclude **2** : to deal with, to take care of, to handle **3** : to dispatch, to send off **4** *fam* : to finish off, to kill — **despacharse** *vr fam* : to gulp down, to polish off

despacho *nm* **1** : dispatch, shipment **2** OFICINA : office, study

despacio *adv* LENTAMENTE, LENTO : slowly, slow ⟨¡despacio! : take it easy!, easy does it!⟩

desparasitar *vt* : to worm (an animal), to delouse

desparpajo *nm fam* **1** : self-confidence, nerve **2** *CA* : confusion, muddle

desparramar *vt* **1** : to spill, to splatter **2** : to spread, to scatter

despatarrarse *vr* : to sprawl (out)

despavorido, -da *adj* : terrified, horrified

despecho *nm* **1** : spite **2 a despecho de** : despite, in spite of

despectivo, -va *adj* **1** : contemptuous, disparaging **2** : derogatory, pejorative

despedazar {21} *vt* : to cut to pieces, to tear apart

despedida *nf* **1** : farewell, good-bye **2 despedida de soltera** : bridal shower

despedir {54} *vt* **1** : to see off, to show out **2** : to dismiss, to fire **3** EMITIR : to give off, to emit ⟨despedir un olor : to give off an odor⟩ — **despedirse** *vr* : to take one's leave, to say good-bye

despegado, -da *adj* **1** : separated, detached **2** : cold, distant

despegar {52} *vt* : to remove, to detach — *vi* : to take off, to lift off, to blast off

despegue *nm* : takeoff, liftoff

despeinado, -da *adj* : disheveled, tousled ⟨estoy despeinada : my hair's a mess⟩

despeinarse *vr* **1** : to mess up one's hair **2** : to become disheveled ⟨me despeiné : my hair got messed up⟩

despejado, -da *adj* **1** : clear, fair **2** : alert, clear-headed **3** : uncluttered, unobstructed

despejar *vt* **1** : to clear, to free **2** : to clarify — *vi* **1** : to clear up **2** : to punt (in sports)

despeje *nm* **1** : clearing **2** : punt (in sports)

despellejar *vt* : to skin (an animal)

despenalizar {21} *vt* : to legalize — **despenalización** *nf*

despensa *nf* **1** : pantry, larder **2** PROVISIONES : provisions *pl*, supplies *pl*

despeñar *vt* : to hurl down

despepitar *vt* : to seed, to remove the seeds from

desperdiciar *vt* **1** DESAPROVECHAR, MALGASTAR : to waste **2** : to miss, to miss out on

desperdicio *nm* **1** : waste **2 desperdicios** *nmpl* RESIDUOS : refuse, scraps, rubbish

desperdigar {52} *vt* DISPERSAR : to disperse, to scatter

desperfecto *nm* **1** DEFECTO : flaw, defect **2** : damage

despertador *nm* : alarm clock

despertar {55} *vi* : to awaken, to wake up — *vt* **1** : to arouse, to wake **2** EVOCAR : to elicit, to evoke — **despertarse** *vr* : to wake (oneself) up

despido *nm* : dismissal, layoff

despierto, -ta *adj* **1** : awake, alert **2** LISTO : clever, sharp ⟨con la mente despierta : with a sharp mind⟩

despilfarrador[1]**, -dora** *adj* : extravagant, wasteful

despilfarrador[2]**, -dora** *n* : spendthrift, prodigal

despilfarrar *vt* MALGASTAR : to squander, to waste

despilfarro *nm* : extravagance, wastefulness

despintar *vt* : to strip the paint from — **despintarse** *vr* : to fade, to wash off, to peel off

despistado[1]**, -da** *adj* **1** DISTRAÍDO : absentminded, forgetful **2** CONFUSO : confused, bewildered

despistado[2]**, -da** *n* : scatterbrain, absentminded person

despistar *vt* : to throw off the track, to confuse — **despistarse** *vr*

despiste *nm* **1** : absentmindedness **2** : mistake, slip

desplantador *nm* : garden trowel

desplante *nm* : insolence, rudeness

desplazamiento *nm* **1** : movement, displacement **2** : journey

desplazar {21} *vt* **1** : to replace, to displace **2** TRASLADAR : to move, to shift

desplegar {49} *vt* **1** : to display, to show, to manifest **2** DESDOBLAR : to unfold, to unfurl **3** : to spread (out) **4** : to deploy

despliegue *nm* **1** : display **2** : deployment

desplomarse *vr* **1** : to plummet, to fall **2** DERRUMBARSE : to collapse, to break down

desplome *nm* **1** : fall, drop **2** : collapse

desplumar *vt* : to pluck (a chicken, etc.)

despoblado[1]**, -da** *adj* : uninhabited, deserted

despoblado[2] *nm* : open country, deserted area

despoblar {19} *vt* : to depopulate

despojar *vt* **1** : to strip, to clear **2** : to divest, to deprive — **despojarse** *vr* **1** ∼ **de** : to remove (clothing) **2** ∼ **de** : to relinquish, to renounce

despojos *nmpl* 1 : remains, scraps 2 : plunder, spoils

desportilladura *nf* : chip, nick

desportillar *vt* : to chip — **desportillarse** *vr*

desposeer {20} *vt* : to dispossess

déspota *nmf* : despot, tyrant

despotismo *nm* : despotism — **despótico, -ca** *adj*

despotricar {72} *vi* : to rant and rave, to complain excessively

despreciable *adj* 1 : despicable, contemptible 2 : negligible ⟨nada despreciable : not inconsiderable, significant⟩

despreciar *vt* DESDEÑAR, MENOSPRECIAR : to despise, to scorn, to disdain

despreciativo, -va *adj* : scornful, disdainful

desprecio *nm* DESDÉN, MENOSPRECIO : disdain, contempt, scorn

desprender *vt* 1 SOLTAR : to detach, to loosen, to unfasten 2 EMITIR : to emit, to give off — **desprenderse** *vr* 1 : to come off, to come undone 2 : to be inferred, to follow 3 ~ **de** : to part with, to get rid of

desprendido, -da *adj* : generous, unselfish, disinterested

desprendimiento *nm* 1 : detachment 2 GENEROSIDAD : generosity 3 **desprendimiento de tierras** : landslide

despreocupación *nf, pl* **-ciones** : indifference, lack of concern

despreocupado, -da *adj* : carefree, easygoing, unconcerned

desprestigiar *vt* DESACREDITAR : to discredit, to disgrace — **desprestigiarse** *vr* : to lose prestige

desprestigio *nm* DESCRÉDITO : discredit, disrepute

desprevenido, -da *adj* DESAPERCIBIDO : unprepared, off guard, unsuspecting

desproporción *nf, pl* **-ciones** : disproportion, disparity

desproporcionado, -da : out of proportion

despropósito *nm* : piece of nonsense, absurdity

desprotegido, -da *adj* : unprotected, vulnerable

desprovisto, -ta *adj* ~ **de** : devoid of, lacking in

después *adv* 1 : afterward, later 2 : then, next 3 ~ **de** : after, next after ⟨después de comer : after eating⟩ 4 **después (de) que** : after ⟨después que lo acabé : after I finished it⟩ 5 **después de todo** : after all 6 **poco después** : shortly after, soon thereafter

despuntado, -da *adj* : blunt, dull

despuntar *vt* : to blunt — *vi* 1 : to dawn 2 : to sprout 3 : to excel, to stand out

desquiciar *vt* 1 : to unhinge (a door) 2 : to drive crazy — **desquiciarse** *vr* : to go crazy

desquitarse *vr* 1 : to get even, to retaliate 2 ~ **con** : to take it out on

desquite *nm* : revenge

desregulación *nf, pl* **-ciones** : deregulation

desregular *vt* : to deregulate

desregularización *nf* → **desregulación**

destacadamente *adv* : outstandingly, prominently

destacado, -da *adj* 1 : outstanding, prominent 2 : stationed, posted

destacamento *nm* : detachment (of troops)

destacar {72} *vt* 1 ENFATIZAR, SUBRAYAR : to emphasize, to highlight, to stress 2 : to station, to post — *vi* : to stand out

destajo *nm* 1 : piecework 2 **a** ~ : by the item, by the job

destapador *nm* : bottle opener

destapar *vt* 1 : to open, to take the top off 2 DESCUBRIR : to reveal, to uncover 3 : to unblock, to unclog

destape *nm* : uncovering, revealing

destartalado, -da *adj* : dilapidated, tumbledown

destellar *vi* 1 : to sparkle, to flash, to glint 2 : to twinkle

destello *nm* 1 : flash, sparkle, twinkle 2 : glimmer, hint

destemplado, -da *adj* 1 : out of tune 2 : irritable, out of sorts 3 : unpleasant (of weather)

desteñir {67} *vi* : to run, to fade — **desteñirse** *vr* DESCOLORARSE : to fade

desterrado[1], -da *adj* : banished, exiled

desterrado[2], -da *n* : exile

desterrar {55} *vt* 1 EXILIAR : to banish, to exile 2 ERRADICAR : to eradicate, to do away with

destetar *vt* : to wean

destiempo *adv* **a** ~ : at the wrong time

destierro *nm* EXILIO : exile

destilación *nf, pl* **-ciones** : distillation

destilador, -dora *n* : distiller

destilar *vt* 1 : to exude 2 : to distill

destilería *nf* : distillery

destinación *nf, pl* **-ciones** DESTINO : destination

destinado, -da *adj* : destined, bound

destinar *vt* 1 : to appoint, to assign 2 ASIGNAR : to earmark, to allot

destinatario, -ria *n* 1 : addressee 2 : payee

destino *nm* 1 : destiny, fate 2 DESTINACIÓN : destination 3 : use 4 : assignment, post

destitución *nf, pl* **-ciones** : dismissal, removal from office

destituir {41} *vt* : to dismiss, to remove from office

destorcer {14} *vt* : to untwist

destornillador *nm* : screwdriver

destornillar *vt* : to unscrew

destrabar *vt* 1 : to untie, to undo, to ease up 2 : to separate

destreza *nf* HABILIDAD : dexterity, skill

destronar *vt* : to depose, to dethrone

destrozado, -da *adj* 1 : ruined, destroyed 2 : devastated, brokenhearted

destrozar {21} *vt* **1** : to smash, to shatter **2** : to destroy, to wreck — **destrozarse** *vr*
destrozo *nm* **1** DAÑO : damage **2** : havoc, destruction
destrucción *nf, pl* **-ciones** : destruction
destructivo, -va *adj* : destructive
destructor¹, -tora *adj* : destructive
destructor² *nm* : destroyer (ship)
destruir {41} *vt* : to destroy — **destruirse** *vr*
desubicado, -da *adj* **1** : out of place **2** : confused, disoriented
desunión *nf, pl* **-niones** : disunity
desunir *vt* : to split, to divide
desusado, -da *adj* **1** INSÓLITO : unusual **2** OBSOLETO : obsolete, disused, antiquated
desuso *nm* : disuse, obsolescence ⟨caer en desuso : to fall into disuse⟩
desvaído, -da *adj* **1** : pale, washed-out **2** : vague, blurred
desvainar *vt* : to shell
desvalido, -da *adj* DESAMPARADO : destitute, helpless
desvalijar *vt* **1** : to ransack **2** : to rob
desvalorización *nf, pl* **-ciones** **1** DEVALUACIÓN : devaluation **2** : depreciation
desvalorizar {21} *vt* : to devalue
desván *nm, pl* **desvanes** ÁTICO, BUHARDILLA : attic
desvanecer {53} *vt* **1** DISIPAR : to make disappear, to dispel **2** : to fade, to blur — **desvanecerse** *vr* **1** : to vanish, to disappear **2** : to fade **3** DESMAYARSE : to faint, to swoon
desvanecimiento *nm* **1** : disappearance **2** DESMAYO : faint **3** : fading
desvariar {85} *vi* **1** DELIRAR : to be delirious **2** : to rave, to talk nonsense
desvarío *nm* DELIRIO : delirium
desvelado, -da *adj* : sleepless
desvelar *vt* **1** : to keep awake **2** REVELAR : to reveal, to disclose — **desvelarse** *vr* **1** : to stay awake **2** : to do one's utmost
desvelo *nm* **1** : sleeplessness **2** **desvelos** *nmpl* : efforts, pains
desvencijado, -da *adj* : dilapidated, rickety
desventaja *nf* : disadvantage, drawback
desventajoso, -sa *adj* : disadvantageous, unfavorable
desventura *nf* INFORTUNIO : misfortune
desventurado, -da *adj* : unfortunate, ill-fated
desvergonzado, -da *adj* : shameless, impudent
desvergüenza *nf* : shamelessness, impudence
desvestir {54} *vt* : to undress — **desvestirse** *vr* : to get undressed
desviación *nf, pl* **-ciones** **1** : deviation, departure **2** : detour, diversion
desviar {85} *vt* **1** : to change the course of, to divert **2** : to turn away, to deflect — **desviarse** *vr* **1** : to branch off **2** APARTARSE : to stray
desvinculación *nf, pl* **-ciones** : dissociation
desvincular *vt* ~ **de** : to separate from, to dissociate from — **desvincularse** *vr*
desvío *nm* **1** : diversion, detour **2** : deviation
desvirtuar {3} *vt* **1** : to impair, to spoil **2** : to detract from **3** : to distort, to misrepresent
detalladamente *adv* : in detail, at great length
detallar *vt* : to detail
detalle *nm* **1** : detail **2 al detalle** : retail
detallista¹ *adj* **1** : meticulous **2** : retail
detallista² *nmf* **1** : perfectionist **2** : retailer
detección *nf, pl* **-ciones** : detection
detectar *vt* : to detect — **detectable** *adj*
detective *nmf* : detective
detector *nm* : detector ⟨detector de mentiras : lie detector⟩
detención *nf, pl* **-ciones** **1** ARRESTO : detention, arrest **2** : stop, halt **3** : delay, holdup
detener {80} *vt* **1** ARRESTAR : to arrest, to detain **2** PARAR : to stop, to halt **3** : to keep, to hold back — **detenerse** *vr* **1** : to stop **2** : to delay, to linger
detenidamente *adv* : thoroughly, at length
detenimiento *nm* **con** ~ : carefully, in detail
detentar *vt* : to hold, to retain
detergente *nm* : detergent
deteriorado, -da *adj* : damaged, worn
deteriorar *vt* ESTROPEAR : to damage, to spoil — **deteriorarse** *vr* **1** : to get damaged, to wear out **2** : to deteriorate, to worsen
deterioro *nm* **1** : deterioration, wear **2** : worsening, decline
determinación *nf, pl* **-ciones** **1** : determination, resolve **2 tomar una determinación** : to make a decision
determinado, -da *adj* **1** : certain, particular **2** : determined, resolute
determinante¹ *adj* : determining, deciding
determinante² *nm* : determinant
determinar *vt* **1** : to determine **2** : to cause, to bring about — **determinarse** *vr* : to make up one's mind, to decide
detestar *vt* : to detest — **detestable** *adj*
detonación *nf, pl* **-ciones** : detonation
detonador *nm* : detonator
detonante¹ *adj* : detonating, explosive
detonante² *nm* **1** → **detonador 2** : catalyst, cause
detonar *vi* : to detonate, to explode
detractor, -tora *n* : detractor, critic
detrás *adv* **1** : behind **2** ~ **de** : in back of **3 por** ~ : from behind
detrimento *nm* : detriment ⟨en detrimento de : to the detriment of⟩
detuvo, etc. → **detener**

deuda *nf* **1** DÉBITO : debt **2 en deuda con** : indebted to
deudo, -da *n* : relative
deudor¹, -dora *adj* : indebted
deudor², -dora *n* : debtor
devaluación *nf*, *pl* **-ciones** DESVALORIZACIÓN : devaluation
devaluar {3} *vt* : to devalue — **devaluarse** *vr* : to depreciate
devanarse *vr* **devanarse los sesos** : to rack one's brains
devaneo *nm* **1** : flirtation, fling **2** : idle pursuit
devastador, -dora *adj* : devastating
devastar *vt* : to devastate — **devastación** *nf*
devenir {87} *vi* **1** : to come about **2 ~ en** : to become, to turn into
devoción *nf*, *pl* **-ciones** : devotion
devolución *nf*, *pl* **-ciones** REEMBOLSO : return, refund
devolver {89} *vt* **1** : to return, to give back **2** REEMBOLSAR : to refund, to pay back **3** : to vomit, to bring up — *vi* : to vomit, to throw up — **devolverse** *vr* : to return, to come back, to go back
devorar *vt* **1** : to devour **2** : to consume
devoto¹, -ta *adj* : devout — **devotamente** *adv*
devoto², -ta *n* : devotee, admirer
di → **dar, decir**
día *nm* **1** : day ⟨todos los días : every day⟩ **2** : daytime, daylight ⟨de día : by day, in the daytime⟩ ⟨en pleno día : in broad daylight⟩ **3 al día** : up-to-date **4 en su día** : in due time
diabetes *nf* : diabetes
diabético, -ca *adj & n* : diabetic
diablillo *nm* : little devil, imp
diablo *nm* DEMONIO : devil
diablura *nf* **1** : prank **2 diabluras** *nfpl* : mischief
diabólico, -ca *adj* : diabolical, diabolic, devilish
diaconisa *nf* : deaconess
diácono *nm* : deacon
diacrítico, -ca *adj* : diacritic, diacritical
diadema *nf* : diadem, crown
diáfano, -na *adj* : diaphanous
diafragma *nm* : diaphragm
diagnosticar {72} *vt* : to diagnose
diagnóstico¹, -ca *adj* : diagnostic
diagnóstico² *nm* : diagnosis
diagonal *adj & nf* : diagonal — **diagonalmente** *adv*
diagrama *nm* **1** : diagram **2 diagrama de flujo** ORGANIGRAMA : flowchart
dial *nm* : dial (on a radio, etc.)
dialecto *nm* : dialect
dialogar {52} *vi* : to have a talk, to converse
diálogo *nm* : dialogue
diamante *nm* : diamond
diametral *adj* : diametric, diametrical — **diametralmente** *adv*
diámetro *nm* : diameter
diana *nf* **1** : target, bull's-eye **2** *or* **toque de diana** : reveille

diapositiva *nf* : slide, transparency
diario¹ *adv* *Mex* : every day, daily
diario², -ria *adj* : daily, everyday — **diariamente** *adv*
diario³ *nm* **1** : diary **2** PERIÓDICO : newspaper
diarrea *nf* : diarrhea
diatriba *nf* : diatribe, tirade
dibujante *nmf* **1** : draftsman *m*, draftswoman *f* **2** CARICATURISTA : cartoonist
dibujar *vt* **1** : to draw, to sketch **2** : to portray, to depict
dibujo *nm* **1** : drawing **2** : design, pattern **3 dibujos animados** : (animated) cartoons
dicción *nf*, *pl* **-ciones** : diction
diccionario *nm* : dictionary
dícese → **decir**
dicha *nf* **1** SUERTE : good luck **2** FELICIDAD : happiness, joy
dicho¹ *pp* → **decir**
dicho², -cha *adj* : said, aforementioned
dicho³ *nm* DECIR : saying, proverb
dichoso, -sa *adj* **1** : blessed **2** FELIZ : happy **3** AFORTUNADO : fortunate, lucky
diciembre *nm* : December
diciendo → **decir**
dictado *nm* : dictation
dictador, -dora *n* : dictator
dictadura *nf* : dictatorship
dictamen *nm*, *pl* **dictámenes** **1** : report **2** : judgment, opinion
dictaminar *vt* : to report — *vi* : to give an opinion, to pass judgment
dictar *vt* **1** : to dictate **2** : to pronounce (a judgment) **3** : to give, to deliver ⟨dictar una conferencia : to give a lecture⟩
dictatorial *adj* : dictatorial
didáctico, -ca *adj* : didactic
diecinueve *adj & nm* : nineteen
diecinueveavo¹, -va *adj* : nineteenth
diecinueveavo² *nm* : nineteenth (fraction)
dieciocho *adj & nm* : eighteen
dieciochoavo¹, -va *or* **dieciochavo, -va** *adj* : eighteenth
dieciochoavo² *or* **dieciochavo** *nm* : eighteenth (fraction)
dieciséis *adj & nm* : sixteen
dieciseisavo¹, -va *adj* : sixteenth
dieciseisavo² *nm* : sixteenth (fraction)
diecisiete *adj & nm* : seventeen
diecisieteavo¹, -va *adj* : seventeenth
diecisieteavo² *nm* : seventeenth
diente *nm* **1** : tooth ⟨diente canino : eyetooth, canine tooth⟩ **2** : tusk, fang **3** : prong, tine **4 diente de león** : dandelion
dieron, etc. → **dar**
diesel ['disɛl] *nm* : diesel
diestra *nf* : right hand
diestramente *adv* : skillfully, adroitly
diestro¹, -tra *adj* **1** : right **2** : skillful, accomplished
diestro² *nm* : bullfighter, matador
dieta *nf* : diet

dietética *nf* : dietetics
dietético, -ca *adj* : dietetic
dietista *nmf* : dietitian
diez *adj & nm, pl* **dieces** : ten
difamación *nf, pl* **-ciones** : defamation, slander
difamar *vt* : to defame, to slander
difamatorio, -ria *adj* : slanderous, defamatory, libelous
diferencia *nf* **1** : difference **2 a diferencia de** : unlike, in contrast to
diferenciación *nf, pl* **-ciones** : differentiation
diferenciar *vt* : to differentiate between, to distinguish — **diferenciarse** *vr* : to differ
diferendo *nm* : dispute, conflict
diferente *adj* DISTINTO : different — **diferentemente** *adv*
diferir {76} *vt* DILATAR, POSPONER : to postpone, to put off — *vi* : to differ
difícil *adj* : difficult, hard
difícilmente *adv* **1** : with difficulty **2** : hardly
dificultad *nf* : difficulty
dificultar *vt* : to make difficult, to obstruct
dificultoso, -sa *adj* : difficult, hard
difteria *nf* : diphtheria
difundir *vt* **1** : to diffuse, to spread out **2** : to broadcast, to spread
difunto, -ta *adj & n* FALLECIDO : deceased
difusión *nf, pl* **-siones 1** : spreading **2** : diffusion (of heat, etc.) **3** : broadcast, broadcasting ⟨los medios de difusión : the media⟩
difuso, -sa *adj* : diffuse, widespread
diga, etc. → **decir**
digerir {76} *vt* : to digest — **digerible** *adj*
digestión *nf, pl* **-tiones** : digestion
digestivo, -va *adj* : digestive
digital¹ *adj* : digital — **digitalmente** *adv*
digital² *nf* **1** DEDALERA : foxglove **2** : digitalis
dígito *nm* : digit
dignarse *vr* : to deign, to condescend ⟨no se dignó contestar : he didn't deign to answer⟩
dignatario, -ria *n* : dignitary
dignidad *nf* **1** : dignity **2** : dignitary
dignificar {72} *vt* : to dignify
digno, -na *adj* **1** HONORABLE : honorable **2** : worthy — **dignamente** *adv*
digresión *nf, pl* **-ciones** : digression
dije *nm* : charm (on a bracelet)
dijo, etc. → **decir**
dilación *nf, pl* **-ciones** : delay
dilapidar *vt* : to waste, to squander
dilatar *vt* **1** : to dilate, to widen, to expand **2** DIFERIR, POSPONER : to put off, to postpone — **dilatarse** *vr* **1** : to expand (of gases, metals, etc.) **2** *Mex* : to take long, to be long
dilatorio, -ria *adj* : dilatory, delaying
dilema *nm* : dilemma
diletante *nmf* : dilettante

diligencia *nf* **1** : diligence, care **2** : promptness, speed **3** : action, step **4** : task, errand **5** : stagecoach **6 diligencias** *nfpl* : judicial procedures, formalities
diligente *adj* : diligent — **diligentemente** *adv*
dilucidar *vt* : to elucidate, to clarify
dilución *nf, pl* **-ciones** : dilution
diluir {41} *vt* : to dilute
diluviar *v impers* : to pour (with rain), to pour down
diluvio *nm* **1** : flood **2** : downpour
dimensión *nf, pl* **-siones** : dimension — **dimensional** *adj*
dimensionar *vt* : to measure, to gauge
diminutivo¹, -va *adj* : diminutive
diminutivo² *nm* : diminutive
diminuto, -ta *adj* : minute, tiny
dimisión *nf, pl* **-siones** : resignation
dimitir *vi* : to resign, to step down
dimos → **dar**
dinámica *nf* : dynamics
dinámico, -ca *adj* : dynamic — **dinámicamente** *adv*
dinamismo *nm* : energy, vigor
dinamita *nf* : dynamite
dinamitar *vt* : to dynamite
dínamo *or* **dinamo** *nm* : dynamo
dinastía *nf* : dynasty
dineral *nm* : fortune, large sum of money
dinero *nm* : money
dinosaurio *nm* : dinosaur
dintel *nm* : lintel
dio, etc. → **dar**
diocesano, -na *adj* : diocesan
diócesis *nfs & pl* : diocese
dios, diosa *n* : god, goddess *f*
Dios *nm* : God
diploma *nm* : diploma
diplomacia *nf* : diplomacy
diplomado¹, -da *adj* : qualified, trained
diplomado² *nm Mex* : seminar
diplomático¹, -ca *adj* : diplomatic — **diplomáticamente** *adv*
diplomático², -ca *n* : diplomat
diptongo *nm* : diphthong
diputación *nf, pl* **-ciones** : deputation, delegation
diputado, -da *n* : delegate, representative
dique *nm* : dike
dirá, etc. → **decir**
dirección *nf, pl* **-ciones 1** : address **2** : direction **3** : management, leadership **4** : steering (of an automobile)
direccional¹ *adj* : directional
direccional² *nf* : directional, turn signal
directa *nf* : high gear
directamente *adv* : straight, directly
directiva *nf* **1** ORDEN : directive **2** DIRECTORIO, JUNTA : board of directors
directivo¹, -va *adj* : executive, managerial
directivo², -va *n* : executive, director
directo, -ta *adj* **1** : direct, straight, immediate **2 en ~** : live (in broadcasting)

director, -tora *n* **1** : director, manager, head **2** : conductor (of an orchestra)
directorial *adj* : managing, executive
directorio *nm* **1** : directory **2** DIRECTIVA, JUNTA : board of directors
directriz *nf, pl* **-trices** : guideline
dirigencia *nf* : leaders *pl*, leadership
dirigente¹ *adj* : directing, leading
dirigente² *nmf* : director, leader
dirigible *nm* : dirigible, blimp
dirigir {35} *vt* **1** : to direct, to lead **2** : to address **3** : to aim, to point **4** : to conduct (music) — **dirigirse** *vr* ~ **a 1** : to go towards **2** : to speak to, to address
dirimir *vt* **1** : to resolve, to settle **2** : to annul, to dissolve (a marriage)
discapacidad *nf* MINUSVALÍA : disability, handicap
discapacitado¹, -da *adj* : disabled, handicapped
discapacitado², -da *n* : disabled person, handicapped person
discar {72} *v* : to dial
discernimiento *nm* : discernment
discernir {25} *v* : to discern, to distinguish
disciplina *nf* : discipline
disciplinar *vt* : to discipline — **disciplinario, -ria** *adj*
discípulo, -la *n* : disciple, follower
disc jockey [ˌdiskˈjoke, -ˈdʒo-] *nmf* : disc jockey
disco *nm* **1** : phonograph record **2** : disc, disk ⟨disco compacto : compact disc⟩ **3** : discus
díscolo, -la *adj* : unruly, disobedient
disconforme *adj* : in disagreement
discontinuidad *nf* : discontinuity
discontinuo, -nua *adj* : discontinuous
discordancia *nf* DESAVENENCIA : conflict, disagreement
discordante *adj* **1** : discordant **2** : conflicting
discordia *nf* : discord
discoteca *nf* **1** : disco, discotheque **2** *CA, Mex* : record store
discreción *nf, pl* **-ciones** : discretion
discrecional *adj* : discretionary
discrepancia *nf* : discrepancy
discrepar *vi* **1** : to disagree **2** : to differ
discreto, -ta *adj* : discreet — **discretamente** *adv*
discriminación *nf, pl* **-ciones** : discrimination
discriminar *vt* **1** : to discriminate against **2** : to distinguish, to differentiate
discriminatorio, -ria *adj* : discriminatory
disculpa *nf* **1** : apology **2** : excuse
disculpable *adj* : excusable
disculpar *vt* : to excuse, to pardon — **disculparse** *vr* : to apologize
discurrir *vi* **1** : to flow **2** : to pass, to go by **3** : to ponder, to reflect
discurso *nm* **1** ORACIÓN : speech, address **2** : discourse, treatise

discusión *nf, pl* **-siones** **1** : discussion **2** ALTERCADO, DISPUTA : argument
discutible *adj* : arguable, debatable
discutidor, -dora *adj* : argumentative
discutir *vt* **1** : to discuss **2** : to dispute — *vi* ALTERCAR : to argue, to quarrel
disecar {72} *vt* **1** : to dissect **2** : to stuff (for preservation)
disección *nf, pl* **-ciones** : dissection
diseminación *nf, pl* **-ciones** : dissemination, spreading
diseminar *vt* : to disseminate, to spread
disensión *nf, pl* **-siones** : dissension, disagreement
disentería *nf* : dysentery
disentir {76} *vi* : to dissent, to disagree
diseñador, -dora *n* : designer
diseñar *vt* **1** : to design, to plan **2** : to lay out, to outline
diseño *nm* : design
disentimiento *nm* : dissent
disertación *nf, pl* **-ciones** **1** : lecture, talk **2** : dissertation
disertar *vi* : to lecture, to give a talk
disfraz *nm, pl* **disfraces** **1** : disguise **2** : costume **3** : front, pretense
disfrazar {21} *vt* **1** : to disguise **2** : to mask, to conceal — **disfrazarse** *vr* : to wear a costume, to be in disguise
disfrutar *vt* : to enjoy — *vi* : to enjoy oneself, to have a good time
disfrute *nm* : enjoyment
disfunción *nf, pl* **-ciones** : dysfunction — **disfuncional** *adj*
disgresión → **digresión**
disgustar *vt* : to upset, to displease, to make angry — **disgustarse** *vr*
disgusto *nm* **1** : annoyance, displeasure **2** : argument, quarrel **3** : trouble, misfortune
disidencia *nf* : dissidence, dissent
disidente *adj & nmf* : dissident
disímbolo, -la *adj Mex* : dissimilar
disímil *adj* : dissimilar
disimulado, -da *adj* **1** : concealed, disguised **2** : furtive, sly
disimular *vi* : to dissemble, to pretend — *vt* : to conceal, to hide
disimulo *nm* **1** : dissembling, pretense **2** : slyness, furtiveness **3** : tolerance
disipar *vt* **1** : to dissipate, to dispel **2** : to squander — **disiparse** *vr*
diskette [diˈskɛt] *nm* : floppy disk, diskette
dislocar {72} *vt* : to dislocate — **dislocación** *nf*
disminución *nf, pl* **-ciones** : decrease, drop, fall
disminuir {41} *vt* REDUCIR : to reduce, to decrease, to lower — *vi* **1** : to lower **2** : to drop, to fall
disociación *nf, pl* **-ciones** : dissociation
disociar *vt* : to dissociate, to separate
disolución *nf, pl* **-ciones** **1** : dissolution, dissolving **2** : breaking up **3** : dissipation
disoluto, -ta *adj* : dissolute, dissipated

disolver {89} vt 1 : to dissolve 2 : to break up — disolverse vr

disonancia nf : dissonance — disonante adj

dispar adj 1 : different, disparate 2 DIVERSO : diverse 3 DESIGUAL : inconsistent

disparado, -da adj salir disparado fam : to take off in a hurry, to rush away

disparar vi 1 : to shoot, to fire 2 Mex fam : to pay — vt 1 : to shoot 2 Mex fam : to treat to, to buy — dispararse vr : to shoot up, to skyrocket

disparatado, -da adj ABSURDO, RIDÍCULO : absurd, ridiculous, crazy

disparate nm : silliness, stupidity ⟨decir disparates : to talk nonsense⟩

disparejo, -ja adj DESIGUAL : uneven

disparidad nf : disparity

disparo nm TIRO : shot

dispendio nm : wastefulness, extravagance

dispendioso, -sa adj : wasteful, extravagant

dispensa nf : dispensation

dispensable adj 1 : dispensable 2 : excusable

dispensar vt 1 : to dispense, to give, to grant 2 EXCUSAR : to excuse, to forgive 3 EXIMIR : to exempt

dispensario nm 1 : dispensary, clinic 2 Mex : dispenser

dispersar vt DESPERDIGAR : to disperse, to scatter

dispersión nf, pl -siones : dispersion

disperso, -sa adj : dispersed, scattered

displicencia nf : indifference, coldness, disdain

displicente adj : indifferent, cold, disdainful

disponer {60} vt 1 : to arrange, to lay out 2 : to stipulate, to order 3 : to prepare — vi ~ de : to have at one's disposal — disponerse vr ~ a : to prepare to, to be about to

disponibilidad nf : availability

disponible adj : available

disposición nf, pl -ciones 1 : disposition 2 : aptitude, talent 3 : order, arrangement 4 : willingness, readiness 5 última disposición : last will and testament

dispositivo nm 1 APARATO, MECANISMO : device, mechanism 2 : force, detachment

dispuesto¹ pp → disponer

dispuesto², -ta adj PREPARADO : ready, prepared, disposed

dispuso, etc. → disponer

disputa nf ALTERCADO, DISCUSIÓN : dispute, argument

disputar vi : to argue, to contend, to vie — vt : to dispute, to question — disputarse vr : to be in competition for ⟨se disputan la corona : they're fighting for the crown⟩

disquera nf : record label, recording company

disquete → diskette

disquisición nf, pl -ciones 1 : formal discourse 2 disquisiciones nfpl : digressions

distancia nf : distance

distanciamiento nm 1 : distancing 2 : rift, estrangement

distanciar vt 1 : to space out 2 : to draw apart — distanciarse vr : to grow apart, to become estranged

distante adj 1 : distant, far-off 2 : aloof

distar vi ~ de : to be far from ⟨dista de ser perfecto : he is far from perfect⟩

diste → dar

distender {56} vt : to distend, to stretch

distensión nf, pl -siones : distension

distinción nf, pl -ciones : distinction

distinguible adj : distinguishable

distinguido, -da adj : distinguished, refined

distinguir {26} vt 1 : to distinguish 2 : to honor — distinguirse vr

distintivo, -va adj : distinctive, distinguishing

distinto, -ta adj 1 DIFERENTE : different 2 CLARO : distinct, clear, evident

distorsión nf, pl -siones : distortion

distorsionar vt : to distort

distracción nf, pl -ciones 1 : distraction, amusement 2 : forgetfulness 3 : oversight

distraer {81} vt 1 : to distract 2 ENTRETENER : to entertain, to amuse — distraerse vr 1 : to get distracted 2 : to amuse oneself

distraídamente adv : absentmindedly

distraído¹ pp → distraer

distraído², -da adj 1 : distracted, preoccupied 2 DESPISTADO : absentminded

distribución nf, pl -ciones : distribution

distribuidor, -dora n : distributor

distribuir {41} vt : to distribute

distributivo, -va adj : distributive

distrital adj : district, of the district

distrito nm : district

distrofia nf : dystrophy ⟨distrofia muscular : muscular dystrophy⟩

disturbio nm : disturbance

disuadir vt : to dissuade, to discourage

disuasión nf, pl -siones : dissuasion

disuasivo, -va adj : deterrent, discouraging

disuasorio, -ria adj : discouraging

disuelto pp → disolver

disyuntiva nf : dilemma

DIU ['diu] nm (dispositivo intrauterino) : IUD, intrauterine device

diurético¹, -ca adj : diuretic

diurético² nm : diuretic

diurno, -na adj : day, daytime

diva nf → divo

divagar {52} vi : to digress

diván nm, pl divanes : divan

divergencia nf : divergence, difference

divergente adj : divergent, differing

divergir {35} vi 1 : to diverge 2 : to differ, to disagree

diversidad *nf* : diversity, variety
diversificación *nf, pl* **-ciones** : diversification
diversificar {72} *vt* : to diversify
diversión *nf, pl* **-siones** ENTRETENIMIENTO : fun, amusement, diversion
diverso, -sa *adj* : diverse, various
divertido, -da *adj* **1** : amusing, funny **2** : entertaining, enjoyable
divertir {76} *vt* ENTRETENER : to amuse, to entertain — **divertirse** *vr* : to have fun, to have a good time
dividendo *nm* : dividend
dividir *vt* **1** : to divide, to split **2** : to distribute, to share out — **dividirse** *vr*
divieso *nm* : boil
divinidad *nf* : divinity
divino, -na *adj* : divine
divisa *nf* **1** : currency **2** LEMA : motto **3** : emblem, insignia
divisar *vt* : to discern, to make out
divisible *adj* : divisible
división *nf, pl* **-siones** : division
divisionismo *nm* : factionalism
divisivo, -va *adj* : divisive
divisor *nm* : denominator
divisorio, -ria *adj* : dividing
divo, -va *n* **1** : prima donna **2** : celebrity, star
divorciado¹, -da *adj* **1** : divorced **2** : split, divided
divorciado², -da *n* : divorcé *m*, divorcée *f*
divorciar *vt* : to divorce — **divorciarse** *vr* : to get a divorce
divorcio *nm* : divorce
divulgación *nf, pl* **-ciones** **1** : spreading, dissemination **2** : popularization
divulgar {52} *vt* **1** : to spread, to circulate **2** REVELAR : to divulge, to reveal **3** : to popularize — **divulgarse** *vr*
dizque *adv* : supposedly, apparently
dobladillar *vt* : to hem
dobladillo *nm* : hem
doblar *vt* **1** : to double **2** PLEGAR : to fold, to bend **3** : to turn ⟨doblar la esquina : to turn the corner⟩ **4** : to dub — *vi* **1** : to turn **2** : to toll, to ring — **doblarse** *vr* **1** : to fold up, to double over **2** : to give in, to yield
doble¹ *adj* : double — **doblemente** *adv*
doble² *nm* **1** : double **2** : toll (of a bell), knell
doble³ *nmf* : stand-in, double
doblegar {52} *vt* **1** : to fold, to crease **2** : to force to yield — **doblegarse** *vr* : to yield, to bow
doblez¹ *nm, pl* **dobleces** : fold, crease
doblez² *nmf* : duplicity, deceitfulness
doce *adj & nm* : twelve
doceavo¹, -va *adj* : twelfth
doceavo² *nm* : twelfth (fraction)
docena *nf* **1** : dozen **2 docena de fraile** : baker's dozen
docencia *nf* : teaching
docente¹ *adj* : educational, teaching
docente² *n* : teacher, lecturer
dócil *adj* : docile — **dócilmente** *adv*

docilidad *nf* : docility
docto, -ta *adj* : learned, erudite
doctor, -tora *n* : doctor
doctorado *nm* : doctorate
doctrina *nf* : doctrine — **doctrinal** *adj*
documentación *nf, pl* **-ciones** : documentation
documental *adj & nm* : documentary
documentar *vt* : to document
documento *nm* : document
dogma *nm* : dogma
dogmático, -ca *adj* : dogmatic
dogmatismo *nm* : dogmatism
dólar *nm* : dollar
dolencia *nf* : ailment, malaise
doler {47} *vi* **1** : to hurt, to ache **2** : to grieve — **dolerse** *vr* **1** : to be distressed **2** : to complain
doliente *nmf* : mourner, bereaved
dolor *nm* **1** : pain, ache ⟨dolor de cabeza : headache⟩ **2** PENA, TRISTEZA : grief, sorrow
dolorido, -da *adj* **1** : sore, aching **2** : hurt, upset
doloroso, -sa *adj* **1** : painful **2** : distressing — **dolorosamente** *adv*
doloso, -sa *adj* : fraudulent — **dolosamente** *adv*
domador, -dora *n* : tamer
domar *vt* : to tame, to break in
domesticado, -da *adj* : domesticated, tame
domesticar {72} *vt* : to domesticate, to tame
doméstico, -ca *adj* : domestic, household
domiciliado, -da *adj* : residing
domiciliario, -ria *adj* **1** : home **2 arresto domiciliario** : house arrest
domiciliarse *vr* RESIDIR : to reside
domicilio *nm* : home, residence ⟨cambio de domicilio : change of address⟩
dominación *nf, pl* **-ciones** : domination
dominancia *nf* : dominance
dominante *adj* **1** : dominant **2** : domineering
dominar *vt* **1** : to dominate **2** : to master, to be proficient at — *vi* : to predominate, to prevail — **dominarse** *vr* : to control oneself
domingo *nm* : Sunday
dominical *adj* : Sunday ⟨periódico dominical : Sunday newspaper⟩
dominicano, -na *adj & n* : Dominican
dominio *nm* **1** : dominion, power **2** : mastery **3** : domain, field
dominó *nm, pl* **-nós** **1** : domino (tile) **2** : dominoes *pl* (game)
domo *nm* : dome
don¹ *nm* **1** : gift, present **2** : talent
don² *nm* **1** : title of courtesy preceding a man's first name **2 don nadie** : nobody, insignificant person
dona *nf Mex* : doughnut, donut
donación *nf, pl* **-ciones** : donation
donador, -dora *n* : donor
donaire *nm* **1** GARBO : grace, poise **2** : witticism

donante *nf* → donador
donar *vt* : to donate
donativo *nm* : donation
doncella *nf* : maiden, damsel
doncellez *nf* : maidenhood
donde[1] *conj* : where, in which ⟨el pueblo donde vivo : the town where I live⟩
donde[2] *prep* : over by ⟨lo encontré donde la silla : I found it over by the chair⟩
dónde *adv* : where ⟨¿dónde está su casa? : where is your house?⟩
dondequiera *adv* 1 : anywhere, no matter where 2 dondequiera que : wherever, everywhere
doña *nf* : title of courtesy preceding a woman's first name
doquier *adv* por ∼ : everywhere, all over
dorado[1], -da *adj* : gold, golden
dorado[2], -da *nm* : gilt
dorar *vt* 1 : to gild 2 : to brown (food)
dormido, -da *adj* 1 : asleep 2 : numb ⟨tiene el pie dormido : her foot's numb, her foot's gone to sleep⟩
dormilón, -lona *n* : sleepyhead, late riser
dormir {27} *vt* : to put to sleep — *vi* : to sleep — dormirse *vr* : to fall asleep
dormitar *vi* : to snooze, to doze
dormitorio *nm* 1 : bedroom 2 : dormitory
dorsal[1] *adj* : dorsal
dorsal[2] *nm* : number (worn in sports)
dorso *nm* 1 : back ⟨el dorso de la mano : the back of the hand⟩ 2 *Mex* : backstroke
dos *adj & nm* : two
doscientos[1], -tas *adj* : two hundred
doscientos[2] *nms & pl* : two hundred
dosel *nm* : canopy
dosificación *nf, pl* -ciones : dosage
dosis *nfs & pl* 1 : dose 2 : amount, quantity
dossier *nm* : dossier
dotación *nf, pl* -ciones 1 : endowment, funding 2 : staff, personnel
dotado, -da *adj* 1 : gifted 2 ∼ de : endowed with, equipped with
dotar *vt* 1 : to provide, to equip 2 : to endow
dote *nf* 1 : dowry 2 dotes *nfpl* : talent, gift
doy → dar
draga *nf* : dredge
dragado *nm* : dredging
dragar {52} *vt* : to dredge
dragón *nm, pl* dragones 1 : dragon 2 : snapdragon
drague, etc. → dragar
drama *nm* : drama
dramático, -ca *adj* : dramatic — dramáticamente *adv*
dramatizar {21} *vt* : to dramatize — dramatización *nf*
dramaturgo, -ga *n* : dramatist, playwright

drástico, -ca *adj* : drastic — drásticamente *adv*
drenaje *nm* : drainage
drenar *vt* : to drain
drene *nm Mex* : drain
driblar *vi* : to dribble (in basketball)
drible *nm* : dribble (in basketball)
droga *nf* : drug
drogadicción *nf, pl* -ciones : drug addiction
drogadicto, -ta *n* : drug addict
drogar {52} *vt* : to drug — drogarse *vr* : to take drugs
drogue, etc. → drogar
droguería *nf* FARMACIA : drugstore
dromedario *nm* : dromedary
dual *adj* : dual
dualidad *nf* : duality
dualismo *nm* : dualism
ducha *nf* : shower ⟨darse una ducha : to take a shower⟩
ducharse *vr* : to take a shower
ducho, -cha *adj* : experienced, skilled, expert
dúctil *adj* : ductile
ducto *nm* 1 : duct, shaft 2 : pipeline
duda *nf* : doubt ⟨no cabe duda : there's no doubt about it⟩
dudar *vt* : to doubt — *vi* ∼ en : to hesitate to ⟨no dudes en pedirme ayuda : don't hesitate to ask me for help⟩
dudoso, -sa *adj* 1 : doubtful 2 : dubious, questionable — dudosamente *adv*
duele, etc. → doler
duelo *nm* 1 : duel 2 LUTO : mourning
duende *nm* 1 : elf, goblin 2 ENCANTO : magic, charm ⟨una bailarina que tiene duende : a dancer with a certain magic⟩
dueño, -ña *n* 1 : owner, proprietor, proprietress *f* 2 : landlord, landlady *f*
duerme, etc. → dormir
dueto *nm* : duet
dulce[1] *adv* : sweetly, softly
dulce[2] *adj* 1 : sweet 2 : mild, gentle, mellow — dulcemente *adv*
dulce[3] *nm* : candy, sweet
dulcería *nf* : candy store
dulcificante *nm* : sweetener
dulzura *nf* 1 : sweetness 2 : gentleness, mellowness
duna *nf* : dune
dúo *nm* : duo, duet
duodécimo[1], -ma *adj* : twelfth
duodécimo[2], -ma *nm* : twelfth (in a series)
dúplex *nms & pl* : duplex apartment
duplicación *nf, pl* -ciones : duplication, copying
duplicado *nm* : duplicate, copy
duplicar {72} *vt* 1 : to double 2 : to duplicate, to copy
duplicidad *nf* : duplicity
duque *nm* : duke
duquesa *nf* : duchess
durabilidad *nf* : durability
durable → duradero

duración *nf, pl* **-ciones** : duration, length
duradero, -ra *adj* : durable, lasting
duramente *adv* **1** : harshly, severely **2** : hard
durante *prep* : during ⟨durante todo el día : all day long⟩ ⟨trabajó durante tres horas : he worked for three hours⟩
durar *vi* : to last, to endure
durazno *nm* **1** : peach **2** : peach tree

dureza *nf* **1** : hardness, toughness **2** : severity, harshness
durmiente[1] *adj* : sleeping
durmiente[2] *nmf* : sleeper
durmió, etc. → **dormir**
duro[1] *adv* : hard ⟨trabajé tan duro : I worked so hard⟩
duro[2]**, -ra** *adj* **1** : hard, tough **2** : harsh, severe

E

e[1] *nf* : fifth letter of the Spanish alphabet
e[2] *conj* (used instead of **y** before words beginning with i- or hi-) : and
ebanista *nmf* : cabinetmaker
ebanistería *nf* : cabinetmaking
ébano *nm* : ebony
ebriedad *nf* EMBRIAGUEZ : inebriation, drunkenness
ebrio, -bria *adj* EMBRIAGADO : inebriated, drunk
ebullición *nf, pl* **-ciones** : boiling
eccéntrico → **excéntrico**
echar *vt* **1** LANZAR : to throw, to cast, to hurl **2** EXPULSAR : to throw out, to expel **3** EMITIR : to emit, give off **4** BROTAR : to sprout, to put forth **5** DESPEDIR : to fire, to dismiss **6** : to put in, to add **7 echar a perder** : to spoil, to ruin **8 echar de menos** : to miss ⟨echan de menos a su madre : they miss their mother⟩ — *vi* **1** : to start off **2** ~ **a** : to begin to — **echarse** *vr* **1** : to throw oneself **2** : to lie down **3** : to put on **4** ~ **a** : to start to **5 echarse a perder** : to go bad, to spoil **6 echárselas de** : to pose as
ecléctico, -ca *adj* : eclectic
eclesiástico[1]**, -ca** *adj* : ecclesiastical, ecclesiastic
eclesiástico[2] *nm* CLÉRIGO : cleric, clergyman
eclipsar *vt* **1** : to eclipse **2** : to outshine, to surpass
eclipse *nm* : eclipse
eco *nm* : echo
ecografía *nf* : ultrasound scanning
ecología *nf* : ecology
ecológico, -ca *adj* : ecological — **ecológicamente** *adv*
ecologista *nmf* : ecologist, environmentalist
ecólogo, -ga *n* : ecologist
economía *nf* **1** : economy **2** : economics
económicamente *adv* : financially
económico, -ca *adj* : economic, economical
economista *nmf* : economist
economizar {21} *vt* **1** : to save, to economize on — *vi* : to save up, to be frugal
ecosistema *nm* : ecosystem
ecuación *nf, pl* **-ciones** : equation
ecuador *nm* : equator

ecuánime *adj* **1** : even-tempered **2** : impartial
ecuanimidad *nf* **1** : equanimity **2** : impartiality
ecuatorial *adj* : equatorial
ecuatoriano, -na *adj & n* : Ecuadorian
ecuestre *adj* : equestrian
ecuménico, -ca *adj* : ecumenical
eczema *nm* : eczema
edad *nf* **1** : age ⟨¿qué edad tiene? : how old is she?⟩ **2** ÉPOCA, ERA : epoch, era
edema *nm* : edema
Edén *nm, pl* Edenes : Eden, paradise
edición *nf, pl* **-ciones** **1** : edition **2** : publication, publishing
edicto *nm* : edict, proclamation
edificación *nf, pl* **-ciones** **1** : edification **2** : construction, building
edificante *adj* : edifying
edificar {72} *vt* **1** : to edify **2** CONSTRUIR : to build, to construct
edificio *nm* : building, edifice
editar *vt* **1** : to edit **2** PUBLICAR : to publish
editor[1]**, -tora** *adj* : publishing ⟨casa editora : publishing house⟩
editor[2]**, -tora** *n* **1** : editor **2** : publisher
editora *nf* : publisher, publishing company
editorial[1] *adj* **1** : publishing **2** : editorial
editorial[2] *nm* : editorial
editorial[3] *nf* : publishing house
editorializar {21} *vi* : to editorialize
edredón *nm, pl* **-dones** COBERTOR, COLCHA : comforter, eiderdown, quilt
educable *adj* : educable, teachable
educación *nf, pl* **-ciones** **1** ENSEÑANZA : education **2** : manners *pl* — **educacional** *adj*
educado, -da *adj* : polite, well-mannered
educador, -dora *n* : educator
educando, -da *n* ALUMNO, PUPILO : pupil, student
educar {72} *vt* **1** : to educate **2** CRIAR : to bring up, to raise **3** : to train — **educarse** *vr* : to be educated
educativo, -va *adj* : educational
efectista *adj* : dramatic, sensational
efectivamente *adv* : really, actually
efectividad *nf* : effectiveness

efectivo¹, -va *adj* **1** : effective **2** : real, actual **3** : permanent, regular (of employment)

efectivo² *nm* : cash

efecto *nm* **1** : effect **2 en ~** : actually, in fact **3 efectos** *nmpl* : goods, property ⟨efectos personales : personal effects⟩

efectuar {3} *vt* : to carry out, to bring about

efervescencia *nf* **1** : effervescence **2** : vivacity, high spirits *pl*

efervescente *adj* **1** : effervescent **2** : vivacious

eficacia *nf* **1** : effectiveness, efficacy **2** : efficiency

eficaz *adj, pl* **-caces 1** : effective **2** EFICIENTE : efficient — **eficazmente** *adv*

eficiencia *nf* : efficiency

eficiente *adj* EFICAZ : efficient — **eficientemente** *adv*

eficientizar {21} *vt Mex* : to streamline, to make more efficient

efigie *nf* : effigy

efímera *nf* : mayfly

efímero, -ra *adj* : ephemeral

efusión *nf, pl* **-siones 1** : effusion **2** : warmth, effusiveness **3 con ~** : effusively

efusivo, -va *adj* : effusive — **efusivamente** *adv*

egipcio, -cia *adj & n* : Egyptian

eglefino *nm* : haddock

ego *nm* : ego

egocéntrico, -ca *adj* : egocentric, self-centered

egoísmo *nm* : selfishness, egoism

egoísta¹ *adj* : selfish, egoistic

egoísta² *nmf* : egoist, selfish person

egotismo *nm* : egotism, conceit

egotista¹ *adj* : egotistic, egotistical, conceited

egotista² *nmf* : egotist, conceited person

egresado, -da *n* : graduate

egresar *vi* : to graduate

egreso *nm* **1** : graduation **2 ingresos y egresos** : income and expenditure

eh *interj* **1** : hey! **2** : eh?, huh?

eje *nm* **1** : axle **2** : axis

ejecución *nf, pl* **-ciones** : execution

ejecutante *nmf* : performer

ejecutar *vt* **1** : to execute, to put to death **2** : to carry out, to perform

ejecutivo, -va *adj & n* : executive

ejecutor, -tora *n* : executor

ejemplar¹ *adj* : exemplary, model

ejemplar² *nm* **1** : copy (of a book, magazine, etc.) **2** : specimen, example

ejemplificar {72} *vt* : to exemplify, to illustrate

ejemplo *nm* **1** : example **2 por ~** : for example **3 dar ejemplo** : to set an example

ejercer {86} *vi* **~ de** : to practice as, to work as — *vt* **1** : to practice **2** : exercise (a right) **3** : to exert

ejercicio *nm* **1** : exercise **2** : practice

ejercitar *vt* **1** : to exercise **2** ADIESTRAR : to drill, to train

ejército *nm* : army

ejidal *adj Mex* : cooperative

ejido *nm* **1** : common land **2** *Mex* : cooperative

ejote *nm Mex* : green bean

el¹ *pron (referring to masculine nouns)* **1** : the one ⟨tengo mi libro y el tuyo : I have my book and yours⟩ ⟨de los cantantes me gusta el de México : I prefer the singer from México⟩ **2 el que** : he who, whoever, the one that ⟨el que vino ayer : the one who came yesterday⟩ ⟨el que trabaja duro estará contento : he who works hard will be happy⟩

el², la *art, pl* **los, las** : the ⟨los niños están en la casa : the boys are in the house⟩ ⟨me duele el pie : my foot hurts⟩

él *pron* : he, him ⟨él es mi amigo : he's my friend⟩ ⟨hablaremos con él : we will speak with him⟩

elaboración *nf, pl* **-ciones 1** PRODUCCIÓN : production, making **2** : preparation, devising

elaborado, -da *adj* : elaborate

elaborar *vt* **1** : to make, to produce **2** : to devise, to draw up

elasticidad *nf* : elasticity

elástico¹, -ca *adj* **1** FLEXIBLE : flexible **2** : elastic

elástico² *nm* **1** : elastic (material) **2** : rubber band

elección *nf, pl* **-ciones 1** SELECCIÓN : choice, selection **2** : election

electivo, -va *adj* : elective

electo, -ta *adj* : elect ⟨el presidente electo : the president-elect⟩

elector, -tora *n* : elector, voter

electorado *nm* : electorate

electoral *adj* : electoral, election

electricidad *nf* : electricity

electricista *nmf* : electrician

eléctrico, -ca *adj* : electric, electrical

electrificar {72} *vt* : to electrify — **electrificación** *nf*

electrizar {21} *vt* : to electrify, to thrill — **electrizante** *adj*

electrocardiógrafo *nm* : electrocardiograph

electrocardiograma *nm* : electrocardiogram

electrocutar *vt* : to electrocute — **electrocución** *nf*

electrodo *nm* : electrode

electrodoméstico *nm* : electric appliance

electroimán *nm, pl* **-manes** : electromagnet

electrólisis *nfs & pl* : electrolysis

electrolito *nm* : electrolyte

electromagnético, -ca *adj* : electromagnetic

electromagnetismo *nm* : electromagnetism

electrón *nm, pl* **-trones** : electron

electrónica *nf* : electronics

electrónico, -ca *adj* : electronic — **electrónicamente** *adv*

elefante · embotellamiento

ESCLAREC-

elefante, -ta n : elephant
elegancia nf : elegance
elegante adj : elegant, smart — **elegantemente** adv
elegía nf : elegy
elegíaco, -ca adj : elegiac
elegibilidad nf : eligibility
elegible adj : eligible
elegido, -da adj 1 : chosen, selected 2 : elected
elegir {28} vt 1 ESCOGER, SELECCIONAR : to choose, to select 2 : to elect
elemental adj 1 : elementary, basic 2 : fundamental, essential
elemento nm : element
elenco nm : cast (of actors)
elepé nm : long-playing record
elevación nf, pl **-ciones** : elevation, height
elevado, -da adj 1 : elevated, lofty 2 : high
elevador nm ASCENSOR : elevator
elevar vt 1 ALZAR : to raise, to lift 2 AUMENTAR : to raise, to increase 3 : to elevate (in a hierarchy), to promote 4 : to present, to submit — **elevarse** vr : to rise
elfo nm : elf
eliminación nf, pl **-ciones** : elimination, removal
eliminar vt 1 : to eliminate, to remove 2 : to do in, to kill
elipse nf : ellipse
elipsis nf : ellipsis
elíptico, -ca adj : elliptical, elliptic
elite or **élite** nf : elite
elixir or **elíxir** nm : elixir
ella pron : she, her ⟨ella es mi amiga : she is my friend⟩ ⟨nos fuimos con ella : we left with her⟩
ello pron : it ⟨es por ello que me voy : that's why I'm going⟩
ellos, ellas pron pl 1 : they, them 2 **de ellos, de ellas** : theirs
elocución nf, pl **-ciones** : elocution
elocuencia nf : eloquence
elocuente adj : eloquent — **elocuentemente** adv
elogiar vt ENCOMIAR : to praise
elogio nm : praise
elote nm 1 Mex : corn, maize 2 CA, Mex : corncob
elucidación nf, pl **-ciones** ESCLARECIMIENTO : elucidation
elucidar vt ESCLARECER : to elucidate
eludir vt EVADIR : to evade, to avoid, to elude
emanación nf, pl **-ciones** : emanation
emanar vi ~ **de** : to emanate from — vt : to exude
emancipar vt : to emancipate — **emancipación** nf
embadurnar vt EMBARRAR : to smear, to daub
embajada nf : embassy
embajador, -dora n : ambassador
embalaje nm : packing, packaging
embalar vt EMPAQUETAR : to pack

embaldosar vt : to tile, to pave with tiles
embalsamar vt : to embalm
embalsar vt : to dam, to dam up
embalse nm : dam, reservoir
embarazada adj ENCINTA, PREÑADA : pregnant, expecting
embarazar {21} vt 1 : to obstruct, to hamper 2 PREÑAR : to make pregnant
embarazo nm : pregnancy
embarazoso, -sa adj : embarrassing, awkward
embarcación nf, pl **-ciones** : boat, craft
embarcadero nm : wharf, pier, jetty
embarcar {72} vi : to embark, to board — vt : to load
embarco nm : embarkation
embargar {52} vt 1 : to seize, to impound 2 : to overwhelm
embargo nm 1 : seizure 2 : embargo 3 **sin ~** : however, nevertheless
embarque nm 1 : embarkation 2 : shipment
embarrancar {72} vi 1 : to run aground 2 : to get bogged down
embarrar vt 1 : to cover with mud 2 EMBADURNAR : to smear
embarullar vt fam : to muddle, to confuse — **embarullarse** vr fam : to get mixed up
embate nm 1 : onslaught 2 : battering (of waves or wind)
embaucador, -dora n : swindler, deceiver
embaucar {72} vt : to trick, to swindle
embeber vt : to absorb, to soak up — vi : to shrink
embelesado, -da adj : spellbound
embelesar vt : to enchant, to captivate
embellecer {53} vt : to embellish, to beautify
embellecimiento nm : beautification, embellishment
embestida nf 1 : charge (of a bull) 2 ARREMETIDA : attack, onslaught
embestir {54} vt : to hit, to run into, to charge at — vi ARREMETER : to charge, to attack
emblanquecer {53} vt BLANQUEAR : to bleach, to whiten — **emblanquecerse** vr : to turn white
emblema nm : emblem
emblemático, -ca adj : emblematic
embolia nf : embolism
émbolo nm : piston
embolsarse vr 1 : to pocket (money) 2 : to collect (payment)
emborracharse vr EMBRIAGARSE : to get drunk
emborronar vt 1 : to blot, to smudge 2 GARABATEAR : to scribble
emboscada nf : ambush
emboscar {72} vt : to ambush — **emboscarse** vr : to lie in ambush
embotadura nf : bluntness, dullness
embotar vt 1 : to dull, to blunt 2 : to weaken, to enervate
embotellamiento nm ATASCO : traffic jam

embotellar *vt* ENVASAR : to bottle
embragar {52} *vi* : to engage the clutch
embrague *nm* : clutch
embravecerse {53} *vr* **1** : to get furious **2** : to get rough ⟨el mar se embraveció : the sea became tempestuous⟩
embriagado, -da *adj* : inebriated, drunk
embriagador, -dora *adj* : intoxicating
embriagarse {52} *vr* EMBORRACHARSE : to get drunk
embriaguez *nf* EBRIEDAD : drunkenness, inebriation
embrión *nm, pl* **embriones** : embryo
embrionario, -ria *adj* : embryonic
embrollo *nm* ENREDO : imbroglio, confusion
embrujar *vt* HECHIZAR : to bewitch
embrujo *nm* : spell, curse
embudo *nm* : funnel
embuste *nm* **1** MENTIRA : lie, fib **2** ENGAÑO : trick, hoax
embustero[1], -ra *adj* : lying, deceitful
embustero[2], -ra *n* : liar, cheat
embutido *nm* **1** : sausage **2** : inlaid work
embutir *vt* **1** : to cram, to stuff, to jam **2** : to inlay
emergencia *nf* **1** : emergency **2** : emergence
emergente *adj* **1** : emergent **2** : consequent, resultant
emerger {15} *vi* : to emerge, to surface
emético[1], -ca *adj* : emetic
emético[2] *nm* : emetic
emigración *nf, pl* **-ciones 1** : emigration **2** : migration
emigrante *adj & nmf* : emigrant
emigrar *vi* **1** : to emigrate **2** : to migrate
eminencia *nf* : eminence
eminente *adj* : eminent, distinguished
eminentemente *adv* : basically, essentially
emisario[1], -ria *n* : emissary
emisario[2] *nm* : outlet (of a body of water)
emisión *nf, pl* **-siones 1** : emission **2** : broadcast **3** : issue ⟨emisión de acciones : stock issue⟩
emisor *nm* TRANSMISOR : television or radio transmitter
emisora *nf* : radio station
emitir *vt* **1** : to emit, to give off **2** : to broadcast **3** : to issue **4** : to cast (a vote)
emoción *nf, pl* **-ciones** : emotion — **emocional** *adj* — **emocionalmente** *adv*
emocionado, -da *adj* **1** : moved, affected by emotion **2** ENTUSIASMADO : excited
emocionante *adj* **1** CONMOVEDOR : moving, touching **2** EXCITANTE : exciting, thrilling
emocionar *vt* **1** CONMOVER : to move, to touch **2** : to excite, to thrill — **emocionarse** *vr*
emotivo, -va *adj* : emotional, moving
empacador, -dora *n* : packer

empacar {72} *vt* **1** EMPAQUETAR : to pack **2** : to bale — *vi* : to pack — **empacarse** *vr* **1** : to balk, to refuse to budge **2** *Col, Mex fam* : to eat ravenously, to devour
empachar *vt* **1** ESTORBAR : to obstruct **2** : to give indigestion to **3** DISFRAZAR : to disguise, to mask — **empacharse** *vr* **1** INDIGESTARSE : to get indigestion **2** AVERGONZARSE : to be embarrassed
empacho *nm* **1** INDIGESTIÓN : indigestion **2** VERGÜENZA : embarrassment **3** **no tener empacho en** : to have no qualms about
empadronarse *vr* : to register to vote
empalagar {52} *vt* **1** : to cloy, to surfeit **2** FASTIDIAR : to annoy, to bother
empalagoso, -sa *adj* MELOSO : cloying, excessively sweet
empalar *vt* : to impale
empalizada *nf* : palisade (fence)
empalmar *vt* **1** : to splice, to link **2** : to combine — *vi* : to meet, to converge
empalme *nm* **1** CONEXIÓN : connection, link **2** : junction
empanada *nf* : pie, turnover
empanadilla *nf* : meat or seafood pie
empanar *vt* : to bread
empantanado, -da *adj* : bogged down, delayed
empañar *vt* **1** : to steam up **2** : to tarnish, to sully
empapado, -da *adj* : soggy, sodden
empapar *vt* MOJAR : to soak, to drench — **empaparse** *vr* **1** : to get soaking wet **2** ~ **de** : to absorb, to be imbued with
empapelar *vt* : to wallpaper
empaque *nm fam* **1** : presence, bearing **2** : pomposity **3** DESCARO : impudence, nerve
empaquetar *vt* EMBALAR : to pack, to package — **empaquetarse** *vr fam* : to dress up
emparedado *nm* : sandwich
emparedar *vt* : to wall in, to confine
emparejar *vt* **1** : to pair, to match up **2** : to make even — *vi* : to catch up — **emparejarse** *vr* : to pair up
emparentado, -da *adj* : related
emparentar {55} *vi* : to become related by marriage
emparrillado *nm Mex* : gridiron (in football)
empastar *vt* **1** : to fill (a tooth) **2** : to bind (a book)
empaste *nm* : filling (of a tooth)
empatar *vt* : to tie, to connect — *vi* : to result in a draw, to be tied — **empatarse** *vr Ven* : to hook up, to link together
empate *nm* : draw, tie
empatía *nf* : empathy
empecinado, -da *adj* TERCO : stubborn
empecinarse *vr* OBSTINARSE : to be stubborn, to persist
empedernido, -da *adj* INCORREGIBLE : hardened, inveterate
empedrado *nm* : paving, pavement

empedrar {55} *vt* : to pave (with stones)
empeine *nm* : instep
empellón *nm, pl* **-llones** : shove, push
empelotado, -da *adj* **1** *Mex fam* : madly in love **2** *fam* : stark naked
empeñado, -da *adj* : determined, committed
empeñar *vt* **1** : to pawn **2** : to pledge, to give (one's word) — **empeñarse** *vr* **1** : to insist stubbornly **2** : to make an effort
empeño *nm* **1** : pledge, commitment **2** : insistence **3** ESFUERZO : effort, determination **4** : pawning ⟨casa de empeños : pawnshop⟩
empeoramiento *nm* : worsening, deterioration
empeorar *vi* : to deteriorate, to get worse — *vt* : to make worse
empequeñecer {53} *vi* : to diminish, to become smaller — *vt* : to minimize, to make smaller
emperador *nm* : emperor
emperatriz *nf, pl* **-trices** : empress
empero *conj* : however, nevertheless
empezar {29} *v* COMENZAR : to start, to begin
empinado, -da *adj* : steep
empinar *vt* ELEVAR : to lift, to raise — **empinarse** *vr* : to stand on tiptoe
empírico, -ca *adj* : empirical — **empíricamente** *adv*
emplasto *nm* : poultice, dressing
emplazamiento *nm* **1** : location, site **2** CITACIÓN : summons, subpoena
emplazar {21} *vt* **1** CONVOCAR : to convene, to summon **2** : to subpoena **3** UBICAR : to place, to position
empleado, -da *n* : employee
empleador, -dora *n* PATRÓN : employer
emplear *vt* **1** : to employ **2** USAR : to use — **emplearse** *vr* **1** : to get a job **2** : to occupy oneself
empleo *nm* **1** OCUPACIÓN : employment, occupation, job **2** : use, usage
empobrecer {53} *vt* : to impoverish — *vi* : to become poor — **empobrecerse** *vr*
empobrecimiento *nm* : impoverishment
empollar *vi* : to brood eggs — *vt* : to incubate
empolvado, -da *adj* **1** : dusty **2** : powdered, powdery
empolvar *vt* **1** : to cover with dust **2** : to powder — **empolvarse** *vr* **1** : to gather dust **2** : to powder one's face
emporio *nm* **1** : center, capital, empire ⟨un emporio cultural : a cultural center⟩ ⟨un emporio financiero : a financial empire⟩ **2** : department store
empotrado, -da *adj* : built-in ⟨armarios empotrados : built-in cabinets⟩
empotrar *vt* : to build into, to embed
emprendedor, -dora *adj* : enterprising
emprender *vt* : to undertake, to begin

empresa *nf* **1** COMPAÑÍA, FIRMA : company, corporation, firm **2** : undertaking, venture
empresariado *nm* **1** : business world **2** : management, managers *pl*
empresarial *adj* : business, managerial, corporate
empresario, -ria *n* **1** : manager **2** : businessman *m*, businesswoman *f* **3** : impresario
empréstito *nm* : loan
empujar *vi* : to push, to shove — *vt* **1** : to push **2** PRESIONAR : to spur on, to press
empuje *nm* : impetus, drive
empujón *nm, pl* **-jones** : push, shove
empuñadura *nf* MANGO : hilt, handle
empuñar *vt* **1** ASIR : to grasp **2 empuñar las armas** : to take up arms
emú *nm* : emu
emular *vt* IMITAR : to emulate — **emulación** *nf*
emulsión *nf, pl* **-siones** : emulsion
emulsionante *nm* : emulsifier
emulsionar *vt* : to emulsify
en *prep* **1** : in ⟨en el bolsillo : in one's pocket⟩ ⟨en una semana : in a week⟩ **2** : on ⟨en la mesa : on the table⟩ **3** : at ⟨en casa : at home⟩ ⟨en el trabajo : at work⟩ ⟨en ese momento : at that moment⟩
enagua *nf* : petticoat, slip
enajenación *nf, pl* **-ciones** **1** : transfer (of property) **2** : alienation **3** : absentmindedness
enajenado, -da *adj* : out of one's mind
enajenar *vt* **1** : to transfer (property) **2** : to alienate **3** : to enrapture — **enajenarse** *vr* **1** : to become estranged **2** : to go mad
enaltecer {53} *vt* : to praise, to extol
enamorado¹, -da *adj* : in love
enamorado², -da *n* : lover, sweetheart
enamoramiento *nm* : infatuation, crush
enamorar *vt* : to enamor, to win the love of — **enamorarse** *vr* : to fall in love
enamoriscarse {72} *vr fam* : to have a crush, to be infatuated
enamorizado, -da *adj* : amorous, passionate
enano¹, -na *adj* : tiny, minute
enano², -na *n* : dwarf, midget
enarbolar *vt* **1** : to hoist, to raise **2** : to brandish
enarcar {72} *vt* : to arch, to raise
enardecer {53} *vt* **1** : to arouse (anger, passions) **2** : to stir up, to excite — **enardecerse** *vr*
encabezado *nm Mex* : headline
encabezamiento *nm* **1** : heading **2** : salutation, opening
encabezar {21} *vt* **1** : to head, to lead **2** : to put a heading on
encabritarse *vr* **1** : to rear up **2** *fam* : to get angry
encadenar *vt* **1** : to chain **2** : to connect, to link **3** INMOVILIZAR : to immobilize

encajar *vi* : to fit, to fit together, to fit in — *vt* **1** : to insert, to stick **2** : to take, to cope with ⟨encajó el golpe : he withstood the blow⟩

encaje *nm* **1** : lace **2** : financial reserve

encajonar *vt* **1** : to box, to crate **2** : to cram in

encalar *vt* : to whitewash

encallar *vi* **1** : to run aground **2** : to get stuck

encallecido, -da *adj* : callused

encamar *vt* : to confine to a bed

encaminado, -da *adj* **1** : on the right track **2** ~ **a** : aimed at, designed to

encaminar *vt* **1** : to direct, to channel **2** : to head in the right direction — **encaminarse** *vr* ~ **a** : to head for, to aim at

encandilar *vt* : to dazzle

encanecer {53} *vi* : to gray, to go gray

encantado, -da *adj* **1** : charmed, bewitched **2** : delighted

encantador¹, -dora *adj* : charming, delightful

encantador², -dora *n* : magician

encantamiento *nm* : enchantment, spell

encantar *vt* **1** : to enchant, to bewitch **2** : to charm, to delight ⟨me encanta esta canción : I love this song⟩

encanto *nm* **1** : charm, fascination **2** HECHIZO : spell **3** : delightful person or thing

encañonar *vt* : to point (a gun) at, to hold up

encapotado, -da *adj* : cloudy, overcast

encapotarse *vr* : to cloud over, to become overcast

encaprichado, -da *adj* : infatuated

encaprichamiento *nm* : infatuation

encapuchado, -da *adj* : hooded

encarado, -da *adj* **estar mal encarado** *fam* : to be ugly-looking, to look mean

encaramar *vt* : to raise, to lift up — **encaramarse** *vr* : to perch

encarar *vt* CONFRONTAR : to face, to confront

encarcelación *nf* → encarcelamiento

encarcelamiento *nm* : incarceration, imprisonment

encarcelar *vt* : to incarcerate, to imprison

encarecer {53} *vt* **1** : to increase, to raise (price, value) **2** : to beseech, to entreat — **encarecerse** *vr* : to become more expensive

encarecidamente *adv* : insistently, urgently

encarecimiento *nm* : increase, rise (in price)

encargado¹, -da *adj* : in charge

encargado², -da *n* : manager, person in charge

encargar {52} *vt* **1** : to put in charge of **2** : to recommend, to advise **3** : to order, to request — **encargarse** *vr* ~ **de** : to take charge of

encargo *nm* **1** : errand **2** : job assignment **3** : order ⟨hecho de encargo : custom-made, made to order⟩

encariñarse *vr* ~ **con** : to become fond of, to grow attached to

encarnación *nf, pl* **-ciones** : incarnation, embodiment

encarnado¹, -da *adj* **1** : incarnate **2** : flesh-colored **3** : red **4** : ingrown

encarnado² *nm* : red

encarnar *vt* : to incarnate, to embody — **encarnarse** *vr* **encarnarse una uña** : to have an ingrown nail

encarnizado, -da *adj* **1** : bloodshot, inflamed **2** : fierce, bloody

encarnizar {21} *vt* : to enrage, to infuriate — **encarnizarse** *vr* : to be brutal, to attack viciously

encarrilar *vt* : to guide, to put on the right track

encasillar *vt* CLASIFICAR : to classify, to pigeonhole, to categorize

encausar *vt* : to prosecute, to charge

encauzar {21} *vt* : to channel, to guide — **encauzarse** *vr*

encebollado, -da *adj* : cooked with onions

encefalitis *nms & pl* : encephalitis

enceguecedor, -dora *n* : blinding

encendedor *nm* : lighter

encender {56} *vi* : to light — *vt* **1** : to light, to set fire to **2** PRENDER : to switch on **3** : to start (a motor) **4** : to arouse, to kindle — **encenderse** *vr* **1** : to get excited **2** : to blush

encendido¹, -da *adj* **1** : burning **2** : flushed **3** : fiery, passionate

encendido² *nm* : ignition

encerado *nm* **1** : waxing, polishing **2** : blackboard

encerar *vt* : to wax, to polish

encerrar {55} *vt* **1** : to lock up, to shut away **2** : to contain, to include **3** : to involve, to entail

encerrona *nf* **1** TRAMPA : trap, setup **2** **prepararle una encerrona a alguien** : to set a trap for someone, to set someone up

encestar *vi* : to make a basket (in basketball)

enchapado *nm* : plating, coating (of metal)

encharcamiento *nm* : flood, flooding

encharcar {72} *vt* : to flood, to swamp — **encharcarse** *vr*

enchilada *nf* : enchilada

enchilar *vt Mex* : to season with chili

enchuecar {72} *vt Chile, Mex fam* : to make crooked, to twist

enchufar *vt* **1** : to plug in **2** : to connect, to fit together

enchufe *nm* **1** : connection **2** : plug, socket

encía *nf* : gum (tissue)

encíclica *nf* : encyclical

enciclopedia *nf* : encyclopedia

enciclopédico, -ca *adj* : encyclopedic

encierro *nm* **1** : confinement **2** : enclosure

encima *adv* **1** : on top, above **2** ADEMÁS : as well, besides **3** ~ **de** : on, on top of, over **4 por encima de** : above, beyond ⟨por encima de la ley : above the law⟩ **5 echarse encima** : to take upon oneself **6 estar encima de** *fam* : to nag, to criticize **7 quitarse de encima** : to get rid of

encina *nf* : evergreen oak

encinta *adj* EMBARAZADA, PREÑADA : pregnant, expecting

enclaustrado, -da *adj* : cloistered, shut away

enclavado, -da *adj* : buried

enclenque *adj* : weak, sickly

encoger {15} *vt* **1** : to shrink, to make smaller **2** : to intimidate — *vi* : to shrink, to contract — **encogerse** *vr* **1** : to shrink **2** : to be intimidated, to cower, to cringe **3 encogerse de hombros** : to shrug (one's shoulders)

encogido, -da *adj* **1** : shriveled, shrunken **2** TÍMIDO : shy, inhibited

encogimiento *nm* **1** : shrinking, shrinkage **2** TIMIDEZ : shyness

encolar *vt* : to paste, to glue

encolerizar {21} *vt* ENFURECER : to enrage, to infuriate — **encolerizarse** *vr*

encomendar {55} *vt* CONFIAR : to entrust, to commend — **encomendarse** *vr*

encomiable *adj* : commendable, praiseworthy

encomiar *vt* ELOGIAR : to praise, to pay tribute to

encomienda *nf* **1** : charge, mission **2** : royal land grant **3** : parcel

encomio *nm* : praise, eulogy

encomioso, -sa *adj* : eulogistic, laudatory

enconar *vt* **1** : to irritate, to anger **2** : to inflame — **enconarse** *vr* **1** : to become heated **2** : to fester

encono *nm* **1** RENCOR : animosity, rancor **2** : inflammation, infection

encontrado, -da *adj* : contrary, opposing

encontrar {19} *vt* **1** HALLAR : to find **2** : to encounter, to meet — **encontrarse** *vr* **1** REUNIRSE : to meet **2** : to clash, to conflict **3** : to be ⟨su abuelo se encuentra mejor : her grandfather is doing better⟩

encorvar *vt* : to bend, to curve — **encorvarse** *vr* : to hunch over, to stoop

encrespar *vt* **1** : to curl, to ruffle, to ripple **2** : to annoy, to irritate — **encresparse** *vr* **1** : to curl one's hair **2** : to become choppy **3** : to get annoyed

encrucijada *nf* : crossroads

encuadernación *nf, pl* **-ciones** : bookbinding

encuadernar *vt* EMPASTAR : to bind (a book)

encuadrar *vt* **1** ENMARCAR : to frame **2** ENCAJAR : to fit, to insert **3** COMPRENDER : to contain, to include

encubierto *pp* → **encubrir**

encubrimiento *nm* : cover-up

encubrir {2} *vt* : to cover up, to conceal

encuentro *nm* **1** : meeting, encounter **2** : conference, congress

encuerado, -da *adj fam* : naked

encuerar *vt fam* : to undress

encuesta *nf* **1** INVESTIGACIÓN, PESQUISA : inquiry, investigation **2** SONDEO : survey

encuestador, -dora *n* : pollster

encuestar *vt* : to poll, to take a survey of

encumbrado, -da *adj* **1** : lofty, high **2** : eminent, distinguished

encumbrar *vt* **1** : to exalt, to elevate **2** : to extol — **encumbrarse** *vr* : to reach the top

encurtir *vt* ESCABECHAR : to pickle

ende *adv* por ~ : therefore, consequently

endeble *adj* : feeble, weak

endeblez *nf* : weakness, frailty

endémico, -ca *adj* : endemic

endemoniado, -da *adj* : fiendish, diabolical

endentecer {53} *vi* : to teethe

enderezar {21} *vt* **1** : to straighten (out) **2** : to stand on end, to put upright

endeudado, -da *adj* : in debt, indebted

endeudamiento *nm* : indebtedness

endeudarse *vr* **1** : to go into debt **2** : to feel obliged

endiabladamente *adv* : extremely, diabolically

endiablado, -da *adj* **1** : devilish, diabolical **2** : complicated, difficult

endibia *or* **endivia** *nf* : endive

endilgar {52} *vt fam* : to spring, to foist ⟨me endilgó la responsabilidad : he saddled me with the responsibility⟩

endocrino, -na *adj* : endocrine

endogamia *nf* : inbreeding

endosar *vt* : to endorse

endoso *nm* : endorsement

endulzante *nm* : sweetener

endulzar {21} *vt* **1** : to sweeten **2** : to soften, to mellow — **endulzarse** *vr*

endurecer {53} *vt* : to harden, to toughen — **endurecerse** *vr*

enebro *nm* : juniper

eneldo *nm* : dill

enema *nm* : enema

enemigo, -ga *adj & n* : enemy

enemistad *nf* : enmity, hostility

enemistar *vt* : to make enemies of — **enemistarse** *vr* ~ **con** : to fall out with

energía *nf* : energy

enérgico, -ca *adj* **1** : energetic, vigorous **2** : forceful, emphatic — **enérgicamente** *adv*

energúmeno, -na *n fam* : lunatic, crazy person

enero *nm* : January

enervar *vt* **1** : to enervate **2** *fam* : to annoy, to get on one's nerves — **enervante** *adj*

enésimo, -ma *adj* : umpteenth, nth

enfadar *vt* **1** : to annoy, to make angry **2** *Mex fam* : to bore — **enfadarse** *vr* : to get angry, to get annoyed

enfado *nm* : anger, annoyance

enfadoso, -sa *adj* : irritating, annoying

enfardar *vt* : to bale

énfasis *nms & pl* : emphasis

enfático, -ca *adj* : emphatic — **enfáticamente** *adv*

enfatizar {21} *vt* DESTACAR, SUBRAYAR : to emphasize

enfermar *vt* : to make sick — *vi* : to fall ill, to get sick — **enfermarse** *vr*

enfermedad *nf* **1** INDISPOSICIÓN : sickness, illness **2** : disease

enfermería *nf* : infirmary

enfermero, -ra *n* : nurse

enfermizo, -za *adj* : sickly

enfermo¹, -ma *adj* : sick, ill

enfermo², -ma *n* **1** : sick person, invalid **2** PACIENTE : patient

enfilar *vt* **1** : to take, to go along ⟨enfiló la carretera de Montevideo : she went up the road to Montevideo⟩ **2** : to line up, to put in a row **3** : to string, to thread **4** : to aim, to direct — *vi* : to make one's way

enflaquecer {53} *vi* : to lose weight, to become thin — *vt* : to emaciate

enfocar {72} *vt* **1** : to focus (on) **2** : to consider, to look at

enfoque *nm* : focus

enfrascamiento *nm* : immersion, absorption

enfrascarse {72} *vr* ~ **en** : to immerse oneself in, to get caught up in

enfrentamiento *nm* : clash, confrontation

enfrentar *vt* : to confront, to face — **enfrentarse** *vr* **1** ~ **con** : to clash with **2** ~ **a** : to face up to

enfrente *adv* **1** DELANTE : in front **2** : opposite

enfriamiento *nm* **1** CATARRO : chill, cold **2** : cooling off, damper

enfriar {85} *vt* **1** : to chill, to cool **2** : to cool down, to dampen — *vi* : to get cold — **enfriarse** *vr* : to get chilled, to catch a cold

enfundar *vt* : to sheathe, to encase

enfurecer {53} *vt* ENCOLERIZAR : to infuriate — **enfurecerse** *vr* : to fly into a rage

enfurecido, -da *adj* : furious, raging

enfurruñarse *vr fam* : to sulk

engalanar *vt* : to decorate, to deck out — **engalanarse** *vr* : to dress up

enganchar *vt* **1** : to hook, to snag **2** : to attach, to hitch up — **engancharse** *vr* **1** : to get snagged, to get hooked **2** : to enlist

enganche *nm* **1** : hook **2** : coupling, hitch **3** *Mex* : down payment

engañar *vt* **1** EMBAUCAR : to trick, to deceive, to mislead **2** : to cheat on, to be unfaithful to — **engañarse** *vr* **1** : to be mistaken **2** : to deceive oneself

engaño *nm* **1** : deception, trick **2** : fake, feint (in sports)

engañoso, -sa *adj* **1** : deceitful **2** : misleading, deceptive

engarrotarse *vr* : to stiffen up, to go numb

engatusamiento *nm* : cajolery

engatusar *vt* : to coax, to cajole

engendrar *vt* **1** : to beget, to father **2** : to give rise to, to engender

engentarse *vr Mex* : to be in a daze

englobar *vt* : to include, to embrace

engomar *vt* : to glue

engordar *vt* : to fatten, to fatten up — *vi* : to gain weight

engorro *nm* : nuisance, bother

engorroso, -sa *adj* : bothersome

engranaje *nm* : gears *pl*, cogs *pl*

engranar *vt* : to mesh, to engage — *vi* : to mesh gears

engrandecer {53} *vt* **1** : to enlarge **2** : to exaggerate **3** : to exalt

engrandecimiento *nm* **1** : enlargement **2** : exaggeration **3** : exaltation

engrane *nm Mex* : cogwheel

engrapadora *nf* : stapler

engrapar *vt* : to staple

engrasar *vt* : to grease, to lubricate

engrase *nm* : greasing, lubrication

engreído, -da *adj* PRESUMIDO, VANIDOSO : vain, conceited, stuck-up

engreimiento *nm* ARROGANCIA : arrogance, conceit

engreír {66} *vt* ENVANECER : to make vain — **engreírse** *vr* : to become conceited

engrosar {19} *vt* : to enlarge, to increase, to swell — *vi* ENGORDAR : to gain weight

engrudo *nm* : paste

engullir {38} *vt* : to gulp down, to gobble up — **engullirse** *vr*

enharinar *vt* : to flour

enhebrar *vt* ENSARTAR : to string, to thread

enhiesto, -ta *adj* **1** : erect, upright **2** : lofty, towering

enhilar *vt* : to thread (a needle, etc.)

enhorabuena *nf* FELICIDADES : congratulations *pl*

enigma *nm* : enigma, mystery

enigmático, -ca *adj* : enigmatic — **enigmáticamente** *adv*

enjabonar *vt* : to soap up, to lather — **enjabonarse** *vr*

enjaezar {21} *vt* : to harness

enjalbegar {52} *vt* : to whitewash

enjambrar *vi* : to swarm

enjambre *nm* **1** : swarm **2** MUCHEDUMBRE : crowd, mob

enjaular *vt* **1** : to cage **2** *fam* : to jail, to lock up

enjuagar {52} *vt* : to rinse — **enjuagarse** *vr* : to rinse out

enjuague *nm* **1** : rinse **2 enjuague bucal** : mouthwash

enjugar {52} *vt* : to wipe away (tears)

enjuiciar *vt* **1** : to indict, to prosecute **2** JUZGAR : to try

enjundioso, -sa *adj* : substantial, weighty

enjuto, -ta *adj* : lean, gaunt

enlace *nm* 1 : bond, link, connection 2 : liaison

enladrillado *nm* : brick paving

enladrillar *vt* : to pave with bricks

enlatar *vt* ENVASAR : to can

enlazar {21} *v* : to join, to link, to fit together

enlistar *vt* : to list — enlistarse *vr* : to enlist

enlodado, -da *adj* BARROSO : muddy

enlodar *vt* 1 : to cover with mud 2 : to stain, to sully — enlodarse *vr*

enlodazar → enlodar

enloquecedor, -dora *adj* : maddening

enloquecer {53} *vt* ALOCAR : to drive crazy — enloquecerse *vr* : to go crazy

enlosado *nm* : flagstone pavement

enlosar *vt* : to pave with flagstone

enlutarse *vr* : to go into mourning

enmaderado *nm* 1 : wood paneling 2 : hardwood floor

enmarañar *vt* 1 : to tangle 2 : to complicate 3 : to confuse, to mix up — enmarañarse *vr*

enmarcar {72} *vt* 1 ENCUADRAR : to frame 2 : to provide the setting for

enmascarar *vt* : to mask, to disguise

enmasillar *vt* : to putty, to caulk

enmendar {55} *vt* 1 : to amend 2 CORREGIR : to emend, to correct 3 COMPENSAR : to compensate for — enmendarse *vr* : to mend one's ways

enmienda *nf* 1 : amendment 2 : correction, emendation

enmohecerse {53} *vr* 1 : to become moldy 2 OXIDARSE : to rust, to become rusty

enmudecer {53} *vt* : to mute, to silence — *vi* : to fall silent

enmugrar *vt* : to soil, to make dirty — enmugrarse *vr* : to get dirty

ennegrecer {53} *vt* : to blacken, to darken — ennegrecerse *vr*

ennoblecer {53} *vt* 1 : to ennoble 2 : to embellish

enojadizo, -za *adj* IRRITABLE : irritable, cranky

enojado, -da *adj* 1 : annoyed 2 : angry, mad

enojar *vt* 1 : to anger 2 : to annoy, to upset — enojarse *vr*

enojo *nm* 1 CÓLERA : anger 2 : annoyance

enojón, -jona *adj, pl* -jones *Chile, Mex fam* : irritable, cranky

enojoso, -sa *adj* FASTIDIOSO, MOLESTOSO : annoying, irritating

enorgullecer {53} *vt* : to make proud — enorgullecerse *vr* : to pride oneself

enorme *adj* INMENSO : enormous, huge — enormemente *adv*

enormidad *nf* 1 : enormity, seriousness 2 : immensity, hugeness

enraizado, -da *adj* : deep-seated, deeply rooted

enraizar {30} *vi* : to take root

enramada *nf* : arbor, bower

enramar *vt* : to cover with branches

enrarecer {53} *vt* : to rarefy — enrarecerse *vr*

enredadera *nf* : climbing plant, vine

enredar *vt* 1 : to tangle up, to entangle 2 : to confuse, to complicate 3 : to involve, to implicate — enredarse *vr*

enredo *nm* 1 EMBROLLO : muddle, confusion 2 MARAÑA : tangle

enredoso, -sa *adj* : complicated, tricky

enrejado *nm* 1 : railing 2 : grating, grille 3 : trellis, lattice

enrevesado, -da *adj* : complicated, involved

enriquecer {53} *vt* : to enrich — enriquecerse *vr* : to get rich

enriquecido, -da *adj* : enriched

enriquecimiento *nm* : enrichment

enrojecer {53} *vt* : to make red, to redden — enrojecerse *vr* : to blush

enrolar *vt* RECLUTAR : to recruit — enrolarse *vr* INSCRIBIRSE : to enlist, to sign up

enrollar *vt* : to roll up, to coil — enrollarse *vr*

enronquecerse {53} *vr* : to become hoarse

enroscar {72} *vt* TORCER : to twist — enroscarse *vr* : to coil, to twine

ensacar {72} *vt* : to bag (up)

ensalada *nf* : salad

ensaladera *nf* : salad bowl

ensalmo *nm* : incantation, spell

ensalzar {21} *vt* 1 : to praise, to extol 2 EXALTAR : to exalt

ensamblaje *nm* : assembly

ensamblar *vt* 1 : to assemble 2 : to join, to fit together

ensanchar *vt* 1 : to widen 2 : to expand, to extend — ensancharse *vr*

ensanche *nm* 1 : widening 2 : expansion, development

ensangrentado, -da *adj* : bloody, bloodstained

ensañarse *vr* : to act cruelly, to be merciless

ensartar *vt* 1 ENHEBRAR : to string, to thread 2 : to skewer, to pierce

ensayar *vi* : to rehearse — *vt* 1 : to try out, to test 2 : to assay

ensayista *nmf* : essayist

ensayo *nm* 1 : essay 2 : trial, test 3 : rehearsal 4 : assay (of metals)

enseguida *adv* INMEDIATAMENTE : right away, immediately, at once

ensenada *nf* : cove, inlet

enseña *nf* 1 INSIGNIA : emblem, insignia 2 : standard, banner

enseñanza *nf* 1 EDUCACIÓN : education 2 : teaching

enseñar *vt* 1 : to teach 2 MOSTRAR : to show, to display — enseñarse *vr* ~ a : to learn to, to get used to

enseres *nmpl* : equipment, furnishings *pl* ⟨enseres domésticos : household goods⟩

ensillar *vt* : to saddle (up)

ensimismado, -da *adj* : absorbed, engrossed

ensimismarse *vr* : to lose oneself in thought

ensoberbecerse {53} *vr* : to become haughty

ensombrecer {53} *vt* : to cast a shadow over, to darken — **ensombrecerse** *vr*

ensoñación *nf, pl* **-ciones** : fantasy

ensopar *vt* 1 : to drench 2 : to dunk, to dip

ensordecedor, -dora *adj* : deafening, thunderous

ensordecer {53} *vt* : to deafen — *vi* : to go deaf

ensuciar *vt* : to soil, to dirty — **ensuciarse** *vr*

ensueño *nm* 1 : daydream, revery 2 FANTASÍA : illusion, fantasy

entablar *vt* 1 : to cover with boards 2 : to initiate, to enter into, to start

entallar *vt* AJUSTAR : to tailor, to fit, to take in — *vi* QUEDAR : to fit

ente *nm* 1 : being, entity 2 : body, organization ⟨ente rector : ruling body⟩ 3 *fam* : eccentric, crackpot

enteco, -ca *adj* : gaunt, frail

entenado, -da *n Mex* : stepchild, stepson *m*, stepdaughter *f*

entender¹ {56} *vt* 1 COMPRENDER : to understand 2 OPINAR : to think, to believe 3 : to mean, to intend 4 DEDUCIR : to infer, to deduce — *vi* 1 : to understand ⟨¡ya entiendo! : now I understand!⟩ 2 ~ **de** : to know about, to be good at 3 ~ **en** : to be in charge of — **entenderse** *vr* 1 : to be understood 2 : to get along well, to understand each other 3 ~ **con** : to deal with

entender² *nm* **a mi entender** : in my opinion

entendible *adj* : understandable

entendido¹, -da *adj* 1 : skilled, expert 2 **tener entendido** : to understand, to be under the impression ⟨teníamos entendido que vendrías : we were under the impression you would come⟩ 3 **darse por entendido** : to go without saying

entendido² *nm* : expert, authority, connoisseur

entendimiento *nm* 1 : intellect, mind 2 : understanding, agreement

enterado, -da *adj* : aware, well-informed ⟨estar enterado de : to be privy to⟩

enteramente *adv* : entirely, completely

enterar *vt* INFORMAR : to inform — **enterarse** *vr* INFORMARSE : to find out, to learn

entereza *nf* 1 INTEGRIDAD : integrity 2 FORTALEZA : fortitude 3 FIRMEZA : resolve

enternecedor, -dora *adj* CONMOVEDOR : touching, moving

enternecer {53} *vt* CONMOVER : to move, to touch

entero¹, -ra *adj* 1 : entire, whole 2 : complete, absolute 3 : intact — **enteramente** *adv*

entero² *nm* 1 : integer, whole number 2 : point (in finance)

enterramiento *nm* : burial

enterrar {55} *vt* : to bury

entibiar *vt* : to cool (down) — **entibiarse** *vr* : to become lukewarm

entidad *nf* 1 ENTE : entity 2 : body, organization 3 : firm, company 4 : importance, significance

entierro *nm* 1 : burial 2 : funeral

entintar *vt* : to ink

entoldado *nm* : awning

entomología *nf* : entomology

entomólogo, -ga *n* : entomologist

entonación *nf, pl* **-ciones** : intonation

entonar *vi* : to be in tune — *vt* 1 : to intone 2 : to tone up

entonces *adv* 1 : then 2 **desde ~** : since then 3 **en aquel entonces** : in those days

entornado, -da *adj* ENTREABIERTO : half-closed, ajar

entornar *vt* ENTREABRIR : to leave ajar

entorno *nm* : surroundings *pl*, environment

entorpecer {53} *vt* 1 : to hinder, to obstruct 2 : to dull — **entorpecerse** *vr* : to dull the senses

entrada *nf* 1 : entrance, entry 2 : ticket, admission 3 : beginning, onset 4 : entrée 5 : cue (in music) 6 **entradas** *nfpl* : income ⟨entradas y salidas : income and expenditures⟩ 7 **tener entradas** : to have a receding hairline

entrado, -da *adj* **entrado en años** : elderly

entramado *nm* : framework

entrampar *vt* 1 ATRAPAR : to entrap, to ensnare 2 ENGAÑAR : to deceive, to trick

entrante *adj* 1 : next, upcoming ⟨el año entrante : next year⟩ 2 : incoming, new ⟨el presidente entrante : the president elect⟩

entraña *nf* 1 MEOLLO : core, heart, crux 2 **entrañas** *nfpl* VÍSCERAS : entrails

entrañable *adj* : close, intimate

entrañar *vt* : to entail, to involve

entrar *vi* 1 : to enter, to go in, to come in 2 : to begin — *vt* 1 : to bring in, to introduce 2 : to access

entre *prep* 1 : between 2 : among

entreabierto¹ *pp* → **entreabrir**

entreabierto², -ta *adj* ENTORNADO : half-open, ajar

entreabrir {2} *vt* ENTORNAR : to leave ajar

entreacto *nm* : intermission, interval

entrecano, -na *adj* : grayish, graying

entrecejo *nm* **fruncir el entrecejo** : to knit one's brows

entrecomillar *vt* : to place in quotation marks

entrecortado, -da *adj* 1 : labored, difficult ⟨respiración entrecortada : shortness of breath⟩ 2 : faltering, hesitant ⟨con la voz entrecortada : with a catch in his voice⟩

entrecruzar {21} *vt* ENTRELAZAR : to interweave, to intertwine — **entrecruzarse** *vr*

entredicho *nm* **1** DUDA : doubt, question **2** : prohibition

entrega *nf* **1** : delivery **2** : handing over, surrender **3** : installment ⟨entrega inicial : down payment⟩

entregar {52} *vt* **1** : to deliver **2** DAR : to give, to present **3** : to hand in, to hand over — **entregarse** *vr* **1** : to surrender, to give in **2** : to devote oneself

entrelazar {21} *vt* ENTRECRUZAR : to interweave, to intertwine

entremedias *adv* **1** : in between, halfway **2** : in the meantime

entremés *nm, pl* **-meses 1** APERITIVO : appetizer, hors d'oeuvre **2** : interlude, short play

entremeterse → **entrometerse**

entremetido *nm* → **entrometido**

entremezclar *vt* : to intermingle

entrenador, -dora *n* : trainer, coach

entrenamiento *nm* : training, drill, practice

entrenar *vt* : to train, to drill, to practice — **entrenarse** *vr* : to train, to spar (in boxing)

entreoír {50} *vt* : to hear indistinctly

entrepierna *nf* **1** : inner thigh **2** : crotch **3** : inseam

entrepiso *nm* ENTRESUELO : mezzanine

entresacar {72} *vt* **1** SELECCIONAR : to pick out, to select **2** : to thin out

entresuelo *nm* ENTREPISO : mezzanine

entretanto¹ *adv* : meanwhile

entretanto² *nm* **en el entretanto** : in the meantime

entretejer *vt* : to interweave

entretela *nf* : facing (of a garment)

entretener {80} *vt* **1** DIVERTIR : to entertain, to amuse **2** DISTRAER : to distract **3** DEMORAR : to delay, to hold up — **entretenerse** *vr* **1** : to amuse oneself **2** : to dally

entretenido, -da *adj* DIVERTIDO : entertaining, amusing

entretenimiento *nm* **1** : entertainment, pastime **2** DIVERSIÓN : fun, amusement

entrever {88} *vt* **1** : to catch a glimpse of **2** : to make out, to see indistinctly

entreverar *vt* : to mix, to intermingle

entrevero *nm* : confusion, disorder

entrevista *nf* : interview

entrevistador, -dora *n* : interviewer

entrevistar *vt* : to interview — **entrevistarse** *vr* REUNIRSE ~ **con** : to meet with

entristecer {53} *vt* : to sadden

entrometerse *vr* : to interfere, to meddle

entrometido, -da *n* : meddler, busybody

entroncar {72} *vt* RELACIONAR : to establish a relationship between, to connect — *vi* **1** : to be related **2** : to link up, to be connected

entronque *nm* **1** : kinship **2** VÍNCULO : link, connection

entuerto *nm* : wrong, injustice

entumecer {53} *vt* : to make numb, to be numb — **entumecerse** *vr* : to go numb, to fall asleep

entumecido, -da *adj* **1** : numb **2** : stiff (of muscles, joints, etc.)

entumecimiento *nm* : numbness

enturbiar *vt* **1** : to cloud **2** : to confuse — **enturbiarse** *vr*

entusiasmar *vt* : to excite, to fill with enthusiasm — **entusiasmarse** *vr* : to get excited

entusiasmo *nm* : enthusiasm

entusiasta¹ *adj* : enthusiastic

entusiasta² *nmf* AFICIONADO : enthusiast

enumerar *vt* : to enumerate — **enumeración** *nf*

enunciación *nf, pl* **-ciones** : enunciation, statement

enunciar *vt* : to enunciate, to state

envainar *vt* : to sheathe

envalentonar *vt* : to make bold, to encourage — **envalentonarse** *vr*

envanecer {53} *vt* ENGREÍR : to make vain — **envanecerse** *vr*

envasar *vt* **1** EMBOTELLAR : to bottle **2** ENLATAR : to can **3** : to pack in a container

envase *nm* **1** : packaging, packing **2** : container **3** LATA : can **4** : empty bottle

envejecer {53} *vt* : to age, to make look old — *vi* : to age, to grow old

envejecido, -da *adj* : aged, old-looking

envejecimiento *nm* : aging

envenenamiento *nm* : poisoning

envenenar *vt* **1** : to poison **2** : to embitter

envergadura *nf* **1** : span, breadth, spread **2** : importance, scope

envés *nm, pl* **enveses** : reverse, opposite side

enviado, -da *n* : envoy, correspondent

enviar {85} *vt* **1** : to send **2** : to ship

envidia *nf* : envy, jealousy

envidiar *vt* : to envy — **envidiable** *adj*

envidioso, -sa *adj* : envious, jealous

envilecer {53} *vt* : to degrade, to debase

envilecimiento *nm* : degradation, debasement

envío *nm* **1** : shipment **2** : remittance

enviudar *vi* : to be widowed, to become a widower

envoltorio *nm* **1** : bundle, package **2** : wrapping, wrapper

envoltura *nf* : wrapper, wrapping

envolver {89} *vt* **1** : to wrap **2** : to envelop, to surround **3** : to entangle, to involve — **envolverse** *vr* **1** : to become involved **2** : to wrap oneself (up)

envuelto *pp* → **envolver**

enyerbar *vt* *Mex* : to bewitch

enyesar *vt* **1** : to plaster **2** ESCAYOLAR : to put in a plaster cast

enzima *nf* : enzyme

éon *nm, pl* **eones** : aeon

eperlano *nm* : smelt (fish)

épico, -ca *adj* : epic
epicúreo[1], -rea *adj* : epicurean
epicúreo[2], -rea *n* : epicure
epidemia *nf* : epidemic
epidémico, -ca *adj* : epidemic
epidermis *nf* : epidermis
epifanía *nf* : feast of the Epiphany (January 6th)
epigrama *nm* : epigram
epilepsia *nf* : epilepsy
epiléptico, -ca *adj & n* : epileptic
epílogo *nm* : epilogue
episcopal *adj* : episcopal
episcopaliano, -na *adj & n* : Episcopalian
episódico, -ca *adj* : episodic
episodio *nm* : episode
epístola *nf* : epistle
epitafio *nm* : epitaph
epíteto *nm* : epithet, name
epítome *nm* : summary, abstract
época *nf* 1 EDAD, ERA, PERÍODO : epoch, age, period 2 : time of year, season 3 de ~ : vintage, antique
epopeya *nf* : epic poem
equidad *nf* JUSTICIA : equity, justice, fairness
equilátero, -ra *adj* : equilateral
equilibrado, -da *adj* : well-balanced
equilibrar *vt* : to balance — equilibrarse *vr*
equilibrio *nm* 1 : balance, equilibrium ⟨perder el equilibrio : to lose one's balance⟩ ⟨equilibrio político : balance of power⟩ 2 : poise, aplomb
equilibrista *nmf* ACRÓBATA, FUNÁMBULO : acrobat, tightrope walker
equino, -na *adj* : equine
equinoccio *nm* : equinox
equipaje *nm* BAGAJE : baggage, luggage
equipamiento *nm* : equipping, equipment
equipar *vt* : to equip — equiparse *vr*
equiparable *adj* : comparable
equiparar *vt* 1 IGUALAR : to put on a same level, to make equal 2 COMPARAR : to compare
equipo *nm* 1 : team, crew 2 : gear, equipment
equitación *nf, pl* -ciones : horseback riding, horsemanship
equitativo, -va *adj* JUSTO : equitable, fair, just — equitativamente *adv*
equivalencia *nf* : equivalence
equivalente *adj & nm* : equivalent
equivaler {84} *vi* : to be equivalent
equivocación *nf, pl* -ciones ERROR : error, mistake
equivocado, -da *adj* : mistaken, wrong — equivocadamente *adv*
equivocar {72} *vt* : to mistake, to confuse — equivocarse *vr* : to make a mistake, to be wrong
equívoco[1], -ca *adj* AMBIGUO : ambiguous, equivocal
equívoco[2] *nm* : misunderstanding
era[1], etc. → ser
era[2] *nf* EDAD, ÉPOCA : era, age

erario *nm* : public treasury
erección *nf, pl* -ciones : erection, raising
eremita *nmf* ERMITAÑO : hermit
ergonomía *nf* : ergonomics
erguido, -da *adj* : erect, upright
erguir {31} *vt* : to raise, to lift up — erguirse *vr* : to straighten up
erial *nm* : uncultivated land
erigir {35} *vt* : to build, to erect — erigirse *vr* ~ en : to set oneself up as
erizado, -da *adj* : bristly
erizarse {21} *vr* : to bristle, to stand on end
erizo *nm* 1 : hedgehog 2 erizo de mar : sea urchin
ermitaño[1], -ña *n* EREMITA : hermit, recluse
ermitaño[2] *nm* : hermit crab
erogación *nf, pl* -ciones : expenditure
erogar {52} *vt* 1 : to pay out 2 : to distribute
erosión *nf, pl* -siones : erosion
erosionar *vt* : to erode
erótico, -ca *adj* : erotic
erotismo *nm* : eroticism
errabundo, -da *adj* ERRANTE, VAGABUNDO : wandering
erradicar {72} *vt* : to eradicate — erradicación *nf*
errado, -da *adj* : wrong, mistaken
errante *adj* ERRABUNDO, VAGABUNDO : errant, wandering
errar {32} *vt* FALLAR : to miss — *vi* 1 DESACERTAR : to be wrong, to be mistaken 2 VAGAR : to wander
errata *nf* : misprint, error
errático, -ca *adj* : erratic — erráticamente *adv*
erróneo, -nea *adj* EQUIVOCADO : erroneous, wrong — erróneamente *adv*
error *nm* EQUIVOCACIÓN : error, mistake
eructar *vi* : to belch, to burp
eructo *nm* : belch, burp
erudición *nf, pl* -ciones : erudition, learning
erudito[1], -ta *adj* LETRADO : erudite, learned
erudito[2], -ta *n* : scholar
erupción *nf, pl* -ciones 1 : eruption 2 SARPULLIDO : rash
eruptivo, -va *adj* : eruptive
es → ser
esbelto, -ta *adj* DELGADO : slender, slim
esbirro *nm* : henchman
esbozar {21} *vt* BOSQUEJAR : to sketch, to outline
esbozo *nm* 1 : sketch 2 : rough draft
escabechar *vt* 1 ENCURTIR : to pickle 2 *fam* : to kill, to rub out
escabeche *nm* : brine (for pickling)
escabechina *nf* MASACRE : massacre, bloodbath
escabel *nm* : footstool
escabroso, -sa *adj* 1 : rugged, rough 2 : difficult, tough 3 : risqué
escabullirse {38} *vr* : to slip away, to escape

escala *nf* 1 : scale 2 ESCALERA : ladder 3 : stopover

escalada *nf* : ascent, climb

escalador, -dora *n* ALPINISTA : mountain climber

escalafón *nm, pl* **-fones** 1 : list of personnel 2 : salary scale, rank

escalar *vt* : to climb, to scale — *vi* 1 : to go climbing 2 : to escalate

escaldar *vt* : to scald

escalera *nf* 1 : ladder ⟨escalera de tijera : stepladder⟩ 2 : stairs *pl*, staircase 3 **escalera mecánica** : escalator

escalfador *nm* : chafing dish

escalfar *vt* : to poach (eggs)

escalinata *nf* : flight of stairs

escalofriante *adj* : horrifying, bloodcurdling

escalofrío *nm* : shiver, chill, shudder

escalón *nm, pl* **-lones** 1 : echelon 2 : step, rung

escalonado, -da *adj* GRADUAL : gradual, staggered

escalonar *vt* 1 : to terrace 2 : to stagger, to alternate

escalpelo *nm* BISTURÍ : scalpel

escama *nf* 1 : scale (of fish or reptiles) 2 : flake (of skin)

escamar *vt* 1 : to scale (fish) 2 : to make suspicious

escamocha *nf Mex* : fruit salad

escamoso, -sa *adj* : scaly

escamotear *vt* 1 : to palm, to conceal 2 *fam* : to lift, to swipe 3 : to hide, to cover up

escandalizar {21} *vt* : to shock, to scandalize — *vi* : to make a fuss — **escandalizarse** *vr* : to be shocked

escándalo *nm* 1 : scandal 2 : scene, commotion

escandaloso, -sa *adj* 1 : shocking, scandalous 2 RUIDOSO : noisy, rowdy 3 : flagrant, outrageous — **escandalosamente** *adv*

escandinavo, -va *adj & n* : Scandinavian

escandir *vt* : to scan (poetry)

escanear *vt* : to scan

escáner *nm* : scanner, scan

escaño *nm* 1 : seat (in a legislative body) 2 BANCO : bench

escapada *nf* HUIDA : flight, escape

escapar *vi* HUIR : to escape, to flee, to run away — **escaparse** *vr* : to escape notice, to leak out

escaparate *nm* 1 : shop window 2 : showcase

escapatoria *nf* 1 : loophole, excuse, pretext ⟨no tener escapatoria : to have no way out⟩ 2 ESCAPADA : escape, flight

escape *nm* 1 FUGA : escape 2 : exhaust (from a vehicle)

escapismo *nm* : escapism

escápula *nf* OMÓPLATO : scapula, shoulder blade

escapulario *nm* : scapular

escarabajo *nm* : beetle

escaramuza *nf* 1 : skirmish 2 : scrimmage

escaramuzar {21} *vi* : to skirmish

escarapela *nf* : rosette (ornament)

escarbar *vt* 1 : to dig, to scratch up 2 : to poke, to pick 3 ~ **en** : to investigate, to pry into

escarcha *nf* 1 : frost 2 *Mex, PRi* : glitter

escarchar *vt* 1 : to frost (a cake) 2 : to candy (fruit)

escardar *vt* 1 : to weed, to hoe 2 : to weed out

escariar *vt* : to ream

escarlata *adj & nf* : scarlet

escarlatina *nf* : scarlet fever

escarmentar {55} *vt* : to punish, to teach a lesson to — *vi* : to learn one's lesson

escarmiento *nm* 1 : lesson, warning 2 CASTIGO : punishment

escarnecer {53} *vt* RIDICULIZAR : to ridicule, to mock

escarnio *nm* : ridicule, mockery

escarola *nf* : escarole

escarpa *nf* : escarpment, steep slope

escarpado, -da *adj* : steep, sheer

escarpia *nf* : hook, spike

escasamente *adv* : scarcely, barely

escasear *vi* : to be scarce, to run short

escasez *nf, pl* **-seces** : shortage, scarcity

escaso, -sa *adj* 1 : scarce, scant 2 ~ **de** : short of

escatimar *vt* : to skimp on, to be sparing with ⟨no escatimar esfuerzos : to spare no effort⟩

escayola *nf* 1 : plaster (for casts) 2 : plaster cast

escayolar *vt* : to put in a plaster cast

escena *nf* 1 : scene 2 : stage

escenario *nm* 1 ESCENA : stage 2 : setting, scene ⟨el escenario del crimen : the scene of the crime⟩

escénico, -ca *adj* 1 : scenic 2 : stage

escenificar {72} *vt* : to stage, to dramatize

escepticismo *nm* : skepticism

escéptico[1]**, -ca** *adj* : skeptical

escéptico[2]**, -ca** *n* : skeptic

escindirse *vr* 1 : to split 2 : to break away

escisión *nf, pl* **-siones** 1 : split, division 2 : excision

esclarecer {53} *vt* 1 ELUCIDAR : to elucidate, to clarify 2 ILUMINAR : to illuminate, to light up

esclarecimiento *nm* ELUCIDACIÓN : elucidation, clarification

esclavitud *nf* : slavery

esclavización *nf, pl* **-ciones** : enslavement

esclavizar {21} *vt* : to enslave

esclavo, -va *n* : slave

esclerosis *nf* **esclerosis múltiple** : multiple sclerosis

esclusa *nf* : floodgate, lock (of a canal)

escoba *nf* : broom

escobilla *nf* : small broom, brush, whisk broom

escobillón *nm, pl* **-llones** : swab

escocer {14} *vi* ARDER : to smart, to sting — **escocerse** *vr* : to be sore

escocés[1], **-cesa** *adj, mpl* **-ceses** 1 : Scottish 2 : tartan, plaid

escocés[2], **-cesa** *n, mpl* **-ceses** : Scottish person, Scot

escocés[3] *nm* 1 : Scots (language) 2 *pl* **-ceses** : Scotch (whiskey)

escofina *nf* : file, rasp

escoger {15} *vt* ELEGIR, SELECCIONAR : to choose, to select

escogido, -da *adj* : choice, select

escolar[1] *adj* : school

escolar[2] *nmf* : student, pupil

escolaridad *nf* : schooling ⟨escolaridad obligatoria : compulsory education⟩

escolarización *nf, pl* **-ciones** : education, schooling

escollo *nm* 1 : reef 2 OBSTÁCULO : obstacle

escolta *nmf* : escort

escoltar *vt* : to escort, to accompany

escombro *nm* 1 : debris, rubbish 2 **escombros** *nmpl* : ruins, rubble

esconder *vt* OCULTAR : to hide, to conceal

escondidas *nfpl* 1 : hide-and-seek 2 **a ∼** : secretly, in secret

escondimiento *nm* : concealment

escondite *nm* 1 ENCONDRIJO : hiding place 2 ESCONDIDAS : hide-and-seek

escondrijo *nm* ESCONDITE : hiding place

escopeta *nf* : shotgun

escoplear *vt* : to chisel (out)

escoplo *nm* : chisel

escora *nf* : list, heeling

escorar *vi* : to list, to heel (of a boat)

escorbuto *nm* : scurvy

escoria *nf* 1 : slag, dross 2 HEZ : dregs *pl*, scum ⟨la escoria de la sociedad : the dregs of society⟩

Escorpio *or* **Escorpión** *nmf* : Scorpio

escorpión *nm, pl* **-piones** ALACRÁN : scorpion

escote *nm* 1 : low neckline 2 **pagar a escote** : to go dutch

escotilla *nf* : hatch, hatchway

escotillón *nf, pl* **-llones** : trapdoor

escozor *nm* : smarting, stinging

escriba *nm* : scribe

escribano, -na *n* 1 : court clerk 2 NOTARIO : notary public

escribir {33} *v* 1 : to write 2 : to spell — **escribirse** *vr* CARTEARSE : to write to one another, to correspond

escrito[1] *pp* → **escribir**

escrito[2], **-ta** *adj* : written

escrito[3] *nm* 1 : written document 2 **escritos** *nmpl* : writings, works

escritor, -tora *n* : writer

escritorio *nm* : desk

escritorzuelo, -la *n* : hack (writer)

escritura *nf* 1 : writing, handwriting 2 : deed 3 **las Escrituras** : the Scriptures

escroto *nm* : scrotum

escrúpulo *nm* : scruple

escrupuloso, -sa *adj* 1 : scrupulous 2 METICULOSO : exact, meticulous — **escrupulosamente** *adv*

escrutador, -dora *adj* : penetrating, searching

escrutar *vt* ESCUDRIÑAR : to scrutinize, to examine closely

escrutinio *nm* : scrutiny

escuadra *nf* 1 : square (instrument) 2 : fleet, squadron

escuadrilla *nf* : squadron, formation, flight

escuadrón *nm, pl* **-drones** : squadron

escuálido, -da *adj* 1 : skinny, scrawny 2 INMUNDO : filthy, squalid

escuchar *vt* 1 : to listen to 2 : to hear — *vi* : to listen — **escucharse** *vr*

escudar *vt* : to shield — **escudarse** *vr* **∼ en** : to hide behind

escudero *nm* : squire

escudo *nm* 1 : shield 2 **escudo de armas** : coat of arms

escudriñar *vt* 1 ESCRUTAR : to scrutinize 2 : to inquire into, to investigate

escuela *nf* : school

escueto, -ta *adj* 1 : plain, simple 2 : succinct, concise — **escuetamente** *adv*

escuincle, -cla *n Mex fam* : child, kid

esculcar {72} *vt* : to search

esculpir *vt* 1 : to sculpt 2 : to carve, to engrave — *vi* : to sculpt

escultor, -tora *n* : sculptor

escultórico, -ca *adj* : sculptural

escultura *nf* : sculpture

escultural *adj* : statuesque

escupidera *nf* : spittoon, cuspidor

escupir *v* : to spit

escupitajo *nm* : spit

escurridizo, -za *adj* : slippery, elusive

escurridor *nm* 1 : dish rack 2 : colander

escurrir *vt* 1 : to wring out 2 : to drain — *vi* 1 : to drain 2 : to drip, to drip-dry — **escurrirse** *vr* : to slip away

ese, esa *adj, mpl* **esos** : that, those

ése, ésa *pron, mpl* **ésos** : that one, those ones *pl*

esencia *nf* : essence

esencial *adj* : essential — **esencialmente** *adv*

esfera *nf* 1 : sphere 2 : face, dial (of a watch)

esférico[1], **-ca** *adj* : spherical

esférico[2] *nm* : ball (in sports)

esfinge *nf* : sphinx

esforzado, -da *adj* 1 : energetic, vigorous 2 VALIENTE : courageous, brave

esforzar {36} *vt* : to strain — **esforzarse** *vr* : to make an effort

esfuerzo *nm* 1 : effort 2 ÁNIMO, VIGOR : spirit, vigor 3 **sin ∼** : effortlessly

esfumar *vt* : to tone down, to soften — **esfumarse** *vr* 1 : to fade away, to vanish 2 *fam* : to take off, to leave

esgrima *nf* : fencing (sport)

esgrimidor, -dora *n* : fencer

esgrimir *vt* 1 : to brandish, to wield 2 : to use, to resort to — *vi* : to fence

esguince *nm* : sprain, strain (of a muscle)
eslabón *nm, pl* **-bones** : link
eslabonar *vt* : to link, to connect, to join
eslavo¹, -va *adj* : Slavic
eslavo², -va *n* : Slav
eslogan *nm, pl* **-lóganes** : slogan
eslovaco, -ca *adj & n* : Slovakian, Slovak
esloveno, -na *adj & nm* : Slovene, Slovenian
esmaltar *vt* : to enamel
esmalte *nm* 1 : enamel 2 **esmalte de uñas** : nail polish
esmerado, -da *adj* : careful, painstaking
esmeralda *nf* : emerald
esmerarse *vr* : to take great pains, to do one's utmost
esmeril *nm* : emery
esmero *nm* : meticulousness, great care
esmoquin *nm, pl* **-quins** : tuxedo
esnob¹ *adj, pl* **esnobs** : snobbish
esnob² *nmf, pl* **esnobs** : snob
esnobismo *nm* : snobbery, snobbishness
eso *pron (neuter)* 1 : that ⟨eso no me gusta : I don't like that⟩ 2 **¡eso es!** : that's it!, that's right! 3 **a eso de** : around ⟨a eso de las tres : around three o'clock⟩ 4 **en ~** : at that point, just then
esófago *nm* : esophagus
esos → ese
ésos → ése
esotérico, -ca *adj* : esoteric — **esotéricamente** *adv*
espabilado, -da *adj* : bright, smart
espabilarse *vr* 1 : to awaken 2 : to get a move on 3 : to get smart, to wise up
espacial *adj* 1 : space 2 : spatial
espaciar *vt* DISTANCIAR : to space out, to spread out
espacio *nm* 1 : space, room 2 : period, length (of time) 3 **espacio exterior** : outer space
espacioso, -sa *adj* : spacious, roomy
espada¹ *nf* 1 : sword 2 **espadas** *nfpl* : spades (in playing cards)
espada² *nf* MATADOR, TORERO : bullfighter, matador
espadaña *nf* 1 : belfry 2 : cattail
espadilla *nf* : scull, oar
espagueti *nm or* **espaguetis** *nmpl* : spaghetti
espalda *nf* 1 : back 2 **espaldas** *nfpl* : shoulders, back 3 **por la espalda** : from behind
espaldarazo *nm* 1 : recognition, support 2 : slap on the back
espaldera *nf* : trellis
espantajo *nm* : scarecrow
espantapájaros *nms & pl* : scarecrow
espantar *vt* ASUSTAR : to scare, to frighten — **espantarse** *vr*
espanto *nm* : fright, fear, horror
espantoso, -sa *adj* 1 : frightening, terrifying 2 : frightful, dreadful

español¹, -ñola *adj* : Spanish
español², -ñola *n* : Spaniard
español³ *nm* CASTELLANO : Spanish (language)
esparadrapo *nm* : adhesive bandage, Band-Aid™
esparcimiento *nm* 1 DIVERSIÓN, RECREO : entertainment, recreation 2 DESCANSO : relaxation 3 DISEMINACIÓN : dissemination, spreading
esparcir {83} *vt* DISPERSAR : to scatter, to spread — **esparcirse** *vr* 1 : to spread out 2 DESCANSARSE : to take it easy 3 DIVERTIRSE : to amuse oneself
espárrago *nm* : asparagus
espartano, -na *adj* : severe, austere
espasmo *nm* : spasm
espasmódico, -ca *adj* : spasmodic
espástico, -ca *adj* : spastic
espátula *nf* : spatula
especia *nf* : spice
especial *adj & nm* : special
especialidad *nf* : specialty
especialista *nmf* : specialist, expert
especialización *nf, pl* **-ciones** : specialization
especializarse {21} *vr* : to specialize
especialmente *adv* : especially, particularly
especie *nf* 1 : species 2 CLASE, TIPO : type, kind, sort
especificación *nf, pl* **-ciones** : specification
especificar {72} *vt* : to specify
específico, -ca *adj* : specific — **específicamente** *adv*
espécimen *nm, pl* **especímenes** : specimen
especioso, -sa *adj* : specious
espectacular *adj* : spectacular — **espectacularmente** *adv*
espectáculo *nm* 1 : spectacle, sight 2 : show, performance
espectador, -dora *n* : spectator, onlooker
espectro *nm* 1 : ghost, specter 2 : spectrum
especulación *nf, pl* **-ciones** : speculation
especulador, -dora *n* : speculator
especular *vi* : to speculate
especulativo, -va *adj* : speculative
espejismo *nm* 1 : mirage 2 : illusion
espejo *nm* : mirror
espejuelos *nmpl* ANTEOJOS : spectacles, glasses
espeluznante *adj* : hair-raising, terrifying
espera *nf* : wait
esperado, -da *adj* : anticipated
esperanza *nf* : hope, expectation
esperanzado, -da *adj* : hopeful
esperanzador, -dora *adj* : encouraging, promising
esperanzar {21} *vt* : to give hope to
esperar *vt* 1 AGUARDAR : to wait for, to await 2 : to expect 3 : to hope ⟨espero poder trabajar : I hope to be able to work⟩ ⟨espero que sí : I hope so⟩ — *vi*

: to wait — **esperarse** *vr* **1** : to expect, to be hoped ⟨como podría esperarse : as would be expected⟩ **2** : to hold on, to hang on ⟨espérate un momento : hold on a minute⟩

esperma *nmf* : sperm

esperpéntico, -ca *adj* GROTESCO : grotesque

esperpento *nm* *fam* MAMARRACHO : sight, fright ⟨voy hecha un esperpento : I really look a sight⟩

espesante *nm* : thickener

espesar *vt* : to thicken — **espesarse** *vr*

espeso, -sa *adj* : thick, heavy, dense

espesor *nm* : thickness, density

espesura *nf* **1** : thickness **2** : thicket

espetar *vt* **1** : to blurt out **2** : to skewer

espía *nmf* : spy

espiar {85} *vt* : to spy on, to observe — *vi* : to spy

espiga *nf* **1** : ear (of wheat) **2** : spike (of flowers)

espigado, -da *adj* : willowy, slender

espigar {52} *vt* : to glean, to gather — **espigarse** *vr* : to grow quickly, to shoot up

espigón *nm*, *pl* **-gones** : breakwater

espina *nf* **1** : thorn **2** : spine ⟨espina dorsal : spinal column⟩ **3** : fish bone

espinaca *nf* **1** : spinach (plant) **2 espinacas** *nfpl* : spinach (food)

espinal *adj* : spinal

espinazo *nm* : backbone

espineta *nf* : spinet

espinilla *nf* **1** BARRO, GRANO : pimple **2** : shin

espino *nm* : hawthorn

espinoso, -sa *adj* **1** : thorny, prickly **2** : bony (of fish) **3** : knotty, difficult

espionaje *nm* : espionage

espiración *nf*, *pl* **-ciones** : exhalation

espiral *adj* & *nf* : spiral

espirar *vt* EXHALAR : to breathe out, to give off — *vi* : to exhale

espiritismo *nm* : spiritualism

espiritista *nmf* : spiritualist

espíritu *nm* **1** : spirit **2** ÁNIMO : state of mind, spirits *pl* **3 el Espíritu Santo** : the Holy Ghost

espiritual *adj* : spiritual — **espiritualmente** *adv*

espiritualidad *nf* : spirituality

espita *nf* : spigot, tap

esplendidez *nf*, *pl* **-deces** ESPLENDOR : magnificence, splendor

espléndido, -da *adj* **1** : splendid, magnificent **2** : generous, lavish — **espléndidamente** *adv*

esplendor *nm* ESPLENDIDEZ : splendor

esplendoroso, -sa *adj* MAGNÍFICO : magnificent, grand

espliego *nm* LAVANDA : lavender

espolear *vt* : to spur on

espoleta *nf* **1** DETONADOR : detonator, fuse **2** : wishbone

espolón *nm*, *pl* **-lones** : spur (of poultry), fetlock (of a horse)

espolvorear *vt* : to sprinkle, to dust

esponja *nf* **1** : sponge **2 tirar la esponja** : to throw in the towel

esponjado, -da *adj* : spongy

esponjoso, -sa *adj* **1** : spongy **2** : soft, fluffy

esponsales *nmpl* : betrothal, engagement

espontaneidad *nf* : spontaneity

espontáneo, -nea *adj* : spontaneous — **espontáneamente** *adv*

espora *nf* : spore

esporádico, -ca *adj* : sporadic — **esporádicamente** *adv*

esposar *vt* : to handcuff

esposas *nfpl* : handcuffs

esposo, -sa *n* : spouse, wife *f*, husband *m*

esprint *nm* : sprint

esprintar *vi* : to sprint

esprínter *nmf* : sprinter

espuela *nf* : spur

espuerta *nf* : two-handled basket

espulgar {52} *vt* **1** : to delouse **2** : to scrutinize

espuma *nf* **1** : foam **2** : lather **3** : froth, head (on beer)

espumar *vi* : to foam, to froth — *vt* : to skim off

espumoso, -sa *adj* : foamy, frothy

espurio, -ria *adj* : spurious

esputar *v* : to expectorate, to spit

esputo *nm* : spit, sputum

esqueje *nm* : cutting (from a plant)

esquela *nf* **1** : note **2** : notice, announcement

esquelético, -ca *adj* : emaciated, skeletal

esqueleto *nm* **1** : skeleton **2** ARMAZÓN : framework

esquema *nf* BOSQUEJO : outline, sketch, plan

esquemático, -ca *adj* : schematic

esquí *nm* **1** : ski **2 esquí acuático** : water ski, waterskiing

esquiador, -dora *n* : skier

esquiar {85} *vi* : to ski

esquife *nm* : skiff

esquila *nf* **1** CENCERRO : cowbell **2** : shearing

esquilar *vt* TRASQUILAR : to shear

esquimal *adj* & *nmf* : Eskimo

esquina *nf* : corner

esquinazo *nm* **1** : corner **2 dar esquinazo a** *fam* : to stand up, to give the slip to

esquirla *nf* : splinter (of bone, glass, etc.)

esquirol *nm* ROMPEHUELGAS : strikebreaker, scab

esquisto *nm* : shale

esquivar *vt* **1** EVADIR : to dodge, to evade **2** EVITAR : to avoid

esquivez *nf*, *pl* **-veces 1** : aloofness **2** TIMIDEZ : shyness

esquivo, -va *adj* **1** HURAÑO : aloof, unsociable **2** : shy **3** : elusive, evasive

esquizofrenia *nf* : schizophrenia

esquizofrénico, -ca *adj* & *n* : schizophrenic

esta *adj* → **este**[1]
ésta → **éste**
estabilidad *nf* : stability
estabilización *nf, pl* **-ciones** : stabilization
estabilizador *nm* : stabilizer
estabilizar {21} *vt* : to stabilize — **estabilizarse** *vr*
estable *adj* : stable, steady
establecer {53} *vt* FUNDAR, INSTITUIR : to establish, to found, to set up — **establecerse** *vr* INSTALARSE : to settle, to establish oneself
establecimiento *nm* 1 : establishing 2 : establishment, institution, office
establo *nm* : stable
estaca *nf* : stake, picket, post
estacada *nf* 1 : picket fence 2 : stockade
estacar {72} *vt* 1 : to stake out 2 : to fasten down with stakes — **estacarse** *vr* : to remain rigid
estación *nf, pl* **-ciones** 1 : station ⟨estación de servicio : service station, gas station⟩ 2 : season
estacional *adj* : seasonal
estacionamiento *nm* 1 : parking 2 : parking lot
estacionar *vt* 1 : to place, to station 2 : to park — **estacionarse** *vr* 1 : to park 2 : to remain stationary
estacionario, -ria *adj* 1 : stationary 2 : stable
estada *nf* : stay
estadía *nf* ESTANCIA : stay, sojourn
estadio *nm* 1 : stadium 2 : phase, stage
estadista *nmf* : statesman
estadística *nf* 1 : statistic, figure 2 : statistics
estadístico[1], **-ca** *adj* : statistical — **estadísticamente** *adv*
estadístico[2], **-ca** *n* : statistician
estado *nm* 1 : state 2 : status ⟨estado civil : marital status⟩ 3 CONDICIÓN : condition
estadounidense *adj & nmf* AMERICANO, NORTEAMERICANO : American
estafa *nf* : swindle, fraud
estafador, -dora *n* : cheat, swindler
estafar *vt* DEFRAUDAR : to swindle, to defraud
estalactita *nf* : stalactite
estalagmita *nf* : stalagmite
estallar *vi* 1 REVENTAR : to burst, to explode, to erupt 2 : to break out
estallido *nm* 1 EXPLOSIÓN : explosion 2 : report (of a gun) 3 : outbreak, outburst
estambre *nm* 1 : worsted (fabric) 2 : stamen
estampa *nf* 1 ILUSTRACIÓN, IMAGEN : printed image, illustration 2 ASPECTO : appearance, demeanor
estampado[1], **-da** *adj* : patterned, printed
estampado[2] *nm* : print, pattern
estampar *vt* : to stamp, to print, to engrave

estampida *nf* : stampede
estampilla *nf* 1 : rubber stamp 2 SELLO, TIMBRE : postage stamp
estancado, -da *adj* : stagnant
estancamiento *nm* : stagnation
estancar {72} *vt* 1 : to dam up, to hold back 2 : to bring to a halt, to deadlock — **estancarse** *vr* 1 : to stagnate 2 : to be brought to a standstill, to be deadlocked
estancia *nf* 1 ESTADÍA : stay, sojourn 2 : ranch, farm
estanciero, -ra *n* : rancher, farmer
estanco, -ca *adj* : watertight
estándar *adj & nm* : standard
estandarización *nf, pl* **-ciones** : standardization
estandarizar {21} *vt* : to standardize
estandarte *nm* : standard, banner
estanque *nm* 1 : pool, pond 2 : tank, reservoir
estante *nm* REPISA : shelf
estantería *nf* : shelves *pl*, bookcase
estaño *nm* : tin
estaquilla *nf* 1 : peg 2 ESPIGA : spike
estar {34} *v aux* : to be ⟨estoy aprendiendo inglés : I'm learning English⟩ ⟨está terminado : it's finished⟩ — *vi* 1 (*indicating a state or condition*) : to be ⟨está muy alto : he's so tall, he's gotten very tall⟩ ⟨¿ya estás mejor? : are you feeling better now?⟩ ⟨estoy casado : I'm married⟩ 2 (*indicating location*) : to be ⟨están en la mesa : they're on the table⟩ ⟨estamos en la página 2 : we're on page 2⟩ 3 : to be at home ⟨¿está María? : is Maria in?⟩ 4 : to remain ⟨estaré aquí 5 días : I'll be here for 5 days⟩ 5 : to be ready, to be done ⟨estará para las diez : it will be ready by ten o'clock⟩ 6 : to agree ⟨¿estamos? : are we in agreement?⟩ ⟨estoy contigo : I'm with you⟩ 7 ¿cómo estás? : how are you? 8 ¡está bien! : all right!, that's fine! 9 ~ a : to cost 10 ~ a : to be ⟨¿a qué día estamos? : what's today's date?⟩ 11 ~ con : to have ⟨está con fiebre : she has a fever⟩ 12 ~ de : to be ⟨estoy de vacaciones : I'm on vacation⟩ ⟨está de director hoy : he's acting as director today⟩ 13 estar bien (mal) : to be well (sick) 14 ~ para : to be in the mood for 15 ~ por : to be in favor of 16 ~ por : to be about to ⟨está por cerrar : it's on the verge of closing⟩ 17 estar de más : to be unnecessary 18 estar que : to be (in a state or condition) ⟨está que echa chispas : he's hopping mad⟩ — **estarse** *vr* QUEDARSE : to stay, to remain ⟨¡estáte quieto! : be still!⟩
estarcir {83} *vt* : to stencil
estatal *adj* : state, national
estática *nf* : static
estático, -ca *adj* : static
estatizar {21} *vt* : to nationalize — **estatización** *nf*
estatua *nf* : statue

estatuilla *nf* : statuette, figurine
estatura *nf* : height, stature ⟨de mediana estatura : of medium height⟩
estatus *nm* : status, prestige
estatutario, -ria *adj* : statutory
estatuto *nm* : statute
este¹, esta *adj, mpl* **estos** : this, these
este² *adj* : eastern, east
este³ *nm* 1 ORIENTE : east 2 : east wind 3 **el Este** : the East, the Orient
éste, ésta *pron, mpl* **éstos** 1 : this one, these ones *pl* 2 : the latter
estela *nf* 1 : wake (of a ship) 2 RASTRO : trail (of dust, smoke, etc.)
estelar *adj* : stellar
estelarizar {21} *vt Mex* : to star in, to be the star of
esténcil *nm* : stencil
estentóreo, -rea *adj* : loud, thundering
estepa *nf* : steppe
éster *nf* : ester
estera *nf* : mat
estercolero *nm* : dunghill
estéreo *adj & nm* : stereo
estereofónico, -ca *adj* : stereophonic
estereotipado, -da *adj* : stereotyped
estereotipar *vt* : to stereotype
estereotipo *nm* : stereotype
estéril *adj* 1 : sterile, germ-free 2 : infertile, barren 3 : futile, vain
esterilidad *nf* 1 : sterility 2 : infertility
esterilizar {21} *vt* 1 : to sterilize, to disinfect 2 : to sterilize (a person), to spay (an animal) — **esterilización** *nf*
esterlina *adj* : sterling
esternón *nm, pl* **-nones** : sternum
estero *nm* : estuary
estertor *nm* : death rattle
estética *nf* : aesthetics
estético, -ca *adj* : aesthetic — **estéticamente** *adv*
estetoscopio *nm* : stethoscope
estibador, -dora *n* : longshoreman, stevedore
estibar *vt* : to load (freight)
estiércol *nm* : dung, manure
estigma *nm* : stigma
estigmatizar {21} *vt* : to stigmatize, to brand
estilarse *vr* : to be in fashion
estilete *nm* : stiletto
estilista *nmf* : stylist
estilizar {21} *vt* : to stylize
estilo *nm* 1 : style 2 : fashion, manner 3 : stylus
estima *nf* ESTIMACIÓN : esteem, regard
estimable *adj* 1 : considerable 2 : estimable, esteemed
estimación *nf, pl* **-ciones** 1 ESTIMA : esteem, regard 2 : estimate
estimado, -da *adj* : esteemed, dear ⟨Estimado señor Ortiz : Dear Mr. Ortiz⟩
estimar *vt* 1 APRECIAR : to esteem, to respect 2 EVALUAR : to estimate, to appraise 3 OPINAR : to consider, to deem
estimulación *nf, pl* **-ciones** : stimulation
estimulante¹ *adj* : stimulating
estimulante² *nm* : stimulant

estimular *vt* 1 : to stimulate 2 : to encourage
estímulo *nm* 1 : stimulus 2 INCENTIVO : incentive, encouragement
estío *nm* : summertime
estipendio *nm* 1 : salary 2 : stipend, remuneration
estipular *vt* : to stipulate — **estipulación** *nf*
estirado, -da *adj* 1 : stretched, extended 2 PRESUMIDO : stuck-up, conceited
estiramiento *nm* 1 : stretching 2 **estiramiento facial** : face-lift
estirar *vt* : to stretch (out), to extend — **estirarse** *vr*
estirón *nm, pl* **-rones** 1 : pull, tug 2 **dar un estirón** : to grow quickly, to shoot up
estirpe *nf* LINAJE : lineage, stock
estival *adj* VERANIEGO : summer
esto *pron (neuter)* 1 : this ⟨¿qué es esto? : what is this?⟩ 2 **en ~** : at this point 3 **por ~** : for this reason
estocada *nf* 1 : final thrust (in bullfighting) 2 : thrust, lunge (in fencing)
estofa *nf* CLASE : class, quality ⟨de baja estofa : low-class, poor-quality⟩
estofado *nm* COCIDO, GUISADO : stew
estofar *vt* GUISAR : to stew
estoicismo *nm* : stoicism
estoico¹, -ca *adj* : stoic, stoical
estoico², -ca *n* : stoic
estola *nf* : stole
estomacal *adj* GÁSTRICO : stomach, gastric
estómago *nm* : stomach
estoniano, -na *adj & n* : Estonian
estonio, -nia *adj & n* : Estonian
estopa *nf* 1 : tow (yarn or cloth) 2 : burlap
estopilla *nf* : cheesecloth
estoque *nm* : rapier, sword
estorbar *vt* OBSTRUIR : to obstruct, to hinder — *vi* : to get in the way
estorbo *nm* 1 : obstacle, hindrance 2 : nuisance
estornino *nm* : starling
estornudar *vi* : to sneeze
estornudo *nm* : sneeze
estos *adj* → **este¹**
éstos → **éste**
estoy → **estar**
estrabismo *nm* : squint
estrado *nm* 1 : dais, platform, bench (of a judge) 2 **estrados** *nmpl* : courts of law
estrafalario, -ria *adj* ESTRAMBÓTICO, EXCÉNTRICO : eccentric, bizarre
estragar {52} *vt* DEVASTAR : to ruin, to devastate
estragón *nm* : tarragon
estragos *nmpl* 1 : ravages, destruction, devastation ⟨los estragos de la guerra : the ravages of war⟩ 2 **hacer estragos** *en or* **causar estragos entre** : to play havoc with
estrambótico, -ca *adj* ESTRAFALARIO, EXCÉNTRICO : eccentric, bizarre

estrangulamiento *nm* : strangling, strangulation
estrangular *vt* AHOGAR : to strangle — **estrangulación** *nf*
estratagema *nf* ARTIMAÑA : stratagem, ruse
estratega *nmf* : strategist
estrategia *nf* : strategy
estratégico, -ca *adj* : strategic, tactical — **estratégicamente** *adv*
estratificación *nf, pl* -**ciones** : stratification
estratificado, -da *adj* : stratified
estrato *nm* : stratum, layer
estratosfera *nf* : stratosphere
estratosférico, -ca *adj* 1 : stratospheric 2 : astronomical, exorbitant
estrechamiento *nm* 1 : narrowing 2 : narrow point 3 : tightening, strengthening (of relations)
estrechar *vt* 1 : to narrow 2 : to tighten, to strengthen (a bond) 3 : to hug, to embrace 4 **estrechar la mano de** : to shake hands with — **estrecharse** *vr*
estrechez *nf, pl* -**checes** 1 : tightness, narrowness 2 **estrecheces** *nfpl* : financial problems
estrecho¹, -cha *adj* 1 : tight, narrow 2 ÍNTIMO : close — **estrechamente** *adv*
estrecho² *nm* : strait, narrows
estrella *nf* 1 ASTRO : star ⟨estrella fugaz : shooting star⟩ 2 : destiny ⟨tener buena estrella : to be born lucky⟩ 3 : movie star 4 **estrella de mar** : starfish
estrellado, -da *adj* 1 : starry 2 : star-shaped 3 **huevos estrellados** : fried eggs
estrellamiento *nm* : crash, collision
estrellar *vt* : to smash, to crash — **estrellarse** *vr* : to crash, to collide
estrellato *nm* : stardom
estremecedor, -dora *adj* : horrifying
estremecer {53} *vt* : to cause to shake — *vi* : to tremble, to shake — **estremecerse** *vr* : to shudder, to shiver (with emotion)
estremecimiento *nm* : trembling, shaking, shivering
estrenar *vt* 1 : to use for the first time 2 : to premiere, to open — **estrenarse** *vr* : to make one's debut
estreno *nm* DEBUT : debut, premiere
estreñimiento *nm* : constipation
estreñirse {67} *vr* : to be constipated
estrépito *nm* ESTRUENDO : clamor, din
estrepitoso, -sa *adj* : clamorous, noisy — **estrepitosamente** *adv*
estrés *nm, pl* **estreses** : stress
estresante *adj* : stressful
estresar *vt* : to stress, to stress out
estría *nf* : fluting, groove
estribación *nf, pl* -**ciones** 1 : spur, ridge 2 **estribaciones** *nfpl* : foothills
estribar *vi* FUNDARSE ~ **en** : to be due to, to stem from
estribillo *nm* : refrain, chorus

estribo *nm* 1 : stirrup 2 : abutment, buttress 3 **perder los estribos** : to lose one's temper
estribor *nm* : starboard
estricnina *nf* : strychnine
estricto, -ta *adj* SEVERO : strict, severe — **estrictamente** *adv*
estridente *adj* : strident, shrill, loud — **estridentemente** *adv*
estrofa *nf* : stanza, verse
estrógeno *nm* : estrogen
estropajo *nm* : scouring pad
estropear *vt* 1 ARRUINAR : to ruin, to spoil 2 : to break, to damage — **estropearse** *vr* 1 : to spoil, to go bad 2 : to break down
estropicio *nm* DAÑO : damage, breakage
estructura *nf* : structure, framework
estructuración *nf, pl* -**ciones** : structuring, structure
estructural *adj* : structural — **estructuralmente** *adv*
estructurar *vt* : to structure, to organize
estruendo *nm* ESTRÉPITO : racket, din, roar
estruendoso, -sa *adj* : resounding, thunderous
estrujar *vt* APRETAR : to press, to squeeze
estuario *nm* : estuary
estuche *nm* : kit, case
estuco *nm* : stucco
estudiado, -da *adj* : affected, mannered
estudiantado *nm* : student body, students *pl*
estudiante *nmf* : student
estudiantil *adj* : student ⟨la vida estudiantil : student life⟩
estudiar *v* : to study
estudio *nm* 1 : study 2 : studio 3 **estudios** *nmpl* : studies, education
estudioso, -sa *adj* : studious
estufa *nf* 1 : stove, heater 2 *Col, Mex* : cooking stove, range
estupefacción *nf, pl* -**ciones** : stupefaction, astonishment
estupefaciente¹ *adj* : narcotic
estupefaciente² *nm* DROGA, NARCÓTICO : drug, narcotic
estupefacto, -ta *adj* : astonished, stunned
estupendo, -da *adj* MARAVILLOSO : stupendous, marvelous — **estupendamente** *adv*
estupidez *nf, pl* -**deces** 1 : stupidity 2 : nonsense
estúpido¹, -da *adj* : stupid — **estúpidamente** *adj*
estúpido², -da *n* IDIOTA : idiot, fool
estupor *nm* 1 : stupor 2 : amazement
esturión *nm, pl* -**riones** : sturgeon
estuvo, etc. → **estar**
etano *nm* : ethane
etanol *nm* : ethanol
etapa *nf* FASE : stage, phase
etcétera¹ : et cetera, and so on
etcétera² *nmf* : et cetera
éter *nm* : ether

117   etéreo · excepcional

etéreo, -rea *adj* : ethereal, heavenly
eternidad *nf* : eternity
eternizar {21} *vt* PERPETUAR : to make eternal, to perpetuate — **eternizarse** *vr fam* : to take forever
eterno, -na *adj* : eternal, endless — **eternamente** *adv*
ética *nf* : ethics
ético, -ca *adj* : ethical — **éticamente** *adv*
etimología *nf* : etymology
etimológico, -ca *adj* : etymological
etimólogo, -ga *n* : etymologist
etíope *adj & nmf* : Ethiopian
etiqueta *nf* **1** : etiquette **2** : tag, label **3 de ~** : formal, dressy
etiquetar *vt* : to label
étnico, -ca *adj* : ethnic
etnología *nf* : ethnology
etnólogo, -ga *n* : ethnologist
eucalipto *nm* : eucalyptus
Eucaristía *nf* : Eucharist, communion
eucarístico, -ca *adj* : eucharistic
eufemismo *nm* : euphemism
eufemístico, -ca *adj* : euphemistic
eufonía *nf* : euphony
eufónico, -ca *adj* : euphonious
euforia *nf* : euphoria, joyousness
eufórico, -ca *adj* : euphoric, exuberant, joyous — **eufóricamente** *adv*
eunuco *nm* : eunuch
europeo, -pea *adj & n* : European
euskera *nm* : Basque (language)
eutanasia *nf* : euthanasia
evacuación *nf, pl* **-ciones** : evacuation
evacuar *vt* **1** : to evacuate, to vacate **2** : to carry out — *vi* : to have a bowel movement
evadir *vt* ELUDIR : to evade, to avoid — **evadirse** *vr* : to escape, to slip away
evaluación *nf, pl* **-ciones** : assessment, evaluation
evaluador, -dora *n* : assessor
evaluar {3} *vt* : to evaluate, to assess, to appraise
evangélico, -ca *adj* : evangelical — **evangélicamente** *adv*
evangelio *nm* : gospel
evangelismo *nm* : evangelism
evangelista *nm* : evangelist
evangelizador, -dora *n* : evangelist, missionary
evaporación *nf, pl* **-ciones** : evaporation
evaporar *vt* : to evaporate — **evaporarse** *vr* ESFUMARSE : to disappear, to vanish
evasión *nf, pl* **-siones** **1** : escape, flight **2** : evasion, dodge
evasiva *nf* : excuse, pretext
evasivo, -va *adj* : evasive
evento *nm* : event
eventual *adj* **1** : possible **2** : temporary ⟨trabajadores eventuales : temporary workers⟩ — **eventualmente** *adv*
eventualidad *nf* : possibility, eventuality
evidencia *nf* **1** : evidence, proof **2 poner en evidencia** : to demonstrate, to make clear

evidenciar *vt* : to demonstrate, to show — **evidenciarse** *vr* : to be evident
evidente *adj* : evident, obvious, clear — **evidentemente** *adv*
eviscerar *vt* : to eviscerate
evitable *adj* : avoidable, preventable
evitar *vt* **1** : to avoid **2** PREVENIR : to prevent **3** ELUDIR : to escape, to elude
evocación *nf, pl* **-ciones** : evocation
evocador, -dora *adj* : evocative
evocar {72} *vt* **1** : to evoke **2** RECORDAR : to recall
evolución *nf, pl* **-ciones** **1** : evolution **2** : development, progress
evolucionar *vi* **1** : to evolve **2** : to change, to develop
evolutivo, -va *adj* : evolutionary
exabrupto *nm* : pointed remark
exacción *nf, pl* **-ciones** : levying, exaction
exacerbar *vt* **1** : to exacerbate, to aggravate **2** : to irritate, to exasperate
exactamente *adv* : exactly
exactitud *nf* PRECISIÓN : accuracy, precision, exactitude
exacto, -ta *adj* PRECISO : accurate, precise, exact
exageración *nf, pl* **-ciones** : exaggeration
exagerado, -da *adj* **1** : exaggerated **2** : excessive — **exageradamente** *adv*
exagerar *v* : to exaggerate
exaltación *nf, pl* **-ciones** **1** : exaltation **2** : excitement, agitation
exaltado[1], -da *adj* : excitable, hotheaded
exaltado[2], -da *n* : hothead
exaltar *vt* **1** ENSALZAR : to exalt, to extol **2** : to excite, to agitate — **exaltarse** *vr* ACALORARSE : to get overexcited
ex–alumno → **alumno**
examen *nm, pl* **exámenes** **1** : examination, test **2** : consideration, investigation
examinar *vt* **1** : to examine **2** INSPECCIONAR : to inspect — **examinarse** *vr* : to take an exam
exánime *adj* **1** : lifeless **2** : exhausted
exasperante *adj* : exasperating
exasperar *vt* IRRITAR : to exasperate, to irritate — **exasperación** *nf*
excavación *nf, pl* **-ciones** : excavation
excavadora *nf* : excavator
excavar *v* : to excavate, to dig
excedente[1] *adj* **1** : excessive **2** : excess, surplus
excedente[2] *nm* : surplus, excess
exceder *vt* : to exceed, to surpass — **excederse** *vr* : to go too far
excelencia *nf* **1** : excellence **2** : excellency ⟨Su Excelencia : His Excellency⟩
excelente *adj* : excellent — **excelentemente** *adv*
excelso, -sa *adj* : lofty, sublime
excentricidad *nf* : eccentricity
excéntrico, -ca *adj & n* : eccentric
excepción *nf, pl* **-ciones** : exception
excepcional *adj* EXTRAORDINARIO : exceptional, extraordinary, rare

excepto *prep* SALVO : except

exceptuar {3} *vt* EXCLUIR : to except, to exclude

excesivo, -va *adj* : excessive — **excesivamente** *adv*

exceso *nm* 1 : excess 2 **excesos** *nmpl* : excesses, abuses 3 **exceso de velocidad** : speeding

excitabilidad *nf* : excitability

excitación *nf, pl* -**ciones** : excitement

excitante *adj* : exciting

excitar *vt* : to excite, to arouse — **excitarse** *vr*

exclamación *nf, pl* -**ciones** : exclamation

exclamar *v* : to exclaim

excluir {41} *vt* EXCEPTUAR : to exclude, to leave out

exclusión *nf, pl* -**siones** : exclusion

exclusividad *nf* 1 : exclusiveness 2 : exclusive rights *pl*

exclusivista *adj & nmf* : exclusivist

exclusivo, -va *adj* : exclusive — **exclusivamente** *adv*

excomulgar {52} *vt* : to excommunicate

excomunión *nf, pl* -**niones** : excommunication

excreción *nf, pl* -**ciones** : excretion

excremento *nm* : excrement

excretar *vt* : to excrete

exculpar *vt* : to exonerate, to exculpate — **exculpación** *nf*

excursión *nf, pl* -**siones** : excursion, outing

excursionista *nmf* 1 : sightseer, tourist 2 : hiker

excusa *nf* 1 PRETEXTO : excuse 2 DISCULPA : apology

excusado *nm Mex* : toilet

excusar *vt* 1 : to excuse 2 : to exempt — **excusarse** *vr* : to apologize, to send one's regrets

execrable *adj* : detestable, abominable

exención *nf, pl* -**ciones** : exemption

exento, -ta *adj* 1 : exempt, free 2 **exento de impuestos** : tax-exempt

exequias *nfpl* FUNERALES : funeral rites

exhalación *nf, pl* -**ciones** 1 : exhalation 2 : shooting star ⟨salió como una exhalación : he took off like a shot⟩

exhalar *vt* ESPIRAR : to exhale, to give off

exhaustivo, -va *adj* : exhaustive — **exhaustivamente** *adv*

exhausto, -ta *adj* AGOTADO : exhausted, worn-out

exhibición *nf, pl* -**ciones** 1 : exhibition, show 2 : showing

exhibir *vt* : to exhibit, to show, to display — **exhibirse** *vr*

exhortación *nf, pl* -**ciones** : exhortation

exhortar *vt* : to exhort

exhumar *vt* DESENTERRAR : to exhume — **exhumación** *nf*

exigencia *nf* : demand, requirement

exigente *adj* : demanding, exacting

exigir {35} *vt* 1 : to demand, to require 2 : to exact, to levy

exiguo, -gua *adj* : meager

exiliado[1], -da *adj* : exiled, in exile

exiliado[2], -da *n* : exile

exiliar *vt* DESTERRAR : to exile, to banish — **exiliarse** *vr* : to go into exile

exilio *nm* DESTIERRO : exile

eximio, -mia *adj* : distinguished, eminent

eximir *vt* EXONERAR : to exempt

existencia *nf* 1 : existence 2 **existencias** *nfpl* MERCANCÍA : goods, stock

existente *adj* 1 : existing, in existence 2 : in stock

existir *vi* : to exist

éxito *nm* 1 TRIUNFO : success, hit 2 **tener éxito** : to be successful

exitoso, -sa *adj* : successful — **exitosamente** *adv*

éxodo *nm* : exodus

exoneración *nf, pl* -**ciones** EXENCIÓN : exoneration, exemption

exonerar *vt* 1 EXIMIR : to exempt, to exonerate 2 DESPEDIR : to dismiss

exorbitante *adj* : exorbitant

exorcismo *nm* : exorcism — **exorcista** *nmf*

exorcizar {21} *vt* : to exorcise

exótico, -ca *adj* : exotic

expandir *vt* EXPANSIONAR : to expand — **expandirse** *vr* : to spread

expansión *nf, pl* -**siones** 1 : expansion, spread 2 DIVERSIÓN : recreation, relaxation

expansionar *vt* EXPANDIR : to expand — **expansionarse** *vr* 1 : to expand 2 DIVERTIRSE : to amuse oneself, to relax

expansivo, -va *adj* : expansive

expatriado, -da *adj & n* : expatriate

expatriarse {85} *vr* 1 EMIGRAR : to emigrate 2 : to go into exile

expectación *nf, pl* -**ciones** : expectation, anticipation

expectante *adj* : expectant

expectativa *nf* 1 : expectation, hope 2 **expectativas** *nfpl* : prospects

expedición *nf, pl* -**ciones** : expedition

expediente *nm* 1 : expedient, means 2 ARCHIVO : file, dossier, record

expedir {54} *vt* 1 EMITIR : to issue 2 DESPACHAR : to dispatch, to send

expedito, -ta *adj* 1 : free, clear 2 : quick, easy

expeler *vt* : to expel, to eject

expendedor, -dora *n* : dealer, seller

expendio *nm* TIENDA : store, shop

expensas *nfpl* 1 : expenses, costs 2 **a expensas de** : at the expense of

experiencia *nf* 1 : experience 2 EXPERIMENTO : experiment

experimentación *nf, pl* -**ciones** : experimentation

experimental *adj* : experimental

experimentar *vi* : to experiment — *vt* 1 : to experiment with, to test out 2 : to experience

experimento *nm* EXPERIENCIA : experiment

experto, -ta *adj & n* : expert
expiación *nf, pl* **-ciones** : expiation, atonement
expiar {85} *vt* : to expiate, to atone for
expiración *nf, pl* **-ciones** VENCIMIENTO : expiration
expirar *vi* **1** FALLECER, MORIR : to pass away, to die **2** : to expire
explanada *nf* : esplanade, promenade
explayar *vt* : to extend — **explayarse** *vr* : to expound, to speak at length
explicable *adj* : explicable, explainable
explicación *nf, pl* **-ciones** : explanation
explicar {72} *vt* : to explain — **explicarse** *vr* : to understand
explicativo, -va *adj* : explanatory
explicitar *vt* : to state explicitly, to specify
explícito, -ta *adj* : explicit — **explícitamente** *adv*
exploración *nf, pl* **-ciones** : exploration
explorador, -dora *n* : explorer, scout
explorar *vt* : to explore — **exploratorio, -ria** *adj*
explosión *nf, pl* **-siones 1** ESTALLIDO : explosion **2** : outburst ⟨una explosión de ira : an outburst of anger⟩
explosionar *vi* : to explode
explosivo, -va *adj* : explosive
explotación *nf, pl* **-ciones 1** : exploitation **2** : operation, running
explotar *vt* **1** : to exploit **2** : to operate, to run — *vi* ESTALLAR, REVENTAR : to explode — **explotable** *adj*
exponencial *adj* : exponential — **exponencialmente** *adv*
exponente *nm* : exponent
exponer {60} *vt* **1** : to exhibit, to show, to display **2** : to explain, to present, to set forth **3** : to expose, to risk — *vi* : to exhibit
exportación *nf, pl* **-ciones 1** : exportation **2 exportaciones** *nfpl* : exports
exportador, -dora *n* : exporter
exportar *vt* : to export — **exportable** *adj*
exposición *nf, pl* **-ciones 1** EXHIBICIÓN : exposition, exhibition **2** : exposure **3** : presentation, statement
expositor, -tora *n* **1** : exhibitor **2** : exponent
exprés *nms & pl* **1** : express, express train **2** : espresso
expresamente *adv* : expressly, on purpose
expresar *vt* : to express — **expresarse** *vr*
expresión *nf, pl* **-siones** : expression
expresivo, -va *adj* **1** : expressive **2** CARIÑOSO : affectionate — **expresivamente** *adv*
expreso[1], -sa *adj* : express, specific
expreso[2] *nm* : express train, express
exprimidor *nm* : squeezer, juicer
exprimir *vt* **1** : to squeeze **2** : to exploit
expropiar *vt* : to expropriate, to commandeer — **expropiación** *nf*
expuesto[1] *pp* → **exponer**
expuesto[2], -ta *adj* **1** : exposed **2** : hazardous, risky

expulsar *vt* : to expel, to eject
expulsión *nf, pl* **-siones** : expulsion
expurgar {52} *vt* : to expurgate
expuso, etc. → **exponer**
exquisitez *nf, pl* **-teces 1** : exquisiteness, refinement **2** : delicacy, special dish
exquisito, -ta *adj* **1** : exquisite **2** : delicious
extasiarse {85} *vr* : to be in ecstasy, to be enraptured
éxtasis *nms & pl* : ecstasy, rapture
extático, -ca *adj* : ecstatic
extemporáneo, -nea *adj* **1** : unseasonable **2** : untimely
extender {56} *vt* **1** : to spread out, to stretch out **2** : to broaden, to expand ⟨extender la influencia : to broaden one's influence⟩ **3** : to draw up (a document), to write out (a check) — **extenderse** *vr* **1** : to spread **2** : to last
extendido, -da *adj* **1** : outstretched **2** : widespread
extensamente *adv* : extensively, at length
extensible *adj* : extensible, extendable
extensión *nf, pl* **-siones 1** : extension, stretching **2** : expanse, spread **3** : extent, range **4** : length, duration
extensivo, -va *adj* **1** : extensive **2 hacer extensivo** : to extend
extenso, -sa *adj* **1** : extensive, detailed **2** : spacious, vast
extenuar {3} *vt* : to exhaust, to tire out — **extenuarse** *vr* — **extenuante** *adj*
exterior[1] *adj* **1** : exterior, external **2** : foreign ⟨asuntos exteriores : foreign affairs⟩
exterior[2] *nm* **1** : outside **2** : abroad
exteriorizar {21} *vt* : to express, to reveal
exteriormente *adv* : outwardly
exterminar *vt* : to exterminate — **exterminación** *nf*
exterminio *nm* : extermination
externar *vt Mex* : to express, to display
externo, -na *adj* : external, outward
extinción *nf, pl* **-ciones** : extinction
extinguidor *nm* : fire extinguisher
extinguir {26} *vt* **1** APAGAR : to extinguish, to put out **2** : to wipe out — **extinguirse** *vr* **1** APAGARSE : to go out, to fade out **2** : to die out, to become extinct
extinto, -ta *adj* : extinct
extintor *nm* : extinguisher
extirpación *n, pl* **-ciones** : removal, excision
extirpar *vt* : to eradicate, to remove, to excise — **extirparse** *vr*
extorsión *nf, pl* **-siones 1** : extortion **2** : harm, trouble
extorsionar *vt* : to extort
extra[1] *adv* : extra
extra[2] *adj* **1** : additional, extra **2** : superior, top-quality
extra[3] *nmf* : extra (in movies)

extra[4] *nm* : extra expense ⟨paga extra : bonus⟩
extracción *nf, pl* **-ciones** : extraction
extracto *nm* **1** : extract ⟨extracto de vainilla : vanilla extract⟩ **2** : abstract, summary
extractor *nm* : extractor
extracurricular *adj* : extracurricular
extradición *nf, pl* **-ciones** : extradition
extraditar *vt* : to extradite
extraer {81} *vt* : to extract
extraído *pp* → **extraer**
extrajudicial *adj* : out-of-court
extramatrimonial *adj* : extramarital
extranjerizante *adj* : foreign-sounding, foreign-looking
extranjero[1], **-ra** *adj* : foreign
extranjero[2], **-ra** *n* : foreigner
extranjero[3] *nm* : foreign countries *pl* ⟨viajó al extranjero : he traveled abroad⟩ ⟨trabajan en el extranjero : they work overseas⟩
extrañamente *adv* : strangely, oddly
extrañamiento *nm* ASOMBRO : amazement, surprise, wonder
extrañar *vt* : to miss (someone) — **extrañarse** *vr* : to be surprised
extrañeza *nf* **1** : strangeness, oddness **2** : surprise
extraño[1], **-ña** *adj* **1** RARO : strange, odd **2** EXTRANJERO : foreign
extraño[2], **-ña** *n* DESCONOCIDO : stranger
extraoficial *adj* OFICIOSO : unofficial — **extraoficialmente** *adv*
extraordinario, -ria *adj* EXCEPCIONAL : extraordinary — **extraordinariamente** *adv*
extrasensorial *adj* : extrasensory ⟨percepción extrasensorial : extrasensory perception⟩
extraterrestre *adj & nmf* : extraterrestrial, alien

extravagancia *nf* : extravagance, outlandishness, flamboyance
extravagante *adj* : extravagant, outrageous, flamboyant
extraviar {85} *vt* **1** : to mislead, to lead astray **2** : to misplace, to lose — **extraviarse** *vr* : to get lost, to go astray
extravío *nm* **1** PÉRDIDA : loss, misplacement **2** : misconduct
extremado, -da *adj* : extreme — **extremadamente** *adv*
extremar *vt* : to carry to extremes — **extremarse** *vr* : to do one's utmost
extremidad *nf* **1** : extremity, tip, edge **2 extremidades** *nfpl* : extremities
extremista *adj & nmf* : extremist
extremo[1], **-ma** *adj* **1** : extreme, utmost **2** EXCESIVO : excessive **3 en caso extremo** : as a last resort
extremo[2] *nm* **1** : extreme, end **2 al extremo de** : to the point of **3 en ∼** : in the extreme
extrovertido[1], **-da** *adj* : extroverted, outgoing
extrovertido[2], **-da** *n* : extrovert
extrudir *vt* : to extrude
exuberancia *nf* **1** : exuberance **2** : luxuriance, lushness
exuberante *adj* : exuberant, luxuriant — **exuberantemente** *adv*
exudar *vt* : to exude
exultación *nf, pl* **-ciones** : exultation, elation
exultante *adj* : exultant, elated — **exultantemente** *adv*
exultar *vi* : to exult, to rejoice
eyacular *vi* : to ejaculate — **eyaculación** *nf*
eyección *nf, pl* **-ciones** : ejection, expulsion
eyectar *vt* : to eject, to expel — **eyectarse** *vr*

F

f *nf* : sixth letter of the Spanish alphabet
fábrica *nf* FACTORÍA : factory
fabricación *nf, pl* **-ciones** : manufacture
fabricante *nmf* : manufacturer
fabricar {72} *vt* MANUFACTURAR : to manufacture, to make
fabril *adj* INDUSTRIAL : industrial, manufacturing
fábula *nf* **1** : fable **2** : fabrication, fib
fabuloso, -sa *adj* **1** : fabulous, fantastic **2** : mythical, fabled
facción *nf, pl* **facciones** **1** : faction **2 facciones** *nfpl* RASGOS : features
faccioso, -sa *adj* : factious
faceta *nf* : facet
facha *nf* : appearance, look ⟨estar hecho una facha : to look a sight⟩
fachada *nf* : facade
facial *adj* : facial

fácil *adj* **1** : easy **2** : likely, probable ⟨es fácil que no pase : it probably won't happen⟩
facilidad *nf* **1** : facility, ease **2 facilidades** *nfpl* : facilities, services **3 facilidades** *nfpl* : opportunities
facilitar *vt* **1** : to facilitate **2** : to provide, to supply
fácilmente *adv* : easily, readily
facsímil *or* **facsímile** *nm* **1** : facsimile, copy **2** : fax
facsimilar *adj* : facsimile
factibilidad *nf* : feasibility
factible *adj* : feasible, practicable
facticio, -cia *adj* : artificial, factitious
factor[1], **-tora** *n* **1** : agent, factor **2** : baggage clerk
factor[2] *nm* ELEMENTO : factor, element
factoría *nf* FÁBRICA : factory
factótum *nm* : factotum

121 — factura · faringe

factura *nf* **1** : making, manufacturing **2** : bill, invoice

facturación *nf, pl* **-ciones 1** : invoicing, billing **2** : check-in

facturar *vt* **1** : to bill, to invoice **2** : to register, to check in

facultad *nf* **1** : faculty, ability ⟨facultades mentales : mental faculties⟩ **2** : authority, power **3** : school (of a university) ⟨facultad de derecho : law school⟩

facultar *vt* : to authorize, to empower

facultativo, -va *adj* **1** OPTATIVO : voluntary, optional **2** : medical ⟨informe facultativo : medical report⟩

faena *nf* : task, job, work ⟨faenas domésticas : housework⟩

faenar *vi* **1** : to work, to labor **2** PESCAR : to fish

fagot *nm* : bassoon

faisán *nm, pl* **faisanes** : pheasant

faja *nf* **1** : sash, belt **2** : girdle **3** : strip (of land)

fajar *vt* **1** : to wrap (a sash or girdle) around **2** : to hit, to thrash — **fajarse** *vr* **1** : to put on a sash or girdle **2** : to come to blows

fajín *nm, pl* **-jines** : sash, belt

fajo *nm* : bundle, sheaf ⟨un fajo de billetes : a wad of cash⟩

falacia *nf* : fallacy

falaz, -laza *adj, mpl* **falaces** FALSO : fallacious, false

falda *nf* **1** : skirt ⟨falda escocesa : kilt⟩ **2** REGAZO : lap (of the body) **3** VERTIENTE : side, slope

faldón *nm, pl* **-dones 1** : tail (of a shirt, etc.) **2** : full skirt **3 faldón bautismal** : christening gown

falible *adj* : fallible

fálico, -ca *adj* : phallic

falla *nf* **1** : flaw, defect **2** : (geological) fault **3** : fault, failing

fallar *vi* **1** FRACASAR : to fail, to go wrong **2** : to rule (in a court of law) — *vt* **1** ERRAR : to miss (a target) **2** : to pronounce judgment on

fallecer {53} *vi* MORIR : to pass away, to die

fallecido, -da *adj & n* DIFUNTO : deceased

fallecimiento *nm* : demise, death

fallido, -da *adj* : failed, unsuccessful

fallo *nm* **1** SENTENCIA : sentence, judgment, verdict **2** : error, fault

falo *nm* : phallus, penis

falsamente *adv* : falsely

falsear *vt* **1** : to falsify, to fake **2** : to distort — *vi* **1** CEDER : to give way **2** : to be out of tune

falsedad *nf* **1** : falseness, hypocrisy **2** MENTIRA : falsehood, lie

falsete *nm* : falsetto

falsificación *nf, pl* **-ciones 1** : counterfeit, forgery **2** : falsification

falsificador, -dora *n* : counterfeiter, forger

falsificar {72} *vt* **1** : to counterfeit, to forge **2** : to falsify

falso, -sa *adj* **1** FALAZ : false, untrue **2** : counterfeit, forged

falta *nf* **1** CARENCIA : lack ⟨hacer falta : to be lacking, to be needed⟩ **2** DEFECTO : defect, fault, error **3** : offense, misdemeanor **4** : foul (in basketball), fault (in tennis)

faltar *vi* **1** : to be lacking, to be needed ⟨me falta tiempo : I don't have enough time⟩ **2** : to be absent, to be missing **3** QUEDAR : to remain, to be left ⟨faltan pocos días para la fiesta : the party is just a few days away⟩ **4 ¡no faltaba más!** : don't mention it!, you're welcome!

falto, -ta *adj* ~ **de** : lacking (in), short of

fama *nf* **1** : fame **2** REPUTACIÓN : reputation **3 de mala fama** : disreputable

famélico, -ca *adj* HAMBRIENTO : starving, famished

familia *nf* **1** : family **2 familia política** : in-laws

familiar[1] *adj* **1** CONOCIDO : familiar **2** : familial, family **3** INFORMAL : informal

familiar[2] *nmf* PARIENTE : relation, relative

familiaridad *nf* **1** : familiarity **2** : informality

familiarizarse {21} *vr* ~ **con** : to familiarize oneself with

famoso[1], **-sa** *adj* CÉLEBRE : famous

famoso[2], **-sa** *n* : celebrity

fanal *nm* **1** : beacon, signal light **2** *Mex* : headlight

fanático, -ca *adj & n* : fanatic

fanatismo *nm* : fanaticism

fandango *nm* : fandango

fanfarria *nf* **1** : (musical) fanfare **2** : pomp, ceremony

fanfarrón[1], **-rrona** *adj, mpl* **-rrones** *fam* : bragging, boastful

fanfarrón[2], **-rrona** *n, mpl* **-rrones** *fam* : braggart

fanfarronada *nf* : boast, bluster

fanfarronear *vi* : to brag, to boast

fango *nm* LODO : mud, mire

fangosidad *nf* : muddiness

fangoso, -sa *adj* LODOSO : muddy

fantasear *vi* : to fantasize, to daydream

fantasía *nf* **1** : fantasy **2** : imagination

fantasioso, -sa *adj* : fanciful

fantasma *nm* : ghost, phantom

fantasmagórico, -ca *adj* : phantasmagoric

fantasmal *adj* : ghostly

fantástico, -ca *adj* **1** : fantastic, imaginary, unreal **2** *fam* : great, fantastic

faquir *nm* : fakir

farándula *nf* : show business, theater

faraón *nm, pl* **faraones** : pharaoh

fardo *nm* **1** : bale **2** : bundle

farfulla *nf* : jabbering

farfullar *v* : to jabber, to gabble

faringe *nf* : pharynx

faríngeo, -gea *adj* : pharyngeal
fariña *nf* : coarse manioc flour
farmacéutico[1], **-ca** *adj* : pharmaceutical
farmacéutico[2], **-ca** *n* : pharmacist
farmacia *nf* : drugstore, pharmacy
fármaco *nm* : medicine, drug
farmacodependencia *nf* : drug addiction
farmacología *nf* : pharmacology
faro *nm* **1** : lighthouse **2** : headlight
farol *nm* **1** : streetlight **2** : lantern, lamp **3** *fam* **4** *Mex* : headlight
farola *nf* **1** : lamppost **2** : streetlight
farolero, -ra *n fam* : bluffer
farra *nf* : spree, revelry
fárrago *nm* REVOLTIJO : hodgepodge, jumble
farsa *nf* **1** : farce **2** : fake, sham
farsante *nmf* CHARLATÁN : charlatan, fraud, phony
fascículo *nm* : fascicle, part (of a publication)
fascinación *nf, pl* **-ciones** : fascination
fascinante *adj* : fascinating
fascinar *vt* **1** : to fascinate **2** : to charm, to captivate
fascismo *nm* : fascism
fascista *adj & nmf* : fascist
fase *nf* : phase, stage
fastidiar *vt* **1** MOLESTAR : to annoy, to bother, to hassle **2** ABURRIR : to bore — *vi* : to be annoying or bothersome
fastidio *nm* **1** MOLESTIA : annoyance, nuisance, hassle **2** ABURRIMIENTO : boredom
fastidioso, -sa *adj* **1** MOLESTO : annoying, bothersome **2** ABURRIDO : boring
fatal *adj* **1** MORTAL : fatal **2** *fam* : awful, terrible **3** : fateful, unavoidable
fatalidad *nf* **1** : fatality **2** DESGRACIA : misfortune, bad luck
fatalismo *nm* : fatalism
fatalista[1] *adj* : fatalistic
fatalista[2] *nmf* : fatalist
fatalmente *adv* **1** : unavoidably **2** : unfortunately
fatídico, -ca *adj* : fateful, momentous
fatiga *nf* CANSANCIO : fatigue
fatigado, -da *adj* AGOTADO : weary, tired
fatigar {52} *vt* CANSAR : to fatigue, to tire — **fatigarse** *vr* : to wear oneself out
fatigoso, -sa *adj* : fatiguing, tiring
fatuidad *nf* **1** : fatuousness **2** VANIDAD : vanity, conceit
fatuo, -tua *adj* **1** : fatuous **2** PRESUMIDO : vain
fauces *nfpl* : jaws *pl*, maw
faul *nm, pl* **fauls** : foul, foul ball
fauna *nf* : fauna
fausto *nm* : splendor, magnificence
favor *nm* **1** : favor **2 a favor de** : in favor of **3 por ~** : please
favorable *adj* : favorable — **favorablemente** *adv*
favorecedor, -dora *adj* : becoming, flattering
favorecer {53} *vt* **1** : to favor **2** : to look well on, to suit

favorecido, -da *adj* **1** : flattering **2** : fortunate
favoritismo *nm* : favoritism
favorito, -ta *adj & n* : favorite
fax *nm* : fax, facsimile
fayuca *nf Mex* **1** : contraband **2** : black market
fayuquero *nm Mex* : smuggler, black marketeer
faz *nf* **1** : face, countenance ⟨la faz de la tierra : the face of the earth⟩ **2** : side (of coins, fabric, etc.)
fe *nf* **1** : faith **2** : assurance, testimony ⟨dar fe de : to bear witness to⟩ **3** : intention, will ⟨de buena fe : bona fide, in good faith⟩
fealdad *nf* : ugliness
febrero *nm* : February
febril *adj* : feverish — **febrilmente** *adv*
fecal *adj* : fecal
fecha *nf* **1** : date **2 fecha de caducidad** *or* **fecha de vencimiento** : expiration date **3 fecha límite** : deadline
fechar *vt* : to date, to put a date on
fechoría *nf* : misdeed
fécula *nf* : starch
fecundar *vt* : to fertilize (an egg) — **fecundación** *nf*
fecundidad *nf* **1** : fecundity, fertility **2** : productiveness
fecundo, -da *adj* FÉRTIL : fertile, fecund
federación *nf, pl* **-ciones** : federation
federal *adj* : federal
federalismo *nm* : federalism
federalista *adj & nmf* : federalist
federar *vt* : to federate
fehaciente *adj* : reliable, irrefutable — **fehacientemente** *adv*
feldespato *nm* : feldspar
felicidad *nf* **1** : happiness **2 ¡felicidades!** : best wishes!, congratulations!, happy birthday!
felicitación *nf, pl* **-ciones 1** : congratulation ⟨¡felicitaciones! : congratulations!⟩ **2** : greeting card
felicitar *vt* CONGRATULAR : to congratulate — **felicitarse** *vr* ~ **de** : to be glad about
feligrés, -gresa *n, mpl* **-greses** : parishioner
feligresía *nf* : parish
felino, -na *adj & n* : feline
feliz *adj, pl* **felices 1** : happy **2 Feliz Navidad** : Merry Christmas
felizmente *adv* **1** : happily **2** : fortunately, luckily
felonía *nf* : felony
felpa *nf* **1** : terry cloth **2** : plush
felpudo *nm* : doormat
femenil *adj* : women's, girls' ⟨futbol femenil : women's soccer⟩
femenino, -na *adj* **1** : feminine **2** : women's ⟨derechos femeninos : women's rights⟩ **3** : female
femineidad *nf* : femininity
feminidad *nf* : femininity
feminismo *nm* : feminism
feminista *adj & nmf* : feminist

femoral *adj* : femoral
fémur *nm* : femur, thighbone
fenecer {53} *vi* **1** : to die, to pass away **2** : to come to an end, to cease
fénix *nm* : phoenix
fenomenal *adj* **1** : phenomenal **2** *fam* : fantastic, terrific — **fenomenalmente** *adv*
fenómeno *nm* **1** : phenomenon **2** : prodigy, genius
feo[1] *adv* : badly, bad
feo[2], **fea** *adj* **1** : ugly **2** : unpleasant, nasty
féretro *nm* ATAÚD : coffin, casket
feria *nf* **1** : fair, market **2** : festival, holiday **3** *Mex* : change (money)
feriado, -da *adj* día feriado : public holiday
ferial *nm* : fairground
fermentar *v* : to ferment — **fermentación** *nf*
fermento *nm* : ferment
ferocidad *nf* : ferocity, fierceness
feroz *adj, pl* **feroces** FIERO : ferocious, fierce — **ferozmente** *adv*
férreo, -rrea *adj* **1** : iron **2** : strong, steely ⟨una voluntad férrea : an iron will⟩ **3** : strict, severe **4** vía férrea : railroad track
ferretería *nf* **1** : hardware store **2** : hardware **3** : foundry, ironworks
férrico, -ca *adj* : ferric
ferrocarril *nm* : railroad, railway
ferrocarrilero → **ferroviario**
ferroso, -sa *adj* : ferrous
ferroviario, -ria *adj* : rail, railroad
ferry *nm, pl* **ferrys** : ferry
fértil *adj* FECUNDO : fertile, fruitful
fertilidad *nf* : fertility
fertilizante[1] *adj* : fertilizing ⟨droga fertilizante : fertility drug⟩
fertilizante[2] *nm* ABONO : fertilizer
fertilizar *vt* ABONAR : to fertilize — **fertilización** *nf*
ferviente *adj* FERVOROSO : fervent
fervor *nm* : fervor, zeal
fervoroso, -sa *adj* FERVIENTE : fervent, zealous
festejar *vt* **1** CELEBRAR : to celebrate **2** AGASAJAR : to entertain, to wine and dine **3** *Mex fam* : to thrash, to beat
festejo *nm* : celebration, festivity
festín *nm, pl* **festines** : banquet, feast
festinar *vt* : to hasten, to hurry up
festival *nm* : festival
festividad *nf* **1** : festivity **2** : (religious) feast, holiday
festivo, -va *adj* **1** : festive **2** día festivo : holiday — **festivamente** *adv*
fetal *adj* : fetal
fetiche *nm* : fetish
fétido, -da *adj* : fetid, foul
feto *nm* : fetus
feudal *adj* : feudal — **feudalismo** *nm*
feudo *nm* **1** : fief **2** : domain, territory
fiabilidad *nf* : reliability, trustworthiness
fiable *adj* : trustworthy, reliable
fiado, -da *adj* : on credit

fiador, -dora *n* : bondsman, guarantor
fiambrería *nf* : delicatessen
fiambres *nfpl* : cold cuts
fianza *nf* **1** CAUCIÓN : bail, bond **2** : surety, deposit
fiar {85} *vt* **1** : to sell on credit **2** : to guarantee — **fiarse** *vr* ∼ **de** : to place trust in
fiasco *nm* FRACASO : fiasco, failure
fibra *nf* **1** : fiber **2** fibra de vidrio : fiberglass
ficción *nf, pl* **ficciones** **1** : fiction **2** : fabrication, lie
ficha *nf* **1** : index card **2** : file, record **3** : token **4** : domino, checker, counter, poker chip
fichar *vt* **1** : to open a file on **2** : to sign up — *vi* : to punch in, to punch out
fichero *nm* **1** : card file **2** : filing cabinet
ficticio, -cia *adj* : fictitious
fidedigno, -na *adj* FIABLE : reliable, trustworthy
fideicomisario, -ria *n* : trustee
fideicomiso *nm* : trusteeship, trust ⟨guardar en fideicomiso : to hold in trust⟩
fidelidad *nf* : fidelity, faithfulness
fideo *nm* : noodle
fiduciario[1], **-ria** *adj* : fiduciary
fiduciario[2], **-ria** *n* : trustee
fiebre *nf* **1** CALENTURA : fever, temperature ⟨fiebre amarilla : yellow fever⟩ ⟨fiebre palúdica : malaria⟩ **2** : fever, excitement
fiel[1] *adj* **1** : faithful, loyal **2** : accurate — **fielmente** *adv*
fiel[2] *nm* **1** : pointer (of a scale) **2 los fieles** : the faithful
fieltro *nm* : felt
fiera *nf* **1** : wild animal, beast **2** : fiend, demon ⟨una fiera para el trabajo : a demon for work⟩
fiereza *nf* : fierceness, ferocity
fiero, -ra *adj* FEROZ : fierce, ferocious
fierro *nm* HIERRO : iron
fiesta *nf* **1** : party, fiesta **2** : holiday, feast day
figura *nf* **1** : figure **2** : shape, form **3** figura retórica : figure of speech
figurado, -da *adj* : figurative — **figuradamente** *adv*
figurar *vi* **1** : to figure, to be included ⟨Rivera figura entre los más grandes pintores de México : Rivera is among Mexico's greatest painters⟩ **2** : to be prominent, to stand out — *vt* : to represent ⟨esta línea figura el horizonte : this line represents the horizon⟩ — **figurarse** *vr* : to imagine, to think ⟨¡figúrate el lío en que se metió! : imagine the mess she got into!⟩
fijación *nf, pl* **-ciones** **1** : fixation, obsession **2** : fixing, establishing **3** : fastening, securing
fijador *nm* **1** : fixative **2** : hair spray

fijamente *adv* : fixedly
fijar *vt* **1** : to fasten, to affix **2** ES-
TABLECER : to establish, to set up **3**
CONCRETAR : to set, to fix ⟨fijar la
fecha : to set the date⟩ — **fijarse** *vr* **1**
: to settle, to become fixed **2** ~ **en** : to
notice, to pay attention to
fijeza *nf* **1** : firmness (of convictions) **2**
: persistence, constancy ⟨mirar con fi-
jeza a : to stare at⟩
fijiano, -na *adj & n* : Fijian
fijo, -ja *adj* **1** : fixed, firm, steady **2** PER-
MANENTE : permanent
fila *nf* **1** HILERA : line, file ⟨ponerse en
fila : to get in line⟩ **2** : rank, row **3 filas** *nfpl* : ranks ⟨cerrar filas : to close
ranks⟩
filamento *nm* : filament
filantropía *nf* : philanthropy
filantrópico, -ca *adj* : philanthropic
filántropo, -pa *n* : philanthropist
filatelia *nf* : philately, stamp collecting
filatelista *nmf* : stamp collector, philat-
elist
fildeador, -dora *n* : fielder
filete *nm* **1** : fillet **2** SOLOMILLO : sirloin **3** : thread (of a screw)
filiación *nf, pl* **-ciones** **1** : affiliation,
connection **2** : particulars *pl,* (police)
description
filial[1] *adj* : filial
filial[2] *nf* : affiliate, subsidiary
filibustero *nm* : freebooter, pirate
filigrana *nf* **1** : filigree **2** : watermark
(on paper)
filipino, -na *adj & n* : Filipino
filmación *nf, pl* **-ciones** : filming, shooting
filmar *vt* : to film, to shoot
filme *or* **film** *nm* PELÍCULA : film, movie
filmina *nf* : slide, transparency
filo *nm* **1** : cutting edge, blade **2** : edge
⟨al filo del escritorio : at the edge of
the desk⟩ ⟨al filo de la medianoche : at
the stroke of midnight⟩
filología *nf* : philology
filólogo, -ga *n* : philologist
filón *nm, pl* **filones** **1** : seam, vein (of
minerals) **2** *fam* : successful business,
gold mine
filoso, -sa *adj* : sharp
filosofar *vi* : to philosophize
filosofía *nf* : philosophy
filosófico, -ca *adj* : philosophic, philosophical — **filosóficamente** *adv*
filósofo, -fa *n* : philosopher
filtración *nf* : seepage, leaking
filtrar *v* : to filter — **filtrarse** *vr* : to seep
through, to leak
filtro *nm* : filter
filudo, -da *adj* : sharp
fin *nm* **1** : end **2** : purpose, aim, objective **3 en** ~ : in short **4 fin de semana** : weekend **5 por** ~ : finally, at
last
finado, -da *adj & n* DIFUNTO : deceased
final[1] *adj* : final, ultimate — **finalmente**
adv

final[2] *nm* : end, conclusion, finale
final[3] *nf* : final, play-off
finalidad *nf* **1** : purpose, aim **2** : finality
finalista *nmf* : finalist
finalización *nf* : completion, end
finalizar {21} *v* : to finish, to end
financiación *nf, pl* **-ciones** : financing,
funding
financiamiento *nm* → **financiación**
financiar *vt* : to finance, to fund
financiero[1], **-ra** *adj* : financial
financiero[2], **-ra** *n* : financier
financista *nmf* : financier
finanzas *nfpl* : finances, finance ⟨altas
finanzas : high finance⟩
finca *nf* **1** : farm, ranch **2** : country
house
fineza *nf* FINURA, REFINAMIENTO : refinement
fingido, -da *adj* : false, feigned
fingimiento *nm* : pretense
fingir {35} *v* : to feign, to pretend
finiquitar *vt* **1** : to settle (an account) **2**
: to conclude, to bring to an end
finiquito *nm* : settlement (of an account)
finito, -ta *adj* : finite
finja, etc. → **fingir**
finlandés, -desa *adj & n* : Finnish
fino, -na *adj* **1** : fine, excellent **2** : delicate, slender **3** REFINADO : refined **4**
: sharp, acute ⟨olfato fino : keen sense
of smell⟩ **5** : subtle
finta *nf* : feint
fintar *or* **fintear** *vi* : to feint
finura *nf* **1** : fineness, high quality **2**
FINEZA, REFINAMIENTO : refinement
fiordo *nm* : fjord
fique *nm* : sisal
firma *nf* **1** : signature **2** : signing **3** EM-
PRESA : firm, company
firmamento *nm* : firmament, sky
firmante *nmf* : signer, signatory
firmar *v* : to sign
firme *adj* **1** : firm, resolute **2** : steady,
stable
firmemente *adv* : firmly
firmeza *nf* **1** : firmness, stability **2**
: strength, resolve
firuletes *nmpl* : frills, adornments
fiscal[1] *adj* : fiscal — **fiscalmente** *adv*
fiscal[2] *nmf* : district attorney, prosecutor
fiscalizar {21} *vt* **1** : to audit, to inspect
2 : to oversee **3** : to criticize
fisco *nm* : national treasury, exchequer
fisgar {52} *vt* HUSMEAR : to pry into, to
snoop on
fisgón, -gona *n, mpl* **fisgones** : snoop,
busybody
fisgonear *vi* : to snoop, to pry
fisgue, etc. → **fisgar**
física *nf* : physics
físico[1], **-ca** *adj* : physical — **físicamente**
adv
físico[2], **-ca** *n* : physicist
físico[3] *nm* : physique, figure
fisiología *nf* : physiology

fisiológico, -ca *adj* : physiological, physiologic

fisiólogo, -ga *n* : physiologist

fisión *nf, pl* **fisiones** : fission — **fisionable** *adj*

fisionomía → **fisonomía**

fisioterapeuta *nmf* : physical therapist

fisioterapia *nf* : physical therapy

fisonomía *nf* : physiognomy, features *pl*

fistol *nm Mex* : tie clip

fisura *nf* : fissure, crevasse

fláccido, -da *or* **flácido, -da** *adj* : flaccid, flabby

flaco, -ca *adj* **1** DELGADO : thin, skinny **2** : feeble, weak ⟨una flaca excusa : a feeble excuse⟩

flagelar *vt* : to flagellate — **flagelación** *nf*

flagelo *nm* **1** : scourge, whip **2** : calamity

flagrante *adj* : flagrant, glaring, blatant — **flagrantemente** *adv*

flama *nf* LLAMA : flame

flamante *adj* **1** : bright, brilliant **2** : brand-new

flamear *vi* **1** LLAMEAR : to flame, to blaze **2** ONDEAR : to flap, to flutter

flamenco¹, -ca *adj* **1** : flamenco **2** : Flemish

flamenco², -ca *n* : Fleming, Flemish person

flamenco³ *nm* **1** : Flemish (language) **2** : flamingo **3** : flamenco (music or dance)

flanco *nm* : flank, side

flanquear *vt* : to flank

flaquear *vi* DECAER : to flag, to weaken

flaqueza *nf* **1** DEBILIDAD : frailty, feebleness **2** : thinness **3** : weakness, failing

flato *nm* : gloom, melancholy

flatulento, -ta *adj* : flatulent — **flatulencia** *nf*

flauta *nf* **1** : flute **2 flauta dulce** : recorder

flautín *nm, pl* **flautines** : piccolo

flautista *nmf* : flute player, flutist

flebitis *nf* : phlebitis

flecha *nf* : arrow

fleco *nm* **1** : bangs *pl* **2** : fringe

flema *nf* : phlegm

flemático, -ca *adj* : phlegmatic, stolid, impassive

flequillo *nm* : bangs *pl*

fletar *vt* **1** : to charter, to hire **2** : to load (freight)

flete *nm* **1** : charter fee **2** : shipping cost **3** : freight, cargo

fletero *nm* : shipper, carrier

flexibilidad *nf* : flexibility

flexibilizar {21} *vt* : to make more flexible

flexible¹ *adj* : flexible

flexible² *nm* **1** : flexible electrical cord **2** : soft hat

flirtear *vi* : to flirt

flojear *vi* **1** DEBILITARSE : to weaken, to flag **2** : to idle, to loaf around

flojedad *nf* : weakness

flojera *nf fam* **1** : lethargy, feeling of weakness **2** : laziness

flojo, -ja *adj* **1** SUELTO : loose, slack **2** : weak, poor ⟨está flojo en las ciencias : he's weak in science⟩ **3** PEREZOSO : lazy

flor *nf* **1** : flower **2 flor de Pascua** : poinsettia

flora *nf* : flora

floración *nf* : flowering ⟨en plena floración : in full bloom⟩

floral *adj* : floral

floreado, -da *adj* : flowered, flowery

florear *vi* FLORECER : to flower, to bloom — *vt* **1** : to adorn with flowers **2** *Mex* : to flatter, to compliment

florecer {53} *vi* **1** : to bloom, to blossom **2** : to flourish, to thrive

floreciente *adj* **1** : flowering **2** PRÓSPERO : flourishing, thriving

florecimiento *nm* : flowering

floreo *nm* : flourish

florería *nf* : flower shop, florist's

florero¹, -ra *n* : florist

florero² *nm* JARRÓN : vase

floresta *nf* **1** : glade, grove **2** BOSQUE : woods

florido, -da *adj* **1** : full of flowers **2** : florid, flowery ⟨escritos floridos : flowery prose⟩

florista *nmf* : florist

floritura *nf* : frill, embellishment

flota *nf* : fleet

flotabilidad *nf* : buoyancy

flotación *nf, pl* **-ciones** : flotation

flotador *nm* **1** : float **2** : life preserver

flotante *adj* : floating, buoyant

flotar *vi* : to float

flote *nm* **a ~** : afloat

flotilla *nf* : flotilla, fleet

fluctuar {3} *vi* **1** : to fluctuate **2** VACILAR : to vacillate — **fluctuación** *nf* — **fluctuante** *adj*

fluidez *nf* **1** : fluency **2** : fluidity

fluido¹, -da *adj* **1** : flowing **2** : fluent **3** : fluid

fluido² *nm* : fluid

fluir {41} *vi* : to flow

flujo *nm* **1** : flow **2** : discharge

flúor *nm* : fluorine

fluoración *nf, pl* **-ciones** : fluoridation

fluorescencia *nf* : fluorescence — **fluorescente** *adj*

fluorizar {21} *vt* : to fluoridate

fluoruro *nm* : fluoride

fluvial *adj* : fluvial, river

fluye, etc. → **fluir**

fobia *nf* : phobia

foca *nf* : seal (animal)

focal *adj* : focal

focha *nf* : coot

foco *nm* **1** : focus **2** : center, pocket **3** : lightbulb **4** : spotlight **5** : headlight

fofo, -fa *adj* **1** ESPONJOSO : soft, spongy **2** : flabby

fogaje *nm* **1** FUEGO : skin eruption, cold sore **2** BOCHORNO : hot and humid weather

fogata *nf* : bonfire
fogón *nm, pl* **fogones** : bonfire
fogonazo *nm* : flash, explosion
fogonero, -ra *n* : stoker (of a furnace), fireman
fogoso, -sa *adj* ARDIENTE : ardent
foguear *vt* : to inure, to accustom
foja *nf* : sheet (of paper)
folículo *nm* : follicle
folio *nm* : folio, leaf
folklore *nm* : folklore
folklórico, -ca *adj* : folk, traditional
follaje *nm* : foliage
folleto *nm* : pamphlet, leaflet, circular
fomentar *vt* **1** : to foment, to stir up **2** PROMOVER : to promote, to foster
fomento *nm* : promotion, encouragement
fonda *nf* **1** POSADA : inn **2** : small restaurant
fondeado, -da *adj fam* : rich, in the money
fondear *vt* **1** : to sound **2** : to sound out, to examine **3** *Mex* : to fund, to finance — *vi* ANCLAR : to anchor — **fondearse** *vr fam* : to get rich
fondeo *nm* **1** : anchoring **2** *Mex* : funding, financing
fondillos *mpl* : seat, bottom (of clothing)
fondo *nm* **1** : bottom **2** : rear, back, end **3** : depth **4** : background **5** : sea bed **6** : fund ⟨fondo de inversiones : investment fund⟩ **7** *Mex* : slip, petticoat **8 fondos** *nmpl* : funds, resources ⟨cheque sin fondos : bounced check⟩ **9 a ~** : thoroughly, in depth **10 en ~** : abreast
fonema *nm* : phoneme
fonética *nf* : phonetics
fonético, -ca *adj* : phonetic
fontanería *nf* PLOMERÍA : plumbing
fontanero, -ra *n* PLOMERO : plumber
footing ['fu,tɪŋ] *nm* : jogging ⟨hacer footing : to jog⟩
foque *nm* : jib
forajido, -da *n* : bandit, fugitive, outlaw
foráneo, -nea *adj* : foreign, strange
forastero, -ra *n* : stranger, outsider
forcejear *vi* : to struggle
forcejeo *nm* : struggle
fórceps *nms & pl* : forceps *pl*
forense *adj* : forensic, legal
forestal *adj* : forest
forja *nf* FRAGUA : forge
forjar *vt* **1** : to forge **2** : to shape, to create ⟨forjar un compromiso : to hammer out a compromise⟩ **3** : to invent, to concoct
forma *nf* **1** : form, shape **2** MANERA, MODO : manner, way **3** : fitness ⟨estar en forma : to be fit, to be in shape⟩ **4 formas** *nfpl* : appearances, conventions
formación *nf, pl* **-ciones 1** : formation **2** : training ⟨formación profesional : vocational training⟩

formal *adj* **1** : formal **2** : serious, dignified **3** : dependable, reliable
formaldehído *nm* : formaldehyde
formalidad *nf* **1** : formality **2** : seriousness, dignity **3** : dependability, reliability
formalizar {21} *vt* : to formalize, to make official
formalmente *adv* : formally
formar *vt* **1** : to form, to make **2** CONSTITUIR : to constitute, to make up **3** : to train, to educate — **formarse** *vr* **1** DESARROLLARSE : to develop, to take shape **2** EDUCARSE : to be educated
formatear *vt* : to format
formativo, -va *adj* : formative
formato *nm* : format
formidable *adj* **1** : formidable, tremendous **2** *fam* : fantastic, terrific
formón *nm, pl* **formones** : chisel
fórmula *nf* : formula
formulación *nf, pl* **-ciones** : formulation
formular *vt* **1** : to formulate, to draw up **2** : to make, to lodge (a protest or complaint)
formulario *nm* : form ⟨rellenar un formulario : to fill out a form⟩
fornicar {72} *vi* : to fornicate — **fornicación** *nf*
fornido, -da *adj* : well-built, burly, hefty
foro *nm* **1** : forum **2** : public assembly, open discussion
forraje *nm* **1** : forage, fodder **2** : foraging **3** *fam* : hodgepodge
forrajear *vi* : to forage
forrar *vt* **1** : to line (a garment) **2** : to cover (a book)
forro *nm* **1** : lining **2** CUBIERTA : book cover
forsitia *nf* : forsythia
fortachón, -chona *adj, pl* **-chones** *fam* : brawny, strong, tough
fortalecer {53} *vt* : to strengthen, to fortify — **fortalecerse** *vr*
fortalecimiento *nm* **1** : strengthening, fortifying **2** : fortifications
fortaleza *nf* **1** : fortress **2** FUERZA : strength **3** : resolution, fortitude
fortificación *nf, pl* **-ciones** : fortification
fortificar {72} *vt* **1** : to fortify **2** : to strengthen
fortín *nm, pl* **fortines** : small fort
fortuito, -ta *adj* : fortuitous
fortuna *nf* **1** SUERTE : fortune, luck **2** RIQUEZA : wealth, fortune
forzar {36} *vt* **1** OBLIGAR : to force, to compel **2** : to force open **3** : to strain ⟨forzar los ojos : to strain one's eyes⟩
forzosamente *adv* **1** : forcibly, by force **2** : necessarily, inevitably ⟨forzosamente tendrán que pagar : they'll have no choice but to pay⟩
forzoso, -sa *adj* **1** : forced, compulsory **2** : necessary, inevitable
fosa *nf* **1** : ditch, pit ⟨fosa séptica : septic tank⟩ **2** TUMBA : grave **3** : cavity ⟨fosas nasales : nasal cavities, nostrils⟩
fosfato *nm* : phosphate

fosforescencia *nf* : phosphorescence —
fosforescente *adj*
fósforo *nm* **1** CERILLA : match **2** : phosphorus
fósil[1] *adj* : fossilized, fossil
fósil[2] *nm* : fossil
fosilizarse {21} *vr* : to fossilize, to become fossilized
foso *nm* **1** FOSA, ZANJA : ditch **2** : pit
(of a theater) **3** : moat
foto *nf* : photo, picture
fotocopia *nf* : photocopy — **fotocopiar**
vt
fotocopiadora *nf* COPIADORA : photocopier
fotoeléctrico, -ca *adj* : photoelectric
fotogénico, -ca *adj* : photogenic
fotografía *nf* **1** : photograph **2** : photography
fotografiar {85} *vt* : to photograph
fotográfico, -ca *adj* : photographic —
fotográficamente *adv*
fotógrafo, -fa *n* : photographer
fotosíntesis *nf* : photosynthesis
fotosintético, -ca *adj* : photosynthetic
fracasado[1] **, -da** *adj* : unsuccessful,
failed
fracasado[2] **, -da** *n* : failure
fracasar *vi* **1** FALLAR : to fail **2** : to fall
through
fracaso *nm* FIASCO : failure
fracción *nf, pl* **fracciones 1** : fraction
2 : part, fragment **3** : faction, splinter
group
fraccionamiento *nm* **1** : division, breaking up **2** *Mex* : residential area, housing development
fraccionar *vt* : to divide, to break up
fraccionario, -ria *adj* : fractional
fractura *nf* **1** : fracture **2 fractura complicada** : compound fracture
fracturarse *vr* QUEBRARSE, ROMPERSE
: to fracture, to break ⟨fracturarse el
brazo : to break one's arm⟩
fragancia *nf* : fragrance, scent
fragante *adj* : fragrant
fragata *nf* : frigate
frágil *adj* **1** : fragile **2** : frail, delicate
fragilidad *nf* **1** : fragility **2** : frailty, delicacy
fragmentar *vt* : to fragment — **fragmentación** *nf*
fragmentario, -ria *adj* : fragmentary,
sketchy
fragmento *nm* **1** : fragment, shard **2**
: bit, snippet **3** : excerpt, passage
fragor *nm* : clamor, din, roar
fragoroso, -sa *adj* : thunderous, deafening
fragoso, -sa *adj* **1** : rough, uneven **2**
: thick, dense
fragua *nf* FORJA : forge
fraguar {10} *vt* **1** : to forge **2** : to conceive, to concoct, to hatch — *vi* : to set,
to solidify
fraile *nm* : friar, monk
frambuesa *nf* : raspberry

francamente *adv* **1** : frankly, candidly
2 REALMENTE : really ⟨es francamente
admirable : it's really impressive⟩
francés[1] **, -cesa** *adj, mpl* **franceses**
: French
francés[2] **, -cesa** *n, mpl* **franceses**
: French person, Frenchman *m*,
Frenchwoman *f*
francés[3] *nm* : French (language)
franciscano, -na *adj & n* : Franciscan
francmasón, -sona *n, mpl* **-sones**
: Freemason — **francmasonería** *f*
franco[1] **, -ca** *adj* **1** CÁNDIDO : frank, candid **2** PATENTE : clear, obvious **3** : free
⟨franco a bordo : free on board⟩
franco[2] *nm* : franc
francotirador, -dora *n* : sniper
franela *nf* : flannel
franja *nf* **1** : stripe, band **2** : border,
fringe
franquear *vt* **1** : to clear **2** ATRAVESAR
: to cross, to go through **3** : to pay the
postage on
franqueo *nm* : postage
franqueza *nf* : frankness
franquicia *nf* **1** EXENCIÓN : exemption
2 : franchise
frasco *nm* : small bottle, flask, vial
frase *nf* **1** : phrase **2** ORACIÓN : sentence
frasear *vt* : to phrase
fraternal *adj* : fraternal, brotherly
fraternidad *nf* **1** : brotherhood **2** : fraternity
fraternizar {21} *vi* : to fraternize — **fraternización** *nf*
fraterno, -na *adj* : fraternal, brotherly
fratricida *adj* : fratricidal
fratricidio *nm* : fratricide
fraude *nm* : fraud
fraudulento, -ta *adj* : fraudulent —
fraudulentamente *adv*
fray *nm* : brother (title of a friar) ⟨Fray
Bartolomé : Brother Bartholomew⟩
frazada *nf* COBIJA, MANTA : blanket
frecuencia *nf* : frequency
frecuentar *vt* : to frequent, to haunt
frecuente *adj* : frequent — **frecuentemente** *adv*
fregadera *nf fam* : hassle, pain in the
neck
fregadero *nm* : kitchen sink
fregado[1] **, -da** *adj fam* : annoying, bothersome
fregado[2] *nm* **1** : scrubbing, scouring **2**
fam : mess, muddle
fregar {49} *vt* **1** : to scrub, to scour, to
wash ⟨fregar los trastes : to do the dish-
es⟩ ⟨fregar el suelo : to scrub the floor⟩
2 *fam* : to annoy — *vi* **1** : to wash the
dishes **2** : to clean, to scrub **3** *fam* : to
be annoying
freidera *nf Mex* : frying pan
freír {37} *vt* : to fry — **freírse** *vr*
frenar *vt* **1** : to brake **2** DETENER : to
curb, to check — *vi* : to apply the
brakes — **frenarse** *vr* : to restrain oneself

frenesí *nm* : frenzy

frenético, -ca *adj* : frantic, frenzied — **frenéticamente** *adv*

freno *nm* **1** : brake **2** : bit (of a bridle) **3** : check, restraint **4 frenos** *nmpl Mex* : braces (for teeth)

frente[1] *nm* **1** : front ⟨al frente de : at the head of⟩ ⟨en frente : in front, opposite⟩ **2** : facade **3** : front line, sphere of activity **4** : front (in meteorology) ⟨frente frío : cold front⟩ **5 hacer frente a** : to face up to, to brave

frente[2] *nf* **1** : forehead, brow **2 frente a frente** : face to face

fresa *nf* **1** : strawberry **2** : drill (in dentistry)

fresco[1]**, -ca** *adj* **1** : fresh **2** : cool **3** *fam* : insolent, nervy

fresco[2] *nm* **1** : coolness **2** : fresh air ⟨al fresco : in the open air, outdoors⟩ **3** : fresco

frescor *nm* : cool air ⟨el frescor de la noche : the cool of the evening⟩

frescura *nf* **1** : freshness **2** : coolness **3** : calmness **4** DESCARO : nerve, audacity

fresno *nm* : ash (tree)

freza *nf* : spawn, roe

frezar {21} *vi* DESOVAR : to spawn

friable *adj* : friable

frialdad *nf* **1** : coldness **2** INDIFERENCIA : indifference, unconcern

fríamente *adv* : coldly, indifferently

fricasé *nm* : fricassee

fricción *nf, pl* **fricciones 1** : friction **2** : rubbing, massage **3** : discord, disagreement ⟨fricción entre los hermanos : friction between the brothers⟩

friccionar *vt* **1** FROTAR : to rub **2** : to massage

friega[1]**, friegue, etc.** → **fregar**

friega[2] *nf* **1** FRICCIÓN : rubdown, massage **2** : annoyance, bother

frigidez *nf* : (sexual) frigidity

frigorífico *nm Spain* : refrigerator

frijol *nm* : bean ⟨frijoles refritos : refried beans⟩

frío[1]**, fría** *adj* **1** : cold **2** INDIFERENTE : cool, indifferent

frío[2] *nm* **1** : cold ⟨hace mucho frío esta noche : it's very cold tonight⟩ **2** INDIFERENCIA : coldness, indifference **3 tener frío** : to feel cold ⟨tengo frío : I'm cold⟩ **4 tomar frío** RESFRIARSE : to catch a cold

friolento, -ta *adj* : sensitive to cold

friolera *nf* (*used ironically or humorously*) : trifling amount ⟨una friolera de mil dólares : a mere thousand dollars⟩

friso *nm* : frieze

fritar *vt* : to fry

frito[1] *pp* → **freír**

frito[2]**, -ta** *adj* **1** : fried **2** *fam* : worn-out, fed up ⟨tener frito a alguien : to get on someone's nerves⟩ **3** *fam* : fast asleep ⟨se quedó frito en el sofá : she fell asleep on the couch⟩

fritura *nf* **1** : frying **2** : fried food

frivolidad *nf* : frivolity

frívolo, -la *adj* : frivolous — **frívolamente** *adv*

fronda *nf* **1** : frond **2 frondas** *nfpl* : foliage

frondoso, -sa *adj* : leafy, luxuriant

frontal *adj* : frontal, head-on ⟨un choque frontal : a head-on collision⟩

frontalmente *adv* : head-on

frontera *nf* : border, frontier

fronterizo, -za *adj* : border, on the border ⟨estados fronterizos : neighboring states⟩

frontispicio *nm* : frontispiece

frotar *vt* **1** : to rub **2** : to strike (a match) — **frotarse** *vr* : to rub (together)

frote *nm* : rubbing, rub

fructífero, -ra *adj* : fruitful, productive

fructificar {72} *vi* **1** : to bear or produce fruit **2** : to be productive

fructuoso, -sa *adj* : fruitful

frugal *adj* : frugal, thrifty — **frugalmente** *adv*

frugalidad *adj* : frugality

frunce *nm* : gather (in cloth), pucker

fruncido *nm* : gathering, shirring

fruncir {83} *vt* **1** : to gather, to shirr **2 fruncir el ceño** : to knit one's brow, to frown **3 fruncir la boca** : to pucker up, to purse one's lips

frunza, etc. → **fruncir**

frustración *nf, pl* **-ciones** : frustration

frustrado, -da *adj* **1** : frustrated **2** : failed, unsuccessful

frustrante *adj* : frustrating

frustrar *vt* : to frustrate, to thwart — **frustrarse** *vr* FRACASAR : to fail, to come to nothing ⟨se frustraron sus esperanzas : his hopes were dashed⟩

fruta *nf* : fruit

frutal[1] *adj* : fruit, fruit-bearing

frutal[2] *nm* : fruit tree

frutilla *nf* : South American strawberry

fruto *nm* **1** : fruit, agricultural product ⟨los frutos de la tierra : the fruits of the earth⟩ **2** : result, consequence ⟨los frutos de su trabajo : the fruits of his labor⟩

fucsia *adj* & *nm* : fuchsia

fue, etc. → **ir, ser**

fuego *nm* **1** : fire **2** : light ⟨¿tienes fuego? : have you got a light?⟩ **3** : flame, burner (on a stove) **4** : ardor, passion **5** FOGAJE : skin eruption, cold sore **6 fuegos artificiales** *nmpl* : fireworks

fuelle *nm* : bellows

fuente *nf* **1** MANANTIAL : spring **2** : fountain **3** ORIGEN : source ⟨fuentes informativas : sources of information⟩ **4** : platter, serving dish

fuera *adv* **1** : outside, out **2** : abroad, away **3 ~ de** : outside of, out of, beyond **4 ~ de** : besides, in addition to ⟨fuera de eso : aside from that⟩ **5 fuera de lugar** : out of place, amiss

fuerce, fuerza etc. → **forzar**

fuero *nm* **1** JURISDICCIÓN : jurisdiction **2** : privilege, exemption **3 fuero interno** : conscience, heart of hearts
fuerte[1] *adv* **1** : strongly, tightly, hard **2** : loudly **3** : abundantly
fuerte[2] *adj* **1** : strong **2** : intense ⟨un fuerte dolor : an intense pain⟩ **3** : loud **4** : extreme, excessive
fuerte[3] *nm* **1** : fort, stronghold **2** : forte, strong point
fuerza *nf* **1** : strength, vigor ⟨fuerza de voluntad : willpower⟩ **2** : force ⟨fuerza bruta : brute force⟩ **3** : power, might ⟨fuerza de brazos : manpower⟩ **4 fuerzas** *nfpl* : forces ⟨fuerzas armadas : armed forces⟩ **5 a fuerza de** : by, by dint of
fuetazo *nm* : lash
fuga *nf* **1** HUIDA : flight, escape **2** : fugue **3** : leak ⟨fuga de gas : gas leak⟩
fugarse {52} *vr* **1** : to escape **2** HUIR : to flee, to run away **3** : to elope
fugaz *adj, pl* **fugaces** : brief, fleeting
fugitivo, -va *adj & n* : fugitive
fulana *nf* : hooker, slut
fulano, -na *n* : so-and-so, what's-his-name, what's-her-name ⟨fulano, mengano, y zutano : Tom, Dick, and Harry⟩ ⟨señora fulana de tal : Mrs. so-and-so⟩
fulcro *nm* : fulcrum
fulgor *nm* : brilliance, splendor
fulgurar *vi* : to shine brightly, to gleam, to glow
fulminante *adj* **1** : fulminating, explosive **2** : devastating, terrible ⟨una mirada fulminante : a withering look⟩
fulminar *vt* **1** : to strike with lightning **2** : to strike down ⟨fulminar a alguien con la mirada : to look daggers at someone⟩
fumador, -dora *n* : smoker
fumar *v* : to smoke
fumble *nm* : fumble (in football)
fumblear *vt* : to fumble (in football)
fumigante *nm* : fumigant
fumigar {52} *vt* : to fumigate — **fumigación** *nf*
funámbulo, -la *n* EQUILIBRISTA : tightrope walker
función *nf, pl* **funciones 1** : function **2** : duty **3** : performance, show
funcional *adj* : functional — **funcionalmente** *adv*
funcionamiento *nm* **1** : functioning **2 en ~** : in operation
funcionar *vi* **1** : to function **2** : to run, to work
funcionario, -ria *n* : civil servant, official
funda *nf* **1** : case, cover, sheath **2** : pillowcase
fundación *nf, pl* **-ciones** : foundation, establishment
fundado, -da *adj* : well-founded, justified
fundador, -dora *n* : founder

fundamental *adj* BÁSICO : fundamental, basic — **fundamentalmente** *adv*
fundamentalismo *nm* : fundamentalism
fundamentalista *nmf* : fundamentalist
fundamentar *vt* **1** : to lay the foundations for **2** : to support, to back up **3** : to base, to found
fundamento *nm* : basis, foundation, groundwork
fundar *vt* **1** ESTABLECER, INSTITUIR : to found, to establish **2** BASAR : to base — **fundarse** *vr* **~ en** : to be based on, to stem from
fundición *nf, pl* **-ciones 1** : founding, smelting **2** : foundry
fundir *vt* **1** : to melt down, to smelt **2** : to fuse, to merge **3** : to burn out (a lightbulb) — **fundirse** *vr* **1** : to fuse together, to blend, to merge **2** : to melt, to thaw **3** : to fade (in television or movies)
fúnebre *adj* **1** : funeral, funereal **2** LÚGUBRE : gloomy, mournful
funeral[1] *adj* : funeral, funerary
funeral[2] *nm* **1** : funeral **2 funerales** *nmpl* EXEQUIAS : funeral rites
funeraria *nf* **1** : funeral home, funeral parlor **2 director de funeraria** : funeral director, undertaker
funerario, -ria *adj* : funeral
funesto, -ta *adj* : terrible, disastrous ⟨consecuencias funestas : disastrous consequences⟩
fungicida[1] *adj* : fungicidal
fungicida[2] *nm* : fungicide
fungir {35} *vi* : to act, to function ⟨fungir de asesor : to act as a consultant⟩
fungoso, -sa *adj* : fungous
funja, etc. → **fungir**
furgón *nm, pl* **furgones 1** : van, truck **2** : freight car, boxcar **3 furgón de cola** : caboose
furgoneta *nf* : van
furia *nf* **1** CÓLERA, IRA : fury, rage **2** : violence, fury ⟨la furia de la tormenta : the fury of the storm⟩
furibundo, -da *adj* : furious
furiosamente *adv* : furiously, frantically
furioso, -sa *adj* **1** AIRADO : furious, irate **2** : intense, violent
furor *nm* **1** : fury, rage **2** : violence (of the elements) **3** : passion, frenzy **4** : enthusiasm ⟨hacer furor : to be all the rage⟩
furtivo, -va *adj* : furtive — **furtivamente** *adv*
furúnculo *nm* DIVIESO : boil
fuselaje *nm* : fuselage
fusible *nm* : (electrical) fuse
fusil *nm* : rifle
fusilar *vt* **1** : to shoot, to execute (by firing squad) **2** *fam* : to plagiarize, to pirate
fusilería *nf* **1** : rifles *pl*, rifle fire **2 descarga de fusilería** : fusillade
fusión *nf, pl* **fusiones 1** : fusion **2** : union, merger

fusionar *vt* **1** : to fuse **2** : to merge, to amalgamate — **fusionarse** *vr*
fusta *nf* : riding crop
fustigar {52} *vt* **1** AZOTAR : to whip, to lash **2** : to upbraid, to berate
futbol *or* fútbol *nm* **1** : soccer **2** futbol americano : football

futbolista *nmf* : soccer player
futesa *nf* **1** : small thing, trifle **2** futesas *nfpl* : small talk
fútil *adj* : trifling, trivial
futurista *adj* : futuristic
futuro¹, -ra *adj* : future
futuro² *nm* PORVENIR : future

G

g *nf* : seventh letter of the Spanish alphabet
gabán *nm*, *pl* gabanes : topcoat, overcoat
gabardina *nf* **1** : gabardine **2** : trench coat, raincoat
gabarra *nf* : barge
gabinete *nm* **1** : cabinet (in government) **2** : study, office (in the home) **3** : (professional) office
gablete *nm* : gable
gabonés, -nesa *adj & n*, *mpl* -neses : Gabonese
gacela *nf* : gazelle
gaceta *nf* : gazette, newspaper
gachas *nfpl* : porridge
gacho, -cha *adj* **1** : drooping, turned downward ⟨*Mex fam* : nasty, awful **3** ir a gachas *fam* : to go on all fours
gaélico¹, -ca *adj* : Gaelic
gaélico² *nm* : Gaelic (language)
gafas *nfpl* ANTEOJOS : eyeglasses, glasses
gaita *nf* : bagpipes *pl*
gajes *nmpl* gajes del oficio : occupational hazards
gajo *nm* **1** : broken branch (of a tree) **2** : cluster, bunch (of fruit) **3** : segment (of citrus fruit)
gala *nf* **1** : gala ⟨vestido de gala : formal dress⟩ ⟨tener algo a gala : to be proud of something⟩ **2** galas *nfpl* : finery, attire
galáctico, -ca *adj* : galactic
galán *nm*, *pl* galanes **1** : ladies' man, gallant **2** : leading man, hero **3** : boyfriend, suitor
galano, -na *adj* **1** : elegant **2** *Mex* : mottled
galante *adj* : gallant, attentive — galantemente *adv*
galantear *vt* **1** CORTEJAR : to court, to woo **2** : to flirt with
galanteo *nm* **1** CORTEJO : courtship **2** : flirtation, flirting
galantería *nf* **1** : gallantry, attentiveness **2** : compliment
galápago *nm* : aquatic turtle
galardón *nm*, *pl* -dones : award, prize
galardonado, -da *adj* : prize-winning
galardonar *vt* : to give an award to
galaxia *nf* : galaxy
galeno *nm fam* : physician, doctor
galeón *nm*, *pl* galeones : galleon
galera *nf* : galley

galería *nf* **1** : gallery, balcony (in a theater) ⟨galería comercial : shopping mall⟩ **2** : corridor, passage
galerón *n*, *mpl* -rones *Mex* : large hall
galés¹, -lesa *adj* : Welsh
galés², -lesa *n*, *mpl* galeses **1** : Welshman *m*, Welshwoman *f* **2** los galeses : the Welsh
galés³ *nm* : Welsh (language)
galgo *nm* : greyhound
galimatías *nms & pl* : gibberish, nonsense
galio *nm* : gallium
gallardete *nm* : pennant, streamer
gallardía *nf* **1** VALENTÍA : bravery **2** APOSTURA : elegance, gracefulness
gallardo, -da *adj* **1** VALIENTE : brave **2** APUESTO : elegant, graceful
gallear *vi* : to show off, to strut around
gallego¹, -ga *adj* **1** : Galician **2** *fam* : Spanish
gallego², -ga *n* **1** : Galician **2** *fam* : Spaniard
galleta *nf* **1** : cookie **2** : cracker
gallina *nf* **1** : hen **2** gallina de Guinea : guinea fowl
gallinazo *nm* : vulture, buzzard
gallinero *nm* : chicken coop, henhouse
gallito, -ta *adj fam* : cocky, belligerent
gallo *nm* **1** : rooster, cock **2** *fam* : squeak or crack in the voice **3** *Mex* : serenade **4** gallo de pelea : gamecock
galo¹, -la *adj* **1** : Gaulish **2** : French
galo², -la *n* : Frenchman *m*, Frenchwoman *f*
galocha *nf* : galosh
galón *nm*, *pl* galones **1** : gallon **2** : stripe (military insignia)
galopada *nf* : gallop
galopante *adj* : galloping ⟨inflación galopante : galloping inflation⟩
galopar *vi* : to gallop
galope *nm* : gallop
galpón *nm*, *pl* galpones : shed, storehouse
galvanizar {21} *vt* : to galvanize — galvanización *nf*
gama *nf* **1** : range, spectrum, gamut **2** → gamo
gamba *nf* : large shrimp, prawn
gamberro, -rra *n Spain* : hooligan, troublemaker
gambiano, -na *adj & n* : Gambian
gambito *nm* : gambit (in chess)
gameto *nm* : gamete

gamo, -ma *n* : fallow deer
gamuza *nf* 1 : suede 2 : chamois
gana *nf* 1 : desire, inclination 2 **de buena gana** : willingly, readily, gladly 3 **de mala gana** : reluctantly, halfheartedly 4 **tener ganas de** : to feel like, to be in the mood for ⟨tengo ganas de bailar : I feel like dancing⟩ 5 **ponerle ganas a algo** : to put effort into something
ganadería *nf* 1 : cattle raising, stockbreeding 2 : cattle ranch 3 GANADO : cattle *pl*, livestock
ganadero¹, -ra *adj* : cattle, ranching
ganadero², -ra *n* : rancher, stockbreeder
ganado *nm* 1 : cattle *pl*, livestock 2 **ganado ovino** : sheep *pl* 3 **ganado porcino** : swine *pl*
ganador¹, -dora *adj* : winning
ganador², -dora *n* : winner
ganancia *nf* 1 : profit 2 **ganancias** *nfpl* : winnings, gains
ganancioso, -sa *adj* : profitable
ganar *vt* 1 : to win 2 : to gain ⟨ganar tiempo : to buy time⟩ 3 : to earn ⟨ganar dinero : to make money⟩ 4 : to acquire, to obtain — *vi* 1 : to win 2 : to profit ⟨salir ganando : to come out ahead⟩ — **ganarse** *vr* 1 : to gain, to win ⟨ganarse a alguien : to win someone over⟩ 2 : to earn ⟨ganarse la vida : to make a living⟩ 3 : to deserve
gancho *nm* 1 : hook 2 : clothes hanger 3 : hairpin, bobby pin 4 *Col* : safety pin
gandul¹ *nm CA, Car, Col* : pigeon pea
gandul², -dula *n fam* : idler, lazybones
gandulear *vi* : to idle, to loaf, to lounge about
ganga *nf* : bargain
ganglio *nm* 1 : ganglion 2 : gland
gangrena *nf* : gangrene — **gangrenoso, -sa** *adj*
gángster *nmf, pl* **gángsters** : gangster
gansada *nf* : silly thing, nonsense
ganso, -sa *n* 1 : goose, gander *m* 2 : idiot, fool
gañido *nm* : yelp (of a dog)
gañir {38} *vi* : to yelp
garabatear *v* : to scribble, to scrawl, to doodle
garabato *nm* 1 : doodle 2 **garabatos** *nmpl* : scribble, scrawl
garaje *nm* : garage
garante *nmf* : guarantor
garantía *nf* 1 : guarantee, warranty 2 : security ⟨garantía de trabajo : job security⟩
garantizar {21} *vt* : to guarantee
garapiña *nf* : pineapple drink
garapiñar *vt* : to candy
garbanzo *nm* : chickpea, garbanzo
garbo *nm* 1 DONAIRE : grace, poise 2 : jauntiness
garboso, -sa *adj* 1 : graceful 2 : elegant, stylish
garceta *nf* : egret

gardenia *nf* : gardenia
garfio *nm* : hook, gaff, grapnel
gargajo *nm fam* : phlegm
garganta *nf* 1 : throat 2 : neck (of a person or a bottle) 3 : ravine, narrow pass
gargantilla *nf* : choker, necklace
gárgara *nf* 1 : gargle, gargling 2 **hacer gárgaras** : to gargle
gargarizar *vi* : to gargle
gárgola *nf* : gargoyle
garita *nf* 1 : cabin, hut 2 : sentry box, lookout post
garoso, -sa *adj Col, Ven* : gluttonous, greedy
garra *nf* 1 : claw 2 : hand, paw 3 **garras** *nfpl* : claws, clutches ⟨caer en las garras de alguien : to fall into someone's clutches⟩
garrafa *nf* : decanter, carafe
garrafal *adj* : terrible, monstrous
garrafón *nm, pl* **-fones** : large decanter, large bottle
garrapata *nf* : tick
garrobo *nm CA* : large lizard, iguana
garrocha *nf* 1 PICA : lance, pike 2 : pole ⟨salto con garrocha : pole vault⟩
garrotazo *nm* : blow (with a club)
garrote *nm* 1 : club, stick 2 *Mex* : brake
garúa *nf* : drizzle
garuar {3} *v impers* LLOVIZNAR : to drizzle
garza *nf* : heron
gas *nm* : gas, vapor, fumes *pl* ⟨gas lagrimógeno : tear gas⟩
gasa *nf* : gauze
gasear *vt* 1 : to gas 2 : to aerate (a liquid)
gaseosa *nf* REFRESCO : soda, soft drink
gaseoso, -sa *adj* 1 : gaseous 2 : carbonated, fizzy
gasoducto *nm* : gas pipeline
gasolina *nf* : gasoline, gas
gasolinera *nf* : gas station, service station
gastado, -da *adj* 1 : spent 2 : worn, worn-out
gastador¹, -dora *adj* : extravagant, spendthrift
gastador², -dora *n* : spendthrift
gastar *vt* 1 : to spend 2 CONSUMIR : to consume, to use up 3 : to squander, to waste 4 : to wear ⟨gasta un bigote : he sports a mustache⟩ — **gastarse** *vr* 1 : to spend, to expend 2 : to run down, to wear out
gasto *nm* 1 : expense, expenditure 2 DETERIORO : wear 3 **gastos generales** *or* **gastos indirectos** : overhead
gástrico, -ca *adj* : gastric
gastritis *nf* : gastritis
gastronomía *nf* : gastronomy
gastronómico, -ca *adj* : gastronomic
gastrónomo, -ma *n* : gourmet
gatas *adv* **andar a gatas** : to crawl, to go on all fours
gatear *vi* 1 : to crawl 2 : to climb, to clamber (up)

gatillero *nm Mex* : gunman
gatillo *nm* : trigger
gatito, -ta *n* : kitten
gato[1], -ta *n* : cat
gato[2] *nm* : jack (for an automobile)
gauchada *nf Arg, Uru* : favor, kindness
gaucho *nm* : gaucho
gaveta *nf* 1 CAJÓN : drawer 2 : till
gavilla *nf* 1 : gang, band 2 : sheaf
gaviota *nf* : gull, seagull
gay ['ge, 'gai] *adj* : gay (homosexual)
gaza *nf* : loop
gazapo *nm* 1 : young rabbit 2 : misprint, error
gazmoñería *nf* MOJIGATERÍA : prudery, primness
gazmoño[1], -ña *adj* : prudish, prim
gazmoño[2], -ña *n* MOJIGATO : prude, prig
gaznate *nm* : throat, gullet
gazpacho *nm* : gazpacho
géiser *or* **géyser** *nm* : geyser
gel *nm* : gel
gelatina *nf* : gelatin
gélido, -da *adj* : icy, freezing cold
gelificarse *vr* : to jell
gema *nf* : gem
gemelo[1], -la *adj & n* MELLIZO : twin
gemelo[2] *nm* 1 : cuff link 2 **gemelos** *nmpl* BINOCULARES : binoculars
gemido *nm* : moan, groan, wail
Géminis *nmf* : Gemini
gemir {54} *vi* : to moan, to groan, to wail
gen *or* **gene** *nm* : gene
gendarme *nmf* POLICÍA : police officer, policeman *m*, policewoman *f*
gendarmería *nf* : police
genealogía *nf* : genealogy
genealógico, -ca *adj* : genealogical
generación *nf, pl* **-ciones** 1 : generation ⟨tercera generación : third generation⟩ 2 : generating, creating 3 : class ⟨la generación del '97 : the class of '97⟩
generacional *adj* : generation, generational
generador *nm* : generator
general[1] *adj* 1 : general 2 **en** ∼ *or por* **lo general** : in general, generally
general[2] *nmf* 1 : general 2 **general de división** : major general
generalidad *nf* 1 : generality, generalization 2 : majority
generalización *nf, pl* **-ciones** 1 : generalization 2 : escalation, spread
generalizado, -da *adj* : generalized, widespread
generalizar {21} *vi* : to generalize — *vt* : to spread, to spread out — **generalizarse** *vr* : to become widespread
generalmente *adv* : usually, generally
generar *vt* : to generate — **generarse** *vr*
genérico, -ca *adj* : generic
género *nm* 1 : genre, class, kind ⟨el género humano : the human race, mankind⟩ 2 : gender (in grammar) 3 **géneros** *nmpl* : goods, commodities
generosidad *nf* : generosity
generoso, -sa *adj* 1 : generous, unselfish 2 : ample — **generosamente** *adv*

genética *nf* : genetics
genético, -ca *adj* : genetic — **genéticamente** *adv*
genetista *nmf* : geneticist
genial *adj* 1 AGRADABLE : genial, pleasant 2 : brilliant ⟨una obra genial : a work of genius⟩ 3 *fam* FORMIDABLE : fantastic, terrific
genialidad *nf* 1 : genius 2 : stroke of genius 3 : eccentricity
genio *nm* 1 : genius 2 : temper, disposition ⟨de mal genio : bad-tempered⟩ 3 : genie
genital *adj* : genital
genitales *nmpl* : genitals, genitalia
genocidio *nm* : genocide
genotipo *nm* : genotype
gente *nf* 1 : people 2 : relatives *pl*, folks *pl* 3 **gente menuda** *fam* : children, kids *pl* 4 **ser buena gente** : to be nice, to be kind
gentil[1] *adj* 1 AMABLE : kind 2 : gentile
gentil[2] *nmf* : gentile
gentileza *nf* 1 AMABILIDAD : kindness 2 CORTESÍA : courtesy
gentilicio, -cia *adj* 1 : national, tribal 2 : family
gentío *nm* MUCHEDUMBRE, MULTITUD : crowd, mob
gentuza *nf* CHUSMA : riffraff, rabble
genuflexión *nf, pl* **-xiones** 1 : genuflection 2 **hacer una genuflexión** : to genuflect
genuino, -na *adj* : genuine — **genuinamente** *adv*
geofísica *nf* : geophysics
geofísico, -ca *adj* : geophysical
geografía *nf* : geography
geográfico, -ca *adj* : geographic, geographical — **geográficamente** *adv*
geógrafo, -fa *n* : geographer
geología *nf* : geology
geológico, -ca *adj* : geologic, geological — **geológicamente** *adv*
geólogo, -ga *n* : geologist
geometría *nf* : geometry
geométrico, -ca *adj* : geometric, geometrical — **geométricamente** *adv*
geopolítica *nf* : geopolitics
geopolítico, -ca *adj* : geopolitical
georgiano, -na *adj & n* : Georgian
geranio *nm* : geranium
gerbo *nm* : gerbil
gerencia *nf* : management, administration
gerencial *adj* : managerial
gerente *nmf* : manager, director
geriatría *nf* : geriatrics
geriátrico, -ca *adj* : geriatric
germanio *nm* : germanium
germano, -na *adj* : Germanic, German
germen *nm, pl* **gérmenes** : germ
germicida *nf* : germicide
germinación *nf, pl* **-ciones** : germination
germinar *vi* : to germinate, to sprout
gerontología *nf* : gerontology
gerundio *nm* : gerund

gesta *nf* : deed, exploit
gestación *nf, pl* **-ciones** : gestation
gesticulación *nf, pl* **-ciones** : gesturing, gesticulation
gesticular *vi* : to gesticulate, to gesture
gestión *nf, pl* **gestiones 1** TRÁMITE : procedure, step **2** ADMINISTRACIÓN : management **3 gestiones** *nfpl* : negotiations
gestionar *vt* **1** : to negotiate, to work towards **2** ADMINISTRAR : to manage, to handle
gesto *nm* **1** ADEMÁN : gesture **2** : facial expression **3** MUECA : grimace
gestor[1], **-tora** *adj* : facilitating, negotiating, managing
gestor[2], **-tora** *n* : facilitator, manager
géyser → **géiser**
ghanés, -nesa *adj & n, mpl* **ghaneses** : Ghanaian
ghetto → **gueto**
giba *nf* **1** : hump (of an animal) **2** : hunchback (of a person)
gibón *nm, pl* **gibones** : gibbon
giboso[1], **-sa** *adj* : hunchbacked, humpbacked
giboso[2], **-sa** *n* : hunchback, humpback
gigabyte *nm* : gigabyte
gigante[1] *adj* : giant, gigantic
gigante[2], **-ta** *n* : giant
gigantesco, -ca *adj* : gigantic, huge
gime, etc. → **gemir**
gimnasia *nf* : gymnastics
gimnasio *nm* : gymnasium, gym
gimnasta *nmf* : gymnast
gimnástico, -ca *adj* : gymnastic
gimotear *vi* LLORIQUEAR : to whine, to whimper
gimoteo *nm* : whimpering
ginebra *nf* : gin
ginecología *nf* : gynecology
ginecológico, -ca *adj* : gynecologic, gynecological
ginecólogo, -ga *n* : gynecologist
ginseng *nm* : ginseng
gira *nf* : tour
giralda *nf* : weather vane
girar *vi* **1** : to turn around, to revolve **2** : to swing around, to swivel — *vt* **1** : to turn, to twist, to rotate **2** : to draft (checks) **3** : to transfer (funds)
girasol *nm* MIRASOL : sunflower
giratorio, -ria *adj* : revolving
giro *nm* **1** VUELTA : turn, rotation **2** : change of direction ⟨giro de 180 grados : U-turn, about-face⟩ **3 giro bancario** : bank draft **4 giro postal** : money order
giroscopio *or* **giróscopo** *nm* : gyroscope
gis *nm Mex* : chalk
gitano, -na *adj & n* : Gypsy
glacial *adj* : glacial, icy — **glacialmente** *adv*
glaciar *nm* : glacier
gladiador *nm* : gladiator
gladiolo *or* **gladíolo** *nm* : gladiolus
glándula *nf* : gland — **glandular** *adj*

glaseado *nm* : glaze, icing
glasear *vt* : to glaze
glaucoma *nm* : glaucoma
glicerina *nf* : glycerin, glycerol
glicinia *nf* : wisteria
global *adj* **1** : global, worldwide **2** : full, comprehensive **3** : total, overall
globalizar {21} *vt* **1** ABARCAR : to include, to encompass **2** : to extend worldwide
globalmente *adv* : globally, as a whole
globo *nm* **1** : globe, sphere **2** : balloon **3 globo ocular** : eyeball
glóbulo *nm* **1** : globule **2** : blood cell, corpuscle
gloria *nf* **1** : glory **2** : fame, renown **3** : delight, enjoyment **4** : star, legend ⟨las glorias del cine : the great names in motion pictures⟩
glorieta *nf* **1** : rotary, traffic circle **2** : bower, arbor
glorificar {72} *vt* ALABAR : to glorify — **glorificación** *nf*
glorioso, -sa *adj* : glorious — **gloriosamente** *adv*
glosa *nf* **1** : gloss **2** : annotation, commentary
glosar *vt* **1** : to gloss **2** : to annotate, to comment on (a text)
glosario *nm* : glossary
glotis *nf* : glottis
glotón[1], **-tona** *adj, mpl* **glotones** : gluttonous
glotón[2], **-tona** *n, mpl* **glotones** : glutton
glotón[3] *nm, pl* **glotones** : wolverine
glotonería *nf* GULA : gluttony
glucosa *nf* : glucose
glutinoso, -sa *adj* : glutinous
gnomo ['nomo] *nm* : gnome
gobernación *nf, pl* **-ciones** : governing, government
gobernador, -dora *n* : governor
gobernante[1] *adj* : ruling, governing
gobernante[2] *nmf* : ruler, leader, governor
gobernar {55} *vt* **1** : to govern, to rule **2** : to steer, to sail (a ship) — *vi* **1** : to govern **2** : to steer
gobierno *nm* : government
goce[1], **etc.** → **gozar**
goce[2] *nm* **1** PLACER : enjoyment, pleasure **2** : use, possession
gol *nm* : goal (in soccer)
golear *vt* : to rout, to score many goals against (in soccer)
goleta *nf* : schooner
golf *nm* : golf
golfista *nmf* : golfer
golfo *nm* : gulf, bay
golondrina *nf* **1** : swallow (bird) **2 golondrina de mar** : tern
golosina *nf* : sweet, snack
goloso, -sa *adj* : fond of sweets ⟨ser goloso : to have a sweet tooth⟩
golpazo *nm* : heavy blow, bang, thump
golpe *nm* **1** : blow ⟨caerle a golpes a alguien : to give someone a beating⟩ **2** : knock **3 de ~** : suddenly **4 de un**

golpe : all at once, in one fell swoop **5**
golpe de estado : coup, coup d'etat **6**
golpe de suerte : stroke of luck
golpeado, -da *adj* **1** : beaten, hit **2** : bruised (of fruit) **3** : dented
golpear *vt* **1** : to beat (up), to hit **2** : to slam, to bang, to strike — *vi* **1** : to knock (at a door) **2** : to beat ⟨la lluvia golpeaba contra el tejado : the rain beat against the roof⟩ — **golpearse** *vr*
golpetear *v* : to knock, to rattle, to tap
golpeteo *nm* : banging, knocking, tapping
goma *nf* **1** : gum ⟨goma de mascar : chewing gum⟩ **2** CAUCHO : rubber ⟨goma espuma : foam rubber⟩ **3** PEGAMENTO : glue **4** : rubber band **5** *Arg* : tire **6** *or* **goma de borrar** : eraser
gomita *nf* : rubber band
gomoso, -sa *adj* : gummy, sticky
góndola *nf* : gondola
gong *nm* : gong
gonorrea *nf* : gonorrhea
gorda *nf Mex* : thick corn tortilla
gordinflón[1], -flona *adj, mpl* **-flones** *fam* : chubby, pudgy
gordinflón[2], -flona *n, mpl* **-flones** *fam* : chubby person
gordo[1], -da *adj* **1** : fat **2** : thick **3** : fatty, greasy, oily **4** : unpleasant ⟨me cae gorda tu tía : I can't stand your aunt⟩
gordo[2], -da *n* : fat person
gordo[3] *nm* **1** GRASA : fat **2** : jackpot
gordura *nf* : fatness, flab
gorgojo *nm* : weevil
gorgotear *vi* : to gurgle, to bubble
gorgoteo *nm* : gurgle
gorila *nm* : gorilla
gorjear *vi* **1** : to chirp, to tweet, to warble **2** : to gurgle
gorjeo *nm* **1** : chirping, warbling **2** : gurgling
gorra *nf* **1** : bonnet **2** : cap **3 de ~** *fam* : for free, at someone else's expense ⟨vivir de gorra : to sponge, to freeload⟩
gorrear *vt fam* : to bum, to scrounge — *vi fam* : to freeload
gorrero, -ra *n fam* : freeloader, sponger
gorrión *nm, pl* **gorriones** : sparrow
gorro *nm* **1** : cap **2 estar hasta el gorro** : to be fed up
gorrón, -rrona *n, mpl* **gorrones** *fam* : freeloader, scrounger
gorronear *vt fam* : to bum, to scrounge — *vi fam* : to freeload
gota *nf* **1** : drop ⟨una gota de sudor : a bead of sweat⟩ ⟨como dos gotas de agua : like two peas in a pod⟩ ⟨sudar la gota gorda : to sweat buckets, to work very hard⟩ **2** : gout
gotear *v* **1** : to drip **2** : to leak — *v impers* LLOVIZNAR : to drizzle
goteo *nm* : drip, dripping
gotera *nf* **1** : leak **2** : stain (from dripping water)
gotero *nm* : (medicine) dropper
gótico, -ca *adj* : Gothic
gourmet *nmf* : gourmet

gozar {21} *vi* **1** : to enjoy oneself, to have a good time **2 ~ de** : to enjoy, to have, to possess ⟨gozar de buena salud : to enjoy good health⟩ **3 ~ con** : to take delight in
gozne *nm* BISAGRA : hinge
gozo *nm* **1** : joy **2** PLACER : enjoyment, pleasure
gozoso, -sa *adj* : joyful
grabación *nf, pl* **-ciones** : recording
grabado *nm* **1** : engraving **2 grabado al aguafuerte** : etching
grabador, -dora *n* : engraver
grabadora *nf* : tape recorder
grabar *vt* **1** : to engrave **2** : to record, to tape — *vi* **grabar al aguafuerte** : to etch — **grabarse** *vr* **grabársele a alguien en la memoria** : to become engraved on someone's mind
gracia *nf* **1** : grace **2** : favor, kindness **3** : humor, wit ⟨su comentario no me hizo gracia : I wasn't amused by his remark⟩ **4 gracias** *nfpl* : thanks ⟨igracias! : thank you!⟩ ⟨dar gracias : to give thanks⟩
grácil *adj* **1** : graceful **2** : delicate, slender, fine
gracilidad *nm* : gracefulness
gracioso, -sa *adj* **1** CHISTOSO : funny, amusing **2** : cute, attractive
grada *nf* **1** : harrow **2** PELDAÑO : step, stair **3 gradas** *nfpl* : bleachers, grandstand
gradación *nf, pl* **-ciones** : gradation, scale
gradar *vt* : to harrow, to hoe
gradería *nf* : tiers *pl*, stands *pl*, rows *pl* (in a theater)
gradiente *nf* : gradient, slope
grado *nm* **1** : degree (in meteorology and mathematics) ⟨grado centígrado : degree centigrade⟩ **2** : extent, level, degree ⟨en grado sumo : greatly, to the highest degree⟩ **3** RANGO : rank **4** : year, class (in education) **5 de buen grado** : willingly, readily
graduable *adj* : adjustable
graduación *nf, pl* **-ciones** **1** : graduation (from a school) **2** GRADO : rank **3** : alcohol content, proof
graduado[1], -da *adj* **1** : graduated **2 lentes graduados** : prescription lenses
graduado[2], -da *n* : graduate
gradual *adj* : gradual — **gradualmente** *adv*
graduar {3} *v* **1** : to regulate, to adjust **2** CALIBRAR : to calibrate, to gauge — **graduarse** *vr* : to graduate (from a school)
graffiti *or* **grafiti** *nmpl* : graffiti *pl*
gráfica *nf* → **gráfico[2]**
gráfico[1], -ca *adj* : graphic — **gráficamente** *adv*
gráfico[2] *nm* **1** : graph, chart **2** : graphic (for a computer, etc.) **3 gráfico de barras** : bar graph
grafismo *nm* : graphics *pl*

grafito *nm* : graphite
gragea *nf* **1** : coated pill or tablet **2 grageas** *nfpl* : sprinkles, jimmies
grajo *nm* : rook (bird)
grama *nf* : grass
gramática *nf* : grammar
gramatical *adj* : grammatical — **gramaticalmente** *adv*
gramo *nm* : gram
gran → **grande**
grana *nf* : scarlet, deep red
granada *nf* **1** : pomegranate **2** : grenade ⟨granada de mano : hand grenade⟩
granadero *nm* **1** : grenadier **2 granaderos** *nmpl Mex* : riot squad
granadino, -na *adj & n* : Grenadian
granado, -da *adj* **1** DISTINGUIDO : distinguished **2** : choice, select
granate *nm* **1** : garnet **2** : deep red, maroon
grande *adj* (**gran** *before singular nouns*) **1** : large, big ⟨un libro grande : a big book⟩ **2** ALTO : tall **3** NOTABLE : great ⟨un gran autor : a great writer⟩ **4** (*indicating intensity*) : great ⟨con gran placer : with great pleasure⟩ **5** : old, grown-up ⟨hijos grandes : grown children⟩
grandeza *nf* **1** MAGNITUD : greatness, size **2** : nobility **3** : generosity, graciousness **4** : grandeur, magnificence
grandilocuencia *nf* : grandiloquence — **grandilocuente** *adj*
grandiosidad *nf* : grandeur
grandioso, -sa *adj* **1** MAGNÍFICO : grand, magnificent **2** : grandiose
granel *adv* **1 a** ∼ : galore, in great quantities **2 a** ∼ : in bulk ⟨vender a granel : to sell in bulk⟩
granero *nm* : barn, granary
granito *nm* : granite
granizada *nf* : hailstorm
granizar {21} *v impers* : to hail
granizo *nm* : hail
granja *nf* : farm
granjear *vt* : to earn, to win — **granjearse** *vr* : to gain, to earn
granjero, -ra *n* : farmer
grano *nm* **1** PARTÍCULA : grain, particle ⟨un grano de arena : a grain of sand⟩ **2** : grain (of rice, etc.), bean (of coffee), seed **3** : grain (of wood or rock) **4** BARRO, ESPINILLA : pimple **5 ir al grano** : to get to the point
granuja *nmf* PILLUELO : rascal, urchin
granular¹ *vt* : to granulate — **granularse** *vr* : to break out in spots
granular² *adj* : granular, grainy
granza *nf* : chaff
grapa *nf* **1** : staple **2** : clamp
grapadora *nf* ENGRAPADORA : stapler
grapar *vt* ENGRAPAR : to staple
grasa *nf* **1** : grease **2** : fat **3** *Mex* : shoe polish
grasiento, -ta *adj* : greasy, oily
graso, -sa *adj* **1** : fatty **2** : greasy, oily
grasoso, -sa *adj* GRASIENTO : greasy, oily

gratificación *nf, pl* **-ciones 1** SATISFACCIÓN : gratification **2** : bonus **3** RECOMPENSA : recompense, reward
gratificar {72} *vt* **1** SATISFACER : to satisfy, to gratify **2** RECOMPENSAR : to reward **3** : to give a bonus to
gratinado, -da *adj* : au gratin
gratis¹ *adv* GRATUITAMENTE : free, for free, gratis
gratis² *adj* GRATUITO : free, gratis
gratitud *nf* : gratitude
grato, -ta *adj* AGRADABLE, PLACENTERO : pleasant, agreeable — **gratamente** *adv*
gratuitamente *adv* **1** : gratuitously **2** GRATIS : free, for free, gratis
gratuito, -ta *adj* **1** : gratuitous, unwarranted **2** GRATIS : free, gratis
grava *nf* : gravel
gravamen *nm, pl* **-vámenes 1** : burden, obligation **2** : (property) tax
gravar *vt* **1** : to burden, to encumber **2** : to levy (a tax)
grave *adj* **1** : grave, important **2** : serious, somber **3** : serious (of an illness)
gravedad *nf* **1** : gravity ⟨centro de gravedad : center of gravity⟩ **2** : seriousness, severity
gravemente *adv* : gravely, seriously
gravilla *nf* : (fine) gravel
gravitación *nf, pl* **-ciones** : gravitation
gravitacional *adj* : gravitational
gravitar *vi* **1** : to gravitate **2** ∼ **sobre** : to rest on **3** ∼ **sobre** : to loom over
gravoso, -sa *adj* **1** ONEROSO : burdensome, onerous **2** : costly
graznar *vi* : to caw, to honk, to quack, to squawk
graznido *nm* : cawing, honking, quacking, squawking
gregario, -ria *adj* : gregarious
gregoriano, -na *adj* : Gregorian
gremial *adj* SINDICAL : union, labor
gremio *nm* SINDICATO : union, guild
greña *nf* **1** : mat, tangle **2 greñas** *nfpl* MELENAS : shaggy hair, mop
greñudo, -da *n* HIPPIE, MELENUDO : longhair, hippie
grey *nf* : congregation, flock
griego¹, -ga *adj & n* : Greek
griego² *nm* : Greek (language)
grieta *nf* : crack, crevice
grifo *nm* **1** : faucet ⟨agua del grifo : tap water⟩ **2** : griffin
grillete *nm* : shackle
grillo *nm* **1** : cricket **2 grillos** *nmpl* : fetters, shackles
grima *nf* **1** : disgust, uneasiness **2 darle grima a alguien** : to get on someone's nerves
gringo, -ga *adj & n* YANQUI : Yankee, gringo
gripa *nf Col, Mex* : flu
gripe *nf* : flu
gris *adj* **1** : gray **2** : overcast, cloudy
grisáceo, -cea *adj* : grayish
gritar *v* : to shout, to scream, to cry
gritería *nf* : shouting, clamor

grito *nm* : shout, scream, cry ⟨a grito pelado : at the top of one's voice⟩
groenlandés, -desa *adj & n* : Greenlander
grogui *adj fam* : dazed, groggy
grosella *nf* 1 : currant 2 **grosella espinosa** : gooseberry
grosería *nf* 1 : insult, coarse language 2 : rudeness, discourtesy
grosero¹, -ra *adj* 1 : rude, fresh 2 : coarse, vulgar
grosero², -ra *n* : rude person
grosor *nm* : thickness
grosso *adj* **a grosso modo** : roughly, broadly, approximately
grotesco, -ca *adj* : grotesque, hideous
grúa *nf* 1 : crane (machine) 2 : tow truck
gruesa *nf* : gross
grueso¹, -sa *adj* 1 : thick, bulky 2 : heavy, big 3 : heavyset, stout
grueso² *nm* 1 : thickness 2 : main body, mass 3 **en ~** : in bulk
grulla *nf* : crane (bird)
grumo *nm* : lump, glob
gruñido *nm* : growl, grunt
gruñir {38} *vi* 1 : to growl, to grunt 2 : to grumble
gruñón¹, -ñona *adj, mpl* **gruñones** *fam* : grumpy, crabby
gruñón², -ñona *n, mpl* **gruñones** *fam* : grumpy person, nag
grupa *nf* : rump, hindquarters *pl*
grupo *nm* : group
gruta *nf* : grotto, cave
guacal *nm Col, Mex, Ven* : crate
guacamayo *nm* : macaw
guacamole *or* **guacamol** *nm* : guacamole
guacamote *nm Mex* : yuca, cassava
guachinango → **huachinango**
guacho, -cha *adj* 1 *Arg, Col, Chile, Peru* : orphaned 2 *Chile, Peru* : odd, unmatched
guadaña *nf* : scythe
guagua *nf* 1 *Arg, Col, Chile, Peru* : baby 2 *Cuba, PRi* : bus
guaira *nf* 1 *CA* : traditional flute 2 *Peru* : smelting furnace
guajiro, -ra *n Cuba* : peasant
guajolote *nm Mex* : turkey
guanábana *nf* : guanabana, soursop (fruit)
guanaco *nm* : guanaco
guandú *nm CA, Car, Col* : pigeon pea
guango, -ga *adj Mex* 1 : loose-fitting, baggy 2 : slack, loose
guano *nm* : guano
guante *nm* 1 : glove ⟨guante de boxeo : boxing glove⟩ 2 **arrojarle el guante (a alguien)** : to throw down the gauntlet (to someone)
guantelete *nm* : gauntlet
guapo, -pa *adj* 1 : handsome, good-looking, attractive 2 : elegant, smart 3 *fam* : bold, dashing
guapura *nf fam* : handsomeness, attractiveness, good looks *pl* ⟨¡qué guapura! : what a vision!⟩

guarache → **huarache**
guarachear *vi Cuba, PRi fam* : to go on a spree, to go out on the town
guaraní¹ *adj & nmf* : Guarani
guaraní² *nm* : Guarani (language of Paraguay)
guarda *nmf* 1 GUARDIÁN : security guard 2 : keeper, custodian
guardabarros *nms & pl* : fender, mudguard
guardabosque *nmf* : forest ranger, gamekeeper
guardacostas¹ *nmfs & pl* : coastguardsman
guardacostas² *nms & pl* : coast guard vessel
guardaespaldas *nmfs & pl* : bodyguard
guardafangos *nms & pl* : fender, mudguard
guardameta *nmf* ARQUERO, PORTERO : goalkeeper, goalie
guardapelo *nm* : locket
guardapolvo *nm* 1 : dustcover 2 : duster, housecoat
guardar *vt* 1 : to guard 2 : to maintain, to preserve 3 CONSERVAR : to put away 4 RESERVAR : to save 5 : to keep (a secret or promise) — **guardarse** *vr* 1 **~ de** : to refrain from 2 **~ de** : to guard against, to be careful not to
guardarropa *nm* 1 : cloakroom, checkroom 2 ARMARIO : closet, wardrobe
guardería *nf* : nursery, day-care center
guardia¹ *nf* 1 : guard, defense 2 : guard duty, watch 3 **en ~** : on guard
guardia² *nmf* 1 : sentry, guardsman, guard 2 : police officer, policeman *m*, policewoman *f*
guardiamarina *nmf* : midshipman
guardián, -diana *n, mpl* **guardianes** 1 GUARDA : security guard, watchman 2 : guardian, keeper 3 **perro guardián** : watchdog
guarecer {53} *vt* : to shelter, to protect — **guarecerse** *vr* : to take shelter
guarida *nf* 1 : den, lair 2 : hideout
guarismo *nm* : figure, numeral
guarnecer {53} *vt* 1 : to adorn 2 : to garnish 3 : to garrison
guarnición *nf, pl* **-ciones** 1 : garnish 2 : garrison 3 : decoration, trimming, setting (of a jewel)
guaro *nm CA* : liquor distilled from sugarcane
guasa *nf fam* 1 : joking, fooling around 2 **de ~** : in jest, as a joke
guasón¹, -sona *adj, mpl* **guasones** *fam* : funny, witty
guasón², -sona *n, mpl* **guasones** *fam* : joker, clown
guatemalteco, -ca *adj & n* : Guatemalan
guau *interj* : wow!
guayaba *nf* : guava (fruit)
gubernamental *adj* : governmental
gubernativo, -va → **gubernamental**
gubernatura *nf Mex* : governing body
guepardo *nm* : cheetah
güero, -ra *adj Mex* : blond, fair

guerra *nf* **1** : war ⟨declarar la guerra : to declare war⟩ ⟨guerra sin cuartel : all-out war⟩ **2** : warfare **3** LUCHA : conflict, struggle
guerrear *vi* : to wage war
guerrero¹, -ra *adj* **1** : war, fighting **2** : warlike
guerrero², -ra *n* : warrior
guerrilla *nf* : guerrilla warfare
guerrillero, -ra *adj & n* : guerrilla
gueto *nm* : ghetto
guía¹ *nf* **1** : directory, guidebook **2** ORIENTACIÓN : guidance, direction ⟨la conciencia me sirve como guía : conscience is my guide⟩
guía² *nmf* : guide, leader ⟨guía de turismo : tour guide⟩
guiar {85} *vt* **1** : to guide, to lead **2** CONDUCIR : to manage — **guiarse** *vr* : to be guided by, to go by
guija *nf* : pebble
guijarro *nm* : pebble
guillotina *nf* : guillotine — **guillotinar** *vt*
guinda¹ *adj & nm Mex* : burgundy (color)
guinda² *nf* : morello (cherry)
guineo *nm Car* : banana
guinga *nf* : gingham
guiñada → **guiño**
guiñar *vi* : to wink
guiño *nm* : wink
guión *nm, pl* **guiones 1** : script, screenplay **2** : hyphen, dash **3** ESTANDARTE : standard, banner
guirnalda *nf* : garland
guisa *nf* **1** : manner, fashion **2 a guisa de** : like, by way of **3 de tal guisa** : in such a way

guisado ESTOFADO *nm* : stew
guisante *nm* : pea
guisar *vt* **1** ESTOFAR : to stew **2** *Spain* : to cook
guiso *nm* **1** : stew **2** : casserole
güisqui → **whisky**
guita *nf* : string, twine
guitarra *nf* : guitar
guitarrista *nmf* : guitarist
gula *nf* GLOTONERÍA : gluttony, greed
gusano *nm* **1** LOMBRIZ : worm, earthworm ⟨gusano de seda : silkworm⟩ **2** : caterpillar, maggot, grub
gustar *vt* **1** : to taste **2** : to like ⟨¿gustan pasar? : would you like to come in?⟩ — *vi* **1** : to be pleasing ⟨me gustan los dulces : I like sweets⟩ ⟨a María le gusta Carlos : Maria is attracted to Carlos⟩ ⟨no me gusta que me griten : I don't like to be yelled at⟩ **2 ~ de** : to like, to enjoy ⟨no gusta de chismes : she doesn't like gossip⟩ **3 como guste** : as you wish, as you like
gustativo, -va *adj* : taste ⟨papilas gustativas : taste buds⟩
gusto *nm* **1** : flavor, taste **2** : taste, style **3** : pleasure, liking **4** : whim, fancy ⟨a gusto : at will⟩ **5 a ~** : comfortable, at ease **6 al gusto** : to taste, as one likes **7 mucho gusto** : pleased to meet you
gustosamente *adv* : gladly
gustoso, -sa *adj* **1** : willing, glad ⟨nuestra empresa participará gustosa : our company will be pleased to participate⟩ **2** : zesty, tasty
gutural *adj* : guttural

H

h *nf* : eighth letter of the Spanish alphabet
ha → **haber**
haba *nf* : broad bean
habanero¹, -ra *adj* : of or from Havana
habanero², -ra *n* : native or resident of Havana
haber¹ {39} *v aux* **1** : have, has ⟨no ha llegado el envío : the shipment hasn't arrived⟩ **2 ~ de** : must ⟨ha de ser tarde : it must be late⟩ — *v impers* **1 hay** : there is, there are ⟨hay dos mensajes : there are two messages⟩ ⟨¿qué hay de nuevo? : what's new?⟩ **2 hay que** : it is necessary ⟨hay que trabajar más rápido : you have to work faster⟩
haber² *nm* **1** : assets *pl* **2** : credit, credit side **3 haberes** *nmpl* : salary, income, remuneration
habichuela *nf* **1** : bean, kidney bean **2** : green bean
hábil *adj* **1** : able, skillful **2** : working ⟨días hábiles : working days⟩
habilidad *nf* CAPACIDAD : ability, skill
habilidoso, -sa *adj* : skillful, clever

habilitación *nf, pl* **-ciones 1** : authorization **2** : furnishing, equipping
habilitar *vt* **1** : to enable, to authorize, to empower **2** : to equip, to furnish
hábilmente *adv* : skillfully, expertly
habitable *adj* : habitable, inhabitable
habitación *nf, pl* **-ciones 1** CUARTO : room **2** DORMITORIO : bedroom **3** : habitation, occupancy
habitante *nmf* : inhabitant, resident
habitar *vt* : to inhabit — *vi* : to reside, to dwell
hábitat *nm, pl* **-tats** : habitat
hábito *nm* **1** : habit, custom **2** : habit (of a monk or nun)
habitual *adj* : habitual, customary — **habitualmente** *adv*
habituar {3} *vt* : to accustom, to habituate — **habituarse** *vr* **~ a** : to get used to, to grow accustomed to
habla *nf* **1** : speech **2** : language, dialect **3 de ~** : speaking ⟨de habla inglesa : English-speaking⟩
hablado, -da *adj* **1** : spoken **2 mal hablado** : foulmouthed

hablador¹, -dora *adj* : talkative
hablador², -dora *n* : chatterbox
habladuría *nf* 1 : rumor 2 **habladurías**
   nfpl : gossip, scandal
hablante *nmf* : speaker
hablar *vi* 1 : to speak, to talk ⟨hablar en
   broma : to be joking⟩ 2 ~ **de** : to mention, to talk about 3 **dar que hablar**
   : to make people talk — *vt* 1 : to speak
   (a language) 2 : to talk about, to discuss ⟨háblalo con tu jefe : discuss it
   with your boss⟩ — **hablarse** *vr* 1 : to
   speak to each other, to be on speaking
   terms 2 **se habla inglés (etc.)** : English (etc.) spoken
habrá, etc. → **haber**
hacedor, -dora *n* : creator, maker, doer
hacendado, -da *n* : landowner
hacer {40} *vt* 1 : to make 2 : to do, to
   perform 3 : to force, to oblige ⟨los hice
   esperar : I made them wait⟩ — *vi* : to
   act ⟨haces bien : you're doing the right
   thing⟩ — *v impers* 1 (*referring to weather*) ⟨hacer frío : to be cold⟩ ⟨hace viento : it's windy⟩ 2 **hace** : ago ⟨hace mucho tiempo : a long time ago, for a long
   time⟩ 3 **no le hace** : it doesn't matter,
   it makes no difference 4 **hacer falta**
   : to be necessary, to be needed — **hacerse** *vr* 1 : to become 2 : to pretend,
   to act, to play ⟨hacerse el tonto : to
   play dumb⟩ 3 : to seem ⟨el examen se
   me hizo difícil : the exam seemed difficult to me⟩ 4 : to get, to grow ⟨se
   hace tarde : it's growing late⟩
hacha *nf* : hatchet, ax
hachazo *nm* : blow, chop (with an ax)
hachís *nm* : hashish
hacia *prep* 1 : toward, towards ⟨hacia
   abajo : downward⟩ ⟨hacia adelante
   : forward⟩ 2 : near, around, about
   ⟨hacia las seis : about six o'clock⟩
hacienda *nf* 1 : estate, ranch, farm 2
   : property 3 : livestock 4 **la Hacienda**
   : department of revenue, tax office
hacinar *vt* 1 : to pile up, to stack 2 : to
   overcrowd — **hacinarse** *vr* : to crowd
   together
hada *nf* : fairy
hado *nm* : destiny, fate
haga, etc. → **hacer**
haitiano, -na *adj & n* : Haitian
hala *interj Spain* 1 (*expressing encouragement or disbelief*) : come on! 2 (*expressing surprise*) : wow! 3 (*expressing
   protest*) : hey!
halagador¹, -dora *adj* : flattering
halagador², -dora *n* : flatterer
halagar {52} *vt* : to flatter, to compliment
halago *nm* : flattery, praise
halagüeño, -ña *adj* 1 : flattering 2 : encouraging, promising
halar *vt CA, Car* → **jalar**
halcón *nm, pl* **halcones** : hawk, falcon
halibut *nm, pl* **-buts** : halibut
hálito *nm* 1 : breath 2 : gentle breeze

hallar *vt* 1 ENCONTRAR : to find 2 DE-
   SCUBRIR : to discover, to find out —
   hallarse *vr* 1 : to be situated, to find
   oneself 2 : to feel ⟨no se halla bien : he
   doesn't feel comfortable, he feels out
   of place⟩
hallazgo *nm* 1 : discovery 2 : find ⟨¡es
   un verdadero hallazgo! : it's a real
   find!⟩
halo *nm* 1 : halo 2 : aura
halógeno *nm* : halogen
hamaca *nf* : hammock
hambre *nf* 1 : hunger 2 : starvation 3
   tener hambre : to be hungry 4 **dar
   hambre** : to make hungry
hambriento, -ta *adj* : hungry, starving
hambruna *nf* : famine
hamburguesa *nf* : hamburger
hampa *nf* : criminal underworld
hampón, -pona *n, mpl* **hampones**
   : criminal, thug
hámster ['xamster] *nm, pl* **hámsters**
   : hamster
han → **haber**
handicap *or* **hándicap** ['handi,kap] *nm,
   pl* **-caps** : handicap (in sports)
hangar *nm* : hangar
hará, etc. → **hacer**
haragán¹, -gana *adj, mpl* **-ganes** : lazy,
   idle
haragán², -gana *n, mpl* **-ganes** HOL-
   GAZÁN : slacker, good-for-nothing
haraganear *vi* : to be lazy, to waste one's
   time
haraganería *nf* : laziness
harapiento, -ta *adj* : ragged, tattered
harapos *nmpl* ANDRAJOS : rags, tatters
hardware ['hard,wer] *nm* : computer
   hardware
harén *nm, pl* **harenes** : harem
harina *nf* 1 : flour 2 **harina de maíz**
   : cornmeal
hartar *vt* 1 : to glut, to satiate 2 FAS-
   TIDIAR : to tire, to irritate, to annoy —
   hartarse *vr* : to be weary, to get fed up
harto¹ *adv* : most, extremely, very
harto², -ta *adj* 1 : full, satiated 2 : fed
   up
hartura *nf* 1 : surfeit 2 : abundance,
   plenty
has → **haber**
hasta¹ *adv* : even
hasta² *prep* 1 : until, up until ⟨hasta entonces : until then⟩ ⟨¡hasta luego! : see
   you later!⟩ 2 : as far as ⟨nos fuimos
   hasta Managua : we went all the way
   to Managua⟩ 3 : up to ⟨hasta cierto
   punto : up to a certain point⟩ 4 **hasta
   que** : until
hastiar {85} *vt* 1 : to make weary, to
   bore 2 : to disgust, to sicken — **has-
   tiarse** *vr* ~ **de** : to get tired of
hastío *nm* 1 TEDIO : tedium 2 REPUG-
   NANCIA : disgust
hato *nm* 1 : flock, herd 2 : bundle (of
   possessions)
hawaiano, -na *adj & n* : Hawaiian
hay → **haber¹**

---

139 · **haya · herraje**

haya¹, etc. → haber
haya² nf : beech (tree and wood)
hayuco nm : beechnut
haz¹ → hacer
haz² nm, pl haces 1 FARDO : bundle 2 : beam (of light)
haz³ nf, pl haces 1 : face 2 haz de la tierra : surface of the earth
hazaña nf PROEZA : feat, exploit
hazmerreír nm fam : laughingstock
he¹ {39} → haber
he² v impers he aquí : here is, here are, behold
hebilla nf : buckle, clasp
hebra nf : strand, thread
hebreo¹, -brea adj & n : Hebrew
hebreo² nm : Hebrew (language)
hecatombe nf 1 MATANZA : massacre 2 : disaster
heces → hez
hechicería nf 1 BRUJERÍA : sorcery, witchcraft 2 : curse, spell
hechicero¹, -ra adj : bewitching, enchanting
hechicero², -ra n : sorcerer, sorceress f
hechizar {21} vt 1 EMBRUJAR : to bewitch 2 CAUTIVAR : to charm
hechizo nm 1 SORTILEGIO : spell, enchantment 2 ENCANTO : charm, fascination
hecho¹ pp → hacer
hecho², -cha adj 1 : made, done 2 : ready-to-wear 3 : complete, finished ⟨hecho y derecho : full-fledged⟩
hecho³ nm 1 : fact 2 : event ⟨hechos históricos : historic events⟩ 3 : act, action 4 de ~ : in fact, in reality
hechura nf 1 : style 2 : craftsmanship, workmanship 3 : product, creation
hectárea nf : hectare
heder {56} vi : to stink, to reek
hediondez nf, pl -deces : stink, stench
hediondo, -da adj MALOLIENTE : foul-smelling, stinking
hedor nm : stench, stink
hegemonía nf 1 : dominance 2 : hegemony (in politics)
helada nf : frost (in meteorology)
heladería nf : ice-cream parlor, ice-cream stand
helado¹, -da adj 1 GÉLIDO : icy, freezing cold 2 CONGELADO : frozen
helado² nm : ice cream
heladora nf CONGELADOR : freezer
helar {55} v CONGELAR : to freeze — v impers : to produce frost ⟨anoche heló : there was frost last night⟩ — helarse vr
helecho nm : fern, bracken
hélice nf 1 : spiral, helix 2 : propeller
helicóptero nm : helicopter
helio nm : helium
helipuerto nm : heliport
hembra adj & nf : female
hemisférico, -ca adj : hemispheric, hemispherical
hemisferio nm : hemisphere
hemofilia nf : hemophilia

hemofílico, -ca adj & n : hemophiliac
hemoglobina nf : hemoglobin
hemorragia nf 1 : hemorrhage 2 hemorragia nasal : nosebleed
hemorroides nfpl ALMORRANAS : hemorrhoids, piles
hemos → haber
henchido, -da adj : swollen, bloated
henchir {54} vt 1 : to stuff, to fill 2 : to swell, to swell up — henchirse vr 1 : to stuff oneself 2 LLENARSE : to fill up, to be full
hender {56} vt : to cleave, to split
hendidura nf : crack, crevice, fissure
henequén nm, pl -quenes : sisal hemp
heno nm : hay
hepatitis nf : hepatitis
heráldica nf : heraldry
heráldico, -ca adj : heraldic
heraldo nm : herald
herbario, -ria adj : herbal
herbicida nm : herbicide, weed killer
herbívoro¹, -ra adj : herbivorous
herbívoro² nm : herbivore
herbolario, -ria n : herbalist
hercio nm : hertz
hercúleo, -lea adj : herculean
heredar vt : to inherit
heredero, -ra n : heir, heiress f
hereditario, -ria adj : hereditary
hereje nmf : heretic
herejía nf : heresy
herencia nf 1 : inheritance 2 : heritage 3 : heredity
herético, -ca adj : heretical
herida nf : injury, wound
herido¹, -da adj 1 : injured, wounded 2 : hurt, offended
herido², -da n : injured person, casualty
herir {76} vt 1 : to injure, to wound 2 : to hurt, to offend
hermafrodita nmf : hermaphrodite
hermanar vt 1 : to unite, to bring together 2 : to match up, to twin (cities)
hermanastro, -tra n : half brother m, half sister f
hermandad nf 1 FRATERNIDAD : brotherhood ⟨hermandad de mujeres : sisterhood, sorority⟩ 2 : association
hermano, -na n : sibling, brother m, sister f
hermético, -ca adj : hermetic, watertight — herméticamente adv
hermoso, -sa adj BELLO : beautiful, lovely — hermosamente adv
hermosura nf BELLEZA : beauty, loveliness
hernia nf : hernia
héroe nm : hero
heroicidad nf : heroism, heroic deed
heroico, -ca adj : heroic — heroicamente adv
heroína nf 1 : heroine 2 : heroin
heroísmo nm : heroism
herpes nms & pl 1 : herpes 2 : shingles
herradura nf : horseshoe
herraje nm : ironwork

herramienta *nf* : tool
herrar {55} *vt* : to shoe (a horse)
herrería *nf* : blacksmith's shop
herrero, -ra *n* : blacksmith
herrumbre *nf* ORÍN : rust
herrumbroso, -sa *adj* OXIDADO : rusty
hertzio *nm* : hertz
hervidero *nm* **1** : mass, swarm **2**
: hotbed (of crime, etc.)
hervidor *nm* : kettle
hervir {76} *vi* **1** BULLIR : to boil, to bubble **2 ~ de** : to teem with, to be swarm-
ing with — *vt* : to boil
hervor *nm* **1** : boiling **2** : fervor, ardor
heterogeneidad *nf* : heterogeneity
heterogéneo, -nea *adj* : heterogeneous
heterosexual *adj & nmf* : heterosexual
heterosexualidad *nf* : heterosexuality
hexágono *nm* : hexagon — **hexagonal**
adj
hez *nf, pl* **heces 1** ESCORIA : scum, dregs
pl **2** : sediment, lees *pl* **3 heces** *nfpl*
: feces, excrement
hiato *nm* : hiatus
hibernar *vi* : to hibernate — **hibernación** *nf*
híbrido[1], -da *adj* : hybrid
híbrido[2] *nm* : hybrid
hicieron, etc. → **hacer**
hidalgo, -ga *n* : nobleman *m,* noblewoman *f*
hidrante *nm* CA, Col : hydrant
hidratar *vt* : to moisturize — **hidratante**
adj
hidrato *nm* **1** : hydrate **2 hidrato de
carbono** : carbohydrate
hidráulico, -ca *adj* : hydraulic
hidroavión *nm, pl* **-viones** : seaplane
hidrocarburo *nm* : hydrocarbon
hidroeléctrico, -ca *adj* : hydroelectric
hidrofobia *nf* RABIA : hydrophobia, rabies
hidrófugo, -ga *adj* : water-repellent
hidrógeno *nm* : hydrogen
hidroplano *nm* : hydroplane
hiede, etc. → **heder**
hiedra *nf* **1** : ivy **2 hiedra venenosa**
: poison ivy
hiel *nf* **1** BILIS : bile **2** : bitterness
hiela, etc. → **helar**
hielo *nm* **1** : ice **2** : coldness, reserve
⟨romper el hielo : to break the ice⟩
hiena *nf* : hyena
hiende, etc. → **hender**
hierba *nf* **1** : herb **2** : grass **3 mala hierba** : weed
hierbabuena *nf* : mint, spearmint
hiere, etc. → **herir**
hierra, etc. → **herrar**
hierro *nm* **1** : iron ⟨hierro fundido : cast
iron⟩ **2** : branding iron
hierve, etc. → **hervir**
hígado *nm* : liver
higiene *nf* : hygiene
higiénico, -ca *adj* : hygienic — **higiéni-
camente** *adv*
higienista *nmf* : hygienist
higo *nm* **1** : fig **2 higo chumbo** : prickly pear (fruit)

higrómetro *nm* : hygrometer
higuera *nf* : fig tree
hijastro, -tra *n* : stepson *m,* stepdaughter *f*
hijo, -ja *n* **1** : son *m,* daughter *f* **2 hijos**
nmpl : children, offspring
híjole *interj Mex* : wow!, good grief!
hilacha *nf* **1** : ravel, loose thread **2
mostrar la hilacha** : to show one's true
colors
hilado *nm* **1** : spinning **2** HILO : yarn,
thread
hilar *vt* **1** : to spin (thread) **2** : to consider, to string together (ideas) — *vi* **1**
: to spin **2 hilar delgado** : to split hairs
hilarante *adj* **1** : humorous, hilarious **2
gas hilarante** : laughing gas
hilaridad *nf* : hilarity
hilera *nf* FILA : file, row, line
hilo *nm* **1** : thread ⟨colgar de un hilo
: to hang by a thread⟩ ⟨hilo dental
: dental floss⟩ **2** LINO : linen **3** : (electric) wire **4** : theme, thread (of a discourse) **5** : trickle (of water, etc.)
hilvanar *vt* **1** : to baste, to tack **2** : to
piece together
himnario *nm* : hymnal
himno *nm* **1** : hymn **2 himno nacional**
: national anthem
hincapié *nm* **hacer hincapié en** : to emphasize, to stress
hincar {72} *vt* CLAVAR : to stick, to
plunge — **hincarse** *vr* **hincarse de
rodillas** : to kneel down, to fall to one's
knees
hinchado, -da *adj* **1** : swollen, inflated
2 : pompous, overblown
hinchar *vt* **1** INFLAR : to inflate **2** : to
exaggerate — **hincharse** *vr* **1** : to swell
up **2** : to become conceited, to swell
with pride
hinchazón *nf, pl* **-zones** : swelling
hinche, etc. → **henchir**
hindi *nm* : Hindi
hindú *adj & nmf* : Hindu
hinduismo *nm* : Hinduism
hiniesta *nf* : broom (plant)
hinojo *nm* **1** : fennel **2 de hinojos** : on
bended knee
hinque, etc. → **hincar**
hipar *vi* : to hiccup
hiperactividad *nf* : hyperactivity
hiperactivo, -va *adj* : hyperactive, overactive
hipérbole *nf* : hyperbole
hiperbólico, -ca *adj* : hyperbolic, exaggerated
hipercrítico, -ca *adj* : hypercritical
hipermetropía *nf* : farsightedness
hipersensibilidad *nf* : hypersensitivity
hipersensible *adj* : hypersensitive
hipertensión *nf, pl* **-siones** : hypertension, high blood pressure
hip–hop [ˌxipˈxop] *nm* : hip-hop (music)
hípico, -ca *adj* : equestrian ⟨concurso
hípico : horse show⟩
hipil → **huipil**
hipnosis *nfs & pl* : hypnosis

hipnótico, -ca *adj* : hypnotic
hipnotismo *nm* : hypnotism
hipnotizador[1], -dora *adj* **1** : hypnotic **2** : spellbinding, mesmerizing
hipnotizador[2], -dora *n* : hypnotist
hipnotizar {21} *vt* : to hypnotize
hipo *nm* : hiccup, hiccups *pl*
hipocampo *nm* : sea horse
hipocondría *nf* : hypochondria
hipocondríaco, -ca *adj & n* : hypochondriac
hipocresía *nf* : hypocrisy
hipócrita[1] *adj* : hypocritical — **hipócritamente** *adv*
hipócrita[2] *nmf* : hypocrite
hipodérmico, -ca *adj* **aguja hipodérmica** : hypodermic needle
hipódromo *nm* : racetrack
hipopótamo *nm* : hippopotamus
hipoteca *nf* : mortgage
hipotecar {72} *vt* **1** : to mortgage **2** : to compromise, to jeopardize
hipotecario, -ria *adj* : mortgage
hipotensión *nf* : low blood pressure
hipotenusa *nf* : hypotenuse
hipótesis *nfs & pl* : hypothesis
hipotético, -ca *adj* : hypothetical — **hipotéticamente** *adv*
hippie *or* **hippy** ['hipi] *nmf, pl* **hippies** [-pis] : hippie
hiriente *adj* : hurtful, offensive
hirió, etc. → **herir**
hirsuto, -ta *adj* **1** : hirsute, hairy **2** : bristly, wiry
hirviente *adj* : boiling
hirvió, etc. → **hervir**
hisopo *nm* **1** : hyssop **2** : cotton swab
hispánico, -ca *adj & n* : Hispanic
hispano[1], -na *adj* : Hispanic ⟨de habla hispana : Spanish-speaking⟩
hispano[2], -na *n* : Hispanic (person)
hispanoamericano[1], -na *adj* LATINOAMERICANO : Latin-American
hispanoamericano[2], -na *n* LATINOAMERICANO : Latin American
hispanohablante[1] *adj* : Spanish-speaking
hispanohablante[2] *nmf* : Spanish speaker
histerectomía *nf* : hysterectomy
histeria *nf* **1** : hysteria **2** : hysterics
histérico, -ca *adj* : hysterical — **histéricamente** *adv*
histerismo *nm* **1** : hysteria **2** : hysterics
historia *nf* **1** : history **2** NARRACIÓN, RELATO : story
historiador, -dora *n* : historian
historial *nm* **1** : record, document **2** CURRÍCULUM : résumé, curriculum vitae
histórico, -ca *adj* **1** : historical **2** : historic, important — **históricamente** *adv*
historieta *nf* : comic strip
histrionismo *nm* : histrionics, acting
hit ['hit] *nm, pl* **hits** **1** ÉXITO : hit, popular song **2** : hit (in baseball)
hito *nm* : milestone, landmark

hizo → **hacer**
hobby ['hɔbi] *nm, pl* **hobbies** [-bis] : hobby
hocico *nm* : snout, muzzle
hockey ['hɔke, -ki] *nm* : hockey
hogar *nm* **1** : home **2** : hearth, fireplace
hogareño, -ña *adj* **1** : home-loving **2** : domestic, homelike
hogaza *nf* : large loaf (of bread)
hoguera *nf* **1** FOGATA : bonfire **2** **morir en la hoguera** : to burn at the stake
hoja *nf* **1** : leaf, petal, blade (of grass) **2** : sheet (of paper), page (of a book) **3** FORMULARIO : form ⟨hoja de pedido : order form⟩ **4** : blade (of a knife) ⟨hoja de afeitar : razor blade⟩
hojalata *nf* : tinplate
hojaldre *nm* : puff pastry
hojarasca *nf* : fallen leaves *pl*
hojear *vt* : to leaf through (a book or magazine)
hojuela *nf* **1** : leaflet, young leaf **2** : flake
hola *interj* : hello!, hi!
holandés[1], -desa *adj, mpl* **-deses** : Dutch
holandés[2], -desa *n, mpl* **-deses** : Dutch person, Dutchman *m*, Dutchwoman *f* ⟨los holandeses : the Dutch⟩
holandés[3] *nm* : Dutch (language)
holgadamente *adv* : comfortably, easily ⟨vivir holgadamente : to be well-off⟩
holgado, -da *adj* **1** : loose, baggy **2** : at ease, comfortable
holganza *nf* : leisure, idleness
holgazán[1], -zana *adj, mpl* **-zanes** : lazy
holgazán[2], -zana *n, mpl* **-zanes** HARAGÁN : slacker, idler
holgazanear *vi* HARAGANEAR : to laze around, to loaf
holgazanería *nf* PEREZA : idleness, laziness
holgura *nf* **1** : looseness **2** COMODIDAD : comfort, ease
holístico, -ca *adj* : holistic
hollar {19} *vt* : to tread on, to trample
hollín *nm, pl* **hollines** TIZNE : soot
holocausto *nm* : holocaust
holograma *nm* : hologram
hombre *nm* **1** : man ⟨el hombre : man, mankind⟩ **2** **hombre de estado** : statesman **3** **hombre de negocios** : businessman **4** **hombre lobo** : werewolf
hombrera *nf* **1** : shoulder pad **2** : epaulet
hombría *nf* : manliness
hombro *nm* : shoulder ⟨encogerse de hombros : to shrug one's shoulders⟩
hombruno, -na *adj* : mannish
homenaje *nm* : homage, tribute ⟨rendir homenaje a : to pay tribute to⟩
homenajear *vt* : to pay homage to, to honor
homeopatía *nf* : homeopathy
homicida[1] *adj* : homicidal, murderous
homicida[2] *nmf* ASESINO : murderer
homicidio *nm* ASESINATO : homicide, murder

homilía *nf* : homily, sermon
homófono *nm* : homophone
homogeneidad *nf* : homogeneity
homogeneización *nf* : homogenization
homogeneizar {21} *vt* : to homogenize
homogéneo, -nea *adj* : homogeneous
homógrafo *nm* : homograph
homologación *nf, pl* **-ciones** 1 : sanctioning, approval 2 : parity
homologar {52} *vt* 1 : to sanction 2 : to bring into line
homólogo[1], -ga *adj* : homologous, equivalent
homólogo[2], -ga *n* : counterpart
homónimo[1], -ma *n* TOCAYO : namesake
homónimo[2] *nm* : homonym
homosexual *adj & nmf* : homosexual
homosexualidad *nf* : homosexuality
honda *nf* : sling
hondo[1] *adv* : deeply
hondo[2], -da *adj* PROFUNDO : deep ⟨en lo más hondo de : in the depths of⟩ — **hondamente** *adv*
hondonada *nf* 1 : hollow, depression 2 : ravine, gorge
hondura *nf* : depth
hondureño, -ña *adj & n* : Honduran
honestidad *nf* 1 : decency, modesty 2 : honesty, uprightness
honesto, -ta *adj* 1 : decent, virtuous 2 : honest, honorable — **honestamente** *adv*
hongo *nm* 1 : fungus 2 : mushroom
honor *nm* 1 : honor ⟨en honor a la verdad : to be quite honest⟩ 2 **honores** *nmpl* : honors ⟨hacer los honores : to do the honors⟩
honorable *adj* HONROSO : honorable — **honorablemente** *adv*
honorario, -ria *adj* : honorary
honorarios *nmpl* : payment, fees (for professional services)
honorífico, -ca *adj* : honorary ⟨mención honorífica : honorable mention⟩
honra *nf* 1 : dignity, self-respect ⟨tener a mucha honra : to take great pride in⟩ 2 : good name, reputation
honradamente *adv* : honestly, decently
honradez *nf, pl* **-deces** : honesty, integrity, probity
honrado, -da *adj* 1 HONESTO : honest, upright 2 : honored
honrar *vt* 1 : to honor 2 : to be a credit to ⟨su generosidad lo honra : his generosity does him credit⟩
honroso, -sa *adj* HONORABLE : honorable — **honrosamente** *adv*
hora *nf* 1 : hour ⟨media hora : half an hour⟩ ⟨a la última hora : at the last minute⟩ ⟨a la hora en punto : on the dot⟩ ⟨horas de oficina : office hours⟩ 2 : time ⟨¿qué hora es? : what time is it?⟩ 3 CITA : appointment
horario *nm* : schedule, timetable, hours *pl* ⟨horario de visita : visiting hours⟩
horca *nf* 1 : gallows *pl* 2 : pitchfork
horcajadas *nfpl* a ~ : astride, astraddle
horcón *nm, pl* **horcones** : wooden post, prop

horda *nf* : horde
horizontal *adj* : horizontal — **horizontalmente** *adv*
horizonte *nm* : horizon, skyline
horma *nf* 1 : shoe tree 2 : shoemaker's last
hormiga *nf* : ant
hormigón *nm, pl* **-gones** CONCRETO : concrete
hormigonera *nf* : cement mixer
hormigueo *nm* 1 : tingling, pins and needles *pl* 2 : uneasiness
hormiguero *nm* 1 : anthill 2 : swarm (of people)
hormona *nf* : hormone — **hormonal** *adj*
hornacina *nf* : niche, recess
hornada *nf* : batch
hornear *vt* : to bake
hornilla *nf* : burner (of a stove)
horno *nm* 1 : oven ⟨horno crematorio : crematorium⟩ ⟨horno de microondas : microwave oven⟩ 2 : kiln
horóscopo *nm* : horoscope
horqueta *nf* 1 : fork (in a river or road) 2 : crotch (in a tree) 3 : small pitchfork
horquilla *nf* 1 : hairpin, bobby pin 2 : pitchfork
horrendo, -da *adj* : horrendous, horrible
horrible *adj* : horrible, dreadful — **horriblemente** *adv*
horripilante *adj* : horrifying, hair-raising
horripilar *vt* : to horrify, to terrify
horror *nm* : horror, dread
horrorizado, -da *adj* : terrified
horrorizar {21} *vt* : to horrify, to terrify — **horrorizarse** *vr*
horroroso, -sa *adj* 1 : horrifying, terrifying 2 : dreadful, bad
hortaliza *nf* 1 : vegetable 2 **hortalizas** *nfpl* : garden produce
hortera *adj Spain fam* : tacky, gaudy
hortícola *adj* : horticultural
horticultor, -ra *n* : horticulturist
horticultura *nf* : horticulture
hosco, -ca *adj* : sullen, gloomy
hospedaje *nm* : lodging, accommodations *pl*
hospedar *vt* : to provide with lodging, to put up — **hospedarse** *vr* : to stay, to lodge
hospicio *nm* : orphanage
hospital *nm* : hospital
hospitalario, -ria *adj* : hospitable
hospitalidad *nf* : hospitality
hospitalización *nf, pl* **-ciones** : hospitalization
hospitalizar {21} *vt* : to hospitalize — **hospitalizarse** *vr*
hostería *nf* POSADA : inn
hostia *nf* : host, Eucharist
hostigamiento *nm* : harassment
hostigar {52} *vt* ACOSAR, ASEDIAR : to harass, to pester
hostil *adj* : hostile

hostilidad *nf* **1** : hostility, antagonism **2 hostilidades** *nfpl* : (military) hostilities

hostilizar {21} *vt* : to harass

hotel *nm* : hotel

hotelero[1], **-ra** *adj* : hotel ⟨la industria hotelera : the hotel business⟩

hotelero[2], **-ra** *n* : hotel manager, hotelier

hoy *adv* **1** : today ⟨hoy mismo : right now, this very day⟩ **2** : now, nowadays ⟨de hoy en adelante : from now on⟩

hoyo *nm* AGUJERO : hole

hoyuelo *nm* : dimple

hoz *nf*, *pl* **hoces** : sickle

hozar {21} *vi* : to root (of a pig)

huachinango *nm Mex* : red snapper

huarache *nm* : huarache sandal

hubo, etc. → **haber**

hueco[1], **-ca** *adj* **1** : hollow, empty **2** : soft, spongy **3** : hollow-sounding, resonant **4** : proud, conceited **5** : superficial

hueco[2] *nm* **1** : hole, hollow, cavity **2** : gap, space **3** : recess, alcove

huele, etc. → **oler**

huelga *nf* **1** PARO : strike **2 hacer huelga** : to strike, to go on strike

huelguista *nmf* : striker

huella[1], **etc.** → **hollar**

huella[2] *nf* **1** : footprint ⟨seguir las huellas de alguien : to follow in someone's footsteps⟩ **2** : mark, impact ⟨dejar huella : to leave one's mark⟩ ⟨sin dejar huella : without a trace⟩ **3 huella digital** *or* **huella dactilar** : fingerprint

huérfano[1], **-na** *adj* **1** : orphan, orphaned **2** : defenseless **3** ~ **de** : lacking, devoid of

huérfano[2], **-na** *n* : orphan

huerta *nf* **1** : large vegetable garden, truck farm **2** : orchard **3** : irrigated land

huerto *nm* **1** : vegetable garden **2** : orchard

hueso *nm* **1** : bone **2** : pit, stone (of a fruit)

huésped[1], **-peda** *n* INVITADO : guest

huésped[2] *nm* : host ⟨organismo huésped : host organism⟩

huestes *nfpl* **1** : followers **2** : troops, army

huesudo, -da *adj* : bony

hueva *nf* : roe, spawn

huevo *nm* : egg ⟨huevos revueltos : scrambled eggs⟩

huida *nf* : flight, escape

huidizo, -za *adj* **1** ESCURRIDIZO : elusive, slippery **2** : shy, evasive

huipil *nm CA, Mex* : traditional sleeveless blouse or dress

huir {41} *vi* **1** ESCAPAR : to escape, to flee **2** ~ **de** : to avoid

huiro *nm Chile, Peru* : seaweed

huizache *nm* : huisache, acacia

hule *nm* **1** : oilcloth, oilskin **2** *Mex* : rubber **3 hule espuma** *Mex* : foam rubber

humanidad *nf* **1** : humanity, mankind **2** : humaneness **3 humanidades** *nfpl* : humanities *pl*

humanismo *nm* : humanism

humanista *nmf* : humanist

humanístico, -ca *adj* : humanistic

humanitario, -ria *adj & n* : humanitarian

humano[1], **-na** *adj* **1** : human **2** BENÉVOLO : humane, benevolent — **humanamente** *adv*

humano[2] *nm* : human being, human

humareda *nf* : cloud of smoke

humeante *adj* **1** : smoky **2** : smoking, steaming

humear *vi* **1** : to smoke **2** : to steam

humectante[1] *adj* : moisturizing

humectante[2] *nm* : moisturizer

humedad *nf* **1** : humidity **2** : dampness, moistness

humedecer {53} *vt* **1** : to humidify **2** : to moisten, to dampen

húmedo, -da *adj* **1** : humid **2** : moist, damp

humidificador *nm* : humidifier

humidificar {72} *vt* : to humidify

humildad *nf* **1** : humility **2** : lowliness

humilde *adj* **1** : humble **2** : lowly ⟨gente humilde : poor people⟩

humildemente *adv* : meekly, humbly

humillación *nf*, *pl* **-ciones** : humiliation

humillante *adj* : humiliating

humillar *vt* : to humiliate — **humillarse** *vr* : to humble oneself ⟨humillarse a hacer algo : to stoop to doing something⟩

humo *nm* **1** : smoke, steam, fumes **2 humos** *nmpl* : airs *pl*, conceit

humor *nm* **1** : humor **2** : mood, temper ⟨está de buen humor : she's in a good mood⟩

humorada *nf* **1** BROMA : joke, witticism **2** : whim, caprice

humorismo *nm* : humor, wit

humorista *nmf* : humorist, comedian, comedienne *f*

humorístico, -ca *adj* : humorous — **humorísticamente** *adv*

humoso, -sa *adj* : smoky, steamy

humus *nm* : humus

hundido, -da *adj* **1** : sunken **2** : depressed

hundimiento *nm* **1** : sinking **2** : collapse, ruin

hundir *vt* **1** : to sink **2** : to destroy, to ruin — **hundirse** *vr* **1** : to sink down **2** : to cave in **3** : to break down, to go to pieces

húngaro[1], **-ra** *adj & n* : Hungarian

húngaro[2] *nm* : Hungarian (language)

huracán *nm*, *pl* **-canes** : hurricane

huraño, -ña *adj* **1** : unsociable, aloof **2** : timid, skittish (of an animal)

hurgar {52} *vt* : to poke, to jab, to rake (a fire) — *vi* ~ **en** : to rummage in, to poke through

hurgue, etc. → **hurgar**

hurón *nm*, *pl* **hurones** : ferret

huronear *vi* : to pry, to snoop

hurra *interj* : hurrah!, hooray!
hurtadillas *nfpl* a ~ : stealthily, on the sly
hurtar *vt* ROBAR : to steal
hurto *nm* 1 : theft, robbery 2 : stolen property, loot
husmear *vt* 1 : to follow the scent of, to track 2 : to sniff out, to pry into — *vi* 1 : to pry, to snoop 2 : to sniff around (of an animal)
huso *nm* 1 : spindle 2 huso horario : time zone
huy *interj* : ow!, ouch!
huye, etc. → huir

I

i *nf* : ninth letter of the Spanish alphabet
iba, etc. → ir
ibérico, -ca *adj* : Iberian
ibero, -ra *or* íbero, -ra *adj & n* : Iberian
iberoamericano, -na *adj* HISPANOAMERICANO, LATINOAMERICANO : Latin-American
ibis *nfs & pl* : ibis
ice, etc. → izar
iceberg *nm, pl* icebergs : iceberg
icono *nm* : icon
iconoclasia *nf* : iconoclasm
iconoclasta *nmf* : iconoclast
ictericia *nf* : jaundice
ida *nf* 1 : going, departure 2 ida y vuelta : round-trip 3 idas y venidas : comings and goings
idea *nf* 1 : idea, notion 2 : opinion, belief 3 PROPÓSITO : intention
ideal *adj & nm* : ideal — idealmente *adv*
idealismo *nm* : idealism
idealista[1] *adj* : idealistic
idealista[2] *nmf* : idealist
idealizar {21} *vt* : to idealize — idealización *nf*
idear *vt* : to devise, to think up
ideario *nm* : ideology
ídem *nm* : idem, the same, ditto
idéntico, -ca *adj* : identical, alike — idénticamente *adv*
identidad *nf* : identity
identificable *adj* : identifiable
identificación *nf, pl* -ciones 1 : identification, identifying 2 : identification document, ID
identificar {72} *vt* : to identify — identificarse *vr* 1 : to identify oneself 2 ~ con : to identify with
ideología *nf* : ideology — ideológicamente *adv*
ideológico, -ca *adj* : ideological
idílico, -ca *adj* : idyllic
idilio *nm* : idyll
idioma *nm* : language ⟨el idioma inglés : the English language⟩
idiomático, -ca *adj* : idiomatic — idiomáticamente *adv*
idiosincrasia *nf* : idiosyncrasy
idiosincrásico, -ca *adj* : idiosyncratic
idiota[1] *adj* : idiotic, stupid, foolish
idiota[2] *nmf* : idiot, foolish person
idiotez *nf, pl* -teces 1 : idiocy 2 : idiotic act or remark ⟨¡no digas idioteces! : don't talk nonsense!⟩
ido *pp* → ir

idólatra[1] *adj* : idolatrous
idólatra[2] *nmf* : idolater
idolatrar *vt* : to idolize
idolatría *nf* : idolatry
ídolo *nm* : idol
idoneidad *nf* : suitability
idóneo, -nea *adj* ADECUADO : suitable, fitting
iglesia *nf* : church
iglú *nm* : igloo
ignición *nf, pl* -ciones : ignition
ignífugo, -ga *adj* : fire-resistant, fireproof
ignominia *nf* : ignominy, disgrace
ignominioso, -sa *adj* : ignominious, shameful
ignorancia *nf* : ignorance
ignorante[1] *adj* : ignorant
ignorante[2] *nmf* : ignorant person, ignoramus
ignorar *vt* 1 : to ignore 2 DESCONOCER : to be unaware of ⟨lo ignoramos por absoluto : we have no idea⟩
ignoto, -ta *adj* : unknown
igual[1] *adv* 1 : in the same way 2 por ~ : equally
igual[2] *adj* 1 : equal 2 IDÉNTICO : the same, alike 3 : even, smooth 4 SEMEJANTE : similar 5 CONSTANTE : constant
igual[3] *nmf* : equal, peer
igualación *nf* 1 : equalization 2 : leveling, smoothing 3 : equating (in mathematics)
igualado, -da *adj* 1 : even (of a score) 2 : level 3 *Mex* : disrespectful
igualar *vt* 1 : to equalize 2 : to tie ⟨igualar el marcador : to even the score⟩
igualdad *nf* 1 : equality 2 UNIFORMIDAD : evenness, uniformity
igualmente *adv* 1 : equally 2 ASIMISMO : likewise
iguana *nf* : iguana
ijada *nf* : flank, loin, side
ijar *nm* → ijada
ilegal[1] *adj* : illegal, unlawful — ilegalmente *adv*
ilegal[2] *nmf* CA, *Mex* : illegal alien
ilegalidad *nf* : illegality, unlawfulness
ilegibilidad *nf* : illegibility
ilegible *adj* : illegible — ilegiblemente *adv*
ilegitimidad *nf* : illegitimacy
ilegítimo, -ma *adj* : illegitimate, unlawful

ileso, -sa *adj* : uninjured, unharmed
ilícito, -ta *adj* : illicit — **ilícitamente** *adv*
ilimitado, -da *adj* : unlimited
ilógico, -ca *adj* : illogical — **ilógicamente** *adv*
iluminación *nf, pl* **-ciones 1** : illumination **2** ALUMBRADO : lighting
iluminado, -da *adj* : illuminated, lighted
iluminar *vt* **1** : to illuminate, to light (up) **2** : to enlighten
ilusión *nf, pl* **-siones 1** : illusion, delusion **2** ESPERANZA : hope ⟨hacerse ilusiones : to get one's hopes up⟩
ilusionado, -da *adj* ESPERANZADO : hopeful, eager
ilusionar *vt* : to build up hope, to excite — **ilusionarse** *vr* : to get one's hopes up
iluso¹, -sa *adj* : naive, gullible
iluso², -sa *n* SOÑADOR : dreamer, visionary
ilusorio, -ria *adj* ENGAÑOSO : illusory, misleading
ilustración *nf, pl* **-ciones 1** : illustration **2** : erudition, learning ⟨la Ilustración : the Enlightenment⟩
ilustrado, -da *adj* **1** : illustrated **2** DOCTO : learned, erudite
ilustrador, -dora *n* : illustrator
ilustrar *vt* **1** : to illustrate **2** ACLARAR, CLARIFICAR : to explain
ilustrativo, -va *adj* : illustrative
ilustre *adj* : illustrious, eminent
imagen *nf, pl* **imágenes** : image, picture
imaginable *adj* : imaginable, conceivable
imaginación *nf, pl* **-ciones** : imagination
imaginar *vt* : to imagine — **imaginarse** *vr* **1** : to suppose, to imagine **2** : to picture
imaginario, -ria *adj* : imaginary
imaginativo, -va *adj* : imaginative — **imaginativamente** *adv*
imaginería *nf* **1** : imagery **2** : image making (in religion)
imán *nm, pl* **imanes** : magnet
imantar *vt* : to magnetize
imbatible *adj* : unbeatable
imbécil¹ *adj* : stupid, idiotic
imbécil² *nmf* **1** : imbecile **2** *fam* : idiot, dope
imborrable *adj* : indelible
imbuir {41} *vt* : to imbue — **imbuirse** *vr*
imitación *nf, pl* **-ciones 1** : imitation **2** : mimicry, impersonation
imitador¹, -dora *adj* : imitative
imitador², -dora *n* **1** : imitator **2** : mimic
imitar *vt* **1** : to imitate, to copy **2** : to mimic, to impersonate
imitativo, -va *adj* → **imitador¹**
impaciencia *nf* : impatience
impacientar *vt* : to make impatient, to exasperate — **impacientarse** *vr*
impaciente *adj* : impatient — **impacientemente** *adv*
impactado, -da *adj* : shocked, stunned
impactante *adj* **1** : shocking **2** : impressive, powerful

impactar *vt* **1** GOLPEAR : to hit **2** IMPRESIONAR : to impact, to affect — **impactarse** *vr*
impacto *nm* **1** : impact, effect **2** : shock, collision
impagable *adj* **1** : unpayable **2** : priceless
impago *nm* : nonpayment
impalpable *adj* INTANGIBLE : impalpable, intangible
impar¹ *adj* : odd ⟨números impares : odd numbers⟩
impar² *nm* : odd number
imparable *adj* : unstoppable
imparcial *adj* : impartial — **imparcialmente** *adv*
imparcialidad *nf* : impartiality
impartir *vt* : to impart, to give
impasible *adj* : impassive, unmoved — **impasiblemente** *adv*
impasse *nm* : impasse
impávido, -da *adj* : undaunted, unperturbed
impecable *adj* INTACHABLE : impeccable, faultless — **impecablemente** *adv*
impedido, -da *adj* : disabled, crippled
impedimento *nm* **1** : impediment, obstacle **2** : disability
impedir {54} *vt* **1** : to prevent, to block **2** : to impede, to hinder
impeler *vt* **1** : to drive, to propel **2** : to impel
impenetrable *adj* : impenetrable — **impenetrabilidad** *nf*
impenitente *adj* : unrepentant, impenitent
impensable *adj* : unthinkable
impensado, -da *adj* : unforeseen, unexpected
imperante *adj* : prevailing
imperar *vi* **1** : to reign, to rule **2** PREDOMINAR : to prevail
imperativo¹, -va *adj* : imperative
imperativo² *nm* : imperative
imperceptible *adj* : imperceptible — **imperceptiblemente** *adv*
imperdible *nm Spain* : safety pin
imperdonable *adj* : unpardonable, unforgivable
imperecedero, -ra *adj* **1** : imperishable **2** INMORTAL : immortal, everlasting
imperfección *nf, pl* **-ciones 1** : imperfection **2** DEFECTO : defect, flaw
imperfecto, -ta *adj* : imperfect, flawed
imperfecto² *nm* : imperfect tense
imperial *adj* : imperial
imperialismo *nm* : imperialism
imperialista *adj & nmf* : imperialist
impericia *nf* : lack of skill, incompetence
imperio *nm* : empire
imperioso, -sa *adj* **1** : imperious **2** : pressing, urgent — **imperiosamente** *adv*
impermeabilizante *adj* : water-repellent
impermeabilizar {21} *vt* : to waterproof
impermeable¹ *adj* **1** : impervious **2** : impermeable, waterproof
impermeable² *nm* : raincoat

impersonal *adj* : impersonal — **impersonalmente** *adv*

impertinencia *nf* INSOLENCIA : impertinence, insolence

impertinente *adj* **1** INSOLENTE : impertinent, insolent **2** INOPORTUNO : inappropriate, uncalled-for **3** IRRELEVANTE : irrelevant

imperturbable *adj* : imperturbable, impassive, stolid

ímpetu *nm* **1** : impetus, momentum **2** : vigor, energy **3** : force, violence

impetuoso, -sa *adj* : impetuous, impulsive — **impetuosamente** *adv*

impiedad *nf* : impiety

impío, -pía *adj* : impious, ungodly

implacable *adj* : implacable, relentless — **implacablemente** *adv*

implantación *nf, pl* **-ciones 1** : implantation **2** ESTABLECIMIENTO : establishment, introduction

implantado, -da *adj* : well-established

implantar *vt* **1** : to implant **2** ESTABLECER : to establish, to introduce — **implantarse** *vr*

implante *nm* : implant

implementar *vt* : to implement — **implementarse** *vr* — **implementación** *nf*

implemento *nm* : implement, tool

implicación *nf, pl* **-ciones** : implication

implicar {72} *vt* **1** ENREDAR, ENVOLVER : to involve, to implicate **2** : to imply

implícito, -ta *adj* : implied, implicit — **implícitamente** *adv*

implorar *vt* : to implore

implosión *nf, pl* **-siones** : implosion — **implosivo, -va** *adj*

implosionar *vi* : to implode

imponderable *adj & nm* : imponderable

imponente *adj* : imposing, impressive

imponer {60} *vt* **1** : to impose **2** : to confer — *vi* : to be impressive, to command respect — **imponerse** *vr* **1** : to take on (a duty) **2** : to assert oneself **3** : to prevail

imponible *adj* : taxable

impopular *adj* : unpopular — **impopularidad** *nf*

importación *nf, pl* **-ciones 1** : importation **2 importaciones** *nfpl* : imports

importado, -da *adj* : imported

importador¹, -dora *adj* : importing

importador², -dora *n* : importer

importancia *nf* : importance

importante *adj* : important — **importantemente** *adv*

importar *vi* : to matter, to be important ⟨no le importa lo que piensen : she doesn't care what they think⟩ — *vt* : to import

importe *nm* **1** : price, cost **2** : sum, amount

importunar *vt* : to bother, to inconvenience — *vi* : to be inconvenient

importuno, -na *adj* **1** : inopportune, inconvenient **2** : bothersome, annoying

imposibilidad *nf* : impossibility

imposibilitado, -da *adj* **1** : disabled, crippled **2 verse imposibilitado** : to be unable (to do something)

imposibilitar *vt* **1** : to make impossible **2** : to disable, to incapacitate — **imposibilitarse** *vr* : to become disabled

imposible *adj* : impossible

imposición *nf, pl* **-ciones 1** : imposition **2** EXIGENCIA : demand, requirement **3** : tax **4** : deposit

impositivo, -va *adj* : tax ⟨tasa impositiva : tax rate⟩

impostor, -tora *n* : impostor

impostura *nf* **1** : fraud, imposture **2** CALUMNIA : slander

impotencia *nf* **1** : impotence, powerlessness **2** : impotence (in medicine)

impotente *adj* **1** : powerless **2** : impotent

impracticable *adj* : impracticable

imprecisión *nf, pl* **-siones 1** : imprecision, vagueness **2** : inaccuracy

impreciso, -sa *adj* **1** : imprecise, vague **2** : inaccurate

impredecible *adj* : unpredictable

impregnar *vt* : to impregnate

imprenta *nf* **1** : printing **2** : printing shop, press

imprescindible *adj* : essential, indispensable

impresentable *adj* : unpresentable, unfit

impresión *nf, pl* **-siones 1** : print, printing **2** : impression, feeling

impresionable *adj* : impressionable

impresionante *adj* : impressive, incredible, amazing — **impresionantemente** *adv*

impresionar *vt* **1** : to impress, to strike **2** : to affect, to move — *vi* : to make an impression — **impresionarse** *vr* : to be affected, to be removed

impresionismo *nm* : impressionism

impresionista¹ *adj* : impressionist, impressionistic

impresionista² *nmf* : impressionist

impreso¹ *pp* → **imprimir**

impreso², -sa *adj* : printed

impreso³ *nm* PUBLICACIÓN : printed matter, publication

impresor, -sora *n* : printer

impresora *nf* : (computer) printer

imprevisible *adj* : unforeseeable

imprevisión *nf, pl* **-siones** : lack of foresight, thoughtlessness

imprevisto¹, -ta *adj* : unexpected, unforeseen

imprevisto² *nm* : unexpected occurrence, contingency

imprimir {42} *vt* **1** : to print **2** : to imprint, to stamp, to impress

improbabilidad *nf* : improbability

improbable *adj* : improbable, unlikely

improcedente *adj* **1** : inadmissible **2** : inappropriate, improper

improductivo, -va *adj* : unproductive

improperio *nm* : affront, insult

impropiedad *nf* : impropriety

impropio, -pia *adj* **1** : improper, incorrect **2** INADECUADO : unsuitable, inappropriate
improvisación *nf, pl* **-ciones** : improvisation, ad-lib
improvisado, -da *adj* : improvised, ad-lib
improvisar *v* : to improvise, to ad-lib
improviso *adj* **de ~** : all of a sudden, unexpectedly
imprudencia *nf* INDISCRECIÓN : imprudence, indiscretion
imprudente *adj* INDISCRETO : imprudent, indiscreet — **imprudentemente** *adv*
impúdico, -ca *adj* : shameless, indecent
impuesto[1] *pp* → **imponer**
impuesto[2] *nm* : tax
impugnar *vt* : to challenge, to contest
impulsar *vt* : to propel, to drive
impulsividad *nf* : impulsiveness
impulsivo, -va *adj* : impulsive — **impulsivamente** *adv*
impulso *nm* **1** : drive, thrust **2** : impulse, urge
impune *adj* : unpunished
impunemente *adv* : with impunity
impunidad *nf* : impunity
impureza *nf* : impurity
impuro, -ra *adj* : impure
impuso, etc. → **imponer**
imputable *adj* ATRIBUIBLE : attributable
imputación *nf, pl* **-ciones** **1** : attribution, imputation **2** : accusation
imputar *vt* ATRIBUIR : to impute, to attribute
inacabable *adj* : endless
inacabado, -da *adj* INCONCLUSO : unfinished
inaccesibilidad *nf* : inaccessibility
inaccesible *adj* **1** : inaccessible **2** : unattainable
inacción *nf, pl* **-ciones** : inactivity, inaction
inaceptable *adj* : unacceptable
inactividad *nf* : inactivity, idleness
inactivo, -va *adj* : inactive, idle
inadaptado[1]**, -da** *adj* : maladjusted
inadaptado[2]**, -da** *n* : misfit
inadecuación *nf, pl* **-ciones** : inadequacy
inadecuado, -da *adj* **1** : inadequate **2** IMPROPIO : inappropriate — **inadecuadamente** *adv*
inadmisible *adj* **1** : inadmissible **2** : unacceptable
inadvertencia *nf* : oversight
inadvertidamente *adv* : inadvertently
inadvertido, -da *adj* **1** : unnoticed ⟨pasar inadvertido : to go unnoticed⟩ **2** DESPISTADO, DISTRAÍDO : inattentive, distracted
inagotable *adj* : inexhaustible
inaguantable *adj* INSOPORTABLE : insufferable, unbearable
inalámbrico, -ca *adj* : wireless, cordless
inalcanzable *adj* : unreachable, unattainable

inalienable *adj* : inalienable
inalterable *adj* **1** : unalterable, unchangeable **2** : impassive **3** : colorfast
inamovible *adj* : immovable, fixed
inanición *nf, pl* **-ciones** : starvation
inanimado, -da *adj* : inanimate
inapelable *adj* : indisputable
inapetencia *nf* : lack of appetite
inaplicable *adj* : inapplicable
inapreciable *adj* **1** : imperceptible, negligible **2** : invaluable
inapropiado, -da *adj* : inappropriate, unsuitable
inarticulado, -da *adj* : inarticulate, unintelligible — **inarticuladamente** *adv*
inasequible *adj* : unattainable, inaccessible
inasistencia *nf* AUSENCIA : absence
inatacable *adj* : unassailable, indisputable
inaudible *adj* : inaudible
inaudito, -ta *adj* : unheard-of, unprecedented
inauguración *nf, pl* **-ciones** : inauguration
inaugural *adj* : inaugural, opening
inaugurar *vt* **1** : to inaugurate **2** : to open
inca *adj & nmf* : Inca
incalculable *adj* : incalculable
incalificable *adj* : indescribable
incandescencia *nf* : incandescence — **incandescente** *adj*
incansable *adj* INFATIGABLE : tireless — **incansablemente** *adv*
incapacidad *nf* **1** : inability, incapacity **2** : disability, handicap
incapacitado, -da *adj* **1** : disqualified **2** : disabled, handicapped
incapacitar *vt* **1** : to incapacitate, to disable **2** : to disqualify
incapaz *adj, pl* **-paces** **1** : incapable, unable **2** : incompetent, inept
incautación *nf, pl* **-ciones** : seizure, confiscation
incautar *vt* CONFISCAR : to confiscate, to seize — **incautarse** *vr*
incauto, -ta *adj* : unwary, unsuspecting
incendiar *vt* : to set fire to, to burn (down) — **incendiarse** *vr* : to catch fire
incendiario[1]**, -ria** *adj* : incendiary, inflammatory
incendiario[2]**, -ria** *n* : arsonist
incendio *nm* **1** : fire **2 incendio premeditado** : arson
incensario *nm* : censer
incentivar *vt* : to encourage, to stimulate
incentivo *nm* : incentive
incertidumbre *nf* : uncertainty, suspense
incesante *adj* : incessant — **incesantemente** *adv*
incesto *nm* : incest
incestuoso, -sa *adj* : incestuous
incidencia *nf* **1** : incident **2** : effect, impact **3 por ~** : by chance, accidentally

incidental *adj* : incidental
incidentalmente *adv* : by chance
incidente *nm* : incident, occurrence
incidir *vi* **1** ~ **en** : to fall into, to enter into ⟨incidimos en el mismo error : we fell into the same mistake⟩ **2** ~ **en** : to affect, to influence, to have a bearing on
incienso *nm* : incense
incierto, -ta *adj* **1** : uncertain **2** : untrue **3** : unsteady, insecure
incineración *nf, pl* **-ciones 1** : incineration **2** : cremation
incinerador *nm* : incinerator
incinerar *vt* **1** : to incinerate **2** : to cremate
incipiente *adj* : incipient
incisión *nf, pl* **-siones** : incision
incisivo¹, -va *adj* : incisive
incisivo² *nm* : incisor
inciso *nm* : digression, aside
incitación *nf, pl* **-ciones** : incitement
incitador¹, -dora *n* : instigator, agitator
incitador², -dora *adj* : provocative
incitante *adj* : provocative
incitar *vt* : to incite, to rouse
incivilizado, -da *adj* : uncivilized
inclemencia *nf* : inclemency, severity
inclemente *adj* : inclement
inclinación *nf, pl* **-ciones 1** PROPENSIÓN : inclination, tendency **2** : incline, slope
inclinado, -da *adj* **1** : sloping **2** : inclined, apt
inclinar *vt* : to tilt, to lean, to incline ⟨inclinar la cabeza : to bow one's head⟩ — **inclinarse** *vr* **1** : to lean, to lean over **2** ~ **a** : to be inclined to
incluir {41} *vt* : to include
inclusión *nf, pl* **-siones** : inclusion
inclusive *adv* : inclusively, up to and including
inclusivo, -va *adj* : inclusive
incluso *adv* **1** AUN : even, in fact ⟨es importante e incluso crucial : it is important and even crucial⟩ **2** : inclusively
incógnita *nf* **1** : unknown quantity (in mathematics) **2** : mystery
incógnito, -ta *adj* **1** : unknown **2 de incógnito** : incognito
incoherencia *nf* : incoherence
incoherente *adj* : incoherent — **incoherentemente** *adv*
incoloro, -ra *adj* : colorless
incombustible *adj* : fireproof
incomible *adj* : inedible
incomodar *vt* **1** : to make uncomfortable **2** : to inconvenience — **incomodarse** *vr* : to put oneself out, to take the trouble
incomodidad *nf* **1** : discomfort, awkwardness **2** MOLESTIA : inconvenience, bother
incómodo, -da *adj* **1** : uncomfortable, awkward **2** INCONVENIENTE : inconvenient
incomparable *adj* : incomparable

incompatibilidad *nf* : incompatibility
incompatible *adj* : incompatible, uncongenial
incompetencia *nf* : incompetence
incompetente *adj & nmf* : incompetent
incompleto, -ta *adj* : incomplete
incomprendido, -da *adj* : misunderstood
incomprensible *adj* : incomprehensible
incomprensión *nf, pl* **-siones** : lack of understanding, incomprehension
incomunicación *nf, pl* **-ciones** : lack of communication
incomunicado, -da *adj* **1** : cut off, isolated **2** : in solitary confinement
inconcebible *adj* : inconceivable, unthinkable — **inconcebiblemente** *adv*
inconcluso, -sa *adj* INACABADO : unfinished
incondicional *adj* : unconditional — **incondicionalmente** *adv*
inconexo, -xa *adj* : unconnected, disconnected
inconfesable *adj* : unspeakable, shameful
inconforme *adj & nmf* : nonconformist
inconformidad *nf* : nonconformity
inconformista *adj & nmf* : nonconformist
inconfundible *adj* : unmistakable, obvious — **inconfundiblemente** *adv*
incongruencia *nf* : incongruity
incongruente *adj* : incongruous
inconmensurable *adj* : vast, immeasurable
inconquistable *adj* : unyielding
inconsciencia *nf* **1** : unconsciousness, unawareness **2** : irresponsibility
inconsciente¹ *adj* **1** : unconscious, unaware **2** : reckless, needless — **inconscientemente** *adv*
inconsciente² *nm* **el inconsciente** : the unconscious
inconsecuente *adj* : inconsistent — **inconsecuencia** *nf*
inconsiderado, -da *adj* : inconsiderate, thoughtless
inconsistencia *nf* : inconsistency
inconsistente *adj* **1** : weak, flimsy **2** : inconsistent, weak (of an argument)
inconsolable *adj* : inconsolable — **inconsolablemente** *adv*
inconstancia *nf* : inconstancy
inconstante *adj* : inconstant, fickle, changeable
inconstitucional *adj* : unconstitutional
inconstitucionalidad *nf* : unconstitutionality
incontable *adj* INNUMERABLE : countless, innumerable
incontenible *adj* : uncontrollable, unstoppable
incontestable *adj* INCUESTIONABLE, INDISCUTIBLE : irrefutable, indisputable
incontinencia *nf* : incontinence — **incontinente** *adj*
incontrolable *adj* : uncontrollable
incontrolado, -da *adj* : uncontrolled, out of control

incontrovertible *adj* : indisputable
inconveniencia *nf* **1** : inconvenience, trouble **2** : unsuitability, inappropriateness **3** : tactless remark
inconveniente[1] *adj* **1** INCÓMODO : inconvenient **2** INAPROPIADO : improper, unsuitable
inconveniente[2] *nm* : obstacle, problem, snag ⟨no tengo inconveniente en hacerlo : I don't mind doing it⟩
incorporación *nf, pl* **-ciones** : incorporation
incorporar *vt* **1** : to incorporate **2** : to add, to include — **incorporarse** *vr* **1** : to sit up **2** ~ **a** : to join
incorpóreo, -rea *adj* : incorporeal, bodiless
incorrección *n, pl* **-ciones** : impropriety, improper word or action
incorrecto, -ta *adj* : incorrect — **incorrectamente** *adv*
incorregible *adj* : incorrigible — **incorregibilidad** *nf*
incorruptible *adj* : incorruptible
incredulidad *nf* : incredulity, skepticism
incrédulo[1]**, -la** *adj* : incredulous, skeptical
incrédulo[2]**, -la** *n* : skeptic
increíble *adj* : incredible, unbelievable — **increíblemente** *adv*
incrementar *vt* : to increase — **incrementarse** *vr*
incremento *nm* AUMENTO : increase
incriminar *vt* : to incriminate — **incriminación** *nf*
incriminatorio, -ria *adj* : incriminating, incriminatory
incruento, -ta *adj* : bloodless
incrustación *nf, pl* **-ciones** : inlay
incrustar *vt* **1** : to embed **2** : to inlay — **incrustarse** *vr* : to become embedded
incubación *nf, pl* **-ciones** : incubation
incubadora *nf* : incubator
incubar *v* : to incubate
incuestionable *adj* INCONTESTABLE, INDISCUTIBLE : unquestionable, indisputable — **incuestionablemente** *adv*
inculcar {72} *vt* : to inculcate, to instill
inculpar *vt* ACUSAR : to accuse, to charge
inculto, -ta *adj* **1** : uncultured, ignorant **2** : uncultivated, fallow
incumbencia *nf* : obligation, responsibility
incumbir *vi* (*3rd person only*) ~ **a** : to be incumbent upon, to be of concern to ⟨a mí no me incumbe : it's not my concern⟩
incumplido, -da *adj* : irresponsible, unreliable
incumplimiento *nm* **1** : nonfulfillment, neglect **2 incumplimiento de contrato** : breach of contract
incumplir *vt* : to fail to carry out, to break (a promise, a contract)
incurable *adj* : incurable
incurrir *vi* **1** ~ **en** : to incur ⟨incurrir en gastos : to incur expenses⟩ **2** ~ **en** : to fall into, to commit ⟨incurrió en un error : he made a mistake⟩

incursión *nf, pl* **-siones** : incursion, raid
incursionar *vi* **1** : to raid **2** ~ **en** : to go into, to enter ⟨el actor incursionó en el baile : the actor worked in dance for awhile⟩
indagación *nf, pl* **-ciones** : investigation, inquiry
indagar {52} *vt* : to inquire into, to investigate
indebido, -da *adj* : improper, undue — **indebidamente** *adv*
indecencia *nf* : indecency, obscenity
indecente *adj* : indecent, obscene
indecible *adj* : indescribable, inexpressible
indecisión *nf, pl* **-siones** : indecision
indeciso, -sa *adj* **1** IRRESOLUTO : indecisive **2** : undecided
indeclinable *adj* : unavoidable
indecoro *nm* : impropriety, indecorousness
indecoroso, -sa *adj* : indecorous, unseemly
indefectible *adj* : unfailing, sure
indefendible *adj* : indefensible
indefenso, -sa *adj* : defenseless, helpless
indefinible *adj* : indefinable
indefinido, -da *adj* **1** : undefined, vague **2** INDETERMINADO : indefinite — **indefinidamente** *adv*
indeleble *adj* : indelible — **indeleblemente** *adv*
indelicado, -da *adj* : indelicate, tactless
indemnización *nf, pl* **-ciones** **1** : indemnity **2 indemnización por despido** : severance pay
indemnizar {21} *vt* : to indemnify, to compensate
independencia *nf* : independence
independiente *adj* : independent — **independientemente** *adv*
independizarse {21} *vr* : to become independent, to gain independence
indescifrable *adj* : indecipherable
indescriptible *adj* : indescribable — **indescriptiblemente** *adv*
indeseable *adj & nmf* : undesirable
indestructible *adj* : indestructible
indeterminación *nf, pl* **-ciones** : indeterminacy
indeterminado, -da *adj* **1** INDEFINIDO : indefinite **2** : indeterminate
indexar *vt* INDICIAR : to index (wages, prices, etc.)
indicación *nf, pl* **-ciones** **1** : sign, signal **2** : direction, instruction **3** : suggestion, hint
indicado, -da *adj* **1** APROPIADO : appropriate, suitable **2** : specified, indicated ⟨al día indicado : on the specified day⟩
indicador *nm* **1** : gauge, dial, meter **2** : indicator ⟨indicadores económicos : economic indicators⟩
indicar {72} *vt* **1** SEÑALAR : to indicate **2** ENSEÑAR, MOSTRAR : to show
indicativo[1]**, -va** *adj* : indicative
indicativo[2] *nm* : indicative (mood)

índice *nm* **1** : index **2** : index finger, forefinger **3** INDICIO : indication

indiciar *vt* : to index (prices, wages, etc.)

indicio *nm* : indication, sign

indiferencia *nf* : indifference

indiferente *adj* **1** : indifferent, unconcerned **2 ser indiferente** : to be of no concern ⟨me es indiferente : it doesn't matter to me⟩

indígena¹ *adj* : indigenous, native

indígena² *nmf* : native

indigencia *nf* MISERIA : poverty, destitution

indigente *adj & nmf* : indigent

indigestarse *vr* **1** EMPACHARSE : to have indigestion **2** *fam* : to nauseate, to disgust ⟨ese tipo se me indigesta : that guy makes me sick⟩

indigestión *nf, pl* **-tiones** EMPACHO : indigestion

indigesto, -ta *adj* : indigestible, difficult to digest

indignación *nf, pl* **-ciones** : indignation

indignado, -da *adj* : indignant

indignante *adj* : outrageous, infuriating

indignar *vt* : to outrage, to infuriate — **indignarse** *vr*

indignidad *nf* : indignity

indigno, -na *adj* : unworthy

índigo *nm* : indigo

indio¹, -dia *adj* **1** : American Indian, Indian, Amerindian **2** : Indian (from India)

indio², -dia *n* **1** : American Indian **2** : Indian (from India)

indirecta *nf* **1** : hint, innuendo **2 echar indirectas** *or* **lanzar indirectas** : to drop a hint, to insinuate

indirecto, -ta *adj* : indirect — **indirectamente** *adv*

indisciplina *nf* : indiscipline, unruliness

indisciplinado, -da *adj* : undisciplined, unruly

indiscreción *nf, pl* **-ciones 1** IMPRUDENCIA : indiscretion **2** : tactless remark

indiscreto, -ta *adj* IMPRUDENTE : indiscreet, imprudent — **indiscretamente** *adv*

indiscriminado, -da *adj* : indiscriminate — **indiscriminadamente** *adv*

indiscutible *adj* INCONTESTABLE, INCUESTIONABLE : indisputable, unquestionable — **indiscutiblemente** *adv*

indispensable *adj* : indispensable — **indispensablemente** *adv*

indisponer {60} *vt* **1** : to spoil, to upset **2** : to make ill — **indisponerse** *vr* **1** : to become ill **2 ~ con** : to fall out with

indisposición *nf, pl* **-ciones** : indisposition, illness

indispuesto, -ta *adj* : unwell, indisposed

indistinguible *adj* : indistinguishable

indistintamente *adv* **1** : indistinctly **2** : indiscriminately

indistinto, -ta *adj* : indistinct, vague, faint

individual *adj* : individual — **individualmente** *adv*

individualidad *nf* : individuality

individualismo *nm* : individualism

individualista¹ *adj* : individualistic

individualista² *nmf* : individualist

individualizar {21} *vt* : to individualize

individuo *nm* : individual, person

indivisible *adj* : indivisible — **indivisibilidad** *nf*

indocumentado, -da *n* : illegal immigrant

índole *nf* **1** : nature, character **2** CLASE, TIPO : sort, kind

indolencia *nf* : indolence, laziness

indolente *adj* : indolent, lazy

indoloro, -ra *adj* : painless

indomable *adj* **1** : indomitable **2** : unruly, unmanageable

indómito, -ta *adj* : indomitable

indonesio, -sia *adj & n* : Indonesian

inducción *nf, pl* **-ciones** : induction

inducir {61} *vt* **1** : to induce, to cause **2** : to infer, to deduce

inductivo, -va *adj* : inductive

indudable *adj* : unquestionable, beyond doubt

indudablemente *adv* : undoubtedly, unquestionably

indulgencia *nf* **1** : indulgence, leniency **2** : indulgence (in religion)

indulgente *adj* : indulgent, lenient

indultar *vt* : to pardon, to reprieve

indulto *nm* : pardon, reprieve

indumentaria *nf* : clothing, attire

industria *nf* : industry

industrial¹ *adj* : industrial

industrial² *nmf* : industrialist, manufacturer

industrialización *nf, pl* **-ciones** : industrialization

industrializar {21} *vt* : to industrialize

industrioso, -sa *adj* : industrious

inédito, -ta *adj* **1** : unpublished **2** : unprecedented

inefable *adj* : ineffable

ineficacia *nf* **1** : inefficiency **2** : ineffectiveness

ineficaz *adj, pl* **-caces 1** : inefficient **2** : ineffective — **ineficazmente** *adv*

ineficiencia *nf* : inefficiency

ineficiente *adj* : inefficient — **ineficientemente** *adv*

inelegancia *nf* : inelegance — **inelegante** *adj*

inelegible *adj* : ineligible — **inelegibilidad** *nf*

ineludible *adj* : inescapable, unavoidable — **ineludiblemente** *adv*

ineptitud *nf* : ineptitude, incompetence

inepto, -ta *adj* : inept, incompetent

inequidad *nf* : inequity

inequitativo, -va *adj* : inequitable

inequívoco, -ca *adj* : unequivocal, unmistakable — **inequívocamente** *adv*

inercia *nf* **1** : inertia **2** : apathy, passivity **3 por ~** : out of habit

inerme *adj* : unarmed, defenseless

inerte *adj* : inert
inescrupuloso, -sa *adj* : unscrupulous
inescrutable *adj* : inscrutable
inesperado, -da *adj* : unexpected — **inesperadamente** *adv*
inestabilidad *nf* : instability, unsteadiness
inestable *adj* : unstable, unsteady
inestimable *adj* : inestimable, invaluable
inevitabilidad *nf* : inevitability
inevitable *adj* : inevitable, unavoidable — **inevitablemente** *adv*
inexactitud *nf* : inaccuracy
inexacto, -ta *adj* : inexact, inaccurate
inexcusable *adj* : inexcusable, unforgivable
inexistencia *nf* : lack, nonexistence
inexistente *adj* : nonexistent
inexorable *adj* : inexorable — **inexorablemente** *adv*
inexperiencia *nf* : inexperience
inexperto, -ta *adj* : inexperienced, unskilled
inexplicable *adj* : inexplicable — **inexplicablemente** *adv*
inexplorado, -da *adj* : unexplored
inexpresable *adj* : inexpressible
inexpresivo, -va *adj* : inexpressive, expressionless
inexpugnable *adj* : impregnable
inextinguible *adj* 1 : inextinguishable 2 : unquenchable
inextricable *adj* : inextricable — **inextricablemente** *adv*
infalibilidad *nf* : infallibility
infalible *adj* : infallible — **infaliblemente** *adv*
infame *adj* 1 : infamous 2 : loathsome, vile ⟨tiempo infame : terrible weather⟩
infamia *nf* : infamy, disgrace
infancia *nf* 1 NIÑEZ : infancy, childhood 2 : children *pl* 3 : beginnings *pl*
infante *nm* 1 : infante, prince 2 : infantryman
infantería *nf* : infantry
infantil *adj* 1 : childish, infantile 2 : child's, children's
infantilismo *nm* 1 : infantilism 2 INMADUREZ : childishness
infarto *nm* : heart attack
infatigable *adj* : indefatigable, tireless — **infatigablemente** *adv*
infección *nf, pl* **-ciones** : infection
infeccioso, -sa *adj* : infectious
infectar *vt* : to infect — **infectarse** *vr*
infecto, -ta *adj* 1 : infected 2 : repulsive, sickening
infecundidad *nf* : infertility
infecundo, -da *adj* : infertile, barren
infelicidad *nf* : unhappiness
infeliz[1] *adj, pl* **-lices** 1 : unhappy 2 : hapless, unfortunate, wretched
infeliz[2] *nmf, pl* **-lices** : wretch
inferencia *nf* : inference
inferior[1] *adj* : inferior, lower
inferior[2] *nmf* : inferior, underling
inferioridad *nf* : inferiority

inferir {76} *vt* 1 DEDUCIR : to infer, to deduce 2 : to cause (harm or injury), to inflict
infernal *adj* : infernal, hellish
infestación *n, pl* **-ciones** : infestation
infestar *vt* 1 : to infest 2 : to overrun, to invade
inficción *nf, pl* **-ciones** *Mex* : pollution
infidelidad *nf* : unfaithfulness, infidelity
infiel[1] *adj* : unfaithful, disloyal
infiel[2] *nmf* : infidel, heathen
infierno *nm* 1 : hell 2 **el quinto infierno** : the middle of nowhere
infiltrar *vt* : to infiltrate — **infiltrarse** *vr* — **infiltración** *nf*
infinidad *nf* 1 : infinity 2 SINFÍN : great number, huge quantity ⟨una infinidad de veces : countless times⟩
infinitesimal *adj* : infinitesimal
infinitivo *nm* : infinitive
infinito[1] *adv* : infinitely, vastly
infinito[2], **-ta** *adj* 1 : infinite 2 : limitless, endless 3 **hasta lo infinito** : ad infinitum — **infinitamente** *adv*
infinito[3] *nm* : infinity
inflable *adj* : inflatable
inflación *nf, pl* **-ciones** : inflation
inflacionario, -ria *adj* : inflationary
inflacionista → **inflacionario**
inflamable *adj* : flammable
inflamación *nf, pl* **-ciones** : inflammation
inflamar *vt* : to inflame
inflamatorio, -ria *adj* : inflammatory
inflar *vt* HINCHAR : to inflate — **inflarse** *vr* 1 : to swell 2 : to become conceited
inflexibilidad *nf* : inflexibility
inflexible *adj* : inflexible, unyielding
inflexión *nf, pl* **-xiones** : inflection
infligir {35} *vt* : to inflict
influencia *nf* INFLUJO : influence
influenciable *adj* : easily influenced, suggestible
influenciar *vt* : to influence
influenza *nf* : influenza
influir {41} *vt* : to influence — *vi* ~ **en** *or* ~ **sobre** : to have an influence on, to affect
influjo *nm* INFLUENCIA : influence
influyente *adj* : influential
información *nf, pl* **-ciones** 1 : information 2 INFORME : report, inquiry 3 NOTICIAS : news
informado, -da *adj* : informed ⟨bien informado : well-informed⟩
informador, -dora *n* : informer, informant
informal *adj* 1 : unreliable (of persons) 2 : informal, casual — **informalmente** *adv*
informalidad *nf* : informality
informante *nmf* : informant
informar *vt* ENTERAR : to inform — *vi* : to report — **informarse** *vr* ENTERARSE : to get information, to find out
informática *nf* : computer science, computing

informativo[1], **-va** *adj* : informative
informativo[2] *nm* : news program, news
informatización *nf, pl* **-ciones** : computerization
informatizar {21} *vt* : to computerize
informe[1] *adj* AMORFO : shapeless, formless
informe[2] *nm* 1 : report 2 : reference (for employment) 3 **informes** *nmpl* : information, data
infortunado, -da *adj* : unfortunate, unlucky
infortunio *nm* 1 DESGRACIA : misfortune 2 CONTRATIEMPO : mishap
infracción *nf, pl* **-ciones** : violation, offense, infraction
infractor, -tora *n* : offender
infraestructura *nf* : infrastructure
infrahumano, -na *adj* : subhuman
infranqueable *adj* 1 : impassable 2 : insurmountable
infrarrojo, -ja *adj* : infrared
infrecuente *adj* : infrequent
infringir {35} *vt* : to infringe, to breach
infructuoso, -sa *adj* : fruitless — **infructuosamente** *adv*
ínfulas *nfpl* 1 : conceit 2 **darse ínfulas** : to put on airs
infundado, -da *adj* : unfounded, baseless
infundio *nm* : false story, lie, tall tale ⟨todo eso son infundios : that's a pack of lies⟩
infundir *vt* 1 : to instill 2 **infundir ánimo a** : to encourage 3 **infundir miedo a** : to intimidate
infusión *nf, pl* **-siones** : infusion
ingeniar *vt* : to devise, to think up — **ingeniarse** *vr* : to manage, to find a way
ingeniería *nf* : engineering
ingeniero, -ra *n* : engineer
ingenio *nm* 1 : ingenuity 2 CHISPA : wit, wits 3 : device, apparatus 4 **ingenio azucarero** : sugar refinery
ingenioso, -sa *adj* 1 : ingenious 2 : clever, witty — **ingeniosamente** *adv*
ingente *adj* : huge, enormous
ingenuidad *nf* : naïveté, ingenuousness
ingenuo[1], **-nua** *adj* CÁNDIDO : naive — **ingenuamente** *adv*
ingenuo[2], **-nua** *n* : naive person
ingerencia → injerencia
ingerir {76} *vt* : to ingest, to consume
ingestión *nf, pl* **-tiones** : ingestion
ingle *nf* : groin
inglés[1], **-glesa** *adj, mpl* **ingleses** : English
inglés[2], **-glesa** *n, mpl* **ingleses** : Englishman *m*, Englishwoman *f*
inglés[3] *nm* : English (language)
inglete *nm* : miter joint
ingobernable *adj* : ungovernable, lawless
ingratitud *nf* : ingratitude
ingrato[1], **-ta** *adj* 1 : ungrateful 2 : thankless
ingrato[2], **-ta** *n* : ingrate
ingrediente *nm* : ingredient

ingresar *vt* 1 : to admit ⟨ingresaron a Luis al hospital : Luis was admitted into the hospital⟩ 2 : to deposit — *vi* 1 : to enter, to go in 2 ~ **en** : to join, to enroll in
ingreso *nm* 1 : entrance, entry 2 : admission 3 **ingresos** *nmpl* : income, earnings *pl*
íngrimo, -ma *adj* : all alone, all by oneself
inhábil *adj* : unskillful, clumsy
inhabilidad *nf* 1 : unskillfulness 2 : unfitness
inhabilitar *vt* 1 : to disqualify, to bar 2 : to disable
inhabitable *adj* : uninhabitable
inhabituado, -da *adj* ~ **a** : unaccustomed to
inhalador *nm* : inhaler
inhalante *nm* : inhalant
inhalar *vt* : to inhale — **inhalación** *nf*
inherente *adj* : inherent
inhibición *nf, pl* **-ciones** COHIBICIÓN : inhibition
inhibir *vt* : to inhibit — **inhibirse** *vr*
inhóspito, -ta *adj* : inhospitable
inhumación *nf, pl* **-ciones** : interment, burial
inhumanidad *nf* : inhumanity
inhumano, -na *adj* : inhuman, cruel, inhumane
inhumar *vt* : to inter, to bury
iniciación *nf, pl* **-ciones** 1 : initiation 2 : introduction
iniciado, -da *n* : initiate
iniciador[1], **-dora** *adj* : initiatory
iniciador[2], **-dora** *n* : initiator, originator
inicial[1] *adj* : initial, original — **inicialmente** *adv*
inicial[2] *nf* : initial (letter)
iniciar *vt* COMENZAR : to initiate, to begin — **iniciarse** *vr*
iniciativa *nf* : initiative
inicio *nm* COMIENZO : beginning
inicuo, -cua *adj* : iniquitous, wicked
inigualado, -da *adj* : unequaled
inimaginable *adj* : unimaginable
inimitable *adj* : inimitable
ininteligible *adj* : unintelligible
ininterrumpido, -da *adj* : uninterrupted, continuous — **ininterrumpidamente** *adv*
iniquidad *nf* : iniquity, wickedness
injerencia *nf* : interference
injerirse {76} *vr* ENTROMETERSE, INMISCUIRSE : to meddle, to interfere
injertar *vt* : to graft
injerto *nm* : graft ⟨injerto de piel : skin graft⟩
injuria *nf* AGRAVIO : affront, insult
injuriar *vt* INSULTAR : to insult, to revile
injurioso, -sa *adj* : insulting, abusive
injusticia *nf* : injustice, unfairness
injustificable *adj* : unjustifiable
injustificadamente *adv* : unjustifiably, unfairly
injustificado, -da *adj* : unjustified, unwarranted

injusto, -ta *adj* : unfair, unjust — **injustamente** *adv*

inmaculado, -da *adj* : immaculate, spotless

inmadurez *nf, pl* **-reces** : immaturity

inmaduro, -ra *adj* 1 : immature 2 : unripe

inmediaciones *nfpl* : environs, surrounding area

inmediatamente *adv* ENSEGUIDA : immediately

inmediatez *nf, pl* **-teces** : immediacy

inmediato, -ta *adj* 1 : immediate 2 CONTIGUO : adjoining 3 de ~ : immediately, right away 4 ~ a : next to, close to

inmejorable *adj* : excellent, unbeatable

inmemorial *adj* : immemorial ⟨tiempos inmemoriales : time immemorial⟩

inmensidad *nf* : immensity, vastness

inmenso, -sa *adj* ENORME : immense, huge, vast — **inmensamente** *adv*

inmensurable *adj* : boundless, immeasurable

inmerecido, -da *adj* : undeserved — **inmerecidamente** *adv*

inmersión *nf, pl* **-siones** : immersion

inmerso, -sa *adj* 1 : immersed 2 : involved, absorbed

inmigración *nf, pl* **-ciones** : immigration

inmigrado, -da *adj & n* : immigrant

inmigrante *adj & nmf* : immigrant

inmigrar *vi* : to immigrate

inminencia *nf* : imminence

inminente *adj* : imminent — **inminentemente** *adv*

inmiscuirse {41} *vr* ENTROMETERSE, INJERIRSE : to meddle, to interfere

inmobiliario, -ria *adj* : real estate, property

inmoderación *n, pl* **-ciones** : immoderation, intemperance

inmoderado, -da *adj* : immoderate, excessive — **inmoderamente** *adv*

inmodestia *nf* : immodesty — **inmodesto, -ta** *adj*

inmolar *vt* : to immolate — **inmolación** *nf*

inmoral *adj* : immoral

inmoralidad *nf* : immorality

inmortal *adj & nmf* : immortal

inmortalidad *nf* : immortality

inmortalizar {21} *vt* : to immortalize

inmotivado, -da *adj* 1 : unmotivated 2 : groundless

inmovible *adj* : immovable, fixed

inmóvil *adj* 1 : still, motionless 2 : steadfast

inmovilidad *nf* : immobility

inmovilizar {21} *vt* : to immobilize

inmueble *nm* : building, property

inmundicia *nf* : dirt, filth, trash

inmundo, -da *adj* : dirty, filthy, nasty

inmune *adj* : immune

inmunidad *nf* : immunity

inmunizar {21} *vt* : to immunize — **inmunización** *nf*

inmunología *nf* : immunology

inmunológico, -ca *adj* : immune ⟨sistema inmunológico : immune system⟩

inmutabilidad *nf* : immutability

inmutable *adj* : immutable, unchangeable

innato, -ta *adj* : innate, inborn

innecesario, -ria *adj* : unnecessary — **innecesariamente** *adv*

innegable *adj* : undeniable

innoble *adj* : ignoble — **innoblemente** *adv*

innovación *nf, pl* **-ciones** : innovation

innovador, -dora *adj* : innovative

innovar *vt* : to introduce — *vi* : to innovate

innumerable *adj* INCONTABLE : innumerable, countless

inobjetable *adj* : indisputable, unobjectionable

inocencia *nf* : innocence

inocente[1] *adj* 1 : innocent 2 INGENUO : naive — **inocentemente** *adv*

inocente[2] *nmf* : innocent person

inocentón[1], -tona *adj, mpl* **-tones** : naive, gullible

inocentón[2], -tona *n, mpl* **-tones** : simpleton, dupe

inocuidad *nf* : harmlessness

inocular *vt* : to inoculate, to vaccinate — **inoculación** *nf*

inocuo, -cua *adj* : innocuous, harmless

inodoro[1], -ra *adj* : odorless

inodoro[2] *nm* : toilet

inofensivo, -va *adj* : inoffensive, harmless

inolvidable *adj* : unforgettable

inoperable *adj* : inoperable

inoperante *adj* : ineffective, inoperative

inopinado, -da *adj* : unexpected — **inopinadamente** *adv*

inoportuno, -na *adj* : untimely, inopportune, inappropriate

inorgánico, -ca *adj* : inorganic

inoxidable *adj* 1 : rustproof 2 acero inoxidable : stainless steel

inquebrantable *adj* : unshakable, unwavering

inquietante *adj* : disturbing, worrisome

inquietar *vt* PREOCUPAR : to disturb, to upset, to worry — **inquietarse** *vr*

inquieto, -ta *adj* 1 : anxious, uneasy, worried 2 : restless

inquietud *nf* 1 : anxiety, uneasiness, worry 2 AGITACIÓN : restlessness

inquilinato *nm* : tenancy

inquilino, -na *n* : tenant, occupant

inquina *nf* 1 : aversion, dislike 2 : ill will ⟨tener inquina a alguien : to have a grudge against someone⟩

inquirir {4} *vi* : to make inquiries — *vt* : to investigate

inquisición *nf, pl* **-ciones** : investigation, inquiry

inquisidor, -dora *adj* : inquisitive

inquisitivo, -va *adj* : inquisitive, curious — **inquisitivamente** *adv*

insaciable *adj* : insatiable

insalubre *adj* 1 : unhealthy 2 ANTIHIGIÉNICO : unsanitary

insalubridad *nf* : unhealthiness

insalvable *adj* : insuperable, insurmountable

insano, -na *adj* **1** LOCO : insane, mad **2** INSALUBRE : unhealthy

insatisfacción *nf, pl* **-ciones** : dissatisfaction

insatisfactorio *nm* : unsatisfactory

insatisfecho, -cha *adj* **1** : dissatisfied **2** : unsatisfied

inscribir {33} *vt* **1** MATRICULAR : to enroll, to register **2** GRABAR : to engrave — **inscribirse** *vr* : to register, to sign up

inscripción *nf, pl* **-ciones 1** MATRÍCULA : enrollment, registration **2** : inscription

inscrito *pp* → **inscribir**

insecticida[1] *adj* : insecticidal

insecticida[2] *nm* : insecticide

insecto *nm* : insect

inseguridad *nf* **1** : insecurity **2** : lack of safety **3** : uncertainty

inseguro, -ra *adj* **1** : insecure **2** : unsafe **3** : uncertain

inseminar *vt* : to inseminate — **inseminación** *nf*

insensatez *nf, pl* **-teces** : foolishness, stupidity

insensato[1], **-ta** *adj* : foolish, senseless

insensato[2], **-ta** *n* : fool

insensibilidad *nf* : insensitivity

insensible *adj* : insensitive, unfeeling

inseparable *adj* : inseparable — **inseparablemente** *adv*

inserción *nf, pl* **-ciones** : insertion

insertar *vt* : to insert

inservible *adj* INÚTIL : useless, unusable

insidia *nf* **1** : snare, trap **2** : malice

insidioso, -sa *adj* : insidious

insigne *adj* : noted, famous

insignia *nf* ENSEÑA : insignia, emblem, badge

insignificancia *nf* **1** : insignificance **2** NIMIEDAD : trifle, triviality

insignificante *adj* : insignificant

insincero, -ra *adj* : insincere — **insinceridad** *nf*

insinuación *nf, pl* **-ciones** : insinuation, hint

insinuante *adj* : suggestive

insinuar {3} *vt* : to insinuate, to hint at — **insinuarse** *vr* **1** ~ **a** : to make advances to **2** ~ **en** : to worm one's way into

insipidez *nf, pl* **-deces** : insipidness, blandness

insípido, -da *adj* : insipid, bland

insistencia *nf* : insistence

insistente *adj* : insistent — **insistentemente** *adv*

insistir *v* : to insist

insociable *adj* : unsociable

insolación *nf, pl* **-ciones** : sunstroke

insolencia *nf* IMPERTINENCIA : insolence

insolente *adj* IMPERTINENTE : insolent

insólito, -ta *adj* : rare, unusual

insoluble *adj* : insoluble — **insolubilidad** *nf*

insolvencia *nf* : insolvency, bankruptcy

insolvente *adj* : insolvent, bankrupt

insomne *adj & nmf* : insomniac

insomnio *nm* : insomnia

insondable *adj* : fathomless, deep

insonorizado, -da *adj* : soundproof

insoportable *adj* INAGUANTABLE : unbearable, intolerable

insoslayable *adj* : unavoidable, inescapable

insospechado, -da *adj* : unexpected, unforeseen

insostenible *adj* : untenable

inspección *nf, pl* **-ciones** : inspection

inspeccionar *vt* : to inspect

inspector, -tora *n* : inspector

inspiración *nf, pl* **-ciones 1** : inspiration **2** INHALACIÓN : inhalation

inspirador, -dora *adj* : inspiring

inspirar *vt* : to inspire — *vi* INHALAR : to inhale

instalación *nf, pl* **-ciones** : installation

instalar *vt* **1** : to install **2** : to instate — **instalarse** *vr* ESTABLECERSE : to settle, to establish oneself

instancia *nf* **1** : petition, request **2 en última instancia** : as a last resort

instantánea *nf* : snapshot

instantáneo, -nea *adj* : instantaneous — **instantáneamente** *adv*

instante *nm* **1** : instant, moment **2 al instante** : immediately **3 a cada instante** : frequently, all the time **4 por instantes** : constantly, incessantly

instar *vt* APREMIAR : to urge, to press — *vi* URGIR : to be urgent or pressing ⟨insta que vayamos pronto : it is imperative that we leave soon⟩

instauración *nf, pl* **-ciones** : establishment

instaurar *vt* : to establish

instigador, -dora *n* : instigator

instigar {52} *vt* : to instigate, to incite

instintivo, -va *adj* : instinctive — **instintivamente** *adv*

instinto *nm* : instinct

institución *nf, pl* **-ciones** : institution

institucional *adj* : institutional — **institucionalmente** *adv*

institucionalización *nf, pl* **-ciones** : institutionalization

institucionalizar {21} *vt* : to institutionalize

instituir {41} *vt* ESTABLECER, FUNDAR : to institute, to establish, to found

instituto *nm* : institute

institutriz *nf, pl* **-trices** : governess *f*

instrucción *nf, pl* **-ciones 1** EDUCACIÓN : education **2 instrucciones** *nfpl* : instructions, directions

instructivo, -va *adj* : instructive, educational

instructor, -tora *n* : instructor

instruir {41} *vt* **1** ADIESTRAR : to instruct, to train **2** ENSEÑAR : to educate, to teach

instrumentación *nf, pl* **-ciones** : orchestration
instrumental *adj* : instrumental
instrumentar *vt* : to orchestrate
instrumentista *nmf* : instrumentalist
instrumento *nm* : instrument
insubordinado, -da *adj* : insubordinate — **insubordinación** *nf*
insubordinarse *vr* : to rebel
insuficiencia *nf* **1** : insufficiency, inadequacy **2 insuficiencia cardíaca** : heart failure
insuficiente *adj* : insufficient, inadequate — **insuficientemente** *adv*
insufrible *adj* : insufferable
insular *adj* : insular
insularidad *nf* : insularity
insulina *nf* : insulin
insulso, -sa *adj* **1** INSÍPIDO : insipid, bland **2** : dull
insultante *adj* : insulting
insultar *vt* : to insult
insulto *nm* : insult
insumos *nmpl* : supplies ⟨insumos agrícolas : agricultural supplies⟩
insuperable *adj* : insuperable, insurmountable
insurgente *adj & nmf* : insurgent — **insurgencia** *nf*
insurrección *nf, pl* **-ciones** : insurrection, uprising
insustancial *adj* : insubstantial, flimsy
insustituible *adj* : irreplaceable
intachable *adj* : irreproachable, faultless
intacto, -ta *adj* : intact
intangible *adj* IMPALPABLE : intangible, impalpable
integración *nf, pl* **-ciones** : integration
integral *adj* **1** : integral, essential **2 pan integral** : whole grain bread
integrante[1] *adj* : integrating, integral
integrante[2] *nmf* : member
integrar *vt* : to make up, to compose — **integrarse** *vr* : to integrate, to fit in
integridad *nf* **1** RECTITUD : integrity, honesty **2** : wholeness, completeness
integrismo *nm* : fundamentalism
integrista *adj & nmf* : fundamentalist
íntegro, -gra *adj* **1** : honest, upright **2** ENTERO : whole, complete **3** : unabridged
intelecto *nm* : intellect
intelectual *adj & nmf* : intellectual — **intelectualmente** *adv*
intelectualidad *nf* : intelligentsia
inteligencia *nf* : intelligence
inteligente *adj* : intelligent — **inteligentemente** *adv*
inteligible *adj* : intelligible — **inteligibilidad** *nf*
intemperancia *adj* : intemperance, excess
intemperie *nf* **1** : bad weather, elements *pl* **2 a la intemperie** : in the open air, outside
intempestivo, -va *adj* : inopportune, untimely — **intempestivamente** *adv*

intención *nf, pl* **-ciones** : intention, plan
intencionado, -da → **intencional**
intencional *adj* : intentional — **intencionalmente** *adv*
intendencia *nf* : management, administration
intendente *nmf* : quartermaster
intensidad *nf* : intensity
intensificación *nf, pl* **-ciones** : intensification
intensificar {72} *vt* : to intensify — **intensificarse** *vr*
intensivo, -va *adj* : intensive — **intensivamente** *adv*
intenso, -sa *adj* : intense — **intensamente** *adv*
intentar *vt* : to attempt, to try
intento *nm* **1** PROPÓSITO : intent, intention **2** TENTATIVA : attempt, try
interacción *nf, pl* **-ciones** : interaction
interactivo, -va *adj* : interactive
interactuar {3} *vi* : to interact
intercalar *vt* : to intersperse, to insert
intercambiable *adj* : interchangeable
intercambiar *vt* CANJEAR : to exchange, to trade
intercambio *nm* CANJE : exchange, trade
interceder *vi* : to intercede
intercepción *nf, pl* **-ciones** : interception
interceptar *vt* **1** : to intercept, to block **2 interceptar las líneas** : to wiretap
intercesión *nf, pl* **-siones** : intercession
intercomunicación *nf, pl* **-ciones** : intercommunication
interconexión *nf, pl* **-xiones** : interconnection
interconfesional *adj* : interdenominational
interdepartamental *adj* : interdepartmental
interdependencia *nf* : interdependence — **interdependiente** *adj*
interdicción *nf, pl* **-ciones** : interdiction, prohibition
interés *nm, pl* **-reses** : interest
interesado, -da *adj* **1** : interested **2** : selfish, self-seeking
interesante *adj* : interesting
interesar *vt* : to interest — *vi* : to be of interest, to be interesting — **interesarse** *vr*
interestatal *adj* : interstate ⟨autopista interestatal : interstate highway⟩
interestelar *adj* : interstellar
interfase → **interfaz**
interfaz *nf, pl* **-faces** : interface
interferencia *nf* : interference, static
interferir {76} *vi* : to interfere, to meddle — *vt* : to interfere with, to obstruct
intergaláctico, -ca *adj* : intergalactic
intergubernamental *adj* : intergovernmental
interín[1] *or* **ínterin** *adv* : meanwhile
interín[2] *or* **ínterin** *nm, pl* **-rines** : meantime, interim ⟨en el interín : in the meantime⟩

interinamente *adv* : temporarily
interino, -na *adj* : acting, temporary, interim
interior[1] *adj* : interior, inner
interior[2] *nm* **1** : interior, inside **2** : inland region
interiormente *adv* : inwardly
interjección *nf, pl* **-ciones** : interjection
interlocutor, -tora *n* : interlocutor, speaker
interludio *nm* : interlude
intermediario, -ria *adj & n* : intermediary, go-between
intermedio[1], **-dia** *adj* : intermediate
intermedio[2] *nm* **1** : intermission **2 por intermedio de** : by means of
interminable *adj* : interminable, endless — **interminablemente** *adv*
intermisión *nf, pl* **-siones** : intermission, pause
intermitente[1] *adj* **1** : intermittent **2** : flashing, blinking (of a light) — **intermitentemente** *adv*
intermitente[2] *nm* : blinker, turn signal
internacional *adj* : international — **internacionalmente** *adv*
internacionalismo *nm* : internationalism
internacionalizar {21} *vt* : to internationalize
internado *nm* : boarding school
internar *vt* : to commit, to confine — **internarse** *vr* **1** : to penetrate, to advance into **2 ~ en** : to go into, to enter
internista *nmf* : internist
interno[1], **-na** *adj* : internal — **internamente** *adv*
interno[2], **-na** *n* **1** : intern **2** : inmate, internee
interpelación *nf, pl* **-ciones** : appeal, plea
interpelar *vt* : to question (formally)
interpersonal *adj* : interpersonal
interpolar *vt* : to insert, to interpolate
interponer {60} *vt* : to interpose — **interponerse** *vr* : to intervene
interpretación *nf, pl* **-ciones** : interpretation
interpretar *vt* **1** : to interpret **2** : to play, to perform
interpretativo, -va *adj* : interpretive
intérprete *nmf* **1** TRADUCTOR : interpreter **2** : performer
interpuesto *pp* → **interponer**
interracial *adj* : interracial
interrelación *nf, pl* **-ciones** : interrelationship
interrelacionar *vi* : to interrelate
interrogación *nf, pl* **-ciones 1** : interrogation, questioning **2 signo de interrogación** : question mark
interrogador, -dora *n* : interrogator, questioner
interrogante[1] *adj* : questioning
interrogante[2] *nm* **1** : question mark **2** : query
interrogar {52} *vt* : to interrogate, to question

interrogativo, -va *adj* : interrogative
interrogatorio *nm* : interrogation, questioning
interrumpir *v* : to interrupt
interrupción *nf, pl* **-ciones** : interruption
interruptor *nm* **1** : (electrical) switch **2** : circuit breaker
intersección *nf, pl* **-ciones** : intersection
intersticio *nm* : interstice — **intersticial** *adj*
interuniversitario, -ria *adj* : intercollegiate
interurbano, -na *adj* **1** : intercity **2** : long-distance ⟨llamadas interurbanas : long-distance calls⟩
intervalo *nm* : interval
intervención *nf, pl* **-ciones 1** : intervention **2** : audit **3 intervención quirúrgica** : operation
intervencionista *adj & nmf* : interventionist
intervenir {87} *vi* **1** : to take part **2** INTERCEDER : to intervene, to intercede — *vt* **1** : to control, to supervise **2** : to audit **3** : to operate on **4** : to tap (a telephone)
interventor, -tora *n* **1** : inspector **2** : auditor, comptroller
intestado, -da *adj* : intestate
intestinal *adj* : intestinal
intestino[1] *nm* : intestine
intimar *vi* **~ con** : to become friendly with — *vt* : to require, to call on
intimidación *nf, pl* **-ciones** : intimidation
intimidad *nf* **1** : intimacy **2** : privacy, private life
intimidar *vt* ACOBARDAR : to intimidate
íntimo, -ma *adj* **1** : intimate, close **2** PRIVADO : private — **íntimamente** *adv*
intitular *vt* : to entitle, to title
intocable *adj* : untouchable
intolerable *adj* : intolerable, unbearable
intolerancia *nf* : intolerance
intolerante[1] *adj* : intolerant
intolerante[2] *nmf* : intolerant person, bigot
intoxicación *nf, pl* **-ciones** : poisoning
intoxicante *nm* : poison
intoxicar {72} *vt* : to poison
intranquilidad *nf* PREOCUPACIÓN : worry, anxiety
intranquilizar {21} *vt* : to upset, to make uneasy — **intranquilizarse** *vr* : to get worried, to be anxious
intranquilo, -la *adj* PREOCUPADO : uneasy, worried
intransigencia *nf* : intransigence
intransigente *adj* : intransigent, unyielding
intransitable *adj* : impassable
intransitivo, -va *adj* : intransitive
intrascendente *adj* : unimportant, insignificant
intratable *adj* **1** : intractable **2** : awkward **3** : unsociable
intravenoso, -sa *adj* : intravenous

intrepidez *nf* : fearlessness
intrépido, -da *adj* : intrepid, fearless
intriga *nf* : intrigue
intrigante *nmf* : schemer
intrigar {52} *v* : to intrigue — **intrigante** *adj*
intrincado, -da *adj* : intricate, involved
intrínseco, -ca *adj* : intrinsic — **intrínsecamente** *adv*
introducción *nf, pl* -ciones : introduction
introducir {61} *vt* 1 : to introduce 2 : to bring in 3 : to insert 4 : to input, to enter — **introducirse** *vr* : to penetrate, to get into
introductorio, -ria *adj* : introductory
intromisión *nf, pl* -siones : interference, meddling
introspección *nf, pl* -ciones : introspection
introspectivo, -va *adj* : introspective
introvertido¹, -da *adj* : introverted
introvertido², -da *n* : introvert
intrusión *nf, pl* -siones : intrusion
intruso¹, -sa *adj* : intrusive
intruso², -sa *n* : intruder
intuición *nf, pl* -ciones : intuition
intuir {41} *vt* 1 : to intuit, to sense
intuitivo, -va *adj* : intuitive — **intuitivamente** *adv*
inundación *nf, pl* -ciones : flood, inundation
inundar *vt* : to flood, to inundate
inusitado, -da *adj* : unusual, uncommon — **inusitadamente** *adv*
inusual *adj* : unusual, uncommon — **inusualmente** *adv*
inútil¹ *adj* INSERVIBLE : useless — **inútilmente** *adv*
inútil² *nmf* : good-for-nothing
inutilidad *nf* : uselessness
inutilizar {21} *vt* 1 : to make useless 2 INCAPACITAR : to disable, to put out of commission
invadir *vt* : to invade
invalidar *vt* : to nullify, to invalidate
invalidez *nf, pl* -deces 1 : invalidity 2 : disablement
inválido, -da *adj & n* : invalid
invalorable *adj* : invaluable
invariable *adj* : invariable — **invariablemente** *adv*
invasión *nf, pl* -siones : invasion
invasivo, -va *adj* : invasive
invasor¹, -sora *adj* : invading
invasor², -sora *n* : invader
invectiva *nf* : invective, abuse
invencibilidad *nf* : invincibility
invencible *adj* 1 : invincible 2 : insurmountable
invención *nf, pl* -ciones 1 INVENTO : invention 2 MENTIRA : fabrication, lie
inventar *vt* 1 : to invent 2 : to fabricate, to make up
inventariar {85} *vt* : to inventory
inventario *nm* : inventory
inventiva *nf* : ingenuity, inventiveness
inventivo, -va *adj* : inventive

invento *nm* INVENCIÓN : invention
inventor, -tora *n* : inventor
invernadero *nm* : greenhouse, hothouse
invernal *adj* : winter, wintry
invernar {55} *vi* 1 : to spend the winter 2 HIBERNAR : to hibernate
inverosímil *adj* : unlikely, far-fetched
inversión *nf, pl* -siones 1 : inversion 2 : investment
inversionista *nmf* : investor
inverso¹, -sa *adj* 1 : inverse, inverted 2 CONTRARIO : opposite 3 a la inversa : on the contrary, vice versa 4 en orden inverso : in reverse order — **inversamente** *adv*
inverso² *n* : inverse
inversor, -sora *n* : investor
invertebrado¹, -da *adj* : invertebrate
invertebrado² *nm* : invertebrate
invertir {76} *vt* 1 : to invert, to reverse 2 : to invest — *vi* : to make an investment — **invertirse** *vr* : to be reversed
investidura *nf* : investiture, inauguration
investigación *nf, pl* -ciones 1 ENCUESTA, INDAGACIÓN : investigation, inquiry 2 : research
investigador¹, -dora *adj* : investigative
investigador², -dora *n* 1 : investigator 2 : researcher
investigar {52} *vt* 1 INDAGAR : to investigate 2 : to research — *vi* ~ sobre : to do research into
investir {54} *vt* 1 : to empower 2 : to swear in, to inaugurate
inveterado, -da *adj* : inveterate, deep-seated
invicto, -ta *adj* : undefeated
invidente¹ *adj* CIEGO : blind, sightless
invidente² *nmf* CIEGO : blind person
invierno *nm* : winter, wintertime
inviolable *adj* : inviolable — **inviolabilidad** *nf*
inviolado, -da *adj* : inviolate, pure
invisibilidad *nf* : invisibility
invisible *adj* : invisible — **invisiblemente** *adv*
invitación *nf, pl* -ciones : invitation
invitado, -da *n* : guest
invitar *vt* : to invite
invocación *nf, pl* -ciones : invocation
invocar {72} *vt* : to invoke, to call on
involucramiento *nm* : involvement
involucrar *vt* : to implicate, to involve — **involucrarse** *vr* : to get involved
involuntario, -ria *adj* : involuntary — **involuntariamente** *adv*
invulnerable *adj* : invulnerable
inyección *nf, pl* -ciones : injection, shot
inyectado, -da *adj* ojos inyectados : bloodshot eyes
inyectar *vt* : to inject
ion *nm* : ion
iónico, -ca *adj* : ionic
ionizar {21} *vt* : to ionize — **ionización** *nf*
ionosfera *nf* : ionosphere
ir {43} *vi* 1 : to go ⟨ir a pie : to go on foot, to walk⟩ ⟨ir a caballo : to ride

horseback⟩ ⟨ir a casa : to go home⟩ **2**
: to lead, to extend, to stretch ⟨el
camino va de Cali a Bogotá : the road
goes from Cali to Bogotá⟩ **3** FUN-
CIONAR : to work, to function ⟨esta
computadora ya no va : this computer
doesn't work anymore⟩ **4** : to get on,
to get along ⟨¿cómo te va? : how are
you?, how's it going?⟩ ⟨el negocio no
va bien : the business isn't doing well⟩
5 : to suit ⟨ese vestido te va bien : that
dress really suits you⟩ **6 ~ con** : to be
⟨ir con prisa : to be in a hurry⟩ **7 ~
por** : to follow, to go along ⟨fueron por
la costa : they followed the shoreline⟩
8 dejarse ir : to let oneself go **9 ir a
parar** : to end up **10 vamos a ver** : let's
see — *v aux* **1** (*with present participle*)
⟨ir caminando : to walk⟩ ⟨¡voy corriendo! : I'll be right there!⟩ **2 ~ a** : to
be going to ⟨voy a hacerlo : I'm going
to do it⟩ ⟨el avión va a despegar : the
plane is about to take off⟩ — **irse** *vr* **1**
: to leave, to go ⟨¡vámonos! : let's go!⟩
⟨todo el mundo se fue : everyone left⟩
2 ESCAPARSE : to leak **3** GASTARSE : to
be used up, to be gone
ira *nf* CÓLERA, FURIA : wrath, anger
iracundo, -da *adj* : irate, angry
iraní *adj & nmf* : Iranian
iraquí *adj & nmf* : Iraqi
irascible *adj* : irascible, irritable — **irascibilidad** *nf*
irga, irgue etc. → **erguir**
iridio *nm* : iridium
iridiscencia *nf* : iridescence — **iridiscente** *adj*
iris *nms & pl* **1** : iris **2 arco iris** : rainbow
irlandés¹, -desa *adj, mpl* **-deses** : Irish
irlandés², -desa *n, pl* **-deses** : Irish person, Irishman *m*, Irishwoman *f*
irlandés³ *nm* : Irish (language)
ironía *nf* : irony
irónico, -ca *adj* : ironic, ironical —
irónicamente *adv*
irracional *adj* : irrational — **irracionalmente** *adv*
irracionalidad *nf* : irrationality
irradiación *nf, pl* **-ciones** : irradiation
irradiar *vt* : to radiate, to irradiate
irrazonable *adj* : unreasonable
irreal *adj* : unreal
irrebatible *adj* : unanswerable, irrefutable
irreconciliable *adj* : irreconcilable
irreconocible *adj* : unrecognizable
irrecuperable *adj* : irrecoverable, irretrievable
irredimible *adj* : irredeemable
irreductible *adj* : unyielding
irreemplazable *adj* : irreplaceable
irreflexión *nf, pl* **-xiones** : thoughtlessness, impetuosity
irreflexivo, -va *adj* : rash, unthinking —
irreflexivamente *adv*
irrefrenable *adj* : uncontrollable, unstoppable ⟨un impulso irrefrenable : an
irresistible urge⟩

irrefutable *adj* : irrefutable
irregular *adj* : irregular — **irregularmente** *adv*
irregularidad *nf* : irregularity
irrelevante *adj* : irrelevant — **irrelevancia** *nf*
irreligioso, -sa *adj* : irreligious
irremediable *adj* : incurable — **irreme-
diablemente** *adv*
irreparable *adj* : irreparable
irreprimible *adj* : irrepressible
irreprochable *adj* : irreproachable
irresistible *adj* : irresistible — **irre-
sistiblemente** *adv*
irresolución *nf, pl* **-ciones** : indecision,
hesitation
irresoluto, -ta *adj* INDECISO : undecided
irrespeto *nm* : disrespect
irrespetuoso, -sa *adj* : disrespectful —
irrespetuosamente *adv*
irresponsabilidad *nf* : irresponsibility
irresponsable *adj* : irresponsible — **irr-
esponsablemente** *adv*
irrestricto, -ta *adj* : unrestricted, unconditional
irreverencia *nf* : disrespect
irreverente *adj* : disrespectful
irreversible *adj* : irreversible
irrevocable *adj* : irrevocable — **irrevo-
cablemente** *adv*
irrigar {52} *vt* : to irrigate — **irrigación**
nf
irrisible *adj* : laughable
irrisión *nf, pl* **-siones** : derision, ridicule
irrisorio, -ria *adj* RISIBLE : ridiculous,
ludicrous
irritabilidad *nf* : irritability
irritable *adj* : irritable
irritación *nf, pl* **-ciones** : irritation
irritante *adj* : irritating
irritar *vt* : to irritate — **irritación** *nf*
irrompible *adj* : unbreakable
irrumpir *vi* **~ en** : to burst into
irrupción *nf, pl* **-ciones** **1** : irruption **2**
: invasion
isla *nf* : island
islámico, -ca *adj* : Islamic, Muslim
islandés¹, -desa *adj, mpl* **-deses** : Icelandic
islandés², -desa *n, mpl* **-deses** : Icelander
islandés³ *nm* : Icelandic (language)
isleño, -ña *n* : islander
islote *nm* : islet
isometría *nfs & pl* : isometrics
isométrico, -ca *adj* : isometric
isósceles *adj* : isosceles ⟨triángulo
isósceles : isosceles triangle⟩
isótopo *nm* : isotope
israelí *adj & nmf* : Israeli
istmo *nm* : isthmus
itacate *nm Mex* : pack, provisions *pl*
italiano¹, -na *adj & n* : Italian
italiano² *nm* : Italian (language)
iterbio *nm* : ytterbium
itinerante *adj* AMBULANTE : traveling,
itinerant
itinerario *nm* : itinerary, route

itrio *nm* : yttrium
izar {21} *vt* : to hoist, to raise ⟨izar la bandera : to raise the flag⟩

izquierda *nf* : left
izquierdista *adj & nmf* : leftist
izquierdo, -da *adj* : left

J

j *nf* : tenth letter of the Spanish alphabet
ja *interj* **1** : ha! **2 ja, ja** : ha-ha!
jabalí *nm* : wild boar
jabalina *nf* : javelin
jabón *nm, pl* **jabones** : soap
jabonar *vt* ENJABONAR : to soap up, to lather — **jabonarse** *vr*
jabonera *nf* : soap dish
jabonoso, -sa *adj* : soapy
jaca *nf* **1** : pony **2** YEGUA : mare
jacal *nm Mex* : shack, hut
jacinto *nm* : hyacinth
jactancia *nf* **1** : boastfulness **2** : boasting, bragging
jactancioso¹, -sa *adj* : boastful
jactancioso², -sa *n* : boaster, braggart
jactarse *vr* : to boast, to brag
jade *nm* : jade
jadear *vi* : to pant, to gasp, to puff — **jadeante** *adj*
jadeo *nm* : panting, gasping, puffing
jaez *nm, pl* **jaeces 1** : harness **2** : kind, sort, ilk **3 jaeces** *nmpl* : trappings
jaguar *nm* : jaguar
jai alai *nm* : jai alai
jaiba *nf* CANGREJO : crab
jalapeño *nm Mex* : jalapeño pepper
jalar *vt* **1** : to pull, to tug **2** *fam* : to attract, to draw in ⟨las ideas nuevas lo jalan : new ideas appeal to him⟩ — *vi* **1** : to pull, to pull together **2** *fam* : to hurry up, to get going **3** *Mex fam* : to be in working order ⟨esta máquina no jala : this machine doesn't work⟩
jalbegue *nm* : whitewash
jalea *nf* : jelly
jalear *vt* : to encourage, to urge on
jaleo *nm* **1** *fam* : uproar, ruckus, racket **2** *fam* : confusion, hassle **3** : cheering and clapping (for a dance)
jalón *nm, pl* **jalones 1** : milestone, landmark **2** TIRÓN : pull, tug
jalonar *vt* : to mark, to stake out
jalonear *vt Mex, Peru fam* : to tug at — *vi* **1** *fam* : to pull, to tug **2** *CA fam* : to haggle
jamaica *nf* : hibiscus
jamaicano, -na → jamaiquino
jamaiquino, -na *adj & n* : Jamaican
jamás *adv* **1** NUNCA : never **2 nunca jamás** *or* **jamás de los jamases** : never ever **3 para siempre jamás** : for ever and ever
jamba *nf* : jamb
jamelgo *nm* : nag (horse)
jamón *nm, pl* **jamones** : ham
Januká *nmf* : Hanukkah
japonés¹, -nesa *adj & n, mpl* **-neses** : Japanese

japonés² *nm, pl* **-neses** : Japanese (language)
jaque *nm* **1** : check (in chess) ⟨jaque mate : checkmate⟩ **2 tener en jaque** : to intimidate, to bully
jaqueca *nf* : headache, migraine
jarabe *nm* **1** : syrup **2** : Mexican folk dance
jarana *nf* **1** *fam* : revelry, partying, spree **2** *fam* : joking, fooling around **3** : small guitar
jaranear *vi fam* : to go on a spree, to party
jarcia *nf* **1** : rigging **2** : fishing tackle
jardín *nm, pl* **jardines 1** : garden **2 jardín de niños** : kindergarten **3 los jardines** *nmpl* : the outfield
jardinería *nf* : gardening
jardinero, -ra *n* **1** : gardener **2** : outfielder (in baseball)
jarra *nf* **1** : pitcher, jug **2** : stein, mug **3 de jarras** *or* **en jarras** : akimbo
jarrete *nm* **1** : back of the knee **2** CORVEJÓN : hock
jarro *nm* **1** : pitcher, jug **2** : mug
jarrón *nm, pl* **jarrones** FLORERO : vase
jaspe *nm* : jasper
jaspeado, -da *adj* **1** VETEADO : streaked, veined **2** : speckled, mottled
jaula *nf* : cage
jauría *nf* : pack of hounds
javanés, -nesa *adj & n* : Javanese
jazmín *nm, pl* **jazmines** : jasmine
jazz ['jas, 'dʒas] *nm* : jazz
jeans ['jins, 'dʒins] *nmpl* : jeans
jeep ['jip, 'dʒip] *nm, pl* **jeeps** : jeep
jefatura *nf* **1** : leadership **2** : headquarters ⟨jefatura de policía : police headquarters⟩
jefe, -fa *n* **1** : chief, head, leader ⟨jefe de bomberos : fire chief⟩ **2** : boss
Jehová *nm* : Jehovah
jején *nm, pl* **jejenes** : gnat, small mosquito
jengibre *nm* : ginger
jeque *nm* : sheikh, sheik
jerarca *nmf* : leader, chief
jerarquía *nf* **1** : hierarchy **2** RANGO : rank
jerárquico, -ca *adj* : hierarchical
jerbo *nm* : gerbil
jerez *nm, pl* **jereces** : sherry
jerga *nf* **1** : jargon, slang **2** : coarse cloth
jerigonza *nf* GALIMATÍAS : mumbo jumbo, gibberish
jeringa *nf* : syringe
jeringar {52} *vt* **1** : to inject **2** *fam* JORO-BAR : to annoy, to pester — *vi fam*

JOROBAR : to be annoying, to be a nuisance

jeringuear → **jeringar**

jeringuilla → **jeringa**

jeroglífico *nm* : hieroglyphic

jersey *nm, pl* **jerseys** 1 : jersey (fabric) 2 *Spain* : sweater

Jesucristo *nm* : Jesus Christ

jesuita *adj & nm* : Jesuit

Jesús *nm* 1 : Jesus 2 **¡Jesús!** : goodness!, good heavens!

jeta *nf* 1 : snout 2 *fam* : face, mug

jíbaro, -ra *adj* 1 : Jivaro 2 : rustic, rural

jibia *nf* : cuttlefish

jícama *nf* : jicama

jícara *nf Mex* : calabash

jilguero *nm* : European goldfinch

jinete *nmf* : horseman, horsewoman *f*, rider

jinetear *vt* 1 : to ride, to perform (on horseback) 2 DOMAR : to break in (a horse) — *vi* CABALGAR : to ride horseback

jingoísmo [jɪŋgoˈizmo, ˌʤɪŋ-] *nm* : jingoism

jingoísta *adj* : jingoist, jingoistic

jiote *nm Mex* : rash

jira *nf* : outing, picnic

jirafa *nf* 1 : giraffe 2 : boom microphone

jirón *nm, pl* **jirones** : shred, rag ⟨hecho jirones : in tatters⟩

jitomate *nm Mex* : tomato

jockey [ˈjɔki, ˈʤɔ-] *nmf, pl* **jockeys** [-kis] : jockey

jocosidad *nf* : humor, jocularity

jocoso, -sa *adj* : playful, jocular — **jocosamente** *adv*

jofaina *nf* : washbowl

jogging [ˈjɔgɪn, ˈʤɔ-] *nm* : jogging

jolgorio *nm* : merrymaking, fun

jonrón *nm, pl* **jonrones** : home run

jordano, -na *adj & n* : Jordanian

jornada *nf* 1 : expedition, day's journey 2 **jornada de trabajo** : working day 3 **jornadas** *nfpl* : conference, congress

jornal *nm* 1 : day's pay 2 **a ~** : by the day

jornalero, -ra *n* : day laborer

joroba *nf* 1 GIBA : hump 2 *fam* : nuisance, pain in the neck

jorobado¹, -da *adj* GIBOSO : hunchbacked, humpbacked

jorobado², -da *n* GIBOSO : hunchback, humpback

jorobar *vt fam* JERINGAR : to bother, to annoy — *vi fam* JERINGAR : to be annoying, to be a nuisance

jorongo *nm Mex* : full-length poncho

jota *nf* 1 : jot, bit ⟨no entiendo ni jota : I don't understand a word of it⟩ ⟨no se ve ni jota : you can't see a thing⟩ 2 : jack (in playing cards)

joven¹ *adj, pl* **jóvenes** 1 : young 2 : youthful

joven² *nmf, pl* **jóvenes** : young man *m*, young woman *f*, young person

jovial *adj* : jovial, cheerful — **jovialmente** *adv*

jovialidad *nf* : joviality, cheerfulness

joya *nf* 1 : jewel, piece of jewelry 2 : treasure, gem ⟨la nueva empleada es una joya : the new employee is a real gem⟩

joyería *nf* 1 : jewelry store 2 : jewelry 3 **joyería de fantasía** : costume jewelry

joyero, -ra *n* : jeweler

juanete *nm* : bunion

jubilación *nf, pl* **-ciones** 1 : retirement 2 PENSIÓN : pension

jubilado¹, -da *adj* : retired, in retirement

jubilado², -da *nmf* : retired person, retiree

jubilar *vt* 1 : to retire, to pension off 2 *fam* : to get rid of, to discard — **jubilarse** *vr* : to retire

jubileo *nm* : jubilee

júbilo *nm* : jubilation, joy

jubiloso, -sa *adj* : jubilant, joyous

judaico, -ca *adj* : Judaic, Jewish

judaísmo *nm* : Judaism

judía *nf* 1 : bean 2 *or* **judía verde** : green bean, string bean

judicatura *nf* 1 : judiciary, judges *pl* 2 : office of judge

judicial *adj* : judicial — **judicialmente** *adv*

judío¹, -día *adj* : Jewish

judío², -día *n* : Jewish person, Jew

judo [ˈjuðo, ˈʤu-] *nm* : judo

juega, juegue, etc. → **jugar**

juego *nm* 1 : play, playing ⟨poner en juego : to bring into play⟩ 2 : game, sport ⟨juego de cartas : card game⟩ ⟨Juegos Olímpicos : Olympic Games⟩ 3 : gaming, gambling ⟨estar en juego : to be at stake⟩ 4 : set ⟨un juego de llaves : a set of keys⟩ 5 **hacer juego** : to go together, to match 6 **juego de manos** : conjuring trick, sleight of hand

juerga *nf* : partying, binge ⟨irse de juerga : to go on a spree⟩

juerguista *nmf* : reveler, carouser

jueves *nms & pl* : Thursday

juez¹ *nmf, pl* **jueces** 1 : judge 2 ÁRBITRO : umpire, referee

juez², jueza *n* → **juez¹**

jugada *nf* 1 : play, move 2 : trick ⟨hacer una mala jugada : to play a dirty trick⟩

jugador, -dora *n* 1 : player 2 : gambler

jugar {44} *vi* 1 : to play ⟨jugar a la pelota : to play ball⟩ 2 APOSTAR : to gamble, to bet 3 : to joke, to kid — *vt* 1 : to play ⟨jugar un papel : to play a role⟩ ⟨jugar una carta : to play a card⟩ 2 : to bet — **jugarse** *vr* 1 : to risk, to gamble away ⟨jugarse la vida : to risk one's life⟩ 2 **jugarse el todo por el todo** : to risk everything

jugarreta *nf fam* : prank, dirty trick

juglar *nm* : minstrel

jugo *nm* **1** : juice **2** : substance, essence ⟨sacarle el jugo a algo : to get the most out of something⟩
jugosidad *nf* : juiciness, succulence
jugoso, -sa *adj* : juicy
juguete *nm* : toy
juguetear *vi* **1** : to play, to cavort, to frolic **2** : to toy, to fiddle
juguetería *nf* : toy store
juguetón, -tona *adj, mpl* **-tones** : playful — **juguetonamente** *adv*
juicio *nm* **1** : good judgment, reason, sense **2** : opinion ⟨a mi juicio : in my opinion⟩ **3** : trial ⟨llevar a juicio : to take to court⟩
juicioso, -sa *adj* : judicious, wise — **juiciosamente** *adv*
julio *nm* : July
juncia *nf* : sedge
junco *nm* **1** : reed, rush **2** : junk (boat)
jungla *nf* : jungle
junio *nm* : June
junquillo *nm* : jonquil
junta *nf* **1** : board, committee ⟨junta directiva : board of directors⟩ **2** REUNIÓN : meeting, session **3** : junta **4** : joint, gasket
juntamente *adv* **1** : jointly, together ⟨juntamente con : together with⟩ **2** : at the same time
juntar *vt* **1** UNIR : to unite, to combine, to put together **2** REUNIR : to collect, to gather together, to assemble **3** : to close partway ⟨juntar la puerta : to leave the door ajar⟩ — **juntarse** *vr* **1** : to join together **2** : to socialize, to get together
junto, -ta *adj* **1** UNIDO : joined, united **2** : close, adjacent ⟨colgaron los dos retratos juntos : they hung the two paintings side by side⟩ **3** (*used adverbially*) : together ⟨llegamos juntos : we arrived together⟩ **4** ~ **a** : next to, alongside of **5** ~ **con** : together with, along with
juntura *nf* : joint, coupling
Júpiter *nm* : Jupiter
jura *nf* : oath, pledge ⟨jura de bandera : pledge of allegiance⟩

jurado¹ *nm* : jury
jurado², -da *n* : juror
juramento *nm* **1** : oath ⟨juramento hipocrático : Hippocratic oath⟩ **2** : swearword, oath
jurar *vt* **1** : to swear ⟨jurar lealtad : to swear loyalty⟩ **2** : to take an oath ⟨el alcalde juró su cargo : the mayor took the oath of office⟩ — *vi* : to curse, to swear
jurídico, -ca *adj* : legal
jurisdicción *nf, pl* **-ciones** : jurisdiction
jurisdiccional *adj* : jurisdictional, territorial
jurisprudencia *nf* : jurisprudence, law
jurista *nmf* : jurist
justa *nf* **1** : joust **2** TORNEO : tournament, competition
justamente *adv* **1** PRECISAMENTE : precisely, exactly **2** : justly, fairly
justar *vi* : to joust
justicia *nf* **1** : justice, fairness ⟨hacerle justicia a : to do justice to⟩ ⟨ser de justicia : to be only fair⟩ **2 la justicia** : the law ⟨tomarse la justicia por su mano : to take the law into one's own hands⟩
justiciero, -ra *adj* : righteous, avenging
justificable *adj* : justifiable
justificación *nf, pl* **-ciones** : justification
justificante *nm* **1** : justification **2** : proof, voucher
justificar {72} *vt* **1** : to justify **2** : to excuse, to vindicate
justo¹ *adv* **1** : justly **2** : right, exactly ⟨justo a tiempo : just in time⟩ **3** : tightly
justo², -ta *adj* **1** : just, fair **2** : right, exact **3** : tight ⟨estos zapatos me quedan muy justos : these shoes are too tight⟩
justo³, -ta *n* : just person ⟨los justos : the just⟩
juvenil *adj* **1** : juvenile, young, youthful **2** ADOLESCENTE : teenage
juventud *nf* **1** : youth **2** : young people
juzgado *nm* TRIBUNAL : court, tribunal
juzgar {52} *vt* **1** : to try, to judge (a case in court) **2** : to pass judgment on **3** CONSIDERAR : to consider, to deem
juzgue, etc. → juzgar

K

k *nf* : eleventh letter of the Spanish alphabet
káiser *nm* : kaiser
kaki → caqui
kaleidoscopio → caleidoscopio
kamikaze *adj & nm* : kamikaze
kampucheano, -na *adj & n* : Kampuchean
kan *nm* : khan
karaoke *nm* : karaoke
karate *or* **kárate** *nm* : karate
kayac *or* **kayak** *nm, pl* **kayacs** *or* **kayaks** : kayak

keniano, -na *adj & n* : Kenyan
kepí *nm* : kepi
kermesse *or* **kermés** [kɛrˈmɛs] *nf, pl* **kermesses** *or* **kermeses** [-ˈmɛses] : charity fair, bazaar
kerosene *or* **kerosén** *or* **keroseno** *nm* : kerosene, paraffin
kibutz *or* **kibbutz** *nms & pl* : kibbutz
kilo *nm* **1** : kilo, kilogram **2** *fam* : large amount
kilobyte [ˌkiloˈbait] *nm* : kilobyte
kilocíclo *nm* : kilocycle
kilogramo *nm* : kilogram

kilohertzio *nm* : kilohertz
kilometraje *nm* : distance in kilometers, mileage
kilométrico, -ca *adj fam* : endless, very long
kilómetro *nm* : kilometer
kilovatio *nm* : kilowatt
kimono *nm* : kimono
kinder ['kɪndɛr] → **kindergarten**
kindergarten [ˌkɪndɛr'gartɛn] *nm, pl* **kindergartens** [-tɛns] : kindergarten, nursery school
kinesiología *nf* : physical therapy

kinesiólogo, -ga *n* : physical therapist
kiosco → **quiosco**
kit *nm, pl* **kits** : kit
kiwi ['kiwi] *nm* **1** : kiwi (bird) **2** : kiwifruit
klaxon → **claxon**
knockout [nɔ'kaut] → **nocaut**
koala *nm* : koala bear
kriptón *nm* : krypton
kurdo¹, -da *adj* : Kurdish
kurdo², -da *n* : Kurd
kuwaití [kuˌwai'ti] *adj & nmf* : Kuwaiti

L

l *nf* : twelfth letter of the Spanish alphabet
la¹ *pron* **1** : her, it ⟨llámala hoy : call her today⟩ ⟨sacó la botella y la abrió : he took out the bottle and opened it⟩ **2** *(formal)* : you ⟨no la vi a usted, Señora Díaz : I didn't see you, Mrs. Díaz⟩ **3** : the one ⟨mi casa y la de la puerta roja : my house and the one with the red door⟩ **4 la que** : the one who
la² *art* → **el²**
laberíntico, -ca *adj* : labyrinthine
laberinto *nm* : labyrinth, maze
labia *nf fam* : gift of gab ⟨tu amigo tiene labia : your friend has a way with words⟩
labial *adj* : labial, lip ⟨lápiz labial : lipstick⟩
labio *nm* **1** : lip **2 labio leporino** : harelip
labor *nf* : work, labor
laborable *adj* **1** : arable **2 día laborable** : workday, business day
laboral *adj* : work, labor ⟨costos laborales : labor costs⟩
laborar *vi* : to work
laboratorio *nm* : laboratory, lab
laboriosidad *nf* : industriousness, diligence
laborioso, -sa *adj* **1** : laborious, hard **2** : industrious, hardworking
labrado¹, -da *adj* **1** : cultivated, tilled **2** : carved, wrought
labrado² *nm* : cultivated field
labrador, -dora *n* : farmer
labranza *nf* : farming
labrar *vt* **1** : to carve, to work (metal) **2** : to cultivate, to till **3** : to cause, to bring about
laca *nf* **1** : lacquer, shellac **2** : hair spray **3 laca de uñas** : nail polish
lacayo *nm* : lackey
lace, etc. → **lazar**
lacear *vt* : to lasso
laceración *nf, pl* **-ciones** : laceration
lacerante *adj* : hurtful, wounding
lacerar *vt* **1** : to lacerate, to cut **2** : to hurt, to wound (one's feelings)
lacio, -cia *adj* **1** : limp, lank **2 pelo lacio** : straight hair

lacónico, -ca *adj* : laconic — **lacónicamente** *adv*
lacra *nf* **1** : scar, mark (on the skin) **2** : stigma, blemish
lacrar *vt* : to seal (with wax)
lacrimógeno, -na *adj* **gas lacrimógeno** : tear gas
lacrimoso, -sa *adj* : tearful, moving
lactancia *nf* **1** : lactation **2** : breastfeeding
lactante *nmf* : nursing infant, suckling
lactar *v* : to breast-feed
lácteo, -tea *adj* **1** : dairy **2 Vía Láctea** : Milky Way
láctico, -ca *adj* : lactic
lactosa *nf* : lactose
ladeado, -da *adj* : crooked, tilted, lopsided
ladear *vt* : to tilt, to tip — **ladearse** *vr* : to bend (over)
ladera *nf* : slope, hillside
ladino¹, -na *adj* **1** : cunning, shrewd **2** *CA, Mex* : mestizo
ladino², -na *n* **1** : trickster **2** *CA, Mex* : Spanish-speaking Indian **3** *CA, Mex* : mestizo
lado *nm* **1** : side **2** PARTE : place ⟨miró por todos lados : he looked everywhere⟩ **3 al lado de** : next to, beside **4 de ~** : tilted, sideways ⟨está de lado : it's lying on its side⟩ **5 hacerse a un lado** : to step aside **6 lado a lado** : side by side **7 por otro lado** : on the other hand
ladrar *vi* : to bark
ladrido *nm* : bark (of a dog), barking
ladrillo *nm* **1** : brick **2** AZULEJO : tile
ladrón, -drona *n, mpl* **ladrones** : robber, thief, burglar
lagartija *nf* : small lizard
lagarto *nm* **1** : lizard **2 lagarto de Indias** : alligator
lago *nm* : lake
lágrima *nf* : tear, teardrop
lagrimear *vi* **1** : to water (of eyes) **2** : to weep easily
laguna *nf* **1** : lagoon **2** : lacuna, gap
laicado *nm* : laity
laico¹, -ca *adj* : lay, secular
laico², -ca *n* : layman *m*, laywoman *f*

laja *nf* : slab
lama[1] *nf* : slime, ooze
lama[2] *nm* : lama
lamber *vt* : to lick
lamé *nm* : lamé
lamentable *adj* **1** : unfortunate, lamentable **2** : pitiful, sad
lamentablemente *adv* : unfortunately, regrettably
lamentación *nf, pl* **-ciones** : lamentation, groaning, moaning
lamentar *vt* **1** : to lament **2** : to regret ⟨lo lamento : I'm sorry⟩ — **lamentarse** *vr* : to grumble, to complain
lamento *nm* : lament, groan, cry
lamer *vt* **1** : to lick **2** : to lap against
lamida *nf* : lick
lámina *nf* **1** PLANCHA : sheet, plate **2** : plate, illustration
laminado[1], **-da** *adj* : laminated
laminado[2] *nm* : laminate
laminar *vt* : to laminate — **laminación** *nf*
lámpara *nf* : lamp
lampiño, -ña *adj* : hairless
lamprea *nf* : lamprey
lana *nf* **1** : wool ⟨lana de acero : steel wool⟩ **2** *Mex fam* : money, dough
lance[1], etc. → lanzar
lance[2] *nm* **1** INCIDENTE : event, incident **2** RIÑA : quarrel **3** : throw, cast (of a net, etc.) **4** : move, play (in a game), throw (of dice)
lancear *vt* : to spear
lanceta *nf* : lancet
lancha *nf* **1** : small boat, launch **2 lancha motora** : motorboat, speedboat
langosta *nf* **1** : lobster **2** : locust
langostino *nm* : prawn, crayfish
languidecer {53} *vi* : to languish
languidez *nf, pl* **-deces** : languor, listlessness
lánguido, -da *adj* : languid, listless — **lánguidamente** *adv*
lanolina *nf* : lanolin
lanudo, -da *adj* : woolly
lanza *nf* : spear, lance
lanzadera *nf* **1** : shuttle (for weaving) **2 lanzadera espacial** : space shuttle
lanzado, -da *adj* **1** : impulsive, brazen **2** : forward, determined ⟨ir lanzado : to hurtle along⟩
lanzador, -dora *n* : thrower, pitcher
lanzallamas *nms & pl* : flamethrower
lanzamiento *nm* **1** : throw **2** : pitch (in baseball) **3** : launching, launch
lanzar {21} *vt* **1** : to throw, to hurl **2** : to pitch **3** : to launch — **lanzarse** *vr* **1** : to throw oneself (at, into) **2 ~ a** : to embark upon, to undertake
laosiano, -na *adj & n* : Laotian
lapicero *nm* **1** : mechanical pencil **2** *CA, Peru* : ballpoint pen
lápida *nf* : marker, tombstone
lapidar *vt* APEDREAR : to stone
lapidario, -ria *adj & n* : lapidary
lápiz *nm, pl* **lápices 1** : pencil **2 lápiz de labios** *or* **lápiz labial** : lipstick

lapón, -pona *adj & n, mpl* **lapones** : Lapp
lapso *nm* : lapse, space (of time)
lapsus *nms & pl* : error, slip
laptop *nm, pl* **laptops** : laptop
laquear *vt* : to lacquer, to varnish, to shellac
largamente *adv* **1** : at length, extensively **2** : easily, comfortably **3** : generously
largar {52} *vt* **1** SOLTAR : to let loose, to release **2** AFLOJAR : to loosen, to slacken **3** *fam* : to give, to hand over **4** *fam* : to hurl, to let fly (insults, etc.) — **largarse** *vr fam* : to scram, to beat it
largo[1], **-ga** *adj* **1** : long **2 a lo largo** : lengthwise **3 a lo largo de** : along **4 a la larga** : in the long run
largo[2] *nm* : length ⟨tres metros de largo : three meters long⟩
largometraje *nm* : feature film
largue, etc. → largar
larguero *nm* : crossbeam
largueza *nf* : generosity, largesse
larguirucho, -cha *adj fam* : lanky
largura *nf* : length
laringe *nf* : larynx
laringitis *nfs & pl* : laryngitis
larva *nf* : larva — **larval** *adj*
las → el[2], los[1]
lasaña *nf* : lasagna
lasca *nf* : chip, chipping
lascivia *nf* : lasciviousness, lewdness
lascivo, -va *adj* : lascivious, lewd — **lascivamente** *adv*
láser *nm* : laser
lasitud *nf* : lassitude, weariness
laso, -sa *adj* : languid, weary
lástima *nf* **1** : compassion, pity **2** PENA : shame, pity ⟨¡qué lástima! : what a shame!⟩
lastimadura *nf* : injury, wound
lastimar *vt* **1** DAÑAR, HERIR : to hurt, to injure **2** AGRAVIAR : to offend — **lastimarse** *vr* : to hurt oneself
lastimero, -ra *adj* : pitiful, wretched
lastimoso, -sa *adj* **1** : shameful **2** : pitiful, terrible
lastrar *vt* **1** : to ballast **2** : to burden, to encumber
lastre *nm* **1** : burden **2** : ballast
lata *nf* **1** : tinplate **2** : tin can **3** *fam* : pest, bother, nuisance **4 dar lata** *fam* : to bother, to annoy
latencia *nf* : latency
latente *adj* : latent
lateral[1] *adj* **1** : lateral, side **2** : indirect — **lateralmente** *adv*
lateral[2] *nm* : end piece, side
látex *nms & pl* : latex
latido *nm* : beat, throb ⟨latido del corazón : heartbeat⟩
latifundio *nm* : large estate
latigazo *nm* : lash (with a whip)
látigo *nm* AZOTE : whip
latín *nm* : Latin (language)
latino[1], **-na** *adj* **1** : Latin **2** *fam* : Latin-American

latino · legua

latino², -na *n fam* : Latin American
latinoamericano¹, -na *adj* HISPANO-AMERICANO : Latin American
latinoamericano, -na *n* : Latin American
latir *vi* **1** : to beat, to throb **2 latirle a uno** *Mex fam* : to have a hunch ⟨me late que no va a venir : I have a feeling he's not going to come⟩
latitud *nf* **1** : latitude **2** : breadth
lato, -ta *adj* **1** : extended, lengthy **2** : broad (in meaning)
latón *nm, pl* **latones** : brass
latoso¹, -sa *adj fam* : annoying, bothersome
latoso², -sa *n fam* : pest, nuisance
latrocinio *nm* : larceny
laúd *nm* : lute
laudable *adj* : laudable, praiseworthy
laudo *nm* : findings, decision
laureado, -da *adj & n* : laureate
laurear *vt* : to award, to honor
laurel *nm* **1** : laurel **2** : bay leaf **3 dormirse en sus laureles** : to rest on one's laurels
lava *nf* : lava
lavable *adj* : washable
lavabo *nm* **1** LAVAMANOS : sink, washbowl **2** : lavatory, toilet
lavadero *nm* : laundry room
lavado *nm* **1** : laundry, wash **2** : laundering ⟨lavado de dinero : money laundering⟩
lavadora *nf* : washing machine
lavamanos *nms & pl* LAVABO : sink, washbowl
lavanda *nf* ESPLIEGO : lavender
lavandería *nf* : laundry (service)
lavandero, -ra *n* : launderer, laundress *f*
lavaplatos *nms & pl* **1** : dishwasher **2** *Chile, Col, Mex* : kitchen sink
lavar *vt* **1** : to wash, to clean **2** : to launder (money) **3 lavar en seco** : to dry-clean — **lavarse** *vr* **1** : to wash oneself **2 lavarse las manos de** : to wash one's hands of
lavativa *nf* : enema
lavatorio *nm* : lavatory, washroom
lavavajillas *nms & pl* : dishwasher
laxante *adj & nm* : laxative
laxitud *nf* : laxity, slackness
laxo, -xa *adj* : lax, slack
lazada *nf* : bow, loop
lazar {21} *vt* : to rope, to lasso
lazo *nm* **1** VÍNCULO : link, bond **2** : bow, ribbon **3** : lasso, lariat
le *pron* **1** : to her, to him, to it ⟨¿qué le dijiste? : what did you tell him?⟩ **2** : from her, from him, from it ⟨el ladrón le robó la cartera : the thief stole his wallet⟩ **3** : for her, for him, for it ⟨cómprale flores a tu mamá : buy your mom some flowers⟩ **4** (*formal*) : to you, for you ⟨le traje un regalo : I brought you a gift⟩
leal *adj* : loyal, faithful — **lealmente** *adv*
lealtad *nf* : loyalty, allegiance

lebrel *nm* : hound
lección *nf, pl* **lecciones** : lesson
lechada *nf* **1** : whitewash **2** : grout
lechal *adj* : suckling, unweaned ⟨cordero lechal : suckling lamb⟩
leche *nf* **1** : milk ⟨leche en polvo : powdered milk⟩ ⟨leche de magnesia : milk of magnesia⟩ **2** : milky sap
lechera *nf* **1** : milk jug **2** : dairymaid *f*
lechería *nf* : dairy store
lechero¹, -ra *adj* : dairy
lechero², -ra *n* : milkman *m*, milk dealer
lecho *nm* **1** : bed ⟨un lecho de rosas : a bed of roses⟩ ⟨lecho de muerte : deathbed⟩ **2** : riverbed **3** : layer, stratum (in geology)
lechón, -chona *n, mpl* **lechones** : suckling pig
lechoso, -sa *adj* : milky
lechuga *nf* : lettuce
lechuza *nf* BÚHO : owl, barn owl
lectivo, -va *adj* : school ⟨año lectivo : school year⟩
lector¹, -tora *adj* : reading ⟨nivel lector : reading level⟩
lector², -tora *n* : reader
lector³ *nm* : scanner, reader ⟨lector óptico : optical scanner⟩
lectura *nf* **1** : reading **2** : reading matter
leer {20} *v* : to read
legación *nf, pl* **-ciones** : legation
legado *nm* **1** : legacy, bequest **2** : legate, emissary
legajo *nm* : dossier, file
legal *adj* : legal, lawful — **legalmente** *adv*
legalidad *nf* : legality, lawfulness
legalista *adj* : legalistic
legalizar {21} *vt* : to legalize — **legalización** *nf*
legar {52} *vt* **1** : to bequeath, to hand down **2** DELEGAR : to delegate
legendario, -ria *adj* : legendary
legible *adj* : legible
legión *nf, pl* **legiones** : legion
legionario, -ria *n* : legionnaire
legislación *nf* **1** : legislation, lawmaking **2** : laws *pl*, legislation
legislador¹, -dora *adj* : legislative
legislador², -dora *n* : legislator
legislar *vi* : to legislate
legislativo, -va *adj* : legislative
legislatura *nf* **1** : legislature **2** : term of office
legitimar *vt* **1** : to legitimize **2** : to authenticate — **legitimación** *nf*
legitimidad *nf* : legitimacy
legítimo, -ma *adj* **1** : legitimate **2** : genuine, authentic — **legítimamente** *adv*
lego¹, -ga *adj* **1** : secular, lay **2** : uninformed, ignorant
lego², -ga *n* : layperson, layman *m*, laywoman *f*
legua *nf* **1** : league **2 notarse a leguas** : to be very obvious ⟨se notaba a leguas : you could tell from a mile away⟩

legue, etc. → **legar**
legumbre *nf* **1** HORTALIZA : vegetable **2** : legume
leíble *adj* : readable
leída *nf* : reading, read ⟨de una leída : in one reading, at one go⟩
leído[1] *pp* → **leer**
leído[2], **-da** *adj* : well-read
lejanía *nf* : remoteness, distance
lejano, -na *adj* : remote, distant, far away
lejía *nf* **1** : lye **2** : bleach
lejos *adv* **1** : far away, distant ⟨a lo lejos : in the distance, far off⟩ ⟨desde lejos : from a distance⟩ **2** : long ago, a long way off ⟨está lejos de los 50 años : he's a long way from 50 years old⟩ **3 de ~** : by far ⟨esta decisión fue de lejos la más fácil : this decision was by far the easiest⟩ **4 ~ de** : far from ⟨lejos de ser reprobado, recibió una nota de B : far from failing, he got a B⟩
lelo, -la *adj* : silly, stupid
lema *nm* : motto, slogan
lencería *nf* : lingerie
lengua *nf* **1** : tongue ⟨morderse la lengua : to bite one's tongue⟩ **2** IDIOMA : language ⟨lengua materna : mother tongue, native language⟩ ⟨lengua muerta : dead language⟩
lenguado *nm* : sole, flounder
lenguaje *nm* **1** : language, speech **2 lenguaje gestual** *or* **lenguaje de gestos** : sign language **3 lenguaje de programación** : programming language
lengüeta *nf* **1** : tongue (of a shoe), tab, flap **2** : reed (of a musical instrument) **3** : barb, point
lengüetada *nf* **beber a lengüetadas** : to lap (up)
lenidad *nf* : leniency
lenitivo, -va *adj* : soothing
lente *nmf* **1** : lens ⟨lentes de contacto : contact lenses⟩ **2 lentes** *nmpl* ANTEOJOS : eyeglasses ⟨lentes de sol : sunglasses⟩
lenteja *nf* : lentil
lentejuela *nf* : sequin, spangle
lentitud *nf* : slowness
lento[1] *adv* DESPACIO : slowly
lento[2], **-ta** *adj* **1** : slow **2** : slow-witted, dull — **lentamente** *adv*
leña *nf* : wood, firewood
leñador, -dora *n* : lumberjack, woodcutter
leñera *nf* : woodshed
leño *nm* : log
leñoso, -sa *adj* : woody
Leo *nmf* : Leo
león, -ona *n, mpl* **leones 1** : lion, lioness *f* **2** (*in various countries*) : puma, cougar
leonado, -da *adj* : tawny
leonino, -na *adj* **1** : leonine **2** : one-sided, unfair
leopardo *nm* : leopard
leotardo *nm* MALLA : leotard, tights *pl*
leperada *nf Mex* : obscenity

lépero, -ra *adj Mex* : vulgar, coarse
lepra *nf* : leprosy
leproso[1], **-sa** *adj* : leprous
leproso[2], **-sa** *n* : leper
lerdo, -da *adj* **1** : clumsy **2** : dull, oafish, slow-witted
les *pron* **1** : to them ⟨dales una propina : give them a tip⟩ **2** : from them ⟨se les privó de su herencia : they were deprived of their inheritance⟩ **3** : for them ⟨les hice sus tareas : I did their homework for them⟩ **4** : to you *pl*, for you *pl* ⟨les compré un regalo : I bought you all a present⟩
lesbiana *nf* : lesbian — **lesbiano, -na** *adj*
lesbianismo *nm* : lesbianism
lesión *nf, pl* **lesiones** HERIDA : lesion, wound, injury ⟨una lesión grave : a serious injury⟩
lesionado, -da *adj* HERIDO : injured, wounded
lesionar *vt* : to injure, to wound — **lesionarse** *vr* : to hurt oneself
lesivo, -va *adj* : harmful, damaging
letal *adj* MORTÍFERO : deadly, lethal — **letalmente** *adv*
letanía *nf* **1** : litany **2** *fam* : spiel, song and dance
letárgico, -ca *adj* : lethargic
letargo *nm* : lethargy, torpor
letón[1], **-tona** *adj & n, mpl* **letones** : Latvian
letón[2] *nm* : Latvian (language)
letra *nf* **1** : letter **2** CALIGRAFÍA : handwriting, lettering **3** : lyrics *pl* **4 al pie de la letra** : word for word, by the book **5 letras** *nfpl* : arts (in education)
letrado[1], **-da** *adj* ERUDITO : learned, erudite
letrado[2], **-da** *n* : attorney-at-law, lawyer
letrero *nm* RÓTULO : sign, notice
letrina *nf* : latrine
letrista *nmf* : lyricist, songwriter
leucemia *nf* : leukemia
leva *nf* : cam
levadizo, -za *adj* **1** : liftable **2 puente levadizo** : drawbridge
levadura *nf* **1** : yeast, leavening **2 levadura en polvo** : baking powder
levantamiento *nm* **1** ALZAMIENTO : uprising **2** : raising, lifting ⟨levantamiento de pesas : weight lifting⟩
levantar *vt* **1** ALZAR : to lift, to raise **2** : to put up, to erect **3** : to call off, to adjourn **4** : to give rise to, to arouse ⟨levantar sospechas : to arouse suspicion⟩ — **levantarse** *vr* **1** : to rise, to stand up **2** : to get out of bed
levar *vt* **levar anclas** : to weigh anchor
leve *adj* **1** : light, slight **2** : trivial, unimportant — **levemente** *adv*
levedad *nf* : lightness
levemente *adv* LIGERAMENTE : lightly, softly
leviatán *nm, pl* **-tanes** : leviathan
léxico[1], **-ca** *adj* : lexical
léxico[2] *nm* : lexicon, glossary
lexicografía *nf* : lexicography

lexicográfico, -ca *adj* : lexicographical, lexicographic
lexicógrafo, -fa *n* : lexicographer
ley *nf* **1** : law ⟨fuera de la ley : outside the law⟩ ⟨la ley de gravedad : the law of gravity⟩ **2** : purity (of metals) ⟨oro de ley : pure gold⟩
leyenda *nf* **1** : legend **2** : caption, inscription
leyó, etc. → leer
liar {85} *vt* **1** ATAR : to bind, to tie (up) **2** : to roll (a cigarette) **3** : to confuse — **liarse** *vr* : to get mixed up
libanés, -nesa *adj & n, mpl* **-neses** : Lebanese
libar *vt* **1** : to suck (nectar) **2** : to sip, to swig (liquor, etc.)
libelo *nm* **1** : libel, lampoon **2** : petition (in court)
libélula *nf* : dragonfly
liberación *nf, pl* **-ciones** : liberation, deliverance ⟨liberación de la mujer : women's liberation⟩
liberado, -da *adj* **1** : liberated ⟨una mujer liberada : a liberated woman⟩ **2** : freed, delivered
liberal *adj & nmf* : liberal
liberalidad *nf* : generosity, liberality
liberalismo *nm* : liberalism
liberalizar {21} *vt* : to liberalize — **liberalización** *nf*
liberar *vt* : to liberate, to free — **liberarse** *vr* : to get free of
liberiano, -na *adj & n* : Liberian
libertad *nf* **1** : freedom, liberty ⟨tomarse la libertad de : to take the liberty of⟩ **2 libertad bajo fianza** : bail **3 libertad condicional** : parole
libertador[1], -dora *adj* : liberating
libertador[2], -dora *n* : liberator
libertar *vt* LIBRAR : to set free
libertario, -ria *adj & n* : libertarian
libertinaje *nm* : licentiousness, dissipation
libertino[1], -na *adj* : licentious, dissolute
libertino[2], -na *n* : libertine
libidinoso, -sa *adj* : lustful, lewd
libido *nf* : libido
libio, -bia *adj & n* : Libyan
libra *nf* **1** : pound **2 libra esterlina** : pound sterling
Libra *nmf* : Libra
libramiento *nm* **1** : liberating, freeing **2** LIBRANZA : order of payment **3** *Mex* : beltway
libranza *nf* : order of payment
librar *vt* **1** LIBERTAR : to deliver, to set free **2** : to wage ⟨librar batalla : to do battle⟩ **3** : to issue ⟨librar una orden : to issue an order⟩ — **librarse** *vr* ~ **de** : to free oneself from, to get out of
libre[1] *adj* **1** : free ⟨un país libre : a free country⟩ ⟨libre de : free from, exempt from⟩ ⟨libre albedrío : free will⟩ **2** DESOCUPADO : vacant **3 día libre** : day off
libre[2] *nm Mex* : taxi
librea *nf* : livery

librecambio *nm* : free trade
libremente *adv* : freely
librería *nf* : bookstore
librero[1], -ra *n* : bookseller
librero[2] *nm Mex* : bookcase
libresco, -ca *adj* : bookish
libreta *nf* CUADERNO : notebook
libretista *nmf* **1** : librettist **2** : scriptwriter
libreto *nm* : libretto, script
libro *nm* **1** : book ⟨libro de texto : textbook⟩ **2 libros** *nmpl* : books (in bookkeeping), accounts ⟨llevar los libros : to keep the books⟩
licencia *nf* **1** : permission **2** : leave, leave of absence **3** : permit, license ⟨licencia de conducir : driver's license⟩
licenciado, -da *n* **1** : university graduate **2** ABOGADO : lawyer
licenciar *vt* **1** : to license, to permit, to allow **2** : to discharge **3** : to grant a university degree to — **licenciarse** *vr* : to graduate
licenciatura *nf* **1** : college degree **2** : course of study (at a college or university)
licencioso, -sa *adj* : licentious, lewd
liceo *nm* : secondary school, high school
licitación *nf, pl* **-ciones** : bid, bidding
licitar *vt* : to bid on
lícito, -ta *adj* **1** : lawful, licit **2** JUSTO : just, fair
licor *nm* **1** : liquor **2** : liqueur
licorera *nf* : decanter
licuado *nm* BATIDO : milk shake
licuadora *nf* : blender
licuar {3} *vt* : to liquefy — **licuarse** *vr*
lid *nf* **1** : fight, combat **2** : argument, dispute **3 lides** *nfpl* : matters, affairs **4 en buena lid** : fair and square
líder[1] *adj* : leading, foremost
líder[2] *nmf* : leader
liderar *vt* DIRIGIR : to lead, to head
liderato *nm* : leadership, leading
liderazgo → liderato
lidiar *vt* : to fight — *vi* BATALLAR, LUCHAR : to struggle, to battle, to wrestle
liebre *nf* : hare
liendre *nf* : nit
lienzo *nm* **1** : linen **2** : canvas, painting **3** : stretch of wall or fencing
liga *nf* **1** ASOCIACIÓN : league **2** GOMITA : rubber band **3** : garter
ligado, -da *adj* : linked, connected
ligadura *nf* **1** ATADURA : tie, bond **2** : ligature
ligamento *nm* : ligament
ligar {52} *vt* : to bind, to tie (up)
ligeramente *adv* **1** : slightly **2** LEVEMENTE : lightly, gently **3** : casually, flippantly
ligereza *nf* **1** : lightness **2** : flippancy **3** : agility
ligero, -ra *adj* **1** : light, lightweight **2** : slight, minor **3** : agile, quick **4** : lighthearted, superficial
lignito *nm* : lignite

ligue, etc. → ligar
lija *nf or* **papel de lija** : sandpaper
lijar *vt* : to sand
lila¹ *adj* : lilac, light purple
lila² *nf* : lilac
lima *nf* **1** : lime (fruit) **2** : file ⟨lima de uñas : nail file⟩
limadora *nf* : polisher
limar *vt* **1** : to file **2** : to polish, to put the final touch on **3** : to smooth over ⟨limar las diferencias : to iron out differences⟩
limbo *nm* **1** : limbo **2** : limb (in botany and astronomy)
limeño¹, -ña *adj* : of or from Lima, Peru
limeño², -ña *n* : person from Lima, Peru
limero *nm* : lime tree
limitación *nf, pl* **-ciones 1** : limitation **2** : limit, restriction ⟨sin limitación : unlimited⟩
limitado, -da *adj* **1** RESTRINGIDO : limited **2** : dull, slow-witted
limitar *vt* RESTRINGIR : to limit, to restrict — *vi* ~ **con** : to border on — **limitarse** *vr* ~ **a** : to limit oneself to
límite *nm* **1** : boundary, border **2** : limit ⟨el límite de mi paciencia : the limit of my patience⟩ ⟨límite de velocidad : speed limit⟩ **3 fecha límite** : deadline
limítrofe *adj* LINDANTE, LINDERO : bordering, adjoining
limo *nm* : slime, mud
limón *nm, pl* **limones 1** : lemon **2** : lemon tree **3 limón verde** *Mex* : lime
limonada *nf* : lemonade
limosna *nf* : alms, charity
limosnear *vi* : to beg (for alms)
limosnero, -ra *n* MENDIGO : beggar
limoso, -sa *adj* : slimy
limpiabotas *nmfs & pl* : bootblack
limpiador¹, -dora *adj* : cleaning
limpiador², -dora *n* : cleaning person, cleaner
limpiamente *adv* : cleanly, honestly, fairly
limpiaparabrisas *nms & pl* : windshield wiper
limpiar *vt* **1** : to clean, to cleanse **2** : to clean up, to remove defects **3** *fam* : to clean out (in a game) **4** *fam* : to swipe, to pinch — *vi* : to clean — **limpiarse** *vr*
limpiavidrios *nmfs & pl Mex* : windshield wiper
límpido, -da *adj* : limpid
limpieza *nf* **1** : cleanliness, tidiness **2** : cleaning **3** HONRADEZ : integrity, honesty **4** DESTREZA : skill, dexterity
limpio¹ *adv* : fairly
limpio², -pia *adj* **1** : clean, neat **2** : honest ⟨un juego limpio : a fair game⟩ **3** : free ⟨limpio de impurezas : pure, free from impurities⟩ **4** : clear, net ⟨ganancia limpia : clear profit⟩
limusina *nf* : limousine
linaje *nm* ABOLENGO : lineage, ancestry
linaza *nf* : linseed
lince *nm* : lynx

linchamiento *nm* : lynching
linchar *vt* : to lynch
lindante *adj* LIMÍTROFE, LINDERO : bordering, adjoining
lindar *vi* **1** ~ **con** : to border, to skirt **2** ~ **con** BORDEAR : to border on, to verge on
linde *nmf* : boundary, limit
lindero¹, -ra *adj* LIMÍTROFE, LINDANTE : bordering, adjoining
lindero² *nm* : boundary, limit
lindeza *nf* **1** : prettiness **2** : clever remark **3 lindezas** *nfpl, (used ironically)* : insults
lindo¹ *adv* **1** : beautifully, wonderfully ⟨canta lindo tu mujer : your wife sings beautifully⟩ **2 de lo lindo** : a lot, a great deal ⟨los zancudos nos picaban de lo lindo : the mosquitoes were biting away at us⟩
lindo², -da *adj* **1** BONITO : pretty, lovely **2** MONO : cute
línea *nf* **1** : line ⟨línea divisoria : dividing line⟩ ⟨línea de banda : sideline⟩ **2** : line, course, position ⟨línea de conducta : course of action⟩ ⟨en líneas generales : in general terms, along general lines⟩ **3** : line, service ⟨línea aérea : airline⟩ ⟨línea telefónica : telephone line⟩
lineal *adj* : linear
linfa *nf* : lymph
linfático, -ca *adj* : lymphatic
lingote *nm* : ingot
lingüista *nmf* : linguist
lingüística *nf* : linguistics
lingüístico, -ca *adj* : linguistic
linimento *nm* : liniment
lino *nm* **1** : linen **2** : flax
linóleo *nm* : linoleum
linterna *nf* **1** : lantern **2** : flashlight
lío *nm fam* **1** : confusion, mess **2** : hassle, trouble, jam ⟨meterse en un lío : to get into a jam⟩ **3** : affair, liaison
liofilizar {21} *vt* : to freeze-dry
lioso, -sa *adj fam* **1** : confusing, muddled **2** : troublemaking
liquen *nm* : lichen
liquidación *nf, pl* **-ciones 1** : liquidation **2** : clearance sale **3** : settlement, payment
liquidar *vt* **1** : to liquefy **2** : to liquidate **3** : to settle, to pay off **4** *fam* : to rub out, to kill
liquidez *nf, pl* **-deces** : liquidity
líquido¹, -da *adj* **1** : liquid, fluid **2** : net ⟨ingresos líquidos : net income⟩
líquido² *nm* **1** : liquid, fluid ⟨líquido de frenos : brake fluid⟩ **2** : ready cash, liquid assets
lira *nf* : lyre
lírica *nf* : lyric poetry
lírico, -ca *adj* : lyric, lyrical
lirio *nm* **1** : iris **2 lirio de los valles** MUGUETE : lily of the valley
lirismo *nm* : lyricism
lirón *nm, pl* **lirones** : dormouse
lisiado¹, -da *adj* : disabled, crippled

lisiado², -da *n* : disabled person, cripple
lisiar *vt* : to cripple, to disable — **lisiarse** *vr*
liso, -sa *adj* **1** : smooth **2** : flat **3** : straight ⟨pelo liso : straight hair⟩ **4** : plain, unadorned ⟨liso y llano : plain and simple⟩
lisonja *nf* : flattery
lisonjear *vt* ADULAR : to flatter
lista *nf* **1** : list **2** : roster, roll ⟨pasar lista : to take attendance⟩ **3** : stripe, strip **4** : menu
listado¹, -da *adj* : striped
listado² *nm* : listing
listar *vt* : to list
listeza *nf* : smartness, alertness
listo, -ta *adj* **1** DISPUESTO, PREPARADO : ready ⟨¿estás listo? : are you ready?⟩ **2** : clever, smart
listón *nm, pl* **listones 1** : ribbon **2** : strip (of wood), lath **3** : high bar (in sports)
lisura *nf* : smoothness
litera *nf* : bunk bed, berth
literal *adj* : literal — **literalmente** *adv*
literario, -ria *adj* : literary
literato, -ta *n* : writer, author
literatura *nf* : literature
litigante *adj & nmf* : litigant
litigar {52} *vi* : to litigate, to be in litigation
litigio *nm* **1** : litigation, lawsuit **2 en ~** : in dispute
litigioso, -sa *adj* : litigious
litio *nm* : lithium
litografía *nf* **1** : lithography **2** : lithograph
litógrafo, -fa *n* : lithographer
litoral¹ *adj* : coastal
litoral² *nm* : shore, seaboard
litosfera *nf* : lithosphere
litro *nm* : liter
lituano¹, -na *adj & n* : Lithuanian
lituano² *nm* : Lithuanian (language)
liturgia *nf* : liturgy
litúrgico, -ca *adj* : liturgical — **litúrgicamente** *adv*
liviandad *nf* LIGEREZA : lightness
liviano, -na *adj* **1** : light, slight **2** INCONSTANTE : fickle
lividez *nf* PALIDEZ : pallor
lívido, -da *adj* **1** AMORATADO : livid **2** PÁLIDO : pallid, extremely pale
living *nm* : living room
llaga *nf* : sore, wound
llama *nf* **1** : flame **2** : llama
llamada *nf* : call ⟨llamada a larga distancia : long-distance call⟩ ⟨llamada al orden : call to order⟩
llamado¹, -da *adj* : named, called ⟨una mujer llamada Rosa : a woman called Rosa⟩
llamado² → **llamamiento**
llamador *nm* : door knocker
llamamiento *nm* : call, appeal
llamar *vt* **1** : to name, to call **2** : to call, to summon **3** : to phone, to call up — **llamarse** *vr* : to be called, to be named ⟨¿cómo te llamas? : what's your name?⟩

llamarada *nf* **1** : flare-up, sudden blaze **2** : flushing (of the face)
llamativo, -va *adj* : flashy, showy, striking
llameante *adj* : flaming, blazing
llamear *vi* : to flame, to blaze
llana *nf* **1** : trowel **2** → **llano²**
llanamente *adv* : simply, plainly, straightforwardly
llaneza *nf* : simplicity, naturalness
llano¹, -na *adj* **1** : even, flat **2** : frank, open **3** LISO : plain, simple
llano² *nm* : plain
llanta *nf* **1** NEUMÁTICO : tire **2** : rim
llantén *nm, pl* **llantenes** : plantain (weed)
llanto *nm* : crying, weeping
llanura *nf* : plain, prairie
llave *nf* **1** : key **2** : faucet **3** INTERRUPTOR : switch **4** : brace (punctuation mark) **5 llave inglesa** : monkey wrench
llavero *nm* : key chain, key ring
llegada *nf* : arrival
llegar {52} *vi* **1** : to arrive, to come **2 ~ a** : to arrive at, to reach, to amount to **3 ~ a** : to manage to ⟨llegó a terminar la novela : she managed to finish the novel⟩ **4 llegar a ser** : to become ⟨llegó a ser un miembro permanente : he became a permanent member⟩
llegue, etc. → **llegar**
llenar *vt* **1** : to fill, to fill up, to fill in **2** : to meet, to fulfill ⟨los regalos no llenaron sus expectativas : the gifts did not meet her expectations⟩ — **llenarse** *vr* : to fill up, to become full
llenito, -ta *adj fam* REGORDETE : chubby, plump
lleno¹, -na *adj* **1** : full, filled **2 de ~** : completely, fully **3 estar lleno de sí mismo** : to be full of oneself
lleno² *nm* **1** *fam* : plenty, abundance **2** : full house, sellout
llevadero, -ra *adj* : bearable
llevar *vt* **1** : to take away, to carry ⟨me gusta, me lo llevo : I like it, I'll take it⟩ **2** : to wear **3** : to take, to lead ⟨llevamos a Pedro al cine : we took Pedro to the movies⟩ **4 llevar a cabo** : to carry out **5 llevar adelante** : to carry on, to keep going — *vi* : to lead ⟨un problema lleva al otro : one problem leads to another⟩ — *v aux* : to have ⟨llevo mucho tiempo buscándolo : I've been looking for it for a long time⟩ ⟨lleva leído medio libro : he's halfway through the book⟩ — **llevarse** *vr* **1** : to take away, to carry off **2** : to get along ⟨siempre nos llevábamos bien : we always got along well⟩
llorar *vi* : to cry, to weep — *vt* : to mourn, to bewail
lloriquear *vi* : to whimper, to whine
lloriqueo *nm* : whimpering, whining
llorón, -rona *n, mpl* **llorones** : crybaby, whiner
lloroso, -sa *adj* : tearful, sad

llovedizo, -za *adj* : rain ⟨agua llovediza : rainwater⟩

llover {47} *v impers* : to rain ⟨está lloviendo : it's raining⟩ ⟨llover a cántaros : to rain cats and dogs⟩ — *vi* : to rain down, to shower ⟨le llovieron regalos : he was showered with gifts⟩

llovizna *nf* : drizzle, sprinkle

lloviznar *v impers* : to drizzle, to sprinkle

llueve, etc. → llover

lluvia *nf* **1** : rain, rainfall **2** : barrage, shower

lluvioso, -sa *adj* : rainy

lo¹ *pron* **1** : him, it ⟨lo vi ayer : I saw him yesterday⟩ ⟨lo entiendo : I understand it⟩ ⟨no lo creo : I don't believe so⟩ **2** (*formal, masculine*) : you ⟨discúlpe, señor, no lo oí : excuse me sir, I didn't hear you⟩ **3 lo que** : what, that which ⟨eso es lo que más le gusta : that's what he likes the most⟩

lo² *art* **1** : the ⟨lo mejor : the best, the best thing⟩ **2** : how ⟨sé lo bueno que eres : I know how good you are⟩

loa *nf* : praise

loable *adj* : laudable, praiseworthy — **loablemente** *adv*

loar *vt* : to praise, to laud

lobato, -ta *n* : wolf cub

lobby *nm* : lobby, pressure group

lobo, -ba *n* : wolf

lóbrego, -ga *adj* SOMBRÍO : gloomy, dark

lobulado, -da *adj* : lobed

lóbulo *nm* : lobe ⟨lóbulo de la oreja : earlobe⟩

locación *nf, pl* **-ciones 1** : location (in moviemaking) **2** *Mex* : place

local¹ *adj* : local — **localmente** *adv*

local² *nm* : premises *pl*

localidad *nf* : town, locality

localización *nf, pl* **-ciones 1** : locating, localization **2** : location

localizar {21} *vt* **1** UBICAR : to locate, to find **2** : to localize — **localizarse** *vr* UBICARSE : to be located ⟨se localiza en el séptimo piso : it is located on the seventh floor⟩

locatario, -ria *n* : tenant

loción *nf, pl* **lociones** : lotion

lócker *nm, pl* **lóckers** : locker

loco¹, -ca *adj* **1** DEMENTE : crazy, insane, mad **2 a lo loco** : wildly, recklessly **3 volverse loco** : to go mad

loco², -ca *n* **1** : crazy person, lunatic **2 hacerse el loco** : to act the fool

locomoción *nf, pl* **-ciones** : locomotion

locomotor, -tora *adj* : locomotive

locomotora *nf* **1** : locomotive **2** : driving force

locuacidad *nf* : loquacity, talkativeness

locuaz *adj, pl* **locuaces** : loquacious, talkative

locución *nf, pl* **-ciones** : locution, phrase ⟨locución adverbial : adverbial phrase⟩

locura *nf* **1** : insanity, madness **2** : crazy thing, folly

locutor, -tora *n* : announcer

lodazal *nm* : bog, quagmire

lodo *nm* BARRO : mud, mire

lodoso, -sa *adj* : muddy

logaritmo *nm* : logarithm

logia *nf* : lodge ⟨logia masónica : Masonic lodge⟩

lógica *nf* : logic

lógico, -ca *adj* : logical — **lógicamente** *adv*

logística *nf* : logistics *pl*

logístico, -ca *adj* : logistic, logistical

logo → logotipo

logotipo *nm* : logo

logrado, -da *adj* : successful, well done

lograr *vt* **1** : to get, to obtain **2** : to achieve, to attain — **lograrse** *vr* : to be successful

logro *nm* : achievement, attainment

loma *nf* : hill, hillock

lombriz *nf, pl* **lombrices** : worm ⟨lombriz de tierra : earthworm, night crawler⟩ ⟨lombriz solitaria : tapeworm⟩ ⟨tener lombrices : to have worms⟩

lomo *nm* **1** : back (of an animal) **2** : loin ⟨lomo de cerdo : pork loin⟩ **3** : spine (of a book) **4** : blunt edge (of a knife)

lona *nf* : canvas

loncha *nf* LONJA, REBANADA : slice

lonche *nm* **1** ALMUERZO : lunch **2** *Mex* : submarine sandwich

lonchería *nf Mex* : luncheonette

londinense¹ *adj* : of or from London

londinense² *nmf* : Londoner

longaniza *nf* : spicy pork sausage

longevidad *nf* : longevity

longevo, -va *adj* : long-lived

longitud *nf* **1** LARGO : length ⟨longitud de onda : wavelength⟩ **2** : longitude

longitudinal *adj* : longitudinal

lonja *nf* LONCHA, REBANADA : slice

lontananza *nf* : background ⟨en lontananza : in the distance, far away⟩

lord *nm, pl* **lores** (*title in England*) : lord

loro *nm* : parrot

los¹, las *pron* **1** : them ⟨hice galletas y se las di a los nuevos vecinos : I made cookies and gave them to the new neighbors⟩ **2** : you ⟨voy a llevarlos a los dos : I am going to take both of you⟩ **3 los que, las que** : those, who, the ones ⟨los que van a cantar deben venir temprano : those who are singing must come early⟩ **4** (*used with* **haber**) ⟨los hay en varios colores : they come in various colors⟩

los² *art* → **el²**

losa *nf* : flagstone, paving stone

loseta *nf* BALDOSA : floor tile

lote *nm* **1** : part, share **2** : batch, lot **3** : plot of land, lot

lotería *nf* : lottery

loto *nm* : lotus

loza *nf* **1** : crockery, earthenware **2** : china

lozanía *nf* **1** : healthiness, robustness **2** : luxuriance, lushness

lozano, -na *adj* **1** : robust, healthy-looking ⟨un rostro lozano : a smooth, fresh face⟩ **2** : lush, luxuriant
LSD *nm* : LSD
lubricante[1] *adj* : lubricating
lubricante[2] *nm* : lubricant
lubricar {72} *vt* : to lubricate, to oil — **lubricación** *nf*
lucero *nm* : bright star ⟨lucero del alba : morning star⟩
lucha *nf* **1** : struggle, fight **2** : wrestling
luchador, -dora *n* **1** : fighter **2** : wrestler
luchar *vi* **1** : to fight, to struggle **2** : to wrestle
luchón, -chona *adj, mpl* **luchones** *Mex* : industrious, hardworking
lucidez *nf, pl* **-deces** : lucidity, clarity
lucido, -da *adj* MAGNÍFICO : magnificent, splendid
lúcido, -da *adj* : lucid
luciérnaga *nf* : firefly, glowworm
lucimiento *nm* **1** : brilliance, splendor, sparkle **2** : triumph, success ⟨salir con lucimiento : to succeed with flying colors⟩
lucio *nm* : pike (fish)
lucir {45} *vi* **1** : to shine **2** : to look good, to stand out **3** : to seem, to appear ⟨ahora luce contento : he looks happy now⟩ — *vt* **1** : to wear, to sport **2** : to flaunt, to show off — **lucirse** *vr* **1** : to distinguish oneself, to excel **2** : to show off
lucrarse *vr* : to make a profit
lucrativo, -va *adj* : lucrative, profitable — **lucrativamente** *adv*
lucro *nm* GANANCIA : profit, gain
luctuoso, -sa *adj* : mournful, tragic
luego[1] *adv* **1** DESPUÉS : then, afterwards **2** : later (on) **3** desde ~ : of course **4** ¡hasta luego! : see you later! **5 luego que** : as soon as **6 luego luego** *Mex fam* : right away, immediately
luego[2] *conj* : therefore ⟨pienso, luego existo : I think, therefore I am⟩
lugar *nm* **1** : place, position ⟨se llevó el primer lugar en su división : she took first place in her division⟩ **2** ESPACIO : space, room **3 dar lugar a** : to give rise to, to lead to **4 en lugar de** : instead of **5 lugar común** : cliché, platitude **6 tener lugar** : to take place
lugareño[1], **-ña** *adj* : village, rural
lugareño[2], **-ña** *n* : villager
lugarteniente *nmf* : lieutenant, deputy
lúgubre *adj* : gloomy, lugubrious
lujo *nm* **1** : luxury **2 de ~** : deluxe
lujoso, -sa *adj* : luxurious
lujuria *nf* : lust, lechery
lujurioso, -sa *adj* : lustful, lecherous
lumbago *nm* : lumbago
lumbar *adj* : lumbar
lumbre *nf* **1** FUEGO : fire **2** : brilliance, splendor **3 poner en la lumbre** : to put on the stove, to warm up
lumbrera *nf* **1** : skylight **2** : vent, port **3** : brilliant person, luminary
luminaria *nf* **1** : altar lamp **2** LUMBRERA : luminary, celebrity
luminiscencia *nf* : luminescence — **luminiscente** *adj*
luminosidad *nf* : luminosity, brightness
luminoso, -sa *adj* : shining, luminous
luna *nf* **1** : moon **2 luna de miel** : honeymoon
lunar[1] *adj* : lunar
lunar[2] *nm* **1** : mole, beauty spot **2** : defect, blemish **3** : polka dot
lunático, -ca *adj & n* : lunatic
lunes *nms & pl* : Monday
luneta *nf* **1** : lens (of eyeglasses) **2** : windshield (of an automobile) **3** : crescent
lupa *nf* : magnifying glass
lúpulo *nm* : hops (plant)
lustrar *vt* : to shine, to polish
lustre *nm* **1** BRILLO : luster, shine **2** : glory, distinction
lustroso, -sa *adj* BRILLOSO : lustrous, shiny
luto *nm* : mourning ⟨estar de luto : to be in mourning⟩
luz *nf, pl* **luces 1** : light **2** : lighting **3** *fam* : electricity **4** : window, opening **5** : light, lamp **6** : span, spread (between supports) **7 a la luz de** : in light of **8 dar a luz** : to give birth **9 traje de luces** : matador's costume
luzca, etc. → lucir

M

m *nf* : thirteenth letter of the Spanish alphabet
macabro, -bra *adj* : macabre
macaco[1], **-ca** *adj* : ugly, misshapen
macaco[2], **-ca** *n* : macaque
macadán *nm, pl* **-danes** : macadam
macana *nf* **1** : club, cudgel **2** *fam* : nonsense, silliness **3** *fam* : lie, fib
macanudo, -da *adj fam* : great, fantastic
macarrón *nm, pl* **-rrones 1** : macaroon **2 macarrones** *nmpl* : macaroni
maceta *nf* **1** : flowerpot **2** : mallet **3** *Mex fam* : head
macetero *nm* **1** : plant stand **2** TIESTO : flowerpot, planter
machacar {72} *vt* **1** : to crush, to grind **2** : to beat, to pound — *vi* : to insist, to go on (about)
machacón, -cona *adj, mpl* **-cones** : insistent, tiresome
machete *nm* : machete
machetear *vt* : to hack with a machete — *vi Mex fam* : to plod, to work tirelessly
machismo *nm* **1** : machismo **2** : male chauvinism
machista *nm* : male chauvinist

macho[1] *adj* **1** : male **2** : macho, virile, tough

macho[2] *nm* **1** : male **2** : he-man

machote *nm* **1** *fam* : tough guy, he-man **2** *CA, Mex* : rough draft, model **3** *Mex* : blank form

machucar {72} *vt* **1** : to pound, to beat, to crush **2** : to bruise

machucón *nm, pl* **-cones 1** MORETÓN : bruise **2** : smashing, pounding

macilento, -ta *adj* : gaunt, wan

macis *nm* : mace (spice)

macizo, -za *adj* **1** : solid ⟨oro macizo : solid gold⟩ **2** : strong, strapping **3** : massive

macrocosmo *nm* : macrocosm

mácula *nf* : blemish, stain

madeja *nf* **1** : skein, hank **2** : tangle (of hair)

madera *nf* **1** : wood **2** : lumber, timber **3 madera dura** *or* **madera noble** : hardwood

maderero, -ra *adj* : timber, lumber

madero *nm* : piece of lumber, plank

madrastra *nf* : stepmother

madrazo *nm Mex fam* : punch, blow ⟨se agarraron a madrazos : they beat each other up⟩

madre *nf* **1** : mother **2 madre política** : mother-in-law **3 la Madre Patria** : the mother country (said of Spain)

madrear *vt Mex fam* : to beat up

madreperla *nf* NÁCAR : mother-of-pearl

madreselva *nf* : honeysuckle

madriguera *nf* : burrow, den, lair

madrileño[1], **-ña** *adj* : of or from Madrid

madrileño[2], **-ña** *n* : person from Madrid

madrina *nf* **1** : godmother **2** : bridesmaid **3** : sponsor

madrugada *nf* **1** : early morning, wee hours **2** ALBA : dawn, daybreak

madrugador, -dora *n* : early riser

madrugar {52} *vi* **1** : to get up early **2** : to get a head start

madurar *v* **1** : to ripen **2** : to mature

madurez *nf, pl* **-reces 1** : maturity **2** : ripeness

maduro, -ra *adj* **1** : mature **2** : ripe

maestría *nf* **1** : mastery, skill **2** : master's degree

maestro[1], **-tra** *adj* **1** : masterly, skilled **2** : chief, main **3** : trained ⟨un elefante maestro : a trained elephant⟩

maestro[2], **-tra** *n* **1** : teacher (in grammar school) **2** : expert, master **3** : maestro

Mafia *nf* : Mafia

mafioso, -sa *n* : mafioso, gangster

magdalena *nf* : bun, muffin

magenta *adj & n* : magenta

magia *nf* : magic

mágico, -ca *adj* : magic, magical — **mágicamente** *adv*

magisterio *nm* **1** : teaching **2** : teachers *pl*, teaching profession

magistrado, -da *n* : magistrate, judge

magistral *adj* **1** : masterful, skillful **2** : magisterial

magistralmente *adv* : masterfully, brilliantly

magistratura *nf* : judgeship, magistracy

magma *nm* : magma

magnanimidad *nf* : magnanimity

magnánimo, -ma *adj* GENEROSO : magnanimous — **magnánimamente** *adv*

magnate *nmf* : magnate, tycoon

magnesia *nf* : magnesia

magnesio *nm* : magnesium

magnético, -ca *adj* : magnetic

magnetismo *nm* : magnetism

magnetizar {21} *vt* : to magnetize

magnetófono *nm* : tape recorder

magnetofónico, -ca *adj* **cinta magnetofónica** : magnetic tape

magnificar {72} *vt* **1** : to magnify **2** EXAGERAR : to exaggerate **3** ENSALZAR : to exalt, to extol, to praise highly

magnificencia *nf* : magnificence, splendor

magnífico, -ca *adj* ESPLENDOROSO : magnificent, splendid — **magníficamente** *adv*

magnitud *nf* : magnitude

magnolia *nf* : magnolia (flower)

magnolio *nm* : magnolia (tree)

mago, -ga *n* **1** : magician **2** : wizard (in folk tales, etc.) **3 los Reyes Magos** : the Magi

magro, -gra *adj* **1** : lean (of meat) **2** : meager

maguey *nm* : maguey

magulladura *nf* MORETÓN : bruise

magullar *vt* : to bruise — **magullarse** *vr*

mahometano[1], **-na** *adj* ISLÁMICO : Islamic, Muslim

mahometano[2], **-na** *n* : Muslim

mahonesa → **mayonesa**

maicena *nf* : cornstarch

mainframe ['mein,freim] *nm* : mainframe

maíz *nm* : corn, maize

maizal *nm* : cornfield

maja *nf* : pestle

majadería *nf* **1** TONTERÍA : stupidity, foolishness **2** *Mex* LEPERADA : insult, obscenity

majadero[1], **-ra** *adj* **1** : foolish, silly **2** *Mex* LÉPERO : crude, vulgar

majadero[2], **-ra** *n* **1** TONTO : fool **2** *Mex* : rude person, boor

majar *vt* : to crush, to mash

majestad *nf* : majesty ⟨Su Majestad : Your Majesty⟩

majestuosamente *adv* : majestically

majestuosidad *nf* : majesty, grandeur

majestuoso, -sa *adj* : majestic, stately

majo, -ja *adj Spain* **1** : nice, likeable **2** GUAPO : attractive, good-looking

mal[1] *adv* **1** : badly, poorly ⟨baila muy mal : he dances very badly⟩ **2** : wrong, incorrectly ⟨me entendió mal : she misunderstood me⟩ **3** : with difficulty, hardly ⟨mal puedo oírte : I can hardly hear you⟩ **4 de mal en peor** : from bad to worse **5 menos mal** : it could have been worse

mal² *adj* → **malo**
mal³ *nm* **1** : evil, wrong **2** DAÑO : harm, damage **3** DESGRACIA : misfortune **4** ENFERMEDAD : illness, sickness
malabar *adj* **juegos malabares** : juggling
malabarista *nmf* : juggler
malaconsejado, -da *adj* : ill-advised
malacostumbrado, -da *adj* CONSENTIDO : spoiled, pampered
malacostumbrar *vt* : to spoil
malagradecido, -da *adj* INGRATO : ungrateful
malaisio → **malasio**
malaquita *nf* : malachite
malaria *nf* PALUDISMO : malaria
malasio, -sia *adj & n* : Malaysian
malauiano, -na *adj & n* : Malawian
malaventura *nf* : misadventure, misfortune
malaventurado, -da *adj* MALHADADO : ill-fated, unfortunate
malayo, -ya *adj & n* : Malay, Malayan
malbaratar *vt* **1** MALGASTAR : to squander **2** : to undersell
malcriado¹, -da *adj* **1** : ill-bred, ill-mannered **2** : spoiled, pampered
malcriado², -da *n* : spoiled brat
maldad *nf* **1** : evil, wickedness **2** : evil deed
maldecir {11} *vt* : to curse, to damn — *vi* **1** : to curse, to swear **2** ~ **de** : to speak ill of, to slander, to defame
maldición *nf, pl* **-ciones** : curse
maldiga, maldijo etc. → **maldecir**
maldito, -ta *adj* **1** : cursed, damned ⟨¡maldita sea! : damn it all!⟩ **2** : wicked
maldoso, -sa *adj Mex* : mischievous
maleable *adj* : malleable
maleante *nmf* : crook, thug
malecón *nm, pl* **-cones** : jetty, breakwater
maleducado, -da *adj* : ill-mannered, rude
maleficio *nm* : curse, hex
maléfico, -ca *adj* : evil, harmful
malentender {56} *vt* : to misunderstand
malentendido *nm* : misunderstanding
malestar *nm* **1** : discomfort **2** IRRITACIÓN : annoyance **3** INQUIETUD : uneasiness, unrest
maleta *nf* : suitcase, bag ⟨haz tus maletas : pack your bags⟩
maletero¹, -ra *n* : porter
maletero² *nm* : trunk (of an automobile)
maletín *nm, pl* **-tines** **1** PORTAFOLIO : briefcase **2** : overnight bag, satchel
malevolencia *nf* : malevolence, wickedness
malévolo, -la *adj* : malevolent, wicked
maleza *nf* **1** : thicket, underbrush **2** : weeds *pl*
malformación *nf, pl* **-ciones** : malformation
malgache *adj & nmf* : Madagascan
malgastar *vt* : to squander (resources), to waste (time, effort)
malhablado, -da *adj* : foul-mouthed

malhadado, -da *adj* MALAVENTURADO : ill-fated
malhechor, -chora *n* : criminal, delinquent, wrongdoer
malherir {76} *vt* : to injure seriously
malhumor *nm* : bad mood, sullenness
malhumorado, -da *adj* : bad-tempered, cross
malicia *nf* **1** : wickedness, malice **2** : mischief, naughtiness **3** : cunning, craftiness
malicioso, -sa *adj* **1** : malicious **2** PÍCARO : mischievous
malignidad *nf* **1** : malignancy **2** MALDAD : evil
maligno, -na *adj* **1** : malignant ⟨un tumor maligno : a malignant tumor⟩ **2** : evil, harmful, malign
malinchismo *nm Mex* : preference for foreign goods or people — **malinchista** *adj*
malintencionado, -da *adj* : malicious, spiteful
malinterpretar *vt* : to misinterpret
malla *nf* **1** : mesh **2** LEOTARDO : leotard, tights *pl* **3** **malla de baño** : bathing suit
mallorquín, -quina *adj & n* : Majorcan
malnutrición *nf, pl* **-ciones** DESNUTRICIÓN : malnutrition
malnutrido, -da *adj* DESNUTRIDO : malnourished, undernourished
malo¹, -la *adj* (**mal** *before masculine singular nouns*) **1** : bad ⟨mala suerte : bad luck⟩ **2** : wicked, naughty **3** : cheap, poor (quality) **4** : harmful ⟨malo para la salud : bad for one's health⟩ **5** (*using the form* **mal**) : unwell ⟨estar mal del corazón : to have heart trouble⟩ **6** **estar de malas** : to be in a bad mood
malo², -la *n* : villain, bad guy (in novels, movies, etc.)
malogrado, -da *adj* : failed, unsuccessful
malograr *vt* **1** : to spoil, to ruin **2** : to waste (an opportunity, time) — **malograrse** *vr* **1** FRACASAR : to fail **2** : to die young
malogro *nm* **1** : untimely death **2** FRACASO : failure
maloliente *adj* HEDIONDO : foul-smelling, smelly
malparado, -da *adj* **salir malparado** *or* **quedar malparado** : to come out of (something) badly, to end up in a bad state
malpensado, -da *adj* : distrustful, suspicious, nasty-minded
malquerencia *nf* AVERSIÓN : ill will, dislike
malquerer {64} *vt* : to dislike
malquiso, etc. → **malquerer**
malsano, -na *adj* : unhealthy
malsonante *adj* : rude, offensive ⟨palabras malsonantes : foul language⟩
malta *nf* : malt
malteada *nf* : malted milk ⟨malteada de chocolate : chocolate malt⟩

maltés, -tesa *adj & n, mpl* **malteses** : Maltese

maltratar *vt* **1** : to mistreat, to abuse **2** : to damage, to spoil

maltrato *nm* : mistreatment, abuse

maltrecho, -cha *adj* : battered, damaged

malucho, -cha *adj fam* : sick, under the weather

malva *adj & nm* : mauve

malvado¹, -da *adj* : evil, wicked

malvado², -da *n* : evildoer, wicked person

malvavisco *nm* : marshmallow

malvender *vt* : to sell at a loss

malversación *nf, pl* **-ciones** : misappropriation (of funds), embezzlement

malversador, -dora *n* : embezzler

malversar *vt* : to embezzle

malvivir *vi* : to live badly, to just scrape by

mamá *nf fam* : mom, mama

mamar *vi* **1** : to suckle **2 darle de mamar a** : to breast-feed — *vt* **1** : to suckle, to nurse **2** : to learn from childhood, to grow up with — **mamarse** *vr fam* : to get drunk

mamario, -ria *adj* : mammary

mamarracho *nm fam* **1** ESPERPENTO : mess, sight **2** : laughingstock, fool **3** : rubbish, junk

mambo *nm* : mambo

mami *nf fam* : mommy

mamífero¹, -ra *adj* : mammalian

mamífero² *nm* : mammal

mamila *nf* **1** : nipple **2** *Mex* : baby bottle, pacifier

mamografía *nf* : mammogram

mamola *nf* : pat, chuck under the chin

mamotreto *nm fam* **1** : huge book, tome **2** ARMATOSTE : hulk, monstrosity

mampara *nf* BIOMBO : screen, room divider

mamparo *nm* : bulkhead

mampostería *nf* : masonry, stonemasonry

mampostero *nm* : mason, stonemason

mamut *nm, pl* **mamuts** : mammoth

maná *nm* : manna

manada *nf* **1** : flock, herd, pack **2** *fam* : horde, mob ⟨llegaron en manada : they came in droves⟩

manantial *nm* **1** FUENTE : spring **2** : source

manar *vi* **1** : to flow **2** : to abound

manatí *nm* : manatee

mancha *nf* **1** : stain, spot, mark ⟨mancha de sangre : bloodstain⟩ **2** : blemish, blot ⟨una mancha en su reputación : a blemish on his reputation⟩ **3** : patch

manchado, -da *adj* : stained

manchar *vt* **1** ENSUCIAR : to stain, to soil **2** DESHONRAR : to sully, to tarnish — **mancharse** *vr* : to get dirty

mancillar *vt* : to sully, to besmirch

manco, -ca *adj* : one-armed, one-handed

mancomunar *vt* : to combine, to pool — **mancomunarse** *vr* : to unite, to join together

mancomunidad *nf* **1** : commonwealth **2** : association, confederation

mancuernas *nfpl* : cuff links

mancuernillas *nf Mex* : cuff links

mandadero, -ra *n* : errand boy *m,* errand girl *f,* messenger

mandado *nm* **1** : order, command **2** : errand ⟨hacer los mandados : to run errands, to go shopping⟩

mandamás *nmf, pl* **-mases** *fam* : boss, bigwig, honcho

mandamiento *nm* **1** : commandment **2** : command, order, warrant ⟨mandamiento judicial : warrant, court order⟩

mandar *vt* **1** ORDENAR : to command, to order **2** ENVIAR : to send ⟨te manda saludos : he sends you his regards⟩ **3** ECHAR : to hurl, to throw **4 ¿mande?** *Mex* : yes?, pardon? — *vi* : to be the boss, to be in charge — **mandarse** *vr Mex* : to take liberties, to take advantage

mandarín *nm* : Mandarin

mandarina *nf* : mandarin orange, tangerine

mandatario, -ria *n* **1** : leader (in politics) ⟨primer mandatario : head of state⟩ **2** : agent (in law)

mandato *nm* **1** : term of office **2** : mandate

mandíbula *nf* **1** : jaw **2** : mandible

mandil *nm* **1** DELANTAL : apron **2** : horse blanket

mandilón *nm, pl* **-lones** *fam* : wimp, coward

mandioca *nf* **1** : manioc, cassava **2** : tapioca

mando *nm* **1** : command, leadership **2** : control (for a device) ⟨mando a distancia : remote control⟩ **3 al mando de** : in charge of **4 al mando de** : under the command of

mandolina *nf* : mandolin

mandón, -dona *adj, mpl* **mandones** : bossy, domineering

mandonear *vt fam* MANGONEAR : to boss around

mandrágora *nf* : mandrake

manecilla *nf* : hand (of a clock), pointer

manejable *adj* **1** : manageable **2** : docile, easily led

manejar *vt* **1** CONDUCIR : to drive (a car) **2** OPERAR : to handle, to operate **3** : to manage **4** : to manipulate (a person) — *vi* : to drive — **manejarse** *vr* **1** COMPORTARSE : to behave **2** : to get along, to manage

manejo *nm* **1** : handling, operation **2** : management

manera *nf* **1** MODO : way, manner, fashion **2 de cualquier manera** *or* **de todas maneras** : anyway, anyhow **3 de manera que** : so, in order that **4 de ninguna manera** : by no means, absolutely not **5 manera de ser** : personality, demeanor

manga *nf* **1** : sleeve **2** MANGUERA : hose
manganeso *nm* : manganese
mangle *nm* : mangrove
mango *nm* **1** : hilt, handle **2** : mango
mangonear *vt fam* : to boss around, to bully — *vi* **1** : to be bossy **2** : to loaf, to fool around
mangosta *nf* : mongoose
manguera *nf* : hose
manguito *nm* **1** : muff **2** : sleeve (of a pipe, etc.), hose (of a car)
maní *nm, pl* **maníes** : peanut
manía *nf* **1** OBSESIÓN : mania, obsession **2** : craze, fad **3** : odd habit, peculiarity **4** : dislike, aversion
maníaco¹, -ca *adj* : maniacal
maníaco², -ca *n* : maniac
maniatar *vt* : to tie the hands of, to manacle
maniático¹, -ca *adj* **1** MANÍACO : maniacal **2** : obsessive **3** : fussy, finicky
maniático², -ca *n* **1** MANÍACO : maniac, lunatic **2** : obsessive person, fanatic **3** : eccentric, crank
manicomio *nm* : insane asylum, madhouse
manicura *nf* : manicure
manicuro, -ra *n* : manicurist
manido, -da *adj* : hackneyed, stale, trite
manifestación *nf, pl* **-ciones 1** : manifestation, sign **2** : demonstration, rally
manifestante *nmf* : demonstrator
manifestar {55} *vt* **1** : to demonstrate, to show **2** : to declare — **manifestarse** *vr* **1** : to be or become evident **2** : to state one's position ⟨se han manifestado a favor del acuerdo : they have declared their support for the agreement⟩ **3** : to demonstrate, to rally
manifiesto¹, -ta *adj* : manifest, evident, clear — **manifiestamente** *adv*
manifiesto² *nm* : manifesto
manija *nf* MANGO : handle
manilla → **manecilla**
manillar *nm* : handlebars *pl*
maniobra *nf* : maneuver, stratagem
maniobrar *v* : to maneuver
manipulación *nf, pl* **-ciones** : manipulation
manipulador¹, -dora *adj* : manipulating, manipulative
manipulador², -dora *n* : manipulator
manipular *vt* **1** : to manipulate **2** MANEJAR : to handle
maniquí¹ *nmf, pl* **-quíes** : mannequin, model
maniquí² *nm, pl* **-quíes** : mannequin, dummy
manirroto¹, -ta *adj* : extravagant
manirroto², -ta *n* : spendthrift
manivela *nf* : crank
manjar *nm* : delicacy, special dish
mano¹ *nf* **1** : hand **2** : coat (of paint or varnish) **3 a** ~ : by hand **4 a** ~ *or* **a la mano** : handy, at hand, nearby **5 darse la mano** : to shake hands **6 de la mano** : hand in hand ⟨la política y la economía van de la mano : politics and economics go hand in hand⟩ **7 de primera mano** : firsthand, at firsthand **8 de segunda mano** : secondhand ⟨ropa de segunda mano : secondhand clothing⟩ **9 mano a mano** : one-on-one **10 mano de obra** : labor, manpower **11 mano de mortero** : pestle **12 echar una mano** : to lend a hand **13 mano negra** *Mex fam* : shady dealings *pl*
mano², -na *n Mex fam* : buddy, pal ⟨¡oye, mano! : hey man!⟩
manojo *nm* PUÑADO : handful, bunch
manopla *nf* **1** : mitten, mitt **2** : brass knuckles *pl*
manosear *vt* **1** : to handle or touch excessively **2** ACARICIAR : to fondle, to caress
manotazo *nm* : slap, smack, swipe
manotear *vi* : to wave one's hands, to gesticulate
mansalva *adv* **a** ~ : at close range
mansarda *nf* BUHARDILLA : attic
mansedumbre *nf* **1** : gentleness, meekness **2** : tameness
mansión *nf, pl* **-siones** : mansion
manso, -sa *adj* **1** : gentle, meek **2** : tame — **mansamente** *adv*
manta *nf* **1** COBIJA, FRAZADA : blanket **2** : poncho **3** *Mex* : coarse cotton fabric
manteca *nf* **1** GRASA : lard, fat **2** : butter
mantecoso, -sa *adj* : buttery
mantel *nm* **1** : tablecloth **2** : altar cloth
mantelería *nf* : table linen
mantener {80} *vt* **1** SUSTENTAR : to support, to feed ⟨mantener uno su familia : to support one's family⟩ **2** CONSERVAR : to keep, to preserve **3** CONTINUAR : to keep up, to sustain ⟨mantener una correspondencia : to keep up a correspondence⟩ **4** AFIRMAR : to maintain, to affirm — **mantenerse** *vr* **1** : to support oneself, to subsist **2 mantenerse firme** : to hold one's ground
mantenimiento *nm* **1** : maintenance, upkeep **2** : sustenance, food **3** : preservation
mantequera *nf* **1** : churn **2** : butter dish
mantequería *nf* **1** : creamery, dairy **2** : grocery store
mantequilla *nf* : butter
mantilla *nf* : mantilla
mantis *nf* **mantis religiosa** : praying mantis
manto *nm* **1** : cloak **2** : mantle (in geology)
mantón *nm, pl* **-tones** CHAL : shawl
mantuvo, etc. → **mantener**
manual¹ *adj* **1** : manual ⟨trabajo manual : manual labor⟩ **2** : handy, manageable — **manualmente** *adv*
manual² *nm* : manual, handbook
manualidades *nfpl* : handicrafts (in schools)
manubrio *nm* **1** : handle, crank **2** : handlebars *pl*

manufactura *nf* **1** FABRICACIÓN : manufacture **2** : manufactured item, product **3** FÁBRICA : factory

manufacturar *vt* FABRICAR : to manufacture

manufacturero¹, -ra *adj* : manufacturing

manufacturero², -ra *n* FABRICANTE : manufacturer

manuscrito¹, -ta *adj* : handwritten

manuscrito² *nm* : manuscript

manutención *nf, pl* **-ciones** : maintenance, support

manzana *nf* **1** : apple **2** CUADRA : block (enclosed by streets or buildings) **3** *or* **manzana de Adán** : Adam's apple

manzanal *nm* **1** : apple orchard **2** MANZANO : apple tree

manzanar *nm* : apple orchard

manzanilla *nf* **1** : chamomile **2** : chamomile tea

manzano *nm* : apple tree

maña *nf* **1** : dexterity, skill **2** : cunning, guile **3 mañas** *or* **malas mañas** *nfpl* : bad habits, vices

mañana *nf* **1** : morning **2** : tomorrow

mañanero, -ra *adj* MATUTINO : morning ⟨rocío mañanero : morning dew⟩

mañanitas *nfpl Mex* : birthday serenade

mañoso, -sa *adj* **1** HÁBIL : skillful **2** ASTUTO : cunning, crafty **3** : fussy, finicky

mapa *nm* CARTA : map

mapache *nm* : raccoon

mapamundi *nm* : map of the world

maqueta *nf* : model, mock-up

maquillador, -dora *n* : makeup artist

maquillaje *nm* : makeup

maquillarse *vr* : to put on makeup, to make oneself up

máquina *nf* **1** : machine ⟨máquina de coser : sewing machine⟩ ⟨máquina de escribir : typewriter⟩ **2** LOCOMOTORA : engine, locomotive **3** : machine (in politics) **4 a toda máquina** : at full speed

maquinación *nf, pl* **-ciones** : machination, scheme, plot

maquinal *adj* : mechanical, automatic — **maquinalmente** *adv*

maquinar *vt* : to plot, to scheme

maquinaria *nf* **1** : machinery **2** : mechanism, works *pl*

maquinilla *nf* **1** : small machine or device **2** *CA, Car* : typewriter

maquinista *nmf* **1** : machinist **2** : railroad engineer

mar *nmf* **1** : sea ⟨un mar agitado : a rough sea⟩ ⟨hacerse a la mar : to set sail⟩ **2 alta mar** : high seas

maraca *nf* : maraca

maraña *nf* **1** : thicket **2** ENREDO : tangle, mess

marasmo *nm* : paralysis, stagnation

maratón *nm, pl* **-tones** : marathon

maravilla *nf* **1** : wonder, marvel ⟨a las mil maravillas : wonderfully, mar-

velously⟩ ⟨hacer maravillas : to work wonders⟩ **2** : marigold

maravillar *vt* ASOMBRAR : to astonish, to amaze — **maravillarse** *vr* : to be amazed, to marvel

maravilloso, -sa *adj* ESTUPENDO : wonderful, marvelous — **maravillosamente** *adv*

marbete *nm* **1** ETIQUETA : label, tag **2** *PRi* : registration sticker (of a car)

marca *nf* **1** : mark **2** : brand, make **3** : trademark ⟨marca registrada : registered trademark⟩ **4** : record (in sports) ⟨batir la marca : to beat the record⟩

marcado, -da *adj* : marked ⟨un marcado contraste : a marked contrast⟩

marcador *nm* **1** TANTEADOR : scoreboard **2** : marker, felt-tipped pen **3 marcador de libros** : bookmark

marcaje *nm* **1** : scoring (in sports) **2** : guarding (in sports)

marcapasos *nms & pl* : pacemaker

marcar {72} *vt* **1** : to mark **2** : to brand (livestock) **3** : to indicate, to show **4** RESALTAR : to emphasize **5** : to dial (a telephone) **6** : to guard (an opponent) **7** ANOTAR : to score (a goal, a point) — *vi* **1** ANOTAR : to score **2** : to dial

marcha *nf* **1** : march **2** : hike, walk ⟨ir de marcha : to go hiking⟩ **3** : pace, speed ⟨a toda marcha : at top speed⟩ **4** : gear (of an automobile) ⟨marcha atrás : reverse, reverse gear⟩ **5 en ~** : in motion, in gear, under way

marchar *vi* **1** IR : to go, to travel **2** ANDAR : to walk **3** FUNCIONAR : to work, to go **4** : to march — **marcharse** *vr* : to leave

marchitar *vi* : to make wither, to wilt — **marchitarse** *vr* **1** : to wither, to shrivel up, to wilt **2** : to languish, to fade away

marchito, -ta *adj* : withered, faded

marcial *adj* : martial, military

marco *nm* **1** : frame, framework **2** : goalposts *pl* **3** AMBIENTE : setting, atmosphere **4** : mark (unit of currency)

marea *nf* : tide

mareado, -da *adj* **1** : dizzy, lightheaded **2** : queasy, nauseous **3** : seasick

marear *vt* **1** : to make sick ⟨los gases me marearon : the fumes made me sick⟩ **2** : to bother, to annoy — **marearse** *vr* **1** : to get sick, to become nauseated **2** : to feel dizzy **3** : to get tipsy

marejada *nf* **1** : surge, swell (of the sea) **2** : undercurrent, ferment, unrest

maremoto *nm* : tidal wave

mareo *nm* **1** : dizzy spell **2** : nausea **3** : seasickness, motion sickness **4** : annoyance, vexation

marfil *nm* : ivory

margarina *nf* : margarine

margarita *nf* **1** : daisy **2** : margarita (cocktail)

margen¹ *nf, pl* **márgenes** : bank (of a river), side (of a street)

margen² *nm, pl* **márgenes 1** : edge, border **2** : margin ⟨margen de ganancia : profit margin⟩

marginación *nf, pl* **-ciones** : marginalization, exclusion

marginado¹, -da *adj* **1** DESHEREDADO : outcast, alienated, dispossessed **2 clases marginadas** : underclass

marginado², -da *n* : outcast, misfit

marginal *adj* : marginal, fringe

marginalidad *nf* : marginality

marginar *vt* : to ostracize, to exclude

mariachi *nm* : mariachi musician or band

maridaje *nm* : marriage, union

maridar *vt* UNIR : to marry, to unite

marido *nm* ESPOSO : husband

marihuana *or* **mariguana** *or* **marijuana** *nf* : marihuana

marimacho *nmf fam* **1** : mannish woman **2** : tomboy

marimba *nf* : marimba

marina *nf* **1** : coast, coastal area **2** : navy, fleet ⟨marina mercante : merchant marine⟩

marinada *nf* : marinade

marinar *vt* : to marinate

marinero¹, -ra *adj* **1** : seaworthy **2** : sea, marine

marinero² *nm* : sailor

marino¹, -na *adj* : marine, sea

marino² *nm* : sailor, seaman

marioneta *nf* TÍTERE : puppet, marionette

mariposa *nf* **1** : butterfly **2 mariposa nocturna** : moth

mariquita¹ *nf* : ladybug

mariquita² *nm fam* : sissy, wimp

mariscal *nm* **1** : marshal **2 mariscal de campo** : field marshal (in the military), quarterback (in football)

marisco *nm* **1** : shellfish **2 mariscos** *nmpl* : seafood

marisma *nf* : marsh, salt marsh

marital *adj* : marital, married ⟨la vida marital : married life⟩

marítimo, -ma *adj* : maritime, shipping ⟨la industria marítima : the shipping industry⟩

marmita *nf* : (cooking) pot

mármol *nm* : marble

marmóreo, -rea *adj* : marble, marmoreal

marmota *nf* **1** : marmot **2 marmota de América** : woodchuck, groundhog

maroma *nf* **1** : rope **2** : acrobatic stunt **3** *Mex* : somersault

marque, etc. → **marcar**

marqués, -quesa *n, mpl* **marqueses** : marquis *m*, marquess *m*, marquise *f*, marchioness *f*

marquesina *nf* : marquee, canopy

marqueta *nf Mex* : block (of chocolate), lump (of sugar or salt)

marranada *nf* **1** : disgusting thing **2** : dirty trick

marrano¹, -na *adj* : filthy, disgusting

marrano², -na *n* **1** CERDO : pig, hog **2** : dirty pig, slob

marrar *vt* : to miss (a target) — *vi* : to fail, to go wrong

marras *nf* **1** : long ago **2 de ~** : said, aforementioned ⟨el individuo de marras : the individual in question⟩

marrasquino *nm* : maraschino

marrón *adj & nm, pl* **marrones** CASTAÑO : brown

marroquí *adj & nmf, pl* **-quíes** : Moroccan

marsopa *nf* : porpoise

marsupial *nm* : marsupial

marta *nf* **1** : marten **2 marta cebellina** : sable (animal)

Marte *nm* : Mars

martes *nms & pl* : Tuesday

martillar *v* : to hammer

martillazo *nm* : blow with a hammer

martillo *nm* **1** : hammer **2 martillo neumático** : jackhammer

martinete *nm* **1** : heron **2** : pile driver

mártir *nmf* : martyr

martirio *nm* **1** : martyrdom **2** : ordeal, torment

martirizar {21} *vt* **1** : to martyr **2** ATORMENTAR : to torment

marxismo *nm* : Marxism

marxista *adj & nmf* : Marxist

marzo *nm* : March

mas *conj* PERO : but

más¹ *adv* **1** : more ⟨¿hay algo más grande? : is there anything bigger?⟩ **2** : most ⟨Luis es el más alto : Luis is the tallest⟩ **3** : longer ⟨el sabor dura más : the flavor lasts longer⟩ **4** : rather ⟨más querría andar : I would rather walk⟩ **5 a ~** : besides, in addition **6 más allá** : further **7 qué ... más ...** : what ..., what a ... ⟨¡qué día más bonito! : what a beautiful day!⟩

más² *adj* **1** : more ⟨dáme dos kilos más : give me two more kilos⟩ **2** : most ⟨la que ganó más dinero : the one who earned the most money⟩ **3** : else ⟨¿quién más quiere vino? : who else wants wine?⟩

más³ *n* : plus sign

más⁴ *prep* : plus ⟨tres más dos es igual a cinco : three plus two equals five⟩

más⁵ *pron* **1** : more ⟨¿tienes más? : do you have more?⟩ **2 a lo más** : at most **3 de ~** : extra, excess **4 más o menos** : more or less, approximately **5 por más que** : no matter how much ⟨por más que corras no llegarás a tiempo : no matter how fast you run you won't arrive on time⟩

masa *nf* **1** : mass, volume ⟨masa atómica : atomic mass⟩ ⟨producción en masa : mass production⟩ **2** : dough, batter **3 masas** *nfpl* : people, masses ⟨las masas populares : the common people⟩ **4 masa harina** *Mex* : corn flour (for tortillas, etc.)

masacrar *vt* : to massacre

masacre *nf* : massacre

masaje *nm* : massage

masajear *vt* : to massage

masajista *nmf* : masseur *m*, masseuse *f*
mascar {72} *v* MASTICAR : to chew
máscara *nf* **1** CARETA : mask **2** : appearance, pretense **3 máscara antigás** : gas mask
mascarada *nf* : masquerade
mascarilla *nf* **1** : mask (in medicine) ⟨mascarilla de oxígeno : oxygen mask⟩ **2** : facial mask (in cosmetology)
mascota *nf* : mascot
masculinidad *nf* : masculinity
masculino, -na *adj* **1** : masculine, male **2** : manly **3** : masculine (in grammar)
mascullar *v* : to mumble, to mutter
masificado, -da *adj* : overcrowded
masilla *nf* : putty
masivamente *adv* : en masse
masivo, -va *adj* : mass ⟨comunicación masiva : mass communication⟩
masón *nm, pl* **masones** FRANCMASÓN : Mason, Freemason
masonería *nf* FRANCMASONERÍA : Masonry, Freemasonry
masónico, -ca *adj* : Masonic
masoquismo *nm* : masochism
masoquista[1] *adj* : masochistic
masoquista[2] *nmf* : masochist
masque, etc. → **mascar**
masticar {72} *v* MASCAR : to chew, to masticate
mástil *nm* **1** : mast **2** ASTA : flagpole **3** : neck (of a stringed instrument)
mastín *nm, pl* **mastines** : mastiff
mástique *nm* : putty, filler
mastodonte *nm* : mastodon
masturbación *nf, pl* **-ciones** : masturbation
masturbarse *vr* : to masturbate
mata *nf* **1** ARBUSTO : bush, shrub **2** : plant ⟨mata de tomate : tomato plant⟩ **3** : sprig, tuft **4 mata de pelo** : mop of hair
matadero *nm* : slaughterhouse, abattoir
matado, -da *adj Mex* : strenuous, exhausting
matador *nm* TORERO : matador, bullfighter
matamoscas *nms & pl* : flyswatter
matanza *nf* MASACRE : slaughter, butchering
matar *vt* **1** : to kill **2** : to slaughter, to butcher **3** APAGAR : to extinguish, to put out (fire, light) **4** : to tone down (colors) **5** : to pass, to waste (time) **6** : to trump (in card games) — *vi* : to kill — **matarse** *vr* **1** : to be killed **2** SUICIDARSE : to commit suicide **3** *fam* : to exhaust oneself ⟨se mató tratando de terminarlo : he knocked himself out trying to finish it⟩
matasanos *nms & pl fam* : quack
matasellar *vt* : to cancel (a stamp), to postmark
matasellos *nms & pl* : postmark
matatena *nf Mex* : jacks
mate[1] *adj* : matte, dull
mate[2] *nm* **1** : maté **2 jaque mate** : checkmate ⟨darle mate a *or* darle jaque mate a : to checkmate⟩

matemática → **matemáticas**
matemáticas *nfpl* : mathematics, math
matemático[1], **-ca** *adj* : mathematical — **matemáticamente** *adv*
matemático[2], **-ca** *n* : mathematician
materia *nf* **1** : matter ⟨materia gris : gray matter⟩ **2** : material ⟨materia prima : raw material⟩ **3** : (academic) subject **4 en materia de** : on the subject of, concerning
material[1] *adj* **1** : material, physical, real **2 daños materiales** : property damage
material[2] *nm* **1** : material ⟨material de construcción : building material⟩ **2** EQUIPO : equipment, gear
materialismo *nm* : materialism
materialista[1] *adj* : materialistic
materialista[2] *nmf* **1** : materialist **2** *Mex* : truck driver
materializar {21} *vt* : to bring to fruition, to realize — **materializarse** *vr* : to materialize, to come into being
materialmente *adv* **1** : materially, physically ⟨materialmente imposible : physically impossible⟩ **2** : really, absolutely
maternal *adj* : maternal, motherly
maternidad *nf* **1** : maternity, motherhood **2** : maternity hospital, maternity ward
materno, -na *adj* : maternal
matinal *adj* MATUTINO : morning ⟨la pálida luz matinal : the pale morning light⟩
matinée *or* **matiné** *nf* : matinee
matiz *nm, pl* **matices** **1** : hue, shade **2** : nuance
matización *nf, pl* **-ciones** **1** : tinting, toning, shading **2** : clarification (of a statement)
matizar {21} *vt* **1** : to tinge, to tint (colors) **2** : to vary, to modulate (sounds) **3** : to qualify (statements)
matón *nm, pl* **matones** : thug, bully
matorral *nm* **1** : thicket **2** : scrub, scrubland
matraca *nf* **1** : rattle, noisemaker **2 dar la matraca a** : to pester, to nag
matriarca *nf* : matriarch
matriarcado *nm* : matriarchy
matrícula *nf* **1** : list, roll, register **2** INSCRIPCIÓN : registration, enrollment **3** : license plate, registration number
matriculación *nf, pl* **-ciones** : matriculation, registration
matricular *vt* **1** INSCRIBIR : to enroll, to register (a person) **2** : to register (a vehicle) — **matricularse** *vr* : to matriculate
matrimonial *adj* : marital, matrimonial ⟨la vida matrimonial : married life⟩
matrimonio *nm* **1** : marriage, matrimony **2** : married couple
matriz *nf, pl* **matrices** **1** : uterus, womb **2** : original, master copy **3** : main office, headquarters **4** : stub (of a check) **5** : matrix ⟨matriz de puntos : dot matrix⟩

matrona *nf* : matron
matronal *adj* : matronly
matutino¹, -na *adj* : morning ⟨la edición matutina : the morning edition⟩
matutino² *nm* : morning paper
maullar {8} *vi* : to meow
maullido *nm* : meow
mauritano, -na *adj & n* : Mauritanian
mausoleo *nm* : mausoleum
maxilar *nm* : jaw, jawbone
máxima *nf* : maxim
máxime *adv* ESPECIALMENTE : especially, principally
maximizar {21} *vt* : to maximize
máximo¹, -ma *adj* : maximum, greatest, highest
máximo² *nm* **1** : maximum **2 al máximo** : to the utmost **3 como ~** : at the most, at the latest
maya¹ *adj & nmf* : Mayan
maya² *nmf* : Maya, Mayan
mayo *nm* : May
mayonesa *nf* : mayonnaise
mayor¹ *adj* **1** (*comparative of* **grande**) : bigger, larger, greater, elder, older **2** (*superlative of* **grande**) : biggest, largest, greatest, eldest, oldest **3** : grown-up, mature **4** : main, major **5 mayor de edad** : of (legal) age **6 al por mayor** *or* **por ~** : wholesale
mayor² *nmf* **1** : major (in the military) **2** : adult
mayoral *nm* CAPATAZ : foreman, overseer
mayordomo *nm* : butler, majordomo
mayoreo *nm* : wholesale
mayores *nmpl* : grown-ups, elders
mayoría *nf* **1** : majority **2 en su mayoría** : on the whole
mayorista¹ *adj* ALMACENISTA : wholesale
mayorista² *nmf* : wholesaler
mayoritariamente *adv* : primarily, chiefly
mayoritario, -ria *adj & n* : majority ⟨un consenso mayoritario : a majority consensus⟩
mayormente *adv* : primarily, chiefly
mayúscula *nf* : capital letter
mayúsculo, -la *adj* **1** : capital, uppercase **2** : huge, terrible ⟨un problema mayúsculo : a huge problem⟩
maza *nf* **1** : mace (weapon) **2** : drumstick **3** *fam* : bore, pest
mazacote *nm* **1** : concrete **2** : lumpy mess (of food) **3** : eyesore, crude work of art
mazapán *nm, pl* **-panes** : marzipan
mazmorra *nf* CALABOZO : dungeon
mazo *nm* **1** : mallet **2** : pestle **3** MANOJO : handful, bunch
mazorca *nf* **1** CHOCLO : cob, ear of corn **2 pelar la mazorca** *Mex fam* : to smile from ear to ear
me *pron* **1** : me ⟨me vieron : they saw me⟩ **2** : to me, for me, from me ⟨dame el libro : give me the book⟩ ⟨me lo compró : he bought it for me⟩ ⟨me robaron la cartera : they stole my pocketbook⟩

3 : myself, to myself, for myself, from myself ⟨me preparé una buena comida : I cooked myself a good dinner⟩ ⟨me equivoqué : I made a mistake⟩
mecánica *nf* : mechanics
mecánico¹, -ca *adj* : mechanical — **mecánicamente** *adv*
mecánico², -ca *n* **1** : mechanic **2** : technician ⟨mecánico dental : dental technician⟩
mecanismo *nm* : mechanism
mecanización *nf, pl* **-ciones** : mechanization
mecanizar {21} *vt* : to mechanize
mecanografía *nf* : typing
mecanografiar {85} *vt* : to type
mecanógrafo, -fa *n* : typist
mecate *nm* CA, Mex, Ven : rope, twine, cord
mecedor *nm* : glider (seat)
mecedora *nf* : rocking chair
mecenas *nmfs & pl* : patron (of the arts), sponsor
mecenazgo *nm* PATROCINIO : sponsorship, patronage
mecer {86} *vt* **1** : to rock **2** COLUMPIAR : to push (on a swing) — **mecerse** *vr* : to rock, to swing, to sway
mecha *nf* **1** : fuse **2** : wick **3 mechas** *nfpl* : highlights (in hair)
mechero *nm* **1** : burner **2** *Spain* : lighter
mechón *nm, pl* **mechones** : lock (of hair)
medalla *nf* : medal, medallion
medallista *nmf* : medalist
medallón *nm, pl* **-llones** **1** : medallion **2** : locket
media *nf* **1** CALCETÍN : sock **2** : average, mean **3 medias** *nfpl* : stockings, hose, tights **4 a medias** : by halves, half and half, halfway ⟨ir a medias : to go halves⟩ ⟨verdad a medias : half-truth⟩
mediación *nf, pl* **-ciones** : mediation
mediado, -da *adj* **1** : half full, half empty, half over **2** : halfway through ⟨mediada la tarea : halfway through the job⟩
mediador, -dora *n* : mediator
mediados *nmpl* **a mediados de** : halfway through, in the middle of ⟨a mediados del mes : towards the middle of the month, mid-month⟩
medialuna *nf* **1** : crescent **2** : croissant, crescent roll
medianamente *adv* : fairly, moderately
medianero, -ra *adj* **1** : dividing **2** : mediating
medianía *nf* **1** : middle position **2** : mediocre person, mediocrity
mediano, -na *adj* **1** : medium, average ⟨la mediana edad : middle age⟩ **2** : mediocre
medianoche *nf* : midnight
mediante *prep* : through, by means of ⟨Dios mediante : God willing⟩
mediar *vi* **1** : to mediate **2** : to be in the middle, to be halfway through **3** : to elapse, to pass ⟨mediaron cinco años entre el inicio de la guerra y el armisti-

cio : five years passed between the start of the war and the armistice⟩ **4** : to be a consideration ⟨media el hecho de que cuesta mucho : one must take into account that it is costly⟩ **5** : to come up, to happen ⟨medió algo urgente : something pressing came up⟩

mediatizar {21} *vt* : to influence, to interfere with

medicación *nf, pl* **-ciones** : medication, treatment

medicamento *nm* : medication, medicine, drug

medicar {72} *vt* : to medicate — **medicarse** *vr* : to take medicine

medicina *nf* : medicine

medicinal *adj* **1** : medicinal **2** : medicated

medicinar *vt* : to give medication to, to dose

medición *nf, pl* **-ciones** : measuring, measurement

médico[1], **-ca** *adj* : medical ⟨una receta médica : a doctor's prescription⟩

médico[2], **-ca** *n* DOCTOR : doctor, physician

medida *nf* **1** : measurement, measure ⟨hecho a medida : custom-made⟩ **2** : measure, step ⟨tomar medidas : to take steps⟩ **3** : moderation, prudence ⟨sin medida : immoderately⟩ **4** : extent, degree ⟨en gran medida : to a great extent⟩

medidor *nm* : meter, gauge

medieval *adj* : medieval — **medievalista** *nmf*

medievo → **medioevo**

medio[1] *adv* **1** : half ⟨está medio dormida : she's half asleep⟩ **2** : rather, kind of ⟨está medio aburrida esta fiesta : this party is rather boring⟩

medio[2], **-dia** *adj* **1** : half ⟨una media hora : half an hour⟩ ⟨medio hermano : half brother⟩ ⟨a media luz : in the half-light⟩ ⟨son las tres y media : it's half past three, it's three-thirty⟩ **2** : midway, halfway ⟨a medio camino : halfway there⟩ **3** : middle ⟨la clase media : the middle class⟩ **4** : average ⟨la temperatura media : the average temperature⟩

medio[3] *nm* **1** CENTRO : middle, center ⟨en medio de : in the middle of, amid⟩ **2** AMBIENTE : milieu, environment **3** : medium, spiritualist **4** : means *pl*, way ⟨por medio de : by means of⟩ ⟨los medios de comunicación : the media⟩ **5 medios** *nmpl* : means, resources

mediocampista *nmf* : midfielder

mediocre *adj* : mediocre, average

mediocridad *nf* : mediocrity

mediodía *nm* : noon, midday

medioevo *nm* : Middle Ages

medir {54} *vt* **1** : to measure **2** : to weigh, to consider ⟨medir los riesgos : to weigh the risks⟩ — *vi* : to measure — **medirse** *vr* : to be moderate, to exercise restraint

meditabundo, -da *adj* PENSATIVO : pensive, thoughtful

meditación *nf, pl* **-ciones** : meditation, thought

meditar *vi* : to meditate, to think ⟨meditar sobre la vida : to contemplate life⟩ — *vt* **1** : to think over, to consider **2** : to plan, to work out

meditativo, -va *adj* : pensive

mediterráneo, -nea *adj* : Mediterranean

medrar *vi* **1** PROSPERAR : to prosper, to thrive **2** AUMENTAR : to increase, to grow

medro *nm* PROSPERIDAD : prosperity, growth

medroso, -sa *adj* : fainthearted, fearful

médula *nf* **1** : marrow, pith **2 médula espinal** : spinal cord

medular *adj* : fundamental, core ⟨el punto medular : the crux of the matter⟩

medusa *nf* : jellyfish, medusa

megabyte *nm* : megabyte

megáfono *nm* : megaphone

megahercio *nm* : megahertz

megahertzio *nm* : megahertz

megatón *nm, pl* **-tones** : megaton

megavatio *nm* : megawatt

mejicano → **mexicano**

mejilla *nf* : cheek

mejillón *nm, pl* **-llones** : mussel

mejor[1] *adv* **1** : better ⟨Carla cocina mejor que Ana : Carla cooks better than Ann⟩ **2** : best ⟨ella es la que lo hace mejor : she's the one who does it best⟩ **3** : rather ⟨mejor morir que rendirme : I'd rather die than give up⟩ **4** : it's better that ... ⟨mejor te vas : you'd better go⟩ **5 a lo mejor** : maybe, perhaps

mejor[2] *adj* **1** (*comparative of* **bueno**) : better ⟨a falta de algo mejor : for lack of something better⟩ **2** (*comparative of* **bien**) : better ⟨está mucho mejor : he's much better⟩ **3** (*superlative of* **bueno**) : best, the better ⟨mi mejor amigo : my best friend⟩ **4** (*superlative of* **bien**) : best, the better ⟨duermo mejor en un clima seco : I sleep best in a dry climate⟩ **5** PREFERIBLE : preferable, better **6 lo mejor** : the best thing, the best part

mejor[3] *nmf* (*with definite article*) : the better (one), the best (one)

mejora *nf* : improvement

mejoramiento *nm* : improvement

mejorana *nf* : marjoram

mejorar *vt* : to improve, to make better — *vi* : to improve, to get better — **mejorarse** *vr*

mejoría *nf* : improvement, betterment

mejunje *nm* : concoction, brew

melancolía *nf* : melancholy, sadness

melancólico, -ca *adj* : melancholy, sad

melanoma *nm* : melanoma

melaza *nf* : molasses

melena *nf* **1** : mane **2** : long hair **3 melenas** *nfpl* GREÑAS : shaggy hair, mop

melenudo[1], **-da** *adj fam* : longhaired
melenudo[2], **-da** *n* GREÑUDO : longhair, hippie
melindres *nmpl* **1** : affectation, airs *pl* **2** : finickiness
melindroso[1], **-sa** *adj* **1** : affected **2** : fussy, finicky
melindroso[2], **-sa** *n* : finicky person, fussbudget
melisa *nf* : lemon balm
mella *nf* **1** : dent, nick **2 hacer mella en** : to have an effect on, to make an impression on
mellado, -da *adj* **1** : chipped, dented **2** : gap-toothed
mellar *vt* : to dent, to nick
mellizo, -za *adj & n* GEMELO : twin
melocotón *nm, pl* **-tones** : peach
melodía *nf* : melody, tune
melódico, -ca *adj* : melodic
melodioso, -sa *adj* : melodious
melodrama *nm* : melodrama
melodramático, -ca *adj* : melodramatic
melón *nm, pl* **melones** : melon, cantaloupe
meloso, -sa *adj* **1** : honeyed, sweet **2** EMPALAGOSO : cloying, saccharine
membrana *nf* **1** : membrane **2 membrana interdigital** : web, webbing (of a bird's foot) — **membranoso, -sa** *adj*
membresía *nf* : membership, members *pl*
membrete *nm* : letterhead, heading
membrillo *nm* : quince
membrudo, -da *adj* FORNIDO : muscular, well-built
memez *nf, pl* **memeces** : stupid thing
memo, -ma *adj* : silly, stupid
memorabilia *nf* : memorabilia
memorable *adj* : memorable
memorándum *or* **memorando** *nm, pl* **-dums** *or* **-dos** **1** : memorandum, memo **2** : memo book, appointment book
memoria *nf* **1** : memory ⟨de memoria : by heart⟩ ⟨hacer memoria : to try to remember⟩ ⟨traer a la memoria : to call to mind⟩ **2** RECUERDO : remembrance, memory ⟨su memoria perdurará para siempre : his memory will live forever⟩ **3** : report ⟨memoria annual : annual report⟩ **4 memorias** *nfpl* : memoirs
memorizar {21} *vt* : to memorize — **memorización** *nf*
mena *nf* : ore
menaje *nm* : household goods *pl*, furnishings *pl*
mención *nf, pl* **-ciones** : mention
mencionar *vt* : to mention, to refer to
mendaz *adj, pl* **mendaces** : mendacious, lying
mendicidad *nf* : begging
mendigar {52} *vi* : to beg — *vt* : to beg for
mendigo, -ga *n* LIMOSNERO : beggar
mendrugo *nm* : crust (of bread)

menear *vt* **1** : to shake (one's head) **2** : to sway, to wiggle (one's hips) **3** : to wag (a tail) **4** : to stir (a liquid) — **menearse** *vr* **1** : to wiggle one's hips **2** : to fidget
meneo *nm* **1** : movement **2** : shake, toss **3** : swaying, wagging, wiggling **4** : stir, stirring
menester *nm* **1** : activity, occupation, duties *pl* **2 ser menester** : to be necessary ⟨es menester que vengas : you must come⟩
mengano, -na → fulano
mengua *nf* **1** : decrease, decline **2** : lack, want **3** : discredit, dishonor
menguar *vt* : to diminish, to lessen — *vi* **1** : to decline, to decrease **2** : to wane — **menguante** *adj*
meningitis *nf* : meningitis
menisco *nm* : meniscus, cartilage
menjurje → mejunje
menopausia *nf* : menopause
menor[1] *adj* **1** (*comparative of* **pequeño**) : smaller, lesser, younger **2** (*superlative of* **pequeño**) : smallest, least, youngest **3** : minor **4 al por menor** : retail **5 ser menor de edad** : to be a minor, to be underage
menor[2] *nmf* : minor, juvenile
menos[1] *adv* **1** : less ⟨llueve menos en agosto : it rains less in August⟩ **2** : least ⟨el coche menos caro : the least expensive car⟩ **3 ~ de** : less than, fewer than
menos[2] *adj* **1** : less, fewer ⟨tengo más trabajo y menos tiempo : I have more work and less time⟩ **2** : least, fewest ⟨la clase que tiene menos estudiantes : the class that has the fewest students⟩
menos[3] *prep* **1** SALVO, EXCEPTO : except **2** : minus ⟨quince menos cuatro son once : fifteen minus four is eleven⟩
menos[4] *pron* **1** : less, fewer ⟨no deberías aceptar menos : you shouldn't accept less⟩ **2 al menos** *or* **por lo menos** : at least **3 a menos que** : unless
menoscabar *vt* **1** : to lessen, to diminish **2** : to disgrace, to discredit **3** PERJUDICAR : to harm, to damage
menoscabo *nm* **1** : lessening, diminishing **2** : disgrace, discredit **3** : harm, damage
menospreciar *vt* **1** DESPRECIAR : to scorn, to look down on **2** : to underestimate, to undervalue
menosprecio *nm* DESPRECIO : contempt, scorn
mensaje *nm* : message
mensajero, -ra *n* : messenger
menso, -sa *adj Mex fam* : foolish, stupid
menstrual *adj* : menstrual
menstruar {3} *vi* : to menstruate — **menstruación** *nf*
mensual *adj* : monthly
mensualidad *nf* **1** : monthly payment, installment **2** : monthly salary
mensualmente *adv* : every month, monthly

mensurable *adj* : measurable

menta *nf* **1** : mint, peppermint **2 menta verde** : spearmint

mentado, -da *adj* **1** : aforementioned **2** FAMOSO : renowned, famous

mental *adj* : mental, intellectual — **mentalmente** *adv*

mentalidad *nf* : mentality

mentar {55} *vt* **1** : to mention, to name **2 mentar la madre a** *fam* : to insult, to swear at

mente *nf* : mind ⟨tener en mente : to have in mind⟩

mentecato¹, -ta *adj* : foolish, simple

mentecato², -ta *n* : fool, idiot

mentir {76} *vi* : to lie

mentira *nf* : lie

mentiroso¹, -sa *adj* EMBUSTERO : lying, untruthful

mentiroso², -sa *n* EMBUSTERO : liar

mentís *nm, pl* **mentises** : denial, repudiation ⟨dar el mentís a : to deny, to refute⟩

mentol *nm* : menthol

mentón *nm, pl* **mentones** BARBILLA : chin

mentor *nm* : mentor, counselor

menú *nm, pl* **menús** : menu

menudear *vi* : to occur frequently — *vt* : to do repeatedly

menudencia *nf* **1** : trifle **2 menudencias** *nfpl* : giblets

menudeo *nm* : retail, retailing

menudillos *nmpl* : giblets

menudo¹, -da *adj* **1** : minute, small **2 a ∼** FRECUENTEMENTE : often, frequently

menudo² *nm* **1** *Mex* : tripe stew **2 menudos** *nmpl* : giblets

meñique *nm or* **dedo meñique** : little finger, pinkie

meollo *nm* **1** MÉDULA : marrow **2** SESO : brains *pl* **3** ENTRAÑA : essence, core ⟨el meollo del asunto : the heart of the matter⟩

mequetrefe *nm fam* : good-for-nothing

mercachifle *nm* : peddler, hawker

mercadeo *nm* : marketing

mercadería *nf* : merchandise, goods *pl*

mercado *nm* : market ⟨mercado de trabajo *or* mercado laboral : labor market⟩ ⟨mercado de valores *or* mercado bursátil : stock market⟩

mercadotecnia *nf* : marketing

mercancía *nf* : merchandise, goods *pl*

mercante *nmf* : merchant, dealer

mercantil *adj* COMERCIAL : commercial, mercantile

merced *nf* **1** : favor **2 ∼ a** : thanks to, due to **3 a merced de** : at the mercy of

mercenario, -ria *adj & n* : mercenary

mercería *nf* : notions store

Mercosur *nm* : economic community consisting of Argentina, Brazil, Paraguay, and Uruguay

mercurio *nm* : mercury

Mercurio *nm* : Mercury (planet)

merecedor, -dora *adj* : deserving, worthy

merecer {53} *vt* : to deserve, to merit — *vi* : to be worthy

merecidamente *adv* : rightfully, deservedly

merecido *nm* : something merited, due ⟨recibieron su merecido : they got their just deserts⟩

merecimiento *nm* : merit, worth

merendar {55} *vi* : to have an afternoon snack — *vt* : to have as an afternoon snack

merendero *nm* **1** : lunchroom, snack bar **2** : picnic area

merengue *nm* **1** : meringue **2** : merengue (dance)

meridiano¹, -na *adj* **1** : midday **2** : crystal clear

meridiano² *nm* : meridian

meridional *adj* SUREÑO : southern

merienda *nf* : afternoon snack, tea

mérito *nm* : merit

meritorio¹, -ria *adj* : deserving, meritorious

meritorio², -ria *n* : intern, trainee

merluza *nf* : hake

merma *nf* **1** : decrease, cut **2** : waste, loss

mermar *vi* : to decrease, to diminish — *vt* : to reduce, to cut down

mermelada *nf* : marmalade, jam

mero¹, -ra *adv Mex fam* **1** : nearly, almost ⟨ya mero me caí : I almost fell⟩ **2** : just, exactly ⟨aquí mero : right here⟩

mero², -ra *adj* **1** : mere, simple **2** *Mex fam* (used as an intensifier) : very ⟨en el mero centro : in the very center of town⟩

mero³ *nm* : grouper

merodeador, -dora *n* **1** : marauder **2** : prowler

merodear *vi* **1** : to maraud, to pillage **2** : to prowl around, to skulk

mes *nm* : month

mesa *nf* **1** : table **2** : committee, board

mesada *nf* : allowance, pocket money

mesarse *vr* : to pull at ⟨mesarse los cabellos : to tear one's hair⟩

mesero, -ra *n* CAMARERO : waiter, waitress *f*

meseta *nf* : plateau, tableland

Mesías *nm* : Messiah

mesón *nm, pl* **mesones** : inn

mesonero, -ra *nm* : innkeeper

mestizo¹, -za *adj* **1** : of mixed ancestry **2** HÍBRIDO : hybrid

mestizo², -za *n* : person of mixed ancestry

mesura *nf* **1** MODERACIÓN : moderation, discretion **2** CORTESÍA : courtesy **3** GRAVEDAD : seriousness, dignity

mesurado, -da *adj* COMEDIDO : moderate, restrained

mesurar *vt* : to moderate, to restrain, to temper — **mesurarse** *vr* : to restrain oneself

meta *nf* : goal, objective

metabólico, -ca *adj* : metabolic
metabolismo *nm* : metabolism
metabolizar {21} *vt* : to metabolize
metafísica *nf* : metaphysics
metafísico, -ca *adj* : metaphysical
metáfora *nf* : metaphor
metafórico, -ca *adj* : metaphoric, metaphorical
metal *nm* **1** : metal **2** : brass section (in an orchestra)
metálico, -ca *adj* : metallic, metal
metalistería *nf* : metalworking
metalurgia *nf* : metallurgy
metalúrgico[1], -ca *adj* : metallurgical
metalúrgico[2], -ca *n* : metallurgist
metamorfosis *nfs & pl* : metamorphosis
metano *nm* : methane
metedura *nf* **metedura de pata** : blunder, faux pas
meteórico, -ca *adj* : meteoric
meteorito *nm* : meteorite
meteoro *nm* : meteor
meteorología *nf* : meteorology
meteorológico, -ca *adj* : meteorologic, meteorological
meteorólogo, -ga *n* : meteorologist
meter *vt* **1** : to put (in) ⟨metieron su dinero en el banco : they put their money in the bank⟩ **2** : to fit, to squeeze ⟨puedes meter dos líneas más en esa página : you can fit two more lines on that page⟩ **3** : to place (in a job) ⟨lo metieron de barrendero : they got him a job as a street sweeper⟩ **4** : to involve ⟨lo metió en un buen lío : she got him in an awful mess⟩ **5** : to make, to cause ⟨meten demasiado ruido : they make too much noise⟩ **6** : to spread (a rumor) **7** : to strike (a blow) **8** : to take up, to take in (clothing) **9 a todo meter** : at top speed — **meterse** *vr* **1** : to get into, to enter **2** *fam* : to meddle ⟨no te metas en lo que no te importa : mind your own business⟩ **3** ~ **con** *fam* : to pick a fight with, to provoke ⟨no te metas conmigo : don't mess with me⟩
metiche[1] *adj Mex fam* : nosy
metiche[2] *nmf Mex fam* : busybody
meticulosidad *nf* : thoroughness, meticulousness
meticuloso, -sa *adj* : meticulous, thorough — **meticulosamente** *adv*
metida *nf* **metida de pata** *fam* : blunder, gaffe, blooper
metódico, -ca *adj* : methodical — **metódicamente** *adv*
metodista *adj & nmf* : Methodist
método *nm* : method
metodología *nf* : methodology
metomentodo *nmf fam* : busybody
metraje *nm* : length (of a film) ⟨de largo metraje : feature-length⟩
metralla *nf* : shrapnel
metralleta *nf* : submachine gun
métrico, -ca *adj* **1** : metric **2 cinta métrica** : tape measure
metro *nm* **1** : meter **2** : subway
metrónomo *nm* : metronome

metrópoli *nf or* **metrópolis** *nfs & pl* : metropolis
metropolitano, -na *adj* : metropolitan
mexicanismo *nm* : Mexican word or expression
mexicano, -na *adj & n* : Mexican
mexicoamericano, -na *adj & n* : Mexican-American
meza, etc. → **mecer**
mezcla *nf* **1** : mixing **2** : mixture, blend **3** : mortar (masonry material)
mezclar *vt* **1** : to mix, to blend **2** : to mix up, to muddle **3** INVOLUCRAR : to involve — **mezclarse** *vr* **1** : to get mixed up (in) **2** : to mix, to mingle (socially)
mezclilla *nf Chile, Mex* : denim ⟨pantalones de mezclilla : jeans⟩
mezcolanza *nf* : jumble, hodgepodge
mezquindad *nf* **1** : meanness, stinginess **2** : petty deed, mean action
mezquino[1], -na *adj* **1** : mean, petty **2** : stingy **3** : paltry
mezquino[2] *nm Mex* : wart
mezquita *nf* : mosque
mezquite *nm* : mesquite
mi *adj* : my
mí *pron* **1** : me ⟨es para mí : it's for me⟩ ⟨a mí no me importa : it doesn't matter to me⟩ **2 mí mismo, mí misma** : myself
miasma *nm* : miasma
miau *nm* : meow
mica *nf* : mica
mico *nm* : monkey, long-tailed monkey
micra *nf* : micron
microbio *nm* : microbe, germ
microbiología *nf* : microbiology
microbiológico, -ca *adj* : microbiological
microbús *nm, pl* **-buses** : minibus
microcomputadora *nf* : microcomputer
microcosmos *nms & pl* : microcosm
microficha *nf* : microfiche
microfilm *nm, pl* **-films** : microfilm
micrófono *nm* : microphone
micrómetro *nm* : micrometer
microonda *nf* : microwave
microondas *nms & pl* : microwave, microwave oven
microordenador *nm Spain* : microcomputer
microorganismo *nm* : microorganism
microprocesador *nm* : microprocessor
microscópico, -ca *adj* : microscopic
microscopio *nm* : microscope
mide, etc. → **medir**
miedo *nm* **1** TEMOR : fear ⟨le tiene miedo al perro : he's scared of the dog⟩ ⟨tenían miedo de hablar : they were afraid to speak⟩ **2 dar miedo** : to frighten
miedoso, -sa *adj* TEMEROSO : fearful
miel *nf* : honey
miembro *nm* **1** : member **2** EXTREMIDAD : limb, extremity
mienta, etc. → **mentar**
miente, etc. → **mentir**

mientras[1] *adv* **1** *or* **mientras tanto** : meanwhile, in the meantime **2 mientras más** : the more ⟨mientras más como, más quiero : the more I eat, the more I want⟩

mientras[2] *conj* **1** : while, as ⟨roncaba mientras dormía : he snored while he was sleeping⟩ **2** : as long as ⟨luchará mientras pueda : he will fight as long as he is able⟩ **3 mientras que** : while, whereas ⟨él es alto mientras que ella es muy baja : he is tall, whereas she is very short⟩

miércoles *nms & pl* : Wednesday

miga *nf* **1** : crumb **2 hacer buenas (malas) migas con** : to get along well (poorly) with

migaja *nf* **1** : crumb **2 migajas** *nfpl* SOBRAS : leftovers, scraps

migración *nf, pl* **-ciones** : migration

migrante *nmf* : migrant

migraña *nf* : migraine

migratorio, -ria *adj* : migratory

mijo *nm* : millet

mil[1] *adj* : thousand

mil[2] *nm* : one thousand, a thousand

milagro *nm* : miracle ⟨de milagro : miraculously⟩

milagroso, -sa *adj* : miraculous, marvelous — **milagrosamente** *adv*

milenio *nm* : millennium

milésimo, -ma *adj* : thousandth — **milésimo** *nm*

milicia *nf* **1** : militia **2** : military service

miligramo *nm* : milligram

mililitro *nm* : milliliter

milímetro *nm* : millimeter

militancia *nf* : militancy

militante[1] *adj* : militant

militante[2] *nmf* : militant, activist

militar[1] *vi* **1** : to serve (in the military) **2** : to be active (in politics)

militar[2] *adj* : military

militar[3] *nmf* SOLDADO : soldier

militarismo *nm* : militarism

militarista *adj & nmf* : militarist

militarizar {21} *vt* : to militarize

milla *nf* : mile

millar *nm* : thousand

millón *nm, pl* **millones** : million

millonario, -ria *n* : millionaire

millonésimo[1], **-ma** *adj* : millionth

millonésimo[2] *nm* : millionth

mil millones *nms & pl* : billion

milpa *nf CA, Mex* : cornfield

milpiés *nms & pl* : millipede

mimar *vt* CONSENTIR : to pamper, to spoil

mimbre *nm* : wicker

mimeógrafo *nm* : mimeograph

mímica *nf* **1** : mime, sign language **2** IMITACIÓN : mimicry

mimo *nm* **1** : pampering, indulgence ⟨hacerle mimos a alguien : to pamper someone⟩ **2** : mime

mimoso, -sa *adj* **1** : fussy, finicky **2** : affectionate, clinging

mina *nf* **1** : mine **2** : lead (for pencils)

minar *vt* **1** : to mine **2** DEBILITAR : to undermine

minarete *nm* ALMINAR : minaret

mineral *adj & nm* : mineral

minería *nf* : mining

minero[1], **-ra** *adj* : mining

minero[2], **-ra** *n* : miner, mine worker

miniatura *nf* : miniature

minicomputadora *nf* : minicomputer

minifalda *nf* : miniskirt

minifundio *nm* : small farm

minimizar {21} *vt* : to minimize

mínimo[1], **-ma** *adj* **1** : minimum ⟨salario mínimo : minimum wage⟩ **2** : least, smallest **3** : very small, minute

mínimo[2] *nm* **1** : minimum, least amount **2** : modicum, small amount **3 como ~** : at least

minino, -na *n fam* : pussy, pussycat

miniserie *nf* : miniseries

ministerial *adj* : ministerial

ministerio *nm* : ministry, department

ministro, -tra *n* : minister, secretary ⟨primer ministro : prime minister⟩ ⟨Ministro de Defensa : Secretary of Defense⟩

minivan [ˌminiˈban, -ˈvan] *nf, pl* **-vanes** : minivan

minoría *nf* : minority

minorista[1] *adj* : retail

minorista[2] *nmf* : retailer

minoritario, -ria *adj* : minority

mintió, etc. → **mentir**

minuciosamente *adv* **1** : minutely **2** : in great detail **3** : thoroughly, meticulously

minucioso, -sa *adj* **1** : minute **2** DETALLADO : detailed **3** : thorough, meticulous

minué *nm* : minuet

minúsculo, -la *adj* DIMINUTO : tiny, miniscule

minusvalía *nf* : disability, handicap

minusválido[1], **-da** *adj* : handicapped, disabled

minusválido[2], **-da** *n* : handicapped person

minuta *nf* **1** BORRADOR : rough draft **2** : bill, fee

minutero *nm* : minute hand

minuto *nm* : minute

mío[1], **mía** *adj* **1** : my, of mine ⟨¡Dios mío! : my God!, good heavens!⟩ ⟨una amiga mía : a friend of mine⟩ **2** : mine ⟨es mío : it's mine⟩

mío[2], **mía** *pron* (*with definite article*) : mine, my own ⟨tus zapatos son iguales a los míos : your shoes are just like mine⟩

miope *adj* : nearsighted, myopic

miopía *nf* : myopia, nearsightedness

mira *nf* **1** : sight (of a firearm or instrument) **2** : aim, objective ⟨con miras a : with the intention of, with a view to⟩ ⟨de amplias miras : broad-minded⟩ ⟨poner la mira en : to aim at, to aspire to⟩

mirada *nf* **1** : look, glance, gaze **2** EX-
PRESIÓN : look, expression ⟨una mira-
da de sorpresa : a look of surprise⟩
mirado, -da *adj* **1** : cautious, careful **2**
: considerate **3 bien mirado** : well
thought of **4 mal mirado** : disliked, dis-
approved of
mirador *nm* : balcony, lookout, vantage
point
miramiento *nm* **1** CONSIDERACIÓN
: consideration, respect **2 sin mi-
ramientos** : without due consideration, carelessly
mirar *vt* **1** : to look at **2** OBSERVAR : to
watch **3** REFLEXIONAR : to consider,
to think over — *vi* **1** : to look **2** : to
face, to overlook **3 ~ por** : to look after, to look out for — **mirarse** *vr* **1** : to
look at oneself **2** : to look at each
other
mirasol *nm* GIRASOL : sunflower
miríada *nf* : myriad
mirlo *nm* : blackbird
mirra *nf* : myrrh
mirto *nm* ARRAYÁN : myrtle
misa *nf* : Mass
misantropía *nf* : misanthropy
misantrópico, -ca *adj* : misanthropic
misántropo, -pa *n* : misanthrope
miscelánea *nf* : miscellany
misceláneo, -nea *adj* : miscellaneous
miserable *adj* **1** LASTIMOSO : miserable,
wretched **2** : paltry, meager **3**
MEZQUINO : stingy, miserly **4** : despicable, vile
miseria *nf* **1** POBREZA : poverty **2** : misery, suffering **3** : pittance, meager
amount
misericordia *nf* COMPASIÓN : mercy,
compassion
misericordioso, -sa *adj* : merciful
mísero, -ra *adj* **1** : wretched, miserable
2 : stingy **3** : paltry, meager
misil *nm* : missile
misión *nf, pl* **misiones** : mission
misionero, -ra *adj & n* : missionary
misiva *nf* : missive, letter
mismísimo, -ma *adj* (*used as an intensifier*) : very, selfsame ⟨el mismísimo día
: that very same day⟩
mismo¹ *adv* (*used as an intensifier*)
: right, exactly ⟨hazlo ahora mismo : do
it right now⟩ ⟨te llamará hoy mismo
: he'll definitely call you today⟩
mismo², -ma *adj* **1** : same **2** (*used as an
intensifier*) : very ⟨en ese mismo mo-
mento : at that very moment⟩ **3** : oneself ⟨lo hizo ella misma : she made it
herself⟩ **4 por lo mismo** : for that reason
misoginia *nf* : misogyny
misógino *nm* : misogynist
misterio *nm* : mystery
misterioso, -sa *adj* : mysterious — **misteriosamente** *adv*
misticismo *nm* : mysticism
místico¹, -ca *adj* : mystic, mystical
místico², -ca *n* : mystic

mitad *nf* **1** : half ⟨mitad y mitad : half
and half⟩ **2** MEDIO : middle ⟨a mitad
de : halfway through⟩ ⟨por la mitad : in
half⟩
mítico, -ca *adj* : mythical, mythic
mitigar {52} *vt* ALIVIAR : to mitigate, to
alleviate — **mitigación** *nf*
mitin *nm, pl* **mítines** : (political) meeting, rally
mito *nm* LEYENDA : myth, legend
mitología *nf* : mythology
mitológico, -ca *adj* : mythological
mitosis *nfs & pl* : mitosis
mitra *nf* : miter (bishop's hat)
mixto, -ta *adj* **1** : mixed, joint **2** : coeducational
mixtura *nf* : mixture, blend
mnemónico, -ca *adj* : mnemonic
mobiliario *nm* : furniture
mocasín *nm, pl* **-sines** : moccasin
mocedad *nf* **1** JUVENTUD : youth **2**
: youthful prank
mochila *nf* MORRAL : backpack, knapsack
moción *nf, pl* **-ciones** **1** MOVIMIENTO
: motion, movement **2** : motion (to a
court or assembly)
moco *nm* **1** : mucus **2** *fam* : snot
⟨limpiarse los mocos : to wipe one's
(runny) nose⟩
mocoso, -sa *n* : kid, brat
moda *nf* **1** : fashion, style **2 a la moda**
or **de ~** : in style, fashionable **3 moda
pasajera** : fad
modales *nmpl* : manners
modalidad *nf* **1** CLASE : kind, type **2**
MANERA : way, manner
modelar *vt* **1** : to model, to mold — **mo-
delarse** *vr* : to model oneself after, to
emulate
modelo¹ *adj* : model ⟨una casa modelo
: a model home⟩
modelo² *nm* : model, example, pattern
modelo³ *nmf* : model, mannequin
módem *or* **modem** [ˈmoðɛm] *nm* : modem
moderación *nf, pl* **-ciones** MESURA
: moderation
moderado, -da *adj & n* : moderate —
moderadamente *adv*
moderador, -dora *n* : moderator, chair
moderar *vt* **1** TEMPERAR : to temper, to
moderate **2** : to curb, to reduce ⟨mod-
erar gastos : to curb spending⟩ **3** PRE-
SIDIR : to chair (a meeting) — **moderarse** *vr* **1** : to restrain oneself **2** : to
diminish, to calm down
modernidad *nf* **1** : modernity, modern-
ness **2** : modern age
modernismo *nm* : modernism
modernista¹ *adj* : modernist, mod-
ernistic
modernista² *nmf* : modernist
modernizar {21} *vt* : to modernize —
modernización *nf*
moderno, -na *adj* : modern, up-to-date
modestia *nf* : modesty

modesto, -ta *adj* : modest — **modesta-mente** *adv*

modificación *nf, pl* **-ciones** : alteration

modificador¹, -dora *adj* : modifying, moderating

modificador² → **modificante**

modificante *nm* : modifier

modificar {72} *vt* ALTERAR : to modify, to alter, to adapt

modismo *nm* : idiom

modista *nmf* **1** : dressmaker **2** : fashion designer

modo *nm* **1** MANERA : way, manner, mode ⟨de un modo u otro : one way or another⟩ ⟨a mi modo de ver : to my way of thinking⟩ **2** : mood (in grammar) **3** : mode (in music) **4 a modo de** : by way of, in the manner of, like ⟨a modo de ejemplo : by way of example⟩ **5 de cualquier modo** : in any case, anyway **6 de modo que** : so, in such a way that **7 de todos modos** : in any case, anyway **8 en cierto modo** : in a way, to a certain extent

modorra *nf* : drowsiness, lethargy

modular¹ *v* : to modulate — **modulación** *nf*

modular² *adj* : modular

módulo *nm* : module, unit

mofa *nf* **1** : mockery, ridicule **2 hacer mofa de** : to make fun of, to ridicule

mofarse *vr* ~ **de** : to scoff at, to make fun of

mofeta *nf* ZORRILLO : skunk

mofle *nm* CA, Mex : muffler (of a car)

moflete *nm fam* : fat cheek

mofletudo, -da *adj fam* : fat-cheeked, chubby

mohín *nm, pl* **mohines** : grimace, face

mohino, -na *adj* : gloomy, melancholy

moho *nm* **1** : mold, mildew **2** : rust

mohoso, -sa *adj* **1** : moldy **2** : rusty

moisés *nm, pl* **moiseses** : bassinet, cradle

mojado¹, -da *adj* : wet

mojado², -da *n Mex fam* : illegal immigrant

mojar *vt* **1** : to wet, to moisten **2** : to dunk — **mojarse** *vr* : to get wet

mojigatería *nf* **1** : hypocrisy **2** GAZMOÑERÍA : primness, prudery

mojigato¹, -ta *adj* : prudish, prim — **mojigatamente** *adv*

mojigato², -ta *n* : prude, prig

mojón *nm, pl* **mojones** : boundary stone, marker

molar *nm* MUELA : molar

molcajete *nm Mex* : mortar

molde *nm* **1** : mold, form **2 letras de molde** : printing, block lettering

moldear *vt* **1** FORMAR : to mold, to shape **2** : to cast

moldura *nf* : molding

mole¹ *nm Mex* **1** : spicy sauce made with chilies and usually chocolate **2** : meat served with mole sauce

mole² *nf* : mass, bulk

molécula *nf* : molecule — **molecular** *adj*

moler {47} *vt* **1** : to grind, to crush **2** CANSAR : to exhaust, to wear out

molestar *vt* **1** FASTIDIAR : to annoy, to bother **2** : to disturb, to disrupt — *vi* : to be a nuisance — **molestarse** *vr* ~ **en** : to take the trouble to

molestia *nf* **1** FASTIDIO : annoyance, bother, nuisance **2** : trouble ⟨se tomó la molestia de investigar : she took the trouble to investigate⟩ **3** MALESTAR : discomfort

molesto, -ta *adj* **1** ENOJADO : bothered, annoyed **2** FASTIDIOSO : bothersome, annoying

molestoso, -sa *adj* : bothersome, annoying

molido, -da *adj* **1** MACHACADO : ground, crushed **2 estar molido** : to be exhausted

molienda *nf* : milling, grinding

molinero, -ra *n* : miller

molinillo *nm* : grinder, mill ⟨molinillo de café : coffee grinder⟩

molino *nm* **1** : mill **2 molino de viento** : windmill

molla *nf* : soft fleshy part, flesh (of fruit), lean part (of meat)

molleja *nf* : gizzard

molusco *nm* : mollusk

momentáneamente *adv* : momentarily

momentáneo, -nea *adj* **1** : momentary **2** TEMPORARIO : temporary

momento *nm* **1** : moment, instant ⟨espera un momentito : wait just a moment⟩ **2** : time, period of time ⟨momentos difíciles : hard times⟩ **3** : present, moment ⟨los atletas del momento : the athletes of the moment, today's popular athletes⟩ **4** : momentum **5 al momento** : right away, at once **6 de** ~ : at the moment, for the moment **7 de un momento a otro** : any time now **8 por momentos** : at times

momia *nf* : mummy

monaguillo *nm* ACÓLITO : altar boy

monarca *nmf* : monarch

monarquía *nf* : monarchy

monárquico, -ca *n* : monarchist

monasterio *nm* : monastery

monástico, -ca *adj* : monastic

mondadientes *nms & pl* PALILLO : toothpick

mondar *vt* : to peel

mondongo *nm* ENTRAÑAS : innards *pl*, insides *pl*, guts *pl*

moneda *nf* **1** : coin **2** : money, currency

monedero *nm* : change purse

monetario, -ria *adj* : monetary, financial

mongol, -gola *adj & n* : Mongol, Mongolian

monitor¹, -tora *n* : instructor (in sports)

monitor² *nm* : monitor ⟨monitor de televisión : television monitor⟩

monitorear *vt* : to monitor

monja *nf* : nun

monje *nm* : monk

mono¹, -na *adj fam* : lovely, pretty, cute, darling

mono², -na n : monkey
monóculo nm : monocle
monogamia nf : monogamy
monógamo, -ma adj : monogamous
monografía nf : monograph
monograma nm : monogram
monolingüe adj : monolingual
monolítico, -ca adj : monolithic
monolito nm : monolith
monólogo nm : monologue
monomanía nf : obsession
monopatín nm, pl -tines 1 : scooter 2 : skateboard
monopolio nm : monopoly
monopolizar {21} vt : to monopolize — monopolización nf
monosilábico, -ca adj : monosyllabic
monosílabo nm : monosyllable
monoteísmo nm : monotheism
monoteísta¹ adj : monotheistic
monoteísta² nmf : monotheist
monotonía nf 1 : monotony 2 : monotone
monótono, -na adj : monotonous — monótonamente adv
monóxido nm : monoxide ⟨monóxido de carbono : carbon monoxide⟩
monserga nf : gibberish, drivel
monstruo nm : monster
monstruosidad nf : monstrosity
monstruoso, -sa adj : monstrous — monstruosamente adv
monta nf 1 : sum, total 2 : importance, value ⟨de poca monta : unimportant, insignificant⟩
montaje nm 1 : assembling, assembly 2 : montage
montante nm : transom, fanlight
montaña nf 1 MONTE : mountain 2 montaña rusa : roller coaster
montañero, -ra n : mountaineer, mountain climber
montañoso, -sa adj : mountainous
montar vt 1 : to mount 2 ESTABLECER : to set up, to establish 3 ARMAR : to assemble, to put together 4 : to edit (a film) 5 : to stage, to put on (a show) 6 : to cock (a gun) 7 montar en bicicleta : to get on a bicycle 8 montar a caballo CABALGAR : to ride horseback
monte nm 1 MONTAÑA : mountain, mount 2 : woodland, scrubland ⟨monte bajo : underbrush⟩ 3 : outskirts (of a town), surrounding country 4 monte de piedad : pawnshop
montés adj, pl monteses : wild (of animals or plants)
montículo nm 1 : mound, heap 2 : hillock, knoll
monto nm : amount, total
montón nm, pl -tones 1 : heap, pile 2 fam : ton, load ⟨un montón de preguntas : a ton of questions⟩ ⟨montones de gente : loads of people⟩
montura nf 1 : mount (horse) 2 : saddle, tack 3 : setting, mounting (of jewelry) 4 : frame (of glasses)

monumental adj fam 1 : tremendous, terrific 2 : massive, huge
monumento nm : monument
monzón nm, pl monzones : monsoon
moño nm 1 : bun (chignon) 2 LAZO : bow, knot ⟨corbata de moño : bow tie⟩
moquear vi : to snivel
moquillo nm : distemper
mora nf 1 : blackberry 2 : mulberry
morada nf RESIDENCIA : dwelling, abode
morado¹, -da adj : purple
morado² nm : purple
morador, -dora n : dweller, inhabitant
moral¹ adj : moral — moralmente adv
moral² nf 1 MORALIDAD : ethics, morality, morals pl 2 ÁNIMO : morale, spirits pl
moraleja nf : moral (of a story)
moralidad nf : morality
moralista¹ adj : moralistic
moralista² nmf : moralist
morar vi : to dwell, to reside
moratoria nf : moratorium
mórbido, -da adj : morbid
morboso, -sa adj : morbid — morbosidad nf
morcilla nf : blood sausage, blood pudding
mordacidad nf : bite, sharpness
mordaz adj : caustic, scathing
mordaza nf 1 : gag 2 : clamp
mordedura nf : bite (of an animal)
morder {47} v : to bite
mordida nf 1 : bite 2 CA, Mex : bribe, payoff
mordisco nm : bite, nibble
mordisquear vt : to nibble (on), to bite
morena nf 1 : moraine 2 : moray (eel)
moreno¹, -na adj 1 : brunette 2 : dark, dark-skinned
moreno², -na n 1 : brunette 2 : dark-skinned person
moretón nm, pl -tones : bruise
morfina nf : morphine
morfología nf : morphology
morgue nf : morgue
moribundo¹, -da adj : dying, moribund
moribundo², -da n : dying person
morillo nm : andiron
morir {46} vi 1 FALLECER : to die 2 APAGARSE : to die out, to go out
mormón, -mona adj & n, pl mormones : Mormon
moro¹, -ra adj : Moorish
moro², -ra n 1 : Moor 2 : Muslim
morosidad nf 1 : delinquency (in payment) 2 : slowness
moroso, -sa adj 1 : delinquent, in arrears ⟨cuentas morosas : delinquent accounts⟩ 2 : slow, sluggish
morral nm MOCHILA : backpack, knapsack
morralla nf 1 : small fish 2 : trash, riffraff 3 Mex : small change
morriña nf : homesickness
morro nm HOCICO : snout

morsa *nf* : walrus
morse *nm* : Morse code
mortaja *nf* SUDARIO : shroud
mortal[1] *adj* 1 : mortal 2 FATAL : fatal, deadly — **mortalmente** *adv*
mortal[2] *nmf* : mortal
mortalidad *nf* : mortality
mortandad *nf* 1 : loss of life, death toll 2 : carnage, slaughter
mortero *nm* : mortar (bowl, cannon, or building material)
mortífero, -ra *adj* LETAL : deadly, fatal
mortificación *nf, pl* **-ciones** 1 : mortification 2 TORMENTO : anguish, torment
mortificar {72} *vt* 1 : to mortify 2 TORTURAR : to trouble, to torment — **mortificarse** *vr* : to be mortified, to feel embarrassed
mosaico *nm* : mosaic
mosca *nf* 1 : fly 2 **mosca común** : housefly
moscada *adj* **nuez moscada** : nutmeg
moscovita *adj & nmf* : Muscovite
mosquearse *vr* 1 : to become suspicious 2 : to take offense
mosquete *nm* : musket
mosquetero *nm* : musketeer
mosquitero *nm* : mosquito net
mosquito *nm* ZANCUDO : mosquito
mostachón *nm, pl* **-chones** : macaroon
mostaza *nf* : mustard
mostrador *nm* : counter (in a store)
mostrar {19} *vt* 1 : to show 2 EXHIBIR : to exhibit, to display — **mostrarse** *vr* : to show oneself, to appear
mota *nf* 1 : fleck, speck 2 : defect, blemish
mote *nm* SOBRENOMBRE : nickname
moteado, -da *adj* : dotted, spotted, dappled
motel *nm* : motel
motín *nm, pl* **motines** 1 : riot 2 : rebellion, mutiny
motivación *nf, pl* **-ciones** : motivation — **motivacional** *adj*
motivar *vt* 1 CAUSAR : to cause 2 IMPULSAR : to motivate
motivo *nm* 1 MÓVIL : motive 2 CAUSA : cause, reason 3 TEMA : theme, motif
moto *nf* : motorcycle, motorbike
motocicleta *nf* : motorcycle
motociclismo *nm* : motorcycling
motociclista *nmf* : motorcyclist
motor[1], **-ra** *adj* MOTRIZ : motor
motor[2] *nm* 1 : motor, engine 2 : driving force, cause
motorista *nmf* : motorist
motriz *adj, pl* **motrices** : driving
motu proprio *adv* **de motu proprio** [de ˈmotuˈproprio] : voluntarily, of one's own accord
mousse [ˈmus] *nmf* : mousse
mover {47} *vt* 1 TRASLADAR : to move, to shift 2 AGITAR : to shake, to nod (the head) 3 ACCIONAR : to power, to drive 4 INDUCIR : to provoke, to cause 5 : to excite, to stir — **moverse** *vr* 1

: to move, to move over 2 : to hurry, to get a move on 3 : to get moving, to make an effort
movible *adj* : movable
movida *nf* : move (in a game)
móvil[1] *adj* : mobile
móvil[2] *nm* 1 MOTIVO : motive 2 : mobile
movilidad *nf* : mobility
movilizar {21} *vt* : to mobilize — **movilización** *nf*
movimiento *nm* : movement, motion ⟨movimiento del cuerpo : bodily movement⟩ ⟨movimiento sindicalista : labor movement⟩
mozo[1], **-za** *adj* : young, youthful
mozo[2], **-za** *n* 1 JOVEN : young man *m*, young woman *f*, youth 2 : helper, servant 3 *Arg, Chile, Col, Peru* : waiter *m*, waitress *f*
mucamo, -ma *n* : servant, maid *f*
muchacha *nf* : maid
muchacho, -cha *n* 1 : kid, boy *m*, girl *f* 2 JOVEN : young man *m*, young woman *f*
muchedumbre *nf* MULTITUD : crowd, multitude
mucho[1] *adv* 1 : much, a lot ⟨mucho más : much more⟩ ⟨le gusta mucho : he likes it a lot⟩ 2 : long, a long time ⟨tardó mucho en venir : he was a long time getting here⟩ 3 **por mucho que** : no matter how much
mucho[2], **-cha** *adj* 1 : a lot of, many, much ⟨mucha gente : a lot of people⟩ ⟨hace mucho tiempo que no lo veo : I haven't seen him in ages⟩ 2 **muchas veces** : often
mucho[3], **-cha** *pron* 1 : a lot, many, much ⟨hay mucho que hacer : there is a lot to do⟩ ⟨muchas no vinieron : many didn't come⟩ 2 **cuando ∼** *or* **como ∼** : at most 3 **con ∼** : by far 4 **ni mucho menos** : not at all, far from it
mucílago *nm* : mucilage
mucosidad *nf* : mucus
mucoso, -sa *adj* : mucous, slimy
muda *nf* 1 : change ⟨muda de ropa : change of clothes⟩ 2 : molt, molting
mudanza *nf* 1 CAMBIO : change 2 TRASLADO : move, moving
mudar *v* 1 CAMBIAR : to change 2 : to molt, to shed — **mudarse** *vr* 1 TRASLADARSE : to move (one's residence) 2 : to change (clothes)
mudo[1], **-da** *adj* 1 SILENCIOSO : silent ⟨el cine mudo : silent films⟩ 2 : mute, dumb
mudo[2], **-da** *n* : mute
mueble *nm* 1 : piece of furniture 2 **muebles** *nmpl* : furniture, furnishings
mueblería *nf* : furniture store
mueca *nf* : grimace, face
muela *nf* 1 : tooth, molar ⟨dolor de muelas : toothache⟩ ⟨muela de juicio : wisdom tooth⟩ 2 : millstone 3 : whetstone
muele, etc. → **moler**

muelle[1] *adj* : soft, comfortable, easy
muelle[2] *nm* **1** : wharf, dock **2** RESORTE
: spring
muérdago *nm* : mistletoe
muerde, etc. → **morder**
muere, etc. → **morir**
muerte *nf* : death
muerto[1] *pp* → **morir**
muerto[2], **-ta** *adj* **1** : dead **2** : lifeless, flat,
dull **3** ~ **de** : dying of ⟨estoy muerto
de hambre : I'm dying of hunger⟩
muerto[3], **-ta** *nm* DIFUNTO : dead person,
deceased
muesca *nf* : nick, notch
muestra[1], **etc.** → **mostrar**
muestra[2] *nf* **1** : sample **2** SEÑAL : sign,
show ⟨una muestra de respeto : a show
of respect⟩ **3** EXPOSICIÓN : exhibition,
exposition **4** : pattern, model
mueve, etc. → **mover**
mugido *nm* : moo, lowing, bellow
mugir {35} *vi* : to moo, to low, to bellow
mugre *nf* SUCIEDAD : grime, filth
mugriento, -ta *adj* : filthy
muguete *nm* : lily of the valley
muja, etc. → **mugir**
mujer *nf* **1** : woman **2** ESPOSA : wife
mulato, -ta *adj & n* : mulatto
muleta *nf* : crutch
mullido, -da *adj* **1** : soft, fluffy **2**
: spongy, springy
mulo, -la *n* : mule
multa *nf* : fine
multar *vt* : to fine
multicolor *adj* : multicolored
multicultural *adj* : multicultural
multidisciplinario, -ria *adj* : multidisci-
plinary
multifacético, -ca *adj* : multifaceted
multifamiliar *adj* : multifamily
multilateral *adj* : multilateral
multimedia *nf* : multimedia
multimillonario, -ria *n* : multimillionaire
multinacional *adj* : multinational
múltiple *adj* : multiple
multiplicación *nf, pl* **-ciones** : multiplication
multiplicar {72} *v* **1** : to multiply **2** : to
increase — **multiplicarse** *vr* : to multiply, to reproduce
multiplicidad *nf* : multiplicity
múltiplo *nm* : multiple
multitud *nf* MUCHEDUMBRE : crowd,
multitude
multiuso, -sa *adj* : multipurpose
multivitamínico, -ca *adj* : multivitamin
mundano, -na *adj* : worldly, earthly
mundial *adj* : world, worldwide
mundialmente *adv* : worldwide, all over
the world

mundo *nm* **1** : world **2 todo el mundo**
: everyone, everybody
municiones *nfpl* : ammunition, munitions
municipal *adj* : municipal
municipio *nm* **1** : municipality **2** AYUN-
TAMIENTO : town council
muñeca *nf* **1** : doll **2** MANIQUÍ : mannequin **3** : wrist
muñeco *nm* **1** : doll, boy doll **2** MARI-
ONETA : puppet
muñón *nm, pl* **muñones** : stump (of an
arm or leg)
mural *adj & nm* : mural
muralista *nmf* : muralist
muralla *nf* : rampart, wall
murciélago *nm* : bat (animal)
murga *nf* : band of street musicians
murió, etc. → **morir**
murmullo *nm* **1** : murmur, murmuring
2 : rustling, rustle ⟨el murmullo de las
hojas : the rustling of the leaves⟩
murmurar *vt* **1** : to murmur, to mutter
2 : to whisper (gossip) — *vi* **1** : to murmur **2** CHISMEAR : to gossip
muro *nm* : wall
musa *nf* : muse
musaraña *nf* : shrew
muscular *adj* : muscular
musculatura *nf* : muscles *pl*, musculature
músculo *nm* : muscle
musculoso, -sa *adj* : muscular, brawny
muselina *nf* : muslin
museo *nm* : museum
musgo *nm* : moss
musgoso, -sa *adj* : mossy
música *nf* : music
musical *adj* : musical — **musicalmente**
adv
músico[1], **-ca** *adj* : musical
músico[2], **-ca** *n* : musician
musitar *vt* : to mumble, to murmur
muslo *nm* : thigh
musulmán, -mana *adj & n, mpl* **-manes**
: Muslim
mutación *nf, pl* **-ciones** : mutation
mutante *adj & nm* : mutant
mutar *v* : to mutate
mutilar *vt* : to mutilate — **mutilación** *nf*
mutis *nm* **1** : exit (in theater) **2** : silence
mutual *adj* : mutual
mutuo, -tua *adj* : mutual, reciprocal —
mutuamente *adv*
muy *adv* **1** : very, quite ⟨es muy inteligente : she's very intelligent⟩ ⟨muy
bien : very well, fine⟩ ⟨eso es muy
americano : that's typically American⟩
2 : too ⟨es muy grande para él : it's too
big for him⟩

N

n *nf* : fourteenth letter of the Spanish alphabet

nabo *nm* : turnip

nácar *nm* MADREPERLA : nacre, mother-of-pearl

nacarado, -da *adj* : pearly

nacer {48} *vi* **1** : to be born ⟨nací en Guatemala : I was born in Guatemala⟩ ⟨no nació ayer : he wasn't born yesterday⟩ **2** : to hatch **3** : to bud, to sprout **4** : to rise, to originate **5 nacer para algo** : to be born to be something **6 volver a nacer** : to have a lucky escape

nacido¹, -da *adj* **1** : born **2 recién nacido** : newborn

nacido², -da *n* **1 los nacidos** : those born (at a particular time) **2 recién nacido** : newborn baby

naciente *adj* **1** : newfound, growing **2** : rising ⟨el sol naciente : the rising sun⟩

nacimiento *nm* **1** : birth **2** : source (of a river) **3** : beginning, origin **4** BELÉN : Nativity scene, crèche

nación *nf, pl* **naciones** : nation, country, people (of a country)

nacional¹ *adj* : national

nacional² *nmf* CIUDADANO : national, citizen

nacionalidad *nf* : nationality

nacionalismo *nm* : nationalism

nacionalista¹ *adj* : nationalist, nationalistic

nacionalista² *nmf* : nationalist

nacionalización *nf, pl* **-ciones** **1** : nationalization **2** : naturalization

nacionalizar {21} *vt* **1** : to nationalize **2** : to naturalize (as a citizen) — **nacionalizarse** *vr*

naco, -ca *adj Mex* : trashy, vulgar, common

nada¹ *adv* : not at all, not in the least ⟨no estamos nada cansados : we are not at all tired⟩

nada² *nf* **1** : nothingness **2** : smidgen, bit ⟨una nada le disgusta : the slightest thing upsets him⟩

nada³ *pron* **1** : nothing ⟨no estoy haciendo nada : I'm not doing anything⟩ **2 casi nada** : next to nothing **3 de ~** : you're welcome **4 dentro de nada** : very soon, in no time **5 nada más** : nothing else, nothing more

nadador, -dora *n* : swimmer

nadar *vi* **1** : to swim **2 ~ en** : to be swimming in, to be rolling in — *vt* : to swim

nadería *nf* : small thing, trifle

nadie *pron* : nobody, no one ⟨no vi a nadie : I didn't see anyone⟩

nadir *nm* : nadir

nado *nm* **1** *Mex* : swimming **2 a ~** : swimming ⟨cruzó el río a nado : he swam across the river⟩

nafta *nf* **1** : naphtha **2** (*in various countries*) : gasoline

naftalina *nf* : naphthalene, mothballs *pl*

náhuatl¹ *adj & nmf, pl* **nahuas** : Nahuatl

náhuatl² *nm* : Nahuatl (language)

nailon → nilón

naipe *nm* : playing card

nalga *nf* **1** : buttock **2 nalgas** *nfpl* : buttocks, bottom

nalgada *nf* : smack on the bottom, spanking

namibio, -bia *adj & n* : Namibian

nana *nf* **1** : lullaby **2** *fam* : grandma **3** *CA, Col, Mex, Ven* : nanny

nanay *interj fam* : no way!, not likely!

naranja¹ *adj & nm* : orange (color)

naranja² *nf* : orange (fruit)

naranjal *nm* : orange grove

naranjo *nm* : orange tree

narcisismo *nm* : narcissism

narcisista¹ *adj* : narcissistic

narcisista² *nmf* : narcissist

narciso *nm* : narcissus, daffodil

narcótico¹, -ca *adj* : narcotic

narcótico² *nm* : narcotic

narcotizar {21} *vt* : to drug, to dope

narcotraficante *nmf* : drug trafficker

narcotráfico *nm* : drug trafficking

narigón, -gona *adj, mpl* **-gones** : big-nosed

narigudo → narigón

nariz *nf, pl* **narices** **1** : nose ⟨sonar(se) la nariz : to blow one's nose⟩ **2** : sense of smell

narración *nf, pl* **-ciones** : narration, account

narrador, -dora *n* : narrator

narrar *vt* : to narrate, to tell

narrativa *nf* : narrative, story

narrativo, -va *adj* : narrative

narval *nm* : narwhal

nasa *nf* : creel

nasal *adj* : nasal

nata *nf* **1** : cream ⟨nata batida : whipped cream⟩ **2** : skin (on boiled milk)

natación *nf, pl* **-ciones** : swimming

natal *adj* : native, natal

natalicio *nm* : birthday ⟨el natalicio de George Washington : George Washington's birthday⟩

natalidad *nf* : birthrate

natillas *nfpl* : custard

natividad *nf* : birth, nativity

nativo, -va *adj & n* : native

nato, -ta *adj* : born, natural

natural¹ *adj* **1** : natural **2** : normal ⟨como es natural : naturally, as expected⟩ **3 ~ de** : native of, from **4 de tamaño natural** : life-size

natural² *nm* **1** CARÁCTER : disposition, temperament **2** : native ⟨un natural de Venezuela : a native of Venezuela⟩

naturaleza *nf* **1** : nature ⟨la madre naturaleza : mother nature⟩ **2** ÍNDOLE : nature, disposition, constitution ⟨la naturaleza humana : human nature⟩ **3 naturaleza muerta** : still life

naturalidad *nf* : simplicity, naturalness
naturalismo *nm* : naturalism
naturalista[1] *adj* : naturalistic
naturalista[2] *nmf* : naturalist
naturalización *nf, pl* **-ciones** : naturalization
naturalizar {21} *vt* : to naturalize — **naturalizarse** *vr* NACIONALIZARSE : to become naturalized
naturalmente *adv* **1** : naturally, inherently **2** : of course
naufragar {52} *vi* **1** : to be shipwrecked **2** FRACASAR : to fail, to collapse
naufragio *nm* **1** : shipwreck **2** FRACASO : failure, collapse
náufrago[1], **-ga** *adj* : shipwrecked, castaway
náufrago[2], **-ga** *n* : shipwrecked person, castaway
náusea *nf* **1** : nausea **2 dar náuseas** : to nauseate, to disgust **3 náuseas matutinas** : morning sickness
nauseabundo, -da *adj* : nauseating, sickening
náutica *nf* : navigation
náutico, -ca *adj* : nautical
nautilo *nm* : nautilus
navaja *nf* **1** : pocketknife, penknife ⟨navaja de muelle : switchblade⟩ **2 navaja de afeitar** : straight razor, razor blade
navajo, -ja *adj & n* : Navajo
naval *adj* : naval
nave *nf* **1** : ship ⟨nave capitana : flagship⟩ ⟨nave espacial : spaceship⟩ **2** : nave ⟨nave lateral : aisle⟩ **3 quemar uno sus naves** : to burn one's bridges
navegabilidad *nf* : navigability
navegable *adj* : navigable
navegación *nf, pl* **-ciones** : navigation
navegante[1] *adj* : sailing, seafaring
navegante[2] *nmf* : navigator
navegar {52} *v* : to navigate, to sail
Navidad *nf* : Christmas, Christmastime ⟨Feliz Navidad : Merry Christmas⟩
navideño, -ña *adj* : Christmas
naviero, -ra *adj* : shipping
náyade *nf* : naiad
nazca, etc. → nacer
nazi *adj & nmf* : Nazi
nazismo *nm* : Nazism
nébeda *nf* : catnip
neblina *nf* : light fog, mist
neblinoso, -sa *adj* : misty, foggy
nebulosa *nf* : nebula
nebulosidad *nf* : mistiness, haziness
nebuloso, -sa *adj* **1** : hazy, misty **2** : nebulous, vague
necedad *nf* : stupidity, foolishness ⟨decir necedades : to talk nonsense⟩
necesariamente *adv* : necessarily
necesario, -ria *adj* **1** : necessary **2 si es necesario** : if need be **3 hacerse necesario** : to be required
neceser *nm* : toilet kit, vanity case
necesidad *nf* **1** : need, necessity **2** : poverty, want **3 necesidades** *nfpl* : hardships **4 hacer sus necesidades** : to relieve oneself

necesitado, -da *adj* : needy
necesitar *vt* **1** : to need **2** : to necessitate, to require — *vi* **~ de** : to have need of
necio[1], **-cia** *adj* **1** : foolish, silly, dumb **2** *fam* : naughty
necio[2], **-cia** *n* ESTÚPIDO : fool, idiot
necrología *nf* : obituary
necrópolis *nfs & pl* : cemetery
néctar *nm* : nectar
nectarina *nf* : nectarine
neerlandés[1], **-desa** *adj, mpl* **-deses** HOLANDÉS : Dutch
neerlandés[2], **-desa** *n, mpl* **-deses** HOLANDÉS : Dutch person, Dutchman *m*
nefando, -da *adj* : unspeakable, heinous
nefario, -ria *adj* : nefarious
nefasto, -ta *adj* **1** : ill-fated, unlucky **2** : disastrous, terrible
negación *nf, pl* **-ciones** **1** : negation, denial **2** : negative (in grammar)
negar {49} *vt* **1** : to deny **2** REHUSAR : to refuse **3** : to disown — **negarse** *vr* **1** : to refuse **2** : to deny oneself
negativa *nf* **1** : denial **2** : refusal
negativo[1], **-va** *adj* : negative
negativo[2] *nm* : negative (of a photograph)
negligé *nm* : negligee
negligencia *nf* : negligence
negligente *adj* : neglectful, negligent — **negligentemente** *adv*
negociable *adj* : negotiable
negociación *nf, pl* **-ciones** **1** : negotiation **2 negociación colectiva** : collective bargaining
negociador, -dora *n* : negotiator
negociante *nmf* : businessman *m*, businesswoman *f*
negociar *vt* : to negotiate — *vi* : to deal, to do business
negocio *nm* **1** : business, place of business **2** : deal, transaction **3 negocios** *nmpl* : commerce, trade, business
negrero, -ra *n* **1** : slave trader **2** *fam* : slave driver, brutal boss
negrita *nf* : boldface (type)
negro[1], **-gra** *adj* **1** : black, dark **2** BRONCEADO : suntanned **3** : gloomy, awful, desperate ⟨la cosa se está poniendo negra : things are looking bad⟩ **4 mercado negro** : black market
negro[2], **-gra** *n* **1** : dark-skinned person, black person **2** *fam* : darling, dear
negro[3] *nm* : black (color)
negrura *nf* : blackness
negruzco, -ca *adj* : blackish
nene, -na *n* : baby, small child
nenúfar *nm* : water lily
neocelandés → neozelandés
neoclasicismo *nm* : neoclassicism
neoclásico, -ca *adj* : neoclassical
neófito, -ta *n* : neophyte, novice
neologismo *nm* : neologism
neón *nm, pl* **neones** : neon
neoyorquino[1], **-na** *adj* : of or from New York

neoyorquino², -na *n* : New Yorker
neozelandés¹, -desa *adj, mpl* **-deses** : of or from New Zealand
neozelandés², -desa *n, mpl* **-deses** : New Zealander
nepalés, -lesa *adj & n, mpl* **-leses** : Nepali
nepotismo *nm* : nepotism
neptunio *nm* : neptunium
Neptuno *nm* : Neptune
nervio *nm* **1** : nerve **2** : tendon, sinew, gristle (in meat) **3** : energy, drive **4** : rib (of a vault) **5 nervios** *nmpl* : nerves ⟨estar mal de los nervios : to be a bundle of nerves⟩ ⟨ataque de nervios : nervous breakdown⟩
nerviosamente *adv* : nervously
nerviosidad → nerviosismo
nerviosismo *nf* : nervousness, anxiety
nervioso, -sa *adj* **1** : nervous, nerve ⟨sistema nervioso : nervous system⟩ **2** : high-strung, restless, anxious ⟨ponerse nervioso : to get nervous⟩ **3** : vigorous, energetic
nervudo, -da *adj* : sinewy, wiry
neta *nf Mex fam* : truth ⟨la neta es que me cae mal : the truth is, I don't like her⟩
netamente *adv* : clearly, obviously
neto, -ta *adj* **1** : net ⟨peso neto : net weight⟩ **2** : clear, distinct
neumático¹, -ca *adj* : pneumatic
neumático² *nm* LLANTA : tire
neumonía *nf* PULMONÍA : pneumonia
neural *adj* : neural
neuralgia *nf* : neuralgia
neuritis *nf* : neuritis
neurología *nf* : neurology
neurológico, -ca *adj* : neurological, neurologic
neurólogo, -ga *n* : neurologist
neurosis *nfs & pl* : neurosis
neurótico, -ca *adj & n* : neurotic
neutral *adj* : neutral
neutralidad *nf* : neutrality
neutralizar {21} *vt* : to neutralize — **neutralización** *nf*
neutro, -tra *adj* **1** : neutral **2** : neuter
neutrón *nm, pl* **neutrones** : neutron
nevada *nf* : snowfall
nevado, -da *adj* **1** : snowcapped **2** : snow-white
nevar {55} *v impers* : to snow
nevasca *nf* : snowstorm, blizzard
nevera *nf* REFRIGERADOR : refrigerator
nevería *nf Mex* : ice cream parlor
nevisca *nf* : light snowfall, flurry
nevoso, -sa *adj* : snowy
nexo *nm* VÍNCULO : link, connection, nexus
ni *conj* **1** : neither, nor ⟨afuera no hace ni frío ni calor : it's neither cold nor hot outside⟩ **2 ni que** : not even if, not as if ⟨ni que me pagaran : not even if they paid me⟩ ⟨ni que fuera (yo) su madre : it's not as if I were his mother⟩ **3 ni siquiera** : not even ⟨ni siquiera nos llamaron : they didn't even call us⟩

nicaragüense *adj & nmf* : Nicaraguan
nicho *nm* : niche
nicotina *nf* : nicotine
nido *nm* **1** : nest **2** : hiding place, den
niebla *nf* : fog, mist
niega, niegue etc. → negar
nieto, -ta *n* **1** : grandson *m*, granddaughter *f* **2 nietos** *nmpl* : grandchildren
nieva, etc. → nevar
nieve *nf* **1** : snow **2** *Cuba, Mex, PRi* : sherbet
nigeriano, -na *adj & n* : Nigerian
nigua *nf* : sand flea, chigger
nihilismo *nm* : nihilism
nilón *or* **nilon** *nm, pl* **nilones** : nylon
nimbo *nm* **1** : halo **2** : nimbus
nimiedad *nf* INSIGNIFICANCIA : trifle, triviality
nimio, -mia *adj* INSIGNIFICANTE : insignificant, trivial
ninfa *nf* : nymph
ningunear *vt Mex fam* : to disrespect
ninguno¹, -na (**ningún** *before masculine singular nouns*) *adj, mpl* **ningunos** : no, none ⟨no es ninguna tonta : she's no fool⟩ ⟨no debe hacerse en ningún momento : that should never be done⟩
ninguno², -na *pron* **1** : neither, none ⟨ninguno de los dos ha vuelto aún : neither one has returned yet⟩ **2** : no one, no other ⟨te quiero más que a ninguna : I love you more than any other⟩
niña *nf* **1** PUPILA : pupil (of the eye) **2 la niña de los ojos** : the apple of one's eye
niñada *nf* **1** : childishness **2** : trifle, silly thing
niñería → niñada
niñero, -ra *n* : baby-sitter, nanny
niñez *nf, pl* **niñeces** INFANCIA : childhood
niño, -ña *n* : child, boy *m*, girl *f*
niobio *nm* : niobium
nipón, -pona *adj & n, mpl* **nipones** JAPONÉS : Japanese
níquel *nm* : nickel
nitidez *nf, pl* **-deces** CLARIDAD : clarity, vividness, sharpness
nítido, -da *adj* CLARO : clear, vivid, sharp
nitrato *nm* : nitrate
nítrico, -ca *adj* **ácido nítrico** : nitric acid
nitrito *nm* : nitrite
nitrógeno *nm* : nitrogen
nitroglicerina *nf* : nitroglycerin
nivel *nm* **1** : level, height ⟨nivel del mar : sea level⟩ **2** : level, standard ⟨nivel de vida : standard of living⟩
nivelar *vt* : to level (out)
nixtamal *nm Mex* : limed corn used for tortillas
no *adv* **1** : no ⟨¿quieres ir al mercado? no, voy más tarde : do you want to go shopping? no, I'm going later⟩ **2** : not ⟨no hagas eso! : don't do that!⟩ ⟨creo que no : I don't think so⟩ **3** : non- ⟨no fumador : non-smoker⟩ **4 ¡como no!** : of course! **5 no bien** : as soon as, no sooner

nobelio *nm* : nobelium
noble¹ *adj* : noble — **noblemente** *adv*
noble² *nmf* : nobleman *m*, noblewoman *f*
nobleza *nf* **1** : nobility **2** HONRADEZ : honesty, integrity
nocaut *nm* : knockout, KO
noche *nf* **1** : night, nighttime, evening **2 buenas noches** : good evening, good night **3 de noche** *or* **por la noche** : at night **4 hacerse de noche** : to get dark
Nochebuena *nf* : Christmas Eve
nochecita *nf* : dusk
Nochevieja *nf* : New Year's Eve
noción *nf, pl* **nociones 1** CONCEPTO : notion, concept **2 nociones** *nfpl* : smattering, rudiments *pl*
nocivo, -va *adj* DAÑINO : harmful, noxious
noctámbulo, -la *n* **1** : sleepwalker **2** : night owl
nocturno¹, -na *adj* : night, nocturnal
nocturno² *nm* : nocturne
nodriza *nf* : wet nurse
nódulo *nm* : nodule
nogal *nm* **1** : walnut tree **2** *Mex* : pecan tree **3 nogal americano** : hickory
nómada¹ *adj* : nomadic
nómada² *nmf* : nomad
nomás *adv* : only, just ⟨lo hice nomás porque sí : I did it just because⟩ ⟨nomás de recordarlo me enojo : I get angry just remembering it⟩ ⟨nomás faltan dos semanas para Navidad : there are only two weeks left till Christmas⟩
nombradía *nf* RENOMBRE : fame, renown
nombrado, -da *adj* : famous, well-known
nombramiento *nm* : appointment, nomination
nombrar *vt* **1** : to appoint **2** : to mention, to name
nombre *nm* **1** : name ⟨nombre de pluma : pseudonym, pen name⟩ ⟨en nombre : on behalf of⟩ ⟨sin nombre : nameless⟩ **2** : noun ⟨nombre propio : proper noun⟩ **3** : fame, renown
nomenclatura *nf* : nomenclature
nomeolvides *nmfs & pl* : forget-me-not
nómina *nf* : payroll
nominación *nf, pl* **-ciones** : nomination
nominal *adj* : nominal — **nominalmente** *adv*
nominar *vt* : to nominate
nominativo¹, -va *adj* : nominative
nominativo² *nm* : nominative (case)
nomo *nm* : gnome
non¹ *adj* IMPAR : odd, not even
non² *nm* : odd number
nonagésimo¹, -ma *adj* : ninetieth, ninety-
nonagésimo², -ma *n* : ninetieth, ninety- (in a series)
nono, -na *adj* : ninth — **nono** *nm*
nopal *nm* : nopal, cactus
nopalitos *nmpl Mex* : pickled cactus leaves
noquear *vt* : to knock out, to KO

norcoreano, -na *adj & n* : North Korean
nordeste¹ *or* **noreste** *adj* **1** : northeastern **2** : northeasterly
nordeste² *or* **noreste** *nm* : northeast
nórdico, -ca *adj & n* **1** ESCANDINAVO : Scandinavian **2** : Norse
noreste → **nordeste**
noria *nf* **1** : waterwheel **2** : Ferris wheel
norirlandés¹, -desa *adj, mpl* **-deses** : Northern Irish
norirlandés², -desa *n, mpl* **-deses** : person from Northern Ireland
norma *nf* **1** : rule, regulation **2** : norm, standard
normal *adj* **1** : normal, usual **2** : standard **3 escuela normal** : teacher-training college
normalidad *nf* : normality, normalcy
normalización *nf, pl* **-ciones** *nf* **1** REGULARIZACIÓN : normalization **2** ESTANDARIZACIÓN : standardization
normalizar {21} *vt* **1** REGULARIZAR : to normalize **2** ESTANDARIZAR : to standardize — **normalizarse** *vr* : to return to normal
normalmente *adv* GENERALMENTE : ordinarily, generally
noroeste¹ *adj* **1** : northwestern **2** : northwesterly
noroeste² *nm* : northwest
norte¹ *adj* : north, northern
norte² *nm* **1** : north **2** : north wind **3** META : aim, objective
norteamericano, -na *adj & n* **1** : North American **2** AMERICANO, ESTADOUNIDENSE : American, native or inhabitant of the United States
norteño¹, -ña *adj* : northern
norteño², -ña *n* : Northerner
noruego¹, -ga *adj & n* : Norwegian
noruego² *nm* : Norwegian (language)
nos *pron* **1** : us ⟨nos enviaron a la frontera : they sent us to the border⟩ **2** : ourselves ⟨nos divertimos muchísimo : we enjoyed ourselves a great deal⟩ **3** : each other, one another ⟨nos vimos desde lejos : we saw each other from far away⟩ **4** : to us, for us, from us ⟨nos lo dio : he gave it to us⟩ ⟨nos lo compraron : they bought it from us⟩
nosotros, -tras *pron* **1** : we ⟨nosotros llegamos ayer : we arrived yesterday⟩ **2** : us ⟨ven con nosotros : come with us⟩ **3 nosotros mismos** : ourselves ⟨lo arreglamos nosotros mismos : we fixed it ourselves⟩
nostalgia *nf* **1** : nostalgia, longing **2** : homesickness
nostálgico, -ca *adj* **1** : nostalgic **2** : homesick
nota *nf* **1** : note, message **2** : announcement ⟨nota de prensa : press release⟩ **3** : grade, mark (in school) **4** : characteristic, feature, touch **5** : note (in music) **6** : bill, check (in a restaurant)

notable *adj* 1 : notable, noteworthy 2 : outstanding

notación *nf, pl* **-ciones** : notation

notar *vt* 1 : to notice ⟨hacer notar algo : to point out something⟩ 2 : to tell ⟨la diferencia se nota inmediatamente : you can tell the difference right away⟩ — **notarse** *vr* 1 : to be evident, to show 2 : to feel, to seem

notario, -ria *n* : notary, notary public

noticia *nf* 1 : news item, piece of news 2 **noticias** *nfpl* : news

noticiero *nm* : news program, newscast

noticioso, -sa *adj* : news ⟨agencia noticiosa : news agency⟩

notificación *nf, pl* **-ciones** : notification

notificar {72} *vt* : to notify, to inform

notoriedad *nf* 1 : knowledge, obviousness 2 : fame, notoriety

notorio, -ria *adj* 1 OBVIO : obvious, evident 2 CONOCIDO : well-known

novato¹, -ta *adj* : inexperienced, new

novato², -ta *n* : beginner, novice

novecientos¹, -tas *adj* : nine hundred

novecientos² *nms & pl* : nine hundred

novedad *nf* 1 : newness, novelty 2 : innovation

novedoso, -sa *adj* : original, novel

novel *adj* NOVATO : inexperienced, new

novela *nf* 1 : novel 2 : soap opera

novelar *vt* : to fictionalize, to make a novel out of

novelesco, -ca *adj* 1 : fictional 2 : fantastic, fabulous

novelista *nmf* : novelist

novena *nf* : novena

noveno, -na *adj* : ninth — **noveno, -na** *n*

noventa *adj & nm* : ninety

noventavo¹, -va *adj* : ninetieth

noventavo² *nm* : ninetieth (fraction)

noviazgo *nm* 1 : courtship, relationship 2 : engagement, betrothal

novicio, -cia *n* 1 : novice (in religion) 2 PRINCIPIANTE : novice, beginner

noviembre *nm* : November

novilla *nf* : heifer

novillada *nf* : bullfight featuring young bulls

novillero, -ra *n* : apprentice bullfighter

novillo *nm* : young bull

novio, -via *n* 1 : boyfriend *m*, girlfriend *f* 2 PROMETIDO : fiancé *m*, fiancée *f* 3 : bridegroom *m*, bride *f*

novocaína *nf* : novocaine

nubarrón *nm, pl* **-rrones** : storm cloud

nube *nf* 1 : cloud ⟨andar en las nubes : to have one's head in the clouds⟩ ⟨por las nubes : sky-high⟩ 2 : cloud (of dust), swarm (of insects, etc.)

nublado¹, -da *adj* 1 NUBOSO : cloudy, overcast 2 : clouded, dim

nublado² *nm* 1 : storm cloud 2 AMENAZA : menace, threat

nublar *vt* 1 : to cloud 2 OSCURECER : to obscure — **nublarse** *vr* : to get cloudy

nubosidad *nf* : cloudiness

nuboso, -sa *adj* NUBLADO : cloudy

nuca *nf* : nape, back of the neck

nuclear *adj* : nuclear

núcleo *nm* 1 : nucleus 2 : center, heart, core

nudillo *nm* : knuckle

nudismo *nm* : nudism

nudista *adj & nmf* : nudist

nudo *nm* 1 : knot ⟨nudo de rizo : square knot⟩ ⟨un nudo en la garganta : a lump in one's throat⟩ 2 : node 3 : junction, hub ⟨nudo de comunicaciones : communication center⟩ 4 : crux, heart (of a problem, etc.)

nudoso, -sa *adj* : knotty, gnarled

nuera *nf* : daughter-in-law

nuestro¹, -tra *adj* : our

nuestro², -tra *pron* (*with definite article*) : ours, our own ⟨el nuestro es más grande : ours is bigger⟩ ⟨es de los nuestros : it's one of ours⟩

nuevamente *adv* : again, anew

nuevas *nfpl* : tidings *pl*

nueve *adj & nm* : nine

nuevecito, -ta *adj* : brand-new

nuevo, -va *adj* 1 : new ⟨una casa nueva : a new house⟩ ⟨¿qué hay de nuevo? : what's new?⟩ 2 **de ~** : again, once more 3 **Nuevo Testamento** : New Testament

nuez *nf, pl* **nueces** 1 : nut 2 : walnut 3 *Mex* : pecan 4 **nuez de Adán** : Adam's apple 5 **nuez moscada** : nutmeg

nulidad *nf* 1 : nullity 2 : incompetent person ⟨¡es una nulidad! : he's hopeless!⟩

nulo, -la *adj* 1 : null, null and void 2 INEPTO : useless, inept ⟨es nula para la cocina : she's hopeless at cooking⟩

numen *nm* : poetic muse, inspiration

numerable *adj* : countable

numeración *nf, pl* **-ciones** 1 : numbering 2 : numbers *pl*, numerals *pl* ⟨numeración romana : Roman numerals⟩

numerador *nm* : numerator

numeral *adj* : numeral

numerar *vt* : to number

numerario, -ria *adj* : long-standing, permanent ⟨profesor numerario : tenured professor⟩

numérico, -ca *adj* : numerical — **numéricamente** *adv*

número *nm* 1 : number ⟨número impar : odd number⟩ ⟨número ordinal : ordinal number⟩ ⟨número arábico : Arabic numeral⟩ ⟨número quebrado : fraction⟩ 2 : issue (of a publication) 3 **sin ~** : countless

numeroso, -sa *adj* : numerous

numismática *nf* : numismatics

nunca *adv* 1 : never, ever ⟨nunca es tarde : it's never too late⟩ ⟨no trabaja casi nunca : he hardly ever works⟩ 2 **nunca más** : never again 3 **nunca jamás** : never ever

nuncio *nm* : harbinger, herald

nupcial *adj* : nuptial, wedding

nupcias *nfpl* : nuptials *pl*, wedding

nutria *nf* **1** : otter **2** : nutria
nutrición *nf, pl* **-ciones** : nutrition, nourishment
nutrido, -da *adj* **1** : nourished ⟨mal nutrido : undernourished, malnourished⟩ **2** : considerable, abundant ⟨de nutrido : full of, abounding in⟩
nutriente *nm* : nutrient
nutrimento *nm* : nutriment
nutrir *vt* **1** ALIMENTAR : to feed, to nourish **2** : to foster, to provide
nutritivo, -va *adj* : nourishing, nutritious

nylon → **nilón**
ñ *nf* : fifteenth letter of the Spanish alphabet
ñame *nm* : yam
ñandú *nm* : rhea
ñapa *nf* : extra amount ⟨de ñapa : for good measure⟩
ñoñear *vi fam* : to whine
ñoño, -ña *adj fam* : whiny, fussy ⟨no seas tan ñoño : don't be such a wimp⟩
ñoquis *nmpl* : gnocchi *pl*
ñu *nm* : gnu, wildebeest

O

o¹ *nf* : sixteenth letter of the Spanish alphabet
o² *conj* (**u** *before words beginning with o- or ho-*) **1** : or ⟨¿vienes con nosotros o te quedas? : are you coming with us or staying?⟩ **2** : either ⟨o vienes con nosotros o te quedas : either you come with us or you stay⟩ **3 o sea** : that is to say, in other words
oasis *nms & pl* : oasis
obcecado, -da *adj* **1** : blinded ⟨obcecado por la ira : blinded by rage⟩ **2** : stubborn, obstinate
obcecar {72} *vt* : to blind (by emotions) — **obcecarse** *vr* : to become stubborn
obedecer {53} *vt* : to obey ⟨obedecer órdenes : to obey orders⟩ ⟨obedece a tus padres : obey your parents⟩ — *vi* **1** : to obey **2** ~ **a** : to respond to **3** ~ **a** : to be due to, to result from
obediencia *nf* : obedience
obediente *adj* : obedient — **obedientemente** *adv*
obelisco *nm* : obelisk
obertura *nf* : overture
obesidad *nf* : obesity
obeso, -sa *adj* : obese
óbice *nm* : obstacle, impediment
obispado *nm* DIÓCESIS : bishopric, diocese
obispo *nm* : bishop
obituario *nm* : obituary
objeción *nf, pl* **-ciones** : objection ⟨ponerle objeciones a algo : to object to something⟩
objetar *v* : to object ⟨no tengo nada que objetar : I have no objections⟩
objetividad *nf* : objectivity
objetivo¹, -va *adj* : objective — **objetivamente** *adv*
objetivo² *nm* **1** META : objective, goal, target **2** : lens
objeto *nm* **1** COSA : object, thing **2** OBJETIVO : objective, purpose ⟨con objeto de : in order to, with the aim of⟩ **3 objeto volador no identificado** : unidentified flying object
objetor, -tora *n* : objector ⟨objetor de conciencia : conscientious objector⟩
oblea *nf* **1** : wafer **2 hecho una oblea** *fam* : skinny as a rail

oblicuo, -cua *adj* : oblique — **oblicuamente** *adv*
obligación *nf, pl* **-ciones 1** DEBER : obligation, duty **2** : bond, debenture
obligado, -da *adj* **1** : obliged **2** : obligatory, compulsory **3** : customary
obligar {52} *vt* : to force, to require, to oblige — **obligarse** *vr* : to commit oneself, to undertake (to do something)
obligatorio, -ria *adj* : mandatory, required, compulsory
obliterar *vt* : to obliterate, to destroy — **obliteración** *nf*
oblongo, -ga *adj* : oblong
obnubilación *nf, pl* **-ciones** : bewilderment, confusion
obnubilar *vt* : to daze, to bewilder
oboe¹ *nm* : oboe
oboe² *nmf* : oboist
obra *nf* **1** : work ⟨obra de arte : work of art⟩ ⟨obra de teatro : play⟩ ⟨obra de consulta : reference work⟩ **2** : deed ⟨una buena obra : a good deed⟩ **3** : construction work **4 obra maestra** : masterpiece **5 obras públicas** : public works **6 por obra de** : thanks to, because of
obrar *vt* : to work, to produce ⟨obrar milagros : to work miracles⟩ — *vi* **1** : to act, to behave ⟨obrar con cautela : to act with caution⟩ **2 obrar en poder de** : to be in possession of
obrero¹, -ra *adj* : working ⟨la clase obrera : the working class⟩
obrero², -ra *n* : worker, laborer
obscenidad *nf* : obscenity
obsceno, -na *adj* : obscene
obscurecer, obscuridad, obscuro → **oscurecer, oscuridad, oscuro**
obsequiar *vt* REGALAR : to give, to present ⟨lo obsequiaron con una placa : they presented him with a plaque⟩
obsequio *nm* REGALO : gift, present
obsequiosidad *nf* : attentiveness, deference
obsequioso, -sa *adj* : obliging, attentive
observable *adj* : observable
observación *nf, pl* **-ciones 1** : observation, watching **2** : remark, comment
observador¹, -dora *adj* : observant

observador², **-dora** *n* : observer, watcher

observancia *nf* : observance

observante *adj* : observant ⟨los judíos observantes : observant Jews⟩

observar *vt* **1** : to observe, to watch ⟨estábamos observando a los niños : we were watching the children⟩ **2** NOTAR : to notice **3** ACATAR : to obey, to abide by **4** COMENTAR : to remark, to comment

observatorio *nm* : observatory

obsesión *nf*, *pl* **-siones** : obsession

obsesionar *vt* : to obsess, to preoccupy excessively — **obsesionarse** *vr*

obsesivo, -va *adj* : obsessive

obseso, -sa *adj* : obsessed

obsolescencia *nf* DESUSO : obsolescence — **obsolescente** *adj*

obsoleto, -ta *adj* DESUSADO : obsolete

obstaculizar {21} *vt* IMPEDIR : to obstruct, to hinder

obstáculo *nm* IMPEDIMENTO : obstacle

obstante¹ *conj* **no obstante** : nevertheless, however

obstante² *prep* **no obstante** : in spite of, despite ⟨mantuvo su inocencia no obstante la evidencia : he maintained his innocence in spite of the evidence⟩

obstar *v impers* ~ **a** *or* ~ **para** : to hinder, to prevent ⟨eso no obsta para que me vaya : that doesn't prevent me from leaving⟩

obstetra *nmf* TOCÓLOGO : obstetrician

obstetricia *nf* : obstetrics

obstétrico, -ca *adj* : obstetric, obstetrical

obstinación *nf*, *pl* **-ciones** **1** TERQUEDAD : obstinacy, stubbornness **2** : perseverance, tenacity

obstinado, -da *adj* **1** TERCO : obstinate, stubborn **2** : persistent — **obstinadamente** *adv*

obstinarse *vr* EMPECINARSE : to be obstinate, to be stubborn

obstrucción *nf*, *pl* **-ciones** : obstruction, blockage

obstruccionismo *nm* : obstructionism, filibustering

obstruccionista *adj* : obstructionist, filibustering

obstructor, -tora *adj* : obstructive

obstruir {41} *vt* BLOQUEAR : to obstruct, to block, to clog — **obstruirse** *vr*

obtención *nf* : obtaining, procurement

obtener {80} *vt* : to obtain, to secure, to get — **obtenible** *adj*

obturador *nm* : shutter (of a camera)

obtuso, -sa *adj* : obtuse

obtuvo, etc. → **obtener**

obús *nm*, *pl* **obuses** **1** : mortar (weapon) **2** : mortar shell

obviar *vt* : to get around (a difficulty), to avoid

obvio, -via *adj* : obvious — **obviamente** *adv*

oca *nf* : goose

ocasión *nf*, *pl* **-siones** **1** : occasion, time **2** : opportunity, chance **3** : bargain **4** **de** ~ : secondhand **5** **aviso de ocasión** *Mex* : classified ad

ocasional *adj* **1** : occasional **2** : chance, fortuitous

ocasionalmente *adv* **1** : occasionally **2** : by chance

ocasionar *vt* CAUSAR : to cause, to occasion

ocaso *nm* **1** ANOCHECER : sunset, sundown **2** DECADENCIA : decline, fall

occidental *adj* : western, occidental

occidente *nm* **1** OESTE, PONIENTE : west **2** **el Occidente** : the West

oceánico, -ca *adj* : oceanic

océano *nm* : ocean

oceanografía *nf* : oceanography

oceanográfico, -ca *adj* : oceanographic

ocelote *nm* : ocelot

ochenta *adj & nm* : eighty

ochentavo¹, -va *adj* : eightieth

ochentavo² *nm* : eightieth (fraction)

ocho *adj & nm* : eight

ochocientos¹, -tas *adj* : eight hundred

ochocientos² *ms & pl* : eight hundred

ocio *nm* **1** : free time, leisure **2** : idleness

ociosidad *nf* : idleness, inactivity

ocioso, -sa *adj* **1** INACTIVO : idle, inactive **2** INÚTIL : pointless, useless

ocre *nm* : ocher

octágono *nm* : octagon — **octagonal** *adj*

octava *nf* : octave

octavo, -va *adj* : eighth — **octavo, -va** *n*

octeto *nm* **1** : octet **2** : byte

octogésimo¹, -ma *adj* : eightieth, eighty-

octogésimo², -ma *n* : eightieth, eighty- (in a series)

octubre *nm* : October

ocular *adj* **1** : ocular, eye ⟨músculos oculares : eye muscles⟩ **2** **testigo ocular** : eyewitness

oculista *nmf* : oculist, ophthalmologist

ocultación *nf*, *pl* **-ciones** : concealment

ocultar *vt* ESCONDER : to conceal, to hide — **ocultarse** *vr*

oculto, -ta *adj* **1** ESCONDIDO : hidden, concealed **2** : occult

ocupación *nf*, *pl* **-ciones** **1** : occupation, activity **2** : occupancy **3** EMPLEO : employment, job

ocupacional *adj* : occupational, job-related

ocupado, -da *adj* **1** : busy **2** : taken ⟨este asiento está ocupado : this seat is taken⟩ **3** : occupied ⟨territorios ocupados : occupied territories⟩ **4** **señal de ocupado** : busy signal

ocupante *nmf* : occupant

ocupar *vt* **1** : to occupy, to take possession of **2** : to hold (a position) **3** : to employ, to keep busy **4** : to fill (space, time) **5** : to inhabit (a dwelling) **6** : to bother, to concern — **ocuparse** *vr* ~ **de 1** : to be concerned with **2** : to take care of

ocurrencia *nf* **1** : occurrence, event **2** : witticism **3** : bright idea

ocurrente *adj* **1** : witty **2** : clever, sharp

ocurrir *vi* : to occur, to happen — **ocurrirse** *vr* ~ **a** : to occur to, to strike ⟨se me ocurrió una mejor idea : a better idea occurred to me⟩

oda *nf* : ode

odiar *vt* ABOMINAR, ABORRECER : to hate

odio *nm* : hate, hatred

odioso, -sa *adj* ABOMINABLE, ABORRECIBLE : hateful, detestable

odisea *nf* : odyssey

odontología *nf* : dentistry, dental surgery

odontólogo, -ga *n* : dentist, dental surgeon

oeste¹ *adj* **1** : west, western ⟨la región oeste : the western region⟩ **2** : westerly

oeste² *nm* **1** : west, West **2** : west wind

ofender *vt* AGRAVIAR : to offend, to insult — *vi* : to offend, to be insulting — **ofenderse** *vr* : to take offense

ofensa *nf* : offense, insult

ofensiva *nf* : offensive ⟨pasar a la ofensiva : to go on the offensive⟩

ofensivo, -va *adj* : offensive, insulting

ofensor, -sora *n* : offender

oferente *nmf* **1** : supplier **2** FUENTE : source ⟨un oferente no identificado : an unidentified source⟩

oferta *nf* **1** : offer **2** : sale, bargain ⟨las camisas están en oferta : the shirts are on sale⟩ **3 oferta y demanda** : supply and demand

ofertar *vt* OFRECER : to offer

oficial¹ *adj* : official — **oficialmente** *adv*

oficial² *nmf* **1** : officer, police officer, commissioned officer (in the military) **2** : skilled worker

oficializar {21} *vt* : to make official

oficiante *nmf* : celebrant

oficiar *vt* **1** : to inform officially **2** : to officiate at, to celebrate (Mass) — *vi* ~ **de** : to act as

oficina *nf* : office

oficinista *nmf* : office worker

oficio *nm* **1** : trade, profession ⟨es electricista de oficio : he's an electrician by trade⟩ **2** : function, role **3** : official communication **4** : experience ⟨tener oficio : to be experienced⟩ **5** : religious ceremony

oficioso, -sa *adj* **1** EXTRAOFICIAL : unofficial **2** : officious — **oficiosamente** *adv*

ofrecer {53} *vt* **1** : to offer **2** : to provide, to give **3** : to present (an appearance, etc.) — **ofrecerse** *vr* **1** : to offer oneself, to volunteer **2** : to open up, to present itself

ofrecimiento *nm* : offer, offering

ofrenda *nf* : offering

oftalmología *nf* : ophthalmology

oftalmólogo, -ga *n* : ophthalmologist

ofuscación *nf, pl* **-ciones** : blindness, confusion

ofuscar {72} *vt* **1** : to blind, to dazzle **2** CONFUNDIR : to bewilder, to confuse — **ofuscarse** *vr* ~ **con** : to be blinded by

ogro *nm* : ogre

ohm *nm, pl* **ohms** : ohm

ohmio → **ohm**

oídas *nfpl* **de** ~ : by hearsay

oído *nm* **1** : ear ⟨oído interno : inner ear⟩ **2** : hearing ⟨duro de oído : hard of hearing⟩ **3 tocar de oído** : to play by ear

oiga, etc. → **oír**

oír {50} *vi* : to hear — *vt* **1** : to hear **2** ESCUCHAR : to listen to **3** : to pay attention to, to heed **4 ¡oye!** *or* **¡oiga!** : listen!, excuse me!, look here!

ojal *nm* : buttonhole

ojalá *interj* **1** : I hope so!, if only!, God willing! **2** : I hope, I wish, hopefully ⟨ojalá que le vaya bien! : I hope things go well for her!⟩ ⟨ojalá no llueva! : hopefully it won't rain!⟩

ojeada *nf* : glimpse, glance ⟨echar una ojeada : to have a quick look⟩

ojear *vt* : to eye, to have a look at

ojete *nm* : eyelet

ojiva *nf* : warhead

ojo *nm* **1** : eye **2** : judgment, sharpness ⟨tener buen ojo para : to be a good judge of, to have a good eye for⟩ **3** : hole (in cheese), eye (in a needle), center (of a storm) **4** : span (of a bridge) **5 a ojos vistas** : openly, publicly **6 andar con ojo** : to be careful **7 ojo de agua** *Mex* : spring, source **8 ¡ojo!** : look out!, pay attention!

ola *nf* **1** : wave **2 ola de calor** : heat wave

oleada *nf* : swell, wave ⟨una oleada de protestas : a wave of protests⟩

oleaje *nm* : waves *pl*, surf

óleo *nm* **1** : oil **2** : oil painting

oleoducto *nm* : oil pipeline

oleoso, -sa *adj* : oily

oler {51} *vt* **1** : to smell **2** INQUIRIR : to pry into, to investigate **3** AVERIGUAR : to smell out, to uncover — *vi* **1** : to smell ⟨huele mal : it smells bad⟩ **2** ~ **a** : to smell like, to smell of ⟨huele a pino : it smells like pine⟩ — **olerse** *vr* : to have a hunch, to suspect

olfatear *vt* **1** : to sniff **2** : to sense, to sniff out

olfativo, -va *adj* : olfactory

olfato *nm* **1** : sense of smell **2** : nose, instinct

oligarquía *nf* : oligarchy

olimpiada *or* **olimpíada** *nf* **1** : Olympiad **2** *or* **olympiadas** *nfpl* : Olympics *pl*

olímpico, -ca *adj* : Olympic

olisquear *vt* : to sniff at

oliva *nf* ACEITUNA : olive ⟨aceite de oliva : olive oil⟩

olivo *nm* : olive tree

olla *nf* **1** : pot ⟨olla de presión : pressure cooker⟩ **2 olla podrida** : Spanish stew

olmeca *adj & nmf* : Olmec
olmo *nm* : elm
olor *nm* : smell, odor
oloroso, -sa *adj* : scented, fragrant
olote *nm Mex* : cob, corncob
olvidadizo, -za *adj* : forgetful, absent-minded
olvidar *vt* **1** : to forget, to forget about ⟨olvida lo que pasó : forget about what happened⟩ **2** : to leave behind ⟨olvidé mi chequera en la casa : I left my checkbook at home⟩ — **olvidarse** *vr* : to forget ⟨se me olvidó mi cuaderno : I forgot my notebook⟩ ⟨se le olvidó llamarme : he forgot to call me⟩
olvido *nm* **1** : forgetfulness **2** : oblivion **3** DESCUIDO : oversight
omaní *adj & nmf* : Omani
ombligo *nm* : navel, belly button
ombudsman *nmfs & pl* : ombudsman
omelette *nmf* : omelet
ominoso, -sa *adj* : ominous — **ominosamente** *adv*
omisión *nf, pl* **-siones** : omission, neglect
omiso, -sa *adj* **1** NEGLIGENTE : neglectful **2 hacer caso omiso de** : to ignore
omitir *vt* **1** : to omit, to leave out **2** : to fail to ⟨omitió dar su nombre : he failed to give his name⟩
ómnibus *n, pl* **-bus** *or* **-buses** : bus, coach
omnipotencia *nf* : omnipotence
omnipotente *adj* TODOPODEROSO : omnipotent, almighty
omnipresencia *nf* : ubiquity, omnipresence
omnipresente *adj* : ubiquitous, omnipresent
omnisciente *adj* : omniscient — **omnisciencia** *nf*
omnívoro, -ra *adj* : omnivorous
omóplato *or* **omoplato** *nm* : shoulder blade
once *adj & nm* : eleven
onceavo[1], -va *adj* : eleventh
onceavo[2] *nm* : eleventh (fraction)
onda *nf* **1** : wave, ripple, undulation ⟨onda sonora : sound wave⟩ **2** : wave (in hair) **3** : scallop (on clothing) **4** *fam* : wavelength, understanding ⟨agarrar la onda : to get the point⟩ ⟨en la onda : on the ball, with it⟩ **5 ¿qué onda?** *fam* : what's happening?, what's up?
ondear *vi* : to ripple, to undulate, to flutter
ondulación *nf, pl* **-ciones** : undulation
ondulado, -da *adj* **1** : wavy ⟨pelo ondulado : wavy hair⟩ **2** : undulating
ondulante *adj* : undulating
ondular *vt* : to wave (hair) — *vi* : to undulate, to ripple
oneroso, -sa *adj* GRAVOSO : onerous, burdensome
ónix *nm* : onyx
onza *nf* : ounce

opacar {72} *vt* **1** : to make opaque or dull **2** : to outshine, to overshadow
opacidad *nf* **1** : opacity **2** : dullness
opaco, -ca *adj* **1** : opaque **2** : dull
ópalo *nm* : opal
opción *nf, pl* **opciones 1** ALTERNATIVA : option, choice **2** : right, chance ⟨tener opción a : to be eligible for⟩
opcional *adj* : optional — **opcionalmente** *adv*
ópera *nf* : opera
operación *nf, pl* **-ciones 1** : operation **2** : transaction, deal
operacional *adj* : operational
operador, -dora *n* **1** : operator **2** : cameraman, projectionist
operante *adj* : operating, working
operar *vt* **1** : to produce, to bring about **2** INTERVENIR : to operate on **3** *Mex* : to operate, to run (a machine) — *vi* **1** : to operate, to function **2** : to deal, to do business — **operarse** *vr* **1** : to come about, to take place **2** : to have an operation
operario, -ria *n* : laborer, worker
operático, -ca → operístico
operativo[1], -va *adj* **1** : operating ⟨capacidad operativa : operating capacity⟩ **2** : operative
operativo[2] *nm* : operation ⟨operativo militar : military operation⟩
opereta *nf* : operetta
operístico, -ca *adj* : operatic
opiato *nm* : opiate
opinable *adj* : arguable
opinar *vi* **1** : to think, to have an opinion **2** : to express an opinion **3 opinar bien de** : to think highly of — *vt* : to think ⟨opinamos lo mismo : we're of the same opinion, we're in agreement⟩
opinión *nf, pl* **-niones** : opinion, belief
opio *nm* : opium
oponente *nmf* : opponent
oponer {60} *vt* **1** CONTRAPONER : to oppose, to place against **2 oponer resistencia** : to resist, to put up a fight — **oponerse** *vr* **~ a** : to object to, to be against
oporto *nm* : port (wine)
oportunamente *adv* **1** : at the right time, opportunely **2** : appropriately
oportunidad *nf* : opportunity, chance
oportunismo *nm* : opportunism
oportunista[1] *adj* : opportunistic
oportunista[2] *nmf* : opportunist
oportuno, -na *adj* **1** : opportune, timely **2** : suitable, appropriate
oposición *nf, pl* **-ciones** : opposition
opositor, -tora *n* ADVERSARIO : opponent
oposum *nm* ZARIGÜEYA : opossum
opresión *nf, pl* **-siones 1** : oppression **2 opresión de pecho** : tightness in the chest
opresivo, -va *adj* : oppressive
opresor[1], -sora *adj* : oppressive
opresor[2], -sora *n* : oppressor

oprimir *vt* **1** : to oppress **2** : to press, to squeeze ⟨oprima el botón : push the button⟩

oprobio *nm* : opprobrium, shame

optar *vi* **1** ~ **por** : to opt for, to choose **2** ~ **a** : to aspire to, to apply for ⟨dos candidatos optan a la presidencia : two candidates are running for president⟩

optativo, -va *adj* FACULTATIVO : optional

óptica *nf* **1** : optics **2** : optician's shop **3** : viewpoint

óptico[1], -ca *adj* : optical, optic

óptico[2], -ca *n* : optician

optimismo *nm* : optimism

optimista[1] *adj* : optimistic

optimista[2] *nmf* : optimist

óptimo, -ma *adj* : optimum, optimal

optometría *nf* : optometry — **optometrista** *nmf*

opuesto[1] *pp* → **oponer**

opuesto[2] *adj* **1** : opposite, contrary **2** : opposed

opulencia *nf* : opulence — **opulento, -ta** *adj*

opus *nm* : opus

opuso, etc. → **oponer**

ora *conj* : now ⟨los matices eran variados, ora verdes, ora ocres : the hues were varied, now green, now ocher⟩

oración *nf, pl* **-ciones 1** DISCURSO : oration, speech **2** PLEGARIA : prayer **3** FRASE : sentence, clause

oráculo *nm* : oracle

orador, -dora *n* : speaker, orator

oral *adj* : oral — **oralmente** *adv*

órale *interj Mex fam* **1** : sure!, OK! ⟨¿los dos por cinco pesos? ¡órale! : both for five pesos? you've got a deal!⟩ **2** : come on! ⟨¡órale, vámonos! : come on, let's go!⟩

orangután *nm, pl* **-tanes** : orangutan

orar *vi* REZAR : to pray

oratoria *nf* : oratory

oratorio *nm* **1** CAPILLA : oratory, chapel **2** : oratorio

orbe *nm* **1** : orb, sphere **2** GLOBO : globe, world

órbita *nf* **1** : orbit **2** : eye socket **3** ÁMBITO : sphere, field

orbitador *nm* : space shuttle, orbiter

orbital *adj* : orbital

orbitar *v* : to orbit

orden[1] *nm, pl* **órdenes 1** : order ⟨todo está en orden : everything's in order⟩ ⟨por orden cronológico : in chronological order⟩ **2 orden del día** : agenda (at a meeting) **3 orden público** : law and order

orden[2] *nf, pl* **órdenes 1** : order ⟨una orden religiosa : a religious order⟩ ⟨una orden de tacos : an order of tacos⟩ **2 orden de compra** : purchase order **3 estar a la orden del día** : to be the order of the day, to be prevalent

ordenación *nf, pl* **-ciones 1** : ordination **2** : ordering, organizing

ordenadamente *adv* : in an orderly fashion, neatly

ordenado, -da *adj* : orderly, neat

ordenador *nm Spain* : computer

ordenamiento *nm* **1** : ordering, organizing **2** : code (of laws)

ordenanza[1] *nf* REGLAMENTO : ordinance, regulation

ordenanza[2] *nm* : orderly (in the armed forces)

ordenar *vt* **1** MANDAR : to order, to command **2** ARREGLAR : to put in order, to arrange **3** : to ordain (a priest)

ordeñar *vt* : to milk

ordeño *nm* : milking

ordinal *nm* : ordinal (number)

ordinariamente *adv* **1** : usually **2** : coarsely

ordinariez *nf* : coarseness, vulgarity

ordinario, -ria *adj* **1** : ordinary **2** : coarse, common, vulgar **3 de ~** : usually

orear *vt* : to air

orégano *nm* : oregano

oreja *nf* : ear

orfanato *nm* : orphanage

orfanatorio *nm Mex* : orphanage

orfebre *nmf* : goldsmith, silversmith

orfebrería *nf* : articles of gold or silver

orfelinato *nm* : orphanage

orgánico, -ca *adj* : organic — **orgánicamente** *adv*

organigrama *nm* : organization chart, flowchart

organismo *nm* **1** : organism **2** : agency, organization

organista *nmf* : organist

organización *nf, pl* **-ciones** : organization

organizador[1], -dora *adj* : organizing

organizador[2], -dora *n* : organizer

organizar {21} *vt* : to organize, to arrange — **organizarse** *vr* : to get organized

organizativo, -va *adj* : organizational

órgano *nm* : organ

orgasmo *nm* : orgasm

orgía *nf* : orgy

orgullo *nm* : pride

orgulloso, -sa *adj* : proud — **orgullosamente** *adv*

orientación *nf, pl* **-ciones 1** : orientation **2** DIRECCIÓN : direction, course **3** GUÍA : guidance, direction

oriental[1] *adj* **1** : eastern **2** : oriental **3** *Arg, Uru* : Uruguayan

oriental[2] *nmf* **1** : Easterner **2** : Oriental **3** *Arg, Uru* : Uruguayan

orientar *vt* **1** : to orient, to position **2** : to guide, to direct — **orientarse** *vr* **1** : to orient oneself, to get one's bearings **2** ~ **hacia** : to turn towards, to lean towards

oriente *nm* **1** : east, East **2 el Oriente** : the Orient

orífice *nmf* : goldsmith

orificio *nm* : orifice, opening

origen *nm, pl* **orígenes 1** : origin **2** : lineage, birth **3 dar origen a** : to give rise to **4 en su origen** : originally

original *adj & nm* : original — **origi-nalmente** *adv*

originalidad *nf* : originality

originar *vt* : to originate, to give rise to — **originarse** *vr* : to originate, to begin

originario, -ria *adj* ~ **de** : native of

originariamente *adv* : originally

orilla *nf* **1** BORDE : border, edge **2** : bank (of a river) **3** : shore

orillar *vt* **1** : to skirt, to go around **2** : to trim, to edge (cloth) **3** : to settle, to wind up **4** *Mex* : to pull over (a vehicle)

orín *nm* **1** HERRUMBRE : rust **2 orines** *nmpl* : urine

orina *nf* : urine

orinación *nf* : urination

orinal *nm* : urinal (vessel)

orinar *vi* : to urinate — **orinarse** *vr* : to wet oneself

oriol *nm* OROPÉNDOLA : oriole

oriundo, -da *adj* ~ **de** : native of

orla *nf* : border, edging

orlar *vt* : to edge, to trim

ornamentación *nf, pl* **-ciones** : ornamentation

ornamental *adj* : ornamental

ornamentar *vt* ADORNAR : to ornament, to adorn

ornamento *nm* : ornament, adornment

ornar *vt* : to adorn, to decorate

ornitología *nf* : ornithology

ornitólogo, -ga *n* : ornithologist

ornitorrinco *nm* : platypus

oro *nm* : gold

orondo, -da *adj* **1** : rounded, potbellied (of a container) **2** *fam* : smug, self-satisfied

oropel *nm* : glitz, glitter, tinsel

oropéndola *nf* : oriole

orquesta *nf* : orchestra — **orquestal** *adj*

orquestar *vt* : to orchestrate — **orquestación** *nf*

orquídea *nf* : orchid

ortiga *nf* : nettle

ortodoncia *nf* : orthodontics

ortodoncista *nmf* : orthodontist

ortodoxia *nf* : orthodoxy

ortodoxo, -xa *adj* : orthodox

ortografía *nf* : orthography, spelling

ortográfico, -ca *adj* : orthographic, spelling

ortopedia *nf* : orthopedics

ortopédico, -ca *adj* : orthopedic

ortopedista *nmf* : orthopedist

oruga *nf* **1** : caterpillar **2** : track (of a tank, etc.)

orzuelo *nm* : sty, stye (in the eye)

os *pron pl* (*objective form of* **vosotros**) *Spain* **1** : you, to you **2** : yourselves, to yourselves **3** : each other, to each other

osa *nf* → **oso**

osadía *nf* **1** VALOR : boldness, daring **2** AUDACIA : audacity, nerve

osado, -da *adj* **1** : bold, daring **2** : audacious, impudent — **osadamente** *adv*

osamenta *nf* : skeletal remains *pl*, bones *pl*

osar *vi* : to dare

oscilación *nf, pl* **-ciones** **1** : oscillation **2** : fluctuation **3** : vacillation, wavering

oscilar *vi* **1** BALANCEARSE : to swing, to sway, to oscillate **2** FLUCTUAR : to fluctuate **3** : to vacillate, to waver

oscuramente *adv* : obscurely

oscurecer {53} *vt* **1** : to darken **2** : to obscure, to confuse, to cloud **3 al oscurecer** : at dusk, at nightfall — *v impers* : to grow dark, to get dark — **oscurecerse** *vr* : to darken, to dim

oscuridad *nf* **1** : darkness **2** : obscurity

oscuro, -ra *adj* **1** : dark **2** : obscure **3 a oscuras** : in the dark, in darkness

óseo, ósea *adj* : skeletal, bony

ósmosis *or* **osmosis** *nf* : osmosis

oso, osa *n* **1** : bear **2 Osa Mayor** : Big Dipper **3 Osa Menor** : Little Dipper **4 oso blanco** : polar bear **5 oso hormiguero** : anteater **6 oso de peluche** : teddy bear

ostensible *adj* : ostensible, apparent — **ostensiblemente** *adv*

ostentación *nf, pl* **-ciones** : ostentation, display

ostentar *vt* **1** : to display, to flaunt **2** POSEER : to have, to hold ⟨ostenta el récord mundial : he holds the world record⟩

ostentoso, -sa *adj* : ostentatious, showy — **ostentosamente** *adv*

osteópata *nmf* : osteopath

osteopatía *n* : osteopathy

osteoporosis *nf* : osteoporosis

ostión *nm, pl* **ostiones** **1** *Mex* : oyster **2** *Chile* : scallop

ostra *nf* : oyster

ostracismo *nm* : ostracism

otear *vt* : to scan, to survey, to look over

otero *nm* : knoll, hillock

otomana *nf* : ottoman (mueble)

otomano, -na *adj & n* : Ottoman

otoñal *adj* : autumn, autumnal

otoño *nm* : autumn, fall

otorgamiento *nm* : granting, awarding

otorgar {52} *vt* **1** : to grant, to award **2** : to draw up, to frame (a legal document)

otro¹, otra *adj* **1** : other **2** : another ⟨en otro juego, ellos ganaron : in another game, they won⟩ **3 otra vez** : again **4 de otra manera** : otherwise **5 otra parte** : elsewhere **6 en otro tiempo** : once, formerly

otro², otra *pron* **1** : another one ⟨dame otro : give me another⟩ **2** : other one ⟨el uno o el otro : one or the other⟩ **3 los otros, las otras** : the others, the rest ⟨me dio una y se quedó con las otras : he gave me one and kept the rest⟩

ovación *nf, pl* **-ciones** : ovation

ovacionar *vt* : to cheer, to applaud

oval → ovalado
ovalado, -da *adj* : oval
óvalo *nm* : oval
ovárico, -ca *adj* : ovarian
ovario *nm* : ovary
oveja *nf* **1** : sheep, ewe **2 oveja negra** : black sheep
overol *nm* : overalls *pl*
ovillar *vt* : to roll into a ball
ovillo *nm* **1** : ball (of yarn) **2** : tangle
ovni *or* OVNI *nm* (*objeto volador no identificado*) : UFO
ovoide *adj* : ovoid, ovoidal
ovulación *nf, pl* **-ciones** : ovulation
ovular *vi* : to ovulate
óvulo *nm* : ovum

oxidación *nf, pl* **-ciones 1** : oxidation **2** : rusting
oxidado, -da *adj* : rusty
oxidar *vt* **1** : to cause to rust **2** : to oxidize — **oxidarse** *vr* : to rust, to become rusty
óxido *nm* **1** HERRUMBRE, ORÍN : rust **2** : oxide
oxigenar *vt* **1** : to oxygenate **2** : to bleach (hair)
oxígeno *nm* : oxygen
oxiuro *nm* : pinworm
oye, etc. → oír
oyente *nmf* **1** : listener **2** : auditor, auditing student
ozono *nm* : ozone

P

p *nf* : seventeenth letter of the Spanish alphabet
pabellón *nm, pl* **-llones 1** : pavilion **2** : summerhouse, lodge **3** : flag (of a vessel)
pabilo *nm* MECHA : wick
paca *nf* FARDO : bale
pacana *nf* : pecan
pacer {48} *v* : to graze, to pasture
paces → paz
pachanga *nf fam* : party, bash
paciencia *nf* : patience
paciente *adj & nmf* : patient — **pacientemente** *adv*
pacificación *nf, pl* **-ciones** : pacification
pacíficamente *adv* : peacefully, peaceably
pacificar {72} *vt* : to pacify, to calm — **pacificarse** *vr* : to calm down, to abate
pacífico, -ca *adj* : peaceful, pacific
pacifismo *nm* : pacifism
pacifista *adj & nmf* : pacifist
pacotilla *nf* de ～ : shoddy, trashy
pactar *vt* : to agree on — *vi* : to come to an agreement
pacto *nm* CONVENIO : pact, agreement
padecer {53} *vt* : to suffer, to endure — *vi* ADOLECER ～ de : to suffer from
padecimiento *nm* **1** : suffering **2** : ailment, condition
padrastro *nm* **1** : stepfather **2** : hangnail
padre¹ *adj Mex fam* : fantastic, great
padre² *nm* **1** : father **2 padres** *nmpl* : parents
padrenuestro *nm* : Lord's Prayer, paternoster
padrino *nm* **1** : godfather **2** : best man **3** : sponsor, patron
padrón *nm, pl* **padrones** : register, roll ⟨padrón municipal : city register⟩
paella *nf* : paella
paga *nf* **1** : payment **2** : pay, wages *pl*
pagadero, -ra *adj* : payable
pagado, -da *adj* **1** : paid **2 pagado de sí mismo** : self-satisfied, smug
pagador, -dora *n* : payer

paganismo *nm* : paganism
pagano, -na *adj & n* : pagan
pagar {52} *vt* : to pay, to pay for, to repay — *vi* : to pay
pagaré *nm* VALE : promissory note, IOU
página *nf* : page
pago *nm* **1** : payment **2 en pago de** : in return for
pagoda *nf* : pagoda
pague, etc. → pagar
país *nm* **1** NACIÓN : country, nation **2** REGIÓN : region, territory
paisaje *nm* : scenery, landscape
paisano, -na *n* COMPATRIOTA : compatriot, fellow countryman
paja *nf* **1** : straw **2** *fam* : trash, tripe
pajar *nm* : hayloft, haystack
pajarera *nf* : aviary
pájaro *nm* : bird ⟨pájaro cantor : songbird⟩ ⟨pájaro bobo : penguin⟩ ⟨pájaro carpintero : woodpecker⟩
pajita *nf* : (drinking) straw
pajote *nm* : straw, mulch
pala *nf* **1** : shovel, spade **2** : blade (of an oar or a rotor) **3** : paddle, racket
palabra *nf* **1** VOCABLO : word **2** PROMESA : word, promise ⟨un hombre de palabra : a man of his word⟩ **3** HABLA : speech **4** : right to speak ⟨tener la palabra : to have the floor⟩
palabrería *nf* : empty talk
palabrota *nf* : swearword
palacio *nm* **1** : palace, mansion **2 palacio de justicia** : courthouse
paladar *nm* **1** : palate **2** GUSTO : taste
paladear *vt* SABOREAR : to savor
paladín *nm, pl* **-dines** : champion, defender
palanca *nf* **1** : lever, crowbar **2** *fam* : leverage, influence **3 palanca de cambio** *or* **palanca de velocidad** : gearshift
palangana *nf* : washbowl
palanqueta *nf* : jimmy, small crowbar
palco *nm* : box (in a theater or stadium)
palear *vt* **1** : to shovel **2** : to paddle
palenque *nm* **1** ESTACADA : stockade, palisade **2** : arena, ring

paleontología *nf* : paleontology
paleontólogo, -ga *n* : paleontologist
palestino, -na *adj & n* : Palestinian
palestra *nf* : arena ⟨salir a la palestra : to join the fray⟩
paleta *nf* **1** : palette **2** : trowel **3** : spatula **4** : blade, vane **5** : paddle **6** *CA, Mex* : lollipop, Popsicle
paletilla *nf* : shoulder blade
paliar *vt* MITIGAR : to alleviate, to palliate
paliativo¹, -va *adj* : palliative
paliativo² *nm* : palliative
palidecer {53} *vi* : to turn pale
palidez *nf, pl* **-deces** : paleness, pallor
pálido, -da *adj* : pale
palillo *nm* **1** MONDADIENTES : toothpick **2 palillos** *nmpl* : chopsticks **3 palillo de tambor** : drumstick
paliza *nf* : beating, pummeling ⟨darle una paliza a : to beat, to thrash⟩
palma *nf* **1** : palm (of the hand) **2** : palm (tree or leaf) **3 batir palmas** : to clap, to applaud **4 llevarse la palma** *fam* : to take the cake
palmada *nf* **1** : pat **2** : slap **3** : clap
palmarés *nm* : record (of achievements)
palmario, -ria *adj* MANIFIESTO : clear, manifest
palmeado, -da *adj* : webbed
palmear *vt* : to slap on the back — *vi* : to clap, to applaud
palmera *nf* : palm tree
palmo *nm* **1** : span, small amount **2 palmo a palmo** : bit by bit, inch by inch **3 dejar con un palmo de narices** : to disappoint
palmotear *vi* : to applaud
palmoteo *nm* : clapping, applause
palo *nm* **1** : stick, pole, post **2** : shaft, handle ⟨palo de escoba : broomstick⟩ **3** : mast, spar **4** : wood **5** : blow (with a stick) **6** : suit (of cards)
paloma *nf* **1** : pigeon, dove **2 paloma mensajera** : carrier pigeon
palomilla *nf* : moth
palomitas *nfpl* : popcorn
palpable *adj* : palpable, tangible
palpar *vt* : to feel, to touch
palpitación *nf, pl* **-ciones** : palpitation
palpitar *vi* : to palpitate, to throb — **palpitante** *adj*
palta *nf* : avocado
paludismo *nm* MALARIA : malaria
palurdo, -da *n* : boor, yokel, bumpkin
pampa *nf* : pampa
pampeano, -na *adj* : pampean, pampas
pampero → **pampeano**
pan *nm* **1** : bread **2** : loaf of bread **3** : cake, bar ⟨pan de jabón : bar of soap⟩ **4 pan dulce** *CA, Mex* : traditional pastry **5 pan tostado** : toast **6 ser pan comido** *fam* : to be a piece of cake, to be a cinch
pana *nf* : corduroy
panacea *nf* : panacea
panadería *nf* : bakery, bread shop
panadero, -ra *n* : baker

panal *nm* : honeycomb
panameño, -ña *adj & n* : Panamanian
pancarta *nf* : placard, sign
pancita *nf Mex* : tripe
páncreas *nms & pl* : pancreas
panda *nmf* : panda
pandeado, -da *adj* : warped
pandearse *vr* **1** : to warp **2** : to bulge, to sag
pandemonio *or* **pandemónium** *nm* : pandemonium
pandereta *nf* : tambourine
pandero *nm* : tambourine
pandilla *nf* **1** : group, clique **2** : gang
panecito *nm* : roll, bread roll
panegírico¹, -ca *adj* : eulogistic, panegyrical
panegírico² *nm* : eulogy, panegyric
panel *nm* : panel — **panelista** *nmf*
panera *nf* : bread box
panfleto *nm* : pamphlet
pánico *nm* : panic
panorama *nm* **1** VISTA : panorama, view **2** : scene, situation ⟨el panorama nacional : the national scene⟩ **3** PERSPECTIVA : outlook
panorámico, -ca *adj* : panoramic
panqueque *nm* : pancake
pantaletas *nfpl* : panties
pantalla *nf* **1** : screen, monitor **2** : lampshade **3** : fan
pantalón *nm, pl* **-lones 1** : pants *pl*, trousers *pl* **2 pantalones vaqueros** : jeans **3 pantalones de mezclilla** *Chile, Mex* : jeans **4 pantalones de montar** : jodhpurs
pantano *nm* **1** : swamp, marsh, bayou **2** : reservoir **3** : obstacle, difficulty
pantanoso, -sa *adj* **1** : marshy, swampy **2** : difficult, thorny
panteón *nm, pl* **-teones 1** CEMENTERIO : cemetery **2** : pantheon, mausoleum
pantera *nf* : panther
pantimedias *nfpl Mex* : panty hose
pantomima *nf* : pantomime
pantorrilla *nf* : calf (of the leg)
pantufla *nf* ZAPATILLA : slipper
panza *nf* BARRIGA : belly, paunch
panzón, -zona *adj, mpl* **panzones** : potbellied, paunchy
pañal *nm* : diaper
pañería *nf* **1** : cloth, material **2** : fabric store
pañito *nm* : doily
paño *nm* **1** : cloth **2** : rag, dust cloth **3 paño de cocina** : dishcloth **4 paño higiénico** : sanitary napkin
pañuelo *nm* **1** : handkerchief **2** : scarf
papa¹ *nm* : pope
papa² *nf* **1** : potato **2 papa dulce** : sweet potato **3 papas fritas** : potato chips, french fries **4 papas a la francesa** *Mex* : french fries
papá *nm fam* **1** : dad, pop **2 papás** *nmpl* : parents, folks
papada *nf* **1** : double chin, jowl **2** : dewlap
papagayo *nm* LORO : parrot

papal *adj* : papal
papalote *nm Mex* : kite
papaya *nf* : papaya
papel *nm* **1** : paper, piece of paper **2** : role, part **3 papel de estaño** : tinfoil **4 papel de empapelar** *or* **papel pintado** : wallpaper **5 papel higiénico** : toilet paper **6 papel de lija** : sandpaper
papeleo *nm* : paperwork, red tape
papelera *nf* : wastebasket
papelería *nf* : stationery store
papelero, -ra *adj* : paper
papeleta *nf* **1** : ballot **2** : ticket, slip
paperas *nfpl* : mumps
papi *nm fam* : daddy, papa
papilla *nf* **1** : pap, mash **2 hacer papilla** : to beat to a pulp
papiro *nm* : papyrus
paquete *nm* BULTO : package, parcel
paquistaní *adj & nmf* : Pakistani
par¹ *adj* : even (in number)
par² *nm* **1** : pair, couple **2** : equal, peer ⟨sin par : matchless, peerless⟩ **3** : par (in golf) **4** : rafter **5 de par en par** : wide open
par³ *nf* : par ⟨por encima de la par : above par⟩ **2 a la par que** : at the same time as, as well as ⟨interesante a la par que instructivo : both interesting and informative⟩
para *prep* **1** : for ⟨para ti : for you⟩ ⟨alta para su edad : tall for her age⟩ ⟨una cita para el lunes : an appointment for Monday⟩ **2** : to, towards ⟨para la derecha : to the right⟩ ⟨van para el río : they're heading towards the river⟩ **3** : to, in order to ⟨lo hace para molestarte : he does it to annoy you⟩ **4** : around, by (a time) ⟨para mañana estarán listos : they'll be ready by tomorrow⟩ **5 para adelante** : forwards **6 para atrás** : backwards **7 para que** : so, so that, in order that ⟨te lo digo para que sepas : I'm telling you so you'll know⟩
parabién *nm, pl* **-bienes** : congratulations *pl*
parábola *nf* **1** : parable **2** : parabola
parabrisas *nms & pl* : windshield
paracaídas *nms & pl* : parachute
paracaidista *nmf* **1** : parachutist **2** : paratrooper
parachoques *nms & pl* : bumper
parada *nf* **1** : stop ⟨parada de autobús : bus stop⟩ **2** : catch, save, parry (in sports) **3** DESFILE : parade
paradero *nm* : whereabouts
paradigma *nm* : paradigm
paradisíaco, -ca *or* **paradisiaco, -ca** *adj* : heavenly
parado, -da *adj* **1** : motionless, idle, stopped **2** : standing (up) **3** : confused, bewildered **4 bien (mal) parado** : in good (bad) shape ⟨salió bien parado : it turned out well for him⟩
paradoja *nf* : paradox
paradójico, -ca *adj* : paradoxical
parafernalia *nf* : paraphernalia

parafina *nf* : paraffin
parafrasear *vt* : to paraphrase
paráfrasis *nfs & pl* : paraphrase
paraguas *nms & pl* : umbrella
paraguayo, -ya *adj & n* : Paraguayan
paraíso *nm* **1** : paradise, heaven **2 paraíso fiscal** : tax shelter
paraje *nm* : spot, place
paralelismo *nm* : parallelism, similarity
paralelo¹, -la *adj* : parallel
paralelo² *nm* : parallel
paralelogramo *nm* : parallelogram
parálisis *nfs & pl* **1** : paralysis **2** : standstill **3 parálisis cerebral** : cerebral palsy
paralítico, -ca *adj & n* : paralytic
paralizar {21} *vt* **1** : to paralyze **2** : to bring to a standstill — **paralizarse** *vr*
parámetro *nm* : parameter
páramo *nm* : barren plateau, moor
parangón *nm, pl* **-gones 1** : comparison **2 sin ~** : incomparable
paraninfo *nm* : auditorium, assembly hall
paranoia *nf* : paranoia
paranoico, -ca *adj & n* : paranoid
parapeto *nm* : parapet, rampart
parapléjico, -ca *adj & n* : paraplegic
parar *vt* **1** DETENER : to stop **2** : to stand, to prop — *vi* **1** CESAR : to stop **2** : to stay, to put up **3 ir a parar** : to end up, to wind up — **pararse** *vr* **1** : to stop **2** ATASCARSE : to stall (out) **3** : to stand up, to get up
pararrayos *nms & pl* : lightning rod
parasitario, -ria *adj* : parasitic
parasitismo *nm* : parasitism
parásito *nm* : parasite
parasol *nm* SOMBRILLA : parasol
parcela *nf* : parcel, tract of land
parcelar *vt* : to parcel (land)
parchar *vt* : to patch, to patch up
parche *nm* : patch
parcial *adj* : partial — **parcialmente** *adv*
parcialidad *nf* : partiality, bias
parco, -ca *adj* **1** : sparing, frugal **2** : moderate, temperate
pardo, -da *adj* : brownish grey
pardusco → pardo
parecer¹ {53} *vi* **1** : to seem, to look, to appear to be ⟨parece bien fácil : it looks very easy⟩ ⟨así parece : so it seems⟩ ⟨pareces una princesa : you look like a princess⟩ **2** : to think, to have an opinion ⟨me parece que sí : I think so⟩ **3** : to like, to be in agreement ⟨si te parece : if you like, if it's all right with you⟩ — **parecerse** *vr* **~ a** : to resemble
parecer² *nm* **1** OPINIÓN : opinion **2** ASPECTO : appearance ⟨al parecer : apparently⟩
parecido¹, -da *adj* **1** : similar, alike **2 bien parecido** : good-looking
parecido² *nm* : resemblance, similarity
pared *nf* : wall
pareja *nf* **1** : couple, pair **2** : partner, mate

parejo, -ja *adj* **1** : even, smooth, level **2** : equal, similar

parentela *nf* : relations *pl*, kinfolk

parentesco *nm* : relationship, kinship

paréntesis *nms & pl* **1** : parenthesis **2** : digression

parentético, -ca *adj* : parenthetic, parenthetical

paria *nmf* : pariah, outcast

paridad *nf* : parity, equality

pariente *nmf* : relative, relation

parir *vi* : to give birth — *vt* : to give birth to, to bear

parking *nm* : parking lot

parlamentar *vi* : to talk, to parley

parlamentario[1], -ria *adj* : parliamentary

parlamentario[2], -ria *n* : member of parliament

parlamento *nm* **1** : parliament **2** : negotiations *pl*, talks *pl*

parlanchín[1], -china *adj, mpl* **-chines** : chatty, talkative

parlanchín[2], -china *n, mpl* **-chines** : chatterbox

parlante *nm* ALTOPARLANTE : loudspeaker

parlotear *vi fam* : to gab, to chat, to prattle

parloteo *nm fam* : prattle, chatter

paro *nm* **1** HUELGA : strike **2** : stoppage, stopping **3 paro forzoso** : layoff

parodia *nf* : parody

parodiar *vt* : to parody

paroxismo *nm* **1** : fit, paroxysm **2** : peak, height ⟨llevaral paroxismo : to carry to the extreme⟩

parpadear *vi* **1** : to blink **2** : to flicker

parpadeo *nm* **1** : blink, blinking **2** : flickering

párpado *nm* : eyelid

parque *nm* **1** : park **2 parque de atracciones** : amusement park

parquear *vt* : to park — **parquearse** *vr*

parqueo *nm* : parking

parquet *or* **parqué** *nm* : parquet

parquímetro *nm* : parking meter

parra *nf* : vine, grapevine

párrafo *nm* : paragraph

parranda *nf fam* : party, spree

parrilla *nf* **1** : broiler, grill **2** : grate

parrillada *nf* BARBACOA : barbecue

párroco *nm* : parish priest

parroquia *nf* **1** : parish **2** : parish church **3** : customers *pl*, clientele

parroquial *adj* : parochial

parroquiano, -na *nm* **1** : parishioner **2** : customer, patron

parsimonia *nf* **1** : calm **2** : parsimony, thrift

parsimonioso, -sa *adj* **1** : calm, unhurried **2** : parsimonious, thrifty

parte[1] *nm* : report, dispatch

parte[2] *nf* **1** : part, share **2** : part, place ⟨en alguna parte : somewhere⟩ ⟨por todas partes : everywhere⟩ **3** : party (in negotiations, etc.) **4 de parte de** : on behalf of **5 ¿de parte de quién?** : may I ask who's calling? **6 tomar parte** : to take part

partero, -ra *n* : midwife

partición *nf, pl* **-ciones** : division, sharing

participación *nf, pl* **-ciones** **1** : participation **2** : share, interest **3** : announcement, notice

participante *nmf* **1** : participant **2** : competitor, entrant

participar *vi* **1** : to participate, to take part **2 ~ en** : to have a share in — *vt* : to announce, to notify

partícipe *nmf* : participant

participio *nm* : participle

partícula *nf* : particle

particular[1] *adj* **1** : particular, specific **2** : private, personal **3** : special, unique

particular[2] *nm* **1** : matter, detail **2** : individual

particularidad *nf* : characteristic, peculiarity

particularizar {21} *vt* **1** : to distinguish, to characterize **2** : to specify

partida *nf* **1** : departure **2** : item, entry **3** : certificate ⟨partida de nacimiento : birth certificate⟩ **4** : game, match, hand **5** : party, group

partidario, -ria *n* : follower, supporter

partido *nm* **1** : (political) party **2** : game, match ⟨partido de futbol : soccer game⟩ **3** APOYO : support, following **4** PROVECHO : profit, advantage ⟨sacar partido de : to profit from⟩

partir *vt* **1** : to cut, to split **2** : to break, to crack **3** : to share (out), to divide — *vi* **1** : to leave, to depart **2 ~ de** : to start from **3 a partir de** : as of, from ⟨a partir de hoy : as of today⟩ — **partirse** *vr* **1** : to smash, to split open **2** : to chap

partisano, -na *adj & n* : partisan

partitura *nf* : (musical) score

parto *nm* **1** : childbirth, delivery, labor ⟨estar de parto : to be in labor⟩ **2** : product, creation, brainchild

parvulario *nm* : nursery school

párvulo, -la *n* : toddler, preschooler

pasa *nf* **1** : raisin **2 pasa de Corinto** : currant

pasable *adj* : passable, tolerable — **pasablemente** *adv*

pasada *nf* **1** : passage, passing **2** : pass, wipe, coat (of paint) **3 de ~** : in passing **4 mala pasada** : dirty trick

pasadizo *nm* : passageway, corridor

pasado[1], -da *adj* **1** : past ⟨el año pasado : last year⟩ ⟨pasado mañana : the day after tomorrow⟩ ⟨pasadas las siete : after seven o'clock⟩ **2** : stale, bad, overripe **3** : old-fashioned, out-of-date **4** : overripe, slightly spoiled

pasado[2] *nm* : past

pasador *nm* **1** : bolt, latch **2** : barrette **3** *Mex* : bobby pin

pasaje *nm* **1** : ticket (for travel) **2** TARIFA : fare **3** : passageway **4** : passengers *pl*

pasajero[1], -ra *adj* : passing, fleeting

pasajero[2], -ra *n* : passenger

pasamanos *nms & pl* **1** : handrail **2** : bannister

pasante *nmf* : assistant

pasaporte *nm* : passport

pasar *vi* **1** : to pass, to go by, to come by **2** : to come in, to enter ⟨¿se puede pasar? : may we come in?⟩ **3** : to happen ⟨¿qué pasa? : what's happening?, what's going on?⟩ **4** : to manage, to get by **5** : to be over, to end **6** ~ **de** : to exceed, to go beyond **7** ~ **por** : to pretend to be — *vt* **1** : to pass, to give ⟨¿me pasas la sal? : would you pass me the salt?⟩ **2** : to pass (a test) **3** : to go over, to cross **4** : to spend (time) **5** : to tolerate **6** : to go through, to suffer **7** : to show (a movie, etc.) **8** : to overtake, to pass, to surpass **9** : to pass over, to wipe up **10 pasarlo bien** *or* **pasarla bien** : to have a good time **11 pasarlo mal** *or* **pasarla mal** : to have a bad time, to have a hard time **12 pasar por alto** : to overlook, to omit — **pasarse** *vr* **1** : to move, to pass, to go away **2** : to slip one's mind, to forget **3** : to go too far

pasarela *nf* **1** : gangplank **2** : footbridge **3** : runway, catwalk

pasatiempo *nm* : pastime, hobby

Pascua *nf* **1** : Easter **2** : Passover **3** : Christmas **4 Pascuas** *nfpl* : Christmas season

pase *nm* **1** PERMISO : pass, permit **2 pase de abordar** *Mex* : boarding pass

pasear *vi* : to take a walk, to go for a ride — *vt* **1** : to take for a walk **2** : to parade around, to show off — **pasearse** *vr* : to walk around

paseo *nm* **1** : walk, stroll **2** : ride **3** EXCURSIÓN : outing, trip **4** : avenue, walk **5** *or* **paseo marítimo** : boardwalk

pasiflora *nf* : passionflower

pasillo *nm* CORREDOR : hallway, corridor, aisle

pasión *nf, pl* **pasiones** : passion

pasional *adj* : passionate ⟨crimen pasional : crime of passion⟩

pasionaria → pasiflora

pasivo[1], **-va** *adj* : passive — **pasivamente** *adv*

pasivo[2] *nm* **1** : liability ⟨activos y pasivos : assets and liabilities⟩ **2** : debit side (of an account)

pasmado, -da *adj* : stunned, flabbergasted

pasmar *vt* : to amaze, to stun — **pasmarse** *vr*

pasmo *nm* **1** : shock, astonishment **2** : wonder, marvel

pasmoso, -sa *adj* : incredible, amazing — **pasmosamente** *adv*

paso[1], **-sa** *adj* : dried ⟨ciruela pasa : prune⟩

paso[2] *nm* **1** : passage, passing ⟨de paso : in passing, on the way⟩ **2** : way, path ⟨abrirse paso : to make one's way⟩ **3** : crossing ⟨paso de peatones : crosswalk⟩ ⟨paso a desnivel : underpass⟩ ⟨paso elevado : overpass⟩ **4** : step

⟨paso a paso : step by step⟩ **5** : pace, gait ⟨a buen paso : quickly, at a good rate⟩

pasta *nf* **1** : paste ⟨pasta de dientes *or* pasta dental : toothpaste⟩ **2** : pasta **3** : pastry dough **4 libro en pasta dura** : hardcover book **5 tener pasta de** : to have the makings of

pastar *vi* : to graze — *vt* : to put to pasture

pastel[1] *adj* : pastel

pastel[2] *nm* **1** : cake ⟨pastel de cumpleaños : birthday cake⟩ **2** : pie, turnover **3** : pastel

pastelería *nf* : pastry shop

pasteurización *nf, pl* **-ciones** : pasteurization

pasteurizar {21} *vt* : to pasteurize

pastilla *nf* **1** COMPRIMIDO, PÍLDORA : pill, tablet **2** : lozenge ⟨pastilla para la tos : cough drop⟩ **3** : cake (of soap), bar (of chocolate)

pastizal *nm* : pasture, grazing land

pasto *nm* **1** : pasture **2** HIERBA : grass, lawn

pastor, -tora *n* **1** : shepherd, shepherdess *f* **2** : minister, pastor

pastoral *adj & nf* : pastoral

pastorear *vt* : to shepherd, to tend

pastorela *nf* **1** : pastoral, pastourelle **2** *Mex* : a traditional Christmas play

pastoso, -sa *adj* **1** : pasty, doughy **2** : smooth, mellow (of sounds)

pata *nf* **1** : paw, leg (of an animal) **2** : foot, leg (of furniture) **3 patas de gallo** : crow's-feet **4 meter la pata** *fam* : to put one's foot in it, to make a blunder

patada *nf* **1** PUNTAPIÉ : kick **2** : stamp (of the foot)

patalear *vi* **1** : to kick **2** : to stamp one's feet

pataleta *nf fam* : tantrum

patán[1] *adj, pl* **patanes** : boorish, crude

patán[2] *nm, pl* **patanes** : boor, lout

patata *nf Spain* : potato

pateador, -dora *n* : kicker (in sports)

patear *vt* : to kick — *vi* : to stamp one's foot

patentar *vt* : to patent

patente[1] *adj* EVIDENTE : obvious, patent — **patentemente** *adv*

patente[2] *nf* : patent

paternal *adj* : fatherly, paternal

paternidad *nf* **1** : fatherhood, paternity **2** : parenthood **3** : authorship

paterno, -na *adj* : paternal ⟨abuela paterna : paternal grandmother⟩

patético, -ca *adj* : pathetic, moving

patetismo *nm* : pathos

patíbulo *nm* : gallows, scaffold

patillas *nfpl* : sideburns

patín *nm, pl* **patines** : skate ⟨patín de ruedas : roller skate⟩

patinador, -dora *n* : skater

patinaje *nm* : skating

patinar *vi* **1** : to skate **2** : to skid, to slip **3** *fam* : to slip up, to blunder

patinazo *nm* **1** : skid **2** *fam* : blunder, slipup

patineta *nf* **1** : scooter **2** : skateboard
patinete *nm* : scooter
patio *nm* **1** : courtyard, patio **2 patio de recreo** : playground
patito, -ta *n* : duckling
pato, -ta *n* **1** : duck **2 pato real** : mallard **3 pagar el pato** *fam* : to take the blame
patología *nf* : pathology
patológico, -ca *adj* : pathological
patólogo, -ga *n* : pathologist
patraña *nf* : tall tale, humbug, nonsense
patria *nf* : native land
patriarca *nm* : patriarch — **patriarcal** *adj*
patriarcado *nm* : patriarchy
patrimonio *nm* : patrimony, legacy
patrio, -tria *adj* **1** : native, home ⟨suelo patrio : native soil⟩ **2** : paternal
patriota[1] *adj* : patriotic
patriota[2] *nmf* : patriot
patriotería *nf* : jingoism, chauvinism
patriotero[1], **-ra** *adj* : jingoistic, chauvinistic
patriotero[2], **-ra** *n* : jingoist, chauvinist
patriótico, -ca *adj* : patriotic
patriotismo *nm* : patriotism
patrocinador, -dora *n* : sponsor, patron
patrocinar *vt* : to sponsor
patrocinio *nm* : sponsorship, patronage
patrón[1], **-trona** *n, mpl* **patrones 1** JEFE : boss **2** : patron saint
patrón[2] *nm, pl* **patrones 1** : standard **2** : pattern (in sewing)
patronal *adj* **1** : management, employers' ⟨sindicato patronal : employers' association⟩ **2** : pertaining to a patron saint ⟨fiesta patronal : patron saint's day⟩
patronato *nm* **1** : board, council **2** : foundation, trust
patrono, -na *n* **1** : employer **2** : patron saint
patrulla *nf* **1** : patrol **2** : police car, cruiser
patrullar *v* : to patrol
patrullero *nm* **1** : police car **2** : patrol boat
paulatino, -na *adj* : gradual
paupérrimo, -ma *adj* : destitute, poverty-stricken
pausa *nf* : pause, break
pausado[1] *adv* : slowly, deliberately ⟨habla más pausado : speak more slowly⟩
pausado[2], **-da** *adj* : slow, deliberate — **pausadamente** *adv*
pauta *nf* **1** : rule, guideline **2** : lines *pl* (on paper)
pava *nf Arg, Bol, Chile* : kettle
pavimentar *vt* : pave
pavimento *nm* : pavement
pavo, -va *n* **1** : turkey **2 pavo real** : peacock **3 comer pavo** : to be a wallflower
pavón *nm, pl* **pavones** : peacock
pavonearse *vr* : to strut, to swagger
pavoneo *nm* : strut, swagger
pavor *nm* TERROR : dread, terror

pavoroso, -sa *adj* ATERRADOR : dreadful, terrifying
payasada *nf* BUFONADA : antic, buffoonery
payasear *vi* : to clown around
payaso, -sa *n* : clown
paz *nf, pl* **paces 1** : peace **2 dejar en paz** : to leave alone **3 hacer las paces** : to make up, to reconcile
pazca, etc. → **pacer**
PC *nmf* : PC, personal computer
peaje *nm* : toll
peatón *nm, pl* **-tones** : pedestrian
peatonal *adj* : pedestrian
peca *nf* : freckle
pecado *nm* : sin
pecador[1], **-dora** *adj* : sinful, sinning
pecador[2], **-dora** *n* : sinner
pecaminoso, -sa *adj* : sinful
pecar {72} *vi* **1** : to sin **2 ∼ de** : to be too much (something) ⟨no pecan de amabilidad : they're not overly friendly⟩
pécari *or* **pecarí** *nm* : peccary
pececillo *nm* : small fish
pecera *nf* : fishbowl, fish tank
pecho *nm* **1** : chest **2** SENO : breast, bosom **3** : heart, courage **4 dar el pecho** : to breast-feed **5 tomar a pecho** : to take to heart
pechuga *nf* : breast (of fowl)
pecoso, -sa *adj* : freckled
pectoral *adj* : pectoral
peculado *nm* : embezzlement
peculiar *adj* **1** CARACTERÍSTICO : particular, characteristic **2** RARO : peculiar, uncommon
peculiaridad *nf* : peculiarity
pecuniario, -ria *adj* : pecuniary
pedagogía *nf* : pedagogy
pedagógico, -ca *adj* : pedagogic, pedagogical
pedagogo, -ga *n* : educator, pedagogue
pedal *nm* : pedal
pedalear *vi* : to pedal
pedante[1] *adj* : pedantic
pedante[2] *nmf* : pedant
pedantería *nf* : pedantry
pedazo *nm* TROZO : piece, bit, chunk ⟨caerse a pedazos : to fall to pieces⟩ ⟨hacer pedazos : to tear into shreds, to smash to pieces⟩
pedernal *nm* : flint
pedestal *nm* : pedestal
pedestre *adj* : commonplace, pedestrian
pediatra *nmf* : pediatrician
pediatría *nf* : pediatrics
pediátrico, -ca *adj* : pediatric
pedido *nm* **1** : order (of merchandise) **2** : request
pedigrí *nm* : pedigree
pedir {54} *vt* **1** : to ask for, to request ⟨le pedí un préstamo a Claudia : I asked Claudia for a loan⟩ **2** : to order (food, merchandise) **3 pedir disculpas** *or* **pedir perdón** : to apologize — *vi* **1** : to order **2** : to beg

pedrada *nf* **1** : blow (with a rock or stone) ⟨la ventana se quebró de una pedrada : the window was broken by a rock⟩ **2** *fam* : cutting remark, dig
pedregal *nm* : rocky ground
pedregoso, -sa *adj* : rocky, stony
pedrera *nf* CANTERA : quarry
pedrería *nf* : precious stones *pl*, gems *pl*
pegado, -da *adj* **1** : glued, stuck, stuck together **2 ~ a** : right next to
pegajoso, -sa *adj* **1** : sticky, gluey **2** : catchy ⟨una tonada pegajosa : a catchy tune⟩
pegamento *nm* : adhesive, glue
pegar {52} *vt* **1** : to glue, to stick, to paste **2** : to attach, to sew on **3** : to infect with, to give ⟨me pegó el resfriado : he gave me his cold⟩ **4** GOLPEAR : to hit, to deal, to strike ⟨me pegaron un puntapié : they gave me a kick⟩ **5** : to give (out with) ⟨pegó un grito : she let out a yell⟩ — *vi* **1** : to adhere, to stick **2 ~ en** : to hit, to strike (against) **3 ~ con** : to match, to go with — **pegarse** *vr* **1** GOLPEARSE : to hit oneself, to hit each other **2** : to stick, to take hold **3** : to be contagious **4** *fam* : to tag along, to stick around
pegote *nm* **1** : sticky mess **2** *Mex* : sticker, adhesive label
pegue, etc. → **pegar**
peinado *nm* : hairstyle, hairdo
peinador, -dora *n* : hairdresser
peinar *vt* : to comb — **peinarse** *vr*
peine *nm* : comb
peineta *nf* : ornamental comb
peladez *nf, pl* **-deces** *Mex fam* : obscenity, bad language
pelado, -da *adj* **1** : bald, hairless **2** : peeled **3** : bare, barren **4** : broke, penniless **5** *Mex fam* : coarse, crude
pelador *nm* : peeler
pelagra *nf* : pellagra
pelaje *nm* : coat (of an animal), fur
pelar *vt* **1** : to peel, to shell **2** : to skin **3** : to pluck **4** : to remove hair from **5** *fam* : to clean out (of money) — **pelarse** *vr* **1** : to peel **2** *fam* : to get a haircut **3** *Mex fam* : to split, to leave
peldaño *nm* **1** : step, stair **2** : rung
pelea *nf* **1** LUCHA : fight **2** : quarrel
pelear *vi* **1** LUCHAR : to fight **2** DISPUTAR : to quarrel — **pelearse** *vr*
peleón, -ona *adj, mpl* **-ones** *Spain* : quarrelsome, argumentative
peleonero, -ra *adj Mex* : quarrelsome
peletería *nf* **1** : fur shop **2** : fur trade
peletero, -ra *n* : furrier
peliagudo, -da *adj* : tricky, difficult, ticklish
pelícano *nm* : pelican
película *nf* **1** : movie, film **2** : (photographic) film **3** : thin covering, layer
peligrar *vi* : to be in danger
peligro *nm* **1** : danger, peril **2** : risk ⟨correr peligro de : to run the risk of⟩
peligroso, -sa *adj* : dangerous, hazardous

pelirrojo[1], -ja *adj* : red-haired, redheaded
pelirrojo[2], -ja *n* : redhead
pellejo *nm* **1** : hide, skin **2 salvar el pellejo** : to save one's neck
pellizcar {72} *vt* **1** : to pinch **2** : to nibble on
pellizco *nm* : pinch
pelo *nm* **1** : hair **2** : fur **3** : pile, nap **4 a pelo** : bareback **5 con pelos y señales** : in great detail **6 no tener pelos en la lengua** : to not mince words, to be blunt **7 tomarle el pelo a alguien** : to tease someone, to pull someone's leg
pelón, -lona *adj, mpl* **pelones 1** : bald **2** *fam* : broke **3** *Mex fam* : tough, difficult
pelota *nf* **1** : ball **2** *fam* : head **3 en pelotas** *fam* : naked **4 pelota vasca** : jai alai **5 pasar la pelota** *fam* : to pass the buck
pelotón *nm, pl* **-tones** : squad, detachment
peltre *nm* : pewter
peluca *nf* : wig
peluche *nm* : plush (fabric)
peludo, -da *adj* : hairy, shaggy, bushy
peluquería *nf* **1** : hairdresser's, barber shop **2** : hairdressing
peluquero, -ra *n* : barber, hairdresser
peluquín *nm, pl* **-quines** TUPÉ : hairpiece, toupee
pelusa *nf* : lint, fuzz
pélvico, -ca *adj* : pelvic
pelvis *nfs & pl* : pelvis
pena *nf* **1** CASTIGO : punishment, penalty ⟨pena de muerte : death penalty⟩ **2** AFLICCIÓN : sorrow, grief ⟨morir de pena : to die of a broken heart⟩ ⟨¡qué pena! : what a shame!, how sad!⟩ **3** DOLOR : pain, suffering **4** DIFICULTAD : difficulty, trouble ⟨a duras penas : with great difficulty⟩ **5** VERGÜENZA : shame, embarrassment **6 valer la pena** : to be worthwhile
penacho *nm* **1** : crest, tuft **2** : plume (of feathers)
penal[1] *adj* : penal
penal[2] *nm* CÁRCEL : prison, penitentiary
penalidad *nf* **1** : hardship **2** : penalty, punishment
penalizar {21} *vt* : to penalize
penalty *nm* : penalty (in sports)
penar *vt* : to punish, to penalize — *vi* : to suffer, to grieve
pendenciero, -ra *adj* : argumentative, quarrelsome
pender *vi* **1** : to hang **2** : to be pending
pendiente[1] *adj* **1** : pending **2 estar pendiente de** : to be watchful of, to be on the lookout for
pendiente[2] *nm Spain* : earring
pendiente[3] *nf* : slope, incline
pendón *nm, pl* **pendones** : banner
péndulo *nm* : pendulum
pene *nm* : penis

penetración *nf, pl* **-ciones 1** : penetration **2** : insight
penetrante *adj* **1** : penetrating, piercing **2** : sharp, acute **3** : deep (of a wound)
penetrar *vi* **1** : to penetrate, to sink in **2** ~ **por** *or* ~ **en** : to pierce, to go in, to enter into ⟨el frío penetra por la ventana : the cold comes right in through the window⟩ — *vt* **1** : to penetrate, to permeate **2** : to pierce ⟨el dolor penetró su corazón : sorrow pierced her heart⟩ **3** : to fathom, to understand
penicilina *nf* : penicillin
península *nf* : peninsula — **peninsular** *adj*
penitencia *nf* : penance, penitence
penitenciaría *nf* : penitentiary
penitente *adj & nmf* : penitent
penol *nm* : yardarm
penoso, -sa *adj* **1** : painful, distressing **2** : difficult, arduous **3** : shy, bashful
pensado, -da *adj* **1 bien pensado** : well thought-out **2 en el momento menos pensado** : when least expected **3 poco pensado** : badly thought-out **4 mal pensado** : evil-minded
pensador, -dora *n* : thinker
pensamiento *nm* **1** : thought **2** : thinking **3** : pansy
pensar {55} *vi* **1** : to think **2** ~ **en** : to think about — *vt* **1** : to think **2** : to think about **3** : to intend, to plan on — **pensarse** *vr* : to think over
pensativo, -va *adj* : pensive, thoughtful
pensión *nf, pl* **pensiones 1** JUBILACIÓN : pension **2** : boarding house **3 pensión alimenticia** : alimony
pensionado, -da *n* → **pensionista**
pensionista *nmf* **1** JUBILADO : pensioner, retiree **2** : boarder, lodger
pentágono *nm* : pentagon — **pentagonal** *adj*
pentagrama *nm* : staff (in music)
penúltimo, -ma *adj* : next to last, penultimate
penumbra *nf* : semidarkness
penuria *nf* **1** ESCASEZ : shortage, scarcity **2** : poverty
peña *nf* : rock, crag
peñasco *nm* : crag, large rock
peñón → **peñasco**
peón *nm, pl* **peones 1** : laborer, peon **2** : pawn (in chess)
peonía *nf* : peony
peor[1] *adv* **1** (*comparative of* **mal**) : worse ⟨se llevan peor que antes : they get along worse than before⟩ **2** (*superlative of* **mal**) : worst ⟨me fue peor que a nadie : I did the worst of all⟩
peor[2] *adj* **1** (*comparative of* **malo**) : worse ⟨es peor que el original : it's worse than the original⟩ **2** (*superlative of* **malo**) : worst ⟨el peor de todos : the worst of all⟩
pepa *nf* : seed, pit (of a fruit)
pepenador, -dora *n CA, Mex* : scavenger
pepenar *vt CA, Mex* : to scavenge, to scrounge

pepinillo *nm* : pickle, gherkin
pepino *nm* : cucumber
pepita *nf* **1** : seed, pip **2** : nugget **3** *Mex* : dried pumpkin seed
peque, etc. → **pecar**
pequeñez *nf, pl* **-ñeces 1** : smallness **2** : trifle, triviality **3 pequeñez de espíritu** : pettiness
pequeño[1], **-ña** *adj* **1** : small, little ⟨un libro pequeño : a small book⟩ **2** : young **3** BAJO : short
pequeño[2], **-ña** *n* : child, little one
pera *nf* : pear
peraltar *vt* : to bank (a road)
perca *nf* : perch (fish)
percal *nm* : percale
percance *nm* : mishap, misfortune
percatarse *vr* ~ **de** : to notice, to become aware of
percebe *nm* : barnacle
percepción *nf, pl* **-ciones 1** : perception **2** : idea, notion **3** COBRO : receipt (of payment), collection
perceptible *adj* : perceptible, noticeable — **perceptiblemente** *adv*
percha *nf* **1** : perch **2** : coat hanger **3** : coatrack, coat hook
perchero *nm* : coatrack
percibir *vt* **1** : to perceive, to notice, to sense **2** : to earn, to draw (a salary)
percudido, -da *adj* : grimy
percudir *vt* : to make grimy — **percudirse** *vr*
percusión *nf, pl* **-siones** : percussion
percusor *or* **percutor** *nm* : hammer (of a firearm)
perdedor[1], **-dora** *adj* : losing
perdedor[2], **-dora** *n* : loser
perder {56} *vt* **1** : to lose **2** : to miss ⟨perdimos la oportunidad : we missed the opportunity⟩ **3** : to waste (time) — *vi* : to lose — **perderse** *vr* EXTRAVIARSE : to get lost, to stray
perdición *nf, pl* **-ciones** : perdition, damnation
pérdida *nf* **1** : loss **2 pérdida de tiempo** : waste of time
perdidamente *adv* : hopelessly
perdido, -da *adj* **1** : lost **2** : inveterate, incorrigible ⟨es un caso perdido : he's a hopeless case⟩ **3** : in trouble, done for **4 de** ~ *Mex fam* : at least
perdigón *nm, pl* **-gones** : shot, pellet
perdiz *nf, pl* **perdices** : partridge
perdón[1] *nm, pl* **perdones** : forgiveness, pardon
perdón[2] *interj* : excuse me!, sorry!
perdonable *adj* : forgivable
perdonar *vt* **1** DISCULPAR : to forgive, to pardon **2** : to exempt, to excuse
perdurable *adj* : lasting
perdurar *vi* : to last, to endure, to survive
perecedero, -ra *adj* : perishable
perecer {53} *vi* : to perish, to die
peregrinación *nf, pl* **-ciones** : pilgrimage
peregrinaje *nm* → **peregrinación**

peregrino[1], **-na** *adj* **1** : unusual, odd **2**
MIGRATORIO : migratory
peregrino[2], **-na** *n* : pilgrim
perejil *nm* : parsley
perenne *adj* : perennial
perentorio, -ria *adj* **1** : peremptory **2**
URGENTE : urgent **3** FIJO : fixed, set
pereza *nf* FLOJERA, HOLGAZANERÍA
: laziness, idleness
perezoso[1], **-sa** *adj* FLOJO, HOLGAZÁN
: lazy
perezoso[2] *nm* : sloth (animal)
perfección *nf, pl* **-ciones** : perfection
perfeccionamiento *nm* : perfecting, refinement
perfeccionar *vt* : to perfect, to refine
perfeccionismo *nm* : perfectionism
perfeccionista *nmf* : perfectionist
perfecto, -ta *adj* : perfect — **perfecta-**
mente *adv*
perfidia *nf* : perfidy, treachery
pérfido, -da *adj* : perfidious
perfil *nm* **1** : profile **2 de ~** : sideways,
from the side **3 perfiles** *nmpl* RASGOS
: features, characteristics
perfilar *vt* : to outline, to define — **per-**
filarse *vr* **1** : to be outlined, to be silhouetted **2** : to take shape
perforación *nf, pl* **-ciones 1** : perforation **2** : drilling
perforadora *nf* **1** : hole punch (for paper) **2** : drill (in mining, etc.)
perforar *vt* **1** : to perforate, to pierce **2**
: to drill, to bore
perfumar *vt* : to perfume, to scent —
perfumarse *vr*
perfume *nm* : perfume, scent
pergamino *nm* : parchment
pérgola *nf* : pergola, arbor
pericia *nf* : skill, expertise
pericial *adj* : expert ⟨testigo pericial : expert witness⟩
perico *nm* COTORRA : small parrot
periferia *nf* : periphery
periférico[1], **-ca** *adj* : peripheral
periférico[2] *nm* **1** *CA, Mex* : beltway **2**
: peripheral
perilla *nf* **1** : goatee **2** : pommel (on a
saddle) **3** *Col, Mex* : knob, handle **4**
perilla de la oreja : earlobe **5 de pe-**
rillas *fam* : handy, just right
perímetro *nm* : perimeter
periódico[1], **-ca** *adj* : periodic — **pe-**
riódicamente *adv*
periódico[2] *nm* DIARIO : newspaper
periodismo *nm* : journalism
periodista *nmf* : journalist
periodístico, -ca *adj* : journalistic, news
período *or* **periodo** *nm* : period
peripecia *nf* VICISITUD : vicissitude, reversal ⟨las peripecias de su carrera : the
ups and downs of her career⟩
periquito *nm* **1** : parakeet **2 periquito**
australiano : budgerigar
periscopio *nm* : periscope
perito, -ta *adj & n* : expert
perjudicar {72} *vt* : to harm, to be detrimental to

perjudicial *adj* : harmful, detrimental
perjuicio *nm* **1** : harm, damage **2 en**
perjuicio de : to the detriment of
perjurar *vi* : to perjure oneself
perjurio *nm* : perjury
perjuro, -ra *n* : perjurer
perla *nf* **1** : pearl **2 de perlas** *fam* : wonderfully ⟨me viene de perlas : it suits
me just fine⟩
permanecer {53} *vi* **1** QUEDARSE : to remain, to stay **2** SEGUIR : to remain, to
continue to be
permanencia *nf* **1** : permanence, continuance **2** ESTANCIA : stay
permanente[1] *adj* **1** : permanent **2** : constant — **permanentemente** *adv*
permanente[2] *nf* : permanent (wave)
permeabilidad *nf* : permeability
permeable *adj* : permeable
permisible *adj* : permissible, allowable
permisividad *nf* : permissiveness
permisivo, -va *adv* : permissive
permiso *nm* **1** : permission **2** : permit,
license **3** : leave, furlough **4 con ~**
: excuse me, pardon me
permitir *vt* : to permit, to allow — **per-**
mitirse *vr*
permuta *nf* : exchange
permutar *vt* INTERCAMBIAR : to exchange
pernicioso, -sa *adj* : pernicious, destructive
pernil *nm* **1** : haunch (of an animal) **2**
: leg (of meat), ham **3** : trouser leg
perno *nm* : bolt, pin
pernoctar *vi* : to stay overnight, to spend
the night
pero[1] *nm* **1** : fault, defect ⟨ponerle per-
os a : to find fault with⟩ **2** : objection
pero[2] *conj* : but
perogrullada *nf* : truism, platitude,
cliché
peroné *nm* : fibula
perorar *vi* : to deliver a speech
perorata *nf* : oration, long-winded
speech
peróxido *nm* : peroxide
perpendicular *adj & nf* : perpendicular
perpetrar *vt* : to perpetrate
perpetuar {3} *vt* ETERNIZAR : to perpetuate
perpetuidad *nf* : perpetuity
perpetuo, -tua *adj* : perpetual — **per-**
petuamente *adv*
perplejidad *nf* : perplexity
perplejo, -ja *adj* : perplexed, puzzled
perrada *nf fam* : dirty trick
perrera *nf* : kennel, dog pound
perrero, -ra *n* : dogcatcher
perrito, -ta *n* CACHORRO : puppy, small
dog
perro, -rra *n* **1** : dog, bitch *f* **2 perro**
caliente : hot dog **3 perro salchicha**
: dachshund **4 perro faldero** : lapdog
5 perro cobrador : retriever
persa[1] *adj & nmf* : Persian
persa[2] *nm* : Persian (language)

persecución *nf, pl* **-ciones 1** : pursuit, chase **2** : persecution

perseguidor, -dora *n* **1** : pursuer **2** : persecutor

perseguir {75} *vt* **1** : to pursue, to chase **2** : to persecute **3** : to pester, to annoy

perseverancia *nf* : perseverance

perseverar *vi* : to persevere

persiana *nf* : blind, venetian blind

persignarse *vr* SANTIGUARSE : to cross oneself, to make the sign of the cross

persistir *vi* : to persist — **persistencia** *nf* — **persistente** *adj*

persona *nf* : person

personaje *nm* **1** : character (in drama or literature) **2** : personage, celebrity

personal[1] *adj* : personal — **personalmente** *adv*

personal[2] *nm* : personnel, staff

personalidad *nf* : personality

personalizar {21} *vt* : to personalize

personificar {72} *vi* : to personify — **personificación** *nf*

perspectiva *nf* **1** : perspective, view **2** : prospect, outlook

perspicacia *nf* : shrewdness, perspicacity, insight

perspicaz *adj, pl* **-caces** : shrewd, perspicacious

persuadir *vt* : to persuade — **persuadirse** *vr* : to become convinced

persuasión *nf, pl* **-siones** : persuasion

persuasivo, -va *adj* : persuasive

pertenecer {53} *vi* : to belong

perteneciente *adj* ~ **a** : belonging to

pertenencia *nf* **1** : membership **2** : ownership **3 pertenencias** *nfpl* : belongings, possessions

pértiga *nf* GARROCHA : pole ⟨salto de pértiga : pole vault⟩

pertinaz *adj, pl* **-naces 1** OBSTINADO : obstinate **2** PERSISTENTE : persistent

pertinencia *nf* : pertinence, relevance — **pertinente** *adj*

pertrechos *nmpl* : equipment, gear

perturbación *nf, pl* **-ciones** : disturbance, disruption

perturbador, -dora *adj* **1** INQUIETANTE : disturbing, troubling **2** : disruptive

perturbar *vt* **1** : to disturb, to trouble **2** : to disrupt

peruano, -na *adj & n* : Peruvian

perversidad *nf* : perversity, depravity

perversión *nf, pl* **-siones** : perversion

perverso, -sa *adj* : wicked, depraved

pervertido[1]**, -da** *adj* DEPRAVADO : perverted, depraved

pervertido[2]**, -da** *n* : pervert

pervertir {76} *vt* : to pervert, to corrupt

pesa *nf* **1** : weight **2 levantamiento de pesas** : weightlifting

pesadamente *adv* **1** : heavily **2** : slowly, clumsily

pesadez *nf, pl* **-deces 1** : heaviness **2** : slowness **3** : tediousness

pesadilla *nf* : nightmare

pesado[1]**, -da** *adj* **1** : heavy **2** : slow **3** : irritating, annoying **4** : tedious, boring **5** : tough, difficult

pesado[2]**, -da** *n fam* : bore, pest

pesadumbre *nf* AFLICCIÓN : grief, sorrow, sadness

pésame *nm* : condolences *pl* ⟨mi más sentido pésame : my heartfelt condolences⟩

pesar[1] *vt* **1** : to weigh **2** EXAMINAR : to consider, to think over — *vi* **1** : to weigh ⟨¿cuánto pesa? : how much does it weigh?⟩ **2** : to be heavy **3** : to weigh heavily, to be a burden ⟨no le pesa : it's not a burden on him⟩ ⟨pesa sobre mi corazón : it weighs upon my heart⟩ **4** INFLUIR : to carry weight, to have bearing **5** (*with personal pronouns*) : to grieve, to sadden ⟨me pesa mucho : I'm very sorry⟩ **6 pese a** : in spite of, despite

pesar[2] *nm* **1** AFLICCIÓN, PENA : sorrow, grief **2** REMORDIMIENTO : remorse **3 a pesar de** : in spite of, despite

pesaroso, -sa *adj* **1** : sad, mournful **2** ARREPENTIDO : sorry, regretful

pesca *nf* : fishing

pescadería *nf* : fish market

pescado *nm* : fish (as food)

pescador, -dora *n* : fisherman *m*, fisherwoman *f*

pescar {72} *vt* **1** : to fish for **2** : to catch **3** *fam* : to get a hold of, to land — *vi* : to fish, to go fishing

pescuezo *nm* : neck

pesebre *nm* : manger

pesero *nm Mex* : minibus

peseta *nf* : peseta (Spanish unit of currency)

pesimismo *nm* : pessimism

pesimista[1] *adj* : pessimistic

pesimista[2] *nmf* : pessimist

pésimo, -ma *adj* : dreadful, abominable

peso *nm* **1** : weight, heaviness **2** : burden, responsibility **3** : weight (in sports) **4** BÁSCULA : scales *pl* **5** : peso

pesque, etc. → **pescar**

pesquería *nf* : fishery

pesquero[1]**, -ra** *adj* : fishing ⟨pueblo pesquero : fishing village⟩

pesquero[2] *nm* : fishing boat

pesquisa *nf* INVESTIGACIÓN : inquiry, investigation

pestaña *nf* **1** : eyelash **2** : flange, rim

pestañear *vi* : to blink

pestañeo *nm* : blink

peste *nf* **1** : plague, pestilence **2** : stench, stink **3** : nuisance, pest

pesticida *nm* : pesticide

pestilencia *nf* **1** : stench, foul odor **2** : pestilence

pestilente *adj* **1** : foul, smelly **2** : pestilent

pestillo *nm* CERROJO : bolt, latch

petaca *nf* **1** *Mex* : suitcase **2 petacas** *nfpl Mex fam* : bottom, behind

pétalo *nm* : petal

petardear *vi* : to backfire

petardeo *nm* : backfiring
petardo *nm* : firecracker
petate *nm Mex* : mat
petición *nf, pl* **-ciones** : petition, request
peticionar *vt* : to petition
peticionario, -ria *n* : petitioner
petirrojo *nm* : robin
peto *nm* : bib (of clothing)
pétreo, -trea *adj* : stone, stony
petrificar {72} *vt* : to petrify
petróleo *nm* : oil, petroleum
petrolero¹, -ra *adj* : oil ⟨industria petrolera : oil industry⟩
petrolero² *nm* : oil tanker
petrolífero, -ra *adj* → **petrolero¹**
petulancia *nf* INSOLENCIA : insolence, petulance
petulante *adj* INSOLENTE : insolent, petulant — **petulantemente** *adv*
petunia *nf* : petunia
peyorativo, -va *adj* : pejorative
pez¹ *nm, pl* **peces** 1 : fish 2 **pez de colores** : goldfish 3 **pez espada** : swordfish 4 **pez gordo** : big shot
pez² *nf, pl* **peces** : pitch, tar
pezón *nm, pl* **pezones** : nipple
pezuña *nf* : hoof ⟨pezuña hendida : cloven hoof⟩
pi *nf* : pi
piadoso, -sa *adj* 1 : compassionate, merciful 2 DEVOTO : pious, devout
pianista *nmf* : pianist, piano player
piano *nm* : piano
piar {85} *vi* : to chirp, to cheep, to tweet
pibe, -ba *n Arg, Uru fam* : kid, child
pica *nf* 1 : pike, lance 2 : goad (in bullfighting) 3 : spade (in playing cards)
picada *nf* 1 : bite, sting (of an insect) 2 : sharp descent
picadillo *nm* 1 : minced meat, hash 2 **hacer picadillo a** : to beat to a pulp
picado, -da *adj* 1 : perforated 2 : minced, chopped 3 : decayed (of teeth) 4 : choppy, rough 5 *fam* : annoyed, miffed
picador *nm* : picador
picadura *nf* 1 : sting, bite 2 : prick, puncture 3 : decay, cavity
picaflor *nm* COLIBRÍ : hummingbird
picana *nf* : goad, prod
picante¹ *adj* 1 : hot, spicy 2 : sharp, cutting 3 : racy, risqué
picante² *nm* 1 : spiciness 2 : hot spices *pl*, hot sauce
picaporte *nm* 1 : latch 2 : door handle 3 ALDABA : door knocker
picar {72} *vt* 1 : to sting, to bite 2 : to peck at 3 : to nibble on 4 : to prick, to puncture, to punch (a ticket) 5 : to grind, to chop 6 : to goad, to incite 7 : to pique, to provoke — *vi* 1 : to itch 2 : to sting 3 : to be spicy 4 : to nibble 5 : to take the bait 6 ~ **en** : to dabble in 7 **picar muy alto** : to aim too high — **picarse** *vr* 1 : to get a cavity, to decay 2 : to get annoyed, to take offense
picardía *nf* 1 : cunning, craftiness 2 : prank, dirty trick

picaresco, -ca *adj* 1 : picaresque 2 : rascally, roguish
pícaro¹, -ra *adj* 1 : mischievous 2 : cunning, sly 3 : off-color, risqué
pícaro², -ra *n* 1 : rogue, scoundrel 2 : rascal
picazón *nf, pl* **-zones** COMEZÓN : itch
picea *nf* : spruce (tree)
pichel *nm* : pitcher, jug
pichón, -chona *n, mpl* **pichones** 1 : young pigeon, squab 2 *Mex fam* : novice, greenhorn
picnic *nm* : picnic
pico *nm* 1 : peak 2 : point, spike 3 : beak, bill 4 : pick, pickax 5 **y pico** : and a little, and a bit ⟨las siete y pico : a little after seven⟩ ⟨dos metros y pico : a bit over two meters⟩
picor *nm* : itch, irritation
picoso, -sa *adj Mex* : very hot, spicy
picota *nf* 1 : pillory, stock 2 **poner a alguien en la picota** : to put someone on the spot
picotada *nf* → **picotazo**
picotazo *nm* : peck (of a bird)
picotear *vt* : to peck — *vi* : to nibble, to pick
pictórico, -ca *adj* : pictorial
picudo, -da *adj* 1 : pointy, sharp 2 ~ **para** *Mex fam* : clever at, good at
pide, etc. → **pedir**
pie *nm* 1 : foot ⟨a pie : on foot⟩ ⟨de pie : on one's feet, standing⟩ 2 : base, bottom, stem, foot ⟨pie de la cama : foot of the bed⟩ ⟨pie de una lámpara : base of a lamp⟩ ⟨pie de la escalera : bottom of the stairs⟩ ⟨pie de una copa : stem of a glass⟩ 3 : foot (in measurement) ⟨pie cuadrado : square foot⟩ 4 : cue (in theater) 5 **dar pie a** : to give cause for, to give rise to 6 **en pie de igualdad** : on equal footing
piedad *nf* 1 COMPASIÓN : mercy, pity 2 DEVOCIÓN : piety, devotion
piedra *nf* 1 : stone 2 : flint (of a lighter) 3 : hailstone 4 **piedra de afilar** : whetstone, grindstone 5 **piedra angular** : cornerstone 6 **piedra arenisca** : sandstone 7 **piedra caliza** : limestone 8 **piedra imán** : lodestone 9 **piedra de molino** : millstone 10 **piedra de toque** : touchstone
piel *nf* 1 : skin 2 CUERO : leather, hide ⟨piel de venado : deerskin⟩ 3 : fur, pelt 4 CÁSCARA : peel, skin 5 **piel de gallina** : goose bumps *pl* ⟨me pone la piel de gallina : it gives me goose bumps⟩
piélago *nm* **el piélago** : the deep, the ocean
piensa, etc. → **pensar**
pienso *nm* : feed, fodder
pierde, etc. → **perder**
pierna *nf* : leg
pieza *nf* 1 ELEMENTO : piece, part, component ⟨vestido de dos piezas : two-piece dress⟩ ⟨pieza de recambio : spare part⟩ ⟨pieza clave : key element⟩ 2 : piece (in chess) 3 OBRA : piece, work

⟨pieza de teatro : play⟩ 4 : room, bedroom

pifia *nf fam* : goof, blunder

pigargo *nm* : osprey

pigmentación *nf, pl* **-ciones** : pigmentation

pigmento *nm* : pigment

pigmeo, -mea *adj & n* : pygmy, Pygmy

pijama *nm* : pajamas *pl*

pila *nf* 1 BATERÍA : battery ⟨pila de linterna : flashlight battery⟩ 2 MONTÓN : pile, heap 3 : sink, basin, font ⟨pila bautismal : baptismal font⟩ ⟨pila para pájaros : birdbath⟩

pilar *nm* 1 : pillar, column 2 : support, mainstay

píldora *nf* PASTILLA : pill

pillaje *nm* : pillage, plunder

pillar *vt* 1 *fam* : to catch ⟨¡cuidado! ¡nos pillarán! : watch out! they'll catch us!⟩ 2 *fam* : to grasp, to catch on ⟨¿no lo pillas? : don't you get it?⟩

pillo[1], -lla *adj* : cunning, crafty

pillo[2], -lla *n* 1 : rascal, brat 2 : rogue, scoundrel

pilluelo, -la *n* : urchin

pilón *nm, pl* **pilones** 1 PILA : basin 2 : pillar, tower (for cables), pylon (of a bridge) 3 *Mex* : extra, lagniappe

pilotar *vt* : to pilot, to drive

pilote *nm* : pile (stake)

pilotear → pilotar

piloto *nm* 1 : pilot, driver 2 : pilot light

piltrafa *nf* 1 : poor quality meat 2 : wretch 3 **piltrafas** *nfpl* : food scraps

pimentero *nm* : pepper shaker

pimentón *nm, pl* **-tones** 1 : paprika 2 : cayenne pepper

pimienta *nf* 1 : pepper (condiment) 2 **pimienta de Jamaica** : allspice

pimiento *nm* : pepper (fruit) ⟨pimiento verde : green pepper⟩

pináculo *nm* 1 : pinnacle (of a building) 2 : peak, acme

pincel *nm* : paintbrush

pincelada *nf* 1 : brushstroke 2 **últimas pinceladas** : final touches

pinchar *vt* 1 PICAR : to puncture (a tire) 2 : to prick, to stick 3 : to goad, to tease, to needle — *vi* 1 : to be prickly 2 : to get a flat tire 3 *fam* : to get beaten, to lose out — **pincharse** *vr* : to give oneself an injection

pinchazo *nm* 1 : prick, jab 2 : puncture, flat tire

pingüe *adj* 1 : rich, huge (of profits) 2 : lucrative

pingüino *nm* : penguin

pininos *or* **pinitos** *nmpl* : first steps ⟨hacer pininos : to take one's first steps, to toddle⟩

pino *nm* : pine, pine tree

pinta *nf* 1 : dot, spot 2 : pint 3 *fam* : aspect, appearance ⟨las peras tienen buena pinta : the pears look good⟩ 4 **pintas** *nfpl Mex* : graffiti

pintadas *nfpl* : graffiti

pintar *vt* 1 : to paint 2 : to draw, to mark 3 : to describe, to depict — *vi* 1 : to paint, to draw 2 : to look ⟨no pinta bien : it doesn't look good⟩ 3 *fam* : to count ⟨aquí no pinta nada : he has no say here⟩ — **pintarse** *vr* 1 MAQUILLARSE : to put on makeup 2 **pintárselas solo** *fam* : to manage by oneself, to know it all

pintarrajear *vt* : to daub (with paint)

pinto, -ta *adj* : speckled, spotted

pintor, -tora *n* 1 : painter 2 **pintor de brocha gorda** : housepainter, dauber

pintoresco, -ca *adj* : picturesque, quaint

pintura *nf* 1 : paint 2 : painting (art, work of art)

pinza *nf* 1 : clothespin 2 : claw, pincer 3 : pleat, dart 4 **pinzas** *nfpl* : tweezers 5 **pinzas** *nfpl* ALICATES : pliers, pincers

pinzón *nm, pl* **pinzones** : finch

piña *nf* 1 : pineapple 2 : pine cone

piñata *nf* : piñata

piñón *nm, pl* **piñones** 1 : pine nut 2 : pinion

pío[1], pía *adj* 1 DEVOTO : pious, devout 2 : piebald, pied, dappled

pío[2] *nm* : peep, tweet, cheep

piocha *nf* 1 : pickax 2 *Mex* : goatee

piojo *nm* : louse

piojoso, -sa *adj* 1 : lousy 2 : filthy

pionero[1], -ra *adj* : pioneering

pionero[2], -ra *n* : pioneer

pipa *nf* : pipe (for smoking)

pipián *nm, pl* **pipianes** *Mex* : a spicy sauce or stew

pipiolo, -la *n fam* 1 : greenhorn, novice 2 : kid, youngster

pique[1], etc. → picar

pique[2] *nm* 1 : pique, resentment 2 : rivalry, competition 3 **a pique de** : about to, on the verge of 4 **irse a pique** : to sink, to founder

piqueta *nf* : pickax

piquete *nm* 1 : picketers *pl*, picket line 2 : squad, detachment 3 *Mex* : prick, jab

piquetear *vt* 1 : to picket 2 *Mex* : to prick, to jab

pira *nf* : pyre

piragua *nf* : canoe — **piragüista** *nmf*

pirámide *nf* : pyramid

piraña *nf* : piranha

pirata[1] *adj* : bootleg, pirated

pirata[2] *nmf* 1 : pirate 2 : bootlegger 3 **pirata aéreo** : hijacker

piratear *vt* 1 : to hijack, to commandeer 2 : to bootleg, to pirate

piratería *nf* : piracy, bootlegging

piromanía *nf* : pyromania

pirómano, -na *n* : pyromaniac

piropo *nm* : flirtatious compliment

pirotecnia *nf* : fireworks *pl*, pyrotechnics *pl*

pirotécnico, -ca *adj* : fireworks, pyrotechnic

pírrico, -ca *adj* : Pyrrhic

pirueta *nf* : pirouette

pirulí *nm* : cone-shaped lollipop

pisada *nf* **1** : footstep **2** HUELLA : footprint

pisapapeles *nms & pl* : paperweight

pisar *vt* **1** : to step on, to set foot in **2** : to walk all over, to mistreat — *vi* : to step, to walk, to tread

piscina *nf* **1** : swimming pool **2** : fish pond

Piscis *nmf* : Pisces

piso *nm* **1** PLANTA : floor, story **2** SUELO : floor **3** *Spain* : apartment

pisotear *vt* **1** : to stamp on, to trample **2** PISAR : to walk all over **3** : to flout, to disregard

pisotón *nm*, *pl* **-tones** : stamp, step ⟨sufrieron empujones y pisotones : they were pushed and stepped on⟩

pista *nf* **1** RASTRO : trail, track ⟨siguen la pista de los sospechosos : they're on the trail of the suspects⟩ **2** : clue **3** CAMINO : road, trail **4** : track, racetrack **5** : ring, arena, rink **6 pista de aterrizaje** : runway, airstrip **7 pista de baile** : dance floor

pistacho *nm* : pistachio

pistilo *nm* : pistil

pistola *nf* **1** : pistol, handgun **2** : spray gun

pistolera *nf* : holster

pistolero *nm* : gunman

pistón *nm*, *pl* **pistones** : piston

pita *nf* **1** : agave **2** : pita fiber **3** : twine

pitar *vi* **1** : to blow a whistle **2** : to whistle, to boo **3** : to beep, to honk, to toot — *vt* : to whistle at, to boo

pitido *nm* **1** : whistle, whistling **2** : beep, honk, toot

pito *nm* **1** SILBATO : whistle **2 no me importa un pito** *fam* : I don't give a damn

pitón *nm*, *pl* **pitones 1** : python **2** : point of a bull's horn

pituitario, -ria *adj* : pituitary

pívot *nmf*, *pl* **pívots** : center (in basketball)

pivote *nm* : pivot

piyama *nmf* : pajamas *pl*

pizarra *nf* **1** : slate **2** : blackboard **3** : scoreboard

pizarrón *nm*, *pl* **-rrones** : blackboard, chalkboard

pizca *nf* **1** : pinch ⟨una pizca de canela : a pinch of cinnamon⟩ **2** : speck, trace ⟨ni pizca : not a bit⟩ **3** *Mex* : harvest

pizcar {72} *vt Mex* : to harvest

pizque, etc. → **pizcar**

pizza [ˈpitsa, ˈpisa] *nf* : pizza

pizzería *nf* : pizzeria, pizza parlor

placa *nf* **1** : sheet, plate **2** : plaque, nameplate **3** : plate (in photography) **4** : badge, insignia **5 placa de matrícula** : license plate, tag **6 placa dental** : plaque, tartar

placebo *nm* : placebo

placenta *nf* : placenta, afterbirth

placentero, -ra *adj* AGRADABLE, GRATO : pleasant, agreeable

placer[1] {57} *vi* GUSTAR : to be pleasing ⟨hazlo como te plazca : do it however you please⟩

placer[2] *nm* **1** : pleasure, enjoyment **2 a ~** : as much as one wants

plácido, -da *adj* TRANQUILO : placid, calm

plaga *nf* **1** : plague, infestation, blight **2** CALAMIDAD : disaster, scourge

plagado, -da *adj* **~ de** : filled with, covered with

plagar {52} *vt* : to plague

plagiar *vt* **1** : to plagiarize **2** SECUESTRAR : to kidnap, to abduct

plagiario, -ria *n* **1** : plagiarist **2** SECUESTRADOR : kidnapper, abductor

plagio *nm* **1** : plagiarism **2** SECUESTRO : kidnapping, abduction

plague, etc. → **plagar**

plan *nm* **1** : plan, strategy, program ⟨plan de inversiones : investment plan⟩ ⟨plan de estudios : curriculum⟩ **2** PLANO : plan, diagram **3** : attitude, intent, purpose ⟨ponte en plan serio : be serious⟩ ⟨estamos en plan de divertirnos : we're looking to have some fun⟩

plana *nf* **1** : page ⟨noticias en primera plana : front-page news⟩ **2 plana mayor** : staff (in the military)

plancha *nf* **1** : iron, ironing **2** : grill, griddle ⟨a la plancha : grilled⟩ **3** : sheet, plate ⟨plancha para hornear : baking sheet⟩ **4** *fam* : blunder, blooper

planchada *nf* : ironing, pressing

planchado *nm* → **planchada**

planchar *v* : to iron

planchazo *nm fam* : goof, blunder

plancton *nm* : plankton

planeación *nf* → **planeamiento**

planeador *nm* : glider (aircraft)

planeamiento *nm* : plan, planning

planear *vt* : to plan — *vi* : to glide (in the air)

planeo *nm* : gliding, soaring

planeta *nm* : planet

planetario[1]**, -ria** *adj* **1** : planetary **2** : global, worldwide

planetario[2] *nm* : planetarium

planicie *nf* : plain

planificación *nf* : planning ⟨planificación familiar : family planning⟩

planificar {72} *vt* : to plan

planilla *nf* **1** LISTA : list **2** NÓMINA : payroll **3** TABLA : chart, table **4** *Mex* : slate, ticket (of candidates) **5 planilla de cálculo** *Arg, Chile* : spreadsheet

plano[1]**, -na** *adj* : flat, level, plane

plano[2] *nm* **1** PLAN : map, plan **2** : plane (surface) **3** NIVEL : level ⟨en un plano personal : on a personal level⟩ **4** : shot (in photography) **5 de ~** : flatly, outright, directly ⟨se negó de plano : he flatly refused⟩

planta *nf* **1** : plant ⟨planta de interior : houseplant⟩ **2** FÁBRICA : plant, factory **3** PISO : floor, story **4** : staff, employees *pl* **5** : sole (of the foot)

plantación *nf, pl* **-ciones 1** : plantation **2** : planting
plantado, -da *adj* **1** : planted **2 dejar plantado** : to stand up (a date), to dump (a lover)
plantar *vt* **1** : to plant, to sow ⟨plantar de flores : to plant with flowers⟩ **2** : to put in, to place **3** *fam* : to plant, to land ⟨plantar un beso : to plant a kiss⟩ **4** *fam* : to leave, to jilt — **plantarse** *vr* **1** : to stand firm **2** *fam* : to arrive, to show up **3** *fam* : to balk
planteamiento *nm* **1** : approach, position ⟨el planteamiento feminista : the feminist viewpoint⟩ **2** : explanation, exposition **3** : proposal, suggestion, plan
plantear *vt* **1** : to set forth, to bring up, to suggest **2** : to establish, to set up **3** : to create, to pose (a problem) — **plantearse** *vr* **1** : to think about **2** : to arise
plantel *nm* **1** : educational institution **2** : staff, team
planteo → **planteamiento**
plantilla *nf* **1** : insole **2** : pattern, template, stencil **3** *Mex, Spain* : staff, roster of employees
plantío *nm* : field (planted with a crop)
plantón *nm, pl* **plantones 1** : seedling **2** : long wait ⟨darle a alguien un plantón : to stand someone up⟩
plañidero[1], -ra *adj* : mournful
plañidero[2], -ra *nf* : hired mourner
plañir {38} *v* : to mourn, to lament
plasma *nm* : plasma
plasmar *vt* : to express, to give form to — **plasmarse** *vr*
plasta *nf* : soft mass, lump
plástica *nf* : modeling, sculpture
plasticidad *nf* : plasticity
plástico[1], -ca *adj* : plastic
plástico[2] *nm* : plastic
plastificar {72} *vt* : to laminate
plata *nf* **1** : silver **2** : money
plataforma *nf* **1** ESTRADO, TARIMA : platform, dais **2** : platform (in politics) **3** : springboard, stepping stone **4 plataforma continental** : continental shelf **5 plataforma de lanzamiento** : launchpad **6 plataforma petrolífera** : oil rig (at sea)
platal *nm* : large sum of money, fortune
platanal *nm* : banana plantation
platanero[1], -ra *adj* : banana, banana-producing
platanero[2], -ra *n* : banana grower
plátano *nm* **1** : banana **2** : plantain **3 plátano macho** *Mex* : plantain
platea *nf* : orchestra, pit (in a theater)
plateado, -da *adj* **1** : silver, silvery **2** : silver-plated
plática *nf* **1** : talk, lecture **2** : chat, conversation
platicar {72} *vi* : to talk, to chat — *vt Mex* : to tell, to say
platija *nf* : flatfish, flounder

platillo *nm* **1** : saucer ⟨platillo volador : flying saucer⟩ **2** : cymbal **3** *Mex* : dish ⟨platillos típicos : local dishes⟩
platino *nm* : platinum
plato *nm* **1** : plate, dish ⟨lavar los platos : to do the dishes⟩ **2** : serving, helping **3** : course (of a meal) **4** : dish ⟨plato típico : typical dish⟩ **5** : home plate (in baseball) **6 plato hondo** : soup bowl
plató *nm* : set (in the movies)
platónico, -ca *adj* : platonic
playa *nf* : beach, seashore
playera *nf* **1** : canvas sneaker **2** *CA, Mex* : T-shirt
plaza *nf* **1** : square, plaza **2** : marketplace **3** : room, space, seat (in a vehicle) **4** : post, position **5 plaza fuerte** : stronghold, fortified city **6 plaza de toros** : bullring
plazca, etc. → **placer**
plazo *nm* **1** : period, term ⟨un plazo de cinco días : a period of five days⟩ ⟨a largo plazo : long-term⟩ **2** ABONO : installment ⟨pagar a plazos : to pay in installments⟩
pleamar *nf* : high tide
plebe *nf* : common people, masses *pl*
plebeyo[1], -ya *adj* : plebeian
plebeyo[2], -ya *n* : plebeian, commoner
plegable *adj* : folding, collapsible
plegadizo → **plegable**
plegar {49} *vt* DOBLAR : to fold, to bend — **plegarse** *vr* : to give in, to yield
plegaria *nf* ORACIÓN : prayer
pleito *nm* **1** : lawsuit **2** : fight, argument, dispute
plenamente *adv* COMPLETAMENTE : fully, completely
plenario, -ria *adj* : plenary, full
plenilunio *nm* : full moon
plenipotenciario, -ria *n* : plenipotentiary
plenitud *nf* : fullness, abundance
pleno, -na *adj* COMPLETO ⟨(often used as an intensifier)⟩ : full, complete ⟨en pleno uso de sus facultades : in full command of his faculties⟩ ⟨en plena noche : in the middle of the night⟩ ⟨en pleno corazón de la ciudad : right in the heart of the city⟩
plétora *nf* : plethora
pleuresía *nf* : pleurisy
pliega, pliegue etc. → **plegar**
pliego *nm* **1** HOJA : sheet of paper **2** : sealed document
pliegue *nm* **1** DOBLEZ : crease, fold **2** : pleat
plisar *vt* : to pleat
plomada *nf* **1** : plumb line **2** : sinker
plomería *nf* FONTANERÍA : plumbing
plomero, -ra *n* FONTANERO : plumber
plomizo, -za *adj* : leaden
plomo *nm* **1** : lead **2** : plumb line **3** : fuse **4** *fam* : bore, drag **5 a ∼** : plumb, straight
plugo, etc. → **placer**
pluma *nf* **1** : feather **2** : pen **3 pluma fuente** : fountain pen

plumaje *nm* : plumage
plumero *nm* : feather duster
plumilla *nf* : nib
plumón *nm, pl* plumones : down
plumoso, -sa *adj* : feathery, downy
plural *adj & nm* : plural
pluralidad *nf* : plurality
pluralizar {21} *vt* : to pluralize
pluriempleado, -da *adj* : holding more
  than one job
pluriempleo *nm* : moonlighting
plus *nm* : bonus
plusvalía *nf* : appreciation, capital gain
Plutón *nm* : Pluto
plutocracia *nf* : plutocracy
plutonio *nm* : plutonium
población *nf, pl* -ciones 1 : population
  2 : city, town, village
poblado¹, -da *adj* 1 : inhabited, populated 2 : full, thick ⟨cejas pobladas
  : bushy eyebrows⟩
poblado² *nm* : village, settlement
poblador, -dora *n* : settler
poblar {19} *vt* 1 : to populate, to inhabit
  2 : to settle, to colonize 3 ~ de : to
  stock with, to plant with — poblarse
  vr : to fill up, to become crowded
pobre¹ *adj* 1 : poor, impoverished 2
  : unfortunate ⟨¡pobre de mí! : poor
  me!⟩ 3 : weak, deficient ⟨una dieta pobre : a poor diet⟩
pobre² *nmf* : poor person ⟨los pobres
  : the poor⟩ ⟨¡pobre! : poor thing!⟩
pobremente *adv* : poorly
pobreza *nf* : poverty
pocilga *nf* CHIQUERO : pigsty, pigpen
pocillo *nm* : small coffee cup, demitasse
poción *nf, pl* pociones : potion
poco¹ *adv* 1 : little, not much ⟨poco
  probable : not very likely⟩ ⟨come poco
  : he doesn't eat much⟩ 2 : a short time,
  a while ⟨tardaremos poco : we won't
  be very long⟩ 3 poco antes : shortly
  before 4 poco después : shortly after
poco², -ca *adj* 1 : little, not much, (a)
  few ⟨tengo poco dinero : I don't have
  much money⟩ ⟨en no pocas ocasiones
  : on more than a few occasions⟩ ⟨poca
  gente : few people⟩ 2 pocas veces
  : rarely
poco³, -ca *pron* 1 : little, few ⟨le falta
  poco para terminar : he's almost fin-
  ished⟩ ⟨uno de los pocos que quedan
  : one of the remaining few⟩ 2 un poco
  : a little, a bit ⟨un poco de vino : a little wine⟩ ⟨un poco extraño : a bit
  strange⟩ 3 a ~ *Mex* (*used to express
  disbelief*) ⟨¿a poco no se te hizo difícil?
  : you mean you didn't find it difficult?⟩
  4 de a poco : little by little 5 hace
  poco : not long ago 6 poco a poco
  : little by little 7 dentro de poco
  : shortly, in a little while 8 por ~
  : nearly, almost
podar *vt* : to prune, to trim
poder¹ {58} *v aux* 1 : to be able to, can
  ⟨no puede hablar : he can't speak⟩ 2
  (*expressing possibility*) : might, may
  ⟨puede llover : it may rain at any mo-

ment⟩ ⟨¿cómo puede ser? : how can
that be?⟩ 3 (*expressing permission*)
  : can, may ⟨¿puedo ir a la fiesta? : can
  I go to the party?⟩ ⟨¿se puede? : may
  I come in?⟩ — *vi* 1 : to beat, to defeat
  ⟨cree que le puede a cualquiera : he
  thinks he can beat anyone⟩ 2 : to be
  possible ⟨¿crees que vendrán? —
  puede (que sí) : do you think they'll
  come? — maybe⟩ 3 ~ con : to cope
  with, to manage ⟨¡no puedo con estos
  niños! : I can't handle these children!⟩
  4 no poder más : to have had enough
  ⟨no puede más : she can't take any-
  more⟩ 5 no poder menos que : to not
  be able to help ⟨no pudo menos que
  asombrarse : she couldn't help but be
  amazed⟩
poder² *nm* 1 : control, power ⟨poder
  adquisitivo : purchasing power⟩ 2 : authority ⟨el poder legislativo : the legis-
  lature⟩ 3 : possession ⟨está en mi
  poder : it's in my hands⟩ 4 : strength,
  force ⟨poder militar : military might⟩
poderío *nm* 1 : power 2 : wealth, influence
poderoso, -sa *adj* 1 : powerful 2
  : wealthy, influential 3 : effective
podiatría *nf* : podiatry
podio *nm* : podium
pódium → podio
podología *nf* : podiatry, chiropody
podólogo, -ga *n* : podiatrist, chiropodist
podrá, etc. → poder
podredumbre *nf* 1 : decay, rottenness
  2 : corruption
podrido, -da *adj* 1 : rotten, decayed 2
  : corrupt
podrir → pudrir
poema *nm* : poem
poesía *nf* 1 : poetry 2 POEMA : poem
poeta *nmf* : poet
poético, -ca *adj* : poetic, poetical
pogrom *nm* : pogrom
póker *or* poker *nm* : poker (card game)
polaco¹, -ca *adj* : Polish
polaco², -ca *n* : Pole, Polish person
polaco³ *nm* : Polish (language)
polar *adj* : polar
polarizar {21} *vt* : to polarize — po-
  larizarse *vr* — polarización *nf*
polea *nf* : pulley
polémica *nf* CONTROVERSIA : controversy, polemics
polémico, -ca *adj* CONTROVERTIDO
  : controversial, polemical
polen *nm, pl* pólenes : pollen
policía¹ *nf* : police
policía² *nmf* : police officer, policeman
  m, policewoman *f*
policíaco, -ca *or* policiaco, -ca *adj* : police ⟨novela policíaca : detective story⟩
policial *adj* : police
poliéster *nm* : polyester
poligamia *nf* : polygamy
polígamo¹, -ma *adj* : polygamous
polígamo², -ma *n* : polygamist
polígono *nm* : polygon — poligonal *adj*

poliinsaturado, -da *adj* : polyunsaturated

polilla *nf* : moth

polimerizar {21} *vt* : to polymerize

polímero *nm* : polymer

polinesio, -sia *adj & n* : Polynesian

polinizar {21} *vt* : to pollinate — **polinización** *nf*

polio *nf* : polio

poliomielitis *nf* : poliomyelitis, polio

polisón *nm, pl* **-sones** : bustle (on clothing)

politécnico, -ca *adj* : polytechnic

politeísmo *nm* : polytheism — **politeísta** *adj & nmf*

política *nf* **1** : politics **2** : policy

políticamente *adv* : politically

político[1]**, -ca** *adj* **1** : political **2** : tactful, politic **3** : by marriage ⟨padre político : father-in-law⟩

político[2]**, -ca** *n* : politician

póliza *nf* : policy ⟨póliza de seguros : insurance policy⟩

polizón *nm, pl* **-zones** : stowaway ⟨viajar de polizón : to stow away⟩

polka *nf* : polka

polla *nf* APUESTA : bet

pollera *nf* **1** : chicken coop **2** : skirt

pollero, -ra *n* **1** : poulterer **2** : poultry farm **3** *Mex fam* COYOTE : smuggler of illegal immigrants

pollito, -ta *n* : chick, young bird, fledgling

pollo, -lla *n* **1** : chicken **2** POLLITO : chick **3** JOVEN : young man *m*, young lady *f*

polluelo *nm* → pollito

polo *nm* **1** : pole ⟨el Polo Norte : the North Pole⟩ ⟨polo negativo : negative pole⟩ **2** : polo (sport) **3** : polo shirt **4** : focal point, center **5 polo opuesto** : exact opposite

polución *nf, pl* **-ciones** CONTAMINACIÓN : pollution

polvareda *nf* **1** : cloud of dust **2** : uproar, fuss

polvera *nf* : compact (for face powder)

polvo *nm* **1** : dust **2** : powder **3 polvos** *nmpl* : face powder **4 polvos de hornear** : baking powder **5 hacer polvo** *fam* : to crush, to shatter ⟨vas a hacer polvo el reloj : you're going to destroy your watch⟩

pólvora *nf* **1** : gunpowder **2** : fireworks *pl*

polvoriento, -ta *adj* : dusty, powdery

polvorín *nm, pl* **-rines** : magazine, storehouse (for explosives)

pomada *nf* : ointment, cream

pomelo *nm* : grapefruit

pómez *nf or* **piedra pómez** : pumice

pomo *nm* **1** : pommel (on a sword) **2** : knob, handle **3** : perfume bottle

pompa *nf* **1** : bubble **2** : pomp, splendor **3 pompas fúnebres** : funeral

pompón *nm, pl* **pompones** BORLA : pom-pom

pomposidad *nf* **1** : pomp, splendor **2** : pomposity, ostentation

pomposo, -sa *adj* : pompous — **pomposamente** *adv*

pómulo *nm* : cheekbone

pon → poner

ponchadura *nf Mex* : puncture, flat (tire)

ponchar *vt* **1** : to strike out (in baseball) **2** *Mex* : to puncture — **poncharse** *vr* **1** *Col, Ven* : to strike out (in baseball) **2** *Mex* : to blow out (of a tire)

ponche *nm* **1** : punch (drink) **2 ponche de huevo** : eggnog

poncho *nm* : poncho

ponderación *nf, pl* **-ciones** **1** : consideration, deliberation **2** : high praise

ponderar *vt* **1** : to weigh, to consider **2** : to speak highly of

pondrá, etc. → poner

ponencia *nf* **1** DISCURSO : paper, presentation, address **2** INFORME : report

ponente *nmf* : speaker, presenter

poner {60} *vt* **1** COLOCAR : to put, to place ⟨pon el libro en la mesa : put the book on the table⟩ **2** AGREGAR, AÑADIR : to put in, to add **3** : to put on (clothes) **4** CONTRIBUIR : to contribute **5** ESCRIBIR : to put in writing ⟨no le puso su nombre : he didn't put his name on it⟩ **6** IMPONER : to set, to impose **7** EXPONER : to put, to expose ⟨lo puso en peligro : she put him in danger⟩ **8** : to prepare, to arrange ⟨poner la mesa : to set the table⟩ **9** : to name ⟨le pusimos Ana : we called her Ana⟩ **10** ESTABLECER : to set up, to establish ⟨puso un restaurante : he opened up a restaurant⟩ **11** INSTALAR : to install, to put in **12** (*with an adjective or adverb*) : to make ⟨siempre lo pones de mal humor : you always put him in a bad mood⟩ **13** : to turn on, to switch on **14** SUPONER : to suppose ⟨pongamos que no viene : supposing he doesn't come⟩ **15** : to lay (eggs) **16** **~ a** : to start (someone doing something) ⟨lo puse a trabajar : I put him to work⟩ **17** **~ de** : to place as ⟨la pusieron de directora : they made her director⟩ **18** **~ en** : to put in (a state or condition) ⟨poner en duda : to call into question⟩ — *vi* **1** : to contribute **2** : to lay eggs — **ponerse** *vr* **1** : to move (into a position) ⟨ponerse de pie : to stand up⟩ **2** : to put on, to wear **3** : to become, to turn ⟨se puso colorado : he turned red⟩ **4** : to set (of the sun or moon)

poni *or* **poney** *nm* : pony

ponga, etc. → poner

poniente *nm* **1** OCCIDENTE : west **2** : west wind

ponqué *nm Col, Ven* : cake

pontifical *adj* : pontifical

pontificar {72} *vi* : to pontificate

pontífice *nm* : pontiff, pope

pontón *nm, pl* **pontones** : pontoon

ponzoña *nf* VENENO : poison — **ponzoñoso, -sa** *adj*

popa *nf* **1** : stern **2 a ~** : astern, abaft, aft
popelín *nm, pl* **-lines** : poplin
popelina *nf* : poplin
popote *nm Mex* : (drinking) straw
populachero, -ra *adj* : common, popular, vulgar
populacho *nm* : rabble, masses *pl*
popular *adj* **1** : popular **2** : traditional **3** : colloquial
popularidad *nf* : popularity
popularizar {21} *vt* : to popularize — **popularizarse** *vr*
populista *adj & nmf* : populist — **populismo** *nm*
populoso, -sa *adj* : populous
popurrí *nm* : potpourri
por *prep* **1** : for, during ⟨se quedaron allí por la semana : they stayed there during the week⟩ ⟨por el momento : for now, at the moment⟩ **2** : around, during ⟨por noviembre empieza a nevar : around November it starts to snow⟩ ⟨por la mañana : in the morning⟩ **3** : around (a place) ⟨debe estar por allí : it must be over there⟩ ⟨por todas partes : everywhere⟩ **4** : by, through, along ⟨por la puerta : through the door⟩ ⟨pasé por tu casa : I stopped by your house⟩ ⟨por la costa : along the coast⟩ **5** : for, for the sake of ⟨lo hizo por su madre : he did it for his mother⟩ ⟨¡por Dios! : for heaven's sake!⟩ **6** : because of, on account of ⟨llegué tarde por el tráfico : I arrived late because of the traffic⟩ ⟨dejar por imposible : to give up as impossible⟩ **7** : per ⟨60 millas por hora : 60 miles per hour⟩ ⟨por docena : by the dozen⟩ **8** : for, in exchange for, instead of ⟨su hermana habló por él : his sister spoke on his behalf⟩ **9** : by means of ⟨hablar por teléfono : to talk on the phone⟩ ⟨por escrito : in writing⟩ **10** : as for ⟨por mí : as far as I'm concerned⟩ **11** : times ⟨tres por dos son seis : three times two is six⟩ **12** SEGÚN : from, according to ⟨por lo que dices : judging from what you're telling me⟩ **13** : as, for ⟨por ejemplo : for example⟩ **14** : by ⟨hecho por mi abuela : made by my grandmother⟩ ⟨por correo : by mail⟩ **15** : for, in order to ⟨lucha por ganar su respeto : he struggles to win her respect⟩ **16 estar por** : to be about to **17 por ciento** : percent **18 por favor** : please **19 por lo tanto** : therefore, consequently **20 ¿por qué?** : why? **21 por que → porque 22 por . . . que** : no matter how ⟨por mucho que intente : no matter how hard I try⟩ **23 por si** *or* **por si acaso** : just in case
porcelana *nf* : china, porcelain
porcentaje *nm* : percentage
porche *nm* : porch
porción *nf, pl* **porciones 1** : portion **2** PARTE : part, share **3** RACIÓN : serving, helping

pordiosear *vi* MENDIGAR : beg
pordiosero, -ra *n* MENDIGO : beggar
porfiado, -da *adj* OBSTINADO, TERCO : obstinate, stubborn — **porfiadamente** *adv*
porfiar {85} *vi* : to insist, to persist
pormenor *nm* DETALLE : detail
pormenorizar {21} *vi* : to go into detail — *vt* : to tell in detail
pornografía *nf* : pornography
pornográfico, -ca *adj* : pornographic
poro *nm* : pore
poroso, -sa *adj* : porous — **porosidad** *nf*
poroto *nm Arg, Chile, Uru* : bean
porque *conj* **1** : because **2** *or* **por que** : in order that
porqué *nm* : reason, cause
porquería *nf* **1** SUCIEDAD : dirt, filth **2** : nastiness, vulgarity **3** : worthless thing, trifle **4** : junk food
porra *nf* **1** : nightstick, club **2** *Mex* : cheer, yell ⟨los aficionados le echaban porras : the fans cheered him on⟩
porrazo *nm* **1** : blow, whack **2 de golpe y porrazo** : suddenly
porrista *nmf* **1** : cheerleader **2** : fan, supporter
portaaviones *nms & pl* : aircraft carrier
portada *nf* **1** : title page **2** : cover **3** : facade, front
portador, -dora *n* : carrier, bearer
portafolio *or* **portafolios** *nm, pl* **-lios 1** MALETÍN : briefcase **2** : portfolio (of investments)
portal *nm* **1** : portal, doorway **2** VESTÍBULO : vestibule, hall
portar *vt* **1** : to carry, to bear **2** : to wear — **portarse** *vr* CONDUCIRSE : to behave ⟨pórtate bien : behave yourself⟩
portátil *adj* : portable
portaviandas *nms & pl* : lunch box
portaviones *nm* → **portaaviones**
portavoz *nmf, pl* **-voces** : spokesperson, spokesman *m*, spokeswoman *f*
portazo *nm* : slam (of a door)
porte *nm* **1** ASPECTO : bearing, demeanor **2** TRANSPORTE : transport, carrying ⟨porte pagado : postage paid⟩
portento *nm* MARAVILLA : marvel, wonder
portentoso, -sa *adj* MARAVILLOSO : marvelous, wonderful
porteño, -ña *adj* : of or from Buenos Aires
portería *nf* **1** ARCO : goal, goalposts *pl* **2** : superintendent's office
portero, -ra *n* **1** ARQUERO : goalkeeper, goalie **2** : doorman *m* **3** : janitor, superintendent
pórtico *nm* : portico
portilla *nf* : porthole
portón *nm, pl* **portones 1** : main door **2** : gate
portugués¹, -guesa *adj & n, mpl* **-gueses** : Portuguese
portugués² *nm* : Portuguese (language)

porvenir *nm* FUTURO : future
pos *adv* **en pos de** : in pursuit of
posada *nf* **1** : inn **2** *Mex* : Advent celebration
posadero, -ra *n* : innkeeper
posar *vi* : to pose — *vt* : to place, to lay — **posarse** *vr* **1** : to land, to light, to perch **2** : to settle, to rest
posavasos *nms & pl* : coaster (for drinks)
posdata → **postdata**
pose *nf* : pose
poseedor, -dora *n* : possessor, holder
poseer {20} *vt* : to possess, to hold, to have
poseído, -da *adj* : possessed
posesión *nf, pl* **-siones** : possession
posesionarse *vr* ~ **de** : to take possession of, to take over
posesivo[1], -va *adj* : possessive
posesivo[2] *nm* : possessive case
posguerra *nf* : postwar period
posibilidad *nf* **1** : possibility **2 posibilidades** *nfpl* : means, income
posibilitar *vt* : to make possible, to permit
posible *adj* : possible — **posiblemente** *adv*
posición *nf, pl* **-ciones 1** : position, place **2** : status, standing **3** : attitude, stance
posicionar *vt* **1** : to position, to place **2** : to establish — **posicionarse** *vr*
positivo[1], -va *adj* : positive
positivo[2] *nm* : print (in photography)
poso *nm* **1** : sediment, dregs *pl* **2** : grounds *pl* (of coffee)
posoperatorio, -ria *adj* : postoperative
posponer {60} *vt* **1** : to postpone **2** : to put behind, to subordinate
pospuso, etc. → **posponer**
posta *nf* : relay race
postal[1] *adj* : postal
postal[2] *nf* : postcard
postdata *nf* : postscript
poste *nm* : post, pole ⟨poste de teléfonos : telephone pole⟩
póster *or* **poster** *nm, pl* **pósters** *or* **posters** : poster, placard
postergación *nf, pl* **-ciones** : postponement, deferring
postergar {52} *vt* **1** : to delay, to postpone **2** : to pass over (an employee)
posteridad *nf* : posterity
posterior *adj* **1** ULTERIOR : later, subsequent **2** TRASERO : back, rear
postgrado *nm* : graduate course
postgraduado, -da *n* : graduate student, postgraduate
postigo *nm* **1** CONTRAVENTANA : shutter **2** : small door, wicket gate
postilla *nf* : scab
postizo, -za *adj* : artificial, false ⟨dentadura postiza : dentures⟩
postnatal *adj* : postnatal
postor, -tora *n* : bidder ⟨mejor postor : highest bidder⟩

postración *nf, pl* **-ciones 1** : prostration **2** ABATIMIENTO : depression
postrado, -da *adj* **1** : prostrate **2 postrado en cama** : bedridden
potranco, -ca *n* → **potro[1]**
postrar *vt* DEBILITAR : to debilitate, to weaken — **postrarse** *vr* : to prostrate oneself
postre *nm* : dessert
postrero, -ra *adj* (**postrer** *before masculine singular nouns*) ÚLTIMO : last
postulación *nf, pl* **-ciones 1** : collection **2** : nomination (of a candidate)
postulado *nm* : postulate, assumption
postulante, -ta *n* **1** : postulant **2** : candidate, applicant
postular *vt* **1** : to postulate **2** : to nominate **3** : to propose — **postularse** *vr* : to run, to be a candidate
póstumo, -ma *adj* : posthumous — **póstumamente** *adv*
postura *nf* **1** : posture, position (of the body) **2** ACTITUD, POSICIÓN : position, stance
potable *adj* : drinkable, potable
potaje *nm* : thick vegetable soup, pottage
potasa *nf* : potash
potasio *nm* : potassium
pote *nm* **1** OLLA : pot **2** : jar, container
potencia *nf* **1** : power ⟨potencias extranjeras : foreign powers⟩ ⟨elevado a la tercera potencia : raised to the third power⟩ **2** : capacity, potency
potencial *adj & nm* : potential
potenciar *vt* : to promote, to foster
potenciómetro *nm* : dimmer, dimmer switch
potentado, -da *n* **1** SOBERANO : potentate, sovereign **2** MAGNATE : tycoon, magnate
potente *adj* **1** : powerful, strong **2** : potent, virile
potestad *nf* **1** AUTORIDAD : authority, jurisdiction **2 patria potestad** : custody, guardianship
potrero *nm* **1** : field, pasture **2** : cattle ranch
potro[1], -tra *n* : colt *m*, filly *f*
potro[2] *nm* **1** : rack (for torture) **2** : horse (in gymnastics)
pozo *nm* **1** : well ⟨pozo de petróleo : oil well⟩ **2** : deep pool (in a river) **3** : mine shaft **4** *Arg, Par, Uru* : pothole **5 pozo séptico** : cesspool
pozole *nm Mex* : spicy stew made with pork and hominy
práctica *nf* **1** : practice, experience **2** EJERCICIO : exercising ⟨la práctica de la medicina : the practice of medicine⟩ **3** APLICACIÓN : application, practice ⟨poner en práctica : to put into practice⟩ **4 prácticas** *nfpl* : training
practicable *adj* : practicable, feasible
prácticamente *adv* : practically
practicante[1] *adj* : practicing ⟨católicos practicantes : practicing Catholics⟩

practicante² *nmf* : practicer, practitioner

practicar {72} *vt* **1** : to practice **2** : to perform, to carry out **3** : to exercise (a profession) — *vi* : to practice

práctico, -ca *adj* : practical, useful

pradera *nf* : grassland, prairie

prado *nm* **1** CAMPO : field, meadow **2** : park

pragmático, -ca *adj* : pragmatic — **pragmáticamente** *adv*

pragmatismo *nm* : pragmatism

preámbulo *nm* **1** INTRODUCCIÓN : preamble, introduction **2** RODEO : evasion ⟨gastar preámbulos : to beat around the bush⟩

prebélico, -ca *adj* : antebellum

prebenda *nf* : privilege, perquisite

precalentar {55} *vt* : to preheat

precariedad *nf* : precariousness

precario, -ria *adj* : precarious — **precariamente** *adv*

precaución *nf, pl* **-ciones 1** : precaution ⟨medidas de precaución : precautionary measures⟩ **2** PRUDENCIA : caution, care ⟨con precaución : cautiously⟩

precautorio, -ria *adj* : precautionary

precaver *vt* PREVENIR : to prevent, to guard against — **precaverse** *vr* PREVENIRSE : to take precautions, to be on guard

precavido, -da *adj* CAUTELOSO : cautious, prudent

precedencia *nf* : precedence, priority

precedente¹ *adj* : preceding, previous

precedente² *nm* : precedent

preceder *v* : to precede

precepto *nm* : rule, precept

preciado, -da *adj* : esteemed, prized, valuable

preciarse *vr* **1** JACTARSE : to boast, to brag **2** ∼ **de** : to pride oneself on

precinto *nm* : seal

precio *nm* **1** : price **2** : cost, sacrifice ⟨a cualquier precio : whatever the cost⟩

preciosidad *nf* : beautiful thing ⟨este vestido es una preciosidad : this dress is lovely⟩

precioso, -sa *adj* **1** HERMOSO : beautiful, exquisite **2** VALIOSO : precious, valuable

precipicio *nm* **1** : precipice **2** RUINA : ruin

precipitación *nf, pl* **-ciones 1** PRISA : haste, hurry, rush **2** : precipitation, rain, snow

precipitado, -da *adj* **1** : hasty, sudden **2** : rash — **precipitadamente** *adv*

precipitar *vt* **1** APRESURAR : to hasten, to speed up **2** ARROJAR : to hurl, to throw — **precipitarse** *vr* **1** APRESURARSE : to rush **2** : to act rashly **3** ARROJARSE : to throw oneself

precisamente *adv* JUSTAMENTE : precisely, exactly

precisar *vt* **1** : to specify, to determine exactly **2** NECESITAR : to need, to require — *vi* : to be necessary

precisión *nf, pl* **-siones 1** EXACTITUD : precision, accuracy **2** CLARIDAD : clarity (of style, etc.) **3** NECESIDAD : necessity ⟨tener precisión de : to have need of⟩

preciso, -sa *adj* **1** EXACTO : precise **2** : very, exact ⟨en ese preciso instante : at that very instant⟩ **3** NECESARIO : necessary

precocidad *nf* : precocity

precocinar *vt* : to precook

preconcebir {54} *vt* : to preconceive

precondición *nf, pl* **-ciones** : precondition

preconizar {21} *vt* **1** : to recommend, to advocate **2** : to extol

precoz *adj, pl* **precoces 1** : precocious **2** : early, premature — **precozmente** *adv*

precursor, -sora *n* : forerunner, precursor

predecesor, -sora *n* ANTECESOR : predecessor

predecir {11} *vt* : to foretell, to predict

predestinado, -da *adj* : predestined, fated

predestinar *vt* : to predestine — **predestinación** *nf*

predeterminar *vt* : to predetermine

prédica *nf* SERMÓN : sermon

predicado *nm* : predicate

predicador, -dora *n* : preacher

predicar {72} *v* : to preach

predicción *nf, pl* **-ciones 1** : prediction **2** PRONÓSTICO : forecast ⟨predicción del tiempo : weather forecast⟩

prediga, predijo etc. → **predecir**

predilección *nf, pl* **-ciones** : predilection, preference

predilecto, -ta *adj* : favorite

predio *nm* : property, piece of land

predisponer {60} *vt* **1** : to predispose, to incline **2** : to prejudice, to bias

predisposición *nf, pl* **-ciones 1** : predisposition, tendency **2** : prejudice, bias

predominante *adj* : predominant — **predominantemente** *adv*

predominar *vi* PREVALECER : to predominate, to prevail

predominio *nm* : predominance, prevalence

preeminente *adj* : preeminent — **preeminencia** *nf*

preescolar *adj & nm* : preschool

preestreno *nm* : preview

prefabricado, -da *adj* : prefabricated

prefacio *nm* : preface

prefecto *nm* : prefect

preferencia *nf* **1** : preference **2** PRIORIDAD : priority **3** **de** ∼ : preferably

preferencial *adj* : preferential

preferente *adj* : preferential, special ⟨trato preferente : special treatment⟩

preferentemente *adv* : preferably

preferible *adj* : preferable
preferido, -da *adj & n* : favorite
preferir {76} *vt* : to prefer
prefigurar *vt* : foreshadow, prefigure
prefijo *nm* : prefix
pregonar *vt* **1** : to proclaim, to announce **2** : to hawk (merchandise) **3** : to extol **4** : to reveal, to disclose
pregunta *nf* **1** : question **2 hacer una pregunta** : to ask a question
preguntar *vt* : to ask, to question — *vi* : to ask, to inquire — **preguntarse** *vr* : to wonder
preguntón, -tona *adj, mpl* **-tones** : inquisitive
prehistórico, -ca *adj* : prehistoric
prejuiciado, -da *adj* : prejudiced
prejuicio *nm* : prejudice
prejuzgar {52} *vt* : to prejudge
prelado *nm* : prelate
preliminar *adj & nm* : preliminary
preludio *nm* : prelude
prematrimonial *adj* : premarital
prematuro, -ra *adj* : premature
premeditación *nf, pl* **-ciones** : premeditation
premeditar *vt* : to premeditate, to plan
premenstrual *adj* : premenstrual
premiado, -da *adj* : winning, prizewinning
premiar *vt* **1** : to award a prize to **2** : to reward
premier *nmf* : premier, prime minister
premio *nm* **1** : prize ⟨premio gordo : grand prize, jackpot⟩ **2** : reward **3** : premium
premisa *nf* : premise, basis
premolar *nm* : bicuspid (tooth)
premonición *nf, pl* **-ciones** : premonition
premura *nf* : haste, urgency
prenatal *adj* : prenatal
prenda *nf* **1** : piece of clothing **2** : security, pledge
prendar *vt* **1** : to charm, to captivate **2** : to pawn, to pledge — **prendarse** *vr* ~ **de** : to fall in love with
prendedor *nm* : brooch, pin
prender *vt* **1** SUJETAR : to pin, to fasten **2** APRESAR : to catch, to apprehend **3** : to light (a cigarette, a match) **4** : to turn on ⟨prende la luz : turn on the light⟩ **5 prender fuego a** : to set fire to — *vi* **1** : to take root **2** : to catch fire **3** : to catch on
prensa *nf* **1** : printing press **2** : press ⟨conferencia de prensa : press conference⟩
prensar *vt* : to press
prensil *adj* : prehensile
preñado, -da *adj* **1** : pregnant **2** ~ **de** : filled with
preñar *vt* EMBARAZAR : to make pregnant
preñez *nf, pl* **preñeces** : pregnancy
preocupación *nf, pl* **-ciones** INQUIETUD : worry, concern
preocupante *adj* : worrisome

preocupar *vt* INQUIETAR : to worry, to concern — **preocuparse** *vr* APURARSE : to worry, to be concerned
preparación *nf, pl* **-ciones 1** : preparation, readiness **2** : education, training **3** : (medicinal) preparation
preparado¹, -da *adj* **1** : ready, prepared **2** : trained
preparado² *nm* : preparation, mixture
preparar *vt* **1** : to prepare, to make ready **2** : to teach, to train, to coach — **prepararse** *vr*
preparativos *nmpl* : preparations
preparatoria *nf Mex* : high school
preparatorio, -ria *adj* : preparatory
preponderante *adj* : preponderant, predominant — **preponderancia** *nf* — **preponderantemente** *adv*
preposición *nf, pl* **-ciones** : preposition — **preposicional** *adj*
prepotente *adj* : arrogant, domineering, overbearing — **prepotencia** *nf*
prerrogativa *nf* : prerogative, privilege
presa *nf* **1** : capture, seizure ⟨hacer presa de : to seize⟩ **2** : catch, prey ⟨presa de : prey to, seized with⟩ **3** : claw, fang **4** DIQUE : dam **5** : morsel, piece (of food)
presagiar *vt* : to presage, to portend
presagio *nm* : omen, portent
presbiterio *nm* : presbytery, sanctuary (of a church)
presbítero *nm* : presbyter
presciencia *nf* : prescience
prescindible *adj* : expendable, dispensable
prescindir *vi* **1** ~ **de** : to do without, to dispense with **2** DESATENDER : to ignore, to disregard **3** OMITIR : to omit, to skip
prescribir {33} *vt* : to prescribe
prescripción *nf, pl* **-ciones** : prescription
prescrito *pp* → **prescribir**
presencia *nf* **1** : presence **2** ASPECTO : appearance
presenciar *vt* : to be present at, to witness
presentable *adj* : presentable
presentación *nf, pl* **-ciones 1** : presentation **2** : introduction **3** : appearance
presentador, -dora *n* : newscaster, anchorman *m*, anchorwoman *f*
presentar *vt* **1** : to present, to show **2** : to offer, to give **3** : to submit (a document), to launch (a product) **4** : to introduce (a person) — **presentarse** *vr* **1** : to show up, to appear **2** : to arise, to come up **3** : to introduce oneself
presente¹ *adj* **1** : present, in attendance **2** : present, current **3 tener presente** : to keep in mind
presente² *nm* **1** : present (time, tense) **2** : one present ⟨entre los presentes se encontraban ... : those present included ...⟩
presentimiento *nm* : premonition, hunch, feeling

presentir {76} *vt* : to sense, to intuit ⟨presentía lo que iba a pasar : he sensed what was going to happen⟩
preservación *nf, pl* **-ciones** : preservation
preservar *vt* **1** : to preserve **2** : to protect
preservativo *nm* CONDÓN : condom
presidencia *nf* **1** : presidency **2** : chairmanship
presidencial *adj* : presidential
presidente, -ta *n* **1** : president **2** : chair, chairperson **3** : presiding judge
presidiario, -ria *n* : convict, prisoner
presidio *nm* : prison, penitentiary
presidir *vt* **1** MODERAR : to preside over, to chair **2** : to dominate, to rule over
presilla *nf* : eye, loop, fastener
presión *nf, pl* **presiones 1** : pressure **2 presión arterial** : blood pressure
presionar *vt* **1** : to pressure **2** : to press, to push — *vi* : to put on the pressure
preso¹, -sa *adj* : imprisoned
preso², -sa *n* : prisoner
prestado, -da *adj* **1** : borrowed, on loan **2 pedir prestado** : to borrow
prestamista *nmf* : moneylender, pawnbroker
préstamo *nm* : loan
prestar *vt* **1** : to lend, to loan **2** : to render (a service), to give (aid) **3 prestar atención** : to pay attention **4 prestar juramento** : to take an oath — **prestarse** *vr* : to lend oneself ⟨se presta a confusiones : it lends itself to confusion⟩
prestatario, -ria *n* : borrower
presteza *nf* : promptness, speed
prestidigitación *nf, pl* **-ciones** : sleight of hand, prestidigitation
prestidigitador, -dora *n* : conjurer, magician
prestigio *nm* : prestige — **prestigioso, -sa** *adj*
presto¹ *adv* : promptly, at once
presto², -ta *adj* **1** : quick, prompt **2** DISPUESTO, PREPARADO : ready
presumido, -da *adj* VANIDOSO : conceited, vain
presumir *vt* SUPONER : to presume, to suppose — *vi* **1** ALARDEAR : to boast, to show off **2 ~ de** : to consider oneself ⟨presume de inteligente : he thinks he's intelligent⟩
presunción *nf, pl* **-ciones 1** SUPOSICIÓN : presumption, supposition **2** VANIDAD : conceit, vanity
presunto, -ta *adj* : presumed, supposed, alleged — **presuntamente** *adv*
presuntuoso, -sa *adj* : conceited
presuponer {60} *vt* : to presuppose
presupuestal *adj* : budget, budgetary
presupuestar *vi* : to budget — *vt* : to budget for
presupuestario, -ria *adj* : budget, budgetary
presupuesto *nm* **1** : budget, estimate **2** : assumption, supposition

presurizar {21} *vt* : to pressurize
presuroso, -sa *adj* : hasty, quick
pretencioso, -sa *adj* : pretentious
pretender *vt* **1** INTENTAR : to attempt, to try ⟨pretendo estudiar : I'm trying to study⟩ **2** AFIRMAR : to claim ⟨pretende ser pobre : he claims he's poor⟩ **3** : to seek, to aspire to ⟨¿qué pretendes tú? : what are you after?⟩ **4** CORTEJAR : to court **5 pretender que** : to expect ⟨¿pretendes que lo crea? : do you expect me to believe you?⟩
pretendiente¹ *nmf* **1** : candidate, applicant **2** : pretender, claimant (to a throne, etc.)
pretendiente² *nm* : suitor
pretensión *nf, pl* **-siones 1** : intention, hope, plan **2** : pretension ⟨sin pretensiones : unpretentious⟩
pretexto *nm* EXCUSA : pretext, excuse
pretil *nm* : parapet, railing
prevalecer {53} *vi* : to prevail, to triumph
prevaleciente *adj* : prevailing, prevalent
prevalerse {84} *vr* **~ de** : to avail oneself of, to take advantage of
prevención *nf, pl* **-ciones 1** : prevention **2** : preparation, readiness **3** : precautionary measure **4** : prejudice, bias
prevenido, -da *adj* **1** PREPARADO : prepared, ready **2** ADVERTIDO : forewarned **3** CAUTELOSO : cautious
prevenir {87} *vt* **1** : to prevent **2** : to warn — **prevenirse** *vr* **~ contra** *or* **~ de** : to take precautions against
preventivo, -va *adj* : preventive, precautionary
prever {88} *vt* ANTICIPAR : to foresee, to anticipate
previo, -via *adj* **1** : previous, prior **2** : after, upon ⟨previo pago : after paying, upon payment⟩
previsible *adj* : foreseeable
previsión *nf, pl* **-siones 1** : foresight **2** : prediction, forecast **3** : precaution
previsor, -sora *adj* : farsighted, prudent
prieto, -ta *adj* **1** : blackish, dark **2** : dark-skinned, swarthy **3** : tight, compressed
prima *nf* **1** : premium **2** : bonus **3 →** **primo**
primacía *nf* **1** : precedence, priority **2** : superiority, supremacy
primado *nm* : primate (bishop)
primario, -ria *adj* : primary
primate *nm* : primate
primavera *nf* **1** : spring (season) **2** PRÍMULA : primrose
primaveral *adj* : spring, springlike
primero¹ *adv* **1** : first **2** : rather, sooner
primero², -ra *adj* (**primer** *before masculine singular nouns*) **1** : first **2** : top, leading **3** : fundamental, basic **4 de primera** : first-rate
primero³, -ra *n* : first
primicia *nf* **1** : first fruits **2** : scoop, exclusive

primigenio, -nia *adj* : original, primary
primitivo, -va *adj* **1** : primitive **2** ORIG-
INAL : original
primo, -ma *n* : cousin
primogénito, -ta *adj & n* : firstborn
primor *nm* **1** : skill, care **2** : beauty, elegance
primordial *adj* **1** : primordial **2** : basic,
fundamental
primoroso, -sa *adj* **1** : exquisite, fine,
delicate **2** : skillful
prímula *nf* : primrose
princesa *nf* : princess
principado *nm* : principality
principal[1] *adj* **1** : main, principal **2**
: foremost, leading
principal[2] *nm* : capital, principal
príncipe *nm* : prince
principesco, -ca *adj* : princely
principiante[1] *adj* : beginning
principiante[2] *nmf* : beginner, novice
principiar *vt* EMPEZAR : to begin
principio *nm* **1** COMIENZO : beginning
2 : principle **3 al principio** : at first **4**
a principios de : at the beginning of ⟨a
principios de agosto : at the beginning
of August⟩ **5 en ~** : in principle
pringar {52} *vt* **1** : to dip (in grease) **2**
: to soil, to spatter (with grease) —
pringarse *vr*
pringoso, -sa *adj* : greasy
pringue[1], etc. → **pringar**
pringue[2] *nm* : grease, drippings *pl*
prior, priora *n* : prior *m*, prioress *f*
priorato *nm* : priory
prioridad *nf* : priority, precedence
prisa *nf* **1** : hurry, rush **2 a ~** *or* **de ~**
: quickly, fast **3 a toda prisa** : as fast
as possible **4 darse prisa** : to hurry **5**
tener prisa : to be in a hurry
prisión *nf, pl* **prisiones 1** CÁRCEL
: prison, jail **2** ENCARCELAMIENTO
: imprisonment
prisionero, -ra *n* : prisoner
prisma *nm* : prism
prismáticos *nmpl* : binoculars
prístino, -na *adj* : pristine
privacidad *nf* : privacy
privación *nf, pl* **-ciones 1** : deprivation
2 : privation, want
privado, -da *adj* : private — **privada-
mente** *adv*
privar *vt* **1** DESPOJAR : to deprive **2** : to
stun, to knock out — **privarse** *vr* : to
deprive oneself
privativo, -va *adj* : exclusive, particular
privilegiado, -da *adj* : privileged
privilegiar *vt* : to grant a privilege to, to
favor
privilegio *nm* : privilege
pro[1] *nm* **1** : pro, advantage ⟨los pros y
contras : the pros and cons⟩ **2 en pro
de** : for, in favor of
pro[2] *prep* : for, in favor of ⟨grupos pro
derechos humanos : groups supporting
human rights⟩
proa *nf* : bow, prow
probabilidad *nf* : probability

probable *adj* : probable, likely
probablemente *adv* : probably
probar {19} *vt* **1** : to demonstrate, to
prove **2** : to test, to try out **3** : to try
on (clothing) **4** : to taste, to sample —
vi : to try — **probarse** *vr* : to try on
(clothing)
probeta *nf* : test tube
probidad *nf* : probity
problema *nm* : problem
problemática *nf* : set of problems ⟨la
problemática que debemos enfrentar
: the problems we must face⟩
proboscide *nf* : proboscis
problemático, -ca *adj* : problematic
procaz *adj, pl* **procaces 1** : insolent, impudent **2** : indecent
procedencia *nf* : origin, source
procedente *adj* **1** : proper, fitting **2 ~
de** : coming from
proceder *vi* **1** AVANZAR : to proceed **2**
: to act, to behave **3** : to be appropriate, to be fitting **4 ~ de** : to originate
from, to come from
procedimiento *nm* : procedure, process
prócer *nmf* : eminent person, leader
procesado, -da *n* : accused, defendant
procesador *nm* : processor ⟨procesador
de textos : word processor⟩
procesamiento *nm* : processing ⟨proce-
samiento de datos : data processing⟩
procesar *vt* **1** : to prosecute, to try **2**
: to process
procesión *nf, pl* **-siones** : procession
proceso *nm* **1** : process **2** : trial, proceedings *pl*
proclama *nf* : proclamation
proclamación *nf, pl* **-ciones** : proclamation
proclamar *vt* : to proclaim — **procla-
marse** *vr*
proclive *adj* **~ a** : inclined to, prone to
proclividad *nf* : proclivity, inclination
procrear *vi* : to procreate — **procreación** *nf*
procurador, -dora *n* ABOGADO : attorney
procurar *vt* **1** INTENTAR : to try, to endeavor **2** CONSEGUIR : to obtain, to
procure **3 procurar hacer** : to manage
to do
prodigar {52} *vt* : to lavish, to be generous with
prodigio *nm* : wonder, marvel
prodigioso, -sa *adj* : prodigious, marvelous
pródigo[1], **-ga** *adj* **1** : generous, lavish **2**
: wasteful, prodigal
pródigo[2], **-ga** *n* : spendthrift, prodigal
producción *nf, pl* **-ciones 1** : production **2 producción en serie** : mass production
producir {61} *vt* **1** : to produce, to make,
to manufacture **2** : to cause, to bring
about **3** : to bear (interest) — **producirse** *vr* : to take place, to occur
productividad *nf* : productivity
productivo, -va *adj* **1** : productive **2** LU-
CRATIVO : profitable

producto *nm* **1** : product **2** : proceeds *pl*, yield
productor, -tora *n* : producer
proeza *nf* HAZAÑA : feat, exploit
profanar *vt* : to profane, to desecrate — **profanación** *nf*
profano[1], **-na** *adj* **1** : profane **2** : worldly, secular
profano[2], **-na** *n* : nonspecialist
profecía *nf* : prophecy
proferir {76} *vt* **1** : to utter **2** : to hurl (insults)
profesar *vt* **1** : to profess, to declare **2** : to practice, to exercise
profesión *nf, pl* **-siones** : profession
profesional *adj & nmf* : professional — **profesionalmente** *adv*
profesionalismo *nm* : professionalism
profesionalizar {21} *vt* : to professionalize
profesionista *nmf Mex* : professional
profesor, -sora *n* **1** MAESTRO : teacher **2** : professor
profesorado *nm* **1** : faculty **2** : teaching profession
profeta *nm* : prophet
profético, -ca *adj* : prophetic
profetisa *nf* : prophetess, prophet
profetizar {21} *vt* : to prophesy
prófugo, -ga *adj & n* : fugitive
profundidad *nf* : depth, profundity
profundizar {21} *vt* **1** : to deepen **2** : to study in depth — *vi* ～ **en** : to go deeply into, to study in depth
profundo, -da *adj* **1** HONDO : deep **2** : profound — **profundamente** *adv*
profusión *nf, pl* **-siones** : abundance, profusion
profuso, -sa *adj* : profuse, abundant, extensive
progenie *nf* : progeny, offspring
progenitor, -tora *n* ANTEPASADO : ancestor, progenitor
progesterona *nf* : progesterone
prognóstico *nm* : prognosis
programa *nm* **1** : program **2** : plan **3** **programa de estudios** : curriculum
programable *adj* : programmable
programación *nf, pl* **-ciones** **1** : programming **2** : planning
programador, -dora *n* : programmer
programar *vt* **1** : to schedule, to plan **2** : to program (a computer, etc.)
progresar *vi* : to progress, to make progress
progresista *adj & nmf* : progressive
progresivo, -va *adj* : progressive, gradual
progreso *nm* : progress
prohibición *nf, pl* **-ciones** : ban, prohibition
prohibir {62} *vt* : to prohibit, to ban, to forbid
prohibitivo, -va *adj* : prohibitive
prohijar {5} *vt* ADOPTAR : to adopt
prójimo *nm* : neighbor, fellow man
prole *nf* : offspring, progeny
proletariado *nm* : proletariat, working class

proletario, -ria *adj & n* : proletarian
proliferar *vi* : to proliferate — **proliferación** *nf*
prolífico, -ca *adj* : prolific
prolijo, -ja *adj* : wordy, long-winded
prólogo *nm* : prologue, preface, foreword
prolongación *nf, pl* **-ciones** : extension, lengthening
prolongar {52} *vt* **1** : to prolong **2** : to extend, to lengthen — **prolongarse** *vr* CONTINUAR : to last, to continue
promediar *vt* **1** : to average **2** : to divide in half — *vi* : to be half over
promedio *nm* **1** : average **2** : middle, midpoint
promesa *nf* : promise
prometedor, -dora *adj* : promising, hopeful
prometer *vt* : to promise — *vi* : to show promise — **prometerse** *vr* COMPROMETERSE : to get engaged
prometido[1], **-da** *adj* : engaged
prometido[2], **-da** *n* NOVIO : fiancé *m*, fiancée *f*
prominente *adj* : prominent — **prominencia** *nf*
promiscuo, -cua *adj* : promiscuous — **promiscuidad** *nf*
promisorio, -ria *adj* **1** : promising **2** : promissory
promoción *nf, pl* **-ciones** **1** : promotion **2** : class, year **3** : play-off (in soccer)
promocionar *vt* : to promote — **promocional** *adj*
promontorio *nm* : promontory, headland
promotor, -tora *n* : promoter
promover {47} *vt* **1** : to promote, to advance **2** FOMENTAR : to foster, to encourage **3** PROVOCAR : to provoke, to cause
promulgación *nf, pl* **-ciones** **1** : enactment **2** : proclamation, enactment
promulgar {52} *vt* **1** : to promulgate, to proclaim **2** : to enact (a law or decree)
prono, -na *adj* : prone
pronombre *nm* : pronoun
pronosticar {72} *vt* : to predict, to forecast
pronóstico *nm* **1** PREDICCIÓN : forecast, prediction **2** : prognosis
prontitud *nf* **1** PRESTEZA : promptness, speed **2 con ～** : promptly, quickly
pronto[1] *adv* **1** : quickly, promptly **2** : soon **3 de ～** : suddenly **4 lo más pronto posible** : as soon as possible **5 tan pronto como** : as soon as
pronto[2], **-ta** *adj* **1** RÁPIDO : quick, speedy, prompt **2** PREPARADO : ready
pronunciación *nf, pl* **-ciones** : pronunciation
pronunciado, -da *adj* **1** : pronounced, sharp, steep **2** : marked, noticeable
pronunciamiento *nm* **1** : pronouncement **2** : military uprising
pronunciar *vt* **1** : to pronounce, to say **2** : to give, to deliver (a speech) **3 pro-**

nunciar un fallo : to pronounce sentence — **pronunciarse** *vr* : to declare oneself
propagación *nf, pl* **-ciones** : propagation, spreading
propaganda *nf* **1** : propaganda **2** PUBLICIDAD : advertising
propagar {52} *vt* **1** : to propagate **2** : to spread, to disseminate — **propagarse** *vr*
propalar *vt* **1** : to divulge **2** : to spread
propano *nm* : propane
propasarse *vr* : to go too far, to overstep one's bounds
propensión *nf, pl* **-siones** INCLINACIÓN : inclination, propensity
propenso, -sa *adj* : prone, susceptible
propiamente *adv* **1** : properly, correctly **2** : exactly, precisely ⟨propiamente dicho : strictly speaking⟩
propiciar *vt* **1** : to propitiate **2** : to favor, to foster
propicio, -cia *adj* : favorable, propitious
propiedad *nf* **1** : property ⟨propiedad privada : private property⟩ **2** : ownership **3** CUALIDAD : property, quality **4** : suitability, appropriateness
propietario[1], -ria *adj* : proprietary
propietario[2], -ria *n* DUEÑO : owner, proprietor
propina *nf* : tip, gratuity
propinar *vt* : to give, to strike ⟨propinar una paliza : to give a beating⟩
propio, -pia *adj* **1** : own ⟨su propia casa : his own house⟩ ⟨sus recursos propios : their own resources⟩ **2** APROPIADO : appropriate, suitable **3** CARACTERÍSTICO : characteristic, typical **4** MISMO : oneself ⟨el propio director : the director himself⟩
proponer {60} *vt* **1** : to propose, to suggest **2** : to nominate — **proponerse** *vr* : to intend, to plan, to set out ⟨lo que se propone lo cumple : he does what he sets out to do⟩
proporción *nf, pl* **-ciones** **1** : proportion **2** : ratio (in mathematics) **3 proporciones** *nfpl* : proportions, size ⟨de grandes proporciones : very large⟩
proporcionado, -da *adj* **1** : proportionate **2** : proportioned ⟨bien proporcionado : well-proportioned⟩ — **proporcionadamente** *adv*
proporcional *adj* : proportional — **proporcionalmente** *adv*
proporcionar *vt* **1** : to provide, to give **2** : to proportion, to adapt
proposición *nf, pl* **-ciones** : proposal, proposition
propósito *nm* **1** INTENCIÓN : purpose, intention **2 a ∼** : by the way **3 a ∼** : on purpose, intentionally
propuesta *nf* PROPOSICIÓN : proposal
propulsar *vt* **1** IMPULSAR : to propel, to drive **2** PROMOVER : to promote, to encourage
propulsión *nf, pl* **-siones** : propulsion
propulsor *nm* : propellant

propuso, etc. → **proponer**
prorrata *nf* **1** : share, quota **2 a ∼** : pro rata, proportionately
prórroga *nf* **1** : extension, deferment **2** : overtime (in sports)
prorrogar {52} *vt* **1** : to extend (a deadline) **2** : to postpone
prorrumpir *vi* : to burst forth, to break out ⟨prorrumpí en lágrimas : I burst into tears⟩
prosa *nf* : prose
prosaico, -ca *adj* : prosaic, mundane
proscribir {33} *v* **1** PROHIBIR : to prohibit, to ban, to proscribe **2** DESTERRAR : to banish, to exile
proscripción *nf, pl* **-ciones** **1** PROHIBICIÓN : ban, proscription **2** DESTIERRO : banishment
proscrito[1] *pp* → **proscribir**
proscrito[2], -ta *n* **1** DESTERRADO : exile **2** : outlaw
prosecución *nf, pl* **-ciones** **1** : continuation **2** : pursuit
proseguir {75} *vt* **1** CONTINUAR : to continue **2** : to pursue (studies, goals) — *vi* : to continue, to go on
prosélito, -ta *n* : proselyte
prospección *nf, pl* **-ciones** : prospecting, exploration
prospectar *vi* : to prospect
prospecto *nm* : prospectus, leaflet, brochure
prosperar *vi* : to prosper, to thrive
prosperidad *nf* : prosperity
próspero, -ra *adj* : prosperous, flourishing
próstata *nf* : prostate
prostitución *nf, pl* **-ciones** : prostitution
prostituir {41} *vt* : to prostitute — **prostituirse** *vr* : to prostitute oneself
prostituto, -ta *n* : prostitute
protagonista *nmf* **1** : protagonist, main character **2** : leader
protagonizar {21} *vt* : to star in
protección *nf, pl* **-ciones** : protection
protector[1], -tora *adj* : protective
protector[2], -tora *n* **1** : protector, guardian **2** : patron
protector[3] *nm* : protector, guard ⟨chaleco protector : chest protector⟩
protectorado *nm* : protectorate
proteger {15} *vt* : to protect, to defend — **protegerse** *vr*
protegido, -da *n* : protégé
proteína *nf* : protein
prótesis *nfs & pl* : prosthesis
protesta *nf* **1** : protest **2** *Mex* : promise, oath
protestante *adj & nmf* : Protestant
protestantismo *nm* : Protestantism
protestar *vi* : to protest, to object — *vt* **1** : to protest, to object to **2** : to declare, to profess
protocolo *nm* : protocol
protón *nm, pl* **protones** : proton
protoplasma *nm* : protoplasm
prototipo *nm* : prototype
protozoario *or* **protozoo** *nm* : protozoan

protuberancia *nf* : protuberance — **protuberante** *adj*
provecho *nm* : benefit, advantage
provechoso, -sa *adj* BENEFICIOSO : beneficial, profitable, useful — **provechosamente** *adv*
proveedor, -dora *n* : provider, supplier
proveer {63} *vt* : to provide, to supply — **proveerse** *vr* ~ **de** : to obtain, to supply oneself with
provenir {87} *vi* ~ **de** : to come from
provenzal[1] *adj* : Provençal
provenzal[2] *nmf* : Provençal
provenzal[3] *nm* : Provençal (language)
proverbio *nm* REFRÁN : proverb — **proverbial** *adj*
providencia *nf* 1 : providence, foresight 2 : Providence, God 3 **providencias** *nfpl* : steps, measures
providencial *adj* : providential
provincia *nf* : province — **provincial** *adj*
provinciano, -na *adj* : provincial, unsophisticated
provisión *nf, pl* **-siones** : provision
provisional *adj* : provisional, temporary
provisionalmente *adv* : provisionally, tentatively
provisorio, -ria *adj* : provisional, temporary
provisto *pp* → **proveer**
provocación *nf, pl* **-ciones** : provocation
provocador[1]**, -dora** *adj* : provocative, provoking
provocador[2]**, -dora** *n* AGITADOR : agitator
provocar {72} *vt* 1 CAUSAR : to provoke, to cause 2 IRRITAR : to provoke, to pique
provocativo, -va *adj* : provocative
proxeneta *nmf* : pimp *m*
próximamente *adv* : shortly, soon
proximidad *nf* 1 : nearness, proximity 2 **proximidades** *nfpl* : vicinity
próximo, -ma *adj* 1 : near, close ⟨la Navidad está próxima : Christmas is almost here⟩ 2 SIGUIENTE : next, following ⟨la próxima semana : the following week⟩
proyección *nf, pl* **-ciones** 1 : projection 2 : showing, screening (of a film) 3 : range, influence, diffusion
proyectar *vt* 1 : to plan 2 LANZAR : to throw, to hurl 3 : to project, to cast (light or shadow) 4 : to show, to screen (a film)
proyectil *nm* : projectile, missile
proyecto *nm* 1 : plan, project 2 **proyecto de ley** : bill
proyector *nm* 1 : projector 2 : spotlight
prudencia *nf* : prudence, care, discretion
prudente *adj* : prudent, sensible, reasonable
prueba[1]**, etc.** → **probar**
prueba[2] *nf* 1 : proof, evidence 2 : trial, test 3 : proof (in printing or photography) 4 : event, qualifying round (in sports) 5 **a prueba de agua** : waterproof 6 **prueba de fuego** : acid test 7 **poner a prueba** : to put to the test

prurito *nm* 1 : itching 2 : desire, urge
psicoanálisis *nm* : psychoanalysis — **psicoanalista** *nmf*
psicoanalítico, -ca *adj* : psychoanalytic
psicoanalizar {21} *vt* : to psychoanalyze
psicología *nf* : psychology
psicológico, -ca *adj* : psychological — **psicológicamente** *adv*
psicólogo, -ga *n* : psychologist
psicópata *nmf* : psychopath
psicopático, -ca *adj* : sycopathic
psicosis *nfs & pl* : psychosis
psicosomático, -ca *adj* : psychosomatic
psicoterapeuta *nmf* : psychotherapist
psicoterapia *nf* : psychotherapy
psicótico, -ca *adj & n* : psychotic
psique *nf* : psyche
psiquiatra *nmf* : psychiatrist
psiquiatría *nf* : psychiatry
psiquiátrico[1]**, -ca** *adj* : psychiatric
psiquiátrico[2] *nm* : mental hospital
psíquico, -ca *adj* : psychic
psiquis *nfs & pl* : psyche
psoriasis *nf* : psoriasis
ptomaína *nf* : ptomaine
púa *nf* 1 : barb ⟨alambre de púas : barbed wire⟩ 2 : tooth (of a comb) 3 : quill, spine
pubertad *nf* : puberty
pubiano → **púbico**
púbico, -ca *adj* : pubic
publicación *nf, pl* **-ciones** : publication
publicar {72} *vt* 1 : to publish 2 DIVULGAR : to divulge, to disclose
publicidad *nf* 1 : publicity 2 : advertising
publicista *nmf* : publicist
publicitar *vt* 1 : to publicize 2 : to advertise
publicitario, -ria *adj* : advertising, publicity ⟨agencia publicitaria : advertising agency⟩
público[1]**, -ca** *adj* : public — **públicamente** *adv*
público[2] *nm* 1 : public 2 : audience, spectators *pl*
puchero *nm* 1 : pot 2 : stew 3 : pout ⟨hacer pucheros : to pout⟩
pucho *nm* 1 : waste, residue 2 : cigarette butt 3 **a puchos** : little by little, bit by bit
púdico, -ca *adj* : chaste, modest
pudiente *adj* 1 : powerful 2 : rich, wealthy
pudín *nm, pl* **pudines** BUDÍN : pudding
pudo, etc. → **poder**
pudor *nm* : modesty, reserve
pudoroso, -sa *adj* : modest, reserved, shy
pudrir {59} *vt* 1 : to rot 2 *fam* : to annoy, to upset — **pudrirse** *vr* 1 : to rot 2 : to languish
pueblerino, -na *adj* : provincial, countrified

puebla, etc. → **poblar**
pueblo *nm* **1** NACIÓN : people **2** : common people **3** ALDEA, POBLADO : town, village
puede, etc. → **poder**
puente *nm* **1** : bridge ⟨puente levadizo : drawbridge⟩ **2** : denture, bridge **3 puente aéreo** : airlift
puerco¹, -ca *adj* : dirty, filthy
puerco², -ca *n* **1** CERDO, MARRANO : pig, hog **2** : pig, dirty or greedy person **3 puerco espín** : porcupine
pueril *adj* : childish, puerile
puerro *nm* : leek
puerta *nf* **1** : door, entrance, gate **2 a puerta cerrada** : behind closed doors
puerto *nm* **1** : port, harbor **2** : mountain pass **3 puerto marítimo** : seaport
puertorriqueño, -ña *adj & n* : Puerto Rican
pues *conj* **1** : since, because, for ⟨no puedo ir, pues no tengo plata : I can't go, since I don't have any money⟩ ⟨lo hace, pues a él le gusta : he does it because he likes to⟩ **2** (*used interjectionally*) : well, then ⟨¡pues claro que sí! : well, of course!⟩ ⟨¡pues no voy! : well then, I'm not going!⟩
puesta *nf* **1** : setting ⟨puesta del sol : sunset⟩ **2** : laying (of eggs) **3 puesta a punto** : tune-up **4 puesta en marcha** : start, starting up
puestero, -ra *n* : seller, vendor
puesto¹ *pp* → **poner**
puesto², -ta *adj* : dressed ⟨bien puesto : well-dressed⟩
puesto³ *nm* **1** LUGAR, SITIO : place, position **2** : position, job **3** : kiosk, stand, stall **4 puesto que** : since, given that
pugilato *nm* BOXEO : boxing, pugilism
pugilista *nm* BOXEADOR : boxer, pugilist
pugna *nf* **1** CONFLICTO, LUCHA : conflict, struggle **2 en ~** : at odds, in conflict
pugnar *vi* LUCHAR : to fight, to strive, to struggle
pugnaz *adj* : pugnacious
pujante *adj* : mighty, powerful
pujanza *nf* : strength, vigor ⟨pujanza económica : economic strength⟩
pulcritud *nf* **1** : neatness, tidiness **2** ESMERO : meticulousness
pulcro, -cra *adj* **1** : clean, neat **2** : exquisite, delicate, refined
pulga *nf* **1** : flea **2 tener malas pulgas** : to be bad-tempered
pulgada *nf* : inch
pulgar *nm* **1** : thumb **2** : big toe
pulir *vt* **1** : to polish, to shine **2** REFINAR : to refine, to perfect
pulla *nf* **1** : cutting remark, dig, gibe **2** : obscenity
pulmón *nm, pl* **pulmones** : lung
pulmonar *adj* : pulmonary
pulmonía *nf* NEUMONÍA : pneumonia
pulpa *nf* : pulp, flesh
pulpería *nf* : small grocery store

púlpito *nm* : pulpit
pulpo *nm* : octopus
pulsación *nf, pl* **-ciones** **1** : beat, pulsation, throb **2** : keystroke
pulsar *vt* **1** APRETAR : to press, to push **2** : to strike (a key) **3** : to assess — *vi* : to beat, to throb
pulsera *nf* : bracelet
pulso *nm* **1** : pulse ⟨tomarle el pulso a alguien : to take someone's pulse⟩ ⟨tomarle el pulso a la opinión : to sound out opinion⟩ **2** : steadiness (of hand) ⟨dibujo a pulso : freehand sketch⟩
pulular *vi* ABUNDAR : to abound, to swarm ⟨en el río pululan los peces : the river is teeming with fish⟩
pulverizador *nm* **1** : atomizer, spray **2** : spray gun
pulverizar {21} *vt* **1** : to pulverize, to crush **2** : to spray
puma *nf* : cougar, puma
puna *nf* : bleak Andean tableland
punción *nf, pl* **punciones** : puncture
punible *adj* : punishable
punitivo, -va *adj* : punitive
punce, etc. → **punzar**
punta *nf* **1** : tip, end ⟨punta del dedo : fingertip⟩ ⟨en la punta de la lengua : at the tip of one's tongue⟩ **2** : point (of a weapon or pencil) ⟨punta de lanza : spearhead⟩ **3** : point, headland **4** : bunch, lot ⟨una punta de ladrones : a bunch of thieves⟩ **5 a punta de** : by, by dint of
puntada *nf* **1** : stitch (in sewing) **2** PUNZADA : sharp pain, stitch, twinge **3** *Mex* : witticism, quip
puntal *nm* **1** : prop, support **2** : stanchion
puntapié *nm* PATADA : kick
puntazo *nm* CORNADA : wound (from a goring)
puntear *vt* **1** : to pluck (a guitar) **2** : to lead (in sports)
puntería *nf* : aim, marksmanship
puntero *nm* **1** : pointer **2** : leader
puntiagudo, -da *adj* : sharp, pointed
puntilla *nf* **1** : lace edging **2** : dagger (in bullfighting) **3 de puntillas** : on tiptoe
puntilloso, -sa *adj* : punctilious
punto *nm* **1** : dot, point **2** : period (in punctuation) **3** : item, question **4** : spot, place **5** : moment, stage, degree **6** : point (in a score) **7** : stitch **8 en ~** : on the dot, sharp ⟨a las dos en punto : at two o'clock sharp⟩ **9 al punto** : at once **10 a punto fijo** : exactly, certainly **11 dos puntos** : colon **12 hasta cierto punto** : up to a point **13 punto decimal** : decimal point **14 punto de vista** : point of view **15 punto y coma** : semicolon **16 y punto** : period ⟨es el mejor que hay y punto : it's the best there is, period⟩ **17 puntos cardinales** : points of the compass

puntuación *nf, pl* **-ciones 1** : punctuation **2** : scoring, score, grade
puntual *adj* **1** : prompt, punctual **2** : exact, accurate — **puntualmente** *adv*
puntualidad *nf* **1** : promptness, punctuality **2** : exactness, accuracy
puntualizar {21} *vt* **1** : to specify, to state **2** : to point out
puntuar {3} *vt* : to punctuate — *vi* : to score points
punzada *nf* : sharp pain, twinge, stitch
punzante *adj* **1** : sharp **2** CÁUSTICO : biting, caustic
punzar {21} *vt* : to pierce, to puncture
punzón *nm, pl* **punzones 1** : awl **2** : hole punch
puñado *nm* **1** : handful **2 a puñados** : lots of, by the handful
puñal *nm* DAGA : dagger
puñalada *nf* : stab, stab wound
puñetazo *nm* : punch (with the fist)
puño *nm* **1** : fist **2** : handful, fistful **3** : cuff (of a shirt) **4** : handle, hilt
pupila *nf* : pupil (of the eye)
pupilo, -la *n* **1** : pupil, student **2** : ward, charge
pupitre *nm* : writing desk
puré *nm* : purée ⟨puré de papas : mashed potatoes⟩
pureza *nf* : purity
purga *nf* **1** : laxative **2** : purge
purgante *adj & nm* : laxative, purgative
purgar {52} *vt* **1** : to purge, to cleanse **2** : to liquidate (in politics) **3** : to give a laxative to — **purgarse** *vr* **1** : to take a laxative **2** ~ **de** : to purge oneself of
purgatorio *nm* : purgatory
purgue, etc. → **purgar**
purificador *nm* : purifier
purificar {72} *vt* : to purify — **purificación** *nf*
puritano¹, -na *adj* : puritanical, puritan
puritano², -na *n* **1** : Puritan **2** : puritan
puro¹ *adv* : sheer, much ⟨de puro terco : out of sheer stubbornness⟩
puro², -ra *adj* **1** : pure ⟨aire puro : fresh air⟩ **2** : plain, simple, sheer ⟨por pura curiosidad : from sheer curiosity⟩ **3** : only, just ⟨emplean puras mujeres : they only employ women⟩ **4 pura sangre** : Thoroughbred horse
puro³ *nm* : cigar
púrpura *nf* : purple
purpúreo, -rea *adj* : purple
purpurina *nf* : glitter (for decoration)
pus *nm* : pus
pusilánime *adj* COBARDE : pusillanimous, cowardly
puso, etc. → **poner**
pústula *nf* : pustule, pimple
puta *nf* : whore, slut
putrefacción *nf, pl* **-ciones** : putrefaction
putrefacto, -ta *adj* **1** PODRIDO : putrid, rotten **2** : decayed
pútrido, -da *adj* : putrid, rotten
puya *nf* **1** : point (of a lance) **2 lanzar una puya** : to gibe, to taunt

Q

q *nf* : eighteenth letter of the Spanish alphabet
que¹ *conj* **1** : that ⟨dice que está listo : he says that he's ready⟩ ⟨espero que lo haga : I hope that he does it⟩ **2** : than ⟨más que nada : more than anything⟩ **3** (*implying permission or desire*) ⟨¡que entre! : send him in!⟩ ⟨¡que te vaya bien! : I wish you well!⟩ **4** (*indicating a reason or cause*) ⟨¡cuidado, que te caes! : be careful, you're about to fall!⟩ ⟨no provoques al perro, que te va a morder : don't provoke the dog or (else) he'll bite⟩ **5 es que** : the thing is that, I'm afraid that **6 yo que tú** : if I were you
que² *pron* **1** : who, that ⟨la niña que viene : the girl who is coming⟩ **2** : whom, that ⟨los alumnos que enseñé : the students that I taught⟩ **3** : that, which ⟨el carro que me gusta : the car that I like⟩ **4 el (la, lo, las, los) que** → **el¹, la¹, lo¹, los¹**
qué¹ *adv* : how, what ⟨¡qué bonito! : how pretty!⟩
qué² *adj* : what, which ⟨¿qué hora es? : what time is it?⟩
qué³ *pron* : what ⟨¿qué quieres? : what do you want?⟩
quebracho *nm* : quebracho (tree)
quebrada *nf* DESFILADERO : ravine, gorge
quebradizo, -za *adj* FRÁGIL : breakable, delicate, fragile
quebrado¹, -da *adj* **1** : bankrupt **2** : rough, uneven **3** ROTO : broken
quebrado² *nm* : fraction
quebrantamiento *nm* **1** : breaking **2** : deterioration, weakening
quebrantar *vt* **1** : to break, to split, to crack **2** : to weaken **3** : to violate (a law or contract)
quebranto *nm* **1** : break, breaking **2** AFLICCIÓN : affliction, grief **3** PÉRDIDA : loss
quebrar {55} *vt* **1** ROMPER : to break **2** DOBLAR : to bend, to twist — *vi* **1** : to go bankrupt **2** : to fall out, to break up — **quebrarse** *vr*
queda *nf* : curfew
quedar *vi* **1** PERMANECER : to remain, to stay **2** : to be ⟨quedamos contentos con las mejoras : we were pleased with the improvements⟩ **3** : to be situated ⟨queda muy lejos : it's very far, it's too far away⟩ **4** : to be left ⟨quedan sólo dos alternativas : there are only two options left⟩ **5** : to fit, to suit ⟨estos zap-

atos no me quedan : these shoes don't fit⟩ **6 quedar bien (mal)** : to turn out well (badly) **7 ~ en** : to agree, to arrange ⟨¿en qué quedamos? : what's the arrangement, then?⟩ — **quedarse** *vr* **1** : to stay ⟨se quedó en casa : she stayed at home⟩ **2** : to keep on ⟨se quedó esperando : he kept on waiting⟩ **3 quedarse atrás** : to stay behind ⟨no quedarse atrás : to be no slouch⟩ **4 ~ con** : to remain ⟨me quedé con hambre después de comer : I was still hungry after I ate⟩

quedo¹ *adv* : softly, quietly

quedo², **-da** *adj* : quiet, still

quehacer *nm* **1** : work **2 quehaceres** *nmpl* : chores

queja *nf* : complaint

quejarse *vr* **1** : to complain **2** : to groan, to moan

quejido *nm* **1** : groan, moan **2** : whine, whimper

quejoso, -sa *adj* : complaining, whining

quejumbroso, -sa *adj* : querulous, whining

quema *nf* **1** FUEGO : fire **2** : burning

quemado, -da *adj* **1** : burned, burnt **2** : annoyed **3** : burned-out

quemador *nm* : burner

quemadura *nf* : burn

quemar *vt* : to burn, to set fire to — *vi* : to be burning hot — **quemarse** *vr*

quemarropa *nf* a ~ : point-blank

quemazón *nf, pl* **-zones 1** : burning **2** : intense heat **3** : itch **4** : cutting remark

quena *nf* : Peruvian reed flute

quepa, etc. → **caber**

querella *nf* **1** : complaint **2** : lawsuit

querellante *nmf* : plaintiff

querellarse *vr* ~ **contra** : to bring suit against, to sue

querer¹ {64} *vt* **1** DESEAR : to want, to desire ⟨quiere ser profesor : he wants to be a teacher⟩ ⟨¿cuánto quieres por esta computadora? : how much do you want for this computer?⟩ **2** : to love, to like, to be fond of ⟨te quiero : I love you⟩ **3** (*indicating a request*) ⟨¿quieres pasarme la leche? : please pass the milk⟩ **4 querer decir** : to mean **5 sin ~** : unintentionally — *vi* : like, want ⟨si quieras : if you like⟩

querer² *nm* : love, affection

querido¹, -da *adj* : dear, beloved

querido², -da *n* : dear, sweetheart

queroseno *nm* : kerosene

querrá, etc. → **querer**

querúbico, -ca *adj* : cherubic

querubín *nm, pl* **-bines** : cherub

quesadilla *nf* : quesadilla

quesería *nf* : cheese shop

queso *nm* : cheese

quetzal *nm* **1** : quetzal (bird) **2** : monetary unit of Guatemala

quicio *nm* **1 estar fuera de quicio** : to be beside oneself **2 sacar de quicio** : to exasperate, to drive crazy

quid *nm* : crux, gist ⟨el quid de la cuestión : the crux of the matter⟩

quiebra¹, etc. → **quebrar**

quiebra² *nf* **1** : break, crack **2** BANCARROTA : failure, bankruptcy

quien *pron, pl* **quienes 1** : who, whom ⟨no sé quien ganará : I don't know who will win⟩ ⟨las personas con quienes trabajo : the people with whom I work⟩ **2** : whoever, whomever ⟨quien quiere salir que salga : whoever wants to can leave⟩ **3** : anyone, some people ⟨hay quienes no están de acuerdo : some people don't agree⟩

quién *pron, pl* **quiénes 1** : who, whom ⟨¿quién sabe? : who knows?⟩ ⟨¿con quién hablo? : with whom am I speaking?⟩ **2 de ~** : whose ⟨¿de quién es este libro? : whose book is this?⟩

quienquiera *pron, pl* **quienesquiera** : whoever, whomever

quiere, etc. → **querer**

quieto, -ta *adj* **1** : calm, quiet **2** INMÓVIL : still

quietud *nf* **1** : calm, tranquility **2** INMOVILIDAD : stillness

quijada *nf* : jaw, jawbone

quijotesco, -ca *adj* : quixotic

quilate *nm* : karat

quilla *nf* : keel

quimera *nf* : chimera, illusion

quimérico, -ca *adj* : chimeric, fanciful

química *nf* : chemistry

químico¹, -ca *adj* : chemical

químico², -ca *n* : chemist

quimioterapia *nf* : chemotherapy

quimono *nm* : kimono

quince *adj & nm* : fifteen

quinceañero, -ra *n* : fifteen-year-old, teenager

quinceavo¹, -va *adj* : fifteenth

quinceavo² *nm* : fifteenth (fraction)

quincena *nf* : two week period, fortnight

quincenal *adj* : bimonthly, twice a month

quincuagésimo¹, -ma *adj* : fiftieth, fifty-

quincuagésimo², -ma *n* : fiftieth, fifty- (in a series)

quingombó *nm* : okra

quiniela *nf* : sports lottery

quinientos¹, -tas *adj* : five hundred

quinientos² *nms & pl* : five hundred

quinina *nf* : quinine

quino *nm* : cinchona

quinqué *nm* : oil lamp

quinquenal *adj* : five-year ⟨un plan quinquenal : a five-year plan⟩

quinta *nf* : country house, villa

quintaesencia *nf* : quintessence — **quintaesencial** *adj*

quintal *nm* : hundredweight

quinteto *nm* : quintet

quintillizo, -za *n* : quintuplet

quinto, -ta *adj* : fifth — **quinto, -ta** *n*

quíntuplo, -la *adj* : quintuple, five-fold

quiosco *nm* **1** : kiosk **2** : newsstand **3 quiosco de música** : bandstand

quirófano *nm* : operating room

quiromancia *nf* : palmistry
quiropráctica *nf* : chiropractic
quiropráctico, -ca *n* : chiropractor
quirúrgico, -ca *adj* : surgical — **quirúrgicamente** *adv*
quiso, etc. → querer
quisquilloso[1], -sa *adj* : fastidious, fussy
quisquilloso[2], -sa *n* : fussy person, fussbudget
quiste *nm* : cyst
quitaesmalte *nm* : nail polish remover
quitamanchas *nms & pl* : stain remover

quitanieves *nms & pl* : snowplow
quitar *vt* 1 : to remove, to take away 2 : to take off (clothes) 3 : to get rid of, to relieve — **quitarse** *vr* 1 : to withdraw, to leave 2 : to take off (one's clothes) 3 ~ **de** : to give up (a habit) 4 **quitar de encima** : to get rid of
quitasol *nm* : parasol
quiteño[1], -ña *adj* : of or from Quito
quiteño[2], -ña *n* : person from Quito
quizá *or* **quizás** *adv* : maybe, perhaps
quórum *nm, pl* **quórums** : quorum

R

r *nf* : nineteenth letter of the Spanish alphabet
rábano *nm* 1 : radish 2 **rábano picante** : horseradish
rabí *nmf, pl* **rabíes** : rabbi
rabia *nf* 1 HIDROFOBIA : rabies, hydrophobia 2 : rage, anger
rabiar *vi* 1 : to rage, to be furious 2 : to be in great pain 3 **a ~ fam** : like crazy, like mad
rabieta *nf* BERRINCHE : tantrum
rabino, -na *n* : rabbi
rabioso, -sa *adj* 1 : enraged, furious 2 : rabid
rabo *nm* 1 COLA : tail 2 **el rabo del ojo** : the corner of one's eye
racha *nf* 1 : gust of wind 2 : run, series, string ⟨racha perdedora : losing streak⟩
racheado, -da *adj* : gusty, windy
racial *adj* : racial
racimo *nm* : bunch, cluster ⟨un racimo de uvas : a bunch of grapes⟩
raciocinio *nm* : reason, reasoning
ración *nf, pl* **raciones** 1 : share, ration 2 PORCIÓN : portion, helping
racional *adj* : rational, reasonable — **racionalmente** *adv*
racionalidad *nf* : rationality
racionalización *nf, pl* **-ciones** : rationalization
racionalizar {21} *vt* 1 : to rationalize 2 : to streamline
racionamiento *nm* : rationing
racionar *vt* : to ration
racismo *nm* : racism
racista *adj & nmf* : racist
radar *nm* : radar
radiación *nf, pl* **-ciones** : radiation, irradiation
radiactividad *nf* : radioactivity
radiactivo, -va *adj* : radioactive
radiador *nm* : radiator
radial *adj* 1 : radial 2 : radio, broadcasting ⟨emisora radial : radio transmitter⟩
radiante *adj* : radiant
radiar *vt* 1 : to radiate 2 : to irradiate 3 : to broadcast (on the radio)
radical[1] *adj* : radical, extreme — **radicalmente** *adv*

radical[2] *nmf* : radical
radicalismo *nm* : radicalism
radicar {72} *vi* 1 : to be found, to lie 2 ARRAIGAR : to take root — **radicarse** *vr* : to settle, to establish oneself
radio[1] *nm* 1 : radius 2 : radium
radio[2] *nmf* : radio
radioactividad *nf* : radioactivity
radioactivo, -va *adj* : radioactive
radioaficionado, -da *n* : ham radio operator
radiodifusión *nf, pl* **-siones** : radio broadcasting
radiodifusora *nf* : radio station
radioemisora *nf* : radio station
radiofaro *nm* : radio beacon
radiofónico, -ca *adj* : radio ⟨estación radiofónica pública : public radio station⟩
radiofrecuencia *nf* : radio frequency
radiografía *nf* : X ray (photograph)
radiografiar {85} *vt* : to x-ray
radiología *nf* : radiology
radiólogo, -ga *n* : radiologist
radón *nm* : radon
raer {65} *vt* RASPAR : to scrape, to scrape off
ráfaga *nf* 1 : gust (of wind) 2 : flash, burst ⟨una ráfaga de luz : a flash of light⟩
raid *nm* CA, Mex fam : lift, ride
raído, -da *adj* : worn, shabby
raiga, etc. → raer
raíz *nf, pl* **raíces** 1 : root 2 : origin, source 3 **a raíz de** : following, as a result of 4 **echar raíces** : to take root
raja *nf* 1 : crack, slit 2 : slice, wedge
rajá *nm* : raja
rajadura *nf* : crack, split
rajar *vt* HENDER : to crack, to split — *vi* 1 *fam* : to chatter 2 *fam* : to boast, to brag — **rajarse** *vr* 1 : to crack, to split open 2 *fam* : to back out
rajatabla *adv* **a ~** : strictly, to the letter
ralea *nf* : kind, sort, ilk ⟨son de la misma valea : they're two of a kind⟩
ralentí *nm* **dejar al ralentí** : to leave (a motor) idling
rallado, -da *adj* 1 : grated 2 **pan rallado** : bread crumbs *pl*
rallador *nm* : grater

rallar *vt* : to grate
ralo, -la *adj* : sparse, thin
RAM *nf* : RAM, random-access memory
rama *nf* : branch
ramaje *nm* : branches *pl*
ramal *nm* **1** : branchline **2** : halter, strap
ramera *nf* : harlot, prostitute
ramificación *nf, pl* **-ciones** : ramification
ramificarse {72} *vr* : to branch out, to divide into branches
ramillete *nm* **1** RAMO : bouquet **2** : select group, cluster
ramo *nm* **1** : branch **2** RAMILLETE : bouquet **3** : division (of science or industry) **4 Domingo de Ramos** : Palm Sunday
rampa *nf* : ramp, incline
rana *nf* **1** : frog **2 rana toro** : bullfrog
ranchera *nf Mex* : traditional folk song
ranchería *nf* : settlement
ranchero, -ra *n* : rancher, farmer
rancho *nm* **1** : ranch, farm **2** : hut **3** : settlement, camp **4** : food, mess (for soldiers, etc.)
rancio, -cia *adj* **1** : aged, mellow (of wine) **2** : ancient, old **3** : rancid
rango *nm* **1** : rank, status **2** : high social standing **3** : pomp, splendor
ranúnculo *nm* : buttercup
ranura *nf* : groove, slot
rap *nm* : rap (music)
rapacidad *nf* : rapacity
rapar *vt* **1** : to crop **2** : to shave
rapaz[1] *adj, pl* **rapaces** : rapacious, predatory
rapaz[2], -paza *n, mpl* **rapaces** : youngster, child
rape *nm* : close haircut
rapé *nm* : snuff
rapero, -ra *n* : rapper, rap artist
rapidez *nf* : rapidity, speed
rápido[1] *adv* : quickly, fast ⟨¡manejas tan rápido! : you drive so fast!⟩
rápido[2], -da *adj* : rapid, quick — **rápidamente** *adv*
rápido[3] *nm* **1** : express train **2 rápidos** *nmpl* : rapids
rapiña *nf* **1** : plunder, pillage **2 ave de rapiña** : bird of prey
raposa *nf* : vixen (fox)
rapsodia *nf* : rhapsody
raptar *vt* SECUESTRAR : to abduct, to kidnap
rapto *nm* **1** SECUESTRO : kidnapping, abduction **2** ARREBATO : fit, outburst
raptor, -tora *n* SECUESTRADOR : kidnapper
raque *nm* : beachcombing
raquero, -ra *n* : beachcomber
raqueta *nf* **1** : racket (in sports) **2** : snowshoe
raquítico, -ca *adj* **1** : scrawny, weak **2** : measly, skimpy
raquitismo *nm* : rickets
raramente *adv* : seldom, rarely
rareza *nf* **1** : rarity **2** : peculiarity, oddity

raro, -ra *adj* **1** EXTRAÑO : odd, strange, peculiar **2** : unusual, rare **3** : exceptional **4 rara vez** : seldom, rarely
ras *nm* **a ras de** : level with
rasar *vt* **1** : to skim, to graze **2** : to level
rascacielos *nms & pl* : skyscraper
rascar {72} *vt* **1** : to scratch **2** : to scrape — **rascarse** *vr* : to scratch an itch
rasgadura *nf* : tear, rip
rasgar {52} *vt* : to rip, to tear — **rasgarse** *vr*
rasgo *nm* **1** : stroke (of a pen) ⟨a grandes rasgos : in broad outlines⟩ **2** CARACTERÍSTICA : trait, characteristic **3** : gesture, deed **4 rasgos** *nmpl* FACCIONES : features
rasgón *nm, pl* **rasgones** : rip, tear
rasgue, etc. → **rasgar**
rasguear *vt* : to strum
rasguñar *vt* **1** : to scratch **2** : to sketch, to outline
rasguño *nm* **1** : scratch **2** : sketch
raso[1], -sa *adj* **1** : level, flat **2 soldado raso** : private (in the army) ⟨los soldados rasos : the ranks⟩
raso[2] *nm* : satin
raspadura *nf* **1** : scratching, scraping **2 raspaduras** *nfpl* : scrapings
raspar *vt* **1** : to scrape **2** : to file down, to smooth — *vi* **1** : to be rough
rasque, etc. → **rascar**
rastra *nf* **1** : harrow **2 a rastras** : by dragging, unwillingly
rastrear *vt* **1** : to track, to trace **2** : to comb, to search **3** : to trawl
rastrero, -ra *adj* **1** : creeping, crawling **2** : vile, despicable
rastrillar *vt* : to rake, to harrow
rastrillo *nm* **1** : rake **2 Mex** : razor
rastro *nm* **1** PISTA : trail, track **2** VESTIGIO : trace, sign
rastrojo *nm* : stubble (of plants)
rasuradora *nf Mex, CA* : electric razor, shaver
rasurar *vt* AFEITAR : to shave — **rasurarse** *vr*
rata[1] *nm fam* : pickpocket, thief
rata[2] *nf* **1** : rat **2 Col, Pan, Peru** : rate, percentage
ratear *vt* : to pilfer, to steal
ratero, -ra *n* : petty thief
ratificación *nf, pl* **-ciones** : ratification
ratificar {72} *vt* **1** : to ratify **2** : to confirm
rato *nm* **1** : while **2 pasar el rato** : to pass the time **3 a cada rato** : all the time, constantly ⟨les sacaba dinero a cada rato : he was always taking money from them⟩ **4 al poco rato** : later, shortly after
ratón[1], -tona *n, mpl* **ratones** **1** : mouse **2 ratón de biblioteca** *fam* : bookworm
ratón[2] *nm, pl* **ratones** **1** : (computer) mouse **2 CoRi** : biceps
ratonera *nf* : mousetrap
raudal *nm* **1** : torrent **2 a raudales** : in abundance

raya¹, etc. → raer

raya² *nf* **1** : line **2** : stripe **3** : skate, ray **4** : part (in the hair) **5** : crease (in clothing)

rayar *vt* **1** ARAÑAR : to scratch **2** : to scrawl on, to mark up ⟨rayaron las paredes : they covered the walls with graffiti⟩ — *vi* **1** : to scratch **2** AMANECER : to dawn, to break ⟨al rayar el alba : at break of day⟩ **3 ~ con** : to be adjacent to, to be next to **4 ~ en** : to border on, to verge on ⟨su respuesta raya en lo ridículo : his answer borders on the ridiculous⟩ — **rayarse** *vr*

rayo *nm* **1** : ray, beam ⟨rayo láser : laser beam⟩ ⟨rayo de gamma : gamma ray⟩ ⟨rayo de sol : sunbeam⟩ **2** RELÁMPAGO : lightning bolt **3 rayo X** : X-ray

rayón *nm, pl* **rayones** : rayon

raza *nf* **1** : race ⟨raza humana : human race⟩ **2** : breed, strain **3 de ~** : thoroughbred, pedigreed

razón *nf, pl* **razones 1** MOTIVO : reason, motive ⟨en razón de : by reason of, because of⟩ **2** JUSTICIA : rightness, justice ⟨tener razón : to be right⟩ **3** : reasoning, sense ⟨perder la razón : to lose one's mind⟩ **4** : ratio, proportion

razonable *adj* : reasonable — **razonablemente** *adv*

razonado, -da *adj* : itemized, detailed

razonamiento *nm* : reasoning

razonar *v* : to reason, to think

reabastecimiento *nm* : replenishment

reabierto *pp* → reabrir

reabrir {2} *vt* : to reopen — **reabrirse** *vr*

reacción *nf, pl* **-ciones 1** : reaction **2 motor a reacción** : jet engine

reaccionar *vi* : to react, to respond

reaccionario, -ria *adj & n* : reactionary

reacio, -cia *adj* : resistant, opposed

reacondicionar *vt* : to recondition

reactivación *nf, pl* **-ciones** : reactivation, revival

reactivar *vt* : to reactivate, revive

reactor *nm* **1** : reactor ⟨reactor nuclear : nuclear reactor⟩ **2** : jet engine **3** : jet airplane, jet

reafirmar *vt* : to reaffirm, to assert, to strengthen

reajustar *vt* : to readjust, to adjust

reajuste *nm* : readjustment ⟨reajuste de precios : price increase⟩

real *adj* **1** : real, true **2** : royal

realce *nm* **1** : embossing, relief **2 dar realce** : to highlight, to bring out

realeza *nf* : royalty

realidad *nf* **1** : reality **2 en ~** : in truth, actually

realinear *vt* : to realign

realismo *nm* **1** : realism **2** : royalism

realista¹ *adj* **1** : realistic **2** : realist **3** : royalist

realista² *nmf* **1** : realist **2** : royalist

realización *nf, pl* **-ciones** : execution, realization

realizar {21} *vt* **1** : to carry out, to execute **2** : to produce, to direct (a film or play) **3** : to fulfill, to achieve **4** : to realize (a profit) — **realizarse** *vr* **1** : to come true **2** : to fulfill oneself

realmente *adv* : really, in reality

realzar {21} *vt* **1** : to heighten, to raise **2** : to highlight, to enhance

reanimación *nf, pl* **-ciones** : revival, resuscitation

reanimar *vt* **1** : to revive, to restore **2** : to resuscitate — **reanimarse** *vr* : to come around, to recover

reanudación *nf, pl* **-ciones** : resumption, renewal

reanudar *vt* : to resume, to renew — **reanudarse** *vr* : to resume, to continue

reaparecer {53} *vi* **1** : to reappear **2** : to make a comeback

reaparición *nf, pl* **-ciones** : reappearance

reapertura *nf* : reopening

reata *nf* **1** : rope **2** *Mex* : lasso, lariat **3 de ~** : single file

reavivar *vt* : to revive, to reawaken

rebaja *nf* **1** : reduction **2** DESCUENTO : discount **3 rebajas** *nfpl* : sale

rebajar *vt* **1** : to reduce, to lower ⟨a precios rebajados : at reduced prices, on sale⟩ **2** : to lessen, to diminish **3** : to humiliate — **rebajarse** *vr* **1** : to humble oneself **2 rebajarse a** : to stoop to

rebanada *nf* : slice

rebañar *vt* : to mop up, to sop up

rebaño *nm* **1** : flock **2** : herd

rebasar *vt* **1** : to surpass, to exceed **2** *Mex* : to pass, to overtake

rebatiña *nf* : scramble, fight (over something)

rebatir *vt* REFUTAR : to refute

rebato *nm* **1** : surprise attack **2 tocar a rebato** : to sound the alarm

rebelarse *vr* : to rebel

rebelde¹ *adj* : rebellious, unruly

rebelde² *nmf* **1** : rebel **2** : defaulter

rebeldía *nf* **1** : rebelliousness **2 en ~** : in default

rebelión *nf, pl* **-liones** : rebellion

rebobinar *vt* : to rewind

reborde *nm* : border, flange, rim

rebosante *adj* : brimming, overflowing ⟨rebosante de salud : brimming with health⟩

rebosar *vi* **1** : to overflow **2 ~ de** : to abound in, to be bursting with — *vt* : to radiate

rebotar *vi* **1** : to bounce **2** : to ricochet, to rebound

rebote *nm* **1** : bounce **2** : rebound, ricochet

rebozar {21} *vt* : to coat in batter

rebozo *nm* **1** : shawl, wrap **2 sin ~** : frankly, openly

rebullir {38} *v* : to move, to stir — **rebullirse** *vr*

rebuscado, -da *adj* : affected, pretentious

rebuscar {72} *vi* : to search thoroughly

rebuznar *vi* : to bray
rebuzno *nm* : bray, braying
recabar *vt* **1** : to gather, to obtain, to collect **2 recabar fondos** : to raise money
recado *nm* **1** : message ⟨mandar recado : to send word⟩ **2** *Spain* : errand
recaer {13} *vi* **1** : to relapse **2 ∼ en** *or* **∼ sobre** : to fall on, to fall to
recaída *nf* : relapse
recaiga, etc. → recaer
recalar *vi* : to arrive
recalcar {72} *vt* : to emphasize, to stress
recalcitrante *adj* : recalcitrant
recalentar {55} *vt* **1** : to reheat, to warm up **2** : to overheat
recámara *nf* **1** *Col, Mex, Pan* : bedroom **2** : chamber (of a firearm)
recamarera *nf Mex* : chambermaid
recambio *nm* **1** : spare part **2** : refill (for a pen, etc.)
recapacitar *vi* **1** : to reconsider **2 ∼ en** : to reflect on, to weigh
recapitular *v* : to recapitulate — **recapitulación** *nf*
recargable *adj* : rechargeable
recargado, -da *adj* : overly elaborate or ornate
recargar {52} *vt* **1** : to recharge **2** : to overload
recargo *nm* : surcharge
recatado, -da *adj* MODESTO : modest, demure
recato *nm* PUDOR : modesty
recaudación *nf, pl* **-ciones 1** : collection **2** : earnings *pl*, takings *pl*
recaudador, -dora *n* **recaudador de impuestos** : tax collector
recaudar *vt* : to collect
recaudo *nm* : safe place ⟨a (buen) recaudo : in safe keeping⟩
recayó, etc. → recaer
rece, etc. → rezar
recelo *nm* : distrust, suspicion
receloso, -sa *adj* : distrustful, suspicious
recepción *nf, pl* **-ciones** : reception
recepcionista *nmf* : receptionist
receptáculo *nm* : receptacle
receptividad *nf* : receptivity, receptiveness
receptivo, -va *adj* : receptive
receptor[1], -tora *adj* : receiving
receptor[2], -tora *n* **1** : recipient **2** : catcher (in baseball), receiver (in football)
receptor[3] *nm* : receiver ⟨receptor de televisión : television set⟩
recesión *nf, pl* **-siones** : recession
recesivo, -va *adj* : recessive
receso *nm* : recess, adjournment
receta *nf* **1** : recipe **2** : prescription
recetar *vt* : to prescribe (medications)
rechazar {21} *vt* **1** : to reject **2** : to turn down, to refuse
rechazo *nm* : rejection, refusal
rechifla *nf* : booing, jeering
rechinar *vi* **1** : to squeak **2** : to grind, to gnash ⟨hacer rechinar los dientes : to grind one's teeth⟩

rechoncho, -cha *adj fam* : chubby, squat
recibidor *nm* : vestibule, entrance hall
recibimiento *nm* : reception, welcome
recibir *vt* **1** : to receive, to get **2** : to welcome — *vi* : to receive visitors — **recibirse** *vr* **∼ de** : to qualify as
recibo *nm* : receipt
reciclable *adj* : recyclable
reciclado → reciclaje
reciclaje *nm* **1** : recycling **2** : retraining
reciclar *vt* **1** : to recycle **2** : to retrain
recién *adv* **1** : newly, recently ⟨recién nacido : newborn⟩ ⟨recién casados : newlyweds⟩ ⟨recién llegado : newcomer⟩ **2** : just, only just ⟨recién ahora me acordé : I just now remembered⟩
reciente *adj* : recent — **recientemente** *adv*
recinto *nm* **1** : enclosure **2** : site, premises *pl*
recio[1] *adv* **1** : strongly, hard **2** : loudly, loud
recio[2], -cia *adj* **1** : severe, harsh **2** : tough, strong
recipiente[1] *nm* : container, receptacle
recipiente[2] *nmf* : recipient
reciprocar {72} *vi* : to reciprocate
reciprocidad *nf* : reciprocity
recíproco, -ca *adj* : reciprocal, mutual
recitación *nf, pl* **-ciones** : recitation, recital
recital *nm* : recital
recitar *vt* : to recite
reclamación *nf, pl* **-ciones 1** : claim, demand **2** QUEJA : complaint
reclamar *vt* **1** EXIGIR : to demand, to require **2** : to claim — *vi* : to complain
reclamo *nm* **1** : bird call, lure **2** : lure, decoy **3** : inducement, attraction **4** : advertisement **5** : complaint
reclinar *vt* : to rest, to lean — **reclinarse** *vr* : to recline, to lean back
recluir {41} *vt* : to confine, to lock up — **recluirse** *vr* : to shut oneself up, to withdraw
reclusión *nf, pl* **-siones** : imprisonment
recluso, -sa *n* **1** : inmate, prisoner **2** SOLITARIO : recluse
recluta *nmf* : recruit, draftee
reclutamiento *nm* : recruitment, recruiting
reclutar *vt* ENROLAR : to recruit, to enlist
recobrar *vt* : to recover, to regain — **recobrarse** *vr* : to recover, to recuperate
recocer {14} *vt* : to overcook, to cook again
recodo *nm* : bend
recogedor *nm* : dustpan
recoger {15} *vt* **1** : to collect, to gather **2** : to get, to retrieve, to pick up **3** : to clean up, to tidy (up)
recogido, -da *adj* : quiet, secluded
recogimiento *nm* **1** : collecting, gathering **2** : withdrawal **3** : absorption, concentration

recolección *nf, pl* **-ciones 1** : collection ⟨recolección de basura : trash pickup⟩ **2** : harvest

recolectar *vt* **1** : to gather, to collect **2** : to harvest, to pick

recomendable *adj* : advisable, recommended

recomendación *nf, pl* **-ciones** : recommendation

recomendar {55} *vt* **1** : to recommend **2** ACONSEJAR : to advise

recompensa *nf* : reward, recompense

recompensar *vt* **1** PREMIAR : to reward **2** : to compensate

reconciliación *nf, pl* **-ciones** : reconciliation

reconciliar *vt* : to reconcile — **reconciliarse** *vr*

recóndito, -ta *adj* **1** : remote, isolated **2** : hidden, recondite **3 en lo más recóndito de** : in the depths of

reconfortar *vt* : to comfort — **reconfortante** *adj*

reconocer {18} *vt* **1** : to recognize **2** : to admit **3** : to examine

reconocible *adj* : recognizable

reconocido, -da *adj* **1** : recognized, accepted **2** : grateful

reconocimiento *nm* **1** : acknowledgment, recognition, avowal **2** : (medical) examination **3** : reconnaissance

reconquista *nf* : reconquest

reconquistar *vt* **1** : to reconquer, to recapture **2** RECUPERAR : to regain, to recover

reconsiderar *vt* : to reconsider — **reconsideración** *nf*

reconstrucción *nf, pl* **-ciones** : reconstruction

reconstruir {41} *vt* : to rebuild, to reconstruct

reconversión *nf, pl* **-siones** : restructuring

reconvertir {76} *vt* **1** : to restructure **2** : to retrain

recopilación *nf, pl* **-ciones 1** : summary **2** : collection, compilation

recopilar *vt* : to compile, to collect

récord *or* **record** ['rɛkɔr] *nm, pl* **récords** *or* **records** [-kɔrs] : record ⟨record mundial : world record⟩ — **récord** *or* **record** *adj*

recordar {19} *vt* **1** : to recall, to remember **2** : to remind — *vi* **1** ACORDARSE : to remember **2** DESPERTAR : to wake up

recordatorio¹, -ria *adj* : commemorative

recordatorio² *nm* : reminder

recorrer *vt* **1** : to travel through, to tour **2** : to cover (a distance) **3** : to go over, to look over

recorrido *nm* **1** : journey, trip **2** : path, route, course **3** : round (in golf)

recortar *vt* **1** : to cut, to reduce **2** : to cut out **3** : to trim, to cut off **4** : to outline — **recortarse** *vr* : to stand out ⟨los árboles se recortaban en el horizonte : the trees were silhouetted against the horizon⟩

recorte *nm* **1** : cut, reduction **2** : clipping ⟨recortes de periódicos : newspaper clippings⟩

recostar {19} *vt* : to lean, to rest — **recostarse** *vr* : to lie down, recline

recoveco *nm* **1** VUELTA : bend, turn **2** : nook, corner **3 recovecos** *nmpl* : intricacies, ins and outs

recreación *nf, pl* **-ciones 1** : re-creation **2** DIVERSIÓN : recreation, entertainment

recrear *vt* **1** : to re-create **2** : to entertain, to amuse — **recrearse** *vr* : to enjoy oneself

recreativo, -va *adj* : recreational

recreo *nm* **1** DIVERSIÓN : entertainment, amusement **2** : recess, break

recriminación *nf, pl* **-ciones** : reproach, recrimination

recriminar *vt* : to reproach — *vi* : to recriminate — **recriminarse** *vr*

recrudecer {53} *v* : to intensify, to worsen — **recrudecerse** *vr*

rectal *adj* : rectal

rectangular *adj* : rectangular

rectángulo *nm* : rectangle

rectificación *nf, pl* **-ciones** : rectification, correction

rectificar {72} *vt* **1** : to rectify, to correct **2** : to straighten (out)

rectitud *nf* **1** : straightness **2** : honesty, rectitude

recto¹ *adv* : straight

recto², -ta *adj* **1** : straight **2** : upright, honorable **3** : sound

recto³ *nm* : rectum

rector¹, -tora *adj* : governing, managing

rector², -tora *nm* : rector

rectoría *nf* : rectory

recubierto *pp* → **recubrir**

recubrir {2} *vt* : to cover, to coat

recuento *nm* : recount, count ⟨un recuento de los votos : a recount of the votes⟩

recuerdo *nm* **1** : memory **2** : souvenir, memento **3 recuerdos** *nmpl* : regards

recular *vi* **1** : to back up **2** REPLEGARSE : to retreat, to fall back **3** RETRACTARSE : to back down

recuperación *nf, pl* **-ciones 1** : recovery, recuperation **2 recuperación de datos** : data retrieval

recuperar *vt* **1** : to recover, to get back, to retrieve **2** : to recuperate **3** : to make up for ⟨recuperar el tiempo perdido : to make up for lost time⟩ — **recuperarse** *vr* ~ **de** : to recover from, to get over

recurrente *adj* : recurrent, recurring

recurrir *vi* **1** ~ **a** : to turn to, to appeal to **2** ~ **a** : to resort to **3** : to appeal (in law)

recurso *nm* **1** : recourse ⟨el último recurso : the last resort⟩ **2** : appeal (in law) **3 recursos** *nmpl* : resources, means ⟨recursos naturales : natural resources⟩

red *nf* **1** : net, mesh **2** : network, system, chain **3** : trap, snare
redacción *nf, pl* **-ciones 1** : writing, composition **2** : editing
redactar *vt* **1** : to write, to draft **2** : to edit
redactor, -tora *n* : editor
redada *nf* **1** : raid **2** : catch, haul
redefinir *vt* : to redefine — **redefinición** *nf*
redención *nf, pl* **-ciones** : redemption
redentor¹, -tora *adj* : redeeming
redentor², -tora *n* : redeemer
redescubierto *pp* → **redescubrir**
redescubrir {2} *vt* : to rediscover
redicho, -cha *adj fam* : affected, pretentious
redil *nm* **1** : sheepfold **2 volver al redil** : to return to the fold
redimir *vt* : to redeem, to deliver (from sin)
rediseñar *vt* : to redesign
redistribuir {41} *vt* : to redistribute — **redistribución** *nf*
rédito *nm* : return, yield
redituar {3} *vt* : to produce, to yield
redoblar *vt* : to redouble, to strengthen — **redoblado, -da** *adj*
redoble *nm* : drum roll
redomado, -da *adj* **1** : sly, crafty **2** : utter, out-and-out
redonda *nf* **1** : region, surrounding area **2 a la redonda** ALREDEDOR : around ⟨de diez millas a la redonda : for ten miles around⟩
redondear *vt* : to round off, to round out
redondel *nm* **1** : ring, circle **2** : bullring, arena
redondez *nf* : roundness
redondo, -da *adj* **1** : round ⟨mesa redonda : round table⟩ **2** : great, perfect ⟨un negocio redondo : an excellent deal⟩ **3** : straightforward, flat ⟨un rechazo redondo : a flat refusal⟩ **4** *Mex* : round-trip **5 en ~** : around
reducción *nf, pl* **-ciones** : reduction, decrease
reducido, -da *adj* **1** : reduced, limited **2** : small
reducir {61} *vt* **1** DISMINUIR : to reduce, to decrease, to cut **2** : to subdue **3** : to boil down — **reducirse** *vr* **~ a** : to come down to, to be nothing more than
redundancia *nf* : redundancy
redundante *adj* : redundant
reedición *nf, pl* **-ciones** : reprint
reelegir {28} *vt* : to reelect — **reelección** *nf*
reembolsable *adj* : refundable
reembolsar *vt* **1** : to refund, to reimburse **2** : to repay
reembolso *nm* : refund, reimbursement
reemplazable *adj* : replaceable
reemplazar {21} *vt* : to replace, to substitute
reemplazo *nm* : replacement, substitution
reencarnación *nf, pl* **-ciones** : reincarnation

reencuentro *nm* : reunion
reestablecer {53} *vt* : to reestablish
reestructurar *vt* : to restructure
reexaminar *vt* : to reexamine
refaccionar *vt* : to repair, to renovate
refacciones *nfpl* : repairs, renovations
referencia *nf* **1** : reference **2 hacer referencia a** : to refer to
referendo → **referéndum**
referéndum *nm, pl* **-dums** : referendum
referente *adj* **~ a** : concerning
réferi *or* **referi** [ˈreferi] *nmf* : referee
referir {76} *vt* **1** : to relate, to tell **2** : to refer ⟨nos refirió al diccionario : she referred us to the dictionary⟩ — **referirse** *vr* **~ a** : to refer to **2 ~ a** : to be concerned, to be in reference to ⟨en lo que se refiere a la educación : as far as education is concerned⟩
refinado¹, -da *adj* : refined
refinado² *nm* : refining
refinamiento *nm* **1** : refining **2** FINURA : refinement
refinanciar *vt* : to refinance
refinar *vt* : to refine
refinería *nf* : refinery
reflectante *adj* : reflective, reflecting
reflector¹, -tora *adj* : reflecting
reflector² *nm* **1** : spotlight, searchlight **2** : reflector
reflejar *vt* : to reflect — **reflejarse** *vr* : to be reflected ⟨la decepción se refleja en su rostro : the disappointment shows on her face⟩
reflejo *nm* **1** : reflection **2** : reflex **3 reflejos** *nmpl* : highlights, streaks (in hair)
reflexión *nf, pl* **-xiones** : reflection, thought
reflexionar *vi* : to reflect, to think
reflexivo, -va *adj* **1** : reflective, thoughtful **2** : reflexive
reflujo *nm* : ebb, ebb tide
reforma *nf* **1** : reform **2** : alteration, renovation
reformador, -dora *n* : reformer
reformar *vt* **1** : to reform **2** : to change, to alter **3** : to renovate, to repair — **reformarse** *vr* : to mend one's ways
reformatorio *nm* : reformatory
reformular *vt* : to reformulate — **reformulación** *nf*
reforzar {36} *vt* **1** : to reinforce, to strengthen **2** : to encourage, to support
refracción *nf, pl* **-ciones** : refraction
refractar *vt* : to refract — **refractarse** *vr*
refractario, -ria *adj* : refractory, obstinate
refrán *nm, pl* **refranes** ADAGIO : proverb, saying
refregar {49} *vt* : to scrub
refrenar *vt* **1** : to rein in (a horse) **2** : to restrain, to check — **refrenarse** *vr* : to restrain oneself
refrendar *vt* **1** : to countersign, to endorse **2** : to stamp (a passport)
refrescante *adj* : refreshing

refrescar {72} *vt* **1** : to refresh, to cool **2** : to brush up (on) **3 refrescar la memoria** : to refresh one's memory — *vi* : to turn cooler

refresco *nm* : refreshment, soft drink

refriega *nf* : skirmish, scuffle

refrigeración *nf*, *pl* **-ciones 1** : refrigeration **2** : air-conditioning

refrigerador *nmf* NEVERA : refrigerator

refrigeradora *nf Col, Peru* : refrigerator

refrigerante *nm* : coolant

refrigerar *vt* **1** : to refrigerate **2** : to air-condition

refrigerio *nm* : snack, refreshments *pl*

refrito¹, -ta *adj* : refried

refrito² *nm* : rehash

refuerzo *nm* : reinforcement, support

refugiado, -da *n* : refugee

refugiar *vt* : to shelter — **refugiarse** *vr* ACOGERSE : to take refuge

refugio *nm* : refuge, shelter

refulgencia *nf* : brilliance, splendor

refulgir {35} *vi* : to shine brightly

refundir *vt* **1** : to recast (metals) **2** : to revise, to rewrite

refunfuñar *vi* : to grumble, to groan

refutar *vt* : to refute — **refutación** *nf*

regadera *nf* **1** : watering can **2** : shower head, shower **3** : sprinkler

regaderazo *nm Mex* : shower

regalar *vt* **1** OBSEQUIAR : to present (as a gift), to give away **2** : to regale, to entertain **3** : to flatter, to make a fuss over — **regalarse** *vr* : to pamper oneself

regalía *nf* : royalty, payment

regaliz *nm*, *pl* **-lices** : licorice

regalo *nm* **1** OBSEQUIO : gift, present **2** : pleasure, comfort **3** : treat

regañadientes *mpl* **a ~** : reluctantly, unwillingly

regañar *vt* : to scold, to give a talking to — *vi* **1** QUEJARSE : to grumble, to complain **2** REÑIR : to quarrel, to argue

regaño *nm fam* : scolding

regañon, -ñona *adj*, *mpl* **-ñones** *fam* : grumpy, irritable

regar {49} *vt* **1** : to irrigate **2** : to water **3** : to wash, to hose down **4** : to spill, to scatter

regata *nf* : regatta, yacht race

regate *nm* : dodge, feint

regatear *vt* **1** : to haggle over **2** ESCATIMAR : to skimp on, to be sparing with — *vi* : to bargain, to haggle

regateo *nm* : bargaining, haggling

regatón *nm*, *pl* **-tones** : ferrule, tip

regazo *nm* : lap (of a person)

regencia *nf* : regency

regenerar *vt* : to regenerate — **regenerarse** *vr* — **regeneración** *nf*

regentar *vt* : to run, to manage

regente *nmf* : regent

regidor, -dora *n* : town councillor

régimen *nm*, *pl* **regímenes 1** : regime **2** : diet **3** : regimen, rules *pl* ⟨régimen de vida : lifestyle⟩

regimiento *nm* : regiment

regio, -gia *adj* **1** : great, magnificent **2** : regal, royal

región *nf*, *pl* **regiones** : region, area

regional *adj* : regional — **regionalmente** *adv*

regir {28} *vt* **1** : to rule **2** : to manage, to run **3** : to control, to govern ⟨las costumbres que rigen la conducta : the customs which govern behavior⟩ — *vi* : to apply, to be in force ⟨las leyes rigen en los tres países : the laws apply in all three countries⟩ — **regirse** *vr* **~ por** : to go by, to be guided by

registrador¹, -dora *adj* **caja registradora** : cash register

registrador², -dora *n* : registrar, recorder

registrar *vt* **1** : to register, to record **2** GRABAR : to record, to tape **3** : to search, to examine — **registrarse** *vr* **1** INSCRIBIRSE : to register **2** OCURRIR : to happen, to occur

registro *nm* **1** : register **2** : registration **3** : registry, record office **4** : range (of a voice or musical instrument) **5** : search

regla *nf* **1** NORMA : rule, regulation **2** : ruler ⟨regla de cálculo : slide rule⟩ **3** MENSTRUACIÓN : period, menstruation

reglamentación *nf*, *pl* **-ciones 1** : regulation **2** : rules *pl*

reglamentar *vt* : to regulate, to set rules for

reglamentario, -ria *adj* : regulation, official ⟨equipo reglamentario : standard equipment⟩

reglamento *nm* : regulations *pl*, rules *pl* ⟨reglamento de tráfico : traffic regulations⟩

regocijar *vt* : to gladden, to delight — **regocijarse** *vr* : to rejoice

regocijo *nm* : delight, rejoicing

regordete, -ta *adj fam* LLENITO : chubby

regresar *vt* DEVOLVER : to give back — *vi* : to return, to come back, to go back

regresión *nf*, *pl* **-siones** : regression, return

regresivo, -va *adj* : regressive

regreso *nm* **1** : return **2 estar de regreso** : to be back, to be home

reguero *nm* **1** : irrigation ditch **2** : trail, trace **3 propagarse como reguero de pólvora** : to spread like wildfire

regulable *adj* : adjustable

regulación *nf*, *pl* **-ciones** : regulation, control

regulador¹, -dora *adj* : regulating, regulatory

regulador² *nm* **1** : regulator, governor **2 regulador de tiro** : damper (in a chimney)

regular¹ *vt* : to regulate, to control

regular² *adj* **1** : regular **2** : fair, OK, so-so **3** : medium, average **4 por lo regular** : in general, generally

regularidad *nf* : regularity

regularización *nf, pl* **-ciones** NORMAL-IZACIÓN : normalization

regularizar {21} *vt* NORMALIZAR : to normalize, to make regular

regularmente *adv* : regularly

regusto *nm* : aftertaste

rehabilitar *vt* **1** : to rehabilitate **2** : to reinstate **3** : renovate, to restore — **rehabilitación** *nf*

rehacer {40} *vt* **1** : to redo **2** : to remake, to repair, to renew — **rehacerse** *vr* **1** : to recover **2** ~ **de** : to get over

rehecho *pp* → **rehacer**

rehén *nm, pl* **rehenes** : hostage

rehicieron, etc. → **rehacer**

rehizo → **rehacer**

rehuir {41} *vt* : to avoid, to shun

rehusar {8} *v* : to refuse

reimprimir *vt* : to reprint

reina *nf* : queen

reinado *nm* : reign

reinante *adj* **1** : reigning **2** : prevailing, current

reinar *vi* **1** : to reign **2** : to prevail

reincidencia *nf* : recidivism, relapse

reincidente *nmf* : backslider, recidivist

reincidir *vi* : to backslide, to retrogress

reincorporar *vt* : to reinstate — **reincorporarse** *vr* ~ **a** : to return to, to rejoin

reiniciar *vt* **1** : to resume, to restart **2** : to reboot (a computer)

reino *nm* : kingdom, realm ⟨reino animal : animal kingdom⟩

reinstalar *vt* **1** : to reinstall **2** : to reinstate

reintegración *nf, pl* **-ciones 1** : reinstatement, reintegration **2** : refund, reimbursement

reintegrar *vt* **1** : to reintegrate, reinstate **2** : to refund, to reimburse — **reintegrarse** *vr* ~ **a** : to return to, to rejoin

reír {66} *vi* : to laugh — *vt* : to laugh at — **reírse** *vr*

reiteración *nf, pl* **-ciones** : reiteration, repetition

reiterado, -da *adj* : repeated ⟨lo explicó en reiteradas ocasiones : he explained it repeatedly⟩ — **reiteradamente** *adv*

reiterar *vt* : to reiterate, to repeat

reiterativo, -va *adj* : repetitive, repetitious

reivindicación *nf, pl* **-ciones 1** : demand, claim **2** : vindication

reivindicar {72} *vt* **1** : to vindicate **2** : to demand, to claim **3** : to restore

reja *nf* **1** : grille, grating ⟨entre rejas : behind bars⟩ **2** : plowshare

rejilla *nf* : grille, grate, screen

rejuvenecer {53} *vt* : to rejuvenate — *vi* : to be rejuvenated — **rejuvenecerse** *vr*

rejuvenecimiento *nm* : rejuvenation

relación *nf, pl* **-ciones 1** : relation, connection, relevance **2** : relationship **3** RELATO : account **4** LISTA : list **5 con relación a** *or* **en relación con** : in re-

lation to, concerning **6 relaciones-públicas** : public relations

relacionar *vt* : to relate, to connect — **relacionarse** *vr* ~ **con** : to be connected to, to be linked with

relajación *nf, pl* **-ciones** : relaxation

relajado, -da *adj* **1** : relaxed, loose **2** : dissolute, depraved

relajante *adj* : relaxing

relajar *vt* : to relax, to slacken — *vi* : to be relaxing — **relajarse** *vr*

relajo *nm* **1** : commotion, ruckus **2** : joke, laugh ⟨lo hizo de relajo : he did it for a laugh⟩

relamerse *vr* : to smack one's lips, to lick one's chops

relámpago *nm* : flash of lightning

relampaguear *vi* : to flash

relanzar {21} *vt* : to relaunch

relatar *vt* : to relate, to tell

relatividad *nf* : relativity

relativo, -va *adj* **1** : relative **2 en lo relativo a** : with regard to, concerning — **relativamente** *adv*

relato *nm* **1** : story, tale **2** : account

releer {20} *vt* : to reread

relegar {52} *vt* **1** : to relegate **2 relegar al olvido** : to consign to oblivion

relevante *adj* : outstanding, important

relevar *vt* **1** : to relieve, to take over from **2** ~ **de** : to exempt from — **relevarse** *vr* : to take turns

relevo *nm* **1** : relief, replacement **2** : relay ⟨carrera de relevos : relay race⟩

relicario *nm* **1** : reliquary **2** : locket

relieve *nm* **1** : relief, projection ⟨mapa en relieve : relief map⟩ ⟨letras en relieve : embossed letters⟩ **2** : prominence, importance **3 poner en relieve** : to highlight, to emphasize

religión *nf, pl* **-giones** : religion

religiosamente *adv* : religiously, faithfully

religioso[1], -sa *adj* : religious

religioso[2], -sa *n* : monk *m*, nun *f*

relinchar *vi* : to neigh, to whinny

relincho *nm* : neigh, whinny

reliquia *nf* **1** : relic **2 reliquia de familia** : family heirloom

rellenar *vt* **1** : to refill **2** : to stuff, to fill **3** : to fill out

relleno[1], -na *adj* : stuffed, filled

relleno[2] *nm* : stuffing, filling

reloj *nm* **1** : clock **2** : watch **3 reloj de arena** : hourglass **4 reloj de pulsera** : wristwatch **5 como un reloj** : like clockwork

relojería *nf* **1** : watchmaker's shop **2** : watchmaking, clockmaking

reluciente *adj* : brilliant, shining

relucir {45} *vi* **1** : to glitter, to shine **2 salir a relucir** : to come to the surface **3 sacar a relucir** : to bring up, to mention

relumbrante *adj* : dazzling

relumbrar *vi* : to shine brightly

relumbrón *nm, pl* **-brones 1** : flash, glare **2 de** ~ : flashy, showy

remachar *vt* **1** : to rivet **2** : to clinch (a nail) **3** : to stress, to drive home — *vi* : to smash, to spike (a ball)

remache *nm* **1** : rivet **2** : smash, spike (in sports)

remanente *nm* **1** : remainder, balance **2** : surplus

remanso *nm* : pool

remar *vi* **1** : to row, to paddle **2** : to struggle, to toil

remarcar {72} *vt* : to emphasize, to stress

rematado, -da *adj* : utter, complete

rematador, -dora *n* : auctioneer

rematar *vt* **1** : to finish off **2** : to auction — *vi* **1** : to shoot **2** : to end

remate *nm* **1** : shot (in sports) **2** : auction **3** : end, conclusion **4 como ~** : to top it off **5 de ~** : completely, utterly

remecer {86} *vt* : to sway, to swing

remedar *vt* **1** IMITAR : to imitate, to copy **2** : to mimic, to ape

remediar *vt* **1** : to remedy, to repair **2** : to help out, to assist **3** EVITAR : to prevent, to avoid

remedio *nm* **1** : remedy, cure **2** : solution **3** : option ⟨no me quedó más remedio : I had no other choice⟩ ⟨no hay remedio : it can't be helped⟩ **4 poner remedio a** : to put a stop to **5 sin ~** : unavoidable, inevitable

remedo *nm* : imitation

rememorar *vi* : to recall ⟨rememorar los viejos tiempos : to reminisce⟩

remendar {55} *vt* **1** : to mend, to patch, to darn **2** : to correct

remero, -ra *n* : rower

remesa *nf* **1** : remittance **2** : shipment

remezón *nm, pl* **-zones** : mild earthquake, tremor

remiendo *nm* **1** : patch **2** : correction

remilgado, -da *adj* **1** : prim, prudish **2** : affected

remilgo *nm* : primness, affectation

reminiscencia *nf* : reminiscence

remisión *nf, pl* **-siones 1** ENVÍO : sending, delivery **2** : remission **3** : reference, cross-reference

remiso, -sa *adj* **1** : lax, remiss **2** : reluctant

remitente[1] *nm* : return address

remitente[2] *nmf* : sender (of a letter, etc.)

remitir *vt* **1** : to send, to remit **2 ~ a** : to refer to, to direct to ⟨nos remitió al diccionario : he referred us to the dictionary⟩ — *vi* : to subside, to let up

remo *nm* **1** : paddle, oar **2** : rowing (sport)

remoción *nf, pl* **-ciones 1** : removal **2** : dismissal

remodelación *nf, pl* **-ciones 1** : remodeling **2** : reorganization, restructuring

remodelar *vt* **1** : to remodel **2** : to restructure

remojar *vt* **1** : to soak, to steep **2** : to dip, to dunk **3** : to celebrate with a drink

remojo *nm* **1** : soaking, steeping **2 poner en remojo** : to soak, to leave soaking

remolacha *nf* : beet

remolcador *nm* : tugboat

remolcar {72} *vt* : to tow, to haul

remolino *nm* **1** : whirlwind **2** : eddy, whirlpool **3** : crowd, throng **4** : cowlick

remolque *nm* **1** : towing, tow **2** : trailer **3 a ~** : in tow

remontar *vt* **1** : to overcome **2** SUBIR : to go up — **remontarse** *vr* **1** : to soar **2 ~ a** : to date from, to go back to

rémora *nf* : obstacle, hindrance

remorder {47} *vt* INQUIETAR : to trouble, to distress

remordimiento *nm* : remorse

remotamente *adv* : remotely, vaguely

remoto, -ta *adj* **1** : remote, unlikely ⟨hay una posibilidad remota : there is a slim possibility⟩ **2** : distant, far-off

remover {47} *vt* **1** : to stir **2** : to move around, to turn over **3** : to stir up **4** : to remove **5** : to dismiss

remozamiento *nm* : renovation

remozar {21} *vt* **1** : to renew, to brighten up **2** : to redo, to renovate

remuneración *nf, pl* **-ciones** : remuneration, pay

remunerar *vt* : to pay, to remunerate

remunerativo, -va *adj* : remunerative

renacer {48} *vi* : to be reborn, to revive

renacimiento *nm* **1** : rebirth, revival **2 el Renacimiento** : the Renaissance

renacuajo *nm* : tadpole, pollywog

renal *adj* : renal, kidney

rencilla *nf* : quarrel

renco, -ca *adj* : lame

rencor *nm* **1** : rancor, enmity, hostility **2 guardar rencor** : to hold a grudge

rencoroso, -sa *adj* : resentful, rancorous

rendición *nf, pl* **-ciones 1** : surrender, submission **2** : yield, return

rendido, -da *adj* **1** : submissive **2** : worn-out, exhausted **3** : devoted

rendija *nf* GRIETA : crack, split

rendimiento *nm* **1** : performance **2** : yield

rendir {54} *vt* **1** : to render, to give ⟨rendir las gracias : to give thanks⟩ ⟨rendir homenaje a : to pay homage to⟩ **2** : to yield **3** CANSAR : to exhaust — *vi* **1** CUNDIR : to progress, to make headway **2** : to last, to go a long way — **rendirse** *vr* : to surrender, to give up

renegado, -da *n* : renegade

renegar {49} *vi* **1 ~ de** : to renounce, to disown, to give up **2 ~ de** : to complain about — *vt* **1** : to deny vigorously **2** : to abhor, to hate

renegociar *vt* : to renegotiate — **renegociación** *nf*

renglón *nm, pl* **renglones 1** : line (of writing) **2** : merchandise, line (of products)

rengo, -ga *adj* : lame
renguear *vi* : to limp
reno *nm* : reindeer
renombrado, -da *adj* : renowned, famous
renombre *nm* NOMBRADÍA : renown, fame
renovable *adj* : renewable
renovación *nf, pl* **-ciones 1** : renewal ⟨renovación de un contrato : renewal of a contract⟩ **2** : change, renovation
renovar {19} *vt* **1** : to renew, to restore **2** : to renovate
renquear *vi* : to limp, to hobble
renquera *nf* COJERA : limp, lameness
renta *nf* **1** : income **2** : rent **3 impuesto sobre la renta** : income tax
rentable *adj* : profitable
rentar *vt* **1** : to produce, to yield **2** ALQUILAR : to rent
renuencia *nf* : reluctance, unwillingness
renuente *adj* : reluctant, unwilling
renuncia *nf* **1** : resignation **2** : renunciation **3** : waiver
renunciar *vi* **1** : to resign **2** ~ **a** : to renounce, to relinquish ⟨renunció al título : he relinquished the title⟩
reñido, -da *adj* **1** : tough, hard-fought **2** : at odds, on bad terms
reñir {67} *vi* **1** : to argue **2** ~ **con** : to fall out with, to go up against — *vt* : to scold, to reprimand
reo, rea *n* **1** : accused, defendant **2** : offender, culprit
reojo *nm* **de** ~ : out of the corner of one's eye ⟨una mirada de reojo : a sidelong glance⟩
reorganizar {21} *vt* : to reorganize — **reorganización** *nf*
repantigarse {52} *vr* : to slouch, to loll about
reparación *nf, pl* **-ciones 1** : reparation, amends **2** : repair
reparar *vt* **1** : to repair, to fix, to mend **2** : to make amends for **3** : to correct **4** : to restore, to refresh — *vi* **1** ~ **en** : to observe, to take notice of **2** ~ **en** : to consider, to think about
reparo *nm* **1** : repair, restoration **2** : reservation, qualm ⟨no tuvieron reparos en decírmelo : they didn't hesitate to tell me⟩ **3 poner reparos a** : to find fault with, to object to
repartición *nf, pl* **-ciones 1** : distribution **2** : department, division
repartidor¹, -dora *adj* : delivery ⟨camión repartidor : delivery truck⟩
repartidor², -dora *n* : delivery person, distributor
repartimiento *nm* → **repartición**
repartir *vt* **1** : to allocate **2** DISTRIBUIR : to distribute, to hand out **3** : to spread
reparto *nm* **1** : allocation **2** : distribution **3** : cast (of characters)
repasar *vt* **1** : to pass by again **2** : to review, to go over **3** : to mend
repaso *nm* **1** : review **2** : mending **3** : checkup, overhaul

repatriar {85} *vt* : to repatriate — **repatriación** *nf*
repavimentar *vt* : to resurface
repelente¹ *adj* : repellent, repulsive
repelente² *nm* : repellent ⟨repelente de insectos : insect repellent⟩
repeler *vt* **1** : to repel, to resist, to repulse **2** : to reject **3** : to disgust ⟨el sabor me repele : I find the taste repulsive⟩
repensar {55} *v* : to rethink, to reconsider
repente *nm* **1** : sudden movement, start ⟨de repente : suddenly⟩ **2** : fit, outburst ⟨un repente de ira : a fit of anger⟩
repentino, -na *adj* : sudden — **repentinamente** *adv*
repercusión *nf, pl* **-siones** : repercussion
repercutir *vi* **1** : to reverberate, to echo **2** ~ **en** : to have effects on, to have repercussions on
repertorio *nm* : repertoire
repetición *nf, pl* **-ciones 1** : repetition **2** : rerun, repeat
repetidamente *adv* : repeatedly
repetido, -da *adj* **1** : repeated, numerous **2 repetidas veces** : repeatedly, time and again
repetir {54} *vt* **1** : to repeat **2** : to have a second helping of — **repetirse** *vr* **1** : to repeat oneself **2** : to recur
repetitivo, -va *adj* : repetitive, repetitious
repicar {72} *vt* : to ring — *vi* : to ring out, to peal
repique *nm* : ringing, pealing
repisa *nf* : shelf, ledge ⟨repisa de chimenea : mantelpiece⟩ ⟨repisa de ventana : windowsill⟩
replantear *vt* : to redefine, to restate — **replantearse** *vr* : to reconsider
replegar {49} *vt* : to fold — **replegarse** *vr* RETIRARSE : to retreat, to withdraw
repleto, -ta *adj* **1** : replete, full **2** ~ **de** : packed with, crammed with
réplica *nf* **1** : reply **2** : replica, reproduction **3** *Chile, Mex* : aftershock
replicación *nf, pl* **-ciones** : replication
replicar {72} *vi* **1** : to reply, to retort **2** : to argue, to answer back
repliegue *nm* **1** : fold **2** : retreat, withdrawal
repollo *nm* COL : cabbage
reponer {60} *vt* **1** : to replace, to put back **2** : to reinstate **3** : to reply — **reponerse** *vr* : to recover
reportaje *nm* : article, story, report
reportar *vt* **1** : to check, to restrain **2** : to bring, to carry, to yield ⟨me reportó numerosos beneficios : it brought me many benefits⟩ **3** : to report — **reportarse** *vr* **1** CONTENERSE : to control oneself **2** PRESENTARSE : to report, to show up
reporte *nm* : report
reportear *vt* : to report on, to cover

reportero, -ra n 1 : reporter 2 **reportero gráfico** : photojournalist
reposado, -da adj : calm
reposar vi 1 : to rest, to repose 2 : to stand, to settle ⟨deje reposar la masa media hora : let the dough stand for half an hour⟩ 3 : to lie, to be buried — **reposarse** vr : to settle
reposición nf, pl **-ciones** 1 : replacement 2 : reinstatement 3 : revival
repositorio nm : repository
reposo nm : repose, rest
repostar vi 1 : to stock up 2 : to refuel
repostería nf 1 : confectioner's shop 2 : pastry-making
repostero, -ra n : confectioner
repreguntar vt : to cross-examine
repreguntas nfpl : cross-examination
reprender vt : to reprimand, to scold
reprensible adj : reprehensible
represa nf : dam
represalia nf 1 : reprisal, retaliation 2 **tomar represalias** : to retaliate
represar vt : to dam
representación nf, pl **-ciones** 1 : representation 2 : performance 3 **en representación de** : on behalf of
representante nmf 1 : representative 2 : performer
representar vt 1 : to represent, to act for 2 : to perform 3 : to look, to appear as 4 : to symbolize, to stand for 5 : to signify, to mean — **representarse** vr : to imagine, to picture
representativo, -va adj : representative
represión nf, pl **-siones** : repression
represivo, -va adj : repressive
reprimenda nf : reprimand
reprimir vt 1 : to repress 2 : to suppress, to stifle
reprobable adj : reprehensible, culpable
reprobación nf : disapproval
reprobar {19} vt 1 DESAPROBAR : to condemn, to disapprove of 2 : to fail (a course)
reprobatorio, -ria adj : disapproving, admonitory
reprochable adj : reprehensible, reproachable
reprochar vt : to reproach — **reprocharse** vr
reproche nm : reproach
reproducción nf, pl **-ciones** : reproduction
reproducir {61} vt : to reproduce — **reproducirse** vr 1 : to breed, to reproduce 2 : to recur
reproductor, -tora adj : reproductive
reptar vi : to crawl, to slither
reptil[1] adj : reptilian
reptil[2] nm : reptile
república nf : republic
republicanismo nm : republicanism
republicano, -na adj & n : republican
repudiar vt : to repudiate — **repudiación** nf
repudio nm : repudiation
repuesto[1] pp → **reponer**

repuesto[2] nm 1 : spare part 2 **de** ∼ : spare ⟨rueda de repuesto : spare wheel⟩
repugnancia nf : repugnance
repugnante adj : repulsive, repugnant, revolting
repugnar vt : to cause repugnance, to disgust — **repugnarse** vr
repujar vt : to emboss
repulsivo, -va adj : repulsive
repuntar vt Arg, Chile : to round up (cattle) — vi : to begin to appear — **repuntarse** vr : to fall out, to quarrel
repuso, etc. → **reponer**
reputación nf, pl **-ciones** : reputation
reputar vt : to consider, to deem
requerir {76} vt 1 : to require, to call for 2 : to summon, to send for
requesón nm, pl **-sones** : curd cheese, cottage cheese
réquiem nm : requiem
requisa nf 1 : requisition 2 : seizure 3 : inspection
requisar vt 1 : to requisition 2 : to seize 3 INSPECCIONAR : to inspect
requisito nm 1 : requirement 2 **requisito previo** : prerequisite
res nf 1 : beast, animal 2 CA, Mex : beef 3 **reses** nfpl : cattle ⟨60 reses : 60 head of cattle⟩
resabio nm 1 VICIO : bad habit, vice 2 DEJO : aftertaste
resaca nf 1 : undertow 2 : hangover
resaltar vi 1 SOBRESALIR : to stand out 2 **hacer resaltar** : to bring out, to highlight — vt : to stress, to emphasize
resarcimiento nm 1 : compensation 2 : reimbursement
resarcir {83} vt : to compensate, to indemnify — **resarcirse** vr ∼ **de** : to make up for
resbaladizo, -za adj 1 RESBALOSO : slippery 2 : tricky, ticklish, delicate
resbalar vi 1 : to slip, to slide 2 : to slip up, to make a mistake 3 : to skid — **resbalarse** vr
resbalón nm, pl **-lones** : slip
resbaloso, -sa adj : slippery
rescatar vt 1 : to rescue, to save 2 : to recover, to get back
rescate nm 1 : rescue 2 : recovery 3 : ransom
rescindir vt : to rescind, to annul, to cancel
rescisión nf, pl **-siones** : annulment, cancellation
rescoldo nm : embers pl
resecar {72} vt : to make dry, to dry up — **resecarse** vr : to dry up
reseco, -ca adj : dry, dried-up
resentido, -da adj : resentful
resentimiento nm : resentment
resentirse {76} vr 1 : to suffer, to be weakened 2 OFENDERSE : to be upset ⟨se resintió porque la insultaron : she got upset when they insulted her, she resented being insulted⟩ 3 ∼ **de** : to feel the effects of

reseña *nf* **1** : report, summary, review **2** : description
reseñar *vt* **1** : to review **2** DESCRIBIR : to describe
reserva *nf* **1** : reservation **2** : reserve **3** : confidence, privacy ⟨con la mayor reserva : in strictest confidence⟩ **4 de** ～ : spare, in reserve **5 reservas** *nfpl* : reservations, doubts
reservación *nf, pl* **-ciones** : reservation
reservado, -da *adj* **1** : reserved, reticent **2** : confidential
reservar *vt* : to reserve — **reservarse** *vr* **1** : to save oneself **2** : to conceal, to keep to oneself
reservorio *nm* : reservoir, reserve
resfriado *nm* CATARRO : cold
resfriar {85} *vt* : to cool — **resfriarse** *vr* **1** : to cool off **2** : to catch a cold
resfrío *nm* : cold
resguardar *vt* : to safeguard, to protect — **resguardarse** *vr*
resguardo *nm* **1** : safeguard, protection **2** : receipt, voucher **3** : border guard, coast guard
residencia *nf* **1** : residence **2** : boarding house
residencial *adj* : residential
residente *adj & nmf* : resident
residir *vi* **1** VIVIR : to reside, to dwell **2** ～ **en** : to lie in, to consist of
residual *adj* : residual
residuo *nm* **1** : residue **2** : remainder **3 residuos** *nmpl* : waste ⟨residuos nucleares : nuclear waste⟩
resignación *nf, pl* **-ciones** : resignation
resignar *vt* : to resign — **resignarse** *vr* ～ **a** : to resign oneself to
resina *nf* **1** : resin **2 resina epoxídica** : epoxy
resistencia *nf* **1** : resistance **2** AGUANTE : endurance, strength, stamina
resistente *adj* **1** : resistant **2** : strong, tough
resistir *vt* **1** : to stand, to bear, to tolerate **2** : to withstand — *vi* : to resist ⟨resistió hasta el último minuto : he held out until the last minute⟩ — **resistirse** *vr* ～ **a** : to be resistant to, to be reluctant
resollar {19} *vi* : to breathe heavily, to wheeze
resolución *nf, pl* **-ciones 1** : resolution, settlement **2** : decision **3** : determination, resolve
resolver {89} *vt* **1** : to resolve, to settle **2** : to decide — **resolverse** *vr* : to make up one's mind
resonancia *nf* **1** : resonance **2** : impact, repercussions *pl*
resonante *adj* **1** : resonant **2** : tremendous, resounding ⟨un éxito resonante : a resounding success⟩
resonar {19} *vi* : to resound, to ring
resoplar *vi* **1** : to puff, to pant **2** : snort
resoplo *nm* **1** : puffing, panting **2** : snort

resorte *nm* **1** MUELLE : spring **2** : elasticity **3** : influence, means *pl* ⟨tocar resortes : to pull strings⟩
resortera *nf Mex* : slingshot
respaldar *vt* : to back, to support, to endorse — **respaldarse** *vr* : to lean back
respaldo *nm* **1** : back (of an object) **2** : support, backing
respectar *vt* : to concern, to relate to ⟨por lo que a mí respecta : as far as I'm concerned⟩
respectivo, -va *adj* : respective — **respectivamente** *adv*
respecto *nm* **1** ～ **a** : in regard to, concerning **2 al respecto** : on this matter, in this respect
respetable *adj* : respectable — **respetabilidad** *nf*
respetar *vt* : to respect
respeto *nm* **1** : respect, consideration **2 respetos** *nmpl* : respects ⟨presentar sus respetos : to pay one's respects⟩
respetuosidad *nf* : respectfulness
respetuoso, -sa *adj* : respectful — **respetuosamente** *adv*
respingo *nm* : start, jump
respiración *nf, pl* **-ciones** : respiration, breathing
respiradero *nm* : vent, ventilation shaft
respirador *nm* : respirator
respirar *v* : to breathe
respiratorio, -ria *adj* : respiratory
respiro *nm* **1** : breath **2** : respite, break
resplandecer {53} *vi* **1** : to shine **2** : to stand out
resplandeciente *adj* **1** : resplendent, shining **2** : radiant
resplandor *nm* **1** : brightness, brilliance, radiance **2** : flash
responder *vt* : to answer — *vi* **1** : to answer, to reply, to respond **2** ～ **a** : to respond to ⟨responder al tratamiento : to respond to treatment⟩ **3** ～ **de** : to answer for, to vouch for (something) **4** ～ **por** : to vouch for (someone)
responsabilidad *nf* : responsibility
responsable *adj* : responsible — **responsablemente** *adv*
respuesta *nf* : answer, response
resquebrajar *vt* : to split, to crack — **resquebrajarse** *vr*
resquemor *nm* : resentment, bitterness
resquicio *nm* **1** : crack **2** : opportunity, chance **3** : trace ⟨sin un resquicio de remordimiento : without a trace of remorse⟩ **4 resquicio legal** : loophole
resta *nf* SUSTRACCIÓN : subtraction
restablecer {53} *vt* : to reestablish, to restore — **restablecerse** *vr* : to recover
restablecimiento *nm* **1** : reestablishment, restoration **2** : recovery
restallar *vi* : to crack, to crackle, to click
restallido *nm* : crack, crackle
restante *adj* **1** : remaining **2 lo restante, los restantes** : the rest
restañar *vt* : to stanch
restar *vt* **1** : to deduct, to subtract ⟨restar un punto : to deduct a point⟩

2 : to minimize, to play down — *vi* : to remain, to be left

restauración *nf, pl* **-ciones** 1 : restoration 2 : catering, food service

restaurante *nm* : restaurant

restaurar *vt* : to restore

restitución *nf, pl* **-ciones** : restitution, return

restituir {41} *vt* : to return, to restore, to reinstate

resto *nm* 1 : rest, remainder 2 **restos** *nmpl* : remains ⟨restos de comida : leftovers⟩ ⟨restos arqueológicos : archeological ruins⟩ 3 **restos mortales** : mortal remains

restorán *nm, pl* **-ranes** : restaurant

restregadura *nf* : scrub, scrubbing

restregar {49} *vt* 1 : to rub 2 : to scrub — **restregarse** *vr*

restricción *nf, pl* **-ciones** : restriction, limitation

restrictivo, -va *adj* : restrictive

restringido, -da *adj* LIMITADO : limited, restricted

restringir {35} *vt* LIMITAR : to restrict, to limit

restructuración *nf* : restructuring

restructurar *vt* : to restructure

resucitación *nf* : resuscitation ⟨resucitación cardiopulmonar : CPR, cardiopulmonary resuscitation⟩

resucitar *vt* 1 : to resuscitate, to revive, to resurrect 2 : to revitalize

resuello *nm* 1 : puffing, heavy breathing, wheezing 2 : break, breather

resuelto¹ *pp* → **resolver**

resuelto², -ta *adj* : determined, resolved, resolute

resulta *nf* 1 : consequence, result 2 **a resultas de** *or* **de resultas de** : as a result of

resultado *nm* : result, outcome

resultante *adj & nf* : resultant

resultar *vi* 1 : to work, to work out ⟨mi idea no resultó : my idea didn't work out⟩ 2 : to prove, to turn out to be ⟨resultó bien simpático : he turned out to be very nice⟩ 3 ~ **en** : to lead to, to result in 4 ~ **de** : to be the result of

resumen *nm, pl* **-súmenes** 1 : summary, summation 2 **en** ~ : in summary, in short

resumidero *nm* : drain

resumir *v* : to summarize, to sum up

resurgimiento *nm* : resurgence

resurgir {35} *vi* : to reappear, to revive

resurrección *nf, pl* **-ciones** : resurrection

retablo *nm* 1 : tableau 2 : altarpiece

retador, -dora *n* : challenger (in sports)

retaguardia *nf* : rear guard

retahíla *nf* : string, series ⟨una retahíla de insultos : a volley of insults⟩

retaliación *nf, pl* **-ciones** : retaliation

retama *nf* : broom (plant)

retar *vt* DESAFIAR : to challenge, to defy

retardante *adj* : retardant

retardar *vt* 1 RETRASAR : to delay, to retard 2 : to postpone

retazo *nm* 1 : remnant, scrap 2 : fragment, piece ⟨retazos de su obra : bits and pieces from his writings⟩

retención *nf, pl* **-ciones** 1 : retention 2 : deduction, withholding

retener {80} *vt* 1 : to retain, to keep 2 : to withhold 3 : to detain

retentivo, -va *adj* : retentive

reticencia *nf* 1 : reluctance, reticence 2 : insinuation

reticente *adj* 1 : reluctant, reticent 2 : insinuating, misleading

retina *nf* : retina

retintín *nm, pl* **-tines** 1 : jingle, jangle 2 **con** ~ : sarcastically

retirada *nf* 1 : retreat ⟨batirse en retirada : to withdraw, to beat a retreat⟩ 2 : withdrawal (of funds) 3 : retirement 4 : refuge, haven

retirado, -da *adj* 1 : remote, distant, far off 2 : secluded, quiet

retirar *vt* 1 : to remove, to take away, to recall 2 : to withdraw, to take out — **retirarse** *vr* 1 REPLEGARSE : to retreat, to withdraw 2 JUBILARSE : to retire

retiro *nm* 1 JUBILACIÓN : retirement 2 : withdrawal, retreat 3 : seclusion

reto *nm* DESAFÍO : challenge, dare

retocar {72} *vt* : to touch up

retoñar *vi* : to sprout

retoño *nm* : sprout, shoot

retoque *nm* : retouching

retorcer {14} *vt* 1 : to twist 2 : to wring — **retorcerse** *vr* 1 : to get twisted, to get tangled up 2 : to squirm, to writhe, to wiggle about

retorcijón *nm, pl* **-jones** : cramp, sharp pain

retorcimiento *nm* 1 : twisting, wringing 2 : deviousness

retórica *nf* : rhetoric

retórico, -ca *adj* : rhetorical — **retóricamente** *adv*

retornar *v* : to return

retorno *nm* : return

retozar {21} *vi* : to frolic, to romp

retozo *nm* : frolicking

retozón, -zona *adj, mpl* **-zones** : playful

retracción *nf, pl* **-ciones** : retraction, withdrawal

retractable *adj* : retractable

retractación *nf, pl* **-ciones** : retraction (of a statement, etc.)

retractarse *vr* 1 : to withdraw, to back down 2 ~ **de** : to take back, to retract

retraer {81} *vt* 1 : to bring back 2 : to dissuade — **retraerse** *vr* 1 RETIRARSE : to withdraw, to retire 2 REFUGIARSE : to take refuge

retraído, -da *adj* : withdrawn, retiring, shy

retraimiento *nm* 1 : shyness, timidity 2 : withdrawal

retrasado, -da *adj* 1 : retarded, mentally slow 2 : behind, in arrears 3

: backward (of a country) **4** : slow (of a watch)

retrasar *vt* **1** DEMORAR, RETARDAR : to delay, to hold up **2** : to put off, to postpone — **retrasarse** *vr* **1** : to be late **2** : to fall behind

retraso *nm* **1** ATRASO : delay, lateness **2 retraso mental** : mental retardation

retratar *vt* **1** : to portray, to depict **2** : to photograph **3** : to paint a portrait of

retrato *nm* **1** : depiction, portrayal **2** : portrait, photograph

retrete *nm* : restroom, toilet

retribución *nf, pl* **-ciones 1** : pay, payment **2** : reward

retribuir {41} *vt* **1** : to pay **2** : to reward

retroactivo, -va *adj* : retroactive — **retroactivamente** *adv*

retroalimentación *nf, pl* **-ciones** : feedback

retroceder *vi* **1** : to move back, to turn back **2** : to back off, to back down **3** : to recoil (of a firearm)

retroceso *nm* **1** : backward movement **2** : backing down **3** : setback, relapse **4** : recoil

retrógrado, -da *adj* **1** : reactionary **2** : retrograde

retropropulsión *nf* : jet propulsion

retrospectiva *nf* : retrospective, hindsight

retrospectivo, -va *adj* **1** : retrospective **2 mirada retrospectiva** : backward glance

retrovisor *nm* : rearview mirror

retruécano *nm* : pun, play on words

retumbar *vi* **1** : to boom, to thunder **2** : to resound, to reverberate

retumbo *nm* : booming, thundering, roll

retuvo, etc. → **retener**

reubicar {72} *vt* : to relocate — **reubicación** *nf*

reuma *or* **reúma** *nmf* → **reumatismo**

reumático, -ca *adj* : rheumatic

reumatismo *nm* : rheumatism

reunión *nf, pl* **-niones 1** : meeting **2** : gathering, reunion

reunir {68} *vt* **1** : to unite, to join, to bring together **2** : to have, to possess ⟨reunieron los requisitos necesarios : they fulfilled the necessary requirements⟩ **3** : to gather, to collect, to raise (funds) — **reunirse** *vr* : to meet

reutilizable *adj* : reusable

reutilizar {21} *vt* : to recycle, to reuse

revalidar *vt* **1** : to confirm, to ratify **2** : to defend (a title)

revaluar {3} *vt* : to reevaluate — **revaluación** *n*

revancha *nf* **1** DESQUITE : revenge, requital **2** : rematch

revelación *nf, pl* **-ciones** : revelation

revelado *nm* : developing (of film)

revelador¹, -dora *adj* : revealing

revelador² *nm* : developer

revelar *vt* **1** : to reveal, to disclose **2** : to develop (film)

revendedor, -dora *n* **1** : scalper **2** DETALLISTA : retailer

revender *vt* **1** : to resell **2** : to scalp

reventa *nf* **1** : resale **2** : scalping

reventar {55} *vi* **1** ESTALLAR, EXPLOTAR : to burst, to blow up **2** ~ **de** : to be bursting with — *vt* **1** : to burst **2** *fam* : to annoy, to rile

reventón *nm, pl* **-tones 1** : burst, bursting **2** : blowout, flat tire **3** *Mex fam* : bash, party

reverberar *vi* : to reverberate — **reverberación** *nf*

reverdecer {53} *vi* **1** : to grow green again **2** : to revive

reverencia *nf* **1** : reverence **2** : bow, curtsy

reverenciar *vt* : to revere, to venerate

reverendo¹, -da *adj* **1** : reverend **2** *fam* : total, absolute ⟨es un reverendo imbécil : he is a complete idiot⟩

reverendo², -da *n* : reverend

reverente *adj* : reverent

reversa *nf Col, Mex* : reverse (gear)

reversible *adj* : reversible

reversión *nf, pl* **-siones** : reversion

reverso *nm* **1** : back, other side **2 el reverso de la medalla** : the complete opposite

revertir {76} *vi* **1** : to revert, to go back **2** ~ **en** : to result in, to end up as

revés *nm, pl* **reveses 1** : back, wrong side **2** : setback, reversal **3** : backhand (in sports) **4 al revés** : the other way around, upside down, inside out **5 al revés de** : contrary to

revestimiento *nm* : covering, facing (of a building)

revestir {54} *vt* **1** : to coat, to cover, to surface **2** : to conceal, to disguise **3** : to take on, to assume ⟨la reunión revistió gravedad : the meeting took on a serious note⟩

revisar *vt* **1** : to examine, to inspect, to check **2** : to check over, to overhaul (machinery) **3** : to revise

revisión *nf, pl* **-siones 1** : revision **2** : inspection, check

revisor, -sora *n* **1** : inspector **2** : conductor (on a train)

revista *nf* **1** : magazine, journal **2** : revue **3 pasar revista** : to review, to inspect

revistar *vt* : to review, to inspect

revitalizar {21} *vt* : to revitalize — **revitalización** *nf*

revivir *vi* : to revive, to come alive again — *vt* : to relive

revocación *nf, pl* **-ciones** : revocation, repeal

revocar {72} *vt* **1** : to revoke, to repeal **2** : to plaster (a wall)

revolcar {82} *vt* : to knock over, to knock down — **revolcarse** *vr* : to roll around, to wallow

revolcón *nm, pl* **-cones** *fam* : tumble, fall

revolotear *vi* : to flutter around, to flit

revoloteo *nm* : fluttering, flitting

revoltijo *nm* **1** FÁRRAGO : mess, jumble **2** *Mex* : traditional seafood dish
revoltoso, -sa *adj* : unruly, rebellious
revolución *nf, pl* **-ciones** : revolution
revolucionar *vt* : to revolutionize
revolucionario, -ria *adj & n* : revolutionary
revolver {89} *vt* **1** : to move about, to mix, to shake, to stir **2** : to upset (one's stomach) **3** : to mess up, to rummage through ⟨revolver la casa : to turn the house upside down⟩ — **revolverse** *vr* **1** : to toss and turn **2** VOLVERSE : to turn around
revólver *nm* : revolver
revoque *nm* : plaster
revuelo *nm* **1** : fluttering **2** : commotion, stir
revuelta *nf* : uprising, revolt
revuelto¹ *pp* → **revolver**
revuelto², -ta *adj* **1** : choppy, rough ⟨mar revuelto : rough sea⟩ **2** : untidy **3 huevos revueltos** : scrambled eggs
rey *nm* : king
reyerta *nf* : brawl, fight
rezagado, -da *n* : straggler, latecomer
rezagar {52} *vt* **1** : to leave behind **2** : to postpone — **rezagarse** *vr* : to fall behind, to lag
rezar {21} *vi* **1** : to pray **2** : to say ⟨como reza el refrán : as the saying goes⟩ **3** ~ **con** : to concern, to have to do with — *vt* : to say, to recite ⟨rezar un Ave María : to say a Hail Mary⟩
rezo *nm* : prayer, praying
rezongar {52} *vi* : to gripe, to grumble
rezumar *v* : to ooze, to leak
ría¹, etc. → **reír**
ría² *nf* : estuary
riachuelo *nm* ARROYO : brook, stream
riada *nf* : flood
ribera *nf* : bank, shore
ribete *nm* **1** : border, trim **2** : frill, adornment **3 ribetes** *nmpl* : hint, touch ⟨tiene sus ribetes de genio : there's a touch of genius in him⟩
ribetear *vt* : to border, to edge, to trim
ricamente *adv* : richly, splendidly
rice, etc. → **rizar**
rico¹, -ca *adj* **1** : rich, wealthy **2** : fertile **3** : luxurious, valuable **4** : delicious **5** : adorable, lovely **6** : great, wonderful
rico², -ca *n* : rich person
ridiculez *nf, pl* **-leces** : ridiculousness, absurdity
ridiculizar {21} *vt* : to ridicule
ridículo¹, -la *adj* ABSURDO, DISPARATADO : ridiculous, ludicrous — **ridículamente** *adv*
ridículo², -la *n* **1 hacer el ridículo** : to make a fool of oneself **2 poner en ridículo** : to ridicule
ríe, etc. → **reír**
riega, riegue etc. → **regar**
riego *nm* : irrigation
riel *nm* : rail, track

rienda *nf* **1** : rein **2 dar rienda suelta a** : to give free rein to **3 llevar las riendas** : to be in charge **4 tomar las riendas** : to take control
riesgo *nm* : risk
riesgoso, -sa *adj* : risky
rifa *nf* : raffle
rifar *vt* : to raffle — *vi* : to quarrel, to fight
rifle *nm* : rifle
rige, rija etc. → **regir**
rigidez *nf, pl* **-deces** **1** : rigidity, stiffness ⟨rigidez cadavérica : rigor mortis⟩ **2** : inflexibility
rígido, -da *adj* **1** : rigid, stiff **2** : strict — **rígidamente** *adv*
rigor *nm* **1** : rigor, harshness **2** : precision, meticulousness **3 de** ~ : usual ⟨la respuesta de rigor : the standard reply⟩ **4 de** ~ : essential, obligatory **5 en** ~ : strictly speaking, in reality
riguroso, -sa *adj* : rigorous — **rigurosamente** *adv*
rima *nf* **1** : rhyme **2 rimas** *nfpl* : verse, poetry
rimar *vi* : to rhyme
rimbombante *adj* **1** : grandiose, showy **2** : bombastic, pompous
rímel *or* **rimel** *nm* : mascara
rin *nm Col, Mex* : wheel, rim (of a tire)
rincón *nm, pl* **rincones** : corner, nook
rinde, etc. → **rendir**
rinoceronte *nm* : rhinoceros
riña *nf* **1** : fight, brawl **2** : dispute, quarrel
riñe, etc. → **reñir**
riñón *nm, pl* **riñones** : kidney
río¹ → **reír**
río² *nm* **1** : river **2** : torrent, stream ⟨un río de lágrimas : a flood of tears⟩
ripio *nm* **1** : debris, rubble **2** : gravel
riqueza *nf* **1** : wealth, riches *pl* **2** : richness **3 riquezas naturales** : natural resources
risa *nf* **1** : laughter, laugh **2 dar risa** : to make laugh ⟨me dio mucha risa : I found it very funny⟩ **3** *fam* **morirse de la risa** : to die laughing, to crack up
risco *nm* : crag, cliff
risible *adj* IRRISORIO : ludicrous, laughable
risita *nf* : giggle, titter, snicker
risotada *nf* : guffaw
ristra *nf* : string, series *pl*
risueño, -ña *adj* **1** : cheerful, pleasant **2** : promising
rítmico, -ca *adj* : rhythmical, rhythmic — **rítmicamente** *adv*
ritmo *nm* **1** : rhythm **2** : pace, tempo ⟨trabajó a ritmo lento : she worked at a slow pace⟩
rito *nm* : rite, ritual
ritual *adj & nm* : ritual — **ritualmente** *adv*
rival *adj & nmf* COMPETIDOR : rival
rivalidad *nf* : rivalry, competition
rivalizar {21} *vi* ~ **con** : to rival, to compete with

rizado, -da *adj* **1** : curly **2** : ridged **3** : ripply, undulating

rizar {21} *vt* **1** : to curl **2** : to ripple, to ruffle (a surface) **3** : to crumple, to fold — **rizarse** *vr* **1** : to frizz **2** : to ripple

rizo *nm* **1** : curl **2** : loop (in aviation)

robalo *or* **róbalo** *nm* : sea bass

robar *vt* **1** : to steal **2** : to rob, to burglarize SECUESTRAR : to abduct, to kidnap **4** : to captivate — *vi* ~ **en** : to break into

roble *nm* : oak

robo *nm* : robbery, theft

robot *nm, pl* **robots** : robot

robótica *nf* : robotics

robustecer {53} *vt* : to grow stronger, to strengthen

robustez *nf* : sturdiness, robustness

robusto, -ta *adj* : robust, sturdy

roca *nf* : rock, boulder

roce¹, etc. → **rozar**

roce² *nm* **1** : rubbing, chafing **2** : brush, graze, touch **3** : close contact, familiarity **4** : friction, disagreement

rociador *nm* : sprinkler

rociar {85} *vt* : to spray, to sprinkle

rocío *nm* **1** : dew **2** : shower, light rain

rock *or* **rock and roll** *nm* : rock, rock and roll

rocola *nf* : jukebox

rocoso, -sa *adj* : rocky

rodada *nf* : track (of a tire), rut

rodado, -da *adj* **1** : wheeled **2** : dappled (of a horse)

rodadura *nf* : rolling, taxiing

rodaja *nf* : round, slice

rodaje *nm* **1** : filming, shooting **2** : breaking in (of a vehicle)

rodamiento *nm* **1** : bearing ⟨rodamiento de bolas : ball bearings⟩ **2** : rolling

rodante *adj* : rolling

rodar {19} *vi* **1** : to roll, to roll down, to roll along ⟨rodé por la escalera : I tumbled down the stairs⟩ ⟨todo rodaba bien : everthing was going along well⟩ **2** GIRAR : to turn, to go around **3** : to move about, to travel ⟨andábamos rodando por todas partes : we drifted along from place to place⟩ — *vt* **1** : to film, to shoot **2** : to break in (a new vehicle)

rodear *vt* **1** : to surround **2** : to round up (cattle) — *vi* **1** : to go around **2** : to beat around the bush — **rodearse** *vr* ~ **de** : to surround oneself with

rodeo *nm* **1** : rodeo, roundup **2** DESVÍO : detour **3** : evasion ⟨andar con rodeos : to beat around the bush⟩ ⟨sin rodeos : without reservations⟩

rodilla *nf* : knee

rodillo *nm* **1** : roller **2** : rolling pin

rododendro *nm* : rhododendron

roedor¹, -dora *adj* : gnawing

roedor² *nm* : rodent

roer {69} *vt* **1** : to gnaw **2** : to eat away at, to torment

rogar {16} *vt* : to beg, to request — *vi* **1** : to beg, to plead **2** : to pray

roiga, etc. → **roer**

rojez *nf* : redness

rojizo, -za *adj* : reddish

rojo¹, -ja *adj* **1** : red **2 ponerse rojo** : to blush

rojo² *nm* : red

rol *nm* **1** : role **2** : list, roll

rollo *nm* **1** : roll, coil ⟨un rollo de cinta : a roll of tape⟩ ⟨en rollo : rolled up⟩ **2** *fam* : roll of fat **3** *fam* : boring speech, lecture

romance *nm* **1** : Romance language **2** : ballad **3** : romance **4 en buen romance** : simply stated, simply put

romano, -na *adj & n* : Roman

romanticismo *nm* : romanticism

romántico, -ca *adj* : romantic — **románticamente** *adv*

rombo *nm* : rhombus

romería *nf* **1** : pilgrimage, procession **2** : crowd, gathering

romero¹, -ra *n* PEREGRINO : pilgrim

romero² *nm* : rosemary

romo, -ma *adj* : blunt, dull

rompecabezas *nms & pl* : puzzle, riddle

rompehielos *nms & pl* : icebreaker (ship)

rompehuelgas *nmfs & pl* ESQUIROL : strikebreaker, scab

rompenueces *nms & pl* : nutcracker

rompeolas *ns & pl* : breakwater, jetty

romper {70} *vt* **1** : to break, to smash **2** : to rip, to tear **3** : to break off (relations), to break (a contract) **4** : to break through, to break down **5** GASTAR : to wear out — *vi* **1** : to break ⟨al romper del día : at the break of day⟩ **2** ~ **a** : to begin to, to burst out with ⟨romper a llorar : to burst into tears⟩ **3** ~ **con** : to break off with

rompope *nm CA, Mex* : drink similar to eggnog

ron *nm* : rum

roncar {72} *vi* **1** : to snore **2** : to roar

ronco, -ca *adj* **1** : hoarse **2** : husky (of the voice) — **roncamente** *adv*

ronda *nf* **1** : beat, patrol **2** : round (of drinks, of negotiations, of a game)

rondar *vt* **1** : to patrol **2** : to hang around ⟨siempre está rondando la calle : he's always hanging around the street⟩ **3** : to be approximately ⟨debe rondar los cincuenta : he must be about 50⟩ — *vi* **1** : to be on patrol **2** : to prowl around, to roam about

ronque, etc. → **roncar**

ronquera *nf* : hoarseness

ronquido *nm* **1** : snore **2** : roar

ronronear *vi* : to purr

ronroneo *nm* : purr, purring

ronzal *nm* : halter (for an animal)

ronzar {21} *v* : to munch, to crunch

roña *nf* **1** : mange **2** : dirt, filth **3** *fam* : stinginess

roñoso, -sa *adj* **1** : mangy **2** : dirty **3** *fam* : stingy

ropa *nf* **1** : clothes *pl,* clothing **2 ropa interior** : underwear

ropaje *nm* : apparel, garments *pl*, regalia
ropero *nm* ARMARIO, CLÓSET : wardrobe, closet
rosa[1] *adj* : rose-colored, pink
rosa[2] *nm* : rose, pink (color)
rosa[3] *nf* : rose (flower)
rosáceo, -cea *adj* : pinkish
rosado[1], **-da** *adj* **1** : pink **2 vino rosado** : rosé
rosado[2] *nm* : pink (color)
rosal *nm* : rosebush
rosario *nm* **1** : rosary **2** : series ⟨un rosario de islas : a string of islands⟩
rosbif *nm* : roast beef
rosca *nf* **1** : thread (of a screw) ⟨una tapa a rosca : a screw top⟩ **2** : ring, coil
roseta *nf* : rosette
rosquilla *nf* : ring-shaped pastry, doughnut
rostro *nm* : face, countenance
rotación *nf*, *pl* **-ciones** : rotation
rotar *vt* : to rotate, to turn — *vi* : to turn, to spin
rotativo[1], **-va** *adj* : rotary
rotativo[2] *nm* : newspaper
rotatorio, -ria *adj* → **rotativo**[1]
roto[1] *pp* → **romper**
roto[2], **-ta** *adj* **1** : broken **2** : ripped, torn
rotonda *nf* **1** : traffic circle, rotary **2** : rotunda
rotor *nm* : rotor
rótula *nf* : kneecap
rotular *vt* **1** : to head, to entitle **2** : to label
rótulo *nm* **1** : heading, title **2** : label, sign
rotundo, -da *adj* **1** REDONDO : round **2** : categorical, absolute ⟨un éxito rotundo : a resounding success⟩ — **rotundamente** *adv*
rotura *nf* : break, tear, fracture
roya *nf* : plant rust
roya, etc. → **roer**
rozado, -da *adj* GASTADO : worn
rozadura *nf* **1** : scratch, abrasion **2** : rubbed spot, sore
rozar {21} *vt* **1** : to chafe, to rub against **2** : to border on, to touch on **3** : to graze, to touch lightly — **rozarse** *vr* ~ **con** *fam* : to rub shoulders with
ruandés, -desa *adj* & *n* : Rwandan
ruano, -na *adj* : roan
rubí *nm*, *pl* **rubíes** : ruby
rubio, -bia *adj* & *n* : blond
rublo *nm* : ruble
rubor *nm* **1** : flush, blush **2** : rouge, blusher
ruborizarse {21} *vr* : to blush
rúbrica *nf* : title, heading
rubricar {72} *vt* **1** : sign with a flourish ⟨firmado y rubricado : signed and sealed⟩ **2** : to endorse, to sanction
rubro *nm* **1** : heading, title **2** : line, area (in business)
rudeza *nf* ASPEREZA : roughness, coarseness

rudimentario, -ria *adj* : rudimentary — **rudimentariamente** *adv*
rudimento *nm* : rudiment, basics *pl*
rudo, -da *adj* **1** : rough, harsh **2** : coarse, unpolished — **rudamente** *adv*
rueda[1], **etc.** → **rodar**
rueda[2] *nf* **1** : wheel **2** RODAJA : round slice **3** : circle, ring **4 rueda de andar** : treadmill **5 rueda de prensa** : press conference **6 ir sobre ruedas** : to go smoothly
ruedita *nf* : caster (on furniture)
ruedo *nm* **1** : bullring, arena **2** : rotation, turn **3** : hem
ruega, ruegue etc. → **rogar**
ruego *nm* : request, appeal, plea
rugido *nm* : roar
rugir {35} *vi* : to roar
ruibarbo *nm* : rhubarb
ruido *nm* : noise, sound
ruidoso, -sa *adj* : loud, noisy — **ruidosamente** *adv*
ruin *adj* **1** : base, despicable **2** : mean, stingy
ruina *nf* **1** : ruin, destruction **2** : downfall, collapse **3 ruinas** *nfpl* : ruins, remains
ruinoso, -sa *adj* **1** : run-down, dilapidated **2** : ruinous, disastrous
ruiseñor *nm* : nightingale
ruja, etc. → **rugir**
ruleta *nf* : roulette
rulo *nm* : curler, roller
rumano, -na *n* : Romanian, Rumanian
rumbo *nm* **1** : direction, course ⟨con rumbo a : bound for, heading for⟩ ⟨perder el rumbo : to go off course, to lose one's bearings⟩ ⟨sin rumbo : aimless, aimlessly⟩ **2** : ostentation, pomp **3** : lavishness, generosity
rumiante *adj* & *nm* : ruminant
rumiar *vt* : to ponder, to mull over — *vi* **1** : to chew the cud **2** : to ruminate, to ponder
rumor *nm* **1** : rumor **2** : murmur
rumorearse *or* **rumorarse** *vr* : to be rumored ⟨se rumorea que se va : rumor has it that she's leaving⟩
rumoroso, -sa *adj* : murmuring, babbling ⟨un arroyo rumoroso : a babbling brook⟩
rupia *nf* : rupee
ruptura *nf* **1** : break **2** : breaking, breach (of a contract) **3** : breaking off, breakup
rural *adj* : rural
ruso[1], **-sa** *adj* & *n* : Russian
ruso[2] *nm* : Russian (language)
rústico[1], **-ca** *adj* : rural, rustic
rústico[2], **-ca** *n* : rustic, country dweller
ruta *nf* : route
rutina *nf* : routine, habit
rutinario, -ria *adj* : routine, ordinary ⟨visita rutinaria : routine visit⟩ — **rutinariamente** *adv*

S

s *nf* : twentieth letter of the Spanish alphabet

sábado *nm* **1** : Saturday **2** : Sabbath

sábalo *nm* : shad

sabana *nf* : savanna

sábana *nf* : sheet, bedsheet

sabandija *nf* BICHO : bug, small reptile, pesky creature

sabático, -ca *adj* : sabbatical

sabedor, -dora *adj* : aware, informed

sabelotodo *nmf fam* : know-it-all

saber¹ {71} *vt* **1** : to know **2** : to know how to, to be able to ⟨sabe tocar el violín : she can play the violin⟩ **3** : to learn, to find out **4** ~ *a* : to wit, namely — *vi* **1** : to know, to suppose **2** : to be informed ⟨supimos del desastre : we heard about the disaster⟩ **3** : to taste ⟨esto no sabe bien : this doesn't taste right⟩ **4** ~ *a* : to taste like ⟨sabe a naranja : it tastes like orange⟩ — **saberse** *vr* : to know ⟨ese chiste no me lo sé : I don't know that joke⟩

saber² *nm* : knowledge, learning

sabiamente *adv* : wisely

sabido, -da *adj* : well-known

sabiduría *nf* **1** : wisdom **2** : learning, knowledge

sabiendas *adv* **1** *a* ~ : knowingly **2** *a* **sabiendas de que** : knowing full well that

sabio¹, -bia *adj* **1** PRUDENTE : wise, sensible **2** DOCTO : learned

sabio², -bia *n* **1** : wise person **2** : savant, learned person

sable *nm* : saber, cutlass

sabor *nm* **1** : flavor, taste **2 sin** ~ : flavorless

saborear *vt* **1** : to taste, to savor **2** : to enjoy, to relish

sabotaje *nm* : sabotage

saboteador, -dora *n* : saboteur

sabotear *vt* : to sabotage

sabrá, etc. → **saber**

sabroso, -sa *adj* **1** RICO : delicious, tasty **2** AGRADABLE : pleasant, nice, lovely

sabueso *nm* **1** : bloodhound **2** *fam* : detective, sleuth

sacacorchos *nms & pl* : corkscrew

sacapuntas *nms & pl* : pencil sharpener

sacar {72} *vt* **1** : to pull out, to take out ⟨saca el pollo del congelador : take the chicken out of the freezer⟩ **2** : to get, to obtain ⟨saqué un 100 en el examen : I got 100 on the exam⟩ **3** : to get out, to extract ⟨le saqué la información : I got the information from him⟩ **4** : to stick out ⟨sacar la lengua : to stick out one's tongue⟩ **5** : to bring out, to introduce ⟨sacar un libro : to publish a book⟩ ⟨sacaron una moda nueva : they introduced a new style⟩ **6** : to take (photos) **7** : to make (copies) — *vi* **1**

: to kick off (in soccer or football) **2** : to serve (in sports)

sacarina *nf* : saccharin

sacarosa *nf* : sucrose

sacerdocio *nm* : priesthood

sacerdotal *adj* : priestly

sacerdote, -tisa *n* : priest *m*, priestess *f*

saciar *vt* **1** HARTAR : to sate, to satiate **2** SATISFACER : to satisfy

saciedad *nf* : satiety

saco *nm* **1** : bag, sack **2** : sac **3** : jacket, sport coat

sacramento *nm* : sacrament — **sacramental** *adj*

sacrificar {72} *vt* : to sacrifice — **sacrificarse** *vr* : to sacrifice oneself, to make sacrifices

sacrificio *nm* : sacrifice

sacrilegio *nm* : sacrilege

sacrílego, -ga *adj* : sacrilegious

sacristán *nm, pl* **-tanes** : sexton, sacristan

sacristía *nf* : sacristy, vestry

sacro, -cra *adj* SAGRADO : sacred ⟨arte sacro : sacred art⟩

sacrosanto, -ta *adj* : sacrosanct

sacudida *nf* **1** : shaking **2** : jerk, jolt, shock **3** : shake-up, upheaval

sacudir *vt* **1** : to shake, to beat **2** : to jerk, to jolt **3** : to dust off **4** CONMOVER : to shake up, to shock — **sacudirse** *vr* : to shake off

sacudón *nm, pl* **-dones** : intense jolt or shake-up

sádico¹, -ca *adj* : sadistic

sádico², -ca *n* : sadist

sadismo *nm* : sadism

safari *nm* : safari

saga *nf* : saga

sagacidad *nf* : sagacity, shrewdness

sagaz *adj, pl* **sagaces** PERSPICAZ : shrewd, discerning, sagacious

Sagitario *nmf* : Sagittarius, Sagittarian

sagrado, -da *adj* : sacred, holy

sainete *nm* : comedy sketch, one-act farce ⟨este proceso es un sainete : these proceedings are a farce⟩

sajar *vt* : to lance, to cut open

sal¹ → **salir**

sal² *nf* **1** : salt **2** *CA, Mex* : misfortune, bad luck

sala *nf* **1** : living room **2** : room, hall ⟨sala de conferencias : lecture hall⟩ ⟨sala de urgencias : emergency room⟩ ⟨sala de baile : ballroom⟩

salado, -da *adj* **1** : salty **2 agua salada** : salt water

salamandra *nf* : salamander

salami *nm* : salami

salar *vt* **1** : to salt **2** : to spoil, to ruin **3** *CoRi, Mex* : to jinx, to bring bad luck

salarial *adj* : salary, salary-related

salario *nm* **1** : salary **2 salario mínimo** : minimum wage

salaz *adj, pl* **salaces** : salacious, lecherous

salchicha *nf* **1** : sausage **2** : frankfurter, wiener

salchichón *nf, pl* **-chones** : a type of deli meat

salchichonería *nf Mex* **1** : delicatessen **2** : cold cuts *pl*

saldar *vt* : to settle, to pay off ⟨saldar una cuenta : to settle an account⟩

saldo *nm* **1** : settlement, payment **2** : balance ⟨saldo de cuenta : account balance⟩ **3** : remainder, leftover merchandise

saldrá, etc. → **salir**

salero *nm* **1** : saltshaker **2** : wit, charm

salga, etc. → **salir**

salida *nf* **1** : exit ⟨salida de emergencia : emergency exit⟩ **2** : leaving, departure **3** SOLUCIÓN : way out, solution **4** : start (of a race) **5** OCURRENCIA : wisecrack, joke **6 salida del sol** : sunrise

saliente[1] *adj* **1** : departing, outgoing **2** : projecting **3** DESTACADO : salient, prominent

saliente[2] *nm* **1** : projection, protrusion **2 ventana en saliente** : bay window

salinidad *nf* : salinity, saltiness

salino, -na *adj* : saline ⟨solución salina : saline solution⟩

salir {73} *vi* **1** : to go out, to come out, to get out ⟨salimos todas las noches : we go out every night⟩ ⟨su libro acaba de salir : her book just came out⟩ **2** PARTIR : to leave, to depart **3** APARECER : to appear ⟨salió en todos los diarios : it came out in all the papers⟩ **4** : to project, to stick out **5** : to cost, to come to **6** RESULTAR : to turn out, to prove **7** : to come up, to occur ⟨salga lo que salga : whatever happens⟩ ⟨salió una oportunidad : an opportunity came up⟩ **8 ~ a** : to take after, to look like, to resemble **9 ~ con** : to go out with, to date — **salirse** *vr* **1** : to escape, to get out, to leak out **2** : to come loose, to come off **3 salirse con la suya** : to get one's own way

saliva *nf* : saliva

salivar *vi* : to salivate

salmo *nm* : psalm

salmón[1] *adj* : salmon-colored

salmón[2] *nm, pl* **salmones** : salmon

salmuera *nf* : brine

salobre *adj* : brackish, briny

salón *nm, pl* **salones** **1** : hall, large room ⟨salón de clase : classroom⟩ ⟨salón de baile : ballroom⟩ **2** : salon ⟨salón de belleza : beauty salon⟩ **3** : parlor, sitting room

salpicadera *nf Mex* : fender

salpicadura *nf* : spatter, splash

salpicar {72} *vt* **1** : to spatter, to splash **2** : to sprinkle, to scatter about

salpimentar {55} *vt* **1** : to season (with salt and pepper) **2** : to spice up

salsa *nf* **1** : sauce ⟨salsa picante : hot sauce⟩ ⟨salsa inglesa : Worcestershire sauce⟩ ⟨salsa tártara : tartar sauce⟩ **2**

: gravy **3** : salsa (music) **4 salsa mexicana** : salsa (sauce)

salsero, -ra *n* : salsa musician

saltador, -dora *n* : jumper

saltamontes *nms & pl* : grasshopper

saltar *vi* **1** BRINCAR : to jump, to leap **2** : to bounce **3** : to come off, to pop out **4** : to shatter, to break **5** : to explode, to blow up — *vt* **1** : to jump, to jump over **2** : to skip, to miss — **saltarse** *vr* OMITIR : to skip, to omit ⟨me salté ese capítulo : I skipped that chapter⟩

saltarín, -rina *adj, mpl* **-rines** : leaping, hopping ⟨frijol saltarín : jumping bean⟩

salteado, -da *adj* **1** : sautéed **2** : jumbled up ⟨los episodios se transmitieron salteados : the episodes were broadcast in random order⟩

salteador *nm* : highwayman

saltear *vt* **1** SOFREÍR : to sauté **2** : to skip around, to skip over

saltimbanqui *nmf* : acrobat

salto *nm* **1** BRINCO : jump, leap, skip **2** : jump, dive (in sports) **3** : gap, omission **4 dar saltos** : to jump up and down **5** *or* **salto de agua** CATARATA : waterfall

saltón, -tona *adj, mpl* **saltones** : bulging, protruding

salubre *adj* : healthful, salubrious

salubridad *nf* : healthfulness, health

salud *nf* **1** : health ⟨buena salud : good health⟩ **2 ¡salud!** : bless you! (when someone sneezes) **3 ¡salud!** : cheers!, to your health!

saludable *adj* **1** SALUBRE : healthful **2** SANO : healthy, well

saludar *vt* **1** : to greet, to say hello to **2** : to salute — **saludarse** *vr*

saludo *nm* **1** : greeting, regards *pl* **2** : salute

salutación *nf, pl* **-ciones** : salutation

salva *nf* **1** : salvo, volley **2 salva de aplausos** : round of applause

salvación *nf, pl* **-ciones** **1** : salvation **2** RESCATE : rescue

salvado *nm* : bran

salvador, -dora *n* **1** : savior, rescuer **2 el Salvador** : the Savior

salvadoreño, -ña *adj & n* : Salvadoran, El Salvadoran

salvaguardar *vt* : to safeguard

salvaguardia *or* **salvaguarda** *nf* : safeguard, defense

salvajada *nf* ATROCIDAD : atrocity, act of savagery

salvaje[1] *adj* **1** : wild ⟨animales salvajes : wild animals⟩ **2** : savage, cruel **3** : primitive, uncivilized

salvaje[2] *nmf* : savage

salvajismo *nm* : savagery

salvamento *nm* **1** : rescuing, lifesaving **2** : salvation **3** : refuge

salvar *vt* **1** : to save, to rescue **2** : to cover (a distance) **3** : to get around (an obstacle), to overcome (a difficulty) **4**

: to cross, to jump across **5 salvando**
: except for, excluding — **salvarse** *vr*
1 : to survive, to escape **2** : to save one's
soul
salvavidas[1] *nms & pl* **1** : life preserver
2 bote salvavidas : lifeboat
salvavidas[2] *nmf* : lifeguard
salvedad *nf* **1** EXCEPCIÓN : exception
2 : proviso, stipulation
salvia *nf* : sage (plant)
salvo[1], **-va** *adj* **1** : unharmed, sound
⟨sano y salvo : safe and sound⟩ **2 a ~**
: safe from danger
salvo[2] *prep* **1** EXCEPTO : except (for),
save ⟨todos asistirán salvo Jaime : all
will attend except for Jaime⟩ **2 salvo
que** : unless ⟨salvo que llueva : unless
it rains⟩
salvoconducto *nm* : safe-conduct
samba *nf* : samba
San *adj* → **santo**[1]
sanar *vt* : to heal, to cure — *vi* : to get
well, to recover
sanatorio *nm* **1** : sanatorium **2** : clinic, private hospital
sanción *nf, pl* **sanciones** : sanction
sancionar *vt* **1** : to penalize, to impose
a sanction on **2** : to sanction, to approve
sancochar *vt* : to parboil
sandalia *nf* : sandal
sándalo *nm* : sandalwood
sandez *nf, pl* **sandeces** ESTUPIDEZ
: nonsense, silly thing to say
sandía *nf* : watermelon
sandwich ['sandwitʃ, 'saŋgwitʃ] *nm, pl*
sandwiches [-dwitʃɛs, -gwi-] EMPARE-
DADO : sandwich
saneamiento *nm* **1** : cleaning up, sanitation **2** : reorganizing, streamlining
sanear *vt* **1** : to clean up, to sanitize **2**
: to reorganize, to streamline
sangrante *adj* **1** : bleeding **2** : flagrant,
blatant
sangrar *vi* : to bleed — *vt* : to indent (a
paragraph, etc.)
sangre *nf* **1** : blood **2 a sangre fría** : in
cold blood **3 a sangre y fuego** : by violent force **4 pura sangre** : thoroughbred
sangría *nf* **1** : bloodletting **2** : sangria
(wine punch) **3** : drain, draining ⟨una
sangría fiscal : a financial drain⟩ **4** : indentation, indenting
sangriento, -ta *adj* **1** : bloody **2** : cruel
sanguijuela *nf* **1** : leech, bloodsucker **2**
: sponger, leech
sanguinario, -ria *adj* : bloodthirsty
sanguíneo, -nea *adj* **1** : blood ⟨vaso
sanguíneo : blood vessel⟩ **2** : sanguine,
ruddy
sanidad *nf* **1** : health **2** : public health,
sanitation
sanitario[1], **-ria** *adj* **1** : sanitary **2** : health
⟨centro sanitario : health center⟩
sanitario[2], **-ria** *n* : sanitation worker
sanitario[3] *nm Col, Mex, Ven* : toilet ⟨los
sanitarios : the toilets, the restroom⟩

sano, -na *adj* **1** SALUDABLE : healthy **2**
: wholesome **3** : whole, intact
santiaguino, -na *adj* : of or from Santi-
ago, Chile
santiamén *nm* **en un santiamén** : in no
time at all
santidad *nf* : holiness, sanctity
santificar {72} *vt* : to sanctify, to consecrate, to hallow
santiguarse {10} *vr* PERSIGNARSE : to
cross oneself
santo[1], **-ta** *adj* **1** : holy, saintly ⟨el Santo Padre : the Holy Father⟩ ⟨una vida
santa : a saintly life⟩ **2 Santo, Santa**
(San *before names of masculine saints
except those beginning with D or T*)
: Saint ⟨Santa Clara : Saint Claire⟩
⟨Santo Tomás : Saint Thomas⟩ ⟨San
Francisco : Saint Francis⟩
santo[2], **-ta** *n* : saint
santo[3] *nm* **1** : saint's day **2** CUMPLE-
AÑOS : birthday
santuario *nm* : sanctuary
santurrón, -rrona *adj, mpl* **-rrones**
: overly pious, sanctimonious — **santurronamente** *adv*
saña *nf* **1** : fury, rage **2** : viciousness
⟨con saña : viciously⟩
sapo *nm* : toad
saque[1], etc. → **sacar**
saque[2] *nm* **1** : kickoff (in soccer or football) **2** : serve, service (in sports)
saqueador, -dora *n* DEPREDADOR
: plunderer, looter
saquear *vt* : to sack, to plunder, to loot
saqueo *nm* DEPREDACIÓN : sacking,
plunder, looting
sarampión *nm* : measles *pl*
sarape *nm CA, Mex* : serape, blanket
sarcasmo *nm* : sarcasm
sarcástico, -ca *adj* : sarcastic
sarcófago *nm* : sarcophagus
sardina *nf* : sardine
sardónico, -ca *adj* : sardonic
sarga *nf* : serge
sargento *nmf* : sergeant
sarna *nf* : mange
sarnoso, -sa *adj* : mangy
sarpullido *nm* ERUPCIÓN : rash
sarro *nm* **1** : deposit, coating **2** : tartar,
plaque
sarta *nf* **1** : string, series (of insults, etc.)
2 : string (of pearls, etc.)
sartén *nmf, pl* **sartenes** **1** : frying pan
2 tener la sartén por el mango : to call
the shots, to be in control
sasafrás *nm* : sassafras
sastre, -tra *n* : tailor
sastrería *nf* **1** : tailoring **2** : tailor's shop
Satanás *or* **Satán** *nm* : Satan, the devil
satánico, -ca *adj* : satanic
satélite *nm* : satellite
satín *or* **satén** *nm, pl* **satines** *or* **satenes**
: satin
satinado, -da *adj* : satiny, glossy
sátira *nf* : satire
satírico, -ca *adj* : satirical, satiric
satirizar {21} *vt* : to satirize

sátiro *nm* : satyr

satisfacción *nf, pl* -ciones : satisfaction

satisfacer {74} *vt* 1 : to satisfy 2 : to fulfill, to meet 3 : to pay, to settle — satisfacerse *vr* 1 : to be satisfied 2 : to take revenge

satisfactorio, -ria *adj* : satisfactory — satisfactoriamente *adv*

satisfecho, -cha *adj* : satisfied, content, pleased

saturación *nf, pl* -ciones : saturation

saturar *vt* 1 : to saturate, to fill up 2 : to satiate, to surfeit

saturnismo *nm* : lead poisoning

Saturno *nm* : Saturn

sauce *nm* : willow

saúco *nm* : elder (tree)

saudí *or* saudita *adj & nmf* : Saudi, Saudi Arabian

sauna *nmf* : sauna

savia *nf* : sap

saxofón *nm, pl* -fones : saxophone

sazón[1] *nf, pl* sazones 1 : flavor, seasoning 2 : ripeness, maturity ⟨en sazón : in season, ripe⟩ 3 a la sazón : at that time, then

sazón[2] *nmf, pl* sazones *Mex* : flavor, seasoning

sazonar *vt* CONDIMENTAR : to season, to spice

scanner *nm* → escáner

sé → saber, ser

se *pron* 1 : to him, to her, to you, to them ⟨se los daré a ella : I'll give them to her⟩ 2 : each other, one another ⟨se abrazaron : they hugged each other⟩ 3 : himself, herself, itself, yourself, yourselves, themselves ⟨se afeitó antes de salir : he shaved before leaving⟩ 4 (*used in passive constructions*) ⟨se dice que es hermosa : they say she's beautiful⟩ ⟨se habla inglés : English spoken⟩

sea, etc. → ser

sebo *nm* 1 : grease, fat 2 : tallow 3 : suet

secado *nm* : drying

secador *nm* : hair dryer

secadora *nf* 1 : dryer, clothes dryer 2 *Mex* : hair dryer

secante *nm* : blotting paper, blotter

secar {72} *v* : to dry — secarse *vr* 1 : to get dry 2 : to dry up

sección *nf, pl* secciones 1 : section ⟨sección transversal : cross section⟩ 2 : department, division

seco, -ca *adj* 1 : dry 2 DISECADO : dried ⟨fruta seca : dried fruit⟩ 3 : thin, lean 4 : curt, brusque 5 : sharp ⟨un golpe seco : a sharp blow⟩ 6 a secas : simply, just ⟨se llama Chico, a secas : he's just called Chico⟩ 7 en ~ : abruptly, suddenly ⟨frenar en seco : to make a sudden stop⟩

secoya *nf* : sequoia, redwood

secreción *nf, pl* -ciones : secretion

secretar *vt* : to secrete

secretaría *nf* 1 : secretariat, administrative department 2 *Mex* : ministry, cabinet office

secretariado *nm* 1 : secretariat 2 : secretarial profession

secretario, -ria *n* : secretary — secretarial *adj*

secreto[1], -ta *adj* 1 : secret 2 : secretive — secretamente *adv*

secreto[2] *nm* 1 : secret 2 : secrecy

secta *nf* : sect

sectario, -ria *adj & n* : sectarian

sector *nm* : sector

secuaz *nmf, pl* secuaces : follower, henchman, underling

secuela *nf* : consequence, sequel ⟨las secuelas de la guerra : the aftermath of the war⟩

secuencia *nf* : sequence

secuestrador, -dora *n* 1 : kidnapper, abductor 2 : hijacker

secuestrar *vt* 1 RAPTAR : to kidnap, to abduct 2 : to hijack, to commandeer 3 CONFISCAR : to confiscate, to seize

secuestro *nm* 1 RAPTO : kidnapping, abduction 2 : hijacking 3 : seizure, confiscation

secular *adj* : secular — secularismo *nm* — secularización *nf*

secundar *vt* : to support, to second

secundaria *nf* 1 : secondary education, high school 2 *Mex* : junior high school, middle school

secundario, -ria *adj* : secondary

secuoya *nf* : sequoia

sed *nf* 1 : thirst ⟨tener sed : to be thirsty⟩ 2 tener sed de : to hunger for, to thirst for

seda *nf* : silk

sedación *nf, pl* -ciones : sedation

sedal *nm* : fishing line

sedán *nm, pl* sedanes : sedan

sedante *adj & nm* CALMANTE : sedative

sedar *vt* : to sedate

sede *nf* 1 : seat, headquarters 2 : venue, site 3 la Santa Sede : the Holy See

sedentario, -ria *adj* : sedentary

sedición *nf, pl* -ciones : sedition — sedicioso, -sa *adj*

sediento, -ta *adj* : thirsty, thirsting

sedimentación *nf, pl* -ciones : sedimentation

sedimentario, -ria *adj* : sedimentary

sedimento *nm* : sediment

sedoso, -sa *adj* : silky, silken

seducción *nf, pl* -ciones : seduction

seducir {61} *vt* 1 : to seduce 2 : to captivate, to charm

seductivo, -va *adj* : seductive

seductor[1], -tora *adj* 1 SEDUCTIVO : seductive 2 ENCANTADOR : charming, alluring

seductor[2], -tora *n* : seducer

segador, -dora *n* : harvester

segar {49} *vt* 1 : to reap, to harvest, to cut 2 : to sever abruptly ⟨una vida segada por la enfermedad : a life cut short by illness⟩

seglar[1] *adj* LAICO : lay, secular

seglar[2] *nm* LAICO : layperson, layman *m*, laywoman *f*

segmentación *nf, pl* **-ciones** : segmentation

segmentado, -da *adj* : segmented

segmento *nm* : segment

segregar {52} *vt* **1** : to segregate **2** SECRETAR : to secrete

seguida *nf* **en** ~ : right away, immediately ⟨vuelvo en seguida : I'll be right back⟩

seguidamente *adv* **1** : next, immediately after **2** : without a break, continuously

seguido¹ *adv* **1** RECTO : straight, straight ahead **2** : often, frequently

seguido², -da *adj* **1** CONSECUTIVO : consecutive, successive ⟨tres días seguidos : three days in a row⟩ **2** : straight, unbroken **3** ~ **por** *or* ~ **de** : followed by

seguidor, -dora *n* : follower, supporter

seguimiento *nm* **1** : following, pursuit **2** : continuation **3** : tracking, monitoring

seguir {75} *vt* **1** : to follow ⟨el sol sigue la lluvia : sunshine follows the rain⟩ ⟨seguiré tu consejo : I'll follow your advice⟩ ⟨me siguieron con la mirada : they followed me with their eyes⟩ **2** : to go along, to keep on ⟨seguimos toda la carretera panamericana : we continued along the PanAmerican Highway⟩ ⟨siguió hablando : he kept on talking⟩ ⟨seguir el curso : to stay on course⟩ **3** : to take (a course, a treatment) — *vi* **1** : to go on, to keep going ⟨sigue adelante : keep going, carry on⟩ **2** : to remain, to continue to be ⟨¿todavía sigues aquí? : you're still here?⟩ ⟨sigue con vida : she's still alive⟩ **3** : to follow, to come after ⟨la frase que sigue : the following sentence⟩

según¹ *adv* : it depends ⟨según y como : it all depends on⟩

según² *conj* **1** COMO, CONFORME : as, just as ⟨según lo dejé : just as I left it⟩ **2** : depending on how ⟨según se vea : depending on how one sees it⟩

según³ *prep* **1** : according to ⟨según los rumores : according to the rumors⟩ **2** : depending on ⟨según los resultados : depending on the results⟩

segundo¹, -da *adj* : second ⟨el segundo lugar : second place⟩

segundo², -da *n* **1** : second (in a series) **2** : second (person), second-in-command

segundo³ *nm* : second ⟨sesenta segundos : sixty seconds⟩

seguramente *adv* **1** : for sure, surely **2** : probably

seguridad *nf* **1** : safety, security **2** : (financial) security ⟨seguridad social : Social Security⟩ **3** CERTEZA : certainty, assurance ⟨con toda seguridad : with complete certainty⟩ **4** : confidence, self-confidence

seguro¹ *adv* : certainly, definitely ⟨va a llover, seguro : it's going to rain for sure⟩ ⟨¡seguro que sí! : of course!⟩

seguro², -ra *adj* **1** : safe, secure **2** : sure, certain ⟨estoy segura que es él : I'm sure that's him⟩ **3** : reliable, trustworthy **4** : self-assured

seguro³ *nm* **1** : insurance ⟨seguro de vida : life insurance⟩ **2** : fastener, clasp **3** *Mex* : safety pin

seis *adj & nm* : six

seiscientos¹, -tas *adj* : six hundred

seiscientos² *nms & pl* : six hundred

selección *nf, pl* **-ciones** **1** ELECCIÓN : selection, choice **2** **selección natural** : natural selection

seleccionar *vt* ELEGIR : to select, to choose

selectivo, -va *adj* : selective — **selectivamente** *adv*

selecto, -ta *adj* **1** : choice, select **2** EXCLUSIVO : exclusive

selenio *nm* : selenium

sellar *vt* **1** : to seal **2** : to stamp

sello *nm* **1** : seal **2** ESTAMPILLA, TIMBRE : postage stamp **3** : hallmark, characteristic

selva *nf* **1** BOSQUE : woods *pl*, forest ⟨selva húmeda : rain forest⟩ **2** JUNGLA : jungle

selvático, -ca *adj* **1** : forest, jungle ⟨sendero selvático : jungle path⟩ **2** : wild

semáforo *nm* **1** : traffic light **2** : stop signal

semana *nf* : week

semanal *adj* : weekly — **semanalmente** *adv*

semanario *nm* : weekly (publication)

semántica *nf* : semantics

semántico, -ca *adj* : semantic

semblante *nm* **1** : countenance, face **2** : appearance, look

semblanza *nf* : biographical sketch, profile

sembrado *nm* : cultivated field

sembrador, -dora *n* : planter, sower

sembradora *nf* : seeder (machine)

sembrar {55} *vt* **1** : to plant, to sow **2** : to scatter, to strew ⟨sembrar el pánico : to spread panic⟩

semejante¹ *adj* **1** PARECIDO : similar, alike **2** TAL : such ⟨nunca he visto cosa semejante : I have never seen such a thing⟩

semejante² *nm* PRÓJIMO : fellowman

semejanza *nf* PARECIDO : similarity, resemblance

semejar *vi* : to resemble, to look like — **semejarse** *vr* : to be similar, to look alike

semen *nm* : semen

semental *nm* : stud (animal) ⟨caballo semental : stallion⟩

semestre *nm* : semester

semicírculo *nm* : semicircle, half circle

semiconductor *nm* : semiconductor

semidiós *nm, pl* **-dioses** : demigod *m*

semifinal *nf* : semifinal

semifinalista¹ *adj* : semifinal

semifinalista² *nmf* : semifinalist

semiformal *adj* : semiformal
semilla *nf* : seed
semillero *nm* **1** : seedbed **2** : hotbed, breeding ground
seminario *nm* **1** : seminary **2** : seminar, graduate course
seminarista *nm* : seminarian
semiprecioso, -sa *adj* : semiprecious
semita¹ *adj* : Semitic
semita² *nmf* : Semite
sémola *nf* : semolina
sempiterno, -na *adj* ETERNO : eternal, everlasting
senado *nm* : senate
senador, -dora *n* : senator
sencillamente *adv* : simply, plainly
sencillez *nf* : simplicity
sencillo¹, -lla *adj* **1** : simple, easy **2** : plain, unaffected **3** : single
sencillo² *nm* **1** : single (recording) **2** : small change (coins) **3** : one-way ticket
senda *nf* CAMINO, SENDERO : path, way
sendero *nm* CAMINO, SENDA : path, way
sendos, -das *adj pl* : each, both ⟨llevaban sendos vestidos nuevos : they were each wearing a new dress⟩
senectud *nf* ANCIANIDAD : old age
senegalés, -lesa *adj & n, mpl* **-leses** : Senegalese
senil *adj* — senile — **senilidad** *nf*
seno *nm* **1** : breast, bosom ⟨los senos : the breasts⟩ ⟨el seno de la familia : the bosom of the family⟩ **2** : sinus **3 seno materno** : womb
sensación *nf, pl* **-ciones 1** IMPRESIÓN : feeling ⟨tener la sensación : to have a feeling⟩ **2** : sensation ⟨causar sensación : to cause a sensation⟩
sensacional *adj* : sensational
sensacionalista *adj* : sensationalistic, lurid
sensatez *nf* **1** : good sense **2 con ~** : sensibly
sensato, -ta *adj* : sensible, sound — **sensatamente** *adv*
sensibilidad *nf* **1** : sensitivity, sensibility **2** SENSACIÓN : feeling
sensibilizar {21} *vt* : to sensitize
sensible *adj* **1** : sensitive **2** APRECIABLE : considerable, significant
sensiblemente *adv* : considerably, significantly
sensiblería *nf* : sentimentality, mush
sensiblero, -ra *adj* : mawkish, sentimental, mushy
sensitivo, -va *adj* **1** : sense ⟨órganos sensitivos : sense organs⟩ **2** : sentient, capable of feeling
sensor *nm* : sensor
sensorial *adj* : sensory
sensual *adj* : sensual, sensuous — **sensualmente** *adv*
sensualidad *nf* : sensuality
sentado, -da *adj* **1** : sitting, seated **2** : established, settled ⟨dar por sentado : to take for granted⟩ ⟨dejar sentado : to make clear⟩ **3** : sensible, steady, judicious

sentar {55} *vt* **1** : to seat, to sit **2** : to establish, to set — *vi* **1** : to suit ⟨ese color te sienta : that color suits you⟩ **2** : to agree with (of food or drink) ⟨las cebollas no me sientan : onions don't agree with me⟩ **3** : to please ⟨le sentó mal el paseo : she didn't enjoy the trip⟩ — **sentarse** *vr* : to sit, to sit down ⟨siéntese, por favor : please have a seat⟩
sentencia *nf* **1** : sentence, judgment **2** : maxim, saying
sentenciar *vt* : to sentence
sentido¹, -da *adj* **1** : heartfelt, sincere ⟨mi más sentido pésame : my sincerest condolences⟩ **2** : touchy, sensitive **3** : offended, hurt
sentido² *nm* **1** : sense ⟨sentido común : common sense⟩ ⟨los cinco sentidos : the five senses⟩ ⟨sin sentido : senseless⟩ **2** CONOCIMIENTO : consciousness **3** SIGNIFICADO : meaning, sense ⟨doble sentido : double entendre⟩ **4** : direction ⟨calle de sentido único : one-way street⟩
sentimental¹ *adj* **1** : sentimental **2** : love, romantic ⟨vida sentimental : love life⟩
sentimental² *nmf* : sentimentalist
sentimentalismo *nm* : sentimentality, sentimentalism
sentimiento *nm* **1** : feeling, emotion **2** PESAR : regret, sorrow
sentir {76} *vt* **1** : to feel, to experience ⟨no siento nada de dolor : I don't feel any pain⟩ ⟨sentía sed : he was feeling thirsty⟩ ⟨sentir amor : to feel love⟩ **2** PERCIBIR : to perceive, to sense ⟨sentir un ruido : to hear a noise⟩ **3** LAMENTAR : to regret, to feel sorry for ⟨lo siento mucho : I'm very sorry⟩ — *vi* **1** : to have feeling, to feel **2 sin ~** : without noticing, inadvertently — **sentirse** *vr* **1** : to feel ⟨¿te sientes mejor? : are you feeling better?⟩ **2** *Chile, Mex* : to take offense
seña *nf* **1** : sign, signal **2 dar señas de** : to show signs of
señal *nf* **1** : signal **2** : sign ⟨señal de tráfico : traffic sign⟩ **3** INDICIO : indication ⟨en señal de : as a token of⟩ **4** VESTIGIO : trace, vestige **5** : scar, mark **6** : deposit, down payment
señalado, -da *adj* : distinguished, notable
señalador *nm* : marker ⟨señalador de libros : bookmark⟩
señalar *vt* **1** INDICAR : to indicate, to show **2** : to mark **3** : to point out, to stress **4** : to fix, to set — **señalarse** *vr* : to distinguish oneself
señor, -ñora *n* **1** : gentleman *m*, man *m*, lady *f*, woman *f*, wife *f* **2** : Sir *m*, Madam *f* ⟨estimados señores : Dear Sirs⟩ **3** : Mr. *m*, Mrs. *f* **4** : lord *m*, lady *f* ⟨el Señor : the Lord⟩
señoría *nf* **1** : lordship **2 Su Señoría** : Your Honor
señorial *adj* : stately, regal

señorío *nm* **1** : manor, estate **2** : dominion, power **3** : elegance, class
señorita *nf* **1** : young lady, young woman **2** : Miss
señuelo *nm* **1** : decoy **2** : bait
sépalo *nm* : sepal
sepa, etc. → **saber**
separación *nf, pl* **-ciones 1** : separation, division **2** : gap, space
separadamente *adv* : separately, apart
separado, -da *adj* **1** : separated **2** : separate ⟨vidas separadas : separate lives⟩ **3 por** ~ : separately
separar *vt* **1** : to separate, to divide **2** : to split up, to pull apart — **separarse** *vr*
sepelio *nm* : interment, burial
sepia[1] *adj & nm* : sepia
sepia[2] *nf* : cuttlefish
septentrional *adj* : northern
séptico, -ca *adj* : septic
septiembre *nm* : September
séptimo[1], **-ma** *adj* : seventh
séptimo[2] *nm* : seventh
septuagésimo[1], **-ma** *adj* : seventieth
septuagésimo[2] *nm* : seventieth
sepulcral *adj* **1** : sepulchral **2** : dismal, gloomy
sepulcro *nm* TUMBA : tomb, sepulchre
sepultar *vt* ENTERRAR : to bury
sepultura *nf* **1** : burial **2** TUMBA : grave, tomb
seque, etc. → **secar**
sequedad *nf* **1** : dryness **2** : brusqueness, curtness
sequía *nf* : drought
séquito *nm* : retinue, entourage
ser[1] {77} *vi* **1** : to be ⟨él es mi hermano : he is my brother⟩ ⟨Camila es linda : Camila is pretty⟩ **2** : to exist, to live ⟨ser, o no ser : to be or not to be⟩ **3** : to take place, to occur ⟨el concierto es el domingo : the concert is on Sunday⟩ **4** (*used with expressions of time, date, season*) ⟨son las diez : it's ten o'clock⟩ ⟨hoy es el 9 : today's the 9th⟩ **5** : to cost, to come to ⟨¿cuánto es? : how much is it?⟩ **6** (*with the future tense*) : to be able to be ⟨¿será posible? : can it be possible?⟩ **7** ~ **de** : to come from ⟨somos de Managua : we're from Managua⟩ **8** ~ **de** : to belong to ⟨ese lápiz es de Juan : that's Juan's pencil⟩ **9 es que** : the thing is that ⟨es que no lo conozco : it's just that I don't know him⟩ **10 ¡sea!** : agreed!, all right! **11 sea...sea** : either...or — *v aux* (*used in passive constructions*) : to be ⟨la cuenta ha sido pagada : the bill has been paid⟩ ⟨él fue asesinado : he was murdered⟩
ser[2] *nm* : being ⟨ser humano : human being⟩
seráfico, -ca *adj* : angelic, seraphic
serbio[1], **-bia** *adj & n* : Serb, Serbian
serbio[2] *nm* : Serbian (language)
serbocroata[1] *adj* : Serbo-Croatian
serbocroata[2] *nm* : Serbo-Croatian (language)

serenar *vt* : to calm, to soothe — **serenarse** *vr* CALMARSE : to calm down
serenata *nf* : serenade
serendipia *nf* : serendipity
serenidad *nf* : serenity, calmness
sereno[1], **-na** *adj* **1** SOSEGADO : serene, calm, composed **2** : fair, clear (of weather) **3** : calm, still (of the sea) — **serenamente** *adv*
sereno[2] *nm* : night watchman
seriado, -da *adj* : serial
serial *nm* : serial (on radio or television)
seriamente *adv* : seriously
serie *nf* **1** : series **2** SERIAL : serial **3 fabricación en serie** : mass production **4 fuera de serie** : extraordinary, amazing
seriedad *nf* **1** : seriousness, earnestness **2** : gravity, importance
serio, -ria *adj* **1** : serious, earnest **2** : reliable, responsible **3** : important **4 en** ~ : seriously, in earnest — **seriamente** *adv*
sermón *nm, pl* **sermones 1** : sermon **2** *fam* : harangue, lecture
sermonear *vt fam* : to harangue, to lecture
serpentear *vi* : to twist, to wind — **serpenteante** *adj*
serpentina *nf* : paper streamer
serpiente *nf* : serpent, snake
serrado, -da *adj* DENTADO : serrated
serranía *nf* : mountainous area
serrano, -na *adj* : from the mountains
serrar {55} *vt* : to saw
serrín *nm, pl* **serrines** : sawdust
serruchar *vt* : to saw up
serrucho *nm* : saw, handsaw
servicentro *nm Peru* : gas station
servicial *adj* : obliging, helpful
servicio *nm* **1** : service **2** SAQUE : serve (in sports) **3 servicios** *nmpl* : restroom
servidor, -dora *n* **1** : servant **2 su seguro servidor** : yours truly (in correspondence)
servidumbre *nf* **1** : servitude **2** : help, servants *pl*
servil *adj* **1** : servile, subservient **2** : menial
servilismo *nm* : servility, subservience
servilleta *nf* : napkin
servir {54} *vt* **1** : to serve, to be of use to **2** : to serve, to wait **3** SURTIR : to fill (an order) — *vi* **1** : to work ⟨mi radio no sirve : my radio isn't working⟩ **2** : to be of use, to be helpful ⟨esa computadora no sirve para nada : that computer's perfectly useless⟩ — **servirse** *vr* **1** : to help oneself to **2** : to be kind enough ⟨sírvase enviarnos un catálogo : please send us a catalog⟩
sésamo *nm* AJONJOLÍ : sesame, sesame seeds *pl*
sesenta *adj & nm* : sixty
sesentavo[1], **-va** *adj* : sixtieth
sesentavo[2] *n* : sixtieth (fraction)
sesgado, -da *adj* **1** : inclined, tilted **2** : slanted, biased

sesgar {52} *vt* **1** : to cut on the bias **2** : to tilt **3** : to bias, to slant
sesgo *nm* : bias
sesgue, etc. → **sesgar**
sesión *nf, pl* **sesiones 1** : session **2** : showing, performance
sesionar *vi* REUNIRSE : to meet, to be in session
seso *nm* **1** : brains, intelligence **2 sesos** *nmpl* : brains (as food)
sesudo, -da *adj* **1** : prudent, sensible **2** : brainy
set *nm, pl* **sets** : set (in tennis)
seta *nf* : mushroom
setecientos[1], **-tas** *adj* : seven hundred
setecientos[2] *nms & pl* : seven hundred
setenta *adj & nm* : seventy
setentavo[1], **-va** *adj* : seventieth
setentavo[2] *nm* : seventieth
setiembre → **septiembre**
seto *nm* **1** : fence, enclosure **2 seto vivo** : hedge
seudónimo *nm* : pseudonym
severidad *nf* **1** : harshness, severity **2** : strictness
severo, -ra *adj* **1** : harsh, severe **2** ES-TRICTO : strict — **severamente** *adv*
sexagésimo[1], **-ma** *adj* : sixtieth, sixty-
sexagésimo[2], **-ma** *n* : sixtieth, sixty- (in a series)
sexismo *nm* : sexism — **sexista** *adj & nmf*
sexo *nm* : sex
sextante *nm* : sextant
sexteto *nm* : sextet
sexto, -ta *adj* : sixth — **sexto, -ta** *n*
sexual *adj* : sexual, sex ⟨educación sexual : sex education⟩ — **sexualmente** *adv*
sexualidad *nf* : sexuality
sexy *adj, pl* **sexy** *or* **sexys** : sexy
shock [ˈʃɔk, ˈtʃɔk] *nm* : shock ⟨estado de shock : state of shock⟩
short *nm, pl* **shorts** : shorts *pl*
show *nm, pl* **shows** : show
si *conj* **1** : if ⟨lo haré si me pagan : I'll do it if they pay me⟩ ⟨si lo supiera te lo diría : if I knew it I would tell you⟩ **2** : whether, if ⟨no importa si funciona o no : it doesn't matter whether it works (or not)⟩ **3** (*expressing desire, protest, or surprise*) ⟨si supiera la verdad : if only I knew the truth⟩ ⟨¡si no quiero! : but I don't want to!⟩ **4 si bien** : although ⟨si bien se ha progresado : although progress has been made⟩ **5 si no** : otherwise, or else ⟨si no, no voy : otherwise I won't go⟩
sí[1] *adv* **1** : yes ⟨sí, gracias : yes, please⟩ ⟨creo que sí : I think so⟩ **2 sí que** : indeed, absolutely ⟨esta vez sí que ganaré : this time I'm sure to win⟩ **3 porque sí** *fam* : because, just because ⟨lo hizo porque sí : she did it just because⟩
sí[2] *nm* : yes ⟨dar el sí : to say yes, to express consent⟩
sí[3] *pron* **1 de por sí** *or* **en sí** : by itself, in itself, per se **2 fuera de sí** : beside

oneself **3 para sí (mismo)** : to himself, to herself, for himself, for herself **4 entre ~** : among themselves
siamés, -mesa *adj & n, mpl* **siameses** : Siamese
sibilante *adj & nf* : sibilant
siciliano, -na *adj & n* : Sicilian
sico- → **psico-**
sicomoro *or* **sicómoro** *nm* : sycamore
SIDA *or* **sida** *nm* (*síndrome de inmunodeficiencia adquirida*) : AIDS
siderurgia *nf* : iron and steel industry
siderúrgico, -ca *adj* : steel, iron ⟨la industria siderúrgica : the steel industry⟩
sidra *nf* : hard cider
siega[1], **siegue, etc.** → **segar**
siega[2] *nf* **1** : harvesting **2** : harvest time **3** : harvested crop
siembra[1], **etc.** → **sembrar**
siembra[2] *nf* **1** : sowing **2** : sowing season **3** SEMBRADO : cultivated field
siempre *adv* **1** : always ⟨siempre tienes hambre : you're always hungry⟩ **2** : still ⟨¿siempre te vas? : are you still going?⟩ **3** *Mex* : after all ⟨siempre no fui : I didn't go after all⟩ **4 siempre que** : whenever, every time ⟨siempre que pasa : every time he walks by⟩ **5 para ~** : forever, for good **6 siempre y cuando** : provided that
sien *nf* : temple (on the forehead)
sienta, etc. → **sentar**
siente, etc. → **sentir**
sierpe *nf* : serpent, snake
sierra[1], **etc.** → **serrar**
sierra[2] *nf* **1** : saw ⟨sierra de vaivén : jigsaw⟩ **2** CORDILLERA : mountain range **3** : mountains *pl* ⟨viven en la sierra : they live in the mountains⟩
siervo, -va *n* **1** : slave **2** : serf
siesta *nf* : nap, siesta
siete *adj & nm* : seven
sífilis *nf* : syphilis
sifón *nm, pl* **sifones** : siphon
siga, sigue etc. → **seguir**
sigilo *nm* : secrecy, stealth
sigiloso, -sa *adj* FURTIVO : furtive, stealthy — **sigilosamente** *adv*
sigla *nf* : acronym, abbreviation
siglo *nm* **1** : century **2** : age ⟨el Siglo de Oro : the Golden Age⟩ ⟨hace siglos que no te veo : I haven't seen you in ages⟩ **3** : world, secular life
signar *vt* : to sign (a treaty or agreement)
signatario, -ria *n* : signatory
significación *nf, pl* **-ciones 1** : significance, importance **2** : signification, meaning
significado *nm* **1** : sense, meaning **2** : significance
significante *adj* : significant
significar {72} *vt* **1** : to mean, to signify **2** : to express, to make known — **significarse** *vr* **1** : to draw attention, to become known **2** : to take a stance
significativo, -va *adj* **1** : significant, important **2** : meaningful — **significativamente** *adv*

signo *nm* **1** : sign ⟨signo de igual : equal sign⟩ ⟨un signo de alegría : a sign of happiness⟩ **2** : (punctuation) mark ⟨signo de interrogación : question mark⟩ ⟨signo de admiración : exclamation point⟩ ⟨signo de intercalación : caret⟩

siguiente *adj* : next, following

sílaba *nf* : syllable

silábico, -ca *adj* : syllabic

silbar *v* : to whistle

silbato *nm* PITO : whistle

silbido *nm* : whistle, whistling

silenciador *nm* **1** : muffler (of an automobile) **2** : silencer

silenciar *vt* **1** : to silence **2** : to muffle

silencio *nm* **1** : silence, quiet ⟨¡silencio! : be quiet!⟩ **2** : rest (in music)

silencioso, -sa *adj* : silent, quiet — **silenciosamente** *adv*

sílice *nf* : silica

silicio *nm* : silicon

silla *nf* **1** : chair **2 silla de ruedas** : wheelchair

sillón *nm, pl* **sillones** : armchair, easy chair

silo *nm* : silo

silueta *nf* **1** : silhouette **2** : figure, shape

silvestre *adj* : wild ⟨flor silvestre : wildflower⟩

silvicultor, -tora *n* : forester

silvicultura *nf* : forestry

sima *nf* ABISMO : chasm, abyss

simbólico, -ca *adj* : symbolic — **simbólicamente** *adj*

simbolismo *nm* : symbolism

simbolizar {21} *vt* : to symbolize

símbolo *nm* : symbol

simetría *nf* : symmetry

simétrico, -ca *adj* : symmetrical, symmetric

simiente *nf* : seed

símil *nm* **1** : simile **2** : analogy, comparison

similar *adj* SEMEJANTE : similar, alike

similitud *nf* : similarity, resemblance

simio *nm* : ape

simpatía *nf* **1** : liking, affection ⟨tomarle simpatía a : to take a liking to⟩ **2** : warmth, friendliness **3** : support, solidarity

simpático, -ca *adj* : nice, friendly, likeable

simpatizante *nf* : sympathizer, supporter

simpatizar {21} *vi* **1** : to get along, to hit it off ⟨simpaticé mucho con él : I really liked him⟩ **2 ~ con** : to sympathize with, to support

simple[1] *adj* **1** SENCILLO : plain, simple, easy **2** : pure, mere ⟨por simple vanidad : out of pure vanity⟩ **3** : simpleminded, foolish

simple[2] *n* : fool, simpleton

simplemente *adv* : simply, merely, just

simpleza *nf* **1** : foolishness, simpleness **2** NECEDAD : nonsense

simplicidad *nf* : simplicity

simplificar {72} *vt* : to simplify — **simplificación** *nf*

simplista *adj* : simplistic

simposio *or* **simposium** *nm* : symposium

simulación *nf, pl* **-ciones** : simulation

simulacro *nm* : imitation, sham ⟨simulacro de juicio : mock trial⟩

simular *vt* **1** : to simulate **2** : to feign, to pretend

simultáneo, -nea *adj* : simultaneous — **simultáneamente** *adv*

sin *prep* **1** : without ⟨sin querer : unintentionally⟩ ⟨sin refinar : unrefined⟩ **2 sin que** : without ⟨lo hicimos sin que él se diera cuenta : we did it without him noticing⟩

sinagoga *nf* : synagogue

sinceridad *nf* : sincerity

sincero, -ra *adj* : sincere, honest, true — **sinceramente** *adv*

síncopa *nf* : syncopation

sincopar *vt* : to syncopate

sincronizar {21} *vt* : to synchronize — **sincronización** *nf*

sindical *adj* GREMIAL : union, labor ⟨representante sindical : union representative⟩

sindicalización *nf, pl* **-ciones** : unionizing, unionization

sindicalizar {21} *vt* : to unionize — **sindicalizarse** *vr* **1** : to form a union **2** : to join a union

sindicar → **sindicalizar**

sindicato *nm* GREMIO : union, guild

síndrome *nm* : syndrome

sinecura *nf* : sinecure

sinfín *nm* : endless number ⟨un sinfín de problemas : no end of problems⟩

sinfonía *nf* : symphony

sinfónica *nf* : symphony orchestra

sinfónico, -ca *adj* : symphonic, symphony

singular[1] *adj* **1** : singular, unique **2** PARTICULAR : peculiar, odd **3** : singular (in grammar) — **singularmente** *adv*

singular[2] *nm* : singular

singularidad *nf* : uniqueness, singularity

singularizar {21} *vt* : to make unique or distinct — **singularizarse** *vr* : to stand out, to distinguish oneself

siniestrado, -da *adj* : damaged, wrecked ⟨zona siniestrada : disaster zone⟩

siniestro[1], -tra *adj* **1** IZQUIERDO : left, left-hand **2** MALVADO : sinister, evil

siniestro[2] *nm* : accident, disaster

sinnúmero → **sinfín**

sino *conj* **1** : but, rather ⟨no será hoy, sino mañana : it won't be today, but tomorrow⟩ **2** EXCEPTO : but, except ⟨no hace sino despertar suspicacias : it does nothing but arouse suspicion⟩

sinónimo[1], -ma *adj* : synonymous

sinónimo[2] *nm* : synonym

sinopsis *nfs & pl* RESUMEN : synopsis, summary

sinrazón *nf, pl* **-zones** : wrong, injustice

sinsabores *nmpl* : woes, troubles
sinsonte *nm* : mockingbird
sintáctico, -ca *adj* : syntactic, syntactical
sintaxis *nfs & pl* : syntax
síntesis *nfs & pl* **1** : synthesis, fusion **2** SINOPSIS : synopsis, summary
sintético, -ca *adj* : synthetic — **sintéticamente** *adv*
sintetizar {21} *vt* **1** : to synthesize **2** RESUMIR : to summarize
sintió, etc. → **sentir**
síntoma *nm* : symptom
sintomático, -ca *adj* : symptomatic
sintonía *nf* **1** : tuning in (of a radio) **2** **en sintonía con** : in tune with, attuned to
sintonizador *nm* : tuner, knob for tuning (of a radio, etc.)
sintonizar {21} *vt* : to tune (in) to — *vi* **1** : to tune in **2** ~ **con** : to be in tune with, to empathize with
sinuosidad *nf* : sinuosity
sinuoso, -sa *adj* **1** : winding, sinuous **2** : devious
sinvergüenza[1] *adj* **1** DESCARADO : shameless, brazen, impudent **2** TRAVIESO : naughty
sinvergüenza[2] *nmf* **1** : rogue, scoundrel **2** : brat, rascal
sionista *adj & nmf* : Zionist — **sionismo** *nm*
siqui- → **psiqui-**
siquiera *adv* **1** : at least ⟨dame siquiera un poquito : at least give me a little bit⟩ **2** (*in negative constructions*) : not even ⟨ni siquiera nos saludaron : they didn't even say hello to us⟩
sirena *nf* **1** : mermaid **2** : siren ⟨sirena de niebla : foghorn⟩
sirio, -ria *adj & n* : Syrian
sirope *nm* : syrup
sirve, etc. → **servir**
sirviente, -ta *n* : servant, maid *f*
sisal *nm* : sisal
sisear *vi* : to hiss
siseo *nm* : hiss
sísmico, -ca *adj* : seismic
sismo *nm* **1** TERREMOTO : earthquake **2** TEMBLOR : tremor
sismógrafo *nm* : seismograph
sistema *nm* : system
sistemático, -ca *adj* : systematic — **sistemáticamente** *adv*
sistematizar {21} *vt* : to systematize
sistémico, -ca *adj* : systemic
sitiar *vt* ASEDIAR : to besiege
sitio *nm* **1** LUGAR : place, site ⟨vámonos a otro sitio : let's go somewhere else⟩ **2** ESPACIO : room, space ⟨hacer sitio a : to make room for⟩ **3** : siege ⟨estado de sitio : state of siege⟩ **4** *Mex* : taxi stand
situación *nf, pl* **-ciones** : situation
situado, -da *adj* : situated, placed
situar {3} *vt* UBICAR : to situate, to place, to locate — **situarse** *vr* **1** : to be placed, to be located **2** : to make a place for oneself, to do well

sketch *nm* : sketch, skit
slip *nm* : briefs *pl*, underpants *pl*
smog *nm* : smog
smoking *nm* ESMOQUIN : tuxedo
snob → **esnob**
so *prep* : under ⟨so pena de : under penalty of⟩
sobaco *nm* : armpit
sobado, -da *adj* **1** : worn, shabby **2** : well-worn, hackneyed
sobar *vt* **1** : to finger, to handle **2** : to knead **3** : to rub, to massage **4** *fam* : to beat, to pummel
soberanía *nf* : sovereignty
soberano, -na *adj & n* : sovereign
soberbia *nf* **1** ORGULLO : pride, arrogance **2** MAGNIFICENCIA : magnificence
soberbio, -bia *adj* **1** : proud, arrogant **2** : grand, magnificent
sobornable *adv* : venal, bribable
sobornar *vt* : to bribe
soborno *nm* **1** : bribery **2** : bribe
sobra *nf* **1** : excess, surplus **2 de** ~ : extra, to spare **3 sobras** *nfpl* : leftovers, scraps
sobrado, -da *adj* : abundant, excessive, more than enough
sobrante[1] *adj* : remaining, superfluous
sobrante[2] *nm* : remainder, surplus
sobrar *vi* : to be in excess, to be superfluous ⟨más vale que sobre a que falte : it's better to have too much than not enough⟩
sobre[1] *nm* **1** : envelope **2** : packet ⟨un sobre de sazón : a packet of seasoning⟩
sobre[2] *prep* **1** : on, on top of ⟨sobre la mesa : on the table⟩ **2** : over, above **3** : about ⟨¿tiene libros sobre Bolivia? : do you have books on Bolivia?⟩ **4 sobre todo** : especially, above all
sobrealimentar *vt* : to overfeed
sobrecalentar {55} *vt* : to overheat — **sobrecalentarse** *vr*
sobrecama *nmf* : bedspread
sobrecargar {52} *vt* : to overload, to overburden, to weigh down
sobrecoger {15} *vt* **1** : to surprise, to startle **2** : to scare — **sobrecogerse** *vr*
sobrecubierta *nf* : dust jacket
sobredosis *nfs & pl* : overdose
sobreentender {56} *vt* : to infer, to understand
sobreestimar *vt* : to overestimate, to overrate
sobreexcitado, -da *adj* : overexcited
sobreexponer {60} *vt* : to overexpose
sobregirar *vt* : to overdraw
sobregiro *nm* : overdraft
sobrehumano, -na *adj* : superhuman
sobrellevar *vt* : to endure, to bear
sobremanera *adv* : exceedingly
sobremesa *nf* : after-dinner conversation
sobrenatural *adj* : supernatural
sobrenombre *nm* APODO : nickname
sobrentender → **sobreentender**

sobrepasar *vt* : to exceed, to surpass —
sobrepasarse *vr* PASARSE : to go too
far

sobrepelliz *nf, pl* **-pellices** : surplice

sobrepeso *nm* **1** : excess weight **2**
: overweight, obesity

sobrepoblación, sobrepoblado → **superpoblación, superpoblado**

sobreponer {60} *vt* **1** SUPERPONER : to
superimpose **2** ANTEPONER : to put
first, to give priority to — **sobrepon-
erse** *vr* **1** : to pull oneself together **2**
~ a : to overcome

sobreprecio *nm* : surcharge

sobreproducción *nf, pl* **-ciones** : over-
production

sobreproducir {61} *vt* : to overproduce

sobreprotector, -tora *adj* : overprotec-
tive

sobreproteger {15} *vt* : to overprotect

sobresaliente[1] *adj* **1** : protruding, projecting **2** : outstanding, noteworthy **3**
: significant, salient

sobresaliente[2] *nmf* : understudy

sobresalir {73} *vi* **1** : to protrude, to jut
out, to project **2** : to stand out, to excel

sobresaltar *vt* : to startle, to frighten —
sobresaltarse *vr*

sobresalto *nm* : start, fright

sobresueldo *nm* : bonus, additional pay

sobretasa *nf* : surcharge ⟨sobretasa a la
gasolina : gas tax⟩

sobretodo *nm* : overcoat

sobrevalorar *or* **sobrevaluar** {3} *vt* : to
overvalue, to overrate

sobrevender *vt* : to oversell

sobrevenir {87} *vi* ACAECER : to take
place, to come about ⟨podrían sobrevenir complicaciones : complications could occur⟩

sobrevivencia → **supervivencia**

sobreviviente → **superviviente**

sobrevivir *vi* : to survive — *vt* : to outlive, to outlast

sobrevolar {19} *vt* : to fly over, to overfly

sobriedad *nf* : sobriety, moderation

sobrino, -na *n* : nephew *m*, niece *f*

sobrio, -bria *adj* : sober — **sobriamente**
adv

socarrón, -rrona *adj, mpl* **-rrones 1**
: sly, cunning **2** : sarcastic

socavar *vt* : to undermine

sociabilidad *nf* : sociability

sociable *adj* : sociable

social *adj* : social — **socialmente** *adv*

socialista *adj & nmf* : socialist — **socialismo** *nm*

sociedad *nf* **1** : society **2** : company,
enterprise **3 sociedad anónima** : incorporated company

socio, -cia *n* **1** : member **2** : partner

socioeconómico, -ca *adj* : socioeconomic

sociología *nf* : sociology

sociológico, -ca *adj* : sociological —
sociológicamente *adv*

sociólogo, -ga *n* : sociologist

socorrer *vt* : to assist, to come to the aid
of

socorrido, -da *adj* ÚTIL : handy, practical

socorrista *nmf* **1** : rescue worker **2**
: lifeguard

socorro *nm* AUXILIO **1** : aid, help
⟨equipo de socorro : rescue team⟩ **2**
¡socorro! : help!

soda *nf* : soda, soda water

sodio *nf* : sodium

soez *adj, pl* **soeces** GROSERO : rude,
vulgar — **soezmente** *adv*

sofá *nm* : couch, sofa

sofistería *nf* : sophistry — **sofista** *nmf*

sofisticación *nf, pl* **-ciones** : sophistication

sofisticado, -da *adj* : sophisticated

sofocante *adj* : suffocating, stifling

sofocar {72} *vt* **1** AHOGAR : to suffocate,
to smother **2** EXTINGUIR : to extinguish, to put out (a fire) **3** APLASTAR
: to crush, to put down ⟨sofocar una
rebelión : to crush a rebellion⟩ — **sofocarse** *vr* **1** : to suffocate **2** *fam* : to
get upset, to get mad

sofreír {66} *vt* : to sauté

sofrito[1], **-ta** *adj* : sautéed

sofrito[2] *nm* : seasoning sauce

softbol *nm* : softball

software *nm* : software

soga *nf* : rope

soja → **soya**

sojuzgar *vt* : to subdue, to conquer, to
subjugate

sol *nm* **1** : sun **2** : Peruvian unit of currency

solamente *adv* SÓLO : only, just

solapa *nf* **1** : lapel (of a jacket) **2** : flap
(of an envelope)

solapado, -da *adj* : secret, underhanded

solapar *vt* : to cover up, to keep secret
— **solaparse** *vr* : to overlap

solar[1] {19} *vt* : to floor, to tile

solar[2] *adj* : solar, sun

solar[3] *nm* **1** TERRENO : lot, piece of
land, site **2** *Cuba, Peru* : tenement
building

solariego, -ga *adj* : ancestral

solaz *nm, pl* **solaces 1** CONSUELO : solace, comfort **2** DESCANSO : relaxation, recreation

solazarse {21} *vr* : to relax, to enjoy oneself

soldado *nm* **1** : soldier **2 soldado raso**
: private, enlisted man

soldador[1], **-dora** *n* : welder

soldador[2] *nm* : soldering iron

soldadura *nf* **1** : welding **2** : soldering,
solder

soldar {19} *vt* **1** : to weld **2** : to solder

soleado, -da *adj* : sunny

soledad *nf* : loneliness, solitude

solemne *adj* : solemn — **solemne-
mente** *adv*

solemnidad *nf* : solemnity

soler {78} *vi* : to be in the habit of, to tend to ⟨solía tomar café por la tarde : she usually drank coffee in the afternoon⟩ ⟨eso suele ocurrir : that frequently happens⟩

solera *nf* **1** : prop, support **2** : tradition

solicitante *nmf* : applicant

solicitar *vt* **1** : to request, to solicit **2** : to apply for ⟨solicitar empleo : to apply for employment⟩

solícito, -ta *adj* : solicitous, attentive, obliging

solicitud *nf* **1** : solicitude, concern **2** : request **3** : application

solidaridad *nf* : solidarity

solidario, -ria *adj* : supportive, united in support ⟨se declararon solidarios con la nueva ley : they declared their support for the new law⟩ ⟨espíritu solidario : spirit of solidarity⟩

solidarizar {21} *vi* : to be in solidarity ⟨solidarizamos con la huelga : we support the strike⟩

solidez *nf* **1** : solidity, firmness **2** : soundness (of an argument, etc.)

solidificar {72} *vt* : to solidify, to make solid — **solidificarse** *vr* — **solidificación** *nf*

sólido¹, -da *adj* **1** : solid, firm **2** : sturdy, well-made **3** : sound, well-founded — **sólidamente** *adv*

sólido² *nm* : solid

soliloquio *nm* : soliloquy

solista *nmf* : soloist

solitaria *nf* TENIA : tapeworm

solitario¹, -ria *adj* **1** : lonely **2** : lone, solitary **3** DESIERTO : deserted, lonely ⟨una calle solitaria : a deserted street⟩

solitario², -ria *n* : recluse, loner

solitario³ *nm* : solitaire

sollozar {21} *vi* : to sob

sollozo *nm* : sob

solo¹, -la *adj* **1** : alone, by oneself **2** : lonely **3** ÚNICO : only, sole, unique ⟨hay un solo problema : there's only one problem⟩ **4 a solas** : alone

solo² *nm* : solo

sólo *adv* SOLAMENTE : just, only ⟨sólo quieren comer : they just want to eat⟩

solomillo *nm* : sirloin, loin

solsticio *nm* : solstice

soltar {19} *vt* **1** : to let go of, to drop **2** : to release, to set free **3** AFLOJAR : to loosen, to slacken

soltería *nf* : bachelorhood, spinsterhood

soltero¹, -ra *adj* : single, unmarried

soltero², -ra *n* **1** : bachelor *m*, single man *m*, single woman *f* **2 apellido de soltera** : maiden name

soltura *nf* **1** : looseness, slackness **2** : fluency (of language) **3** : agility, ease of movement

soluble *adj* : soluble — **solubilidad** *nf*

solución *nf, pl* **-ciones 1** : solution (in a liquid) **2** : answer, solution

solucionar *vt* RESOLVER : to solve, to resolve — **solucionarse** *vr*

solvencia *nf* **1** : solvency **2** : settling, payment (of debts) **3** : reliability ⟨solvencia moral : trustworthiness⟩

solvente¹ *adj* **1** : solvent **2** : reliable, trustworthy

solvente² *nm* : solvent

somalí *adj & nmf* : Somalian

sombra *nf* **1** : shadow **2** : shade **3 sombras** *nfpl* : darkness, shadows *pl* **4 sin sombra de duda** : without a shadow of a doubt

sombreado, -da *adj* **1** : shady **2** : shaded, darkened

sombrear *vt* : to shade

sombrerero, -ra *n* : milliner, hatter

sombrero *nm* **1** : hat **2 sin ~** : bareheaded **3 sombrero hongo** : derby

sombrilla *nf* : parasol, umbrella

sombrío, -bría *adj* LÓBREGO : dark, somber, gloomy — **sombríamente** *adv*

someramente *adv* : cursorily, summarily

somero, -ra *adj* : superficial, cursory, shallow

someter *vt* **1** : to subjugate, to conquer **2** : to subordinate **3** : to subject (to treatment or testing) **4** : to submit, to present — **someterse** *vr* **1** : to submit, to yield **2** : to undergo

sometimiento *nm* **1** : submission, subjection **2** : presentation

somnífero¹, -ra *adj* : soporific

somnífero² *nm* : sleeping pill

somnolencia *nf* : drowsiness, sleepiness

somnoliento, -ta *adj* : drowsy, sleepy

somorgujo *or* **somormujo** *nm* : loon, grebe

somos → **ser¹**

son¹ → **ser**

son² *nm* **1** : sound ⟨al son de la trompeta : at the sound of the trumpet⟩ **2** : news, rumor **3 en son de** : as, in the manner of, by way of ⟨en son de broma : as a joke⟩ ⟨en son de paz : in peace⟩

sonado, -da *adj* : celebrated, famous, much-discussed

sonaja *nf* : rattle

sonajero *nm* : rattle (toy)

sonámbulo, -la *n* : sleepwalker

sonar¹ {19} *vi* **1** : to sound ⟨suena bien : it sounds good⟩ **2** : to ring (bells) **3** : to look or sound familiar ⟨me suena ese nombre : that name rings a bell⟩ **4 ~ a** : to sound like — *vt* **1** : to ring **2** : to blow (a trumpet, a nose) — **sonarse** *vr* : to blow one's nose

sonar² *nm* : sonar

sonata *nf* : sonata

sonda *nf* **1** : sounding line **2** : probe **3** CATÉTER : catheter

sondar *vt* **1** : to sound, to probe (in medicine, drilling, etc.) **2** : to probe, to explore (outer space)

sondear *vt* **1** : to sound **2** : to probe **3** : to sound out, to test (opinions, markets)

sondeo *nm* **1** : sounding, probing **2** : drilling **3** ENCUESTA : survey, poll
soneto *nm* : sonnet
sónico, -ca *adj* : sonic
sonido *nm* : sound
sonoridad *nf* : sonority, resonance
sonoro, -ra *adj* **1** : resonant, sonorous, voiced (in linguistics) **2** : resounding, loud **3 banda sonora** : soundtrack
sonreír {66} *vi* : to smile
sonriente *adj* : smiling
sonrisa *nf* : smile
sonrojar *vt* : to cause to blush — **sonrojarse** *vr* : to blush
sonrojo *nm* RUBOR : blush
sonrosado, -da *adj* : rosy, pink
sonsacar {72} *vt* : to wheedle, to extract
sonsonete *nm* **1** : tapping **2** : drone **3** : mocking tone
soñador¹, -dora *adj* : dreamy
soñador², -dora *n* : dreamer
soñar {19} *v* **1** : to dream **2 ~ con** : to dream about **3 soñar despierto** : to daydream
soñoliento, -ta *adj* : sleepy, drowsy
sopa *nf* **1** : soup **2 estar hecho una sopa** : to be soaked to the bone
sopera *nf* : soup tureen
sopesar *vt* : to weigh, to evaluate
soplar *vi* : to blow — *vt* : to blow on, to blow out, to blow off
soplete *nm* : blowtorch
soplido *nm* : puff
soplo *nm* : puff, gust
soplón, -plona *n, mpl* **soplones** *fam* : tattletale, sneak
sopor *nm* SOMNOLENCIA : drowsiness, sleepiness
soporífero, -ra *adj* : soporific
soportable *adj* : bearable, tolerable
soportar *vt* **1** SOSTENER : to support, to hold up **2** RESISTIR : to withstand, to resist **3** AGUANTAR : to bear, to tolerate
soporte *nm* : base, stand, support
soprano *nmf* : soprano
sor *nf* : Sister (religious title)
sorber *vt* **1** : to sip, to suck in **2** : to absorb, to soak up
sorbete *nm* : sherbet
sorbo *nm* **1** : sip, gulp, swallow **2 beber a sorbos** : to sip
sordera *nf* : deafness
sordidez *nf, pl* **-deces** : sordidness, squalor
sórdido, -da *adj* : sordid, dirty, squalid
sordina *nf* : mute (for a musical instrument)
sordo, -da *adj* **1** : deaf **2** : muted, muffled
sordomudo, -da *n* : deaf-mute
sorgo *nm* : sorghum
soriasis *nfs & pl* : psoriasis
sorna *nf* : sarcasm, mocking tone
sorprendente *adj* : surprising — **sorprendentemente** *adv*
sorprender *vt* : to surprise — **sorprenderse** *vr*

sorpresa *nf* : surprise
sorpresivo, -va *adj* **1** : surprising, surprise **2** IMPREVISTO : sudden, unexpected
sortear *vt* **1** RIFAR : to raffle, to draw lots for **2** : to dodge, to avoid
sorteo *nm* : drawing, raffle
sortija *nf* **1** ANILLO : ring **2** : curl, ringlet
sortilegio *nm* **1** HECHIZO : spell, charm **2** HECHICERÍA : sorcery
SOS *nm* : SOS
sosegado, -da *adj* SERENO : calm, tranquil, serene
sosegar {49} *vt* : to calm, to pacify — **sosegarse** *vr*
sosiego *nm* : tranquillity, serenity, calm
soslayar *vt* ESQUIVAR : to dodge, to evade
soslayo *nm* **de ~** : obliquely, sideways ⟨mirar de soslayo : to look askance⟩
soso, -sa *adj* **1** INSÍPIDO : bland, flavorless **2** ABURRIDO : dull, boring
sospecha *nf* : suspicion
sospechar *vt* : to suspect — *vi* : to be suspicious
sospechosamente *adv* : suspiciously
sospechoso¹, -sa *adj* : suspicious, suspect
sospechoso², -sa *n* : suspect
sostén *nm, pl* **sostenes 1** APOYO : support **2** : sustenance **3** : brassiere, bra
sostener {80} *vt* **1** : to support, to hold up **2** : to hold ⟨sostenme la puerta : hold the door for me⟩ ⟨sostener una conversación : to hold a conversation⟩ **3** : to sustain, to maintain — **sostenerse** *vr* **1** : to stand, to hold oneself up **2** : to continue, to remain
sostenible *adj* : sustainable, tenable
sostenido¹, -da *adj* **1** : sustained, prolonged **2** : sharp (in music)
sostenido² *nm* : sharp (in music)
sostuvo, etc. → **sostener**
sotana *nf* : cassock
sótano *nm* : basement
sotavento *nm* : lee ⟨a sotavento : leeward⟩
soterrar {55} *vt* **1** : to bury **2** : to conceal, to hide away
soto *nm* : grove, copse
souvenir *nm, pl* **-nirs** RECUERDO : souvenir, memento
soviético, -ca *adj* : Soviet
soy → **ser**
soya *nf* : soy, soybean
spaghetti → **espagueti**
sport [ɛ'spor] *adj* : sport, casual
sprint [ɛ'sprin, -'sprint] *nm* : sprint — **sprinter** *nmf*
squash [ɛ'skwaʃ, -'skwatʃ] *nm* : squash (sport)
Sr. *nm* : Mr.
Sra. *nf* : Mrs., Ms.
Srta. *or* **Srita.** *nf* : Miss, Ms.
standard → **estándar**
stress → **estrés**
su *adj* **1** : his, her, its, their, one's ⟨su libro : her book⟩ ⟨sus consecuencias

: its consequences⟩ 2 (*formal*) : your ⟨tómese su medicina, señor : take your medicine, sir⟩

suave *adj* 1 BLANDO : soft 2 LISO : smooth 3 : gentle, mild 4 *Mex fam* : great, fantastic

suavemente *adv* : smoothly, gently, softly

suavidad *nf* : softness, smoothness, mellowness

suavizante *nm* : softener, fabric softener

suavizar {21} *vt* 1 : to soften, to smooth out 2 : to tone down — **suavizarse** *vr*

subacuático, -ca *adj* : underwater

subalterno¹, -na *adj* 1 SUBORDINADO : subordinate 2 SECUNDARIO : secondary

subalterno², -na *n* SUBORDINADO : subordinate

subarrendar {55} *vt* : to sublet

subasta *nf* : auction

subastador, -dora *n* : auctioneer

subastar *vt* : to auction, to auction off

subcampeón, -peona *n, mpl* **-peones** : runner-up

subcomité *nm* : subcommittee

subconsciente *adj & nm* : subconscious — **subconscientemente** *adv*

subcontratar *vt* : to subcontract

subcontratista *nmf* : subcontractor

subcultura *nf* : subculture

subdesarrollado, -da *adj* : underdeveloped

subdirector, -tora *n* : assistant manager

súbdito, -ta *n* : subject (of a monarch)

subdividir *vt* : to subdivide

subdivisión *nf, pl* **-siones** : subdivision

subestimar *vt* : to underestimate, to undervalue

subexponer {60} *vt* : to underexpose

subexposición *nf, pl* **-ciones** : underexposure

subgrupo *nm* : subgroup

subibaja *nm* : seesaw

subida *nf* 1 : ascent, climb 2 : rise, increase 3 : slope, hill ⟨ir de subida : to go uphill⟩

subido, -da *adj* 1 : intense, strong ⟨amarillo subido : bright yellow⟩ 2 **subido de tono** : risqué

subir *vt* 1 : to bring up, to take up 2 : to climb, to go up 3 : to raise — *vi* 1 : to go up, to come up 2 : to rise, to increase 3 : to be promoted 4 ~ **a** : to get on, to mount ⟨subir a un tren : to get on a train⟩ — **subirse** *vr* 1 : to climb (up) 2 : to pull up (clothing) 3 **subirse a la cabeza** : to go to one's head

súbito, -ta *adj* 1 REPENTINO : sudden 2 **de** ~ : all of a sudden, suddenly — **súbitamente** *adv*

subjetivo, -va *adj* : subjective — **subjetivamente** *adv* — **subjetividad** *nf*

subjuntivo¹, -va *adj* : subjunctive

subjuntivo² *nm* : subjunctive

sublevación *nf, pl* **-ciones** ALZAMIENTO : uprising, rebellion

sublevar *vt* : to incite to rebellion — **sublevarse** *vr* : to rebel, to rise up

sublimar *vt* : to sublimate — **sublimación** *nf*

sublime *adj* : sublime

submarinismo *nm* : scuba diving

submarinista *nmf* : scuba diver

submarino¹, -na *adj* : submarine, undersea

submarino² *nm* : submarine

suboficial *nmf* : noncommissioned officer, petty officer

subordinado, -da *adj & n* : subordinate

subordinar *vt* : to subordinate — **subordinarse** *vr* — **subordinación** *nf*

subproducto *nm* : by-product

subrayar *vt* 1 : to underline, to underscore 2 ENFATIZAR : to highlight, to emphasize

subrepticio, -cia *adj* : surreptitious — **subrepticiamente** *adv*

subsahariano, -na *adj* : sub-Saharan

subsanar *vt* 1 RECTIFICAR : to rectify, to correct 2 : to overlook, to excuse 3 : to make up for

subscribir → **suscribir**

subsecretario, -ria *n* : undersecretary

subsecuente *adj* : subsequent — **subsecuentemente** *adv*

subsidiar *vt* : to subsidize

subsidiaria *nf* : subsidiary

subsidio *nm* : subsidy

subsiguiente *adj* : subsequent

subsistencia *nf* 1 : subsistence 2 : sustenance

subsistir *vi* 1 : to subsist, to live 2 : to endure, to survive

substancia → **sustancia**

subteniente *nmf* : second lieutenant

subterfugio *nm* : subterfuge

subterráneo¹, -nea *adj* : underground, subterranean

subterráneo² *nm* 1 : underground passage, tunnel 2 *Arg, Uru* : subway

subtítulo *nm* : subtitle, subheading

subtotal *nm* : subtotal

suburbano, -na *adj* : suburban

suburbio *nm* 1 : suburb 2 : slum (outside a city)

subvención *nf, pl* **-ciones** : subsidy, grant

subvencionar *vt* : to subsidize

subversivo, -va *adj & n* : subversive — **subversión** *nf*

subvertir {76} *vt* : to subvert

subyacente *adj* : underlying

subyugar {52} *vt* : to subjugate — **subyugación** *nf*

succión *nf, pl* **succiones** : suction

succionar *vt* : to suck up, to draw in

sucedáneo *nm* : substitute ⟨sucedáneo de azúcar : sugar substitute⟩

suceder *vi* 1 OCURRIR : to happen, to occur ⟨¿qué sucede? : what's going on?⟩ ⟨suceda lo que suceda : come what may⟩ 2 ~ **a** : to follow, to succeed ⟨suceder al trono : to succeed to the throne⟩ ⟨a la primavera sucede el verano : summer follows spring⟩

sucesión *nf, pl* **-siones 1** : succession **2** : sequence, series **3** : issue, heirs *pl*

sucesivamente *adv* : successively, consecutively ⟨y así sucesivamente : and so on⟩

sucesivo, -va *adj* : successive ⟨en los días sucesivos : in the days that followed⟩

suceso *nm* **1** : event, happening, occurrence **2** : incident, crime

sucesor, -sora *n* : successor

suciedad *nf* **1** : dirtiness, filthiness **2** MUGRE : dirt, filth

sucinto, -ta *adj* CONCISO : succinct, concise — **sucintamente** *adv*

sucio, -cia *adj* : dirty, filthy

sucre *nm* : Ecuadoran unit of currency

suculento, -ta *adj* : succulent

sucumbir *vi* : to succumb

sucursal *nf* : branch (of a business)

sudadera *nf* : sweatshirt

sudado, -da → **sudoroso**

sudafricano, -na *adj & n* : South African

sudamericano, -na *adj & n* : South American

sudanés, -nesa *adj & n, mpl* **-neses** : Sudanese

sudar *vi* TRANSPIRAR : to sweat, to perspire

sudario *nm* : shroud

sudeste → **sureste**

sudoeste → **suroeste**

sudor *nm* TRANSPIRACIÓN : sweat, perspiration

sudoroso, -sa *adj* : sweaty

sueco¹, -ca *adj* : Swedish

sueco², -ca *n* : Swede

sueco³ *nm* : Swedish (language)

suegro, -gra *n* **1** : father-in-law *m,* mother-in-law *f* **2 suegros** *nmpl* : in-laws

suela *nf* : sole (of a shoe)

suelda, etc. → **soldar**

sueldo *nm* : salary, wage

suele, etc. → **soler**

suelo *nm* **1** : ground ⟨caerse al suelo : to fall down, to hit the ground⟩ **2** : floor, flooring **3** TIERRA : soil, land

suelta, etc. → **soltar**

suelto¹, -ta *adj* : loose, free, unattached

suelto² *nm* : loose change

suena, etc. → **sonar**

sueña, etc. → **soñar**

sueño *nm* **1** : dream **2** : sleep ⟨perder el sueño : to lose sleep⟩ **3** : sleepiness ⟨tener sueño : to be sleepy⟩

suero *nm* **1** : serum **2** : whey

suerte *nf* **1** FORTUNA : luck, fortune ⟨tener suerte : to be lucky⟩ ⟨por suerte : luckily⟩ **2** DESTINO : fate, destiny, lot **3** CLASE, GÉNERO : sort, kind ⟨toda suerte de cosas : all kinds of things⟩

suertudo, -da *adj fam* : lucky

suéter *nm* : sweater

suficiencia *nf* **1** : adequacy, sufficiency **2** : competence, fitness **3** : smugness, self-satisfaction

suficiente *adj* **1** BASTANTE : enough, sufficient ⟨tener suficiente : to have

enough⟩ **2** : suitable, fit **3** : smug, complacent

suficientemente *adv* : sufficiently, enough

sufijo *nm* : suffix

suflé *nm* : soufflé

sufragar {52} *vt* **1** AYUDAR : to help out, to support **2** : to defray (costs) — *vi* : to vote

sufragio *nm* : suffrage, vote

sufrido, -da *adj* **1** : long-suffering, patient **2** : sturdy, serviceable (of clothing)

sufrimiento *nm* : suffering

sufrir *vt* **1** : to suffer ⟨sufrir una pérdida : to suffer a loss⟩ **2** : to tolerate, to put up with ⟨ella no lo puede sufrir : she can't stand him⟩ — *vi* : to suffer

sugerencia *nf* : suggestion

sugerir {76} *vt* **1** PROPONER, RECOMENDAR : to suggest, to recommend, to propose **2** : to suggest, to bring to mind

sugestión *nf, pl* **-tiones** : suggestion, prompting ⟨poder de sugestión : power of suggestion⟩

sugestionable *adj* : suggestible, impressionable

sugestionar *vt* : to influence, to sway — **sugestionarse** *vr* ~ **con** : to talk oneself into, to become convinced of

sugestivo, -va *adj* **1** : suggestive **2** : interesting, stimulating

suicida¹ *adj* : suicidal

suicida² *nmf* : suicide victim, suicide

suicidarse *vr* : to commit suicide

suicidio *nm* : suicide

suite *nf* : suite

suizo, -za *adj & n* : Swiss

sujeción *nf, pl* **-ciones 1** : holding, fastening **2** : subjection

sujetador *nm* **1** : fastener **2** : holder ⟨sujetador de tazas : cup holder⟩

sujetalibros *nms & pl* : bookend

sujetapapeles *nms & pl* CLIP : paper clip

sujetar *vt* **1** : to hold on to, to steady, to hold down **2** FIJAR : to fasten, to attach **3** DOMINAR : to subdue, to conquer — **sujetarse** *vr* **1** : to hold on, to hang on **2** ~ **a** : to abide by

sujeto¹, -ta *adj* **1** : secure, fastened **2** ~ **a** : subject to

sujeto² *nm* **1** INDIVIDUO : individual, character **2** : subject (in grammar)

sulfúrico, -ca *adj* : sulfuric

sulfuro *nm* : sulfur

sultán *nm, pl* **sultanes** : sultan

suma *nf* **1** CANTIDAD : sum, quantity **2** : addition

sumamente *adv* : extremely, exceedingly

sumar *vt* **1** : to add, to add up **2** : to add up to, to total — *vi* : to add up — **sumarse** *vr* ~ **a** : to join

sumario¹, -ria *adj* SUCINTO : succinct, summary — **sumariamente** *adv*

sumario² *nm* : summary

sumergir {35} vt : to submerge, to immerse, to plunge — **sumergirse** vr
sumersión nf, pl **-siones** : submersion, immersion
sumidero nm : drain, sewer
suministrar vt : to supply, to provide
suministro nm : supply, provision
sumir vt SUMERGIR : to plunge, to immerse, to sink — **sumirse** vr
sumisión nf, pl **-siones** 1 : submission 2 : submissiveness
sumiso, -sa adj : submissive, acquiescent, docile
sumo, -ma adj 1 : extreme, great, high ⟨la suma autoridad : the highest authority⟩ 2 **a lo sumo** : at the most — **sumamente** adv
suntuoso, -sa adj : sumptuous, lavish — **suntuosamente** adv
supeditar vt SUBORDINAR : to subordinate — **supeditación** nf
super[1] or **súper** adj fam : super, great
super[2] nm SUPERMERCADO : market, supermarket
superable adj : surmountable
superabundancia nf : overabundance, superabundance — **superabundante** adj
superar vt 1 : to surpass, to exceed 2 : to overcome, to surmount — **superarse** vr : to improve oneself
superávit nm, pl **-vit** or **-vits** : surplus
superchería nf : trickery, fraud
supercomputadora nf : supercomputer
superestructura nf : superstructure
superficial adj : superficial — **superficialmente** adv
superficialidad nf : superficiality
superficie nf 1 : surface 2 : area ⟨la superficie de un triángulo : the area of a triangle⟩
superfluidad nf : superfluity
superfluo, -flua adj : superfluous
superintendente nmf : supervisor, superintendent
superior[1] adj 1 : superior 2 : upper ⟨nivel superior : upper level⟩ 3 : higher ⟨educación superior : higher education⟩ 4 **~ a** : above, higher than, in excess of
superior[2] nm : superior
superioridad nf : superiority
superlativo[1], **-va** adj : superlative
superlativo[2] nm : superlative
supermercado nm : supermarket
superpoblación nf, pl **-ciones** : overpopulation
superpoblado, -da adj : overpopulated
superponer {60} vt : to superimpose
superpotencia nf : superpower
superproducción → **sobreproducción**
supersónico, -ca adj : supersonic
superstición nf, pl **-ciones** : superstition
supersticioso, -sa adj : superstitious
supervisar vt : to supervise, to oversee
supervisión nf, pl **-siones** : supervision
supervisor, -sora n : supervisor, overseer

supervivencia nf : survival
superviviente nmf : survivor
supino, -na adj : supine
suplantar vt : to supplant, to replace
suplemental → **suplementario**
suplementario, -ria adj : supplementary, additional, extra
suplemento nm : supplement
suplencia nf : substitution, replacement
suplente adj & nmf : substitute ⟨equipo suplente : replacement team⟩
supletorio, -ria adj : extra, additional ⟨teléfono supletorio : extension phone⟩ ⟨cama supletoria : spare bed⟩
súplica nf : plea, entreaty
suplicar {72} vt IMPLORAR, ROGAR : to entreat, to implore, to supplicate
suplicio nm TORMENTO : ordeal, torture
suplir vt 1 COMPENSAR : to make up for, to compensate for 2 REEMPLAZAR : to replace, to substitute
supo, etc. → **saber**
suponer {60} vt 1 PRESUMIR : to suppose, to assume ⟨supongo que sí : I guess so, I suppose so⟩ ⟨se supone que van a llegar mañana : they're supposed to arrive tomorrow⟩ 2 : to imply, to suggest 3 : to involve, to entail ⟨el éxito supone mucho trabajo : success involves a lot of work⟩
suposición nf, pl **-ciones** PRESUNCIÓN : supposition, assumption
supositorio nm : suppository
supremacía nf : supremacy
supremo, -ma adj : supreme
supresión nf, pl **-siones** 1 : suppression, elimination 2 : deletion
suprimir vt 1 : to suppress, to eliminate 2 : to delete
supuestamente adv : supposedly, allegedly
supuesto, -ta adj 1 : supposed, alleged 2 **por ~** : of course, absolutely
supurar vi : to ooze, to discharge
supuso, etc. → **suponer**
sur[1] adj : southern, southerly, south
sur[2] nm 1 : south, South 2 : south wind
surafricano, -na → **sudafricano**
suramericano, -na → **sudamericano**
surcar {72} vt 1 : to plow (through) 2 : to groove, to score, to furrow
surco nm : groove, furrow, rut
sureño[1], **-ña** adj : southern, Southern
sureño[2], **-ña** n : Southerner
sureste[1] adj 1 : southeast, southeastern 2 : southeasterly
sureste[2] nm : southeast, Southeast
surf nm : surfing
surfear vi : to surf
surfing → **surf**
surfista nmf : surfer
surgimiento nm : rise, emergence
surgir {35} vi : to rise, to arise, to emerge
suroeste[1] adj 1 : southwest, southwestern 2 : southwesterly
suroeste[2] nm : southwest, Southwest
surtido[1], **-da** adj 1 : assorted, varied 2 : stocked, provisioned

surtido² *nm* : assortment, selection
surtidor *nm* **1** : jet, spout **2** *Arg, Chile, Spain* : gas pump
surtir *vt* **1** : to supply, to provide ⟨surtir un pedido : to fill an order⟩ **2 surtir efecto** : to have an effect — *vi* : to spout, to spurt up — **surtirse** *vr* : to stock up
susceptible *adj* : susceptible, sensitive — **susceptibilidad** *nf*
suscitar *vt* : to provoke, to give rise to
suscribir {33} *vt* **1** : to sign (a formal document) **2** : to endorse, to sanction — **suscribirse** *vr* ~ **a** : to subscribe to
suscripción *nf, pl* **-ciones 1** : subscription **2** : endorsement, sanction **3** : signing
suscriptor, -tora *n* : subscriber
susodicho, -cha *adj* : aforementioned, aforesaid
suspender *vt* **1** COLGAR : to suspend, to hang **2** : to suspend, to discontinue **3** : to suspend, to dismiss
suspensión *nf, pl* **-siones** : suspension
suspenso *nm* : suspense
suspicacia *nf* : suspicion, mistrust
suspicaz *adj, pl* **-caces** DESCONFIADO : suspicious, wary
suspirar *vi* : to sigh
suspiro *nm* : sigh
surque, etc. → **surcar**
suscrito *pp* → **suscribir**
sustancia *nf* **1** : substance **2 sin** ~ : shallow, lacking substance
sustancial *adj* **1** : substantial **2** ESENCIAL, FUNDAMENTAL : essential, fundamental — **sustancialmente** *adv*
sustancioso, -sa *adj* **1** NUTRITIVO : hearty, nutritious **2** : substantial, solid
sustantivo *nm* : noun

sustentación *nf, pl* **-ciones** SOSTÉN : support
sustentar *vt* **1** : to support, to hold up **2** : to sustain, to nourish **3** : to maintain, to hold (an opinion) — **sustentarse** *vr* : to support oneself
sustento *nm* **1** : means of support, livelihood **2** : sustenance, food
sustitución *nf, pl* **-ciones** : replacement, substitution
sustituir {41} *vt* **1** : to replace, to substitute for **2** : to stand in for
sustituto, -ta *n* : substitute, stand-in
susto *nm* : fright, scare
sustracción *nf, pl* **-ciones 1** RESTA : subtraction **2** : theft
sustraer {81} *vt* **1** : to remove, to take away **2** RESTAR : to subtract **3** : to steal — **sustraerse** *vr* ~ **a** : to avoid, to evade
susurrar *vi* **1** : to whisper **2** : to murmur **3** : to rustle (leaves, etc.) — *vt* : to whisper
susurro *nm* **1** : whisper **2** : murmur **3** : rustle, rustling
sutil *adj* **1** : delicate, thin, fine **2** : subtle
sutileza *nf* **1** : delicacy **2** : subtlety
sutura *nf* : suture
suturar *vt* : to suture
suyo¹, -ya *adj* **1** : his, her, its, theirs ⟨los libros suyos : his books⟩ ⟨un amigo suyo : a friend of hers⟩ ⟨esta casa es suya : this house is theirs⟩ **2** (*formal*) : yours ⟨¿este abrigo es suyo, señor? : is this your coat, sir?⟩
suyo², -ya *pron* **1** : his, hers, theirs ⟨mi guitarra y la suya : my guitar and hers⟩ ⟨ellos trajeron las suyas : they brought theirs, they brought their own⟩ **2** (*formal*) : yours ⟨usted olvidó la suya : you forgot yours⟩
switch *nm* : switch

T

t *nf* : twenty-first letter of the Spanish alphabet
taba *nf* : anklebone
tabacalero¹, -ra *adj* : tobacco ⟨industria tabacalera : tobacco industry⟩
tabacalero², -ra *n* : tobacco grower
tabaco *nm* : tobacco
tábano *nm* : horsefly
taberna *nf* : tavern, bar
tabernáculo *nm* : tabernacle
tabicar {72} *vt* : to wall up
tabique *nm* : thin wall, partition
tabla *nf* **1** : table, list ⟨tabla de multiplicar : multiplication table⟩ **2** : board, plank, slab ⟨tabla de planchar : ironing board⟩ **3** : plot, strip (of land) **4 tablas** *nfpl* : stage, boards *pl*
tablado *nm* **1** : floor **2** : platform, scaffold **3** : stage
tablero *nm* **1** : bulletin board **2** : board (in games) ⟨tablero de ajedrez : chess-

board⟩ ⟨tablero de damas : checkerboard⟩ **3** PIZARRA : blackboard **4** : switchboard **5 tablero de instrumentos** : dashboard, instrument panel
tableta *nf* **1** COMPRIMIDO, PÍLDORA : tablet, pill **2** : bar (of chocolate)
tabletear *vi* : to rattle, to clack
tableteo *nm* : clack, rattling
tablilla *nf* **1** : small board or tablet **2** : bulletin board **3** : splint
tabloide *nm* : tabloid
tablón *nm, pl* **tablones 1** : plank, beam **2 tablón de anuncios** : bulletin board
tabú¹ *adj* : taboo
tabú² *nm, pl* **tabúes** *or* **tabús** : taboo
tabulador *nm* : tabulator
tabular¹ *vt* : to tabulate
tabular² *adj* : tabular
taburete *nm* : footstool, stool
tacañería *nf* : miserliness, stinginess

tacaño¹, -ña *adj* MEZQUINO : stingy, miserly
tacaño², -ña *n* : miser, tightwad
tacha *nf* 1 : flaw, blemish, defect 2 **poner tacha a** : to find fault with 3 **sin ~** : flawless
tachadura *nf* : erasure, correction
tachar *vt* 1 : to cross out, to delete 2 **~ de** : to accuse of, to label as ⟨lo tacharon de mentiroso : they accused him of being a liar⟩
tachón *nm, pl* **tachones** : stud, hobnail
tachonar *vt* : to stud
tachuela *nf* : tack, hobnail, stud
tácito, -ta *adj* : tacit, implicit — **tácitamente** *adv*
taciturno, -na *adj* 1 : taciturn 2 : sullen, gloomy
tacle *nm* : tackle
taclear *vt* : to tackle (in football)
taco *nm* 1 : wad, stopper, plug 2 : pad (of paper) 3 : cleat 4 : heel (of a shoe) 5 : cue (in billiards) 6 : light snack, bite 7 : taco
tacón *nm, pl* **tacones** : heel (of a shoe) ⟨de tacón alto : high-heeled⟩
táctica *nf* : tactic, tactics *pl*
táctico¹, -ca *adj* : tactical
táctico², -ca *n* : tactician
táctil *adj* : tactile
tacto *nm* 1 : touch, touching, feel 2 DELICADEZA : tact
tafetán *nm, pl* **-tanes** : taffeta
tahúr *nm, pl* **tahúres** : gambler
tailandés¹, -desa *adj & n, pl* **-deses** : Thai
tailandés² *nm* : Thai (language)
taimado, -da *adj* 1 : crafty, sly 2 *Chile* : sullen, sulky
tajada *nf* 1 : slice 2 **sacar tajada** *fam* : to get one's share
tajante *adj* 1 : cutting, sharp 2 : decisive, categorical
tajantemente *adj* : emphatically, categorically
tajar *vt* : to cut, to slice
tajo *nm* 1 : cut, slash, gash 2 ESCARPA : steep cliff
tal¹ *adv* 1 : so, in such a way 2 **tal como** : just as ⟨tal como lo hice : just the way I did it⟩ 3 **con tal que** : provided that, as long as 4 **¿qué tal?** : how are you?, how's it going?
tal² *adj* 1 : such, such a 2 **tal vez** : maybe, perhaps
tal³ *pron* 1 : such a one, someone 2 : such a thing, something 3 **tal para cual** : two of a kind
tala *nf* : felling (of trees)
taladrar *vt* : to drill
taladro *nm* : drill, auger ⟨taladro eléctrico : power drill⟩
talante *nm* 1 HUMOR : mood, disposition 2 VOLUNTAD : will, willingness
talar *vt* 1 : to cut down, to fell 2 DEVASTAR : to devastate, to destroy
talco *nm* 1 : talc 2 : talcum powder
talego *nm* : sack

talento *nm* : talent, ability
talentoso, -sa *adj* : talented, gifted
talismán *nm, pl* **-manes** AMULETO : talisman, charm
talla *nf* 1 ESTATURA : height 2 : size (in clothing) 3 : stature, status 4 : sculpture, carving
tallar *vt* 1 : to sculpt, to carve 2 : to measure (someone's height) 3 : to deal (cards)
tallarín *nf, pl* **-rines** : noodle
talle *nm* 1 : size 2 : waist, waistline 3 : figure, shape
taller *nm* 1 : shop, workshop 2 : studio (of an artist)
tallo *nm* : stalk, stem ⟨tallo de maíz : cornstalk⟩
talón *nm, pl* **talones** 1 : heel (of the foot) 2 : stub (of a check) 3 **talón de Aquiles** : Achilles' heel
talud *nm* : slope, incline
tamal *nm* : tamale
tamaño¹, -ña *adj* : such a big ⟨¿crees tamaña mentira? : do you believe such a lie?⟩
tamaño² *nm* 1 : size 2 **de tamaño natural** : life-size
tamarindo *nm* : tamarind
tambalearse *vr* 1 : to teeter 2 : to totter, to stagger, to sway — **tambaleante** *adj*
tambaleo *nm* : staggering, lurching, swaying
también *adv* : too, as well, also
tambor *nm* : drum
tamborilear *vi* : to drum, to tap
tamborileo *nm* : tapping, drumming
tamiz *nm* : sieve
tamizar {21} *vt* : to sift
tampoco *adv* : neither, not either ⟨ni yo tampoco : me neither⟩
tampón *nm, pl* **tampones** 1 : ink pad 2 : tampon
tam-tam *nm* : tom-tom
tan *adv* 1 : so, so very ⟨no es tan difícil : it is not that difficult⟩ 2 : as ⟨tan pronto como : as soon as⟩ 3 **tan siquiera** : at least, at the least 4 **tan sólo** : only, merely
tanda *nf* 1 : turn, shift 2 : batch, lot, series
tándem *nm* 1 : tandem (bicycle) 2 : duo, pair
tangente *adj & nf* : tangent — **tangencial** *adj*
tangible *adj* : tangible
tango *nm* : tango
tanino *nm* : tannin
tanque *nm* 1 : tank, reservoir 2 : tanker, tank (vehicle)
tanteador *nm* MARCADOR : scoreboard
tantear *vt* 1 : to feel, to grope 2 : to size up, to weigh — *vi* 1 : to keep score 2 : to feel one's way
tanteo *nm* 1 : estimate, rough calculation 2 : testing, sizing up 3 : scoring
tanto¹ *adv* 1 : so much ⟨tanto mejor : so much the better⟩ 2 : so long ⟨¿por qué

te tardaste tanto? : why did you take so long?⟩

tanto², -ta *adj* **1** : so much, so many, such ⟨no hagas tantas preguntas : don't ask so many questions⟩ ⟨tiene tanto encanto : he has such charm, he's so charming⟩ **2** : as much, as many ⟨come tantos dulces como yo : she eats as many sweets as I do⟩ **3** : odd, however many ⟨cuarenta y tantos años : forty-odd years⟩

tanto³ *nm* **1** : certain amount **2** : goal, point (in sports) **3 al tanto** : abreast, in the picture **4 un tanto** : somewhat, rather ⟨un tanto cansado : rather tired⟩

tanto⁴, -ta *pron* **1** : so much, so many ⟨tiene tanto que hacer : she has so much to do⟩ ⟨¡no me des tantos! : don't give me so many!⟩ **2 entre ~** : meanwhile **3 por lo tanto** : therefore

tañer {79} *vt* **1** : to ring (a bell) **2** : to play (a musical instrument)

tañido *nm* **1** CAMPANADA : ring, peal, toll **2** : sound (of an instrument)

tapa *nf* **1** : cover, top, lid **2** *Spain* : bar snack

tapacubos *nms & pl* : hubcap

tapadera *nf* **1** : cover, lid **2** : front, cover (for an organization or person)

tapar *vt* **1** CUBRIR : to cover, to cover up **2** OBSTRUIR : to block, to obstruct — **taparse** *vr*

tapete *nm* **1** : small rug, mat **2** : table cover **3 poner sobre el tapete** : to bring up for discussion

tapia *nf* : (adobe) wall, garden wall

tapiar *vt* **1** : to wall in **2** : to enclose, to block off

tapicería *nf* **1** : upholstery **2** TAPIZ : tapestry

tapicero, -ra *n* : upholsterer

tapioca *nf* : tapioca

tapir *nm* : tapir

tapiz *nm, pl* **tapices** : tapestry

tapizar {21} *vt* **1** : to upholster **2** : to cover, to carpet

tapón *nm, pl* **tapones** **1** : cork **2** : bottle cap **3** : plug, stopper

tapujo *nm* **1** : deceit, pretension **2 sin tapujos** : openly, frankly

taquigrafía *nf* : stenography, shorthand

taquigráfico, -ca *adj* : stenographic

taquígrafo, -fa *n* : stenographer

taquilla *nf* **1** : box office, ticket office **2** : earnings *pl*, take

taquillero, -ra *adj* : box-office, popular ⟨un éxito taquillero : a box-office success⟩

tarántula *nf* : tarantula

tararear *vt* : to hum

tardanza *nf* : lateness, delay

tardar *vi* **1** : to delay, to take a long time **2** : to be late **3 a más tardar** : at the latest — *vt* DEMORAR : to take (time) ⟨tarda una hora : it takes an hour⟩

tarde¹ *adv* **1** : late **2 tarde o temprano** : sooner or later

tarde² *nf* **1** : afternoon, evening **2 ¡buenas tardes!** : good afternoon!, good evening! **3 en la tarde** *or* **por la tarde** : in the afternoon, in the evening

tardío, -día *adj* : late, tardy

tardo, -da *adj* : slow

tarea *nf* **1** : task, job **2** : homework

tarifa *nf* **1** : rate ⟨tarifas postales : postal rates⟩ **2** : fare (for transportation) **3** : price list **4** ARANCEL : duty

tarima *nf* PLATAFORMA : dais, platform, stage

tarjeta *nf* : card ⟨tarjeta de crédito : credit card⟩ ⟨tarjeta postal : postcard⟩

tarro *nm* **1** : jar, pot **2** *Arg, Chile* : can, tin

tarta *nf* **1** : tart **2** : cake

tartaleta *nf* : tart

tartamudear *vi* : to stammer, to stutter

tartamudeo *nm* : stammer, stammering

tartán *nm, pl* **tartanes** : tartan, plaid

tártaro *nm* : tartar

tasa *nf* **1** : rate ⟨tasa de desempleo : unemployment rate⟩ **2** : tax, fee **3** : appraisal, valuation

tasación *nf, pl* **-ciones** : appraisal, assessment

tasador, -dora *n* : assessor, appraiser

tasar *vt* **1** VALORAR : to appraise, to value **2** : to set the price of **3** : to ration, to limit

tasca *nf* : cheap bar, dive

tatuaje *nm* : tattoo, tattooing

tatuar {3} *vt* : to tattoo

taurino, -na *adj* : bull, bullfighting

Tauro *nmf* : Taurus

tauromaquia *nf* : (art of) bullfighting

taxi *nm, pl* **taxis** : taxi, taxicab

taxidermia *nf* : taxidermy

taxidermista *nmf* : taxidermist

taxímetro *nm* : taximeter

taxista *nmf* : taxi driver

taza *nf* **1** : cup **2** : cupful **3** : (toilet) bowl **4** : basin (of a fountain)

tazón *nm, pl* **tazones** **1** : bowl **2** : large cup, mug

te *pron* **1** : you ⟨te quiero : I love you⟩ **2** : for you, to you, from you ⟨me gustaría dártelo : I would like to give it to you⟩ **3** : yourself, for yourself, to yourself, from yourself ⟨¡cálmate! : calm yourself!⟩ ⟨¿te guardaste uno? : did you keep one for yourself?⟩ **4** : thee

té *nm* **1** : tea **2** : tea party

tea *nf* : torch

teatral *adj* : theatrical — **teatralmente** *adv*

teatro *nm* **1** : theater **2 hacer teatro** : to put on an act, to exaggerate

teca *nf* : teak

techado *nm* **1** : roof **2 bajo techado** : under cover, indoors

techar *vt* : to roof, to shingle

techo *nm* **1** TEJADO : roof **2** : ceiling **3** : upper limit, ceiling

techumbre *nf* : roofing

tecla *nf* **1** : key (of a musical instrument or a machine) **2 dar en la tecla** : to hit the nail on the head

teclado *nm* : keyboard
teclear *vt* : to type in, to enter
técnica *nf* **1** : technique, skill **2** : technology
técnico[1], **-ca** *adj* : technical — **técnicamente** *adv*
técnico[2], **-ca** *n* : technician, expert, engineer
tecnología *nf* : technology
tecnológico, -ca *adj* : technological — **tecnológicamente** *adv*
tecolote *nm Mex* : owl
tedio *nm* : tedium, boredom
tedioso, -sa *adj* : tedious, boring — **tediosamente** *adv*
teja *nf* : tile
tejado *nm* TECHO : roof
tejedor, -dora *n* : weaver
tejer *vt* **1** : to knit, to crochet **2** : to weave **3** FABRICAR : to concoct, to make up, to fabricate
tejido *nm* **1** TELA : fabric, cloth **2** : weave, texture **3** : tissue ⟨tejido muscular : muscle tissue⟩
tejo *nm* **1** : yew **2** : hopscotch (children's game)
tejón *nm, pl* **tejones** : badger
tela *nf* **1** : fabric, cloth, material **2 tela de araña** : spiderweb **3 poner en tela de juicio** : to call into question, to doubt
telar *nm* : loom
telaraña *nf* : spiderweb, cobweb
tele *nf fam* : TV, television
telecomunicación *nf, pl* **-ciones** : telecommunication
teleconferencia *nf* : teleconference
teledifusión *nf, pl* **-siones** : television broadcasting
teledirigido, -da *adj* : remote-controlled
telefonear *v* : to telephone, to call
telefónico, -ca *adj* : phone, telephone ⟨llamada telefónica : phone call⟩
telefonista *nmf* : telephone operator
teléfono *nm* **1** : telephone **2 llamar por teléfono** : to telephone, to make a phone call
telegrafiar {85} *v* : to telegraph
telegráfico, -ca *adj* : telegraphic
telégrafo *nm* : telegraph
telegrama *nm* : telegram
telenovela *nf* : soap opera
telepatía *nf* : telepathy
telepático, -ca *adj* : telepathic — **telepáticamente** *adv*
telescópico, -ca *adj* : telescopic
telescopio *nm* : telescope
telespectador, -dora *n* : television viewer
telesquí *nm, pl* **-squís** : ski lift
televidente *nmf* : television viewer
televisar *vt* : to televise
televisión *nf, pl* **-siones** : television, TV
televisivo, -va *adj* : television ⟨serie televisiva : television series⟩
televisor *nm* : television set
telón *nm, pl* **telones 1** : curtain (in the-ater) **2 telón de fondo** : backdrop, background

tema *nm* **1** ASUNTO : theme, topic, subject **2** MOTIVO : motif, central theme
temario *nm* **1** : set of topics (for study) **2** : agenda
temática *nf* : subject matter
temático, -ca *adj* : thematic
temblar {55} *vi* **1** : to tremble, to shake, to shiver ⟨le temblaban las rodillas : his knees were shaking⟩ **2** : to shudder, to be afraid ⟨tiemblo con sólo pensarlo : I shudder to think of it⟩
temblor *nm* **1** : shaking, trembling **2** : tremor, earthquake
tembloroso, -sa *adj* : tremulous, trembling, shaking ⟨con la voz temblorosa : with a shaky voice⟩
temer *vt* : to fear, to dread — *vi* : to be afraid
temerario, -ria *adj* : reckless, rash — **temerariamente** *adv*
temeridad *nf* **1** : temerity, recklessness, rashness **2** : rash act
temeroso, -sa *adj* MIEDOSO : fearful, frightened
temible *adj* : fearsome, dreadful
temor *nm* MIEDO : fear, dread
témpano *nm* : ice floe
temperamento *nm* : temperament — **temperamental** *adj*
temperancia *nf* : temperance
temperar *vt* MODERAR : to temper, to moderate — *vi* : to have a change of air
temperatura *nf* : temperature
tempestad *nf* **1** : storm, tempest **2 tempestad de arena** : sandstorm
tempestuoso, -sa *adj* : tempestuous, stormy
templado, -da *adj* **1** : temperate, mild **2** : moderate, restrained **3** : warm, lukewarm **4** VALIENTE : courageous, bold
templanza *nf* **1** : temperance, moderation **2** : mildness (of weather)
templar *vt* **1** : to temper (steel) **2** : to restrain, to moderate **3** : to tune (a musical instrument) **4** : to warm up, to cool down — **templarse** *vr* **1** : to be moderate **2** : to warm up, to cool down
temple *nm* **1** : temper (of steel, etc.) **2** HUMOR : mood ⟨de buen temple : in a good mood⟩ **3** : tuning **4** VALOR : courage
templo *nm* **1** : temple **2** : church, chapel
tempo *nm* : tempo (in music)
temporada *nf* **1** : season, time ⟨temporada de béisbol : baseball season⟩ **2** : period, spell ⟨por temporadas : on and off⟩
temporal[1] *adj* **1** : temporal **2** : temporary
temporal[2] *nm* **1** : storm **2 capear el temporal** : to weather the storm
temporalmente *adv* : temporarily
temporario, -ria *adj* : temporary — **temporariamente** *adv*
temporero[1], **-ra** *adj* : temporary, seasonal

temporero², **-ra** *n* : temporary or seasonal worker

temporizador *nm* : timer

tempranero, **-ra** *adj* **1** : early **2** : early-rising

temprano¹ *adv* : early ⟨lo más temprano posible : as soon as possible⟩

temprano², **-na** *adj* : early ⟨la parte temprana del siglo : the early part of the century⟩

ten → **tener**

tenacidad *nf* : tenacity, perseverance

tenaz *adj*, *pl* **tenaces 1** : tenacious, persistent **2** : strong, tough

tenaza *nf*, *or* **tenazas** *nfpl* **1** : pliers, pincers **2** : tongs **3** : claw (of a crustacean)

tenazmente *adv* : tenaciously

tendedero *nm* : clothesline

tendencia *nf* **1** PROPENSIÓN : tendency, inclination **2** : trend

tendencioso, **-sa** *adj* : tendentious, biased

tendente → **tendiente**

tender {56} *vt* **1** EXTENDER : to spread out, to lay out **2** : to hang out (clothes) **3** : to lay (cables, etc.) **4** : to set (a trap) — *vi* ~ **a** : to tend to, to have a tendency towards — **tenderse** *vr* : to stretch out, to lie down

tendero, **-ra** *n* : shopkeeper, storekeeper

tendido *nm* **1** : laying (of cables, etc.) **2** : seats *pl*, section (at a bullfight)

tendiente *adj* ~ **a** : aimed at, designed to

tendón *nm*, *pl* **tendones** : tendon

tenebrosidad *nf* : darkness, gloom

tendrá, etc. → **tener**

tenebroso, **-sa** *adj* **1** OSCURO : gloomy, dark **2** SINIESTRO : sinister

tenedor¹, **-dora** *n* **1** : holder **2 tenedor de libros, tenedora de libros** : bookkeeper

tenedor² *nm* : table fork

tenencia *nf* **1** : possession, holding **2** : tenancy **3** : tenure

tener {80} *vt* **1** : to have ⟨tiene ojos verdes : she has green eyes⟩ ⟨tengo mucho que hacer : I have a lot to do⟩ ⟨tiene veinte años : he's twenty years old⟩ ⟨tiene un metro de largo : it's one meter long⟩ **2** : to hold ⟨ten esto un momento : hold this for a moment⟩ **3** : to feel, to make ⟨tengo frío : I'm cold⟩ ⟨eso nos tiene contentos : that makes us happy⟩ **4** ~ **por** : to think, to consider ⟨me tienes por loco : you think I'm crazy⟩ — *v aux* **1 tener que** : to have to ⟨tengo que salir : I have to leave⟩ ⟨tiene que estar aquí : it has to be here, it must be here⟩ **2** (*with past participle*) ⟨tenía pensado escribirte : I've been thinking of writing to you⟩ — **tenerse** *vr* **1** : to stand up **2** ~ **por** : to consider oneself ⟨me tengo por afortunado : I consider myself lucky⟩

tenería *nf* CURTIDURÍA : tannery

tenga, etc. → **tener**

tenia *nf* SOLITARIA : tapeworm

teniente *nmf* **1** : lieutenant **2 teniente coronel** : lieutenant colonel

tenis *nms & pl* **1** : tennis **2 tenis** *nmpl* : sneakers *pl*

tenista *nmf* : tennis player

tenor *nm* **1** : tenor **2** : tone, sense

tensar *vt* **1** : to tense, to make taut **2** : to draw (a bow) — **tensarse** *vr* : to become tense

tensión *nf*, *pl* **tensiones 1** : tension, tautness **2** : stress, strain **3 tensión arterial** : blood pressure

tenso, **-sa** *adj* : tense

tentación *nf*, *pl* **-ciones** : temptation

tentáculo *nm* : tentacle, feeler

tentador¹, **-dora** *adj* : tempting

tentador², **-dora** *n* : tempter, temptress *f*

tentar {55} *vt* **1** TOCAR : to feel, to touch **2** PROBAR : to test, to try **3** ATRAER : to tempt, to entice

tentativa *nf* : attempt, try

tentempié *nm fam* : snack, bite

tenue *adj* **1** : tenuous **2** : faint, weak, dim **3** : light, fine **4** : thin, slender

teñir {67} *vt* **1** : to dye **2** : to stain

teodolito *nm* : theodolite, transit (for surveying)

teología *nf* : theology

teológico, **-ca** *adj* : theological

teólogo, **-ga** *n* : theologian

teorema *nm* : theorem

teoría *nf* : theory

teórico¹, **-ca** *adj* : theoretical — **teóricamente** *adv*

teórico², **-ca** *n* : theorist

teorizar {21} *vi* : to theorize

tepe *nm* : sod, turf

teponaztle *nm Mex* : traditional drum

tequila *nm* : tequila

terapeuta *nmf* : therapist

terapéutica *nf* : therapeutics

terapéutico, **-ca** *adj* : therapeutic

terapia *nf* **1** : therapy **2 terapia intensiva** : intensive care

tercer → **tercero**

tercermundista *adj* : third-world

tercero¹, **-ra** *adj* (**tercer** *before masculine singular nouns*) **1** : third **2 el Tercer Mundo** : the Third World

tercero², **-ra** *n* : third (in a series)

terceto *nm* **1** : tercet, triplet (in literature) **2** : trio (in music)

terciar *vt* **1** : to place diagonally **2** : to divide into three parts — *vi* **1** : to mediate **2** ~ **en** : to take part in

terciario, **-ria** *adj* : tertiary

tercio¹, **-cia** → **tercero**

tercio² *nm* : third ⟨dos tercios : two thirds⟩

terciopelo *nm* : velvet

terco, **-ca** *adj* OBSTINADO : obstinate, stubborn

tergiversación *nf*, *pl* **-ciones** : distortion

tergiversar *vt* : to distort, to twist

termal *adj* : thermal, hot

termas *nfpl* : hot springs

térmico, **-ca** *adj* : thermal, heat ⟨energía térmica : thermal energy⟩

terminación *nf, pl* -ciones : termination, conclusion

terminal[1] *adj* : terminal — terminalmente *adv*

terminal[2] *nm* (*in some regions f*) : (electric or electronic) terminal

terminal[3] *nf* (*in some regions m*) : terminal, station

terminante *adj* : final, definitive, categorical — terminantemente *adv*

terminar *vt* 1 CONCLUIR : to end, to conclude 2 ACABAR : to complete, to finish off — *vi* 1 : to finish 2 : to stop, to end — terminarse *vr* 1 : to run out 2 : to come to an end

término *nm* 1 CONCLUSIÓN : end, conclusion 2 : term, expression 3 : period, term of office 4 término medio : happy medium 5 términos *nmpl* : terms, specifications ⟨los términos del acuerdo : the terms of the agreement⟩

terminología *nf* : terminology

termita *nf* : termite

termo *nm* : thermos

termodinámica *nf* : thermodynamics

termómetro *nm* : thermometer

termostato *nm* : thermostat

ternera *nf* : veal

ternero, -ra *n* : calf

terno *nm* 1 : set of three 2 : three-piece suit

ternura *nf* : tenderness

terquedad *nf* OBSTINACIÓN : obstinacy, stubbornness

terracota *nf* : terra-cotta

terraplén *nm, pl* -plenes : terrace, embankment

terráqueo, -quea *adj* 1 : earth 2 globo terráqueo : the earth, globe (of the earth)

terrateniente *nmf* : landowner

terraza *nf* 1 : terrace, veranda 2 : balcony (in a theater) 3 : terrace (in agriculture)

terremoto *nm* : earthquake

terrenal *adj* : worldly, earthly

terreno *nm* 1 : terrain 2 SUELO : earth, ground 3 : plot, tract of land 4 perder terreno : to lose ground 5 preparar el terreno : to pave the way

terrestre *adj* : terrestrial

terrible *adj* : terrible, horrible — terriblemente *adv*

terrier *nmf* : terrier

territorial *adj* : territorial

territorio *nm* : territory

terrón *nm, pl* terrones 1 : clod (of earth) 2 terrón de azúcar : lump of sugar

terror *nm* : terror

terrorífico, -ca *adj* : horrific, terrifying

terrorismo *nm* : terrorism

terrorista *adj & nmf* : terrorist

terroso, -sa *adj* : earthy ⟨colores terrosos : earthy colors⟩

terruño *nm* : native land, homeland

terso, -sa *adj* 1 : smooth 2 : glossy, shiny 3 : polished, flowing (of a style)

tersura *nf* 1 : smoothness 2 : shine

tertulia *nf* : gathering, group ⟨tertulia literaria : literary circle⟩

tesauro *nm* : thesaurus

tesis *nfs & pl* : thesis

tesón *nm* : persistence, tenacity

tesonero, -ra *adj* : persistent, tenacious

tesorería *nf* : treasurer's office

tesorero, -ra *n* : treasurer

tesoro *nm* 1 : treasure 2 : thesaurus

test *nm* : test

testaferro *nm* : figurehead

testamentario[1], -ria *adj* : testamentary

testamentario[2], -ria *n* ALBACEA : executor, executrix *f*

testamento *nm* : testament, will

testar *vi* : to draw up a will

testarudo, -da *adj* : stubborn, pigheaded

testículo *nm* : testicle

testificar {72} *v* : to testify

testigo *nmf* : witness

testimonial *adj* 1 : testimonial 2 : token

testimoniar *vi* : to testify

testimonio *nm* : testimony, statement

teta *nf* : teat

tétano *or* tétanos *nm* : tetanus, lockjaw

tetera *nf* 1 : teapot 2 : teakettle

tetilla *nf* 1 : teat 2 : nipple

tetina *nf* : nipple (on a bottle)

tétrico, -ca *adj* : somber, gloomy

textil *adj & nm* : textile

texto *nm* : text

textual *adj* : literal, exact — textualmente *adv*

textura *nf* : texture

tez *nf, pl* teces : complexion, coloring

ti *pron* 1 : you ⟨es para ti : it's for you⟩ 2 ti mismo, ti misma : yourself 3 : thee

tía → tío

tiamina *nf* : thiamine

tianguis *nm Mex* : open-air market

tibetano[1], -na *adj & n* : Tibetan

tibetano[2] *nm* : Tibetan (language)

tibia *nf* : tibia

tibieza *nf* 1 : tepidness 2 : halfheartedness

tibio, -bia *adj* 1 : lukewarm, tepid 2 : cool, unenthusiastic

tiburón *nm, pl* -rones 1 : shark 2 : raider (in finance)

tic *nm* 1 : click, tick 2 tic nervioso : tic

tico, -ca *adj & n fam* : Costa Rican

tictac *nm* 1 : ticking, tick-tock 2 hacer tictac : to tick

tiembla, etc. → temblar

tiempo *nm* 1 : time ⟨justo a tiempo : just in time⟩ ⟨perder tiempo : to waste time⟩ ⟨tiempo libre : spare time⟩ 2 : period, age ⟨en los tiempos que corren : nowadays⟩ 3 : season, moment ⟨antes de tiempo : prematurely⟩ 4 : weather ⟨hace buen tiempo : the weather is fine, it's nice outside⟩ 5 : tempo (in music) 6 : half (in sports) 7 : tense (in grammar)

tienda *nf* 1 : store, shop 2 *or* tienda de campaña : tent

tiende, etc. → tender

tiene, etc. → **tener**

tienta[1], etc. → **tentar**

tienta[2] *nf* **andar a tientas** : to feel one's way, to grope around

tiernamente *adv* : tenderly

tierno, -na *adj* **1** : affectionate, tender **2** : tender, young

tierra *nf* **1** : land **2** SUELO : ground, earth **3** : country, homeland, soil **4 tierra natal** : native land **5 tierras altas** : highlands **6 la Tierra** : the Earth

tieso, -sa *adj* **1** : stiff, rigid **2** : upright, erect

tiesto *nm* **1** : potsherd **2** MACETA : flowerpot

tiesura *nf* : stiffness, rigidity

tifoidea *nf* : typhoid

tifoideo, -dea *adj* : typhoid ⟨fiebre tifoidea : typhoid fever⟩

tifón *nm, pl* **tifones** : typhoon

tifus *nm* : typhus

tigre, -gresa *n* **1** : tiger, tigress *f* **2** : jaguar

tijera *nf* **1** *or* **tijeras** *nfpl* : scissors **2 de ~** : folding ⟨escalera de tijera : stepladder⟩

tijereta *nf* : earwig

tijeretada *nf or* **tijeretazo** *nm* : cut, snip

tildar *vt* **~ de** : to brand as, to call ⟨lo tildaron de traidor : they branded him as a traitor⟩

tilde *nf* **1** : accent mark **2** : tilde (accent over *ñ*)

tilo *nm* : linden (tree)

timador, -dora *n* : swindler

timar *vt* : to swindle, to cheat

timbal *nm* **1** : kettledrum **2 timbales** *nmpl* : timpani

timbre *nm* **1** : bell ⟨tocar el timbre : to ring the doorbell⟩ **2** : tone, timbre **3** SELLO : seal, stamp **4** *CA, Mex* : postage stamp

timidez *nf* : timidity, shyness

tímido, -da *adj* : timid, shy — **tímidamente** *adv*

timo *nm fam* : swindle, trick, hoax

timón *nm, pl* **timones** : rudder ⟨estar al timón : to beat the helm⟩

timonel *nm* : helmsman, coxswain

timorato, -ta *adj* **1** : timorous **2** : sanctimonious

tímpano *nm* **1** : eardrum **2 tímpanos** *nmpl* : timpani, kettledrums

tina *nf* **1** BAÑERA : tub, bathtub **2** : vat

tinaco *nm Mex* : water tank

tinieblas *nfpl* **1** OSCURIDAD : darkness **2** : ignorance

tino *nm* **1** : good judgment, sense **2** : tact, sensitivity, insight

tinta *nf* : ink

tinte *nm* **1** : dye, coloring **2** : overtone ⟨tintes raciales : racial overtones⟩

tintero *nm* **1** : inkwell **2 quedarse en el tintero** : to remain unsaid

tintinear *vt* : to jingle, to clink, to tinkle

tintineo *nm* : clink, jingle, tinkle

tinto, -ta *adj* **1** : dyed, stained ⟨tinto en sangre : bloodstained⟩ **2** : red (of wine)

tintorería *nf* : dry cleaner (service)

tintura *nf* **1** : dye, tint **2** : tincture ⟨tintura de yodo : tincture of iodine⟩

tiña *nf* : ringworm

tiñe, etc. → **teñir**

tío, tía *n* : uncle *m*, aunt *f*

tiovivo *nm* : merry-go-round

tipi *nm* : tepee

típico, -ca *adj* : typical — **típicamente** *adv*

tipificar {72} *vt* **1** : to classify, to categorize **2** : to typify

tiple *nm* : soprano

tipo[1] *nm* **1** CLASE : type, kind, sort **2** : figure, build, appearance **3** : rate ⟨tipo de interés : interest rate⟩ **4** : (printing) type, typeface **5** : style, model ⟨un vestido tipo 60's : a 60's-style dress⟩

tipo[2], **-pa** *n fam* : guy *m*, gal *f*, character

tipografía *nf* : typography, printing

tipográfico, -ca *adj* : typographic, typographical

tipógrafo, -fa *n* : printer, typographer

tique *or* **tiquet** *nm* **1** : ticket **2** : receipt

tira *nf* **1** : strip, strap **2 tira cómica** : comic, comic strip

tirabuzón *nf, pl* **-zones** : corkscrew

tirada *nf* **1** : throw **2** : distance, stretch **3** IMPRESIÓN : printing, issue

tiradero *nm Mex* **1** : dump **2** : mess, clutter

tirador[1] *nm* : handle, knob

tirador[2], **-dora** *n* : marksman *m*, markswoman *f*

tiragomas *nms & pl* : slingshot

tiranía *nf* : tyranny

tiránico, -ca *adj* : tyrannical

tiranizar {21} *vt* : to tyrannize

tirano[1], **-na** *adj* : tyrannical, despotic

tirano[2], **-na** *n* : tyrant

tirante[1] *adj* **1** : tense, strained **2** : taut

tirante[2] *nm* **1** : shoulder strap **2 tirantes** *nmpl* : suspenders

tirantez *nf* **1** : tautness **2** : tension, friction, strain

tirar *vt* **1** : to throw, to hurl, to toss **2** BOTAR : to throw away, to throw out, to waste **3** DERRIBAR : to knock down **4** : to shoot, to fire, to launch **5** : to take (a photo) **6** : to print, to run off — *vi* **1** : to pull, to draw **2** : to shoot **3** : to attract **4** : to get by, to manage ⟨va tirando : he's getting along, he's managing⟩ **5 ~ a** : to tend towards, to be rather ⟨tira a picante : it's a bit spicy⟩ — **tirarse** *vr* **1** : to throw oneself **2** *fam* : to spend (time)

tiritar *vi* : to shiver, to tremble

tiro *nm* **1** BALAZO, DISPARO : shot, gunshot **2** : shot, kick (in sports) **3** : flue **4** : team (of horses, etc.) **5 a ~** : within range **6 al tiro** : right away **7 tiro de gracia** : coup de grace, death blow

tiroideo, -dea *adj* : thyroid

tiroides *nmf* : thyroid, thyroid gland — **tiroides** *adj*

tirolés, -lesa *adj* : Tyrolean
tirón *nm, pl* **tirones 1** : pull, tug, yank **2 de un tirón** : all at once, in one go
tiroteo *nm* **1** : shooting **2** : gunfight, shoot-out
tirria *nf* **tener tirria a** *fam* : to have a grudge against
titánico, -ca *adj* : titanic, huge
titanio *nm* : titanium
títere *nm* : puppet
tití *nm* : marmoset
titilar *vi* : to twinkle, to flicker
titileo *nm* : twinkle, flickering
titiritero, -ra *n* **1** : puppeteer **2** : acrobat
titubear *vi* **1** : to hesitate **2** : to stutter, to stammer — **titubeante** *adj*
titubeo *nm* **1** : hesitation **2** : stammering
titulado, -da *adj* **1** : titled, entitled **2** : qualified
titular[1] *vt* : to title, to entitle — **titularse** *vr* **1** : to be called, to be entitled **2** : to receive a degree
titular[2] *adj* : titular, official
titular[3] *nm* : headline
titular[4] *nmf* **1** : owner, holder **2** : officeholder, incumbent
titularidad *nf* **1** : ownership, title **2** : position, office (with a title) **3** : starting position (in sports)
título *nm* **1** : title **2** : degree, qualification **3** : security, bond **4 a título de** : by way of, in the capacity of
tiza *nf* : chalk
tiznar *vt* : to blacken (with soot, etc.)
tizne *nm* HOLLÍN : soot
tiznón *nm, pl* **tiznones** : stain, smudge
tlapalería *nf Mex* : hardware store
TNT *nm* (trinitrotolueno) : TNT
toalla *nf* : towel
toallita *nf* : washcloth
tobillo *nm* : ankle
tobogán *nm, pl* **-ganes 1** : toboggan, sled **2** : slide, chute
tocadiscos *nms & pl* : record player, phonograph
tocado[1], **-da** *adj* **1** : bad, bruised (of fruit) **2** *fam* : touched, not all there
tocado[2] *nm* : headdress
tocador[1] *nm* **1** : dressing table, vanity table **2 artículos de tocador** : toiletries
tocador[2], **-dora** *n* : player (of music)
tocante *adj* ~ **a** : with regard to, regarding
tocar {72} *vt* **1** : to touch, to feel, to handle **2** : to touch on, to refer to **3** : to concern, to affect **4** : to play (a musical instrument) — *vi* **1** : to knock, to ring ⟨tocar a la puerta : to rap on the door⟩ **2** — **en** : to touch on, to border on ⟨eso toca en lo ridículo : that's almost ludicrous⟩ **3 tocarle a** : to fall to, to be up to, to be one's turn ⟨¿a quién le toca manejar? : whose turn is it to drive?⟩
tocayo, -ya *n* : namesake
tocineta *nf Col, Ven* : bacon
tocino *nm* **1** : bacon **2** : salt pork

tocología *nf* OBSTETRICIA : obstetrics
tocólogo, -ga *n* OBSTETRA : obstetrician
tocón *nm, pl* **tocones** CEPA : stump (of a tree)
todavía *adv* **1** AÚN : still, yet ⟨todavía puedes verlo : you can still see it⟩ **2** : even ⟨todavía más rápido : even faster⟩ **3 todavía no** : not yet
todo[1], **-da** *adj* **1** : all, whole, entire ⟨con toda sinceridad : with all sincerity⟩ ⟨toda la comunidad : the whole community⟩ **2** : every, each ⟨a todo nivel : at every level⟩ **3** : maximum ⟨a toda velocidad : at top speed⟩ **4 todo el mundo** : everyone, everybody
todo[2] *nm* : whole
todo[3], **-da** *pron* **1** : everything, all, every bit ⟨lo sabe todo : he knows it all⟩ ⟨es todo un soldado : he's every inch a soldier⟩ **2 todos, -das** *pl* : everybody, everyone, all
todopoderoso, -sa *adj* OMNIPOTENTE : almighty, all-powerful
toga *nf* **1** : toga **2** : gown, robe (for magistrates, etc.)
toldo *nm* : awning, canopy
tolerable *adj* : tolerable — **tolerablemente** *adv*
tolerancia *nf* : tolerance, toleration
tolerante *adj* : tolerant — **tolerantemente** *adv*
tolerar *vt* : to tolerate
tolete *nm* : oarlock
tolva *nf* : hopper (container)
toma *nf* **1** : taking, seizure, capture **2** DOSIS : dose **3** : take, shot **4 toma de corriente** : wall socket, outlet **5 toma y daca** : give-and-take
tomar *vt* **1** : to take ⟨tomé el libro : I took the book⟩ ⟨tomar un taxi : to take a taxi⟩ ⟨tomar una foto : to take a photo⟩ ⟨toma dos años : it takes two years⟩ ⟨tomaron medidas drásticas : they took drastic measures⟩ **2** BEBER : to drink **3** CAPTURAR : to capture, to seize **4 tomar el sol** : to sunbathe **5 tomar tierra** : to land — *vi* : to drink (alcohol) — **tomarse** *vr* **1** : to take ⟨tomarse la molestia de : to take the trouble to⟩ **2** : to drink, to eat, to have
tomate *nm* : tomato
tomillo *nm* : thyme
tomo *nm* : volume, tome
ton *nm* **sin ton ni son** : without rhyme or reason
tonada *nf* **1** : tune, song **2** : accent
tonalidad *nf* : tonality
tonel *nm* BARRICA : barrel, cask
tonelada *nf* : ton
tonelaje *nm* : tonnage
tónica *nf* **1** : tonic (water) **2** : tonic (in music) **3** : trend, tone ⟨dar la tónica : to set the tone⟩
tónico[1], **-ca** *adj* : tonic
tónico[2] *nm* : tonic ⟨tónico capilar : hair tonic⟩
tono *nm* **1** : tone ⟨tono muscular : muscle tone⟩ **2** : shade (of colors) **3** : key (in music)

tontamente *adv* : foolishly, stupidly
tontear *vi* **1** : to fool around, to play the fool **2** : to flirt
tontería *nf* **1** : foolishness **2** : stupid remark or action **3 decir tonterías** : to talk nonsense
tonto¹, -ta *adj* **1** : dumb, stupid **2** : silly **3 a tontas y a locas** : without thinking, haphazardly
tonto², -ta *n* : fool, idiot
topacio *nm* : topaz
toparse *vr* ~ **con** : to bump into, to run into, to come across ⟨me topé con algunas dificultades : I ran into some problems⟩
tope *nm* **1** : limit, end ⟨hasta el tope : to the limit, to the brim⟩ **2** : stop, check, buffer ⟨tope de puerta : doorstop⟩ **3** : bump, collision **4** *Mex* : speed bump
tópico¹, -ca *adj* **1** : topical, external **2** : trite, commonplace
tópico² *nm* **1** : topic, subject **2** : cliché, trite expression
topo *nm* **1** : mole (animal) **2** *fam* : clumsy person, blunderer
topografía *nf* : topography
topográfico, -ca *adj* : topographic, topographical
topógrafo, -fa *n* : topographer
toque¹, etc. → **tocar**
toque² *nm* **1** : touch ⟨el último toque : the finishing touch⟩ ⟨un toque de color : a touch of color⟩ **2** : ringing, peal, chime **3** *Mex* : shock, jolt **4 toque de queda** : curfew **5 toque de diana** : reveille
toquetear *vt* : to touch, to handle, to finger
tórax *nm* : thorax
torbellino *nm* : whirlwind
torcedura *nf* **1** : twisting, buckling **2** : sprain
torcer {14} *vt* **1** : to bend, to twist **2** : to sprain **3** : to turn (a corner) **4** : to wring, to wring out **5** : to distort — *vi* : to turn — **torcerse** *vr*
torcido, -da *adj* **1** : twisted, crooked **2** : devious
tordo *nm* ZORZAL : thrush
torear *vt* **1** : to fight (bulls) **2** : to dodge, to sidestep
toreo *nm* : bullfighting
torero, -ra *n* MATADOR : bullfighter, matador
tormenta *nf* **1** : storm ⟨tormenta de nieve : snowstorm⟩ **2** : turmoil, frenzy
tormento *nm* **1** : torment, anguish **2** : torture
tormentoso, -sa *adj* : stormy, turbulent
tornado *nm* : tornado
tornamesa *nmf* : turntable
tornar *vt* **1** : to return, to give back **2** : to make, to render — *vi* : to go back — **tornarse** *vr* : to become, to turn into
tornasol *nm* **1** : reflected light **2** : sunflower **3** : litmus
tornear *vt* : to turn (in carpentry)
torneo *nm* : tournament

tornillo *nm* **1** : screw **2 tornillo de banco** : vise
torniquete *nm* **1** : tourniquet **2** : turnstile
torno *nm* **1** : lathe **2** : winch **3 torno de banco** : vise **4 en torno a** : around, about ⟨en torno a este asunto : about this issue⟩ ⟨en torno suyo : around him⟩
toro *nm* : bull
toronja *nf* : grapefruit
toronjil *nm* : balm, lemon balm
torpe *adj* **1** DESMAÑADO : clumsy, awkward **2** : stupid, dull — **torpemente** *adv*
torpedear *vt* : to torpedo
torpedo *nm* : torpedo
torpeza *nf* **1** : clumsiness, awkwardness **2** : stupidity **3** : blunder
torre *nf* **1** : tower ⟨torre de perforación : oil rig⟩ **2** : turret **3** : rook, castle (in chess)
torrencial *adj* : torrential — **torrencialmente** *adv*
torrente *nm* **1** : torrent **2 torrente sanguíneo** : bloodstream
torreón *nm, pl* **-rreones** : tower (of a castle)
torreta *nf* : turret (of a tank, ship, etc.)
tórrido, -da *adj* : torrid
torsión *nf, pl* **torsiones** : torsion — **torsional** *adj*
torso *nm* : torso, trunk
torta *nf* **1** : torte, cake **2** *Mex* : sandwich
tortazo *nm fam* : blow, wallop
tortilla *nf* **1** : tortilla **2** *or* **tortilla de huevo** : omelet
tórtola *nf* : turtledove
tortuga *nf* **1** : turtle, tortoise **2 tortuga de agua dulce** : terrapin **3 tortuga boba** : loggerhead
tortuoso, -sa *adj* : tortuous, winding
tortura *nf* : torture
torturador, -dora *n* : torturer
torturar *vt* : to torture, to torment
torvo, -va *adj* : grim, stern, baleful
torzamos, etc. → **torcer**
tos *nf* **1** : cough **2 tos ferina** : whooping cough
tosco, -ca *adj* : rough, coarse
toser *vi* : to cough
tosquedad *nf* : crudeness, coarseness, roughness
tostada *nf* **1** : piece of toast **2** : tostada
tostador *nm* **1** : toaster **2** : roaster (for coffee)
tostar {19} *vt* **1** : to toast **2** : to roast (coffee) **3** : to tan — **tostarse** *vr* : to get a tan
tostón *nm, pl* **tostones** *Car* : fried plantain chip
total¹ *adv* : in the end, so ⟨total, que no fui : in short, I didn't go⟩
total² *adj & nm* : total — **totalmente** *adv*
totalidad *nf* : totality, whole
totalitario, -ria *adj & n* : totalitarian
totalitarismo *nm* : totalitarianism

totalizar {21} *vt* : total, to add up to
tótem *nm, pl* **tótems** : totem
totopo *nm CA, Mex* : tortilla chip
totuma *nf* : calabash
tour [ˈtur] *nm, pl* **tours** : tour, excursion
toxicidad *nf* : toxicity
tóxico[1], **-ca** *adj* : toxic, poisonous
tóxico[2] *nm* : poison
toxicomanía *nf* : drug addiction
toxicómano, -na *n* : drug addict
toxina *nf* : toxin
tozudez *nf* : stubbornness, obstinacy
tozudo, -da *adj* : stubborn, obstinate —
  tozudamente *adv*
traba *nf* **1** : tie, bond **2** : obstacle, hindrance
trabajador[1], **-dora** *adj* : hardworking
trabajador[2], **-dora** *n* : worker
trabajar *vi* **1** : to work ⟨trabaja mucho : he works hard⟩ ⟨trabajo de secretaria : I work as a secretary⟩ **2** : to strive ⟨trabajan por mejores oportunidades : they're striving for better opportunities⟩ **3** : to act, to perform ⟨trabajar en una película : to be in a movie⟩ — *vt* **1** : to work (metal) **2** : to knead **3** : to till **4** : to work on ⟨tienes que trabajar el español : you need to work on your Spanish⟩
trabajo *nm* **1** : work, job **2** LABOR : labor, work ⟨tengo mucho trabajo : I have a lot of work to do⟩ **3** TAREA : task **4** ESFUERZA : effort **5 costar trabajo** : to be difficult **6 tomarse el trabajo** : to take the trouble **7 trabajo en equipo** : teamwork **8 trabajos** *nmpl* : hardships, difficulties
trabajoso, -sa *adj* LABORIOSO : laborious — **trabajosamente** *adv*
trabalenguas *nms & pl* : tongue twister
trabar *vt* **1** : to join, to connect **2** : to impede, to hold back **3** : to strike up (a conversation), to form (a friendship) **4** : to thicken (sauces) — **trabarse** *vr* **1** : to jam **2** : to become entangled **3** : to be tongue-tied, to stammer
trabucar {72} *vt* : to confuse, to mix up
trabuco *nm* : blunderbuss
tracalero, -ra *adj Mex* : dishonest, tricky
tracción *nf* : traction
trace, etc. → trazar
tracto *nm* : tract
tractor *nm* : tractor
tradición *nf, pl* **-ciones** : tradition
tradicional *adj* : traditional — **tradicionalmente** *adv*
traducción *nf, pl* **-ciones** : translation
traducible *adj* : translatable
traducir {61} *vt* **1** : to translate **2** : to convey, to express — **traducirse** *vr* ~ **en** : to result in
traductor, -tora *n* : translator
traer {81} *vt* **1** : to bring ⟨trae una ensalada : bring a salad⟩ **2** CAUSAR : to cause, to bring about ⟨el problema puede traer graves consecuencias : the problem could have serious consequences⟩ **3** : to carry, to have ⟨todos los periódicos traían las mismas noti-

cias : all of the newspapers carried the same news⟩ **4** LLEVAR : to wear —
traerse *vr* **1** : to bring along **2 traérselas** : to be difficult
traficante *nmf* : dealer, trafficker
traficar {72} *vi* **1** : to trade, to deal **2** ~ **con** : to traffic in
tráfico *nm* **1** : trade **2** : traffic
tragaluz *nf, pl* **-luces** : skylight, fanlight
tragar {52} *v* : to swallow — **tragarse** *vr*
tragedia *nf* : tragedy
trágico, -ca *adj* : tragic — **trágicamente** *adv*
trago *nm* **1** : swallow, swig **2** : drink, liquor **3 trago amargo** : hard time
trague, etc. → tragar
traición *nf, pl* **traiciones 1** : treason **2** : betrayal, treachery
traicionar *vt* : to betray
traicionero, -ra → traidor
traidor[1], **-dora** *adj* : traitorous, treasonous
traidor[2], **-dora** *n* : traitor
traiga, etc. → traer
trailer *or* **trailer** *nm* : trailer
trailla *nf* **1** : leash **2** : harrow
traje *nm* **1** : suit **2** : dress **3** : costume **4 traje de baño** : bathing suit
trajín *nm, pl* **trajines 1** : transport **2** *fam* : hustle and bustle
trajinar *vt* : to transport, to carry — *vi* : to rush around
trajo, etc. → traer
trama *nf* **1** : plot **2** : weave, weft (fabric)
tramar *vt* **1** : to plot, to plan **2** : to weave
tramitar *vt* : to transact, to negotiate, to handle
trámite *nm* : procedure, step
tramo *nm* **1** : stretch, section **2** : flight (of stairs)
trampa *nf* **1** : trap **2 hacer trampas** : to cheat
trampear *vt* : to cheat
trampero, -ra *n* : trapper
trampilla *nf* : trapdoor
trampolín *nm, pl* **-lines 1** : diving board **2** : trampoline **3** : springboard ⟨un trampolín al éxito : a springboard to success⟩
tramposo[1], **-sa** *adj* : crooked, cheating
tramposo[2], **-sa** *n* : cheat, swindler
tranca *nf* **1** : stick, club **2** : bar, crossbar
trancar {72} *vt* : to bar (a door or window)
trancazo *nm* GOLPE : blow, hit
trance *nm* **1** : critical juncture, tough time **2** : trance **3 en trance de** : in the process of ⟨en trance de extinción : on the verge of extinction⟩
tranco *nm* **1** : stride **2** UMBRAL : threshold
tranque, etc. → trancar
tranquilidad *nf* : tranquility, peace
tranquilizador, -dora *adj* **1** : soothing **2** : reassuring
tranquilizante[1] *adj* **1** : reassuring **2** : tranquilizing

tranquilizante[2] *nm* : tranquilizer

tranquilizar {21} *vt* CALMAR : to calm down, to soothe ⟨tranquilizar la conciencia : to ease the conscience⟩ — **tranquilizarse** *vr*

tranquilo, -la *adj* CALMO : calm, tranquil ⟨una vida tranquila : a quiet life⟩ — **tranquilamente** *adv*

transacción *nf, pl* **-ciones** : transaction

transar *vi* TRANSIGIR : to give way, to compromise — *vt* : to buy and sell

transatlántico[1], **-ca** *adj* : transatlantic

transatlántico[2] *nm* : ocean liner

transbordador *nm* **1** : ferry **2 transbordador espacial** : space shuttle

transbordar *v* : to transfer

transbordo *nm* : transfer

transcendencia → **trascendencia**

transcender → **trascender**

transcribir {33} *vt* : to transcribe

transcrito *pp* → **transcribir**

transcripción *nf, pl* **-ciones** : transcription

transcurrir *vi* : to elapse, to pass

transcurso *nm* : course, progression ⟨en el transcurso de cien años : over the course of a hundred years⟩

transeúnte *nmf* **1** : passerby **2** : transient

transferencia *nf* : transfer, transference

transferir {76} *vt* TRASLADAR : to transfer — **transferible** *adj*

transfigurar *vt* : to transfigure, to transform — **transfiguración** *nf*

transformación *nf, pl* **-ciones** : transformation, conversion

transformador *nm* : transformer

transformar *vt* **1** CONVERTIR : to convert **2** : to transform, to change, to alter — **transformarse** *vr*

transfusión *nf, pl* **-siones** : transfusion

transgredir {1} *vt* : to transgress — **transgresión** *nf*

transgresor, -sora *n* : transgressor

transición *nf, pl* **-ciones** : transition ⟨período de transición : transition period⟩

transido, -da *adj* : overcome, beset ⟨transido de dolor : racked with pain⟩

transigir {35} *vi* **1** : to give in, to compromise **2** ~ **con** : to tolerate, to put up with

transistor *nm* : transistor

transitable *adj* : passable

transitar *vi* : to go, to pass, to travel ⟨transitar por la ciudad : to travel through the city⟩

transitivo, -va *adj* : transitive

tránsito *nm* **1** TRÁFICO : traffic ⟨hora de máximo tránsito : rush hour⟩ **2** : transit, passage, movement **3** : death, passing

transitorio, -ria *adj* **1** : transitory **2** : provisional, temporary — **transitoriamente** *adv*

translúcido, -da *adj* : translucent

translucir → **traslucir**

transmisible *adj* : transmissible

transmisión *nf, pl* **-siones** **1** : transmission, broadcast **2** : transfer **3** : transmission (of an automobile)

transmisor *nm* : transmitter

transmitir *vt* **1** : to transmit, to broadcast **2** : to pass on, to transfer — *vi* : to transmit, to broadcast

transparencia *nf* : transparency

transparentar *vt* : to reveal, to betray — **transparentarse** *vr* **1** : to be transparent **2** : to show through

transparente[1] *adj* : transparent — **transparentemente** *adv*

transparente[2] *nm* : shade, blind

transpiración *nf, pl* **-ciones** SUDOR : perspiration, sweat

transpirado, -da *adj* : sweaty

transpirar *vi* **1** SUDAR : to perspire, to sweat **2** : to transpire

transplantar, transplante → **trasplantar, trasplante**

transponer {60} *vt* **1** : to transpose, to move about **2** TRASPLANTAR : to transplant — **transponerse** *vr* **1** OCULTARSE : to hide **2** PONERSE : to set, to go down (of the sun or moon) **3** DORMITAR : to doze off

transportación *nf, pl* **-ciones** : transportation

transportador *nm* **1** : protractor **2** : conveyor

transportar *vt* **1** : to transport, to carry **2** : to transpose (music) — **transportarse** *vr* : to get carried away

transporte *nm* : transport, transportation

transportista *nmf* : hauler, carrier, trucker

transpuso, etc. → **transponer**

transversal *adj* : transverse, cross ⟨corte transversal : cross section⟩

transversalmente *adv* : obliquely

transverso, -sa *adj* : transverse

tranvía *nm* : streetcar, trolley

trapeador *nm* : mop

trapear *vt* : to mop

trapecio *nm* **1** : trapezoid **2** : trapeze

trapezoide *nm* : trapezoid

trapo *nm* **1** : cloth, rag ⟨trapo de polvo : dust cloth⟩ **2 soltar el trapo** : to burst into tears **3 trapos** *nmpl fam* : clothes

tráquea *nf* : trachea, windpipe

traquetear *vi* : to clatter, to jolt

traqueteo *nm* **1** : jolting **2** : clattering, clatter

tras *prep* **1** : after ⟨día tras día : day after day⟩ ⟨uno tras otro : one after another⟩ **2** : behind ⟨tras la puerta : behind the door⟩

trasbordar, trasbordo → **transbordar, transbordo**

trascendencia *nf* **1** : importance, significance **2** : transcendence

trascendental *adj* **1** : transcendental **2** : important, momentous

trascendente *adj* **1** : important, significant **2** : transcendent

trascender {56} *vi* **1** : to leak out, to become known **2** : to spread, to have a wide effect **3** ~ **a** : to smell of ⟨la casa trascendía a flores : the house smelled of flowers⟩ **4** ~ **de** : to transcend, to go beyond — *vt* : to transcend

trasero[1], **-ra** *adj* POSTERIOR : rear, back

trasero[2] *nm* : buttocks

trasfondo *nm* **1** : background, backdrop **2** : undertone, undercurrent

trasformación → **transformación**

trasgo *nm* : goblin, imp

trasgredir → **transgredir**

trasladar *vt* **1** TRANSFERIR : to transfer, to move **2** POSPONER : to postpone **3** TRADUCIR : to translate **4** COPIAR : to copy, to transcribe — **trasladarse** *vr* MUDARSE : to move, to relocate

traslado *nm* **1** : transfer, move **2** : copy

traslapar *vt* : to overlap — **traslaparse** *vr*

traslapo *nm* : overlap

traslúcido, -da → **translúcido**

traslucir {45} *vi* : to reveal, to show — **traslucirse** *vr* : to show through

trasmano *nm* **a** ~ : out of the way, out of reach

trasmisión, trasmitir → **transmisión, transmitir**

trasnochar *vi* : to stay up all night

trasparencia *nf* **trasparente** → **transparencia, transparente**

traspasar *vt* **1** PERFORAR : to pierce, to go through **2** : to go beyond ⟨traspasar los límites : to overstep the limits⟩ **3** ATRAVESAR : to cross, to go across **4** : to sell, to transfer

traspaso *nm* : transfer, sale

traspié *nm* **1** : stumble **2** : blunder

traspiración → **transpiración**

trasplantar *vt* : to transplant

trasplante *nm* : transplant

trasponer → **transponer**

trasportar → **transportar**

trasquilar *vt* ESQUILAR : to shear

traste *nm* **1** : fret (on a guitar) **2** *CA, Mex, PRi* : kitchen utensil ⟨lavar los trastes : to do the dishes⟩ **3 dar al traste con** : to ruin, to destroy **4 irse al traste** : to fall through

trastornar *vt* : to disturb, to upset, to disrupt — **trastornarse** *vr*

trastorno *nm* **1** : disorder ⟨trastorno mental : mental disorder⟩ **2** : disturbance, upset

trastos *nmpl* **1** : implements, utensils **2** *fam* : pieces of junk, stuff

trasunto *nm* : image, likeness

tratable *adj* **1** : friendly, sociable **2** : treatable

tratado *nm* **1** : treatise **2** : treaty

tratamiento *nm* : treatment

tratante *nmf* : dealer, trader

tratar *vi* **1** ~ **con** : to deal with, to have contact with ⟨no trato mucho con los clientes : I don't have much contact with customers⟩ **2** ~ **de** : to try to ⟨estoy tratando de comer : I am trying to

eat⟩ **3** ~ **de** *or* ~ **sobre** : to be about, to concern ⟨el libro trata de las plantas : the book is about plants⟩ **4** ~ **en** : to deal in ⟨trata en herramientas : he deals in tools⟩ — *vt* **1** : to treat ⟨tratan bien a sus empleados : they treat their employees well⟩ **2** : to handle ⟨trató el tema con delicadeza : he handled the subject tactfully⟩ — **tratarse** *vr* ~ **de** : to be about, to concern

trato *nm* **1** : deal, agreement **2** : relationship, dealings *pl* **3** : treatment ⟨malos tratos : ill-treatment⟩

trauma *nm* : trauma

traumático, -ca *adj* : traumatic — **traumáticamente** *adv*

traumatismo *nm* : injury ⟨traumatismo cervical : whiplash⟩

través *nm* **1 a través de** : across, through **2 al través** : crosswise, across **3 de través** : sideways

travesaño *nm* **1** : crossbar **2** : crossbeam, crosspiece, transom (of a window)

travesía *nf* : voyage, crossing (of the sea)

travesura *nf* **1** : prank, mischievous act **2 travesuras** *nfpl* : mischief

travieso, -sa *adj* : mischievous, naughty — **traviesamente** *adv*

trayecto *nm* **1** : journey **2** : route **3** : trajectory, path

trayectoria *nf* : course, path, trajectory

trayendo → **traer**

traza *nf* **1** DISEÑO : design, plan **2** : appearance

trazado *nm* **1** BOSQUEJO : outline, sketch **2** PLAN : plan, layout

trazar {21} *vt* **1** : to trace **2** : to draw up, to devise **3** : to outline, to sketch

trazo *nm* **1** : stroke, line **2** : sketch, outline

trébol *nm* **1** : clover, shamrock **2** : club (playing card)

trece *adj & nm* : thirteen

treceavo[1], **-va** *adj* : thirteenth

treceavo[2] *nm* : thirteenth (fraction)

trecho *nm* **1** : stretch, period ⟨de trecho en trecho : at intervals⟩ **2** : distance, space

tregua *nf* **1** : truce **2** : lull, respite **3 sin** ~ : relentless, unrelenting

treinta *adj & nm* : thirty

treintavo[1], **-va** *adj* : thirtieth

treintavo[2] *nm* : thirtieth (fraction)

tremendo, -da *adj* **1** : tremendous, enormous **2** : terrible, dreadful **3** *fam* : great, super

trementina *nf* AGUARRÁS : turpentine

trémulo, -la *adj* **1** : trembling, shaky **2** : flickering

tren *nm* **1** : train **2** : set, assembly ⟨tren de aterrizaje : landing gear⟩ **3** : speed, pace ⟨a todo tren : at top speed⟩

trence, etc. → **trenzar**

trenza *nf* : braid, pigtail

trenzar {21} *vt* : to braid — **trenzarse** *vr* : to get involved

trepador, -dora *adj* : climbing ⟨rosal trepador : rambling rose⟩

trepadora *nf* **1** : climbing plant, climber **2** : nuthatch

trepar *vi* **1** : to climb ⟨trepar a un árbol : to climb up a tree⟩ **2** : to creep, to spread (of a plant)

trepidación *nf, pl* **-ciones** : vibration

trepidante *adj* **1** : vibrating **2** : fast, frantic

trepidar *vi* **1** : to shake, to vibrate **2** : to hesitate, to waver

tres *adj & nm* : three

trescientos¹, -tas *adj* : three hundred

trescientos² *nms & pl* : three hundred

treta *nf* : trick, ruse

tríada *nf* : triad

triángulo *nm* : triangle — **triangular** *adj*

tribal *adj* : tribal

tribu *nf* : tribe

tribulación *nf, pl* **-ciones** : tribulation

tribuna *nf* **1** : dais, platform **2** : stands *pl*, bleachers *pl*, grandstand

tribunal *nm* : court, tribunal

tributar *vt* : to pay, to render — *vi* : to pay taxes

tributario¹, -ria *adj* : tax ⟨evasión tributaria : tax evasion⟩

tributario² *nm* : tributary

tributo *nm* **1** : tax **2** : tribute

triciclo *nm* : tricycle

tricolor *adj* : tricolor, tricolored

tridente *nm* : trident

tridimensional *adj* : three-dimensional, 3-D

trienal *adj* : triennial

trifulca *nf fam* : row, ruckus

trigésimo¹, -ma *adj* : thirtieth, thirty-

trigésimo², -ma *n* : thirtieth, thirty- (in a series)

trigo *nm* **1** : wheat **2 trigo rubión** : buckwheat

trigonometría *nf* : trigonometry

trigueño, -ña *adj* **1** : light brown (of hair) **2** MORENO : dark, olive-skinned

trillado, -da *adj* : trite, hackneyed

trilladora *nf* : thresher, threshing machine

trillar *vt* : to thresh

trillizo, -za *n* : triplet

trilogía *nf* : trilogy

trimestral *adj* : quarterly — **trimestralmente** *adv*

trinar *vi* **1** : to thrill **2** : to warble

trinchar *vt* : to carve, to cut up

trinchera *nf* **1** : trench, ditch **2** : trench coat

trineo *nm* : sled, sleigh

trinidad *nf* **la Trinidad** : the Trinity

trino *nm* : trill, warble

trinquete *nm* : ratchet

trío *nm* : trio

tripa *nf* **1** INTESTINO : gut, intestine **2 tripas** *nfpl fam* : belly, tummy, insides *pl* ⟨dolerle a uno las tripas : to have a stomach ache⟩

tripartito, -ta *adj* : tripartite

triple *adj & nm* : triple

triplicado *nm* : triplicate

triplicar {72} *vt* : to triple, to treble

trípode *nm* : tripod

tripulación *nf, pl* **-ciones** : crew

tripulante *nmf* : crew member

tripular *vt* : to man

tris *nm* **estar en un tris de** : to be within an inch of, to be very close to

triste *adj* **1** : sad, gloomy ⟨ponerse triste : to become sad⟩ **2** : desolate, dismal ⟨una perspectiva triste : a dismal outlook⟩ **3** : sorry, sorry-looking ⟨la triste verdad : the sorry truth⟩

tristeza *nf* DOLOR : sadness, grief

tristón, -tona *adj, mpl* **-tones** : melancholy, downhearted

tritón *nm, pl* **tritones** : newt

triturar *vt* : to crush, to grind

triunfal *adj* : triumphal, triumphant — **triunfalmente** *adv*

triunfante *adj* : triumphant, victorious

triunfar *vi* : to triumph, to win

triunfo *nm* **1** : triumph, victory **2** ÉXITO : success **3** : trump (in card games)

triunvirato *nm* : triumvirate

trivial *adj* **1** : trivial **2** : trite, commonplace

trivialidad *nf* : triviality

triza *nf* **1** : shred, bit **2 hacer trizas** : to tear into shreds, to smash to pieces

trocar {82} *vt* **1** CAMBIAR : to exchange, to trade **2** CAMBIAR : to change, to alter, to transform **3** CONFUNDIR : to confuse, to mix up

trocha *nf* : path, trail

troce, etc. → **trozar**

trofeo *nm* : trophy

tromba *nf* **1** : whirlwind **2 tromba de agua** : downpour, cloudburst

trombón *nm, pl* **trombones 1** : trombone **2** : trombonist — **trombonista** *nmf*

trombosis *nf* : thrombosis

trompa *nf* **1** : trunk (of an elephant), proboscis (of an insect) **2** : horn ⟨trompa de caza : hunting horn⟩ **3** : tube, duct (in the body)

trompada *nf fam* **1** : punch, blow **2** : bump, collision (of persons)

trompeta *nf* : trumpet

trompetista *nmf* : trumpet player, trumpeter

trompo *nm* : spinning top

tronada *nf* : thunderstorm

tronar {19} *vi* **1** : to thunder, to roar **2** : to be furious, to rage **3** *CA, Mex fam* : to shoot — *v impers* : to thunder ⟨está tronando : it's thundering⟩

tronchar *vt* **1** : to snap, to break off **2** : to cut off (relations)

tronco *nm* **1** : trunk (of a tree) **2** : log **3** : torso

trono *nm* **1** : throne **2** *fam* : toilet

tropa *nf* **1** : troop, soldiers *pl* **2** : crowd, mob **3** : herd (of livestock)

tropel *nm* : mob, swarm

tropezar {29} *vi* **1** : to trip, to stumble **2** : to slip up, to blunder **3** ~ **con** : to run into, to bump into **4** ~ **con** : to come up against (a problem)

tropezón *nm, pl* **-zones 1** : stumble **2** : mistake, slip

tropical *adj* : tropical

trópico *nm* **1** : tropic ⟨trópico de Cáncer : tropic of Cancer⟩ **2 el trópico** : the tropics

tropiezo *nm* **1** CONTRATIEMPO : snag, setback **2** EQUIVOCACIÓN : mistake, slip

troqué, etc. → **trocar**

troquel *nm* : die (for stamping)

trotamundos *nmf* : globe-trotter

trotar *vi* **1** : to trot **2** : to jog **3** *fam* : to rush about

trote *nm* **1** : trot **2** *fam* : rush, bustle **3 de ~** : durable, for everyday use

trovador, -dora *n* : troubadour

trozar {21} *vt* : to cut up, to dice

trozo *nm* **1** PEDAZO : piece, bit, chunk **2** : passage, extract

trucha *nf* : trout

truco *nm* **1** : trick **2** : knack

truculento, -ta *adj* : horrifying, gruesome

trueca, trueque etc. → **trocar**

truena, etc. → **tronar**

trueno *nm* : thunder

trueque *nm* : barter, exchange

trufa *nf* : truffle

truncar {72} *vt* **1** : to truncate, to cut short **2** : to thwart, to frustrate ⟨truncó sus esperanzas : she shattered their hopes⟩

trunco, -ca *adj* **1** : truncated **2** : unfinished, incomplete

trunque, etc. → **truncar**

tu *adj* **1** : your ⟨tu vestido : your dress⟩ ⟨toma tus vitaminas : take your vitamins⟩ **2** : thy

tú *pron* **1** : you ⟨tú eres mi hijo : you are my son⟩ **2** : thou

tuba *nf* : tuba

tubérculo *nm* : tuber

tuberculosis *nf* : tuberculosis

tuberculoso, -sa *adj* : tuberculous, tubercular

tubería *nf* : pipes *pl*, tubing

tuberoso, -sa *adj* : tuberous

tubo *nm* **1** : tube ⟨tubo de ensayo : test tube⟩ **2** : pipe ⟨tubo de desagüe : drainpipe⟩ **3 tubo digestivo** : alimentary canal

tubular *adj* : tubular

tuerca *nf* : nut ⟨tuercas y tornillos : nuts and bolts⟩

tuerce, etc. → **torcer**

tuerto, -ta *adj* : one-eyed, blind in one eye

tuerza, etc. → **torcer**

tuesta, etc. → **tostar**

tuétano *nm* : marrow

tufo *nm* **1** : fume, vapor **2** *fam* : stench, stink

tugurio *nm* : hovel

tulipán *nm, pl* **-panes** : tulip

tumba *nf* **1** SEPULCRO : tomb **2** FOSA : grave **3** : felling of trees

tumbar *vt* **1** : to knock down **2** : to fell, to cut down — *vi* : to fall down —
tumbarse *vr* ACOSTARSE : to lie down

tumbo *nm* **1** : tumble, fall **2 dar tumbos** : to jolt, to bump around

tumor *nm* : tumor

túmulo *nm* : burial mound

tumulto *nm* **1** ALBOROTO : commotion, tumult **2** MOTÍN : riot **3** MULTITUD : crowd

tumultuoso, -sa *adj* : tumultuous

tuna *nf* : prickly pear (fruit)

tundra *nf* : tundra

tunecino, -na *adj & n* : Tunisian

túnel *nm* : tunnel

tungsteno *nm* : tungsten

túnica *nf* : tunic

tupé *nm* PELUQUÍN : toupee

tupido, -da *adj* **1** DENSO : dense, thick **2** OBSTRUIDO : obstructed, blocked up

turba *nf* **1** : peat **2** : mob, throng

turbación *nf, pl* **-ciones 1** : disturbance **2** : alarm, concern **3** : confusion

turbante *nm* : turban

turbar *vt* **1** : to disturb, to disrupt **2** : to worry, to upset **3** : to confuse

turbina *nf* : turbine

turbio, -bia *adj* **1** : cloudy, murky, turbid **2** : dim, blurred **3** : shady, crooked

turbopropulsor *nm* : turboprop

turborreactor *nm* : turbojet

turbulencia *nf* : turbulence

turbulento, -ta *adj* : turbulent

turco[1], -ca *adj* : Turkish

turco[2], -ca *n* : Turk

turco[3] *nm* : Turkish (language)

turgente *adj* : turgid, swollen

turismo *nm* : tourism, tourist industry

turista *nmf* : tourist, vacationer

turístico, -ca *adj* : tourist, travel

turnar *vi* : to take turns, to alternate

turno *nm* **1** : turn ⟨ya te tocará tu turno : you'll get your turn⟩ **2** : shift, duty ⟨turno de noche : night shift⟩ **3 por turno** : alternately

turón *nm, pl* **turones** : polecat

turquesa *nf* : turquoise

turrón *nm, pl* **turrones** : nougat

tusa *nf* : corn husk

tutear *vt* : to address as *tú*

tutela *nf* **1** : guardianship **2** : tutelage, protection

tuteo *nm* : addressing as *tú*

tutor, -tora *n* **1** : tutor **2** : guardian

tuvo, etc. → **tener**

tuyo[1], -ya *adj* : yours, of yours ⟨un amigo tuyo : a friend of yours⟩ ⟨¿es tuya esta casa? : is this house yours?⟩

tuyo[2], -ya *pron* **1** : yours ⟨ése es el tuyo : that one is yours⟩ ⟨trae la tuya : bring your own⟩ **2 los tuyos** : your relations, your friends ⟨¿vendrán los tuyos? : are your folks coming?⟩

tweed ['twið] *nm* : tweed

U

u¹ *nf* : twenty-second letter of the Spanish alphabet

u² *conj* (*used instead of* o *before words beginning with* o- *or* ho-) : or

ualabí *nm* : wallaby

uapití *nm* : American elk, wapiti

ubicación *nf, pl* -ciones : location, position

ubicar {72} *vt* 1 SITUAR : to place, to put, to position 2 LOCALIZAR : to locate, to find — ubicarse *vr* 1 LOCALIZARSE : to be placed, to be located 2 SITUARSE : to position oneself

ubicuidad *nf* OMNIPRESENCIA : ubiquity

ubicuo, -cua *adj* OMNIPRESENTE : ubiquitous

ubre *nf* : udder

ucraniano¹, -na *adj & n* : Ukranian

ucraniano² *nm* : Ukranian (language)

Ud., Uds. → usted

ufanarse *vr* ~ de : to boast about, to pride oneself on

ufano, -na *adj* 1 ORGULLOSO : proud 2 : self-satisfied, smug

ugandés, -desa *adj & n, mpl* -deses : Ugandan

ukelele *nm* : ukulele

úlcera *nf* : ulcer — ulceroso, -sa *adj*

ulcerar *vt* : to ulcerate — ulcerarse *vr* — ulceración *nf*

ulceroso, -sa *adj* : ulcerous

ulterior *adj* : later, subsequent — ulteriormente *adv*

últimamente *adv* : lately, recently

ultimar *vt* 1 CONCLUIR : to complete, to finish, to finalize 2 MATAR : to kill

ultimátum *nm, pl* -tums : ultimatum

último, -ma *adj* 1 : last, final ⟨la última galleta : the last cookie⟩ ⟨en último caso : as a last resort⟩ 2 : last, latest, most recent ⟨su último viaje a España : her last trip to Spain⟩ ⟨en los últimos años : in recent years⟩ 3 por ~ : finally

ultrajar *vt* INSULTAR : to offend, to outrage, to insult

ultraje *nm* INSULTO : outrage, insult

ultramar *nm* de ~ *or* en ~ : overseas, abroad

ultranza *nf* 1 a ~ : to the extreme ⟨lo defendió a ultranza : she defended him fiercely⟩ 2 a ~ : extreme, out-and-out ⟨perfeccionismo a ultranza : rabid perfectionism⟩

ultrarrojo, -ja *adj* : infrared

ultravioleta *adj* : ultraviolet

ulular *vi* 1 : to hoot 2 : to howl, to wail

ululato *nm* : hoot (of an owl), wail (of a person)

umbilical *adj* : umbilical ⟨cordón umbilical : umbilical cord⟩

umbral *nm* : threshold, doorstep

un¹ *adj* → uno¹

un², una *art, mpl* unos 1 : a, an 2 unos *or* unas *pl* : some, a few ⟨hace unas se-

manas : a few weeks ago⟩ 3 unos *or* unas *pl* : about, approximately ⟨unos veinte años antes : about twenty years before⟩

unánime *adj* : unanimous — unánimemente *adv*

unanimidad *nf* 1 : unanimity 2 por ~ : unanimously

unción *nf, pl* -ciones : unction

uncir {83} *vt* : to yoke

undécimo¹, -ma *adj* : eleventh

undécimo², -ma *n* : eleventh (in a series)

ungir {35} *vt* : to anoint

ungüento *nm* : ointment, salve

únicamente *adv* : only, solely

unicelular *adj* : unicellular

único¹, -ca *adj* 1 : only, sole 2 : unique, extraordinary

único², -ca *n* : only one ⟨los únicos que vinieron : the only ones who showed up⟩

unicornio *nm* : unicorn

unidad *nf* 1 : unity 2 : unit

unidireccional *adj* : unidirectional

unido, -da *adj* 1 : joined, united 2 : close ⟨unos amigos muy unidos : very close friends⟩

unificar {72} *vt* : to unify — unificación *nf*

uniformado, -da *adj* : uniformed

uniformar *vt* ESTANDARIZAR : to standardize, to make uniform

uniforme¹ *adj* : uniform — uniformemente *adv*

uniforme² *nm* : uniform

uniformidad *nf* : uniformity

unilateral *adj* : unilateral — unilateralmente *adv*

unión *nf, pl* uniones 1 : union 2 JUNTURA : joint, coupling

unir *vt* 1 JUNTAR : to unite, to join, to link 2 COMBINAR : to combine, to blend — unirse *vr* 1 : to join together 2 : to combine, to mix together 3 ~ a : to join ⟨se unieron al grupo : they joined the group⟩

unísono *nm* : unison ⟨al unísono : in unison⟩

unitario, -ria *adj* : unitary, unit ⟨precio unitario : unit price⟩

universal *adj* : universal — universalmente *adv*

universidad *nf* : university

universitario¹, -ria *adj* : university, college

universitario², -ria *n* : university student, college student

universo *nm* : universe

unja, etc. → ungir

uno¹, una *adj* (un *before masculine singular nouns*) : one ⟨una silla : one chair⟩ ⟨tiene treinta y un años : he's thirty-one years old⟩ ⟨el tomo uno : volume one⟩

uno² *nm* : one, number one

uno³, una *pron* **1** : one (number) ⟨uno por uno : one by one⟩ ⟨es la una : it's one o'clock⟩ **2** : one (person or thing) ⟨una es mejor que las otras : one (of them) is better than the others⟩ ⟨hacerlo uno mismo : to do it oneself⟩ **3 unos, unas** *pl* : some (ones), some people **4 uno y otro** : both **5 unos y otros** : all of them **6 el uno al otro** : one another, each other ⟨se enseñaron los unos a los otros : they taught each other⟩

untar *vt* **1** : to anoint **2** : to smear, to grease **3** : to bribe

unza, etc. → **uncir**

uña *nf* **1** : fingernail, toenail **2** : claw, hoof, stinger

uranio *nm* : uranium

Urano *nm* : Uranus

urbanidad *nf* : urbanity, courtesy

urbanización *nf, pl* **-ciones** : housing development, residential area

urbanizar {21} *vt* : to develop (an area)

urbano, -na *adj* **1** : urban **2** CORTÉS : urbane, polite

urbe *nf* : large city, metropolis

urdimbre *nf* : warp (in a loom)

urdu *nm* : Urdu

uretra *nf* : urethra

urgencia *nf* **1** : urgency **2** EMERGENCIA : emergency

urgente *adj* : urgent — **urgentemente** *adv*

urgir {35} *v impers* : to be urgent, to be pressing ⟨me urge localizarlo : I urgently need to find him⟩ ⟨el tiempo urge : time is running out⟩

urinario¹, -ria *adj* : urinary

urinario² *nm* : urinal (place)

urja, etc. → **urgir**

urna *nf* **1** : urn **2** : ballot box ⟨acudir a las urnas : to go to the polls⟩

urogallo *nm* : grouse (bird)

urraca *nf* **1** : magpie **2 urraca de América** : blue jay

urticaria *nf* : hives

uruguayo, -ya *adj & n* : Uruguayan

usado, -da *adj* **1** : used, secondhand **2** : worn, worn-out

usanza *nf* : custom, usage

usar *vt* **1** EMPLEAR, UTILIZAR : to use, to make use of **2** CONSUMIR : to consume, to use (up) **3** LLEVAR : to wear **4 de usar y tirar** : disposable — **usarse** *vr* **1** : to be used **2** : to be in fashion

uso *nm* **1** EMPLEO, UTILIZACIÓN : use ⟨de uso personal : for personal use⟩ ⟨hacer uso de : to make use of⟩ **2** : wear ⟨uso y desgaste : wear and tear⟩ **3** USANZA : custom, usage, habit ⟨al uso de : in the manner of, in the style of⟩

usted *pron* **1** (*formal form of address in most countries; often written as Ud. or Vd.*) : you **2 ustedes** *pl* (*often written as Uds. or Vds.*) : you, all of you

usual *adj* : usual, common, normal ⟨poco usual : not very common⟩ — **usualmente** *adv*

usuario, -ria *n* : user

usura *nf* : usury — **usurario, -ria** *adj*

usurero, -ra *n* : usurer

usurpador, -dora *n* : usurper

usurpar *vt* : to usurp — **usurpación** *nf*

utensilio *nm* : utensil, tool

uterino, -na *adj* : uterine

útero *nm* : uterus, womb

útil *adj* : useful, handy, helpful

útiles *nmpl* : implements, tools

utilidad *nf* **1** : utility, usefulness **2 utilidades** *nfpl* : profits

utilitario, -ria *adj* : utilitarian

utilizable *adj* : usable, fit for use

utilización *nf, pl* **-ciones** : utilization, use

utilizar {21} *vt* : to use, to utilize

útilmente *adv* : usefully

utopía *nf* : utopia

utópico, -ca *adj* : utopian

uva *nf* : grape

uvular *adj* : uvular

V

v *nf* : twenty-third letter of the Spanish alphabet

va → **ir**

vaca *nf* : cow

vacación *nf, pl* **-ciones 1** : vacation ⟨dos semanas de vacaciones : two weeks of vacation⟩ **2 estar de vacaciones** : to be on vacation **3 irse de vacaciones** : to go on vacation

vacacionar *vi Mex* : to vacation

vacacionista *nmf CA, Mex* : vacationer

vacante¹ *adj* : vacant, empty

vacante² *nf* : vacancy (for a job)

vaciado *nm* : cast, casting ⟨vaciado de yeso : plaster cast⟩

vaciar {85} *vt* **1** : to empty, to empty out, to drain **2** AHUECAR : to hollow out **3** : to cast (in a mold) — *vi* ~ **en** : to flow into, to empty into

vacilación *nf, pl* **-ciones** : hesitation, vacillation

vacilante *adj* **1** : hesitant, unsure **2** : shaky, unsteady **3** : flickering

vacilar *vi* **1** : to hesitate, to vacillate, to waver **2** : to be unsteady, to wobble **3** : to flicker **4** *fam* : to joke, to fool around

vacío¹, -cía *adj* **1** : vacant **2** : empty **3** : meaningless

vacío² *nm* **1** : emptiness, void **2** : space, gap **3** : vacuum **4 hacerle el vacío a alguien** : to ostracize someone, to give someone the cold shoulder

vacuidad *nf* : vacuity, vacuousness

vacuna *nf* : vaccine
vacunación *nf, pl* -**ciones** INOCU-
LACIÓN : vaccination, inoculation
vacunar *vt* INOCULAR : to vaccinate, to
inoculate
vacuno¹, -na *adj* : bovine ⟨ganado vacuno : beef cattle⟩
vacuno² *nm* : bovine
vacuo, -cua *adj* : empty, shallow, inane
vadear *vt* : to ford, to wade across
vado *nm* : ford
vagabundear *vi* : to wander, to roam
about
vagabundo¹, -da *adj* 1 ERRANTE : wandering 2 : stray
vagabundo², -da *n* : vagrant, bum,
vagabond
vagamente *adv* : vaguely
vagancia *nf* 1 : vagrancy 2 PEREZA
: laziness, idleness
vagar {52} *vi* ERRAR : to roam, to wander
vagina *nf* : vagina — **vaginal** *adj*
vago¹, -ga *adj* 1 : vague 2 PEREZOSO
: lazy, idle
vago², -ga *n* 1 : idler, loafer 2 VAGA-
BUNDO : vagrant, bum
vagón *nm, pl* **vagones** : car (of a train)
vague, etc. → **vagar**
vaguear *vi* 1 : to loaf, to lounge around
2 VAGAR : to wander
vaguedad *nf* : vagueness
vahído *nm* : dizzy spell
vaho *nm* 1 : breath 2 : vapor, steam (on
glass, etc.)
vaina *nf* 1 : sheath, scabbard 2 : pod
(of a pea or bean) 3 *fam* : nuisance,
bother
vainilla *nf* : vanilla
vaivén *nm, pl* **vaivenes** 1 : swinging,
swaying, rocking 2 : change, fluctuation ⟨los vaivenes de la vida : life's ups
and downs⟩
vajilla *nf* : dishes *pl*, set of dishes
valdrá, etc. → **valer**
vale *nm* 1 : voucher 2 PAGARÉ : promissory note, IOU
valedero, -ra *adj* : valid
valentía *nf* : courage, valor
valer {84} *vt* 1 : to be worth ⟨valen una
fortuna : they're worth a fortune⟩ ⟨no
vale protestar : there's no point in
protesting⟩ ⟨valer la pena : to be worth
the trouble⟩ 2 : to cost ⟨¿cuánto vale?
: how much does it cost?⟩ 3 : to earn,
to gain ⟨le valió una reprimenda : it
earned him a reprimand⟩ 4 : to protect, to aid ⟨¡válgame Dios! : God help
me!⟩ 5 : to be equal to — *vi* 1 : to have
value ⟨sus consejos no valen para nada
: his advice is worthless⟩ 2 : to be valid,
to count ⟨eso no vale! : that doesn't
count!⟩ 3 **hacerse valer** : to assert oneself 4 **más vale** : it's better ⟨más vale
que te vayas : you'd better go⟩ —
valerse *vr* 1 ~ **de** : to take advantage
of 2 **valerse solo** *or* **valerse por sí mismo** : to look after oneself 3 *Mex* : to
be fair ⟨no se vale : it's not fair⟩

valeroso, -sa *adj* : brave, valiant
valet ['balet, -'le] *nm* : jack (in playing
cards)
valga, etc. → **valer**
valía *nf* : value, worth
validar *vt* : to validate — **validación** *nf*
validez *nf* : validity
válido, -da *adj* : valid
valiente *adj* 1 : brave, valiant 2 (*used
ironically*) : fine, great ⟨¡valiente amiga! : what a fine friend!⟩ — **valientemente** *adv*
valija *nf* : suitcase, valise
valioso, -sa *adj* PRECIOSO : valuable,
precious
valla *nf* 1 : fence, barricade 2 : hurdle
(in sports) 3 : obstacle, hindrance
vallar *vt* : to fence, to put a fence around
valle *nm* : valley, vale
valor *nm* 1 : value, worth, importance
2 CORAJE : courage, valor 3 **valores**
nmpl : values, principles 4 **valores**
nmpl : securities, bonds 5 **sin** ~
: worthless
valoración *nf, pl* -**ciones** 1 EVALU-
ACIÓN : valuation, appraisal, assessment 2 APRECIACIÓN : appreciation
valorar *vt* 1 EVALUAR : to evaluate, to
appraise, to assess 2 APRECIAR : to value, to appreciate
valorizarse {21} *vr* : to appreciate, to increase in value — **valorización** *nf*
vals *nm* : waltz
valsar *vi* : to waltz
valuación *nf, pl* -**ciones** : valuation, appraisal
valuar {3} *vt* : to value, to appraise, to
assess
válvula *nf* 1 : valve 2 **válvula reguladora** : throttle
vamos → **ir**
vampiro *nm* : vampire
van → **ir**
vanadio *nm* : vanadium
vanagloriarse *vr* : to boast, to brag
vanamente *adv* : vainly, in vain
vandalismo : vandalism
vándalo *nm* : vandal — **vandalismo** *nm*
vanguardia *nf* 1 : vanguard 2 : avante-
garde 3 **a la vanguardia** : at the forefront
vanidad *nf* : vanity
vanidoso, -sa *adj* PRESUMIDO : vain,
conceited
vano, -na *adj* 1 INÚTIL : vain, useless 2
: vain, worthless ⟨vanas promesas
: empty promises⟩ 3 **en** ~ : in vain,
of no avail
vapor *nm* 1 : vapor, steam 2 : steamer,
steamship 3 **al vapor** : steamed
vaporizador *nm* : vaporizer
vaporizar {21} *vt* : to vaporize — **vaporizarse** *vr* — **vaporización** *nf*
vaporoso, -sa *adj* 1 : vaporous 2
: sheer, airy
vapulear *vt* : to beat, to thrash
vaquero¹, -ra *adj* : cowboy ⟨pantalón vaquero : jeans⟩

vaquero², **-ra** *n* : cowboy *m*, cowgirl *f*
vaqueros *nmpl* JEANS : jeans
vaquilla *nf* : heifer
vara *nf* 1 : pole, stick, rod 2 : staff (of office) 3 : lance, pike (in bullfighting) 4 : yardstick 5 **vara de oro** : goldenrod
varado, -da *adj* 1 : beached, aground 2 : stranded
varar *vt* : to beach (a ship), to strand — *vi* : to run aground
variable *adj & nf* : variable — **variabilidad** *nf*
variación *nf, pl* **-ciones** : variation
variado, -da *adj* : varied, diverse
variante *adj & nf* : variant
varianza *nf* : variance
variar {85} *vt* 1 : to change, to alter 2 : to diversify — *vi* 1 : to vary, to change 2 **variar de opinión** : to change one's mind
varicela *nf* : chicken pox
varices *or* **várices** *nfpl* : varicose veins
varicoso, -sa *adj* : varicose
variedad *nf* DIVERSIDAD : variety, diversity
varilla *nf* 1 : rod, bar 2 : spoke (of a wheel) 3 : rib (of an umbrella)
vario, -ria *adj* 1 : varied, diverse 2 : variegated, motley 3 : changeable 4 **varios, varias** *pl* : various, several
variopinto, -ta *adj* : diverse, assorted, motley
varita *nf* : wand ⟨varita mágica : magic wand⟩
varón *nm, pl* **varones** 1 HOMBRE : man, male 2 NIÑO : boy
varonil *adj* 1 : masculine, manly 2 : mannish
vas → **ir**
vasallo *nm* : vassal — **vasallaje** *nm*
vasco¹, -ca *adj & n* : Basque
vasco² *nm* : Basque (language)
vascular *adj* : vascular
vasija *nf* : container, vessel
vaso *nm* 1 : glass, tumbler 2 : glassful 3 : vessel ⟨vaso sanguíneo : blood vessel⟩
vástago *nm* 1 : offspring, descendant 2 : shoot (of a plant)
vastedad *nf* : vastness, immensity
vasto, -ta *adj* : vast, immense
vataje *nm* : wattage
vaticinar *vt* : to predict, to foretell
vaticinio *nm* : prediction, prophecy
vatio *nm* : watt
vaya, etc. → **ir**
Vd., Vds. → **usted**
ve, etc. → **ir, ver**
vea, etc. → **ver**
vecinal *adj* : local
vecindad *nf* 1 : neighborhood, vicinity 2 **casa de vecindad** : tenement
vecindario *nm* 1 : neighborhood, area 2 : residents *pl*
vecino, -na *n* 1 : neighbor 2 : resident, inhabitant
veda *nf* 1 PROHIBICIÓN : prohibition 2 : closed season (for hunting or fishing)

vedar *vt* 1 : to prohibit, to ban 2 IMPEDIR : to impede, to prevent
vega *nf* : fertile lowland
vegetación *nf, pl* **-ciones** 1 : vegetation 2 **vegetaciones** *nfpl* : adenoids
vegetal *adj & nm* : vegetable, plant
vegetar *vi* : to vegetate
vegetarianismo *nm* : vegetarianism
vegetariano, -na *adj & n* : vegetarian
vegetativo, -va *adj* : vegetative
vehemente *adj* : vehement — **vehemencia** *nf*
vehículo *nm* : vehicle — **vehicular** *adj*
veía, etc. → **ver**
veinte *adj & nm* : twenty
veinteavo¹, -va *adj* : twentieth
veinteavo² *nm* : twentieth (fraction)
veintena *nf* : group of twenty, score ⟨una veintena de participantes : about twenty participants⟩
vejación *nf, pl* **-ciones** : ill-treatment, humiliation
vejar *vt* : to mistreat, to ridicule, to harass
vejete *nm* : old fellow, codger
vejez *nf* : old age
vejiga *nf* 1 : bladder 2 AMPOLLA : blister
vela *nf* 1 VIGILIA : wakefulness ⟨pasé la noche en vela : I stayed awake all night⟩ 2 : watch, vigil, wake 3 : candle 4 : sail
velada *nf* : evening party, soirée
velado, -da *adj* 1 : veiled, hidden 2 : blurred 3 : muffled
velador¹, -dora *n* : guard, night watchman
velador² *nm* 1 : candlestick 2 : night table
velar *vt* 1 : to hold a wake over 2 : to watch over, to sit up with 3 : to blur, to expose (a photo) 4 : to veil, to conceal — *vi* 1 : to stay awake 2 ~ **por** : to watch over, to look after
velatorio *nm* VELORIO : wake (for the dead)
veleidad *nf* 1 : fickleness 2 : whim, caprice
veleidoso, -sa : fickle, capricious
velero *nm* 1 : sailing ship 2 : sailboat
veleta *nf* : weather vane
vello *nm* 1 : body hair 2 : down, fuzz
vellocino *nm* : fleece
vellón *nm, pl* **vellones** 1 : fleece, sheepskin 2 *PRi* : nickel (coin)
vellosidad *nf* : downiness, hairiness
velloso, -sa *adj* : downy, fluffy, hairy
velo *nm* : veil
velocidad *nf* 1 : speed, velocity ⟨velocidad máxima : speed limit⟩ 2 MARCHA : gear (of an automobile)
velocímetro *nm* : speedometer
velocista *nmf* : sprinter
velorio *nm* VELATORIO : wake (for the dead)
velour *nm* : velour, velours
veloz *adj, pl* **veloces** : fast, quick, swift — **velozmente** *adv*
ven → **venir**

vena *nf* **1** : vein ⟨vena yugular : jugular vein⟩ **2** : vein, seam, lode **3** : grain (of wood) **4** : style ⟨en vena lírica : in a lyrical vein⟩ **5** : strain, touch ⟨una vena de humor : a touch of humor⟩ **6** : mood

venado *nm* **1** : deer **2** : venison

venal *adj* : venal — **venalidad** *nf*

vencedor, -dora *n* : winner, victor

vencejo *nm* : swift (bird)

vencer {86} *vt* **1** DERROTAR : to vanquish, to defeat **2** SUPERAR : to overcome, to surmount — *vi* **1** GANAR : to win, to triumph **2** CADUCAR : to expire ⟨el plazo vence el jueves : the deadline is Thursday⟩ **3** : to fall due, to mature — **vencerse** *vr* **1** DOMINARSE : to control oneself **2** : to break, to collapse

vencido, -da *adj* **1** : defeated **2** : expired **3** : due, payable **4 darse por vencido** : to give up

vencimiento *nm* **1** : defeat **2** : expiration **3** : maturity (of a loan)

venda *nf* : bandage

vendaje *nm* : bandage, dressing

vendar *vt* **1** : to bandage **2 vendar los ojos** : to blindfold

vendaval *nm* : gale, strong wind

vendedor, -dora *n* : salesperson, salesman *m*, saleswoman *f*

vender *vt* **1** : to sell **2** : to sell out, to betray — **venderse** *vr* **1** : to be sold ⟨se vende : for sale⟩ **2** : to sell out

vendetta *nf* : vendetta

vendible *adj* : salable, marketable

vendimia *nf* : grape harvest

vendrá, etc. → venir

veneno *nm* **1** : poison **2** : venom

venenoso, -sa *adj* : poisonous, venomous

venerable *adj* : venerable

veneración *nf*, *pl* **-ciones** : veneration, reverence

venerar *vt* : to venerate, to revere

venéreo, -rea *adj* : venereal

venero *nm* **1** VENA : seam, lode, vein **2** MANANTIAL : spring **3** FUENTE : origin, source

venezolano, -na *adj & n* : Venezuelan

venga, etc. → venir

vengador, -dora *n* : avenger

venganza *nf* : vengeance, revenge

vengar {52} *vt* : to avenge — **vengarse** *vr* : to get even, to revenge oneself

vengativo, -va *adj* : vindictive, vengeful

vengue, etc. → vengar

venia *nf* **1** PERMISO : permission, leave **2** PERDÓN : pardon **3** : bow (of the head)

venial *adj* : venial

venida *nf* **1** LLEGADA : arrival, coming **2** REGRESO : return **3 idas y venidas** : comings and goings

venidero, -ra *adj* : coming, future

venir {87} *vi* **1** : to come ⟨lo vi venir : I saw him coming⟩ ⟨¡venga! : come on!⟩ **2** : to arrive ⟨vinieron en coche : they came by car⟩ **3** : to come, to originate ⟨sus zapatos vienen de Italia : her shoes

are from Italy⟩ **4** : to come, to be available ⟨viene envuelto en plástico : it comes wrapped in plastic⟩ **5** : to come back, to return **6** : to affect, to overcome ⟨me vino un vahído : a dizzy spell came over me⟩ **7** : to fit ⟨te viene un poco grande : it's a little big for you⟩ **8** (*with the present participle*) : to have been ⟨viene entrenando diariamente : he's been training daily⟩ **9** ~ **a** (*with the infinitive*) : to end up, to turn out ⟨viene a ser lo mismo : it comes out the same⟩ **10 que viene** : coming, next ⟨el año que viene : next year⟩ **11 venir bien** : to be suitable, to be just right —
venirse *vr* **1** : to come, to arrive **2** : to come back **3 venirse abajo** : to fall apart, to collapse

venta *nf* **1** : sale **2 venta al por menor** *or* **venta al detalle** : retail sales

ventaja *nf* **1** : advantage **2** : lead, head start **3 ventajas** *nfpl* : perks, extras

ventajoso, -sa *adj* **1** : advantageous **2** : profitable — **ventajosamente** *adv*

ventana *nf* **1** : window (of a building) **2 ventana de la nariz** : nostril

ventanal *nm* : large window

ventanilla *nf* **1** : window (of a vehicle or airplane) **2** : ticket window, box office

ventero, -ra *n* : innkeeper

ventilación *nf*, *pl* **-ciones** : ventilation

ventilador *nm* **1** : ventilator **2** : fan

ventilar *vt* **1** : to ventilate, to air out **2** : to air, to discuss **3** : to make public, to reveal — **ventilarse** *vr* : to get some air

ventisca *nf* : snowstorm, blizzard

ventisquero *nm* : snowdrift

ventosear *vi* : to break wind

ventosidad *nf* : wind, flatulence

ventoso, -sa *adj* : windy

ventrículo *nm* : ventricle

ventrílocuo, -cua *n* : ventriloquist

ventriloquia *nf* : ventriloquism

ventura *nf* **1** : fortune, luck, chance **2** : happiness **3 a la ventura** : at random, as it comes

venturoso, -sa *adj* **1** AFORTUNADO : fortunate, lucky **2** : successful

Venus *nm* : Venus

venza, etc. → vencer

ver[1] {88} *vt* **1** : to see ⟨vimos la película : we saw the movie⟩ **2** ENTENDER : to understand ⟨ya lo veo : now I get it⟩ **3** EXAMINAR : to examine, to look into ⟨lo veré : I'll take a look at it⟩ **4** JUZGAR : to see, to judge ⟨a mi manera de ver : to my way of thinking⟩ **5** VISITAR : to meet with, to visit **6** AVERIGUAR : to find out **7 a ver** *or* **vamos a ver** : let's see — *vi* **1** : to see **2** ENTERARSE : to learn, to find out **3** ENTENDER : to understand — **verse** *vr* **1** HALLARSE : to find oneself **2** PARECER : to look, to appear **3** ENCONTRARSE : to see each other, to meet

ver[2] *nm* **1** : looks *pl*, appearance **2** : opinion ⟨a mi ver : in my view⟩

vera *nf* : side ⟨a la vera del camino : alongside the road⟩
veracidad *nf* : truthfulness, veracity
veranda *nf* : veranda
veraneante *nmf* : summer vacationer
veranear *vi* : to spend the summer
veraniego, -ga *adj* **1** ESTIVAL : summer ⟨el sol veraniego : the summer sun⟩ **2** : summery
verano *nm* : summer
veras *nfpl* de ~ : really, truly
veraz *adj*, *pl* **veraces** : truthful, veracious
verbal *adj* : verbal — **verbalmente** *adv*
verbalizar {21} *vt* : to verbalize, to express
verbena *nf* **1** FIESTA : festival, fair **2** : verbena, vervain
verbigracia *adv* : for example
verbo *nm* : verb
verborrea *nf* : verbiage
verbosidad *nf* : verbosity, wordiness
verboso, -sa *adj* : verbose, wordy
verdad *nf* **1** : truth **2** de ~ : really, truly **3** ¿verdad? : right?, isn't that so?
verdaderamente *adv* : really, truly
verdadero, -dera *adj* **1** REAL, VERÍDICO : true, real **2** AUTÉNTICO : genuine
verde[1] *adj* **1** : green (in color) **2** : green, unripe **3** : inexperienced, green **4** : dirty, risqué
verde[2] *nm* : green
verdear *vi* : to turn green, to become verdant
verdín *nm*, *pl* **verdines** : slime, scum
verdor *nm* **1** : greenness **2** : verdure
verdoso, -sa *adj* : greenish
verdugo *nm* **1** : executioner, hangman **2** : tyrant
verdugón *nm*, *pl* **-gones** : welt, wheal
verdura *nf* : vegetable(s), green(s)
vereda *nf* **1** SENDA : path, trail **2** : sidewalk, pavement
veredicto *nm* : verdict
verga *nf* : spar, yard (of a ship)
vergonzoso, -sa *adj* **1** : disgraceful, shameful **2** : bashful, shy — **vergonzosamente** *adv*
vergüenza *nf* **1** : disgrace, shame **2** : embarrassment **3** : bashfulness, shyness
vericueto *nm* : rough terrain
verídico, -ca *adj* **1** REAL, VERDADERO : true, real **2** VERAZ : truthful
verificación *nf*, *pl* **-ciones 1** : verification **2** : testing, checking
verificador, -dora *n* : inspector, tester
verificar {72} *vt* **1** : to verify, to confirm **2** : to test, to check **3** : to carry out, to conduct — **verificarse** *vr* **1** : to take place, to occur **2** : to come true
verja *nf* **1** : rails *pl* (of a fence) **2** : grating, grille **3** : gate
vermut *nm*, *pl* **vermuts** : vermouth
vernáculo, -la *adj* : vernacular
vernal *adj* : vernal, spring
verosímil *adj* **1** : probable, likely **2** : credible, realistic

verosimilitud *nf* **1** : probability, likeliness **2** : verisimilitude
verraco *nm* : boar
verruga *nf* : wart
versado, -da *adj* ~ **en** : versed in, knowledgeable about
versar *vi* ~ **sobre** : to deal with, to be about
versátil *adj* **1** : versatile **2** : fickle
versatilidad *nf* **1** : versatility **2** : fickleness
versículo *nm* : verse (in the Bible)
versión *nf*, *pl* **versiones 1** : version **2** : translation
verso *nm* : verse
versus *prep* : versus, against
vértebra *nf* : vertebra — **vertebral** *adj*
vertebrado[1], **-da** *adj* : vertebrate
vertebrado[2] *nm* : vertebrate
vertedero *nm* **1** : garbage dump **2** DESAGÜE : drain, outlet
verter {56} *vt* **1** : to pour **2** : to spill, to shed **3** : to empty out **4** : to express, to voice **5** : to translate, to render — *vi* : to flow
vertical *adj* & *nf* : vertical — **verticalmente** *adv*
vértice *nm* : vertex, apex
vertido *nm* : spilling, spill
vertiente *nf* **1** : slope **2** : aspect, side, element
vertiginoso, -sa *adj* : vertiginous — **vertiginosamente** *adv*
vértigo *nm* : vertigo, dizziness
vesícula *nf* **1** : vesicle **2 vesícula biliar** : gallbladder
vesicular *adj* : vesicular
vestíbulo *nm* : vestibule, hall, lobby, foyer
vestido *nm* **1** : dress, costume, clothes *pl* **2** : dress (garment)
vestidor *nm* : dressing room
vestiduras *nfpl* **1** : clothing, raiment, regalia **2** *or* **vestiduras sacerdotales** : vestments
vestigio *nm* : vestige, sign, trace
vestimenta *nf* ROPA : clothing, clothes *pl*
vestir {54} *vt* **1** : to dress, to clothe **2** LLEVAR : to wear **3** ADORNAR : to decorate, to dress up — *vi* **1** : to dress ⟨vestir bien : to dress well⟩ **2** : to look good, to suit the occasion — **vestirse** *vr* **1** : to get dressed **2** ~ **de** : to dress up as ⟨se vistieron de soldados : they dressed up as soldiers⟩ **3** ~ **de** : to wear, to dress in
vestuario *nm* **1** : wardrobe **2** : dressing room, locker room
veta *nf* **1** : grain (in wood) **2** : vein, seam, lode **3** : trace, streak ⟨una veta de terco : a stubborn streak⟩
vetar *vt* : to veto
veteado, -da *adj* : streaked, veined
veterano, -na *adj* & *n* : veteran
veterinaria *nf* : veterinary medicine
veterinario[1], **-ria** *adj* : veterinary
veterinario[2], **-ria** *n* : veterinarian

veto *nm* : veto

vetusto, -ta *adj* ANTIGUO : ancient, very old

vez *nf, pl* **veces** **1** : time, occasion ⟨a la vez : at the same time⟩ ⟨a veces : at times, occasionally⟩ ⟨de vez en cuando : from time to time⟩ **2** (*with numbers*) : time ⟨una vez : once⟩ ⟨de una vez : all at once⟩ ⟨de una vez para siempre : once and for all⟩ ⟨dos veces : twice⟩ **3** : turn ⟨a su vez : in turn⟩ ⟨en vez de : instead of⟩ ⟨hacer las veces de : to act as, to stand in for⟩

vía[1] *nf* **1** RUTA, CAMINO : road, route, way ⟨Vía Láctea : Milky Way⟩ **2** MEDIO : means, way ⟨por vía oficial : through official channels⟩ **3** : track, line (of a railroad) **4** : tract, passage ⟨por vía oral : orally⟩ **5 en vías de** : in the process of ⟨en vías de solución : on the road to a solution⟩ **6 por ~** : by (in transportation) ⟨por vía aérea : by air, airmail⟩

vía[2] *prep* : via

viable *adj* : viable, feasible — **viabilidad** *nf*

viaducto *nm* : viaduct

viajante *mf* : traveling salesman, traveling saleswoman

viajar *vi* : to travel, to journey

viaje *nm* : trip, journey ⟨viaje de negocios : business trip⟩

viajero[1]**, -ra** *adj* : traveling

viajero[2]**, -ra** *n* **1** : traveler **2** PASAJERO : passenger

vial *adj* : road, traffic

viático *nm* : travel allowance, travel expenses *pl*

víbora *nf* : viper

vibración *nf, pl* **-ciones** : vibration

vibrador *nm* : vibrator

vibrante *adj* **1** : vibrant **2** : vibrating

vibrar *vi* : to vibrate

vibratorio, -ria *adj* : vibratory

vicario, -ria *n* : vicar

vicealmirante *nmf* : vice admiral

vicepresidente, -ta *n* : vice president — **vicepresidencia** *nf*

viceversa *adv* : vice versa, conversely

viciado, -da *adj* : stuffy, close

viciar *vt* **1** : to corrupt **2** : to invalidate **3** FALSEAR : to distort **4** : to pollute, to adulterate

vicio *nm* **1** : vice, depravity **2** : bad habit **3** : defect, blemish

vicioso, -sa *adj* : depraved, corrupt

vicisitud *nf* : vicissitude

víctima *nf* : victim

victimario, -ria *n* ASESINO : killer, murderer

victimizar {21} *vt Arg, Mex* : to victimize

victoria *nf* : victory — **victorioso, -sa** *adj* — **victoriosamente** *adv*

victoriano, -na *adj* : Victorian

vid *nf* : vine, grapevine

vida *nf* **1** : life ⟨la vida cotidiana : everyday life⟩ **2** : life span, lifetime **3** BI-

OGRAFÍA : biography, life **4** : way of life, lifestyle **5** : livelihood ⟨ganarse la vida : to earn one's living⟩ **6** VIVEZA : liveliness **7 media vida** : half-life

vidente *nmf* **1** : psychic, clairvoyant **2** : sighted person

video *or* **vídeo** *nm* : video

videocasete *or* **videocassette** *nm* : videocassette

videocasetera *or* **videocassettera** *nf* : videocassette recorder, VCR

videocinta *nf* : videotape

videograbar *vt* : to videotape

vidriado *nm* : glaze

vidriar *vt* : to glaze (pottery, tile, etc.)

vidriera *nf* **1** : stained-glass window **2** : glass door or window **3** : store window

vidriero, -ra *n* : glazier

vidrio *nm* **1** : glass, piece of glass **2** : windowpane

vidrioso, -sa *adj* **1** : brittle, fragile **2** : slippery **3** : glassy, glazed (of eyes) **4** : touchy, delicate

vieira *nf* **1** : scallop **2** : scallop shell

viejo[1]**, -ja** *adj* **1** ANCIANO : old, elderly **2** ANTIGUO : former, longstanding ⟨viejas tradiciones : old traditions⟩ ⟨viejos amigos : old friends⟩ **3** GASTADO : old, worn, worn-out

viejo[2]**, -ja** *n* ANCIANO : old man *m,* old woman *f*

viene, etc. → **venir**

viento *nm* **1** : wind **2 hacer viento** : to be windy **3 contra viento y marea** : against all odds **4 viento alisio** : trade wind **5 viento en popa** : splendidly, successfully

vientre *nm* **1** : abdomen, belly **2** : womb **3** : bowels *pl*

viernes *nms & pl* : Friday

vierte, etc. → **verter**

vietnamita[1] *adj & nmf* : Vietnamese

vietnamita[2] *nm* : Vietnamese (language)

viga *nf* **1** : beam, rafter, girder **2 viga voladiza** : cantilever

vigencia *nf* **1** : validity **2** : force, effect ⟨entrar en vigencia : to go into effect⟩

vigente *adj* : valid, in force

vigésimo[1]**, -ma** *adj* : twentieth, twenty- ⟨la vigésima segunda edición : the twenty-second edition⟩

vigésimo[2]**, -ma** *n* : twentieth, twenty- (in a series)

vigía *nmf* : lookout

vigilancia *nf* : vigilance, watchfulness ⟨bajo vigilancia : under surveillance⟩

vigilante[1] *adj* : vigilant, watchful

vigilante[2] *nmf* : watchman, guard

vigilar *vt* **1** CUIDAR : to look after, to keep an eye on **2** GUARDAR : to watch over, to guard — *vi* **1** : to be watchful **2** : to keep watch

vigilia *nf* **1** VELA : wakefulness **2** : night work **3** : vigil (in religion)

vigor *nm* **1** : vigor, energy, strength **2** VIGENCIA : force, effect

vigorizante *adj* : invigorating

vigorizar {21} *vt* : to strengthen, to invigorate
vigoroso, -sa *adj* : vigorous — **vigorosamente** *adv*
VIH *nm* (*virus de inmunodeficiencia humana*) : HIV
vikingo, -ga *adj & n* : Viking
vil *adj* : vile, despicable
vileza *nf* **1** : vileness **2** : despicable action, villainy
vilipendiar *vt* : to vilify, to revile
villa *nf* **1** : town, village **2** : villa
villancico *nm* : carol, Christmas carol
villano, -na *n* **1** : villain **2** : peasant
vilo *nm* **1 en ~** : in the air **2 en ~** : uncertain, in suspense
vinagre *nm* : vinegar
vinagrera *nf* : cruet (for vinegar)
vinatería *nf* : wine shop
vinculación *nf, pl* **-ciones 1** : linking **2** RELACIÓN : bond, link, connection
vincular *vt* CONECTAR, RELACIONAR : to tie, to link, to connect
vínculo *nm* LAZO : tie, link, bond
vindicación *nf, pl* **-ciones** : vindication
vindicar *vt* **1** : to vindicate **2** : to avenge
vinilo *nm* : vinyl
vino¹, etc. → **venir**
vino² *nm* : wine
viña *nf* : vineyard
viñedo *nm* : vineyard
vio, etc. → **ver**
viola *nf* : viola
violación *nf, pl* **-ciones 1** : violation, offense **2** : rape
violador¹, -dora *n* : violator, offender
violador² *nm* : rapist
violar *vt* **1** : to rape **2** : to violate (a law or right) **3** PROFANAR : to desecrate
violencia *nf* : violence
violentamente *adv* : by force, violently
violentar *vt* **1** FORZAR : to break open, to force **2** : to distort (words or ideas) — **violentarse** *vr* : to force oneself
violento, -ta *adj* **1** : violent **2** EMBARAZOSO, INCÓMODO : awkward, embarrassing
violeta¹ *adj & nm* : violet (color)
violeta² *nf* : violet (flower)
violín *nm, pl* **-lines** : violin
violinista *nmf* : violinist
violonchelo *nm* : cello, violoncello
violonchelista *nmf* : cellist
VIP *nmf, pl* **VIPs** : VIP
vira *nf* : welt (of a shoe)
virago *nf* : virago, shrew
viraje *nm* **1** : turn, swerve **2** : change
viral *adj* : viral
virar *vi* : to tack, to turn, to veer
virgen¹ *adj* : virgin ⟨lana virgen : virgin wool⟩
virgen² *nmf, pl* **vírgenes** : virgin ⟨la Santísima Virgen : the Blessed Virgin⟩
virginal *adj* : virginal, chaste
virginidad *nf* : virginity
Virgo *nmf* : Virgo
vírico, -ca *adj* : viral
viril *adj* : virile — **virilidad** *nf*

virrey, -rreina *n* : viceroy *m*, vicereine *f*
virtual *adj* : virtual — **virtualmente** *adv*
virtud *nf* **1** : virtue **2 en virtud de** : by virtue of
virtuosismo *nm* : virtuosity
virtuoso¹, -sa *adj* : virtuous — **virtuosamente** *adv*
virtuoso², -sa *n* : virtuoso
viruela *nf* **1** : smallpox **2** : pockmark
virulencia *nf* : virulence
virulento, -ta *adj* : virulent
virus *nm* : virus
viruta *nf* : shaving
visa *nf* : visa
visado *nm Spain* : visa
visaje *nm* : face, grimace ⟨hacer visajes : to make faces⟩
visceral *adj* : visceral
vísceras *nfpl* : viscera, entrails
visconde, -desa *n* : viscount *m*, viscountess *f*
viscosidad *nf* : viscosity
viscoso, -sa *adj* : viscous
visera *nf* : visor
visibilidad *nf* : visibility
visible *adj* : visible — **visiblemente** *adv*
visión *nf, pl* **visiones 1** : vision, eyesight **2** : view, perspective **3** : vision, illusion ⟨ver visiones : to be seeing things⟩
visionario, -ria *adj & n* : visionary
visita *nf* **1** : visit, call **2** : visitor **3 ir de visita** : to go visiting
visitador, -dora *n* : visitor, frequent caller
visitante¹ *adj* : visiting
visitante² *nmf* : visitor
visitar *vt* : to visit
vislumbrar *vt* **1** : to discern, to make out **2** : to begin to see, to have an inkling of
vislumbre *nf* : glimmer, gleam
viso *nm* **1** APARIENCIA : appearance ⟨tener visos de : to seem, to show signs of⟩ **2** DESTELLO : glint, gleam **3** : sheen, iridescence
visón *nm, pl* **visones** : mink
víspera *nf* **1** : eve, day before **2 vísperas** *nfpl* : vespers
vista *nf* **1** VISIÓN : vision, eyesight **2** MIRADA : look, gaze, glance **3** PANORAMA : view, vista, panorama **4** : hearing (in court) **5 a primera vista** : at first sight **6 en vista de** : in view of **7 hacer la vista gorda** : to turn a blind eye **8 ¡hasta la vista!** : so long!, see you! **9 perder de vista** : to lose sight of **10 punto de vista** : point of view
vistazo *nm* : glance, look
viste, etc. → **ver¹, vestir**
visto¹ *pp* → **ver**
visto², -ta *adj* **1** : obvious, clear **2** : in view of, considering **3 estar bien visto** : to be approved of **4 estar mal visto** : to be frowned upon **5 por lo visto** : apparently **6 nunca visto** : unheard-of **7 visto que** : since, given that
visto³ *nm* **visto bueno** : approval

vistoso, -sa *adj* : colorful, bright
visual *adj* : visual — **visualmente** *adv*
visualización *nf, pl* **-ciones** : visualization
visualizar {21} *vt* **1** : to visualize **2** : to display (on a screen)
vital *adj* **1** : vital **2** : lively, dynamic
vitalicio, -cia *adj* : life, lifetime
vitalidad *nf* : vitality
vitamina *nf* : vitamin
vitamínico, -ca *adj* : vitamin ⟨complejos vitamínicos : vitamin compounds⟩
vitorear *vt* : to cheer, to acclaim
vitral *nm* : stained-glass window
vítreo, -rea *adj* : vitreous, glassy
vitrina *nf* **1** : showcase, display case **2** : store window
vitriolo *nm* : vitriol
vituperar *vt* : to condemn, to vituperate against
vituperio *nm* : vituperation, censure
viudez *nf* : widowerhood, widowhood
viudo, -da *n* : widower *m*, widow *f*
vivacidad *nf* VIVEZA : vivacity, liveliness
vivamente *adv* **1** : in a lively manner **2** : vividly **3** : strongly, acutely ⟨se lo recomendamos vivamente : we strongly recommend it⟩
vivaque *nm* : bivouac
vivaquear *vi* : to bivouac
vivar *vi* : to cheer
vivaz *adj, pl* **vivaces 1** : lively, vivacious **2** : clever, sharp **3** : perennial
víveres *nmpl* : provisions, supplies, food
vivero *nm* **1** : nursery (for plants) **2** : hatchery, fish farm
viveza *nf* **1** VIVACIDAD : liveliness **2** BRILLO : vividness, brightness **3** ASTUCIA : cleverness, sharpness
vívido, -da *adj* : vivid, lively
vividor, -dora *n* : sponger, parasite
vivienda *nf* **1** : housing **2** MORADA : dwelling, home
viviente *adj* : living
vivificar {72} *vt* : to vivify, to give life to
vivir[1] *vi* **1** : to live, to be alive **2** SUBSISTIR : to subsist, to make a living **3** RESIDIR : to reside **4** : to spend one's life ⟨vive para trabajar : she lives to work⟩ **5** ~ **de** : to live on — *vt* **1** : to live ⟨vivir su vida : to live one's life⟩ **2** EXPERIMENTAR : to go through, to experience
vivir[2] *nm* **1** : life, lifestyle **2 de mal vivir** : disreputable
vivisección *nf, pl* **-ciones** : vivisection
vivo, -va *adj* **1** : alive **2** INTENSO : vivid, bright, intense **3** ANIMADO : lively, vivacious **4** ASTUTO : sharp, clever **5 en** ~ : live ⟨transmisión en vivo : live broadcast⟩ **6 al rojo vivo** : red-hot
vizconde, -desa *n* : viscount *m*, viscountess *f*
vocablo *nm* PALABRA : word
vocabulario *nm* : vocabulary
vocación *nf, pl* **-ciones** : vocation
vocacional *adj* : vocational
vocal[1] *adj* : vocal

vocal[2] *nmf* : member (of a committee, board, etc.)
vocal[3] *nf* : vowel
vocalista *nmf* CANTANTE : singer, vocalist
vocalizar {21} *vi* : to vocalize
vocear *v* : to shout
vocerío *nm* : clamor, shouting
vocero, -ra *n* PORTAVOZ : spokesperson, spokesman *m*, spokeswoman *f*
vociferante *adj* : vociferous
vociferar *vi* GRITAR : to shout, to yell
vodevil *nm* : vaudeville
vodka *nm* : vodka
voladizo[1], **-za** *adj* : projecting
voladizo[2] *nm* : projection
volador, -dora *adj* : flying
volando *adv* : quickly, in a hurry
volante[1] *adj* : flying
volante[2] *nm* **1** : steering wheel **2** FOLLETO : flier, circular **3** : shuttlecock **4** : flywheel **5** : balance wheel (of a watch) **6** : ruffle, flounce
volar {19} *vi* **1** : to fly **2** CORRER : to hurry, to rush ⟨el tiempo vuela : time flies⟩ ⟨pasar volando : to fly past⟩ **3** DIVULGARSE : to spread ⟨unos rumores volaban : rumors were spreading around⟩ **4** DESAPARECER : to disappear ⟨el dinero ya voló : the money's already gone⟩ — *vt* **1** : to blow up, to demolish **2** : to irritate
volátil *adj* : volatile — **volatilidad** *nf*
volatilizar {21} *vt* : to volatize — **volatilizarse** *vr*
volcán *nm, pl* **volcanes** : volcano
volcánico, -ca *adj* : volcanic
volcar {82} *vt* **1** : to upset, to knock over, to turn over **2** : to empty out **3** : to make dizzy **4** : to cause a change of mind in **5** : to irritate — *vi* **1** : to overturn, to tip over **2** : to capsize — **volcarse** *vr* **1** : to overturn **2** : to do one's utmost
volea *nf* : volley (in sports)
volear *vi* : to volley (in sports)
voleibol *nm* : volleyball
voleo *nm* **al voleo** : haphazardly, at random
volframio *nm* : wolfram, tungsten
volición *nf, pl* **-ciones** : volition
volqué, etc. → **volcar**
voltaje *nm* : voltage
voltear *vt* **1** : to turn over, to turn upside down **2** : to reverse, to turn inside out **3** : to turn ⟨voltear la cara : to turn one's head⟩ **4** : to knock down — *vi* **1** : to roll over, to do somersaults **2** : to turn ⟨volteó a la izquierda : he turned left⟩ — **voltearse** *vr* **1** : to turn around **2** : to change one's allegiance
voltereta *nf* : somersault, tumble
voltio *nm* : volt
volubilidad *nf* : fickleness, changeableness
voluble *adj* : fickle, changeable
volumen *nm, pl* **-lúmenes 1** TOMO : volume, book **2** : capacity, size, bulk **3** CANTIDAD : amount ⟨el volumen de

ventas : the volume of sales⟩ **4** : volume, loudness

voluminoso, -sa *adj* : voluminous, massive, bulky

voluntad *nf* **1** : will, volition **2** DESEO : desire, wish **3** INTENCIÓN : intention **4 a voluntad** : at will **5 buena voluntad** : good will **6 mala voluntad** : ill will **7 fuerza de voluntad** : will-power

voluntario¹, -ria *adj* : voluntary — **voluntariamente** *adv*

voluntario², -ria *n* : volunteer

voluntarioso, -sa *adj* **1** : stubborn **2** : willing, eager

voluptuosidad *nf* : voluptuousness

voluptuoso, -sa *adj* : voluptuous — **voluptuosamente** *adv*

voluta *nf* : spiral, column (of smoke)

volver {89} *vi* **1** : to return, to come or go back ⟨volver a casa : to return home⟩ **2** : to revert ⟨volver al tema : to get back to the subject⟩ **3 ∼ a** : to do again ⟨volvieron a llamar : they called again⟩ **4 volver en sí** : to come to, to regain consciousness — *vt* **1** : to turn, to turn over, to turn inside out **2** : to return, to repay, to restore **3** : to cause, to make ⟨la volvía loca : it was driving her crazy⟩ — **volverse** *vr* **1** : to become ⟨se volvió deprimido : he became depressed⟩ **2** : to turn around

vomitar *vi* : to vomit — *vt* **1** : to vomit **2** : to spew out (lava, etc.)

vómito *nm* **1** : vomiting **2** : vomit

voracidad *nf* : voracity

vorágine *nf* : whirlpool, maelstrom

voraz *adj, pl* **voraces** : voracious — **vorazmente** *adv*

vórtice *nm* **1** : whirlpool, vortex **2** TORBELLINO : whirlwind

vos *pron* (*in some regions of Latin America*) : you

vosear *vt* : to address as *vos*

vosotros, -tras *pron pl Spain* **1** : you, yourselves **2** : ye

votación *nf, pl* **-ciones** : vote, voting

votante *nmf* : voter

votar *vi* : to vote — *vt* : to vote for

votivo, -va *adj* : votive

voto *nm* **1** : vote **2** : vow (in religion) **3 votos** *nmpl* : good wishes

voy → ir

voz *nf, pl* **voces 1** : voice **2** : opinion, say **3** GRITO : shout, yell **4** : sound **5** VOCABLO : word, term **6** : rumor **7 a**

voz en cuello : at the top of one's lungs **8 dar voces** : to shout **9 en voz alta** : aloud, in a loud voice **10 en voz baja** : softly, in a low voice

vudú *nm* : voodoo

vuelco *nm* : upset, overturning ⟨me dio un vuelco el corazón : my heart skipped a beat⟩

vuela, etc. → volar

vuelca, vuelque etc. → volcar

vuelo *nm* **1** : flight, flying ⟨alzar el vuelo : to take flight⟩ **2** : flight (of an aircraft) ⟨vuelo espacial : space flight⟩ **3** : flare, fullness (of clothing) **4 al vuelo** : on the wing

vuelta *nf* **1** GIRO : turn ⟨se dio la vuelta : he turned around⟩ **2** REVOLUCIÓN : circle, revolution ⟨dio la vuelta al mundo : she went around the world⟩ ⟨las ruedas daban vueltas : the wheels were spinning⟩ **3** : flip, turn ⟨le dio la vuelta : she flipped it over⟩ **4** : bend, curve ⟨a la vuelta de la esquina : around the corner⟩ **5** REGRESO : return ⟨de ida y vuelta : round trip⟩ ⟨a vuelta de correo : return mail⟩ **6** : round, lap (in sports or games) **7** PASEO : walk, drive, ride ⟨dio una vuelta : he went for a walk⟩ **8** DORSO, REVÉS : back, other side ⟨a la vuelta : on the back⟩ **9** : cuff (of pants) **10 darle vueltas** : to think over **11 estar de vuelta** : to be back

vuelto *pp* **→ volver**

vuelve, etc. → volver

vuestro¹, -stra *adj Spain* : your, of yours ⟨vuestros coches : your cars⟩ ⟨una amiga vuestra : a friend of yours⟩

vuestro², -stra *pron Spain, (with definite article)* : yours ⟨la vuestra es más grande : yours is bigger⟩ ⟨esos son los vuestros : those are yours⟩

vulcanizar {21} *vt* : to vulcanize

vulgar *adj* **1** : common **2** : vulgar

vulgaridad *nf* : vulgarity

vulgarismo *nm* : vulgarism

vulgarizar {21} *vt* : to vulgarize, to popularize

vulgarmente *adv* : vulgarly, popularly

vulgo *nm* **el vulgo** : the masses, common people

vulnerable *adj* : vulnerable — **vulnerabilidad** *nf*

vulnerar *vt* **1** : to injure, to damage (one's reputation or honor) **2** : to violate, to break (a law or contract)

W

w *nf* : twenty-fourth letter of the Spanish alphabet

wafle *nm* : waffle

waflera *nf* : waffle iron

wapití *nm* : wapiti, elk

whisky *nm, pl* **whiskys** *or* **whiskies** : whiskey

wigwam *nm* : wigwam

X

x *nf* : twenty-fifth letter of the Spanish alphabet
xenofobia *nf* : xenophobia
xenófobo¹, -ba *adj* : xenophobic
xenófobo², -ba *n* : xenophobe
xenón *nm* : xenon
xerocopiar *vt* : to photocopy, to xerox
xilófono *nm* : xylophone

Y

y¹ *nf* : twenty-sixth letter of the Spanish alphabet
y² *conj* (**e** *before words beginning with i- or hi-*) **1** : and ⟨mi hermano y yo : my brother and I⟩ ⟨¿y los demás? : and (what about) the others?⟩ **2** (*used in numbers*) ⟨cincuenta y cinco : fifty-five⟩ **3** *fam* : well ⟨y por supuesto : well, of course⟩
ya¹ *adv* **1** : already ⟨ya terminó : she's finished already⟩ **2** : now, right now ⟨¡hazlo ya! : do it now!⟩ ⟨ya mismo : right away⟩ **3** : later, soon ⟨ya iremos : we'll go later on⟩ **4** : no longer, anymore ⟨ya no fuma : he no longer smokes⟩ **5** (*used for emphasis*) ⟨¡ya lo sé! : I know!⟩ ⟨ya lo creo : of course⟩ **6 no ya** : not only ⟨no ya lloran sino gritan : they're not only crying but screaming⟩ **7 ya que** : now that, since ⟨ya que sabe la verdad : now that she knows the truth⟩
ya² *conj* **ya . . . ya** : whether . . . or, first . . . then ⟨ya le gusta, ya no : first he likes it, then he doesn't⟩
yac *nm* : yak
yacer {90} *vi* : to lie ⟨en esta tumba yacen sus abuelos : his grandparents lie in this grave⟩
yacimiento *nm* : bed, deposit ⟨yacimiento petrolífero : oil field⟩
yaga, etc. → **yacer**
yanqui *adj & nmf* : Yankee
yarda *nf* : yard
yate *nm* : yacht
yaz, yazca, yazga etc. → **yacer**
yedra *nf* : ivy
yegua *nf* : mare
yelmo *nm* : helmet
yema *nf* **1** : bud, shoot **2** : yolk (of an egg) **3 yema del dedo** : fingertip
yemenita *adj & nmf* : Yemenite
yen *nm* : yen (currency)
yendo → **ir**

yerba *nf* **1** *or* **yerba mate** : maté **2** → **hierba**
yerga, yergue etc. → **erguir**
yermo¹, -ma *adj* : barren, deserted
yermo² *nm* : wasteland
yerno *nm* : son-in-law
yerra, etc. → **errar**
yerro *nm* : blunder, mistake
yerto, -ta *adj* : rigid, stiff
yesca *nf* : tinder
yeso *nm* **1** : plaster **2** : gypsum
yo¹ *nm* : ego, self
yo² *pron* **1** : I **2** : me ⟨todos menos yo : everyone except me⟩ ⟨tan bajo como yo : as short as me⟩ **3 soy yo** : it is I, it's me
yodado, -da *adj* : iodized
yodo *nm* : iodine
yoduro *nm* : iodide
yoga *nm* : yoga
yogui *nm* : yogi
yogurt *or* **yogur** *nm* : yogurt
yola *nf* : yawl
yoyo *or* **yoyó** *nm* : yo-yo
yuca *nf* **1** : yucca (plant) **2** : cassava, manioc
yucateco¹, -ca *adj* : of or from the Yucatán
yucateco², -ca *n* : person from the Yucatán
yudo → **judo**
yugo *nm* : yoke
yugoslavo, -va *adj & n* : Yugoslavian
yugular *adj* : jugular ⟨vena yugular : jugular vein⟩
yungas *nfpl Bol, Chile, Peru* : warm tropical valleys
yunque *nm* : anvil
yunta *nf* : yoke, team (of oxen)
yuppy *nmf, pl* **yuppies** : yuppie
yute *nm* : jute
yuxtaponer {60} *vt* : to juxtapose — **yuxtaposición** *nf*

Z

z *nf* : twenty-seventh letter of the Spanish alphabet
zacate *nm CA, Mex* **1** : grass, forage **2** : hay
zafacón *nm, pl* **-cones** *Car* : wastebasket
zafar *vt* : to loosen, to untie — **zafarse** *vr* **1** : to loosen up, to come undone **2** : to get free of
zafio, -fia *adj* : coarse, crude
zafiro *nm* : sapphire
zaga *nf* **1** : defense (in sports) **2 a la zaga** *or* **en ~** : behind, in the rear
zagual *nm* : paddle (of a canoe)

zaguán *nm, pl* **zaguanes** : front hall, vestibule
zaherir {76} *vt* **1** : to criticize sharply **2** : to wound, to mortify
zahones *nmpl* : chaps
zaino, -na *adj* : chestnut (color)
zalamería *nf* : flattery, sweet talk
zalamero[1]**, -ra** *adj* : flattering, fawning
zalamero[2]**, -ra** *n* : flatterer
zambiano, -na *adj & nmf* : Zambian
zambullida *nf* : dive, plunge
zambullirse {38} *vr* : to dive, to plunge
zanahoria *nf* : carrot
zancada *nf* : stride, step
zancadilla **1** : trip, stumble **2** *fam* : trick, ruse
zancos *nmpl* : stilts
zancuda *nf* : wading bird
zancudo *nm* MOSQUITO : mosquito
zángano *nm* : drone, male bee
zanja *nf* : ditch, trench
zanjar *vt* ACLARAR : to settle, to clear up, to resolve
zapallo *nm Arg, Chile, Peru, Uru* : pumpkin
zapapico *nm* : pickax
zapata *nf* : brake shoe
zapatería *nf* **1** : shoemaker's, shoe factory **2** : shoe store
zapatero[1]**, -ra** *adj* : dry, tough, poorly cooked
zapatero[2]**, -ra** *n* : shoemaker, cobbler
zapatilla *nf* **1** PANTUFLA : slipper **2** *or* **zapatilla de deporte** : sneaker
zapato *nm* : shoe
zar, zarina *n* : czar *m*, czarina *f*
zarandear *vt* **1** : to sift, to sieve **2** : to shake, to jostle, to jiggle
zarapito *nm* : curlew
zarcillo *nm* **1** : earring **2** : tendril (of a plant)
zarigüeya *nf* : opossum
zarista *adj & nmf* : czarist
zarpa *nf* : paw
zarpar *vi* : to set sail, to raise anchor
zarza *nf* : bramble, blackberry bush
zarzamora *nf* **1** : blackberry **2** : bramble, blackberry bush

zarzaparrilla *nf* : sarsaparilla
zepelín *nm, pl* **-lines** : zeppelin
zigoto *nm* : zygote
zigzag *nm, pl* **zigzags** *or* **zigzagues** : zigzag
zigzaguear *vi* : to zigzag
zimbabuense *adj & nmf* : Zimbabwean
zinc *nm* : zinc
zinnia *nf* : zinnia
zíper *nm CA, Mex* : zipper
zircón *nm, pl* **zircones** : zircon
zócalo *nm Mex* : main square
zodíaco *or* **zodiaco** *nm* : zodiac — **zodíacal** *adj*
zombi *or* **zombie** *nmf* : zombie
zona *nf* : zone, district, area
zonzo[1]**, -za** *adj* : stupid, silly
zonzo[2]**, -za** *n* : idiot, nitwit
zoo *nm* : zoo
zoología *nf* : zoology
zoológico[1]**, -ca** *adj* : zoological
zoológico[2] *nm* : zoo
zoólogo, -ga *n* : zoologist
zoom *nm* : zoom lens
zopilote *nm CA, Mex* : buzzard
zoquete *nmf fam* : oaf, blockhead
zorrillo *nm* MOFETA : skunk
zorro[1]**, -rra** *adj* : sly, crafty
zorro[2]**, -rra** *n* **1** : fox, vixen **2** : sly crafty person
zorzal *nm* : thrush
zozobra *nf* : anxiety, worry
zozobrar *vi* : to capsize
zueco *nm* : clog (shoe)
zulú[1] *adj & nmf* : Zulu
zulú[2] *nm* : Zulu (language)
zumaque *nm* : sumac
zumbar *vi* : to buzz, to hum — *vt fam* **1** : to hit, to thrash **2** : to make fun of
zumbido *nm* : buzzing, humming
zumo *nf* JUGO : juice
zurcir {83} *vt* : to darn, to mend
zurdo[1]**, -da** *adj* : left-handed
zurdo[2]**, -da** *n* : left-handed person
zurza, etc. → **zurcir**
zutano, -na → **fulano**

English–Spanish
Dictionary

A

a¹ [ˈeɪ] *n, pl* **a's** *or* **as** [ˈeɪz] : primera letra del alfabeto inglés

a² [ə, ˈeɪ] *art* (**an** [ən, ˈæn] before vowel or silent h) **1** : un *m*, una *f* ⟨a house : una casa⟩ ⟨half an hour : media hora⟩ ⟨what a surprise! : ¡qué sorpresa!⟩ **2** PER : por, a la, al ⟨30 kilometers an hour : 30 kilómetros por hora⟩ ⟨twice a month : dos veces al mes⟩

aardvark [ˈɑrdˌvɑrk] *n* : oso *m* hormiguero

aback [əˈbæk] *adv* **1** : por sorpresa **2 to be taken aback** : quedarse desconcertado

abacus [ˈæbəkəs] *n, pl* **abaci** [ˈæbəˌsaɪ, -ˌkiː] *or* **abacuses** : ábaco *m*

abaft [əˈbæft] *adv* : a popa

abalone [ˌæbəˈloːni] *n* : abulón *m*, oreja *f* marina

abandon¹ [əˈbændən] *vt* **1** DESERT, FORSAKE : abandonar, desamparar (a alguien), desertar de (algo) **2** GIVE UP, SUSPEND : renunciar a, suspender ⟨he abandoned the search : suspendió la búsqueda⟩ **3** EVACUATE, LEAVE : abandonar, evacuar, dejar ⟨to abandon ship : abandonar el buque⟩ **4 to abandon oneself** : entregarse, abandonarse

abandon² *n* : desenfreno *m* ⟨with wild abandon : desenfrenadamente⟩

abandoned [əˈbændənd] *adj* **1** DESERTED : abandonado **2** UNRESTRAINED : desenfrenado, desinhibido

abandonment [əˈbændənmənt] *n* : abandono *m*, desamparo *m*

abase [əˈbeɪs] *vt* **abased; abasing** : degradar, humillar, rebajar

abash [əˈbæʃ] *vt* : avergonzar, abochornar

abashed [əˈbæʃt] *adj* : avergonzado

abate [əˈbeɪt] *vi* **abated; abating** : amainar, menguar, disminuir

abattoir [ˈæbəˌtwɑr] *n* : matadero *m*

abbess [ˈæbɪs, -ˌbɛs, -bəs] *n* : abadesa *f*

abbey [ˈæbi] *n, pl* **-beys** : abadía *f*

abbot [ˈæbət] *n* : abad *m*

abbreviate [əˈbriːviˌeɪt] *vt* **-ated; -ating** : abreviar

abbreviation [əˌbriːviˈeɪʃən] *n* : abreviación *f*, abreviatura *f*

ABC's [ˌeɪˌbiːˈsiːz] *npl* : abecé *m*

abdicate [ˈæbdɪˌkeɪt] *v* **-cated; -cating** : abdicar

abdication [ˌæbdɪˈkeɪʃən] *n* : abdicación *f*

abdomen [ˈæbdəmən, æbˈdoːmən] *n* : abdomen *m*, vientre *m*

abdominal [æbˈdɑmənəl] *adj* : abdominal — **abdominally** *adv*

abduct [æbˈdʌkt] *vt* : raptar, secuestrar

abduction [æbˈdʌkʃən] *n* : rapto *m*, secuestro *m*

abductor [æbˈdʌktər] *n* : raptor *m*, -tora *f*; secuestrador *m*, -dora *f*

abed [əˈbɛd] *adv & adj* : en cama

aberrant [æˈbɛrənt, ˈæbərənt] *adj* **1** ABNORMAL : anormal, aberrante **2** ATYPICAL : anómalo, atípico

aberration [ˌæbəˈreɪʃən] *n* **1** : aberración *f* **2** DERANGEMENT : perturbación *f* mental

abet [əˈbɛt] *vt* **abetted; abetting** ASSIST : ayudar ⟨to aid and abet : ser cómplice de⟩

abeyance [əˈbeɪənts] *n* : desuso *m*, suspensión *f*

abhor [əbˈhɔr, æb-] *vt* **-horred; -horring** : abominar, aborrecer

abhorrence [əbˈhɔrənts, æb-] *n* : aborrecimiento *m*, odio *m*

abhorrent [əbˈhɔrənt, æb-] *adj* : abominable, aborrecible, odioso

abide [əˈbaɪd] *v* **abode** [əˈboːd] *or* **abided; abiding** *vt* STAND : soportar, tolerar ⟨I can't abide them : no los puedo ver⟩ — *vi* **1** ENDURE : quedar, permanecer **2** DWELL : morar, residir **3 to abide by** : atenerse a

ability [əˈbɪləti] *n, pl* **-ties 1** CAPABILITY : aptitud *f*, capacidad *f*, facultad *f* **2** COMPETENCE : competencia *f* **3** TALENT : talento *m*, don *m*, habilidad *f*

abject [ˈæbˌdʒɛkt, æbˈ-] *adj* **1** WRETCHED : miserable, desdichado **2** HOPELESS : abatido, desesperado **3** SERVILE : servil ⟨abject flattery : halagos serviles⟩ — **abjectly** *adv*

abjure [æbˈdʒʊr] *vt* **-jured; -juring** : abjurar de

ablaze [əˈbleɪz] *adj* **1** BURNING : ardiendo, en llamas **2** RADIANT : resplandeciente, radiante

able [ˈeɪbəl] *adj* **abler; ablest 1** CAPABLE : capaz, hábil **2** COMPETENT : competente

ablution [əˈbluːʃən] *n* : ablución *f* ⟨to perform one's ablutions : lavarse⟩

ably [ˈeɪbli] *adv* : hábilmente, eficientemente

abnormal [æbˈnɔrməl] *adj* : anormal — **abnormally** *adv*

abnormality [ˌæbnərˈmæləti, -nɔr-] *n, pl* **-ties** : anormalidad *f*

aboard¹ [əˈbord] *adv* : a bordo

aboard² *prep* : a bordo de

abode¹ → **abide**

abode² [əˈboːd] *n* : morada *f*, residencia *f*, vivienda *f*

abolish [əˈbɑlɪʃ] *vt* : abolir, suprimir

abolition [ˌæbəˈlɪʃən] *n* : abolición *f*, supresión *f*

abominable [əˈbɑmənəbəl] *adj* DETESTABLE : abominable, aborrecible, espantoso

abominate [əˈbɑməˌneɪt] *vt* **-nated; -nating** : abominar, aborrecer

abomination [əˌbɑməˈneɪʃən] *n* : abominación *f*

aboriginal [ˌæbəˈrɪdʒənəl] *adj* : aborigen, indígena

aborigine [ˌæbəˈrɪdʒəni] *n* NATIVE : aborigen *mf*, indígena *mf*

abort [ə'bɔrt] *vt* **1** : abortar (en medicina) **2** CALL OFF : suspender, abandonar — *vi* : abortar, hacerse un aborto

abortion [ə'bɔrʃən] *n* : aborto *m*

abortive [ə'bɔrtɪv] *adj* UNSUCCESSFUL : fracasado, frustrado, malogrado

abound [ə'baʊnd] *vi* **to abound in** : abundar en, estar lleno de

about¹ [ə'baʊt] *adv* **1** APPROXIMATELY : aproximadamente, casi, más o menos **2** AROUND : por todas partes, alrededor ⟨the children are running about : los niños están corriendo por todas partes⟩ **3 to be about to** : estar a punto de **4 to be up and about** : estar levantado

about² *prep* **1** AROUND : alrededor de **2** CONCERNING : de, acerca de, sobre ⟨he always talks about politics : siempre habla de política⟩

above¹ [ə'bʌv] *adv* **1** OVERHEAD : por encima, arriba **2** : más arriba ⟨as stated above : como se indica más arriba⟩

above² *adj* : anterior, antedicho ⟨for the above reasons : por las razones antedichas⟩

above³ *prep* **1** OVER : encima de, arriba de, sobre **2** : superior a, por encima de ⟨he's above those things : él está por encima de esas cosas⟩ **3** : más de, superior a ⟨he earns above $50,000 : gana más de $50,000⟩ ⟨a number above 10 : un número superior a 10⟩ **4 above all** : sobre todo

aboveboard¹ [ə'bʌv'bord, -ˌbord] *adv* **open and aboveboard** : sin tapujos

aboveboard² *adj* : legítimo, sincero

abrade [ə'breɪd] *vt* **abraded; abrading 1** ERODE : erosionar, corroer **2** SCRAPE : escoriar, raspar

abrasion [ə'breɪʒən] *n* **1** SCRAPE, SCRATCH : raspadura *f*, rasguño *m* **2** EROSION : erosión *f*

abrasive¹ [ə'breɪsɪv] *adj* **1** ROUGH : abrasivo, áspero **2** BRUSQUE, IRRITATING : brusco, irritante

abrasive² *n* : abrasivo *m*

abreast [ə'brest] *adv* **1** : en fondo, al lado ⟨to march three abreast : marchar de tres en fondo⟩ **2 to keep abreast** : mantenerse al día

abridge [ə'brɪdʒ] *vt* **abridged; abridging** : compendiar, resumir

abridgment *or* **abridgement** [ə'brɪdʒmənt] *n* : compendio *m*, resumen *m*

abroad [ə'brɔd] *adv* **1** ABOUT, WIDELY : por todas partes, en todas direcciones ⟨the news spread abroad : la noticia corrió por todas partes⟩ **2** OVERSEAS : en el extranjero, en el exterior

abrogate ['æbrəˌgeɪt] *vt* **-gated; -gating** : abrogar

abrupt [ə'brʌpt] *adj* **1** SUDDEN : abrupto, repentino, súbito **2** BRUSQUE, CURT : brusco, cortante — **abruptly** *adv*

abscess ['æbˌses] *n* : absceso *m*

abscond [æb'skɑnd] *vi* : huir, fugarse

absence ['æbsənts] *n* **1** : ausencia *f* (de una persona) **2** LACK : falta *f*, carencia *f*

absent¹ [æb'sɛnt] *vt* **to absent oneself** : ausentarse

absent² ['æbsənt] *adj* : ausente

absentee [ˌæbsən'ti:] *n* : ausente *mf*

absentminded [ˌæbsənt'maɪndəd] *adj* : distraído, despistado

absentmindedly [ˌæbsənt'maɪndədli] *adv* : distraídamente

absentmindedness [ˌæbsənt'maɪndədnəs] *n* : distracción *f*, despiste *m*

absolute ['æbsəˌlu:t, ˌæbsə'lu:t] *adj* **1** COMPLETE, PERFECT : completo, pleno, perfecto **2** UNCONDITIONAL : absoluto, incondicional **3** DEFINITE : categórico, definitivo

absolutely ['æbsəˌlu:tli, ˌæbsə'lu:tli] *adv* **1** COMPLETELY : completamente, absolutamente **2** CERTAINLY : desde luego ⟨do you agree? absolutely! : ¿estás de acuerdo? ¡desde luego!⟩

absolution [ˌæbsə'lu:ʃən] *n* : absolución *f*

absolutism ['æbsəˌlu:ˌtɪzəm] *n* : absolutismo *m*

absolve [əb'zɑlv, æb-, -'sɑlv] *vt* **-solved; -solving** : absolver, perdonar

absorb [əb'zɔrb, æb-, -'sɔrb] *vt* **1** : absorber, embeber (un líquido), amortiguar (un golpe, la luz) **2** ENGROSS : absorber **3** ASSIMILATE : asimilar

absorbed [əb'zɔrbd, æb-, -'sɔrbd] *adj* ENGROSSED : absorto, ensimismado

absorbency [əb'zɔrbəntsi, æb-, -'sɔr-] *n* : absorbencia *f*

absorbent [əb'zɔrbənt, æb-, -'sɔr-] *adj* : absorbente

absorbing [əb'zɔrbɪŋ, æb-, -'sɔr-] *adj* : absorbente, fascinante

absorption [əb'zɔrpʃən, æb-, -'sɔrp-] *n* **1** : absorción *f* **2** CONCENTRATION : concentración *f*

abstain [əb'steɪn, æb-] *vi* : abstenerse

abstainer [əb'steɪnər, æb-] *n* : abstemio *m*, -mia *f*

abstemious [æb'sti:miəs] *adj* : abstemio, sobrio — **abstemiously** *adv*

abstention [əb'stɛntʃən, æb-] *n* : abstención *f*

abstinence ['æbstənənts] *n* : abstinencia *f*

abstract¹ [æb'strækt, 'æbˌ-] *vt* **1** EXTRACT : abstraer, extraer **2** SUMMARIZE : compendiar, resumir

abstract² *adj* : abstracto — **abstractly** [æb'stræktli, 'æbˌ-] *adv*

abstract³ ['æbˌstrækt] *n* : resumen *m*, compendio *m*, sumario *m*

abstraction [æb'strækʃən] *n* **1** : abstracción *f*, idea *f* abstracta **2** ABSENTMINDEDNESS : distracción *f*

abstruse [əb'stru:s, æb-] *adj* : abstruso, recóndito — **abstrusely** *adv*

absurd [əb'sərd, -'zərd] *adj* : absurdo, ridículo, disparatado — **absurdly** *adv*

absurdity [əb'sərdəṭi, -'zər-] *n, pl* **-ties 1**
: absurdo *m* **2** NONSENSE : disparate
m, despropósito *m*

abundance [ə'bʌndənts] *n* : abundancia
f

abundant [ə'bʌndənt] *adj* : abundante,
cuantioso, copioso

abundantly [ə'bʌndəntli] *adv* : abundantemente, en abundancia

abuse[1] [ə'bju:z] *vt* **abused; abusing 1**
MISUSE : abusar de **2** MISTREAT : maltratar **3** REVILE : insultar, injuriar,
denostar

abuse[2] [ə'bju:s] *n* **1** MISUSE : abuso *m*
2 MISTREATMENT : abuso *m*, maltrato
m **3** INSULTS : insultos *mpl*, imprope-
rios *mpl* ⟨a string of abuse : una serie
de improperios⟩

abuser [ə'bju:zər] *n* : abusador *m*, -dora
f

abusive [ə'bju:sɪv] *adj* **1** ABUSING : abusivo **2** INSULTING : ofensivo, injurioso,
insultante — **abusively** *adv*

abut [ə'bʌt] *v* **abutted; abutting** *vt* : bordear — *vi* **to abut on** : colindar con

abutment [ə'bʌtmənt] *n* **1** BUTTRESS
: contrafuerte *m*, estribo *m* **2** CLOSE-
NESS : contigüidad *f*

abysmal [ə'bɪzməl] *adj* **1** DEEP : abismal, insondable **2** TERRIBLE : atroz,
desastroso

abysmally [ə'bɪzməli] *adv* : desastrosa-
mente, terriblemente

abyss [ə'bɪs, 'æbɪs] *n* : abismo *m*, sima
f

acacia [ə'keɪʃə] *n* : acacia *f*

academic[1] [ˌækə'dɛmɪk] *adj* **1** : académico **2** THEORETICAL : teórico —
academically [-mɪkli] *adv*

academic[2] *n* : académico *m*, -ca *f*

academician [ˌækədə'mɪʃən] *n* → **academic**

academy [ə'kædəmi] *n, pl* **-mies** : academia *f*

acanthus [ə'kænθəs] *n* : acanto *m*

accede [æk'si:d] *vi* **-ceded; -ceding 1**
AGREE : acceder, consentir **2** ASCEND
: subir, acceder ⟨he acceded to the
throne : subió al trono⟩

accelerate [ɪk'sɛlə,reɪt, æk-] *v* **-ated;
-ating** *vt* : acelerar, apresurar — *vi*
: acelerar (dícese de un carro)

acceleration [ɪkˌsɛlə'reɪʃən, æk-] *n*
: aceleración *f*

accelerator [ɪk'sɛlə,reɪṭər, æk-] *n* : acelerador *m*

accent[1] ['æk,sɛnt, æk'sɛnt] *vt* : acentuar

accent[2] ['æk,sɛnt, -sənt] *n* **1** : acento *m*
2 EMPHASIS, STRESS : énfasis *m*, acento *m*

accentuate [ɪk'sɛntʃu,eɪt, æk-] *vt* **-ated;
-ating** : acentuar, poner énfasis en

accept [ɪk'sɛpt, æk-] *vt* **1** : aceptar **2** AC-
KNOWLEDGE : admitir, reconocer

acceptability [ɪkˌsɛptə'bɪləṭi, æk-] *n*
: aceptabilidad *f*

acceptable [ɪk'sɛptəbəl, æk-] *adj*
: aceptable, admisible — **acceptably**
[-bli] *adv*

acceptance [ɪk'sɛptənts, æk-] *n* : aceptación *f*, aprobación *f*

access[1] ['æk,sɛs] *vt* : obtener acceso a,
entrar a

access[2] *n* : acceso *m*

accessibility [ɪkˌsɛsə'bɪləṭi] *n, pl* **-ties**
: accesibilidad *f*

accessible [ɪk'sɛsəbəl, æk-] *adj* : accesible, asequible

accession [ɪk'sɛʃən, æk-] *n* **1** : ascenso
f, subida *f* (al trono, etc.) **2** ACQUISI-
TION : adquisición *f*

accessory[1] [ɪk'sɛsəri, æk-] *adj* : auxiliar

accessory[2] *n, pl* **-ries 1** : accesorio *m*,
complemento *m* **2** ACCOMPLICE : cómplice *mf*

accident ['æksədənt] *n* **1** MISHAP : accidente *m* **2** CHANCE : casualidad *f*

accidental [ˌæksə'dɛntəl] *adj* : accidental, casual, imprevisto, fortuito

accidentally [ˌæksə'dɛntəli, -'dɛntli] *adv*
1 BY CHANCE : por casualidad **2** UN-
INTENTIONALLY : sin querer, involuntariamente

acclaim[1] [ə'kleɪm] *vt* : aclamar, elogiar

acclaim[2] *n* : aclamación *f*, elogio *m*

acclamation [ˌæklə'meɪʃən] *n* : aclamación *f*

acclimate ['æklə,meɪt, ə'klaɪmət] → **acclimatize**

acclimatize [ə'klaɪmə,taɪz] *v* **-tized;
-tizing** *vt* **1** : aclimatar **2 to acclimatize oneself** : aclimatarse

accolade ['ækə,leɪd, -,lɑd] *n* **1** PRAISE
: elogio *m* **2** AWARD : galardón *m*

accommodate [ə'kɑmə,deɪt] *vt* **-dated;
-dating 1** ADAPT : acomodar, adaptar
2 SATISFY : tener en cuenta, satisfacer
3 HOLD : dar cabida a, tener cabida
para

accommodation [əˌkɑmə'deɪʃən] *n* **1**
: adaptación *f*, adecuación *f* **2 accommodations** *npl* LODGING : alojamiento *m*, hospedaje *m*

accompaniment [ə'kʌmpənəmənt,
-'kɑm-] *n* : acompañamiento *m*

accompanist [ə'kʌmpənɪst, -'kɑm-] *n*
: acompañante *mf*

accompany [ə'kʌmpəni, -'kɑm-] *vt*
-nied; -nying : acompañar

accomplice [ə'kɑmpləs, -'kʌm-] *n* : cómplice *mf*

accomplish [ə'kɑmplɪʃ, -'kʌm-] *vt* : efectuar, realizar, lograr, llevar a cabo

accomplished [ə'kɑmplɪʃt, -'kʌm-] *adj*
: consumado, logrado

accomplishment [ə'kɑmplɪʃmənt,
-'kʌm-] *n* **1** ACHIEVEMENT : logro *m*,
éxito *m* **2** SKILL : destreza *f*, habilidad
f

accord[1] [ə'kɔrd] *vt* GRANT : conceder,
otorgar — *vi* **to accord with** : concordar con, conformarse con

accord[2] *n* **1** AGREEMENT : acuerdo *m*,
convenio *m* **2** VOLITION : voluntad *f*

⟨on one's own accord⟩ : voluntariamente, de motu proprio⟩
accordance [əˈkɔrdənts] *n* **1** ACCORD
: acuerdo *m*, conformidad *f* **2 in accordance with** : conforme a, según, de
acuerdo con
accordingly [əˈkɔrdɪŋli] *adv* **1** CORRE-
SPONDINGLY : en consecuencia **2** CON-
SEQUENTLY : por consiguiente, por lo
tanto
according to [əˈkɔrdɪŋ] *prep* : según, de
acuerdo con, conforme a
accordion [əˈkɔrdiən] *n* : acordeón *m*
accordionist [əˈkɔrdiənɪst] *n* : acordeonista *mf*
accost [əˈkɔst] *vt* : abordar, dirigirse a
account¹ [əˈkaʊnt] *vt* : considerar, estimar ⟨he accounts himself lucky : se
considera afortunado⟩ — *vi* **to account for** : dar cuenta de, explicar
account² *n* **1** : cuenta *f* ⟨savings account
: cuenta de ahorros⟩ **2** EXPLANATION
: versión *f*, explicación *f* **3** REPORT : relato *m*, informe *m* **4** IMPORTANCE : importancia *f* ⟨to be of no account : no
tener importancia⟩ **5 on account of**
BECAUSE OF : a causa de, debido a, por
6 on no account : de ninguna manera
accountability [ə,kaʊntəˈbɪləti] *n* : responsabilidad *f*
accountable [əˈkaʊntəbəl] *adj* : responsable
accountant [əˈkaʊntənt] *n* : contador *m*,
-dora *f*; contable *mf Spain*
accounting [əˈkaʊntɪŋ] *n* : contabilidad
f
accoutrements *or* **accouterments** [ə-
ˈkuːtrəmənts, -ˈkuːtər-] *npl* **1** EQUIP-
MENT : equipo *m*, avíos *mpl* **2** ACCES-
SORIES : accesorios *mpl* **3** TRAPPINGS
: símbolos *mpl* ⟨the accoutrements of
power : los símbolos del poder⟩
accredit [əˈkrɛdət] *vt* : acreditar, autorizar
accreditation [ə,krɛdəˈteɪʃən] *n* : acreditación *f*, homologación *f*
accretion [əˈkriːʃən] *n* **1** : acrecentamiento *m* (proceso) **2** : acreción *f*,
acrecencia *f* (producto)
accrual [əˈkruːəl] *n* : incremento *m*, acumulación *f*
accrue [əˈkruː] *vi* **-crued; -cruing** : acumularse, aumentarse
accumulate [əˈkjuːmjə,leɪt] *v* **-lated;
-lating** *vt* : acumular, amontonar — *vi*
: acumularse, amontonarse
accumulation [ə,kjuːmjəˈleɪʃən] *n* : acumulación *f*, amontonamiento *m*
accuracy [ˈækjərəsi] *n* : exactitud *f*, precisión *f*
accurate [ˈækjərət] *adj* : exacto, correcto, fiel, preciso — **accurately** *adv*
accusation [,ækjəˈzeɪʃən] *n* : acusación
f
accusatory [əˈkjuːzə,tɔri] *adj* : acusatorio
accuse [əˈkjuːz] *vt* **-cused; -cusing**
: acusar, delatar, denunciar

accused [əˈkjuːzd] *ns & pl* DEFENDANT
: acusado *m*, -da *f*
accuser [əˈkjuːzər] *n* : acusador *m*, -dora
f
accustom [əˈkʌstəm] *vt* : acostumbrar,
habituar
ace [ˈeɪs] *n* : as *m*
acerbic [əˈsərbɪk, æ-] *adj* : acerbo, mordaz
acetate [ˈæsə,teɪt] *n* : acetato *m*
acetic [əˈsiːtɪk] *adj* : acético
acetone [ˈæsə,toːn] *n* : acetona *f*
acetylene [əˈsɛtələn, -tə,liːn] *n* : acetileno *m*
ache¹ [ˈeɪk] *vi* **ached; aching 1** : doler
2 to ache for : anhelar, ansiar
ache² *n* : dolor *m*
achieve [əˈtʃiːv] *vt* **achieved; achieving**
: lograr, alcanzar, conseguir, realizar
achievement [əˈtʃiːvmənt] *n* : logro *m*,
éxito *m*, realización *f*
acid¹ [ˈæsəd] *adj* **1** SOUR : ácido, agrio
2 CAUSTIC, SHARP : acerbo, mordaz —
acidly *adv*
acid² *n* : ácido *m*
acidic [əˈsɪdɪk, æ-] *adj* : ácido
acidity [əˈsɪdəti, æ-] *n*, *pl* **-ties** : acidez *f*
acknowledge [ɪkˈnɑlɪdʒ, æk-] *vt* **-edged;
-edging 1** ADMIT : reconocer, admitir
2 RECOGNIZE : reconocer **3 to acknowledge receipt of** : acusar recibo
de
acknowledgment [ɪkˈnɑlɪdʒmənt, æk-] *n*
1 RECOGNITION : reconocimiento *m* **2**
THANKS : agradecimiento *m*
acme [ˈækmi] *n* : colmo *m*, apogeo *m*,
cúspide *f*
acne [ˈækni] *n* : acné *m*
acolyte [ˈækə,laɪt] *n* : acólito *m*
acorn [ˈeɪ,kɔrn, -kərn] *n* : bellota *f*
acoustic [əˈkuːstɪk] *or* **acoustical**
[-stɪkəl] *adj* : acústico — **acoustically**
adv
acoustics [əˈkuːstɪks] *ns & pl* : acústica
f
acquaint [əˈkweɪnt] *vt* **1** INFORM : enterar, informar **2** FAMILIARIZE : familiarizar **3 to be acquainted with**
: conocer a (una persona), estar al tanto de (un hecho)
acquaintance [əˈkweɪntənts] *n* **1**
KNOWLEDGE : conocimiento *m* **2**
: conocido *m*, -da *f* ⟨friends and ac-
quaintances : amigos y conocidos⟩
acquiesce [,ækwiˈɛs] *vi* **-esced; -escing**
: consentir, conformarse
acquiescence [,ækwiˈɛsənts] *n* : consentimiento *m*, aquiescencia *f*
acquire [əˈkwaɪr] *vt* **-quired; -quiring**
: adquirir, obtener
acquisition [,ækwəˈzɪʃən] *n* : adquisición *f*
acquisitive [əˈkwɪzətɪv] *adj* : adquisitivo, codicioso
acquit [əˈkwɪt] *vt* **-quitted; -quitting 1**
: absolver, exculpar **2 to acquit oneself** : comportarse, defenderse
acquittal [əˈkwɪtəl] *n* : absolución *f*, exculpación *f*

acre ['eɪkər] *n* : acre *m*

acreage ['eɪkərɪʤ] *n* : superficie *f* en acres

acrid ['ækrəd] *adj* **1** BITTER : acre **2** CAUSTIC : acre, mordaz — **acridly** *adv*

acrimonious [ˌækrə'mo:niəs] *adj* : áspero, cáustico, sarcástico

acrimony ['ækrəˌmo:ni] *n, pl* **-nies** : acrimonia *f*

acrobat ['ækrəˌbæt] *n* : acróbata *mf*, saltimbanqui *mf*

acrobatic [ˌækrə'bætɪk] *adj* : acrobático

acrobatics [ˌækrə'bætɪks] *ns & pl* : acrobacia *f*

acronym ['ækrəˌnɪm] *n* : acrónimo *m*

across¹ [ə'krɔs] *adv* **1** CROSSWISE : al través **2** : a través, del otro lado ⟨he's already across : ya está del otro lado⟩ **3** : de ancho ⟨40 feet across : 40 pies de ancho⟩

across² *prep* **1** : al otro lado de ⟨across the street : al otro lado de la calle⟩ **2** : a través de ⟨a log across the road : un tronco a través del camino⟩

acrylic [ə'krɪlɪk] *n* : acrílico *m*

act¹ ['ækt] *vi* **1** PERFORM : actuar, interpretar **2** FEIGN, PRETEND : fingir, simular **3** BEHAVE : comportarse **4** FUNCTION : actuar, servir, funcionar **5** : tomar medidas ⟨he acted to save the business : tomó medidas para salvar el negocio⟩ **6 to act as** : servir de, hacer de

act² *n* **1** DEED : acto *m*, hecho *m*, acción *f* **2** DECREE : ley *f*, decreto *m* **3** : acto *m* (en una obra de teatro), número *m* (en un espectáculo) **4** PRETENSE : fingimiento *m*

action ['ækʃən] *n* **1** DEED : acción *f*, acto *m*, hecho *m* **2** BEHAVIOR : actuación *f*, comportamiento *m* **3** LAWSUIT : demanda *f* **4** MOVEMENT : movimiento *m* **5** COMBAT : combate *m* **6** PLOT : acción *f*, trama *f* **7** MECHANISM : mecanismo *m*

activate ['æktəˌveɪt] *vt* **-vated; -vating** : activar

activation [ˌæktə'veɪʃən] *n* : activación *f*

active ['æktɪv] *adj* **1** MOVING : activo, en movimiento **2** LIVELY : vigoroso, enérgico **3** : en actividad ⟨an active volcano : un volcán en actividad⟩ **4** OPERATIVE : vigente

actively ['æktɪvli] *adv* : activamente, enérgicamente

activist ['æktɪvɪst] *n* : activista *mf* — **activist** *adj*

activity [æk'tɪvəti] *n, pl* **-ties 1** MOVEMENT : actividad *f*, movimiento *m* **2** VIGOR : vigor *m*, energía *f* **3** OCCUPATION : actividad *f*, ocupación *f*

actor ['æktər] *n* : actor *m*, artista *mf*

actress ['æktrəs] *n* : actriz *f*

actual ['æktʃuəl] *adj* : real, verdadero

actuality [ˌæktʃu'æləti] *n, pl* **-ties** : realidad *f*

actually ['æktʃuəli, -ʃəli] *adv* : realmente, en realidad

actuary ['æktʃuˌeri] *n, pl* **-aries** : actuario *m*, -ria *f* de seguros

acumen [ə'kju:mən] *n* : perspicacia *f*

acupuncture ['ækjuˌpʌŋktʃər] *n* : acupuntura *f*

acute [ə'kju:t] *adj* **acuter; acutest 1** SHARP : agudo **2** PERCEPTIVE : perspicaz, sagaz **3** KEEN : fino, muy desarrollado, agudo ⟨an acute sense of smell : un fino olfato⟩ **4** SEVERE : grave **5 acute angle** : ángulo *m* agudo

acutely [ə'kju:tli] *adv* : intensamente ⟨to be acutely aware : estar perfectamente consciente⟩

acuteness [ə'kju:tnəs] *n* : agudeza *f*

ad ['æd] → **advertisement**

adage ['ædɪʤ] *n* : adagio *m*, refrán *m*, dicho *m*

adamant ['ædəmənt, -ˌmænt] *adj* : firme, categórico, inflexible — **adamantly** *adv*

Adam's apple ['ædəmz] *n* : nuez *f* de Adán

adapt [ə'dæpt] *vt* : adaptar, ajustar — *vi* : adaptarse

adaptability [əˌdæptə'bɪləti] *n* : adaptabilidad *f*, flexibilidad *f*

adaptable [ə'dæptəbəl] *adj* : adaptable, amoldable

adaptation [ˌæˌdæp'teɪʃən, -dəp-] *n* **1** : adaptación *f*, modificación *f* **2** VERSION : versión *f*

adapter [ə'dæptər] *n* : adaptador *m*

add ['æd] *vt* **1** : añadir, agregar ⟨to add a comment : añadir una observación⟩ **2** : sumar ⟨add these numbers : suma estos números⟩ — *vi* : sumar (en total)

adder ['ædər] *n* : víbora *f*

addict¹ [ə'dɪkt] *vt* : causar adicción en

addict² ['ædɪkt] *n* **1** : adicto *m*, -ta *f* **2 drug addict** : drogadicto *m*, -ta *f*; toxicómano *m*, -na *f*

addiction [ə'dɪkʃən] *n* **1** : adicción *f*, dependencia *f* **2 drug addiction** : drogadicción *f*

addictive [ə'dɪktɪv] *adj* : adictivo

addition [ə'dɪʃən] *n* **1** : adición *f*, añadidura *f* **2 in ~** : además, también

additional [ə'dɪʃənəl] *adj* : extra, adicional, de más

additionally [ə'dɪʃənəli] *adv* : además, adicionalmente

additive ['ædətɪv] *n* : aditivo *m*

addle ['ædəl] *vt* **-dled; -dling** : confundir, enturbiar

address¹ [ə'drɛs] *vt* **1** : dirigirse a, pronunciar un discurso ante ⟨to address a jury : dirigirse a un jurado⟩ **2** : dirigir, ponerle la dirección a ⟨to address a letter : dirigir una carta⟩

address² [ə'drɛs, 'æˌdrɛs] *n* **1** SPEECH : discurso *m*, alocución *f* **2** : dirección *f* (de una residencia, etc.)

addressee [ˌæˌdrɛ'si:, ə-] *n* : destinatario *m*, -ria *f*

adduce [ə-'du:s, 'dju:s] *vt* **-duced; -duc-ing** : aducir

adenoids ['æd,nɔɪd, -dən,ɔɪd] *npl* : adenoides *fpl*

adept [ə'dɛpt] *adj* : experto, hábil — **adeptly** *adv*

adequacy ['ædɪkwəsi] *n, pl* **-cies** : cantidad *f* suficiente

adequate ['ædɪkwət] *adj* **1** SUFFICIENT : adecuado, suficiente **2** ACCEPTABLE, PASSABLE : adecuado, aceptable

adequately ['ædɪkwətli] *adv* : suficientemente, apropiadamente

adhere [æd'hɪr, əd-] *vi* **-hered; -hering 1** STICK : pegarse, adherirse **2 to adhere to** : adherirse a (una política, etc.), cumplir con (una promesa)

adherence [æd'hɪrənts, əd-] *n* : adhesión *f*, adherencia *f*, observancia *f* (de una ley, etc.)

adherent¹ [æd'hɪrənt, əd-] *adj* : adherente, adhesivo, pegajoso

adherent² *n* : adepto *m*, -ta *f*; partidario *m*, -ria *f*

adhesion [æd'hi:ʒən, əd-] *n* : adhesión *f*

adhesive¹ [æd'hi:sɪv, əd-, -zɪv] *adj* : adhesivo

adhesive² *n* : adhesivo *m*, pegamento *m*

adjacent [ə'ʤeɪsənt] *adj* : adyacente, colindante, contiguo

adjective ['æʤɪktɪv] *n* : adjetivo *m* — **adjectival** [,æʤɪk'taɪvəl] *adj*

adjoin [ə'ʤɔɪn] *vt* : lindar con, colindar con

adjoining [ə'ʤɔɪnɪŋ] *adj* : contiguo, colindante

adjourn [ə'ʤərn] *vt* : levantar, suspender ⟨the meeting is adjourned : se levanta la sesión⟩ — *vi* : aplazarse

adjournment [ə'ʤərnmənt] *n* : suspensión *f*, aplazamiento *m*

adjudicate [ə'ʤu:dɪ,keɪt] *vt* **-cated; -cating** : juzgar, arbitrar

adjudication [ə,ʤu:dɪ'keɪʃən] *n* **1** JUDGING : arbitrio *m* (judicial) **2** JUDGMENT : fallo *m*

adjunct ['æ,ʤʌŋkt] *n* : adjunto *m*, complemento *m*

adjust [ə'ʤʌst] *vt* : ajustar, arreglar, regular — *vi* **to adjust to** : adaptarse a

adjustable [ə'ʤʌstəbəl] *adj* : ajustable, regulable, graduable

adjustment [ə'ʤʌstmənt] *n* : ajuste *m*, modificación *f*

ad–lib¹ ['æd'lɪb] *v* **-libbed; -libbing** : improvisar

ad–lib² *adj* : improvisado

administer [æd'mɪnəstər, əd-] *vt* : administrar

administration [æd,mɪnə'streɪʃən, əd-] *n* **1** MANAGING : administración *f*, dirección *f* **2** GOVERNMENT, MANAGEMENT : administración *f*, gobierno *m*

administrative [æd'mɪnə,streɪtɪv, əd-] *adj* : administrativo — **administratively** *adv*

administrator [æd'mɪnə,streɪtər, əd-] *n* : administrador *m*, -dora *f*

admirable ['ædmərəbəl] *adj* : admirable, loable — **admirably** *adv*

admiral ['ædmərəl] *n* : almirante *mf*

admiration [,ædmə'reɪʃən] *n* : admiración *f*

admire [æd'maɪr] *vt* **-mired; -miring** : admirar

admirer [æd'maɪrər] *n* : admirador *m*, -dora *f*

admiring [æd'maɪrɪŋ] *adj* : admirativo, de admiración

admiringly [æd'maɪrɪŋli] *adv* : con admiración

admissible [æd'mɪsəbəl] *adj* : admisible, aceptable

admission [æd'mɪʃən] *n* **1** ADMITTANCE : entrada *f*, admisión *f* **2** ACKNOWLEDGMENT : reconocimiento *m*, admisión *f*

admit [æd'mɪt, əd-] *vt* **-mitted; -mitting 1** : admitir, dejar entrar ⟨the museum admits children : el museo deja entrar a los niños⟩ **2** ACKNOWLEDGE : reconocer, admitir

admittance [æd'mɪtənts, əd-] *n* : admisión *f*, entrada *f*, acceso *m*

admittedly [æd'mɪtədli, əd-] *adv* : la verdad es que, lo cierto es que ⟨admittedly we went too fast : la verdad es que fuimos demasiado de prisa⟩

admonish [æd'mɑnɪʃ, əd-] *vt* : amonestar, reprender

admonition [,ædmə'nɪʃən] *n* : admonición *f*

ado [ə'du:] *n* **1** FUSS : ruido *m*, alboroto *m* **2** TROUBLE : dificultad *f*, lío *m* **3** without further ado : sin más preámbulos

adobe [ə'do:bi] *n* : adobe *m*

adolescence [,ædəl'ɛsənts] *n* : adolescencia *f*

adolescent¹ [,ædəl'ɛsənt] *adj* : adolescente, de adolescencia

adolescent² *n* : adolescente *mf*

adopt [ə'dɑpt] *vt* : adoptar

adoption [ə'dɑpʃən] *n* : adopción *f*

adoptive [ə'dɑptɪv] *adj* : adoptivo

adorable [ə'dorəbəl] *adj* : adorable, encantador

adorably [ə'dorəbli] *adv* : de manera adorable

adoration [,ædə'reɪʃən] *n* : adoración *f*

adore [ə'dor] *vt* **adored; adoring 1** WORSHIP : adorar **2** LOVE : querer, adorar **3** LIKE : encantarle (algo a uno), gustarle mucho (algo a uno) ⟨I adore your new dress : me encanta tu vestido nuevo⟩

adorn [ə'dɔrn] *vt* : adornar, ornar, engalanar

adornment [ə'dɔrnmənt] *n* : adorno *m*, decoración *f*

adrenaline [ə'drɛnələn] *n* : adrenalina *f*

adrift [ə'drɪft] *adj & adv* : a la deriva

adroit [ə'drɔɪt] *adj* : diestro, hábil — **adroitly** *adv*

adroitness [ə'drɔɪtnəs] *n* : destreza *f*, habilidad *f*

adult[1] [ə'dʌlt, 'æ,dʌlt] *adj* : adulto
adult[2] *n* : adulto *m*, -ta *f*
adulterate [ə'dʌltə,reɪt] *vt* -ated; -ating : adulterar
adulterous [ə'dʌltərəs] *adj* : adúltero
adultery [ə'dʌltəri] *n*, *pl* -teries : adulterio *m*
adulthood [ə'dʌlt,hʊd] *n* : adultez *f*, edad *f* adulta
advance[1] [æd'vænts, əd-] *v* -vanced; -vancing *vt* 1 : avanzar, adelantar ⟨to advance troops : avanzar las tropas⟩ 2 PROMOTE : ascender, promover 3 PROPOSE : proponer, presentar 4 : adelantar, anticipar ⟨they advanced me next month's salary : me adelantaron el sueldo del próximo mes⟩ — *vi* 1 PROCEED : avanzar, adelantarse 2 PROGRESS : progresar
advance[2] *adj* : anticipado ⟨advance notice : previo aviso⟩
advance[3] *n* 1 PROGRESSION : avance *m* 2 PROGRESS : adelanto *m*, mejora *f*, progreso *m* 3 RISE : aumento *m*, alza *f* 4 LOAN : anticipo *m*, préstamo *m* 5 in ∼ : por adelantado
advanced [æd'væntst, əd-] *adj* 1 DEVELOPED : avanzado, desarrollado 2 PRECOCIOUS : adelantado, precoz 3 HIGHER : superior
advancement [æd'væntsmənt, əd-] *n* 1 FURTHERANCE : fomento *m*, adelantamiento *m*, progreso *m* 2 PROMOTION : ascenso *m*
advantage [əd'væntɪdʒ, æd-] *n* 1 SUPERIORITY : ventaja *f*, superioridad *f* 2 GAIN : provecho *m*, partido *m* 3 to take advantage of : aprovecharse de
advantageous [,æd,væn'teɪdʒəs, -vən-] *adj* : ventajoso, provechoso — **advantageously** *adv*
advent ['æd,vɛnt] *n* 1 **Advent** : Adviento *m* 2 ARRIVAL : advenimiento *m*, venida *f*
adventure [æd'vɛntʃər, əd-] *n* : aventura *f*
adventurer [æd'vɛntʃərər, əd-] *n* : aventurero *m*, -ra *f*
adventurous [æd'vɛntʃərəs, əd-] *adj* 1 : intrépido, aventurero ⟨an adventurous traveler : un viajero intrépido⟩ 2 RISKY : arriesgado, aventurado
adverb ['æd,vərb] *n* : adverbio *m* — **adverbial** [æd'vərbiəl] *adj*
adversary ['ædvər,sɛri] *n*, *pl* -saries : adversario *m*, -ria *f*
adverse [æd'vərs, 'æd,] *adj* 1 OPPOSING : opuesto, contrario 2 UNFAVORABLE : adverso, desfavorable — **adversely** *adv*
adversity [æd'vərsəti, əd-] *n*, *pl* -ties : adversidad *f*
advertise ['ædvər,taɪz] *v* -tised; -tising *vt* : anunciar, hacerle publicidad a — *vi* : hacer publicidad, hacer propaganda
advertisement ['ædvər,taɪzmənt; æd 'vərtəzmənt] *n* : anuncio *m*

advertiser ['ædvər,taɪzər] *n* : anunciante *mf*
advertising ['ædvər,taɪzɪŋ] *n* : publicidad *f*, propaganda *f*
advice [æd'vaɪs] *n* : consejo *m*, recomendación *f* ⟨take my advice : sigue mis consejos⟩
advisability [æd,vaɪzə'bɪləti, əd-] *n* : conveniencia *f*
advisable [æd'vaɪzəbəl, əd-] *adj* : aconsejable, recomendable, conveniente
advise [æd'vaɪz, əd-] *v* -vised; -vising *vt* 1 COUNSEL : aconsejar, asesorar 2 RECOMMEND : recomendar 3 INFORM : informar, notificar — *vi* : dar consejo
adviser *or* **advisor** [æd'vaɪzər, əd-] *n* : consejero *m*, -ra *f*; asesor *m*, -sora *f*
advisory [æd'vaɪzəri, əd-] *adj* 1 : consultivo 2 in an advisory capacity : como asesor
advocacy ['ædvəkəsi] *n* : promoción *f*, apoyo *m*
advocate[1] ['ædvə,keɪt] *vt* -cated; -cating : recomendar, abogar por, ser partidario de
advocate[2] ['ædvəkət] *n* : defensor *m*, -sora *f*; partidario *m*, -ria *f*
adze ['ædz] *n* : azuela *f*
aeon ['iːən, 'iː,ɑn] *n* : eón *m*, siglo *m*, eternidad *f*
aerate ['ær,eɪt] *vt* -ated; -ating : gasear (un líquido), oxigenar (la sangre)
aerial[1] ['æriəl] *adj* : aéreo
aerial[2] *n* : antena *f*
aerie ['æri, 'ɪri, 'eɪəri] *n* : aguilera *f*
aerobic [,ær'oːbɪk] *adj* : aerobio, aeróbico ⟨aerobic exercises : ejercicios aeróbicos⟩
aerobics [,ær'oːbɪks] *ns & pl* : aeróbic *m*
aerodynamic [,æro:daɪ'næmɪk] *adj* : aerodinámico — **aerodynamically** [-mɪkli] *adv*
aerodynamics [,æro:daɪ'næmɪks] *n* : aerodinámica *f*
aeronautical [,ærə'nɔtɪkəl] *adj* : aeronáutico
aeronautics [,ærə'nɔtɪks] *n* : aeronáutica *f*
aerosol ['ærə,sɔl] *n* : aerosol *m*
aerospace[1] ['æro:,speɪs] *adj* : aeroespacial
aerospace[2] *n* : espacio *m*
aesthetic [ɛs'θɛtɪk] *adj* : estético — **aesthetically** [-tɪkli] *adv*
aesthetics [ɛs'θɛtɪks] *n* : estética *f*
afar [ə'fɑr] *adv* : lejos, a lo lejos
affability [,æfə'bɪləti] *n* : afabilidad *f*
affable ['æfəbəl] *adj* : afable — **affably** *adv*
affair [ə'fær] *n* 1 MATTER : asunto *m*, cuestión *f*, caso *m* 2 EVENT : ocasión *f*, acontecimiento *m* 3 LIAISON : amorío *m*, aventura *f* 4 business affairs : negocios *mpl* 5 current affairs : actualidades *fpl*
affect [ə'fɛkt, æ-] *vt* 1 INFLUENCE, TOUCH : afectar, tocar 2 FEIGN : fingir

affectation [ˌæˌfɛkˈteɪʃən] *n* : afectación *f*

affected [əˈfɛktəd, æ-] *adj* **1** FEIGNED : afectado, fingido **2** MOVED : conmovido

affecting [əˈfɛktɪŋ, æ-] *adj* : conmovedor

affection [əˈfɛkʃən] *n* : afecto *m*, cariño *m*

affectionate [əˈfɛkʃənət] *adj* : afectuoso, cariñoso — **affectionately** *adv*

affidavit [ˌæfəˈdeɪvət, ˈæfə-] *n* : declaración *f* jurada, affidávit *m*

affiliate¹ [əˈfɪliˌeɪt] *v* -ated; -ating *vt* : afiliar, asociar ⟨to be affiliated with : estar afiliado a⟩

affiliate² [əˈfɪliət] *n* : afiliado *m*, -da *f* (persona), filial *f* (organización)

affiliation [əˌfɪliˈeɪʃən] *n* : afiliación *f*, filiación *f*

affinity [əˈfɪnəti] *n*, *pl* -ties : afinidad *f*

affirm [əˈfərm] *vt* : afirmar, aseverar, declarar

affirmation [ˌæfərˈmeɪʃən] *n* : afirmación *f*, aserto *m*, declaración *f*

affirmative¹ [əˈfərmətɪv] *adj* : afirmativo ⟨affirmative action : acción afirmativa⟩

affirmative² *n* **1** : afirmativa *f* **2 to answer in the affirmative** : responder afirmativamente, dar una respuesta afirmativa

affix [əˈfɪks] *vt* : fijar, poner, pegar

afflict [əˈflɪkt] *vt* **1** : afligir, aquejar **2 to be afflicted with** : padecer de, sufrir de

affliction [əˈflɪkʃən] *n* **1** TRIBULATION : aflicción *f*, tribulación *f* **2** AILMENT : enfermedad *f*, padecimiento *m*

affluence [ˈæˌfluːənts; æˈfluː-, ə-] *n* : afluencia *f*, abundancia *f*, prosperidad *f*

affluent [ˈæˌfluːənt; æˈfluː-, ə-] *adj* : próspero, adinerado

afford [əˈford] *vt* **1** : tener los recursos para, permitirse el lujo de ⟨I can afford it : puedo permitírmelo, tengo con que comprarlo⟩ **2** PROVIDE : ofrecer, proporcionar, dar

affront¹ [əˈfrʌnt] *vt* : afrentar, insultar, ofender

affront² *n* : afrenta *f*, insulto *m*, ofensa *f*

Afghan [ˈæfˌgæn, -gən] *n* : afgano *m*, -na *f* — **Afghan** *adj*

afire [əˈfaɪr] *adj* : ardiendo, en llamas

aflame [əˈfleɪm] *adj* : llameante, en llamas

afloat [əˈfloːt] *adv & adj* : a flote

afoot [əˈfʊt] *adj* **1** WALKING : a pie, andando **2** UNDER WAY : en marcha ⟨something suspicious is afoot : algo sospechoso se está tramando⟩

aforementioned [əˈforˈmɛntʃənd] *adj* : antedicho, susodicho

aforesaid [əˈforˌsɛd] *adj* : antes mencionado, antedicho

afraid [əˈfreɪd] *adj* **1 to be afraid** : tener miedo **2 to be afraid that** : temerse que ⟨I'm afraid not : me temo que no⟩

afresh [əˈfrɛʃ] *adv* **1** : de nuevo, otra vez **2 to start afresh** : volver a empezar

African [ˈæfrɪkən] *n* : africano *m*, -na *f* — **African** *adj*

Afro–American¹ [ˌæfroəˈmɛrɪkən] *adj* : afroamericano *m*, -na *f*

Afro–American² *n* : afroamericano

aft [ˈæft] *adv* : a popa

after¹ [ˈæftər] *adv* **1** AFTERWARD : después **2** BEHIND : detrás, atrás

after² *adj* : posterior, siguiente ⟨in after years : en los años posteriores⟩

after³ *conj* : después de, después de que ⟨after we ate : después de que comimos, después de comer⟩

after⁴ *prep* **1** FOLLOWING : después de, tras ⟨after Saturday : después del sábado⟩ ⟨day after day : día tras día⟩ **2** BEHIND : tras de, después de ⟨I ran after the dog : corrí tras del perro⟩ **3** CONCERNING : por ⟨they asked after you : preguntaron por ti⟩ **4 after all** : después de todo

aftereffect [ˈæftərɪˌfɛkt] *n* : efecto *m* secundario

afterlife [ˈæftərˌlaɪf] *n* : vida *f* venidera, vida *f* después de la muerte

aftermath [ˈæftərˌmæθ] *n* : consecuencias *fpl*, resultados *mpl*

afternoon [ˌæftərˈnuːn] *n* : tarde *f*

aftertaste [ˈæftərˌteɪst] *n* : resabio *m*, regusto *m*

afterthought [ˈæftərˌθɔt] *n* : ocurrencia *f* tardía, idea *f* tardía

afterward [ˈæftərwərd] *or* **afterwards** [-wərdz] *adv* : después, luego ⟨soon afterward : poco después⟩

again [əˈgɛn, -ˈgɪn] *adv* **1** ANEW, OVER : de nuevo, otra vez **2** BESIDES : además **3 then again** : por otra parte ⟨I may stay, then again I may not : puede ser que me quede, por otra parte, puede que no⟩

against [əˈgɛntst, -ˈgɪntst] *prep* **1** TOUCHING : contra ⟨against the wall : contra la pared⟩ **2** OPPOSING : contra, en contra de ⟨I will vote against the proposal : votaré en contra de la propuesta⟩ ⟨against the grain : a contrapelo⟩

agape [əˈgeɪp] *adj* : boquiabierto

agate [ˈægət] *n* : ágata *f*

age¹ [ˈeɪdʒ] *vi* **aged; aging** : envejecer, madurar

age² *n* **1** : edad *f* ⟨ten years of age : diez años de edad⟩ ⟨to be of age : ser mayor de edad⟩ **2** PERIOD : era *f*, siglo *m*, época *f* **3 old age** : vejez *f* **4 ages** *npl* : siglos *mpl*, eternidad *f*

aged *adj* **1** [ˈeɪdʒəd, ˈeɪdʒd] OLD : anciano, viejo, vetusto **2** [ˈeɪdʒd] (*indicating a specified age*) ⟨a girl aged 10 : una niña de 10 años de edad⟩

ageless [ˈeɪdʒləs] *adj* **1** YOUTHFUL : eternamente joven **2** TIMELESS : eterno, perenne

agency [ˈeɪdʒəntsi] *n*, *pl* -cies **1** : agencia *f*, oficina *f* ⟨travel agency : agencia de viajes⟩ **2 through the agency of** : a través de, por medio de

agenda [ə'dʒɛndə] *n* : agenda *f*, orden *m* del día

agent ['eɪdʒənt] *n* **1** MEANS : agente *m*, medio *m*, instrumento *m* **2** REPRESENTATIVE : agente *mf*, representante *mf*

aggravate ['ægrə‚veɪt] *vt* **-vated; -vating 1** WORSEN : agravar, empeorar **2** ANNOY : irritar, exasperar

aggravation [‚ægrə'veɪʃən] *n* **1** WORSENING : empeoramiento *m* **2** ANNOYANCE : molestia *f*, irritación *f*, exasperación *f*

aggregate¹ ['ægrɪ‚geɪt] *vt* **-gated; -gating** : juntar, sumar

aggregate² ['ægrɪgət] *adj* : total, global, conjunto

aggregate³ ['ægrɪgət] *n* **1** CONGLOMERATE : agregado *m*, conglomerado *m* **2** WHOLE : total *m*, conjunto *m*

aggression [ə'grɛʃən] *n* **1** ATTACK : agresión *f* **2** AGGRESSIVENESS : agresividad *f*

aggressive [ə'grɛsɪv] *adj* : agresivo — **aggressively** *adv*

aggressiveness [ə'grɛsɪvnəs] *n* : agresividad *f*

aggressor [ə'grɛsər] *n* : agresor *m*, -sora *f*

aggrieved [ə'gri:vd] *adj* : ofendido, herido

aghast [ə'gæst] *adj* : espantado, aterrado, horrorizado

agile ['ædʒəl] *adj* : ágil

agility [ə'dʒɪləti] *n, pl* **-ties** : agilidad *f*

agitate ['ædʒə‚teɪt] *v* **-tated; -tating** *vt* **1** SHAKE : agitar **2** UPSET : inquietar, perturbar — *vi* **to agitate against** : hacer campaña en contra de

agitation [‚ædʒə'teɪʃən] *n* : agitación *f*, inquietud *f*

agitator ['ædʒə‚teɪtər] *n* : agitador *m*, -dora *f*

agnostic [æg'nɑstɪk] *n* : agnóstico *m*, -ca

ago [ə'go:] *adv* : hace ⟨two years ago : hace dos años⟩ ⟨long ago : hace tiempo, hace mucho tiempo⟩

agog [ə'gɑg] *adj* : ansioso, curioso

agonize ['ægə‚naɪz] *vi* **-nized; -nizing** : tormentarse, angustiarse

agonizing ['ægə‚naɪzɪŋ] *adj* : angustioso, terrible — **agonizingly** [-zɪŋli] *adv*

agony ['ægəni] *n, pl* **-nies 1** PAIN : dolor *m* **2** ANGUISH : angustia *f*

agrarian [ə'grɛriən] *adj* : agrario

agree [ə'gri:] *v* **agreed; agreeing** *vt* ACKNOWLEDGE : estar de acuerdo ⟨he agreed that I was right : estuvo de acuerdo en que tenía razón⟩ — *vi* **1** CONCUR : estar de acuerdo **2** CONSENT : ponerse de acuerdo **3** TALLY : concordar **4 to agree with** : sentarle bien (a alguien) ⟨this climate agrees with me : este clima me sienta bien⟩

agreeable [ə'gri:əbəl] *adj* **1** PLEASING : agradable, simpático **2** WILLING : dispuesto **3** AGREEING : de acuerdo, conforme

agreeably [ə'gri:əbli] *adv* : agradablemente

agreement [ə'gri:mənt] *n* **1** : acuerdo *m*, conformidad *f* ⟨in agreement with : de acuerdo con⟩ **2** CONTRACT, PACT : acuerdo *m*, pacto *m*, convenio *m* **3** CONCORD, HARMONY : concordia *f*

agriculture ['ægrɪ‚kʌltʃər] *n* : agricultura *f* — **agricultural** [‚ægrɪ'kʌltʃərəl] *adj*

aground [ə'graʊnd] *adj* : encallado, varado

ahead [ə'hɛd] *adv* **1** : al frente, delante, adelante ⟨he walked ahead : caminó delante⟩ **2** BEFOREHAND : por adelantado, con antelación **3** LEADING : a la delantera **4 to get ahead** : adelantar, progresar

ahead of *prep* **1** : al frente de, delante de, antes de **2 to get ahead of** : adelantarse a

ahoy [ə'hɔɪ] *interj* **ship ahoy!** : ¡barco a la vista!

aid¹ ['eɪd] *vt* : ayudar, auxiliar

aid² *n* **1** HELP : ayuda *f*, asistencia *f* **2** ASSISTANT : asistente *mf*

aide ['eɪd] *n* : ayudante *mf*

AIDS ['eɪdz] *n* : SIDA *m*, sida *m*

ail ['eɪl] *vt* : molestar, afligir — *vi* : sufrir, estar enfermo

aileron ['eɪlə‚rɑn] *n* : alerón *m*

ailment ['eɪlmənt] *n* : enfermedad *f*, dolencia *f*, achaque *m*

aim¹ ['eɪm] *vt* **1** : apuntar (un arma), dirigir (una observación) **2** INTEND : proponerse, querer ⟨he aims to do it tonight : se propone hacerlo esta noche⟩ — *vi* **1** POINT : apuntar **2 to aim at** : aspirar a

aim² *n* **1** MARKSMANSHIP : puntería *f* **2** GOAL : propósito *m*, objetivo *m*, fin *m*

aimless ['eɪmləs] *adj* : sin rumbo, sin objeto

aimlessly ['eɪmləsli] *adv* : sin rumbo, sin objeto

air¹ ['ær] *vt* **1** : airear, ventilar ⟨to air out a mattress : airear un colchón⟩ **2** EXPRESS : airear, manifestar, comunicar **3** BROADCAST : transmitir, emitir

air² *n* **1** : aire *m* **2** MELODY : aire *m* **3** APPEARANCE : aire *m*, aspecto *m* **4 airs** *npl* : aires *mpl*, afectación *f* **5 by ~** : por avión (dícese de una carta), en avión (dícese de una persona) **6 to be on the air** : estar en el aire, estar emitiendo

airborne ['ær‚born] *adj* **1** : aerotransportado ⟨airborne troops : tropas aerotransportadas⟩ **2** FLYING : volando, en el aire

air–condition [‚ærkən'dɪʃən] *vt* : climatizar, condicionar con el aire

air conditioner [‚ærkən'dɪʃənər] *n* : acondicionador *m* de aire

air–conditioning [ˌærkən'dɪʃənɪŋ] *n*
: aire *m* acondicionado

aircraft ['ær,kræft] *ns & pl* **1** : avión *m*,
aeronave *f* **2 aircraft carrier** : portaaviones *m*

airfield ['ær,fi:ld] *n* : aeródromo *m*, campo *m* de aviación

air force *n* : fuerza *f* aérea

airlift ['ær,lɪft] *n* : puente *m* aéreo, transporte *m* aéreo

airline ['ær,laɪn] *n* : aerolínea *f*, línea *f*
aérea

airliner ['ær,laɪnər] *n* : avión *m* de pasajeros

airmail[1] ['ær,meɪl] *vt* : enviar por vía
aérea

airmail[2] *n* : correo *m* aéreo

airman ['ærmən] *n, pl* **-men** [-mən,
-,mɛn] **1** AVIATOR : aviador *m*, -dora *f*
2 : soldado *m* de la fuerza aérea

airplane ['ær,pleɪn] *n* : avión *m*

airport ['ær,port] *n* : aeropuerto *m*

airship ['ær,ʃɪp] *n* : dirigible *m*, zepelín
m

airstrip ['ær,strɪp] *n* : pista *f* de aterrizaje

airtight ['ær'taɪt] *adj* : hermético, herméticamente cerrado

airwaves ['ær,weɪvz] *npl* : radio *m*, televisión *f*

airy ['æri] *adj* **airier** [-iər]; **-est 1** DELI-
CATE, LIGHT : delicado, ligero **2**
BREEZY : aireado, bien ventilado

aisle ['aɪl] *n* : pasillo *m*, nave *f* lateral (de
una iglesia)

ajar [ə'dʒar] *adj* : entreabierto, entornado

akimbo [ə'kɪmbo] *adj & adv* : en jarras

akin [ə'kɪn] *adj* **1** RELATED : emparentado **2** SIMILAR : semejante,
parecido

alabaster ['ælə,bæstər] *n* : alabastro *m*

alacrity [ə'lækrəti] *n* : presteza *f*, prontitud *f*

alarm[1] [ə'larm] *vt* **1** WARN : alarmar,
alertar **2** FRIGHTEN : asustar

alarm[2] *n* **1** WARNING : alarma *f*, alerta *f*
2 APPREHENSION, FEAR : aprensión *f*,
inquietud *f*, temor *m* **3 alarm clock**
: despertador *m*

alarming [ə'larmɪŋ] *adj* : alarmante

alas [ə'læs] *interj* : ¡ay!

Albanian [æl'beɪniən] *n* : albanés *m*,
-nesa *f* — **Albanian** *adj*

albatross ['ælbə,trɔs] *n, pl* **-tross** *or*
-trosses : albatros *m*

albeit [ɔl'bi:ət, æl-] *conj* : aunque

albino [æl'baɪno] *n, pl* **-nos** : albino *m*,
-na *f*

album ['ælbəm] *n* : álbum *m*

albumen [æl'bju:mən] *n* **1** : clara *f* de
huevo **2** → **albumin**

albumin [æl'bju:mən] *n* : albúmina *f*

alchemist ['ælkəmɪst] *n* : alquimista *mf*

alchemy ['ælkəmi] *n, pl* **-mies** : alquimia
f

alcohol ['ælkə,hɔl] *n* **1** ETHANOL : alcohol *m*, etanol *m* **2** LIQUOR : alcohol
m, bebidas *fpl* alcohólicas

alcoholic[1] [ˌælkə'hɔlɪk] *adj* : alcohólico

alcoholic[2] *n* : alcohólico *m*, -ca *f*

alcoholism ['ælkəhɔ,lɪzəm] *n* : alcoholismo *m*

alcove ['æl,ko:v] *n* : nicho *m*, hueco *m*

alderman ['ɔldərmən] *n, pl* **-men** [-mən,
-,mɛn] : concejal *mf*

ale ['eɪl] *n* : cerveza *f*

alert[1] [ə'lərt] *vt* : alertar, poner sobre aviso

alert[2] *adj* **1** WATCHFUL : alerta, vigilante
2 QUICK : listo, vivo

alert[3] *n* : alerta *f*, alarma *f*

alertly [ə'lərtli] *adv* : con listeza

alertness [ə'lərtnəs] *n* **1** WATCHFUL-
NESS : vigilancia *f* **2** ASTUTENESS : listeza *f*, viveza *f*

alfalfa [æl'fælfə] *n* : alfalfa *f*

alga ['ælgə] *n, pl* **-gae** ['æl,dʒi:] : alga *f*

algebra ['ældʒəbrə] *n* : álgebra *m*

algebraic [ˌældʒə'breɪk] *adj* : algebraico
— **algebraically** [-ɪkli] *adv*

Algerian [æl'dʒɪriən] *n* : argelino *m*, -na
f — **Algerian** *adj*

algorithm ['ælgə,rɪðəm] *n* : algoritmo *m*

alias[1] ['eɪliəs] *adv* : alias

alias[2] *n* : alias *m*

alibi[1] ['ælə,baɪ] *vi* : ofrecer una coartada

alibi[2] *n* **1** : coartada *f* **2** EXCUSE : pretexto *m*, excusa *f*

alien[1] ['eɪliən] *adj* **1** STRANGE : ajeno,
extraño **2** FOREIGN : extranjero, foráneo **3** EXTRATERRESTRIAL : extraterrestre

alien[2] *n* **1** FOREIGNER : extranjero *m*,
-ra *f*; forastero *m*, -ra *f* **2** EXTRATER-
RESTRIAL : extraterrestre *mf*

alienate ['eɪliə,neɪt] *vt* **-ated; -ating 1** ES-
TRANGE : alienar, enajenar **2 to alien-
ate oneself** : alejarse, distanciarse

alienation [ˌeɪliə'neɪʃən] *n* : alienación *f*,
enajenación *f*

alight [ə'laɪt] *vi* **1** DISMOUNT : bajarse,
apearse **2** LAND : posarse, aterrizar

align [ə'laɪn] *vt* : alinear

alignment [ə'laɪnmənt] *n* : alineación *f*,
alineamiento *m*

alike[1] [ə'laɪk] *adv* : igual, del mismo
modo

alike[2] *adj* : igual, semejante, parecido

alimentary [ˌælə'mɛntəri] *adj* **1** : alimenticio **2 alimentary canal** : tubo *m*
digestivo

alimony ['ælə,mo:ni] *n, pl* **-nies** : pensión *f* alimenticia

alive [ə'laɪv] *adj* **1** LIVING : vivo, viviente
2 LIVELY : animado, activo **3** ACTIVE
: vigente, en uso **4** AWARE : consciente
⟨alive to the danger : consciente del
peligro⟩

alkali ['ælkə,laɪ] *n, pl* **-lies** [-,laɪz] *or* **-lis**
[-,laɪz] : álcali *m*

alkaline ['ælkələn, -,laɪn] *adj* : alcalino

all[1] ['ɔl] *adv* **1** COMPLETELY : todo, completamente **2** : igual ⟨the score is 14 all
: es 14 iguales, están empatados a 14⟩

3 all the better : tanto mejor **4 all the more** : aún más, todavía más

all² *adj* : todo ⟨all the children : todos los niños⟩ ⟨in all likelihood : con toda probabilidad, con la mayor probabilidad⟩

all³ *pron* **1** : todo, -da ⟨they ate it all : lo comieron todo⟩ ⟨that's all : eso es todo⟩ ⟨enough for all : suficiente para todos⟩ **2 all in all** : en general **3 not at all** (*in negative constructions*) : en absoluto, para nada

Allah [ˈɑlɑ, ɑˈlɑ] *n* : Alá *m*

all–around [ˌɔləˈraʊnd] *adj* : completo, amplio

allay [əˈleɪ] *vt* **1** ALLEVIATE : aliviar, mitigar **2** CALM : aquietar, calmar

allegation [ˌælɪˈgeɪʃən] *n* : alegato *m*, acusación *f*

allege [əˈlɛdʒ] *vt* **-leged; -leging 1** : alegar, afirmar **2 to be alleged** : decirse, pretenderse ⟨she is alleged to be wealthy : se dice que es adinerada⟩

alleged [əˈlɛdʒd, əˈlɛdʒəd] *adj* : presunto, supuesto

allegedly [əˈlɛdʒədli] *adv* : supuestamente, según se alega

allegiance [əˈliːdʒənts] *n* : lealtad *f*, fidelidad *f*

allegorical [ˌæləˈgɔrɪkəl] *adj* : alegórico

allegory [ˈæləˌgori] *n, pl* **-ries** : alegoría *f*

alleluia [ˌɑləˈluːjə, ˌæ-] → **hallelujah**

allergen [ˈælərdʒən] *n* : alérgeno *m*

allergic [əˈlərdʒɪk] *adj* : alérgico

allergy [ˈælərdʒi] *n, pl* **-gies** : alergia *f*

alleviate [əˈliːviˌeɪt] *vt* **-ated; -ating** : aliviar, mitigar, paliar

alleviation [əˌliːviˈeɪʃən] *n* : alivio *m*

alley [ˈæli] *n, pl* **-leys 1** : callejón *m* **2 bowling alley** : bolera *f*

alliance [əˈlaɪənts] *n* : alianza *f*, coalición *f*

alligator [ˈæləˌgeɪtər] *n* : caimán *m*

alliteration [əˌlɪtəˈreɪʃən] *n* : aliteración *f*

allocate [ˈæləˌkeɪt] *vt* **-cated; -cating** : asignar, adjudicar

allocation [ˌæləˈkeɪʃən] *n* : asignación *f*, reparto *m*, distribución *f*

allot [əˈlɑt] *vt* **-lotted; -lotting** : repartir, distribuir, asignar

allotment [əˈlɑtmənt] *n* : reparto *m*, asignación *f*, distribución *f*

allow [əˈlaʊ] *vt* **1** PERMIT : permitir, dejar **2** ALLOT : conceder, dar **3** ADMIT, CONCEDE : admitir, conceder — *vi* **to allow for** : tener en cuenta

allowable [əˈlaʊəbəl] *adj* **1** PERMISSIBLE : permisible, lícito **2** : deducible ⟨allowable expenditure : gasto deducible⟩

allowance [əˈlaʊənts] *n* **1** : complemento *m* (para gastos, etc.), mesada *f* (para niños) **2 to make allowance(s)** : tener en cuenta, disculpar

alloy [ˈæˌlɔɪ] *n* : aleación *f*

all–purpose [ˈɔlˈpərpəs] *adj* : multiuso ⟨all-purpose flour : harina común⟩

all right¹ *adv* **1** YES : sí, por supuesto **2** WELL : bien ⟨I did all right : me fue bien⟩ **3** DEFINITELY : bien, ciertamente, sin duda ⟨he's sick all right : está bien enfermo⟩

all right² *adj* **1** OK : bien ⟨are you all right? : ¿estás bien?⟩ **2** SATISFACTORY : bien, bueno ⟨your work is all right : tu trabajo es bueno⟩

all–round [ˌɔlˈraʊnd] → **all–around**

allspice [ˈɔlspaɪs] *n* : pimienta *f* de Jamaica

allude [əˈluːd] *vi* **-luded; -luding** : aludir, referirse

allure¹ [əˈlʊr] *vt* **-lured; -luring** : cautivar, atraer

allure² *n* : atractivo *m*, encanto *m*

allusion [əˈluːʒən] *n* : alusión *f*

ally¹ [əˈlaɪ, ˈæˌlaɪ] *vi* **-lied; -lying** : aliarse

ally² [ˈæˌlaɪ, əˈlaɪ] *n* : aliado *m*, -da *f*

almanac [ˈɔlməˌnæk, ˈæl-] *n* : almanaque *m*

almighty [ɔlˈmaɪti] *adj* : omnipotente, todopoderoso

almond [ˈɑmənd, ˈɑl-, ˈæ-, ˈæl-] *n* : almendra *f*

almost [ˈɔlˌmoːst, ɔlˈmoːst] *adv* : casi, prácticamente

alms [ˈɑmz, ˈɑlmz, ˈælmz] *ns & pl* : limosna *f*, caridad *f*

aloe [ˈæloː] *n* : áloe *m*

aloft [əˈlɔft] *adv* : en alto, en el aire

alone¹ [əˈloːn] *adv* : sólo, solamente, únicamente

alone² *adj* : solo ⟨they're alone in the house : están solos en la casa⟩

along¹ [əˈlɔŋ] *adv* **1** FORWARD : adelante ⟨farther along : más adelante⟩ ⟨move along! : ¡circulen, por favor!⟩ **2 to bring along** : traer **3 ~ with** : con, junto con **4 all along** : desde el principio

along² *prep* **1** : por, a lo largo de ⟨along the coast : a lo largo de la costa⟩ **2** : en, en el curso de, por ⟨along the way : en el curso del viaje⟩

alongside¹ [əˌlɔŋˈsaɪd] *adv* : al costado, al lado

alongside² *or* **alongside of** *prep* : junto a, al lado de

aloof [əˈluːf] *adj* : distante, reservado

aloofness [əˈluːfnəs] *n* : reserva *f*, actitud *f* distante

aloud [əˈlaʊd] *adv* : en voz alta

alpaca [ælˈpækə] *n* : alpaca *f*

alphabet [ˈælfəˌbɛt] *n* : alfabeto *m*

alphabetical [ˌælfəˈbɛtɪkəl] *or* **alphabetic** [-ˈbɛtɪk] *adj* : alfabético — **alphabetically** [-tɪkli] *adv*

alphabetize [ˈælfəbəˌtaɪz] *vt* **-ized; -izing** : alfabetizar, poner en orden alfabético

alpine [ˈælˌpaɪn] *adj* : alpino

already [ɔlˈrɛdi] *adv* : ya

also [ˈɔlˌsoː] *adv* : también, además

altar [ˈɔltər] *n* : altar *m*

alter [ˈɔltər] *vt* : alterar, cambiar, modificar

alteration [ˌɔltəˈreɪʃən] *n* : alteración *f*, cambio *m*, modificación *f*
altercation [ˌɔltərˈkeɪʃən] *n* : altercado *m*, disputa *f*
alternate¹ [ˈɔltərˌneɪt] *v* **-nated; -nating** : alternar
alternate² [ˈɔltərnət] *adj* **1** : alterno ⟨alternate cycles of inflation and depression : ciclos alternos de inflación y depresión⟩ **2** : uno sí y otro no ⟨he cooks on alternate days : cocina un día sí y otro no⟩
alternate³ [ˈɔltərnət] *n* : suplente *mf*; sustituto *m*, -ta *f*
alternately [ˈɔltərnətli] *adv* : alternativamente, por turno
alternating current [ˈɔltərˌneɪtɪŋ] *n* : corriente *f* alterna
alternation [ˌɔltərˈneɪʃən] *n* : alternancia *f*, rotación *f*
alternative¹ [ɔlˈtərnətɪv] *adj* : alternativo
alternative² *n* : alternativa *f*
alternator [ˈɔltərˌneɪtər] *n* : alternador *m*
although [ɔlˈðoː] *conj* : aunque, a pesar de que
altitude [ˈæltəˌtuːd, -ˌtjuːd] *n* : altitud *f*, altura *f*
alto [ˈælˌtoː] *n, pl* **-tos** : alto *mf*, contralto *mf*
altogether [ˌɔltəˈgɛðər] *adv* **1** COMPLETELY : completamente, totalmente, del todo **2** ON THE WHOLE : en suma, en general
altruism [ˈæltruˌɪzəm] *n* : altruismo *m*
altruistic [ˌæltruˈɪstɪk] *adj* : altruista — **altruistically** [-tɪkli] *adv*
alum [ˈæləm] *n* : alumbre *m*
aluminum [əˈluːmənəm] *n* : aluminio *m*
alumna [əˈlʌmnə] *n, pl* **-nae** [-ˌniː] : exalumna *f*
alumnus [əˈlʌmnəs] *n, pl* **-ni** [-ˌnaɪ] : exalumno *m*
always [ˈɔlwiz, -ˌweɪz] *adv* **1** INVARIABLY : siempre, invariablemente **2** FOREVER : para siempre
am → be
amalgam [əˈmælgəm] *n* : amalgama *f*
amalgamate [əˈmælgəˌmeɪt] *vt* **-ated; -ating** : amalgamar, unir, fusionar
amalgamation [əˌmælgəˈmeɪʃən] *n* : fusión *f*, unión *f*
amaryllis [ˌæməˈrɪləs] *n* : amarilis *f*
amass [əˈmæs] *vt* : amasar, acumular
amateur [ˈæməˌtʃər, -tər, -ˌtur, -ˌtjur] *n* **1** : amateur *mf* **2** BEGINNER : principiante *mf*; aficionado *m*, -da *f*
amateurish [ˌæməˈtʃərɪʃ, -ˌtər-, -ˌtur-, -ˌtjur-] *adj* : amateur, inexperto
amaze [əˈmeɪz] *vt* **amazed; amazing** : asombrar, maravillar, pasmar
amazement [əˈmeɪzmənt] *n* : asombro *m*, sorpresa *f*
amazing [əˈmeɪzɪŋ] *adj* : asombroso, sorprendente — **amazingly** [-zɪŋli] *adv*
Amazon [ˈæməˌzan] *n* : amazona *f* (en mitología)
Amazonian [ˌæməˈzoːniən] *adj* : amazónico

ambassador [æmˈbæsədər] *n* : embajador *m*, -dora *f*
amber [ˈæmbər] *n* : ámbar *m*
ambergris [ˈæmbərˌgrɪs, -ˌgriːs] *n* : ámbar *m* gris
ambidextrous [ˌæmbɪˈdɛkstrəs] *adj* : ambidextro — **ambidextrously** *adv*
ambience *or* **ambiance** [ˈæmbiənts, ˈambiˌants] *n* : ambiente *m*, atmósfera *f*
ambiguity [ˌæmbəˈgjuːəti] *n, pl* **-ties** : ambigüedad *f*
ambiguous [æmˈbɪgjuəs] *adj* : ambiguo
ambition [æmˈbɪʃən] *n* : ambición *f*
ambitious [æmˈbɪʃəs] *adj* : ambicioso — **ambitiously** *adv*
ambivalence [æmˈbɪvələnts] *n* : ambivalencia *f*
ambivalent [æmˈbɪvələnt] *adj* : ambivalente
amble¹ [ˈæmbəl] *vi* **-bled; -bling** : ir tranquilamente, pasearse despreocupadamente
amble² *n* : paseo *m* tranquilo
ambulance [ˈæmbjələnts] *n* : ambulancia *f*
ambush¹ [ˈæmˌbuʃ] *vt* : emboscar
ambush² *n* : emboscada *f*, celada *f*
ameliorate [əˈmiːljəˌreɪt] *v* **-rated; -rating** IMPROVE : mejorar
amelioration [əˌmiːljəˈreɪʃən] *n* : mejora *f*
amen [ˈeɪmɛn, ˈa-] *interj* : amén
amenable [əˈmiːnəbəl, -ˈmɛ-] *adj* RESPONSIVE : susceptible, receptivo, sensible
amend [əˈmɛnd] *vt* **1** IMPROVE : mejorar, enmendar **2** CORRECT : enmendar, corregir
amendment [əˈmɛndmənt] *n* : enmienda *f*
amends [əˈmɛndz] *ns & pl* : compensación *f*, reparación *f*, desagravio *m*
amenity [əˈmɛnəti, -ˈmiː-] *n, pl* **-ties 1** PLEASANTNESS : lo agradable, amenidad *f* **2 amenities** *npl* : servicios *mpl*, comodidades *fpl*
American [əˈmɛrɪkən] *n* : americano *m*, -na *f* — **American** *adj*
American Indian *n* : indio *m* (americano), india *f* (americana)
amethyst [ˈæməθəst] *n* : amatista *f*
amiability [ˌeɪmiːəˈbɪləti] *n* : amabilidad *f*, afabilidad *f*
amiable [ˈeɪmiːəbəl] *adj* : amable, afable — **amiably** [-bli] *adv*
amicable [ˈæmɪkəbəl] *adj* : amigable, amistoso, cordial — **amicably** [-bli] *adv*
amid [əˈmɪd] *or* **amidst** [əˈmɪdst] *prep* : en medio de, entre
amino acid [əˈmiːno] *n* : aminoácido *m*
amiss¹ [əˈmɪs] *adv* : mal, fuera de lugar ⟨to take amiss : tomar a mal, llevar a mal⟩
amiss² *adj* **1** WRONG : malo, inoportuno **2 there's something amiss** : pasa algo, algo anda mal
ammeter [ˈæˌmiːtər] *n* : amperímetro *m*

ammonia [ə'mo:njə] n : amoníaco m
ammunition [ˌæmjə'nɪʃən] n 1 : municiones fpl 2 ARGUMENTS : argumentos
mpl
amnesia [æm'ni:ʒə] n : amnesia f
amnesty ['æmnəsti] n, pl -ties : amnistía
f
amoeba [ə'mi:bə] n, pl -bas or -bae [-ˌbi:]
: ameba f
amoebic [ə'mi:bɪk] adj : amébico
amok [ə'mʌk, -'mɑk] adv to run amok
: correr a ciegas, enloquecerse, desbocarse (dícese de la economía, etc.)
among [ə'mʌŋ] prep : entre
amoral [eɪ'mɔrəl] adj : amoral
amorous ['æmərəs] adj 1 PASSIONATE
: enamoradizo, apasionado 2 ENAM-
ORED : enamorado 3 LOVING
: amoroso, cariñoso
amorously ['æmərəsli] adv : con cariño
amorphous [ə'mɔrfəs] adj : amorfo, informe
amortize ['æmərˌtaɪz, ə'mɔr-] vt -tized;
-tizing : amortizar
amount[1] [ə'maʊnt] vi to amount to 1
: equivaler a, significar ⟨that amounts
to treason : eso equivale a la traición⟩
2 : ascender (a) ⟨my debts amount to
$2000 : mis deudas ascienden a $2000⟩
amount[2] n : cantidad f, suma f
ampere ['æmˌpɪr] n : amperio m
ampersand ['æmpərˌsænd] n : el signo
&
amphetamine [æm'fɛtəˌmi:n] n : anfetamina f
amphibian [æm'fɪbiən] n : anfibio m
amphibious [æm'fɪbiəs] adj : anfibio
amphitheater ['æmfəˌθi:ətər] n : anfiteatro m
ample ['æmpəl] adj -pler; -plest 1
LARGE, SPACIOUS : amplio, extenso,
grande 2 ABUNDANT : abundante, generoso
amplifier ['æmpləˌfaɪər] n : amplificador
m
amplify ['æmpləˌfaɪ] vt -fied; -fying : amplificar
amply ['æmpli] adv : ampliamente,
abundantemente, suficientemente
amputate ['æmpjəˌteɪt] vt -tated; -tating
: amputar
amputation [ˌæmpjə'teɪʃən] n : amputación f
amuck [ə'mʌk] → amok
amulet ['æmjələt] n : amuleto m, talismán m
amuse [ə'mju:z] vt amused; amusing 1
ENTERTAIN : entretener, distraer 2
: hacer reír, divertir ⟨the joke amused
us : la broma nos hizo reír⟩
amusement [ə'mju:zmənt] n 1 ENTER-
TAINMENT : diversión f, entretenimiento m, pasatiempo m 2 LAUGHTER
: risa f
an art → a[2]
anachronism [ə'nækrəˌnɪzəm] n : anacronismo m
anachronistic [əˌnækrə'nɪstɪk] adj : anacrónico

anaconda [ˌænə'kɑndə] n : anaconda f
anagram ['ænəˌgræm] n : anagrama m
anal ['eɪnəl] adj : anal
analgesic [ˌænəl'dʒi:zɪk, -sɪk] n : analgésico m
analog ['ænəˌlɔg] adj : analógico
analogical [ˌænə'lɑdʒɪkəl] adj : analógico — analogically [-kli] adv
analogous [ə'næləgəs] adj : análogo
analogy [ə'nælədʒi] n, pl -gies : analogía
f
analysis [ə'næləsəs] n, pl -yses [-ˌsi:z] 1
: análisis m 2 PSYCHOANALYSIS : psicoanálisis m
analyst ['ænəlɪst] n 1 : analista mf 2 PSY-
CHOANALYST : psicoanalista mf
analytic [ˌænə'lɪtɪk] or analytical [-tɪkəl]
adj : analítico — analytically [-tɪkli]
adv
analyze ['ænəˌlaɪz] vt -lyzed; -lyzing
: analizar
anarchic [æ'nɑrkɪk] adj : anárquico —
anarchically [-kɪkli] adv
anarchism ['ænərˌkɪzəm, -nɑr-] n : anarquismo m
anarchist ['ænərkɪst, -nɑr-] n : anarquista mf
anarchy ['ænərki, -nɑr-] n : anarquía f
anathema [ə'næθəmə] n : anatema m
anatomic [ˌænə'tɑmɪk] or anatomical
[-mɪkəl] adj : anatómico — anatomi-
cally [-mɪkli] adv
anatomy [ə'nætəmi] n, pl -mies : anatomía f
ancestor ['ænˌsɛstər] n : antepasado m,
-da f; antecesor m, -sora f
ancestral [æn'sɛstrəl] adj : ancestral, de
los antepasados
ancestry ['ænˌsɛstri] n 1 DESCENT : ascendencia f, linaje m, abolengo m 2 AN-
CESTORS : antepasados mpl, -das fpl
anchor[1] ['æŋkər] vt 1 MOOR : anclar,
fondear 2 FASTEN : sujetar, asegurar,
fijar
anchor[2] n 1 : ancla f 2 : presentador m,
-dora f (en televisión)
anchorage ['æŋkərɪdʒ] n : anclaje m
anchovy ['ænˌtʃo:vi, æn'tʃo:-] n, pl -vies
or -vy : anchoa f
ancient ['eɪntʃənt] adj 1 : antiguo ⟨an-
cient history : historia antigua⟩ 2 OLD
: viejo
ancients ['eɪntʃənts] npl : los antiguos
mpl
and ['ænd] conj 1 : y (e before words beginning with i- or hi-) 2 : con ⟨ham and
eggs : huevos con jamón⟩ 3 : a ⟨go and
see : ve a ver⟩ 4 : de ⟨try and finish it
soon : trata de terminarlo pronto⟩
Andalusian [ˌændə'lu:ʒən] n : andaluz
m, -luza f — Andalusian adj
Andean ['ændiən] adj : andino
andiron ['ænˌdaɪərn] n : morillo m
Andorran [æn'dɔrən] n : andorrano m,
-na f — Andorran adj
androgynous [æn'drɑdʒənəs] adj : andrógino
anecdotal [ˌænɪk'do:t̬əl] adj : anecdótico

anecdote ['ænɪkˌdoːt] n : anécdota f
anemia [ə'niːmiə] n : anemia f
anemic [ə'niːmɪk] adj : anémico
anemone [ə'nɛmən i] n : anémona f
anesthesia [ˌænəs'θiːʒə] n : anestesia f
anesthetic[1] [ˌænəs'θɛtɪk] adj : anestésico
anesthetic[2] n : anestésico m
anesthetist [ə'nɛsθətɪst] n : anestesista mf
anesthetize [ə'nɛsθəˌtaɪz] vt -tize; -tized : anestesiar
aneurysm ['ænjəˌrɪzəm] n : aneurisma mf
anew [ə'nuː, -'njuː] adv : de nuevo, otra vez, nuevamente
angel ['eɪndʒəl] n : ángel m
angelic [æn'dʒɛlɪk] or angelical [-lɪkəl] adj : angélico, angelical — angelically [-lɪkli] adv
anger[1] ['æŋgər] vt : enojar, enfadar
anger[2] n : enojo m, enfado m, ira f, cólera f, rabia f
angina [æn'dʒaɪnə] n : angina f
angle[1] ['æŋgəl] v angled; angling vt DIRECT, SLANT : orientar, dirigir — vi FISH : pescar (con caña)
angle[2] n 1 : ángulo m 2 POINT OF VIEW : perspectiva f, punto m de vista
angler ['æŋglər] n : pescador m, -dora f
Anglican ['æŋglɪkən] n : anglicano m, -na f — Anglican adj
Anglo–Saxon[1] [ˌæŋglo'sæksən] adj : anglosajón
Anglo–Saxon[2] n : anglosajón m, -jona f
Angolan [æŋ'goːlən, æn-] n : angoleño m, -ña f — Angolan adj
angora [æŋ'gorə, æn-] n : angora f
angrily ['æŋgrəli] adv : furiosamente, con ira
angry ['æŋgri] adj -grier; -est : enojado, enfadado, furioso
anguish ['æŋgwɪʃ] n : angustia f, congoja f
anguished ['æŋgwɪʃt] adj : angustiado, acongojado
angular ['æŋgjələr] adj : angular (dícese de las formas), anguloso (dícese de las caras)
animal ['ænəməl] n 1 : animal m 2 BRUTE : bruto m, -ta f
animate[1] ['ænəˌmeɪt] vt -mated; -mating : animar
animate[2] ['ænəmət] adj : animado
animated ['ænəˌmeɪtəd] adj 1 LIVELY : animado, vivo, vivaz 2 animated cartoon : dibujos mpl animados
animation [ˌænə'meɪʃən] n : animación f
animosity [ˌænə'mɑsəti] n, pl -ties : animosidad f, animadversión f
anise ['ænəs] n : anís m
aniseed ['ænəsˌsiːd] n : anís m, semilla f de anís
ankle ['æŋkəl] n : tobillo m
anklebone ['æŋkəlˌboːn] n : taba f
annals ['ænəlz] npl : anales mpl, crónica f
anneal [ə'niːl] vt 1 TEMPER : templar 2 STRENGTHEN : fortalecer

annex[1] [ə'nɛks, 'æˌnɛks] vt : anexar
annex[2] ['æˌnɛks, -nɪks] n : anexo m, anejo m
annexation [ˌæˌnɛk'seɪʃən] n : anexión f
annihilate [ə'naɪəˌleɪt] vt -lated; -lating : aniquilar
annihilation [əˌnaɪə'leɪʃən] n : aniquilación f, aniquilamiento m
anniversary [ˌænə'vərsəri] n, pl -ries : aniversario m
annotate ['ænəˌteɪt] vt -tated; -tating : anotar
annotation [ˌænə'teɪʃən] n : anotación f
announce [ə'naʊnts] vt -nounced; -nouncing : anunciar
announcement [ə'naʊntsmənt] n : anuncio m
announcer [ə'naʊntsər] n : anunciador m, -dora f; comentarista mf; locutor m, -tora f
annoy [ə'nɔɪ] vt : molestar, fastidiar, irritar
annoyance [ə'nɔɪənts] n 1 IRRITATION : irritación f, fastidio m 2 NUISANCE : molestia f, fastidio m
annoying [ə'nɔɪɪŋ] adj : molesto, fastidioso, engorroso — annoyingly [-ɪŋli] adv
annual[1] ['ænjʊəl] adj : anual — annually adv
annual[2] n 1 : planta f anual 2 YEARBOOK : anuario m
annuity [ə'nuːəti] n, pl -ties : anualidad f
annul [ə'nʌl] vt annulled; annulling : anular, invalidar
annulment [ə'nʌlmənt] n : anulación f
anode ['æˌnoːd] n : ánodo m
anoint [ə'nɔɪnt] vt : ungir
anomalous [ə'nɑmələs] adj : anómalo
anomaly [ə'nɑməli] n, pl -lies : anomalía f
anonymity [ˌænə'nɪməti] n : anonimato m
anonymous [ə'nɑnəməs] adj : anónimo — anonymously adv
anorexia [ˌænə'rɛksiə] n : anorexia f
anorexic [ˌænə'rɛksɪk] adj : anoréxico
another[1] [ə'nʌðər] adj : otro
another[2] pron : otro, otra
answer[1] ['æntsər] vt 1 : contestar (a), responder (a) <to answer the telephone : contestar el teléfono> 2 FULFILL : satisfacer 3 to answer for : ser responsable de, pagar por <she'll answer for that mistake : pagará por ese error> — vi : contestar, responder
answer[2] n 1 REPLY : respuesta f, contestación f 2 SOLUTION : solución f
answerable ['æntsərəbəl] adj : responsable
ant ['ænt] n : hormiga f
antacid [ænt'æsəd, 'ænˌtæ-] n : antiácido m
antagonism [æn'tægəˌnɪzəm] n : antagonismo m, hostilidad f
antagonist [æn'tægənɪst] n : antagonista mf

antagonistic [æn͵tægə'nɪstɪk] *adj* : antagonista, hostil

antagonize [æn'tægə͵naɪz] *vt* **-nized; -nizing** : antagonizar

antarctic [ænt'ɑrktɪk, -'ɑrṭɪk] *adj* : antártico

antarctic circle *n* : círculo *m* antártico

anteater ['ænt͵iːtər] *n* : oso *m* hormiguero

antebellum [͵æntɪ'bɛləm] *adj* : prebélico

antecedent¹ [͵æntə'siːdənt] *adj* : antecedente, precedente

antecedent² *n* : antecedente *mf*; precursor *m*, -sora *f*

antelope ['æntəl͵oːp] *n, pl* **-lope** *or* **-lopes** : antílope *m*

antenna [æn'tɛnə] *n, pl* **-nae** [-͵niː, -͵naɪ] *or* **-nas** : antena *f*

anterior [æn'tɪriər] *adj* : anterior

anthem ['ænθəm] *n* : himno *m* ⟨national anthem : himno nacional⟩

anther ['ænθər] *n* : antera *f*

anthill ['ænt͵hɪl] *n* : hormiguero *m*

anthology [æn'θɑləʤi] *n, pl* **-gies** : antología *f*

anthracite ['ænθrə͵saɪt] *n* : antracita *f*

anthropoid¹ ['ænθrə͵pɔɪd] *adj* : antropoide

anthropoid² *n* : antropoide *mf*

anthropological [͵ænθrəpə'lɑʤɪkəl] *adj* : antropológico

anthropologist [͵ænθrə'pɑləʤɪst] *n* : antropólogo *m*, -ga *f*

anthropology [͵ænθrə'pɑləʤi] *n* : antropología *f*

antiabortion [͵æntiə'bɔrʃən, ͵æntaɪ-] *adj* : antiaborto

antiaircraft [͵ænti'ær͵kræft, ͵æntaɪ-] *adj* : antiaéreo

anti–American [͵æntiə'mɛrɪkən, ͵æntaɪ-] *adj* : antiamericano

antibiotic¹ [͵æntibaɪ'ɑtɪk, ͵æntaɪ-, -bi-] *adj* : antibiótico

antibiotic² *n* : antibiótico *m*

antibody ['ænti͵bɑdi] *n, pl* **-bodies** : anticuerpo *m*

antic¹ ['æntɪk] *adj* : extravagante, juguetón

antic² *n* : payasada *f*, travesura *f*

anticipate [æn'tɪsə͵peɪt] *vt* **-pated; -pating 1** FORESEE : anticipar, prever **2** EXPECT : esperar, contar con

anticipation [æn͵tɪsə'peɪʃən] *n* **1** FORESIGHT : previsión *f* **2** EXPECTATION : anticipación *f*, expectación *f*, esperanza *f*

anticipatory [æn'tɪsəpə͵tori] *adj* : en anticipación, en previsión

anticlimactic [͵æntiklaɪ'mæktɪk] *adj* : anticlimático, decepcionante

anticlimax [͵ænti'klaɪ͵mæks] *n* : anticlímax *m*

anticommunism [͵ænti'kɑmjə͵nɪzəm, ͵æntaɪ-] *n* : anticomunismo *m*

anticommunist¹ [͵ænti'kɑmjənɪst, ͵æntaɪ-] *adj* : anticomunista

anticommunist² *n* : anticomunista *mf*

antidemocratic [͵ænti͵dɛmə'krætɪk, ͵æntaɪ-] *adj* : antidemocrático

antidepressant [͵æntidi'prɛsənt] *n* : antidepresivo *m* — **antidepressant** *adj*

antidote ['ænti͵doːt] *n* : antídoto *m*

antidrug [͵ænti'drʌg, ͵æntaɪ-; 'ænti͵drʌg, 'æntaɪ-] *adj* : antidrogas

antifascist [͵ænti'fæʃɪst, ͵æntaɪ-] *adj* : antifascista

antifeminist [͵ænti'fɛmənɪst, ͵æntaɪ-] *adj* : antifeminista

antifreeze ['ænti͵friːz] *n* : anticongelante *m*

antigen ['æntɪʤən, -͵ʤɛn] *n* : antígeno *m*

antihistamine [͵ænti'hɪstə͵miːn, -mən] *n* : antihistamínico *m*

anti–imperialism [͵æntiɪm'pɪriə͵lɪzəm, ͵æntaɪ-] *n* : antiimperialismo *m*

anti–imperialist [͵æntiɪm'pɪriəlɪst, ͵æntaɪ-] *adj* : antiimperialista

anti–inflammatory [͵ætiɪn'flæmətori] *adj* : antiinflamatorio

anti–inflationary [͵æntiɪn'fleɪʃə͵nɛri, ͵æntaɪ-] *adj* : antiinflacionario

antimony ['æntə͵moːni] *n* : antimonio *m*

antipathy [æn'tɪpəθi] *n, pl* **-thies** : antipatía *f*, aversión *f*

antiperspirant [͵ænti'pərspərənt, ͵æntaɪ-] *n* : antitranspirante *m*

antiquarian¹ [͵æntə'kwɛriən] *adj* : antiguo, anticuario ⟨an antiquarian book : un libro antiguo⟩

antiquarian² *n* : anticuario *m*, -ria *f*

antiquary ['æntə͵kwɛri] *n* → **antiquarian²**

antiquated ['æntə͵kweɪṭəd] *adj* : anticuado, pasado de moda

antique¹ [æn'tiːk] *adj* **1** OLD : antiguo, de época ⟨an antique mirror : un espejo antiguo⟩ **2** OLD-FASHIONED : anticuado, pasado de moda

antique² *n* : antigüedad *f*

antiquity [æn'tɪkwəṭi] *n, pl* **-ties** : antigüedad

antirevolutionary [͵ænti͵rɛvə'luː͵ʃə͵nɛri, ͵æntaɪ-] *adj* : antirrevolucionario

anti–Semitic [͵æntisə'mɪtɪk, ͵æntaɪ-] *adj* : antisemita

anti–Semitism [͵ænti'sɛmə͵tɪzəm, ͵æntaɪ-] *n* : antisemitismo *m*

antiseptic¹ [͵æntə'sɛptɪk] *adj* : antiséptico — **antiseptically** [-tɪkli] *adv*

antiseptic² *n* : antiséptico *m*

antismoking [͵ænti'smoː͵kɪŋ, ͵æntaɪ-] *adj* : antitabaco

antisocial [͵ænti'soː͵ʃəl, ͵æntaɪ-] *adj* **1** : antisocial **2** UNSOCIABLE : poco sociable

antitheft [͵ænti'θɛft, ͵æntaɪ-] *adj* : antirrobo

antithesis [æn'tɪθəsɪs] *n, pl* **-eses** [-͵siːz] : antítesis *f*

antitoxin [͵ænti'tɑksən, ͵æntaɪ-] *n* : antitoxina *f*

antitrust [͵ænti'trʌst, ͵æntaɪ-] *adj* : antimonopolista

antler ['æntlər] *n* : asta *f*, cuerno *m*

antonym ['æntə,nɪm] *n* : antónimo *m*

anus ['eɪnəs] *n* : ano *m*

anvil ['ænvəl, -vɪl] *n* : yunque *m*

anxiety [æŋk'zaɪəti] *n, pl* **-eties 1** UNEASINESS : inquietud *f*, preocupación *f*, ansiedad *f* **2** APPREHENSION : ansiedad *f*, angustia *f*

anxious ['æŋkʃəs] *adj* **1** WORRIED : inquieto, preocupado, ansioso **2** WORRISOME : preocupante, inquietante **3** EAGER : ansioso, deseoso

anxiously ['æŋkʃəsli] *adv* : con inquietud, con ansiedad

any¹ ['ɛni] *adv* **1** : algo ⟨is it any better? : ¿está (algo) mejor?⟩ **2** : para nada ⟨it is not any good : no sirve para nada⟩

any² *adj* **1** : alguno ⟨is there any doubt? : ¿hay alguna duda?⟩ ⟨call me if you have any questions : llámeme si tiene alguna pregunta⟩ **2** : cualquier ⟨I can answer any question : puedo responder a cualquier pregunta⟩ **3** : todo ⟨in any case : en todo caso⟩ **4** : ningún ⟨he would not accept it under any circumstances : no lo aceptaría bajo ninguna circunstancia⟩

any³ *pron* **1** : alguno *m*, -na *f* ⟨are there any left? : ¿queda alguno?⟩ **2** : ninguno *m*, -na *f* ⟨I don't want any : no quiero ninguno⟩

anybody ['ɛni,bʌdi, -,bɑ-] → **anyone**

anyhow ['ɛni,haʊ] *adv* **1** HAPHAZARDLY : de cualquier manera **2** IN ANY CASE : de todos modos, en todo caso

anymore [ɛni'mor] *adv* **1** : ya, ya más ⟨he doesn't dance anymore : ya no baila más⟩ **2** : todavía ⟨do they sing anymore? : ¿cantan todavía?⟩

anyone ['ɛni,wʌn] *pron* **1** : alguien ⟨is anyone here? : ¿hay alguien aquí?⟩ ⟨if anyone wants to come : si alguno quiere venir⟩ **2** : cualquiera ⟨anyone can play : cualquiera puede jugar⟩ **3** : nadie ⟨I don't want anyone here : no quiero a nadie aquí⟩

anyplace ['ɛni,pleɪs] → **anywhere**

anything ['ɛni,θɪŋ] *pron* **1** : algo, alguna cosa ⟨do you want anything? : ¿quieres algo?, ¿quieres alguna cosa?⟩ **2** : nada ⟨hardly anything : casi nada⟩ **3** : cualquier cosa ⟨I eat anything : como de todo⟩

anytime ['ɛni,taɪm] *adv* : en cualquier momento, a cualquier hora, cuando sea

anyway ['ɛni,weɪ] → **anyhow**

anywhere ['ɛni,hwɛr] *adv* **1** : en algún sitio, en alguna parte ⟨do you see it anywhere? : ¿lo ves en alguna parte?⟩ **2** : en ningún sitio, por ninguna parte ⟨I can't find it anywhere : no puedo encontrarlo por ninguna parte⟩ **3** : en cualquier parte, dondequiera, donde sea ⟨put it anywhere : ponlo dondequiera⟩

aorta [eɪ'ɔrtə] *n, pl* **-tas** *or* **-tae** [-ṭi, -ṭaɪ] : aorta *f*

Apache [ə'pætʃi] *n, pl* **Apache** *or* **Apaches** : apache *mf*

apart [ə'pɑrt] *adv* **1** SEPARATELY : aparte, separadamente **2** ASIDE : aparte, a un lado **3 to fall apart** : deshacerse, hacerse pedazos **4 to take apart** : desmontar, desmantelar

apartheid [ə'pɑr,teɪt, -,taɪt] *n* : apartheid *m*

apartment [ə'pɑrtmənt] *n* : apartamento *m*, departamento *m*, piso *m Spain*

apathetic [,æpə'θɛṭɪk] *adj* : apático, indiferente — **apathetically** [-ṭɪkli] *adv*

apathy ['æpəθi] *n* : apatía *f*, indiferencia *f*

ape¹ ['eɪp] *vt* **aped; aping** : imitar, remedar

ape² *n* : simio *m*; mono *m*, -na *f*

aperitif [ə,pɛrə'tiːf] *n* : aperitivo *m*

aperture ['æpərtʃər, -,tʃʊr] *n* : abertura *f*, rendija *f*, apertura *f* (en fotografía)

apex ['eɪ,pɛks] *n, pl* **apexes** *or* **apices** ['eɪpə,siːz, 'æ-] : ápice *m*, cúspide *f*, cima *f*

aphid ['eɪfɪd, 'æ-] *n* : áfido *m*

aphorism ['æfə,rɪzəm] *n* : aforismo *m*

aphrodisiac [,æfrə'diːzi,æk, -'dɪ-] *n* : afrodisíaco *m*

apiary ['eɪpi,ɛri] *n, pl* **-aries** : apiario *m*, colmenar *m*

apiece [ə'piːs] *adv* : cada uno

aplenty [ə'plɛnti] *adj* : en abundancia

aplomb [ə'plɑm, -'plʌm] *n* : aplomo *m*

apocalypse [ə'pɑkə,lɪps] *n* : apocalipsis *m*

apocalyptic [ə,pɑkə'lɪptɪk] *adj* : apocalíptico

apocrypha [ə'pɑkrəfə] *n* : textos *mpl* apócrifos

apocryphal [ə'pɑkrəfəl] *adj* : apócrifo

apologetic [ə,pɑlə'dʒɛṭɪk] *adj* : lleno de disculpas

apologetically [ə,pɑlə'dʒɛṭɪkli] *adv* : disculpándose, con aire de disculpas

apologize [ə'pɑlə,dʒaɪz] *vi* **-gized; -gizing** : disculparse, pedir perdón

apology [ə'pɑlədʒi] *n, pl* **-gies** : disculpa *f*, excusa *f*

apoplectic [,æpə'plɛktɪk] *adj* : apoplético

apoplexy ['æpə,plɛksi] *n* : apoplejía *f*

apostasy [ə'pɑstəsi] *n, pl* **-sies** : apostasía *f*

apostate [ə'pɑs,teɪt] *n* : apóstata *mf*

apostle [ə'pɑsəl] *n* : apóstol *m*

apostolic [,æpə'stɑlɪk] *adj* : apostólico

apostrophe [ə'pɑstrə,fiː] *n* : apóstrofo *m* (ortográfico)

apothecary [ə'pɑθə,kɛri] *n, pl* **-caries** : boticario *m*, -ria *f*

appall [ə'pɔl] *vt* : consternar, horrorizar

apparatus [,æpə'ræṭəs, -'reɪ-] *n, pl* **-tuses** *or* **-tus** : aparato *m*, equipo *m*

apparel [ə'pærəl] *n* : atavío *m*, ropa *f*

apparent [ə'pærənt] *adj* **1** VISIBLE : visible **2** OBVIOUS : claro, evidente, manifiesto **3** SEEMING : aparente, ostensible

apparently [ə'pærəntli] *adv* : aparentemente, al parecer

apparition [ˌæpə'rɪʃən] *n* : aparición *f*, visión *f*

appeal[1] [ə'pi:l] *vt* : apelar ⟨to appeal a decision : apelar contra una decisión⟩ — *vi* **1 to appeal for** : pedir, solicitar **2 to appeal to** : atraer a ⟨that doesn't appeal to me : eso no me atrae⟩

appeal[2] *n* **1** : apelación *f* (en derecho) **2** PLEA : ruego *m*, súplica *f* **3** ATTRACTION : atracción *f*, atractivo *m*, interés *m*

appear [ə'pɪr] *vi* **1** : aparecer, aparecerse, presentarse ⟨he suddenly appeared : apareció de repente⟩ **2** COME OUT : aparecer, salir, publicarse **3** : comparecer (ante el tribunal), actuar (en el teatro) **4** SEEM : parecer

appearance [ə'pɪrənts] *n* **1** APPEARING : aparición *f*, presentación *f*, comparecencia *f* (ante un tribunal), publicación *f* (de un libro) **2** LOOK : apariencia *f*, aspecto *m*

appease [ə'pi:z] *vt* **-peased; -peasing 1** CALM, PACIFY : aplacar, apaciguar, sosegar **2** SATISFY : satisfacer, mitigar

appeasement [ə'pi:zmənt] *n* : aplacamiento *m*, apaciguamiento *m*

append [ə'pɛnd] *vt* : agregar, añadir, adjuntar

appendage [ə'pɛndɪʤ] *n* **1** ADDITION : apéndice *m*, añadidura *f* **2** LIMB : miembro *m*, extremidad *f*

appendectomy [ˌæpən'dɛktəmi] *n, pl* **-mies** : apendicectomía *f*

appendicitis [ə,pɛndə'saɪtəs] *n* : apendicitis *f*

appendix [ə'pɛndɪks] *n, pl* **-dixes** *or* **-dices** [-də,si:z] : apéndice *m*

appetite ['æpə,taɪt] *n* **1** CRAVING : apetito *m*, deseo *m*, ganas *fpl* **2** PREFERENCE : gusto *m*, preferencia *f* ⟨the cultural appetites of today : los gustos culturales de hoy⟩

appetizer ['æpə,taɪzər] *n* : aperitivo *m*, entremés *m*, botana *f Mex*, tapa *f Spain*

appetizing ['æpə,taɪzɪŋ] *adj* : apetecible, apetitoso — **appetizingly** [-zɪŋli] *adv*

applaud [ə'plɔd] *v* : aplaudir

applause [ə'plɔz] *n* : aplauso *m*

apple ['æpəl] *n* : manzana *f*

appliance [ə'plaɪənts] *n* **1** : aparato *m* **2 household appliance** : electrodoméstico *m*, aparato *m* electrodoméstico

applicability [ˌæplɪkə'bɪləti, ə,plɪkə-] *n* : aplicabilidad *f*

applicable ['æplɪkəbəl, ə'plɪkə-] *adj* : aplicable, pertinente

applicant ['æplɪkənt] *n* : solicitante *mf*, aspirante *mf*, postulante *mf*; candidato *m*, -ta *f*

application [ˌæplə'keɪʃən] *n* **1** USE : aplicación *f*, empleo *m*, uso *m* **2** DILIGENCE : aplicación *f*, diligencia *f*, dedicación *f* **3** REQUEST : solicitud *f*, petición *f*, demanda *f*

applicator ['æplə,keɪtər] *n* : aplicador *m*

appliqué[1] [ˌæplə'keɪ] *vt* : decorar con apliques

appliqué[2] *n* : aplique *m*

apply [ə'plaɪ] *v* **-plied; -plying** *vt* **1** : aplicar (una sustancia, los frenos, el conocimiento) **2 to apply oneself** : dedicarse, aplicarse — *vi* **1** : aplicarse, referirse ⟨the rules apply to everyone : las reglas se aplican a todos⟩ **2 to apply for** : solicitar, pedir

appoint [ə'pɔɪnt] *vt* **1** NAME : nombrar, designar **2** FIX, SET : fijar, señalar, designar ⟨to appoint a date : fijar una fecha⟩ **3** EQUIP : equipar ⟨a well-appointed office : una oficina bien equipada⟩

appointee [ə,pɔɪn'ti:, ,æ-] *n* : persona *f* designada

appointment [ə'pɔɪntmənt] *n* **1** APPOINTING : nombramiento *m*, designación *f* **2** ENGAGEMENT : cita *f*, hora *f* **3** POST : puesto *m*

apportion [ə'porʃən] *vt* : distribuir, repartir

apportionment [ə'porʃənmənt] *n* : distribución *f*, repartición *f*, reparto *m*

apposite ['æpəzət] *adj* : apropiado, oportuno, pertinente — **appositely** *adv*

appraisal [ə'preɪzəl] *n* : evaluación *f*, valoración *f*, tasación *f*, apreciación *f*

appraise [ə'preɪz] *vt* **-praised; -praising** : evaluar, valorar, tasar, apreciar

appraiser [ə'preɪzər] *n* : tasador *m*, -dora *f*

appreciable [ə'pri:ʃəbəl, -'prɪʃiə-] *adj* : apreciable, sensible, considerable — **appreciably** [-bli] *adv*

appreciate [ə'pri:ʃi,eɪt, -'prɪ-] *v* **-ated; -ating** *vt* **1** VALUE : apreciar, valorar **2** : agradecer ⟨we appreciate his frankness : agradecemos su franqueza⟩ **3** UNDERSTAND : darse cuenta de, entender — *vi* : apreciarse, valorizarse

appreciation [ə,pri:ʃi'eɪʃən, -,prɪ-] *n* **1** GRATITUDE : agradecimiento *m*, reconocimiento *m* **2** VALUING : apreciación *f*, valoración *f*, estimación *f* ⟨art appreciation : apreciación artística⟩ **3** UNDERSTANDING : comprensión *f*, entendimiento *m*

appreciative [ə'pri:ʃətɪv, -'prɪ-; ə'pri:ʃi,eɪ-] *adj* **1** : apreciativo ⟨an appreciative audience : un público apreciativo⟩ **2** GRATEFUL : agradecido **3** ADMIRING : de admiración

apprehend [ˌæprɪ'hɛnd] *vt* **1** ARREST : aprehender, detener, arrestar **2** DREAD : temer **3** COMPREHEND : comprender, entender

apprehension [ˌæprɪ'hɛnʧən] *n* **1** ARREST : arresto *m*, detención *f*, aprehensión *f* **2** ANXIETY : aprensión *f*, ansiedad *f*, temor *m* **3** UNDERSTANDING : comprensión *f*, percepción *f*

apprehensive [ˌæprɪ'hɛntsɪv] *adj* : aprensivo, inquieto — **apprehensively** *adv*

apprentice¹ [ə'prɛntɪs] *vt* **-ticed; -ticing** : colocar de aprendiz

apprentice² *n* : aprendiz *m*, -diza *f*

apprenticeship [ə'prɛntɪsˌʃɪp] *n* : aprendizaje *f*

apprise [ə'praɪz] *vt* **-prised; -prising** : informar, avisar

approach¹ [ə'proːʧ] *vt* **1** NEAR : acercarse a **2** APPROXIMATE : aproximarse a **3** : abordar, dirigirse a ⟨I approached my boss with the proposal : me dirigí a mi jefe con la propuesta⟩ **4** TACKLE : abordar, enfocar, considerar — *vi* : acercarse, aproximarse

approach² *n* **1** NEARING : acercamiento *m*, aproximación *f* **2** POSITION : enfoque *m*, planteamiento *m* **3** OFFER : propuesta *f*, oferta *f* **4** ACCESS : acceso *m*, vía *f* de acceso

approachable [ə'proːʧəbəl] *adj* : accesible, asequible

approbation [ˌæprə'beɪʃən] *n* : aprobación *f*

appropriate¹ [ə'proːpriˌeɪt] *vt* **-ated; -ating 1** SEIZE : apropiarse de **2** ALLOCATE : destinar, asignar

appropriate² [ə'proːpriət] *adj* : apropiado, adecuado, idóneo — **appropriately** *adv*

appropriateness [ə'proːpriətnəs] *n* : idoneidad *f*, propiedad *f*

appropriation [əˌproːpri'eɪʃən] *n* **1** SEIZURE : apropiación *f* **2** ALLOCATION : asignación *f*

approval [ə'pruːvəl] *n* **1** : aprobación *f*, visto *m* bueno **2 on approval** : a prueba

approve [ə'pruːv] *vt* **-proved; -proving 1** : aprobar, sancionar, darle el visto bueno a **2 to approve of** : consentir en, aprobar ⟨he doesn't approve of smoking : está en contra del tabaco⟩

approximate¹ [ə'praksəˌmeɪt] *vt* **-mated; -mating** : aproximarse a, acercarse a

approximate² [ə'praksəmət] *adj* : aproximado

approximately [ə'praksəmətli] *adv* : aproximadamente, más o menos

approximation [əˌpraksə'meɪʃən] *n* : aproximación *f*

appurtenance [ə'pərtənənts] *n* : accesorio *m*

apricot ['æprəˌkat, 'eɪ-] *n* : albaricoque *m*, chabacano *m* *Mex*

April ['eɪprəl] *n* : abril *m*

apron ['eɪprən] *n* : delantal *m*, mandil *m*

apropos¹ [ˌæprə'poː, 'æprəˌpoː] *adv* : a propósito

apropos² *adj* : pertinente, oportuno, acertado

apropos of *prep* : a propósito de

apt ['æpt] *adj* **1** FITTING : apto, apropiado, acertado, oportuno **2** LIABLE : propenso, inclinado **3** CLEVER, QUICK : listo, despierto

aptitude ['æptəˌtuːd, -ˌtjuːd] *n* **1** : aptitud *f*, capacidad *f* ⟨aptitude test : prueba de aptitud⟩ **2** TALENT : talento *m*, facilidad *f*

aptly ['æptli] *adv* : acertadamente

aqua ['ækwə, 'ɑ-] *n* : color *m* aguamarina

aquarium [ə'kwæriəm] *n, pl* **-iums** *or* **-ia** [-iə] : acuario *m*

Aquarius [ə'kwæriəs] *n* : Acuario *mf*

aquatic [ə'kwɑtɪk, -'kwæ-] *adj* : acuático

aqueduct ['ækwəˌdʌkt] *n* : acueducto *m*

aqueous ['eɪkwiəs, 'æ-] *adj* : acuoso

aquiline ['ækwəˌlaɪn, -lən] *adj* : aguileño

Arab¹ ['ærəb] *adj* : árabe

Arab² *n* : árabe *mf*

arabesque [ˌærə'bɛsk] *n* : arabesco *m*

Arabian¹ [ə'reɪbiən] *adj* : árabe

Arabian² *n* → **Arab²**

Arabic¹ ['ærəbɪk] *adj* : árabe

Arabic² *n* : árabe *m* (idioma)

arable ['ærəbəl] *adj* : arable, cultivable

arbiter ['arbəˌtər] *n* : árbitro *m*, -tra *f*

arbitrary ['arbəˌtreri] *adj* : arbitrario — **arbitrarily** [ˌarbə'trɛrəli] *adv*

arbitrate ['arbəˌtreɪt] *v* **-trated; -trating** : arbitrar

arbitration [ˌarbə'treɪʃən] *n* : arbitraje *m*

arbitrator ['arbəˌtreɪtər] *n* : árbitro *m*, -tra *f*

arbor ['arbər] *n* : cenador *m*, pérgola *f*

arboreal [ar'boriəl] *adj* : arbóreo

arc¹ ['ark] *vi* **arced; arcing** : formar un arco

arc² *n* : arco *m*

arcade [ar'keɪd] *n* **1** ARCHES : arcada *f* **2** MALL : galería *f* comercial

arcane [ar'keɪn] *adj* : arcano, secreto, misterioso

arch¹ ['arʧ] *vt* : arquear, enarcar — *vi* : formar un arco, arquearse

arch² *adj* **1** CHIEF : principal **2** MISCHIEVOUS : malicioso, pícaro

arch³ *n* : arco *m*

archaeological [ˌarkiə'ladʒɪkəl] *adj* : arqueológico

archaeologist [ˌarki'alədʒɪst] *n* : arqueólogo *m*, -ga *f*

archaeology *or* **archeology** [ˌarki'alədʒi] *n* : arqueología *f*

archaic [ar'keɪɪk] *adj* : arcaico — **archaically** [-ɪkli] *adv*

archangel ['arkˌeɪndʒəl] *n* : arcángel *m*

archbishop [arʧ'bɪʃəp] *n* : arzobispo *m*

archdiocese [arʧ'daɪəsəs, -ˌsiːz, -ˌsiːs] *n* : archidiócesis *f*

archer ['arʧər] *n* : arquero *m*, -ra *f*

archery ['arʧəri] *n* : tiro *m* al arco

archetypal [ˌarki'taɪpəl] *adj* : arquetípico

archetype ['arkiˌtaɪp] *n* : arquetipo *m*

archipelago [ˌarkə'pɛləˌgoː, ˌarʧə-] *n, pl* **-goes** *or* **-gos** [-goːz] : archipiélago *m*

architect ['arkəˌtɛkt] *n* : arquitecto *m*, -ta *f*

architectural [ˌarkə'tɛktʃərəl] *adj* : arquitectónico — **architecturally** *adv*

architecture ['arkəˌtɛktʃər] *n* : arquitectura *f*

archive ['arˌkaɪv] *n or* **archives** ['arˌkaɪvz] *npl* : archivo *m*

archivist [ˈɑrkəvɪst, -ˌkaɪ-] n : archivero m, -ra f; archivista mf
archway [ˈɑrtʃˌweɪ] n : arco m, pasadizo m abovedado
arctic [ˈɑrktɪk, ˈɑrt-] adj 1 : ártico ⟨arctic regions : zonas árticas⟩ 2 FRIGID : glacial
arctic circle n : círculo m ártico
ardent [ˈɑrdənt] adj 1 PASSIONATE : ardiente, fogoso, apasionado 2 FERVENT : ferviente, fervoroso — **ardently** adv
ardor [ˈɑrdər] n : ardor m, pasión f, fervor m
arduous [ˈɑrdʒuəs] adj : arduo, duro, riguroso — **arduously** adv
arduousness [ˈɑrdʒuəsnəs] n : dureza f, rigor m
are → **be**
area [ˈæriə] n 1 SURFACE : área f, superficie f 2 REGION : área f, región f, zona f 3 FIELD : área f, terreno m, campo m (de conocimiento)
area code n : código m de la zona, prefijo m Spain
arena [əˈriːnə] n 1 : arena f, estadio m ⟨sports arena : estadio deportivo⟩ 2 : arena f, ruedo m ⟨the political arena : el ruedo político⟩
Argentine [ˈɑrdʒənˌtaɪn, -ˌtiːn] or **Argentinean** or **Argentinian** [ˌɑrdʒənˈtɪniən] n : argentino m, -na f — **Argentine** or **Argentinean** or **Argentinian** adj
argon [ˈɑrˌgɑn] n : argón m
argot [ˈɑrgət, -ˌgoː] n : argot m
arguable [ˈɑrgjuəbəl] adj : discutible
argue [ˈɑrˌgjuː] v -gued; -guing vi 1 REASON : argüir, argumentar, razonar 2 DISPUTE : discutir, pelear(se), alegar — vt 1 SUGGEST : sugerir 2 MAINTAIN : alegar, argüir, sostener 3 DISCUSS : discutir, debatir
argument [ˈɑrgjəmənt] n 1 REASONING : argumento m, razonamiento m 2 DISCUSSION : discusión f, debate m 3 QUARREL : pelea f, riña f, disputa f
argumentative [ˌɑrgjəˈmɛntətɪv] adj : discutidor
argyle [ˈɑrˌgaɪl] n : diseño m de rombos
aria [ˈɑriə] n : aria f
arid [ˈærəd] adj : árido
aridity [əˈrɪdəti, æ-] n : aridez f
Aries [ˈɛriːz, -iˌiːz] n : Aries mf
arise [əˈraɪz] vi **arose** [əˈroːz]; **arisen** [əˈrɪzən]; **arising** 1 ASCEND : ascender, subir, elevarse 2 ORIGINATE : originarse, surgir, presentarse 3 GET UP : levantarse
aristocracy [ˌærəˈstɑkrəsi] n, pl -cies : aristocracia f
aristocrat [əˈrɪstəˌkræt] n : aristócrata mf
aristocratic [əˌrɪstəˈkrætɪk] adj : aristocrático, noble
arithmetic¹ [ˌærɪθˈmɛtɪk] or **arithmetical** [-tɪkəl] adj : aritmético
arithmetic² [əˈrɪθməˌtɪk] n : aritmética f
ark [ˈɑrk] n : arca f

arm¹ [ˈɑrm] vt : armar — vi : armarse
arm² n 1 : brazo m (del cuerpo o de un sillón), manga f (de una prenda) 2 BRANCH : rama f, sección f 3 WEAPON : arma f ⟨to take up arms : tomar las armas⟩ 4 → **coat of arms**
armada [ɑrˈmɑdə, -ˈmeɪ-] n : armada f, flota f
armadillo [ˌɑrməˈdɪlo] n, pl -los : armadillo m
armament [ˈɑrməmənt] n : armamento m
armchair [ˈɑrmˌtʃɛr] n : butaca f, sillón m
armed [ˈɑrmd] adj 1 : armado ⟨armed robbery : robo a mano armada⟩ 2 **armed forces** : fuerzas fpl armadas
Armenian [ɑrˈmiːniən] n : armenio m, -nia f — **Armenian** adj
armistice [ˈɑrməstɪs] n : armisticio m
armor [ˈɑrmər] n : armadura f, coraza f
armored [ˈɑrmərd] adj : blindado, acorazado
armory [ˈɑrməri] n, pl -mories : arsenal m (almacén), armería f (museo), fábrica f de armas
armpit [ˈɑrmˌpɪt] n : axila f, sobaco m
army [ˈɑrmi] n, pl -mies 1 : ejército m (militar) 2 MULTITUDE : legión f, multitud f, ejército m
aroma [əˈroːmə] n : aroma f
aromatic [ˌærəˈmætɪk] adj : aromático
around¹ [əˈraʊnd] adv 1 : de circunferencia ⟨a tree three feet around : un árbol de tres pies de circunferencia⟩ 2 : alrededor, a la redonda ⟨for miles around : por millas a la redonda⟩ ⟨all around : por todos lados, todo alrededor⟩ 3 : por ahí ⟨they're somewhere around : deben estar por ahí⟩ 4 APPROXIMATELY : más o menos, aproximadamente ⟨around 5 o'clock : a eso de las 5⟩ 5 **to turn around** : darse la vuelta, voltearse
around² prep 1 SURROUNDING : alrededor de, en torno a 2 THROUGH : por, en ⟨he traveled around Mexico : viajó por México⟩ ⟨around the house : en casa⟩ 3 : a la vuelta de ⟨around the corner : a la vuelta de la esquina⟩ 4 NEAR : alrededor de, cerca de
arousal [əˈraʊzəl] n : excitación f
arouse [əˈraʊz] vt **aroused; arousing** 1 AWAKE : despertar 2 EXCITE : despertar, suscitar, excitar
arraign [əˈreɪn] vt : hacer comparecer (ante un tribunal)
arraignment [əˈreɪnmənt] n : orden m de comparecencia, acusación f
arrange [əˈreɪndʒ] vt **-ranged; -ranging** 1 ORDER : arreglar, poner en orden, disponer 2 SETTLE : arreglar, fijar, concertar 3 ADAPT : arreglar, adaptar
arrangement [əˈreɪndʒmənt] n 1 ORDER : arreglo m, orden m 2 ARRANGING : disposición f ⟨floral arrangement : arreglo floral⟩ 3 AGREEMENT : arreglo m, acuerdo m, convenio m 4 **arrange-**

ments *npl* : preparativos *mpl*, planes *mpl*

array¹ [ə'reɪ] *vt* **1** ORDER : poner en orden, presentar, formar **2** GARB : vestir, ataviar, engalanar

array² *n* **1** ORDER : orden *m*, formación *f* **2** ATTIRE : atavío *m*, galas *mpl* **3** RANGE, SELECTION : selección *f*, serie *f*, gama *f* ⟨an array of problems : una serie de problemas⟩

arrears [ə'rɪrz] *npl* : atrasos *mpl* ⟨to be in arrears : estar atrasado en los pagos⟩

arrest¹ [ə'rɛst] *vt* **1** APPREHEND : arrestar, detener **2** CHECK, STOP : detener, parar

arrest² *n* **1** APPREHENSION : arresto *m*, detención *f* ⟨under arrest : detenido⟩ **2** STOPPING : paro *m*

arrival [ə'raɪvəl] *n* : llegada *f*, venida *f*, arribo *m*

arrive [ə'raɪv] *vi* **-rived; -riving 1** COME : llegar, arribar **2** SUCCEED : triunfar, tener éxito

arrogance ['ærəgənts] *n* : arrogancia *f*, soberbia *f*, altanería *f*, altivez *f*

arrogant ['ærəgənt] *adj* : arrogante, soberbio, altanero, altivo — **arrogantly** *adv*

arrogate ['ærə,geɪt] *vt* **-gated; -gating to arrogate to oneself** : arrogarse

arrow ['æro] *n* : flecha *f*

arrowhead ['æro,hɛd] *n* : punta *f* de flecha

arroyo [ə'rɔɪo] *n* : arroyo *m*

arsenal ['arsənəl] *n* : arsenal *m*

arsenic ['arsənɪk] *n* : arsénico *m*

arson ['arsən] *n* : incendio *m* premeditado

arsonist ['arsənɪst] *n* : incendiario *m*, -ria *f*; pirómano *m*, -na *f*

art ['art] *n* **1** : arte *m* **2** SKILL : destreza *f*, habilidad *f*, maña *f* **3 arts** *npl* : letras *fpl* (en la educación) **4 fine arts** : bellas artes *fpl*

arterial [ar'tɪriəl] *adj* : arterial

arteriosclerosis [ar,tɪrioskləˈro:sɪs] *n* : arteriosclerosis *f*

artery ['artəri] *n, pl* **-teries 1** : arteria *f* **2** THOROUGHFARE : carretera *f* principal, arteria *f*

artesian well [ar'ti:ʒən] *n* : pozo *m* artesiano

artful ['artfəl] *adj* **1** INGENIOUS : ingenioso, diestro **2** CRAFTY : astuto, taimado, ladino, artero — **artfully** *adv*

arthritic [ar'θrɪtɪk] *adj* : artrítico

arthritis [ar'θraɪtəs] *n, pl* **-tides** [ar-'θrɪtə,di:z] : artritis *f*

arthropod ['arθrə,pad] *n* : artrópodo *m*

artichoke ['artə,tʃo:k] *n* : alcachofa *f*

article ['artɪkəl] *n* **1** ITEM : artículo *m*, objeto *m* **2** ESSAY : artículo *m* **3** CLAUSE : artículo *m*, cláusula *f* **4** : artículo *m* ⟨definite article : artículo determinado⟩

articulate¹ [ar'tɪkjə,leɪt] *vt* **-lated; -lating 1** UTTER : articular, enunciar, expresar **2** CONNECT : articular (en anatomía)

articulate² [ar'tɪkjələt] *adj* **to be articulate** : poder articular palabras, expresarse bien

articulately [ar'tɪkjələtli] *adv* : elocuentemente, con fluidez

articulateness [ar'tɪkjələtnəs] *n* : elocuencia *f*, fluidez *f*

articulation [ar,tɪkjə'leɪʃən] *n* **1** JOINT : articulación *f* **2** UTTERANCE : articulación *f*, declaración *f* **3** ENUNCIATION : articulación *f*, pronunciación *f*

artifact ['artə,fækt] *n* : artefacto *m*

artifice ['artəfəs] *n* : artificio *m*

artificial [,artə'fɪʃəl] *adj* **1** SYNTHETIC : artificial, sintético **2** FEIGNED : artificial, falso, afectado

artificially [,artə'fɪʃəli] *adv* : artificialmente, con afectación

artillery [ar'tɪləri] *n, pl* **-leries** : artillería *f*

artisan ['artəzən, -sən] *n* : artesano *m*, -na *f*

artist ['artɪst] *n* : artista *mf*

artistic [ar'tɪstɪk] *adj* : artístico — **artistically** [-tɪkli] *adv*

artistry ['artəstri] *n* : maestría *f*, arte *m*

artless ['artləs] *adj* : sencillo, natural, ingenuo, cándido — **artlessly** *adv*

artlessness ['artləsnəs] *n* : ingenuidad *f*, candidez *f*

arty ['arti] *adj* **artier; -est** : pretenciosamente artístico

as¹ ['æz] *adv* **1** : tan, tanto ⟨this one's not as difficult : éste no es tan difícil⟩ **2** : como ⟨some trees, as oak and pine : algunos árboles, como el roble y el pino⟩

as² *conj* **1** LIKE : como, igual que **2** WHEN, WHILE : cuando, mientras, a la vez que **3** BECAUSE : porque **4** THOUGH : aunque, por más que ⟨strange as it may appear : por extraño que parezca⟩ **5 as is** : tal como está

as³ *prep* **1** : de ⟨I met her as a child : la conocí de pequeña⟩ **2** LIKE : como ⟨behave as a man : compórtate como un hombre⟩

as⁴ *pron* : que ⟨in the same building as my brother : en el mismo edificio que mi hermano⟩

asbestos [æz'bɛstəs, æs-] *n* : asbesto *m*, amianto *m*

ascend [ə'sɛnd] *vi* : ascender, subir — *vt* : subir, subir a, escalar

ascendancy [ə'sɛndəntsi] *n* : ascendiente *m*, predominio *m*

ascendant¹ [ə'sɛndənt] *adj* **1** RISING : ascendente **2** DOMINANT : superior, dominante

ascendant² *n* **to be in the ascendant** : estar en alza, ir ganando predominio

ascension [ə'sɛnʃən] *n* : ascensión *f*

ascent [ə'sɛnt] *n* **1** RISE : ascensión *f*, subida *f*, ascenso *m* **2** SLOPE : cuesta *f*, pendiente *f*

ascertain [,æsər'teɪn] *vt* : determinar, establecer, averiguar

ascertainable [,æsər'teɪnəbəl] *adj* : determinable, averiguable

ascetic[1] [ə'sɛtɪk] *adj* : ascético
ascetic[2] *n* : asceta *mf*
asceticism [ə'sɛtə,sɪzəm] *n* : ascetismo *m*
ascribable [ə'skraɪbəbəl] *adj* : atribuible, imputable
ascribe [ə'skraɪb] *vt* **-cribed; -cribing** : atribuir, imputar
aseptic [eɪ'sɛptɪk] *adj* : aséptico
asexual [,eɪ'sɛkʃʊəl] *adj* : asexual
as for *prep* CONCERNING : en cuanto a, respecto a, para
ash ['æʃ] *n* **1** : ceniza *f* ⟨to reduce to ashes : reducir a cenizas⟩ **2** : fresno *m* (árbol)
ashamed [ə'ʃeɪmd] *adj* : avergonzado, abochornado, apenado — **ashamedly** [ə'ʃeɪmədli] *adv*
ashen ['æʃən] *adj* : lívido, ceniciento, pálido
ashore [ə'ʃor] *adv* **1** : en tierra **2 to go ashore** : desembarcar
ashtray ['æʃ,treɪ] *n* : cenicero *m*
Asian[1] ['eɪʒən, -ʃən] *adj* : asiático
Asian[2] *n* : asiático *m*, -ca *f*
aside [ə'saɪd] *adv* **1** : a un lado ⟨to step aside : hacerse a un lado⟩ **2** : de lado, aparte ⟨jesting aside : bromas aparte⟩ **3 to set aside** : guardar, apartar, reservar
aside from *prep* **1** BESIDES : además de **2** EXCEPT : aparte de, menos
as if *conj* : como si
asinine ['æsən,aɪn] *adj* : necio, estúpido
ask ['æsk] *vt* **1** : preguntar ⟨ask him if he's coming : pregúntale si viene⟩ **2** REQUEST : pedir, solicitar ⟨to ask a favor : pedir un favor⟩ **3** INVITE : invitar — *vi* **1** INQUIRE : preguntar ⟨I asked about her children : pregunté por sus niños⟩ **2** REQUEST : pedir ⟨we asked for help : pedimos ayuda⟩
askance [ə'skænts] *adv* **1** SIDELONG : de reojo, de soslayo **2** SUSPICIOUSLY : con recelo, con desconfianza
askew [ə'skju:] *adj* : torcido, ladeado
asleep [ə'sli:p] *adj* **1** : dormido, durmiendo **2 to fall asleep** : quedarse dormido
as of *prep* : desde, a partir de
asparagus [ə'spærəgəs] *n* : espárrago *m*
aspect ['æ,spɛkt] *n* : aspecto *m*
aspen ['æspən] *n* : álamo *m* temblón
asperity [æ'spɛrəṭi, ə-] *n, pl* **-ties** : aspereza *f*
aspersion [ə'spərʒən] *n* : difamación *f*, calumnia *f*
asphalt ['æs,fɔlt] *n* : asfalto *m*
asphyxia [æ'sfɪksiə, ə-] *n* : asfixia *f*
asphyxiate [æ'sfɪksi,eɪt] *v* **-ated; -ating** *vt* : asfixiar — *vi* : asfixiarse
asphyxiation [æ,sfɪksi'eɪʃən] *n* : asfixia *f*
aspirant ['æspərənt, ə'spaɪrənt] *n* : aspirante *mf*, pretendiente *mf*
aspiration [,æspə'reɪʃən] *n* **1** DESIRE : aspiración *f*, anhelo *m*, ambición *f* **2** BREATHING : aspiración *f*

aspire [ə'spaɪr] *vi* **-pired; -piring** : aspirar
aspirin ['æsprən, 'æspə-] *n, pl* **aspirin** *or* **aspirins** : aspirina *f*
ass ['æs] *n* **1** : asno *m* **2** IDIOT : imbécil *mf*, idiota *mf*
assail [ə'seɪl] *vt* : atacar, asaltar
assailant [ə'seɪlənt] *n* : asaltante *mf*, atacante *mf*
assassin [ə'sæsən] *n* : asesino *m*, -na *f*
assassinate [ə'sæsən,eɪt] *vt* **-nated; -nating** : asesinar
assassination [ə,sæsən'eɪʃən] *n* : asesinato *m*
assault[1] [ə'sɔlt] *vt* : atacar, asaltar, agredir
assault[2] *n* : ataque *m*, asalto *m*, agresión *f*
assay[1] [æ'seɪ, 'æ,seɪ] *vt* : ensayar
assay[2] ['æ,seɪ, æ'seɪ] *n* : ensayo *m*
assemble [ə'sɛmbəl] *v* **-bled; -bling** *vt* **1** GATHER : reunir, recoger, juntar **2** CONSTRUCT : ensamblar, montar, construir — *vi* : reunirse, congregarse
assembly [ə'sɛmbli] *n, pl* **-blies 1** MEETING : reunión *f* **2** CONSTRUCTING : ensamblaje *m*, montaje *m*
assemblyman [ə'sɛmblimən] *n, pl* **-men** [-mən, -,mɛn] : asambleísta *m*
assemblywoman [ə'sɛmbli,wʊmən] *n, pl* **-women** [-,wɪmən] : asambleísta *f*
assent[1] [ə'sɛnt] *vi* : asentir, consentir
assent[2] *n* : asentimiento *m*, aprobación *f*
assert [ə'sərt] *vt* **1** AFFIRM : afirmar, aseverar, mantener **2 to assert oneself** : imponerse, hacerse valer
assertion [ə'sərʃən] *n* : afirmación *f*, aseveración *f*, aserto *m*
assertive [ə'sərṭɪv] *adj* : firme, enérgico
assertiveness [ə'sərṭɪvnəs] *n* : seguridad *f* en sí mismo
assess [ə'sɛs] *vt* **1** IMPOSE : gravar (un impuesto), imponer **2** EVALUATE : evaluar, valorar, aquilatar
assessment [ə'sɛsmənt] *n* : evaluación *f*, valoración *f*
assessor [ə'sɛsər] *n* : evaluador *m*, -dora *f*; tasador *m*, -dora *f*
asset ['æ,sɛt] *n* **1** : ventaja *f*, recurso *m* **2 assets** *npl* : bienes *mpl*, activo *m* ⟨assets and liabilities : activo y pasivo⟩
assiduous [ə'sɪdʒuəs] *adj* : diligente, aplicado, asiduo — **assiduously** *adv*
assign [ə'saɪn] *vt* **1** APPOINT : designar, nombrar **2** ALLOT : asignar, señalar **3** ATTRIBUTE : atribuir, dar, conceder
assignment [ə'saɪnmənt] *n* **1** TASK : función *f*, tarea *f*, misión *f* **2** HOMEWORK : tarea *f*, asignación *f* *PRi*, deberes *mpl* *Spain* **3** APPOINTMENT : nombramiento *m* **4** ALLOCATION : asignación *f*
assimilate [ə'sɪmə,leɪt] *v* **-lated; -lating** *vt* : asimilar — *vi* : adaptarse, integrarse
assimilation [ə,sɪmə'leɪʃən] *n* : asimilación *f*
assist[1] [ə'sɪst] *vt* : asistir, ayudar
assist[2] *n* : asistencia *f*, contribución *f*

assistance [ə'sɪstənts] *n* : asistencia *f*, ayuda *f*, auxilio *m*

assistant [ə'sɪstənt] *n* : ayudante *mf*, asistente *mf*

associate[1] [ə'so:ʃi,eɪt, -si-] *v* **-ated; -ating** *vt* **1** CONNECT, RELATE : asociar, relacionar **2 to be associated with** : estar relacionado con, estar vinculado a — *vi* **to associate with** : relacionarse con, frecuentar

associate[2] [ə'so:ʃiət, -siət] *n* : asociado *m*, -da *f*; colega *mf*; socio *m*, -cia *f*

association [ə,so:ʃi'eɪʃən, -si-] *n* **1** ORGANIZATION : asociación *f*, sociedad *f* **2** RELATIONSHIP : asociación *f*, relación *f*

as soon as *conj* : en cuanto, tan pronto como

assorted [ə'sɔrtəd] *adj* : surtido

assortment [ə'sɔrtmənt] *n* : surtido *m*, variedad *f*, colección *f*

assuage [ə'sweɪdʒ] *vt* **-suaged; -suaging 1** EASE : aliviar, mitigar **2** CALM : calmar, aplacar **3** SATISFY : saciar, satisfacer

assume [ə'su:m] *vt* **-sumed; -suming 1** SUPPOSE : suponer, asumir **2** UNDERTAKE : asumir, encargarse de **3** TAKE ON : adquirir, adoptar, tomar ⟨to assume importance : tomar importancia⟩ **4** FEIGN : adoptar, afectar, simular

assumption [ə'sʌmpʃən] *n* : asunción *f*, presunción *f*

assurance [ə'ʃʊrənts] *n* **1** CERTAINTY : certidumbre *f*, certeza *f* **2** CONFIDENCE : confianza *f*, aplomo *m*, seguridad *f*

assure [ə'ʃʊr] *vt* **-sured; -suring** : asegurar, garantizar ⟨I assure you that I'll do it : te aseguro que lo haré⟩

assured [ə'ʃʊrd] *adj* **1** CERTAIN : seguro, asegurado **2** CONFIDENT : confiado, seguro de sí mismo

aster ['æstər] *n* : aster *m*

asterisk ['æstə,rɪsk] *n* : asterisco *m*

astern [ə'stərn] *adv* **1** BEHIND : detrás, a popa **2** BACKWARDS : hacia atrás

asteroid ['æstə,rɔɪd] *n* : asteroide *m*

asthma ['æzmə] *n* : asma *m*

asthmatic [æz'mætɪk] *adj* : asmático

as though → **as if**

astigmatism [ə'stɪgmə,tɪzəm] *n* : astigmatismo *m*

as to *prep* **1** ABOUT : sobre, acerca de **2** → **according to**

astonish [ə'stɑnɪʃ] *vt* : asombrar, sorprender, pasmar

astonishing [ə'stɑnɪʃɪŋ] *adj* : asombroso, sorprendente, increíble — **astonishingly** *adv*

astonishment [ə'stɑnɪʃmənt] *n* : asombro *m*, estupefacción *f*, sorpresa *f*

astound [ə'staʊnd] *vt* : asombrar, pasmar, dejar estupefacto

astounding [ə'staʊndɪŋ] *adj* : asombroso, pasmoso — **astoundingly** *adv*

astraddle [ə'strædəl] *adv* : a horcajadas

astral ['æstrəl] *adj* : astral

astray [ə'streɪ] *adv & adj* : perdido, extraviado, descarriado

astride [ə'straɪd] *adv* : a horcajadas

astringency [ə'strɪndʒəntsi] *n* : astringencia *f*

astringent[1] [ə'strɪndʒənt] *adj* : astringente

astringent[2] *n* : astringente *m*

astrologer [ə'strɑlədʒər] *n* : astrólogo *m*, -ga *f*

astrological [,æstrə'lɑdʒɪkəl] *adj* : astrológico

astrology [ə'strɑlədʒi] *n* : astrología *f*

astronaut ['æstrə,nɔt] *n* : astronauta *mf*

astronautic [,æstrə'nɔtɪk] *or* **astronautical** [-tɪkəl] *adj* : astronáutico

astronautics [,æstrə'nɔtɪks] *ns & pl* : astronáutica *f*

astronomer [ə'strɑnəmər] *n* : astrónomo *m*, -ma *f*

astronomical [,æstrə'nɑmɪkəl] *adj* **1** : astronómico **2** ENORMOUS : astronómico, enorme, gigantesco

astronomy [ə'strɑnəmi] *n, pl* **-mies** : astronomía *f*

astute [ə'stu:t, -'stju:t] *adj* : astuto, sagaz, perspicaz — **astutely** *adv*

astuteness [ə'stu:tnəs, -'stju:t-] *n* : astucia *f*, sagacidad *f*, perspicacia *f*

asunder [ə'sʌndər] *adv* : en dos, en pedazos ⟨to tear asunder : hacer pedazos⟩

as well as[1] *conj* : tanto como

as well as[2] *prep* BESIDES : además de, aparte de

as yet *adv* : aún, todavía

asylum [ə'saɪləm] *n* **1** REFUGE : refugio *m*, santuario *m*, asilo *m* **2 insane asylum** : manicomio *m*

asymmetrical [,eɪsə'mɛtrɪkəl] *or* **asymmetric** [-'mɛtrɪk] *adj* : asimétrico

asymmetry [,eɪ'sɪmətri] *n* : asimetría *f*

at ['æt] *prep* **1** : en ⟨at the top : en lo alto⟩ ⟨at peace : en paz⟩ ⟨at Ann's house : en casa de Ana⟩ **2** : a ⟨at the rear : al fondo⟩ ⟨at 10 o'clock : a las diez⟩ **3** : por ⟨at last : por fin⟩ ⟨to be surprised at something : sorprenderse por algo⟩ **4** : de ⟨he's laughing at you : está riéndose de ti⟩ **5** : para ⟨you're good at this : eres bueno para esto⟩

at all *adv* : en absoluto, para nada

ate → **eat**

atheism ['eɪθi,ɪzəm] *n* : ateísmo *m*

atheist ['eɪθiɪst] *n* : ateo *m*, atea *f*

atheistic [,eɪθi'ɪstɪk] *adj* : ateo

athlete ['æθ,li:t] *n* : atleta *mf*

athletic [æθ'lɛtɪk] *adj* : atlético

athletics [æθ'lɛtɪks] *ns & pl* : atletismo *m*

Atlantic [ət'læntɪk, æt-] *adj* : atlántico

atlas ['ætləs] *n* : atlas *m*

ATM [,eɪ,ti:'ɛm] *n* : cajero *m* automático

atmosphere ['ætmə,sfɪr] *n* **1** AIR : atmósfera *f*, aire *m* **2** AMBIENCE : ambiente *m*, atmósfera *f*, clima *m*

atmospheric [,ætmə'sfɪrɪk, -'sfɛr-] *adj* : atmosférico — **atmospherically** [-ɪkli] *adv*

atoll ['æ‚tɔl, 'eɪ-, -‚tɑl] *n* : atolón *m*
atom ['æt̬əm] *n* **1** : átomo *m* **2** SPECK : ápice *m*, pizca *f*
atomic [ə'tɑmɪk] *adj* : atómico
atomic bomb *n* : bomba *f* atómica
atomizer ['æt̬ə‚maɪzər] *n* : atomizador *m*, pulverizador *m*
atone [ə'to:n] *vt* **atoned; atoning to atone for** : expiar
atonement [ə'to:nmənt] *n* : expiación *f*, desagravio *m*
atop¹ [ə'tɑp] *adj* : encima
atop² *prep* : encima de, sobre
atrium ['eɪtriəm] *n*, *pl* **atria** [-triə] *or* **atriums 1** : atrio *m* **2** : aurícula *f* (del corazón)
atrocious [ə'tro:ʃəs] *adj* : atroz — **atrociously** *adv*
atrocity [ə'trɑsət̬i] *n*, *pl* **-ties** : atrocidad *f*
atrophy¹ ['ætrəfi] *vt* **-phied; -phying** : atrofiar
atrophy² *n*, *pl* **-phies** : atrofia *f*
attach [ə'tætʃ] *vt* **1** FASTEN : sujetar, atar, amarrar, pegar **2** JOIN : juntar, adjuntar **3** ATTRIBUTE : dar, atribuir ⟨I attached little importance to it : le di poca importancia⟩ **4** SEIZE : embargar **5 to become attached to someone** : encariñarse con alguien
attaché [‚ætə'ʃeɪ, ‚æ‚tæ-, ə‚tæ-] *n* : agregado *m*, -da *f*
attachment [ə'tætʃmənt] *n* **1** ACCESSORY : accesorio *m* **2** CONNECTION : conexión *f*, acoplamiento *m* **3** FONDNESS : apego *m*, cariño *m*, afición *f*
attack¹ [ə'tæk] *vt* **1** ASSAULT : atacar, asaltar, agredir **2** TACKLE : acometer, combatir, enfrentarse con
attack² *n* **1** : ataque *m*, asalto *m*, acometida *f* ⟨to launch an attack : lanzar un ataque⟩ **2** : ataque *m*, crisis *f* ⟨heart attack : ataque cardíaco, infarto⟩ ⟨attack of nerves : crisis nerviosa⟩
attacker [ə'tækər] *n* : asaltante *mf*
attain [ə'teɪn] *vt* **1** ACHIEVE : lograr, conseguir, alcanzar, realizar **2** REACH : alcanzar, llegar a
attainable [ə'teɪnəbəl] *adj* : alcanzable, realizable, asequible
attainment [ə'teɪnmənt] *n* : logro *m*, consecución *f*, realización *f*
attempt¹ [ə'tɛmpt] *vt* : intentar, tratar de
attempt² *n* : intento *m*, tentativa *f*
attend [ə'tɛnd] *vt* **1** : asistir a ⟨to attend a meeting : asistir a una reunión⟩ **2** : atender, ocuparse de, cuidar ⟨to attend a patient : atender a un paciente⟩ **3** HEED : atender a, hacer caso de **4** ACCOMPANY : acompañar
attendance [ə'tɛndənts] *n* **1** ATTENDING : asistencia *f* **2** TURNOUT : concurrencia *f*
attendant¹ [ə'tɛndənt] *adj* : concomitante, inherente
attendant² *n* : asistente *mf*, acompañante *mf*, guarda *mf*

attention [ə'tɛntʃən] *n* **1** : atención *f* **2 to pay attention** : prestar atención, hacer caso **3 to stand at attention** : estar firme
attentive [ə'tɛntɪv] *adj* : atento — **attentively** *adv*
attentiveness [ə'tɛntɪvnəs] *n* **1** THOUGHTFULNESS : cortesía *f*, consideración *f* **2** CONCENTRATION : atención *f*, concentración *f*
attest [ə'tɛst] *vt* : atestiguar, dar fe de
attestation [‚æ‚ts'teɪʃən] *n* : testimonio *m*
attic ['ætɪk] *n* : ático *m*, desván *m*, buhardilla *f*
attire¹ [ə'taɪr] *vt* **-tired; -tiring** : ataviar
attire² *n* : atuendo *m*, atavío *m*
attitude ['æt̬ə‚tu:d, -‚tju:d] *n* **1** FEELING : actitud *f* **2** POSTURE : postura *f*
attorney [ə'tərni] *n*, *pl* **-neys** : abogado *m*, -da *f*
attract [ə'trækt] *vt* **1** : atraer **2 to attract attention** : llamar la atención
attraction [ə'trækʃən] *n* : atracción *f*, atractivo *m*
attractive [ə'træktɪv] *adj* : atractivo, atrayente
attractively [ə'træktɪvli] *adv* : de manera atractiva, de buen gusto, hermosamente
attractiveness [ə'træktɪvnəs] *n* : atractivo *m*
attributable [ə'trɪbjʊt̬əbəl] *adj* : atribuible, imputable
attribute¹ [ə'trɪ‚bju:t] *vt* **-tributed; -tributing** : atribuir
attribute² ['ætrə‚bju:t] *n* : atributo *m*, cualidad *f*
attribution [‚ætrə'bju:ʃən] *n* : atribución *f*
attune [ə'tu:n, -'tju:n] *vt* **-tuned; -tuning 1** ADAPT : adaptar, adecuar **2 to be attuned to** : estar en armonía con
atypical [‚eɪ'tɪpɪkəl] *adj* : atípico
auburn ['ɔbərn] *adj* : castaño rojizo
auction¹ ['ɔkʃən] *vt* : subastar, rematar
auction² *n* : subasta *f*, remate *m*
auctioneer [‚ɔkʃə'nɪr] *n* : subastador *m*, -dora *f*; rematador *m*, -dora *f*
audacious [ɔ'deɪʃəs] *adj* : audaz, atrevido
audacity [ɔ'dæsət̬i] *n*, *pl* **-ties** : audacia *f*, atrevimiento *m*, descaro *m*
audible ['ɔdəbəl] *adj* : audible — **audibly** [-bli] *adv*
audience ['ɔdiənts] *n* **1** INTERVIEW : audiencia *f* **2** PUBLIC : audiencia *f*, público *m*, auditorio *m*, espectadores *mpl*
audio¹ ['ɔdi‚o:] *adj* : de sonido, de audio
audio² *n* : audio *m*
audiovisual [‚ɔdio'vɪʒʊəl] *adj* : audiovisual
audit¹ ['ɔdət] *vt* **1** : auditar (finanzas) **2** : asistir como oyente a (una clase o un curso)
audit² *n* : auditoría *f*
audition¹ [ɔ'dɪʃən] *vi* : hacer una audición

audition · average

312

audition² *n* : audición *f*

auditor [ˈɔdətər] *n* **1** : auditor *m*, -tora *f* (de finanzas) **2** STUDENT : oyente *mf*

auditorium [ˌɔdəˈtoriəm] *n, pl* **-riums** *or* **-ria** [-riə] : auditorio *m*, sala *f*

auditory [ˈɔdəˌtori] *adj* : auditivo

auger [ˈɔgər] *n* : taladro *m*, barrena *f*

augment [ɔgˈmɛnt] *vt* : aumentar, incrementar

augmentation [ˌɔgmənˈteɪʃən] *n* : aumento *m*, incremento *m*

augur¹ [ˈɔgər] *vt* : augurar, presagiar — *vi* **to augur well** : ser de buen agüero

augur² *n* : augur *m*

augury [ˈɔgjʊri, -gər-] *n, pl* **-ries** : augurio *m*, presagio *m*, agüero *m*

august [ɔˈgʌst] *adj* : augusto

August [ˈɔgəst] *n* : agosto *m*

auk [ˈɔk] *n* : alca *f*

aunt [ˈænt, ˈɑnt] *n* : tía *f*

aura [ˈɔrə] *n* : aura *f*

aural [ˈɔrəl] *adj* : auditivo

auricle [ˈɔrɪkəl] *n* : aurícula *f*

aurora borealis [əˈrorəˌboriˈæləs] *n* : aurora *f* boreal

auspices [ˈɔspəsəz, -ˌsiːz] *npl* : auspicios *mpl*

auspicious [ɔˈspɪʃəs] *adj* : prometedor, propicio, de buen augurio

austere [ɔˈstɪr] *adj* : austero, severo, adusto — **austerely** *adv*

austerity [ɔˈstɛrəti] *n, pl* **-ties** : austeridad *f*

Australian [ɔˈstreɪljən] *n* : australiano *m*, -na *f* — **Australian** *adj*

Austrian [ˈɔstriən] *n* : austriaco *m*, -ca *f* — **Austrian** *adj*

authentic [əˈθɛntɪk, ɔ-] *adj* : auténtico, genuino — **authentically** [-tɪkli] *adv*

authenticate [əˈθɛntɪˌkeɪt, ɔ-] *vt* **-cated; -cating** : autenticar, autentificar

authenticity [ˌɔθɛnˈtɪsəti] *n* : autenticidad *f*

author [ˈɔθər] *n* **1** WRITER : escritor *m*, -tora *f*; autor *m*, -tora *f* **2** CREATOR : autor *m*, -tora *f*; creador *m*, -dora *f*; artífice *mf*

authoritarian [ɔˌθɔrəˈtɛriən, ə-] *adj* : autoritario

authoritative [əˈθɔrəˌteɪtɪv, ɔ-] *adj* **1** RELIABLE : fidedigno, autorizado **2** DICTATORIAL : autoritario, dictatorial, imperioso

authoritatively [əˈθɔrəˌteɪtɪvli, ɔ-] *adv* **1** RELIABLY : con autoridad **2** DICTATORIALLY : de manera autoritaria

authority [əˈθɔrəti, ɔ-] *n, pl* **-ties 1** EXPERT : autoridad *f*; experto *m*, -ta *f* **2** POWER : autoridad *f*, poder *m* **3** AUTHORIZATION : autorización *f*, licencia *f* **4 the authorities** : las autoridades **5 on good authority** : de buena fuente

authorization [ˌɔθərəˈzeɪʃən] *n* : autorización *f*

authorize [ˈɔθəˌraɪz] *vt* **-rized; -rizing** : autorizar, facultar

authorship [ˈɔθərˌʃɪp] *n* : autoría *f*

autism [ˈɔˌtɪzəm] *n* : autismo *m*

autistic [ɔˈtɪstɪk] *adj* : autista

auto [ˈɔto] → **automobile**

autobiographical [ˌɔtoˌbaɪəˈgræfɪkəl] *adj* : autobiográfico

autobiography [ˌɔtobaɪˈɑgrəfi] *n, pl* **-phies** : autobiografía *f*

autocracy [ɔˈtɑkrəsi] *n, pl* **-cies** : autocracia *f*

autocrat [ˈɔtəˌkræt] *n* : autócrata *mf*

autocratic [ˌɔtəˈkrætɪk] *adj* : autocrático — **autocratically** [-tɪkli] *adv*

autograph¹ [ˈɔtəˌgræf] *vt* : autografiar

autograph² *n* : autógrafo *m*

automaker [ˈɔtoːmeɪkər] *n* : fabricante *mf* de autos, automotriz *f*

automate [ˈɔtəˌmeɪt] *vt* **-mated; -mating** : automatizar

automatic [ˌɔtəˈmætɪk] *adj* : automático — **automatically** [-tɪkli] *adv*

automation [ˌɔtəˈmeɪʃən] *n* : automatización *f*

automaton [ɔˈtɑməˌtɑn] *n, pl* **-atons** *or* **-ata** [-tə, -ˌtɑ] : autómata *m*

automobile [ˌɔtəmoˈbiːl, -ˈmoːˌbiːl] *n* : automóvil *m*, auto *m*, carro *m*, coche *m*

automotive [ˌɔtəˈmoːtɪv] *adj* : automotor

autonomous [ɔˈtɑnəməs] *adj* : autónomo — **autonomously** *adv*

autonomy [ɔˈtɑnəmi] *n, pl* **-mies** : autonomía *f*

autopsy [ˈɔˌtɑpsi, -təp-] *n, pl* **-sies** : autopsia *f*

autumn [ˈɔtəm] *n* : otoño *m*

autumnal [ɔˈtʌmnəl] *adj* : otoñal

auxiliary¹ [ɔgˈzɪljəri, -ˈzɪləri] *adj* : auxiliar

auxiliary² *n, pl* **-ries** : auxiliar *mf*, ayudante *mf*

avail¹ [əˈveɪl] *vt* **to avail oneself** : aprovecharse, valerse

avail² *n* **1** : provecho *m*, utilidad *f* **2 to no avail** : en vano **3 to be of no avail** : no servir de nada, ser inútil

availability [əˌveɪləˈbɪləti] *n, pl* **-ties** : disponibilidad *f*

available [əˈveɪləbəl] *adj* : disponible

avalanche [ˈævəˌlæntʃ] *n* : avalancha *f*, alud *m*

avarice [ˈævərəs] *n* : avaricia *f*, codicia *f*

avaricious [ˌævəˈrɪʃəs] *adj* : avaricioso, codicioso

avenge [əˈvɛndʒ] *vt* **avenged; avenging** : vengar

avenger [əˈvɛndʒər] *n* : vengador *m*, -dora *f*

avenue [ˈævəˌnuː, -ˌnjuː] *n* **1** : avenida *f* **2** MEANS : vía *f*, camino *m*

average¹ [ˈævrɪdʒ, ˈævə-] *vt* **-aged; -aging 1** : hacer un promedio de ⟨he averages 8 hours a day : hace un promedio de 8 horas diarias⟩ **2** : calcular el promedio de, promediar (en matemáticas)

average² *adj* **1** MEAN : medio ⟨the average temperature : la temperatura media⟩ **2** ORDINARY : común, ordinario ⟨the average man : el hombre común⟩

average³ *n* : promedio *m*

averse [ə'vərs] *adj* : reacio, opuesto

aversion [ə'vərʒən] *n* : aversión *f*

avert [ə'vərt] *vt* **1** : apartar, desviar ⟨he averted his eyes from the scene : apartó los ojos de la escena⟩ **2** AVOID, PREVENT : evitar, prevenir

aviary ['eɪviˌɛri] *n, pl* **-aries** : pajarera *f*

aviation [ˌeɪvi'eɪʃən] *n* : aviación *f*

aviator ['eɪviˌeɪtər] *n* : aviador *m*, -dora *f*

avid ['ævɪd] *adj* **1** GREEDY : ávido, codicioso **2** ENTHUSIASTIC : ávido, entusiasta, ferviente — **avidly** *adv*

avocado [ˌævə'kɑdo, ˌɑvə-] *n, pl* **-dos** : aguacate *m*, palta *f*

avocation [ˌævə'keɪʃən] *n* : pasatiempo *m*, afición *f*

avoid [ə'vɔɪd] *vt* **1** SHUN : evitar, eludir **2** FORGO : evitar, abstenerse de ⟨I always avoided gossip : siempre evitaba los chismes⟩ **3** EVADE : evitar ⟨if I can avoid it : si puedo evitarlo⟩

avoidable [ə'vɔɪdəbəl] *adj* : evitable

avoidance [ə'vɔɪdənts] *n* : el evitar

avoirdupois [ˌævərdə'pɔɪz] *n* : sistema *m* inglés de pesos y medidas

avow [ə'vaʊ] *vt* : reconocer, confesar

avowal [ə'vaʊəl] *n* : reconocimiento *m*, confesión *f*

await [ə'weɪt] *vt* : esperar

awake¹ [ə'weɪk] *v* **awoke** [ə'wo:k]; **awoken** [ə'wo:kən] *or* **awaked; awaking** : despertar

awake² *adj* : despierto

awaken [ə'weɪkən] → **awake¹**

award¹ [ə'wɔrd] *vt* : otorgar, conceder, conferir

award² *n* **1** PRIZE : premio *m*, galardón *m* **2** MEDAL : condecoración *f*

aware [ə'wær] *adj* : consciente ⟨to be aware of : darse cuenta de, estar consciente de⟩

awareness [ə'wærnəs] *n* : conciencia *f*, conocimiento *m*

awash [ə'wɔʃ] *adj* : inundado

away¹ [ə'weɪ] *adv* **1** : de aquí ⟨go away! : ¡fuera de aquí!, ¡vete!⟩ **2** : de distancia ⟨10 miles away : 10 millas de distancia, queda a 10 millas⟩ **3 far away** : lejos, a lo lejos **4 right away** : en segui-

da, ahora mismo **5 to be away** : estar ausente, estar de viaje **6 to give away** : regalar (una posesión), revelar (un secreto) **7 to go away** : irse, largarse **8 to put away** : guardar **9 to turn away** : volver la cara

away² *adj* **1** ABSENT : ausente ⟨away for the week : ausente por la semana⟩ **2 away game** : partido *m* que se juega fuera

awe¹ ['ɔ] *vt* **awed; awing** : abrumar, asombrar, impresionar

awe² *n* : asombro *m*

awesome ['ɔsəm] *adj* **1** IMPOSING : imponente, formidable **2** AMAZING : asombroso

awestruck ['ɔˌstrʌk] *adj* : asombrado

awful ['ɔfəl] *adj* **1** AWESOME : asombroso **2** DREADFUL : horrible, terrible, atroz **3** ENORMOUS : enorme, tremendo ⟨an awful lot of people : muchísima gente, la mar de gente⟩

awfully ['ɔfəli] *adv* **1** EXTREMELY : terriblemente, extremadamente **2** BADLY : muy mal, espantosamente

awhile [ə'hwaɪl] *adv* : un rato, algún tiempo

awkward ['ɔkwərd] *adj* **1** CLUMSY : torpe, desmañado **2** EMBARRASSING : embarazoso, delicado — **awkwardly** *adv*

awkwardness ['ɔkwərdnəs] *n* **1** CLUMSINESS : torpeza *f* **2** INCONVENIENCE : incomodidad *f*

awl ['ɔl] *n* : punzón *m*

awning ['ɔnɪŋ] *n* : toldo *m*

awry [ə'raɪ] *adj* **1** ASKEW : torcido **2 to go awry** : salir mal, fracasar

ax *or* **axe** ['æks] *n* : hacha *m*

axiom ['æksiəm] *n* : axioma *m*

axiomatic [ˌæksiə'mætɪk] *adj* : axiomático

axis ['æksɪs] *n, pl* **axes** [-ˌsi:z] : eje *m*

axle ['æksəl] *n* : eje *m*

aye¹ ['aɪ] *adv* : sí

aye² *n* : sí *m*

azalea [ə'zeɪljə] *n* : azalea *f*

azimuth ['æzəməθ] *n* : azimut *m*, acimut *m*

Aztec ['æzˌtɛk] *n* : azteca *mf*

azure¹ ['æʒər] *adj* : azur, celeste

azure² *n* : azur *m*

B

b ['bi:] *n, pl* **b's** *or* **bs** ['bi:z] : segunda letra del alfabeto inglés

babble¹ ['bæbəl] *vi* **-bled; -bling** **1** PRATTLE : balbucear **2** CHATTER : charlatanear, parlotear *fam* **3** MURMUR : murmurar

babble² *n* : balbuceo *m* (de bebé), parloteo *m* (de adultos), murmullo *m* (de voces, de un arroyo)

babe ['beɪb] *n* → **baby³**

babel ['beɪbəl, 'bæ-] *n* : babel *f*, caos *m*

baboon [bæ'bu:n] *n* : babuino *m*

baby¹ ['beɪbi] *vt* **-bied; -bying** : mimar, consentir

baby² *adj* **1** : de niño ⟨a baby carriage : un cochecito⟩ ⟨baby talk : habla infantil⟩ **2** TINY : pequeño, minúsculo

baby³ *n, pl* **-bies** : bebé *m*; niño *m*, -ña *f*

babyhood ['beɪbiˌhʊd] *n* : niñez *f*, primera infancia *f*

babyish ['beɪbiɪʃ] *adj* : infantil, pueril

baby–sit [ˈbeɪbiˌsɪt] *vi* **-sat** [-ˌsæt]; **-sitting** : cuidar niños, hacer de canguro *Spain*

baby–sitter [ˈbeɪbiˌsɪtər] *n* : niñero *m*, -ra *f*; canguro *mf Spain*

baccalaureate [ˌbækəˈlɔriət] *n* : licenciatura *f*

bachelor [ˈbætʃələr] *n* **1** : soltero *m* **2** : licenciado *m*, -da *f* ⟨bachelor of arts degree : licenciatura en filosofía y letras⟩

bacillus [bəˈsɪləs] *n, pl* **-li** [-ˌlaɪ] : bacilo *m*

back¹ [ˈbæk] *vt* **1** *or* **to back up** SUPPORT : apoyar, respaldar **2** *or* **to back up** REVERSE : darle marcha atrás a (un vehículo) **3** : estar detrás de, formar el fondo de ⟨trees back the garden : unos árboles están detrás del jardín⟩ — *vi* **1** *or* **to back up** : retroceder **2 to back away** : echarse atrás **3 to back down** *or* **to back out** : volverse atrás, echarse para atrás

back² *adv* **1** : atrás, hacia atrás, detrás ⟨to move back : moverse atrás⟩ ⟨back and forth : de acá para allá⟩ **2** AGO : atrás, antes, ya ⟨some years back : unos años atrás, ya unos años⟩ ⟨10 months back : hace diez meses⟩ **3** : de vuelta, de regreso ⟨we're back : estamos de vuelta⟩ ⟨she ran back : volvió corriendo⟩ ⟨to call back : llamar de nuevo⟩

back³ *adj* **1** REAR : de atrás, posterior, trasero **2** OVERDUE : atrasado **3 back pay** : atrasos *mpl*

back⁴ *n* **1** : espalda *f* (de un ser humano), lomo *m* (de un animal) **2** : respaldo *m* (de una silla), espalda *f* (de ropa) **3** REVERSE : reverso *m*, dorso *m*, revés *m* **4** REAR : fondo *m*, parte *f* de atrás **5** : defensa *mf* (en deportes)

backache [ˈbækˌeɪk] *n* : dolor *m* de espalda

backbite [ˈbækˌbaɪt] *v* **-bit** [-ˌbɪt]; **-bitten** [-ˌbɪtən]; **-biting** *vt* : calumniar, hablar mal de — *vi* : murmurar

backbiter [ˈbækˌbaɪtər] *n* : calumniador *m*, -dora *f*

backbone [ˈbækˌboːn] *n* **1** : columna *f* vertebral **2** FIRMNESS : firmeza *f*, carácter *m*

backdrop [ˈbækˌdrɑp] *n* : telón *m* de fondo

backer [ˈbækər] *n* **1** SUPPORTER : partidario *m*, -ria *f* **2** SPONSOR : patrocinador *m*, -dora *f*

backfire¹ [ˈbækˌfaɪr] *vi* **-fired; -firing 1** : petardear (dícese de un automóvil) **2** FAIL : fallar, salir el tiro por la culata

backfire² *n* : petardeo *m*, explosión *f*

background [ˈbækˌgraʊnd] *n* **1** : fondo *m* (de un cuadro, etc.), antecedentes *mpl* (de una situación) **2** EXPERIENCE, TRAINING : experiencia *f* profesional, formación *f*

backhand¹ [ˈbækˌhænd] *adv* : de revés, con el revés

backhand² *n* : revés *m*

backhanded [ˈbækˌhændəd] *adj* **1** : dado con el revés, de revés **2** INDIRECT : indirecto, ambiguo

backing [ˈbækɪŋ] *n* **1** SUPPORT : apoyo *m*, respaldo *m* **2** REINFORCEMENT : refuerzo *m* **3** SUPPORTERS : partidarios *mpl*, -rias *fpl*

backlash [ˈbækˌlæʃ] *n* : reacción *f* violenta

backlog [ˈbækˌlɔg] *n* : atraso *m*, trabajo *m* acumulado

backpack¹ [ˈbækˌpæk] *vi* : viajar con mochila

backpack² *n* : mochila *f*

backrest [ˈbækˌrɛst] *n* : respaldo *m*

backside [ˈbækˌsaɪd] *n* : trasero *m*

backslide [ˈbækˌslaɪd] *vi* **-slid** [-ˌslɪd]; **-slid** *or* **-slidden** [-ˌslɪdən]; **-sliding** : recaer, reincidir

backstage [ˌbækˈsteɪdʒ, ˈbækˌ-] *adv & adj* : entre bastidores

backtrack [ˈbækˌtræk] *vi* : dar marcha atrás, volverse atrás

backup [ˈbækˌʌp] *n* **1** SUPPORT : respaldo *m*, apoyo *m* **2** : copia *f* de seguridad (para computadoras)

backward¹ [ˈbækwərd] *or* **backwards** [-wərdz] *adv* **1** : hacia atrás **2** : de espaldas ⟨he fell backwards : se cayó de espaldas⟩ **3** : al revés ⟨you're doing it backwards : lo estás haciendo al revés⟩ **4 to bend over backwards** : hacer todo lo posible

backward² *adj* **1** : hacia atrás ⟨a backward glance : una mirada hacia atrás⟩ **2** RETARDED : retrasado **3** SHY : tímido **4** UNDERDEVELOPED : atrasado

backwardness [ˈbækwərdnəs] *n* : atraso *m* (dícese de una región), retraso *m* (dícese de una persona)

backwoods [ˌbækˈwʊdz] *npl* : monte *m*, región *f* alejada

bacon [ˈbeɪkən] *n* : tocino *m*, tocineta *f Col, Ven*, bacon *m Spain*

bacterial [bækˈtɪriəl] *adj* : bacteriano

bacteriologist [bækˌtɪriˈɑlədʒɪst] *n* : bacteriólogo *m*, -ga *f*

bacteriology [bækˌtɪriˈɑlədʒi] *n* : bacteriología *f*

bacterium [bækˈtɪriəm] *n, pl* **-ria** [-iə] : bacteria *f*

bad¹ [ˈbæd] *adv* → **badly**

bad² *adj* **1** : malo **2** ROTTEN : podrido **3** SERIOUS, SEVERE : grave **4** DEFECTIVE : defectuoso ⟨a bad check : un cheque sin fondos⟩ **5** HARMFUL : perjudicial **6** CORRUPT, EVIL : malo, corrompido **7** NAUGHTY : travieso **8 from bad to worse** : de mal en peor **9 too bad!** : ¡qué lástima!

bad³ *n* : lo malo ⟨the good and the bad : lo bueno y lo malo⟩

bade → **bid**

badge [ˈbædʒ] *n* : insignia *f*, botón *m*, chapa *f*

badger¹ [ˈbædʒər] *vt* : fastidiar, acosar, importunar

badger² *n* : tejón *m*
badly ['bædli] *adv* **1** : mal **2** URGENTLY : mucho, con urgencia **3** SEVERELY : gravemente
badminton ['bæd,mɪntən, -,mɪt-] *n* : bádminton *m*
badness ['bædnəs] *n* : maldad *f*
baffle¹ ['bæfəl] *vi* **-fled; -fling 1** PERPLEX : desconcertar, confundir **2** FRUSTRATE : frustrar
baffle² *n* : deflector *m*, bafle *m* (acústico)
bafflement ['bæfəlmənt] *n* : desconcierto *m*, confusión *f*
bag¹ ['bæg] *v* **bagged; bagging** *vi* SAG : formar bolsas — *vt* **1** : ensacar, poner en una bolsa **2** : cobrar (en la caza), cazar
bag² *n* **1** : bolsa *f*, saco *m* **2** HANDBAG : cartera *f*, bolso *m*, bolsa *f Mex* **3** SUITCASE : maleta *f*, valija *f*
bagatelle [,bægə'tɛl] *n* : bagatela *f*
bagel ['beɪgəl] *n* : rosquilla *f* de pan
baggage ['bægɪʤ] *n* : equipaje *m*
baggy ['bægi] *adj* **-gier; -est** : holgado, ancho
bagpipe ['bæg,paɪp] *n or* **bagpipes** ['bæg,paɪps] *npl* : gaita *f*
bail¹ ['beɪl] *vt* **1** : achicar (agua de un bote) **2 to bail out** : poner en libertad (de una cárcel) bajo fianza **3 to bail out** EXTRICATE : sacar de apuros
bail² *n* : fianza *f*, caución *f*
bailiff ['beɪləf] *n* : alguacil *mf*
bailiwick ['beɪli,wɪk] *n* : dominio *m*
bailout ['beɪl,aʊt] *n* : rescate *m* (financiero)
bait¹ ['beɪt] *vt* **1** : cebar (un anzuelo o cepo) **2** HARASS : acosar
bait² *n* : cebo *m*, carnada *f*
bake¹ ['beɪk] *vt* **baked; baking** : hornear, hacer al horno
bake² *n* : fiesta con platos hechos al horno
baker ['beɪkər] *n* : panadero *m*, -ra *f*
baker's dozen *n* : docena *f* de fraile
bakery ['beɪkəri] *n, pl* **-ries** : panadería *f*
bakeshop ['beɪk,ʃɑp] *n* : pastelería *f*, panadería *f*
baking powder *n* : levadura *f* en polvo
baking soda → **sodium bicarbonate**
balance¹ ['bælənts] *v* **-anced; -ancing** *vt* **1** : hacer el balance de (una cuenta) ⟨to balance the books : cuadrar las cuentas⟩ **2** EQUALIZE : balancear, equilibrar **3** HARMONIZE : armonizar — *vi* : balancearse
balance² *n* **1** SCALES : balanza *f*, báscula *f* **2** COUNTERBALANCE : contrapeso *m* **3** EQUILIBRIUM : equilibrio *m* **4** REMAINDER : balance *m*, resto *m*
balanced ['bæləntst] *adj* : equilibrado, balanceado
balcony ['bælkəni] *n, pl* **-nies 1** : balcón *m*, terraza *f* (de un edificio) **2** : galería *f* (de un teatro)

bald ['bɔld] *adj* **1** : calvo, pelado, pelón **2** PLAIN : simple, puro ⟨the bald truth : la pura verdad⟩
balding ['bɔldɪŋ] *adj* : quedándose calvo
baldly ['bɔldli] *adv* : sin reparos, sin rodeos, francamente
baldness ['bɔldnəs] *n* : calvicie *f*
bale¹ ['beɪl] *vt* **baled; baling** : empacar, hacer balas de
bale² *n* : bala *f*, fardo *m*, paca *f*
baleful ['beɪlfəl] *adj* **1** DEADLY : mortífero **2** SINISTER : siniestro, funesto, torvo ⟨a baleful glance : una mirada torva⟩
balk¹ ['bɔk] *vt* : obstaculizar, impedir — *vi* **1** : plantarse *fam* (dícese de un caballo, etc.) **2 to balk at** : resistirse a, mostrarse reacio a
balk² *n* : obstáculo *m*
Balkan ['bɔlkən] *adj* : balcánico
balky ['bɔki] *adj* **balkier; -est** : reacio, obstinado, terco
ball¹ ['bɔl] *vt* : apelotonar, ovillar
ball² *n* **1** : pelota *f*, bola *f*, balón *m*, ovillo *m* (de lana) **2** : juego *m* con pelota o bola **3** DANCE : baile *m*, baile *m* de etiqueta
ballad ['bæləd] *n* : romance *m*, balada *f*
balladeer [,bælə'dɪr] *n* : cantante *mf* de baladas
ballast¹ ['bæləst] *vt* : lastrar
ballast² *n* : lastre *m*
ball bearing *n* : cojinete *m* de bola
ballerina [,bælə'ri:nə] *n* : bailarina *f*
ballet [bæ'leɪ, 'bæ,leɪ] *n* : ballet *m*
ballistic [bə'lɪstɪk] *adj* : balístico
ballistics [bə'lɪstɪks] *ns & pl* : balística *f*
balloon¹ [bə'lu:n] *vi* **1** : viajar en globo **2** SWELL : hincharse, inflarse
balloon² *n* : globo *m*
balloonist [bə'lu:nɪst] *n* : aeróstata *mf*
ballot¹ ['bælət] *vi* : votar
ballot² *n* **1** : papeleta *f* (de voto) **2** BALLOTING : votación *f* **3** VOTE : voto *m*
ballpoint pen ['bɔl,pɔɪnt] *n* : bolígrafo *m*
ballroom ['bɔl,ru:m, -,rʊm] *n* : sala *f* de baile
ballyhoo ['bæli,hu:] *n* : propaganda *f*, publicidad *f*, bombo *m fam*
balm ['bɑm, 'bɑlm] *n* : bálsamo *m*, ungüento *m*
balmy ['bɑmi, 'bɑl-] *adj* **balmier; -est 1** MILD : templado, agradable **2** SOOTHING : balsámico **3** CRAZY : chiflado *fam*, chalado *fam*
baloney [bə'lo:ni] *n* NONSENSE : tonterías *fpl*, estupideces *fpl*
balsa ['bɔlsə] *n* : balsa *f*
balsam ['bɔlsəm] *n* **1** : bálsamo *m* **2** *or* **balsam fir** : abeto *m* balsámico
Baltic ['bɔltɪk] *adj* : báltico
baluster ['bæləstər] *n* : balaustre *m*
balustrade ['bælə,streɪd] *n* : balaustrada *f*
bamboo [bæm'bu:] *n* : bambú *m*
bamboozle [bæm'bu:zəl] *vt* **-zled; -zling** : engañar, embaucar

ban¹ ['bæn] *vt* **banned; banning** : prohibir, proscribir

ban² *n* : prohibición *f*, proscripción *f*

banal [bə'nɑl, bə'næl, 'beɪnəl] *adj* : banal, trivial

banality [bə'næləṭi] *n, pl* **-ties** : banalidad *f*, trivialidad *f*

banana [bə'nænə] *n* : banano *m*, plátano *m*, banana *f*, cambur *m Ven*, guineo *m Car*

band¹ ['bænd] *vt* **1** BIND : fajar, atar **2 to band together** : unirse, juntarse

band² *n* **1** STRIP : banda *f*, cinta *f* (de un sombrero, etc.) **2** STRIPE : franja *f* **3** : banda *f* (de radiofrecuencia) **4** RING : anillo *m* **5** GROUP : banda *f*, grupo *m*, conjunto *m* ⟨jazz band : conjunto de jazz⟩

bandage¹ ['bændɪʤ] *vt* **-daged; -daging** : vendar

bandage² *n* : vendaje *m*, venda *f*

bandanna *or* **bandana** [bæn'dænə] *n* : pañuelo *m* (de colores)

bandit ['bændət] *n* : bandido *m*, -da *f*; bandolero *m*, -ra *f*

banditry ['bændətri] *n* : bandolerismo *m*, bandidaje *m*

bandstand ['bænd,stænd] *n* : quiosco *m* de música

bandwagon ['bænd,wægən] *n* **1** : carroza *f* de músicos **2 to jump on the bandwagon** : subirse al carro, seguir la moda

bandy¹ ['bændi] *vt* **-died; -dying 1** EXCHANGE : intercambiar **2 to bandy about** : circular, propagar

bandy² *adj* : arqueado, torcido ⟨bandy-legged : de piernas arqueadas⟩

bane ['beɪn] *n* **1** POISON : veneno *m* **2** RUIN : ruina *f*, pesadilla *f*

baneful ['beɪnfəl] *adj* : nefasto, funesto

bang¹ ['bæŋ] *vt* **1** STRIKE : golpear, darse ⟨he banged his elbow against the door : se dio con el codo en la puerta⟩ **2** SLAM : cerrar (la puerta) con un portazo — *vi* **1** SLAM : cerrarse de un golpe **2 to bang on** : aporrear, golpear ⟨she was banging on the table : aporreaba la mesa⟩

bang² *adv* : directamente, exactamente

bang³ *n* **1** BLOW : golpe *m*, porrazo *m*, trancazo *m* **2** EXPLOSION : explosión *f*, estallido *m* **3** SLAM : portazo *m* **4 bangs** *npl* : flequillo *m*, fleco *m*

Bangladeshi [,bɑŋglə'dɛʃi, ,bæŋ-, ,bʌŋ-, -'deɪ-] *n* : bangladesí *mf* — **Bangladeshi** *adj*

bangle ['bæŋgəl] *n* : brazalete *m*, pulsera *f*

banish ['bænɪʃ] *vt* **1** EXILE : desterrar, exiliar **2** EXPEL : expulsar

banishment ['bænɪʃmənt] *n* **1** EXILE : destierro *m*, exilio *m* **2** EXPULSION : expulsión *f*

banister ['bænəstər] *n* **1** BALUSTER : balaustre *m* **2** HANDRAIL : pasamanos *m*, barandilla *f*, barandal *m*

banjo ['bæn,ʤo:] *n, pl* **-jos** : banjo *m*

bank¹ ['bæŋk] *vt* **1** TILT : peraltar (una carretera), ladear (un avión) **2** HEAP : amontonar **3** : cubrir (un fuego) **4** : depositar (dinero en un banco) — *vi* **1** : ladearse (dícese de un avión) **2** : tener una cuenta (en un banco) **3 to bank on** : contar con

bank² *n* **1** MASS : montón *m*, montículo *m*, masa *f* **2** : orilla *f*, ribera *f* (de un río) **3** : peralte *m* (de una carretera) **4** : banco *m* ⟨World Bank : Banco Mundial⟩ ⟨banco de sangre : blood bank⟩

bankbook ['bæŋk,bʊk] *n* : libreta *f* bancaria, libreta *f* de ahorros

banker ['bæŋkər] *n* : banquero *m*, -ra *f*

banking ['bæŋkɪŋ] *n* : banca *f*

bankrupt¹ ['bæŋ,krʌpt] *vt* : hacer quebrar, llevar a la quiebra, arruinar

bankrupt² *adj* **1** : en bancarrota, en quiebra **2** ~ **of** LACKING : carente de, falto de

bankrupt³ *n* : fallido *m*, -da *f*; quebrado *m*, -da *f*

bankruptcy ['bæŋ,krʌptsi] *n, pl* **-cies** : ruina *f*, quiebra *f*, bancarrota *f*

banner¹ ['bænər] *adj* : excelente

banner² *n* : estandarte *m*, bandera *f*

banns ['bænz] *npl* : amonestaciones *fpl*

banquet¹ ['bæŋkwət] *vi* : celebrar un banquete

banquet² *n* : banquete *m*

banter¹ ['bæntər] *vi* : bromear, hacer bromas

banter² *n* : bromas *fpl*

baptism ['bæp,tɪzəm] *n* : bautismo *m*

baptismal [bæp'tɪzməl] *adj* : bautismal

Baptist ['bæptɪst] *n* : bautista *mf* — **Baptist** *adj*

baptize [bæp'taɪz, 'bæp,taɪz] *vt* **-tized; -tizing** : bautizar

bar¹ ['bɑr] *vt* **barred; barring 1** OBSTRUCT : obstruir, bloquear **2** EXCLUDE : excluir **3** PROHIBIT : prohibir **4** SECURE : atrancar, asegurar ⟨bar the door! : ¡atranca la puerta!⟩

bar² *n* **1** : barra *f*, barrote *m* (de una ventana), tranca *f* (de una puerta) **2** BARRIER : barrera *f*, obstáculo *m* **3** LAW : abogacía *f* **4** STRIPE : franja *f* **5** COUNTER : mostrador *m*, barra *f* **6** TAVERN : bar *m*, taberna *f*

bar³ *prep* **1** : excepto, con excepción de **2 bar none** : sin excepción

barb ['bɑrb] *n* **1** POINT : púa *f*, lengüeta *f* **2** GIBE : pulla *f*

barbarian¹ [bɑr'bæriən] *adj* **1** : bárbaro **2** CRUDE : tosco, bruto

barbarian² *n* : bárbaro *m*, -ra *f*

barbaric [bɑr'bærɪk] *adj* **1** PRIMITIVE : primitivo **2** CRUEL : brutal, cruel

barbarity [bɑr'bærəṭi] *n, pl* **-ties** : barbaridad *f*

barbarous ['bɑrbərəs] *adj* **1** UNCIVILIZED : bárbaro **2** MERCILESS : despiadado, cruel

barbarously ['bɑrbərəsli] *adv* : bárbaramente

barbecue¹ ['bɑrbɪ,kjuː] *vt* **-cued; -cuing** : asar a la parrilla
barbecue² *n* : barbacoa *f*, parrillada *f*
barbed ['bɑrbd] *adj* **1** : con púas ⟨barbed wire : alambre de púas⟩ **2** BITING : mordaz
barber ['bɑrbər] *n* : barbero *m*, -ra *f*
barbiturate [bɑr'bɪtʃərət] *n* : barbitúrico *m*
bard ['bɑrd] *n* : bardo *m*
bare¹ ['bær] *vt* **bared; baring** : desnudar
bare² *adj* **1** NAKED : desnudo **2** EXPOSED : descubierto, sin protección **3** EMPTY : desprovisto, vacío **4** MINIMUM : mero, mínimo ⟨the bare necessities : las necesidades mínimas⟩ **5** PLAIN : puro, sencillo
bareback ['bær,bæk] *or* **barebacked** [-,bækt] *adv & adj* : a pelo
barefaced ['bær,feɪst] *adj* : descarado
barefoot ['bær,fʊt] *or* **barefooted** [-,fʊtəd] *adv & adj* : descalzo
bareheaded ['bær,hɛdəd] *adv & adj* : sin sombrero, con la cabeza descubierta
barely ['bærli] *adv* : apenas, por poco
bareness ['bærnəs] *n* : desnudez *f*
bargain¹ ['bɑrgən] *vi* HAGGLE : regatear, negociar — *vt* BARTER : trocar, cambiar
bargain² *n* **1** AGREEMENT : acuerdo *m*, convenio *m* ⟨to strike a bargain : cerrar un trato⟩ **2** : ganga *f* ⟨bargain price : precio de ganga⟩
barge¹ ['bɑrdʒ] *vi* **barged; barging 1** : mover con torpeza **2 to barge in** : entrometerse, interrumpir
barge² *n* : barcaza *f*, gabarra *f*
bar graph *n* : gráfico *m* de barras
baritone ['bærə,toːn] *n* : barítono *m*
barium ['bæriəm] *n* : bario *m*
bark¹ ['bɑrk] *vi* : ladrar — *vt or* **to bark out** : gritar ⟨to bark out an order : dar una orden a gritos⟩
bark² *n* **1** : ladrido *m* (de un perro) **2** : corteza *f* (de un árbol) **3** *or* **barque** : tipo de embarcación con velas de proa y popa
barley ['bɑrli] *n* : cebada *f*
barn ['bɑrn] *n* : granero *m* (para cosechas), establo *m* (para ganado)
barnacle ['bɑrnɪkəl] *n* : percebe *m*
barnyard ['bɑrn,jɑrd] *n* : corral *m*
barometer [bə'rɑmətər] *n* : barómetro *m*
barometric [,bærə'mɛtrɪk] *adj* : barométrico
baron ['bærən] *n* **1** : barón *m* **2** TYCOON : magnate *mf*
baroness ['bærənɪs, -nəs, -,nɛs] *n* : baronesa *f*
baronet [,bærə'nɛt, 'bærənət] *n* : baronet *m*
baronial [bə'roːniəl] *adj* **1** : de barón **2** STATELY : señorial, majestuoso
baroque [bə'roːk, -'rɑk] *adj* : barroco
barracks ['bærəks] *ns & pl* : cuartel *m*
barracuda [,bærə'kuːdə] *n, pl* **-da** *or* **-das** : barracuda *f*

barrage [bə'rɑʒ, -'rɑdʒ] *n* **1** : descarga *f* (de artillería) **2** DELUGE : aluvión *m* ⟨a barrage of questions : un aluvión de preguntas⟩
barred ['bɑrd] *adj* : excluido, prohibido
barrel¹ ['bærəl] *v* **-reled** *or* **-relled; -reling** *or* **-relling** *vt* : embarrilar — *vi* : ir disparado
barrel² *n* **1** : barril *m*, tonel *m* **2** : cañón *m* (de un arma de fuego), cilindro *m* (de una cerradura)
barren ['bærən] *adj* **1** STERILE : estéril (dícese de las plantas o la mujer), árido (dícese del suelo) **2** DESERTED : yermo, desierto
barrette [bɑ'rɛt, bə-] *n* : pasador *m*, broche *m* para el cabello
barricade¹ ['bærə,keɪd, ,bærə'-] *vt* **-caded; -cading** : cerrar con barricadas
barricade² *n* : barricada *f*
barrier ['bæriər] *n* **1** : barrera *f* **2** OBSTACLE : obstáculo *m*, impedimento *m*
barring ['bɑrɪŋ] *prep* : excepto, salvo, a excepción de
barrio ['bɑrio, 'bær-] *n* : barrio *m*
barroom ['bɑr,ruːm, -,rʊm] *n* : bar *m*
barrow ['bær,oː] → **wheelbarrow**
bartender ['bɑr,tɛndər] *n* : camarero *m*, -ra *f*; barman *m*
barter¹ ['bɑrtər] *vt* : cambiar, trocar
barter² *n* : trueque *m*, permuta *f*
basalt [bə'sɔlt, 'beɪ,-] *n* : basalto *m*
base¹ ['beɪs] *vt* **based; basing** : basar, fundamentar, establecer
base² *adj* **baser; basest 1** : de baja ley (dícese de un metal) **2** CONTEMPTIBLE : vil, despreciable
base³ *n, pl* **bases** : base *f*
baseball ['beɪs,bɔl] *n* : beisbol *m*, béisbol *m*
baseless ['beɪsləs] *adj* : infundado
basely ['beɪsli] *adv* : vilmente
basement ['beɪsmənt] *n* : sótano *m*
baseness ['beɪsnəs] *n* : vileza *f*, bajeza *f*
bash¹ ['bæʃ] *vt* : golpear violentamente
bash² *n* **1** BLOW : golpe *m*, porrazo *m*, madrazo *m* *Mex fam* **2** PARTY : fiesta *f*, juerga *f fam*
bashful ['bæʃfəl] *adj* : tímido, vergonzoso, penoso
bashfulness ['bæʃfəlnəs] *n* : timidez *f*
basic ['beɪsɪk] *adj* **1** FUNDAMENTAL : básico, fundamental **2** RUDIMENTARY : básico, elemental **3** : básico (en química)
basic² *n* : fundamento *m*, rudimento *m*
basically ['beɪsɪkli] *adv* : fundamentalmente
basil ['beɪzəl, 'bæzəl] *n* : albahaca *f*
basilica [bə'sɪlɪkə] *n* : basílica *f*
basin ['beɪsən] *n* **1** WASHBOWL : palangana *f*, lavamanos *m*, lavabo *m* **2** : cuenca *f* (de un río)
basis ['beɪsəs] *n, pl* **bases** [-,siːz] **1** BASE : base *f*, pilar *m* **2** FOUNDATION : fundamento *m*, base *f* **3 on a weekly basis** : semanalmente

bask ['bæsk] *vi* : disfrutar, deleitarse ⟨to bask in the sun : disfrutar del sol⟩

basket ['bæskət] *n* : cesta *f*, cesto *m*, canasta *f*

basketball ['bæskət,bɔl] *n* : baloncesto *m*, basquetbol *m*

bas–relief [,bɑrɪ'liːf] *n* : bajorrelieve *m*

bass[1] ['bæs] *n, pl* **bass** *or* **basses** : róbalo *m* (pesca)

bass[2] ['beɪs] *n* : bajo *m* (tono, voz, cantante)

bass drum *n* : bombo *m*

basset hound ['bæsət,haʊnd] *n* : basset *m*

bassinet [,bæsə'nɛt] *n* : moisés *m*, cuna *f*

bassist ['beɪsɪst] *n* : bajista *mf*

bassoon [bə'suːn, bæ-] *n* : fagot *m*

bass viol ['beɪs'vaɪəl, -,oːl] → **double bass**

bastard[1] ['bæstərd] *adj* : bastardo

bastard[2] *n* : bastardo *m*, -da *f*

bastardize ['bæstər,daɪz] *vt* **-ized; -izing** DEBASE : degradar, envilecer

baste ['beɪst] *vt* **basted; basting 1** STITCH : hilvanar **2** : bañar (con su jugo durante la cocción)

bastion ['bæstʃən] *n* : bastión *m*, baluarte *m*

bat[1] ['bæt] *vt* **batted; batting 1** HIT : batear **2 without batting an eye** : sin pestañear

bat[2] *n* **1** : murciélago *m* (animal) **2** : bate *m* ⟨baseball bat : bate de beisbol⟩

batch ['bætʃ] *n* : hornada *f*, tanda *f*, grupo *m*, cantidad *f*

bate ['beɪt] *vt* **bated; bating 1** : aminorar, reducir **2 with bated breath** : con ansiedad, aguantando la respiración

bath ['bæθ, 'bɑθ] *n, pl* **baths** ['bæðz, 'bæθs, 'bɑðz, 'bɑθs] **1** BATHING : baño *m* ⟨to take a bath : bañarse⟩ **2** : baño *m* (en fotografía, etc.) **3** BATHROOM : baño *m*, cuarto *m* de baño **4** SPA : balneario *m* **5** LOSS : pérdida *f*

bathe ['beɪð] *v* **bathed; bathing** *vt* **1** WASH : bañar, lavar **2** SOAK : poner en remojo **3** FLOOD : inundar ⟨to bathe with light : inundar de luz⟩ — *vi* : bañarse, ducharse

bather ['beɪðər] *n* : bañista *mf*

bathrobe ['bæθ,roːb] *n* : bata *f* (de baño)

bathroom ['bæθ,ruːm, -,rʊm] *n* : baño *m*, cuarto *m* de baño

bathtub ['bæθ,tʌb] *n* : bañera *f*, tina *f* (de baño)

batiste [bə'tiːst] *n* : batista *f*

baton [bə'tɑn] *n* : batuta *f*, bastón *m*

battalion [bə'tæljən] *n* : batallón *m*

batten ['bætən] *vt* **to batten down the hatches** : cerrar las escotillas

batter[1] ['bætər] *vt* **1** BEAT : aporrear, golpear **2** MISTREAT : maltratar

batter[2] *n* **1** : masa *f* para rebozar **2** HITTER : bateador *m*, -dora *f*

battering ram *n* : ariete *m*

battery ['bætəri] *n, pl* **-teries 1** : lesiones *fpl* ⟨assault and battery : agresión con

lesiones⟩ **2** ARTILLERY : batería *f* **3** : batería *f*, pila *f* (de electricidad) **4** SERIES : serie *f*

batting ['bætɪŋ] *n* **1** *or* **cotton batting** : algodón *m* en láminas **2** : bateo *m* (en beisbol)

battle[1] ['bætəl] *vi* **-tled; -tling** : luchar, pelear

battle[2] *n* : batalla *f*, lucha *f*, pelea *f*

battle–ax ['bætəl,æks] *n* : hacha *f* de guerra

battlefield ['bætəl,fiːld] *n* : campo *m* de batalla

battlements ['bætəlmənts] *npl* : almenas *fpl*

battleship ['bætəl,ʃɪp] *n* : acorazado *m*

batty ['bæti] *adj* **-tier; -est** : chiflado *fam*, chalado *fam*

bauble ['bɔbəl] *n* : chuchería *f*, baratija *f*

Bavarian [bə'vɛriən] *n* : bávaro *m*, -ra *f* — **Bavarian** *adj*

bawdiness ['bɔdinəs] *n* : picardía *f*

bawdy ['bɔdi] *adj* **bawdier; -est** : subido de tono, verde, colorado *Mex*

bawl[1] ['bɔl] *vi* : llorar a gritos

bawl[2] *n* : grito *m*, alarido *m*

bawl out *vt* SCOLD : regañar

bay[1] ['beɪ] *vi* HOWL : aullar

bay[2] *adj* : castaño, zaino (dícese de los caballos)

bay[3] *n* **1** : bahía *f* ⟨Bay of Campeche : Bahía de Campeche⟩ **2** *or* **bay horse** : caballo *m* castaño **3** LAUREL : laurel *m* **4** HOWL : aullido *m* **5** : saliente *m* ⟨bay window : ventana en saliente⟩ **6** COMPARTMENT : área *f*, compartimento *m* **7 at** ~ : acorralado

bayberry ['beɪ,bɛri] *n, pl* **-ries** : arrayán *m* brabántico

bayonet[1] [,beɪə'nɛt, 'beɪə,nɛt] *vt* **-neted; -neting** : herir *o* matar) con bayoneta

bayonet[2] *n* : bayoneta *f*

bayou ['baɪ,uː, -,oː] *n* : pantano *m*

bazaar [bə'zɑr] *n* **1** : bazar *m* **2** SALE : venta *f* benéfica

bazooka [bə'zuːkə] *n* : bazuca *f*

BB ['bi:bi] *n* : balín *m*

be ['bi:] *v* **was** ['wəz, 'wɑz]; **were** ['wər]; **been** ['bɪn]; **being; am** ['æm]; **is** ['ɪz]; **are** ['ɑr] *vi* **1** (*expressing equality*) : ser ⟨José is a doctor : José es doctor⟩ ⟨I'm Ann's sister : soy la hermana de Ana⟩ **2** (*expressing quality*) : ser ⟨the tree is tall : el árbol es alto⟩ ⟨you're silly! : ¡eres tonto!⟩ **3** (*expressing origin or possession*) : ser ⟨she's from Managua : es de Managua⟩ ⟨it's mine : es mío⟩ **4** (*expressing location*) : estar ⟨my mother is at home : mi madre está en casa⟩ ⟨the cups are on the table : las tazas están en la mesa⟩ **5** (*expressing existence*) : ser, existir ⟨to be or not to be : ser, o no ser⟩ ⟨I think, therefore I am : pienso, luego existo⟩ **6** (*expressing a state of being*) : estar, tener ⟨how are you? : ¿cómo estás?⟩ ⟨I'm cold : tengo frío⟩ ⟨she's 10 years old : tiene 10 años⟩ ⟨they're both sick : están enfermos los dos⟩ — v impers **1** (*indicating time*) : ser ⟨it's eight o'clock : son las ocho⟩ ⟨it's Friday : hoy es viernes⟩ **2** (*indicating a condition*) : hacer, estar ⟨it's sunny : hace sol⟩ ⟨it's very dark outside : está bien oscuro afuera⟩ — v aux **1** (*expressing progression*) : estar ⟨what are you doing?—I'm working : ¿qué haces?—estoy trabajando⟩ **2** (*expressing occurrence*) : ser ⟨it was finished yesterday : fue acabado ayer, se acabó ayer⟩ ⟨it was cooked in the oven : se cocinó en el horno⟩ **3** (*expressing possibility*) : poderse ⟨can she be trusted? : ¿se puede confiar en ella?⟩ **4** (*expressing obligation*) : deber ⟨you are to stay here : debes quedarte aquí⟩ ⟨he was to come yesterday : se esperaba que viniese ayer⟩

beach¹ [ˈbiːtʃ] vt : hacer embarrancar, hacer varar, hacer encallar

beach² n : playa f

beachcomber [ˈbiːtʃˌkoːmər] n : raquero m, -ra f

beachhead [ˈbiːtʃˌhɛd] n : cabeza f de playa

beacon [ˈbiːkən] n : faro m

bead¹ [ˈbiːd] vi : formarse en gotas

bead² n **1** : cuenta f **2** DROP : gota f **3 beads** npl NECKLACE : collar m

beady [ˈbiːdi] adj **beadier; -est 1** : de forma de cuenta **2 beady eyes** : ojos mpl pequeños y brillantes

beagle [ˈbiːgəl] n : beagle m

beak [ˈbiːk] n : pico m

beaker [ˈbiːkər] n **1** CUP : taza f alta **2** : vaso m de precipitados (en un laboratorio)

beam¹ [ˈbiːm] vi **1** SHINE : brillar **2** SMILE : sonreír radiantemente — vt BROADCAST : transmitir, emitir

beam² n **1** : viga f, barra f **2** RAY : rayo m, haz m de luz **3** : haz m de radiofaro (para guiar pilotos, etc.)

bean [ˈbiːn] n **1** : habichuela f, frijol m **2 broad bean** : haba f **3 string bean** : judía f

bear¹ [ˈbær] v **bore** [ˈbor]; **borne** [ˈbɔrn]; **bearing** vt **1** CARRY : llevar, portar **2** : dar a luz a (un niño) **3** PRODUCE : dar (frutas, cosechas) **4** ENDURE, SUPPORT : soportar, resistir, aguantar — vi **1** TURN : doblar, dar la vuelta ⟨bear right : doble a la derecha⟩ **2 to bear up** : resistir

bear² n, pl **bears** or **bear** : oso m, osa f

bearable [ˈbærəbəl] adj : soportable

beard [ˈbɪrd] n **1** : barba f **2** : arista f (de plantas)

bearded [ˈbɪrdəd] adj : barbudo, de barba

bearer [ˈbærər] n : portador m, -dora f

bearing [ˈbærɪŋ] n **1** CONDUCT, MANNERS : comportamiento m, modales mpl **2** SUPPORT : soporte f **3** SIGNIFICANCE : relación f, importancia f ⟨to have no bearing on : no tener nada que ver con⟩ **4** : cojinete m, rodamiento m

(de una máquina) **5** COURSE, DIRECTION : dirección f, rumbo m ⟨to get one's bearings : orientarse⟩

beast [ˈbiːst] n **1** : bestia f, fiera f ⟨beast of burden : animal de carga⟩ **2** BRUTE : bruto m, -ta f; bestia mf

beastly [ˈbiːstli] adj : detestable, repugnante

beat¹ [ˈbiːt] v **beat; beaten** [ˈbiːtən] or **beat; beating** vt **1** STRIKE : golpear, pegar, darle una paliza (a alguien) **2** DEFEAT : vencer, derrotar **3** AVOID : anticiparse a, evitar ⟨to beat the crowd : evitar el gentío⟩ **4** MASH, WHIP : batir — vi THROB : palpitar, latir

beat² adj EXHAUSTED : derrengado, muy cansado ⟨I'm beat! : ¡estoy molido!⟩

beat³ n **1** : golpe m, redoble m (de un tambor), latido m (del corazón) **2** RHYTHM : ritmo m, tiempo m

beater [ˈbiːtər] n **1** : batidor m, -dora f **2** EGGBEATER : batidor m

beatific [ˌbiːəˈtɪfɪk] adj : beatífico

beatitude [biˈætəˌtuːd] n **1** : beatitud f **2 the Beatitudes** : las bienaventuranzas

beau [ˈboː] n, pl **beaux** or **beaus** : pretendiente m, galán m

beautification [ˌbjuːtəfəˈkeɪʃən] n : embellecimiento m

beautiful [ˈbjuːtɪfəl] adj : hermoso, bello, lindo, precioso

beautifully [ˈbjuːtɪfəli] adv **1** ATTRACTIVELY : hermosamente **2** EXCELLENTLY : maravillosamente, excelentemente

beauty [ˈbjuːti] n, pl **-ties** : belleza f, hermosura f, beldad f

beauty shop or **beauty salon** n : salón m de belleza

beaver [ˈbiːvər] n : castor m

because [bɪˈkʌz, -ˈkɔz] conj : porque

because of prep : por, a causa de, debido a

beck [ˈbɛk] n **to be at the beck and call of** : estar a la entera disposición de, estar sometido a la voluntad de

beckon [ˈbɛkən] vi **to beckon to someone** : hacerle señas a alguien

become [bɪˈkʌm] v **-came** [-ˈkeɪm]; **-come; -coming** vi : hacerse, volverse, ponerse ⟨he became famous : se hizo famoso⟩ ⟨to become sad : ponerse triste⟩ ⟨to become accustomed to : acostumbrarse a⟩ — vt **1** BEFIT : ser apropiado para **2** SUIT : favorecer, quedarle bien (a alguien) ⟨that dress becomes you : ese vestido te favorece⟩

becoming [bɪˈkʌmɪŋ] adj **1** SUITABLE : apropiado **2** FLATTERING : favorecedor

bed¹ [ˈbɛd] v **bedded; bedding** vt : acostar — vi : acostarse

bed² n **1** : cama f, lecho m **2** : cauce m (de un río), fondo m (del mar) **3** : arriate m (para plantas) **4** LAYER, STRATUM : estrato m, capa f

bedbug ['bɛd,bʌg] *n* : chinche *f*

bedclothes ['bɛd,kloːðz, -,kloːz] *npl* : ropa *f* de cama, sábanas *fpl*

bedding ['bɛdɪŋ] *n* **1** → **bedclothes 2** : cama *f* (para animales)

bedeck [bɪ'dɛk] *vt* : adornar, engalanar

bedevil [bɪ'dɛvəl] *vt* -**iled** *or* -**illed**; -**iling** *or* -**illing** : acosar, plagar

bedlam ['bɛdləm] *n* : locura *f*, caos *m*, alboroto *m*

bedraggled [bɪ'drægəld] *adj* : desaliñado, despeinado

bedridden ['bɛd,rɪdən] *adj* : postrado en cama

bedrock ['bɛd,rak] *n* : lecho *m* de roca

bedroom ['bɛd,ruːm, -,rʊm] *n* : dormitorio *m*, habitación *f*, pieza *f*, recámara *f Col, Mex, Pan*

bedspread ['bɛd,sprɛd] *n* : cubrecama *m*, colcha *f*, cobertor *m*

bee ['biː] *n* **1** : abeja *f* (insecto) **2** GATHERING : círculo *m*, reunión *f*

beech ['biːtʃ] *n, pl* **beeches** *or* **beech** : haya *f*

beechnut ['biːtʃ,nʌt] *n* : hayuco *m*

beef¹ ['biːf] *vt* **to beef up** : fortalecer, reforzar — *vi* COMPLAIN : quejarse

beef² *n, pl* **beefs** ['biːfs] *or* **beeves** ['biːvz] : carne *f* de vaca, carne *f* de res *CA, Mex*

beefsteak ['biːf,steɪk] *n* : filete *m*, bistec *m*

beehive ['biː,haɪv] *n* : colmena *f*

beekeeper ['biː,kiːpər] *n* : apicultor *m*, -tora *f*

beeline ['biː,laɪn] *n* **to make a beeline for** : ir derecho a, ir directo hacia

been → **be**

beep¹ ['biːp] *v* : pitar

beep² *n* : pitido *m*

beeper ['biːpər] *n* : busca *m*, buscapersonas *m*

beer ['bɪr] *n* : cerveza *f*

beeswax ['biːz,wæks] *n* : cera *f* de abejas

beet ['biːt] *n* : remolacha *f*, betabel *m Mex*

beetle ['biːtəl] *n* : escarabajo *m*

befall [bɪ'fɔl] *v* -**fell** [-'fɛl]; -**fallen** [-'fɔlən] *vt* : sucederle a, acontecerle a — *vi* : acontecer

befit [bɪ'fɪt] *vt* -**fitted**; -**fitting** : convenir a, ser apropiado para

before¹ [bɪ'for] *adv* **1** : antes ⟨before and after : antes y después⟩ **2** : anterior ⟨the month before : el mes anterior⟩

before² *conj* : antes que ⟨he would die before surrendering : moriría antes que rendirse⟩

before³ *prep* **1** : antes de ⟨before eating : antes de comer⟩ **2** : delante de, ante ⟨I stood before the house : estaba parada delante de la casa⟩ ⟨before the judge : ante el juez⟩

beforehand [bɪ'for,hænd] *adv* : antes, por adelantado, de antemano, con anticipación

befriend [bɪ'frɛnd] *vt* : hacerse amigo de

befuddle [bɪ'fʌdəl] *vt* -**dled**; -**dling** : aturdir, ofuscar, confundir

beg ['bɛg] *v* **begged**; **begging** *vt* : pedir, mendigar, suplicar ⟨I begged him to go : le supliqué que fuera⟩ — *vi* : mendigar, pedir limosna

beget [bɪ'gɛt] *vt* -**got** [-'gat]; -**gotten** [-'gatən] *or* -**got**; -**getting** : engendrar

beggar ['bɛgər] *n* : mendigo *m*, -ga *f*; pordiosero *m*, -ra *f*

begin [bɪ'gɪn] *v* -**gan** [-'gæn]; -**gun** [-'gʌn]; -**ginning** *vt* : empezar, comenzar, iniciar — *vi* **1** START : empezar, comenzar, iniciarse **2** ORIGINATE : nacer, originarse **3 to begin with** : en primer lugar, para empezar

beginner [bɪ'gɪnər] *n* : principiante *mf*

beginning [bɪ'gɪnɪŋ] *n* : principio *m*, comienzo *m*

begone [bɪ'gɔn] *interj* : ¡fuera de aquí!

begonia [bɪ'goːnjə] *n* : begonia *f*

begrudge [bɪ'grʌdʒ] *vt* -**grudged**; -**grudging 1** : dar de mala gana **2** ENVY : envidiar, resentir

beguile [bɪ'gaɪl] *vt* -**guiled**; -**guiling 1** DECEIVE : engañar **2** AMUSE : divertir, entretener

behalf [bɪ'hæf, -'haf] *n* **1** : favor *m*, beneficio *m*, parte *f* **2 on behalf of** *or* **in behalf of** : de parte de, en nombre de

behave [bɪ'heɪv] *vi* -**haved**; -**having** : comportarse, portarse

behavior [bɪ'heɪvjər] *n* : comportamiento *m*, conducta *f*

behead [bɪ'hɛd] *vt* : decapitar

behest [bɪ'hɛst] *n* **1** : mandato *m*, orden *f* **2 at the behest of** : a instancia de

behind¹ [bɪ'haɪnd] *adv* : atrás, detrás ⟨to fall behind : quedarse atrás⟩

behind² *prep* **1** : atrás de, detrás de, tras ⟨behind the house : detrás de la casa⟩ ⟨one behind another : uno tras otro⟩ **2** : atrasado con, después de ⟨behind schedule : atrasado con el trabajo⟩ ⟨I arrived behind the others : llegué después de los otros⟩ **3** SUPPORTING : en apoyo de, detrás

behind³ [bɪ'haɪnd, 'biː,haɪnd] *n* : trasero *m*

behold [bɪ'hoːld] *vt* -**held**; -**holding** : contemplar

beholder [bɪ'hoːldər] *n* : observador *m*, -dora *f*

behoove [bɪ'huːv] *vt* -**hooved**; -**hooving** : convenirle a, corresponderle a ⟨it behooves us to help him : nos conviene ayudarlo⟩

beige¹ ['beɪʒ] *adj* : beige

beige² *n* : beige *m*

being ['biːɪŋ] *n* **1** EXISTENCE : ser *m*, existencia *f* **2** CREATURE : ser *m*, ente *m*

belabor [bɪ'leɪbər] *vt* **to belabor the point** : extenderse sobre el tema

belated [bɪ'leɪtəd] *adj* : tardío, retrasado

belch¹ ['bɛltʃ] *vi* **1** BURP : eructar **2** EXPEL : expulsar, arrojar

belch² *n* : eructo *m*

beleaguer [bɪˈliːgər] *vt* **1** BESIEGE : asediar, sitiar **2** HARASS : fastidiar, molestar

belfry [ˈbɛlfri] *n, pl* **-fries** : campanario *m*

Belgian [ˈbɛldʒən] *n* : belga *mf* — **Belgian** *adj*

belie [bɪˈlaɪ] *vt* **-lied; -lying 1** MISREPRESENT : falsear, ocultar **2** CONTRADICT : contradecir, desmentir

belief [bəˈliːf] *n* **1** TRUST : confianza *f* **2** CONVICTION : creencia *f*, convicción *f* **3** FAITH : fe *f*

believable [bəˈliːvəbəl] *adj* : verosímil, creíble

believe [bəˈliːv] *v* **-lieved; -lieving** : creer

believer [bəˈliːvər] *n* **1** : creyente *mf* **2** : partidario *m*, -ria *f*; entusiasta *mf* ⟨she's a great believer in vitamins : ella es una gran partidaria de las vitaminas⟩

belittle [bɪˈlɪtəl] *vt* **-littled; -littling 1** DISPARAGE : menospreciar, denigrar, rebajar **2** MINIMIZE : minimizar, quitar importancia a

Belizean [bəˈliːziən] *n* : beliceño *m*, -ña *f* — **Belizean** *adj*

bell[1] [ˈbɛl] *vt* : ponerle un cascabel a

bell[2] *n* : campana *f*, cencerro *m* (para una vaca o cabra), cascabel *m* (para un gato), timbre *m* (de teléfono, de la puerta)

belle [ˈbɛl] *n* : belleza *f*, beldad *f*

bellhop [ˈbɛlˌhɑp] *n* : botones *m*

bellicose [ˈbɛlɪˌkoːs] *adj* : belicoso *m* — **bellicosity** [ˌbɛlɪˈkɑsəti] *n*

belligerence [bəˈlɪdʒərənts] *n* : agresividad *f*, beligerancia *f*

belligerent[1] [bəˈlɪdʒərənt] *adj* : agresivo, beligerante

belligerent[2] *n* : beligerante *mf*

bellow[1] [ˈbɛˌloː] *vi* : bramar, mugir — *vt* : gritar

bellow[2] *n* : bramido *m*, grito *m*

bellows [ˈbɛˌloːz] *ns & pl* : fuelle *m*

bellwether [ˈbɛlˌwɛðər] *n* : líder *mf*

belly[1] [ˈbɛli] *vi* **-lied; -lying** SWELL : hincharse, inflarse

belly[2] *n, pl* **-lies** : abdomen *m*, vientre *m*, barriga *f*, panza *f*

belong [bɪˈlɔŋ] *vi* **1** : pertenecer (a), ser propiedad (de) ⟨it belongs to her : pertenece a ella, es suyo, es de ella⟩ **2** : ser parte (de), ser miembro (de) ⟨he belongs to the club : es miembro del club⟩ **3** : deber estar, ir ⟨your coat belongs in the closet : tu abrigo va en el ropero⟩

belongings [bɪˈlɔŋɪŋz] *npl* : pertenencias *fpl*, efectos *mpl* personales

beloved[1] [bɪˈlʌvəd, -ˈlʌvd] *adj* : querido, amado

beloved[2] *n* : amado *m*, -da *f*; enamorado *m*, -da *f*; amor *m*

below[1] [bɪˈloː] *adv* : abajo

below[2] *prep* **1** : abajo de, debajo de ⟨below the window : debajo de la ventana⟩ **2** : por debajo de, bajo ⟨below average : por debajo del promedio⟩ ⟨5 degrees below zero : 5 grados bajo cero⟩

belt[1] [ˈbɛlt] *vt* **1** : ceñir con un cinturón, ponerle un cinturón a **2** THRASH : darle una paliza a, darle un trancazo a

belt[2] *n* **1** : cinturón *m*, cinto *m* (para el talle) **2** BAND, STRAP : cinta *f*, correa *f*, banda *f Mex* **3** AREA : frente *m*, zona *f*

beltway [ˈbɛltˌweɪ] *n* : carretera *f* de circunvalación; periférico *m* CA, Mex; libramiento *m* Mex

bemoan [bɪˈmoːn] *vt* : lamentarse de

bemuse [bɪˈmjuːz] *vt* **-mused; -musing 1** BEWILDER : confundir, desconcertar **2** ENGROSS : absorber

bench [ˈbɛntʃ] *n* **1** SEAT : banco *m*, escaño *m*, banca *f* **2** : estrado *m* (de un juez) **3** COURT : tribunal *m*

bend[1] [ˈbɛnd] *v* **bent** [ˈbɛnt;]; **bending** *vt* : torcer, doblar, curvar, flexionar — *vi* **1** : torcerse, agacharse ⟨to bend over : inclinarse⟩ **2** TURN : torcer, hacer una curva

bend[2] *n* **1** TURN : vuelta *f*, recodo *m* **2** CURVE : curva *f*, ángulo *m*, codo *m*

beneath[1] [bɪˈniːθ] *adv* : bajo, abajo, debajo

beneath[2] *prep* : bajo de, abajo de, por bajo

benediction [ˌbɛnəˈdɪkʃən] *n* : bendición *f*

benefactor [ˈbɛnəˌfæktər] *n* : benefactor *m*, -tora *f*

beneficence [bəˈnɛfəsənts] *n* : beneficencia *f*

beneficent [bəˈnɛfəsənt] *adj* : benéfico, caritativo

beneficial [ˌbɛnəˈfɪʃəl] *adj* : beneficioso, provechoso — **beneficially** *adv*

beneficiary [ˌbɛnəˈfɪʃiˌɛri, -ˈfɪʃəri] *n, pl* **-ries** : beneficiario *m*, -ria *f*

benefit[1] [ˈbɛnəfɪt] *vt* : beneficiar — *vi* : beneficiarse

benefit[2] *n* **1** ADVANTAGE : beneficio *m*, ventaja *f*, provecho *m* **2** AID : asistencia *f*, beneficio *m* **3** : función *f* benéfica (para recaudar fondos)

benevolence [bəˈnɛvələnts] *n* : bondad *f*, benevolencia *f*

benevolent [bəˈnɛvələnt] *adj* : benévolo, bondadoso — **benevolently** *adv*

Bengali [bɛnˈgɔli, bɛŋ-] *n* **1** : bengalí *mf* **2** : bengalí *m* (idioma) — **Bengali** *adj*

benign [bɪˈnaɪn] *adj* **1** GENTLE, KIND : benévolo, amable **2** FAVORABLE : propicio, favorable **3** MILD : benigno ⟨a benign tumor : un tumor benigno⟩

Beninese [bəˌnɪˈniːz, -ˌniː-, -ˈniːs; ˌbnɪˈ-] *n* : beninés *m*, -nesa *f* — **Beninese** *adj*

bent [ˈbɛnt] *n* : aptitud *f*, inclinación *f*

benumb [bɪˈnʌm] *vt* : entumecer

benzene [ˈbɛnˌziːn] *n* : benceno *m*

bequeath [bɪˈkwiːθ, -ˈkwiːð] *vt* : legar, dejar en testamento

bequest [bɪˈkwɛst] *n* : legado *m*

berate [bɪˈreɪt] *vt* **-rated; -rating** : reprender, regañar

bereaved[1] [bɪˈriːvd] *adj* : que está de luto, afligido (por la muerte de alguien)

bereaved² *n* **the bereaved** : los deudos del difunto (o de la difunta)
bereavement [bɪˈriːvmənt] *n* **1** SORROW : dolor *m*, pesar *m* **2** LOSS : pérdida *f*
bereft [bɪˈrɛft] *adj* : privado, desprovisto
beret [bəˈreɪ] *n* : boina *f*
beriberi [ˌbɛriˈbɛri] *n* : beriberi *m*
berm [ˈbərm] *n* : arcén *m*
berry [ˈbɛri] *n*, *pl* **-ries** : baya *f*
berserk [bərˈsərk, -ˈzərk] *adj* **1** : enloquecido **2 to go beserk** : volverse loco
berth¹ [ˈbərθ] *vi* : atracar
berth² *n* **1** DOCK : atracadero *m* **2** ACCOMMODATION : litera *f*, camarote *m* **3** POSITION : trabajo *m*, puesto *m*
beryl [ˈbɛrəl] *n* : berilo *m*
beseech [bɪˈsiːtʃ] *vt* **-seeched** *or* **-sought** [-ˈsɔt]; **-seeching** : suplicar, implorar, rogar
beset [bɪˈsɛt] *vt* **-set; -setting 1** HARASS : acosar **2** SURROUND : rodear
beside [bɪˈsaɪd] *prep* : al lado de, junto a
besides¹ [bɪˈsaɪdz] *adv* **1** ALSO : además, también, aparte **2** MOREOVER : además, por otra parte
besides² *prep* **1** : además de, aparte de ⟨six others besides you : seis otros además de ti⟩ **2** EXCEPT : excepto, fuera de, aparte de
besiege [bɪˈsiːdʒ] *vt* **-sieged; -sieging** : asediar, sitiar, cercar
besmirch [bɪˈsmərtʃ] *vt* : ensuciar, mancillar
best¹ [ˈbɛst] *vt* : superar, ganar a
best² *adv* (*superlative of* **well**) : mejor ⟨as best I can : lo mejor que puedo⟩
best³ *adj* (*superlative of* **good**) : mejor ⟨my best friend : mi mejor amigo⟩
best⁴ *n* **1 the best** : lo mejor, el mejor, la mejor, los mejores, las mejores **2 at ~** : a lo más **3 to do one's best** : hacer todo lo posible
bestial [ˈbɛstʃəl, ˈbiːs-] *adj* **1** : bestial **2** BRUTISH : brutal, salvaje
best man *n* : padrino *m*
bestow [bɪˈstoː] *vt* : conferir, otorgar, conceder
bestowal [bɪˈstoːəl] *n* : concesión *f*, otorgamiento *m*
bet¹ [ˈbɛt] *v* **bet; betting** *vt* : apostar — *vi* **to bet on** : apostarle a
bet² *n* : apuesta *f*
betoken [bɪˈtoːkən] *vt* : denotar, ser indicio de
betray [bɪˈtreɪ] *vt* **1** : traicionar ⟨to betray one's country : traicionar uno a su patria⟩ **2** DIVULGE, REVEAL : delatar, revelar ⟨to betray a secret : revelar un secreto⟩
betrayal [bɪˈtreɪəl] *n* : traición *f*, delación *f*, revelación *f* ⟨betrayal of trust : abuso de confianza⟩
betrothal [bɪˈtroːðəl, -ˈtrɔ-] *n* : esponsales *mpl*, compromiso *m*
betrothed [bɪˈtroːðd, -ˈtrɔθt] *n* FIANCÉ : prometido *m*, -da *f*

better¹ [ˈbɛtər] *vt* **1** IMPROVE : mejorar **2** SURPASS : superar
better² *adv* (*comparative of* **well**) **1** : mejor **2** MORE : más ⟨better than 50 miles : más de 50 millas⟩
better³ *adj* (*comparative of* **good**) **1** : mejor ⟨the weather is better today : hace mejor tiempo hoy⟩ ⟨I was sick, but now I'm better : estuve enfermo, pero ahora estoy mejor⟩ **2** : mayor ⟨the better part of a month : la mayor parte de un mes⟩
better⁴ *n* **1** : el mejor, la mejor ⟨the better of the two : el mejor de los dos⟩ **2 to get the better of** : vencer a, quedar por encima de, superar
betterment [ˈbɛtərmənt] *n* : mejoramiento *m*, mejora *f*
bettor *or* **better** [ˈbɛtər] *n* : apostador *m*, -dora *f*
between¹ [bɪˈtwiːn] *adv* **1** : en medio, por lo medio **2 in ~** : intermedio
between² *prep* : entre
bevel¹ [ˈbɛvəl] *v* **-eled** *or* **-elled; -eling** *or* **-elling** *vt* : biselar — *vi* INCLINE : inclinarse
bevel² *n* : bisel *m*
beverage [ˈbɛvrɪdʒ, ˈbɛvə-] *n* : bebida *f*
bevy [ˈbɛvi] *n*, *pl* **bevies** : grupo *m* (de personas), bandada *f* (de pájaros)
bewail [bɪˈweɪl] *vt* : lamentarse de, llorar
beware [bɪˈwær] *vi* **to beware of** : tener cuidado con ⟨beware of the dog! : ¡cuidado con el perro!⟩ — *vt* : guardarse de, cuidarse de
bewilder [bɪˈwɪldər] *vt* : desconcertar, dejar perplejo
bewilderment [bɪˈwɪldərmənt] *n* : desconcierto *m*, perplejidad *f*
bewitch [bɪˈwɪtʃ] *vt* **1** : hechizar, embrujar **2** CHARM : cautivar, encantar
bewitchment [bɪˈwɪtʃmənt] *n* : hechizo *m*
beyond¹ [biˈjɑnd] *adv* **1** FARTHER, LATER : más allá, más lejos (en el espacio), más adelante (en el tiempo) **2** MORE : más ⟨$50 and beyond : $50 o más⟩
beyond² *n* **the beyond** : el más allá, lo desconocido
beyond³ *prep* **1** : más allá de ⟨beyond the frontier : más allá de la frontera⟩ **2** : fuera de ⟨beyond one's reach : fuera de su alcance⟩ **3** BESIDES : además de
biannual [ˌbaɪˈænjʊəl] *adj* : bianual — **biannually** *adv*
bias¹ [ˈbaɪəs] *vt* **-ased** *or* **-assed; -asing** *or* **-assing 1** : predisponer, sesgar, influir en, afectar **2 to be biased against** : tener prejuicio contra
bias² *n* **1** : sesgo *m*, bies *m* (en la costura) **2** PREJUDICE : prejuicio *m* **3** TENDENCY : inclinación *f*, tendencia *f*
biased [ˈbaɪəst] *adj* : tendencioso, parcial
bib [ˈbɪb] *n* **1** : peto *m* **2** : babero *m* (para niños)
Bible [ˈbaɪbəl] *n* : Biblia *f*
biblical [ˈbɪblɪkəl] *adj* : bíblico

bibliographer [ˌbɪbliˈɑgrəfər] *n* : bibliógrafo *m*, -fa *f*
bibliographic [ˌbɪbliəˈgræfɪk] *adj* : bibliográfico
bibliography [ˌbɪbliˈɑgrəfi] *n*, *pl* **-phies** : bibliografía *f*
bicameral [ˌbaɪˈkæmərəl] *adj* : bicameral
bicarbonate [ˌbaɪˈkɑrbənət, -ˌneɪt] *n* : bicarbonato *m*
bicentennial [ˌbaɪsɛnˈtɛniəl] *n* : bicentenario *m*
biceps [ˈbaɪˌsɛps] *ns & pl* : bíceps *m*
bicker[1] [ˈbɪkər] *vi* : pelear, discutir, reñir
bicker[2] *n* : pelea *f*, riña *f*, discusión *f*
bicuspid [baɪˈkʌspɪd] *n* : premolar *m*, diente *m* bicúspide
bicycle[1] [ˈbaɪsɪkəl, -ˌsɪ-] *vi* **-cled; -cling** : ir en bicicleta
bicycle[2] *n* : bicicleta *f*
bicycling [ˈbaɪsɪkəlɪŋ] *n* : ciclismo *m*
bicyclist [ˈbaɪsɪkəlɪst] *n* : ciclista *mf*
bid[1] [ˈbɪd] *vt* **bade** [ˈbæd, ˈbeɪd] *or* **bid; bidden** [ˈbɪdən] *or* **bid; bidding 1** ORDER : pedir, mandar **2** INVITE : invitar **3** SAY : dar, decir ⟨to bid good evening : dar las buenas noches⟩ ⟨to bid farewell to : decir adiós a⟩ **4** : ofrecer (en una subasta), declarar (en juegos de cartas)
bid[2] *n* **1** OFFER : oferta *f* (en una subasta), declaración *f* (en juegos de cartas) **2** INVITATION : invitación *f* **3** ATTEMPT : intento *m*, tentativa *f*
bidder [ˈbɪdər] *n* : postor *m*, -tora *f*
bide [ˈbaɪd] *v* **bode** [ˈboːd] *or* **bided; bided; biding** *vt* : esperar, aguardar ⟨to bide one's time : esperar el momento oportuno⟩ — *vi* DWELL : morar, vivir
biennial [baɪˈɛniəl] *adj* : bienal — **biennially** *adv*
bier [ˈbɪr] *n* **1** STAND : andas *fpl* **2** COFFIN : ataúd *m*, féretro *m*
bifocals [ˈbaɪˌfoːkəlz] *npl* : lentes *mpl* bifocales, bifocales *mpl*
big [ˈbɪg] *adj* **bigger; biggest 1** LARGE : grande **2** PREGNANT : embarazada **3** IMPORTANT, MAJOR : importante, grande ⟨a big decision : una gran decisión⟩ **4** POPULAR : popular, famoso, conocido
bigamist [ˈbɪgəmɪst] *n* : bígamo *m*, -ma *f*
bigamous [ˈbɪgəməs] *adj* : bígamo
bigamy [ˈbɪgəmi] *n* : bigamia *f*
Big Dipper → **dipper**
bighorn [ˈbɪgˌhɔrn] *n*, *pl* **-horn** *or* **-horns** *or* **bighorn sheep** : oveja *f* salvaje de las montañas
bight [ˈbaɪt] *n* : bahía *f*, ensenada *f*, golfo *m*
bigot [ˈbɪgət] *n* : intolerante *mf*
bigoted [ˈbɪgətəd] *adj* : intolerante, prejuiciado, fanático
bigotry [ˈbɪgətri] *n*, *pl* **-tries** : intolerancia *f*
big shot *n* : pez *m* gordo *fam*, mandamás *mf*

bigwig [ˈbɪgˌwɪg] → **big shot**
bike [ˈbaɪk] *n* **1** : bicicleta *f*, bici *f fam* **2** : motocicleta *f*, moto *f*
bikini [bəˈkiːni] *n* : bikini *m*
bilateral [baɪˈlætərəl] *adj* : bilateral — **bilaterally** *adv*
bile [ˈbaɪl] *n* **1** : bilis *f* **2** IRRITABILITY : mal genio *m*
bilingual [baɪˈlɪŋgwəl] *adj* : bilingüe
bilious [ˈbɪliəs] *adj* **1** : bilioso **2** IRRITABLE : bilioso, colérico
bilk [ˈbɪlk] *vt* : burlar, estafar, defraudar
bill[1] [ˈbɪl] *vt* : pasarle la cuenta a — *vi* : acariciar ⟨to bill and coo : acariciarse⟩
bill[2] *n* **1** LAW : proyecto *m* de ley, ley *f* **2** INVOICE : cuenta *f*, factura *f* **3** POSTER : cartel *m* **4** PROGRAM : programa *m* (del teatro) **5** : billete *m* ⟨a five-dollar bill : un billete de cinco dólares⟩ **6** BEAK : pico *m*
billboard [ˈbɪlˌbɔrd] *n* : cartelera *f*
billet[1] [ˈbɪlət] *vt* : acuartelar, alojar
billet[2] *n* : alojamiento *m*
billfold [ˈbɪlˌfoːld] *n* : billetera *f*, cartera *f*
billiards [ˈbɪljərdz] *n* : billar *m*
billion [ˈbɪljən] *n*, *pl* **billions** *or* **billion** : mil millones *mpl*
billow[1] [ˈbɪlo] *vi* : hincharse, inflarse
billow[2] *n* **1** WAVE : ola *f* **2** CLOUD : nube *f* ⟨a billow of smoke : un nube de humo⟩
billowy [ˈbɪlowi] *adj* : ondulante
billy goat [ˈbɪliˌgoːt] *n* : macho *m* cabrío
bin [ˈbɪn] *n* : cubo *m*, cajón *m*
binary [ˈbaɪnəri, -ˌnɛri] *adj* : binario *m*
bind [ˈbaɪnd] *vt* **bound** [ˈbaʊnd]; **binding 1** TIE : atar, amarrar **2** OBLIGATE : obligar **3** UNITE : aglutinar, ligar, unir **4** BANDAGE : vendar **5** : encuadernar (un libro)
binder [ˈbaɪndər] *n* **1** FOLDER : carpeta *f* **2** : encuadernador *m*, -dora *f* (de libros)
binding [ˈbaɪndɪŋ] *n* **1** : encuadernación *f* (de libros) **2** COVER : cubierta *f*, forro *m*
binge [ˈbɪndʒ] *n* : juerga *f*, parranda *f fam*
bingo [ˈbɪŋˌgoː] *n*, *pl* **-gos** : bingo *m*
binocular [baɪˈnɑkjələr, bə-] *adj* : binocular
binoculars [bəˈnɑkjələrz, baɪ-] *npl* : binoculares *mpl*
biochemical[1] [ˌbaɪoˈkɛmɪkəl] *adj* : bioquímico
biochemical[2] *n* : bioquímico *m*
biochemist [ˌbaɪoˈkɛmɪst] *n* : bioquímico *m*, -ca *f*
biochemistry [ˌbaɪoˈkɛməstri] *n* : bioquímica *f*
biodegradable [ˌbaɪodɪˈgreɪdəbəl] *adj* : biodegradable
biodegradation [ˌbaɪodɛgrəˈdeɪʃən] *n* : biodegradación *f*
biodegrade [ˌbaɪodɪˈgreɪd] *vi* **-graded; -grading** : biodegradarse

biodiversity [ˌbaɪodə'vərsəti, -daɪ-] *n, pl* **-ties** : bioversidad *f*

biographer [baɪ'ɑgrəfər] *n* : biógrafo *m*, -fa *f*

biographical [ˌbaɪə'græfɪkəl] *adj* : biográfico

biography [baɪ'ɑgrəfi, bi:-] *n, pl* **-phies** : biografía *f*

biologic [ˌbaɪə'lɑʤɪk] *or* **biological** [-ʤɪkəl] *adj* : biológico

biologist [baɪ'ɑləʤɪst] *n* : biólogo *m*, -ga *f*

biology [baɪ'ɑləʤi] *n* : biología *f*

biophysical [ˌbaɪo'fɪzɪkəl] *adj* : biofísico

biophysicist [ˌbaɪo'fɪzəsɪst] *n* : biofísico *m*, -ca *f*

biophysics [ˌbaɪo'fɪzɪks] *ns & pl* : biofísica *f*

biopsy ['baɪˌɑpsi] *n, pl* **-sies** : biopsia *f*

biosphere ['baɪəˌsfɪr] *n* : biosfera *f*, biósfera *f*

biotechnology [ˌbaɪotɛk'nɑləʤi] *n* : biotecnología *f*

biotic [baɪ'ɑtɪk] *adj* : biótico

bipartisan [baɪ'pɑrtəzən, -sən] *adj* : bipartidista, de dos partidas

biped ['baɪˌpɛd] *n* : bípedo *m*

birch ['bərʧ] *n* : abedul *m*

bird ['bərd] *n* : pájaro *m* (pequeño), ave *f* (grande)

birdbath ['bərdˌbæθ, -ˌbɑθ] *n* : pila *f* para pájaros

bird dog *n* : perro *m*, -rra *f* de caza

bird of prey *n* : ave *f* rapaz, ave *f* de presa

birdseed ['bərdˌsi:d] *n* : alpiste *m*

bird's–eye ['bərdzˌaɪ] *adj* **1** : visto desde arriba ⟨bird's-eye view : vista aérea⟩ **2** CURSORY : rápido, somero

birth ['bərθ] *n* **1** : nacimiento *m*, parto *m* **2** ORIGIN : origen *m*, nacimiento *m*

birthday ['bərθˌdeɪ] *n* : cumpleaños *m*, aniversario *m*

birthmark ['bərθˌmɑrk] *n* : mancha *f* de nacimiento

birthplace ['bərθˌpleɪs] *n* : lugar *m* de nacimiento

birthrate ['bərθˌreɪt] *n* : índice *m* de natalidad

birthright ['bərθˌraɪt] *n* : derecho *m* de nacimiento

biscuit ['bɪskət] *n* : bizcocho *m*

bisect ['baɪˌsɛkt, ˌbaɪ'-] *vt* : bisecar

bisexual [ˌbaɪ'sɛkʃuəl] *adj* : bisexual

bishop ['bɪʃəp] *n* **1** : obispo *m* **2** : alfil *m* (en ajedrez)

bismuth ['bɪzməθ] *n* : bismuto *m*

bison ['baɪzən, -sən] *ns & pl* : bisonte *m*

bistro ['bi:stro, 'bɪs-] *n, pl* **-tros** : bar *m*, restaurante *m* pequeño

bit ['bɪt] *n* **1** FRAGMENT, PIECE : pedazo *m*, trozo *m* ⟨a bit of luck : un poco de suerte⟩ **2** : freno *m*, bocado *m* (de una brida) **3** : broca *f* (de un taladro) **4** : bit *m* (de información)

bitch¹ ['bɪʧ] *vi* COMPLAIN : quejarse, reclamar

bitch² *n* : perra *f*

bite¹ ['baɪt] *v* **bit** ['bɪt]; **bitten** ['bɪtən]; **biting** *vt* **1** : morder **2** STING : picar **3** PUNCTURE : punzar, pinchar **4** GRIP : agarrar — *vi* **1** : morder ⟨that dog bites : ese perro muerde⟩ **2** STING : picar (dícese de un insecto), cortar (dícese del viento) **3** : picar ⟨the fish are biting now : ya están picando los peces⟩ **4** GRAB : agarrarse

bite² *n* **1** BITING : mordisco *m*, dentellada *f* **2** SNACK : bocado *m* ⟨a bite to eat : algo de comer⟩ **3** : picadura *f* (de un insecto), mordedura *f* (de un animal) **4** SHARPNESS : mordacidad *f*, penetración *f*

biting *adj* **1** PENETRATING : cortante, penetrante **2** CAUSTIC : mordaz, sarcástico

bitter ['bɪtər] *adj* **1** ACRID : amargo, acre **2** PENETRATING : cortante, penetrante ⟨bitter cold : frío glacial⟩ **3** HARSH : duro, amargo ⟨to the bitter end : hasta el final⟩ **4** INTENSE, RELENTLESS : intenso, extremo, implacable ⟨bitter hatred : odio implacable⟩

bitterly ['bɪtərli] *adv* : amargamente

bitterness ['bɪtərnəs] *n* : amargura *f*

bittersweet ['bɪtərˌswi:t] *adj* : agridulce

bivalve ['baɪˌvælv] *n* : bivalvo *m* — **bivalve** *adj*

bivouac¹ ['bɪvəˌwæk, 'bɪvˌwæk] *vi* **-ouacked; -ouacking** : acampar, vivaquear

bivouac² *n* : vivaque *m*

bizarre [bə'zɑr] *adj* : extraño, singular, estrafalario, estrambótico — **bizarrely** *adv*

blab ['blæb] *vi* **blabbed; blabbing** : parlotear *fam*, cotorrear *fam*

black¹ ['blæk] *vt* : ennegrecer

black² *adj* **1** : negro (color, raza) **2** SOILED : sucio **3** DARK : oscuro, negro **4** WICKED : malvado, perverso, malo **5** GLOOMY : negro, sombrío, deprimente

black³ *n* **1** : negro *m* (color) **2** : negro *m*, -gra *f* (persona)

black–and–blue [ˌblækən'blu:] *adj* : amoratado

blackball ['blækˌbɔl] *vt* **1** OSTRACIZE : hacerle el vacío a, aislar **2** BOYCOTT : boicotear

blackberry ['blækˌbɛri] *n, pl* **-ries** : mora *f*

blackbird ['blækˌbərd] *n* : mirlo *m*

blackboard ['blækˌbɔrd] *n* : pizarra *f*, pizarrón *m*

blacken ['blækən] *vt* **1** BLACK : ennegrecer **2** DEFAME : deshonrar, difamar, manchar

blackhead ['blækˌhɛd] *n* : espinilla *f*, punto *m* negro

black hole *n* : agujero *m* negro

blackjack ['blækˌʤæk] *n* **1** : cachiporra *f* (arma) **2** : veintiuna *f* (juego de cartas)

blacklist¹ ['blækˌlɪst] *vt* : poner en la lista negra

blacklist² *n* : lista *f* negra
blackmail¹ ['blæk,meɪl] *vt* : chantajear, hacer chantaje a
blackmail² *n* : chantaje *m*
blackmailer ['blæk,meɪlər] *n* : chantajista *mf*
blackout ['blæk,aʊt] *n* **1** : apagón *m* (de poder eléctrico) **2** FAINT : desmayo *m*, desvanecimiento *m*
black out *vt* : dejar sin luz — *vi* FAINT : perder el conocimiento, desmayarse
blacksmith ['blæk,smɪθ] *n* : herrero *m*
blacktop ['blæk,tɑp] *n* : asfalto *m*
bladder ['blædər] *n* : vejiga *f*
blade ['bleɪd] *n* : hoja *f* (de un cuchillo), cuchilla *f* (de un patín), pala *f* (de un remo o una hélice), brizna *f* (de hierba)
blamable ['bleɪməbəl] *adj* : culpable
blame¹ ['bleɪm] *vt* **blamed; blaming** : culpar, echar la culpa a
blame² *n* : culpa *f*
blameless ['bleɪmləs] *adj* : intachable, sin culpa, inocente — **blamelessly** *adv*
blameworthiness ['bleɪm,wərðinəs] *n* : culpa *f*, culpabilidad *f*
blameworthy ['bleɪm,wərði] *adj* : culpable, reprochable, censurable
blanch ['blæntʃ] *vt* WHITEN : blanquear — *vi* PALE : palidecer
bland ['blænd] *adj* : soso, insulso, desabrido ⟨a bland smile : una sonrisa insulsa⟩ ⟨a bland diet : una dieta fácil de digerir⟩
blandishments ['blændɪʃmənts] *npl* : lisonjas *fpl*, halagos *mpl*
blandly ['blændli] *adv* : de manera insulsa
blandness ['blændnəs] *n* : lo insulso, lo desabrido
blank¹ ['blæŋk] *vt* OBLITERATE : borrar
blank² *adj* **1** DAZED : perplejo, desconcertado **2** EXPRESSIONLESS : sin expresión, inexpresivo **3** : en blanco (dícese de un papel), liso (dícese de una pared) **4** EMPTY : vacío, en blanco ⟨a blank stare : una mirada vacía⟩ ⟨his mind went blank : se quedó en blanco⟩
blank³ *n* **1** SPACE : espacio *m* en blanco **2** FORM : formulario *m* **3** CARTRIDGE : cartucho *m* de fogueo **4** *or* **blank key** : llave *f* ciega
blanket¹ ['blæŋkət] *vt* : cubrir
blanket² *adj* : global
blanket³ *n* : manta *f*, cobija *f*, frazada *f*
blankly ['blæŋkli] *adv* : sin comprender
blankness ['blæŋknəs] *n* **1** PERPLEXITY : desconcierto *m*, perplejidad *f* **2** EMPTINESS : vacío *m*, vacuidad *f*
blare¹ ['blær] *vi* **blared; blaring** : resonar
blare² *n* : estruendo *m*
blarney ['blɑrni] *n* : labia *f fam*
blasé [blɑ'zeɪ] *adj* : displicente, indiferente
blaspheme [blæs'fi:m, 'blæs,-] *vi* **-phemed; -pheming** : blasfemar
blasphemer [blæs'fi:mər, 'blæs,-] *n* : blasfemo *m*, -ma *f*

blasphemous ['blæsfəməs] *adj* : blasfemo
blasphemy ['blæsfəmi] *n, pl* **-mies** : blasfemia *f*
blast¹ ['blæst] *vt* **1** BLOW UP : volar, hacer volar **2** ATTACK : atacar, arremeter contra
blast² *n* **1** GUST : ráfaga *f* **2** EXPLOSION : explosión *f*
blast–off ['blæst,ɔf] *n* : despegue *m*
blast off *vi* : despegar
blatant ['bleɪtənt] *adj* : descarado — **blatantly** ['bleɪtəntli] *adv*
blaze¹ ['bleɪz] *v* **blazed; blazing** *vi* SHINE : arder, brillar, resplandecer — *vt* MARK : marcar, señalar ⟨to blaze a trail : abrir un camino⟩
blaze² *n* **1** FIRE : fuego *m* **2** BRIGHTNESS : resplandor *m*, brillantez *f* **3** OUTBURST : arranque *m* ⟨a blaze of anger : un arranque de cólera⟩ **4** DISPLAY : alarde *m*, llamarada *f* ⟨a blaze of color : un derroche de color⟩
blazer ['bleɪzər] *n* : chaqueta *f* deportiva, blazer *m*
bleach¹ ['bli:tʃ] *vt* : blanquear, decolorar
bleach² *n* : lejía *f*, blanqueador *m*
bleachers ['bli:tʃərz] *ns & pl* : gradas *fpl*, tribuna *f* descubierta
bleak ['bli:k] *adj* **1** DESOLATE : inhóspito, sombrío, desolado **2** DEPRESSING : deprimente, triste, sombrío
bleakly ['bli:kli] *adv* : sombríamente
bleakness ['bli:knəs] *n* : lo inhóspito, lo sombrío
blear ['blɪr] *adj* : empañado, nublado
bleary ['blɪri] *adj* **1** : adormilado, fatigado **2 bleary–eyed** : con los ojos nublados
bleat¹ ['bli:t] *vi* : balar
bleat² *n* : balido *m*
bleed ['bli:d] *v* **bled** ['bɛld]; **bleeding** *vi* **1** : sangrar **2** GRIEVE : sufrir, afligirse **3** EXUDE : exudar (dícese de una planta), correrse (dícese de los colores) — : sangrar (a una persona), purgar (frenos) **2 to bleed someone dry** : sacarle todo el dinero a alguien
blemish¹ ['blɛmɪʃ] *vt* : manchar, marcar
blemish² *n* : imperfección *f*, mancha *f*, marca *f*
blend¹ ['blɛnd] *vt* **1** MIX : mezclar **2** COMBINE : combinar, aunar
blend² *n* : mezcla *f*, combinación *f*
blender ['blɛndər] *n* : licuadora *f*
bless ['blɛs] *vt* **blessed** ['blɛst]; **blessing 1** CONSECRATE : bendecir, consagrar **2** : bendecir ⟨may God bless you! : ¡que Dios te bendiga!⟩ **3 to bless with** : dotar de **4 to bless oneself** : santiguarse
blessed ['blɛsəd] *or* **blest** ['blɛst] *adj* : bienaventurado, bendito, dichoso
blessedly ['blɛsədli] *adv* : felizmente, alegremente, afortunadamente
blessing ['blɛsɪŋ] *n* **1** : bendición *f* **2** APPROVAL : aprobación *f*, consentimiento *m*

blew → blow

blight¹ ['blaɪt] *vt* : arruinar, infestar

blight² *n* **1** : añublo *m* **2** PLAGUE : peste *f*, plaga *f* **3** DECAY : deterioro *m*, ruina *f*

blimp ['blɪmp] *n* : dirigible *m*

blind¹ ['blaɪnd] *vt* **1** : cegar, dejar ciego **2** DAZZLE : deslumbrar

blind² *adj* **1** SIGHTLESS : ciego **2** INSENSITIVE : ciego, insensible, sin razón **3** CLOSED : sin salida ⟨blind alley : callejón sin salida⟩

blind³ *n* **1** : persiana *f* (para una ventana) **2** COVER : escondite *m*, escondrijo *m*

blinders ['blaɪndərz] *npl* : anteojeras *fpl*

blindfold¹ ['blaɪnd,foːld] *vt* : vendar los ojos

blindfold² *n* : venda *f* (para los ojos)

blinding ['blaɪndɪŋ] *adj* : enceguecedor, cegador ⟨with blinding speed : con una rapidez inusitada⟩

blindly ['blaɪndli] *adv* : a ciegas, ciegamente

blindness ['blaɪndnəs] *n* : ceguera *f*

blink¹ ['blɪŋk] *vi* **1** WINK : pestañear, parpadear **2** : brillar intermitentemente

blink² *n* : pestañeo *m*, parpadeo *m*

blinker ['blɪŋkər] *n* : intermitente *m*, direccional *f*

bliss ['blɪs] *n* **1** HAPPINESS : dicha *f*, felicidad *f* absoluta **2** PARADISE : paraíso *m*

blissful ['blɪsfəl] *adj* : dichoso, feliz — **blissfully** *adv*

blister¹ ['blɪstər] *vi* : ampollarse

blister² *n* : ampolla *f* (en la piel o una superficie), burbuja *f* (en una superficie)

blithe ['blaɪθ, 'blaɪð] *adj* **blither; blithest** **1** CAREFREE : despreocupado **2** CHEERFUL : alegre, risueño — **blithely** *adv*

blitz¹ ['blɪts] *vt* **1** BOMBARD : bombardear **2** : atacar con rapidez

blitz² *n* **1** : bombardeo *m* aéreo **2** CAMPAIGN : ataque *m*, acometida *f*

blizzard ['blɪzərd] *n* : tormenta *f* de nieve, ventisca *f*

bloat ['bloːt] *vi* : hincharse, inflarse

blob ['blab] *n* : gota *f*, mancha *f*, borrón *m*

bloc ['blak] *n* : bloque *m*

block¹ ['blak] *vt* **1** OBSTRUCT : obstruir, bloquear **2** CLOG : atascar, atorar

block² *n* **1** PIECE : bloque *m* ⟨building blocks : cubos de construcción⟩ ⟨auction block : plataforma de subastas⟩ ⟨starting block : taco de salida⟩ **2** OBSTRUCTION : obstrucción *f*, bloqueo *m* **3** : cuadra *f*, manzana *f* (de edificios) ⟨to go around the block : dar la vuelta a la cuadra⟩ **4** BUILDING : edificio *m* (de apartamentos, oficinas, etc.) **5** GROUP, SERIES : serie *f*, grupo *m* ⟨a block of tickets : una serie de entradas⟩ **6 block and tackle** : aparejo *m* de poleas

blockade¹ [bla'keɪd] *vt* **-aded; -ading** : bloquear

blockade² *n* : bloqueo *m*

blockage ['blakɪʤ] *n* : bloqueo *m*, obstrucción *f*

blockhead ['blak,hɛd] *n* : bruto *m*, -ta *f*; estúpido *m*, -da *f*

blond¹ *or* **blonde** ['bland] *adj* : rubio, güero *Mex*, claro (dícese de la madera)

blond² *or* **blonde** *n* : rubio *m*, -bia *f*; güero *m*, -ra *f* *Mex*

blood ['blʌd] *n* **1** : sangre *f* **2** LIFEBLOOD : vida *f*, alma *f* **3** LINEAGE : linaje *m*, sangre *f*

blood bank *n* : banco *m* de sangre

bloodcurdling ['blʌd,kərdəlɪŋ] *adj* : espeluznante, aterrador

blooded ['blʌdəd] *adj* : de sangre ⟨cold-blooded animal : animal de sangre fría⟩

bloodhound ['blʌd,haʊnd] *n* : sabueso *m*

bloodless ['blʌdləs] *adj* **1** : incruento, sin derramamiento de sangre **2** LIFELESS : desanimado, insípido, sin vida

bloodmobile ['blʌdmo,biːl] *n* : unidad *f* móvil para donantes de sangre

blood pressure *n* : tensión *f*, presión *f* (arterial)

bloodshed ['blʌd,ʃɛd] *n* : derramamiento *m* de sangre

bloodshot ['blʌd,ʃat] *adj* : inyectado de sangre

bloodstain ['blʌd,steɪn] *n* : mancha *f* de sangre

bloodstained ['blʌd,steɪnd] *adj* : manchado de sangre

bloodstream ['blʌd,striːm] *n* : torrente *m* sanguíneo, corriente *f* sanguínea

bloodsucker ['blʌd,sʌkər] *n* : sanguijuela *f*

bloodthirsty ['blʌd,θərsti] *adj* : sanguinario

blood vessel *n* : vaso *m* sanguíneo

bloody ['blʌdi] *adj* **bloodier; -est** : ensangrentado, sangriento

bloom¹ ['bluːm] *vi* **1** FLOWER : florecer **2** MATURE : madurar

bloom² *n* **1** FLOWER : flor *f* ⟨to be in bloom : estar en flor⟩ **2** FLOWERING : floración *f* ⟨in full bloom : en plena floración⟩ **3** : rubor *m* (de la tez) ⟨in the bloom of youth : en plena juventud, en la flor de la vida⟩

bloomers ['bluːmərz] *npl* : bombachos *mpl*

blooper ['bluːpər] *n* : metedura *f* de pata *fam*

blossom¹ ['blasəm] *vi* : florecer, dar flor

blossom² *n* : flor *f*

blot¹ ['blat] *vt* **blotted; blotting** **1** SPOT : emborronar, borronear **2** DRY : secar

blot² *n* **1** STAIN : mancha *f*, borrón *m* **2** BLEMISH : mancha *f*, tacha *f*

blotch¹ ['blatʃ] *vt* : emborronar, borronear

blotch² *n* : mancha *f*, borrón *m*

blotchy ['blatʃi] *adj* **blotchier; -est** : lleno de manchas

blotter ['blɑʈər] *n* : hoja *f* de papel secante, secante *m*

blouse ['blaʊs, 'blaʊz] *n* : blusa *f*

blow¹ ['blo:] *v* **blew** ['blu:]; **blown** ['blo:n]; **blowing** *vi* **1** : soplar, volar ⟨the wind is blowing hard : el viento está soplando con fuerza⟩ ⟨it blew out the door : voló por la puerta⟩ ⟨the window blew shut : se cerró la ventana⟩ **2** SOUND : sonar ⟨the whistle blew : sonó el silbato⟩ **3 to blow out** : fundirse (dícese de un fusible eléctrico), reventarse (dícese de una llanta) **4 to blow off** : dejar plantado (a alguien), flatar a (una cita, etc.) — *vt* **1** : soplar, echar ⟨to blow smoke : echar humo⟩ **2** SOUND : tocar, sonar **3** SHAPE : soplar, dar forma a ⟨to blow glass : soplar vidrio⟩ **4** BUNGLE : echar a perder

blow² *n* **1** PUFF : soplo *m*, soplido *m* **2** GALE : vendaval *f* **3** HIT, STROKE : golpe *m* **4** CALAMITY : golpe *m*, desastre *m* **5 to come to blows** : llegar a las manos

blower ['blo:ər] *n* FAN : ventilador *m*

blowout ['blo:,aʊt] *n* : reventón *m*

blowtorch ['blo:,tɔrʧ] *n* : soplete *m*

blow up *vi* EXPLODE : estallar, hacer explosión — *vt* BLAST : volar, hacer volar

blubber¹ ['blʌbər] *vi* : lloriquear

blubber² *n* : esperma *f* de ballena

bludgeon ['blʌʤən] *vt* : aporrear

blue¹ ['blu:] *adj* **bluer; bluest 1** : azul **2** MELANCHOLY : melancólico, triste

blue² *n* : azul *m*

blueberry ['blu:,bɛri] *n, pl* **-ries** : arándano *m*

bluebird ['blu:,bərd] *n* : azulejo *m*

blue cheese *n* : queso *m* azul

blueprint ['blu:,prɪnt] *n* **1** : plano *m*, proyecto *m*, cianotipo *m* **2** PLAN : anteproyecto *m*, programa *m*

blues ['blu:z] *npl* **1** DEPRESSION : depresión *f*, melancolía *f* **2** : blues *m* ⟨to sing the blues : cantar blues⟩

bluff¹ ['blʌf] *vi* : hacer un farol, blofear *Col, Mex*

bluff² *adj* **1** STEEP : escarpado **2** FRANK : campechano, franco, directo

bluff³ *n* **1** : farol *m*, blof *m Col, Mex* **2** CLIFF : acantilado *m*, risco *m*

bluing *or* **blueing** ['blu:ɪŋ] *n* : añil *m*, azulete *m*

bluish ['blu:ɪʃ] *adj* : azulado

blunder¹ ['blʌndər] *vi* **1** STUMBLE : tropezar, dar traspiés **2** ERR : cometer un error, tropezar, meter la pata *fam*

blunder² *n* : error *m*, fallo *m* garrafal, metedura *f* de pata *fam*

blunderbuss ['blʌndər,bʌs] *n* : trabuco *m*

blunt¹ ['blʌnt] *vt* : despuntar (aguja o lápiz), desafilar (cuchillo o tijeras), suavizar (crítica)

blunt² *adj* **1** DULL : desafilado, despuntado **2** DIRECT : directo, franco, categórico

bluntly ['blʌntli] *adv* : sin rodeos, francamente, bruscamente

bluntness ['blʌntnəs] *n* **1** DULLNESS : falta *f* de filo, embotadura *f* **2** FRANKNESS : franqueza *f*

blur¹ ['blər] *vt* **blurred; blurring** : desdibujar, hacer borroso

blur² *n* **1** SMEAR : mancha *f*, borrón *m* **2** : aspecto *m* borroso ⟨everything was just a blur : todo se volvió borroso⟩

blurb ['blərb] *n* : propaganda *f*, nota *f* publicitaria

blurry ['bləri] *adj* : borroso

blurt ['blərt] *vt* : espetar, decir impulsivamente

blush¹ ['blʌʃ] *vi* : ruborizarse, sonrojarse, hacerse colorado

blush² *n* : rubor *m*, sonrojo *m*

bluster¹ ['blʌstər] *vi* **1** BLOW : soplar con fuerza **2** BOAST : fanfarronear, echar bravatas

bluster² *n* : fanfarronada *f*, bravatas *fpl*

blustery ['blʌstəri] *adj* : borrascoso, tempestuoso

boa ['bo:ə] *n* : boa *f*

boar ['bor] *n* : cerdo *m* macho, verraco *m*

board¹ ['bord] *vt* **1** : embarcarse en, subir a bordo de (una nave o un avión), subir a (un tren o carro) **2** LODGE : hospedar, dar hospedaje con comidas a **3 to board up** : cerrar con tablas

board² *n* **1** PLANK : tabla *f*, tablón *m* **2** : tablero *m* ⟨chessboard : tablero de ajedrez⟩ **3** MEALS : comida *f* ⟨board and lodging : comida y alojamiento⟩ **4** COMMITTEE, COUNCIL : junta *f*, consejo *m*

boarder ['bordər] *n* LODGER : huésped *m*, -peda *f*

boardinghouse ['bordɪŋ,haʊs] *n* : casa *f* de huéspedes

boarding school *n* : internado *m*

boardwalk ['bord,wɔk] *n* : paseo *m* marítimo

boast¹ ['bo:st] *vi* : alardear, presumir, jactarse

boast² *n* : jactancia *f*, alarde *m*

boaster ['bo:stər] *n* : presumido *m*, -da *f*; fanfarrón *m*, -rrona *f fam*

boastful ['bo:stfəl] *adj* : jactancioso, fanfarrón *m*

boastfully ['bo:stfəli] *adv* : de manera jactanciosa

boat¹ ['bo:t] *vt* : transportar en barco, poner a bordo

boat² *n* : barco *m*, embarcación *f*, bote *m*, barca *f*

boatman ['bo:tmən] *n, pl* **-men** [-mən, -,mɛn] : barquero *m*

boatswain ['bo:sən] *n* : contramaestre *m*

bob¹ ['bɑb] *v* **bobbed; bobbing** *vi* **1** : balancearse, mecerse ⟨to bob up and down : subir y bajar⟩ **2** *or* **to bob up** APPEAR : presentarse, surgir — *vt* **1** : inclinar (la cabeza o el cuerpo) **2** CUT : cortar, recortar ⟨she bobbed her hair : se cortó el pelo⟩

bob² *n* **1** : inclinación *f* (de la cabeza, del cuerpo), sacudida *f* **2** FLOAT : flotador *m*, corcho *m* (de pesca) **3** : pelo *m* corto

bobbin ['babən] *n* : bobina *f*, carrete *m*

bobby pin ['babi,pɪn] *n* : horquilla *f*

bobcat ['bab,kæt] *n* : lince *m* rojo

bobolink ['babə,lɪŋk] *n* : tordo *m* arrocero

bobsled ['bab,slɛd] *n* : bobsleigh *m*

bobwhite ['bab,hwaɪt] *n* : codorniz *f* (del Nuevo Mundo)

bode¹ ['bo:d] *v* **boded; boding** *vt* : presagiar, augurar — *vi* **to bode well** : ser de buen agüero

bode² → bide

bodice ['badəs] *n* : corpiño *m*

bodied ['badid] *adj* : de cuerpo ⟨lean-bodied : de cuerpo delgado⟩ ⟨able-bodied : no discapacitado⟩

bodiless ['badiləs, 'badələs] *adj* : incorpóreo

bodily¹ ['badəli] *adv* : en peso ⟨to lift someone bodily : levantar a alguien en peso⟩

bodily² *adj* : corporal, del cuerpo ⟨bodily harm : daños corporales⟩

body ['badi] *n, pl* **bodies 1** : cuerpo *m*, organismo *m* **2** CORPSE : cadáver *m* **3** PERSON : persona *f*, ser *m* humano **4** : nave *f* (de una iglesia), carrocería *f* (de un automóvil), fuselaje *m* (de un avión), casco *m* (de una nave) **5** COLLECTION, MASS : conjunto *m*, grupo *m*, masa *f* ⟨in a body : todos juntos, en masa⟩ **6** ORGANIZATION : organismo *m*, organización *f*

bodyguard ['badi,gard] *n* : guardaespaldas *mf*

bog¹ ['bag, 'bɔg] *vt* **bogged; bogging** : empantanar, inundar ⟨to get bogged down : empantanarse⟩

bog² *n* : lodazal *m*, ciénaga *f*, cenagal *m*

bogey ['bugi, 'bo:-] *n, pl* **-geys** : terror *m*, coco *m fam*

boggle ['bagəl] *vi* **-gled; -gling** : quedarse atónito, quedarse pasmado ⟨the mind boggles! : ¡es increíble!⟩

boggy ['bagi, 'bɔ-] *adj* **boggier; -est** : cenagoso

bogus ['bo:gəs] *adj* : falso, fingido, falaz

bohemian [bo:'hi:miən] *n* : bohemio *m*, -mia *f* — **bohemian** *adj*

boil¹ ['bɔɪl] *vi* **1 : hervir 2 to make one's blood boil** : hervirle la sangre a uno — *vt* **1** : hervir, hacer hervir ⟨to boil water : hervir agua⟩ **2** : cocer, hervir ⟨to boil potatoes : cocer papas⟩

boil² *n* **1** BOILING : hervor *m* **2** : furúnculo *m*, divieso *m* (en medicina)

boiler ['bɔɪlər] *n* : caldera *f*

boisterous ['bɔɪstərəs] *adj* : bullicioso, escandaloso — **boisterously** *adv*

bold ['bo:ld] *adj* **1** COURAGEOUS : valiente **2** INSOLENT : insolente, descarado **3** DARING : atrevido, audaz — **boldly** *adv*

boldface ['bo:ld,feɪs] *or* **boldface type** *n* : negrita *f*

boldness ['bo:ldnəs] *n* **1** COURAGE : valor *m*, coraje *m* **2** INSOLENCE : atrevimiento *m*, insolencia *f*, descaro *m* **3** DARING : audacia *f*

bolero [bə'lɛro] *n, pl* **-ros** : bolero *m*

Bolivian [bə'lɪviən] *n* : boliviano *m*, -na *f* — **Bolivian** *adj*

boll ['bo:l] *n* : cápsula *f* (del algodón)

boll weevil *n* : gorgojo *m* del algodón

bologna [bə'lo:ni] *n* : salchicha *f* ahumada

bolster¹ ['bo:lstər] *vt* **-stered; -stering** : reforzar, reafirmar ⟨to bolster morale : levantar la moral⟩

bolster² *n* : cabezal *m*, almohadón *m*

bolt¹ ['bo:lt] *vt* **1** : atornillar, sujetar con pernos ⟨bolted to the floor : sujetado con pernos al suelo⟩ **2** : cerrar con pestillo, echar el cerrojo a ⟨to bolt the door : echar el cerrojo a la puerta⟩ **3 to bolt down** : engullir ⟨she bolted down her dinner : engulló su comida⟩ — *vi* : echar a correr, salir corriendo ⟨he bolted from the room : salió corriendo de la sala⟩

bolt² *n* **1** LATCH : pestillo *m*, cerrojo *m* **2** : tornillo *m*, perno *m* ⟨nuts and bolts : tuercas y tornillos⟩ **3** : rollo *m* ⟨a bolt of cloth : un rollo de tela⟩ **4 lightning bolt** : relámpago *m*, rayo *m*

bomb¹ ['bam] *vt* : bombardear

bomb² *n* : bomba *f*

bombard [bam'bard, bəm-] *vt* : bombardear

bombardier [,bambə'dɪr] *n* : bombardero *m*, -ra *f*

bombardment [bam'bardmənt] *n* : bombardeo *m*

bombast ['bam,bæst] *n* : grandilocuencia *f*, ampulosidad *f*

bombastic [bam'bæstɪk] *adj* : grandilocuente, ampuloso, bombástico

bomber ['bamər] *n* : bombardero *m*

bombproof ['bam,pru:f] *adj* : a prueba de bombas

bombshell ['bam,ʃɛl] *n* : bomba *f* ⟨a political bombshell : una bomba política⟩

bona fide ['bo:nə,faɪd, 'ba-; ,bo:nə'faɪdi] *adj* **1** : de buena fe ⟨a bona fide offer : una oferta de buena fe⟩ **2** GENUINE : genuino, auténtico

bonanza [bə'nænzə] *n* : bonanza *f*

bonbon ['ban,ban] *n* : bombón *m*

bond¹ ['band] *vt* **1** INSURE : dar fianza a, asegurar **2** STICK : adherir, pegar — *vi* : adherirse, pegarse

bond² *n* **1** LINK, TIE : vínculo *m*, lazo *m* **2** BAIL : fianza *f*, caución *f* **3** : bono *m* ⟨stocks and bonds : acciones y bonos⟩ **4 bonds** *npl* FETTERS : cadenas *fpl*

bondage ['bandɪdʒ] *n* : esclavitud *f*

bondholder ['band,ho:ldər] *n* : tenedor *m*, -dora *f* de bonos

bondsman ['bandzmən] *n, pl* **-men** [-mən, -,mn] **1** SLAVE : esclavo *m* **2** SURETY : fiador *m*, -dora *f*

bone¹ ['bo:n] *vt* **boned; boning** : deshuesar

bone² *n* : hueso *m*
boneless ['bo:nləs] *adj* : sin huesos, sin espinas
boner ['bo:nər] *n* : metedura *f* de pata, metida *f* de pata
bonfire ['bɑn,faɪr] *n* : hoguera *f*, fogata *f*, fogón *m*
bonito [bə'ni:t̬o] *n*, *pl* **-tos** *or* **-to** : bonito *m*
bonnet ['bɑnət] *n* : sombrero *m* (de mujer), gorra *f* (de niño)
bonus ['bo:nəs] *n* **1** : prima *f*, bonificación *f* (pagado al empleado) **2** ADVANTAGE, BENEFIT : beneficio *m*, provecho *m*
bony ['bo:ni] *adj* **bonier; -est** : huesudo
boo¹ ['bu:] *vt* : abuchear
boo² *n*, *pl* **boos** : abucheo *m*
booby ['bu:bi] *n*, *pl* **-bies** : bobo *m*, -ba *f*; tonto *m*, -ta *f*
book¹ ['bʊk] *vt* : reservar ⟨to book a flight : reservar un vuelo⟩
book² *n* **1** : libro *m* **2 the Book** : la Biblia **3 by the book** : según las reglas
bookcase ['bʊk,keɪs] *n* : estantería *f*, librero *m* Mex
bookend ['bʊk,ɛnd] *n* : sujetalibros *m*
bookie ['bʊki] → **bookmaker**
bookish ['bʊkɪʃ] *adj* : libresco
bookkeeper ['bʊk,ki:pər] *n* : tenedor *m*, -dora *f* de libros; contable *mf* Spain
bookkeeping ['bʊk,ki:pɪŋ] *n* : contabilidad *f*, teneduría *f* de libros
booklet ['bʊklət] *n* : folleto *m*
bookmaker ['bʊk,meɪkər] *n* : corredor *m*, -dora *f* de apuestas
bookmark ['bʊk,mɑrk] *n* : señalador *m* de libros, marcador *m* de libros
bookseller ['bʊk,slər] *n* : librero *m*, -ra *f*
bookshelf ['bʊk,ʃɛlf] *n*, *pl* **-shelves 1** : estante *m* **2 bookshelves** *npl* : estantería *f*
bookstore ['bʊk,stor] *n* : librería *f*
bookworm ['bʊk,wərm] *n* : ratón *m* de biblioteca *fam*
boom¹ ['bu:m] *vi* **1** THUNDER : tronar, resonar **2** FLOURISH, PROSPER : estar en auge, prosperar
boom² *n* **1** BOOMING : bramido *m*, estruendo *m* **2** FLOURISHING : auge *m* ⟨population boom : auge de población⟩
boomerang ['bu:mə,ræŋ] *n* : bumerán *m*
boon¹ ['bu:n] *adj* **boon companion** : amigo *m*, -ga *f* del alma
boon² *n* : ayuda *f*, beneficio *m*, adelanto *m*
boondocks ['bu:n,dɑks] *npl* : área *f* rural remota, región *f* alejada
boor ['bʊr] *n* : grosero *m*, -ra *f*
boorish ['bʊrɪʃ] *adj* : grosero
boost¹ ['bu:st] *vt* **1** LIFT : levantar, alzar **2** INCREASE : aumentar, incrementar **3** PROMOTE : promover, fomentar, hacer publicidad por

boost² *n* **1** THRUST : impulso *m*, empujón *m* **2** ENCOURAGEMENT : estímulo *m*, aliento *m* **3** INCREASE : aumento *m*, incremento *m*
booster ['bu:stər] *n* **1** SUPPORTER : partidario *m*, -ria *f* **2 booster rocket** : cohete *m* propulsor **3 booster shot** : vacuna *f* de refuerzo
boot¹ ['bu:t] *vt* KICK : dar una patada a, patear
boot² *n* **1** : bota *f*, botín *m* **2** KICK : puntapié *m*, patada *f*
bootee *or* **bootie** ['bu:t̬i] *n* : botita *f*, botín *m*
booth ['bu:θ] *n*, *pl* **booths** ['bu:ðz, 'bu:θs] : cabina *f* (de teléfono, de votar), caseta *f* (de información), barraca *f* (a una feria)
bootlegger ['bu:t̬,lɛgər] *n* : contrabandista *mf* del alcohol
booty ['bu:t̬i] *n*, *pl* **-ties** : botín *m*
booze ['bu:z] *n* *fam* : alcohol *m*
borax ['bor,æks] *n* : bórax *m*
border¹ ['bordər] *vt* **1** EDGE : ribetear, bordear **2** BOUND : limitar con, lindar con — *vi* VERGE : rayar, lindar ⟨that borders on absurdity : eso raya en el absurdo⟩
border² *n* **1** EDGE : borde *m*, orilla *f* **2** TRIM : ribete *m* **3** FRONTIER : frontera *f*
bore¹ ['bor] *vt* **bored; boring 1** PIERCE : taladrar, perforar ⟨to bore metals : taladrar metales⟩ **2** OPEN : hacer, abrir ⟨to bore a tunnel : abrir un túnel⟩ **3** WEARY : aburrir
bore² → **bear¹**
bore³ *n* **1** : pesado *m*, -da *f* (persona aburrida) **2** TEDIOUSNESS : pesadez *f*, lo aburrido **3** DIAMETER : calibre *m*
boredom ['bordəm] *n* : aburrimiento *m*
boring ['borɪŋ] *adj* : aburrido, pesado
born ['born] *adj* **1** : nacido **2** : nato ⟨she's a born singer : es una cantante nata⟩ ⟨he's a born leader : nació para mandar⟩
borne *pp* → **bear¹**
boron ['bor,ɑn] *n* : boro *m*
borough ['bəro] *n* : distrito *m* municipal
borrow ['bɑro] *vt* **1** : pedir prestado, tomar prestado **2** APPROPRIATE : apropiarse de, adoptar
borrower ['bɑrəwər] *n* : prestatario *m*, -ria *f*
Bosnian ['bɑzniən, 'bɔz-] *n* : bosnio *m*, -nia *f* — **Bosnian** *adj*
bosom¹ ['bʊzəm, 'bu:-] *adj* : íntimo
bosom² *n* **1** CHEST : pecho *m* **2** BREAST : pecho *m*, seno *m* **3** CLOSENESS : seno *m* ⟨in the bosom of her family : en el seno de su familia⟩
bosomed ['bʊzəmd, 'bu:-] *adj* : con busto ⟨big-bosomed : con mucho busto⟩
boss¹ ['bɔs] *vt* **1** SUPERVISE : dirigir, supervisar **2 to boss around** : mandonear *fam*, mangonear *fam*
boss² *n* : jefe *m*, -fa *f*; patrón *m*, -trona *f*
bossy ['bɔsi] *adj* **bossier; -est** : mandón *fam*, autoritario, dominante

botanist ['bɑtənɪst] *n* : botánico *m*, -ca *f*
botany ['bɑtəni] *n* : botánica *f* — **botanical** [bə'tænɪkəl] *adj*
botch¹ ['bɑtʃ] *vt* : hacer una chapuza de, estropear
botch² *n* : chapuza *f*
both¹ ['bo:θ] *adj* : ambos, los dos, las dos ⟨both books : ambos libros, los dos libros⟩
both² *conj* : tanto como ⟨both Ann and her mother are tall : tanto Ana como su madre son altas⟩
both³ *pron* : ambos *m*, -bas *f*; los dos, las dos
bother¹ ['bɑðər] *vt* **1** IRK : preocupar ⟨nothing's bothering me : nada me preocupa⟩ ⟨what's bothering him? : ¿qué le pasa?⟩ **2** PESTER : molestar, fastidiar — *vi* **to bother to** : molestarse en, tomar la molestia de
bother² *n* **1** TROUBLE : molestia *f*, problemas *mpl* **2** ANNOYANCE : molestia *f*, fastidio *m*
bothersome ['bɑðərsəm] *adj* : molesto, fastidioso
bottle¹ ['bɑtəl] *vt* **bottled; bottling** : embotellar, envasar
bottle² *n* : botella *f*, frasco *m*
bottleneck ['bɑtəl,nɛk] *n* **1** : cuello *m* de botella (en un camino) **2** : embotellamiento *m*, atasco *m* (de tráfico) **3** OBSTACLE : obstáculo *m*
bottom¹ ['bɑtəm] *adj* : más bajo, inferior, de abajo
bottom² *n* **1** : fondo *m* (de una caja, de una taza, del mar), pie *m* (de una escalera, una página, una montaña), asiento *m* (de una silla), parte *f* de abajo (de una pila) **2** CAUSE : origen *m*, causa *f* ⟨to get to the bottom of : llegar al fondo de⟩ **3** BUTTOCKS : trasero *m*, nalgas *fpl*
bottomless ['bɑtəmləs] *adj* : sin fondo, sin límites
botulism ['bɑtʃə,lɪzəm] *n* : botulismo *m*
boudoir [bə'dwar, bʊ-; 'bu:,-, 'bʊ-] *n* : tocador *m*
bough ['baʊ] *n* : rama *f*
bought → **buy¹**
bouillon ['bu:,jan; 'bʊl,jan, -jən] *n* : caldo *m*
boulder ['bo:ldər] *n* : canto *m* rodado, roca *f* grande
boulevard ['bʊlə,vard, 'bu:-] *n* : bulevar *m*, boulevard *m*
bounce¹ ['baʊnts] *v* **bounced; bouncing** *vt* : hacer rebotar — *vi* : rebotar
bounce² *n* : rebote *m*
bouncy ['baʊntsi] *adj* **bouncier; -est 1** LIVELY : vivo, exuberante, animado **2** RESILIENT : elástico, flexible **3** : que rebota (dícese de una pelota)
bound¹ ['baʊnd] *vt* : delimitar, rodear — *vi* LEAP : saltar, dar brincos
bound² *adj* **1** OBLIGED : obligado **2** : encuadernado, empastado ⟨a book bound in leather : un libro encuadernado en cuero⟩ **3** DETERMINED : de-

cidido, empeñado **4 to be bound to** : ser seguro que, tener que, no caber duda que ⟨it was bound to happen : tenía que suceder⟩ **5 bound for** : con rumbo a ⟨bound for Chicago : con rumbo a Chicago⟩ ⟨to be homeward bound : ir camino a casa⟩
bound³ *n* **1** LIMIT : límite *m* **2** LEAP : salto *m*, brinco *m*
boundary ['baʊndri, -dəri] *n, pl* **-aries** : límite *m*, línea *f* divisoria, linde *mf*
boundless ['baʊndləs] *adj* : sin límites, infinito
bounteous ['baʊntiəs] *adj* **1** GENEROUS : generoso **2** ABUNDANT : copioso, abundante — **bounteously** *adv*
bountiful ['baʊntɪfəl] *adj* **1** GENEROUS, LIBERAL : munificente, pródigo, generoso **2** ABUNDANT : copioso, abundante
bounty ['baʊnti] *n, pl* **-ties 1** GENEROSITY : generosidad *f*, munificencia *f* **2** REWARD : recompensa *f*
bouquet [bo:'keɪ, bu:-] *n* **1** : ramo *m*, ramillete *m* **2** FRAGRANCE : bouquet *m*, aroma *m*
bourbon ['bərbən, 'bʊr-] *n* : bourbon *m*, whisky *m* americano
bourgeois¹ ['bʊrʒ,wa, bʊrʒ'wa] *adj* : burgués
bourgeois² *n* : burgués *m*, -guesa *f*
bourgeoisie [,bʊrʒ,wa'zi] *n* : burguesía *f*
bout ['baʊt] *n* **1** : encuentro *m*, combate *m* (en deportes) **2** ATTACK : ataque *m* (de una enfermedad) **3** PERIOD, SPELL : período *m* (de actividad)
boutique [bu:'ti:k] *n* : boutique *f*
bovine¹ ['bo:,vaɪn, -,vi:n] *adj* : bovino, vacuno
bovine² *n* : bovino *m*
bow¹ ['baʊ] *vi* **1** : hacer una reverencia, inclinarse **2** SUBMIT : ceder, resignarse, someterse — *vt* LOWER : inclinar, bajar **2** BEND : doblar
bow² ['baʊ] *n* **1** BOWING : reverencia *f*, inclinación *f* **2** : proa *f* (de un barco)
bow³ ['bo:] *vi* CURVE : arquearse, doblarse
bow⁴ ['bo:] *n* **1** ARCH, CURVE : arco *m*, curva *f* **2** : arco *m* (arma o vara para tocar varios instrumentos de música) **3** : lazo *m*, moño *m* ⟨to tie a bow : hacer un moño⟩
bowels ['baʊəls] *npl* **1** INTESTINES : intestinos *mpl* **2** : entrañas *fpl* ⟨in the bowels of the earth : en las entrañas de la tierra⟩
bower ['baʊər] *n* : enramada *f*
bowl¹ ['bo:l] *vi* : jugar a los bolos
bowl² *n* : tazón *m*, cuenco *m*
bowler ['bo:lər] *n* : jugador *m*, -dora *f* de bolos
bowling ['bo:lɪŋ] *n* : bolos *mpl*
box¹ ['bɑks] *vt* **1** PACK : empaquetar, embalar, encajonar **2** SLAP : bofetear, cachetear — *vi* : boxear

box² *n* **1** CONTAINER : caja *f*, cajón *m* **2** COMPARTMENT : compartimento *m*, palco *m* (en el teatro) **3** SLAP : bofetada *f*, cachetada *f* **4** : boj *m* (planta)

boxcar [ˈbɑksˌkɑr] *n* : vagón *m* de carga, furgón *m*

boxer [ˈbɑksər] *n* : boxeador *m*, -dora *f*

boxing [ˈbɑksɪŋ] *n* : boxeo *m*

box office *n* : taquilla *f*, boletería *f*

boxwood [ˈbɑksˌwʊd] *n* : boj *m*

boy [ˈbɔɪ] *n* **1** : chico *m*, muchacho *m* **2** *or* **little boy** : niño *m*, chico *m* **3** SON : hijo *m*

boycott¹ [ˈbɔɪˌkɑt] *vt* : boicotear

boycott² *n* : boicot *m*

boyfriend [ˈbɔɪˌfrɛnd] *n* **1** FRIEND : amigo *m* **2** SWEETHEART : novio *m*

boyhood [ˈbɔɪˌhʊd] *n* : niñez *f*

boyish [ˈbɔɪʃ] *adj* : de niño, juvenil

bra [ˈbrɑ] → **brassiere**

brace¹ [ˈbreɪs] *v* **braced; bracing** *vt* **1** PROP UP, SUPPORT : apuntalar, apoyar, sostener **2** INVIGORATE : vigorizar **3** REINFORCE : reforzar — *vi* **to brace oneself** PREPARE : prepararse

brace² *n* **1** : berbiquí *m* ⟨brace and bit : berbiquí y barrena⟩ **2** CLAMP, REINFORCEMENT : abrazadera *f*, refuerzo *m* **3** : llave *f* (signo de puntuación) **4** **braces** *npl* : aparatos *mpl* (de ortodoncia), frenos *mpl* Mex

bracelet [ˈbreɪslət] *n* : brazalete *m*, pulsera *f*

bracken [ˈbrækən] *n* : helecho *m*

bracket¹ [ˈbrækət] *vt* **1** SUPPORT : asegurar, apuntalar **2** : poner entre corchetes **3** CATEGORIZE, GROUP : catalogar, agrupar

bracket² *n* **1** SUPPORT : soporte *m* **2** : corchete *m* (marca de puntuación) **3** CATEGORY, CLASS : clase *f*, categoría *f*

brackish [ˈbrækɪʃ] *adj* : salobre

brad [ˈbræd] *n* : clavo *m* con cabeza pequeña, clavito *m*

brag¹ [ˈbræg] *vi* **bragged; bragging** : alardear, fanfarronear, jactarse

brag² *n* : alarde *m*, jactancia *f*, fanfarronada *f*

braggart [ˈbrægərt] *n* : fanfarrón *m*, -rrona *f fam*; jactancioso *m*, -sa *f*

braid¹ [ˈbreɪd] *vt* : trenzar

braid² *n* : trenza *f*

braille [ˈbreɪl] *n* : braille *m*

brain¹ [ˈbreɪn] *vt* : romper la crisma a, aplastar el cráneo a

brain² *n* **1** : cerebro *m* **2 brains** *npl* INTELLECT : inteligencia *f*, sesos *mpl*

brainless [ˈbreɪnləs] *adj* : estúpido, tonto

brainstorm [ˈbreɪnˌstɔrm] *n* : idea *f* brillante, idea *f* genial

brainy [ˈbreɪni] *adj* **brainier; -est** : inteligente, listo

braise [ˈbreɪz] *vt* **braised; braising** : cocer a fuego lento, estofar

brake¹ [ˈbreɪk] *v* **braked; braking** : frenar

brake² *n* : freno *m*

bramble [ˈbræmbəl] *n* : zarza *f*, zarzamora *f*

bran [ˈbræn] *n* : salvado *m*

branch¹ [ˈbræntʃ] *vi* **1** : echar ramas (dícese de una planta) **2** DIVERGE : ramificarse, separarse

branch² *n* **1** : rama *f* (de una planta) **2** EXTENSION : ramal *m* (de un camino, un ferrocarril, un río), rama *f* (de una familia o un campo de estudiar), sucursal *f* (de una empresa), agencia *f* (del gobierno)

brand¹ [ˈbrænd] *vt* **1** : marcar (ganado) **2** LABEL : tachar, tildar ⟨they branded him as a liar : lo tacharon de mentiroso⟩

brand² *n* **1** : marca *f* (de ganado) **2** STIGMA : estigma *m* **3** MAKE : marca *f* ⟨brand name : marca de fábrica⟩

brandish [ˈbrændɪʃ] *vt* : blandir

brand-new [ˈbrændˈnuː, -ˈnjuː] *adj* : nuevo, flamante

brandy [ˈbrændi] *n*, *pl* **-dies** : brandy *m*

brash [ˈbræʃ] *adj* **1** IMPULSIVE : impulsivo, impetuoso **2** BRAZEN : excesivamente desenvuelto, descarado

brass [ˈbræs] *n* **1** : latón *m* **2** GALL, NERVE : descaro *m*, cara *f fam* **3** OFFICERS : mandamases *mpl fam*

brassiere [brəˈzɪr, brɑ-] *n* : sostén *m*, brasier *m* Col, Mex

brassy [ˈbræsi] *adj* **brassier; -est** : dorado

brat [ˈbræt] *n* : mocoso *m*, -sa *f*; niño *m* mimado, niña *f* mimada

bravado [brəˈvɑdo] *n*, *pl* **-does** *or* **-dos** : bravuconadas *fpl*, bravatas *fpl*

brave¹ [ˈbreɪv] *vt* **braved; braving** : afrontar, hacer frente a

brave² *adj* **braver; bravest** : valiente, valeroso — **bravely** *adv*

brave³ *n* : guerrero *m* indio

bravery [ˈbreɪvəri] *n* : valor *m*, valentía *f*

bravo [ˈbrɑˌvoː] *n*, *pl* **-vos** : bravo *m*

brawl¹ [ˈbrɔl] *vi* : pelearse, pegarse

brawl² *n* : pelea *f*, reyerta *f*

brawn [ˈbrɔn] *n* : fuerza *f* muscular

brawny [ˈbrɔni] *adj* **brawnier; -est** : musculoso

bray¹ [ˈbreɪ] *vi* : rebuznar

bray² *n* : rebuzno *m*

brazen [ˈbreɪzən] *adj* **1** : de latón **2** BOLD : descarado, directo

brazenly [ˈbreɪzənli] *adv* : descaradamente, insolentemente

brazenness [ˈbreɪzənnəs] *n* : descaro *m*, atrevimiento *m*

brazier [ˈbreɪzər] *n* : brasero *m*

Brazilian [brəˈzɪljən] *n* : brasileño *m*, -ña *f* — **Brazilian** *adj*

Brazil nut [brəˈzɪlˌnʌt] *n* : nuez *f* de Brasil

breach¹ [ˈbriːtʃ] *vt* **1** PENETRATE : abrir una brecha en, penetrar **2** VIOLATE : infringir, violar

breach² *n* **1** VIOLATION : infracción *f*, violación *f* ⟨breach of trust : abuso de confianza⟩ **2** GAP, OPENING : brecha *f*

bread¹ ['brɛd] *vt* : empanar
bread² *n* : pan *m*
breadth ['brɛtθ] *n* : ancho *m*, anchura *f*
breadwinner ['brɛd,wɪnər] *n* : sostén *m* de la familia
break¹ ['breɪk] *v* broke ['bro:k]; broken ['bro:kən]; breaking *vt* 1 SMASH : romper, quebrar 2 VIOLATE : infringir, violar, romper 3 SURPASS : batir, superar 4 CRUSH, RUIN : arruinar, deshacer, destrozar ⟨to break one's spirit : quebrantar su espíritu⟩ 5 : dar, comunicar ⟨to break the news : dar las noticias⟩ 6 INTERRUPT : cortar, interrumpir — *vi* 1 : romperse, quebrarse ⟨my calculator broke : se me rompió la calculadora⟩ 2 DISPERSE : dispersarse, despejarse 3 : estallar (dícese de una tormenta), romper (dícese del día) 4 CHANGE : cambiar (dícese del tiempo o de la voz) 5 DECREASE : bajar ⟨my fever broke : me bajó la fiebre⟩ 6 : divulgarse, revelarse ⟨the news broke : la noticia se divulgó⟩ 7 to break into : forzar, abrir 8 to break out of : escaparse de 9 to break through : penetrar
break² *n* 1 : ruptura *f*, rotura *f*, fractura *f* (de un hueso), claro *m* (entre las nubes), cambio *m* (del tiempo) 2 CHANCE : oportunidad *f* ⟨a lucky break : un golpe de suerte⟩ 3 REST : descanso *m* ⟨to take a break : tomar(se) un descanso⟩
breakable ['breɪkəbəl] *adj* : quebradizo, frágil
breakage ['breɪkɪdʒ] *n* 1 BREAKING : rotura *f* 2 DAMAGE : destrozos *mpl*, daños *mpl*
breakdown ['breɪk,daʊn] *n* 1 : avería *f* (de máquinas), interrupción *f* (de comunicaciones), fracaso *m* (de negociaciones) 2 ANALYSIS : análisis *m*, desglose *m* 3 *or* nervous breakdown : crisis *f* nerviosa
break down *vi* 1 : estropearse, descomponerse ⟨the machine broke down : la máquina se descompuso⟩ 2 FAIL : fracasar 3 CRY : echarse a llorar — *vt* 1 DESTROY : derribar, echar abajo 2 OVERCOME : vencer (la resistencia), disipar (sospechas) 3 ANALYZE : analizar, descomponer
breaker ['breɪkər] *n* 1 WAVE : ola *f* grande 2 : interruptor *m* automático (de electricidad)
breakfast¹ ['brɛkfəst] *vi* : desayunar
breakfast² *n* : desayuno *m*
breakneck ['breɪk,nɛk] *adj* at breakneck speed : a una velocidad vertiginosa
break out *vi* 1 : salirse ⟨she broke out in spots : le salieron granos⟩ 2 ERUPT : estallar (dícese de una guerra, la violencia, etc.) 3 ESCAPE : fugarse, escaparse
breakup ['breɪk,əp] *n* 1 DIVISION : desintegración *f* 2 : ruptura *f*

break up *vt* 1 DIVIDE : dividir 2 : disolver (una muchedumbre, una pelea, etc.) — *vi* 1 BREAK : romperse 2 SEPARATE : deshacerse, separarse ⟨I broke up with him : terminé con él⟩
breast ['brɛst] *n* 1 : pecho *m*, seno *m* (de una mujer) 2 CHEST : pecho *m*
breastbone ['brɛst,bo:n] *n* : esternón *m*
breast–feed ['brɛst,fi:d] *vt* -fed [-,fɛd]; -feeding : amamantar, darle de mamar (a un niño)
breath ['brɛθ] *n* 1 BREATHING : aliento *m* ⟨to hold one's breath : aguantar la respiración⟩ 2 BREEZE : soplo *m* ⟨a breath of fresh air : un soplo de aire fresco⟩
breathe ['bri:ð] *v* breathed; breathing *vi* 1 : respirar 2 LIVE : vivir, respirar — *vt* 1 : respirar, aspirar ⟨to breathe fresh air : respirar el aire fresco⟩ 2 UTTER : decir ⟨I won't breathe a word of this : no diré nada de esto⟩
breathless ['brɛθləs] *adj* : sin aliento, jadeante
breathlessly ['brɛθləsli] *adv* : entrecortadamente, jadeando
breathlessness ['brɛθləsnəs] *n* : dificultad *f* al respirar
breathtaking ['brɛθ,teɪkɪŋ] *adj* IMPRESSIVE : impresionante, imponente
breeches ['brɪtʃəz, 'bri:-] *npl* : pantalones *mpl*, calzones *mpl*, bombachos *mpl*
breed¹ ['bri:d] *v* bred ['brɛd]; breeding *vt* 1 : criar (animales) 2 ENGENDER : engendrar, producir ⟨familiarity breeds contempt : la confianza hace perder el respeto⟩ 3 RAISE, REAR : criar, educar — *vi* REPRODUCE : reproducirse
breed² *n* 1 : variedad *f* (de plantas), raza *f* (de animales) 2 CLASS : clase *f*, tipo *m*
breeder ['bri:dər] *n* : criador *m*, -dora *f* (de animales); cultivador *m*, -dora *f* (de plantas)
breeze¹ ['bri:z] *vi* breezed; breezing : pasar con ligereza ⟨to breeze in : entrar como si nada⟩
breeze² *n* : brisa *f*, soplo *m* (de aire)
breezy ['bri:zi] *adj* breezier; -est 1 AIRY, WINDY : aireado, ventoso 2 LIVELY : animado, alegre 3 NONCHALANT : despreocupado
brethren → brother
brevity ['brɛvəti] *n, pl* -ties : brevedad *f*, concisión *f*
brew¹ ['bru:] *vt* 1 : fabricar, elaborar (cerveza) 2 FOMENT : tramar, maquinar, fomentar — *vi* 1 : fabricar cerveza 2 : amenazar ⟨a storm is brewing : una tormenta amenaza⟩
brew² *n* 1 BEER : cerveza *f* 2 POTION : brebaje *m*
brewer ['bru:ər] *n* : cervecero *m*, -ra *f*
brewery ['bru:əri, 'bruri] *n, pl* -eries : cervecería *f*
briar ['braɪər] → brier

bribe¹ ['braɪb] *vt* **bribed; bribing**
: sobornar, cohechar, coimear *Arg,
Chile, Peru*
bribe² *n* : soborno *m*, cohecho *m*, coima
f Arg, Chile, Peru, mordida *f CA, Mex*
bribery ['braɪbəri] *n, pl* **-eries** : soborno
m, cohecho *m*, coima *f*, mordida *f CA,
Mex*
bric-a-brac ['brɪkə‚bræk] *npl* : baratijas *fpl*, chucherías *fpl*
brick¹ ['brɪk] *vt* **to brick up** : tabicar,
tapiar
brick² *n* : ladrillo *m*
bricklayer ['brɪk‚leɪər] *n* : albañil *mf*
bricklaying ['brɪk‚leɪɪŋ] *n* : albañilería *f*
bridal ['braɪdəl] *adj* : nupcial, de novia
bride ['braɪd] *n* : novia *f*
bridegroom ['braɪd‚gruːm] *n* : novio *m*
bridesmaid ['braɪdz‚meɪd] *n* : dama *f* de
honor
bridge¹ ['brɪdʒ] *vt* **bridged; bridging 1**
: tender un puente sobre **2 to bridge
the gap** : salvar las diferencias
bridge² *n* **1** : puente *m* **2** : caballete *m*
(de la nariz) **3** : puente *m* de mando
(de un barco) **4** DENTURE : puente *m*
(dental) **5** : bridge *m* (juego de naipes)
bridle¹ ['braɪdəl] *v* **-dled; -dling** *vt* **1** : em-
bridar (un caballo) **2** RESTRAIN : re-
frenar, dominar, contener — *vi* **to bridle at** : molestarse por, picarse por
bridle² *n* : brida *f*
brief¹ ['briːf] *vt* : dar órdenes a, instruir
brief² *adj* : breve, sucinto, conciso
brief³ *n* **1** : resumen *m*, sumario *m* **2**
briefs *npl* : calzoncillos *mpl*
briefcase ['briːf‚keɪs] *n* : portafolio *m*,
maletín *m*
briefly ['briːfli] *adv* : brevemente, por
poco tiempo ⟨to speak briefly : dis-
cursar en pocas palabras⟩
brier ['braɪər] *n* **1** BRAMBLE : zarza *f*,
rosal *m* silvestre **2** HEATH : brezo *m*
veteado
brig ['brɪg] *n* **1** : bergantín *m* (barco) **2**
: calabozo *m* (en un barco)
brigade [brɪ'geɪd] *n* : brigada *f*
brigadier general [‚brɪgə'dɪr] *n* : general *m* de brigada
brigand ['brɪgənd] *n* : bandolero *m*, -ra
f; forajido *m*, -da *f*
bright ['braɪt] *adj* **1** : brillante (dícese
del sol, de los ojos), vivo (dícese de un
color), claro, fuerte **2** CHEERFUL : alegre, animado ⟨bright and early : muy
temprano⟩ **3** INTELLIGENT : listo, inteligente ⟨a bright idea : una idea lu-
minosa⟩
brighten ['braɪtən] *vt* **1** ILLUMINATE
: iluminar **2** ENLIVEN : alegrar, animar
— *vi* **1** : hacerse más brillante **2 to
brighten up** : animarse, alegrarse,
mejorar
brightly ['braɪtli] *adv* : vivamente, intensamente, alegremente
brightness ['braɪtnəs] *n* **1** LUMINOSITY
: luminosidad *f*, brillantez *f*, resplandor
m, brillo *m* **2** CHEERFULNESS : alegría
f, ánimo *m*

brilliance ['brɪljənts] *n* **1** BRIGHTNESS
: resplandor *m*, fulgor *m*, brillo *m*, brillantez *f* **2** INTELLIGENCE : inteligencia *f*, brillantez *f*
brilliancy ['brɪljəntsi] → **brilliance**
brilliant ['brɪljənt] *adj* : brillante
brilliantly ['brɪljəntli] *adv* : brillantemente, con brillantez
brim¹ ['brɪm] *vi* **brimmed; brimming 1**
or **to brim over** : desbordarse, rebosar
2 to brim with tears : llenarse de lágrimas
brim² *n* **1** : ala *f* (de un sombrero) **2**
: borde *m* (de una taza o un vaso)
brimful ['brɪm'fʊl] *adj* : lleno hasta el
borde, repleto, rebosante
brimless ['brɪmləs] *adj* : sin ala
brimstone ['brɪm‚stoːn] *n* : azufre *m*
brindled ['brɪndəld] *adj* : manchado,
pinto
brine ['braɪn] *n* **1** : salmuera *f*, escabeche
m (para encurtir) **2** OCEAN : océano
m, mar *m*
bring ['brɪŋ] *vt* **brought** ['brɔt]; **bringing
1** CARRY : traer ⟨bring me some coffee
: tráigame un café⟩ **2** PRODUCE : traer,
producir, conseguir ⟨his efforts will
bring him success : sus esfuerzos le
conseguirán el éxito⟩ **3** PERSUADE
: convencer, persuadir **4** YIELD
: rendir, alcanzar, venderse por ⟨to
bring a good price : alcanzar un precio
alto⟩ **5 to bring to an end** : terminar
(con) **6 to bring to light** : sacar a la luz
bring about *vt* : ocasionar, provocar, determinar
bring forth *vt* PRODUCE : producir
bring out *vt* : sacar, publicar (un libro,
etc.)
bring to *vt* REVIVE : resucitar
bring up *vt* **1** REAR : criar **2** MENTION
: sacar, mencionar
brininess ['braɪnɪnəs] *n* : salinidad *f*
brink ['brɪŋk] *n* : borde *m*
briny ['braɪni] *adj* **brinier; -est** : salobre
briquette *or* **briquet** [brɪ'kɛt] *n* : briqueta *f*
brisk ['brɪsk] *adj* **1** LIVELY : rápido,
enérgico, brioso **2** INVIGORATING
: fresco, estimulante
brisket ['brɪskət] *n* : falda *f*
briskly ['brɪskli] *adv* : rápidamente,
enérgicamente, con brío
briskness ['brɪsknəs] *n* : brío *m*, rapidez
f
bristle¹ ['brɪsəl] *vi* **-tled; -tling 1**
: erizarse, ponerse de punta **2** : enfurecerse, enojarse ⟨she bristled at the
suggestion : se enfureció ante tal sug-
erencia⟩ **3** : estar plagado, estar repleto ⟨a city bristling with tourists : una
ciudad repleta de turistas⟩
bristle² *n* : cerda *f* (de un animal), pelo
m (de una planta)
bristly ['brɪsəli] *adj* **bristlier; -est**
: áspero y erizado
British¹ ['brɪtɪʃ] *adj* : británico
British² *n* **the British** *npl* : los británicos

brittle ['brɪtəl] *adj* -tler; -tlest : frágil, quebradizo

brittleness ['brɪtəlnəs] *n* : fragilidad *f*

broach ['broːtʃ] *vt* BRING UP : mencionar, abordar, sacar

broad ['brɔd] *adj* **1** WIDE : ancho **2** SPACIOUS : amplio, extenso **3** FULL : pleno ⟨in broad daylight : en pleno día⟩ **4** OBVIOUS : claro, evidente **5** TOLERANT : tolerante, liberal **6** GENERAL : general **7** ESSENTIAL : principal, esencial ⟨the broad outline : los rasgos esenciales⟩

broadcast¹ ['brɔd,kæst] *vt* -cast; -casting **1** SCATTER : esparcir, diseminar **2** CIRCULATE, SPREAD : divulgar, difundir, propagar **3** TRANSMIT : transmitir, emitir

broadcast² *n* **1** TRANSMISSION : transmisión *f*, emisión *f* **2** PROGRAM : programa *m*, emisión *f*

broadcaster ['brɔd,kæstər] *n* : presentador *m*, -dora *f*; locutor *m*, -tora *f*

broadcloth ['brɔd,klɔθ] *n* : paño *m* fino

broaden ['brɔdən] *vt* : ampliar, ensanchar — *vi* : ampliarse, ensancharse

broadloom ['brɔd,luːm] *adj* : tejido en telar ancho

broadly ['brɔdli] *adv* **1** GENERALLY : en general, aproximadamente **2** WIDELY : extensivamente

broad-minded ['brɔd'maɪndəd] *adj* : tolerante, de amplias miras

broad-mindedness [brɔd'maɪndədnəs] *n* : tolerancia *f*

broadside ['brɔd,saɪd] *n* **1** VOLLEY : andanada *f* **2** ATTACK : ataque *m*, invectiva *f*, andanada *f*

brocade [bro'keɪd] *n* : brocado *m*

broccoli ['brɑkəli] *n* : brócoli *m*, brécol *m*

brochure [bro'ʃʊr] *n* : folleto *m*

brogue ['broːg] *n* : acento *m* irlandés

broil¹ ['brɔɪl] *vt* : asar a la parrilla

broil² *n* : asado *m*

broiler ['brɔɪlər] *n* **1** GRILL : parrilla *f* **2** : pollo *m* para asar

broke¹ ['broːk] → **break¹**

broke² *adj* : pelado, arruinado ⟨to go broke : arruinarse, quebrar⟩

broken ['broːkən] *adj* **1** DAMAGED, SHATTERED : roto, quebrado, fracturado **2** IRREGULAR, UNEVEN : accidentado, irregular, recortado **3** VIOLATED : roto, quebrantado **4** INTERRUPTED : interrumpido, descontinuo **5** CRUSHED : abatido, quebrantado ⟨a broken man : un hombre destrozado⟩ **6** IMPERFECT : mal ⟨to speak broken English : hablar el inglés con dificultad⟩

brokenhearted [,broːkən'hɑrtəd] *adj* : descorazonado, desconsolado

broker¹ ['broːkər] *vt* : hacer corretaje de

broker² *n* **1** : agente *mf*; corredor *m*, -dora *f* **2** → **stockbroker**

brokerage ['broːkərɪdʒ] *n* : corretaje *m*, agencia *f* de corredores

bromine ['broː,miːn] *n* : bromo *m*

bronchitis [brɑn'kaɪtəs, brɑn-] *n* : bronquitis *f*

bronze¹ ['brɑnz] *vt* bronzed; bronzing : broncear

bronze² *n* : bronce *m*

brooch ['broːtʃ, 'bruːtʃ] *n* : broche *m*, prendedor *m*

brood¹ ['bruːd] *vt* **1** INCUBATE : empollar, incubar **2** PONDER : sopesar, considerar — *vi* **1** INCUBATE : empollar **2** REFLECT : rumiar, reflexionar **3** WORRY : ponerse melancólico, inquietarse

brood² *adj* : de cría

brood³ *n* : nidada *f* (de pájaros), camada *f* (de mamíferos)

brooder ['bruːdər] *n* **1** THINKER : pensador *m*, -dora *f* **2** INCUBATOR : incubadora *f*

brook¹ ['brʊk] *vt* TOLERATE : tolerar, admitir

brook² *n* : arroyo *m*

broom ['bruːm, 'brʊm] *n* **1** : retama *f*, hiniesta *f* **2** : escoba *f* (para barrer)

broomstick ['bruːm,stɪk, 'brʊm-] *n* : palo *m* de escoba

broth ['brɔθ] *n, pl* **broths** ['brɔθs, 'brɔðz] : caldo *m*

brothel ['brɑθəl, 'brɔ-] *n* : burdel *m*

brother ['brʌðər] *n, pl* **brothers** *also* **brethren** ['brɔðrən, -ðərn] **1** : hermano *m* **2** KINSMAN : pariente *m*, familiar *m*

brotherhood ['brʌðər,hʊd] *n* **1** FELLOWSHIP : fraternidad *f* **2** ASSOCIATION : hermandad *f*

brother-in-law ['brʌðərɪn,lɔ] *n, pl* **brothers-in-law** : cuñado *m*

brotherly ['brʌðərli] *adj* : fraternal

brought → **bring**

brow ['braʊ] *n* **1** EYEBROW : ceja *f* **2** FOREHEAD : frente *f* **3** : cima *f* ⟨the brow of a hill : la cima de una colina⟩

browbeat ['braʊ,biːt] *vt* -beat; -beaten [-,biːtən] *or* -beat; -beating : intimidar

brown¹ ['braʊn] *vt* **1** : dorar (en cocina) **2** TAN : broncear — *vi* **1** : dorarse (en cocina) **2** TAN : broncearse

brown² *adj* : marrón, café, castaño (dícese del pelo), moreno (dícese de la piel)

brown³ *n* : marrón *m*, café *m*

brownish ['braʊnɪʃ] *adj* : pardo

browse ['braʊz] *vi* browsed; browsing **1** GRAZE : pacer **2** LOOK : mirar, echar un vistazo

bruin ['bruːɪn] *n* BEAR : oso *m*

bruise¹ ['bruːz] *vt* bruised; bruising **1** : contusionar, machucar, magullar (a una persona) **2** DAMAGE : magullar, dañar (frutas) **3** CRUSH : majar **4** HURT : herir (los sentimientos)

bruise² *n* : moretón *m*, cardenal *m*, magulladura *f* (dícese de frutas)

brunch ['brʌntʃ] *n* : combinación *f* de desayuno y almuerzo

brunet¹ *or* **brunette** [bru'nɛt] *adj* : moreno

brunet² *or* **brunette** *n* : moreno *m*, -na *f*

brunt ['brʌnt] *n* **to bear the brunt of** : llevar el peso de, aguantar el mayor impacto de

brush¹ ['brʌʃ] *vt* **1** : cepillar ⟨to brush one's teeth : cepillarse uno los dientes⟩ **2** SWEEP : barrer, quitar con un cepillo **3** GRAZE : rozar **4 to brush off** DISREGARD : hacer caso omiso de, ignorar — *vi* **to brush up on** : repasar, refrescar, dar un repaso a

brush² *n* **1** *or* **brushwood** ['brʌʃ,wʊd] : broza *f* **2** SCRUB, UNDERBRUSH : maleza *f* **3** : cepillo *m*, pincel *m* (de artista), brocha *f* (de pintor) **4** TOUCH : roce *m* **5** SKIRMISH : escaramuza *f*

brush–off ['brʌʃ,ɔf] *n* **to give the brush–off to** : dar calabazas a

brusque ['brʌsk] *adj* : brusco — **brusquely** *adv*

brussels sprout ['brʌsəlz,spraut] *n* : col *f* de Bruselas

brutal ['bruːt̬əl] *adj* : brutal, cruel, salvaje — **brutally** *adv*

brutality [bruːˈtæləti] *n, pl* **-ties** : brutalidad *f*

brutalize ['bruːt̬əl,aɪz] *vt* **-ized; -izing** : brutalizar, maltratar

brute¹ ['bruːt] *adj* : bruto ⟨brute force : fuerza bruta⟩

brute² *n* **1** BEAST : bestia *f*, animal *m* **2** : bruto *m*, -ta *f*; bestia *mf* (persona)

brutish ['bruːt̬ɪʃ] *adj* **1** : de animal **2** CRUEL : brutal, salvaje **3** STUPID : bruto, estúpido

bubble¹ ['bʌbəl] *vi* **-bled; -bling** : burbujear ⟨to bubble over with joy : rebosar de alegría⟩

bubble² *n* : burbuja *f*

bubbly ['bʌbəli] *adj* **bubblier; -est 1** BUBBLING : burbujeante **2** LIVELY : vivaz, lleno de vida

bubonic plague [buːˈbɑnɪk, ˈbjuː-] *n* : peste *f* bubónica

buccaneer [,bʌkəˈnɪr] *n* : bucanero *m*

buck¹ ['bʌk] *vi* **1** : corcovear (dícese de un caballo o un burro) **2** JOLT : dar sacudidas **3 to buck against** : resistirse a, rebelarse contra **4 to buck up** : animarse, levantar el ánimo — *vt* OPPOSE : oponerse a, ir en contra de

buck² *n, pl* **buck** *or* **bucks 1** : animal *m* macho, ciervo *m* (macho) **2** DOLLAR : dólar *m* **3 to pass the buck** *fam* : pasar la pelota *fam*

bucket ['bʌkət] *n* : balde *m*, cubo *m*, cubeta *f Mex*

bucketful ['bʌkət,fʊl] *n* : balde *m* lleno

buckle¹ ['bʌkəl] *v* **-led; -ling** *vt* **1** FASTEN : abrochar **2** BEND, TWIST : combar, torcer — *vi* **1** BEND, TWIST : combarse, torcerse, doblarse (dícese de las rodillas) **2 to buckle down** : ponerse a trabajar con esmero **3 to buckle up** : abrocharse

buckle² *n* **1** : hebilla *f* **2** TWISTING : torcedura *f*

buckshot ['bʌk,ʃɑt] *n* : perdigón *m*

buckskin ['bʌk,skɪn] *n* : gamuza *f*

bucktooth ['bʌk,tuːθ] *n* : diente *m* saliente, diente *m* salido

buckwheat ['bʌk,ʰwiːt] *n* : trigo *m* rubión, alforfón *m*

bucolic [bjuːˈkɑlɪk] *adj* : bucólico

bud¹ ['bʌd] *v* **budded; budding** *vt* GRAFT : injertar — *vi* : brotar, hacer brotes

bud² *n* : brote *m*, yema *f*, capullo *m* (de una flor)

Buddhism ['buː,dɪzəm, 'buː-] *n* : budismo *m*

Buddhist ['buː,dɪst, 'buː-] *n* : budista *mf* — **Buddhist** *adj*

buddy ['bʌdi] *n, pl* **-dies** : amigo *m*, -ga *f*; compinche *mf fam*; cuate *m*, -ta *f Mex fam*

budge ['bʌdʒ] *vi* **budged; budging 1** MOVE : moverse, desplazarse **2** YIELD : ceder

budget¹ ['bʌdʒət] *vt* : presupuestar (gastos), asignar (dinero) — *vi* : presupuestar, planear el presupuesto

budget² *n* : presupuesto

budgetary ['bʌdʒə,teri] *adj* : presupuestario

buff¹ ['bʌf] *vt* POLISH : pulir, sacar brillo a, lustrar

buff² *adj* : beige, amarillento

buff³ *n* **1** : beige *m*, amarillento *m* **2** ENTHUSIAST : aficionado *m*, -da *f*; entusiasta *mf*

buffalo ['bʌfə,loː] *n, pl* **-lo** *or* **-loes 1** : búfalo *m* **2** BISON : bisonte *m*

buffer ['bʌfər] *n* **1** BARRIER : barrera *f* ⟨buffer state : estado tapón⟩ **2** SHOCK ABSORBER : amortiguador *m*

buffet¹ ['bʌfət] *vt* : golpear, zarandear, sacudir

buffet² *n* BLOW : golpe *m*

buffet³ [,bʌˈfeɪ, ,buː-] *n* **1** : bufete *m*, bufé *m* (comida) **2** SIDEBOARD : aparador *m*

buffoon [,bʌˈfuːn] *n* : bufón *m*, -fona *f*; payaso *m*, -sa *f*

buffoonery [,bʌˈfuːnəri] *n, pl* **-eries** : bufonada *f*, payasada *f*

bug¹ ['bʌg] *vt* **bugged; bugging 1** PESTER : fastidiar, molestar **2** : ocultar micrófonos en

bug² *n* **1** INSECT : bicho *m*, insecto *m* **2** DEFECT : defecto *m*, falla *f*, problema *m* **3** GERM : microbio *m*, virus *m* **4** MICROPHONE : micrófono *m*

bugaboo ['bʌgə,buː] → **bogey**

bugbear ['bʌg,bær] *n* : pesadilla *f*, coco *m*

buggy ['bʌgi] *n, pl* **-gies** : calesa *f* (tirada por caballos), cochecito *m* (para niños)

bugle ['bjuːgəl] *n* : clarín *m*, corneta *f*

bugler ['bjuːgələr] *n* : corneta *mf*

build¹ ['bɪld] *v* **built** ['bɪlt]; **building** *vt* **1** CONSTRUCT : construir, edificar, ensamblar, levantar **2** DEVELOP : desarrollar, elaborar, forjar **3** INCREASE : incrementar, aumentar — *vi* **to build up** : aumentar, intensificar

build² *n* PHYSIQUE : físico *m*, complexión *f*

builder ['bɪldər] *n* : constructor *m*, -tora *f*; contratista *mf*

building ['bɪldɪŋ] *n* **1** EDIFICE : edificio *m* **2** CONSTRUCTION : construcción *f*

built–in ['bɪlt'ɪn] *adj* **1** : empotrado ⟨built-in cabinets : armarios empotrados⟩ **2** INHERENT : incorporado, intrínseco

bulb ['bʌlb] *n* **1** : bulbo *m* (de una planta), cabeza *f* (de ajo), cubeta *f* (de un termómetro) **2** LIGHTBULB : bombilla *f*, foco *m*, bombillo *m CA, Col, Ven*

bulbous ['bʌlbəs] *adj* : bulboso

Bulgarian [bʌl'gæriən, bʊl-] *n* **1** : búlgaro *m*, -ra *f* **2** : búlgaro *m* (idioma) — **Bulgarian** *adj*

bulge[1] ['bʌlʤ] *vi* **bulged; bulging** : abultar, sobresalir

bulge[2] *n* : bulto *m*, protuberancia *f*

bulk[1] ['bʌlk] *vt* : hinchar — *vi* EXPAND, SWELL : ampliarse, hincharse

bulk[2] *n* **1** SIZE, VOLUME : volumen *m*, tamaño *m* **2** FIBER : fibra *f* **3** MASS : mole *f* **4 the bulk of** : la mayor parte de **5 in ∼** : en grandes cantidades

bulkhead ['bʌlk,hɛd] *n* : mamparo *m*

bulky ['bʌlki] *adj* **bulkier; -est** : voluminoso, grande

bull[1] ['bʊl] *adj* : macho

bull[2] *n* **1** : toro *m*, macho *m* (de ciertas especies) **2** : bula *f* (papal) **3** DECREE : decreto *m*, edicto *m*

bulldog ['bʊl,dɔg] *n* : bulldog *m*

bulldoze ['bʊl,do:z] *vt* **-dozed; -dozing 1** LEVEL : nivelar (el terreno), derribar (un edificio) **2** FORCE : forzar ⟨he bulldozed his way through : se abrió paso a codazos⟩

bulldozer ['bʊl,do:zər] *n* : bulldozer *m*

bullet ['bʊlət] *n* : bala *f*

bulletin ['bʊlətən, -lətən] *n* **1** NOTICE : comunicado *m*, anuncio *m*, boletín *m* **2** NEWSLETTER : boletín *m* (informativo)

bulletin board *n* : tablón *m* de anuncios

bulletproof ['bʊlət,pru:f] *adj* : antibalas, a prueba de balas

bullfight ['bʊl,faɪt] *n* : corrida *f* (de toros)

bullfighter ['bʊl,faɪtər] *n* : torero *m*, -ra *f*; matador *m*

bullfrog ['bʊl,frɔg] *n* : rana *f* toro

bullheaded ['bʊl'hɛdəd] *adj* : testarudo

bullion ['bʊljən] *n* : oro *m* en lingotes, plata *f* en lingotes

bullock ['bʊlək] *n* **1** STEER : buey *m*, toro *m* castrado **2** : toro *m* joven, novillo *m*

bull's–eye ['bʊlz,aɪ] *n, pl* **bull's–eyes** : diana *f*, blanco *m*

bully[1] ['bʊli] *vt* **-lied; -lying** : intimidar, amedrentar, mangonear

bully[2] *n, pl* **-lies** : matón *m*; bravucón *m*, -cona *f*

bulrush ['bʊl,rʌʃ] *n* : especie *f* de junco

bulwark ['bʊl,wərk, -,wɔrk; 'bʌl,wərk] *n* : baluarte *m*, bastión *f*

bum[1] ['bʌm] *v* **bummed; bumming** *vi* **to bum around** : vagabundear, vagar — *vt* : gorronear *fam*, sablear *fam*

bum[2] *adj* : inútil, malo ⟨a bum rap : una acusación falsa⟩

bum[3] *n* **1** LOAFER : vago *m*, -ga *f* **2** HOBO, TRAMP : vagabundo *m*, -da *f*

bumblebee ['bʌmbəl,bi:] *n* : abejorro *m*

bump[1] ['bʌmp] *vt* : chocar contra, golpear contra, dar ⟨to bump one's head : darse (un golpe) en la cabeza⟩ — *vi* **to bump into** MEET : encontrarse con, tropezarse con

bump[2] *n* **1** BULGE : bulto *m*, protuberancia *f* **2** IMPACT : golpe *m*, choque *m* **3** JOLT : sacudida *f*

bumper[1] ['bʌmpər] *adj* : extraordinario, récord ⟨a bumper crop : una cosecha abundante⟩

bumper[2] *n* : parachoques *mpl*

bumpkin ['bʌmpkən] *n* : palurdo *m*, -da *f*

bumpy ['bʌmpi] *adj* **bumpier; -est** : desigual, lleno de baches (dícese de un camino), agitado (dícese de un vuelo en avión)

bun ['bʌn] *n* : bollo *m*

bunch[1] ['bʌntʃ] *vt* : agrupar, amontonar — *vi* **to bunch up** : amontonarse, agruparse, fruncirse (dícese de una tela)

bunch[2] *n* : grupo *m*, montón *m*, ramo *m* (de flores)

bundle[1] ['bʌndəl] *vt* **-dled; -dling** : liar, atar

bundle[2] *n* **1** : fardo *m*, atado *m*, bulto *m*, haz *m* (de palos) **2** PARCEL : paquete *m* **3** LOAD : montón *m* ⟨a bundle of money : un montón de dinero⟩

bungalow ['bʌŋgə,lo:] *n* : tipo de casa de un solo piso

bungle[1] ['bʌŋgəl] *vt* **-gled; -gling** : echar a perder, malograr

bungle[2] *n* : chapuza *f*, desatino *m*

bungler ['bʌŋgələr] *n* : chapucero *m*, -ra *f*; inepto *m*, -ta *f*

bunion ['bʌnjən] *n* : juanete *m*

bunk[1] ['bʌŋk] *vi* : dormir (en una litera)

bunk[2] *n* **1** *or* **bunk bed** : litera *f* **2** NONSENSE : tonterías *fpl*, bobadas *fpl*

bunker ['bʌŋkər] *n* **1** : carbonera *f* (en un barco) **2** SHELTER : búnker *m*

bunny ['bʌni] *n, pl* **-nies** : conejo *m*, -ja *f*

buoy[1] ['bu:i, 'bɔi] *vt* **to buoy up 1** : mantener a flote **2** CHEER, HEARTEN : animar, levantar el ánimo a

buoy[2] *n* : boya *f*

buoyancy ['bɔiəntsi, 'bu:jən-] *n* **1** : flotabilidad *f* **2** OPTIMISM : confianza *f*, optimismo *m*

buoyant ['bɔiənt, 'bu:jənt] *adj* : boyante, flotante

bur *or* **burr** ['bər] *n* : abrojo *m* (de una planta)

burden[1] ['bərdən] *vt* : cargar, oprimir

burden[2] *n* : carga *f*, peso *m*

burdensome ['bərdənsəm] *adj* : oneroso

burdock ['bər,dɑk] *n* : bardana *f*

bureau ['bjuro] *n* **1** CHEST OF DRAWERS : cómoda *f* **2** DEPARTMENT : departamento *m* (del gobierno) **3** AGENCY

: agencia *f* ⟨travel bureau : agencia de viajes⟩

bureaucracy ['bjʊ'rɑkrəsi] *n, pl* **-cies** : burocracia *f*

bureaucrat ['bjʊrə,kræt] *n* : burócrata *mf*

bureaucratic [,bjʊrə'kræṭık] *adj* : burocrático

burgeon ['bərdʒən] *vi* : florecer, retoñar, crecer

burglar ['bərglər] *n* : ladrón *m*, -drona *f*

burglarize ['bərglə,raız] *vt* **-ized; -izing** : robar

burglary ['bərgləri] *n, pl* **-glaries** : robo *m*

burgle ['bərgəl] *vt* **-gled; -gling** : robar

burgundy ['bərgəndi] *n, pl* **-dies** : borgoña *m*, vino *m* de Borgoña

burial ['beriəl] *n* : entierro *m*, sepelio *m*

burlap ['bər,læp] *n* : arpillera *f*

burlesque[1] [bər'lesk] *vt* **-lesqued; -lesquing** : parodiar

burlesque[2] *n* **1** PARODY : parodia *f* **2** REVUE : revista *f* (musical)

burly ['bərli] *adj* **-lier; -liest** : fornido, corpulento, musculoso

Burmese [,bər'miːz, -'miːs] *n* : birmano *m*, -na *f* — **Burmese** *adj*

burn[1] ['bərn] *v* **burned** ['bərnd, 'bərnt] *or* **burnt** ['bərnt]; **burning** *vt* **1** : quemar, incendiar ⟨to burn a building : incendiar un edificio⟩ ⟨I burned my hand : me quemé la mano⟩ **2** CONSUME : usar, gastar, consumir — *vi* **1** : arder (dícese de un fuego o un edificio), quemarse (dícese de la comida, etc.) **2** : estar prendido, estar encendido ⟨we left the lights burning : dejamos las luces encendidas⟩ **3 to burn out** : consumirse, apagarse **4 to burn with** : arder de ⟨he was burning with jealousy : ardía de celos⟩

burn[2] *n* : quemadura *f*

burner ['bərnər] *n* : quemador *m*

burnish ['bərnıʃ] *vt* : bruñir

burp[1] ['bərp] *vi* : eructar — *vt* : hacer eructar

burp[2] *n* : eructo *m*

burr → **bur**

burro ['bəro, 'bʊr-] *n, pl* **-os** : burro *m*

burrow[1] ['bəro] *vi* **1** : cavar, hacer una madriguera **2 to burrow into** : hurgar en — *vt* : cavar, excavar

burrow[2] *n* : madriguera *f*, conejera *f* (de un conejo)

bursar ['bərsər] *n* : administrador *m*, -dora *f*

bursitis [bər'saiṭəs] *n* : bursitis *f*

burst[1] ['bərst] *v* **burst; bursting** *vi* **1** : reventarse (dícese de una llanta o un globo), estallar (dícese de obuses o fuegos artificiales), romperse (dícese de un dique) **2 to burst in** : irrumpir en **3 to burst into** : empezar a, echar a ⟨to burst into tears : echarse a llorar⟩ — *vt* : reventar

burst[2] *n* **1** EXPLOSION : estallido *m*, explosión *f*, reventón *m* (de una llanta) **2** OUTBURST : arranque *m* (de actividad,

de velocidad), arrebato *m* (de ira), salva *f* (de aplausos)

Burundian [bʊ'ruːndiən, -'rʊn-] *n* : burundés *m*, -desa *f* — **Burundian** *adj*

bury ['beri] *vt* **buried; burying 1** INTER : enterrar, sepultar **2** HIDE : esconder, ocultar **3 to bury oneself in** : enfrascarse en

bus[1] ['bʌs] *v* **bused** *or* **bussed** ['bʌst]; **busing** *or* **bussing** *vt* : transportar en autobús — *vi* : viajar en autobús

bus[2] *n* : autobús *m*, bus *m*, camión *m Mex*, colectivo *m Arg, Bol, Peru*

busboy ['bʌs,bɔɪ] *n* : ayudante *mf* de camarero

bush ['bʊʃ] *n* **1** SHRUB : arbusto *m*, mata *f* **2** THICKET : maleza *f*, matorral *m*

bushel ['bʊʃəl] *n* : medida *f* de áridos igual a 35.24 litros

bushing ['bʊʃıŋ] *n* : cojinete *m*

bushy ['bʊʃi] *adj* **bushier; -est** : espeso, poblado ⟨bushy eyebrows : cejas pobladas⟩

busily ['bızəli] *adv* : afanosamente, diligentemente

business ['bıznəs, -nəz] *n* **1** OCCUPATION : ocupación *f*, oficio *m* **2** DUTY, MISSION : misión *f*, deber *m*, responsabilidad *f* **3** ESTABLISHMENT, FIRM : empresa *f*, firma *f*, negocio *m*, comercio *m* **4** COMMERCE : negocios *mpl*, comercio *m* **5** AFFAIR, MATTER : asunto *m*, cuestión *f*, cosa *f* ⟨it's none of your business : no es asunto tuyo⟩

businessman ['bıznəs,mæn, -nəz-] *n, pl* **-men** [-mən, -,mɛn] : empresario *m*, hombre *m* de negocios

businesswoman ['bıznəs,wʊmən, -nəz-] *n, pl* **-women** [-,wımən] : empresaria *f*, mujer *f* de negocios

bust[1] ['bʌst] *vt* **1** BREAK, SMASH : romper, estropear, destrozar **2** TAME : domar, amansar (un caballo) — *vi* : romperse, estropearse

bust[2] *n* **1** : busto *m* (en la escultura) **2** BREASTS : pecho *m*, senos *mpl*, busto *m*

bustle[1] ['bʌsəl] *vi* **-tled; -tling to bustle about** : ir y venir, trajinar, ajetrearse

bustle[2] *n* **1** *or* **hustle and bustle** : bullicio *m*, ajetreo *m* **2** : polisón *m* (en la ropa feminina)

busy[1] ['bızi] *vt* **busied; busying to busy oneself with** : ocuparse con, ponerse a, entretenerse con

busy[2] *adj* **busier; -est 1** OCCUPIED : ocupado, atareado ⟨he's busy working : está ocupado en su trabajo⟩ ⟨the telephone was busy : el teléfono estaba ocupado⟩ **2** BUSTLING : concurrido, animado ⟨a busy street : una calle concurrida, una calle con mucho tránsito⟩

busybody ['bızi,bɑdi] *n, pl* **-bodies** : entrometido *m*, -da *f*; metiche *mf fam*; metomentodo *mf*

but[1] ['bʌt] *conj* **1** THAT : que ⟨there is no doubt but he is lazy : no cabe duda

que sea perezoso⟩ **2** WITHOUT : sin que
3 NEVERTHELESS : pero, no obstante,
sin embargo ⟨I called her but she did-
n't answer : la llamé pero no contestó⟩
4 YET : pero ⟨he was poor but proud
: era pobre pero orgulloso⟩
but² *prep* EXCEPT : excepto, menos
⟨everyone but Carlos : todos menos
Carlos⟩ ⟨the last but one : el penúlti-
mo⟩
butcher¹ ['bʊtʃər] *vt* **1** SLAUGHTER
: matar (animales) **2** KILL : matar, asesinar, masacrar **3** BOTCH : estropear,
hacer una chapuza
butcher² *n* **1** : carnicero *m*, -ra *f* **2**
KILLER : asesino *m*, -na *f* **3** BUNGLER
: chapucero *m*, -ra *f*
butler ['bʌtlər] *n* : mayordomo *m*
butt¹ ['bʌt] *vt* **1** : embestir (con los cuernos), darle un cabezazo a **2** ABUT : colindar con, bordear — *vi* **to butt in 1**
INTERRUPT : interrumpir **2** MEDDLE
: entrometerse, meterse
butt² *n* **1** BUTTING : embestida *f* (de cuernos), cabezazo *m* **2** TARGET : blanco
m ⟨the butt of their jokes : el blanco
de sus bromas⟩ **3** BOTTOM, END : extremo *m*, culata *f* (de un rifle), colilla *f*
(de un cigarrillo)
butte ['bjuːt] *n* : colina *f* empinada y ais-
lada
butter¹ ['bʌtər] *vt* **1** : untar con mantequilla **2 to butter up** : halagar
butter² *n* : mantequilla *f*
buttercup ['bʌtərˌkʌp] *n* : ranúnculo *m*
butterfat ['bʌtərˌfæt] *n* : grasa *f* de la
leche
butterfly ['bʌtərˌflaɪ] *n, pl* **-flies** : mariposa *f*
buttermilk ['bʌtərˌmɪlk] *n* : suero *m* de
la leche
butternut ['bʌtərˌnʌt] *n* : nogal *m* ceniciento (árbol)
butterscotch ['bʌtərˌskɑtʃ] *n* : caramelo
m duro hecho con mantequilla
buttery ['bʌtəri] *adj* : mantecoso
buttocks ['bʌtəks, -ˌtaks] *npl* : nalgas *fpl*,
trasero *m*
button¹ ['bʌtən] *vt* : abrochar, abotonar
— *vi* : abrocharse, abotonarse
button² *n* : botón *m*
buttonhole¹ ['bʌtənˌhoːl] *vt* **-holed;**
-holing : acorralar
buttonhole² *n* : ojal *m*
buttress¹ ['bʌtrəs] *vt* : apoyar, reforzar
buttress² *n* **1** : contrafuerte *m* (en la arquitectura) **2** SUPPORT : apoyo *m*,
sostén *m*

buxom ['bʌksəm] *adj* : con mucho busto, con mucho pecho
buy¹ ['baɪ] *vt* **bought** ['bɔt]; **buying**
: comprar
buy² *n* BARGAIN : compra *f*, ganga *f*
buyer ['baɪər] *n* : comprador *m*, -dora *f*
buzz¹ ['bʌz] *vi* : zumbar (dícese de un insecto), sonar (dícese de un teléfono o
un despertador)
buzz² *n* **1** : zumbido *m* (de insectos) **2**
: murmullo *m*, rumor *m* (de voces)
buzzard ['bʌzərd] *n* VULTURE : buitre *m*,
zopilote *m* CA, Mex
buzzer ['bʌzər] *n* : timbre *m*, chicharra *f*
buzzword ['bʌzˌwərd] *n* : palabra *f* de
moda
by¹ ['baɪ] *adv* **1** NEAR : cerca ⟨he lives
close by : vive muy cerca⟩ **2 to stop
by** : pasar por casa, hacer una visita **3
to go by** : pasar ⟨they rushed by
: pasaron corriendo⟩ **4 to put by**
: reservar, poner a un lado **5 by and
by** : poco después, dentro de poco **6
by and large** : en general
by² *prep* **1** NEAR : cerca de, al lado de,
junto a **2** VIA : por ⟨she left by the door
: salió por la puerta⟩ **3** PAST : por, por
delante de ⟨they walked by him
: pasaron por delante de él⟩ **4** DURING
: de, durante ⟨by night : de noche⟩ **5**
(*in expressions of time*) : para ⟨we'll be
there by ten : estaremos allí para las
diez⟩ ⟨by then : para entonces⟩ **6** (*indicating cause or agent*) : por, de, a
⟨built by the Romans : construido por
los romanos⟩ ⟨a book by Borges : un
libro de Borges⟩ ⟨made by hand : hecho a mano⟩
by and by *adv* : dentro de poco
bygone¹ ['baɪˌgɔn] *adj* : pasado
bygone² *n* **let bygones be bygones** : lo
pasado, pasado está
bylaw *or* **byelaw** ['baɪˌlɔ] *n* : norma *f*,
reglamento *m*
by–line ['baɪˌlaɪn] *n* : data *f*
bypass¹ ['baɪˌpæs] *vt* : evitar
bypass² *n* **1** BELTWAY : carretera *f* de
circunvalación **2** DETOUR : desvío *m*
by–product ['baɪˌprɑdəkt] *n* : subproducto *m*, producto *m* derivado
bystander ['baɪˌstændər] *n* : espectador
m, -dora *f*
byte ['baɪt] *n* : byte *m*
byway ['baɪˌweɪ] *n* : camino *m* (apartado), carretera *f* secundaria
byword ['baɪˌwərd] *n* **1** PROVERB
: proverbio *m*, refrán *m* **2 to be a byword for** : estar sinónimo de

C

c ['si:] *n, pl* **c's** *or* **cs** : tercera letra del alfabeto inglés

cab ['kæb] *n* **1** TAXI : taxi *m* **2** : cabina *f* (de un camión o una locomotora) **3** CARRIAGE : coche *m* de caballos

cabal [kə'bɑl, -'bæl] *n* **1** INTRIGUE, PLOT : conspiración *f*, complot *m*, intriga *f* **2** : grupo *m* de conspiradores

cabaret [ˌkæbə'reɪ] *n* : cabaret *m*

cabbage ['kæbɪʤ] *n* : col *f*, repollo *m*

cabbie *or* **cabby** ['kæbi] *n* : taxista *mf*

cabin ['kæbən] *n* **1** HUT : cabaña *f*, choza *f*, barraca *f* **2** STATEROOM : camarote *m* **3** : cabina *f* (de un automóvil o avión)

cabinet ['kæbnət] *n* **1** CUPBOARD : armario *m* **2** : gabinete *m*, consejo *m* de ministros **3** **medicine cabinet** : botiquín *m*

cabinetmaker ['kæbnətˌmeɪkər] *n* : ebanista *mf*

cabinetmaking ['kæbnətˌmeɪkɪŋ] *n* : ebanistería *f*

cable¹ ['keɪbəl] *vt* **-bled; -bling** : enviar un cable, telegrafiar

cable² *n* **1** : cable *m* (para colgar o sostener algo) **2** : cable *m* eléctrico **3** → **cablegram**

cablegram ['keɪbəlˌgræm] *n* : telegrama *m*, cable *m*

caboose [kə'bu:s] *n* : furgón *m* de cola, cabús *m Mex*

cabstand ['kæbˌstænd] *n* : parada *f* de taxis

cacao [kə'kaʊ, -'keɪo] *n, pl* **cacaos** : cacao *m*

cache¹ ['kæʃ] *vt* **cached; caching** : esconder, guardar en un escondrijo

cache² *n* **1** : escondite *m*, escondrijo *m* ⟨cache of weapons : escondite de armas⟩ **2** : caché *m* ⟨cache memory : memoria cache⟩

cachet [kæ'ʃeɪ] *n* : caché *m*, prestigio *m*

cackle¹ ['kækəl] *vi* **-led; -ling 1** CLUCK : cacarear **2** : reírse o carcajearse estridentemente ⟨he was cackling with delight : estaba carcajeándose de gusto⟩

cackle² *n* **1** : cacareo *m* (de una polla) **2** LAUGH : risa *f* estridente

cacophony [kæ'kɑfəni, -'kɔ-] *n, pl* **-nies** : cacofonía *f*

cactus ['kæktəs] *n, pl* **cacti** [-ˌtaɪ] *or* **-tus-es** : cacto *m*, cactus *m*

cadaver [kə'dævər] *n* : cadáver *m*

cadaverous [kə'dævərəs] *adj* : cadavérico

caddie¹ *or* **caddy** ['kædi] *vi* **caddied; caddying** : trabajar de caddie, hacer de caddie

caddie² *or* **caddy** *n, pl* **-dies** : caddie *mf*

caddy ['kædi] *n, pl* **-dies** : cajita *f* para té

cadence ['keɪdənts] *n* : cadencia *f*, ritmo *m*

cadenced ['keɪdəntst] *adj* : cadencioso, rítmico

cadet [kə'dɛt] *n* : cadete *mf*

cadmium ['kædmiəm] *n* : cadmio *m*

cadre ['kæˌdreɪ, 'kɑ-, -ˌdri:] *n* : cuadro *m* (de expertos)

café [kæ'feɪ, kə-] *n* : café *m*, cafetería *f*

cafeteria [ˌkæfə'tɪriə] *n* : cafetería *f*, restaurante *m* de autoservicio

caffeine [kæ'fi:n] *n* : cafeína *f*

cage¹ ['keɪʤ] *vt* **caged; caging** : enjaular

cage² *n* : jaula *f*

cagey ['keɪʤi] *adj* **-gier; -est 1** CAUTIOUS : cauteloso, reservado **2** SHREWD : astuto, vivo — **cagily** [-ʤəli] *adv*

caisson ['keɪˌsɑn, -sən] *n* **1** : cajón *m* de municiones **2** : cajón *m* hidráulico

cajole [kə'ʤo:l] *vt* **-joled; -joling** : engatusar

cajolery [kə'ʤo:ləri] *n* : engatusamiento *m*

cake¹ ['keɪk] *v* **caked; caking** *vt* : cubrir ⟨caked with mud : cubierto de barro⟩ — *vi* : endurecerse

cake² *n* **1** : torta *f*, bizcocho *m*, pastel *m* **2** : pastilla *f* (de jabón) **3 to take the cake** : llevarse la palma, ser el colmo

calabash ['kæləˌbæʃ] *n* : calabaza *f*

calamari [ˌkɑlə'mɑri] *ns & pl* : calamares *mpl*

calamine ['kæləˌmaɪn] *n* : calamina *f* ⟨calamine lotion : loción de calamina⟩

calamitous [kə'læmətəs] *adj* : desastroso, catastrófico, calamitoso — **calamitously** *adv*

calamity [kə'læməti] *n, pl* **-ties** : desastre *m*, desgracia *f*, calamidad *f*

calcium ['kælsiəm] *n* : calcio *m*

calcium carbonate ['kɑrbəˌneɪt, -nət] *n* : carbonato *m* de calcio

calculable ['kælkjələbəl] *adj* : calculable, computable

calculate ['kælkjəˌleɪt] *v* **-lated; -lating** *vt* **1** COMPUTE : calcular, computar **2** ESTIMATE : calcular, creer **3** INTEND : planear, tener la intención de ⟨I calculated on spending $100 : planeaba gastar $100⟩ — *vi* : calcular, hacer cálculos

calculated ['kælkjəˌleɪtəd] *adj* **1** ESTIMATED : calculado **2** DELIBERATE : intencional, premeditado, deliberado

calculating ['kælkjəˌleɪtɪŋ] *adj* SHREWD : calculador, astuto

calculation [ˌkælkjə'leɪʃən] *n* : cálculo *m*

calculator ['kælkjəˌleɪtər] *n* : calculadora *f*

calculus ['kælkjələs] *n, pl* **-li** [-ˌlaɪ] **1** : cálculo *m* ⟨differential calculus : cálculo diferencial⟩ **2** TARTAR : sarro *m* (dental)

caldron ['kɔldrən] → **cauldron**

calendar ['kæləndər] *n* **1** : calendario *m* **2** SCHEDULE : calendario *m*, programa *m*, agenda *f*

calf ['kæf, 'kaf] *n, pl* **calves** ['kævz, 'kavz] **1** : becerro *m*, -rra *f*; ternero *m*, -ra *f* (de vacunos) **2** : cría *f* (de otros mamíferos) **3** : pantorrilla *f* (de la pierna)

calfskin ['kæf,skın] *n* : piel *f* de becerro

caliber *or* **calibre** ['kæləbər] *n* **1** : calibre *m* ⟨a .38 caliber gun : una pistola de calibre .38⟩ **2** ABILITY : calibre *m*, valor *m*, capacidad *f*

calibrate ['kælə,breıt] *vt* -**brated**; -**brating** : calibrar (armas), graduar (termómetros)

calibration [,kælə'breıʃən] *n* : calibrado *m*, calibración *f*

calico ['kælı,ko:] *n, pl* -**coes** *or* -**cos 1** : calicó *m*, percal *m* **2** *or* **calico cat** : gato *m* manchado

calipers ['kæləpərz] *npl* : calibrador *m*

caliph *or* **calif** ['keıləf, 'kæ-] *n* : califa *m*

calisthenics [,kæləs'θenıks] *ns & pl* : calistenia *f*

calk ['kɔk] → **caulk**

call[1] ['kɔl] *vi* **1** CRY, SHOUT : gritar, vociferar **2** VISIT : hacer (una) visita, visitar **3 to call for** : exigir, requerir, necesitar ⟨it calls for patience : requiere mucha paciencia⟩ — *vt* **1** SUMMON : llamar, convocar **2** TELEPHONE : llamar por teléfono, telefonear **3** NAME : llamar, apodar

call[2] *n* **1** SHOUT : grito *m*, llamada *f* **2** : grito *m* (de un animal), reclamo *m* (de un pájaro) **3** SUMMONS : llamada *f* **4** DEMAND : llamado *m*, petición *f* **5** VISIT : visita *f* **6** DECISION : decisión *f* (en deportes) **7** *or* **telephone call** : llamada *f* (telefónica)

call down *vt* REPRIMAND : reprender, reñir

caller ['kɔlər] *n* **1** VISITOR : visita *f* **2** : persona *f* que llama (por teléfono)

calligraphy [kə'lıgrəfi] *n, pl* -**phies** : caligrafía *f*

calling ['kɔlıŋ] *n* : vocación *f*, profesión *f*

calliope [kə'laıə,pi:, 'kæli,o:p] *n* : órgano *m* de vapor

call off *vt* CANCEL : cancelar, suspender

callous[1] ['kæləs] *vt* : encallecer

callous[2] *adj* **1** CALLUSED : calloso, encallecido **2** UNFEELING : insensible, desalmado, cruel

callously ['kæləsli] *adv* : cruelmente, insensiblemente

callousness ['kæləsnəs] *n* : insensibilidad *f*, crueldad *f*

callow ['kælo] *adj* : inexperto, inmaduro

callus ['kæləs] *n* : callo *m*

callused ['kæləst] *adj* : encallecido, calloso

calm[1] ['kam, 'kalm] *vt* : tranquilizar, calmar, sosegar — *vi* : tranquilizarse, calmarse ⟨calm down! : ¡tranquilízate!⟩

calm[2] *adj* **1** TRANQUIL : calmo, tranquilo, sereno, ecuánime **2** STILL : en calma (dícese del mar), sin viento (dícese del aire)

calm[3] *n* : tranquilidad *f*, calma *f*

calmly ['kamli, 'kalm-] *adv* : con calma, tranquilamente

calmness ['kamnəs, 'kalm-] *n* : calma *f*, tranquilidad *f*

caloric [kə'lɔrık] *adj* : calórico (dícese de los alimentos), calorífico (dícese de la energía)

calorie ['kæləri] *n* : caloría *f*

calumniate [kə'lʌmni,eıt] *vt* -**ated**; -**ating** : calumniar, difamar

calumny ['kæləmni] *n, pl* -**nies** : calumnia *f*, difamación *f*

calve ['kæv, 'kav] *vi* **calved**; **calving** : parir (dícese de los mamíferos)

calves → **calf**

calypso [kə'lıp,so:] *n, pl* -**sos** : calipso *m*

calyx ['keılıks, 'kæ-] *n, pl* -**lyxes** *or* -**lyces** [-lə,si:z] : cáliz *m*

cam ['kæm] *n* : leva *f*

camaraderie [,kam'radəri, ,kæm-; ,kamə'ra-] *n* : compañerismo *m*, camaradería *f*

Cambodian [kæm'bo:diən] *n* : camboyano *m*, -na *f* — **Cambodian** *adj*

came → **come**

camel ['kæməl] *n* : camello *m*

camellia [kə'mi:ljə] *n* : camelia *f*

cameo ['kæmi,o:] *n, pl* -**eos 1** : camafeo *m* **2** *or* **cameo performance** : actuación *f* especial

camera ['kæmrə, 'kæmərə] *n* : cámara *f*, máquina *f* fotográfica

Cameroonian [,kæmə'ru:niən] *n* : camerunés *m*, -nesa *f*

camouflage[1] ['kæmə,flaʒ, -,flaʤ] *vt* -**flaged**; -**flaging** : camuflajear, camuflar

camouflage[2] *n* : camuflaje *m*

camp[1] ['kæmp] *vi* : acampar, ir de camping

camp[2] *n* **1** : campamento *m* **2** FACTION : campo *m*, bando *m* ⟨in the same camp : del mismo bando⟩ **3 to pitch camp** : acampar, poner el campamento **4 to break camp** : levantar el campamento

campaign[1] [kæm'peın] *vi* : hacer (una) campaña

campaign[2] *n* : campaña *f*

campanile [,kæmpə'ni:,li:, -'ni:l] *n, pl* -**niles** *or* -**nili** [-'ni:,li:] : campanario *m*

camper ['kæmpər] *n* **1** : campista *mf* (persona) **2** : cámper *m* (vehículo)

campground ['kæmp,graund] *n* : campamento *m*, camping *m*

camphor ['kæmpfər] *n* : alcanfor *m*

campsite ['kæmp,saıt] *n* : campamento *m*, camping *m*

campus ['kæmpəs] *n* : campus *m*, recinto *m* universitario

can[1] ['kæn] *v aux, past* **could** ['kʊd]; *present s & pl* **can 1** : poder ⟨could you help me? : ¿podría ayudarme?⟩ **2** : saber ⟨she can't drive yet : todavía no sabe manejar⟩ **3** MAY : poder, tener permiso para ⟨can I sit down? : ¿puedo sentarme?⟩ **4** : poder ⟨it can't be! : ¡no puede ser!⟩ ⟨where can they be? : ¿dónde estarán?⟩

can² [ˈkæn] *vt* **canned; canning 1** : enlatar, envasar ⟨to can tomatoes : enlatar tomates⟩ **2** DISMISS, FIRE : despedir, echar

can³ *n* : lata *f*, envase *m*, cubo *m* ⟨a can of beer : una lata de cerveza⟩ ⟨garbage can : cubo de basura⟩

Canadian [kəˈneɪdiən] *n* : canadiense *mf* — **Canadian** *adj*

canal [kəˈnæl] *n* **1** : canal *m*, tubo *m* ⟨alimentary canal : tubo digestivo⟩ **2** : canal *m* ⟨Panama Canal : Canal de Panamá⟩

canapé [ˈkænəpi, -ˌpeɪ] *n* : canapé *m*

canary [kəˈnɛri] *n, pl* **-naries** : canario *m*

cancel [ˈkænt̮səl] *vt* **-celed** *or* **-celled; -celing** *or* **-celling** : cancelar

cancellation [ˌkænt̮səˈleɪʃən] *n* : cancelación *f*

cancer [ˈkænt̮sər] *n* : cáncer *m*

Cancer *n* : Cáncer *mf*

cancerous [ˈkænt̮sərəs] *adj* : canceroso

candelabrum [ˌkændəˈlabrəm, -ˈlæ-] *or* **candelabra** [-brə] *n, pl* **-bra** *or* **-bras** : candelabro *m*

candid [ˈkændɪd] *adj* **1** FRANK : franco, sincero, abierto **2** : natural, espontáneo (en la fotografía)

candidacy [ˈkændədəsi] *n, pl* **-cies** : candidatura *f*

candidate [ˈkændəˌdeɪt, -dət] *n* : candidato *m*, -ta *f*

candidly [ˈkændɪdli] *adv* : con franqueza

candied [ˈkændid] *adj* : confitado

candle [ˈkændəl] *n* : vela *f*, candela *f*, cirio *m* (ceremonial)

candlestick [ˈkændəlˌstɪk] *n* : candelero *m*

candor [ˈkændər] *n* : franqueza *f*

candy [ˈkændi] *n, pl* **-dies** : dulce *m*, caramelo *m*

cane¹ [ˈkeɪn] *vt* **caned; caning 1** : tapizar (muebles) con mimbre **2** FLOG : azotar con una vara

cane² *n* **1** : bastón *m* (para andar), vara *f* (para castigar) **2** REED : caña *f*, mimbre *m* (para muebles)

canine¹ [ˈkeɪˌnaɪn] *adj* : canino

canine² *n* **1** DOG : canino *m*; perro *m*, -rra *f* **2** *or* **canine tooth** : colmillo *m*, diente *m* canino

canister [ˈkænəstər] *n* : lata *f*, bote *m*

canker [ˈkæŋkər] *n* : úlcera *f* bucal

cannery [ˈkænəri] *n, pl* **-ries** : fábrica *f* de conservas

cannibal [ˈkænəbəl] *n* : caníbal *mf*; antropófago *m*, -ga *f*

cannibalism [ˈkænəbəˌlɪzəm] *n* : canibalismo *m*, antropofagia *f*

cannibalize [ˈkænəbəˌlaɪz] *vt* **-ized; -izing** : canibalizar

cannily [ˈkænəli] *adv* : astutamente, sagazmente

cannon [ˈkænən] *n, pl* **-nons** *or* **-non** : cañón *m*

cannot (can not) [ˈkænˌɑt, kəˈnɑt] → **can¹**

canny [ˈkæni] *adj* **-nier; -est** SHREWD : astuto, sagaz

canoe¹ [kəˈnuː] *vt* **-noed; -noeing** : ir en canoa

canoe² *n* : canoa *f*, piragua *f*

canon [ˈkænən] *n* **1** : canon *m* ⟨canon law : derecho canónico⟩ **2** WORKS : canon *m* ⟨the canon of American literature : el canon de la literatura americana⟩ **3** : canónigo *m* (de una catedral) **4** STANDARD : canon *m*, norma *f*

canonical [kəˈnɑnɪkəl] *adj* : canónico

canonize [ˈkænəˌnaɪz] *vt* **-ized; -izing** : canonizar

canopy [ˈkænəpi] *n, pl* **-pies** : dosel *m*, toldo *m*

cant¹ [ˈkænt] *vt* TILT : ladear, inclinar — *vi* **1** SLANT : ladearse, inclinarse, escorar (dícese de un barco) **2** : hablar insinceramente

cant² *n* **1** SLANT : plano *m* inclinado **2** JARGON : jerga *f* **3** : palabras *fpl* insinceras

can't [ˈkænt, ˈkant] (*contraction* of **can not**) → **can¹**

cantaloupe [ˈkæntəlˌoːp] *n* : melón *m*, cantalupo *m*

cantankerous [kænˈtæŋkərəs] *adj* : irritable, irascible — **cantankerously** *adv*

cantankerousness [kænˈtæŋkərəsnəs] *n* : irritabilidad *f*, irascibilidad *f*

cantata [kənˈtɑtə] *n* : cantata *f*

canteen [kænˈtiːn] *n* **1** FLASK : cantimplora *f* **2** CAFETERIA : cantina *f*, comedor *m* **3** : club *m* para actividades sociales y recreativas

canter¹ [ˈkæntər] *vi* : ir a medio galope

canter² *n* : medio galope *m*

cantilever [ˈkæntəˌliːvər, -ˌlɛvər] *n* **1** : viga *f* voladiza **2 cantilever bridge** : puente *m* voladizo

canto [ˈkænˌtoː] *n, pl* **-tos** : canto *m*

canton [ˈkæntən, -ˌtɑn] *n* : cantón *m*

Cantonese [ˌkæntənˈiːz, -ˈiːs] *n* **1** : cantonés *m*, -nesa *f* **2** : cantonés *m* (idioma) — **Cantonese** *adj*

cantor [ˈkæntər] *n* : solista *mf*

canvas [ˈkænvəs] *n* **1** : lona *f* **2** SAILS : velas *fpl* (de un barco) **3** : lienzo *m*, tela *f* (de pintar) **4** PAINTING : pintura *f*, óleo *m*, cuadro *m*

canvass¹ [ˈkænvəs] *vt* **1** SOLICIT : solicitar votos o pedidos de, hacer campaña entre **2** SOUND OUT : sondear (opiniones, etc.)

canvass² *n* SURVEY : sondeo *m*, encuesta *f*

canyon [ˈkænjən] *n* : cañón *m*

cap¹ [ˈkæp] *vt* **capped; capping 1** COVER : tapar (un recipiente), enfundar (un diente), cubrir (una montaña) **2** CLIMAX : coronar, ser el punto culminante de ⟨to cap it all off : para colmo⟩ **3** LIMIT : limitar, poner un tope a

cap² *n* **1** : gorra *f*, gorro *m*, cachucha *f* *Mex* ⟨baseball cap : gorra de béisbol⟩

2 COVER, TOP : tapa *f*, tapón *m* (de botellas), corcholata *f Mex* 3 LIMIT : tope *m*, límite *m*

capability [ˌkeɪpəˈbɪləti] *n*, *pl* **-ties** : capacidad *f*, habilidad *f*, competencia *f*

capable [ˈkeɪpəbəl] *adj* : competente, capaz, hábil — **capably** [-bli] *adv*

capacious [kəˈpeɪʃəs] *adj* : amplio, espacioso, de gran capacidad

capacity[1] [kəˈpæsəti] *adj* : completo, total ⟨a capacity crowd : un lleno completo⟩

capacity[2] *n*, *pl* **-ties** 1 ROOM, SPACE : capacidad *f*, cabida *f*, espacio *m* 2 CAPABILITY : habilidad *f*, competencia *f* 3 FUNCTION, ROLE : calidad *f*, función *f* ⟨in his capacity as ambassador : en su calidad de embajador⟩

cape [ˈkeɪp] *n* 1 : capa *f* 2 : cabo *m* ⟨Cape Horn : el Cabo de Hornos⟩

caper[1] [ˈkeɪpər] *vi* : dar saltos, correr y brincar

caper[2] *n* 1 : alcaparra *f* ⟨olives and capers : aceitunas y alcaparras⟩ 2 ANTIC, PRANK : broma *f*, travesura *f* 3 LEAP : brinco *m*, salto *m*

Cape Verdean [ˈkeɪpˈvərdiən] *n* : caboverdiano *m*, -na *f* — **Cape Verdean** *adj*

capful [ˈkæpˌfʊl] *n* : tapa *f*, tapita *f*

capillary[1] [ˈkæpəˌlɛri] *adj* : capilar

capillary[2] *n*, *pl* **-ries** : capilar *m*

capital[1] [ˈkæpətəl] *adj* 1 : capital ⟨capital punishment : pena capital⟩ 2 : mayúsculo (dícese de las letras) 3 : de capital ⟨capital assets : activo fijo⟩ ⟨capital gain : ganancia de capital, plusvalía⟩ 4 EXCELLENT : excelente, estupendo

capital[2] *n* 1 *or* **capital city** : capital *f*, sede *f* del gobierno 2 WEALTH : capital *m* 3 *or* **capital letter** : mayúscula *f* 4 : capitel *m* (de una columna)

capitalism [ˈkæpətəlˌɪzəm] *n* : capitalismo *m*

capitalist[1] [ˈkæpətəlɪst] *or* **capitalistic** [ˌkæpətəlˈɪstɪk] *adj* : capitalista

capitalist[2] *n* : capitalista *mf*

capitalization [ˌkæpətələˈzeɪʃən] *n* : capitalización *f*

capitalize [ˈkæpətəlˌaɪz] *v* **-ized; -izing** *vt* 1 FINANCE : capitalizar, financiar 2 : escribir con mayúscula — *vi* to **capitalize on** : sacar partido de, aprovechar

capitol [ˈkæpətəl] *n* : capitolio *m*

capitulate [kəˈpɪtʃəˌleɪt] *vi* **-lated; -lating** : capitular

capitulation [kəˌpɪtʃəˈleɪʃən] *n* : capitulación *f*

capon [ˈkeɪˌpɑn, -pən] *n* : capón *m*

cappuccino [ˌkɑpəˈtʃiːnoː] *n* : capuchino *m* (café)

caprice [kəˈpriːs] *n* : capricho *m*, antojo *m*

capricious [kəˈprɪʃəs, -ˈpriː-] *adj* : caprichoso — **capriciously** *adv*

Capricorn [ˈkæprɪˌkɔrn] *n* : Capricornio *mf*

capsize [ˈkæpˌsaɪz, kæpˈsaɪz] *v* **-sized; -sizing** *vi* : volcar, volcarse — *vt* : hacer volcar

capstan [ˈkæpstən, -ˌstæn] *n* : cabrestante *m*

capsule [ˈkæpsəl, -ˌsuːl] *n* 1 : cápsula *f* (en la farmacéutica y botánica) 2 **space capsule** : cápsula *f* espacial

captain[1] [ˈkæptən] *vt* : capitanear

captain[2] *n* 1 : capitán *m*, -tana *f* 2 HEADWAITER : jefe *m*, -fa *f* de comedor 3 **captain of industry** : magnate *mf*

caption[1] [ˈkæpʃən] *vt* : ponerle una leyenda a (una ilustración), titular (un artículo), subtitular (una película)

caption[2] *n* 1 HEADING : titular *m*, encabezamiento *m* 2 : leyenda *f* (al pie de una ilustración) 3 SUBTITLE : subtítulo *m*

captivate [ˈkæptəˌveɪt] *vt* **-vated; -vating** CHARM : cautivar, hechizar, encantar

captivating [ˈkæptəˌveɪtɪŋ] *adj* : cautivador, hechicero, encantador

captive[1] [ˈkæptɪv] *adj* : cautivo

captive[2] *n* : cautivo *m*, -va *f*

captivity [kæpˈtɪvəti] *n* : cautiverio *m*

captor [ˈkæptər] *n* : captor *m*, -tora *f*

capture[1] [ˈkæpʃər] *vt* **-tured; -turing** 1 SEIZE : capturar, apresar 2 CATCH : captar ⟨to capture one's interest : captar el interés de uno⟩

capture[2] *n* : captura *f*, apresamiento *m*

car [ˈkɑr] *n* 1 AUTOMOBILE : automóvil *m*, coche *m*, carro *m* 2 : vagón *m*, coche *m* (de un tren) 3 : cabina *f* (de un ascensor)

carafe [kəˈræf, -ˈrɑf] *n* : garrafa *f*

caramel [ˈkɑrməl; ˈkærəməl, -ˌmɛl] *n* 1 : caramelo *m*, azúcar *f* quemada 2 *or* **caramel candy** : caramelo *m*, dulce *m* de leche

carat [ˈkærət] *n* : quilate *m*

caravan [ˈkærəˌvæn] *n* : caravana *f*

caraway [ˈkærəˌweɪ] *n* : alcaravea *f*

carbine [ˈkɑrˌbaɪn, -ˌbiːn] *n* : carabina *f*

carbohydrate [ˌkɑrboˈhaɪˌdreɪt, -drət] *n* : carbohidrato *m*, hidrato *m* de carbono

carbon [ˈkɑrbən] *n* 1 : carbono *m* 2 → **carbon paper** 3 → **carbon copy**

carbonated [ˈkɑrbəˌneɪtəd] *adj* : carbonatado (dícese del agua), gaseoso (dícese de las bebidas)

carbon copy *n* 1 : copia *f* al carbón 2 DUPLICATE : duplicado *m*, copia *f* exacta

carbon paper *n* : papel *m* carbón

carbuncle [ˈkɑrˌbʌŋkəl] *n* : carbunco *m*

carburetor [ˈkɑrbəˌreɪtər, -bjə-] *n* : carburador *m*

carcass [ˈkɑrkəs] *n* : cuerpo *m* (de un animal muerto)

carcinogen [kɑrˈsɪnədʒən, ˈkɑrsənəˌdʒɛn] *n* : carcinógeno *m*, cancerígeno *m*

carcinogenic [ˌkɑrsənoˈdʒɛnɪk] *adj* : carcinogénico

carcinoma [ˌkɑrsəˈnoːmə] *n* : carcinoma *m*

343

card · carry

card¹ [ˈkɑrd] *vt* : cardar (fibras)
card² *n* **1** : carta *f*, naipe *m* ⟨to play cards : jugar a las cartas⟩ ⟨a deck of cards : una baraja⟩ **2** : tarjeta *f* ⟨birthday card : tarjeta de cumpleaños⟩ ⟨business card : tarjeta (de visita)⟩
cardboard [ˈkɑrdˌbord] *n* : cartón *m*, cartulina *f*
cardiac [ˈkɑrdiˌæk] *adj* : cardíaco, cardiaco
cardigan [ˈkɑrdɪgən] *n* : cárdigan *m*, chaqueta *f* de punto
cardinal¹ [ˈkɑrdənəl] *adj* FUNDAMENTAL : cardinal, fundamental
cardinal² *n* : cardenal *m*
cardinal number *n* : número *m* cardinal
cardinal point *n* : punto *m* cardinal
cardiologist [ˌkɑrdiˈɑləʤɪst] *n* : cardiólogo *m*, -ga *f*
cardiology [ˌkɑrdiˈɑləʤi] *n* : cardiología *f*
cardiovascular [ˌkɑrdioˈvæskjələr] *adj* : cardiovascular
care¹ [ˈkær] *v* **cared; caring** *vi* **1** : importarle a uno ⟨they don't care : no les importa⟩ **2** : preocuparse, inquietarse ⟨she cares about the poor : se preocupa por los pobres⟩ **3 to care for** TEND : cuidar (de), atender, encargarse de **4 to care for** CHERISH : querer, sentir cariño por **5 to care for** LIKE : gustarle (algo a uno) ⟨I don't care for your attitude : tu actitud no me agrada⟩ — *vt* WISH : desear, querer ⟨if you care to go : si deseas ir⟩
care² *n* **1** ANXIETY : inquietud *f*, preocupación *f* **2** CAREFULNESS : cuidado *m*, atención *f* ⟨handle with care : manejar con cuidado⟩ **3** CHARGE : cargo *m*, cuidado *m* **4 to take care of** : cuidar (de), atender, encargarse de
careen [kəˈriːn] *vi* **1** SWAY : oscilar, balancearse **2** CAREER : ir a toda velocidad
career¹ [kəˈrɪr] *vi* : ir a toda velocidad
career² *n* VOCATION : vocación *f*, profesión *f*, carrera *f*
carefree [ˈkærˌfriː, ˈkær-] *adj* : despreocupado
careful [ˈkærfəl] *adj* **1** CAUTIOUS : cuidadoso, cauteloso **2** PAINSTAKING : cuidadoso, esmerado, meticuloso
carefully [ˈkærfəli] *adv* : con cuidado, cuidadosamente
carefulness [ˈkærfəlnəs] *n* **1** CAUTION : cuidado *m*, cautela *f* **2** METICULOUSNESS : esmero *m*, meticulosidad *f*
caregiver [ˈkærˌgɪvər] *n* : persona *f* que cuida a niños o enfermos
careless [ˈkærləs] *adj* : descuidado, negligente — **carelessly** *adv*
carelessness [ˈkærləsnəs] *n* : descuido *m*, negligencia *f*
caress¹ [kəˈrɛs] *vt* : acariciar
caress² *n* : caricia *f*
caret [ˈkærət] *n* : signo *m* de intercalación
caretaker [ˈkɛrˌteɪkər] *n* : conserje *mf*; velador *m*, -dora *f*

cargo [ˈkɑrˌgoː] *n, pl* **-goes** *or* **-gos** : cargamento *m*, carga *f*
Caribbean [ˌkærəˈbiːən, kəˈrɪbiən] *adj* : caribeño ⟨the Caribbean Sea : el mar Caribe⟩
caribou [ˈkærəˌbuː] *n, pl* **-bou** *or* **-bous** : caribú *m*
caricature¹ [ˈkærɪkəˌʧʊr] *vt* **-tured; -turing** : caricaturizar
caricature² *n* : caricatura *f*
caricaturist [ˈkærɪkəˌʧʊrɪst] *n* : caricaturista *mf*
caries [ˈkærˌiːz] *ns & pl* : caries *f*
carillon [ˈkærəˌlɑn] *n* : carillón *m*
carmine [ˈkɑrmən, -ˌmaɪn] *n* : carmín *m*
carnage [ˈkɑrnɪʤ] *n* : matanza *f*, carnicería *f*
carnal [ˈkɑrnəl] *adj* : carnal
carnation [kɑrˈneɪʃən] *n* : clavel *m*
carnival [ˈkɑrnəvəl] *n* : carnaval *m*, feria *f*
carnivore [ˈkɑrnəˌvor] *n* : carnívoro *m*
carnivorous [kɑrˈnɪvərəs] *adj* : carnívoro
carol¹ [ˈkærəl] *vi* **-oled** *or* **-olled; -oling** *or* **-olling** : cantar villancicos
carol² *n* : villancico *m*
caroler *or* **caroller** [ˈkærələr] *n* : persona *f* que canta villancicos
carom¹ [ˈkærəm] *vi* **1** REBOUND : rebotar ⟨the bullet caromed off the wall : la bala rebotó contra el muro⟩ **2** : hacer carambola (en billar)
carom² *n* : carambola *f*
carouse [kəˈraʊz] *vt* **-roused; -rousing** : irse de parranda, irse de juerga
carousel *or* **carrousel** [ˌkærəˈsɛl, ˈkærə-] *n* : carrusel *m*, tiovivo *m*
carouser [kəˈraʊzər] *n* : juerguista *mf*
carp¹ [ˈkɑrp] *vi* **1** COMPLAIN : quejarse **2 to carp at** : criticar
carp² *n, pl* **carp** *or* **carps** : carpa *f*
carpel [ˈkɑrpəl] *n* : carpelo *m*
carpenter [ˈkɑrpəntər] *n* : carpintero *m*, -ra *f*
carpentry [ˈkɑrpəntri] *n* : carpintería *f*
carpet¹ [ˈkɑrpət] *vt* : alfombrar
carpet² *n* : alfombra *f*
carpeting [ˈkɑrpətɪŋ] *n* : alfombrado *m*
carport [ˈkɑrˌport] *n* : cochera *f*, garaje *m* abierto
carriage [ˈkærɪʤ] *n* **1** TRANSPORT : transporte *m* **2** POSTURE : porte *m*, postura *f* **3 horse–drawn carriage** : carruaje *m*, coche *m* **4 baby carriage** : cochecito *m*
carrier [ˈkæriər] *n* **1** : transportista *mf*, empresa *f* de transportes **2** : portador *m*, -dora *f* (de una enfermedad) **3 air-craft carrier** : portaaviones *m*
carrier pigeon : paloma *f* mensajera
carrion [ˈkæriən] *n* : carroña *f*
carrot [ˈkærət] *n* : zanahoria *f*
carry [ˈkæri] *v* **-ried; -rying** *vt* **1** TRANSPORT : llevar, cargar, transportar (cargamento), conducir (electricidad), portar (un virus) ⟨to carry a bag : cargar una bolsa⟩ ⟨to carry money : llevar dinero encima, traer dinero consi-

go〉 **2** BEAR : soportar, aguantar, resistir (peso) **3** STOCK : vender, tener en abasto **4** ENTAIL : llevar, implicar, acarrear **5** WIN : ganar (una elección o competición), aprobar (una moción) **6 to carry oneself** : portarse, comportarse 〈he carried himself honorably : se comportó dignamente〉 — *vi* : oírse, proyectarse 〈her voice carries well : su voz se puede oír desde lejos〉

carryall [ˈkæri₁ɔl] *n* : bolsa *f* de viaje

carry away *vt* **to get carried away** : exaltarse, entusiasmarse

carry on *vt* CONDUCT : realizar, ejercer, mantener 〈to carry on research : realizar investigaciones〉 〈to carry on a correspondence : mantener una correspondencia〉 — *vi* **1** : portarse de manera escandalosa o inapropiada 〈it's embarrassing how he carries on : su manera de comportarse da vergüenza〉 **2** CONTINUE : seguir, continuar

carry out *vt* **1** PERFORM : llevar a cabo, realizar **2** FULFILL : cumplir

cart¹ [ˈkɑrt] *vt* : acarrear, llevar

cart² *n* : carreta *f*, carro *m*

cartel [kɑrˈtɛl] *n* : cártel *m*

cartilage [ˈkɑrt̬əlɪdʒ] *n* : cartílago *m*

cartilaginous [₁kɑrt̬əlˈædʒənəs] *adj* : cartilaginoso

cartographer [kɑrˈtɑgrəfər] *n* : cartógrafo *m*, -fa *f*

cartography [kɑrˈtɑgrəfi] *n* : cartografía *f*

carton [ˈkɑrt̬ən] *n* : caja *f* de cartón

cartoon [kɑrˈtuːn] *n* **1** : chiste *m* (gráfico), caricatura *f* 〈a political cartoon : un chiste político〉 **2** COMIC STRIP : tira *f* cómica, historieta *f* **3** *or* **animated cartoon** : dibujo *m* animado

cartoonist [kɑrˈtuːnɪst] *n* : caricaturista *mf*, dibujante *mf* (de chistes)

cartridge [ˈkɑrtrɪdʒ] *n* : cartucho *m*

carve [ˈkɑrv] *vt* **carved; carving 1** : tallar (madera), esculpir (piedra), grabar 〈he carved his name in the bark : grabó su nombre en la corteza〉 **2** SLICE : cortar, trinchar (carne)

cascade¹ [kæsˈkeɪd] *vi* **-caded; -cading** : caer en cascada

cascade² *n* : cascada *f*, salto *m* de agua

case¹ [ˈkeɪs] *vt* **cased; casing 1** BOX, PACK : embalar, encajonar **2** INSPECT : observar, inspeccionar (antes de cometer un delito)

case² *n* **1** : caso *m* 〈an unusual case : un caso insólito〉 〈ablative case : caso ablativo〉 〈a case of the flu : un caso de gripe〉 **2** BOX : caja *f* **3** CONTAINER : funda *f*, estuche *m* **4 in any case** : de todos modos, en cualquier caso **5 in case** : como precaución 〈just in case : por si acaso〉 **6 in case of** : en caso de

casement [ˈkeɪsmənt] *n* : ventana *f* con bisagras

cash¹ [ˈkæʃ] *vt* : convertir en efectivo, cobrar, cambiar (un cheque)

cash² *n* : efectivo *m*, dinero *m* en efectivo

cashew [ˈkæ₁ʃuː, kəˈʃuː] *n* : anacardo *m*

cashier¹ [kæˈʃɪr] *vt* : destituir, despedir

cashier² *n* : cajero *m*, -ra *f*

cashmere [ˈkæʒ₁mɪr, ˈkæʃ-] *n* : cachemir *m*

casino [kəˈsiː₁noː] *n*, *pl* **-nos** : casino *m*

cask [ˈkæsk] *n* : tonel *m*, barrica *f*, barril *m*

casket [ˈkæskət] *n* COFFIN : ataúd *m*, féretro *m*

cassava [kəˈsɑvə] *n* : mandioca *f*, yuca *f*

casserole [ˈkæsə₁roːl] *n* **1** : cazuela *f* **2** : guiso *m*, guisado *m* 〈tuna casserole : guiso de atún〉

cassette [kəˈsɛt, kæ-] *n* : cassette *mf*

cassock [ˈkæsək] *n* : sotana *f*

cast¹ [ˈkæst] *vt* **cast; casting 1** THROW : tirar, echar, arrojar 〈the die is cast : la suerte está echada〉 **2** : depositar (un voto) **3** : asignar (papeles en una obra de teatro) **4** MOLD : moldear, fundir, vaciar **5 to cast off** ABANDON : desamparar, abandonar

cast² *n* **1** THROW : lance *m*, lanzamiento *m* **2** APPEARANCE : aspecto *m*, forma *f* **3** : elenco *m*, reparto *m* (de una obra de teatro) **4 plaster cast** : molde *m* de yeso, escayola *f*

castanets [₁kæstəˈnɛts] *npl* : castañuelas *fpl*

castaway¹ [ˈkæstə₁weɪ] *adj* : náufrago

castaway² *n* : náufrago *m*, -ga *f*

caste [ˈkæst] *n* : casta *f*

caster [ˈkæstər] *n* : ruedita *f* (de un mueble)

castigate [ˈkæstə₁geɪt] *vt* **-gated; -gating** : castigar severamente, censurar, reprobar

Castilian [kæˈstɪljən] *n* **1** : castellano *m*, -na *f* **2** : castellano *m* (idioma) — **Castilian** *adj*

cast iron *n* : hierro *m* fundido

castle [ˈkæsəl] *n* **1** : castillo *m* **2** : torre *f* (en ajedrez)

cast–off [ˈkæst₁ɔf] *adj* : desechado

castoff [ˈkæst₁ɔf] *n* : desecho *m*

castrate [ˈkæs₁treɪt] *vt* **-trated; -trating** : castrar

castration [kæˈstreɪʃən] *n* : castración *f*

casual [ˈkæʒuəl] *adj* **1** FORTUITOUS : casual, fortuito **2** INDIFFERENT : indiferente, despreocupado **3** INFORMAL : informal — **casually** [ˈkæʒuəli, ˈkæʒəli] *adv*

casualness [ˈkæʒuəlnəs] *n* **1** FORTUITOUSNESS : casualidad *f* **2** INDIFFERENCE : indiferencia *f*, despreocupación *f* **3** INFORMALITY : informalidad *f*

casualty [ˈkæʒuəlti, ˈkæʒəl-] *n*, *pl* **-ties 1** ACCIDENT : accidente *m* serio, desastre *m* **2** VICTIM : víctima *f*; baja *f*; herido *m*, -da *f*

cat [ˈkæt] *n* : gato *m*, -ta *f*

cataclysm [ˈkæt̬ə₁klɪzəm] *n* : cataclismo *m*

cataclysmal [ˌkæt̬ə'klɪzməl] *or* **cataclysmic** [ˌkæt̬ə'klɪzmɪk] *adj* : catastrófico

catacombs ['kæt̬əˌko:mz] *npl* : catacumbas *fpl*

Catalan ['kæt̬ələn, -ˌlæn] *n* **1** : catalán *m*, catalana *f* **2** : catalán *m* (idioma) — **Catalan** *adj*

catalog¹ *or* **catalogue** ['kæt̬əˌlɔg] *vt* -loged *or* -logued; -loging *or* -loguing : catalogar

catalog² *n* : catálogo *m*

catalyst ['kæt̬ələst] *n* : catalizador *m*

catalytic [ˌkæt̬əl'ɪt̬ɪk] *adj* : catalítico

catamaran [ˌkæt̬əmə'ræn, 'kæt̬əməˌræn] *n* : catamarán *m*

catapult¹ ['kæt̬əˌpʌlt, -ˌpʊlt] *vt* : catapultar

catapult² *n* : catapulta *f*

cataract ['kæt̬əˌrækt] *n* : catarata *f*

catarrh [kə'tɑr] *n* : catarro *m*

catastrophe [kə'tæstrəˌfi:] *n* : catástrofe *f*

catastrophic [ˌkæt̬ə'strɑfɪk] *adj* : catastrófico — **catastrophically** [-fɪkli] *adv*

catcall ['kætˌkɔl] *n* : rechifla *f*, abucheo *m*

catch¹ ['kætʃ, 'kɛtʃ] *v* **caught** ['kɔt]; **catching** *vt* **1** CAPTURE, TRAP : capturar, agarrar, atrapar, coger **2** : agarrar, pillar *fam*, tomar de sorpresa ⟨they caught him red-handed : lo pillaron con las manos en la masa⟩ **3** GRASP : agarrar, captar **4** ENTANGLE : enganchar, enredar **5** : tomar (un tren, etc.) **6** : contagiarse de ⟨to catch a cold : contagiarse de un resfriado, resfriarse⟩ — *vi* **1** GRASP : agarrar **2** HOOK : engancharse **3** IGNITE : prender, agarrar

catch² *n* **1** CATCHING : captura *f*, atrapada *f*, parada *f* (de una pelota) **2** : redada *f* (de pescado), presa *f* (de caza) ⟨he's a good catch : es un buen partido⟩ **3** LATCH : pestillo *m*, pasador *m* **4** DIFFICULTY, TRICK : problema *m*, trampa *f*, truco *m*

catcher ['kætʃər, 'kɛ-] *n* : catcher *mf*; receptor *m*, -tora *f* (en béisbol)

catching ['kætʃɪŋ, 'kɛ-] *adj* : contagioso

catchup ['kætʃəp, 'kɛ-] → ketchup

catchword ['kætʃˌwərd, 'kɛtʃ-] *n* : eslogan *m*, lema *m*

catchy ['kætʃi, 'kɛ-] *adj* **catchier; -est** : pegajoso ⟨a catchy song : una canción pegajosa⟩

catechism ['kæt̬əˌkɪzəm] *n* : catecismo *m*

categorical [ˌkæt̬ə'gɔrɪkəl] *adj* : categórico, absoluto, rotundo — **categorically** [-kli] *adv*

categorize ['kæt̬ɪgəˌraɪz] *vt* -rized; -rizing : clasificar, catalogar

category ['kæt̬əˌgori] *n, pl* -ries : categoría *f*, género *m*, clase *f*

cater ['keɪt̬ər] *vi* **1** : proveer alimentos (para fiestas, bodas, etc.) **2 to cater to** : atender a ⟨to cater to all tastes : atender a todos los gustos⟩

catercorner¹ ['kæt̬iˌkɔrnər, 'kæt̬ə-, 'kɪt̬i-] *or* **cater–cornered** [-ˌkɔrnərd] *adv* : diagonalmente, en diagonal

catercorner² *or* **cater–cornered** *adj* : diagonal

caterer ['keɪt̬ərər] *n* : proveedor *m*, -dora *f* de comida

caterpillar ['kæt̬ərˌpɪlər] *n* : oruga *f*

catfish ['kætˌfɪʃ] *n* : bagre *m*

catgut ['kætˌgʌt] *n* : cuerda *f* de tripa

catharsis [kə'θɑrsɪs] *n, pl* **catharses** [-ˌsi:z] : catarsis *f*

cathartic¹ [kə'θɑrt̬ɪk] *adj* : catártico

cathartic² *n* : purgante *m*

cathedral [kə'θi:drəl] *n* : catedral *f*

catheter ['kæθət̬ər] *n* : catéter *m*, sonda *f*

cathode ['kæˌθo:d] *n* : cátodo *m*

catholic ['kæθəlɪk] *adj* **1** BROAD, UNIVERSAL : liberal, universal **2 Catholic** : católico

Catholic *n* : católico *m*, -ca *f*

Catholicism [kə'θɑləˌsɪzəm] *n* : catolicismo *m*

catlike ['kætˌlaɪk] *adj* : gatuno, felino

catnap¹ ['kætˌnæp] *vi* -napped; -napping : tomarse una siestecita

catnap² *n* : siesta *f* breve, siestecita *f*

catnip ['kætˌnɪp] *n* : nébeda *f*

catsup ['kɛtʃəp, 'kætsəp] → ketchup

cattail ['kætˌteɪl] *n* : espadaña *f*, anea *f*

cattiness ['kæt̬inəs] *n* : malicia *f*

cattle ['kæt̬əl] *npl* : ganado *m*, reses *fpl*

cattleman ['kæt̬əlmən, -ˌmæn] *n, pl* -men [-mən, -ˌmɛn] : ganadero *m*

catty ['kæt̬i] *adj* -tier; -est : malicioso, malintencionado

catwalk ['kætˌwɔk] *n* : pasarela *f*

Caucasian¹ [kɔ'keɪʒən] *adj* : caucásico

Caucasian² *n* : caucásico *m*, -ca *f*

caucus ['kɔkəs] *n* : junta *f* de políticos

caught → catch

cauldron ['kɔldrən] *n* : caldera *f*

cauliflower ['kɑlɪˌflaʊər, 'kɔ-] *n* : coliflor *f*

caulk¹ ['kɔk] *vt* : calafatear (un barco), enmasillar (una grieta)

caulk² *n* : masilla *f*

causal ['kɔzəl] *adj* : causal

causality [kɔ'zæləti] *n* : causalidad *f*

cause¹ ['kɔz] *vt* **caused; causing** : causar, provocar, ocasionar

cause² *n* **1** ORIGIN : causa *f*, origen *m* **2** REASON : causa *f*, razón *f*, motivo *m* **3** LAWSUIT : litigio *m*, pleito *m* **4** MOVEMENT : causa *f*, movimiento *m*

causeless ['kɔzləs] *adj* : sin causa

causeway ['kɔzˌweɪ] *n* : camino *m* elevado

caustic ['kɔstɪk] *adj* **1** CORROSIVE : cáustico, corrosivo **2** BITING : mordaz, sarcástico

cauterize ['kɔt̬əˌraɪz] *vt* -ized; -izing : cauterizar

caution¹ ['kɔʃən] *vt* : advertir

caution² *n* **1** WARNING : advertencia *f*, aviso *m* **2** CARE, PRUDENCE : precaución *f*, cuidado *m*, cautela *f*

cautionary ['kɔʃə,nɛri] *adv* : admonitorio ⟨cautionary tale : cuento moral⟩
cautious ['kɔʃəs] *adj* : cauteloso, cuidadoso, precavido
cautiously ['kɔʃəsli] *adv* : cautelosamente, con precaución
cautiousness ['kɔʃəsnəs] *n* : cautela *f*, precaución *f*
cavalcade [,kævəl'keɪd, 'kævəl,-] *n* 1 : cabalgata *f* 2 SERIES : serie *f*
cavalier[1] [,kævə'lɪr] *adj* : altivo, desdeñoso — **cavalierly** *adv*
cavalier[2] *n* : caballero *m*
cavalry ['kævəlri] *n, pl* **-ries** : caballería *f*
cave[1] ['keɪv] *vi* **caved; caving** *or* **to cave in** : derrumbarse
cave[2] *n* : cueva *f*
cavern ['kævərn] *n* : caverna *f*
cavernous ['kævərnəs] *adj* : cavernoso — **cavernously** *adv*
caviar *or* **caviare** ['kævi,ɑr, 'kɑ-] *n* : caviar *m*
cavity ['kævəti] *n, pl* **-ties** 1 HOLE : cavidad *f*, hueco *m* 2 CARIES : caries *f*
cavort [kə'vɔrt] *vi* : brincar, hacer cabriolas
caw[1] ['kɔ] *vi* : graznar
caw[2] *n* : graznido *m*
cayenne pepper [,kaɪ'ɛn, ,keɪ-] *n* : pimienta *f* cayena, pimentón *m*
CD [,si:'di:] *n* : CD *m*, disco *m* compacto
CD–ROM [,si:,di:'rɑm] *n* : CD-ROM *m*
cease ['si:s] *v* **ceased; ceasing** *vt* : dejar de ⟨they ceased bickering : dejaron de discutir⟩ — *vi* : cesar, pasarse
ceaseless ['si:sləs] *adj* : incesante, continuo
cedar ['si:dər] *n* : cedro *m*
cede ['si:d] *vt* **ceded; ceding** : ceder, conceder
ceiling ['si:lɪŋ] *n* 1 : techo *m*, cielo *m* raso 2 LIMIT : límite *m*, tope *m*
celebrant ['sɛləbrənt] *n* : celebrante *mf*, oficiante *mf*
celebrate ['sɛlə,breɪt] *v* **-brated; -brating** *vt* 1 : celebrar, oficiar ⟨to celebrate Mass : celebrar la misa⟩ 2 : celebrar, festejar ⟨we're celebrating our anniversary : estamos celebrando nuestro aniversario⟩ 3 EXTOL : alabar, ensalzar, exaltar — *vi* : estar de fiesta, divertirse
celebrated ['sɛlə,breɪtəd] *adj* : célebre, famoso, renombrado
celebration [,sɛlə'breɪʃən] *n* : celebración *f*, festejos *mpl*
celebrity [sə'lɛbrəti] *n, pl* **-ties** 1 RENOWN : fama *f*, renombre *m*, celebridad *f* 2 PERSONALITY : celebridad *f*, personaje *m*
celery ['sɛləri] *n, pl* **-eries** : apio *m*
celestial [sə'lɛstʃəl, -'lstiəl] *adj* 1 : celeste 2 HEAVENLY : celestial, paradisiaco
celibacy ['sɛləbəsi] *n* : celibato *m*
celibate[1] ['sɛləbət] *adj* : célibe
celibate[2] *n* : célibe *mf*

cell ['sɛl] *n* 1 : célula *f* (de un organismo) 2 : celda *f* (en una cárcel, etc.) 3 : elemento *m* (de una pila)
cellar ['sɛlər] *n* 1 BASEMENT : sótano *m* 2 : bodega *f* (de vinos)
cellist ['tʃɛlɪst] *n* : violonchelista *mf*
cello ['tʃɛ,lo:] *n, pl* **-los** : violonchelo *m*
cellophane ['sɛlə,feɪn] *n* : celofán *m*
cell phone *n* : teléfono *m* celular
cellular ['sɛljələr] *adj* : celular
celluloid ['sɛljə,lɔɪd] *n* : celuloide *m*
cellulose ['sɛljə,lo:s] *n* : celulosa *f*
Celsius ['sɛlsiəs] *adj* : centígrado ⟨100 degrees Celsius : 100 grados centígrados⟩
Celt ['kɛlt, 'sɛlt] *n* : celta *mf*
Celtic[1] ['kɛltɪk, 'sɛl-] *adj* : celta
Celtic[2] *n* : celta *m*
cement[1] [sɪ'mɛnt] *vi* : unir o cubrir algo con cemento, cementar
cement[2] *n* 1 : cemento *m* 2 GLUE : pegamento *m*
cemetery ['sɛmə,tɛri] *n, pl* **-teries** : cementerio *m*, panteón *m*
censer ['sɛntsər] *n* : incensario *m*
censor[1] ['sɛntsər] *vt* : censurar
censor[2] *n* : censor *m*, -sora *f*
censorious [sɛn'soriəs] *adj* : de censura, crítico
censorship ['sɛntsər,ʃɪp] *n* : censura *f*
censure[1] ['sɛntʃər] *vt* **-sured; -suring** : censurar, criticar, reprobar — **censurable** [-tʃərəbəl] *adj*
censure[2] *n* : censura *f*, reproche *m* oficial
census ['sɛntsəs] *n* : censo *m*
cent ['sɛnt] *n* : centavo *m*
centaur ['sɛn,tɔr] *n* : centauro *m*
centennial[1] [sɛn'tɛniəl] *adj* : del centenario
centennial[2] *n* : centenario *m*
center[1] ['sɛntər] *vt* 1 : centrar 2 CONCENTRATE : concentrar, fijar, enfocar — *vi* : centrarse, enfocarse
center[2] *n* 1 : centro *m* ⟨center of gravity : centro de gravedad⟩ 2 : centro *mf* (en futbol americano), pívot *mf* (en basquetbol)
centerpiece ['sɛntər,pi:s] *n* : centro *m* de mesa
centigrade ['sɛntə,greɪd, 'sɑn-] *adj* : centígrado
centigram ['sɛntə,græm, 'sɑn-] *n* : centigramo *m*
centimeter ['sɛntə,mi:tər, 'sɑn-] *n* : centímetro *m*
centipede ['sɛntə,pi:d] *n* : ciempiés *m*
central ['sɛntrəl] *adj* 1 : céntrico, central ⟨in a central location : en un lugar céntrico⟩ 2 MAIN, PRINCIPAL : central, fundamental, principal
Central American[1] *adj* : centroamericano
Central American[2] *n* : centroamericano *m*, -na *f*
centralization [,sɛntrələ'zeɪʃən] *n* : centralización *f*
centralize ['sɛntrə,laɪz] *vt* **-ized; -izing** : centralizar

centrally ['sɛntrəli] *adv* 1 **centrally heated** : con calefacción central 2 **centrally located** : céntrico, en un lugar céntrico

centre ['sɛntər] → **center**

centrifugal [sɛn'trɪfjəgəl, -'trɪfɪ-] *adj* : centrífugo

centrifugal force *n* : fuerza *f* centrífuga

century ['sɛnt∫əri] *n, pl* -ries : siglo *m*

ceramic[1] [sə'ræmɪk] *adj* : de cerámica

ceramic[2] *n* 1 : objeto *m* de cerámica, cerámica *f* 2 ceramics *npl* : cerámica *f*

cereal[1] ['sɪriəl] *adj* : cereal

cereal[2] *n* : cereal *m*

cerebellum [ˌsɛrə'bɛləm] *n, pl* -bellums *or* -bella [-'bɛlə] : cerebelo *m*

cerebral [sə'ri:brəl, 'sɛrə-] *adj* : cerebral

cerebral palsy *n* : parálisis *f* cerebral

cerebrum [sə'ri:brəm, 'sɛrə-] *n, pl* -brums *or* -bra [-brə] : cerebro *m*

ceremonial[1] [ˌsɛrə'mo:niəl] *adj* : ceremonial

ceremonial[2] *n* : ceremonial *m*

ceremonious [ˌsɛrə'mo:niəs] *adj* 1 FORMAL : ceremonioso, formal 2 CEREMONIAL : ceremonial

ceremony ['sɛrəˌmo:ni] *n, pl* -nies : ceremonia *f*

cerise [sə'ri:s] *n* : rojo *m* cereza

certain[1] ['sərtən] *adj* 1 DEFINITE : cierto, determinado ⟨a certain percentage : un porcentaje determinado⟩ 2 TRUE : cierto, con certeza ⟨I don't know for certain : no sé exactamente⟩ 3 : cierto, alguno ⟨it has a certain charm : tiene cierta gracia⟩ 4 INEVITABLE : seguro, inevitable 5 ASSURED : seguro, asegurado ⟨she's certain to do well : seguro que le irá bien⟩

certain[2] *pron* : ciertos *pl*, algunos *pl* ⟨certain of my friends : algunos de mis amigos⟩

certainly ['sərtənli] *adv* 1 DEFINITELY : ciertamente, seguramente 2 OF COURSE : por supuesto

certainty ['sərtənti] *n, pl* -ties : certeza *f*, certidumbre *f*, seguridad *f*

certifiable [ˌsərtə'faɪəbəl] *adj* : certificable

certificate [sər'tɪfɪkət] *n* : certificado *m*, acta *f* ⟨birth certificate : acta de nacimiento⟩

certification [ˌsərtəfə'keɪʃən] *n* : certificación *f*

certify ['sərtəˌfaɪ] *vt* -fied; -fying 1 VERIFY : certificar, verificar, confirmar 2 ENDORSE : endosar, aprobar oficialmente

certitude ['sərtəˌtu:d, -ˌtju:d] *n* : certeza *f*, certidumbre *f*

cervical ['sərvɪkəl] *adj* 1 : cervical (dícese del cuello) 2 : del cuello del útero

cervix ['sərvɪks] *n, pl* -vices [-və-ˌsi:z] *or* -vixes 1 NECK : cerviz *f* 2 *or* uterine cervix : cuello *m* del útero

cesarean[1] [sɪ'zæriən] *adj* : cesáreo

cesarean[2] *n* : cesárea *f*

cesium ['si:ziəm] *n* : cesio *m*

cessation [sɛ'seɪʃən] *n* : cesación *f*, cese *m*

cesspool ['sɛsˌpu:l] *n* : pozo *m* séptico

Chadian ['t∫ædiən] *n* : chadiano *m*, -na *f* — **Chadian** *adj*

chafe ['t∫eɪf] *v* **chafed; chafing** *vi* : enojarse, irritarse — *vt* : rozar

chaff ['t∫æf] *n* 1 : barcia *f*, granzas *fpl* 2 **to separate the wheat from the chaff** : separar el grano de la paja

chafing dish ['t∫eɪfɪŋˌdɪ∫] *n* : escalfador *m*

chagrin[1] [∫ə'grɪn] *vt* : desilusionar, avergonzar

chagrin[2] *n* : desilusión *f*, disgusto *m*

chain[1] ['t∫eɪn] *vt* : encadenar

chain[2] *n* 1 : cadena *f* ⟨steel chain : cadena de acero⟩ ⟨restaurant chain : cadena de restaurantes⟩ 2 SERIES : serie *f* ⟨chain of events : serie de eventos⟩ 3 **chains** *npl* FETTERS : grillos *mpl*

chair[1] ['t∫er] *vt* : presidir, moderar

chair[2] *n* 1 : silla *f* 2 CHAIRMANSHIP : presidencia *f* 3 → **chairman, chairwoman**

chairman ['t∫ermən] *n, pl* -men [-mən, -ˌmɛn] : presidente *m*

chairmanship ['t∫ermənˌ∫ɪp] *n* : presidencia *f*

chairwoman ['t∫erˌwʊmən] *n, pl* -women [-ˌwɪmən] : presidenta *f*

chaise longue ['∫eɪz'lɔŋ] *n, pl* **chaise longues** [-lɔŋ, -'lɔŋz] : chaise longue *f*

chalet [∫æ'leɪ] *n* : chalet *m*, chalé *m*

chalice ['t∫ælɪs] *n* : cáliz *m*

chalk[1] ['t∫ɔk] *vt* : escribir con tiza

chalk[2] *n* 1 LIMESTONE : creta *f*, caliza *f* 2 : tiza *f*, gis *m Mex* (para escribir)

chalkboard ['t∫ɔkˌbɔrd] → **blackboard**

chalk up *vt* 1 ASCRIBE : atribuir, adscribir 2 SCORE : apuntarse, anotarse (una victoria, etc.)

chalky ['t∫ɔki] *adj* **chalkier; -est** 1 : calcáreo 2 PALE : pálido 3 POWDERY : polvoriento

challenge[1] ['t∫ælɪndʒ] *vt* -lenged; -lenging 1 DISPUTE : disputar, cuestionar, poner en duda 2 DARE : desafiar, retar 3 STIMULATE : estimular, incentivar

challenge[2] *n* : reto *m*, desafío *m*

challenger ['t∫ælɪndʒər] *n* : retador *m*, -dora *f*; contendiente *mf*

chamber ['t∫eɪmbər] *n* 1 ROOM : cámara *f*, sala *f* ⟨the senate chamber : la cámara del senado⟩ 2 : recámara *f* (de un arma de fuego), cámara *f* (de combustión) 3 : cámara *f* ⟨chamber of commerce : cámara de comercio⟩ 4 **chambers** *npl or* **judge's chambers** : despacho *m* del juez

chambermaid ['t∫eɪmbərˌmeɪd] *n* : camarera *f*

chamber music *n* : música *f* de cámara

chameleon [kə'mi:ljən, -liən] *n* : camaleón *m*

chamois ['ʃæmi] *n, pl* **chamois** [-mi, -miz] : gamuza *f*

champ[1] ['tʃæmp, 'tʃamp] *vi* 1 : masticar ruidosamente 2 **to champ at the bit** : impacientarse, comerle a uno la impaciencia

champ[2] ['tʃæmp] *n* : campeón *m*, -peona *f*

champagne [ʃæm'peɪn] *n* : champaña *m*, champán *m*

champion[1] ['tʃæmpiən] *vt* : defender, luchar por (una causa)

champion[2] *n* 1 ADVOCATE, DEFENDER : paladín *m*; campeón *m*, -peona *f*; defensor *m*, -sora *f* 2 WINNER : campeón *m*, -peona *f* ⟨world champion : campeón mundial⟩

championship ['tʃæmpiən,ʃɪp] *n* : campeonato *m*

chance[1] ['tʃænts] *v* **chanced; chancing** *vi* 1 HAPPEN : ocurrir por casualidad 2 **to chance upon** : encontrar por casualidad — *vt* RISK : arriesgar

chance[2] *adj* : fortuito, casual ⟨a chance encounter : un encuentro casual⟩

chance[3] *n* 1 FATE, LUCK : azar *m*, suerte *f*, fortuna *f* 2 OPPORTUNITY : oportunidad *f*, ocasión *f* 3 PROBABILITY : probabilidad *f*, posibilidad *f* 4 RISK : riesgo *m* 5 : boleto *m* (de una rifa o lotería) 6 **by chance** : por casualidad

chancellor ['tʃæntsələr] *n* 1 : canciller *m* 2 : rector *m*, -tora *f* (de una universidad)

chancre ['ʃæŋkər] *n* : chancro *m*

chancy ['tʃæntsi] *adj* **chancier; -est** : riesgoso, arriesgado

chandelier [,ʃændə'lɪr] *n* : araña *f* de luces

change[1] ['tʃeɪndʒ] *v* **changed; changing** *vt* 1 ALTER : cambiar, alterar, modificar 2 EXCHANGE : cambiar de, intercambiar ⟨to change places : cambiar de sitio⟩ — *vi* 1 VARY : cambiar, variar, transformarse ⟨you haven't changed : no has cambiado⟩ 2 **to change clothes** : cambiarse (de ropa)

change[2] *n* 1 ALTERATION : cambio *m* 2 : cambio *m*, vuelto *m* ⟨two dollars change : dos dólares de vuelto⟩ 3 COINS : cambio *m*, monedas *fpl*

changeable ['tʃeɪndʒəbəl] *adj* : cambiante, variable

changeless ['tʃeɪndʒləs] *adj* : invariable, constante

changer ['tʃeɪndʒər] *n* 1 : cambiador *m* ⟨record changer : cambiador de discos⟩ 2 *or* **money changer** : cambista *mf* (de dinero)

channel[1] ['tʃænəl] *vt* **-neled** *or* **-nelled; -neling** *or* **-nelling** : encauzar, canalizar

channel[2] *n* 1 RIVERBED : cauce *m* 2 STRAIT : canal *m*, estrecho *m* ⟨English Channel : Canal de la Mancha⟩ 3 COURSE, MEANS : vía *f*, conducto *m* ⟨the usual channels : las vías normales⟩ 4 : canal *m* (de televisión)

chant[1] ['tʃænt] *v* : salmodiar, cantar

chant[2] *n* 1 : salmodia *f* 2 **Gregorian chant** : canto *m* gregoriano

Chanukah ['xɑnəkə, 'hɑ-] → **Hanukkah**

chaos ['keɪˌɑs] *n* : caos *m*

chaotic [keɪ'ɑtɪk] *adj* : caótico — **chaotically** [-tɪkli] *adv*

chap[1] ['tʃæp] *vi* **chapped; chapping** : partirse, agrietarse

chap[2] *n* FELLOW : tipo *m*, hombre *m*

chapel ['tʃæpəl] *n* : capilla *f*

chaperon[1] *or* **chaperone** ['ʃæpə,roːn] *vt* **-oned; -oning** : ir de chaperón, acompañar

chaperon[2] *or* **chaperone** *n* : chaperón *m*, -rona *f*; acompañante *mf*

chaplain ['tʃæplɪn] *n* : capellán *m*

chapter ['tʃæptər] *n* 1 : capítulo *m* (de un libro) 2 BRANCH : sección *f*, división *f* (de una organización)

char ['tʃar] *vt* **charred; charring** 1 BURN : carbonizar 2 SCORCH : chamuscar

character ['kærɪktər] *n* 1 LETTER, SYMBOL : carácter *m* ⟨Chinese characters : caracteres chinos⟩ 2 DISPOSITION : carácter *m*, personalidad *f* ⟨of good character : de buena reputación⟩ 3 : tipo *m*, personaje *m* peculiar ⟨he's quite a character! : ¡él es algo serio!⟩ 4 : personaje *m* (ficticio)

characteristic[1] [,kærɪktə'rɪstɪk] *adj* : característico, típico — **characteristically** [-tɪkli] *adv*

characteristic[2] *n* : característica *f*

characterization [,kærɪktərə'zeɪʃən] *n* : caracterización *f*

characterize ['kærɪktə,raɪz] *vt* **-ized; -izing** : caracterizar

charades [ʃə'reɪdz] *ns & pl* : charada *f*

charcoal ['tʃar,koːl] *n* : carbón *m*

chard ['tʃard] → **Swiss chard**

charge[1] ['tʃardʒ] *v* **charged; charging** *vt* 1 : cargar ⟨to charge the batteries : cargar las pilas⟩ 2 ENTRUST : encomendar, encargar 3 COMMAND : ordenar, mandar 4 ACCUSE : acusar ⟨charged with robbery : acusado de robo⟩ 5 : cargar a una cuenta, comprar a crédito — *vi* 1 : cargar (contra el enemigo) ⟨charge! : ¡a la carga!⟩ 2 : cobrar ⟨they charge too much : cobran demasiado⟩

charge[2] *n* 1 : carga *f* (eléctrica) 2 BURDEN : carga *f*, peso *m* 3 RESPONSIBILITY : cargo *m*, responsabilidad *f* ⟨to take charge of : hacerse cargo de⟩ 4 ACCUSATION : cargo *m*, acusación *f* 5 COST : costo *m*, cargo *m*, precio *m* 6 ATTACK : carga *f*, ataque *m*

charge card → **credit card**

chargeable ['tʃardʒəbəl] *adj* 1 : acusable, perseguible (dícese de un delito) 2 ~ **to** : a cargo de (una cuenta)

charger ['tʃardʒər] *n* : corcel *m*, caballo *m* (de guerra)

chariot ['tʃæriət] *n* : carro *m* (de guerra)

charisma [kə'rɪzmə] *n* : carisma *m*

charismatic [,kærəz'mætɪk] *adj* : carismático

349

charitable · check

charitable ['tʃærətəbəl] *adj* **1** GENER-
OUS : caritativo ⟨a charitable organization : una organización benéfica⟩ **2**
KIND, UNDERSTANDING : generoso,
benévolo, comprensivo — **charitably**
[-bli] *adv*

charitableness ['tʃærətəbəlnəs] *n* : caridad *f*

charity ['tʃærəti] *n, pl* **-ties 1** GENEROS-
ITY : caridad *f* **2** ALMS : caridad *f*,
limosna *f* **3** : organización *f* benéfica,
obra *f* de beneficencia

charlatan ['ʃarlətən] *n* : charlatán *m*,
-tana *f*; farsante *mf*

charley horse ['tʃarli,hɔrs] *n* : calambre
m

charm[1] ['tʃarm] *vt* : encantar, cautivar,
fascinar

charm[2] *n* **1** AMULET : amuleto *m*, talismán *m* **2** ATTRACTION : encanto *m*,
atractivo *m* ⟨it has a certain charm
: tiene cierto atractivo⟩ **3** : dije *m*, colgante *m* ⟨charm bracelet : pulsera de
dijes⟩

charmer ['tʃarmər] *n* : persona *f* encantadora

charming ['tʃarmɪŋ] *adj* : encantador,
fascinante

chart[1] ['tʃart] *vt* **1** : trazar un mapa de,
hacer un gráfico de **2** PLAN : trazar,
planear ⟨to chart a course : trazar un
derrotero⟩

chart[2] *n* **1** MAP : carta *f*, mapa *m* **2** DI-
AGRAM : gráfico *m*, cuadro *m*, tabla *f*

charter[1] ['tʃartər] *vt* **1** : establecer los estatutos de (una organización) **2** RENT
: alquilar, fletar

charter[2] *n* **1** STATUTES : estatutos *mpl*
2 CONSTITUTION : carta *f*, constitución
f

chartreuse [ʃar'truːz, -'truːs] *n* : color *m*
verde-amarillo intenso

chary ['tʃæri] *adj* **charier; -est 1** WARY
: cauteloso, precavido **2** SPARING : parco

chase[1] ['tʃeɪs] *vt* **chased; chasing 1**
PURSUE : perseguir, ir a la caza de **2**
DRIVE : ahuyentar, echar ⟨he chased
the dog from the garden : ahuyentó al
perro del jardín⟩ **3** : grabar (metales)

chase[2] *n* **1** PURSUIT : persecución *f*,
caza *f* **2 the chase** HUNTING : caza *f*

chaser ['tʃeɪsər] *n* **1** PURSUER : perseguidor *m*, -dora *f* **2** : bebida *f* que se
toma después de un trago de licor

chasm ['kæzəm] *n* : abismo *m*, sima *f*

chassis ['tʃæsi, 'ʃæsi] *n, pl* **chassis** [-siz]
: chasis *m*, armazón *m*

chaste ['tʃeɪst] *adj* **chaster; -est 1** : casto **2** MODEST : modesto, puro **3** AUS-
TERE : austero, sobrio

chastely ['tʃeɪstli] *adv* : castamente

chasten ['tʃeɪsən] *vt* : castigar, sancionar

chasteness ['tʃeɪstnəs] *n* **1** MODESTY
: modestia *f*, castidad *f* **2** AUSTERITY
: sobriedad *f*, austeridad *f*

chastise ['tʃæs,taɪz, tʃæs'-] *vt* **-tised;
-tising 1** REPRIMAND : reprender, corregir, reprobar **2** PUNISH : castigar

chastisement ['tʃæs,taɪzmənt, tʃæs'taɪz-
, 'tʃæstəz-] *n* : castigo *m*, corrección *f*

chastity ['tʃæstəti] *n* : castidad *f*, decencia *f*, modestia *f*

chat[1] ['tʃæt] *vi* **chatted; chatting** : charlar, platicar

chat[2] *n* : charla *f*, plática *f*

château [ʃæ'toː] *n, pl* **-teaus** [-'toːz] *or*
-teaux [-'toː, -'toːz] : mansión *f*
campestre

chattel ['tʃætəl] *n* : bienes *fpl* muebles,
enseres *mpl*

chatter[1] ['tʃætər] *vi* **1** : castañetear
(dícese de los dientes) **2** GAB : parlotear
fam, cotorrear *fam*

chatter[2] *n* **1** CHATTERING : castañeteo
m (de dientes) **2** GABBING : parloteo
m fam, cotorreo *m fam*, cháchara *f fam*

chatterbox ['tʃætər,baks] *n* : parlanchín
m, -china *f*; charlatán *m*, -tana *f*;
hablador *m*, -dora *f*

chatty ['tʃæti] *adj* **chattier; chattiest 1**
TALKATIVE : parlanchín, charlatán **2**
CONVERSATIONAL : familiar, conversador ⟨a chatty letter : una carta llena
de noticias⟩

chauffeur[1] ['ʃoːfər, ʃo'fər] *vi* : trabajar
de chofer privado — *vt* : hacer de
chofer para

chauffeur[2] *n* : chofer *m* privado

chauvinism ['ʃoːvə,nɪzəm] *n* : chauvinismo *m*, patriotería *f*

chauvinist ['ʃoːvənɪst] *n* : chauvinista
mf; patriotero *m*, -ra *f*

chauvinistic [,ʃoːvə'nɪstɪk] *adj* : chauvinista, patriotero

cheap[1] ['tʃiːp] *adv* : barato ⟨to sell cheap
: vender barato⟩

cheap[2] *adj* **1** INEXPENSIVE : barato,
económico **2** SHODDY : barato, mal hecho **3** STINGY : tacaño, agarrado *fam*,
codo *Mex*

cheapen ['tʃiːpən] *vt* : degradar, rebajar

cheaply ['tʃiːpli] *adv* : barato, a precio
bajo

cheapness ['tʃiːpnəs] *n* **1** : baratura *f*,
precio *m* bajo **2** STINGINESS : tacañería
f

cheapskate ['tʃiːp,skeɪt] *n* : tacaño *m*,
-ña *f*; codo *m*, -da *f Mex*

cheat[1] ['tʃiːt] *vt* : defraudar, estafar, engañar — *vi* : hacer trampa

cheat[2] *n* **1** CHEATING : engaño *m*,
fraude *m*, trampa *f* **2** → **cheater**

cheater ['tʃiːtər] *n* : estafador *m*, -dora *f*;
tramposo *m*, -sa *f*

check[1] ['tʃɛk] *vt* **1** HALT : frenar, parar,
detener **2** RESTRAIN : refrenar, contener, reprimir **3** VERIFY : verificar,
comprobar **4** INSPECT : revisar,
chequear, inspeccionar **5** MARK : marcar, señalar **6** : chequear, facturar
(maletas, equipaje) **7** CHECKER : marcar con cuadros **8 to check in** : registrarse en un hotel **9 to check out** : irse
de un hotel

check² *n* **1** HALT : detención *f* súbita, parada *f* **2** RESTRAINT : control *m*, freno *m* **3** INSPECTION : inspección *f*, verificación *f*, chequeo *m* **4** : cheque *m* ⟨to pay by check : pagar con cheque⟩ **5** VOUCHER : resguardo *m*, comprobante *m* **6** BILL : cuenta *f* (en un restaurante) **7** SQUARE : cuadro *m* **8** MARK : marca *f* **9** : jaque *m* (en ajedrez)

checkbook ['tʃɛk,bʊk] *n* : chequera *f*

checker¹ ['tʃɛkər] *vt* : marcar con cuadros

checker² *n* **1** : pieza *f* (en el juego de damas) **2** : verificador *m*, -dora *f* **3** CASHIER : cajero *m*, -ra *f*

checkerboard ['tʃɛkər,bord] *n* : tablero *m* de damas

checkers ['tʃɛkərz] *n* : damas *fpl*

checkmate¹ ['tʃɛk,meɪt] *vt* **-mated; -mating 1** : dar jaque mate a (en ajedrez) **2** THWART : frustrar, arruinar

checkmate² *n* : jaque mate *m*

checkout ['tʃɛk,aʊt] *n or* **checkout counter** : caja *f*

checkpoint ['tʃɛk,pɔɪnt] *n* : puesto *m* de control

checkup ['tʃɛk,ʌp] *n* : examen *m* médico, chequeo *m*

cheddar ['tʃɛdər] *n* : queso *m* Cheddar

cheek ['tʃi:k] *n* **1** : mejilla *f*, cachete *m* **2** IMPUDENCE : insolencia *f*, descaro *m*

cheekbone ['tʃi:k,bo:n] *n* : pómulo *m*

cheeky ['tʃi:ki] *adj* **cheekier; -est** : descarado, insolente, atrevido

cheep¹ ['tʃi:p] *vi* : piar

cheep² *n* : pío *m*

cheer¹ ['tʃɪr] *vt* **1** ENCOURAGE : alentar, animar **2** GLADDEN : alegrar, levantar el ánimo a **3** ACCLAIM : aclamar, vitorear, echar porras a

cheer² *n* **1** CHEERFULNESS : alegría *f*, buen humor *m*, jovialidad *f* **2** APPLAUSE : aclamación *f*, ovación *f*, aplausos *mpl* ⟨three cheers for the chief! : ¡viva el jefe!⟩ **3 cheers!** : ¡salud!

cheerful ['tʃɪrfəl] *adj* : alegre, de buen humor

cheerfully ['tʃɪrfəli] *adv* : alegremente, jovialmente

cheerfulness ['tʃɪrfəlnəs] *n* : buen humor *m*, alegría *f*

cheerily ['tʃɪrəli] *adv* : alegremente

cheeriness ['tʃɪrinəs] *n* : buen humor *m*, alegría *f*

cheerleader ['tʃɪr,li:dər] *n* : porrista *mf*

cheerless ['tʃɪrləs] *adj* BLEAK : triste, sombrío

cheerlessly ['tʃɪrləsli] *adv* : desanimadamente

cheery ['tʃɪri] *adj* **cheerier; -est** : alegre, de buen humor

cheese ['tʃi:z] *n* : queso *m*

cheesecloth ['tʃi:z,klɔθ] *n* : estopilla *f*

cheesy ['tʃi:zi] *adj* **cheesier; -est 1** : a queso **2** : que contiene queso **3** CHEAP : barato, de mala calidad

cheetah ['tʃi:tʃə] *n* : guepardo *m*

chef ['ʃɛf] *n* : chef *m*

chemical¹ ['kɛmɪkəl] *adj* : químico — **chemically** [-mɪkli] *adv*

chemical² *n* : sustancia *f* química

chemise [ʃə'mi:z] *n* **1** : camiseta *f*, prenda *f* interior de una pieza **2** : vestido *m* holgado

chemist ['kɛmɪst] *n* : químico *m*, -ca *f*

chemistry ['kɛmɪstri] *n, pl* **-tries** : química *f*

chemotherapy [,ki:mo'θɛrəpi, ,kɛmo-] *n, pl* **-pies** : quimioterapia *f*

chenille [ʃə'ni:l] *n* : felpilla *f*

cherish ['tʃɛrɪʃ] *vt* **1** VALUE : apreciar, valorar **2** HARBOR : abrigar, albergar

cherry ['tʃɛri] *n, pl* **-ries 1** : cereza *f* (fruta) **2** : cerezo *m* (árbol)

cherub ['tʃɛrəb] *n* **1** *pl* **-ubim** ['tʃɛrə,bɪm, 'tʃɛrjə-]** ANGEL : ángel *m*, querubín *m* **2** *pl* **-ubs** : niño *m* regordete, niña *f* regordeta

cherubic [tʃə'ru:bɪk] *adj* : querúbico, angelical

chess ['tʃɛs] *n* : ajedrez *m*

chessboard ['tʃɛs,bord] *n* : tablero *m* de ajedrez

chessman ['tʃɛsmən, -,mæn] *n, pl* **-men** [-mən, -,mɛn] : pieza *f* de ajedrez

chest ['tʃɛst] *n* **1** : cofre *m*, baúl *m* **2** : pecho *m* ⟨chest pains : dolores de pecho⟩

chestnut ['tʃɛst,nʌt] *n* **1** : castaña *f* (fruto) **2** : castaño *m* (árbol)

chest of drawers *n* : cómoda *f*

chevron ['ʃɛvrən] *n* : galón *m* (de un oficial militar)

chew¹ ['tʃu:] *vt* : masticar, mascar

chew² *n* : algo que se masca (como tabaco)

chewable ['tʃu:əbəl] *adj* : masticable

chewing gum *n* : goma *f* de mascar, chicle *m*

chewy ['tʃu:i] *adj* **chewier; -est 1** : fibroso (dícese de las carnes o los vegetales) **2** : pegajoso, chicloso (dícese de los dulces)

chic¹ ['ʃi:k] *adj* : chic, elegante, de moda

chic² *n* : chic *m*, elegancia *f*

Chicano [tʃɪ'kɑno] *n* : chicano *m*, -na *f* — **Chicano** *adj*

chick ['tʃɪk] *n* : pollito *m*, -ta *f*; polluelo *m*, -la *f*

chicken ['tʃɪkən] *n* **1** FOWL : pollo *m* **2** COWARD : cobarde *mf*

chickenhearted ['tʃɪkən,hɑrtəd] *n* : miedoso, cobarde

chicken pox *n* : varicela *f*

chickpea ['tʃɪk,pi:] *n* : garbanzo *m*

chicle ['tʃɪkəl] *n* : chicle *m* (resina)

chicory ['tʃɪkəri] *n, pl* **-ries 1** : endibia *f* (para ensaladas) **2** : achicoria *f* (aditivo de café)

chide ['tʃaɪd] *vt* **chid** ['tʃɪd] *or* **chided; chid** *or* **chidden** ['tʃɪdən] *or* **chided; chiding** ['tʃaɪdɪŋ] : regañar, reprender

chief¹ ['tʃi:f] *adj* : principal, capital ⟨chief negotiator : negociador en jefe⟩ — **chiefly** *adv*

chief² *n* : jefe *m*, -fa *f*

chieftain [ˈtʃiːftən] *n* : jefe *m*, -fa *f* (de una tribu)

chiffon [ʃɪˈfɑn, ˈʃɪˌ-] *n* : chifón *m*

chigger [ˈtʃɪɡər] *n* : nigua *f*

chignon [ˈʃiːnˌjɑn, -ˌjɔn] *n* : moño *m*, chongo *m Mex*

chilblain [ˈtʃɪlˌbleɪn] *n* : sabañón *m*

child [ˈtʃaɪld] *n, pl* **children** [ˈtʃɪldrən] **1** BABY, YOUNGSTER : niño *m*, -ña *f*; criatura *f* **2** OFFSPRING : hijo *m*, -ja *f*; progenie *f*

childbearing[1] [ˈtʃaɪlbɛrɪŋ] *adj* : relativo al parto ⟨of childbearing age : en edad fértil⟩

childbearing[2] → **childbirth**

childbirth [ˈtʃaɪldˌbərθ] *n* : parto *m*

childhood [ˈtʃaɪldˌhʊd] *n* : infancia *f*, niñez *f*

childish [ˈtʃaɪldɪʃ] *adj* : infantil, inmaduro — **childishly** *adv*

childishness [ˈtʃaɪldɪʃnəs] *n* : infantilismo *m*, inmadurez *f*

childless [ˈtʃaɪldləs] *adj* : sin hijos

childlike [ˈtʃaɪldˌlaɪk] *adj* : infantil, inocente ⟨a childlike imagination : una imaginación infantil⟩

childproof [ˈtʃaɪldˌpruːf] *adj* : a prueba de niños

Chilean [ˈtʃɪliən, tʃɪˈleɪən] *n* : chileno *m*, -na *f* — **Chilean** *adj*

chili *or* **chile** *or* **chilli** [ˈtʃɪli] *n, pl* **chilies** *or* **chiles** *or* **chillies 1** *or* **chili pepper** : chile *m*, ají *m* **2** : chile *m* con carne

chill[1] [ˈtʃɪl] *v* : enfriar

chill[2] *adj* : frío, gélido ⟨a chill wind : un viento frío⟩

chill[3] *n* **1** CHILLINESS : fresco *m*, frío *m* **2** SHIVER : escalofrío *m* **3** DAMPER : enfriamiento *m*, frío *m* ⟨to cast a chill over : enfriar⟩

chilliness [ˈtʃɪlinəs] *n* : frío *m*, fresco *m*

chilly [ˈtʃɪli] *adj* **chillier; -est** : frío ⟨it's chilly tonight : hace frío esta noche⟩

chime[1] [ˈtʃaɪm] *v* **chimed; chiming** *vt* : hacer sonar (una campana) — *vi* : sonar una campana, dar campanadas

chime[2] *n* **1** BELLS : juego *m* de campanitas sintonizadas, carillón *m* **2** PEAL : tañido *m*, campanada *f*

chime in *vi* : meterse en una conversación

chimera *or* **chimaera** [kaɪˈmɪrə, kə-] *n* : quimera *f*

chimney [ˈtʃɪmni] *n, pl* **-neys** : chimenea *f*

chimney sweep *n* : deshollinador *m*, -dora *f*

chimp [ˈtʃɪmp, ˈʃɪmp] → **chimpanzee**

chimpanzee [ˌtʃɪmˌpænˈziː, ˌʃɪm-; tʃɪmˈpænzi, ʃɪm-] *n* : chimpancé *m*

chin [ˈtʃɪn] *n* : barbilla *f*, mentón *m*, barba *f*

china [ˈtʃaɪnə] *n* **1** PORCELAIN : porcelana *f*, loza *f* **2** CROCKERY, TABLEWARE : loza *f*, vajilla *f*

chinchilla [tʃɪnˈtʃɪlə] *n* : chinchilla *f*

Chinese [ˈtʃaɪˈniːz, -ˈniːs] *n* **1** : chino *m*, -na *f* **2** : chino *m* (idioma) — **Chinese** *adj*

chink [ˈtʃɪŋk] *n* : grieta *f*, abertura *f*

chintz [ˈtʃɪnts] *n* : chintz *m*, chinz *m*

chip[1] [ˈtʃɪp] *v* **chipped; chipping** *vt* : desportillar, desconchar, astillar (madera) — *vi* : desportillarse, desconcharse, descascararse (dícese de la pintura, etc.)

chip[2] *n* **1** : astilla *f* (de madera o vidrio), lasca *f* (de piedra) ⟨he's a chip off the old block : de tal palo, tal astilla⟩ **2** : bocado *m* pequeño (en rodajas o rebanadas) ⟨tortilla chips : totopos, tortillitas tostadas⟩ **3** : ficha *f* (de póker, etc.) **4** NICK : desportilladura *f*, mella *f* **5** : chip *m* ⟨memory chip : chip de memoria⟩

chip in *v* CONTRIBUTE : contribuir

chipmunk [ˈtʃɪpˌmʌŋk] *n* : ardilla *f* listada

chipper [ˈtʃɪpər] *adj* : alegre y vivaz

chiropodist [kəˈrɑpədɪst, ʃə-] *n* : podólogo *m*, -ga *f*

chiropody [kəˈrɑpədi, ʃə-] *n* : podología *f*

chiropractic [ˈkaɪrəˌpræktɪk] *n* : quiropráctica *f*

chiropractor [ˈkaɪrəˌpræktər] *n* : quiropráctico *m*, -ca *f*

chirp[1] [ˈtʃərp] *vi* : gorjear (dícese de los pájaros), chirriar (dícese de los grillos)

chirp[2] *n* : gorjeo *m* (de un pájaro), chirrido *m* (de un grillo)

chisel[1] [ˈtʃɪzəl] *vt* **-eled** *or* **-elled; -eling** *or* **-elling 1** : cincelar, tallar, labrar **2** CHEAT : estafar, defraudar

chisel[2] *n* : cincel *m* (para piedras y metales), escoplo *m* (para madera), formón *m*

chiseler [ˈtʃɪzələr] *n* SWINDLER : estafador *m*, -dora *f*; fraude *mf*

chit [ˈtʃɪt] *n* : resguardo *m*, recibo *m*

chitchat [ˈtʃɪtˌtʃæt] *n* : cotorreo *m*, charla *f*

chivalric [ʃəˈvælrɪk] → **chivalrous**

chivalrous [ˈʃɪvəlrəs] *adj* **1** KNIGHTLY : caballeresco, relativo a la caballería **2** GENTLEMANLY : caballeroso, honesto, cortés

chivalrousness [ˈʃɪvəlrəsnəs] *n* : caballerosidad *f*, cortesía *f*

chivalry [ˈʃɪvəlri] *n, pl* **-ries 1** KNIGHTHOOD : caballería *f* **2** CHIVALROUSNESS : caballerosidad *f*, nobleza *f*, cortesía *f*

chive [ˈtʃaɪv] *n* : cebollino *m*

chloride [ˈklorˌaɪd] *n* : cloruro *m*

chlorinate [ˈklorəˌneɪt] *vt* **-nated; -nating** : clorar

chlorination [ˌklorəˈneɪʃən] *n* : cloración *f*

chlorine [ˈklorˌiːn] *n* : cloro *m*

chloroform [ˈklorəˌfɔrm] *n* : cloroformo *m*

chlorophyll [ˈklorəˌfɪl] *n* : clorofila *f*

chock–full [ˈtʃɑkˈfʊl, ˈtʃʌk-] *adj* : colmado, repleto

chocolate [ˈtʃɑkələt, ˈtʃɔk-] *n* **1** : chocolate *m* **2** BONBON : bombón *m* **3** : color *m* chocolate, marrón *m*

choice¹ [ˈtʃɔɪs] *adj* **choicer; -est** : selecto, escogido, de primera calidad
choice² *n* **1** CHOOSING : elección *f*, selección *f* **2** OPTION : elección *f*, opción *f* ⟨I have no choice : no tengo alternativa⟩ **3** PREFERENCE : preferencia *f*, elección *f* **4** VARIETY : surtido *m*, selección *f* ⟨a wide choice : un gran surtido⟩
choir [ˈkwaɪr] *n* : coro *m*
choirboy [ˈkwaɪrˌbɔɪ] *n* : niño *m* de coro
choke¹ [ˈtʃoːk] *v* **choked; choking** *vt* **1** ASPHYXIATE, STRANGLE : sofocar, asfixiar, ahogar, estrangular **2** BLOCK : tapar, obstruir — *vi* **1** SUFFOCATE : asfixiarse, sofocarse, ahogarse, atragantarse (con comida) **2** CLOG : taparse, obstruirse
choke² *n* **1** CHOKING : estrangulación *f* **2** : choke *m* (de un motor)
choker [ˈtʃoːkər] *n* : gargantilla *f*
cholera [ˈkɑlərə] *n* : cólera *m*
cholesterol [kəˈlɛstəˌrɔl] *n* : colesterol *m*
choose [ˈtʃuːz] *v* **chose** [ˈtʃoːz]; **chosen** [ˈtʃoːzən]; **choosing** *vt* **1** SELECT : escoger, elegir ⟨choose only one : escoja sólo uno⟩ **2** DECIDE : decidir ⟨he chose to leave : decidió irse⟩ **3** PREFER : preferir ⟨which one do you choose? : ¿cuál prefiere?⟩ — *vi* : escoger ⟨much to choose from : mucho de donde escoger⟩
choosy *or* **choosey** [ˈtʃuːzi] *adj* **choosier; -est** : exigente, remilgado
chop¹ [ˈtʃɑp] *vt* **chopped; chopping 1** MINCE : picar, cortar, moler (carne) **2 to chop down** : cortar, talar (un árbol)
chop² *n* **1** CUT : hachazo *m* (con una hacha), tajo *m* (con una cuchilla) **2** BLOW : golpe *m* (penetrante) ⟨karate chop : golpe de karate⟩ **3** : chuleta *f* ⟨pork chops : chuletas de cerdo⟩
chopper [ˈtʃɑpər] → **helicopter**
choppy [ˈtʃɑpi] *adj* **choppier; -est 1** : agitado, picado (dícese del mar) **2** DISCONNECTED : incoherente, inconexo
chops [ˈtʃɑps] *npl* **1** : quijada *f*, mandíbula *f*, boca *f* (de una persona) **2 to lick one's chops** : relamerse
chopsticks [ˈtʃɑpˌstɪks] *npl* : palillos *mpl*
choral [ˈkorəl] *adj* : coral
chorale [kəˈræl, -ˈrɑl] *n* **1** : coral *f* (composición musical vocal) **2** CHOIR, CHORUS : coral *f*, coro *m*
chord [ˈkɔrd] *n* **1** : acorde *m* (en música) **2** : cuerda *f* (en anatomía o geometría)
chore [ˈtʃor] *n* **1** TASK : tarea *f* rutinaria **2** BOTHER, NUISANCE : lata *f fam*, fastidio *m* **3 chores** *npl* WORK : quehaceres *mpl*, faenas *fpl*
choreograph [ˈkoriəˌgræf] *vt* : coreografiar
choreographer [ˌkoriˈɑgrəfər] *n* : coreógrafo *m*, -fa *f*
choreographic [ˌkoriəˈgræfɪk] *adj* : coreográfico
choreography [ˌkoriˈɑgrəfi] *n, pl* **-phies** : coreografía *f*

chorister [ˈkorəstər] *n* : corista *mf*
chortle¹ [ˈtʃɔrtəl] *vi* **-tled; -tling** : reírse (con satisfacción o júbilo)
chortle² *n* : risa *f* (de satisfacción o júbilo)
chorus¹ [ˈkorəs] *vt* : corear
chorus² *n* **1** : coro *m* (grupo o composición musical) **2** REFRAIN : coro *m*, estribillo *m*
chose → **choose**
chosen [ˈtʃoːzən] *adj* : elegido, selecto
chow [ˈtʃaʊ] *n* **1** FOOD : comida *f* **2** : chow-chow *m* (perro)
chowder [ˈtʃaʊdər] *n* : sopa *f* de pescado
Christ [ˈkraɪst] *n* **1** : Cristo *m* **2 for Christ's sake** : ¡por Dios!
christen [ˈkrɪsən] *vt* **1** BAPTIZE : bautizar **2** NAME : bautizar con el nombre de
Christendom [ˈkrɪsəndəm] *n* : cristiandad *f*
christening [ˈkrɪsənɪŋ] *n* : bautismo *m*, bautizo *m*
Christian¹ [ˈkrɪstʃən] *adj* : cristiano
Christian² *n* : cristiano *m*, -na *f*
Christianity [ˌkrɪstʃiˈænəti, ˌkrɪsˈtʃæ-] *n* : cristianismo *m*
Christian name *n* : nombre *m* de pila
Christmas [ˈkrɪsməs] *n* : Navidad *f* ⟨Christmas season : las Navidades⟩
chromatic [kroˈmætɪk] *adj* : cromático ⟨chromatic scale : escala cromática⟩
chrome [ˈkroːm] *n* : cromo *m* (metal)
chromium [ˈkroːmiəm] *n* : cromo *m* (elemento)
chromosome [ˈkroːməˌsoːm, -ˌzoːm] *n* : cromosoma *m*
chronic [ˈkrɑnɪk] *adj* : crónico — **chronically** [-nɪkli] *adv*
chronicle¹ [ˈkrɑnɪkəl] *vt* **-cled; -cling** : escribir (una crónica o historia)
chronicle² *n* : crónica *f*, historia *f*
chronicler [ˈkrɑnɪklər] *n* : historiador *m*, -dora *f*; cronista *mf*
chronological [ˌkrɑnəlˈɑdʒɪkəl] *adj* : cronológico — **chronologically** [-kli] *adv*
chronology [krəˈnɑlədʒi] *n, pl* **-gies** : cronología *f*
chronometer [krəˈnɑmətər] *n* : cronómetro *m*
chrysalis [ˈkrɪsələs] *n, pl* **chrysalides** [krɪˈsæləˌdiːz] *or* **chrysalises** : crisálida *f*
chrysanthemum [krɪˈsæntθəməm] *n* : crisantemo *m*
chubbiness [ˈtʃʌbinəs] *n* : gordura *f*
chubby [ˈtʃʌbi] *adj* **-bier; -est** : gordito, regordete, rechoncho
chuck¹ [ˈtʃʌk] *vt* **1** TOSS : tirar, lanzar, aventar *Col, Mex* **2 to chuck under the chin** : hacer la mamola
chuck² *n* **1** PAT : mamola *f*, palmada *f* **2** TOSS : lanzamiento *m* **3** *or* **chuck steak** : corte *m* de carne de res
chuckle¹ [ˈtʃʌkəl] *vi* **-led; -ling** : reírse entre dientes
chuckle² *n* : risita *f*, risa *f* ahogada

chug¹ [ˈtʃʌg] *vi* **chugged; chugging** : resoplar, traquetear

chug² *n* : resoplido *m*, traqueteo *m*

chum¹ [ˈtʃʌm] *vi* **chummed; chumming** : ser camaradas, ser cuates *Mex fam*

chum² *n* : amigo *m*, -ga *f*; camarada *mf*; compinche *mf fam*

chummy [ˈtʃʌmi] *adj* **-mier; -est** : amistoso ⟨they're very chummy : son muy amigos⟩

chump [ˈtʃʌmp] *n* : tonto *m*, -ta *f*; idiota *mf*

chunk [ˈtʃʌŋk] *n* **1** PIECE : cacho *m*, pedazo *m*, trozo *m* **2** : cantidad *f* grande ⟨a chunk of money : mucho dinero⟩

chunky [ˈtʃʌŋki] *adj* **chunkier; -est 1** STOCKY : fornido, robusto **2** : que contiene pedazos

church [ˈtʃərtʃ] *n* **1** : iglesia *f* ⟨to go to church : ir a la iglesia⟩ **2** CHRISTIANS : iglesia *f*, conjunto *m* de fieles cristianos **3** DENOMINATION : confesión *f*, secta *f* **4** CONGREGATION : feligreses *mpl*, fieles *mpl*

churchgoer [ˈtʃərtʃˌgoːər] *n* : practicante *mf*

churchyard [ˈtʃərtʃˌjɑrd] *n* : cementerio *m* (junto a una iglesia)

churn¹ [ˈtʃərn] *vt* **1** : batir (crema), hacer (mantequilla) **2** : agitar con fuerza, revolver — *vi* : agitarse, arremolinarse

churn² *n* : mantequera *f*

chute [ˈʃuːt] *n* : conducto *m* inclinado, vertedero *m* (para basuras)

chutney [ˈtʃʌtni] *n, pl* **-neys** : chutney *m*

chutzpah [ˈhʊtspə, ˈxʊt-, -ˌspɑ] *n* : descaro *m*, frescura *f*, cara *f fam*

cicada [səˈkeɪdə, -ˈkɑ-] *n* : cigarra *f*, chicharra *f*

cider [ˈsaɪdər] *n* **1** : jugo *m* (de manzana, etc.) **2 hard cider** : sidra *f*

cigar [sɪˈgɑr] *n* : puro *m*, cigarro *m*

cigarette [ˌsɪgəˈret, ˈsɪgəˌret] *n* : cigarrillo *m*, cigarro *m*

cilantro [sɪˈlɑntroː, -ˈlæn-] *n* : cilantro *m*

cinch¹ [ˈsɪntʃ] *vt* **1** : cinchar (un caballo) **2** ASSURE : asegurar

cinch² *n* **1** : cincha *f* (para caballos) **2** : algo fácil o seguro ⟨it's a cinch : es bien fácil, es pan comido⟩

cinchona [sɪnˈkoːnə] *n* : quino *m*

cinder [ˈsɪndər] *n* **1** EMBER : brasa *f*, ascua *f* **2 cinders** *npl* ASHES : cenizas *fpl*

cinema [ˈsɪnəmə] *n* : cine *m*

cinematic [ˌsɪnəˈmætɪk] *adj* : cinematográfico

cinnamon [ˈsɪnəmən] *n* : canela *f*

cipher [ˈsaɪfər] *n* **1** ZERO : cero *m* **2** CODE : cifra *f*, clave *f*

circa [ˈsərkə] *prep* : alrededor de, hacia ⟨circa 1800 : hacia el año 1800⟩

circle¹ [ˈsərkəl] *v* **-cled; -cling** *vt* **1** : encerrar en un círculo, poner un círculo alrededor de **2** : girar alrededor de, dar vueltas a ⟨we circled the building twice : le dimos vueltas al edificio dos veces⟩ — *vi* : dar vueltas

circle² *n* **1** : círculo *m* **2** CYCLE : ciclo *m* ⟨to come full circle : volver al punto de partida⟩ **3** GROUP : círculo *m*, grupo *m* (social)

circuit [ˈsərkət] *n* **1** BOUNDARY : circuito *m*, perímetro *m* (de una zona o un territorio) **2** TOUR : circuito *m*, recorrido *m*, tour *m* **3** : circuito *m* (eléctrico) ⟨a short circuit : un cortocircuito⟩

circuitous [ˌsərˈkjuːətəs] *adj* : sinuoso, tortuoso

circuitry [ˈsərkətri] *n, pl* **-ries** : sistema *m* de circuitos

circular¹ [ˈsərkjələr] *adj* ROUND : circular, redondo

circular² *n* : circular *f*

circulate [ˈsərkjəˌleɪt] *v* **-lated; -lating** *vi* : circular — *vt* **1** : circular (noticias, etc.) **2** DISSEMINATE : hacer circular, divulgar

circulation [ˌsərkjəˈleɪʃən] *n* : circulación *f*

circulatory [ˈsərkjələˌtori] *adj* : circulatorio

circumcise [ˈsərkəmˌsaɪz] *vt* **-cised; -cising** : circuncidar

circumcision [ˌsərkəmˈsɪʒən, ˈsərkəmˌ-] *n* : circuncisión *f*

circumference [sərˈkʌmpfrənts] *n* : circunferencia *f*

circumflex [ˈsərkəmˌfleks] *n* : acento *m* circunflejo

circumlocution [ˌsərkəmloˈkjuːʃən] *n* : circunlocución *f*

circumnavigate [ˌsərkəmˈnævəˌgeɪt] *vt* **-gated; -gating** : circunnavegar

circumscribe [ˈsərkəmˌskraɪb] *vt* **-scribed; -scribing 1** : circunscribir, trazar una figura alrededor de **2** LIMIT : circunscribir, limitar

circumspect [ˈsərkəmˌspekt] *adj* : circunspecto, prudente, cauto

circumspection [ˌsərkəmˈspekʃən] *n* : circunspección *f*, cautela *f*

circumstance [ˈsərkəmˌstænts] *n* **1** EVENT : circunstancia *f*, acontecimiento *m* **2 circumstances** *npl* SITUATION : circunstancias *fpl*, situación *f* ⟨under the circumstances : dadas las circunstancias⟩ ⟨under no circumstances : de ninguna manera, bajo ningún concepto⟩ **3 circumstances** *npl* : situación *f* económica

circumstantial [ˌsərkəmˈstæntʃəl] *adj* : circunstancial

circumvent [ˌsərkəmˈvent] *vt* : evadir, burlar (una ley o regla), sortear (una responsabilidad o dificultad)

circumvention [ˌsərkəmˈventʃən] *n* : evasión *f*

circus [ˈsərkəs] *n* : circo *m*

cirrhosis [səˈroːsɪs] *n, pl* **-rhoses** [-ˈroːˌsiːz] : cirrosis *f*

cirrus [ˈsɪrəs] *n, pl* **-ri** [ˈsɪrˌaɪ] : cirro *m*

cistern [ˈsɪstərn] *n* : cisterna *f*, aljibe *m*

citadel [ˈsɪtədəl, -ˌdɛl] *n* FORTRESS : ciudadela *f*, fortaleza *f*

citation [saɪ'teɪʃən] *n* **1** SUMMONS : emplazamiento *m*, citación *f*, convocatoria *f* (judicial) **2** QUOTATION : cita *f* **3** COMMENDATION : elogio *m*, mención *f* (de honor)

cite ['saɪt] *vt* **cited; citing 1** ARRAIGN, SUBPOENA : emplazar, citar, hacer comparecer (ante un tribunal) **2** QUOTE : citar **3** COMMEND : elogiar, honrar (oficialmente)

citizen ['sɪtəzən] *n* : ciudadano *m*, -na *f*

citizenry ['sɪtəzənri] *n, pl* **-ries** : ciudadanía *f*, conjunto *m* de ciudadanos

citizenship ['sɪtəzən,ʃɪp] *n* : ciudadanía *f* ⟨Nicaraguan citizenship : ciudadanía nicaragüense⟩

citron ['sɪtrən] *n* : cidra *f*

citrus ['sɪtrəs] *n, pl* **-rus** *or* **-ruses** : cítrico *m*

city ['sɪti] *n, pl* **cities** : ciudad *f*

civic ['sɪvɪk] *adj* : cívico

civics ['sɪvɪks] *ns & pl* : civismo *m*

civil ['sɪvəl] *adj* **1** : civil ⟨civil law : derecho civil⟩ **2** POLITE : civil, cortés

civilian [sə'vɪljən] *n* : civil *mf* ⟨soldiers and civilians : soldados y civiles⟩

civility [sə'vɪləti] *n, pl* **-ties** : cortesía *f*, educación *f*

civilization [,sɪvələ'zeɪʃən] *n* : civilización *f*

civilize ['sɪvə,laɪz] *vt* **-lized; -lizing** : civilizar — **civilized** *adj*

civil liberties *npl* : derechos *mpl* civiles

civilly ['sɪvəli] *adv* : cortésmente

civil rights *npl* : derechos *mpl* civiles

civil service *n* : administración *f* pública

civil war *n* : guerra *f* civil

clack[1] ['klæk] *vi* : tabletear

clack[2] *n* : tableteo *m*

clad ['klæd] *adj* **1** CLOTHED : vestido **2** COVERED : cubierto

claim[1] ['kleɪm] *vt* **1** DEMAND : reclamar, reivindicar ⟨she claimed her rights : reclamó sus derechos⟩ **2** MAINTAIN : afirmar, sostener ⟨they claim it's theirs : sostienen que es suyo⟩

claim[2] *n* **1** DEMAND : demanda *f*, reclamación *f* **2** DECLARATION : declaración *f*, afirmación *f* **3 to stake a claim** : reclamar, reivindicar

claimant ['kleɪmənt] *n* : demandante *mf* (ante un juez), pretendiente *mf* (al trono, etc.)

clairvoyance [klær'vɔɪənts] *n* : clarividencia *f*

clairvoyant[1] [klær'vɔɪənt] *adj* : clarividente

clairvoyant[2] *n* : clarividente *mf*

clam ['klæm] *n* : almeja *f*

clamber ['klæmbər] *vi* : treparse o subirse torpemente

clammy ['klæmi] *adj* **-mier; -est** : húmedo y algo frío

clamor[1] ['klæmər] *vi* : gritar, clamar

clamor[2] *n* : clamor *m*

clamorous ['klæmərəs] *adj* : clamoroso, ruidoso, estrepitoso

clamp[1] ['klæmp] *vt* : sujetar con abrazaderas

clamp[2] *n* : abrazadera *f*

clan ['klæn] *n* : clan *m*

clandestine [klæn'dɛstɪn] *adj* : clandestino, secreto

clang[1] ['klæŋ] *vi* : hacer resonar (dícese de un objeto metálico)

clang[2] *n* : ruido *m* metálico fuerte

clangor ['klæŋər, -gər] *n* : estruendo *m* metálico

clank[1] ['klæŋk] *vi* : producir un ruido metálico seco

clank[2] *n* : ruido *m* metálico seco

clannish ['klænɪʃ] *adj* : exclusivista

clap[1] ['klæp] *v* **clapped; clapping** *vt* **1** SLAP, STRIKE : golpear ruidosamente, dar una palmada ⟨to clap one's hands : batir palmas, dar palmadas⟩ **2** APPLAUD : aplaudir — *vi* APPLAUD : aplaudir

clap[2] *n* **1** SLAP : palmada *f*, golpecito *m* **2** NOISE : ruido *m* seco ⟨a clap of thunder : un trueno⟩

clapboard ['klæbərd, 'klæp,bord] *n* : tabla *f* de madera (para revestir muros)

clapper ['klæpər] *n* : badajo *m* (de una campana)

clarification [,klærəfə'keɪʃən] *n* : clarificación *f*

clarify ['klærə,faɪ] *vt* **-fied; -fying 1** EXPLAIN : aclarar **2** : clarificar (un líquido)

clarinet [,klærə'nɛt] *n* : clarinete *m*

clarion ['klæriən] *adj* : claro y sonoro

clarity ['klærəti] *n* : claridad *f*, nitidez *f*

clash[1] ['klæʃ] *vi* **1** : sonar, chocarse ⟨the cymbals clashed : los platillos sonaron⟩ **2** : chocar, enfrentarse ⟨the students clashed with the police : los estudiantes se enfrentaron con la policía⟩ **3** CONFLICT : estar en conflicto, oponerse **4** : desentonar (dícese de los colores), coincidir (dícese de los datos)

clash[2] *n* **1** : ruido *m* (producido por un choque) **2** CONFLICT, CONFRONTATION : enfrentamiento *m*, conflicto *m*, choque *m* **3** : desentono *m* (de colores), coincidencia *f* (de datos)

clasp[1] ['klæsp] *vt* **1** FASTEN : sujetar, abrochar **2** EMBRACE, GRASP : agarrar, sujetar, abrazar

clasp[2] *n* **1** FASTENING : broche *m*, cierre *m* **2** EMBRACE, SQUEEZE : apretón *m*, abrazo *m*

class[1] ['klæs] *vt* : clasificar, catalogar

class[2] *n* **1** KIND, TYPE : clase *f*, tipo *m*, especie *f* **2** : clase *f*, rango *m* social ⟨the working class : la clase obrera⟩ **3** LESSON : clase *f*, curso *m* ⟨English class : clase de inglés⟩ **4** : conjunto *m* de estudiantes, clase *f* ⟨the class of '97 : la promoción del 97⟩

classic[1] ['klæsɪk] *adj* : clásico

classic[2] *n* : clásico *m*, obra *f* clásica

classical ['klæsɪkəl] *adj* : clásico — **classically** [-kli] *adv*

classicism ['klæsə,sɪzəm] *n* : clasicismo *m*

classification [,klæsəfə'keɪʃən] *n* : clasificación *f*

classified ['klæsə,faɪd] *adj* **1** : clasificado ⟨classified ads : avisos clasificados⟩ **2** RESTRICTED : confidencial, secreto ⟨classified documents : documentos secretos⟩

classify ['klæsə,faɪ] *vt* **-fied; -fying** : clasificar, catalogar

classless ['klæsləs] *adj* : sin clases

classmate ['klæs,meɪt] *n* : compañero *m*, -ra *f* de clase

classroom ['klæs,ru:m] *n* : aula *f*, salón *m* de clase

clatter¹ ['klæt̬ər] *vi* : traquetear, hacer ruido

clatter² *n* : traqueteo *m*, ruido *m*, estrépito *m*

clause ['klɔz] *n* : cláusula *f*

claustrophobia [,klɔstrə'fo:biə] *n* : claustrofobia *f*

claustrophobic [,klɔstrə'fo:bɪk] *adj* : claustrofóbico

clavicle ['klævɪkəl] *n* : clavícula *f*

claw¹ ['klɔ] *v* : arañar

claw² *n* : garra *f*, uña *f* (de un gato), pinza *f* (de un crustáceo)

clay ['kleɪ] *n* : arcilla *f*, barro *m*

clayey ['kleɪi] *adj* : arcilloso

clean¹ ['kli:n] *vt* : limpiar, lavar, asear

clean² *adv* : limpio, limpiamente ⟨to play clean : jugar limpio⟩

clean³ *adj* **1** : limpio **2** UNADULTERATED : puro **3** IRREPROACHABLE : intachable, sin mancha ⟨to have a clean record : no tener antecedentes penales⟩ **4** DECENT : decente **5** COMPLETE : completo, absoluto ⟨a clean break with the past : un corte radical con el pasado⟩

cleaner ['kli:nər] *n* **1** : limpiador *m*, -dora *f* **2** : producto *m* de limpieza **3** DRY CLEANER : tintorería *f* (servicio)

cleanliness ['klɛnlinəs] *n* : limpieza *f*, aseo *m*

cleanly¹ ['kli:nli] *adv* : limpiamente, con limpieza

cleanly² ['klɛnli] *adj* **-lier; -est** : limpio, pulcro

cleanness ['kli:nnəs] *n* : limpieza *f*

cleanse ['klɛnz] *vt* **cleansed; cleansing** : limpiar, purificar

cleanser ['klɛnzər] *n* : limpiador *m*, purificador *m*

clear¹ ['klɪr] *vt* **1** CLARIFY : aclarar, clarificar (un líquido) **2** : despejar (una superficie), desatascar (un tubo), desmontar (una selva) ⟨to clear the table : levantar la mesa⟩ ⟨to clear one's throat : carraspear, aclararse la voz⟩ **3** EXONERATE : absolver, limpiar el nombre de **4** EARN : ganar, sacar (una ganancia de) **5** : pasar sin tocar ⟨he cleared the hurdle : saltó por encima de la valla⟩ **6 to clear up** RESOLVE : aclarar, resolver, esclarecer — *vi* **1**

DISPERSE : irse, despejarse, disiparse **2** : ser compensado (dícese de un cheque) **3 to clear up** : despejar (dícese del tiempo), mejorarse (dícese de una enfermedad)

clear² *adv* : claro, claramente

clear³ *adj* **1** BRIGHT : claro, lúcido **2** FAIR : claro, despejado **3** TRANSPARENT : transparente, translúcido **4** EVIDENT, UNMISTAKABLE : evidente, claro, obvio **5** CERTAIN : seguro **6** UNOBSTRUCTED : despejado, libre

clear⁴ *n* **1 in the clear** : inocente, libre de toda sospecha **2 in the clear** SAFE : fuera de peligro

clearance ['klɪrənts] *n* **1** CLEARING : despeje *m* **2** SPACE : espacio *m* (libre), margen *m* **3** AUTHORIZATION : autorización *f*, despacho *m* (de la aduana)

clearing ['klɪrɪŋ] *n* : claro *m* (de un bosque)

clearly ['klɪrli] *adv* **1** DISTINCTLY : claramente, directamente **2** OBVIOUSLY : obviamente, evidentemente

cleat ['kli:t] *n* **1** : taco *m* **2 cleats** *npl* : zapatos *mpl* deportivos (con tacos)

cleavage ['kli:vɪʤ] *n* **1** CLEFT : hendidura *f*, raja *f* **2** : escote *m* (del busto)

cleave¹ ['kli:v] *vi* **cleaved** ['kli:vd] *or* **clove** ['klo:v]; **cleaving** ADHERE : adherirse, unirse

cleave² *vt* **cleaved; cleaving** SPLIT : hender, dividir, partir

cleaver ['kli:vər] *n* : cuchilla *f* de carnicero

clef ['klɛf] *n* : clave *f*

cleft ['klɛft] *n* : hendidura *f*, raja *f*, grieta *f*

clemency ['klɛməntsi] *n* : clemencia *f*

clement ['klɛmənt] *adj* **1** MERCIFUL : clemente, piadoso **2** MILD : clemente, apacible

clench ['klɛntʃ] *vt* **1** CLUTCH : agarrar **2** TIGHTEN : apretar (el puño, los dientes)

clergy ['klərʤi] *n*, *pl* **-gies** : clero *m*

clergyman ['klərʤimən] *n*, *pl* **-men** [-mən, -,mɛn] : clérigo *m*

cleric ['klɛrɪk] *n* : clérigo *m*, -ga *f*

clerical ['klɛrɪkəl] *adj* **1** : clerical ⟨a clerical collar : un alzacuello⟩ **2** : de oficina ⟨clerical staff : personal de oficina⟩

clerk¹ ['klərk, *Brit* 'klɑrk] *vi* : trabajar de oficinista, trabajar de dependiente

clerk² *n* **1** : funcionario *m*, -ria *f* (de una oficina gubernamental) **2** : oficinista *mf*, empleado *m*, -da *f* de oficina **3** SALESPERSON : dependiente *m*, -ta *f*

clever ['klɛvər] *adj* **1** SKILLFUL : ingenioso, hábil **2** SMART : listo, inteligente, astuto

cleverly ['klɛvərli] *adv* **1** SKILLFULLY : ingeniosamente, hábilmente **2** INTELLIGENTLY : inteligentemente

cleverness ['klɛvərnəs] *n* **1** SKILL : ingenio *m*, habilidad *f* **2** INTELLIGENCE : inteligencia *f*

clew ['klu:] → **clue**

cliché [kliˈʃeɪ] *n* : cliché *m*, tópico *m*

click¹ ['klɪk] *vt* **1** : chasquear (los dedos, etc.) ⟨to click one's heels : dar un taconazo⟩ **2** : hacer clic en (un botón, etc.) — *vi* **1** : hacer clic **2** SNAP : chasquear **3** SUCCEED : tener éxito **4** GET ALONG : congeniar, llevarse bien

click² *n* : chasquido *m* (de los dedos, etc.), clic *m* (de un botón, etc.)

client ['klaɪənt] *n* : cliente *m*, -ta *f*

clientele [ˌklaɪənˈtɛl, ˌkliː-] *n* : clientela *f*

cliff ['klɪf] *n* : acantilado *m*, precipicio *m*, risco *m*

climate ['klaɪmət] *n* : clima *m*

climatic [klaɪˈmætɪk, klə-] *adj* : climático

climax¹ ['klaɪˌmæks] *vi* : llegar al punto culminante, culminar — *vt* : ser el punto culminante de

climax² *n* : clímax *m*, punto *m* culminante

climb¹ ['klaɪm] *vt* : escalar, trepar a, subir a ⟨to climb a mountain : escalar una montaña⟩ — *vi* **1** RISE : subir, ascender ⟨prices are climbing : los precios están subiendo⟩ **2** : subirse, treparse ⟨to climb up a tree : treparse a un árbol⟩

climb² *n* : ascenso *m*, subida *f*

climber ['klaɪmər] *n* **1** : escalador *m*, -dora *f* ⟨a mountain climber : un alpinista⟩ **2** : trepadora *f* (planta)

clinch¹ ['klɪntʃ] *vt* **1** FASTEN, SECURE : remachar (un clavo), afianzar, abrochar **2** SETTLE : decidir, cerrar ⟨to clinch the title : ganar el título⟩

clinch² *n* : abrazo *m*, clinch *m* (en el boxeo)

clincher ['klɪntʃər] *n* : argumento *m* decisivo

cling ['klɪŋ] *vi* clung ['klʌŋ]; clinging **1** STICK : adherirse, pegarse **2** : aferrarse, agarrarse ⟨he clung to the railing : se aferró a la barandilla⟩

clinic ['klɪnɪk] *n* : clínica *f*

clinical ['klɪnɪkəl] *adj* : clínico — **clinically** [-kli] *adv*

clink¹ ['klɪŋk] *vi* : tintinear

clink² *n* : tintineo *m*

clip¹ ['klɪp] *vt* clipped; clipping **1** CUT : cortar, recortar **2** HIT : golpear, dar un puñetazo a **3** FASTEN : sujetar (con un clip)

clip² *n* **1** → **clippers** **2** BLOW : golpe *m*, puñetazo *m* **3** PACE : paso *m* rápido **4** FASTENER : clip *m* ⟨a paper clip : un sujetapapeles⟩

clipper ['klɪpər] *n* **1** : clíper *m* (buque de vela) **2** clippers *npl* : tijeras *fpl* ⟨nail clippers : cortauñas⟩

clique ['kliːk, 'klɪk] *n* : grupo *m* exclusivo, camarilla *f* (de políticos)

clitoris ['klɪtərəs, klɪˈtɔrɪs] *n, pl* clitorides [-'tɔrəˌdiːz] : clítoris *m*

cloak¹ ['klo:k] *vt* : encubrir, envolver (en un manto de)

cloak² *n* : capa *f*, capote *m*, manto *m* ⟨under the cloak of darkness : al amparo de la oscuridad⟩

clobber ['klabər] *vt* : dar una paliza a

clock¹ ['klak] *vt* : cronometrar

clock² *n* **1** : reloj *m* (de pared), cronómetro *m* (en deportes o competencias) **2** around the clock : las veinticuatro horas

clockwise ['klak,waɪz] *adv & adj* : en la dirección de las manecillas del reloj

clockwork ['klak,wərk] *n* : mecanismo *m* de relojería

clod ['klad] *n* **1** : terrón *m* **2** OAF : zoquete *mf*

clog¹ ['klag] *v* clogged; clogging *vt* **1** HINDER : estorbar, impedir **2** BLOCK : atascar, tapar — *vi* : atascarse, taparse

clog² *n* **1** OBSTACLE : traba *f*, impedimento *m*, estorbo *m* **2** : zueco *m* (zapato)

cloister¹ ['klɔɪstər] *vt* : enclaustrar

cloister² *n* : claustro *m*

clone ['klo:n] *n* **1** : clon *m* (de un organismo) **2** COPY : copia *f*, reproducción *f*

close¹ ['klo:z] *v* closed; closing *vt* : cerrar — *vi* **1** : cerrarse, cerrar **2** TERMINATE : concluirse, terminar **3** to close in APPROACH : acercarse, aproximarse

close² ['klo:s] *adv* : cerca, de cerca

close³ *adj* closer; closest **1** CONFINING : restrictivo, estrecho **2** SECRETIVE : reservado **3** STRICT : estricto, detallado **4** STUFFY : cargado, bochornoso (dícese del tiempo) **5** TIGHT : apretado, entallado, ceñido ⟨it's a close fit : es muy apretado⟩ **6** NEAR : cercano, próximo **7** INTIMATE : íntimo ⟨close friends : amigos íntimos⟩ **8** ACCURATE : fiel, exacto **9** : reñido ⟨a close election : una elección muy reñida⟩

close⁴ ['klo:z] *n* : fin *m*, final *m*, conclusión *f*

closely ['klo:sli] *adv* : cerca, de cerca

closeness ['klo:snəs] *n* **1** NEARNESS : cercanía *f*, proximidad *f* **2** INTIMACY : intimidad *f*

closet¹ ['klazət] *vt* to be closeted with : estar encerrado con

closet² *n* : armario *m*, guardarropa *f*, clóset *m*

closure ['klo:ʒər] *n* **1** CLOSING, END : cierre *m*, clausura *f*, fin *m* **2** FASTENER : cierre *m*

clot¹ ['klat] *v* clotted; clotting *vt* : coagular, cuajar — *vi* : cuajarse, coagularse

clot² *n* : coágulo *m*

cloth ['klɔθ] *n, pl* cloths ['klɔðz, 'klɔθs] **1** FABRIC : tela *f* **2** RAG : trapo *m* **3** TABLECLOTH : mantel *m*

clothe ['klo:ð] *vt* clothed *or* clad ['klæd]; clothing DRESS : vestir, arropar, ataviar

clothes ['klo:z, 'klo:ðz] *npl* **1** CLOTHING : ropa *f* **2** BEDCLOTHES : ropa *f* de cama

clothespin ['klo:z,pɪn] *n* : pinza *f* (para la ropa)

clothing [ˈkloːðɪŋ] *n* : ropa *f*, indumentaria *f*

cloud¹ [ˈklaʊd] *vt* : nublar, oscurecer — *vi* **to cloud over** : nublarse

cloud² *n* : nube *f*

cloudburst [ˈklaʊd‚bərst] *n* : chaparrón *m*, aguacero *m*

cloudless [ˈklaʊdləs] *adj* : despejado, claro

cloudy [ˈklaʊdi] *adj* **cloudier; -est** : nublado, nuboso

clout¹ [ˈklaʊt] *vt* : bofetear, dar un tortazo a

clout² *n* **1** BLOW : golpe *m*, tortazo *m fam* **2** INFLUENCE : influencia *f*, palanca *f fam*

clove¹ [ˈkloːv] *n* **1** : diente *m* (de ajo) **2** : clavo *m* (especia)

clove² → **cleave**

cloven hoof [ˈkloːvən] *n* : pezuña *f* hendida

clover [ˈkloːvər] *n* : trébol *m*

cloverleaf [ˈkloːvər‚liːf] *n, pl* **-leafs** *or* **-leaves** [-‚liːvz] : intersección *f* en trébol

clown¹ [ˈklaʊn] *vi* : payasear, bromear ⟨stop clowning around : déjate de payasadas⟩

clown² *n* : payaso *m*, -sa *f*

clownish [ˈklaʊnɪʃ] *adj* **1** : de payaso **2** BOORISH : grosero — **clownishly** *adv*

cloying [ˈklɔɪɪŋ] *adj* : empalagoso, meloso

club¹ [ˈklʌb] *vt* **clubbed; clubbing** : aporrear, dar garrotazos a

club² *n* **1** CUDGEL : garrote *m*, porra *f* **2** : palo *m* ⟨golf club : palo de golf⟩ **3** : trébol *m* (naipe) **4** ASSOCIATION : club *m*

clubfoot [ˈklʌb‚fʊt] *n, pl* **-feet** : pie *m* deforme

clubhouse [ˈklʌb‚haʊs] *n* : sede *f* de un club

cluck¹ [ˈklʌk] *vi* : cloquear, cacarear

cluck² *n* : cloqueo *m*, cacareo *m*

clue¹ [ˈkluː] *vt* **clued; clueing** *or* **cluing** *or* **to clue in** : dar una pista a, informar

clue² *n* : pista *f*, indicio *m*

clump¹ [ˈklʌmp] *vi* **1** : caminar con pisadas fuertes **2** LUMP : agruparse, aglutinarse — *vt* : amontonar

clump² *n* **1** : grupo *m* (de arbustos o árboles), terrón *m* (de tierra) **2** : pisada *f* fuerte

clumsily [ˈklʌmzəli] *adv* : torpemente, sin gracia

clumsiness [ˈklʌmzinəs] *n* : torpeza *f*

clumsy [ˈklʌmzi] *adj* **-sier; -est** **1** AWKWARD : torpe, desmañado **2** TACTLESS : carente de tacto, poco delicado

clung → **cling**

clunky [ˈklʌŋki] *adj* : torpe, poco elegante

cluster¹ [ˈklʌstər] *vt* : agrupar, juntar — *vi* : agruparse, apiñarse, arracimarse

cluster² *n* : grupo *m*, conjunto *m*, racimo *m* (de uvas)

clutch¹ [ˈklʌtʃ] *vt* : agarrar, asir — *vi* **to clutch at** : tratar de agarrar

clutch² *n* **1** GRASP, GRIP : agarre *m*, apretón *m* **2** : embrague *m*, clutch *m* (de una máquina) **3** **clutches** *npl* : garras *fpl* ⟨he fell into their clutches : cayó en sus garras⟩

clutter¹ [ˈklʌtər] *vt* : atiborrar o atestar de cosas, llenar desordenadamente

clutter² *n* : desorden *m*, revoltijo *m*

coach¹ [ˈkoːtʃ] *vt* : entrenar (atletas, artistas), preparar (alumnos)

coach² *n* **1** CARRIAGE : coche *m*, carruaje *m*, carroza *f* **2** : vagón *m* de pasajeros (de un tren) **3** BUS : autobús *m*, ómnibus *m* **4** : pasaje *m* aéreo de segunda clase **5** TRAINER : entrenador *m*, -dora *f*

coagulate [koˈægjə‚leɪt] *v* **-lated; -lating** *vt* : coagular, cuajar — *vi* : coagularse, cuajarse

coal [ˈkoːl] *n* **1** EMBER : ascua *f*, brasa *f* **2** : carbón *m* ⟨a coal mine : una mina de carbón⟩

coalesce [‚koːəˈlɛs] *vi* **-alesced; -alescing** : unirse

coalition [‚koːəˈlɪʃən] *n* : coalición *f*

coarse [ˈkors] *adj* **coarser; -est** **1** : grueso (dícese de la arena o la sal), basto (dícese de las telas), áspero (dícese de la piel) **2** CRUDE, ROUGH : basto, tosco, ordinario **3** VULGAR : grosero — **coarsely** *adv*

coarsen [ˈkorsən] *vt* : hacer áspero o basto — *vi* : volverse áspero o basto

coarseness [ˈkorsnəs] *n* : aspereza *f*, tosquedad *f*

coast¹ [ˈkoːst] *vi* : deslizarse, rodar sin impulso

coast² *n* : costa *f*, litoral *m*

coastal [ˈkoːstəl] *adj* : costero

coaster [ˈkoːstər] *n* : posavasos *m*

coast guard *n* : guardia *f* costera, guardacostas *mpl*

coastline [ˈkoːst‚laɪn] *n* : costa *f*

coat¹ [ˈkoːt] *vt* : cubrir, revestir, bañar (en un líquido)

coat² *n* **1** : abrigo *m* ⟨a sport coat : una chaqueta, un saco⟩ **2** : pelaje *m* (de animales) **3** LAYER : capa *f*, mano *f* (de pintura)

coating [ˈkoːtɪŋ] *n* : capa *f*

coat of arms *n* : escudo *m* de armas

coax [ˈkoːks] *vt* : engatusar, persuadir

cob [ˈkɑb] → **corncob**

cobalt [ˈkoː‚bɔlt] *n* : cobalto *m*

cobble [ˈkɑbəl] *vt* **cobbled; cobbling** **1** : fabricar o remendar (zapatos) **2 to cobble together** : improvisar, hacer apresuradamente

cobbler [ˈkɑblər] *n* **1** SHOEMAKER : zapatero *m*, -ra *f* **2 fruit cobbler** : tarta *f* de fruta

cobblestone [ˈkɑbəl‚stoːn] *n* : adoquín *m*

cobra [ˈkoːbrə] *n* : cobra *f*

cobweb [ˈkɑb‚wɛb] *n* : telaraña *f*

coca [ˈkoːkə] *n* : coca *f*

cocaine [ko:'keɪn, 'ko:ˌkeɪn] *n* : cocaína *f*

cock¹ ['kɑk] *vt* **1** : ladear ⟨to cock one's head : ladear la cabeza⟩ **2** : montar, amartillar (un arma de fuego)

cock² *n* **1** ROOSTER : gallo *m* **2** FAUCET : grifo *m*, llave *f* **3** : martillo *m* (de un arma de fuego)

cockatoo ['kɑkəˌtu:] *n, pl* **-toos** : cacatúa *f*

cockeyed ['kɑkˌaɪd] *adj* **1** ASKEW : ladeado, torcido, chueco **2** ABSURD : disparatado, absurdo

cockfight ['kɑkˌfaɪt] *n* : pelea *f* de gallos

cockiness ['kɑkinəs] *n* : arrogancia *f*

cockle ['kɑkəl] *n* : berberecho *m*

cockpit ['kɑkˌpɪt] *n* : cabina *f*

cockroach ['kɑkˌro:ʧ] *n* : cucaracha *f*

cocktail ['kɑkˌteɪl] *n* **1** : coctel *m*, cóctel *m* **2** APPETIZER : aperitivo *m*

cocky ['kɑki] *adj* **cockier; -est** : creído, engreído

cocoa ['ko:ˌko:] *n* **1** CACAO : cacao *m* **2** : cocoa *f*, chocolate *m* (bebida)

coconut ['ko:kəˌnʌt] *n* : coco *m*

cocoon [kə'ku:n] *n* : capullo *m*

cod ['kɑd] *n, pl* **cod** : bacalao *m*

coddle ['kɑdəl] *vt* **-dled; -dling** : mimar, consentir

code ['ko:d] *n* **1** : código *m* ⟨civil code : código civil⟩ **2** : código *m*, clave *f* ⟨secret code : clave secreta⟩

codeine ['ko:ˌdi:n] *n* : codeína *f*

codex ['ko:ˌdɛks] *n, pl* **-dexes** [-ˌdɛksəz] *or* **-dices** [-dəˌsi:z] : códice *m*

codger ['kɑʤər] *n* : viejo *m*, vejete *m*

codify ['kɑdəˌfaɪ, 'ko:-] *vt* **-fied; -fying** : codificar

coeducation [ˌko:ˌɛʤə'keɪʃən] *n* : coeducación *f*, enseñanza *f* mixta

coeducational [ˌko:ˌɛʤə'keɪʃənəl] *adj* : mixto

coefficient [ˌko:ə'fɪʃənt] *n* : coeficiente *m*

coerce [ko'ərs] *vt* **-erced; -ercing** : coaccionar, forzar, obligar

coercion [ko'ərʒən, -ʃən] *n* : coacción *f*

coercive [ko'ərsɪv] *adj* : coactivo

coexist [ˌko:ɪg'zɪst] *vi* : coexistir

coexistence [ˌko:ɪg'zɪstəns] *n* : coexistencia *f*

coffee ['kɔfi] *n* : café *m*

coffeepot ['kɔfiˌpɑt] *n* : cafetera *f*

coffee table *n* : mesa *f* de centro

coffer ['kɔfər] *n* : cofre *m*

coffin ['kɔfən] *n* : ataúd *m*, féretro *m*

cog ['kɑg] *n* : diente *m* (de una rueda dentada)

cogent ['ko:ʤənt] *adj* : convincente, persuasivo

cogitate ['kɑʤəˌteɪt] *vi* **-tated; -tating** : reflexionar, meditar, discurrir

cogitation [ˌkɑʤə'teɪʃən] *n* : reflexión *f*, meditación *f*

cognac ['ko:nˌjæk] *n* : coñac *m*

cognate ['kɑgˌneɪt] *adj* : relacionado, afín

cognition [kɑg'nɪʃən] *n* : cognición *f*

cognitive ['kɑgnətɪv] *adj* : cognitivo

cogwheel ['kɑgˌʍi:l] *n* : rueda *f* dentada

cohabit [ˌko:'hæbət] *vi* : cohabitar

cohere [ko'hɪr] *vi* **-hered; -hering** **1** ADHERE : adherirse, pegarse **2** : ser coherente o congruente

coherence [ko'hɪrənts] *n* : coherencia *f*, congruencia *f*

coherent [ko'hɪrənt] *adj* : coherente, congruente — **coherently** *adv*

cohesion [ko'hi:ʒən] *n* : cohesión *f*

cohesive [ko:'hi:sɪv, -zɪv] *adj* : cohesivo

cohort ['ko:ˌhɔrt] *n* **1** : cohorte *f* (de soldados) **2** COMPANION : compañero *m*, -ra *f*; colega *mf*

coiffure [kwɑ'fjur] *n* : peinado *m*

coil¹ ['kɔɪl] *vt* : enrollar — *vi* : enrollarse, enroscarse

coil² *n* : rollo *m* (de cuerda, etc.), espiral *f* (de humo)

coin¹ ['kɔɪn] *vt* **1** MINT : acuñar (moneda) **2** INVENT : acuñar, crear, inventar ⟨to coin a phrase : como se suele decir⟩

coin² *n* : moneda *f*

coincide [ˌko:ɪn'saɪd, 'ko:ɪnˌsaɪd] *vi* **-cided; -ciding** : coincidir

coincidence [ko'ɪntsədənts] *n* : coincidencia *f*, casualidad *f* ⟨what a coincidence! : ¡qué casualidad!⟩

coincident [ko'ɪntsədənt] *adj* : coincidente, concurrente

coincidental [ko,ɪntsə'dɛntəl] *adj* : casual, accidental, fortuito

coitus ['ko:ətəs] *n* : coito *m*

coke ['ko:k] *n* : coque *m*

colander ['kɑləndər, 'kʌ-] *n* : colador *m*

cold¹ ['ko:ld] *adj* : frío ⟨it's cold out : hace frío⟩ ⟨a cold reception : una fría recepción⟩ ⟨in cold blood : a sangre fría⟩

cold² *n* **1** : frío *m* ⟨to feel the cold : sentir frío⟩ **2** : resfriado *m*, catarro *m* ⟨to catch a cold : resfriarse⟩

cold–blooded ['ko:ld'blʌdəd] *adj* **1** CRUEL : cruel, despiadado **2** : de sangre fría (dícese de los reptiles, etc.)

coldly ['ko:ldli] *adv* : fríamente, con frialdad

coldness ['ko:ldnəs] *n* : frialdad *f* (de una persona o una actitud), frío *m* (de la temperatura)

coleslaw ['ko:lˌslɔ] *n* : ensalada *f* de col

colic ['kɑlɪk] *n* : cólico *m*

coliseum [ˌkɑlə'si:əm] *n* : coliseo *m*, arena *f*

collaborate [kə'læbəˌreɪt] *vi* **-rated; -rating** : colaborar

collaboration [kəˌlæbə'reɪʃə n] *n* : colaboración *f*

collaborator [kə'læbəˌreɪtər] *n* **1** COLLEAGUE : colaborador *m*, -dora *f* **2** TRAITOR : colaboracionista *mf*

collage [kə'lɑʒ] *n* : collage *m*

collapse¹ [kə'læps] *vi* **-lapsed; -lapsing** **1** : derrumbarse, desplomarse, hundirse ⟨the building collapsed : el edificio se derrumbó⟩ **2** FALL : desplomarse, caerse ⟨he collapsed on the bed : se desplomó en la cama⟩ ⟨to collapse with laughter : morirse de risa⟩ **3** FAIL : fracasar, quebrar, arruinarse **4** FOLD : plegarse

collapse² *n* **1** FALL : derrumbe *m*, desplome *m* **2** BREAKDOWN, FAILURE : fracaso *m*, colapso *m* (físico), quiebra *f* (económica)

collapsible [kə'læpsəbəl] *adj* : plegable

collar¹ ['kɑlər] *vt* : agarrar, atrapar

collar² *n* : cuello *m*

collarbone ['kɑlər,boːn] *n* : clavícula *f*

collate [kə'leɪt; 'kɑ,leɪt, 'koː-] *vt* -**lated**; -**lating 1** COMPARE : cotejar, comparar **2** : ordenar, recopilar (páginas)

collateral¹ [kə'lætərəl] *adj* : colateral

collateral² *n* : garantía *f*, fianza *f*, prenda *f*

colleague ['kɑ,liːg] *n* : colega *mf*; compañero *m*, -ra *f*

collect¹ [kə'lɛkt] *vt* **1** GATHER : recopilar, reunir, recoger ⟨she collected her thoughts : puso en orden sus ideas⟩ **2** : coleccionar, juntar ⟨to collect stamps : coleccionar timbres⟩ **3** : cobrar (una deuda), recaudar (un impuesto) **4** DRAW : cobrar, percibir (un sueldo, etc.) — *vi* **1** ACCUMULATE : acumularse, juntarse **2** CONGREGATE : congregarse, reunirse

collect² *adv & adj* : por cobrar, a cobro revertido

collectible *or* **collectable** [kə'lɛktəbəl] *adj* : coleccionable

collection [kə'lɛkʃən] *n* **1** COLLECTING : colecta *f* (de contribuciones), cobro *m* (de deudas), recaudación *f* (de impuestos) **2** GROUP : colección *f* (de objetos), grupo *m* (de personas)

collective¹ [kə'lɛktɪv] *adj* : colectivo — **collectively** *adv*

collective² *n* : colectivo *m*

collector [kə'lɛktər] *n* **1** : coleccionista *mf* (de objetos) **2** : cobrador *m*, -dora *f* (de deudas)

college ['kɑlɪʤ] *n* **1** : universidad *f* **2** : colegio *m* (de electores o profesionales)

collegiate [kə'liːʤət] *adj* : universitario

collide [kə'laɪd] *vi* -**lided**; -**liding** : chocar, colisionar, estrellarse

collie ['kɑli] *n* : collie *mf*

collision [kə'lɪʒən] *n* : choque *m*, colisión *f*

colloquial [kə'loːkwiəl] *adj* : coloquial

colloquialism [kə'loːkwiə,lɪzəm] *n* : expresión *f* coloquial

collusion [kə'luː:ʒən] *n* : colusión *f*

cologne [kə'loːn] *n* : colonia *f*

Colombian [kə'lʌmbiən] *n* : colombiano *m*, -na *f* — **Colombian** *adj*

colon¹ ['koːlən] *n*, *pl* **colons** *or* **cola** [-lə] : colon *m* (de los intestinos)

colon² *n*, *pl* **colons** : dos puntos *mpl* (signo ortográfico)

colonel ['kərnəl] *n* : coronel *m*

colonial¹ [kə'loːniəl] *adj* : colonial

colonial² *n* : colono *m*, -na *f*

colonist ['kɑlənɪst] *n* : colono *m*, -na *f*; colonizador *m*, -dora *f*

colonization [,kɑlənə'zeɪʃən] *n* : colonización *f*

colonize ['kɑlə,naɪz] *vt* -**nized**; -**nizing 1** : establecer una colonia en **2** SETTLE : colonizar

colonnade [,kɑlə'neɪd] *n* : columnata *f*

colony ['kɑləni] *n*, *pl* -**nies** : colonia *f*

color¹ ['kʌlər] *vt* **1** : colorear, pintar **2** INFLUENCE : influir en, influenciar — *vi* BLUSH : sonrojarse, ruborizarse

color² *n* **1** : color *m* ⟨primary colors : colores primarios⟩ **2** INTEREST, VIVIDNESS : color *m*, colorido *m* ⟨local color : color local⟩

coloration [kələ'reɪʃən] *n* : coloración *f*

color–blind ['kʌlər,blaɪnd] *adj* : daltónico

color blindness *n* : daltonismo *m*

colored ['kʌlərd] *adj* **1** : de color (dícese de los objetos) **2** : de color, negro (dícese de las personas)

colorfast ['kʌlər,fæst] *adj* : que no se destiñe

colorful ['kʌlərfəl] *adj* **1** : lleno de colorido, de colores vivos **2** PICTURESQUE, STRIKING : pintoresco, llamativo

coloring ['kələrɪŋ] *n* **1** : color *m*, colorido *m* **2 food coloring** : colorante *m*

colorless ['kʌlərləs] *adj* **1** : incoloro, sin color **2** DULL : soso, aburrido

colossal [kə'lɑsəl] *adj* : colosal

colossus [kə'lɑsəs] *n*, *pl* -**si** [-,saɪ] : coloso *m*

colt ['koːlt] *n* : potro *m*, potranco *m*

column ['kɑləm] *n* : columna *f*

columnist ['kɑləmnɪst, -ləmɪst] *n* : columnista *mf*

coma ['koːmə] *n* : coma *m*, estado *m* de coma

Comanche [kə'mænʧi] *n* : comanche *mf* — **Comanche** *adj*

comatose ['koːmə,toːs, 'kɑ-] *adj* : comatoso, en estado de coma

comb¹ ['koːm] *vt* **1** : peinar (el pelo) **2** SEARCH : peinar, rastrear, registrar a fondo

comb² *n* **1** : peine *m* **2** : cresta *f* (de un gallo)

combat¹ [kəm'bæt, 'kɑm,bæt] *vt* -**bated** *or* -**batted**; -**bating** *or* -**batting** : combatir, luchar contra

combat² ['kɑm,bæt] *n* : combate *m*, lucha *f*

combatant [kəm'bætənt] *n* : combatiente *mf*

combative [kəm'bætɪv] *adj* : combativo

combination [,kɑmbə'neɪʃən] *n* : combinación *f*

combine¹ [kəm'baɪn] *v* -**bined**; -**bining** *vt* : combinar, aunar — *vi* : combinarse, mezclarse

combine² ['kɑm,baɪn] *n* **1** ALLIANCE : alianza *f* comercial o política **2** HARVESTER : cosechadora *f*

combustible [kəm'bʌstəbəl] *adj* : inflamable, combustible

combustion [kəm'bʌstʃən] *n* : combustión *f*

come ['kʌm] *vi* **came** ['keɪm]; **come**; **coming 1** APPROACH : venir, aproximarse ⟨here they come : acá vienen⟩ **2** ARRIVE : venir, llegar, alcanzar ⟨they came yesterday : vinieron ayer⟩ **3** ORIGINATE : venir, provenir ⟨this wine comes from France : este vino viene de Francia⟩ **4** AMOUNT : llegar, ascender ⟨the investment came to two million : la inversión llegó a dos millones⟩ **5 to come clean** : confesar, desahogar la conciencia **6 to come into** ACQUIRE : adquirir ⟨to come into a fortune : heredar una fortuna⟩ **7 to come off** SUCCEED : tener éxito, ser un éxito **8 to come out** : salir, aparecer, publicarse **9 to come to** REVIVE : recobrar el conocimiento, volver en sí **10 to come to pass** HAPPEN : acontecer **11 to come to terms** : llegar a un acuerdo

comeback ['kʌm,bæk] *n* **1** RETORT : réplica *f*, respuesta *f* **2** RETURN : retorno *m*, regreso *m* ⟨the champion announced his comeback : el campeón anunció su regreso⟩

come back *vi* **1** RETORT : replicar, contestar **2** RETURN : volver ⟨come back here! : ¡vuelve acá!⟩ ⟨that style's coming back : ese estilo está volviendo⟩

comedian [kə'mi:diən] *n* : cómico *m*, -ca *f*; humorista *mf*

comedienne [kə,mi:di'ɛn] *n* : cómica *f*, humorista *f*

comedy ['kɑmədi] *n, pl* **-dies** : comedia *f*

comely ['kʌmli] *adj* **-lier; -est** : bello, bonito

comet ['kɑmət] *n* : cometa *m*

comfort¹ ['kʌmpfərt] *vt* **1** CHEER : confortar, alentar **2** CONSOLE : consolar

comfort² *n* **1** CONSOLATION : consuelo *m* **2** WELL-BEING : confort *m*, bienestar *m* **3** CONVENIENCE : comodidad *f* ⟨the comforts of home : las comodidades del hogar⟩

comfortable ['kʌmpfərtəbəl, 'kʌmpftə-] *adj* : cómodo, confortable — **comfortably** ['kʌmpfərtəbli, 'kʌmpftə-] *adv*

comforter ['kʌmpfərtər] *n* QUILT : edredón *m*, cobertor *m*

comic¹ ['kɑmɪk] *adj* : cómico, humorístico

comic² *n* **1** COMEDIAN : cómico *m*, -ca *f*; humorista *mf* **2** *or* **comic book** : historieta *f*, cómic *m*

comical ['kɑmɪkəl] *adj* : cómico, gracioso, chistoso

comic strip *n* : tira *f* cómica, historieta *f*

coming ['kʌmɪŋ] *adj* : siguiente, próximo, que viene

comma ['kɑmə] *n* : coma *f*

command¹ [kə'mænd] *vt* **1** ORDER : ordenar, mandar **2** CONTROL, DIRECT : comandar, tener el mando de — *vi* **1** : dar órdenes **2** GOVERN : estar al mando *m*, gobernar

command² *n* **1** CONTROL, LEADERSHIP : mando *m*, control *m*, dirección *f* **2** ORDER : orden *f*, mandato *m* **3** MASTERY : maestría *f*, destreza *f*, dominio *m* **4** : tropa *f* asignada a un comandante

commandant ['kɑmən,dɑnt, -,dænt] *n* : comandante *mf*

commandeer [,kɑmən'dɪr] *vt* : piratear, secuestrar (un vehículo, etc.)

commander [kə'mændər] *n* : comandante *mf*

commandment [kə'mændmənt] *n* : mandamiento *m*, orden *f* ⟨the Ten Commandments : los diez mandamientos⟩

commando [kə'mændo:] *n* : comando *m*

commemorate [kə'mɛmə,reɪt] *vt* **-rated; -rating** : conmemorar

commemoration [kə,mɛmə'reɪʃən] *n* : conmemoración *f*

commemorative [kə'mɛmrətɪv, -'mɛmə,reɪtɪv] *adj* : conmemorativo

commence [kə'mɛnts] *v* **-menced; -mencing** *vt* : iniciar, comenzar — *vi* : iniciarse, comenzar

commencement [kə'mɛntsmənt] *n* **1** BEGINNING : inicio *m*, comienzo *m* **2** : ceremonia *f* de graduación

commend [kə'mɛnd] *vt* **1** ENTRUST : encomendar **2** RECOMMEND : recomendar **3** PRAISE : elogiar, alabar

commendable [kə'mɛndəbəl] *adj* : loable, meritorio, encomiable

commendation [,kɑmən'deɪʃən, -,mɛn-] *n* : elogio *m*, encomio *m*

commensurate [kə'mɛntsərət, -'mɛntʃurət] *adj* : proporcionado ⟨commensurate with : en proporción a⟩

comment¹ ['kɑ,mɛnt] *vi* **1** : hacer comentarios **2 to comment on** : comentar, hacer observaciones sobre

comment² *n* : comentario *m*, observación *f*

commentary ['kɑmən,tɛri] *n, pl* **-taries** : comentario *m*, crónica *f* (deportiva)

commentator ['kɑmən,teɪtər] *n* : comentarista *mf*, cronista *mf* (de deportes)

commerce ['kɑmərs] *n* : comercio *m*

commercial¹ [kə'mərʃəl] *adj* : comercial — **commercially** *adv*

commercial² *n* : comercial *m*

commercialize [kə'mərʃə,laɪz] *vt* **-ized; -izing** : comercializar

commiserate [kə'mɪzə,reɪt] *vi* **-ated; -ating** : compadecerse, consolarse

commiseration [kə,mɪzə'reɪʃən] *n* : conmiseración *f*

commission¹ [kə'mɪʃən] *vt* **1** : nombrar (un oficial) **2** : comisionar, encargar ⟨to commission a painting : encargar una pintura⟩

commission² *n* **1** : nombramiento *m* (al grado de oficial) **2** COMMITTEE : comisión *f*, comité *m* **3** COMMITTING : comisión *f*, realización *f* (de un acto) **4** PERCENTAGE : comisión *f* ⟨sales commissions : comisiones de venta⟩

commissioned officer *n* : oficial *mf*

commissioner [kə'mɪʃənər] *n* **1** : comisionado *m*, -da *f*; miembro de una comisión **2** : comisario *m*, -ria *f* (de policía, etc.)

commit [kə'mɪt] *vt* **-mitted; -mitting 1** ENTRUST : encomendar, confiar **2** CONFINE : internar (en un hospital), encarcelar (en una prisión) **3** PERPETRATE : cometer ⟨to commit a crime : cometer un crimen⟩ **4 to commit oneself** : comprometerse

commitment [kə'mɪtmənt] *n* **1** RESPONSIBILITY : compromiso *m*, responsabilidad *f* **2** DEDICATION : dedicación *f*, devoción *f* ⟨commitment to the cause : devoción a la causa⟩

committee [kə'mɪti] *n* : comité *m*

commodious [kə'mo:diəs] *adj* SPACIOUS : amplio, espacioso

commodity [kə'madəti] *n, pl* **-ties** : artículo *m* de comercio, mercancía *f*, mercadería *f*

commodore ['kamə,dor] *n* : comodoro *m*

common¹ ['kamən] *adj* **1** PUBLIC : común, público ⟨the common good : el bien común⟩ **2** SHARED : común ⟨a common interest : un interés común⟩ **3** GENERAL : común, general ⟨it's common knowledge : todo el mundo lo sabe⟩ **4** ORDINARY : ordinario, común y corriente ⟨the common man : el hombre medio, el hombre de la calle⟩

common² *n* **1** : tierra *f* comunal **2 in ~** : en común

common cold *n* : resfriado *m* común

common denominator *n* : denominador *m* común

commoner ['kamənər] *n* : plebeyo *m*, -ya *f*

commonly ['kamənli] *adv* **1** FREQUENTLY : comúnmente, frecuentemente **2** USUALLY : normalmente

common noun *n* : nombre *m* común

commonplace¹ ['kamən,pleɪs] *adj* : común, ordinario

commonplace² *n* : cliché *m*, tópico *m*

common sense *n* : sentido *m* común

commonwealth ['kamən,welθ] *n* : entidad *f* política ⟨the British Commonwealth : la Mancomunidad Británica⟩

commotion [kə'mo:ʃən] *n* **1** RUCKUS : alboroto *m*, jaleo *m*, escándalo *m* **2** STIR, UPSET : revuelo *m*, conmoción *f*

communal [kə'mju:nəl] *adj* : comunal

commune¹ [kə'mju:n] *vi* **-muned; -muning** : estar en comunión

commune² ['ka,mju:n, kə'mju:n] *n* : comuna *f*

communicable [kə'mju:nɪkəbəl] *adj* CONTAGIOUS : transmisible, contagioso

communicate [kə'mju:nə,keɪt] *v* **-cated; -cating** *vt* **1** CONVEY : comunicar, expresar, hacer saber **2** TRANSMIT : transmitir (una enfermedad), contagiar — *vi* : comunicarse, expresarse

communication [kə,mju:nə'keɪʃən] *n* : comunicación *f*

communicative [kə'mju:nɪ,keɪtɪv, -kətɪv] *adj* : comunicativo

communion [kə'mju:njən] *n* **1** SHARING : comunión *f* **2 Communion** : comunión *f*, eucaristía *f*

communiqué [kə'mju:nə,keɪ, -,mju:nə'keɪ] *n* : comunicado *m*

communism *or* **Communism** ['kamjə,nɪzəm] *n* : comunismo *m*

communist¹ *or* **Communist** ['kamjə,nɪst] *adj* : comunista ⟨the Communist Party : el Partido Comunista⟩

communist² *or* **Communist** *n* : comunista *mf*

communistic *or* **Communistic** [,kamjə'nɪstɪk] *adj* : comunista

community [kə'mju:nəti] *n, pl* **-ties** : comunidad *f*

commute [kə'mju:t] *v* **-muted; -muting** *vt* REDUCE : conmutar, reducir (una sentencia) — *vi* : viajar de la residencia al trabajo

commuter [kə'mju:tər] *n* : persona *f* que viaja diariamente al trabajo

compact¹ [kəm'pækt, 'kam,pækt] *vt* : compactar, consolidar, comprimir

compact² [kəm'pækt, 'kam,pækt] *adj* **1** DENSE, SOLID : compacto, macizo, denso **2** CONCISE : breve, conciso

compact³ ['kam,pækt] *n* **1** AGREEMENT : acuerdo *m*, pacto *m* **2** : polvera *f*, estuche *m* de maquillaje **3** *or* **compact car** : auto *m* compacto

compact disc ['kam,pækt'dɪsk] *n* : disco *m* compacto, compact disc *m*

compactly [kəm'pæktli, 'kam,pækt-] *adv* **1** DENSELY : densamente, macizamente **2** CONCISELY : concisamente, brevemente

companion [kəm'pænjən] *n* **1** COMRADE : compañero *m*, -ra *f*; acompañante *mf* **2** MATE : pareja *f* (de un zapato, etc.)

companionable [kəm'pænjənəbəl] *adj* : sociable, amigable

companionship [kəm'pænjən,ʃɪp] *n* : compañerismo *m*, camaradería *f*

company ['kʌmpəni] *n, pl* **-nies 1** FIRM : compañía *f*, empresa *f* **2** GROUP : compañía *f* (de actores o soldados) **3** GUESTS : visita *f* ⟨we have company : tenemos visita⟩

comparable ['kampərəbəl] *adj* : comparable, parecido

comparative¹ [kəm'pærətɪv] *adj* RELATIVE : comparativo, relativo — **comparatively** *adv*

comparative² *n* : comparativo *m*

compare[1] [kəm'pær] v **-pared; -paring** vt : comparar — vi **to compare with** : poder comparar con, tener comparación con

compare[2] n : comparación f ⟨beyond compare : sin igual, sin par⟩

comparison [kəm'pærəsən] n : comparación f

compartment [kəm'pɑrtmənt] n : compartimento m, compartimiento m

compass ['kʌmpəs, 'kɑm-] n **1** RANGE, SCOPE : alcance m, extensión f, límites mpl **2** : compás m (para trazar circunferencias) **3** : compás m, brújula f ⟨the points of the compass : los puntos cardinales⟩

compassion [kəm'pæʃən] n : compasión f, piedad f, misericordia f

compassionate [kəm'pæʃənət] adj : compasivo

compatibility [kəm,pætə'bɪləti] n : compatibilidad f

compatible [kəm'pætəbəl] adj : compatible, afín

compatriot [kəm'peɪtriət, -'pæ-] n : compatriota mf; paisano m, -na f

compel [kəm'pɛl] vt **-pelled; -pelling** : obligar, compeler

compelling [kəm'pɛlɪŋ] adj **1** FORCEFUL : fuerte **2** ENGAGING : absorbente **3** PERSUASIVE : persuasivo, convincente

compendium [kəm'pɛndiəm] n, pl **-diums** or **-dia** [-diə] : compendio m

compensate ['kɑmpən,seɪt] v **-sated; -sating** vi **to compensate for** : compensar — vt : indemnizar, compensar

compensation [,kɑmpən'seɪʃən] n : compensación f, indemnización f

compensatory [kəm'pɛntsə,tori] adj : compensatorio

compete [kəm'pi:t] vi **-peted; -peting** : competir, contender, rivalizar

competence ['kɑmpətənts] n : competencia f, aptitud f

competency ['kɑmpətəntsi] → **competence**

competent ['kɑmpətənt] adj : competente, capaz

competition [,kɑmpə'tɪʃən] n : competencia f, concurso m

competitive [kəm'pɛtətɪv] adj : competitivo

competitor [kəm'pɛtətər] n : competidor m, -dora f

compilation [,kɑmpə'leɪʃən] n : recopilación f, compilación f

compile [kəm'paɪl] vt **-piled; -piling** : compilar, recopilar

complacency [kəm'pleɪsəntsi] n : satisfacción f consigo mismo, suficiencia f

complacent [kəm'pleɪsənt] adj : satisfecho de sí mismo, suficiente

complain [kəm'pleɪn] vi **1** GRIPE : quejarse, regañar, rezongar **2** PROTEST : reclamar, protestar

complaint [kəm'pleɪnt] n **1** GRIPE : queja f **2** AILMENT : afección f, dolencia f

3 ACCUSATION : reclamo m, acusación f

complement[1] ['kɑmplə,mɛnt] vt : complementar

complement[2] ['kɑmpləmənt] n : complemento m

complementary [,kɑmplə'mɛntəri] adj : complementario

complete[1] [kəm'pli:t] vt **-pleted; -pleting 1** : completar, hacer entero ⟨this piece completes the collection : esta pieza completa la colección⟩ **2** FINISH : completar, acabar, terminar ⟨she completed her studies : completó sus estudios⟩

complete[2] adj **-pleter; -est 1** WHOLE : completo, entero, íntegro **2** FINISHED : terminado, acabado **3** TOTAL : completo, total, absoluto

completely [kəm'pli:tli] adv : completamente, totalmente

completion [kəm'pli:ʃən] n : finalización f, cumplimiento m

complex[1] [kɑm'plɛks, kəm-; 'kɑm,plɛks] adj : complejo, complicado

complex[2] ['kɑm,plɛks] n : complejo m

complexion [kəm'plɛkʃən] n : cutis m, tez f ⟨of dark complexion : de tez morena⟩

complexity [kəm'plɛksəti, kɑm-] n, pl **-ties** : complejidad f

compliance [kəm'plaɪənts] n : conformidad f ⟨in compliance with the law : conforme a la ley⟩

compliant [kəm'plaɪənt] adj : dócil, sumiso

complicate ['kɑmplə,keɪt] vt **-cated; -cating** : complicar

complicated ['kɑmplə,keɪtəd] adj : complicado

complication [,kɑmplə'keɪʃən] n : complicación f

complicity [kəm'plɪsəti] n, pl **-ties** : complicidad f

compliment[1] ['kɑmplə,mɛnt] vt : halagar, florear Mex

compliment[2] ['kɑmpləmənt] n **1** : halago m, cumplido m **2 compliments** npl : saludos mpl ⟨give them my compliments : déles saludos de mi parte⟩

complimentary [,kɑmplə'mɛntəri] adj **1** FLATTERING : halagador, halagüeño **2** FREE : de cortesía, gratis

comply [kəm'plaɪ] vi **-plied; -plying** : cumplir, acceder, obedecer

component[1] [kəm'po:nənt, 'kɑm-,po:-] adj : componente

component[2] n : componente m, elemento m, pieza f

compose [kəm'po:z] vt **-posed; -posing 1** : componer, crear ⟨to compose a melody : componer una melodía⟩ **2** CALM : calmar, serenar ⟨to compose oneself : serenarse⟩ **3** CONSTITUTE : constar, componer ⟨to be composed of : constar de⟩ **4** : componer (un texto a imprimirse)

composer [kəm'po:zər] n : compositor m, -tora f

composite¹ [kam'pazət, kəm-; 'kam-pəzət] *adj* : compuesto (de varias partes)

composite² *n* : compuesto *m*, mezcla *f*

composition [ˌkampə'zɪʃən] *n* **1** MAKE-UP : composición *f* **2** ESSAY : ensayo *m*, trabajo *m*

compost ['kam,po:st] *n* : abono *m* vegetal

composure [kəm'po:ʒər] *n* : compostura *f*, serenidad *f*

compound¹ [kam'paʊnd, kəm-; 'kam-ˌpaʊnd] *vt* **1** COMBINE, COMPOSE : combinar, componer **2** AUGMENT : agravar, aumentar ⟨to compound a problem : agravar un problema⟩

compound² ['kam,paʊnd; kam'paʊnd, kəm-] *adj* : compuesto ⟨compound interest : interés compuesto⟩

compound³ ['kam,paʊnd] *n* **1** MIXTURE : compuesto *m*, mezcla *f* **2** ENCLOSURE : recinto *m* (de residencias, etc.)

compound fracture *n* : fractura *f* complicada

comprehend [ˌkamprɪ'hɛnd] *vt* **1** UNDERSTAND : comprender, entender **2** INCLUDE : comprender, incluir, abarcar

comprehensible [ˌkamprɪ'hɛntsəbəl] *adj* : comprensible

comprehension [ˌkamprɪ'hɛntʃən] *n* : comprensión *f*

comprehensive [ˌkamprɪ'hɛntsɪv] *adj* **1** INCLUSIVE : inclusivo, exhaustivo **2** BROAD : extenso, amplio

compress¹ [kəm'prɛs] *vt* : comprimir

compress² ['kam,prɛs] *n* : compresa *f*

compression [kəm'prɛʃən] *n* : compresión *f*

compressor [kəm'prɛsər] *n* : compresor *m*

comprise [kəm'praɪz] *vt* **-prised; -prising 1** INCLUDE : comprender, incluir **2** : componerse de, constar de ⟨the installation comprises several buildings : la instalación está compuesta de varios edificios⟩

compromise¹ ['kamprə,maɪz] *v* **-mised; -mising** *vi* : transigir, avenirse — *vt* JEOPARDIZE : comprometer, poner en peligro

compromise² *n* : acuerdo *m* mutuo, compromiso *m*

comptroller [kən'tro:lər, 'kamp-ˌtro:-] *n* : contralor *m*, -lora *f*; interventor *m*, -tora *f*

compulsion [kəm'pʌlʃən] *n* **1** COERCION : coacción *f* **2** URGE : compulsión *f*, impulso *m*

compulsive [kəm'pʌlsɪv] *adj* : compulsivo

compulsory [kəm'pʌlsəri] *adj* : obligatorio

compunction [kəm'pʌŋkʃən] *n* **1** QUALM : reparo *m*, escrúpulo *m* **2** REMORSE : remordimiento *m*

computation [ˌkampjʊ'teɪʃən] *n* : cálculo *m*, cómputo *m*

compute [kəm'pju:t] *vt* **-puted; -puting** : computar, calcular

computer [kəm'pju:ṭər] *n* : computadora *f*, computador *m*, ordenador *m* *Spain*

computerize [kəm'pju:ṭə,raɪz] *vt* **-ized; -izing** : computarizar, informatizar

comrade ['kam,ræd] *n* : camarada *mf*; compañero *m*, -ra *f*

con¹ ['kan] *vt* **conned; conning** SWINDLE : estafar, timar

con² *adv* : contra

con³ *n* : contra *m* ⟨the pros and cons : los pros y los contras⟩

concave [kan'keɪv, 'kan,keɪv] *adj* : cóncavo

conceal [kən'si:l] *vt* : esconder, ocultar, disimular

concealment [kən'si:lmənt] *n* : escondimiento *m*, ocultación *f*

concede [kən'si:d] *vt* **-ceded; -ceding 1** ALLOW, GRANT : conceder **2** ADMIT : conceder, reconocer ⟨to concede defeat : reconocer la derrota⟩

conceit [kən'si:t] *n* : engreimiento *m*, presunción *f*

conceited [kən'si:ṭəd] *adj* : presumido, engreído, presuntuoso

conceivable [kən'si:vəbəl] *adj* : concebible, imaginable

conceivably [kən'si:vəbli] *adv* : posiblemente, de manera concebible

conceive [kən'si:v] *v* **-ceived; -ceiving** *vi* : concebir, embarazarse — *vt* IMAGINE : concebir, imaginar

concentrate¹ ['kantsən,treɪt] *v* **-trated; -trating** *vt* : concentrar — *vi* : concentrarse

concentrate² *n* : concentrado *m*

concentration [ˌkantsən'treɪʃən] *n* : concentración *f*

concentric [kən'sɛntrɪk] *adj* : concéntrico

concept ['kan,spt] *n* : concepto *m*, idea *f*

conception [kən'sɛpʃən] *n* **1** : concepción *f* (de un bebé) **2** IDEA : concepto *m*, idea *f*

concern¹ [kən'sərn] *vt* **1** : tratarse de, tener que ver con ⟨the novel concerns a sailor : la novela se trata de un marinero⟩ **2** INVOLVE : concernir, incumbir a, afectar ⟨that does not concern me : eso no me incumbe⟩

concern² *n* **1** AFFAIR : asunto *m* **2** WORRY : inquietud *f*, preocupación *f* **3** BUSINESS : negocio *m*

concerned [kən'sərnd] *adj* **1** ANXIOUS : preocupado, ansioso **2** INTERESTED, INVOLVED : interesado, afectado

concerning [kən'sərnɪŋ] *prep* REGARDING : con respecto a, acerca de, sobre

concert ['kan,sərt] *n* **1** AGREEMENT : concierto *m*, acuerdo *m* **2** : concierto *m* (musical)

concerted [kən'sərṭəd] *adj* : concertado, coordinado ⟨to make a concerted effort : coordinar los esfuerzos⟩

concertina [ˌkantsər'ti:nə] *n* : concertina *f*

concerto [kən'tʃɛrtoː] *n, pl* **-ti** [-ti, -ˌtiː] *or* **-tos** : concierto *m* ⟨violin concerto : concierto para violín⟩

concession [kən'sɛʃən] *n* : concesión *f*

conch ['kaŋk, 'kantʃ] ['kaŋks] *or* **conches** ['kantʃəz] : caracol *m* (animal), caracola *f* (concha)

conciliatory [kən'sɪliəˌtori] *adj* : conciliador, conciliatorio

concise [kən'saɪs] *adj* : conciso, breve — **concisely** *adv*

conclave ['kanˌkleɪv] *n* : cónclave *m*

conclude [kən'kluːd] *v* **-cluded; -cluding** *vt* **1** END : concluir, finalizar ⟨to conclude a meeting : concluir una reunión⟩ **2** DECIDE : concluir, llegar a la conclusión de — *vi* END : concluir, terminar

conclusion [kən'kluːʒən] *n* **1** INFERENCE : conclusión *f* **2** END : fin *m*, final *m*

conclusive [kən'kluːsɪv] *adj* : concluyente, decisivo — **conclusively** *adv*

concoct [kən'kakt, kan-] *vt* **1** PREPARE : preparar, confeccionar **2** DEVISE : inventar, tramar

concoction [kən'kakʃən] *n* : invención *f*, mejunje *m*, brebaje *m*

concomitant [kən'kamətənt] *adj* : concomitante

concord ['kanˌkɔrd, 'kaŋ-] *n* **1** HARMONY : concordia *f*, armonía *f* **2** AGREEMENT : acuerdo *m*

concordance [kən'kɔrdənts] *n* : concordancia *f*

concourse ['kanˌkors] *n* : explanada *f*, salón *m* (para pasajeros)

concrete[1] ['kanˌkriːt, 'kanˌkriːt] *adj* **1** REAL : concreto ⟨concrete objects : objetos concretos⟩ **2** SPECIFIC : determinado, específico **3** : de concreto, de hormigón ⟨concrete walls : paredes de concreto⟩

concrete[2] ['kanˌkriːt, kan'kriːt] *n* : concreto *m*, hormigón *m*

concur [kən'kər] *vi* **concurred; concurring 1** COINCIDE : concurrir, coincidir **2** AGREE : concurrir, estar de acuerdo

concurrent [kən'kərənt] *adj* : concurrente, simultáneo

concussion [kən'kʌʃən] *n* : conmoción *f* cerebral

condemn [kən'dɛm] *vt* **1** CENSURE : condenar, reprobar, censurar **2** : declarar insalubre (alimentos), declarar ruinoso (un edificio) **3** SENTENCE : condenar ⟨condemned to death : condenado a muerte⟩

condemnation [ˌkanˌdɛm'neɪʃən] *n* : condena *f*, reprobación *f*

condensation [ˌkanˌdɛn'seɪʃən, -dən-] *n* : condensación *f*

condense [kən'dɛnts] *v* **-densed; -densing** *vt* **1** ABRIDGE : condensar, resumir **2** : condensar (vapor, etc.) — *vi* : condensarse

condescend [ˌkandɪ'sɛnd] *vi* **1** DEIGN : condescender, dignarse **2** **to condescend to someone** : tratar a alguien con condescendencia

condescension [ˌkandɪ'sɛntʃən] *n* : condescendencia *f*

condiment ['kandəmənt] *n* : condimento *m*

condition[1] [kən'dɪʃən] *vt* **1** DETERMINE : condicionar, determinar **2** : acondicionar (el pelo o el aire), poner en forma (el cuerpo)

condition[2] *n* **1** STIPULATION : condición *f*, estipulación *f* ⟨on the condition that : a condición de que⟩ **2** STATE : condición *f*, estado *m* ⟨in poor condition : en malas condiciones⟩ **3 conditions** *npl* : condiciones *fpl*, situación *f* ⟨working conditions : condiciones del trabajo⟩

conditional [kən'dɪʃənəl] *adj* : condicional — **conditionally** *adv*

conditioner [kən'dɪʃənər] *n* : acondicionador *m*

condo ['kandoː] → **condominium**

condolence [kən'doːlənts] *n* **1** SYMPATHY : condolencia *f* **2 condolences** *npl* : pésame *m*

condom ['kandəm] *n* : condón *m*

condominium [ˌkandə'mɪniəm] *n, pl* **-ums** : condominio *m*

condone [kən'doːn] *vt* **-doned; -doning** : aprobar, perdonar, tolerar

condor ['kandər, -ˌdɔr] *n* : cóndor *m*

conducive [kən'duːsɪv, -'djuː-] *adj* : propicio, favorable

conduct[1] [kən'dʌkt] *vt* **1** GUIDE : guiar, conducir ⟨to conduct a tour : guiar una visita⟩ **2** DIRECT : conducir, dirigir ⟨to conduct an orchestra : dirigir una orquesta⟩ **3** CARRY OUT : realizar, llevar a cabo ⟨to conduct an investigation : llevar a cabo una investigación⟩ **4** TRANSMIT : conducir, transmitir (calor, electricidad, etc.) **5 to conduct oneself** BEHAVE : conducirse, comportarse

conduct[2] ['kanˌdʌkt] *n* **1** MANAGEMENT : conducción *f*, dirección *f*, manejo *m* ⟨the conduct of foreign affairs : la conducción de asuntos exteriores⟩ **2** BEHAVIOR : conducta *f*, comportamiento *m*

conduction [kən'dʌkʃən] *n* : conducción *f*

conductivity [ˌkanˌdʌk'tɪvəti] *n, pl* **-ties** : conductividad *f*

conductor [kən'dʌktər] *n* **1** : conductor *m*, -tora *f*; revisor *m*, -sora *f* (en un tren); cobrador *m*, -dora *f* (en un bus); director *m*, -tora *f* (de una orquesta) **2** : conductor *m* (de electricidad, etc.)

conduit ['kanˌduːət, -ˌdjuː-] *n* : conducto *m*, canal *m*, vía *f*

cone ['koːn] *n* **1** : piña *f* (fruto de las coníferas) **2** : cono *m* (en geometría) **3 ice–cream cone** : cono *m*, barquillo *m*, cucurucho *m*

confection [kən'fɛkʃən] *n* : dulce *m*

confectioner [kən'fɛkʃənər] *n* : confitero *m*, -ra *f*

confederacy [kən'fɛdərəsi] *n, pl* **-cies** : confederación *f*

confederate[1] [kən'fɛdə,reɪt] *v* **-ated;** **-ating** *vt* : unir, confederar — *vi* : confederarse, aliarse

confederate[2] [kən'fɛdərət] *adj* : confederado

confederate[3] *n* : cómplice *mf*; aliado *m*, -da *f*

confederation [kən,fɛdə'reɪʃən] *n* : confederación *f*, alianza *f*

confer [kən'fər] *v* **-ferred; -ferring** *vt* : conferir, otorgar — *vi* **to confer with** : consultar

conference ['kɑnfrənts, -fərənts] *n* : conferencia *f* ⟨press conference : conferencia de prensa⟩

confess [kən'fɛs] *vt* : confesar — *vi* **1** : confesar ⟨the prisoner confessed : el detenido confesó⟩ **2** : confesarse (en religión)

confession [kən'fɛʃən] *n* : confesión *f*

confessional [kən'fɛʃənəl] *n* : confesionario *m*

confessor [kən'fɛsər] *n* : confesor *m*

confetti [kən'fɛṭi] *n* : confeti *m*

confidant ['kɑnfə,dɑnt, -,dænt] *n* : confidente *mf*

confide [kən'faɪd] *v* **-fided; -fiding** : confiar

confidence ['kɑnfədənts] *n* **1** TRUST : confianza *f* **2** SELF-ASSURANCE : confianza *f* en sí mismo, seguridad *f* en sí mismo **3** SECRET : confidencia *f*, secreto *m*

confident ['kɑnfədənt] *adj* **1** SURE : seguro **2** SELF-ASSURED : confiado, seguro de sí mismo

confidential [,kɑnfə'dɛnʧəl] *adj* : confidencial — **confidentially** [,kɑnfə-'dɛnʧəli] *adv*

confidently ['kɑnfədəntli] *adv* : con seguridad, con confianza

configuration [kən,fɪgjə'reɪʃən] *n* : configuración *f*

confine [kən'faɪn] *vt* **-fined; -fining 1** LIMIT : confinar, restringir, limitar **2** IMPRISON : recluir, encarcelar, encerrar

confinement [kən'faɪnmənt] *n* : confinamiento *m*, reclusión *f*, encierro *m*

confines ['kɑn,faɪnz] *npl* : límites *mpl*, confines *mpl*

confirm [kən'fərm] *vt* **1** RATIFY : ratificar **2** VERIFY : confirmar, verificar **3** : confirmar (en religión)

confirmation [,kɑnfər'meɪʃən] *n* : confirmación *f*

confiscate ['kɑnfə,skeɪt] *vt* **-cated;** **-cating** : confiscar, incautar, decomisar

confiscation [,kɑnfə'skeɪʃən] *n* : confiscación *f*, incautación *f*, decomiso *m*

conflagration [,kɑnflə'greɪʃən] *n* : conflagración *f*

conflict[1] [kən'flɪkt] *vi* : estar en conflicto, oponerse

conflict[2] ['kɑn,flɪkt] *n* : conflicto *m* ⟨to be in conflict : estar en desacuerdo⟩

confluence ['kɑn,flu:ənts, kən'flu:ənts] *n* : confluencia *f*

conform [kən'fɔrm] *vi* **1** ACCORD, COMPLY : ajustarse, adaptarse, conformarse ⟨it conforms with our standards : se ajusta a nuestras normas⟩ **2** CORRESPOND : corresponder, encajar ⟨to conform to the truth : corresponder a la verdad⟩

conformity [kən'fɔrməṭi] *n, pl* **-ties** : conformidad *f*

confound [kən'faʊnd, kɑn-] *vt* : confundir, desconcertar

confront [kən'frʌnt] *vt* : afrontar, enfrentarse a, encarar

confrontation [,kɑnfrən'teɪʃən] *n* : enfrentamiento *m*, confrontación *f*

confuse [kən'fju:z] *vt* **-fused; -fusing 1** PUZZLE : confundir, enturbiar **2** COMPLICATE : confundir, enredar, complicar ⟨to confuse the issue : complicar las cosas⟩

confusing [kən'fju:zɪŋ] *adj* : complicado, que confunde

confusion [kən'fju:ʒən] *n* **1** PERPLEXITY : confusión *f* **2** MESS, TURMOIL : confusión *f*, embrollo *m*, lío *m fam*

congeal [kən'ʤi:l] *vi* **1** FREEZE : congelarse **2** COAGULATE, CURDLE : coagularse, cuajarse

congenial [kən'ʤi:niəl] *adj* : agradable, simpático

congenital [kən'ʤɛnəṭəl] *adj* : congénito

congest [kən'ʤɛst] *vt* **1** : congestionar (en la medicina) **2** OVERCROWD : abarrotar, atestar, congestionar (el tráfico) — *vi* : congestionarse

congestion [kən'ʤɛsʧən] *n* : congestión *f*

conglomerate[1] [kən'glɑmərət] *adj* : conglomerado

conglomerate[2] [kən'glɑmərət] *n* : conglomerado *m*

conglomeration [kən,glɑmə'reɪʃən] *n* : conglomerado *m*, acumulación *f*

Congolese [,kɑŋgə'li:z, -'li:s] *n* : congoleño *m*, -ña *f* — **Congolese** *adj*

congratulate [kən'græʤə,leɪt, -'græʧə-] *vt* **-lated; -lating** : felicitar

congratulation [kən,græʤə'leɪʃən, -,græʧə-] *n* : felicitación *f* ⟨congratulations! : ¡felicidades!, ¡enhorabuena!⟩

congregate ['kɑŋgrɪ,geɪt] *v* **-gated;** **-gating** *vi* : congregar, reunir — *vi* : congregarse, reunirse

congregation [,kɑŋgrɪ'geɪʃən] *n* **1** GATHERING : congregación *f*, fieles *mpl* (a un servicio religioso) **2** PARISHIONERS : feligreses *mpl*

congress ['kɑŋgrəs] *n* : congreso *m*

congressional [kən'grɛʃənəl, kɑn-] *adj* : del congreso

congressman ['kɑŋgrəsmən] *n, pl* **-men** [-mən, -,mɛn] : congresista *m*, diputado *m*

congresswoman ['kɑŋgrəs,wʊmən] *n*, *pl* **-women** [-,wɪmən] : congresista *f*, diputada *f*

congruence [kən'gru:ənts, 'kɑŋgru-ənts] *n* : congruencia *f*

congruent [kən'gru:ənt, 'kɑŋgruənt] *adj* : congruente

conic ['kɑnɪk] → **conical**

conical ['kɑnɪkəl] *adj* : cónico

conifer ['kɑnəfər, 'ko:-] *n* : conífera *f*

coniferous [ko:'nɪfərəs, kə-] *adj* : conífero

conjecture¹ [kən'ʤɛktʃər] *v* **-tured; -turing** : conjeturar

conjecture² *n* : conjetura *f*, presunción *f*

conjugal ['kɑnʤɪgəl, kən'ʤu:-] *adj* : conyugal

conjugate ['kɑnʤə,geɪt] *vt* **-gated; -gating** : conjugar

conjugation [,kɑnʤə'geɪʃən] *n* : conjugación *f*

conjunction [kən'ʤʌŋkʃən] *n* : conjunción *f* ⟨in conjunction with : en combinación con⟩

conjure ['kɑnʤər, 'kʌn-] *v* **-jured; -juring** *vt* **1** ENTREAT : rogar, suplicar **2 to conjure up** : hacer aparecer (apariciones), evocar (memorias, etc.) — *vi* : practicar la magia

conjurer *or* **conjuror** ['kɑnʤərər, 'kʌn-] *n* : mago *m*, -ga *f*; prestidigitador *m*, -dora *f*

connect [kə'nɛkt] *vi* : conectar, enlazar, empalmar, comunicarse — *vt* **1** JOIN, LINK : conectar, unir, juntar, vincular **2** RELATE : relacionar, asociar (ideas)

connection [kə'nɛkʃən] *n* : conexión *f*, enlace *m* ⟨professional connections : relaciones profesionales⟩

connective [kə'nɛktɪv] *adj* : conectivo, conjuntivo ⟨connective tissue : tejido conjuntivo⟩

connector [kə'nɛktər] *n* : conector *m*

connivance [kə'naɪvənts] *n* : connivencia *f*, complicidad *f*

connive [kə'naɪv] *vi* **-nived; -niving** CONSPIRE, PLOT : actuar en connivencia, confabularse, conspirar

connoisseur [,kɑnə'sər, -'sʊr] *n* : conocedor *m*, -dora *f*; entendido *m*, -da *f*

connotation [,kɑnə'teɪʃən] *n* : connotación *f*

connote [kə'no:t] *vt* **-noted; -noting** : connotar

conquer ['kɑŋkər] *vt* : conquistar, vencer

conqueror ['kɑŋkərər] *n* : conquistador *m*, -dora *f*

conquest ['kɑn,kwɛst, 'kɑŋ-] *n* : conquista *f*

conscience ['kɑntʃənts] *n* : conciencia *f*, consciencia *f* ⟨to have a clear conscience : tener la conciencia limpia⟩

conscientious [,kɑntʃi'ɛntʃəs] *adj* : concienzudo — **conscientiously** *adv*

conscious ['kɑntʃəs] *adj* **1** AWARE : consciente ⟨to become conscious of : darse cuenta de⟩ **2** ALERT, AWAKE : consciente **3** INTENTIONAL : intencional, deliberado

consciously ['kɑntʃəsli] *adv* INTENTIONALLY : intencionalmente, deliberadamente, a propósito

consciousness ['kɑntʃəsnəs] *n* **1** AWARENESS : conciencia *f*, consciencia *f* **2** : conocimiento *m* ⟨to lose consciousness : perder el conocimiento⟩

conscript¹ [kən'skrɪpt] *vt* : reclutar, alistar, enrolar

conscript² ['kɑn,skrɪpt] *n* : conscripto *m*, -ta *f*; recluta *mf*

consecrate ['kɑntsə,kreɪt] *vt* **-crated; -crating** : consagrar

consecration [,kɑntsə'kreɪʃən] *n* : consagración *f*, dedicación *f*

consecutive [kən'sɛkjətɪv] *adj* : consecutivo, seguido ⟨on five consecutive days : cinco días seguidos⟩

consecutively [kən'sɛkjətɪvli] *adv* : consecutivamente

consensus [kən'sɛntsəs] *n* : consenso *m*

consent¹ [kən'sɛnt] *vi* **1** AGREE : acceder, ponerse de acuerdo **2 to consent to do something** : consentir en hacer algo

consent² *n* : consentimiento *m*, permiso *m* ⟨by common consent : de común acuerdo⟩

consequence ['kɑntsə,kwɛnts, -kwənts] *n* **1** RESULT : consecuencia *f*, secuela *f* **2** IMPORTANCE : importancia *f*, trascendencia *f*

consequent ['kɑntsəkwənt, -,kwɛnt] *adj* : consiguiente

consequential [,kɑntsə'kwɛntʃəl] *adj* **1** CONSEQUENT : consiguiente **2** IMPORTANT : importante, trascendente, trascendental

consequently ['kɑntsəkwəntli, -,kwɛnt-] *adv* : por consiguiente, por ende, por lo tanto

conservation [,kɑntsər'veɪʃən] *n* : conservación *f*, protección *f*

conservationist [,kɑntsər'veɪʃənɪst] *n* : conservacionista *mf*

conservatism [kən'sərvə,tɪzəm] *n* : conservadurismo *m*

conservative¹ [kən'sərvətɪv] *adj* **1** : conservador **2** CAUTIOUS : moderado, cauteloso ⟨a conservative estimate : un cálculo moderado⟩

conservative² *n* : conservador *m*, -dora *f*

conservatory [kən'sərvə,tori] *n*, *pl* **-ries** : conservatorio *m*

conserve¹ [kən'sərv] *vt* **-served; -serving** : conservar, preservar

conserve² ['kɑn,sərv] *n* PRESERVES : confitura *f*

consider [kən'sɪdər] *vt* **1** CONTEMPLATE : considerar, pensar en ⟨we'd considered attending : habíamos pensado en asistir⟩ **2** : considerar, tener en cuenta ⟨consider the consequences : considera las consecuencias⟩ **3** JUDGE, REGARD : considerar, estimar

considerable [kən'sɪdərəbəl] *adj* : considerable — **considerably** [-bli] *adv*

considerate [kən'sɪdərət] *adj* : considerado, atento

consideration [kən,sɪdə'reɪʃən] *n* : consideración *f* ⟨to take into consideration : tener en cuenta⟩

considering [kən'sɪdərɪŋ] *prep* : teniendo en cuenta, visto

consign [kən'saɪn] *vt* 1 COMMIT, ENTRUST : confiar, encomendar 2 TRANSFER : consignar, transferir 3 SEND : consignar, enviar (mercancía)

consignment [kən'saɪnmənt] *n* 1 : envío *m*, remesa *f* 2 on ~ : en consignación

consist [kən'sɪst] *vi* 1 LIE : consistir ⟨success consists in hard work : el éxito consiste en trabajar duro⟩ 2 : constar, componerse ⟨the set consists of 5 pieces : el juego se compone de 5 piezas⟩

consistency [kən'sɪstəntsi] *n, pl* **-cies** 1 : consistencia *f* (de una mezcla o sustancia) 2 COHERENCE : coherencia *f* 3 UNIFORMITY : regularidad *f*, uniformidad *f*

consistent [kən'sɪstənt] *adj* 1 COMPATIBLE : compatible, coincidente ⟨consistent with policy : coincidente con la política⟩ 2 UNIFORM : uniforme, constante, regular — **consistently** [kən'sɪstəntli] *adv*

consolation [,kɑntsə'leɪʃə n] *n* 1 : consuelo *m* 2 **consolation prize** : premio *m* de consolación

console[1] [kən'so:l] *vt* **-soled; -soling** : consolar

console[2] ['kɑn,so:l] *n* : consola *f*

consolidate [kən'sɑlə,deɪt] *vt* **-dated; -dating** : consolidar, unir

consolidation [kən,sɑlə'deɪʃən] *n* : consolidación *f*

consommé [,kɑntsə'meɪ] *n* : consomé *m*

consonant ['kɑntsənənt] *n* : consonante *m*

consort[1] [kən'sɔrt] *vi* : asociarse, relacionarse, tener trato ⟨to consort with criminals : tener trato con criminales⟩

consort[2] ['kɑn,sɔrt] *n* : consorte *mf*

consortium [kən'sɔrʃəm] *n, pl* **-tia** [-ʃə] *or* **-tiums** [-ʃəmz] : consorcio *m*

conspicuous [kən'spɪkjuəs] *adj* 1 OBVIOUS : visible, evidente 2 STRIKING : llamativo

conspicuously [kən'spɪkjuəsli] *adv* : de manera llamativa

conspiracy [kən'spɪrəsi] *n, pl* **-cies** : conspiración *f*, complot *m*, confabulación *f*

conspirator [kən'spɪrətər] *n* : conspirador *m*, -dora *f*

conspire [kən'spaɪr] *vi* **-spired; -spiring** : conspirar, confabularse

constable ['kɑntstəbəl, 'kʌntstə-] *n* : agente *mf* de policía (en un pueblo)

constancy ['kɑntstəntsi] *n, pl* **-cies** : constancia *f*

constant[1] ['kɑntstənt] *adj* 1 FAITHFUL : leal, fiel 2 INVARIABLE : constante, invariable 3 CONTINUAL : constante, continuo

constant[2] *n* : constante *f*

constantly ['kɑntstəntli] *adv* : constantemente, continuamente

constellation [,kɑntstə'leɪʃən] *n* : constelación *f*

consternation [,kɑntstər'neɪʃən] *n* : consternación *f*

constipate ['kɑntstə,peɪt] *vt* **-pated; -pating** : estreñir

constipation [kɑntstə'peɪʃən] *n* : estreñimiento *m*, constipación *f* (de vientre)

constituency [kən'stɪtʃuəntsi] *n, pl* **-cies** 1 : distrito *m* electoral 2 : residentes *mpl* de un distrito electoral

constituent[1] [kən'stɪtʃuənt] *adj* 1 COMPONENT : constituyente, componente 2 : constituyente, constitutivo ⟨a constituent assembly : una asamblea constituyente⟩

constituent[2] *n* 1 COMPONENT : componente *m* 2 ELECTOR, VOTER : elector *m*, -tora *f*; votante *mf*

constitute ['kɑntstə,tu:t, -,tju:t] *vt* **-tuted; -tuting** 1 ESTABLISH : constituir, establecer 2 COMPOSE, FORM : constituir, componer

constitution [,kɑntstə'tu:ʃən, -'tju:-] *n* : constitución *f*

constitutional [,kɑntstə'tu:ʃənəl, -'tju:-] *adj* : constitucional

constitutionality [,kɑntstə,tu:ʃə'næləti, -,tju:-] *n* : constitucionalidad *f*

constrain [kən'streɪn] *vt* 1 COMPEL : constreñir, obligar 2 CONFINE : constreñir, limitar, restringir 3 RESTRAIN : contener, refrenar

constraint [kən'streɪnt] *n* : restricción *f*, limitación *f*

constrict [kən'strɪkt] *vt* : estrechar, apretar, comprimir

constriction [kən'strɪkʃən] *n* : estrechamiento *m*, compresión *f*

construct [kən'strʌkt] *vt* : construir

construction [kən'strʌkʃən] *n* : construcción *f*

constructive [kən'strʌktɪv] *adj* : constructivo

construe [kən'stru:] *vt* **-strued; -struing** : interpretar

consul ['kɑntsəl] *n* : cónsul *mf*

consular ['kɑntsələr] *adj* : consular

consulate ['kɑntsələt] *n* : consulado *m*

consult [kən'sʌlt] *vt* : consultar — *vi* **to consult with** : consultar con, solicitar la opinión de

consultant [kən'sʌltənt] *n* : consultor *m*, -tora *f*; asesor *m*, -sora *f*

consultation [,kɑntsəl'teɪʃən] *n* : consulta *f*

consumable [kən'su:məbəl] *adj* : consumible

consume [kən'su:m] *vt* **-sumed; -suming** : consumir, usar, gastar

consumer [kən'suːmər] *n* : consumidor *m*, -dora *f*

consummate¹ ['kɑntsə,meɪt] *vt* **-mated; -mating** : consumar

consummate² [kən'sʌmət, 'kɑntsə-mət] *adj* : consumado, perfecto

consummation [,kɑntsə'meɪʃən] *n* : consumación *f*

consumption [kən'sʌmpʃən] *n* **1** USE : consumo *m*, uso *m* ⟨consumption of electricity : consumo de electricidad⟩ **2** TUBERCULOSIS : tisis *f*, consunción *f*

contact¹ ['kɑn,tækt, kən'-] *vt* : ponerse en contacto con, contactar (con)

contact² ['kɑn,tækt] *n* **1** TOUCHING : contacto *m* ⟨to come into contact with : entrar en contacto con⟩ **2** TOUCH : contacto *m*, comunicación *f* ⟨to lose contact with : perder contacto con⟩ **3** CONNECTION : contacto *m* (en negocios) **4** → **contact lens**

contact lens ['kɑn,tækt'lɛnz] *n* : lente *mf* de contacto, pupilente *m Mex*

contagion [kən'teɪʤən] *n* : contagio *m*

contagious [kən'teɪʤəs] *adj* : contagioso

contain [kən'teɪn] *vt* **1** : contener **2 to contain oneself** : contenerse

container [kən'teɪnər] *n* : recipiente *m*, envase *m*

containment [kən'teɪnmənt] *n* : contención *f*

contaminant [kən'tæmənənt] *n* : contaminante *m*

contaminate [kən'tæmə,neɪt] *vt* **-nated; -nating** : contaminar

contamination [kən,tæmə'neɪʃən] *n* : contaminación *f*

contemplate ['kɑntəm,pleɪt] *v* **-plated; -plating** *vt* **1** VIEW : contemplar **2** PONDER : contemplar, considerar **3** CONSIDER, PROPOSE : proponerse, proyectar, pensar en ⟨to contemplate a trip : pensar en viajar⟩ — *vi* MEDITATE : meditar

contemplation [,kɑntəm'pleɪʃən] *n* : contemplación *f*

contemplative [kən'tɛmplətɪv, 'kɑntəm,pleɪtɪv] *adj* : contemplativo

contemporaneous [kən,tɛmpə'reɪniəs] *adj* → **contemporary¹**

contemporary¹ [kən'tɛmpə,rɛri] *adj* : contemporáneo

contemporary² *n, pl* **-raries** : contemporáneo *m*, -nea *f*

contempt [kən'tɛmpt] *n* **1** DISDAIN : desprecio *m*, desdén *m* ⟨to hold in contempt : despreciar⟩ **2** : desacato *m* (ante un tribunal)

contemptible [kən'tɛmptəbəl] *adj* : despreciable, vil

contemptuous [kən'tɛmptʃuəs] *adj* : despectivo, despreciativo, desdeñoso

contemptuously [kən'tɛmptʃuəsli] *adv* : despectivamente, con desprecio

contend [kən'tɛnd] *vi* **1** STRUGGLE : luchar, lidiar, contender ⟨to contend with a problem : lidiar con un proble-

ma⟩ **2** COMPETE : competir ⟨to contend for a position : competir por un puesto⟩ — *vt* **1** ARGUE, MAINTAIN : argüir, sostener, afirmar ⟨he contended that he was right : afirmó que tenía razón⟩ **2** CONTEST : protestar contra (una decisión, etc.), disputar

contender [kən'tɛndər] *n* : contendiente *mf*; aspirante *mf*; competidor *m*, -dora *f*

content¹ [kən'tɛnt] *vt* SATISFY : contentar, satisfacer

content² *adj* : conforme, contento, satisfecho

content³ *n* CONTENTMENT : contento *m*, satisfacción *f* ⟨to one's heart's content : hasta quedar satisfecho, a más no poder⟩

content⁴ ['kɑn,tɛnt] *n* **1** MEANING : contenido *m*, significado *m* **2** PROPORTION : contenido *m*, proporción *f* ⟨fat content : contenido de grasa⟩ **3 contents** *npl* : contenido *m*, sumario *m* (de un libro) ⟨table of contents : índice de materias⟩

contented [kən'tɛntəd] *adj* : conforme, satisfecho ⟨a contented smile : una sonrisa de satisfacción⟩

contentedly [kən'tɛntədli] *adv* : con satisfacción

contention [kən'tɛntʃən] *n* **1** DISPUTE : disputa *f*, discusión *f* **2** COMPETITION : competencia *f*, contienda *f* **3** OPINION : argumento *m*, opinión *f*

contentious [kən'tɛntʃəs] *adj* : disputador, pugnaz, combativo

contentment [kən'tɛntmənt] *n* : satisfacción *f*, contento *m*

contest¹ [kən'tɛst] *vt* : disputar, cuestionar, impugnar ⟨to contest a will : impugnar un testamento⟩

contest² ['kɑn,tɛst] *n* **1** STRUGGLE : lucha *f*, contienda *f* **2** GAME : concurso *m*, competencia *f*

contestable [kən'tɛstəbəl] *adj* : discutible, cuestionable

contestant [kən'tɛstənt] *n* : concursante *mf*; competidor *m*, -dora *f*

context ['kɑn,tɛkst] *n* : contexto *m*

contiguous [kən'tɪgjuəs] *adj* : contiguo

continence ['kɑntənənts] *n* : continencia *f*

continent¹ ['kɑntənənt] *adj* : continente

continent² *n* : continente *m* — **continental** [,kɑntən'ɛntəl] *adj*

contingency [kən'tɪnʤəntsi] *n, pl* **-cies** : contingencia *f*, eventualidad *f*

contingent¹ [kən'tɪnʤənt] *adj* **1** POSSIBLE : contingente, eventual **2** ACCIDENTAL : fortuito, accidental **3 to be contingent on** : depender de, estar sujeto a

contingent² *n* : contingente *m*

continual [kən'tɪnjuəl] *adj* : continuo, constante — **continually** [kən-'tɪnjuəli, -'tɪnjəli] *adv*

continuance [kən'tɪnjuənts] *n* **1** CONTINUATION : continuación *f* **2** DURA-

TION : duración *f* **3** : aplazamiento *m* (de un proceso)

continuation [kən‚tɪnju'eɪʃən] *n* : continuación *f*, prolongación *f*

continue [kən'tɪnju:] *v* **-tinued; -tinuing** *vi* **1** CARRY ON : continuar, seguir, proseguir ⟨please continue : continúe, por favor⟩ **2** ENDURE, LAST : continuar, prolongarse, durar **3** RESUME : continuar, reanudarse — *vt* **1** : continuar, seguir ⟨she continued writing : continuó escribiendo⟩ **2** RESUME : continuar, reanudar **3** EXTEND, PROLONG : continuar, prolongar

continuity [‚kɑntə-'nu:əti, -'nju:-] *n, pl* **-ties** : continuidad *f*

continuous [kən'tɪnjuəs] *adj* : continuo — **continuously** *adv*

contort [kən'tɔrt] *vt* : torcer, retorcer, contraer (el rostro) — *vi* : contraerse, demudarse

contortion [kən'tɔrʃən] *n* : contorsión *f*

contour [ˈkɑn‚tʊr] *n* **1** OUTLINE : contorno *m* **2 contours** *npl* SHAPE : forma *f*, curvas *fpl* **3 contour map** : mapa *m* topográfico

contraband [ˈkɑntrə‚bænd] *n* : contrabando *m*

contraception [‚kɑntrə'sɛpʃən] *n* : anticoncepción *f*, contracepción *f*

contraceptive¹ [‚kɑntrə'sɛptɪv] *adj* : anticonceptivo, contraceptivo

contraceptive² *n* : anticonceptivo *m*, contraceptivo *m*

contract¹ [kən'trækt, **1** *usu* ˈkɑn‚trækt] *vt* **1** : contratar (servicios profesionales) **2** : contraer (una enfermedad, una deuda) **3** TIGHTEN : contraer (un músculo) **4** SHORTEN : contraer (una palabra) — *vi* : contraerse, reducirse

contract² [ˈkɑn‚trækt] *n* : contrato *m*

contraction [kən'trækʃən] *n* : contracción *f*

contractor [ˈkɑn‚træktər, kən'træk-] *n* : contratista *mf*

contractual [kən'træktʃuəl] *adj* : contractual — **contractually** *adv*

contradict [‚kɑntrə'dɪkt] *vt* : contradecir, desmentir

contradiction [‚kɑntrə'dɪkʃən] *n* : contradicción *f*

contradictory [‚kɑntrə'dɪktəri] *adj* : contradictorio

contralto [kən'træl‚to:] *n, pl* **-tos** : contralto *m* (voz), contralto *mf* (vocalista)

contraption [kən'træpʃən] *n* DEVICE : aparato *m*, artefacto *m*

contrary¹ [ˈkɑn‚treri, **2** *often* kən-'treri] *adj* **1** OPPOSITE : contrario, opuesto **2** BALKY, STUBBORN : terco, testarudo **3 contrary to** : al contrario de, en contra de ⟨contrary to the facts : en contra de los hechos⟩

contrary² [ˈkɑn‚treri] *n, pl* **-traries 1** OPPOSITE : lo contrario, lo opuesto **2 on the contrary** : al contrario, todo lo contrario

contrast¹ [kən'træst] *vi* DIFFER : contrastar, diferir — *vt* COMPARE : contrastar, comparar

contrast² [ˈkɑn‚træst] *n* : contraste *m*

contravene [‚kɑntrə'vi:n] *vt* **-vened; -vening** : contravenir, infringir

contribute [kən'trɪbjət] *v* **-uted; -uting** *vt* : contribuir, aportar (dinero, bienes, etc.) — *vi* : contribuir

contribution [‚kɑntrə'bju:ʃən] *n* : contribución *f*

contributor [kən'trɪbjətər] *n* : contribuidor *m*, -dora *f*; colaborador *m*, -dora *f* (en periodismo)

contrite [ˈkɑn‚traɪt, kən'traɪt] *adj* REPENTANT : contrito, arrepentido

contrition [kən'trɪʃən] *n* : contrición *f*, arrepentimiento *m*

contrivance [kən'traɪvənts] *n* **1** DEVICE : aparato *m*, artefacto *m* **2** SCHEME : artimaña *f*, treta *f*, ardid *m*

contrive [kən'traɪv] *vt* **-trived; -triving 1** DEVISE : idear, ingeniar, maquinar **2** MANAGE : lograr, ingeniárselas para ⟨she contrived a way out of the mess : se las ingenió para salir del enredo⟩

control¹ [kən'tro:l] *vt* **-trolled; -trolling** : controlar, dominar

control² *n* **1** : control *m*, dominio *m*, mando *m* ⟨to be under control : estar bajo control⟩ **2** RESTRAINT : control *m*, limitación *f* ⟨birth control : control natal⟩ **3** : control *m*, dispositivo *m* de mando ⟨remote control : control remoto⟩

controllable [kən'tro:ləbəl] *adj* : controlable

controller [kən'tro:lər, ˈkɑn‚-] *n* **1** → **comptroller 2** : controlador *m*, -dora *f* ⟨air traffic controller : controlador aéreo⟩

controversial [‚kɑntrə'vərʃəl, -siəl] *adj* : controvertido ⟨a controversial decision : una decisión controvertida⟩

controversy [ˈkɑntrə‚vərsi] *n, pl* **-sies** : controversia *f*

controvert [ˈkɑntrə‚vərt, ‚kɑntrə'-] *vt* : controvertir, contradecir

contusion [kən'tu:ʒən, -tju:-] *n* BRUISE : contusión *f*, moretón *m*

conundrum [kə'nʌndrəm] *n* RIDDLE : acertijo *m*, adivinanza *f*

convalesce [‚kɑnvə'lɛs] *vi* **-lesced; -lescing** : convalecer

convalescence [‚kɑnvə'lɛsənts] *n* : convalecencia *f*

convalescent¹ [‚kɑnvə'lɛsənt] *adj* : convaleciente

convalescent² *n* : convaleciente *mf*

convection [kən'vɛkʃən] *n* : convección *f*

convene [kən'vi:n] *v* **-vened; -vening** *vt* : convocar — *vi* : reunirse

convenience [kən'vi:njənts] *n* **1** : conveniencia *f* ⟨at your convenience : cuando le resulte conveniente⟩ **2** AMENITY : comodidad *f* ⟨modern conveniences : comodidades modernas⟩

convenience store *n* : tienda *f* de conveniencia

convenient [kən'vi:njənt] *adj* : conveniente, cómodo — **conveniently** *adv*

convent ['kɑnvənt, -ˌvɛnt] *n* : convento *m*

convention [kən'vɛntʃən] *n* **1** PACT : convención *f*, convenio *m*, pacto *m* ⟨the Geneva Convention : la Convención de Ginebra⟩ **2** MEETING : convención *f*, congreso *m* **3** CUSTOM : convención *f*, convencionalismo *m*

conventional [kən'vɛntʃənəl] *adj* : convencional — **conventionally** *adv*

converge [kən'vərdʒ] *vi* **-verged; -verging** : converger, convergir

convergence [kən'vərdʒənts] *n* : convergencia *f*

convergent [kən'vərdʒənt] *adj* : convergente

conversant [kən'vərsənt] *adj* **conversant with** : versado con, experto en

conversation [ˌkɑnvər'seɪʃən] *n* : conversación *f*

conversational [ˌkɑnvər'seɪʃənəl] *adj* : familiar ⟨a conversational style : un estilo familiar⟩

converse¹ [kən'vərs] *vi* **-versed; -versing** : conversar

converse² [kən'vərs, 'kɑnˌvərs] *adj* : contrario, opuesto, inverso

conversely [kən'vərsli, 'kɑnˌvərs-] *adv* : a la inversa

conversion [kən'vərʒən] *n* **1** CHANGE : conversión *f*, transformación *f*, cambio *m* **2** : conversión *f* (a una religión)

convert¹ [kən'vərt] *vt* **1** : convertir (a una religión o un partido) **2** CHANGE : convertir, cambiar — *vi* : convertirse

convert² ['kɑnˌvərt] *n* : converso *m*, -sa *f*

converter *or* **convertor** [kən'vərtər] *n* : convertidor *m*

convertible¹ [kən'vərtəbəl] *adj* : convertible

convertible² *n* : convertible *m*, descapotable *m*

convex [kɑn'vɛks, 'kɑnˌ-, kən'-] *adj* : convexo

convey [kən'veɪ] *vt* **1** TRANSPORT : transportar, conducir **2** TRANSMIT : transmitir, comunicar, expresar (noticias, ideas, etc.)

conveyance [kən'veɪənts] *n* **1** TRANSPORT : transporte *m*, transportación *f* **2** COMMUNICATION : transmisión *f*, comunicación *f* **3** TRANSFER : transferencia *f*, traspaso *m* (de una propiedad)

conveyor [kən'veɪər] *n* : transportador *m*, -dora *f* ⟨conveyor belt : cinta transportadora⟩

convict¹ [kən'vɪkt] *vt* : declarar culpable

convict² ['kɑnˌvɪkt] *n* : preso *m*, -sa *f*; presidiario *m*, -ria *f*; recluso *m*, -sa *f*

conviction [kən'vɪkʃən] *n* **1** : condena *f* (de un acusado) **2** BELIEF : convicción *f*, creencia *f*

convince [kən'vɪnts] *vt* **-vinced; -vincing** : convencer

convincing [kən'vɪntsɪŋ] *adj* : convincente, persuasivo

convincingly [kən'vɪntsɪŋli] *adv* : de forma convincente

convivial [kən'vɪvjəl, -'vɪviəl] *adj* : jovial, festivo, alegre

conviviality [kənˌvɪvi'æləti] *n, pl* **-ties** : jovialidad *f*

convoke [kən'vo:k] *vt* **-voked; -voking** : convocar

convoluted ['kɑnvəˌlu:təd] *adj* : intrincado, complicado

convoy ['kɑnˌvɔɪ] *n* : convoy *m*

convulse [kən'vʌls] *v* **-vulsed; -vulsing** *vt* : convulsionar ⟨convulsed with laughter : muerto de risa⟩ — *vi* : sufrir convulsiones

convulsion [kən'vʌlʃən] *n* : convulsión *f*

convulsive [kən'vʌlsɪv] *adj* : convulsivo — **convulsively** *adv*

coo¹ ['ku:] *vi* : arrullar

coo² *n* : arrullo *m* (de una paloma)

cook¹ ['kʊk] *vi* : cocinar — *vt* **1** : preparar (comida) **2 to cook up** CONCOCT : inventar, tramar

cook² *n* : cocinero *m*, -ra *f*

cookbook ['kʊkˌbʊk] *n* : libro *m* de cocina

cookery ['kʊkəri] *n, pl* **-eries** : cocina *f*

cookie *or* **cooky** ['kʊki] *n, pl* **-ies** : galleta *f* (dulce)

cooking ['kʊkɪŋ] *n* **1** COOKERY : cocina *f* **2** : cocción *f*, cocimiento *m* ⟨cooking time : tiempo de cocción⟩

cookout ['kʊkˌaʊt] *n* : comida *f* al aire libre

cool¹ ['ku:l] *vt* : refrescar, enfriar — *vi* **1** : refrescarse, enfriarse ⟨the pie is cooling : el pastel se está enfriando⟩ **2** : calmarse, tranquilizarse ⟨his anger cooled : su ira se calmó⟩

cool² *adj* **1** : fresco, frío ⟨cool weather : tiempo fresco⟩ **2** CALM : tranquilo, sereno **3** ALOOF : frío, distante

cool³ *n* **1** : fresco *m* ⟨the cool of the evening : el fresco de la tarde⟩ **2** COMPOSURE : calma *f*, serenidad *f*

coolant ['ku:lənt] *n* : refrigerante *m*

cooler ['ku:lər] *n* : nevera *f* portátil

coolie ['ku:li] *n* : culi *m*

coolly ['ku:lli] *adv* **1** CALMLY : con calma, tranquilamente **2** COLDLY : fríamente, con frialdad

coolness ['ku:lnəs] *n* **1** : frescura *f*, frescor *m* ⟨the coolness of the evening : el frescor de la noche⟩ **2** CALMNESS : tranquilidad *f*, serenidad *f* **3** COLDNESS, INDIFFERENCE : frialdad *f*, indiferencia *f*

coop¹ ['ku:p, 'kʊp] *vt or* **to coop up** : encerrar ⟨cooped up in the house : encerrado en la casa⟩

coop² *n* : gallinero *m*

co-op ['ko:ˌɑp] *n* → **cooperative²**

cooperate [ko'ɑpəˌreɪt] *vi* **-ated; -ating** : cooperar, colaborar

cooperation [ko͜ͺɑpəˈreɪʃən] *n* : cooperación *f*, colaboración *f*
cooperative[1] [koˈɑpərətɪv, -ˈɑpəˌreɪtɪv] *adj* : cooperativo
cooperative[2] [koˈɑpərətɪv] *n* : cooperativa *f*
co–opt [koˈɑpt] *vt* 1 : nombrar como miembro, cooptar 2 APPROPRIATE : apropiarse de
coordinate[1] [koˈɔrdənˌeɪt] *v* -nated; -nating *vt* : coordinar — *vi* : coordinarse, combinar, acordar
coordinate[2] [koˈɔrdənət] *adj* 1 COORDINATED : coordinado 2 EQUAL : igual, semejante
coordinate[3] [koˈɔrdənət] *n* : coordenada *f*
coordination [koͺɔrdənˈeɪʃən] *n* : coordinación *f*
coordinator [koˈɔrdənˌeɪtər] *n* : coordinador *m*, -dora *f*
cop[1] [ˈkɑp] → **police officer**
cope [ˈkoːp] *vi* **coped; coping** 1 : arreglárselas 2 **to cope with** : hacer frente a, poder con ⟨I can't cope with all this! : ¡no puedo con todo esto!⟩
copier [ˈkɑpiər] *n* : copiadora *f*, fotocopiadora *f*
copilot [ˈkoːˌpaɪlət] *n* : copiloto *m*
copious [ˈkoːpiəs] *adj* : copioso, abundante — **copiously** *adv*
copiousness [ˈkoːpiəsnəs] *n* : abundancia *f*
copper [ˈkɑpər] *n* : cobre *m*
coppery [ˈkɑpəri] *adj* : cobrizo
copra [ˈkoːprə, ˈkɑ-] *n* : copra *f*
copse [ˈkɑps] *n* THICKET : soto *m*, matorral *m*
copulate [ˈkɑpjəˌleɪt] *vi* -lated; -lating : copular
copulation [ͺkɑpjəˈleɪʃən] *n* : cópula *f*, relaciones *fpl* sexuales
copy[1] [ˈkɑpi] *vt* **copied; copying** 1 DUPLICATE : hacer una copia de, duplicar, reproducir 2 IMITATE : copiar, imitar
copy[2] *n, pl* **copies** 1 : copia *f*, duplicado *m* (de un documento), reproducción *f* (de una obra de arte) 2 : ejemplar *m* (de un libro), número *m* (de una revista) 3 TEXT : manuscrito *m*, texto *m*
copyright[1] [ˈkɑpiˌraɪt] *vt* : registrar los derechos de
copyright[2] *n* : derechos *mpl* de autor
coral[1] [ˈkɔrəl] *adj* : de coral ⟨a coral reef : un arrecife de coral⟩
coral[2] *n* : coral *m*
coral snake *n* : serpiente *f* de coral
cord [ˈkɔrd] *n* 1 ROPE, STRING : cuerda *f*, cordón *m*, cordel *m* 2 : cuerda *f*, cordón *m*, médula *f* (en la anatomía) ⟨vocal cords : cuerdas vocales⟩ 3 : cuerda *f* ⟨a cord of firewood : una cuerda de leña⟩ 4 *or* **electric cord** : cable *m* eléctrico
cordial[1] [ˈkɔrdʒəl] *adj* : cordial — **cordially** *adv*
cordial[2] *n* : cordial *m*

cordiality [ͺkɔrdʒiˈæləti] *n* : cordialidad *f*
cordless [ˈkɔrdləs] *adj* : inalámbrico
cordon[1] [ˈkɔrdən] *vt* **to cordon off** : acordonar
cordon[2] *n* : cordón *m*
corduroy [ˈkɔrdəˌrɔɪ] *n* 1 : pana *f* 2 **corduroys** *npl* : pantalones *mpl* de pana
core[1] [ˈkor] *vt* **cored; coring** : quitar el corazón a (una fruta)
core[2] *n* 1 : corazón *m*, centro *m* (de algunas frutas) 2 CENTER : núcleo *m*, centro *m* 3 ESSENCE : núcleo *m*, meollo *m* ⟨to the core : hasta la médula⟩
coriander [ˈkoriͺændər] *n* : cilantro *m*
cork[1] [ˈkɔrk] *vt* : ponerle un corcho a
cork[2] *n* : corcho *m*
corkscrew [ˈkɔrkˌskruː] *n* : tirabuzón *m*, sacacorchos *m*
cormorant [ˈkɔrmərənt, -ͺrænt] *n* : cormorán *m*
corn[1] [ˈkɔrn] *vt* : conservar en salmuera ⟨corned beef : carne en conserva⟩
corn[2] *n* 1 GRAIN : grano *m* 2 : maíz *m*, elote *m* *Mex* ⟨corn tortillas : tortillas de maíz⟩ 3 : callo *m* ⟨corn plaster : emplasto para callos⟩
corncob [ˈkɔrnˌkɑb] *n* : mazorca *f* (de maíz), choclo *m*, elote *m* *CA, Mex*
cornea [ˈkɔrniə] *n* : córnea *f*
corner[1] [ˈkɔrnər] *vt* 1 TRAP : acorralar, arrinconar 2 MONOPOLIZE : monopolizar, acaparar (un mercado) — *vi* : tomar una curva, doblar una esquina (en un automóvil)
corner[2] *n* 1 ANGLE : rincón *m*, esquina *f*, ángulo *m* ⟨the corner of a room : el rincón de una sala⟩ ⟨all corners of the world : todos los rincones del mundo⟩ ⟨to cut corners : atajar, economizar esfuerzos⟩ 2 INTERSECTION : esquina *f* 3 IMPASSE, PREDICAMENT : aprieto *m*, impasse *m* ⟨to be backed into a corner : estar acorralado⟩
cornerstone [ˈkɔrnərˌstoːn] *n* : piedra *f* angular
cornet [kɔrˈnɛt] *n* : corneta *f*
cornfield [ˈkɔrnˌfiːld] *n* : maizal *m*; milpa *f* *CA, Mex*
cornice [ˈkɔrnɪs] *n* : cornisa *f*
cornmeal [ˈkɔrnˌmiːl] *n* : harina *f* de maíz
cornstalk [ˈkɔrnˌstɔk] *n* : tallo *m* del maíz
cornstarch [ˈkɔrnˌstɑrtʃ] *n* : maicena *f*, almidón *m* de maíz
cornucopia [ͺkɔrnəˈkoːpiə, -njə-] *n* : cornucopia *f*
corolla [kəˈrɑlə] *n* : corola *f*
corollary [ˈkɔrəͺlɛri] *n, pl* -laries : corolario *m*
corona [kəˈroːnə] *n* : corona *f* (del sol)
coronary[1] [ˈkɔrəͺnɛri] *adj* : coronario
coronary[2] *n, pl* -naries 1 : trombosis *f* coronaria 2 HEART ATTACK : infarto *m*, ataque *m* al corazón
coronation [ͺkɔrəˈneɪʃən] *n* : coronación *f*

coroner ['kɔrənər] *n* : médico *m* forense
corporal[1] ['kɔrpərəl] *adj* : corporal ⟨corporal punishment : castigos corporales⟩
corporal[2] *n* : cabo *m*
corporate ['kɔrpərət] *adj* : corporativo, empresarial
corporation [ˌkɔrpə'reɪʃən] *n* : sociedad *f* anónima, corporación *f*, empresa *f*
corporeal [kɔr'pɔriəl] *adj* **1** PHYSICAL : corpóreo **2** MATERIAL : material, tangible — **corporeally** *adv*
corps ['kor] *n, pl* **corps** ['korz] : cuerpo *m* ⟨medical corps : cuerpo médico⟩ ⟨diplomatic corps : cuerpo diplomático⟩
corpse ['kɔrps] *n* : cadáver *m*
corpulence ['kɔrpjələnts] *n* : obesidad *f*, gordura *f*
corpulent ['kɔrpjələnt] *adj* : obeso, gordo
corpuscle ['kɔr,pʌsəl] *n* : corpúsculo *m*, glóbulo *m* (sanguíneo)
corral[1] [kə'ræl] *vt* **-ralled; -ralling** : acorralar, encorralar (ganado)
corral[2] *n* : corral *m*
correct[1] [kə'rɛkt] *vt* **1** RECTIFY : corregir, rectificar **2** REPRIMAND : corregir, reprender
correct[2] *adj* **1** ACCURATE, RIGHT : correcto, exacto ⟨to be correct : estar en lo cierto⟩ **2** PROPER : correcto, apropiado
correction [kə'rɛkʃən] *n* : corrección *f*
corrective [kə'rɛktɪv] *adj* : correctivo
correctly [kə'rɛktli] *adv* : correctamente
correctness [kə'rɛk(t)nəs] *n* **1** ACCURACY : exactitud *f* **2** PROPRIETY : corrección *f*
correlate ['kɔrə,leɪt] *vt* **-lated; -lating** : relacionar, poner en correlación
correlation [ˌkɔrə'leɪʃən] *n* : correlación *f*
correspond [ˌkɔrə'spɑnd] *vi* **1** MATCH : corresponder, concordar, coincidir **2** WRITE : corresponderse, escribirse
correspondence [ˌkɔrə'spɑndənts] *n* : correspondencia *f*
correspondent [ˌkɔrə'spɑndənt] *n* : corresponsal *mf*
corresponding [kɔrə'spɑndɪŋ, kɑr-] *adj* : correspondiente
correspondingly [ˌkɔrə'spɑndɪŋli] *adv* : en consecuencia, de la misma manera
corridor ['kɔrədər, -,dɔr] *n* : corredor *m*, pasillo *m*
corroborate [kə'rɑbə,reɪt] *vt* **-rated; -rating** : corroborar
corroboration [kə,rɑbə'reɪʃən] *n* : corroboración *f*
corrode [kə'ro:d] *v* **-roded; -roding** *vt* : corroer — *vi* : corroerse
corrosion [kə'ro:ʒən] *n* : corrosión *f*
corrosive [kə'ro:sɪv] *adj* : corrosivo
corrugate ['kɔrə,geɪt] *vt* **-gated; -gating** : ondular, acanalar, corrugar

corrugated ['kɔrə,geɪtəd] *adj* : ondulado, acanalado ⟨corrugated cardboard : cartón ondulado⟩
corrupt[1] [kə'rʌpt] *vt* **1** PERVERT : corromper, pervertir, degradar (información) **2** BRIBE : sobornar
corrupt[2] *adj* : corrupto, corrompido
corruptible [kə'rʌptəbəl] *adj* : corruptible
corruption [kə'rʌpʃən] *n* : corrupción *f*
corsage [kɔr'sɑʒ, -'sɑʤ] *n* : ramillete *m* que se lleva como adorno
corset ['kɔrsət] *n* : corsé *m*
cortex ['kɔr,tɛks] *n, pl* **-tices** ['kɔrtə,si:z] *or* **-texes** : corteza *f* ⟨cerebral cortex : corteza cerebral⟩
cortisone ['kɔrtə,so:n, -zo:n] *n* : cortisona *f*
cosmetic[1] [kɑz'mɛtɪk] *adj* : cosmético
cosmetic[2] *n* : cosmético *m*
cosmic ['kɑzmɪk] *adj* **1** : cósmico ⟨cosmic ray : rayo cósmico⟩ **2** VAST : grandioso, inmenso, vasto
cosmonaut ['kɑzmə,nɔt] *n* : cosmonauta *mf*
cosmopolitan[1] [ˌkɑzmə'pɑlətən] *adj* : cosmopolita
cosmopolitan[2] *n* : cosmopolita *mf*
cosmos ['kɑzməs, -,mo:s, -,mɑs] *n* : cosmos *m*, universo *m*
cost[1] ['kɔst] *v* **cost; costing** *vt* : costar ⟨how much does it cost? : ¿cuánto cuesta?, ¿cuánto vale?⟩ — *vi* : costar ⟨these cost more : éstos cuestan más⟩
cost[2] *n* : costo *m*, precio *m*, coste *m* ⟨cost of living : costo de vida⟩ ⟨victory at all costs : victoria a toda costa⟩
Costa Rican[1] [ˌkɑstə'ri:kən] *adj* : costarricense
Costa Rican[2] *n* : costarricense *mf*
costly ['kɔstli] *adj* : costoso, caro
costume ['kɑs,tu:m, -,tju:m] *n* **1** : traje *m* ⟨national costume : traje típico⟩ **2** : disfraz *m* ⟨costume party : fiesta de disfraces⟩ **3** OUTFIT : vestimenta *f*, traje *m*, conjunto *m*
cosy ['ko:zi] → **cozy**
cot ['kɑt] *n* : catre *m*
coterie ['ko:ṭə,ri, ˌko:ṭə'-] *n* : tertulia *f*, círculo *m* (social)
cottage ['kɑṭɪʤ] *n* : casita *f* (de campo)
cottage cheese *n* : requesón *m*
cotton ['kɑtən] *n* : algodón *m*
cottonmouth ['kɑtən,maʊθ] → **moccasin**
cottonseed ['kɑtən,si:d] *n* : semilla *f* de algodón
cotton swab → **swab**
cottontail ['kɑtən,teɪl] *n* : conejo *m* de cola blanca
couch[1] ['kaʊʧ] *vt* : expresar, formular ⟨couched in strong language : expresado en lenguaje enérgico⟩
couch[2] *n* SOFA : sofá *m*
couch potato *n* : haragán *m*, -gana *f*; vago *m*, -ga *f*
cougar ['ku:gər] *n* : puma *m*
cough[1] ['kɔf] *vi* : toser

cough² *n* : tos *f*
could ['kʊd] → **can**
council ['kaʊntsəl] *n* **1** : concejo *m* ⟨city council : concejo municipal, ayuntamiento⟩ **2** MEETING : concejo *m*, junta *f* **3** BOARD : consejo *m* **4** : concilio *m* (eclesiástico)
councillor *or* **councilor** ['kaʊntsələr] *n* : concejal *m*, -jala *f*
councilman ['kaʊntsəlmən] *n, pl* **-men** [-mən, -ˌmɛn] : concejal *m*
councilwoman ['kaʊntsəlˌwʊmən] *n, pl* **-women** [-ˌwɪmən] : concejala *f*
counsel¹ ['kaʊntsəl] *v* **-seled** *or* **-selled**; **-seling** *or* **-selling** *vt* ADVISE : aconsejar, asesorar, recomendar — *vi* CONSULT : consultar
counsel² *n* **1** ADVICE : consejo *m*, recomendación *f* **2** CONSULTATION : consulta *f* **3** counsel *ns & pl* LAWYER : abogado *m*, -da *f*
counselor *or* **counsellor** ['kaʊntsələr] *n* : consejero *m*, -ra *f*; consultor *m*, -tora *f*; asesor *m*, -sora *f*
count¹ ['kaʊnt] *vt* : contar, enumerar — *vi* **1** : contar ⟨to count out loud : contar en voz alta⟩ **2** MATTER : contar, valer, importar ⟨that's what counts : eso es lo que cuenta⟩ **3 to count on** : contar con
count² *n* **1** COMPUTATION : cómputo *m*, recuento *m*, cuenta *f* ⟨to lose count : perder la cuenta⟩ **2** CHARGE : cargo *m* ⟨two counts of robbery : dos cargos de robo⟩ **3** : conde *m* (noble)
countable ['kaʊntəbəl] *adj* : numerable
countdown ['kaʊntˌdaʊn] *n* : cuenta *f* atrás
countenance¹ ['kaʊntənənts] *vt* **-nanced; -nancing** : permitir, tolerar
countenance² *n* FACE : semblante *m*, rostro *m*
counter¹ ['kaʊntər] *vt* **1** → **counteract 2** OPPOSE : oponerse a, resistir — *vi* RETALIATE : responder, contraatacar
counter² *adv* **counter to** : contrario a, en contra de
counter³ *adj* : contrario, opuesto
counter⁴ *n* **1** PIECE : ficha *f* (de un juego) **2** : mostrador *m* (de un negocio), ventanilla *f* (en un banco) **3** : contador *m* (aparato) **4** COUNTERBALANCE : fuerza *f* opuesta, contrapeso *m*
counteract [ˌkaʊntər'ækt] *vt* : contrarrestar
counterattack ['kaʊntərəˌtæk] *n* : contraataque *m*
counterbalance¹ [ˌkaʊntər'bælənts] *vt* **-anced; -ancing** : contrapesar
counterbalance² ['kaʊntərˌbælənts] *n* : contrapeso *m*
counterclockwise [ˌkaʊntər'klɑkˌwaɪz] *adv & adj* : en el sentido opuesto al de las manecillas del reloj
counterfeit¹ ['kaʊntərˌfɪt] *vt* **1** : falsificar (dinero) **2** PRETEND : fingir, aparentar
counterfeit² *adj* : falso, inauténtico
counterfeit³ *n* : falsificación *f*

counterfeiter ['kaʊntərˌfɪtər] *n* : falsificador *m*, -dora *f*
countermand ['kaʊntərˌmænd, ˌkaʊntər'-] *vt* : contramandar
countermeasure ['kaʊntərˌmɛʒər] *n* : contramedida *f*
counterpart ['kaʊntərˌpɑrt] *n* : homólogo *m*, contraparte *f Mex*
counterpoint ['kaʊntərˌpɔɪnt] *n* : contrapunto *m*
counterproductive [ˌkaʊntərprə'dʌktɪv] *adj* : contraproducente
counterrevolution [ˌkaʊntərˌrɛvə-'luːʃən] *n* : contrarrevolución *f*
counterrevolutionary¹ [ˌkaʊntərˌrɛvə-'luːʃənˌɛri] *adj* : contrarrevolucionario
counterrevolutionary² *n, pl* **-ries** : contrarrevolucionario *m*, -ria *f*
countersign ['kaʊntərˌsaɪn] *n* : contraseña *f*
countess ['kaʊntɪs] *n* : condesa *f*
countless ['kaʊntləs] *adj* : incontable, innumerable
country¹ ['kʌntri] *adj* : campestre, rural
country² *n, pl* **-tries 1** NATION : país *m*, nación *f*, patria *f* ⟨country of origin : país de origen⟩ ⟨love of one's country : amor a la patria⟩ **2** : campo *m* ⟨they left the city for the country : se fueron de la ciudad al campo⟩
countryman ['kʌntrimən] *n, pl* **-men** [-mən, -ˌmɛn] : compatriota *mf*; paisano *m*, -na *f*
countryside ['kʌntriˌsaɪd] *n* : campo *m*, campiña *f*
county ['kaʊnti] *n, pl* **-ties** : condado *m*
coup ['kuː] *n, pl* **coups** [-z] **1** : golpe *m* maestro **2** *or* **coup d'etat** : golpe *m* (de estado), cuartelazo *m*
coupe ['kuːp] *n* : cupé *m*
couple¹ ['kʌpəl] *vt* **-pled; -pling** : acoplar, enganchar, conectar
couple² *n* **1** PAIR : par *m* ⟨a couple of hours : un par de horas, unas dos horas⟩ **2** : pareja *f* ⟨a young couple : una pareja joven⟩
coupling ['kʌpliŋ] *n* : acoplamiento *m*
coupon ['kuːˌpɑn, 'kjuː-] *n* : cupón *m*
courage ['kərɪdʒ] *n* : valor *m*, valentía *f*, coraje *m*
courageous [kə'reɪdʒəs] *adj* : valiente, valeroso
courier ['kʊriər, 'kəriər] *n* : mensajero *m*, -ra *f*
course¹ ['kors] *vi* **coursed; coursing** : correr (a toda velocidad)
course² *n* **1** PROGRESS : curso *m*, transcurso *m* ⟨to run its course : seguir su curso⟩ **2** DIRECTION : rumbo *m* (de un avión), derrota *f*, derrotero *m* (de un barco) **3** PATH, WAY : camino *m*, vía *f* ⟨course of action : línea de conducta⟩ **4** : plato *m* (de una cena) ⟨the main course : el plato principal⟩ **5** : curso *m* (académico) **6 of course** : desde luego, por supuesto ⟨yes, of course! : ¡claro que sí!⟩

court¹ ['kort] *vt* WOO : cortejar, galantear

court² *n* **1** PALACE : palacio *m* **2** RETINUE : corte *f*, séquito *m* **3** COURTYARD : patio *m* **4** : cancha *f* (de tenis, baloncesto, etc.) **5** TRIBUNAL : corte *f*, tribunal *m* ⟨the Supreme Court : la Corte Suprema⟩

courteous ['kərṭiəs] *adj* : cortés, atento, educado — **courteously** *adv*

courtesan ['korṭəzən, 'kər-] *n* : cortesana *f*

courtesy ['kərṭəsi] *n, pl* **-sies** : cortesía *f*

courthouse ['kort,haʊs] *n* : palacio *m* de justicia, juzgado *m*

courtier ['korṭiər, 'kortjər] *n* : cortesano *m*, -na *f*

courtly ['kortli] *adj* **-lier; -est** : distinguido, elegante, cortés

court–martial¹ ['kort,marʃəl] *vt* : someter a consejo de guerra

court–martial² *n, pl* **courts–martial** ['korts,marʃəl] : consejo *m* de guerra

court order *n* : mandamiento *m* judicial

courtroom ['kort,ru:m] *n* : tribunal *m*, corte *f*

courtship ['kort,ʃɪp] *n* : cortejo *m*, noviazgo *m*

courtyard ['kort,jard] *n* : patio *m*

cousin ['kʌzən] *n* : primo *m*, -ma *f*

couture [ku:'tʊr] *n* : industria *f* de la moda ⟨haute couture : alta costura⟩

cove ['ko:v] *n* : ensenada *f*, cala *f*

covenant ['kʌvənənt] *n* : pacto *m*, contrato *m*

cover¹ ['kʌvər] *vt* **1** : cubrir, tapar ⟨cover your head : tápate la cabeza⟩ ⟨covered with mud : cubierto de lodo⟩ **2** HIDE, PROTECT : encubrir, proteger **3** TREAT : tratar **4** INSURE : asegurar, cubrir

cover² *n* **1** SHELTER : cubierta *f*, abrigo *m*, refugio *m* ⟨to take cover : ponerse a cubierto⟩ ⟨under cover of darkness : al amparo de la oscuridad⟩ **2** LID, TOP : cubierta *f*, tapa *f* **3** : cubierta *f* (de un libro), portada *f* (de una revista) **4** **covers** *npl* BEDCLOTHES : ropa *f* de cama, cobijas *fpl*, mantas *fpl*

coverage ['kʌvərɪʤ] *n* : cobertura *f*

coverlet ['kʌvərlət] *n* : cobertor *m*

covert¹ ['ko:,vərt, 'kʌvərt] *adj* : encubierto, secreto ⟨covert operations : operaciones encubiertas⟩

covert² ['kʌvərt, 'ko:-] *n* THICKET : espesura *f*, maleza *f*

cover–up ['kʌvər,ʌp] *n* : encubrimiento *m* (de algo ilícito)

covet ['kʌvət] *vt* : codiciar

covetous ['kʌvəṭəs] *adj* : codicioso

covey ['kʌvi] *n, pl* **-eys 1** : bandada *f* pequeña (de codornices, etc.) **2** GROUP : grupo *m*

cow¹ ['kaʊ] *vt* : intimidar, acobardar

cow² *n* : vaca *f*, hembra *f* (de ciertas especies)

coward ['kaʊərd] *n* : cobarde *mf*

cowardice ['kaʊərdɪs] *n* : cobardía *f*

cowardly ['kaʊərdli] *adj* : cobarde

cowboy ['kaʊ,bɔɪ] *n* : vaquero *m*, cowboy *m*

cower ['kaʊər] *vi* : encogerse (de miedo), acobardarse

cowgirl ['kaʊ,gərl] *n* : vaquera *f*

cowherd ['kaʊ,hərd] *n* : vaquero *m*, -ra *f*

cowhide ['kaʊ,haɪd] *n* : cuero *m*, piel *f* de vaca

cowl ['kaʊl] *n* : capucha *f* (de un monje)

cowlick ['kaʊ,lɪk] *n* : remolino *m*

cowpuncher ['kaʊ,pʌnʧər] → **cowboy**

cowslip ['kaʊ,slɪp] *n* : prímula *f*, primavera *f*

coxswain ['kaksən, -,sweɪn] *n* : timonel *m*

coy ['kɔɪ] *adj* **1** SHY : tímido, cohibido **2** COQUETTISH : coqueto

coyote [kaɪ'o:ṭi, 'kaɪ,o:t] *n, pl* **coyotes** *or* **coyote** : coyote *m*

cozy ['ko:zi] *adj* **-zier; -est** : acogedor, cómodo

CPU [,si:,pi:'ju:] *n* (central processing unit) : CPU *f*

crab ['kræb] *n* : cangrejo *m*, jaiba *f*

crabby ['kræbi] *adj* **-bier; -est** : gruñón, malhumorado

crabgrass ['kræb,græs] *n* : garranchuelo *m*

crack¹ ['kræk] *vi* **1** : chasquear, restallar ⟨the whip cracked : el látigo restalló⟩ **2** SPLIT : rajarse, resquebrajarse, agrietarse **3** : quebrarse (dícese de la voz) — *vt* **1** : restallar, chasquear (un látigo, etc.) **2** SPLIT : rajar, agrietar, resquebrajar **3** BREAK : romper (un huevo), cascar (nueces), forzar (una caja fuerte) **4** SOLVE : resolver, descifrar (un código)

crack² *adj* FIRST-RATE : buenísimo, de primera

crack³ *n* **1** : chasquido *m*, restallido *m*, estallido *m* (de un arma de fuego), crujido *m* (de huesos) ⟨a crack of thunder : un trueno⟩ **2** WISECRACK : chiste *m*, ocurrencia *f*, salida *f* **3** CREVICE : raja *f*, grieta *f*, fisura *f* **4** BLOW : golpe *m* **5** ATTEMPT : intento *m*

crackdown ['kræk,daʊn] *n* : medidas *fpl* enérgicas

crack down *vt* : tomar medidas enérgicas

cracker ['krækər] *n* : galleta *f* (de soda, etc.)

crackle¹ ['krækəl] *vi* **-led; -ling** : crepitar, chisporrotear

crackle² *n* : crujido *m*, chisporroteo *m*

crackpot ['kræk,pat] *n* : excéntrico *m*, -ca *f*; chiflado *m*, -da *f*

crack–up ['kræk,ʌp] *n* **1** CRASH : choque *m*, estrellamiento *m* **2** BREAKDOWN : crisis *f* nerviosa

crack up *vt* **1** : estrellar (un vehículo) **2** : hacer reír **3** : elogiar ⟨it isn't all that it's cracked up to be : no es tan bueno como se dice⟩ — *vi* **1** : estrellarse **2** LAUGH : echarse a reír

cradle¹ [ˈkreɪdəl] *vt* **-dled; -dling** : acunar, mecer (a un niño)
cradle² *n* : cuna *f*
craft [ˈkræft] *n* **1** TRADE : oficio *m* ⟨the craft of carpentry : el oficio de carpintero⟩ **2** CRAFTSMANSHIP, SKILL : arte *m*, artesanía *f*, destreza *f* **3** CRAFTINESS : astucia *f*, maña *f* **4** *pl usually* **craft** BOAT : barco *m*, embarcación *f* **5** *pl usually* **craft** AIRCRAFT : avión *m*, aeronave *f*
craftiness [ˈkræftinəs] *n* : astucia *f*, maña *f*
craftsman [ˈkræftsmən] *n, pl* **-men** [-mən, -ˌmɛn] : artesano *m*, -na *f*
craftsmanship [ˈkræftsmənˌʃɪp] *n* : artesanía *f*, destreza *f*
crafty [ˈkræfti] *adj* **craftier; -est** : astuto, taimado
crag [ˈkræg] *n* : peñasco *m*
craggy [ˈkrægi] *adj* **-gier; -est** : peñascoso
cram [ˈkræm] *v* **crammed; cramming** *vt* **1** JAM : embutir, meter **2** STUFF : atiborrar, abarrotar ⟨crammed with people : atiborrado de gente⟩ — *vi* : estudiar a última hora, memorizar (para un examen)
cramp¹ [ˈkræmp] *vt* **1** : dar calambre en **2** RESTRICT : limitar, restringir, entorpecer ⟨to cramp someone's style : cortarle el vuelo a alguien⟩ — *vi or* **to cramp up** : acalambrarse
cramp² *n* **1** SPASM : calambre *m*, espasmo *m* (de los músculos) **2 cramps** *npl* : retorcijones *mpl* ⟨stomach cramps : retorcijones de estómago⟩
cranberry [ˈkrænˌbɛri] *n, pl* **-berries** : arándano *m* (rojo y agrio)
crane¹ [ˈkreɪn] *vt* **craned; craning** : estirar ⟨to crane one's neck : estirar el cuello⟩
crane² *n* **1** : grulla *f* (ave) **2** : grúa *f* (máquina)
cranial [ˈkreɪniəl] *adj* : craneal, craneano
cranium [ˈkreɪniəm] *n, pl* **-niums** *or* **-nia** [-niə] : cráneo *m*
crank¹ [ˈkræŋk] *vt or* **to crank up** : arrancar (con una manivela)
crank² *n* **1** : manivela *f*, manubrio *m* **2** ECCENTRIC : excéntrico *m*, -ca *f*
cranky [ˈkræŋki] *adj* **crankier; -est** : irritable, malhumorado, enojadizo
cranny [ˈkræni] *n, pl* **-nies** : grieta *f* ⟨every nook and cranny : todos los rincones⟩
crash¹ [ˈkræʃ] *vi* **1** SMASH : caerse con estrépito, estrellarse **2** COLLIDE : estrellarse, chocar **3** BOOM, RESOUND : retumbar, resonar — *vt* **1** SMASH : estrellar **2 to crash a party** : colarse en una fiesta **3 to crash one's car** : tener un accidente
crash² *n* **1** DIN : estrépito *m* **2** COLLISION : choque *m*, colisión *f* ⟨car crash : accidente automovilístico⟩ **3** FAILURE : quiebra *f* (de un negocio), crac *m* (de la bolsa)

crass [ˈkræs] *adj* : grosero, de mal gusto
crate¹ [ˈkreɪt] *vt* **crated; crating** : empacar en un cajón
crate² *n* : cajón *m* (de madera)
crater [ˈkreɪtər] *n* : cráter *m*
cravat [krəˈvæt] *n* : corbata *f*
crave [ˈkreɪv] *vt* **craved; craving** : ansiar, apetecer, tener muchas ganas de
craven [ˈkreɪvən] *adj* : cobarde, pusilánime
craving [ˈkreɪvɪŋ] *n* : ansia *f*, antojo *m*, deseo *m*
crawfish [ˈkrɔˌfɪʃ] → **crayfish**
crawl¹ [ˈkrɔl] *vi* **1** CREEP : arrastrarse, gatear (dícese de un bebé) **2** TEEM : estar plagado
crawl² *n* : paso *m* lento
crayfish [ˈkreɪˌfɪʃ] *n* **1** : ástaco *m* (de agua dulce) **2** : langostino *m* (de mar)
crayon [ˈkreɪˌɑn, -ən] *n* : crayón *m*
craze [ˈkreɪz] *n* : moda *f* pasajera, manía *f*
crazed [ˈkreɪzd] *adj* : enloquecido
crazily [ˈkreɪzəli] *adv* : locamente, erráticamente, insensatamente
craziness [ˈkreɪzinəs] *n* : locura *f*, demencia *f*
crazy [ˈkreɪzi] *adj* **-zier; -est** **1** INSANE : loco, demente ⟨to go crazy : volverse loco⟩ **2** ABSURD, FOOLISH : loco, insensato, absurdo **3 like crazy** : como loco **4 to be crazy about** : estar loco por
creak¹ [ˈkrik] *vi* : chirriar, rechinar, crujir
creak² *n* : chirrido *m*, crujido *m*
creaky [ˈkriki] *adj* **creakier; -est** : chirriante, que cruje
cream¹ [ˈkrim] *vt* **1** BEAT, MIX : batir, mezclar (azúcar y mantequilla, etc.) **2** : preparar (alimentos) con crema
cream² *n* **1** : crema *f* (de leche) **2** LOTION : crema *f*, loción *f* **3** ELITE : crema *f*, elite *f* ⟨the cream of the crop : la crema y nata, lo mejor⟩
creamery [ˈkrimməri] *n, pl* **-eries** : fábrica *f* de productos lácteos
creamy [ˈkrimi] *adj* **creamier; -est** : cremoso
crease¹ [ˈkris] *vt* **creased; creasing** **1** : plegar, poner una raya en (pantalones) **2** WRINKLE : arrugar
crease² *n* : pliegue *m*, doblez *m*, raya *f* (de pantalones)
create [kriˈeɪt] *vt* **-ated; -ating** : crear, hacer
creation [kriˈeɪʃən] *n* : creación *f*
creative [kriˈeɪtɪv] *adj* : creativo, original ⟨creative people : personas creativas⟩ ⟨a creative work : un obra original⟩
creatively [kriˈeɪtɪvli] *adv* : creativamente, con originalidad
creativity [ˌkriˌeɪˈtɪvəti] *n* : creatividad *f*
creator [kriˈeɪtər] *n* : creador *m*, -dora *f*
creature [ˈkriˌtʃər] *n* : ser *m* viviente, criatura *f*, animal *m*

credence [ˈkriːdən/s] n : crédito m
credentials [krɪˈden/fəlz] npl : referencias fpl oficiales, cartas fpl credenciales
credibility [ˌkrɛdəˈbɪləʧi] n : credibilidad f
credible [ˈkrɛdəbəl] adj : creíble
credit¹ [ˈkrɛdɪt] vt **1** BELIEVE : creer, dar crédito a **2** : ingresar, abonar ⟨to credit $100 to an account : ingresar $100 en (una) cuenta⟩ **3** ATTRIBUTE : atribuir ⟨they credit the invention to him : a él se le atribuye el invento⟩
credit² n **1** : saldo m positivo, saldo m a favor (de una cuenta) **2** : crédito m ⟨to buy on credit : comprar a crédito⟩ ⟨credit card : tarjeta de crédito⟩ **3** CREDENCE : crédito m ⟨I gave credit to everything he said : di crédito a todo lo que dijo⟩ **4** RECOGNITION : reconocimiento m **5** : orgullo m, honor m ⟨she's a credit to the school : ella es el orgullo de la escuela⟩
creditable [ˈkrɛdɪtəbəl] adj : encomiable, loable — **creditably** [-bli] adv
credit card n : tarjeta de crédito
creditor [ˈkrɛdɪtər] n : acreedor m, -dora f
credo [ˈkriːdoː, ˈkreɪ-] n : credo m
credulity [krɪˈduːləti, -ˈdjuː-] n : credulidad f
credulous [ˈkrɛdʒələs] adj : crédulo
creed [ˈkriːd] n : credo m
creek [ˈkriːk, ˈkrɪk] n : arroyo m, riachuelo m
creel [ˈkriːl] n : nasa f, cesta f (de pescador)
creep¹ [ˈkriːp] vi **crept** [ˈkrɛpt]; **creeping 1** CRAWL : arrastrarse, gatear **2** : moverse lentamente o sigilosamente ⟨he crept out of the house : salió sigilosamente de la casa⟩ **3** SPREAD : trepar (dícese de una planta)
creep² n **1** CRAWL : paso m lento **2** : asqueroso m, -sa f **3 creeps** npl : escalofríos mpl ⟨that gives me the creeps : eso me da escalofríos⟩
creeper [ˈkriːpər] n : planta f trepadora, trepadora f
creepy [ˈkriːpi] adj **1** SPOOKY : espeluznante **2** UNPLEASANT : asqueroso
cremate [ˈkriːˌmeɪt] vt -mated; -mating : cremar
cremation [krɪˈmeɪʃən] n : cremación f
Creole [ˈkriːˌoːl] n **1** : criollo m, criolla f **2** : criollo m (idioma) — **Creole** adj
creosote [ˈkriːəˌsoːt] n : creosota f
crepe or **crêpe** [ˈkreɪp] n **1** : crespón m (tela) **2** PANCAKE : crepe mf, crepa f Mex
crescendo [krɪˈʃɛnˌdoː] n, pl -dos or -does : crescendo m
crescent [ˈkrɛsənt] n : creciente m
crest [ˈkrɛst] n **1** : cresta f, penacho m (de un ave) **2** PEAK, TOP : cresta f (de una ola), cima f (de una colina) **3** : emblema m (sobre un escudo de armas)
crestfallen [ˈkrɛstˌfɔlən] adj : alicaído, abatido

cretin [ˈkriːtən] n : cretino m, -na f
crevasse [krɪˈvæs] n : grieta f, fisura f
crevice [ˈkrɛvɪs] n : grieta f, hendidura f
crew [ˈkruː] n **1** : tripulación f (de una nave) **2** TEAM : equipo m (de trabajadores o atletas)
crib [ˈkrɪb] n **1** MANGER : pesebre m **2** GRANARY : granero m **3** : cuna f (de un bebé)
crick [ˈkrɪk] n : calambre m, espasmo m muscular
cricket [ˈkrɪkət] n **1** : grillo m (insecto) **2** : críquet m (juego)
crime [ˈkraɪm] n **1** : crimen m, delito m ⟨to commit a crime : cometer un delito⟩ **2** : crimen m, delincuencia f ⟨organized crime : crimen organizado⟩
criminal¹ [ˈkrɪmənəl] adj : criminal
criminal² n : criminal mf, delincuente mf
crimp [ˈkrɪmp] vt : ondular, rizar (el pelo), arrugar (una tela, etc.)
crimson [ˈkrɪmzən] n : carmesí m
cringe [ˈkrɪnʤ] vi **cringed; cringing** : encogerse
crinkle¹ [ˈkrɪŋkəl] v **-kled; -kling** vt : arrugar — vi : arrugarse
crinkle² n : arruga f
crinkly [ˈkrɪŋkəli] adj : arrugado
cripple¹ [ˈkrɪpəl] vt **-pled; -pling 1** DISABLE : lisiar, dejar inválido **2** INCAPACITATE : inutilizar, incapacitar
cripple² n : lisiado m, -da f
crisis [ˈkraɪsɪs] n, pl **crises** [-ˌsiːz] : crisis f
crisp¹ [ˈkrɪsp] vt : tostar, hacer crujiente
crisp² adj **1** CRUNCHY : crujiente, crocante **2** FIRM, FRESH : firme, fresco ⟨crisp lettuce : lechuga fresca⟩ **3** LIVELY : vivaz, alegre ⟨a crisp tempo : un ritmo alegre⟩ **4** INVIGORATING : fresco, vigorizante ⟨the crisp autumn air : el fresco aire otoñal⟩ — **crisply** adv
crisp³ n : postre m de fruta (con pedacitos de masa dulce por encima)
crispy [ˈkrɪspi] adj **crispier; -est** : crujiente ⟨crispy potato chips : papitas crujientes⟩
crisscross [ˈkrɪsˌkrɔs] vt : entrecruzar
criterion [kraɪˈtɪriən] n, pl **-ria** [-iə] : criterio m
critic [ˈkrɪtɪk] n **1** : crítico m, -ca f (de las artes) **2** FAULTFINDER : detractor m, -tora f; criticón m, -cona f
critical [ˈkrɪtɪkəl] adj : crítico
critically [ˈkrɪtɪkli] adv : críticamente ⟨critically ill : gravemente enfermo⟩
criticism [ˈkrɪtəˌsɪzəm] n : crítica f
criticize [ˈkrɪtəˌsaɪz] vt -cized; -cizing **1** EVALUATE, JUDGE : criticar, analizar, evaluar **2** CENSURE : criticar, reprobar
critique [krɪˈtiːk] n : crítica f, evaluación f
croak¹ [ˈkroːk] vi : croar
croak² n : croar m, canto m (de la rana)
Croatian [kroˈeɪʃən] n : croata mf — **Croatian** adj

crochet[1] [kro:'ʃeɪ] v : tejer al croché
crochet[2] n : croché m, crochet m
crock ['krɑk] n : vasija f de barro
crockery ['krɑkəri] n : vajilla f (de barro)
crocodile ['krɑkə,daɪl] n : cocodrilo m
crocus ['kro:kəs] n, pl **-cuses** : azafrán m
croissant [krə'sɑnt] n : croissant m
crone ['kro:n] n : vieja f arpía, vieja f bruja
crony ['kro:ni] n, pl **-nies** : amigote m fam; compinche mf fam
crook[1] ['krʊk] vt : doblar (el brazo o el dedo)
crook[2] n 1 STAFF : cayado m (de pastor), báculo m (de obispo) 2 THIEF : ratero m, -ra f; ladrón m, -drona f
crooked ['krʊkəd] adj 1 BENT : chueco, torcido 2 DISHONEST : deshonesto
crookedness ['krʊkədnəs] n 1 : lo torcido, lo chueco 2 DISHONESTY : falta f de honradez
croon ['kru:n] v : cantar suavemente
crop[1] ['krɑp] v **cropped; cropping** vt TRIM : recortar, cortar — vi **to crop up** : aparecer, surgir ⟨these problems keep cropping up : estos problemas no cesan de surgir⟩
crop[2] n 1 : buche m (de un ave o insecto) 2 WHIP : fusta f (de jinete) 3 HARVEST : cosecha f, cultivo m
croquet [,kro:'keɪ] n : croquet m
croquette [kro:'kɛt] n : croqueta f
cross[1] ['krɔs] vt 1 : cruzar, atravesar ⟨to cross the street : cruzar la calle⟩ ⟨several canals cross the city : varios canales atraviesan la ciudad⟩ 2 CANCEL : tachar, cancelar ⟨he crossed his name off the list : tachó su nombre de la planilla⟩ 3 INTERBREED : cruzar (en genética)
cross[2] adj 1 : que atraviesa ⟨cross ventilation : ventilación que atraviesa un cuarto⟩ 2 CONTRARY : contrario, opuesto ⟨cross purposes : objetivos opuestos⟩ 3 ANGRY : enojado, de mal humor
cross[3] n 1 : cruz f ⟨the sign of the cross : la señal de la cruz⟩ 2 : cruza f (en biología)
crossbones ['krɔs,bo:nz] npl 1 : huesos mpl cruzados 2 → **skull**
crossbow ['krɔs,bo:] n : ballesta f
crossbreed ['krɔs,bri:d] vt **-bred** [-,brɛd]; **-breeding** : cruzar
crosscurrent ['krɔs,kərənt] n : contracorriente f
cross–examination [,krɔsɪg,zæmə-'neɪʃən] n : repreguntas fpl, interrogatorio m
cross–examine [,krɔsɪg'zæmən] vt **-ined; -ining** : repreguntar
cross–eyed ['krɔs,aɪd] adj : bizco
crossing ['krɔsɪŋ] n 1 INTERSECTION : cruce m, paso m ⟨pedestrian crossing : paso de peatones⟩ 2 VOYAGE : travesía f (del mar)

crossly ['krɔsli] adv : con enojo, con enfado
cross–reference [,krɔs'rɛfrənts, -'rɛfə-rənts] n : referencia f, remisión f
crossroads ['krɔs,ro:dz] n : cruce m, encrucijada f, crucero m Mex
cross section n 1 SECTION : corte m transversal 2 SAMPLE : muestra f representativa ⟨a cross section of the population : una muestra representativa de la población⟩
crosswalk ['krɔs,wɔk] n : cruce m peatonal, paso m de peatones
crossways ['krɔs,weɪz] → **crosswise**
crosswise[1] ['krɔs,waɪz] adv : transversalmente, diagonalmente
crosswise[2] adj : transversal, diagonal
crossword puzzle ['krɔs,wərd] n : crucigrama m
crotch ['krɑtʃ] n : entrepierna f
crotchety ['krɑtʃəti] adj CRANKY : malhumorado, irritable, enojadizo
crouch ['kraʊtʃ] vi : agacharse, ponerse de cuclillas
croup ['kru:p] n : crup m
crouton ['kru:,tɑn] n : crutón m
crow[1] ['kro:] vi 1 : cacarear, cantar (como un cuervo) 2 BRAG : alardear, presumir
crow[2] n 1 : cuervo m (ave) 2 : cantar m (del gallo)
crowbar ['kro:,bɑr] n : palanca f
crowd[1] ['kraʊd] vi : aglomerarse, amontonarse — vt : atestar, atiborrar, llenar
crowd[2] n : multitud f, muchedumbre f, gentío m
crown[1] ['kraʊn] vt : coronar
crown[2] n : corona f
crow's nest n : cofa f
crucial ['kru:ʃəl] adj : crucial, decisivo
crucible ['kru:səbəl] n : crisol m
crucifix ['kru:sə,fɪks] n : crucifijo m
crucifixion [,kru:sə'fɪkʃən] n : crucifixión f
crucify ['kru:sə,faɪ] vt **-fied; -fying** : crucificar
crude ['kru:d] adj **cruder; -est** 1 RAW, UNREFINED : crudo, sin refinar ⟨crude oil : petróleo crudo⟩ 2 VULGAR : grosero, de mal gusto 3 ROUGH : tosco, burdo, rudo
crudely ['kru:dli] adv 1 VULGARLY : groseramente 2 ROUGHLY : burdamente, de manera rudimentaria
crudity ['kru:dəti] n, pl **-ties** 1 VULGARITY : grosería f 2 COARSENESS, ROUGHNESS : tosquedad f, rudeza f
cruel ['kru:əl] adj **-eler** or **-eller; -elest** or **-ellest** : cruel
cruelly ['kru:əli] adv : cruelmente
cruelty ['kru:əlti] n, pl **-ties** : crueldad f
cruet ['kru:ɪt] n : vinagrera f, aceitera f
cruise[1] ['kru:z] vi **cruised; cruising** 1 : hacer un crucero 2 : navegar o conducir a una velocidad constante ⟨cruising speed : velocidad de crucero⟩
cruise[2] n : crucero m

cruiser ['kru:zər] *n* **1** WARSHIP : crucero *m*, buque *m* de guerra **2** : patrulla *f* (de policía)

crumb ['krʌm] *n* : miga *f*, migaja *f*

crumble ['krʌmbəl] *v* **-bled; -bling** *vt* : desmigajar, desmenuzar — *vi* : desmigajarse, desmoronarse, desmenuzarse

crumbly ['krʌmbli] *adj* : que se desmenuza fácilmente, friable

crumple ['krʌmpəl] *v* **-pled; -pling** *vt* RUMPLE : arrugar — *vi* **1** WRINKLE : arrugarse **2** COLLAPSE : desplomarse

crunch¹ ['krʌntʃ] *vt* **1** : ronzar (con los dientes) **2** : hacer crujir (con los pies, etc.) — *vi* : crujir

crunch² *n* : crujido *m*

crunchy ['krʌntʃi] *adj* **crunchier; -est** : crujiente

crusade¹ [kru:'seɪd] *vi* **-saded; -sading** : hacer una campaña (a favor de o contra algo)

crusade² *n* **1** : campaña *f* (de reforma, etc.) **2** **Crusade** : cruzada *f*

crusader [kru:'seɪdər] *n* **1** : cruzado *m* (en la Edad Media) **2** : campeón *m*, -peona *f* (de una causa)

crush¹ ['krʌʃ] *vt* **1** SQUASH : aplastar, apachurrar **2** GRIND, PULVERIZE : triturar, machacar **3** SUPPRESS : aplastar, suprimir

crush² *n* **1** CROWD, MOB : gentío *m*, multitud *f*, aglomeración *f* **2** INFATUATION : enamoramiento *m*

crushing ['krʌʃɪŋ] *adj* : aplastante, abrumador

crust ['krʌst] *n* **1** : corteza *f*, costra *f* (de pan) **2** : tapa *f* de masa, pasta *f* (de un pastel) **3** LAYER : capa *f*, corteza *f* ⟨the earth's crust : la corteza terrestre⟩

crustacean [ˌkrʌs'teɪʃən] *n* : crustáceo *m*

crusty ['krʌsti] *adj* **crustier; -est 1** : de corteza dura **2** CROSS, GRUMPY : enojado, malhumorado

crutch ['krʌtʃ] *n* : muleta *f*

crux ['krʌks, 'krʊks] *n, pl* **cruxes** : quid *m*, esencia *f*, meollo *m* ⟨the crux of the problem : el quid del problema⟩

cry¹ ['kraɪ] *vi* **cried; crying 1** SHOUT : gritar ⟨they cried for more : a gritos pidieron más⟩ **2** WEEP : llorar

cry² *n, pl* **cries 1** SHOUT : grito *m* **2** WEEPING : llanto *m* **3** : chillido *m* (de un animal)

crybaby ['kraɪˌbeɪbi] *n, pl* **-bies** : llorón *m*, -rona *f*

crypt ['krɪpt] *n* : cripta *f*

cryptic ['krɪptɪk] *adj* : enigmático, críptico

crystal ['krɪstəl] *n* : cristal *m*

crystalline ['krɪstəlɪn] *adj* : cristalino

crystallize ['krɪstəˌlaɪz] *v* **-lized; -lizing** *vt* : cristalizar, materializar ⟨to crystallize one's thoughts : cristalizar uno sus pensamientos⟩ — *vi* : cristalizarse

cub ['kʌb] *n* : cachorro *m*

Cuban ['kju:bən] *n* : cubano *m*, -na *f* — **Cuban** *adj*

cubbyhole ['kʌbiˌho:l] *n* : chiribitil *m*

cube¹ ['kju:b] *vt* **cubed; cubing 1** : elevar (un número) al cubo **2** : cortar en cubos

cube² *n* **1** : cubo *m* **2 ice cube** : cubito *m* de hielo **3 sugar cube** : terrón *m* de azúcar

cubic ['kju:bɪk] *adj* : cúbico

cubicle ['kju:bɪkəl] *n* : cubículo *m*

cuckoo¹ ['ku:ˌku:, 'kʊ-] *adj* : loco, chiflado

cuckoo² *n, pl* **-oos** : cuco *m*, cuclillo *m*

cucumber ['kju:ˌkʌmbər] *n* : pepino *m*

cud ['kʌd] *n* **to chew the cud** : rumiar

cuddle ['kʌdəl] *v* **-dled; -dling** *vi* : abrazarse tiernamente, acurrucarse — *vt* : abrazar

cudgel¹ ['kʌdʒəl] *vt* **-geled** *or* **-gelled; -geling** *or* **-gelling** : apalear, aporrear

cudgel² *n* : garrote *m*, porra *f*

cue¹ ['kju:] *vt* **cued; cuing** *or* **cueing** : darle el pie a, darle la señal a

cue² *n* **1** SIGNAL : señal *f*, pie *m* (en teatro), entrada *f* (en música) **2** : taco *m* (de billar)

cuff¹ ['kʌf] *vt* : bofetear, cachetear

cuff² *n* **1** : puño *m* (de una camisa), vuelta *f* (de pantalones) **2** SLAP : bofetada *f*, cachetada *f* **3 cuffs** *npl* HANDCUFFS : esposas *fpl*

cuisine [kwɪ'zi:n] *n* : cocina *f* ⟨Mexican cuisine : la cocina mexicana⟩

culinary ['kʌləˌnɛri, 'kju:lə-] *adj* : culinario

cull ['kʌl] *vt* : seleccionar, entresacar

culminate ['kʌlməˌneɪt] *vi* **-nated; -nating** : culminar

culmination [ˌkʌlmə'neɪʃən] *n* : culminación *f*, punto *m* culminante

culpable ['kʌlpəbəl] *adj* : culpable

culprit ['kʌlprɪt] *n* : culpable *mf*

cult ['kʌlt] *n* : culto *m*

cultivate ['kʌltəˌveɪt] *vt* **-vated; -vating 1** TILL : cultivar, labrar **2** FOSTER : cultivar, fomentar **3** REFINE : cultivar, refinar ⟨to cultivate the mind : cultivar la mente⟩

cultivation [ˌkʌltə'veɪʃən] *n* **1** : cultivo *m* ⟨under cultivation : en cultivo⟩ **2** CULTURE, REFINEMENT : cultura *f*, refinamiento *m*

cultural ['kʌltʃərəl] *adj* : cultural — **culturally** *adv*

culture ['kʌltʃər] *n* **1** CULTIVATION : cultivo *m* **2** REFINEMENT : cultura *f*, educación *f*, refinamiento *m* **3** CIVILIZATION : cultura *f*, civilización *f* ⟨the Incan culture : la cultura inca⟩

cultured ['kʌltʃərd] *adj* **1** EDUCATED, REFINED : culto, educado, refinado **2** : de cultivo, cultivado ⟨cultured pearls : perlas de cultivo⟩

culvert ['kʌlvərt] *n* : alcantarilla *f*

cumbersome ['kʌmbərsəm] *adj* : torpe y pesado, difícil de manejar

cumin ['kʌmən] *n* : comino *m*

cumulative ['kju:mjələˌtɪv, -ˌleɪtɪv] *adj* : acumulativo

cumulus [ˈkjuːmjələs] *n, pl* **-li** [-ˌlaɪ, -ˌliː] : cúmulo *m*

cunning[1] [ˈkʌnɪŋ] *adj* **1** CRAFTY : astuto, taimado **2** CLEVER : ingenioso, hábil **3** CUTE : mono, gracioso, lindo

cunning[2] *n* **1** SKILL : habilidad *f* **2** CRAFTINESS : astucia *f*, maña *f*

cup[1] [ˈkʌp] *vt* **cupped; cupping** : ahuecar (las manos)

cup[2] *n* **1** : taza *f* ⟨a cup of coffee : una taza de café⟩ **2** CUPFUL : taza *f* **3** : media pinta *f* (unidad de medida) **4** GOBLET : copa *f* **5** TROPHY : copa *f*, trofeo *m*

cupboard [ˈkʌbərd] *n* : alacena *f*, armario *m*

cupcake [ˈkʌpˌkeɪk] *n* : pastelito *m*

cupful [ˈkʌpˌfʊl] *n* : taza *f*

cupola [ˈkjuːpələ, -ˌloː] *n* : cúpula *f*

cur [ˈkər] *n* : perro *m* callejero, perro *m* corriente *Mex*

curate [ˈkjʊrət] *n* : cura *m*, párroco *m*

curator [ˈkjʊrˌeɪtər, kjuˈreɪtər] *n* : conservador *m*, -dora *f* (de un museo); director *m*, -tora *f* (de un zoológico)

curb[1] [ˈkərb] *vt* : refrenar, restringir, controlar

curb[2] *n* **1** RESTRAINT : freno *m*, control *m* **2** : borde *m* de la acera

curd [ˈkərd] *n* : cuajada *f*

curdle [ˈkərdəl] *v* **-dled; -dling** *vi* : cuajarse — *vt* : cuajar ⟨to curdle one's blood : helarle la sangre a uno⟩

cure[1] [ˈkjʊr] *vt* **cured; curing 1** HEAL : curar, sanar **2** REMEDY : remediar **3** PROCESS : curar (alimentos, etc.)

cure[2] *n* **1** RECOVERY : curación *f*, recuperación *f* **2** REMEDY : cura *f*, remedio *m*

curfew [ˈkərˌfjuː] *n* : toque *m* de queda

curio [ˈkjʊriˌoː] *n, pl* **-rios** : curiosidad *f*, objeto *m* curioso

curiosity [ˌkjʊriˈɑsəti] *n, pl* **-ties** : curiosidad *f*

curious [ˈkjʊriəs] *adj* **1** INQUISITIVE : curioso **2** STRANGE : curioso, raro

curl[1] [ˈkərl] *vt* **1** : rizar, ondular (el pelo) **2** COIL : enrollar **3** TWIST : torcer ⟨to curl one's lip : hacer una mueca⟩ — *vi* **1** : rizarse, ondularse **2 to curl up** : acurrucarse (con un libro, etc.)

curl[2] *n* **1** RINGLET : rizo *m* **2** COIL : espiral *f*, rosca *f*

curler [ˈkərlər] *n* : rulo *m*

curlew [ˈkərˌluː, ˈkərlˌjuː] *n, pl* **-lews** *or* **-lew** : zarapito *m*

curly [ˈkərli] *adj* **curlier; -est** : rizado, crespo

currant [ˈkərənt] *n* **1** : grosella *f* (fruta) **2** RAISIN : pasa *f* de Corinto

currency [ˈkərənsi] *n, pl* **-cies 1** PREVALENCE, USE : uso *m*, aceptación *f*, difusión *f* ⟨to be in currency : estar en uso⟩ **2** MONEY : moneda *f*, dinero *m*

current[1] [ˈkərənt] *adj* **1** PRESENT : actual ⟨current events : actualidades⟩ **2** PREVALENT : corriente, común — **currently** *adv*

current[2] *n* : corriente *f*

curriculum [kəˈrɪkjələm] *n, pl* **-la** [-lə] : currículum *m*, currículo *m*, programa *m* de estudio

curriculum vitae [ˈviːˌtaɪ, ˈvaɪˌti] *n, pl* **curricula vitae** : currículum *m*, currículo *m*

curry[1] [ˈkəri] *vt* **-ried; -rying 1** GROOM : almohazar (un caballo) **2** : condimentar con curry **3 to curry favor** : congraciarse (con alguien)

curry[2] *n, pl* **-ries** : curry *m*

curse[1] [ˈkərs] *v* **cursed; cursing** *vt* **1** DAMN : maldecir **2** INSULT : injuriar, insultar, decir malas palabras a **3** AFFLICT : afligir — *vi* : maldecir, decir malas palabras

curse[2] *n* **1** : maldición *f* ⟨to put a curse on someone : echarle una maldición a alguien⟩ **2** AFFLICTION : maldición *f*, aflicción *f*, cruz *f*

cursor [ˈkərsər] *n* : cursor *m*

cursory [ˈkərsəri] *adj* : rápido, superficial, somero

curt [ˈkərt] *adj* : cortante, brusco, seco — **curtly** *adv*

curtail [kərˈteɪl] *vt* : acortar, limitar, restringir

curtailment [kərˈteɪlmənt] *n* : restricción *f*, limitación *f*

curtain [ˈkərtən] *n* : cortina *f* (de una ventana), telón *m* (en un teatro)

curtness [ˈkərtnəs] *n* : brusquedad *f*, sequedad *f*

curtsy[1] *or* **curtsey** [ˈkərtsi] *vt* **-sied** *or* **-seyed; -sying** *or* **-seying** : hacer una reverencia

curtsy[2] *or* **curtsey** *n, pl* **-sies** *or* **-seys** : reverencia *f*

curvature [ˈkərvəˌtʃʊr] *n* : curvatura *f*

curve[1] [ˈkərv] *v* **curved; curving** *vi* : torcerse, describir una curva — *vt* : encorvar

curve[2] *n* : curva *f*

cushion[1] [ˈkʊʃən] *vt* **1** : poner cojines o almohadones a **2** SOFTEN : amortiguar, mitigar, suavizar ⟨to cushion a blow : amortiguar un golpe⟩

cushion[2] *n* **1** : cojín *m*, almohadón *m* **2** PROTECTION : colchón *m*, protección *f*

cusp [ˈkʌsp] *n* : cúspide *f* (de un diente), cuerno *m* (de la luna)

cuspid [ˈkʌspɪd] *n* : diente *m* canino, colmillo *m*

custard [ˈkʌstərd] *n* : natillas *fpl*

custodian [ˌkʌˈstoːdiən] *n* : custodio *m*, -dia *f*; guardián, -diana *f*

custody [ˈkʌstədi] *n, pl* **-dies** : custodia *f*, cuidado *m* ⟨to be in custody : estar detenido⟩

custom[1] [ˈkʌstəm] *adj* : a la medida, a la orden

custom[2] *n* **1** : costumbre *f*, tradición *f* **2 customs** *npl* : aduana *f*

customarily [ˌkʌstəˈmɛrəli] *adv* : habitualmente, normalmente, de costumbre

customary [ˈkʌstəˌmɛri] *adj* **1** TRADITIONAL : tradicional **2** USUAL : habitual, de costumbre
customer [ˈkʌstəmər] *n* : cliente *m*, -ta *f*
custom–made [ˈkʌstəmˈmeɪd] *adj* : hecho a la medida
cut¹ [ˈkʌt] *v* **cut; cutting** *vt* **1** : cortar ⟨to cut paper : cortar papel⟩ **2** : cortarse ⟨to cut one's finger : cortarse uno el dedo⟩ **3** TRIM : cortar, recortar ⟨to have one's hair cut : cortarse el pelo⟩ **4** INTERSECT : cruzar, atravesar **5** SHORTEN : acortar, abreviar **6** REDUCE : reducir, rebajar ⟨to cut prices : rebajar los precios⟩ **7 to cut one's teeth** : salirle los dientes a uno — *vi* **1** : cortar, cortarse **2 to cut in** : entrometerse
cut² *n* **1** : corte *m* ⟨a cut of meat : un corte de carne⟩ **2** SLASH : tajo *m*, corte *m*, cortadura *f* **3** REDUCTION : rebaja *f*, reducción *f* ⟨a cut in the rates : una rebaja en las tarifas⟩
cute [ˈkjuːt] *adj* **cuter; -est** : mono *fam*, lindo
cuticle [ˈkjuːtɪkəl] *n* : cutícula *f*
cutlass [ˈkʌtləs] *n* : alfanje *m*
cutlery [ˈkʌtləri] *n* : cubiertos *mpl*
cutlet [ˈkʌtlət] *n* : chuleta *f*
cutter [ˈkʌtər] *n* **1** : cortadora *f* (implemento) **2** : cortador *m*, -dora *f* (persona) **3** : cúter *m* (embarcación)
cutthroat [ˈkʌtˌθroːt] *adj* : despiadado, desalmado ⟨cutthroat competition : competencia feroz⟩
cutting¹ [ˈkʌtɪŋ] *adj* **1** : cortante ⟨a cutting wind : un viento cortante⟩ **2** CAUSTIC : mordaz

cutting² *n* : esqueje *m* (de una planta)
cuttlefish [ˈkʌtəlˌfɪʃ] *n*, *pl* **-fish** *or* **-fishes** : jibia *f*, sepia *f*
cyanide [ˈsaɪəˌnaɪd, -nɪd] *n* : cianuro *m*
cycle¹ [ˈsaɪkəl] *vi* **-cled; -cling** : andar en bicicleta, ir en bicicleta
cycle² *n* **1** : ciclo *m* ⟨life cycle : ciclo de vida, ciclo vital⟩ **2** BICYCLE : bicicleta *f* **3** MOTORCYCLE : motocicleta *f*
cyclic [ˈsaɪklɪk, ˈsɪ-] *or* **cyclical** [-klɪkəl] *adj* : cíclico
cyclist [ˈsaɪklɪst] *n* : ciclista *mf*
cyclone [ˈsaɪˌkloːn] *n* **1** : ciclón *m* **2** TORNADO : tornado *m*
cyclopedia *or* **cyclopaedia** [ˌsaɪkləˈpiːdiə] → **encyclopedia**
cylinder [ˈsɪləndər] *n* : cilindro *m*
cylindrical [səˈlɪndrɪkəl] *adj* : cilíndrico
cymbal [ˈsɪmbəl] *n* : platillo *m*, címbalo *m*
cynic [ˈsɪnɪk] *n* : cínico *m*, -ca *f*
cynical [ˈsɪnɪkəl] *adj* : cínico
cynicism [ˈsɪnəˌsɪzəm] *n* : cinismo *m*
cypress [ˈsaɪprəs] *n* : ciprés *m*
Cypriot [ˈsɪpriət, -ˌat] *n* : chipriota *mf* — **Cypriot** *adj*
cyst [ˈsɪst] *n* : quiste *m*
cytoplasm [ˈsaɪtoˌplæzəm] *n* : citoplasma *m*
czar [ˈzɑr, ˈsɑr] *n* : zar *m*
czarina [zɑˈriːnə, sɑ-] *n* : zarina *f*
Czech [ˈtʃɛk] *n* **1** : checo *m*, -ca *f* **2** : checo *m* (idioma) — **Czech** *adj*
Czechoslovak [ˌtʃɛkoˈsloːˌvak, -ˌvæk] *or* **Czechoslovakian** [-sloˈvɑkiən, -ˈvæ-] *n* : checoslovaco *m*, -ca *f* — **Czechoslovak** *or* **Czechoslovakian** *adj*

D

d [ˈdiː] *n*, *pl* **d's** *or* **ds** [ˈdiːz] : cuarta letra del alfabeto inglés
dab¹ [ˈdæb] *vt* **dabbed; dabbing** : darle toques ligeros a, aplicar suavemente
dab² *n* **1** BIT : toque *m*, pizca *f*, poco *m* ⟨a dab of ointment : un toque de ungüento⟩ **2** PAT : toque *m* ligero, golpecito *m*
dabble [ˈdæbəl] *v* **-bled; -bling** *vt* SPATTER : salpicar — *vi* **1** SPLASH : chapotear **2** TRIFLE : jugar, interesarse superficialmente
dabbler [ˈdæbələr] *n* : diletante *mf*
dachshund [ˈdɑksˌhʊnt, -ˌhʊnd; ˈdɑksənt, -sənd] *n* : perro *m* salchicha
dad [ˈdæd] *n* : papá *m fam*
daddy [ˈdædi] *n*, *pl* **-dies** : papi *m fam*
daffodil [ˈdæfəˌdɪl] *n* : narciso *m*
daft [ˈdæft] *adj* : tonto, bobo
dagger [ˈdægər] *n* : daga *f*, puñal *m*
dahlia [ˈdæljə, ˈdɑl-, ˈdeɪl-] *n* : dalia *f*
daily¹ [ˈdeɪli] *adv* : a diario, diariamente
daily² *adj* : diario, cotidiano
daily³ *n*, *pl* **-lies** : diario *m*, periódico *m*
daintily [ˈdeɪntəli] *adv* : delicadamente, con delicadeza

daintiness [ˈdeɪntinəs] *n* : delicadeza *f*, finura *f*
dainty¹ [ˈdeɪnti] *adj* **-tier; -est 1** DELICATE : delicado **2** FASTIDIOUS : remilgado, melindroso **3** DELICIOUS : exquisito, sabroso
dainty² *n*, *pl* **-ties** DELICACY : exquisitez *f*, manjar *m*
dairy [ˈdæri] *n*, *pl* **-ies 1** *or* **dairy store** : lechería *f* **2** *or* **dairy farm** : granja *f* lechera
dairymaid [ˈdæriˌmeɪd] *n* : lechera *f*
dairyman [ˈdærimən, -ˌmæn] *n*, *pl* **-men** [-mən, -ˌmɛn] : lechero *m*
dais [ˈdeɪəs] *n* : tarima *f*, estrado *m*
daisy [ˈdeɪzi] *n*, *pl* **-sies** : margarita *f*
dale [ˈdeɪl] *n* : valle *m*
dally [ˈdæli] *vi* **-lied; -lying 1** TRIFLE : juguetear **2** DAWDLE : entretenerse, perder tiempo
dalmatian [dælˈmeɪʃən, dɔl-] *n* : dálmata *m*
dam¹ [ˈdæm] *vt* **dammed; damming** : represar, embalsar
dam² *n* **1** : represa *f*, dique *m* **2** : madre *f* (de animales domésticos)

damage[1] ['dæmɪʤ] *vt* **-aged; -aging** : dañar (un objeto o una máquina), perjudicar (la salud o una reputación)

damage[2] *n* **1** : daño *m*, perjuicio *m* **2 damages** *npl* : daños y perjuicios *mpl*

damaging ['dæməʤɪŋ] *adj* : perjudicial

damask ['dæməsk] *n* : damasco *m*

dame ['deɪm] *n* LADY : dama *f*, señora *f*

damn[1] ['dæm] *vt* **1** CONDEMN : condenar **2** CURSE : maldecir

damn[2] *or* **damned** ['dæmd] *adj* : condenado *fam*, maldito *fam*

damn[3] *n* : pito *m*, bledo *m*, comino *m* ⟨it's not worth a damn : no vale un pito⟩ ⟨I don't give a damn : me importa un comino⟩

damnable ['dæmnəbəl] *adj* : condenable, detestable

damnation [dæm'neɪʃən] *n* : condenación *f*

damned[1] ['dæmd] *adv* VERY : muy

damned[2] *adj* **1** → **damnable 2** REMARKABLE : extraordinario

damp[1] ['dæmp] *vt* → **dampen**

damp[2] *adj* : húmedo

damp[3] *n* MOISTURE : humedad *f*

dampen ['dæmpən] *vt* **1** MOISTEN : humedecer **2** DISCOURAGE : desalentar, desanimar

damper ['dæmpər] *n* **1** : regulador *m* de tiro (de una chimenea) **2** : sordina *f* (de un piano) **3 to put a damper on** : desanimar, apagar (el entusiasmo), enfriar

dampness ['dæmpnəs] *n* : humedad *f*

damsel ['dæmzəl] *n* : damisela *f*

dance[1] ['dænts] *v* **danced; dancing** : bailar

dance[2] *n* : baile *m*

dancer ['dæntsər] *n* : bailarín *m*, -rina *f*

dandelion ['dændəl,aɪən] *n* : diente *m* de león

dandruff ['dændrəf] *n* : caspa *f*

dandy[1] ['dændi] *adj* **-dier; -est** : excelente, magnífico, macanudo *fam*

dandy[2] *n, pl* **-dies 1** FOP : dandi *m* **2** : algo *m* excelente ⟨this new program is a dandy : este programa nuevo es algo excelente⟩

Dane ['deɪn] *n* : danés *m*, -nesa *f*

danger ['deɪnʤər] *n* : peligro *m*

dangerous ['deɪnʤərəs] *adj* : peligroso

dangle ['dæŋgəl] *v* **-gled; -gling** *vi* HANG : colgar, pender — *vt* **1** SWING : hacer oscilar **2** PROFFER : ofrecer (como incentivo) **3 to keep someone dangling** : dejar a alguien en suspenso

Danish[1] ['deɪnɪʃ] *adj* : danés

Danish[2] *n* : danés *m* (idioma)

dank ['dæŋk] *adj* : frío y húmedo

dapper ['dæpər] *adj* : pulcro, atildado

dappled ['dæpəld] *adj* : moteado ⟨a dappled horse : un caballo rodado⟩

dare[1] ['dær] *v* **dared; daring** *vi* : osar, atreverse ⟨how dare you! : ¡cómo te atreves!⟩ — *vt* **1** CHALLENGE : desafiar, retar **2 to dare to do something** : atreverse a hacer algo, osar hacer algo

dare[2] *n* : desafío *m*, reto *m*

daredevil ['dær,dɛvəl] *n* : persona *f* temeraria

daring[1] ['dærɪŋ] *adj* : osado, atrevido, audaz

daring[2] *n* : arrojo *m*, coraje *m*, audacia *f*

dark ['dɑrk] *adj* **1** : oscuro (dícese del ambiente o de los colores), moreno (dícese del pelo o de la piel) **2** SOMBER : sombrío, triste

darken ['dɑrkən] *vt* **1** DIM : oscurecer **2** SADDEN : entristecer — *vi* : ensombrecerse, nublarse

darkly ['dɑrkli] *adv* **1** DIMLY : oscuramente **2** GLOOMILY : tristemente **3** MYSTERIOUSLY : misteriosamente, enigmáticamente

darkness ['dɑrknəs] *n* : oscuridad *f*, tinieblas *f*

darling[1] ['dɑrlɪŋ] *adj* **1** BELOVED : querido, amado **2** CHARMING : encantador, mono *fam*

darling[2] *n* **1** BELOVED : querido *m*, -da *f*; amado *m*, -da *f*; cariño *m*, -ña *f* **2** FAVORITE : preferido *m*, -da *f*; favorito *m*, -ta *f*

darn[1] ['dɑrn] *vt* : zurcir

darn[2] *n* **1** : zurcido *m* **2** → **damn**[3]

dart[1] ['dɑrt] *vt* THROW : lanzar, tirar — *vi* DASH : lanzarse, precipitarse

dart[2] *n* **1** : dardo *m* **2 darts** *npl* : juego *m* de dardos

dash[1] ['dæʃ] *vt* **1** SMASH : romper, estrellar **2** HURL : arrojar, lanzar **3** SPLASH : salpicar **4** FRUSTRATE : frustrar **5 to dash off** : hacer (algo) rápidamente — *vi* **1** SMASH : romperse, estrellarse **2** DART : lanzarse, irse apresuradamente

dash[2] *n* **1** BURST, SPLASH : arranque *m*, salpicadura *f* (de aguas) **2** : guión *m* largo (signo de puntuación) **3** DROP : gota *f*, pizca *f* **4** VERVE : brío *m* **5** RACE : carrera *f* ⟨a 100-meter dash : una carrera de 100 metros⟩ **6 to make a dash for it** : precipitarse (hacia), echarse a correr **7** → **dashboard**

dashboard ['dæʃ,bord] *n* : tablero *m* de instrumentos

dashing ['dæʃɪŋ] *adj* : gallardo, apuesto

data ['deɪtə, 'dæ-, 'dɑ-] *ns & pl* : datos *mpl*, información *f*

database ['deɪtə,beɪs, 'dæ-, 'dɑ-] *n* : base *f* de datos

date[1] ['deɪt] *v* **dated; dating** *vt* **1** : fechar (una carta, etc.), datar (un objeto) ⟨it was dated June 9 : estaba fechada el 9 de junio⟩ **2** : salir con ⟨she's dating my brother : sale con mi hermano⟩ — *vi* : datar

date[2] *n* **1** : fecha *f* ⟨to date : hasta la fecha⟩ **2** EPOCH, PERIOD : época *f*, período *m* **3** APPOINTMENT : cita *f* **4** COMPANION : acompañante *mf* **5** : dátil *m* (fruta)

dated ['deɪtəd] *adj* OUT-OF-DATE : anticuado, pasado de moda

datum ['deɪtəm, 'dæ-, 'dɑ-] *n, pl* **-ta** [-t̬ə] *or* **-tums** : dato *m*

daub¹ ['dɔb] *vt* : embadurnar

daub² *n* : mancha *f*

daughter ['dɔt̬ər] *n* : hija *f*

daughter–in–law ['dɔt̬ərɪn,lɔ] *n, pl* **daughters–in–law** : nuera *f*, hija *f* política

daunt ['dɔnt] *vt* : amilanar, acobardar, intimidar

dauntless ['dɔntləs] *adj* : intrépido, impávido

davenport ['dævən,port] *n* : sofá *m*

dawdle ['dɔdəl] *vi* **-dled; -dling** **1** DALLY : demorarse, entretenerse, perder tiempo **2** LOITER : vagar, holgazanear, haraganear

dawn¹ ['dɔn] *vi* **1** : amanecer, alborear, despuntar ⟨Saturday dawned clear and bright : el sábado amaneció claro y luminoso⟩ **2 to dawn on** : hacerse obvio ⟨it dawned on me that she was right : me di cuenta de que tenía razón⟩

dawn² *n* **1** DAYBREAK : amanecer *m*, alba *f* **2** BEGINNING : albor *m*, comienzo *m* ⟨the dawn of history : los albores de la historia⟩ **3 from dawn to dusk** : de sol a sol

day ['deɪ] *n* **1** : día *m* **2** DATE : fecha *f* **3** TIME : día *m*, tiempo *m* ⟨in olden days : intaño⟩ **4** WORKDAY : jornada *f* laboral

daybreak ['deɪ,breɪk] *n* : alba *f*, amanecer *m*

day care *n* : servicio *m* de guardería infantil

daydream¹ ['deɪ,dri:m] *vi* : soñar despierto, fantasear

daydream² *n* : ensueño *m*, ensoñación *f*, fantasía *f*

daylight ['deɪ,laɪt] *n* **1** : luz *f* del día ⟨in broad daylight : a plena luz del día⟩ **2** → daybreak **3** → daytime

daylight saving time *n* : hora *f* de verano

daytime ['deɪ,taɪm] *n* : horas *fpl* diurnas, día *m*

daze¹ ['deɪz] *vt* **dazed; dazing** **1** STUN : aturdir **2** DAZZLE : deslumbrar, ofuscar

daze² *n* **1** : aturdimiento *m* **2 in a daze** : aturdido, atontado

dazzle¹ ['dæzəl] *vt* **-zled; -zling** : deslumbrar, ofuscar

dazzle² *n* : resplandor *m*, brillo *m*

DDT [,di:,di:'ti:] *n* : DDT *m*

deacon ['di:kən] *n* : diácono *m*

dead¹ ['dɛd] *adv* **1** ABRUPTLY : repentinamente, súbitamente ⟨to stop dead : parar en seco⟩ **2** ABSOLUTELY : absolutamente ⟨I'm dead certain : estoy absolutamente seguro⟩ **3** DIRECTLY : justo ⟨dead ahead : justo adelante⟩

dead² *adj* **1** LIFELESS : muerto **2** NUMB : entumecido **3** INDIFFERENT : indiferente, frío **4** INACTIVE : inactivo ⟨a dead volcano : un volcán inactivo⟩ **5** : desconectado (dícese del teléfono),

descargado (dícese de una batería) **6** EXHAUSTED : agotado, derrengado, muerto **7** OBSOLETE : obsoleto, muerto ⟨a dead language : una lengua muerta⟩ **8** EXACT : exacto ⟨in the dead center : justo en el blanco⟩

dead³ *n* **1 the dead** : los muertos **2 in the dead of night** : a las altas horas de la noche **3 in the dead of winter** : en pleno invierno

deadbeat ['dɛd,bi:t] *n* **1** LOAFER : vago *m*, -ga *f*; holgazán *m*, -zana *f* **2** FREELOADER : gorrón *m*, -rrona *f fam*; gorrero *m*, -ra *f fam*

deaden ['dɛdən] *vt* **1** : atenuar (un dolor), entorpecer (sensaciones) **2** DULL : deslustrar **3** DISPIRIT : desanimar **4** MUFFLE : amortiguar, reducir (sonidos)

dead–end ['dɛd'ɛnd] *adj* **1** : sin salida ⟨dead-end street : calle sin salida⟩ **2** : sin futuro ⟨a dead-end job : un trabajo sin porvenir⟩

dead end *n* : callejón *m* sin salida

dead heat *n* : empate *m*

deadline ['dɛd,laɪn] *n* : fecha *f* límite, fecha *f* tope, plazo *m* (determinado)

deadlock¹ ['dɛd,lɑk] *vt* : estancar — *vi* : estancarse, llegar a punto muerto

deadlock² *n* : punto *m* muerto, impasse *m*

deadly¹ ['dɛdli] *adv* : extremadamente, sumamente ⟨deadly serious : muy en serio⟩

deadly² *adj* **-lier; -est** **1** LETHAL : mortal, letal, mortífero **2** ACCURATE : certero, preciso ⟨a deadly aim : una puntería infalible⟩ **3** CAPITAL : capital ⟨the seven deadly sins : los siete pecados capitales⟩ **4** DULL : funesto, aburrido **5** EXTREME : extremo, absoluto ⟨a deadly calm : una calma absoluta⟩

deadpan¹ ['dɛd,pæn] *adv* : de manera inexpresiva, sin expresión

deadpan² *adj* : inexpresivo, impasible

deaf ['dɛf] *adj* : sordo

deafen ['dɛfən] *vt* **-ened; -ening** : ensordecer

deafening ['dɛfənɪŋ] *adj* : ensordecedor

deaf–mute ['dɛf'mju:t] *n* : sordomudo *m*, -da *f*

deafness ['dɛfnəs] *n* : sordera *f*

deal¹ ['di:l] *v* **dealt; dealing** *vt* **1** APPORTION : repartir ⟨to deal justice : repartir la justicia⟩ **2** DISTRIBUTE : repartir, dar (naipes) **3** DELIVER : asestar, propinar ⟨to deal a blow : asestar un golpe⟩ — *vi* **1** : dar, repartir (en juegos de naipes) **2 to deal in** : comerciar en, traficar con (drogas) **3 to deal with** CONCERN : tratar de, tener que ver con ⟨the book deals with poverty : el libro trata de la pobreza⟩ **4 to deal with** HANDLE : tratar (con), encargarse de **5 to deal with** TREAT : tratar ⟨the judge dealt with him severely : el juez lo trató con severidad⟩ **6 to deal with** ACCEPT : aceptar (una situación o desgracia)

deal² *n* **1** : reparto *m* (de naipes) **2** AGREEMENT, TRANSACTION : trato *m*, acuerdo *m*, transacción *f* **3** TREATMENT : trato *m* ⟨he got a raw deal : le hicieron una injusticia⟩ **4** BARGAIN : ganga *f*, oferta *f* **5 a good deal** *or a* **great deal** : mucho, una gran cantidad
dealer ['di:lər] *n* : comerciante *mf*, traficante *mf*
dealership ['di:lər,ʃɪp] *n* : concesión *f*
dealings ['di:lɪŋz] *npl* **1** : relaciones *fpl* (personales) **2** TRANSACTIONS : negocios *mpl*, transacciones *fpl*
dean ['di:n] *n* **1** : deán *m* (del clero) **2** : decano *m*, -na *f* (de una facultad o profesión)
dear¹ ['dɪr] *adj* **1** ESTEEMED, LOVED : querido, estimado ⟨a dear friend : un amigo querido⟩ ⟨Dear Sir : Estimado Señor⟩ **2** COSTLY : caro, costoso
dear² *n* : querido *m*, -da *f*; amado *m*, -da *f*
dearly ['dɪrli] *adv* **1** : mucho ⟨I love them dearly : los quiero mucho⟩ **2** : caro ⟨to pay dearly : pagar caro⟩
dearth ['dərθ] *n* : escasez *f*, carestía *f*
death ['dɛθ] *n* **1** : muerte *f*, fallecimiento *m* ⟨to be the death of : matar⟩ **2** FATALITY : víctima *f* (mortal); muerto *m*, -ta *f* **3** END : fin *m* ⟨the death of civilization : el fin de la civilización⟩
deathbed ['dɛθ,bɛd] *n* : lecho *m* de muerte
deathblow ['dɛθ,blo:] *n* : golpe *m* mortal
deathless ['dɛθləs] *adj* : eterno, inmortal
deathly ['dɛθli] *adj* : de muerte, sepulcral (dícese del silencio), cadavérico (dícese de la palidez)
debacle [dɪ'bakəl, -'bæ-] *n* : desastre *m*, debacle *m*, fiasco *m*
debar [dɪ'bar] *vt* **-barred; -barring** : excluir, prohibir
debase [dɪ'beɪs] *vt* **-based; -basing** : degradar, envilecer
debasement [dɪ'beɪsmənt] *n* : degradación *f*, envilecimiento *m*
debatable [dɪ'beɪt̬əbəl] *adj* : discutible
debate¹ [dɪ'beɪt] *vt* **-bated; -bating** : debatir, discutir
debate² *n* : debate *m*, discusión *f*
debauch [dɪ'bɔtʃ] *vt* : pervertir, corromper
debauchery [dɪ'bɔtʃəri] *n, pl* **-eries** : libertinaje *m*, disipación *f*, intemperancia *f*
debilitate [dɪ'bɪlə,teɪt] *vt* **-tated; -tating** : debilitar
debility [dɪ'bɪləti] *n, pl* **-ties** : debilidad *f*
debit¹ ['dɛbɪt] *vt* : adeudar, cargar, debitar
debit² *n* : débito *m*, cargo *m*, debe *m*
debonair [,dɛbə'nær] *adj* : elegante y desenvuelto, apuesto
debris [də'bri:, deɪ-; 'deɪ,bri:] *n, pl* **-bris** ['bri:z, -,bri:z] **1** RUBBLE, RUINS : es-

combros *mpl*, ruinas *fpl*, restos *mpl* **2** RUBBISH : basura *f*, deshechos *mpl*
debt ['dɛt] *n* **1** : deuda *f* ⟨to pay a debt : saldar una deuda⟩ **2** INDEBTEDNESS : endeudamiento *m*
debtor ['dɛt̬ər] *n* : deudor *m*, -dora *f*
debunk [di'bʌŋk] *vt* DISCREDIT : desacreditar, desprestigiar
debut¹ [deɪ'bju:, 'deɪ,bju:] *vi* : debutar
debut² *n* **1** : debut *m* (de un actor), estreno *m* (de una obra) **2** : debut *m*, presentación *f* (en sociedad)
debutante ['dɛbju,tɑnt] *n* : debutante *f*
decade ['dɛ,keɪd, dɛ'keɪd] *n* : década *f*
decadence ['dɛkədənts] *n* : decadencia *f*
decadent ['dɛkədənt] *adj* : decadente
decaf¹ ['di:,kæf] → **decaffeinated**
decaf² *n* : café *m* descafeinado
decaffeinated [di'kæfə,neɪt̬əd] *adj* : descafeinado
decal ['di:,kæl, dɪ'kæl] *n* : calcomanía *f*
decamp [di'kæmp] *vi* : irse, largarse *fam*
decant [di'kænt] *vt* : decantar
decanter [di'kæntər] *n* : licorera *f*, garrafa *f*
decapitate [di'kæpə,teɪt] *vt* **-tated; -tating** : decapitar
decay¹ [di'keɪ] *vi* **1** DECOMPOSE : descomponerse, pudrirse **2** DETERIORATE : deteriorarse **3** : cariarse (dícese de los dientes)
decay² *n* **1** DECOMPOSITION : descomposición *f* **2** DECLINE, DETERIORATION : decadencia *f*, deterioro *m* **3** : caries *f* (de los dientes)
decease¹ [di'si:s] *vi* **-ceased; -ceasing** : morir, fallecer
decease² *n* : fallecimiento *m*, defunción *f*, deceso *m*
deceit [di'si:t] *n* **1** DECEPTION : engaño *m* **2** DISHONESTY : deshonestidad *f*
deceitful [di'si:tfəl] *adj* : falso, embustero, engañoso, mentiroso
deceitfully [di'si:tfəli] *adv* : con engaño, con falsedad
deceitfulness [di'si:tfəlnəs] *n* : falsedad *f*, engaño *m*
deceive [di'si:v] *vt* **-ceived; -ceiving** : engañar, burlar
deceiver [di'si:vər] *n* : impostor *m*, -tora *f*
decelerate [di'sɛlə,reɪt] *vi* **-ated; -ating** : reducir la velocidad, desacelerar
December [di'sɛmbər] *n* : diciembre *m*
decency ['di:səntsi] *n, pl* **-cies** : decencia *f*, decoro *m*
decent ['di:sənt] *adj* **1** CORRECT, PROPER : decente, decoroso, correcto **2** CLOTHED : vestido, presentable **3** MODEST : púdico, modesto **4** ADEQUATE : decente, adecuado ⟨decent wages : paga adecuada⟩
decently ['di:səntli] *adv* : decentemente
decentralize [di'sɛntrə,laɪz] *v* **-lized** [-,laɪzd]; **-lizing** [-,laɪzɪŋ] *vt* : descentralizar — *vi* : descentralizarse
deception [di'sɛpʃən] *n* : engaño *m*

deceptive [dɪ'sɛptɪv] *adj* : engañoso, falaz — **deceptively** *adv*

decibel ['dɛsəbəl, -ˌbɛl] *n* : decibelio *m*

decide [dɪ'saɪd] *v* **-cided; -ciding** *vt* **1** CONCLUDE : decidir, llegar a la conclusión de ⟨he decided what to do : decidió qué iba a hacer⟩ **2** DETERMINE : decidir, determinar ⟨one blow decided the fight : un solo golpe determinó la pelea⟩ **3** CONVINCE : decidir ⟨her pleas decided me to help : sus súplicas me decidieron a ayudarla⟩ **4** RESOLVE : resolver — *vi* : decidirse

decided [dɪ'saɪdəd] *adj* **1** UNQUESTIONABLE : indudable **2** RESOLUTE : decidido, resuelto — **decidedly** *adv*

deciduous [dɪ'sɪdʒuəs] *adj* : caduco, de hoja caduca

decimal¹ ['dɛsəməl] *adj* : decimal

decimal² *n* : número *m* decimal

decipher [dɪ'saɪfər] *vt* : descifrar — **decipherable** [-əbəl] *adj*

decision [dɪ'sɪʒən] *n* : decisión *f*, determinación *f* ⟨to make a decision : tomar una decisión⟩

decisive [dɪ'saɪsɪv] *adj* **1** DECIDING : decisivo ⟨the decisive vote : el voto decisivo⟩ **2** CONCLUSIVE : decisivo, concluyente, contundente ⟨a decisive victory : una victoria contundente⟩ **3** RESOLUTE : decidido, resuelto, firme

decisively [dɪ'saɪsɪvli] *adv* : con decisión, de manera decisiva

decisiveness [dɪ'saɪsɪvnəs] *n* **1** FORCEFULNESS : contundencia *f* **2** RESOLUTION : firmeza *f*, decisión *f*, determinación *f*

deck¹ ['dɛk] *vt* **1** FLOOR : tumbar, derribar ⟨she decked him with one blow : lo tumbó de un solo golpe⟩ **2 to deck out** : adornar, engalanar

deck² *n* **1** : cubierta *f* (de un barco) **2** *or* **deck of cards** : baraja *f* (de naipes)

declaim [dɪ'kleɪm] *v* : declamar

declaration [ˌdɛklə'reɪʃən] *n* : declaración *f*, pronunciamiento *m* (oficial)

declare [dɪ'klær] *vt* **-clared; -claring** : declarar, manifestar ⟨to declare war : declarar la guerra⟩ ⟨they declared their support : manifestaron su apoyo⟩

decline¹ [dɪ'klaɪn] *v* **-clined; -clining** *vi* **1** DESCEND : descender **2** DETERIORATE : deteriorarse, decaer ⟨her health is declining : su salud se está deteriorando⟩ **3** DECREASE : disminuir, decrecer, decaer **4** REFUSE : rehusar — *vt* **1** INFLECT : declinar **2** REFUSE, TURN DOWN : declinar, rehusar

decline² *n* **1** DETERIORATION : decadencia *f*, deterioro *m* **2** DECREASE : disminución *f*, descenso *m* **3** SLOPE : declive *m*, pendiente *f*

decode [dɪ'ko:d] *vt* **-coded; -coding** : descifrar (un mensaje), descodificar (una señal)

decoder [dɪ'ko:dər] *n* : descodificador *m*

decompose [ˌdi:kəm'po:z] *v* **-posed; -posing** *vt* **1** BREAK DOWN : descomponer **2** ROT : descomponer, pudrir — *vi* : descomponerse, pudrirse

decomposition [ˌdi:ˌkɑmpə'zɪʃən] *n* : descomposición *f*

decongestant [ˌdi:kən'dʒɛstənt] *n* : descongestionante *m*

decor *or* **décor** [deɪ'kɔr, 'deɪˌkɔr] *n* : decoración *f*

decorate ['dɛkəˌreɪt] *vt* **-rated; -rating 1** ADORN : decorar, adornar **2** : condecorar ⟨he was decorated for bravery : lo condecoraron por valor⟩

decoration [ˌdɛkə'reɪʃən] *n* **1** ADORNMENT : decoración *f*, adorno *m* **2** : condecoración *f* (de honor)

decorative ['dɛkərətɪv, -ˌreɪ-] *adj* : decorativo, ornamental, de adorno

decorator ['dɛkəˌreɪtər] *n* : decorador *m*, -dora *f*

decorum [dɪ'kɔrəm] *n* : decoro *m*

decoy¹ ['di:ˌkɔɪ, dɪ'-] *vt* : atraer (con señuelo)

decoy² *n* : señuelo *m*, reclamo *m*, cimbel *m*

decrease¹ [dɪ'kri:s] *v* **-creased; -creasing** *vi* : decrecer, disminuir, bajar — *vt* : reducir, disminuir

decrease² ['di:ˌkri:s] *n* : disminución *f*, descenso *m*, bajada *f*

decree¹ [dɪ'kri:] *vt* **-creed; -creeing** : decretar

decree² *n* : decreto *m*

decrepit [dɪ'krɛpɪt] *adj* **1** FEEBLE : decrépito, débil **2** DILAPIDATED : deteriorado, ruinoso

decry [dɪ'kraɪ] *vt* **-cried; -crying** : censurar, criticar

dedicate ['dɛdɪˌkeɪt] *vt* **-cated; -cating 1** : dedicar ⟨she dedicated the book to Carlos : le dedicó el libro a Carlos⟩ **2** : consagrar, dedicar ⟨to dedicate one's life : consagrar uno su vida⟩

dedication [ˌdɛdɪ'keɪʃən] *n* **1** DEVOTION : dedicación *f*, devoción *f* **2** : dedicatoria *f* (de un libro, una canción, etc.) **3** CONSECRATION : dedicación *f*

deduce [dɪ'du:s, -'dju:s] *vt* **-duced; -ducing** : deducir, inferir

deduct [dɪ'dʌkt] *vt* : deducir, descontar, restar

deductible [dɪ'dʌktəbəl] *adj* : deducible

deduction [dɪ'dʌkʃən] *n* : deducción *f*

deed¹ ['di:d] *vt* : ceder, transferir

deed² *n* **1** ACT : acto *m*, acción *f*, hecho *m* ⟨a good deed : una buena acción⟩ **2** FEAT : hazaña *f*, proeza *f* **3** TITLE : escritura *f*, título *m*

deem ['di:m] *vt* : considerar, juzgar

deep¹ ['di:p] *adv* : hondo, profundamente ⟨to dig deep : cavar hondo⟩

deep² *adj* **1** : hondo, profundo ⟨the deep end : la parte honda⟩ ⟨a deep wound : una herida profunda⟩ **2** WIDE : ancho **3** INTENSE : profundo, intenso **4** DARK : intenso, subido ⟨deep red : rojo subido⟩ **5** LOW : profundo ⟨a deep tone

: un tono profundo⟩ 6 ABSORBED : absorto ⟨deep in thought : absorto en la meditación⟩

deep³ *n* 1 the deep : lo profundo, el piélago 2 the deep of night : lo más profundo de la noche

deepen ['di:pən] *vt* 1 : ahondar, profundizar 2 INTENSIFY : intensificar — *vi* 1 : hacerse más profundo 2 INTENSIFY : intensificarse

deeply ['di:pli] *adv* : hondo, profundamente ⟨I'm deeply sorry : lo siento sinceramente⟩

deep–seated ['di:p'si:təd] *adj* : profundamente arraigado, enraizado

deer ['dɪr] *ns & pl* : ciervo *m*, venado *m*

deerskin ['dɪr₁skɪn] *n* : piel *f* de venado

deface [di'feɪs] *vt* -faced; -facing MAR : desfigurar

defacement [di'feɪsmənt] *n* : desfiguración *f*

defamation [₁dɛfə'meɪʃən] *n* : difamación *f*

defamatory [di'fæmə₁tori] *adj* : difamatorio

defame [di'feɪm] *vt* -famed; -faming : difamar, calumniar

default¹ [di'fɔlt, 'di:₁fɔlt] *vi* 1 : no cumplir (con una obligación), no pagar 2 : no presentarse (en un tribunal)

default² *n* 1 NEGLECT : omisión *f*, negligencia *f* 2 NONPAYMENT : impago *m*, falta *f* de pago 3 to win by default : ganar por abandono

defaulter [di'fɔltər] *n* : moroso *m*, -sa *f*; rebelde *mf* (en un tribunal)

defeat¹ [di'fi:t] *vt* 1 FRUSTRATE : frustrar 2 BEAT : vencer, derrotar

defeat² *n* : derrota *f*, rechazo *m* (de legislación), fracaso *m* (de planes, etc.)

defecate ['dɛfi₁keɪt] *vi* -cated; -cating : defecar

defect¹ [di'fɛkt] *vi* : desertar

defect² ['di:₁fɛkt, di'fɛkt] *n* : defecto *m*

defection [di'fɛkʃən] *n* : deserción *f*, defección *f*

defective [di'fɛktɪv] *adj* 1 FAULTY : defectuoso 2 DEFICIENT : deficiente

defector [di'fɛktər] *n* : desertor *m*, -tora *f*

defend [di'fɛnd] *vt* : defender

defendant [di'fɛndənt] *n* : acusado *m*, -da *f*; demandado *m*, -da *f*

defender [di'fɛndər] *n* 1 ADVOCATE : defensor *m*, -sora *f* 2 : defensa *mf* (en deportes)

defense [di'fɛnts, 'di:₁fɛnts] *n* : defensa *f*

defenseless [di'fɛntsləs] *adj* : indefenso

defensive¹ [di'fɛntsɪv] *adj* : defensivo

defensive² *n* on the defensive : a la defensiva

defer [di'fər] *v* -ferred; -ferring *vt* POSTPONE : diferir, aplazar, posponer — *vi* to defer to : deferir a

deference ['dɛfərənts] *n* : deferencia *f*

deferential [₁dɛfə'rɛntʃəl] *adj* : respetuoso

deferment [di'fərmənt] *n* : aplazamiento *m*

defiance [di'faɪənts] *n* : desafío *m*

defiant [di'faɪənt] *adj* : desafiante, insolente

deficiency [di'fɪʃəntsi] *n, pl* -cies : deficiencia *f*, carencia *f*

deficient [di'fɪʃənt] *adj* : deficiente, carente

deficit ['dɛfəsɪt] *n* : déficit *m*

defile [di'faɪl] *vt* -filed; -filing 1 DIRTY : ensuciar, manchar 2 CORRUPT : corromper 3 DESECRATE, PROFANE : profanar 4 DISHONOR : deshonrar

defilement [di'faɪlmənt] *n* 1 DESECRATION : profanación *f* 2 CORRUPTION : corrupción *f* 3 CONTAMINATION : contaminación *f*

define [di'faɪn] *vt* -fined; -fining 1 BOUND : delimitar, demarcar 2 CLARIFY : aclarar, definir 3 : definir ⟨to define a word : definir una palabra⟩

definite ['dɛfənɪt] *adj* 1 CERTAIN : definido, determinado 2 CLEAR : claro, explícito 3 UNQUESTIONABLE : seguro, incuestionable

definite article *n* : artículo *m* definido

definitely ['dɛfənɪtli] *adv* 1 DOUBTLESSLY : indudablemente, sin duda 2 DEFINITIVELY : definitivamente, seguramente

definition [₁dɛfə'nɪʃən] *n* : definición *f*

definitive [di'fɪnətɪv] *adj* 1 CONCLUSIVE : definitivo, decisivo 2 AUTHORITATIVE : de autoridad, autorizado

deflate [di'fleɪt] *v* -flated; -flating *vt* 1 : desinflar (una llanta, etc.) 2 REDUCE : rebajar ⟨to deflate one's ego : bajarle los humos a uno⟩ — *vi* : desinflarse

deflation [di'fleɪʃən] *n* 1 : desinflación *f* (de una llanta, etc.) 2 : deflación *f* (económica)

deflect [di'flɛkt] *vt* : desviar — *vi* : desviarse

defoliant [di'fo:liənt] *n* : defoliante *m*

deforestation [di₁forə'steɪʃən] *n* : deforestación *f*, desforestación *f*

deform [di'fɔrm] *vt* : deformar

deformation [₁di:₁fɔr'meɪʃən] *n* : deformación *f*

deformed [di'fɔrmd] *adj* : deforme

deformity [di'fɔrməti] *n, pl* -ties : deformidad *f*

defraud [di'frɔd] *vt* : estafar, defraudar

defray [di'freɪ] *vt* : sufragar, costear

defrost [di'frɔst] *vt* : descongelar, deshelar — *vi* : descongelarse, deshelarse

deft ['dɛft] *adj* : hábil, diestro — **deftly** *adv*

defunct [di'fʌŋkt] *adj* 1 DECEASED : difunto, fallecido 2 EXTINCT : extinto, fenecido

defuse [di'fju:z] *vt* : desactivar ⟨to defuse the situation : reducir las tensiones⟩

defy [di'faɪ] *vt* -fied; -fying 1 CHALLENGE : desafiar, retar 2 DISOBEY : desobedecer 3 RESIST : resistir, hacer imposible, hacer inútil

degenerate¹ [di'dʒɛnə,reɪt] *vi* **-ated; -ating** : degenerar

degenerate² [di'dʒɛnərət] *adj* : degenerado

degeneration [di,dʒɛnə'reɪʃən] *n* : degeneración *f*

degenerative [di'dʒɛnərətɪv] *adj* : degenerative

degradation [,dɛgrə'deɪʃən] *n* : degradación *f*

degrade [di'greɪd] *vt* **-graded; -grading** 1 : degradar, envilecer 2 **to degrade oneself** : rebajarse

degrading [di'greɪdɪŋ] *adj* : degradante

degree [di'gri:] *n* 1 EXTENT : grado *m* ⟨a third degree burn : una quemadura de tercer grado⟩ 2 : título *m* (de enseñanza superior) 3 : grado *m* (de un círculo, de la temperatura) 4 **by degrees** : gradualmente, poco a poco

dehydrate [di'haɪ,dreɪt] *v* **-drated; -drating** *vt* : deshidratar — *vi* : deshidratarse

dehydration [,di:haɪ'dreɪʃən] *n* : deshidratación *f*

deice [,di:'aɪs] *vt* **-iced; -icing** : deshelar, descongelar

deify ['di:ə,faɪ, 'deɪ-] *vt* **-fied; -fying** : deificar

deign ['deɪn] *vi* : dignarse, condescender

deity ['di:əti, 'deɪ-] *n, pl* **-ties** 1 **the Deity** : Dios *m* 2 GOD, GODDESS : deidad *f*; dios *m*, diosa *f*

dejected [di'dʒɛktəd] *adj* : abatido, desalentado, desanimado

dejection [di'dʒɛkʃən] *n* : abatimiento *m*, desaliento *m*, desánimo *m*

delay¹ [di'leɪ] *vt* 1 POSTPONE : posponer, postergar 2 HOLD UP : retrasar, demorar — *vi* : tardar, demorar

delay² *n* 1 LATENESS : tardanza *f* 2 HOLDUP : demora *f*, retraso *m*

delectable [di'lɛktəbəl] *adj* 1 DELICIOUS : delicioso, exquisito 2 DELIGHTFUL : encantador

delegate¹ ['dɛlɪ,geɪt] *v* **-gated; -gating** : delegar

delegate² ['dɛlɪgət, -,geɪt] *n* : delegado *m*, -da *f*

delegation [,dɛlɪ'geɪʃən] *n* : delegación *f*

delete [di'li:t] *vt* **-leted; -leting** : suprimir, tachar, eliminar

deletion [di'li:ʃən] *n* : supresión *f*, tachadura *f*, eliminación *f*

deli ['dɛli] → **delicatessen**

deliberate¹ [di'lɪbə,reɪt] *v* **-ated; -ating** *vt* : deliberar sobre, reflexionar sobre, considerar — *vi* : deliberar

deliberate² [di'lɪbərət] *adj* 1 CONSIDERED : reflexionado, premeditado 2 INTENTIONAL : deliberado, intencional 3 SLOW : lento, pausado

deliberately [di'lɪbərətli] *adv* 1 INTENTIONALLY : adrede, a propósito 2 SLOWLY : pausadamente, lentamente

deliberation [di,lɪbə'reɪʃən] *n* 1 CONSIDERATION : deliberación *f*, consideración *f* 2 SLOWNESS : lentitud *f*

delicacy ['dɛlɪkəsi] *n, pl* **-cies** 1 : manjar *m*, exquisitez *f* ⟨caviar is a real delicacy : el caviar es un verdadero manjar⟩ 2 FINENESS : delicadeza *f* 3 FRAGILITY : fragilidad *f*

delicate ['dɛlɪkət] *adj* 1 SUBTLE : delicado ⟨a delicate fragrance : una fragancia delicada⟩ 2 DAINTY : delicado, primoroso, fino 3 FRAGILE : frágil 4 SENSITIVE : delicado ⟨a delicate matter : un asunto delicado⟩

delicately ['dɛlɪkətli] *adv* : delicadamente, con delicadeza

delicatessen [,dɛlɪkə'tɛsən] *n* : charcutería *f*, fiambrería *f*, salchichonería *f* Mex

delicious [di'lɪʃəs] *adj* : delicioso, exquisito, rico — **deliciously** *adv*

delight¹ [di'laɪt] *vt* : deleitar, encantar — *vi* **to delight in** : deleitarse con, complacerse en

delight² *n* 1 JOY : placer *m*, deleite *m*, gozo *m* 2 : encanto *m* ⟨your garden is a delight : su jardín es un encanto⟩

delightful [di'laɪtfəl] *adj* : delicioso, encantador

delightfully [di'laɪtfəli] *adv* : de manera encantadora, de maravilla

delineate [di'lɪni,eɪt] *vt* **-eated; -eating** : delinear, trazar, bosquejar

delinquency [di'lɪŋkwəntsi] *n, pl* **-cies** : delincuencia *f*

delinquent¹ [di'lɪŋkwənt] *adj* 1 : delincuente 2 OVERDUE : vencido y sin pagar, moroso

delinquent² *n* : delincuente *mf* ⟨juvenile delinquent : delincuente juvenil⟩

delirious [di'lɪriəs] *adj* : delirante ⟨delirious with joy : loco de alegría⟩

delirium [di'lɪriəm] *n* : delirio *m*, desvarío *m*

deliver [di'lɪvər] *vt* 1 FREE : liberar, librar 2 DISTRIBUTE, HAND : entregar, repartir 3 : asistir en el parto de (un niño) 4 : pronunciar ⟨to deliver a speech : pronunciar un discurso⟩ 5 PROJECT : despachar, lanzar ⟨he delivered a fast ball : lanzó un pelota rápida⟩ 6 DEAL : propinar, asestar ⟨to deliver a blow : asestar un golpe⟩

deliverance [di'lɪvərənts] *n* : liberación *f*, rescate *m*, salvación *f*

deliverer [di'lɪvərər] *n* RESCUER : libertador *m*, -dora *f*; salvador *m*, -dora *f*

delivery [di'lɪvəri] *n, pl* **-eries** 1 LIBERATION : liberación *f* 2 : entrega *f*, reparto *m* ⟨cash on delivery : entrega contra reembolso⟩ ⟨home delivery : servicio a domicilio⟩ 3 CHILDBIRTH : parto *m*, alumbramiento *m* 4 SPEECH : expresión *f* oral, modo *m* de hablar 5 THROW : lanzamiento *m*

dell ['dɛl] *n* : hondonada *f*, valle *m* pequeño

delta ['dɛltə] *n* : delta *m*

delude [di'lu:d] *vt* **-luded; -luding** 1 : engañar 2 **to delude oneself** : engañarse

deluge¹ ['dɛlˌjuːʤ, -ˌjuːʒ] *vt* **-uged;
-uging 1** FLOOD : inundar **2** OVER-
WHELM : abrumar ⟨deluged with re-
quests : abrumado de pedidos⟩
deluge² *n* **1** FLOOD : inundación *f* **2**
DOWNPOUR : aguacero *m* **3** BARRAGE
: aluvión *m*
delusion [dɪ'luːʒən] *n* **1** : ilusión *f*
(falsa) **2 delusions of grandeur**
: delirios *mpl* de grandeza
deluxe [di'lʌks, -'lʊks] *adj* : de lujo
delve ['dɛlv] *vi* **delved; delving 1** DIG
: escarbar **2 to delve into** PROBE
: cavar en, ahondar en
demagogue ['dɛməˌgɑg] *n* : demagogo
m, demagoga *f*
demand¹ [di'mænd] *vt* : demandar, exigir, reclamar
demand² *n* **1** REQUEST : petición *f*, pedido *m*, demanda *f* ⟨by popular demand : a petición del público⟩ **2** CLAIM
: reclamación *f*, exigencia *f* **3** MARKET
: demanda *f* ⟨supply and demand : la
oferta y la demanda⟩
demanding [di'mændɪŋ] *adj* : exigente
demarcation [ˌdiː-ˌmɑr'keɪʃən] *n* : demarcación *f*, deslinde *m*
demean [di'miːn] *vt* : degradar, rebajar
demeanor [di'miːnər] *n* : comportamiento *m*, conducta *f*
demented [di'mɛntəd] *adj* : demente,
loco
dementia [di'mɛntʃə] *n* : demencia *f*
demerit [di'mɛrət] *n* : demérito *m*
demigod ['dɛmiˌgɑd, -ˌgɔd] *n* : semidiós
m
demise [di'maɪz] *n* **1** DEATH : fallecimiento *m*, deceso *m* **2** END : hundimiento *m*, desaparición *f* (de una institución, etc.)
demitasse ['dɛmiˌtæs, -ˌtɑs] *n* : taza *f* pequeña (de café)
demobilization [diˌmoːbələ'zeɪʃən] *n*
: desmovilización *f*
demobilize [di'moːbəˌlaɪz] *vt* **-lized;
-lizing** : desmovilizar
democracy [di'mɑkrəsi] *n, pl* **-cies**
: democracia *f*
democrat ['dɛməˌkræt] *n* : demócrata
mf
democratic [ˌdɛmə'krætɪk] *adj* : democrático — **democratically** [-ˌtɪkli] *adv*
demographic [dɛmə'græfɪk] *adj* : demográfico
demolish [di'mɑlɪʃ] *vt* **1** RAZE : demoler, derribar, arrasar **2** DESTROY : destruir, destrozar
demolition [ˌdɛmə'lɪʃən, ˌdiː-] *n* : demolición *f*, derribo *m*
demon ['diːmən] *n* : demonio *m*, diablo
m
demonstrably [di'mɑnstrəbli] *adv* : manifiestamente, claramente
demonstrate ['dɛmənˌstreɪt] *vt* **-strated;
-strating 1** SHOW : demostrar **2** PROVE
: probar, demostrar **3** EXPLAIN : explicar, ilustrar

demonstration [ˌdɛmən'streɪʃən] *n* **1**
SHOW : muestra *f*, demostración *f* **2**
RALLY : manifestación *f*
demonstrative [di'mɑnstrətɪv] *adj* **1**
EFFUSIVE : efusivo, expresivo,
demostrativo **2** : demostrativo (en
lingüística) ⟨demonstrative pronoun
: pronombre demostrativo⟩
demonstrator ['dɛmənˌstreɪtər] *n* **1**
: demostrador *m*, -dora *f* (de productos) **2** PROTESTER : manifestante *mf*
demoralize [di'mɔrəˌlaɪz] *vt* **-ized; -izing**
: desmoralizar
demote [di'moːt] *vt* **-moted; -moting**
: degradar, bajar de categoría
demotion [di'moːʃən] *n* : degradación *f*,
descenso *m* de categoría
demur [di'mər] *vi* **-murred; -murring 1**
OBJECT : oponerse **2 to demur at** : ponerle objeciones a (algo)
demure [di'mjʊr] *adj* : recatado, modesto — **demurely** *adv*
den ['dɛn] *n* **1** LAIR : cubil *m*, madriguera *f* **2** HIDEOUT : guarida *f* **3**
STUDY : estudio *m*, gabinete *m*
denature [di'neɪtʃər] *vt* **-tured; -turing**
: desnaturalizar
denial [di'naɪəl] *n* **1** REFUSAL : rechazo
m, denegación *f*, negativa *f* **2** REPUDI-
ATION : negación *f* (de una creencia,
etc.), rechazo *m*
denigrate ['dɛnɪˌgreɪt] *vt* **-grated; -grat-
ing** : denigrar
denim ['dɛnəm] *n* **1** : tela *f* vaquera,
mezclilla *f* *Chile, Mex* **2 denims** *npl* →
jeans
denizen ['dɛnəzən] *n* : habitante *mf*;
morador *m*, -dora *f*
denomination [dɪˌnɑmə'neɪʃən] *n* **1**
FAITH : confesión *f*, fe *f* **2** VALUE : denominación *f*, valor *m* (de una moneda)
denominator [dɪ'nɑməˌneɪtər] *n* : denominador *m*
denote [di'noːt] *vt* **-noted; -noting 1** IN-
DICATE, MARK : indicar, denotar, se-
ñalar **2** MEAN : significar
denouement [ˌdeɪnu'mɑ] *n* : desenlace
m
denounce [di'naʊnts] *vt* **-nounced;
-nouncing 1** CENSURE : denunciar,
censurar **2** ACCUSE : denunciar,
acusar, delatar
dense ['dɛnts] *adj* **denser; -est 1** THICK
: espeso, denso ⟨dense vegetation : vegetación densa⟩ ⟨a dense fog : una
niebla espesa⟩ **2** STUPID : estúpido,
burro *fam*
densely ['dɛntsli] *adv* **1** THICKLY : densamente **2** STUPIDLY : torpemente
denseness ['dɛntsnəs] *n* **1** → **density 2**
STUPIDITY : estupidez *f*
density ['dɛntsəti] *n, pl* **-ties** : densidad
f
dent¹ ['dɛnt] *vt* : abollar, mellar
dent² *n* : abolladura *f*, mella *f*
dental ['dɛntəl] *adj* : dental
dental floss *n* : hilo *m* dental

dentifrice ['dɛntəfrɪs] *n* : dentífrico *m*, pasta *f* de dientes

dentist ['dɛntɪst] *n* : dentista *mf*

dentistry ['dɛntɪstri] *n* : odontología *f*

dentures ['dɛntʃərz] *npl* : dentadura *f* postiza

denude [di'nu:d, -'nju:d] *vt* -nuded; -nuding STRIP : desnudar, despojar

denunciation [di,nʌntsi'eɪʃən] *n* : denuncia *f*, acusación *f*

deny [di'naɪ] *vt* -nied; -nying 1 REFUTE : desmentir, negar 2 DISOWN, REPUDIATE : negar, renegar de 3 REFUSE : denegar 4 to deny oneself : privarse, sacrificarse

deodorant [di'o:dərənt] *n* : desodorante *m*

deodorize [di'o:də,raɪz] *vt* -ized; -izing : desodorizar

depart [di'pɑrt] *vt* : salirse de — *vi* 1 LEAVE : salir, partir, irse 2 DIE : morir

department [di'pɑrtmənt] *n* 1 DIVISION : sección *f* (de una tienda, una organización, etc.), departamento *m* (de una empresa, una universidad, etc.), ministerio *m* (del gobierno) 2 PROVINCE, SPHERE : esfera *f*, campo *m*, competencia *f*

departmental [di,pɑrt'mɛntəl, ,di:-] *adj* : departamental

department store *n* : grandes almacenes *mpl*

departure [di'pɑrtʃər] *n* 1 LEAVING : salida *f*, partida *f* 2 DEVIATION : desviación *f*

depend [di'pɛnd] *vi* 1 RELY : contar (con), confiar (en) ⟨depend on me! : ¡cuenta conmigo!⟩ 2 to depend on : depender de ⟨success depends on hard work : el éxito depende de trabajar duro⟩ 3 that depends : según, eso depende

dependable [di'pɛndəbəl] *adj* : responsable, digno de confianza, fiable

dependence [di'pɛndənts] *n* : dependencia *f*

dependency [di'pɛndəntsi] *n, pl* -cies 1 → dependence 2 : posesión *f* (de una unidad política)

dependent[1] [di'pɛndənt] *adj* : dependiente

dependent[2] *n* : persona *f* a cargo de alguien

depict [di'pɪkt] *vt* 1 PORTRAY : representar 2 DESCRIBE : describir

depiction [di'pɪkʃən] *n* : representación *f*, descripción *f*

deplete [di'pli:t] *vt* -pleted; -pleting 1 EXHAUST : agotar 2 REDUCE : reducir

depletion [di'pli:ʃən] *n* 1 EXHAUSTION : agotamiento *m* 2 REDUCTION : reducción *f*, disminución *f*

deplorable [di'plorəbəl] *adj* 1 CONTEMPTIBLE : deplorable, despreciable 2 LAMENTABLE : lamentable

deplore [di'plor] *vt* -plored; -ploring 1 REGRET : deplorar, lamentar 2 CONDEMN : condenar, deplorar

deploy [di'plɔɪ] *vt* : desplegar

deployment [di'plɔɪmənt] *n* : despliegue *m*

deport [di'port] *vt* 1 EXPEL : deportar, expulsar (de un país) 2 to deport oneself BEHAVE : comportarse

deportation [,di:,por'teɪʃən] *n* : deportación *f*

depose [di'po:z] *vt* -posed; -posing : deponer

deposit[1] [di'pazət] *vt* -ited; -iting : depositar

deposit[2] *n* 1 : depósito *m* (en el banco) 2 DOWN PAYMENT : entrega *f* inicial 3 : depósito *m*, yacimiento *m* (en geología)

deposition [,dɛpə'zɪʃən] *n* TESTIMONY : deposición *f*

depositor [di'pazətər] *n* : depositante *mf*

depository [di'pazə,tori] *n, pl* -ries : almacén *m*, depósito *m*

depot [*in sense 1 usu* 'dɛ,po:, *2 usu* 'di:-] *n* 1 STOREHOUSE : almacén *m*, depósito *m* 2 STATION, TERMINAL : terminal *mf*, estación *f* (de autobuses, ferrocarriles, etc.)

deprave [di'preɪv] *vt* -praved; -praving : depravar, pervertir

depraved [di'preɪvd] *adj* : depravado, degenerado

depravity [di'prævəti] *n, pl* -ties : depravación *f*

depreciate [di'pri:ʃi,eɪt] *v* -ated; -ating *vt* 1 DEVALUE : depreciar, devaluar 2 DISPARAGE : menospreciar, despreciar — *vi* : depreciarse, devaluarse

depreciation [di,pri:ʃi'eɪʃən] *n* : depreciación *f*, devaluación *f*

depress [di'prɛs] *vt* 1 PRESS, PUSH : apretar, presionar, pulsar 2 REDUCE : reducir, hacer bajar (precios, ventas, etc.) 3 SADDEN : deprimir, abatir, entristecer 4 DEVALUE : depreciar

depressant[1] [di'prɛsənt] *adj* : depresivo

depressant[2] *n* : depresivo *m*

depressed [di'prɛst] *adj* 1 DEJECTED : deprimido, abatido 2 : deprimido, en crisis (dícese de la economía)

depressing [di'prɛsɪŋ] *adj* : deprimente, triste

depression [di'prɛʃən] *n* 1 DESPONDENCY : depresión *f*, abatimiento *m* 2 : depresión (en una superficie) 3 RECESSION : depresión *f* económica, crisis *f*

deprivation [,dɛprə'veɪʃən] *n* : privación *f*

deprive [di'praɪv] *vt* -prived; -priving : privar

depth ['dɛpθ] *n, pl* **depths** ['dɛpθs, 'dɛps] : profundidad *f*, fondo *m* ⟨to study in depth : estudiar a fondo⟩ ⟨in the depths of winter : en pleno invierno⟩

deputize ['dɛpjʊ,taɪz] *vt* -tized; -tizing : nombrar como segundo

deputy ['dɛpjʊti] *n, pl* -ties : suplente *mf*, sustituto *m*, -ta *f*

derail [di'reɪl] *v* : descarrilar

derailment [dɪ'reɪlmənt] *n* : descarrilamiento *m*

derange [dɪ'reɪndʒ] *vt* **-ranged; -ranging** **1** DISARRANGE : desarreglar, desordenar **2** DISTURB, UPSET : trastornar, perturbar **3** MADDEN : enloquecer, volver loco

derangement [dɪ'reɪndʒmənt] *n* **1** DISTURBANCE, UPSET : trastorno *m* **2** INSANITY : locura *f*, perturbación *f* mental

derby ['dərbi] *n, pl* **-bies** **1** : derby *m* ⟨the Kentucky Derby : el Derby de Kentucky⟩ **2** : sombrero *m* hongo

deregulate [dɪ'rɛɡjʊ,leɪt] *vt* **-lated; -lating** : desregular

deregulation [dɪ,rɛɡjʊ'leɪʃən] *n* : desregulación *f*

derelict[1] ['dɛrə,lɪkt] *adj* **1** ABANDONED : abandonado, en ruinas **2** REMISS : negligente, remiso

derelict[2] *n* **1** : propiedad *f* abandonada **2** VAGRANT : vagabundo *m*, -da *f*

deride [dɪ'raɪd] *vt* **-rided; -riding** : ridiculizar, burlarse de

derision [dɪ'rɪʒən] *n* : escarnio *m*, irrisión *f*, mofa *f*

derisive [dɪ'raɪsɪv] *adj* : burlón

derivation [,dɛrə'veɪʃən] *n* : derivación *f*

derivative[1] [dɪ'rɪvətɪv] *adj* **1** DERIVED : derivado **2** BANAL : carente de originalidad, banal

derivative[2] *n* : derivado *m*

derive [dɪ'raɪv] *v* **-rived; -riving** *vt* **1** OBTAIN : obtener, sacar **2** DEDUCE : deducir, inferir — *vi* : provenir, derivar, proceder

dermatologist [,dərmə'talədʒɪst] *n* : dermatólogo *m*, -ga *f*

dermatology [,dərmə'talədʒi] *n* : dermatología *f*

derogatory [dɪ'ragə,tori] *adj* : despectivo, despreciativo

derrick ['dɛrɪk] *n* **1** CRANE : grúa *f* **2** : torre *f* de perforación (sobre un pozo de petróleo)

descend [dɪ'sɛnd] *vt* : descender, bajar — *vi* **1** : descender, bajar ⟨he descended from the platform : descendió del estrado⟩ **2** DERIVE : descender, provenir **3** STOOP : rebajarse ⟨I descended to his level : me rebajé a su nivel⟩ **4** **to descend upon** : caer sobre, invadir

descendant[1] [dɪ'sɛndənt] *adj* : descendente

descendant[2] *n* : descendiente *mf*

descent [dɪ'sɛnt] *n* **1** : bajada *f*, descenso *m* ⟨the descent from the mountain : el descenso de la montaña⟩ **2** ANCESTRY : ascendencia *f*, linaje *f* **3** SLOPE : pendiente *f*, cuesta *f* **4** FALL : caída *f* **5** ATTACK : incursión *f*, ataque *m*

describe [dɪ'skraɪb] *vt* **-scribed; -scribing** : describir

description [dɪ'skrɪpʃən] *n* : descripción *f*

descriptive [dɪ'skrɪptɪv] *adj* : descriptivo ⟨descriptive adjective : adjetivo calificativo⟩

desecrate ['dɛsɪ,kreɪt] *vt* **-crated; -crating** : profanar

desecration [,dɛsɪ'kreɪʃən] *n* : profanación *f*

desegregate [di'sɛɡrə,ɡeɪt] *vt* **-gated; -gating** : eliminar la segregación racial de

desegregation [di,sɛɡrə'ɡeɪʃən] *n* : eliminación *f* de la segregación racial

desert[1] [dɪ'zərt] *vt* : abandonar (una persona o un lugar), desertar de (una causa, etc.) — *vi* : desertar

desert[2] ['dɛzərt] *adj* : desierto ⟨a desert island : una isla desierta⟩

desert[3] *n* **1** ['dɛzərt] : desierto *m* (en geografía) **2** [dɪ'zərt] → **deserts**

deserter [dɪ'zərtər] *n* : desertor *m*, -tora *f*

desertion [dɪ'zərʃən] *n* : abandono *m*, deserción *f* (militar)

deserts [dɪ'zərts] *npl* : merecido *m* ⟨to get one's just deserts : llevarse uno su merecido⟩

deserve [dɪ'zərv] *vt* **-served; -serving** : merecer, ser digno de

deserving [dɪ'zərvɪŋ] *adj* : meritorio ⟨deserving of : digno de⟩

desiccate ['dɛsɪ,keɪt] *vt* **-cated; -cating** : desecar, deshidratar

design[1] [dɪ'zaɪn] *vt* **1** DEVISE : diseñar, concebir, idear **2** PLAN : proyectar **3** SKETCH : trazar, bosquejar

design[2] *n* **1** PLAN, SCHEME : plan *m*, proyecto *m* ⟨by design : a propósito, intencionalmente⟩ **2** SKETCH : diseño *m*, bosquejo *m* **3** PATTERN, STYLE : diseño *m*, estilo *m* **4** **designs** *npl* INTENTIONS : propósitos *mpl*, designios *mpl*

designate ['dɛzɪɡ,neɪt] *vt* **-nated; -nating** **1** INDICATE, SPECIFY : indicar, especificar **2** APPOINT : nombrar, designar

designation [,dɛzɪɡ'neɪʃən] *n* **1** NAMING : designación *f* **2** NAME : denominación *f*, nombre *m* **3** APPOINTMENT : designación *f*, nombramiento *m*

designer [dɪ'zaɪnər] *n* : diseñador *m*, -dora *f*

desirability [dɪ,zaɪrə'bɪləti] *n, pl* **-ties** **1** ADVISABILITY : conveniencia *f* **2** ATTRACTIVENESS : atractivo *m*

desirable [dɪ'zaɪrəbəl] *adj* **1** ADVISABLE : conveniente, aconsejable **2** ATTRACTIVE : deseable, atractivo

desire[1] [dɪ'zaɪr] *vt* **-sired; -siring** **1** WANT : desear **2** REQUEST : rogar, solicitar

desire[2] *n* : deseo *m*, anhelo *m*, ansia *m*

desist [dɪ'sɪst, -'zɪst] *vi* **to desist from** : desistir de, abstenerse de

desk ['dɛsk] *n* : escritorio *m*, pupitre *m* (en la escuela)

desktop ['dɛsk,tap] *adj* : de escritorio

desolate[1] ['dɛsə,leɪt, -zə-] *vt* **-lated; -lating** : devastar, desolar

desolate² ['dɛsələt, -zə-] *adj* **1** BARREN : desolado, desierto, yermo **2** DISCONSOLATE : desconsolado, desolado

desolation [ˌdɛsə'leɪʃən, -zə-] *n* : desolación *f*

despair¹ [di'spær] *vi* : desesperar, perder las esperanzas

despair² *n* : desesperación *f*, desesperanza *f*

desperate ['dɛspərət] *adj* **1** HOPELESS : desesperado, sin esperanzas **2** RASH : desesperado, precipitado **3** SERIOUS, URGENT : grave, urgente, apremiante ⟨a desperate need : una necesidad apremiante⟩

desperately ['dɛspərətli] *adv* : desesperadamente, urgentemente

desperation [ˌdɛspə'reɪʃən] *n* : desesperación *f*

despicable [di'spɪkəbəl, 'dɛspɪ-] *adj* : vil, despreciable, infame

despise [di'spaɪz] *vt* **-spised; -spising** : despreciar

despite [də'spaɪt] *prep* : a pesar de, aún con

despoil [di'spɔɪl] *vt* : saquear

despondency [di'spɑndən*t*si] *n* : desaliento *m*, desánimo *m*, depresión *f*

despondent [di'spɑndənt] *adj* : desalentado, desanimado

despot ['dɛspət, -ˌpɑt] *n* : déspota *mf*; tirano *m*, -na *f*

despotic [dɛs'pɑtɪk] *adj* : despótico

despotism ['dɛspəˌtɪzəm] *n* : despotismo *m*

dessert [di'zərt] *n* : postre *m*

destination [ˌdɛstə'neɪʃən] *n* : destino *m*, destinación *f*

destined ['dɛstənd] *adj* **1** FATED : predestinado **2** BOUND : destinado, con destino (a), con rumbo (a)

destiny ['dɛstəni] *n, pl* **-nies** : destino *m*

destitute ['dɛstəˌtuːt, -ˌtjuːt] *adj* **1** LACKING : carente, desprovisto **2** POOR : indigente, en miseria

destitution [ˌdɛstə'tuːʃən, -'tjuː-] *n* : indigencia *f*, miseria *f*

destroy [di'strɔɪ] *vt* **1** KILL : matar **2** DEMOLISH : destruir, destrozar

destroyer [di'strɔɪər] *n* : destructor *m* (buque)

destructible [di'strʌktəbəl] *adj* : destructible

destruction [di'strʌkʃən] *n* : destrucción *f*, ruina *f*

destructive [di'strʌktɪv] *adj* : destructor, destructivo

desultory ['dɛsəlˌtori] *adj* **1** AIMLESS : sin rumbo, sin objeto **2** DISCONNECTED : inconexo

detach [di'tætʃ] *vt* : separar, quitar, desprender

detached [di'tætʃt] *adj* **1** SEPARATE : separado, suelto **2** ALOOF : distante, indiferente **3** IMPARTIAL : imparcial, objetivo

detachment [di'tætʃmənt] *n* **1** SEPARATION : separación *f* **2** DETAIL : destacamento *m* (de tropas) **3** ALOOFNESS : reserva *f*, indiferencia *f* **4** IMPARTIALITY : imparcialidad *f*

detail¹ [di'teɪl, 'diːˌteɪl] *vt* : detallar, exponer en detalle

detail² *n* **1** : detalle *m*, pormenor *m* **2** : destacamento *m* (de tropas)

detailed [di'teɪld, 'diːˌteɪld] *adj* : detallado, minucioso

detain [di'teɪn] *vt* **1** HOLD : detener **2** DELAY : entretener, demorar, retrasar

detect [di'tɛkt] *vt* : detectar, descubrir

detection [di'tɛkʃən] *n* : descubrimiento *m*

detective [di'tɛktɪv] *n* : detective *mf* ⟨private detective : detective privado⟩

detector [di'tɛktər] *n* : detector *m*

detention [di'tɛnʃən] *n* : detención *m*

deter [di'tər] *vt* **-terred; -terring** : disuadir, impedir

detergent [di'tərdʒənt] *n* : detergente *m*

deteriorate [di'tɪriəˌreɪt] *vi* **-rated; -rating** : deteriorarse, empeorar

deterioration [diˌtɪriə'reɪʃən] *n* : deterioro *m*, empeoramiento *m*

determinant¹ [di'tərmənənt] *adj* : determinante

determinant² *n* **1** : factor *m* determinante **2** : determinante *m* (en matemáticas)

determination [diˌtərmə'neɪʃən] *n* **1** DECISION : determinación *f*, decisión *f* **2** RESOLUTION : resolución *f*, determinación *f* ⟨with grim determination : con una firme resolución⟩

determine [di'tərmən] *vt* **-mined; -mining 1** ESTABLISH : determinar, establecer **2** SETTLE : decidir **3** FIND OUT : averiguar **4** BRING ABOUT : determinar

determined [di'tərmənd] *adj* RESOLUTE : decidido, resuelto

deterrent [di'tərənt] *n* : medida *f* disuasiva

detest [di'tɛst] *vt* : detestar, odiar, aborrecer

detestable [di'tɛstəbəl] *adj* : detestable, odioso, aborrecible

dethrone [di'θroːn] *vt* **-throned; -throning** : destronar

detonate ['dɛtənˌeɪt] *v* **-nated; -nating** *vt* : hacer detonar — *vi* : detonar, estallar

detonation [ˌdɛtə'neɪʃən] *n* : detonación *f*

detour¹ ['diːˌtur, di'tur] *vi* : desviarse

detour² *n* : desvío *m*, rodeo *m*

detract [di'trækt] *vi* **to detract from** : restarle valor a, quitarle méritos a

detractor [di'træktər] *n* : detractor *m*, -tora *f*

detriment ['dɛtrəmənt] *n* : detrimento *m*, perjuicio *m*

detrimental [ˌdɛtrə'mɛntəl] *adj* : perjudicial — **detrimentally** *adv*

devaluation [diˌvæljuˈeɪʃən] *n* : devaluación *f*

devalue [di'væljuː] *vt* **-ued; -uing** : devaluar, depreciar

devastate ['dɛvə,steɪt] *vt* **-tated; -tating** : devastar, arrasar, asolar

devastation [,dɛvə'steɪʃən] *n* : devastación *f*, estragos *mpl*

develop [dɪ'vɛləp] *vt* **1** FORM, MAKE : desarrollar, elaborar, formar **2** : revelar (en fotografía) **3** FOSTER : desarrollar, fomentar **4** EXPLOIT : explotar (recursos), urbanizar (un área) **5** ACQUIRE : adquirir ⟨to develop an interest : adquirir un interés⟩ **6** CONTRACT : contraer (una enfermedad) — *vi* **1** GROW : desarrollarse **2** ARISE : aparecer, surgir

developed [dɪ'vɛləpt] *adj* : avanzado, desarrollado

developer [dɪ'vɛləpər] *n* **1** : inmobiliaria *f*, urbanizadora *f* **2** : revelador *m* (en fotografía)

development [dɪ'vɛləpmənt] *n* **1** : desarrollo *m* ⟨physical development : desarrollo físico⟩ **2** : urbanización *f* (de un área), explotación *f* (de recursos), creación *f* (de inventos) **3** EVENT : acontecimiento *m*, suceso *m* ⟨to await developments : esperar acontecimientos⟩

deviant ['di:viənt] *adj* : desviado, anormal

deviate ['di:vi,eɪt] *v* **-ated; -ating** *vi* : desviarse, apartarse — *vt* : desviar

deviation [,di:vi'eɪʃən] *n* : desviación *f*

device [dɪ'vaɪs] *n* **1** MECHANISM : dispositivo *m*, aparato *m*, mecanismo *m* **2** EMBLEM : emblema *m*

devil[1] ['dɛvəl] *vt* **-iled** *or* **-illed; -iling** *or* **-illing** **1** : sazonar con picante y especias **2** PESTER : molestar

devil[2] *n* **1** SATAN : el diablo, Satanás *m* **2** DEMON : diablo *m*, demonio *m* **3** FIEND : persona *f* diabólica; malvado *m*, -da *f*

devilish ['dɛvəlɪʃ] *adj* : diabólico

devilry ['dɛvəlri] *n, pl* **-ries** : diabluras *fpl*, travesuras *fpl*

devious ['di:viəs] *adj* **1** CRAFTY : taimado, artero **2** WINDING : tortuoso, sinuoso

devise [dɪ'vaɪz] *vt* **-vised; -vising** **1** INVENT : idear, concebir, inventar **2** PLOT : tramar

devoid [dɪ'vɔɪd] *adj* ~ **of** : carente de, desprovisto de

devote [dɪ'vo:t] *vt* **-voted; -voting** **1** DEDICATE : consagrar, dedicar ⟨to devote one's life : dedicar uno su vida⟩ **2 to devote oneself** : dedicarse

devoted [dɪ'vo:təd] *adj* **1** FAITHFUL : leal, fiel **2 to be devoted to someone** : tenerle mucho cariño a alguien

devotee [,dɛvə'ti:, -'teɪ] *n* : devoto *m*, -ta *f*

devotion [dɪ'vo:ʃən] *n* **1** DEDICATION : dedicación *f*, devoción *f* **2 devotions** PRAYERS : oraciones *fpl*, devociones *fpl*

devour [dɪ'vauər] *vt* : devorar

devout [dɪ'vaut] *adj* **1** PIOUS : devoto, piadoso **2** EARNEST, SINCERE : sincero, ferviente — **devoutly** *adv*

devoutness [dɪ'vautnəs] *n* : devoción *f*, piedad *f*

dew ['du:, 'dju:] *n* : rocío *m*

dewlap ['du:,læp, 'dju-] *n* : papada *f*

dew point *n* : punto *m* de condensación

dewy ['du:i, 'dju:i] *adj* **dewier; -est** : cubierto de rocío

dexterity [dɛk'stɛrəti] *n, pl* **-ties** : destreza *f*, habilidad *f*

dexterous ['dɛkstrəs] *adj* : diestro, hábil

dexterously ['dɛkstrəsli] *adv* : con destreza, con habilidad, hábilmente

dextrose ['dɛk,stro:s] *n* : dextrosa *f*

diabetes [,daɪə'bi:,tiz] *n* : diabetes *f*

diabetic[1] [,daɪə'bɛtɪk] *adj* : diabético

diabetic[2] *n* : diabético *m*, -ca *f*

diabolic [,daɪə'balɪk] *or* **diabolical** [-lɪkəl] *adj* : diabólico, satánico

diacritical mark [,daɪə'krɪtɪkəl] *n* : signo *m* diacrítico

diadem ['daɪə,dɛm, -dəm] *n* : diadema *f*

diagnose ['daɪɪg,no:s, ,daɪɪg'no:s] *vt* **-nosed; -nosing** : diagnosticar

diagnosis [,daɪɪg'no:sɪs] *n, pl* **-noses** [-'no:,si:z] : diagnóstico *m*

diagnostic [,daɪɪg'nastɪk] *adj* : diagnóstico

diagonal[1] [daɪ'ægənəl] *adj* : diagonal, en diagonal

diagonal[2] *n* : diagonal *f*

diagonally [daɪ'ægənəli] *adv* : diagonalmente, en diagonal

diagram[1] ['daɪə,græm] *vt* **-gramed** *or* **-grammed; -graming** *or* **-gramming** : hacer un diagrama de

diagram[2] *n* : diagrama *m*, gráfico *m*, esquema *m*

dial[1] ['daɪl] *v* **dialed** *or* **dialled; dialing** *or* **dialling** : marcar, discar

dial[2] *n* : esfera *f* (de un reloj), dial *m* (de un radio), disco *m* (de un teléfono)

dialect ['daɪə,lɛkt] *n* : dialecto *m*

dialogue ['daɪə,lɔg] *n* : diálogo *m*

diameter [daɪ'æmətər] *n* : diámetro *m*

diamond ['daɪmənd, 'daɪə-] *n* **1** : diamante *m*, brillante *m* ⟨a diamond necklace : un collar de brillantes⟩ **2** : rombo *m*, forma *f* de rombo **3** : diamante *m* (en naipes) **4** INFIELD : cuadro *m*, diamante *m* (en béisbol)

diaper ['daɪpər, 'daɪə-] *n* : pañal *m*

diaphragm ['daɪə,fræm] *n* : diafragma *m*

diarrhea [,daɪə'ri:ə] *n* : diarrea *f*

diary ['daɪəri] *n, pl* **-ries** : diario *m*

diatribe ['daɪə,traɪb] *n* : diatriba *f*

dice[1] ['daɪs] *vt* **diced; dicing** : cortar en cubos

dice[2] *ns & pl* **1** → **die**[2] **2** : dados *mpl* (juego)

dicker ['dɪkər] *vt* : regatear

dictate[1] ['dɪk,teɪt, dɪk'teɪt] *v* **-tated; -tating** *vt* **1** : dictar ⟨to dictate a letter : dictar una carta⟩ **2** ORDER : mandar, ordenar — *vi* : dar órdenes

dictate² ['dık₁teɪt] *n* **1** : mandato *m*, orden *f* **2 dictates** *npl* : dictados *mpl* ⟨the dictates of conscience : los dictados de la conciencia⟩

dictation [dık'teɪʃən] *n* : dictado *m*

dictator ['dık₁teɪtər] *n* : dictador *m*, -dora *f*

dictatorial [₁dıktə'toriəl] *adj* : dictatorial — **dictatorially** *adv*

dictatorship [dık'teɪtər₁ʃıp, 'dık₁-] *n* : dictadura *f*

diction ['dıkʃən] *n* **1** : lenguaje *m*, estilo *m* **2** ENUNCIATION : dicción *f*, articulación *f*

dictionary ['dıkʃə₁nɛri] *n, pl* **-naries** : diccionario *m*

did → **do**

didactic [daɪ'dæktık] *adj* : didáctico

die¹ ['daɪ] *vi* **died** ['daɪd]; **dying** ['daɪɪŋ] **1** : morir **2** CEASE : morir, morirse ⟨a dying civilization : una civilización moribunda⟩ **3** STOP : apagarse, dejar de funcionar ⟨the motor died : el motor se apagó⟩ **4 to die down** SUBSIDE : amainar, disminuir **5 to die out** : extinguirse **6 to be dying for** *or* **to be dying to** : morirse por ⟨I'm dying to leave : me muero por irme⟩

die² ['daɪ] *n, pl* **dice** ['daɪs] : dado *m*

die³ *n, pl* **dies** ['daɪz] **1** STAMP : troquel *m*, cuño *m* **2** MOLD : matriz *f*, molde *m*

diesel ['di:zəl, -səl] *n* : diesel *m*

diet¹ ['daɪət] *vi* : ponerse a régimen, hacer dieta

diet² *n* : régimen *m*, dieta *f*

dietary ['daɪə₁tɛri] *adj* : alimenticio, dietético

dietitian *or* **dietician** [₁daɪə'tıʃən] *n* : dietista *mf*

differ ['dıfər] *vi* **-ferred; -ferring 1** : diferir, diferenciarse **2** VARY : variar **3** DISAGREE : discrepar, diferir, no estar de acuerdo

difference ['dıfrənts, 'dıfərənts] *n* : diferencia *f*

different ['dıfrənt, 'dıfərənt] *adj* : distinto, diferente

differentiate [₁dıfə'rɛntʃi₁eɪt] *v* **-ated; -ating** *vt* **1** : hacer diferente **2** DISTINGUISH : distinguir, diferenciar — *vi* : distinguir

differentiation [₁dıfə₁rɛntʃi'eɪʃən] *n* : diferenciación *f*

differently ['dıfrəntli, 'dıfərənt-] *adv* : de otra manera, de otro modo, distintamente

difficult ['dıfı₁kʌlt] *adj* : difícil

difficulty ['dıfı₁kʌlti] *n, pl* **-ties 1** : dificultad *f* **2** PROBLEM : problema *f*, dificultad *f*

diffidence ['dıfədənts] *n* **1** SHYNESS : retraimiento *m*, timidez *f*, apocamiento *m* **2** RETICENCE : reticencia *f*

diffident ['dıfədənt] *adj* **1** SHY : tímido, apocado, inseguro **2** RESERVED : reservado

diffuse¹ [dı'fju:z] *v* **-fused; -fusing** *vt* : difundir, esparcir — *vi* : difundirse, esparcirse

diffuse² [dı'fju:s] *adj* **1** WORDY : prolijo, verboso **2** WIDESPREAD : difuso

diffusion [dı'fju:ʒən] *n* : difusión *f*

dig¹ ['dıg] *v* **dug** ['dʌg]; **digging** *vt* **1** : cavar, excavar ⟨to dig a hole : cavar un hoyo⟩ **2** EXTRACT : sacar ⟨to dig up potatoes : sacar papas del suelo⟩ **3** POKE, THRUST : clavar, hincar ⟨he dug me in the ribs : me dio un codazo en las costillas⟩ **4 to dig up** DISCOVER : descubrir, sacar a luz — *vi* : cavar, excavar

dig² *n* **1** POKE : codazo *m* **2** GIBE : pulla *f* **3** EXCAVATION : excavación *f*

digest¹ [daɪ'ʤɛst, dı-] *vt* **1** ASSIMILATE : digerir, asimilar **2** : digerir (comida) **3** SUMMARIZE : compendiar, resumir

digest² ['daɪ₁ʤɛst] *n* : compendio *m*, resumen *m*

digestible [daɪ'ʤɛstəbəl, dı-] *adj* : digerible

digestion [daɪ'ʤɛstʃən, dı-] *n* : digestión *f*

digestive [daɪ'ʤɛstıv, dı-] *adj* : digestivo ⟨the digestive system : el sistema digestivo⟩

digit ['dıʤət] *n* **1** NUMERAL : dígito *m*, número *m* **2** FINGER, TOE : dedo *m*

digital ['dıʤətəl] *adj* : digital — **digitally** *adv*

dignified ['dıgnə₁faɪd] *adj* : digno, decoroso

dignify ['dıgnə₁faɪ] *vt* **-fied; -fying** : dignificar, honrar

dignitary ['dıgnə₁tɛri] *n, pl* **-taries** : dignatario *m*, -ria *f*

dignity ['dıgnəti] *n, pl* **-ties** : dignidad *f*

digress [daɪ'grɛs, də-] *vi* : desviarse del tema, divagar

digression [daɪ'grɛʃən, də-] *n* : digresión *f*

dike *or* **dyke** ['daɪk] *n* : dique *m*

dilapidated [də'læpə₁deɪtəd] *adj* : ruinoso, desvencijado, destartalado

dilapidation [də₁læpə'deɪʃən] *n* : deterioro *m*, estado *m* ruinoso

dilate [daɪ'leɪt, 'daɪ₁leɪt] *v* **-lated; -lating** *vt* : dilatar — *vi* : dilatarse

dilemma [dı'lɛmə] *n* : dilema *m*

dilettante ['dılə₁tɑnt, -₁tænt] *n, pl* **-tantes** [-₁tɑnts, -₁tænts] *or* **-tanti** [₁dılə'tɑnti, -'tæn-] : diletante *mf*

diligence ['dıləʤənts] *n* : diligencia *f*, aplicación *f*

diligent ['dıləʤənt] *adj* : diligente ⟨a diligent search : una búsqueda minuciosa⟩ — **diligently** *adv*

dill ['dıl] *n* : eneldo *m*

dillydally ['dıli₁dæli] *vi* **-lied; lying** : demorarse, perder tiempo

dilute [daɪ'lu:t, də-] *vt* **-luted; -luting** : diluir, aguar

dilution [daɪ'lu:ʃən, də-] *n* : dilución *f*

dim¹ ['dım] *v* **dimmed; dimming** *vt* : atenuar (la luz), nublar (la vista), borrar (la memoria), opacar (una superficie) — *vi* : oscurecerse, apagarse

dim² *adj* **dimmer; dimmest 1** FAINT : oscuro, tenue (dícese de la luz), nublado (dícese de la vista), borrado (dícese de la memoria) **2** DULL : deslustrado **3** STUPID : tonto, torpe

dime ['daim] *n* : moneda *f* de diez centavos

dimension [də'mɛntʃən, dai-] *n* **1** : dimensión *f* **2 dimensions** *npl* EXTENT, SCOPE : dimensiones *fpl*, extensión *f*, medida *f*

diminish [də'mɪnɪʃ] *vt* LESSEN : disminuir, reducir, amainar — *vi* DWINDLE, WANE : menguar, reducirse

diminutive [də'mɪnjʊt̬ɪv] *adj* : diminutivo, minúsculo

dimly ['dɪmli] *adv* : indistintamente, débilmente

dimmer ['dɪmər] *n* : potenciómetro *m*, conmutador *m* de luces (en automóviles)

dimness ['dɪmnəs] *n* : oscuridad *f*, debilidad *f* (de la vista), imprecisión *f* (de la memoria)

dimple ['dɪmpəl] *n* : hoyuelo *m*

din ['dɪn] *n* : estrépito *m*, estruendo *m*

dine ['daɪn] *vi* **dined; dining** : cenar

diner ['daɪnər] *n* **1** : comensal *mf* (persona) **2** : vagón *m* restaurante (en un tren) **3** : cafetería *f*, restaurante *m* barato

dinghy ['dɪŋi, 'dɪŋgi, 'dɪŋki] *n, pl* **-ghies** : bote *m*

dinginess ['dɪndʒinəs] *n* **1** DIRTINESS : suciedad *f* **2** SHABBINESS : lo gastado, lo deslucido

dingy ['dɪndʒi] *adj* **-gier; -est 1** DIRTY : sucio **2** SHABBY : gastado, deslucido

dinner ['dɪnər] *n* : cena *f*, comida *f*

dinosaur ['daɪnə‚sɔr] *n* : dinosaurio *m*

dint ['dɪnt] *n* **by dint of** : a fuerza de

diocese ['daɪəsəs, -‚siːz, -‚siːs] *n, pl* **-ceses** ['daɪəsəsəz] : diócesis *f*

dip¹ ['dɪp] *v* **dipped; dipping** *vt* **1** DUNK, PLUNGE : sumergir, mojar, meter **2** LADLE : servir con cucharón **3** LOWER : bajar, arriar (una bandera) — *vi* **1** DESCEND, DROP : bajar en picada, descender **2** SLOPE : bajar, inclinarse

dip² *n* **1** SWIM : chapuzón *m* **2** DROP : descenso *m*, caída *f* **3** SLOPE : cuesta *f*, declive *m* **4** SAUCE : salsa *f*

diphtheria [dɪf'θɪriə] *n* : difteria *f*

diphthong ['dɪf‚θɔŋ] *n* : diptongo *m*

diploma [də'ploːmə] *n, pl* **-mas** : diploma *m*

diplomacy [də'ploːməsi] *n* **1** : diplomacia *f* **2** TACT : tacto *m*, discreción *f*

diplomat ['dɪplə‚mæt] *n* **1** : diplomático *m*, -ca *f* (en relaciones internacionales) **2** : persona *f* diplomática

diplomatic [‚dɪplə'mæt̬ɪk] *adj* : diplomático ⟨diplomatic immunity : inmunidad diplomática⟩

dipper ['dɪpər] *n* **1** LADLE : cucharón *m*, cazo *m* **2 Big Dipper** : Osa *f* Mayor **3 Little Dipper** : Osa *f* Menor

dire ['daɪr] *adj* **direr; direst 1** HORRIBLE : espantoso, terrible, horrendo **2** EXTREME : extremo ⟨dire poverty : pobreza extrema⟩

direct¹ [də'rɛkt, daɪ-] *vt* **1** ADDRESS : dirigir, mandar **2** AIM, POINT : dirigir **3** GUIDE : indicarle el camino (a alguien), orientar **4** MANAGE : dirigir ⟨to direct a film : dirigir una película⟩ **5** COMMAND : ordenar, mandar

direct² *adv* : directamente

direct³ *adj* **1** STRAIGHT : directo **2** FRANK : franco

direct current *n* : corriente *f* continua

direction [də'rɛkʃən, daɪ-] *n* **1** SUPERVISION : dirección *f* **2** INSTRUCTION, ORDER : instrucción *f*, orden *f* **3** COURSE : dirección *f*, rumbo *m* ⟨to change direction : cambiar de dirección⟩ **4 to ask directions** : pedir indicaciones

directional [də'rɛkʃənəl, daɪ-] *adj* : direccional

directive [də'rɛktɪv, daɪ-] *n* : directiva *f*

directly [də'rɛktli, daɪ-] *adv* **1** STRAIGHT : directamente ⟨directly north : directamente al norte⟩ **2** FRANKLY : francamente **3** EXACTLY : exactamente, justo ⟨directly opposite : justo enfrente⟩ **4** IMMEDIATELY : en seguida, inmediatamente

directness [də'rɛktnəs, daɪ-] *n* : franqueza *f*

director [də'rɛktər, daɪ-] *n* **1** : director *m*, -tora *f* **2 board of directors** : junta *f* directiva, directorio *m*

directory [də'rɛktəri, daɪ-] *n, pl* **-ries** : guía *f*, directorio *m* ⟨telephone directory : directorio telefónico⟩

dirge ['dərdʒ] *n* : canto *m* fúnebre

dirigible ['dɪrədʒəbəl, də'rɪdʒə-] *n* : dirigible *m*, zepelín *m*

dirt ['dərt] *n* **1** FILTH : suciedad *f*, mugre *f*, porquería *f* **2** SOIL : tierra *f*

dirtiness ['dərt̬inəs] *n* : suciedad *f*

dirty¹ ['dərt̬i] *vt* **dirtied; dirtying** : ensuciar, manchar

dirty² *adj* **dirtier; -est 1** SOILED, STAINED : sucio, manchado **2** DISHONEST : sucio, deshonesto ⟨a dirty player : un jugador tramposo⟩ ⟨a dirty trick : una mala pasada⟩ **3** INDECENT : indecente, cochino ⟨a dirty joke : un chiste verde⟩

disability [‚dɪsə'bɪləti] *n, pl* **-ties** : minusvalía *f*, discapacidad *f*, invalidez *f*

disable [dɪs'eɪbəl] *vt* **-abled; -abling** : dejar inválido, inutilizar, incapacitar

disabled [dɪs'eɪbəld] *adj* : minusválido, discapacitado

disabuse [‚dɪsə'bjuːz] *vt* **-bused; -busing** : desengañar, sacar del error

disadvantage [‚dɪsəd'væntɪdʒ] *n* : desventaja *f*

disadvantageous [‚dɪs‚æd‚væn'teɪ-dʒəs] *adj* : desventajoso, desfavorable

disagree [ˌdɪsəˈgriː] *vi* **1** DIFFER : discrepar, no coincidir **2** DISSENT : disentir, discrepar, no estar de acuerdo

disagreeable [ˌdɪsəˈgriːbəl] *adj* : desagradable

disagreement [ˌdɪsəˈgriːmənt] *n* **1** : desacuerdo *m* **2** DISCREPANCY : discrepancia *f* **3** ARGUMENT : discusión *f*, altercado *m*, disputa *f*

disappear [ˌdɪsəˈpɪr] *vi* : desaparecer, desvanecerse ⟨to disappear from view : perderse de vista⟩

disappearance [ˌdɪsəˈpɪrənts] *n* : desaparición *f*

disappoint [ˌdɪsəˈpɔɪnt] *vt* : decepcionar, defraudar, fallar

disappointing [ˌdɪsəˈpɔɪntɪŋ] *adj* : decepcionante

disappointment [ˌdɪsəˈpɔɪntmənt] *n* : decepción *f*, desilusión *f*, chasco *m*

disapproval [ˌdɪsəˈpruːvəl] *n* : desaprobación *f*

disapprove [ˌdɪsəˈpruːv] *vi* **-proved; -proving** : desaprobar, estar en contra

disapprovingly [ˌdɪsəˈpruːvɪŋli] *adv* : con desaprobación

disarm [dɪsˈɑrm] *vt* : desarmar

disarmament [dɪsˈɑrməmənt] *n* : desarme *m* ⟨nuclear disarmament : desarme nuclear⟩

disarrange [ˌdɪsəˈreɪndʒ] *vt* **-ranged; -ranging** : desarreglar, desordenar

disarray [ˌdɪsəˈreɪ] *n* : desorden *m*, confusión *f*, desorganización *f*

disaster [dɪˈzæstər] *n* : desastre *m*, catástrofe *f*

disastrous [dɪˈzæstrəs] *adj* : desastroso

disband [dɪsˈbænd] *vt* : disolver — *vi* : disolverse, dispersarse

disbar [dɪsˈbɑr] *vt* **-barred; -barring** : prohibir de ejercer la abogacía

disbelief [ˌdɪsbɪˈliːf] *n* : incredulidad *f*

disbelieve [ˌdɪsbɪˈliːv] *v* **-lieved; -lieving** : no creer, dudar

disburse [dɪsˈbərs] *vt* **-bursed; -bursing** : desembolsar

disbursement [dɪsˈbərsmənt] *n* : desembolso *m*

disc → **disk**

discard [dɪsˈkɑrd, ˈdɪsˌkɑrd] *vt* : desechar, deshacerse de, botar — *vi* : descartarse (en juegos de naipes)

discern [dɪˈsərn, -ˈzərn] *vt* : discernir, distinguir, percibir

discernible [dɪˈsərnəbəl, -ˈzər-] *adj* : perceptible, visible

discernment [dɪˈsərnmənt, -ˈzərn-] *n* : discernimiento *m*, criterio *m*

discharge¹ [dɪsˈtʃɑrdʒ, ˈdɪsˌ-] *v* **-charged; -charging 1** UNLOAD : descargar (carga), desembarcar (pasajeros) **2** SHOOT : descargar, disparar **3** FREE : liberar, poner en libertad **4** DISMISS : despedir **5** EMIT : despedir (humo, etc.), descargar (electricidad) **6** : cumplir con (una obligación), saldar (una deuda) — *vi* **1** : descargarse (dícese de una batería) **2** OOZE : supurar

discharge² [ˈdɪsˌtʃɑrdʒ, dɪsˈ-] *n* **1** EMISSION : descarga *f* (de electricidad), emisión *f* (de gases) **2** DISMISSAL : despido *m* (del empleo), baja *f* (del ejército) **3** SECRETION : secreción *f*

disciple [dɪˈsaɪpəl] *n* : discípulo *m*, -la *f*

discipline¹ [ˈdɪsəplən] *vt* **-plined; -plining 1** PUNISH : castigar, sancionar (a los empleados) **2** CONTROL : disciplinar **3 to discipline oneself** : disciplinarse

discipline² *n* **1** FIELD : disciplina *f*, campo *m* **2** TRAINING : disciplina *f* **3** PUNISHMENT : castigo *m* **4** SELF-CONTROL : dominio *m* de sí mismo

disc jockey *n* : disc jockey *mf*

disclaim [dɪsˈkleɪm] *vt* DENY : negar

disclose [dɪsˈkloːz] *vt* **-closed; -closing** : revelar, poner en evidencia

disclosure [dɪsˈkloːʒər] *n* : revelación *f*

disco [ˈdɪskoː] *n* **1** → **discotheque 2** or **disco music** : disco *f*, música *f* disco

discolor [dɪsˈkʌlər] *vt* **1** BLEACH : decolorar **2** FADE : desteñir **3** STAIN : manchar — *vi* : decolorarse, desteñirse

discoloration [dɪsˌkʌləˈreɪʃən] *n* **1** FADING : decoloración *f* **2** STAIN : mancha *f*

discomfort [dɪsˈkʌmfərt] *n* **1** PAIN : molestia *f*, malestar *m* **2** UNEASINESS : inquietud *f*

disconcert [ˌdɪskənˈsərt] *vt* : desconcertar

disconcerting [ˌdɪskənˈsərtɪŋ] *adj* : desconcertante

disconnect [ˌdɪskəˈnɛkt] *vt* : desconectar

disconnected [ˌdɪskəˈnɛktəd] *adj* : inconexo

disconsolate [dɪsˈkɑntsələt] *adj* : desconsolado

discontent [ˌdɪskənˈtɛnt] *n* : descontento *m*

discontented [ˌdɪskənˈtɛntəd] *adj* : descontento

discontinue [ˌdɪskənˈtɪnˌjuː] *vt* **-ued; -uing** : suspender, descontinuar

discontinuity [ˌdɪskɑntəˈnuːəti, -ˈnjuː-] *n, pl* **-ties** : discontinuidad *f*

discontinuous [ˌdɪskənˈtɪnjəwəs] *adj* : discontinuo

discord [ˈdɪsˌkɔrd] *n* **1** STRIFE : discordia *f*, discordancia *f* **2** : disonancia *f* (en música)

discordant [dɪsˈkɔrdənt] *adj* : discordante, discorde — **discordantly** *adv*

discotheque [ˈdɪskəˌtɛk, ˌdɪskəˈtɛk] *n* : discoteca *f*

discount¹ [ˈdɪsˌkaʊnt, dɪsˈ-] *vt* **1** REDUCE : descontar, rebajar (precios) **2** DISREGARD : descartar, ignorar

discount² [ˈdɪsˌkaʊnt] *n* : descuento *m*, rebaja *f*

discourage [dɪsˈkərɪdʒ] *vt* **-aged; -aging 1** DISHEARTEN : desalentar, desanimar **2** DISSUADE : disuadir

discouragement [dɪsˈkərɪdʒmənt] *n* : desánimo *m*, desaliento *m*

discouraging [dɪs'kərədʒɪŋ] *adj* : desalentador
discourse[1] [dɪs'kors] *vi* **-coursed; -coursing** : disertar, conversar
discourse[2] ['dɪs,kors] *n* **1** TALK : conversación *f* **2** SPEECH, TREATISE : discurso *m*, tratado *m*
discourteous [dɪs'kərtiəs] *adj* : descortés — **discourteously** *adv*
discourtesy [dɪs'kərtəsi] *n, pl* **-sies** : descortesía *f*
discover [dɪs'kʌvər] *vt* : descubrir
discoverer [dɪs'kʌvərər] *n* : descubridor *m*, -dora *f*
discovery [dɪs'kʌvəri] *n, pl* **-ries** : descubrimiento *m*
discredit[1] [dɪs'krɛdət] *vt* **1** DISBELIEVE : no creer, dudar **2** : desacreditar, desprestigiar, poner en duda ⟨they discredited his research : desacreditaron sus investigaciones⟩
discredit[2] *n* **1** DISREPUTE : descrédito *m*, desprestigio *m* **2** DOUBT : duda *f*
discreet [dɪs'kri:t] *adj* : discreto — **discreetly** *adv*
discrepancy [dɪs'krɛpəntsi] *n, pl* **-cies** : discrepancia *f*
discretion [dɪs'krɛʃən] *n* **1** CIRCUMSPECTION : discreción *f*, circunspección *f* **2** JUDGMENT : discernimiento *m*, criterio *m*
discretionary [dɪs'krɛʃə,nɛri] *adj* : discrecional
discriminate [dɪs'krɪmə,neɪt] *v* **-nated; -nating** *vt* DISTINGUISH : distinguir, discriminar, diferenciar — *vi* : discriminar ⟨to discriminate against women : discriminar a las mujeres⟩
discrimination [dɪs,krɪmə'neɪʃən] *n* **1** PREJUDICE : discriminación *f* **2** DISCERNMENT : discernimiento *m*
discriminatory [dɪs'krɪmənə,tori] *adj* : discriminatorio
discus ['dɪskəs] *n, pl* **-cuses** [-kəsəz] : disco *m*
discuss [dɪs'kʌs] *vt* : hablar de, discutir, tratar (de)
discussion [dɪs'kʌʃən] *n* : discusión *f*, debate *m*, conversación *f*
disdain[1] [dɪs'deɪn] *vt* : desdeñar, despreciar ⟨they disdained to reply : no se dignaron a responder⟩
disdain[2] *n* : desdén *m*
disdainful [dɪs'deɪnfəl] *adj* : desdeñoso — **disdainfully** *adv*
disease [dɪ'zi:z] *n* : enfermedad *f*, mal *m*, dolencia *f*
diseased [dɪ'zi:zd] *adj* : enfermo
disembark [,dɪsɪm'bark] *v* : desembarcar
disembarkation [dɪs,ɛm,bar'keɪʃən] *n* : desembarco *m*, desembarque *m*
disembodied [,dɪsɪm'badid] *adj* : incorpóreo
disenchant [,dɪsɪn'tʃænt] *vt* : desilusionar, desencantar, desengañar
disenchantment [,dɪsɪn'tʃæntmənt] *n* : desencanto *m*, desilusión *f*

disengage [,dɪsɪn'geɪdʒ] *vt* **-gaged; -gaging 1** : soltar, desconectar (un mecanismo) **2 to disengage the clutch** : desembragar
disentangle [,dɪsɪn'tæŋgəl] *vt* **-gled; -gling** UNTANGLE : desenredar, desenmarañar
disfavor [dɪs'feɪvər] *n* : desaprobación *f*
disfigure [dɪs'fɪgjər] *vt* **-ured; -uring** : desfigurar (a una persona), afear (un edificio, un área)
disfigurement [dɪs'fɪgjərmənt] *n* : desfiguración *f*, afeamiento *m*
disfranchise [dɪs'fræn,tʃaɪz] *vt* **-chised; -chising** : privar del derecho a votar
disgrace[1] [dɪs'kreɪs] *vt* **-graced; -gracing** : deshonrar
disgrace[2] *n* **1** DISHONOR : desgracia *f*, deshonra *f* **2** SHAME : vergüenza *f* ⟨he's a disgrace to his family : es una vergüenza para su familia⟩
disgraceful [dɪs'kreɪsfəl] *adj* : vergonzoso, deshonroso, ignominioso
disgracefully [dɪs'kreɪsfəli] *adv* : vergonzosamente
disgruntle [dɪs'grʌntəl] *vt* **-tled; -tling** : enfadar, contrariar
disguise[1] [dɪs'skaɪz] *vt* **-guised; -guising 1** : disfrazar, enmascarar (el aspecto) **2** CONCEAL : encubrir, disimular
disguise[2] *n* : disfraz *m*
disgust[1] [dɪs'kʌst] *vt* : darle asco (a alguien), asquear, repugnar ⟨that disgusts me : eso me da asco⟩
disgust[2] *n* : asco *m*, repugnancia *f*
disgusting [dɪs'kʌstɪŋ] *adj* : asqueroso, repugnante — **disgustingly** *adv*
dish[1] ['dɪʃ] *vt* SERVE : servir
dish[2] *n* **1** : plato *m* ⟨the national dish : el plato nacional⟩ **2** PLATE : plato *m* ⟨to wash the dishes : lavar los platos⟩ **3 serving dish** : fuente *f*
dishcloth ['dɪʃ,klɔθ] *n* : paño *m* de cocina (para secar), trapo *m* de fregar (para lavar)
dishearten [dɪs'hartən] *vt* : desanimar, desalentar
dishevel [dɪ'ʃɛvəl] *vt* **-eled** *or* **-elled; -eling** *or* **-elling** : desarreglar, despeinar (el pelo)
disheveled *or* **dishevelled** [dɪ'ʃɛvəld] *adj* : despeinado (dícese del pelo), desarreglado, desaliñado
dishonest [dɪs'anəst] *adj* : deshonesto, fraudulento — **dishonestly** *adv*
dishonesty [dɪs'anəsti] *n, pl* **-ties** : deshonestidad *f*, falta *f* de honradez
dishonor[1] [dɪs'anər] *vt* : deshonrar
dishonor[2] *n* : deshonra *f*
dishonorable [dɪs'anərəbəl] *adj* : deshonroso — **dishonorably** [-bli] *adv*
dishrag ['dɪʃ,ræg] → **dishcloth**
dishwasher ['dɪʃ,wɔʃər] *n* : lavaplatos *m*, lavavajillas *m*
disillusion [,dɪsə'lu:ʒən] *vt* : desilusionar, desencantar, desengañar
disillusionment [,dɪsə'lu:ʒənmənt] *n* : desilusión *f*, desencanto *m*

disinclination [dɪsˌɪnkləˈneɪʃən, -ˌɪŋ-] *n* : aversión *f*

disinclined [ˌdɪsɪnˈklaɪnd] *adv* : poco dispuesto

disinfect [ˌdɪsɪnˈfɛkt] *vt* : desinfectar

disinfectant¹ [ˌdɪsɪnˈfɛktənt] *adj* : desinfectante

disinfectant² *n* : desinfectante *m*

disinherit [ˌdɪsɪnˈhɛrət] *vt* : desheredar

disintegrate [dɪsˈɪntəˌgreɪt] *v* **-grated; -grating** *vt* : desintegrar, deshacer — *vi* : desintegrarse, deshacerse

disintegration [dɪsˌɪntəˈgreɪʃən] *n* : desintegración *f*

disinterested [dɪsˈɪntərəstəd, -ˌrɛs-] *adj* **1** INDIFFERENT : indiferente **2** IMPARTIAL : imparcial, desinteresado

disinterestedness [dɪsˈɪntərəstədnəs, -ˌrɛs-] *n* : desinterés *m*

disjointed [dɪsˈʤɔɪntəd] *adj* : inconexo, incoherente

disk *or* **disc** [ˈdɪsk] *n* : disco *m*

disk drive *n* : unidad *f* de disco

diskette [ˌdɪsˈkɛt] *n* : diskette *m*, disquete *m*

dislike¹ [dɪsˈlaɪk] *vt* **-liked; -liking** : tenerle aversión a (algo), tenerle antipatía (a alguien), no gustarle (algo a uno)

dislike² *n* : aversión *f*, antipatía *f*

dislocate [ˈdɪsloˌkeɪt, dɪsˈlo-] *vt* **-cated; -cating** : dislocar

dislocation [ˌdɪsloˈkeɪʃən] *n* : dislocación *f*

dislodge [dɪsˈlɑʤ] *vt* **-lodged; -lodging** : sacar, desalojar, desplazar

disloyal [dɪsˈlɔɪəl] *adj* : desleal

disloyalty [dɪsˈlɔɪəlti] *n, pl* **-ties** : deslealtad *f*

dismal [ˈdɪzməl] *adj* **1** GLOOMY : sombrío, lúgubre, tétrico **2** DEPRESSING : deprimente, triste

dismantle [dɪsˈmæntəl] *vt* **-tled; -tling** : desmantelar, desmontar, desarmar

dismay¹ [dɪsˈmeɪ] *vt* : consternar

dismay² *n* : consternación *f*

dismember [dɪsˈmɛmbər] *vt* : desmembrar

dismiss [dɪsˈmɪs] *vt* **1** : dejar salir, darle permiso (a alguien) para retirarse **2** DISCHARGE : despedir, destituir **3** REJECT : descartar, desechar, rechazar

dismissal [dɪsˈmɪsəl] *n* **1** : permiso *m* para retirarse **2** DISCHARGE : despido *m* (de un empleado), destitución *f* (de un funcionario) **3** REJECTION : rechazo *m*

dismount [dɪsˈmaʊnt] *vi* : desmontar, bajarse, apearse

disobedience [ˌdɪsəˈbiːdiənts] *n* : desobediencia *f* — **disobedient** [-ənt] *adj*

disobey [ˌdɪsəˈbeɪ] *v* : desobedecer

disorder¹ [dɪsˈɔrdər] *vt* : desordenar, desarreglar

disorder² *n* **1** DISARRAY : desorden *m* **2** UNREST : disturbios *mpl*, desórdenes *mpl* **3** AILMENT : afección *f*, indisposición *f*, dolencia *f*

disorderly [dɪsˈɔrdərli] *adj* **1** UNTIDY : desordenado, desarreglado **2** UNRULY : indisciplinado, alborotado **3** **disorderly conduct** : conducta *f* escandalosa

disorganization [dɪsˌɔrgənəˈzeɪʃən] *n* : desorganización *f*

disorganize [dɪsˈɔrgəˌnaɪz] *vt* **-nized; -nizing** : desorganizar

disorient [dɪsˈoriˌɛnt] *vt* : desorientar

disown [dɪsˈoːn] *vt* : renegar de, repudiar

disparage [dɪsˈpærɪʤ] *vt* **-aged; -aging** : menospreciar, denigrar

disparagement [dɪsˈpærɪʤmənt] *n* : menosprecio *m*

disparate [ˈdɪspərət, dɪsˈpærət] *adj* : dispar, diferente

disparity [dɪsˈpærəti] *n, pl* **-ties** : disparidad *f*

dispassionate [dɪsˈpæʃənət] *adj* : desapasionado, imparcial — **dispassionately** *adv*

dispatch¹ [dɪsˈpætʃ] *vt* **1** SEND : despachar, enviar **2** KILL : despachar, matar **3** HANDLE : despachar

dispatch² *n* **1** SENDING : envío *m*, despacho *m* **2** MESSAGE : despacho *m*, reportaje *m* (de un periodista), parte *m* (en el ejército) **3** PROMPTNESS : prontitud *f*, rapidez *f*

dispel [dɪsˈpɛl] *vt* **-pelled; -pelling** : disipar, desvanecer

dispensable [dɪˈspɛntsəbəl] *adj* : prescindible

dispensation [ˌdɪspɛnˈseɪʃən] *n* EXEMPTION : exención *m*, dispensa *f*

dispense [dɪsˈpɛnts] *v* **-pensed; -pensing** *vt* **1** DISTRIBUTE : repartir, distribuir, dar **2** ADMINISTER, BESTOW : administrar (justicia), conceder (favores, etc.) **3** : preparar y despachar (medicamentos) — *vi* **to dispense with** : prescindir de

dispenser [dɪsˈpɛntsər] *n* : dispensador *m*, distribuidor *m* automático

dispersal [dɪsˈpərsəl] *n* : dispersión *f*

disperse [dɪsˈpərs] *v* **-persed; -persing** *vt* : dispersar, diseminar — *vi* : dispersarse

dispersion [dɪˈspərʒən] *n* : dispersión *f*

dispirit [dɪˈspɪrət] *vt* : desalentar, desanimar

displace [dɪsˈpleɪs] *vt* **-placed; -placing** **1** : desplazar (un líquido, etc.) **2** REPLACE : reemplazar

displacement [dɪsˈpleɪsmənt] *n* **1** : desplazamiento *m* (de personas) **2** REPLACEMENT : sustitución *f*, reemplazo *m*

display¹ [dɪsˈpleɪ] *vt* : exponer, exhibir, mostrar

display² *n* **1** : muestra *f*, exposición *f*, alarde *m* **2** : visualizador *m* (de una computadora)

displease [dɪsˈpliːz] *vt* **-pleased; -pleasing** : desagradar a, disgustar, contrariar

displeasure [dɪs'plɛʒər] *n* : desagrado *m*
disposable [dɪs'po:zəbəl] *adj* 1 : desechable ⟨disposable diapers : pañales desechables⟩ 2 AVAILABLE : disponible
disposal [dɪs'po:zəl] *n* 1 PLACEMENT : disposición *f*, colocación *f* 2 REMOVAL : eliminación *f* 3 to have at one's disposal : disponer de, tener a su disposición
dispose [dɪs'po:z] *v* **-posed; -posing** *vt* 1 ARRANGE : disponer, colocar 2 INCLINE : predisponer — *vi* 1 to dispose of DISCARD : desechar, deshacerse de 2 to dispose of HANDLE : despachar
disposition [,dɪspə'zɪʃən] *n* 1 ARRANGEMENT : disposición *f* 2 TENDENCY : predisposición *f*, inclinación *f* 3 TEMPERAMENT : temperamento *m*, carácter *m*
dispossess [,dɪspə'zɛs] *vt* : deposeer
disproportion [,dɪsprə'porʃən] *n* : desproporción *f*
disproportionate [,dɪsprə'porʃənət] *adj* : desproporcionado — **disproportionately** *adv*
disprove [dɪs'pru:v] *vt* **-proved; -proving** : rebatir, refutar
disputable [dɪs'pju:təbəl, 'dɪspjutəbəl] *adj* : disputable, discutible
dispute¹ [dɪs'pju:t] *v* **-puted; -puting** *vt* 1 QUESTION : discutir, cuestionar 2 OPPOSE : combatir, resistir — *vi* ARGUE, DEBATE : discutir
dispute² *n* 1 DEBATE : debate *m*, discusión *f* 2 QUARREL : disputa *f*, discusión *f*
disqualification [dɪs,kwɑləfə'keɪʃən] *n* : descalificación *f*
disqualify [dɪs'kwɑlə,faɪ] *vt* **-fied; -fying** : descalificar, inhabilitar
disquiet¹ [dɪs'kwaɪət] *vt* : inquietar
disquiet² *n* : ansiedad *f*, inquietud *f*
disregard¹ [,dɪsrɪ'gɑrd] *vt* : ignorar, no prestar atención a
disregard² *n* : indiferencia *f*
disrepair [,dɪsrɪ'pær] *n* : mal estado *m*
disreputable [dɪs'rɛpjutəbəl] *adj* : de mala fama (dícese de una persona o un lugar), vergonzoso (dícese de la conducta)
disreputably [dɪs'rɛpjutəbli] *adv* : vergonzosamente
disrepute [,dɪsrɪ'pju:t] *n* : descrédito *m*, mala fama *f*, deshonra *f*
disrespect [,dɪsrɪ'spɛkt] *n* : falta *f* de respeto
disrespectful [,dɪsrɪ'spɛktfəl] *adj* : irrespetuoso — **disrespectfully** *adv*
disrobe [dɪs'ro:b] *v* **-robed; -robing** : desvestir, desnudar — *vi* : desvestirse, desnudarse
disrupt [dɪs'rʌpt] *vt* : trastornar, perturbar
disruption [dɪs'rʌpʃən] *n* : trastorno *m*
disruptive [dɪs'rʌptɪv] *adj* : perjudicial, perturbador — **disruptively** *adv*
dissatisfaction [dɪs,sætəs'fækʃən] *n* : descontento *m*, insatisfacción *f*

dissatisfied [dɪs'sætəs,faɪd] *adj* : descontento, insatisfecho
dissatisfy [dɪs'sætəs,faɪ] *vt* **-fied; -fying** : no contentar, no satisfacer
dissect [dɪ'sɛkt] *vt* : disecar
dissection [dɪ'sɛkʃən] *n* : disección *f*
dissemble [dɪ'sɛmbəl] *v* **-bled; -bling** *vt* HIDE : ocultar, disimular — *vi* PRETEND : fingir, disimular
disseminate [dɪ'sɛmə,neɪt] *vt* **-nated; -nating** : diseminar, difundir, divulgar
dissemination [dɪ,sɛmə'neɪʃən] *n* : diseminación *f*, difusión *f*
dissension [dɪ'sɛnʃən] *n* : disensión *f*, desacuerdo *m*
dissent¹ [dɪ'sɛnt] *vi* : disentir
dissent² *n* : disentimiento *m*, disensión *f*
dissertation [,dɪsər'teɪʃən] *n* 1 DISCOURSE : disertación *f*, discurso *m* 2 THESIS : tesis *f*
disservice [dɪs'sərvɪs] *n* : perjuicio *m*
dissident¹ ['dɪsədənt] *adj* : disidente
dissident² *n* : disidente *mf*
dissimilar [dɪ'sɪmələr] *adj* : distinto, diferente, disímil
dissipate ['dɪsə,peɪt] *vt* **-pated; -pating** 1 DISPERSE : disipar, dispersar 2 SQUANDER : malgastar, desperdiciar, derrochar, disipar
dissipation [,dɪsə'peɪʃən] *n* : disipación *f*, libertinaje *m*
dissociate [dɪ'so:ʃi,eɪt, -si-] *v* **-ated [-,eɪtəd]; -ating [-,eɪtɪŋ]** *vt* : disociar ⟨to disassociate oneself : disociarse⟩ — *vi* : disociarse
dissociation [dɪ,so:ʃi'eɪʃən, -si-] *n* : disociación *f*
dissolute ['dɪsə,lu:t] *adj* : disoluto
dissolution [,dɪsə'lu:ʃən] *n* : disolución *f*
dissolve [dɪ'zɑlv] *v* **-solved; -solving** *vt* : disolver — *vi* : disolverse
dissonance ['dɪsənənts] *n* : disonancia *f*
dissuade [dɪ'sweɪd] *vt* **-suaded; -suading** : disuadir
distance¹ ['dɪstənts] *vt* **-tanced [-təntst]; -tancing [-təntsɪŋ]** to distance oneself : distanciarse
distance² *n* 1 : distancia *f* ⟨the distance between two points : la distancia entre dos puntos⟩ ⟨in the distance : a lo lejos⟩ 2 RESERVE : actitud *f* distante, reserva *f* ⟨to keep one's distance : guardar las distancias⟩
distant ['dɪstənt] *adj* 1 FAR : distante, lejano 2 REMOTE : distante, lejano, remoto 3 ALOOF : distante, frío
distantly ['dɪstəntli] *adv* 1 LOOSELY : aproximadamente, vagamente 2 COLDLY : fríamente, con frialdad
distaste [dɪs'teɪst] *n* : desagrado *m*, aversión *f*
distasteful [dɪs'teɪstfəl] *adj* : desagradable, de mal gusto
distemper [dɪs'tɛmpər] *n* : moquillo *m*
distend [dɪs'tɛnd] *vt* : dilatar, hinchar — *vi* : dilatarse, hincharse

distill [dɪ'stɪl] vt : destilar

distillation [ˌdɪstə'leɪʃən] n : destilación f

distiller [dɪ'stɪlər] n : destilador m, -dora f

distillery [dɪ'stɪləri] n, pl **-ries** [-riz] : destilería f

distinct [dɪ'stɪŋkt] adj **1** DIFFERENT : distinto, diferente **2** CLEAR, UNMISTAKABLE : marcado, claro, evidente ⟨a distinct possibility : una clara posibilidad⟩

distinction [dɪ'stɪŋkʃən] n **1** DIFFERENTIATION : distinción f **2** DIFFERENCE : diferencia f **3** EXCELLENCE : distinción f, excelencia f ⟨a writer of distinction : un escritor destacado⟩

distinctive [dɪ'stɪŋktɪv] adj : distintivo, característico — **distinctively** adv

distinctiveness [dɪ'stɪŋktɪvnəs] n : peculiaridad f

distinctly [dɪ'stɪŋktli] adv : claramente, con claridad

distinguish [dɪs'tɪŋgwɪʃ] vt **1** DIFFERENTIATE : distinguir, diferenciar **2** DISCERN : distinguir ⟨he distinguished the sound of the piano : distinguió el sonido del piano⟩ **3 to distinguish oneself** : señalarse, distinguirse — vi DISCRIMINATE : distinguir

distinguishable [dɪs'tɪŋgwɪʃəbəl] adj : distinguible

distinguished [dɪs'tɪŋgwɪʃt] adj : distinguido

distort [dɪ'stɔrt] vt **1** MISREPRESENT : distorsionar, tergiversar **2** DEFORM : distorsionar, deformar

distortion [dɪ'stɔrʃən] n : distorsión f, deformación f, tergiversación f

distract [dɪ'strækt] vt : distraer, entretener

distracted [dɪ'stræktəd] adj : distraído

distraction [dɪ'strækʃən] n **1** INTERRUPTION : distracción f, interrupción f **2** CONFUSION : confusión f **3** AMUSEMENT : diversión f, entretenimiento m, distracción f

distraught [dɪ'strɔt] adj : afligido, turbado

distress¹ [dɪ'strɛs] vt : afligir, darle pena (a alguien), hacer sufrir

distress² n **1** SORROW : dolor m, angustia f, aflicción f **2** PAIN : dolor m **3 in ∼** : en peligro

distressful [dɪ'strɛsfəl] adj : doloroso, penoso

distribute [dɪ'strɪˌbjuːt, -bjʊt] vt **-uted; -uting** : distribuir, repartir

distribution [ˌdɪstrə'bjuːʃən] n : distribución f, reparto m

distributive [dɪ'strɪbjʊtɪv] adj : distributivo

distributor [dɪ'strɪbjʊtər] n : distribuidor m, -dora f

district ['dɪsˌtrɪkt] n **1** REGION : región f, zona f, barrio m (de una ciudad) **2** : distrito m (zona política)

distrust¹ [dɪs'trʌst] vt : desconfiar de

distrust² n : desconfianza f, recelo m

distrustful [dɪs'trʌstfəl] adj : desconfiado, receloso, suspicaz

disturb [dɪ'stərb] vt **1** BOTHER : molestar, perturbar ⟨sorry to disturb you : perdone la molestia⟩ **2** DISARRANGE : desordenar **3** WORRY : inquietar, preocupar **4 to disturb the peace** : alterar el orden público

disturbance [dɪ'stərbənts] n **1** COMMOTION : alboroto m, disturbio m **2** INTERRUPTION : interrupción f

disuse [dɪs'juːs] n : desuso m

ditch¹ ['dɪtʃ] vt **1** : cavar zanjas en **2** DISCARD : deshacerse de, botar

ditch² n : zanja f, fosa f, cuneta f (en una carretera)

dither ['dɪðər] n **to be in a dither** : estar nervioso, ponerse como loco

ditto ['dɪtoː] n, pl **-tos 1** : lo mismo, ídem m **2 ditto marks** : comillas fpl

ditty ['dɪti] n, pl **-ties** : canción f corta y simple

diurnal [daɪ'ərnəl] adj **1** DAILY : diario, cotidiano **2** : diurno ⟨a diurnal animal : un animal diurno⟩

divan ['daɪˌvæn, dɪ'-] n : diván m

dive¹ ['daɪv] vi **dived** or **dove** ['doːv]; **dived; diving 1** PLUNGE : tirarse al agua, zambullirse, dar un clavado **2** SUBMERGE : sumergirse **3** DROP : bajar en picada (dícese de un avión), caer en picada

dive² n **1** PLUNGE : zambullida f, clavado m (en el agua) **2** DESCENT : descenso m en picada **3** BAR, JOINT : antro m

diver ['daɪvər] n : saltador m, -dora f; clavadista mf

diverge [də'vərdʒ, daɪ-] vi **-verged; -verging 1** SEPARATE : divergir, separarse **2** DIFFER : divergir, discrepar

divergence [də'vərdʒənts, daɪ-] n : divergencia f — **divergent** [-ənt] adj

diverse [daɪ'vərs, də-, 'daɪˌvərs] adj : diverso, variado

diversification [daɪˌvərsəfə'keɪʃən, də-] n : diversificación f

diversify [daɪ'vərsəˌfaɪ, də-] vt **-fied; -fying** : diversificar, variar

diversion [daɪ'vərʒən, də-] n **1** DEVIATION : desviación f **2** AMUSEMENT, DISTRACTION : diversión f, distracción f, entretenimiento m

diversity [daɪ'vərsəti, də-] n, pl **-ties** : diversidad f

divert [də'vərt, daɪ-] vt **1** DEFLECT : desviar **2** DISTRACT : distraer **3** AMUSE : divertir, entretener

divest [daɪ'vɛst, də-] vt **1** UNDRESS : desnudar, desvestir **2 to divest of** : despojar de

divide [də'vaɪd] v **-vided; -viding** vt **1** HALVE : dividir, partir por la mitad **2** SHARE : repartir, dividir **3** : dividir (números) — vi : dividirse, dividir (en matemáticas)

dividend ['dıvə₁dɛnd, -dənd] n 1 : dividendo m (en finanzas) 2 BONUS : beneficío m, provecho m 3 : dividendo m (en matemáticas)

divider [dı'vaıdər] n 1 : separador m (para ficheros, etc.) 2 or room divider : mampara f, biombo m

divination [₁dıvə'neıʃən] n : adivinación f

divine¹ [də'vaın] adj -viner; -est 1 : divino 2 SUPERB : divino, espléndido — **divinely** adv

divine² n : clérigo m, eclesiástico m

divinity [də'vınəti] n, pl -ties : divinidad f

divisible [dı'vızəbəl] adj : divisible

division [dı'vıʒən] n 1 DISTRIBUTION : división f, reparto m ⟨division of labor : distribución del trabajo⟩ 2 PART : división f, sección f 3 : división f (en matemáticas)

divisive [də'vaısıv] adj : divisivo

divisor [dı'vaızər] n : divisor m

divorce¹ [də'vors] v -vorced; -vorcing vt : divorciar — vi : divorciarse

divorce² n : divorcio m

divorcé [dı₁vor'seı, -'si:; -'vor₁-] n : divorciado m

divorcée [dı₁vor'seı, -'si:; -'vor₁-] n : divorciada f

divulge [də'vʌlʤ, daı-] vt -vulged; -vulging : revelar, divulgar

dizzily ['dızəli] adv : vertiginosamente

dizziness ['dızinəs] n : mareo m, vahído m, vértigo m

dizzy ['dızi] adj dizzier; -est 1 : mareado ⟨I feel dizzy : estoy mareado⟩ 2 : vertiginoso ⟨a dizzy speed : una velocidad vertiginosa⟩

DNA [₁di:₁ɛn'eı] n : ADN m

do ['du:] v did ['dıd]; done ['dʌn]; doing; does ['dʌz] vt 1 CARRY OUT, PERFORM : hacer, realizar, llevar a cabo ⟨she did her best : hizo todo lo posible⟩ 2 PREPARE : preparar, hacer ⟨do your homework : haz tu tarea⟩ 3 ARRANGE : arreglar, peinar (el pelo) 4 to do in RUIN : estropear, arruinar 5 to do in KILL : matar, liquidar fam — vi 1 : hacer ⟨you did well : hiciste bien⟩ 2 FARE : estar, ir, andar ⟨how are you doing? : ¿cómo estás?, ¿cómo te va?⟩ 3 FINISH : terminar ⟨now I'm done : ya terminé⟩ 4 SERVE : servir, ser suficiente, alcanzar ⟨this will do for now : esto servirá por el momento⟩ 5 to do away with ABOLISH : abolir, suprimir 6 to do away with KILL : eliminar, matar 7 to do by TREAT : tratar ⟨he does well by her : él la trata bien⟩ — v aux 1 (used in interrogative sentences and negative statements) ⟨do you know her? : ¿la conoces?⟩ ⟨I don't like that : a mí no me gusta eso⟩ 2 (used for emphasis) ⟨I do hope you'll come : espero que vengas⟩ 3 (used as a substitute verb to avoid repetition) ⟨do you speak English? yes, I do : ¿habla inglés? sí⟩

docile ['dasəl] adj : dócil, sumiso

dock¹ ['dak] vt 1 CUT : cortar 2 : descontar dinero (de un sueldo) — vi ANCHOR, LAND : fondear, atracar

dock² n 1 PIER : atracadero m 2 WHARF : muelle m 3 : banquillo m de los acusados (en un tribunal)

doctor¹ ['daktər] vt 1 TREAT : tratar, curar 2 ALTER : adulterar, alterar, falsificar (un documento)

doctor² n 1 : doctor m, -tora f ⟨Doctor of Philosophy : doctor en filosofía⟩ 2 PHYSICIAN : médico m, -ca f; doctor m, -tora f

doctorate ['daktərət] n : doctorado m

doctrine ['daktrın] n : doctrina f

document¹ ['dakju₁mɛnt] vt : documentar

document² ['dakjumənt] n : documento m

documentary¹ [₁dakju'mɛntəri] adj : documental

documentary² n, pl -ries : documental m

documentation [₁dakjumən'teıʃən] n : documentación f

dodge¹ ['daʤ] v dodged; dodging vt : esquivar, eludir, evadir (impuestos) — vi : echarse a un lado

dodge² n 1 RUSE : truco m, treta f, artimaña f 2 EVASION : regate m, evasión f

dodo ['do:₁do:] n, pl -does or -dos : dodo m

doe ['do:] n, pl does or doe : gama f, cierva f

doer ['du:ər] n : hacedor m, -dora f

does → do

doff ['daf, 'dɔf] vt : quitarse ⟨to doff one's hat : quitarse el sombrero⟩

dog¹ ['dɔg, 'dag] vt dogged; dogging : seguir de cerca, perseguir, acosar ⟨to dog someone's footsteps : seguir los pasos de alguien⟩ ⟨dogged by bad luck : perseguido por la mala suerte⟩

dog² n : perro m, -rra f

dogcatcher ['dɔg₁kæʧər] n : perrero m, -ra f

dog–eared ['dɔg₁ırd] adj : con las esquinas dobladas

dogged ['dɔgəd] adj : tenaz, terco, obstinado

doggy ['dɔgi] n, pl doggies : perrito m, -ta f

doghouse ['dɔg₁haus] n : casita f de perro

dogma ['dɔgmə] n : dogma m

dogmatic [dɔg'mætık] adj : dogmático

dogmatism ['dɔgmə₁tızəm] n : dogmatismo m

dogwood ['dɔg₁wud] n : cornejo m

doily ['dɔıli] n, pl -lies : pañito m

doings ['du:ıŋz] npl : eventos mpl, actividades fpl

doldrums ['do:ldrəmz, 'dal-] npl 1 : zona f de las calmas ecuatoriales 2 to be in the doldrums : estar abatido (dícese de una persona), estar estancado (dícese de una empresa)

dole ['do:l] *n* **1** ALMS : distribución *f* a los necesitados, limosna *f* **2** : subsidios *mpl* de desempleo

doleful ['do:lfəl] *adj* : triste, lúgubre

dolefully ['do:lfəli] *adv* : con pesar, de manera triste

dole out *vt* **doled out; doling out** : repartir

doll ['dɑl, 'dɔl] *n* : muñeco *m*, -ca *f*

dollar ['dɑlər] *n* : dólar *m*

dolly ['dɑli] *n, pl* **-lies 1** → **doll 2** : plataforma *f* rodante

dolphin ['dɑlfən, 'dɔl-] *n* : delfín *m*

dolt ['do:lt] *n* : imbécil *mf*; tonto *m*, -ta *f*

domain [do'meɪn, də-] *n* **1** TERRITORY : dominio *m*, territorio *m* **2** FIELD : campo *m*, esfera *f*, ámbito *m* ⟨the domain of art : el ámbito de las artes⟩

dome ['do:m] *n* : cúpula *f*, bóveda *f*

domestic[1] [də'mɛstɪk] *adj* **1** HOUSEHOLD : doméstico, casero **2** : nacional, interno ⟨domestic policy : política interna⟩ **3** TAME : domesticado

domestic[2] *n* : empleado *m* doméstico, empleada *f* doméstica

domestically [də'mɛstɪkli] *adv* : domésticamente

domesticate [də'mɛstɪˌkeɪt] *vt* **-cated; -cating** : domesticar

domicile ['dɑməˌsaɪl, 'do:-; 'dɑməsɪl] *n* : domicilio *m*

dominance ['dɑmənənts] *n* : dominio *m*, dominación *f*

dominant ['dɑmənənt] *adj* : dominante

dominate ['dɑməˌneɪt] *v* **-nated; -nating** : dominar

domination [ˌdɑmə'neɪʃən] *n* : dominación *f*

domineer [ˌdɑmə'nɪr] *vt* : dominar sobre, avasallar, tiranizar

Dominican [də'mɪnɪkən] *n* : dominicano *m*, -na *f* — **Dominican** *adj*

dominion [də'mɪnjən] *n* **1** POWER : dominio *m* **2** DOMAIN, TERRITORY : dominio *m*, territorio *m*

domino ['dɑməˌno:] *n, pl* **-noes** *or* **-nos 1** : dominó *m* **2 dominoes** *npl* : dominó *m* (juego)

don ['dɑn] *vt* **donned; donning** : ponerse

donate ['do:ˌneɪt, do:'-] *vt* **-nated; -nating** : donar, hacer un donativo de

donation [do:'neɪʃən] *n* : donación *f*, donativo *m*

done[1] ['dʌn] → **do**

done[2] *adj* **1** FINISHED : terminado, acabado, concluido **2** COOKED : cocinado

donkey ['dɑŋki, 'dʌŋ-] *n, pl* **-keys** : burro *m*, asno *m*

donor ['do:nər] *n* : donante *mf*; donador *m*, -dora *f*

don't ['do:nt] (*contraction* of **do not**) → **do**

doodle[1] ['du:dəl] *v* **-dled; -dling** : garabatear

doodle[2] *n* : garabato *m*

doom[1] ['du:m] *vt* : condenar

doom[2] *n* **1** JUDGMENT : sentencia *f*, condena *f* **2** DEATH : muerte *f* **3** FATE : destino *m* **4** RUIN : perdición *f*, ruina *f*

door ['dor] *n* : puerta *f*

doorbell ['dorˌbɛl] *n* : timbre *m*

doorknob ['dorˌnɑb] *n* : pomo *m*, perilla *f*

doorman ['dormən] *n, pl* **-men** [-mən, -ˌmɛn] : portero *m*

doormat ['dorˌmæt] *n* : felpudo *m*

doorstep ['dorˌstɛp] *n* : umbral *m*

doorway ['dorˌweɪ] *n* : entrada *f*, portal *m*

dope[1] ['do:p] *vt* **doped; doping** : drogar, narcotizar

dope[2] *n* **1** DRUG : droga *f*, estupefaciente *m*, narcótico *m* **2** IDIOT : idiota *mf*; tonto *m*, -ta *f* **3** INFORMATION : información *f*

dormant ['dɔrmənt] *adj* : inactivo, latente

dormer ['dɔrmər] *n* : buhardilla *f*

dormitory ['dɔrməˌtori] *n, pl* **-ries** : dormitorio *m*, residencia *f* de estudiantes

dormouse ['dɔrˌmaʊs] *n* : lirón *m*

dorsal ['dɔrsəl] *adj* : dorsal — **dorsally** *adv*

dory ['dori] *n, pl* **-ries** : bote *m* de fondo plano

dosage ['do:sɪdʒ] *n* : dosis *f*

dose[1] ['do:s] *vt* **dosed; dosing** : medicinar

dose[2] *n* : dosis *f*

dossier ['dɔsˌjeɪ, 'dɑs-] *n* : dossier *m*

dot[1] ['dɑt] *vt* **dotted; dotting 1** : poner el punto sobre (una letra) **2** SCATTER : esparcir, salpicar

dot[2] *n* : punto *m* ⟨at six on the dot : a las seis en punto⟩ ⟨dots and dashes : puntos y rayas⟩

dote ['do:t] *vi* **doted; doting** : chochear

double[1] ['dʌbəl] *v* **-bled; -bling** *vt* **1** : doblar, duplicar (una cantidad), redoblar (esfuerzos) **2** FOLD : doblar, plegar **3 to double one's fist** : apretar el puño — *vi* **1** : doblarse, duplicarse **2 to double over** : retorcerse

double[2] *adj* : doble — **doubly** *adv*

double[3] *n* : doble *mf*

double bass *n* : contrabajo *m*

double–cross [ˌdʌbəl'krɔs] *vt* : traicionar

double–crosser [ˌdʌbəl'krɔsər] *n* : traidor *m*, -dora *f*

double–jointed [ˌdʌbəl'dʒɔɪntəd] *adj* : con articulaciones dobles

double–talk ['dʌbəlˌtɔk] *n* : ambigüedades *fpl*, lenguaje *m* con doble sentido

doubt[1] ['daʊt] *vt* **1** QUESTION : dudar de, cuestionar **2** DISTRUST : desconfiar de **3** : dudar, creer poco probable ⟨I doubt it very much : lo dudo mucho⟩

doubt[2] *n* **1** UNCERTAINTY : duda *f*, incertidumbre *f* **2** DISTRUST : desconfianza *f* **3** SKEPTICISM : duda *f*, escepticismo *m*

doubtful ['daʊtfəl] *adj* **1** QUESTIONABLE : dudoso **2** UNCERTAIN : dudoso, incierto

doubtfully ['daʊtfəli] *adv* : dudosamente, sin estar convencido

doubtless ['daʊtləs] *or* **doubtlessly** *adv* : sin duda

douche¹ ['duːʃ] *vt* **douched; douching** : irrigar

douche² *n* : ducha *f*, irrigación *f*

dough ['doː] *n* : masa *f*

doughnut *or* **donut** ['doːˌnʌt] *n* : rosquilla *f*, dona *f Mex*

doughty ['daʊti] *adj* **-tier; -est** : fuerte, valiente

dour ['daʊər, 'dʊr] *adj* **1** STERN : severo, adusto **2** SULLEN : hosco, taciturno — **dourly** *adv*

douse ['daʊs, 'daʊz] *vt* **doused; dousing 1** DRENCH : empapar, mojar **2** EXTINGUISH : extinguir, apagar

dove¹ ['doːv] → **dive**

dove² ['dʌv] *n* : paloma *f*

dovetail ['dʌvˌteɪl] *vi* : encajar, enlazar

dowdy ['daʊdi] *adj* **dowdier; -est** : sin gracia, poco elegante

dowel ['daʊəl] *n* : clavija *f*

down¹ ['daʊn] *vt* **1** FELL : tumbar, derribar, abatir **2** DEFEAT : derrotar

down² *adv* **1** DOWNWARD : hacia abajo **2 to lie down** : acostarse, echarse **3 to put down (money)** : pagar un depósito (de dinero) **4 to sit down** : sentarse **5 to take down, to write down** : apuntar, anotar

down³ *adj* **1** DESCENDING : de bajada ⟨the down elevator : el ascensor de bajada⟩ **2** REDUCED : reducido, rebajado ⟨attendance is down : la concurrencia ha disminuido⟩ **3** DOWNCAST : abatido, deprimido

down⁴ *n* **1** : plumón *m* **2** : down *m* (en deportes) **3 ups and downs** : altibajos *mpl*

down⁵ *prep* **1** : (hacia) abajo ⟨down the mountain : montaña abajo⟩ ⟨I walked down the stairs : bajé por la escalera⟩ **2** ALONG : por, a lo largo de ⟨we ran down the beach : corrimos por la playa⟩ **3** : a través de ⟨down the years : a través de los años⟩

downcast ['daʊnˌkæst] *adj* **1** SAD : triste, abatido **2 with downcast eyes** : con los ojos bajos, con los ojos mirando al suelo

downfall ['daʊnˌfɔl] *n* : ruina *f*, perdición *f*

downgrade¹ ['daʊnˌgreɪd] *vt* **-graded; -grading** : bajar de categoría

downgrade² *n* : bajada *f*

downhearted ['daʊnˌhɑrtəd] *adj* : desanimado, descorazonado

downhill ['daʊnˌhɪl] *adv & adj* : cuesta abajo

download¹ ['daʊnˌloːd] *vt* : descargar (un archivo)

download² *n* : descarga *f* (de archivos, etc.)

down payment *n* : entrega *f* inicial

downplay ['daʊnˌpleɪ] *vt* : minimizar

downpour ['daʊnˌpor] *n* : aguacero *m*, chaparrón *m*

downright¹ ['daʊnˌraɪt] *adv* THOROUGHLY : absolutamente, completamente

downright² *adj* : patente, manifiesto, absoluto ⟨a downright refusal : un rechazo categórico⟩

downside ['daʊnˌsaɪd] *n* : desventaja *f*

downstairs¹ ['daʊn'stærz] *adv* : abajo

downstairs² ['daʊn'stærz] *adj* : del piso de abajo

downstairs³ ['daʊn'stærz, -ˌstærz] *n* : planta *f* baja

downstream ['daʊn'striːm] *adv* : río abajo

down-to-earth [ˌdaʊntuˈərθ] *adj* : práctico, realista

downtown¹ [ˌdaʊn'taʊn] *adv* : hacia el centro, al centro, en el centro (de la ciudad)

downtown² *adj* : del centro (de la ciudad) ⟨downtown Chicago : el centro de Chicago⟩

downtown³ [ˌdaʊn'taʊn, 'daʊnˌtaʊn] *n* : centro *m* (de la ciudad)

downtrodden ['daʊnˌtrɑdən] *adj* : oprimido

downward ['daʊnwərd] *or* **downwards** [-wərdz] *adv & adj* : hacia abajo

downwind ['daʊn'wɪnd] *adv & adj* : en la dirección del viento

downy ['daʊni] *adj* **downier; -est 1** : cubierto de plumón, plumoso **2** VELVETY : aterciopelado, velloso

dowry ['daʊri] *n, pl* **-ries** : dote *f*

doze¹ ['doːz] *vi* **dozed; dozing** : dormitar

doze² *n* : sueño *m* ligero, cabezada *f*

dozen ['dʌzən] *n, pl* **dozens** *or* **dozen** : docena *f*

drab ['dræb] *adj* **drabber; drabbest 1** BROWNISH : pardo **2** DULL, LACKLUSTER : monótono, gris, deslustrado

draft¹ ['dræft, 'draft] *vt* **1** CONSCRIPT : reclutar **2** COMPOSE, SKETCH : hacer el borrador de, redactar

draft² *adj* **1** : de barril ⟨draft beer : cerveza de barril⟩ **2** : de tiro ⟨draft horses : caballos de tiro⟩

draft³ *n* **1** HAULAGE : tiro *m* **2** DRINK, GULP : trago *m* **3** OUTLINE, SKETCH : bosquejo *m*, borrador *m*, versión *f* **4** : corriente *f* de aire, chiflón *m*, tiro *m* (de una chimenea) **5** CONSCRIPTION : conscripción *f* **6 bank draft** : giro *m* bancario, letra *f* de cambio

draftee [dræfˈtiː] *n* : recluta *mf*

draftsman ['dræftsmən] *n, pl* **-men** [-mən, -ˌmen] : dibujante *mf*

drafty ['dræfti] *adj* **draftier; -est** : con corrientes de aire

drag¹ ['dræg] *v* **dragged; dragging** *vt* **1** HAUL : arrastrar, jalar **2** DREDGE : dragar — *vi* **1** TRAIL : arrastrarse **2** LAG : rezagarse **3** : hacerse pesado, hacerse largo ⟨the day dragged on : el día se hizo largo⟩

drag² *n* **1** RESISTANCE : resistencia *f* (aerodinámica) **2** HINDRANCE : traba *f*, estorbo *m* **3** BORE : pesadez *f*, plomo *m fam*

dragnet ['dræg,nɛt] *n* **1** : red *f* barredera (en pesca) **2** : operativo *m* policial de captura

dragon ['drægən] *n* : dragón *m*

dragonfly ['drægən,flaɪ] *n, pl* **-flies** : libélula *f*

drain¹ ['dreɪn] *vt* **1** EMPTY : vaciar, drenar **2** EXHAUST : agotar, consumir — *vi* **1** : escurrir, escurrirse ⟨the dishes are draining : los platos están escurriéndose⟩ **2** EMPTY : desaguar **3 to drain away** : irse agotando

drain² *n* **1** : desagüe *m* **2** SEWER : alcantarilla *f* **3** GRATING : sumidero *m*, resumidero *m*, rejilla *f* **4** EXHAUSTION : agotamiento *m*, disminución *f* (de energía, etc.) ⟨to be a drain on : agotar, consumir⟩ **5 to throw down the drain** : tirar por la ventana

drainage ['dreɪnɪʤ] *n* : desagüe *m*, drenaje *m*

drainpipe ['dreɪn,paɪp] *n* : tubo *m* de desagüe, caño *m*

drake ['dreɪk] *n* : pato *m* (macho)

drama ['drɑmə, 'dræ-] *n* **1** THEATER : drama *m*, teatro *m* **2** PLAY : obra *f* de teatro, drama *m*

dramatic [drə'mæṭɪk] *adj* : dramático — **dramatically** [-ṭɪkli] *adv*

dramatist ['dræmətɪst, 'drɑ-] *n* : dramaturgo *m*, -ga *f*

dramatization [,dræmətə'zeɪʃən, ,drɑ-] *n* : dramatización *f*

dramatize ['dræmə,taɪz, 'drɑ-] *vt* **-tized; -tizing** : dramatizar

drank → **drink**

drape¹ ['dreɪp] *vt* **draped; draping 1** COVER : cubrir (con tela) **2** HANG : drapear, disponer los pliegues de

drape² *n* **1** HANG : caída *f* **2 drapes** *npl* : cortinas *fpl*

drapery ['dreɪpəri] *n, pl* **-eries 1** CLOTH : pañería *f*, tela *f* para cortinas **2 draperies** *npl* : cortinas *fpl*

drastic ['dræstɪk] *adj* **1** HARSH, SEVERE : drástico, severo **2** EXTREME : radical, excepcional — **drastically** [-ṭɪkli] *adv*

draught ['dræft, 'drɑft] *n* → **draft³**

draughty ['drɑfti] → **drafty**

draw¹ ['drɔ] *v* **drew** ['dru:]; **drawn** ['drɔn]; **drawing** *vt* **1** PULL : tirar de, jalar, correr (cortinas) **2** ATTRACT : atraer **3** PROVOKE : provocar, suscitar **4** INHALE : aspirar ⟨to draw breath : respirar⟩ **5** EXTRACT : sacar, extraer **6** TAKE : sacar ⟨to draw a number : sacar un número⟩ **7** COLLECT : cobrar, percibir (un sueldo, etc.) **8** BEND : tensar (un arco) **9** TIE : empatar (en deportes) **10** SKETCH : dibujar, trazar **11** FORMULATE : sacar, formular, llegar a ⟨to draw a conclusion : llegar a

una conclusión⟩ **12 to draw out** : hacer hablar (sobre algo), hacer salir de sí mismo **13 to draw up** DRAFT : redactar — *vi* **1** SKETCH : dibujar **2** TUG : tirar, jalar **3 to draw near** : acercarse **4 to draw to a close** : terminar, finalizar **5 to draw up** STOP : parar

draw² *n* **1** DRAWING, RAFFLE : sorteo *m* **2** TIE : empate *m* **3** ATTRACTION : atracción *f* **4** PUFF : chupada *f* (de un cigarrillo, etc.)

drawback ['drɔ,bæk] *n* : desventaja *f*, inconveniente *m*

drawbridge ['drɔ,brɪʤ] *n* : puente *m* levadizo

drawer ['drɔr, 'drɔər] *n* **1** ILLUSTRATOR : dibujante *mf* **2** : gaveta *f*, cajón *m* (en un mueble) **3 drawers** *npl* UNDERPANTS : calzones *mpl*

drawing ['drɔɪŋ] *n* **1** LOTTERY : sorteo *m*, lotería *f* **2** SKETCH : dibujo *m*, bosquejo *m*

drawl¹ ['drɔl] *vi* : hablar arrastrando las palabras

drawl² *n* : habla *f* lenta y con vocales prolongadas

dread¹ ['drɛd] *vt* : tenerle pavor a, temer

dread² *adj* : pavoroso, aterrado

dread³ *n* : pavor *m*, temor *m*

dreadful ['drɛdfəl] *adj* **1** DREAD : pavoroso **2** TERRIBLE : espantoso, atroz, terrible — **dreadfully** *adv*

dream¹ ['dri:m] *v* **dreamed** ['drɛmpt, 'dri:md] *or* **dreamt** ['drɛmpt]; **dreaming** *vi* **1** : soñar ⟨to dream about : soñar con⟩ **2** FANTASIZE : fantasear — *vt* **1** : soñar **2** IMAGINE : imaginarse **3 to dream up** : inventar, idear

dream² *n* **1** : sueño *m*, ensueño *m* **2 bad dream** NIGHTMARE : pesadilla *f*

dreamer ['dri:mər] *n* : soñador *m*, -dora *f*

dreamlike ['dri:m,laɪk] *adj* : de ensueño

dreamy ['dri:mi] *adj* **dreamier; -est 1** DISTRACTED : soñador, distraído **2** DREAMLIKE : de ensueño **3** MARVELOUS : maravilloso

drearily ['drɪrəli] *adv* : sombríamente

dreary ['drɪri] *adj* **-rier; -est** : deprimente, lóbrego, sombrío

dredge¹ ['drɛʤ] *vt* **dredged; dredging 1** DIG : dragar **2** COAT : espolvorear, enharinar

dredge² *n* : draga *f*

dredger ['drɛʤər] *n* : draga *f*

dregs ['drɛgz] *npl* **1** LEES : posos *mpl*, heces *fpl* (de un líquido) **2** : heces *fpl*, escoria *f* ⟨the dregs of society : la escoria de la sociedad⟩

drench ['drɛntʃ] *vt* : empapar, mojar, calar

dress¹ ['drɛs] *vt* **1** CLOTHE : vestir **2** DECORATE : decorar, adornar **3** : preparar (pollo o pescado), aliñar (ensalada) **4** : curar, vendar (una herida) **5** FERTILIZE : abonar (la tierra) — *vi* **1** : vestirse **2 to dress up** : ataviarse, engalanarse, ponerse de etiqueta

dress² *n* **1** APPAREL : indumentaria *f*, ropa *f* **2** : vestido *m*, traje *m* (de mujer)

dresser ['drɛsər] *n* : cómoda *f* con espejo

dressing ['drɛsɪŋ] *n* **1** : vestirse *m* **2** : aderezo *m*, aliño *m* (de ensalada), relleno *m* (de pollo) **3** BANDAGE : vendaje *m*, gasa *f*

dressmaker ['drɛs,meɪkər] *n* : modista *mf*

dressmaking ['drɛs,meɪkɪŋ] *n* : costura *f*

dressy ['drɛsi] *adj* **dressier; -est** : de mucho vestir, elegante

drew → **draw**

dribble¹ ['drɪbəl] *vi* **-bled; -bling 1** DRIP : gotear **2** DROOL : babear **3** : driblar (en basquetbol)

dribble² *n* **1** TRICKLE : goteo *m*, hilo *m* **2** DROOL : baba *f* **3** : drible *m* (en basquetbol)

drier → dry², dryer

driest *adj* → **dry²**

drift¹ ['drɪft] *vi* **1** : dejarse llevar por la corriente, ir a la deriva (dícese de un bote), ir sin rumbo (dícese de una persona) **2** ACCUMULATE : amontonarse, acumularse, apilarse

drift² *n* **1** DRIFTING : deriva *f* **2** HEAP, MASS : montón *m* (de arena, etc.), ventisquero *m* (de nieve) **3** MEANING : sentido *m*

drifter ['drɪftər] *n* : vagabundo *m*, -da *f*

driftwood ['drɪft,wʊd] *n* : madera *f* flotante

drill¹ ['drɪl] *vt* **1** BORE : perforar, taladrar **2** INSTRUCT : instruir por repetición — *vi* **1** TRAIN : entrenarse **2 to drill for oil** : perforar en busca de petróleo

drill² *n* **1** : taladro *m*, barrena *f* **2** EXERCISE, PRACTICE : ejercicio *m*, instrucción *f*

drily → dryly

drink¹ ['drɪŋk] *v* **drank** ['dræŋk]; **drunk** ['drʌŋk] *or* **drank; drinking** *vt* **1** IMBIBE : beber, tomar **2 to drink up** ABSORB : absorber — *vi* **1** : beber **2** : beber alcohol, tomar

drink² *n* **1** : bebida *f* **2** : bebida *f* alcohólica

drinkable ['drɪŋkəbəl] *adj* : potable

drinker ['drɪŋkər] *n* : bebedor *m*, -dora *f*

drip¹ ['drɪp] *vi* **dripped; dripping** : gotear, chorrear

drip² *n* **1** DROP : gota *f* **2** DRIPPING : goteo *m*

drive¹ ['draɪv] *v* **drove** ['droːv]; **driven** ['drɪvən]; **driving** *vt* **1** IMPEL : impeler, impulsar **2** OPERATE : guiar, conducir, manejar (un vehículo) **3** COMPEL : obligar, forzar **4** : clavar, hincar ⟨to drive a stake : clavar una estaca⟩ **5** *or* **to drive away** : ahuyentar, echar **6 to drive crazy** : volver loco — *vi* : manejar, conducir ⟨do you know how to drive? : ¿sabes manejar?⟩

drive² *n* **1** RIDE : paseo *m* en coche **2** CAMPAIGN : campaña *f* ⟨fund-raising drive : campaña para recaudar fondos⟩ **3** DRIVEWAY : camino *m* de entrada, entrada *f* **4** TRANSMISSION : transmisión *f* ⟨front-wheel drive : tracción delantera⟩ **5** ENERGY : dinamismo *m*, energía *f* **6** INSTINCT, NEED : instinto *m*, necesidad *f* básica **7** → **disk drive**

drivel ['drɪvəl] *n* : tontería *f*, estupidez *f*

driver ['draɪvər] *n* : conductor *m*, -tora *f*; chofer *m*

driveway ['draɪv,weɪ] *n* : camino *m* de entrada, entrada *f* (para coches)

drizzle¹ ['drɪzəl] *vi* **-zled; -zling** : lloviznar, garuar

drizzle² *n* : llovizna *f*, garúa *f*

droll ['droːl] *adj* : cómico, gracioso, chistoso — **drolly** *adv*

dromedary ['drɑmə,dɛri] *n*, *pl* **-daries** : dromedario *m*

drone¹ ['droːn] *vi* **droned; droning 1** BUZZ : zumbar **2** MURMUR : hablar con monotonía, murmurar

drone² *n* **1** : zángano *m* (abeja) **2** FREELOADER : gorrón *m*, -rrona *f fam*; parásito *m*, -ta *f* **3** BUZZ, HUM : zumbido *m*, murmullo *m*

drool¹ ['druːl] *vi* : babear

drool² *n* : baba *f*

droop¹ ['druːp] *vi* **1** HANG : inclinarse (dícese de la cabeza), encorvarse (dícese de los escombros), marchitarse (dícese de las flores) **2** FLAG : decaer, flaquear ⟨his spirits drooped : se desanimó⟩

droop² *n* : inclinación *f*, caída *f*

drop¹ ['drɑp] *v* **dropped; dropping** *vt* **1** : dejar caer, soltar ⟨she dropped the glass : se le cayó el vaso⟩ ⟨to drop a hint : dejar caer una indirecta⟩ **2** SEND : mandar ⟨drop me a line : mándame unas líneas⟩ **3** ABANDON : abandonar, dejar ⟨to drop the subject : cambiar de tema⟩ **4** LOWER : bajar ⟨he dropped his voice : bajó la voz⟩ **5** OMIT : omitir **6 to drop off** : dejar — *vi* **1** DRIP : gotear **2** FALL : caer(se) **3** DECREASE, DESCEND : bajar, descender ⟨the wind dropped : amainó el viento⟩ **4 to drop back** *or* **to drop behind** : rezagarse, quedarse atrás **5 to drop by** *or* **to drop in** : pasar

drop² *n* **1** : gota *f* (de líquido) **2** DECLINE : caída *f*, bajada *f*, descenso *m* **3** INCLINE : caída *f*, pendiente *f* ⟨a 20-foot drop : una caída de 20 pies⟩ **4** SWEET : pastilla *f*, dulce *m* **5 drops** *npl* : gotas *fpl* (de medicina)

droplet ['drɑplət] *n* : gotita *f*

dropper ['drɑpər] *n* : gotero *m*, cuentagotas *m*

dross ['drɑs, 'drɔs] *n* : escoria *f*

drought ['draʊt] *n* : sequía *f*

drove¹ → **drive**

drove² ['droːv] *n* : multitud *f*, gentío *m*, manada *f* (de ganado) ⟨in droves : en manada⟩

drown ['draʊn] *vt* **1** : ahogar **2** INUN-
DATE : anegar, inundar **3 to drown out**
: ahogar — *vi* : ahogarse
drowse[1] ['draʊz] *vi* **drowsed; drowsing**
DOZE : dormitar
drowse[2] *n* : sueño *m* ligero, cabezada *f*
drowsiness ['draʊzinəs] *n* : somnolencia *f*, adormecimiento *m*
drowsy ['draʊzi] *adj* **drowsier; -est**
: somnoliento, soñoliento
drub ['drʌb] *vt* **drubbed; drubbing 1**
BEAT, THRASH : golpear, apalear **2** DE-
FEAT : derrotar por completo
drudge[1] ['drʌdʒ] *vi* **drudged; drudging**
: trabajar como esclavo, trabajar duro
drudge[2] *n* : esclavo *m*, -va *f* del trabajo
drudgery ['drʌdʒəri] *n, pl* **-eries** : trabajo *m* pesado
drug[1] ['drʌg] *vt* **drugged; drugging**
: drogar, narcotizar
drug[2] *n* **1** MEDICATION : droga *f*, medicina *f*, medicamento *m* **2** NARCOTIC
: narcótico *m*, estupefaciente *m*, droga
f
druggist ['drʌgist] *n* : farmacéutico *m*,
-ca *f*
drugstore ['drʌg,stor] *n* : farmacia *f*,
botica *f*, droguería *f*
drum[1] ['drʌm] *v* **drummed; drumming**
vt : meter a fuerza ⟨he drummed it into
my head : me lo metió en la cabeza a
fuerza⟩ — *vi* : tocar el tambor
drum[2] *n* **1** : tambor *m* **2** : bidón *m* ⟨oil
drum : bidón de petróleo⟩
drummer ['drʌmər] *n* : baterista *mf*
drumstick ['drʌm,stik] *n* **1** : palillo *m*
(de tambor), baqueta *f* **2** : muslo *m* de
pollo
drunk[1] *pp* → **drink**[1]
drunk[2] ['drʌŋk] *adj* : borracho, embriagado, ebrio
drunk[3] *n* : borracho *m*, -cha *f*
drunkard ['drʌŋkərd] *n* : borracho *m*,
-cha *f*
drunken ['drʌŋkən] *adj* : borracho,
ebrio ⟨drunken driver : conductor
ebrio⟩ ⟨drunken brawl : pleito de bo-
rrachos⟩
drunkenly ['drʌŋkənli] *adv* : como un
borracho
drunkenness ['drʌŋkənnəs] *n* : borrachera *f*, embriaguez *f*, ebriedad *f*
dry[1] ['drai] *v* **dried; drying** *vt* : secar —
vi : secarse
dry[2] *adj* **drier; driest 1** : seco **2** THIRSTY
: sediento **3** : donde la venta de bebidas
alcohólicas está prohibida ⟨a dry county : un condado seco⟩ **4** DULL : aburrido, árido **5** : seco (dícese del vino),
brut (dícese de la champaña)
dry–clean ['drai,kli:n] *v* : limpiar en seco
dry cleaner *n* : tintorería *f* (servicio)
dry cleaning *n* : limpieza *f* en seco
dryer ['draiər] *n* **1 hair dryer** : secador
m **2 clothes dryer** : secadora *f*
dry goods *npl* : artículos *mpl* de confección
dry ice *n* : hielo *m* seco

dryly ['draili] *adv* : secamente
dryness ['drainəs] *n* : sequedad *f*, aridez
f
dual ['du:əl, 'dju:-] *adj* : doble
dualism ['du:ə,lizəm] *n* : dualismo *m*
dub ['dʌb] *vt* **dubbed; dubbing 1** CALL
: apodar **2** : doblar (una película),
mezclar (una grabación)
dubious ['du:biəs, 'dju:-] *adj* **1** UNCER-
TAIN : dudoso, indeciso **2** QUESTION-
ABLE : sospechoso, dudoso, discutible
dubiously ['du:biəsli, 'dju:-] *adv* **1** UN-
CERTAINLY : dudosamente, con desconfianza **2** SUSPICIOUSLY : de modo
sospechoso, con recelo
duchess ['dʌtʃəs] *n* : duquesa *f*
duck[1] ['dʌk] *vt* **1** LOWER : agachar, bajar (la cabeza) **2** PLUNGE : zambullir
3 EVADE : eludir, evadir — *vi* **to duck
down** : agacharse
duck[2] *n, pl* **duck** *or* **ducks** : pato *m*,
-ta *f*
duckling ['dʌkliŋ] *n* : patito *m*, -ta *f*
duct ['dʌkt] *n* : conducto *m*
ductile ['dʌktəl] *adj* : dúctil
dude ['du:d, 'dju:d] *n* **1** DANDY : dandi
m, dandy *m* **2** GUY : tipo *m*
due[1] ['du:, 'dju:] *adv* : justo a, derecho
hacia ⟨due north : derecho hacia el
norte⟩
due[2] *adj* **1** PAYABLE : pagadero, sin pagar **2** APPROPRIATE : debido, apropiado ⟨after due consideration : con las
debidas consideraciones⟩ **3** EXPECTED
: esperado ⟨the train is due soon : esperamos el tren muy pronto, el tren
debe llegar pronto⟩ **4 due to** : debido
a, por
due[3] *n* **1 to give someone his (her) due**
: darle a alguien su merecido **2 dues**
npl : cuota *f*
duel[1] ['du:əl, 'dju:-] *vi* : batirse en duelo
duel[2] *n* : duelo *m*
duet ['du:'ɛt, dju-] *n* : dúo *m*
due to *prep* : debido a
dug → **dig**
dugout ['dʌg,aʊt] *n* **1** CANOE : piragua
f **2** SHELTER : refugio *m* subterráneo
duke ['du:k, 'dju:k] *n* : duque *m*
dull[1] ['dʌl] *vt* **1** DIM : opacar, quitar el
brillo a, deslustrar **2** BLUNT : embotar
(un filo), entorpecer (los sentidos),
aliviar (el dolor), amortiguar (sonidos)
dull[2] *adj* **1** STUPID : torpe, lerdo, lento
2 BLUNT : desafilado, despuntado **3**
LACKLUSTER : sin brillo, deslustrado **4**
BORING : aburrido, soso, pesado —
dully *adv*
dullness ['dʌlnəs] *n* **1** STUPIDITY : estupidez *f* **2** : embotamiento *m* (de los
sentidos) **3** MONOTONY : monotonía *f*,
insipidez *f* **4** : falta *f* de brillo **5** BLUNT-
NESS : falta *f* de filo, embotadura *f*
duly ['du:li, 'dju:-] *adv* PROPERLY : debidamente, a su debido tiempo
dumb ['dʌm] *adj* **1** MUTE : mudo **2** STU-
PID : estúpido, tonto, bobo — **dumbly**
adv

dumbbell ['dʌm,bɛl] *n* **1** WEIGHT : pesa *f* **2** : estúpido *m*, -da *f*

dumbfound *or* **dumfound** [,dʌm-'faʊnd] *vt* : dejar atónito, dejar sin habla

dummy ['dʌmi] *n, pl* **-mies 1** SHAM : imitación *f*, sustituto *m* **2** PUPPET : muñeco *m* **3** MANNEQUIN : maniquí *m* **4** IDIOT : tonto *m*, -ta *f*; idiota *mf*

dump[1] ['dʌmp] *vt* : descargar, verter

dump[2] *n* **1** : vertedero *m*, tiradero *m* *Mex* **2 down in the dumps** : triste, deprimido

dumpling ['dʌmplɪŋ] *n* : bola *f* de masa hervida

dumpy ['dʌmpi] *adj* **dumpier; -est** : rechoncho, regordete

dun[1] ['dʌn] *vt* **dunned; dunning** : apremiar (a un deudor)

dun[2] *adj* : pardo (color)

dunce ['dʌnts] *n* : estúpido *m*, -da *f*; burro *m*, -rra *f fam*

dune ['du:n, 'dju:n] *n* : duna *f*

dung ['dʌŋ] *n* **1** FECES : excrementos *mpl* **2** MANURE : estiércol *m*

dungaree [,dʌŋɡə'ri:] *n* **1** DENIM : tela *f* vaquera, mezclilla *f Chile, Mex* **2 dungarees** *npl* : pantalones *mpl* de trabajo hechos de tela vaquera

dungeon ['dʌndʒən] *n* : mazmorra *f*, calabozo *m*

dunk ['dʌŋk] *vt* : mojar, ensopar

duo ['du:o:, 'dju:-] *n, pl* **duos** : dúo *m*, par *m*

dupe[1] ['du:p, dju:p] *vt* **duped; duping** : engañar, embaucar

dupe[2] *n* : inocentón *m*, -tona *f*; simple *mf*

duplex[1] ['du:,plɛks, 'dju:-] *adj* : doble

duplex[2] *n* : casa *f* de dos viviendas, dúplex *m*

duplicate[1] ['du:plɪ,keɪt, 'dju:-] *vt* **-cated; -cating 1** COPY : duplicar, hacer copias de **2** REPEAT : repetir, reproducir

duplicate[2] ['du:plɪkət, 'dju:-] *adj* : duplicado ⟨a duplicate invoice : una factura por duplicado⟩

duplicate[3] ['du:plɪkət, 'dju:-] *n* : duplicado *m*, copia *f*

duplication [,du:plɪ'keɪʃən, ,dju:-] *n* **1** DUPLICATING : duplicación *f*, repetición *f* (de esfuerzos) **2** DUPLICATE : copia *f*, duplicado *m*

duplicity [dʊ'plɪsəti, ,dju:-] *n, pl* **-ties** : duplicidad *f*

durability [,dʊrə'bɪləti, ,djʊr-] *n* : durabilidad *f* (de un producto) permanencia *f*

durable ['dʊrəbəl, 'djʊr-] *adj* : duradero

duration [dʊ'reɪʃən, dju-] *n* : duración *f*

duress [dʊ'rɛs, dju-] *n* : coacción *f*

during ['dʊrɪŋ, 'djʊr-] *prep* : durante

dusk ['dʌsk] *n* : anochecer *m*, crepúsculo *m*

dusky ['dʌski] *adj* **duskier; -est** : oscuro (dícese de los colores)

dust[1] ['dʌst] *vt* **1** : quitar el polvo de **2** SPRINKLE : espolvorear

dust[2] *n* : polvo *m*

duster ['dʌstər] *n* **1** *or* **dust cloth** : trapo *m* de polvo **2** HOUSECOAT : guardapolvo *m* **3 feather duster** : plumero *m*

dustpan ['dʌst,pæn] *n* : recogedor *m*

dusty ['dʌsti] *adj* **dustier; -est** : cubierto de polvo, polvoriento

Dutch[1] ['dʌtʃ] *adj* : holandés

Dutch[2] *n* **1** : holandés *m* (idioma) **2 the Dutch** *npl* : los holandeses

Dutch treat *n* : invitación o pago a escote

dutiful ['du:tɪfəl, 'dju:-] *adj* : motivado por sus deberes, responsable

duty ['du:ti, 'dju:-] *n, pl* **-ties 1** OBLIGATION : deber *m*, obligación *f*, responsabilidad *f* **2** TAX : impuesto *m*, arancel *m*

DVD [,di:,vi:'di:] *n* : DVD *m*

dwarf[1] ['dwɔrf] *vt* **1** STUNT : arrestar el crecimiento de **2** : hacer parecer pequeño

dwarf[2] *n, pl* **dwarfs** ['dwɔrfs] *or* **dwarves** ['dwɔrvz] : enano *m*, -na *f*

dwell ['dwɛl] *vi* **dwelled** *or* **dwelt** ['dwɛlt]; **dwelling 1** RESIDE : residir, morar, vivir **2 to dwell on** : pensar demasiado en, insistir en

dweller ['dwɛlər] *n* : habitante *mf*

dwelling ['dwɛlɪŋ] *n* : morada *f*, vivienda *f*, residencia *f*

dwindle ['dwɪndəl] *vi* **-dled; -dling** : menguar, reducirse, disminuir

dye[1] ['daɪ] *vt* **dyed; dyeing** : teñir

dye[2] *n* : tintura *f*, tinte *m*

dying → **die**

dyke → **dike**

dynamic [daɪ'næmɪk] *adj* : dinámico

dynamics [daɪ'næmɪks] *npl* : dinámica *f*

dynamite[1] ['daɪnə,maɪt] *vt* **-mited; -miting** : dinamitar

dynamite[2] *n* : dinamita *f*

dynamo ['daɪnə,mo:] *n, pl* **-mos** : dínamo *m*, generador *m* de electricidad

dynasty ['daɪnəsti, -,næs-] *n, pl* **-ties** : dinastía *f*

dysentery ['dɪsən,tɛri] *n, pl* **-teries** : disentería *f*

dysfunction [dɪs'fʌŋkʃən] *n* : disfunción *f*

dystrophy ['dɪstrəfi] *n, pl* **-phies 1** : distrofia *f* **2** → **muscular dystrophy**

E

e [ˈiː] *n, pl* **e's** *or* **es** [ˈiːz] : quinta letra del alfabeto inglés
each[1] [ˈiːtʃ] *adv* : cada uno, por persona ⟨they cost $10 each : costaron $10 cada uno⟩
each[2] *adj* : cada ⟨each student : cada estudiante⟩ ⟨each and every one : todos sin excepción⟩
each[3] *pron* **1** : cada uno *m*, cada una *f* ⟨each of us : cada uno de nosotros⟩ **2** **each other** : el uno al otro, mutuamente ⟨we are helping each other : nos ayudamos el uno al otro⟩ ⟨they love each other : se aman⟩
eager [ˈiːgər] *adj* **1** ENTHUSIASTIC : entusiasta, ávido, deseoso **2** ANXIOUS : ansioso, impaciente
eagerly [ˈiːgərli] *adv* : con entusiasmo, ansiosamente
eagerness [ˈiːgərnəs] *n* : entusiasmo *m*, deseo *m*, impaciencia *f*
eagle [ˈiːgəl] *n* : águila *f*
ear [ˈɪr] *n* **1** : oído *m*, oreja *f* ⟨inner ear : oído interno⟩ ⟨big ears : orejas grandes⟩ **2 ear of corn** : mazorca *f*, choclo *m*
earache [ˈɪrˌeɪk] *n* : dolor *m* de oído
eardrum [ˈɪrˌdrʌm] *n* : tímpano *m*
earl [ˈərl] *n* : conde *m*
earlobe [ˈɪrˌloːb] *n* : lóbulo *m* de la oreja, perilla *f* de la oreja
early[1] [ˈərli] *adv* **earlier; -est** : temprano, pronto ⟨he arrived early : llegó temprano⟩ ⟨as early as possible : lo más pronto posible, cuanto antes⟩ ⟨ten minutes early : diez minutos de adelanto⟩
early[2] *adj* **earlier; -est 1** (*referring to a beginning*) : primero ⟨the early stages : las primeras etapas⟩ ⟨in early May : a principios de mayo⟩ **2** (*referring to antiquity*) : primitivo, antiguo ⟨early man : el hombre primitivo⟩ ⟨early painting : la pintura antigua⟩ **3** (*referring to a designated time*) : temprano, antes de la hora, prematuro ⟨he was early : llegó temprano⟩ ⟨early fruit : frutas tempraneras⟩ ⟨an early death : una muerte prematura⟩
earmark [ˈɪrˌmɑrk] *vt* : destinar ⟨earmarked funds : fondos destinados⟩
earn [ˈərn] *vt* **1** : ganar ⟨to earn money : ganar dinero⟩ **2** DESERVE : ganarse, merecer
earnest[1] [ˈərnəst] *adj* : serio, sincero
earnest[2] *n* **in ~** : en serio, de verdad ⟨we began in earnest : empezamos de verdad⟩
earnestly [ˈərnəstli] *adv* **1** SERIOUSLY : con seriedad, en serio **2** FERVENTLY : de todo corazón
earnestness [ˈərnəstnəs] *n* : seriedad *f*, sinceridad *f*
earnings [ˈərnɪŋz] *npl* : ingresos *mpl*, ganancias *fpl*, utilidades *fpl*
earphone [ˈɪrˌfoːn] *n* : audífono *m*

earring [ˈɪrˌrɪŋ] *n* : zarcillo *m*, arete *m*, aro *m Arg, Chile, Uru*, pendiente *m Spain*
earshot [ˈɪrˌʃɑt] *n* : alcance *m* del oído
earth [ˈərθ] *n* **1** LAND, SOIL : tierra *f*, suelo *m* **2 the Earth** : la Tierra
earthen [ˈərθən, -ðən] *adj* : de tierra, de barro
earthenware [ˈərθənˌwær, -ðən-] *n* : loza *f*, vajillas *fpl* de barro
earthly [ˈərθli] *adj* : terrenal, mundano
earthquake [ˈərθˌkweɪk] *n* : terremoto *m*, temblor *m*
earthworm [ˈərθˌwərm] *n* : lombriz *f* (de tierra)
earthy [ˈərθi] *adj* **earthier; -est 1** : terroso ⟨earthy colors : colores terrosos⟩ **2** DOWN-TO-EARTH : realista, práctico, llano **3** COARSE, CRUDE : basto, grosero, tosco ⟨earthy jokes : chistes groseros⟩
earwax [ˈɪrˌwæks] *n* → **wax**[2]
earwig [ˈɪrˌwɪg] *n* : tijereta *f*
ease[1] [ˈiːz] *v* **eased; easing** *vt* **1** ALLEVIATE : aliviar, calmar, hacer disminuir **2** LOOSEN, RELAX : aflojar (una cuerda), relajar (restricciones), descargar (tensiones) **3** FACILITATE : facilitar — *vi* : calmarse, relajarse
ease[2] *n* **1** CALM, RELIEF : tranquilidad *f*, comodidad *f*, desahogo *m* **2** FACILITY : facilidad *f* **3 at ~** : relajado, cómodo ⟨to put someone at ease : tranquilizar a alguien⟩
easel [ˈiːzəl] *n* : caballete *m*
easily [ˈiːzəli] *adv* **1** : fácilmente, con facilidad **2** UNQUESTIONABLY : con mucho, de lejos
easiness [ˈiːzinəs] *n* : facilidad *f*, soltura *f*
east[1] [ˈiːst] *adv* : al este
east[2] *adj* : este, del este, oriental ⟨east winds : vientos del este⟩
east[3] *n* **1** : este *m* **2 the East** : el Oriente
Easter [ˈiːstər] *n* : Pascua *f* (de Resurrección)
easterly [ˈiːstərli] *adv & adj* : del este
eastern [ˈiːstərn] *adj* **1** : Oriental, del Este ⟨Eastern Europe : Europa del Este⟩ **2** : oriental, este
Easterner [ˈiːstərnər] *n* : habitante *mf* del este
eastward [ˈiːstwərd] *adv & adj* : hacia el este
easy [ˈiːzi] *adj* **easier; -est 1** : fácil **2** LENIENT : indulgente
easygoing [ˌiːziˈgoːɪŋ] *adj* : acomodaticio, tolerante, poco exigente
eat [ˈiːt] *v* **ate** [ˈeɪt]; **eaten** [ˈiːtən]; **eating** *vt* **1** : comer **2** CONSUME : consumir, gastar, devorar ⟨expenses ate up profits : los gastos devoraron las ganancias⟩ **3** CORRODE : corroer — *vi* **1** : comer **2 to eat away at** *or* **to eat into** : comerse **3 to eat out** : comer fuera

eatable[1] [ˈiːṭəbəl] *adj* : comestible, comible *fam*

eatable[2] *n* **1** : algo para comer **2 eatables** *npl* : comestibles *mpl*, alimentos *mpl*

eater [ˈiːṭər] *n* : comedor *m*, -dora *f*

eaves [ˈiːvz] *npl* : alero *m*

eavesdrop [ˈiːvzˌdrɑp] *vi* **-dropped; -dropping** : escuchar a escondidas

eavesdropper [ˈiːvzˌdrɑpər] *n* : persona *f* que escucha a escondidas

ebb[1] [ˈɛb] *vi* **1** : bajar, menguar (dícese de la marea) **2** DECLINE : decaer, disminuir

ebb[2] *n* **1** : reflujo *m* (de una marea) **2** DECLINE : decadencia *f*, declive *m*, disminución *f*

ebony[1] [ˈɛbəni] *adj* **1** : de ébano **2** BLACK : de color ébano, negro

ebony[2] *n*, *pl* **-nies** : ébano *m*

ebullience [ɪˈbʊljənts, -ˈbʌl-] *n* : efervescencia *f*, vivacidad *f*

ebullient [ɪˈbʊljənt, -ˈbʌl-] *adj* : efervescente, vivaz

eccentric[1] [ɪkˈsɛntrɪk] *adj* **1** : excéntrico ⟨an eccentric wheel : una rueda excéntrica⟩ **2** ODD, SINGULAR : excéntrico, extraño, raro — **eccentrically** [-trɪkli] *adv*

eccentric[2] *n* : excéntrico *m*, -ca *f*

eccentricity [ˌɛkˌsɛnˈtrɪsəṭi] *n*, *pl* **-ties** : excentricidad *f*

ecclesiastic [ɪˌkliːziˈæstɪk] *n* : eclesiástico *m*, clérigo *m*

ecclesiastical [ɪˌkliːziˈæstɪkəl] *or* **ecclesiastic** *adj* : eclesiástico — **ecclesiastically** *adv*

echelon [ˈɛʃəˌlɑn] *n* **1** : escalón *m* (de tropas o aviones) **2** LEVEL : nivel *m*, esfera *f*, estrato *m*

echo[1] [ˈɛˌkoː] *v* **echoed; echoing** *vi* : hacer eco, resonar — *vt* : repetir

echo[2] *n*, *pl* **echoes** : eco *m*

éclair [eɪˈklær, i-] *n* : pastel *m* relleno de crema

eclectic [ɛˈklɛktɪk, ɪ-] *adj* : ecléctico

eclipse[1] [ɪˈklɪps] *vt* **eclipsed; eclipsing** : eclipsar

eclipse[2] *n* : eclipse *m*

ecological [ˌiːkəˈlɑdʒɪkəl, ˌɛkə-] *adj* : ecológico — **ecologically** *adv*

ecologist [iˈkɑlədʒɪst, ɛ-] *n* : ecólogo *m*, -ga *f*

ecology [iˈkɑlədʒi, ɛ-] *n*, *pl* **-gies** : ecología *f*

economic [ˌiːkəˈnɑmɪk, ˌɛkə-] *adj* : económico

economical [ˌiːkəˈnɑmɪkəl, ˌɛkə-] *adj* : económico — **economically** *adv*

economics [ˌiːkəˈnɑmɪks, ˌɛkə-] *n* : economía *f*

economist [iˈkɑnəmɪst] *n* : economista *mf*

economize [iˈkɑnəˌmaɪz] *v* **-mized; -mizing** : economizar, ahorrar

economy [iˈkɑnəmi] *n*, *pl* **-mies** **1** : economía *f*, sistema *m* económico **2** THRIFT : economía *f*, ahorro *m*

ecosystem [ˈiːkoˌsɪstəm] *n* : ecosistema *m*

ecru [ˈɛˌkruː, ˈeɪ-] *n* : color *m* crudo

ecstasy [ˈɛkstəsi] *n*, *pl* **-sies** : éxtasis *m*

ecstatic [ɛkˈstæṭɪk, ɪk-] *adj* : extático

ecstatically [ɛkˈstæṭɪkli, ɪk-] *adv* : con éxtasis, con gran entusiasmo

Ecuadoran [ˌɛkwəˈdorən] *or* **Ecuadorean** *or* **Ecuadorian** [-ˈdoriən] *n* : ecuatoriano *m*, -na *f* — **Ecuadorean** *or* **Ecuadorian** *adj*

ecumenical [ˌɛkjʊˈmnɪkəl] *adj* : ecuménico

eczema [ɪgˈziːmə, ˈɛgzəmə, ˈɛksə-] *n* : eczema *m*

eddy[1] [ˈɛdi] *vi* **eddied; eddying** : arremolinarse, hacer remolinos

eddy[2] *n*, *pl* **-dies** : remolino *m*

edema [ɪˈdiːmə] *n* : edema *m*

Eden [ˈiːdən] *n* : Edén *m*

edge[1] [ˈɛdʒ] *v* **edged; edging** *vt* **1** BORDER : bordear, ribetear, orlar **2** SHARPEN : afilar, aguzar **3** *or* **to edge one's way** : avanzar poco a poco **4 to edge out** : derrotar por muy poco — *vi* ADVANCE : ir avanzando (poco a poco)

edge[2] *n* **1** : filo *m* (de un cuchillo) **2** BORDER : borde *m*, orilla *f*, margen *m* **3** ADVANTAGE : ventaja *f*

edger [ˈɛdʒər] *n* : cortabordes *m*

edgewise [ˈɛdʒˌwaɪz] *adv* SIDEWAYS : de lado, de canto

edginess [ˈɛdʒinəs] *n* : tensión *f*, nerviosismo *m*

edgy [ˈɛdʒi] *adj* **edgier; -est** : tenso, nervioso

edible [ˈɛdəbəl] *adj* : comestible

edict [ˈiːˌdɪkt] *n* : edicto *m*, mandato *m*, orden *f*

edification [ˌɛdəfəˈkeɪʃən] *n* : edificación *f*, instrucción *f*

edifice [ˈɛdəfɪs] *n* : edificio *m*

edify [ˈɛdəˌfaɪ] *vt* **-fied; -fying** : edificar

edit [ˈɛdɪt] *vt* **1** : editar, redactar, corregir **2** *or* **to edit out** DELETE : recortar, cortar

edition [ɪˈdɪʃən] *n* : edición *f*

editor [ˈɛdɪṭər] *n* : editor *m*, -tora *f*; redactor *m*, -tora *f*

editorial[1] [ˌɛdɪˈtoriəl] *adj* **1** : de redacción **2** : editorial ⟨an editorial comment : un comentario editorial⟩

editorial[2] *n* : editorial *m*

editorship [ˈɛdəṭərˌʃɪp] *n* : dirección *f*

educable [ˈɛdʒəkəbəl] *adj* : educable

educate [ˈɛdʒəˌkeɪt] *vt* **-cated; -cating 1** TEACH : educar, enseñar **2** INSTRUCT : formar, educar, instruir **3** INFORM : informar, concientizar

education [ˌɛdʒəˈkeɪʃən] *n* : educación *f*

educational [ˌɛdʒəˈkeɪʃənəl] *adj* **1** : docente, de enseñanza ⟨an educational institution : una institución docente⟩ **2** PEDAGOGICAL : pedagógico **3** INSTRUCTIONAL : educativo, instructivo

educator [ˈɛdʒəˌkeɪṭər] *n* : educador *m*, -dora *f*

eel [ˈiːl] *n* : anguila *f*

eerie ['ɪri] *adj* **-rier; -est 1** SPOOKY : que da miedo, espeluznante **2** GHOSTLY : fantasmagórico

eerily ['ɪrəli] *adv* : de manera extraña y misteriosa

efface [ɪ'feɪs, -] *vt* **-faced; -facing** : borrar

effect¹ [ɪ'fɛkt] *vt* **1** CARRY OUT : efectuar, llevar a cabo **2** ACHIEVE : lograr, realizar

effect² *n* **1** RESULT : efecto *m*, resultado *m*, consecuencia *f* ⟨to no effect : sin resultado⟩ **2** MEANING : sentido *m* ⟨something to that effect : algo por el estilo⟩ **3** INFLUENCE : efecto *m*, influencia *f* **4 effects** *npl* BELONGINGS : efectos *mpl*, pertenencias *fpl* **5 to go into effect** : entrar en vigor **6 in ∼** REALLY : en realidad, efectivamente

effective [ɪ'fɛktɪv] *adj* **1** EFFECTUAL : efectivo, eficaz **2** OPERATIVE : vigente — **effectively** *adv*

effectiveness [ɪ'fɛktɪvnəs] *n* : eficacia *f*, efectividad *f*

effectual [ɪ'fɛktʃuəl] *adj* : eficaz, efectivo — **effectually** *adv*

effeminate [ə'fɛmənət] *adj* : afeminado

effervesce [ˌɛfər'vɛs] *vi* **-vesced; -vescing 1** : estar en efervescencia, burbujear (dícese de líquidos) **2** : estar eufórico, estar muy animado (dícese de las personas)

effervescence [ˌɛfər'vɛsənts] *n* **1** : efervescencia *f* **2** LIVELINESS : vivacidad *f*

effervescent [ˌɛfər'vɛsənt] *adj* **1** : efervescente **2** LIVELY, VIVACIOUS : vivaz, animado

effete [ɛ'fi:t, ɪ-] *adj* **1** WORN-OUT : desgastado, agotado **2** DECADENT : decadente **3** EFFEMINATE : afeminado

efficacious [ˌɛfə'keɪʃəs] *adj* : eficaz, efectivo

efficacy ['ɛfɪkəsi] *n, pl* **-cies** : eficacia *f*

efficiency [ɪ'fɪʃəntsi] *n, pl* **-cies** : eficiencia *f*

efficient [ɪ'fɪʃənt] *adj* : eficiente — **efficiently** *adv*

effigy ['ɛfədʒi] *n, pl* **-gies** : efigie *f*

effluent ['ɛˌfluːənt, ɛ'fluː-] *n* : efluente *m* — **effluent** *adj*

effort ['ɛfərt] *n* **1** EXERTION : esfuerzo *m* **2** ATTEMPT : tentativa *f*, intento *m* ⟨it's not worth the effort : no vale la pena⟩

effortless ['ɛfərtləs] *adj* : fácil, sin esfuerzo

effortlessly ['ɛfərtləsli] *adv* : sin esfuerzo, fácilmente

effrontery [ɪ'frʌntəri] *n, pl* **-teries** : insolencia *f*, desfachatez *f*, descaro *m*

effusion [ɪ'fjuːʒən, ɛ-] *n* : efusión *f*

effusive [ɪ'fjuːsɪv, ɛ-] *adj* : efusivo — **effusively** *adv*

egg¹ ['ɛg] *vt* **to egg on** : incitar, azuzar, provocar

egg² *n* **1** : huevo *m* **2** OVUM : óvulo *m*

eggbeater ['ɛgˌbiːtər] *n* : batidor *m* (de huevos)

eggnog ['ɛgˌnɑg] *n* : ponche *m* de huevo, rompope *m CA, Mex*

eggplant ['ɛgˌplænt] *n* : berenjena *f*

eggshell ['ɛgˌʃl] *n* : cascarón *m*

ego ['iːˌgoː] *n, pl* **egos 1** SELF-ESTEEM : amor *m* propio **2** SELF : ego *m*, yo *m*

egocentric [ˌiːgoː'sɛntrɪk] *adj* : egocéntrico

egoism ['iːgoːˌwɪzəm] *n* : egoísmo *m*

egoist ['iːgoːwɪst] *n* : egoísta *mf*

egoistic [ˌiːˌgoː'wɪstɪk] *adj* : egoísta

egotism ['iːgəˌtɪzəm] *n* : egotismo *m*

egotist ['iːgətɪst] *n* : egotista *mf*

egotistic [ˌiːgə'tɪstɪk] *or* **egotistical** [-'tɪstɪkəl] *adj* : egotista — **egotistically** *adv*

egregious [ɪ'griːdʒəs] *adj* : atroz, flagrante, mayúsculo — **egregiously** *adv*

egress ['iːˌgrɛs] *n* : salida *f*

egret ['iːˌgrət, -ˌgrɛt] *n* : garceta *f*

Egyptian [ɪ'dʒɪpʃən] *n* **1** : egipcio *m*, -cia *f* **2** : egipcio *m* (idioma) — **Egyptian** *adj*

eiderdown ['aɪdərˌdaʊn] *n* **1** : plumón *m* **2** COMFORTER : edredón *m*

eight¹ ['eɪt] *adj* : ocho

eight² *n* : ocho *m*

eight hundred¹ *adj* : ochocientos

eight hundred² *n* : ochocientos *m*

eighteen¹ [eɪt'tiːn] *adj* : dieciocho

eighteen² *n* : dieciocho *m*

eighteenth¹ [eɪt'tiːnθ] *adj* : decimoctavo

eighteenth² *n* **1** : decimoctavo *m*, -va *f* (en una serie) **2** : dieciochoavo *m*, dieciochoava parte *f*

eighth¹ ['eɪtθ] *adj* : octavo

eighth² *n* **1** : octavo *m*, -va *f* (en una serie) **2** : octavo *m*, octava parte *f*

eightieth¹ ['eɪtiəθ] *adj* : octogésimo

eightieth² *n* **1** : octogésimo *m*, -ma *f* (en una serie) **2** : ochentavo *m*, ochentava parte *f*

eighty¹ ['eɪti] *adj* : ochenta

eighty² *n, pl* **eighties 1** : ochenta *m* **2 the eighties** : los ochenta *mpl*

either¹ ['iːðər, 'aɪ-] *adj* **1** : cualquiera (de los dos) ⟨we can watch either movie : podemos ver cualquiera de las dos películas⟩ **2** : ninguno de los dos ⟨she wasn't in either room : no estaba en ninguna de las dos salas⟩ **3** EACH : cada ⟨on either side of the street : a cada lado de la calle⟩

either² *pron* **1** : cualquiera *mf* (de los dos) ⟨either is fine : cualquiera de los dos está bien⟩ **2** : ninguno *m*, -na *f* (de los dos) ⟨I don't like either : no me gusta ninguno⟩ **3** : algún *m*, alguna *f* ⟨is either of you interested? : ¿está alguno de ustedes (dos) interesado?⟩

either³ *conj* **1** : o, u ⟨either David or Daniel could go : puede ir (o) David o Daniel⟩ **2** : ni ⟨we won't watch either this movie or the other : no veremos ni esta película ni la otra⟩

ejaculate [i'dʒækjəˌleɪt] *v* **-lated; -lating** *vt* **1** : eyacular **2** EXCLAIM : exclamar — *vi* : eyacular

ejaculation [iˌd͡ʒækjə'leɪʃən] *n* **1** : eyaculación *f* (en fisiología) **2** EXCLAMATION : exclamación *f*

eject [i'd͡ʒɛkt] *vt* : expulsar, expeler

ejection [i'd͡ʒɛkʃən] *n* : expulsión *f*

eke ['iːk] *vt* **eked; eking** *or* **to eke out** : ganar a duras penas

elaborate[1] [i'læbəˌreɪt] *v* **-rated; -rating** *vt* : elaborar, idear, desarrollar — *vi* **to elaborate on** : ampliar, entrar en detalles

elaborate[2] [i'læbərət] *adj* **1** DETAILED : detallado, minucioso, elaborado **2** COMPLICATED : complicado, intrincado, elaborado — **elaborately** *adv*

elaboration [iˌlæbə'reɪʃən] *n* : elaboración *f*

elapse [i'læps] *vi* **elapsed; elapsing** : transcurrir, pasar

elastic[1] [i'læstɪk] *adj* : elástico

elastic[2] *n* **1** : elástico *m* **2** RUBBER BAND : goma *f*, gomita *f*, elástico *m*, liga *f*

elasticity [iˌlæs'tɪsəti, ˌiːˌlæs-] *n*, *pl* **-ties** : elasticidad *f*

elate [i'leɪt] *vt* **elated; elating** : alborozar, regocijar

elation [i'leɪʃən] *n* : euforia *f*, júbilo *m*, alborozo *m*

elbow[1] ['ɛlˌboː] *vt* : darle un codazo a

elbow[2] *n* : codo *m*

elder[1] ['ɛldər] *adj* : mayor

elder[2] *n* **1 to be someone's elder** : ser mayor que alguien **2** : anciano *m*, -na *f* (de un pueblo o una tribu) **3** : miembro *m* del consejo (en varias religiones)

elderberry ['ɛldərˌbɛri] *n*, *pl* **-berries** : baya *f* de saúco (fruta), saúco *m* (árbol)

elderly ['ɛldərli] *adj* : mayor, de edad, anciano

eldest ['ɛldəst] *adj* : mayor, de más edad

elect[1] [i'lɛkt] *vt* : elegir

elect[2] *adj* : electo ⟨the president-elect : el presidente electo⟩

elect[3] *npl* **the elect** : los elegidos *mpl*

election [i'lɛkʃən] *n* : elección *f*

elective[1] [i'lɛktɪv] *adj* **1** : electivo **2** OPTIONAL : facultativo, optativo

elective[2] *n* : asignatura *f* electiva

elector [i'lɛktər] *n* : elector *m*, -tora *f*

electoral [i'lɛktərəl] *adj* : electoral

electorate [i'lɛktərət] *n* : electorado *m*

electric [i'lɛktrɪk] *adj* **1** *or* **electrical** [-trɪkəl] : eléctrico **2** THRILLING : electrizante, emocionante

electrician [iˌlɛk'trɪʃən] *n* : electricista *mf*

electricity [iˌlɛk'trɪsəti] *n*, *pl* **-ties** : electricidad *f* **2** CURRENT : corriente *m* eléctrica

electrification [iˌlɛktrəfə'keɪʃən] *n* : electrificación *f*

electrify [i'lɛktrəˌfaɪ] *vt* **-fied; -fying 1** : electrificar **2** THRILL : electrizar, emocionar

electrocardiogram [iˌlɛktro'kardiəˌgræm] *n* : electrocardiograma *m*

electrocardiograph [iˌlɛktro'kardiəˌgræf] *n* : electrocardiógrafo *m*

electrocute [i'lɛktrəˌkjuːt] *vt* **-cuted; -cuting** : electrocutar

electrocution [iˌlɛktrə'kjuːʃən] *n* : electrocución *f*

electrode [i'lɛkˌtroːd] *n* : electrodo *m*

electrolysis [iˌlɛk'traləsɪs] *n* : electrólisis *f*

electrolyte [i'lɛktrəˌlaɪt] *n* : electrolito *m*

electromagnet [iˌlɛktro'mægnət] *n* : electroimán *m*

electromagnetic [iˌlɛktromæg'nɛtɪk] *adj* : electromagnético — **electromagnetically** [-tɪkli] *adv*

electromagnetism [iˌlɛktro'mægnəˌtɪzəm] *n* : electromagnetismo *m*

electron [i'lɛkˌtran] *n* : electrón *m*

electronic [iˌlɛk'tranɪk] *adj* : electrónico — **electronically** [-nɪkli] *adv*

electronic mail *n* : correo *m* electrónico

electronics [iˌlɛk'tranɪks] *n* : electrónica *f*

electroplate [i'lɛktrəˌpleɪt] *vt* **-plated; plating** : galvanizar mediante electrólisis

elegance ['ɛligənʧ] *n* : elegancia *f*

elegant ['ɛligənt] *adj* : elegante — **elegantly** *adv*

elegy ['ɛlədʒi] *n*, *pl* **-gies** : elegía *f*

element ['ɛləmənt] *n* **1** COMPONENT : elemento *m*, factor *m* **2** : elemento *m* (en la química) **3** MILIEU : elemento *m*, medio *m* ⟨to be in one's element : estar en su elemento⟩ **4 elements** *npl* RUDIMENTS : elementos *mpl*, rudimentos *mpl*, bases *fpl* **5 the elements** WEATHER : los elementos *mpl*

elemental [ˌɛlə'mɛntəl] *adj* **1** BASIC : elemental, primario **2** : elemental (dícese de los elementos químicos)

elementary [ˌɛlə'mɛntri] *adj* **1** SIMPLE : elemental, simple, fundamental **2** : de enseñanza primaria

elementary school *n* : escuela *f* primaria

elephant ['ɛləfənt] *n* : elefante *m*, -ta *f*

elevate ['ɛləˌveɪt] *vt* **-vated; -vating 1** RAISE : elevar, levantar, alzar **2** EXALT, PROMOTE : elevar, exaltar, ascender **3** ELATE : alborozar, regocijar

elevation [ˌɛlə'veɪʃən] *n* **1** : elevación *f* **2** ALTITUDE : altura *f*, altitud *f* **3** PROMOTION : ascenso *m*

elevator ['ɛləˌveɪtər] *n* : ascensor *m*, elevador *m*

eleven[1] [i'lɛvən] *adj* : once

eleven[2] *n* : once *m*

eleventh[1] [i'lɛvənθ] *adj* : undécimo

eleventh[2] *n* **1** : undécimo *m*, -ma *f* (en una serie) **2** : onceavo *m*, onceava parte *f*

elf ['ɛlf] *n*, *pl* **elves** ['ɛlvz] : elfo *m*, geniecillo *m*, duende *m*

elfin ['ɛlfən] *adj* **1** : de elfo, menudo **2** ENCHANTING, MAGIC : mágico, encantador

elfish ['ɛlfɪʃ] *adj* **1** : de elfo **2** MISCHIEVOUS : travieso

elicit [i'lɪsət] *vt* : provocar

eligibility [ˌɛləʤə'bɪləṭi] *n, pl* **-ties** : elegibilidad *f*

eligible ['ɛləʤəbəl] *adj* **1** QUALIFIED : elegible **2** SUITABLE : idóneo

eliminate [ɪ'lɪmə,neɪt] *vt* **-nated; -nating** : eliminar

elimination [ɪˌlɪmə'neɪʃən] *n* : eliminación *f*

elite [eɪ'liːt, i-] *n* : elite *f*

elixir [i'lɪksər] *n* : elixir *m*

elk ['ɛlk] *n* : alce *m* (de Europa), uapití *m* (de América)

ellipse [ɪ'lɪps, -] *n* : elipse *f*

ellipsis [ɪ'lɪpsəs, -] *n, pl* **-lipses** [-ˌsiːz] **1** : elipsis *f* **2** : puntos *mpl* suspensivos (en la puntuación)

elliptical [ɪ'lɪptɪkəl, -] *or* **elliptic** [-tɪk] *adj* : elíptico

elm ['ɛlm] *n* : olmo *m*

elocution [ˌɛlə'kjuːʃən] *n* : elocución *f*

elongate [i'lɔŋˌgeɪt] *vt* **-gated; -gating** : alargar

elongation [ˌiːˌlɔŋ'geɪʃən] *n* : alargamiento *m*

elope [i'loːp] *vi* **eloped; eloping** : fugarse

elopement [i'loːpmənt] *n* : fuga *f*

eloquence ['ɛləkwənts] *n* : elocuencia *f*

eloquent ['ɛləkwənt] *adj* : elocuente — **eloquently** *adv*

El Salvadoran [ˌɛlˌsælvə'dorən] *n* : salvadoreño *m*, -ña *f* — **El Salvadoran** *adj*

else¹ ['ɛls] *adv* **1** DIFFERENTLY : de otro modo, de otra manera ⟨how else? : ¿de qué otro modo?⟩ **2** ELSEWHERE : de otro sitio, de otro lugar ⟨where else? : ¿en qué otro sitio?⟩ **3** *or* **else** OTHERWISE : si no, de lo contrario

else² *adj* **1** OTHER : otro ⟨anyone else : cualquier otro⟩ ⟨everyone else : todos los demás⟩ ⟨nobody else : ningún otro, nadie más⟩ ⟨somebody else : otra persona⟩ **2** MORE : más ⟨nothing else : nada más⟩ ⟨what else? : ¿qué más?⟩

elsewhere ['ɛlsˌhwɛr] *adv* : en otra parte, en otro sitio, en otro lugar

elucidate [i'luːsəˌdeɪt] *vt* **-dated; -dating** : dilucidar, elucidar, esclarecer

elucidation [iˌluːsə'deɪʃən] *n* : elucidación *f*, esclarecimiento *m*

elude [i'luːd] *vt* **eluded; eluding** : eludir, evadir

elusive [i'luːsɪv] *adj* **1** EVASIVE : evasivo, esquivo **2** SLIPPERY : huidizo, escurridizo **3** FLEETING, INTANGIBLE : impalpable, fugaz

elusively [i'luːsɪvli] *adv* : de manera esquiva

elves → **elf**

emaciate [i'meɪʃiˌeɪt] *vt* **-ated; -ating** : enflaquecer

emaciation [iˌmeɪsiˈeɪʃən, -ʃi-] *n* : enflaquecimiento *m*, escualidez *f*, delgadez *f* extrema

e-mail ['iːˌmeɪl] *n* : e-mail *m*

emanate ['ɛməˌneɪt] *v* **-nated; -nating** *vi* : emanar, provenir, proceder — *vt* : emanar

emanation [ˌɛmə'neɪʃən] *n* : emanación *f*

emancipate [i'mæntsəˌpeɪt] *vt* **-pated; -pating** : emancipar

emancipation [iˌmæntsə'peɪʃən] *n* : emancipación *f*

emasculate [i'mæskjəˌleɪt] *vt* **-lated; -lating** **1** CASTRATE : castrar, emascular **2** WEAKEN : debilitar

embalm [ɪm'bam, ɛm-, -'balm] *vt* : embalsamar

embankment [ɪm'bæŋkmənt, ɛm-] *n* : terraplén *m*, muro *m* de contención

embargo¹ [ɪm'bargo, ɛm-] *vt* **-goed; -going** : imponer un embargo sobre

embargo² *n, pl* **-goes** : embargo *m*

embark [ɪm'bark, ɛm-] *vt* : embarcar — *vi* **1** : embarcarse **2 to embark on** START : emprender, embarcarse en

embarkation [ˌɛmˌbar'keɪʃən] *n* : embarque *m*, embarco *m*

embarrass [ɪm'bærəs, ɛm-] *vt* : avergonzar, abochornar

embarrassing [ɪm'bærəsɪŋ, ɛm-] *adj* : embarazoso, violento

embarrassment [ɪm'bærəsmənt, ɛm-] *n* : vergüenza *f*, pena *f*

embassy ['ɛmbəsi] *n, pl* **-sies** : embajada *f*

embed [ɪm'bɛd, ɛm-] *vt* **-bedded; -bedding** : incrustar, empotrar, grabar (en la memoria)

embellish [ɪm'bɛlɪʃ, ɛm-] *vt* : adornar, embellecer

embellishment [ɪm'bɛlɪʃmənt, ɛm-] *n* : adorno *m*

ember ['ɛmbər] *n* : ascua *f*, brasa *f*

embezzle [ɪm'bɛzəl, ɛm-] *vt* **-zled; -zling** : desfalcar, malversar

embezzlement [ɪm'bɛzəlmənt, ɛm-] *n* : desfalco *m*, malversación *f*

embezzler [ɪm'bɛzələr, ɛm-] *n* : desfalcador *m*, -dora *f*; malversador *m*, -dora *f*

embitter [ɪm'bɪṭər, ɛm-] *vt* : amargar

emblem ['ɛmbləm] *n* : emblema *m*, símbolo *m*

emblematic [ˌɛmblə'mæṭɪk] *adj* : emblemático, simbólico

embodiment [ɪm'badɪmənt, ɛm-] *n* : encarnación *f*, personificación *f*

embody [ɪm'badi, ɛm-] *vt* **-bodied; -bodying** : encarnar, personificar

emboss [ɪm'bas, ɛm-, -'bɔs] *vt* : repujar, grabar en relieve

embrace¹ [ɪm'breɪs, ɛm-] *vt* **-braced; -bracing** **1** HUG : abrazar **2** ADOPT, TAKE ON : adoptar, aceptar **3** INCLUDE : abarcar, incluir

embrace² *n* : abrazo *m*

embroider [ɪm'brɔɪdər, ɛm-] *vt* : bordar (una tela), adornar (una historia)

embroidery [ɪm'brɔɪdəri, ɛm-] *n, pl* **-deries** : bordado *m*

embroil [ɪm'brɔɪl, ɛm-] *vt* : embrollar, enredar

embryo ['ɛmbriˌoː] *n, pl* **embryos** : embrión *m*

embryonic [ˌɛmbri'ɑnɪk] *adj* : embrionario

emend [i'mɛnd] *vt* : enmendar, corregir

emendation [ˌiːˌmɛn'deɪʃən] *n* : enmienda *f*

emerald[1] ['ɛmrəld, 'ɛmə-] *adj* : verde esmeralda

emerald[2] *n* : esmeralda *f*

emerge [i'mərdʒ] *vi* **emerged; emerging** : emerger, salir, aparecer, surgir

emergence [i'mərdʒənts] *n* : aparición *f*, surgimiento *m*

emergency [i'mərdʒəntsi] *n*, *pl* **-cies** : emergencia *f*

emergent [i'mərdʒənt] *adj* : emergente

emery ['ɛməri] *n*, *pl* **-eries** : esmeril *m*

emetic[1] [i'mɛtɪk] *adj* : vomitivo, emético

emetic[2] *n* : vomitivo *m*, emético *m*

emigrant ['ɛmɪgrənt] *n* : emigrante *mf*

emigrate ['ɛməˌgreɪt] *vi* **-grated; -grating** : emigrar

emigration [ˌɛmə'greɪʃən] *n* : emigración *f*

eminence ['ɛmənənts] *n* **1** PROMINENCE : eminencia *f*, prestigio *m*, renombre *m* **2** DIGNITARY : eminencia *f*; dignatario *m*, -ria *f* ⟨Your Eminence : Su Eminencia⟩

eminent ['ɛmənənt] *adj* : eminente, ilustre

eminently ['ɛmənəntli] *adv* : sumamente

emissary ['ɛməˌsɛri] *n*, *pl* **-saries** : emisario *m*, -ria *f*

emission [i'mɪʃən] *n* : emisión *f*

emit [i'mɪt] *vt* **emitted; emitting** : emitir, despedir, producir

emote [i'moːt] *vi* **emoted; emoting** : exteriorizar las emociones

emotion [i'moːʃən] *n* : emoción *f*, sentimiento *m*

emotional [i'moːʃənəl] *adj* **1** : emocional, afectivo ⟨an emotional reaction : una reacción emocional⟩ **2** MOVING : emocionante, emotivo, conmovedor

emotionally [i'moːʃənəli] *adv* : emocionalmente

empathy ['ɛmpəθi] *n* : empatía *f*

emperor ['ɛmpərər] *n* : emperador *m*

emphasis ['ɛmfəsɪs] *n*, *pl* **-phases** [-ˌsiːz] : énfasis *m*, hincapié *m*

emphasize ['ɛmfəˌsaɪz] *vt* **-sized; -sizing** : enfatizar, destacar, subrayar, hacer hincapié en

emphatic [ɪm'fætɪk, ɛm-] *adj* : enfático, enérgico, categórico — **emphatically** [-ɪkli] *adv*

empire ['ɛmˌpaɪr] *n* : imperio *m*

empirical [ɪm'pɪrɪkəl, ɛm-] *adj* : empírico — **empirically** [-ɪkli] *adv*

employ[1] [ɪm'plɔɪ, ɛm-] *vt* **1** USE : usar, utilizar **2** HIRE : contratar, emplear **3** OCCUPY : ocupar, dedicar, emplear

employ[2] [ɪm'plɔɪ, ɛm-; 'ɪmˌ-, 'ɛmˌ-] *n* **1** : puesto *m*, cargo *m*, ocupación *f* **2 to be in the employ of** : estar al servicio de, trabajar para

employee [ɪmˌplɔɪ'iː, ɛm-, -'plɔɪˌiː] *n* : empleado *m*, -da *f*

employer [ɪm'plɔɪər, ɛm-] *n* : patrón *m*, -trona *f*; empleador *m*, -dora *f*

employment [ɪm'plɔɪmənt, ɛm-] *n* : trabajo *m*, empleo *m*

empower [ɪm'pauər, ɛm-] *vt* : facultar, autorizar, conferirle poder a

empowerment [ɪm'pauərmənt, ɛm-] *n* : autorización *f*

empress ['ɛmprəs] *n* : emperatriz *f*

emptiness ['ɛmptinəs] *n* : vacío *m*, vacuidad *f*

empty[1] ['ɛmpti] *v* **-tied; -tying** *vt* : vaciar — *vi* : desaguar (dícese de un río)

empty[2] *adj* **emptier; -est 1** : vacío **2** VACANT : desocupado, libre **3** MEANINGLESS : vacío, hueco, vano

empty–handed [ˌɛmpti'hændəd] *adj* : con las manos vacías

empty–headed [ˌɛmpti'hɛdəd] *adj* : cabeza hueca, tonto

emu ['iːˌmjuː] *n* : emú *m*

emulate ['ɛmjəˌleɪt] *vt* **-lated; -lating** : emular

emulation [ˌɛmjə'leɪʃən] *n* : emulación *f*

emulsifier [ɪ'mʌlsəˌfaɪər] *n* : emulsionante *m*

emulsify [ɪ'mʌlsəˌfaɪ] *vt* **-fied; -fying** : emulsionar

emulsion [ɪ'mʌlʃən] *n* : emulsión *f*

enable [ɪ'neɪbəl, ɛ-] *vt* **-abled; -abling 1** EMPOWER : habilitar, autorizar, facultar **2** PERMIT : hacer posible, posibilitar, permitir

enact [ɪ'nækt, ɛ-] *vt* **1** : promulgar (un ley o decreto) **2** : representar (un papel en el teatro)

enactment [ɪ'næktmənt, ɛ-] *n* : promulgación *f*

enamel[1] [ɪ'næməl] *vt* **-eled** *or* **-elled; -eling** *or* **-elling** : esmaltar

enamel[2] *n* : esmalte *m*

enamor [ɪ'næmər] *vt* **1** : enamorar **2 to be enamored of** : estar enamorado de (una persona), estar entusiasmado con (algo)

encamp [ɪn'kæmp, ɛn-] *vi* : acampar

encampment [ɪn'kæmpmənt, ɛn-] *n* : campamento *m*

encase [ɪn'keɪs, ɛn-] *vt* **-cased; -casing** : encerrar, revestir

encephalitis [ɪnˌsɛfə'laɪtəs, ɛn-] *n*, *pl* **-litides** ['lɪtəˌdiːz] : encefalitis *f*

enchant [ɪn'tʃænt, ɛn-] *vt* **1** BEWITCH : hechizar, encantar, embrujar **2** CHARM, FASCINATE : cautivar, fascinar, encantar

enchanting [ɪn'tʃæntɪŋ, ɛn-] *adj* : encantador

enchanter [ɪn'tʃæntər, ɛn-] *n* SORCERER : mago *m*, encantador *m*

enchantment [ɪn'tʃæntmənt, ɛn-] *n* **1** SPELL : encanto *m*, hechizo *m* **2** CHARM : encanto *m*

enchantress [ɪn'tʃæntrəs, ɛn-] *n* **1** SORCERESS : maga *f*, hechicera *f* **2** CHARMER : mujer *f* cautivadora

encircle [ɪn'sərkəl, ɛn-] *vt* **-cled; -cling** : rodear, ceñir, cercar

enclose [ɪn'kloːz, ɛn-] *vt* **-closed; -closing 1** SURROUND : encerrar, cercar, rodear **2** INCLUDE : incluir, adjuntar, acompañar ⟨please find enclosed : le enviamos adjunto⟩

enclosure [ɪn'kloːʒər, ɛn-] *n* **1** ENCLOSING : encierro *m* **2** : cercado *m* (de terreno), recinto *m* ⟨an enclosure for the press : un recinto para la prensa⟩ **3** ADJUNCT : anexo *m* (con una carta), documento *m* adjunto

encode [ɪn'koːd, ɛn-] *vt* : cifrar (mensajes, etc.), codificar (en informática)

encompass [ɪn'kʌmpəs, ɛn-, -'kɑm-] *vt* **1** SURROUND : circundar, rodear **2** INCLUDE : abarcar, comprender

encore ['ɑn,kor] *n* : bis *m*, repetición *f*

encounter[1] [ɪn'kaʊntər, ɛn-] *vt* **1** MEET : encontrar, encontrarse con, toparse con, tropezar con **2** FIGHT : combatir, luchar contra

encounter[2] *n* : encuentro *m*

encourage [ɪn'kərɪdʒ, ɛn-] *vt* **-aged; -aging 1** HEARTEN, INSPIRE : animar, alentar **2** FOSTER : fomentar, promover

encouragement [ɪn'kərɪdʒmənt, ɛn-] *n* : ánimo *m*, aliento *m*

encouraging [ɪn'kərədʒɪŋ, ɛn-] *adj* : alentador, esperanzador

encroach [ɪn'kroːtʃ, ɛn-] *vi* **to encroach on** : invadir, abusar (derechos), quitar (tiempo)

encroachment [ɪn'kroːtʃmənt, ɛn-] *n* : invasión *f*, usurpación *f*

encrust [ɪn'krʌst, ɛn-] *vt* **1** : recubrir con una costra **2** INLAY : incrustar ⟨encrusted with gems : incrustado de gemas⟩

encumber [ɪn'kʌmbər, ɛn-] *vt* **1** BLOCK : obstruir, estorbar **2** BURDEN : cargar, gravar

encumbrance [ɪn'kʌmbrənts, ɛn-] *n* : estorbo *m*, carga *f*, gravamen *m*

encyclopedia [ɪn,saɪklə'piːdiə, ɛn-] *n* : enciclopedia *f*

encyclopedic [ɪn,saɪklə'piːdɪk, ɛn-] *adj* : enciclopédico

end[1] ['ɛnd] *vt* **1** STOP : terminar, poner fin a **2** CONCLUDE : concluir, terminar — *vi* : terminar(se), acabar, concluir(se)

end[2] *n* **1** EXTREMITY : extremo *m*, final *m*, punta *f* **2** CONCLUSION : fin *m*, final *m* **3** AIM : fin *m*

endanger [ɪn'deɪndʒər, ɛn-] *vt* : poner en peligro

endear [ɪn'dɪr, ɛn-] *vt* **to endear oneself to** : ganarse la simpatía de, granjearse el cariño de

endearment [ɪn'dɪrmənt, ɛn-] *n* : expresión *f* de cariño

endeavor[1] [ɪn'dɛvər, ɛn-] *vt* : intentar, esforzarse por ⟨he endeavored to improve his work : intentó por mejorar su trabajo⟩

endeavor[2] *n* : intento *m*, esfuerzo *m*

endemic [ɛn'dɛmɪk, ɪn-] *adj* : endémico

ending ['ɛndɪŋ] *n* **1** CONCLUSION : final *m*, desenlace *m* **2** SUFFIX : sufijo *m*, terminación *f*

endive ['ɛn,daɪv, ,ɑn'diːv] *n* : endibia *f*, endivia *f*

endless ['ɛndləs] *adj* **1** INTERMINABLE : interminable, inacabable, sin fin **2** INNUMERABLE : innumerable, incontable

endlessly ['ɛndləsli] *adv* : interminablemente, eternamente, sin parar

endocrine ['ɛndəkrən, -,kraɪn, -,kriːn] *adj* : endocrino

endorse [ɪn'dors, ɛn-] *vt* **-dorsed; -dorsing 1** SIGN : endosar, firmar **2** APPROVE : aprobar, sancionar

endorsement [ɪn'dorsmənt, ɛn-] *n* **1** SIGNATURE : endoso *m*, firma *f* **2** APPROVAL : aprobación *f*, aval *m*

endow [ɪn'daʊ, ɛn-] *vt* : dotar

endowment [ɪn'daʊmənt, ɛn-] *n* **1** FUNDING : dotación *f* **2** DONATION : donación *f*, legado *m* **3** ATTRIBUTE, GIFT : atributo *m*, dotes *fpl*

endurable [ɪn'dʊrəbəl, ɛn-, -'djʊr-] *adj* : tolerable, soportable

endurance [ɪn'dʊrənts, ɛn-, -'djʊr-] *n* : resistencia *f*, aguante *m*

endure [ɪn'dʊr, ɛn-, -'djʊr] *v* **-dured; -during** *vt* **1** BEAR : resistir, soportar, aguantar **2** TOLERATE : tolerar, soportar — *vi* LAST : durar, perdurar

enema ['ɛnəmə] *n* : enema *m*, lavativa *f*

enemy ['ɛnəmi] *n, pl* **-mies** : enemigo *m*, -ga *f*

energetic [,ɛnər'dʒɛtɪk] *adj* : enérgico, vigoroso — **energetically** [-tɪkli] *adv*

energize ['ɛnər,dʒaɪz] *vt* **-gized; -gizing 1** ACTIVATE : activar **2** INVIGORATE : vigorizar

energy ['ɛnərdʒi] *n, pl* **-gies 1** VITALITY : energía *f*, vitalidad *f* **2** EFFORT : esfuerzo *m*, energías *fpl* **3** POWER : energía *f* ⟨atomic energy : energía atómica⟩

enervate ['ɛnər,veɪt] *vt* **-vated; -vating** : enervar, debilitar

enfold [ɪn'foːld, ɛn-] *vt* : envolver

enforce [ɪn'fors, ɛn-] *vt* **-forced; -forcing 1** : hacer respetar, hacer cumplir (una ley, etc.) **2** IMPOSE : imponer ⟨to enforce obedience : imponer la obediencia⟩

enforcement [ɪn'forsmənt, ɛn-] *n* : imposición *f*

enfranchise [ɪn'fræn,tʃaɪz, ɛn-] *vt* **-chised; -chising** : conceder el voto a

enfranchisement [ɪn'fræn,tʃaɪzmənt, ɛn-] *n* : concesión *f* del voto

engage [ɪn'geɪdʒ, ɛn-] *v* **-gaged; -gaging** *vt* **1** ATTRACT : captar, atraer, llamar ⟨to engage one's attention : captar la atención⟩ **2** MESH : engranar ⟨to engage the clutch : embragar⟩ **3** COMMIT : comprometer ⟨to get engaged : comprometerse⟩ **4** HIRE : contratar **5** : entablar combate con (un enemigo)

— *vi* **1** PARTICIPATE : participar **2 to engage in combat** : entrar en combate

engagement [ɪn'geɪʤmənt, ɛn-] *n* **1** APPOINTMENT : cita *f*, hora *f* **2** BETROTHAL : compromiso *m*

engaging [ɪn'geɪʤɪŋ, ɛn-] *adj* : atractivo, encantador, interesante

engender [ɪn'ʤɛndər, ɛn-] *vt* **-dered; -dering** : engendrar

engine ['ɛnʤən] *n* **1** MOTOR : motor *m* **2** LOCOMOTIVE : locomotora *f*, máquina *f*

engineer[1] [ˌɛnʤə'nɪr] *vt* **1** : diseñar, construir (un sistema, un mecanismo, etc.) **2** CONTRIVE : maquinar, tramar, fraguar

engineer[2] *n* **1** : ingeniero *m*, -ra *f* **2** : maquinista *mf* (de locomotoras)

engineering [ˌɛnʤə'nɪrɪŋ] *n* : ingeniería *f*

English[1] ['ɪŋglɪʃ, 'ɪŋlɪʃ] *adj* : inglés

English[2] *n* **1** : inglés *m* (idioma) **2 the English** : los ingleses

Englishman ['ɪŋglɪʃmən, 'ɪŋlɪʃ-] *n, pl* **-men** [-mən, -ˌmɛn] : inglés *m*

Englishwoman ['ɪŋglɪʃˌwumən, 'ɪŋlɪʃ-] *n, pl* **-women** [-ˌwɪmən] : inglesa *f*

engrave [ɪn'greɪv, ɛn-] *vt* **-graved; -graving** : grabar

engraver [ɪn'greɪvər, ɛn-] *n* : grabador *m*, -dora *f*

engraving [ɪn'greɪvɪŋ, ɛn-] *n* : grabado *m*

engross [ɪn'gro:s, ɛn-] *vt* : absorber

engrossed [ɪn'gro:st, ɛn-] *adj* : absorto

engrossing [ɪn'gro:sɪŋ, ɛn-] *adj* : fascinante, absorbente

engulf [ɪn'gʌlf, ɛn-] *vt* : envolver, sepultar

enhance [ɪn'hænts, ɛn-] *vt* **-hanced; -hancing** : realzar, aumentar, mejorar

enhancement [ɪn'hæntsmənt, ɛn-] *n* : mejora *f*, realce *m*, aumento *m*

enigma [ɪ'nɪgmə] *n* : enigma *m*

enigmatic [ˌɛnɪg'mætɪk, ˌiːnɪg-] *adj* : enigmático — **enigmatically** [-tɪkli] *adv*

enjoin [ɪn'ʤɔɪn, ɛn-] *vt* **1** COMMAND : ordenar, imponer **2** FORBID : prohibir, vedar

enjoy [ɪn'ʤɔɪ, ɛn-] *vt* **1** : disfrutar, gozar de ⟨did you enjoy the book? : ¿te gustó el libro?⟩ ⟨to enjoy good health : gozar de buena salud⟩ **2 to enjoy oneself** : divertirse, pasarlo bien

enjoyable [ɪn'ʤɔɪəbəl, ɛn-] *adj* : agradable, placentero, divertido

enjoyment [ɪn'ʤɔɪmənt, ɛn-] *n* : placer *m*, goce *m*, disfrute *m*, deleite *m*

enlarge [ɪn'lɑrʤ, ɛn-] *v* **-larged; -larging** *vt* : extender, agrandar, ampliar — *vi* **1** : ampliarse **2 to enlarge upon** : extenderse sobre, entrar en detalles sobre

enlargement [ɪn'lɑrʤmənt, ɛn-] *n* : expansión *f*, ampliación *f* (dícese de fotografías)

enlarger [ɪn'lɑrʤər, ɛn-] *n* : ampliadora *f*

enlighten [ɪn'laɪtən, ɛn-] *vt* : iluminar, aclarar

enlightenment [ɪn'laɪtənmənt, ɛn-] *n* **1** : ilustración *f* ⟨the Enlightenment : la Ilustración⟩ **2** CLARIFICATION : aclaración *f*

enlist [ɪn'lɪst, ɛn-] *vt* **1** ENROLL : alistar, reclutar **2** SECURE : conseguir ⟨to enlist the support of : conseguir el apoyo de⟩ — *vi* : alistarse

enlisted man [ɪn'lɪstəd, ɛn-] *n* : soldado *m* raso

enlistment [ɪn'lɪstmənt, ɛn-] *n* : alistamiento *m*, reclutamiento *m*

enliven [ɪn'laɪvən, ɛn-] *vt* : animar, alegrar, darle vida a

enmity ['ɛnməti] *n, pl* **-ties** : enemistad *f*, animadversión *f*

ennoble [ɪ'no:bəl, ɛ-] *vt* **-bled; -bling** : ennoblecer

ennui [ˌɑn'wiː] *n* : hastío *m*, tedio *m*, fastidio *m*, aburrimiento *m*

enormity [ɪ'nɔrməti] *n, pl* **-ties** **1** ATROCITY : atrocidad *f*, barbaridad *f* **2** IMMENSITY : enormidad *f*, inmensidad *f*

enormous [ɪ'nɔrməs] *adj* : enorme, inmenso, tremendo — **enormously** *adv*

enough[1] [ɪ'nʌf] *adv* **1** : bastante, suficientemente **2 fair enough!** : ¡está bien!, ¡de acuerdo! **3 strangely enough** : por extraño que parezca **4 sure enough** : en efecto, sin duda alguna **5 well enough** : muy bien, bastante bien

enough[2] *adj* : bastante, suficiente ⟨do we have enough chairs? : ¿tenemos suficientes sillas?⟩

enough[3] *pron* : (lo) suficiente, (lo) bastante ⟨enough to eat : lo suficiente para comer⟩ ⟨it's not enough : no basta⟩ ⟨I've had enough! : ¡estoy harto!, ¡está bueno ya!⟩

enquire [ɪn'kwaɪr, ɛn-] **enquiry** ['ɪnˌkwaɪri, 'ɛn-, -kwəri; ɪn'kwaɪri, ɛn'-] → **inquire, inquiry**

enrage [ɪn'reɪʤ, ɛn-] *vt* **-raged; -raging** : enfurecer, encolerizar

enraged [ɪn'reɪʤd, ɛn-] *adj* : enfurecido, furioso

enrich [ɪn'rɪʧ, ɛn-] *vt* : enriquecer

enrichment [ɪn'rɪʧmənt, ɛn-] *n* : enriquecimiento *m*

enroll *or* **enrol** [ɪn'ro:l, ɛn-] *v* **-rolled; -rolling** *vt* : matricular, inscribir — *vi* : matricularse, inscribirse

enrollment [ɪn'ro:lmənt, ɛn-] *n* : matrícula *f*, inscripción *f*

en route [ɑ'ruːt, ɛn'raut] *adv* : de camino, por el camino

ensconce [ɪn'skɑnts, ɛn-] *vt* **-sconced; -sconcing** : acomodar, instalar, establecer cómodamente

ensemble [ɑn'sɑmbəl] *n* : conjunto *m*

enshrine [ɪn'ʃraɪn, ɛn-] *vt* **-shrined; -shrining** : conservar religiosamente, preservar

ensign ['ɛntsən, 'ɛnˌsaɪn] *n* **1** FLAG : enseña *f*, pabellón *m* **2** : alférez *mf* (de fragata)

enslave [ɪn'sleɪv, ɛn-] *vt* **-slaved; -slaving** : esclavizar

enslavement [ɪn'sleɪvmənt, ɛn-] *n* : esclavización *f*

ensnare [ɪn'snær, ɛn-] *vt* **-snared; -snaring** : atrapar

ensue [ɪn'su:, ɛn-] *vi* **-sued; -suing** : seguir, resultar

ensure [ɪn'ʃʊr, ɛn-] *vt* **-sured; -suring** : asegurar, garantizar

entail [ɪn'teɪl, ɛn-] *vt* : implicar, suponer, conllevar

entangle [ɪn'tæŋgəl, ɛn-] *vt* **-gled; -gling** : enredar

entanglement [ɪn'tæŋgəlmənt, ɛn-] *n* : enredo *m*

enter ['ɛntər] *vt* **1** : entrar en, entrar a **2** BEGIN : entrar en, comenzar, iniciar **3** RECORD : anotar, inscribir, dar entrada a ⟨to enter data : introducir datos⟩ **4** JOIN : entrar en, alistarse en, hacerse socio de — *vi* **1** : entrar **2 to enter into** : entrar en, firmar (un acuerdo), entablar (negociaciones, etc.)

enterprise ['ɛntər,praɪz] *n* **1** UNDERTAKING : empresa *f* **2** BUSINESS : empresa *f*, firma *f* **3** INITIATIVE : iniciativa *f*, empuje *m*

enterprising ['ɛntər,praɪzɪŋ] *adj* : emprendedor

entertain [,ɛntər'teɪn] *vt* **1** : recibir, agasajar ⟨to entertain guests : tener invitados⟩ **2** CONSIDER : considerar, contemplar **3** AMUSE : entretener, divertir

entertainer [,ɛntər'teɪnər] *n* : artista *mf*

entertaining [,ɛntər'teɪnɪŋ] *adj* : entretenido, divertido

entertainment [,ɛntər'teɪnmənt] *n* : entretenimiento *m*, diversión *f*

enthrall *or* **enthral** [ɪn'θrɔl, ɛn-] *vt* **-thralled; -thralling** : cautivar, embelesar

enthuse [ɪn'θuiz, ɛn-] *v* **-thused; -thusing** *vt* **1** EXCITE : entusiasmar **2** : decir con entusiasmo — *vi* **to enthuse over** : hablar con entusiasmo sobre

enthusiasm [ɪn'θu:zi,æzəm, ɛn-, -'θju:-] *n* : entusiasmo *m*

enthusiast [ɪn'θu:zi,æst, ɛn-, -'θju:-, -əst] *n* : entusiasta *mf*; aficionado *m*, -da *f*

enthusiastic [ɪn,θu:zi'æstɪk, ɛn-, -,θju:-] *adj* : entusiasta, aficionado

enthusiastically [ɪn,θu:zi'æstɪkli, ɛn-, -,θju:-] *adv* : con entusiasmo

entice [ɪn'taɪs, ɛn-] *vt* **-ticed; -ticing** : atraer, tentar

enticement [ɪn'taɪsmənt, ɛn-] *n* : tentación *f*, atracción *f*, señuelo *m*

entire [ɪn'taɪr, ɛn-] *adj* : entero, completo

entirely [ɪn'taɪrli, ɛn-] *adv* : completamente, totalmente

entirety [ɪn'taɪrti, ɛn-, -'taɪrəti] *n, pl* **-ties** : totalidad *f*

entitle [ɪn'taɪtəl, ɛn-] *vt* **-tled; -tling 1** NAME : titular, intitular **2** : dar derecho a ⟨it entitles you to enter free : le da derecho a entrar gratis⟩ **3 to be entitled to** : tener derecho a

entitlement [ɪn'taɪtəlmənt, ɛn-] *n* RIGHT : derecho *m*

entity ['ɛntəti] *n, pl* **-ties** : entidad *f*, ente *m*

entomologist [,ɛntə'malədʒɪst] *n* : entomólogo *m*, -ga *f*

entomology [,ɛntə'malədʒi] *n* : entomología *f*

entourage [,antu'raʒ] *n* : séquito *m*

entrails ['ɛn,treɪlz, -trəlz] *npl* : entrañas *fpl*, vísceras *fpl*

entrance¹ [ɪn'trænts, ɛn-] *vt* **-tranced; -trancing** : encantar, embelesar, fascinar

entrance² ['ɛntrənts] *n* **1** ENTERING : entrada *f* ⟨to make an entrance : entrar en escena⟩ **2** ENTRY : entrada *f*, puerta *f* **3** ADMISSION : entrada *f*, ingreso *m* ⟨entrance examination : examen de ingreso⟩

entrant ['ɛntrənt] *n* : candidato *m*, -ta *f* (en un examen); participante *mf* (en un concurso)

entrap [ɪn'træp, ɛn-] *vt* **-trapped; -trapping** : atrapar, entrampar, hacer caer en una trampa

entrapment [ɪn'træpmənt, ɛn-] *n* : captura *f*

entreat [ɪn'tri:t, ɛn-] *vt* : suplicar, rogar

entreaty [ɪn'tri:ti, ɛn-] *n, pl* **-treaties** : ruego *m*, súplica *f*

entrée *or* **entree** ['an,treɪ, ,an'-] *n* : plato *m* principal

entrench [ɪn'trɛntʃ, ɛn-] *vt* **1** FORTIFY : atrincherar (una posición militar) **2** : consolidar, afianzar ⟨firmly entrenched in his job : afianzado en su puesto⟩

entrepreneur [,antrəprə'nər, -'njʊr] *n* : empresario *m*, -ria *f*

entrust [ɪn'trʌst, ɛn-] *vt* : confiar, encomendar

entry ['ɛntri] *n, pl* **-tries 1** ENTRANCE : entrada *f* **2** NOTATION : entrada *f*, anotación *f*

entwine [ɪn'twaɪn, ɛn-] *vt* **-twined; -twining** : entrelazar, entretejer, entrecruzar

enumerate [ɪ'nu:mə,reɪt, ɛ-, -'nju:-] *vt* **-ated; -ating 1** LIST : enumerar **2** COUNT : contar, enumerar

enumeration [ɪ,nu:mə'reɪʃən, ɛ-, -,nju:-] *n* : enumeración *f*, lista *f*

enunciate [i'nʌntsi,eɪt, ɛ-] *vt* **-ated; -ating 1** STATE : enunciar, decir **2** PRONOUNCE : articular, pronunciar

enunciation [i,nʌntsi'eɪʃən, ɛ-] *n* **1** STATEMENT : enunciación *f*, declaración *f* **2** ARTICULATION : articulación *f*, pronunciación *f*, dicción *f*

envelop [ɪn'vləp, ɛn-] *vt* : envolver, cubrir

envelope ['ɛnvə,lo:p, 'an-] *n* : sobre *m*

enviable ['ɛnviəbəl] *adj* : envidiable

envious ['ɛnviəs] *adj* : envidioso — **enviously** *adv*

environment [ɪn'vaɪrənmənt, ɛn-, -'vaɪərn-] *n* : medio *m* (ambiente), ambiente *m*, entorno *m*

environmental [ɪn,vaɪrən'mɛntəl, ɛn-, -,vaɪərn-] *adj* : ambiental

environmentalist [ɪn,vaɪrən'mɛntəlɪst, ɛn-, -,vaɪərn-] *n* : ecologista *mf*

environs [ɪn'vaɪrənz, ɛn-, -'vaɪərnz] *npl* : alrededores *mpl*, entorno *m*, inmediaciones *fpl*

envisage [ɪn'vɪzɪʤ, ɛn-] *vt* **-aged; -aging 1** IMAGINE : imaginarse, concebir **2** FORESEE : prever

envision [ɪn'vɪʒən, ɛn-] *vt* : imaginar

envoy ['ɛn,vɔɪ, 'ɑn-] *n* : enviado *m*, -da *f*

envy[1] ['ɛnvi] *vt* **-vied; -vying** : envidiar

envy[2] *n, pl* **envies** : envidia *f*

enzyme ['ɛn,zaɪm] *n* : enzima *f*

eon ['i:ən, i:,ɑn] → **aeon**

epaulet [,pə'lɛt] *n* : charretera *f*

ephemeral [ɪ'fɛmərəl, -'fi:-] *adj* : efímero, fugaz

epic[1] ['ɛpɪk] *adj* : épico

epic[2] *n* : poema *m* épico, epopeya *f*

epicure ['ɛpɪ,kjʊr] *n* : epicúreo *m*, -rea *f*; gastrónomo *m*, -ma *f*

epicurean [,ɛpɪkjʊ'ri:ən, -'kjʊriən] *adj* : epicúreo

epidemic[1] [,ɛpə'dɛmɪk] *adj* : epidémico

epidemic[2] *n* : epidemia *f*

epidermis [,ɛpə'dərməs] *n* : epidermis *f*

epigram ['ɛpə,græm] *n* : epigrama *m*

epilepsy ['ɛpə,lɛpsi] *n, pl* **-sies** : epilepsia *f*

epileptic[1] [,ɛpə'lɛptɪk] *adj* : epiléptico

epileptic[2] *n* : epiléptico *m*, -ca *f*

epilogue ['ɛpə,lɔg, -,lɑg] *n* : epílogo *m*

epiphany [ɪ'pɪfəni] *n, pl* **-nies 1 Epiphany** : Epifanía *f* **2 to have an epiphany** : tener una revelación

episcopal [ɪ'pɪskəpəl] *adj* : episcopal

Episcopalian [ɪ,pɪskə'peɪljən] *n* : episcopalista *mf*; episcopaliano *m*, -na *f*

episode ['ɛpə,so:d] *n* : episodio *m*

episodic [,ɛpə'sɑdɪk] *adj* : episódico

epistle [ɪ'pɪsəl] *n* : epístola *f*, carta *f*

epitaph ['ɛpə,tæf] *n* : epitafio *m*

epithet ['ɛpə,θɛt, -θət] *n* : epíteto *m*

epitome [ɪ'pɪtəmi] *n* **1** SUMMARY : epítome *m*, resumen *m* **2** EMBODIMENT : personificación *f*

epitomize [ɪ'pɪtə,maɪz] *vt* **-mized; -mizing 1** SUMMARIZE : resumir **2** EMBODY : ser la personificación de, personificar

epoch ['ɛpək, 'ɛ,pɑk, 'i:,pɑk] *n* : época *f*, era *f*

epoxy [ɪ'pɑksi] *n, pl* **epoxies** : resina *f* epoxídica

equable ['ɛkwəbəl, 'i:-] *adj* **1** CALM, STEADY : ecuánime **2** UNIFORM : estable (dícese de la temperatura), constante (dícese del clima), uniforme

equably ['ɛkwəbli, 'i:-] *adv* : con ecuanimidad

equal[1] ['i:kwəl] *vt* **equaled** *or* **equalled; equaling** *or* **equalling 1** : ser igual a

⟨two plus three equals five : dos más tres es igual a cinco⟩ **2** MATCH : igualar

equal[2] *adj* **1** SAME : igual **2** ADEQUATE : adecuado, capaz

equal[3] *n* : igual *mf*

equality [ɪ'kwɑləti] *n, pl* **-ties** : igualdad *f*

equalize ['i:kwə,laɪz] *vt* **-ized; -izing** : igualar, equiparar

equally ['i:kwəli] *adv* : igualmente, por igual

equanimity [,i:kwə'nɪməti, ,ɛ-] *n, pl* **-ties** : ecuanimidad *f*

equate [ɪ'kweɪt] *vt* **equated; equating** : equiparar, identificar

equation [ɪ'kweɪʒən] *n* : ecuación *f*

equator [ɪ'kweɪtər] *n* : ecuador *m*

equatorial [,i:kwə'toriəl, ,ɛ-] *adj* : ecuatorial

equestrian[1] [ɪ'kwɛstriən, ɛ-] *adj* : ecuestre

equestrian[2] *n* : jinete *mf*, caballista *mf*

equilateral [,i:kwə'lætərəl, ,ɛ-] *adj* : equilátero

equilibrium [,i:kwə'lɪbriəm, ,ɛ-] *n, pl* **-riums** *or* **-ria** [-briə] : equilibrio *m*

equine ['i:,kwaɪn, 'ɛ-] *adj* : equino, hípico

equinox ['i:kwə,nɑks, 'ɛ-] *n* : equinoccio *m*

equip [ɪ'kwɪp] *vt* **equipped; equipping 1** FURNISH : equipar **2** PREPARE : preparar

equipment [ɪ'kwɪpmənt] *n* : equipo *m*

equitable ['ɛkwətəbəl] *adj* : equitativo, justo, imparcial

equity ['ɛkwəti] *n, pl* **-ties 1** FAIRNESS : equidad *f*, imparcialidad *f* **2** VALUE : valor *m* líquido

equivalence [ɪ'kwɪvələn*t*s] *n* : equivalencia *f*

equivalent[1] [ɪ'kwɪvələnt] *adj* : equivalente

equivalent[2] *n* : equivalente *m*

equivocal [ɪ'kwɪvəkəl] *adj* **1** AMBIGUOUS : equívoco, ambiguo **2** QUESTIONABLE : incierto, dudoso, sospechoso

equivocate [ɪ'kwɪvə,keɪt] *vi* **-cated; -cating** : usar lenguaje equívoco, andarse con evasivas

equivocation [ɪ,kwɪvə'keɪʃən] *n* : evasiva *f*, subterfugio *m*

era ['ɪrə, 'ɛrə, 'i:rə] *n* : era *f*, época *f*

eradicate [ɪ'rædə,keɪt] *vt* **-cated; -cating** : erradicar

erase [ɪ'reɪs] *vt* **erased; erasing** : borrar

eraser [ɪ'reɪsər] *n* : goma *f* de borrar, borrador *m*

erasure [ɪ'reɪʃər] *n* : tachadura *f*

ere[1] ['ɛr] *conj* : antes de que

ere[2] *prep* **1** : antes de **2 ere long** : dentro de poco

erect[1] [ɪ'rɛkt] *vt* **1** CONSTRUCT : erigir, construir **2** RAISE : levantar **3** ESTABLISH : establecer

erect[2] *adj* : erguido, derecho, erecto

erection [ɪˈrɛkʃən] *n* **1** : erección *f* (en fisiología) **2** BUILDING : construcción *f*

ergonomics [ˌərgəˈnɑmɪks] *npl* : ergonomía *f*

ermine [ˈərmən] *n* : armiño *m*

erode [ɪˈroːd] *vt* **eroded; eroding** : erosionar (el suelo), corroer (metales)

erosion [ɪˈroːʒən] *n* : erosión *f*, corrosión *f*

erotic [ɪˈrɑtɪk] *adj* : erótico — **erotically** [-tɪkli] *adv*

eroticism [ɪˈrɑtəˌsɪzəm] *n* : erotismo *m*

err [ˈɛr, ˈər] *vi* : cometer un error, equivocarse, errar

errand [ˈɛrənd] *n* : mandado *m*, encargo *m*, recado *m Spain* ⟨an errand of mercy : una misión de caridad⟩

errant [ˈɛrənt] *adj* **1** WANDERING : errante **2** ASTRAY : descarriado

erratic [ɪˈrætɪk] *adj* **1** INCONSISTENT : errático, irregular, inconsistente **2** ECCENTRIC : excéntrico, raro

erratically [ɪˈrætɪkli] *adv* : erráticamente, de manera irregular

erroneous [ɪˈroːniəs, ɛ-] *adj* : erróneo — **erroneously** *adv*

error [ˈɛrər] *n* : error *m*, equivocación *f* ⟨to be in error : estar equivocado⟩

ersatz [ˈɛrˌsɑts, ˈərˌsæts] *adj* : artificial, sustituto

erstwhile [ˈərstˌʍaɪl] *adj* : antiguo

erudite [ˈɛrəˌdaɪt, ˈɛrju-] *adj* : erudito, letrado

erudition [ˌɛrəˈdɪʃən, ˌɛrju-] *n* : erudición *f*

erupt [ɪˈrʌpt] *vi* **1** : hacer erupción (dícese de un volcán o un sarpullido) **2** : estallar (dícese de la cólera o la violencia)

eruption [ɪˈrʌpʃən] *n* : erupción *f*, estallido *m*

eruptive [ɪˈrʌptɪv] *adj* : eruptivo

escalate [ˈɛskəˌleɪt] *v* **-lated; -lating** *vt* : intensificar (un conflicto), aumentar (precios) — *vi* : intensificarse, aumentarse

escalation [ˌɛskəˈleɪʃən] *n* : intensificación *f*, escalada *f*, aumento *m*, subida *f*

escalator [ˈɛskəˌleɪtər] *n* : escalera *f* mecánica

escapade [ˈɛskəˌpeɪd] *n* : aventura *f*

escape¹ [ɪˈskeɪp, ɛ-] *v* **-caped; -caping** *vt* : escaparse de, librarse de, evitar — *vi* : escaparse, fugarse, huir

escape² *n* **1** FLIGHT : fuga *f*, huida *f*, escapada *f* **2** LEAKAGE : escape *m*, fuga *f* **3** : escapatoria *f*, evasión *f* ⟨to have no escape : no tener escapatoria⟩ ⟨escape from reality : evasión de la realidad⟩

escapee [ɪˌskeɪˈpiː, ˌɛ-] *n* : fugitivo *m*, -va *f*

escarole [ˈɛskəˌroːl] *n* : escarola *f*

escarpment [ɪsˈkɑrpmənt, ɛs-] *n* : escarpa *f*, escarpadura *f*

eschew [ɛˈʃuː, ɪsˈtʃuː] *vt* : evitar, rehuir, abstenerse de

escort¹ [ɪˈskɔrt, ɛ-] *vt* **1** : escoltar ⟨to escort a ship : escoltar un barco⟩ **2** ACCOMPANY : acompañar

escort² [ˈɛsˌkɔrt] *n* **1** : escolta *f* ⟨armed escort : escolta armada⟩ **2** COMPANION : acompañante *mf*; compañero *m*, -ra *f*

escrow [ˈɛsˌkroː] *n* **in escrow** : en depósito, en custodia de un tercero

Eskimo [ˈɛskəˌmoː] *n* **1** : esquimal *mf* **2** : esquimal *m* (idioma) — **Eskimo** *adj*

esophagus [ɪˈsɑfəgəs, iː-] *n*, *pl* **-gi** [-ˌgaɪ, -ˌdʒaɪ] : esófago *m*

esoteric [ˌɛsəˈtɛrɪk] *adj* : esotérico, hermético

especially [ɪˈspeʃəli] *adv* : especialmente, particularmente

espionage [ˈɛspiəˌnɑʒ, -ˌnɑdʒ] *n* : espionaje *m*

espouse [ɪˈspaʊz, ɛ-] *vt* **espoused; espousing 1** MARRY : casarse con **2** ADOPT, ADVOCATE : apoyar, adherirse a, adoptar

espresso [ɛˈsprɛˌsoː] *n*, *pl* **-sos** : café *m* exprés

essay¹ [ˈɛseɪ, ˈɛˌseɪ] *vt* : intentar, tratar

essay² [ˈɛˌseɪ] *n* **1** COMPOSITION : ensayo *m*, trabajo *m* **2** ATTEMPT : intento *m*

essayist [ˈɛˌseɪɪst] *n* : ensayista *mf*

essence [ˈɛsənts] *n* **1** CORE : esencia *f*, núcleo *m*, meollo *m* ⟨in essence : esencialmente⟩ **2** EXTRACT : esencia *f*, extracto *m* **3** PERFUME : esencia *f*, perfume *m*

essential¹ [ɪˈsɛnʃəl] *adj* : esencial, imprescindible, fundamental — **essentially** *adv*

essential² *n* : elemento *m* esencial, lo imprescindible

establish [ɪˈstæblɪʃ, ɛ-] *vt* **1** FOUND : establecer, fundar **2** SET UP : establecer, instaurar, instituir **3** PROVE : demostrar, probar

establishment [ɪˈstæblɪʃmənt, ɛ-] *n* **1** ESTABLISHING : establecimiento *m*, fundación *f*, instauración *f* **2** BUSINESS : negocio *m*, establecimiento *m* **3 the Establishment** : la clase dirigente

estate [ɪˈsteɪt, ɛ-] *n* **1** POSSESSIONS : bienes *mpl*, propiedad *f*, patrimonio *m* **2** PROPERTY : hacienda *f*, finca *f*, propiedad *f*

esteem¹ [ɪˈstiːm, ɛ-] *vt* : estimar, apreciar

esteem² *n* : estima *f*, aprecio *m*

ester [ˈɛstər] *n* : éster *m*

esthetic [ɛsˈθɛtɪk] → **aesthetic**

estimable [ˈɛstəməbəl] *adj* : estimable

estimate¹ [ˈɛstəˌmeɪt] *vt* **-mated; -mating** : calcular, estimar

estimate² [ˈɛstəmət] *n* **1** : cálculo *m* aproximado ⟨to make an estimate : hacer un cálculo⟩ **2** ASSESSMENT : valoración *f*, estimación *f*

estimation [ˌɛstəˈmeɪʃən] *n* **1** JUDGMENT : juicio *m*, opinión *f* ⟨in my estimation : en mi opinión, según mis cálculos⟩ **2** ESTEEM : estima *f*, aprecio *m*

estimator [ˈɛstəˌmeɪtər] *n* : tasador *m*, -dora *f*
Estonian [ɛˈstoːniən] *n* : estonio *m*, -nia *f* — **Estonian** *adj*
estrange [ɪˈstreɪndʒ, ɛ-] *vt* **-tranged; -tranging** : enajenar, apartar, alejar
estrangement [ɪˈstreɪndʒmənt, ɛ-] *n* : alejamiento *m*, distanciamiento *m*
estrogen [ˈɛstrədʒən] *n* : estrógeno *m*
estrus [ˈɛstrəs] *n* : celo *m*
estuary [ˈɛstʃuˌwɛri] *n, pl* **-aries** : estuario *m*, -ría *f*
et cetera [ɛtˈsɛtərə, -ˈsɛtrə] : etcétera
etch [ˈɛtʃ] *v* : grabar al aguafuerte
etching [ˈɛtʃɪŋ] *n* : aguafuerte *m*, grabado *m* al aguafuerte
eternal [ɪˈtərnəl, iː-] *adj* **1** EVERLASTING : eterno **2** INTERMINABLE : constante, incesante
eternally [ɪˈtərnəli, iː-] *adv* : eternamente, para siempre
eternity [ɪˈtərnəti, iː-] *n, pl* **-ties** : eternidad *f*
ethane [ˈɛˌθeɪn] *n* : etano *m*
ethanol [ˈɛθəˌnɔl, -ˌnoːl] *n* : etanol *m*
ether [ˈiːθər] *n* : éter *m*
ethereal [ɪˈθɪriəl, iː-] *adj* **1** CELESTIAL : etéreo, celeste **2** DELICATE : delicado
ethical [ˈɛθɪkəl] *adj* : ético — **ethically** *adv*
ethics [ˈɛθɪks] *ns & pl* **1** : ética *f* **2** MORALITY : ética *f*, moral *f*, moralidad *f*
Ethiopian [ˌiːθiˈoːpiən] *n* : etíope *mf* — **Ethiopian** *adj*
ethnic [ˈɛθnɪk] *adj* : étnico
ethnologist [ɛθˈnalədʒɪst] *n* : etnólogo *m*, -ga *f*
ethnology [ɛθˈnalədʒi] *n* : etnología *f*
etiquette [ˈɛtɪkət, -ˌkɛt] *n* : etiqueta *f*, protocolo *m*
etymological [ˌɛtəməˈladʒɪkəl] *adj* : etimológico
etymology [ˌɛtəˈmalədʒi] *n, pl* **-gies** : etimología *f*
eucalyptus [ˌjuːkəˈlɪptəs] *n, pl* **-ti** [-ˌtaɪ] *or* **-tuses** [-təsəz] : eucalipto *m*
Eucharist [ˈjuːkərɪst] *n* : Eucaristía *f*
eulogize [ˈjuːləˌdʒaɪz] *vt* **-gized; -gizing** : elogiar, encomiar
eulogy [ˈjuːlədʒi] *n, pl* **-gies** : elogio *m*, encomio *m*, panegírico *m*
eunuch [ˈjuːnək] *n* : eunuco *m*
euphemism [ˈjuːfəˌmɪzəm] *n* : eufemismo *m*
euphemistic [ˌjuːfəˈmɪstɪk] *adj* : eufemístico
euphony [ˈjuːfəni] *n, pl* **-nies** : eufonía *f*
euphoria [juˈforiə] *n* : euforia *f*
euphoric [juˈforɪk] *adj* : eufórico
European [ˌjurəˈpiːən] *n* : europeo *m*, europea *f* — **European** *adj*
euthanasia [ˌjuːθəˈneɪʒə, -ʒiə] *n* : eutanasia *f*
evacuate [ɪˈvækjuˌeɪt] *v* **-ated; -ating** *vt* VACATE : evacuar, desalojar — *vi* WITHDRAW : retirarse

evacuation [ɪˌvækjuˈeɪʃən] *n* : evacuación *f*, desalojo *m*
evade [ɪˈveɪd] *vt* **evaded; evading** : evadir, eludir, esquivar
evaluate [ɪˈvæljuˌeɪt] *vt* **-ated; -ating** : evaluar, valorar, tasar
evaluation [ɪˌvæljuˈeɪʃən] *n* : evaluación *f*, valoración *f*, tasación *f*
evangelical [ˌiːˌvænˈdʒɛlɪkəl, ˌɛvən-] *adj* : evangélico
evangelist [ɪˈvændʒəlɪst] *n* **1** : evangelista *m* **2** PREACHER : predicador *m*, -dora *f*
evaporate [ɪˈvæpəˌreɪt] *vi* **-rated; -rating** **1** VAPORIZE : evaporarse **2** VANISH : evaporarse, desvanecerse, esfumarse
evaporation [ɪˌvæpəˈreɪʃən] *n* : evaporación *f*
evasion [ɪˈveɪʒən] *n* : evasión *f*
evasive [ɪˈveɪsɪv] *adj* : evasivo
evasiveness [ɪˈveɪsɪvnəs] *n* : carácter *m* evasivo
eve [ˈiːv] *n* **1** : víspera *f* ⟨on the eve of the festivities : en vísperas de las festividades⟩ **2** → **evening**
even[1] [ˈiːvən] *vt* **1** LEVEL : allanar, nivelar, emparejar **2** EQUALIZE : igualar, equilibrar — *vi* **to even out** : nivelarse, emparejarse
even[2] *adv* **1** : hasta, incluso ⟨even a child can do it : hasta un niño puede hacerlo⟩ ⟨he looked content, even happy : se le veía satisfecho, incluso feliz⟩ **2** (*in negative constructions*) : ni siquiera ⟨he didn't even try : ni siquiera lo intentó⟩ **3** (*in comparisons*) : aún, todavía ⟨even better : aún mejor, todavía mejor⟩ **4 even if** : aunque **5 even so** : aun así **6 even though** : aun cuando, a pesar de que
even[3] *adj* **1** SMOOTH : uniforme, liso, parejo **2** FLAT : plano, llano **3** EQUAL : igual, igualado ⟨an even score : un marcador igualado⟩ **4** REGULAR : regular, constante ⟨an even pace : un ritmo constante⟩ **5** EXACT : exacto, justo **6** : par ⟨even number : número par⟩ **7 to be even** : estar en paz, estar a mano **8 to get even** : desquitarse, vengarse
evening [ˈiːvnɪŋ] *n* : tarde *f*, noche *f* ⟨in the evening : por la noche⟩
evenly [ˈiːvənli] *adv* **1** UNIFORMLY : de modo uniforme, de manera constante **2** FAIRLY : igualmente, equitativamente
evenness [ˈiːvənnəs] *n* : uniformidad *f*, igualdad *f*, regularidad *f*
event [ɪˈvɛnt] *n* **1** : acontecimiento *m*, suceso *m*, prueba *f* (en deportes) **2 in the event that** : en caso de que
eventful [ɪˈvɛntfəl] *adj* : lleno de incidentes, memorable
eventual [ɪˈvɛntʃuəl] *adj* : final, consiguiente
eventuality [ɪˌvɛntʃuˈæləti] *n, pl* **-ties** : eventualidad *f*
eventually [ɪˈvɛntʃuəli] *adv* : al fin, con el tiempo, algún día

ever ['ɛvər] *adv* **1** ALWAYS : siempre ⟨as ever : como siempre⟩ ⟨ever since : desde entonces⟩ **2** (*in questions*) : alguna vez, algún día ⟨have you ever been to Mexico? : ¿has estado en México alguna vez?⟩ **3** (*in negative constructions*) : nunca ⟨doesn't he ever work? : ¿es que nunca trabaja?⟩ ⟨nobody ever helps me : nadie nunca me ayuda⟩ **4** (*in comparisons*) : nunca ⟨better than ever : mejor que nunca⟩ **5** (*as intensifier*) ⟨I'm ever so happy! : ¡estoy tan y tan feliz!⟩ ⟨he looks ever so angry : parece estar muy enojado⟩

evergreen¹ ['ɛvər,gri:n] *adj* : de hoja perenne

evergreen² *n* : planta *f* de hoja perenne

everlasting [,ɛvər'læstɪŋ] *adj* : eterno, perpetuo, imperecedero

evermore [,ɛvər'mor] *adv* : eternamente

every ['ɛvri] *adj* **1** EACH : cada ⟨every time : cada vez⟩ ⟨every other house : cada dos casas⟩ **2** ALL : todo ⟨every month : todos los meses⟩ ⟨every woman : toda mujer, todas las mujeres⟩ **3** COMPLETE : pleno, entero ⟨to have every confidence : tener plena confianza⟩

everybody ['ɛvri,bʌdi, -,ba-] *pron* : todos *mpl*, -das *fpl*; todo el mundo

everyday [,ɛvri'deɪ, 'ɛvri,-] *adj* : cotidiano, diario, corriente ⟨everyday clothes : ropa de todos los días⟩

everyone ['ɛvri,wʌn] → **everybody**

everything ['ɛvri,θɪŋ] *pron* : todo

everywhere ['ɛvri,hwɛr] *adv* : en todas partes, por todas partes, dondequiera ⟨I looked everywhere : busqué en todas partes⟩ ⟨everywhere we go : dondequiera que vayamos⟩

evict [ɪ'vɪkt] *vt* : desalojar, desahuciar

eviction [ɪ'vɪkʃən] *n* : desalojo *m*, desahucio *m*

evidence ['ɛvədənts] *n* **1** INDICATION : indicio *m*, señal *m* ⟨to be in evidence : estar a la vista⟩ **2** PROOF : evidencia *f*, prueba *f* **3** TESTIMONY : testimonio *m*, declaración *f* ⟨to give evidence : declarar como testigo, prestar declaración⟩

evident ['ɛvɪdənt] *adj* : evidente, patente, manifiesto

evidently ['ɛvɪdəntli, ,ɛvi'dɛntli] *adv* **1** CLEARLY : claramente, obviamente **2** APPARENTLY : aparentemente, evidentemente, al parecer

evil¹ ['i:vəl, -vɪl] *adj* **eviler** *or* **eviller**; **evilest** *or* **evillest** **1** WICKED : malvado, malo, maligno **2** HARMFUL : nocivo, dañino, pernicioso **3** UNPLEASANT : desagradable ⟨an evil odor : un olor horrible⟩

evil² *n* **1** WICKEDNESS : mal *m*, maldad *f* **2** MISFORTUNE : desgracia *f*, mal *m*

evildoer [,i:vəl'du:ər, ,i:vɪl-] *n* : malvado *m*, -da *f*

evince [ɪ'vɪnts] *vt* **evinced**; **evincing** : mostrar, manifestar, revelar

eviscerate [ɪ'vɪsə,reɪt] *vt* **-ated**; **-ating** : eviscerar, destripar (un pollo, etc.)

evocation [,i:vo'keɪʃən, ,ɛ-] *n* : evocación *f*

evocative [i'vɑkətɪv] *adj* : evocador

evoke [i'vo:k] *vt* **evoked**; **evoking** : evocar, provocar

evolution [,ɛvə'lu:ʃən, ,i:-] *n* : evolución *f*, desarrollo *m*

evolutionary [,ɛvə'lu:ʃə,nɛri, ,i:-] *adj* : evolutivo

evolve [i'vɑlv] *vi* **evolved**; **evolving** : evolucionar, desarrollarse

ewe ['ju:] *n* : oveja *f*

exacerbate [ɪg'zæsər,beɪt] *vt* **-bated**; **-bating** : exacerbar

exact¹ [ɪg'zækt, ɛ-] *vt* : exigir, imponer, arrancar

exact² *adj* : exacto, preciso — **exactly** *adv*

exacting [ɪ'zæktɪŋ, ɛg-] *adj* : exigente, riguroso

exactitude [ɪg'zæktə,tu:d, ɛg-, -,tju:d] *n* : exactitud *f*, precisión *f*

exaggerate [ɪg'zædʒə,reɪt, ɛg-] *v* **-ated**; **-ating** : exagerar

exaggerated [ɪg'zædʒə,reɪtəd, ɛg-] *adj* : exagerado — **exaggeratedly** *adv*

exaggeration [ɪg,zædʒə'reɪʃən, ɛg-] *n* : exageración *f*

exalt [ɪg'zɔlt, ɛg-] *vt* : exaltar, ensalzar, glorificar

exaltation [,ɛg,zɔl'teɪʃən, ,ɛk,sɔl-] *n* : exaltación *f*

exam [ɪg'zæm, ɛg-] → **examination**

examination [ɪg,zæmə'neɪʃən, ɛg-] *n* **1** TEST : examen *m* **2** INSPECTION : inspección *f*, revisión *f* **3** INVESTIGATION : examen *m*, estudio *m*

examine [ɪg'zæmən, ɛg-] *vt* **-ined**; **-ining** **1** TEST : examinar **2** INSPECT : inspeccionar, revisar **3** STUDY : examinar

example [ɪg'zæmpəl, ɛg-] *n* : ejemplo *m* ⟨for example : por ejemplo⟩ ⟨to set an example : dar ejemplo⟩

exasperate [ɪg'zæspə,reɪt, ɛg-] *vt* **-ated**; **-ating** : exasperar, sacar de quicio

exasperation [ɪg,zæspə'reɪʃən, ɛg-] *n* : exasperación *f*

excavate ['ɛkskə,veɪt] *vt* **-vated**; **-vating** : excavar

excavation [,ɛkskə'veɪʃən] *n* : excavación *f*

exceed [ɪk'si:d, ɛk-] *vt* **1** SURPASS : exceder, rebasar, sobrepasar **2** : exceder de, sobrepasar ⟨not exceeding two months : que no exceda de dos meses⟩

exceedingly [ɪk'si:dɪŋli, ɛk-] *adv* : extremadamente, sumamente

excel [ɪk'sɛl, ɛk-] *v* **-celled**; **-celling** *vi* : sobresalir, descollar, lucirse — *vt* : superar

excellence ['ɛksələnts] *n* : excelencia *f*

excellency ['ɛksələntsi] *n*, *pl* **-cies** : excelencia *f* ⟨His Excellency : Su Excelencia⟩

excellent ['ɛksələnt] *adj* : excelente, sobresaliente — **excellently** *adv*

except[1] [ɪk'sɛpt] *vt* : exceptuar, excluir
except[2] *conj* : pero, si no fuera por
except[3] *prep* : excepto, menos, salvo ⟨everyone except Carlos : todos menos Carlos⟩
exception [ɪk'sɛpʃən] *n* **1** : excepción *f* **2 to take exception to** : ofenderse por, objetar a
exceptional [ɪk'sɛpʃənəl] *adj* : excepcional, extraordinario — **exceptionally** *adv*
excerpt[1] [ɛk'sərpt, ɛg'zərpt, 'ɛk͵-, 'g͵-] *vt* : escoger, seleccionar
excerpt[2] ['ɛk͵sərpt, 'ɛg͵zərpt] *n* : pasaje *m*, selección *f*
excess[1] ['ɛk͵sɛs, ɪk'sɛs] *adj* **1** : excesivo, de sobra **2 excess baggage** : exceso *m* de equipaje
excess[2] [ɪk'sɛs, 'ɛk͵sɛs] *n* **1** SUPERFLUITY : exceso *m*, superfluidad *f* ⟨an excess of energy : un exceso de energía⟩ **2** SURPLUS : excedente *m*, sobrante *m* ⟨in excess of : superior a⟩
excessive [ɪk'sɛsɪv, ɛk-] *adj* : excesivo, exagerado, desmesurado — **excessively** *adv*
exchange[1] [ɪks'tʃeɪndʒ, ɛks-; 'ɛks͵tʃeɪndʒ] *vt* **-changed; -changing** : cambiar, intercambiar, canjear
exchange[2] *n* **1** : cambio *m*, intercambio *m*, canje *m* **2 stock exchange** : bolsa *f* (de valores)
exchangeable [ɪks'tʃeɪndʒəbəl, ɛks-] *adj* : canjeable
excise[1] [ɪk'saɪz, ɛk-] *vt* **-cised; -cising** : extirpar
excise[2] ['ɛk͵saɪz] *n* **excise tax** : impuesto *m* interno, impuesto *m* sobre el consumo
excision [ɪk'sɪʒən, ɛk-] *n* : extirpación *f*, excisión *f*
excitability [ɪk͵saɪtə'bɪləti, ɛk-] *n* : excitabilidad *f*
excitable [ɪk'saɪtəbəl, ɛk-] *adj* : excitable
excitation [͵ɛk͵saɪ'teɪʃən] *n* : excitación *f*
excite [ɪk'saɪt, ɛk-] *vt* **-cited; -citing 1** AROUSE, STIMULATE : excitar, mover, estimular **2** ANIMATE : entusiasmar, animar **3** EVOKE, PROVOKE : provocar, despertar, suscitar ⟨to excite curiosity : despertar la curiosidad⟩
excited [ɪk'saɪtəd, ɛk-] *adj* **1** STIMULATED : excitado, estimulado **2** ENTHUSIASTIC : entusiasmado, emocionado
excitedly [ɪk'saɪtədli, ɛk-] *adv* : con excitación, con entusiasmo
excitement [ɪk'saɪtmənt, ɛk-] *n* **1** ENTHUSIASM : entusiasmo *m*, emoción *f* **2** AGITATION : agitación *f*, alboroto *m*, conmoción *f* **3** AROUSAL : excitación *f*
exciting [ɪk'saɪtɪŋ, ɛk-] *adj* **1** : emocionante **2** AROUSING : excitante
exclaim [ɪks'kleɪm, ɛk-] *v* : exclamar
exclamation [͵ɛksklə'meɪʃən] *n* : exclamación *f*
exclamation point *n* : signo *m* de admiración

exclamatory [ɪks'klæmə͵tori, ɛks-] *adj* : exclamativo
exclude [ɪks'klu:d, ɛks-] *vt* **-cluded; -cluding 1** BAR : excluir, descartar, no admitir **2** EXPEL : expeler, expulsar
exclusion [ɪks'klu:ʒən, ɛks-] *n* : exclusión *f*
exclusive[1] [ɪks'klu:sɪv, ɛks-] *adj* **1** SOLE : exclusivo, único **2** SELECT : exclusivo, selecto
exclusive[2] *n* : exclusiva *f*
exclusively [ɪks'klu:sɪvli, ɛks-] *adv* : exclusivamente, únicamente
exclusiveness [ɪks'klu:sɪvnəs, ɛks-] *n* : exclusividad *f*
excommunicate [͵ɛkskə'mju:nə͵keɪt] *vt* **-cated; -cating** : excomulgar
excommunication [͵ɛkskə͵mju:nə'keɪʃən] *n* : excomunión *f*
excrement ['ɛkskrəmənt] *n* : excremento *m*
excrete [ɪk'skri:t, ɛk-] *vt* **-creted; -creting** : excretar
excretion [ɪk'skri:ʃən, ɛk-] *n* : excreción *f*
excruciating [ɪk'skru:ʃi͵eɪtɪŋ, ɛk-] *adj* : insoportable, atroz, terrible — **excruciatingly** *adv*
exculpate ['ɛkskəl͵peɪt] *vt* **-pated; -pating** : exculpar
excursion [ɪk'skərʒən, ɛk-] *n* **1** OUTING : excursión *f*, paseo *m* **2** DIGRESSION : digresión *f*
excuse[1] [ɪk'skju:z, ɛk-] *vt* **-cused; -cusing 1** PARDON : disculpar, perdonar ⟨excuse me : con permiso, perdóneme, perdón⟩ **2** EXEMPT : eximir, disculpar **3** JUSTIFY : excusar, justificar
excuse[2] [ɪk'skju:s, ɛk-] *n* **1** JUSTIFICATION : excusa *f*, justificación *f* **2** PRETEXT : pretexto *m* **3 to make one's excuses to someone** : pedirle disculpas a alguien
execute ['ɛksɪ͵kju:t] *vt* **-cuted; -cuting 1** CARRY OUT : ejecutar, llevar a cabo, desempeñar **2** ENFORCE : ejecutar, cumplir (un testamento, etc.) **3** KILL : ejecutar, ajusticiar
execution [͵ɛksɪ'kju:ʃən] *n* **1** PERFORMANCE : ejecución *f*, desempeño *m* **2** IMPLEMENTATION : cumplimiento *m* **3** : ejecución *f* (por un delito)
executioner [͵ɛksɪ'kju:ʃənər] *n* : verdugo *m*
executive[1] [ɪg'zɛkjətɪv, ɛg-] *adj* : ejecutivo
executive[2] *n* : ejecutivo *m*, -va *f*
executor [ɪg'zɛkjətər, ɛg-] *n* : albacea *m*, testamentario *m*
executrix [ɪg'zɛkjə͵trɪks, ɛg-] *n, pl* **executrices** [-͵zɛkjə'traɪ͵si:z] *or* **executrixes** [-'zɛkjə͵trɪksəz] : albacea *f*, testamentaria *f*
exemplary [ɪg'zɛmpləri, ɛg-] *adj* : ejemplar
exemplify [ɪg'zɛmplə͵faɪ, ɛg-] *vt* **-fied; -fying** : ejemplificar, ilustrar, demostrar

exempt · expedient

exempt¹ [ɪgˈzɛmpt, ɛg-] *vt* : eximir, dispensar, exonerar

exempt² *adj* : exento, eximido

exemption [ɪgˈzɛmpʃən, ɛg-] *n* : exención *f*

exercise¹ [ˈɛksərˌsaɪz] *v* **-cised; -cising** *vt* **1** : ejercitar (el cuerpo) **2** USE : ejercer, hacer uso de — *vi* : hacer ejercicio

exercise² *n* **1** : ejercicio *m* **2 exercises** *npl* WORKOUT : ejercicios *mpl* físicos **3 exercises** *npl* CEREMONY : ceremonia *f*

exert [ɪgˈzərt, ɛg-] *vt* **1** : ejercer, emplear **2 to exert oneself** : esforzarse

exertion [ɪgˈzərʃən, ɛg-] *n* **1** USE : ejercicio *m* (de autoridad, etc.), uso *m* (de fuerza, etc.) **2** EFFORT : esfuerzo *m*, empeño *m*

exhalation [ˌɛksəˈleɪʃən, ˌɛkshə-] *n* : exhalación *f*, espiración *f*

exhale [ɛksˈheɪl] *v* **-haled; -haling** *vt* **1** : exhalar, espirar **2** EMIT : exhalar, despedir, emitir — *vi* : espirar

exhaust¹ [ɪgˈzɔst, ɛg-] *vt* **1** DEPLETE : agotar **2** TIRE : cansar, fatigar, agotar **3** EMPTY : vaciar

exhaust² *n* **1 exhaust fumes** : gases *mpl* de escape **2 exhaust pipe** : tubo *m* de escape **3 exhaust system** : sistema *m* de escape

exhausted [ɪgˈzɔstəd, ɛg-] *adj* : agotado, derrengado

exhausting [ɪgˈzɔstɪŋ, ɛg-] *adj* : extenuante, agotador

exhaustion [ɪgˈzɔstʃən, ɛg-] *n* : agotamiento *m*

exhaustive [ɪgˈzɔstɪv, ɛg-] *adj* : exhaustivo

exhibit¹ [ɪgˈzɪbət, ɛg-] *vt* **1** DISPLAY : exhibir, exponer **2** PRODUCE, SHOW : mostrar, presentar

exhibit² *n* **1** OBJECT : objeto *m* expuesto **2** EXHIBITION : exposición *f*, exhibición *f* **3** EVIDENCE : prueba *f* instrumental

exhibition [ˌɛksəˈbɪʃən] *n* **1** : exposición *f*, exhibición *f* **2 to make an exhibition of oneself** : dar el espectáculo, hacer el ridículo

exhibitor [ɪgˈzɪbətər] *n* : expositor *m*, -tora *f*

exhilarate [ɪgˈzɪləˌreɪt, ɛg-] *vt* **-rated; -rating** : alegrar, levantar el ánimo de

exhilaration [ɪgˌzɪləˈreɪʃən, ɛg-] *n* : alegría *f*, regocijo *m*, júbilo *m*

exhort [ɪgˈzɔrt, ɛg-] *vt* : exhortar

exhortation [ˌɛkˌsɔrˈteɪʃən, -sər-; ˌɛgˌzɔr-] *n* : exhortación *f*

exhumation [ˌɛksjuˈmeɪʃən, -hju-; ˌɛgzu-, -zju-] *n* : exhumación *f*

exhume [ɪgˈzuːm, -ˈzjuːm; ɪksˈjuːm, -ˈhjuːm] *vt* **-humed; -huming** : exhumar, desenterrar

exigencies [ˈɛksɪʤənˌsiz, ɪgˈzɪʤənˌsiːz] *npl* : exigencias *fpl*

exile¹ [ˈɛgˌzaɪl, ˈɛkˌsaɪl] *vt* **exiled; exiling** : exiliar, desterrar

exile² *n* **1** BANISHMENT : exilio *m*, destierro *m* **2** OUTCAST : exiliado *m*, -da *f*; desterrado *m*, -da *f*

exist [ɪgˈzɪst, ɛg-] *vi* **1** BE : existir **2** LIVE : subsistir, vivir

existence [ɪgˈzɪstənts, ɛg-] *n* : existencia *f*

existent [ɪgˈzɪstənt, ɛg-] *adj* : existente

existing [ɪgˈzɪstɪŋ] *adj* : existente

exit¹ [ˈɛgzət, ˈɛksət] *vi* : salir, hacer mutis (en el teatro) — *vt* : salir de

exit² *n* **1** DEPARTURE : salida *f*, partida *f* **2** EGRESS : salida *f* ⟨emergency exit : salida de emergencia⟩

exodus [ˈɛksədəs] *n* : éxodo *m*

exonerate [ɪgˈzɑnəˌreɪt, ɛg-] *vt* **-ated; -ating** : exonerar, disculpar, absolver

exoneration [ɪgˌzɑnəˈreɪʃən, ɛg-] *n* : exoneración *f*

exorbitant [ɪgˈzɔrbətənt, ɛg-] *adj* : exorbitante, excesivo

exorcise [ˈɛkˌsɔrˌsaɪz, -sər-] *vt* **-cised; -cising** : exorcizar

exorcism [ˈɛksərˌsɪzəm] *n* : exorcismo *m*

exotic¹ [ɪgˈzɑtɪk, ɛg-] *adj* : exótico — **exotically** [-ɪkli] *adv*

exotic² *n* : planta *f* exótica

expand [ɪkˈspænd, ɛk-] *vt* **1** ENLARGE : expandir, dilatar, aumentar, ampliar **2** EXTEND : extender — *vi* **1** ENLARGE : ampliarse, extenderse **2** : expandirse, dilatarse (dícese de los metales, gases, etc.)

expanse [ɪkˈspænts, ɛk-] *n* : extensión *f*

expansion [ɪkˈspænʃən, ɛk-] *n* **1** ENLARGEMENT : expansión *f*, ampliación *f* **2** EXPANSE : extensión *f*

expansive [ɪkˈspænsɪv, ɛk-] *adj* **1** : expansivo **2** OUTGOING : expansivo, comunicativo **3** AMPLE : ancho, amplio — **expansively** *adv*

expansiveness [ɪkˈspæntsɪvnəs, ɛk-] *n* : expansibilidad *f*

expatriate¹ [ɛksˈpeɪtriˌeɪt] *vt* **-ated; -ating** : expatriar

expatriate² [ɛksˈpeɪtriət, -ˌeɪt] *adj* : expatriado

expatriate³ [ɛksˈpeɪtriət, -ˌeɪt] *n* : expatriado *m*, -da *f*

expect [ɪkˈspɛkt, ɛk-] *vt* **1** SUPPOSE : suponer, imaginarse **2** ANTICIPATE : esperar **3** COUNT ON, REQUIRE : contar con, esperar — *vi* **to be expecting** : estar embarazada

expectancy [ɪkˈspɛktəntsi, ɛk-] *n, pl* **-cies** : expectativa *f*, esperanza *f*

expectant [ɪkˈspɛktənt, ɛk-] *adj* **1** ANTICIPATING : expectante **2** EXPECTING : futuro ⟨expectant mother : futura madre⟩

expectantly [ɪkˈspɛktəntli, ɛk-] *adv* : con expectación

expectation [ˌɛkˌspɛkˈteɪʃən] *n* **1** ANTICIPATION : expectación *f* **2** EXPECTANCY : expectativa *f*

expedient¹ [ɪkˈspiːdiənt, ɛk-] *adj* : conveniente, oportuno

expedient² *n* : expediente *m*, recurso *m*

expedite ['ɛkspə,daɪt] *vt* **-dited; -diting 1** FACILITATE : facilitar, dar curso a **2** HASTEN : acelerar

expedition [,ɛkspə'dɪʃən] *n* : expedición *f*

expeditious [,ɛkspə'dɪʃəs] *adj* : pronto, rápido

expel [ɪk'spɛl, ɛk-] *vt* **-pelled; -pelling** : expulsar, expeler

expend [ɪk'spɛnd, ɛk-] *vt* **1** DISBURSE : gastar, desembolsar **2** CONSUME : consumir, agotar

expendable [ɪk'spɛndəbəl, ɛk-] *adj* : prescindible

expenditure [ɪk'spɛndɪtʃər, ɛk-, -,tʃʊr] *n* : gasto *m*

expense [ɪk'spɛnts, ɛk-] *n* **1** COST : gasto *m* **2 expenses** *npl* : gastos *mpl*, expensas *fpl* **3 at the expense of** : a expensas de

expensive [ɪk'spɛntsɪv, ɛk-] *adj* : costoso, caro — **expensively** *adv*

experience[1] [ɪk'spɪriənts, ɛk-] *vt* **-enced; -encing** : experimentar (sentimientos), tener (dificultades), sufrir (una pérdida)

experience[2] *n* : experiencia *f*

experienced [ɪk'spɪriəntst, ɛk-] *adj* : con experiencia, experimentado

experiment[1] [ɪk'spɛrəmənt, ɛk-, -'spɪr-] *vi* : experimentar, hacer experimentos

experiment[2] *n* : experimento *m*

experimental [ɪk,spɛrə'mntəl, ɛk-, -,spɪr-] *adj* : experimental — **experimentally** *adv*

experimentation [ɪk,spɛrəmən'teɪʃən, ɛk-, -,spɪr-] *n* : experimentación *f*

expert[1] ['ɛk,spərt, ɪk'spərt] *adj* : experto, de experto, pericial (dícese de un testigo) — **expertly** *adv*

expert[2] ['ɛk,spərt] *n* : experto *m*, -ta *f*; perito *m*, -ta *f*; especialista *mf*

expertise [,ɛkspər'tiːz] *n* : pericia *f*, competencia *f*

expiate ['ɛkspi,eɪt] *vt* **-ated; -ating** : expiar

expiation [,ɛkspi'eɪʃən] *n* : expiación *f*

expiration [,ɛkspə'reɪʃən] *n* **1** EXHALATION : exhalación *f*, espiración *f* **2** DEATH : muerte *f* **3** TERMINATION : vencimiento *m*, caducidad *f*

expire [ɪk'spaɪr, ɛk-] *vi* **-pired; -piring 1** EXHALE : espirar **2** DIE : expirar, morir **3** TERMINATE : caducar, vencer

explain [ɪk'spleɪn, ɛk-] *vt* : explicar

explanation [,ɛksplə'neɪʃən] *n* : explicación *f*

explanatory [ɪk'splænə,tori, ɛk-] *adj* : explicativo, aclaratorio

expletive ['ɛksplətɪv] *n* : improperio *m*, palabrota *f fam*, grosería *f*

explicable [ɛk'splɪkəbəl, 'ɛksplɪ-] *adj* : explicable

explicit [ɪk'splɪsət, ɛk-] *adj* : explícito, claro, categórico, rotundo — **explicitly** *adv*

explicitness [ɪk'splɪsətnəs, ɛk-] *n* : claridad *f*, carácter *m* explícito

explode [ɪk'sploːd, ɛk-] *v* **-ploded; -ploding** *vt* **1** BURST : hacer explosionar, hacer explotar **2** REFUTE : rebatir, refutar, desmentir — *vi* **1** BURST : explotar, estallar, reventar **2** SKYROCKET : dispararse

exploit[1] [ɪk'sploɪt, ɛk-] *vt* : explotar, aprovecharse de

exploit[2] ['ɛk,sploɪt] *n* : hazaña *f*, proeza *f*

exploitation [,ɛk,sploɪ'teɪʃən] *n* : explotación *f*

exploration [,ɛksplə'reɪʃən] *n* : exploración *f*

exploratory [ɪk'splorə,tori, ɛk-] *adj* : exploratorio

explore [ɪk'splor, ɛk-] *vt* **-plored; -ploring** : explorar, investigar, examinar

explorer [ɪk'splorər, ɛk-] *n* : explorador *m*, -dora *f*

explosion [ɪk'sploːʒən, ɛk-] *n* : explosión *f*, estallido *m*

explosive[1] [ɪk'sploːsɪv, ɛk-] *adj* : explosivo, fulminante — **explosively** *adv*

explosive[2] *n* : explosivo *m*

exponent [ɪk'spoːnənt, 'ɛk,spo-] *n* **1** : exponente *m* **2** ADVOCATE : defensor *m*, -sora *f*; partidario *m*, -ria *f*

exponential [,ɛkspə'nɛntʃəl] *adj* : exponencial — **exponentially** *adv*

export[1] [ɛk'sport, 'ɛk,sport] *vt* : exportar

export[2] ['ɛk,sport] *n* **1** : artículo *m* de exportación **2** → **exportation**

exportation [,ɛk,spor'teɪʃən] *n* : exportación *f*

exporter [ɛk'sportər, 'ɛk,spor-] *n* : exportador *m*, -dora *f*

expose [ɪk'spoːz, ɛk-] *vt* **-posed; -posing 1** : exponer (al peligro, a los elementos, a una enfermedad) **2** : exponer (una película a la luz) **3** DISCLOSE : descubrir, revelar, poner en evidencia **4** UNMASK : desenmascarar

exposé *or* **expose** [,ɛkspo'zeɪ] *n* : exposición *f* (de hechos), revelación *f* (de un escándalo)

exposed [ɪk'spoːzd, ɛk-] *adj* : descubierto, sin protección

exposition [,ɛkspə'zɪʃən] *n* : exposición *f*

exposure [ɪk'spoːʒər, ɛk-] *n* **1** : exposición *f* **2** CONTACT : exposición *f*, experiencia *f*, contacto *m* **3** UNMASKING : desenmascaramiento *m* **4** ORIENTATION : orientación *f* ⟨a room with a northern exposure : una sala orientada al norte⟩

expound [ɪk'spaʊnd, ɛk-] *vt* : exponer, explicar — *vi* : hacer comentarios detallados

express[1] [ɪk'sprɛs, ɛk-] *vt* **1** SAY : expresar, comunicar **2** SHOW : expresar, manifestar, externar *Mex* **3** SQUEEZE : exprimir ⟨to express the juice from a lemon : exprimir el jugo de un limón⟩

express[2] *adv* : por correo exprés, por correo urgente

express³ *adj* **1** EXPLICIT : expreso, manifiesto **2** SPECIFIC : específico ⟨for that express purpose : con ese fin específico⟩ **3** RAPID : expreso, rápido

express⁴ *n* **1** : correo *m* exprés, correo *m* urgente **2** : expreso *m* (tren)

expression [ɪk'sprɛʃən, ɛk-] *n* **1** UTTERANCE : expresión *f* ⟨freedom of expression : libertad de expresión⟩ **2** : expresión *f* (en la matemática) **3** PHRASE : frase *f*, expresión *f* **4** LOOK : expresión *f*, cara *f*, gesto *m* ⟨with a sad expression : con un gesto de tristeza⟩

expressionless [ɪk'sprɛʃənləs, ɛk-] *adj* : inexpresivo

expressive [ɪk'sprɛsɪv, ɛk-] *adj* : expresivo

expressway [ɪk'sprɛs,weɪ, ɛk-] *n* : autopista *f*

expulsion [ɪk'spʌlʃən, ɛk-] *n* : expulsión *f*

expurgate ['ɛkspər,geɪt] *vt* **-gated; -gating** : expurgar

exquisite [ɛk'skwɪzət, 'ɛk,skwɪ-] *adj* **1** FINE : exquisito, delicado, primoroso **2** INTENSE : intenso, extremo

extant ['ɛkstənt, ɛk'stænt] *adj* : existente

extemporaneous [ɛk,stɛmpə'reɪniəs] *adj* : improvisado — **extemporaneously** *adv*

extend [ɪk'stɛnd, ɛk-] *vt* **1** STRETCH : extender, tender **2** PROLONG : prolongar, prorrogar **3** ENLARGE : agrandar, ampliar, aumentar **4** PROFFER : extender, dar, ofrecer — *vi* : extenderse

extended [ɪk'stɛndəd, ɛk-] *adj* LENGTHY : prolongado, largo

extension [ɪk'stɛntʃən, ɛk-] *n* **1** EXTENDING : extensión *f*, ampliación *f*, prórroga *f*, prolongación *f* **2** ANNEX : ampliación *f*, anexo *m* **3** : extensión *f* (de teléfono)

extensive [ɪk'stɛntsɪv, ɛk-] *adj* : extenso, vasto, amplio — **extensively** *adv*

extent [ɪk'stɛnt, ɛk-] *n* **1** SIZE : extensión *f*, magnitud *f* **2** DEGREE, SCOPE : alcance *m*, grado *m* ⟨to a certain extent : hasta cierto punto⟩

extenuate [ɪk'stɛnjə,weɪt, ɛk-] *vt* **-ated; -ating** : atenuar, aminorar, mitigar ⟨extenuating circumstances : circunstancias atenuantes⟩

extenuation [ɪk,stɛnjə'weɪʃən, ɛk-] *n* : atenuación *f*, aminoración *f*

exterior¹ [ɛk'stɪriər] *adj* : exterior

exterior² *n* : exterior *m*

exterminate [ɪk'stərmə,neɪt, ɛk-] *vt* **-nated; -nating** : exterminar

extermination [ɪk,stərmə'neɪʃən, ɛk-] *n* : exterminación *f*, exterminio *m*

exterminator [ɪk'stərmə,neɪtər, ɛk-] *n* : exterminador *m*, -dora *f*

external [ɪk'stərnəl, ɛk-] *adj* : externo, exterior — **externally** *adv*

extinct [ɪk'stɪŋkt, ɛk-] *adj* : extinto

extinction [ɪk'stɪŋkʃən, ɛk-] *n* : extinción *f*

extinguish [ɪk'stɪŋgwɪʃ, ɛk-] *vt* : extinguir, apagar

extinguisher [ɪk'stɪŋgwɪʃər, ɛk-] *n* : extinguidor *m*, extintor *m*

extirpate ['ɛkstər,peɪt] *vt* **-pated; -pating** : extirpar, exterminar

extol [ɪk'stoːl, ɛk-] *vt* **-tolled; -tolling** : exaltar, ensalzar, alabar

extort [ɪk'stɔrt, ɛk-] *vt* : extorsionar

extortion [ɪk'stɔrʃən, ɛk-] *n* : extorsión *f*

extra¹ ['ɛkstrə] *adv* : extra, más, extremadamente, super ⟨extra special : super especial⟩

extra² *adj* **1** ADDITIONAL : adicional, suplementario, de más **2** SUPERIOR : superior

extra³ *n* : extra *m*

extract¹ [ɪk'strækt, ɛk-] *vt* : extraer, sacar

extract² ['ɛk,strækt] *n* **1** EXCERPT : pasaje *m*, selección *f*, trozo *m* **2** : extracto *m* ⟨vanilla extract : extracto de vainilla⟩

extraction [ɪk'strækʃən, ɛk-] *n* : extracción *f*

extractor [ɪk'stræktər, ɛk-] *n* : extractor *m*

extracurricular [,ɛkstrəkə'rɪkjələr] *adj* : extracurricular

extradite ['ɛkstrə,daɪt] *vt* **-dited; -diting** : extraditar

extradition [,ɛkstrə'dɪʃən] *n* : extradición *f*

extramarital [,ɛkstrə'mærətəl] *adj* : extramatrimonial

extraneous [ɛk'streɪniəs] *adj* **1** OUTSIDE : extrínseco, externo **2** SUPERFLUOUS : superfluo, ajeno — **extraneously** *adv*

extraordinary [ɪk'strɔrdən,ɛri, ,ɛkstrə-'ɔrd-] *adj* : extraordinario, excepcional — **extraordinarily** [ɪk,strɔrdən'ɛrəli, ,ɛkstrə,ɔrd-] *adv*

extrasensory [,ɛkstrə'sɛntsəri] *adj* : extrasensorial

extraterrestrial¹ [,ɛkstrətə'rɛstriəl] *adj* : extraterrestre

extraterrestrial² *n* : extraterrestre *mf*

extravagance [ɪk'strævɪgənts, ɛk-] *n* **1** EXCESS : exceso *m*, extravagancia *f* **2** WASTEFULNESS : derroche *m*, despilfarro *m* **3** LUXURY : lujo *m*

extravagant [ɪk'strævɪgənt, ɛk-] *adj* **1** EXCESSIVE : excesivo, extravagante **2** WASTEFUL : despilfarrador, derrochador, gastador **3** EXORBITANT : costoso, exorbitante

extravagantly [ɪk'strævɪgəntli, ɛk-] *adv* **1** LAVISHLY : a lo grande **2** EXCESSIVELY : exageradamente, desmesuradamente

extravaganza [ɪk,strævə'gænzə, ɛk-] *n* : gran espectáculo *m*

extreme¹ [ɪk'striːm, ɛk-] *adj* **1** UTMOST : extremo, sumo ⟨of extreme importance : de suma importancia⟩ **2** INTENSE : intenso, extremado ⟨extreme cold : frío extremado⟩ **3** EXCESSIVE : excesivo, extremo ⟨extreme views : opiniones extremas⟩ ⟨extreme measures : medidas excepcionales, medidas drásticas⟩ **4** OUTERMOST : extremo ⟨the extreme north : el norte extremo⟩

extreme² n **1** : extremo m **2 in the extreme** : en extremo, en sumo grado

extremely [ɪk'stri:mli, ɛk-] adv : sumamente, extremadamente, terriblemente

extremist [ɪk'stri:mɪst, ɛk-] n : extremista mf — **extremist** adj

extremity [ɪk'strɛməṭi, ɛk-] n, pl **-ties 1** EXTREME : extremo m **2 extremities** npl LIMBS : extremidades fpl

extricate ['ɛkstrə,keɪt] vt **-cated; -cating** : librar, sacar

extrinsic [ɪk'strɪnzɪk, -'strɪntsɪk] adj : extrínseco

extrovert ['ɛkstrə,vərt] n : extrovertido m, -da f

extroverted ['ɛkstrə,vərṭəd] adj : extrovertido

extrude [ɪk'stru:d, ɛk-] vt **-truded; -truding** : extrudir, expulsar

exuberance [ɪg'zu:bərənts, ɛg-] n **1** JOYOUSNESS : euforia f, exaltación f **2** VIGOR : exuberancia f, vigor m

exuberant [ɪg'zu:bərənt, ɛg-] adj **1** JOYOUS : eufórico **2** LUSH : exuberante — **exuberantly** adv

exude [ɪg'zu:d, ɛg-] vt **-uded; -uding 1** OOZE : rezumar, exudar **2** EMANATE : emanar, irradiar

exult [ɪg'zʌlt, ɛg-] vi : exultar, regocijarse

exultant [ɪg'zʌltənt, ɛg-] adj : exultante, jubiloso — **exultantly** adv

exultation [,ɛksəl'teɪʃən, ,ɛgzəl-] n : exultación f, júbilo m, alborozo m

eye¹ ['aɪ] vt **eyed; eyeing** or **eying** : mirar, observar

eye² n **1** : ojo m **2** VISION : visión f, vista f, ojo m ⟨a good eye for bargains : un buen ojo para las gangas⟩ **3** GLANCE : mirada f, ojeada f **4** ATTENTION : atención f ⟨to catch one's eye : llamar la atención⟩ **5** POINT OF VIEW : punto m de vista ⟨in the eyes of the law : según la ley⟩ **6** : ojo m (de una aguja, una papa, una tormenta)

eyeball ['aɪ,bɔl] n : globo m ocular

eyebrow ['aɪ,braʊ] n : ceja f

eyedropper ['aɪ,drɑpər] n : cuentagotas f

eyeglasses ['aɪ,glæsəz] npl : anteojos mpl, lentes mpl, espejuelos mpl, gafas fpl

eyelash ['aɪ,læʃ] n : pestaña f

eyelet ['aɪlət] n : ojete m

eyelid ['aɪ,lɪd] n : párpado m

eye–opener ['aɪo:pənər] n : revelación f, sorpresa f

eye–opening ['aɪo:pənɪŋ] adj : revelador

eyepiece ['aɪ,pi:s] n : ocular m

eyesight ['aɪ,saɪt] n : vista f, visión f

eyesore ['aɪ,sor] n : monstruosidad f, adefesio m

eyestrain ['aɪ,streɪn] n : fatiga f visual, vista f cansada

eyetooth ['aɪ,tu:θ] n : colmillo m

eyewitness ['aɪ'wɪtnəs] n : testigo mf ocular, testigo mf presencial

eyrie ['aɪri] → **aerie**

F

f ['ɛf] n, pl **f's** or **fs** ['ɛfs] : sexta letra del alfabeto inglés

fable ['feɪbəl] n : fábula f

fabled ['feɪbəld] adj : legendario, fabuloso

fabric ['fæbrɪk] n **1** MATERIAL : tela f, tejido m **2** STRUCTURE : estructura f ⟨the fabric of society : la estructura de la sociedad⟩

fabricate ['fæbrɪ,keɪt] vt **-cated; -cating 1** CONSTRUCT, MANUFACTURE : construir, fabricar **2** INVENT : inventar (excusas o mentiras)

fabrication [,fæbrɪ'keɪʃən] n **1** LIE : mentira f, invención f **2** MANUFACTURE : fabricación f

fabulous ['fæbjələs] adj **1** LEGENDARY : fabuloso, legendario **2** INCREDIBLE : increíble, fabuloso ⟨fabulous wealth : riqueza fabulosa⟩ **3** WONDERFUL : magnífico, estupendo, fabuloso — **fabulously** adv

facade [fə'sɑd] n : fachada f

face¹ ['feɪs] v **faced; facing** vt **1** LINE : recubrir (una superficie), forrar (ropa) **2** CONFRONT : enfrentarse a, afrontar, hacer frente a ⟨to face the music : afrontar las consecuencias⟩ ⟨to face the facts : aceptar la realidad⟩ **3** : estar de cara a, estar enfrente de ⟨she's facing her brother : está de cara a su hermano⟩ **4** OVERLOOK : dar a — vi : mirar (hacia), estar orientado (a)

face² n **1** : cara f, rostro m ⟨he told me to my face : me lo dijo a la cara⟩ **2** EXPRESSION : cara f, expresión f ⟨to pull a long face : poner mala cara⟩ **3** GRIMACE : mueca f ⟨to make faces : hacer muecas⟩ **4** APPEARANCE : fisonomía f, aspecto m ⟨the face of society : la fisonomía de la sociedad⟩ **5** EFFRONTERY : desfachatez f **6** PRESTIGE : prestigio m ⟨to lose face : desprestigiarse⟩ **7** FRONT, SIDE : cara f (de una moneda), esfera f (de un reloj), fachada f (de un edificio), pared f (de una montaña) **8** SURFACE : superficie f, faz f (de la tierra), cara f (de la luna) **9 in the face of** DESPITE : en medio de, en visto de, ante

facedown ['feɪs,daʊn] adv : boca abajo

faceless ['feɪsləs] adj ANONYMOUS : anónimo

face–lift ['feɪs,lɪft] n **1** : estiramiento m

facial **2** RENOVATION : renovación *f*, remozamiento *m*

facet ['fæsət] *n* **1** : faceta *f* (de una piedra) **2** ASPECT : faceta *f*, aspecto *m*

facetious [fə'si:ʃəs] *adj* : gracioso, burlón, bromista

facetiously [fə'si:ʃəsli] *adv* : en tono de burla

facetiousness [fə'si:ʃəsnəs] *n* : jocosidad *f*

face–to–face *adv & adj* : cara a cara

faceup ['feɪsˌʌp] *adv* : boca arriba

face value *n* : valor *m* nominal

facial[1] ['feɪʃəl] *adj* : de la cara, facial

facial[2] *n* : tratamiento *m* facial, limpieza *f* de cutis

facile ['fæsəl] *adj* SUPERFICIAL : superficial, simplista

facilitate [fə'sɪləˌteɪt] *vt* **-tated; -tating** : facilitar

facility [fə'sɪləti] *n, pl* **-ties 1** EASE : facilidad *f* **2** CENTER, COMPLEX : centro *m*, complejo *m* **3 facilities** *npl* AMENITIES : comodidades *fpl*, servicios *mpl*

facing ['feɪsɪŋ] *n* **1** LINING : entretela *f* (de una prenda) **2** : revestimiento *m* (de un edificio)

facsimile [fæk'sɪməli] *n* : facsímile *m*, facsímil *m*

fact ['fækt] *n* **1** : hecho *m* ⟨as a matter of fact : de hecho⟩ **2** INFORMATION : información *f*, datos *mpl* ⟨facts and figures : datos y cifras⟩ **3** REALITY : realidad *f* ⟨in fact : en realidad⟩

faction ['fækʃən] *n* : facción *m*, bando *m*

factional ['fækʃənəl] *adj* : entre facciones

factious ['fækʃəs] *adj* : faccioso, contencioso

factitious [fæk'tɪʃəs] *adj* : artificial, facticio

factor ['fæktər] *n* : factor *m*

factory ['fæktəri] *n, pl* **-ries** : fábrica *f*

factual ['fæktʃuəl] *adj* : basado en hechos, objetivo

factually ['fæktʃuəli] *adv* : en cuanto a los hechos

faculty ['fækəlti] *n, pl* **-ties 1** : facultad *f* ⟨the faculty of sight : las facultades visuales, el sentido de la vista⟩ **2** APTITUDE : aptitud *f*, facilidad *f* **3** TEACHERS : cuerpo *m* docente

fad ['fæd] *n* : moda *f* pasajera, manía *f*

fade ['feɪd] *v* **faded; fading** *vi* **1** WITHER : debilitarse (dícese de las personas), marchitarse (dícese de las flores y las plantas) **2** DISCOLOR : desteñirse, decolorarse **3** DIM : apagarse (dícese de la luz), perderse (dícese de los sonidos), fundirse (dícese de las imágenes) **4** VANISH : desvanecerse, decaer — *vt* DISCOLOR : desteñir

fag ['fæg] *vt* **fagged; fagging** EXHAUST : cansar, fatigar

fagot *or* **faggot** ['fægət] *n* : haz *m* de leña

Fahrenheit ['færənˌhaɪt] *adj* : Fahrenheit

fail[1] ['feɪl] *vi* **1** WEAKEN : fallar, deteriorarse **2** STOP : fallar, detenerse ⟨his heart failed : le falló el corazón⟩ **3** : fracasar, fallar ⟨her plan failed : su plan fracasó⟩ ⟨the crops failed : se perdió la cosecha⟩ **4** : quebrar ⟨a business about to fail : una empresa a punto de quebrar⟩ **5 to fail in** : faltar a, no cumplir con ⟨to fail in one's duties : faltar a sus deberes⟩ — *vt* **1** FLUNK : reprobar (un examen) **2** : fallar ⟨words fail me : las palabras me fallan, no encuentro palabras⟩ **3** DISAPPOINT : fallar, decepcionar ⟨don't fail me! : ¡no me falles!⟩

fail[2] *n* : fracaso *m*

failing ['feɪlɪŋ] *n* : defecto *m*

failure ['feɪljər] *n* **1** : fracaso *m*, malogro *m* ⟨crop failure : pérdida de la cosecha⟩ ⟨heart failure : insuficiencia cardíaca⟩ ⟨engine failure : falla mecánica⟩ **2** BANKRUPTCY : bancarrota *f*, quiebra *f* **3** : fracaso *m* (persona) ⟨he was a failure as a manager : como gerente, fue un fracaso⟩

faint[1] ['feɪnt] *vi* : desmayarse

faint[2] *adj* **1** COWARDLY, TIMID : cobarde, tímido **2** DIZZY : mareado ⟨faint with hunger : desfallecido de hambre⟩ **3** SLIGHT : leve, ligero, vago ⟨I haven't the faintest idea : no tengo la más mínima idea⟩ **4** INDISTINCT : tenue, indistinto, apenas perceptible

faint[3] *n* : desmayo *m*

fainthearted ['feɪnt'hɑrtəd] *adj* : cobarde, pusilánime

faintly ['feɪntli] *adv* : débilmente, ligeramente, levemente

faintness ['feɪntnəs] *n* **1** INDISTINCTNESS : lo débil, falta *f* de claridad **2** FAINTING : desmayo *m*, desfallecimiento *m*

fair[1] ['fær] *adj* **1** ATTRACTIVE, BEAUTIFUL : bello, hermoso, atractivo **2** (*relating to weather*) : bueno, despejado ⟨fair weather : tiempo despejado⟩ **3** JUST : justo, imparcial **4** ALLOWABLE : permisible **5** BLOND, LIGHT : rubio (dícese del pelo), blanco (dícese de la tez) **6** ADEQUATE : bastante, adecuado ⟨fair to middling : mediano, regular⟩ **7 fair game** : presa *f* fácil **8 to play fair** : jugar limpio

fair[2] *n* : feria *f*

fairground ['fær,graʊnd] *n* : parque *m* de diversiones

fairly ['færli] *adv* **1** IMPARTIALLY : imparcialmente, limpiamente, equitativamente **2** QUITE : bastante **3** MODERATELY : medianamente

fairness ['færnəs] *n* **1** IMPARTIALITY : imparcialidad *f*, justicia *f* **2** LIGHTNESS : blancura *f* (de la piel), lo rubio (del pelo)

fairy ['færi] *n, pl* **fairies 1** : hada *f* **2 fairy tale** : cuento *m* de hadas

fairyland ['færi,lænd] *n* **1** : país *m* de las hadas **2** : lugar *m* encantador

faith ['feɪθ] *n*, *pl* **faiths** ['feɪθs, 'feɪðz] 1
BELIEF : fe *f* 2 ALLEGIANCE : lealtad *f*
3 CONFIDENCE, TRUST : confianza *f*, fe
f 4 RELIGION : religión *f*
faithful ['feɪθfəl] *adj* : fiel — **faithfully**
adv
faithfulness ['feɪθfəlnəs] *n* : fidelidad *f*
faithless ['feɪθləs] *adj* 1 DISLOYAL
: desleal 2 : infiel (en la religión) —
faithlessly *adv*
faithlessness ['feɪθləsnəs] *n* : deslealtad
f
fake[1] ['feɪk] *v* **faked; faking** *vt* 1 FALSI-
FY : falsificar, falsear 2 FEIGN : fingir
— *vi* 1 PRETEND : fingir 2 : hacer un
engaño, hacer una finta (en deportes)
fake[2] *adj* : falso, fingido, postizo
fake[3] *n* 1 IMITATION : imitación *f*, falsificación *f* 2 IMPOSTOR : impostor *m*,
-tora *f*; charlatán *m*, -tana *f*; farsante *mf*
3 FEINT : engaño *m*, finta *f* (en deportes)
faker ['feɪkər] *n* : impostor *m*, -tora *f*;
charlatán *m*, -tana *f*; farsante *mf*
fakir [fə'kɪr, 'feɪkər] *n* : faquir *m*
falcon ['fælkən, 'fɔl-] *n* : halcón *m*
falconry ['fælkənri, 'fɔl-] *n* : cetrería *f*
fall[1] ['fɔl] *vi* **fell** ['fɛl]; **fallen** [fɔlən]; **falling**
1 : caer, caerse ⟨to fall out of bed : caer
de la cama⟩ ⟨to fall down : caerse⟩ 2
HANG : caer 3 DESCEND : caer (dícese
de la lluvia o de la noche), bajar (dícese
de los precios), descender (dícese de la
temperatura) 4 : caer (a un enemigo),
rendirse ⟨the city fell : la ciudad se
rindió⟩ 5 OCCUR : caer ⟨Christmas
falls on a Friday : la Navidad cae en
viernes⟩ 6 **to fall asleep** : dormirse,
quedarse dormido 7 **to fall from grace**
SIN : perder la gracia 8 **to fall sick** : caer
enfermo, enfermarse 9 **to fall through**
: fracasar, caer en la nada 10 **to fall to**
: tocar a, corresponder a ⟨the task fell
to him : le tocó hacerlo⟩
fall[2] *n* 1 TUMBLE : caída *f* ⟨to break one's
fall : frenar uno su caída⟩ ⟨a fall of
three feet : una caída de tres pies⟩ 2
FALLING : derrumbe *m* (de rocas),
aguacero *m* (de lluvia), nevada *f* (de
nieve), bajada *f* (de precios), disminución *f* (de cantidades) 3 AUTUMN
: otoño *m* 4 DOWNFALL : caída *f*, ruina *f* 5 **falls** *npl* WATERFALL : cascada
f, catarata *f*
fallacious [fə'leɪʃəs] *adj* : erróneo, engañoso, falaz
fallacy ['fæləsi] *n*, *pl* **-cies** : falacia *f*
fall back *vi* 1 RETREAT : retirarse, replegarse 2 **to fall back on** : recurrir a
fall guy *n* SCAPEGOAT : chivo *m* expiatorio
fallible ['fæləbəl] *adj* : falible
fallout ['fɔl,aʊt] *n* 1 : lluvia *f* radioacti-
va 2 CONSEQUENCES : secuelas *fpl*,
consecuencias *fpl*
fallow[1] ['fælo] *vt* : barbechar
fallow[2] *adj* **to lie fallow** : estar en barbecho

fallow[3] *n* : barbecho *m*
false ['fɔls] *adj* **falser; falsest** 1 UNTRUE
: falso 2 ERRONEOUS : erróneo, equiv-
ocado 3 FAKE : falso, postizo 4 UN-
FAITHFUL : infiel 5 FRAUDULENT
: fraudulento ⟨under false pretenses
: por fraude⟩
falsehood ['fɔls,hʊd] *n* : mentira *f*, falsedad *f*
falsely ['fɔlsli] *adv* : falsamente, con
falsedad
falseness ['fɔlsnəs] *n* : falsedad *f*
falsetto [fɔl'sɛto:] *n*, *pl* **-tos** : falsete *m*
falsification [,fɔlsəfə'keɪʃən] *n* : falsificación *f*, falseamiento *m*
falsify ['fɔlsə,faɪ] *vt* **-fied; fying** : falsificar, falsear
falsity ['fɔlsəti] *n*, *pl* **-ties** : falsedad *f*
falter ['fɔltər] *vi* **-tered; -tering** 1 TOT-
TER : tambalearse 2 STAMMER
: titubear, tartamudear 3 WAVER : vacilar
faltering ['fɔltərɪŋ] *adj* : titubeante, vacilante
fame ['feɪm] *n* : fama *f*
famed ['feɪmd] *adj* : famoso, célebre,
afamado
familial [fə'mɪljəl, -liəl] *adj* : familiar
familiar[1] [fə'mɪljər] *adj* 1 KNOWN : familiar, conocido ⟨to be familiar with
: estar familiarizado con⟩ 2 INFORMAL
: familiar, informal 3 INTIMATE : íntimo, de confianza 4 FORWARD : confianzudo, atrevido — **familiarly** *adv*
familiar[2] *n* : espíritu *m* guardián
familiarity [fə,mɪli'ærəti, -,mɪl'jær-] *n*, *pl*
-ties 1 KNOWLEDGE : conocimiento
m, familiaridad *f* 2 INFORMALITY, IN-
TIMACY : confianza *f*, familiaridad *f* 3
FORWARDNESS : exceso *m* de confianza, descaro *m*
familiarize [fə'mɪljə,raɪz] *vt* **-ized; -izing**
1 : familiarizar 2 **to familiarize one-
self** : familiarizarse
family ['fæmli, 'fæmə-] *n*, *pl* **-lies** : familia *f*
family room *n* : living *m*, sala *f* (informal)
family tree *n* : árbol *m* genealógico
famine ['fæmən] *n* : hambre *f*, hambruna
f
famish ['fæmɪʃ] *vi* **to be famished** : estar famélico, estar hambriento, morir
de hambre *fam*
famous ['feɪməs] *adj* : famoso
famously ['feɪməsli] *adv* **to get on famously** : llevarse de maravilla
fan[1] ['fæn] *vt* **fanned; fanning** 1
: abanicar (a una persona), avivar (un
fuego) 2 STIMULATE : avivar, estimular
fan[2] *n* 1 : ventilador *m*, abanico *m* 2
ADMIRER, ENTHUSIAST : aficionado
m, -da *f*; entusiasta *mf*; admirador *m*,
-dora *f*
fanatic[1] [fə'nætɪk] *or* **fanatical** [-tɪ-kəl]
adj : fanático
fanatic[2] *n* : fanático *m*, -ca *f*

fanaticism [fə'næt̬ə,sɪzəm] *n* : fanatismo *m*

fanciful ['fænt̬sɪfəl] *adj* **1** CAPRICIOUS : caprichoso, fantástico, extravagante **2** IMAGINATIVE : imaginativo — **fancifully** *adv*

fancy¹ ['fænt̬si] *vt* **-cied; -cying 1** IMAGINE : imaginarse, figurarse ⟨fancy that! : ¡figúrate!, ¡imagínate!⟩ **2** CRAVE : apetecer, tener ganas de

fancy² *adj* **-cier; -est 1** ELABORATE : elaborado **2** LUXURIOUS : lujoso, elegante — **fancily** ['fænt̬səli] *adv*

fancy³ *n, pl* **-cies 1** LIKING : gusto *m*, afición *f* **2** WHIM : antojo *m*, capricho *m* **3** IMAGINATION : fantasía *f*, imaginación *f*

fandango [fæn'dæŋgo] *n, pl* **-gos** : fandango *m*

fanfare ['fæn,fær] *n* : fanfarria *f*

fang ['fæŋ] *n* : colmillo *m* (de un animal), diente *m* (de una serpiente)

fanlight ['fæn,laɪt] *n* : tragaluz *m*

fantasia [fæn'teɪʒə, -ziə; ,fæntə-'zi:ə] *n* : fantasía *f*

fantasize ['fænt̬ə,saɪz] *vi* **-sized; -sizing** : fantasear

fantastic [fæn'tæstɪk] *adj* **1** UNBELIEVABLE : fantástico, increíble, extraño **2** ENORMOUS : fabuloso, inmenso ⟨fantastic sums : sumas fabulosas⟩ **3** WONDERFUL : estupendo, fantástico, bárbaro *fam*, macanudo *fam* — **fantastically** [-tɪkli] *adv*

fantasy ['fænt̬əsi] *n, pl* **-sies** : fantasía *f*

far¹ ['far] *adv* **farther** ['farðər] *or* **further** ['fər-]; **farthest** *or* **furthest** [-ðəst] **1** : lejos ⟨far from here : lejos de aquí⟩ ⟨to go far : llegar lejos⟩ ⟨as far as Chicago : hasta Chicago⟩ ⟨far away : a lo lejos⟩ **2** MUCH : muy, mucho ⟨far bigger : mucho más grande⟩ ⟨far superior : muy superior⟩ ⟨it's by far the best : es con mucho el mejor⟩ **3** (*expressing degree or extent*) ⟨the results are far off : salieron muy inexactos los resultados⟩ ⟨to go so far as : decir tanto como⟩ ⟨to go far enough : tener el alcance necesario⟩ **4** (*expressing progress*) ⟨the work is far advanced : el trabajo está muy avanzado⟩ ⟨to take (something) too far : llevar (algo) demasiado lejos⟩ **5 far and wide** : por todas partes **6 far from it!** : ¡todo lo contrario! **7 so far** : hasta ahora, todavía

far² *adj* **farther** *or* **further; farthest** *or* **furthest 1** REMOTE : lejano, remoto ⟨the Far East : el Lejano Oriente, el Extremo Oriente⟩ ⟨a far country : un país lejano⟩ **2** LONG : largo ⟨a far journey : un viaje largo⟩ **3** EXTREME : extremo ⟨the far right : la extrema derecha⟩ ⟨at the far end of the room : en el otro extremo de la sala⟩

faraway ['farə,weɪ] *adj* : remoto, lejano

farce ['fars] *n* : farsa *f*

farcical ['farsɪkəl] *adj* : absurdo, ridículo

fare¹ ['fær] *vi* **fared; faring** : ir, salir ⟨how did you fare? : ¿cómo te fue?⟩

fare² *n* **1** : pasaje *m*, billete *m*, boleto *m* ⟨half fare : medio pasaje⟩ **2** FOOD : comida *f*

farewell¹ [fær'wɛl] *adj* : de despedida

farewell² *n* : despedida *f*

far–fetched ['far'fɛtʃt] *adj* : improbable, exagerado

farina [fə'ri:nə] *n* : harina *f*

farm¹ ['farm] *vt* **1** : cultivar, labrar **2** : criar (animales) — *vi* : ser agricultor

farm² *n* : granja *f*, hacienda *f*, finca *f*, estancia *f*

farmer ['farmər] *n* : agricultor *m*, granjero *m*

farmhand ['farm,hænd] *n* : peón *m*

farmhouse ['farm,haʊs] *n* : granja *f*, vivienda *f* del granjero, casa *f* de hacienda

farming ['farmɪŋ] *n* : labranza *f*, cultivo *m*, crianza *f* (de animales)

farmland ['farm,lænd] *n* : tierras *fpl* de labranza

farmyard ['farm,jard] *n* : corral *m*

far–off ['far,ɔf, -'ɔf] *adj* : remoto, distante, lejano

far–reaching ['far'ri:tʃɪŋ] *adj* : de gran alcance

farsighted ['far,saɪt̬əd] *adj* **1** : hipermétrope **2** JUDICIOUS : con visión de futuro, previsor, precavido

farsightedness ['far,saɪt̬ədnəs] *n* **1** : hipermetropía *f* **2** PRUDENCE : previsión *f*

farther¹ ['farðər] *adv* **1** AHEAD : más lejos (en el espacio), más adelante (en el tiempo) **2** MORE : más

farther² *adj* : más lejano, más remoto

farthermost ['farðər,mo:st] *adj* : (el) más lejano

farthest¹ ['farðəst] *adv* **1** : lo más lejos ⟨I jumped farthest : salté lo más lejos⟩ **2** : lo más avanzado ⟨he progressed farthest : progresó al punto más avanzado⟩ **3** : más ⟨the farthest developed plan : el plan más desarrollado⟩

farthest² *adj* : más lejano

fascicle ['fæsɪkəl] *n* : fascículo *m*

fascinate ['fæsən,eɪt] *vt* **-nated; -nating** : fascinar, cautivar

fascinating ['fæsən,eɪt̬ɪŋ] *adj* : fascinante

fascination [,fæsən'eɪʃən] *n* : fascinación *f*

fascism ['fæʃ,ɪzəm] *n* : fascismo *m*

fascist¹ ['fæʃɪst] *adj* : fascista

fascist² *n* : fascista *mf*

fashion¹ ['fæʃən] *vt* : formar, moldear

fashion² *n* **1** MANNER : manera *f*, modo *m* **2** CUSTOM : costumbre *f* **3** STYLE : moda *f*

fashionable ['fæʃənəbəl] *adj* : de moda, chic

fashionably ['fæʃənəbli] *adv* : a la moda

fast¹ ['fæst] *vi* : ayunar

fast² *adv* **1** SECURELY : firmemente, seguramente ⟨to hold fast : agarrarse bien⟩ **2** RAPIDLY : rápidamente, rápi-do, de prisa **3 to run fast** : ir adelan-tado (dícese de un reloj) **4** SOUNDLY : profundamente ⟨fast asleep : profun-damente dormido⟩

fast³ *adj* **1** SECURE : firme, seguro ⟨to make fast : amarrar (un barco)⟩ **2** FAITHFUL : leal ⟨fast friends : amigos leales⟩ **3** RAPID : rápido, veloz **4** : ade-lantado ⟨my watch is fast : tengo el reloj adelantado⟩ **5** DEEP : profundo ⟨a fast sleep : un sueño profundo⟩ **6** COLORFAST : inalterable, que no des-tiñe **7** DISSOLUTE : extravagante, disi-pado, disoluto

fast⁴ *n* : ayuno *m*

fasten [ˈfæsən] *vt* **1** ATTACH : sujetar, atar **2** FIX : fijar ⟨to fasten one's eyes on : fijar los ojos en⟩ **3** SECURE : abrochar (ropa o cinturones), atar (cordones), cerrar (una maleta) — *vi* : abrocharse, cerrar

fastener [ˈfæsənər] *n* : cierre *m*, sujeta-dor *m*

fastening [ˈfæsəniŋ] *n* : cierre *m*, suje-tador *m*

fast food *n* : comida *f* rápida

fastidious [fæsˈtɪdiəs] *adj* : quisquilloso, exigente — **fastidiously** *adv*

fat¹ [ˈfæt] *adj* **fatter; fattest 1** OBESE : gordo, obeso **2** THICK : grueso

fat² *n* : grasa *f*

fatal [ˈfeɪtəl] *adj* **1** DEADLY : mortal **2** ILL-FATED : malhadado, fatal **3** MO-MENTOUS : fatídico

fatalism [ˈfeɪtəlˌɪzəm] *n* : fatalismo *m*

fatalist [ˈfeɪtəlɪst] *n* : fatalista *mf*

fatalistic [ˌfeɪtəlˈɪstɪk] *adj* : fatalista

fatality [feɪˈtæləti, fə-] *n, pl* **-ties** : vícti-ma *f* mortal

fatally [ˈfeɪtəli] *adv* : mortalmente

fate [ˈfeɪt] *n* **1** DESTINY : destino *m* **2** END, LOT : final *m*, suerte *f*

fated [ˈfeɪtəd] *adj* : predestinado

fateful [ˈfeɪtfəl] *adj* **1** MOMENTOUS : fatídico, aciago **2** PROPHETIC : profético — **fatefully** *adv*

father¹ [ˈfɑðər] *vt* : engendrar

father² *n* **1** : padre *m* ⟨my father and my mother : mi padre y mi madre⟩ ⟨Fa-ther Smith : el padre Smith⟩ **2 the Fa-ther** GOD : el Padre, Dios *m*

fatherhood [ˈfɑðərˌhʊd] *n* : paternidad *f*

father-in-law [ˈfɑðərɪnˌlɔ] *n, pl* **fa-thers-in-law** : suegro *m*

fatherland [ˈfɑðərˌlænd] *n* : patria *f*

fatherless [ˈfɑðərləs] *adj* : huérfano de padre, sin padre

fatherly [ˈfɑðərli] *adj* : paternal

fathom¹ [ˈfæðəm] *vt* UNDERSTAND : en-tender, comprender

fathom² *n* : braza *f*

fatigue¹ [fəˈtiːg] *vt* **-tigued; -tiguing** : fatigar, cansar

fatigue² *n* : fatiga *f*

fatness [ˈfætnəs] *n* : gordura *f* (de una persona o un animal), grosor *m* (de un objeto)

fatten [ˈfætən] *vt* : engordar, cebar

fatty [ˈfæti] *adj* **fattier; -est** : graso, gra-soso, adiposo (dícese de los tejidos)

fatuous [ˈfætʃuəs] *adj* : necio, fatuo — **fatuously** *adv*

faucet [ˈfɔsət] *n* : llave *f*, canilla *f Arg, Uru*, grifo *m*

fault¹ [ˈfɔlt] *vt* : encontrar defectos a

fault² *n* **1** SHORTCOMING : defecto *m*, falta *f* **2** DEFECT : falta *f*, defecto *m*, falla *f* **3** BLAME : culpa *f* **4** FRACTURE : falla *f* (geológica)

faultfinder [ˈfɔltˌfaɪndər] *n* : criticón *m*, -cona *f*

faultfinding [ˈfɔltˌfaɪndɪŋ] *n* : crítica *f*

faultless [ˈfɔltləs] *adj* : sin culpa, sin im-perfecciones, impecable

faultlessly [ˈfɔltləsli] *adv* : impecable-mente, perfectamente

faulty [ˈfɔlti] *adj* **faultier; -est** : defectu-oso, imperfecto — **faultily** [ˈfɔltəli] *adv*

fauna [ˈfɔnə] *n* : fauna *f*

faux [ˈfo] *adj* : de imitación

faux pas [ˌfoːˈpɑ] *n, pl* **faux pas** [*same or* -ˈpɑz] : metedura *f* de pata *fam*

favor¹ [ˈfeɪvər] *vt* **1** SUPPORT : estar a fa-vor de, ser partidario de, apoyar **2** OBLIGE : hacerle un favor a **3** PREFER : preferir **4** RESEMBLE : parecerse a, salir a

favor² *n* : favor *m* ⟨in favor of : a favor de⟩ ⟨an error in his favor : un error a su favor⟩

favorable [ˈfeɪvərəbəl] *adj* : favorable, propicio

favorably [ˈfeɪvərəbli] *adv* : favorable-mente, bien

favorite¹ [ˈfeɪvərət] *adj* : favorito, preferido

favorite² *n* : favorito *m*, -ta *f*; preferido *m*, -da *f*

favoritism [ˈfeɪvərəˌtɪzəm] *n* : fa-voritismo *m*

fawn¹ [ˈfɔn] *vi* : adular, lisonjear

fawn² *n* : cervato *m*

fax [ˈfæks] *n* : facsímil *m*, facsímile *m*

faze [ˈfeɪz] *vt* **fazed; fazing** : desconcer-tar, perturbar

fear¹ [ˈfɪr] *vt* : temer, tener miedo de — *vi* : temer

fear² *n* : miedo *m*, temor *m* ⟨for fear of : por temor a⟩

fearful [ˈfɪrfəl] *adj* **1** FRIGHTENING : es-pantoso, aterrador, horrible **2** FRIGHT-ENED : temeroso, miedoso

fearfully [ˈfɪrfəli] *adv* **1** EXTREMELY : ex-tremadamente, terriblemente **2** TIMID-LY : con temor

fearless [ˈfɪrləs] *adj* : intrépido, impávi-do

fearlessly [ˈfɪrləsli] *adv* : sin temor

fearlessness [ˈfɪrləsnəs] *n* : intrepidez *f*, impavidez *f*

fearsome [ˈfɪrsəm] *adj* : aterrador

feasibility [ˌfiːzəˈbɪləti] *n* : viabilidad *f*, factibilidad *f*

feasible [ˈfiːzəbəl] *adj* : viable, factible, realizable

feast¹ ['fi:st] *vi* : banquetear — *vt* **1** : agasajar, festejar **2 to feast one's eyes on** : regalarse la vista con

feast² *n* **1** BANQUET : banquete *m*, festín *m* **2** FESTIVAL : fiesta *f*

feat ['fi:t] *n* : proeza *f*, hazaña *f*

feather¹ ['fɛðər] *vt* **1** : emplumar **2 to feather one's nest** : hacer su agosto

feather² *n* **1** : pluma *f* **2 a feather in one's cap** : un triunfo personal

feathered ['fɛðərd] *adj* : con plumas

feathery ['fɛðəri] *adj* **1** DOWNY : plumoso **2** LIGHT : liviano

feature¹ ['fi:tʃər] *v* **-tured; -turing** *vt* **1** IMAGINE : imaginarse **2** PRESENT : presentar — *vi* : figurar

feature² *n* **1** CHARACTERISTIC : característica *f*, rasgo *m* **2** : largometraje *m* (en el cine), artículo *m* (en un periódico), documental *m* (en la televisión) **3 features** *npl* : rasgos *mpl*, facciones *fpl* ⟨delicate features : facciones delicadas⟩

February ['fɛbjʊ̩ri, 'fɛbʊ-, 'fbrʊ-] *n* : febrero *m*

fecal ['fi:kəl] *adj* : fecal

feces ['fi:ˌsi:z] *npl* : heces *fpl*, excrementos *mpl*

feckless ['fɛkləs] *adj* : irresponsable

fecund ['fɛkənd, 'fi:-] *adj* : fecundo

fecundity [fɪ'kʌndəti, fɛ-] *n* : fecundidad *f*

federal ['fɛdrəl, -dərəl] *adj* : federal

federalism ['fɛdrə̩lɪzəm, -dərə-] *n* : federalismo *m*

federalist¹ ['fɛdrəlɪst, -dərə-] *adj* : federalista

federalist² *n* : federalista *mf*

federate ['fɛdə̩reɪt] *vt* **-ated; -ating** : federar

federation [ˌfɛdə'reɪʃən] *n* : federación *f*

fedora [fɪ'dorə] *n* : sombrero *m* flexible de fieltro

fed up *adj* : harto

fee ['fi:] *n* **1** : honorarios *mpl* (a un médico, un abogado, etc.) **2 entrance fee** : entrada *f*

feeble ['fi:bəl] *adj* **-bler; -blest 1** WEAK : débil, endeble **2** INEFFECTIVE : flojo, pobre, poco convincente

feebleminded [ˌfi:bəl'maɪndəd] *adj* **1** : débil mental **2** FOOLISH, STUPID : imbécil, tonto

feebleness ['fi:bəlnəs] *n* : debilidad *f*

feebly ['fi:bli] *adv* : débilmente

feed¹ ['fi:d] *v* **fed** ['fɛd]; **feeding** *vt* **1** : dar de comer a, nutrir, alimentar (a una persona) **2** : alimentar (un fuego o una máquina), proveer (información), introducir (datos) — *vi* : comer, alimentarse

feed² *n* **1** NOURISHMENT : alimento *m* **2** FODDER : pienso *m*

feedback ['fi:dˌbæk] *n* **1** : realimentación *f* (electrónica) **2** RESPONSE : reacción *f*

feeder ['fi:dər] *n* : comedero *m* (para animales)

feel¹ ['fi:l] *v* **felt** ['fɪlt]; **feeling** *vi* **1** : sentirse, encontrarse ⟨I feel tired : me siento cansada⟩ ⟨he feels hungry : tiene hambre⟩ ⟨she feels like a fool : se siente como una idiota⟩ ⟨to feel like doing something : tener ganas de hacer algo⟩ **2** SEEM : parecer ⟨it feels like spring : parece primavera⟩ **3** THINK : parecerse, opinar, pensar ⟨how does he feel about that? : ¿qué opina él de eso?⟩ — *vt* **1** TOUCH : tocar, palpar **2** SENSE : sentir ⟨to feel the cold : sentir el frío⟩ **3** CONSIDER : sentir, creer, considerar ⟨to feel (it) necessary : creer necesario⟩

feel² *n* **1** SENSATION, TOUCH : sensación *f*, tacto *m* **2** ATMOSPHERE : ambiente *m*, atmósfera *f* **3 to have a feel for** : tener un talento especial para

feeler ['fi:lər] *n* : antena *f*, tentáculo *m*

feeling ['fi:lɪŋ] *n* **1** SENSATION : sensación *f*, sensibilidad *f* **2** EMOTION : sentimiento *m* **3** OPINION : opinión *f* **4 feelings** *npl* SENSIBILITIES : sentimientos *mpl* ⟨to hurt someone's feelings : herir los sentimientos de alguien⟩

feet → **foot**

feign ['feɪn] *vt* : simular, aparentar, fingir

feint¹ ['feɪnt] *vi* : fintar, fintear

feint² *n* : finta *f*

feldspar ['fɛldˌspar] *n* : feldespato *m*

felicitate [fɪ'lɪsə̩teɪt] *vt* **-tated; -tating** : felicitar, congratular

felicitation [fɪˌlɪsə'teɪʃən] *n* : felicitación *f*

felicitous [fɪ'lɪsətəs] *adj* : acertado, oportuno

feline¹ ['fi:ˌlaɪn] *adj* : felino

feline² *n* : felino *m*, -na *f*

fell¹ ['fɛl] *vt* : talar (un árbol), derribar (a una persona)

fell² → **fall**

fellow ['fɛˌlo:] *n* **1** COMPANION : compañero *m*, -ra *f*; camarada *mf* **2** ASSOCIATE : socio *m*, -cia *f* **3** MAN : tipo *m*, hombre *m*

fellowman [ˌfɛlo'mæn] *n, pl* **-men** : prójimo *m*, semejante *m*

fellowship ['fɛloˌʃɪp] *n* **1** COMPANIONSHIP : camaradería *f*, compañerismo *m* **2** ASSOCIATION : fraternidad *f* **3** GRANT : beca *f* (de investigación)

felon ['fɛlən] *n* : malhechor *m*, -chora *f*; criminal *mf*

felonious [fə'lo:niəs] *adj* : criminal

felony ['fɛləni] *n, pl* **-nies** : delito *m* grave

felt¹ ['fɛlt] *n* : fieltro *m*

felt² → **feel**

female¹ ['fi:ˌmeɪl] *adj* : femenino

female² *n* **1** : hembra *f* (de animal) **2** WOMAN : mujer *f*

feminine ['fɛmənən] *adj* : femenino

femininity [ˌfɛmə'nɪnəti] *n* : feminidad *f*, femineidad *f*

feminism ['fɛmə̩nɪzəm] *n* : feminismo *m*

feminist¹ ['fɛmənɪst] *adj* : feminista

feminist² *n* : feminista *mf*

femoral ['fɛmərəl] *adj* : femoral
femur ['fiːmər] *n, pl* **femurs** *or* **femora** ['fɛmərə] : fémur *m*
fence¹ ['fɛnts] *v* **fenced; fencing** *vt* : vallar, cercar — *vi* : hacer esgrima
fence² *n* : cerca *f*, valla *f*, cerco *m*
fencer ['fɛntsər] *n* : esgrimista *mf*; esgrimidor *m*, -dora *f*
fencing ['fɛntsɪŋ] *n* **1** : esgrima *m* (deporte) **2** : materiales *mpl* para cercas **3** ENCLOSURE : cercado *m*
fend ['fɛnd] *vt* **to fend off** : rechazar (un enemigo), parar (un golpe), eludir (una pregunta) — *vi* **to fend for oneself** : arreglárselas sólo, valerse por sí mismo
fender ['fɛndər] *n* : guardabarros *mpl*, salpicadera *f Mex*
fennel ['fɛnəl] *n* : hinojo *m*
ferment¹ [fər'mɛnt] *v* : fermentar
ferment² ['fər,mɛnt] *n* **1** : fermento *m* (en la química) **2** TURMOIL : agitación *f*, conmoción *f*
fermentation [,fərmən'teɪʃən, -,mɛn-] *n* : fermentación *f*
fern ['fərn] *n* : helecho *m*
ferocious [fə'roːʃəs] *adj* : feroz — **ferociously** *adv*
ferociousness [fə'roːʃəsnəs] *n* : ferocidad *f*
ferocity [fə'rasəti] *n* : ferocidad *f*
ferret¹ ['fɛrət] *vi* SNOOP : hurgar, husmear — *vt* **to ferret out** : descubrir
ferret² *n* : hurón *m*
ferric ['fɛrɪk] *or* **ferrous** ['fɛrəs] *adj* : férrico
Ferris wheel ['fɛrɪs] *n* : noria *f*
ferry¹ ['fɛri] *vt* **-ried; -rying** : llevar, transportar
ferry² *n, pl* **-ries** : transbordador *m*, ferry *m*
ferryboat ['fɛri,boːt] *n* : transbordador *m*, ferry *m*
fertile ['fərtəl] *adj* : fértil, fecundo
fertility [fər'tɪləti] *n* : fertilidad *f*
fertilization [,fərtələ'zeɪʃən] *n* : fertilización *f* (del suelo), fecundación (de un huevo)
fertilize ['fərtəl,aɪz] *vt* **-ized; -izing 1** : fecundar (un huevo) **2** : fertilizar, abonar (el suelo)
fertilizer ['fərtəl,aɪzər] *n* : fertilizante *m*, abono *m*
fervent ['fərvənt] *adj* : ferviente, fervoroso, ardiente — **fervently** *adv*
fervid ['fərvɪd] *adj* : ardiente, apasionado — **fervidly** *adv*
fervor ['fərvər] *n* : fervor *m*, ardor *m*
fester ['fɛstər] *vi* : enconarse, supurar
festival ['fɛstəvəl] *n* : fiesta *f*, festividad *f*, festival *m*
festive ['fɛstɪv] *adj* : festivo — **festively** *adv*
festivity [fɛs'tɪvəti] *n, pl* **-ties** : festividad *f*, celebración *f*
festoon¹ [fɛs'tuːn] *vt* : adornar, engalanar
festoon² *n* GARLAND : guirnalda *f*
fetal ['fiːtəl] *adj* : fetal

fetch ['fɛtʃ] *vt* **1** BRING : traer, recoger, ir a buscar **2** REALIZE : realizar, venderse por ⟨the jewelry fetched $10,000 : las joyas se vendieron por $10,000⟩
fetching ['fɛtʃɪŋ] *adj* : atractivo, encantador
fête¹ ['feɪt, 'fɛt] *vt* **fêted; fêting** : festejar, agasajar
fête² *n* : fiesta *f*
fetid ['fɛtəd] *adj* : fétido
fetish ['fɛtɪʃ] *n* : fetiche *m*
fetlock ['fɛt,lak] *n* : espolón *m*
fetter ['fɛtər] *vt* : encadenar, poner grillos a
fetters ['fɛtərz] *npl* : grillos *mpl*, grilletes *mpl*, cadenas *fpl*
fettle ['fɛtəl] *n* **in fine fettle** : en buena forma, en plena forma
fetus ['fiːtəs] *n* : feto *m*
feud¹ ['fjuːd] *vi* : pelear, contender
feud² *n* : contienda *f*, enemistad *f* (heredada)
feudal ['fjuːdəl] *adj* : feudal
feudalism ['fjuːdəl,ɪzəm] *n* : feudalismo *m*
fever ['fiːvər] *n* : fiebre *f*, calentura *f*
feverish ['fiːvərɪʃ] *adj* **1** : afiebrado, con fiebre, febril **2** FRANTIC : febril, frenético
few¹ ['fjuː] *adj* : pocos ⟨with few exceptions : con pocas excepciones⟩ ⟨a few times : varias veces⟩
few² *pron* **1** : pocos ⟨few (of them) were ready : pocos estaban listos⟩ **2 a few** : algunos, unos cuantos **3 few and far between** : contados
fewer ['fjuːər] *pron* : menos ⟨the fewer the better : cuantos menos mejor⟩
fez ['fɛz] *n, pl* **fezzes** : fez *m*
fiancé [,fiː,ɑn'seɪ, ,fiː'ɑn,seɪ] *n* : prometido *m*, novio *m*
fiancée [,fiː,ɑn'seɪ, ,fiː'ɑn,seɪ] *n* : prometida *f*, novia *f*
fiasco [fi'æs,koː] *n, pl* **-coes** : fiasco *m*, fracaso *m*
fiat ['fiː,ɑt, -,æt, -ət; 'faɪət, -,æt] *n* : decreto *m*, orden *m*
fib¹ ['fɪb] *vi* **fibbed; fibbing** : decir mentirillas
fib² *n* : mentirilla *f*, bola *f fam*
fibber ['fɪbər] *n* : mentirosillo *m*, -lla *f*; cuentista *mf fam*
fiber *or* **fibre** ['faɪbər] *n* : fibra *f*
fiberboard ['faɪbər,bord] *n* : cartón *m* madera
fiberglass ['faɪbər,glæs] *n* : fibra *f* de vidrio
fibrillate ['fɪbrə,leɪt, 'faɪ-] *vi* **-lated; -lating** : fibrilar
fibrillation [,fɪbrə'leɪʃən, ,faɪ-] *n* : fibrilación *f*
fibrous ['faɪbrəs] *adj* : fibroso
fibula ['fɪbjələ] *n, pl* **-lae** [-,liː; -,laɪ] *or* **-las** : peroné *m*
fickle ['fɪkəl] *adj* : inconstante, voluble, veleidoso
fickleness ['fɪkəlnəs] *n* : volubilidad *f*, inconstancia *f*, veleidad *f*

fiction ['fɪkʃən] *n* : ficción *f*
fictional ['fɪkʃənəl] *adj* : ficticio
fictitious [fɪk'tɪʃəs] *adj* **1** IMAGINARY : ficticio, imaginario **2** FALSE : falso, ficticio
fiddle[1] ['fɪdəl] *vi* **-dled; -dling 1** : tocar el violín **2 to fiddle with** : juguetear con, toquetear
fiddle[2] *n* : violín *m*
fiddler ['fɪdlər, 'fɪdələr] *n* : violinista *mf*
fiddlesticks ['fɪdəl‚stɪks] *interj* : ¡tonterías!
fidelity [fə'dɛləti, faɪ-] *n, pl* **-ties** : fidelidad *f*
fidget[1] ['fɪdʒət] *vi* **1** : moverse, estarse inquieto **2 to fidget with** : juguetear con
fidget[2] *n* **1** : persona *f* inquieta **2 fidgets** *npl* RESTLESSNESS : inquietud *f*
fidgety ['fɪdʒəti] *adj* : inquieto
fiduciary[1] [fə'du:ʃi‚ɛri, -'dju:-, -ʃəri] *adj* : fiduciario
fiduciary[2] *n, pl* **-ries** : fiduciario *m*, -ria *f*
field[1] ['fi:ld] *vt* : interceptar y devolver (una pelota), presentar (un candidato), sortear (una pregunta)
field[2] *adj* : de campaña, de campo ⟨field hospital : hospital de campaña⟩ ⟨field goal : gol de campo⟩ ⟨field trip : viaje de estudio⟩
field[3] *n* **1** : campo *m* (de cosechas, de batalla, de magnetismo) **2** : campo *m*, cancha *f* (en deportes) **3** : campo *m* (de trabajo), esfera *f* (de actividades)
fielder ['fi:ldər] *n* : jugador *m*, -dora *f* de campo; fildeador *m*, -dora *f*
field glasses *n* : binoculares *mpl*, gemelos *mpl*
fiend ['fi:nd] *n* **1** DEMON : demonio *m* **2** EVILDOER : persona *f* maligna; malvado *m*, -da *f* **3** FANATIC : fanático *m*, -ca *f*
fiendish ['fi:ndɪʃ] *adj* : diabólico — **fiendishly** *adv*
fierce ['fɪrs] *adj* **fiercer; -est 1** FEROCIOUS : fiero, feroz **2** HEATED : acalorado **3** INTENSE : intenso, violento, fuerte — **fiercely** *adv*
fierceness ['fɪrsnəs] *n* **1** FEROCITY : ferocidad *f*, fiereza *f* **2** INTENSITY : intensidad *f*, violencia *f*
fieriness ['faɪərinəs] *n* : pasión *f*, ardor *m*
fiery ['faɪəri] *adj* **fierier; -est 1** BURNING : ardiente, llameante **2** GLOWING : encendido **3** PASSIONATE : acalorado, ardiente, fogoso
fiesta [fi'ɛstə] *n* : fiesta *f*
fife ['faɪf] *n* : pífano *m*
fifteen[1] [fɪf'ti:n] *adj* : quince
fifteen[2] *n* : quince *m*
fifteenth[1] [fɪf'ti:nθ] *adj* : decimoquinto
fifteenth[2] *n* **1** : decimoquinto *m*, -ta *f* (en una serie) **2** : quinceavo *m*, quinceava parte *f*
fifth[1] ['fɪfθ] *adj* : quinto

fifth[2] *n* **1** : quinto *m*, -ta *f* (en una serie) **2** : quinto *m*, quinta parte *f* **3** : quinta *f* (en la música)
fiftieth[1] ['fɪftiəθ] *adj* : quincuagésimo
fiftieth[2] *n* **1** : quincuagésimo *m*, -ma *f* (en una serie) **2** : cincuentavo *m*, cincuentava parte *f*
fifty[1] ['fɪfti] *adj* : cincuenta
fifty[2] *n, pl* **-ties** : cincuenta *m*
fifty–fifty[1] [‚fɪfti'fɪfti] *adv* : a medias, mitad y mitad
fifty–fifty[2] *adj* **to have a fifty–fifty chance** : tener un cincuenta por ciento de posibilidades
fig ['fɪg] *n* : higo *m*
fight[1] ['faɪt] *v* **fought** ['fɔt]; **fighting** *vi* : luchar, combatir, pelear — *vt* : luchar contra, combatir contra
fight[2] *n* **1** COMBAT : lucha *f*, pelea *f*, combate *m* **2** MATCH : pelea *f*, combate *m* (en boxeo) **3** QUARREL : disputa *f*, pelea *f*, pleito *m*
fighter ['faɪtər] *n* **1** COMBATANT : luchador *m*, -dora *f*; combatiente *mf* **2** BOXER : boxeador *m*, -dora *f*
figment ['fɪgmənt] *n* **figment of the imagination** : producto *m* de la imaginación
figurative ['fɪgjərətɪv, -gə-] *adj* : figurado, metafórico
figuratively ['fɪgjərətɪvli, -gə-] *adv* : en sentido figurado, de manera metafórica
figure[1] ['fɪgjər, -gər] *v* **-ured; -uring** *vt* **1** CALCULATE : calcular **2** ESTIMATE : figurarse, calcular ⟨he figured it was possible : se figuró que era posible⟩ — *vi* **1** FEATURE, STAND OUT : figurar, destacar **2 that figures!** : ¡obvio!, ¡no me extraña nada!
figure[2] *n* **1** DIGIT : número *m*, cifra *f* **2** PRICE : precio *m*, cifra *f* **3** PERSONAGE : figura *f*, personaje *m* **4** : figura *f*, tipo *m*, físico *m* ⟨to have a good figure : tener buen tipo, tener un buen físico⟩ **5** DESIGN, OUTLINE : figura *f* **6 figures** *npl* : aritmética *f*
figurehead ['fɪgjər‚hɛd, -gər-] *n* : testaferro *m*, líder *mf* sin poder
figure of speech *n* : figura *f* retórica, figura *f* de hablar
figure out *vt* **1** UNDERSTAND : entender **2** RESOLVE : resolver (un problema, etc.)
figurine [‚fɪgjə'ri:n] *n* : estatuilla *f*
Fijian ['fi:ʤiən, fɪ'ji:ən] *n* : fijiano *m*, -na *f* — **Fijian** *adj*
filament ['fɪləmənt] *n* : filamento *m*
filbert ['fɪlbərt] *n* : avellana *f*
filch ['fɪltʃ] *vt* : hurtar, birlar *fam*
file[1] ['faɪl] *v* **filed; filing** *vt* **1** CLASSIFY : clasificar **2** : archivar (documentos) **3** SUBMIT : presentar ⟨to file charges : presentar cargos⟩ **4** SMOOTH : limar — *vi* : desfilar, entrar (o salir) en fila
file[2] *n* **1** : lima *f* ⟨nail file : lima de uñas⟩ **2** DOCUMENTS : archivo *m* **3** LINE : fila *f*

filial ['fɪliəl, 'fɪljəl] *adj* : filial
filibuster¹ ['fɪlə,bʌstər] *vi* : practicar el obstruccionismo
filibuster² *n* : obstruccionismo *m*
filibusterer ['fɪlə,bʌstərər] *n* : obstruccionista *mf*
filigree ['fɪlə,gri:] *n* : filigrana *f*
Filipino [,fɪlə'pi:no:] *n* : filipino *m*, -na *f* — **Filipino** *adj*
fill¹ ['fɪl] *vt* **1** : llenar, ocupar ⟨to fill a cup : llenar una taza⟩ ⟨to fill a room : ocupar una sala⟩ **2** STUFF : rellenar **3** PLUG : tapar, rellenar, empastar (un diente) **4** SATISFY : cumplir con, satisfacer **5** *or* **to fill out** : llenar, re-llenar ⟨to fill out a form : rellenar un formulario⟩
fill² *n* **1** FILLING, STUFFING : relleno *m* **2 to eat one's fill** : comer lo suficiente **3 to have one's fill of** : estar harto de
filler ['fɪlər] *n* : relleno *m*
fillet¹ ['fɪlət, fɪ'leɪ, 'fɪ,leɪ] *vt* : cortar en filetes
fillet² *n* : filete *m*
fill in *vt* INFORM : informar, poner al corriente — *vi* **to fill in for** : reemplazar a
filling ['fɪlɪŋ] *n* **1** : relleno *m* **2** : empaste *m* (de un diente)
filling station → **gas station**
filly ['fɪli] *n*, *pl* **-lies** : potra *f*, potranca *f*
film¹ ['fɪlm] *vt* : filmar — *vi* : rodar
film² *n* **1** COATING : capa *f*, película *f* **2** : película *f* (fotográfica) **3** MOVIE : película *f*, filme *m*
filmmaker ['fɪlm,meɪkər] *n* : cineasta *mf*
filmy ['fɪlmi] *adj* **filmier; -est 1** GAUZY : diáfano, vaporoso **2** : cubierto de una película
filter¹ ['fɪltər] *vt* : filtrar
filter² *n* : filtro *m*
filth ['fɪlθ] *n* : mugre *f*, porquería *f*, roña *f*
filthiness ['fɪlθinəs] *n* : suciedad *f*
filthy ['fɪlθi] *adj* **filthier; -est 1** DIRTY : mugriento, sucio **2** OBSCENE : obsceno, indecente
filtration [fɪl'treɪʃən] *n* : filtración *f*
fin ['fɪn] *n* **1** : aleta *f* **2** : alerón *m* (de un automóvil o un avión)
finagle [fə'neɪgəl] *vt* **-gled; -gling** : arreglárselas para conseguir
final¹ ['faɪnəl] *adj* **1** DEFINITIVE : definitivo, final, inapelable **2** ULTIMATE : final **3** LAST : último, final
final² *n* **1** : final *f* (en deportes) **2 finals** *npl* : exámenes *mpl* finales
finale [fɪ'næli, -'nɑ-] *n* : final *m* ⟨grand finale : final triunfal⟩
finalist ['faɪnəlɪst] *n* : finalista *mf*
finality [faɪ'næləti, fə-] *n, pl* **-ties** : finalidad *f*
finalize ['faɪnəl,aɪz] *vt* **-ized; -izing** : finalizar
finally ['faɪnəli] *adv* **1** LASTLY : por último, finalmente **2** EVENTUALLY : por fin, al final **3** DEFINITIVELY : definitivamente

finance¹ [fə'nænts, 'faɪ,nænts] *vt* **-nanced; -nancing** : financiar
finance² *n* **1** : finanzas *fpl* **2 finances** *npl* RESOURCES : recursos *mpl* financieros
financial [fə'næntʃəl, faɪ-] *adj* : financiero, económico
financially [fə'næntʃəli, faɪ-] *adv* : económicamente
financier [,fɪnən'sɪr, ,faɪ,næn-] *n* : financiero *m*, -ra *f*; financista *mf*
financing [fə'næntsɪŋ, 'faɪ,næntsɪŋ] *n* : financiación *f*, financiamiento *m*
finch ['fɪntʃ] *n* : pinzón *m*
find¹ ['faɪnd] *vt* **found** ['faʊnd]; **finding 1** LOCATE : encontrar, hallar ⟨I can't find it : no lo encuentro⟩ ⟨to find one's way : encontrar el camino, orientarse⟩ **2** DISCOVER, REALIZE : descubrir, darse cuenta de ⟨he found it difficult : descubrió que era difícil⟩ **3** DECLARE : declarar, hallar ⟨they found him guilty : lo declararon culpable⟩
find² *n* : hallazgo *m*
finder ['faɪndər] *n* : descubridor *m*, -dora *f*
finding ['faɪndɪŋ] *n* **1** FIND : hallazgo *m* **2 findings** *npl* : conclusiones *fpl*
find out *vt* DISCOVER : descubrir, averiguar — *vi* LEARN : enterarse
fine¹ ['faɪn] *vt* **fined; fining** : multar
fine² *adj* **finer; -est 1** PURE : puro (dícese del oro y de la plata) **2** THIN : fino, delgado **3** : fino ⟨fine sand : arena fina⟩ **4** SMALL : pequeño, minúsculo ⟨fine print : letras minúsculas⟩ **5** SUBTLE : sutil, delicado **6** EXCELLENT : excelente, magnífico, selecto **7** FAIR : bueno ⟨it's a fine day : hace buen tiempo⟩ **8** EXQUISITE : exquisito, delicado, fino **9 fine arts** : bellas artes *fpl*
fine³ *n* : multa *f*
finely ['faɪnli] *adv* **1** EXCELLENTLY : con arte **2** ELEGANTLY : elegantemente **3** PRECISELY : con precisión **4 to chop finely** : picar muy fino, picar en trozos pequeños
fineness ['faɪnnəs] *n* **1** EXCELLENCE : excelencia *f* **2** ELEGANCE : elegancia *f*, refinamiento *m* **3** DELICACY : delicadeza *f*, lo fino **4** PRECISION : precisión *f* **5** SUBTLETY : sutileza *f* **6** PURITY : ley *f* (de oro y plata)
finery ['faɪnəri] *n* : galas *fpl*, adornos *mpl*
finesse¹ [fə'nɛs] *vt* **-nessed; -nessing** : ingeniar
finesse² *n* **1** REFINEMENT : refinamiento *m*, finura *f* **2** TACT : delicadeza *f*, tacto *m*, diplomacia *f* **3** CRAFTINESS : astucia *f*
finger¹ ['fɪŋgər] *vt* **1** HANDLE : tocar, toquetear **2** ACCUSE : acusar, delatar
finger² *n* : dedo *m*
fingerling ['fɪŋgərlɪŋ] *n* : pez *m* pequeño y joven
fingernail ['fɪŋgər,neɪl] *n* : uña *f*
fingerprint¹ ['fɪŋgər,prɪnt] *vt* : tomar las huellas digitales a

fingerprint² *n* : huella *f* digital
fingertip ['fɪŋɡər,tɪp] *n* : punta *f* del dedo, yema *f* del dedo
finicky ['fɪnɪki] *adj* : maniático, melindroso, mañoso
finish¹ ['fɪnɪʃ] *vt* **1** COMPLETE : acabar, terminar **2** : aplicar un acabado a (muebles, etc.)
finish² *n* **1** END : fin *m*, final *m* **2** REFINEMENT : refinamiento *m* **3** : acabado *m* ⟨a glossy finish : un acabado brillante⟩
finite ['faɪ,naɪt] *adj* : finito
fink ['fɪŋk] *n* : mequetrefe *mf fam*
Finn ['fɪn] *n* : finlandés *m*, -desa *f*
Finnish¹ ['fɪnɪʃ] *adj* : finlandés
Finnish² *n* : finlandés *m* (idioma)
fiord [fi'ɔrd] → **fjord**
fir ['fər] *n* : abeto *m*
fire¹ ['faɪr] *vt* **fired; firing 1** IGNITE, KINDLE : encender **2** ENLIVEN : animar, avivar **3** DISMISS : despedir **4** SHOOT : disparar **5** BAKE : cocer (cerámica)
fire² *n* **1** : fuego *m* **2** BURNING : incendio *m* ⟨fire alarm : alarma contra incendios⟩ ⟨to be on fire : estar en llamas⟩ **3** ENTHUSIASM : ardor *m*, entusiasmo *m* **4** SHOOTING : disparos *mpl*, fuego *m*
firearm ['faɪr,ɑrm] *n* : arma *f* de fuego
fireball ['faɪr,bɔl] *n* **1** : bola *f* de fuego **2** METEOR : bólido *m*
firebreak ['faɪr,breɪk] *n* : cortafuegos *m*
firebug ['faɪr,bʌɡ] *n* : pirómano *m*, -na *f*; incendiario *m*, -ria *f*
firecracker ['faɪr,krækər] *n* : petardo *m*
fire escape *n* : escalera *f* de incendios
firefighter ['faɪr,faɪtər] *n* : bombero *m*, -ra *f*
firefly ['faɪr,flaɪ] *n, pl* **-flies** : luciérnaga *f*
fireman ['faɪrmən] *n, pl* **-men** [-mən, -,mɛn] **1** FIREFIGHTER : bombero *m*, -ra *f* **2** STOKER : fogonero *m*, -ra *f*
fireplace ['faɪr,pleɪs] *n* : hogar *m*, chimenea *f*
fireproof¹ ['faɪr,pru:f] *vt* : hacer incombustible
fireproof² *adj* : incombustible, ignífugo
fireside¹ ['faɪr,saɪd] *adj* : informal ⟨fireside chat : charla informal⟩
fireside² *n* **1** HEARTH : chimenea *f*, hogar *m* **2** HOME : hogar *m*, casa *f*
firewall ['faɪr,wɔl] *n* : cortafuegos *m*
firewood ['faɪr,wʊd] *n* : leña *f*
fireworks ['faɪr,wərks] *npl* : fuegos *mpl* artificiales, pirotecnia *f*
firm¹ ['fərm] *vt or* **to firm up** : endurecer
firm² *adj* **1** VIGOROUS : fuerte, vigoroso **2** SOLID, UNYIELDING : firme, duro, sólido **3** UNCHANGING : firme, inalterable **4** RESOLUTE : firme, resuelto
firm³ *n* : empresa *f*, firma *f*, compañía *f*
firmament ['fərməmənt] *n* : firmamento *m*
firmly ['fərmli] *adv* : firmemente
firmness ['fərmnəs] *n* : firmeza *f*
first¹ ['fərst] *adv* **1** : primero ⟨finish your homework first : primero termina tu tarea⟩ ⟨first and foremost : ante todo⟩ ⟨first of all : en primer lugar⟩ **2** : por primera vez ⟨I saw it first in Boston : lo vi por primera vez en Boston⟩
first² *adj* **1** : primero ⟨the first time : la primera vez⟩ ⟨at first sight : a primera vista⟩ ⟨in the first place : en primer lugar⟩ ⟨the first ten applicants : los diez primeros candidatos⟩ **2** FOREMOST : principal, primero ⟨first tenor : tenor principal⟩
first³ *n* **1** : primero *m*, -ra *f* **2** *or* **first gear** : primera *f* **3** at ~ : al principio
first aid *n* : primeros auxilios *mpl*
first-class¹ ['fərst'klæs] *adv* : en primera ⟨to travel first-class : viajar en primera⟩
first-class² *adj* : de primera
first class *n* : primera clase *f*
firsthand¹ ['fərst'hænd] *adv* : directamente
firsthand² *adj* : de primera mano
first lieutenant *n* : teniente *mf*; teniente primero *m*, teniente primera *f*
firstly ['fərstli] *adv* : primeramente, principalmente, en primer lugar
first-rate¹ ['fərst'reɪt] *adv* : muy bien
first-rate² *adj* : de primera, de primera clase
first sergeant *n* : sargento *mf*
firth ['fərθ] *n* : estuario *m*
fiscal ['fɪskəl] *adj* : fiscal — **fiscally** *adv*
fish¹ ['fɪʃ] *vi* **1** : pescar **2 to fish for** SEEK : buscar, rebuscar ⟨to fish for compliments : andar a la caza de cumplidos⟩ — *vt* : pescar
fish² *n, pl* **fish** *or* **fishes** : pez *m* (vivo), pescado *m* (para comer)
fisherman ['fɪʃərmən] *n, pl* **-men** [-mən, -,mɛn] : pescador *m*, -dora *f*
fishery ['fɪʃəri] *n, pl* **-eries 1** → **fishing 2** : zona *f* pesquera, pesquería *f*
fishhook ['fɪʃ,hʊk] *n* : anzuelo *m*
fishing ['fɪʃɪŋ] *n* : pesca *f*, industria *f* pesquera
fishing pole *n* : caña *f* de pescar
fish market *n* : pescadería *f*
fishy ['fɪʃi] *adj* **fishier; -est 1** : a pescado ⟨a fishy taste : un sabor a pescado⟩ **2** QUESTIONABLE : dudoso, sospechoso ⟨there's something fishy going on : aquí hay gato encerrado⟩
fission ['fɪʃən, -ʒən] *n* : fisión *f*
fissure ['fɪʃər] *n* : fisura *f*, hendidura *f*
fist ['fɪst] *n* : puño *m*
fistful ['fɪst,fʊl] *n* : puñado *m*
fisticuffs ['fɪstɪ,kʌfs] *npl* : lucha *f* a puñetazos
fit¹ ['fɪt] *v* **fitted; fitting** *vt* **1** MATCH : corresponder a, coincidir con ⟨the punishment fits the crime : el castigo corresponde al crimen⟩ **2** : quedar ⟨the dress doesn't fit me : el vestido no me queda⟩ **3** GO : caber, encajar en ⟨her key fits the lock : su llave encaja en la cerradura⟩ **4** INSERT, INSTALL : poner, colocar **5** ADAPT : adecuar, ajustar, adaptar **6** *or* **to fit out** EQUIP : equipar

— *vi* **1** : quedar, entallar ⟨these pants don't fit : estos pantalones no me quedan⟩ **2** CONFORM : encajar, cuadrar **3 to fit in** : encajar, estar integrado

fit² *adj* **fitter; fittest 1** SUITABLE : adecuado, apropiado, conveniente **2** QUALIFIED : calificado, competente **3** HEALTHY : sano, en forma

fit³ *n* **1** ATTACK : ataque *m*, acceso *m*, arranque *m* **2 to be a good fit** : quedar bien **3 to be a tight fit** : ser muy entallado (de ropa), estar apretado (de espacios)

fitful ['fɪtfəl] *adj* : irregular, intermitente — **fitfully** *adv*

fitness ['fɪtnəs] *n* **1** HEALTH : salud *f*, buena forma *f* (física) **2** SUITABILITY : idoneidad *f*

fitting¹ ['fɪʈɪŋ] *adj* : adecuado, apropiado

fitting² *n* : accesorio *m*

five¹ ['faɪv] *adj* : cinco

five² *n* : cinco *m*

five hundred¹ *adj* : quinientos

five hundred² *n* : quinientos *m*

fix¹ ['fɪks] *vt* **1** ATTACH, SECURE : sujetar, asegurar, fijar **2** ESTABLISH : fijar, concretar, establecer **3** REPAIR : arreglar, reparar **4** PREPARE : preparar ⟨to fix dinner : preparar la cena⟩ **5** : arreglar, amañar ⟨to fix a race : arreglar una carrera⟩ **6** RIVET : fijar (los ojos, la mirada, etc.)

fix² *n* **1** PREDICAMENT : aprieto *m*, apuro *m* **2** : posición *f* ⟨to get a fix on : establecer la posición de⟩

fixate ['fɪk,seɪt] *vi* **-ated; -ating** : obsesionarse

fixation [fɪk'seɪʃən] *n* : fijación *f*, obsesión *f*

fixed ['fɪkst] *adj* **1** STATIONARY : estacionario, inmóvil **2** UNCHANGING : fijo, inalterable **3** INTENT : fijo ⟨a fixed stare : una mirada fija⟩ **4 to be comfortably fixed** : estar en posición acomodada

fixedly ['fɪksədli] *adv* : fijamente

fixedness ['fɪksədnəs, 'fɪkst-] *n* : rigidez *f*

fixture ['fɪkstʃər] *n* **1** : parte *f* integrante, elemento *m* fijo **2 fixtures** *npl* : instalaciones *fpl* (de una casa)

fizz¹ ['fɪz] *vi* : burbujear

fizz² *n* : efervescencia *f*, burbujeo *m*

fizzle¹ ['fɪzəl] *vi* **-zled; -zling 1** FIZZ : burbujear **2** FAIL : fracasar

fizzle² *n* : fracaso *m*, fiasco *m*

fjord [fi'ɔrd] *n* : fiordo *m*

flab ['flæb] *n* : gordura *f*

flabbergast ['flæbər,gæst] *vt* : asombrar, pasmar, dejar atónito

flabby ['flæbi] *adj* **-bier; -est** : blando, fofo, aguado *CA*, *Col*, *Mex*

flaccid ['flæksəd, 'flæsəd] *adj* : fláccido

flag¹ ['flæg] *vi* **flagged; flagging 1** : hacer señales con banderas **2** WEAKEN : flaquear, desfallecer

flag² *n* : bandera *f*, pabellón *m*, estandarte *m*

flagon ['flægən] *n* : jarra *f* grande

flagpole ['flæg,po:l] *n* : asta *f*, mástil *m*

flagrant ['fleɪgrənt] *adj* : flagrante — **flagrantly** *adv*

flagship ['flæg,ʃɪp] *n* : buque *m* insignia

flagstaff ['flæg,stæf] → **flagpole**

flagstone ['flæg,sto:n] *n* : losa *f*, piedra *f*

flail¹ ['fleɪl] *vt* **1** : trillar (grano) **2** : sacudir, agitar (los brazos)

flail² *n* : mayal *m*

flair ['flær] *n* : don *m*, facilidad *f*

flak ['flæk] *ns & pl* **1** : fuego *m* antiaéreo **2** CRITICISM : críticas *fpl*

flake¹ ['fleɪk] *vi* **flaked; flaking** : desmenuzarse, pelarse (dícese de la piel)

flake² *n* : copo *m* (de nieve), escama *f* (de la piel), astilla *f* (de madera)

flamboyance [flæm'bɔɪənts] *n* : extravagancia *f*, rimbombancia *f*

flamboyant [flæm'bɔɪənt] *adj* : exuberante, extravagante, rimbombante

flame¹ ['fleɪm] *vi* **flamed; flaming 1** BLAZE : arder, llamear **2** GLOW : brillar, encenderse

flame² *n* BLAZE : llama *f* ⟨to burst into flames : estallar en llamas⟩ ⟨to go up in flame : incendiarse⟩

flamethrower ['fleɪm,θro:ər] *n* : lanzallamas *m*

flamingo [flə'mɪŋgo] *n*, *pl* **-gos** : flamenco *m*

flammable ['flæməbəl] *adj* : inflamable, flamable

flange ['flændʒ] *n* : reborde *m*, pestaña *f*

flank¹ ['flæŋk] *vt* **1** : flanquear (para defender o atacar) **2** BORDER, LINE : bordear

flank² *n* : ijada *f* (de un animal), costado *m* (de una persona), falda *f* (de una colina), flanco *m* (de un cuerpo de soldados)

flannel ['flænəl] *n* : franela *f*

flap¹ ['flæp] *v* **flapped; flapping** *vi* **1** : aletear ⟨the bird was flapping (its wings) : el pájaro aleteaba⟩ **2** FLUTTER : ondear, agitarse — *vt* : batir, agitar

flap² *n* **1** FLAPPING : aleteo *m*, aletazo *m* (de alas) **2** : soplada *f* (de un sobre), hoja *f* (de una mesa), faldón *m* (de una chaqueta)

flapjack ['flæp,dʒæk] → **pancake**

flare¹ ['flær] *vi* **flared; flaring 1** FLAME, SHINE : llamear, brillar **2 to flare up** : estallar, explotar (de cólera)

flare² *n* **1** FLASH : destello *m* **2** SIGNAL : (luz *f* de) bengala *f* **3 solar flare** : erupción *f* solar

flash¹ ['flæʃ] *vi* **1** SHINE, SPARKLE : destellar, brillar, relampaguear **2** : pasar como un relámpago ⟨an idea flashed through my mind : una idea me cruzó la mente como un relámpago⟩ — *vt* : despedir, lanzar (una luz), transmitir (un mensaje)

flash² *adj* SUDDEN : repentino
flash³ *n* **1** : destello *m* (de luz), fogonazo *m* (de una explosión) **2 flash of lightning** : relámpago *m* **3 in a flash** : de repente, de un abrir y cerrar los ojos
flashback ['flæʃ,bæk] *n* : flashback *m*
flashiness ['flæʃinəs] *n* : ostentación *f*
flashlight ['flæʃ,laɪt] *n* : linterna *f*
flashy ['flæʃi] *adj* **flashier; -est** : llamativo, ostentoso
flask ['flæsk] *n* : frasco *m*
flat¹ ['flæt] *vt* **flatted; flatting 1** FLATTEN : aplanar, achatar **2** : bajar de tono (en música)
flat² *adv* **1** EXACTLY : exactamente ⟨in ten minutes flat : en diez minutos exactos⟩ **2** : desafinado, demasiado bajo (en la música)
flat³ *adj* **flatter; flattest 1** EVEN, LEVEL : plano, llano **2** SMOOTH : liso **3** DEFINITE : categórico, rotundo, explícito ⟨a flat refusal : una negativa categórica⟩ **4** DULL : aburrido, soso, monótono (dícese la voz) **5** DEFLATED : desinflado, pinchado, ponchado *Mex* **6** : bemol (en música) ⟨to sing flat : cantar desafinado⟩
flat⁴ *n* **1** PLAIN : llano *m*, terreno *m* llano **2** : bemol *m* (en la música) **3** APARTMENT : apartamento *m*, departamento *m* **4** *or* **flat tire** : pinchazo *m*, ponchadura *f Mex*
flatbed ['flæt,bɛd] *n* : camión *m* de plataforma
flatcar ['flæt,kɑr] *n* : vagón *m* abierto
flatfish ['flæt,fɪʃ] *n* : platija *f*
flat–footed ['flæt,fʊtəd, ,flæt'-] *adj* : de pies planos
flatly ['flætli] *adv* DEFINITELY : categóricamente, rotundamente
flatness ['flætnəs] *n* **1** EVENNESS : lo llano, lisura *f*, uniformidad *f* **2** DULLNESS : monotonía *f*
flat–out ['flæt'aʊt] *adj* **1** : frenético, a toda máquina ⟨a flat-out effort : un esfuerzo frenético⟩ **2** CATEGORICAL : descarado, rotundo, categórico
flatten ['flætən] *vt* : aplanar, achatar
flatter ['flætər] *vt* **1** OVERPRAISE : adular **2** COMPLIMENT : halagar **3** : favorecer ⟨the photo flatters you : la foto te favorece⟩
flatterer ['flætərər] *n* : adulador *m*, -dora *f*
flattering ['flætərɪŋ] *adj* **1** COMPLIMENTARY : halagador **2** BECOMING : favorecedor
flattery ['flætəri] *n*, *pl* **-ries** : halagos *mpl*
flatulence ['flætʃələnts] *n* : flatulencia *f*, ventosidad *f*
flatulent ['flætʃələnt] *adj* : flatulento
flatware ['flæt,wær] *n* : cubertería *f*, cubiertos *mpl*
flaunt¹ ['flɔnt] *vt* : alardear, hacer alarde de
flaunt² *n* : alarde *m*, ostentación *f*
flavor¹ ['fleɪvər] *vt* : dar sabor a, sazonar

flavor² *n* **1** : gusto *m*, sabor *m* **2** FLAVORING : sazón *f*, condimento *m*
flavorful ['fleɪvərfəl] *adj* : sabroso
flavoring ['fleɪvərɪŋ] *n* : condimento *m*, sazón *f*
flavorless ['fleɪvərləs] *adj* : sin sabor
flaw ['flɔ] *n* : falla *f*, defecto *m*, imperfección *f*
flawed ['flɔd] *adj* : imperfecto, con defectos
flawless ['flɔləs] *adj* : impecable, perfecto — **flawlessly** *adv*
flax ['flæks] *n* : lino *m*
flaxen ['flæksən] *adj* : rubio, blondo (dícese del pelo)
flay ['fleɪ] *vt* **1** SKIN : desollar, despellejar **2** VILIFY : criticar con dureza, vilipendiar
flea ['fli:] *n* : pulga *f*
fleck¹ ['flɛk] *vt* : salpicar
fleck² *n* : mota *f*, pinta *f*
fledgling ['flɛdʒlɪŋ] *n* : polluelo *m*, pollito *m*
flee ['fli:] *v* **fled** ['flɛd]; **fleeing** *vi* : huir, escapar(se) — *vt* : huir de
fleece¹ ['fli:s] *vt* **fleeced; fleecing 1** SHEAR : esquilar, trasquilar **2** SWINDLE : estafar, defraudar
fleece² *n* : lana *f*, vellón *m*
fleet¹ ['fli:t] *vi* : moverse con rapidez
fleet² *adj* SWIFT : rápido, veloz
fleet³ *n* : flota *f*
fleet admiral *n* : almirante *mf*
fleeting ['fli:tɪŋ] *adj* : fugaz, breve
flesh ['flɛʃ] *n* **1** : carne *f* (de seres humanos y animales) **2** : pulpa *f* (de frutas)
flesh out *vt* : desarrollar, darle cuerpo a
fleshy ['flɛʃi] *adj* **fleshier; -est** : gordo (dícese de las personas), carnoso (dícese de la fruta)
flew → fly
flex ['flɛks] *vt* : doblar, flexionar
flexibility [,flɛksə'bɪləti] *n*, *pl* **-ties** : flexibilidad *f*, elasticidad *f*
flexible ['flɛksəbəl] *adj* : flexible — **flexibly** [-bli] *adv*
flick¹ ['flɪk] *vt* : dar un capirotazo a (con el dedo) ⟨to flick a switch : darle al interruptor⟩ — *vi* **1** FLIT : revolotear **2 to flick through** : hojear (un libro)
flick² *n* : coletazo *m* (de una cola), capirotazo *m* (de un dedo)
flicker¹ ['flɪkər] *vi* **1** FLUTTER : revolotear, aletear **2** BLINK, TWINKLE : parpadear, titilar
flicker² *n* **1** : parpadeo *m*, titileo *m* **2** HINT, TRACE : indicio *m*, rastro *m* ⟨a flicker of hope : un rayo de esperanza⟩
flier ['flaɪər] *n* **1** AVIATOR : aviador *m*, -dora *f* **2** CIRCULAR : folleto *m* publicitario, circular *f*
flight ['flaɪt] *n* **1** : vuelo *m* (de aves o aviones), trayectoria *f* (de proyectiles) **2** TRIP : vuelo *m* **3** FLOCK, SQUADRON : bandada *f* (de pájaros), escuadrilla *f* (de aviones) **4** ESCAPE : huida *f*, fuga

f **5 flight of fancy** : ilusiones *fpl*, fantasía *f* **6 flight of stairs** : tramo *m*
flight attendant *n* : auxiliar *mf* de vuelo
flightless ['flaɪtləs] *adj* : no volador
flighty ['flaɪti] *adj* **flightier; -est** : caprichoso, frívolo
flimsy [flɪmzi] *adj* **flimsier; -est** **1** LIGHT, THIN : ligero, fino **2** WEAK : endeble, poco sólido **3** IMPLAUSIBLE : pobre, flojo, poco convincente ⟨a flimsy excuse : una excusa floja⟩
flinch ['flɪntʃ] *vi* **1** WINCE : estremecerse **2** RECOIL : recular, retroceder
fling¹ ['flɪŋ] *vt* **flung** ['flʌŋ]; **flinging** **1** THROW : lanzar, tirar, arrojar **2 to fling oneself** : lanzarse, tirarse, precipitarse
fling² *n* **1** THROW : lanzamiento *m* **2** ATTEMPT : intento *m* **3** AFFAIR : aventura *f* **4** BINGE : juerga *f*
flint ['flɪnt] *n* : pedernal *m*
flinty ['flɪnti] *adj* **flintier; -est** **1** : de pedernal **2** STERN, UNYIELDING : severo, inflexible
flip¹ ['flɪp] *v* **flipped; flipping** *vt* **1** TOSS : tirar ⟨to flip a coin : echar a cara o cruz⟩ **2** OVERTURN : dar la vuelta a, voltear — *vi* **1** : moverse bruscamente **2 to flip through** : hojear (un libro)
flip² *adj* : insolente, descarado
flip³ *n* **1** FLICK : capirotazo *m*, golpe *m* ligero **2** SOMERSAULT : voltereta *f*
flip–flop ['flɪp,flɑp] *n* **1** REVERSAL : giro *m* radical **2** THONG : chancla *f*, chancleta *f*
flippancy ['flɪpəntsi] *n*, *pl* **-cies** : ligereza *f*, falta *f* de seriedad
flippant ['flɪpənt] *adj* : ligero, frívolo, poco serio
flipper ['flɪpər] *n* : aleta *f*
flirt¹ ['flərt] *vi* **1** : coquetear, flirtear **2** TRIFLE : jugar ⟨to flirt with death : jugar con la muerte⟩
flirt² *n* : coqueto *m*, -ta *f*
flirtation [,flər'teɪʃən] *n* : devaneo *m*, coqueteo *m*
flirtatious [,flər'teɪʃəs] *adj* : insinuante, coqueto
flit ['flɪt] *vi* **flitted; flitting** **1** : revolotear **2 to flit about** : ir y venir rápidamente
float¹ ['floːt] *vi* **1** : flotar **2** WANDER : vagar, errar — *vt* **1** : poner a flote, hacer flotar (un barco) **2** LAUNCH : hacer flotar (una empresa) **3** ISSUE : emitir (acciones en la bolsa)
float² *n* **1** : flotador *m*, corcho *m* (para pescar) **2** BUOY : boya *f* **3** : carroza *f* (en un desfile)
floating ['floːtɪŋ] *adj* : flotante
flock¹ ['flɑk] *vi* **1** : moverse en rebaño **2** CONGREGATE : congregarse, reunirse
flock² *n* : rebaño *m* (de ovejas), bandada *f* (de pájaros)
floe ['floː] *n* : témpano *m* de hielo
flog ['flɑg] *vt* **flogged; flogging** : azotar, fustigar
flood¹ ['flʌd] *vt* : inundar, anegar

flood² *n* **1** INUNDATION : inundación *f* **2** TORRENT : avalancha *f*, diluvio *m*, torrente *m* ⟨a flood of tears : un mar de lágrimas⟩
floodlight ['flʌd,laɪt] *n* : foco *m*
floodwater ['flʌd,wɔtər] *n* : crecida *f*, creciente *f*
floor¹ ['flor] *vt* **1** : solar, poner suelo a (una casa o una sala) **2** KNOCK DOWN : derribar, echar al suelo **3** NONPLUS : desconcertar, confundir, dejar perplejo
floor² *n* **1** : suelo *m*, piso *m* ⟨dance floor : pista de baile⟩ **2** STORY : piso *m*, planta *f* ⟨ground floor : planta baja⟩ ⟨second floor : primer piso⟩ **3** : mínimo *m* (de sueldos, precios, etc.)
floorboard ['flor,bord] *n* : tabla *f* del suelo, suelo *m*, piso *m*
flooring ['florɪŋ] *n* : entarimado *m*
flop¹ ['flɑp] *vi* **flopped; flopping** **1** FLAP : golpearse, agitarse **2** COLLAPSE : dejarse caer, desplomarse **3** FAIL : fracasar
flop² *n* **1** FAILURE : fracaso *m* **2 to take a flop** : caerse
floppy ['flɑpi] *adj* **-pier; -est** **1** : blando, flexible **2 floppy disk** : diskette *m*, disquete *m*
flora ['florə] *n* : flora *f*
floral ['florəl] *adj* : floral, floreado
florid ['florɪd] *adj* **1** FLOWERY : florido **2** REDDISH : rojizo
florist ['florɪst] *n* : florista *mf*
floss¹ ['flɔs] *vi* : limpiarse los dientes con hilo dental
floss² *n* **1** : hilo *m* de seda (de bordar) **2** → **dental floss**
flotation [flo'teɪʃən] *n* : flotación *f*
flotilla [flo'tɪlə] *n* : flotilla *f*
flotsam ['flɑtsəm] *n* **1** : restos *mpl* flotantes (en el mar) **2 flotsam and jetsam** : desechos *mpl*, restos *mpl*
flounce¹ ['flaʊnts] *vi* **flounced; flouncing** : moverse haciendo aspavientos ⟨she flounced into the room : entró en la sala haciendo aspavientos⟩
flounce² *n* **1** RUFFLE : volante *m* **2** FLOURISH : aspaviento *m*
flounder¹ ['flaʊndər] *vi* **1** STRUGGLE : forcejear **2** STUMBLE : no saber qué hacer o decir, perder el hilo (en un discurso)
flounder² *n*, *pl* **flounder** *or* **flounders** : platija *f*
flour¹ ['flaʊər] *vt* : enharinar
flour² *n* : harina *f*
flourish¹ ['flərɪʃ] *vi* THRIVE : florecer, prosperar, crecer (dícese de las plantas) — *vt* BRANDISH : blandir
flourish² *n* : floritura *f*, floreo *m*
flourishing ['flərɪʃɪŋ] *adj* : floreciente, próspero
flout ['flaʊt] *vt* : desacatar, burlarse de
flow¹ ['floː] *vi* **1** COURSE : fluir, manar, correr **2** CIRCULATE : circular, correr ⟨traffic is flowing smoothly : el tránsito está circulando con fluidez⟩

flow · fo'c'sle

flow² *n* **1** FLOWING : flujo *m*, circulación *f* **2** STREAM : corriente *f*, chorro *m*

flower¹ ['flauər] *vi* : florecer, florear

flower² *n* : flor *f*

flowered ['flauərd] *adj* : florido, floreado

floweriness ['flauərinəs] *n* : floritura *f*

flowering¹ ['flauəriŋ] *adj* : floreciente

flowering² *n* : floración *f*, florecimiento *m*

flowerpot ['flauər,pɑt] *n* : maceta *f*, tiesto *m*, macetero *m*

flowery ['flauəri] *adj* **1** : florido **2** FLOWERED : floreado, de flores

flowing ['flo:iŋ] *adj* : fluido, corriente

flown → **fly**

flu ['flu:] *n* : gripe *f*, gripa *f* *Col, Mex*

fluctuate ['flʌktʃu,eit] *vi* **-ated; -ating** : fluctuar

fluctuation [,flʌktʃu'eiʃən] *n* : fluctuación *f*

flue ['flu:] *n* : tiro *m*, salida *f* de humos

fluency ['flu:ən̩si] *n* : fluidez *f*, soltura *f*

fluent ['flu:ənt] *adj* : fluido

fluently ['flu:əntli] *adv* : con soltura, con fluidez

fluff¹ ['flʌf] *vt* **1** : mullir ⟨to fluff up the pillows : mullir las almohadas⟩ **2** BUNGLE : echar a perder, equivocarse

fluff² *n* **1** FUZZ : pelusa *f* **2** DOWN : plumón *m*

fluffy ['flʌfi] *adj* **fluffier; -est 1** DOWNY : lleno de pelusa, velloso **2** SPONGY : esponjoso

fluid¹ ['flu:id] *adj* : fluido

fluid² *n* : fluido *m*, líquido *m*

fluidity [flu'idəti] *n* : fluidez *f*

fluid ounce *n* : onza *f* líquida (29.57 mililitros)

fluke ['flu:k] *n* : golpe *m* de suerte, chiripa *f*, casualidad *f*

flung → **fling**

flunk ['flʌŋk] *vt* FAIL : reprobar — *vi* : salir reprobando

fluorescence [,flur'ɛsənts, ,flɔr-] *n* : fluorescencia *f*

fluorescent [,flur'ɛsənt, ,flɔr-] *adj* : fluorescente

fluoridate ['flɔrə,deit, 'flur-] *vt* **-dated; -dating** : fluorizar

fluoridation [,flɔrə'deiʃən, ,flur-] *n* : fluorización *f*, fluoración *f*

fluoride ['flɔr,aid, 'flur-] *n* : fluoruro *m*

fluorine ['flur,i:n] *n* : flúor *m*

fluorocarbon [,flɔro'karbən, ,flur-] *n* : fluorocarbono *m*

flurry ['fləri] *n, pl* **-ries 1** GUST : ráfaga *f* **2** SNOWFALL : nevisca *f* **3** BUSTLE : frenesí *m*, bullicio *m* **4** BARRAGE : aluvión *m*, oleada *f* ⟨a flurry of questions : un aluvión de preguntas⟩

flush¹ ['flʌʃ] *vt* **1** : limpiar con agua ⟨to flush the toilet : jalar la cadena⟩ **2** RAISE : hacer salir, levantar (en la caza) — *vi* BLUSH : ruborizarse, sonrojarse

flush² *adv* : al mismo nivel, a ras

flush³ *adj* **1** *or* **flushed** ['flʌʃt] : colorado, rojo, encendido (dícese de la

cara) **2** FILLED : lleno a rebosar **3** ABUNDANT : copioso, abundante **4** AFFLUENT : adinerado **5** ALIGNED, SMOOTH : alineado, liso **6** flush against : pegado a, contra

flush⁴ *n* **1** FLOW, JET : chorro *m*, flujo *m* rápido **2** SURGE : arrebato *m*, arranque *m* ⟨a flush of anger : un arrebato de cólera⟩ **3** BLUSH : rubor *m*, sonrojo *m* **4** GLOW : resplandor *m*, flor *f* ⟨the flush of youth : la flor de la juventud⟩ ⟨in the flush of victory : en la euforia del triunfo⟩

fluster¹ ['flʌstər] *vt* : poner nervioso, aturdir

fluster² *n* : agitación *f*, confusión *f*

flute ['flu:t] *n* : flauta *f*

fluted ['flu:təd] *adj* **1** GROOVED : estriado, acanalado **2** WAVY : ondulado

fluting ['flu:tiŋ] *n* : estrías *fpl*

flutist ['flu:tist] *n* : flautista *mf*

flutter¹ ['flʌtər] *vi* **1** : revolotear (dícese de un pájaro), ondear (dícese de una bandera), palpitar con fuerza (dícese del corazón) **2 to flutter about** : ir y venir, revolotear — *vt* : sacudir, batir

flutter² *n* **1** FLUTTERING : revoloteo *m*, aleteo *m* **2** COMMOTION, STIR : revuelo *m*, agitación *f*

flux ['flʌks] *n* **1** : flujo *m* (en física y medicina) **2** CHANGE : cambio *m* ⟨to be in a state of flux : estar cambiando continuamente⟩

fly¹ ['flai] *v* **flew** ['flu:]; **flown** ['flo:n]; **flying** *vi* **1** : volar (dícese de los pájaros, etc.) **2** TRAVEL : volar (dícese de los aviones), ir en avión (dícese de los pasajeros) **3** FLOAT : flotar, ondear **4** FLEE : huir, escapar **5** RUSH : correr, irse volando **6** PASS : pasar (volando) ⟨how time flies! : ¡cómo pasa el tiempo!⟩ **7 to fly open** : abrir de golpe — *vt* : pilotar (un avión), hacer volar (una cometa)

fly² *n, pl* **flies 1** : mosca *f* ⟨to drop like flies : caer como moscas⟩ **2** : bragueta *f* (de pantalones, etc.)

flyer → **flier**

flying saucer *n* : platillo *m* volador

flypaper ['flai,peipər] *n* : papel *m* matamoscas

flyspeck ['flai,spɛk] *n* **1** : excremento *m* de mosca **2** SPECK : motita *f*, puntito *m*

flyswatter ['flai,swɑtər] *n* : matamoscas *m*

flywheel ['flai,hwi:l] *n* : volante *m*

foal¹ ['fo:l] *vi* : parir

foal² *n* : potro *m*, -tra *f*

foam¹ ['fo:m] *vi* : hacer espuma

foam² *n* : espuma *f*

foamy ['fo:mi] *adj* **foamier; -est** : espumoso

focal ['fo:kəl] *adj* **1** : focal, central **2 focal point** : foco *m*, punto *m* de referencia

fo'c'sle ['fo:ksəl] → **forecastle**

focus¹ ['fo:kəs] *v* **-cused** *or* **-cussed; -cusing** *or* **-cussing** *vt* **1** : enfocar (un instrumento) **2** CONCENTRATE : concentrar, centrar — *vi* : enfocar, fijar la vista

focus² *n, pl* **-ci** ['fo:ˌsaɪ, -ˌkaɪ] **1** : foco *m* ⟨to be in focus : estar enfocado⟩ **2** FOCUSING : enfoque *m* **3** CENTER : centro *m*, foco *m*

fodder ['fɑdər] *n* : pienso *m*, forraje *m*

foe ['fo:] *n* : enemigo *m*, -ga *f*

fog¹ ['fɔg, 'fɑg] *v* **fogged; fogging** *vt* : empañar — *vi* **to fog up** : empañarse

fog² *n* : niebla *f*, neblina *f*

foggy ['fɔgi, 'fɑ-] *adj* **foggier; -est** : nebuloso, brumoso

foghorn ['fɔgˌhɔrn, 'fɑg-] *n* : sirena *f* de niebla

fogy ['fo:gi] *n, pl* **-gies** : carca *mf fam*, persona *f* chapada a la antigua

foible ['fɔɪbəl] *n* : flaqueza *f*, debilidad *f*

foil¹ ['fɔɪl] *vt* : frustrar, hacer fracasar

foil² *n* **1** : lámina *f* de metal, papel *m* de aluminio **2** CONTRAST : contraste *m*, complemento *m* **3** SWORD : florete *m* (en esgrima)

foist ['fɔɪst] *vt* : encajar, endilgar *fam*, colocar

fold¹ ['fo:ld] *vt* **1** BEND : doblar, plegar **2** CLASP : cruzar (brazos), enlazar (manos), plegar (alas) **3** EMBRACE : estrechar, abrazar **4 to fold in** : incorporar ⟨fold in the cream : incorpore la crema⟩ — *vi* **1** FAIL : fracasar **2 to fold up** : doblarse, plegarse

fold² *n* **1** SHEEPFOLD : redil *m* (para ovejas) **2** FLOCK : rebaño *m* ⟨to return to the fold : volver al redil⟩ **3** CREASE : pliegue *m*, doblez *m*

folder ['fo:ldər] *n* **1** CIRCULAR : circular *f*, folleto *m* **2** BINDER : carpeta *f*

foliage ['fo:liɪʤ, -liʤ] *n* : follaje *m*

folio ['fo:liˌo:] *n, pl* **-lios** : folio *m*

folk¹ ['fo:k] *adj* : popular, folklórico ⟨folk customs : costumbres populares⟩ ⟨folk dance : danza folklórica⟩

folk² *n, pl* **folk** *or* **folks 1** PEOPLE : gente *f* **2 folks** *npl* : familia *f*, padres *mpl*

folklore ['fo:kˌlor] *n* : folklore *m*

folklorist ['fo:kˌlorɪst] *n* : folklorista *mf*

folksy ['fo:ksi] *adj* **folksier; -est** : campechano

follicle ['fɑlɪkəl] *n* : folículo *m*

follow ['fɑlo] *vt* **1** : seguir ⟨follow the guide : siga al guía⟩ ⟨she followed the road : siguió el camino, continuó por el camino⟩ **2** PURSUE : perseguir, seguir **3** OBEY : seguir, cumplir, observar **4** UNDERSTAND : entender — *vi* **1** : seguir **2** UNDERSTAND : entender **3 it follows that . . .** : se deduce que . . .

follower ['fɑloər] *n* : seguidor *m*, -dora *f*

following¹ ['fɑloɪŋ] *adj* NEXT : siguiente

following² *n* FOLLOWERS : seguidores *mpl*

following³ *prep* AFTER : después de

follow through *vi* **to follow through with** : continuar con, realizar

follow up *vt* : seguir (una sugerencia, etc.), investigar (una huella)

folly ['fɑli] *n, pl* **-lies** : locura *f*, desatino *m*

foment [fo'mɛnt] *vt* : fomentar

fond ['fɑnd] *adj* **1** LOVING : cariñoso, tierno **2** PARTIAL : aficionado **3** FERVENT : ferviente, fervoroso

fondle ['fɑndəl] *vt* **-dled; -dling** : acariciar

fondly ['fɑndli] *adv* : cariñosamente, afectuosamente

fondness ['fɑndnəs] *n* **1** LOVE : cariño *m* **2** LIKING : afición *f*

fondue [fɑn'du:, -'dju:] *n* : fondue *f*

font ['fɑnt] *n* **1** *or* **baptismal font** : pila *f* bautismal **2** FOUNTAIN : fuente *f*

food ['fu:d] *n* : comida *f*, alimento *m*

food chain *n* : cadena *f* alimenticia

foodstuffs ['fu:dˌstʌfs] *npl* : comestibles *mpl*

fool¹ ['fu:l] *vi* **1** JOKE : bromear, hacer el tonto **2** TOY : jugar, juguetear ⟨don't fool with the computer : no juegues con la computadora⟩ **3 to fool around** : perder el tiempo ⟨he fools around instead of working : pierde el tiempo en vez de trabajar⟩ — *vt* DECEIVE : engañar, burlar

fool² *n* **1** IDIOT : idiota *mf*; tonto *m*, -ta *f*; bobo *m*, -ba *f* **2** JESTER : bufón *m*, -fona *f*

foolhardiness ['fu:lˌhɑrdinəs] *n* : imprudencia *f*

foolhardy ['fu:lˌhɑrdi] *adj* RASH : imprudente, temerario, precipitado

foolish ['fu:lɪʃ] *adj* **1** STUPID : insensato, estúpido **2** SILLY : idiota, tonto

foolishly ['fu:lɪʃli] *adv* : tontamente

foolishness ['fu:lɪʃnəs] *n* : insensatez *f*, estupidez *f*, tontería *f*

foolproof ['fu:lˌpru:f] *adj* : infalible

foot ['fʊt] *n, pl* **feet** ['fi:t] : pie *m*

footage ['fʊtɪʤ] *n* : medida *f* en pies, metraje *m* (en el cine)

football ['fʊtˌbɔl] *n* : futbol *m* americano, fútbol *m* americano

footbridge ['fʊtˌbrɪʤ] *n* : pasarela *f*, puente *m* peatonal

foothills ['fʊtˌhɪlz] *npl* : estribaciones *fpl*

foothold ['fʊtˌho:ld] *n* **1** : punto *m* de apoyo **2 to gain a foothold** : afianzarse en una posición

footing ['fʊtɪŋ] *n* **1** BALANCE : equilibrio *m* **2** FOOTHOLD : punto *m* de apoyo **3** BASIS : base *f* ⟨on an equal footing : en igualdad⟩

footlights ['fʊtˌlaɪts] *npl* : candilejas *fpl*

footlocker ['fʊtˌlɑkər] *n* : baúl *m* pequeño, cofre *m*

footloose ['fʊtˌlu:s] *adj* : libre y sin compromiso

footman ['fʊtmən] *n, pl* **-men** [-mən, -ˌmɛn] : lacayo *m*

footnote ['fʊtˌno:t] *n* : nota *f* al pie de la página

footpath ['fʊtˌpæθ] *n* : sendero *m*, senda *f*, vereda *f*

footprint ['fʊt,prɪnt] *n* : huella *f*
footrace ['fʊt,reɪs] *n* : carrera *f* pedestre
footrest ['fʊt,rɛst] *n* : apoyapiés *m*, reposapiés *m*
footstep ['fʊt,stɛp] *n* 1 STEP : paso *m* 2 FOOTPRINT : huella *f*
footstool ['fʊt,stuːl] *n* : taburete *m*, escabel *m*
footwear ['fʊt,wær] *n* : calzado *m*
footwork ['fʊt,wərk] *n* : juego *m* de piernas, juego *m* de pies
fop ['fɑp] *n* : petimetre *m*, dandi *m*
for¹ ['fɔr] *conj* : puesto que, porque
for² *prep* 1 (*indicating purpose*) : para, de ⟨clothes for children : ropa para niños⟩ ⟨it's time for dinner : es la hora de comer⟩ 2 BECAUSE OF : por ⟨for fear of : por miedo de⟩ 3 (*indicating a recipient*) : para, por ⟨a gift for you : un regalo para ti⟩ 4 (*indicating support*) : por ⟨he fought for his country : luchó por su patria⟩ 5 (*indicating a goal*) : por, para ⟨a cure for cancer : una cura para el cáncer⟩ ⟨for your own good : por tu propio bien⟩ 6 (*indicating correspondence or exchange*) : por, para ⟨I bought it for $5 : lo compré por $5⟩ ⟨a lot of trouble for nothing : mucha molestia para nada⟩ 7 AS FOR : para, con respecto a 8 (*indicating duration*) : durante, por ⟨he's going for two years : se va por dos años⟩ ⟨I spoke for ten minutes : hablé (durante) diez minutos⟩ ⟨she has known it for three months : lo sabe desde hace tres meses⟩
forage¹ ['fɔrɪdʒ] *v* -aged; -aging *vi* : hurgar (en busca de alimento) — *vt* : buscar (provisiones)
forage² *n* : forraje *m*
foray ['fɔr,eɪ] *n* : incursión *f*
forbear¹ [fɔr'bær] *vi* -bore [-'bor]; -borne [-'born]; -bearing 1 ABSTAIN : abstenerse 2 : tener paciencia
forbear² → forbear
forbearance [fɔr'bærənts] *n* 1 ABSTAINING : abstención *f* 2 PATIENCE : paciencia *f*
forbid [fər'bɪd] *vt* -bade [-'bæd, -'beɪd]; -bidden [-'bɪdən]; -bidding 1 PROHIBIT : prohibir 2 PREVENT : impedir
forbidding [fər'bɪdɪŋ] *adj* 1 IMPOSING : imponente 2 DISAGREEABLE : desagradable, ingrato 3 GRIM : severo
force¹ ['fors] *vt* forced; forcing 1 COMPEL : obligar, forzar 2 : forzar ⟨to force open the window : forzar la ventana⟩ ⟨to force a lock : forzar una cerradura⟩ 3 IMPOSE : imponer, obligar
force² *n* 1 : fuerza *f* 2 by force : por la fuerza 3 in force : en vigor, en vigencia
forced ['forst] *adj* : forzado, forzoso
forceful ['forsfəl] *adj* : fuerte, energético, contundente
forcefully ['forsfəli] *adv* : con energía, con fuerza
forcefulness ['forsfəlnəs] *n* : contundencia *f*, fuerza *f*

forceps ['fɔrsəps, -,sɛps] *ns & pl* : fórceps *m*
forcible ['fɔrsəbəl] *adj* 1 FORCED : forzoso 2 CONVINCING : contundente, convincente — forcibly [-bli] *adv*
ford¹ ['ford] *vt* : vadear
ford² *n* : vado *m*
fore¹ ['for] *adv* 1 FORWARD : hacia adelante 2 fore and aft : de popa a proa
fore² *adj* 1 FORWARD : delantero, de adelante 2 FORMER : anterior
fore³ *n* 1 : frente *m*, delantera *f* 2 to come to the fore : empezar a destacar, saltar a primera plana
fore-and-aft ['forən'æft, -ənd-] *adj* : longitudinal
forearm ['for,ɑrm] *n* : antebrazo *m*
forebear ['for,bær] *n* : antepasado *m*, -da *f*
foreboding [for'bo:dɪŋ] *n* : premonición *f*, presentimiento *m*
forecast¹ ['for,kæst] *vt* -cast; -casting : pronosticar, predecir
forecast² *n* : predicción *f*, pronóstico *m*
forecastle ['fo:ksəl] *n* : castillo *m* de proa
foreclose [for'klo:z] *vt* -closed; -closing : ejecutar (una hipoteca)
forefather ['for,fɑðər] *n* : antepasado *m*, ancestro *m*
forefinger ['for,fɪŋgər] *n* : índice *m*, dedo *m* índice
forefoot ['for,fʊt] *n* : pata *f* delantera
forefront ['for,frʌnt] *n* : frente *m*, vanguardia *f* ⟨in the forefront : a la vanguardia⟩
forego [for'go:] *vt* -went; -gone; -going 1 PRECEDE : preceder 2 → forgo
foregoing [for'go:ɪŋ] *adj* : precedente, anterior
foregone [for'gɔn] *adj* : previsto ⟨a foregone conclusion : un resultado inevitable⟩
foreground ['for,graʊnd] *n* : primer plano *m*
forehand¹ ['for,hænd] *adj* : directo, derecho
forehand² *n* : golpe *m* del derecho
forehead ['fɔrəd, 'for,hɛd] *n* : frente *f*
foreign ['fɔrən] *adj* 1 : extranjero, exterior ⟨foreign countries : países extranjeros⟩ ⟨foreign trade : comercio exterior⟩ 2 ALIEN : ajeno, extraño ⟨foreign to their nature : ajeno a su carácter⟩ ⟨a foreign body : un cuerpo extraño⟩
foreigner ['fɔrənər] *n* : extranjero *m*, -ra *f*
foreknowledge [for'nɑlɪdʒ] *n* : conocimiento *m* previo
foreleg ['for,lɛg] *n* : pata *f* delantera
foreman ['formən] *n*, *pl* -men [-mən, -,mɛn] : capataz *mf* ⟨foreman of the jury : presidente del jurado⟩
foremost¹ ['for,mo:st] *adv* : en primer lugar
foremost² *adj* : más importante, principal, grande
forenoon ['for,nuːn] *n* : mañana *m*

forensic [fə'rɛn*t*sɪk] *adj* **1** RHETORICAL : retórico, de argumentación **2** : forense ⟨forensic medicine : medicina forense⟩

foreordain [ˌfɔrɔr'deɪn] *vt* : predestinar, predeterminar

forequarter ['fɔrˌkwɔrtər] *n* : cuarto *m* delantero

forerunner ['fɔrˌrʌnər] *n* : precursor *m*, -sora *f*

foresee [fɔr'si:] *vt* **-saw; -seen; -seeing** : prever

foreseeable [fɔr'si:əbəl] *adj* : previsible ⟨in the foreseeable future : en el futuro inmediato⟩

foreshadow [fɔr'ʃædo:] *vt* : anunciar, prefigurar

foresight ['fɔrˌsaɪt] *n* : previsión *f*

foresighted ['fɔrˌsaɪtəd] *adj* : previsto

forest ['fɔrəst] *n* : bosque *m* (en zonas templadas), selva *f* (en zonas tropicales)

forestall [fɔr'stɔl] *vt* **1** PREVENT : prevenir, impedir **2** PREEMPT : adelantarse a

forested ['fɔrəstəd] *adj* : arbolado

forester ['fɔrəstər] *n* : silvicultor *m*, -tora *f*

forestland ['fɔrəstˌlænd] *n* : zona *f* boscosa

forest ranger → **ranger**

forestry ['fɔrəstri] *n* : silvicultura *f*, ingeniería *f* forestal

foreswear → **forswear**

foretaste¹ ['fɔrˌteɪst] *vt* **-tasted; -tasting** : anticipar

foretaste² *n* : anticipo *m*

foretell [fɔr'tɛl] *vt* **-told; -telling** : predecir, pronosticar, profetizar

forethought ['fɔrˌθɔt] *n* : previsión *f*, reflexión *f* previa

forever [fɔr'ɛvər] *adv* **1** PERPETUALLY : para siempre, eternamente **2** CONTINUALLY : siempre, constantemente

forevermore [fɔrˌɛvər'mor] *adv* : por siempre jamás

forewarn [fɔr'wɔrn] *vt* : prevenir, advertir

foreword ['fɔrwərd] *n* : prólogo *m*

forfeit¹ ['fɔrfət] *vt* : perder el derecho a

forfeit² *n* **1** FINE, PENALTY : multa *f* **2** : prenda *f* (en un juego)

forge¹ ['fɔrʤ] *v* **forged; forging** *vt* **1** : forjar (metal o un plan) **2** COUNTERFEIT : falsificar — *vi* **to forge ahead** : avanzar, seguir adelante

forge² *n* : forja *f*

forger ['fɔrʤər] *n* : falsificador *m*, -dora *f*

forgery ['fɔrʤəri] *n, pl* **-eries** : falsificación *f*

forget [fər'gɛt] *v* **-got** [-'gɑt]; **-gotten** [-'gɑtən] *or* **-got; -getting** *vt* : olvidar — *vi* **to forget about** : olvidarse de, no acordarse de

forgetful [fər'gɛtfəl] *adj* : olvidadizo

forget–me–not [fər'gɛtmiˌnɑt] *n* : nomeolvides *mf*

forgettable [fər'gɛtəbəl] *adj* : poco memorable

forgivable [fər'gɪvəbəl] *adj* : perdonable

forgive [fər'gɪv] *vt* **-gave** [-'geɪv]; **-given** [-'gɪvən]; **-giving** : perdonar

forgiveness [fər'gɪvnəs] *n* : perdón *m*

forgiving [fər'gɪvɪŋ] *adj* : indulgente, comprensivo, clemente

forgo *or* **forego** [fɔr'go:] *vt* **-went; -gone; -going** : privarse de, renunciar a

fork¹ ['fɔrk] *vi* : ramificarse, bifurcarse — *vt* **1** : levantar (con un tenedor, una horca, etc.) **2 to fork over** : desembolsar

fork² *n* **1** : tenedor *m* (utensilio de cocina) **2** PITCHFORK : horca *f*, horquilla *f* **3** : bifurcación *f* (de un río o camino), horqueta *f* (de un árbol)

forked ['fɔrkt, 'fɔrkəd] *adj* : bífido, ahorquillado

forklift ['fɔrkˌlɪft] *n* : carretilla *f* elevadora

forlorn [fɔr'lɔrn] *adj* **1** DESOLATE : abandonado, desolado, desamparado **2** SAD : triste **3** DESPERATE : desesperado

forlornly [fɔr'lɔrnli] *adv* **1** SADLY : con tristeza **2** HALFHEARTEDLY : sin ánimo

form¹ ['fɔrm] *vt* **1** FASHION, MAKE : formar **2** DEVELOP : moldear, desarrollar **3** CONSTITUTE : constituir, formar **4** ACQUIRE : adquirir (un hábito), formar (una idea) — *vi* : tomar forma, formarse

form² *n* **1** SHAPE : forma *f*, figura *f* **2** MANNER : manera *f*, forma *f* **3** DOCUMENT : formulario *m* **4** : forma *f* ⟨in good form : en buena forma⟩ ⟨true to form : en forma consecuente⟩ **5** MOLD : molde *m* **6** KIND, VARIETY : clase *f*, tipo *m* **7** : forma *f* (en gramática) ⟨plural forms : formas plurales⟩

formal¹ ['fɔrməl] *adj* **1** CEREMONIOUS : formal, de etiqueta, ceremonioso **2** OFFICIAL : formal, oficial, de forma

formal² *n* **1** BALL : baile *m* formal, baile *m* de etiqueta **2** *or* **formal dress** : traje *m* de etiqueta

formaldehyde [fɔr'mældəˌhaɪd] *n* : formaldehído *m*

formality [fɔr'mæləti] *n, pl* **-ties** : formalidad *f*

formalize ['fɔrməˌlaɪz] *vt* **-ized; -izing** : formalizar

formally ['fɔrməli] *adv* : formalmente

format¹ ['fɔrˌmæt] *vt* **-matted; -matting** : formatear

format² *n* : formato *m*

formation [fɔr'meɪʃən] *n* **1** FORMING : formación *f* **2** SHAPE : forma *f* **3 in formation** : en formación

formative ['fɔrmətɪv] *adj* : formativo

former ['fɔrmər] *adj* **1** PREVIOUS : antiguo, anterior ⟨the former president : el antiguo presidente⟩ **2** : primero (de dos)

formerly ['fɔrmərli] *adv* : anteriormente, antes

formidable ['fɔrmədəbəl, fɔr'mɪdə-] *adj*
: formidable — **formidably** *adv*

formless ['fɔrmləs] *adj* : informe, amorfo

formula ['fɔrmjələ] *n, pl* -**las** *or* -**lae** [-ˌliː,
-ˌlaɪ] **1** : fórmula *f* **2 baby formula**
: preparado *m* para biberón

formulate ['fɔrmjəˌleɪt] *vt* -**lated; -lating**
: formular, hacer

formulation [ˌfɔrmjə'leɪʃən] *n* : formulación *f*

fornicate ['fɔrnəˌkeɪt] *vi* -**cated; -cating**
: fornicar

fornication [ˌfɔrnə'keɪʃən] *n* : fornicación *f*

forsake [fər'seɪk] *vt* -**sook** [-'sʊk];
-**saken** [-'seɪkən]; -**saking 1** ABANDON
: abandonar, desamparar **2** RELIN-
QUISH : renunciar a

forswear [fɔr'swær] *v* -**swore; -sworn;
-swearing** *vt* RENOUNCE : renunciar a
— *vi* : perjurar

forsythia [fər'sɪθiə] *n* : forsitia *f*

fort ['fɔrt] *n* **1** STRONGHOLD : fuerte *m*,
fortaleza *f*, fortín *m* **2** BASE : base *f* militar

forte ['fɔrt, 'fɔrˌteɪ] *n* : fuerte *m*

forth ['fɔrθ] *adv* **1** : adelante ⟨from this
day forth : de hoy en adelante⟩ **2 and
so forth** : etcétera

forthcoming [fɔrθ'kʌmɪŋ, 'fɔrθˌ-] *adj* **1**
COMING : próximo **2** DIRECT, OPEN
: directo, franco, comunicativo

forthright ['fɔrθˌraɪt] *adj* : directo, franco — **forthrightly** *adv*

forthrightness ['fɔrθˌraɪtnəs] *n* : franqueza *f*

forthwith [fɔrθ'wɪθ, -'wɪð] *adv* : inmediatamente, en el acto, enseguida

fortieth¹ ['fɔrtiəθ] *adj* : cuadragésimo

fortieth² *n* **1** : cuadragésimo *m*, -ma *f*
(en una serie) **2** : cuarentavo *m*,
cuarentava parte *f*

fortification [ˌfɔrtəfə'keɪʃən] *n* : fortificación *f*

fortify ['fɔrtəˌfaɪ] *vt* -**fied; -fying** : fortificar

fortitude ['fɔrtəˌtuːd, -ˌtjuːd] *n* : fortaleza
f, valor *m*

fortnight ['fɔrtˌnaɪt] *n* : quince días *mpl*,
dos semanas *fpl*

fortnightly¹ ['fɔrtˌnaɪtli] *adv* : cada
quince días

fortnightly² *adj* : quincenal

fortress ['fɔrtrəs] *n* : fortaleza *f*

fortuitous [fɔr'tuːətəs, -'tjuː-] *adj* : fortuito, accidental

fortunate ['fɔrtʃənət] *adj* : afortunado

fortunately ['fɔrtʃənətli] *adv* : afortunadamente, con suerte

fortune ['fɔrtʃən] *n* **1** : fortuna *f* ⟨to seek
one's fortune : buscar uno su fortuna⟩
2 LUCK : suerte *f*, fortuna *f* **3** DESTINY,
FUTURE : destino *m*, buenaventura *f* **4**
: dineral *m*, platal *m* ⟨she spent a fortune : se gastó un dineral⟩

fortune–teller ['fɔrtʃənˌtɛlər] *n* : adivino
m, -na *f*

fortune–telling ['fɔrtʃənˌtɛlɪŋ] *n* : adivinación *f*

forty¹ ['fɔrti] *adj* : cuarenta

forty² *n, pl* **forties** : cuarenta *m*

forum ['fɔrəm] *n, pl* -**rums** : foro *m*

forward¹ ['fɔrwərd] *vt* **1** PROMOTE : promover, adelantar, fomentar **2** SEND
: remitir, enviar

forward² *adv* **1** : adelante, hacia adelante ⟨to go forward : irse adelante⟩ **2
from this day forward** : de aquí en adelante

forward³ *adj* **1** : hacia adelante, delantero **2** BRASH : atrevido, descarado

forward⁴ *n* : delantero *m*, -ra *f* (en deportes)

forwarder ['fɔrwərdər] *n* : agencia *f* de
transportes, agente *mf* expedidor

forwardness ['fɔrwərdnəs] *n* : atrevimiento *m*, descaro *m*

forwards ['fɔrwərdz] *adv* → **forward²**

fossil¹ ['fɑsəl] *adj* : fósil

fossil² *n* : fósil *m*

fossilize ['fɑsəˌlaɪz] *vt* -**ized; -izing** : fos-
ilizar — *vi* : fosilizarse

foster¹ ['fɔstər] *vt* : promover, fomentar

foster² *adj* : adoptivo ⟨foster child : niño
adoptivo⟩

fought → **fight**

foul¹ ['faʊl] *vi* : cometer faltas (en deportes) — *vt* **1** DIRTY, POLLUTE : contaminar, ensuciar **2** TANGLE : enredar

foul² *adv* **1** → **foully 2** : contra las reglas

foul³ *adj* **1** REPULSIVE : asqueroso, repugnante **2** CLOGGED : atascado, obstruido **3** TANGLED : enredado **4** OB-
SCENE : obsceno **5** BAD : malo ⟨foul
weather : mal tiempo⟩ **6** : antirreglamentario (en deportes)

foul⁴ *n* : falta *f*, faul *m*

foully ['faʊli] *adv* : asquerosamente

foulmouthed ['faʊlˌmæuːðd, -ˌmauːθd]
adj : malhablado

foulness ['faʊlnəs] *n* **1** DIRTINESS : suciedad *f* **2** INCLEMENCY : inclemencia
f **3** OBSCENITY : obscenidad *f*, grosería
f

foul play *n* : actos *mpl* criminales

foul–up ['faʊlˌʌp] *n* : lío *m*, confusión *f*,
desastre *m*

foul up *vt* SPOIL : estropear, arruinar —
vi BUNGLE : echar todo a perder

found¹ → **find**

found² ['faʊnd] *vt* : fundar, establecer

foundation [faʊn'deɪʃən] *n* **1** FOUND-
ING : fundación *f* **2** BASIS : fundamento
m, base *f* **3** INSTITUTION : fundación *f*
4 : cimientos *mpl* (de un edificio)

founder¹ ['faʊndər] *vi* SINK : hundirse,
irse a pique

founder² *n* : fundador *m*, -dora *f*

founding ['faʊndɪŋ] *adj* : fundador ⟨the
founding fathers : los fundadores⟩

foundling ['faʊndlɪŋ] *n* : expósito *m*, -ta
f

foundry ['faʊndri] *n, pl* -**dries** : fundición *f*

fount ['faʊnt] *n* SOURCE : fuente *f*, origen *m*

fountain ['faʊntən] *n* **1** SPRING : fuente *f*, manantial *m* **2** SOURCE : fuente *f*, origen *m* **3** JET : chorro *m* (de agua), surtidor *m*

fountain pen *n* : pluma *f* fuente

four¹ ['for] *adj* : cuatro

four² *n* **1** : cuatro *m* **2 on all fours** : a gatas

fourfold ['for,fo:ld, -'fo:ld] *adj* : cuadruple

four hundred¹ *adj* : cuatrocientos

four hundred² *n* : cuatrocientos *m*

fourscore ['for'skor] *adj* EIGHTY : ochenta *m*

fourteen¹ [for'ti:n] *adj* : catorce

fourteen² *n* : catorce *m*

fourteenth¹ [for'ti:nθ] *adj* : decimocuarto

fourteenth² *n* **1** : decimocuarto *m*, -ta *f* (en una serie) **2** : catorceavo *m*, catorceava parte *f*

fourth¹ ['forθ] *adj* : cuarto

fourth² *n* **1** : cuarto *m*, -ta *f* (en una serie) **2** : cuarto *m*, cuarta parte *f*

fowl ['faʊl] *n*, *pl* **fowl** *or* **fowls 1** BIRD : ave *f* **2** CHICKEN : pollo *m*

fox¹ ['faks] *vt* **1** TRICK : engañar **2** BAFFLE : confundir

fox² *n*, *pl* **foxes** : zorro *m*, -ra *f*

foxglove ['faks,glʌv] *n* : dedalera *f*, digital *f*

foxhole ['faks,ho:l] *n* : hoyo *m* para atrincherarse, trinchera *f* individual

foxy ['faksi] *adj* **foxier; -est** SHREWD : astuto

foyer ['fɔɪər, 'fɔɪ,jeɪ] *n* : vestíbulo *m*

fracas ['freɪkəs, 'fræ-] *n*, *pl* **-cases** [-kəsəz] : altercado *m*, pelea *f*, reyerta *f*

fraction ['frækʃən] *n* **1** : fracción *f*, quebrado *m* **2** PORTION : porción *f*, parte *f*

fractional ['frækʃənəl] *adj* **1** : fraccionario **2** TINY : minúsculo, mínimo, insignificante

fractious ['frækʃəs] *adj* **1** UNRULY : rebelde **2** IRRITABLE : malhumorado, irritable

fracture¹ ['fræktʃər] *vt* **-tured; -turing** : fracturar

fracture² *n* **1** : fractura *f* (de un hueso) **2** CRACK : fisura *f*, grieta *f*, falla *f* (geológica)

fragile ['frædʒəl, -,dʒaɪl] *adj* : frágil

fragility [frə'dʒɪləti] *n*, *pl* **-ties** : fragilidad *f*

fragment¹ ['fræg,mɛnt] *vt* : fragmentar — *vi* : fragmentarse, hacerse añicos

fragment² ['frægmənt] *n* : fragmento *m*, trozo *m*, pedazo *m*

fragmentary ['frægmən,tɛri] *adj* : fragmentario, incompleto

fragmentation [,frægmən'teɪʃən, -,mn-] *n* : fragmentación *f*

fragrance ['freɪgrənts] *n* : fragancia *f*, aroma *m*

fragrant ['freɪgrənt] *adj* : fragante, aromático — **fragrantly** *adv*

frail ['freɪl] *adj* : débil, delicado

frailty ['freɪlti] *n*, *pl* **-ties** : debilidad *f*, flaqueza *f*

frame¹ ['freɪm] *vt* **framed; framing 1** FORMULATE : formular, elaborar **2** BORDER : enmarcar, encuadrar **3** INCRIMINATE : incriminar

frame² *n* **1** BODY : cuerpo *m* **2** : armazón *f* (de un edificio, un barco, o un avión), bastidor *m* (de un automóvil), cuadro *m* (de una bicicleta), marco *m* (de un cuadro, una ventana, una puerta, etc.) **3 frames** *npl* : armazón *mf*, montura *f* (para anteojos) **4 frame of mind** : estado *m* de ánimo

framework ['freɪm,wərk] *n* **1** SKELETON, STRUCTURE : armazón *f*, estructura *f* **2** BASIS : marco *m*

franc ['fræŋk] *n* : franco *m*

franchise ['fræn,tʃaɪz] *n* **1** LICENSE : licencia *f* exclusiva, concesión *f* (en comercio) **2** SUFFRAGE : sufragio *m*

franchisee [,fræn,tʃaɪ'zi:, -tʃə-] *n* : concesionario *m*, -ria *f*

Franciscan [fræn'sɪskən] *n* : franciscano *m*, -na *f* — **Franciscan** *adj*

frank¹ ['fræŋk] *vt* : franquear

frank² *adj* : franco, sincero, cándido — **frankly** *adv*

frank³ *n* : franqueo *m* (de correo)

frankfurter ['fræŋkfərtər, -,fər-] *or* **frankfurt** [-fərt] *n* : salchicha *f* (de Frankfurt, de Viena), perro *m* caliente

frankincense ['fræŋkən,sɛnts] *n* : incienso *m*

frankness ['fræŋknəs] *n* : franqueza *f*, sinceridad *f*, candidez *f*

frantic ['fræntɪk] *adj* : frenético, desesperado — **frantically** *adv*

fraternal [frə'tərnəl] *adj* : fraterno, fraternal

fraternity [frə'tərnəti] *n*, *pl* **-ties** : fraternidad *f*

fraternization [,frætərnə'zeɪʃən] *n* : fraternización *f*, confraternización *f*

fraternize ['frætər,naɪz] *vi* **-nized; -nizing** : fraternizar, confraternizar

fratricidal [,frætrə'saɪdəl] *adj* : fratricida

fratricide ['frætrə,saɪd] *n* : fratricidio *m*

fraud ['frɔd] *n* **1** DECEPTION, SWINDLE : fraude *m*, estafa *f*, engaño *m* **2** IMPOSTOR : impostor *m*, -tora *f*; farsante *mf*

fraudulent ['frɔdʒələnt] *adj* : fraudulento — **fraudulently** *adv*

fraught ['frɔt] *adj* **fraught with** : lleno de, cargado de

fray¹ ['freɪ] *vt* **1** WEAR : desgastar, deshilachar **2** IRRITATE : crispar, irritar (los nervios) — *vi* : desgastarse, deshilacharse

fray² *n* : pelea *f* ⟨to join the fray : salir a la palestra⟩ ⟨to return to the fray : volver a la carga⟩

frazzle¹ ['fræzəl] *vt* **-zled; -zling 1** FRAY : desgastar, deshilachar **2** EXHAUST : agotar, fatigar

frazzle² *n* EXHAUSTION : agotamiento *m*

freak ['fri:k] *n* **1** ODDITY : ejemplar *m* anormal, fenómeno *m*, rareza *f* **2** EN-THUSIAST : entusiasta *mf*

freakish ['fri:kɪʃ] *adj* : extraño, estrafalario, raro

freak out *vi* : ponerse como loco — *vt* : darle un ataque (a alguien)

freckle¹ ['frɛkəl] *vi* **-led; -ling** : cubrirse de pecas

freckle² *n* : peca *f*

free¹ ['fri:] *vt* **freed; freeing 1** LIBERATE : libertar, liberar, poner en libertad **2** RELIEVE, RID : librar, eximir **3** RE-LEASE, UNTIE : desatar, soltar **4** UN-CLOG : desatascar, destapar

free² *adv* **1** FREELY : libremente **2** GRATIS : gratuitamente, gratis

free³ *adj* **freer; freest 1** : libre ⟨free as a bird : libre como un pájaro⟩ **2** EX-EMPT : libre ⟨tax-free : libre de impuestos⟩ **3** GRATIS : gratuito, gratis **4** VOLUNTARY : espontáneo, voluntario, libre **5** UNOCCUPIED : desocupado, libre **6** LOOSE : suelto

freebooter ['fri:,bu:tər] *n* : pirata *mf*

freeborn ['fri:'bɔrn] *adj* : nacido libre

freedom ['fri:dəm] *n* : libertad *f*

free—for—all ['fri:fər,ɔl] *n* : pelea *f*, batalla *f* campal

freelance¹ ['fri:,lænts] *vi* **-lanced; -lanc-ing** : trabajar por cuenta propia

freelance² *adj* : por cuenta propia, independiente

freeload ['fri:,lo:d] *vi* : gorronear *fam*, gorrear *fam*

freeloader ['fri:,lo:dər] *n* : gorrón *m*, -rrona *f*; gorrero *m*, -ra *f*; vividor *m*, -dora *f*

freely ['fri:li] *adv* **1** FREE : libremente **2** GRATIS : gratis, gratuitamente

freestanding ['fri:'stændɪŋ] *adj* : de pie, no empotrado, independiente

freeway ['fri:,weɪ] *n* : autopista *f*

freewill ['fri:,wɪl] *adj* : de propia voluntad

free will *n* : libre albedrío *m*, propia voluntad *f*

freeze¹ ['fri:z] *v* **froze** ['fro:z]; **frozen** ['fro:zən]; **freezing** *vi* **1** : congelarse, helarse ⟨the water froze in the lake : el agua se congeló en el lago⟩ ⟨my blood froze : se me heló la sangre⟩ ⟨I'm freezing : me estoy helando⟩ **2** STOP : quedarse inmóvil — *vt* : helar, congelar (líquidos), congelar (alimentos, precios, activos)

freeze² *n* **1** FROST : helada *f* **2** FREEZ-ING : congelación *f*, congelamiento *m*

freeze—dried ['fri:z'draɪd] *adj* : liofilizado

freeze—dry ['fri:z'draɪ] *vt* **-dried; -drying** : liofilizar

freezer ['fri:zər] *n* : congelador *m*

freezing ['fri:zɪŋ] *adj* : helando ⟨it's freezing! : ¡hace un frío espantoso!⟩

freezing point *n* : punto *m* de congelación

freight¹ ['freɪt] *vt* : enviar como carga

freight² *n* **1** SHIPPING, TRANSPORT : transporte *m*, porte *m*, flete *m* **2** GOODS : mercancías *fpl*, carga *f*

freighter ['freɪtər] *n* : carguero *m*, buque *m* de carga

French¹ ['frɛntʃ] *adj* : francés

French² *n* **1** : francés *m* (idioma) **2 the French** *npl* : los franceses

french fries ['frɛntʃ,fraɪz] *npl* : papas *fpl* fritas

Frenchman ['frɛntʃmən] *n, pl* **-men** [-mən, -,mɛn] : francés *m*

Frenchwoman ['frɛntʃ,wʊmən] *n, pl* **-women** [-,wɪmən] : francesa *f*

frenetic [frɪ'nɛtɪk] *adj* : frenético — **fre-netically** [-tɪkli] *adv*

frenzied ['frɛnzid] *adj* : frenético

frenzy ['frɛnzi] *n, pl* **-zies** : frenesí *m*

frequency ['fri:kwəntsi] *n, pl* **-cies** : frecuencia *f*

frequent¹ [fri'kwɛnt, 'fri:kwɛnt] *vt* : frecuentar

frequent² ['fri:kwɛnt] *adj* : frecuente — **frequently** *adv*

fresco ['frɛs,ko:] *n, pl* **-coes** : fresco *m*

fresh ['frɛʃ] *adj* **1** : dulce ⟨freshwater : agua dulce⟩ **2** PURE : puro *m* **3** : fresco ⟨fresh fruits : frutas frescas⟩ **4** CLEAN, NEW : limpio, nuevo ⟨fresh clothes : ropa limpia⟩ ⟨fresh evidence : evidencia nueva⟩ **5** REFRESHED : fresco, descansado **6** IMPERTINENT : descarado, impertinente

freshen ['frɛʃən] *vt* : refrescar, arreglar — *vi* **to freshen up** : arreglarse, lavarse

freshet ['frɛʃət] *n* : arroyo *m* desbordado

freshly ['frɛʃli] *adv* : recientemente, recién

freshman ['frɛʃmən] *n, pl* **-men** [-mən, -,mɛn] : estudiante *mf* de primer año universitario

freshness ['frɛʃnəs] *n* : frescura *f*

freshwater ['frɛʃ,wɔtər] *n* : agua *f* dulce

fret¹ ['frɛt] *vi* **fretted; fretting** : preocuparse, inquietarse

fret² *n* **1** VEXATION : irritación *f*, molestia *f* **2** WORRY : preocupación *f* **3** : traste *m* (de un instrumento musical)

fretful ['frɛtfəl] *adj* : fastidioso, quejoso, neurótico

fretfully ['frɛtfəli] *adv* : ansiosamente, fastidiosamente, inquieto

fretfulness ['frɛtfəlnəs] *n* : inquietud *f*, irritabilidad *f*

friable ['fraɪəbəl] *adj* : friable, pulverizable

friar ['fraɪər] *n* : fraile *m*

fricassee¹ ['frɪkə,si:, ,frɪkə'si:] *vt* **-seed; -seeing** : cocinar al fricasé

fricassee² *n* : fricasé *m*

friction ['frɪkʃən] *n* **1** RUBBING : fricción *f* **2** CONFLICT : fricción *f*, roce *m*

Friday ['fraɪ,deɪ, -di] *n* : viernes *m*

fridge ['frɪdʒ] → refrigerator

friend ['frɛnd] *n* : amigo *m*, -ga *f*
friendless ['frɛndləs] *adj* : sin amigos
friendliness ['frɛndlinəs] *n* : simpatía *f*, amabilidad *f*
friendly ['frɛndli] *adj* **-lier; -est 1** : simpático, amable, de amigo ⟨a friendly child : un niño simpático⟩ ⟨friendly advice : consejo de amigo⟩ **2** : agradable, acogedor ⟨a friendly atmosphere : un ambiente agradable⟩ **3** GOOD-NATURED : amigable, amistoso ⟨friendly competition : competencia amistosa⟩
friendship ['frɛnd,ʃɪp] *n* : amistad *f*
frieze ['fri:z] *n* : friso *m*
frigate ['frɪgət] *n* : fragata *f*
fright ['fraɪt] *n* : miedo *m*, susto *m*
frighten ['fraɪtən] *vt* : asustar, espantar
frightened ['fraɪtənd] *adj* : asustado, temeroso
frightening ['fraɪtənɪŋ] *adj* : espantoso, aterrador
frightful ['fraɪtfəl] *adj* **1** → **frightening 2** TREMENDOUS : espantoso, tremendo
frightfully ['fraɪtfəli] *adv* : terriblemente, tremendamente
frigid ['frɪʤɪd] *adj* : glacial, extremadamente frío
frigidity [frɪ'ʤɪdəti] *n* **1** COLDNESS : frialdad *f* **2** : frigidez *f* (sexual)
frill ['frɪl] *n* **1** RUFFLE : volante *m* **2** EMBELLISHMENT : floritura *f*, adorno *m*
frilly ['frɪli] *adj* **frillier; -est 1** RUFFLY : con volantes **2** OVERDONE : recargado
fringe¹ ['frɪnʤ] *vt* **fringed; fringing** : orlar, bordear
fringe² *n* **1** BORDER : fleco *m*, orla *f* **2** EDGE : periferia *f*, margen *m* **3 fringe benefits** : incentivos *mpl*, extras *mpl*
frisk ['frɪsk] *vi* FROLIC : retozar, juguetear — *vt* SEARCH : cachear, registrar
friskiness ['frɪskɪnəs] *n* : vivacidad *f*
frisky ['frɪski] *adj* **friskier; -est** : retozón, juguetón
fritter¹ ['frɪtər] *vt* : desperdiciar, malgastar ⟨I frittered away the money : malgasté el dinero⟩
fritter² *n* : buñuelo *m*
frivolity [frɪ'vɑləti] *n, pl* **-ties** : frivolidad *f*
frivolous ['frɪvələs] *adj* : frívolo, de poca importancia
frivolously ['frɪvələsli] *adv* : frívolamente, a la ligera
frizz ['frɪz] *vi* : rizarse, encresparse, ponerse chino *Mex*
frizz² *n* : rizos *mpl* muy apretados
frizzy ['frɪzi] *adj* **frizzier; -est** : rizado, crespo, chino *Mex*
fro ['fro:] *adv* **to and fro** : de aquí para allá, de un lado para otro
frock ['frɑk] *n* DRESS : vestido *m*
frog ['frɔg, 'frɑg] *n* **1** : rana *f* **2** FASTENER : alamar *m* **3 to have a frog in one's throat** : tener carraspera
frogman ['frɔg,mæn, 'frɑg-, -mən] *n, pl* **-men** [-mən, -,mɛn] : hombre *m* rana, submarinista *mf*

frolic¹ ['frɑlɪk] *vi* **-icked; -icking** : retozar, juguetear
frolic² *n* FUN : diversión *f*
frolicsome ['frɑlɪksəm] *adj* : juguetón
from ['frʌm, 'frɑm] *prep* **1** (*indicating a starting point*) : desde, de, a partir de ⟨from Cali to Bogota : de Cali a Bogotá⟩ ⟨where are you from? : ¿de dónde eres?⟩ ⟨from that time onward : desde entonces⟩ ⟨from tomorrow : a partir de mañana⟩ **2** (*indicating a source or sender*) : de ⟨a letter from my friend : una carta de mi amiga⟩ ⟨a quote from Shakespeare : una cita de Shakespeare⟩ **3** (*indicating distance*) : de ⟨10 feet from the entrance : a 10 pies de la entrada⟩ **4** (*indicating a cause*) : de ⟨red from crying : rojos de llorar⟩ ⟨he died from the cold : murió del frío⟩ **5** OFF, OUT OF : de ⟨she took it from the drawer : lo sacó del cajón⟩ **6** (*with adverbs or adverbial phrases*) : de, desde ⟨from above : desde arriba⟩ ⟨from among : de entre⟩
frond ['frɑnd] *n* : fronda *f*, hoja *f*
front¹ ['frʌnt] *vi* **1** FACE : dar, estar orientado ⟨the house fronts north : la casa da al norte⟩ **2** : servir de pantalla ⟨he fronts for his boss : sirve de pantalla para su jefe⟩
front² *adj* : delantero, de adelante, primero ⟨the front row : la primera fila⟩
front³ *n* **1** : frente *m*, parte *f* de adelante, delantera *f* ⟨the front of the class : el frente de la clase⟩ ⟨at the front of the train : en la parte delantera del tren⟩ **2** AREA, ZONE : frente *m*, zona *f* ⟨the Eastern front : el frente oriental⟩ ⟨on the educational front : en el frente de la enseñanza⟩ **3** FACADE : fachada *f* (de un edificio o una persona) **4** : frente *m* (en meteorología)
frontage ['frʌntɪʤ] *n* : fachada *f*, frente *m*
frontal ['frʌntəl] *adj* : frontal, de frente
frontier [,frʌn'tɪr] *n* : frontera *f*
frontiersman [,frʌn'tɪrzmən] *n, pl* **-men** [-mən, -,mɛn] : hombre *m* de la frontera
frontispiece ['frʌntəs,pi:s] *n* : frontispicio *m*
frost¹ ['frɔst] *vt* **1** FREEZE : helar **2** ICE : escarchar (pasteles)
frost² *n* **1** : helada *f* (en meteorología) **2** : escarcha *f* (frost on the window : escarcha en la ventana)
frostbite ['frɔst,baɪt] *n* : congelación *f*
frostbitten ['frɔst,bɪtən] *adj* : congelado (dícese de una persona), quemado (dícese de una planta)
frosting ['frɔstɪŋ] *n* ICING : glaseado *m*, betún *m* Mex
frosty ['frɔsti] *adj* **frostier; -est 1** CHILLY : helado, frío **2** COOL, UNFRIENDLY : frío, glacial
froth ['frɔθ] *n, pl* **froths** ['frɔθs, 'frɔðz] : espuma *f*

frothy ['frɔθi] *adj* **frothier; -est** : espumoso

frown[1] ['fraʊn] *vi* **1** : fruncir el ceño, fruncir el entrecejo **2 to frown at** : mirar (algo) con ceño, mirar (a alguien) con ceño

frown[2] *n* : ceño *m* (fruncido)

frowsy *or* **frowzy** ['fraʊzi] *adj* **frowsier** *or* **frowzier; -est** : desaliñado, desaseado

froze → **freeze**

frozen → **freeze**

frugal ['fru:gəl] *adj* : frugal, ahorrativo, parco — **frugally** *adv*

frugality [fru'gæləti] *n* : frugalidad *f*

fruit[1] ['fru:t] *vi* : dar fruto

fruit[2] *n* **1** : fruta *f* (término genérico), fruto *m* (término particular) **2 fruits** *npl* REWARDS : frutos *mpl* ⟨the fruits of his labor : los frutos de su trabajo⟩

fruitcake ['fru:t,keɪk] *n* : pastel *m* de frutas

fruitful ['fru:tfəl] *adj* : fructífero, provechoso

fruition [fru'ɪʃən] *n* **1** : cumplimiento *m*, realización *f* **2 to bring to fruition** : realizar

fruitless ['fru:tləs] *adj* : infructuoso, inútil — **fruitlessly** *adv*

fruity ['fru:ti] *adj* **fruitier; -est** : (con sabor) a fruta

frumpy ['frʌmpi] *adj* **frumpier; -est** : anticuado y sin atractivo

frustrate ['frʌs,treɪt] *vt* **-trated; -trating** : frustrar

frustrating ['frʌs,treɪtɪŋ] *adj* : frustrante — **frustratingly** *adv*

frustration [,frʌs'treɪʃən] *n* : frustración *f*

fry[1] ['fraɪ] *vt* **fried; frying** : freír

fry[2] *n, pl* **fries 1** : fritura *f*, plato *m* frito **2** : fiesta *f* en que se sirven frituras **3** *pl* **fry** : alevín *m* (pez)

frying pan *n* : sartén *mf*

fuchsia ['fju:ʃə] *n* **1** : fucsia *f* (planta) **2** : fucsia *m* (color)

fuddle ['fʌdəl] *vt* **-dled; -dling** : confundir, atontar

fuddy-duddy ['fʌdi,dʌdi] *n, pl* **-dies** : persona *f* chapada a la antigua, carca *mf*

fudge[1] ['fʌʤ] *vt* **fudged; fudging 1** FALSIFY : amañar, falsificar **2** DODGE : esquivar

fudge[2] *n* : dulce *m* blando de chocolate y leche

fuel[1] ['fju:əl] *vt* **-eled** *or* **-elled; -eling** *or* **-elling 1** : abastecer de combustible **2** STIMULATE : estimular

fuel[2] *n* : combustible *m*, carburante *m* (para motores)

fugitive[1] ['fju:ʤətɪv] *adj* **1** RUNAWAY : fugitivo **2** FLEETING : efímero, pasajero, fugaz

fugitive[2] *n* : fugitivo *m*, -va *f*

fugue ['fju:g] *n* : fuga *f*

fulcrum ['fʊlkrəm, 'fʌl-] *n, pl* **-crums** *or* **-cra** [-krə] : fulcro *m*

fulfill *or* **fulfil** [fʊl'fɪl] *vt* **-filled; -filling 1** PERFORM : cumplir con, realizar, llevar a cabo **2** SATISFY : satisfacer

fulfillment [fʊl'fɪlmənt] *n* **1** PERFORMANCE : cumplimiento *m*, ejecución *f* **2** SATISFACTION : satisfacción *f*, realización *f*

full[1] ['fʊl, 'fʌl] *adv* **1** VERY : muy ⟨full well : muy bien, perfectamente⟩ **2** ENTIRELY : completamente ⟨she swung full around : giró completamente⟩ **3** DIRECTLY : de lleno, directamente ⟨he looked me full in the face : me miró directamente a la cara⟩

full[2] *adj* **1** FILLED : lleno **2** COMPLETE : completo, detallado **3** MAXIMUM : todo, pleno ⟨at full speed : a toda velocidad⟩ ⟨in full bloom : en plena flor⟩ **4** PLUMP : redondo, llenito *fam*, regordete *fam* ⟨a full face : una cara redonda⟩ ⟨a full figure : un cuerpo llenito⟩ **5** AMPLE : amplio ⟨a full skirt : una falda amplia⟩

full[3] *n* **1 to pay in full** : pagar en su totalidad **2 to the full** : al máximo

full-fledged [fʊl'flɛʤd] *adj* : hecho y derecho

fullness ['fʊlnəs] *n* **1** ABUNDANCE : plenitud *f*, abundancia *f* **2** : amplitud *f* (de una falda)

fully ['fʊli] *adv* **1** COMPLETELY : completamente, totalmente **2** : al menos, por lo menos ⟨fully half of them : al menos la mitad de ellos⟩

fulsome ['fʊlsəm] *adj* : excesivo, exagerado, efusivo

fumble[1] ['fʌmbəl] *v* **-bled; -bling** *vt* **1** : dejar caer, fumblear **2 to fumble one's way** : ir a tientas — *vi* **1** GROPE : hurgar, tantear **2 to fumble with** : manejar con torpeza

fumble[2] *n* : fumble *m* (en futbol americano)

fume[1] ['fju:m] *vi* **fumed; fuming 1** SMOKE : echar humo, humear **2** : estar furioso

fume[2] *n* : gas *m*, humo *m*, vapor *m*

fumigate ['fju:mə,geɪt] *vt* **-gated; -gating** : fumigar

fumigation [,fju:mə'geɪʃən] *n* : fumigación *f*

fun[1] ['fʌn] *adj* : divertido, entretenido

fun[2] *n* **1** AMUSEMENT : diversión *f*, entretenimiento *m* **2** ENJOYMENT : disfrute *m* **3 to have fun** : divertirse **4 to make fun of** : reírse de, burlarse de

function[1] ['fʌŋkʃən] *vi* : funcionar, desempeñarse, servir

function[2] *n* **1** PURPOSE : función *f* **2** GATHERING : reunión *f* social, recepción *f* **3** CEREMONY : ceremonia *f*, acto *m*

functional ['fʌŋkʃənəl] *adj* : funcional — **functionally** *adv*

functionary ['fʌŋkʃə,neri] *n, pl* **-aries** : funcionario *m*, -ria *f*

fund[1] ['fʌnd] *vt* : financiar

fund² *n* **1** SUPPLY : reserva *f*, cúmulo *m* **2** : fondo *m* ⟨investment fund : fondo de inversiones⟩ **3 funds** *npl* RESOURCES : fondos *mpl*
fundamental¹ [ˌfʌndə'mɛntəl] *adj* **1** BASIC : fundamental, básico **2** PRINCIPAL : esencial, principal **3** INNATE : innato, intrínseco
fundamental² *n* : fundamento *m*
fundamentalism [ˌfʌndə'mɛntəlˌɪzəm] *n* : integrismo *m*, fundamentalismo *m*
fundamentalist [ˌfʌndə'mɛntəlɪst] *n* : integrista *mf*, fundamentalista *mf* — **fundamentalist** *adj*
fundamentally [ˌfʌndə'mɛntəli] *adv* : fundamentalmente, básicamente
funding ['fʌndɪŋ] *n* : financiación *f*
fund–raiser ['fʌndˌreɪzər] *n* : función *f* para recaudar fondos
funeral¹ ['fjuːnərəl] *adj* **1** : funeral, funerario, fúnebre ⟨funeral procession : cortejo fúnebre⟩ **2 funeral home** : funeraria *f*
funeral² *n* : funeral *m*, funerales *mpl*
funereal [fju'nɪriəl] *adj* : fúnebre
fungal ['fʌŋgəl] *adj* : de hongos, micótico
fungicidal [ˌfʌndʒə'saɪdəl, ˌfʌŋgə-] *adj* : fungicida
fungicide ['fʌndʒəˌsaɪd, 'fʌŋgə-] *n* : fungicida *m*
fungous ['fʌŋgəs] *adj* : fungoso
fungus ['fʌŋgəs] *n*, *pl* **fungi** ['fʌnˌdʒaɪ, 'fʌnˌgaɪ] : hongo *m*
funk ['fʌŋk] *n* **1** FEAR : miedo *m* **2** DEPRESSION : depresión *f*
funky ['fʌŋki] *adj* **funkier; -est** ODD, QUAINT : raro, extraño, original
funnel¹ ['fʌnəl] *vt* **-neled; -neling** CHANNEL : canalizar, encauzar
funnel² *n* **1** : embudo *m* **2** SMOKESTACK : chimenea *f* (de un barco o vapor)
funnies ['fʌniz] *npl* : tiras *fpl* cómicas
funny ['fʌni] *adj* **funnier; -est 1** AMUSING : divertido, cómico **2** STRANGE : extraño, raro
fur¹ ['fər] *adj* : de piel
fur² *n* **1** : pelaje *m*, piel *f* **2** : prenda *f* de piel
furbish ['fərbɪʃ] *vt* : pulir, limpiar
furious ['fjuriəs] *adj* **1** ANGRY : furioso **2** FRANTIC : violento, frenético, vertiginoso (dícese de la velocidad)
furiously ['fjuriəsli] *adv* **1** ANGRILY : furiosamente **2** FRANTICALLY : frenéticamente
furlong ['fərˌlɔŋ] *n* : estadio *m* (201.2 m)
furlough¹ ['fərˌloː] *vt* : dar permiso a, dar licencia a
furlough² *n* LEAVE : permiso *m*, licencia *f*
furnace ['fərnəs] *n* : horno *m*
furnish ['fərnɪʃ] *vt* **1** SUPPLY : proveer, suministrar **2** : amueblar ⟨furnished apartment : departamento amueblado⟩
furnishings ['fərnɪʃɪŋz] *npl* **1** ACCESSORIES : accesorios *mpl* **2** FURNITURE : muebles *mpl*, mobiliario *m*

furniture ['fərnɪtʃər] *n* : muebles *mpl*, mobiliario *m*
furor ['fjurˌɔr, -ər] *n* **1** RAGE : furia *f*, rabia *f* **2** UPROAR : escándalo *m*, jaleo *m*, alboroto *m*
furrier ['fəriər] *n* : peletero *m*, -ra *f*
furrow¹ ['fəroː] *vt* **1** : surcar **2 to furrow one's brow** : fruncir el ceño
furrow² *n* **1** GROOVE : surco *m* **2** WRINKLE : arruga *f*, surco *m*
furry ['fəri] *adj* **furrier; -est** : peludo (dícese de un animal), peluche (dícese de un objeto)
further¹ ['fərðər] *vt* : promover, fomentar
further² *adv* **1** FARTHER : más lejos, más adelante **2** MOREOVER : además **3** MORE : más ⟨I'll consider it further in the morning : lo consideraré más en la mañana⟩
further³ *adj* **1** FARTHER : más lejano **2** ADDITIONAL : adicional, más
furtherance ['fərðərənts] *n* : promoción *f*, fomento *m*, adelantamiento *m*
furthermore ['fərðərˌmor] *adv* : además
furthermost ['fərðərˌmoːst] *adj* : más lejano, más distante
furthest ['fərðəst] → **farthest¹, farthest²**
furtive ['fərtɪv] *adj* : furtivo, sigiloso — **furtively** *adv*
furtiveness ['fərtɪvnəs] *n* STEALTH : sigilo *m*
fury ['fjuri] *n*, *pl* **-ries 1** RAGE : furia *f*, ira *f* **2** VIOLENCE : furia *f*, furor *m*
fuse¹ ['fjuːz] *n* **or fuze** *vt* **fused** *or* **fuzed; fusing** *or* **fuzing** : equipar con un fusible
fuse² *v* **fused; fusing** *vt* **1** SMELT : fundir **2** MERGE : fusionar, fundir — *vi* : fundirse, fusionarse
fuse³ *n* : fusible *m*
fuselage ['fjuːsəˌlɑʒ, -zə-] *n* : fuselaje *m*
fusillade ['fjuːsəˌlɑd, -ˌleɪd, ˌfjuːsə'-, -zə-] *n* : descarga *f* de fusilería
fusion ['fjuːʒən] *n* : fusión *f*
fuss¹ ['fʌs] *vi* **1** WORRY : preocuparse **2 to fuss with** : juguetear con, toquetear **3 to fuss over** : mimar
fuss² *n* **1** COMMOTION : alboroto *m*, escándalo *m* **2** ATTENTION : atenciones *fpl* **3** COMPLAINT : quejas *fpl*
fussbudget ['fʌsˌbʌdʒət] *n* : quisquilloso *m*, -sa *f*; melindroso *m*, -sa *f*
fussiness ['fʌsinəs] *n* **1** IRRITABILITY : irritabilidad *f* **2** ORNATENESS : lo recargado **3** METICULOUSNESS : meticulosidad *f*
fussy ['fʌsi] *adj* **fussier; -est 1** IRRITABLE : irritable, nervioso **2** OVERELABORATE : recargado **3** METICULOUS : meticuloso **4** FASTIDIOUS : quisquilloso, exigente
futile ['fjuːtəl, 'fjuːˌtaɪl] *adj* : inútil, vano
futility [fju'tɪləti] *n*, *pl* **-ties** : inutilidad *f*
future¹ ['fjuːtʃər] *adj* : futuro
future² *n* : futuro *m*
futuristic [ˌfjuːtʃə'rɪstɪk] *adj* : futurista
fuze → **fuse¹**

fuzz ['fʌz] *n* : pelusa *f*
fuzziness ['fʌzinəs] *n* **1** DOWNINESS : vellosidad *f* **2** INDISTINCTNESS : falta *f* de claridad

fuzzy ['fʌzi] *adj* **fuzzier; -est 1** FLUFFY, FURRY : con pelusa, peludo **2** INDISTINCT : indistinto ⟨a fuzzy image : una imagen borrosa⟩

G

g ['ʤi:] *n, pl* **g's** *or* **gs** ['ʤi:z] : séptima letra del alfabeto inglés
gab[1] ['gæb] *vi* **gabbed; gabbing** : charlar, cotorrear *fam*, parlotear *fam*
gab[2] *n* CHATTER : cotorreo *m fam*, parloteo *m fam*
gabardine ['gæbər,di:n] *n* : gabardina *f*
gabby ['gæbi] *adj* **gabbier; -est** : hablador, parlanchín
gable ['geibəl] *n* : hastial *m*, aguilón *m*
Gabonese [,gæbə'ni:z, -'ni:s] *n* : gabonés *m*, -nesa *f* — **Gabonese** *adj*
gad ['gæd] *vi* **gadded; gadding** WANDER : deambular, vagar, callejear
gadfly ['gæd,flaɪ] *n, pl* **-flies 1** : tábano *m* (insecto) **2** FAULTFINDER : criticón *m*, -cona *f fam*
gadget ['gæʤət] *n* : artilugio *m*, aparato *m*
gadgetry ['gæʤətri] *n* : artilugios *mpl*, aparatos *mpl*
Gaelic ['geilɪk, 'gæ] *n* : gaélico *m* (idioma) — **Gaelic** *adj*
gaff ['gæf] *n* **1** : garfio *m* **2** → **gaffe**
gaffe ['gæf] *n* : metedura *f* de pata *fam*
gag[1] ['gæg] *v* **gagged; gagging** *vt* : amordazar ⟨to tie up and gag : atar y amordazar⟩ — *vi* **1** CHOKE : atragantarse **2** RETCH : hacer arcadas
gag[2] *n* **1** : mordaza *f* (para la boca) **2** JOKE : chiste *m*
gage → **gauge**
gaggle ['gægəl] *n* : bandada *f*, manada *f* (de gansos)
gaiety ['geiəti] *n, pl* **-eties 1** MERRYMAKING : juerga *f* **2** MERRIMENT : alegría *f*, regocijo *m*
gaily ['geili] *adv* : alegremente
gain[1] ['gein] *vt* **1** ACQUIRE, OBTAIN : ganar, obtener, adquirir, conseguir ⟨to gain knowledge : adquirir conocimientos⟩ ⟨to gain a victory : obtener una victoria⟩ **2** REACH : alcanzar, llegar a **3** INCREASE : ganar, aumentar ⟨to gain weight : aumentar de peso⟩ **4** : adelantarse, ganar ⟨the watch gains two minutes a day : el reloj se adelanta dos minutos por día⟩ — *vi* **1** PROFIT : beneficiarse **2** INCREASE : aumentar
gain[2] *n* **1** PROFIT : beneficio *m*, ganancia *f*, lucro *m*, provecho *m* **2** INCREASE : aumento *m*
gainful ['geinfəl] *adj* : lucrativo, beneficioso, provechoso ⟨gainful employment : trabajo remunerado⟩
gait ['geit] *n* : paso *m*, andar *m*, manera *f* de caminar
gal ['gæl] *n* : muchacha *f*
gala[1] ['geilə, 'gæ-, 'gɑ-] *adj* : de gala

gala[2] *n* : gala *f*, fiesta *f*
galactic [gə'læktɪk] *adj* : galáctico
galaxy ['gæləksi] *n, pl* **-axies** : galaxia *f*
gale ['geil] *n* **1** WIND : vendaval *f*, viento *m* fuerte **2 gales of laughter** : carcajadas *fpl*
gall[1] ['gɔl] *vt* **1** CHAFE : rozar **2** IRRITATE, VEX : irritar, molestar
gall[2] *n* **1** BILE : bilis *f*, hiel *f* **2** INSOLENCE : audacia *f*, insolencia *f*, descaro *m* **3** SORE : rozadura *f* (de un caballo) **4** : agalla *f* (de una planta)
gallant ['gælənt] *adj* **1** BRAVE : valiente, gallardo **2** CHIVALROUS, POLITE : galante, cortés
gallantry ['gæləntri] *n, pl* **-ries** : galantería *f*, caballerosidad *f*
gallbladder ['gɔl,blædər] *n* : vesícula *f* biliar
galleon ['gæljən] *n* : galeón *m*
gallery ['gæləri] *n, pl* **-leries 1** BALCONY : galería *f* (para espectadores) **2** CORRIDOR : pasillo *m*, galería *f*, corredor *m* **3** : galería *f* (para exposiciones)
galley ['gæli] *n, pl* **-leys** : galera *f*
gallium ['gæliəm] *n* : galio *m*
gallivant ['gælə,vænt] *vi* : callejear
gallon ['gælən] *n* : galón *m*
gallop[1] ['gæləp] *vi* : galopar
gallop[2] *n* : galope *m*
gallows ['gæ,lo:z] *n, pl* **-lows** *or* **-lowses** [-,lo:zəz] : horca *f*
gallstone ['gɔl,sto:n] *n* : cálculo *m* biliar
galore [gə'lor] *adj* : en abundancia ⟨bargains galore : muchísimas gangas⟩
galoshes [gə'lɑʃəz] *npl* : galochas *fpl*, chanclos *mpl*
galvanize ['gælvən,aɪz] *vt* **-nized; -nizing 1** STIMULATE : estimular, excitar, impulsar **2** : galvanizar (metales)
Gambian ['gæmbiən] *n* : gambiano *m*, -na *f* — **Gambian** *adj*
gambit ['gæmbɪt] *n* **1** : gambito *m* (en ajedrez) **2** STRATAGEM : estratagema *f*, táctica *f*
gamble[1] ['gæmbəl] *v* **-bled; -bling** *vi* : jugar, arriesgarse — *vt* **1** BET, WAGER : apostar, jugarse **2** RISK : arriesgar
gamble[2] *n* **1** BET : apuesta *f* **2** RISK : riesgo *m*
gambler ['gæmbələr] *n* : jugador *m*, -dora *f*
gambling ['gæmbəliŋ] *n* : juego *m*
gambol ['gæmbəl] *vi* **-boled** *or* **-bolled; -boling** *or* **-bolling** FROLIC : retozar, juguetear
game[1] ['geim] *adj* **1** READY : listo, dispuesto ⟨we're game for anything : es-

tamos listos para lo que sea⟩ **2** LAME
: cojo
game² *n* **1** AMUSEMENT : juego *m*, diversión *f* **2** CONTEST : juego *m*, partido
m, concurso *m* **3** : caza *f* ⟨big game
: caza mayor⟩
gamecock [ˈɡeɪmˌkɑk] *n* : gallo *m* de pelea
gamekeeper [ˈɡeɪmˌkiːpər] *n* : guardabosque *mf*
gamely [ˈɡeɪmli] *adv* : animosamente
gamma ray [ˈɡæmə] *n* : rayo *m* gamma
gamut [ˈɡæmət] *n* : gama *f*, espectro *m*
⟨to run the gamut : pasar por toda la
gama⟩
gamy *or* **gamey** [ˈɡeɪmi] *adj* **gamier; -est**
: con sabor de animal de caza, fuerte
gander [ˈɡændər] *n* **1** : ganso *m* (animal) **2** GLANCE : mirada *f*, vistazo *m*,
ojeada *f*
gang¹ [ˈɡæŋ] *vi* **to gang up** : agruparse,
unirse
gang² *n* : banda *f*, pandilla *f*
gangling [ˈɡæŋɡlɪŋ] *adj* LANKY : larguirucho *fam*
ganglion [ˈɡæŋɡliən] *n, pl* **-glia** [-gliə]
: ganglio *m*
gangplank [ˈɡæŋˌplæŋk] *n* : pasarela *f*
gangrene [ˈɡæŋˌɡriːn, ˈɡæn-; ˈɡæŋˈ-,
ɡæn¹-] *n* : gangrena *f*
gangrenous [ˈɡæŋɡrənəs] *adj* : gangrenoso
gangster [ˈɡæŋstər] *n* : gángster *mf*
gangway [ˈɡæŋˌweɪ] *n* **1** : pasarela *f* **2**
gangway! : ¡abran paso!
gap [ˈɡæp] *n* **1** BREACH, OPENING : espacio *m*, brecha *f*, abertura *f* **2** GORGE
: desfiladero *m*, barranco *m* **3** : laguna *f* ⟨a gap in my education : una laguna en mi educación⟩ **4** INTERVAL
: pausa *f*, intervalo *m* **5** DISPARITY
: brecha *f*, disparidad *f*
gape¹ [ˈɡeɪp] *vi* **gaped; gaping 1** OPEN
: abrirse, estar abierto **2** STARE : mirar fijamente con la boca abierta, mirar boquiabierto
gape² *n* **1** OPENING : abertura *f*, brecha
f **2** STARE : mirada *f* boquiabierta
garage¹ [ɡəˈrɑʒ, -ˈrɑdʒ] *vt* **-raged;**
-raging : dejar en un garaje
garage² *n* : garaje *m*, cochera *f*
garb¹ [ˈɡɑrb] *vt* : vestir, ataviar
garb² *n* : vestimenta *f*, atuendo *f*
garbage [ˈɡɑrbɪdʒ] *n* : basura *f*, desechos
mpl
garbageman [ˈɡɑrbɪdʒmən] *n, pl* **-men**
[-mən, -ˌmɛn] : basurero *m*
garble [ˈɡɑrbəl] *vt* **-bled; -bling** : tergiversar, distorsionar
garbled [ˈɡɑrbəld] *adj* : incoherente, incomprensible
garden¹ [ˈɡɑrdən] *vi* : trabajar en el
jardín
garden² *n* : jardín *m*
gardener [ˈɡɑrdənər] *n* : jardinero *m*, -ra
f
gardenia [ɡɑrˈdiːnjə] *n* : gardenia *f*
gardening [ˈɡɑrdənɪŋ] *n* : jardinería *f*

gargantuan [ɡɑrˈɡænʧuən] *adj* : gigantesco, colosal
gargle¹ [ˈɡɑrɡəl] *vi* **-gled; -gling** : hacer
gárgaras, gargarizar
gargle² *n* : gárgara *f*
gargoyle [ˈɡɑrˌɡɔɪl] *n* : gárgola *f*
garish [ˈɡærɪʃ] *adj* GAUDY : llamativo,
chillón, charro — **garishly** *adv*
garland¹ [ˈɡɑrlənd] *vt* : adornar con
guirnaldas
garland² *n* : guirnalda *f*
garlic [ˈɡɑrlɪk] *n* : ajo *m*
garment [ˈɡɑrmənt] *n* : prenda *f*
garner [ˈɡɑrnər] *vt* : recoger, cosechar
garnet [ˈɡɑrnət] *n* : granate *m*
garnish¹ [ˈɡɑrnɪʃ] *vt* : aderezar, guarnecer
garnish² *n* : aderezo *m*, guarnición *f*
garret [ˈɡærət] *n* : buhardilla *f*, desván
m
garrison¹ [ˈɡærəsən] *vt* **1** QUARTER
: acuartelar (tropas) **2** OCCUPY : guarnecer, ocupar (con tropas)
garrison² *n* **1** : guarnición *f* (ciudad) **2**
FORT : fortaleza *f*, poste *m* militar
garrulous [ˈɡærələs] *adj* : charlatán, parlanchín, garlero *Col fam*
garter [ˈɡɑrtər] *n* : liga *f*
gas¹ [ˈɡæs] *v* **gassed; gassing** *vt* : gasear
— *vi* **to gas up** : llenar el tanque con
gasolina
gas² *n, pl* **gases** [ˈɡæsəz] **1** : gas *m* ⟨tear
gas : gas lacrimógeno⟩ **2** GASOLINE
: gasolina *f*
gaseous [ˈɡæsəs, ˈɡæsiəs] *adj* : gaseoso
gash¹ [ˈɡæʃ] *vt* : hacer un tajo en, cortar
gash² *n* : cuchillada *f*, tajo *m*
gasket [ˈɡæskət] *n* : junta *f*
gas mask *n* : máscara *f* antigás
gasoline [ˈɡæsəˌliːn, ˌɡæsəˈ-] *n* : gasolina *f*, nafta *f*
gasp¹ [ˈɡæsp] *vi* **1** : boquear ⟨to gasp
with surprise : gritar de asombro⟩ **2**
PANT : jadear, respirar con dificultad
gasp² *n* **1** : boqueada *f* ⟨a gasp of surprise : un grito sofocado⟩ **2** PANTING
: jadeo *m*
gas station *n* : estación *f* de servicio,
gasolinera *f*
gastric [ˈɡæstrɪk] *adj* : gástrico ⟨gastric
juice : jugo gástrico⟩
gastronomic [ˌɡæstrəˈnɑmɪk] *adj* : gastronómico
gastronomy [ɡæsˈtrɑnəmi] *n* : gastronomía *f*
gate [ˈɡeɪt] *n* : portón *m*, verja *f*, puerta
f
gatekeeper [ˈɡeɪtˌkiːpər] *n* : guarda *mf*;
guardián *m*, -diana *f*
gateway [ˈɡeɪtˌweɪ] *n* : puerta *f* (de acceso), entrada *f*
gather [ˈɡæðər] *vt* **1** ASSEMBLE : juntar,
recoger, reunir **2** HARVEST : recoger,
cosechar **3** : fruncir (una tela) **4** IN-
FER : deducir, suponer
gathering [ˈɡæðərɪŋ] *n* : reunión *f*
gauche [ˈɡoːʃ] *adj* : torpe, falto de tacto

gaudy ['gɔdi] *adj* **gaudier; -est** : chillón, llamativo
gauge¹ ['geɪʤ] *vt* **gauged; gauging 1** MEASURE : medir **2** ESTIMATE, JUDGE : estimar, evaluar, juzgar
gauge² *n* **1** : indicador *m* ⟨pressure gauge : indicador de presión⟩ **2** CALIBER : calibre *m* **3** INDICATION : indicio *m*, muestra *f*
gaunt ['gɔnt] *adj* : demacrado, enjuto, descarnado
gauntlet ['gɔntlət] *n* : guante *m* ⟨to run the gauntlet of : exponerse a⟩
gauze ['gɔz] *n* : gasa *f*
gauzy ['gɔzi] *adj* **gauzier; -est** : diáfano, vaporoso
gave → **give**
gavel ['gævəl] *n* : martillo *m* (de un juez, un subastador, etc.)
gawk ['gɔk] *vi* GAPE : mirar boquiabierto
gawky ['gɔki] *adj* **gawkier; -est** : desmañado, torpe, desgarbado
gay ['geɪ] *adj* **1** MERRY : alegre **2** BRIGHT, COLORFUL : vistoso, vivo **3** HOMOSEXUAL : homosexual
gaze¹ ['geɪz] *vi* **gazed; gazing** : mirar (fijamente)
gaze² *n* : mirada *f* (fija)
gazelle [gə'zɛl] *n* : gacela *f*
gazette [gə'zɛt] *n* : gaceta *f*
gazetteer [ˌgæzə'tɪr] *n* : diccionario *m* geográfico
gear¹ ['gɪr] *vt* ADAPT, ORIENT : adaptar, ajustar, orientar ⟨a book geared to children : un libro adaptado a los niños⟩ — *vi* **to gear up** : prepararse
gear² *n* **1** CLOTHING : ropa *f* **2** BELONGINGS : efectos *mpl* personales **3** EQUIPMENT, TOOLS : equipo *m*, aparejo *m*, herramientas *fpl* ⟨fishing gear : aparejo de pescar⟩ ⟨landing gear : tren de aterrizaje⟩ **4** COGWHEEL : rueda *f* dentada **5** : marcha *f*, velocidad *f* (de un vehículo) ⟨to put in gear : poner en marcha⟩ ⟨to change gear(s) : cambiar de velocidad⟩
gearshift ['gɪrˌʃɪft] *n* : palanca *f* de cambio, palanca *f* de velocidad
geek ['giːk] *n fam* : intelectual *mf*
geese → **goose**
Geiger counter ['gaɪgərˌkaʊntər] *n* : contador *m* Geiger
gel ['ʤɛl] *n* : gel *m*
gelatin ['ʤɛlətən] *n* : gelatina *f*
gem ['ʤɛm] *n* : joya *f*, gema *f*, alhaja *f*
Gemini ['ʤɛməˌnaɪ] *n* : Géminis *mf*
gemstone ['ʤɛmˌstoːn] *n* : piedra *f* (semipreciosa o preciosa), gema *f*
gender ['ʤɛndər] *n* **1** SEX : sexo *m* **2** : género *m* (en la gramática)
gene ['ʤiːn] *n* : gen *m*, gene *m*
genealogical [ˌʤiːniə'lɑʤɪkəl] *adj* : genealógico
genealogy [ˌʤiːni'ɑləʤi, ˌʤɛ-, -'æ-] *n, pl* **-gies** : genealogía *f*
genera → **genus**

general¹ ['ʤɛnrəl, 'ʤɛnə-] *adj* : general ⟨in general : en general, por lo general⟩
general² *n* : general *mf*
generality [ˌʤɛnə'ræləti] *n, pl* **-ties** : generalidad *f*
generalization [ˌʤɛnrələ'zeɪʃən, ˌʤɛnərə-] *n* : generalización *f*
generalize ['ʤɛnrəˌlaɪz, 'ʤɛnərə-] *v* **-ized; -izing** : generalizar
generally ['ʤɛnrəli, 'ʤɛnərə-] *adv* : generalmente, por lo general, en general
generate ['ʤɛnəˌreɪt] *vt* **-ated; -ating** : generar, producir
generation [ˌʤɛnə'reɪʃən] *n* : generación *f*
generator ['ʤɛnəˌreɪtər] *n* : generador *m*
generic [ʤə'nɛrɪk] *adj* : genérico
generosity [ˌʤɛnə'rɑsəti] *n, pl* **-ties** : generosidad *f*
generous ['ʤɛnərəs] *adj* **1** OPENHANDED : generoso, dadivoso, desprendido **2** ABUNDANT, AMPLE : abundante, amplio, generoso — **generously** *adv*
genetic [ʤə'nɛtɪk] *adj* : genético — **genetically** [-tɪkli] *adv*
geneticist [ʤə'nɛtəsɪst] *n* : genetista *mf*
genetics [ʤə'nɛtɪks] *n* : genética *f*
genial ['ʤiːniəl] *adj* GRACIOUS : simpático, cordial, afable — **genially** *adv*
geniality [ˌʤiːni'æləti] *n* : simpatía *f*, afabilidad *f*
genie ['ʤiːni] *n* : genio *m*
genital ['ʤɛnətəl] *adj* : genital
genitals ['ʤɛnətəlz] *npl* : genitales *mpl*
genius ['ʤiːnjəs] *n* : genio *m*
genocide ['ʤɛnəˌsaɪd] *n* : genocidio *m*
genre ['ʒɑnrə, 'ʒɑr] *n* : género *m*
genteel [ʤɛn'tiːl] *adj* : cortés, fino, refinado
gentile¹ ['ʤɛnˌtaɪl] *adj* : gentil
gentile² *n* : gentil *mf*
gentility [ʤɛn'tɪləti] *n, pl* **-ties 1** : nobleza *f* (de nacimiento) **2** POLITENESS, REFINEMENT : cortesía *f*, refinamiento *m*
gentle ['ʤɛntəl] *adj* **-tler; -tlest 1** NOBLE : bien nacido, noble **2** DOCILE : dócil, manso **3** KINDLY : bondadoso, amable **4** MILD : suave, apacible ⟨a gentle breeze : una brisa suave⟩ **5** SOFT : suave (dícese de un sonido), ligero (dícese del tacto) **6** MODERATE : moderado, gradual ⟨a gentle slope : una cuesta gradual⟩
gentleman ['ʤɛntəlmən] *n, pl* **-men** [-mən, -ˌmɛn] : caballero *m*, señor *m*
gentlemanly ['ʤɛntəlmənli] *adj* : caballeroso
gentleness ['ʤɛntəlnəs] *n* : delicadeza *f*, suavidad *f*, ternura *f*
gentlewoman ['ʤɛntəlˌwʊmən] *n, pl* **-women** [-ˌwɪmən] : dama *f*, señora *f*
gently ['ʤɛntli] *adv* **1** CAREFULLY, SOFTLY : con cuidado, suavemente, ligeramente **2** KINDLY : amablemente, con delicadeza

gentry ['ʤɛntri] *n, pl* **-tries** : aristocracia *f*

genuflect ['ʤɛnjʊˌflɛkt] *vi* : doblar la rodilla, hacer una genuflexión

genuflection [ˌʤɛnjʊ'flɛkʃən] *n* : genuflexión *f*

genuine ['ʤɛnjuwən] *adj* **1** AUTHENTIC, REAL : genuino, verdadero, auténtico **2** SINCERE : sincero — **genuinely** *adv*

genus ['ʤi:nəs] *n, pl* **genera** ['ʤɛ-nərə] : género *m*

geographer [ʤi'ɑgrəfər] *n* : geógrafo *m*, -fa *f*

geographical [ˌʤi:ə'græfɪkəl] *or* **geographic** [-fɪk] *adj* : geográfico — **geographically** [-fɪkli] *adv*

geography [ʤi'ɑgrəfi] *n, pl* **-phies** : geografía *f*

geologic [ˌʤi:ə'lɑʤɪk] *or* **geological** [-ʤɪkəl] *adj* : geológico — **geologically** [-ʤɪkli] *adv*

geologist [ʤi'ɑləʤɪst] *n* : geólogo *m*, -ga *f*

geology [ʤi'ɑləʤi] *n* : geología *f*

geometric [ˌʤi:ə'mɛtrɪk] *or* **geometrical** [-trɪkəl] *adj* : geométrico

geometry [ʤi'ɑmətri] *n, pl* **-tries** : geometría *f*

geopolitical [ˌʤi:opə'lɪţɪkəl] *adj* : geopolítico

Georgian ['ʤɔrʤən] *n* **1** : georgiano *m* (idioma) **2** : georgiano *m*, -na *f* — **Georgian** *adj*

geranium [ʤə'reɪniəm] *n* : geranio *m*

gerbil ['ʤərbəl] *n* : jerbo *m*, gerbo *m*

geriatric [ˌʤɛri'ætrɪk] *adj* : geriátrico

geriatrics [ˌʤɛri'ætrɪks] *n* : geriatría *f*

germ ['ʤərm] *n* **1** MICROORGANISM : microbio *m*, germen *m* **2** BEGINNING : germen *m*, principio *m* ⟨the germ of a plan : el germen de un plan⟩

German ['ʤərmən] *n* **1** : alemán *m*, -mana *f* **2** : alemán *m* (idioma) — **German** *adj*

germane [ʤər'meɪn] *adj* : relevante, pertinente

Germanic[1] [ʤər'mænɪk] *adj* : germánico, germano

Germanic[2] *n* : germánico *m* (idioma)

germanium [ʤər'meɪniəm] *n* : germanio *m*

germ cell *n* : célula *f* germen

germicide ['ʤərməˌsaɪd] *n* : germicida *m*

germinate ['ʤərməˌneɪt] *v* **-nated; -nating** *vi* : germinar — *vt* : hacer germinar

germination [ˌʤərmə'neɪʃən] *n* : germinación *f*

gerund ['ʤɛrənd] *n* : gerundio *m*

gestation [ʤɛ'steɪʃən] *n* : gestación *f*

gesture[1] ['ʤɛsʧər] *vi* **-tured; -turing** : gesticular, hacer gestos

gesture[2] *n* **1** : gesto *m*, ademán *m* **2** SIGN, TOKEN : gesto *m*, señal *f* ⟨a gesture of friendship : una señal de amistad⟩

get ['gɛt] *v* **got** ['gɑt]; **got** *or* **gotten** ['gɑtən]; **getting** *vt* **1** OBTAIN : conseguir, obtener, adquirir **2** RECEIVE : recibir ⟨to get a letter : recibir una carta⟩ **3** EARN : ganar ⟨he gets $10 an hour : gana $10 por hora⟩ **4** FETCH : traer ⟨get me my book : tráigame el libro⟩ **5** CATCH : tomar (un tren, etc.), agarrar (una pelota, una persona, etc.) **6** CONTRACT : contagiarse de, contraer ⟨she got the measles : le dio el sarampión⟩ **7** PREPARE : preparar (una comida) **8** PERSUADE : persuadir, mandar a hacer ⟨I got him to agree : logré convencerlo⟩ **9** (*to cause to be*) ⟨to get one's hair cut : cortarse el pelo⟩ **10** UNDERSTAND : entender ⟨now I get it! : ¡ya entiendo!⟩ **11 to have got** : tener ⟨I've got a headache : tengo un dolor de cabeza⟩ **12 to have got to** : tener que ⟨you've got to come : tienes que venir⟩ — *vi* **1** BECOME : ponerse, volverse, hacerse ⟨to get angry : ponerse furioso, enojarse⟩ **2** GO, MOVE : ir, avanzar ⟨he didn't get far : no avanzó mucho⟩ **3** ARRIVE : llegar ⟨to get home : llegar a casa⟩ **4 to get to be** : llegar a ser ⟨she got to be the director : llegó a ser directora⟩ **5 to get ahead** : adelantarse, progresar **6 to get along** : llevarse bien (con alguien), congeniar **7 to get by** MANAGE : arreglárselas **8 to get over** OVERCOME : superar, consolarse de **9 to get together** MEET : reunirse **10 to get up** : levantarse

getaway ['gɛţəˌweɪ] *n* ESCAPE : fuga *f*, huida *f*, escapada *f*

geyser ['gaɪzər] *n* : géiser *m*

Ghanaian ['gɑniən, 'gæ-] *n* : ghanés *m*, -nesa *f* — **Ghanaian** *adj*

ghastly ['gæstli] *adj* **-lier; -est 1** HORRIBLE : horrible, espantoso **2** PALE : pálido, cadavérico

gherkin ['gərkən] *n* : pepinillo *m*

ghetto ['gɛţo:] *n, pl* **-tos** *or* **-toes** : gueto *m*

ghost ['go:st] *n* **1** : fantasma *f*, espectro *m* **2 the Holy Ghost** : el Espíritu Santo

ghostly ['go:stli] *adv* : fantasmal

ghoul ['gu:l] *n* **1** : demonio *m* necrófago **2** : persona *f* de gustos macabros

GI ['ʤi:'aɪ] *n, pl* **GI's** *or* **GIs** : soldado *m* estadounidense

giant[1] ['ʤaɪənt] *adj* : gigante, gigantesco, enorme

giant[2] *n* : gigante *m*, -ta *f*

gibberish ['ʤɪbəriʃ] *n* : galimatías *m*, jerigonza *f*

gibbon ['gɪbən] *n* : gibón *m*

gibe[1] ['ʤaɪb] *vi* **gibed; gibing** : mofarse, burlarse

gibe[2] *n* : pulla *f*, burla *f*, mofa *f*

giblets ['ʤɪbləts] *npl* : menudos *mpl*, menudencias *fpl*

giddiness ['gɪdinəs] *n* **1** DIZZINESS : vértigo *m*, mareo *m* **2** SILLINESS : frivolidad *f*, estupidez *f*

giddy ['gɪdi] *adj* **-dier; -est 1** DIZZY : mareado, vertiginoso **2** FRIVOLOUS, SILLY : frívolo, tonto

gift ['gɪft] *n* **1** TALENT : don *m*, talento *m*, dotes *fpl* **2** PRESENT : regalo *m*, obsequio *m*

gifted ['gɪftəd] *adj* TALENTED : talentoso

gig ['gɪg] *vi* : trabajo *m* (de duración limitada) ⟨to play a gig : tocar en un concierto⟩

gigabyte ['dʒɪgə,baɪt, 'gɪ-] *n* : gigabyte *m*

gigantic [dʒaɪ'gæntɪk] *adj* : gigantesco, enorme, colosal

giggle¹ ['gɪgəl] *vi* **-gled; -gling** : reírse tontamente

giggle² *n* : risita *f*, risa *f* tonta

gild ['gɪld] *vt* **gilded** *or* **gilt** ['gɪlt]; **gilding** : dorar

gill ['gɪl] *n* : agalla *f*, branquia *f*

gilt¹ ['gɪlt] *adj* : dorado

gilt² *n* : dorado *m*

gimlet ['gɪmlət] *n* **1** : barrena *f* (herramienta) **2** : bebida *f* de vodka o ginebra y limón

gimmick ['gɪmɪk] *n* **1** GADGET : artilugio *m* **2** CATCH : engaño *m*, trampa *f* **3** SCHEME, TRICK : ardid *m*, truco *m*

gin ['dʒɪn] *n* **1** : desmotadora *f* (de algodón) **2** : ginebra *f* (bebida alcohólica)

ginger ['dʒɪndʒər] *n* : jengibre *m*

ginger ale *n* : ginger ale *m*, gaseosa *f* de jengibre

gingerbread ['dʒɪndʒər,brɛd] *n* : pan *m* de jengibre

gingerly ['dʒɪndʒərli] *adv* : con cuidado, cautelosamente

gingham ['gɪŋəm] *n* : guinga *f*

ginseng ['dʒɪn,sɪŋ, -,sɛŋ] *n* : ginseng *m*

giraffe [dʒə'ræf] *n* : jirafa *f*

gird ['gərd] *vt* **girded** *or* **girt** ['gərt]; **girding 1** BIND : ceñir, atar **2** ENCIRCLE : rodear **3 to gird oneself** : prepararse

girder ['gərdər] *n* : viga *f*

girdle¹ ['gərdəl] *vt* **-dled; -dling 1** GIRD : ceñir, atar **2** SURROUND : rodear, circundar

girdle² *n* : faja *f*

girl ['gərl] *n* **1** : chica *f*, muchacha *f* **2** *or* **little girl** : niña *f*, chica *f* **3** SWEETHEART : novia *f* **4** DAUGHTER : hija *f*

girlfriend ['gərl,frɛnd] *n* : novia *f*, amiga *f*

girlhood ['gərl,hʊd] *n* : niñez *f*, juventud *f* (de una muchacha)

girlish ['gərlɪʃ] *adj* : de niña

girth ['gərθ] *n* **1** : circunferencia *f* (de un árbol, etc.), cintura *f* (de una persona) **2** CINCH : cincha *f* (para caballos, etc.)

gist ['dʒɪst] *n* : quid *m*, meollo *m*

give¹ ['gɪv] *v* **gave** ['geɪv]; **given** ['gɪvən]; **giving** *vt* **1** HAND, PRESENT : dar, regalar, obsequiar ⟨give it to me : dámelo⟩ ⟨they gave him a gold watch : le regalaron un reloj de oro⟩ **2** PAY : dar, pagar ⟨I'll give you $10 for this one : te daré $10 por éste⟩ **3** UTTER : dar, pronunciar ⟨to give a shout : dar un grito⟩ ⟨to give a speech : pronunciar un discurso⟩ ⟨to give a verdict : dictar sentencia⟩ **4** PROVIDE : dar ⟨to give one's word : dar uno su palabra⟩ ⟨to give a party : dar una fiesta⟩ **5** CAUSE : dar, causar, ocasionar ⟨to give trouble : causar problemas⟩ ⟨to give someone to understand : darle a entender a alguien⟩ **6** GRANT : dar, otorgar ⟨to give permission : dar permiso⟩ — *vi* **1** : hacer regalos **2** YIELD : ceder, romperse ⟨it gave under the weight of the crowd : cedió bajo el peso de la muchedumbre⟩ **3 to give in** *or* **to give up** SURRENDER : rendirse, entregarse **4 to give out** : agotarse, acabarse ⟨the supplies gave out : las provisiones se agotaron⟩

give² *n* FLEXIBILITY : flexibilidad *f*, elasticidad *f*

giveaway ['gɪvə,weɪ] *n* **1** : revelación *f* involuntaria **2** GIFT : regalo *m*, obsequio *m*

given ['gɪvən] *adj* **1** INCLINED : dado, inclinado ⟨he's given to quarreling : es muy dado a discutir⟩ **2** SPECIFIC : dado, determinado ⟨at a given time : en un momento dado⟩

given name *n* : nombre *m* de pila

give up *vt* : dejar, renunciar a, abandonar ⟨to give up smoking : dejar de fumar⟩

gizzard ['gɪzərd] *n* : molleja *f*

glacial ['gleɪʃəl] *adj* : glacial — **glacially** *adv*

glacier ['gleɪʃər] *n* : glaciar *m*

glad ['glæd] *adj* **gladder; gladdest 1** PLEASED : alegre, contento ⟨she was glad I came : se alegró de que haya venido⟩ ⟨glad to meet you! : ¡mucho gusto!⟩ **2** HAPPY, PLEASING : feliz, agradable ⟨glad tidings : buenas nuevas⟩ **3** WILLING : dispuesto, gustoso ⟨I'll be glad to do it : lo haré con mucho gusto⟩

gladden ['glædən] *vt* : alegrar

glade ['gleɪd] *n* : claro *m*

gladiator ['glædi,eɪtər] *n* : gladiador *m*

gladiolus [,glædi'o:ləs] *n*, *pl* **-li** [-li, -,laɪ] : gladiolo *m*, gladíolo *m*

gladly ['glædli] *adv* : con mucho gusto

gladness ['glædnəs] *n* : alegría *f*, gozo *m*

glamor *or* **glamour** ['glæmər] *n* : atractivo *m*, hechizo *m*, encanto *m*

glamorous ['glæmərəs] *adj* : atractivo, encantador

glance¹ ['glænts] *vi* **glanced; glancing 1** RICOCHET : rebotar ⟨it glanced off the wall : rebotó en la pared⟩ **2 to glance at** : mirar, echar un vistazo a **3 to glance away** : apartar los ojos

glance² *n* : mirada *f*, vistazo *m*, ojeada *f*

gland ['glænd] *n* : glándula *f*

glandular ['glændʒʊlər] *adj* : glandular

glare¹ ['glær] *vi* **glared; glaring 1** SHINE : brillar, relumbrar **2** STARE : mirar con ira, lanzar una mirada feroz

glare² *n* **1** BRIGHTNESS : resplandor *m*, luz *f* deslumbrante **2** : mirada *f* feroz

glaring [ˈglærɪŋ] *adj* **1** BRIGHT : deslumbrante, brillante **2** FLAGRANT, OBVIOUS : flagrante, manifiesto ⟨a glaring error : un error que salta a la vista⟩

glass [ˈglæs] *n* **1** : vidrio *m*, cristal *m* ⟨stained glass : vidrio de color⟩ **2** : vaso *m* ⟨a glass of milk : un vaso de leche⟩ **3 glasses** *npl* SPECTACLES : gafas *fpl*, anteojos *mpl*, lentes *mpl*, espejuelos *mpl*

glassblowing [ˈglæsˌbloːɪŋ] *n* : soplado *m* del vidrio

glassful [ˈglæsˌfʊl] *n* : vaso *m*, copa *f*

glassware [ˈglæsˌwær] *n* : cristalería *f*

glassy [ˈglæsi] *adj* **glassier; -est 1** VITREOUS : vítreo **2** : vidrioso ⟨glassy eyes : ojos vidriosos⟩

glaucoma [glaʊˈkoːmə, glɔ-] *n* : glaucoma *m*

glaze¹ [ˈgleɪz] *vt* **glazed; glazing 1** : ponerle vidrios a (una ventana, etc.) **2** : vidriar (cerámica) **3** : glasear (papel, verduras, etc.)

glaze² *n* : vidriado *m*, glaseado *m*, barniz *m*

glazier [ˈgleɪʒər] *n* : vidriero *m*, -ra *f*

gleam¹ [ˈgliːm] *vi* : brillar, destellar, relucir

gleam² *n* **1** LIGHT : luz *f* (oscura) **2** GLINT : destello *m* **3** GLIMMER : rayo *m*, vislumbre *f* ⟨a gleam of hope : un rayo de esperanza⟩

glean [ˈgliːn] *vt* : recoger, espigar

glee [ˈgliː] *n* : alegría *f*, júbilo *m*, regocijo *m*

gleeful [ˈgliːfəl] *adj* : lleno de alegría

glen [ˈglɛn] *n* : cañada *f*

glib [ˈglɪb] *adj* **glibber; glibbest 1** : simplista ⟨a glib reply : una respuesta simplista⟩ **2** : con mucha labia (dícese de una persona)

glibly [ˈglɪbli] *adv* : con mucha labia

glide¹ [ˈglaɪd] *vi* **glided; gliding** : deslizarse (en una superficie), planear (en el aire)

glide² *n* : planeo *m*

glider [ˈglaɪdər] *n* **1** : planeador *m* (aeronave) **2** : mecedor *m* (tipo de columpio)

glimmer¹ [ˈglɪmər] *vi* : brillar con luz trémula

glimmer² *n* **1** : luz *f* trémula, luz *f* tenue **2** GLEAM : rayo *m*, vislumbre *f* ⟨a glimmer of understanding : un rayo de entendimiento⟩

glimpse¹ [ˈglɪmps] *vt* **glimpsed; glimpsing** : vislumbrar, entrever

glimpse² *n* : mirada *f* breve ⟨to catch a glimpse of : alcanzar a ver, vislumbrar⟩

glint¹ [ˈglɪnt] *vi* GLEAM, SPARKLE : destellar, fulgurar

glint² *n* **1** SPARKLE : destello *m*, centelleo *m* **2 to have a glint in one's eye** : chispearle los ojos a uno

glisten¹ [ˈglɪsən] *vi* : brillar, centellear

glisten² *n* : brillo *m*, centelleo *m*

glitch [ˈglɪtʃ] *n* **1** MALFUNCTION : mal funcionamiento *m* **2** SNAG : problema *m*, complicación *f*

glitter¹ [ˈglɪt̬ər] *vi* **1** SPARKLE : destellar, relucir, brillar **2** FLASH : relampaguear ⟨his eyes glittered in anger : le relampagueaban los ojos de ira⟩

glitter² *n* **1** BRIGHTNESS : brillo *m* **2** : purpurina *f* (para decoración)

glitz [ˈglɪts] *n* : oropel *m*

gloat [ˈgloːt] *vi* **to gloat over** : regodearse en

glob [ˈglɑb] *n* : plasta *f*, masa *f*, grumo *m*

global [ˈgloːbəl] *adj* **1** SPHERICAL : esférico **2** WORLDWIDE : global, mundial — **globally** *adv*

globe [ˈgloːb] *n* **1** SPHERE : esfera *f*, globo *m* **2** EARTH : globo *m*, Tierra *f* **3** : globo *m* terráqueo (modelo de la Tierra)

globe–trotter [ˈgloːbˌtrɑt̬ər] *n* : trotamundos *mf*

globular [ˈglɑbjʊlər] *adj* : globular

globule [ˈglɑˌbjuːl] *n* : glóbulo *m*

gloom [ˈgluːm] *n* **1** DARKNESS : penumbra *f*, oscuridad *f* **2** MELANCHOLY : melancolía *f*, tristeza *f*

gloomily [ˈgluːməli] *adv* : tristemente

gloomy [ˈgluːmi] *adj* **gloomier; -est 1** DARK : oscuro, tenebroso ⟨gloomy weather : tiempo gris⟩ **2** MELANCHOLY : melancólico **3** PESSIMISTIC : pesimista **4** DEPRESSING : deprimente, lúgubre

glorification [ˌglorəfəˈkeɪʃən] *n* : glorificación *f*

glorify [ˈglorəˌfaɪ] *vt* **-fied; -fying** : glorificar

glorious [ˈgloriəs] *adj* **1** ILLUSTRIOUS : glorioso, ilustre **2** MAGNIFICENT : magnífico, espléndido, maravilloso — **gloriously** *adv*

glory¹ [ˈglori] *vi* **-ried; -rying** EXULT : exultar, regocijarse

glory² *n, pl* **-ries 1** RENOWN : gloria *f*, fama *f*, honor *m* **2** PRAISE : gloria *f* ⟨glory to God : gloria a Dios⟩ **3** MAGNIFICENCE : magnificencia *f*, esplendor *m*, gloria *f* **4 to be in one's glory** : estar uno en su gloria

gloss¹ [ˈglɔs, ˈglɑs] *vt* **1** EXPLAIN : glosar, explicar **2** POLISH : lustrar, pulir **3 to gloss over** : quitarle importancia a, minimizar

gloss² *n* **1** SHINE : lustre *m*, brillo *m* **2** EXPLANATION : glosa *f*, explicación *f* breve **3** → **glossary**

glossary [ˈglɔsəri, ˈglɑ-] *n, pl* **-ries** : glosario *m*

glossy [ˈglɔsi, ˈglɑ-] *adj* **glossier; -est** : brillante, lustroso, satinado (dícese del papel)

glove [ˈglʌv] *n* : guante *m*

glow¹ [ˈgloː] *vi* **1** SHINE : brillar, resplandecer **2** BRIM : rebosar ⟨to glow with health : rebosar de salud⟩

glow[2] *n* **1** BRIGHTNESS : resplandor *m*, brillo *m*, luminosidad *f* **2** FEELING : sensación *f* (de bienestar), oleada *f* (de sentimiento) **3** INCANDESCENCE : incandescencia *f*

glower ['glaʊər] *vi* : fruncir el ceño

glowworm ['gloˌwərm] *n* : luciérnaga *f*

glucose ['gluːˌkoːs] *n* : glucosa *f*

glue[1] ['gluː] *vt* **glued; gluing** *or* **glueing** : pegar, encolar

glue[2] *n* : pegamento *m*, cola *f*

gluey ['gluːi] *adj* **gluier; -est** : pegajoso

glum ['glʌm] *adj* **glummer; glummest** **1** SULLEN : hosco, sombrío **2** DREARY, GLOOMY : sombrío, triste, melancólico

glut[1] ['glʌt] *vt* **glutted; glutting 1** SATIATE : saciar, hartar **2** : inundar (el mercado)

glut[2] *n* : exceso *m*, superabundancia *f*

glutinous ['gluːtənəs] *adj* STICKY : pegajoso, glutinoso

glutton ['glʌtən] *n* : glotón *m*, -tona *f*

gluttonous ['glʌtənəs] *adj* : glotón

gluttony ['glʌtəni] *n*, *pl* **-tonies** : glotonería *f*, gula *f*

gnarled ['nɑrld] *adj* **1** KNOTTY : nudoso **2** TWISTED : retorcido

gnash ['næʃ] *vt* : hacer rechinar (los dientes)

gnat ['næt] *n* : jején *m*

gnaw ['nɔ] *vt* : roer

gnome ['noːm] *n* : gnomo *m*

gnu ['nuː, 'njuː] *n*, *pl* **gnu** *or* **gnus** : ñu *m*

go[1] ['goː] *v* **went** ['wɛnt]; **gone** ['gɔn, 'gɑn]; **going; goes** ['goːz] *vi* **1** PROCEED : ir ⟨to go slow : ir despacio⟩ ⟨to go shopping : ir de compras⟩ **2** LEAVE : irse, marcharse, salir ⟨let's go! : ¡vámonos!⟩ ⟨the train went on time : el tren salió a tiempo⟩ **3** DISAPPEAR : desaparecer, pasarse, irse ⟨her fear is gone : se le ha pasado el miedo⟩ ⟨my pen is gone! : ¡mi pluma desapareció!⟩ **4** EXTEND : ir, extenderse, llegar ⟨this road goes to the river : este camino se extiende hasta el río⟩ ⟨to go from top to bottom : ir de arriba abajo⟩ **5** FUNCTION : funcionar, marchar ⟨the car won't go : el coche no funciona⟩ ⟨to get something going : poner algo en marcha⟩ **6** SELL : venderse ⟨it goes for $15 : se vende por $15⟩ **7** PROGRESS : ir, andar, seguir ⟨my exam went well : me fue bien en el examen⟩ ⟨how did the meeting go? : ¿qué tal la reunión?⟩ **8** BECOME : volverse, quedarse ⟨he's going crazy : está volviéndose loco⟩ ⟨the tire went flat : la llanta se desinfló⟩ **9** FIT : caber ⟨it will go through the door : cabe por la puerta⟩ **10** **anything goes!** : ¡todo vale! **11 to go** : faltar ⟨only 10 days to go : faltan sólo 10 días⟩ **12 to go back on** : faltar uno a (su promesa) **13 to go bad** SPOIL : estropearse, echarse a perder **14 to go for** : interesarse uno en, gustarle a uno (algo, alguien) ⟨I don't go for that : eso

no me interesa⟩ **15 to go off** EXPLODE : estallar **16 to go with** MATCH : armonizar con, hacer juego con — *v aux* **to be going to** : ir a ⟨I'm going to write a letter : voy a escribir una carta⟩ ⟨it's not going to last : no va a durar⟩

go[2] *n*, *pl* **goes 1** ATTEMPT : intento *m* ⟨to have a go at : intentar, probar⟩ **2** SUCCESS : éxito *m* **3** ENERGY : energía *f*, empuje *m* ⟨to be on the go : no parar, no descansar⟩

goad[1] ['goːd] *vt* : aguijonear (un animal), incitar (a una persona)

goad[2] *n* : aguijón *m*

goal ['goːl] *n* **1** : gol *m* (en deportes) ⟨to score a goal : anotar un gol⟩ **2** *or* **goalposts** : portería *f* **3** AIM, OBJECTIVE : meta *m*, objetivo *m*

goalie ['goːli] → **goalkeeper**

goalkeeper ['goːlˌkiːpər] *n* : portero *m*, -ra *f*; guardameta *mf*; arquero *m*, -ra *f*

goaltender ['goːlˌtɛndər] → **goalkeeper**

goat ['goːt] *n* **1** : cabra *f* (hembra) **2 billy goat** : macho *m* cabrío, chivo *m*

goatee [goːˈtiː] *n* : barbita *f* de chivo, piocha *f Mex*

goatskin ['goːtˌskɪn] *n* : piel *f* de cabra

gob ['gɑb] *n* : masa *f*, grumo *m*

gobble ['gɑbəl] *v* **-bled; -bling; -bling up** : tragar, engullir — *vi* : hacer ruidos de pavo

gobbledygook ['gɑbəldiˌgʊk, -ˌguːk] *n* GIBBERISH : jerigonza *f*

go-between ['goːbɪˌtwiːn] *n* : intermediario *m*, -ria *f*; mediador *m*, -dora *f*

goblet ['gɑblət] *n* : copa *f*

goblin ['gɑblən] *n* : duende *m*, trasgo *m*

god ['gɑd, 'gɔd] *n* **1** : dios *m* **2 God** : Dios *m*

godchild ['gɑdˌtʃaɪld, 'gɔd-] *n*, *pl* **-children** : ahijado *m*, -da *f*

goddess ['gɑdəs, 'gɔ-] *n* : diosa *f*

godfather ['gɑdˌfɑðər, 'gɔd-] *n* : padrino *m*

godless ['gɑdləs, 'gɔd-] *adj* : ateo

godlike ['gɑdˌlaɪk, 'gɔd-] *adj* : divino

godly ['gɑdli, 'gɔd-] *adj* **-lier; -est 1** DIVINE : divino **2** DEVOUT, PIOUS : piadoso, devoto, beato

godmother ['gɑdˌmʌðər, 'gɔd-] *n* : madrina *f*

godparents ['gɑdˌpærənts, 'gɔd-] *npl* : padrinos *mpl*

godsend ['gɑdˌsɛnd, 'gɔd-] *n* : bendición *f*, regalo *m* divino

goes → **go**

go-getter ['goːˌgɛtər] *n* : persona *f* ambiciosa, buscavidas *mf fam*

goggle ['gɑgəl] *vi* **-gled; -gling** : mirar con ojos desorbitados

goggles ['gɑgəlz] *npl* : gafas *fpl* (protectoras), anteojos *mpl*

goings-on [ˌgoːɪŋzˈɑn, -ˈɔn] *npl* : sucesos *mpl*, ocurrencias *fpl*

goiter ['gɔɪtər] *n* : bocio *m*

gold ['goːld] *n* : oro *m*

golden ['goːldən] *adj* **1** : (hecho) de oro **2** : dorado, de color oro ⟨golden hair

: pelo rubio⟩ **3** FLOURISHING, PROS-
PEROUS : dorado, próspero ⟨golden
years : años dorados⟩ **4** FAVORABLE
: favorable, excelente ⟨a golden opportunity : una excelente oportu-
nidad⟩

goldenrod ['go:ldən,rɑd] *n* : vara *f* de
oro

golden rule *n* : regla *f* de oro

goldfinch ['go:ld,fɪntʃ] *n* : jilguero *m*

goldfish ['go:ld,fɪʃ] *n* : pez *m* de colores

goldsmith ['go:ld,smɪθ] *n* : orífice *mf*,
orfebre *mf*

golf[1] ['gɑlf, 'gɔlf] *vi* : jugar (al) golf

golf[2] *n* : golf *m*

golfer ['gɑlfər, 'gɔl-] *n* : golfista *mf*

gondola ['gɑndələ, gɑn'do:lə] *n* : góndola *f*

gone ['gɔn] *adj* **1** DEAD : muerto **2** PAST
: pasado, ido **3** LOST : perdido, desaparecido **4 to be far gone** : estar muy
avanzado **5 to be gone on** : estar loco
por

goner ['gɔnər] *n* **to be a goner** : estar en
las últimas

gong ['gɔŋ, 'gɑŋ] *n* : gong *m*

gonorrhea [,gɑnə'ri:ə] *n* : gonorrea *f*

good[1] ['gʊd] *adv* **1** (*used as an intensifier*) : bien ⟨a good strong rope : una
cuerda bien fuerte⟩ **2** WELL : bien

good[2] *adj* **better** ['bɛt̬ər]; **best** ['bɛst] **1**
PLEASANT : bueno, agradable ⟨good
news : buenas noticias⟩ ⟨to have a good
time : divertirse⟩ **2** BENEFICIAL
: bueno, beneficioso ⟨good for a cold
: beneficioso para los resfriados⟩ ⟨it's
good for you : es bueno para uno⟩ **3**
FULL : completo, entero ⟨a good hour
: una hora entera⟩ **4** CONSIDERABLE
: bueno, bastante ⟨a good many people : muchísima gente, un buen
número de gente⟩ **5** ATTRACTIVE, DE-
SIRABLE : bueno, bien ⟨a good salary
: un buen sueldo⟩ ⟨to look good
: quedar bien⟩ **6** KIND, VIRTUOUS
: bueno, amable ⟨she's a good person
: es buena gente⟩ ⟨that's good of you!
: ¡qué amable!⟩ ⟨good deeds : buenas
obras⟩ **7** SKILLED : bueno, hábil ⟨to
be good at : tener facilidad para⟩ **8**
SOUND : bueno, sensato ⟨good advice
: buenos consejos⟩ **9** (*in greetings*)
: bueno ⟨good morning : buenos días⟩
⟨good afternoon (evening) : buenas
tardes⟩ ⟨good night : buenas noches⟩

good[3] *n* **1** RIGHT : bien *m* ⟨to do good
: hacer el bien⟩ **2** GOODNESS : bondad
f **3** BENEFIT : bien *m*, provecho *m* ⟨it's
for your own good : es por tu propio
bien⟩ **4 goods** *npl* PROPERTY : efectos
mpl personales, posesiones *fpl* **5 goods**
npl WARES : mercancía *f*, mercadería *f*,
artículos *mpl* **6 for ~** : para siempre

good–bye *or* **good–by** [gʊd'baɪ] *n*
: adiós *m*

good–for–nothing ['gʊdfər,nʌθɪŋ] *n*
: inútil *mf*; haragán *m*, -gana *f*; holgazán
m, -zana *f*

Good Friday *n* : Viernes *m* Santo

good–hearted ['gʊd'hɑrt̬əd] *adj* : bondadoso, benévolo, de buen corazón

good–looking ['gʊd'lʊkɪŋ] *adj* : bello,
bonito, guapo

goodly ['gʊdli] *adj* **-lier; -est** : considerable, importante ⟨a goodly number
: un número considerable⟩

good–natured ['gʊd'neɪtʃərd] *adj* : amigable, amistoso, bonachón *fam*

goodness ['gʊdnəs] *n* **1** : bondad *f* **2
thank goodness!** : ¡gracias a Dios!,
¡menos mal!

good–tempered ['gʊd'tɛmpərd] *adj* : de
buen genio

goodwill [,gʊd'wɪl] *n* **1** BENEVOLENCE
: benevolencia *f*, buena voluntad *f* **2**
: buen nombre *m* (de comercios),
renombre *m* comercial

goody ['gʊdi] *n*, *pl* **goodies** : cosa *f* rica
para comer, golosina *f*

gooey ['gu:i] *adj* **gooier; gooiest** : pegajoso

goof[1] ['gu:f] *vi* **1 to goof off** : holgazanear **2 to goof around** : hacer tonterías **3 to goof up** BLUNDER : cometer un error

goof[2] *n* **1** : bobo *m*, -ba *f*; tonto *m*, -ta *f*
2 BLUNDER : error *m*, planchazo *m fam*

goofy ['gu:fi] *adj* **goofier; -est** SILLY
: tonto, bobo

goose ['gu:s] *n*, *pl* **geese** ['gi:s] : ganso
m, -sa *f*; ánsar *m*; oca *f*

gooseberry ['gu:s,bɛri:, 'gu:z-] *n*, *pl*
-berries : grosella *f* espinosa

goose bumps *npl* : carne *f* de gallina

gooseflesh ['gu:s,flɛʃ] → **goose bumps**

goose pimples → **goose bumps**

gopher ['go:fər] *n* : taltuza *f*

gore[1] ['gor] *vt* **gored; goring** : cornear

gore[2] *n* BLOOD : sangre *f*

gorge[1] ['gɔrdʒ] *vt* **gorged; gorging 1** SA-
TIATE : saciar, hartar **2 to gorge oneself** : hartarse, atiborrarse, atracarse
fam

gorge[2] *n* RAVINE : desfiladero *m*

gorgeous ['gɔrdʒəs] *adj* : hermoso, espléndido, magnífico

gorilla [gə'rɪlə] *n* : gorila *m*

gory ['gori] *adj* **gorier; -est** BLOODY
: sangriento

gosling ['gɑzlɪŋ, 'gɔz-] *n* : ansarino *m*

gospel ['gɑspəl] *n* **1** *or* **Gospel** : evangelio *m* ⟨the four Gospels : los cuatro
evangelios⟩ **2 the gospel truth** : el
evangelio, la pura verdad

gossamer ['gɑsəmər, 'gɑzə-] *adj* : tenue,
sutil ⟨gossamer wings : alas tenues⟩

gossip[1] ['gɑsɪp] *vi* : chismear, contar
chismes

gossip[2] *n* **1** : chismoso *m*, -sa *f* (persona) **2** RUMOR : chisme *m*, rumor *m*

gossipy ['gɑsɪpi] *adj* : chismoso

got → get

Gothic ['gɑθɪk] *adj* : gótico

gotten → get

gouge[1] ['gaʊdʒ] *vt* **gouged; gouging 1**
: excavar, escoplear (con una gubia) **2**
SWINDLE : estafar, extorsionar

gouge² *n* **1** CHISEL : gubia *f*, formón *m* **2** GROOVE : ranura *f*, hoyo *m* (hecho por un formón)

goulash ['guːˌlɑʃ, -ˌlæʃ] *n* : estofado *m*, guiso *m* al estilo húngaro

gourd ['gord, 'gurd] *n* : calabaza *f*

gourmand ['gurˌmɑnd] *n* **1** GLUTTON : glotón *m*, -tona *f* **2** → **gourmet**

gourmet ['gurˌmeɪ, gurˈmeɪ] *n* : gourmet *mf*; gastrónomo *m*, -ma *f*

gout ['gaut] *n* : gota *f*

govern ['gʌvərn] *vt* **1** RULE : gobernar **2** CONTROL, DETERMINE : determinar, controlar, guiar **3** RESTRAIN : dominar (las emociones, etc.) — *vi* : gobernar

governess ['gʌvərnəs] *n* : institutriz *f*

government ['gʌvərmənt] *n* : gobierno *m*

governmental [ˌgʌvərˈmɛntəl] *adj* : gubernamental, gubernativo

governor ['gʌvənər, 'gʌvərnər] *n* **1** : gobernador *m*, - dora *f* (de un estado, etc.) **2** : regulador *m* (de una máquina)

governorship ['gʌvənərˌʃɪp, 'gʌvərnər-] *n* : cargo *m* de gobernador

gown ['gaun] *n* **1** : vestido *m* ⟨evening gown : traje de fiesta⟩ **2** : toga *f* (de magistrados, clérigos, etc.)

grab¹ ['græb] *v* **grabbed; grabbing** *vt* SNATCH : agarrar, arrebatar — *vi* : agarrarse

grab² *n* **1 to make a grab for** : tratar de agarrar **2 up for grabs** : disponible, libre

grace¹ ['greɪs] *vt* **graced; gracing 1** HONOR : honrar **2** ADORN : adornar, embellecer

grace² *n* **1** : gracia *f* ⟨by the grace of God : por la gracia de Dios⟩ **2** BLESSING : bendición *f* (de la mesa) **3** RESPITE : plazo *m*, gracia *f* ⟨a five days' grace (period) : un plazo de cinco días⟩ **4** GRACIOUSNESS : gentileza *f*, cortesía *f* **5** ELEGANCE : elegancia *f*, gracia *f* **6 to be in the good graces of** : estar en buenas relaciones con **7 with good grace** : de buena gana

graceful ['greɪsfəl] *adj* : lleno de gracia, garboso, grácil

gracefully ['greɪsfəli] *adv* : con gracia, con garbo

gracefulness ['greɪsfəlnəs] *n* : gracilidad *f*, apostura *f*, gallardía *f*

graceless ['greɪsləs] *adj* **1** DISCOURTEOUS : descortés **2** CLUMSY, INELEGANT : torpe, desgarbado, poco elegante

gracious ['greɪʃəs] *adj* : cortés, gentil, cordial

graciously ['greɪʃəsli] *adv* : gentilmente

graciousness ['greɪʃəsnəs] *n* : gentileza *f*

gradation [greɪˈdeɪʃən, grə-] *n* : gradación *f*

grade¹ ['greɪd] *vt* **graded; grading 1** SORT : clasificar **2** LEVEL : nivelar **3** : calificar (exámenes, alumnos)

grade² *n* **1** QUALITY : categoría *f*, calidad *f* **2** RANK : grado *m*, rango *m* (mil-

itar) **3** YEAR : grado *m*, curso *m*, año *m* ⟨sixth grade : el sexto grado⟩ **4** MARK : nota *f*, calificación *f* (en educación) **5** SLOPE : cuesta *f*, pendiente *f*, gradiente *f*

grade school → **elementary school**

gradient ['greɪdiənt] *n* : gradiente *f*

gradual ['grædʒuəl] *adj* : gradual, paulatino

gradually ['grædʒuəli, 'grædʒəli] *adv* : gradualmente, poco a poco

graduate¹ ['grædʒuˌeɪt] *v* **-ated; -ating** *vi* : graduarse, licenciarse — *vt* : graduar ⟨a graduated thermometer : un termómetro graduado⟩

graduate² ['grædʒuət] *adj* : de postgrado ⟨graduate course : curso de postgrado⟩

graduate³ *n* **1** : licenciado *m*, -da *f*; graduado *m*, -da *f* (de la universidad) **2** : bachiller *mf* (de la escuela secundaria)

graduate student *n* : postgraduado *m*, -da *f*

graduation [ˌgrædʒuˈeɪʃən] *n* : graduación *f*

graffiti [grəˈfiːtˌi, græ-] *npl* : pintadas *fpl*, graffiti *mpl*

graft¹ ['græft] *vt* : injertar

graft² *n* **1** : injerto *m* ⟨skin graft : injerto cutáneo⟩ **2** CORRUPTION : soborno *m* (político), ganancia *f* ilegal

grain ['greɪn] *n* **1** : grano *m* ⟨a grain of corn : un grano de maíz⟩ ⟨like a grain of sand : como grano de arena⟩ **2** CEREALS : cereales *mpl* **3** : veta *f*, vena *f*, grano *m* (de madera) **4** SPECK, TRACE : pizca *f*, ápice *m* ⟨a grain of truth : una pizca de verdad⟩ **5** grano *m* (unidad de peso)

gram ['græm] *n* : gramo *m*

grammar ['græmər] *n* : gramática *f*

grammar school → **elementary school**

grammatical [grəˈmætɪkəl] *adj* : gramatical — **grammatically** [-kli] *adv*

granary ['greɪnəri, 'græ-] *n*, *pl* **-ries** : granero *m*

grand ['grænd] *adj* **1** FOREMOST : grande **2** IMPRESSIVE : impresionante, magnífico ⟨a grand view : una vista magnífica⟩ **3** LAVISH : grandioso, suntuoso, lujoso ⟨to live in a grand manner : vivir a lo grande⟩ **4** FABULOUS : fabuloso, magnífico ⟨to have a grand time : pasarlo estupendamente, pasarlo en grande⟩ **5 grand total** : total *m*, suma *f* total

grandchild ['grændˌtʃaɪld] *n*, *pl* **-children** : nieto *m*, -ta *f*

granddaughter ['grændˌdɔtər] *n* : nieta *f*

grandeur ['grændʒər] *n* : grandiosidad *f*, esplendor *m*

grandfather ['grændˌfɑðər] *n* : abuelo *m*

grandiose ['grændiˌoːs, ˌgrændiˈ-] *adj* **1** IMPOSING : imponente, grandioso **2** POMPOUS : pomposo, presuntuoso

grandma ['grænˌmɑ, -ˌmɔ] *n* : abuelita *f*, nana *f*

grandmother ['grænd,mʌðər] *n* : abuela *f*

grandpa ['græm,pɑ, -,pɔ] *n* : abuelito *m*

grandparents ['grænd,pærənts] *npl* : abuelos *mpl*

grandson ['grænd,sʌn] *n* : nieto *m*

grandstand ['grænd,stænd] *n* : tribuna *f*

granite ['grænɪt] *n* : granito *m*

grant¹ ['grænt] *vt* **1** ALLOW : conceder ⟨to grant a request : conceder una petición⟩ **2** BESTOW : conceder, dar, otorgar ⟨to grant a favor : otorgar un favor⟩ **3** ADMIT : reconocer, admitir ⟨I'll grant that he's clever : reconozco que es listo⟩ **4 to take for granted** : dar (algo) por sentado

grant² *n* **1** GRANTING : concesión *f*, otorgamiento *m* **2** SCHOLARSHIP : beca *f* **3** SUBSIDY : subvención *f*

granular ['grænjʊlər] *adj* : granular

granulated ['grænjʊ,leɪţəd] *adj* : granulado

grape ['greɪp] *n* : uva *f*

grapefruit ['greɪp,fru:t] *n* : toronja *f*, pomelo *m*

grapevine ['greɪp,vaɪn] *n* **1** : vid *f*, parra *f* **2 through the grapevine** : por vías secretas ⟨I heard it through the grapevine : me lo contaron⟩

graph ['græf] *n* : gráfica *f*, gráfico *m*

graphic ['græfɪk] *adj* **1** VIVID : vívido, gráfico **2 graphic arts** : artes gráficas

graphically ['græfɪkli] *adv* : gráficamente

graphite ['græ,faɪt] *n* : grafito *m*

grapnel ['græpnəl] *n* : rezón *f*

grapple ['græpəl] *v* **-pled; -pling** *vt* GRIP : agarrar (con un garfio) — *vi* STRUGGLE : forcejear, luchar (con un problema, etc.)

grasp¹ ['græsp] *vt* **1** GRIP, SEIZE : agarrar, asir **2** COMPREHEND : entender, comprender — *vi* **to grasp at** : aprovechar

grasp² *n* **1** GRIP : agarre *m* **2** CONTROL : control *m*, garras *fpl* **3** REACH : alcance *m* ⟨within your grasp : a su alcance⟩ **4** UNDERSTANDING : comprensión *f*, entendimiento *m*

grass ['græs] *n* **1** : hierba *f* (planta) **2** PASTURE : pasto *m*, zacate *m* CA, Mex **3** LAWN : césped *m*, pasto *m*

grasshopper ['græs,hɑpər] *n* : saltamontes *m*

grassland ['græs,lænd] *n* : pradera *f*

grassy ['græsi] *adj* **grassier; -est** : cubierto de hierba

grate¹ ['greɪt] *v* **grated; -ing** *vt* **1** : rallar (en cocina) **2** SCRAPE : rascar **3 to grate one's teeth** : hacer rechinar los dientes — *vi* **1** RASP, SQUEAK : chirriar **2** IRRITATE : irritar ⟨to grate on one's nerves : crisparle los nervios a uno⟩

grate² *n* **1** : parrilla *f* (para cocinar) **2** GRATING : reja *f*, rejilla *f*, verja *f* (en una ventana)

grateful ['greɪtfəl] *adj* : agradecido

gratefully ['greɪtfəli] *adv* : con agradecimiento

gratefulness ['greɪtfəlnəs] *n* : gratitud *f*, agradecimiento *m*

grater ['greɪţər] *n* : rallador *m*

gratification [,græţəfə'keɪʃən] *n* : gratificación *f*

gratify ['græţə,faɪ] *vt* **-fied; -fying 1** PLEASE : complacer **2** SATISFY : satisfacer, gratificar

grating ['greɪţɪŋ] *n* : reja *f*, rejilla *f*

gratis¹ ['græţəs, 'greɪ-] *adv* : gratis, gratuitamente

gratis² *adj* : gratis, gratuito

gratitude ['græţə,tu:d, -,tju:d] *n* : gratitud *f*, agradecimiento *m*

gratuitous [grə'tu:əţəs] *adj* : gratuito

gratuity [grə'tu:əţi] *n, pl* **-ities** TIP : propina *f*

grave¹ ['greɪv] *adj* **graver; -est 1** IMPORTANT : grave, de mucha gravedad **2** SERIOUS, SOLEMN : grave, serio

grave² *n* : tumba *f*, sepultura *f*

gravel ['grævəl] *n* : grava *f*, gravilla *f*

gravelly ['grævəli] *adj* **1** : de grava **2** HARSH : áspero (dícese de la voz)

gravely ['greɪvli] *adv* : gravemente

gravestone ['greɪv,sto:n] *n* : lápida *f*

graveyard ['greɪv,jɑrd] *n* CEMETERY : cementerio *m*, panteón *m*, camposanto *m*

gravitate ['grævə,teɪt] *vi* **-tated; -tating** : gravitar

gravitation [,grævə'teɪʃən] *n* : gravitación *f*

gravitational [,grævə'teɪʃənəl] *adj* : gravitacional

gravity ['grævəţi] *n, pl* **-ties 1** SERIOUSNESS : gravedad *f*, seriedad *f* **2** : gravedad *f* ⟨the law of gravity : la ley de la gravedad⟩

gravy ['greɪvi] *n, pl* **-vies** : salsa *f* (preparada con el jugo de la carne asada)

gray¹ ['greɪ] *vt* : hacer gris — *vi* : encanecer, ponerse gris

gray² *adj* **1** : gris (dícese del color) **2** : cano, canoso ⟨gray hair : pelo canoso⟩ ⟨to go gray : volverse cano⟩ **3** DISMAL, GLOOMY : gris, triste

gray³ *n* : gris *m*

grayish ['greɪɪʃ] *adj* : grisáceo

graze ['greɪz] *v* **grazed; grazing** *vi* : pastar, pacer — *vt* **1** : pastorear (ganado) **2** BRUSH : rozar **3** SCRATCH : raspar

grease¹ ['gri:s, 'gri:z] *vt* **greased; greasing** : engrasar, lubricar

grease² ['gri:s] *n* : grasa *f*

greasy ['gri:si, -zi] *adj* **greasier; -est 1** : grasiento **2** OILY : graso, grasoso

great ['greɪt] *adj* **1** LARGE : grande ⟨a great mountain : una montaña grande⟩ ⟨a great crowd : una gran muchedumbre⟩ **2** INTENSE : intenso, fuerte, grande ⟨great pain : gran dolor⟩ **3** EMINENT : grande, eminente, distinguido ⟨a great poet : un gran poeta⟩ **4** EXCELLENT, TERRIFIC : excelente, estupendo, fabuloso ⟨to have a great time : pasarlo en grande⟩ **5 a great while** : mucho tiempo

great–aunt [ˌgreɪtˈænt, -ˈant] *n* : tía *f* abuela

greater [ˈgreɪtər] (*comparative* of **great**) : mayor

greatest [ˈgreɪtəst] (*superlative* of **great**) : el mayor, la mayor

great–grandchild [ˌgreɪtˈgrænd-ˌtʃaɪld] *n, pl* **-children** [-ˌtʃɪldrən] : bisnieto *m*, -ta *f*

great–grandfather [ˌgreɪtˈgrænd-ˌfɑðər] *n* : bisabuelo *m*

great–grandmother [ˌgreɪtˈgrænd-ˌmʌðər] *n* : bisabuela *f*

greatly [ˈgreɪtli] *adv* **1** MUCH : mucho, sumamente ⟨to be greatly improved : haber mejorado mucho⟩ **2** VERY : muy ⟨greatly superior : muy superior⟩

greatness [ˈgreɪtnəs] *n* : grandeza *f*

great–uncle [ˌgreɪtˈʌŋkəl] *n* : tío *m* abuelo

grebe [ˈgriːb] *n* : somorgujo *m*

greed [ˈgriːd] *n* **1** AVARICE : avaricia *f*, codicia *f* **2** GLUTTONY : glotonería *f*, gula *f*

greedily [ˈgriːdəli] *adv* : con avaricia, con gula

greediness [ˈgriːdinəs] → **greed**

greedy [ˈgriːdi] *adj* **greedier; -est** **1** AVARICIOUS : codicioso, avaricioso **2** GLUTTONOUS : glotón

Greek [ˈgriːk] *n* **1** : griego *m*, -ga *f* **2** : griego *m* (idioma) — **Greek** *adj*

green¹ [ˈgriːn] *adj* **1** : verde (dícese del color) **2** UNRIPE : verde, inmaduro **3** INEXPERIENCED : verde, novato

green² *n* **1** : verde *m* **2 greens** *npl* VEGETABLES : verduras *fpl*

greenery [ˈgriːnəri] *n, pl* **-eries** : plantas *fpl* verdes, vegetación *f*

greenhorn [ˈgriːnˌhorn] *n* : novato *m*, -ta *f*

greenhouse [ˈgriːnˌhaʊs] *n* : invernadero *m*

greenhouse effect : efecto *m* invernadero

greenish [ˈgriːnɪʃ] *adj* : verdoso

Greenlander [ˈgriːnləndər, -ˌlæn-] *n* : groenlandés *m*, -desa *f*

greenness [ˈgriːnnəs] *n* **1** : verdor *m* **2** INEXPERIENCE : inexperiencia *f*

green thumb *n* **to have a green thumb** : tener buena mano para las plantas

greet [ˈgriːt] *vt* **1** : saludar ⟨to greet a friend : saludar a un amigo⟩ **2** : acoger, recibir ⟨they greeted him with boos : lo recibieron con abucheos⟩

greeting [ˈgriːtɪŋ] *n* **1** : saludo *m* **2 greetings** *npl* REGARDS : saludos *mpl*, recuerdos *mpl*

gregarious [grɪˈgæriəs] *adj* : gregario (dícese de los animales), sociable (dícese de las personas) — **gregariously** *adv*

gregariousness [grɪˈgæriəsnəs] *n* : sociabilidad *f*

gremlin [ˈgrɛmlən] *n* : duende *m*

grenade [grəˈneɪd] *n* : granada *f*

Grenadian [grəˈneɪdiən] *n* : granadino *m*, -na *f* — **Grenadian** *adj*

grew → **grow**

grey → **gray**

greyhound [ˈgreɪˌhaʊnd] *n* : galgo *m*

grid [ˈgrɪd] *n* **1** GRATING : rejilla *f* **2** NETWORK : red *f* (de electricidad, etc.) **3** : cuadriculado *m* (de un mapa)

griddle [ˈgrɪdəl] *n* : plancha *f*

griddle cake → **pancake**

gridiron [ˈgrɪdˌaɪərn] *n* **1** GRILL : parrilla *f* **2** : campo *m* de futbol americano

gridlock [ˈgrɪdˌlɑk] *n* : atasco *m* completo (de una red de calles)

grief [ˈgriːf] *n* **1** SORROW : dolor *m*, pena *f* **2** ANNOYANCE, TROUBLE : problemas *mpl*, molestia *f*

grievance [ˈgriːvənts] *n* COMPLAINT : queja *f*

grieve [ˈgriːv] *v* **grieved; grieving** *vt* DISTRESS : afligir, entristecer, apenar — *vi* **1** : sufrir, afligirse **2 to grieve for** *or* **to grieve over** : llorar, lamentar

grievous [ˈgriːvəs] *adj* **1** OPPRESSIVE : gravoso, opresivo, severo **2** GRAVE, SERIOUS : grave, severo, doloroso

grievously [ˈgriːvəsli] *adv* : gravemente, de gravedad

grill¹ [ˈgrɪl] *vt* **1** : asar (a la parrilla) **2** INTERROGATE : interrogar

grill² *n* **1** : parrilla *f* (para cocinar) **2** : parrillada *f* (comida) **3** RESTAURANT : grill *m*

grille *or* **grill** [ˈgrɪl] *n* : reja *f*, enrejado *m*

grim [ˈgrɪm] *adj* **grimmer; grimmest** **1** CRUEL : cruel, feroz **2** STERN : adusto, severo ⟨a grim expression : un gesto severo⟩ **3** GLOOMY : sombrío, deprimente **4** SINISTER : macabro, siniestro **5** UNYIELDING : inflexible, persistente ⟨with grim determination : con una voluntad de hierro⟩

grimace¹ [ˈgrɪməs, grɪˈmeɪs] *vi* **-maced; -macing** : hacer muecas

grimace² *n* : mueca *f*

grime [ˈgraɪm] *n* : mugre *f*, suciedad *f*

grimly [ˈgrɪmli] *adv* **1** STERNLY : severamente **2** RESOLUTELY : inexorablemente

grimy [ˈgraɪmi] *adj* **grimier; -est** : mugriento, sucio

grin¹ [ˈgrɪn] *vi* **grinned; grinning** : sonreír abiertamente

grin² *n* : sonrisa *f* abierta

grind¹ [ˈgraɪnd] *v* **ground** [ˈgraʊnd]; **grinding** *vt* **1** CRUSH : moler, machacar, triturar **2** SHARPEN : afilar **3** POLISH : pulir, esmerilar (lentes, espejos) **4 to grind one's teeth** : rechinarle los dientes a uno **5 to grind down** OPPRESS : oprimir, agobiar — *vi* **1** : funcionar con dificultad, rechinar ⟨to grind to a halt : pararse poco a poco, llegar a un punto muerto⟩ **2** STUDY : estudiar mucho

grind² *n* : trabajo *m* pesado ⟨the daily grind : la rutina diaria⟩

grinder ['graɪndər] *n* : molinillo *m* ⟨coffee grinder : molinillo de café⟩

grindstone ['graɪnd‚sto:n] *n* : piedra *m* de afilar

grip¹ ['grɪp] *vt* **gripped; gripping 1** GRASP : agarrar, asir **2** HOLD, INTEREST : captar el interés de

grip² *n* **1** GRASP : agarre *m*, asidero *m* ⟨to have a firm grip on something : agarrarse bien de algo⟩ **2** CONTROL, HOLD : control *m*, dominio *m* ⟨to lose one's grip on : perder el control de⟩ ⟨inflation tightened its grip on the economy : la inflación se afianzó en su dominio de la economía⟩ **3** UNDERSTANDING : comprensión *f*, entendimiento *m* ⟨to come to grips with : llegar a entender⟩ **4** HANDLE : asidero *m*, empuñadura *f* (de un arma)

gripe¹ ['graɪp] *v* **griped; griping** *vt* IRRITATE, VEX : irritar, fastidiar, molestar — *vi* COMPLAIN : quejarse, rezongar

gripe² *n* : queja *f*

grippe ['grɪp] *n* : influenza *f*, gripe *f*, gripa *f Col, Mex*

grisly ['grɪzli] *adj* **-lier; -est** : horripilante, horroroso, truculento

grist ['grɪst] *n* : molienda *f* ⟨it's all grist for the mill : todo ayuda, todo es provechoso⟩

gristle ['grɪsəl] *n* : cartílago *m*

gristly ['grɪsli] *adj* **-tlier; -est** : cartilaginoso

grit¹ ['grɪt] *vt* **gritted; gritting** : hacer rechinar (los dientes, etc.)

grit² *n* **1** SAND : arena *f* **2** GRAVEL : grava *f* **3** COURAGE : valor *m*, coraje *m* **4 grits** *npl* : sémola *f* de maíz

gritty ['grɪti] *adj* **-tier; -est 1** : arenoso ⟨a gritty surface : una superficie arenosa⟩ **2** PLUCKY : valiente

grizzled ['grɪzəld] *adj* : entrecano

grizzly bear ['grɪzli] *n* : oso *m* pardo

groan¹ ['gro:n] *vi* **1** MOAN : gemir, quejarse **2** CREAK : crujir

groan² *n* **1** MOAN : gemido *m*, quejido *m* **2** CREAK : crujido *m*

grocer ['gro:sər] *n* : tendero *m*, -ra *f*

grocery ['gro:səri, -ʃəri] *n, pl* **-ceries 1** *or* **grocery store** : tienda *f* de comestibles, tienda *f* de abarrotes **2 groceries** *npl* : comestibles *mpl*, abarrotes *mpl*

groggy ['grɑgi] *adj* **-gier; -est** : atontado, grogui, tambaleante

groin ['grɔɪn] *n* : ingle *f*

grommet ['grɑmət, 'grʌ-] *n* : arandela *f*

groom¹ ['gru:m, 'grʊm] *vt* **1** : cepillar, almohazar (un animal) **2** : arreglar, cuidar ⟨well-groomed : bien arreglado⟩ **3** PREPARE : preparar

groom² *n* **1** : mozo *m*, -za *f* de cuadra **2** BRIDEGROOM : novio *m*

groove¹ ['gru:v] *vt* **grooved; grooving** : acanalar, hacer ranuras en, surcar

groove² *n* **1** FURROW, SLOT : ranura *f*, surco *m* **2** RUT : rutina *f*

grope ['gro:p] *v* **groped; groping** *vi* : andar a tientas, tantear ⟨he groped for the switch : buscó el interruptor a tientas⟩ — *vt* **to grope one's way** : avanzar a tientas

gross¹ ['gro:s] *vt* : tener entrada bruta de, recaudar en bruto

gross² *adj* **1** FLAGRANT : flagrante, grave ⟨a gross error : un error flagrante⟩ ⟨a gross injustice : una injusticia grave⟩ **2** FAT : muy gordo, obeso **3** : bruto ⟨gross national product : producto nacional bruto⟩ **4** COARSE, VULGAR : grosero, basto

gross³ *n* **1** *pl* **gross** : gruesa *f* (12 docenas) **2** *or* **gross income** : ingresos *mpl* brutos

grossly ['gro:sli] *adv* **1** EXTREMELY : extremadamente ⟨grossly unfair : totalmente injusto⟩ **2** CRUDELY : groseramente

grotesque [gro:'tɛsk] *adj* : grotesco

grotesquely [gro:'tɛskli] *adv* : de forma grotesca

grotto ['grɑto:] *n, pl* **-toes** : gruta *f*

grouch¹ ['graʊʧ] *vi* : refunfuñar, rezongar

grouch² *n* **1** COMPLAINT : queja *f* **2** GRUMBLER : gruñón *m*, -ñona *f*; cascarrabias *mf fam*

grouchy ['graʊʧi] *adj* **grouchier; -est** : malhumorado, gruñón

ground¹ ['graʊnd] *vt* **1** BASE : fundar, basar **2** INSTRUCT : enseñar los conocimientos básicos a ⟨to be well grounded in : ser muy entendido en⟩ **3** : conectar a tierra (un aparato eléctrico) **4** : varar, hacer encallar (un barco) **5** : restringir (un avión o un piloto) a la tierra

ground² *n* **1** EARTH, SOIL : suelo *m*, tierra *f* ⟨to dig (in) the ground : cavar la tierra⟩ ⟨to fall to the ground : caerse al suelo⟩ **2** LAND, TERRAIN : terreno *m* ⟨hilly ground : terreno alto⟩ ⟨to lose ground : perder terreno⟩ **3** BASIS, REASON : razón *f*, motivo *m* ⟨grounds for complaint : motivos de queja⟩ **4** BACKGROUND : fondo *m* **5** FIELD : campo *m*, plaza *f* ⟨parade ground : plaza de armas⟩ **6** : tierra *f* (para electricidad) **7 grounds** *npl* PREMISES : recinto *m*, terreno *m* **8 grounds** *npl* DREGS : posos *mpl* (de café)

ground³ → **grind**

groundhog ['graʊnd‚hɔg] *n* : marmota *f* (de América)

groundless ['graʊndləs] *adj* : infundado

groundwork ['graʊnd‚wərk] *n* **1** FOUNDATION : fundamento *m*, base *f* **2** PREPARATION : trabajo *m* preparatorio

group¹ ['gru:p] *vt* : agrupar

group² *n* : grupo *m*, agrupación *f*, conjunto *m*, compañía *f*

grouper ['gru:pər] *n* : mero *m*

grouse¹ ['graʊs] *vi* **groused; grousing** : quejarse, rezongar, refunfuñar

grouse² *n, pl* **grouse** *or* **grouses** : urogallo *m* (ave)

grout ['graʊt] *n* : lechada *f*

grove ['gro:v] *n* : bosquecillo *m*, arboleda *f*, soto *m*

grovel ['grɑvəl, 'grʌ-] *vi* **-eled** *or* **-elled; -eling** *or* **-elling 1** CRAWL : arrastrarse **2** : humillarse, postrarse ⟨to grovel before someone : postrarse ante alguien⟩

grow ['gro:] *v* **grew** ['gru:]; **grown** ['gro:n]; **growing** *vi* **1** : crecer ⟨palm trees grow on the islands : las palmas crecen en las islas⟩ ⟨my hair grows very fast : mi pelo crece muy rápido⟩ **2** DEVELOP, MATURE : desarrollarse, madurar **3** INCREASE : crecer, aumentar **4** BECOME : hacerse, volverse, ponerse ⟨she was growing angry : se estaba poniendo furiosa⟩ ⟨to grow dark : oscurecerse⟩ **5 to grow up** : hacerse mayor ⟨grow up! : ¡no seas niño!⟩ — *vt* **1** CULTIVATE, RAISE : cultivar **2** : dejar crecer ⟨to grow one's hair : dejarse crecer el pelo⟩

grower ['gro:ər] *n* : cultivador *m*, -dora *f*

growl¹ ['graʊl] *vi* : gruñir (dícese de un animal), refunfuñar (dícese de una persona)

growl² *n* : gruñido *m*

grown–up¹ ['gro:n,ʌp] *adj* : adulto, mayor

grown–up² *n* : adulto *m*, -ta *f*; persona *f* mayor

growth ['gro:θ] *n* **1** : crecimiento *m* ⟨to stunt one's growth : detener el crecimiento⟩ **2** INCREASE : aumento *m*, crecimiento *m*, expansión *f* **3** DEVELOPMENT : desarrollo *m* ⟨economic growth : desarrollo económico⟩ ⟨a five days' growth of beard : una barba de cinco días⟩ **4** LUMP, TUMOR : bulto *m*, tumor *m*

grub¹ ['grʌb] *vi* **grubbed; grubbing 1** DIG : escarbar **2** RUMMAGE : hurgar, buscar **3** DRUDGE : trabajar duro

grub² *n* **1** : larva *f* ⟨beetle grub : larva del escarabajo⟩ **2** DRUDGE : esclavo *m*, -va *f* del trabajo **3** FOOD : comida *f*

grubby ['grʌbi] *adj* **grubbier; -est** : mugriento, sucio

grudge¹ ['grʌʤ] *vt* **grudged; grudging** : resentir, envidiar

grudge² *n* : rencor *m*, resentimiento *m* ⟨to hold a grudge : guardar rencor⟩

grueling *or* **gruelling** ['gru:lɪŋ, 'gru:ə-] *adj* : extenuante, agotador, duro

gruesome ['gru:səm] *adj* : horripilante, truculento, horroroso

gruff ['grʌf] *adj* **1** BRUSQUE : brusco ⟨a gruff reply : una respuesta brusca⟩ **2** HOARSE : ronco — **gruffly** *adv*

grumble¹ ['grʌmbəl] *vi* **-bled; -bling 1** COMPLAIN : refunfuñar, rezongar, quejarse **2** RUMBLE : hacer un ruido sordo, retumbar (dícese del trueno)

grumble² *n* **1** COMPLAINT : queja *f* **2** RUMBLE : ruido *m* sordo, estruendo *m*

grumbler ['grʌmbələr] *n* : gruñón *m*, -ñona *f*

grumpy ['grʌmpi] *adj* **grumpier; -est** : malhumorado, gruñón

grungy ['grʌnʤi] *adj* : sucio

grunt¹ ['grʌnt] *vi* : gruñir

grunt² *n* : gruñido *m*

guacamole [,gwɑkə'mo:li] *n* : guacamole *m*, guacamol *m*

guarantee¹ [,gærən'ti:] *vt* **-teed; -teeing 1** PROMISE : asegurar, prometer **2** : poner bajo garantía, garantizar (un producto o servicio)

guarantee² *n* **1** PROMISE : garantía *f*, promesa *f* ⟨lifetime guarantee : garantía de por vida⟩ **2** → **guarantor**

guarantor [,gærən'tɔr] *n* : garante *mf*; fiador *m*, -dora *f*

guaranty [,gærən'ti:] → **guarantee**

guard¹ ['gɑrd] *vt* **1** DEFEND, PROTECT : defender, proteger **2** : guardar, vigilar, custodiar ⟨to guard the frontier : vigilar la frontera⟩ ⟨she guarded my secret well : guardó bien mi secreto⟩ — *vi* **to guard against** : protegerse contra, evitar

guard² *n* **1** WATCHMAN : guarda *mf* ⟨security guard : guarda de seguridad⟩ **2** VIGILANCE : guardia *f*, vigilancia *f* ⟨to be on guard : estar en guardia⟩ ⟨to let one's guard down : bajar la guardia⟩ **3** SAFEGUARD : salvaguardia *f*, dispositivo *m* de seguridad (en una máquina) **4** PRECAUTION : precaución *f*, protección *f*

guardhouse ['gɑrd,haʊs] *n* : cuartel *m* de la guardia

guardian ['gɑrdiən] *n* **1** PROTECTOR : guardián *m*, -diana *f*; custodio *m*, -dia *f* **2** : tutor *m*, -tora *f* (de un niño)

guardianship ['gɑrdiən,ʃɪp] *n* : custodia *f*, tutela *f*

Guatemalan [,gwɑtə'mɑlən] *n* : guatemalteco *m*, -ca *f* — **Guatemalan** *adj*

guava ['gwɑvə] *n* : guayaba *f*

gubernatorial [,gu:bənə'tori:əl, ,gju:-] *adj* : del gobernador

guerrilla *or* **guerilla** [gə'rɪlə] *n* : guerrillero *m*, -ra *f*

guess¹ ['gɛs] *vt* **1** CONJECTURE : adivinar, conjeturar ⟨guess what happened! : ¡adivina lo que pasó!⟩ **2** SUPPOSE : pensar, creer, suponer ⟨I guess so : supongo que sí⟩ **3** : adivinar correctamente, acertar ⟨to guess the answer : acertar la respuesta⟩ — *vi* : adivinar

guess² *n* : conjetura *f*, suposición *f*

guesswork ['gɛs,wərk] *n* : suposiciones *fpl*, conjeturas *fpl*

guest ['gɛst] *n* : huésped *mf*; invitado *m*, -da *f*

guffaw¹ [gə'fɔ] *vi* : reírse a carcajadas, carcajearse *fam*

guffaw² [gə'fɔ, 'gʌ,fɔ] *n* : carcajada *f*, risotada *f*

guidance ['gaɪdənts] *n* : orientación *f*, consejos *mpl*

guide¹ ['gaɪd] *vt* **guided; guiding 1** DI-RECT, LEAD : guiar, dirigir, conducir **2** ADVISE, COUNSEL : aconsejar, orientar

guide² *n* : guía *f*

guidebook ['gaɪd,bʊk] *n* : guía *f* (para viajeros)

guideline ['gaɪd,laɪn] *n* : pauta *f*, directriz *f*

guild ['gɪld] *n* : gremio *m*, sindicato *m*, asociación *f*

guile ['gaɪl] *n* : astucia *f*, engaño *m*

guileless ['gaɪlləs] *adj* : inocente, cándido, sin malicia

guillotine¹ ['gɪlə,tiːn, 'giːjə,-] *vt* **-tined; -tining** : guillotinar

guillotine² *n* : guillotina *f*

guilt ['gɪlt] *n* : culpa *f*, culpabilidad *f*

guilty ['gɪlti] *adj* **guiltier; -est** : culpable

guinea fowl ['gɪni] *n* : gallina *f* de Guinea

guinea pig *n* : conejillo *m* de Indias, cobaya *f*

guise ['gaɪz] *n* : apariencia *f*, aspecto *m*, forma *f*

guitar [gə'tɑr, gɪ-] *n* : guitarra *f*

guitarist [gə'tɑrɪst, gɪ-] *n* : guitarrista *mf*

gulch ['gʌltʃ] *n* : barranco *m*, quebrada *f*

gulf ['gʌlf] *n* **1** : golfo *m* ⟨the Gulf of Mexico : el Golfo de México⟩ **2** GAP : brecha *f* ⟨the gulf between generations : la brecha entre las generaciones⟩ **3** CHASM : abismo *m*

gull ['gʌl] *n* : gaviota *f*

gullet ['gʌlət] *n* : garganta *f*

gullible ['gʌlɪbəl] *adj* : crédulo

gully ['gʌli] *n, pl* **-lies** : barranco *m*, hondonada *f*

gulp¹ ['gʌlp] *vt* **1** : engullir, tragar ⟨he gulped down the whiskey : engulló el whisky⟩ **2** SUPPRESS : suprimir, reprimir, tragar ⟨to gulp down a sob : reprimir un sollozo⟩ — *vi* : tragar saliva, tener un nudo en la garganta

gulp² *n* : trago *m*

gum ['gʌm] *n* **1** CHEWING GUM : goma *f* de mascar, chicle *m* **2 gums** *npl* : encías *fpl*

gumbo ['gʌm,boː] *n* : sopa *f* de quingombó

gumdrop ['gʌm,drɑp] *n* : pastilla *f* de goma

gummy ['gʌmi] *adj* **gummier; -est** : gomoso

gumption ['gʌmpʃən] *n* : iniciativa *f*, agallas *fpl fam*

gun¹ ['gʌn] *vt* **gunned; gunning 1** *or to* **gun down** : matar a tiros, asesinar **2** : acelerar (rápidamente) ⟨to gun the engine : acelerar el motor⟩

gun² *n* **1** CANNON : cañón *m* **2** FIREARM : arma *f* de fuego **3** SPRAY GUN : pistola *f* **4 to jump the gun** : adelantarse, salir antes de tiempo

gunboat ['gʌn,boːt] *n* : cañonero *m*

gunfight ['gʌn,faɪt] *n* : tiroteo *m*, balacera *f*

gunfire ['gʌn,faɪr] *n* : disparos *mpl*

gunman ['gʌnmən] *n, pl* **-men** [-mən, -,men] : pistolero *m*, gatillero *m* Mex

gunner ['gʌnər] *n* : artillero *m*, -ra *f*

gunnysack ['gʌni,sæk] *n* : saco *m* de yute

gunpowder ['gʌn,paʊdər] *n* : pólvora *f*

gunshot ['gʌn,ʃɑt] *n* : disparo *m*, tiro *m*, balazo *m*

gunwale ['gʌnəl] *n* : borda *f*

guppy ['gʌpi] *n, pl* **-pies** : lebistes *m*

gurgle¹ ['gərgəl] *vi* **-gled; -gling 1** : borbotar, gorgotear (dícese de un líquido) **2** : gorjear (dícese de un niño)

gurgle² *n* **1** : borboteo *m*, gorgoteo *m* (de un líquido) **2** : gorjeo *m* (de un niño)

gush ['gʌʃ] *vi* **1** SPOUT : surgir, salir a chorros, chorrear **2** : hablar con entusiasmo efusivo ⟨she gushed with praise : se deshizo en elogios⟩

gust ['gʌst] *n* : ráfaga *f*, racha *f*

gusto ['gʌs,toː] *n, pl* **gustoes** : entusiasmo *m* ⟨with gusto : con deleite, con ganas⟩

gusty ['gʌsti] *adj* **gustier; -est** : racheado

gut¹ ['gʌt] *vt* **gutted; gutting 1** EVIS-CERATE : destripar (un pollo, etc.), limpiar (un pescado) **2** : destruir el interior de (un edificio)

gut² *n* **1** INTESTINE : intestino *m* **2 guts** *npl* INNARDS : tripas *fpl fam*, entrañas *fpl* **3 guts** *npl* COURAGE : valentía *f*, agallas *fpl*

gutter ['gʌtər] *n* **1** : canal *mf*, canaleta *f* (de un techo) **2** : cuneta *f*, arroyo *m* (de una calle)

guttural ['gʌtərəl] *adj* : gutural

guy ['gaɪ] *n* **1** *or* **guyline** : cuerda *f* tensora, cable *m* **2** FELLOW : tipo *m*, hombre *m*

guzzle ['gʌzəl] *vt* **-zled; -zling** : chupar, tragarse

gym ['dʒɪm] → **gymnasium**

gymnasium [dʒɪm'neɪziəm, -ʒəm] *n, pl* **-siums** *or* **-sia** [-ziːə, -ʒə] : gimnasio *m*

gymnast ['dʒɪmnəst, -,næst] *n* : gimnasta *mf*

gymnastic [dʒɪm'næstɪk] *adj* : gimnástico

gymnastics [dʒɪm'næstɪks] *ns & pl* : gimnasia *f*

gynecologist [,gaɪnə'kɑlədʒɪst, ,dʒɪnə-] *n* : ginecólogo *m*, -ga *f*

gynecology [,gaɪnə'kɑlədʒi, ,dʒɪnə-] *n* : ginecología *f*

gyp¹ ['dʒɪp] *vt* **gypped; gypping** : estafar, timar

gyp² *n* **1** SWINDLER : estafador *m*, -dora *f* **2** FRAUD, SWINDLE : estafa *f*, timo *m* fam

gypsum ['dʒɪpsəm] *n* : yeso *m*

Gypsy ['dʒɪpsi] *n, pl* **-sies** : gitano *m*, -na *f*

gyrate ['dʒaɪ,reɪt] *vi* **-rated; -rating** : girar, rotar

gyration [dʒaɪ'reɪʃən] *n* : giro *m*, rotación *f*

gyroscope ['dʒaɪrə,skoːp] *n* : giroscopio *m*, giróscopo *m*

H

h ['eɪtʃ] *n, pl* **h's** *or* **hs** ['eɪtʃəz] : octava letra del alfabeto inglés

ha ['hɑ] *interj* : ¡ja!

haberdashery ['hæbər,dæʃəri] *n, pl* **-eries** : tienda *f* de ropa para caballeros

habit ['hæbɪt] *n* **1** CUSTOM : hábito *m*, costumbre *f* **2** : hábito *m* (de un monje o una religiosa) **3** ADDICTION : dependencia *f*, adicción *f*

habitable ['hæbɪtəbəl] *adj* : habitable

habitat ['hæbɪ,tæt] *n* : hábitat *m*

habitation [,hæbɪ'teɪʃən] *n* **1** OCCUPANCY : habitación *f* **2** RESIDENCE : residencia *f*, morada *f*

habit–forming ['hæbɪt,fɔrmɪŋ] *adj* : que crea dependencia

habitual [hə'bɪtʃuəl] *adj* **1** CUSTOMARY : habitual, acostumbrado **2** INVETERATE : incorregible, empedernido — **habitually** *adv*

habituate [hə'bɪtʃu,eɪt] *vt* **-ated; -ating** : habituar, acostumbrar

hack¹ ['hæk] *vt* : cortar, tajear (a hachazos, etc.) ⟨to hack one's way : abrirse paso⟩ — *vi* **1** : hacer tajos **2** COUGH : toser

hack² *n* **1** CHOP : hachazo *m*, tajo *m* **2** HORSE : caballo *m* de alquiler **3** WRITER : escritor *m*, -tora *f* a sueldo; escritorzuelo *m*, -la *f* **4** COUGH : tos *f* seca

hackles ['hækəlz] *npl* **1** : pluma *f* erizada (de un ave), pelo *m* erizado (de un perro, etc.) **2 to get one's hackles up** : ponerse furioso

hackney ['hækni] *n, pl* **-neys** : caballo *m* de silla, caballo *m* de tiro

hackneyed ['hæknid] *adj* TRITE : trillado, gastado

hacksaw ['hæk,sɔ] *n* : sierra *f* para metales

had → **have**

haddock ['hædək] *ns & pl* : eglefino *m*

hadn't ['hædənt] (*contraction of* **had not**) → **have**

haft ['hæft] *n* : mango *m*, empuñadura *f*

hag ['hæg] *n* **1** WITCH : bruja *f*, hechicera *f* **2** CRONE : vieja *f* fea

haggard ['hægərd] *adj* : demacrado, macilento — **haggardly** *adv*

haggle ['hægəl] *vi* **-gled; -gling** : regatear

ha–ha [,hɑ'hɑ, 'hɑ'hɑ] *interj* : ¡ja, ja!

hail¹ ['heɪl] *vt* **1** GREET : saludar **2** SUMMON : llamar ⟨to hail a taxi : llamar un taxi⟩ — *vi* : granizar (en meteorología)

hail² *n* **1** : granizo *m* **2** BARRAGE : aluvión *m*, lluvia *f*

hail³ *interj* : ¡salve!

hailstone ['heɪl,stoːn] *n* : granizo *m*, piedra *f* de granizo

hailstorm ['heɪl,stɔrm] *n* : granizada *f*

hair ['hær] *n* **1** : pelo *m*, cabello *m* ⟨to get one's hair cut : cortarse el pelo⟩ **2** : vello *m* (en las piernas, etc.)

hairbreadth ['hær,brɛdθ] *or* **hairsbreadth** ['hærz-] *n* **by a hairbreadth** : por un pelo

hairbrush ['hær,brʌʃ] *n* : cepillo *m* (para el pelo)

haircut ['hær,kʌt] *n* : corte *m* de pelo

hairdo ['hær,duː] *n, pl* **-dos** : peinado *m*

hairdresser ['hær,drɛsər] *n* : peluquero *m*, -ra *f*

hairiness ['hærinəs] *n* : vellosidad *f*

hairless ['hærləs] *adj* : sin pelo, calvo, pelón

hairline ['hær,laɪn] *n* **1** : línea *f* delgada **2** : nacimiento *m* del pelo ⟨to have a receding hairline : tener entradas⟩

hairpin ['hær,pɪn] *n* : horquilla *f*

hair–raising ['hær,reɪzɪŋ] *adj* : espeluznante

hair spray *n* : laca *f*, fijador *m* (para el pelo)

hairstyle ['hær,staɪl] *n* : peinado *m*

hairy ['hæri] *adj* **hairier; -est** : peludo, velludo

Haitian ['heɪʃən, 'heɪtiən] *n* : haitiano *m*, -na *f* — **Haitian** *adj*

hake ['heɪk] *n* : merluza *f*

hale¹ ['heɪl] *vt* **haled; haling** : arrastrar, halar ⟨to hale to court : arrastrar al tribunal⟩

hale² *adj* : saludable, robusto

half¹ ['hæf, 'hɑf] *adv* : medio, a medias ⟨half cooked : medio cocido⟩

half² *adj* : medio, a medias ⟨a half hour : una media hora⟩ ⟨a half truth : una verdad a medias⟩

half³ *n, pl* **halves** ['hævz, 'hɑvz] **1** : mitad *f* ⟨half of my friends : la mitad de mis amigos⟩ ⟨in half : por la mitad⟩ **2** : tiempo *m* (en deportes)

half brother *n* : medio hermano *m*, hermanastro *m*

halfhearted ['hæf'hɑrtəd] *adj* : sin ánimo, poco entusiasta

halfheartedly ['hæf'hɑrtədli] *adv* : con poco entusiasmo, sin ánimo

half–life ['hæf,laɪf] *n, pl* **half–lives** : media vida *f*

half sister *n* : media hermana *f*, hermanastra *f*

halfway¹ ['hæf'weɪ] *adv* : a medio camino, a mitad de camino

halfway² *adj* : medio, intermedio ⟨a halfway point : un punto intermedio⟩

half–wit ['hæf,wɪt] *n* : tonto *m*, -ta *f*; imbécil *mf*

half–witted ['hæf,wɪtəd] *adj* : estúpido

halibut ['hælɪbət] *ns & pl* : halibut *m*

hall ['hɔl] *n* **1** BUILDING : residencia *f* estudiantil, facultad *f* (de una universidad) **2** VESTIBULE : entrada *f*, vestíbulo *m*, zaguán *m* **3** CORRIDOR : corredor *m*, pasillo *m* **4** AUDITORIUM : sala *f*, salón *m* ⟨concert hall : sala de conciertos⟩ **5 city hall** : ayuntamiento *m*

hallelujah [,hælə'luːjə, ,hɑ-] *interj* : ¡aleluya!

hallmark ['hɔl,mɑrk] *n* : sello *m* (distintivo)

hallow ['hæ,lo:] *vt* : santificar, consagrar

hallowed ['hæ,lo:d, 'hæ,lo:əd, 'hɑ,lo:d] *adj* : sagrado

Halloween [,hælə'wi:n, ,hɑ-] *n* : víspera *f* de Todos los Santos

hallucinate [hæ'lu:sən,eɪt] *vi* **-nated; -nating** : alucinar

hallucination [hə,lu:sən'eɪʃən] *n* : alucinación *f*

hallucinatory [hə'lu:sənə,tori] *adj* : alucinante

hallucinogen [hə'lu:sənədʒən] *n* : alucinógeno *m*

hallucinogenic [hə,lu:sənə'dʒɛnɪk] *adj* : alucinógeno

hallway ['hɔl,weɪ] *n* **1** ENTRANCE : entrada *f* **2** CORRIDOR : corredor *m*, pasillo *m*

halo ['heɪ,lo:] *n, pl* **-los** *or* **-loes** : aureola *f*, halo *m*

halt¹ ['hɔlt] *vi* : detenerse, pararse — *vt* **1** STOP : detener, parar (a una persona) **2** INTERRUPT : interrumpir (una actividad)

halt² *n* **1** : alto *m*, parada *f* **2 to come to a halt** : pararse, detenerse

halter ['hɔltər] *n* **1** : cabestro *m*, ronzal *m* (para un animal) **2** : blusa *f* sin espalda

halting ['hɔltɪŋ] *adj* HESITANT : vacilante, titubeante — **haltingly** *adv*

halve ['hæv, 'hɑv] *vt* **halved; halving 1** DIVIDE : partir por la mitad **2** REDUCE : reducir a la mitad

halves → **half**

ham ['hæm] *n* **1** : jamón *m* **2** *or* **ham actor** : comicastro *m*, -tra *f* **3** *or* **ham radio operator** : radioaficionado *m*, -da *f* **4 hams** *npl* HAUNCHES : ancas *fpl*

hamburger ['hæm,bərgər] *or* **hamburg** [-,bərg] *n* **1** : carne *f* molida **2** : hamburguesa *f* (emparedado)

hamlet ['hæmlət] *n* VILLAGE : aldea *f*, poblado *m*

hammer¹ ['hæmər] *vt* **1** STRIKE : clavar, golpear **2** NAIL : clavar, martillar **3 to hammer out** NEGOTIATE : elaborar, negociar, llegar a — *vi* : martillar, golpear

hammer² *n* **1** : martillo *m* **2** : percusor *m*, percutor *m* (de un arma de fuego)

hammock ['hæmək] *n* : hamaca *f*

hamper¹ ['hæmpər] *vt* : obstaculizar, dificultar

hamper² *n* : cesto *m*, canasta *f*

hamster ['hæmpstər] *n* : hámster *m*

hamstring ['hæm,strɪŋ] *vt* **-strung** [-,strʌŋ]; **-stringing 1** : cortarle el tendón del corvejón a (un animal) **2** INCAPACITATE : incapacitar, inutilizar

hand¹ ['hænd] *vt* : pasar, dar, entregar

hand² *n* **1** : mano *f* ⟨made by hand : hecho a mano⟩ **2** POINTER : manecilla *f*, aguja *f* (de un reloj o instrumento) **3** SIDE : lado *m* ⟨on the other hand : por otro lado⟩ **4** HANDWRITING : letra *f*, escritura *f* **5** APPLAUSE : aplauso *m* **6** : mano *f*, cartas *fpl* (en juegos de naipes)

7 WORKER : obrero *m*, -ra *f*; trabajador *m*, -dora *f* **8 to ask for someone's hand (in marriage)** : pedir la mano de alguien **9 to lend a hand** : echar una mano

handbag ['hænd,bæg] *n* : cartera *f*, bolso *m*, bolsa *f Mex*

handball ['hænd,bɔl] *n* : frontón *m*, pelota *f*

handbill ['hænd,bɪl] *n* : folleto *m*, volante *m*

handbook ['hænd,bʊk] *n* : manual *m*

handcuff ['hænd,kʌf] *vt* : esposar, ponerle esposas (a alguien)

handcuffs ['hænd,kʌfs] *npl* : esposas *fpl*

handful ['hænd,fʊl] *n* : puñado *m*

handgun ['hænd,gʌn] *n* : pistola *f*, revólver *m*

handheld ['hænd,hɛld] *adj* : de mano

handicap¹ ['hændi,kæp] *vt* **-capped; -capping 1** : asignar un handicap a (en deportes) **2** HAMPER : obstaculizar, poner en desventaja

handicap² *n* **1** DISABILITY : minusvalía *f*, discapacidad *f* **2** DISADVANTAGE : desventaja *f*, handicap *m* (en deportes)

handicapped ['hændi,kæpt] *adj* DISABLED : minusválido, discapacitado

handicraft ['hændi,kræft] *n* : artesanía *f*

handily ['hændəli] *adv* EASILY : fácilmente, con facilidad

handiwork ['hændi,wərk] *n* **1** WORK : trabajo *m* **2** CRAFTS : artesanías *fpl*

handkerchief ['hæŋkərtʃəf, -,tʃi:f] *n, pl* **-chiefs** : pañuelo *m*

handle¹ ['hændəl] *v* **-dled; -dling** *vt* **1** TOUCH : tocar **2** MANAGE : tratar, manejar, despachar **3** SELL : comerciar con, vender — *vi* : responder, conducirse (dícese de un vehículo)

handle² *n* : asa *m*, asidero *m*, mango *m* (de un cuchillo, etc.), pomo *m* (de una puerta), tirador *m* (de un cajón)

handlebars ['hændəl,bɑrz] *npl* : manubrio *m*, manillar *m*

handler ['hændələr] *n* : cuidador *m*, -dora *f*

handling ['hændəlɪŋ] *n* **1** MANAGEMENT : manejo *m* **2** TOUCHING : manoseo *m* **3 shipping and handling** : porte *m*, transporte *m*

handmade ['hænd,meɪd] *adj* : hecho a mano

hand—me—downs ['hændmi,daʊnz] *npl* : ropa *f* usada

handout ['hænd,aʊt] *n* **1** AID : dádiva *f*, limosna *f* **2** LEAFLET : folleto *m*

handpick ['hænd'pɪk] *vt* : seleccionar con cuidado

handrail ['hænd,reɪl] *n* : pasamanos *m*, barandilla *f*, barandal *m*

handsaw ['hænd,sɔ] *n* : serrucho *m*

hands down *adv* **1** EASILY : con facilidad **2** UNQUESTIONABLY : con mucho, de lejos

handshake ['hænd,ʃeɪk] *n* : apretón *m* de manos

handsome ['hænʦəm] *adj* **-somer; -est**
1 ATTRACTIVE : apuesto, guapo, atractivo **2** GENEROUS : generoso **3** SIZABLE : considerable
handsomely ['hænʦəmli] *adv* **1** ELEGANTLY : elegantemente **2** GENEROUSLY : con generosidad
handspring ['hænd,sprɪŋ] *n* : voltereta *f*
handstand ['hænd,stænd] *n* **to do a handstand** : pararse de manos
hand–to–hand ['hænʦtə'hænd] *adj* : cuerpo a cuerpo
handwriting ['hænd,raɪʦɪŋ] *n* : letra *f*, escritura *f*
handwritten ['hænd,rɪtən] *adj* : escrito a mano
handy ['hændi] *adj* **handier; -est 1** NEARBY : a mano, cercano **2** USEFUL : útil, práctico **3** DEXTROUS : hábil
hang¹ ['hæŋ] *v* **hung** ['hʌŋ]; **hanging** *vt* **1** SUSPEND : colgar, tender, suspender **2** *past tense often* **hanged** EXECUTE : colgar, ahorcar **3 to hang one's head** : bajar la cabeza — *vi* **1** FALL : caer (dícese de las telas y la ropa) **2** DANGLE : colgar **3** HOVER : flotar, sostenerse en el aire **4** : ser ahorcado **5** DROOP : inclinarse **6 to hang up** : colgar ⟨he hung up on me : me colgó⟩
hang² *n* **1** DRAPE : caída *f* **2 to get the hang of something** : agarrarle la onda a algo
hangar ['hæŋər, 'hæŋgər] *n* : hangar *m*
hanger ['hæŋər] *n* : percha *f*, gancho *m* (para ropa)
hangman ['hæŋmən] *n*, *pl* **-men** [-mən, -,mɛn] : verdugo *m*
hangnail ['hæŋ,neɪl] *n* : padrastro *m*
hangout ['hæŋ,aʊt] *n* : lugar *m* popular, sitio *m* muy frecuentado
hangover ['hæŋ,oːvər] *n* : resaca *f*
hank ['hæŋk] *n* : madeja *f*
hanker ['hæŋkər] *vi* **to hanker for** : tener ansias de, tener ganas de
hankering ['hæŋkərɪŋ] *n* : ansia *f*, anhelo *m*
hansom ['hænʦəm] *n* : coche *m* de caballos
Hanukkah ['xɑnəkə, 'hɑ-] *n* : Januká, Hanukkah
haphazard [hæp'hæzərd] *adj* : casual, fortuito, al azar — **haphazardly** *adv*
hapless ['hæpləs] *adj* UNFORTUNATE : desafortunado, desventurado — **haplessly** *adv*
happen ['hæpən] *vi* **1** OCCUR : pasar, ocurrir, suceder, tener lugar **2** BEFALL : pasar, acontecer ⟨what happened to her? : ¿qué le ha pasado?⟩ **3** CHANCE : resultar, ocurrir por casualidad ⟨it happened that I wasn't home : resulta que estaba fuera de casa⟩ ⟨he happens to be right : da la casualidad de que tiene razón⟩
happening ['hæpənɪŋ] *n* : suceso *m*, acontecimiento *m*
happiness ['hæpinəs] *n* : felicidad *f*, dicha *f*

happy ['hæpi] *adj* **-pier; -est 1** JOYFUL : feliz, contento, alegre **2** FORTUNATE : afortunado, feliz — **happily** [-pəli] *adv*
happy–go–lucky ['hæpigoː'lʌki] *adj* : despreocupado
harangue¹ [hə'ræŋ] *vt* **-rangued; -ranguing** : arengar
harangue² *n* : arenga *f*
harass [hə'ræs, 'hærəs] *vt* **1** BESIEGE, HOUND : acosar, asediar, hostigar **2** ANNOY : molestar
harassment [hə'ræsmənt, 'hærəsmənt] *n* : acoso *m*, hostigamiento *m* ⟨sexual harrassment : acoso sexual⟩
harbinger ['harbɪndʒər] *n* **1** HERALD : heraldo *m*, precursor *m* **2** OMEN : presagio *m*
harbor¹ ['harbər] *vt* **1** SHELTER : dar refugio a, albergar **2** CHERISH, KEEP : abrigar, guardar, albergar ⟨to harbor doubts : guardar dudas⟩
harbor² *n* **1** REFUGE : refugio *m* **2** PORT : puerto *m*
hard¹ ['hard] *adv* **1** FORCEFULLY : fuerte, con fuerza ⟨the wind blew hard : el viento sopló fuerte⟩ **2** STRENUOUSLY : duro, mucho ⟨to work hard : trabajar duro⟩ **3 to take something hard** : tomarse algo muy mal, estar muy afectado por algo
hard² *adj* **1** FIRM, SOLID : duro, firme, sólido **2** DIFFICULT : difícil, arduo **3** SEVERE : severo, duro ⟨a hard winter : un invierno severo⟩ **4** UNFEELING : insensible, duro **5** DILIGENT : diligente ⟨to be a hard worker : ser muy trabajador⟩ **6 hard liquor** : bebidas *fpl* fuertes **7 hard water** : agua *f* dura
hardcover ['hard,kʌvər] *adj* : de pasta dura, de tapa dura
hard disk *n* : disco *m* duro
hard drive → **hard disk**
harden ['hardən] *vt* : endurecer
hardheaded [,hard'hɛdəd] *adj* **1** STUBBORN : testarudo, terco **2** REALISTIC : realista, práctico — **hardheadedly** *adv*
hard–hearted [,hard'hartəd] *adj* : despiadado, insensible — **hard–heartedly** *adv*
hard–heartedness [,hard'hartədnəs] *n* : dureza *f* de corazón
hardly ['hardli] *adv* **1** SCARCELY : apenas, casi ⟨I hardly knew her : apenas la conocía⟩ ⟨hardly ever : casi nunca⟩ **2** NOT : difícilmente, poco, no ⟨they can hardly blame me! : ¡difícilmente pueden echarme la culpa!⟩ ⟨it's hardly likely : es poco probable⟩
hardness ['hardnəs] *n* **1** FIRMNESS : dureza *f* **2** DIFFICULTY : dificultad *f* **3** SEVERITY : severidad *f*
hardship ['hard,ʃɪp] *n* : dificultad *f*, privación *f*
hardware ['hard,wær] *n* **1** TOOLS : ferretería *f* **2** : hardware *m* (de una computadora)
hardwood ['hard,wʊd] *n* : madera *f* dura, madera *f* noble

hardworking ['hɑrd'wərkɪŋ] *adj* : trabajador

hardy ['hɑrdi] *adj* **-dier; -est** : fuerte, robusto, resistente (dícese de las plantas) — **hardily** [-dəli] *adv*

hare ['hær] *n, pl* **hare** *or* **hares** : liebre *f*

harebrained ['hær₁breɪnd] *adj* : estúpido, absurdo, disparatado

harelip ['hær₁lɪp] *n* : labio *m* leporino

harem ['hærəm] *n* : harén *m*

hark ['hɑrk] *vi* **1** (*used only in the imperative*) LISTEN : escuchar **2 hark back** RETURN : volver **3 hark back** RECALL : recordar

harlequin ['hɑrlɪkən, -kwən] *n* : arlequín *m*

harm[1] ['hɑrm] *vt* : hacerle daño a, perjudicar

harm[2] *n* : daño *m*, perjuicio *m*

harmful ['hɑrmfəl] *adj* : dañino, perjudicial — **harmfully** *adv*

harmless ['hɑrmləs] *adj* : inofensivo, inocuo — **harmlessly** *adv*

harmlessness ['hɑrmləsnəs] *n* : inocuidad *f*

harmonic [hɑr'mɑnɪk] *adj* : armónico — **harmonically** [-nɪkli] *adv*

harmonica [hɑr'mɑnɪkə] *n* : armónica *f*

harmonious [hɑr'mo:niəs] *adj* : armonioso — **harmoniously** *adv*

harmonize ['hɑrmə₁naɪz] *v* **-nized; -nizing** : armonizar

harmony ['hɑrməni] *n, pl* **-nies** : armonía *f*

harness[1] ['hɑrnəs] *vt* **1** : enjaezar (un animal) **2** UTILIZE : utilizar, aprovechar

harness[2] *n* : arreos *mpl*, guarniciones *fpl*, arnés *m*

harp[1] ['hɑrp] *vi* **to harp on** : insistir sobre, machacar sobre

harp[2] *n* : arpa *m*

harpist ['hɑrpɪst] *n* : arpista *mf*

harpoon[1] [hɑr'pu:n] *vt* : arponear

harpoon[2] *n* : arpón *m*

harpsichord ['hɑrpsɪ₁kɔrd] *n* : clavicémbalo *m*

harrow[1] ['hær₁o:] *vt* **1** CULTIVATE : gradar, labrar (la tierra) **2** TORMENT : atormentar

harrow[2] *n* : grada *f*, rastra *f*

harry ['hæri] *vt* **-ried; -rying** HARASS : acosar, hostigar

harsh ['hɑrʃ] *adj* **1** ROUGH : áspero **2** SEVERE : duro, severo **3** : discordante (dícese de los sonidos) — **harshly** *adv*

harshness ['hɑrʃnəs] *n* **1** ROUGHNESS : aspereza *f* **2** SEVERITY : dureza *f*, severidad *f*

harvest[1] ['hɑrvəst] *v* : cosechar

harvest[2] *n* **1** HARVESTING : siega *f*, recolección *f* **2** CROP : cosecha *f*

harvester ['hɑrvəstər] *n* : segador *m*, -dora *f*; cosechadora *f* (máquina)

has → **have**

hash[1] ['hæʃ] *vt* **1** MINCE : picar **2 to hash over** DISCUSS : discutir, repasar

hash[2] *n* **1** : picadillo *m* (comida) **2** JUMBLE : revoltijo *m*, fárrago *m*

hasn't ['hæzənt] (*contraction* of **has not**) → **has**

hasp ['hæsp] *n* : picaporte *m*, pestillo *m*

hassle[1] ['hæsəl] *vt* **-sled; -sling** : fastidiar, molestar

hassle[2] *n* **1** ARGUMENT : discusión *f*, disputa *f*, bronca *f* **2** FIGHT : pelea *f*, riña *f* **3** BOTHER, TROUBLE : problemas *mpl*, lío *m*

hassock ['hæsək] *n* **1** CUSHION : almohadón *m*, cojín *m* **2** FOOTSTOOL : escabel *m*

haste ['heɪst] *n* **1** : prisa *f*, apuro *m* **2 to make haste** : darse prisa, apurarse

hasten ['heɪsən] *vt* : acelerar, precipitar — *vi* : apresurarse, apurarse

hasty ['heɪsti] *adj* **hastier; -est 1** HURRIED, QUICK : rápido, apresurado, apurado **2** RASH : precipitado — **hastily** [-təli] *adv*

hat ['hæt] *n* : sombrero *m*

hatch[1] ['hæʧ] *vt* **1** : incubar, empollar (huevos) **2** DEVISE : idear, tramar — *vi* : salir del cascarón

hatch[2] *n* : escotilla *f*

hatchery ['hæʧəri] *n, pl* **-ries** : criadero *m*

hatchet ['hæʧət] *n* : hacha *f*

hatchway ['hæʧ₁weɪ] *n* : escotilla *f*

hate[1] ['heɪt] *vt* **hated; hating** : odiar, aborrecer, detestar

hate[2] *n* : odio *m*

hateful ['heɪtfəl] *adj* : odioso, aborrecible, detestable — **hatefully** *adv*

hatred ['heɪtrəd] *n* : odio *m*

hatter ['hætər] *n* : sombrerero *m*, -ra *f*

haughtiness ['hɔtinəs] *n* : altanería *f*, altivez *f*

haughty ['hɔti] *adj* **-tier; -est** : altanero, altivo — **haughtily** [-təli] *adv*

haul[1] ['hɔl] *vt* **1** DRAG, PULL : arrastrar, jalar **2** TRANSPORT : transportar

haul[2] *n* **1** PULL : tirón *m*, jalón *m* **2** CATCH : redada *f* **3** JOURNEY : viaje *m*, trayecto *m* ⟨it's a long haul : es un trayecto largo⟩

haulage ['hɔlɪʤ] *n* : transporte *m*, tiro *m*

hauler ['hɔlər] *n* : transportista *mf*

haunch ['hɔnʧ] *n* **1** HIP : cadera *f* **2 haunches** *npl* HINDQUARTERS : ancas *fpl*, cuartos *mpl* traseros

haunt[1] ['hɔnt] *vt* **1** : aparecer en (dícese de un fantasma) **2** FREQUENT : frecuentar, rondar **3** PREOCCUPY : perseguir, obsesionar

haunt[2] *n* : guarida *f* (de animales o ladrones), lugar *m* predilecto

haunting ['hɔntɪŋ] *adj* : obsesionante, evocador — **hauntingly** *adv*

haute ['o:t] *adj* **1** : de moda, de categoría **2 haute couture** [₁o:tku'tur] : alta costura *f* **3 haute cuisine** [₁o:tkwɪ'zi:n] : alta cocina *f*

have ['hæv, *in sense 3 as an auxiliary verb usu* 'hæf] *v* **had** ['hæd]; **having; has** ['hæz, *in sense 3 as an auxiliary verb usu* 'hæs] *vt* **1** POSSESS : tener ⟨do you have

change? : ¿tienes cambio?⟩ **2** EXPERI-
ENCE, UNDERGO : tener, experimentar, sufrir ⟨I have a toothache : tengo
un dolor de muelas⟩ **3** INCLUDE : tener, incluir ⟨April has 30 days : abril
tiene 30 días⟩ **4** CONSUME : comer,
tomar **5** RECEIVE : tener, recibir ⟨he
had my permission : tenía mi permiso⟩
6 ALLOW : permitir, dejar ⟨I won't have
it! : ¡no lo permitiré!⟩ **7** HOLD : hacer
⟨to have a party : dar una fiesta⟩ ⟨to
have a meeting : convocar una re-
unión⟩ **8** HOLD : tener ⟨he had me in
his power : me tenía en su poder⟩ **9**
BEAR : tener (niños) **10** (*indicating
causation*) ⟨she had a dress made
: mandó hacer un vestido⟩ ⟨to have
one's hair cut : cortarse el pelo⟩ — *v
aux* **1** : haber ⟨she has been very busy
: ha estado muy ocupada⟩ ⟨I've lived
here three years : hace tres años que
vivo aquí⟩ **2** (*used in tags*) ⟨you've finished, haven't you? : ha terminado,
¿no?⟩ **3 to have to** : deber, tener que
⟨we have to leave : tenemos que salir⟩
haven ['heɪvən] *n* : refugio *m*
havoc ['hævək] *n* **1** DESTRUCTION : estragos *mpl*, destrucción *f* **2** CHAOS,
DISORDER : desorden *m*, caos *m*
Hawaiian[1] [hə'waɪən] *adj* : hawaiano
Hawaiian[2] *n* : hawaiano *m*, -na *f*
hawk[1] ['hɔk] *vt* : pregonar, vender (mercancías) en la calle
hawk[2] *n* : halcón *m*
hawker ['hɔkər] *n* : vendedor *m*, -dora *f*
ambulante
hawthorn ['hɔ,θɔrn] *n* : espino *m*
hay ['heɪ] *n* : heno *m*
hay fever *n* : fiebre *f* del heno
hayloft ['heɪ,lɔft] *n* : pajar *m*
hayseed ['heɪ,si:d] *n* : palurdo *m*, -da *f*
haystack ['heɪ,stæk] *n* : almiar *m*
haywire ['heɪ,waɪr] *adj* : descompuesto,
desbaratado ⟨to go haywire : estro-
pearse⟩
hazard[1] ['hæzərd] *vt* : arriesgar, aventurar
hazard[2] *n* **1** DANGER : peligro *m*, riesgo *m* **2** CHANCE : azar *m*
hazardous ['hæzərdəs] *adj* : arriesgado,
peligroso
haze[1] ['heɪz] *vt* **hazed; hazing** : abrumar, acosar
haze[2] *n* : bruma *f*, neblina *f*
hazel ['heɪzəl] *n* **1** : avellano *m* (árbol)
2 : color *m* avellana
hazelnut ['heɪzəl,nʌt] *n* : avellana *f*
haziness ['heɪzinəs] *n* **1** MISTINESS
: nebulosidad *f* **2** VAGUENESS
: vaguedad *f*
hazy ['heɪzi] *adj* **hazier; -est 1** MISTY
: brumoso, neblinoso, nebuloso **2**
VAGUE : vago, confuso
he ['hi:] *pron* : él
head[1] ['hɛd] *vt* **1** LEAD : encabezar **2**
DIRECT : dirigir — *vi* : dirigirse
head[2] *adj* MAIN : principal ⟨the head office : la oficina central, la sede⟩

head[3] *n* **1** : cabeza *f* ⟨from head to foot
: de pies a cabeza⟩ **2** MIND : mente *f*,
cabeza *f* **3** TIP, TOP : cabeza *f* (de un
clavo, un martillo, etc.), cabecera *f* (de
una mesa o un río), punta *f* (de una
flecha), flor *m* (de un repollo, etc.), encabezamiento *m* (de una carta, etc.),
espuma *f* (de cerveza) **4** DIRECTOR,
LEADER : director *m*, -tora *f*; jefe *m*, -fa
f; cabeza *f* (de una familia) **5** : cara *f*
(de una moneda) ⟨heads or tails : cara
o cruz⟩ **6** : cabeza *f* ⟨500 head of cattle : 500 cabezas de ganado⟩ ⟨$10 a
head : $10 por cabeza⟩ **7 to come to
a head** : llegar a un punto crítico
headache ['hɛd,eɪk] *n* : dolor *m* de
cabeza, jaqueca *f*
headband ['hɛd,bænd] *n* : cinta *f* del
pelo
headdress ['hɛd,drɛs] *n* : tocado *m*
headfirst ['hɛd'fərst] *adv* : de cabeza
headgear ['hɛd,gɪr] *n* : gorro *m*, casco
m, sombrero *m*
heading ['hɛdɪŋ] *n* **1** DIRECTION : dirección *f* **2** TITLE : encabezamiento *m*,
título *m* **3** : membrete *m* (de una carta)
headland ['hɛdlənd, -,lænd] *n* : cabo *m*
headlight ['hɛd,laɪt] *n* : faro *m*, foco *m*,
farol *m Mex*
headline ['hɛd,laɪn] *n* : titular *m*
headlong[1] ['hɛd'lɔŋ] *adv* **1** HEADFIRST
: de cabeza **2** HASTILY : precipitadamente
headlong[2] ['hɛd,lɔŋ] *adj* : precipitado
headmaster ['hɛd,mæstər] *n* : director
m
headmistress ['hɛd,mɪstrəs, -'mɪs-] *n*
: directora *f*
head-on ['hɛd'ɑn, -'ɔn] *adv & adj* : de
frente
headphones ['hɛd,fo:nz] *npl* : audífonos
mpl, cascos *mpl*
headquarters ['hɛd,kwɔrtərz] *ns & pl* **1**
SEAT : oficina *f* central, sede *f* **2** : cuartel *m* general (de los militares)
headrest ['hɛd,rɛst] *n* : apoyacabezas *m*
headship ['hɛd,ʃɪp] *n* : dirección *f*
head start *n* : ventaja *f*
headstone ['hɛd,sto:n] *n* : lápida *f*
headstrong ['hɛd'strɔŋ] *adj* : testarudo,
obstinado, empecinado
headwaiter ['hɛd'weɪtər] *n* : jefe *m*, -fa *f*
de comedor
headwaters ['hɛd,wɔtərz, -,wɑ-] *npl*
: cabecera *f*
headway ['hɛd,weɪ] *n* : progreso *m* ⟨to
make headway against : avanzar con-
tra⟩
heady ['hɛdi] *adj* **headier; -est 1** IN-
TOXICATING : embriagador, excitante
2 SHREWD : astuto, sagaz
heal ['hi:l] *vt* : curar, sanar — *vi* **1** : sanar, curarse **2 to heal up** : cicatrizarse
healer ['hi:lər] *n* **1** : curandero *m*, -dera
f **2** : curador *m*, -dora *f* (cosa)
health ['hɛlθ] *n* : salud *f*

healthful ['hɛlθfəl] *adj* : saludable, salubre — **healthfully** *adv*
healthy ['hɛlθi] *adj* **healthier; -est** : sano, bien — **healthily** [-θəli] *adv*
heap[1] ['hi:p] *vt* **1** PILE : amontonar, apilar **2** SHOWER : colmar
heap[2] *n* : montón *m*, pila *f*
hear ['hɪr] *v* **heard** ['hərd]; **hearing** *vt* **1** : oír ⟨do you hear me? : ¿me oyes?⟩ **2** HEED : oír, prestar atención a **3** LEARN : oír, enterarse de — *vi* **1** : oír ⟨to hear about : oír hablar de⟩ **2 to hear from** : tener noticias de
hearing ['hɪrɪŋ] *n* **1** : oído *m* ⟨hard of hearing : duro de oído⟩ **2** : vista *f* (en un tribunal) **3** ATTENTION : consideración *f*, oportunidad *f* de expresarse **4** EARSHOT : alcance *m* del oído
hearing aid *n* : audífono *m*
hearken ['hɑrkən] *vt* : escuchar
hearsay ['hɪr,seɪ] *n* : rumores *mpl*
hearse ['hərs] *n* : coche *m* fúnebre
heart ['hɑrt] *n* **1** : corazón *m* **2** CENTER, CORE : corazón *m*, centro *m* ⟨the heart of the matter : el meollo del asunto⟩ **3** FEELINGS : corazón *m*, sentimientos *mpl* ⟨a broken heart : un corazón destrozado⟩ ⟨to have a good heart : tener buen corazón⟩ ⟨to take something to heart : tomarse algo a pecho⟩ **4** COURAGE : valor *m*, corazón *m* ⟨to take heart : animarse, cobrar ánimos⟩ **5 hearts** *npl* : corazones *mpl* (en juegos de naipes) **6 by heart** : de memoria
heartache ['hɑrt,eɪk] *n* : pena *f*, angustia *f*
heart attack *n* : infarto *m*, ataque *m* al corazón
heartbeat ['hɑrt,bi:t] *n* : latido *m* (del corazón)
heartbreak ['hɑrt,breɪk] *n* : congoja *f*, angustia *f*
heartbreaking ['hɑrt,breɪkɪŋ] *adj* : desgarrador, que parte el corazón
heartbroken ['hɑrt,bro:kən] *adj* : desconsolado, destrozado
heartburn ['hɑrt,bərn] *n* : acidez *f* estomacal
hearten ['hɑrtən] *vt* : alentar, animar
heartfelt ['hɑrt,fɛlt] *adj* : sentido
hearth ['hɑrθ] *n* : hogar *m*, chimenea *f*
heartily ['hɑrtəli] *adv* **1** ENTHUSIASTICALLY : de buena gana, con entusiasmo **2** TOTALLY : totalmente, completamente
heartless ['hɑrtləs] *adj* : desalmado, despiadado, cruel
heartsick ['hɑrt,sɪk] *adj* : abatido, desconsolado
heartstrings ['hɑrt,strɪŋz] *npl* : fibras *fpl* del corazón
heartwarming ['hɑrt,wɔrmɪŋ] *adj* : conmovedor, emocionante
hearty ['hɑrti] *adj* **heartier; -est 1** CORDIAL, WARM : cordial, caluroso **2** STRONG : fuerte ⟨to have a hearty appetite : ser de buen comer⟩ **3** SUBSTANTIAL : abundante, sustancioso ⟨a

hearty breakfast : un desayuno abundante⟩
heat[1] ['hi:t] *vt* : calentar
heat[2] *n* **1** WARMTH : calor *m* **2** HEATING : calefacción *f* **3** EXCITEMENT : calor *m*, entusiasmo *m* ⟨in the heat of the moment : en el calor del momento⟩ **4** ESTRUS : celo *m*
heated ['hi:təd] *adj* **1** WARMED : calentado **2** IMPASSIONED : acalorado, apasionado
heater ['hi:tər] *n* : calentador *m*, estufa *f*, calefactor *m*
heath ['hi:θ] *n* **1** MOOR : brezal *m*, páramo *m* **2** HEATHER : brezo *m*
heathen[1] ['hi:ðən] *adj* : pagano
heathen[2] *n, pl* **-thens** *or* **-then** : pagano *m*, -na *f*; infiel *mf*
heather ['hɛðər] *n* : brezo *m*
heave[1] ['hi:v] *v* **heaved** *or* **hove** ['ho:v]; **heaving** *vt* **1** LIFT, RAISE : levantar con esfuerzo **2** HURL : lanzar, tirar **3 to heave a sigh** : echar un suspiro, suspirar — *vi* **1** : subir y bajar, palpitar (dícese del pecho) **2 to heave up** RISE : levantarse
heave[2] *n* **1** EFFORT : gran esfuerzo *m* (para levantar algo) **2** THROW : lanzamiento *m*
heaven ['hɛvən] *n* **1** : cielo *m* ⟨for heaven's sake : por Dios⟩ **2 heavens** *npl* SKY : cielo *m* ⟨the heavens opened up : empezó a llover a cántaros⟩
heavenly ['hɛvənli] *adj* **1** : celestial, celeste **2** DELIGHTFUL : divino, encantador
heavily ['hɛvəli] *adv* **1** : pesadamente, con mucho peso **2** LABORIOUSLY : trabajosamente, penosamente **3** : mucho
heaviness ['hɛvinəs] *n* : peso *m*, pesadez *f*
heavy ['hɛvi] *adj* **heavier; -est 1** WEIGHTY : pesado **2** DENSE, THICK : denso, espeso, grueso **3** BURDENSOME : oneroso, gravoso **4** PROFOUND : profundo **5** SLUGGISH : lento, tardo **6** STOUT : corpulento **7** SEVERE : severo, duro, fuerte
heavy-duty ['hɛvi'du:ti, -'dju:-] *adj* : muy resistente, fuerte
heavyweight ['hɛvi,weɪt] *n* : peso *m* pesado (en deportes)
Hebrew[1] ['hi:,bru:] *adj* : hebreo
Hebrew[2] *n* **1** : hebreo *m*, -brea *f* **2** : hebreo *m* (idioma)
heck ['hɛk] *n* : ¡caramba!, ¡caray! ⟨a heck of a lot : un montón⟩ ⟨what the heck is . . . ? : ¿que diablos es . . . ?⟩
heckle ['hɛkəl] *vt* **-led; -ling** : interrumpir (a un orador)
hectare ['hɛk,tær] *n* : hectárea *f*
hectic ['hɛktɪk] *adj* : agitado, ajetreado — **hectically** [-tɪkli] *adv*
he'd ['hi:d] (*contraction* of **he had** *or* **he would**) → **have, would**
hedge[1] ['hɛdʒ] *v* **hedged; hedging** *vt* **1** : cercar con un seto **2 to hedge one's bet** : cubrirse — *vi* **1** : dar rodeos, con-

testar con evasivas **2 to hedge against** : cubrirse contra, protegerse contra
hedge² *n* **1** : seto *m* vivo **2** SAFEGUARD : salvaguardia *f*, protección *f*
hedgehog ['hɛdʒ,hɔg, -hag] *n* : erizo *m*
heed¹ ['hi:d] *vt* : prestar atención a, hacer caso de
heed² *n* : atención *f*
heedless ['hi:dləs] *adj* : descuidado, despreocupado, inconsciente ⟨to be heedless of : hacer caso omiso de⟩ — **heedlessly** *adv*
heel¹ ['hi:l] *vi* : inclinarse
heel² *n* : talón *m* (del pie), tacón *m* (de calzado)
heft ['hɛft] *vt* : sopesar
hefty ['hɛfti] *adj* **heftier; -est** : robusto, fornido, pesado
hegemony [hɪˈdʒɛməni] *n, pl* **-nies** : hegemonía *f*
heifer ['hɛfər] *n* : novilla *f*
height ['haɪt] *n* **1** PEAK : cumbre *f*, cima *f*, punto *m* alto ⟨at the height of her career : en la cumbre de su carrera⟩ ⟨the height of stupidity : el colmo de la estupidez⟩ **2** TALLNESS : estatura *f* (de una persona), altura *f* (de un objeto) **3** ALTITUDE : altura *f*
heighten ['haɪtən] *vt* **1** : hacer más alto **2** INTENSIFY : aumentar, intensificar — *vi* : aumentarse, intensificarse
heinous ['heɪnəs] *adj* : atroz, abominable, nefando
heir ['ær] *n* : heredero *m*, -ra *f*
heiress ['ærəs] *n* : heredera *f*
heirloom ['ær,lu:m] *n* : reliquia *f* de familia
held → **hold**
helicopter ['hɛlə,kɑptər] *n* : helicóptero *m*
helium ['hi:liəm] *n* : helio *m*
helix ['hi:lɪks] *n, pl* **helices** ['hɛlə,si:z, 'hi:-] *or* **helixes** ['hi:lɪksəz] : hélice *f*
hell ['hɛl] *n* : infierno *m*
he'll ['hi:l, 'hɪl] (*contraction of* **he shall** *or* **he will**) → **shall, will**
hellish ['hɛlɪʃ] *adj* : horroroso, infernal
hello [hə'lo:, hɛ-] *interj* : ¡hola!
helm ['hɛlm] *n* **1** : timón *m* **2 to take the helm** : tomar el mando
helmet ['hɛlmət] *n* : casco *m*
help¹ ['hɛlp] *vt* **1** AID, ASSIST : ayudar, auxiliar, socorrer, asistir **2** ALLEVIATE : aliviar **3** SERVE : servir ⟨help yourself! : ¡sírvete!⟩ **4** AVOID : evitar ⟨it can't be helped : no lo podemos evitar, no hay más remedio⟩ ⟨I couldn't help smiling : no pude menos que sonreír⟩
help² *n* **1** ASSISTANCE : ayuda *f* ⟨help! : ¡socorro!, ¡auxilio!⟩ **2** STAFF : personal *m* (en una oficina), servicio *m* doméstico
helper ['hɛlpər] *n* : ayudante *mf*
helpful ['hɛlpfəl] *adj* **1** OBLIGING : servicial, amable, atento **2** USEFUL : útil, práctico — **helpfully** *adv*
helpfulness ['hɛlpfəlnəs] *n* **1** KINDNESS : bondad *f*, amabilidad *f* **2** USEFULNESS : utilidad *f*

helping ['hɛlpɪŋ] *n* : porción *f*
helpless ['hɛlpləs] *adj* **1** POWERLESS : incapaz, impotente **2** DEFENSELESS : indefenso
helplessly ['hɛlpləsli] *adv* : en vano, inútilmente
helplessness ['hɛlpləsnəs] *n* POWERLESSNESS : incapacidad *f*, impotencia *f*
helter-skelter [ˌhɛltərˈskɛltər] *adv* : atropelladamente, precipitadamente
hem¹ ['hɛm] *vt* **hemmed; hemming 1** : dobladillar **2 to hem in** : encerrar
hem² *n* : dobladillo *m*, bastilla *f*
hemisphere ['hɛmə,sfɪr] *n* : hemisferio *m*
hemispheric [ˌhɛməˈsfɪrɪk, -ˈsfɪr-] *or* **hemispherical** [-ɪkəl] *adj* : hemisférico
hemlock ['hɛm,lɑk] *n* : cicuta *f*
hemoglobin ['hi:mə,glo:bən] *n* : hemoglobina *f*
hemophilia [ˌhi:məˈfɪliə] *n* : hemofilia *f*
hemorrhage¹ ['hɛmərɪdʒ] *vi* **-rhaged; -rhaging** : sufrir una hemorragia
hemorrhage² *n* : hemorragia *f*
hemorrhoids ['hɛmə,rɔɪdz, 'hɛm-,rɔɪdz] *npl* : hemorroides *fpl*, almorranas *fpl*
hemp ['hɛmp] *n* : cáñamo *m*
hen ['hɛn] *n* : gallina *f*
hence ['hɛnts] *adv* **1** : de aquí, de ahí ⟨10 years hence : de aquí a 10 años⟩ ⟨a dog bit me, hence my dislike of animals : un perro me mordió, de ahí mi aversión a los animales⟩ **2** THEREFORE : por lo tanto, por consiguiente
henceforth ['hɛnts,forθ, ˌhɛnts'-] *adv* : de ahora en adelante
henchman ['hɛntʃmən] *n, pl* **-men** [-mən, -ˌmɛn] : secuaz *mf*, esbirro *m*
henpeck ['hɛn,pɛk] *vt* : dominar (al marido)
hepatitis [ˌhɛpə'taɪtəs] *n, pl* **-titides** [-'tɪtə,di:z] : hepatitis *f*
her¹ ['hər] *adj* : su, sus, de ella ⟨her house : su casa, la casa de ella⟩
her² ['hər, ər] *pron* **1** (*used as direct object*) : la ⟨I saw her yesterday : la vi ayer⟩ **2** (*used as indirect object*) : le, se ⟨he gave her the book : le dio el libro⟩ ⟨he sent it to her : se lo mandó⟩ **3** (*used as object of a preposition*) : ella ⟨we did it for her : lo hicimos por ella⟩ ⟨taller than her : más alto que ella⟩
herald¹ ['hɛrəld] *vt* ANNOUNCE : anunciar, proclamar
herald² *n* **1** MESSENGER : heraldo *m* **2** HARBINGER : precursor *m*
heraldic [hɛ'rældɪk, hə-] *adj* : heráldico
heraldry ['hɛrəldri] *n, pl* **-ries** : heráldica *f*
herb ['ərb, 'hərb] *n* : hierba *f*
herbal ['ərbəl, 'hər-] *adj* : herbario
herbicide ['ərbə,saɪd, 'hər-] *n* : herbicida *m*
herbivore ['ərbə,vor, 'hər-] *n* : herbívoro *m*
herbivorous [ˌər'bɪvərəs, ˌhər-] *adj* : herbívoro
herculean [ˌhərkjə'li:ən, ˌhər'kju:-liən] *adj* : hercúleo, sobrehumano

herd¹ ['hərd] *vt* : reunir en manada, conducir en manada — *vi* : ir en manada (dícese de los animales), apiñarse (dícese de la gente)

herd² *n* : manada *f*

herder ['hərdər] → **herdsman**

herdsman ['hərdzmən] *n, pl* **-men** [-mən, -ˌmɛn] : vaquero *m* (de ganado), pastor *m* (de ovejas)

here ['hɪr] *adv* 1 : aquí, acá ⟨come here! : ¡ven acá!⟩ ⟨right here : aquí mismo⟩ 2 NOW : en este momento, ahora, ya ⟨here he comes : ya viene⟩ ⟨here it's three o'clock (already) : ahora son las tres⟩ 3 : en este punto ⟨here we agree : estamos de acuerdo en este punto⟩ 4 **here you are!** : ¡toma!

hereabouts ['hɪrəˌbaʊts] *or* **hereabout** [-ˌbaʊt] *adv* : por aquí (cerca)

hereafter¹ [hɪr'æftər] *adv* 1 : de aquí en adelante, a continuación 2 : en el futuro

hereafter² *n* **the hereafter** : el más allá

hereby [hɪr'baɪ] *adv* : por este medio

hereditary [hə'rɛdəˌtɛri] *adj* : hereditario

heredity [hə'rɛdəti] *n* : herencia *f*

herein [hɪr'ɪn] *adv* : aquí

hereof [hɪr'ʌv] *adv* : de aquí

hereon [hɪr'an, -'ɔn] *adv* : sobre esto

heresy ['hɛrəsi] *n, pl* **-sies** : herejía *f*

heretic ['hɛrəˌtɪk] *n* : hereje *mf*

heretical [hə'rɛtɪkəl] *adj* : herético

hereto [hɪr'tuː] *adv* : a esto

heretofore ['hɪrtəˌfor] *adv* HITHERTO : hasta ahora

hereunder [hɪr'ʌndər] *adv* : a continuación, abajo

hereupon [hɪrə'pan, -'pɔn] *adv* : con esto, en ese momento

herewith [hɪr'wɪθ] *adv* : adjunto

heritage ['hɛrəṭɪdʒ] *n* : patrimonio *m* (nacional)

hermaphrodite [hər'mæfrəˌdaɪt] *n* : hermafrodita *mf*

hermetic [hər'mɛtɪk] *adj* : hermético — **hermetically** [-ṭɪkli] *adv*

hermit ['hərmət] *n* : ermitaño *m*, -ña *f*; eremita *mf*

hernia ['hərniə] *n, pl* **-nias** *or* **-niae** [-niˌiː, -niˌaɪ] : hernia *f*

hero ['hiːˌroː, 'hɪrˌoː] *n, pl* **-roes** 1 : héroe *m* 2 PROTAGONIST : protagonista *mf*

heroic [hɪ'roːɪk] *adj* : heroico — **heroically** [-ɪkli] *adv*

heroics [hɪ'roːɪks] *npl* : actos *mpl* heroicos

heroin ['hɛroən] *n* : heroína *f*

heroine ['hɛroən] *n* 1 : heroína *f* 2 PROTAGONIST : protagonista *f*

heroism ['hɛroˌɪzəm] *n* : heroísmo *m*

heron ['hɛrən] *n* : garza *f*

herpes ['hərˌpiːz] *n* : herpes *m*

herring ['hɛrɪŋ] *n, pl* **-ring** *or* **-rings** : arenque *m*

hers ['hərz] *pron* : suyo, -ya; suyos, -yas; de ella ⟨these shoes are hers : estos zapatos son suyos⟩ ⟨hers are bigger : los de ella son más grandes⟩

herself [hər'slf] *pron* 1 (*used reflexively*) : se ⟨she dressed herself : se vistió⟩ 2 (*used emphatically*) : ella misma ⟨she fixed it herself : lo arregló ella misma, lo arregló por sí sola⟩

hertz ['hərts, 'hɪrts] *ns & pl* : hercio *m*

he's ['hiːz] (*contraction of* **he is** *or* **he has**) → **be, have**

hesitancy ['hɛzətəntsi] *n, pl* **-cies** : vacilación *f*, titubeo *m*, indecisión *f*

hesitant ['hɛzətənt] *adj* : titubeante, vacilante — **hesitantly** *adv*

hesitate ['hɛzəˌteɪt] *vi* **-tated; -tating** : vacilar, titubear

hesitation [ˌhɛzə'teɪʃən] *n* : vacilación *f*, indecisión *f*, titubeo *m*

heterogeneous [ˌhɛtərə'dʒiːniəs, -njəs] *adj* : heterogéneo

heterosexual¹ [ˌhɛtəro'skʃuəl] *adj* : heterosexual

heterosexual² *n* : heterosexual *mf*

heterosexuality [ˌhɛtəroˌskʃu'æləti] *n* : heterosexualidad *f*

hew ['hjuː] *v* **hewed; hewed** *or* **hewn** ['hjuːn]; **hewing** *vt* 1 CUT : cortar, talar (árboles) 2 SHAPE : labrar, tallar — *vi* CONFORM : conformarse, ceñirse

hex¹ ['hɛks] *vt* : hacerle un maleficio (a alguien)

hex² *n* : maleficio *m*

hexagon ['hɛksəˌgan] *n* : hexágono *m*

hexagonal [hɛk'sægənəl] *adj* : hexagonal

hey ['heɪ] *interj* : ¡eh!, ¡oye!

heyday ['heɪˌdeɪ] *n* : auge *m*, apogeo *m*

hi ['haɪ] *interj* : ¡hola!

hiatus [haɪ'eɪtəs] *n* 1 : hiato *m* 2 PAUSE : pausa *f*

hibernate ['haɪbərˌneɪt] *vi* **-nated; -nating** : hibernar, invernar

hibernation [ˌhaɪbər'neɪʃən] *n* : hibernación *f*

hiccup¹ ['hɪkəp] *vi* **-cuped; -cuping** : hipar, tener hipo

hiccup² *n* : hipo *m* ⟨to have the hiccups : tener hipo⟩

hick ['hɪk] *n* BUMPKIN : palurdo *m*, -da *f*

hickory ['hɪkəri] *n, pl* **-ries** : nogal *m* americano

hidden ['hɪdən] *adj* : oculto

hide¹ ['haɪd] *v* **hid** ['hɪd]; **hidden** ['hɪdən] *or* **hid; hiding** *vt* 1 CONCEAL : esconder 2 : ocultar ⟨to hide one's motives : ocultar sus motivos⟩ 3 SCREEN : tapar, no dejar ver — *vi* : esconderse

hide² *n* : piel *f*, cuero *m* ⟨to save one's hide : salvar el pellejo⟩

hide–and–seek ['haɪdənd'siːk] *n* **to play hide–and–seek** : jugar a las escondidas

hidebound ['haɪdˌbaʊnd] *adj* : rígido, conservador

hideous ['hɪdiəs] *adj* : horrible, horroroso, espantoso — **hideously** *adv*

hideout ['haɪdˌaʊt] *n* : guarida *f*, escondrijo *m*

hierarchical [ˌhaɪə'rarkɪkəl] *adj* : jerárquico

hierarchy [ˈhaɪəˌrɑrki] *n, pl* **-chies** : jerarquía *f*

hieroglyphic [ˌhaɪərəˈglɪfɪk] *n* : jeroglífico *m*

hi–fi [ˈhaɪˈfaɪ] *n* **1** → **high fidelity 2** : equipo *m* de alta fidelidad

high¹ [ˈhaɪ] *adv* : alto

high² *adj* **1** TALL : alto ⟨a high wall : una pared alta⟩ **2** ELEVATED : alto, elevado ⟨high prices : precios elevados⟩ ⟨high blood pressure : presión alta⟩ **3** GREAT, IMPORTANT : grande, importante, alto ⟨a high number : un número grande⟩ ⟨high society : alta sociedad⟩ ⟨high hopes : grandes esperanzas⟩ **4** : alto (en música) **5** INTOXICATED : borracho, drogado

high³ *n* **1** : récord *m*, punto *m* máximo ⟨to reach an all-time high : batir el récord⟩ **2** : zona *f* de alta presión (en meteorología) **3** *or* **high gear** : directa *f* **4 on high** : en las alturas

highbrow [ˈhaɪˌbraʊ] *n* : intelectual *mf*

higher [ˈhaɪər] *adj* : superior

high fidelity *n* : alta fidelidad *f*

high–flown [ˈhaɪˈfloːn] *adj* : altisonante

high–handed [ˈhaɪˈhændəd] *adj* : arbitrario

highlands [ˈhaɪləndz] *npl* : tierras *fpl* altas, altiplano *m*

highlight¹ [ˈhaɪˌlaɪt] *vt* **1** EMPHASIZE : destacar, poner en relieve, subrayar **2** : ser el punto culminante de

highlight² *n* : punto *m* culminante

highly [ˈhaɪli] *adv* **1** VERY : muy, sumamente **2** FAVORABLY : muy bien ⟨to speak highly of : hablar muy bien de⟩ ⟨to think highly of : tener en mucho a⟩

highness [ˈhaɪnəs] *n* **1** HEIGHT : altura *f* **2 Highness** : Alteza *f* ⟨Your Royal Highness : Su Alteza Real⟩

high–pitched [ˈhaɪˈpɪtʃt] *adj* : agudo

high–rise [ˈhaɪˌraɪz] *adj* : alto, de muchas plantas

high school *n* : escuela *f* superior, escuela *f* secundaria

high seas *npl* : alta mar *f*

high–spirited [ˈhaɪˈspɪrətəd] *adj* : vivaz, muy animado, brioso

high–strung [ˌhaɪˈstrʌŋ] *adj* : nervioso, excitable

highway [ˈhaɪˌweɪ] *n* : carretera *f*

highwayman [ˈhaɪˌweɪmən] *n, pl* **-men** [-mən, -ˌmɛn] : salteador *m* (de caminos), bandido *m*

hijack¹ [ˈhaɪˌdʒæk] *vt* : secuestrar

hijack² *n* : secuestro *m*

hijacker [ˈhaɪˌdʒækər] *n* : secuestrador *m*, -dora *f*

hike¹ [ˈhaɪk] *v* **hiked; hiking** *vi* : hacer una caminata — *vt* RAISE : subir

hike² *n* **1** : caminata *f*, excursión *f* **2** INCREASE : subida *f* (de precios)

hiker [ˈhaɪkər] *n* : excursionista *mf*

hilarious [hɪˈlæriəs, haɪ-] *adj* : muy divertido, hilarante

hilarity [hɪˈlærəti, haɪ-] *n* : hilaridad *f*

hill [ˈhɪl] *n* **1** : colina *f*, cerro *m* **2** SLOPE : cuesta *f*, pendiente *f*

hillbilly [ˈhɪlˌbɪli] *n, pl* **-lies** : palurdo *m*, -da *f* (de las montañas)

hillock [ˈhɪlək] *n* : loma *f*, altozano *m*, otero *m*

hillside [ˈhɪlˌsaɪd] *n* : ladera *f*, cuesta *f*

hilltop [ˈhɪlˌtɑp] *n* : cima *f*, cumbre *f*

hilly [ˈhɪli] *adj* **hillier; -est** : montañoso, accidentado

hilt [ˈhɪlt] *n* : puño *m*, empuñadura *f*

him [ˈhɪm, əm] *pron* **1** (*used as direct object*) : lo ⟨I found him : lo encontré⟩ **2** (*used as indirect object*) : le, se ⟨we gave him a present : le dimos un regalo⟩ ⟨I sent it to him : se lo mandé⟩ **3** (*used as object of a preposition*) : él ⟨she was thinking of him : pensaba en él⟩ ⟨younger than him : más joven que él⟩

himself [hɪmˈsɛlf] *pron* **1** (*used reflexively*) : se ⟨he washed himself : se lavó⟩ **2** (*used emphatically*) : él mismo ⟨he did it himself : lo hizo él mismo, lo hizo por sí solo⟩

hind¹ [ˈhaɪnd] *adj* : trasero, posterior ⟨hind legs : patas traseras⟩

hind² *n* : cierva *f*

hinder [ˈhɪndər] *vt* : dificultar, impedir, estorbar

Hindi [ˈhɪndiː] *n* : hindi *m*

hindquarters [ˈhaɪndˌkwɔrtərz] *npl* : cuartos *mpl* traseros

hindrance [ˈhɪndrənts] *n* : estorbo *m*, obstáculo *m*, impedimento *m*

hindsight [ˈhaɪndˌsaɪt] *n* : retrospectiva *f* ⟨with the benefit of hindsight : en retrospectiva, con la perspectiva que da la experiencia⟩

Hindu¹ [ˈhɪnˌduː] *adj* : hindú

Hindu² *n* : hindú *mf*

Hinduism [ˈhɪnduːˌɪzəm] *n* : hinduismo *m*

hinge¹ [ˈhɪndʒ] *v* **hinged; hinging** *vt* : unir con bisagras — *vi* **to hinge on** : depender de

hinge² *n* : bisagra *f*, gozne *m*

hint¹ [ˈhɪnt] *vt* : insinuar, dar a entender — *vi* : soltar indirectas

hint² *n* **1** INSINUATION : insinuación *f*, indirecta *f* **2** TIP : consejo *m*, sugerencia *f* **3** TRACE : pizca *f*, indicio *m*

hinterland [ˈhɪntərˌlænd, -lənd] *n* : interior *m* (de un país)

hip [ˈhɪp] *n* : cadera *f*

hip–hop [ˈhɪpˌhɑp] *n* : hip-hop *m*

hippie [ˈhɪpi] *n* : hippie *mf*, hippy *mf*

hippopotamus [ˌhɪpəˈpɑtəməs] *n, pl* **-muses** *or* **-mi** [-ˌmaɪ] : hipopótamo *m*

hippo [ˈhɪpoː] *n, pl* **hippos** → **hippopotamus**

hire¹ [ˈhaɪr] *vt* **hired; hiring 1** EMPLOY : contratar, emplear **2** RENT : alquilar, arrendar

hire² *n* **1** RENT : alquiler *m* ⟨for hire : se alquila⟩ **2** WAGES : paga *f*, sueldo *m* **3** EMPLOYEE : empleado *m*, -da *f*

his¹ [ˈhɪz, ɪz] *adj* : su, sus, de él ⟨his hat : su sombrero, el sombrero de él⟩

his² *pron* : suyo, -ya; suyos, suyas; de él ⟨the decision is his : la decisión es suya⟩ ⟨it's his, not hers : es de él, no de ella⟩

Hispanic¹ [hɪ'spænɪk] *adj* : hispano, hispánico

Hispanic² *n* : hispano *m*, -na *f*; hispánico *m*, -ca *f*

hiss¹ ['hɪs] *vi* : sisear, silbar — *vt* : decir entre dientes

hiss² *n* : siseo *m*, silbido *m*

historian [hɪ'stɔriən] *n* : historiador *m*, -dora *f*

historic [hɪ'stɔrɪk] *or* **historical** [-ɪkəl] *adj* : histórico — **historically** [-ɪkli] *adv*

history ['hɪstəri] *n, pl* **-ries** 1 : historia *f* 2 RECORD : historial *m*

histrionics [ˌhɪstri'anɪks] *ns & pl* : histrionismo *m*

hit¹ ['hɪt] *v* **hit; hitting** *vt* 1 STRIKE : golpear, pegar, batear (una pelota) ⟨he hit the dog : le pegó al perro⟩ 2 : chocar contra, dar con, dar en (el blanco) ⟨the car hit a tree : el coche chocó contra un árbol⟩ 3 AFFECT : afectar ⟨the news hit us hard : la noticia nos afectó mucho⟩ 4 ENCOUNTER : tropezar con, toparse con ⟨to hit a snag : tropezar con un obstáculo⟩ 5 REACH : llegar a, alcanzar ⟨the price hit $10 a pound : el precio alcanzó los $10 dólares por libra⟩ ⟨to hit town : llegar a la ciudad⟩ ⟨to hit the headlines : ser noticia⟩ **6 to hit on** *or* **to hit upon** : dar con — *vi* : golpear

hit² *n* 1 BLOW : golpe *m* 2 : impacto *m* (de un arma) 3 SUCCESS : éxito *m*

hitch¹ ['hɪtʃ] *vt* 1 : mover con sacudidas 2 ATTACH : enganchar, atar, amarrar 3 → **hitchhike** 4 **to hitch up** : subirse (los pantalones, etc.)

hitch² *n* 1 JERK : tirón *m*, jalón *m* 2 OBSTACLE : obstáculo *m*, impedimento *m*, tropiezo *m*

hitchhike ['hɪtʃˌhaɪk] *vi* **-hiked; -hiking** : hacer autostop, ir de aventón *Col, Mex fam*

hitchhiker ['hɪtʃˌhaɪkər] *n* : autostopista *mf*

hither ['hɪðər] *adv* : acá, por aquí

hitherto ['hɪðərˌtu:, ˌhɪðər'-] *adv* : hasta ahora

hitter ['hɪtər] *n* BATTER : bateador *m*, -dora *f*

HIV [ˌeɪtʃˌaɪ'vi:] *n* (*h*uman *i*mmunodeficiency *v*irus) : VIH *m*, virus *m* del sida

hive ['haɪv] *n* 1 : colmena *f* 2 SWARM : enjambre *m* 3 : lugar *m* muy activo ⟨a hive of activity : un hervidero de actividad⟩

hives ['haɪvz] *ns & pl* : urticaria *f*

hoard¹ ['hɔrd] *vt* : acumular, atesorar

hoard² *n* : tesoro *m*, reserva *f*, provisión *f*

hoarfrost ['hɔrˌfrɔst] *n* : escarcha *f*

hoarse ['hɔrs] *adj* **hoarser; -est** : ronco — **hoarsely** *adv*

hoarseness ['hɔrsnəs] *n* : ronquera *f*

hoary ['hɔri] *adj* **hoarier; -est** 1 : cano, canoso 2 OLD : vetusto, antiguo

hoax¹ ['ho:ks] *vt* : engañar, embaucar, bromear

hoax² *n* : engaño *m*, broma *f*

hobble¹ ['habəl] *v* **-bled; -bling** *vi* LIMP : cojear, renguear — *vt* : manear (un animal)

hobble² *n* 1 LIMP : cojera *f*, rengo *m* 2 : maniota *f* (para un animal)

hobby ['habi] *n, pl* **-bies** : pasatiempo *m*, afición *f*

hobgoblin ['habˌgablən] *n* : duende *m*

hobnail ['habˌneɪl] *n* : tachuela *f*

hobnob ['habˌnab] *vi* **-nobbed; -nobbing** : codearse

hobo ['ho:ˌbo:] *n, pl* **-boes** : vagabundo *m*, -da *f*

hock¹ ['hak] *vt* PAWN : empeñar

hock² *n* **in hock** : empeñado

hockey ['haki] *n* : hockey *m*

hodgepodge ['hadʒˌpadʒ] *n* : mezcolanza *f*

hoe¹ ['ho:] *vt* **hoed; hoeing** : azadonar

hoe² *n* : azada *f*, azadón *m*

hog¹ ['hɔg, 'hag] *vt* **hogged; hogging** : acaparar, monopolizar

hog² *n* 1 PIG : cerdo *m*, -da *f* 2 GLUTTON : glotón *m*, -tona *f*

hogshead ['hɔgzˌhed, 'hagz-] *n* : tonel *m*

hoist¹ ['hɔɪst] *vt* : levantar, alzar, izar (una bandera, una vela)

hoist² *n* : grúa *f*

hold¹ ['ho:ld] *v* **held** ['held]; **holding** *vt* 1 POSSESS : tener ⟨to hold office : ocupar un puesto⟩ 2 RESTRAIN : detener, controlar ⟨to hold one's temper : controlar su mal genio⟩ 3 CLASP, GRASP : agarrar, coger ⟨to hold hands : agarrarse de la mano⟩ 4 : sujetar, mantener fijo ⟨hold this nail for me : sujétame este clavo⟩ 5 CONTAIN : contener, dar cabida a 6 SUPPORT : aguantar, sostener 7 REGARD : considerar, tener ⟨he held me responsible : me consideró responsable⟩ 8 CONDUCT : celebrar (una reunión), realizar (un evento), mantener (una conversación) — *vi* 1 : aguantar, resistir ⟨the rope will hold : la cuerda resistirá⟩ 2 : ser válido, valer ⟨my offer still holds : mi oferta todavía es válida⟩ **3 to hold forth** : perorar, arengar **4 to hold to** : mantenerse firme en **5 to hold with** : estar de acuerdo con

hold² *n* 1 GRIP : agarre *m*, llave *f* (en deportes) 2 CONTROL : control *m*, dominio *m* ⟨to get hold of oneself : controlarse⟩ 3 DELAY : demora *f* ⟨to put on hold : suspender temporalmente⟩ 4 : bodega *f* (en un barco o un avión) 5 **to get hold of** : conseguir, localizar

holder ['ho:ldər] *n* : poseedor *m*, -dora *f*; titular *mf*

holdings ['ho:ldɪŋz] *npl* : propiedades *fpl*

hold out *vi* 1 LAST : aguantar, durar 2 RESIST : resistir

holdup ['ho:ldˌʌp] *n* 1 ROBBERY : atraco *m* 2 DELAY : retraso *m*, demora *f*

hold up *vt* 1 ROB : robarle (a alguien), atracar, asaltar 2 DELAY : retrasar

hole ['ho:l] *n* : agujero *m*, hoyo *m*

holiday ['hɑlə,deɪ] n 1 : día m feriado, fiesta f 2 VACATION : vacaciones fpl
holiness ['ho:linəs] n 1 : santidad f 2 His Holiness : Su Santidad
holistic [ho:'lɪstɪk] adj : holístico
holler¹ ['hɑlər] vi : gritar, chillar
holler² n : grito m, chillido m
hollow¹ ['hɑ,lo:] vt or to hollow out : ahuecar
hollow² adj -lower; -est 1 : hueco, hundido (dícese de las mejillas, etc.), cavernoso (dícese de un sonido) 2 EMPTY, FALSE : vacío, falso
hollow³ n 1 CAVITY : hueco m, depresión f, cavidad f 2 VALLEY : hondonada f, valle m
hollowness ['hɑ,lo:nəs] n 1 HOLLOW : hueco m, cavidad f 2 FALSENESS : falsedad f 3 EMPTINESS : vacuidad f
holly ['hɑli] n, pl -lies : acebo m
hollyhock ['hɑli,hɑk] n : malvarrosa f
holocaust ['hɑlə,kɔst, 'ho:-, 'hɔ-] n : holocausto m
hologram ['ho:lə,græm, 'hɑ-] n : holograma m
holster ['ho:lstər] n : pistolera f
holy ['ho:li] adj -lier; -est : santo, sagrado
Holy Ghost → Holy Spirit
Holy Spirit n the Holy Spirit : el Espíritu Santo
homage ['ɑmɪʤ, 'hɑ-] n : homenaje m
home ['ho:m] n 1 : casa f, hogar m, domicilio m ⟨to feel at home : sentirse en casa⟩ 2 INSTITUTION : residencia f, asilo m
homecoming ['ho:m,kʌmɪŋ] n : regreso m (a casa)
homegrown ['ho:m'gro:n] adj 1 : de cosecha propia 2 LOCAL : local
homeland ['ho:m,lænd] n : patria f, tierra f natal, terruño m
homeless ['ho:mləs] adj : sin hogar, sin techo
homely ['ho:mli] adj -lier; -est 1 DOMESTIC : casero, hogareño 2 UGLY : feo, poco atractivo
homemade ['ho:m'meɪd] adj : casero, hecho en casa
homemaker ['ho:m,meɪkər] n : ama f de casa, persona f que se ocupa de la casa
home plate n : base f del bateador
home run n : jonrón m
homesick ['ho:m,sɪk] adj : nostálgico ⟨to be homesick : echar de menos a la familia⟩
homesickness ['ho:m,sɪknəs] n : nostalgia f, morriña f
homespun ['ho:m,spʌn] adj : simple, sencillo
homestead ['ho:m,stɛd] n : estancia f, hacienda f
homeward¹ ['ho:mwərd] or homewards [-wərdz] adv : de vuelta a casa, hacia casa
homeward² adj : de vuelta, de regreso
homework ['ho:m,wərk] n : tarea f, deberes mpl Spain, asignación f PRi

homey ['ho:mi] adj homier; -est : hogareño
homicidal [,hɑmə'saɪdəl, ,ho:-] adj : homicida
homicide ['hɑmə,saɪd, 'ho:-] n : homicidio m
hominy ['hɑməni] n : maíz m descascarillado
homogeneity [,ho:məʤə'ni:əti, -'neɪ-] n, pl -ties : homogeneidad f
homogeneous [,ho:mə'ʤi:niəs, -njəs] adj : homogéneo — homogeneously adv
homogenize [ho:'mɑʤə,naɪz, hə-] vt -nized; -nizing : homogeneizar
homograph ['hɑmə,græf, 'ho:-] n : homógrafo m
homologous [ho:'mɑləgəs, hə-] adj : homólogo
homonym ['hɑmə,nɪm, 'ho:-] n : homónimo m
homophone ['hɑmə,fo:n, 'ho:-] n : homófono m
homosexual¹ [,ho:mə'sɛkʃuəl] adj : homosexual
homosexual² n : homosexual mf
homosexuality [,ho:mə,sɛkʃu'æləti] n : homosexualidad f
honcho ['hɑn,tʃo:] n : pez m gordo ⟨the head honcho : el jefe⟩
Honduran [hɑn'dʊrən, -'djʊr-] n : hondureño m, -ña f — Honduran adj
hone ['ho:n] vt honed; honing : afilar
honest ['ɑnəst] adj : honesto, honrado — honestly adv
honesty ['ɑnəsti] n, pl -ties : honestidad f, honradez f
honey ['hʌni] n, pl -eys : miel f
honeybee ['hʌni,bi:] n : abeja f
honeycomb ['hʌni,ko:m] n : panal m
honeymoon¹ ['hʌni,mu:n] vi : pasar la luna de miel
honeymoon² n : luna f de miel
honeysuckle ['hʌni,sʌkəl] n : madreselva f
honk¹ ['hɑŋk, 'hɔŋk] vi 1 : graznar (dícese del ganso) 2 : tocar la bocina (dícese de un vehículo), pitar
honk² n : graznido m (del ganso), bocinazo m (de un vehículo)
honor¹ ['ɑnər] vt 1 RESPECT : honrar 2 : cumplir con ⟨to honor one's word : cumplir con su palabra⟩ 3 : aceptar (un cheque, etc.)
honor² n 1 : honor m ⟨in honor of : en honor de⟩ 2 honors npl AWARDS : honores mpl, condecoraciones fpl 3 Your Honor : Su Señoría
honorable ['ɑnərəbəl] adj : honorable, honroso — honorably [-bli] adv
honorary ['ɑnə,rɛri] adj : honorario
hood ['hʊd] n 1 : capucha f 2 : capó m, bonete m Car (de un automóvil)
hooded ['hʊdəd] adj : encapuchado
hoodlum ['hʊdləm, 'hu:d-] n THUG : maleante mf, matón m
hoodwink ['hʊd,wɪŋk] vt : engañar

hoof ['huf, 'hu:f] *n, pl* **hooves** ['huvz, 'hu:vz] *or* **hoofs** : pezuña *f*, casco *m*
hoofed ['huft, 'hu:ft] *adj* : ungulado
hook¹ ['huk] *vt* : enganchar — *vi* : abrocharse, engancharse
hook² *n* : gancho *m*, percha *f*
hooked ['hukt] *adj* **1** : en forma de gancho **2 to be hooked on** : estar enganchado a
hooker ['hukər] *n* : prostituta *f*, fulana *f fam*
hookworm ['huk,wərm] *n* : anquilostoma *m*
hooligan ['hu:lɪgən] *n* : gamberro *m*, -rra *f*
hoop ['hu:p] *n* : aro *m*
hooray [hu'reɪ] → **hurrah**
hoot¹ ['hu:t] *vi* **1** SHOUT : gritar ⟨to hoot with laughter : morirse de risa, reírse a carcajadas⟩ **2** : ulular (dícese de un búho), tocar la bocina (dícese de un vehículo), silbar (dícese de un tren o un barco)
hoot² *n* **1** : ululato *m* (de un búho), silbido *m* (de un tren), bocinazo *m* (de un vehículo) **2** GUFFAW : carcajada *f*, risotada *f* **3 I don't give a hoot** : me vale un comino, me importa un pito
hop¹ ['hap] *vi* **hopped; hopping** : brincar, saltar
hop² *n* **1** LEAP : salto *m*, brinco *m* **2** FLIGHT : vuelo *m* corto **3** : lúpulo *m* (planta)
hope¹ ['ho:p] *v* **hoped; hoping** *vi* : esperar — *vt* : esperar que ⟨we hope she comes : esperamos que venga⟩ ⟨I hope not : espero que no⟩
hope² *n* : esperanza *f*
hopeful ['ho:pfəl] *adj* : esperanzado — **hopefully** *adv*
hopeless ['ho:pləs] *adj* **1** DESPAIRING : desesperado **2** IMPOSSIBLE : imposible ⟨a hopeless case : un caso perdido⟩
hopelessly ['ho:pləsli] *adv* **1** : sin esperanzas, desesperadamente **2** COMPLETELY : totalmente, completamente **3** IMPOSSIBLY : imposiblemente
hopelessness ['ho:pləsnəs] *n* : desesperanza *f*
hopper ['hapər] *n* : tolva *f*
hopscotch ['hap,skatʃ] *n* : tejo *m*
horde ['hord] *n* : horda *f*, multitud *f*
horizon [hə'raɪzən] *n* : horizonte *m*
horizontal [,hɔrə'zantəl] *adj* : horizontal — **horizontally** *adv*
hormone ['hɔr,mo:n] *n* : hormona *f* — **hormonal** [hɔr'mo:nəl] *adj*
horn ['hɔrn] *n* **1** : cuerno *m* (de un toro, una vaca, etc.) **2** : cuerno *m*, trompa *f* (instrumento musical) **3** : bocina *f*, claxon *m* (de un vehículo)
horned ['hɔrnd, 'hɔrnəd] *adj* : cornudo, astado, con cuernos
hornet ['hɔrnət] *n* : avispón *m*
horny ['hɔrni] *adj* **hornier; -est 1** CALLOUS : calloso **2** LUSTFUL *fam* : caliente *fam*
horoscope ['hɔrə,sko:p] *n* : horóscopo *m*

horrendous [hɔ'rɛndəs] *adj* : horrendo, horroroso, atroz
horrible ['hɔrəbəl] *adj* : horrible, espantoso, horroroso — **horribly** [-bli] *adv*
horrid ['hɔrɪd] *adj* : horroroso, horrible — **horridly** *adv*
horrific [hə'rɪfɪk] *adj* : terrorífico, horroroso
horrify ['hɔrə,faɪ] *vt* **-fied; -fying** : horrorizar
horrifying ['hɔrə,faɪɪŋ] *adj* : horripilante, horroroso
horror ['hɔrər] *n* : horror *m*
hors d'oeuvre [ɔr'dərv] *n, pl* **hors d'oeuvres** [-'dərvz] : entremés *m*
horse ['hɔrs] *n* : caballo *m*
horseback ['hɔrs,bæk] *n* **on ~** : a caballo
horse chestnut *n* : castaña *f* de Indias
horsefly ['hɔrs,flaɪ] *n, pl* **-flies** : tábano *m*
horsehair ['hɔrs,hær] *n* : crin *f*
horseman ['hɔrsmən] *n, pl* **-men** [-mən, -,men] : jinete *m*, caballista *m*
horsemanship ['hɔrsmən,ʃɪp] *n* : equitación *f*
horseplay ['hɔrs,pleɪ] *n* : payasadas *fpl*
horsepower ['hɔrs,pauər] *n* : caballo *m* de fuerza
horseradish ['hɔrs,rædɪʃ] *n* : rábano *m* picante
horseshoe ['hɔrs,ʃu:] *n* : herradura *f*
horsewhip ['hɔrs,hwɪp] *vt* **-whipped; -whipping** : azotar, darle fuetazos (a alguien)
horsewoman ['hɔrs,wumən] *n, pl* **-women** [-,wɪmən] : amazona *f*, jinete *f*, caballista *f*
horsey *or* **horsy** ['hɔrsi] *adj* **horsier; -est** : relacionado a los caballos, caballar
horticultural [,hɔrtə'kʌltʃərəl] *adj* : hortícola
horticulture ['hɔrtə,kʌltʃər] *n* : horticultura *f*
hose¹ ['ho:z] *vt* **hosed; hosing** : regar o lavar con manguera
hose² *n* **1** *pl* **hose** SOCKS : calcetines *mpl*, medias *fpl* **2** *pl* **hose** STOCKINGS : medias *fpl* **3** *pl* **hoses** : manguera *f*, manga *f*
hosiery ['ho:ʒəri, 'ho:zə-] *n* : calcetería *f*, medias *fpl*
hospice ['haspəs] *n* : hospicio *m*
hospitable [ha'spɪtəbəl, 'has,pɪ-] *adj* : hospitalario — **hospitably** [-bli] *adv*
hospital ['has,pɪtəl] *n* : hospital *m*
hospitality [,haspə'tæləti] *n, pl* **-ties** : hospitalidad *f*
hospitalization [,has,pɪtələ'zeɪʃən] *n* : hospitalización *f*
hospitalize ['has,pɪtəl,aɪz] *vt* **-ized; -izing** : hospitalizar
host¹ ['ho:st] *vt* : presentar (un programa de televisión, etc.)
host² *n* **1** : anfitrión *m*, -triona *f* (en la casa, a un evento); presentador *m*, -dora *f* (de un programa de televisión, etc.) **2** *or* **host organism** : huésped *m*

3 TROOPS : huestes *fpl* 4 MULTITUDE : multitud *f* ⟨for a host of reasons : por muchas razones⟩ 5 EUCHARIST : hostia *f*, Eucaristía *f*

hostage ['hɑstɪdʒ] *n* : rehén *m*

hostel ['hɑstəl] *n* : albergue *m* juvenil

hostess ['ho:stɪs] *n* : anfitriona *f* (en la casa), presentadora *f* (de un programa)

hostile ['hɑstəl, -,taɪl] *adj* : hostil — **hostilely** *adv*

hostility [hɑs'tɪləti] *n, pl* -**ties** : hostilidad *f*

hot ['hɑt] *adj* **hotter; hottest** 1 : caliente, cálido, caluroso ⟨hot water : agua caliente⟩ ⟨a hot climate : un clima cálido⟩ ⟨a hot day : un día caluroso⟩ 2 ARDENT, FIERY : ardiente, acalorado ⟨to have a hot temper : tener mal genio⟩ 3 SPICY : picante 4 FRESH : reciente, nuevo ⟨hot news : noticias de última hora⟩ 5 EAGER : ávido 6 STOLEN : robado

hot air *n* : palabrería *f*

hotbed ['hɑt,bɛd] *n* 1 : semillero *m* (de plantas) 2 : hervidero *m*, semillero *m* (de crimen, etc.)

hot dog *n* : perro *m* caliente

hotel [ho:'tɛl] *n* : hotel *m*

hothead ['hɑt,hɛd] *n* : exaltado *m*, -da *f*

hotheaded ['hɑt'hɛdəd] *adj* : exaltado

hothouse ['hɑt,haʊs] *n* : invernadero *m*

hot plate *n* : placa *f* (de cocina)

hot rod *n* : coche *m* con motor modificado

hot water *n* **to get into hot water** : meterse en un lío

hound[1] ['haʊnd] *vt* : acosar, perseguir

hound[2] *n* : perro *m* (de caza)

hour ['aʊər] *n* : hora *f*

hourglass ['aʊər,glæs] *n* : reloj *m* de arena

hourly ['aʊərli] *adv & adj* : cada hora, por hora

house[1] ['haʊz] *vt* **housed; housing** : albergar, alojar, hospedar

house[2] ['haʊs] *n, pl* **houses** ['haʊzəz, -səz] 1 HOME : casa *f* 2 : cámara *f* (del gobierno) 3 BUSINESS : casa *f*, empresa *f*

houseboat ['haʊs,bo:t] *n* : casa *f* flotante

housebroken ['haʊs,bro:kən] *adj* : enseñado

housefly ['haʊs,flaɪ] *n, pl* -**flies** : mosca *f* común

household[1] ['haʊs,ho:ld] *adj* 1 DOMESTIC : doméstico, de la casa 2 FAMILIAR : conocido por todos

household[2] *n* : casa *f*, familia *f*

householder ['haʊs,ho:ldər] *n* : dueño *m*, -ña *f* de casa

housekeeper ['haʊs,ki:pər] *n* : ama *f* de llaves

housekeeping ['haʊs,ki:pɪŋ] *n* : gobierno *m* de la casa, quehaceres *mpl* domésticos

housemaid ['haʊs,meɪd] *n* : criada *f*, mucama *f*, muchacha *f*, sirvienta *f*

housewarming ['haʊs,wɔrmɪŋ] *n* : fiesta *f* de estreno de una casa

housewife ['haʊs,waɪf] *n, pl* -**wives** : ama *f* de casa

housework ['haʊs,wərk] *n* : faenas *fpl* domésticas, quehaceres *mpl* domésticos

housing ['haʊzɪŋ] *n* 1 HOUSES : vivienda *f* 2 COVERING : caja *f* protectora

hove → **heave**

hovel ['hʌvəl, 'hɑ-] *n* : casucha *f*, tugurio *m*

hover ['hʌvər, 'hɑ-] *vi* 1 : cernerse, sostenerse en el aire 2 **to hover about** : rondar

how ['haʊ] *adv* 1 : cómo ⟨how are you? : ¿cómo estás?⟩ ⟨I don't know how to fix it : no se cómo arreglarlo⟩ 2 : qué ⟨how beautiful! : ¡qué bonito!⟩ 3 : cuánto ⟨how old are you? : ¿cuántos años tienes?⟩ 4 **how about . . . ?** : ¿qué te parece . . . ?

however[1] [haʊ'ɛvər] *adv* 1 : por mucho que, por más que ⟨however hot it is : por mucho calor que haga⟩ 2 NEVERTHELESS : sin embargo, no obstante

however[2] *conj* : comoquiera que, de cualquier manera que

howl[1] ['haʊl] *vi* : aullar

howl[2] *n* : aullido *m*, alarido *m*

hub ['hʌb] *n* 1 CENTER : centro *m* 2 : cubo *m* (de una rueda)

hubbub ['hʌ,bʌb] *n* : algarabía *f*, alboroto *m*, jaleo *m*

hubcap ['hʌb,kæp] *n* : tapacubos *m*

huckster ['hʌkstər] *n* : buhonero *m*, -ra *f*; vendedor *m*, -dora *f* ambulante

huddle[1] ['hʌdəl] *vi* -**dled; -dling** 1 : apiñarse, amontonarse 2 **to huddle together** : acurrucarse

huddle[2] *n* : grupo *m* (cerrado) ⟨to go into a huddle : conferenciar en secreto⟩

hue ['hju:] *n* : color *m*, tono *m*

huff ['hʌf] *n* : enojo *m*, enfado *m* ⟨to be in a huff : estar enojado⟩

huffy ['hʌfi] *adj* **huffier; -est** : enojado, enfadado

hug[1] ['hʌg] *vt* **hugged; hugging** 1 EMBRACE : abrazar 2 : ir pegado a ⟨the road hugs the river : el camino está pegado al río⟩

hug[2] *n* : abrazo *m*

huge ['hju:dʒ] *adj* **huger; hugest** : inmenso, enorme — **hugely** *adv*

hulk ['hʌlk] *n* 1 : persona *f* fornida 2 : casco *m* (barco), armatoste *m* (edificio, etc.)

hulking ['hʌlkɪŋ] *adj* : grandote *fam*, pesado

hull[1] ['hʌl] *vt* : pelar

hull[2] *n* 1 HUSK : cáscara *f* 2 : casco *m* (de un barco, un avión, etc.)

hullabaloo ['hʌləbə,lu:] *n, pl* -**loos** : alboroto *m*, jaleo *m*

hum[1] ['hʌm] *v* **hummed; humming** *vi* 1 BUZZ : zumbar 2 : estar muy activo, moverse ⟨to hum with activity : bullir de actividad⟩ — *vt* : tararear (una melodía)

hum² *n* : zumbido *m*, murmullo *m*

human¹ ['hju:mən, 'ju:-] *adj* : humano — **humanly** *adv*

human² *n* : ser *m* humano

humane [hju:'meɪn, ju:-] *adj* : humano, humanitario — **humanely** *adv*

humanism ['hju:mə,nɪzəm, 'ju:-] *n* : humanismo *m*

humanist¹ ['hju:mənɪst, 'ju:-] *n* : humanista *mf*

humanist² *or* **humanistic** [,hju:mə-'nɪstɪk, ,ju:-] *adj* : humanístico

humanitarian¹ [hju:,mænə'triən, ju:-] *adj* : humanitario

humanitarian² *n* : humanitario *m*, -ria *f*

humanity [hju:'mænəti, ju:-] *n, pl* **-ties** : humanidad *f*

humankind ['hju:mən'kaɪnd, 'ju:-] *n* : género *m* humano

humble¹ ['hʌmbəl] *vt* **-bled; -bling 1** : humillar **2 to humble oneself** : humillarse

humble² *adj* **-bler; -blest** : humilde, modesto — **humbly** ['hʌmbli] *adv*

humbug ['hʌm,bʌɡ] *n* **1** FRAUD : charlatán *m*, -tana *f*; farsante *mf* **2** NONSENSE : patrañas *fpl*, tonterías *fpl*

humdrum ['hʌm,drʌm] *adj* : monótono, rutinario

humid ['hju:məd, 'ju:-] *adj* : húmedo

humidifier [hju:'mɪdə,faɪər, ju:-] *n* : humidificador *m*

humidify [hju:'mɪdə,faɪ, ju:-] *vt* **-fied; -fying** : humidificar

humidity [hju:'mɪdəti, ju:-] *n, pl* **-ties** : humedad *f*

humiliate [hju:'mɪli,eɪt, ju:-] *vt* **-ated; -ating** : humillar

humiliating [hju:'mɪli,eɪtɪŋ, ju:-] *adj* : humillante

humiliation [hju:,mɪli'eɪʃən, ju:-] *n* : humillación *f*

humility [hju:'mɪləti, ju:-] *n* : humildad *f*

hummingbird ['hʌmɪŋ,bərd] *n* : colibrí *m*, picaflor *m*

hummock ['hʌmək] *n* : montículo *m*

humor¹ ['hju:mər, 'ju:-] *vt* : seguir el humor a, complacer

humor² *n* : humor *m*

humorist ['hju:mərɪst, 'ju:-] *n* : humorista *mf*

humorless ['hju:mərləs, 'ju:-] *adj* : sin sentido del humor ⟨a humorless smile : una sonrisa forzada⟩

humorous ['hju:mərəs, 'ju:-] *adj* : humorístico, cómico — **humorously** *adv*

hump ['hʌmp] *n* : joroba *f*, giba *f*

humpback ['hʌmp,bæk] *n* **1** HUMP : joroba *f*, giba *f* **2** HUNCHBACK : jorobado *m*, -da *f*; giboso *m*, -sa *f*

humpbacked ['hʌmp,bækt] *adj* : jorobado, giboso

humus ['hju:məs, 'ju:-] *n* : humus *m*

hunch¹ ['hʌntʃ] *vt* : encorvar — *vi or* **to hunch up** : encorvarse

hunch² *n* PREMONITION : presentimiento *m*

hunchback ['hʌntʃ,bæk] *n* **1** HUMP : joroba *f*, giba *f* **2** HUMPBACK : jorobado *m*, -da *f*; giboso *m*, -sa *f*

hunchbacked ['hʌntʃ,bækt] *adj* : jorobado, giboso

hundred¹ ['hʌndrəd] *adj* : cien, ciento

hundred² *n, pl* **-dreds** *or* **-dred** : ciento *m*

hundredth¹ ['hʌndrədθ] *adj* : centésimo

hundredth² *n* **1** : centésimo *m*, -ma *f* (en una serie) **2** : centésimo *m*, centésima parte *f*

hung → **hang**

Hungarian [hʌŋ'gæriən] *n* **1** : húngaro *m*, -ra *f* **2** : húngaro *m* (idioma) — **Hungarian** *adj*

hunger¹ ['hʌŋgər] *vi* **1** : tener hambre **2 to hunger for** : ansiar, anhelar

hunger² *n* : hambre *m*

hungrily ['hʌŋgrəli] *adv* : ávidamente

hungry ['hʌŋgri] *adj* **-grier; -est 1** : hambriento **2 to be hungry** : tener hambre

hunk ['hʌŋk] *n* : trozo *m*, pedazo *m*

hunt¹ ['hʌnt] *vt* **1** PURSUE : cazar **2 to hunt for** : buscar

hunt² *n* **1** PURSUIT : caza *f*, cacería *f* **2** SEARCH : búsqueda *f*, busca *f*

hunter ['hʌntər] *n* : cazador *m*, -dora *f*

hunting ['hʌntɪŋ] *n* : caza *f* ⟨to go hunting : ir de caza⟩

hurdle¹ ['hərdəl] *vt* **-dled; -dling** : saltar, salvar (un obstáculo)

hurdle² *n* : valla *f* (en deportes), obstáculo *m*

hurl ['hərl] *vt* : arrojar, tirar, lanzar

hurrah [hu'rɑ, -'rɔ] *interj* : ¡hurra!

hurricane ['hərə,keɪn] *n* : huracán *m*

hurried ['hərid] *adj* : apresurado, precipitado

hurriedly ['hərədli] *adv* : apresuradamente, de prisa

hurry¹ ['həri] *v* **-ried; -rying** *vi* : apurarse, darse prisa, apresurarse — *vt* : apurar, darle prisa (a alguien)

hurry² *n* : prisa *f*, apuro *f*

hurt¹ ['hərt] *v* **hurt; hurting** *vt* **1** INJURE : hacer daño a, herir, lastimar ⟨to hurt oneself : hacerse daño⟩ **2** DISTRESS, OFFEND : hacer sufrir, ofender, herir — *vi* : doler ⟨my foot hurts : me duele el pie⟩

hurt² *n* **1** INJURY : herida *f* **2** DISTRESS, PAIN : dolor *m*, pena *f*

hurtful ['hərtfəl] *adj* : hiriente, doloroso

hurtle ['hərtəl] *vi* **-tled; -tling** : lanzarse, precipitarse

husband¹ ['hʌzbənd] *vt* : economizar, bien administrar

husband² *n* : esposo *m*, marido *m*

husbandry ['hʌzbəndri] *n* **1** MANAGEMENT, THRIFT : economía *f*, buena administración *f* **2** AGRICULTURE : agricultura *f* ⟨animal husbandry : cría de animales⟩

hush¹ ['hʌʃ] *vt* **1** SILENCE : hacer callar, acallar **2** CALM : calmar, apaciguar

hush² *n* : silencio *m*

hush–hush ['hʌʃ,hʌʃ, ,hʌʃ'hʌʃ] *adj*
: muy secreto, confidencial
husk[1] ['hʌsk] *vt* : descascarar
husk[2] *n* : cáscara *f*
huskily ['hʌskəli] *adv* : con voz ronca
husky[1] ['hʌski] *adj* **-kier; -est 1** HOARSE
: ronco **2** BURLY : fornido
husky[2] *n, pl* **-kies** : perro *m*, -rra *f* esquimal
hustle[1] ['həsəl] *v* **-tled; -tling** *vt* : darle prisa (a alguien), apurar ⟨they hustled me in : me hicieron entrar a empujones⟩ — *vi* : apurarse, ajetrearse
hustle[2] *n* BUSTLE : ajetreo *m*
hut ['hʌt] *n* : cabaña *f*, choza *f*, barraca *f*
hutch ['hʌtʃ] *n* **1** CUPBOARD : alacena *f* **2** rabbit hutch : conejera *f*
hyacinth ['haɪə,sɪnθ] *n* : jacinto *m*
hybrid[1] ['haɪbrɪd] *adj* : híbrido
hybrid[2] *n* : híbrido *m*
hydrant ['haɪdrənt] *n* : boca *f* de riego, hidrante *m CA, Col* ⟨fire hydrant : boca de incendios⟩
hydraulic [haɪ'drɔlɪk] *adj* : hidráulico — **hydraulically** *adv*
hydrocarbon [,haɪdro'kɑrbən] *n* : hidrocarburo *m*
hydrochloric acid [,haɪdro'klorɪk] : ácido *m* clorhídrico
hydroelectric [,haɪdroɪ'lɛktrɪk] *adj* : hidroeléctrico
hydrogen ['haɪdrədʒən] *n* : hidrógeno *m*
hydrogen bomb *n* : bomba *f* de hidrógeno
hydrogen peroxide *n* : agua *f* oxigenada, peróxido *m* de hidrógeno
hydrophobia [,haɪdrə'fo:biə] *n* : hidrofobia *f*, rabia *f*
hydroplane ['haɪdrə,pleɪn] *n* : hidroplano *m*
hyena [haɪ'i:nə] *n* : hiena *f*
hygiene ['haɪ,dʒi:n] *n* : higiene *f*
hygienic [haɪ'dʒɛnɪk, -'dʒi:-; ,haɪ-dʒi'nɪk] *adj* : higiénico — **hygienically** [-nɪkli] *adv*
hygienist [haɪ'dʒi:nɪst, -'dʒɛ-; 'haɪ-,dʒi:-] *n* : higienista *mf*
hygrometer [haɪ'grɑmətər] *n* : higrómetro *m*
hymn ['hɪm] *n* : himno *m*

hymnal ['hɪmnəl] *n* : himnario *m*
hype ['haɪp] *n* : bombo *m* publicitario
hyperactive [,haɪpər'æktɪv] *adj* : hiperactivo
hyperactivity [,haɪpər,æk'tɪvəti] *n, pl* **-ties** : hiperactividad *f*
hyperbole [haɪ'pərbəli] *n* : hipérbole *f*
hyperbolic [,haɪpər'bɑlɪk] *adj* : hiperbólico
hypercritical [,haɪpər'krɪtəkəl] *adj* : hipercrítico
hypersensitivity [,haɪpər,sɛntsə'tɪ-vəti] *n* : hipersensibilidad *f*
hypertension ['haɪpər,tɛntʃən] *n* : hipertensión *f*
hyphen ['haɪfən] *n* : guión *m*
hyphenate ['haɪfən,eɪt] *vt* **-ated; -ating** : escribir con guión
hypnosis [hɪp'no:sɪs] *n, pl* **-noses** [-,si:z] : hipnosis *f*
hypnotic [hɪp'nɑtɪk] *adj* : hipnótico, hipnotizador
hypnotism ['hɪpnə,tɪzəm] *n* : hipnotismo *m*
hypnotize ['hɪpnə,taɪz] *vt* **-tized; -tizing** : hipnotizar
hypochondria [,haɪpə'kɑndriə] *n* : hipocondría *f*
hypochondriac [,haɪpə'kɑndri,æk] *n* : hipocondríaco *m*, -ca *f*
hypocrisy [hɪp'ɑkrəsi] *n, pl* **-sies** : hipocresía *f*
hypocrite ['hɪpə,krɪt] *n* : hipócrita *mf*
hypocritical [,hɪpə'krɪtɪkəl] *adj* : hipócrita
hypodermic[1] [,haɪpə'dərmɪk] *adj* : hipodérmico
hypodermic[2] *n* : aguja *f* hipodérmica
hypotenuse [haɪ'pɑtən,u:s, -,u:z, -,ju:s, -,ju:z] *n* : hipotenusa *f*
hypothesis [haɪ'pɑθəsɪs] *n, pl* **-eses** [-,si:z] : hipótesis *f*
hypothetical [,haɪpə'θɛtɪkəl] *adj* : hipotético — **hypothetically** [-tɪkli] *adv*
hysteria [hɪs'tɛriə, -tɪr-] *n* : histeria *f*, histerismo *m*
hysterical [hɪs'tɛrɪkəl] *adj* : histérico — **hysterically** [-ɪkli] *adv*
hysterics [hɪs'tɛrɪks] *n* : histeria *f*, histerismo *m*

I

i ['aɪ] *n, pl* **i's** *or* **is** ['aɪz] : novena letra del alfabeto inglés
I ['aɪ] *pron* : yo
Iberian [aɪ'bɪriən] *adj* : ibérico
ibis ['aɪbəs] *n, pl* **ibis** *or* **ibises** : ibis *f*
ice[1] ['aɪs] *v* **iced; icing** *vt* **1** FREEZE : congelar, helar **2** CHILL : enfriar **3** to ice a cake : escarchar un pastel — *vi* : helarse, congelarse
ice[2] *n* **1** : hielo *m* **2** SHERBET : sorbete *m*, nieve *f Cuba, Mex, PRi*

iceberg ['aɪs,bərg] *n* : iceberg *m*
icebox ['aɪs,bɑks] → **refrigerator**
icebreaker ['aɪs,breɪkər] *n* : rompehielos *m*
ice cap *n* : casquete *m* glaciar
ice-cold ['aɪs'ko:ld] *adj* : helado
ice cream *n* : helado *m*, mantecado *m PRi*
Icelander ['aɪs,lændər, -lən-] *n* : islandés *m*, -desa *f*
Icelandic[1] [aɪs'lændɪk] *adj* : islandés

Icelandic² *n* : islandés *m* (idioma)
ice–skate ['aɪsˌskeɪt] *vi* **-skated; -skating** : patinar
ice skater *n* : patinador *m*, -dora *f*
ichthyology [ˌɪkthiˈɑləʤi] *n* : ictiología *f*
icicle ['aɪˌsɪkəl] *n* : carámbano *m*
icily ['aɪsəli] *adv* : fríamente, con frialdad ⟨he stared at me icily : me fijó la mirada con mucha frialdad⟩
icing ['aɪsɪŋ] *n* : glaseado *m*, betún *m Mex*
icon ['aɪˌkɑn, -kən] *n* : icono *m*
iconoclasm [aɪˈkɑnəˌklæzəm] *n* : iconoclasia *f*
iconoclast [aɪˈkɑnəˌklæst] *n* : iconoclasta *mf*
icy ['aɪsi] *adj* **icier; -est 1** : cubierto de hielo ⟨an icy road : una carretera cubierta de hielo⟩ **2** FREEZING : helado, gélido, glacial **3** ALOOF : frío, distante
id ['ɪd] *n* : id *m*
I'd ['aɪd] (*contraction of* **I should** *or* **I would**) → **should, would**
idea [aɪˈdiːə] *n* : idea *f*
ideal¹ [aɪˈdiːəl] *adj* : ideal
ideal² *n* : ideal *m*
idealism [aɪˈdiːəˌlɪzəm] *n* : idealismo *m*
idealist [aɪˈdiːəlɪst] *n* : idealista *mf*
idealistic [aɪˌdiːəˈlɪstɪk] *adj* : idealista
idealistically [aɪˌdiːəˈlɪstɪkli] *adv* : con idealismo
idealization [aɪˌdiːələˈzeɪʃən] *n* : idealización *f*
idealize [aɪˈdiːəˌlaɪz] *vt* **-ized; -izing** : idealizar
ideally [aɪˈdiːəli] *adv* : perfectamente
identical [aɪˈdɛntɪkəl] *adj* : idéntico — **identically** [-tɪkli] *adv*
identifiable [aɪˌdɛntəˈfaɪəbəl] *adj* : identificable
identification [aɪˌdɛntəfəˈkeɪʃən] *n* **1** : identificación *f* **2 identification card** : carnet *m*, cédula *f* de identidad, identificación *f*
identify [aɪˈdɛntəˌfaɪ] *v* **-fied; -fying** *vt* : identificar — *vi* **to identify with** : identificarse con
identity [aɪˈdɛntəti] *n, pl* **-ties** : identidad *f*
ideological [ˌaɪdiəˈlɑʤɪkəl, ˌɪ-] *adj* : ideológico — **ideologically** [-ʤɪkli] *adv*
ideology [ˌaɪdiˈɑləʤi, ˌɪ-] *n, pl* **-gies** : ideología *f*
idiocy ['ɪdiəsi] *n, pl* **-cies 1** : idiotez *f* **2** NONSENSE : estupidez *f*, tontería *f*
idiom ['ɪdiəm] *n* **1** LANGUAGE : lenguaje *m* **2** EXPRESSION : modismo *m*, expresión *f* idiomática
idiomatic [ˌɪdiəˈmætɪk] *adj* : idiomático
idiosyncrasy [ˌɪdioˈsɪŋkrəsi] *n, pl* **-sies** : idiosincrasia *f*
idiosyncratic [ˌɪdiosɪnˈkrætɪk] *adj* : idiosincrásico — **idiosyncratically** [-tɪkli] *adv*
idiot ['ɪdiət] *n* **1** : idiota *mf* (en medicina) **2** FOOL : idiota *mf*; tonto *m*, -ta *f*; imbécil *mf fam*

idiotic [ˌɪdiˈɑtɪk] *adj* : estúpido, idiota
idiotically [ˌɪdiˈɑtɪkli] *adv* : estúpidamente
idle¹ ['aɪdəl] *v* **idled; idling** *vi* **1** LOAF : holgazanear, flojear, haraganear **2** : andar al ralentí (dícese de un automóvil), marchar en vacío (dícese de una máquina) — *vt* : dejar sin trabajo
idle² *adj* **idler; idlest 1** VAIN : frívolo, vano, infundado ⟨idle curiosity : pura curiosidad⟩ **2** INACTIVE : inactivo, parado, desocupado **3** LAZY : holgazán, haragán, perezoso
idleness ['aɪdəlnəs] *n* **1** INACTIVITY : inactividad *f*, ociosidad *f* **2** LAZINESS : holgazanería *f*, flojera *f*, pereza *f*
idler ['aɪdələr] *n* : haragán *m*, -gana *f*; holgazán *m*, -zana *f*
idly ['aɪdəli] *adv* : ociosamente
idol ['aɪdəl] *n* : ídolo *m*
idolater *or* **idolator** [aɪˈdɑlətər] *n* : idólatra *mf*
idolatrous [aɪˈdɑlətrəs] *adj* : idólatra
idolatry [aɪˈdɑlətri] *n, pl* **-tries** : idolatría *f*
idolize ['aɪdəˌlaɪz] *vt* **-ized; -izing** : idolatrar
idyll ['aɪdəl] *n* : idilio *m*
idyllic [aɪˈdɪlɪk] *adj* : idílico
if ['ɪf] *conj* **1** : si ⟨I would do it if I could : lo haría si pudiera⟩ ⟨if so : si es así⟩ ⟨as if : como si⟩ ⟨if I were you : yo que tú⟩ **2** WHETHER : si ⟨I don't know if they're ready : no sé si están listos⟩ **3** THOUGH : aunque, si bien ⟨it's pretty, if somewhat old-fashioned : es lindo aunque algo anticuado⟩
igloo ['ɪˌgluː] *n, pl* **-loos** : iglú *m*
ignite [ɪgˈnaɪt] *v* **-nited; -niting** *vt* : prenderle fuego a, encender — *vi* : prender, encenderse
ignition [ɪgˈnɪʃən] *n* **1** IGNITING : ignición *f*, encendido *m* **2** *or* **ignition switch** : encendido *m*, arranque *m* ⟨to turn on the ignition : arrancar el motor⟩
ignoble [ɪgˈnoːbəl] *adj* : innoble — **ignobly** *adv*
ignominious [ˌɪgnəˈmɪniəs] *adj* : ignominioso, deshonroso — **ignominiously** *adv*
ignominy ['ɪgnəˌmɪni] *n, pl* **-nies** : ignominia *f*
ignoramus [ˌɪgnəˈreɪməs] *n* : ignorante *mf*; bestia *mf*; bruto *m*, -ta *f*
ignorance ['ɪgnərənts] *n* : ignorancia *f*
ignorant ['ɪgnərənt] *adj* **1** : ignorante **2 to be ignorant of** : no ser consciente de, desconocer, ignorar
ignorantly ['ɪgnərəntli] *adv* : ignorantemente, con ignorancia
ignore [ɪgˈnor] *vt* **-nored; -noring** : ignorar, hacer caso omiso de, no hacer caso de
iguana [ɪˈgwɑnə] *n* : iguana *f*, garrobo *f CA*
ilk ['ɪlk] *n* : tipo *m*, clase *f*, índole *f*
ill¹ ['ɪl] *adv* **worse** ['wərs]; **worst** ['wərst] : mal ⟨to speak ill of : hablar mal de⟩

⟨he can ill afford to fail : mal puede permitirse el lujo de fracasar⟩

ill² *adj* **worse; worst 1** SICK : enfermo **2** BAD : malo ⟨ill luck : mala suerte⟩

ill³ *n* **1** EVIL : mal *m* **2** MISFORTUNE : mal *m*, desgracia *f* **3** AILMENT : enfermedad *f*

I'll [ˈaɪl] (*contraction of* **I shall** *or* **I will**) → **shall, will**

illegal [ɪlˈliːɡəl] *adj* : ilegal — **illegally** *adv*

illegality [ˌɪliˈɡæləti] *n* : ilegalidad *f*

illegibility [ɪlˌlɛdʒəˈbɪləti] *n, pl* **-ties** : ilegibilidad *f*

illegible [ɪlˈlɛdʒəbəl] *adj* : ilegible — **illegibly** [-bli] *adv*

illegitimacy [ˌɪlɪˈdʒɪtəməsi] *n* : ilegitimidad *f*

illegitimate [ˌɪlɪˈdʒɪtəmət] *adj* **1** BASTARD : ilegítimo, bastardo **2** UNLAWFUL : ilegítimo, ilegal — **illegitimately** *adv*

ill–fated [ˈɪlˈfeɪtəd] *adj* : malhadado, infortunado, desventurado

illicit [ɪlˈlɪsət] *adj* : ilícito — **illicitly** *adv*

illiteracy [ɪlˈlɪtərəsi] *n, pl* **-cies** : analfabetismo *m*

illiterate¹ [ɪlˈlɪtərət] *adj* : analfabeto

illiterate² *n* : analfabeto *m*, -ta *f*

ill–mannered [ˌɪlˈmanərd] *adj* : descortés, maleducado

ill–natured [ˌɪlˈneɪtʃərd] *adj* : desagradable, de mal genio

ill–naturedly [ˌɪlˈneɪtʃərdli] *adv* : desagradablemente

illness [ˈɪlnəs] *n* : enfermedad *f*

illogical [ɪlˈlɑdʒɪkəl] *adj* : ilógico — **illogically** [-kli] *adv*

ill–tempered [ˌɪlˈtempərd] → **ill–natured**

ill–treat [ˌɪlˈtriːt] *vt* : maltratar

ill–treatment [ˌɪlˈtriːtmənt] *n* : maltrato *m*

illuminate [ɪˈluːməˌneɪt] *vt* **-nated; -nating 1** : iluminar, alumbrar **2** ELUCIDATE : esclarecer, elucidar

illumination [ɪˌluːməˈneɪʃən] *n* **1** LIGHTING : iluminación *f*, luz *f* **2** ELUCIDATION : esclarecimiento *m*, elucidación *f*

ill–use [ˈɪlˈjuːz] → **ill–treat**

illusion [ɪˈluːʒən] *n* : ilusión *f*

illusory [ɪˈluːsəri, -zəri] *adj* : engañoso, ilusorio

illustrate [ˈɪləsˌtreɪt] *v* **-trated; -trating** : ilustrar

illustration [ˌɪləsˈtreɪʃən] *n* **1** PICTURE : ilustración *f* **2** EXAMPLE : ejemplo *m*, ilustración *f*

illustrative [ɪˈlʌstrətɪv, ˈɪləˌstreɪtɪv] *adj* : ilustrativo — **illustratively** *adv*

illustrator [ˈɪləˌstreɪtər] *n* : ilustrador *m*, -dora *f*; dibujante *mf*

illustrious [ɪˈlʌstriəs] *adj* : ilustre, eminente, glorioso

illustriousness [ɪˈlʌstriəsnəs] *n* : eminencia *f*, prestigio *m*

ill will *n* : animosidad *f*, malquerencia *f*, mala voluntad *f*

I'm [ˈaɪm] (*contraction of* **I am**) → **be**

image¹ [ˈɪmɪdʒ] *vt* **-aged; -aging** : imaginar, crear una imagen de

image² *n* : imagen *f*

imagery [ˈɪmɪdʒri] *n, pl* **-eries 1** IMAGES : imágenes *fpl* **2** : imaginería *f* (en el arte)

imaginable [ɪˈmædʒənəbəl] *adj* : imaginable — **imaginably** [-bli] *adv*

imaginary [ɪˈmædʒəˌneri] *adj* : imaginario

imagination [ɪˌmædʒəˈneɪʃən] *n* : imaginación *f*

imaginative [ɪˈmædʒənətɪv, -əˌneɪtɪv] *adj* : imaginativo — **imaginatively** *adv*

imagine [ɪˈmædʒən] *vt* **-ined; -ining** : imaginar(se)

imbalance [ɪmˈbælənts] *n* : desajuste *m*, desbalance *m*, desequilibrio *m*

imbecile¹ [ˈɪmbəsəl, -ˌsɪl] *or* **imbecilic** [ˌɪmbəˈsɪlɪk] *adj* : imbécil, estúpido

imbecile² *n* **1** : imbécil *mf* (en medicina) **2** FOOL : idiota *mf*; imbécil *mf fam*; estúpido *m*, -da *f*

imbecility [ˌɪmbəˈsɪləti] *n, pl* **-ties** : imbecilidad *f*

imbibe [ɪmˈbaɪb] *v* **-bibed; -bibing** *vt* **1** DRINK : beber **2** ABSORB : absorber, embeber — *vi* : beber

imbue [ɪmˈbjuː] *vt* **-bued; -buing** : imbuir

imitate [ˈɪməˌteɪt] *vt* **-tated; -tating** : imitar, remedar

imitation¹ [ˌɪməˈteɪʃən] *adj* : de imitación, artificial

imitation² *n* : imitación *f*

imitative [ˈɪməˌteɪtɪv] *adj* : imitativo, imitador, poco original

imitator [ˈɪməˌteɪtər] *n* : imitador *m*, -dora *f*

immaculate [ɪˈmækjələt] *adj* **1** PURE : inmaculado, puro **2** FLAWLESS : impecable, intachable — **immaculately** *adv*

immaterial [ˌɪməˈtɪriəl] *adj* **1** INCORPOREAL : incorpóreo **2** UNIMPORTANT : irrelevante, sin importancia

immature [ˌɪməˈtʃʊr, -ˈtjʊr, -ˈtʊr] *adj* : inmaduro, verde (dícese de la fruta)

immaturity [ˌɪməˈtʃʊrəti, -ˈtjʊr-, -ˈtʊr-] *n, pl* **-ties** : inmadurez *f*, falta *f* de madurez

immeasurable [ɪˈmɛʒərəbəl] *adj* : inconmensurable, incalculable — **immeasurably** [-bli] *adv*

immediacy [ɪˈmiːdiəsi] *n* : inmediatez *f*

immediate [ɪˈmiːdiət] *adj* **1** INSTANT : inmediato, instantáneo ⟨immediate relief : alivio instantáneo⟩ **2** DIRECT : inmediato, directo ⟨the immediate cause of death : la causa directa de la muerte⟩ **3** URGENT : urgente, apremiante **4** CLOSE : cercano, próximo, inmediato ⟨her immediate family : sus familiares más cercanos⟩ ⟨in the immediate vicinity : en los alrededores, en las inmediaciones⟩

immediately [ɪˈmiːdiətli] *adv* : inmediatamente, enseguida

immemorial [ˌɪməˈmoriəl] *adj* : in-memorial

immense [ɪˈmɛnts] *adj* : inmenso, enorme — **immensely** *adv*

immensity [ɪˈmɛntsəṭi] *n, pl* **-ties** : inmensidad *f*

immerse [ɪˈmərs] *vt* **-mersed; -mersing** 1 SUBMERGE : sumergir 2 **to immerse oneself in** : enfrascarse en

immersion [ɪˈmərʒən] *n* 1 : inmersión *f* (en un líquido) 2 : enfrascamiento *m* (en una actividad)

immigrant [ˈɪmɪgrənt] *n* : inmigrante *mf*

immigrate [ˈɪməˌgreɪt] *vi* **-grated; -grating** : inmigrar

immigration [ˌɪməˈgreɪʃən] *n* : inmigración *f*

imminence [ˈɪmənənts] *n* : inminencia *f*

imminent [ˈɪmənənt] *adj* : inminente — **imminently** *adv*

immobile [ɪˈmoːbəl] *adj* 1 FIXED, IMMOVABLE : inmovible, fijo 2 MOTIONLESS : inmóvil

immobility [ˌɪmoˈbɪləṭi] *n, pl* **-ties** : inmovilidad *f*

immobilize [ɪˈmoːbəˌlaɪz] *vt* **-lized; -lizing** : inmovilizar, paralizar

immoderate [ɪˈmɑdərət] *adj* : inmoderado, desmesurado, desmedido, excesivo — **immoderately** *adv*

immodest [ɪˈmɑdəst] *adj* 1 INDECENT : inmodesto, indecente, impúdico 2 CONCEITED : inmodesto, presuntuoso, engreído — **immodestly** *adv*

immodesty [ɪˈmɑdəsti] *n* : inmodestia *f*

immoral [ɪˈmorəl] *adj* : inmoral

immorality [ˌɪmoˈræləṭi, ˌɪmə-] *n, pl* **-ties** : inmoralidad *f*

immorally [ɪˈmorəli] *adv* : de manera inmoral

immortal[1] [ɪˈmortəl] *adj* : inmortal

immortal[2] *n* : inmortal *mf*

immortality [ˌɪˌmorˈtæləṭi] *n* : inmortalidad *f*

immortalize [ɪˈmortəlˌaɪz] *vt* **-ized; -izing** : inmortalizar

immovable [ɪˈmuːvəbəl] *adj* 1 FIXED : fijo, inmovible 2 UNYIELDING : inflexible

immune [ɪˈmjuːn] *adj* 1 : inmune ⟨immune to smallpox : inmune a la viruela⟩ 2 EXEMPT : exento, inmune

immune system *n* : sistema *m* inmunológico

immunity [ɪˈmjuːnəṭi] *n, pl* **-ties** 1 : inmunidad *f* 2 EXEMPTION : exención *f*

immunization [ˌɪmjʊnəˈzeɪʃən] *n* : inmunización *f*

immunize [ˈɪmjʊˌnaɪz] *vt* **-nized; -nizing** : inmunizar

immunology [ˌɪmjʊˈnɑləʤi] *n* : inmunología *f*

immutable [ɪˈmjuːṭəbəl] *adj* : inmutable

imp [ˈɪmp] *n* RASCAL : diablillo *m*; pillo *m*, -lla *f*

impact[1] [ɪmˈpækt] *vt* 1 STRIKE : chocar con, impactar 2 AFFECT : afectar, impactar, impresionar — *vi* 1 STRIKE : hacer impacto, golpear 2 **to impact on** : tener un impacto sobre

impact[2] [ˈɪmˌpækt] *n* 1 COLLISION : impacto *m*, choque *m*, colisión *f* 2 EFFECT : efecto *m*, impacto *m*, consecuencias *fpl*

impacted [ɪmˈpæktəd] *adj* : impactado, incrustado (dícese de los dientes)

impair [ɪmˈpær] *vt* : perjudicar, dañar, afectar

impairment [ɪmˈpærmənt] *n* : perjuicio *m*, daño *m*

impala [ɪmˈpɑlə, -ˈpæ-] *n, pl* **impalas** *or* **impala** : impala *m*

impale [ɪmˈpeɪl] *vt* **-paled; -paling** : empalar

impanel [ɪmˈpænəl] *vt* **-eled** *or* **-elled; eling** *or* **-elling** : elegir (un jurado)

impart [ɪmˈpɑrt] *vt* 1 CONVEY : impartir, dar, conferir 2 DISCLOSE : revelar, divulgar

impartial [ɪmˈpɑrʃəl] *adj* : imparcial — **impartially** *adv*

impartiality [ɪmˌpɑrʃiˈæləṭi] *n, pl* **-ties** : imparcialidad *f*

impassable [ɪmˈpæsəbəl] *adj* : infranqueable, intransitable — **impassably** [-bli] *adv*

impasse [ˈɪmˌpæs] *n* 1 DEADLOCK : impasse *m*, punto *m* muerto 2 DEAD END : callejón *m* sin salida

impassioned [ɪmˈpæʃənd] *adj* : apasionado, vehemente

impassive [ɪmˈpæsɪv] *adj* : impasible, indiferente

impassively [ɪmˈpæsɪvli] *adv* : impasiblemente, sin emoción

impatience [ɪmˈpeɪʃənts] *n* : impaciencia *f*

impatient [ɪmˈpeɪʃənt] *adj* : impaciente — **impatiently** *adv*

impeach [ɪmˈpiːtʃ] *vt* : destituir (a un funcionario) de su cargo

impeachment [ɪmˈpiːtʃmənt] *n* 1 ACCUSATION : acusación *f* 2 DISMISSAL : destitución *f*

impeccable [ɪmˈpɛkəbəl] *adj* : impecable — **impeccably** [-bli] *adv*

impecunious [ˌɪmpɪˈkjuːniəs] *adj* : falto de dinero

impede [ɪmˈpiːd] *vt* **-peded; -peding** : impedir, dificultar, obstaculizar

impediment [ɪmˈpɛdəmənt] *n* 1 HINDRANCE : impedimento *m*, obstáculo *m* 2 **speech impediment** : defecto *m* del habla

impel [ɪmˈpɛl] *vt* **-pelled; -pelling** : impeler

impend [ɪmˈpɛnd] *vi* : ser inminente

impenetrable [ɪmˈpɛnətrəbəl] *adj* 1 : impenetrable ⟨an impenetrable forest : una selva impenetrable⟩ 2 INSCRUTABLE : incomprensible, inescrutable, impenetrable — **impenetrably** [-bli] *adv*

impenitent [ɪmˈpɛnətənt] *adj* : impenitente

imperative[1] [ɪm'pɛrətɪv] *adj* **1** AUTHOR-ITATIVE : imperativo, imperioso **2** NECESSARY : imprescindible — **imperatively** *adv*

imperative[2] *n* : imperativo *m*

imperceptible [ˌɪmpər'sɛptəbəl] *adj* : imperceptible — **imperceptibly** [-bli] *adv*

imperfect [ɪm'pərfɪkt] *adj* : imperfecto, defectuoso — **imperfectly** *adv*

imperfection [ˌɪmˌpər'fɪkʃən] *n* : imperfección *f*, defecto *m*

imperial [ɪm'pɪriəl] *adj* **1** : imperial **2** SOVEREIGN : soberano **3** IMPERIOUS : imperioso, señorial

imperialism [ɪm'pɪriəˌlɪzəm] *n* : imperialismo *m*

imperialist[1] [ɪm'pɪriəlɪst] *adj* : imperialista

imperialist[2] *n* : imperialista *mf*

imperialistic [ɪmˌpɪriːəˈlɪstɪk] *adj* : imperialista

imperil [ɪm'pɛrəl] *vt* **-iled** *or* **-illed; -iling** *or* **-illing** : poner en peligro

imperious [ɪm'pɪriəs] *adj* : imperioso — **imperiously** *adv*

imperishable [ɪm'pɛrɪʃəbəl] *adj* : imperecedero

impermanent [ɪm'pərmənənt] *adj* : pasajero, inestable, efímero — **impermanently** *adv*

impermeable [ɪm'pərmiəbəl] *adj* : impermeable

impersonal [ɪm'pərsənəl] *adj* : impersonal — **impersonally** *adv*

impersonate [ɪm'pərsənˌeɪt] *vt* **-ated; -ating** : hacerse pasar por, imitar

impersonation [ɪmˌpərsən'eɪʃən] *n* : imitación *f*

impersonator [ɪm'pərsənˌeɪtər] *n* : imitador *m*, -dora *f*

impertinence [ɪm'pərtənənts] *n* : impertinencia *f*

impertinent [ɪm'pərtənənt] *adj* **1** IRRELEVANT : impertinente, irrelevante **2** INSOLENT : impertinente, insolente

impertinently [ɪm'pərtənəntli] *adv* : con impertinencia, impertinentemente

imperturbable [ˌɪmpər'tərbəbəl] *adj* : imperturbable

impervious [ɪm'pərviəs] *adj* **1** IMPENETRABLE : impermeable **2** INSENSITIVE : insensible ⟨impervious to criticism : insensible a la crítica⟩

impetuosity [ɪmˌpɛtʃuˈasəti] *n, pl* **-ties** : impetuosidad *f*

impetuous [ɪm'pɛtʃuəs] *adj* : impetuoso, impulsivo

impetuously [ɪm'pɛtʃuəsli] *adv* : de manera impulsiva, impetuosamente

impetus ['ɪmpətəs] *n* : ímpetu *m*, impulso *m*

impiety [ɪm'paɪəti] *n, pl* **-ties** : impiedad *f*

impinge [ɪm'pɪndʒ] *vi* **-pinged; -pinging** **1 to impinge on** AFFECT : afectar a, incidir en **2 to impinge on** VIOLATE : violar, vulnerar

impious ['ɪmpiəs, ɪm'paɪəs] *adj* : impío, irreverente

impish ['ɪmpɪʃ] *adj* MISCHIEVOUS : pícaro, travieso

impishly ['ɪmpɪʃli] *adv* : con picardía

implacable [ɪm'plækəbəl] *adj* : implacable — **implacably** [-bli] *adv*

implant[1] [ɪm'plænt] *vt* **1** INCULCATE, INSTILL : inculcar, implantar **2** INSERT : implantar, insertar

implant[2] ['ɪmˌplænt] *n* : implante *m* (de pelo), injerto *m* (de piel)

implantation [ˌɪmˌplæn'teɪʃən] *n* : implantación *f*

implausibility [ɪmˌplɔzə'bɪləti] *n, pl* **-ties** : inverosimilitud *f*

implausible [ɪm'plɔzəbəl] *adj* : inverosímil, poco convincente

implement[1] ['ɪmpləˌmnt] *vt* : poner en práctica, implementar

implement[2] ['ɪmpləmənt] *n* : utensilio *m*, instrumento *m*, implemento *m*

implementation [ˌɪmpləmən'teɪʃən] *n* : implementación *f*, ejecución *f*, cumplimiento *m*

implicate ['ɪmpləˌkeɪt] *vt* **-cated; -cating** : implicar, involucrar

implication [ˌɪmplə'keɪʃən] *n* **1** CONSEQUENCE : implicación *f*, consecuencia *f* **2** INFERENCE : insinuación *f*, inferencia *f*

implicit [ɪm'plɪsət] *adj* **1** IMPLIED : implícito, tácito **2** ABSOLUTE : absoluto, completo ⟨implicit faith : fe ciega⟩ — **implicitly** *adv*

implied [ɪm'plaɪd] *adj* : implícito, tácito

implode [ɪm'ploːd] *vi* **-ploded; -ploding** : implosionar

implore [ɪm'plor] *vt* **-plored; -ploring** : implorar, suplicar

implosion [ɪm'ploːʒən] *n* : implosión *f*

imply [ɪm'plaɪ] *vt* **-plied; -plying** **1** SUGGEST : insinuar, dar a entender **2** INVOLVE : implicar, suponer ⟨rights imply obligations : los derechos implican unas obligaciones⟩

impolite [ˌɪmpə'laɪt] *adj* : descortés, maleducado

impoliteness [ˌɪmpə'laɪtnəs] *n* : descortesía *f*, falta *f* de educación

impolitic [ɪm'paləˌtɪk] *adj* : imprudente, poco político

imponderable[1] [ɪm'pandərəbəl] *adj* : imponderable

imponderable[2] *n* : imponderable *m*

import[1] [ɪm'port] *vt* **1** SIGNIFY : significar **2** : importar ⟨to import foreign cars : importar autos extranjeros⟩

import[2] ['ɪmˌport] *n* **1** SIGNIFICANCE : importancia *f*, significación *f* **2** → **importation**

importance [ɪm'portənts] *n* : importancia *f*

important [ɪm'portənt] *adj* : importante

importantly [ɪm'portəntli] *adv* **1** : con importancia **2 more importantly** : lo que es más importante

importation [ˌɪmˌpor'teɪʃən] *n* : importación *f*

importer [ɪm'portər] *n* : importador *m*, -dora *f*

importunate [ɪm'pɔrtʃənət] *adj* : importuno, insistente

importune [ˌɪmpər'tu:n, -'tju:n; ɪm'pɔrtʃən] *vt* **-tuned; -tuning** : importunar, implorar

impose [ɪm'po:z] *v* **-posed; -posing** *vt* : imponer ⟨to impose a tax : imponer un impuesto⟩ — *vi* **to impose on** : abusar de, molestar ⟨to impose on her kindness : abusar de su bondad⟩

imposing [ɪm'po:zɪŋ] *adj* : imponente, impresionante

imposition [ˌɪmpə'zɪʃən] *n* : imposición *f*

impossibility [ɪmˌpasə'bɪləti] *n, pl* **-ties** : imposibilidad *f*

impossible [ɪm'pasəbəl] *adj* **1** : imposible ⟨an impossible task : una tarea imposible⟩ ⟨to make life impossible for : hacerle la vida imposible a⟩ **2** UNACCEPTABLE : inaceptable

impossibly [ɪm'pasəbli] *adv* : imposiblemente, increíblemente

impostor *or* **imposter** [ɪm'pastər] *n* : impostor *m*, -tora *f*

impotence ['ɪmpətəns] *n* : impotencia *f*

impotency ['ɪmpətənsi] → **impotence**

impotent ['ɪmpətənt] *adj* : impotente

impound [ɪm'paʊnd] *vt* : incautar, embargar, confiscar

impoverish [ɪm'pavərɪʃ] *vt* : empobrecer

impoverishment [ɪm'pavərɪʃmənt] *n* : empobrecimiento *m*

impracticable [ɪm'præktɪkəbəl] *adj* : impracticable

impractical [ɪm'præktɪkəl] *adj* : poco práctico

imprecise [ˌɪmprɪ'saɪs] *adj* : impreciso

imprecisely [ˌɪmprɪ'saɪsli] *adv* : con imprecisión

impreciseness [ˌɪmprɪ'saɪsnəs] → **imprecision**

imprecision [ˌɪmprɪ'sɪʒən] *n* : imprecisión *f*, falta de precisión *f*

impregnable [ɪm'prɛgnəbəl] *adj* : inexpugnable, impenetrable, inconquistable

impregnate [ɪm'prɛgˌneɪt] *vt* **-nated; -nating 1** FERTILIZE : fecundar **2** PERMEATE, SATURATE : impregnar, empapar, saturar

impresario [ˌɪmprə'sari‚o, -'sær-] *n, pl* **-rios** : empresario *m*, -ria *f*

impress [ɪm'prɛs] *vt* **1** IMPRINT : imprimir, estampar **2** : impresionar, causar impresión a ⟨I was not impressed : no me hizo buena impresión⟩ **3 to impress (something) on someone** : recalcarle (algo) a alguien — *vi* : impresionar, hacer una impresión

impression [ɪm'prɛʃən] *n* **1** IMPRINT : marca *f*, huella *f*, molde *m* (de los dientes) **2** EFFECT : impresión *f*, efecto *m*, impacto *m* **3** PRINTING : impresión *f* **4** NOTION : impresión *f*, noción *f*

impressionable [ɪm'prɛʃənəbəl] *adj* : impresionable

impressionism [ɪm'prɛʃə‚nɪzəm] *n* : impresionismo *m*

impressionist [ɪm'prɛʃənɪst] *n* : impresionista *mf* — **impressionist** *adj*

impressive [ɪm'prɛsɪv] *adj* : impresionante — **impressively** *adv*

impressiveness [ɪm'prɛsɪvnəs] *n* : calidad de ser impresionante

imprint¹ [ɪm'prɪnt, 'ɪm‚-] *vt* : imprimir, estampar

imprint² ['ɪm‚prɪnt] *n* : marca *f*, huella *f*

imprison [ɪm'prɪzən] *vt* **1** JAIL : encarcelar, aprisionar **2** CONFINE : recluir, encerrar

imprisonment [ɪm'prɪzənmənt] *n* : encarcelamiento *m*

improbability [ɪmˌprabə'bɪləti] *n, pl* **-ties** : improbabilidad *f*, inverosimilitud *f*

improbable [ɪm'prabəbəl] *adj* : improbable, inverosímil

impromptu¹ [ɪm'pramp‚tu:, -‚tju:] *adv* : sin preparación, espontáneamente

impromptu² *adj* : espontáneo, improvisado

impromptu³ *n* : improvisación *f*

improper [ɪm'prapər] *adj* **1** INCORRECT : incorrecto, impropio **2** INDECOROUS : indecoroso

improperly [ɪm'praprli] *adv* : incorrectamente, indebidamente

impropriety [ˌɪmprə'praɪəti] *n, pl* **-eties 1** INDECOROUSNESS : indecoro *m*, falta *f* de decoro **2** ERROR : impropiedad *f*, incorrección *f*

improve [ɪm'pru:v] *v* **-proved; -proving** : mejorar

improvement [ɪm'pru:vmənt] *n* : mejoramiento *m*, mejora *f*

improvidence [ɪm'pravədənts] *n* : imprevisión *f*

improvisation [ɪmˌpravə'zeɪʃən, ˌɪmprəvə-] *n* : improvisación *f*

improvise ['ɪmprə‚vaɪz] *v* **-vised; -vising** : improvisar

imprudence [ɪm'pru:dənts] *n* : imprudencia *f*, indiscreción *f*

imprudent [ɪm'pru:dənt] *adj* : imprudente, indiscreto

impudence ['ɪmpjədənts] *n* : insolencia *f*, descaro *m*

impudent ['ɪmpjədənt] *adj* : insolente, descarado — **impudently** *adv*

impugn [ɪm'pju:n] *vt* : impugnar

impulse ['ɪm‚pʌls] *n* **1** : impulso *m* **2 on impulse** : sin reflexionar

impulsive [ɪm'pʌlsɪv] *adj* : impulsivo — **impulsively** *adv*

impulsiveness [ɪm'pʌlsɪvnəs] *n* : impulsividad *f*

impunity [ɪm'pju:nəti] *n* **1** : impunidad *f* **2 with impunity** : impunemente

impure [ɪm'pjʊr] *adj* **1** : impuro ⟨impure thoughts : pensamientos impuros⟩ **2** CONTAMINATED : con impurezas, impuro

impurity [ɪm'pjʊrəti] *n, pl* **-ties** : impureza *f*

impute [ɪm'pjuːt] *vt* **-puted; -puting** AT-TRIBUTE : imputar, atribuir

in¹ ['ɪn] *adv* **1** INSIDE : dentro, adentro ⟨let's go in : vamos adentro⟩ **2** HAR-VESTED : recogido ⟨the crops are in : las cosechas ya están recogidas⟩ **3 to be in** : estar ⟨is Linda in? : ¿está Linda?⟩ **4 to be in** : estar en poder ⟨the Democrats are in : los demócratas están en el poder⟩ **5 to be in for** : ser objeto de, estar a punto de ⟨they're in for a treat : los van a agasajar⟩ ⟨he's in for a surprise : se va a llevar una sorpresa⟩ **6 to be in on** : participar en, tomar parte en

in² *adj* **1** INSIDE : interior ⟨the in part : la parte interior⟩ **2** FASHIONABLE : de moda

in³ *prep* **1** (*indicating location or position*) ⟨in the lake : en el lago⟩ ⟨a pain in the leg : un dolor en la pierna⟩ ⟨in the sun : al sol⟩ ⟨in the rain : bajo la lluvia⟩ ⟨the best restaurant in Buenos Aires : el mejor restaurante de Buenos Aires⟩ **2** INTO : en, a ⟨he broke it in pieces : lo rompió en pedazos⟩ ⟨she went in the house : se metió a la casa⟩ **3** DURING : por, durante ⟨in the afternoon : por la tarde⟩ **4** WITHIN : dentro de ⟨I'll be back in a week : vuelvo dentro de una semana⟩ **5** (*indicating manner*) : en, con, de ⟨in Spanish : en español⟩ ⟨written in pencil : escrito con lápiz⟩ ⟨in this way : de esta manera⟩ **6** (*indicating states or circumstances*) ⟨to be in luck : tener suerte⟩ ⟨to be in love : estar enamorado⟩ ⟨to be in a hurry : tener prisa⟩ **7** (*indicating purpose*) : en ⟨in reply : en respuesta, como réplica⟩

in⁴ *n* **ins and outs** : pormenores *mpl*

inability [ˌɪnə'bɪləti] *n, pl* **-ties** : incapacidad *f*

inaccessibility [ˌɪnɪkˌsɛsə'bɪləti] *n, pl* **-ties** : inaccesibilidad *f*

inaccessible [ˌɪnɪk'sɛsəbəl] *adj* : inaccesible

inaccuracy [ɪn'ækjərəsi] *n, pl* **-cies 1** : inexactitud *f* **2** MISTAKE : error *m*

inaccurate [ɪn'ækjərət] *n* : inexacto, erróneo, incorrecto

inaccurately [ɪn'ækjərətli] *adv* : incorrectamente, con inexactitud

inaction [ɪn'ækʃən] *n* : inactividad *f*, inacción *f*

inactive [ɪn'æktɪv] *adj* : inactivo

inactivity [ˌɪnˌæk'tɪvəti] *n, pl* **-ties** : inactividad *f*, ociosidad *f*

inadequacy [ɪn'ædɪkwəsi] *n, pl* **-cies 1** INSUFFICIENCY : insuficiencia *f* **2** IN-COMPETENCE : ineptitud *f*, incompetencia *f*

inadequate [ɪn'ædɪkwət] *adj* **1** INSUF-FICIENT : insuficiente, inadecuado **2** INCOMPETENT : inepto, incompetente

inadmissible [ˌɪnæd'mɪsəbəl] *adj* : inadmisible

inadvertent [ˌɪnəd'vərtənt] *adj* : inadvertido, involuntario — **inadvertently** *adv*

inadvisable [ˌɪnæd'vaɪzəbəl] *adj* : desaconsejable

inalienable [ɪn'eɪljənəbəl, -'eɪliənə-] *adj* : inalienable

inane [ɪ'neɪn] *adj* **inaner; -est** : estúpido, idiota, necio

inanimate [ɪn'ænəmət] *adj* : inanimado, exánime

inanity [ɪ'nænəti] *n, pl* **-ties 1** STUPIDI-TY : estupidez *f* **2** NONSENSE : idiotez *f*, disparate *m*

inapplicable [ɪn'æplɪkəbəl, ˌɪnə-'plɪkə-bəl] *adj* IRRELEVANT : inaplicable, irrelevante

inappreciable [ˌɪnə'priːʃəbəl] *adj* : inapreciable, imperceptible

inappropriate [ˌɪnə'proːpriət] *adj* : inapropiado, inadecuado, impropio

inappropriateness [ˌɪnə'proːpriətnəs] *n* : lo inapropiado, impropiedad *f*

inapt [ɪn'æpt] *adj* **1** UNSUITABLE : inadecuado, inapropiado **2** INEPT : inepto

inarticulate [ˌɪnɑr'tɪkjələt] *adj* : inarticulado, incapaz de expresarse

inarticulately [ˌɪnɑr'tɪkjələtli] *adv* : inarticuladamente

inasmuch as [ˌɪnæz'mʌtʃæz] *conj* : ya que, dado que, puesto que

inattention [ˌɪnə'tɛntʃən] *n* : falta *f* de atención, distracción *f*

inattentive [ˌɪnə'tɛntɪv] *adj* : distraído, despistado

inattentively [ˌɪnə'tɛntɪvli] *adv* : distraídamente, sin prestar atención

inaudible [ɪn'ɔdəbəl] *adj* : inaudible

inaudibly [ɪn'ɔdəbli] *adv* : de forma inaudible

inaugural¹ [ɪ'nɔgjərəl, -gərəl] *adj* : inaugural, de investidura

inaugural² *n* **1** *or* **inaugural address** : discurso *m* de investidura **2** INAU-GURATION : investidura *f* (de una persona)

inaugurate [ɪ'nɔgjə̩reɪt, -gə-] *vt* **-rated; -rating 1** BEGIN : inaugurar **2** INDUCT : investir ⟨to inaugurate the president : investir al presidente⟩

inauguration [ɪˌnɔgjə'reɪʃən, -gə-] *n* **1** : inauguración *f* (de un edificio, un sistema, etc.) **2** : investidura *f* (de una persona)

inauspicious [ˌɪnə'spɪʃəs] *adj* : desfavorable, poco propicio

inborn ['ɪn'bɔrn] *adj* **1** CONGENITAL, IN-NATE : innato, congénito **2** HEREDI-TARY : hereditario

inbred ['ɪn'brɛd] *adj* **1** : engendrado por endogamia **2** INNATE : innato

inbreed ['ɪn'briːd] *vt* **-bred; -breeding** : engendrar por endogamia

inbreeding ['ɪn'briːdɪŋ] *n* : endogamia *f*

Inca ['ɪŋkə] *n* : inca *mf*

incalculable [ɪn'kælkjələbəl] *adj* : incalculable — **incalculably** [-bli] *adv*

incandescence [ˌɪnkənˈdɛsənts] *n* : incandescencia *f*
incandescent [ˌɪnkənˈdɛsənt] *adj* **1** : incandescente **2** BRILLIANT : brillante
incantation [ˌɪnˌkænˈteɪʃən] *n* : conjuro *m*, ensalmo *m*
incapable [ɪnˈkeɪpəbəl] *adj* : incapaz
incapacitate [ˌɪnkəˈpæsəˌteɪt] *vt* **-tated; -tating** : incapacitar
incapacity [ˌɪnkəˈpæsəṭi] *n, pl* **-ties** : incapacidad *f*
incarcerate [ɪnˈkɑrsəˌreɪt] *vt* **-ated; -ating** : encarcelar
incarceration [ɪnˌkɑrsəˈreɪʃən] *n* : encarcelamiento *m*, encarcelación *f*
incarnate¹ [ɪnˈkɑrˌneɪt] *vt* **-nated; -nating** : encarnar
incarnate² [ɪnˈkɑrnət, -ˌneɪt] *adj* : encarnado
incarnation [ˌɪnˌkɑrˈneɪʃən] *n* : encarnación *f*
incendiary¹ [ɪnˈsɛndiˌri] *adj* : incendiario
incendiary² *n, pl* **-aries** : incendiario *m*, -ria *f*; pirómano *m*, -na *f*
incense¹ [ɪnˈsɛnts] *vt* **-censed; -censing** : indignar, enfadar, enfurecer
incense² [ˈɪnˌsɛnts] *n* : incienso *m*
incentive [ɪnˈsɛntɪv] *n* : incentivo *m*, aliciente *m*, motivación *f*, acicate *m*
inception [ɪnˈsɛpʃən] *n* : comienzo *m*, principio *m*
incessant [ɪnˈsɛsənt] *adj* : incesante, continuo — **incessantly** *adv*
incest [ˈɪnˌsɛst] *n* : incesto *m*
incestuous [ɪnˈsɛstʃuəs] *adj* : incestuoso
inch¹ [ˈɪntʃ] *v* : avanzar poco a poco
inch² *n* **1** : pulgada *f* **2 every inch** : absoluto, seguro ⟨every inch a winner : un seguro ganador⟩ **3 within an inch of** : a punto de
incidence [ˈɪntsədənts] *n* **1** FREQUENCY : frecuencia *f*, índice *m* ⟨a high incidence of crime : un alto índice de crímenes⟩ **2 angle of incidence** : ángulo *m* de incidencia
incident¹ [ˈɪntsədənt] *adj* : incidente
incident² *n* : incidente *m*, incidencia *f*, episodio *m* (en una obra de ficción)
incidental¹ [ˌɪntsəˈdɛntəl] *adj* **1** SECONDARY : incidental, secundario **2** ACCIDENTAL : casual, fortuito
incidental² *n* **1** : algo incidental **2 incidentals** *npl* : imprevistos *mpl*
incidentally [ˌɪntsəˈdɛntəli, -ˈdɛntli] *adv* **1** BY CHANCE : incidentalmente, casualmente **2** BY THE WAY : a propósito, por cierto
incinerate [ɪnˈsɪnəˌreɪt] *vt* **-ated; -ating** : incinerar
incinerator [ɪnˈsɪnəˌreɪṭər] *n* : incinerador *m*
incipient [ɪnˈsɪpiənt] *adj* : incipiente, naciente
incise [ɪnˈsaɪz] *vt* **-cised; -cising** **1** ENGRAVE : grabar, cincelar, inscribir **2** : hacer una incisión en
incision [ɪnˈsɪʒən] *n* : incisión *f*

incisive [ɪnˈsaɪsɪv] *adj* : incisivo, penetrante
incisively [ɪnˈsaɪsɪvli] *adv* : con agudeza
incisor [ɪnˈsaɪzər] *n* : incisivo *m*
incite [ɪnˈsaɪt] *vt* **-cited; -citing** : incitar, instigar
incitement [ɪnˈsaɪtmənt] *n* : incitación *f*
inclemency [ɪnˈklɛməntsi] *n, pl* **-cies** : inclemencia *f*
inclement [ɪnˈklɛmənt] *adj* : inclemente, tormentoso
inclination [ˌɪnkləˈneɪʃən] *n* **1** PROPENSITY : inclinación *f*, tendencia *f* **2** DESIRE : deseo *m*, ganas *fpl* **3** BOW : inclinación *f*
incline¹ [ɪnˈklaɪn] *v* **-clined; -clining** *vi* **1** SLOPE : inclinarse **2** TEND : inclinarse, tender ⟨he is inclined to be late : tiende a llegar tarde⟩ — *vt* **1** LOWER : inclinar, bajar ⟨to incline one's head : bajar la cabeza⟩ **2** SLANT : inclinar **3** PREDISPOSE : predisponer
incline² [ˈɪnˌklaɪn] *n* : inclinación *f*, pendiente *f*
inclined [ɪnˈklaɪnd] *adj* **1** SLOPING : inclinado **2** PRONE : prono, dispuesto, dado
inclose, inclosure → enclose, enclosure
include [ɪnˈkluːd] *vt* **-cluded; -cluding** : incluir, comprender
inclusion [ɪnˈkluːʒən] *n* : inclusión *f*
inclusive [ɪnˈkluːsɪv] *adj* : inclusivo
incognito [ˌɪnˌkɑgˈniːˌṭo, ɪnˈkɑgnəˌtoː] *adv & adj* : de incógnito
incoherence [ˌɪnkoˈhɪrənts, -ˈhɛr-] *n* : incoherencia *f*
incoherent [ˌɪnkoˈhɪrənt, -ˈhɛr-] *adj* : incoherente — **incoherently** *adv*
incombustible [ˌɪnkəmˈbʌstəbəl] *adj* : incombustible
income [ˈɪnˌkʌm] *n* : ingresos *mpl*, entradas *fpl*
income tax *n* : impuesto *m* sobre la renta
incoming [ˈɪnˌkʌmɪŋ] *adj* **1** ARRIVING : que se recibe (dícese del correo), que llega (dícese de las personas), ascendente (dícese de la marea) **2** NEW : nuevo, entrante ⟨the incoming president : el nuevo presidente⟩ ⟨the incoming year : el año entrante⟩
incommunicado [ˌɪnkəˌmjuːnəˈkɑdo] *adj* : incomunicado
incomparable [ɪnˈkɑmpərəbəl] *adj* : incomparable, sin igual
incompatible [ˌɪnkəmˈpæṭəbəl] *adj* : incompatible
incompetence [ɪnˈkɑmpəṭənts] *n* : incompetencia *f*, impericia *f*, ineptitud *f*
incompetent [ɪnˈkɑmpəṭənt] *adj* : incompetente, inepto, incapaz
incomplete [ˌɪnkəmˈpliːt] *adj* : incompleto — **incompletely** *adv*
incomprehensible [ˌɪnˌkɑmpriˈhɛntsəbəl] *adj* : incomprensible
inconceivable [ˌɪnkənˈsiːvəbəl] *adj* **1** INCOMPREHENSIBLE : incomprensible **2** UNBELIEVABLE : inconcebible, increíble

inconceivably [ˌɪnkən'si:vəbli] *adv* : inconcebiblemente, increíblemente
inconclusive [ˌɪnkən'klu:sɪv] *adj* : inconcluyente, no decisivo
incongruity [ˌɪnkən'gru:əţi, -ˌkɑn-] *n, pl* **-ties** : incongruencia *f*
incongruous [ɪn'kɑŋgruəs] *adj* : incongruente, inapropiado, fuera de lugar
incongruously [ɪn'kɑŋgruəsli] *adv* : de manera incongruente, inapropiadamente
inconsequential [ˌɪnˌkɑnsə'kwentʃəl] *adj* : intrascendente, de poco importancia
inconsiderable [ˌɪnkən'sɪdərəbəl] *adj* : insignificante
inconsiderate [ˌɪnkən'sɪdərət] *adj* : desconsiderado, sin consideración — **inconsiderately** *adv*
inconsistency [ˌɪnkən'sɪstənṭsi] *n, pl* **-cies** : inconsecuencia *f*, inconsistencia *f*
inconsistent [ˌɪnkən'sɪstənt] *adj* : inconsecuente, inconsistente
inconsolable [ˌɪnkən'so:ləbəl] *adj* : inconsolable — **inconsolably** [-bli] *adv*
inconspicuous [ˌɪnkən'spɪkjuəs] *adj* : discreto, no conspicuo, que no llama la atención
inconspicuously [ˌɪnkən'spɪkjuəsli] *adv* : discretamente, sin llamar la atención
incontestable [ˌɪnkən'testəbəl] *adj* : incontestable, indiscutible — **incontestably** [-bli] *adv*
incontinence [ɪn'kɑntənənṭs] *n* : incontinencia *f*
incontinent [ɪn'kɑntənənt] *adj* : incontinente
inconvenience¹ [ˌɪnkən'vi:njənṭs] *vt* **-nienced; -niencing** : importunar, incomodar, molestar
inconvenience² *n* : incomodidad *f*, molestia *f*
inconvenient [ˌɪnkən'vi:njənt] *adj* : inconveniente, importuno, incómodo — **inconveniently** *adv*
incorporate [ɪn'kɔrpəˌreɪt] *vt* **-rated; -rating 1** INCLUDE : incorporar, incluir **2** : incorporar, constituir en sociedad (dícese de un negocio)
incorporation [ɪnˌkɔrpə'reɪʃən] *n* : incorporación *f*
incorporeal [ˌɪnˌkɔr'poriəl] *adj* : incorpóreo
incorrect [ˌɪnkə'rekt] *adj* **1** INACCURATE : incorrecto **2** WRONG : equivocado, erróneo **3** IMPROPER : impropio — **incorrectly** *adv*
incorrigible [ɪn'kɔrəʤəbəl] *adj* : incorregible
incorruptible [ˌɪnkə'rʌptəbəl] *adj* : incorruptible
increase¹ [ɪn'kri:s, 'ɪnˌkri:s] *v* **-creased; -creasing** *vi* GROW : aumentar, crecer, subir (dícese de los precios) — *vt* AUGMENT : aumentar, acrecentar
increase² ['ɪnˌkri:s, ɪn'kri:s] *n* : aumento *m*, incremento *m*, subida *f* (de precios)

increasing [ɪn'kri:sɪŋ, 'ɪnˌkri:sɪŋ] *adj* : creciente
increasingly [ɪn'kri:sɪŋli] *adv* : cada vez más
incredible [ɪn'krɛdəbəl] *adj* : increíble — **incredibly** [-bli] *adv*
incredulity [ˌɪnkrɪ'du:ləţi, -'dju:-] *n* : incredulidad *f*
incredulous [ɪn'krɛʤələs] *adj* : incrédulo, escéptico
incredulously [ɪn'krɛʤələsli] *adv* : con incredulidad
increment ['ɪŋkrəmənt, 'ɪn-] *n* : incremento *m*, aumento *m*
incremental [ˌɪŋkrə'mentəl, ˌɪn-] *adj* : de incremento
incriminate [ɪn'krɪməˌneɪt] *vt* **-nated; -nating** : incriminar
incrimination [ɪnˌkrɪmə'neɪʃən] *n* : incriminación *f*
incriminatory [ɪn'krɪmənəˌtori] *adj* : incriminatorio
incubate ['ɪŋkjuˌbeɪt, 'ɪn-] *v* **-bated; -bating** *vt* : incubar, empollar — *vi* : incubar(se), empollar
incubation [ˌɪŋkju'beɪʃən, ˌɪn-] *n* : incubación *f*
incubator ['ɪŋkjuˌbeɪţər, 'ɪn-] *n* : incubadora *f*
inculcate [ɪn'kʌlˌkeɪt, 'ɪnˌkʌl-] *vt* **-cated; -cating** : inculcar
incumbency [ɪn'kʌmbənṭsi] *n, pl* **-cies 1** OBLIGATION : incumbencia *f* **2** : mandato *m* (en la política)
incumbent¹ [ɪn'kʌmbənt] *adj* : obligatorio
incumbent² *n* : titular *mf*
incur [ɪn'kər] *vt* **incurred; incurring** : provocar (al enojo), incurrir en (gastos, obligaciones)
incurable [ɪn'kjurəbəl] *adj* : incurable, sin remedio
incursion [ɪn'kərʒən] *n* : incursión *f*
indebted [ɪn'dɛţəd] *adj* **1** : endeudado **2 to be indebted to** : estar en deuda con, estarle agradecido a
indebtedness [ɪn'dɛţədnəs] *n* : endeudamiento *m*
indecency [ɪn'di:sənṭsi] *n, pl* **-cies** : indecencia *f*
indecent [ɪn'di:sənt] *adj* : indecente — **indecently** *adv*
indecipherable [ˌɪndɪ'saɪfərəbəl] *adj* : indescifrable
indecision [ˌɪndɪ'sɪʒən] *n* : indecisión *f*, irresolución *f*
indecisive [ˌɪndɪ'saɪsɪv] *adj* **1** INCONCLUSIVE : indeciso, que no es decisivo **2** IRRESOLUTE : indeciso, irresoluto, vacilante **3** INDEFINITE : indefinido — **indecisively** *adv*
indecorous [ɪn'dɛkərəs, ˌɪndɪ'korəs] *adj* : indecoroso — **indecorously** *adv*
indecorousness [ɪn'dɛkərəsnəs, ˌɪndɪ'korəs-] *n* : indecoro *m*
indeed [ɪn'di:d] *adv* **1** TRULY : verdaderamente, de veras **2** (*used as intensifier*) ⟨thank you very much indeed

: muchísimas gracias⟩ **3** OF COURSE : claro, por supuesto

indefatigable [ˌɪndɪˈfætɪɡəbəl] *adj* : incansable, infatigable — **indefatigably** [-bli] *adv*

indefensible [ˌɪndɪˈfɛntsəbəl] *adj* **1** VULNERABLE : indefendible, vulnerable **2** INEXCUSABLE : inexcusable

indefinable [ˌɪndɪˈfaɪnəbəl] *adj* : indefinible

indefinite [ɪnˈdɛfənət] *adj* **1** : indefinido, indeterminado ⟨indefinite pronouns : pronombres indefinidos⟩ **2** VAGUE : vago, impreciso

indefinitely [ɪnˈdɛfənətli] *adv* : indefinidamente, por un tiempo indefinido

indelible [ɪnˈdɛləbəl] *adj* : indeleble, imborrable — **indelibly** [-bli] *adv*

indelicacy [ɪnˈdɛləkəsi] *n* : falta *f* de delicadeza

indelicate [ɪnˈdɛlɪkət] *adj* **1** IMPROPER : indelicado, indecoroso **2** TACTLESS : indiscreto, falto de tacto

indemnify [ɪnˈdɛmnəˌfaɪ] *vt* **-fied; -fying 1** INSURE : asegurar **2** COMPENSATE : indemnizar, compensar

indemnity [ɪnˈdɛmnəti] *n, pl* **-ties 1** INSURANCE : indemnidad *f* **2** COMPENSATION : indemnización *f*

indent [ɪnˈdɛnt] *vt* : sangrar (un párrafo)

indentation [ˌɪnˌdɛnˈteɪʃən] *n* **1** NOTCH : muesca *f*, mella *f* **2** INDENTING : sangría *f* (de un párrafo)

indenture¹ [ɪnˈdɛntʃər] *vt* **-tured; -turing** : ligar por contrato

indenture² *n* : contrato de aprendizaje

independence [ˌɪndəˈpɛndənts] *n* : independencia *f*

Independence Day *n* : día *m* de la Independencia (4 de julio en los EE.UU.)

independent¹ [ˌɪndəˈpɛndənt] *adj* : independiente — **independently** *adv*

independent² *n* : independiente *mf*

indescribable [ˌɪndɪˈskraɪbəbəl] *adj* : indescriptible, incalificable — **indescribably** [-bli] *adv*

indestructibility [ˌɪndɪˌstrʌktəˈbɪləti] *n* : indestructibilidad *f*

indestructible [ˌɪndɪˈstrʌktəbəl] *adj* : indestructible

indeterminate [ˌɪndɪˈtərmənət] *adj* **1** VAGUE : vago, impreciso, indeterminado **2** INDEFINITE : indeterminado, indefinido

index¹ [ˈɪnˌdɛks] *vt* **1** : ponerle un índice a (un libro o una revista) **2** : incluir en un índice ⟨all proper names are indexed : todos los nombres propios están incluidos en el índice⟩ **3** INDICATE : indicar, señalar **4** REGULATE : indexar, indiciar ⟨to index prices : indiciar los precios⟩

index² *n, pl* **-dexes** *or* **-dices** [ˈɪndəˌsiːz] **1** : índice *m* (de un libro, de precios) **2** INDICATION : indicio *m*, índice *m*, señal *f* ⟨an index of her character : una señal de su carácter⟩

index finger *n* FOREFINGER : dedo *m* índice

Indian [ˈɪndiən] *n* **1** : indio *m*, -dia *f* **2** → **American Indian** — **Indian** *adj*

indicate [ˈɪndəˌkeɪt] *vt* **-cated; -cating 1** POINT OUT : indicar, señalar **2** SHOW, SUGGEST : ser indicio de, ser señal de **3** EXPRESS : expresar, señalar **4** REGISTER : marcar, poner (una medida, etc.)

indication [ˌɪndəˈkeɪʃən] *n* : indicio *m*, señal *f*

indicative [ɪnˈdɪkətɪv] *adj* : indicativo

indicator [ˈɪndəˌkeɪtər] *n* : indicador *m*

indict [ɪnˈdaɪt] *vt* : acusar, procesar (por un crimen)

indictment [ɪnˈdaɪtmənt] *n* : acusación *f*

indifference [ɪnˈdɪfrənts, -ˈdɪfə-] *n* : indiferencia *f*

indifferent [ɪnˈdɪfrənt, -ˈdɪfə-] *adj* **1** UNCONCERNED : indiferente **2** MEDIOCRE : mediocre

indifferently [ɪnˈdɪfrəntli, -ˈdɪfə-] *adv* **1** : con indiferencia, indiferentemente **2** SO-SO : de modo regular, más o menos

indigence [ˈɪndɪdʒənts] *n* : indigencia *f*

indigenous [ɪnˈdɪdʒənəs] *adj* : indígena, nativo

indigent [ˈɪndɪdʒənt] *adj* : indigente, pobre

indigestible [ˌɪndaɪˈdʒɛstəbəl, -dɪ-] *adj* : difícil de digerir

indigestion [ˌɪndaɪˈdʒɛstʃən, -dɪ-] *n* : indigestión *f*, empacho *m*

indignant [ɪnˈdɪɡnənt] *adj* : indignado

indignantly [ɪnˈdɪɡnəntli] *adv* : con indignación

indignation [ˌɪndɪɡˈneɪʃən] *n* : indignación *f*

indignity [ɪnˈdɪɡnəti] *n, pl* **-ties** : indignidad *f*

indigo [ˈɪndɪˌɡoː] *n, pl* **-gos** *or* **-goes** : añil *m*, índigo *m*

indirect [ˌɪndəˈrɛkt, -daɪ-] *adj* : indirecto — **indirectly** *adv*

indiscernible [ˌɪndɪˈsərnəbəl, -ˈzər-] *adj* : imperceptible

indiscreet [ˌɪndɪˈskriːt] *adj* : indiscreto, imprudente — **indiscreetly** *adv*

indiscretion [ˌɪndɪˈskrɛʃən] *n* : indiscreción *f*, imprudencia *f*

indiscriminate [ˌɪndɪˈskrɪmənət] *adj* : indiscriminado

indiscriminately [ˌɪndɪˈskrɪmənətli] *adv* : sin discriminación, sin discernimiento

indispensable [ˌɪndɪˈspɛntsəbəl] *adj* : indispensable, necesario, imprescindible — **indispensably** [-bli] *adv*

indisposed [ˌɪndɪˈspoːzd] *adj* **1** ILL : indispuesto, enfermo **2** AVERSE, DISINCLINED : opuesto, reacio ⟨to be indisposed toward working : no tener ganas de trabajar⟩

indisputable [ˌɪndɪˈspjuːtəbəl, ɪnˈdɪspjuːtə-] *adj* : indiscutible, incuestionable, incontestable — **indisputably** [-bli] *adv*

indistinct [ˌɪndɪ'stɪŋkt] *adj* : indistinto — **indistinctly** *adv*
indistinctness [ˌɪndɪ'stɪŋktnəs] *n* : falta *f* de claridad
indistinguishable [ˌɪndɪ'stɪŋgwɪʃəbəl] *adj* : indistinguible
individual[1] [ˌɪndə'vɪdʒuəl] *adj* **1** PERSONAL : individual, personal ⟨individual traits : características personales⟩ **2** SEPARATE : individual, separado **3** PARTICULAR : particular, propio
individual[2] *n* : individuo *m*
individualism [ˌɪndə'vɪdʒəwəˌlɪzəm] *n* : individualismo *m*
individualist [ˌɪndə'vɪdʒuəlɪst] *n* : individualista *mf*
individuality [ˌɪndəˌvɪdʒu'æləti] *n, pl* **-ties** : individualidad *f*
individually [ˌɪndə'vɪdʒuəli, -dʒəli] *adv* : individualmente
indivisible [ˌɪndɪ'vɪzəbəl] *adj* : indivisible
indoctrinate [ɪn'dɑktrəˌneɪt] *vt* **-nated; -nating 1** TEACH : enseñar, instruir **2** PROPAGANDIZE : adoctrinar
indoctrination [ɪnˌdɑktrə'neɪʃən] *n* : adoctrinamiento *m*
indolence ['ɪndələnts] *n* : indolencia *f*
indolent ['ɪndələnt] *adj* : indolente
indomitable [ɪn'dɑmətəbəl] *adj* : invencible, indomable, indómito — **indomitably** [-bli] *adv*
Indonesian [ˌɪndo'niːʒən, -ʃən] *n* : indonesio *m*, -sia *f* — **Indonesian** *adj*
indoor ['ɪn'dor] *adj* : interior (dícese de las plantas), para estar en casa (dícese de la ropa), cubierto (dícese de las piscinas, etc.), bajo techo (dícese de los deportes)
indoors ['ɪn'dorz] *adv* : adentro, dentro
indubitable [ɪn'duːbətəbəl, -'djuː-] *adj* : indudable, incuestionable, indiscutible
indubitably [ɪn'duːbətəbli, -'djuː-] *adv* : indudablemente
induce [ɪn'duːs, -'djuːs] *vt* **-duced; -ducing 1** PERSUADE : persuadir, inducir **2** CAUSE : inducir, provocar ⟨to induce labor : provocar un parto⟩
inducement [ɪn'duːsmənt, -'djuː-] *n* **1** INCENTIVE : incentivo *m*, aliciente *m* **2** : inducción *f*, provocación *f* (de un parto)
induct [ɪn'dʌkt] *vt* **1** INSTALL : instalar, investir **2** ADMIT : admitir (como miembro) **3** CONSCRIPT : reclutar (al servicio militar)
inductee [ɪnˌdʌk'tiː] *n* : recluta *mf*, conscripto *m*, -ta *f*
induction [ɪn'dʌkʃən] *n* **1** INTRODUCTION : iniciación *f*, introducción *f* **2** : inducción *f* (en la lógica o la electricidad)
inductive [ɪn'dʌktɪv] *adj* : inductivo
indulge [ɪn'dʌldʒ] *v* **-dulged; -dulging** *vt* **1** GRATIFY : gratificar, satisfacer **2** SPOIL : consentir, mimar — *vi* **to indulge in** : permitirse

indulgence [ɪn'dʌldʒənts] *n* **1** SATISFYING : satisfacción *f*, gratificación *f* **2** HUMORING : complacencia *f*, indulgencia *f* **3** SPOILING : consentimiento *m* **4** : indulgencia *f* (en la religión)
indulgent [ɪn'dʌldʒənt] *adj* : indulgente, consentido — **indulgently** *adv*
industrial [ɪn'dʌstriəl] *adj* : industrial — **industrially** *adv*
industrialist [ɪn'dʌstriəlɪst] *n* : industrial *mf*
industrialization [ɪnˌdʌstriələ'zeɪ-ʃən] *n* : industrialización *f*
industrialize [ɪn'dʌstriəˌlaɪz] *vt* **-ized; -izing** : industrializar
industrious [ɪn'dʌstriəs] *adj* : diligente, industrioso, trabajador
industriously [ɪn'dʌstriəsli] *adv* : con diligencia, con aplicación
industriousness [ɪn'dʌstriəsnəs] *n* : diligencia *f*, aplicación *f*
industry ['ɪndəstri] *n, pl* **-tries 1** DILIGENCE : diligencia *f*, aplicación *f* **2** : industria *f* ⟨the steel industry : la industria siderúrgica⟩
inebriated [ɪ'niːbriˌeɪtəd] *adj* : ebrio, embriagado
inebriation [ɪˌniːbri'eɪʃən] *n* : ebriedad *f*, embriaguez *f*
ineffable [ɪn'efəbəl] *adj* : inefable — **ineffably** [-bli] *adv*
ineffective [ˌɪnɪ'fɛktɪv] *adj* **1** INEFFECTUAL : ineficaz, inútil **2** INCAPABLE : incompetente, ineficiente, incapaz
ineffectively [ˌɪnɪ'fɛktɪvli] *adv* : ineficazmente, infructuosamente
ineffectual [ˌɪnɪ'fɛktʃuəl] *adj* : inútil, ineficaz — **ineffectually** *adv*
inefficiency [ˌɪnɪ'fɪʃəntsi] *n, pl* **-cies** : ineficiencia *f*, ineficacia *f*
inefficient [ˌɪnɪ'fɪʃənt] *adj* **1** : ineficiente, ineficaz **2** INCAPABLE, INCOMPETENT : incompetente, incapaz — **inefficiently** *adv*
inelegance [ɪn'ɛləgənts] *n* : inelegancia *f*
inelegant [ɪn'ɛləgənt] *adj* : inelegante, poco elegante
ineligibility [ɪnˌɛlədʒə'bɪləti] *n* : inelegibilidad *f*
ineligible [ɪn'ɛlədʒəbəl] *adj* : inelegible
inept [ɪ'ɛnpt] *adj* : inepto ⟨inept at : incapaz para⟩
ineptitude [ɪ'ɛnptəˌtuːd, -ˌtjuːd] *n* : ineptitud *f*, incompetencia *f*, incapacidad *f*
inequality [ˌɪnɪ'kwɑləti] *n, pl* **-ties** : desigualdad *f*
inert [ɪ'nərt] *adj* **1** INACTIVE : inerte, inactivo **2** SLUGGISH : lento
inertia [ɪ'nərʃə] *n* : inercia *f*
inescapable [ˌɪnɪ'skeɪpəbəl] *adj* : inevitable, ineludible — **inescapably** [-bli] *adv*
inessential [ˌɪnɪ'sɛntʃəl] *adj* : que no es esencial, innecesario
inestimable [ɪn'ɛstəməbəl] *adj* : inestimable, inapreciable

inevitability [ɪnˌɛvət̬əˈbɪlət̬i] *n, pl* **-ties** : inevitabilidad *f*

inevitable [ɪnˈɛvət̬əbəl] *adj* : inevitable — **inevitably** [-bli] *adv*

inexact [ˌɪnɪgˈzækt] *adj* : inexacto

inexactly [ˌɪnɪgˈzæktli] *adv* : sin exactitud

inexcusable [ˌɪnɪkˈskju:zəbəl] *adj* : inexcusable, imperdonable — **inexcusably** [-bli] *adv*

inexhaustible [ˌɪnɪgˈzɔstəbəl] *adj* **1** INDEFATIGABLE : infatigable, incansable **2** ENDLESS : inagotable — **inexhaustibly** [-bli] *adv*

inexorable [ɪnˈɛksərəbəl] *adj* : inexorable — **inexorably** [-bli] *adv*

inexpensive [ˌɪnɪkˈspɛntsɪv] *adj* : barato, económico

inexperience [ˌɪnɪkˈspɪriənts] *n* : inexperiencia *f*

inexperienced [ˌɪnɪkˈspɪriəntst] *adj* : inexperto, novato

inexplicable [ˌɪnɪkˈsplɪkəbəl] *adj* : inexplicable — **inexplicably** [-bli] *adv*

inexpressible [ˌɪnɪkˈsprɛsəbəl] *adj* : inexpresable, inefable

inextricable [ˌɪnɪkˈstrɪkəbəl, ɪˈnɛk-ˌstrɪ-] *adj* : inextricable — **inextricably** [-bli] *adv*

infallibility [ɪnˌfæləˈbɪlət̬i] *n* : infalibilidad *f*

infallible [ɪnˈfæləbəl] *adj* : infalible — **infallibly** [-bli] *adv*

infamous [ˈɪnfəməs] *adj* : infame — **infamously** *adv*

infamy [ˈɪnfəmi] *n, pl* **-mies** : infamia *f*

infancy [ˈɪnfəntsi] *n, pl* **-cies** : infancia *f*

infant [ˈɪnfənt] *n* : bebé *m*; niño *m*, -ña *f*

infantile [ˈɪnfənˌtaɪl, -t̬əl, -ˌti:l] *adj* : infantil, pueril

infantile paralysis → **poliomyelitis**

infantry [ˈɪnfəntri] *n, pl* **-tries** : infantería *f*

infatuated [ɪnˈfætʃuˌeɪt̬əd] *adj* **to be infatuated with** : estar encaprichado con

infatuation [ɪnˌfætʃuˈeɪʃən] *n* : encaprichamiento *m*, enamoramiento *m*

infect [ɪnˈfɛkt] *vt* : infectar, contagiar

infection [ɪnˈfɛkʃən] *n* : infección *f*, contagio *m*

infectious [ɪnˈfɛkʃəs] *adj* : infeccioso, contagioso

infer [ɪnˈfər] *vt* **inferred; inferring 1** DEDUCE : deducir, inferir **2** SURMISE : concluir, suponer, tener entendido **3** IMPLY : sugerir, insinuar

inference [ˈɪnfərənts] *n* : deducción *f*, inferencia *f*, conclusión *f*

inferior¹ [ɪnˈfɪriər] *adj* : inferior, malo

inferior² *n* : inferior *mf*

inferiority [ɪnˌfɪriˈɔrət̬i] *n, pl* **-ties** : inferioridad *f* ⟨inferiority complex : complejo de inferioridad⟩

infernal [ɪnˈfərnəl] *adj* **1** : infernal ⟨infernal fires : fuegos infernales⟩ **2** DIABOLICAL : infernal, diabólico **3** DAMNABLE : maldito, condenado

inferno [ɪnˈfərˌno:] *n, pl* **-nos** : infierno *m*

infertile [ɪnˈfərt̬əl, -ˌtaɪl] *adj* : estéril, infecundo

infertility [ˌɪnfərˈtɪlət̬i] *n* : esterilidad *f*, infecundidad *f*

infest [ɪnˈfɛst] *vt* : infestar, plagar

infestation [ˌɪnˌfɛsˈteɪʃən] *n* : infestación *f*, plaga *f*

infidel [ˈɪnfədəl, -ˌdɛl] *n* : infiel *mf*

infidelity [ˌɪnfəˈdɛlət̬i, -far-] *n, pl* **-ties 1** UNFAITHFULNESS : infidelidad *f* **2** DISLOYALTY : deslealtad *f*

infield [ˈɪnˌfi:ld] *n* : cuadro *m*, diamante *m*

infiltrate [ɪnˈfɪlˌtreɪt, ˈɪnfɪl-] *v* **-trated; -trating** *vt* : infiltrar — *vi* : infiltrarse

infiltration [ˌɪnfɪlˈtreɪʃən] *n* : infiltración *f*

infinite [ˈɪnfənət] *adj* **1** LIMITLESS : infinito, sin límites **2** VAST : infinito, vasto, extenso

infinitely [ˈɪnfənətli] *adv* : infinitamente

infinitesimal [ˌɪnˌfɪnəˈtɛsəməl] *adj* : infinitésimo, infinitesimal — **infinitesimally** *adv*

infinitive [ɪnˈfɪnət̬ɪv] *n* : infinitivo *m*

infinity [ɪnˈfɪnət̬i] *n, pl* **-ties 1** : infinito *m* (en matemáticas, etc.) **2** : infinidad *f* ⟨an infinity of stars : una infinidad de estrellas⟩

infirm [ɪnˈfərm] *adj* **1** FEEBLE : enfermizo, endeble **2** INSECURE : inseguro

infirmary [ɪnˈfərməri] *n, pl* **-ries** : enfermería *f*, hospital *m*

infirmity [ɪnˈfərmət̬i] *n, pl* **-ties 1** FRAILTY : debilidad *f*, endeblez *f* **2** AILMENT : enfermedad *f*, dolencia *f* ⟨the infirmities of age : los achaques de la vejez⟩

inflame [ɪnˈfleɪm] *v* **-flamed; -flaming** *vt* **1** KINDLE : inflamar, encender **2** : inflamar (una herida) **3** STIR UP : encender, provocar, inflamar — *vi* : inflamarse

inflammable [ɪnˈflæməbəl] *adj* **1** FLAMMABLE : inflamable **2** IRASCIBLE : irascible, explosivo

inflammation [ˌɪnfləˈmeɪʃən] *n* : inflamación *f*

inflammatory [ɪnˈflæməˌtori] *adj* : inflamatorio, incendiario

inflatable [ɪnˈfleɪt̬əbəl] *adj* : inflable

inflate [ɪnˈfleɪt] *vt* **-flated; -flating** : inflar, hinchar

inflation [ɪnˈfleɪʃən] *n* : inflación *f*

inflationary [ɪnˈfleɪʃəˌnɛri] *adj* : inflacionario, inflacionista

inflect [ɪnˈflɛkt] *vt* **1** CONJUGATE, DECLINE : conjugar, declinar **2** MODULATE : modular (la voz)

inflection [ɪnˈflɛkʃən] *n* : inflexión *f*

inflexibility [ɪnˌflɛksəˈbɪlət̬i] *n, pl* **-ties** : inflexibilidad *f*

inflexible [ɪnˈflɛksɪbəl] *adj* : inflexible

inflict [ɪnˈflɪkt] *vt* **1** : infligir, causar, imponer **2 to inflict oneself on** : imponer uno su presencia (a alguien)

infliction [ɪnˈflɪkʃən] *n* : imposición *f*

influence · initial

486

influence¹ [ˈɪnˌfluːənts, ɪnˈfluːənts] vt **-enced; -encing** : influenciar, influir en

influence² n 1 : influencia f, influjo m ⟨to exert influence over : ejercer influencia sobre⟩ ⟨the influence of gravity : el influjo de la gravedad⟩ 2 **under the influence** : bajo la influencia del alcohol, embriagado

influential [ˌɪnfluˈɛntʃəl] adj : influyente

influenza [ˌɪnfluˈɛnzə] n : gripe f, influenza f, gripa f Col, Mex

influx [ˈɪnˌflʌks] n : afluencia f (de gente), entrada f (de mercancías), llegada f (de ideas)

inform [ɪnˈfɔrm] vt : informar, notificar, avisar — vi **to inform on** : delatar, denunciar

informal [ɪnˈfɔrməl] adj 1 UNCEREMONIOUS : sin ceremonia, sin etiqueta 2 CASUAL : informal, familiar (dícese del lenguaje) 3 UNOFFICIAL : extraoficial

informality [ˌɪnfɔrˈmæləti, -fər-] n, pl **-ties** : informalidad f, familiaridad f, falta f de ceremonia

informally [ɪnˈfɔrməli] adv : sin ceremonias, de manera informal, informalmente

informant [ɪnˈfɔrmənt] n : informante mf; informador m, -dora f

information [ˌɪnfərˈmeɪʃən] n : información f

informative [ɪnˈfɔrmətɪv] adj : informativo, instructivo

informer [ɪnˈfɔrmər] n : informante mf; informador m, -dora f

infraction [ɪnˈfrækʃən] n : infracción f, violación f, transgresión f

infrared [ˌɪnfrəˈrɛd] adj : infrarrojo

infrastructure [ˈɪnfrəˌstrʌktʃər] n : infraestructura f

infrequent [ɪnˈfriːkwənt] adj : infrecuente, raro

infrequently [ɪnˈfriːkwəntli] adv : raramente, con poca frecuencia

infringe [ɪnˈfrɪndʒ] v **-fringed; -fringing** vt : infringir, violar — vi **to infringe on** : abusar de, violar

infringement [ɪnˈfrɪndʒmənt] n 1 VIOLATION : violación f (de la ley), incumplimiento m (de un contrato) 2 ENCROACHMENT : usurpación f (de derechos, etc.)

infuriate [ɪnˈfjʊriˌeɪt] vt **-ated; -ating** : enfurecer, poner furioso

infuriating [ɪnˈfjʊriˌeɪtɪŋ] adj : indignante, exasperante

infuse [ɪnˈfjuːz] vt **-fused; -fusing** 1 INSTILL : infundir 2 STEEP : hacer una infusión de

infusion [ɪnˈfjuːʒən] n : infusión f

ingenious [ɪnˈdʒiːnjəs] adj : ingenioso — **ingeniously** adv

ingenue or **ingénue** [ˈɑndʒəˌnuː, ˈæn-; ˈæʒə-, ˈɑ-] n : ingenua f

ingenuity [ˌɪndʒəˈnuːəti, -ˈnjuː-] n, pl **-ities** : ingenio

ingenuous [ɪnˈdʒɛnjuəs] adj 1 FRANK : cándido, franco 2 NAIVE : ingenuo — **ingenuously** adv

ingenuousness [ɪnˈdʒɛnjuəsnəs] n 1 FRANKNESS : candidez f, candor m 2 NAÏVETÉ : ingenuidad f

ingest [ɪnˈdʒɛst] vt : ingerir

ingestion [ɪnˈdʒɛstʃən] n : ingestión f

inglorious [ɪnˈgloriəs] adj : deshonroso, ignominioso

ingot [ˈɪŋgət] n : lingote m

ingrained [ɪnˈgreɪnd] adj : arraigado

ingrate [ˈɪnˌgreɪt] n : ingrato m, -ta f

ingratiate [ɪnˈgreɪʃiˌeɪt] vt **-ated; -ating** : conseguir la benevolencia de ⟨to ingratiate oneself with someone : congraciarse con alguien⟩

ingratiating [ɪnˈgreɪʃiˌeɪtɪŋ] adj : halagador, zalamero, obsequioso

ingratitude [ɪnˈgrætəˌtuːd, -ˌtjuːd] n : ingratitud f

ingredient [ɪnˈgriːdiənt] n : ingrediente m, componente m

ingrown [ˈɪnˌgroːn] adj 1 : crecido hacia adentro 2 **ingrown toenail** : uña f encarnada

inhabit [ɪnˈhæbət] vt : vivir en, habitar, ocupar

inhabitable [ɪnˈhæbətəbəl] adj : habitable

inhabitant [ɪnˈhæbətənt] n : habitante mf

inhalant [ɪnˈheɪlənt] n : inhalante m

inhalation [ˌɪnhəˈleɪʃən, ˌɪnə-] n : inhalación f

inhale [ɪnˈheɪl] v **-haled; -haling** vt : inhalar, aspirar — vi : inspirar

inhaler [ɪnˈheɪlər] n : inhalador m

inhere [ɪnˈhɪr] vi **-hered; -hering** : ser inherente

inherent [ɪnˈhɪrənt, -ˈhɛr-] adj : inherente, intrínseco — **inherently** adv

inherit [ɪnˈhɛrət] vt : heredar

inheritance [ɪnˈhɛrətənts] n : herencia f

inheritor [ɪnˈhɛrətər] n : heredero m, -da f

inhibit [ɪnˈhɪbət] vt IMPEDE : inhibir, impedir

inhibition [ˌɪnhəˈbɪʃən, ˌɪnə-] n : inhibición f, cohibición f

inhuman [ɪnˈhjuːmən, -ˈjuː-] adj : inhumano, cruel — **inhumanly** adv

inhumane [ˌɪnhjuˈmeɪn, -ju-] adj INHUMAN : inhumano, cruel

inhumanity [ˌɪnhjuˈmænəti, -ju-] n, pl **-ties** : inhumanidad f, crueldad f

inimical [ɪˈnɪmɪkəl] adj 1 UNFAVORABLE : adverso, desfavorable 2 HOSTILE : hostil — **inimically** adv

inimitable [ɪˈnɪmətəbəl] adj : inimitable

iniquitous [ɪˈnɪkwətəs] adj : inicuo, malvado

iniquity [ɪˈnɪkwəti] n, pl **-ties** : iniquidad f

initial¹ [ɪˈnɪʃəl] vt **-tialed** or **-tialled; -tialing** or **-tialling** : poner las iniciales a, firmar con las iniciales

initial² adj : inicial, primero — **initially** adv

initial³ *n* : inicial *f*

initiate¹ [ɪˈnɪʃiˌeɪt] *vt* **-ated; -ating 1** BE-GIN : comenzar, iniciar **2** INDUCT : instruir **3** INTRODUCE : introducir, instruir

initiate² [ɪˈnɪʃiət] *n* : iniciado *m*, -da *f*

initiation [ɪˌnɪʃiˈeɪʃən] *n* : iniciación *f*

initiative [ɪˈnɪʃətɪv] *n* : iniciativa *f*

initiatory [ɪˈnɪʃiəˌtori] *adj* **1** INTRODUCTORY : introductorio **2** : de iniciación ⟨initiatory rites : ritos de iniciación⟩

inject [ɪnˈdʒɛkt] *vt* : inyectar

injection [ɪnˈdʒɛkʃən] *n* : inyección *f*

injudicious [ˌɪndʒʊˈdɪʃəs] *adj* : imprudente, indiscreto, poco juicioso

injunction [ɪnˈdʒʌŋkʃən] *n* **1** ORDER : orden *f*, mandato *m* **2** COURT ORDER : mandamiento *m* judicial

injure [ˈɪndʒər] *vt* **-jured; -juring 1** WOUND : herir, lesionar **2** HURT : lastimar, dañar, herir **3 to injure oneself** : hacerse daño

injurious [ɪnˈdʒʊriəs] *adj* : perjudicial ⟨injurious to one's health : perjudicial a la salud⟩

injury [ˈɪndʒəri] *n*, *pl* **-ries 1** WRONG : mal *m*, injusticia *f* **2** DAMAGE, HARM : herida *f*, daño *m*, perjuicio *m*

injustice [ɪnˈdʒʌstəs] *n* : injusticia *f*

ink¹ [ˈɪŋk] *vt* : entintar

ink² *n* : tinta *f*

inkling [ˈɪŋklɪŋ] *n* : presentimiento *m*, indicio *m*, sospecha *f*

inkwell [ˈɪŋkˌwɛl] *n* : tintero *m*

inky [ˈɪŋki] *adj* **1** : manchado de tinta **2** BLACK : negro, impenetrable ⟨inky darkness : negra oscuridad⟩

inland¹ [ˈɪnˌlænd, -lənd] *adv* : hacia el interior, tierra adentro

inland² *adj* : interior

inland³ *n* : interior *m*

in–law [ˈɪnˌlɔ] *n* **1** : pariente *m* político **2 in–laws** *npl* : suegros *mpl*

inlay¹ [ɪnˈleɪ, ˈɪnˌleɪ] *vt* **-laid** [-ˈleɪd, -ˌleɪd]; **-laying** : incrustar, taracear

inlay² [ˈɪnˌleɪ] *n* **1** : incrustación *f* **2** : empaste *m* (de un diente)

inlet [ˈɪnˌlɛt, -lət] *n* : cala *f*, ensenada *f*

inmate [ˈɪnˌmeɪt] *n* : paciente *mf* (en un hospital); preso *m*, -sa *f* (en una prisión); interno *m*, -na *f* (en un asilo)

in memoriam [ˌɪnməˈmoriəm] *prep* : en memoria de

inmost [ˈɪnˌmoːst] → **innermost**

inn [ˈɪn] *n* **1** : posada *f*, hostería *f*, fonda *f* **2** TAVERN : taberna *f*

innards [ˈɪnərdz] *npl* : entrañas *fpl*, tripas *fpl fam*

innate [ɪˈneɪt] *adj* **1** INBORN : innato **2** INHERENT : inherente

inner [ˈɪnər] *adj* : interior, interno

innermost [ˈɪnərˌmoːst] *adj* : más íntimo, más profundo

innersole [ˈɪnərˈsoːl] → **insole**

inning [ˈɪnɪŋ] *n* : entrada *f*

innkeeper [ˈɪnˌkiːpər] *n* : posadero *m*, -ra *f*

innocence [ˈɪnəsən*t*s] *n* : inocencia *f*

innocent¹ [ˈɪnəsənt] *adj* : inocente — **innocently** *adv*

innocent² *n* : inocente *mf*

innocuous [ɪˈnɑkjəwəs] *adj* **1** HARMLESS : inocuo **2** INOFFENSIVE : inofensivo

innovate [ˈɪnəˌveɪt] *vi* **-vated; -vating** : innovar

innovation [ˌɪnəˈveɪʃən] *n* : innovación *f*, novedad *f*

innovative [ˈɪnəˌveɪtɪv] *adj* : innovador

innovator [ˈɪnəˌveɪtər] *n* : innovador *m*, -dora *f*

innuendo [ˌɪnjʊˈɛndo] *n*, *pl* **-dos** or **-does** : insinuación *f*, indirecta *f*

innumerable [ɪˈnuːmərəbəl, -ˈnjuː-] *adj* : innumerable

inoculate [ɪˈnɑkjəˌleɪt] *vt* **-lated; -lating** : inocular

inoculation [ɪˌnɑkjəˈleɪʃən] *n* : inoculación *f*

inoffensive [ˌɪnəˈfɛn*t*sɪv] *adj* : inofensivo

inoperable [ɪnˈɑpərəbəl] *adj* : inoperable

inoperative [ɪnˈɑpərətɪv, -ˌreɪ-] *adj* : inoperante

inopportune [ɪnˌɑpərˈtuːn, -ˈtjuːn] *adj* : inoportuno — **inopportunely** *adv*

inordinate [ɪnˈɔrdənət] *adj* : excesivo, inmoderado, desmesurado — **inordinately** *adv*

inorganic [ˌɪnˌɔrˈgænɪk] *adj* : inorgánico

inpatient [ˈɪnˌpeɪʃənt] *n* : paciente *mf* hospitalizado

input¹ [ˈɪnˌpʊt] *vt* **inputted** or **input; inputting** : entrar (datos, información)

input² *n* **1** CONTRIBUTION : aportación *f*, contribución *f* **2** ENTRY : entrada *f* (de datos) **3** ADVICE, OPINION : consejos *mpl*, opinión *f*

inquest [ˈɪnˌkwɛst] *n* INQUIRY, INVESTIGATION : investigación *f*, averiguación *f*, pesquisa *f* (judicial)

inquire [ɪnˈkwaɪr] *v* **-quired; -quiring** *vt* : preguntar, informarse de, inquirir ⟨he inquired how to get in : preguntó como entrar⟩ — *vi* **1** ASK : preguntar, informarse ⟨to inquire about : informarse sobre⟩ ⟨to inquire after (someone) : preguntar por (alguien)⟩ **2 to inquire into** INVESTIGATE : investigar, inquirir sobre

inquiringly [ɪnˈkwaɪrɪŋli] *adv* : inquisitivamente

inquiry [ˈɪnˌkwaɪri, ɪnˈkwaɪri; ˈɪnkwəri, ˈɪŋ-] *n*, *pl* **-ries 1** QUESTION : pregunta *f* ⟨to make inquiries about : pedir información sobre⟩ **2** INVESTIGATION : investigación *f*, inquisición *f*, pesquisa *f*

inquisition [ˌɪnkwəˈzɪʃən, ˌɪŋ-] *n* **1** : inquisición *f*, interrogatorio *m*, investigación *f* **2 the Inquisition** : la Inquisición *f*

inquisitive [ɪnˈkwɪzətɪv] *adj* : inquisidor, inquisitivo, curioso — **inquisitively** *adv*

inquisitiveness [ɪnˈkwɪzətɪvnəs] *n* : curiosidad *f*

inquisitor [ɪnˈkwɪzətər] *n* : inquisidor *m*, -dora *f*; interrogador *m*, -dora *f*

inroad [ˈɪnˌroːd] *n* **1** ENCROACHMENT, INVASION : invasión *f*, incursión *f* **2 to make inroads into** : ocupar parte de (un tiempo), agotar parte de (ahorros, recursos), invadir (un territorio)

insane [ɪnˈseɪn] *adj* **1** MAD : loco, demente ⟨to go insane : volverse loco⟩ **2** ABSURD : absurdo, insensato ⟨an insane scheme : un proyecto insensato⟩

insanely [ɪnˈseɪnli] *adv* : como un loco ⟨insanely suspicious : loco de recelo⟩

insanity [ɪnˈsænəti] *n*, *pl* **-ties 1** MADNESS : locura *f* **2** FOLLY : locura *f*, insensatez *f*

insatiable [ɪnˈseɪʃəbəl] *adj* : insaciable — **insatiably** [-bli] *adv*

inscribe [ɪnˈskraɪb] *vt* **-scribed; -scribing 1** ENGRAVE : inscribir, grabar **2** ENROLL : inscribir **3** DEDICATE : dedicar (un libro)

inscription [ɪnˈskrɪpʃən] *n* : inscripción *f* (en un monumento), dedicación *f* (en un libro), leyenda *f* (de una ilustración, etc.)

inscrutable [ɪnˈskruːt̬əbəl] *adj* : inescrutable, misterioso — **inscrutably** [-bli] *adv*

inseam [ˈɪnˌsiːm] *n* : entrepierna *f*

insect [ˈɪnˌsɛkt] *n* : insecto *m*

insecticidal [ɪnˌsɛktəˈsaɪd̬əl] *adj* : insecticida

insecticide [ɪnˈsɛktəˌsaɪd] *n* : insecticida *m*

insecure [ˌɪnsɪˈkjʊr] *adj* : inseguro, poco seguro — **insecurely** *adv*

insecurely [ˌɪnsɪˈkjʊrli] *adv* : inseguramente

insecurity [ˌɪnsɪˈkjʊrəti] *n*, *pl* **-ties** : inseguridad *f*

inseminate [ɪnˈsɛməˌneɪt] *vt* **-nated; -nating** : inseminar

insemination [ɪnˌsɛməˈneɪʃən] *n* : inseminación *f*

insensibility [ɪnˌsɛntsəˈbɪləti] *n*, *pl* **-ties** : insensibilidad *f*

insensible [ɪnˈsɛntsəbəl] *adj* **1** UNCONSCIOUS : inconsciente, sin conocimiento **2** NUMB : insensible, entumecido **3** UNAWARE : inconsciente

insensitive [ɪnˈsɛntsət̬ɪv] *adj* : insensible

insensitivity [ɪnˌsɛntsəˈtɪvət̬i] *n*, *pl* **-ties** : insensibilidad *f*

inseparable [ɪnˈsɛpərəbəl] *adj* : inseparable

insert¹ [ɪnˈsərt] *vt* **1** : insertar, introducir, poner, meter ⟨insert your key in the lock : mete tu llave en la cerradura⟩ **2** INTERPOLATE : interpolar, intercalar

insert² [ˈɪnˌsərt] *n* : inserción *f*, hoja *f* insertada (en una revista, etc.)

insertion [ɪnˈsərʃən] *n* : inserción *f*

inset [ˈɪnˌsɛt] *n* : página *f* intercalada (en un libro), entredós *m* (de encaje en la ropa)

inshore¹ [ˈɪnˈʃor] *adv* : hacia la costa

inshore² *adj* : cercano a la costa, costero ⟨inshore fishing : pesca costera⟩

inside¹ [ɪnˈsaɪd, ˈɪnˌsaɪd] *adv* : adentro, dentro ⟨to run inside : correr para adentro⟩ ⟨inside and out : por dentro y por fuera⟩

inside² *adj* **1** : interior, de adentro, de dentro ⟨the inside lane : el carril interior⟩ **2** : confidencial ⟨inside information : información confidencial⟩

inside³ *n* **1** : interior *m*, parte *f* de adentro **2 insides** *npl* BELLY, GUTS : tripas *fpl fam* **3 inside out** : al revés

inside⁴ *prep* **1** : al interior de **2** WITHIN : dentro de **3** (*referring to time*) : en menos de ⟨inside an hour : en menos de una hora⟩

inside of *prep* INSIDE : dentro de

insider [ɪnˈsaɪdər] *n* : persona *f* enterada

insidious [ɪnˈsɪdiəs] *adj* : insidioso — **insidiously** *adv*

insidiousness [ɪnˈsɪdiəsnəs] *n* : insidia *f*

insight [ˈɪnˌsaɪt] *n* : perspicacia *f*, penetración *f*

insightful [ɪnˈsaɪtfəl] *adj* : perspicaz

insignia [ɪnˈsɪgniə] *or* **insigne** [-ˌniː] *n*, *pl* **-nia** *or* **-nias** : insignia *f*, enseña *f*

insignificance [ˌɪnsɪgˈnɪfɪkənts] *n* : insignificancia *f*

insignificant [ˌɪnsɪgˈnɪfɪkənt] *adj* : insignificante

insincere [ˌɪnsɪnˈsɪr] *adj* : insincero, poco sincero

insincerely [ˌɪnsɪnˈsɪrli] *adv* : con poca sinceridad

insincerity [ˌɪnsɪnˈsɛrət̬i, -ˈsɪr-] *n*, *pl* **-ties** : insinceridad *f*

insinuate [ɪnˈsɪnjuˌeɪt] *vt* **-ated; -ating** : insinuar

insinuation [ɪnˌsɪnjuˈeɪʃən] *n* : insinuación *f*

insipid [ɪnˈsɪpəd] *adj* : insípido

insist [ɪnˈsɪst] *v* : insistir

insistence [ɪnˈsɪstənts] *n* : insistencia *f*

insistent [ɪnˈsɪstənt] *adj* : insistente — **insistently** *adv*

insofar as [ˌɪnsoˈfɑræz] *conj* : en la medida en que, en tanto que, en cuanto a

insole [ˈɪnˌsoːl] *n* : plantilla *f*

insolence [ˈɪntsələnts] *n* : insolencia *f*

insolent [ˈɪntsələnt] *adj* : insolente

insolubility [ɪnˌsaljuˈbɪləti] *n* : insolubilidad *f*

insoluble [ɪnˈsaljubəl] *adj* : insoluble

insolvency [ɪnˈsalvəntsi] *n*, *pl* **-cies** : insolvencia *f*

insolvent [ɪnˈsalvənt] *adj* : insolvente

insomnia [ɪnˈsamniə] *n* : insomnio *m*

insomuch as [ˌɪnsoˈmʌtʃæz] → **inasmuch as**

insomuch that *conj* SO : así que, de manera que

inspect [ɪnˈspɛkt] *vt* : inspeccionar, examinar, revisar

inspection [ɪnˈspɛkʃən] *n* : inspección *f*, examen *m*, revisión *f*, revista *f* (de tropas)

inspector [ɪn'spɛktər] *n* : inspector *m*, -tora *f*

inspiration [ˌɪntspə'reɪʃən] *n* : inspiración *f*

inspirational [ˌɪntspə'reɪʃənəl] *adj* : inspirador

inspire [ɪn'spaɪr] *v* **-spired; -spiring** *vt* 1 INHALE : inhalar, aspirar 2 STIMULATE : estimular, animar, inspirar 3 INSTILL : inspirar, infundir — *vi* : inspirar

instability [ˌɪntstə'bɪləti] *n, pl* **-ties** : inestabilidad *f*

install [ɪn'stɔl] *vt* **-stalled; -stalling** 1 : instalar ⟨to install the new president : instalar el presidente nuevo⟩ ⟨to install a fan : montar un abanico⟩ 2 to **install oneself** : instalarse

installation [ˌɪntstə'leɪʃən] *n* : instalación *f*

installment [ɪn'stɔlmənt] *n* 1 : plazo *m*, cuota *f* ⟨to pay in four installments : pagar a cuatro plazos⟩ 2 : entrega *f* (de una publicación o telenovela) 3 INSTALLATION : instalación *f*

instance [ˈɪntstənts] *n* 1 INSTIGATION : instancia *f* 2 EXAMPLE : ejemplo *m* ⟨for instance : por ejemplo⟩ 3 OCCASION : instancia *f*, caso *m*, ocasión *f* ⟨he prefers, in this instance, to remain anonymous : en este caso prefiere quedarse anónimo⟩

instant¹ [ˈɪntstənt] *adj* 1 IMMEDIATE : inmediato, instantáneo ⟨an instant reply : una respuesta inmediata⟩ 2 : instantáneo ⟨instant coffee : café instantáneo⟩

instant² *n* : momento *m*, instante *m*

instantaneous [ˌɪntstən'teɪniəs] *adj* : instantáneo

instantaneously [ˌɪntstən'teɪniəsli] *adv* : instantáneamente, al instante

instantly [ˈɪntstəntli] *adv* : al instante, instantáneamente

instead [ɪn'stɛd] *adv* 1 : en cambio, en lugar de eso, en su lugar ⟨Dad was going, but Mom went instead : papá iba a ir, pero mamá fue en su lugar⟩ 2 RATHER : al contrario

instead of *prep* : en vez de, en lugar de

instep [ˈɪnˌstɛp] *n* : empeine *m*

instigate [ˈɪntstəˌgeɪt] *vt* **-gated; -gating** INCITE, PROVOKE : instigar, incitar, provocar, fomentar

instigation [ˌɪntstə'geɪʃən] *n* : instancia *f*, incitación *f*

instigator [ˈɪntstəˌgeɪtər] *n* : instigador *m*, -dora *f*; incitador *m*, -dora *f*

instill [ɪn'stɪl] *vt* **-stilled; -stilling** : inculcar, infundir

instinct [ˈɪnˌstɪŋkt] *n* 1 TALENT : instinto *m*, don *m* ⟨an instinct for the right word : un don para escoger la palabra apropiada⟩ 2 : instinto *m* ⟨maternal instincts : instintos maternales⟩

instinctive [ɪn'stɪŋktɪv] *adj* : instintivo

instinctively [ɪn'stɪŋktɪvli] *adv* : instintivamente, por instinto

instinctual [ɪn'stɪŋktʃuəl] *adj* : instintivo

institute¹ [ˈɪntstəˌtuːt, -ˌtjuːt] *vt* **-tuted; -tuting** 1 ESTABLISH : establecer, instituir, fundar 2 INITIATE : iniciar, empezar, entablar

institute² *n* : instituto *m*

institution [ˌɪntstə'tuːʃən, -'tjuː-] *n* 1 ESTABLISHING : institución *f*, establecimiento *m* 2 CUSTOM : institución *f*, tradición *f* ⟨the institution of marriage : la institución del matrimonio⟩ 3 ORGANIZATION : institución *f*, organismo *m* 4 ASYLUM : asilo *m*

institutional [ˌɪntstə'tuːʃənəl, -'tjuː-] *adj* : institucional

institutionalize [ˌɪntstə'tuːʃənəˌlaɪz, -'tjuː-] *vt* **-ized; -izing** 1 : institucionalizar ⟨institutionalized values : valores institucionalizados⟩ 2 : internar ⟨institutionalized orphans : huérfanos internados⟩

instruct [ɪn'strʌkt] *vt* 1 TEACH, TRAIN : instruir, adiestrar, enseñar 2 COMMAND : mandar, ordenar, dar instrucciones a

instruction [ɪn'strʌkʃən] *n* 1 TEACHING : instrucción *f*, enseñanza *f* 2 COMMAND : orden *f*, instrucción *f* 3 **instructions** *npl* DIRECTIONS : instrucciones *fpl*, modo *m* de empleo

instructional [ɪn'strʌkʃənəl] *adj* : instructivo, educativo

instructive [ɪn'strʌktɪv] *adj* : instructivo

instructor [ɪn'strʌktər] *n* : instructor *m*, -tora *f*

instrument [ˈɪntstrəmənt] *n* : instrumento *m*

instrumental [ˌɪntstrə'mɛntəl] *adj* : instrumental

instrumentalist [ˌɪntstrə'mɛntəlɪst] *n* : instrumentista *mf*

insubordinate [ˌɪnsə'bɔrdənət] *adj* : insubordinado

insubordination [ˌɪnsəˌbɔrdən'eɪʃən] *n* : insubordinación *f*

insubstantial [ˌɪnsəb'stæntʃəl] *adj* : insustancial, poco nutritivo (dícese de una comida), poco sólido (dícese de una estructura o un argumento)

insufferable [ɪn'sʌfərəbəl] *adj* UNBEARABLE : insufrible, intolerable, inaguantable, insoportable — **insufferably** [-bli] *adv*

insufficiency [ˌɪnsə'fɪʃəntsi] *n, pl* **-cies** : insuficiencia *f*

insufficient [ˌɪnsə'fɪʃənt] *adj* : insuficiente — **insufficiently** *adv*

insular [ˈɪntsʊlər, -sjʊ-] *adj* 1 : isleño (dícese de la gente), insular (dícese del clima) ⟨insular residents : residentes de la isla⟩ 2 NARROW-MINDED : de miras estrechas

insularity [ˌɪntsʊ'lærəti, -sjʊ-] *n* : insularidad *f*

insulate [ˈɪntsəˌleɪt] *vt* **-lated; -lating** : aislar

insulation [ˌɪntsə'leɪʃən] *n* : aislamiento *m*

insulator [ˈɪntsəˌleɪtər] *n* : aislador *m* (pieza), aislante *m* (material)

insulin [ˈɪnʦələn] *n* : insulina *f*
insult¹ [ɪnˈsʌlt] *vt* : insultar, ofender, injuriar
insult² [ˈɪnˌsʌlt] *n* : insulto *m*, injuria *f*, agravio *m*
insulting [ɪnˈsʌltɪŋ] *adj* : ofensivo, injurioso, insultante
insultingly [ɪnˈsʌltɪŋli] *adv* : ofensivamente, de manera insultante
insuperable [ɪnˈsuːpərəbəl] *adj* : insuperable — **insuperably** [-bli] *adv*
insurable [ɪnˈʃʊrəbəl] *adj* : asegurable
insurance [ɪnˈʃʊrənʦ, ˈɪnˌʃʊr-] *n* : seguro *m* ⟨life insurance : seguro de vida⟩ ⟨insurance company : compañía de seguros⟩
insure [ɪnˈʃʊr] *vt* **-sured; -suring 1** UNDERWRITE : asegurar **2** ENSURE : asegurar, garantizar
insured [ɪnˈʃʊrd] *n* : asegurado *m*, -da *f*
insurer [ɪnˈʃʊrər] *n* : asegurador *m*, -dora *f*
insurgent¹ [ɪnˈsərʤənt] *adj* : insurgente
insurgent² *n* : insurgente *mf*
insurmountable [ˌɪnsərˈmaʊntəbəl] *adj* : insuperable, insalvable — **insurmountably** [-bli] *adv*
insurrection [ˌɪnsəˈrɛkʃən] *n* : insurrección *f*, levantamiento *m*, alzamiento *m*
intact [ɪnˈtækt] *adj* : intacto
intake [ˈɪnˌteɪk] *n* **1** OPENING : entrada *f*, toma *f* ⟨fuel intake : toma de combustible⟩ **2** : entrada *f* (de agua o aire), consumo *m* (de sustancias nutritivas) **3** intake of breath : inhalación *f*
intangible [ɪnˈtænʤəbəl] *adj* : intangible, impalpable — **intangibly** [-bli] *adv*
integer [ˈɪntɪʤər] *n* : entero *m*
integral [ˈɪntɪɡrəl] *adj* : integral, esencial
integrate [ˈɪntəˌɡreɪt] *v* **-grated; -grating** *vt* **1** UNITE : integrar, unir **2** DESEGREGATE : eliminar la segregación de — *vi* : integrarse
integration [ˌɪntəˈɡreɪʃən] *n* : integración *f*
integrity [ɪnˈtɛɡrəti] *n* : integridad *f*
intellect [ˈɪntəlˌɛkt] *n* : intelecto *m*, inteligencia *f*, capacidad *f* intelectual
intellectual¹ [ˌɪntəˈlɛkʧʊəl] *adj* : intelectual — **intellectually** *adv*
intellectual² *n* : intelectual *mf*
intellectualism [ˌɪntəˈlɛkʧʊəˌlɪzəm] *n* : intelectualismo *m*
intelligence [ɪnˈtɛləʤənʦ] *n* **1** : inteligencia *f* **2** INFORMATION, NEWS : inteligencia *f*, información *f*, noticias *fpl*
intelligent [ɪnˈtɛləʤənt] *adj* : inteligente — **intelligently** *adv*
intelligentsia [ɪnˌtɛləˈʤɛnʦiə, -ˈɡɛn-] *ns & pl* : intelectualidad *f*
intelligibility [ɪnˌtɛləʤəˈbɪləti] *n* : inteligibilidad *f*
intelligible [ɪnˈtɛləʤəbəl] *adj* : inteligible, comprensible — **intelligibly** [-bli] *adv*
intemperance [ɪnˈtɛmpərənʦ] *n* : inmoderación *f*, intemperancia *f*

intemperate [ɪnˈtɛmpərət] *adj* : excesivo, inmoderado, desmedido
intend [ɪnˈtɛnd] *vt* **1** MEAN : querer decir ⟨that's not what I intended : eso no es lo que quería decir⟩ **2** PLAN : planear, proyectar, proponerse ⟨I intend to finish by Thursday : me propongo acabar para el jueves⟩
intended [ɪnˈtɛndəd] *adj* **1** PLANNED : previsto, proyectado **2** INTENTIONAL : intencional, deliberado
intense [ɪnˈtɛnʦ] *adj* **1** EXTREME : intenso, extremo ⟨intense pain : dolor intenso⟩ **2** : profundo, intenso ⟨to my intense relief : para mi alivio profundo⟩ ⟨intense enthusiasm : entusiasmo ardiente⟩
intensely [ɪnˈtɛnʦli] *adv* : sumamente, profundamente, intensamente
intensification [ɪnˌtɛnʦəfəˈkeɪʃən] *n* : intensificación *f*
intensify [ɪnˈtɛnʦəˌfaɪ] *v* **-fied; -fying** *vt* **1** STRENGTHEN : intensificar, redoblar ⟨to intensify one's efforts : redoblar uno sus esfuerzos⟩ **2** SHARPEN : intensificar, agudizar (dolor, ansiedad) — *vi* : intensificarse, hacerse más intenso
intensity [ɪnˈtɛnʦəti] *n*, *pl* **-ties** : intensidad *f*
intensive [ɪnˈtɛnʦɪv] *adj* : intensivo — **intensively** *adv*
intent¹ [ɪnˈtɛnt] *adj* **1** FIXED : concentrado, fijo ⟨an intent stare : una mirada fija⟩ **2 intent on** *or* **intent upon** : resuelto a, atento a
intent² *n* **1** PURPOSE : intención *f*, propósito *m* **2 for all intents and purposes** : a todos los efectos, prácticamente
intention [ɪnˈtɛnʃən] *n* : intención *f*, propósito *m*
intentional [ɪnˈtɛnʃənəl] *adj* : intencional, deliberado
intentionally [ɪnˈtɛnʃənəli] *adv* : a propósito, adrede
intently [ɪnˈtɛntli] *adv* : atentamente, fijamente
inter [ɪnˈtər] *vt* **-terred; -terring** : enterrar, inhumar
interact [ˌɪntərˈækt] *vi* : interactuar, actuar recíprocamente, relacionarse
interaction [ˌɪntərˈækʃən] *n* : interacción *f*, interrelación *f*
interactive [ˌɪntərˈæktɪv] *adj* : interactivo
interbreed [ˌɪntərˈbriːd] *v* **-bred** [-ˈbrɛd]; **-breeding** *vt* : cruzar — *vi* : cruzarse
intercalate [ɪnˈtərkəˌleɪt] *vt* **-lated; -lating** : intercalar
intercede [ˌɪntərˈsiːd] *vi* **-ceded; -ceding** : interceder
intercept [ˌɪntərˈsɛpt] *vt* : interceptar
interception [ˌɪntərˈsɛpʃən] *n* : intercepción *f*
intercession [ˌɪntərˈsɛʃən] *n* : intercesión *f*

interchange[1] [ˌɪntər'tʃeɪndʒ] *vt* **-changed; -changing** : intercambiar
interchange[2] ['ɪntərˌtʃeɪndʒ] *n* **1** EXCHANGE : intercambio *m*, cambio *m* **2** JUNCTION : empalme *m*, enlace *m* de carreteras
interchangeable [ˌɪntər'tʃeɪndʒəbəl] *adj* : intercambiable
intercity ['ɪntər'sɪti] *adj* : interurbano
intercollegiate [ˌɪntərkə'li:dʒət, -dʒiət] *adj* : interuniversitario
interconnect [ˌɪntərkə'nɛkt] *vt* **1** : conectar, interconectar (en tecnología) **2** RELATE : interrelacionar — *vi* **1** : conectar **2** : interrelacionarse
intercontinental [ˌɪntərˌkɑntən'nɛtəl] *adj* : intercontinental
intercourse ['ɪntərˌkors] *n* **1** RELATIONS : relaciones *fpl*, trato *m* **2** COPULATION : acto *m* sexual, relaciones *fpl* sexuales, coito *m*
interdenominational [ˌɪntərdɪˌnɑmə'neɪʃənəl] *adj* : interconfesional
interdepartmental [ˌɪntərdɪˌpɑrt'mɛntəl, -ˌdi:-] *adj* : interdepartamental
interdependence [ˌɪntərdɪ'pɛndənts] *n* : interdependencia *f*
interdependent [ˌɪntərdɪ'pɛndənt] *adj* : interdependiente
interdict [ˌɪntər'dɪkt] *vt* **1** PROHIBIT : prohibir **2** : cortar (las líneas de comunicación o provisión del enemigo)
interest[1] ['ɪntrəst, -təˌrɛst] *vt* : interesar
interest[2] *n* **1** SHARE, STAKE : interés *m*, participación *f* **2** BENEFIT : provecho *m*, beneficio *m*, interés *m* ⟨in the public interest : en el interés público⟩ **3** CHARGE : interés *m*, cargo *m* ⟨compound interest : interés compuesto⟩ **4** CURIOSITY : interés *m*, curiosidad *f* **5** COLOR : color *m*, interés *m* ⟨places of local interest : lugares de color local⟩ **6** HOBBY : afición *f*
interesting ['ɪntrəstɪŋ, -təˌrɛstɪŋ] *adj* : interesante — **interestingly** *adv*
interface ['ɪntərˌfeɪs] *n* **1** : punto *m* de contacto ⟨oil-water interface : punto de contacto entre el agua y el aceite⟩ **2** : interfaz *f* (de una computadora), interfase *f*
interfere [ˌɪntər'fɪr] *vi* **-fered; -fering 1** INTERPOSE : interponerse, hacer interferencia ⟨to interfere with a play : obstruir una jugada⟩ **2** MEDDLE : entrometerse, interferir, intervenir **3 to interfere with** DISRUPT : afectar (una actividad), interferir (la radiotransmisión) **4 to interfere with** TOUCH : tocar ⟨someone interfered with my papers : alguien tocó mis papeles⟩
interference [ˌɪntər'fɪrənts] *n* : interferencia *f*, intromisión *f*
intergalactic [ˌɪntərgə'læktɪk] *adj* : intergaláctico
intergovernmental [ˌɪntərˌgʌvər-'mɛntəl, -vərn-] *adj* : intergubernamental
interim[1] ['ɪntərəm] *adj* : interino, provisional

interim[2] *n* **1** : interín *m*, intervalo *m* **2 in the interim** : en el interín, mientras tanto
interior[1] [ɪn'tɪriər] *adj* : interior
interior[2] *n* : interior *m*
interject [ˌɪntər'dʒɛkt] *vt* : interponer, agregar
interjection [ˌɪntər'dʒɛkʃən] *n* **1** : interjección *f* (en lingüística) **2** EXCLAMATION : exclamación *f* **3** INTERPOSITION, INTERRUPTION : interposición *f*, interrupción *f*
interlace [ˌɪntər'leɪs] *vt* **-laced; -lacing 1** INTERWEAVE : entrelazar **2** INTERSPERSE : intercalar
interlock [ˌɪntər'lɑk] *vt* **1** UNITE : trabar, unir **2** ENGAGE, MESH : engranar — *vi* : entrelazarse, trabarse
interloper [ˌɪntər'lo:pər] *n* **1** INTRUDER : intruso *m*, -sa *f* **2** MEDDLER : entrometido *m*, -da *f*
interlude ['ɪntərˌlu:d] *n* **1** INTERVAL : intervalo *m*, intermedio *m* (en el teatro) **2** : interludio *m* (en música)
intermarriage [ˌɪntər'mærɪdʒ] *n* **1** : matrimonio *m* mixto (entre miembros de distintas razas o religiones) **2** : matrimonio *m* entre miembros del mismo grupo
intermarry [ˌɪntər'mæri] *vi* **-married; -marrying 1** : casarse (con miembros de otros grupos) **2** : casarse entre sí (con miembros del mismo grupo)
intermediary[1] [ˌɪntər'mi:diˌɛri] *adj* : intermediario
intermediary[2] *n*, *pl* **-aries** : intermediario *m*, -ria *f*
intermediate[1] [ˌɪntər'mi:diət] *adj* : intermedio
intermediate[2] *n* GO-BETWEEN : intermediario *m*, -ria *f*; mediador *m*, -dora *f*
interment [ɪn'tərmənt] *n* : entierro *m*
interminable [ɪn'tərmənəbəl] *adj* : interminable, constante — **interminably** [-bli] *adv*
intermingle [ˌɪntər'mɪŋgəl] *vt* **-mingled; -mingling** : entremezclar, mezclar — *vi* : entremezclarse
intermission [ˌɪntər'mɪʃən] *n* : intermisión *f*, intervalo *m*, intermedio *m*
intermittent [ˌɪntər'mɪtənt] *adj* : intermitente — **intermittently** *adv*
intermix [ˌɪntər'mɪks] *vt* : entremezclar
intern[1] ['ɪnˌtərn, ɪn'tərn] *vt* : confinar (durante la guerra) — *vi* : servir de interno, hacer las prácticas
intern[2] ['ɪnˌtərn] *n* : interno *m*, -na *f*
internal [ɪn'tərnəl] *adj* : interno, interior ⟨internal bleeding : hemorragia interna⟩ ⟨internal affairs : asuntos interiores, asuntos domésticos⟩ — **internally** *adv*
international [ˌɪntər'næʃənəl] *adj* : internacional — **internationally** *adv*
internationalize [ˌɪntər'næʃənəˌlaɪz] *vt* **-ized; -izing** : internacionalizar
internee [ˌɪnˌtər'ni:] *n* : interno *m*, -na *f*
Internet ['ɪntərˌnɛt] *n* : Internet *mf*

internist ['ɪn,tərnɪst] *n* : internista *mf*
interpersonal [,ɪntər'pərsənəl] *adj* : interpersonal
interplay ['ɪntər,pleɪ] *n* : interacción *f*, juego *m*
interpolate [ɪn'tərpə,leɪt] *vt* **-lated; -lating** : interpolar
interpose [,ɪntər'po:z] *v* **-posed; -posing** *vt* : interponer, interrumpir con — *vi* : interponerse
interposition [,ɪntərpə'zɪʃən] *n* : interposición *f*
interpret [ɪn'tərprət] *vt* : interpretar
interpretation [ɪn,tərprə'teɪʃən] *n* : interpretación *f*
interpretative [ɪn'tərprə,teɪtɪv] *adj* : interpretativo
interpreter [ɪn'tərprətər] *n* : intérprete *mf*
interpretive [ɪn'tərprətɪv] *adj* : interpretativo
interracial [,ɪntər'reɪʃəl] *adj* : interracial
interrelate [,ɪntərɪ'leɪt] *v* **-related; -relating** : interrelacionar
interrelationship [,ɪntərɪ'leɪʃən,ʃɪp] *n* : interrelación *f*
interrogate [ɪn'terə,geɪt] *vt* **-gated; -gating** : interrogar, someter a un interrogatorio
interrogation [ɪn,terə'geɪʃən] *n* : interrogación *f*
interrogative[1] [,ɪntə'ragətɪv] *adj* : interrogativo
interrogative[2] *n* : interrogativo *m*
interrogator [ɪn'terə,geɪtər] *n* : interrogador *m*, -dora *f*
interrogatory [,ɪntə'ragə,tɔri] *adj* → **interrogative**[1]
interrupt [,ɪntə'rʌpt] *v* : interrumpir
interruption [,ɪntə'rʌpʃən] *n* : interrupción *f*
intersect [,ɪntər'sɛkt] *vt* : cruzar, cortar — *vi* : cruzarse (dícese de los caminos), intersectarse (dícese de las líneas o figuras), cortarse
intersection [,ɪntər'sɛkʃən] *n* : intersección *f*, cruce *m*
intersperse [,ɪntər'spərs] *vt* **-spersed; -spersing** : intercalar, entremezclar
interstate [,ɪntər'steɪt] *adj* : interestatal
interstellar [,ɪntər'stɛlər] *adj* : interestelar
interstice [ɪn'tərstəs] *n, pl* **-stices** [-stə,si:z, -stəsəz] : intersticio *m*
intertwine [,ɪntər'twaɪn] *vi* **-twined; -twining** : entrelazarse
interval ['ɪntərvəl] *n* : intervalo *m*
intervene [,ɪntər'vi:n] *vi* **-vened; -vening** **1** ELAPSE : transcurrir, pasar ⟨the intervening years : los años intermediarios⟩ **2** INTERCEDE : intervenir, interceder, mediar
intervention [,ɪntər'vɛntʃən] *n* : intervención *f*
interview[1] ['ɪntər,vju:] *vt* : entrevistar — *vi* : hacer entrevistas
interview[2] *n* : entrevista *f*
interviewer ['ɪntər,vju:ər] *n* : entrevistador *m*, -dora *f*

interweave [,ɪntər'wi:v] *v* **-wove** [-'wo:v]; **-woven** [-'wo:vən]; **-weaving** *vt* : entretejer, entrelazar — *vi* INTERTWINE : entrelazarse, entretejerse
interwoven [,ɪntər'wo:vən] *adj* : entretejido
intestate [ɪn'tɛs,teɪt, -tət] *adj* : intestado
intestinal [ɪn'tɛstənəl] *adj* : intestinal
intestine [ɪn'tɛstən] *n* **1** : intestino *m* **2 small intestine** : intestino *m* delgado **3 large intestine** : intestino *m* grueso
intimacy ['ɪntəməsi] *n, pl* **-cies 1** CLOSENESS : intimidad *f* **2** FAMILIARITY : familiaridad *f*
intimate[1] ['ɪntə,meɪt] *vt* **-mated; -mating** : insinuar, dar a entender
intimate[2] ['ɪntəmət] *adj* **1** CLOSE : íntimo, de confianza ⟨intimate friends : amigos íntimos⟩ **2** PRIVATE : íntimo, privado ⟨intimate clubs : clubes íntimos⟩ **3** INNERMOST, SECRET : íntimo, secreto ⟨intimate fantasies : fantasías secretas⟩
intimate[3] *n* : amigo *m* íntimo, amiga *f* íntima
intimidate [ɪn'tɪmə,deɪt] *vt* **-dated; -dating** : intimidar
intimidation [ɪn,tɪmə'deɪʃən] *n* : intimidación *f*
into ['ɪn,tu:] *prep* **1** (*indicating motion*) : en, a, contra, dentro de ⟨she got into bed : se metió en la cama⟩ ⟨to get into a plane : subir a un avión⟩ ⟨he crashed into the wall : chocó contra la pared⟩ ⟨looking into the sun : mirando al sol⟩ **2** (*indicating state or condition*) : a, en ⟨to burst into tears : echarse a llorar⟩ ⟨the water turned into ice : el agua se convirtió en hielo⟩ ⟨to translate into English : traducir al inglés⟩ **3** (*indicating time*) ⟨far into the night : hasta bien entrada la noche⟩ ⟨he's well into his eighties : tiene los ochenta bien cumplidos⟩ **4** (*in mathematics*) ⟨3 into 12 is 4 : 12 dividido por 3 es 4⟩
intolerable [ɪn'tɑlərəbəl] *adj* : intolerable — **intolerably** [-bli] *adv*
intolerance [ɪn'tɑlərənts] *n* : intolerancia *f*
intolerant [ɪn'tɑlərənt] *adj* : intolerante
intonation [,ɪntoʊ'neɪʃən] *n* : entonación *f*
intone [ɪn'to:n] *vt* **-toned; -toning** : entonar
intoxicant [ɪn'tɑksɪkənt] *n* : bebida *f* alcohólica
intoxicate [ɪn'tɑksə,keɪt] *vt* **-cated; -cating** : emborrachar, embriagar
intoxicated [ɪn'tɑksə,keɪtəd] *adj* : borracho, embriagado
intoxicating [ɪn'tɑksə,keɪtɪŋ] *adj* : embriagador
intoxication [ɪn,tɑksə'keɪʃən] *n* : embriaguez *f*
intractable [ɪn'træktəbəl] *adj* : obstinado, intratable
intramural [,ɪntrə'mjʊrəl] *adj* : interno, dentro de la universidad

intransigence [ɪnˈtrænt͡sədʒənt͡s, -ˈtrænzə-] *n* : intransigencia *f*

intransigent [ɪnˈtrænt͡sədʒənt, -ˈtrænzə-] *adj* : intransigente

intransitive [ɪnˈtrænt͡sətɪv, -ˈtrænzə-] *adj* : intransitivo

intravenous [ˌɪntrəˈviːnəs] *adj* : intravenoso — **intravenously** *adv*

intrepid [ɪnˈtrɛpəd] *adj* : intrépido

intricacy [ˈɪntrɪkəsi] *n, pl* **-cies** : complejidad *f*, lo intrincado

intricate [ˈɪntrɪkət] *adj* : intrincado, complicado — **intricately** *adv*

intrigue¹ [ɪnˈtriːg] *v* **-trigued; -triguing** : intrigar

intrigue² [ˈɪnˌtriːg, ɪnˈtriːg] *n* : intriga *f*

intriguing [ɪnˈtriːgɪŋ] *adj* : intrigante, fascinante

intrinsic [ɪnˈtrɪnzɪk, -ˈtrɪnt͡sɪk] *adj* : intrínseco, esencial — **intrinsically** [-zɪkli, -sɪ-] *adv*

introduce [ˌɪntrəˈduːs, -ˈdjuːs] *vt* **-duced; -ducing 1** : presentar ⟨let me introduce my father : permítame presentar a mi padre⟩ **2** : introducir (algo nuevo), lanzar (un producto), presentar (una ley), proponer (una idea o un tema)

introduction [ˌɪntrəˈdʌkʃən] *n* : introducción *f*, presentación *f*

introductory [ˌɪntrəˈdʌktəri] *adj* : introductorio, preliminar, de introducción

introspection [ˌɪntrəˈspɛkʃən] *n* : introspección *f*

introspective [ˌɪntrəˈspɛktɪv] *adj* : introspectivo — **introspectively** *adv*

introvert [ˈɪntrəˌvərt] *n* : introvertido *m*, -da *f*

introverted [ˈɪntrəˌvərtəd] *adj* : introvertido

intrude [ɪnˈtruːd] *v* **-truded; -truding** *vi* **1** INTERFERE : inmiscuirse, entrometerse **2** DISTURB, INTERRUPT : molestar, estorbar, interrumpir — *vt* : introducir por fuerza

intruder [ɪnˈtruːdər] *n* : intruso *m*, -sa *f*

intrusion [ɪnˈtruːʒən] *n* : intrusión *f*

intrusive [ɪnˈtruːsɪv] *adj* : intruso

intuit [ɪnˈtuːɪt, -ˈtjuː-] *vt* : intuir

intuition [ˌɪntuˈɪʃən, -tjʊ-] *n* : intuición *f*

intuitive [ɪnˈtuːətɪv, -ˈtjuː-] *adj* : intuitivo — **intuitively** *adv*

inundate [ˈɪnənˌdeɪt] *vt* **-dated; -dating** : inundar

inundation [ˌɪnənˈdeɪʃən] *n* : inundación *f*

inure [ɪˈnʊr, -ˈnjʊr] *vt* **-ured; -uring** : acostumbrar, habituar

invade [ɪnˈveɪd] *vt* **-vaded; -vading** : invadir

invader [ɪnˈveɪdər] *n* : invasor *m*, -sora *f*

invalid¹ [ɪnˈvæləd] *adj* : inválido, nulo

invalid² [ˈɪnvələd] *adj* : inválido, discapacitado

invalid³ [ˈɪnvələd] *n* : inválido *m*, -da *f*

invalidate [ɪnˈvæləˌdeɪt] *vt* **-dated; -dating** : invalidar

invalidity [ˌɪnvəˈlɪdəti] *n, pl* **-ties** : invalidez *f*, falta de validez *f*

invaluable [ɪnˈvæljəbəl, -ˈvæljʊə-] *adj* : invalorable, inestimable, inapreciable

invariable [ɪnˈværiəbəl] *adj* : invariable, constante — **invariably** [-bli] *adv*

invasion [ɪnˈveɪʒən] *n* : invasión *f*

invasive [ɪnˈveɪsɪv] *adj* : invasivo

invective [ɪnˈvɛktɪv] *n* : invectiva *f*, improperio *m*, vituperio *m*

inveigh [ɪnˈveɪ] *vi* **to inveigh against** : arremeter contra, lanzar invectivas contra

inveigle [ɪnˈveɪgəl, -ˈviː-] *vt* **-gled; -gling** : engatusar, embaucar, persuadir con engaños

invent [ɪnˈvɛnt] *vt* : inventar

invention [ɪnˈvɛntʃən] *n* : invención *f*, invento *m*

inventive [ɪnˈvɛntɪv] *adj* : inventivo

inventiveness [ɪnˈvɛntɪvnəs] *n* : ingenio *m*, inventiva *f*

inventor [ɪnˈvɛntər] *n* : inventor *m*, -tora *f*

inventory¹ [ˈɪnvənˌtɔri] *vt* **-ried; -rying** : inventariar

inventory² *n, pl* **-ries 1** LIST : inventario *m* **2** STOCK : existencias *fpl*

inverse¹ [ɪnˈvərs, ˈɪnˌvərs] *adj* : inverso — **inversely** *adv*

inverse² *n* : inverso *m*

inversion [ɪnˈvərʒən] *n* : inversión *f*

invert [ɪnˈvərt] *vt* : invertir

invertebrate¹ [ɪnˈvərtəbrət, -ˌbreɪt] *adj* : invertebrado

invertebrate² *n* : invertebrado *m*

invest [ɪnˈvɛst] *vt* **1** AUTHORIZE : investir, autorizar **2** CONFER : conferir **3** : invertir, dedicar ⟨he invested his savings in stocks : invirtió sus ahorros en acciones⟩ ⟨to invest one's time : dedicar uno su tiempo⟩

investigate [ɪnˈvɛstəˌgeɪt] *v* **-gated; -gating** : investigar

investigation [ɪnˌvɛstəˈgeɪʃən] *n* : investigación *f*, estudio *m*

investigative [ɪnˈvɛstəˌgeɪtɪv] *adj* : investigador

investigator [ɪnˈvɛstəˌgeɪtər] *n* : investigador *m*, -dora *f*

investiture [ɪnˈvɛstəˌt͡ʃʊr, -t͡ʃər] *n* : investidura *f*

investment [ɪnˈvɛstmənt] *n* : inversión *f*

investor [ɪnˈvɛstər] *n* : inversor *m*, -sora *f*; inversionista *mf*

inveterate [ɪnˈvɛtərət] *adj* **1** DEEP-SEATED : inveterado, enraizado **2** HABITUAL : empedernido, incorregible

invidious [ɪnˈvɪdiəs] *adj* **1** OBNOXIOUS : repugnante, odioso **2** UNJUST : injusto — **invidiously** *adv*

invigorate [ɪnˈvɪgəˌreɪt] *vt* **-rated; -rating** : vigorizar, animar

invigorating [ɪnˈvɪgəˌreɪtɪŋ] *adj* : vigorizante, estimulante

invigoration [ɪnˌvɪgəˈreɪʃən] *n* : animación *f*

invincibility [ɪnˌvɪnt͡səˈbɪləti] *n* : invencibilidad *f*

invincible [ɪn'vɪntsəbəl] *adj* : invencible — **invincibly** [-bli] *adv*
inviolable [ɪn'vaɪələbəl] *adj* : inviolable
inviolate [ɪn'vaɪələt] *adj* : inviolado, puro
invisibility [ɪn,vɪzə'bɪləṭi] *n* : invisibilidad *f*
invisible [ɪn'vɪzəbəl] *adj* : invisible — **invisibly** [-bli] *adv*
invitation [,ɪnvə'teɪʃən] *n* : invitación *f*
invite [ɪn'vaɪt] *vt* **-vited; -viting 1** ATTRACT : atraer, tentar ⟨a book that invites interest : un libro que atrae el interés⟩ **2** PROVOKE : provocar, buscar ⟨to invite trouble : buscarse problemas⟩ **3** ASK : invitar ⟨we invited them for dinner : los invitamos acenar⟩ **4** SOLICIT : solicitar, buscar (preguntas, comentarios, etc.)
inviting [ɪn'vaɪṭɪŋ] *adj* : atractivo, atrayente
invocation [,ɪnvə'keɪʃən] *n* : invocación *f*
invoice[1] ['ɪn,vɔɪs] *vt* **-voiced; -voicing** : facturar
invoice[2] *n* : factura *f*
invoke [ɪn'voːk] *vt* **-voked; -voking 1** : invocar, apelar a ⟨she invoked our aid : apeló a nuestra ayuda⟩ **2** CITE : invocar, citar ⟨to invoke a precedent : invocar un precedente⟩ **3** CONJURE UP : hacer aparecer, invocar
involuntary [ɪn'vɑlən,teri] *adj* : involuntario — **involuntarily** [ɪn-,vɑlən'trəli] *adv*
involve [ɪn'vɑlv] *vt* **-volved; -volving 1** ENGAGE : ocupar (con una tarea, etc.) **2** IMPLICATE : involucrar, enredar, implicar ⟨to be involved in a crime : estar involucrado en un crimen⟩ **3** CONCERN : concernir, afectar **4** CONNECT : conectar, relacionar **5** ENTAIL, INCLUDE : suponer, incluir, consistir en ⟨what does the job involve? : ¿en qué consiste el trabajo?⟩ **6 to be involved with someone** : tener una relación (amorosa) con alguien
involved [ɪn'vɑlvd] *adj* **1** COMPLEX, INTRICATE : complicado, complejo **2** CONCERNED : interesado, afectado
involvement [ɪn'vɑlvmənt] *n* **1** PARTICIPATION : participación *f*, complicidad *f* **2** RELATIONSHIP : relación *f*
invulnerable [ɪn'vʌlnərəbəl] *adj* : invulnerable
inward[1] ['ɪnwərd] *or* **inwards** [-wərdz] *adv* : hacia adentro, hacia el interior
inward[2] *adj* INSIDE : interior, interno
inwardly ['ɪnwərdli] *adv* **1** MENTALLY, SPIRITUALLY : por dentro **2** INTERNALLY : internamente, interiormente **3** PRIVATELY : para sus adentros, para sí
iodide ['aɪə,daɪd] *n* : yoduro *m*
iodine ['aɪə,daɪn, -dən] *n* : yodo *m*, tintura *f* de yodo
iodize ['aɪə,daɪz] *vt* **-dized; -dizing** : yodar

ion ['aɪən, 'aɪ,ɑn] *n* : ion *m*
ionic [aɪ'ɑnɪk] *adj* : iónico
ionize ['aɪə,naɪz] *v* **ionized; ionizing** : ionizar
ionosphere [aɪ'ɑnə,sfɪr] *n* : ionosfera *f*
iota [aɪ'oːṭə] *n* : pizca *f*, ápice *m*
IOU [,aɪ,oʻju:] *n* : pagaré *m*, vale *m*
IPA [,aɪ,pi:'eɪ] *n* International Phonetic Alphabet : AFI *m*
IQ [,aɪ'kju:] *n* (intelligence quotient) : CI *m*, coeficiente *m* intelectual
Iranian [ɪ'reɪniən, -'ræ-, -'rɑ-; aɪ'-] *n* : iraní *mf* — **Iranian** *adj*
Iraqi [ɪ'rɑki:] *n* : iraquí *mf* — **Iraqi** *adj*
irascibility [ɪ,ræsə'bɪləṭi] *n* : irascibilidad *f*
irascible [ɪ'ræsəbəl] *adj* : irascible
irate [aɪ'reɪt] *adj* : furioso, airado, iracundo — **irately** *adv*
ire ['aɪr] *n* : ira *f*, cólera *f*
iridescence [,ɪrə'dɛsənts] *n* : iridiscencia *f*
iridescent [,ɪrə'dɛsənt] *adj* : iridiscente
iridium [ɪ'rɪdiəm] *n* : iridio *m*
iris ['aɪrəs] *n, pl* **irises** *or* **irides** ['aɪrə,di:z, 'ɪr-] **1** : iris *m* (del ojo) **2** : lirio *m* (planta)
Irish[1] ['aɪrɪʃ] *adj* : irlandés
Irish[2] **1** : irlandés *m* (idioma) **2 the Irish** *npl* : los irlandeses
Irishman ['aɪrɪʃmən] *n, pl* **-men** : irlandés *m*
Irishwoman ['aɪrɪʃ,wumən] *n, pl* **-women** : irlandesa *f*
irk ['ərk] *vt* : fastidiar, irritar, preocupar
irksome ['ərksəm] *adj* : irritante, fastidioso — **irksomely** *adv*
iron[1] ['aɪərn] *v* : planchar
iron[2] *n* **1** : hierro *m*, fierro *m* ⟨a will of iron : una voluntad de hierro, una voluntad férrea⟩ **2** : plancha *f* (para planchar la ropa)
ironclad ['aɪərn'klæd] *adj* **1** : acorazado, blindado **2** STRICT : riguroso, estricto
ironic [aɪ'rɑnɪk] *or* **ironical** [-nɪkəl] *adj* : irónico — **ironically** [-kli] *adv*
ironing ['aɪərnɪŋ] *n* **1** PRESSING : planchada *f* **2** : ropa *f* para planchar
ironing board *n* : tabla *f* (de planchar)
ironwork ['aɪərn,wərk] *n* **1** : obra *f* de hierro **2 ironworks** *npl* : fundición *f*
ironworker ['aɪərn,wərkər] *n* : fundidor *m*, -dora *f*
irony ['aɪrəni] *n, pl* **-nies** : ironía *f*
irradiate [ɪ'reɪdi,eɪt] *vt* **-ated; -ating** : irradiar, radiar
irradiation [ɪ,reɪdi'eɪʃən] *n* : irradiación *f*, radiación *f*
irrational [ɪ'ræʃənəl] *adj* : irracional — **irrationally** *adv*
irrationality [ɪ,ræʃə'næləṭi] *n, pl* **-ties** : irracionalidad *f*
irreconcilable [ɪ,rɛkən'saɪləbəl] *adj* : irreconciliable
irrecoverable [,ɪrɪ'kʌvərəbəl] *adj* : irrecuperable — **irrecoverably** [-bli] *adv*

irredeemable [ˌɪrɪ'di:məbəl] *adj* **1** : irredimible (dícese de un bono) **2** HOPELESS : irremediable, irreparable

irreducible [ˌɪrɪ'du:səbəl, -'dju:-] *adj* : irreducible — **irreducibly** [-bli] *adv*

irrefutable [ˌɪrɪ'fju:təbəl, ɪr'rɛfjə-] *adj* : irrefutable

irregular¹ [ɪ'rɛgjələr] *adj* : irregular — **irregularly** *adv*

irregular² *n* **1** : soldado *m* irregular **2 irregulars** *npl* : artículos *mpl* defectuosos

irregularity [ɪˌrɛgjə'lærəti] *n, pl* **-ties** : irregularidad *f*

irrelevance [ɪ'rɛləvənts] *n* : irrelevancia *f*

irrelevant [ɪ'rɛləvənt] *adj* : irrelevante

irreligious [ˌɪrɪ'lɪʤəs] *adj* : irreligioso

irreparable [ɪ'rɛpərəbəl] *adj* : irreparable

irreplaceable [ˌɪrɪ'pleɪsəbəl] *adj* : irreemplazable, insustituible

irrepressible [ˌɪrɪ'prɛsəbəl] *adj* : incontenible, incontrolable

irreproachable [ɪr'pro:ʧəbəl] *adj* : irreprochable, intachable

irresistible [ˌɪrɪ'zɪstəbəl] *adj* : irresistible — **irresistibly** [-bli] *adv*

irresolute [ɪ'rɛzəˌlu:t] *adj* : irresoluto, indeciso

irresolutely [ɪ'rɛzəˌlu:tli, -ˌrzə'lu:t-] *adv* : de manera indecisa

irresolution [ɪˌrɛzə'lu:ʃən] *n* : irresolución *f*

irrespective of [ˌɪrɪ'spɛktɪvəv] *prep* : sin tomar en consideración, sin tener en cuenta

irresponsibility [ˌɪrɪˌspanⁿsə'bɪləti] *n, pl* **-ties** : irresponsabilidad *f*, falta *f* de responsabilidad

irresponsible [ˌɪrɪ'spanⁿsəbəl] *adj* : irresponsable — **irresponsibly** [-bli] *adv*

irretrievable [ˌɪrɪ'tri:vəbəl] *adj* : IRRECOVERABLE : irrecuperable

irreverence [ɪ'rɛvərənts] *n* : irreverencia *f*, falta *f* de respeto

irreverent [ɪ'rɛvərənt] *adj* : irreverente, irrespetuoso

irreversible [ˌɪrɪ'vərsəbəl] *adj* : irreversible

irrevocable [ɪ'rɛvəkəbəl] *adj* : irrevocable — **irrevocably** [-bli] *adv*

irrigate [ˈɪrəˌgeɪt] *vt* **-gated; -gating** : irrigar, regar

irrigation [ˌɪrə'geɪʃən] *n* : irrigación *f*, riego *m*

irritability [ˌɪrətə'bɪləti] *n, pl* **-ties** : irritabilidad *f*

irritable [ˈɪrətəbəl] *adj* : irritable, colérico

irritably [ˈɪrətəbli] *adv* : con irritación

irritant¹ [ˈɪrətənt] *adj* : irritante

irritant² *n* : agente *m* irritante

irritate [ˈɪrəˌteɪt] *vt* **-tated; -tating 1** ANNOY : irritar, molestar **2** : irritar (en medicina)

irritating [ˈɪrəˌteɪtɪŋ] *adj* : irritante

irritatingly [ˈɪrəˌteɪtɪŋli] *adv* : de modo irritante, fastidiosamente

irritation [ˌɪrə'teɪʃən] *n* : irritación *f*

is → **be**

Islam [ɪs'lɑm, ɪz-, -'læm; 'ɪsˌlɑm, 'ɪz-, -ˌlæm] *n* : el Islam

Islamic [ɪs'lɑmɪk, ɪz-, -'læ-] *adj* : islámico

island [ˈaɪlənd] *n* : isla *f*

islander [ˈaɪləndər] *n* : isleño *m*, -ña *f*

isle [ˈaɪl] *n* : isla *f*, islote *m*

islet [ˈaɪlət] *n* : islote *m*

isolate [ˈaɪsəˌleɪt] *vt* **-lated; -lating** : aislar

isolated [ˈaɪsəˌleɪtəd] *adj* : aislado, solo

isolation [ˌaɪsə'leɪʃən] *n* : aislamiento *m*

isometric [ˌaɪsə'mɛtrɪk] *adj* : isométrico

isometrics [ˌaɪsə'mɛtrɪks] *ns & pl* : isometría *f*

isosceles [aɪ'sɑsəˌli:z] *adj* : isósceles

isotope [ˈaɪsəˌto:p] *n* : isótopo *m*

Israeli [ɪz'reɪli] *n* : israelí *mf* — **Israeli** *adj*

issue¹ [ˈɪˌʃu:] *v* **-sued; -suing** *vi* **1** EMERGE : emerger, salir, fluir **2** DESCEND : descender (dícese de los padres o antepasados específicos) **3** EMANATE, RESULT : emanar, surgir, resultar — *vt* **1** EMIT : emitir **2** DISTRIBUTE : emitir, distribuir ⟨to issue a new stamp : emitir un sello nuevo⟩ **3** PUBLISH : publicar

issue² *n* **1** EMERGENCE, FLOW : emergencia *f*, flujo *m* **2** PROGENY : descendencia *f*, progenie *f* **3** OUTCOME, RESULT : desenlace *m*, resultado *m*, consecuencia *f* **4** MATTER, QUESTION : asunto *m*, cuestión *f* **5** PUBLICATION : publicación *f*, distribución *f*, emisión *f* **6** : número *m* (de un periódico o una revista)

isthmus [ˈɪsməs] *n* : istmo *m*

it [ˈɪt] *pron* **1** (*as subject; generally omitted*) : él, ella, ello ⟨it's a big building : es un edificio grande⟩ ⟨who was it? : ¿quién era?⟩ **2** (*as indirect object*) : le ⟨I'll give it some water : voy a darle agua⟩ **3** (*as direct object*) : lo, la ⟨give it to me : dámelo⟩ **4** (*as object of a preposition; generally omitted*) : él, ella, ello ⟨behind it : detrás, detrás de él⟩ **5** (*in impersonal constructions*) ⟨it's raining : está lloviendo⟩ ⟨it's 8 o'clock : son las ocho⟩ **6** (*as the implied subject or object of a verb*) ⟨it is necessary to study : es necesario estudiar⟩ ⟨to give it all one's got : dar lo mejor de sí⟩

Italian [ɪ'tæljən, aɪ-] *n* **1** : italiano *m*, -na *f* **2** : italiano *m* (idioma) — **Italian** *adj*

italic¹ [ɪ'tælɪk, aɪ-] *adj* : en cursiva, en bastardilla

italic² *n* : cursiva *f*, bastardilla *f*

italicize [ɪ'tælə,saɪz, aɪ-] *vt* **-cized; -cizing** : poner en cursiva

itch¹ [ˈɪʧ] *vi* **1** : picar ⟨her arm itched : le pica el brazo⟩ **2** : morirse ⟨they were itching to go outside : se morían por salir⟩ — *vt* : dar picazón, hacer picar

itch² *n* **1** ITCHING : picazón *f*, picor *m*, comezón *f* **2** RASH : sarpullido *m*, erupción *f* **3** DESIRE : ansia *f*, deseo *m*

itchy ['ɪtʃi] *adj* **itchier; -est** : que pica, que da comezón

it'd ['ɪtəd] (*contraction of* it had *or* it would) → have, would

item ['aɪtəm] *n* **1** OBJECT : artículo *m*, pieza *f* ⟨item of clothing : prenda de vestir⟩ **2** : punto *m* (en una agenda), número *m* (en el teatro), ítem *m* (en un documento) **3** news item : noticia *f*

itemize ['aɪtə,maɪz] *vt* **-ized; -izing** : detallar, enumerar, listar

itinerant [aɪ'tɪnərənt] *adj* : itinerante, ambulante

itinerary [aɪ'tɪnə,rɛri] *n, pl* **-aries** : itinerario *m*

it'll ['ɪtəl] (*contraction of* it shall *or* it will) → shall, will

its ['ɪts] *adj* : su, sus ⟨its kennel : su perrera⟩ ⟨a city and its inhabitants : una ciudad y sus habitantes⟩

it's ['ɪts] (*contraction of* it is *or* it has) → be, have

itself [ɪt'sɛlf] *pron* **1** (*used reflexively*) : se ⟨the cat gave itself a bath : el gato se bañó⟩ **2** (*used for emphasis*) : (él) mismo, (ella) misma, sí (mismo), solo ⟨he is courtesy itself : es la misma cortesía⟩ ⟨in and of itself : por sí mismo⟩ ⟨it opened by itself : se abrió solo⟩

IUD [,aɪ,ju:'di:] *n* intrauterine device : DIU *m*, dispositivo *m* intrauterino

I've ['aɪv] (*contraction of* I have) → have

ivory ['aɪvəri] *n, pl* **-ries 1** : marfil *m* **2** : color *m* de marfil

ivy ['aɪvi] *n, pl* **ivies 1** : hiedra *f*, yedra *f* **2** → poison ivy

J

j ['dʒeɪ] *n, pl* **j's** *or* **js** ['dʒeɪz] : décima letra del alfabeto inglés

jab¹ ['dʒæb] *v* **jabbed; jabbing** *vt* **1** PUNCTURE : clavar, pinchar **2** POKE : dar, golpear (con la punta de algo) ⟨he jabbed me in the ribs : me dio un codazo en las costillas⟩ — *vi* to jab at : dar, golpear

jab² *n* **1** PRICK : pinchazo *m* **2** POKE : golpe *m* abrupto

jabber¹ ['dʒæbər] *v* : farfullar

jabber² *n* : galimatías *m*, farfulla *f*

jack¹ ['dʒæk] *vt* to jack up **1** : levantar (con un gato) **2** INCREASE : subir, aumentar

jack² *n* **1** : gato *m*, cric *m* ⟨hydraulic jack : gato hidráulico⟩ **2** FLAG : pabellón *m* **3** SOCKET : enchufe *m* hembra **4** : jota *f*, valet *m* ⟨jack of hearts : jota de corazones⟩ **5** jacks *npl* : cantillos *mpl*

jackal ['dʒækəl] *n* : chacal *m*

jackass ['dʒæk,æs] *n* : asno *m*, burro *m*

jacket ['dʒækət] *n* **1** : chaqueta *f* **2** COVER : sobrecubierta *f* (de un libro), carátula *f* (de un disco)

jackhammer ['dʒæk,hæmər] *n* : martillo *m* neumático

jack–in–the–box ['dʒækɪndə,baks] *n* : caja *f* de sorpresa

jackknife¹ ['dʒæk,naɪf] *vi* **-knifed; -knifing** : doblarse como una navaja, plegarse

jackknife² *n* : navaja *f*

jack–of–all–trades *n* : persona *f* que sabe un poco de todo, persona *f* de muchos oficios

jack–o'–lantern ['dʒækə,læntərn] *n* : linterna *f* hecha de una calabaza

jackpot ['dʒæk,pat] *n* **1** : primer premio *m*, gordo *m* **2** to hit the jackpot : sacarse la lotería, sacarse el gordo

jackrabbit ['dʒæk,ræbət] *n* : liebre *f* grande de Norteamérica

jade ['dʒeɪd] *n* : jade *m*

jaded ['dʒeɪdəd] *adj* **1** TIRED : agotado **2** BORED : hastiado

jagged ['dʒægəd] *adj* : dentado, mellado

jaguar ['dʒæg,war, 'dʒægjʊ,war] *n* : jaguar *m*

jai alai ['haɪ,laɪ] *n* : jai alai *m*, pelota *f* vasca

jail¹ ['dʒeɪl] *vt* : encarcelar

jail² *n* : cárcel *f*

jailbreak ['dʒeɪl,breɪk] *n* : fuga *f*, huida *f* (de la cárcel)

jailer *or* **jailor** ['dʒeɪlər] *n* : carcelero *m*, -ra *f*

jalapeño [,halə'peɪnjo, ,hæ-, -'pi:no] *n* : jalapeño *m*

jalopy [dʒə'lapi] *n, pl* **-lopies** : cacharro *m fam*, carro *m* destartalado

jalousie ['dʒæləsi] *n* : celosía *f*

jam¹ ['dʒæm] *v* **jammed; jamming** *vt* **1** CRAM : apiñar, embutir **2** BLOCK : atascar, atorar **3** to jam on the brakes : frenar en seco — *vi* STICK : atascarse, atrancarse

jam² *n* **1** *or* **traffic jam** : atasco *m*, embotellamiento *m* (de tráfico) **2** PREDICAMENT : lío *m*, aprieto *m*, apuro *m* **3** : mermelada *f* ⟨strawberry jam : mermelada de fresa⟩

Jamaican [dʒə'meɪkən] *n* : jamaiquino *m*, -na *f*; jamaicano *m*, -na *f* — Jamaican *adj*

jamb ['dʒæm] *n* : jamba *f*

jamboree [,dʒæmbə'ri:] *n* : fiesta *f* grande

jangle¹ ['dʒæŋgəl] *v* **-gled; -gling** *vi* : hacer un ruido metálico — *vt* **1** : hacer sonar **2** to jangle one's nerves : irritar, crispar

jangle² *n* : ruido *m* metálico

janitor ['dʒænətər] *n* : portero *m*, -ra *f*; conserje *mf*

January ['dʒænju,ɛri] *n* : enero *m*

Japanese [,dʒæpə'ni:z, -'ni:s] *n* **1**

: japonés *m*, -nesa *f* **2** : japonés *m* (idioma) — **Japanese** *adj*

jar¹ [ˈdʒɑr] *v* **jarred; jarring** *vi* **1** GRATE : chirriar **2** CLASH : desentonar **3** SHAKE : sacudirse **4 to jar on** : crispar, enervar — *vt* JOLT : sacudir

jar² *n* **1** GRATING : chirrido *m* **2** JOLT : vibración *f*, sacudida *f* **3** : tarro *m*, bote *m*, pote *m* ⟨a jar of honey : un tarro de miel⟩

jargon [ˈdʒɑrgən] *n* : jerga *f*

jasmine [ˈdʒæzmən] *n* : jazmín *m*

jasper [ˈdʒæspər] *n* : jaspe *m*

jaundice [ˈdʒɔndɪs] *n* : ictericia *f*

jaundiced [ˈdʒɔndɪst] *adj* **1** : ictérico **2** EMBITTERED, RESENTFUL : amargado, resentido, negativo ⟨with a jaundiced eye : con una actitud de cinismo⟩

jaunt [ˈdʒɔnt] *n* : excursión *f*, paseo *m*

jauntily [ˈdʒɔntəli] *adv* : animadamente

jauntiness [ˈdʒɔntinəs] *n* : animación *f*, vivacidad *f*

jaunty [ˈdʒɔnti] *adj* **-tier; -est 1** SPRIGHTLY : animado, alegre **2** RAKISH : desenvuelto, desenfadado

Javanese [ˌdʒævəˈniːz, ˌdʒɑ-, -ˈniːs] *n* **1** : javanés *m* (idioma) **2** : javanés *m*, -nesa *f* — **Javanese** *adj*

javelin [ˈdʒævələn] *n* : jabalina *f*

jaw¹ [ˈdʒɔ] *vi* GAB : cotorrear *fam*, parlotear *fam*

jaw² *n* **1** : mandíbula *f*, quijada *f* **2** : mordaza *f* (de una herramienta) **3 the jaws of death** : las garras *f* de la muerte

jawbone [ˈdʒɔˌboːn] *n* : mandíbula *f*

jay [ˈdʒeɪ] *n* : arrendajo *m*, chara *f Mex*, azulejo *m Mex*

jaybird [ˈdʒeɪˌbərd] → **jay**

jaywalk [ˈdʒeɪˌwɔk] *vi* : cruzar la calle sin prudencia

jaywalker [ˈdʒeɪˌwɔkər] *n* : peatón *m* imprudente

jazz¹ [ˈdʒæz] *vt* **to jazz up** : animar, alegrar

jazz² *n* : jazz *m*

jazzy [ˈdʒæzi] *adj* **jazzier; -est 1** : con ritmo de jazz **2** FLASHY, SHOWY : llamativo, ostentoso

jealous [ˈdʒɛləs] *adj* : celoso, envidioso — **jealously** *adv*

jealousy [ˈdʒɛləsi] *n* : celos *mpl*, envidia *f*

jeans [ˈdʒiːnz] *npl* : jeans *mpl*, vaqueros *mpl*

jeep [ˈdʒiːp] *n* : jeep *m*

jeer¹ [ˈdʒɪr] *vi* **1** BOO : abuchear **2** SCOFF : mofarse, burlarse — *vt* RIDICULE : mofarse de, burlarse de

jeer² *n* **1** : abucheo *m* **2** TAUNT : mofa *f*, burla *f*

Jehovah [dʒɪˈhoːvə] *n* : Jehová *m*

jell [ˈdʒɛl] *vi* **1** SET : gelificarse, cuajar **2** FORM : cuajar, formarse (una idea, etc.)

jelly¹ [ˈdʒɛli] *v* **jellied; jellying** *vi* **1** JELL : gelificarse, cuajar **2** : hacer jalea — *vt* : gelificar

jelly² *n, pl* **-lies 1** : jalea *f* **2** GELATIN : gelatina *f*

jellyfish [ˈdʒɛliˌfɪʃ] *n* : medusa *f*

jeopardize [ˈdʒɛpərˌdaɪz] *vt* **-dized; -dizing** : arriesgar, poner en peligro

jeopardy [ˈdʒɛpərdi] *n* : peligro *m*, riesgo *m*

jerk¹ [ˈdʒərk] *vt* **1** JOLT : sacudir **2** TUG, YANK : darle un tirón a — *vi* JOLT : dar sacudidas ⟨the train jerked along : el tren iba moviéndose a sacudidas⟩

jerk² *n* **1** TUG : tirón *m*, jalón *m* **2** JOLT : sacudida *f* brusca **3** FOOL : estúpido *m*, -da *f*; idiota *mf*

jerkin [ˈdʒərkən] *n* : chaqueta *f* sin mangas, chaleco *m*

jerky [ˈdʒərki] *adj* **jerkier; -est 1** : espasmódico (dícese de los movimientos) **2** CHOPPY : inconexo (dícese de la prosa) — **jerkily** [-kəli] *adv*

jerry-built [ˈdʒɛriˌbɪlt] *adj* : mal construido, chapucero

jersey [ˈdʒərzi] *n, pl* **-seys** : jersey *m*

jest¹ [ˈdʒɛst] *vi* : bromear

jest² *n* : broma *f*, chiste *m*

jester [ˈdʒɛstər] *n* : bufón *m*, -fona *f*

Jesuit [ˈdʒɛzuət] *n* : jesuita *m* — **Jesuit** *adj*

Jesus [ˈdʒiːzəs, -zəz] *n* **1** : Jesús *m* **2 Jesus Christ** : Jesucristo *m* **3 Jesus (Christ)!** *fam* : ¡por Dios!

jet¹ [ˈdʒɛt] *v* **jetted; jetting** *vt* SPOUT : arrojar a chorros — *vi* **1** GUSH : salir a chorros, chorrear **2** FLY : viajar en avión, volar

jet² *n* **1** STREAM : chorro *m* **2** *or* **jet airplane** : avión *m* a reacción, reactor *m* **3** : azabache *m* (mineral) **4 jet engine** : reactor *m*, motor *m* a reacción **5 jet lag** : desajuste *m* de horario (debido a un vuelo largo)

jet-propelled *adj* : a reacción

jetsam [ˈdʒɛtsəm] *n* **flotsam and jetsam** : restos *mpl*, desechos *mpl*

jettison [ˈdʒɛtəsən] *vt* **1** : echar al mar **2** DISCARD : desechar, deshacerse de

jetty [ˈdʒɛti] *n, pl* **-ties 1** PIER, WHARF : desembarcadero *m*, muelle *m* **2** BREAKWATER : malecón *m*, rompeolas *m*

Jew [ˈdʒuː] *n* : judío *m*, -día *f*

jewel [ˈdʒuːəl] *n* **1** : joya *f*, alhaja *f* **2** GEM : piedra *f* preciosa, gema *f* **3** : rubí *m* (de un reloj) **4** TREASURE : joya *f*, tesoro *m*

jeweler *or* **jeweller** [ˈdʒuːələr] *n* : joyero *m*, -ra *f*

jewelry [ˈdʒuːəlri] *n* : joyas *fpl*, alhajas *fpl*

Jewish [ˈdʒuːɪʃ] *adj* : judío

jib [ˈdʒɪb] *n* : foque *m* (de un barco)

jibe [ˈdʒaɪb] *vi* **jibed; jibing** AGREE : concordar

jiffy [ˈdʒɪfi] *n, pl* **-fies** : santiamén *m*, segundo *m*, momento *m*

jig¹ [ˈdʒɪg] *vi* **jigged; jigging** : bailar la giga

jig² *n* **1** : giga *f* **2 the jig is up** : se acabó la fiesta

jigger [ˈdʒɪgər] *n* : medida de 1 a 2 onzas (para licores)

jiggle¹ ['dʒɪgəl] *v* **-gled; -gling** *vt* : agitar
o sacudir ligeramente — *vi* : agitarse,
vibrar
jiggle² *n* : sacudida *f*, vibración *f*
jigsaw ['dʒɪg,sɔ] *n* **1** : sierra *f* de vaivén
2 jigsaw puzzle : rompecabezas *m*
jilt ['dʒɪlt] *vt* : dejar plantado, dar calabazas a
jimmy¹ ['dʒɪmi] *vt* **-mied; -mying** : forzar
con una palanqueta
jimmy² *n, pl* **-mies** : palanqueta *f*
jingle¹ ['dʒɪŋgəl] *v* **-gled; -gling** *vi* : tintinear — *vt* : hacer sonar
jingle² *n* **1** TINKLE : tintineo *m*, retintín
m **2** : canción *f* rimada
jingoism ['dʒɪŋgo,ɪzəm] *n* : jingoísmo *m*,
patriotería *f*
jingoistic [,dʒɪŋgo'ɪstɪk] *or* **jingoist**
['dʒɪŋgoɪst] *adj* : jingoísta, patriotero
jinx¹ ['dʒɪŋks] *vt* : traer mala suerte a,
salar *CoRi, Mex*
jinx² *n* **1** : cenizo *m*, -za *f* **2 to put a jinx
on** : echarle el mal de ojo a
jitters ['dʒɪtərz] *npl* : nervios *mpl* ⟨he got
the jitters : se puso nervioso⟩
jittery ['dʒɪtəri] *adj* : nervioso
job ['dʒab] *n* **1** : trabajo *m* ⟨he did odd
jobs for her : le hizo algunos trabajos⟩
2 CHORE, TASK : tarea *f*, quehacer *m* **3**
EMPLOYMENT : trabajo *m*, empleo *m*,
puesto *m*
jobber ['dʒabər] *n* MIDDLEMAN : intermediario *m*, -ria *f*
jock ['dʒak] *n* : deportista *mf*, atleta *mf*
jockey¹ ['dʒaki] *v* **-eyed; -eying** *vt* **1** MA-
NIPULATE : manipular **2** MANEUVER
: maniobrar — *vi* to jockey for posi-
tion : maniobrar para conseguir algo
jockey² *n, pl* **-eys** : jockey *mf*
jocose [dʒo'ko:s] *adj* : jocoso
jocular ['dʒakjulər] *adj* : jocoso — **joc-
ularly** *adv*
jocularity [,dʒakju'lærəti] *n* : jocosidad *f*
jodhpurs ['dʒadpərz] *npl* : pantalones
mpl de montar
jog¹ ['dʒag] *v* **jogged; jogging** *vt* **1**
NUDGE : dar, empujar, codear **2 to jog
one's memory** : refrescar la memoria
— *vi* **1** RUN : correr despacio, trotar,
hacer footing (como ejercicio) **2**
TRUDGE : andar a trote corto
jog² *n* **1** PUSH, SHAKE : empujoncito *m*,
sacudida *f* leve **2** TROT : trote *m* corto, footing *m* (en deportes) **3** TWIST
: recodo *m*, vuelta *f*, curva *f*
jogger ['dʒagər] *n* : persona *f* que hace
footing
join ['dʒɔɪn] *vt* **1** CONNECT, LINK : unir,
juntar ⟨to join in marriage : unir en
matrimonio⟩ **2** ADJOIN : lindar con,
colindar con **3** MEET : reunirse con,
encontrarse con ⟨we joined them for
lunch : nos reunimos con ellos para al-
morzar⟩ **4** : hacerse socio de (una organización), afiliarse a (un partido), entrar en (una empresa) — *vi* **1** UNITE
: unirse **2** MERGE : empalmar (dícese
de las carreteras), confluir (dícese de

los ríos) **3 to join up** : hacerse socio,
enrolarse
joiner ['dʒɔɪnər] *n* **1** CARPENTER
: carpintero *m*, -ra *f* **2** : persona *f* que
se une a varios grupos
joint¹ ['dʒɔɪnt] *adj* : conjunto, colectivo,
mutuo ⟨a joint effort : un esfuerzo con-
junto⟩ — **jointly** *adv*
joint² *n* **1** : articulación *f*, coyuntura *f*
⟨out of joint : dislocado⟩ **2** ROAST
: asado *m* **3** JUNCTURE : juntura *f*,
unión *f* **4** DIVE : antro *m*, tasca *f*
joist ['dʒɔɪst] *n* : viga *f*
joke¹ ['dʒo:k] *vi* **joked; joking** : bromear
joke² *n* **1** STORY : chiste *m* **2** PRANK
: broma *f*
joker ['dʒo:kər] *n* **1** PRANKSTER : bromista *mf* **2** : comodín *m* (en los naipes)
jokingly ['dʒo:kɪŋli] *adv* : en broma
jollity ['dʒaləti] *n, pl* **-ties** MERRIMENT
: alegría *f*, regocijo *m*
jolly ['dʒali] *adj* **-lier; -est** : alegre, jovial
jolt¹ ['dʒo:lt] *vi* JERK : dar tumbos, dar
sacudidas — *vt* : sacudir
jolt² *n* **1** JERK : sacudida *f* brusca **2**
SHOCK : golpe *m* (emocional)
jonquil ['dʒankwɪl] *n* : junquillo *m*
Jordanian [dʒɔr'deɪniən] *n* : jordano *m*,
-na *f* — **Jordanian** *adj*
josh ['dʒaʃ] *vt* TEASE : tomarle el pelo (a
alguien) — *vi* JOKE : bromear
jostle ['dʒasəl] *v* **-tled; -tling** *vi* **1** SHOVE
: empujar, dar empellones **2** CONTEND
: competir — *vt* **1** SHOVE : empujar **2
to jostle one's way** : abrirse paso a empellones
jot¹ ['dʒat] *vt* **jotted; jotting** : anotar,
apuntar ⟨jot it down : apúntalo⟩
jot² *n* BIT : ápice *m*, jota *f*, pizca *f*
jounce¹ ['dʒaʊnts] *v* **jounced; jouncing**
vt JOLT : sacudir — *vi* : dar tumbos, dar
sacudidas
jounce² *n* JOLT : sacudida *f*, tumbo *m*
journal ['dʒərnəl] *n* **1** DIARY : diario *m*
2 PERIODICAL : revista *f*, publicación *f*
periódica **3** NEWSPAPER : periódico *m*,
diario *m*
journalism ['dʒərnəl,ɪzəm] *n* : periodismo *m*
journalist ['dʒərnəlɪst] *n* : periodista *mf*
journalistic [,dʒərnəl'ɪstɪk] *adj* : periodístico
journey¹ ['dʒərni] *vi* **-neyed; -neying** : viajar
journey² *n, pl* **-neys** : viaje *m*
journeyman ['dʒərnimən] *n, pl* **-men**
[-mən, -,mn] : oficial *m*
joust¹ ['dʒaʊst] *vi* : justar
joust² *n* : justa *f*
jovial ['dʒo:viəl] *adj* : jovial — **jovially**
adv
joviality [,dʒo:vi'æləti] *n* : jovialidad *f*
jowl ['dʒaʊl] *n* **1** JAW : mandíbula *f* **2**
CHEEK : mejilla *f*, cachete *m*
joy ['dʒɔɪ] *n* **1** HAPPINESS : gozo *m*, alegría *f*, felicidad *f* **2** DELIGHT : placer
m, deleite *m* ⟨the child is a real joy : el
niño es un verdadero placer⟩

joyful ['dʒɔɪfəl] *adj* : gozoso, alegre, feliz — **joyfully** *adv*

joyless ['dʒɔɪləs] *adj* : sin alegría, triste

joyous ['dʒɔɪəs] *adj* : alegre, feliz, eufórico — **joyously** *adv*

joyousness ['dʒɔɪəsnəs] *n* : alegría *f*, felicidad *f*, euforia *f*

joyride ['dʒɔɪˌraɪd] *n* : paseo *m* temerario e irresponsable (en coche)

joystick ['dʒɔɪˌstɪk] *n* : joystick *m*

jubilant ['dʒuːbələnt] *adj* : jubiloso, alborozado — **jubilantly** *adv*

jubilation [ˌdʒuːbə'leɪʃən] *n* : júbilo *m*

jubilee ['dʒuːbəˌliː] *n* **1** : quincuagésimo aniversario *m* **2** CELEBRATION : celebración *f*, festejos *mpl*

Judaic [dʒu'deɪɪk] *adj* : judaico

Judaism ['dʒuːdəˌɪzəm, 'dʒuːdi-, 'dʒuːˌdeɪ-] *n* : judaísmo *m*

judge¹ ['dʒʌdʒ] *vt* **judged; judging 1** ASSESS : evaluar, juzgar **2** DEEM : juzgar, considerar **3** TRY : juzgar (ante el tribunal) **4 judging by** : a juzgar por

judge² *n* **1** : juez *mf*, jueza *f* **2 to be a good judge of** : saber juzgar a, entender mucho de

judgment *or* **judgement** ['dʒʌdʒmənt] *n* **1** RULING : fallo *m*, sentencia *f* **2** OPINION : opinión *f* **3** DISCERNMENT : juicio *m*, discernimiento *m*

judgmental [ˌdʒʌdʒ'mntəl] *adj* : crítico — **judgmentally** *adv*

judicature ['dʒuːdɪkəˌtʃʊr] *n* : judicatura *f*

judicial [dʒu'dɪʃəl] *adj* : judicial — **judicially** *adv*

judiciary¹ [dʒu'dɪʃiˌri, -'dɪʃəri] *adj* : judicial

judiciary² *n* **1** JUDICATURE : judicatura *f* **2** : poder *m* judicial

judicious [dʒu'dɪʃəs] *adj* SOUND, WISE : juicioso, sensato — **judiciously** *adv*

judo ['dʒuːˌdoː] *n* : judo *m*

jug ['dʒʌg] *n* **1** : jarra *f*, jarro *m*, cántaro *m* **2** JAIL : cárcel *f*, chirona *f fam*

juggernaut ['dʒʌgərˌnɔt] *n* : gigante *m*, fuerza *f* irresistible ⟨a political juggernaut : un gigante político⟩

juggle ['dʒʌgəl] *v* **-gled; -gling** *vt* **1** : hacer juegos malabares con **2** MANIPULATE : manipular, jugar con — *vi* : hacer juegos malabares

juggler ['dʒʌglər] *n* : malabarista *mf*

jugular ['dʒʌgjʊlər] *adj* : yugular ⟨jugular vein : vena yugular⟩

juice ['dʒuːs] *n* **1** : jugo *m* (de carne, de frutas) *m*, zumo *m* (de frutas) **2** ELECTRICITY : electricidad *f*, luz *f*

juicer ['dʒuːsər] *n* : exprimidor *m*

juiciness ['dʒuːsinəs] *n* : jugosidad *f*

juicy ['dʒuːsi] *adj* **juicier; -est 1** SUCCULENT : jugoso, suculento **2** PROFITABLE : jugoso, lucrativo **3** RACY : picante

jukebox ['dʒuːkˌbɑks] *n* : rocola *f*, máquina *f* de discos

julep ['dʒuːləp] *n* : bebida *f* hecha con whisky americano y menta

July [dʒu'laɪ] *n* : julio *m*

jumble¹ ['dʒʌmbəl] *vt* **-bled; -bling** : mezclar, revolver

jumble² *n* : revoltijo *m*, fárrago *m*, embrollo *m*

jumbo¹ ['dʒʌmˌboː] *adj* : gigante, enorme, de tamaño extra grande

jumbo² *n, pl* **-bos** : coloso *m*, cosa *f* de tamaño extra grande

jump¹ ['dʒʌmp] *vi* **1** LEAP : saltar, brincar **2** START : levantarse de un salto, sobresaltarse **3** MOVE, SHIFT : moverse, pasar ⟨to jump from job to job : pasar de un empleo a otro⟩ **4** INCREASE, RISE : dar un salto, aumentarse de golpe, subir bruscamente **5** BUSTLE : animarse, ajetrearse **6 to jump to conclusions** : sacar conclusiones precipitadas — *vt* **1** : saltar ⟨to jump a fence : saltar una valla⟩ **2** SKIP : saltarse **3** ATTACK : atacar, asaltar **4 to jump the gun** : precipitarse

jump² *n* **1** LEAP : salto *m* **2** START : sobresalto *m*, respingo *m* **3** INCREASE : subida *f* brusca, aumento *m* **4** ADVANTAGE : ventaja *f* ⟨we got the jump on them : les llevamos la ventaja⟩

jumper ['dʒʌmpər] *n* **1** : saltador *m*, -dora *f* (en deportes) **2** : jumper *m*, vestido *m* sin mangas

jumpy ['dʒʌmpi] *adj* **jumpier; -est** : asustadizo, nervioso

junction ['dʒʌŋkʃən] *n* **1** JOINING : unión *f* **2** : cruce *m* (de calles), empalme *m* (de un ferrocarril), confluencia *f* (de ríos)

juncture ['dʒʌŋktʃər] *n* **1** UNION : juntura *f*, unión *f* **2** MOMENT, POINT : coyuntura *f* ⟨at this juncture : en esta coyuntura, en este momento⟩

June ['dʒuːn] *n* : junio *m*

jungle ['dʒʌŋgəl] *n* : jungla *f*, selva *f*

junior¹ ['dʒuːnjər] *adj* **1** YOUNGER : más joven ⟨John Smith, Junior : John Smith, hijo⟩ **2** SUBORDINATE : subordinado, subalterno

junior² *n* **1** : persona *f* de menor edad ⟨she's my junior : es menor que yo⟩ **2** SUBORDINATE : subalterno *m*, -na *f*; subordinado *m*, -da *f* **3** : estudiante *mf* de penúltimo año

juniper ['dʒuːnəpər] *n* : enebro *m*

junk¹ ['dʒʌŋk] *vt* : echar a la basura

junk² *n* **1** RUBBISH : desechos *mpl*, desperdicios *mpl* **2** STUFF : trastos *mpl fam*, cachivaches *mpl fam* **3 piece of junk** : cacharro *m*, porquería *f*

junket ['dʒʌŋkət] *n* : viaje *m* (pagado con dinero público)

junta ['hʊntə, 'dʒʌn-, 'hʌn-] *n* : junta *f* militar

Jupiter ['dʒuːpətər] *n* : Júpiter *m*

jurisdiction [ˌdʒʊrəs'dɪkʃən] *n* : jurisdicción *f*

jurisprudence [ˌdʒʊrəs'pruːdənts] *n* : jurisprudencia *f*

jurist ['dʒʊrɪst] *n* : jurista *mf*; magistrado *m*, -da *f*

juror ['ʤʊrər] *n* : jurado *m*, -da *f*
jury ['ʤʊri] *n, pl* **-ries** : jurado *m*
just¹ ['ʤʌst] *adv* **1** EXACTLY : justo, precisamente, exactamente **2** POSSIBLY : posiblemente ⟨it just might work : tal vez resulte⟩ **3** BARELY : justo, apenas ⟨just in time : justo a tiempo⟩ **4** ONLY : sólo, solamente, nada más ⟨just us : sólo nosotros⟩ **5** QUITE : muy, simplemente ⟨it's just horrible! : ¡qué horrible!⟩ **6 to have just (done something)** : acabar de (hacer algo) ⟨he just called : acaba de llamar⟩
just² *adj* : justo — **justly** *adv*
justice ['ʤʌstɪs] *n* **1** : justicia *f* **2** JUDGE : juez *mf*, jueza *f*

justification [‚ʤʌstəfə'keɪʃən] *n* : justificación *f*
justify ['ʤʌstə‚faɪ] *vt* **-fied; -fying** : justificar — **justifiable** [‚ʤʌstə-'faɪəbəl] *adj*
jut ['ʤʌt] *vi* **jutted; jutting** : sobresalir
jute ['ʤu:t] *n* : yute *m*
juvenile¹ ['ʤu:və‚naɪl, -vənəl] *adj* **1** : juvenil ⟨juvenile delinquent : delincuente juvenil⟩ ⟨juvenile court : tribunal de menores⟩ **2** CHILDISH : infantil
juvenile² *n* : menor *mf*
juxtapose ['ʤʌkstə‚po:z] *vt* **-posed; -posing** : yuxtaponer
juxtaposition [‚ʤʌkstəpə'zɪʃən] *n* : yuxtaposición *f*

K

k ['keɪ] *n, pl* **k's** *or* **ks** ['keɪz] : undécima letra del alfabeto inglés
kaiser ['kaɪzər] *n* : káiser *m*
kale ['keɪl] *n* : col *f* rizada
kaleidoscope [kə'laɪdə‚sko:p] *n* : calidoscopio *m*
kamikaze [‚kɑmɪ'kɑzi] *n* : kamikaze *m* — **kamikaze** *adj*
kangaroo [‚kæŋgə'ru:] *n, pl* **-roos** : canguro *m*
kaolin ['keɪələn] *n* : caolín *m*
karaoke [‚kæri'o:ki] *n* : karaoke *m*
karat ['kærət] *n* : quilate *m*
karate [kə'rɑṭi] *n* : karate *m*
katydid ['keɪṭi‚dɪd] *n* : saltamontes *m*
kayak ['kaɪ‚æk] *n* : kayac *m*, kayak *m*
keel¹ ['ki:l] *vi* **to keel over** : volcar (dícese de un barco), desplomarse (dícese de una persona)
keel² *n* : quilla *f*
keen ['ki:n] *adj* **1** SHARP : afilado, filoso ⟨a keen blade : una hoja afilada⟩ **2** PENETRATING : cortante, penetrante ⟨a keen wind : un viento cortante⟩ **3** ENTHUSIASTIC : entusiasta **4** ACUTE : agudo, fino ⟨keen hearing : oído fino⟩ ⟨keen intelligence : inteligencia aguda⟩
keenly ['ki:nli] *adv* **1** ENTHUSIASTICALLY : con entusiasmo **2** INTENSELY : vivamente, profundamente ⟨keenly aware of : muy consciente de⟩
keenness ['ki:nnəs] *n* **1** SHARPNESS : lo afilado, lo filoso **2** ENTHUSIASM : entusiasmo *m* **3** ACUTENESS : agudeza *f*
keep¹ ['ki:p] *v* **kept** ['kpt]; **keeping** *vt* **1** : cumplir (la palabra a uno), acudir a (una cita) **2** OBSERVE : observar (una fiesta) **3** GUARD : guardar, cuidar **4** CONTINUE : mantener ⟨to keep silence : mantener silencio⟩ **5** SUPPORT : mantener (una familia) **6** RAISE : criar (animales) **7** : llevar, escribir (un diario, etc.) **8** RETAIN : guardar, conservar, quedarse con **9** STORE : guardar **10** DETAIN : hacer quedar, detener **11** PRESERVE : guardar ⟨to keep a secret : guardar un secreto⟩ — *vi* **1** : conser-

varse (dícese de los alimentos) **2** CONTINUE : seguir, no dejar ⟨he keeps on pestering us : no deja de molestarnos⟩ **3 to keep from** : abstenerse de ⟨I couldn't keep from laughing : no podía contener la risa⟩
keep² *n* **1** TOWER : torreón *m* (de un castillo), torre *f* del homenaje **2** SUSTENANCE : manutención *f*, sustento *m* **3 for keeps** : para siempre
keeper ['ki:pər] *n* **1** : guarda *mf* (en un zoológico); conservador *m*, -dora *f* (en un museo) **2** GAMEKEEPER : guardabosque *mf*
keeping ['ki:pɪŋ] *n* **1** CONFORMITY : conformidad *f*, acuerdo *m* ⟨in keeping with : de acuerdo con⟩ **2** CARE : cuidado *m* ⟨in the keeping of : al cuidado de⟩
keepsake ['ki:p‚seɪk] *n* : recuerdo *m*
keep up *vt* CONTINUE, MAINTAIN : mantener, seguir con — *vi* **1** : mantenerse al corriente ⟨he kept up with the news : se mantenía al tanto de las noticias⟩ **2** CONTINUE : continuar **3 to keep up with someone** : mantener contacto con alguien
keg ['kɛg] *n* : barril *m*
kelp ['kɛlp] *n* : alga *f* marina
ken ['kɛn] *n* **1** SIGHT : vista *f*, alcance *m* de la vista **2** UNDERSTANDING : comprensión *f*, alcance *m* del conocimiento ⟨it's beyond his ken : no lo puede entender⟩
kennel ['kɛnəl] *n* : caseta *f* para perros, perrera *f*
Kenyan ['kɛnjən, 'ki:n-] *n* : keniano *m*, -na *f* — **Kenyan** *adj*
kept → **keep**
kerchief ['kərtʃəf, -‚tʃi:f] *n* : pañuelo *m*
kernel ['kərnəl] *n* **1** : almendra *f* (de semillas y nueces) **2** : grano *m* (de cereales) **3** CORE : meollo *m* ⟨a kernel of truth : un fondo de verdad⟩
kerosene *or* **kerosine** ['kɛrə‚si:n, ‚kɛrə'-] *n* : queroseno *m*, kerosén *m*, kerosene *m*

ketchup ['kɛtʃəp, 'kæ-] *n* : salsa *f* catsup

kettle ['kɛtəl] *n* **1** : hervidor *m*, pava *f Arg, Bol, Chile* **2** → **teakettle**

kettledrum ['kɛtəl,drʌm] *n* : timbal *m*

key¹ ['ki:] *vt* **1** ATTUNE : adaptar, adecuar **2 to key up** : poner nervioso, inquietar

key² *adj* : clave, fundamental

key³ *n* **1** : llave *f* **2** SOLUTION : clave *f*, soluciones *fpl* **3** : tecla *f* (de un piano o una máquina) **4** : tono *m*, tonalidad *f* (en la música) **5** ISLET, REEF : cayo *m*, islote *m*

keyboard ['ki:,bord] *n* : teclado *m*

keyhole ['ki:,ho:l] *n* : bocallave *f*, ojo *m* (de una cerradura)

keynote¹ ['ki:,no:t] *vt* **-noted; -noting 1** : establecer la tónica de (en música) **2** : pronunciar el discurso principal de

keynote² *n* **1** : tónica *f* (en música) **2** : idea *f* fundamental

keystone ['ki:,sto:n] *n* : clave *f*, dovela *f*

keystroke ['ki:,stro:k] *n* : pulsación *f* (de tecla)

khaki ['kæki, 'kɑ-] *n* : caqui *m*

khan ['kɑn, 'kæn] *n* : kan *m*

kibbutz [kə'bʊts, -'bu:ts] *n, pl* **-butzim** [-,bʊt'si:m, -,bu:t-] : kibutz *m*

kibitz ['kɪbɪts] *vi* : dar consejos molestos

kibitzer ['kɪbɪtsər, kɪ'bɪt-] *n* : persona *f* que da consejos molestos

kick¹ ['kɪk] *vi* **1** : dar patadas (dícese de una persona), cocear (dícese de un animal) **2** PROTEST : patalear, protestar **3** RECOIL : dar un culatazo (dícese de un arma de fuego) — *vt* : patear, darle una patada (a alguien)

kick² *n* **1** : patada *f*, puntapié *m*, coz *f* (de un animal) **2** RECOIL : culatazo *m* (de un arma de fuego) **3** : fuerza *f* ⟨a drink with a kick : una bebida fuerte⟩

kicker ['kɪkər] *n* : pateador *m*, -dora *f* (en deportes)

kickoff ['kɪk,ɔf] *n* : saque *m* (inicial)

kick off *vi* **1** : hacer el saque inicial (en deportes) **2** BEGIN : empezar — *vt* : empezar

kid¹ ['kɪd] *v* **kidded; kidding** *vt* **1** FOOL : engañar **2** TEASE : tomarle el pelo (a alguien) — *vi* JOKE : bromear ⟨I'm only kidding : lo digo en broma⟩

kid² *n* **1** : chivo *m*, -va *f*; cabrito *m*, -ta *f* **2** CHILD : chico *m*, -ca *f*; niño *m*, -ña *f*

kidder ['kɪdər] *n* : bromista *mf*

kiddingly ['kɪdɪŋli] *adv* : en broma

kidnap ['kɪd,næp] *vt* **-napped** *or* **-naped** [-,næpt]; **-napping** *or* **-naping** [-,næpɪŋ] : secuestrar, raptar

kidnapper *or* **kidnaper** ['kɪd,næpər] *n* : secuestrador *m*, -dora *f*; raptor *m*, -tora *f*

kidnapping ['kɪd,næpɪŋ] *n* : secuestro *m*

kidney ['kɪdni] *n, pl* **-neys** : riñón *m*

kidney bean *n* : frijol *m*

kill¹ ['kɪl] *vt* **1** : matar **2** END : acabar con, poner fin a **3 to kill time** : matar el tiempo

kill² *n* **1** KILLING : matanza *f* **2** PREY : presa *f*

killer ['kɪlər] *n* : asesino *m*, -na *f*

killjoy ['kɪl,dʒɔɪ] *n* : aguafiestas *mf*

kiln ['kɪl, 'kɪln] *n* : horno *m*

kilo ['ki:,lo:] *n, pl* **-los** : kilo *m*

kilobyte ['kɪlə,baɪt] *n* : kilobyte *m*

kilocycle ['kɪlə,saɪkəl] *n* : kilociclo *m*

kilogram ['kɪlə,græm, 'ki:-] *n* : kilogramo *m*

kilohertz ['kɪlə,hərts] *n* : kilohertzio *m*

kilometer [kɪ'lɑmətər, 'kɪlə,mi:-] *n* : kilómetro *m*

kilowatt ['kɪlə,wɑt] *n* : kilovatio *m*

kilt ['kɪlt] *n* : falda *f* escocesa

kilter ['kɪltər] *n* **1** ORDER : buen estado *m* **2 out of kilter** : descompuesto, estropeado

kimono [kə'mo:no, -nə] *n, pl* **-nos** : kimono *m*, quimono *m*

kin ['kɪn] *n* : familiares *mpl*, parientes *mpl*

kind¹ ['kaɪnd] *adj* : amable, bondadoso, benévolo

kind² *n* **1** ESSENCE : esencia *f* ⟨a difference in degree, not in kind : una diferencia cuantitativa y no cualitativa⟩ **2** CATEGORY : especie *f*, género *m* **3** TYPE : clase *f*, tipo *m*, índole *f*

kindergarten ['kɪndər,gartən, -dən] *n* : kinder, kindergarten *m*, jardín *m* de infantes, jardín *m* de niños *Mex*

kindhearted [,kaɪnd'hartəd] *adj* : bondadoso, de buen corazón

kindle ['kɪndəl] *v* **-dled; -dling** *vt* **1** IGNITE : encender **2** AROUSE : despertar, suscitar — *vi* : encenderse

kindliness ['kaɪndlinəs] *n* : bondad *f*

kindling ['kɪndlɪŋ, 'kɪndlən] *n* : astillas *fpl*, leña *f*

kindly¹ ['kaɪndli] *adv* **1** AMIABLY : amablemente, bondadosamente **2** COURTEOUSLY : cortésmente, con cortesía ⟨we kindly ask you not smoke : les rogamos que no fumen⟩ **3** PLEASE : por favor **4 to take kindly to** : aceptar de buena gana

kindly² *adj* **-lier; -est** : bondadoso, amable

kindness ['kaɪndnəs] *n* : bondad *f*

kind of *adv* SOMEWHAT : un tanto, algo

kindred¹ ['kɪndrəd] *adj* SIMILAR : similar, afín ⟨kindred spirits : almas gemelas⟩

kindred² *n* **1** FAMILY : familia *f*, parentela *f* **2** → **kin**

kinfolk ['kɪn,fo:k] *or* **kinfolks** [-,fo:ks] *npl* → **kin**

king ['kɪŋ] *n* : rey *m*

kingdom ['kɪŋdəm] *n* : reino *m*

kingfisher ['kɪŋ,fɪʃər] *n* : martín *m* pescador

kingly ['kɪŋli] *adj* **-lier; -est** : regio, real

king-size ['kɪŋ,saɪz] *or* **king-sized** [-,saɪzd] *adj* : de tamaño muy grande, extra largo (dícese de cigarrillos)

kink ['kɪŋk] *n* **1** : rizo *m* (en el pelo), vuelta *f* (en una cuerda) **2** CRAMP

: calambre *m* ⟨to have a kink in the neck : tener tortícolis⟩

kinky ['kɪŋki] *adj* **-kier; -est** : rizado (dícese del pelo), enroscado (dícese de una cuerda)

kinship ['kɪn,ʃɪp] *n* : parentesco *m*

kinsman ['kɪnzmən] *n, pl* **-men** [-mən, -,mɛn] : familiar *m*, pariente *m*

kinswoman ['kɪnz,wʊmən] *n, pl* **-women** [-,wɪmən] : familiar *f*, pariente *f*

kiosk ['ki:,ɑsk] *n* : quiosco *m*

kipper ['kɪpər] *n* : arenque *m* ahumado

kiss¹ ['kɪs] *vt* : besar — *vi* : besarse

kiss² *n* : beso *m*

kit ['kɪt] *n* **1** SET : juego *m*, kit *m* **2** CASE : estuche *m*, caja *f* **3** first–aid kit : botiquín *m* **4** tool kit : caja *f* de herramientas **5** travel kit : neceser *m*

kitchen ['kɪtʃən] *n* : cocina *f*

kite ['kaɪt] *n* **1** : milano *m* (ave) **2** : cometa *f*, papalote *m Mex* ⟨to fly a kite : hacer volar una cometa⟩

kith ['kɪθ] *n* : amigos *mpl* ⟨kith and kin : amigos y parientes⟩

kitten ['kɪtən] *n* : gatito *m*, -ta *f*

kitty ['kɪti] *n, pl* **-ties 1** FUND, POOL : bote *m*, fondo *m* común **2** CAT : gato *m*, gatito *m*

kitty–corner ['kɪti,kɔrnər] *or* **kitty-cornered** [-nərd] → **catercorner**

kiwi ['ki:,wi:] *n* : kiwi *m*

kleptomania [,klɛptə'meɪniə] *n* : cleptomanía *f*

kleptomaniac [,klɛptə'meɪni,æk] *n* : cleptómano *m*, -na *f*

knack ['næk] *n* : maña *f*, facilidad *f*

knapsack ['næp,sæk] *n* : mochila *f*, morral *m*

knave ['neɪv] *n* : bellaco *m*, pícaro *m*

knead ['ni:d] *vt* **1** : amasar, sobar **2** MASSAGE : masajear

knee ['ni:] *n* : rodilla *f*

kneecap ['ni:,kæp] *n* : rótula *f*

kneel ['ni:l] *vi* **knelt** ['nɛlt] *or* **kneeled** ['ni:ld]; **kneeling** : arrodillarse, ponerse de rodillas

knell ['nɛl] *n* : doble *m*, toque *m* ⟨death knell : toque de difuntos⟩

knew → **know**

knickers ['nɪkərz] *npl* : pantalones *mpl* bombachos de media pierna

knickknack ['nɪk,næk] *n* : chuchería *f*, baratija *f*

knife¹ ['naɪf] *vt* **knifed** ['naɪft]; **knifing** : acuchillar, apuñalar

knife² *n, pl* **knives** ['naɪvz] : cuchillo *m*

knight¹ ['naɪt] *vt* : conceder el título de *Sir* a

knight² *n* **1** : caballero *m* ⟨knight errant : caballero andante⟩ **2** : caballo *m* (en ajedrez) **3** : uno que tiene el título de *Sir*

knighthood ['naɪt,hʊd] *n* **1** : caballería *f* **2** : título *m* de *Sir*

knightly ['naɪtli] *adj* : caballeresco

knit¹ ['nɪt] *v* **knit** *or* **knitted** ['nɪtəd]; **knitting** *vt* **1** UNITE : unir, enlazar **2** : tejer ⟨to knit a sweater : tejer un suéter⟩ **3**

to knit one's brows : fruncir el ceño — *vi* **1** : tejer **2** : soldarse (dícese de los huesos)

knit² *n* : prenda *f* tejida

knitter ['nɪtər] *n* : tejedor *m*, -dora *f*

knob ['nɑb] *n* **1** LUMP : bulto *m*, protuberancia *f* **2** HANDLE : perilla *f*, tirador *m*, botón *m*

knobbed ['nɑbd] *adj* **1** KNOTTY : nudoso **2** : que tiene perilla o botón

knobby ['nɑbi] *adj* **knobbier; -est 1** KNOTTY : nudoso **2** knobby knees : rodillas *fpl* huesudas

knock¹ ['nɑk] *vt* **1** HIT, RAP : golpear, golpetear **2** : hacer chocar ⟨they knocked heads : se dieron en la cabeza⟩ **3** CRITICIZE : criticar — *vi* **1** RAP : dar un golpe, llamar (a la puerta) **2** COLLIDE : darse, chocar

knock² *n* : golpe *m*, llamada *f* (a la puerta), golpeteo *m* (de un motor)

knock down *vt* : derribar, echar al suelo

knocker ['nɑkər] *n* : aldaba *f*, llamador *m*

knock–kneed ['nɑk'ni:d] *adj* : patizambo

knockout ['nɑk,aʊt] *n* : nocaut *m*, knockout *m* (en deportes)

knock out *vt* : dejar sin sentido, poner fuera de combate (en el boxeo)

knoll ['no:l] *n* : loma *f*, otero *m*, montículo *m*

knot¹ ['nɑt] *v* **knotted; knotting** *vt* : anudar — *vi* : anudarse

knot² *n* **1** : nudo *m* (en cordel o madera), nódulo *m* (en los músculos) **2** CLUSTER : grupo *m* **3** : nudo *m* (unidad de velocidad)

knotty ['nɑti] *adj* **-tier; -est 1** GNARLED : nudoso **2** COMPLEX : espinoso, enredado, complejo

know ['no:] *v* **knew** ['nu:, 'nju:]; **known** ['no:n]; **knowing** *vt* **1** : saber ⟨he knows the answer : sabe la respuesta⟩ **2** : conocer (a una persona, un lugar) ⟨do you know Julia? : ¿conoces a Julia?⟩ **3** RECOGNIZE : reconocer **4** DISCERN, DISTINGUISH : distinguir, discernir **5** to know how to : saber ⟨I don't know how to dance : no sé bailar⟩ — *vi* : saber

knowable ['no:əbəl] *adj* : conocible

knowing ['no:ɪŋ] *adj* **1** KNOWLEDGEABLE : informado ⟨a knowing look : una mirada de complicidad⟩ **2** ASTUTE : astuto **3** DELIBERATE : deliberado, intencional

knowingly ['no:ɪŋli] *adv* **1** : con complicidad ⟨she smiled knowingly : sonrió con una mirada de complicidad⟩ **2** DELIBERATELY : a sabiendas, adrede, a propósito

know–it–all ['no:ɪt,ɔl] *n* : sabelotodo *mf fam*

knowledge ['nɑlɪdʒ] *n* **1** AWARENESS : conocimiento *m* **2** LEARNING : conocimientos *mpl*, saber *m*

knowledgeable ['nɑlɪdʒəbəl] *adj* : informado, entendido, enterado

known ['noːn] *adj* : conocido, familiar
knuckle ['nʌkəl] *n* : nudillo *m*
koala [ko'walə] *n* : koala *m*
kohlrabi [ˌkoːl'rɑbi, -'ræ-] *n, pl* **-bies** : colinabo *m*
Koran [kə'rɑn, -'ræn] *n* **the Koran** : el Corán
Korean [kə'riːən] *n* **1** : coreano *m*, -na *f* **2** : coreano *m* (idioma) — **Korean** *adj*
kosher ['koːʃər] *adj* : aprobado por la ley judía

kowtow [ˌkaʊ'taʊ, 'kaʊˌtaʊ] *vi* **to kowtow to** : humillarse ante, doblegarse ante
krypton ['krɪpˌtɑn] *n* : criptón *m*
kudos ['kjuːˌdɑs, 'kuː-, -ˌdoːz] *n* : fama *f*, renombre *m*
kumquat ['kʌmˌkwɑt] *n* : naranjita *f* china
Kurd ['kʊrd, 'kərd] *n* : kurdo *m*, -da *f*
Kurdish ['kʊrdɪʃ, 'kər-] *adj* : kurdo
Kuwaiti [kʊ'weɪtᵢ] *n* : kuwaití *mf* — **Kuwaiti** *adj*

L

l ['ɛl] *n, pl* **l's** *or* **ls** ['lz] : duodécima letra del alfabeto inglés
lab ['læb] → **laboratory**
label¹ ['leɪbəl] *vt* **-beled** *or* **-belled; -beling** *or* **-belling** **1** : etiquetar, poner etiqueta a **2** BRAND, CATEGORIZE : calificar, tildar, tachar ⟨they labeled him as a fraud : lo calificaron de farsante⟩
label² *n* **1** : etiqueta *f*, rótulo *m* **2** DESCRIPTION : calificación *f*, descripción *f* **3** BRAND : marca *f*
labial ['leɪbiəl] *adj* : labial
labor¹ ['leɪbər] *vi* **1** WORK : trabajar **2** STRUGGLE : avanzar penosamente (dícese de una persona), funcionar con dificultad (dícese de un motor) **3 to labor under a delusion** : hacerse ilusiones, tener una falsa impresión — *vt* BELABOR : insistir en, extenderse sobre
labor² *n* **1** EFFORT, WORK : trabajo *m*, esfuerzos *mpl* **2** : parto *m* ⟨to be in labor : estar de parto⟩ **3** TASK : tarea *f*, labor *m* **4** WORKERS : mano *f* de obra
laboratory ['læbrəˌtori, lə'bɔrə-] *n, pl* **-ries** : laboratorio *m*
Labor Day *n* : Día *m* del Trabajo
laborer ['leɪbərər] *n* : peón *m*; trabajador *m*, -dora *f*
laborious [lə'boriəs] *adj* : laborioso, difícil
laboriously [lə'boriəsli] *adv* : laboriosamente, trabajosamente
labor union → **union**
labyrinth ['læbəˌrɪnθ] *n* : laberinto *m*
lace¹ ['leɪs] *vt* **laced; lacing** **1** TIE : acordonar, atar los cordones de **2** : adornar de encaje ⟨I laced the dress in white : adorné el vestido de encaje blanco⟩ **3** SPIKE : echar licor a
lace² *n* **1** : encaje *m* **2** SHOELACE : cordón *m* (de zapatos), agujeta *f* Mex
lacerate ['læsəˌreɪt] *vt* **-ated; -ating** : lacerar
laceration [ˌlæsə'reɪʃən] *n* : laceración *f*
lack¹ ['læk] *vt* : carecer de, no tener ⟨she lacks patience : carece de paciencia⟩ — *vi* : faltar ⟨they lack for nothing : no les falta nada⟩
lack² *n* : falta *f*, carencia *f*
lackadaisical [ˌlækə'deɪzɪkəl] *adj*

: apático, indiferente, lánguido — **lackadaisically** [-kli] *adv*
lackey ['læki] *n, pl* **-eys** **1** FOOTMAN : lacayo *m* **2** TOADY : adulador *m*, -dora *f*
lackluster ['lækˌlʌstər] *adj* **1** DULL : sin brillo, apagado, deslustrado **2** MEDIOCRE : deslucido, mediocre
laconic [lə'kɑnɪk] *adj* : lacónico — **laconically** [-nɪkli] *adv*
lacquer¹ ['lækər] *vt* : laquear, pintar con laca
lacquer² *n* : laca *f*
lacrosse [lə'krɔs] *n* : lacrosse *f*
lactic acid ['læktɪk] *n* : ácido *m* láctico
lacuna [lə'kuːnə, -'kjuː-] *n, pl* **-nae** [-ˌniː, -ˌnaɪ] *or* **-nas** : laguna *f*
lacy ['leɪsi] *adj* **lacier; -est** : de encaje, como de encaje
lad ['læd] *n* : muchacho *m*, niño *m*
ladder ['lædər] *n* : escalera *f*
laden ['leɪdən] *adj* : cargado
ladle¹ ['leɪdəl] *vt* **-dled; -dling** : servir con cucharón
ladle² *n* : cucharón *m*, cazo *m*
lady ['leɪdi] *n, pl* **-dies** **1** : señora *f*, dama *f* **2** WOMAN : mujer *f*
ladybird ['leɪdiˌbərd] *n* → **ladybug**
ladybug ['leɪdiˌbʌg] *n* : mariquita *f*
lag¹ ['læg] *vi* **lagged; lagging** : quedarse atrás, retrasarse, rezagarse
lag² *n* **1** DELAY : retraso *m*, demora *f* **2** INTERVAL : lapso *m*, intervalo *m*
lager ['lɑgər] *n* : cerveza *f* rubia
laggard¹ ['lægərd] *adj* : retardado, retrasado
laggard² *n* : rezagado *m*, -da *f*
lagoon [lə'guːn] *n* : laguna *f*
laid → **lay¹**
laid-back ['leɪd'bæk] *adj* : tranquilo, relajado
lain *pp* → **lie¹**
lair ['lær] *n* : guarida *f*, madriguera *f*
laissez-faire [ˌlɛˌseɪ'fær, ˌleɪˌzeɪ-] *n* : liberalismo *m* económico
laity ['leɪəti] *n* **the laity** : los laicos, el laicado
lake ['leɪk] *n* : lago *m*
lama ['lɑmə] *n* : lama *m*
lamb ['læm] *n* **1** : cordero *m*, borrego *m* (animal) **2** : carne *f* de cordero

lambaste [læm'beɪst] *or* **lambast** [-'bæst] *vt* **-basted; -basting 1** BEAT, THRASH : golpear, azotar, darle una paliza (a alguien) **2** CENSURE : arremeter contra, censurar

lame¹ ['leɪm] *vt* **lamed; laming** : lisiar, hacer cojo

lame² *adj* **lamer; lamest 1** : cojo, renco, rengo **2** WEAK : pobre, débil, poco convincente ⟨a lame excuse : una excusa débil⟩

lamé [lɑ'meɪ, læ-] *n* : lamé *m*

lame duck *n* : persona *f* sin poder ⟨a lame-duck President : un presidente saliente⟩

lamely ['leɪmli] *adv* : sin convicción

lameness ['leɪmnəs] *n* **1** : cojera *f*, renquera *f* **2** : falta *f* de convicción, debilidad *f*, pobreza *f* ⟨the lameness of her response : la pobreza de su respuesta⟩

lament¹ [lə'mɛnt] *vt* **1** MOURN : llorar, llorar por **2** DEPLORE : lamentar, deplorar — *vi* : llorar

lament² *n* : lamento *m*

lamentable ['læməntəbəl, lə'mɛntə-] *adj* : lamentable, deplorable — **lamentably** [-bli] *adv*

lamentation [,læmən'teɪʃən] *n* : lamentación *f*, lamento *m*

laminate¹ ['læmə,neɪt] *vt* **-nated; -nating** : laminar

laminate² ['læmənət] *n* : laminado *m*

laminated ['læmə,neɪtəd] *adj* : laminado

lamp ['læmp] *n* : lámpara *f*

lampoon¹ [læm'puːn] *vt* : satirizar

lampoon² *n* : sátira *f*

lamprey ['læmpri] *n*, *pl* **-preys** : lamprea *f*

lance¹ ['lænts] *vt* **lanced; lancing** : abrir con lanceta, sajar

lance² *n* : lanza *f*

lance corporal *n* : cabo *m* interino, soldado *m* de primera clase

lancet ['læntsət] *n* : lanceta *f*

land¹ ['lænd] *vt* **1** : desembarcar (pasajeros de un barco), hacer aterrizar (un avión) **2** CATCH : pescar, sacar (un pez) del agua **3** GAIN, SECURE : conseguir, ganar ⟨to land a job : conseguir empleo⟩ **4** DELIVER : dar, asestar ⟨he landed a punch : asestó un puñetazo⟩ — *vi* **1** : aterrizar, tomar tierra, atracar ⟨the plane just landed : el avión acaba de aterrizar⟩ ⟨the ship landed an hour ago : el barco atracó hace una hora⟩ **2** ALIGHT : posarse, aterrizar ⟨to land on one's feet : caer de pie⟩

land² *n* **1** GROUND : tierra *f* ⟨dry land : tierra firme⟩ **2** TERRAIN : terreno *m* **3** NATION : país *m*, nación *f* **4** DOMAIN : mundo *m*, dominio *m* ⟨the land of dreams : el mundo de los sueños⟩

landfill ['lænd,fɪl] *n* : vertedero *m* (de basuras)

landing ['lændɪŋ] *n* **1** : aterrizaje *m* (de aviones), desembarco *m* (de barcos) **2** : descansillo *m* (de una escalera)

landing field *n* : campo *m* de aterrizaje

landing strip → airstrip

landlady ['lænd,leɪdi] *n*, *pl* **-dies** : casera *f*, dueña *f*, arrendadora *f*

landless ['lændləs] *adj* : sin tierra

landlocked ['lænd,lɑkt] *adj* : sin salida al mar

landlord ['lænd,lɔrd] *n* : dueño *m*, casero *m*, arrendador *m*

landlubber ['lænd,lʌbər] *n* : marinero *m* de agua dulce

landmark ['lænd,mɑrk] *n* **1** : señal *f* (geográfica), punto *m* de referencia **2** MILESTONE : hito *m* ⟨a landmark in our history : un hito en nuestra historia⟩ **3** MONUMENT : monumento *m* histórico

landowner ['lænd,oːnər] *n* : hacendado *m*, -da *f*; terrateniente *mf*

landscape¹ ['lænd,skeɪp] *vt* **-scaped; -scaping** : ajardinar

landscape² *n* : paisaje *m*

landslide ['lænd,slaɪd] *n* **1** : desprendimiento *m* de tierras, derrumbe *m* **2 landslide victory** : victoria *f* arrolladora

landward ['lændwərd] *adv* : en dirección de la tierra, hacia tierra

lane ['leɪn] *n* **1** PATH, WAY : camino *m*, sendero *m* **2** : carril *m* (de una carretera)

language ['læŋgwɪdʒ] *n* **1** : idioma *m*, lengua *f* ⟨the English language : el idioma inglés⟩ **2** : lenguaje *m* ⟨body language : lenguaje corporal⟩

languid ['læŋgwɪd] *adj* : lánguido — **languidly** *adv*

languish ['læŋgwɪʃ] *vi* **1** WEAKEN : languidecer, debilitarse **2** PINE : consumirse, suspirar (por) ⟨to languish for love : suspirar por el amor⟩ ⟨he languished in prison : estuvo pudriéndose en la cárcel⟩

languor ['læŋgər] *n* : languidez *f*

languorous ['læŋgərəs] *adj* : lánguido — **languorously** *adv*

lank ['læŋk] *adj* **1** THIN : delgado, larguirucho *fam* **2** LIMP : lacio

lanky ['læŋki] *adj* **lankier; -est** : delgado, larguirucho *fam*

lanolin ['lænəlɪn] *n* : lanolina *f*

lantern ['læntərn] *n* : linterna *f*, farol *m*

Laotian [leɪ'oːʃən, 'lauʃən] *n* : laosiano *m*, -na *f* — **Laotian** *adj*

lap¹ ['læp] *v* **lapped; lapping** *vt* **1** FOLD : plegar, doblar **2** WRAP : envolver **3** : lamer, besar ⟨waves were lapping the shore : las olas lamían la orilla⟩ **4 to lap up** : beber a lengüetadas (como un gato) — *vi* OVERLAP : traslaparse

lap² *n* **1** : falda *f*, regazo *m* (del cuerpo) **2** OVERLAP : traslapo *m* **3** : vuelta *f* (en deportes) **4** STAGE : etapa *f* (de un viaje)

lapdog ['læp,dɔg] *n* : perro *m* faldero

lapel [lə'pɛl] *n* : solapa *f*

Lapp ['læp] *n* : lapón *m*, -pona *f* — **Lapp** *adj*

lapse¹ ['læps] *vi* **lapsed; lapsing 1** FALL, SLIP : caer ⟨to lapse into bad habits : caer en malos hábitos⟩ ⟨to lapse into unconsciousness : perder el conocimiento> <to lapse into silence : quedarse callado> **2** FADE : decaer, desvanecerse <her dedication lapsed : su dedicación se desvaneció> **3** CEASE : cancelarse, perderse **4** ELAPSE : transcurrir, pasar **5** EXPIRE : caducar

lapse² *n* **1** SLIP : lapsus *m*, desliz *m*, falla *f* <a lapse of memory : una falla de memoria> **2** INTERVAL : lapso *m*, intervalo *m*, período *m* **3** EXPIRATION : caducidad *f*

laptop¹ [ˈlæpˌtɑp] *adj* : portátil, laptop

laptop² *n* : laptop *m*

larboard [ˈlɑrbərd] *n* : babor *m*

larcenous [ˈlɑrsənəs] *adj* : de robo

larceny [ˈlɑrsəni] *n*, *pl* **-nies** : robo *m*, hurto *m*

larch [ˈlɑrtʃ] *n* : alerce *f*

lard [ˈlɑrd] *n* : manteca *f* de cerdo

larder [ˈlɑrdər] *n* : despensa *f*, alacena *f*

large [ˈlɑrdʒ] *adj* **larger; largest 1** BIG : grande **2** COMPREHENSIVE : amplio, extenso **3 by and large** : por lo general

largely [ˈlɑrdʒli] *adv* : en gran parte, en su mayoría

largeness [ˈlɑrdʒnəs] *n* : lo grande

largesse *or* **largess** [lɑrˈʒes, -ˈdʒes] *n* : generosidad *f*, largueza *f*

lariat [ˈlæriət] *n* : lazo *m*

lark [ˈlɑrk] *n* **1** FUN : diversión *f* <what a lark! : ¡qué divertido!> **2** : alondra *f* (pájaro)

larva [ˈlɑrvə] *n*, *pl* **-vae** [-ˌviː, -ˌvaɪ] : larva *f* — **larval** [-vəl] *adj*

laryngitis [ˌlærənˈdʒaɪtəs] *n* : laringitis *f*

larynx [ˈlærɪŋks] *n*, *pl* **-rynges** [ləˈrɪnˌdʒiːz] *or* **-ynxes** [ˈlærɪŋksəz] : laringe *f*

lasagna [ləˈzɑnjə] *n* : lasaña *f*

lascivious [ləˈsɪviəs] *adj* : lascivo

lasciviousness [ləˈsɪviəsnəs] *n* : lascivia *f*, lujuria *f*

laser [ˈleɪzər] *n* : láser *m*

laser disc *n* : disco *m* láser

lash¹ [ˈlæʃ] *vt* **1** WHIP : azotar **2** BIND : atar, amarrar

lash² *n* **1** WHIP : látigo *m* **2** STROKE : latigazo *m* **3** EYELASH : pestaña *f*

lass [ˈlæs] *or* **lassie** [ˈlæsi] *n* : muchacha *f*, chica *f*

lassitude [ˈlæsəˌtuːd, -ˌtjuːd] *n* : lasitud *f*

lasso¹ [ˈlæˌsoː, læˈsuː] *vt* : lazar

lasso² *n*, *pl* **-sos** *or* **-soes** : lazo *m*, reata *f Mex*

last¹ [ˈlæst] *vi* **1** CONTINUE : durar <how long will it last? : ¿cuánto durará?> **2** ENDURE : aguantar, durar **3** SURVIVE : durar, sobrevivir **4** SUFFICE : durar, bastar — *vt* **1** : durar <it will last a lifetime : durará toda la vida> **2 to last out** : aguantar

last² *adv* **1** : en último lugar, al último <we came in last : llegamos en último lugar> **2** : por última vez, la última vez <I saw him last in Bogota : lo vi por última vez en Bogotá> **3** FINALLY : por último, en conclusión

last³ *adj* **1** FINAL : último, final **2** PREVIOUS : pasado <last year : el año pasado>

last⁴ *n* **1** : el último, la última, lo último <at last : por fin, al fin, finalmente> **2** : horma *f* (de zapatero)

lasting [ˈlæstɪŋ] *adj* : perdurable, duradero, estable

lastly [ˈlæstli] *adv* : por último, finalmente

latch¹ [ˈlætʃ] *vt* : cerrar con picaporte

latch² *n* : picaporte *m*, pestillo *m*, pasador *m*

late¹ [ˈleɪt] *adv* **later; latest 1** : tarde <to arrive late : llegar tarde> <to sleep late : dormir hasta tarde> **2** : a última hora, a finales <late in the month : a finales del mes> **3** RECENTLY : recién, últimamente <as late as last year : todavía en el año pasado>

late² *adj* **later; latest 1** TARDY : tardío, de retraso <to be late : llegar tarde> **2** : avanzado <because of the late hour : a causa de la hora avanzada> **3** DECEASED : difunto, fallecido **4** RECENT : reciente, último <our late quarrel : nuestra última pelea>

latecomer [ˈleɪtˌkʌmər] *n* : rezagado *m*, -da *f*

lately [ˈleɪtli] *adv* : recientemente, últimamente

lateness [ˈleɪtnəs] *n* **1** DELAY : retraso *m*, atraso *m*, tardanza *f* **2** : lo avanzado (de la hora)

latent [ˈleɪtənt] *adj* : latente — **latently** *adv*

lateral [ˈlætərəl] *adj* : lateral — **laterally** *adv*

latex [ˈleɪˌteks] *n*, *pl* **-tices** [ˈleɪtəˌsiːz, ˈlætə-] *or* **-texes** : látex *m*

lath [ˈlæθ, ˈlæð] *n*, *pl* **laths** *or* **lath** : listón *m*

lathe [ˈleɪð] *n* : torno *m*

lather¹ [ˈlæðər] *vt* : enjabonar — *vi* : espumar, hacer espuma

lather² *n* **1** : espuma *f* (de jabón) **2** : sudor *m* (de caballo) **3 to get into a lather** : ponerse histérico

Latin¹ *adj* : latino

Latin² *n* **1** : latín *m* (idioma) **2** → **Latin American**

Latin–American [ˈlætənəˈmrikən] *adj* : latinoamericano

Latin American *n* : latinoamericano *m*, -na *f*

latitude [ˈlætəˌtuːd, -ˌtjuːd] *n* : latitud *f*

latrine [ləˈtriːn] *n* : letrina *f*

latte [ˈlɑˌteɪ] *n* : café *m* con leche

latter¹ [ˈlætər] *adj* **1** SECOND : segundo **2** LAST : último

latter² *pron* **the latter** : éste, ésta, éstos *pl*, éstas *pl*

lattice [ˈlætəs] *n* : enrejado *m*, celosía *f*

Latvian [ˈlætviən] *n* : letón *m*, -tona *f* — **Latvian** *adj*

laud¹ [ˈlɔd] *vt* : alabar, loar

laud² *n* : alabanza *f*, loa *f*

laudable ['lɔdəbəl] *adj* : loable — **laudably** [-bli] *adv*

laugh¹ ['læf] *vi* : reír, reírse

laugh² *n* **1** LAUGHTER : risa *f* **2** JOKE : chiste *m*, broma *f* ⟨he did it for a laugh : lo hizo en broma, lo hizo para divertirse⟩

laughable ['læfəbəl] *adj* : risible, de risa

laughingstock ['læfɪŋˌstɑk] *n* : hazmerreír *m*

laughter ['læftər] *n* : risa *f*, risas *fpl*

launch¹ ['lɔntʃ] *vt* **1** HURL : lanzar **2** : botar (un barco) **3** START : iniciar, empezar

launch² *n* **1** : lancha *f* (bote) **2** LAUNCHING : lanzamiento *m*

launder ['lɔndər] *vt* **1** : lavar y planchar (ropa) **2** : blanquear, lavar (dinero)

launderer ['lɔndərər] *n* : lavandero *m*, -ra *f*

laundress ['lɔndrəs] *n* : lavandera *f*

laundry ['lɔndri] *n, pl* **laundries 1** : ropa *f* sucia, ropa *f* para lavar ⟨to do the laundry : lavar la ropa⟩ **2** : lavandería *f* (servicio de lavar)

laureate ['lɔriət] *n* : laureado *m*, -da *f* ⟨poet laureate : poeta laureado⟩

laurel ['lɔrəl] *n* **1** : laurel *m* (planta) **2 laurels** *npl* : laureles *mpl* ⟨to rest on one's laurels : dormirse uno en sus laureles⟩

lava ['lɑvə, 'læ-] *n* : lava *f*

lavatory ['lævəˌtori] *n, pl* **-ries** : baño *m*, cuarto *m* de baño

lavender ['lævəndər] *n* : lavanda *f*, espliego *m*

lavish¹ ['lævɪʃ] *vt* : prodigar (a), colmar (de)

lavish² *adj* **1** EXTRAVAGANT : pródigo, generoso, derrochador **2** ABUNDANT : abundante **3** LUXURIOUS : lujoso, espléndido

lavishly ['lævɪʃli] *adv* : con generosidad, espléndidamente ⟨to live lavishly : vivir a lo grande⟩

lavishness ['lævɪʃnəs] *n* : generosidad *f*, esplendidez *f*

law ['lɔ] *n* **1** : ley *f* ⟨to break the law : violar la ley⟩ **2** : derecho *m* ⟨criminal law : derecho criminal⟩ **3** : abogacía *f* ⟨to practice law : ejercer la abogacía⟩

law–abiding ['lɔəˌbaɪdɪŋ] *adj* : observante de la ley

lawbreaker ['lɔˌbreɪkər] *n* : infractor *m*, -tora *f* de la ley

lawful ['lɔfəl] *adj* : legal, legítimo, lícito — **lawfully** *adv*

lawgiver ['lɔˌgɪvər] *n* : legislador *m*, -dora *f*

lawless ['lɔləs] *adj* : anárquico, ingobernable — **lawlessly** *adv*

lawlessness ['lɔləsnəs] *n* : anarquía *f*, desorden *m*

lawmaker ['lɔˌmeɪkər] *n* : legislador *m*, -dora *f*

lawman ['lɔmən] *n, pl* **-men** [-mən, -ˌmen] : agente *m* del orden

lawn ['lɔn] *n* : césped *m*, pasto *m*

lawn mower *n* : cortadora *f* de césped

lawsuit ['lɔˌsuːt] *n* : pleito *m*, litigio *m*, demanda *f*

lawyer ['lɔɪər, 'lɔjər] *n* : abogado *m*, -da *f*

lax ['læks] *adj* : laxo, relajado — **laxly** *adv*

laxative ['læksətɪv] *n* : laxante *m*

laxity ['læksəti] *n* : relajación *f*, descuido *m*, falta *f* de rigor

lay¹ ['leɪ] *vt* **laid** ['leɪd]; **laying 1** PLACE, PUT : poner, colocar ⟨she laid it on the table : lo puso en la mesa⟩ ⟨to lay eggs : poner huevos⟩ **2** : hacer ⟨to lay a bet : hacer una apuesta⟩ **3** IMPOSE : imponer ⟨to lay a tax : imponer un impuesto⟩ ⟨to lay the blame on : echarle la culpa a⟩ **4 to lay out** PRESENT : presentar, exponer ⟨he laid out his plan : presentó su proyecto⟩ **5 to lay out** DESIGN : diseñar (el trazado de)

lay² → **lie¹**

lay³ *adj* SECULAR : laico, lego

lay⁴ *n* **1** : disposición *f*, configuración *f* ⟨the lay of the land : la configuración del terreno⟩ **2** BALLAD : romance *m*, balada *f*

layer ['leɪər] *n* **1** : capa *f* (de pintura, etc.), estrato *m* (de roca) **2** : gallina *f* ponedora

layman ['leɪmən] *n, pl* **-men** [-mən, -ˌmen] : laico *m*, lego *m*

layoff ['leɪˌɔf] *n* : despido *m*

lay off *vt* : despedir

layout ['leɪˌaʊt] *n* : disposición *f*, distribución *f* (de una casa, etc.), trazado *m* (de una ciudad)

lay up *vt* **1** STORE : guardar, almacenar **2 to be laid up** : estar enfermo, tener que guardar cama

laywoman ['leɪˌwʊmən] *n, pl* **-women** [-ˌwɪmən] : laica *f*, lega *f*

laziness ['leɪzinəs] *n* : pereza *f*, flojera *f*

lazy ['leɪzi] *adj* **-zier; -est** : perezoso, holgazán — **lazily** ['leɪzəli] *adv*

leach ['liːtʃ] *vt* : filtrar

lead¹ ['liːd] *vt* **led** ['led]; **leading 1** GUIDE : conducir, llevar, guiar **2** DIRECT : dirigir **3** HEAD : encabezar, ir al frente de **4 to lead to** : resultar en, llevar a ⟨it only leads to trouble : sólo resulta en problemas⟩

lead² *n* : delantera *f*, primer lugar *m* ⟨to take the lead : tomar la delantera⟩

lead³ ['led] *n* **1** : plomo *m* (metal) **2** : mina *f* (de lápiz) **3 lead poisoning** : saturnismo *m*

leaden ['ledən] *adj* **1** : plomizo ⟨a leaden sky : un ciel plomizo⟩ **2** HEAVY : pesado

leader ['liːdər] *n* : jefe *m*, -fa *f*; líder *mf*; dirigente *mf*; gobernante *mf*

leadership ['liːdərˌʃɪp] *n* : mando *m*, dirección *f*

leaf¹ ['liːf] *vi* **1** : echar hojas (dícese de un árbol) **2 to leaf through** : hojear (un libro)

leaf² *n, pl* **leaves** ['li:vz] **1** : hoja *f* (de plantas o libros) **2 to turn over a new leaf** : hacer borrón y cuenta nueva

leafless ['li:fləs] *adj* : sin hojas, pelado

leaflet ['li:flət] *n* : folleto *m*

leafy ['li:fi] *adj* **leafier; -est** : frondoso

league¹ ['li:g] *v* **leagued; leaguing** *vt* : aliar, unir — *vi* : aliarse, unirse

league² *n* **1** : legua *f* (medida de distancia) **2** ASSOCIATION : alianza *f*, sociedad *f*, liga *f*

leak¹ ['li:k] *vt* **1** : perder, dejar escapar (un líquido o un gas) **2** : filtrar (información) — *vi* **1** : gotear, escaparse, fugarse (dícese de un líquido o un gas) **2** : hacer agua (dícese de un bote) **3** : filtrarse, divulgarse (dícese de información)

leak² *n* **1** HOLE : agujero *m* (en recipientes), gotera *f* (en un tejado) **2** ESCAPE : fuga *f*, escape *m* **3** : filtración *f* (de información)

leakage ['li:kɪʤ] *n* : escape *m*, fuga *f*

leaky ['li:ki] *adj* **leakier; -est** : agujereado (dícese de un recipiente), que hace agua (dícese de un bote), con goteras (dícese de un tejado)

lean¹ ['li:n] *vi* **1** BEND : inclinarse, ladearse **2** RECLINE : reclinarse **3** RELY : apoyarse (en), depender (de) **4** INCLINE, TEND : inclinarse, tender — *vt* : apoyar

lean² *adj* **1** THIN : delgado, flaco **2** : sin grasa, magro (dícese de la carne)

leanness ['li:nnəs] *n* : delgadez *f*

lean–to ['li:n,tu:] *n* : cobertizo *m*

leap¹ ['li:p] *vi* **leaped** ['li:pt, 'lɛpt] *or* **leapt; leaping** : saltar, brincar

leap² *n* : salto *m*, brinco *m*

leap year *n* : año *m* bisiesto

learn ['lərn] *vt* **1** : aprender ⟨to learn to sing : aprender a cantar⟩ **2** MEMORIZE : aprender de memoria **3** DISCOVER : saber, enterarse de — *vi* **1** : aprender ⟨to learn from experience : aprender por experiencia⟩ **2** FIND OUT : enterarse, saber

learned ['lərnəd] *adj* : erudito

learner ['lərnər] *n* : principiante *mf*, estudiante *mf*

learning ['lərnɪŋ] *n* : erudición *f*, saber *m*

lease¹ ['li:s] *vt* **leased; leasing** : arrendar

lease² *n* : contrato *m* de arrendamiento

leash¹ ['li:ʃ] *vt* : atraillar (un animal)

leash² *n* : traílla *f*

least¹ ['li:st] *adv* : menos ⟨when least expected : cuando menos se espera⟩

least² *adj* (*superlative of* **little**) : menor, más mínimo

least³ *n* **1** : lo menos ⟨at least : por lo menos⟩ **2 to say the least** : por no decir más

leather ['lɛðər] *n* : cuero *m*

leathery ['lɛðəri] *adj* : curtido (dícese de la piel), correoso (dícese de la carne)

leave¹ ['li:v] *v* **left** ['lɛft]; **leaving** *vt* **1** BEQUEATH : dejar, legar **2** DEPART : dejar, salir(se) de **3** ABANDON : abandonar, dejar **4** FORGET : dejar, olvidarse de ⟨I left the books at the library : dejé los libros en la biblioteca⟩ **5 to be left** : quedar ⟨it's all I have left : es todo lo que me queda⟩ **6 to be left over** : sobrar **7 to leave out** : omitir, excluir — *vi* : irse, salir, partir, marcharse ⟨she left yesterday morning : se fue ayer por la mañana⟩

leave² *n* **1** PERMISSION : permiso *m* ⟨by your leave : con su permiso⟩ **2 or leave of absence** : permiso *m*, licencia *f* ⟨maternity leave : licencia por maternidad⟩ **3 to take one's leave** : despedirse

leaven ['lɛvən] *n* : levadura *f*

leaves → **leaf**²

leaving ['li:vɪŋ] *n* **1** : salida *f*, partida *f* **2 leavings** *npl* : restos *mpl*, sobras *fpl*

Lebanese [,lɛbə'ni:z, -'ni:s] *n* : libanés *m*, -nesa *f* — **Lebanese** *adj*

lecherous ['lɛtʃərəs] *adj* : lascivo, libidinoso — **lecherously** *adv*

lechery ['lɛtʃəri] *n* : lascivia *f*, lujuria *f*

lecture¹ ['lɛktʃər] *v* **-tured; -turing** *vi* : dar clase, dictar clase, dar una conferencia — *vt* SCOLD : sermonear, echar una reprimenda a, regañar

lecture² *n* **1** : conferencia *f* **2** REPRIMAND : reprimenda *f*

lecturer ['lɛktʃərər] *n* **1** SPEAKER : conferenciante *mf* **2** TEACHER : profesor *m*, -sora *f*

led → **lead**¹

ledge ['lɛʤ] *n* : repisa *f* (de una pared), antepecho *m* (de una ventana), saliente *m* (de una montaña)

ledger ['lɛʤər] *n* : libro *m* mayor, libro *m* de contabilidad

lee¹ ['li:] *adj* : de sotavento

lee² *n* : sotavento *m*

leech ['li:tʃ] *n* : sanguijuela *f*

leek ['li:k] *n* : puerro *m*

leer¹ ['lɪr] *vi* : mirar con lascivia

leer² *n* : mirada *f* lasciva

leery ['lɪri] *adj* : receloso

lees ['li:z] *npl* : posos *mpl*, heces *fpl*

leeward¹ ['li:wərd, 'lu:ərd] *adj* : de sotavento

leeward² *n* : sotavento *m*

leeway ['li:,weɪ] *n* : libertad *f*, margen *m*

left¹ ['lɛft] *adv* : hacia la izquierda

left² → **leave**¹

left³ *adj* : izquierdo

left⁴ *n* : izquierda *f* ⟨on the left : a la izquierda⟩

left–hand ['lɛft'hand] *adj* **1** : de la izquierda **2** → **left–handed**

left–handed ['lɛft'handəd] *adj* **1** : zurdo (dícese de una persona) **2** : con doble sentido ⟨a left-handed compliment : un cumplido a medias⟩

leftist ['lɛftɪst] *n* : izquierdista *mf* — **leftist** *adj*

leftover ['lɛft,o:vər] *adj* : sobrante, que sobra

leftovers ['lɛft,oːvərz] *npl* : restos *mpl*, sobras *fpl*
left wing *n* the left wing : la izquierda
left–winger ['lɛft'wɪŋər] *n* : izquierdista *mf*
leg ['lɛg] *n* 1 : pierna *f* (de una persona, de carne, de ropa), pata *f* (de un animal, de muebles) 2 STAGE : etapa *f* (de un viaje), vuelta *f* (de una carrera)
legacy ['lɛgəsi] *n, pl* **-cies** : legado *m*, herencia *f*
legal ['liːgəl] *adj* 1 : legal, jurídico ⟨legal advisor : asesor jurídico⟩ ⟨the legal profession : la abogacía⟩ 2 LAWFUL : legítimo, legal
legalistic [,liːgə'lɪstɪk] *adj* : legalista
legality [li'gæləti] *n, pl* **-ties** : legalidad *f*
legalize ['liːgə,laɪz] *vt* **-ized; -izing** : legalizar
legally ['liːgəli] *adv* : legalmente
legate ['lɛgət] *n* : legado *m*
legation [lɪ'geɪʃən] *n* : legación *f*
legend ['lɛdʒənd] *n* 1 STORY : leyenda *f* 2 INSCRIPTION : leyenda *f*, inscripción *f* 3 : signos *mpl* convencionales (en un mapa)
legendary ['lɛdʒən,dɛri] *adj* : legendario
legerdemain [,lɛdʒərdə'meɪn] → **sleight of hand**
leggings ['lɛgɪŋz, 'lɛgənz] *npl* : mallas *fpl*
legibility [,lɛdʒə'bɪləti] *n* : legibilidad *f*
legible ['lɛdʒəbəl] *adj* : legible
legibly ['lɛdʒəbli] *adv* : de manera legible
legion ['liːdʒən] *n* : legión *f*
legionnaire [,liːdʒə'nær] *n* : legionario *m*, -ria *f*
legislate ['lɛdʒəs,leɪt] *vi* **-lated; -lating** : legislar
legislation [,lɛdʒəs'leɪʃən] *n* : legislación *f*
legislative ['lɛdʒəs,leɪtɪv] *adj* : legislativo, legislador
legislator ['lɛdʒəs,leɪtər] *n* : legislador *m*, -dora *f*
legislature ['lɛdʒəs,leɪtʃər] *n* : asamblea *f* legislativa
legitimacy [lɪ'dʒɪtəməsi] *n* : legitimidad *f*
legitimate [lɪ'dʒɪtəmət] *adj* 1 VALID : legítimo, válido, justificado 2 LAWFUL : legítimo, legal
legitimately [lɪ'dʒɪtəmətli] *adv* : legítimamente
legitimize [lɪ'dʒɪtə,maɪz] *vt* **-mized; -mizing** : legitimar, hacer legítimo
legume ['lɛ,gjuːm, lɪ'gjuːm] *n* : legumbre *f*
leisure ['liːʒər, 'lɛ-] *n* 1 : ocio *m*, tiempo *m* libre ⟨a life of leisure : una vida de ocio⟩ 2 to take one's leisure : reposar 3 at your leisure : cuando te venga bien, cuando tengas tiempo
leisurely ['liːʒərli, 'lɛ-] *adj & adv* : lento, sin prisas
lemming ['lɛmɪŋ] *n* : lemming *m*

lemon ['lɛmən] *n* : limón *m*
lemonade [,lɛmə'neɪd] *n* : limonada *f*
lemony ['lɛməni] *adj* : a limón
lend ['lɛnd] *vt* **lent** ['lɛnt]; **lending** 1 : prestar ⟨to lend money : prestar dinero⟩ 2 GIVE : dar ⟨it lends force to his criticism : da fuerza a su crítica⟩ 3 to lend oneself : prestarse a
length ['lɛŋkθ] *n* 1 : longitud *f*, largo *m* ⟨10 feet in length : 10 pies de largo⟩ 2 DURATION : duración *f* 3 : trozo *m* (de madera), corte *m* (de tela) 4 to go to any lengths : hacer todo lo posible 5 at ~ : extensamente ⟨to speak at length : hablar largo y tendido⟩
lengthen ['lɛŋkθən] *vt* 1 : alargar ⟨can they lengthen the dress? : ¿se puede alargar el vestido?⟩ 2 EXTEND, PROLONG : prolongar, extender — *vi* : alargarse, crecer ⟨the days are lengthening : los días están creciendo⟩
lengthways ['lɛŋkθ,weɪz] → **lengthwise**
lengthwise ['lɛŋkθ,waɪz] *adv* : a lo largo, longitudinalmente
lengthy ['lɛŋkθi] *adj* **lengthier; -est** 1 OVERLONG : largo y pesado 2 EXTENDED : prolongado, largo
leniency ['liːniənsi] *n, pl* **-cies** : lenidad *f*, indulgencia *f*
lenient ['liːniənt] *adj* : indulgente, poco severo
leniently ['liːniəntli] *adv* : con lenidad, con indulgencia
lens ['lɛnz] *n* 1 : cristalino *m* (del ojo) 2 : lente *mf* (de un instrumento o una cámara) 3 → **contact lens**
lent → **lend**
Lent ['lɛnt] *n* : Cuaresma *f*
lentil ['lɛntəl] *n* : lenteja *f*
Leo ['liːoː] *n* : Leo *mf*
leopard ['lɛpərd] *n* : leopardo *m*
leotard ['liːə,tɑrd] *n* : leotardo *m*, malla *f*
leper ['lɛpər] *n* : leproso *m*, -sa *f*
leprechaun ['lɛprə,kɑn] *n* : duende *m* (irlandés)
leprosy ['lɛprəsi] *n* : lepra *f* — **leprous** ['lɛprəs] *adj*
lesbian¹ ['lɛzbiən] *adj* : lesbiano
lesbian² *n* : lesbiana *f*
lesbianism ['lɛzbiə,nɪzəm] *n* : lesbianismo *m*
lesion ['liːʒən] *n* : lesión *f*
less¹ ['lɛs] *adv* (*comparative of* **little¹**) : menos ⟨the less you know, the better : cuanto menos sepas, mejor⟩ ⟨less and less : cada vez menos⟩
less² *adj* (*comparative of* **little²**) : menos ⟨less than three : menos de tres⟩ ⟨less money : menos dinero⟩ ⟨nothing less than perfection : nada menos que la perfección⟩
less³ *pron* : menos ⟨I'm earning less : estoy ganando menos⟩
less⁴ *prep* : menos ⟨one month less two days : un mes menos dos días⟩
lessee [lɛ'siː] *n* : arrendatario *m*, -ria *f*
lessen ['lɛsən] *vt* : disminuir, reducir — *vi* : disminuir, reducirse

lesser [ˈlɛsər] *adj* : menor ⟨to a lesser degree : en menor grado⟩
lesson [ˈlɛsən] *n* **1** CLASS : clase *f*, curso *m* **2** : lección *f* ⟨the lessons of history : las lecciones de la historia⟩
lessor [ˈlɛˌsɔr, lˈsɔr] *n* : arrendador *m*, -dora *f*
lest [ˈlɛst] *conj* : para (que) no ⟨lest we forget : para que no olvidemos⟩
let [ˈlɛt] *vt* **let; letting 1** ALLOW : dejar, permitir ⟨let me see it : déjame verlo⟩ **2** MAKE : hacer ⟨let me know : házmelo saber, avísame⟩ ⟨let them wait : que esperen, haz que esperen⟩ **3** RENT : alquilar ⟨*used in the first person plural imperative*⟩ ⟨let's go! : ¡vamos!, ¡vámonos!⟩ ⟨let us pray : oremos⟩ **5 to let down** DISAPPOINT : fallar **6 to let off** FORGIVE : perdonar **7 to let out** REVEAL : revelar **8 to let up** ABATE : amainar, disminuir ⟨the pace never lets up : el ritmo nunca disminuye⟩
letdown *n* : chasco *m*, decepción *f*
lethal [ˈli:θəl] *adj* : letal — **lethally** *adv*
lethargic [lɪˈθɑrdʒɪk] *adj* : letárgico
lethargy [ˈlɛθərdʒi] *n* : letargo *m*
let on *vi* **1** ADMIT : reconocer ⟨don't let on! : ¡no digas nada!⟩ **2** PRETEND : fingir
let's [ˈlɛts] (*contraction of* **let us**) → **let**
letter[1] [ˈlɛtər] *vt* : marcar con letras, inscribir letras en
letter[2] *n* **1** : letra *f* (del alfabeto) **2** : carta *f* ⟨a letter to my mother : una carta a mi madre⟩ **3 letters** *npl* ARTS : letras *fpl* **4 to the letter** : al pie de la letra
lettering [ˈlɛtərɪŋ] *n* : letra *f*
lettuce [ˈlɛtəs] *n* : lechuga *f*
leukemia [lu:ˈki:miə] *n* : leucemia *f*
levee [ˈlɛvi] *n* : dique *m*
level[1] [ˈlɛvəl] *vt* **-eled** *or* **-elled; -eling** *or* **-elling 1** FLATTEN : nivelar, aplanar **2** AIM : apuntar (una pistola), dirigir (una acusación) **3** RAZE : rasar, arrasar
level[2] *adj* **1** EVEN : llano, plano, parejo **2** CALM : tranquilo ⟨to keep a level head : no perder la cabeza⟩
level[3] *n* : nivel *m*
leveler [ˈlɛvələr] *n* : nivelador *m*, -dora *f*
levelheaded [ˈlɛvəlˈhɛdəd] *adj* : sensato, equilibrado
levelly [ˈlɛvəli] *adv* CALMLY : con ecuanimidad *f*, con calma
levelness [ˈlɛvəlnəs] *n* : uniformidad *f*
lever [ˈlɛvər, ˈli:-] *n* : palanca *f*
leverage [ˈlɛvərɪdʒ, ˈli:-] *n* **1** : apalancamiento *m* (en física) **2** INFLUENCE : influencia *f*, palanca *f fam*
leviathan [lɪˈvaɪəθən] *n* : leviatán *m*, gigante *m*
levity [ˈlɛvəti] *n* : ligereza *f*, frivolidad *f*
levy[1] [ˈlɛvi] *vt* **levied; levying 1** IMPOSE : imponer, exigir, gravar (un impuesto) **2** COLLECT : recaudar (un impuesto)
levy[2] *n, pl* **levies** : impuesto *m*, gravamen *m*
lewd [ˈlu:d] *adj* : lascivo — **lewdly** *adv*
lewdness [ˈlu:dnəs] *n* : lascivia *f*

lexical [ˈlɛksikəl] *adj* : léxico
lexicographer [ˌlɛksəˈkɑgrəfər] *n* : lexicógrafo *m*, -fa *f*
lexicographical [ˌlɛksəkoˈgræfikəl] *or* **lexicographic** [-ˈgræfɪk] *adj* : lexicográfico
lexicography [ˌlɛksəˈkɑgrəfi] *n* : lexicografía *f*
lexicon [ˈlɛksɪˌkɑn] *n, pl* **-ica** [-kə] *or* **-icons** : léxico *m*, lexicón *m*
liability [ˌlaɪəˈbɪləti] *n, pl* **-ties 1** RESPONSIBILITY : responsabilidad *f* **2** SUSCEPTIBILITY : propensión *f* **3** DRAWBACK : desventaja *f* **4 liabilities** *npl* DEBTS : deudas *fpl*, pasivo *m*
liable [ˈlaɪəbəl] *adj* **1** RESPONSIBLE : responsable **2** SUSCEPTIBLE : propenso **3** PROBABLE : probable ⟨it's liable to happen : es probable que suceda⟩
liaison [ˈli:əˌzɑn, liˈeɪ-] *n* **1** CONNECTION : enlace *m*, relación *f* **2** AFFAIR : amorío *m*, aventura *f*
liar [ˈlaɪər] *n* : mentiroso *m*, -sa *f*; embustero *m*, -ra *f*
libel[1] [ˈlaɪbəl] *vt* **-beled** *or* **-belled; -beling** *or* **-belling** : difamar, calumniar
libel[2] *n* : difamación *f*, calumnia *f*
libeler [ˈlaɪbələr] *n* : difamador *m*, -dora *f*; calumniador *m*, -dora *f*; libelista *mf*
libelous *or* **libellous** [ˈlaɪbələs] *adj* : difamatorio, calumnioso, injurioso
liberal[1] [ˈlɪbrəl, ˈlɪbərəl] *adj* **1** TOLERANT : liberal, tolerante **2** GENEROUS : generoso **3** ABUNDANT : abundante **4 liberal arts** : humanidades *fpl*, artes *fpl* liberales
liberal[2] *n* : liberal *mf*
liberalism [ˈlɪbrəˌlɪzəm, ˈlɪbərə-] *n* : liberalismo *m*
liberality [ˌlɪbəˈræləti] *n, pl* **-ties** : liberalidad *f*, generosidad *f*
liberalize [ˈlɪbrəˌlaɪz, ˈlɪbərə-] *vt* **-ized; -izing** : liberalizar
liberally [ˈlɪbrəli, ˈlɪbərə-] *adv* **1** GENEROUSLY : generosamente **2** ABUNDANTLY : abundantemente **3** FREELY : libremente
liberate [ˈlɪbəˌreɪt] *vt* **-ated; -ating** : liberar, libertar
liberation [ˌlɪbəˈreɪʃən] *n* : liberación *f*
liberator [ˈlɪbəˌreɪtər] *n* : libertador *m*, -dora *f*
Liberian [laɪˈbɪriən] *n* : liberiano *m*, -na *f* — **Liberian** *adj*
libertine [ˈlɪbərˌti:n] *n* : libertino *m*, -na *f*
liberty [ˈlɪbərti] *n, pl* **-ties 1** : libertad *f* **2 to take the liberty of** : tomarse la libertad de **3 to take liberties with** : tomarse confianzas con, tomarse libertades con
libido [ləˈbi:do:, -ˈbaɪ-] *n, pl* **-dos** : libido *f* — **libidinous** [ləˈbɪdənəs] *adj*
Libra [ˈli:brə] *n* : Libra *mf*
librarian [laɪˈbrɛriən] *n* : bibliotecario *m*, -ria *f*
library [ˈlaɪˌbrɛri] *n, pl* **-braries** : biblioteca *f*

librettist ['lɪ'brɛtɪst] n : libretista mf
libretto [lɪ'brɛto] n, pl **-tos** or **-ti** [-ṭi:] : libreto m
Libyan ['lɪbiən] n : libio m, -bia f — **Libyan** adj
lice → **louse**
license¹ ['laɪsənts] vt **licensed; licensing** : licenciar, autorizar, dar permiso a
license² or **licence** n **1** PERMISSION : licencia f, permiso m **2** PERMIT : licencia f, carnet m Spain ⟨driver's license : licencia de conducir⟩ **3** FREEDOM : libertad f **4** LICENTIOUSNESS : libertinaje m
licentious [laɪ'sɛntʃəs] adj : licencioso, disoluto — **licentiously** adv
licentiousness [laɪ'sɛntʃəsnəs] n : libertinaje m
lichen ['laɪkən] n : liquen m
licit ['lɪsət] adj : lícito
lick¹ ['lɪk] vt **1** : lamer **2** BEAT : darle una paliza (a alguien)
lick² n **1** : lamida f, lengüetada f ⟨a lick of paint : una mano de pintura⟩ **2** BIT : pizca f, ápice m **3 a lick and a promise** : una lavada a la carrera
licorice ['lɪkərɪʃ, -rəs] n : regaliz m, dulce m de regaliz
lid ['lɪd] n **1** COVER : tapa f **2** EYELID : párpado m
lie¹ ['laɪ] vi **lay** ['leɪ]; **lain** ['leɪn]; **lying** ['laɪɪŋ] **1** : acostarse, echarse ⟨I lay down : me acosté⟩ **2** : estar, estar situado, encontrarse ⟨the book lay on the table : el libro estaba en la mesa⟩ ⟨the city lies to the south : la ciudad se encuentra al sur⟩ **3** CONSIST : consistir **4 to lie in** : residir en ⟨the power lies in the people : el poder reside en el pueblo⟩
lie² vi **lied; lying** ['laɪɪŋ] : mentir
lie³ n **1** UNTRUTH : mentira f ⟨to tell lies : decir mentiras⟩ **2** POSITION : posición f
liege ['li:dʒ] n : señor m feudal
lien ['li:n, 'li:ən] n : derecho m de retención
lieutenant [lu:'tɛnənt] n : teniente mf
lieutenant colonel n : teniente mf coronel
lieutenant commander n : capitán m, -tana f de corbeta
lieutenant general n : teniente mf general
life ['laɪf] n, pl **lives** ['laɪvz] **1** : vida f ⟨plant life : la vida vegetal⟩ **2** EXISTENCE : vida f, existencia f **3** BIOGRAPHY : biografía f, vida f **4** DURATION : duración f, vida f **5** LIVELINESS : vivacidad f, animación f
lifeblood ['laɪf,blʌd] n : parte f vital, sustento m
lifeboat ['laɪf,bo:t] n : bote m salvavidas
lifeguard ['laɪf,gard] n : socorrista mf, salvavidas mf
lifeless ['laɪfləs] adj : sin vida, muerto
lifelike ['laɪf,laɪk] adj : que parece vivo, natural, verosímil

lifelong ['laɪf'lɔŋ] adj : de toda la vida ⟨a lifelong friend : un amigo de toda la vida⟩
life preserver n : salvavidas m
lifesaver ['laɪf,seɪvər] n **1** : salvación f **2** → **lifeguard**
lifesaving ['laɪf,seɪvɪŋ] n : socorrismo m
lifestyle ['laɪf,staɪl] n : estilo m de vida
lifetime ['laɪf,taɪm] n : vida f, curso m de la vida
lift¹ ['lɪft] vt **1** RAISE : levantar, alzar, subir **2** END : levantar ⟨to lift a ban : levantar una prohibición⟩ — vi **1** RISE : levantarse, alzarse **2** CLEAR UP : despejar ⟨the fog lifted : se disipó la niebla⟩
lift² n **1** LIFTING : levantamiento m, alzamiento m **2** BOOST : impulso m, estímulo m **3 to give someone a lift** : llevar en coche a alguien
liftoff ['lɪft,ɔf] n : despegue m
ligament ['lɪgəmənt] n : ligamento m
ligature ['lɪgə,tʃʊr, -tʃər] n : ligadura f
light¹ ['laɪt] v **lit** ['lɪt] or **lighted; lighting** vt **1** ILLUMINATE : iluminar, alumbrar **2** IGNITE : encender, prenderle fuego a — vi : encenderse, prender
light² vi **lighted** or **lit** ['lɪt]; **lighting 1** LAND, SETTLE : posarse **2** DISMOUNT : bajarse, apearse
light³ ['laɪt] adv **1** LIGHTLY : suavemente, ligeramente **2 to travel light** : viajar con poco equipaje
light⁴ adj **1** LIGHTWEIGHT : ligero, liviano, poco pesado **2** EASY : fácil, ligero, liviano ⟨light reading : lectura fácil⟩ **3** GENTLE, MILD : fino, suave, leve ⟨a light breeze : una brisa suave⟩ ⟨a light rain : una lluvia fina⟩ **4** FRIVOLOUS : de poca importancia, superficial **5** BRIGHT : bien iluminado, claro **6** PALE : claro ⟨dícese de los colores), rubio (dícese del pelo⟩
light⁵ n **1** ILLUMINATION : luz f **2** DAYLIGHT : luz f del día **3** DAWN : amanecer m, madrugada f **4** LAMP : lámpara f ⟨to turn on off the light : apagar la luz⟩ **5** ASPECT : aspecto m ⟨in a new light : con otros ojos⟩ ⟨in the light of : en vista de, a la luz de⟩ **6** MATCH : fósforo m, cerillo m **7 to bring to light** : sacar a (la) luz
lightbulb ['laɪt,bʌlb] n : bombilla f, foco m, bombillo m CA, Col, Ven
lighten ['laɪtən] vt **1** ILLUMINATE : iluminar, dar más luz a **2** : aclararse (el pelo) **3** : aligerar (una carga, etc.) **4** RELIEVE : aliviar **5** GLADDEN : alegrar ⟨it lightened his heart : alegró su corazón⟩
lighter ['laɪtər] n : encendedor m
lighthearted ['laɪt'hartəd] adj : alegre, despreocupado, desenfadado — **lightheartedly** adv
lightheartedness ['laɪt'harṭədnəs] n : desenfado m, alegría f
lighthouse ['laɪt,haʊs] n : faro m

lighting [ˈlaɪtɪŋ] *n* : iluminación *f*
lightly [ˈlaɪtli] *adv* **1** GENTLY : suavemente **2** SLIGHTLY : ligeramente **3** FRIVOLOUSLY : a la ligera **4 to let off lightly** : tratar con indulgencia
lightness [ˈlaɪtnəs] *n* **1** BRIGHTNESS : luminosidad *f*, claridad *f* **2** GENTLENESS : ligereza *f*, suavidad *f*, delicadeza *f* **3** : ligereza *f*, liviandad *f* (de peso)
lightning [ˈlaɪtnɪŋ] *n* : relámpago *m*, rayo *m*
lightning bug → **firefly**
lightproof [ˈlaɪtˌpruːf] *adj* : impenetrable por la luz, opaco
lightweight [ˈlaɪtˈweɪt] *adj* : ligero, liviano, de poco peso
light–year [ˈlaɪtˌjɪr] *n* : año *m* luz
lignite [ˈlɪɡˌnaɪt] *n* : lignito *m*
likable *or* **likeable** [ˈlaɪkəbəl] *adj* : simpático, agradable
like[1] [ˈlaɪk] *v* **liked; liking** *vt* **1** : agradar, gustarle (algo a uno) ⟨he likes rice : le gusta el arroz⟩ ⟨she doesn't like flowers : a ella no le gustan las flores⟩ ⟨I like you : me caes bien⟩ **2** WANT : querer, desear ⟨I'd like a hamburger : quiero una hamburguesa⟩ ⟨he would like more help : le gustaría tener más ayuda⟩ — *vi* : querer ⟨do as you like : haz lo que quieras⟩
like[2] *adj* : parecido, semejante, similar
like[3] *n* **1** PREFERENCE : preferencia *f*, gusto *m* **2 the like** : cosa *f* parecida, cosas *fpl* por el estilo ⟨I've never seen the like : nunca he visto cosa parecida⟩
like[4] *conj* **1** AS IF : como si ⟨they looked at me like I was crazy : se me quedaron mirando como si estuviera loca⟩ **2** AS : como, igual que ⟨she doesn't love you like I do : ella no te quiere como yo⟩
like[5] *prep* **1** : como, parecido a ⟨she acts like my mother : se comporta como mi madre⟩ ⟨he looks like me : se parece a mí⟩ **2** : propio de, típico de ⟨that's just like her : eso es muy típico de ella⟩ **3** : como ⟨animals like cows : animales como vacas⟩ **4 like this, like that** : así ⟨do it like that : hazlo así⟩
likelihood [ˈlaɪkliˌhʊd] *n* : probabilidad *f* ⟨in all likelihood : con toda probabilidad⟩
likely[1] [ˈlaɪkli] *adv* : probablemente ⟨most likely he's sick : lo más probable es que esté enfermo⟩ ⟨they're likely to come : es probable que vengan⟩
likely[2] *adj* **-lier; -est** **1** PROBABLE : probable ⟨to be likely to : ser muy probable que⟩ **2** SUITABLE : apropiado, adecuado **3** BELIEVABLE : verosímil, creíble **4** PROMISING : prometedor
liken [ˈlaɪkən] *vt* : comparar
likeness [ˈlaɪknəs] *n* **1** SIMILARITY : semejanza *f*, parecido *m* **2** PORTRAIT : retrato *m*
likewise [ˈlaɪkˌwaɪz] *adv* **1** SIMILARLY : de la misma manera, asimismo **2** ALSO : también, además, asimismo

liking [ˈlaɪkɪŋ] *n* **1** FONDNESS : afición *f* (por una cosa), simpatía *f* (por una persona) **2** TASTE : gusto *m* ⟨is it to your liking? : ¿te gusta?⟩
lilac [ˈlaɪlək, -ˌlæk, -ˌlɑk] *n* : lila *f*
lilt [ˈlɪlt] *n* : cadencia *f*, ritmo *m* alegre
lily [ˈlɪli] *n*, *pl* **lilies 1** : lirio *m*, azucena *f* **2 lily of the valley** : lirio *m* de los valles, muguete *m*
lima bean [ˈlaɪmə] *n* : frijol *m* de media luna
limb [ˈlɪm] *n* **1** APPENDAGE : miembro *m*, extremidad *f* **2** BRANCH : rama *f*
limber[1] [ˈlɪmbər] *vi* *or* **to limber up** : calentarse, prepararse
limber[2] *adj* : ágil (dícese de las personas), flexible (dícese de los objetos)
limbo [ˈlɪmˌboː] *n*, *pl* **-bos 1** : limbo *m* (en la religión) **2** OBLIVION : olvido *m* ⟨the project is in limbo : el proyecto ha caído en el olvido⟩
lime [ˈlaɪm] *n* **1** : cal *f* (óxido) **2** : lima *f* (fruta), limón *m* verde *Mex*
limelight [ˈlaɪmˌlaɪt] *n* **to be in the limelight** : ser el centro de atención, estar en el candelero
limerick [ˈlɪmərɪk] *n* : poema *m* jocoso de cinco versos
limestone [ˈlaɪmˌstoːn] *n* : piedra *f* caliza, caliza *f*
limit[1] [ˈlɪmət] *vt* : limitar, restringir
limit[2] *n* **1** MAXIMUM : límite *m*, máximo *m* ⟨speed limit : límite de velocidad⟩ **2 limits** *npl* : límites *mpl*, confines *mpl* ⟨city limits : límites de la ciudad⟩ **3 that's the limit!** : ¡eso es el colmo!
limitation [ˌlɪməˈteɪʃən] *n* : limitación *f*, restricción *f*
limited [ˈlɪmətəd] *adj* : limitado, restringido
limitless [ˈlɪmətləs] *adj* : ilimitado, sin límites
limousine [ˈlɪməˌziːn, ˌlɪməˈ-] *n* : limusina *f*
limp[1] [ˈlɪmp] *vi* : cojear
limp[2] *adj* **1** FLACCID : fláccido **2** LANK : lacio (dícese del pelo) **3** WEAK : débil ⟨to feel limp : sentirse desfallecer, sentirse sin fuerzas⟩
limp[3] *n* : cojera *f*
limpid [ˈlɪmpəd] *adj* : límpido, claro
limply [ˈlɪmpli] *adv* : sin fuerzas
limpness [ˈlɪmpnəs] *n* : flaccidez *f*, debilidad *f*
linden [ˈlɪndən] *n* : tilo *m*
line[1] [ˈlaɪn] *v* **lined; lining** *vt* **1** : forrar, cubrir ⟨to line a dress : forrar un vestido⟩ ⟨to line the walls : cubrir las paredes⟩ **2** MARK : rayar, trazar líneas en **3** BORDER : bordear **4** ALIGN : alinear — *vi* **to line up** : ponerse in fila, hacer cola
line[2] *n* **1** CORD, ROPE : cuerda *f* **2** WIRE : cable *m* ⟨power line : cable eléctrico⟩ **3** : línea *f* (de teléfono) **4** ROW : fila *f*, hilera *f* **5** NOTE : nota *f*, líneas *fpl* ⟨drop me a line : mándame unas líneas⟩ **6** COURSE : línea *f* ⟨line of inquiry : línea

de investigación⟩ **7** AGREEMENT : conformidad *f* ⟨to be in line with : ser conforme a⟩ ⟨to fall into line : estar de acuerdo⟩ **8** OCCUPATION : ocupación *f*, rama *f*, especialidad *f* **9** LIMIT : línea *f*, límite *m* ⟨dividing line : línea divisoria⟩ ⟨to draw the line : fijar límites⟩ **10** SERVICE : línea *f* ⟨bus line : línea de autobuses⟩ **11** MARK : línea *f*, arruga *f* (de la cara)

lineage ['lɪniɪʤ] *n* : linaje *m*, abolengo *m*

lineal ['lɪniəl] *adj* : en línea directa

lineaments ['lɪniəmənts] *npl* : facciones *fpl* (de la cara), rasgos *mpl*

linear ['lɪniər] *adj* : lineal

linen ['lɪnən] *n* : lino *m*

liner ['laɪnər] *n* **1** LINING : forro *m* **2** SHIP : buque *m*, transatlántico *m*

lineup ['laɪn,əp] *n* **1** : fila *f* de sospechosos **2** : formación *f* (en deportes) **3** ALIGNMENT : alineación *f*

linger ['lɪŋgər] *vi* **1** TARRY : quedarse, entretenerse, rezagarse **2** PERSIST : persistir, sobrevivir

lingerie [,lɑndʒə'reɪ, ,lænʒə'riː] *n* : ropa *f* íntima femenina, lencería *f*

lingo ['lɪŋgo] *n, pl* **-goes 1** LANGUAGE : idioma *m* **2** JARGON : jerga *f*

linguist ['lɪŋgwɪst] *n* : lingüista *mf*

linguistic [lɪŋ'gwɪstɪk] *adj* : lingüístico

linguistics [lɪŋ'gwɪstɪks] *n* : lingüística *f*

liniment ['lɪnəmənt] *n* : linimento *m*

lining ['laɪnɪŋ] *n* : forro *m*

link¹ ['lɪŋk] *vt* : unir, enlazar, conectar — *vi* **to link up** : unirse, conectar

link² *n* **1** : eslabón *m* (de una cadena) **2** BOND : conexión *f*, lazo *m*, vínculo *m*

linkage ['lɪŋkɪʤ] *n* : conexión *f*, unión *f*, enlace *m*

linoleum [lə'noːliəm] *n* : linóleo *m*

linseed oil ['lɪn,siːd] *n* : aceite *m* de linaza

lint ['lɪnt] *n* : pelusa *f*

lintel ['lɪntəl] *n* : dintel *m*

lion ['laɪən] *n* : león *m*

lioness ['laɪənɪs] *n* : leona *f*

lionize ['laɪə,naɪz] *vt* **-ized; -izing** : tratar a una persona como muy importante

lip ['lɪp] *n* **1** : labio *m* **2** EDGE, RIM : pico *m* (de una jarra), borde *m* (de una taza)

lipreading ['lɪp,riːdɪŋ] *n* : lectura *f* de los labios

lipstick ['lɪp,stɪk] *n* : lápiz *m* de labios, barra *f* de labios

liquefy ['lɪkwə,faɪ] *v* **-fied; -fying** *vt* : licuar — *vi* : licuarse

liqueur [lɪ'kur, -'kər, -'kjur] *n* : licor *m*

liquid¹ ['lɪkwəd] *adj* : líquido

liquid² *n* : líquido *m*

liquidate ['lɪkwə,deɪt] *vt* **-dated; -dating** : liquidar

liquidation [,lɪkwə'deɪʃən] *n* : liquidación *f*

liquidity [lɪk'wɪdəti] *n* : liquidez *f*

liquor ['lɪkər] *n* : alcohol *m*, bebidas *fpl* alcohólicas, licor *m*

lisp¹ ['lɪsp] *vi* : cecear

lisp² *n* : ceceo *m*

lissome ['lɪsəm] *adj* **1** FLEXIBLE : flexible **2** LITHE : ágil y grácil

list¹ ['lɪst] *vt* **1** ENUMERATE : hacer una lista de, enumerar **2** INCLUDE : poner en una lista, incluir — *vi* : escorar (dícese de un barco)

list² *n* **1** ENUMERATION : lista *f* **2** SLANT : escora *f*, inclinación *f*

listen ['lɪsən] *vi* **1** : escuchar, oír **2 to listen to** HEED : prestar atención a, hacer caso de, escuchar **3 to listen to reason** : atender a razones

listener ['lɪsənər] *n* : oyente *mf*, persona *f* que sabe escuchar

listless ['lɪstləs] *adj* : lánguido, apático — **listlessly** *adv*

listlessness ['lɪstləsnəs] *n* : apatía *f*, languidez *f*, desgana *f*

lit ['lɪt] → **light**

litany ['lɪtəni] *n, pl* **-nies** : letanía *f*

liter ['liːtər] *n* : litro *m*

literacy ['lɪtərəsi] *n* : alfabetismo *m*

literal ['lɪtərəl] *adj* : literal — **literally** *adv*

literary ['lɪtə,rri] *adj* : literario

literate ['lɪtərət] *adj* : alfabetizado

literature ['lɪtərə,tʃur, -'tʃər] *n* : literatura *f*

lithe ['laɪð, 'laɪθ] *adj* : ágil y grácil

lithesome ['laɪðsəm, 'laɪθ-] → **lissome**

lithium ['lɪθiəm] *n* : litio *m*

lithograph ['lɪθə,græf] *n* : litografía *f*

lithographer [lɪ'θɑgrəfər, 'lɪθə-,græfər] *n* : litógrafo *m*, -fa *f*

lithography [lɪ'θɑgrəfi] *n* : litografía *f*

lithosphere ['lɪθə,sfɪr] *n* : litosfera *f*

Lithuanian [,lɪθə'weɪniən] *n* **1** : lituano *m* (idioma) **2** : lituano *m*, -na *f* — **Lithuanian** *adj*

litigant ['lɪtɪgənt] *n* : litigante *mf*

litigate ['lɪtə,geɪt] *vi* **-gated; -gating** : litigar

litigation [,lɪtə'geɪʃən] *n* : litigio *m*

litmus paper ['lɪtməs] *n* : papel *m* de tornasol

litter¹ ['lɪtər] *vt* : tirar basura en, ensuciar — *vi* : tirar basura

litter² *n* **1** : camada *f*, cría *f* ⟨a litter of kittens : una cría de gatitos⟩ **2** STRETCHER : camilla *f* **3** RUBBISH : basura *f* **4** : arena *f* higiénica (para gatos)

little¹ ['lɪtəl] *adv* **less** ['lɛs]; **least** ['liːst] **1** : poco ⟨she sings very little : canta muy poco⟩ **2 little did I know that . . .** : no tenía la menor idea de que . . . **3 as little as possible** : lo menos posible

little² *adj* **littler** *or* **less** ['lɛs] *or* **lesser** ['lɛsər]; **littlest** *or* **least** ['liːst] **1** SMALL : pequeño **2** : poco ⟨they speak little Spanish : hablan poco español⟩ ⟨little by little : poco a poco⟩ **3** TRIVIAL : sin importancia, trivial

little³ *n* **1** : poco *m* ⟨little has changed : poco ha cambiado⟩ **2 a little** : un poco, algo ⟨it's a little surprising : es algo sorprendente⟩

Little Dipper → **dipper**

liturgical [lə'tərʤɪkəl] *adj* : litúrgico — **liturgically** [-kli] *adv*

liturgy [ˈlɪṭərdʒi] *n, pl* **-gies** : liturgia *f*
livable [ˈlɪvəbəl] *adj* : habitable
live[1] [ˈlɪv] *vi* **lived; living 1** EXIST : vivir ⟨as long as I live : mientras viva⟩ ⟨to live from day to day : vivir al día⟩ **2** : llevar una vida, vivir ⟨he lived simply : llevó una vida sencilla⟩ **3** SUBSIST : mantenerse, vivir **4** RESIDE : vivir, residir
live[2] [ˈlaɪv] *adj* **1** LIVING : vivo **2** BURNING : encendido ⟨a live coal : una brasa⟩ **3** : con corriente ⟨live wires : cables con corriente⟩ **4** : cargado, sin estallar ⟨a live bomb : una bomba sin estallar⟩ **5** CURRENT : de actualidad ⟨a live issue : un asunto de actualidad⟩ **6** : en vivo, en directo ⟨a live interview : una entrevista en vivo⟩
livelihood [ˈlaɪvliˌhʊd] *n* : sustento *m*, vida *f*, medio *m* de vida
liveliness [ˈlaɪvlinəs] *n* : animación *f*, vivacidad *f*
livelong [ˈlɪvˈlɔŋ] *adj* : entero, completo
lively [ˈlaɪvli] *adj* **-lier; -est** : animado, vivaz, vivo, enérgico
liven [ˈlaɪvən] *vt* : animar — *vi* : animarse
liver [ˈlɪvər] *n* : hígado *m*
livery [ˈlɪvəri] *n, pl* **-eries** : librea *f*
lives → **life**
livestock [ˈlaɪvˌstɑk] *n* : ganado *m*
live wire *n* : persona *f* vivaz y muy activa
livid [ˈlɪvəd] *adj* **1** BLACK-AND-BLUE : amoratado **2** PALE : lívido **3** ENRAGED : furioso
living[1] [ˈlɪvɪŋ] *adj* : vivo
living[2] *n* **to make a living** : ganarse la vida
living room *n* : living *m*, sala *f* de estar
lizard [ˈlɪzərd] *n* : lagarto *m*
llama [ˈlɑmə, ˈjɑ-] *n* : llama *f*
load[1] [ˈloːd] *vt* : cargar, embarcar
load[2] *n* **1** CARGO : carga *f* **2** WEIGHT : peso *m* **3** BURDEN : carga *f*, peso *m* **4 loads** *npl* : montón *m*, pila *f*, cantidad *f* ⟨loads of work : un montón de trabajo⟩
loaf[1] [ˈloːf] *vi* : holgazanear, flojear, haraganear
loaf[2] *n, pl* **loaves** [ˈloːvz] **1** : pan *m*, pan *m* de molde, barra *f* de pan **2 meat loaf** : pan *m* de carne
loafer [ˈloːfər] *n* : holgazán *m*, -zana *f*; haragán *m*, -gana *f*; vago *m*, -ga *f*
loam [ˈloːm] *n* : marga *f*, suelo *m*
loan[1] [ˈloːn] *vt* : prestar
loan[2] *n* : préstamo *m*, empréstito *m* (del banco)
loath [ˈloːθ, ˈloːð] *adj* : poco dispuesto ⟨I am loath to say it : me resisto a decirlo⟩
loathe [ˈloːð] *vt* **loathed; loathing** : odiar, aborrecer
loathing [ˈloːðɪŋ] *n* : aversión *f*, odio *m*, aborrecimiento *m*
loathsome [ˈloːθsəm, ˈloːð-] *adj* : odioso, repugnante
lob[1] [ˈlɑb] *vt* **lobbed; lobbing** : hacerle un globo (a otro jugador)

lob[2] *n* : globo *m* (en deportes)
lobby[1] [ˈlɑbi] *v* **-bied; -bying** *vt* : presionar, ejercer presión sobre — *vi* **to lobby for** : presionar para (lograr algo)
lobby[2] *n, pl* **-bies 1** FOYER : vestíbulo *m* **2** LOBBYISTS : grupo *m* de presión, lobby *m*
lobbyist [ˈlɑbiɪst] *n* : miembro *m* de un lobby
lobe [ˈloːb] *n* : lóbulo *m*
lobed [ˈloːbd] *adj* : lobulado
lobotomy [ləˈbɑṭəmi, lo-] *n, pl* **-mies** : lobotomía *f*
lobster [ˈlɑbstər] *n* : langosta *f*
local[1] [ˈloːkəl] *adj* : local
local[2] *n* **1** : anestesia *f* local **2 the locals** : los vecinos del lugar, los habitantes
locale [loˈkæl] *n* : lugar *m*, escenario *m*
locality [loˈkæləṭi] *n, pl* **-ties** : localidad *f*
localize [ˈloːkəˌlaɪz] *vt* **-ized; -izing** : localizar
locally [ˈloːkəli] *adv* : en la localidad, en la zona
locate [ˈloːˌkeɪt, loˈkeɪt] *v* **-cated; -cating** *vt* **1** POSITION : situar, ubicar **2** FIND : localizar, ubicar — *vi* SETTLE : establecerse
location [loˈkeɪʃən] *n* **1** POSITION : posición *f*, emplazamiento *m*, ubicación *f* **2** PLACE : lugar *m*, sitio *m*
lock[1] [ˈlɑk] *vt* **1** FASTEN : cerrar **2** CONFINE : encerrar ⟨they locked me in the room : me encerraron en la sala⟩ **3** IMMOBILIZE : bloquear (una rueda) — *vi* **1** : cerrarse (dícese de una puerta) **2** : trabarse, bloquearse (dícese de una rueda)
lock[2] *n* **1** : mechón *m* (de pelo) **2** FASTENER : cerradura *f*, cerrojo *m*, chapa *f* **3** : esclusa *f* (de un canal)
locker [ˈlɑkər] *n* : armario *m*, cajón *m* con llave, lócker *m*
locket [ˈlɑkət] *n* : medallón *m*, guardapelo *m*, relicario *m*
lockjaw [ˈlɑkˌjɔ] *n* : tétano *m*
lockout [ˈlɑkˌaʊt] *n* : cierre *m* patronal, lockout *m*
locksmith [ˈlɑkˌsmɪθ] *n* : cerrajero *m*, -ra *f*
lockup [ˈlɑkˌʌp] *n* JAIL : cárcel *f*
locomotion [ˌloːkəˈmoːʃən] *n* : locomoción *f*
locomotive[1] [ˌloːkəˈmoːṭɪv] *adj* : locomotor
locomotive[2] *n* : locomotora *f*
locust [ˈloːkəst] *n* **1** : langosta *f*, chapulín *m* CA, Mex **2** CICADA : cigarra *f*, chicharra *f* **3** : acacia *f* blanca (árbol)
locution [loˈkjuːʃən] *n* : locución *f*
lode [ˈloːd] *n* : veta *f*, vena *f*, filón *m*
lodestar [ˈloːdˌstɑr] *n* : estrella *f* polar
lodestone [ˈloːdˌstoːn] *n* : piedra *f* imán
lodge[1] [ˈlɑdʒ] *v* **lodged; lodging** *vt* **1** HOUSE : hospedar, alojar **2** FILE : presentar ⟨to lodge a complaint : presentar una demanda⟩ — *vi* **1** : posarse, meterse ⟨the bullet lodged in the door

: la bala se incrustó en la puerta⟩ 2
STAY : hospedarse, alojarse

lodge² *n* 1 : pabellón *m*, casa *f* de campo ⟨hunting lodge : refugio de caza⟩ 2
: madriguera *f* (de un castor) 3 : logia
f ⟨Masonic lodge : logia masónica⟩

lodger [ˈlɑʤər] *n* : inquilino *m*, -na *f*;
huésped *m*, -peda *f*

lodging [ˈlɑʤɪŋ] *n* 1 : alojamiento *m* 2
lodgings *npl* ROOMS : habitaciones *fpl*

loft [ˈlɔft] *n* 1 ATTIC : desván *m*, ático *m*,
buhardilla *f* 2 : loft *m* (en un depósito
comercial) 3 HAYLOFT : pajar *m* 4
: galería *f* ⟨choir loft : galería del coro⟩

loftily [ˈlɔftəli] *adv* : altaneramente, con
altivez

loftiness [ˈlɔftinəs] *n* 1 NOBILITY : nobleza *f* 2 ARROGANCE : altanería *f*, arrogancia *f* 3 HEIGHT : altura *f*, elevación *f*

lofty [ˈlɔfti] *adj* **loftier; -est** 1 NOBLE
: noble, elevado 2 HAUGHTY : altivo,
arrogante, altanero 3 HIGH : majestuoso, elevado

log¹ [ˈlɔg, ˈlɑg] *vi* **logged; logging** 1 : talar (árboles) 2 RECORD : registrar, anotar 3 **to log on** : entrar (al sistema) 4
to log off : salir (del sistema)

log² *n* 1 : tronco *m*, leño *m* 2 RECORD
: diario *m*

logarithm [ˈlɔgəˌrɪðəm, ˈlɑ-] *n* : logaritmo *m*

logger [ˈlɔgər, ˈlɑ-] *n* : leñador *m*, -dora
f

loggerhead [ˈlɔgərˌhd, ˈlɑ-] *n* 1 : tortuga *f* boba 2 **to be at loggerheads** : estar en pugna, estar en desacuerdo

logic [ˈlɑʤɪk] *n* : lógica *f* — **logical**
[ˈlɑʤɪkəl] *adj* — **logically** [-kli] *adv*

logistic [ləˈʤɪstɪk, lo-] *adj* : logístico

logistics [ləˈʤɪstɪks, lo-] *ns & pl* : logística *f*

logo [ˈloːˌgoː] *n*, *pl* **logos** [-ˌgoːz] : logotipo *m*

loin [ˈlɔɪn] *n* 1 : lomo *m* ⟨pork loin
: lomo de cerdo⟩ 2 **loins** *npl* : lomos
mpl ⟨to gird one's loins : prepararse
para la lucha⟩

loiter [ˈlɔɪtər] *vi* : vagar, perder el tiempo

loll [ˈlɑl] *vi* 1 SLOUCH : repantigarse 2
IDLE : holgazanear, hacer el vago

lollipop *or* **lollypop** [ˈlɑliˌpɑp] *n* : dulce
m en palito, chupete *m* *Chile, Peru*,
paleta *f* *CA, Mex*

lone [ˈloːn] *adj* 1 SOLITARY : solitario 2
ONLY : único

loneliness [ˈloːnlinəs] *n* : soledad *f*

lonely [ˈloːnli] *adj* **-lier; -est** 1 SOLITARY
: solitario, aislado 2 LONESOME : solo
⟨to feel lonely : sentirse muy solo⟩

loner [ˈloːnər] *n* : solitario *m*, -ria *f*; recluso *m*, -sa *f*

lonesome [ˈloːnsəm] *adj* : solo, solitario

long¹ [ˈlɔŋ] *vi* 1 **to long for** : añorar, desear, anhelar 2 **to long to** : anhelar, estar deseando ⟨they longed to see her
: estaban deseando verla, tenían
muchas ganas de verla⟩

long² *adv* 1 : mucho, mucho tiempo ⟨it
didn't take long : no llevó mucho tiempo⟩ ⟨will it last long? : ¿va a durar mucho?⟩ 2 **all day long** : todo el día 3 **as
long as** *or* **so long as** : mientras, con
tal que 4 **long before** : mucho antes 5
so long! : ¡hasta luego!, ¡adiós!

long³ *adj* **longer** [ˈlɔŋgər]; **longest**
[ˈlɔŋgəst] 1 (*indicating length*)) : largo
⟨the dress is too long : el vestido es demasiado largo⟩ ⟨a long way from : bastante lejos de⟩ ⟨in the long run : a la
larga⟩ 2 (*indicating time*)) : largo, prolongado ⟨a long illness : una enfermedad prolongada⟩ ⟨a long walk : un
paseo largo⟩ ⟨at long last : por fin⟩ 3
to be long on : estar cargado de

long⁴ *n* 1 **before long** : dentro de poco
2 **the long and the short** : lo esencial,
lo fundamental

longevity [lɑnˈʤvəti] *n* : longevidad *f*

longhand [ˈlɔŋˌhænd] *n* : escritura *f* a
mano, escritura *f* cursiva

longhorn [ˈlɔŋˌhorn] *n* : longhorn *mf*

longing [ˈlɔŋɪŋ] *n* : vivo deseo *m*, ansia *f*,
anhelo *m*

longingly [ˈlɔŋɪŋlli] *adv* : ansiosamente,
con ansia

longitude [ˈlɑnʤəˌtuːd, -ˌtjuːd] *n* : longitud *f*

longitudinal [ˌlɑnʤəˈtuːdənəl, -ˈtjuː-]
adj : longitudinal — **longitudinally** *adv*

long–lived [ˈlɔŋˈlɪvd, -ˈlaɪvd] *adj* : longevo

longshoreman [ˈlɔŋˈʃormən] *n*, *pl* **-men**
[-mən, -ˌmɛn] : estibador *m*, -dora *f*

long–standing [ˈlɔŋˈstændɪŋ] *adj* : de
larga data

long–suffering [ˈlɔŋˈsʌfərɪŋ] *adj* : paciente, sufrido

look¹ [ˈlʊk] *vi* 1 GLANCE : mirar ⟨to look
out the window : mirar por la ventana⟩
2 INVESTIGATE : buscar, mirar ⟨look
in the closet : busca en el closet⟩ ⟨look
before you leap : mira lo que haces⟩ 3
SEEM : parecer ⟨he looks happy
: parece estar contento⟩ ⟨I look like my
mother : me parezco a mi madre⟩ 4 **to
look after** : cuidar, cuidar de 5 **to look
for** EXPECT : esperar 6 **to look for** SEEK
: buscar — *vt* : mirar

look² *n* 1 GLANCE : mirada *f* 2 EXPRESSION : cara *f* ⟨a look of disapproval : una cara de desaprobación⟩ 3
ASPECT : aspecto *m*, apariencia *f*, aire
m 4 **looks** *npl* : belleza *f*

lookout [ˈlʊkˌaʊt] *n* 1 : centinela *mf*,
vigía *mf* 2 **to be on the lookout for** : estar al acecho de, andar a la caza de

loom¹ [ˈluːm] *vi* 1 : aparecer, surgir ⟨the
city loomed up in the distance : la ciudad surgió en la distancia⟩ 2 IMPEND
: amenazar, ser inminente 3 **to loom
large** : cobrar mucha importancia

loom² *n* 1 : telar *m*

loon [ˈluːn] *n* : somorgujo *m*, somormujo *m*

loony *or* **looney** [ˈluːni] *adj* **-nier; -est**
: loco, chiflado *fam*

loop¹ [ˈluːp] *vt* **1** : hacer lazadas con **2 to loop around** : pasar alrededor de — *vi* **1** : rizar el rizo (dícese de un avión) **2** : serpentear (dícese de una carretera)

loop² *n* **1** : lazada *f* (en hilo o cuerda) **2** BEND : curva *f* **3** CIRCUIT : circuito *m* cerrado **4** : rizo *m* (en la aviación) ⟨to loop the loop : rizar el rizo⟩

loophole [ˈluːpˌhoːl] *n* : escapatoria *f*, pretexto *m*

loose¹ [ˈluːs] *vt* **loosed; loosing 1** RELEASE : poner en libertad, soltar **2** UNTIE : deshacer, desatar **3** DISCHARGE, UNLEASH : descargar, desatar

loose² → **loosely**

loose³ *adj* **looser; -est 1** INSECURE : flojo, suelto, poco seguro ⟨a loose tooth : un diente flojo⟩ **2** ROOMY : suelto, holgado ⟨loose clothing : ropa holgada⟩ **3** OPEN : suelto, abierto ⟨loose soil : suelo suelto⟩ ⟨a loose weave : una tejida abierta⟩ **4** FREE : suelto ⟨to break loose : soltarse⟩ **5** SLACK : flojo, flexible **6** APPROXIMATE : libre, aproximado ⟨a loose translation : una traducción aproximada⟩

loosely [ˈluːsli] *adv* **1** : sin apretar **2** ROUGHLY : aproximadamente, más o menos

loosen [ˈluːsən] *vt* : aflojar

loose–leaf [ˈluːsˌliːf] *adj* : de hojas sueltas

looseness [ˈluːsnəs] *n* **1** : aflojamiento *m*, holgura *f* (de ropa) **2** IMPRECISION : imprecisión *f*

loot¹ [ˈluːt] *vt* : saquear, robar

loot² *n* : botín *m*

looter [ˈluːtər] *n* : saqueador *m*, -dora *f*

lop [ˈlɑp] *vt* **lopped; lopping** : cortar, podar

lope¹ [ˈloːp] *vi* **loped; loping** : correr a paso largo

lope² *n* : paso *m* largo

lopsided [ˈlɑpˌsaɪdəd] *adj* **1** CROOKED : torcido, chueco, ladeado **2** ASYMETRICAL : asimétrico

loquacious [loˈkweɪʃəs] *adj* : locuaz

lord [ˈlɔrd] *n* **1** : señor *m*, noble *m* **2** : lord *m* (en la Gran Bretaña) **3 the Lord** : el Señor **4 good Lord!** : ¡Dios mío!

lordly [ˈlɔrdli] *adj* **-lier; -est** HAUGHTY : arrogante, altanero

lordship [ˈlɔrdˌʃɪp] *n* : señoría *f*

Lord's Supper *n* : Eucaristía *f*

lore [ˈlor] *n* : saber *m* popular, tradición *f*

lose [ˈluːz] *v* **lost** [ˈlɔst]; **losing** [ˈluːzɪŋ] *vt* **1** : perder ⟨I lost my umbrella : perdí mi paraguas⟩ ⟨to lose blood : perder sangre⟩ ⟨to lose one's voice : quedarse fónico⟩ ⟨to have nothing to lose : no tener nada que perder⟩ ⟨to lose no time : no perder tiempo⟩ ⟨to lose weight : perder peso, adelgazar⟩ ⟨to lose one's temper : perder los estribos, enojarse, enfadarse⟩ ⟨to lose sight of : perder de vista⟩ **2** : costar, hacer perder ⟨the errors lost him his job : los errores le costaron su empleo⟩ **3** : atrasar ⟨my watch loses 5 minutes a day : mi reloj atrasa 5 minutos por día⟩ **4 to lose oneself** : perderse, ensimismarse — *vi* **1** : perder ⟨we lost to the other team : perdimos contra el otro equipo⟩ **2** : atrasarse ⟨the clock loses time : el reloj se atrasa⟩

loser [ˈluːzər] *n* : perdedor *m*, -dora *f*

loss [ˈlɔs] *n* **1** LOSING : pérdida *f* ⟨loss of memory : pérdida de memoria⟩ ⟨to sell at a loss : vender con pérdida⟩ ⟨to be at a loss to : no saber como⟩ **2** DEFEAT : derrota *f*, juego *m* perdido **3 losses** *npl* DEATHS : muertos *mpl*

lost [ˈlɔst] *adj* **1** : perdido ⟨a lost cause : una causa perdida⟩ ⟨lost in thought : absorto⟩ **2 to get lost** : perderse **3 to make up for lost time** : recuperar el tiempo perdido

lot [ˈlɑt] *n* **1** DRAWING : sorteo *m* ⟨by lot : por sorteo⟩ **2** SHARE : parte *f*, porción *f* **3** FATE : suerte *f* **4** LAND, PLOT : terreno *m*, solar *m*, lote *m*, parcela *f* ⟨parking lot : estacionamiento⟩ **5 a lot of** *or* **lots of** : mucho, un montón de, bastante ⟨lots of books : un montón de libros, muchos libros⟩ ⟨a lot of people : mucha gente⟩

loth [ˈloːθ, ˈloːð] → **loath**

lotion [ˈloːʃən] *n* : loción *f*

lottery [ˈlɑtəri] *n, pl* **-teries** : lotería *f*

lotus [ˈloːtəs] *n* : loto *m*

loud¹ [ˈlaʊd] *adv* : alto, fuerte ⟨out loud : en voz alta⟩

loud² *adj* **1** : alto, fuerte ⟨a loud voice : una voz alta⟩ **2** NOISY : ruidoso ⟨a loud party : una fiesta ruidosa⟩ **3** FLASHY : llamativo, chillón

loudly [ˈlaʊdli] *adv* : alto, fuerte, en voz alta

loudness [ˈlaʊdnəs] *n* : volumen *m*, fuerza *f* (del ruido)

loudspeaker [ˈlaʊdˌspiːkər] *n* : altavoz *m*, altoparlante *m*

lounge¹ [ˈlaʊndʒ] *vi* **lounged; lounging** : holgazanear, gandulear

lounge² *n* : salón *m*, sala *f* de estar

louse [ˈlaʊs] *n, pl* **lice** [ˈlaɪs] : piojo *m*

lousy [ˈlaʊzi] *adj* **lousier; -est 1** : piojoso, lleno de piojos **2** BAD : pésimo, muy malo

lout [ˈlaʊt] *n* : bruto *m*, patán *m*

louver *or* **louvre** [ˈluːvər] *n* : persiana *f*, listón *m* de persiana

lovable [ˈlʌvəbəl] *adj* : adorable, amoroso, encantador

love¹ [ˈlʌv] *v* **loved; loving** *vt* **1** : querer, amar ⟨I love you : te quiero⟩ **2** ENJOY : encantarle a alguien, ser (muy) aficionado a, gustarle mucho a uno (algo) ⟨she loves flowers : le encantan las flores⟩ ⟨he loves golf : es muy aficionado al golf⟩ ⟨I'd love to go with you : me gustaría mucho acompañarte⟩ — *vi* : querer, amar

love² *n* **1** : amor *m*, cariño *m* ⟨to be in love with : estar enamorado de⟩ ⟨to fall

in love with : enamorarse de〉 **2** EN-
THUSIASM, INTEREST : amor *m*, afición
m, gusto *m* 〈love of music : afición a
la música〉 **3** BELOVED : amor *m*; amado *m*, -da *f*; enamorado *m*, -da *f*
loveless ['lʌvləs] *adj* : sin amor
loveliness ['lʌvlinəs] *n* : belleza *f*, hermosura *f*
lovelorn ['lʌv,lɔrn] *adj* : herido de amor,
perdidamente enamorado
lovely ['lʌvli] *adj* **-lier; -est** : hermoso,
bello, lindo, precioso
lover ['lʌvər] *n* : amante *mf* (de personas); aficionado *m*, -da *f* (a alguna actividad)
loving ['lʌviŋ] *adj* : amoroso, cariñoso
lovingly ['lʌviŋli] *adv* : cariñosamente
low¹ ['loː] *vi* : mugir
low² *adv* : bajo, profundo 〈to aim low
: apuntar bajo〉 〈to lie low : mantenerse escondido〉 〈to turn the lights
down low : bajar las luces〉
low³ *adj* **lower** ['loːər], **-est** **1** : bajo 〈a
low building : un edificio bajo〉 〈a low
bow : una profunda reverencia〉 **2**
SOFT : bajo, suave 〈in a low voice : en
voz baja〉 **3** SHALLOW : bajo, poco profundo **4** HUMBLE : humilde, modesto
5 DEPRESSED : deprimido, bajo de
moral **6** INFERIOR : bajo, inferior **7**
UNFAVORABLE : mal 〈to have a low
opinion of him : tener un mal concepto de él〉 **8 to be low on** : tener poco
de, estar escaso de
low⁴ *n* **1** : punto *m* bajo 〈to reach an all-
time low : estar más bajo que nunca〉
2 *or* **low gear** : primera velocidad *f* **3**
: mugido *m* (de una vaca)
lowbrow ['loː,braʊ] *n* : persona *f* inculta
lower¹ ['loːər] *vt* **1** DROP : bajar 〈to lower one's voice : bajar la voz〉 **2** : arriar, bajar 〈to lower the flag : arriar la
bandera〉 **3** REDUCE : reducir, bajar **4**
to lower oneself : rebajarse
lower² ['loːər] *adj* : inferior, más bajo, de
abajo
lowland ['loːlənd, -,lænd] *n* : tierras *fpl*
bajas
lowly ['loːli] *adj* **-lier; -est** : humilde,
modesto
loyal ['lɔɪəl] *adj* : leal, fiel — **loyally** *adv*
loyalist ['lɔɪəlɪst] *n* : partidario *m*, -ria *f*
del régimen
loyalty ['lɔɪəlti] *n*, *pl* **-ties** : lealtad *f*, fidelidad *f*
lozenge ['lazəndʒ] *n* : pastilla *f*
LSD [,ɛl,ɛs'diː] *n* : LSD *m*
lubricant ['luːbrɪkənt] *n* : lubricante *m*
lubricate ['luːbrɪ,keɪt] *vt* **-cated; -cating**
: lubricar — **lubrication** [,luːbrɪ-
'keɪʃən] *n*
lucid ['luːsəd] *adj* : lúcido, claro — **lu-
cidly** *adv*
lucidity [luː'sɪdəti] *n* : lucidez *f*
luck ['lʌk] *n* **1** : suerte *f* **2 to have bad
luck** : tener mala suerte **3 good luck!**
: ¡(buena) suerte!
luckily ['lʌkəli] *adv* : afortunadamente,
por suerte

luckless ['lʌkləs] *adj* : desafortunado
lucky ['lʌki] *adj* **luckier; -est** **1** : afortunado, que tiene suerte 〈a lucky
woman : una mujer afortunada〉 **2**
FORTUITOUS : fortuito, de suerte **3** OP-
PORTUNE : oportuno **4** : de (la) suerte
〈lucky number : número de la suerte〉
lucrative ['luːkrətɪv] *adj* : lucrativo,
provechoso — **lucratively** *adv*
ludicrous ['luːdəkrəs] *adj* : ridículo, absurdo — **ludicrously** *adv*
ludicrousness ['luːdəkrəsnəs] *n* : ridiculez *f*, absurdo *m*
lug ['lʌg] *vt* **lugged; lugging** : arrastrar,
transportar con dificultad
luggage ['lʌgɪdʒ] *n* : equipaje *m*
lugubrious [lʊ'guːbriəs] *adj* : lúgubre —
lugubriously *adv*
lukewarm ['luːk'wɔrm] *adj* **1** TEPID
: tibio **2** HALFHEARTED : poco entusiasta
lull¹ ['lʌl] *vt* **1** CALM, SOOTHE : calmar,
sosegar **2 to lull to sleep** : arrullar,
adormecer
lull² *n* : calma *f*, pausa *f*
lullaby ['lʌlə,baɪ] *n*, *pl* **-bies** : canción *f*
de cuna, arrullo *m*, nana *f*
lumber¹ ['lʌmbər] *vt* : aserrar (madera)
— *vi* : moverse pesadamente
lumber² *n* : madera *f*
lumberjack ['lʌmbər,dʒæk] *n* : leñador
m, -dora *f*
lumberyard ['lʌmbər,jard] *n* : almacén
m de maderas
luminary ['luːmə,nɛri] *n*, *pl* **-naries**
: lumbrera *f*, luminaria *f*
luminescence [,luːmə'nɛsənts] *n* : luminiscencia *f* — **luminescent** [-'nɛs-
ənt] *adj*
luminosity [,luːmə'nɑsəti] *n*, *pl* **-ties**
: luminosidad *f*
luminous ['luːmənəs] *adj* : luminoso —
luminously *adv*
lump¹ ['lʌmp] *vt* *or* **to lump together**
: juntar, agrupar, amontonar — *vi*
CLUMP : agruparse, aglutinarse
lump² *n* **1** GLOB : grumo *m* **2** PIECE
: pedazo *m*, trozo *m*, terrón *m* 〈a lump
of coal : un trozo de carbón〉 〈a lump
of sugar : un terrón de azúcar〉 **3**
SWELLING : bulto *m*, hinchazón *f*,
protuberancia *f* **4 to have a lump in
one's throat** : tener un nudo en la garganta
lumpy ['lʌmpi] *adj* **lumpier; -est** **1**
: lleno de grumos (dícese de una salsa)
2 UNEVEN : desigual, disparejo
lunacy ['luːnəsi] *n*, *pl* **-cies** : locura *f*
lunar ['luːnər] *adj* : lunar
lunatic¹ ['luːnə,tɪk] *adj* : lunático, loco
lunatic² *n* : loco *m*, -ca *f*
lunch¹ ['lʌntʃ] *vi* : almorzar, comer
lunch² *n* : almuerzo *m*, comida *f*, lonche
m
luncheon ['lʌntʃən] *n* **1** : comida *f*, almuerzo *m* **2 luncheon meat** : fiambres
fpl

lung [ˈlʌŋ] *n* : pulmón *m*
lunge¹ [ˈlʌndʒ] *vi* **lunged; lunging 1**
  THRUST : atacar (en la esgrima) **2 to
  lunge forward** : arremeter, lanzarse
lunge² *n* **1** : arremetida *f*, embestida *f* **2**
  : estocada *f* (en la esgrima)
lurch¹ [ˈlərtʃ] *vi* **1** PITCH : cabecear, dar
  bandazos, dar sacudidas **2** STAGGER
  : tambalearse
lurch² *n* **1** : sacudida *f*, bandazo *m* (de
  un vehículo) **2** : tambaleo *m* (de una
  persona)
lure¹ [ˈlʊr] *vt* **lured; luring** : atraer
lure² *n* **1** ATTRACTION : atractivo *m* **2**
  ENTICEMENT : señuelo *m*, aliciente
  m **3** BAIT : cebo *m* artificial (en la
  pesca)
lurid [ˈlʊrəd] *adj* **1** GRUESOME : espeluznante, horripilante **2** SENSA-
  TIONAL : sensacionalista, chocante **3**
  GAUDY : chillón
lurk [ˈlərk] *vi* : estar al acecho
luscious [ˈlʌʃəs] *adj* **1** DELICIOUS : delicioso, exquisito **2** SEDUCTIVE : seductor, cautivador
lush [ˈlʌʃ] *adj* **1** LUXURIANT : exuberante, lozano **2** LUXURIOUS : suntuoso,
  lujoso
lust¹ [ˈlʌst] *vi* **to lust after** : desear (a una
  persona), codiciar (riquezas, etc.)
lust² *n* **1** LASCIVIOUSNESS : lujuria *f*, lascivia *f* **2** CRAVING : deseo *m*, ansia *f*,
  anhelo *m*
luster *or* **lustre** [ˈlʌstər] *n* **1** GLOSS,
SHEEN : lustre *m*, brillo *m* **2** SPLEN-
  DOR : lustre *m*, esplendor *m*
lusterless [ˈlʌstərləs] *adj* : deslustrado,
  sin brillo
lustful [ˈlʌstfəl] *adj* : lujurioso, lascivo,
  lleno de deseo
lustrous [ˈlʌstrəs] *adj* : brillante, brilloso, lustroso
lusty [ˈlʌsti] *adj* **lustier; -est** : fuerte, robusto, vigoroso — **lustily** [ˈlʌstəli] *adv*
lute [ˈluːt] *n* : laúd *m*
luxuriant [ˌlʌgˈʒʊriənt, ˌlʌkˈʃʊr-] *adj* **1**
  : exuberante, lozano (dícese de las
  plantas) **2** : abundante y hermoso
  (dícese del pelo) — **luxuriantly** *adv*
luxuriate [ˌlʌgˈʒʊriˌeɪt, ˌlʌkˈʃʊr-] *vi*
  -ated; -ating 1 : disfrutar **2 to luxuriate in** : deleitarse con
luxurious [ˌlʌgˈʒʊriəs, ˌlʌkˈʃʊr-] *adj* : lujoso, suntuoso — **luxuriously** *adv*
luxury [ˈlʌkʃəri, ˈlʌgʒə-] *n*, *pl* **-ries** : lujo
  m
lye [ˈlaɪ] *n* : lejía *f*
lying → **lie¹, lie²**
lymph [ˈlɪmpf] *n* : linfa *f*
lymphatic [lɪmˈfætɪk] *adj* : linfático
lynch [ˈlɪntʃ] *vt* : linchar
lynx [ˈlɪŋks] *n*, *pl* **lynx** *or* **lynxes** : lince
  m
lyre [ˈlaɪr] *n* : lira *f*
lyric¹ [ˈlɪrɪk] *adj* : lírico
lyric² *n* **1** : poema *m* lírico **2 lyrics** *npl*
  : letra *f* (de una canción)
lyrical [ˈlɪrɪkəl] *adj* : lírico, elocuente

M

m [ˈɛm] *n*, *pl* **m's** *or* **ms** [ˈɛmz] : deci-
  motercera letra del alfabeto inglés
ma'am [ˈmæm] → **madam**
macabre [məˈkɑb, -ˈkɑbər, -ˈkɑbrə] *adj*
  : macabro
macadam [məˈkædəm] *n* : macadán *m*
macaroni [ˌmækəˈroːni] *n* : macarrones
  mpl
macaroon [ˌmækəˈruːn] *n* : macarrón *m*,
  mostachón *m*
macaw [məˈkɔ] *n* : guacamayo *m*
mace [ˈmeɪs] *n* **1** : maza *f* (arma o símbolo) **2** : macis *f* (especia)
machete [məˈʃɛti] *n* : machete *m*
machination [ˌmækəˈneɪʃən, ˌmæʃə-] *n*
  : maquinación *f*, intriga *f*
machine¹ [məˈʃiːn] *vt* **-chined; -chining**
  : trabajar a máquina
machine² *n* **1** : máquina *f* ⟨machine
  shop : taller de máquinas⟩ ⟨machine
  language : lenguaje de la máquina⟩ **2**
  : aparato *m*, maquinaria *f* (en política)
machine gun *n* : ametralladora *f*
machinery [məˈʃiːnəri] *n*, *pl* **-eries 1**
  : maquinaria *f* **2** WORKS : mecanismo
  m
machinist [məˈʃiːnɪst] *n* : maquinista *mf*
machismo [mɑˈtʃiːzmoː] *n* : machismo
  m, masculinidad *f*
macho [ˈmɑtʃoː] *adj* : machote, macho
mackerel [ˈmækərəl] *n*, *pl* **-el** *or* **-els** : caballa *f*
mackinaw [ˈmækəˌnɔ] *n* : chaqueta *f* escocesa de lana
mad [ˈmæd] *adj* **madder; maddest 1** IN-
  SANE : loco, demente **2** RABID : rabioso **3** FOOLISH : tonto, insensato **4**
  ANGRY : enojado, furioso **5** CRAZY
  : loco ⟨I'm mad about you : estoy loco
  por ti⟩
Madagascan [ˌmædəˈgæskən] *n* : malgache *mf* — **Madagascan** *adj*
madam [ˈmædəm] *n*, *pl* **mesdames**
  [meɪˈdɑm, -ˈdæm] : señora *f*
madcap¹ [ˈmædˌkæp] *adj* ZANY : alocado, disparatado
madcap² *n* : alocado *m*, -da *f*
madden [ˈmædən] *vt* : enloquecer, enfurecer
maddening [ˈmædənɪŋ] *adj* : enloquecedor, exasperante ⟨I find it maddening : me saca de quicio⟩
made → **make¹**
madhouse [ˈmædˌhaʊs] *n* : manicomio
  m ⟨the office was a madhouse : la oficina parecía una casa de locos⟩
madly [ˈmædli] *adv* : como un loco, locamente

madman ['mæd₁mæn, -mən] *n, pl* **-men** [-mən, -₁mɛn] : loco *m*, demente *m*

madness ['mædnəs] *n* : locura *f*, demencia *f*

madwoman ['mæd₁wʊmən] *n, pl* **-women** [-₁wɪmən] : loca *f*, demente *f*

maelstrom ['meɪlstrəm] *n* : remolino *m*, vorágine *f*

maestro ['maɪ₁stro:] *n, pl* **-stros** *or* **-stri** [-₁stri:] : maestro *m*

Mafia ['mɑfiə] *n* : Mafia *f*

magazine ['mægə₁zi:n] *n* **1** STOREHOUSE : almacén *m*, polvorín *m* (de explosivos) **2** PERIODICAL : revista *f* **3** : cargador *m* (de un arma de fuego)

magenta [mə'ʤɛntə] *n* : magenta *f*, color *m* magenta

maggot ['mægət] *n* : gusano *m*

magic[1] ['mæʤɪk] *or* **magical** ['mæʤɪkəl] *adj* : mágico

magic[2] *n* : magia *f*

magically ['mæʤɪkli] *adv* : mágicamente ⟨they magically appeared : aparecieron como por arte de magia⟩

magician [mə'ʤɪʃən] *n* **1** SORCERER : mago *m*, -ga *f* **2** CONJURER : prestidigitador *m*, -dora *f*; mago *m*, -ga *f*

magistrate ['mæʤə₁streɪt] *n* : magistrado *m*, -da *f*

magma ['mægmə] *n* : magma *m*

magnanimity [₁mægnə'nɪməti] *n, pl* **-ties** : magnanimidad *f*

magnanimous [mæg'nænəməs] *adj* : magnánimo, generoso — **magnanimously** *adv*

magnate ['mæg₁neɪt, -nət] *n* : magnate *mf*

magnesium [mæg'ni:ziəm, -ʒəm] *n* : magnesio *m*

magnet ['mægnət] *n* : imán *m*

magnetic [mæg'nɛtɪk] *adj* : magnético — **magnetically** [-tɪkli] *adv*

magnetic field *n* : campo *m* magnético

magnetism ['mægnə₁tɪzəm] *n* : magnetismo *m*

magnetize ['mægnə₁taɪz] *vt* **-tized; -tizing 1** : magnetizar, imantar **2** ATTRACT : magnetizar, atraer

magnification [₁mægnəfə'keɪʃən] *n* : aumento *m*, ampliación *f*

magnificence [mæg'nɪfəsənts] *n* : magnificencia *f*

magnificent [mæg'nɪfəsənt] *adj* : magnífico — **magnificently** *adv*

magnify ['mægnə₁faɪ] *vt* **-fied; -fying 1** ENLARGE : ampliar **2** EXAGGERATE : magnificar, exagerar

magnifying glass *n* : lupa *f*

magnitude ['mægnə₁tu:d, -₁tju:d] *n* **1** GREATNESS : magnitud *f*, grandeza *f* **2** QUANTITY : cantidad *f* **3** IMPORTANCE : magnitud *f*, envergadura *f*

magnolia [mæg'no:ljə] *n* : magnolia *f* (flor), magnolio *m* (árbol)

magpie ['mæg₁paɪ] *n* : urraca *f*

mahogany [mə'hɑgəni] *n, pl* **-nies** : caoba *f*

maid ['meɪd] *n* **1** MAIDEN : doncella *f* **2** *or* **maidservant** ['meɪd₁sərvənt] : sirvienta *f*, muchacha *f*, mucama *f*, criada *f*

maiden[1] ['meɪdən] *adj* **1** UNMARRIED : soltera **2** FIRST : primero ⟨maiden voyage : primera travesía⟩

maiden[2] *n* : doncella *f*

maidenhood ['meɪdən₁hʊd] *n* : doncellez *f*

maiden name *n* : nombre *m* de soltera

mail[1] ['meɪl] *vt* : enviar por correo, echar al correo

mail[2] *n* **1** : correo *m* ⟨airmail : correo aéreo⟩ **2** : malla *f* ⟨coat of mail : cota de malla⟩

mailbox ['meɪl₁bɑks] *n* : buzón *m*

mailman ['meɪl₁mæn, -mən] *n, pl* **-men** [-mən, -₁mɛn] : cartero *m*

maim ['meɪm] *vt* : mutilar, desfigurar, lisiar

main[1] ['meɪn] *adj* : principal, central ⟨the main office : la oficina central⟩

main[2] *n* **1** HIGH SEAS : alta mar *f* **2** : tubería *f* principal (de agua o gas), cable *m* principal (de un circuito) **3** with might and main : con todas sus fuerzas

mainframe ['meɪn₁freɪm] *n* : mainframe *m*, computadora *f* central

mainland ['meɪn₁lænd, -lənd] *n* : continente *m*

mainly ['meɪnli] *adv* **1** PRINCIPALLY : principalmente, en primer lugar **2** MOSTLY : principalmente, en la mayor parte

mainstay ['meɪn₁steɪ] *n* : pilar *m*, sostén *m* principal

mainstream[1] ['meɪn₁stri:m] *adj* : dominante, corriente, convencional

mainstream[2] *n* : corriente *f* principal

maintain [meɪn'teɪn] *vt* **1** SERVICE : dar mantenimiento a (una máquina) **2** PRESERVE : mantener, conservar ⟨to maintain silence : guardar silencio⟩ **3** SUPPORT : mantener, sostener **4** ASSERT : mantener, sostener, afirmar

maintenance ['meɪntənənts] *n* : mantenimiento *m*

maize ['meɪz] *n* : maíz *m*

majestic [mə'ʤɛstɪk] *adj* : majestuoso — **majestically** [-tɪkli] *adv*

majesty ['mæʤəsti] *n, pl* **-ties 1** : majestad *f* ⟨Your Majesty : su Majestad⟩ **2** SPLENDOR : majestuosidad *f*, esplendor *m*

major[1] ['meɪʤər] *vi* **-jored; -joring** : especializarse

major[2] *adj* **1** GREATER : mayor **2** NOTEWORTHY : mayor, notable **3** SERIOUS : grave **4** : mayor (en la música)

major[3] *n* **1** : mayor *mf*, comandante *mf* (en las fuerzas armadas) **2** : especialidad *f* (universitaria)

Majorcan [mə'ʤɔrkən, mə-, -'jɔr-] *n* : mallorquín *m*, -quina *f* — **Majorcan** *adj*

major general *n* : general *mf* de división

majority [mə'dʒɔrəti] *n, pl* **-ties** 1
ADULTHOOD : mayoría *f* de edad 2
: mayoría *f*, mayor parte *f* ⟨the vast majority : la inmensa mayoría⟩
make¹ ['meɪk] *v* **made** ['meɪd;]; **making**
vt 1 CREATE : hacer ⟨to make noise
: hacer ruido⟩ 2 FASHION, MANUFACTURE : hacer, fabricar ⟨she made a
dress : hizo un vestido⟩ 3 DEVISE,
FORM : desarrollar, elaborar, formar 4
CONSTITUTE : hacer, constituir ⟨made
of stone : hecho de piedra⟩ 5 PREPARE
: hacer, preparar 6 RENDER : hacer,
poner ⟨it makes him nervous : lo pone
nervioso⟩ ⟨to make someone happy
: hacer feliz a alguien⟩ ⟨it made me sad
: me dio pena⟩ 7 PERFORM : hacer ⟨to
make a gesture : hacer un gesto⟩ 8
COMPEL : hacer, forzar, obligar 9
EARN : ganar ⟨to make a living : ganarse la vida⟩ — *vi* 1 HEAD : ir, dirigirse ⟨we made for home : nos fuimos
a casa⟩ 2 **to make do** : arreglárselas 3
to make good REPAY : pagar 4 **to make
good** SUCCEED : tener éxito
make² *n* BRAND : marca *f*
make–believe¹ [ˌmeɪkbə'li:v] *adj* : imaginario
make–believe² *n* : fantasía *f*, invención
f ⟨a world of make-believe : un mundo de ensueño⟩
make out *vt* 1 WRITE : hacer (un cheque)
2 DISCERN : distinguir, divisar 3 UNDERSTAND : comprender, entender —
vi : arreglárselas ⟨how did you make
out? : ¿qué tal te fue?⟩
maker ['meɪkər] *n* : fabricante *mf*
makeshift ['meɪkˌʃɪft] *adj* : provisional,
improvisado
makeup ['meɪkˌʌp] *n* 1 COMPOSITION
: composición *f* 2 CHARACTER : carácter *m*, temperamento *m* 3 COSMETICS
: maquillaje *m*
make up *vt* 1 INVENT : inventar 2 : recuperar ⟨she made up the time : recuperó las horas perdidas⟩ — *vi* RECONCILE : hacer las paces, reconciliarse
making ['meɪkɪŋ] *n* 1 : creación *f*, producción *f* ⟨in the making : en ciernes⟩
2 **to have the makings of** : tener
madera de (dícese de personas), tener
los ingredientes para
maladjusted [ˌmælə'dʒʌstəd] *adj* : inadaptado
malady ['mælədi] *n, pl* **-dies** : dolencia
f, enfermedad *f*, mal *m*
malaise [mə'leɪz, mæ-] *n* : malestar *m*
malapropism ['mæləˌprɑˌpɪzəm] *n* : uso
m incorrecto y cómico de una palabra
malaria [mə'lɛriə] *n* : malaria *f*, paludismo *m*
malarkey [mə'lɑrki] *n* : tonterías *fpl*, estupideces *fpl*
Malawian [mə'lɑwiən] *n* : malauiano *m*,
-na *f* — **Malawian** *adj*
Malay [mə'leɪ, 'meɪˌleɪ] *n* 1 *or* **Malayan**
[mə'leɪən, meɪ-; 'meɪˌleɪən] : malayo *m*,

-ya *f* 2 : malayo *m* (idioma) — **Malay**
or **Malayan** *adj*
Malaysian [mə'leɪʒən, -ʃən] *n* : malasio
m, -sia *f*; malaisio *m*, -sia *f* — **Malaysian**
adj
male¹ ['meɪl] *adj* 1 : macho 2 MASCULINE : masculino
male² *n* : macho *m* (de animales o plantas), varón *m* (de personas)
malefactor ['mæləˌfæktər] *n* : malhechor *m*, -chora *f*
maleness ['meɪlnəs] *n* : masculinidad *f*
malevolence [mə'lɛvələnts] *n* : malevolencia *f*
malevolent [mə'lɛvələnt] *adj* : malévolo
malformation [ˌmælfɔr'meɪʃən] *n* : malformación *f*
malformed [mæl'fɔrmd] *adj* : mal formado, deforme
malfunction¹ [mæl'fʌŋkʃən] *vi* : funcionar mal
malfunction² *n* : mal funcionamiento *m*
malice ['mæləs] *n* 1 : malicia *f*, malevolencia *f* 2 **with malice aforethought**
: con premeditación
malicious [mə'lɪʃəs] *adj* : malicioso,
malévolo — **maliciously** *adv*
malign¹ [mə'laɪn] *vt* : calumniar, difamar
malign² *adj* : maligno
malignancy [mə'lɪgnəntsi] *n, pl* **-cies**
: malignidad *f*
malignant [mə'lɪgnənt] *adj* : maligno
malinger [mə'lɪŋgər] *vi* : fingirse enfermo
malingerer [mə'lɪŋgərər] *n* : uno que se
finge enfermo
mall ['mɔl] *n* 1 PROMENADE : alameda
f, paseo *m* (arbolado) 2 : centro *m* comercial ⟨shopping mall : galería comercial⟩
mallard ['mælərd] *n, pl* **-lard** *or* **-lards**
: pato *m* real, ánade *mf* real
malleable ['mæliəbəl] *adj* : maleable
mallet ['mælət] *n* : mazo *m*
malnourished [mæl'nərɪʃt] *adj* : desnutrido, malnutrido
malnutrition [ˌmælnʊ'trɪʃən, -njʊ-] *n*
: desnutrición *f*, malnutrición *f*
malodorous [mæl'o:dərəs] *adj* : maloliente
malpractice [ˌmæl'præktəs] *n* : mala
práctica *f*, negligencia *f*
malt ['mɔlt] *n* : malta *f*
maltreat [mæl'tri:t] *vt* : maltratar
mama *or* **mamma** ['mɑmə] *n* : mamá *f*
mammal ['mæməl] *n* : mamífero *m*
mammalian [mə'meɪliən, mæ-] *adj*
: mamífero
mammary ['mæməri] *adj* 1 : mamario
2 **mammary gland** : glándula mamaria
mammogram ['mæməˌgræm] *n* : mamografía *f*
mammoth¹ ['mæməθ] *adj* : colosal, gigantesco
mammoth² *n* : mamut *m*
man¹ ['mæn] *vt* **manned; manning** : tripular (un barco o avión), encargarse de
(un servicio)

man² *n, pl* **men** ['mɛn] **1** PERSON : hombre *m*, persona *f* **2** MALE : hombre *m* **3** MANKIND : humanidad *f*

manacles ['mænɪkəlz] *npl* HANDCUFFS : esposas *fpl*

manage ['mænɪdʒ] *v* **-aged; -aging** *vt* **1** HANDLE : controlar, manejar **2** DIRECT : administrar, dirigir **3** CONTRIVE : lograr, ingeniárselas para — *vi* COPE : arreglárselas

manageable ['mænɪdʒəbəl] *adj* : manejable

management ['mænɪdʒmənt] *n* **1** DIRECTION : administración *f*, gestión *f*, dirección *f* **2** HANDLING : manejo *m* **3** MANAGERS : dirección *f*, gerencia *f*

manager ['mænɪdʒər] *n* : director *m*, -tora *f*; gerente *mf*; administrador *m*, -dora *f*

managerial [,mænə'dʒɪriəl] *adj* : directivo, gerencial

mandarin ['mændərən] *n* **1** : mandarín *m* **2** *or* **mandarin orange** : mandarina *f*

mandate ['mæn,deɪt] *n* : mandato *m*

mandatory ['mændə,tori] *adj* : obligatorio

mandible ['mændəbəl] *n* : mandíbula *f*

mandolin [,mændə'lɪn, 'mændələn] *n* : mandolina *f*

mane ['meɪn] *n* : crin *f* (de un caballo), melena *f* (de un león o una persona)

maneuver¹ [mə'nu:vər, -'nju:-] *vt* **1** PLACE, POSITION : maniobrar, posicionar, colocar **2** MANIPULATE : manipular, maniobrar — *vi* : maniobrar

maneuver² *n* : maniobra *f*

manfully ['mænfəli] *adj* : valientemente

manganese ['mæŋgə,ni:z, -,ni:s] *n* : manganeso *m*

mange ['meɪndʒ] *n* : sarna *f*

manger ['meɪndʒər] *n* : pesebre *m*

mangle ['mæŋgəl] *vt* **-gled; -gling 1** CRUSH, DESTROY : aplastar, despedazar, destrozar **2** MUTILATE : mutilar ⟨to mangle a text : mutilar un texto⟩

mango ['mæŋ,go:] *n, pl* **-goes** : mango *m*

mangrove ['mæn,gro:v, 'mæŋ-] *n* : mangle *m*

mangy ['meɪndʒi] *adj* **mangier; -est 1** : sarnoso **2** SHABBY : gastado

manhandle ['mæn,hændəl] *vt* **-dled; -dling** : maltratar, tratar con poco cuidado

manhole ['mæn,ho:l] *n* : boca *f* de alcantarilla

manhood ['mæn,hʊd] *n* **1** : madurez *f* (de un hombre) **2** COURAGE, MANLINESS : hombría *f*, valor *m* **3** MEN : hombres *mpl*

manhunt ['mæn,hʌnt] *n* : búsqueda *f* (de un criminal)

mania ['meɪniə, -njə] *n* : manía *f*

maniac ['meɪni,æk] *n* : maníaco *m*, -ca *f*; maniático *m*, -ca *f*

maniacal [mə'naɪəkəl] *adj* : maníaco, maniaco

manicure¹ ['mænə,kjʊr] *vt* **-cured; -curing 1** : hacer la manicura a **2** TRIM : recortar

manicure² *n* : manicura *f*

manicurist ['mænə,kjʊrɪst] *n* : manicuro *m*, -ra *f*

manifest¹ ['mænə,fɛst] *vt* : manifestar

manifest² *adj* : manifiesto, patente — **manifestly** *adv*

manifestation [,mænəfə'steɪʃən] *n* : manifestación *f*

manifesto [,mænə'fɛs,to:] *n, pl* **-tos** *or* **-toes** : manifiesto *m*

manifold¹ ['mænə,fo:ld] *adj* : diverso, variado

manifold² *n* : colector *m* (de escape)

manipulate [mə'nɪpjə,leɪt] *vt* **-lated; -lating** : manipular

manipulation [mə,nɪpjə'leɪʃən] *n* : manipulación *f*

manipulative [mə'nɪpjə,leɪtɪv, -lətɪv] *adj* : manipulador

mankind ['mæn'kaɪnd, ,kaɪnd] *n* : género *m* humano, humanidad *f*

manliness ['mænlinəs] *n* : hombría *f*, masculinidad *f*

manly ['mænli] *adj* **-lier; -est** : varonil, viril

man-made ['mæn'meɪd] *adj* : artificial ⟨man-made fabrics : telas sintéticas⟩

manna ['mænə] *n* : maná *m*

mannequin ['mænɪkən] *n* **1** DUMMY : maniquí *m* **2** MODEL : modelo *mf*

manner ['mænər] *n* **1** KIND, SORT : tipo *m*, clase *f* **2** WAY : manera *f*, modo *m* **3** STYLE : estilo *m* (artístico) **4** **manners** *npl* CUSTOMS : costumbres *fpl* ⟨Victorian manners : costumbres victorianas⟩ **5** **manners** *npl* ETIQUETTE : modales *mpl*, educación *f*, etiqueta *f* ⟨good manners : buenos modales⟩

mannered ['mænərd] *adj* **1** AFFECTED, ARTIFICIAL : amanerado, afectado **2** **well-mannered** : educado, cortés **3** → **ill-mannered**

mannerism ['mænə,rɪzəm] *n* : peculiaridad *f*, gesto *m* particular

mannerly ['mænərli] *adj* : cortés, bien educado

mannish ['mænɪʃ] *adj* : masculino, hombruno

man-of-war [,mænə'wɔr, -əv'wɔr] *n, pl* **men-of-war** [,mɛn-] WARSHIP : buque *m* de guerra

manor ['mænər] *n* **1** : casa *f* solariega, casa *f* señorial **2** ESTATE : señorío *m*

manpower ['mæn,paʊər] *n* : personal *m*, mano *f* de obra

mansion ['mæntʃən] *n* : mansión *f*

manslaughter ['mæn,slɔtər] *n* : homicidio *m* sin premeditación

mantel ['mæntəl] *n* : repisa *f* de chimenea

mantelpiece ['mæntəl,pi:s] → **mantel**

mantis ['mæntəs] *n, pl* **-tises** *or* **-tes** ['mæn,ti:z] : mantis *f* religiosa

mantle ['mæntəl] *n* : manto *m*

manual[1] ['mænjʊəl] *adj* : manual — **manually** *adv*

manual[2] *n* : manual *m*

manufacture[1] [ˌmænjə'fæktʃər] *vt* **-tured; -turing** 1 : fabricar, manufacturar, confeccionar (ropa), elaborar (comestibles)

manufacture[2] *n* : manufactura *f*, fabricación *f*, confección *f* (de ropa), elaboración *f* (de comestibles)

manufacturer [ˌmænjə'fæktʃərər] *n* : fabricante *m*; manufacturero *m*, -ra *f*

manure [mə'nʊr, -'njʊr] *n* : estiércol *m*

manuscript ['mænjəˌskrɪpt] *n* : manuscrito *m*

many[1] ['mɛni] *adj* **more** ['mor]; **most** ['mo:st] : muchos

many[2] *pron* : muchos *pl*, -chas *pl*

map[1] ['mæp] *vt* **mapped; mapping** 1 : trazar el mapa de 2 PLAN : planear, proyectar ⟨to map out a program : planear un programa⟩

map[2] *n* : mapa *m*

maple ['meɪpəl] *n* : arce *m*

mar ['mar] *vt* **marred; marring** 1 SPOIL : estropear, echar a perder 2 DEFACE : desfigurar

maraschino [ˌmærə'ski:no:, -'ʃi:-] *n, pl* **-nos** : cereza *f* al marrasquino

marathon ['mærəˌθan] *n* 1 RACE : maratón *m* 2 CONTEST : competencia *f* de resistencia

maraud [mə'rɔd] *vi* : merodear

marauder [mə'rɔdər] *n* : merodeador *m*, -dora *f*

marble ['marbəl] *n* 1 : mármol *m* 2 : canica *f* ⟨to play marbles : jugar a las canicas⟩

march[1] ['martʃ] *vi* 1 : marchar, desfilar ⟨they marched past the grandstand : desfilaron ante la tribuna⟩ 2 : caminar con resolución ⟨she marched right up to him : se le acercó sin vacilación⟩

march[2] *n* 1 MARCHING : marcha *f* 2 PASSAGE : paso *m* (del tiempo) 3 PROGRESS : avance *m*, progreso *m* 4 : marcha *f* (en música)

March ['martʃ] *n* : marzo *m*

marchioness ['marʃənɪs] *n* : marquesa *f*

Mardi Gras ['mardiˌgra] *n* : martes *m* de Carnaval

mare ['mær] *n* : yegua *f*

margarine ['mardʒərən] *n* : margarina *f*

margin ['mardʒən] *n* : margen *m*

marginal ['mardʒənəl] *adj* 1 : marginal 2 MINIMAL : mínimo — **marginally** *adv*

marigold ['mærəˌgo:ld] *n* : maravilla *f*, caléndula *f*

marijuana [ˌmærə'hwanə] *n* : marihuana *f*

marina [mə'ri:nə] *n* : puerto *m* deportivo

marinade [ˌmærə'nad] *n* : adobo *m*, marinada *f*

marinate ['mærəˌneɪt] *vt* **-nated; -nating** : marinar

marine[1] [mə'ri:n] *adj* 1 : marino ⟨marine life : vida marina⟩ 2 NAUTICAL : náutico, marítimo 3 : de la infantería de marina

marine[2] *n* : soldado *m* de marina

mariner ['mærɪnər] *n* : marinero *m*, marino *m*

marionette [ˌmæriə'nɛt] *n* : marioneta *f*, títere *m*

marital ['mærətəl] *adj* 1 : matrimonial 2 **marital status** : estado *m* civil

maritime ['mærəˌtaɪm] *adj* : marítimo

marjoram ['mardʒərəm] *n* : mejorana *f*

mark[1] ['mark] *vt* 1 : marcar 2 CHARACTERIZE : caracterizar 3 SIGNAL : señalar 4 NOTICE : prestar atención a, hacer caso de 5 **to mark off** : demarcar, delimitar

mark[2] *n* 1 TARGET : blanco *m* 2 : marca *f*, señal *f* ⟨put a mark where you left off : pon una señal donde terminaste⟩ 3 INDICATION : señal *f*, indicio *m* 4 GRADE : nota *f* 5 IMPRINT : huella *f*, marca *f* 6 BLEMISH : marca *f*, imperfección *f*

marked ['markt] *adj* : marcado, notable — **markedly** ['markədli] *adv*

marker ['markər] *n* : marcador *m*

market[1] ['markət] *vt* : poner en venta, comercializar

market[2] *n* 1 MARKETPLACE : mercado *m* ⟨the open market : el mercado libre⟩ 2 DEMAND : demanda *f*, mercado *m* 3 STORE : tienda *f* 4 → **stock market**

marketable ['markətəbəl] *adj* : vendible

marketing ['markətɪŋ] *n* : mercadotecnia *f*, mercadeo *m*

marketplace ['markətˌpleɪs] *n* : mercado *m*

marksman ['marksmən] *n, pl* **-men** [-mən, -ˌmɛn] : tirador *m*

marksmanship ['marksmənˌʃɪp] *n* : puntería *f*

marlin ['marlɪn] *n* : marlín *m*

marmalade ['marməˌleɪd] *n* : mermelada *f*

marmoset ['marməˌsɛt] *n* : tití *m*

marmot ['marmət] *n* : marmota *f*

maroon[1] [mə'ru:n] *vt* : abandonar, aislar

maroon[2] *n* : rojo *m* oscuro, granate *m*

marquee [mar'ki:] *n* : marquesina *f*

marquess ['markwɪs] *or* **marquis** ['markwɪs, mar'ki:] *n, pl* **-quesses** *or* **-quises** [-'ki:z, -'ki:zəz] *or* **-quis** [-'ki:, -'ki:z] : marqués *m*

marquise [mar'ki:z] → **marchioness**

marriage ['mærɪdʒ] *n* 1 : matrimonio *m* 2 WEDDING : casamiento *m*, boda *f*

marriageable ['mærɪdʒəbəl] *adj* **of marriageable age** : de edad de casarse

married ['mærid] *adj* 1 : casado 2 **to get married** : casarse

marrow ['mæro:] *n* : médula *f*, tuétano *m*

marry ['mæri] *vt* **-ried; -rying** 1 : casar ⟨the priest married them : el cura los casó⟩ 2 : casarse con ⟨she married John : se casó con John⟩

Mars ['mɑrz] n : Marte m
marsh ['mɑrʃ] n 1 : pantano m 2 **salt marsh** : marisma f
marshal[1] ['mɑrʃəl] vt **-shaled** or **-shalled; -shaling** or **-shalling** 1 : poner en orden, reunir 2 USHER : conducir
marshal[2] n 1 : maestro m de ceremonias 2 : mariscal m (en el ejército); jefe m, -fa f (de la policía, de los bomberos, etc.)
marshmallow ['mɑrʃ,mɛlo:, -,mælo:] n : malvavisco m
marshy ['mɑrʃi] adj **marshier; -est** : pantanoso
marsupial [mɑr'su:piəl] n : marsupial m
mart ['mɑrt] n MARKET : mercado m
marten ['mɑrtən] n, pl **-ten** or **-tens** : marta f
martial ['mɑrʃəl] adj : marcial
martin ['mɑrtən] n 1 SWALLOW : golondrina f 2 SWIFT : vencejo m
martyr[1] ['mɑrtər] vt : martirizar
martyr[2] n : mártir mf
martyrdom ['mɑrtərdəm] n : martirio m
marvel[1] ['mɑrvəl] vi **-veled** or **-velled; -veling** or **-velling** : maravillarse
marvel[2] n : maravilla f
marvelous ['mɑrvələs] or **marvellous** adj : maravilloso — **marvelously** adv
Marxism ['mɑrk,sɪzəm] n : marxismo m
Marxist[1] ['mɑrksɪst] adj : marxista
Marxist[2] n : marxista mf
mascara [mæs'kærə] n : rímel m, rimel m
mascot ['mæs,kɑt, -kət] n : mascota f
masculine ['mæskjələn] adj : masculino
masculinity [,mæskjə'lɪnəti] n : masculinidad f
mash[1] ['mæʃ] vt 1 : hacer puré de (papas, etc.) 2 CRUSH : aplastar, majar
mash[2] n 1 FEED : afrecho m 2 : malta f (para hacer bebidas alcohólicas) 3 PASTE, PULP : papilla f, pasta f
mask[1] ['mæsk] vt 1 CONCEAL, DISGUISE : enmascarar, ocultar 2 COVER : cubrir, tapar
mask[2] n : máscara f, careta f, mascarilla f (de un cirujano o dentista)
masochism ['mæsə,kɪzəm, 'mæzə-] n : masoquismo m
masochist ['mæsə,kɪst, 'mæzə-] n : masoquista mf
masochistic [,mæsə'kɪstɪk, ,mæzə-] adj : masoquista
mason ['meɪsən] n 1 BRICKLAYER : albañil mf 2 or **stonemason** ['sto:n,-] : mampostero m, cantero m
masonry ['meɪsənri] n, pl **-ries** 1 BRICKLAYING : albañilería f 2 or **stonemasonry** ['sto:n,-] : mampostería f
masquerade[1] [,mæskə'reɪd] vi **-aded; -ading** 1 : disfrazarse (de), hacerse pasar (por) 2 : asistir a una mascarada
masquerade[2] n 1 : mascarada f, baile m de disfraces 2 FACADE : farsa f, fachada f
mass[1] ['mæs] vi : concentrarse, juntarse en masa — vt : concentrar

mass[2] n 1 : masa f ⟨atomic mass : masa atómica⟩ 2 BULK : mole f, volumen m 3 MULTITUDE : cantidad f, montón m (de cosas), multitud f (de gente) 4 **the masses** : las masas, el pueblo, el populacho
Mass ['mæs] n : misa f
massacre[1] ['mæsɪkər] vt **-cred; -cring** : masacrar
massacre[2] n : masacre f
massage[1] [mə'sɑʒ, -'sɑʤ] vt **-saged; -saging** : masajear
massage[2] n : masaje m
masseur [mæ'sər] n : masajista m
masseuse [mæ'søz, -'su:z] n : masajista f
massive ['mæsɪv] adj 1 BULKY : voluminoso, macizo 2 HUGE : masivo, enorme — **massively** adv
mast ['mæst] n : mástil m, palo m
master[1] ['mæstər] vt 1 SUBDUE : dominar 2 : llegar a dominar ⟨she mastered French : llegó a dominar el francés⟩
master[2] n 1 TEACHER : maestro m, profesor m 2 EXPERT : experto m, -ta f; maestro m, -tra f 3 : amo m (de animales o esclavos), señor m (de la casa) 4 **master's degree** : maestría f
masterful ['mæstərfəl] adj 1 IMPERIOUS : autoritario, imperioso, dominante 2 SKILLFUL : magistral — **masterfully** adv
masterly ['mæstərli] adj : magistral
mastermind ['mæstər,maɪnd] n : cerebro m, artífice mf
masterpiece ['mæstər,pi:s] n : obra f maestra
masterwork ['mæstər,wərk] → **masterpiece**
mastery ['mæstəri] n 1 DOMINION : dominio m, autoridad f 2 SUPERIORITY : superioridad f 3 EXPERTISE : maestría f
masticate ['mæstə,keɪt] v **-cated; -cating** : masticar
mastiff ['mæstɪf] n : mastín m
mastodon ['mæstə,dɑn] n : mastodonte m
masturbate ['mæstər,beɪt] v **-bated; bating** vi : masturbarse — vt : masturbar
masturbation [,mæstər'beɪʃən] n : masturbación f
mat[1] ['mæt] v **matted; matting** vt TANGLE : enmarañar — vi : enmarañarse
mat[2] n 1 : estera f 2 TANGLE : maraña f 3 PAD : colchoneta f (de gimnasia) 4 or **matt** or **matte** ['mæt] FRAME : marco m (de cartón)
mat[3] → **matte**
matador ['mætə,dɔr] n : matador m
match[1] ['mæʧ] vt 1 PIT : enfrentar, oponer 2 EQUAL, FIT : igualar, corresponder a, coincidir con 3 : combinar con, hacer juego con ⟨her shoes match her dress : sus zapatos hacen juego con su vestido⟩ — vi 1 CORRESPOND : concordar, coincidir 2 : hacer juego ⟨with a tie to match : con una corbata que hace juego⟩

match² *n* **1** EQUAL : igual *mf* ⟨he's no match for her : no puede competir con ella⟩ **2** FIGHT, GAME : partido *m*, combate *m* (en boxeo) **3** MARRIAGE : matrimonio *m*, casamiento *m* **4** : fósforo *m*, cerilla *f*, cerillo *m in various countries*⟩ ⟨he lit a match : encendió un fósforo⟩ **5 to be a good match** : hacer buena pareja (dícese de las personas), hacer juego (dícese de la ropa)

matchless ['mætʃləs] *adj* : sin igual, sin par

matchmaker ['mætʃ,meɪkər] *n* : casamentero *m*, -ra *f*

mate¹ ['meɪt] *v* **mated; mating** *vi* **1** FIT : encajar **2** PAIR : emparejarse **3** (*relating to animals*) : aparearse, copular — *vt* : aparear, acoplar (animales)

mate² *n* **1** COMPANION : compañero *m*, -ra *f*; camarada *mf* **2** : macho *m*, hembra *f* (de animales) **3** : oficial *mf* (de un barco) ⟨first mate : primer oficial⟩ **4** : compañero *m*, -ra *f*; pareja *f* (de un zapato, etc.)

material¹ [mə'tɪriəl] *adj* **1** PHYSICAL : material, físico ⟨the material world : el mundo material⟩ ⟨material needs : necesidades materiales⟩ **2** IMPORTANT : importante, esencial **3 material evidence** : prueba *f* sustancial

material² *n* **1** : material *m* **2** CLOTH : tejido *m*, tela *f*

materialism [mə'tɪriə,lɪzəm] *n* : materialismo *m*

materialist [mə'tɪriəlɪst] *n* : materialista *mf*

materialistic [mə,tɪriə'lɪstɪk] *adj* : materialista

materialize [mə'tɪriə,laɪz] *v* **-ized; -izing** *vt* : materializar, hacer aparecer — *vi* : materializarse, aparecer

maternal [mə'tərnəl] *adj* MOTHERLY : maternal — **maternally** *adv*

maternity¹ [mə'tərnəti] *adj* : de maternidad ⟨maternity clothes : ropa de futura mamá⟩ ⟨maternity leave : licencia por maternidad⟩

maternity² *n, pl* **-ties** : maternidad *f*

math ['mæθ] → **mathematics**

mathematical [,mæθə'mætɪkəl] *adj* : matemático — **mathematically** *adv*

mathematician [,mæθəmə'tɪʃən] *n* : matemático *m*, -ca *f*

mathematics [,mæθə'mætɪks] *ns & pl* : matemáticas *fpl*, matemática *f*

matinee *or* **matinée** [,mætən'eɪ] *n* : matiné *f*

matriarch ['meɪtri,ɑrk] *n* : matriarca *f*

matriarchy ['meɪtri,ɑrki] *n, pl* **-chies** : matriarcado *m*

matriculate [mə'trɪkjə,leɪt] *v* **-lated; -lating** *vt* : matricular — *vi* : matricularse

matriculation [mə,trɪkjə'leɪʃən] *n* : matrícula *f*, matriculación *f*

matrimony ['mætrə,mo:ni] *n* : matrimonio *m* — **matrimonial** [,mætrə'mo:niəl] *adj*

matrix ['meɪtrɪks] *n, pl* **-trices** ['meɪtrə,si:z, 'mæ-] *or* **-trixes** ['meɪtrɪksəz] : matriz *f*

matron ['meɪtrən] *n* : matrona *f*

matronly ['meɪtrənli] *adj* : de matrona, matronal

matte ['mæt] *adj* : mate, de acabado mate

matter¹ ['mæt̬ər] *vi* : importar ⟨it doesn't matter : no importa⟩

matter² *n* **1** QUESTION : asunto *m*, cuestión *f* ⟨a matter of taste : una cuestión de gusto⟩ **2** SUBSTANCE : materia *f*, sustancia *f* **3 matters** *npl* CIRCUMSTANCES : situación *f*, cosas *fpl* ⟨to make matters worse : para colmo de males⟩ **4 to be the matter** : pasar ⟨what's the matter? : ¿qué pasa?⟩ **5 as a matter of fact** : en efecto, en realidad **6 for that matter** : de hecho **7 no matter how much** : por mucho que

matter-of-fact ['mæt̬ərəv'fækt] *adj* : práctico, realista

mattress ['mætrəs] *n* : colchón *m*

mature¹ [mə'tʊr, -'tjʊr, -'tʃʊr] *vi* **-tured; -turing 1** : madurar **2** : vencer ⟨when does the loan mature? : ¿cuándo vence el préstamo?⟩

mature² *adj* **-turer; -est 1** : maduro **2** DUE : vencido

maturity [mə'tʊrət̬i, -'tjʊr-, -'tʃʊr-] *n* : madurez *f*

maudlin ['mɔdlɪn] *adj* : sensiblero

maul¹ ['mɔl] *vt* **1** BEAT : golpear, pegar **2** MANGLE : mutilar **3** MANHANDLE : maltratar

maul² *n* MALLET : mazo *m*

Mauritanian [,mɔrə'teɪniən] *n* : mauritano *m*, -na *f* — **Mauritanian** *adj*

mausoleum [,mɔsə'li:əm, ,mɔzə-] *n, pl* **-leums** *or* **-lea** [-'li:ə] : mausoleo *m*

mauve ['mo:v, 'mɔv] *n* : malva *m*

maven *or* **mavin** ['meɪvən] *n* EXPERT : experto *m*, -ta *f*

maverick ['mævrɪk, 'mævə-] *n* **1** : ternero *m* sin marcar **2** NONCONFORMIST : inconformista *mf*, disidente *mf*

mawkish ['mɔkɪʃ] *adj* : sensiblero

maxim ['mæksəm] *n* : máxima *f*

maximize ['mæksə,maɪz] *vt* **-mized; -mizing** : maximizar, llevar al máximo

maximum¹ ['mæksəməm] *adj* : máximo

maximum² *n, pl* **-ma** ['mæksəmə] *or* **-mums** : máximo *m*

may ['meɪ] *v aux, past* **might** ['maɪt] *present s & pl* **may 1** (*expressing permission*) : poder ⟨you may go : puedes ir⟩ **2** (*expressing possibility or probability*) : poder ⟨you may be right : puede que tengas razón⟩ ⟨it may happen occasionally : puede pasar de vez en cuando⟩ **3** (*expressing desires, intentions, or contingencies*) ⟨may the best man win : que gane el mejor⟩ ⟨I laugh that I may not weep : me río para no llorar⟩ ⟨come what may : pase lo que pase⟩

May ['meɪ] *n* : mayo *m*

Maya ['maɪə] or **Mayan** ['maɪən] n : maya mf — **Maya** or **Mayan** adj

maybe ['meɪbi] adv PERHAPS : quizás, tal vez

mayfly ['meɪˌflaɪ] n, pl **-flies** : efímera f

mayhem ['meɪˌhɛm, 'meɪəm] n 1 MUTILATION : mutilación f 2 DEVASTATION : estragos mpl

mayonnaise ['meɪəˌneɪz] n : mayonesa f

mayor ['meɪər, 'mɛr] n : alcalde m, -desa f

mayoral ['meɪərəl, 'mɛrəl] adj : de alcalde

maze ['meɪz] n : laberinto m

me ['mi:] pron 1 : me ⟨she called me : me llamó⟩ ⟨give it to me : dámelo⟩ 2 (after a preposition) : mí ⟨for me : para mí⟩ ⟨with me : conmigo⟩ 3 (after conjunctions and verbs) : yo ⟨it's me : soy yo⟩ ⟨as big as me : tan grande como yo⟩ 4 (emphatic use) : yo ⟨me, too! : ¡yo también!⟩ ⟨who, me? : ¿quién, yo?⟩

meadow ['mɛdo:] n : prado m, pradera f

meadowland ['mɛdoˌlænd] n : pradera f

meadowlark ['mɛdoˌlɑrk] n : pájaro m cantor con el pecho amarillo

meager or **meagre** ['mi:gər] adj 1 THIN : magro, flaco 2 POOR, SCANTY : exiguo, escaso, pobre

meagerly ['mi:gərli] adv : pobremente

meagerness ['mi:gərnəs] n : escasez f, pobreza f

meal ['mi:l] n 1 : comida f ⟨a hearty meal : una comida sustanciosa⟩ 2 : harina f (de maíz, etc.)

mealtime ['mi:lˌtaɪm] n : hora f de comer

mean¹ ['mi:n] vt **meant** ['mɛnt]; **meaning** 1 INTEND : querer, pensar, tener la intención de ⟨I didn't mean to do it : lo hice sin querer⟩ ⟨what do you mean to do? : ¿qué piensas hacer?⟩ 2 SIGNIFY : querer decir, significar ⟨what does that mean? : ¿qué quiere decir eso?⟩ 3 : importar ⟨health means everything : lo que más importa es la salud⟩

mean² adj 1 HUMBLE : humilde 2 NEGLIGIBLE : despreciable ⟨it's no mean feat : no es poca cosa⟩ 3 STINGY : mezquino, tacaño 4 CRUEL : malo, cruel ⟨to be mean to someone : tratar mal a alguien⟩ 5 AVERAGE, MEDIAN : medio

mean³ n 1 MIDPOINT : término m medio 2 AVERAGE : promedio m, media f aritmética 3 **means** npl WAY : medio m, manera f, vía f 4 **means** npl RESOURCES : medios mpl, recursos mpl 5 **by all means** : por supuesto, cómo no 6 **by means of** : por medio de 7 **by no means** : de ninguna manera, de ningún modo

meander [mi'ændər] vi **-dered; -dering** 1 WIND : serpentear 2 WANDER : vagar, andar sin rumbo fijo

meaning ['mi:nɪŋ] n 1 : significado m, sentido m ⟨double meaning : doble sentido⟩ 2 INTENT : intención f, propósito m

meaningful ['mi:nɪŋfəl] adj : significativo — **meaningfully** adv

meaningless ['mi:nɪŋləs] adj : sin sentido

meanness ['mi:nnəs] n 1 CRUELTY : crueldad f, mezquindad f 2 STINGINESS : tacañería f

meantime¹ ['mi:nˌtaɪm] adv → **meanwhile¹**

meantime² n 1 : interín m 2 **in the meantime** : entretanto, mientras tanto

meanwhile¹ ['mi:nˌhwaɪl] adv : entretanto, mientras tanto

meanwhile² n → **meantime²**

measles ['mi:zəlz] ns & pl : sarampión m

measly ['mi:zli] adj **-slier; -est** : miserable, mezquino

measurable ['mɛʒərəbəl, 'meɪ-] adj : mensurable — **measurably** [-bli] adv

measure¹ ['mɛʒər, 'meɪ-] v **-sured; -suring** : medir ⟨he measured the table : midió la mesa⟩ ⟨it measures 15 feet tall : mide 15 pies de altura⟩

measure² n 1 AMOUNT : medida f, cantidad f ⟨in large measure : en gran medida⟩ ⟨a full measure : una cantidad exacta⟩ ⟨a measure of proficiency : una cierta competencia⟩ ⟨for good measure : de ñapa, por añadidura⟩ 2 DIMENSIONS, SIZE : medida f, tamaño m 3 RULER : regla f ⟨tape measure : cinta métrica⟩ 4 MEASUREMENT : medida f ⟨cubic measure : medida de capacidad⟩ 5 MEASURING : medición f 6 **measures** npl : medidas fpl ⟨security measures : medidas de seguridad⟩

measureless ['mɛʒərləs, 'meɪ-] adj : inmensurable

measurement ['mɛʒərmənt, 'meɪ-] n 1 MEASURING : medición f 2 DIMENSION : medida f

measure up vi **to measure up to** : estar a la altura de

meat ['mi:t] n 1 FOOD : comida f 2 : carne f ⟨meat and fish : carne y pescado⟩ 3 SUBSTANCE : sustancia f, esencia f ⟨the meat of the story : la sustancia del cuento⟩

meatball ['mi:tˌbɔl] n : albóndiga f

meaty ['mi:ti] adj **meatier; -est** : con mucha carne, carnoso

mechanic [mɪ'kænɪk] n : mecánico m, -ca f

mechanical [mɪ'kænɪkəl] adj : mecánico — **mechanically** adv

mechanics [mɪ'kænɪks] ns & pl 1 : mecánica f ⟨fluid mechanics : la mecánica de fluidos⟩ 2 MECHANISMS : mecanismos mpl, aspectos mpl prácticos

mechanism ['mɛkəˌnɪzəm] n : mecanismo m

mechanization [ˌmɛkənə'zeɪʃən] n : mecanización f

mechanize [ˈmɛkəˌnaɪz] vt **-nized;
-nizing** : mecanizar
medal [ˈmɛdəl] n : medalla f, condecoración f
medalist [ˈmɛdəlɪst] or **medallist** n
: medallista mf
medallion [məˈdæljən] n : medallón m
meddle [ˈmɛdəl] vi **-dled; -dling** : meterse, entrometerse
meddler [ˈmɛdələr] n : entrometido m,
-da f
meddlesome [ˈmɛdəlsəm] adj : entrometido
media [ˈmiːdiə] npl : medios mpl de comunicación
median¹ [ˈmiːdiən] adj : medio
median² n : valor m medio
mediate [ˈmiːdiˌeɪt] vi **-ated; -ating** : mediar
mediation [ˌmiːdiˈeɪʃən] n : mediación f
mediator [ˈmiːdiˌeɪtər] n : mediador m,
-dora f
medical [ˈmɛdɪkəl] adj : médico
medicate [ˈmɛdəˌkeɪt] vt **-cated; -cating** : medicar ⟨medicated powder : polvos medicinales⟩
medication [ˌmɛdəˈkeɪʃən] n **1** TREATMENT : tratamiento m, medicación f **2**
MEDICINE : medicamento m ⟨to be on medication : estar medicado⟩
medicinal [məˈdɪsənəl] adj : medicinal
medicine [ˈmɛdəsən] n **1** MEDICATION
: medicina f, medicamento m **2** : medicina f ⟨he's studying medicine : estudia medicina⟩
medicine man n : hechicero m
medieval or **mediaeval** [mɪˈdiːvəl, ˌmiː-,
ˌm-, -diˈiːvəl] adj : medieval
mediocre [ˌmiːdiˈoːkər] adj : mediocre
mediocrity [ˌmiːdiˈɑkrəti] n, pl **-ties**
: mediocridad f
meditate [ˈmɛdəˌteɪt] vi **-tated; -tating**
: meditar
meditation [ˌmɛdəˈteɪʃən] n : meditación f
meditative [ˈmɛdəˌteɪtɪv] adj : meditabundo
medium¹ [ˈmiːdiəm] adj : mediano ⟨of medium height : de estatura mediana,
de estatura regular⟩
medium² n, pl **-diums** or **-dia** [ˈmiː-diə]
1 MEAN : punto m medio, término m medio ⟨happy medium : justo medio⟩
2 MEANS : medio m **3** SUBSTANCE
: medio m, sustancia f ⟨a viscous medium : un medio viscoso⟩ **4** : medio m
de comunicación **5** : medio m (artístico)
medley [ˈmɛdli] n, pl **-leys** : popurrí m
(de canciones)
meek [ˈmiːk] adj **1** LONG-SUFFERING
: paciente, sufrido **2** SUBMISSIVE : sumiso, dócil, manso
meekly [ˈmiːkli] adv : dócilmente
meekness [ˈmiːknəs] n : mansedumbre f, docilidad f
meet¹ [ˈmiːt] v met [ˈmɛt]; **meeting** vt **1**
ENCOUNTER : encontrarse con **2** JOIN

: unirse con **3** CONFRONT : enfrentarse
a **4** SATISFY : satisfacer, cumplir con
⟨to meet costs : pagar los gastos⟩ **5**
: conocer ⟨I met his sister : conocí a su hermana⟩ — vi ASSEMBLE : reunirse,
congregarse
meet² n : encuentro m
meeting [ˈmiːtɪŋ] n **1** : reunión f ⟨to open the meeting : abrir la sesión⟩ **2**
ENCOUNTER : encuentro m **3** : entrevista f (formal)
meetinghouse [ˈmiːtɪŋˌhaʊs] n : iglesia f
(de ciertas confesiones protestantes)
megabyte [ˈmɛgəˌbaɪt] n : megabyte m
megahertz [ˈmɛgəˌhərts, -ˌhrts] n : megahercio m
megaphone [ˈmɛgəˌfoːn] n : megáfono m
melancholy¹ [ˈmɛlənˌkɑli] adj : melancólico, triste, sombrío
melancholy² n, pl **-cholies** : melancolía f
melanoma [ˌmɛləˈnoːmə] n, pl **-mas**
: melanoma m
meld [ˈmɛld] vt : fusionar, unir — vi : fusionarse, unirse
melee [ˈmeɪˌleɪ, meɪˈleɪ] n BRAWL : reyerta f, riña f, pelea f
meliorate [ˈmiːljəˌreɪt, ˈmiːliə-] → ameliorate
mellow¹ [ˈmɛloː] vt : suavizar, endulzar
— vi : suavizarse, endulzarse
mellow² adj **1** RIPE : maduro **2** MILD
: apacible ⟨a mellow character : un carácter apacible⟩ ⟨mellow wines : vinos añejos⟩ **3** : suave, dulce ⟨mellow colors : colores suaves⟩ ⟨mellow tones
: tonos dulces⟩
mellowness [ˈmɛlonəs] n : suavidad f,
dulzura f
melodic [məˈlɑdɪk] adj : melódico —
melodically [-dɪkli] adv
melodious [məˈloːdiəs] adj : melodioso
— **melodiously** adv
melodiousness [məˈloːdiəsnəs] n : calidad f de melódico
melodrama [ˈmɛləˌdrɑmə, -ˌdræ-] n
: melodrama m
melodramatic [ˌmɛlədrəˈmætɪk] adj
: melodramático — **melodramatically**
[-tɪkli] adv
melody [ˈmɛlədi] n, pl **-dies** : melodía f,
tonada f
melon [ˈmɛlən] n : melón m
melt [ˈmɛlt] vt **1** : derretir, disolver **2**
SOFTEN : ablandar ⟨it melted his heart
: ablandó su corazón⟩ — vi **1** : derretirse, disolverse **2** SOFTEN : ablandarse
3 DISAPPEAR : desvanecerse, esfumarse
⟨the clouds melted away : las nubes se desvanecieron⟩
melting point n : punto m de fusión
member [ˈmɛmbər] n **1** LIMB : miembro m **2** : miembro m (de un grupo); socio m, -cia f (de un club) **3** PART : miembro m, parte f
membership [ˈmɛmbərˌʃɪp] n **1** : membresía f ⟨application for membership

: solicitud de entrada⟩ **2** MEMBERS
: membresía f, miembros mpl, socios
mpl

membrane ['mɛmˌbreɪn] n : membrana
f — **membranous** ['mɛmbrə-nəs] adj

memento [mɪ'mɛnˌtoː] n, pl **-tos** or **-toes**
: recuerdo m

memo ['mɛmoː] n, pl **memos** : memorándum m

memoirs ['mɛmˌwɑrz] npl : memorias
fpl, autobiografía f

memorabilia [ˌmɛmərə'bɪliə, -'bɪljə] npl
1 : objetos mpl de interés histórico **2**
MEMENTOS : recuerdos mpl

memorable ['mɛmərəbəl] adj : memorable, notable — **memorably** [-blɪ] adv

memorandum [ˌmɛmə'rændəm] n, pl
-dums or **-da** [-də] : memorándum m

memorial[1] [mə'moriəl] adj : conmemorativo

memorial[2] n : monumento m conmemorativo

Memorial Day n : el último lunes de
mayo (observado en Estados Unidos
como día feriado para conmemorar a
los caídos en guerra)

memorialize [mə'moriəˌlaɪz] vt **-ized;**
-izing COMMEMORATE : conmemorar

memorization [ˌmɛmərə'zeɪʃən] n
: memorización f

memorize ['mɛməˌraɪz] vt **-rized; -rizing**
: memorizar, aprender de memoria

memory ['mɛmri, 'mɛmə-] n, pl **-ries 1**
: memoria f ⟨he has a good memory
: tiene buena memoria⟩ **2** RECOLLEC-
TION : recuerdo m **3** COMMEMORA-
TION : memoria f, conmemoración f

men → **man**[2]

menace[1] ['mɛnəs] vt **-aced; -acing 1**
THREATEN : amenazar **2** ENDANGER
: poner en peligro

menace[2] n : amenaza f

menacing ['mɛnəsɪŋ] adj : amenazador,
amenazante

menagerie [mə'næʤəri, -'næʒəri] n
: colección f de animales salvajes

mend[1] ['mɛnd] vt **1** CORRECT : enmendar, corregir ⟨to mend one's ways
: enmendarse⟩ **2** REPAIR : remendar,
arreglar, reparar — vi HEAL : curarse

mend[2] n : remiendo m

mendicant ['mɛndɪkənt] n BEGGAR
: mendigo m, -ga f

menhaden [mɛn'heɪdən, mən-] ns & pl
: pez m de la misma familia que los
arenques

menial[1] ['miːniəl] adj : servil, bajo

menial[2] n : sirviente m, -ta f

meningitis [ˌmɛnən'ʤaɪtəs] n, pl
-gitides [-'ʤɪtəˌdiːz] : meningitis f

menopause ['mɛnəˌpɔz] n : menopausia
f

menorah [mə'norə] n : candelabro m
(usado en los oficios religiosos judíos)

menstrual ['mɛnstruəl] adj : menstrual

menstruate ['mɛnstruˌeɪt] vi **-ated; -at-**
ing : menstruar

menstruation [ˌmɛnstru'eɪʃən] n : menstruación f

mental ['mɛntəl] adj : mental ⟨mental
hospital : hospital psiquiátrico⟩ —
mentally adv

mentality [mɛn'tæləti] n, pl **-ties** : mentalidad f

menthol ['mɛnˌθɔl, -ˌθoːl] n : mentol m

mentholated [ˌmɛnθəˌleɪtəd] adj : men-
tolado

mention[1] ['mɛntʃən] vt : mencionar,
mentar, referirse a ⟨don't mention it!
: ¡de nada!, ¡no hay de qué!⟩

mention[2] n : mención f

mentor ['mɛnˌtor, 'mɛntər] n : mentor m

menu ['mɛnˌjuː] n **1** : menú m, carta f
(en un restaurante) **2** : menú m (de
computadoras)

meow[1] [mi:'aʊ] vi : maullar

meow[2] n : maullido m, miau m

mercantile ['mərkənˌtiːl, -ˌtaɪl] adj : mercantil

mercenary[1] ['mərsəˌnɛri] adj : mercenario

mercenary[2] n, pl **-naries** : mercenario
m, -ria f

merchandise ['mərtʃənˌdaɪz, -ˌdaɪs] n
: mercancía f, mercadería f

merchandiser ['mərtʃənˌdaɪzər] n : comerciante mf; vendedor m, -dora f

merchant ['mərtʃənt] n : comerciante mf

merchant marine n : marina f mercante

merciful ['mərsɪfəl] adj : misericordioso,
clemente

mercifully ['mərsɪfli] adv **1** : con misericordia, con compasión **2** FORTU-
NATELY : afortunadamente

merciless ['mərsɪləs] adj : despiadado —
mercilessly adv

mercurial [ˌmər'kjʊriəl] adj TEMPERA-
MENTAL : temperamental, volátil

mercury ['mərkjəri] n, pl **-ries** : mercurio m

Mercury n : Mercurio m

mercy ['mərsi] n, pl **-cies 1** CLEMENCY
: misericordia f, clemencia f **2** BLESS-
ING : bendición f

mere ['mɪr] adj, superlative **merest**
: mero, simple

merely ['mɪrli] adv : solamente, simplemente

merge ['mərʤ] v **merged; merging** vi
: unirse, fusionarse (dícese de las com-
pañías), confluir (dícese de los ríos, las
calles, etc.) — vt : unir, fusionar, combinar

merger ['mərʤər] n : unión f, fusión f

meridian [mə'rɪdiən] n : meridiano m

meringue [mə'ræŋ] n : merengue m

merino [mə'riːno] n, pl **-nos 1** : merino
m, -na f **2** or **merino wool** : lana f merino

merit[1] ['mɛrət] vt : merecer, ser digno de

merit[2] n : mérito m, valor m

meritorious [ˌmɛrə'toriəs] adj : meritorio

mermaid ['mərˌmeɪd] n : sirena f

merriment ['mɛrimənt] n : alegría f, júbilo m, regocijo m

merry ['mɛri] *adj* -rier; -est : alegre —
merrily ['mɛrəli] *adv*
merry–go–round ['mɛrigo,raʊnd] *n*
: carrusel *m*, tiovivo *m*
merrymaker ['mɛri,meɪkər] *n* : juerguista *mf*
merrymaking ['mɛri,meɪkɪŋ] *n* : juerga
f
mesa ['meɪsə] *n* : mesa *f*
mesdames → madam, Mrs.
mesh[1] ['mɛʃ] *vi* 1 ENGAGE : engranar
(dícese de las piezas mecánicas) 2 TAN-
GLE : enredarse 3 COORDINATE : coordinarse, combinar
mesh[2] *n* 1 : malla *f* ⟨wire mesh : malla
metálica⟩ 2 NETWORK : red *f* 3 MESH-
ING : engranaje *m* ⟨in mesh : engrana-
do⟩
mesmerize ['mɛzmə,raɪz] *vt* -ized;
-izing 1 HYPNOTIZE : hipnotizar 2
FASCINATE : cautivar, embelesar, fascinar
mess[1] ['mɛs] *vt* 1 SOIL : ensuciar 2 to
mess up DISARRANGE : desordenar,
desarreglar 3 to mess up BUNGLE
: echar a perder — *vi* 1 PUTTER : entretenerse 2 INTERFERE : meterse, entrometerse ⟨don't mess with me : no te
metas conmigo⟩
mess[2] *n* 1 : rancho *m* (para soldados,
etc.) 2 DISORDER : desorden *m* ⟨your
room is a mess : tienes el cuarto hecho
un desastre⟩ 3 CONFUSION, TURMOIL
: confusión *f*, embrollo *m*, lío *m fam*
message ['mɛsɪdʒ] *n* : mensaje *m*, recado *m*
messenger ['mɛsəndʒər] *n* : mensajero
m, -ra *f*
Messiah [mə'saɪə] *n* : Mesías *m*
Messrs. → Mr.
messy ['mɛsi] *adj* messier; -est UNTIDY
: desordenado, sucio
met → meet
metabolic [,mɛtə'balɪk] *adj* : metabólico
metabolism [mə'tæbə,lɪzəm] *n* : metabolismo *m*
metabolize [mə'tæbə,laɪz] *vt* -lized;
-lizing : metabolizar
metal ['mɛtəl] *n* : metal *m*
metallic [mə'tælɪk] *adj* : metálico
metallurgical [,mɛtəl'ərdʒɪkəl] *adj* : metalúrgico
metallurgy ['mɛtəl,ərdʒi] *n* : metalurgia
f
metalwork ['mɛtəl,wərk] *n* : objeto *m* de
metal
metalworking ['mɛtəl,wərkɪŋ] *n* : metalistería *f*
metamorphosis [,mɛtə'mɔrfəsɪs] *n, pl*
-phoses [-,si:z] : metamorfosis *f*
metaphor ['mɛtə,fɔr, -fər] *n* : metáfora
f
metaphoric [,mɛtə'fɔrɪk] *or* metaphorical [-ɪkəl] *adj* : metafórico
metaphysical [,mɛtə'fɪzəkəl] *adj*
: metafísico
metaphysics [,mɛtə'fɪzɪks] *n* : metafísica *f*

mete ['mi:t] *vt* meted; meting ALLOT
: repartir, distribuir ⟨to mete out punishment : imponer castigos⟩
meteor ['mi:tiər, -ti:,ɔr] *n* : meteoro *m*
meteoric [,mi:ti'ɔrɪk] *adj* : meteórico
meteorite ['mi:tiə,raɪt] *n* : meteorito *m*
meteorologic [,mi:tiərə'ladʒɪk] *or* meteorological [-'ladʒɪkəl] *adj* : meteorológico
meteorologist [,mi:tiə'ralədʒɪst] *n* : meteorólogo *m*, -ga *f*
meteorology [,mi:tiə'ralədʒi] *n* : meteorología *f*
meter ['mi:tər] *n* 1 : metro *m* ⟨it measures 2 meters : mide 2 metros⟩ 2 : contador *m*, medidor *m* (de electricidad,
etc.) ⟨parking meter : parquímetro⟩ 3
: metro *m* (en literatura o música)
methane ['mɛ,θeɪn] *n* : metano *m*
method ['mɛθəd] *n* : método *m*
methodical [mə'θadɪkəl] *adj* : metódico
— methodically *adv*
Methodist ['mɛθədɪst] *n* : metodista *mf*
— Methodist *adj*
methodology [,mɛθə'dalədʒi] *n, pl* -gies
: metodología *f*
meticulous [mə'tɪkjələs] *adj* : meticuloso — meticulously *adv*
meticulousness [mə'tɪkjələsnəs] *n*
: meticulosidad *f*
metric ['mɛtrɪk] *or* metrical [-trɪkəl] *adj*
: métrico
metric system *n* : sistema *m* métrico
metronome ['mɛtrə,no:m] *n*
: metrónomo *m*
metropolis [mə'trapələs] *n* : metrópoli
f, metrópolis *f*
metropolitan [,mɛtrə'palətən] *adj* : metropolitano
mettle ['mɛtəl] *n* : temple *m*, valor *m* ⟨on
one's mettle : dispuesto a mostrar su
valía⟩
Mexican ['mɛksɪkən] *n* : mexicano *m*,
-na *f* — Mexican *adj*
mezzanine ['mɛzə,ni:n, ,mɛzə'ni:n] *n* 1
: entrepiso *m*, entresuelo *m* 2 : primer
piso *m* (de un teatro)
miasma [mar'æzmə] *n* : miasma *m*
mica ['maɪkə] *n* : mica *f*
mice → mouse
micro ['maɪkro] *adj* : muy pequeño, microscópico
microbe ['maɪ,kro:b] *n* : microbio *m*
microbiology [,maɪkrobaɪ'alədʒi] *n* : microbiología *f*
microchip ['maɪkro,tʃɪp] *n* : microchip
m
microcomputer ['maɪkrokəm,pju:tər] *n*
: microcomputadora *f*
microcosm ['maɪkro,kazəm] *n* : micro-
cosmo *m*
microfilm ['maɪkro,fɪlm] *n* : microfilm
m
micrometer [maɪ'kramətər] *n* : micrómetro *m*
micron ['maɪ,kran] *n* : micrón *m*
microorganism [,maɪkro'ɔrgə,nɪzəm] *n*
: microorganismo *m*, microbio *m*

microphone ['maɪkrə,fo:n] *n* : micrófono *m*

microprocessor ['maɪkro,prɑ,ssər] *n* : microprocesador *m*

microscope ['maɪkrə,sko:p] *n* : microscopio *m*

microscopic [,maɪkrə'skɑpɪk] *adj* : microscópico

microscopy [maɪ'krɑskəpi] *n* : microscopía *f*

microwave ['maɪkrə,weɪv] *n* **1** : microonda *f* **2** *or* **microwave oven** : microondas *m*

mid ['mɪd] *adj* : medio ⟨mid morning : a media mañana⟩ ⟨in mid-August : a mediados de agosto⟩ ⟨in mid ocean : en alta mar⟩

midair ['mɪd'ær] *n* **in ~** : en el aire ⟨to catch in midair : agarrar al vuelo⟩

midday ['mɪd'deɪ] *n* NOON : mediodía *m*

middle¹ ['mɪdəl] *adj* **1** CENTRAL : medio, del medio, de en medio **2** INTERMEDIATE : intermedio, mediano ⟨middle age : la mediana edad⟩

middle² *n* **1** CENTER : medio *m*, centro *m* ⟨fold it down the middle : dóblalo por la mitad⟩ **2 in the middle of** : en medio de (un espacio), a mitad de (una actividad) ⟨in the middle of the month : a mediados del mes⟩

Middle Ages *npl* : Edad *f* Media

middle class *n* : clase *f* media

middleman ['mɪdəl,mæn] *n*, *pl* **-men** [-mən, -,mɛn] : intermediario *m*, -ria *f*

middling ['mɪdlɪŋ, -lən] *adj* **1** MEDIUM, MIDDLE : mediano **2** MEDIOCRE : mediocre, regular

midfielder ['mɪd,fi:ldər] *n* : mediocampista *mf*

midge ['mɪdʒ] *n* : mosca *f* pequeña

midget ['mɪdʒət] *n* **1** : enano *m*, -na *f* (persona) **2** : cosa *f* diminuta

midland ['mɪdlənd, -,lænd] *n* : región *f* central (de un país)

midnight ['mɪd,naɪt] *n* : medianoche *f*

midpoint ['mɪd,pɔɪnt] *n* : punto *m* medio, término *m* medio

midriff ['mɪd,rɪf] *n* : diafragma *m*

midshipman ['mɪd,ʃɪpmən, ,mɪd'ʃɪp-] *n*, *pl* **-men** [-mən, -,mɛn] : guardiamarina *m*

midst¹ ['mɪdst] *n* : medio *m* ⟨in our midst : entre nosotros⟩ ⟨in the midst of : en medio de⟩

midst² *prep* : entre

midstream ['mɪd'stri:m, -,stri:m] *n* : medio *m* de la corriente ⟨in the midstream of his career : en medio de su carrera⟩

midsummer ['mɪd'sʌmər, -,sʌ-] *n* : pleno verano *m*

midtown ['mɪd,taʊn] *n* : centro *m* (de una ciudad)

midway ['mɪd,weɪ] *adv* HALFWAY : a mitad de camino

midweek ['mɪd,wi:k] *n* : medio *m* de la semana ⟨in midweek : a media semana⟩

midwife ['mɪd,waɪf] *n*, *pl* **-wives** [-,waɪvz] : partera *f*, comadrona *f*

midwinter ['mɪd'wɪntər, -,win-] *n* : pleno invierno *m*

midyear ['mɪd,jɪr] *n* : medio *m* del año ⟨at midyear : a mediados del año⟩

mien ['mi:n] *n* : aspecto *m*, porte *m*, semblante *m*

miff ['mɪf] *vt* : ofender

might¹ ['maɪt] (*used to express permission or possibility or as a polite alternative to* **may**) → **may** ⟨it might be true : podría ser verdad⟩ ⟨might I speak with Sarah? : ¿se puede hablar con Sarah?⟩

might² *n* : fuerza *f*, poder *m*

mightily ['maɪtəli] *adv* : con mucha fuerza, poderosamente

mighty¹ ['maɪti] *adv* VERY : muy ⟨mighty good : muy bueno, buenísimo⟩

mighty² *adj* **mightier; -est 1** POWERFUL : poderoso, potente **2** GREAT : grande, imponente

migraine ['maɪ,greɪn] *n* : jaqueca *f*, migraña *f*

migrant ['maɪgrənt] *n* : trabajador *m*, -dora *f* ambulante

migrate ['maɪ,greɪt] *vi* **-grated; -grating** : emigrar

migration [maɪ'greɪʃən] *n* : migración *f*

migratory ['maɪgrə,tori] *adj* : migratorio

mild ['maɪld] *adj* **1** GENTLE : apacible, suave ⟨a mild disposition : un temperamento suave⟩ **2** LIGHT : leve, ligero ⟨a mild punishment : un castigo leve, un castigo poco severo⟩ **3** TEMPERATE : templado (dícese del clima) **— mildly** *adv*

mildew¹ ['mɪl,du:, -,dju:] *vi* : enmohecerse

mildew² *n* : moho *m*

mildness ['maɪldnəs] *n* : apacibilidad *f*, suavidad *f*

mile ['maɪl] *n* : milla *f*

mileage ['maɪlɪdʒ] *n* **1** ALLOWANCE : viáticos *mpl* (pagados por milla recorrida) **2** : distancia *f* recorrida (en millas), kilometraje *m*

milestone ['maɪl,sto:n] *n* LANDMARK : hito *m*, jalón *m* ⟨a milestone in his life : un hito en su vida⟩

milieu [mi:l'ju:, -'jø] *n*, *pl* **-lieus** *or* **-lieux** [-'ju:z, -'jø] SURROUNDINGS : entorno *m*, medio *m*, ambiente *m*

militant¹ ['mɪlətənt] *adj* : militante, combativo

militant² *n* : militante *mf*

militarism ['mɪlətə,rɪzəm] *n* : militarismo *m*

militaristic [,mɪlətə'rɪstɪk] *adj* : militarista

military¹ ['mɪlə,teri] *adj* : militar

military² *n* **the military** : las fuerzas armadas

militia [mə'lɪʃə] *n* : milicia *f*

milk¹ ['mɪlk] *vt* **1** : ordeñar (una vaca, etc.) **2** EXPLOIT : explotar milk² *n* : leche *f*

milkman ['mɪlk,mæn, -mən] *n, pl* -men [-mən, -,men] : lechero *m*

milk shake *n* : batido *m*, licuado *m*

milkweed ['mɪlk,wi:d] *n* : algodoncillo *m*

milky ['mɪlki] *adj* milkier; -est : lechoso

Milky Way *n* : Vía *f* Láctea

mill¹ ['mɪl] *vt* : moler (granos), fresar (metales), acordonar (monedas) — *vi* to mill about : arremolinarse

mill² *n* 1 : molino *m* (para moler granos) 2 FACTORY : fábrica *f* ⟨textile mill : fábrica textil⟩ 3 GRINDER : molinillo *m*

millennium [mə'lɛniəm] *n, pl* -nia [-niə] *or* -niums : milenio *m*

miller ['mɪlər] *n* : molinero *m*, -ra *f*

millet ['mɪlət] *n* : mijo *m*

milligram ['mɪlə,græm] *n* : miligramo *m*

milliliter ['mɪlə,li:tər] *n* : mililitro *m*

millimeter ['mɪlə,mi:tər] *n* : milímetro *m*

milliner ['mɪlənər] *n* : sombrerero *m*, -ra *f* (de señoras)

millinery ['mɪlə,nɛri] *n* : sombreros *mpl* de señora

million¹ ['mɪljən] *adj* a million : un millón de

million² *n, pl* millions *or* million : millón *m*

millionaire [,mɪljə'nær, 'mɪljə,nær] *n* : millonario *m*, -ria *f*

millionth¹ ['mɪljənθ] *adj* : millonésimo

millionth² *n* : millonésimo *m*

millipede ['mɪlə,pi:d] *n* : milpiés *m*

millstone ['mɪl,sto:n] *n* : rueda *f* de molino, muela *f*

mime¹ ['maɪm] *v* mimed; miming *vt* MIMIC : imitar, remedar — *vi* PANTOMIME : hacer la mímica

mime² *n* 1 : mimo *mf* 2 PANTOMIME : pantomima *f*

mimeograph ['mɪmiə,græf] *n* : mimeógrafo *m*

mimic¹ ['mɪmɪk] *vt* -icked; -icking : imitar, remedar

mimic² *n* : imitador *m*, -dora *f*

mimicry ['mɪmɪkri] *n, pl* -ries : mímica *f*, imitación *f*

minaret [,mɪnə'rɛt] *n* : alminar *m*, minarete *m*

mince ['mɪnts] *v* minced; mincing *vt* 1 CHOP : picar, moler (carne) 2 not to mince one's words : no tener uno pelos en la lengua — *vi* : caminar de manera afectada

mincemeat ['mɪnts,mi:t] *n* : mezcla *f* de fruta picada, sebo, y especias

mind¹ ['maɪnd] *vt* 1 TEND : cuidar, atender ⟨mind the children : cuida a los niños⟩ 2 OBEY : obedecer 3 : preocuparse por, sentirse molestado por ⟨I don't mind his jokes : sus bromas no me molestan⟩ 4 : tener cuidado con ⟨mind the ladder! : ¡cuidado con la escalera!⟩ — *vi* 1 OBEY : obedecer 2 CARE : importarle a uno ⟨I don't mind : no me importa, me es igual⟩

mind² *n* 1 MEMORY : memoria *f*, recuerdo *m* ⟨keep it in mind : téngalo en cuenta⟩ 2 : mente *f* ⟨the mind and the body : la mente y el cuerpo⟩ 3 INTENTION : intención *f*, propósito *m* ⟨to have a mind to do something : tener intención de hacer algo⟩ 4 : razón *f* ⟨he's out of his mind : está loco⟩ 5 OPINION : opinión *f* ⟨to change one's mind : cambiar de opinión⟩ 6 INTELLECT : capacidad *f* intelectual

minded ['maɪndəd] *adj* 1 (*used in combination*) ⟨narrow-minded : de mentalidad cerrada⟩ ⟨health-minded : preocupado por la salud⟩ 2 INCLINED : inclinado

mindful ['maɪndfəl] *adj* AWARE : consciente — mindfully *adv*

mindless ['maɪndləs] *adj* 1 SENSELESS : estúpido, sin sentido ⟨mindless violence : violencia sin sentido⟩ 2 HEEDLESS : inconsciente

mindlessly ['maɪndləsli] *adv* 1 SENSELESSLY : sin sentido 2 HEEDLESSLY : inconscientemente

mine¹ ['maɪn] *vt* mined; mining 1 : extraer (oro, etc.) 2 : minar (con artefactos explosivos)

mine² *n* : mina *f* ⟨gold mine : mina de oro⟩

mine³ *pron* : mío, mía ⟨that one's mine : ése es el mío⟩ ⟨some friends of mine : unos amigos míos⟩

minefield ['maɪn,fi:ld] *n* : campo *m* de minas

miner ['maɪnər] *n* : minero *m*, -ra *f*

mineral ['mɪnərəl] *n* : mineral *m* — mineral *adj*

mineralogy [,mɪnə'rɑləʤi, -'ræ-] *n* : mineralogía *f*

mingle ['mɪŋgəl] *v* -gled; -gling *vt* MIX : mezclar — *vi* 1 MIX : mezclarse 2 CIRCULATE : circular

miniature¹ ['mɪniə,ʧur, 'mɪni,ʧur, -ʧər] *adj* : en miniatura, diminuto

miniature² *n* : miniatura *f*

minibus ['mɪni,bʌs] *n* : microbús *m*, pesera *f Mex*

minicomputer ['mɪnikəm,pju:tər] *n* : minicomputadora *f*

minimal ['mɪnəməl] *adj* : mínimo

minimally ['mɪnəməli] *adv* : en grado mínimo

minimize ['mɪnə,maɪz] *vt* -mized; -mizing : minimizar

minimum¹ ['mɪnəməm] *adj* : mínimo

minimum² *n, pl* -ma ['mɪnəmə] *or* -mums : mínimo *m*

miniseries ['mɪni,sɪri:z] *n* : miniserie *f*

miniskirt ['mɪni,skərt] *n* : minifalda *f*

minister¹ ['mɪnəstər] *vi* to minister to : cuidar (de), atender a

minister² *n* 1 : pastor *m*, -tora *f* (de una iglesia) 2 : ministro *m*, -tra *f* (en política)

ministerial [,mɪnə'stɪriəl] *adj* : ministerial

ministry ['mɪnəstri] *n, pl* -tries 1 : ministerio *m* (en política) 2 : sacerdocio *m* (en el catolicismo), clerecía *f* (en el protestantismo)

minivan ['mɪni,væn] *n* : minivan *f*

mink ['mɪŋk] *n*, *pl* **mink** *or* **minks** : visón *m*

minnow ['mɪno:] *n*, *pl* **-nows** : pececillo *m* de agua dulce

minor[1] ['maɪnər] *adj* : menor

minor[2] *n* **1** : menor *mf* (de edad) **2** : asignatura *f* secundaria (de estudios)

minority [mə'nɔrəti, maɪ-] *n*, *pl* **-ties** : minoría *f*

minstrel ['mɪntstrəl] *n* : juglar *m*, trovador *m* (en el medioevo)

mint[1] ['mɪnt] *vt* : acuñar

mint[2] *adj* : sin usar ⟨in mint condition : como nuevo⟩

mint[3] *n* **1** : menta *f* ⟨mint tea : té de menta⟩ **2** : pastilla *f* de menta **3** : casa *f* de la moneda ⟨the U.S. Mint : la casa de la moneda de los EE.UU.⟩ **4** FORTUNE : dineral *m*, fortuna *f*

minuet [,mɪnju'et] *n* : minué *m*

minus[1] ['maɪnəs] *n* **1** : cantidad *f* negativa **2 minus sign** : signo *m* de menos

minus[2] *prep* **1** : menos ⟨four minus two : cuatro menos dos⟩ **2** WITHOUT : sin ⟨minus his hat : sin su sombrero⟩

minuscule *or* **miniscule** ['mɪnəs,kju:l, mɪ'nʌs-] *adj* : minúsculo

minute[1] [maɪ'nu:t, mɪ-, -'nju:t] *adj* **-nuter; -est 1** TINY : diminuto, minúsculo **2** DETAILED : minucioso

minute[2] ['mɪnət] *n* **1** : minuto *m* ⟨ten minutes late : diez minutos de retraso⟩ **2** MOMENT : momento *m* **3 minutes** *npl* : actas *fpl* (de una reunión)

minutely [maɪ'nu:tli, mɪ-, -'nju:t-] *adv* : minuciosamente

miracle ['mɪrɪkəl] *n* : milagro *m*

miraculous [mə'rækjələs] *adj* : milagroso — **miraculously** *adv*

mirage [mɪ'rɑʒ, *chiefly Brit* 'mɪr,ɑʒ] *n* : espejismo *m*

mire[1] ['maɪr] *vi* **mired; miring** : atascarse

mire[2] *n* **1** MUD : barro *m*, lodo *m* **2** : atolladero *m* ⟨stuck in a mire of debt : agobiado por la deuda⟩

mirror[1] ['mɪrər] *vt* : reflejar

mirror[2] *n* : espejo *m*

mirth ['mərθ] *n* : alegría *f*, regocijo *m*

mirthful ['mərθfəl] *adj* : alegre, regocijado

misadventure [,mɪsəd'ventʃər] *n* : malaventura *f*, desventura *f*

misanthrope ['mɪsən,θro:p] *n* : misántropo *m*, -pa *f*

misanthropic [,mɪsən'θrɑpɪk] *adj* : misantrópico

misanthropy [mɪ'sænθrəpi] *n* : misantropía *f*

misapprehend [,mɪs,æprə'hend] *vt* : entender mal

misapprehension [,mɪs,æprə'hentʃən] *n* : malentendido *m*

misappropriate [,mɪsə'pro:pri,eɪt] *vt* **-ated; -ating** : malversar

misbegotten [,mɪsbi'gɑtən] *adj* **1** ILLEGITIMATE : ilegítimo **2** : mal concebido ⟨misbegotten laws : leyes mal concebidas⟩

misbehave [,mɪsbi'heɪv] *vi* **-haved; -having** : portarse mal

misbehavior [,mɪsbi'heɪvjər] *n* : mala conducta *f*

miscalculate [mɪs'kælkjə,leɪt] *v* **-lated; -lating** : calcular mal

miscalculation [mɪs,kælkjə'leɪʃən] *n* : error *m* de cálculo, mal cálculo *m*

miscarriage [,mɪs'kærɪdʒ, 'mɪs,kærɪdʒ] *n* **1** : aborto *m* **2** FAILURE : fracaso *m*, malogro *m* ⟨a miscarriage of justice : una injusticia, un error judicial⟩

miscarry [,mɪs'kæri, 'mɪs,kæri] *vi* **-ried; -rying 1** ABORT : abortar **2** FAIL : malograrse, fracasar

miscellaneous [,mɪsə'leɪniəs] *adj* : misceláneo

miscellany ['mɪsə,leɪni] *n*, *pl* **-nies** : miscelánea *f*

mischance [mɪs'tʃænts] *n* : desgracia *f*, infortunio *m*, mala suerte *f*

mischief ['mɪstʃəf] *n* : diabluras *fpl*, travesuras *fpl*

mischievous [mɪs'tʃəvəs] *adj* : travieso, pícaro

mischievously [mɪs'tʃəvəsli] *adv* : de manera traviesa

misconception [,mɪskən'sepʃən] *n* : concepto *m* erróneo, idea *f* falsa

misconduct [mɪs'kɑndəkt] *n* : mala conducta *f*

misconstrue [,mɪskən'stru:] *vt* **-strued; -struing** : malinterpretar

misdeed [mɪs'di:d] *n* : fechoría *f*

misdemeanor [,mɪsdɪ'mi:nər] *n* : delito *m* menor

miser ['maɪzər] *n* : avaro *m*, -ra *f*; tacaño *m*, -ña *f*

miserable ['mɪzərəbəl] *adj* **1** UNHAPPY : triste, desdichado **2** WRETCHED : miserable, desgraciado ⟨a miserable hut : una choza miserable⟩ **3** UNPLEASANT : desagradable, malo ⟨miserable weather : tiempo malísimo⟩ **4** CONTEMPTIBLE : despreciable, mísero ⟨for a miserable $10 : por unos míseros diez dólares⟩

miserably ['mɪzərəbli] *adv* **1** SADLY : tristemente **2** WRETCHEDLY : miserablemente, lamentablemente **3** UNFORTUNATELY : desgraciadamente

miserly ['maɪzərli] *adj* : avaro, tacaño

misery ['mɪzəri] *n*, *pl* **-eries** : miseria *f*, sufrimiento *m*

misfire [mɪs'faɪr] *vi* **-fired; -firing** : fallar

misfit ['mɪs,fɪt] *n* : inadaptado *m*, -da *f*

misfortune [mɪs'fɔrtʃən] *n* : desgracia *f*, desventura *f*, infortunio *m*

misgiving [mɪs'gɪvɪŋ] *n* : duda *f*, recelo *m*

misguided [mɪs'gaɪdəd] *adj* : desacertado, equivocado, mal informado

mishap ['mɪs,hæp] *n* : contratiempo *m*, percance *m*, accidente *m*

misinform [,mɪsɪn'fɔrm] *vt* : informar mal

misinterpret [,mɪsɪn'tərprət] *vt* : malinterpretar

misinterpretation [ˌmɪsɪnˌtərprəˈteɪ-ʃən] *n* : mala interpretación *f*, malentendido *m*

misjudge [mɪsˈdʒʌdʒ] *vt* **-judged; -judging** : juzgar mal

mislay [mɪsˈleɪ] *vt* **-laid** [-leɪd]; **-laying** : extraviar, perder

mislead [mɪsˈliːd] *vt* **-led** [-ˈlɛd]; **-leading** : engañar

misleading [mɪsˈliːdɪŋ] *adj* : engañoso

mismanage [mɪsˈmænɪdʒ] *vt* **-aged; -aging** : administrar mal

mismanagement [mɪsˈmænɪdʒmənt] *n* : mala administración *f*

misnomer [mɪsˈnoːmər] *n* : nombre *m* inapropiado

misogynist [mɪˈsɑdʒənɪst] *n* : misógino *m*

misogyny [məˈsɑdʒəni] *n* : misoginia *f*

misplace [mɪsˈpleɪs] *vt* **-placed; -placing** : extraviar, perder

misprint [ˈmɪsˌprɪnt, mɪsˈ-] *n* : errata *f*, error *m* de imprenta

mispronounce [ˌmɪsprəˈnaʊnts] *vt* **-nounced; -nouncing** : pronunciar mal

mispronunciation [ˌmɪsprəˌnʌntsiˈeɪʃən] *n* : pronunciación *f* incorrecta

misquote [mɪsˈkwoːt] *vt* **-quoted; -quoting** : citar incorrectamente

misread [mɪsˈriːd] *vt* **-read; -reading 1** : leer mal ⟨she misread the sentence : leyó mal la frase⟩ **2** MISUNDERSTAND : malinterpretar ⟨they misread his intention : malinterpretaron su intención⟩

misrepresent [ˌmɪsˌrprɪˈzɛnt] *vt* : distorsionar, falsear, tergiversar

misrule[1] [mɪsˈruːl] *vt* **-ruled; -ruling** : gobernar mal

misrule[2] *n* : mal gobierno *m*

miss[1] [ˈmɪs] *vt* **1** : errar, faltar ⟨to miss the target : no dar en el blanco⟩ **2** : no encontrar, perder ⟨they missed each other : no se encontraron⟩ ⟨I missed the plane : perdí el avión⟩ **3** : echar de menos, extrañar ⟨we miss him a lot : lo echamos mucho de menos⟩ **4** OVERLOOK : pasar por alto, perder (una oportunidad, etc.) **5** AVOID : evitar ⟨they just missed hitting the tree : por muy poco chocan contra el árbol⟩ **6** OMIT : saltarse ⟨he missed breakfast : se saltó el desayuno⟩

miss[2] *n* **1** : fallo *m* (de un tiro, etc.) **2** FAILURE : fracaso *m* **3** : señorita *f* ⟨Miss Jones called us : nos llamó la señorita Jones⟩ ⟨excuse me, miss : perdone, señorita⟩

missal [ˈmɪsəl] *n* : misal *m*

misshapen [mɪsˈʃeɪpən] *adj* : deforme

missile [ˈmɪsəl] *n* **1** : misil *m* ⟨guided missile : misil guiado⟩ **2** PROJECTILE : proyectil *m*

missing [ˈmɪsɪŋ] *adj* **1** ABSENT : ausente ⟨who's missing? : ¿quién falta?⟩ **2** LOST : perdido, desaparecido ⟨missing persons : los desaparecidos⟩

mission [ˈmɪʃən] *n* **1** : misión *f* (mandada por una iglesia) **2** DELEGATION : misión *f*, delegación *f*, embajada *f* **3** TASK : misión *f*

missionary[1] [ˈmɪʃəˌnɛri] *adj* : misionero

missionary[2] *n, pl* **-aries** : misionero *m*, -ra *f*

missive [ˈmɪsɪv] *n* : misiva *f*

misspell [mɪsˈspɛl] *vt* : escribir mal

misspelling [mɪsˈspɛlɪŋ] *n* : falta *f* de ortografía

misstep [ˈmɪsˌstɛp] *n* : traspié *m*, tropezón *m*

mist [ˈmɪst] *n* **1** HAZE : neblina *f*, niebla *f* **2** SPRAY : rocío *m*

mistake[1] [mɪˈsteɪk] *vt* **-took** [-ˈstʊk]; **-taken** [-ˈsteɪkən]; **-taking 1** MISINTERPRET : malinterpretar **2** CONFUSE : confundir ⟨he mistook her for Clara : la confundió con Clara⟩

mistake[2] *n* **1** MISUNDERSTANDING : malentendido *m*, confusión *f* **2** ERROR : error *m* ⟨I made a mistake : me equivoqué, cometí un error⟩

mistaken [mɪˈsteɪkən] *adj* WRONG : equivocado — **mistakenly** *adv*

mister [ˈmɪstər] *n* : señor *m* ⟨watch out, mister : cuidado, señor⟩

mistiness [ˈmɪstinəs] *n* : nebulosidad *f*

mistletoe [ˈmɪsəlˌtoː] *n* : muérdago *m*

mistreat [mɪsˈtriːt] *vt* : maltratar

mistreatment [mɪsˈtriːtmənt] *n* : maltrato *m*, abuso *m*

mistress [ˈmɪstrəs] *n* **1** : dueña *f*, señora *f* (de una casa) **2** LOVER : amante *f*

mistrust[1] [mɪsˈtrʌst] *vt* : desconfiar de

mistrust[2] *n* : desconfianza *f*

mistrustful [mɪsˈtrʌstfəl] *adj* : desconfiado

misty [ˈmɪsti] *adj* **mistier; -est 1** : neblinoso, nebuloso **2** TEARFUL : lloroso

misunderstand [ˌmɪsˌʌndərˈstænd] *vt* **-stood** [-ˈstʊd]; **-standing 1** : entender mal **2** MISINTERPRET : malinterpretar ⟨don't misunderstand me : no me malinterpretes⟩

misunderstanding [ˌmɪsˌʌndərˈstændɪŋ] *n* **1** MISINTERPRETATION : malentendido *m* **2** DISAGREEMENT, QUARREL : disputa *f*, discusión *f*

misuse[1] [mɪsˈjuːz] *vt* **-used; -using 1** : emplear mal **2** ABUSE, MISTREAT : abusar de, maltratar

misuse[2] [mɪsˈjuːs] *n* **1** : mal empleo *m*, mal uso *m* **2** WASTE : derroche *m*, despilfarro *m* **3** ABUSE : abuso *m*

mite [ˈmaɪt] *n* **1** : ácaro *m* **2** BIT : poco *m* ⟨a mite tired : un poquito cansado⟩

miter *or* **mitre** [ˈmaɪtər] *n* **1** : mitra *f* (de un obispo) **2** *or* **miter joint** : inglete *m*

mitigate [ˈmɪtəˌgeɪt] *vt* **-gated; -gating** : mitigar, aliviar

mitigation [ˌmɪtəˈgeɪʃən] *n* : mitigación *f*, alivio *m*

mitosis [maɪˈtoːsɪs] *n, pl* **-toses** [-ˌsiːz] : mitosis *f*

mitt [ˈmɪt] *n* : manopla *f*, guante *m* (de béisbol)

mitten ['mɪtən] *n* : manopla *f*, mitón *m*

mix¹ ['mɪks] *vt* **1** COMBINE : mezclar **2** STIR : remover, revolver **3 to mix up** CONFUSE : confundir — *vi* : mezclarse

mix² *n* : mezcla *f*

mixer ['mɪksər] *n* **1** : batidora *f* (de la cocina) **2 cement mixer** : hormigonera *f*

mixture ['mɪkstʃər] *n* : mezcla *f*

mix–up ['mɪks,ʌp] *n* CONFUSION : confusión *f*, lío *m fam*

mnemonic [nɪ'manɪk] *adj* : mnemónico

moan¹ ['mo:n] *vi* : gemir

moan² *n* : gemido *m*

moat ['mo:t] *n* : foso *m*

mob¹ ['mab] *vt* **mobbed; mobbing 1** ATTACK : atacar en masa **2** HOUND : acosar, rodear

mob² *n* **1** THRONG : multitud *f*, turba *f*, muchedumbre *f* **2** GANG : pandilla *f*

mobile¹ ['mo:bəl, -,bi:l, -,baɪl] *adj* : móvil ⟨mobile home : caravana, casa rodante⟩

mobile² ['mo,bi:l] *n* : móvil *m*

mobility [mo'bɪlət̬i] *n* : movilidad *f*

mobilize ['mo:bə,laɪz] *vt* **-lized; -lizing** : movilizar

moccasin ['makəsən] *n* **1** : mocasín *m* **2** *or* **water moccasin** : serpiente *f* venenosa de Norteamérica

mocha ['mo:kə] *n* **1** : mezcla *f* de café y chocolate **2** : color *m* chocolate

mock¹ ['mak, 'mɔk] *vt* **1** RIDICULE : burlarse de, mofarse de **2** MIMIC : imitar, remedar (de manera burlona)

mock² *adj* **1** SIMULATED : simulado **2** PHONY : falso

mockery ['makəri, 'mɔ-] *n, pl* **-eries 1** JEER, TAUNT : burla *f*, mofa *f* ⟨to make a mockery of : burlarse de⟩ **2** FAKE : imitación *f* (burlona)

mockingbird ['makɪŋ,bərd, 'mɔ-] *n* : sinsonte *m*

mode ['mo:d] *n* **1** FORM : modo *m*, forma *f* **2** MANNER : modo *m*, manera *f*, estilo *m* **3** FASHION : moda *f*

model¹ ['madəl] *v* **-eled** *or* **-elled; -eling** *or* **-elling** *vt* SHAPE : modelar — *vi* : trabajar de modelo

model² *adj* **1** EXEMPLARY : modelo, ejemplar ⟨a model student : un estudiante modelo⟩ **2** MINIATURE : en miniatura

model³ *n* **1** PATTERN : modelo *m* **2** MINIATURE : modelo *m*, miniatura *f* **3** EXAMPLE : modelo *m*, ejemplo *m* **4** MANNEQUIN : modelo *mf* **5** DESIGN : modelo *m* ⟨the '97 model : el modelo '97⟩

modem ['mo:dəm, -,dɛm] *n* : módem *m*

moderate¹ ['madə,reɪt] *v* **-ated; -ating** *vt* : moderar, temperar — *vi* **1** CALM : moderarse, calmarse **2** : fungir como moderador (en un debate, etc.)

moderate² ['madərət] *adj* : moderado

moderate³ ['madərət] *n* : moderado *m*, -da *f*

moderately ['madərətli] *adv* **1** : con moderación **2** FAIRLY : medianamente

moderation [,madə'reɪʃən] *n* : moderación *f*

moderator ['madə,reɪt̬ər] *n* : moderador *m*, -dora *f*

modern ['madərn] *adj* : moderno

modernism ['madər,nɪzəm] *n* : modernismo *m*

modernist ['madərnɪst] *n* : modernista *mf* — **modernist** *adj*

modernity [mə'dərnət̬i] *n* : modernidad *f*

modernization [,madərnə'zeɪʃən] *n* : modernización *f*

modernize ['madər,naɪz] *v* **-ized; -izing** *vt* : modernizar — *vi* : modernizarse

modest ['madəst] *adj* **1** HUMBLE : modesto **2** DEMURE : recatado, pudoroso **3** MODERATE : modesto, moderado — **modestly** *adv*

modesty ['madəsti] *n* : modestia *f*

modicum ['madɪkəm] *n* : mínimo *m*, pizca *f*

modification [,madəfə'keɪʃən] *n* : modificación *f*

modifier ['madə,faɪər] *n* : modificante *m*, modificador *m*

modify ['madə,faɪ] *vt* **-fied; -fying** : modificar, calificar (en gramática)

modish ['mo:dɪʃ] *adj* STYLISH : a la moda, de moda

modular ['madʒələr] *adj* : modular

modulate ['madʒə,leɪt] *vt* **-lated; -lating** : modular

modulation [,madʒə'leɪʃən] *n* : modulación *f*

module ['madʒu:l] *n* : módulo *m*

mogul ['mo:gəl] *n* : magnate *mf*; potentado *m*, -da *f*

mohair ['mo:,hær] *n* : mohair *m*

moist ['mɔɪst] *adj* : húmedo

moisten ['mɔɪsən] *vt* : humedecer

moistness ['mɔɪstnəs] *n* : humedad *f*

moisture ['mɔɪstʃər] *n* : humedad *f*

moisturize ['mɔɪstʃə,raɪz] *vt* **-ized; -izing** : humedecer (el aire), humectar (la piel)

moisturizer ['mɔɪtʃə,raɪzər] *n* : crema *f* hidratante, crema *f* humectante

molar ['mo:lər] *n* : muela *f*, molar *m*

molasses [mə'læsəz] *n* : melaza *f*

mold¹ ['mo:ld] *vt* : moldear, formar (carácter, etc.) — *vi* : enmohecerse ⟨the bread will mold : el pan se enmohecerá⟩

mold² *n* **1** *or* **leaf mold** : mantillo *m* **2** FORM : molde *m* ⟨to break the mold : romper el molde⟩ **3** FUNGUS : moho *m*

molder ['mo:ldər] *vi* CRUMBLE : desmoronarse

molding ['mo:ldɪŋ] *n* : moldura *f* (en arquitectura)

moldy ['mo:ldi] *adj* **moldier; -est** : mohoso

mole ['mo:l] *n* **1** : lunar *m* (en la piel) **2** : topo *m* (animal)

molecule ['malɪˌkju:l] *n* : molécula *f* — **molecular** [mə'lɛkjələr] *adj*

molehill ['mo:lˌhɪl] *n* : topera *f*

molest [mə'lɛst] *vt* **1** ANNOY, DISTURB : molestar **2** : abusar (sexualmente)

mollify ['maləˌfaɪ] *vt* -**fied**; -**fying** : apaciguar, aplacar

mollusk *or* **mollusc** ['maləsk] *n* : molusco *m*

mollycoddle ['malɪˌkadəl] *vt* -**dled**; -**dling** PAMPER : consentir, mimar

molt ['mo:lt] *vi* : mudar, hacer la muda

molten ['mo:ltən] *adj* : fundido

mom ['mam, 'mʌm] *n* : mamá *f*

moment ['mo:mənt] *n* **1** INSTANT : momento *m* ⟨one moment, please : un momento, por favor⟩ **2** TIME : momento *m* ⟨at the moment : de momento, actualmente⟩ ⟨from that moment : desde entonces⟩ **3** IMPORTANCE : importancia *f* ⟨of great moment : de gran importancia⟩

momentarily [ˌmo:mən'tɛrəli] *adv* **1** : momentáneamente **2** SOON : dentro de poco, pronto

momentary ['mo:mənˌtɛri] *adj* : momentáneo

momentous [mo'mɛntəs] *adj* : de suma importancia, fatídico

momentum [mo'mɛntəm] *n, pl* -**ta** [-tə] *or* -**tums** **1** : momento *m* (en física) **2** IMPETUS : ímpetu *m*, impulso *m*

mommy ['mami, 'mʌ-] *n* : mami *f*

monarch ['maˌnark, -nərk] *n* : monarca *mf*

monarchism ['maˌnarˌkɪzəm, -nər-] *n* : monarquismo *m*

monarchist ['maˌnarkɪst, -nər-] *n* : monárquico *m*, -ca *f*

monarchy ['maˌnarki, -nər-] *n, pl* -**chies** : monarquía *f*

monastery ['manəˌstɛri] *n, pl* -**teries** : monasterio *m*

monastic [mə'næstɪk] *adj* : monástico — **monastically** [-tɪkli] *adv*

Monday ['mʌnˌdeɪ, -di] *n* : lunes *m*

monetary ['manəˌtɛri, 'mʌnə-] *adj* : monetario

money ['mʌni] *n, pl* -**eys** *or* -**ies** ['mʌniz] : dinero *m*, plata *f*

moneyed ['mʌnid] *adj* : adinerado

moneylender ['mʌniˌlɛndər] *n* : prestamista *mf*

money order *n* : giro *m* postal

Mongol ['maŋgəl, -ˌgo:l] → **Mongolian**

Mongolian [man'go:liən, maŋ-] *n* : mongol *m*, -gola *f* — **Mongolian** *adj*

mongoose ['maŋˌgu:s, 'maŋ-] *n, pl* -**gooses** : mangosta *f*

mongrel ['maŋgrəl, 'mʌŋ-] *n* **1** : perro *m* mestizo, perro *m* corriente *Mex* **2** HYBRID : híbrido *m*

monitor¹ ['manətər] *vt* : controlar, monitorear

monitor² *n* **1** : ayudante *mf* (en una escuela) **2** : monitor *m* (de una computadora, etc.)

monk ['mʌŋk] *n* : monje *m*

monkey¹ ['mʌŋki] *vi* -**keyed**; -**keying** **1 to monkey around** : hacer payasadas, payasear **2 to monkey with** : juguetear con

monkey² *n, pl* -**keys** : mono *m*, -na *f*

monkeyshines ['mʌŋkiˌʃaɪnz] *npl* PRANKS : picardías *fpl*, travesuras *fpl*

monkey wrench *n* : llave *f* inglesa

monocle ['manɪkəl] *n* : monóculo *m*

monogamous [mə'nagəməs] *adj* : monógamo

monogamy [mə'nagəmi] *n* : monogamia *f*

monogram¹ ['manəˌgræm] *vt* -**grammed**; -**gramming** : marcar con monograma ⟨monogrammed towels : toallas con monograma⟩

monogram² *n* : monograma *m*

monograph ['manəˌgræf] *n* : monografía *f*

monolingual [ˌmanə'lɪŋgwəl] *adj* : monolingüe

monolith ['manəˌlɪθ] *n* : monolito *m*

monolithic [ˌmanə'lɪθɪk] *adj* : monolítico

monologue ['manəˌlɔg] *n* : monólogo *m*

monoplane ['manəˌpleɪn] *n* : monoplano *m*

monopolize [mə'napəˌlaɪz] *vt* -**lized**; -**lizing** : monopolizar

monopoly [mə'napəli] *n, pl* -**lies** : monopolio *m*

monosyllabic [ˌmanosə'læbɪk] *adj* : monosilábico

monosyllable ['manoˌsɪləbəl] *n* : monosílabo *m*

monotheism ['manoθi:ˌɪzəm] *n* : monoteísmo *m*

monotheistic [ˌmanoθi:'ɪstɪk] *adj* : monoteísta

monotone ['manəˌto:n] *n* : voz *f* monótona

monotonous [mə'natənəs] *adj* : monótono — **monotonously** *adv*

monotony [mə'natəni] *n* : monotonía *f*, uniformidad *f*

monoxide [mə'nakˌsaɪd] *n* : monóxido *m*

monsoon [man'su:n] *n* : monzón *m*

monster ['manstər] *n* : monstruo *m*

monstrosity [man'strasəti] *n, pl* -**ties** : monstruosidad *f*

monstrous ['manstrəs] *adj* : monstruoso — **monstrously** *adv*

montage [man'taʒ] *n* : montaje *m*

month ['mʌnθ] *n* : mes *m*

monthly¹ ['mʌnθli] *adv* : mensualmente

monthly² *adj* : mensual

monthly³ *n, pl* -**lies** : publicación *f* mensual

monument ['manjəmənt] *n* : monumento *m*

monumental [ˌmanjə'mɛntəl] *adj* : monumental — **monumentally** *adv*

moo¹ ['mu:] *vi* : mugir

moo² *n* : mugido *m*

mood ['mu:d] *n* : humor *m* ⟨to be in a good mood : estar de buen humor⟩ ⟨to be in the mood for : tener ganas de⟩ ⟨to be in no mood for : no estar para⟩

moodiness ['muːdinəs] *n* **1** SADNESS : melancolía *f*, tristeza *f* **2** : cambios *mpl* de humor, carácter *m* temperamental

moody ['muːdi] *adj* **moodier; -est 1** GLOOMY : melancólico, deprimido **2** TEMPERAMENTAL : temperamental, de humor variable

moon ['muːn] *n* : luna *f*

moonbeam ['muːnˌbiːm] *n* : rayo *m* de luna

moonlight[1] ['muːnˌlaɪt] *vi* : estar pluriempleado

moonlight[2] *n* : claro *m* de luna, luz *f* de la luna

moonlit ['muːnˌlɪt] *adj* : iluminado por la luna ⟨a moonlit night : una noche de luna⟩

moonshine ['muːnˌʃaɪn] *n* **1** MOONLIGHT : luz *f* de la luna **2** NONSENSE : disparates *mpl*, tonterías *fpl* **3** : whisky *m* destilado ilegalmente

moor[1] ['mʊr, 'mɔr] *vt* : amarrar

moor[2] *n* : brezal *m*, páramo *m*

Moor ['mʊr] *n* : moro *m*, -ra *f*

mooring ['mʊrɪŋ, 'mɔr-] *n* DOCK : atracadero *m*

Moorish ['mʊrɪʃ] *adj* : moro

moose ['muːs] *ns & pl* : alce *m* (norteamericano)

moot ['muːt] *adj* DEBATABLE : discutible

mop[1] ['mɑp] *vt* **mopped; mopping** : trapear

mop[2] *n* : trapeador *m*

mope ['moːp] *vi* **moped; moping** : andar deprimido, quedar abatido

moped ['moːˌped] *n* : ciclomotor *m*

moraine [mə'reɪn] *n* : morena *f*

moral[1] ['mɔrəl] *adj* : moral ⟨moral judgment : juicio moral⟩ ⟨moral support : apoyo moral⟩ — **morally** *adv*

moral[2] *n* **1** : moraleja *f* (de un cuento, etc.) **2 morals** *npl* : moral *f*, moralidad *f*

morale [mə'ræl] *n* : moral *f*

moralist ['mɔrəlɪst] *n* : moralista *mf*

moralistic [ˌmɔrə'lɪstɪk] *adj* : moralista

morality [mə'ræləti] *n, pl* **-ties** : moralidad *f*

morass [mə'ræs] *n* **1** SWAMP : ciénaga *f*, pantano *m* **2** CONFUSION, MESS : lío *m fam*, embrollo *m*

moratorium [ˌmɔrə'tɔriəm] *n, pl* **-riums** *or* **-ria** [-iə] : moratoria *f*

moray ['mɔrˌeɪ, mə'reɪ] *n* : morena *f*

morbid ['mɔrbɪd] *adj* **1** : mórbido, morboso (en medicina) **2** GRUESOME : morboso, horripilante

morbidity [mɔr'bɪdəti] *n, pl* **-ties** : morbosidad *f*

more[1] ['mor] *adv* : más ⟨what more can I say? : ¿qué más puedo decir?⟩ ⟨more important : más importante⟩ ⟨once more : una vez más⟩

more[2] *adj* : más ⟨nothing more than that : nada más que eso⟩ ⟨more work : más trabajo⟩

more[3] *n* : más *m* ⟨the more you eat, the more you want : cuanto más comes, tanto más quieres⟩

more[4] *pron* : más ⟨more were found : se encontraron más⟩

moreover [mor'oːvər] *adv* : además

mores ['mɔrˌeɪz, -iːz] *npl* CUSTOMS : costumbres *fpl*, tradiciones *fpl*

morgue ['mɔrg] *n* : morgue *f*

moribund ['mɔrəˌbʌnd] *adj* : moribundo

Mormon ['mɔrmən] *n* : mormón *m*, -mona *f* — **Mormon** *adj*

morn ['mɔrn] → **morning**

morning ['mɔrnɪŋ] *n* : mañana *f* ⟨good morning! : ¡buenos días!⟩

Moroccan [mə'rɑkən] *n* : marroquí *mf* — **Moroccan** *adj*

moron ['morˌɑn] *n* **1** : retrasado *m*, -da *f* mental **2** DUNCE : estúpido *m*, -da *f*; tonto *m*, -ta *f*

morose [mə'roːs] *adj* : hosco, sombrío — **morosely** *adv*

moroseness [mə'roːsnəs] *n* : malhumor *m*

morphine ['mɔrˌfiːn] *n* : morfina *f*

morphology [mɔr'fɑlədʒi] *n, pl* **-gies** : morfología *f*

morrow ['mɑroː] *n* : día *m* siguiente

Morse code ['mɔrs] *n* : código *m* morse

morsel ['mɔrsəl] *n* **1** BITE : bocado *m* **2** FRAGMENT : pedazo *m*

mortal[1] ['mɔrtəl] *adj* : mortal ⟨mortal blow : golpe mortal⟩ ⟨mortal fear : miedo mortal⟩ — **mortally** *adv*

mortal[2] *n* : mortal *mf*

mortality [mɔr'tæləti] *n* : mortalidad *f*

mortar ['mɔrtər] *n* **1** : mortero *m*, molcajete *m Mex* ⟨mortar and pestle : mortero y maja⟩ **2** : mortero *m* ⟨mortar shell : granada de mortero⟩ **3** CEMENT : mortero *m*, argamasa *f*

mortgage[1] ['mɔrgɪdʒ] *vt* **-gaged; -gaging** : hipotecar

mortgage[2] *n* : hipoteca *f*

mortification [ˌmɔrtəfə'keɪʃən] *n* **1** : mortificación *f* **2** HUMILIATION : humillación *f*, vergüenza *f*

mortify ['mɔrtəˌfaɪ] *vt* **-fied; -fying 1** : mortificar (en religión) **2** HUMILIATE : humillar, avergonzar

mortuary ['mɔrtʃəˌweri] *n, pl* **-aries** FUNERAL HOME : funeraria *f*

mosaic [mo'zeɪɪk] *n* : mosaico *m*

Moslem ['mɑzləm] → **Muslim**

mosque ['mɑsk] *n* : mezquita *f*

mosquito [mə'skiːˌto] *n, pl* **-toes** : mosquito *m*, zancudo *m*

moss ['mɔs] *n* : musgo *m*

mossy ['mɔsi] *adj* **-ier; -est** : musgoso

most[1] ['moːst] *adv* : más ⟨the most interesting book : el libro más interesante⟩

most[2] *adj* **1** : la mayoría de, la mayor parte de ⟨most people : la mayoría de la gente⟩ **2** GREATEST : más (dícese de los números), mayor (dícese de las cantidades) ⟨the most ability : la mayor capacidad⟩

most³ *n* : más *m*, máximo *m* ⟨the most I can do : lo más que puedo hacer⟩ ⟨three weeks at the most : tres semanas como máximo⟩

most⁴ *pron* : la mayoría, la mayor parte ⟨most will go : la mayoría irá⟩

mostly ['moːstli] *adv* MAINLY : en su mayor parte, principalmente

mote ['moːt] *n* SPECK : mota *f*

motel [moˈtɛl] *n* : motel *m*

moth ['mɔθ] *n* : palomilla *f*, polilla *f*

mother¹ ['mʌðər] *vt* **1** BEAR : dar a luz a **2** PROTECT : cuidar de, proteger

mother² *n* : madre *f*

motherhood ['mʌðər,hʊd] *n* : maternidad *f*

mother–in–law ['mʌðərɪn,lɔ] *n*, *pl* **mothers–in–law** : suegra *f*

motherland ['mʌðər,lænd] *n* : patria *f*

motherly ['mʌðərli] *adj* : maternal

mother–of–pearl [,mʌðərəvˈpərl] *n* : nácar *m*, madreperla *f*

motif [moˈtiːf] *n* : motivo *m*

motion¹ ['moːʃən] *vt* : hacerle señas (a alguien) ⟨she motioned us to come in : nos hizo señas para que entráramos⟩

motion² *n* **1** MOVEMENT : movimiento *m* ⟨to set in motion : poner en marcha⟩ **2** PROPOSAL : moción *f* ⟨to second a motion : apoyar una moción⟩

motionless ['moːʃənləs] *adj* : inmóvil, quieto

motion picture *n* MOVIE : película *f*

motivate ['moːtə,veɪt] *vt* **-vated; -vating** : motivar, mover, inducir

motivation [,moːtəˈveɪʃən] *n* : motivación *f*

motive¹ ['moːtɪv] *adj* : motor ⟨motive power : fuerza motriz⟩

motive² *n* : motivo *m*, móvil *m*

motley ['mɑtli] *adj* : abigarrado, variopinto

motor¹ ['moːtər] *vi* : viajar en coche

motor² *n* : motor *m*

motorbike ['moːtər,baɪk] *n* : motocicleta *f* (pequeña), moto *f*

motorboat ['moːtər,boːt] *n* : bote *m* a motor, lancha *f* motora

motorcar ['moːtər,kɑr] *n* : automóvil *m*

motorcycle ['moːtər,saɪkəl] *n* : motocicleta *f*

motorcyclist ['moːtər,saɪkəlɪst] *n* : motociclista *mf*

motorist ['moːtərɪst] *n* : automovilista *mf*, motorista *mf*

mottle ['mɑtəl] *vt* **-tled; -tling** : manchar, motear ⟨mottled skin : piel manchada⟩ ⟨a mottled surface : una superficie moteada⟩

motto ['mɑto] *n*, *pl* **-toes** : lema *m*

mould ['moːld] → **mold**

mound ['maʊnd] *n* **1** PILE : montón *m* **2** KNOLL : montículo *m* **3 burial mound** : túmulo *m*

mount¹ ['maʊnt] *vt* **1** : montar a (un caballo), montar en (una bicicleta), subir a **2** : montar (artillería, etc.) — *vi* INCREASE : aumentar

mount² *n* **1** SUPPORT : soporte *m* **2** HORSE : caballería *f*, montura *f* **3** MOUNTAIN : monte *m*, montaña *f*

mountain ['maʊntən] *n* : montaña *f*

mountaineer [,maʊntənˈɪr] *n* : alpinista *mf*; montañero *m*, -ra *f*

mountaineering [,maʊntənˈɪrɪŋ] *n* : alpinismo *m*

mountainous ['maʊntənəs] *adj* : montañoso

mountaintop ['maʊntən,tɑp] *n* : cima *f*, cumbre *f*

mourn ['morn] *vt* : llorar (por), lamentar ⟨to mourn the death of : llorar la muerte de⟩ — *vi* : llorar, estar de luto

mourner ['mornər] *n* : doliente *mf*

mournful ['mornfəl] *adj* **1** SORROWFUL : lloroso, plañidero, triste **2** GLOOMY : deprimente, entristecedor — **mournfully** *adv*

mourning ['mornɪŋ] *n* : duelo *m*, luto *m*

mouse ['maʊs] *n*, *pl* **mice** ['maɪs] **1** : ratón *m*, -tona *f* **2** : ratón *m* (de una computadora)

mousetrap ['maʊs,træp] *n* : ratonera *f*

mousse ['muːs] *n* : mousse *mf*

moustache ['mʌ,stæʃ, məˈstæʃ] → **mustache**

mouth¹ ['maʊð] *vt* **1** : decir con poca sinceridad, repetir sin comprensión **2** : articular en silencio ⟨she mouthed the words : formó las palabras con los labios⟩

mouth² ['maʊθ] *n* : boca *f* (de una persona o un animal), entrada *f* (de un túnel), desembocadura *f* (de un río)

mouthful ['maʊθ,fʊl] *n* : bocado *m* (de comida), bocanada *f* (de líquido o humo)

mouthpiece ['maʊθ,piːs] *n* : boquilla *f* (de un instrumento musical)

mouthwash ['maʊθ,wɔʃ, -,wɑʃ] *n* : enjuague *m* bucal

movable ['muːvəbəl] *or* **moveable** *adj* : movible, móvil

move¹ ['muːv] *v* **moved; moving** *vi* **1** GO : ir **2** RELOCATE : mudarse, trasladarse **3** STIR : moverse ⟨don't move! : ¡no te muevas!⟩ **4** ACT : actuar — *vt* **1** : mover ⟨move it over there : ponlo allí⟩ ⟨he kept moving his feet : no dejaba de mover los pies⟩ **2** INDUCE, PERSUADE : inducir, persuadir, mover **3** TOUCH : conmover ⟨it moved him to tears : lo hizo llorar⟩ **4** PROPOSE : proponer

move² *n* **1** MOVEMENT : movimiento *m* **2** RELOCATION : mudanza *f* (de casa), traslado *m* **3** STEP : paso *m* ⟨a good move : un paso acertado⟩

movement ['muːvmənt] *n* : movimiento *m*

mover ['muːvər] *n* : persona *f* que hace mudanzas

movie ['muːvi] *n* **1** : película *f* **2 movies** *npl* : cine *m*

moving ['muːvɪŋ] *adj* **1** : en movimiento ⟨a moving target : un blanco móvil⟩

2 TOUCHING : conmovedor, emocionante

mow¹ ['moː] *vt* **mowed; mowed** *or* **mown** ['moːn]; **mowing** : cortar (la hierba)

mow² ['mau] *n* : pajar *m*

mower ['moːər] → **lawn mower**

Mr. ['mɪstər] *n, pl* **Messrs.** ['mɛsərz] : señor *m*

Mrs. ['mɪsəz, -səs, *esp South* 'mɪzəz, -zəs] *n, pl* **Mesdames** [meɪ'dɑm, -'dæm] : señora *f*

Ms. ['mɪz] *n* : señora *f*, señorita *f*

much¹ ['mʌtʃ] *adv* **more** ['mor]; **most** ['moːst] : mucho ⟨I'm much happier : estoy mucho más contenta⟩ ⟨she talks as much as I do : habla tanto como yo⟩

much² *adj* **more; most** : mucho ⟨it has much validity : tiene mucha validez⟩ ⟨too much time : demasiado tiempo⟩

much³ *pron* : mucho, -cha ⟨I don't need much : no necesito mucho⟩

mucilage ['mjuːsəlɪdʒ] *n* : mucílago *m*

muck ['mʌk] *n* **1** MANURE : estiércol *m* **2** DIRT, FILTH : mugre *f*, suciedad *f* **3** MIRE, MUD : barro *m*, fango *m*, lodo *m*

mucous ['mjuːkəs] *adj* : mucoso ⟨mucous membrane : membrana mucosa⟩

mucus ['mjuːkəs] *n* : mucosidad *f*

mud ['mʌd] *n* : barro *m*, fango *m*, lodo *m*

muddle¹ ['mʌdəl] *v* **-dled; -dling** *vt* **1** CONFUSE : confundir **2** BUNGLE : echar a perder, malograr — *vi* : andar confundido ⟨to muddle through : arreglárselas⟩

muddle² *n* : confusión *f*, embrollo *m*, lío *m*

muddleheaded [,mʌdəl'hɛdəd, 'mʌdəl,-] *adj* CONFUSED : confuso, despistado

muddy¹ ['mʌdi] *vt* **-died; -dying** : llenar de barro

muddy² *adj* **-dier; -est** : barroso, fangoso, lodoso, enlodado ⟨you're all muddy : estás cubierto de barro⟩

muff¹ ['mʌf] *vt* BUNGLE : echar a perder, fallar (un tiro, etc.)

muff² *n* : manguito *m*

muffin ['mʌfən] *n* : magdalena *f*, mantecada *f Mex*

muffle ['mʌfəl] *vt* **-fled; -fling 1** ENVELOP : cubrir, tapar **2** DEADEN : amortiguar (un sonido)

muffler ['mʌflər] *n* **1** SCARF : bufanda *f* **2** : silenciador *m*, mofle *m CA, Mex* (de un automóvil)

mug¹ ['mʌg] *v* **mugged; mugging** *vi* : posar (con afectación), hacer muecas ⟨mugging for the camera : haciendo muecas para la cámara⟩ — *vt* ASSAULT : asaltar, atracar

mug² *n* CUP : tazón *m*

mugger ['mʌgər] *n* : atracador *m*, -dora *f*

mugginess ['mʌginəs] *n* : bochorno *m*

muggy ['mʌgi] *adj* **-gier; -est** : bochornoso

mulatto [muˈlɑto, -ˈlæ-] *n, pl* **-toes** *or* **-tos** : mulato *m*, -ta *f*

mulberry ['mʌl,bɛri] *n, pl* **-ries** : morera *f* (árbol), mora *f* (fruta)

mulch¹ ['mʌltʃ] *vt* : cubrir con pajote

mulch² *n* : pajote *m*

mule ['mjuːl] *n* **1** : mula *f* **2** : obstinado *m*, -da *f*; terco *m*, -ca *f*

mulish ['mjuːlɪʃ] *adj* : obstinado, terco

mull ['mʌl] *vt* **to mull over** : reflexionar sobre

mullet ['mʌlət] *n, pl* **-let** *or* **-lets** : mújol *m*, múgil *m*

multicolored [,mʌlti'kʌlərd, ,mʌltaɪ-] *adj* : multicolor, abigarrado

multicultural [,mʌlti'kʌltʃərəl] *adj* : multicultural

multifaceted [,mʌlti'fæsətəd, ,mʌltaɪ-] *adj* : multifacético

multifamily [,mʌlti'fæmli, ,mʌltaɪ-] *adj* : multifamiliar

multifarious [,mʌltə'færiəs] *adj* DIVERSE : diverso, variado

multilateral [,mʌlti'lætərəl, ,mʌltaɪ-] *adj* : multilateral

multimedia [,mʌlti'miːdiə, ,mʌltaɪ-] *adj* : multimedia

multimillionaire [,mʌlti,mɪljə'nær, ,mʌltaɪ-, -'mɪljə,nær] *adj* : multimillonario

multinational [,mʌlti'næʃənəl, ,mʌltaɪ-] *adj* : multinacional

multiple¹ ['mʌltəpəl] *adj* : múltiple

multiple² *n* : múltiplo *m*

multiple sclerosis [sklə'roːsɪs] *n* : esclerosis *f* múltiple

multiplication [,mʌltəplə'keɪʃən] *n* : multiplicación *f*

multiplicity [,mʌltə'plɪsəti] *n, pl* **-ties** : multiplicidad *f*

multiplier ['mʌltə,plaɪər] *n* : multiplicador *m* (en matemáticas)

multiply ['mʌltə,plaɪ] *v* **-plied; -plying** *vt* : multiplicar — *vi* : multiplicarse

multipurpose [,mʌlti'pərpəs, ,mʌltaɪ-] *adj* : multiuso

multitude ['mʌltə,tuːd, -,tjuːd] *n* **1** CROWD : multitud *f*, muchedumbre *f* **2** HOST : multitud *f*, gran cantidad *f* ⟨a multitude of ideas : numerosas ideas⟩

multivitamin [,mʌlti'vaɪtəmən, ,mʌltaɪ-] *adj* : multivitamínico

mum¹ ['mʌm] *adj* SILENT : callado

mum² *n* → **chrysanthemum**

mumble¹ ['mʌmbəl] *v* **-bled; -bling** *vt* : mascullar, musitar — *vi* : mascullar, hablar entre dientes, murmurar

mumble² *n* **to speak in a mumble** : hablar entre dientes

mummy ['mʌmi] *n, pl* **-mies** : momia *f*

mumps ['mʌmps] *ns & pl* : paperas *fpl*

munch ['mʌntʃ] *v* : mascar, masticar

mundane [,mʌn'deɪn, 'mʌn,-] *adj* **1** EARTHLY, WORLDLY : mundano, terrenal **2** COMMONPLACE : rutinario, ordinario

municipal [mjuˈnɪsəpəl] *adj* : municipal

municipality [mjuˌnɪsə'pæləti] *n, pl* **-ties** : municipio *m*

munitions [mjuˈnɪʃənz] *npl* : municiones *fpl*

mural[1] [ˈmjʊrəl] *adj* : mural
mural[2] [ˈmjʊrəlɪst] *n* : mural *m*
murder[1] [ˈmərdər] *vt* : asesinar, matar —
  vi : matar
murder[2] *n* : asesinato *m*, homicidio *m*
murderer [ˈmərdərər] *n* : asesino *m*, -na
  f; homicida *mf*
murderess [ˈmərdərɪs, -dəˌrɛs, -dərəs] *n*
  : asesina *f*, homicida *f*
murderous [ˈmərdərəs] *adj* : asesino,
  homicida
murk [ˈmərk] *n* DARKNESS : oscuridad *f*,
  tinieblas *fpl*
murkiness [ˈmərkinəs] *n* : oscuridad *f*,
  tenebrosidad *f*
murky [ˈmərki] *adj* **-kier; -est** : oscuro,
  tenebroso
murmur[1] [ˈmərmər] *vi* **1** DRONE : murmurar **2** GRUMBLE : refunfuñar, regañar, rezongar — *vt* MUMBLE : murmurar
murmur[2] *n* **1** COMPLAINT : queja *f* **2**
  DRONE : murmullo *m*, rumor *m*
muscle[1] [ˈmʌsəl] *vi* **-cled; -cling** : meterse ⟨to muscle in on : meterse por la
  fuerza en, entrometerse en⟩
muscle[2] *n* **1** : músculo *m* **2** STRENGTH
  : fuerza *f*
muscular [ˈmʌskjələr] *adj* **1** : muscular
  ⟨muscular tissue : tejido muscular⟩ **2**
  BRAWNY : musculoso
muscular dystrophy *n* : distrofia *f* muscular
musculature [ˈmʌskjələˌtʃʊr, -tʃər] *n*
  : musculatura *f*
muse[1] [ˈmjuːz] *vi* **mused; musing** PON-
  DER, REFLECT : cavilar, meditar, reflexionar
muse[2] *n* : musa *f*
museum [mjʊˈziːəm] *n* : museo *m*
mush [ˈmʌʃ] *n* **1** : gachas *fpl* (de maíz)
  2 SENTIMENTALITY : sensiblería *f*
mushroom[1] [ˈmʌʃˌruːm, -ˌrʊm] *vi* GROW,
  MULTIPLY : crecer rápidamente, multiplicarse
mushroom[2] *n* : hongo *m*, champiñón *m*,
  seta *f*
mushy [ˈmʌʃi] *adj* **mushier; -est 1** SOFT
  : blando **2** MAWKISH : sensiblero
music [ˈmjuːzɪk] *n* : música *f*
musical[1] [ˈmjuːzɪkəl] *adj* : musical, de
  música — **musically** *adv*
musical[2] *n* : comedia *f* musical
music box *n* : cajita *f* de música
musician [mjʊˈzɪʃən] *n* : músico *m*, -ca
  f
musk [ˈmʌsk] *n* : almizcle *m*
musket [ˈmʌskət] *n* : mosquete *m*
musketeer [ˌmʌskəˈtɪr] *n* : mosquetero
  m
muskrat [ˈmʌskˌræt] *n, pl* **-rat** *or* **-rats**
  : rata *f* almizclera
Muslim[1] [ˈmʌzləm, ˈmʊs-, ˈmuːz-] *adj*
  : musulmán
Muslim[2] *n* : musulmán *m*, -mana *f*
muslin [ˈmʌzlən] *n* : muselina *f*
muss[1] [ˈmʌs] *vt* : desordenar, despeinar
  (el pelo)

muss[2] *n* : desorden *m*
mussel [ˈmʌsəl] *n* : mejillón *m*
must[1] [ˈmʌst] *v aux* **1** (*expressing obligation or necessity*) : deber, tener que
  ⟨you must stop : debes parar⟩ ⟨we
  must obey : tenemos que obedecer⟩ **2**
  (*expressing probability*) : deber (de),
  haber de ⟨you must be tired : debes de
  estar cansado⟩ ⟨it must be late : ha de
  ser tarde⟩
must[2] *n* : necesidad *f* ⟨exercise is a must
  : el ejercicio es imprescindible⟩
mustache [ˈmʌˌstæʃ, mʌˈstæʃ] *n* : bigote
  m, bigotes *mpl*
mustang [ˈmʌˌstæŋ] *n* : mustang *m*
mustard [ˈmʌstərd] *n* : mostaza *f*
muster[1] [ˈmʌstər] *vt* **1** ASSEMBLE : reunir **2 to muster up** : armarse de, cobrar (valor, fuerzas, etc.)
muster[2] *n* **1** INSPECTION : revista *f* (de
  tropas) ⟨it didn't pass muster : no re-
  sistió un examen minucioso⟩ **2** COL-
  LECTION : colección *f*
mustiness [ˈmʌstinəs] *n* : lo mohoso
musty [ˈmʌsti] *adj* **mustier; -est** : mohoso, que huele a moho, que huele a
  encerrado
mutant[1] [ˈmjuːtənt] *adj* : mutante
mutant[2] *n* : mutante *m*
mutate [ˈmjuːˌteɪt] *vi* **-tated; -tating 1**
  : mutar (genéticamente) **2** CHANGE
  : transformarse
mutation [mjuːˈteɪʃən] *n* : mutación *f*
  (genética)
mute[1] [ˈmjuːt] *vt* **muted; muting** MUF-
  FLE : amortiguar, ponerle sordina a (un
  instrumento musical)
mute[2] *adj* **muter; mutest** : mudo —
  mutely *adv*
mute[3] *n* **1** : mudo *m*, -da *f* (persona) **2**
  : sordina *f* (para un instrumento musi-
  cal)
mutilate [ˈmjuːtəˌleɪt] *vt* **-lated; -lating**
  : mutilar
mutilation [ˌmjuːtəˈleɪʃən] *n* : mutilación
  f
mutineer [ˌmjuːtənˈɪr] *n* : amotinado *m*,
  -da *f*
mutinous [ˈmjuːtənəs] *adj* : amotinado
mutiny[1] [ˈmjuːtəni] *vi* **-nied; -nying**
  : amotinarse
mutiny[2] *n, pl* **-nies** : amotinamiento *m*,
  motín *m*
mutt [ˈmʌt] *n* MONGREL : perro *m* mestizo, perro *m* corriente *Mex*
mutter [ˈmʌtər] *vi* **1** MUMBLE : mascullar, hablar entre dientes, murmurar
  2 GRUMBLE : refunfuñar, regañar, rezongar
mutton [ˈmʌtən] *n* : carne *f* de carnero
mutual [ˈmjuːtʃʊəl] *adj* **1** : mutuo ⟨mu-
  tual respect : respeto mutuo⟩ **2** COM-
  MON : común ⟨a mutual friend : un
  amigo común⟩
mutually [ˈmjuːtʃʊəli, -tʃəli] *adv* **1** : mutuamente ⟨mutually beneficial : mutuamente beneficioso⟩ **2** JOINTLY
  : conjuntamente

muzzle¹ ['mʌzəl] *vt* **-zled; -zling** : ponerle un bozal a (un animal), amordazar
muzzle² *n* **1** SNOUT : hocico *m* **2** : bozal *m* (para un perro, etc.) **3** : boca *f* (de un arma de fuego)
my¹ ['maɪ] *adj* : mi ⟨my parents : mis padres⟩
my² *interj* : ¡caramba!, ¡Dios mío!
myopia [maɪ'o:piə] *n* : miopía *f*
myopic [maɪ'o:pɪk, -'ɑ-] *adj* : miope
myriad¹ ['mɪriəd] *adj* INNUMERABLE : innumerable
myriad² *n* : miríada *f*
myrrh ['mər] *n* : mirra *f*
myrtle ['mərtəl] *n* : mirto *m*, arrayán *m*
myself [maɪ'sɛlf] *pron* **1** (*used reflexively*) : me ⟨I washed myself : me lavé⟩ **2** (*used for emphasis*) : yo mismo, yo misma ⟨I did it myself : lo hice yo mismo⟩
mysterious [mɪ'stɪriəs] *adj* : misterioso — **mysteriously** *adv*
mysteriousness [mɪ'stɪriəsnəs] *n* : lo misterioso
mystery ['mɪstəri] *n, pl* **-teries** : misterio *m*
mystic¹ ['mɪstɪk] *adj* : místico
mystic² *n* : místico *m*, -ca *f*
mystical ['mɪstɪkəl] *adj* : místico — **mystically** *adv*
mysticism ['mɪstə,sɪzəm] *n* : misticismo *m*
mystify ['mɪstə,faɪ] *vt* **-fied; -fying** : dejar perplejo, confundir
mystique [mɪ'sti:k] *n* : aura *f* de misterio
myth ['mɪθ] *n* : mito *m*
mythic ['mɪθɪk] *adj* : mítico
mythical ['mɪθɪkəl] *adj* : mítico
mythological [,mɪθə'lɑʤɪkəl] *adj* : mitológico
mythology [mɪ'θɑləʤi] *n, pl* **-gies** : mitología *f*

N

n ['ɛn] *n, pl* **n's** *or* **ns** ['ɛnz] : decimocuarta letra del alfabeto inglés
nab ['næb] *vt* **nabbed; nabbing** : prender, pillar *fam*, pescar *fam*
nadir ['neɪdər, 'neɪ,dɪr] *n* : nadir *m*, punto *m* más bajo
nag¹ ['næg] *v* **nagged; nagging** *vi* **1** COMPLAIN : quejarse, rezongar **2 to nag at** HASSLE : molestar, darle (la) lata (a alguien) — *vt* **1** PESTER : molestar, fastidiar **2** SCOLD : regañar, estarle encima a *fam*
nag² *n* **1** GRUMBLER : gruñón *m*, -ñona *f* **2** HORSE : jamelgo *m*
naiad ['neɪæd, 'naɪ-, -,æd] *n, pl* **-iads** *or* **-iades** [-ə,di:z] : náyade *f*
nail¹ ['neɪl] *vt* : clavar, sujetar con clavos
nail² *n* **1** FINGERNAIL : uña *f* ⟨nail file : lima (de uñas)⟩ ⟨nail polish : laca de uñas⟩ **2** : clavo *m* ⟨to hit the nail on the head : dar en el clavo⟩
naive *or* **naïve** [nɑ'i:v] *adj* **-iver; -est 1** INGENUOUS : ingenuo, cándido **2** GULLIBLE : crédulo
naively [nɑ'i:vli] *adv* : ingenuamente
naïveté [,nɑ,i:və'teɪ, nɑ'i:və,-] *n* : ingenuidad *f*
naked ['neɪkəd] *adj* **1** UNCLOTHED : desnudo **2** UNCOVERED : desenvainado (dícese de una espada), pelado (dícese de los árboles), expuesto al aire (dícese de una llama) **3** OBVIOUS, PLAIN : manifiesto, puro, desnudo ⟨the naked truth : la pura verdad⟩ **4 to the naked eye** : a simple vista
nakedly ['neɪkədli] *adv* : manifiestamente
nakedness ['neɪkədnəs] *n* : desnudez *f*
name¹ ['neɪm] *vt* **named; naming 1** CALL : llamar, bautizar, ponerle nombre a **2** MENTION : mentar, mencionar, dar el nombre de ⟨they have named a

suspect : han dado el nombre de un sospechoso⟩ **3** APPOINT : nombrar **4 to name a price** : fijar un precio
name² *adj* **1** KNOWN : de nombre ⟨name brand : marca conocida⟩ **2** PROMINENT : de renombre, de prestigio
name³ *n* **1** : nombre *m* ⟨what is your name? : ¿cómo se llama?⟩ **2** SURNAME : apellido *m* **3** EPITHET : epíteto *m* ⟨to call somebody names : llamar a alguien de todo⟩ **4** REPUTATION : fama *f*, reputación *f* ⟨to make a name for oneself : darse a conocer, hacerse famoso⟩
nameless ['neɪmləs] *adj* **1** ANONYMOUS : anónimo **2** INDESCRIBABLE : indecible, indescriptible
namelessly ['neɪmləsli] *adv* : anónimamente
namely ['neɪmli] *adv* : a saber
namesake ['neɪm,seɪk] *n* : tocayo *m*, -ya *f*; homónimo *m*, -ma *f*
Namibian [nə'mɪbiən] *n* : namibio *m*, -bia *f* — **Namibian** *adj*
nanny ['næni] *n, pl* **nannies** : niñera *f*; nana *f* CA, Col, Mex, Ven
nap¹ ['næp] *vi* **napped; napping 1** : dormir, dormir la siesta **2 to be caught napping** : estar desprevenido
nap² *n* **1** SLEEP : siesta *f* ⟨to take a nap : echarse una siesta⟩ **2** FUZZ, PILE : pelo *m*, pelusa *f* (de telas)
nape ['neɪp, 'næp] *n* : nuca *f*, cerviz *f*, cogote *m*
naphtha ['næfθə] *n* : nafta *f*
napkin ['næpkən] *n* : servilleta *f*
narcissism ['nɑrsə,sɪzəm] *n* : narcisismo *m*
narcissist ['nɑrsəsɪst] *n* : narcisista *mf*
narcissistic [,nɑrsə'sɪstɪk] *adj* : narcisista
narcissus [nɑr'sɪsəs] *n, pl* **-cissus** *or*

-cissuses *or* -cissi [-'sɪˌsaɪ, -ˌsiː] : narciso *m*
narcotic¹ [nɑr'kɑtɪk] *adj* : narcótico
narcotic² *n* : narcótico *m*, estupefaciente *m*
narrate ['nærˌeɪt] *vt* -rated; -rating : narrar, relatar
narration [næ'reɪʃən] *n* : narración *f*
narrative¹ ['nærətɪv] *adj* : narrativo
narrative² *n* : narración *f*, narrativa *f*, relato *m*
narrator ['nærˌeɪtər] *n* : narrador *m*, -dora *f*
narrow¹ ['nærˌoː] *vi* : estrecharse, angostarse ⟨the river narrowed : el río se estrechó⟩ — *vt* 1 : estrechar, angostar 2 LIMIT : restringir, limitar ⟨to narrow the search : limitar la búsqueda⟩
narrow² *adj* 1 : estrecho, angosto 2 LIMITED : estricto, limitado ⟨in the narrowest sense of the word : en el sentido más estricto de la palabra⟩ 3 to have a narrow escape : escapar por un pelo
narrowly ['næroli] *adv* 1 BARELY : por poco 2 CLOSELY : de cerca
narrow–minded [ˌnæroˈmaɪndəd] *adj* : de miras estrechas
narrowness ['næronəs] *n* : estrechez *f*
narrows ['næroːz] *npl* STRAIT : estrecho *m*
narwhal ['nɑrˌhwɑl, 'nɑrwəl] *n* : narval *m*
nasal ['neɪzəl] *adj* : nasal, gangoso ⟨a nasal voice : una voz gangosa⟩
nasally ['neɪzəli] *adv* 1 : por la nariz 2 : con voz gangosa
nastily ['næstəli] *adv* : con maldad, cruelmente
nastiness ['næstinəs] *n* : porquería *f*
nasturtium [nəˈstərʃəm, næ-] *n* : capuchina *f*
nasty ['næsti] *adj* -tier; -est 1 FILTHY : sucio, mugriento 2 OBSCENE : obsceno 3 MEAN, SPITEFUL : malo, malicioso 4 UNPLEASANT : desagradable, feo 5 REPUGNANT : asqueroso, repugnante ⟨a nasty smell : un olor asqueroso⟩
natal ['neɪtəl] *adj* : natal
nation ['neɪʃən] *n* : nación *f*
national¹ ['næʃənəl] *adj* : nacional
national² *n* : ciudadano *m*, -na *f*; nacional *mf*
nationalism ['næʃənəˌlɪzəm] *n* : nacionalismo *m*
nationalist¹ ['næʃənəlɪst] *adj* : nacionalista
nationalist² *n* : nacionalista *mf*
nationalistic [ˌnæʃənəˈlɪstɪk] *adj* : nacionalista
nationality [ˌnæʃəˈnæləti] *n, pl* -ties : nacionalidad *f*
nationalization [ˌnæʃənələˈzeɪʃən] *n* : nacionalización *f*
nationalize ['næʃənəˌlaɪz] *vt* -ized; -izing : nacionalizar
nationally ['næʃənəli] *adv* : a escala nacional, a nivel nacional

nationwide ['neɪʃənˈwaɪd] *adj* : en toda la nación, por todo el país
native¹ ['neɪtɪv] *adj* 1 INNATE : innato 2 : natal ⟨her native city : su ciudad natal⟩ 3 INDIGENOUS : indígena, autóctono
native² *n* 1 ABORIGINE : nativo *m*, -va *f*; indígena *mf* 2 : natural *m* ⟨he's a native of Mexico : es natural de México⟩
Native American → American Indian
nativity [nəˈtɪvəti, neɪ-] *n, pl* -ties 1 BIRTH : navidad *f* 2 the Nativity : la Natividad, la Navidad
natty ['næti] *adj* -tier; -est : elegante, garboso
natural¹ ['nætʃərəl] *adj* 1 : natural, de la naturaleza ⟨natural woodlands : bosques naturales⟩ ⟨natural childbirth : parto natural⟩ 2 INNATE : innato, natural 3 UNAFFECTED : natural, sin afectación 4 LIFELIKE : natural, vivo
natural² *n* to be a natural : tener un talento innato (para algo)
natural gas *n* : gas *m* natural
natural history *n* : historia *f* natural
naturalism ['nætʃərəˌlɪzəm] *n* : naturalismo *m*
naturalist ['nætʃərəlɪst] *n* : naturalista *mf* — naturalist *adj*
naturalistic [ˌnætʃərəˈlɪstɪk] *adj* : naturalista
naturalization [ˌnætʃərələˈzeɪʃən] *n* : naturalización *f*
naturalize ['nætʃərəˌlaɪz] *vt* -ized; -izing : naturalizar
naturally ['nætʃərəli] *adv* 1 INHERENTLY : naturalmente, intrínsecamente 2 UNAFFECTEDLY : de manera natural 3 OF COURSE : por supuesto, naturalmente
naturalness ['nætʃərəlnəs] *n* : naturalidad *f*
natural science *n* : ciencias *fpl* naturales
nature ['neɪtʃər] *n* 1 : naturaleza *f* ⟨the laws of nature : las leyes de la naturaleza⟩ 2 KIND, SORT : índole *f*, clase *f* ⟨things of this nature : cosas de esta índole⟩ 3 DISPOSITION : carácter *m*, natural *m*, naturaleza *f* ⟨it is his nature to be friendly : es de natural simpático⟩ ⟨human nature : la naturaleza humana⟩
naught ['nɔt] *n* 1 : nada *f* ⟨to come to naught : reducirse a nada, fracasar⟩ 2 ZERO : cero *m*
naughtily ['nɔtəli] *adv* : traviesamente, con malicia
naughtiness ['nɔtinəs] *n* : mala conducta *f*, travesuras *fpl*, malicia *f*
naughty ['nɔti] *adj* -tier; -est 1 MISCHIEVOUS : travieso, pícaro 2 RISQUÉ : picante, subido de tono
nausea ['nɔziə, 'nɔʃə] *n* 1 SICKNESS : náuseas *fpl* 2 DISGUST : asco *m*
nauseate ['nɔziˌeɪt, -ʒi-, -si-, -ʃi-] *vt* -ated; -ating 1 SICKEN : darle náuseas (a alguien) 2 DISGUST : asquear, darle asco (a alguien)

nauseating *adj* : nauseabundo, repugnante

nauseatingly ['nɔzi,eɪtɪŋli, -ʒi-, -si-, -ʃi-] *adv* : hasta el punto de dar asco ⟨nauseatingly sweet : tan dulce que da asco⟩

nauseous ['nɔʃəs, -ziəs] *adj* **1** SICK : mareado, con náuseas **2** SICKENING : nauseabundo

nautical ['nɔtɪkəl] *adj* : náutico

nautilus ['nɔtələs] *n, pl* **-luses** *or* **-li** [-,laɪ, -,li:] : nautilo *m*

Navajo ['nævə,hoʊ, 'nɑ-] *n* : navajo *m*, -ja *f* — **Navajo** *adj*

naval ['neɪvəl] *adj* : naval

nave ['neɪv] *n* : nave *f*

navel ['neɪvəl] *n* : ombligo *m*

navigability [,nævɪgə'bɪləti] *n* : navegabilidad *f*

navigable ['nævɪgəbəl] *adj* : navegable

navigate ['nævə,geɪt] *v* **-gated; -gating** *vi* : navegar — *vt* **1** STEER : gobernar (un barco), pilotar (un avión) **2** : navegar por (un río, etc.)

navigation [,nævə'geɪʃən] *n* : navegación *f*

navigator ['nævə,geɪtər] *n* : navegante *mf*

navy ['neɪvi] *n, pl* **-vies 1** FLEET : flota *f* **2** : marina *f* de guerra, armada *f* ⟨the United States Navy : la armada de los Estados Unidos⟩ **3** *or* **navy blue** : azul *m* marino

nay[1] ['neɪ] *adv* : no

nay[2] *n* : no *m*, voto *m* en contra

Nazi ['nɑtsi, 'næt-] *n* : nazi *mf*

Nazism ['nɑt,sɪzəm, 'næt-] *or* **Naziism** ['nɑtsi,ɪzəm, 'næt-] *n* : nazismo *m*

Neanderthal man [ni'ændər,θɔl, -,tɔl] *n* : hombre *m* de Neanderthal

near[1] ['nɪr] *vt* **1** : acercarse a ⟨the ship is nearing port : el barco se está acercando al puerto⟩ **2** : estar a punto de ⟨she is nearing graduation : está a punto de graduarse⟩

near[2] *adv* **1** CLOSE : cerca ⟨my family lives quite near : mi familia vive muy cerca⟩ **2** NEARLY : casi ⟨I came near to finishing : casi terminé⟩

near[3] *adj* **1** CLOSE : cercano, próximo **2** SIMILAR : parecido, semejante

near[4] *prep* : cerca de

nearby[1] [nɪr'baɪ, 'nɪr,baɪ] *adv* : cerca

nearby[2] *adj* : cercano

nearly ['nɪrli] *adv* **1** ALMOST : casi ⟨nearly asleep : casi dormido⟩ **2 not nearly** : ni con mucho, ni mucho menos ⟨it was not nearly so bad as I had expected : no fue ni con mucho tan malo como esperaba⟩

nearness ['nɪrnəs] *n* : proximidad *f*

nearsighted ['nɪr,saɪtəd] *adj* : miope, corto de vista

nearsightedly ['nɪr,saɪtədli] *adv* : con miopía

nearsightedness ['nɪr,saɪtədnəs] *n* : miopía *f*

neat ['ni:t] *adj* **1** CLEAN, ORDERLY : ordenado, pulcro, limpio **2** UNDILUTED

: solo, sin diluir **3** SIMPLE, TASTEFUL : sencillo y de buen gusto **4** CLEVER : hábil, ingenioso ⟨a neat trick : un truco ingenioso⟩

neatly ['ni:tli] *adv* **1** TIDILY : ordenadamente **2** CLEVERLY : ingeniosamente

neatness ['ni:tnəs] *n* : pulcritud *f*, limpieza *f*, orden *m*

nebula ['nɛbjələ] *n, pl* **-lae** [-,li:, -,laɪ] : nebulosa *f*

nebulous ['nɛbjələs] *adj* : nebuloso, vago

necessarily [,nɛsə'sɛrəli] *adv* : necesariamente, forzosamente

necessary[1] ['nɛsə,sɛri] *adj* **1** INEVITABLE : inevitable **2** COMPULSORY : necesario, obligatorio **3** ESSENTIAL : imprescindible, preciso, necesario

necessary[2] *n, pl* **-saries** : lo esencial, lo necesario

necessitate [nɪ'sɛsə,teɪt] *vt* **-tated; -tating** : necesitar, requerir

necessity [nɪ'sɛsəti] *n, pl* **-ties 1** NEED : necesidad *f* **2** REQUIREMENT : requisito *m* indispensable **3** POVERTY : indigencia *f*, necesidad *f* **4** INEVITABILITY : inevitabilidad *f*

neck[1] ['nɛk] *vi* : besuquearse

neck[2] *n* **1** : cuello *m* (de una persona), pescuezo *m* (de un animal) **2** COLLAR : cuello *m* **3** : cuello *m* (de una botella), mástil *m* (de una guitarra)

neckerchief ['nɛkərtʃəf, -,tʃi:f] *n, pl* **-chiefs** [-tʃəfs, -,tʃi:fs] : pañuelo *m* (para el cuello), mascada *f Mex*

necklace ['nɛkləs] *n* : collar *m*

neckline ['nɛk,laɪn] *n* : escote *m*

necktie ['nɛk,taɪ] *n* : corbata *f*

nectar ['nɛktər] *n* : néctar *m*

nectarine [,nɛktə'ri:n] *n* : nectarina *f*

née *or* **nee** ['neɪ] *adj* : de soltera ⟨Mrs. Smith, née Whitman : la señora Smith, de soltera Whitman⟩

need[1] ['ni:d] *vt* **1** : necesitar ⟨I need your help : necesito su ayuda⟩ ⟨I need money : me falta dinero⟩ **2** REQUIRE : requerir, exigir ⟨that job needs patience : ese trabajo exige paciencia⟩ **3 to need to** : tener que ⟨he needs to study : tiene que estudiar⟩ ⟨they need to be scolded : hay que reprenderlos⟩ — *v aux* **1** MUST : tener que, deber ⟨need you shout? : ¿tienes que gritar?⟩ **2 to be needed** : hacer falta ⟨you needn't worry : no hace falta que te preocupes, no hay por qué preocuparse⟩

need[2] *n* **1** NECESSITY : necesidad *f* ⟨in case of need : en caso de necesidad⟩ **2** LACK : falta *f* ⟨the need for better training : la falta de mejor capacitación⟩ ⟨to be in need : necesitar⟩ **3** POVERTY : necesidad *f*, indigencia *f* **4 needs** *npl* : requisitos *mpl*, carencias *fpl*

needful ['ni:dfəl] *adj* : necesario

needle[1] ['ni:dəl] *vt* **-dled; -dling** : pinchar

needle[2] *n* **1** : aguja *f* ⟨to thread a needle : enhebrar una aguja⟩ ⟨knitting needle : aguja de tejer⟩ **2** POINTER : aguja *f*, indicador *m*

needlepoint [ˈniːdəlˌpɔint] *n* **1** LACE : encaje *m* de mano **2** EMBROIDERY : bordado *m* en cañamazo

needless [ˈniːdləs] *adj* : innecesario

needlessly [ˈniːdləsli] *adv* : sin ninguna necesidad, innecesariamente

needlework [ˈniːdəlˌwərk] *n* : bordado *m*

needn't [ˈniːdənt] (*contraction of* **need not**) → **need**

needy[1] [ˈniːdi] *adj* **needier; -est** : necesitado

needy[2] *n* **the needy** : los necesitados *mpl*

nefarious [nɪˈfæriəs] *adj* : nefario, nefando, infame

negate [nɪˈgeit] *vt* **-gated; -gating** **1** DENY : negar **2** NULLIFY : invalidar, anular

negation [nɪˈgeiʃən] *n* : negación *f*

negative[1] [ˈnɛgət̬ɪv] *adj* : negativo

negative[2] *n* **1** : negación *f* (en lingüística) **2** : negativa *f* ⟨to answer in the negative : contestar con una negativa⟩ **3** : término *m* negativo (en matemáticas) **4** : negativo *m*, imagen *f* en negativo (en fotografía)

negatively [ˈnɛgət̬ɪvli] *adv* : negativamente

neglect[1] [nɪˈglɛkt] *vt* **1** : desatender, descuidar ⟨to neglect one's health : descuidar la salud⟩ **2** : no cumplir con, faltar a ⟨to neglect one's obligations : faltar uno a sus obligaciones⟩ ⟨he neglected to tell me : omitió decírmelo⟩

neglect[2] *n* **1** : negligencia *f*, descuido *m*, incumplimiento *m* ⟨through neglect : por negligencia⟩ ⟨neglect of duty : incumplimiento del deber⟩ **2 in a state of neglect** : abandonado, descuidado

neglectful [nɪˈglɛktfəl] *adj* : descuidado *m*

negligee [ˌnɛgləˈʒei] *n* : negligé *m*

negligence [ˈnɛglɪdʒənts] *n* : descuido *m*, negligencia *f*

negligent [ˈnɛglɪdʒənt] *adj* : negligente, descuidado — **negligently** *adv*

negligible [ˈnɛglɪdʒəbəl] *adj* : insignificante, despreciable

negotiable [nɪˈgoʊʃəbəl, -ʃiə-] *adj* : negociable

negotiate [nɪˈgoʊʃiˌeit] *v* **-ated; -ating** *vi* : negociar — *vt* **1** : negociar, gestionar ⟨to negotiate a treaty : negociar un tratado⟩ **2** : salvar, franquear ⟨they negotiated the obstacles : salvaron los obstáculos⟩ ⟨to negotiate a turn : tomar una curva⟩

negotiation [nɪˌgoʊʃiˈeiʃən, -siˈei-] *n* : negociación *f*

negotiator [nɪˈgoʊʃiˌeit̬ər, -siˌei-] *n* : negociador *m*, -dora *f*

Negro [ˈniːˌgroʊ] *n*, *pl* **-groes** : negro *m*, -gra *f*

neigh[1] [ˈnei] *vi* : relinchar

neigh[2] *n* : relincho *m*

neighbor[1] [ˈneibər] *vt* : ser vecino de, estar junto a ⟨her house neighbors mine : su casa está junto a la mía⟩ — *vi* : estar cercano, lindar, colindar ⟨her land neighbors on mine : sus tierras lindan con las mías⟩

neighbor[2] *n* **1** : vecino *m*, -na *f* **2 love thy neighbor** : ama a tu prójimo

neighborhood [ˈneibərˌhʊd] *n* **1** : barrio *m*, vecindad *f*, vecindario *m* **2 in the neighborhood of** : alrededor de, cerca de

neighborly [ˈneibərli] *adv* : amable, de buena vecindad

neither[1] [ˈniːðər, ˈnai-] *adj* : ninguno (de los dos)

neither[2] *conj* **1** : ni ⟨neither asleep nor awake : ni dormido ni despierto⟩ **2** NOR : ni (tampoco) ⟨I'm not asleep—neither am I : no estoy dormido—ni yo tampoco⟩

neither[3] *pron* : ninguno

nemesis [ˈnɛməsɪs] *n*, *pl* **-eses** [-ˌsiːz] **1** RIVAL : rival *mf* **2** RETRIBUTION : justo castigo *m*

Neoclassical [ˌniːoʊˈklæsɪkəl] *adj* : neoclásico

neologism [niˈɑləˌdʒɪzəm] *n* : neologismo *m*

neon[1] [ˈniːˌɑn] *adj* : de neón ⟨neon sign : letrero de neón⟩

neon[2] *n* : neón *m*

neophyte [ˈniːəˌfait] *n* : neófito *m*, -ta *f*

Nepali [nəˈpɔli, -ˈpɑ-, -ˈpæ-] *n* : nepalés *m*, -lesa *f* — **Nepali** *adj*

nephew [ˈnɛˌfjuː, *chiefly British* ˈnɛˌvjuː] *n* : sobrino *m*

nepotism [ˈnɛpəˌtɪzəm] *n* : nepotismo *m*

Neptune [ˈnɛpˌtuːn, -ˌtjuːn] *n* : Neptuno *m*

nerd [ˈnərd] *n* : ganso *m*, -sa *f*

nerve [ˈnərv] *n* **1** : nervio *m* **2** COURAGE : coraje *m*, valor *m*, fuerza *f* de la voluntad ⟨to lose one's nerve : perder el valor⟩ **3** AUDACITY, GALL : atrevimiento *m*, descaro *m* ⟨of all the nerve! : ¡qué descaro!⟩ **4 nerves** *npl* : nervios *mpl* ⟨a fit of nerves : un ataque de nervios⟩

nervous [ˈnərvəs] *adj* **1** : nervioso ⟨the nervous system : el sistema nervioso⟩ **2** EXCITABLE : nervioso, excitable ⟨to get nervous : excitarse, ponerse nervioso⟩ **3** FEARFUL : miedoso, temeroso

nervously [ˈnərvəsli] *adv* : nerviosamente

nervousness [ˈnərvəsnəs] *n* : nerviosismo *m*, nerviosidad *f*, ansiedad *f*

nervy [ˈnərvi] *adj* **nervier; -est** **1** COURAGEOUS : valiente **2** IMPUDENT : atrevido, descarado, fresco *fam* **3** NERVOUS : nervioso

nest[1] [ˈnɛst] *vi* : anidar

nest[2] *n* **1** : nido *m* (de un ave), avispero *m* (de una avispa), madriguera *f* (de un animal) **2** REFUGE : nido *m*, refugio *m* **3** SET : juego *m* ⟨a nest of tables : un juego de mesitas⟩

nestle [ˈnɛsəl] *vi* **-tled; -tling** : acurrucarse, arrimarse cómodamente

net¹ ['nɛt] *vt* **netted; netting 1** CATCH : pescar, atrapar con una red **2** CLEAR : ganar neto ⟨they netted $5000 : ganaron $5000 netos⟩ **3** YIELD : producir neto

net² *adj* : neto ⟨net weight : peso neto⟩ ⟨net gain : ganancia neta⟩

net³ *n* : red *f*, malla *f*

nether ['nɛðər] *adj* **1** : inferior, más bajo **2 the nether regions** : el infierno

nettle¹ ['nɛtəl] *vt* **-tled; -tling** : irritar, provocar, molestar

nettle² *n* : ortiga *f*

network ['nɛt,wərk] *n* **1** SYSTEM : red *f* **2** CHAIN : cadena *f* ⟨a network of supermarkets : una cadena de supermercados⟩

neural ['nʊrəl, 'njʊr-] *adj* : neural

neuralgia [nʊ'rældʒə, njʊ-] *n* : neuralgia *f*

neuritis [nʊ'raɪtəs, njʊ-] *n, pl* **-ritides** [-'rɪtə,di:z] *or* **-ritises** : neuritis *f*

neurological [,nʊrə'lɑdʒɪkəl, ,njʊr-] *or* **neurologic** [,nʊrə'lɑdʒɪk, ,njʊr-] *adj* : neurológico

neurologist [nʊ'rɑlədʒɪst, njʊ-] *n* : neurólogo *m*, -ga *f*

neurology [nʊ'rɑlədʒi, njʊ-] *n* : neurología *f*

neurosis [nʊ'ro:sɪs, njʊ-] *n, pl* **-roses** [-,si:z] : neurosis *f*

neurotic¹ [nʊ'rɑtɪk, njʊ-] *adj* : neurótico

neurotic² *n* : neurótico *m*, -ca *f*

neuter¹ ['nu:tər, 'nju:-] *vt* : castrar

neuter² *adj* : neutro

neutral¹ ['nu:trəl, 'nju:-] *adj* **1** IMPARTIAL : neutral, imparcial ⟨to remain neutral : permanecer neutral⟩ **2** : neutro ⟨a neutral color : un color neutro⟩ **3** : neutro (en la química o la electricidad)

neutral² *n* : punto *m* muerto (de un automóvil)

neutrality [nu:'træləti:, nju:-] *n* : neutralidad *f*

neutralization [,nu:trələ'zeɪʃən, ,nju:-] *n* : neutralización *f*

neutralize ['nu:trə,laɪz, 'nju:-] *vt* **-ized; -izing** : neutralizar

neutron ['nu:,trɑn, 'nju:-] *n* : neutrón *m*

never ['nɛvər] *adv* **1** : nunca, jamás ⟨he never studies : nunca estudia⟩ **2 never again** : nunca más, nunca jamás **3 never mind** : no importa

nevermore [,nɛvər'mor] *adv* : nunca más

nevertheless [,nɛvərðə'lɛs] *adv* : sin embargo, no obstante

new ['nu:, 'nju:] *adj* **1** : nuevo ⟨a new dress : un vestido nuevo⟩ **2** RECENT : nuevo, reciente ⟨what's new? : ¿qué hay de nuevo?⟩ ⟨a new arrival : un recién llegado⟩ **3** DIFFERENT : nuevo, distinto ⟨this problem is new : este problema es distinto⟩ ⟨new ideas : ideas nuevas⟩ **4 like new** : como nuevo

newborn ['nu:,bɔrn, 'nju:-] *adj* : recién nacido

newcomer ['nu:,kʌmər, 'nju:-] *n* : recién llegado *m*, recién llegada *f*

newfangled ['nu:'fæŋgəld, 'nju:-] *adj* : novedoso

newfound ['nu:'faʊnd, 'nju:-] *adj* : recién descubierto

newly ['nu:li, 'nju:-] *adv* : recién, recientemente

newlywed ['nu:li,wɛd, 'nju:-] *n* : recién casado *m*, -da *f*

new moon *n* : luna *f* nueva

newness ['nu:nəs, 'nju:-] *n* : novedad *f*

news ['nu:z, 'nju:z] *n* : noticias *fpl*

newscast ['nu:z,kæst, 'nju:z-] *n* : noticiero *m*, informativo *m*

newscaster ['nu:z,kæstər, 'nju:z-] *n* : presentador *m*, -dora *f*; locutor *m*, -tora *f*

newsletter ['nu:z,lɛtər, 'nju:z-] *n* : boletín *m* informativo

newsman ['nu:zmən, 'nju:z-, -,mæn] *n, pl* **-men** [-mən, -,mɛn] : periodista *m*, reportero *m*

newspaper ['nu:z,peɪpər, 'nju:z-] *n* : periódico *m*, diario *m*

newspaperman ['nu:z,peɪpər,mæn, 'nju:z-] *n, pl* **-men** [-mən, -,mɛn] **1** REPORTER : periodista *m*, reportero *m* **2** : dueño *m* de un periódico

newsprint ['nu:z,prɪnt, 'nju:z-] *n* : papel *m* de prensa

newsstand ['nu:z,stænd, 'nju:z-] *n* : quiosco *m*, puesto *m* de periódicos

newswoman ['nu:z,wʊmən, 'nju:z-] *n, pl* **-women** [-,wɪmən] : periodista *f*, reportera *f*

newsworthy ['nu:z,wərði, 'nju:z-] *adj* : de interés periodístico

newsy ['nu:zi:, 'nju:-] *adj* **newsier; -est** : lleno de noticias

newt ['nu:t, 'nju:t] *n* : tritón *m*

New Testament *n* : Nuevo Testamento *m*

New Year *n* : Año *m* Nuevo

New Year's Day *n* : día *m* del Año Nuevo

New Yorker [nu:'jɔrkər, nju:-] *n* : neoyorquino *m*, -na *f*

New Zealander [nu:'zi:ləndər, nju:-] *n* : neozelandés *m*, -desa *f*

next¹ ['nɛkst] *adv* **1** AFTERWARD : después, luego ⟨what will you do next? : ¿qué harás después?⟩ **2** NOW : después, ahora, entonces ⟨next I will sing a song : ahora voy a cantar una canción⟩ **3** : la próxima vez ⟨when next we meet : la próxima vez que nos encontremos⟩

next² *adj* **1** ADJACENT : contiguo, de al lado **2** COMING : que viene, próximo ⟨next Friday : el viernes que viene⟩ **3** FOLLOWING : siguiente ⟨the next year : el año siguiente⟩

next–door ['nɛkst'dor] *adj* : de al lado

next to¹ *adv* ALMOST : casi, prácticamente ⟨next to impossible : casi imposible⟩

next to² *prep* : junto a, al lado de

nexus [ˈnɛksəs] *n* : nexo *m*

nib [ˈnɪb] *n* : plumilla *f*

nibble¹ [ˈnɪbəl] *v* **-bled; -bling** *vt* : pellizcar, mordisquear, picar — *vi* : picar

nibble² *n* : mordisco *m*

Nicaraguan [ˌnɪkəˈrɑɡwən] *n* : nicaragüense *mf* — **Nicaraguan** *adj*

nice [ˈnaɪs] *adj* **nicer; nicest 1** REFINED : pulido, refinado **2** SUBTLE : fino, sutil **3** PLEASING : agradable, bueno, lindo ⟨nice weather : buen tiempo⟩ **4** RESPECTABLE : bueno, decente **5 nice and** : bien, muy ⟨nice and hot : bien caliente⟩ ⟨nice and slow : despacito⟩

nicely [ˈnaɪsli] *adv* **1** KINDLY : amablemente **2** POLITELY : con buenos modales **3** ATTRACTIVELY : de buen gusto

niceness [ˈnaɪsnəs] *n* : simpatía *f*, amabilidad *f*

nicety [ˈnaɪsəṭi] *n, pl* **-ties 1** DETAIL, SUBTLETY : sutileza *f*, detalle *m* **2 niceties** *npl* : lujos *mpl*, detalles *mpl*

niche [ˈnɪtʃ] *n* **1** RECESS : nicho *m*, hornacina *f* **2** : nicho *m*, hueco *m* ⟨to make a niche for oneself : hacerse un hueco, encontrarse una buena posición⟩

nick¹ [ˈnɪk] *vt* : cortar, hacer una muesca en

nick² *n* **1** CUT : corte *m*, muesca *f* **2 in the nick of time** : en el momento crítico, justo a tiempo

nickel [ˈnɪkəl] *n* **1** : níquel *m* **2** : moneda *f* de cinco centavos

nickname¹ [ˈnɪkˌneɪm] *vt* **-named; -naming** : apodar

nickname² *n* : apodo *m*, mote *m*, sobrenombre *m*

nicotine [ˈnɪkəˌtiːn] *n* : nicotina *f*

niece [ˈniːs] *n* : sobrina *f*

Nigerian [naɪˈdʒɪriən] *n* : nigeriano *m*, -na *f* — **Nigerian** *adj*

niggardly [ˈnɪɡərdli] *adj* : mezquino, tacaño

niggling [ˈnɪɡəlɪŋ] *adj* **1** PETTY : insignificante **2** PERSISTENT : constante, persistente ⟨a niggling doubt : una duda constante⟩

nigh¹ [ˈnaɪ] *adv* **1** NEARLY : casi **2 to draw nigh** : acercarse, avecinarse

nigh² *adj* : cercano, próximo

night¹ [ˈnaɪt] *adj* : nocturno, de la noche ⟨the night sky : el cielo nocturno⟩ ⟨night shift : turno de la noche⟩

night² *n* **1** EVENING : noche *f* ⟨at night : de noche⟩ ⟨last night : anoche⟩ ⟨tomorrow night : mañana por la noche⟩ **2** DARKNESS : noche *f*, oscuridad *f* ⟨night fell : cayó la noche⟩

nightclothes [ˈnaɪtˌkloːðz, -ˌkloːz] *npl* : ropa *f* de dormir

nightclub [ˈnaɪtˌklʌb] *n* : cabaret *m*, club *m* nocturno

night crawler [ˈnaɪtˌkrɔlər] *n* EARTHWORM : lombriz *f* (de tierra)

nightfall [ˈnaɪtˌfɔl] *n* : anochecer *m*

nightgown [ˈnaɪtˌɡaʊn] *n* : camisón *m* (de noche)

nightingale [ˈnaɪtənˌɡeɪl, ˈnaɪtɪŋ-] *n* : ruiseñor *m*

nightly¹ [ˈnaɪtli] *adv* : cada noche, todas las noches

nightly² *adj* : de todas las noches

nightmare [ˈnaɪtˌmær] *n* : pesadilla *f*

nightmarish [ˈnaɪtˌmærɪʃ] *adj* : de pesadilla

night owl *n* : noctámbulo *m*, -la *f*

nightshade [ˈnaɪtˌʃeɪd] *n* : hierba *f* mora

nightshirt [ˈnaɪtˌʃərt] *n* : camisa *f* de dormir

nightstick [ˈnaɪtˌstɪk] *n* : porra *f*

nighttime [ˈnaɪtˌtaɪm] *n* : noche *f*

nihilism [ˈnaɪəˌlɪzəm] *n* : nihilismo *m*

nil [ˈnɪl] *n* : nada *f*, cero *m*

nimble [ˈnɪmbəl] *adj* **-bler; -blest 1** AGILE : ágil **2** CLEVER : hábil, ingenioso

nimbleness [ˈnɪmbəlnəs] *n* : agilidad *f*

nimbly [ˈnɪmbli] *adv* : con agilidad, ágilmente

nincompoop [ˈnɪnkəmˌpuːp, ˈnɪŋ-] *n* FOOL : tonto *m*, -ta *f*; bobo *m*, -ba *f*

nine¹ [ˈnaɪn] *adj* **1** : nueve **2 nine times out of ten** : casi siempre

nine² *n* : nueve *m*

nine hundred¹ *adj* : novecientos

nine hundred² *n* : novecientos *m*

ninepins [ˈnaɪnˌpɪnz] *n* : bolos *mpl*

nineteen¹ [naɪnˈtiːn] *adj* : diecinueve

nineteen² *n* : diecinueve *m*

nineteenth¹ [naɪnˈtiːnθ] *adj* : decimonoveno, decimonono ⟨the nineteenth century : el siglo diecinueve⟩

nineteenth² *n* **1** : decimonoveno *m*, -na *f*; decimonono *m*, -na *f* (en una serie) **2** : diecinueveavo *m*, diecinueveava parte *f*

ninetieth¹ [ˈnaɪntiəθ] *adj* : nonagésimo

ninetieth² *n* **1** : nonagésimo *m*, -ma *f* (en una serie) **2** : noventavo *m*, noventava parte *f*

ninety¹ [ˈnaɪnti] *adj* : noventa

ninety² *n, pl* **-ties** : noventa *m*

ninth¹ [ˈnaɪnθ] *adj* : noveno

ninth² *n* **1** : noveno *m*, -na *f* (en una serie) **2** : noveno *m*, novena parte *f*

ninny [ˈnɪni] *n, pl* **ninnies** FOOL : tonto *m*, -ta *f*; bobo *m*, -ba *f*

nip¹ [ˈnɪp] *vt* **nipped; nipping 1** PINCH : pellizcar **2** BITE : morder, mordisquear **3 to nip in the bud** : cortar de raíz

nip² *n* **1** TANG : sabor *m* fuerte **2** PINCH : pellizco *m* **3** NIBBLE : mordisco *m* **4** SWALLOW : trago *m*, traguito *m* **5 there's a nip in the air** : hace fresco

nipple [ˈnɪpəl] *n* : pezón *m* (de una mujer), tetilla *f* (de un hombre)

nippy [ˈnɪpi] *adj* **-pier; -est 1** SHARP : fuerte, picante **2** CHILLY : frío ⟨it's nippy today : hoy hace frío⟩

nit [ˈnɪt] *n* : liendre *f*

nitrate [ˈnaɪˌtreɪt] *n* : nitrato *m*

nitric acid [ˈnaɪtrɪk] *n* : ácido *m* nítrico

nitrite [ˈnaɪˌtraɪt] *n* : nitrito *m*

nitrogen [ˈnaɪtrədʒən] *n* : nitrógeno *m*

nitroglycerin *or* **nitroglycerine** [ˌnaɪtroˈɡlɪsərən] *n* : nitroglicerina *f*

nitwit ['nɪt,wɪt] *n* : zonzo *m*, -za *f*; bobo *m*, -ba *f*
no[1] ['no:] *adv* : no ⟨are you leaving?— no : ¿te vas?—no⟩ ⟨no less than : no menos de⟩ ⟨to say no : decir que no⟩ ⟨like it or no : quieras o no quieras⟩
no[2] *adj* 1 : ninguno ⟨it's no trouble : no es ningún problema⟩ ⟨she has no money : no tiene dinero⟩ 2 (*indicating a small amount*) ⟨we'll be there in no time : llegamos dentro de poco, no tardamos nada⟩ 3 (*expressing a negation*) ⟨he's no liar : no es mentiroso⟩
no[3] *n, pl* **noes** *or* **nos** ['no:z] 1 DENIAL : no *m* ⟨I won't take no for an answer : no aceptaré un no por respuesta⟩ 2 : voto *m* en contra ⟨the noes have it : se ha rechazado la moción⟩
nobility [no'bɪləti] *n* : nobleza *f*
noble[1] ['no:bəl] *adj* **-bler; -blest** 1 ILLUSTRIOUS : noble, glorioso 2 ARISTOCRATIC : noble 3 STATELY : majestuoso, magnífico 4 LOFTY : noble, elevado ⟨noble sentiments : sentimientos elevados⟩
noble[2] *n* : noble *mf*, aristócrata *mf*
nobleman ['no:bəlmən] *n, pl* **-men** [-mən, -,mɛn] : noble *m*, aristócrata *m*
nobleness ['no:bəlnəs] *n* : nobleza *f*
noblewoman ['no:bəl,wʊmən] *n, pl* **-women** [-,wɪmən] : noble *f*, aristócrata *f*
nobly ['no:bli] *adv* : noblemente
nobody[1] ['no:bədi, -,badi] *n, pl* **-bodies** : don nadie *m* ⟨he's a mere nobody : es un don nadie⟩
nobody[2] *pron* : nadie
nocturnal [nak'tərnəl] *adj* : nocturno
nocturne ['nak,tərn] *n* : nocturno *m*
nod[1] ['nad] *v* **nodded; nodding** *vi* 1 : saludar con la cabeza, asentir con la cabeza 2 **to nod off** : dormirse, quedarse dormido — *vt* : inclinar (la cabeza) ⟨to nod one's head in agreement : asentir con la cabeza⟩
nod[2] *n* : saludo *m* con la cabeza, señal *m* con la cabeza, señal *m* de asentimiento
node ['no:d] *n* : nudo *m* (de una planta)
nodule ['nɑ,ʤu:l] *n* : nódulo *m*
noel [no'ɛl] *n* 1 CAROL : villancico *m* de Navidad 2 **Noel** CHRISTMAS : Navidad *f*
noes → no[3]
noise[1] ['nɔɪz] *vt* **noised; noising** : rumorear, publicar
noise[2] *n* : ruido *m*
noiseless ['nɔɪzləs] *adj* : silencioso, sin ruido
noiselessly ['nɔɪzləsli] *adv* : silenciosamente
noisemaker ['nɔɪz,meɪkər] *n* : matraca *f*
noisiness ['nɔɪzinəs] *n* : ruido *m*
noisome ['nɔɪsəm] *adj* : maloliente, fétido
noisy ['nɔɪzi] *adj* **noisier; -est** : ruidoso — **noisily** ['nɔɪzəli] *adv*
nomad[1] ['no:,mæd] → **nomadic**

nomad[2] *n* : nómada *mf*
nomadic [no'mædɪk] *adj* : nómada
nomenclature ['no:mən,kleɪtʃər] *n* : nomenclatura *f*
nominal ['nɑmənəl] *adj* 1 : nominal ⟨the nominal head of his party : el jefe nominal de su partido⟩ 2 TRIFLING : insignificante
nominally ['nɑmənəli] *adv* : sólo de nombre, nominalmente
nominate ['nɑmə,neɪt] *vt* **-nated; -nating** 1 PROPOSE : proponer (como candidato), nominar 2 APPOINT : nombrar
nomination [,nɑmə'neɪʃən] *n* 1 PROPOSAL : propuesta *f*, postulación *f* 2 APPOINTMENT : nombramiento *m*
nominative[1] ['nɑmənətɪv] *adj* : nominativo
nominative[2] *n or* **nominative case** : nominativo *m*
nominee [,nɑmə'ni:] *n* : candidato *m*, -ta *f*
nonaddictive [,nɑnə'dɪktɪv] *adj* : que no crea dependencia
nonalcoholic [,nɑn,ælkə'hɔlɪk] *adj* : sin alcohol, no alcohólico
nonaligned [,nɑnə'laɪnd] *adj* : no alineado
nonbeliever [,nɑnbə'li:vər] *n* : no creyente *mf*
nonbreakable [,nɑn'breɪkəbəl] *adj* : irrompible
nonce ['nɑnts] *n* **for the nonce** : por el momento
nonchalance [,nɑnʃə'lants] *n* : indiferencia *f*, despreocupación *f*
nonchalant [,nɑnʃə'lant] *adj* : indiferente, despreocupado, impasible
nonchalantly [,nɑnʃə'lantli] *adv* : con aire despreocupado, con indiferencia
noncombatant [,nɑnkəm'bætənt, -'kɑmbə-] *n* : no combatiente *mf*
noncommissioned officer [,nɑnkə'mɪʃənd] *n* : suboficial *mf*
noncommittal [,nɑnkə'mɪtəl] *adj* : evasivo, que no se compromete
nonconductor [,nɑnkən'dʌktər] *n* : aislante *m*
nonconformist [,nɑnkən'fɔrmɪst] *n* : inconformista *mf*, inconforme *mf*
nonconformity [,nɑnkən'fɔrməti] *n* : inconformidad *f*, no conformidad *f*
noncontagious [,nɑnkən'teɪʤəs] *adj* : no contagioso
nondenominational [,nɑndɪ,nɑmə'neɪʃənəl] *adj* : no sectario
nondescript [,nɑndɪ'skrɪpt] *adj* : anodino, soso
nondiscriminatory [,nɑndɪ'skrɪmənə,tori] *adj* : no discriminatorio
nondrinker [,nɑn'drɪŋkər] *n* : abstemio *m*, -mia *f*
none[1] ['nʌn] *adv* : de ninguna manera, de ningún modo, nada ⟨he was none too happy : no se sintió nada contento⟩ ⟨I'm none the worse for it : no estoy peor por ello⟩ ⟨none too soon : a buena hora⟩

none² *pron* : ninguno, ninguna
nonentity [ˌnɑnˈɛntəti] *n, pl* **-ties** : persona *f* insignificante, nulidad *f*
nonessential [ˌnɑnɪˈsɛntʃəl] *adj* : secundario, no esencial
nonessentials [ˌnɑnɪˈsɛntʃəlz] *npl* : cosas *fpl* secundarias, cosas *fpl* accesorias
nonetheless [ˌnʌnðəˈlɛs] *adv* : sin embargo, no obstante
nonexistence [ˌnɑnɪgˈzɪstənts] *n* : inexistencia *f*
nonexistent [ˌnɑnɪgˈzɪstənt] *adj* : inexistente
nonfat [ˌnɑnˈfæt] *adj* : sin grasa
nonfattening [ˌnɑnˈfætənɪŋ] *adj* : que no engorda
nonfiction [ˌnɑnˈfɪkʃən] *n* : no ficción *f*
nonflammable [ˌnɑnˈflæməbəl] *adj* : no inflamable
nonintervention [ˌnɑnˌɪntərˈvɛntʃən] *n* : no intervención *f*
nonmalignant [ˌnɑnməˈlɪgnənt] *adj* : no maligno, benigno
nonnegotiable [ˌnɑnnɪˈgoːʃəbəl, -ʃiə-] *adj* : no negociable
nonpareil¹ [ˌnɑnpəˈrɛl] *adj* : sin parangón, sin par
nonpareil² *n* : persona *f* sin igual, cosa *f* sin par
nonpartisan [ˌnɑnˈpɑrt̬əzən, -sən] *adj* : imparcial
nonpaying [ˌnɑnˈpeɪɪŋ] *adj* : que no paga
nonpayment [ˌnɑnˈpeɪmənt] *n* : impago *m*, falta *f* de pago
nonperson [ˌnɑnˈpərsən] *n* : persona *f* sin derechos
nonplus [ˌnɑnˈplʌs] *vt* **-plussed; -plussing** : confundir, desconcertar, dejar perplejo
nonprescription [ˌnɑnprɪˈskrɪpʃən] *adj* : disponible sin receta del médico
nonproductive [ˌnɑnprəˈdʌktɪv] *adj* : improductivo
nonprofit [ˌnɑnˈprɑfət] *adj* : sin fines lucrativos
nonproliferation [ˌnɑnprəˌlɪfəˈreɪʃən] *adj* : no proliferación
nonresident [ˌnɑnˈrɛzədənt, -ˌdɛnt] *n* : no residente *mf*
nonscheduled [ˌnɑnˈskɛˌdʒuːld] *adj* : no programado, no regular
nonsectarian [ˌnɑnˌsɛkˈtæriən] *adj* : no sectario
nonsense [ˈnɑnˌsɛnts, ˈnɑntsənts] *n* : tonterías *fpl*, disparates *mpl*
nonsensical [nɑnˈsɛntsɪkəl] *adj* ABSURD : absurdo, disparatado — **nonsensically** [-kli] *adv*
nonsmoker [ˌnɑnˈsmoːkər] *n* : no fumador *m*, -dora *f*; persona *f* que no fuma
nonstandard [ˌnɑnˈstændərd] *adj* : no regular, no estándar
nonstick [ˌnɑnˈstɪk] *adj* : antiadherente
nonstop¹ [ˌnɑnˈstɑp] *adv* : sin parar ⟨he talked nonstop : habló sin parar⟩
nonstop² *adj* : directo, sin escalas ⟨nonstop flight : vuelo directo⟩

nonsupport [ˌnɑnsəˈpɔrt] *n* : falta *f* de manutención
nontaxable [ˌnɑnˈtæksəbəl] *adj* : exento de impuestos
nontoxic [ˌnɑnˈtɑksɪk] *adj* : no tóxico
nonviolence [ˌnɑnˈvaɪlənts, -ˈvaɪə-] *n* : no violencia *f*
nonviolent [ˌnɑnˈvaɪlənt, -ˈvaɪə-] *adj* : pacífico, no violento
noodle [ˈnuːdəl] *n* : fideo *m*, tallarín *m*
nook [ˈnʊk] *n* : rincón *m*, recoveco *m*, escondrijo *m* ⟨in every nook and cranny : en todos los rincones⟩
noon [ˈnuːn] *n* : mediodía *m*
noonday [ˈnuːnˌdeɪ] *n* : mediodía *m* ⟨the noonday sun : el sol de mediodía⟩
no one *pron* NOBODY : nadie
noontime [ˈnuːnˌtaɪm] *n* : mediodía *m*
noose [ˈnuːs] *n* **1** LASSO : lazo *m* **2** hangman's noose : dogal *m*, soga *f*
nor [ˈnɔr] *conj* : ni ⟨neither good nor bad : ni bueno ni malo⟩ ⟨nor I! : ¡ni yo tampoco!⟩
Nordic [ˈnɔrdɪk] *adj* : nórdico
norm [ˈnɔrm] *n* **1** STANDARD : norma *f*, modelo *m* **2** CUSTOM, RULE : regla *f* general, lo normal
normal [ˈnɔrməl] *adj* : normal — **normally** *adv*
normalcy [ˈnɔrməlsi] *n* : normalidad *f*
normality [nɔrˈmæləti] *n* : normalidad *f*
normalize [ˈnɔrməˌlaɪz] *vt* : normalizar
Norse [ˈnɔrs] *adj* : nórdico
north¹ [ˈnɔrθ] *adv* : al norte
north² *adj* : norte, del norte ⟨the north coast : la costa del norte⟩
north³ *n* **1** : norte *m* **2 the North** : el Norte *m*
North American *n* : norteamericano *m*, -na *f* — **North American** *adj*
northbound [ˈnɔrθˌbaʊnd] *adv* : con rumbo al norte
northeast¹ [nɔrθˈiːst] *adv* : hacia el nordeste
northeast² *adj* : nordeste, del nordeste
northeast³ *n* : nordeste *m*, noreste *m*
northeasterly¹ [nɔrθˈiːstərli] *adv* : hacia el nordeste
northeasterly² *adj* : nordeste, del nordeste
northeastern [nɔrθˈiːstərn] *adj* : nordeste, del nordeste
northerly¹ [ˈnɔrðərli] *adv* : hacia el norte
northerly² *adj* : del norte ⟨a northerly wind : un viento del norte⟩
northern [ˈnɔrðərn] *adj* : norte, norteño, septentrional
Northerner [ˈnɔrðərnər] *n* : norteño *m*, -ña *f*
northern lights → aurora borealis
North Pole : Polo *m* Norte
North Star *n* : estrella *f* polar
northward [ˈnɔrθwərd] *adv & adj* : hacia el norte
northwest¹ [nɔrθˈwɛst] *adv* : hacia el noroeste
northwest² *adj* : del noroeste
northwest³ *n* : noroeste *m*

northwesterly[1] [nɔrθ'wɛstərli] *adv* : hacia el noroeste

northwesterly[2] *adj* : del noroeste

northwestern [nɔrθ'wɛstərn] *adj* : noroeste, del noroeste

Norwegian [nɔr'wi:dʒən] *n* **1** : noruego *m*, -ga *f* **2** : noruego *m* (idioma) — **Norwegian** *adj*

nose[1] ['no:z] *v* **nosed; nosing** *vt* **1** SMELL : olfatear **2** : empujar con el hocico ⟨the dog nosed open the bag : el perro abrió el saco con el hocico⟩ **3** EDGE, MOVE : mover poco a poco — *vi* **1** PRY : entrometerse, meter las narices **2** EDGE : avanzar poco a poco

nose[2] *n* **1** : nariz *f* (de una persona), hocico *m* (de un animal) ⟨to blow one's nose : sonarse las narices⟩ **2** SMELL : olfato *m*, sentido *m* del olfato **3** FRONT : parte *f* delantera, nariz *f* (de un avión), proa *f* (de un barco) **4 to follow one's nose** : dejarse guiar por el instinto

nosebleed ['no:z,bli:d] *n* : hemorragia *f* nasal

nosedive ['no:z,daɪv] *n* **1** : descenso *m* en picada (de un avión) **2** : caída *f* súbita (de precios, etc.)

nose–dive ['no:z,daɪv] *vi* : descender en picada, caer en picada

nostalgia [nɑ'stældʒə, nə-] *n* : nostalgia *f*

nostalgic [nɑ'stældʒɪk, nə-] *adj* : nostálgico

nostril ['nɑstrəl] *n* : ventana *f* de la nariz

nostrum ['nɑstrəm] *n* : panacea *f*

nosy *or* **nosey** ['no:zi] *adj* **nosier; -est** : entrometido

not ['nɑt] *adv* **1** (*used to form a negative*) : no ⟨she is not tired : no está cansada⟩ ⟨not to say something would be wrong : no decir nada sería injusto⟩ **2** (*used to replace a negative clause*) : no ⟨are we going or not? : ¿vamos a ir o no?⟩ ⟨of course not! : ¡claro que no!⟩

notable[1] ['no:təbəl] *adj* **1** NOTEWORTHY : notable, de notar **2** DISTINGUISHED, PROMINENT : distinguido, destacado

notable[2] *n* : persona *f* importante, personaje *m*

notably ['no:təbli] *adv* : notablemente, particularmente

notarize ['no:tə,raɪz] *vt* **-rized; -rizing** : autenticar, autorizar

notary public ['no:təri] *n, pl* **-ries publics** *or* **-ry publics** : notario *m*, -ria *f*; escribano *m*, -na *f*

notation [no'teɪʃən] *n* **1** NOTE : anotación *f*, nota *f* **2** : notación *f* ⟨musical notation : notación musical⟩

notch[1] ['nɑtʃ] *vt* : hacer una muesca en, cortar

notch[2] *n* : muesca *f*, corte *m*

note[1] ['no:t] *vt* **noted; noting 1** NOTICE : notar, observar, tomar nota de **2** RECORD : anotar, apuntar

note[2] *n* **1** : nota *f* (musical) **2** COMMENT : nota *f*, comentario *m* **3** LETTER : nota *f*, cartita *f* **4** PROMINENCE : prestigio *m* ⟨a musician of note : un músico destacado⟩ **5** ATTENTION : atención *f* ⟨to take note of : prestar atención a⟩

notebook ['no:t,bʊk] *n* **1** : libreta *f*, cuaderno *m* **2** : notebook *m* (computadora)

noted ['no:təd] *adj* EMINENT : renombrado, eminente, celebrado

noteworthy ['no:t,wərði] *adj* : notable, de notar, de interés

nothing[1] ['nʌθɪŋ] *adv* **1** : de ninguna manera ⟨nothing daunted, we carried on : sin amilanarnos, seguimos adelante⟩ **2 nothing like** : no ... en nada ⟨he's nothing like his brother : no se parece en nada a su hermano⟩

nothing[2] *n* **1** NOTHINGNESS : nada *f* **2** ZERO : cero *m* **3** : persona *f* de poca importancia, cero *m* **4** TRIFLE : nimiedad *f*

nothing[3] *pron* : nada ⟨there's nothing better : no hay nada mejor⟩ ⟨nothing else : nada más⟩ ⟨nothing but : solamente⟩ ⟨they mean nothing to me : ellos me son indiferentes⟩

nothingness ['nʌθɪŋnəs] *n* **1** VOID : vacío *m*, nada *f* **2** NONEXISTENCE : inexistencia *f* **3** TRIFLE : nimiedad *f*

notice[1] ['no:tɪs] *vt* **-ticed; -ticing** : notar, observar, advertir, darse cuenta de

notice[2] *n* **1** NOTIFICATION : aviso *m*, notificación *f* **2** ATTENTION : atención *f* ⟨to take notice of : prestar atención a⟩

noticeable ['no:tɪsəbəl] *adj* : evidente, perceptible — **noticeably** [-bli] *adv*

notification [,no:təfə'keɪʃən] *n* : notificación *f*, aviso *m*

notify ['no:tə,faɪ] *vt* **-fied; -fying** : notificar, avisar

notion ['no:ʃən] *n* **1** IDEA : idea *f*, noción *f* **2** WHIM : capricho *m*, antojo *m* **3 notions** *npl* : artículos *mpl* de mercería

notoriety [,no:tə'raɪəti] *n* : mala fama *f*, notoriedad *f*

notorious [no'to:riəs] *adj* : de mala fama, célebre, bien conocido

notwithstanding[1] [,nɑtwɪθ'stændɪŋ, -wɪð-] *adv* NEVERTHELESS : no obstante, sin embargo

notwithstanding[2] *conj* : a pesar de que

notwithstanding[3] *prep* : a pesar de, no obstante

nougat ['nu:gət] *n* : turrón *m*

nought ['nɔt, 'nɑt] → **naught**

noun ['naʊn] *n* : nombre *m*, sustantivo *m*

nourish ['nərɪʃ] *vt* **1** FEED : alimentar, nutrir, sustentar **2** FOSTER : fomentar, alentar

nourishing ['nərɪʃɪŋ] *adj* : alimenticio, nutritivo

nourishment ['nərɪʃmənt] *n* : nutrición *f*, alimento *m*, sustento *m*

novel[1] ['nɑvəl] *adj* : original, novedoso

novel[2] *n* : novela *f*
novelist ['nɑvəlɪst] *n* : novelista *mf*
novelty ['nɑvəlti] *n, pl* **-ties 1** : novedad *f* **2 novelties** *npl* TRINKETS : baratijas *fpl*, chucherías *fpl*
November [no'vɛmbər] *n* : noviembre *m*
novice ['nɑvɪs] *n* : novato *m*, -ta *f*; principiante *mf*; novicio *m*, -cia *f*
now[1] ['naʊ] *adv* **1** PRESENTLY : ahora, ya, actualmente ⟨from now on : de ahora en adelante⟩ ⟨long before now : ya hace tiempo⟩ ⟨now and then : de vez en cuando⟩ **2** IMMEDIATELY : ahora (mismo), inmediatamente ⟨do it right now! : ¡hazlo ahora mismo!⟩ **3** THEN : ya, entonces ⟨now they were ready : ya estaban listos⟩ **4** (*used to introduce a question, a command, or a transition*) ⟨now hear this! : ¡presten atención!⟩ ⟨now what do you think of that? : ¿qué piensas de eso?⟩
now[2] *n* (*indicating the present time*) ⟨until now : hasta ahora⟩ ⟨by now : ya⟩ ⟨ten years from now : dentro de 10 años⟩
now[3] *conj* **now that** : ahora que, ya que
nowadays ['naʊə,deɪz] *adv* : hoy en día, actualmente, en la actualidad
nowhere[1] ['no:,hwɛr] *adv* **1** : en ninguna parte, a ningún lado ⟨nowhere to be found : en ninguna parte, por ningún lado⟩ ⟨you're going nowhere : no estás yendo a ningún lado, no estás yendo a ninguna parte⟩ **2 nowhere near** : ni con mucho, nada cerca ⟨it's nowhere near here : no está nada cerca de aquí⟩
nowhere[2] *n* **1** : ninguna parte *f* **2 out of nowhere** : de la nada
noxious ['nɑkʃəs] *adj* : nocivo, dañino, tóxico
nozzle ['nɑzəl] *n* : boca *f*
nuance ['nu:,ɑnts, 'nju:-] *n* : matiz *m*
nub ['nʌb] *n* **1** KNOB, LUMP : protuberancia *f*, nudo *m* **2** GIST : quid *m*, meollo *m*
nuclear ['nu:kliər, 'nju:-] *adj* : nuclear
nucleus ['nu:kliəs, 'nju:-] *n, pl* **-clei** [-kli,aɪ] : núcleo *m*
nude[1] ['nu:d, 'nju:d] *adj* **nuder; nudest** : desnudo
nude[2] *n* : desnudo *m*
nudge[1] ['nʌdʒ] *vt* **nudged; nudging** : darle con el codo (a alguien)
nudge[2] *n* : toque *m* que se da con el codo
nudism ['nu:,dɪzəm, 'nju:-] *n* : nudismo *m*
nudist ['nu:dɪst, 'nju:-] *n* : nudista *mf*
nudity ['nu:dəti, 'nju:-] *n* : desnudez *f*
nugget ['nʌgət] *n* : pepita *f*
nuisance ['nu:sənts, 'nju:-] *n* **1** BOTHER : fastidio *m*, molestia *f*, lata *f* **2** PEST : pesado *m*, -da *f fam*
null ['nʌl] *adj* : nulo ⟨null and void : nulo y sin efecto⟩
nullify ['nʌlə,faɪ] *vt* **-fied; -fying** : invalidar, anular
nullity ['nʌləti] *n, pl* **-ties** : nulidad *f*
numb[1] ['nʌm] *vt* : entumecer, adormecer

numb[2] *adj* : entumecido, dormido ⟨numb with fear : paralizado de miedo⟩
number[1] ['nʌmbər] *vt* **1** COUNT, INCLUDE : contar, incluir **2** : numerar ⟨number the pages : numera las páginas⟩ **3** TOTAL : ascender a, sumar
number[2] *n* **1** : número *m* ⟨in round numbers : en números redondos⟩ ⟨telephone number : número de teléfono⟩ **2 a number of** : varios, unos pocos, unos cuantos
numberless ['nʌmbərləs] *adj* : innumerable, sin número
numbness ['nʌmnəs] *n* : entumecimiento *m*
numeral ['nu:mərəl, 'nju:-] *n* : número *m* ⟨Roman numeral : número romano⟩
numerator ['nu:mə,reɪtər, 'nju:-] *n* : numerador *m*
numeric [nʊ'mɛrɪk, nju-] *adj* : numérico
numerical [nʊ'mɛrɪkəl, nju-] *adj* : numérico — **numerically** [-kli] *adv*
numerous ['nu:mərəs, 'nju:-] *adj* : numeroso
numismatics [,nu:məz'mætɪks, ,nju:-] *n* : numismática *f*
numskull ['nʌm,skʌl] *n* : tonto *m*, -ta *f*; mentecato *m*, -ta *f*; zoquete *m fam*
nun ['nʌn] *n* : monja *f*
nuptial ['nʌpʃəl] *adj* : nupcial
nuptials ['nʌpʃəlz] *npl* WEDDING : nupcias *fpl*, boda *f*
nurse[1] ['nərs] *vt* **nursed; nursing 1** SUCKLE : amamantar **2** : cuidar (de), atender ⟨to nurse the sick : cuidar a los enfermos⟩ ⟨to nurse a cold : curarse de un resfriado⟩
nurse[2] *n* **1** : enfermero *m*, -ra *f* **2** → **nursemaid**
nursemaid ['nərs,meɪd] *n* : niñera *f*
nursery ['nərsəri] *n, pl* **-eries 1** *or* day nursery : guardería *f* **2** : vivero *m* (de plantas)
nursing home *n* : hogar *m* de ancianos, clínica *f* de reposo
nurture[1] ['nərtʃər] *vt* **-tured; -turing 1** FEED, NOURISH : nutrir, alimentar **2** EDUCATE : criar, educar **3** FOSTER : alimentar, fomentar
nurture[2] *n* **1** UPBRINGING : crianza *f*, educación *f* **2** FOOD : alimento *m*
nut ['nʌt] *n* **1** : nuez *f* **2** : tuerca *f* ⟨nuts and bolts : tuercas y tornillos⟩ **3** LUNATIC : loco *m*, -ca *f*; chiflado *m*, -da *f fam* **4** ENTHUSIAST : fanático *m*, -ca *f*; entusiasta *mf*
nutcracker ['nʌt,krækər] *n* : cascanueces *m*
nuthatch ['nʌt,hætʃ] *n* : trepador *m*
nutmeg ['nʌt,mɛg] *n* : nuez *f* moscada
nutrient ['nu:triənt, 'nju:-] *n* : nutriente *m*, alimento *m* nutritivo
nutriment ['nu:trəmənt, 'nju:-] *n* : nutrimento *m*
nutrition [nʊ'trɪʃən, nju-] *n* : nutrición *f*
nutritional [nʊ'trɪʃənəl, nju-] *adj* : alimenticio
nutritious [nʊ'trɪʃəs, nju-] *adj* : nutritivo, alimenticio

nuts ['nʌts] *adj* **1** FANATICAL : fanático **2** CRAZY : loco, chiflado *fam*
nutshell ['nʌt,ʃel] *n* **1** : cáscara *f* de nuez **2 in a nutshell** : en pocas palabras
nutty ['nʌti] *adj* **-tier; -tiest** : loco, chiflado *fam*

nuzzle ['nʌzəl] *v* **-zled; -zling** *vi* NESTLE : acurrucarse, arrimarse — *vt* : acariciar con el hocico
nylon ['naɪ,lɑn] *n* **1** : nilón *m* **2 nylons** *npl* : medias *fpl* de nilón
nymph ['nɪmpf] *n* : ninfa *f*

O

o ['o:] *n, pl* **o's** *or* **os** ['o:z] **1** : decimoquinta letra del alfabeto inglés **2** ZERO : cero *m*
O ['o:] → **oh**
oaf ['o:f] *n* : zoquete *m*; bruto *m*, -ta *f*
oafish ['o:fɪʃ] *adj* : torpe, lerdo
oak ['o:k] *n, pl* **oaks** *or* **oak** : roble *m*
oaken ['o:kən] *adj* : de roble
oar ['or] *n* : remo *m*
oarlock ['or,lɑk] *n* : tolete *m*, escálamo *m*
oasis [o'eɪsɪs] *n, pl* **oases** [-,si:z] : oasis *m*
oat ['o:t] *n* : avena *f*
oath ['o:θ] *n, pl* **oaths** ['o:ðz, 'o:θs] **1** : juramento *m* ⟨to take an oath : prestar juramento⟩ **2** SWEARWORD : mala palabra *f*, palabrota *f*
oatmeal ['o:t,mi:l] *n* : avena *f* ⟨instant oatmeal : avena instantánea⟩
obdurate ['ɑbdʊrət, -djʊ-] *adj* : inflexible, firme, obstinado
obedience [o'bi:diənts] *n* : obediencia *f*
obedient [o'bi:diənt] *adj* : obediente — **obediently** *adv*
obelisk ['ɑbə,lɪsk] *n* : obelisco *m*
obese [o'bi:s] *adj* : obeso
obesity [o'bi:səti] *n* : obesidad *f*
obey [o'beɪ] *v* **obeyed; obeying** : obedecer ⟨to obey the law : cumplir la ley⟩
obfuscate ['ɑbfə,skeɪt] *vt* **-cated; -cating** : ofuscar, confundir
obituary [ə'bɪtʃu,ɛri] *n, pl* **-aries** : obituario *m*, necrología *f*
object¹ [əb'dʒɛkt] *vt* : objetar — *vi* : oponerse, poner reparos, hacer objeciones
object² ['ɑbdʒɪkt] *n* **1** : objeto *m* **2** OBJECTIVE, PURPOSE : objetivo *m*, propósito *m* **3** : complemento *m* (en gramática)
objection [əb'dʒɛkʃən] *n* : objeción *f*
objectionable [əb'dʒɛkʃənəbəl] *adj* : ofensivo, indeseable — **objectionably** [-bli] *adv*
objective¹ [əb'dʒɛktɪv] *adj* **1** IMPARTIAL : objetivo, imparcial **2** : de complemento, directo (en gramática)
objective² *n* **1** : objetivo *m* **2** *or* **objective case** : acusativo *m*
objectively [əb'dʒɛktɪvli] *adv* : objetivamente
objectivity [,ɑb,dʒɛk'tɪvəti] *n, pl* **-ties** : objetividad *f*
obligate ['ɑblə,geɪt] *vt* **-gated; -gating** : obligar
obligation [,ɑblə'geɪʃən] *n* : obligación *f*

obligatory [ə'blɪgə,tori] *adj* : obligatorio
oblige [ə'blaɪdʒ] *vt* **obliged; obliging 1** COMPEL : obligar **2** : hacerle un favor (a alguien), complacer ⟨to oblige a friend : hacerle un favor a un amigo⟩ **3 to be much obliged** : estar muy agradecido
obliging [ə'blaɪdʒɪŋ] *adj* : servicial, complaciente — **obligingly** *adv*
oblique [o'bli:k] *adj* **1** SLANTING : oblicuo **2** INDIRECT : indirecto — **obliquely** *adv*
obliterate [ə'blɪtə,reɪt] *vt* **-ated; -ating 1** ERASE : obliterar, borrar **2** DESTROY : destruir, eliminar
obliteration [ə,blɪtə'reɪʃən] *n* : obliteración *f*
oblivion [ə'blɪviən] *n* : olvido *m*
oblivious [ə'blɪviəs] *adj* : inconsciente — **obliviously** *adv*
oblong¹ ['ɑ,blɔŋ] *adj* : oblongo
oblong² *n* : figura *f* oblonga, rectángulo *m*
obnoxious [ɑb'nɑkʃəs, əb-] *adj* : repugnante, odioso — **obnoxiously** *adv*
oboe ['o:,bo:] *n* : oboe *m*
oboist ['o:,boɪst] *n* : oboe *mf*
obscene [ɑb'si:n, əb-] *adj* : obsceno, indecente — **obscenely** *adv*
obscenity [ɑb'sɛnəti, əb-] *n, pl* **-ties** : obscenidad *f*
obscure¹ [ɑb'skjʊr, əb-] *vt* **-scured; -scuring 1** CLOUD, DIM : oscurecer, nublar **2** HIDE : ocultar
obscure² *adj* **1** DIM : oscuro **2** REMOTE, SECLUDED : recóndito **3** VAGUE : oscuro, confuso, vago **4** UNKNOWN : desconocido ⟨an obscure poet : un poeta desconocido⟩ — **obscurely** *adv*
obscurity [ɑb'skjʊrəti, əb-] *n, pl* **-ties** : oscuridad *f*
obsequious [əb'si:kwiəs] *adj* : servil, excesivamente atento
observable [əb'zɜrvəbəl] *adj* : observable, perceptible
observance [əb'zɜrvənts] *n* **1** FULFILLMENT : observancia *f*, cumplimiento *m* **2** PRACTICE : práctica *f*
observant [əb'zɜrvənt] *adj* : observador
observation [,ɑbsər'veɪʃən, -zər-] *n* : observación *f*
observatory [əb'zɜrvə,tori] *n, pl* **-ries** : observatorio *m*
observe [əb'zɜrv] *v* **-served; -serving** *vt* **1** OBEY : observar, obedecer **2** CELEBRATE : celebrar, guardar (una práctica religiosa) **3** WATCH : observar, mi-

rar **4** REMARK : observar, comentar — *vi* LOOK : mirar

observer [ab'zərvər] *n* : observador *m*, -dora *f*

obsess [əb'sɛs] *vt* : obsesionar

obsession [ab'sɛʃən, əb-] *n* : obsesión *f*

obsessive [ab'sɛsɪv, əb-] *adj* : obsesivo — **obsessively** *adv*

obsolescence [ˌabsə'lɛsənts] *n* : obsolescencia *f*

obsolescent [ˌabsə'lɛsənt] *adj* : obsolescente ⟨to become obsolescent : caer en desuso⟩

obsolete [ˌabsə'liːt, 'absəˌ-] *adj* : obsoleto, anticuado

obstacle ['abstɪkəl] *n* : obstáculo *m*, impedimento *m*

obstetric [əb'stɛtrɪk] *or* **obstetrical** [-trɪkəl] *adj* : obstétrico

obstetrician [ˌabstə'trɪʃən] *n* : obstetra *mf*; tocólogo *m*, -ga *f*

obstetrics [əb'stɛtrɪks] *ns & pl* : obstetricia *f*, tocología *f*

obstinacy ['abstənəsi] *n, pl* **-cies** : obstinación *f*, terquedad *f*

obstinate ['abstənət] *adj* : obstinado, terco — **obstinately** *adv*

obstreperous [əb'strɛpərəs] *adj* **1** CLAMOROUS : ruidoso, clamoroso **2** UNRULY : rebelde, indisciplinado

obstruct [əb'strʌkt] *vt* : obstruir, bloquear

obstruction [əb'strʌkʃən] *n* : obstrucción *f*, bloqueo *m*

obstructive [əb'strəktɪv] *adj* : obstructor

obtain [əb'teɪn] *vt* : obtener, conseguir — *vi* PREVAIL : imperar, prevalecer

obtainable [əb'teɪnəbəl] *adj* : obtenible, asequible

obtrude [əb'truːd] *v* **-truded; -truding** *vt* **1** EXTRUDE : expulsar **2** IMPOSE : imponer — *vi* INTRUDE : inmiscuirse, entrometerse

obtrusive [əb'truːsɪv] *adj* **1** IMPERTINENT, MEDDLESOME : impertinente, entrometido **2** PROTRUDING : prominente

obtuse [ab'tuːs, əb-, -'tjuːs] *adj* : obtuso, torpe

obtuse angle *n* : ángulo obtuso

obviate ['abviˌeɪt] *vt* **-ated; -ating** : obviar, evitar

obvious ['abviəs] *adj* : obvio, evidente, manifiesto

obviously ['abviəsli] *adv* **1** CLEARLY : obviamente, evidentemente **2** OF COURSE : claro, por supuesto

occasion¹ [ə'keɪʒən] *vt* : ocasionar, causar

occasion² *n* **1** OPPORTUNITY : oportunidad *f*, ocasión *f* **2** CAUSE : motivo *m*, razón *f* **3** INSTANCE : ocasión *f* **4** EVENT : ocasión *f*, acontecimiento *m* **5 on ~** : de vez en cuando, ocasionalmente

occasional [ə'keɪʒənəl] *adj* : ocasional

occasionally [ə'keɪʒənəli] *adv* : de vez en cuando, ocasionalmente

occidental [ˌaksə'dɛntəl] *adj* : oeste, del oeste, occidental

occult¹ [ə'kʌlt, 'aˌkʌlt] *adj* **1** HIDDEN, SECRET : oculto, secreto **2** ARCANE : arcano, esotérico

occult² *n* **the occult** : las ciencias ocultas

occupancy ['akjəpəntsi] *n, pl* **-cies** : ocupación *f*, habitación *f*

occupant ['akjəpənt] *n* : ocupante *mf*

occupation [ˌakjə'peɪʃən] *n* : ocupación *f*, profesión *f*, oficio *m*

occupational [ˌakjə'peɪʃənəl] *adj* : ocupacional

occupy ['akjəˌpaɪ] *vt* **-pied; -pying** : ocupar

occur [ə'kər] *vi* **occurred; occurring 1** EXIST : encontrarse, existir **2** HAPPEN : ocurrir, acontecer, suceder, tener lugar **3** : ocurrirse ⟨it occurred to him that . . . : se le ocurrió que . . . ⟩

occurrence [ə'kərənts] *n* : acontecimiento *m*, suceso *m*, ocurrencia *f*

ocean ['oːʃən] *n* : océano *m*

oceanic [ˌoːʃi'ænɪk] *adj* : oceánico

oceanography [ˌoːʃə'nagrəfi] *n* : oceanografía *f*

ocelot ['asəˌlat, 'oː-] *n* : ocelote *m*

ocher *or* **ochre** ['oːkər] *n* : ocre *m*

o'clock [ə'klak] *adv* (*used in telling time*) ⟨it's ten o'clock : son las diez⟩ ⟨at six o'clock : a las seis⟩

octagon ['aktəˌgan] *n* : octágono *m*

octagonal [ak'tægənəl] *adj* : octagonal

octave ['aktɪv] *n* : octava *f*

October [ak'toːbər] *n* : octubre *m*

octopus ['aktəˌpus, -pəs] *n, pl* **-puses** *or* **-pi** [-ˌpaɪ] : pulpo *m*

ocular ['akjələr] *adj* : ocular

oculist ['akjəlɪst] *n* **1** OPHTHALMOLOGIST : oftalmólogo *m*, -ga *f*; oculista *mf* **2** OPTOMETRIST : optometrista *mf*

odd ['ad] *adj* **1** : sin pareja, suelto ⟨an odd sock : un calcetín sin pareja⟩ **2** UNEVEN : impar ⟨odd numbers : números impares⟩ **3** : y pico, y tantos ⟨forty odd years ago : hace cuarenta y pico años⟩ **4** : alguno, uno que otro ⟨odd jobs : algunos trabajos⟩ **5** STRANGE : extraño, raro

oddball ['adˌbɔl] *n* : excéntrico *m*, -ca *f*; persona *f* rara

oddity ['adəti] *n, pl* **-ties** : rareza *f*, cosa *f* rara

oddly ['adli] *adv* : de manera extraña

oddness ['adnəs] *n* : rareza *f*, excentricidad *f*

odds ['adz] *npl* **1** CHANCES : probabilidades *fpl* **2** : puntos *mpl* de ventaja (de una apuesta) **3 to be at odds** : estar en desacuerdo

odds and ends *npl* : costillas *fpl*, cosas *fpl* sueltas, cachivaches *mpl*

ode ['oːd] *n* : oda *f*

odious ['oːdiəs] *adj* : odioso — **odiously** *adv*

odor ['oːdər] *n* : olor *m*

odorless ['oːdərləs] *adj* : inodoro, sin olor

odorous [ˈoːdərəs] *adj* : oloroso
odyssey [ˈɑdəsi] *n, pl* **-seys** : odisea *f*
o'er [ˈor] → **over**
of [ˈʌv, ˈəv] *prep* **1** FROM : de ⟨a man of the city : un hombre de la ciudad⟩ **2** (*indicating character or background*) : de ⟨a woman of great ability : una mujer de gran capacidad⟩ **3** (*indicating cause*) : de ⟨he died of the flu : murió de la gripe⟩ **4** BY : de ⟨the works of Shakespeare : las obras de Shakespeare⟩ **5** (*indicating contents, material, or quantity*) : de ⟨a house of wood : una casa de madera⟩ ⟨a glass of water : un vaso de agua⟩ **6** (*indicating belonging or connection*) : de ⟨the front of the house : el frente de la casa⟩ **7** ABOUT : sobre, de ⟨tales of the West : los cuentos del Oeste⟩ **8** (*indicating a particular example*) : de ⟨the city of Caracas : la ciudad de Caracas⟩ **9** FOR : por, a ⟨love of country : amor por la patria⟩ **10** (*indicating time or date*) ⟨five minutes of ten : las diez menos cinco⟩ ⟨the eighth of April : el ocho de abril⟩
off¹ [ˈɔf] *adv* **1** (*indicating change of position or state*) ⟨to march off : marcharse⟩ ⟨he dozed off : se puso a dormir⟩ **2** (*indicating distance in space or time*) ⟨some miles off : a varias millas⟩ ⟨the holiday is three weeks off : faltan tres semanas para la fiesta⟩ **3** (*indicating removal*) ⟨the knob came off : se le cayó el pomo⟩ **4** (*indicating termination*) ⟨shut the television off : apaga la televisión⟩ **5** (*indicating suspension of work*) ⟨to take a day off : tomarse un día de descanso⟩ **6 off and on** : de vez en cuando
off² *adj* **1** FARTHER : más remoto, distante ⟨the off side of the building : el lado distante del edificio⟩ **2** STARTED : empezado ⟨to be off on a spree : irse de juerga⟩ **3** OUT : apagado ⟨the light is off : la luz está apagada⟩ **4** CANCELED : cancelado, suspendido **5** INCORRECT : erróneo, incorrecto **6** REMOTE : remoto, lejano ⟨an off chance : una posibilidad remota⟩ **7** FREE : libre ⟨I'm off today : hoy estoy libre⟩ **8 to be well off** : vivir con desahogo, tener bastante dinero
off³ *prep* **1** (*indicating physical separation*) : de ⟨she took it off the table : lo tomó de la mesa⟩ ⟨a shop off the main street : una tienda al lado de la calle principal⟩ **2** : a la costa de, a expensas de ⟨he lives off his sister : vive a expensas de su hermana⟩ **3** (*indicating the suspension of an activity*) ⟨to be off duty : estar libre⟩ ⟨he's off liquor : ha dejado el alcohol⟩ **4** BELOW : por debajo de ⟨he's off his game : está por debajo de su juego normal⟩
offal [ˈɔfəl] *n* **1** RUBBISH, WASTE : desechos *mpl*, desperdicios *mpl* **2** VISCERA : vísceras *fpl*, asaduras *fpl*

offend [əˈfɛnd] *vt* **1** VIOLATE : violar, atentar contra **2** HURT : ofender ⟨to be easily offended : ser muy susceptible⟩
offender [əˈfɛndər] *n* : delincuente *mf*; infractor *m*, -tora *f*
offense *or* **offence** [əˈfɛns, ˈɔˌfɛns] *n* **1** INSULT : ofensa *f*, injuria *f*, agravio *m* ⟨to take offense : ofenderse⟩ **2** ASSAULT : ataque *m* **3** : ofensiva *f* (en deportes) **4** CRIME, INFRACTION : infracción *f*, delito *m*
offensive¹ [əˈfɛnsɪv, ˈɔˌfɛnt-] *adj* : ofensivo — **offensively** *adv*
offensive² *n* : ofensiva *f*
offer¹ [ˈɔfər] *vt* **1** : ofrecer ⟨they offered him the job : le ofrecieron el puesto⟩ **2** PROPOSE : proponer, sugerir **3** SHOW : ofrecer, mostrar ⟨to offer resistance : ofrecer resistencia⟩
offer² *n* : oferta *f*, ofrecimiento *m*, propuesta *f*
offering [ˈɔfərɪŋ] *n* : ofrenda *f*
offhand¹ [ˈɔfˈhænd] *adv* : sin preparación, sin pensarlo
offhand² *adj* **1** IMPROMPTU : improvisado **2** ABRUPT : brusco
office [ˈɔfəs] *n* **1** : cargo *m* ⟨to run for office : presentarse como candidato⟩ **2** : oficina *f*, despacho *m*, gabinete *m* (en la casa) ⟨office hours : horas de oficina⟩
officeholder [ˈɔfəsˌhoːldər] *n* : titular *mf*
officer [ˈɔfəsər] *n* **1** *or* **police officer** : policía *mf*, agente *mf* de policía **2** OFFICIAL : oficial *mf*; funcionario *m*, -ria *f*; director *m*, -tora *f* (en una empresa) **3** COMMISSIONED OFFICER : oficial *mf*
official¹ [əˈfɪʃəl] *adj* : oficial — **officially** *adv*
official² *n* : funcionario *m*, -ria *f*; oficial *mf*
officiate [əˈfɪʃiˌeɪt] *v* **-ated; -ating** *vi* **1** : arbitrar (en deportes) **2 to officiate at** : oficiar, celebrar — *vt* : arbitrar
officious [əˈfɪʃəs] *adj* : oficioso
offing [ˈɔfɪŋ] *n* **in the offing** : en perspectiva
offset [ˈɔfˌsɛt] *vt* **-set; -setting** : compensar
offshoot [ˈɔfˌʃuːt] *n* **1** OUTGROWTH : producto *m*, resultado *m* **2** BRANCH, SHOOT : retoño *m*, rama *f*, vástago *m* (de una planta)
offshore¹ [ˈɔfˈʃor] *adv* : a una distancia de la costa
offshore² *adj* **1** : de (la) tierra ⟨an offshore wind : un viento que sopla de tierra⟩ **2** : (de) costa afuera, cercano a la costa ⟨an offshore island : una isla costera⟩
offspring [ˈɔfˌsprɪŋ] *ns & pl* **1** YOUNG : crías *fpl* (de los animales) **2** PROGENY : prole *f*, progenie *f*
off-white [ˈɔfˈhwaɪt] *adj* : blancuzco
often [ˈɔfən, ˈɔftən] *adv* : muchas veces, a menudo, seguido

oftentimes ['ɔfən̩ₜtaɪmz, 'ɔftən-] *or* **oft-times** ['ɔftₜtaɪms] → **often**
ogle ['o:gəl] *vt* **ogled; ogling** : comerse con los ojos, quedarse mirando a
ogre ['o:gər] *n* : ogro *m*
oh ['o:] *interj* : ¡oh!, ¡ah!, ¡ay! ⟨oh, of course : ah, por supuesto⟩ ⟨oh no! : ¡ay no!⟩ ⟨oh really? : ¿de veras?⟩
ohm ['o:m] *n* : ohm *m*, ohmio *m*
oil¹ ['ɔɪl] *vt* : lubricar, engrasar, aceitar
oil² *n* **1** : aceite *m* **2** PETROLEUM : petróleo *m* **3** *or* **oil painting** : óleo *m*, pintura *f* al óleo **4** *or* **oil paint(s)** : óleo *m*
oilcloth ['ɔɪl̩klɔθ] *n* : hule *m*
oiliness ['ɔɪlinəs] *n* : lo aceitoso
oilskin ['ɔɪl̩skɪn] *n* **1** : hule *m* **2 oilskins** *npl* : impermeable *m*
oily ['ɔɪli] *adj* **oilier; -est** : aceitoso, grasiento, grasoso ⟨oily fingers : dedos grasientos⟩
ointment ['ɔɪntmənt] *n* : ungüento *m*, pomada *f*
OK¹ [ₒo:'keɪ] *vt* **OK'd** *or* **okayed** [ₒo:'keɪd]; **OK'ing** *or* **okaying** APPROVE, AUTHORIZE : dar el visto bueno a, autorizar, aprobar
OK² *or* **okay** [ₒo:'keɪ] *adv* **1** WELL : bien **2** YES : sí, por supuesto
OK³ *adj* : bien ⟨he's OK : está bien⟩ ⟨it's OK with me : estoy de acuerdo⟩
OK⁴ *n* : autorización *f*, visto *m* bueno
okra ['o:krə, *South also* -kri] *n* : quingombó *m*
old¹ ['o:ld] *adj* **1** ANCIENT : antiguo ⟨old civilizations : civilizaciones antiguas⟩ **2** FAMILIAR : viejo ⟨old friends : viejos amigos⟩ ⟨the same old story : el mismo cuento⟩ **3** (*indicating a certain age*) ⟨he's ten years old : tiene diez años (de edad)⟩ **4** AGED : viejo, anciano ⟨an old woman : una anciana⟩ **5** FORMER : antiguo ⟨her old neighborhood : su antiguo barrio⟩ **6** WORN-OUT : viejo, gastado
old² *n* **1 the old** : los viejos, los ancianos **2 in the days of old** : antaño, en los tiempos antiguos
olden ['o:ldən] *adj* : de antaño, de antigüedad
old-fashioned ['o:ld'fæʃənd] *adj* : anticuado, pasado de moda
old maid *n* **1** SPINSTER : soltera *f* **2** FUSSBUDGET : maniático *m*, -ca *f*; melindroso *m*, -sa *f*
Old Testament *n* : Antiguo Testamento *m*
old-time ['o:ld'taɪm] *adj* : antiguo
old-timer ['o:ld'taɪmər] *n* **1** VETERAN : veterano *m*, -na *f* **2** *or* **oldster** : anciano *m*, -na *f*
old-world ['o:ld'wərld] *adj* : pintoresco (de antaño)
oleander ['o:li,ændər] *n* : adelfa *f*
oleomargarine [ₒo:lio'mɑrdʒərən] → **margarine**
olfactory [ɑl'fæktəri, ol-] *adj* : olfativo
oligarchy ['ɑlə,gɑrki, 'o:lə-] *n, pl* **-chies** : oligarquía *f*

olive ['ɑlɪv, -ləv] *n* **1** : aceituna *f*, oliva *f* (fruta) **2** : olivo *m* (árbol) **3** *or* **olive green** : color *m* aceituna, verde *m* oliva
Olmec ['ɑl̩mɛk, 'o:l-] *n* : olmeca *mf* — **Olmec** *adj*
Olympic [ə'lɪmpɪk, o-] *adj* : olímpico
Olympic Games *npl* : Juegos *mpl* Olímpicos
Olympics [ə'lɪmpɪks, o-] *npl* : olimpiadas *fpl*
Omani [o'mɑni, -'mæ-] *n* : omaní *mf* — **Omani** *adj*
ombudsman ['ɑm̩bʊdzmən, ɑm-'bʊdz-] *n, pl* **-men** [-mən, -ₜmɛn] : ombudsman *m*
omelet *or* **omelette** ['ɑmlət, 'ɑmə-] *n* : omelette *mf*, tortilla *f* (de huevo)
omen ['o:mən] *n* : presagio *m*, augurio *m*, agüero *m*
ominous ['ɑmənəs] *adj* : ominoso, agorero, de mal agüero
ominously ['ɑmənəsli] *adv* : de manera amenazadora
omission [o'mɪʃən] *n* : omisión *f*
omit [o'mɪt] *vt* **omitted; omitting 1** LEAVE OUT : omitir, excluir **2** NEGLECT : omitir ⟨they omitted to tell us : omitieron decírnoslo⟩
omnipotence [ɑm'nɪpətənts] *n* : omnipotencia *f* — **omnipotent** [ɑm'nɪpətənt] *adj*
omnipresent [ₜɑmnɪ'prɛzənt] *adj* : omnipresente
omniscient [ɑm'nɪʃənt] *adj* : omnisciente
omnivorous [ɑm'nɪvərəs] *adj* **1** : omnívoro **2** AVID : ávido, voraz
on¹ ['ɑn, 'ɔn] *adv* **1** (*indicating contact with a surface*) ⟨put the top on : pon la tapa⟩ ⟨he has a hat on : lleva un sombrero puesto⟩ **2** (*indicating forward movement*) ⟨from that moment on : a partir de ese momento⟩ ⟨farther on : más adelante⟩ **3** (*indicating operation or an operating position*) ⟨turn the light on : prende la luz⟩
on² *adj* **1** (*being in operation*) ⟨the radio is on : el radio está prendido⟩ **2** (*taking place*) ⟨the game is on : el juego ha comenzado⟩ **3 to be on to** : estar enterado de
on³ *prep* **1** (*indicating position*) : en, sobre, encima de ⟨on the table : en (sobre, encima de) la mesa⟩ ⟨shadows on the wall : sombras en la pared⟩ ⟨on horseback : a caballo⟩ **2** AT, TO : a ⟨on the right : a la derecha⟩ **3** ABOARD, IN : en, a ⟨on the plane : en el avión⟩ ⟨he got on the train : subió al tren⟩ **4** (*indicating time*) ⟨she worked on Saturdays : trabajaba los sábados⟩ ⟨every hour on the hour : a la hora en punto⟩ **5** (*indicating means or agency*) : por ⟨he cut himself on a tin can : se cortó con una lata⟩ ⟨to talk on the telephone : hablar por teléfono⟩ **6** (*indicating a state or process*) : en ⟨on fire : en llamas⟩ ⟨on the increase : en aumen-

to⟩ **7** (*indicating connection or membership*) : en ⟨on a committee : en una comisión⟩ **8** (*indicating an activity*) ⟨on vacation : de vacaciones⟩ ⟨on a diet : a dieta⟩ **9** ABOUT, CONCERNING : sobre ⟨a book on insects : un libro sobre insectos⟩ ⟨reflect on that : reflexiona sobre eso⟩

once¹ [ˈwʌnts] *adv* **1** : una vez ⟨once a month : una vez al mes⟩ ⟨once and for all : de una vez por todas⟩ **2** EVER : alguna vez **3** FORMERLY : antes, anteriormente

once² *adj* FORMER : antiguo

once³ *n* **1** : una vez **2** at ~ SIMULTANEOUSLY : al mismo tiempo, simultáneamente **3** at ~ IMMEDIATELY : inmediatamente, en seguida

once⁴ *conj* : una vez que, tan pronto como

once–over [ˌwʌnts'oːvər, 'wʌnts₁-] *n* **to give someone the once–over** : echarle un vistazo a alguien

oncoming [ˈɑnˌkʌmɪŋ, 'ɔn-] *adj* : que viene

one¹ [ˈwʌn] *adj* **1** (*being a single unit*) : un, una ⟨he only wants one apple : sólo quiere una manzana⟩ **2** (*being a particular one*) : un, una ⟨he arrived early one morning : llegó temprano una mañana⟩ **3** (*being the same*) : mismo, misma ⟨they're all members of one team : todos son miembros del mismo equipo⟩ ⟨one and the same thing : la misma cosa⟩ **4** SOME : alguno, alguna; un, una ⟨I'll see you again one day : algún día te veré otra vez⟩ ⟨at one time or another : en una u otra ocasión⟩

one² *n* **1** : uno *m* (número) **2** (*indicating the first of a set or series*) ⟨from day one : desde el primer momento⟩ **3** (*indicating a single person or thing*) ⟨the one (girl) on the right : la de la derecha⟩ ⟨he has the one but needs the other : tiene uno pero necesita el otro⟩

one³ *pron* **1** : uno, una ⟨one of his friends : una de sus amigas⟩ ⟨one never knows : uno nunca sabe, nunca se sabe⟩ ⟨to cut one's finger : cortarse el dedo⟩ **2 one and all** : todos, todo el mundo **3 one another** : el uno al otro, se ⟨they loved one another : se amaban⟩ **4 that one** : aquél, aquella **5 which one?** : ¿cuál?

one–on–one [ˌwʌnɔn'wʌn, -ɑn-] *adj* : uno a uno — **one–on–one** *adv*

onerous [ˈɑnərəs, 'oːnə-] *adj* : oneroso, gravoso

oneself [ˌwʌn'sɛlf] *pron* **1** (*used reflexively or for emphasis*) : se, sí mismo, uno mismo ⟨to control oneself : controlarse⟩ ⟨to talk to oneself : hablarse a sí mismo⟩ ⟨to do it oneself : hacérselo uno mismo⟩ **2 by ~** : solo

one–sided [ˈwʌn'saɪdəd] *adj* **1** : de un solo lado **2** LOPSIDED : asimétrico **3** BIASED : parcial, tendencioso **4** UNILATERAL : unilateral

onetime [ˈwʌn'taɪm] *adj* FORMER : antiguo

one–way [ˈwʌn'weɪ] *adj* **1** : de sentido único, de una sola dirección ⟨a one-way street : una calle de sentido único⟩ **2** : de ida, sencillo ⟨a one-way ticket : un boleto de ida⟩

ongoing [ˈɑnˌgoːɪŋ] *adj* **1** CONTINUING : en curso, corriente **2** DEVELOPING : en desarrollo

onion [ˈʌnjən] *n* : cebolla *f*

online [ˈɔn'laɪn, 'ɑn-] *adj* : en línea

onlooker [ˈɔnˌlʊkər, 'ɑn-] *n* : espectador *m*, -dora *f*, circunstante *mf*

only¹ [ˈoːnli] *adv* **1** MERELY : sólo, solamente, nomás ⟨for only two dollars : por tan sólo dos dólares⟩ ⟨only once : sólo una vez, no más de una vez⟩ ⟨I only did it to help : lo hice por ayudar nomás⟩ **2** SOLELY : únicamente, sólo, solamente ⟨only he knows it : solamente él lo sabe⟩ **3** (*indicating a result*) ⟨it will only cause him problems : no hará más que crearle problemas⟩ **4 if only** : ojalá, por lo menos ⟨if only it were true! : ¡ojalá sea cierto!⟩ ⟨if he could only dance : si por lo menos pudiera bailar⟩

only² *adj* : único ⟨an only child : un hijo único⟩ ⟨the only chance : la única oportunidad⟩

only³ *conj* BUT : pero ⟨I would go, only I'm sick : iría, pero estoy enfermo⟩

onset [ˈɑnˌsɛt] *n* : comienzo *m*, llegada *f*

onslaught [ˈɑnˌslɔt, 'ɔn-] *n* : arremetida *f*, embestida *f*, embate *m*

onto [ˈɑnˌtuː, 'ɔn-] *prep* : sobre

onus [ˈoːnəs] *n* : responsabilidad *f*, carga *f*

onward¹ [ˈɑnwərd, 'ɔn-] *or* **onwards** *adv* FORWARD : adelante, hacia adelante

onward² *adj* : hacia adelante

onyx [ˈɑnɪks] *n* : ónix *m*

ooze¹ [ˈuːz] *v* **oozed; oozing** *vi* : rezumar — *vt* **1** : rezumar **2** EXUDE : irradiar, rebosar ⟨to ooze confidence : irradiar confianza⟩

ooze² *n* SLIME : cieno *m*, limo *m*

opacity [oˈpæsəti] *n, pl* **-ties** : opacidad *f*

opal [ˈoːpəl] *n* : ópalo *m*

opaque [oˈpeɪk] *adj* **1** : opaco **2** UNCLEAR : poco claro

open¹ [ˈoːpən] *vt* **1** : abrir ⟨open the door : abre la puerta⟩ **2** UNCOVER : destapar **3** UNFOLD : desplegar, abrir **4** CLEAR : abrir (un camino, etc.) **5** INAUGURATE : abrir (una tienda), inaugurar (una exposición, etc.) **6** INITIATE : iniciar, entablar, abrir ⟨to open the meeting : abrir la sesión⟩ ⟨to open a discussion : entablar un debate⟩ — *vi* **1** : abrirse **2** BEGIN : empezar, comenzar

open² *adj* **1** : abierto ⟨an open window : una ventana abierta⟩ **2** FRANK : abierto, franco, directo **3** UNCOV-

ERED : descubierto, abierto **4** EX-
TENDED : extendido, abierto ⟨with
open arms : con los brazos abiertos⟩ **5**
UNRESTRICTED : libre, abierto **6** UN-
DECIDED : pendiente, por decidir, sin
resolver ⟨an open question : una
cuestión pendiente⟩ **7** AVAILABLE : vacante, libre ⟨the job is open : el puesto
está vacante⟩
open³ *n* **in the open 1** OUTDOORS : al
aire libre **2** KNOWN : conocido, saca-
do a la luz
open–air [ˈoːpənˈær] *adj* OUTDOOR : al
aire libre
open–and–shut [ˈoːpənəndˈʃʌt] *adj*
: claro, evidente ⟨an open-and-shut
case : un caso muy claro⟩
opener [ˈoːpənər] *n* : destapador *m*,
abrelatas *m*, abridor *m*
openhanded [ˌoːpənˈhændəd] *adj* : generoso, liberal
openhearted [ˌoːpənˈhɑrtəd] *adj* **1**
FRANK : franco, sincero **2** : generoso,
de gran corazón
opening [ˈoːpənɪŋ] *n* **1** BEGINNING
: comienzo *m*, principio *m*, apertura *f*
2 APERTURE : abertura *f*, brecha *f*, claro
m (en el bosque) **3** OPPORTUNITY
: oportunidad *f*
openly [ˈoːpənli] *adv* **1** FRANKLY : abiertamente, francamente **2** PUBLICLY
: públicamente, declaradamente
openness [ˈoːpənnəs] *n* : franqueza *f*
opera [ˈɑprə, ˈɑpərə] *n* **1** : ópera *f* **2** →
opus
opera glasses *npl* : gemelos *mpl* de
teatro
operate [ˈɑpəˌreɪt] *v* **-ated; -ating** *vi* **1**
ACT, FUNCTION : operar, funcionar, ac-
tuar **2 to operate on (someone)** : operar a (alguien) — *vt* **1** WORK : operar, manejar, hacer funcionar (una
máquina) **2** MANAGE : manejar, administrar (un negocio)
operatic [ˌɑpəˈrætɪk] *adj* : operístico
operation [ˌɑpəˈreɪʃən] *n* **1** FUNCTION-
ING : funcionamiento *m* **2** USE : uso
m, manejo *m* (de máquinas) **3**
SURGERY : operación *f*, intervención *f*
quirúrgica
operational [ˌɑpəˈreɪʃənəl] *adj* : operacional, de operación
operative [ˈɑpərətɪv, -ˌreɪ-] *adj* **1** OPER-
ATING : vigente, en vigor **2** WORKING
: operativo **3** SURGICAL : quirúrgico
operator [ˈɑpəˌreɪtər] *n* : operador *m*,
-dora *f*
operetta [ˌɑpəˈrɛtə] *n* : opereta *f*
ophthalmologist [ˌɑf,θælˈmɑlədʒɪst,
-θəˈmɑ-] *n* : oftalmólogo *m*, -ga *f*
ophthalmology [ˌɑf,θælˈmɑlədʒi,
-θəˈmɑ-] *n* : oftalmología *f*
opiate [ˈoːpiət, -piˌeɪt] *n* : opiato *m*
opinion [əˈpɪnjən] *n* : opinión *f*
opinionated [əˈpɪnjəˌneɪtəd] *adj* : testarudo, dogmático
opium [ˈoːpiəm] *n* : opio *m*
opossum [əˈpɑsəm] *n* : zarigüeya *f*, oposum *m*

opponent [əˈpoːnənt] *n* : oponente *mf*;
opositor *m*, -tora *f*; contrincante *mf* (en
deportes)
opportune [ˌɑpərˈtuːn, -ˈtjuːn] *adj*
: oportuno — **opportunely** *adv*
opportunist [ˌɑpərˈtuːnɪst, -ˈtjuː-] *n*
: oportunista *mf*
opportunistic [ˌɑpərtuˈnɪstɪk, -tju-] *adj*
: oportunista *mf*
opportunity [ˌɑpərˈtuːnəti, -ˈtjuː-] *n, pl*
-ties : oportunidad *f*, ocasión *f*, chance
m, posibilidades *fpl*
oppose [əˈpoːz] *vt* **-posed; -posing 1** : ir
en contra de, oponerse a ⟨good oppos-
es evil : el bien se opone al mal⟩ **2** COM-
BAT : luchar contra, combatir, resistir
opposite¹ [ˈɑpəzət] *adv* : enfrente
opposite² *adj* **1** FACING : de enfrente
⟨the opposite side : el lado de enfrente⟩
2 CONTRARY : opuesto, contrario ⟨in
opposite directions : en direcciones
contrarias⟩ ⟨the opposite sex : el sexo
opuesto, el otro sexo⟩
opposite³ *n* : lo contrario, lo opuesto
opposite⁴ *prep* : enfrente de, frente a
opposition [ˌɑpəˈzɪʃən] *n* **1** : oposición
f, resistencia *f* **2 in opposition to**
AGAINST : en contra de
oppress [əˈprɛs] *vt* **1** PERSECUTE
: oprimir, perseguir **2** BURDEN
: oprimir, agobiar
oppression [əˈprɛʃən] *n* : opresión *f*
oppressive [əˈprɛsɪv] *adj* **1** HARSH
: opresivo, severo **2** STIFLING : agobiante, sofocante ⟨oppressive heat
: calor sofocante⟩
oppressor [əˈprɛsər] *n* : opresor *m*, -sora
f
opprobrium [əˈproːbriəm] *n* : oprobio *m*
opt [ˈɑpt] *vi* : optar
optic [ˈɑptɪk] *or* **optical** [-tɪkəl] *adj* : óptico
optical disk *n* : disco *m* óptico
optician [ɑpˈtɪʃən] *n* : óptico *m*, -ca *f*
optics [ˈɑptɪks] *npl* : óptica *f*
optimal [ˈɑptəməl] *adj* : óptimo
optimism [ˈɑptəˌmɪzəm] *n* : optimismo
m
optimist [ˈɑptəmɪst] *n* : optimista *mf*
optimistic [ˌɑptəˈmɪstɪk] *adj* : optimista
optimistically [ˌɑptəˈmɪstɪkli] *adv* : con
optimismo, positivamente
optimum¹ [ˈɑptəməm] *adj* → **optimal**
optimum² *n, pl* **-ma** [ˈɑptəmə] : lo óptimo, lo ideal
option [ˈɑpʃən] *n* : opción *f* ⟨she has no
option : no tiene más remedio⟩
optional [ˈɑpʃənəl] *adj* : facultativo, optativo
optometrist [ɑpˈtɑmətrɪst] *n* : optometrista *mf*
optometry [ɑpˈtɑmətri] *n* : optometría *f*
opulence [ˈɑpjələnts] *n* : opulencia *f*
opulent [ˈɑpjələnt] *adj* : opulento
opus [ˈoːpəs] *n, pl* **opera** [ˈoːpərə, ˈɑpə-]
: opus *m*, obra *f* (de música)
or [ˈɔr] *conj* **1** (*indicating an alternative*)
: o (*u before words beginning with o or
ho*) ⟨coffee or tea : café o té⟩ ⟨one day

or another : un día u otro⟩ 2 (*following a negative*) : ni ⟨he didn't have his keys or his wallet : no llevaba ni sus llaves ni su billetera⟩
oracle ['ɔrəkəl] *n* : oráculo *m*
oral ['ɔrəl] *adj* : oral — **orally** *adv*
orange ['ɔrɪndʒ] *n* 1 : naranja *f*, china *f PRi* (fruto) 2 : naranja *m* (color), color *m* de china *PRi*
orangeade [ˌɔrɪndʒ'eɪd] *n* : naranjada *f*
orangutan [ə'ræŋəˌtæn, -'ræŋgə-, -ˌtæn] *n* : orangután *m*
oration [ə'reɪʃən] *n* : oración *f*, discurso *m*
orator ['ɔrətər] *n* : orador *m*, -dora *f*
oratorio [ˌɔrə'toriˌo:] *n, pl* **-rios** : oratorio *m*
oratory ['ɔrəˌtori] *n, pl* **-ries** : oratoria *f*
orb ['ɔrb] *n* : orbe *m*
orbit¹ ['ɔrbət] *vt* 1 CIRCLE : girar alrededor de, orbitar 2 : poner en órbita (un satélite, etc.) — *vi* : orbitar
orbit² *n* : órbita *f*
orbital ['ɔrbətəl] *adj* : orbital
orchard ['ɔrtʃərd] *n* : huerto *m*
orchestra ['ɔrkəstrə] *n* : orquesta *f*
orchestral [ɔr'kɛstrəl] *adj* : orquestal
orchestrate ['ɔrkəˌstreɪt] *vt* **-trated; -trating** 1 : orquestar, instrumentar (en música) 2 ORGANIZE : arreglar, organizar
orchestration [ˌɔrkə'streɪʃən] *n* : orquestación *f*
orchid ['ɔrkɪd] *n* : orquídea *f*
ordain [ɔr'deɪn] *vt* 1 : ordenar (en religión) 2 DECREE : decretar, ordenar
ordeal [ɔr'di:l, 'ɔrˌdi:l] *n* : prueba *f* dura, experiencia *f* terrible
order¹ ['ɔrdər] *vt* 1 ORGANIZE : arreglar, ordenar, poner en orden 2 COMMAND : ordenar, mandar 3 REQUEST : pedir, encargar ⟨to order a meal : pedir algo de comer⟩ — *vi* : hacer un pedido
order² *n* 1 : orden *f* ⟨a religious order : una orden religiosa⟩ 2 COMMAND : orden *f*, mandato *m* ⟨to give an order : dar una orden⟩ 3 REQUEST : orden *f*, pedido *m* ⟨purchase order : orden de compra⟩ 4 ARRANGEMENT : orden *m* ⟨in chronological order : por orden cronológico⟩ 5 DISCIPLINE : orden *m* ⟨law and order : el orden público⟩ 6 **in order to** : para 7 **out of order** : descompuesto, averiado 8 **orders** *npl or* **holy orders** : órdenes *fpl* sagradas
orderliness ['ɔrdərlinəs] *n* : orden *m*
orderly¹ ['ɔrdərli] *adj* 1 METHODICAL : ordenado, metódico 2 PEACEFUL : pacífico, disciplinado
orderly² *n, pl* **-lies** 1 : ordenanza *m* (en el ejército) 2 : camillero *m* (en un hospital)
ordinal ['ɔrdənəl] *n or* **ordinal number** : ordinal *m*, número *m* ordinal
ordinance ['ɔrdənənts] *n* : ordenanza *f*, reglamento *m*
ordinarily [ˌɔrdən'ɛrəli] *adv* : ordinariamente, por lo general

ordinary ['ɔrdənˌɛri] *adj* 1 NORMAL, USUAL : normal, usual 2 AVERAGE : común y corriente, normal 3 MEDIOCRE : mediocre, ordinario
ordination [ˌɔrdən'eɪʃən] *n* : ordenación *f*
ordnance ['ɔrdnənts] *n* : artillería *f*
ore ['or] *n* : mineral *m* (metalífero), mena *f*
oregano [ə'rɛgəˌno:] *n* : orégano *m*
organ ['ɔrgən] *n* 1 : órgano *m* (instrumento) 2 : órgano *m* (del cuerpo) 3 PERIODICAL : publicación *f* periódica, órgano *m*
organic [ɔr'gænɪk] *adj* : orgánico — **organically** *adv*
organism ['ɔrgəˌnɪzəm] *n* : organismo *m*
organist ['ɔrgənɪst] *n* : organista *mf*
organization [ˌɔrgənə'zeɪʃən] *n* 1 ORGANIZING : organización *f* 2 BODY : organización *f*, organismo *m*
organizational [ˌɔrgənə'zeɪʃənəl] *adj* : organizativo
organize ['ɔrgəˌnaɪz] *vt* **-nized; -nizing** : organizar, arreglar, poner en orden
organizer ['ɔrgəˌnaɪzər] *n* : organizador *m*, -dora *f*
orgasm ['ɔrˌgæzəm] *n* : orgasmo *m*
orgy ['ɔrdʒi] *n, pl* **-gies** : orgía *f*
orient ['oriˌɛnt] *vt* : orientar
Orient *n* **the Orient** : el Oriente
oriental [ˌori'ɛntəl] *adj* : del Oriente, oriental
Oriental *n* : oriental *mf*
orientation [ˌoriən'teɪʃən] *n* : orientación *f*
orifice ['ɔrəfəs] *n* : orificio *m*
origin ['ɔrədʒən] *n* 1 ANCESTRY : origen *m*, ascendencia *f* 2 SOURCE : origen *m*, raíz *f*, fuente *f*
original¹ [ə'rɪdʒənəl] *adj* : original
original² *n* : original *m*
originality [əˌrɪdʒə'næləti] *n* : originalidad *f*
originally [ə'rɪdʒənəli] *adv* 1 AT FIRST : al principio, originariamente 2 CREATIVELY : originalmente, con originalidad
originate [ə'rɪdʒəˌneɪt] *v* **-nated; -nating** *vt* : originar, iniciar, crear — *vi* 1 BEGIN : originarse, empezar 2 COME : provenir, proceder, derivarse
originator [ə'rɪdʒəˌneɪtər] *n* : creador *m*, -dora *f*; inventor *m*, -tora *f*
oriole ['oriˌo:l, -iəl] *n* : oropéndola *f*
ornament¹ ['ɔrnəmənt] *vt* : adornar, decorar, ornamentar
ornament² *n* : ornamento *m*, adorno *m*, decoración *f*
ornamental [ˌɔrnə'mɛntəl] *adj* : ornamental, de adorno, decorativo
ornamentation [ˌɔrnəmən'teɪʃən, -mɛn-] *n* : ornamentación *f*
ornate [ɔr'neɪt] *adj* : elaborado, recargado
ornery ['ɔrnəri, 'ɑrnəri] *adj* **ornerier; -est** : de mal genio, malhumorado
ornithologist [ˌɔrnə'θɑlədʒɪst] *n* : ornitólogo *m*, -ga *f*

ornithology [ˌɔrnəˈθɑlədʒi] *n, pl* **-gies** : ornitología *f*

orphan¹ [ˈɔrfən] *vt* : dejar huérfano

orphan² *n* : huérfano *m*, -na *f*

orphanage [ˈɔrfənɪdʒ] *n* : orfelinato *m*, orfanato *m*

orthodontics [ˌɔrθəˈdɑntɪks] *n* : ortodoncia *f*

orthodontist [ˌɔrθəˈdɑntɪst] *n* : ortodoncista *mf*

orthodox [ˈɔrθəˌdɑks] *adj* : ortodoxo

orthodoxy [ˈɔrθəˌdɑksi] *n, pl* **-doxies** : ortodoxia *f*

orthographic [ˌɔrθəˈgræfɪk] *adj* : ortográfico

orthography [ɔrˈθɑgrəfi] *n, pl* **-phies** SPELLING : ortografía *f*

orthopedic [ˌɔrθəˈpiːdɪk] *adj* : ortopédico

orthopedics [ˌɔrθəˈpiːdɪks] *ns & pl* : ortopedia *f*

orthopedist [ˌɔrθəˈpiːdɪst] *n* : ortopedista *mf*

oscillate [ˈɑsəˌleɪt] *vi* **-lated; -lating** : oscilar

oscillation [ˌɑsəˈleɪʃən] *n* : oscilación *f*

osmosis [ɑzˈmoːsɪs, ɑs-] *n* : ósmosis *f*, osmosis *f*

osprey [ˈɑspri, -ˌpreɪ] *n* : pigargo *m*

ostensible [ɑˈstɛntsəbəl] *adj* APPARENT : aparente, ostensible — **ostensibly** [-bli] *adv*

ostentation [ˌɑstənˈteɪʃən] *n* : ostentación *f*, boato *m*

ostentatious [ˌɑstənˈteɪʃəs] *adj* : ostentoso — **ostentatiously** *adv*

osteopath [ˈɑstiəˌpæθ] *n* : osteópata *f*

osteopathy [ˌɑstiˈɑpəθi] *n* : osteopatía *f*

osteoporosis [ˌɑstiopəˈroːsɪs] *n, pl* **-roses** [-ˌsiːz] : osteoporosis *f*

ostracism [ˈɑstrəˌsɪzəm] *n* : ostracismo *m*

ostracize [ˈɑstrəˌsaɪz] *vt* **-cized; -cizing** : condenar al ostracismo, marginar, aislar

ostrich [ˈɑstrɪtʃ, ˈɔs-] *n* : avestruz *m*

other¹ [ˈʌðər] *adv* **other than** : aparte de, fuera de

other² *adj* : otro ⟨the other boys : los otros muchachos⟩ ⟨smarter than other people : más inteligente que los demás⟩ ⟨on the other hand : por otra parte, por otro lado⟩ ⟨every other day : cada dos días⟩

other³ *pron* : otro, otra ⟨one in front of the other : uno tras otro⟩ ⟨myself and three others : yo y tres otros, yo y tres más⟩ ⟨somewhere or other : en alguna parte⟩

otherwise¹ [ˈʌðərˌwaɪz] *adv* **1** DIFFERENTLY : de otro modo, de manera distinta ⟨he could not act otherwise : no pudo actuar de manera distinta⟩ **2** : eso aparte, por lo demás ⟨I'm dizzy, but otherwise I'm fine : estoy mareado pero, por lo demás, estoy bien⟩ **3** OR ELSE : de lo contrario, si no ⟨do what I tell you, otherwise you'll be sorry : haz

lo que te digo, de lo contrario, te arrepentirás⟩

otherwise² *adj* : diferente, distinto ⟨the facts are otherwise : la realidad es diferente⟩

otter [ˈɑtər] *n* : nutria *f*

Ottoman [ˈɑtəmən] *n* **1** : otomano *m*, -na *f* **2** : otomana *f* (mueble) — **Ottoman** *adj*

ouch [ˈaʊtʃ] *interj* : ¡ay!, ¡huy!

ought [ˈɔt] *v aux* : deber ⟨you ought to take care of yourself : deberías cuidarte⟩

oughtn't [ˈɔtənt] (*contraction of* **ought not**) → **ought**

ounce [ˈaʊnts] *n* : onza *f*

our [ˈɑr, ˈaʊr] *adj* : nuestro

ours [ˈaʊrz, ˈɑrz] *pron* : nuestro, nuestra ⟨a cousin of ours : un primo nuestro⟩

ourselves [ɑrˈsɛlvz, aʊr-] *pron* **1** (*used reflexively*) : nos, nosotros ⟨we amused ourselves : nos divertimos⟩ ⟨we were always thinking of ourselves : siempre pensábamos en nosotros⟩ **2** (*used for emphasis*) : nosotros mismos, nosotras mismas ⟨we did it ourselves : lo hicimos nosotros mismos⟩

oust [ˈaʊst] *vt* : desbancar, expulsar

ouster [ˈaʊstər] *n* : expulsión *f* (de un país, etc.), destitución *f* (de un puesto)

out¹ [ˈaʊt] *vi* : revelarse, hacerse conocido

out² *adv* **1** (*indicating direction or movement*) : para afuera ⟨she opened the door and looked out : abrió la puerta y miró para afuera⟩ **2** (*indicating a location away from home or work*) : fuera, afuera ⟨to eat out : comer afuera⟩ **3** (*indicating loss of control or possession*) ⟨they let the secret out : sacaron el secreto a la luz⟩ **4** (*indicating completion or discontinuance*) ⟨his money ran out : se le acabó el dinero⟩ ⟨to turn out the light : apagar la luz⟩ **5** OUTSIDE : fuera, afuera ⟨out in the garden : afuera en el jardín⟩ **6** ALOUD : en voz alta, en alto ⟨to cry out : gritar⟩

out³ *adj* **1** EXTERNAL : externo, exterior **2** OUTLYING : alejado, distante ⟨the out islands : las islas distantes⟩ **3** ABSENT : ausente **4** UNFASHIONABLE : fuera de moda **5** EXTINGUISHED : apagado

out⁴ *prep* **1** (*used to indicate an outward movement*) : por ⟨I looked out the window : miré por la ventana⟩ ⟨she ran out the door : corrió por la puerta⟩ **2** → **out of**

out-and-out [ˈaʊtənˈaʊt] *adj* UTTER : redomado, absoluto

outboard motor [ˈaʊtˌbord] *n* : motor *m* fuera de borde

outbound [ˈaʊtˌbaʊnd] *adj* : que sale, de salida

outbreak [ˈaʊtˌbreɪk] *n* : brote *m* (de una enfermedad), comienzo *m* (de guerra), ola *f* (de violencia), erupción *f* (de granos)

outbuilding ['aʊt,bɪldɪŋ] *n* : edificio *m* anexo

outburst ['aʊt,bərst] *n* : arranque *m*, arrebato *m*

outcast ['aʊt,kæst] *n* : marginado *m*, -da *f*; paria *mf*

outcome ['aʊt,kʌm] *n* : resultado *m*, desenlace *m*, consecuencia *f*

outcrop ['aʊt,krɑp] *n* : afloramiento *m*

outcry ['aʊt,kraɪ] *n, pl* **-cries** : clamor *m*, protesta *f*

outdated [,aʊt'deɪtəd] *adj* : anticuado, fuera de moda

outdistance [,aʊt'dɪstənts] *vt* **-tanced; -tancing** : aventajar, dejar atrás

outdo [,aʊt'du:] *vt* **-did** [-'dɪd]; **-done** [-'dʌn]; **-doing; -does** [-'dʌz] : superar

outdoor ['aʊt'dor] *adj* : al aire libre ⟨outdoor sports : deportes al aire libre⟩ ⟨outdoor clothing : ropa de calle⟩

outdoors¹ ['aʊt'dorz] *adv* : afuera, al aire libre

outdoors² *n* : aire *m* libre

outer ['aʊtər] *adj* **1** : exterior, externo **2 outer space** : espacio *m* exterior

outermost ['aʊtər,mo:st] *adj* : más remoto, más exterior, extremo

outfield ['aʊt,fi:ld] *n* **the outfield** : los jardines

outfielder ['aʊt,fi:ldər] *n* : jardinero *m*, -ra *f*

outfit¹ ['aʊt,fɪt] *vt* **-fitted; -fitting** EQUIP : equipar

outfit² *n* **1** EQUIPMENT : equipo *m* **2** COSTUME, ENSEMBLE : traje *m*, conjunto *m* **3** GROUP : conjunto *m*

outgo ['aʊt,go:] *n, pl* **outgoes** : gasto *m*

outgoing ['aʊt,go:ɪŋ] *adj* **1** OUTBOUND : que sale **2** DEPARTING : saliente ⟨an outgoing president : un presidente saliente⟩ **3** EXTROVERTED : extrovertido, expansivo

outgrow [,aʊt'gro:] *vt* **-grew** [-'gru:]; **-grown** [-'gro:n]; **-growing 1** : crecer más que ⟨that tree outgrew all the others : ese árbol creció más que todos los otros⟩ **2 to outgrow one's clothes** : quedarle pequeña la ropa a uno

outgrowth ['aʊt,gro:θ] *n* **1** OFFSHOOT : brote *m*, vástago *m* (de una planta) **2** CONSEQUENCE : consecuencia *f*, producto *m*, resultado *m*

outing ['aʊtɪŋ] *n* : excursión *f*

outlandish [aʊt'lændɪʃ] *adj* : descabellado, muy extraño

outlast [,aʊt'læst] *vt* : durar más que

outlaw¹ ['aʊt,lɔ] *vt* : hacerse ilegal, declarar fuera de la ley, prohibir

outlaw² *n* : bandido *m*, -da *f*; bandolero *m*, -ra *f*; forajido *m*, -da *f*

outlay ['aʊt,leɪ] *n* : gasto *m*, desembolso *m*

outlet ['aʊt,lɛt, -lət] *n* **1** EXIT : salida *f*, escape *m* ⟨electrical outlet : toma de corriente⟩ **2** RELIEF : desahogo *m* **3** MARKET : mercado *m*, salida *f*

outline¹ ['aʊt,laɪn] *vt* **-lined; -lining 1** SKETCH : diseñar, esbozar, bosquejar **2** DEFINE, EXPLAIN : perfilar, delinear, explicar ⟨she outlined our responsibilities : delineó nuestras responsabilidades⟩

outline² *n* **1** PROFILE : perfil *m*, silueta *f*, contorno *m* **2** SKETCH : bosquejo *m*, boceto *m* **3** SUMMARY : esquema *m*, resumen *m*, sinopsis *m* ⟨an outline of world history : un esquema de la historia mundial⟩

outlive [,aʊt'lɪv] *vt* **-lived; -living** : sobrevivir a

outlook ['aʊt,lʊk] *n* **1** VIEW : vista *f*, panorama *f* **2** POINT OF VIEW : punto *m* de vista **3** PROSPECTS : perspectivas *fpl*

outlying ['aʊt,laɪŋ] *adj* : alejado, distante, remoto ⟨the outlying areas : las afueras⟩

outmoded [,aʊt'mo:dəd] *adj* : pasado de moda, anticuado

outnumber [,aʊt'nʌmbər] *vt* : superar en número a, ser más numeroso de

out of *prep* **1** (*indicating direction or movement from within*) : de, por ⟨we ran out of the house : salimos corriendo de la casa⟩ ⟨to look out of the window : mirar por la ventana⟩ **2** (*being beyond the limits of*) ⟨out of control : fuera de control⟩ ⟨to be out of sight : desaparecer de vista⟩ **3** OF : de ⟨one out of four : uno de cada cuatro⟩ **4** (*indicating absence or loss*) : sin ⟨out of money : sin dinero⟩ ⟨we're out of matches : nos hemos quedado sin fósforos⟩ **5** BECAUSE OF : por ⟨out of curiosity : por curiosidad⟩ **6** FROM : de ⟨made out of plastic : hecho de plástico⟩

out-of-date [,aʊtəv'deɪt] *adj* : anticuado, obsoleto, pasado de moda

out-of-door [,aʊtəv'dor] *or* **out-of-doors** [-'dorz] → **outdoor**

out-of-doors *n* → **outdoors²**

outpatient ['aʊt,peɪʃənt] *n* : paciente *m* externo, paciente *f* externa

outpost ['aʊt,po:st] *n* : puesto *m* avanzado

output¹ ['aʊt,pʊt] *vt* **-putted** *or* **-put; -putting** : producir

output² *n* : producción *f* (de una fábrica), rendimiento *m* (de una máquina), productividad *f* (de una persona)

outrage¹ ['aʊt,reɪʤ] *vt* **-raged; -raging 1** INSULT : ultrajar, injuriar **2** INFURIATE : indignar, enfurecer

outrage² *n* **1** ATROCITY : atropello *m*, atrocidad *f*, atentado *m* **2** SCANDAL : escándalo *m* **3** ANGER : ira *f*, furia *f*

outrageous [,aʊt'reɪʤəs] *adj* **1** SCANDALOUS : escandaloso, ofensivo, atroz **2** UNCONVENTIONAL : poco convencional, extravagante **3** EXORBITANT : exorbitante, excesivo (dícese de los precios, etc.)

outright¹ [,aʊt'raɪt] *adv* **1** COMPLETELY : por completo, totalmente ⟨to sell outright : vender por completo⟩ ⟨he refused it outright : lo rechazó rotundamente〉 **2** DIRECTLY : directamente, sin reserva **3** INSTANTLY : al instante, en el acto

outright² [ˈaʊtˌraɪt] *adj* **1** COMPLETE : completo, absoluto, categórico ⟨an outright lie : una mentira absoluta⟩ **2** : sin reservas ⟨an outright gift : un regalo sin reservas⟩

outset [ˈaʊtˌsɛt] *n* : comienzo *m*, principio *m*

outshine [ˌaʊtˈʃaɪn] *vt* **-shone** [-ˈʃoːn, -ˈʃɑn] *or* **-shined; -shining** : eclipsar

outside¹ [ˌaʊtˈsaɪd, ˈaʊtˌ-] *adv* : fuera, afuera

outside² *adj* **1** : exterior, externo ⟨the outside edge : el borde exterior⟩ ⟨outside influences : influencias externas⟩ **2** REMOTE : remoto ⟨an outside chance : una posibilidad remota⟩

outside³ *n* **1** EXTERIOR : parte *f* de afuera, exterior *m* **2** MOST : máximo *m* ⟨three weeks at the outside : tres semanas como máximo⟩ **3 from the outside** : desde afuera, desde fuera

outside⁴ *prep* : fuera de, afuera de ⟨outside my window : fuera de mi ventana⟩ ⟨outside regular hours : fuera del horario normal⟩ ⟨outside the law : afuera de la ley⟩

outside of *prep* **1** → **outside⁴ 2** → **besides²**

outsider [ˌaʊtˈsaɪdər] *n* : forastero *m*, -ra *f*

outskirts [ˈaʊtˌskərts] *npl* : afueras *fpl*, alrededores *mpl*

outsmart [ˌaʊtˈsmɑrt] → **outwit**

outspoken [ˌaʊtˈspoːkən] *adj* : franco, directo

outstanding [ˌaʊtˈstændɪŋ] *adj* **1** UNPAID : pendiente **2** NOTABLE : destacado, notable, excepcional, sobresaliente

outstandingly [ˌaʊtˈstændɪŋli] *adv* : excepcionalmente

outstretched [ˌaʊtˈstrɛtʃt] *adj* : extendido

outstrip [ˌaʊtˈstrɪp] *vt* **-stripped** *or* **-stript** [-ˈstrɪpt]; **-stripping 1** : aventajar, dejar atrás ⟨he outstripped the other runners : aventajó a los otros corredores⟩ **2** SURPASS : aventajar, sobrepasar

outward¹ [ˈaʊtwərd] *or* **outwards** [-wərdz] *adv* : hacia afuera, hacia el exterior

outward² *adj* **1** : hacia afuera ⟨an outward flow : un flujo hacia afuera⟩ **2** : externo ⟨outward beauty : belleza externa⟩

outwardly [ˈaʊtwərdli] *adv* **1** EXTERNALLY : exteriormente **2** APPARENTLY : aparentemente ⟨outwardly friendly : aparentemente simpático⟩

outwit [ˌaʊtˈwɪt] *vt* **-witted; -witting** : ser más listo que

ova → **ovum**

oval¹ [ˈoːvəl] *adj* : ovalado, oval

oval² *n* : óvalo *m*

ovarian [oˈværiən] *adj* : ovárico

ovary [ˈoːvəri] *n, pl* **-ries** : ovario *m*

ovation [oˈveɪʃən] *n* : ovación *f*

oven [ˈʌvən] *n* : horno *m*

over¹ [ˈoːvər] *adv* **1** (*indicating movement across*) ⟨he flew over to London : voló a Londres⟩ ⟨come on over! : ¡ven acá!⟩ **2** (*indicating an additional amount*) ⟨the show ran 10 minutes over : el espectáculo terminó 10 minutos de tarde⟩ **3** ABOVE, OVERHEAD : por encima **4** AGAIN : otra vez, de nuevo ⟨over and over : una y otra vez⟩ ⟨to start over : volver a empezar⟩ **5 all over** EVERYWHERE : por todas partes **6 to fall over** : caerse **7 to turn over** : poner boca abajo, voltear

over² *adj* **1** HIGHER, UPPER : superior **2** REMAINING : sobrante, que sobra **3** ENDED : terminado, acabado ⟨the work is over : el trabajo está terminado⟩

over³ *prep* **1** ABOVE : encima de, arriba de, sobre ⟨over the fireplace : encima de la chimenea⟩ ⟨the hawk flew over the hills : el halcón voló sobre los cerros⟩ **2** : más de ⟨over $50 : más de $50⟩ **3** ALONG : por, sobre ⟨to glide over the ice : deslizarse sobre el hielo⟩ **4** (*indicating motion through a place or thing*) ⟨they showed me over the house : me mostraron la casa⟩ **5** ACROSS : por encima de, sobre ⟨he jumped over the ditch : saltó por encima de la zanja⟩ **6** UPON : sobre ⟨a cape over my shoulders : una capa sobre los hombros⟩ **7** ON : por ⟨to speak over the telephone : hablar por teléfono⟩ **8** DURING : en, durante ⟨over the past 25 years : durante los últimos 25 años⟩ **9** BECAUSE OF : por ⟨they fought over the money : se pelearon por el dinero⟩

overabundance [ˌoːvərəˈbʌndənts] *n* : superabundancia *f*

overabundant [ˌoːvərəˈbʌndənt] *adj* : superabundante

overactive [ˌoːvərˈæktɪv] *adj* : hiperactivo

overall [ˌoːvərˈɔl] *adj* : total, global, de conjunto

overalls [ˈoːvərˌɔlz] *npl* : overol *m*

overawe [ˌoːvərˈɔ] *vt* **-awed; -awing** : intimidar, impresionar

overbearing [ˌoːvərˈbærɪŋ] *adj* : dominante, imperioso, prepotente

overblown [ˌoːvərˈbloːn] *adj* **1** INFLATED : inflado, exagerado **2** BOMBASTIC : grandilocuente, rimbombante

overboard [ˈoːvərˌbord] *adv* : por la borda, al agua

overburden [ˌoːvərˈbərdən] *vt* : sobrecargar, agobiar

overcast [ˈoːvərˌkæst] *adj* CLOUDY : nublado

overcharge [ˌoːvərˈtʃɑrdʒ] *vt* **-charged; -charging** : cobrarle de más (a alguien)

overcoat [ˈoːvərˌkoːt] *n* : abrigo *m*

overcome [ˌoːvərˈkʌm] *v* **-came** [-ˈkeɪm]; **-come; -coming** *vt* **1** CON-

QUER : vencer, derrotar, superar **2**
OVERWHELM : abrumar, agobiar — *vi*
: vencer
overconfidence [ˌoːvərˈkɑnfədənts] *n*
: exceso *m* de confianza
overconfident [ˌoːvərˈkɑnfədənt] *adj*
: demasiado confiado
overcook [ˌoːvərˈkʊk] *vt* : recocer, cocer
demasiado
overcrowded [ˌoːvərˈkraʊdəd] *adj* **1**
PACKED : abarrotado, atestado de
gente **2** OVERPOPULATED : superpoblado
overdo [ˌoːvərˈduː] *vt* **-did** [-ˈdɪd]; **-done**
[-ˈdʌn]; **-doing; -does** [-ˈdʌz] **1** : hacer demasiado **2** EXAGGERATE : exagerar **3** OVERCOOK : recocer
overdose [ˈoːvərˌdoːs] *n* : sobredosis *f*
overdraft [ˈoːvərˌdræft] *n* : sobregiro *m*,
descubierto *m*
overdraw [ˌoːvərˈdrɔ] *vt* **-drew** [-ˈdruː];
-drawn [-ˈdrɔn]; **-drawing 1** : sobregirar ⟨my account is overdrawn : tengo
la cuenta en descubierto⟩ **2** EXAG-
GERATE : exagerar
overdue [ˌoːvərˈduː] *adj* **1** UNPAID : vencido y sin pagar **2** TARDY : de retraso,
tardío
overeat [ˌoːvərˈiːt] *vi* **-ate** [-ˈeɪt]; **-eaten**
[-ˈiːtən]; **-eating** : comer demasiado
overelaborate [ˌoːvərɪˈlæbərət] *adj* : recargado
overestimate [ˌoːvərˈɛstəˌmeɪt] *vt*
-mated; -mating : sobreestimar
overexcited [ˌoːvərɪkˈsaɪtəd] *adj* : sobreexcitado
overexpose [ˌoːvərɪkˈspoːz] *vt* **-posed;
-posing** : sobreexponer
overfeed [ˌoːvərˈfiːd] *vt* **-fed** [-ˈfɛd];
-feeding : sobrealimentar
overflow[1] [ˌoːvərˈfloː] *vt* **1** : desbordar **2**
INUNDATE : inundar — *vi* : desbor-
darse, rebosar
overflow[2] [ˈoːvərˌfloː] *n* **1** : derrame *m*,
desbordamiento *m* (de un río) **2** SUR-
PLUS : exceso *m*, excedente *m*
overfly [ˌoːvərˈflaɪ] *vt* **-flew** [-ˈfluː];
-flown [-ˈfloːn]; **-flying** : sobrevolar
overgrown [ˌoːvərˈgroːn] *adj* **1** : cubierto ⟨overgrown with weeds : cubierto de malas hierbas⟩ **2** : demasiado grande
overhand[1] [ˈoːvərˌhænd] *adv* : por encima de la cabeza
overhand[2] *adj* : por lo alto (tirada)
overhang[1] [ˌoːvərˈhæŋ] *v* **-hung** [-ˈhʌŋ];
-hanging *vt* **1** : sobresalir por encima
de **2** THREATEN : amenazar — *vi* : sobresalir
overhang[2] [ˈoːvərˌhæŋ] *n* : saliente *mf*
overhaul [ˌoːvərˈhɔl] *vt* **1** : revisar ⟨to
overhaul an engine : revisar un motor⟩
2 OVERTAKE : adelantar
overhead[1] [ˌoːvərˈhɛd] *adv* : por encima,
arriba, por lo alto
overhead[2] [ˈoːvərˌhɛd] *adj* : de arriba
overhead[3] [ˈoːvərˌhɛd] *n* : gastos *mpl*
generales

overhear [ˌoːvərˈhɪr] *vt* **-heard; -hearing**
: oír por casualidad
overheat [ˌoːvərˈhiːt] *vt* : recalentar, sobrecalentar, calentar demasiado
overjoyed [ˌoːvərˈdʒɔɪd] *adj* : rebosante
de alegría
overkill [ˈoːvərˌkɪl] *n* : exceso *m*, excedente *m*
overland[1] [ˈoːvərˌlænd, -lənd] *adv* : por
tierra
overland[2] *adj* : terrestre, por tierra
overlap[1] [ˌoːvərˈlæp] *v* **-lapped; -lapping**
vt : traslapar — *vi* : traslaparse, solaparse
overlap[2] [ˈoːvərˌlæp] *n* : traslapo *m*
overlay[1] [ˌoːvərˈleɪ] *vt* **-laid** [-ˈleɪd];
-laying : recubrir, revestir
overlay[2] [ˈoːvərˌleɪ] *n* : revestimiento *m*
overload [ˌoːvərˈloːd] *vt* : sobrecargar
overlong [ˌoːvərˈlɔŋ] *adj* : excesivamente largo, largo y pesado
overlook [ˌoːvərˈlʊk] *vt* **1** INSPECT : inspeccionar, revisar **2** : tener vista a, dar
a ⟨a house overlooking the valley : una
casa que tiene vista al valle⟩ **3** MISS
: pasar por alto **4** EXCUSE : dejar pasar,
disculpar
overly [ˈoːvərli] *adv* : demasiado
overnight[1] [ˌoːvərˈnaɪt] *adv* **1** : por la
noche, durante la noche **2** : de la noche
a la mañana ⟨we can't do it overnight
: no podemos hacerlo de la noche a la
mañana⟩
overnight[2] [ˈoːvərˈnaɪt] *adj* **1** : de noche
⟨an overnight stay : una estancia de
una noche⟩ ⟨an overnight bag : una
bolsa de viaje⟩ **2** SUDDEN : repentino
overpass [ˈoːvərˌpæs] *n* : paso *m* elevado, paso *m* a desnivel *Mex*
overpopulated [ˌoːvərˈpɑpjəˌleɪtəd] *adj*
: sobrepoblado
overpower [ˌoːvərˈpaʊər] *vt* **1** CON-
QUER, SUBDUE : vencer, superar **2**
OVERWHELM : abrumar, agobiar
⟨overpowered by the heat : sofocado
por el calor⟩
overpraise [ˌoːvərˈpreɪz] *vt* **-praised;
-praising** : adular
overrate [ˌoːvərˈreɪt] *vt* **-rated; -rating**
: sobrevalorar, sobrevaluar
override [ˌoːvərˈraɪd] *vt* **-rode** [-ˈroːd];
-ridden [-ˈrɪdən]; **-riding 1** : predominar sobre, contar más que ⟨hunger
overrode our manners : el hambre pre-
dominó sobre los modales⟩ **2** ANNUL
: anular, invalidar ⟨to override a veto
: anular un veto⟩
overrule [ˌoːvərˈruːl] *vt* **-ruled; -ruling**
: anular (una decisión), desautorizar
(una persona), denegar (un pedido)
overrun [ˌoːvərˈrʌn] *v* **-ran** [-ˈræn];
-running *vt* **1** INVADE : invadir **2** IN-
FEST : infestar, plagar **3** EXCEED : exceder, rebasar — *vi* : rebasar el tiempo previsto
overseas[1] [ˌoːvərˈsiːz] *adv* : en el extranjero ⟨to travel overseas : viajar al
extranjero⟩

overseas² ['oːvərˌsiːz] *adj* : extranjero, exterior

oversee [ˌoːvərˈsiː] *vt* **-saw** [-'sɔ]; **-seen** [-'siːn]; **-seeing** SUPERVISE : supervisar

overseer ['oːvərˌsiːər] *n* : supervisor *m*, -sora *f*; capataz *mf*

overshadow [ˌoːvərˈʃæˌdoː] *vt* **1** DARKEN : oscurecer, ensombrecer **2** ECLIPSE, OUTSHINE : eclipsar

overshoe ['oːvərˌʃuː] *n* : chanclo *m*

overshoot [ˌoːvərˈʃuːt] *vt* **-shot** [-'ʃɑt]; **-shooting** : pasarse de ⟨to overshoot the mark : pasarse de la raya⟩

oversight ['oːvərˌsaɪt] *n* : descuido *m*, inadvertencia *f*

oversleep [ˌoːvərˈsliːp] *vi* **-slept** [-'slɛpt]; **-sleeping** : no despertarse a tiempo, quedarse dormido

overspread [ˌoːvərˈsprɛd] *vt* **-spread; -spreading** : extenderse sobre

overstaffed [ˌoːvərˈstæft] *adj* : con exceso de personal

overstate [ˌoːvərˈsteɪt] *vt* **-stated; -stating** EXAGGERATE : exagerar

overstatement [ˌoːvərˈsteɪtmənt] *n* : exageración *f*

overstep [ˌoːvərˈstɛp] *vt* **-stepped; -stepping** EXCEED : sobrepasar, traspasar, exceder

overt [oːˈvərt, 'oːˌvərt] *adj* : evidente, manifiesto, patente

overtake [ˌoːvərˈteɪk] *vt* **-took** [-'tʊk]; **-taken** [-'teɪkən]; **-taking** : pasar, adelantar, rebasar *Mex*

overthrow¹ [ˌoːvərˈθroː] *vt* **-threw** [-'θruː]; **-thrown** [-'θroːn]; **-throwing 1** OVERTURN : dar la vuelta a, volcar **2** DEFEAT, TOPPLE : derrocar, derribar, deponer

overthrow² ['oːvərˌθroː] *n* : derrocamiento *m*, caída *f*

overtime ['oːvərˌtaɪm] *n* **1** : horas *fpl* extras (de trabajo) **2** : prórroga *f* (en deportes)

overtly [oːˈvərtli, 'oːˌvərt-] *adv* OPENLY : abiertamente

overtone ['oːvərˌtoːn] *n* **1** : armónico *m* (en música) **2** HINT, SUGGESTION : tinte *m*, insinuación *f*

overture ['oːvərˌtʃʊr, -tʃər] *n* **1** PROPOSAL : propuesta *f* **2** : obertura *f* (en música)

overturn [ˌoːvərˈtərn] *vt* **1** UPSET : dar la vuelta a, volcar **2** NULLIFY : anular, invalidar — *vi* TURN OVER : volcar, dar un vuelco

overuse [ˌoːvərˈjuːz] *vt* **-used; -using** : abusar de

overview ['oːvərˌvjuː] *n* : resumen *m*, visión *f* general

overweening [ˌoːvərˈwiːnɪŋ] *adj* **1** ARROGANT : arrogante, soberbio **2** IMMODERATE : desmesurado

overweight [ˌoːvərˈweɪt] *adj* : demasiado gordo, demasiado pesado

overwhelm [ˌoːvərˈhwɛlm] *vt* **1** CRUSH, DEFEAT : aplastar, arrollar **2** SUBMERGE : inundar, sumergir **3** OVERPOWER : abrumar, agobiar ⟨overwhelmed by remorse : abrumado de remordimiento⟩

overwhelming [ˌoːvərˈhwɛlmɪŋ] *adj* **1** CRUSHING : abrumador, apabullante **2** SWEEPING : arrollador, aplastante ⟨an overwhelming majority : una mayoría aplastante⟩

overwork [ˌoːvərˈwərk] *vt* **1** : hacer trabajar demasiado **2** OVERUSE : abusar de — *vi* : trabajar demasiado

overwrought [ˌoːvərˈrɔt] *adj* : alterado, sobreexcitado

ovoid ['oːˌvɔɪd] *or* **ovoidal** [oːˈvɔɪdəl] *adj* : ovoide

ovulate ['ɑvjəˌleɪt, 'oː-] *vi* **-lated; -lating** : ovular

ovulation [ˌɑvjəˈleɪʃən, ˌoː-] *n* : ovulación *f*

ovum ['oːvəm] *n, pl* **ova** [-və] : óvulo *m*

owe ['oː] *vt* **owed; owing** : deber ⟨you owe me $10 : me debes $10⟩ ⟨he owes his wealth to his father : le debe su riqueza a su padre⟩

owing to *prep* : debido a

owl ['aʊl] *n* : búho *m*, lechuza *f*, tecolote *m Mex*

own¹ ['oːn] *vt* **1** POSSESS : poseer, tener, ser dueño de **2** ADMIT : reconocer, admitir — *vi* **to own up** : reconocer (algo), admitir (algo)

own² *adj* : propio, personal, particular ⟨his own car : su propio coche⟩

own³ *pron* **my; (your, his/her, our, their); own** : el mío, la mía; el tuyo, la tuya; el suyo, la suya; el nuestro, la nuestra ⟨to each his own : cada uno a lo suyo⟩ ⟨money of my own : mi propio dinero⟩ ⟨to be on one's own : estar solo⟩

owner ['oːnər] *n* : dueño *m*, -ña *f*; propietario *m*, -ria *f*

ownership ['oːnərˌʃɪp] *n* : propiedad *f*

ox ['ɑks] *n, pl* **oxen** ['ɑksən] : buey *m*

oxidation [ˌɑksəˈdeɪʃən] *n* : oxidación *f*

oxide ['ɑkˌsaɪd] *n* : óxido *m*

oxidize ['ɑksəˌdaɪz] *vt* **-dized; -dizing** : oxidar

oxygen ['ɑksɪdʒən] *n* : oxígeno *m*

oyster ['ɔɪstər] *n* : ostra *f*, ostión *m Mex*

ozone ['oːˌzoːn] *n* : ozono *m*

P

p ['pi:] *n, pl* **p's** *or* **ps** ['pi:z] : decimosexta letra del alfabeto inglés

pace¹ ['peɪs] *v* **paced; pacing** *vi* : caminar, ir y venir — *vt* **1** : caminar por ⟨she paced the floor : caminaba de un lado a otro del cuarto⟩ **2 to pace a runner** : marcarle el ritmo a un corredor

pace² *n* **1** STEP : paso *m* **2** RATE : paso *m*, ritmo *m* ⟨to set the pace : marcar el paso, marcar la pauta⟩

pacemaker ['peɪsˌmeɪkər] *n* : marcapasos *m*

pacific [pəˈsɪfɪk] *adj* : pacífico

pacifier ['pæsəˌfaɪər] *n* : chupete *m*, chupón *m*, mamila *f Mex*

pacifism ['pæsəˌfɪzəm] *n* : pacifismo *m*

pacifist ['pæsəfɪst] *n* : pacifista *mf*

pacify ['pæsəˌfaɪ] *vt* **-fied; -fying 1** SOOTHE : apaciguar, pacificar **2** : pacificar (un país, una región, etc.)

pack¹ ['pæk] *vt* **1** PACKAGE : empaquetar, embalar, envasar **2** : empacar, meter (en una maleta) ⟨to pack one's bag : hacer la maleta⟩ **3** FILL : llenar, abarrotar ⟨a packed theater : un teatro abarrotado⟩ **4 to pack off** SEND : mandar — *vi* : empacar, hacer las maletas

pack² *n* **1** BUNDLE : bulto *m*, fardo *m* **2** BACKPACK : mochila *f* **3** PACKAGE : paquete *m*, cajetilla *f* (de cigarrillos, etc.) **4** : manada *f* (de lobos, etc.), jauría *f* (de perros) ⟨a pack of thieves : una pandilla de ladrones⟩

package¹ ['pækɪdʒ] *vt* **-aged; -aging** : empaquetar, embalar

package² *n* : paquete *m*, bulto *m*

packaging ['pækɪdʒɪŋ] *n* **1** : embalaje *m* **2** WRAPPING : envoltorio *m*

packer ['pækər] *n* : empacador *m*, -dora *f*

packet ['pækət] *n* : paquete *m*

packing ['pækɪŋ] *n* : embalaje *m*

pact ['pækt] *n* : pacto *m*, acuerdo *m*

pad¹ ['pæd] *vt* **padded; padding 1** FILL, STUFF : rellenar, acolchar (una silla, una pared) **2** : meter paja en, rellenar ⟨to pad a speech : rellenar un discurso⟩

pad² *n* **1** CUSHION : almohadilla *f* ⟨a shoulder pad : una hombrera⟩ **2** TABLET : bloc *m* (de papel) **3** *or* **lily pad** : hoja *f* grande (de un nenúfar) **4 ink pad** : tampón *m* **5 launching pad** : plataforma *f* (de lanzamiento)

padding ['pædɪŋ] *n* **1** FILLING : relleno *m* **2** : paja *f* (en un discurso, etc.)

paddle¹ ['pædəl] *v* **-dled; -dling** *vt* **1** : hacer avanzar (una canoa) con canalete **2** HIT : azotar, darle nalgadas a (con una pala o paleta) — *vi* **1** : remar (en una canoa) **2** SPLASH : chapotear, mojarse los pies

paddle² *n* **1** : canalete *m*, zagual *m* (de una canoa, etc.) **2** : pala *f*, paleta *f* (en deportes)

paddock ['pædək] *n* **1** PASTURE : potrero *m* **2** : paddock *m*, cercado *m* (en un hipódromo)

paddy ['pædi] *n, pl* **-dies** : arrozal *m*

padlock¹ ['pædˌlɑk] *vt* : cerrar con candado

padlock² *n* : candado *m*

pagan¹ ['peɪgən] *adj* : pagano

pagan² *n* : pagano *m*, -na *f*

paganism ['peɪgənˌɪzəm] *n* : paganismo *m*

page¹ ['peɪdʒ] *vt* **paged; paging** : llamar por altavoz

page² *n* **1** BELLHOP : botones *m* **2** : página *f* (de un libro, etc.)

pageant ['pædʒənt] *n* **1** SPECTACLE : espectáculo *m* **2** PROCESSION : desfile *m*

pageantry ['pædʒəntri] *n* : pompa *f*, fausto *m*

pager ['peɪdʒər] *n* BEEPER : buscapersonas *m*

pagoda [pəˈgoːdə] *n* : pagoda *f*

paid → **pay**

pail ['peɪl] *n* : balde *m*, cubo *m*, cubeta *f Mex*

pailful ['peɪlˌfʊl] *n* : balde *m*, cubo *m*, cubeta *f Mex*

pain¹ ['peɪn] *vt* : doler

pain² *n* **1** PENALTY : pena *f* ⟨under pain of death : so pena de muerte⟩ **2** SUFFERING : dolor *m*, malestar *m*, pena *f* (mental) **3 pains** *npl* EFFORT : esmero *m*, esfuerzo *m* ⟨to take pains : esmerarse⟩

painful ['peɪnfəl] *adj* : doloroso — **painfully** *adv*

painkiller ['peɪnˌkɪlər] *n* : analgésico *m*

painless ['peɪnləs] *adj* : indoloro, sin dolor

painlessly ['peɪnləsli] *adv* : sin dolor

painstaking ['peɪnˌsteɪkɪŋ] *adj* : esmerado, cuidadoso, meticuloso — **painstakingly** *adv*

paint¹ ['peɪnt] *v* : pintar

paint² *n* : pintura *f*

paintbrush ['peɪntˌbrʌʃ] *n* : pincel *m* (de un artista), brocha *f* (para pintar casas, etc.)

painter ['peɪntər] *n* : pintor *m*, -tora *f*

painting ['peɪntɪŋ] *n* : pintura *f*

pair¹ ['pær] *vt* : emparejar, poner en parejas — *vi* : emparejarse

pair² *n* : par *m* (de objetos), pareja *f* (de personas o animales) ⟨a pair of scissors : unas tijeras⟩

pajamas [pəˈdʒɑməz, -ˈdʒæ-] *npl* : pijama *m*, piyama *mf*

Pakistani [ˌpækɪˈstæni, ˌpɑkɪˈstɑni] *n* : paquistaní *mf* — **Pakistani** *adj*

pal ['pæl] *n* : amigo *m*, -ga *f*; compinche *mf fam*; chamo *m*, -ma *f Ven fam*; cuate *m*, -ta *f Mex*

palace ['pæləs] *n* : palacio *m*

palatable ['pælətəbəl] *adj* : sabroso

palate ['pælət] *n* **1** : paladar *m* (de la boca) **2** TASTE : paladar *m*, gusto *m*

palatial [pə'leɪʃəl] *adj* : suntuoso, espléndido
palaver [pə'lævər, -'lɑ-] *n* : palabrería *f*
pale¹ ['peɪl] *v* **paled; paling** *vi* : palidecer — *vt* : hacer pálido
pale² *adj* **paler; palest 1** : pálido ⟨to turn pale : palidecer, ponerse pálido⟩ **2** : claro (dícese de los colores)
paleness ['peɪlnəs] *n* : palidez *f*
paleontologist [ˌpeɪliˌɑn'tɑlədʒɪst] *n* : paleontólogo *m*, -ga *f*
paleontology [ˌpeɪliˌɑn'tɑlədʒi] *n* : paleontología *f*
Palestinian [ˌpælə'stɪniən] *n* : palestino *m*, -na *f* — **Palestinian** *adj*
palette ['pælət] *n* : paleta *f* (para mezclar pigmentos)
palisade [ˌpælə'seɪd] *n* **1** FENCE : empalizada *f*, estacada *f* **2** CLIFFS : acantilado *m*
pall¹ ['pɔl] *vi* : perder su sabor, dejar de gustar
pall² *n* **1** : paño *m* mortuorio (sobre un ataúd) **2** COVER : cortina *f* (de humo, etc.) **3 to cast a pall over** : ensombrecer
pallbearer ['pɔl,berər] *n* : portador *m*, -dora *f* del féretro
pallet ['pælət] *n* **1** BED : camastro *m* **2** PLATFORM : plataforma *f* de carga
palliative ['pæli,eɪt̬ɪv, 'pælja̬t̬ɪv] *adj* : paliativo
pallid ['pæləd] *adj* : pálido
pallor ['pælər] *n* : palidez *f*
palm¹ ['pɑm, 'pɑlm] *vt* **1** CONCEAL : escamotear (un naipe, etc.) **2 to palm off** : encajar, endilgar *fam* ⟨he palmed it off on me : me lo endilgó⟩
palm² *n* **1** *or* **palm tree** : palmera *f* **2** : palma *f* (de la mano)
Palm Sunday *n* : Domingo *m* de Ramos
palomino [ˌpælə'miːˌnoː] *n, pl* **-nos** : caballo *m* de color dorado
palpable ['pælpəbəl] *adj* : palpable — **palpably** [-bli] *adv*
palpitate ['pælpə,teɪt] *vi* **-tated; -tating** : palpitar
palpitation [ˌpælpə'teɪʃən] *n* : palpitación *f*
palsy ['pɔlzi] *n, pl* **-sies 1** : parálisis *f* **2** → **cerebral palsy**
paltry ['pɔltri] *adj* **-trier; -est** : mísero, mezquino, insignificante ⟨a paltry excuse : una mala excusa⟩
pampas ['pæmpəz, 'pɑmpəs] *npl* : pampa *f*
pamper ['pæmpər] *vt* : mimar, consentir, chiquear *Mex*
pamphlet ['pæmɸflət] *n* : panfleto *m*, folleto *m*
pan¹ ['pæn] *vt* **panned; panning** CRITICIZE : poner por los suelos — *vi* **to pan for gold** : cribar el oro con batea, lavar oro
pan² *n* **1** : cacerola *f*, cazuela *f* **2 frying pan** : sartén *mf*, freidera *f Mex*
panacea [ˌpænə'siːə] *n* : panacea *f*

Panamanian [ˌpænə'meɪniən] *n* : panameño *m*, -ña *f* — **Panamanian** *adj*
pancake ['pæn,keɪk] *n* : panqueque *m*
pancreas ['pæŋkriəs, 'pæn-] *n* : páncreas *m*
panda ['pændə] *n* : panda *mf*
pandemonium [ˌpændə'moːniəm] *n* : pandemonio *m*, pandemónium *m*
pander ['pændər] *vi* **to pander to** : satisfacer, complacer (a alguien) ⟨to pander to popular taste : satisfacer el gusto popular⟩
pane ['peɪn] *n* : cristal *m*, vidrio *m*
panel¹ ['pænəl] *vt* **-eled** *or* **-elled; -eling** *or* **-elling** : adornar con paneles
panel² *n* **1** : lista *f* de nombres (de un jurado, etc.) **2** GROUP : panel *m*, grupo *m* ⟨discussion panel : panel de discusión⟩ **3** : panel *m* (de una pared, etc.) **4 instrument panel** : tablero *m* de instrumentos
paneling ['pænəlɪŋ] *n* : paneles *mpl*
pang ['pæŋ] *n* : puntada *f*, punzada *f*
panic¹ ['pænɪk] *v* **-icked; -icking** *vt* : llenar de pánico — *vi* : ser presa de pánico
panic² *n* : pánico *m*
panicky ['pænɪki] *adj* : presa de pánico
panorama [ˌpænə'ræmə, -'rɑ-] *n* : panorama *m*
panoramic [ˌpænə'ræmɪk, -'rɑ-] *adj* : panorámico
pansy ['pænzi] *n, pl* **-sies** : pensamiento *m*
pant¹ ['pænt] *vi* : jadear, resoplar
pant² *n* : jadeo *m*, resoplo *m*
pantaloons [ˌpæntə'luːnz] → **pants**
pantheon ['pæntθiˌɑn, -ən] *n* : panteón *m*
panther ['pænθər] *n* : pantera *f*
panties ['pæntiz] *npl* : calzones *mpl*; pantaletas *fpl Mex, Ven*; bragas *fpl Spain*
pantomime¹ ['pæntə,maɪm] *v* **-mimed; -miming** *vt* : representar mediante la pantomima — *vi* : hacer la mímica
pantomime² *n* : pantomima *f*
pantry ['pæntri] *n, pl* **-tries** : despensa *f*
pants ['pænts] *npl* **1** TROUSERS : pantalón *m*, pantalones *mpl* **2** → **panties**
panty hose ['pænti] *ns & pl* : medias *fpl*, panties *mfpl*, pantimedias *fpl Mex*
pap ['pæp] *n* : papilla *f* (para bebés, etc.)
papa ['pɑpə] *n* : papá *m*
papal ['peɪpəl] *adj* : papal
papaya [pə'paɪə] *n* : papaya *f* (fruta)
paper¹ ['peɪpər] *vt* WALLPAPER : empapelar
paper² *adj* : de papel
paper³ *n* **1** : papel *m* ⟨a piece of paper : un papel⟩ **2** DOCUMENT : papel *m*, documento *m* **3** NEWSPAPER : periódico *m*, diario *m*
paperback ['peɪpər,bæk] *n* : libro *m* en rústica
paper clip *n* : clip *m*, sujetapapeles *m*
paperweight ['peɪpər,weɪt] *n* : pisapapeles *m*

paperwork ['peɪpərˌwərk] *n* : papeleo *m*
papery ['peɪpəri] *adj* : parecido al papel
papier–mâché [ˌpeɪpərməˈʃeɪ, ˌpæ-ˌpjeɪmæˈʃeɪ] *n* : papel *m* maché
papoose [pæˈpuːs, pə-] *n* : niño *m*, -ña *f* de los indios norteamericanos
paprika [pəˈpriːkə, pæ-] *n* : pimentón *m*, paprika *f*
papyrus [pəˈpaɪrəs] *n, pl* **-ruses** *or* **-ri** [-ˌri, -ˌraɪ] : papiro *m*
par ['pɑr] *n* **1** VALUE : valor *m* (nominal), par *f* ⟨below par : debajo de la par⟩ **2** EQUALITY : igualdad *f* ⟨to be on a par with : estar al mismo nivel que⟩ **3** : par *m* (en golf)
parable ['pærəbəl] *n* : parábola *f*
parabola [pəˈræbələ] *n* : parábola *f* (en matemáticas)
parachute[1] ['pærəˌʃuːt] *vi* **-chuted; -chuting** : lanzarse en paracaídas
parachute[2] *n* : paracaídas *m*
parachutist ['pærəˌʃuːtɪst] *n* : paracaidista *mf*
parade[1] [pəˈreɪd] *vi* **-raded; -rading 1** MARCH : desfilar **2** SHOW OFF : pavonearse, lucirse
parade[2] *n* **1** PROCESSION : desfile *m* **2** DISPLAY : alarde *m*
paradigm ['pærəˌdaɪm] *n* : paradigma *m*
paradise ['pærəˌdaɪs, -ˌdaɪz] *n* : paraíso *m*
paradox ['pærəˌdɑks] *n* : paradoja *f*
paradoxical [ˌpærəˈdɑksɪkəl] *adj* : paradójico — **paradoxically** *adv*
paraffin ['pærəfən] *n* : parafina *f*
paragon ['pærəˌgɑn, -gən] *n* : dechado *m*
paragraph[1] ['pærəˌgræf] *vt* : dividir en párrafos
paragraph[2] *n* : párrafo *m*, acápite *m*
Paraguayan [ˌpærəˈgwaɪən, -ˈgweɪ-] *n* : paraguayo *m*, -ya *f* — **Paraguayan** *adj*
parakeet ['pærəˌkiːt] *n* : periquito *m*
paralegal [ˌpærəˈliːgəl] *n* : asistente *mf* de abogado
parallel[1] ['pærəˌlɛl, -ləl] *vt* **1** MATCH, RESEMBLE : ser paralelo a, ser análogo a, corresponder con **2** : extenderse en línea paralela con ⟨the road parallels the river : el camino se extiende a lo largo del río⟩
parallel[2] *adj* : paralelo
parallel[3] *n* **1** : línea *f* paralela, superficie *f* paralela **2** : paralelo *m* (en geografía) **3** SIMILARITY : paralelismo *m*, semejanza *f*
parallelogram [ˌpærəˈlɛləˌgræm] *n* : paralelogramo *m*
paralysis [pəˈræləsɪs] *n, pl* **-yses** [-ˌsiːz] : parálisis *f*
paralyze ['pærəˌlaɪz] *vt* **-lyzed; -lyzing** : paralizar
parameter [pəˈræmətər] *n* : parámetro *m*
paramount ['pærəˌmaʊnt] *adj* : supremo ⟨of paramount importance : de suma importancia⟩
paranoia [ˌpærəˈnɔɪə] *n* : paranoia *f*

paranoid ['pærəˌnɔɪd] *adj* : paranoico
parapet ['pærəpət, -ˌpɛt] *n* : parapeto *m*
paraphernalia [ˌpærəfəˈneɪljə, -fər-] *ns & pl* : parafernalia *f*
paraphrase[1] ['pærəˌfreɪz] *vt* **-phrased; -phrasing** : parafrasear
paraphrase[2] *n* : paráfrasis *f*
paraplegic[1] [ˌpærəˈpliːdʒɪk] *adj* : parapléjico
paraplegic[2] *n* : parapléjico *m*, -ca *f*
parasite ['pærəˌsaɪt] *n* : parásito *m*
parasitic [ˌpærəˈsɪtɪk] *adj* : parasitario
parasol ['pærəˌsɔl] *n* : sombrilla *f*, quitasol *m*, parasol *m*
paratrooper ['pærəˌtruːpər] *n* : paracaidista *mf* (militar)
parboil ['pɑrˌbɔɪl] *vt* : sancochar, cocer a medias
parcel[1] ['pɑrsəl] *vt* **-celed** *or* **-celled; -celing** *or* **-celling** *or* **to parcel out** : repartir, parcelar (tierras)
parcel[2] *n* **1** LOT : parcela *f*, lote *m* **2** PACKAGE : paquete *m*, bulto *m*
parch ['pɑrtʃ] *vt* : resecar
parchment ['pɑrtʃmənt] *n* : pergamino *m*
pardon[1] ['pɑrdən] *vt* **1** FORGIVE : perdonar, disculpar ⟨pardon me! : ¡perdone!, ¡disculpe la molestia!⟩ **2** REPRIEVE : indultar (a un delincuente)
pardon[2] *n* **1** FORGIVENESS : perdón *m* **2** REPRIEVE : indulto *m*
pardonable ['pɑrdənəbəl] *adj* : perdonable, disculpable
pare ['pær] *vt* **pared; paring 1** PEEL : pelar **2** TRIM : recortar **3** REDUCE : reducir ⟨he pared it (down) to 50 pages : lo redujo a 50 páginas⟩
parent ['pærənt] *n* **1** : madre *f*, padre *m* **2 parents** *npl* : padres *mpl*
parentage ['pærəntɪdʒ] *n* : linaje *m*, abolengo *m*, origen *m*
parental [pəˈrɛntəl] *adj* : de los padres
parenthesis [pəˈrɛnθəsɪs] *n, pl* **-theses** [-ˌsiːz] : paréntesis *m*
parenthetic [ˌpærənˈθɛtɪk] *or* **parenthetical** [-tɪkəl] *adj* : parentético — **parenthetically** [-tɪkli] *adv*
parenthood ['pærəntˌhʊd] *n* : paternidad *f*
parfait [pɑrˈfeɪ] *n* : postre *m* elaborado con frutas y helado
pariah [pəˈraɪə] *n* : paria *mf*
parish ['pærɪʃ] *n* : parroquia *f*
parishioner [pəˈrɪʃənər] *n* : feligrés *m*, -gresa *f*
parity ['pærəti] *n, pl* **-ties** : paridad *f*
park[1] ['pɑrk] *vt* : estacionar, parquear, aparcar *Spain* — *vi* : estacionarse, parquearse, aparcar *Spain*
park[2] *n* : parque *m*
parka ['pɑrkə] *n* : parka *f*
parking ['pɑrkɪŋ] *n* : estacionamiento *m*, aparcamiento *m Spain*
parkway ['pɑrkˌweɪ] *n* : carretera *f* ajardinada, bulevar *m*
parley[1] ['pɑrli] *vi* : parlamentar, negociar

parley[2] *n, pl* **-leys** : negociación *f*, parlamento *m*
parliament [ˈpɑrləmənt, ˈpɑrljə-] *n* : parlamento *m*
parliamentary [ˌpɑrləˈmɛntəri, ˌpɑrljə-] *adj* : parlamentario
parlor [ˈpɑrlər] *n* **1** : sala *f*, salón *m* (en una casa) **2** : salón *m* ⟨beauty parlor : salón de belleza⟩ **3 funeral parlor** : funeraria *f*
parochial [pəˈroːkiəl] *adj* **1** : parroquial **2** PROVINCIAL : pueblerino, de miras estrechas
parody[1] [ˈpærədi] *vt* **-died; -dying** : parodiar
parody[2] *n, pl* **-dies** : parodia *f*
parole [pəˈroːl] *n* : libertad *f* condicional
paroxysm [ˈpærəkˌsɪzəm, pəˈrɑk-] *n* : paroxismo *m*
parquet [ˈpɑrˌkeɪ, pɑrˈkeɪ] *n* : parquet *m*, parqué *m*
parrakeet → **parakeet**
parrot [ˈpærət] *n* : loro *m*, papagayo *m*
parry[1] [ˈpæri] *v* **-ried; -rying** *vi* : parar un golpe — *vt* EVADE : esquivar (una pregunta, etc.)
parry[2] *n, pl* **-ries** : parada *f*
parsimonious [ˌpɑrsəˈmoːniəs] *adj* : tacaño, mezquino
parsley [ˈpɑrsli] *n* : perejil *m*
parsnip [ˈpɑrsnɪp] *n* : chirivía *f*
parson [ˈpɑrsən] *n* : pastor *m*, -tora *f*; clérigo *m*
parsonage [ˈpɑrsənɪʤ] *n* : rectoría *f*, casa *f* del párroco
part[1] [ˈpɑrt] *vi* **1** SEPARATE : separarse, despedirse ⟨we should part as friends : debemos separarnos amistosamente⟩ **2** OPEN : abrirse ⟨the curtains parted : las cortinas se abrieron⟩ **3 to part with** : deshacerse de — *vt* **1** SEPARATE : separar **2 to part one's hair** : hacerse la raya, peinarse con raya
part[2] *n* **1** SECTION, SEGMENT : parte *f*, sección *f* **2** PIECE : pieza *f* (de una máquina, etc.) **3** ROLE : papel *m* **4** : raya *f* (del pelo)
partake [pɑrˈteɪk, pər-] *vi* **-took** [-ˈtʊk]; **-taken** [-ˈteɪkən]; **-taking 1 to partake of** CONSUME : comer, beber, tomar **2 to partake in** : participar en (una actividad, etc.)
partial [ˈpɑrʃəl] *adj* **1** BIASED : parcial, tendencioso **2** INCOMPLETE : parcial, incompleto **3 to be partial to** : ser aficionado a
partiality [ˌpɑrʃiˈæləti] *n, pl* **-ties** : parcialidad *f*
partially [ˈpɑrʃəli] *adv* : parcialmente
participant [pərˈtɪsəpənt, pɑr-] *n* : participante *mf*
participate [pərˈtɪsəˌpeɪt, pɑr-] *vi* **-pated; -pating** : participar
participation [pərˌtɪsəˈpeɪʃən, pɑr-] *n* : participación *f*
participle [ˈpɑrtəˌsɪpəl] *n* : participio *m*
particle [ˈpɑrtɪkəl] *n* : partícula *f*
particular[1] [pərˈtɪkjələr] *adj* **1** SPECIFIC : particular, en particular ⟨this partic-

ular person : esta persona en particular⟩ **2** SPECIAL : particular, especial ⟨with particular emphasis : con un énfasis especial⟩ **3** FUSSY : exigente, maniático ⟨to be very particular : ser muy especial⟩ ⟨I'm not particular : me da igual⟩
particular[2] *n* **1** DETAIL : detalle *m*, sentido *m* **2 in particular** : en particular, en especial
particularly [pərˈtɪkjələrli] *adv* **1** ESPECIALLY : particularmente, especialmente **2** SPECIFICALLY : específicamente, en especial
partisan [ˈpɑrtəzən, -sən] *n* **1** ADHERENT : partidario *m*, -ria *f* **2** GUERRILLA : partisano *m*, -na *f*; guerrillero *m*, -ra *f*
partition[1] [pərˈtɪʃən, pɑr-] *vt* : dividir ⟨to partition off (a room) : dividir (una habitación) con un tabique⟩
partition[2] *n* **1** DISTRIBUTION : partición *f*, división *f*, reparto *m* **2** DIVIDER : tabique *m*, mampara *f*, biombo *m*
partly [ˈpɑrtli] *adv* : en parte, parcialmente
partner [ˈpɑrtnər] *n* **1** COMPANION : compañero *m*, -ra *f* **2** : pareja *f* (en un juego, etc.) ⟨dancing partner : pareja de baile⟩ **3** SPOUSE : cónyuge *mf* **4** *or* **business partner** : socio *m*, -cia *f*; asociado *m*, -da *f*
partnership [ˈpɑrtnərˌʃɪp] *n* **1** ASSOCIATION : asociación *f*, compañerismo *m* **2** : sociedad *f* (de negociantes) ⟨to form a partnership : asociarse⟩
part of speech : categoría *f* gramatical
partridge [ˈpɑrtrɪʤ] *n, pl* **-tridge** *or* **-tridges** : perdiz *f*
party [ˈpɑrti] *n, pl* **-ties 1** : partido *m* (político) **2** PARTICIPANT : parte *f*, participante *mf* **3** GROUP : grupo *m* (de personas) **4** GATHERING : fiesta *f* ⟨to throw a party : dar una fiesta⟩
parvenu [ˈpɑrvəˌnuː, -ˌnjuː] *n* : advenedizo *m*, -za *f*
pass[1] [ˈpæs] *vi* **1** : pasar, cruzarse ⟨a car passed by : pasó un coche⟩ ⟨we passed in the hallway : nos cruzamos en el pasillo⟩ **2** CEASE : pasarse ⟨the pain passed : se pasó el dolor⟩ **3** ELAPSE : pasar, transcurrir **4** PROCEED : pasar ⟨let me pass : déjame pasar⟩ **5** HAPPEN : pasar, ocurrir **6** : pasar, aprobar (en un examen) **7** RULE : fallar ⟨the jury passed on the case : el jurado falló en el caso⟩ **8** *or* **to pass down** : pasar ⟨the throne passed to his son : el trono pasó a su hijo⟩ **9 to let pass** OVERLOOK : pasar por alto **10 to pass as** : pasar por **11 to pass away** *or* **to pass on** DIE : fallecer, morir — *vt* **1** : pasar por ⟨they passed the house : pasaron por la casa⟩ **2** OVERTAKE : pasar, adelantar **3** SPEND : pasar (tiempo) **4** HAND : pasar ⟨pass me the salt : pásame la sal⟩ **5** : aprobar (un examen, una ley)

pass[2] *n* **1** CROSSING, GAP : paso *m*, desfiladero *m*, puerto *m* ⟨mountain pass : puerto de montaña⟩ **2** PERMIT : pase *m*, permiso *m* **3** : pase *m* (en deportes) **4** SITUATION : situación *f* (difícil) ⟨things have come to a pretty pass! : ¡hasta dónde hemos llegado!⟩

passable [ˈpæsəbəl] *adj* **1** ADEQUATE : adecuado, pasable **2** : transitable (dícese de un camino, etc.)

passably [ˈpæsəbli] *adv* : pasablemente

passage [ˈpæsɪʤ] *n* **1** PASSING : paso *m* ⟨the passage of time : el paso del tiempo⟩ **2** PASSAGEWAY : pasillo *m* (dentro de un edificio), pasaje *m* (entre edificios) **3** VOYAGE : travesía *f* (por el mar), viaje *m* ⟨to grant safe passage : dar un salvoconducto⟩ **4** SECTION : pasaje *m* (en música o literatura)

passageway [ˈpæsɪʤˌwei] *n* : pasillo *m*, pasadizo *m*, corredor *m*

passbook [ˈpæsˌbʊk] *n* BANKBOOK : libreta *f* de ahorros

passé [pæˈsei] *adj* : pasado de moda

passenger [ˈpæsənʤər] *n* : pasajero *m*, -ra *f*

passerby [ˌpæsərˈbai, ˈpæsərˌ-] *n, pl* **passersby** : transeúnte *mf*

passing [ˈpæsɪŋ] *n* DEATH : fallecimiento *m*

passion [ˈpæʃən] *n* : pasión *f*, ardor *m*

passionate [ˈpæʃənət] *adj* **1** IRASCIBLE : irascible, iracundo **2** ARDENT : apasionado, ardiente, ferviente, fogoso

passionately [ˈpæʃənətli] *adv* : apasionadamente, fervientemente, con pasión

passive[1] [ˈpæsɪv] *adj* : pasivo — **passively** *adv*

passive[2] *n* : voz *f* pasiva (en gramática)

passivity [pæˈsɪvəti] *n* : pasividad *f*

Passover [ˈpæsˌoːvər] *n* : Pascua *f* (en el judaísmo)

passport [ˈpæsˌport] *n* : pasaporte *m*

password [ˈpæsˌwərd] *n* : contraseña *f*

past[1] [ˈpæst] *adv* : por delante ⟨he drove past : pasamos en coche⟩

past[2] *adj* **1** AGO : hace ⟨10 years past : hace 10 años⟩ **2** LAST : último ⟨the past few months : los últimos meses⟩ **3** BYGONE : pasado ⟨in past times : en tiempos pasados⟩ **4** : pasado (en gramática)

past[3] *n* : pasado *m*

past[4] *prep* **1** BY : por, por delante de ⟨he ran past the house : pasó por la casa corriendo⟩ **2** BEYOND : más allá de ⟨just past the corner : un poco más allá de la esquina⟩ ⟨we went past the exit : pasamos la salida⟩ **3** AFTER : después de ⟨past noon : después del mediodía⟩ ⟨half past two : las dos y media⟩

pasta [ˈpɑstə, ˈpæs-] *n* : pasta *f*

paste[1] [ˈpeist] *vt* **pasted; pasting** : pegar (con engrudo)

paste[2] *n* **1** : pasta *f* ⟨tomato paste : pasta de tomate⟩ **2** : engrudo *m* (para pegar)

pasteboard [ˈpeistˌbord] *n* : cartón *m*, cartulina *f*

pastel [pæˈstɛl] *n* : pastel *m* — **pastel** *adj*

pasteurization [ˌpæstʃərəˈzeiʃən, ˌpæstjə-] *n* : pasteurización *f*

pasteurize [ˈpæstʃəˌraiz, ˈpæstjə-] *vt* **-ized; -izing** : pasteurizar

pastime [ˈpæsˌtaim] *n* : pasatiempo *m*

pastor [ˈpæstər] *n* : pastor *m*, -tora *f*

pastoral [ˈpæstərəl] *adj* : pastoral

past participle *n* : participio *m* pasado

pastry [ˈpeistri] *n, pl* **-ries 1** DOUGH : pasta *f*, masa *f* **2 pastries** *npl* : pasteles *mpl*

pasture[1] [ˈpæstʃər] *v* **-tured; -turing** *vi* GRAZE : pacer, pastar — *vt* : apacentar, pastar

pasture[2] *n* : pastizal *m*, potrero *m*, pasto *m*

pasty [ˈpeisti] *adj* **pastier; -est 1** : pastoso (en consistencia) **2** PALLID : pálido

pat[1] [ˈpæt] *vt* **patted; patting** : dar palmaditas a, tocar

pat[2] *adv* : de memoria ⟨to have down pat : saberse de memoria⟩

pat[3] *adj* **1** APT : apto, apropiado **2** GLIB : fácil **3** UNYIELDING : firme ⟨to stand pat : mantenerse firme⟩

pat[4] *n* **1** TAP : golpecito *m*, palmadita *f* ⟨a pat on the back : una palmadita en la espalda⟩ **2** CARESS : caricia *f* **3** : porción *f* ⟨a pat of butter : una porción de mantequilla⟩

patch[1] [ˈpætʃ] *vt* **1** MEND, REPAIR : remendar, parchar, ponerle un parche a **2 to patch together** IMPROVISE : confeccionar, improvisar **3 to patch up** : arreglar ⟨they patched things up : hicieron las paces⟩

patch[2] *n* **1** : parche *m*, remiendo *m* (para la ropa) ⟨eye patch : parche para el ojo⟩ **2** PIECE : mancha *f*, trozo *m* ⟨a patch of sky : un trozo de cielo⟩ **3** PLOT : parcela *f*, terreno *m* ⟨cabbage patch : parcela de repollos⟩

patchwork [ˈpætʃˌwərk] *n* : labor *f* de retazos

patchy [ˈpætʃi] *adj* **patchier; -est 1** IRREGULAR : irregular, desigual **2** INCOMPLETE : parcial, incompleto

patent[1] [ˈpætənt] *vt* : patentar

patent[2] [ˈpætənt, ˈpeit-] *adj* **1** OBVIOUS : patente, evidente **2** [ˈpæt-] PATENTED : patentado

patent[3] [ˈpætənt] *n* : patente *f*

patently [ˈpætəntli] *adv* : patentemente, evidentemente

paternal [pəˈtərnəl] *adj* **1** FATHERLY : paternal **2** : paterno ⟨paternal grandfather : abuelo paterno⟩

paternity [pəˈtərnəti] *n* : paternidad *f*

path [ˈpæθ, ˈpɑθ] *n* **1** TRACK, TRAIL : camino *m*, sendero *m*, senda *f* **2** COURSE, ROUTE : recorrido *m*, trayecto *m*, trayectoria *f*

pathetic [pəˈθɛtɪk] *adj* : patético — **pathetically** [-tɪkli] *adv*

pathological [ˌpæθəˈlɑʤɪkəl] *adj* : patológico

pathologist [pə'θɑlədʒɪst] n : patólogo m, -ga f
pathology [pə'θɑlədʒi] n, pl **-gies** : patología f
pathos ['peɪ,θɑs, 'pæ-, -,θɔs] n : patetismo m
pathway ['pæθ,weɪ] n : camino m, sendero m, senda f, vereda f
patience ['peɪʃənts] n : paciencia f
patient¹ ['peɪʃənt] adj : paciente — **patiently** adv
patient² n : paciente mf
patio ['pæti,oː] n, pl **-tios** : patio m
patriarch ['peɪtri,ɑrk] n : patriarca m
patriarchy ['peɪtri,ɑrki] n, pl **-chies** : patriarcado m
patrimony ['pætrə,moːni] n, pl **-nies** : patrimonio m
patriot ['peɪtriət] n : patriota mf
patriotic [,peɪtri'ɑtɪk] adj : patriótico — **patriotically** adv
patriotism ['peɪtriə,tɪzəm] n : patriotismo m
patrol¹ [pə'troːl] v **-trolled; -trolling** : patrullar
patrol² n : patrulla f
patrolman [pə'troːlmən] n, pl **-men** [-mən, -,mɛn] : policía mf, guardia mf
patron ['peɪtrən] n **1** SPONSOR : patrocinador m, -dora f **2** CUSTOMER : cliente m, -ta f **3** or **patron saint** : patrono m, -na f
patronage ['peɪtrənɪdʒ, 'pæ-] n **1** SPONSORSHIP : patrocinio m **2** CLIENTELE : clientela f **3** : influencia f (política)
patronize ['peɪtrə,naɪz, 'pæ-] vt **-ized; -izing 1** SPONSOR : patrocinar **2** : ser cliente de (un negocio) **3** : tratar con condescendencia
patter¹ ['pætər] vi **1** TAP : golpetear, tamborilear (dícese de la lluvia) **2 to patter about** : corretear (con pasos ligeros)
patter² n **1** TAPPING : golpeteo m, tamborileo m (de la lluvia), correteo m (de pies) **2** CHATTER : palabrería f, parloteo m fam
pattern¹ ['pætərn] vt **1** BASE : basar (en un modelo) **2 to pattern after** : hacer imitación de
pattern² n **1** MODEL : modelo m, patrón m (de costura) **2** DESIGN : diseño m, dibujo m, estampado m (de tela) **3** NORM, STANDARD : pauta f, norma f, patrón m
patty ['pæti] n, pl **-ties** : porción f de carne picada (u otro alimento) en forma de ruedita ⟨a hamburger patty : una hamburguesa⟩
paucity ['pɔsəti] n : escasez f
paunch ['pɔntʃ] n : panza f, barriga f
pauper ['pɔpər] n : pobre mf, indigente mf
pause¹ ['pɔz] vi **paused; pausing** : hacer una pausa, pararse (brevemente)
pause² n : pausa f
pave ['peɪv] vt **paved; paving** : pavimentar ⟨to pave with stones : empedrar⟩

pavement ['peɪvmənt] n : pavimento m, empedrado m
pavilion [pə'vɪljən] n : pabellón m
paving ['peɪvɪŋ] → **pavement**
paw¹ ['pɔ] vt : tocar, manosear, sobar
paw² n : pata f, garra f, zarpa f
pawn¹ ['pɔn] vt : empeñar, prendar
pawn² n **1** PLEDGE, SECURITY : prenda f **2** PAWNING : empeño m **3** : peón m (en ajedrez)
pawnbroker ['pɔn,broːkər] n : prestamista mf
pawnshop ['pɔn,ʃɑp] n : casa f de empeños, monte m de piedad
pay¹ ['peɪ] v **paid** ['peɪd]; **paying** vt **1** : pagar (una cuenta, a un empleado, etc.) **2 to pay attention** : poner atención, prestar atención, hacer caso **3 to pay back** : pagar, devolver ⟨she paid them back : les devolvió el dinero⟩ ⟨I'll pay you back for what you did! : ¡me las pagarás!⟩ **4 to pay off** SETTLE : saldar, cancelar (una deuda, etc.) **5 to pay one's respects** : presentar uno sus respetos **6 to pay a visit** : hacer una visita — vi : valer la pena ⟨crime doesn't pay : no hay crimen sin castigo⟩
pay² n : paga f
payable ['peɪəbəl] adj DUE : pagadero
paycheck ['peɪ,tʃɛk] n : sueldo m, cheque m del sueldo
payee [peɪ'iː] n : beneficiario m, -ria f (de un cheque, etc.)
payment ['peɪmənt] n **1** : pago m **2** INSTALLMENT : plazo m, cuota f **3** REWARD : recompensa f
payoff ['peɪ,ɔf] n **1** REWARD : recompensa f **2** PROFIT : ganancia f **3** BRIBE : soborno m
payroll ['peɪ,roːl] n : nómina f
PC [,piː'siː] n, pl **PCs** or **PC's** : PC mf, computadora f personal
pea ['piː] n : chícharo m, guisante m, arveja f
peace ['piːs] n **1** : paz f ⟨peace treaty : tratado de paz⟩ ⟨peace and tranquility : paz y tranquilidad⟩ **2** ORDER : orden m (público)
peaceable ['piːsəbəl] adj : pacífico — **peaceably** [-bli] adv
peaceful ['piːsfəl] adj **1** PEACEABLE : pacífico **2** CALM, QUIET : tranquilo, sosegado — **peacefully** adv
peacemaker ['piːs,meɪkər] n : conciliador m, -dora f; mediador m, -dora f
peach ['piːtʃ] n : durazno m, melocotón m
peacock ['piː,kɑk] n : pavo m real
peak¹ ['piːk] vi : alcanzar su nivel máximo
peak² adj : máximo
peak³ n **1** POINT : punta f **2** CREST, SUMMIT : cima f, cumbre f **3** APEX : cúspide f, apogeo m, nivel m máximo
peaked ['piːkəd] adj SICKLY : pálido
peal¹ ['piːl] vi : repicar
peal² n : repique m, tañido m (de campanada) ⟨peals of laughter : carcajadas⟩

peanut ['pi:ˌnʌt] *n* : maní *m*, cacahuate *m Mex*, cacahuete *m Spain*
pear ['pær] *n* : pera *f*
pearl ['pərl] *n* : perla *f*
pearly ['pərli] *adj* **pearlier; -est** : nacarado
peasant ['pɛzənt] *n* : campesino *m*, -na *f*
peat ['pi:t] *n* : turba *f*
pebble ['pɛbəl] *n* : guijarro *m*, piedrecita *f*, piedrita *f*
pecan [pɪ'kɑn, -'kæn, 'pi:ˌkæn] *n* : pacana *f*, nuez *f Mex*
peccadillo [ˌpɛkə'dɪlo] *n*, *pl* **-loes** *or* **-los** : pecadillo *m*
peccary ['pɛkəri] *n*, *pl* **-ries** : pécari *m*, pecarí *m*
peck[1] ['pɛk] *vt* : picar, picotear
peck[2] *n* **1** : medida *f* de áridos equivalente a 8.810 litros **2** : picotazo *m* (de un pájaro) ⟨a peck on the cheek : un besito en la mejilla⟩
pectoral ['pɛktərəl] *adj* : pectoral
peculiar [pɪ'kju:ljər] *adj* **1** DISTINCTIVE : propio, peculiar, característico ⟨peculiar to this area : propio de esta zona⟩ **2** STRANGE : extraño, raro — **peculiarly** *adv*
peculiarity [pɪˌkju:l'jærəti, -ˌkju:li'ær-] *n*, *pl* **-ties 1** DISTINCTIVENESS : peculiaridad *f* **2** ODDITY, QUIRK : rareza *f*, idiosincrasia *f*, excentricidad *f*
pecuniary [pɪ'kju:niˌeri] *adj* : pecuniario
pedagogical [ˌpɛdə'gɑʤɪkəl, -'go:-] *adj* : pedagógico
pedagogy ['pɛdəˌgo:ʤi, -ˌgɑ-] *n* : pedagogía *f*
pedal[1] ['pɛdəl] *v* **-aled** *or* **-alled; -aling** *or* **-alling** *vi* : pedalear — *vt* : darle a los pedales de
pedal[2] *n* : pedal *m*
pedant ['pɛdənt] *n* : pedante *mf*
pedantic [pɪ'dæntɪk] *adj* : pedante
pedantry ['pɛdəntri] *n*, *pl* **-ries** : pedantería *f*
peddle ['pɛdəl] *vt* **-dled; -dling** : vender (en las calles)
peddler ['pɛdlər] *n* : vendedor *m*, -dora *f* ambulante; mercachifle *m*
pedestal ['pɛdəstəl] *n* : pedestal *m*
pedestrian[1] [pə'dɛstriən] *adj* **1** COMMONPLACE : pedestre, ordinario **2** : de peatón, peatonal ⟨pedestrian crossing : paso de peatones⟩
pedestrian[2] *n* : peatón *m*, -tona *f*
pediatric [ˌpi:di'ætrɪk] *adj* : pediátrico
pediatrician [ˌpi:diə'trɪʃən] *n* : pediatra *mf*
pediatrics [ˌpi:di'ætrɪks] *ns & pl* : pediatría *f*
pedigree ['pɛdəˌgri:] *n* **1** FAMILY TREE : árbol *m* genealógico **2** LINEAGE : pedigrí *m* (de un animal), linaje *m* (de una persona)
peek[1] ['pi:k] *vi* **1** PEEP : espiar, mirar furtivamente **2** GLANCE : echar un vistazo
peek[2] *n* **1** : miradita *f* (furtiva) **2** GLANCE : vistazo *m*, ojeada *f*

peel[1] ['pi:l] *vt* **1** : pelar (fruta, etc.) **2** *or* **to peel away** : quitar — *vi* : pelarse (dícese de la piel), desconcharse (dícese de la pintura)
peel[2] *n* : cáscara *f*
peep[1] ['pi:p] *vi* **1** PEEK : espiar, mirar furtivamente **2** CHEEP : piar **3 to peep out** SHOW : asomarse
peep[2] *n* **1** CHEEP : pío *m* (de un pajarito) **2** GLANCE : vistazo *m*, ojeada *f*
peer[1] ['pɪr] *vi* : mirar detenidamente, mirar con atención
peer[2] *n* **1** EQUAL : par *m*, igual *mf* **2** NOBLE : noble *mf*
peerage ['pɪrɪʤ] *n* : nobleza *f*
peerless ['pɪrləs] *adj* : sin par, incomparable
peeve[1] ['pi:v] *vt* **peeved; peeving** : fastidiar, irritar, molestar
peeve[2] *n* : queja *f*
peevish ['pi:vɪʃ] *adj* : quejoso, fastidioso — **peevishly** *adv*
peevishness ['pi:vɪʃnəs] *n* : irritabilidad *f*
peg[1] ['pɛg] *vt* **pegged; pegging 1** PLUG : tapar (con una clavija) **2** FASTEN, FIX : sujetar (con estaquillas) **3 to peg out** MARK : marcar (con estaquillas)
peg[2] *n* : estaquilla *f* (para clavar), clavija *f* (para tapar)
pejorative [pɪ'ʤɔrətɪv] *adj* : peyorativo — **pejoratively** *adv*
pelican ['pɛlɪkən] *n* : pelícano *m*
pellagra [pə'lægrə, -'leɪ-] *n* : pelagra *f*
pellet ['pɛlət] *n* **1** BALL : bolita *f* ⟨food pellet : bolita de comida⟩ **2** SHOT : perdigón *m*
pell—mell ['pɛl'mɛl] *adv* : desordenadamente, atropelladamente
pelt[1] ['pɛlt] *vt* **1** THROW : lanzar, tirar (algo a alguien) **2 to pelt with stones** : apedrear — *vi* BEAT : golpear con fuerza ⟨the rain was pelting down : llovía a cántaros⟩
pelt[2] *n* : piel *f*, pellejo *m*
pelvic ['pɛlvɪk] *adj* : pélvico
pelvis ['pɛlvɪs] *n*, *pl* **-vises** *or* **-ves** ['pɛlˌvi:z] : pelvis *f*
pen[1] ['pɛn] *vt* **penned; penning 1** *or* **pen in** : encerrar (animales) **2** WRITE : escribir
pen[2] *n* **1** CORRAL : corral *m*, redil *m* (para ovejas) **2** : pluma *f* ⟨fountain pen : pluma fuente⟩ ⟨ballpoint pen : bolígrafo⟩
penal ['pi:nəl] *adj* : penal
penalize ['pi:nəlˌaɪz, 'pɛn-] *vt* **-ized; -izing** : penalizar, sancionar, penar
penalty ['pɛnəlti] *n*, *pl* **-ties 1** PUNISHMENT : pena *f*, castigo *m* **2** DISADVANTAGE : desventaja *f*, castigo *m*, penalty *m* (en deportes) **3** FINE : multa *f*
penance ['pɛnənts] *n* : penitencia *f*
pence → penny
penchant ['pɛntʃənt] *n* : inclinación *f*, afición *f*

pencil¹ [ˈpɛntsəl] *vt* **-ciled** *or* **-cilled; -cil-ing** *or* **-cilling** : escribir con lápiz, dibujar con lápiz

pencil² *n* : lápiz *m*

pendant [ˈpɛndənt] *n* : colgante *m*

pending¹ [ˈpɛndɪŋ] *adj* : pendiente

pending² *prep* **1** DURING : durante **2** AWAITING : en espera de

pendulum [ˈpɛndʒələm, -djʊləm] *n* : péndulo *m*

penetrate [ˈpɛnəˌtreɪt] *vt* **-trated; -trating** : penetrar

penetrating [ˈpɛnəˌtreɪtɪŋ] *adj* : penetrante, cortante

penetration [ˌpɛnəˈtreɪʃən] *n* : penetración *f*

penguin [ˈpɛŋgwɪn, ˈpɛn-] *n* : pingüino *m*

penicillin [ˌpɛnəˈsɪlən] *n* : penicilina *f*

peninsula [pəˈnɪntsələ, -ˈnɪntʃʊlə] *n* : península *f*

penis [ˈpiːnəs] *n, pl* **-nes** [-ˌniːz] *or* **-nises** : pene *m*

penitence [ˈpɛnətənts] *n* : arrepentimiento *m*, penitencia *f*

penitent¹ [ˈpɛnətənt] *adj* : arrepentido, penitente

penitent² *n* : penitente *mf*

penitentiary [ˌpɛnəˈtɛnt ʃəri] *n, pl* **-ries** : penitenciaría *f*, prisión *m*, presidio *m*

penmanship [ˈpɛnmənˌʃɪp] *n* : escritura *f*, caligrafía *f*

pen name *n* : seudónimo *m*

pennant [ˈpɛnənt] *n* : gallardete *m* (de un barco), banderín *m*

penniless [ˈpɛniləs] *adj* : sin un centavo

penny [ˈpɛni] *n, pl* **-nies** *or* **pence** [ˈpɛnts] **1** : penique *m* (del Reino Unido) **2** *pl* **-nies** CENT : centavo *m* (de los Estados Unidos)

pension¹ [ˈpɛnʃən] *vt or* **to pension off** : jubilar

pension² *n* : pensión *m*, jubilación *f*

pensive [ˈpɛntsɪv] *adj* : pensativo, meditabundo — **pensively** *adv*

pent [ˈpɛnt] *adj* : encerrado ⟨pent-up feelings : emociones reprimidas⟩

pentagon [ˈpɛntəˌgɑn] *n* : pentágono *m*

pentagonal [pɛnˈtægənəl] *adj* : pentagonal

penthouse [ˈpɛntˌhaʊs] *n* : ático *m*, penthouse *m*

penultimate [pɪˈnʌltəmət] *adj* : penúltimo

penury [ˈpɛnjəri] *n* : penuria *f*, miseria *f*

peon [ˈpiːˌɑn, -ən] *n, pl* **-ons** *or* **-ones** [peɪˈoːniːz] : peón *m*

peony [ˈpiːəni] *n, pl* **-nies** : peonía *f*

people¹ [ˈpiːpəl] *vt* **-pled; -pling** : poblar

people² *ns & pl* **1** **people** *npl* : gente *f*, personas *fpl* ⟨people like him : él le cae bien a la gente⟩ ⟨many people : mucha gente, muchas personas⟩ **2** *pl* **peoples** : pueblo *m* ⟨the Cuban people : el pueblo cubano⟩

pep¹ [ˈpɛp] *vt* **pepped; pepping** *or* **to pep up** : animar

pep² *n* : energía *f*, vigor *m*

pepper¹ [ˈpɛpər] *vt* **1** : añadir pimienta a **2** RIDDLE : acribillar (a balazos) **3** SPRINKLE : salpicar ⟨peppered with quotations : salpicado de citas⟩

pepper² *n* **1** : pimienta *f* (condimento) **2** : pimiento *m*, pimentón *m* (fruta) **3** → **chili**

peppermint [ˈpɛpərˌmɪnt] *n* : menta *f*

peppery [ˈpɛpəri] *adj* : picante

peppy [ˈpɛpi] *adj* **peppier; -est** : lleno de energía, vivaz

peptic [ˈpɛptɪk] *adj* **peptic ulcer** : úlcera *f* estomacal

per [ˈpər] *prep* **1** : por ⟨miles per hour : millas por hora⟩ **2** ACCORDING TO : según ⟨per his specifications : según sus especificaciones⟩

per annum [pərˈænəm] *adv* : al año, por año

percale [ˌpərˈkeɪl, ˈpər-ˌ; ˌpərˈkæl] *n* : percal *m*

per capita [pərˈkæpɪtə] *adv & adj* : per cápita

perceive [pərˈsiːv] *vt* **-ceived; -ceiving 1** REALIZE : percatarse de, concientizarse de, darse cuenta de **2** NOTE : percibir, notar

percent¹ [pərˈsɛnt] *adv* : por ciento

percent² *n, pl* **-cent** *or* **-cents 1** : por ciento ⟨10 percent of the population : el 10 por ciento de la población⟩ **2** → **percentage**

percentage [pərˈsɛntɪdʒ] *n* : porcentaje *m*

perceptible [pərˈsɛptəbəl] *adj* : perceptible — **perceptibly** [-bli] *adv*

perception [pərˈsɛpʃən] *n* **1** : percepción *f* ⟨color perception : la percepción de los colores⟩ **2** INSIGHT : perspicacia *f* **3** IDEA : idea *f*, imagen *f*

perceptive [pərˈsɛptɪv] *adj* : perspicaz

perceptively [pərˈsɛptɪvli] *adv* : con perspicacia

perch¹ [ˈpərtʃ] *vi* **1** ROOST : posarse **2** SIT : sentarse (en un sitio elevado) — *vt* PLACE : posar, colocar

perch² *n* **1** ROOST : percha *f* (para los pájaros) **2** *pl* **perch** *or* **perches** : perca *f* (pez)

percolate [ˈpərkəˌleɪt] *vi* **-lated; -lating** : colarse, filtrarse ⟨percolated coffee : café filtrado⟩

percolator [ˈpərkəˌleɪtər] *n* : cafetera *f* de filtro

percussion [pərˈkʌʃən] *n* **1** STRIKING : percusión *f* **2** *or* **percussion instruments** : instrumentos *mpl* de percusión

peremptory [pəˈrɛmptəri] *adj* : perentorio

perennial¹ [pəˈrɛniəl] *adj* **1** : perenne, vivaz ⟨perennial flowers : flores perennes⟩ **2** RECURRENT : perenne, continuo ⟨a perennial problem : un problema eterno⟩

perennial² *n* : planta *f* perenne, planta *f* vivaz

perfect¹ [pərˈfɛkt] *vt* : perfeccionar

perfect² ['pərfɪkt] *adj* : perfecto — **perfectly** *adv*

perfection [pər'fɛkʃən] *n* : perfección *f*

perfectionist [pər'fɛkʃnɪst] *n* : perfeccionista *mf*

perfidious [pər'fɪdiəs] *adj* : pérfido

perforate ['pərfə,reɪt] *vt* **-rated; -rating** : perforar

perforation [,pərfə'reɪʃən] *n* : perforación *f*

perform [pər'fɔrm] *vt* **1** CARRY OUT : realizar, hacer, desempeñar **2** PRESENT : representar, dar (una obra teatral, etc.) — *vi* : actuar (en una obra teatral), cantar (en una ópera, etc.), tocar (en un concierto, etc.), bailar (en un ballet, etc.)

performance [pər'fɔrmənts] *n* **1** EXECUTION : ejecución *f*, realización *f*, desempeño *m*, rendimiento *m* **2** INTERPRETATION : interpretación *f* ⟨his performance of Hamlet : su interpretación de Hamlet⟩ **3** PRESENTATION : representación *f* (de una obra teatral), función *f*

performer [pər'fɔrmər] *n* : artista *mf*; actor *m*, -triz *f*; intérprete *mf* (de música)

perfume¹ [pər'fju:m, 'pər,-] *vt* **-fumed; -fuming** : perfumar

perfume² ['pər,fju:m, pər'-] *n* : perfume *m*

perfunctory [pər'fʌŋktəri] *adj* : mecánico, superficial, somero

perhaps [pər'hæps] *adv* : tal vez, quizá, quizás

peril ['pɛrəl] *n* : peligro *m*

perilous ['pɛrələs] *adj* : peligroso — **perilously** *adv*

perimeter [pə'rɪmətər] *n* : perímetro *m*

period ['pɪriəd] *n* **1** : punto *m* (en puntuación) **2** : período *m* ⟨a two-hour period : un período de dos horas⟩ **3** STAGE : época *f* (histórica), fase *f*, etapa *f*

periodic [,pɪri'ɑdɪk] *or* **periodical** [-dɪkəl] *adj* : periódico — **periodically** [-dɪkli] *adv*

periodical [,pɪri'ɑdɪkəl] *n* : publicación *f* periódica, revista *f*

peripheral [pə'rɪfərəl] *adj* : periférico

periphery [pə'rɪfəri] *n, pl* **-eries** : periferia *f*

periscope ['pɛrə,sko:p] *n* : periscopio *m*

perish ['pɛrɪʃ] *vi* DIE : perecer, morirse

perishable¹ ['pɛrɪʃəbəl] *adj* : perecedero

perishable² *n* : producto *m* perecedero

perjure ['pərdʒər] *vt* **-jured; -juring** (*used in law*) **to perjure oneself** : perjurar, perjurarse

perjury ['pərdʒəri] *n* : perjurio *m*

perk¹ ['pərk] *vt* **1** : levantar (las orejas, etc.) **2** *or* **to perk up** FRESHEN : arreglar — *vi* **to perk up** : animarse, reanimarse

perk² *n* : extra *m*

perky ['pərki] *adj* **perkier; -est** : animado, alegre, lleno de vida

permanence ['pərmənənts] *n* : permanencia *f*

permanent¹ ['pərmənənt] *adj* : permanente — **permanently** *adv*

permanent² *n* : permanente *f*

permeability [,pərmiə'bɪləti] *n* : permeabilidad *f*

permeable ['pərmiəbəl] *adj* : permeable

permeate ['pərmi,eɪt] *v* **-ated; -ating** *vt* **1** PENETRATE : penetrar, impregnar **2** PERVADE : penetrar, difundirse por — *vi* : penetrar

permissible [pər'mɪsəbəl] *adj* : permisible, lícito

permission [pər'mɪʃən] *n* : permiso *m*

permissive [pər'mɪsɪv] *adj* : permisivo

permit¹ [pər'mɪt] *vt* **-mitted; -mitting** : permitir, dejar ⟨weather permitting : si el tiempo lo permite⟩

permit² ['pər,mɪt, pər'-] *n* : permiso *m*, licencia *f*

pernicious [pər'nɪʃəs] *adj* : pernicioso

peroxide [pə'rɑk,saɪd] *n* **1** : peróxido *m* **2** → hydrogen peroxide

perpendicular¹ [,pərpən'dɪkjələr] *adj* **1** VERTICAL : vertical **2** : perpendicular ⟨perpendicular lines : líneas perpendiculares⟩ — **perpendicularly** *adv*

perpendicular² *n* : perpendicular *f*

perpetrate ['pərpə,treɪt] *vt* **-trated; -trating** : perpetrar, cometer (un delito)

perpetrator ['pərpə,treɪtər] *n* : autor *m*, -tora *f* (de un delito)

perpetual [pər'pɛtʃuəl] *adj* **1** EVERLASTING : perpetuo, eterno **2** CONTINUAL : perpetuo, continuo, constante

perpetually [pər'pɛtʃuəli, -tʃəli] *adv* : para siempre, eternamente

perpetuate [pər'pɛtʃu,eɪt] *vt* **-ated; -ating** : perpetuar

perpetuity [,pərpə'tu:əti, -'tju:-] *n, pl* **-ties** : perpetuidad *f*

perplex [pər'plɛks] *vt* : dejar perplejo, confundir

perplexed [pər'plɛkst] *adj* : perplejo

perplexity [pər'plɛksəti] *n, pl* **-ties** : perplejidad *f*, confusión *f*

persecute ['pərsɪ,kju:t] *vt* **-cuted; -cuting** : perseguir

persecution [,pərsɪ'kju:ʃən] *n* : persecución *f*

perseverance [,pərsə'vɪrənts] *n* : perseverancia *f*

persevere [,pərsə'vɪr] *vi* **-vered; -vering** : perseverar

Persian ['pərʒən] *n* **1** : persa *mf* **2** : persa *m* (idioma) — **Persian** *adj*

persist [pər'sɪst] *vi* : persistir

persistence [pər'sɪstənts] *n* **1** CONTINUATION : persistencia *f* **2** TENACITY : perseverancia *f*, tenacidad *f*

persistent [pər'sɪstənt] *adj* : persistente — **persistently** *adv*

person ['pərsən] *n* **1** HUMAN, INDIVIDUAL : persona *f*, individuo *m*, ser *m* humano **2** : persona *f* (en gramática) **3** **in person** : en persona

personable ['pərsənəbəl] *adj* : agradable

personage ['pərsənidʒ] *n* : personaje *m*
personal ['pərsənəl] *adj* **1** OWN, PRIVATE : personal, particular, privado ⟨for personal reasons : por razones personales⟩ **2** : en persona ⟨to make a personal appearance : presentarse en persona, hacerse acto de presencia⟩ **3** : íntimo, personal ⟨personal hygiene : higiene personal⟩ **4** INDISCREET, PRYING : indiscreto, personal
personal computer *n* : computadora *f* personal, ordenador *m* personal *Spain*
personal digital assistant *n* : asistente *m* personal digital
personality [,pərsən'æləti] *n, pl* **-ties 1** DISPOSITION : personalidad *f*, temperamento *m* **2** CELEBRITY : personalidad *f*, personaje *m*, celebridad *f*
personalize ['pərsənə,laɪz] *vt* **-ized; -izing** : personalizar
personally ['pərsənəli] *adv* **1** : personalmente, en persona ⟨I'll do it personally : lo haré personalmente⟩ **2** : como persona ⟨personally she's very amiable : como persona es muy amable⟩ **3** : personalmente ⟨personally, I don't believe it : yo, personalmente, no me lo creo⟩
personification [pər,sanəfə'keɪʃən] *n* : personificación *f*
personify [pər'sanə,faɪ] *vt* **-fied; -fying** : personificar
personnel [,pərsən'ɛl] *n* : personal *m*
perspective [pər'spɛktɪv] *n* : perspectiva *f*
perspicacious [,pərspə'keɪʃəs] *adj* : perspicaz
perspiration [,pərspə'reɪʃən] *n* : transpiración *f*, sudor *m*
perspire [pər'spaɪr] *vi* **-spired; -spiring** : transpirar, sudar
persuade [pər'sweɪd] *vt* **-suaded; -suading** : persuadir, convencer
persuasion [pər'sweɪʒən] *n* : persuasión *f*
persuasive [pər'sweɪsɪv, -zɪv] *adj* : persuasivo — **persuasively** *adv*
persuasiveness [pər'sweɪsɪvnəs, -zɪv-] *n* : persuasión *f*
pert ['pərt] *adj* **1** SAUCY : descarado, impertinente **2** JAUNTY : alegre, animado ⟨a pert little hat : un sombrero coqueto⟩
pertain [pər'teɪn] *vi* **1** BELONG : pertenecer (a) **2** RELATE : estar relacionado (con)
pertinence ['pərtənənts] *n* : pertinencia *f*
pertinent ['pərtənənt] *adj* : pertinente
perturb [pər'tərb] *vt* : perturbar
perusal [pə'ru:zəl] *n* : lectura *f* cuidadosa
peruse [pə'ru:z] *vt* **-rused; -rusing 1** READ : leer con cuidado **2** SCAN : recorrer con la vista ⟨he perused the newspaper : echó un vistazo al periódico⟩

Peruvian [pə'ru:viən] *n* : peruano *m*, -na *f* — **Peruvian** *adj*
pervade [pər'veɪd] *vt* **-vaded; -vading** : penetrar, difundirse por
pervasive [pər'veɪsɪv, -zɪv] *adj* : penetrante
perverse [pər'vərs] *adj* **1** CORRUPT : perverso, corrompido **2** STUBBORN : obstinado, porfiado, terco (sin razón) — **perversely** *adv*
perversion [pər'vərʒən] *n* : perversión *f*
perversity [pər'vərsəti] *n, pl* **-ties 1** CORRUPTION : corrupción *f* **2** STUBBORNNESS : obstinación *f*, terquedad *f*
pervert[1] [pər'vərt] *vt* **1** DISTORT : pervertir, distorsionar **2** CORRUPT : pervertir, corromper
pervert[2] ['pər,vərt] *n* : pervertido *m*, -da *f*
pesky ['pɛski] *adj* : molestoso, molesto
peso ['peɪ,so:] *n, pl* **-sos** : peso *m*
pessimism ['pɛsə,mɪzəm] *n* : pesimismo *m*
pessimist ['pɛsəmɪst] *n* : pesimista *mf*
pessimistic [,pɛsə'mɪstɪk] *adj* : pesimista
pest ['pɛst] *n* **1** NUISANCE : peste *f*; latoso *m*, -sa *f fam* ⟨to be a pest : dar (la) lata⟩ **2** : insecto *m* nocivo, animal *m* nocivo ⟨the squirrels were pests : las ardillas eran una plaga⟩
pester ['pɛstər] *vt* **-tered; -tering** : molestar, fastidiar
pesticide ['pɛstə,saɪd] *n* : pesticida *m*
pestilence ['pɛstələnts] *n* : pestilencia *f*, peste *f*
pestle ['pɛsəl, 'pɛstəl] *n* : mano *f* de mortero, mazo *m*, maja *f*
pet[1] ['pɛt] *vt* **petted; petting** : acariciar
pet[2] *n* **1** : animal *m* doméstico **2** FAVORITE : favorito *m*, -ta *f*
petal ['pɛtəl] *n* : pétalo *m*
petite [pə'ti:t] *adj* : pequeña, menuda, chiquita
petition[1] [pə'tɪʃən] *vt* : peticionar
petition[2] *n* : petición *f*
petitioner [pə'tɪʃənər] *n* : peticionario *m*, -ria *f*
petrify ['pɛtrə,faɪ] *vt* **-fied; -fying** : petrificar
petroleum [pə'tro:liəm] *n* : petróleo *m*
petticoat ['pɛti,ko:t] *n* : enagua *f*, fondo *m Mex*
pettiness ['pɛtinəs] *n* **1** INSIGNIFICANCE : insignificancia *f* **2** MEANNESS : mezquindad *f*
petty ['pɛti] *adj* **-tier; -est 1** MINOR : menor ⟨petty cash : dinero para gastos menores⟩ **2** INSIGNIFICANT : insignificante, trivial, nimio **3** MEAN : mezquino
petty officer *n* : suboficial *mf*
petulance ['pɛtʃələnts] *n* : irritabilidad *f*, mal genio *m*
petulant ['pɛtʃələnt] *adj* : irritable, de mal genio
petunia [pɪ'tu:njə, -'tju:-] *n* : petunia *f*
pew ['pju:] *n* : banco *m* (de iglesia)

pewter ['pju:tǝr] *n* : peltre *m*
pH [ˌpi:'eɪtʃ] *n* : pH *m*
phallic ['fælɪk] *adj* : fálico
phallus ['fæləs] *n, pl* **-li** ['fæˌlaɪ] *or* **-luses** : falo *m*
phantasy ['fæntəsi] → **fantasy**
phantom ['fæntəm] *n* : fantasma *m*
pharaoh ['fɛrˌo:, 'feɪˌro:] *n* : faraón *m*
pharmaceutical [ˌfɑrmə'su:ṭɪkəl] *adj* : farmacéutico
pharmacist ['fɑrməsɪst] *n* : farmacéutico *m*, -ca *f*
pharmacology [ˌfɑrmə'kɑləʤi] *n* : farmacología *f*
pharmacy ['fɑrməsi] *n, pl* **-cies** : farmacia *f*
pharynx ['færɪŋks] *n, pl* **pharynges** [fə'rɪnˌʤi:z] : faringe *f*
phase¹ ['feɪz] *vt* **phased; phasing 1** SYNCHRONIZE : sincronizar, poner en fase **2** STAGGER : escalonar **3 to phase in** : introducir progresivamente **4 to phase out** : retirar progresivamente, dejar de producir
phase² *n* **1** : fase *f* (de la luna, etc.) **2** STAGE : fase *f*, etapa *f*
pheasant ['fɛzənt] *n, pl* **-ant** *or* **-ants** : faisán *m*
phenomenal [fɪ'nɑmənəl] *adj* : extraordinario, excepcional
phenomenon [fɪ'nɑməˌnɑn, -nən] *n, pl* **-na** [-nə] *or* **-nons 1** : fenómeno *m* **2** *pl* **-nons** PRODIGY : fenómeno *m*, prodigio *m*
philanthropic [ˌfɪlən'θrɑpɪk] *adj* : filantrópico
philanthropist [fə'læntθrəpɪst] *n* : filántropo *m*, -pa *f*
philanthropy [fə'læntθrəpi] *n, pl* **-pies** : filantropía *f*
philately [fə'lætəli] *n* : filatelia *f*
philodendron [ˌfɪlə'dɛndrən] *n, pl* **-drons** *or* **-dra** [-drə] : arácea *f*
philosopher [fə'lɑsəfər] *n* : filósofo *m*, -fa *f*
philosophic [ˌfɪlə'sɑfɪk] *or* **philosophical** [-fɪkəl] *adj* : filosófico — **philosophically** [-kli] *adv*
philosophize [fə'lɑsəˌfaɪz] *vi* **-phized; -phizing** : filosofar
philosophy [fə'lɑsəfi] *n, pl* **-phies** : filosofía *f*
phlebitis [flɪ'baɪṭəs] *n* : flebitis *f*
phlegm ['flɛm] *n* : flema *f*
phlox ['flɑks] *n, pl* **phlox** *or* **phloxes** : polemonio *m*
phobia ['fo:biə] *n* : fobia *f*
phoenix ['fi:nɪks] *n* : fénix *m*
phone¹ ['fo:n] *v* → **telephone¹**
phone² *n* → **telephone²**
phoneme ['fo:ˌni:m] *n* : fonema *m*
phonetic [fə'nɛṭɪk] *adj* : fonético
phonetics [fə'nɛṭɪks] *n* : fonética *f*
phonics ['fɑnɪks] *n* : método *m* fonético de aprender a leer
phonograph ['fo:nəˌgræf] *n* : fonógrafo *m*, tocadiscos *m*
phony¹ *or* **phoney** ['fo:ni] *adj* **-nier; -est** : falso

phony² *or* **phoney** *n, pl* **-nies** : farsante *mf*; charlatán *m*, -tana *f*
phosphate ['fɑsˌfeɪt] *n* : fosfato *m*
phosphorescence [ˌfɑsfə'rɛsənts] *n* : fosforescencia *f*
phosphorescent [ˌfɑsfə'rɛsənt] *adj* : fosforescente — **phosphorescently** *adv*
phosphorus ['fɑsfərəs] *n* : fósforo *m*
photo ['fo:ṭo:] *n, pl* **-tos** : foto *f*
photocopier ['fo:ṭoˌkɑpiər] *n* : fotocopiadora *f*
photocopy¹ ['fo:ṭoˌkɑpi] *vt* **-copied; -copying** : fotocopiar
photocopy² *n, pl* **-copies** : fotocopia *f*
photoelectric [ˌfo:ṭoɪ'lɛktrɪk] *adj* : fotoeléctrico
photogenic [ˌfo:ṭə'ʤɛnɪk] *adj* : fotogénico
photograph¹ ['fo:ṭəˌgræf] *vt* : fotografiar
photograph² *n* : fotografía *f*, foto *f* ⟨to take a photograph of : tomarle una fotografía a, tomar una fotografía de⟩
photographer [fə'tɑgrəfər] *n* : fotógrafo *m*, -fa *f*
photographic [ˌfo:ṭə'græfɪk] *adj* : fotográfico — **photographically** [-fɪkli] *adv*
photography [fə'tɑgrəfi] *n* : fotografía *f*
photosynthesis [ˌfo:ṭo'sɪntθəsɪs] *n* : fotosíntesis *f*
photosynthetic [ˌfo:ṭosɪn'θɛṭɪk] *adj* : fotosintético, de fotosíntesis
phrase¹ ['freɪz] *vt* **phrased; phrasing** : expresar
phrase² *n* : frase *f*, locución *f* ⟨to coin a phrase : para decirlo así⟩
phylum ['faɪləm] *n, pl* **-la** [-lə] : phylum *m*
physical¹ ['fɪzɪkəl] *adj* **1** : físico ⟨physical laws : leyes físicas⟩ **2** MATERIAL : material, físico **3** BODILY : físico, corpóreo — **physically** [-kli] *adv*
physical² *n* CHECKUP : chequeo *m*, reconocimiento *m* médico
physician [fə'zɪʃən] *n* : médico *m*, -ca *f*
physicist ['fɪzəsɪst] *n* : físico *m*, -ca *f*
physics ['fɪzɪks] *ns & pl* : física *f*
physiognomy [ˌfɪzi'ɑgnəmi] *n, pl* **-mies** : fisonomía *f*
physiological ['fɪziə'lɑʤɪkəl] *or* **physiologic** [-ʤɪk] *adj* : fisiológico
physiologist [ˌfɪzi'ɑləʤɪst] *n* : fisiólogo *m*, -ga *f*
physiology [ˌfɪzi'ɑləʤi] *n* : fisiología *f*
physique [fə'zi:k] *n* : físico *m*
pi ['paɪ] *n, pl* **pis** ['paɪz] : pi *f*
pianist ['pi:ænɪst, 'pi:ənɪst] *n* : pianista *mf*
piano [pi'æno:] *n, pl* **-anos** : piano *m*
piazza [pi'æzə, -'ɑtsə] *n, pl* **-zas** *or* **-ze** [-'ɑtˌseɪ] : plaza *f*
picaresque [ˌpɪkə'rɛsk, ˌpi:-] *adj* : picaresco
picayune [ˌpɪki'ju:n] *adj* : trivial, nimio, insignificante
piccolo ['pɪkəˌlo:] *n, pl* **-los** : flautín *m*
pick¹ ['pɪk] *vt* **1** : picar, labrar (con un pico) ⟨he picked the hard soil : picó la

tierra dura⟩ **2** : quitar, sacar (poco a
poco) ⟨to pick meat off the bones
: quitar pedazos de carne de los hue-
sos⟩ **3** : recoger, arrancar (frutas, flores, etc.) **4** SELECT : escoger, elegir **5**
PROVOKE : provocar ⟨to pick a quar-
rel : buscar pleito, buscar pelea⟩ **6 to
pick a lock** : forzar una cerradura **7 to
pick someone's pocket** : robarle algo
del bolsillo de alguien ⟨someone
picked my pocket! : ¡me robaron la
cartera del bolsillo!⟩ — *vi* **1** NIBBLE
: picar, picotear **2 to pick and choose**
: ser exigente **3 to pick at** : tocar, rascarse (una herida, etc.) **4 to pick on**
TEASE : mofarse de, atormentar

pick² *n* **1** CHOICE : selección *f* **2** BEST
: lo mejor ⟨the pick of the crop : la crema y nata⟩ **3 → pickax**

pickax [ˈpɪkˌæks] *n* : pico *m*, zapapico
m, piqueta *f*

pickerel [ˈpɪkərəl] *n, pl* **-el** *or* **-els** : lucio
m pequeño

picket¹ [ˈpɪkət] *v* : piquetear

picket² *n* **1** STAKE : estaca *f* **2** STRIKER
: huelguista *mf*, integrante *mf* de un piquete

pickle¹ [ˈpɪkəl] *vt* **-led; -ling** : encurtir,
escabechar

pickle² *n* **1** BRINE : escabeche *m* **2**
GHERKIN : pepinillo *m* (encurtido) **3**
JAM, TROUBLE : lío *m*, apuro *m*

pickpocket [ˈpɪkˌpɑkət] *n* : carterista *mf*

pickup [ˈpɪkˌəp] *n* **1** IMPROVEMENT
: mejora *f* **2** *or* **pickup truck** : camioneta *f*

pick up *vt* **1** LIFT : levantar **2** TIDY : arreglar, ordenar — *vi* IMPROVE : mejo-
rar

picnic¹ [ˈpɪkˌnɪk] *vi* **-nicked; -nicking** : ir
de picnic

picnic² *n* : picnic *m*

pictorial [pɪkˈtoriəl] *adj* : pictórico

picture¹ [ˈpɪktʃər] *vt* **-tured; -turing 1**
DEPICT : representar **2** IMAGINE
: imaginarse ⟨can you picture it? : ¿te
lo puedes imaginar?⟩

picture² *n* **1** : cuadro *m* (pintado o dibu-
jado), ilustración *f*, fotografía *f* **2** DE-
SCRIPTION : descripción *f* **3** IMAGE
: imagen *f* ⟨he's the picture of his father : es la viva imagen de su padre⟩ **4**
MOVIE : película *f*

picturesque [ˌpɪktʃəˈrɛsk] *adj* : pintoresco

pie [ˈpaɪ] *n* : pastel *m* (con fruta o carne),
empanada *f* (con carne)

piebald [ˈpaɪˌbɔld] *adj* : picazo, pío

piece¹ [ˈpiːs] *vt* **pieced; piecing 1** PATCH
: parchar, arreglar **2 to piece together** : construir pieza por pieza

piece² *n* **1** FRAGMENT : trozo *m*, pedazo *m* **2** COMPONENT : pieza *f* ⟨a three-
piece suit : un traje de tres piezas⟩ **3**
UNIT : pieza *f* ⟨a piece of fruit : una
(pieza de) fruta⟩ **4** WORK : obra *f*, pieza
f (de música, etc.) **5** (*in board games*)
: ficha *f*, pieza *f*, figura *f* (en ajedrez)

piecemeal¹ [ˈpiːsˌmiːl] *adv* : poco a poco,
por partes

piecemeal² *adj* : hecho poco a poco,
poco sistemático

pied [ˈpaɪd] *adj* : pío

pier [ˈpɪr] *n* **1** : pila *f* (de un puente) **2**
WHARF : muelle *m*, atracadero *m*, embarcadero *m* **3** PILLAR : pilar *m*

pierce [ˈpɪrs] *vt* **pierced; piercing 1** PEN-
ETRATE : atravesar, traspasar, penetrar
(en) ⟨the bullet pierced his leg : la bala
le atravesó la pierna⟩ ⟨to pierce one's
heart : traspasarle el corazón a uno⟩ **2**
PERFORATE : perforar, agujerear (las
orejas, etc.) **3 to pierce the silence**
: desgarrar el silencio

piety [ˈpaɪəti] *n, pl* **-eties** : piedad *f*

pig [ˈpɪg] *n* **1** HOG, SWINE : cerdo *m*, -da
f; puerco *m*, -ca *f* **2** SLOB : persona *f*
desaliñada; cerdo *m*, -da *f* **3** GLUTTON
: glotón *m*, -tona *f* **4** *or* **pig iron** : lingote *m* de hierro

pigeon [ˈpɪdʒən] *n* : paloma *f*

pigeonhole [ˈpɪdʒən͵hoːl] *n* : casilla *f*

pigeon–toed [ˈpɪdʒən͵toːd] *adj* : pat-
ituerto

piggish [ˈpɪgɪʃ] *adj* **1** GREEDY : glotón
2 DIRTY : cochino, sucio

piggyback [ˈpɪgi͵bæk] *adv & adj* : a cuestas

pigheaded [ˈpɪg͵hɛdəd] *adj* : terco, obstinado

piglet [ˈpɪglət] *n* : cochinillo *m*; lechón
m, -chona *f*

pigment [ˈpɪgmənt] *n* : pigmento *m*

pigmentation [͵pɪgmənˈteɪʃən] *n* : pigmentación *f*

pigmy → pygmy

pigpen [ˈpɪg͵pɛn] *n* : chiquero *m*, pocilga *f*

pigsty [ˈpɪg͵staɪ] **→ pigpen**

pigtail [ˈpɪg͵teɪl] *n* : coleta *f*, trenza *f*

pike [ˈpaɪk] *n, pl* **pike** *or* **pikes 1** : lucio
m (pez) **2** LANCE : pica *f* **3 → turnpike**

pile¹ [ˈpaɪl] *v* **piled; piling** *vt* : amontonar,
apilar — *vi* **to pile up** : amontonarse,
acumularse

pile² *n* **1** STAKE : pilote *m* **2** HEAP : montón *m*, pila *f* **3** NAP : pelo *m* (de telas)

piles [ˈpaɪlz] *npl* HEMORRHOIDS : hemorroides *fpl*, almorranas *fpl*

pilfer [ˈpɪlfər] *vt* : robar (cosas pe-
queñas), ratear

pilgrim [ˈpɪlgrəm] *n* : peregrino *m*, -na *f*

pilgrimage [ˈpɪlgrəmɪdʒ] *n* : peregrinación *f*

pill [ˈpɪl] *n* : pastilla *f*, píldora *f*

pillage¹ [ˈpɪlɪdʒ] *vt* **-laged; -laging**
: saquear

pillage² *n* : saqueo *m*

pillar [ˈpɪlər] *n* : pilar *m*, columna *f*

pillory [ˈpɪləri] *n, pl* **-ries** : picota *f*

pillow [ˈpɪˌloː] *n* : almohada *f*

pillowcase [ˈpɪˌloːˌkeɪs] *n* : funda *f*

pilot¹ [ˈpaɪlət] *vt* : pilotar, pilotear

pilot² *n* : piloto *mf*

pilot light *n* : piloto *m*

pimento [pəˈmɛn͵toː] **→ pimiento**

pimiento [pə'mɛn,toː, -'mjɛn-] *n*, *pl* **-tos** : pimiento *m* morrón

pimp ['pɪmp] *n* : proxeneta *m*

pimple ['pɪmpəl] *n* : grano *m*

pimply ['pɪmpəli] *adj* **-plier; -est** : cubierto de granos

pin¹ ['pɪn] *vt* **pinned; pinning 1** FASTEN : prender, sujetar (con alfileres) **2** HOLD, IMMOBILIZE : inmovilizar, sujetar **3 to pin one's hopes on** : poner sus esperanzas en

pin² *n* **1** : alfiler *m* ⟨safety pin : alfiler de gancho⟩ ⟨a bobby pin : una horquilla⟩ **2** BROOCH : alfiler *m*, broche *m*, prendedor *m* **3** *or* **bowling pin** : bolo *m*

pinafore ['pɪnə,for] *n* : delantal *m*

pincer ['pɪntsər] *n* **1** CLAW : pinza *f* (de una langosta, etc.) **2 pincers** *npl* : pinzas *fpl*, tenazas *fpl*, tenaza *f*

pinch¹ ['pɪntʃ] *vt* **1** : pellizcar ⟨she pinched my cheek : me pellizcó el cachete⟩ **2** STEAL : robar — *vi* : apretar ⟨my shoes pinch : me aprietan los zapatos⟩

pinch² *n* **1** EMERGENCY : emergencia *f* ⟨in a pinch : en caso necesario⟩ **2** PAIN : dolor *m*, tormento *m* **3** SQUEEZE : pellizco *m* (con los dedos) **4** BIT : pizca *f*, pellizco *m* ⟨a pinch of cinnamon : una pizca de canela⟩

pinch hitter *n* **1** SUBSTITUTE : sustituto *m*, -ta *f* **2** : bateador *m* emergente (en beisbol)

pincushion ['pɪn,kuʃən] *n* : acerico *m*, alfiletero *m*

pine¹ ['paɪn] *vi* **pined; pining 1 to pine away** : languidecer, consumirse **2 to pine for** : añorar, suspirar por

pine² *n* **1** : pino *m* (árbol) **2** : madera *f* de pino

pineapple ['paɪn,æpəl] *n* : piña *f*, ananá *m*, ananás *m*

ping–pong ['pɪŋ,pɑŋ, -,pɔŋ] *n* : ping-pong *m*

pinion¹ ['pɪnjən] *vt* : sujetar los brazos de, inmovilizar

pinion² *n* : piñón *m*

pink¹ ['pɪŋk] *adj* : rosa, rosado

pink² *n* **1** : clavelito *m* (flor) **2** : rosa *m*, rosado *m* (color) **3 to be in the pink** : estar en plena forma, rebosar de salud

pinkeye ['pɪŋk,aɪ] *n* : conjuntivitis *f* aguda

pinkish ['pɪŋkɪʃ] *adj* : rosáceo

pinnacle ['pɪnɪkəl] *n* **1** : pináculo *m* (de un edificio) **2** PEAK : cima *f*, cumbre *f* (de una montaña) **3** ACME : pináculo *m*, cúspide *f*, apogeo *m*

pinpoint ['pɪn,pɔɪnt] *vt* : precisar, localizar con precisión

pint ['paɪnt] *n* : pinta *f*

pinto ['pɪn,toː] *n*, *pl* **pintos** : caballo *m* pinto

pinworm ['pɪn,wərm] *n* : oxiuro *m*

pioneer¹ [,paɪə'nɪr] *vt* : promover, iniciar, introducir

pioneer² *n* : pionero *m*, -ra *f*

pious ['paɪəs] *adj* **1** DEVOUT : piadoso, devoto **2** SANCTIMONIOUS : beato

piously ['paɪəsli] *adv* **1** DEVOUTLY : piadosamente **2** SANCTIMONIOUSLY : santurronamente

pipe¹ ['paɪp] *v* **piped; piping** *vi* : hablar en voz chillona — *vt* **1** PLAY : tocar (el caramillo o la flauta) **2** : conducir por tuberías ⟨to pipe water : transportar el agua por tubería⟩

pipe² *n* **1** : caramillo *m* (instrumento musical) **2** BAGPIPE : gaita *f* **3** : tubo *m*, caño *m* ⟨gas pipes : tubería de gas⟩ **4** : pipa *f* (para fumar)

pipeline ['paɪp,laɪn] *n* **1** : conducto *m*, oleoducto *m* (para petróleo), gasoducto *m* (para gas) **2** CONDUIT : vía *f* (de información, etc.)

piper ['paɪpər] *n* : músico *m*, -ca *f* que toca el caramillo o la gaita

piping ['paɪpɪŋ] *n* **1** : música *f* del caramillo o de la gaita **2** TRIM : cordoncillo *m*, ribete *m* con cordón

piquant ['piːkənt, 'pɪkwənt] *adj* **1** SPICY : picante **2** INTRIGUING : intrigante, estimulante

pique¹ ['piːk] *vt* **piqued; piquing 1** IRRITATE : picar, irritar **2** AROUSE : despertar (la curiosidad, etc.)

pique² *n* : pique *m*, resentimiento *m*

piracy ['paɪrəsi] *n*, *pl* **-cies** : piratería *f*

piranha [pə'rɑnə, -'rɑnjə, -'rænjə] *n* : piraña *f*

pirate¹ ['paɪrət] *n* : pirata *mf*

pirate² *vt* **-rated; -rating** : piratear (software, etc.)

pirouette [,pɪrə'wɛt] *n* : pirueta *f*

pis → pi

Pisces ['paɪ,siːz, 'pɪ-; 'pɪs,keɪs] *n* : Piscis *mf*

pistachio [pə'stæʃi,oː, -'stɑ-] *n*, *pl* **-chios** : pistacho *m*

pistil ['pɪstəl] *n* : pistilo *m*

pistol ['pɪstəl] *n* : pistola *f*

piston ['pɪstən] *n* : pistón *m*, émbolo *m*

pit¹ ['pɪt] *v* **pitted; pitting** *vt* **1** : marcar de hoyos, picar (una superficie) **2** : deshuesar (una fruta) **3 to pit against** : enfrentar a, oponer a — *vi* : quedar marcado

pit² *n* **1** HOLE : fosa *f*, hoyo *m* ⟨a bottomless pit : un pozo sin fondo⟩ **2** MINE : mina *f* **3** : foso *m* ⟨orchestra pit : foso orquestal⟩ **4** POCKMARK : marca *f* (en la cara), cicatriz *f* de viruela **5** STONE : hueso *m*, pepa *f* (de una fruta) **6 pit of the stomach** : boca *f* del estómago

pitch¹ ['pɪtʃ] *vt* **1** SET UP : montar, armar (una tienda) **2** THROW : lanzar, arrojar **3** ADJUST, SET : dar el tono de (un discurso, un instrumento musical) — *vi* **1** *or* **pitch forward** FALL : caerse **2** LURCH : cabecear (dícese de un barco o un avión), dar bandazos

pitch² *n* **1** LURCHING : cabezada *f*, cabeceo *m* (de un barco o un avión) **2** SLOPE : (grado de) inclinación *f*, pendiente *f* **3** : tono *m* (en música) ⟨perfect pitch : oído absoluto⟩ **4** THROW : lanzamiento *m* **5** DEGREE : grado *m*, nivel *m*, punto *m* ⟨the excitement reached a high pitch : la excitación llegó a un punto culminante⟩ **6** *or* **sales pitch** : presentación *f* (de un vendedor) **7** TAR : pez *f*, brea *f*

pitcher ['pɪtʃər] *n* **1** JUG : jarra *f*, jarro *m*, cántaro *m*, pichel *m* **2** : lanzador *m*, -dora *f* (en béisbol, etc.)

pitchfork ['pɪtʃ,fɔrk] *n* : horquilla *f*, horca *f*

piteous ['pɪtiəs] *adj* : lastimoso, lastimero — **piteously** *adv*

pitfall ['pɪt,fɔl] *n* : peligro *m* (poco obvio), dificultad *f*

pith ['pɪθ] *n* **1** : médula *f* (de una planta) **2** CORE : meollo *m*, entraña *f*

pithy ['pɪθi] *adj* **pithier; -est** : conciso y sustancioso ⟨pithy comments : comentarios sucintos⟩

pitiable ['pɪtiəbəl] → **pitiful**

pitiful ['pɪtifəl] *adj* **1** LAMENTABLE : lastimero, lastimoso, lamentable **2** CONTEMPTIBLE : despreciable, lamentable — **pitifully** [-fli] *adv*

pitiless ['pɪtiləs] *adj* : despiadado — **pitilessly** *adv*

pittance ['pɪtənts] *n* : miseria *f*

pituitary [pə'tu:ə,tɛri, -'tju:-] *adj* : pituitario

pity¹ ['pɪti] *vt* **pitied; pitying** : compadecer, compadecerse de

pity² *n*, *pl* **pities** **1** COMPASSION : compasión *f*, piedad *f* **2** SHAME : lástima *f*, pena *f* ⟨what a pity! : ¡qué lástima!⟩

pivot¹ ['pɪvət] *vi* **1** : girar sobre un eje **2 to pivot on** : girar sobre, depender de

pivot² *n* : pivote *m*

pivotal ['pɪvətəl] *adj* : fundamental, central

pixie *or* **pixy** ['pɪksi] *n*, *pl* **pixies** : elfo *m*, hada *f*

pizza ['pi:tsə] *n* : pizza *f*

pizzazz *or* **pizazz** [pə'zæz] *n* **1** GLAMOR : encanto *m* **2** VITALITY : animación *f*, vitalidad *f*

placard ['plæ,kɑrd, -,kɑrd] *n* POSTER : cartel *m*, póster *m*, afiche *m*

placate ['pleɪ,keɪt, 'plæ-] *vt* **-cated; -cating** : aplacar, apaciguar

place¹ ['pleɪs] *vt* **placed; placing** **1** PUT, SET : poner, colocar **2** SITUATE : situar, ubicar, emplazar ⟨to be well placed : estar bien situado⟩ ⟨to place in a job : colocar en un trabajo⟩ **3** IDENTIFY, RECALL : identificar, ubicar, recordar ⟨I can't place him : no lo ubico⟩ **4 to place an order** : hacer un pedido

place² *n* **1** SPACE : sitio *m*, lugar *m* ⟨there's no place to sit : no hay sitio para sentarse⟩ **2** LOCATION, SPOT : lugar *m*, sitio *m*, parte *f* ⟨place of work : lugar de trabajo⟩ ⟨our summer place : nuestra casa de verano⟩ ⟨all over the place : por todas partes⟩ **3** RANK : lugar *m*, puesto *m* ⟨he took first place : ganó el primer lugar⟩ **4** POSITION : lugar *m* ⟨everything in its place : todo en

su debido lugar⟩ ⟨to feel out of place : sentirse fuera de lugar⟩ **5** SEAT : asiento *m*, cubierto *m* (a la mesa) **6** JOB : puesto *m* **7** ROLE : papel *m*, lugar *m* ⟨to change places : cambiarse los papeles⟩ **8 to take place** : tener lugar **9 to take the place of** : sustituir a

placebo [plə'si:,bo:] *n*, *pl* **-bos** : placebo *m*

placement ['pleɪsmənt] *n* : colocación *f*

placenta [plə'sɛntə] *n*, *pl* **-tas** *or* **-tae** [-ti, -,taɪ] : placenta *f*

placid ['plæsəd] *adj* : plácido, tranquilo — **placidly** *adv*

plagiarism ['pleɪdʒə,rɪzəm] *n* : plagio *m*

plagiarist ['pleɪdʒərɪst] *n* : plagiario *m*, -ria *f*

plagiarize ['pleɪdʒə,raɪz] *vt* **-rized; -rizing** : plagiar

plague¹ ['pleɪg] *vt* **plagued; plaguing** **1** AFFLICT : plagar, afligir **2** HARASS : acosar, atormentar

plague² *n* **1** : plaga *f* (de insectos, etc.) **2** : peste *f* (en medicina)

plaid¹ ['plæd] *adj* : escocés, de cuadros ⟨a plaid skirt : una falda escocesa⟩

plaid² *n* TARTAN : tela *f* escocesa, tartán *m*

plain¹ ['pleɪn] *adj* **1** SIMPLE, UNADORNED : liso, sencillo, sin adornos **2** CLEAR : claro ⟨in plain language : en palabras claras⟩ **3** FRANK : franco, puro ⟨the plain truth : la pura verdad⟩ **4** HOMELY : ordinario, poco atractivo **5 in plain sight** : a la vista de todos

plain² *n* : llanura *f*, llano *m*, planicie *f*

plainly ['pleɪnli] *adv* **1** CLEARLY : claramente **2** FRANKLY : francamente, con franqueza **3** SIMPLY : sencillamente

plaintiff ['pleɪntɪf] *n* : demandante *mf*

plaintive ['pleɪntɪv] *adj* MOURNFUL : lastimero, plañidero

plait¹ ['pleɪt, 'plæt] *vt* **1** PLEAT : plisar **2** BRAID : trenzar

plait² *n* **1** PLEAT : pliegue *m* **2** BRAID : trenza *f*

plan¹ ['plæn] *v* **planned; planning** *vt* **1** : planear, proyectar, planificar ⟨to plan a trip : planear un viaje⟩ ⟨to plan a city : planificar una ciudad⟩ **2** INTEND : tener planeado, proyectar — *vi* : hacer planes

plan² *n* **1** DIAGRAM : plano *m*, esquema *m* **2** SCHEME : plan *m*, proyecto *m*, programa *m* ⟨to draw up a plan : elaborar un proyecto⟩

plane¹ ['pleɪn] *vt* **planed; planing** : cepillar (madera)

plane² *adj* : plano

plane³ *n* **1** : plano *m* (en matemáticas, etc.) **2** LEVEL : nivel *m* **3** : cepillo *m* (de carpintero) **4** → **airplane**

planet ['plænət] *n* : planeta *f*

planetarium [,plænə'tɛriəm] *n*, *pl* **-iums** *or* **-ia** [-iə] : planetario *m*

planetary ['plænə,tɛri] *adj* : planetario

plank ['plæŋk] *n* **1** BOARD : tablón *m*, tabla *f* **2** : artículo *m*, punto *m* (de una plataforma política)

plankton ['plæŋktən] *n* : plancton *m*

plant¹ ['plænt] *vt* **1** : plantar, sembrar (semillas) ⟨planted with flowers : plantado de flores⟩ **2** PLACE : plantar, colocar ⟨to plant an idea : inculcar una idea⟩

plant² *n* **1** : planta *f* ⟨leafy plants : plantas frondosas⟩ **2** FACTORY : planta *f*, fábrica *f* ⟨hydroelectric plant : planta hidroeléctrica⟩ **3** MACHINERY : maquinaria *f*, equipo *m*

plantain ['plæntən] *n* **1** : llantén *m* (mala hierba) **2** : plátano *m*, plátano *m* macho *Mex* (fruta)

plantation [plæn'teɪʃən] *n* : plantación *f*, hacienda *f* ⟨a coffee plantation : un cafetal⟩

planter ['plæntər] *n* **1** : hacendado *m*, -da *f* (de una hacienda) **2** FLOWERPOT : tiesto *m*, maceta *f*

plaque ['plæk] *n* **1** TABLET : placa *f* **2** : placa *f* (dental)

plasma ['plæzmə] *n* : plasma *m*

plaster¹ ['plæstər] *vt* **1** : enyesar, revocar (con yeso) **2** COVER : cubrir, llenar ⟨a wall plastered with notices : una pared cubierta de avisos⟩

plaster² *n* **1** : yeso *m*, revoque *m* (para paredes, etc.) **2** : escayola *f*, yeso *m* (en medicina) **3 plaster of Paris** ['pærɪs] : yeso *m* mate

plaster cast *n* : vaciado *m* de yeso

plasterer ['plæstərər] *n* : revocador *m*, -dora *f*

plastic¹ ['plæstɪk] *adj* **1** : de plástico **2** PLIABLE : plástico, flexible **3 plastic surgery** : cirugía *f* plástica

plastic² *n* : plástico *m*

plasticity [plæ'stɪsəti] *n, pl* **-ties** : plasticidad *f*

plate¹ ['pleɪt] *vt* **plated; plating** : chapar (en metal)

plate² *n* **1** PLAQUE, SHEET : placa *f* ⟨a steel plate : una placa de acero⟩ **2** UTENSILS : vajilla *f* (de metal) ⟨silver plate : vajilla de plata⟩ **3** DISH : plato *m* **4** DENTURES : dentadura *f* postiza **5** ILLUSTRATION : lámina *f* (en un libro) **6 license plate** : matrícula *f*, placa *f* de matrícula

plateau [plæ'to:] *n, pl* **-teaus** *or* **-teaux** [-'to:z] : meseta *f*

platform ['plæt,fɔrm] *n* **1** STAGE : plataforma *f*, estrado *m*, tribuna *f* **2** : andén *m* (de una estación de ferrocarril) **3 political platform** : plataforma *f* política, programa *m* electoral

plating ['pleɪtɪŋ] *n* **1** : enchapado *m* **2 silver plating** : plateado *m*

platinum ['plætənəm] *n* : platino *m*

platitude ['plætə,tu:d, -,tju:d] *n* : lugar *m* común, perogrullada *f*

platonic [plə'tɑnɪk] *adj* : platónico

platoon [plə'tu:n] *n* : sección *f* (en el ejército)

platter ['plætər] *n* : fuente *f*

platypus ['plætɪpəs, -,pʊs] *n, pl* **platypuses** *or* **platypi** [-,paɪ, -,pi:] : ornitorrinco *m*

plausibility [,plɔzə'bɪləti] *n, pl* **-ties** : credibilidad *f*, verosimilitud *f*

plausible ['plɔzəbəl] *adj* : creíble, convincente, verosímil — **plausibly** [-bli] *adv*

play¹ ['pleɪ] *vi* **1** : jugar ⟨to play with a doll : jugar con una muñeca⟩ ⟨to play with an idea : darle vueltas a una idea⟩ **2** FIDDLE, TOY : jugar, juguetear ⟨don't play with your food : no juegues con la comida⟩ **3** : tocar ⟨to play in a band : tocar en un grupo⟩ **4** : actuar (en una obra de teatro) — *vt* **1** : jugar (un deporte, etc.), jugar a (un juego), jugar contra (un contrincante) **2** : tocar (música o un instrumento) **3** PERFORM : interpretar, hacer el papel de (un carácter), representar (una obra de teatro) ⟨she plays the lead : hace el papel principal⟩ **4 to play back** : poner (una grabación) **5 to play down** : minimizar **6 to play up** : resaltar

play² *n* **1** GAME, RECREATION : juego *m* ⟨children at play : niños jugando⟩ ⟨a play on words : un juego de palabras⟩ **2** ACTION : juego *m* ⟨the ball is in play : la pelota está en juego⟩ ⟨to bring into play : poner en juego⟩ **3** DRAMA : obra *f* de teatro, pieza *f* (de teatro) **4** MOVEMENT : juego *m* (de la luz, una brisa, etc.) **5** SLACK : juego *m* ⟨there's not enough play in the wheel : la rueda no da lo suficiente⟩

playacting ['pleɪˌæktɪŋ] *n* : actuación *f*, teatro *m*

player ['pleɪər] *n* **1** : jugador *m*, -dora *f* (en un juego) **2** ACTOR : actor *m*, actriz *f* **3** MUSICIAN : músico *m*, -ca *f*

playful ['pleɪfəl] *adj* **1** FROLICSOME : juguetón **2** JOCULAR : jocoso — **playfully** *adv*

playfulness ['pleɪfəlnəs] *n* : lo juguetón, jocosidad *f*, alegría *f*

playground ['pleɪˌgraʊnd] *n* : patio *m* de recreo, jardín *m* para jugar

playhouse ['pleɪˌhaʊs] *n* **1** THEATER : teatro *m* **2** : casita *f* de juguete

playing card *n* : naipe *m*, carta *f*

playmate ['pleɪˌmeɪt] *n* : compañero *m*, -ra *f* de juego

play-off ['pleɪˌɔf] *n* : desempate *m*

playpen ['pleɪˌpɛn] *n* : corral *m* (para niños)

plaything ['pleɪˌθɪŋ] *n* : juguete *m*

playwright ['pleɪˌraɪt] *n* : dramaturgo *m*, -ga *f*

plaza ['plæzə, 'plɑ-] *n* **1** SQUARE : plaza *f* **2 shopping plaza** MALL : centro *m* comercial

plea ['pli:] *n* **1** : acto *m* de declararse ⟨he entered a plea of guilty : se declaró culpable⟩ **2** APPEAL : ruego *m*, súplica *f*

plead ['pli:d] *v* **pleaded** *or* **pled** ['plɛd]; **pleading** *vi* **1** : declararse (culpable o inocente) **2 to plead for** : suplicar, implorar — *vt* **1** : alegar, pretextar ⟨he pleaded illness : pretextó la enfermedad⟩ **2 to plead a case** : defender un caso

pleasant ['plɛzənt] *adj* : agradable, grato, bueno — **pleasantly** *adv*

pleasantness ['plɛzəntnəs] *n* : lo agradable, amenidad *f*

pleasantries ['plɛzəntriz] *npl* : cumplidos *mpl*, cortesías *fpl* ⟨to exchange pleasantries : intercambiar cumplidos⟩

please¹ ['pli:z] *v* **pleased; pleasing** *vt* 1 GRATIFY : complacer ⟨please yourself! : ¡cómo quieras!⟩ 2 SATISFY : contentar, satisfacer — *vi* 1 SATISFY : complacer, agradar ⟨anxious to please : deseoso de complacer⟩ 2 LIKE : querer ⟨do as you please : haz lo que quieras, haz lo que te parezca⟩

please² *adv* : por favor

pleased ['pli:zd] *adj* : contento, satisfecho, alegre

pleasing ['pli:zɪŋ] *adj* : agradable — **pleasingly** *adv*

pleasurable ['plɛʒərəbəl] *adj* PLEASANT : agradable

pleasure ['plɛʒər] *n* 1 WISH : deseo *m*, voluntad *f* ⟨at your pleasure : cuando guste⟩ 2 ENJOYMENT : placer *m*, disfrute *m*, goce *m* ⟨with pleasure : con mucho gusto⟩ 3 : placer *m*, gusto *m* ⟨it's a pleasure to be here : me da gusto estar aquí⟩ ⟨the pleasures of reading : los placeres de leer⟩

pleat¹ ['pli:t] *vt* : plisar

pleat² *n* : pliegue *m*

plebeian [plɪ'biən] *adj* : ordinario, plebeyo

pledge¹ ['plɛdʒ] *vt* **pledged; pledging** 1 PAWN : empeñar, prendar 2 PROMISE : prometer, jurar

pledge² *n* 1 SECURITY : garantía *f*, prenda *f* 2 PROMISE : promesa *f*

plenteous ['plɛntiəs] *adj* : copioso, abundante

plentiful ['plɛntɪfəl] *adj* : abundante — **plentifully** [-fli] *adv*

plenty ['plɛnti] *n* : abundancia *f* ⟨plenty of time : tiempo de sobra⟩ ⟨plenty of visitors : muchos visitantes⟩

plethora ['plɛθərə] *n* : plétora *f*

pleurisy ['plʊrəsi] *n* : pleuresía *f*

pliable ['plaɪəbəl] *adj* : flexible, maleable

pliant ['plaɪənt] → **pliable**

pliers ['plaɪərz] *npl* : alicates *mpl*, pinzas *fpl*

plight ['plaɪt] *n* : situación *f* difícil, apuro *m*

plod ['plɑd] *vi* **plodded; plodding** 1 TRUDGE : caminar pesadamente y lentamente 2 DRUDGE : trabajar laboriosamente

plot¹ ['plɑt] *v* **plotted; plotting** *vt* 1 DEVISE : tramar 2 to plot out : trazar, determinar (una posición, etc.) — *vi* CONSPIRE : conspirar

plot² *n* 1 LOT : terreno *m*, parcela *f*, lote *m* 2 STORY : argumento *m* (en el teatro), trama *f* (en un libro, etc.) 3 CONSPIRACY, INTRIGUE : complot *m*, intriga *f*

plotter ['plɑtər] *n* : conspirador *m*, -dora *f*; intrigante *mf*

plow¹ *or* **plough** ['plaʊ] *vt* 1 : arar (la tierra) 2 **to plow the seas** : surcar los mares

plow² *or* **plough** *n* 1 : arado *m* 2 → **snowplow**

plowshare ['plaʊˌʃɛr] *n* : reja *f* del arado

ploy ['plɔɪ] *n* : estratagema *f*, maniobra *f*

pluck¹ ['plʌk] *vt* 1 PICK : arrancar 2 : desplumar (un pollo, etc.) — *vi* **to pluck at** : tirar de

pluck² *n* 1 TUG : tirón *m* 2 COURAGE, SPIRIT : valor *m*, ánimo *m*

plucky ['plʌki] *adj* **pluckier; -est** : valiente, animoso

plug¹ ['plʌɡ] *vt* **plugged; plugging** 1 BLOCK : tapar 2 PROMOTE : hacerle publicidad a, promocionar 3 **to plug in** : enchufar

plug² *n* 1 STOPPER : tapón *m* 2 : enchufe *m* (eléctrico) 3 ADVERTISEMENT : publicidad *f*, propaganda *f*

plum ['plʌm] *n* 1 : ciruela *f* (fruta) 2 : color *m* ciruela 3 PRIZE : premio *m*, algo muy atractivo

plumage ['plu:mɪdʒ] *n* : plumaje *m*

plumb¹ ['plʌm] *vt* 1 : aplomar ⟨to plumb a wall : aplomar una pared⟩ 2 SOUND : sondear, sondar

plumb² *adv* 1 VERTICALLY : a plomo, verticalmente 2 EXACTLY : justo, exactamente 3 COMPLETELY : completamente, absolutamente ⟨plumb crazy : loco de remate⟩

plumb³ *adj* : a plomo

plumb⁴ *n or* **plumb line** : plomada *f*

plumber ['plʌmər] *n* : plomero *m*, -ra *f*; fontanero *m*, -ra *f*

plumbing ['plʌmɪŋ] *n* 1 : plomería *f*, fontanería *f* (trabajo del plomero) 2 PIPES : cañería *f*, tubería *f*

plume ['plu:m] *n* 1 FEATHER : pluma *f* 2 TUFT : penacho *m* (en un sombrero, etc.)

plumed ['plu:md] *adj* : con plumas ⟨white-plumed birds : aves de plumaje blanco⟩

plummet ['plʌmət] *vi* : caer en picada, desplomarse

plump¹ ['plʌmp] *vi or* **to plump down** : dejarse caer (pesadamente)

plump² *adv* 1 STRAIGHT : a plomo 2 DIRECTLY : directamente, sin rodeos ⟨he ran plump into the door : dio de cara con la puerta⟩

plump³ *adj* : llenito *fam*, regordete *fam*, rechoncho *fam*

plumpness ['plʌmpnəs] *n* : gordura *f*

plunder¹ ['plʌndər] *vi* : saquear, robar

plunder² *n* : botín *m*

plunderer ['plʌndərər] *n* : saqueador *m*, -dora *f*

plunge¹ ['plʌndʒ] *v* **plunged; plunging** *vt* 1 IMMERSE : sumergir 2 THRUST : hundir, clavar — *vi* 1 DIVE : zambullirse (en el agua) 2 : meterse precipitadamente o violentamente ⟨they plunged into war : se enfrascaron en una guerra⟩ ⟨he plunged into depression : cayó en la depresión⟩ 3 DESCEND : descender en picada ⟨the road plunges dizzily : la calle desciende vertiginosamente⟩

plunge² n 1 DIVE : zambullida f 2 DROP : descenso m abrupto ⟨the plunge in prices : el desplome de los precios⟩

plural¹ ['plʊrəl] adj : plural

plural² n : plural m

plurality [plʊ'ræləti] n, pl **-ties** : pluralidad f

pluralize ['plʊrə,laɪz] vt **-ized; -izing** : pluralizar

plus¹ ['plʌs] adj 1 POSITIVE : positivo ⟨a plus factor : un factor positivo⟩ 2 (indicating a quantity in addition) ⟨a grade of C plus : una calificación entre C y B⟩ ⟨a salary of $30,000 plus : un sueldo de más de $30,000⟩

plus² n 1 or **plus sign** : más m, signo m de más 2 ADVANTAGE : ventaja f

plus³ prep : más (en matemáticas)

plus⁴ conj AND : y

plush¹ ['plʌʃ] adj 1 : afelpado 2 LUXURIOUS : lujoso

plush² n : felpa f, peluche m

plushy ['plʌʃi] adj **plushier; -est** : lujoso

Pluto ['plu:to:] n : Plutón m

plutocracy [plu:'takrəsi] n, pl **-cies** : plutocracia f

plutonium [plu:'to:niəm] n : plutonio m

ply¹ ['plaɪ] v **plied; plying** vt 1 USE, WIELD : manejar ⟨to ply an ax : manejar un hacha⟩ 2 PRACTICE : ejercer ⟨to ply a trade : ejercer un oficio⟩ 3 **to ply with questions** : acosar con preguntas

ply² n, pl **plies** 1 LAYER : chapa f (de madera), capa f (de papel) 2 STRAND : cabo m (de hilo, etc.)

plywood ['plaɪ,wʊd] n : contrachapado m

pneumatic [nʊ'mætɪk, njʊ-] adj : neumático

pneumonia [nʊ'mo:njə, njʊ-] n : pulmonía f, neumonía f

poach ['po:tʃ] vt 1 : cocer a fuego lento ⟨to poach an egg : escalfar un huevo⟩ 2 **to poach game** : cazar ilegalmente — vi : cazar ilegalmente

poacher ['po:tʃər] n : cazador m furtivo, cazadora f furtiva

pock ['pak] n 1 PUSTULE : pústula f 2 → pockmark

pocket¹ ['pakət] vt 1 : meterse en el bolsillo ⟨he pocketed the pen : se metió la pluma en el bolsillo⟩ 2 STEAL : embolsarse

pocket² n 1 : bolsillo m, bolsa f Mex ⟨a coat pocket : el bolsillo de un abrigo⟩ ⟨air pockets : bolsas de aire⟩ 2 CENTER : foco m, centro m ⟨a pocket of resistance : un foco de resistencia⟩

pocketbook ['pakət,bʊk] n 1 PURSE : cartera f, bolso m, bolsa f Mex 2 MEANS : recursos mpl

pocketknife ['pakət,naɪf] n, pl **-knives** : navaja f

pocket–size ['pakət'saɪz] adj : de bolsillo

pockmark ['pak,mark] n : cicatriz f de viruela, viruela f

pod ['pad] n : vaina f ⟨pea pod : vaina de guisantes⟩

podiatrist [pə'daɪətrɪst, po-] n : podólogo m, -ga f

podiatry [pə'daɪətri, po-] n : podología f, podiatría f

podium ['po:diəm] n, pl **-diums** or **-dia** [-diə] : podio m, estrado m, tarima f

poem ['po:əm] n : poema m, poesía f

poet ['po:ət] n : poeta mf

poetic [po'ɛtɪk] or **poetical** [-tɪkəl] adj : poético

poetry ['po:ətri] n : poesía f

pogrom ['po:grəm, pə'gram, 'pagrəm] n : pogrom m

poignancy ['pɔɪnjəntsi] n, pl **-cies** : lo conmovedor

poignant ['pɔɪnjənt] adj 1 PAINFUL : penoso, doloroso ⟨poignant grief : profundo dolor⟩ 2 TOUCHING : conmovedor, emocionante

poinsettia [pɔɪn'sɛtiə, -'sɛtə] n : flor f de Nochebuena

point¹ ['pɔɪnt] vt 1 SHARPEN : afilar (la punta de) 2 INDICATE : señalar, indicar ⟨to point the way : señalar el camino⟩ 3 AIM : apuntar 4 **to point out** : señalar, indicar — vi 1 **to point at** : señalar (con el dedo) 2 **to point to** INDICATE : señalar, indicar

point² n 1 ITEM : punto m ⟨the main points : los puntos principales⟩ 2 QUALITY : cualidad f ⟨her good points : sus buenas cualidades⟩ ⟨it's not his strong point : no es su (punto) fuerte⟩ 3 (indicating a chief idea or meaning) ⟨it's beside the point : no viene al caso⟩ ⟨to get to the point : ir al grano⟩ ⟨to stick to the point : no salirse del tema⟩ 4 PURPOSE : fin m, propósito m ⟨there's no point to it : no vale la pena, no sirve para nada⟩ 5 PLACE : punto m, lugar m ⟨points of interest : puntos interesantes⟩ 6 : punto m (en una escala) ⟨boiling point : punto de ebullición⟩ 7 MOMENT : momento m, coyuntura f ⟨at this point : en este momento⟩ 8 TIP : punta f 9 HEADLAND : punta f, cabo m 10 PERIOD : punto m (marca de puntuación) 11 UNIT : punto m ⟨he scored 15 points : ganó 15 puntos⟩ ⟨shares fell 10 points : las acciones bajaron 10 enteros⟩ 12 **compass points** : puntos mpl cardinales 13 **decimal point** : punto m decimal, coma f

point–blank¹ ['pɔɪnt'blæŋk] adv 1 : a quemarropa ⟨to shoot point-blank : disparar a quemarropa⟩ 2 BLUNTLY, DIRECTLY : a bocajarro, sin rodeos, francamente

point–blank² adj 1 : a quemarropa ⟨point-blank shots : disparos a quemarropa⟩ 2 BLUNT, DIRECT : directo, franco

pointed ['pɔɪntəd] *adj* **1** POINTY : puntiagudo **2** PERTINENT : atinado **3** CONSPICUOUS : marcado, manifiesto

pointedly ['pɔɪntədli] *adv* : intencionadamente, directamente

pointer ['pɔɪntər] *n* **1** STICK : puntero *m* (para maestros, etc.) **2** INDICATOR, NEEDLE : indicador *m*, aguja *f* **3** : perro *m* de muestra **4** HINT, TIP : consejo *m*

pointless ['pɔɪntləs] *adj* : inútil, ocioso, vano ⟨it's pointless to continue : no tiene sentido continuar⟩

point of view *n* : perspectiva *f*, punto *m* de vista

pointy ['pɔɪnti] *adj* : puntiagudo

poise¹ ['pɔɪz] *vt* **poised; poising** BALANCE : equilibrar, balancear

poise² *n* : aplomo *m*, compostura *f*

poison¹ ['pɔɪzən] *vt* **1** : envenenar, intoxicar **2** CORRUPT : corromper

poison² *n* : veneno *m*

poison ivy *n* : hiedra *f* venenosa

poisonous ['pɔɪzənəs] *adj* : venenoso, tóxico, ponzoñoso

poke¹ ['po:k] *v* **poked; poking** *vt* **1** JAB : golpear (con la punta de algo), dar ⟨he poked me with his finger : me dio con el dedo⟩ **2** THRUST : introducir, asomar ⟨I poked my head out the window : asomé la cabeza por la ventana⟩ — *vi* **1 to poke around** RUMMAGE : hurgar **2 to poke along** DAWDLE : demorarse, entretenerse

poke² *n* : golpe *m* abrupto (con la punta de algo)

poker ['po:kər] *n* **1** : atizador *m* (para el fuego) **2** : póker *m*, poker *m* (juego de naipes)

polar ['po:lər] *adj* : polar

polar bear *n* : oso *m* blanco

Polaris [po'lærɪs, -'lɑr-] → **North Star**

polarize ['po:lə,raɪz] *vt* **-ized; -izing** : polarizar

pole ['po:l] *n* **1** : palo *m*, poste *m*, vara *f* ⟨telephone pole : poste de teléfonos⟩ **2** : polo *m* ⟨the South Pole : el Polo Sur⟩ **3** : polo *m* (eléctrico o magnético)

Pole ['po:l] *n* : polaco *m*, -ca *f*

polecat ['po:l,kæt] *n, pl* **polecats** *or* **polecat** **1** : turón *m* (de Europa) **2** SKUNK : mofeta *f*, zorrillo *m*

polemical [pə'lɛmɪkəl] *adj* : polémico

polemics [pə'lɛmɪks] *ns & pl* : polémica *f*

polestar ['po:l,stɑr] → **North Star**

police¹ [pə'li:s] *vt* **-liced; -licing** : mantener el orden en ⟨to police the streets : patrullar las calles⟩

police² *ns & pl* **1** : policía *f* (organización) **2** POLICE OFFICERS : policías *mfpl*

policeman [pə'li:smən] *n, pl* **-men** [-mən, -ˌmɛn] : policía *m*

police officer *n* : policía *mf*, agente *mf* de policía

policewoman [pə'li:s,wʊmən] *n, pl* **-women** [-ˌwɪmən] : policía *f*, mujer *f* policía

policy ['pɑləsi] *n, pl* **-cies** **1** : política *f* ⟨foreign policy : política exterior⟩ **2** *or* **insurance policy** : póliza *f* de seguros, seguro *m*

polio¹ ['po:li,o:] *adj* : de polio ⟨polio vaccine : vacuna contra la polio⟩

polio² *n* → **poliomyelitis**

poliomyelitis [ˌpo:li,o:ˌmaɪə'laɪtəs] *n* : poliomielitis *f*, polio *f*

polish¹ ['pɑlɪʃ] *vt* **1** : pulir, lustrar, sacar brillo a ⟨to polish one's nails : pintarse las uñas⟩ **2** REFINE : pulir, perfeccionar

polish² *n* **1** LUSTER : brillo *m*, lustre *m* **2** REFINEMENT : refinamiento *m* **3** : betún *m* (para zapatos), cera *f* (para suelos y muebles), esmalte *m* (para las uñas)

Polish¹ ['po:lɪʃ] *adj* : polaco

Polish² *n* : polaco *m* (idioma)

polite [pə'laɪt] *adj* **-liter; -est** : cortés, correcto, educado

politely [pə'laɪtli] *adv* : cortésmente, correctamente, con buenos modales

politeness [pə'laɪtnəs] *n* : cortesía *f*

politic ['pɑlə,tɪk] *adj* : diplomático, prudente

political [pə'lɪtɪkəl] *adj* : político — **politically** [-tɪkli] *adv*

politician [ˌpɑlə'tɪʃən] *n* : político *m*, -ca *f*

politics ['pɑlə,tɪks] *ns & pl* : política *f*

polka ['po:lkə, 'po:kə] *n* : polka *f*

polka dot ['po:kə,dɑt] *n* : lunar *m* (en un diseño)

poll¹ ['po:l] *vt* **1** : obtener (votos) ⟨she polled over 1000 votes : obtuvo más de 1000 votos⟩ **2** CANVASS : encuestar, sondear — *vi* : obtener votos

poll² *n* **1** SURVEY : encuesta *f*, sondeo *m* **2 polls** *npl* : urnas *fpl* ⟨to go to the polls : acudir a las urnas, ir a votar⟩

pollen ['pɑlən] *n* : polen *m*

pollinate ['pɑlə,neɪt] *vt* **-nated; -nating** : polinizar

pollination [ˌpɑlə'neɪʃən] *n* : polinización *f*

pollster ['po:lstər] *n* : encuestador *m*, -dora *f*

pollutant [pə'lu:tənt] *n* : contaminante *m*

pollute [pə'lu:t] *vt* **-luted; -luting** : contaminar

pollution [pə'lu:ʃən] *n* : contaminación *f*

pollywog *or* **polliwog** ['pɑli,wɔg] *n* TADPOLE : renacuajo *m*

polo ['po:,lo:] *n* : polo *m*

poltergeist ['po:ltər,gaɪst] *n* : poltergeist *m*, fantasma *m* travieso

polyester ['pɑli,ɛstər, ˌpɑli'-] *n* : poliéster *m*

polygamous [pə'lɪgəməs] *adj* : polígamo

polygamy [pə'lɪgəmi] *n* : poligamia *f*

polygon ['pɑli,gɑn] *n* : polígono *m*

polymer ['pɑləmər] *n* : polímero *m*

Polynesian [ˌpɑlə'niːʒən, -ʃən] *n* : polinesio *m*, -sia *f* — **Polynesian** *adj*

polyunsaturated [ˌpɑliˌʌn'sætʃə-ˌreɪtəd] *adj* : poliinsaturado

pomegranate ['pɑməˌgrænət, 'pɑmˌgrænət] *n* : granada *f* (fruta)

pommel¹ ['pʌməl] *vt* → **pummel**

pommel² ['pʌməl, 'pɑ-] *n* **1** : pomo *m* (de una espada) **2** : perilla *f* (de una silla de montar)

pomp ['pɑmp] *n* **1** SPLENDOR : pompa *f*, esplendor *m* **2** OSTENTATION : boato *m*, ostentación *f*

pom–pom ['pɑmˌpɑm] *n* : borla *f*, pompón *m*

pomposity [pɑm'pɑsəṭi] *n, pl* **-ties** : pomposidad *f*

pompous ['pɑmpəs] *adj* : pomposo — **pompously** *adv*

poncho ['pɑnˌtʃoː] *n, pl* **-chos** : poncho *m*

pond ['pɑnd] *n* : charca *f* (natural), estanque *m* (artificial)

ponder ['pɑndər] *vt* : reflexionar, considerar — *vi* **to ponder over** : reflexionar sobre, sopesar

ponderous ['pɑndərəs] *adj* : pesado

pontiff ['pɑntɪf] *n* POPE : pontífice *m*

pontificate [pɑn'tɪfəˌkeɪt] *vi* **-cated; -cating** : pontificar

pontoon [pɑn'tuːn] *n* : pontón *m*

pony ['poːni] *n, pl* **-nies** : poni *m*, poney *m*, jaca *f*

ponytail ['poːniˌteɪl] *n* : cola *f* de caballo, coleta *f*

poodle ['puːdəl] *n* : caniche *m*

pool¹ ['puːl] *vt* : mancomunar, hacer un fondo común de

pool² *n* **1** : charca *f* ⟨a swimming pool : una piscina⟩ **2** PUDDLE : charco *m* **3** RESERVE, SUPPLY : fondo *m* común (de recursos), reserva *f* **4** : billar *m* (juego)

poor ['pʊr, 'por] *adj* **1** : pobre ⟨poor people : los pobres⟩ **2** SCANTY : pobre, escaso ⟨poor attendance : baja asistencia⟩ **3** UNFORTUNATE : pobre ⟨poor thing! : ¡pobrecito!⟩ **4** BAD : malo ⟨to be in poor health : estar mal de salud⟩

poorly ['pʊrli, 'por-] *adv* : mal

pop¹ ['pɑp] *v* **popped; popping** *vi* **1** BURST : reventarse, estallar **2** : ir, venir, o aparecer abruptamente ⟨he popped into the house : se metió en la casa⟩ ⟨a menu pops up : aparece un menú⟩ **3** **to pop out** PROTRUDE : salirse, saltarse ⟨my eyes popped out of my head : se me saltaban los ojos⟩ — *vt* **1** BURST : reventar **2** : hacer o meter abruptamente ⟨he popped it into his mouth : se lo metió en la boca⟩

pop² *adj* : popular ⟨pop music : música popular⟩

pop³ *n* **1** : estallido *m* pequeño (de un globo, etc.) **2** SODA : refresco *m*, gaseosa *f*

popcorn ['pɑpˌkorn] *n* : palomitas *fpl* (de maíz)

pope ['poːp] *n* : papa *m* ⟨Pope John : el Papa Juan⟩

poplar ['pɑplər] *n* : álamo *m*

poplin ['pɑplɪn] *n* : popelín *m*, popelina *f*

poppy ['pɑpi] *n, pl* **-pies** : amapola *f*

populace ['pɑpjələs] *n* **1** MASSES : pueblo *m* **2** POPULATION : población *f*

popular ['pɑpjələr] *adj* **1** : popular ⟨the popular vote : el voto popular⟩ **2** COMMON : generalizado, común ⟨popular beliefs : creencias generalizadas⟩ **3** : popular, de gran popularidad ⟨a popular singer : un cantante popular⟩

popularity [ˌpɑpjə'lærəṭi] *n* : popularidad *f*

popularize ['pɑpjələˌraɪz] *vt* **-ized; -izing** : popularizar

popularly ['pɑpjələrli] *adv* : popularmente, vulgarmente

populate ['pɑpjəˌleɪt] *vt* **-lated; -lating** : poblar

population [ˌpɑpjə'leɪʃən] *n* : población *f*

populist ['pɑpjəlɪst] *n* : populista *mf* — **populist** *adj*

populous ['pɑpjələs] *adj* : populoso

porcelain ['porsələn] *n* : porcelana *f*

porch ['portʃ] *n* : porche *m*

porcupine ['porkjəˌpaɪn] *n* : puerco *m* espín

pore¹ ['por] *vi* **pored; poring** **1** GAZE : mirar (con atención) **2** **to pore over** : leer detenidamente, estudiar

pore² *n* : poro *m*

pork ['pork] *n* : carne *f* de cerdo, carne *f* de puerco

pornographic [ˌpornə'græfɪk] *adj* : pornográfico

pornography [por'nɑgrəfi] *n* : pornografía *f*

porous ['porəs] *adj* : poroso

porpoise ['porpəs] *n* **1** : marsopa *f* **2** DOLPHIN : delfín *m*

porridge ['porɪdʒ] *n* : sopa *f* espesa de harina, gachas *fpl*

port¹ ['port] *adj* : de babor ⟨on the port side : a babor⟩

port² *n* **1** HARBOR : puerto *m* **2** ORIFICE : orificio *m* (de una válvula, etc.) **3** : puerto *m* (de una computadora) **4** PORTHOLE : portilla *f* **5** *or* **port side** : babor *m* (de un barco) **6** : oporto *m* (vino)

portable ['portəbəl] *adj* : portátil

portal ['portəl] *n* : portal *m*

portend [por'tɛnd] *vt* : presagiar, augurar

portent ['porˌtɛnt] *n* : presagio *m*, augurio *m*

portentous [por'tɛntəs] *adj* : profético, que presagia

porter ['portər] *n* : maletero *m*, mozo *m* (de estación)

portfolio [port'foːliˌo] *n, pl* **-lios** **1** FOLDER : cartera *f* (para llevar papeles), carpeta *f* **2** : cartera *f* (diplomática) **3 investment portfolio** : cartera de inversiones

porthole ['pɔrt,hoːl] *n* : portilla *f* (de un barco), ventanilla *f* (de un avión)

portico ['pɔrtɪ,ko] *n, pl* **-coes** *or* **-cos** : pórtico *m*

portion[1] ['pɔrʃən] *vt* DISTRIBUTE : repartir

portion[2] *n* PART, SHARE : porción *f*, parte *f*

portly ['pɔrtli] *adj* **-lier; -est** : corpulento

portrait ['pɔrtrət, -,treɪt] *n* : retrato *m*

portray [pɔr'treɪ] *vt* **1** DEPICT : representar, retratar **2** DESCRIBE : describir **3** PLAY : interpretar (un personaje)

portrayal [pɔr'treɪəl] *n* **1** REPRESENTATION : representación *f* **2** PORTRAIT : retrato *m*

Portuguese [,pɔrtʃə'giːz, -'giːs] *n* **1** : portugués *m*, -guesa *f* (persona) **2** : portugués *m* (idioma) — **Portuguese** *adj*

pose[1] ['poːz] *v* **posed; posing** *vt* PRESENT : plantear (una pregunta, etc.), representar (una amenaza) — *vi* **1** : posar (para una foto, etc.) **2 to pose as** : hacerse pasar por

pose[2] *n* **1** : pose *f* ⟨to strike a pose : asumir una pose⟩ **2** PRETENSE : pose *f*, afectación *f*

posh ['pɑʃ] *adj* : elegante, de lujo

position[1] [pə'zɪʃən] *vt* : colocar, situar, ubicar

position[2] *n* **1** APPROACH, STANCE : posición *f*, postura *f*, planteamiento *m* **2** LOCATION : posición *f*, ubicación *f* **3** STATUS : posición *f* (en una jerarquía) **4** JOB : puesto *m*

positive ['pɑzətɪv] *adj* **1** DEFINITE : incuestionable, inequívoco ⟨positive evidence : pruebas irrefutables⟩ **2** CONFIDENT : seguro **3** : positivo (en gramática, matemáticas, y física) **4** AFFIRMATIVE : positivo, afirmativo ⟨a positive response : una respuesta positiva⟩

positively ['pɑzətɪvli] *adv* **1** FAVORABLY : favorablemente **2** OPTIMISTICALLY : positivamente **3** DEFINITELY : definitivamente, en forma concluyente **4** (*used for emphasis*) : realmente, verdaderamente ⟨it's positively awful! : ¡es verdaderamente malo!⟩

possess [pə'zɛs] *vt* **1** HAVE, OWN : poseer, tener **2** SEIZE : apoderarse de ⟨he was possessed by fear : el miedo se apoderó de él⟩

possession [pə'zɛʃən] *n* **1** POSSESSING : posesión *f* **2** : posesión *f* (por un demonio, etc.) **3 possessions** *npl* PROPERTY : bienes *mpl*, propiedad *f*

possessive[1] [pə'zɛsɪv] *adj* **1** : posesivo (en gramática) **2** JEALOUS : posesivo, celoso

possessive[2] *n or* **possessive case** : posesivo *m*

possessor [pə'zɛsər] *n* : poseedor *m*, -dora *f*

possibility [,pɑsə'bɪləti] *n, pl* **-ties** : posibilidad *f*

possible ['pɑsəbəl] *adj* : posible

possibly ['pɑsəbli] *adv* **1** CONCEIVABLY : posiblemente ⟨it can't possibly be true! : ¡no puede ser!⟩ **2** PERHAPS : quizás, posiblemente

possum ['pɑsəm] → **opossum**

post[1] ['poːst] *vt* **1** MAIL : echar al correo, mandar por correo **2** ANNOUNCE : anunciar ⟨they've posted the grades : han anunciado las notas⟩ **3** AFFIX : fijar, poner (noticias, etc.) **4** STATION : apostar **5 to keep (someone) posted** : tener al corriente (a alguien)

post[2] *n* **1** POLE : poste *m*, palo *m* **2** STATION : puesto *m* **3** CAMP : puesto *m* (militar) **4** JOB, POSITION : puesto *m*, empleo *m*, cargo *m*

postage ['poːstɪdʒ] *n* : franqueo *m*

postal ['poːstəl] *adj* : postal

postcard ['poːst,kɑrd] *n* : postal *f*, tarjeta *f* postal

poster ['poːstər] *n* : póster *m*, cartel *m*, afiche *m*

posterior[1] [pɑ'stɪriər, po-] *adj* : posterior

posterior[2] *n* BUTTOCKS : trasero *m*, nalgas *fpl*, asentaderas *fpl*

posterity [pɑ'stɛrəti] *n* : posteridad *f*

postgraduate[1] [,poːst'grædʒuət] *adj* : de postgrado

postgraduate[2] *n* : postgraduado *m*, -da *f*

posthaste ['poːst'heɪst] *adv* : a toda prisa

posthumous ['pɑstʃəməs] *adj* : póstumo — **posthumously** *adv*

postman ['poːstmən, -,mæn] → **mailman**

postmark[1] ['poːst,mɑrk] *vt* : matasellar

postmark[2] *n* : matasellos *m*

postmaster ['poːst,mæstər] *n* : administrador *m*, -dora *f* de correos

postmodern [,poːst'mɑdərn] *adj* : posmoderno

postmortem [,poːst'mɔrtəm] *n* : autopsia *f*

postnatal [,poːst'neɪtəl] *adj* : postnatal ⟨postnatal depression : depresión posparto⟩

post office *n* : correo *m*, oficina *f* de correos

postoperative [,poːst'ɑpərətɪv, -,reɪ-] *adj* : posoperatorio

postpaid [,poːst'peɪd] *adv* : con franqueo pagado

postpone [poːst'poːn] *vt* **-poned; -poning** : postergar, aplazar, posponer

postponement [poːst'poːnmənt] *n* : postergación *f*, aplazamiento *m*

postscript ['poːst,skrɪpt] *n* : postdata *f*, posdata *f*

postulate ['pɑstʃə,leɪt] *vt* **-lated; -lating** : postular

posture[1] ['pɑstʃər] *vi* **-tured; -turing** : posar, asumir una pose

posture[2] *n* : postura *f*

postwar [,poːst'wɔr] *adj* : de (la) posguerra

posy ['po:zi] *n, pl* **-sies 1** FLOWER : flor *f* **2** BOUQUET : ramo *m*, ramillete *m*
pot¹ ['pɑt] *vt* **potted; potting** : plantar (en una maceta)
pot² *n* **1** : olla *f* (de cocina) **2 pots and pans** : cacharros *mpl*
potable ['po:təbəl] *adj* : potable
potash ['pɑt,æʃ] *n* : potasa *f*
potassium [pə'tæsiəm] *n* : potasio *m*
potato [pə'teɪto] *n, pl* **-toes** : papa *f*, patata *f* *Spain*
potato chips *npl* : papas *fpl* fritas (de bolsa)
potbellied ['pɑt,bɛlid] *adj* : panzón, barrigón *fam*
potbelly ['pɑt,bɛli] *n* : panza *f*, barriga *f*
potency ['po:təntsi] *n, pl* **-cies 1** POWER : fuerza *f*, potencia *f* **2** EFFECTIVENESS : eficacia *f*
potent ['po:tənt] *adj* **1** POWERFUL : potente, poderoso **2** EFFECTIVE : eficaz ⟨a potent medicine : una medicina bien fuerte⟩
potential¹ [pə'tɛntʃəl] *adj* : potencial, posible
potential² *n* **1** : potencial *m* ⟨growth potential : potencial de crecimiento⟩ ⟨a child with potential : un niño que promete⟩ **2** : potencial *m* (eléctrico) — **potentially** *adv*
potful ['pɑt,fʊl] *n* : contenido *m* de una olla ⟨a potful of water : una olla de agua⟩
pothole ['pɑt,ho:l] *n* : bache *m*
potion ['po:ʃən] *n* : brebaje *m*, poción *f*
potluck ['pɑt,lʌk] *n* **to take potluck** : tomar lo que haya
potpourri [,po:pʊ'ri:] *n* : popurrí *m*
potshot ['pɑt,ʃɑt] *n* **1** : tiro *m* al azar ⟨to take potshots at : disparar al azar a⟩ **2** CRITICISM : crítica *f* (hecha al azar)
potter ['pɑtər] *n* : alfarero *m*, -ra *f*
pottery ['pɑtəri] *n, pl* **-teries** : cerámica *f*
pouch ['paʊtʃ] *n* **1** BAG : bolsa *f* pequeña **2** : bolsa *f* (de un animal)
poultice ['po:ltəs] *n* : emplasto *m*, cataplasma *f*
poultry ['po:ltri] *n* : aves *fpl* de corral
pounce ['paʊnts] *vi* **pounced; pouncing** : abalanzarse
pound¹ ['paʊnd] *vt* **1** CRUSH : machacar, machucar, majar **2** BEAT : golpear, machacar ⟨she pounded the lessons into them : les machacaba las lecciones⟩ ⟨he pounded home his point : les hizo entender su razonamiento⟩ — *vi* **1** BEAT : palpitar (dícese del corazón) **2** RESOUND : retumbar, resonar **3** : andar con paso pesado ⟨we pounded through the mud : caminamos pesadamente por el barro⟩
pound² *n* **1** : libra *f* (unidad de peso) **2** : libra *f* (unidad monetaria) **3 dog pound** : perrera *f*
pour ['por] *vt* **1** : echar, verter, servir (bebidas) ⟨pour it into a pot : viértalo

en una olla⟩ **2** : proveer con abundancia ⟨they poured money into it : le invirtieron mucho dinero⟩ **3 to pour out** : dar salida a ⟨he poured out his feelings to her : se desahogó con ella⟩ — *vi* **1** FLOW : manar, fluir, salir ⟨blood was pouring from the wound : la sangre le salía de la herida⟩ **2 it's pouring (outside)** : está lloviendo a cántaros
pout¹ ['paʊt] *vi* : hacer pucheros
pout² *n* : puchero *m*
poverty ['pɑvərti] *n* : pobreza *f*, indigencia *f*
powder¹ ['paʊdər] *vt* **1** : empolvar ⟨to powder one's face : empolvarse la cara⟩ **2** PULVERIZE : pulverizar
powder² *n* : polvo *m*, polvos *mpl*
powdery ['paʊdəri] *adj* : polvoriento, como polvo
power¹ ['paʊər] *vt* : impulsar, propulsar
power² *n* **1** AUTHORITY : poder *m*, autoridad *f* ⟨executive powers : poderes ejecutivos⟩ **2** ABILITY : capacidad *f*, poder *m* **3** : potencia *f* (política) ⟨foreign powers : potencias extranjeras⟩ **4** STRENGTH : fuerza *f* **5** : potencia *f* (en física y matemáticas)
powerful ['paʊərfəl] *adj* : poderoso, potente — **powerfully** *adv*
powerhouse ['paʊər,haʊs] *n* : persona *f* dinámica
powerless ['paʊərləs] *adj* : impotente
power plant *n* : central *f* eléctrica
powwow ['paʊ,waʊ] *n* : conferencia *f*
pox ['pɑks] *n, pl* **pox** *or* **poxes 1** CHICKEN POX : varicela *f* **2** SYPHILIS : sífilis *f*
practicable ['præktɪkəbəl] *adj* : practicable, viable, factible
practical ['præktɪkəl] *adj* : práctico
practicality [,præktɪ'kæləti] *n, pl* **-ties** : factibilidad *f*, viabilidad *f*
practical joke *n* : broma *f* (pesada)
practically ['præktɪkli] *adv* **1** : de manera práctica **2** ALMOST : casi, prácticamente
practice¹ *or* **practise** ['præktəs] *vt* **-ticed** *or* **-tised; -ticing** *or* **-tising 1** : practicar ⟨he practiced his German on us : practicó el alemán con nosotros⟩ ⟨to practice politeness : practicar la cortesía⟩ **2** : ejercer ⟨to practice medicine : ejercer la medicina⟩
practice² *n* **1** USE : práctica *f* ⟨to put into practice : poner en práctica⟩ **2** CUSTOM : costumbre *f* ⟨it's a common practice here : por aquí se acostumbra hacerlo⟩ **3** TRAINING : práctica *f* **4** : ejercicio *m* (de una profesión)
practitioner [præk'tɪʃənər] *n* **1** : profesional *mf* **2 general practitioner** : médico *m*, -ca *f*
pragmatic [præg'mætɪk] *adj* : pragmático — **pragmatically** *adv*
pragmatism ['prægmə,tɪzəm] *n* : pragmatismo
prairie ['prɛri] *n* : pradera *f*, llanura *f*

praise¹ ['preɪz] *vt* **praised; praising** : elogiar, alabar ⟨to praise God : alabar a Dios⟩

praise² *n* : elogio *m*, alabanza *f*

praiseworthy ['preɪz,wərði] *adj* : digno de alabanza, loable

prance¹ ['prænʦ] *vi* **pranced; prancing** **1** : hacer cabriolas, cabriolar ⟨a prancing horse : un caballo haciendo cabriolas⟩ **2** SWAGGER : pavonearse

prance² *n* : cabriola *f*

prank ['præŋk] *n* : broma *f*, travesura *f*

prankster ['præŋkstər] *n* : bromista *mf*

prattle¹ ['prætəl] *vt* **-tled; -tling** : parlotear *fam*, cotorrear *fam*, balbucear (como un niño)

prattle² *n* : parloteo *m fam*, cotorreo *m fam*, cháchara *f fam*

prawn ['prɔn] *n* : langostino *m*, camarón *m*, gamba *f*

pray ['preɪ] *vt* ENTREAT : rogar, suplicar — *vi* : rezar

prayer ['prɛr] *n* **1** : plegaria *f*, oración *f* ⟨to say one's prayers : orar, rezar⟩ ⟨the Lord's Prayer : el Padrenuestro⟩ **2** PRAYING : rezo *m*, oración *f* ⟨to kneel in prayer : arrodillarse para rezar⟩

praying mantis → mantis

preach ['pri:ʧ] *vi* : predicar — *vt* ADVOCATE : abogar por ⟨to preach cooperation : promover la cooperación⟩

preacher ['pri:ʧər] *n* **1** : predicador *m*, -dora *f* **2** MINISTER : pastor *m*, -tora *f*

preamble ['pri:,æmbəl] *n* : preámbulo *m*

prearrange [,pri:ə'reɪnʤ] *vt* **-ranged; -ranging** : arreglar de antemano

precarious [prɪ'kæriəs] *adj* : precario — **precariously** *adv*

precariousness [prɪ'kæriəsnəs] *n* : precariedad *f*

precaution [prɪ'kɔʃən] *n* : precaución *f*

precautionary [prɪ'kɔʃə,nɛri] *adj* : preventivo, cautelar, precautorio

precede [prɪ'si:d] *v* **-ceded; -ceding** : preceder a

precedence ['prɛsədənʦ, prɪ'si:dənʦ] *n* : precedencia *f*

precedent ['prɛsədənt] *n* : precedente *m*

precept ['pri:,sɛpt] *n* : precepto *m*

precinct ['pri:,sɪŋkt] *n* **1** DISTRICT : distrito *m* (policial, electoral, etc.) **2** **precincts** *npl* PREMISES : recinto *m*, predio *m*, límites *mpl* (de una ciudad)

precious ['prɛʃəs] *adj* **1** : precioso ⟨precious gems : piedras preciosas⟩ **2** DEAR : querido **3** AFFECTED : afectado

precipice ['prɛsəpəs] *n* : precipicio *m*

precipitate [prɪ'sɪpə,teɪt] *v* **-tated; -tating** *vt* **1** HASTEN, PROVOKE : precipitar, provocar **2** HURL : arrojar **3** : precipitar (en química) — *vi* : precipitarse (en química), condensarse (en meteorología)

precipitation [prɪ,sɪpə'teɪʃən] *n* **1** HASTE : precipitación *f*, prisa *f* **2** : precipitaciones *fpl* (en meteorología)

precipitous [prɪ'sɪpətəs] *adj* **1** HASTY, RASH : precipitado **2** STEEP : escarpa-

do, empinado ⟨a precipitous drop : una caída vertiginosa⟩

précis [preɪ'si:] *n, pl* **précis** [-'si:z] : resumen *m*

precise [prɪ'saɪs] *adj* **1** DEFINITE : preciso, explícito **2** EXACT : exacto, preciso ⟨precise calculations : cálculos precisos⟩ — **precisely** *adv*

preciseness [prɪ'saɪsnəs] *n* : precisión *f*, exactitud *f*

precision [prɪ'sɪʒən] *n* : precisión *f*

preclude [prɪ'klu:d] *vt* **-cluded; -cluding** : evitar, impedir, excluir (una posibilidad, etc.)

precocious [prɪ'ko:ʃəs] *adj* : precoz — **precociously** *adv*

precocity [prɪ'kɑsəʈi] *n* : precocidad *f*

preconceive [,pri:kən'si:v] *vt* **-ceived; -ceiving** : preconcebir

preconception [,pri:kən'spʃən] *n* : idea *f* preconcebida

precondition [,pri:kən'dɪʃən] *n* : precondición *f*, condición *f* previa

precook [,pri:'kʊk] *vt* : precocinar

precursor [prɪ'kərsər] *n* : precursor *m*, -sora *f*

predator ['prɛdəʈər] *n* : depredador *m*, -dora *f*

predatory ['prɛdə,tori] *adj* : depredador

predecessor ['prɛdə,sɛsər, 'pri:-] *n* : antecesor *m*, -sora *f*; predecesor *m*, -sora *f*

predestination [prɪ,dɛstə'neɪʃən] *n* : predestinación *f*

predestine [prɪ'dɛstən] *vt* **-tined; -tining** : predestinar

predetermine [,pri:dɪ'tərmən] *vt* **-mined; -mining** : predeterminar

predicament [prɪ'dɪkəmənt] *n* : apuro *m*, aprieto *m*

predicate¹ ['prɛdə,keɪt] *vt* **-cated; -cating** **1** AFFIRM : afirmar, aseverar **2 to be predicated on** : estar basado en

predicate² ['prɛdɪkət] *n* : predicado *m*

predict [prɪ'dɪkt] *vt* : pronosticar, predecir

predictable [prɪ'dɪktəbəl] *adj* : previsible — **predictably** [-bli] *adv*

prediction [prɪ'dɪkʃən] *n* : pronóstico *m*, predicción *f*

predilection [,prɛdəl'ɛkʃən, ,pri:-] *n* : predilección *f*

predispose [,pri:dɪ'spo:z] *vt* **-posed; -posing** : predisponer

predisposition [,pri:,dɪspə'zɪʃən] *n* : predisposición *f*

predominance [prɪ'dɑmənənʦ] *n* : predominio *m*

predominant [prɪ'dɑmənənt] *adj* : predominante — **predominantly** *adv*

predominate [prɪ'dɑmə,neɪt] *vt* **-nated; -nating** **1** : predominar (en cantidad) **2** PREVAIL : prevalecer

preeminence [prɪ'ɛmənənʦ] *n* : preeminencia *f*

preeminent [prɪ'ɛmənənt] *adj* : preeminente

preeminently [prɪ'ɛmənəntli] *adv* : especialmente

preempt [pri'ɛmpt] *vt* **1** APPROPRIATE : apoderarse de, apropiarse de **2** : reemplazar (un programa de televisión, etc.) **3** FORESTALL : adelantarse a (un ataque, etc.)

preen ['pri:n] *vt* : arreglarse (el pelo, las plumas, etc.)

prefabricated [ˌpri:'fæbrəˌkeɪtəd] *adj* : prefabricado

preface ['prɛfəs] *n* : prefacio *m*, prólogo *m*

prefatory ['prɛfəˌtori] *adj* : preliminar

prefer [pri'fər] *vt* **-ferred; -ferring 1** : preferir ⟨I prefer coffee : prefiero café⟩ **2 to prefer charges against** : presentar cargos contra

preferable ['prɛfərəbəl] *adj* : preferible

preferably ['prɛfərəbli] *adv* : preferentemente, de preferencia

preference ['prɛfrənts, 'prɛfər-] *n* : preferencia *f*, gusto *m*

preferential [ˌprɛfə'rɛntʃəl] *adj* : preferencial, preferente

prefigure [pri'fɪgjər] *vt* **-ured; -uring** FORESHADOW : prefigurar, anunciar

prefix ['pri:ˌfɪks] *n* : prefijo *m*

pregnancy ['prɛgnəntsi] *n, pl* **-cies** : embarazo *m*, preñez *f*

pregnant ['prɛgnənt] *adj* **1** : embarazada (dícese de una mujer), preñada (dícese de un animal) **2** MEANINGFUL : significativo

preheat [ˌpri:'hi:t] *vt* : precalentar

prehensile [pri'hɛntsəl, -'hɛnˌsaɪl] *adj* : prensil

prehistoric [ˌpri:hɪs'tɔrɪk] *or* **prehistorical** [-ɪkəl] *adj* : prehistórico

prejudge [ˌpri:'dʒʌdʒ] *vt* **-judged; -judging** : prejuzgar

prejudice¹ ['prɛdʒədəs] *vt* **-diced; -dicing 1** DAMAGE : perjudicar **2** BIAS : predisponer, influir en

prejudice² *n* **1** DAMAGE : perjuicio *m* (en derecho) **2** BIAS : prejuicio *m*

prelate ['prɛlət] *n* : prelado *m*

preliminary¹ [pri'lɪməˌnɛri] *adj* : preliminar

preliminary² *n, pl* **-naries 1** : preámbulo *m*, preludio *m* **2 preliminaries** *npl* : preliminares *mpl*

prelude ['prɛˌlu:d, 'prɛlˌju:d; 'preɪˌlu:d, 'pri:-] *n* : preludio *m*

premarital [ˌpri:'mærətəl] *adj* : prematrimonial

premature [ˌpri:mə'tʊr, -'tjʊr, -'tʃʊr] *adj* : prematuro — **prematurely** *adv*

premeditate [pri'mɛdəˌteɪt] *vt* **-tated; -tating** : premeditar

premeditation [priˌmɛdə'teɪʃən] *n* : premeditación *f*

premenstrual [pri'mɛntstruəl] *adj* : premenstrual

premier¹ [pri'mɪr, -'mjɪr; 'pri:miər] *adj* : principal

premier² *n* PRIME MINISTER : primer ministro *m*, primera ministra *f*

premiere¹ [prɪ'mjɛr, -'mɪr] *vt* **-miered; -miering** : estrenar

premiere² *n* : estreno *m*

premise ['prɛmɪs] *n* **1** : premisa *f* ⟨the premise of his arguments : la premisa de sus argumentos⟩ **2 premises** *npl* : recinto *m*, local *m*

premium ['pri:miəm] *n* **1** BONUS : prima *f* **2** SURCHARGE : recargo *m* ⟨to sell at a premium : vender (algo) muy caro⟩ **3 insurance premium** : prima *f* (de seguros) **4 to set a premium on** : darle un gran valor (a algo)

premonition [ˌpri:mə'nɪʃən, ˌprɛmə-] *n* : presentimiento *m*, premonición *f*

prenatal [ˌpri:'neɪtəl] *adj* : prenatal

preoccupation [priˌakjə'peɪʃən] *n* : preocupación *f*

preoccupied [pri'akjəˌpaɪd] *adj* : abstraído, ensimismado, preocupado

preoccupy [pri'akjəˌpaɪ] *vt* **-pied; -pying** : preocupar

preparation [ˌprɛpə'reɪʃən] *n* **1** PREPARING : preparación *f* **2** MIXTURE : preparado *m* ⟨a preparation for burns : un preparado para quemaduras⟩ **3 preparations** *npl* ARRANGEMENTS : preparativos *mpl*

preparatory [pri'pærəˌtori] *adj* : preparatorio

prepare [pri'pær] *v* **-pared; -paring** *vt* : preparar — *vi* : prepararse

prepay [ˌpri:'peɪ] *vt* **-paid; -paying** : pagar por adelantado

preponderance [pri'pandərənts] *n* : preponderancia *f*

preponderant [pri'pandərənt] *adj* : preponderante — **preponderantly** *adv*

preposition [ˌprɛpə'zɪʃən] *n* : preposición *f*

prepositional [ˌprɛpə'zɪʃənəl] *adj* : preposicional

prepossessing [ˌpri:pə'zɛsɪŋ] *adj* : atractivo, agradable

preposterous [pri'pastərəs] *adj* : absurdo, ridículo

prerequisite¹ [pri'rɛkwəzət] *adj* : necesario, esencial

prerequisite² *n* : condición *f* necesario, requisito *m* previo

prerogative [pri'ragətɪv] *n* : prerrogativa *f*

presage ['prɛsɪdʒ, pri'seɪdʒ] *vt* **-saged; -saging** : presagiar

preschool ['pri:ˌsku:l] *adj* : preescolar ⟨preschool students : estudiantes de preescolar⟩

prescribe [pri'skraɪb] *vt* **-scribed; -scribing 1** ORDAIN : prescribir, ordenar **2** : recetar (medicinas, etc.)

prescription [pri'skrɪpʃən] *n* : receta *f*

presence ['prɛzənts] *n* : presencia *f*

present¹ [pri'zɛnt] *vt* **1** INTRODUCE : presentar ⟨to present oneself : presentarse⟩ **2** : presentar (una obra de teatro, etc.) **3** GIVE : entregar (un regalo, etc.), regalar, obsequiar **4** SHOW : presentar, ofrecer ⟨it presents a lovely view : ofrece una vista muy linda⟩

present² ['prɛzənt] *adj* **1** : actual ⟨present conditions : condiciones actuales⟩

2 : presente ⟨all the students were present : todos los estudiantes estaban presentes⟩

present³ [ˈprɛzənt] *n* **1** GIFT : regalo *m*, obsequio *m* **2** : presente *m* ⟨at present : en este momento⟩ **3** *or* **present tense** : presente *m*

presentable [priˈzɛntəbəl] *adj* : presentable

presentation [ˌpriːzɛnˈteɪʃən, ˌprɛzən-] *n* : presentación *f* ⟨presentation ceremony : ceremonia de entrega⟩

presentiment [priˈzɛntəmənt] *n* : presentimiento *m*, premonición *f*

presently [ˈprɛzəntli] *adv* **1** SOON : pronto, dentro de poco **2** NOW : actualmente, ahora

present participle *n* : participio *m* presente, participio *m* activo

preservation [ˌprɛzərˈveɪʃən] *n* : conservación *f*, preservación *f*

preservative [priˈzərvəṭɪv] *n* : conservante *m*

preserve¹ [priˈzərv] *vt* **-served; -serving** **1** PROTECT : proteger, preservar **2** : conservar (los alimentos, etc.) **3** MAINTAIN : conservar, mantener

preserve² *n* **1** *or* **preserves** *npl* : conserva *f* ⟨peach preserves : duraznos en conserva⟩ **2** : coto *m* ⟨game preserve : coto de caza⟩

preside [priˈzaɪd] *vi* **-sided; -siding** **1 to preside over** : presidir ⟨he presided over the meeting : presidió la reunión⟩ **2 to preside over** : supervisar ⟨she presides over the department : dirige el departamento⟩

presidency [ˈprɛzədənˌtsi] *n, pl* **-cies** : presidencia *f*

president [ˈprɛzədənt] *n* : presidente *m*, -ta *f*

presidential [ˌprɛzəˈdɛntʃəl] *adj* : presidencial

press¹ [ˈprɛs] *vt* **1** PUSH : apretar **2** SQUEEZE : apretar, prensar (frutas, flores, etc.) **3** IRON : planchar (ropa) **4** URGE : instar, apremiar ⟨he pressed me to come : insistió en que viniera⟩ — *vi* **1** PUSH : apretar ⟨press hard : aprieta con fuerza⟩ **2** CROWD : apiñarse **3** : abrirse paso ⟨I pressed through the crowd : me abrí paso entre el gentío⟩ **4** URGE : presionar

press² *n* **1** CROWD : multitud *f* **2** : imprenta *f*, prensa *f* ⟨to go to press : entrar en prensa⟩ **3** URGENCY : urgencia *f*, prisa *f* **4** PRINTER, PUBLISHER : imprenta *f*, editorial *f* **5 the press** : la prensa ⟨freedom of the press : libertad de prensa⟩

pressing [ˈprɛsɪŋ] *adj* URGENT : urgente

pressure¹ [ˈprɛʃər] *vt* **-sured; -suring** : presionar, apremiar

pressure² *n* **1** : presión *f* ⟨to be under pressure : estar bajo presión⟩ **2** → **blood pressure**

pressurize [ˈprɛʃəˌraɪz] *vt* **-ized; -izing** : presurizar

prestige [prɛˈstiːʒ, -ˈstiːdʒ] *n* : prestigio *m*

prestigious [prɛˈstɪdʒəs] *adj* : prestigioso

presto [ˈprɛsˌtoː] *adv* : de pronto

presumably [priˈzuːməbli] *adv* : es de suponer, supuestamente ⟨presumably, he's guilty : supone que es culpable⟩

presume [priˈzuːm] *vt* **-sumed; -suming** **1** ASSUME, SUPPOSE : suponer, asumir, presumir **2 to presume to** : atreverse a, osar

presumption [priˈzʌmpʃən] *n* **1** AUDACITY : atrevimiento *m*, osadía *f* **2** ASSUMPTION : presunción *f*, suposición *f*

presumptuous [priˈzʌmptʃuəs] *adj* : descarado, atrevido

presuppose [ˌpriːsəˈpoːz] *vt* **-posed; -posing** : presuponer

pretend [priˈtɛnd] *vt* **1** CLAIM : pretender **2** FEIGN : fingir, simular — *vi* : fingir

pretender [priˈtɛndər] *n* : pretendiente *mf* (al trono, etc.)

pretense *or* **pretence** [ˈpriːˌtɛnts, priˈtɛnts] *n* **1** CLAIM : afirmación *f* (falsa), pretensión *f* **2** FEIGNING : fingimiento *m*, simulación *f* ⟨to make a pretense of doing something : fingir hacer algo⟩ ⟨a pretense of order : una apariencia de orden⟩ **3** PRETEXT : pretexto *m* ⟨under false pretenses : con pretextos falsos, de manera fraudulenta⟩

pretension [priˈtɛntʃən] *n* **1** CLAIM : pretensión *f*, afirmación *f* **2** ASPIRATION : aspiración *f*, ambición *f* **3** PRETENTIOUSNESS : pretensiones *fpl*, presunción *f*

pretentious [priˈtɛntʃəs] *adj* : pretencioso

pretentiousness [priˈtɛntʃəsnəs] *n* : presunción *f*, pretensiones *fpl*

pretext [ˈpriːˌtɛkst] *n* : pretexto *m*, excusa *f*

prettily [ˈprɪṭəli] *adv* : atractivamente

prettiness [ˈprɪṭinəs] *n* : lindeza *f*

pretty¹ [ˈprɪṭi] *adv* : bastante, bien ⟨it's pretty obvious : está bien claro⟩ ⟨it's pretty much the same : es más o menos igual⟩

pretty² *adj* **-tier; -est** : bonito, lindo, guapo ⟨a pretty girl : una muchacha guapa⟩ ⟨what a pretty dress! : ¡qué vestido más lindo!⟩

pretzel [ˈprɛtsəl] *n* : galleta *f* salada (en forma de nudo)

prevail [priˈveɪl] *vi* **1** TRIUMPH : prevalecer **2** PREDOMINATE : predominar **3 to prevail upon** : persuadir, convencer ⟨I prevailed upon her to sing : la convencí para que cantara⟩

prevailing [priˈveɪlɪŋ] *adj* : imperante, prevaleciente

prevalence [ˈprɛvələnts] *n* : preponderancia *f*, predominio *m*

prevalent [ˈprɛvələnt] *adj* **1** COMMON : común y corriente, general **2** WIDESPREAD : extendido

prevaricate [prɪˈværəˌkeɪt] *vi* **-cated; -cating** LIE : mentir

prevarication [prɪˌværəˈkeɪʃən] *n* : mentira *f*

prevent [prɪˈvɛnt] *vt* **1** AVOID : prevenir, evitar ⟨steps to prevent war : medidas para evitar la guerra⟩ **2** HINDER : impedir

preventable [prɪˈvɛntəbəl] *adj* : evitable

preventative [prɪˈvɛntətɪv] → **preventive**

prevention [prɪˈvɛntʃən] *n* : prevención *f*

preventive [prɪˈvɛntɪv] *adj* : preventivo

preview [ˈpriːˌvju] *n* : preestreno *m*

previous [ˈpriːviəs] *adj* : previo, anterior ⟨previous knowledge : conocimientos previos⟩ ⟨the previous day : el día anterior⟩ ⟨in the previous year : en el año pasado⟩

previously [ˈpriːviəsli] *adv* : antes

prewar [ˌpriːˈwɔr] *adj* : de antes de la guerra

prey [ˈpreɪ] *n, pl* **preys** : presa *f*

prey on *vt* **1** : cazar, alimentarse de ⟨it preys on fish : se alimenta de peces⟩ **2 to prey on one's mind** : hacer presa en alguien, atormentar a alguien

price¹ [ˈpraɪs] *vt* **priced; pricing** : poner un precio a

price² *n* : precio *m* ⟨peace at any price : la paz a toda costa⟩

priceless [ˈpraɪsləs] *adj* : inestimable, inapreciable

pricey [ˈpraɪsi] *adj* : caro

prick¹ [ˈprɪk] *vt* **1** : pinchar **2 to prick up one's ears** : levantar las orejas — *vi* : pinchar

prick² *n* **1** STAB : pinchazo *m* ⟨a prick of conscience : un remordimiento⟩ **2** → **pricker**

pricker [ˈprɪkər] *n* THORN : espina *f*

prickle¹ [ˈprɪkəl] *vi* **-led; -ling** : sentir un cosquilleo, tener un hormigueo

prickle² *n* **1** : espina *f* (de una planta) **2** TINGLE : cosquilleo *m*, hormigueo *m*

prickly [ˈprɪkəli] *adj* **1** THORNY : espinoso **2** : que pica ⟨a prickly sensation : un hormigueo⟩

prickly pear *n* : tuna *f*

pride¹ [ˈpraɪd] *vt* **prided; priding** : estar orgulloso de ⟨to pride oneself on : preciarse de, enorgullecerse de⟩

pride² *n* : orgullo *m*

priest [ˈpriːst] *n* : sacerdote *m*, cura *m*

priestess [ˈpriːstɪs] *n* : sacerdotisa *f*

priesthood [ˈpriːstˌhʊd] *n* : sacerdocio *m*

priestly [ˈpriːstli] *adj* : sacerdotal

prig [ˈprɪg] *n* : mojigato *m*, -ta *f*; gazmoño *m*, -ña *f*

prim [ˈprɪm] *adj* **primmer; primmest** **1** PRISSY : remilgado **2** PRUDISH : mojigato, gazmoño

primarily [praɪˈmɛrəli] *adv* : principalmente, fundamentalmente

primary¹ [ˈpraɪˌmɛri, ˈpraɪməri] *adj* **1** FIRST : primario **2** PRINCIPAL : principal **3** BASIC : fundamental

primary² *n, pl* **-ries** : elección *f* primaria

primary color *n* : color *m* primario

primary school → **elementary school**

primate *n* **1** [ˈpraɪˌmeɪt, -mət] : primado *m* (obispo) **2** [-ˌmeɪt] : primate *m* (animal)

prime¹ [ˈpraɪm] *vt* **primed; priming** **1** : cebar ⟨to prime a pump : cebar una bomba⟩ **2** PREPARE : preparar (una superficie para pintar) **3** COACH : preparar (a un testigo, etc.)

prime² *adj* **1** CHIEF, MAIN : principal, primero **2** EXCELLENT : de primera (categoría), excelente

prime³ *n* **the prime of one's life** : la flor de la vida

prime minister *n* : primer ministro *m*, primera ministra *f*

primer¹ [ˈprɪmər] *n* **1** READER : cartilla *f* **2** MANUAL : manual *m*

primer² [ˈpraɪmər] *n* **1** : cebo *m* (para explosivos) **2** : base *f* (de pintura)

prime time *n* : horas *fpl* de mayor audiencia

primeval [praɪˈmiːvəl] *adj* : primitivo, primigenio

primitive [ˈprɪmətɪv] *adj* : primitivo

primly [ˈprɪmli] *adv* : mojigatamente

primness [ˈprɪmnəs] *n* : mojigatería *f*, gazmoñería *f*

primordial [praɪˈmɔrdiəl] *adj* : primordial, fundamental

primp [ˈprɪmp] *vi* : arreglarse, acicalarse

primrose [ˈprɪmˌroːz] *n* : primavera *f*, prímula *f*

prince [ˈprɪnts] *n* : príncipe *m*

princely [ˈprɪntsli] *adj* : principesco

princess [ˈprɪntsəs, ˈprɪnˌsɛs] *n* : princesa *f*

principal¹ [ˈprɪntsəpəl] *adj* : principal — **principally** *adv*

principal² *n* **1** PROTAGONIST : protagonista *mf* **2** : director *m*, -tora *f* (de una escuela) **3** CAPITAL : principal *m*, capital *m* (en finanzas)

principality [ˌprɪntsəˈpæləti] *n, pl* **-ties** : principado *m*

principle [ˈprɪntsəpəl] *n* : principio *m*

print¹ [ˈprɪnt] *vt* : imprimir (libros, etc.) — *vi* : escribir con letra de molde

print² *n* **1** IMPRESSION : marca *f*, huella *f*, impresión *f* **2** : texto *m* impreso ⟨to be out of print : estar agotado⟩ **3** LETTERING : letra *f* **4** ENGRAVING : grabado *m* **5** : copia *f* (en fotografía) **6** : estampado *m* (de tela)

printer [ˈprɪntər] *n* **1** : impresor *m*, -sora *f* (persona) **2** : impresora *f* (máquina)

printing [ˈprɪntɪŋ] *n* **1** : impresión *f* (acto) ⟨the third printing : la tercera tirada⟩ **2** : imprenta *f* (profesión) **3** LETTERING : letras *fpl* de molde

printing press *n* : prensa *f*

print out *vt* : imprimir (de una computadora)

printout [ˈprɪntˌaʊt] *n* : copia *f* impresa (de una computadora)

prior [ˈpraɪər] *adj* **1** : previo **2 prior to** : antes de

priority [praɪ'ɔrəti] *n, pl* **-ties** : prioridad *f*

priory ['praɪəri] *n, pl* **-ries** : priorato *m*

prism ['prɪzəm] *n* : prisma *m*

prison [-'prɪzən] *n* : prisión *f*, cárcel *f*

prisoner ['prɪzənər] *n* : preso *m*, -sa *f*; recluso *m*, -sa *f* ⟨prisoner of war : prisionero de guerra⟩

prissy ['prɪsi] *adj* **-sier; -est** : remilgado, melindroso

pristine ['prɪsˌtiːn, prɪs'-] *adj* : puro, prístino

privacy ['praɪvəsi] *n, pl* **-cies** : privacidad *f*

private[1] ['praɪvət] *adj* **1** PERSONAL : privado, particular ⟨private property : propiedad privada⟩ **2** INDEPENDENT : privado, independiente ⟨private studies : estudios privados⟩ **3** SECRET : secreto **4** SECLUDED : aislado, privado — **privately** *adv*

private[2] *n* : soldado *m* raso

privateer [ˌpraɪvə'tɪr] *n* : corsario *m*

privation [praɪ'veɪʃən] *n* : privación *f*

privilege ['prɪvlɪʤ, 'prɪvə-] *n* : privilegio *m*

privileged ['prɪvlɪʤd, 'prɪvə-] *adj* : privilegiado

privy[1] ['prɪvi] *adj* **to be privy to** : estar enterado de

privy[2] *n, pl* **privies** : excusado *m*, retrete *m* (exterior)

prize[1] ['praɪz] *vt* **prized; prizing** : valorar, apreciar

prize[2] *adj* **1** : premiado ⟨a prize stallion : un semental premiado⟩ **2** OUTSTANDING : de primera, excepcional

prize[3] *n* **1** AWARD : premio *m* ⟨third prize : el tercer premio⟩ **2** : joya *f*, tesoro *m* ⟨he's a real prize : es un tesoro⟩

prizefighter ['praɪzˌfaɪtər] *n* : boxeador *m*, -dora *f* profesional

prizewinning ['praɪzˌwɪnɪŋ] *adj* : premiado

pro[1] ['proː] *adv* : a favor

pro[2] *adj* → **professional**[1]

pro[3] *n* **1** : pro *m* ⟨the pros and cons : los pros y los contras⟩ **2** → **professional**[2]

probability [ˌprɑbə'brlɪti] *n, pl* **-ties** : probabilidad *f*

probable ['prɑbəbəl] *adj* : probable — **probably** [-bli] *adv*

probate[1] ['proːˌbeɪt] *vt* **-bated; -bating** : autenticar (un testamento)

probate[2] *n* : autenticación *f* (de un testamento)

probation [proˈbeɪʃən] *n* **1** : período *m* de prueba (para un empleado, etc.) **2** : libertad *f* condicional (para un preso)

probationary [proˈbeɪʃəˌneri] *adj* : de prueba

probe[1] ['proːb] *vt* **probed; probing 1** : sondar (en medicina y tecnología) **2** INVESTIGATE : investigar, sondear

probe[2] *n* **1** : sonda *f* (en medicina, etc.) ⟨space probe : sonda espacial⟩ **2** INVESTIGATION : investigación *f*, sondeo *m*

probity ['proːbəti] *n* : probidad *f*

problem[1] ['prɑbləm] *adj* : difícil

problem[2] *n* : problema *m*

problematic [ˌprɑblə'mætɪk] *or* **problematical** [-ˌtɪkəl] *adj* : problemático

proboscis [prə'bɑsɪs] *n, pl* **-cises** *also* **-cides** [-səˌdiːz] : probóscide *f*

procedural [prə'siːʤərəl] *adj* : de procedimiento

procedure [prə'siːʤər] *n* : procedimiento *m* ⟨administrative procedures : trámites administrativos⟩

proceed [proˈsiːd] *vi* **1** : proceder ⟨to proceed to do something : proceder a hacer algo⟩ **2** CONTINUE : continuar, proseguir, seguir ⟨he proceeded to the next phase : pasó a la segunda fase⟩ **3** ADVANCE : avanzar ⟨as the conference proceeded : mientras seguía avanzando la conferencia⟩ ⟨the road proceeds south : la calle sigue hacia el sur⟩

proceeding [proˈsiːdɪŋ] *n* **1** PROCEDURE : procedimiento *m* **2 proceedings** *npl* EVENTS : acontecimientos *mpl* **3 proceedings** *npl* MINUTES : actas *fpl* (de una reunión, etc.)

proceeds ['proːˌsiːdz] *npl* : ganancias *fpl*

process[1] ['prɑˌsɛs, 'proː-] *vt* : procesar, tratar

process[2] *n, pl* **-cesses** ['prɑˌsɛsəz, 'proː-, -səsəz, -səˌsiːz] **1** : proceso *m* ⟨the process of elimination : el proceso de eliminación⟩ **2** METHOD : proceso *m*, método *m* ⟨manufacturing processes : procesos industriales⟩ **3** : acción *f* judicial ⟨due process of law : el debido proceso (de la ley)⟩ **4** SUMMONS : citación *f* **5** PROJECTION : protuberancia *f* (anatómica) **6 in the process of** : en vías de ⟨in the process of repair : en reparaciones⟩

procession [prə'sɛʃən] *n* : procesión *f*, desfile *m* ⟨a funeral procession : un cortejo fúnebre⟩

processional [prə'sɛʃənəl] *n* : himno *m* para una procesión

processor ['prɑˌsɛsər, 'proː-, -səsər] *n* **1** : procesador *m* (de una computadora) **2 food processor** : procesador *m* de alimentos

proclaim [proˈkleɪm] *vt* : proclamar

proclamation [ˌprɑklə'meɪʃən] *n* : proclamación *f*

proclivity [proˈklɪvəti] *n, pl* **-ties** : proclividad *f*

procrastinate [prə'kræstəˌneɪt] *vi* **-nated; -nating** : demorar, aplazar las responsabilidades

procrastination [prəˌkræstə'neɪʃən] *n* : aplazamiento *m*, demora *f*, dilación *f*

procreate ['proːkriˌeɪt] *vi* **-ated; -ating** : procrear

procreation [ˌproːkri'eɪʃən] *n* : procreación *f*

proctor[1] ['prɑktər] *vt* : supervisar (un examen)

proctor[2] *n* : supervisor *m*, -sora *f* (de un examen)

procure [prəˈkjʊr] *vt* **-cured; -curing 1** OBTAIN : procurar, obtener **2** BRING ABOUT : provocar, lograr, conseguir

procurement [prəˈkjʊrmənt] *n* : obtención *f*

prod[1] [ˈprɑd] *vt* **prodded; prodding 1** JAB, POKE : pinchar, golpear (con la punta de algo) **2** GOAD : incitar, estimular

prod[2] *n* **1** JAB, POKE : golpe *m* (con la punta de algo), pinchazo *m* **2** STIMULUS : estímulo *m* **3 cattle prod** : picana *f*, aguijón *m*

prodigal[1] [ˈprɑdɪgəl] *adj* SPENDTHRIFT : pródigo, despilfarrador, derrochador

prodigal[2] *n* : pródigo *m*, -ga *f*; derrochador *m*, -dora *f*

prodigious [prəˈdɪdʒəs] *adj* **1** MARVELOUS : prodigioso, maravilloso **2** HUGE : enorme, vasto ⟨prodigious sums : muchísimo dinero⟩ — **prodigiously** *adv*

prodigy [ˈprɑdədʒi] *n, pl* **-gies** : prodigio *m* ⟨child prodigy : niño prodigio⟩

produce[1] [prəˈduːs, -ˈdjuːs] *vt* **-duced; -ducing 1** EXHIBIT : presentar, mostrar **2** YIELD : producir **3** CAUSE : producir, causar **4** CREATE : producir ⟨to produce a poem : escribir un poema⟩ **5** : poner en escena (una obra de teatro), producir (una película)

produce[2] [ˈprɑˌduːs, ˈproː-, -ˌdjuːs] *n* : productos *mpl* agrícolas

producer [prəˈduːsər, -ˈdjuː-] *n* : productor *m*, -tora *f*

product [ˈprɑˌdʌkt] *n* : producto *m*

production [prəˈdʌkʃən] *n* : producción *f*

productive [prəˈdʌktɪv] *adj* : productivo

productivity [ˌproːˌdʌkˈtɪvəti, ˌprɑ-] *n* : productividad *f*

profane[1] [proˈfeɪn] *vt* **-faned; -faning** : profanar

profane[2] *adj* **1** SECULAR : profano **2** IRREVERENT : irreverente, impío

profanity [proˈfænəti] *n, pl* **-ties 1** IRREVERENCE : irreverencia *f*, impiedad *f* **2** : blasfemias *fpl*, obscenidades *fpl* ⟨don't use profanity : no digas blasfemias⟩

profess [prəˈfɛs] *vt* **1** DECLARE : declarar, manifestar **2** CLAIM : pretender **3** : profesar (una religión, etc.)

professedly [prəˈfɛsədli] *adv* **1** OPENLY : declaradamente **2** ALLEGEDLY : supuestamente

profession [prəˈfɛʃən] *n* : profesión *f*

professional[1] [prəˈfɛʃənəl] *adj* : profesional — **professionally** *adv*

professional[2] *n* : profesional *mf*

professionalism [prəˈfɛʃənəˌlizəm] *n* : profesionalismo *m*

professor [prəˈfɛsər] *n* : profesor *m* (universitario), profesora *f* (universitaria); catedrático *m*, -ca *f*

proffer [ˈprɑfər] *vt* **-fered; -fering** : ofrecer, dar

proficiency [prəˈfɪʃəntsi] *n* : competencia *f*, capacidad *f*

proficient [prəˈfɪʃənt] *adj* : competente, experto — **proficiently** *adv*

profile [ˈproːˌfaɪl] *n* : perfil *m* ⟨a portrait in profile : un retrato de perfil⟩ ⟨to keep a low profile : no llamar la atención, hacerse pasar desapercibido⟩

profit[1] [ˈprɑfət] *vi* : sacar provecho (de), beneficiarse (de)

profit[2] *n* **1** ADVANTAGE : provecho *m*, partido *m*, beneficio *m* **2** GAIN : beneficio *m*, utilidad *f*, ganancia *f* ⟨to make a profit : sacar beneficios⟩

profitable [ˈprɑfətəbəl] *adj* : rentable, lucrativo — **profitably** [-bli] *adv*

profitless [ˈprɑfətləs] *adj* : infructuoso, inútil

profligate [ˈprɑflɪgət, -ˌgeɪt] *adj* **1** DISSOLUTE : disoluto, licencioso **2** SPENDTHRIFT : despilfarrador, derrochador, pródigo

profound [prəˈfaʊnd] *adj* : profundo

profoundly [prəˈfaʊndli] *adv* : profundamente, en profundidad

profundity [prəˈfʌndəti] *n, pl* **-ties** : profundidad *f*

profuse [prəˈfjuːs] *adj* **1** COPIOUS : profuso, copioso **2** LAVISH : pródigo — **profusely** *adv*

profusion [prəˈfjuːʒən] *n* : abundancia *f*, profusión *f*

progenitor [proˈdʒɛnətər] *n* : progenitor *m*, -tora *f*

progeny [ˈprɑdʒəni] *n, pl* **-nies** : progenie *f*

progesterone [proˈdʒɛstəˌroːn] *n* : progesterona *f*

prognosis [prɑgˈnoːsɪs] *n, pl* **-noses** [-ˌsiːz] : pronóstico *m* (médico)

program[1] [ˈproːˌgræm, -grəm] *vt* **-grammed** *or* **-gramed; -gramming** *or* **-graming** : programar

program[2] *n* : programa *m*

programmable [ˈproːˌgræməbəl] *adj* : programable

programmer [ˈproːˌgræmər] *n* : programador *m*, -dora *f*

programming [ˈproːˌgræmɪŋ] *n* : programación *f*

progress[1] [prəˈgrɛs] *vi* **1** PROCEED : progresar, adelantar **2** IMPROVE : mejorar

progress[2] [ˈprɑgrəs, -ˌgrɛs] *n* **1** ADVANCE : progreso *m*, adelanto *m*, avance *m* ⟨to make progress : hacer progresos⟩ **2** BETTERMENT : mejora *f*, mejoramiento *m*

progression [prəˈgrɛʃən] *n* **1** ADVANCE : avance *m* **2** SEQUENCE : desarrollo *m* (de eventos)

progressive [prəˈgrɛsɪv] *adj* **1** : progresista ⟨a progressive society : una sociedad progresista⟩ **2** : progresivo ⟨a progressive disease : una enfermedad progresiva⟩ **3** *or* **Progressive** : progresista (en política) **4** : progresivo (en gramática)

progressively [prə'grɛsɪvli] *adv* : progresivamente, poco a poco

prohibit [pro'hɪbət] *vt* : prohibir

prohibition [ˌpro:ə'bɪʃən, ˌpro:hə-] *n* : prohibición *f*

prohibitive [pro'hɪbətɪv] *adj* : prohibitivo

project[1] [prə'dʒɛkt] *vt* **1** PLAN : proyectar, planear **2** : proyectar (imágenes, misiles, etc.) — *vi* PROTRUDE : sobresalir, salir

project[2] ['prɑˌdʒɛkt, -dʒɪkt] *n* : proyecto *m*, trabajo *m* (de un estudiante) ⟨research project : proyecto de investigación⟩

projectile [prə'dʒɛktəl, -ˌtaɪl] *n* : proyectil *m*

projection [prə'dʒɛkʃən] *n* **1** PLAN : plan *m*, proyección *f* **2** : proyección *f* (de imágenes, misiles, etc.) **3** PROTRUSION : saliente *m*

projector [prə'dʒɛktər] *n* : proyector *m*

proletarian[1] [ˌpro:lə'tɛriən] *adj* : proletario

proletarian[2] *n* : proletario *m*, -ria *f*

proletariat [ˌpro:lə'tɛriət] *n* : proletariado *m*

proliferate [prə'lɪfəˌreɪt] *vi* **-ated; -ating** : proliferar

proliferation [prəˌlɪfə'reɪʃən] *n* : proliferación *f*

prolific [prə'lɪfɪk] *adj* : prolífico

prologue ['pro:ˌlɔg] *n* : prólogo *m*

prolong [prə'lɔŋ] *vt* : prolongar

prolongation [ˌpro:ˌlɔŋ'geɪʃən] *n* : prolongación *f*

prom ['prɑm] *n* : baile *m* formal (de un colegio)

promenade[1] [ˌprɑmə'neɪd, -'nɑd] *vi* **-naded; -nading** : pasear, pasearse, dar un paseo

promenade[2] *n* : paseo *m*

prominence ['prɑmənən*t*s] *n* **1** PROJECTION : prominencia *f* **2** EMINENCE : eminencia *f*, prestigio *m*

prominent ['prɑmənənt] *adj* **1** OUTSTANDING : prominente, destacado **2** PROJECTING : prominente, saliente

prominently ['prɑmənəntli] *adv* : destacadamente, prominentemente

promiscuity [ˌprɑmɪs'kju:əti] *n, pl* **-ties** : promiscuidad *f*

promiscuous [prə'mɪskjʊəs] *adj* : promiscuo — **promiscuously** *adv*

promise[1] ['prɑməs] *v* **-ised; -ising** : prometer

promise[2] *n* **1** : promesa *f* ⟨he kept his promise : cumplió su promesa⟩ **2 to show promise** : prometer

promising ['prɑməsɪŋ] *adj* : prometedor

promissory ['prɑməˌsori] *adj* : que promete ⟨a promissory note : un pagaré⟩

promontory ['prɑmənˌtori] *n, pl* **-ries** : promontorio *m*

promote [prə'mo:t] *vt* **-moted; -moting** **1** : ascender (a un alumno o un empleado) **2** ADVERTISE : promocionar,

hacerle publicidad a **3** FURTHER : promover, fomentar

promoter [prə'mo:tər] *n* : promotor *m*, -tora *f*; empresario *m*, -ria *f* (en deportes)

promotion [prə'mo:ʃən] *n* **1** : ascenso *m* (de un alumno o un empleado) **2** FURTHERING : promoción *f*, fomento *m* **3** ADVERTISING : publicidad *f*, propaganda *f*

promotional [prə'mo:ʃənəl] *adj* : promocional

prompt[1] ['prɑmpt] *vt* **1** INDUCE : provocar (una cosa), inducir (a una persona) ⟨curiosity prompted me to ask you : la curiosidad me indujo a preguntarle⟩ **2** : apuntar (a un actor, etc.)

prompt[2] *adj* : pronto, rápido ⟨prompt payment : pago puntual⟩

prompter ['prɑmptər] *n* : apuntador *m*, -dora *f* (en teatro)

promptly ['prɑmptli] *adv* : inmediatamente, rápidamente

promptness ['prɑmptnəs] *n* : prontitud *f*, rapidez *f*

promulgate ['prɑməlˌgeɪt] *vt* **-gated; -gating** : promulgar

prone ['pro:n] *adj* **1** LIABLE : propenso, proclive ⟨accident-prone : propenso a los accidentes⟩ **2** : boca abajo, decúbito prono ⟨in a prone position : en decúbito prono⟩

prong ['prɔŋ] *n* : punta *f*, diente *m*

pronoun ['pro:ˌnaʊn] *n* : pronombre *m*

pronounce [prə'naʊn*t*s] *vt* **-nounced; -nouncing** **1** : pronunciar ⟨how do you pronounce your name? : ¿cómo se pronuncia su nombre?⟩ **2** DECLARE : declarar **3 to pronounce sentence** : dictar sentencia, pronunciar un fallo

pronounced [prə'naʊn*t*st] *adj* MARKED : pronunciado, marcado

pronouncement [prə'naʊn*t*smənt] *n* : declaración *f*

pronunciation [prəˌnʌntsi'eɪʃən] *n* : pronunciación *f*

proof[1] ['pru:f] *adj* : a prueba ⟨proof against tampering : a prueba de manipulación⟩

proof[2] *n* : prueba *f*

proofread ['pru:fˌri:d] *v* **-read; -reading** *vt* : corregir — *vi* : corregir pruebas

proofreader ['pru:fˌri:dər] *n* : corrector *m*, -tora *f* (de pruebas)

prop[1] ['prɑp] *vt* **propped; propping** **1 to prop against** : apoyar contra **2 to prop up** SUPPORT : apoyar, apuntalar, sostener **3 to prop up** SUSTAIN : alentar (a alguien), darle ánimo (a alguien)

prop[2] *n* **1** SUPPORT : puntal *m*, apoyo *m*, soporte *m* **2** : accesorio *m* (en teatro)

propaganda [ˌprɑpə'gændə, ˌpro:-] *n* : propaganda *f*

propagandize [ˌprɑpə'gænˌdaɪz, ˌpro:-] *v* **-dized; -dizing** *vt* : someter a propaganda — *vi* : hacer propaganda

propagate ['prɑpə,geɪt] v **-gated; -gating** vi : propagarse — vt : propagar
propagation [,prɑpə'geɪʃən] n : propagación f
propane ['pro:,peɪn] n : propano m
propel [prə'pɛl] vt **-pelled; -pelling** : impulsar, propulsar, impeler
propellant or **propellent** [prə'pɛlənt] n : propulsor m
propeller [prə'pɛlər] n : hélice f
propensity [prə'pɛntsəṭi] n, pl **-ties** : propensión f, tendencia f, inclinación f
proper ['prɑpər] adj **1** RIGHT, SUITABLE : apropiado, adecuado **2** : propio, mismo ⟨the city proper : la propia ciudad⟩ **3** CORRECT : correcto **4** GENTEEL : fino, refinado, cortés **5** OWN, SPECIAL : propio ⟨proper name : nombre propio⟩ — **properly** adv
property ['prɑpərṭi] n, pl **-ties 1** CHARACTERISTIC : característica f, propiedad f **2** POSSESSIONS : propiedad f **3** BUILDING : inmueble m **4** LAND, LOT : terreno m, lote m, parcela f **5** PROP : accesorio m (en teatro)
prophecy ['prɑfəsi] n, pl **-cies** : profecía f, vaticinio m
prophesy ['prɑfə,saɪ] v **-sied; -sying** vt **1** FORETELL : profetizar (como profeta) **2** PREDICT : profetizar, predecir, vaticinar — vi : hacer profecías
prophet ['prɑfət] n : profeta m, profetisa f
prophetic [prə'fɛṭɪk] or **prophetical** [-ṭɪkəl] adj : profético — **prophetically** [-ṭɪkli] adv
propitiate [pro'pɪʃi,eɪt] vt **-ated; -ating** : propiciar
propitious [prə'pɪʃəs] adj : propicio
proponent [prə'po:nənt] n : defensor m, -sora f; partidario m, -ria f
proportion¹ [prə'porʃən] vt : proporcionar ⟨well-proportioned : de buenas proporciones⟩
proportion² n **1** RATIO : proporción f **2** SYMMETRY : proporción f, simetría f ⟨out of proportion : desproporcionado⟩ **3** SHARE : parte f **4** proportions npl SIZE : dimensiones fpl
proportional [prə'porʃənəl] adj : proporcional — **proportionally** adv
proportionate [prə'porʃənət] adj : proporcional — **proportionately** adv
proposal [prə'po:zəl] n **1** PROPOSITION : propuesta f, proposición f ⟨marriage proposal : propuesta de matrimonio⟩ **2** PLAN : proyecto m, propuesta f
propose [prə'po:z] v **-posed; -posing** vi : proponer matrimonio — vt **1** INTEND : pensar, proponerse **2** SUGGEST : proponer
proposition [,prɑpə'zɪʃən] n **1** PROPOSAL : proposición f, propuesta f **2** STATEMENT : proposición f
propound [prə'paund] vt : proponer, exponer
proprietary [prə'praɪə,tɛri] adj : propietario, patentado

proprietor [prə'praɪəṭər] n : propietario m, -ria f
propriety [prə'praɪəṭi] n, pl **-eties 1** DECORUM : decencia f, decoro m **2** **proprieties** npl CONVENTIONS : convenciones fpl, cánones mpl sociales
propulsion [prə'pʌlʃən] n : propulsión f
prosaic [pro'zeɪɪk] adj : prosaico
proscribe [pro'skraɪb] vt **-scribed; -scribing** : proscribir
prose ['pro:z] n : prosa f
prosecute ['prɑsɪ,kju:t] vt **-cuted; -cuting 1** CARRY OUT : llevar a cabo **2** : procesar, enjuiciar ⟨prosecuted for fraud : procesado por fraude⟩
prosecution [,prɑsɪ'kju:ʃən] n **1** : procesamiento m ⟨the prosecution of forgers : el procesamiento de falsificadores⟩ **2** PROSECUTORS : acusación f ⟨witness for the prosecution : testigo de cargo⟩
prosecutor ['prɑsɪ,kju:ṭər] n : acusador m, -dora f; fiscal mf
prospect¹ ['prɑ,spɛkt] vi : prospectar (el terreno) ⟨to prospect for gold : buscar oro⟩
prospect² n **1** VISTA : vista f, panorama m **2** POSSIBILITY : posibilidad f **3** OUTLOOK : perspectiva f **4** : posible cliente m, -ta f ⟨a salesman looking for prospects : un vendedor buscando nuevos clientes⟩
prospective [prə'spɛktɪv, 'prɑ,spɛk-] adj **1** EXPECTANT : futuro ⟨prospective mother : futura madre⟩ **2** POTENTIAL : potencial, posible ⟨prospective employee : posible empleado⟩
prospector ['prɑ,spɛktər, prɑ'spɛk-] n : prospector m, -tora f; explorador m, -dora f
prospectus [prə'spɛktəs] n : prospecto m
prosper ['prɑspər] vi : prosperar
prosperity [prɑ'spɛrəṭi] n : prosperidad f
prosperous ['prɑspərəs] adj : próspero
prostate ['prɑ,steɪt] n : próstata f
prosthesis [prɑs'θi:sɪs, 'prɑsθə-] n, pl **-theses** [-,si:z] : prótesis f
prostitute¹ ['prɑstə,tu:t, -,tju:t] vt **-tuted; -tuting 1** : prostituir **2 to prostitute oneself** : prostituirse
prostitute² n : prostituto m, -ta f
prostitution [,prɑstə'tu:ʃən, -'tju:-] n : prostitución f
prostrate¹ ['prɑ,streɪt] vt **-trated; -trating 1** : postrar **2 to prostrate oneself** : postrarse
prostrate² adj : postrado
prostration [prɑ'streɪʃən] n : postración f
protagonist [pro'tægənɪst] n : protagonista mf
protect [prə'tɛkt] vt : proteger
protection [prə'tɛkʃən] n : protección f
protective [prə'tɛktɪv] adj : protector
protector [prə'tɛktər] n **1** : protector m, -tora f (persona) **2** GUARD : protector m (aparato)

protectorate [prə'tɛktərət] *n* : protectorado *m*

protégé ['pro:tˌɛˌʒeɪ] *n* : protegido *m*, -da *f*

protein ['pro:ˌti:n] *n* : proteína *f*

protest[1] ['pro:ˌtɛst] *vt* 1 ASSERT : afirmar, declarar 2 : protestar ⟨they protested the decision : protestaron (por) la decisión⟩ — *vi* **to protest against** : protestar contra

protest[2] ['pro:ˌtɛst] *n* 1 DEMONSTRATION : manifestación *f* (de protesta) ⟨a public protest : una manifestación pública⟩ 2 COMPLAINT : queja *f*, protesta *f*

Protestant ['prɑtəstənt] *n* : protestante *mf*

Protestantism ['prɑtəstənˌtɪzəm] *n* : protestantismo *m*

protocol ['pro:təˌkɔl] *n* : protocolo *m*

proton ['pro:ˌtɑn] *n* : protón *m*

protoplasm ['pro:təˌplæzəm] *n* : protoplasma *m*

prototype ['pro:təˌtaɪp] *n* : prototipo *m*

protozoan [ˌpro:təˈzo:ən] *n* : protozoario *m*, protozoo *m*

protract [pro'trækt] *vt* : prolongar

protractor [pro'træktər] *n* : transportador *m* (instrumento)

protrude [pro'tru:d] *vi* **-truded; -truding** : salir, sobresalir

protrusion [pro'tru:ʒən] *n* : protuberancia *f*, saliente *m*

protuberance [pro'tu:bərənts, -'tju:-] *n* : protuberancia *f*

proud ['praʊd] *adj* 1 HAUGHTY : altanero, orgulloso, arrogante 2 : orgulloso ⟨she was proud of her work : estaba orgullosa de su trabajo⟩ ⟨too proud to beg : demasiado orgulloso para rogar⟩ 3 GLORIOUS : glorioso — **proudly** *adv*

prove ['pru:v] *v* **proved; proved** *or* **proven** ['pru:vən]; **proving** *vt* 1 TEST : probar 2 DEMONSTRATE : probar, demostrar — *vi* : resultar ⟨it proved effective : resultó efectivo⟩

Provençal [ˌpro:vɑn'sɑl, ˌprɑvɑn-] *n* 1 : provenzal *mf* 2 : provenzal *m* (idioma) — **Provençal** *adj*

proverb ['prɑˌvərb] *n* : proverbio *m*, refrán *m*

proverbial [prə'vərbiəl] *adj* : proverbial

provide [prə'vaɪd] *v* **-vided; -viding** *vt* 1 STIPULATE : estipular 2 **to provide with** : proveer de, proporcionar — *vi* 1 : proveer ⟨the Lord will provide : el Señor proveerá⟩ 2 **to provide for** SUPPORT : mantener 3 **to provide for** ANTICIPATE : hacer previsiones para, prever

provided [prə'vaɪdəd] *or* **provided that** *conj* : con tal (de) que, siempre que

providence ['prɑvədənts] *n* 1 PRUDENCE : previsión *f*, prudencia *f* 2 **Providence** : providencia *f* ⟨divine providence : la Divina Providencia⟩ 3 **Providence** GOD : Providencia *f*

provident ['prɑvədənt] *adj* 1 PRUDENT : previsor, prudente 2 FRUGAL : frugal, ahorrativo

providential [ˌprɑvə'dɛntʃəl] *adj* : providencial

provider [prə'vaɪdər] *n* 1 PURVEYOR : proveedor *m*, -dora *f* 2 BREADWINNER : sostén *m* (económico)

providing that → **provided**

province ['prɑvɪnts] *n* 1 : provincia *f* (de un país) ⟨to live in the provinces : vivir en las provincias⟩ 2 FIELD, SPHERE : campo *m*, competencia *f* ⟨it's not in my province : no es de mi competencia⟩

provincial [prə'vɪntʃəl] *adj* 1 : provincial ⟨provincial government : gobierno provincial⟩ 2 : provinciano, pueblerino ⟨a provincial mentality : una mentalidad provinciana⟩

provision[1] [prə'vɪʒən] *vt* : aprovisionar, abastecer

provision[2] *n* 1 PROVIDING : provisión *f*, suministro *m* 2 STIPULATION : condición *f*, salvedad *f*, estipulación *f* 3 **provisions** *npl* : despensa *f*, víveres *mpl*, provisiones *fpl*

provisional [prə'vɪʒənəl] *adj* : provisional, provisorio — **provisionally** *adv*

proviso [prə'vaɪˌzo:] *n, pl* **-sos** *or* **-soes** : condición *f*, salvedad *f*, estipulación *f*

provocation [ˌprɑvə'keɪʃən] *n* : provocación *f*

provocative [prə'vɑkətɪv] *adj* : provocador, provocativo ⟨a provocative article : un artículo que hace pensar⟩

provoke [prə'vo:k] *vt* **-voked; -voking** : provocar

prow ['praʊ] *n* : proa *f*

prowess ['praʊəs] *n* 1 VALOR : valor *m*, valentía *f* 2 SKILL : habilidad *f*, destreza *f*

prowl ['praʊl] *vi* : merodear, rondar — *vt* : rondar por

prowler ['praʊlər] *n* : merodeador *m*, -dora *f*

proximity [prɑk'sɪməti] *n* : proximidad *f*

proxy ['prɑksi] *n, pl* **proxies** 1 : poder *m* (de actuar en nombre de alguien) ⟨by proxy : por poder⟩ 2 AGENT : apoderado *m*, -da *f*; representante *mf*

prude ['pru:d] *n* : mojigato *m*, -ta *f*; gazmoño *m*, -ña *f*

prudence ['pru:dənts] *n* 1 SHREWDNESS : prudencia *f*, sagacidad *f* 2 CAUTION : prudencia *f*, cautela *f* 3 THRIFTINESS : frugalidad *f*

prudent ['pru:dənt] *adj* 1 SHREWD : prudente, sagaz 2 CAUTIOUS, FARSIGHTED : prudente, previsor, precavido 3 THRIFTY : frugal, ahorrativo — **prudently** *adv*

prudery ['pru:dəri] *n, pl* **-eries** : mojigatería *f*, gazmoñería *f*

prudish ['pru:dɪʃ] *adj* : mojigato, gazmoño

prune¹ ['pru:n] *vt* **pruned; pruning** : podar (arbustos, etc.), acortar (un texto), recortar (gastos, etc.)

prune² *n* : ciruela *f* pasa

prurient ['prʊriənt] *adj* : lascivo

pry ['praɪ] *v* **pried; prying** *vi* : curiosear, huronear ⟨to pry into other people's business : meterse uno en lo que no le importa⟩ — *vt* **or to pry open** : abrir (con una palanca), apalancar

psalm ['sɑm, 'sɑlm] *n* : salmo *m*

pseudonym ['su:də,nɪm] *n* : seudónimo *m*

psoriasis [sə'raɪəsɪs] *n* : soriasis *f*, psoriasis *f*

psyche ['saɪki] *n* : psique *f*, psiquis *f*

psychedelic¹ [,saɪkə'dɛlɪk] *adj* : psicodélico

psychedelic² *n* : droga *f* psicodélica

psychiatric [,saɪki'ætrɪk] *adj* : psiquiátrico, siquiátrico

psychiatrist [sə'kaɪətrɪst, saɪ-] *n* : psiquiatra *mf*, siquiatra *mf*

psychiatry [sə'kaɪətri, saɪ-] *n* : psiquiatría *f*, siquiatría *f*

psychic¹ ['saɪkɪk] *adj* **1** : psíquico, síquico (en psicología) **2** CLAIRVOYANT : clarividente

psychic² *n* : vidente *mf*, clarividente *mf*

psychoanalysis [,saɪkoə'næləsɪs] *n, pl* **-yses** : psicoanálisis *m*, sicoanálisis *m*

psychoanalyst [,saɪko'ænəlɪst] *n* : psicoanalista *mf*, sicoanalista *mf*

psychoanalytic [,saɪko,ænəl'ɪtɪk] *adj* : psicoanalítico, sicoanalítico

psychoanalyze [,saɪko'ænəl,aɪz] *vt* **-lyzed; -lyzing** : psicoanalizar, sicoanalizar

psychological [,saɪkə'lɑdʒɪkəl] *adj* : psicológico, sicológico — **psychologically** *adv*

psychologist [saɪ'kɑlədʒɪst] *n* : psicólogo *m*, -ga *f*; sicólogo *m*, -ga *f*

psychology [saɪ'kɑlədʒi] *n, pl* **-gies** : psicología *f*, sicología *f*

psychopath ['saɪkə,pæθ] *n* : psicópata *mf*, sicópata *mf*

psychopathic [,saɪkə'pæθɪk] *adj* : psicopático, sicopático

psychosis [saɪ'ko:sɪs] *n, pl* **-choses** [-'ko:,si:z] : psicosis *f*, sicosis *f*

psychosomatic [,saɪkəsə'mætɪk] *adj* : psicosomático, sicosomático

psychotherapist [,saɪko'θɛrəpɪst] *n* : psicoterapeuta *mf*, sicoterapeuta *mf*

psychotherapy [,saɪko'θɛrəpi] *n, pl* **-pies** : psicoterapia *f*, sicoterapia *f*

psychotic¹ [saɪ'kɑtɪk] *adj* : psicótico, sicótico

psychotic² *n* : psicótico *m*, -ca *f*; sicótico *m*, -ca *f*

puberty ['pju:bərti] *n* : pubertad *f*

pubic ['pju:bɪk] *adj* : pubiano, púbico

public¹ ['pʌblɪk] *adj* : público — **publicly** *adv*

public² *n* : público *m*

publication [,pʌblə'keɪʃən] *n* : publicación *f*

publicist ['pʌbləsɪst] *n* : publicista *mf*

publicity [pə'blɪsəti] *n* : publicidad *f*

publicize ['pʌblə,saɪz] *vt* **-cized; -cizing** : publicitar

public school *n* : escuela *f* pública

publish ['pʌblɪʃ] *vt* : publicar

publisher ['pʌblɪʃər] *n* : casa *f* editorial (compañía); editor *m*, -tora *f* (persona)

publishing ['pʌblɪʃɪŋ] *n* : industria *f* editorial

pucker¹ ['pʌkər] *vt* : fruncir, arrugar — *vi* : arrugarse

pucker² *n* : arruga *f*, frunce *m*, fruncido *m*

pudding ['pʊdɪŋ] *n* : budín *m*, pudín *m*

puddle ['pʌdəl] *n* : charco *m*

pudgy ['pʌdʒi] *adj* **pudgier; -est** : regordete *fam*, rechoncho *fam*, gordinflón *fam*

puerile ['pjʊrəl] *adj* : pueril

Puerto Rican¹ [,pwɛrtə'ri:kən, ,porʧə-] *adj* : puertorriqueño

Puerto Rican² *n* : puertorriqueño *m*, -ña *f*

puff¹ ['pʌf] *vi* **1** BLOW : soplar **2** PANT : resoplar, jadear **3 to puff up** SWELL : hincharse — *vt* **1** BLOW : soplar ⟨to puff smoke : echar humo⟩ **2** INFLATE : inflar, hinchar ⟨to puff out one's cheeks : inflar las mejillas⟩

puff² *n* **1** GUST : soplo *m*, ráfaga *f*, bocanada *f* (de humo) **2** DRAW : chupada *f* (a un cigarrillo) **3** SWELLING : hinchazón *f* **4 cream puff** : pastelito *m* de crema **5 powder puff** : borla *f*

puffy ['pʌfi] *adj* **puffier; -est 1** SWOLLEN : hinchado, inflado **2** SPONGY : esponjoso, suave

pug ['pʌg] *n* **1** : doguillo *m* (perro) **2 or pug nose** : nariz *f* achatada

pugnacious [,pʌg'neɪʃəs] *adj* : pugnaz, agresivo

puke ['pju:k] *vi* **puked; puking** : vomitar, devolver

pull¹ ['pʊl, 'pʌl] *vt* **1** DRAW, TUG : tirar de, jalar **2** EXTRACT : sacar, extraer ⟨to pull teeth : sacar muelas⟩ ⟨to pull a gun on : amenazar a (alguien) con pistola⟩ **3** TEAR : desgarrarse (un músculo, etc.) **4 to pull down** : bajar, echar abajo, derribar (un edificio) **5 to pull in** ATTRACT : atraer (una muchedumbre, etc.) ⟨to pull in votes : conseguir votos⟩ **6 to pull off** REMOVE : sacar, quitar **7 to pull oneself together** : calmarse, tranquilizarse **8 to pull up** RAISE : levantar, subir — *vi* **1** DRAW, TUG : tirar, jalar **2** (*indicating movement in a specific direction*) ⟨they pulled in front of us : se nos metieron delante⟩ ⟨to pull to a stop : pararse⟩ **3 to pull through** RECOVER : recobrarse, reponerse **4 to pull together** COOPERATE : trabajar juntos, cooperar

pull² *n* **1** TUG : tirón *m*, jalón *m* ⟨he gave it a pull : le dio un tirón⟩ **2** ATTRACTION : atracción *f*, fuerza *f* ⟨the pull of gravity : la fuerza de la gravedad⟩ **3**

INFLUENCE : influencia *f* **4** HANDLE : tirador *m* (de un cajón, etc.) **5** bell **pull** : cuerda *f*

pullet ['pʊlət] *n* : polla *f*, gallina *f* (joven)

pulley ['pʊli] *n*, *pl* **-leys** : polea *f*

pullover ['pʊl.o:vər] *n* : suéter *m*

pulmonary ['pʊlmə.neri, 'pʌl-] *adj* : pulmonar

pulp ['pʌlp] *n* **1** : pulpa *f* (de una fruta, etc.) **2** MASH : papilla *f*, pasta *f* ⟨wood pulp : pasta de papel, pulpa de papel⟩ ⟨to beat to a pulp : hacer papilla (a alguien)⟩ **3** : pulpa *f* (de los dientes)

pulpit ['pʊl.pɪt] *n* : púlpito *m*

pulsate ['pʌl.seɪt] *vi* **-sated; -sating 1** BEAT : latir, palpitar **2** VIBRATE : vibrar

pulsation [.pʌl'seɪʃən] *n* : pulsación *f*

pulse ['pʌls] *n* : pulso *m*

pulverize ['pʌlvə.raɪz] *vt* **-ized; -izing** : pulverizar

puma ['pu:mə, 'pju:-] *n* : puma *m*; león *m*, leona *f* (in various countries)

pumice ['pʌməs] *n* : piedra *f* pómez

pummel ['pʌməl] *vt* **-meled; -meling** : aporrear, apalear

pump[1] ['pʌmp] *vt* **1** : bombear ⟨to pump water : bombear agua⟩ ⟨to pump (up) a tire : inflar una llanta⟩ **2** : mover (una manivela, un pedal, etc.) de arriba abajo ⟨to pump someone's hand : darle un fuerte apretón de manos (a alguien)⟩ **3** to pump out : sacar, vaciar (con una bomba)

pump[2] *n* **1** : bomba *f* ⟨water pump : bomba de agua⟩ **2** SHOE : zapato *m* de tacón

pumpernickel ['pʌmpər.nɪkəl] *n* : pan *m* negro de centeno

pumpkin ['pʌmpkɪn, 'pʌŋkən] *n* : calabaza *f*, zapallo *m* *Arg, Chile, Peru, Uru*

pun[1] ['pʌn] *vi* **punned; punning** : hacer juegos de palabras

pun[2] *n* : juego *m* de palabras, albur *m Mex*

punch[1] ['pʌntʃ] *vt* **1** HIT : darle un puñetazo (a alguien), golpear ⟨she punched him in the nose : le dio un puñetazo en la nariz⟩ **2** PERFORATE : perforar (papel, etc.), picar (un boleto)

punch[2] *n* **1** : perforadora *f* ⟨paper punch : perforadora de papel⟩ **2** BLOW : golpe *m*, puñetazo *m* **3** : ponche *m* ⟨fruit punch : ponche de frutas⟩

punctilious [pəŋk'tɪliəs] *adj* : puntilloso

punctual ['pʌŋktʃʊəl] *adj* : puntual

punctuality [.pʌŋktʃʊ'æləti] *n* : puntualidad *f*

punctually ['pʌŋktʃʊəli] *adv* : puntualmente, a tiempo

punctuate ['pʌŋktʃʊ.eɪt] *vt* **-ated; -ating** : puntuar

punctuation [.pʌŋktʃʊ'eɪʃən] *n* : puntuación *f*

puncture[1] ['pʌŋktʃər] *vt* **-tured; -turing** : pinchar, punzar, perforar, ponchar *Mex*

puncture[2] *n* : pinchazo *m*, ponchadura *f Mex*

pundit ['pʌndɪt] *n* : experto *m*, -ta *f*

pungency ['pʌndʒəntsi] *n* : acritud *f*, acrimonia *f*

pungent ['pʌndʒənt] *adj* : acre

punish ['pʌnɪʃ] *vt* : castigar

punishable ['pʌnɪʃəbəl] *adj* : punible

punishment ['pʌnɪʃmənt] *n* : castigo *m*

punitive ['pju:nətɪv] *adj* : punitivo

punt[1] ['pʌnt] *vt* : impulsar (un barco) con una pértiga — *vi* : despejar (en deportes)

punt[2] *n* **1** : batea *f* (barco) **2** : patada *f* de despeje (en deportes)

puny ['pju:ni] *adj* **-nier; -est** : enclenque, endeble

pup ['pʌp] *n* : cachorro *m*, -rra *f* (de un perro); cría *f* (de otros animales)

pupa ['pju:pə] *n*, *pl* **-pae** [-pi, -.paɪ] *or* **-pas** : crisálida *f*, pupa *f*

pupil ['pju:pəl] *n* **1** : alumno *m*, -na *f* (de colegio) **2** : pupila *f* (del ojo)

puppet ['pʌpət] *n* : títere *m*, marioneta *f*

puppy ['pʌpi] *n*, *pl* **-pies** : cachorro *m*, -rra *f*

purchase[1] ['pərtʃəs] *vt* **-chased; -chasing** : comprar

purchase[2] *n* **1** PURCHASING : compra *f*, adquisición *f* **2** : compra *f* ⟨last-minute purchases : compras de última hora⟩ **3** GRIP : agarre *m*, asidero *m* ⟨she got a firm purchase on the wheel : se agarró bien del volante⟩

purchase order *n* : orden *f* de compra

pure ['pjʊr] *adj* **purer; purest** : puro

puree[1] [pjʊ'reɪ, -'ri:] *vt* **-reed; -reeing** : hacer un puré con

puree[2] *n* : puré *m*

purely ['pjʊrli] *adv* **1** WHOLLY : puramente, completamente ⟨purely by chance : por pura casualidad⟩ **2** SIMPLY : sencillamente, meramente

purgative ['pərgətɪv] *n* : purgante *m*

purgatory ['pərgə.tori] *n*, *pl* **-ries** : purgatorio *m*

purge[1] ['pərdʒ] *vt* **purged; purging** : purgar

purge[2] *n* : purga *f*

purification [.pjʊrəfə'keɪʃən] *n* : purificación *f*

purify ['pjʊrə.faɪ] *vt* **-fied; -fying** : purificar

puritan ['pjʊrətən] *n* : puritano *m*, -na *f* — **puritan** *adj*

puritanical [.pjʊːrə'tænɪkəl] *adj* : puritano

purity ['pjʊrəti] *n* : pureza *f*

purl[1] ['pərl] *v* : tejer al revés, tejer del revés

purl[2] *n* : punto *m* del revés

purloin [pər'lɔɪn, 'pər.lɔɪn] *vt* : hurtar, robar

purple ['pərpəl] *n* : morado *m*, color *m* púrpura

purport [pər'port] *vt* : pretender ⟨to purport to be : pretender ser⟩

purpose ['pərpəs] *n* **1** INTENTION : propósito *m*, intención *f* ⟨on purpose

: a propósito, adrede⟩ **2** FUNCTION : función *f* **3** RESOLUTION : resolución *f*, determinación *f*

purposeful ['pərpəsfəl] *adj* : determinado, decidido, resuelto

purposefully ['pərpəsfəli] *adv* : decididamente, resueltamente

purposely ['pərpəsli] *adv* : intencionadamente, a propósito, adrede

purr¹ ['pər] *vi* : ronronear

purr² *n* : ronroneo *m*

purse¹ ['pərs] *vt* **pursed; pursing** : fruncir ⟨to purse one's lips : fruncir la boca⟩

purse² *n* **1** HANDBAG : cartera *f*, bolso *m*, bolsa *f Mex* ⟨a change purse : un monedero⟩ **2** FUNDS : fondos *mpl* **3** PRIZE : premio *m*

pursue [pər'su:] *vt* **-sued; -suing 1** CHASE : perseguir **2** SEEK : buscar, tratar de encontrar ⟨to pursue pleasure : buscar el placer⟩ **3** FOLLOW : seguir ⟨the road pursues a northerly course : el camino sigue hacia el norte⟩ **4** : dedicarse a ⟨to pursue a hobby : dedicarse a un pasatiempo⟩

pursuer [pər'su:ər] *n* : perseguidor *m*, -dora *f*

pursuit [pər'su:t] *n* **1** CHASE : persecución *f* **2** SEARCH : búsqueda *f*, busca *f* **3** ACTIVITY : actividad *f*, pasatiempo *m*

purveyor [pər'veɪər] *n* : proveedor *m*, -dora *f*

pus ['pʌs] *n* : pus *m*

push¹ ['pʊʃ] *vt* **1** SHOVE : empujar **2** PRESS : apretar, pulsar ⟨push that button : aprieta ese botón⟩ **3** PRESSURE, URGE : presionar **4 to push around** BULLY : intimidar, mangonear — *vi* **1** SHOVE : empujar **2** INSIST : insistir, presionar **3 to push off** LEAVE : marcharse, irse, largarse *fam* **4 to push on** PROCEED : seguir

push² *n* **1** SHOVE : empujón *m* **2** DRIVE : empuje *m*, energía *f*, dinamismo *m* **3** EFFORT : esfuerzo *m*

push–button ['pʊʃ'bʌtən] *adj* : de botones

pushcart ['pʊʃ,kɑrt] *n* : carretilla *f* de mano

pushy ['pʊʃi] *adj* **pushier; -est** : mandón, prepotente

pussy ['pʊsi] *n, pl* **pussies** : gatito *m*, -ta *f*; minino *m*, -na *f*

pussy willow *n* : sauce *m* blanco

pustule ['pʌs,tʃu:l] *n* : pústula *f*

put ['pʊt] *v* **put; putting** *vt* **1** PLACE : poner, colocar ⟨put it on the table : ponlo en la mesa⟩ **2** INSERT : meter **3** (*indicating causation of a state or feeling*) : poner ⟨it put her in a good mood : la puso de buen humor⟩ ⟨to put into effect : poner en práctica⟩ **4** IMPOSE : imponer ⟨they put a tax on it : lo gravaron con un impuesto⟩ **5** SUBJECT : someter, poner ⟨to put to the test : poner a prueba⟩ ⟨to put to death : ejecutar⟩ **6** EXPRESS : expresar, decir ⟨he put it

simply : lo dijo sencillamente⟩ **7** APPLY : aplicar ⟨to put one's mind to something : proponerse hacer algo⟩ **8** SET : poner ⟨I put him to work : lo puse a trabajar⟩ **9** ATTACH : dar ⟨to put a high value on : dar gran valor a⟩ **10** PRESENT : presentar, exponer ⟨to put a question to someone : hacer una pregunta a alguien⟩ — *vi* **1 to put to sea** : hacerse a la mar **2 to put up with** : aguantar, soportar

put away *vt* **1** KEEP : guardar **2** *or to* **put aside** : dejar a un lado

put by *vt* SAVE : ahorrar

put down *vt* **1** SUPPRESS : aplastar, suprimir **2** ATTRIBUTE : atribuir ⟨she put it down to luck : lo atribuyó a la suerte⟩

put in *vi* : presentarse ⟨I've put in for the position : me presenté para el puesto⟩ — *vt* DEVOTE : dedicar (unas horas, etc.)

put off *vt* DEFER : aplazar, posponer

put on *vt* **1** ASSUME : afectar, adoptar **2** PRODUCE : presentar (una obra de teatro, etc.) **3** WEAR : ponerse

put out *vt* INCONVENIENCE : importunar, incomodar

putrefy ['pju:trə,faɪ] *v* **-fied; -fying** *vt* : pudrir — *vi* : pudrirse

putrid ['pju:trɪd] *adj* : putrefacto, pútrido

putter ['pʌtər] *vi or* **to putter around** : entretenerse

putty¹ ['pʌti] *vt* **-tied; -tying** : poner masilla en

putty² *n, pl* **-ties** : masilla *f*

put up *vt* **1** LODGE : alojar **2** CONTRIBUTE : contribuir, pagar

puzzle¹ ['pʌzəl] *vt* **-zled; -zling 1** CONFUSE : confundir, dejar perplejo **2 to puzzle out** : dar vueltas a, tratar de resolver

puzzle² *n* **1** : rompecabezas *m* ⟨a crossword puzzle : un crucigrama⟩ **2** MYSTERY : misterio *m*, enigma *m*

puzzlement ['pʌzəlmənt] *n* : desconcierto *m*, perplejidad *f*

pygmy¹ ['pɪgmi] *adj* : enano, pigmeo

pygmy² *n, pl* **-mies 1** DWARF : enano *m*, -na *f* **2 Pygmy** : pigmeo *m*, -mea *f*

pylon ['paɪ,lɑn, -lɑn] *n* **1** : torre *f* de conducta eléctrica **2** : pilón *m* (de un puente)

pyramid ['pɪrə,mɪd] *n* : pirámide *f*

pyre ['paɪr] *n* : pira *f*

pyromania [,paɪro'meɪniə] *n* : piromanía *f*

pyromaniac [,paɪro'meɪni,æk] *n* : pirómano *m*, -na *f*

pyrotechnics [,paɪrə'tɛknɪks] *npl* **1** FIREWORKS : fuegos *mpl* artificiales **2** DISPLAY, SHOW : espectáculo *m*, muestra *f* de virtuosismo ⟨computer pyrotechnics : efectos especiales hechos por computadora⟩

python ['paɪ,θɑn, -θən] *n* : pitón *f*, serpiente *f* pitón

Q

q ['kju:] *n, pl* **q's** *or* **qs** ['kju:z] : decimoséptima letra del alfabeto inglés

quack¹ ['kwæk] *vi* : graznar

quack² *n* **1** : graznido *m* (de pato) **2** CHARLATAN : curandero *m*, -ra *f*; matasanos *m fam*

quadrangle ['kwɑ,dræŋgəl] *n* **1** COURTYARD : patio *m* interior **2** → **quadrilateral**

quadrant ['kwɑdrənt] *n* : cuadrante *m*

quadrilateral [,kwɑdrə'lætərəl] *n* : cuadrilátero *m*

quadruped ['kwɑdrə,pɛd] *n* : cuadrúpedo *m*

quadruple [kwɑ'dru:pəl, -'drʌ-; 'kwɑdrə-] *v* **-pled; -pling** *vt* : cuadruplicar — *vi* : cuadruplicarse

quadruplet [kwɑ'dru:plət, -'drʌ-; 'kwɑdrə-] *n* : cuatrillizo *m*, -za *f*

quagmire ['kwæg,maɪr, 'kwɑg-] *n* **1** : lodazal *m*, barrizal *m* **2** PREDICAMENT : atolladero *m*

quail¹ ['kweɪl] *vi* : encogerse, acobardarse

quail² *n, pl* **quail** *or* **quails** : codorniz *f*

quaint ['kweɪnt] *adj* **1** ODD : extraño, curioso **2** PICTURESQUE : pintoresco — **quaintly** *adv*

quaintness ['kweɪntnəs] *n* : rareza *f*, lo curioso

quake¹ ['kweɪk] *vi* **quaked; quaking** : temblar

quake² *n* : temblor *m*, terremoto *m*

qualification [,kwɑləfə'keɪʃən] *n* **1** LIMITATION, RESERVATION : reserva *f*, limitación *f* ⟨without qualification : sin reservas⟩ **2** REQUIREMENT : requisito *m* **3** **qualifications** *npl* ABILITY : aptitud *f*, capacidad *f*

qualified ['kwɑlə,faɪd] *adj* : competente, capacitado

qualifier ['kwɑlə,faɪər] *n* **1** : clasificado *m*, -da *f* (en deportes) **2** : calificativo *m* (en gramática)

qualify ['kwɑlə,faɪ] *v* **-fied; -fying** *vt* **1** : matizar ⟨to qualify a statement : matizar una declaración⟩ **2** MODIFY : calificar (en gramática) **3** : habilitar ⟨the certificate qualified her to teach : el certificado la habilitó para enseñar⟩ — *vi* **1** : obtener el título, recibirse ⟨to qualify as an engineer : recibirse de ingeniero⟩ **2** : clasificarse (en deportes)

quality ['kwɑləti] *n, pl* **-ties 1** NATURE : carácter *m* **2** ATTRIBUTE : cualidad *f* **3** GRADE : calidad *f* ⟨of good quality : de buena calidad⟩

qualm ['kwɑm, 'kwɑlm, 'kwɔm] *n* **1** MISGIVING : duda *f*, aprensión *f* **2** RESERVATION, SCRUPLE : escrúpulo *m*, reparo *m*

quandary ['kwɑndri] *n, pl* **-ries** : dilema *m*

quantitative ['kwɑntə,teɪtɪv] *adj* : cuantitativo

quantity ['kwɑntəti] *n, pl* **-ties** : cantidad *f*

quantum¹ ['kwɑntəm] *n* : cuanto *m* (en física)

quantum² *adj* : cuántico

quantum theory ['kwɑntəm] *n* : teoría *f* cuántica

quarantine¹ ['kwɔrən,ti:n] *vt* **-tined; -tining** : poner en cuarentena

quarantine² *n* : cuarentena *f*

quarrel¹ ['kwɔrəl] *vi* **-reled** *or* **-relled; -reling** *or* **-relling** : pelearse, reñir, discutir

quarrel² *n* : pelea *f*, riña *f*, disputa *f*

quarrelsome ['kwɔrəlsəm] *adj* : pendenciero, discutidor

quarry¹ ['kwɔri] *vt* **quarried; quarrying 1** EXTRACT : extraer, sacar ⟨to quarry marble : extraer mármol⟩ **2** EXCAVATE : excavar ⟨to quarry a hill : excavar un cerro⟩

quarry² *n, pl* **quarries 1** PREY : presa *f* **2** *or* **stone quarry** : cantera *f*

quart ['kwɔrt] *n* : cuarto *m* de galón

quarter¹ ['kwɔrtər] *vt* **1** : dividir en cuatro partes **2** LODGE : alojar, acuartelar (tropas)

quarter² *n* **1** : cuarto *m*, cuarta parte *f* ⟨a foot and a quarter : un pie y cuarto⟩ ⟨a quarter after three : las tres y cuarto⟩ **2** : moneda *f* de 25 centavos, cuarto *m* de dólar **3** DISTRICT : barrio *m* ⟨business quarter : barrio comercial⟩ **4** PLACE : parte *f* ⟨from all quarters : de todas partes⟩ ⟨at close quarters : de muy cerca⟩ **5** MERCY : clemencia *f*, cuartel *m* ⟨to give no quarter : no dar cuartel⟩ **6 quarters** *npl* LODGING : alojamiento *m*, cuartel *m* (militar)

quarterback ['kwɔrtər,bæk] *n* : mariscal *m* de campo

quarterly¹ ['kwɔrtərli] *adv* : cada tres meses, trimestralmente

quarterly² *adj* : trimestral

quarterly³ *n, pl* **-lies** : publicación *f* trimestral

quartermaster ['kwɔrtər,mæstər] *n* : intendente *mf*

quartet [kwɔr'tɛt] *n* : cuarteto *m*

quartz ['kwɔrts] *n* : cuarzo *m*

quash ['kwɑʃ, 'kwɔʃ] *vt* **1** ANNUL : anular **2** QUELL : sofocar, aplastar

quaver¹ ['kweɪvər] *vi* **1** SHAKE : temblar ⟨her voice was quavering : le temblaba la voz⟩ **2** TRILL : trinar

quaver² *n* : temblor *m* (de la voz)

quay ['ki:, 'keɪ, 'kweɪ] *n* : muelle *m*

queasiness ['kwi:zinəs] *n* : mareo *m*, náusea *f*

queasy ['kwi:zi] *adj* **-sier; -est** : mareado

queen ['kwi:n] *n* : reina *f*

queenly ['kwi:nli] *adj* **-lier; -est** : de reina, regio

queer ['kwɪr] *adj* : extraño, raro, curioso — **queerly** *adv*

quell ['kwɛl] *vt* : aplastar, sofocar

quench ['kwɛntʃ] *vt* **1** EXTINGUISH : apagar, sofocar **2** SATISFY : saciar, satisfacer (la sed)

querulous ['kwɛrələs, 'kwɛrjələs, 'kwɪr-] *adj* : quejumbroso, quejoso — **querulously** *adv*

query¹ ['kwɪri, 'kwɛr-] *vt* **-ried; -rying 1** ASK : preguntar, interrogar ⟨we queried the professor : preguntamos al profesor⟩ **2** QUESTION : cuestionar, poner en duda ⟨to query a matter : cuestionar un asunto⟩

query² *n, pl* **-ries 1** QUESTION : pregunta *f* **2** DOUBT : duda *f*

quest¹ ['kwɛst] *v* : buscar

quest² *n* : búsqueda *f*

question¹ ['kwɛstʃən] *vt* **1** ASK : preguntar **2** DOUBT : poner en duda, cuestionar **3** INTERROGATE : interrogar — *vi* INQUIRE : inquirir, preguntar

question² *n* **1** QUERY : pregunta *f* **2** ISSUE : asunto *m*, problema *f*, cuestión *f* **3** POSSIBILITY : posibilidad *f* ⟨it's out of the question : es indiscutible⟩ **4** DOUBT : duda *f* ⟨to call into question : poner en duda⟩

questionable ['kwɛstʃənəbəl] *adj* : dudoso, discutible, cuestionable ⟨questionable results : resultados discutibles⟩ ⟨questionable motives : motivos sospechosos⟩

questioner ['kwɛstʃənər] *n* : interrogador *m*, -dora *f*

question mark *n* : signo *m* de interrogación

questionnaire [ˌkwɛstʃə'nær] *n* : cuestionario *m*

queue¹ ['kju:] *vi* **queued; queuing** *or* **queueing** : hacer cola

queue² *n* **1** PIGTAIL : coleta *f*, trenza *f* **2** LINE : cola *f*, fila *f*

quibble¹ ['kwɪbəl] *vi* **-bled; -bling** : quejarse por nimiedades, andar con sutilezas

quibble² *n* : objeción *f* de poca monta, queja *f* insignificante

quick¹ ['kwɪk] *adv* : rápidamente

quick² *adj* **1** RAPID : rápido **2** ALERT, CLEVER : listo, vivo, agudo **3 a quick temper** : un genio vivo

quick³ *n* **1** FLESH : carne *f* viva **2 to cut someone to the quick** : herir a alguien en lo más vivo

quicken ['kwɪkən] *vt* **1** REVIVE : resucitar **2** AROUSE : estimular, despertar **3** HASTEN : acelerar ⟨she quickened her pace : aceleró el paso⟩

quickly ['kwɪkli] *adv* : rápidamente, rápido, de prisa

quickness ['kwɪknəs] *n* : rapidez *f*

quicksand ['kwɪkˌsænd] *n* : arena *f* movediza

quicksilver ['kwɪkˌsɪlvər] *n* : mercurio *m*, azogue *m*

quick–tempered ['kwɪk'tɛmpərd] *adj* : irascible, de genio vivo

quick–witted ['kwɪk'wɪtəd] *adj* : agudo

quiet¹ ['kwaɪət] *vt* **1** SILENCE : hacer callar, acallar **2** CALM : calmar, tranquilizar — *vi* **to quiet down** : calmarse, tranquilizarse

quiet² *adv* : silenciosamente ⟨a quiet-running engine : un motor silencioso⟩

quiet³ *adj* **1** CALM : tranquilo, calmoso **2** MILD : sosegado, suave ⟨a quiet disposition : un temperamento sosegado⟩ **3** SILENT : silencioso **4** UNOBTRUSIVE : discreto **5** SECLUDED : aislado ⟨a quiet nook : un rincón aislado⟩ — **quietly** *adv*

quiet⁴ *n* **1** CALM : calma *f*, tranquilidad *f* **2** SILENCE : silencio *m*

quietness ['kwaɪətnəs] *n* : suavidad *f*, tranquilidad *f*, quietud *f*

quietude ['kwaɪəˌtu:d, -ˌtju:d] *n* : quietud *f*, reposo *m*

quill ['kwɪl] *n* **1** SPINE : púa *f* (de un puerco espín) **2** : pluma *f* (para escribir)

quilt¹ ['kwɪlt] *vt* : acolchar

quilt² *n* : colcha *f*, edredón *m*

quince ['kwɪnts] *n* : membrillo *m*

quinine ['kwaɪˌnaɪn] *n* : quinina *f*

quintessence [kwɪn'tɛsənts] *n* : quintaesencia *f*

quintet [kwɪn'tɛt] *n* : quinteto *m*

quintuple [kwɪn'tu:pəl, -'tju:-, -'tʌ-; 'kwɪntə-] *adj* : quíntuplo

quintuplet [kwɪn'tʌplət, -'tu:-, -'tju:-; 'kwɪntə-] *n* : quintillizo *m*, -za *f*

quip¹ ['kwɪp] *vi* **quipped; quipping** : bromear

quip² *n* : ocurrencia *f*, salida *f*

quirk ['kwərk] *n* : peculiaridad *f*, rareza *f* ⟨a quirk of fate : un capricho del destino⟩

quirky ['kwərki] *adj* **-kier; -est** : peculiar, raro

quit ['kwɪt] *v* **quit; quitting** *vt* : dejar, abandonar ⟨to quit smoking : dejar de fumar⟩ — *vi* **1** STOP : parar **2** RESIGN : dimitir, renunciar

quite ['kwaɪt] *adv* **1** COMPLETELY : completamente, totalmente **2** RATHER : bastante ⟨quite near : bastante cerca⟩

quits ['kwɪts] *adj* **to call it quits** : quedar en paz

quitter ['kwɪtər] *n* : derrotista *mf*

quiver¹ ['kwɪvər] *vi* : temblar, estremecerse, vibrar

quiver² *n* **1** : carcaj *m*, aljaba *f* (para flechas) **2** TREMBLING : temblor *m*, estremecimiento *m*

quixotic [kwɪk'sɑtɪk] *adj* : quijotesco

quiz¹ ['kwɪz] *vt* **quizzed; quizzing** : interrogar, hacer una prueba a (en el colegio)

quiz² *n, pl* **quizzes** : examen *m* corto, prueba *f*

quizzical ['kwɪzɪkəl] *adj* **1** TEASING : burlón **2** CURIOUS : curioso, interrogativo

quorum ['kworəm] *n* : quórum *m*

quota ['kwo:t̬ə] *n* : cuota *f*, cupo *m*
quotable ['kwo:t̬əbəl] *adj* : citable
quotation [kwo'teɪʃən] *n* **1** CITATION
: cita *f* **2** ESTIMATE : presupuesto *m*,
estimación *f* **3** PRICE : cotización *f*
quotation marks *npl* : comillas *fpl*

quote[1] ['kwo:t] *vt* **quoted; quoting 1**
CITE : citar **2** VALUE : cotizar (en finanzas)
quote[2] *n* **1** → **quotation 2 quotes** *npl*
→ **quotation marks**
quotient ['kwo:ʃənt] *n* : cociente *m*

R

r ['ɑr] *n, pl* **r's** *or* **rs** ['ɑrz] : decimoctava
letra del alfabeto inglés
rabbi ['ræˌbaɪ] *n* : rabino *m*, -na *f*
rabbit ['ræbət] *n, pl* **-bit** *or* **-bits** : conejo *m*, -ja *f*
rabble ['ræbəl] *n* **1** MASSES : populacho
m **2** RIFFRAFF : chusma *f*, gentuza *f*
rabid ['ræbɪd] *adj* **1** : rabioso, afectado
con la rabia **2** FURIOUS : furioso **3**
FANATIC : fanático
rabies ['reɪbi:z] *ns & pl* : rabia *f*
raccoon [ræ'ku:n] *n, pl* **-coon** *or* **-coons**
: mapache *m*
race[1] ['reɪs] *vi* **raced; racing 1** : correr,
competir (en una carrera) **2** RUSH : ir
a toda prisa, ir corriendo
race[2] *n* **1** CURRENT : corriente *f* (de
agua) **2** : carrera *f* ⟨dog race : carrera
de perros⟩ ⟨the presidential race : la
carrera presidential⟩ **3** : raza *f* ⟨the
black race : la raza negra⟩ ⟨the human
race : el género humano⟩
racecourse ['reɪsˌkors] *n* : pista *f* (de carreras)
racehorse ['reɪsˌhors] *n* : caballo *m* de
carreras
racer ['reɪsər] *n* : corredor *m*, -dora *f*
racetrack ['reɪsˌtræk] *n* : pista *f* (de carreras)
racial ['reɪʃəl] *adj* : racial — **racially** *adv*
racism ['reɪˌsɪzəm] *n* : racismo *m*
racist ['reɪsɪst] *n* : racista *mf*
rack[1] ['ræk] *vt* **1** : atormentar ⟨racked
with pain : atormentado por el dolor⟩
2 to rack one's brains : devanarse los
sesos
rack[2] *n* **1** SHELF, STAND : estante *m* ⟨a
luggage rack : un portaequipajes⟩ ⟨a
coatrack : un perchero, una percha⟩ **2**
: potro *m* (instrumento de tortura)
racket ['rækət] *n* **1** : raqueta *f* (en deportes) **2** DIN : estruendo *m*, bulla *f*,
jaleo *m fam* **3** SWINDLE : estafa *f*, timo
m fam
racketeer [ˌrækə'tɪr] *n* : estafador *m*,
-dora *f*
raconteur [ˌræˌkɑn'tər] *n* : anecdotista
mf
racy ['reɪsi] *adj* **racier; -est** : subido de
tono, picante
radar ['reɪˌdɑr] *n* : radar *m*
radial ['reɪdiəl] *adj* : radial
radiance ['reɪdiənts] *n* : resplandor *m*
radiant ['reɪdiənt] *adj* : radiante — **radiantly** *adv*
radiate ['reɪdiˌeɪt] *v* **-ated; -ating** *vt* : irradiar, emitir ⟨to radiate heat : irradi-

ar el calor⟩ ⟨to radiate happiness : rebosar de alegría⟩ — *vi* **1** : irradiar **2**
SPREAD : salir, extenderse ⟨to radiate
(out) from the center : salir del centro⟩
radiation [ˌreɪdi'eɪʃən] *n* : radiación *f*
radiator ['reɪdiˌeɪt̬ər] *n* : radiador *m*
radical[1] ['rædɪkəl] *adj* : radical — **radically** [-kli] *adv*
radical[2] *n* : radical *mf*
radicalism ['rædɪkəˌlɪzəm] *n* : radicalismo *m*
radii → **radius**
radio[1] ['reɪdiˌo:] *v* : llamar por radio,
transmitir por radio
radio[2] *n, pl* **-dios** : radio *m* (aparato), radio *f* (emisora, radiodifusión)
radioactive ['reɪdio'æktɪv] *adj* : radiactivo, radioactivo
radioactivity [ˌreɪdioˌæk'tɪvət̬i] *n, pl*
-ties : radiactividad *f*, radioactividad *f*
radiologist [ˌreɪdi'ɑləʤɪst] *n* : radiólogo
m, -ga *f*
radiology [ˌreɪdi'ɑləʤi] *n* : radiología *f*
radish ['rædɪʃ] *n* : rábano *m*
radium ['reɪdiəm] *n* : radio *m*
radius ['reɪdiəs] *n, pl* **radii** [-diˌaɪ] : radio
m
radon ['reɪˌdɑn] *n* : radón *m*
raffle[1] ['ræfəl] *vt* **-fled; -fling** : rifar,
sortear
raffle[2] *n* : rifa *f*, sorteo *m*
raft ['ræft] *n* **1** : balsa *f* ⟨rubber rafts
: balsas de goma⟩ **2** LOT, SLEW : montón *m* ⟨a raft of documents : un montón de documentos⟩
rafter ['ræftər] *n* : par *m*, viga *f*
rag ['ræg] *n* **1** CLOTH : trapo *m* **2 rags**
npl TATTERS : harapos *mpl*, andrajos
mpl
ragamuffin ['rægəˌmʌfən] *n* : pilluelo *m*,
-la *f*
rage[1] ['reɪʤ] *vi* **raged; raging 1** : estar
furioso, rabiar ⟨to fly into a rage : enfurecerse⟩ **2** : bramar, hacer estragos
⟨the wind was raging : el viento bramaba⟩ ⟨flu raged through the school : la
gripe hizo estragos por el colegio⟩
rage[2] *n* **1** ANGER : furia *f*, ira *f*, cólera *f*
2 FAD : moda *f*, furor *m*
ragged ['rægəd] *adj* **1** UNEVEN : irregular, desigual **2** TORN : hecho jirones
3 TATTERED : andrajoso, harapiento
ragout [ræ'gu:] *n* : ragú *m*, estofado *m*
ragtime ['rægˌtaɪm] *n* : ragtime *m*
ragweed ['rægˌwi:d] *n* : ambrosía *f*
raid[1] ['reɪd] *vt* **1** : invadir, hacer una incursión en ⟨raided by enemy troops

: invadido por tropas enemigas⟩ **2**
: asaltar, atracar ⟨the gang raided the
warehouse : la pandilla asaltó el al-
macén⟩ **3** : allanar, hacer una redada
en ⟨police raided the house : la policía
allanó la vivienda⟩

raid² n **1** : invasión f (militar) **2** : asalto
m (por delincuentes) **3** : redada f, allanamiento m (por la policía)

raider ['reɪdər] n **1** ATTACKER : asaltante
mf; invasor m, -sora f **2 corporate
raider** : tiburón m

rail¹ ['reɪl] vi **1 to rail against** REVILE
: denostar contra **2 to rail at** SCOLD
: regañar, reprender

rail² n **1** BAR : barra f, barrera f **2**
HANDRAIL : pasamanos m, barandilla
f **3** TRACK : riel m (para ferrocarriles)
4 RAILROAD : ferrocarril m

railing ['reɪlɪŋ] n **1** : baranda f (de un
balcón, etc.) **2** RAILS : verja f

raillery ['reɪləri] n, pl **-leries** : bromas f pl

railroad ['reɪl,ro:d] n : ferrocarril m

railway ['reɪl,weɪ] → **railroad**

raiment ['reɪmənt] n : vestiduras f pl

rain¹ ['reɪn] vi **1** : llover ⟨it's raining : está
lloviendo⟩ **2 to rain down** SHOWER
: llover ⟨insults rained down on him : le
llovieron los insultos⟩

rain² n : lluvia f

rainbow ['reɪn,bo:] n : arco m iris

raincoat ['reɪn,ko:t] n : impermeable m

raindrop ['reɪn,drɑp] n : gota f de lluvia

rainfall ['reɪn,fɔl] n : lluvia f, precipitación f

rainstorm ['reɪn,stɔrm] n : temporal m
(de lluvia)

rainwater ['reɪn,wɔtər] n : agua f de lluvia

rainy ['reɪni] adj **rainier; -est** : lluvioso

raise¹ ['reɪz] vt **raised; raising 1** LIFT
: levantar, subir, alzar ⟨to raise one's
spirits : levantarle el ánimo a alguien⟩
2 ERECT : levantar, erigir **3** COLLECT
: recaudar ⟨to raise money : recaudar
dinero⟩ **4** REAR : criar ⟨to raise one's
children : criar uno a sus niños⟩ **5**
GROW : cultivar **6** INCREASE : aumentar, subir **7** PROMOTE : ascender **8**
PROVOKE : provocar ⟨it raised a laugh
: provocó una risa⟩ **9** BRING UP : sacar
(temas, objeciones, etc.)

raise² n : aumento m

raisin ['reɪzən] n : pasa f

raja or **rajah** ['rɑdʒə, -,dʒɑ, -,ʒɑ] n : rajá
m

rake¹ ['reɪk] v **raked; raking** vt **1** : rastrillar ⟨to rake leaves : rastrillar las ho-
jas⟩ **2** SWEEP : barrer ⟨raked with gunfire : barrido con metralla⟩ — vi **to rake
through** : revolver, hurgar en

rake² n **1** : rastrillo m **2** LIBERTINE : libertino m, -na f; calavera m

rakish ['reɪkɪʃ] adj **1** JAUNTY : desenvuelto, desenfadado **2** DISSOLUTE
: libertino, disoluto

rally¹ ['ræli] v **-lied; -lying** vi **1** MEET,
UNITE : reunirse, congregarse **2** RE-

COVER : recuperarse — vt **1** ASSEMBLE
: reunir (tropas, etc.) **2** RECOVER : recobrar (la fuerza, el ánimo, etc.)

rally² n, pl **-lies** : reunión f, mitin m, manifestación f

ram¹ ['ræm] v **rammed; ramming** vt **1**
DRIVE : hincar, clavar ⟨he rammed it
into the ground : lo hincó en la tierra⟩
2 SMASH : estrellar, embestir — vi COL-
LIDE : chocar (contra), estrellarse

ram² n **1** : carnero m (animal) **2 battering ram** : ariete m

RAM ['ræm] n : RAM f

ramble¹ ['ræmbəl] vi **-bled; -bling 1**
WANDER : pasear, deambular **2 to ram-
ble on** : divagar, perder el hilo **3**
SPREAD : trepar (dícese de una planta)

ramble² n : paseo m, excursión f

rambler ['ræmblər] n **1** WALKER : excursionista mf **2** ROSE : rosa f trepadora

rambunctious [ræm'bʌŋkʃəs] adj UN-
RULY : alborotado

ramification [,ræməfə'keɪʃən] n : ramificación f

ramify ['ræmə,faɪ] vi **-fied; -fying** : ramificarse

ramp ['ræmp] n : rampa f

rampage¹ ['ræm,peɪdʒ, ræm'peɪdʒ] vi
-paged; -paging : andar arrasando
todo, correr destrozando

rampage² ['ræm,peɪdʒ] n : alboroto m,
frenesí m (de violencia)

rampant ['ræmpənt] adj : desenfrenado

rampart ['ræm,pɑrt] n : terraplén m, muralla f

ramrod ['ræm,rɑd] n : baqueta f

ramshackle ['ræm,ʃækəl] adj : destartalado

ran → **run**

ranch ['ræntʃ] n **1** : hacienda f, rancho
m, finca f ganadera **2** FARM : granja f
⟨fruit ranch : granja de frutas⟩

rancher ['ræntʃər] n : estanciero m, -ra
f; ranchero m, -ra f

rancid ['rænt̬səd] adj : rancio

rancor ['ræŋkər] n : rencor m

random ['rændəm] adj **1** : fortuito,
aleatorio **2 at ~** : al azar — **randomly** adv

rang → **ring**

range¹ ['reɪndʒ] v **ranged; ranging** vt
ARRANGE : alinear, ordenar, arreglar
— vi **1** ROAM : deambular ⟨to range
through the town : deambular por el
pueblo⟩ **2** EXTEND : extenderse ⟨the
results range widely : los resultados se
extienden mucho⟩ **3** VARY : variar
⟨discounts range from 20% to 40% : los
descuentos varían entre 20% y 40%⟩

range² n **1** ROW : fila f, hilera f ⟨a mountain range : una cordillera⟩ **2** GRASS-
LAND : pradera f, pampa f **3** STOVE
: cocina f **4** VARIETY : variedad f, gama
f **5** SPHERE : ámbito m, esfera f, campo m **6** REACH : registro m (de la voz),
alcance m (de un arma de fuego) **7
shooting range** : campo m de tiro

ranger ['reɪndʒər] *n or* **forest ranger**
: guardabosque *mf*
rangy ['reɪndʒi] *adj* **rangier; -est** : alto y
delgado
rank¹ ['ræŋk] *vt* **1** RANGE : alinear, ordenar, poner en fila **2** CLASSIFY : clasificar — *vi* **1 to rank above** : ser superior a **2 to rank among** : encontrarse
entre, figurar entre
rank² *adj* **1** LUXURIANT : lozano, exuberante (dícese de una planta) **2**
SMELLY : fétido, maloliente **3** OUT-
RIGHT : completo, absoluto ⟨a rank injustice : una injusticia manifiesta⟩
rank³ *n* **1** LINE, ROW : fila *f* ⟨to close
ranks : cerrar filas⟩ **2** GRADE, POSI-
TION : grado *m*, rango *m* (militar) ⟨to
pull rank : abusar de su autoridad⟩ **3**
CLASS : categoría *f*, clase *f* **4 ranks** *npl*
: soldados *mpl* rasos
rank and file *n* **1** RANKS : soldados *mpl*
rasos **2** : bases *fpl* (de un partido, etc.)
rankle ['ræŋkəl] *v* **-kled; -kling** *vi* : doler — *vt* : irritar, herir
ransack ['ræn,sæk] *vt* : revolver, desvalijar, registrar de arriba abajo
ransom¹ ['ræntsəm] *vt* : rescatar, pagar
un rescate por
ransom² *n* : rescate *m*
rant ['rænt] *vi or* **to rant and rave**
: despotricar, desvariar
rap¹ ['ræp] *v* **rapped; rapping** *vt* **1**
KNOCK : golpetear, dar un golpe en **2**
CRITICIZE : criticar — *vi* **1** CHAT : charlar, cotorrear *fam* **2** KNOCK : dar un
golpe
rap² *n* **1** BLOW, KNOCK : golpe *m*,
golpecito *m* **2** CHAT : charla *f* **3** *or* **rap**
music : rap *m* **4 to take the rap** : pagar el pato *fam*
rapacious [rə'peɪʃəs] *adj* **1** GREEDY
: avaricioso, codicioso **2** PREDATORY
: rapaz, de rapiña **3** RAVENOUS : voraz
rape¹ ['reɪp] *vt* **raped; raping** : violar
rape² *n* **1** : colza *f* (planta) **2** : violación
f (de una persona)
rapid ['ræpɪd] *adj* : rápido — **rapidly** *adv*
rapidity [rə'pɪdəti] *n* : rapidez *f*
rapids ['ræpɪdz] *npl* : rápidos *mpl*
rapier ['reɪpiər] *n* : estoque *m*
rapist ['reɪpɪst] *n* : violador *m*, -dora *f*
rapper ['ræpər] *n* : cantante *mf* de rap;
rapero *m*, -ra *f*
rapport [ræ'por] *n* : relación *f* armo-
niosa, entendimiento *m*
rapt ['ræpt] *adj* : absorto, embelesado
rapture ['ræptʃər] *n* : éxtasis *m*
rapturous ['ræptʃərəs] *adj* : extasiado,
embelesado
rare ['rær] *adj* **rarer; rarest 1** RAREFIED
: enrarecido **2** FINE : excelente, excepcional ⟨a rare talent : un talento ex-
cepcional⟩ **3** UNCOMMON : raro, poco
común **4** : poco cocido (dícese de la
carne)
rarefy ['rærə,faɪ] *vt* **-fied; -fying** : rari-
ficar, enrarecer

rarely ['rærli] *adv* SELDOM : pocas veces,
rara vez
raring ['ræran, -ɪŋ] *adj* : lleno de entusiasmo, con muchas ganas
rarity ['rærəti] *n*, *pl* **-ties** : rareza *f*
rascal ['ræskəl] *n* : pillo *m*, -lla *f*; pícaro
m, -ra *f*
rash¹ ['ræʃ] *adj* : imprudente, precipitado — **rashly** *adv*
rash² *n* : sarpullido *m*, erupción *f*
rashness ['ræʃnəs] *n* : precipitación *f*,
impetuosidad *f*
rasp¹ ['ræsp] *vt* **1** SCRAPE : raspar, es-
cofinar **2 to rasp out** : decir en voz
áspera
rasp² *n* : escofina *f*
raspberry ['ræz,bɛri] *n*, *pl* **-ries** : frambuesa *f*
rat ['ræt] *n* : rata *f*
ratchet ['rætʃət] *n* : trinquete *m*
rate¹ ['reɪt] *vt* **rated; rating 1** CONSID-
ER, REGARD : considerar, estimar **2**
DESERVE : merecer
rate² *n* **1** PACE, SPEED : velocidad *f*, ritmo *m* ⟨at this rate : a este paso⟩ **2**
: índice *m*, tasa *f* ⟨birth rate : índice de
natalidad⟩ ⟨interest rate : tasa de in-
terés⟩ **3** CHARGE, PRICE : precio *m*,
tarifa *f*
rather ['ræðər, 'rʌ-, 'rɑ-] *adv* **1** (*indicating preference*) ⟨she would rather stay
in the house : preferiría quedarse en
casa⟩ ⟨I'd rather not : mejor que no⟩
2 (*indicating preciseness*) ⟨my father, or
rather my stepfather : mi padre, o
mejor dicho mi padrastro⟩ **3** INSTEAD
: sino que, más que, al contrario ⟨I'm
not pleased; rather I'm disappointed
: no estoy satisfecho, sino desilusiona-
do⟩ **4** SOMEWHAT : algo, un tanto
⟨rather strange : un poco extraño⟩ **5**
QUITE : bastante ⟨rather difficult : bastante difícil⟩
ratification [,rætəfə'keɪʃən] *n* : ratificación *f*
ratify ['rætə,faɪ] *vt* **-fied; -fying** : ratificar
rating ['reɪtɪŋ] *n* **1** STANDING : clasificación *f*, posición *f* **2 ratings** *npl*
: índice *m* de audiencia
ratio ['reɪʃio] *n*, *pl* **-tios** : proporción *f*,
relación *f*
ration¹ ['ræʃən, 'reɪʃən] *vt* : racionar
ration² *n* **1** : ración *f* **2 rations** *npl* PRO-
VISIONS : víveres *mpl*
rational ['ræʃənəl] *adj* : racional, razonable, lógico — **rationally** *adv*
rationale [,ræʃə'næl] *n* **1** EXPLANATION
: explicación *f* **2** BASIS : base *f*, razones
fpl
rationality [,ræʃə'næləti] *n*, *pl* **-ties**
: racionalidad *f*
rationalization [,ræʃənələ'zeɪʃən] *n*
: racionalización *f*
rationalize ['ræʃənə,laɪz] *vt* **-ized; -izing**
: racionalizar
rattle¹ ['rætəl] *v* **-tled; -tling** *vi* **1** CLAT-
TER : traquetear, hacer ruido **2 to rat-
tle on** CHATTER : parlotear *fam* — *vt*

1 : hacer sonar, agitar ⟨the wind rattled the door : el viento sacudió la puerta⟩ **2** DISCONCERT, WORRY : desconcertar, poner nervioso **3 to rattle off** : despachar, recitar, decir de corrido

rattle² *n* **1** CLATTER : traqueteo *m*, ruido *m* **2** *or* **baby's rattle** : sonajero *m* **3** : cascabel *m* (de una culebra)

rattler ['ræṭələr] → **rattlesnake**

rattlesnake ['ræṭəl,sneɪk] *n* : serpiente *f* de cascabel

ratty ['ræṭi] *adj* **rattier; -est** : raído, andrajoso

raucous ['rɔkəs] *adj* **1** HOARSE : ronco **2** BOISTEROUS : escandaloso, bullicioso — **raucously** *adv*

ravage¹ ['rævɪdʒ] *vt* **-aged; -aging** : devastar, arrasar, hacer estragos

ravage² *n* : destrozo *m*, destrucción *f* ⟨the ravages of war : los estragos de la guerra⟩

rave ['reɪv] *vi* **raved; raving 1** : delirar, desvariar ⟨to rave like a maniac : desvariar como un loco⟩ **2 to rave about** : hablar con entusiasmo sobre, entusiasmarse por

ravel ['rævəl] *v* **-eled** *or* **-elled; -eling** *or* **-elling** *vt* UNRAVEL : desenredar, desenmarañar — *vi* FRAY : deshilacharse

raven ['reɪvən] *n* : cuervo *m*

ravenous ['rævənəs] *adj* : hambriento, voraz — **ravenously** *adv*

ravine [rə'viːn] *n* : barranco *m*, quebrada *f*

ravish ['rævɪʃ] *vt* **1** PLUNDER : saquear **2** ENCHANT : embelesar, cautivar, encantar

raw ['rɔ] *adj* **rawer; rawest 1** UNCOOKED : crudo **2** UNTREATED : sin tratar, sin refinar, puro ⟨raw data : datos en bruto⟩ ⟨raw materials : materias primas⟩ **3** INEXPERIENCED : novato, inexperto **4** OPEN : abierto, en carne viva ⟨a raw sore : una llaga abierta⟩ **5** : frío y húmedo ⟨a raw day : un día crudo⟩ **6** UNFAIR : injusto ⟨a raw deal : un trato injusto, una injusticia⟩

rawhide ['rɔ,haɪd] *n* : cuero *m* sin curtir

ray ['reɪ] *n* **1** : rayo *m* (de la luz, etc.) ⟨a ray of hope : un resquicio de esperanza⟩ **2** : raya *f* (pez)

rayon ['reɪ,ɑn] *n* : rayón *m*

raze ['reɪz] *vt* **razed; razing** : arrasar, demoler

razor ['reɪzər] *n* **1** *or* **straight razor** : navaja *f* (de afeitar) **2** *or* **safety razor** : maquinilla *f* de afeitar, rastrillo *m Mex* **3** SHAVER : afeitadora *f*, rasuradora *f*

reach¹ ['riːtʃ] *vt* **1** EXTEND : extender, alargar ⟨to reach out one's hand : extender la mano⟩ **2** : alcanzar ⟨I couldn't reach the apple : no pude alcanzar la manzana⟩ **3** : llegar a, llegar hasta ⟨the shadow reached the wall : la sombra llegó hasta la pared⟩ **4** CONTACT : contactar, ponerse en contacto con — *vi* **1** *or* **to reach out** : extender la mano **2** STRETCH : extenderse **3 to**

reach for : tratar de agarrar

reach² *n* : alcance *m*, extensión *f*

react [ri'ækt] *vi* : reaccionar

reaction [ri'ækʃən] *n* : reacción *f*

reactionary¹ [ri'ækʃə,nɛri] *adj* : reaccionario

reactionary² *n, pl* **-ries** : reaccionario *m*, -ria *f*

reactor [ri'æktər] *n* : reactor *m* ⟨nuclear reactor : reactor nuclear⟩

read¹ ['riːd] *v* **read** ['rɛd]; **reading** *vt* **1** : leer ⟨to read a story : leer un cuento⟩ **2** INTERPRET : interpretar ⟨it can be read two ways : se puede interpretar de dos maneras⟩ **3** : decir, poner ⟨the sign read "No smoking" : el letrero decía "No Fumar"⟩ **4** : marcar ⟨the thermometer reads 70° : el termómetro marca 70°⟩ — *vi* **1** : leer ⟨he can read : sabe leer⟩ **2** SAY : decir ⟨the list reads as follows : la lista dice lo siguiente⟩

read² *n* **to be a good read** : ser una lectura amena

readable ['riːdəbəl] *adj* : legible — **readably** [-bli] *adv*

reader ['riːdər] *n* : lector *m*, -tora *f*

readily ['rɛdəli] *adv* **1** WILLINGLY : de buena gana, con gusto **2** EASILY : fácilmente, con facilidad

readiness ['rɛdinəs] *n* **1** WILLINGNESS : buena disposición *f* **2 to be in readiness** : estar preparado

reading ['riːdɪŋ] *n* : lectura *f*

readjust [,riːə'dʒʌst] *vt* : reajustar — *vi* : volverse a adaptar

readjustment [,riːə'dʒʌstmənt] *n* : reajuste *m*

ready¹ ['rɛdi] *vt* **readied; readying** : preparar

ready² *adj* **readier; -est 1** PREPARED : listo, preparado **2** WILLING : dispuesto **3** : a punto de ⟨ready to cry : a punto de llorar⟩ **4** AVAILABLE : disponible ⟨ready cash : efectivo⟩ **5** QUICK : vivo, agudo ⟨a ready wit : un ingenio agudo⟩

ready–made ['rɛdi'meɪd] *adj* : preparado, confeccionado

reaffirm [,riːə'fərm] *vt* : reafirmar

real¹ ['riːl] *adv* VERY : muy ⟨we had a real good time : lo pasamos muy bien⟩

real² *adj* **1** : inmobiliario ⟨real property : bien inmueble, bien raíz⟩ **2** GENUINE : auténtico, genuino **3** ACTUAL, TRUE : real, verdadero ⟨a real friend : un verdadero amigo⟩ **4 for real** SERIOUSLY : de veras, de verdad

real estate *n* : propiedad *f* inmobiliaria, bienes *mpl* raíces

realign [,riːə'laɪn] *vt* : realinear

realignment [,riːə'laɪnmənt] *n* : realineamiento *m*

realism ['riːə,lɪzəm] *n* : realismo *m*

realist ['riːəlɪst] *n* : realista *mf*

realistic [,riːə'lɪstɪk] *adj* : realista

realistically [,riːə'lɪstɪkli] *adv* : de manera realista

reality [ri'æləti] *n, pl* **-ties** : realidad *f*
realizable [ˌri:ə'laɪzəbəl] *adj* : realizable, alcanzable
realization [ˌri:ələ'zeɪʃən] *n* : realización *f*
realize ['ri:ə,laɪz] *vt* **-ized; -izing 1** AC-COMPLISH : realizar, llevar a cabo **2** GAIN : obtener, realizar, sacar ⟨to realize a profit : realizar beneficios⟩ **3** UNDERSTAND : darse cuenta de, saber
really ['rɪli, 'ri:-] *adv* **1** ACTUALLY : de verdad, en realidad **2** TRULY : verdaderamente, realmente **3** FRANKLY : francamente, en serio
realm ['rɛlm] *n* **1** KINGDOM : reino *m* **2** SPHERE : esfera *f*, campo *m*
ream¹ ['ri:m] *vt* : escariar
ream² *n* **1** : resma *f* (de papel) **2 reams** *npl* LOADS : montones *mpl*
reap ['ri:p] *v* : cosechar
reaper ['ri:pər] *n* **1** : cosechador *m*, -dora *f* (persona) **2** : cosechadora *f* (máquina)
reappear [ˌri:ə'pɪr] *vi* : reaparecer
reappearance [ˌri:ə'pɪrənts] *n* : reaparición *f*
rear¹ ['rɪr] *vt* **1** LIFT, RAISE : levantar **2** BREED, BRING UP : criar — *vi or* **to rear up** : encabritarse
rear² *adj* : trasero, posterior, de atrás
rear³ *n* **1** BACK : parte *f* de atrás ⟨to bring up the rear : cerrar la marcha⟩ **2 or rear end** : trasero *m*
rear admiral *n* : contraalmirante *mf*
rearrange [ˌri:ə'reɪndʒ] *vt* **-ranged; -ranging** : colocar de otra manera, volver a arreglar, reorganizar
rearview mirror ['rɪr,vju:-] *n* : retrovisor *m*
reason¹ ['ri:zən] *vt* THINK : pensar — *vi* : razonar ⟨I can't reason with her : no puedo razonar con ella⟩
reason² *n* **1** CAUSE, GROUND : razón *f*, motivo *m* ⟨the reason for his trip : el motivo de su viaje⟩ ⟨for this reason : por esta razón, por lo cual⟩ ⟨the reason why : la razón por la cual, el porqué⟩ **2** SENSE : razón *f* ⟨to lose one's reason : perder los sesos⟩ ⟨to listen to reason : avenirse a razones⟩
reasonable ['ri:zənəbəl] *adj* **1** SENSIBLE : razonable **2** INEXPENSIVE : barato, económico
reasonably ['ri:zənəbli] *adv* **1** SENSIBLY : razonablemente **2** FAIRLY : bastante
reasoning ['ri:zənɪŋ] *n* : razonamiento *m*, raciocinio *m*, argumentos *mpl*
reassess [ˌri:ə'sɛs] *vt* : revaluar, reconsiderar
reassurance [ˌri:ə'ʃurənts] *n* : consuelo *m*, palabras *fpl* alentadoras
reassure [ˌri:ə'ʃur] *vt* **-sured; -suring** : tranquilizar
reassuring [ˌri:ə'ʃurɪŋ] *adj* : tranquilizador
reawaken [ˌri:ə'weɪkən] *vt* : volver a despertar, reavivar
rebate ['ri:,beɪt] *n* : reembolso *m*, devolución *f*

rebel¹ [rɪ'bɛl] *vi* **-belled; -belling** : rebelarse, sublevarse
rebel² ['rɛbəl] *adj* : rebelde
rebel³ ['rɛbəl] *n* : rebelde *mf*
rebellion [rɪ'bɛljən] *n* : rebelión *f*
rebellious [rɪ'bɛljəs] *adj* : rebelde
rebelliousness [rɪ'bɛljəsnəs] *n* : rebeldía *f*
rebirth [ˌri:'bərθ] *n* : renacimiento *m*
reboot [ri:'bu:t] *vt* : reiniciar (una computadora)
reborn [ri:'bɔrn] *adj* **to be reborn** : renacer
rebound¹ ['ri:,baund, ˌri:'baund] *vi* : rebotar
rebound² ['ri:,baund] *n* : rebote *m*
rebuff¹ [rɪ'bʌf] *vt* : desairar, rechazar
rebuff² *n* : desaire *m*, rechazo *m*
rebuild [ˌri:'bɪld] *vt* **-built [-'bɪlt]; -building** : reconstruir
rebuke¹ [rɪ'bju:k] *vt* **-buked; -buking** : reprender, regañar
rebuke² *n* : reprimenda *f*, reproche *m*
rebut [rɪ'bʌt] *vt* **-butted; -butting** : rebatir, refutar
rebuttal [rɪ'bʌtəl] *n* : refutación *f*
recalcitrant [rɪ'kælsətrənt] *adj* : recalcitrante
recall¹ [rɪ'kɔl] *vt* **1** : llamar, retirar ⟨recalled to active duty : llamado al servicio activo⟩ **2** REMEMBER : recordar, acordarse de **3** REVOKE : revocar
recall² [rɪ'kɔl, 'ri:ˌkɔl] *n* **1** : retirada *f* (de personas o mercancías) **2** MEMORY : memoria *f* ⟨to have total recall : poder recordar todo⟩
recant [rɪ'kænt] *vt* : retractarse de — *vi* : retractarse, renegar
recapitulate [ˌri:kə'pɪtʃəˌleɪt] *v* **-lated; -lating** : resumir, recapitular
recapture [ˌri:'kæptʃər] *vt* **-tured; -turing 1** REGAIN : volver a tomar, reconquistar **2** RELIVE : revivir (la juventud, etc.)
recast [ri:'kæst] *vt* **-cast; -casting 1** : refundir (metales) **2** REWRITE : refundir, modificar
recede [rɪ'si:d] *vi* **-ceded; -ceding 1** WITHDRAW : retirarse, retroceder **2** FADE : desvanecerse, alejarse **3** SLANT : inclinarse **4 to have a receding hairline** : tener entradas
receipt [rɪ'si:t] *n* **1** : recibo *m* **2 receipts** *npl* : ingresos *mpl*, entradas *fpl*
receivable [rɪ'si:vəbəl] *adj* **accounts receivable** : cuentas por cobrar
receive [rɪ'si:v] *vt* **-ceived; -ceiving 1** GET : recibir ⟨to receive a letter : recibir una carta⟩ ⟨to receive a blow : recibir un golpe⟩ **2** WELCOME : acoger, recibir ⟨to receive guests : tener invitados⟩ **3** : recibir, captar (señales de radio)
receiver [rɪ'si:vər] *n* **1** : receptor *m*, -tora *f* (en futbol americano) **2** : receptor *m* (de radio o televisión) **3 telephone receiver** : auricular *m*
recent ['ri:sənt] *adj* : reciente — **recently** *adv*

receptacle [rɪ'sɛptɪkəl] *n* : receptáculo *m*, recipiente *m*

reception [rɪ'sɛpʃən] *n* : recepción *f*

receptionist [rɪ'sɛpʃənɪst] *n* : recepcionista *mf*

receptive [rɪ'sɛptɪv] *adj* : receptivo

receptivity [ˌriːˌsɛp'tɪvəti] *n* : receptividad *f*

recess¹ ['riːˌsɛs, rɪ'sɛs] *vt* **1** : poner en un hueco ⟨recessed lighting : iluminación empotrada⟩ **2** ADJOURN : suspender, levantar

recess² *n* **1** ALCOVE : hueco *m*, nicho *m* **2** BREAK : receso *m*, descanso *m*, recreo *m* (en el colegio)

recession [rɪ'sɛʃən] *n* : recesión *f*, depresión *f* económica

recessive [rɪ'sɛsɪv] *adj* : recesivo

recharge [ˌriː'tʃardʒ] *vt* **-charged; -charging** : recargar

rechargeable [ˌriː'tʃardʒəbəl] *adj* : recargable

recipe ['rɛsəˌpiː] *n* : receta *f*

recipient [rɪ'sɪpiənt] *n* : recipiente *mf*

reciprocal [rɪ'sɪprəkəl] *adj* : recíproco

reciprocate [rɪ'sɪprəˌkeɪt] *vi* **-cated; -cating** : reciprocar

reciprocity [ˌrɛsə'prasəti] *n, pl* **-ties** : reciprocidad *f*

recital [rɪ'saɪtəl] *n* **1** PERFORMANCE : recital *m* **2** ENUMERATION : relato *m*, enumeración *f*

recitation [ˌrɛsə'teɪʃən] *n* : recitación *f*

recite [rɪ'saɪt] *vt* **-cited; -citing 1** : recitar (un poema, etc.) **2** RECOUNT : narrar, relatar, enumerar

reckless ['rɛkləs] *adj* : imprudente, temerario — **recklessly** *adv*

recklessness ['rɛkləsnəs] *n* : imprudencia *f*, temeridad *f*

reckon ['rɛkən] *vt* **1** CALCULATE : calcular, contar **2** CONSIDER : considerar

reckoning ['rɛkənɪŋ] *n* **1** CALCULATION : cálculo *m* **2** SETTLEMENT : ajuste *m* de cuentas ⟨day of reckoning : día del juicio final⟩

reclaim [rɪ'kleɪm] *vt* **1** : ganar, sanear ⟨to reclaim marshy land : sanear las tierras pantanosas⟩ **2** RECOVER : recobrar, reciclar ⟨to reclaim old tires : reciclar llantas desechadas⟩ **3** REGAIN : reclamar, recuperar ⟨to reclaim one's rights : reclamar uno sus derechos⟩

recline [rɪ'klaɪn] *vi* **-clined; -clining 1** LEAN : reclinarse **2** REPOSE : recostarse

recluse ['rɛˌkluːs, rɪ'kluːs] *n* : solitario *m*, -ria *f*

recognition [ˌrɛkɪg'nɪʃən] *n* : reconocimiento *m*

recognizable ['rɛkəgˌnaɪzəbəl] *adj* : reconocible

recognize ['rɛkɪgˌnaɪz] *vt* **-nized; -nizing** : reconocer

recoil¹ [rɪ'kɔɪl] *vi* : retroceder, dar un culatazo

recoil² ['riːˌkɔɪl, rɪ'-] *n* : retroceso *m*, culatazo *m*

recollect [ˌrɛkə'lɛkt] *v* : recordar

recollection [ˌrɛkə'lɛkʃən] *n* : recuerdo *m*

recommend [ˌrɛkə'mɛnd] *vt* **1** : recomendar ⟨she recommended the medicine : recomendó la medicina⟩ **2** ADVISE, COUNSEL : aconsejar, recomendar

recommendation [ˌrɛkəmən'deɪʃən] *n* : recomendación *f*

recompense¹ ['rɛkəmˌpɛnts] *vt* **-pensed; -pensing** : indemnizar, recompensar

recompense² *n* : indemnización *f*, compensación *f*

reconcile ['rɛkənˌsaɪl] *v* **-ciled; -ciling** *vt* **1** : reconciliar (personas), conciliar (ideas, etc.) **2 to reconcile oneself to** : resignarse a — *vi* MAKE UP : reconciliarse, hacer las paces

reconciliation [ˌrɛkənˌsɪli'eɪʃən] *n* : reconciliación *f* (con personas), conciliación *f* (con ideas, etc.)

recondite ['rɛkənˌdaɪt, rɪ'kan-] *adj* : recóndito, abstruso

recondition [ˌriːkən'dɪʃən] *vt* : reacondicionar

reconnaissance [rɪ'kanəzənts, -sənts] *n* : reconocimiento *m*

reconnoiter *or* **reconnoitre** [ˌriːkə'nɔɪtər, ˌrɛkə-] *v* **-tered** *or* **-tred; -tering** *or* **-tring** *vt* : reconocer — *vi* : hacer un reconocimiento

reconsider [ˌriːkən'sɪdər] *vt* : reconsiderar, repensar

reconsideration [ˌriːkənˌsɪdə'reɪʃən] *n* : reconsideración *f*

reconstruct [ˌriːkən'strʌkt] *vt* : reconstruir

reconstruction [ˌriːkən'strʌkʃən] *n* : reconstrucción *f*

record¹ [rɪ'kɔrd] *vt* **1** WRITE DOWN : anotar, apuntar **2** REGISTER : registrar, hacer constar **3** INDICATE : marcar (una temperatura, etc.) **4** TAPE : grabar

record² ['rɛkərd] *n* **1** DOCUMENT : registro *m*, documento *m* oficial **2** HISTORY : historial *m* ⟨a good academic record : un buen historial académico⟩ ⟨criminal record : antecedentes penales⟩ **3** : récord *m* ⟨the world record : el récord mundial⟩ **4** : disco *m* (de música, etc.) ⟨to make a record : grabar un disco⟩

recorder [rɪ'kɔrdər] *n* **1** : flauta *f* dulce (instrumento de viento) **2** tape **recorder** : grabadora *f*

recording [rɪ'kɔrdɪŋ] *n* : grabación *f*

recount¹ [rɪ'kaʊnt] *vt* **1** NARRATE : narrar, relatar **2** : volver a contar (votos, etc.)

recount² ['riːˌkaʊnt, ˌriː'-] *n* : recuento *m*

recoup [rɪ'kuːp] *vt* : recuperar, recobrar

recourse ['riːˌkors, rɪ'-] *n* : recurso *m* ⟨to have recourse to : recurrir a⟩

recover [rɪ'kʌvər] *vt* REGAIN : recobrar — *vi* RECUPERATE : recuperarse

recovery [rɪˈkʌvəri] *n, pl* **-eries** : recuperación *f*

re–create [ˌriːkriˈeɪt] *vt* **-ated; -ating** : recrear

recreation [ˌrɛkriˈeɪʃən] *n* : recreo *m*, esparcimiento *m*, diversión *f*

recreational [ˌrɛkriˈeɪʃənəl] *adj* : recreativo, de recreo

recrimination [rɪˌkrɪməˈneɪʃən] *n* : recriminación *f*

recruit[1] [rɪˈkruːt] *vt* : reclutar

recruit[2] *n* : recluta *mf*

recruitment [rɪˈkruːtmənt] *n* : reclutamiento *m*, alistamiento *m*

rectal [ˈrɛktəl] *adj* : rectal

rectangle [ˈrɛkˌtæŋɡəl] *n* : rectángulo *m*

rectangular [rɛkˈtæŋɡjələr] *adj* : rectangular

rectify [ˈrɛktəˌfaɪ] *vt* **-fied; -fying** : rectificar

rectitude [ˈrɪktəˌtuːd, -ˌtjuːd] *n* : rectitud *f*

rector [ˈrɛktər] *n* : rector *m*, -tora *f*

rectory [ˈrɛktəri] *n, pl* **-ries** : rectoría *f*

rectum [ˈrɛktəm] *n, pl* **-tums** *or* **-ta** [-tə] : recto *m*

recuperate [rɪˈkuːpəˌreɪt, -ˈkjuː-] *v* **-ated; -ating** *vt* : recuperar — *vi* : recuperarse, restablecerse

recuperation [rɪˌkuːpəˈreɪʃən, -ˌkjuː-] : recuperación *f*

recur [rɪˈkər] *vi* **-curred; -curring** : volver a ocurrir, volver a producirse, repetirse

recurrence [rɪˈkərənts] *n* : repetición *f*, reaparición *f*

recurrent [rɪˈkərənt] *adj* : recurrente, que se repite

recyclable [riˈsaɪkələbəl] *adj* : reciclable

recycle [riˈsaɪkəl] *vt* **-cled; -cling** : reciclar

recycling [riˈsaɪkəlɪŋ] *n* : reciclaje *m*

red[1] [ˈrɛd] *adj* **1** : rojo, colorado ⟨to be red in the face : ponerse colorado⟩ ⟨to have red hair : ser pelirrojo⟩ **2** COMMUNIST : rojo, comunista

red[2] *n* **1** : rojo *m*, colorado *m* **2 Red** COMMUNIST : comunista *mf*

red blood cell *n* : glóbulo *m* rojo

red–blooded [ˈrɛdˈblʌdəd] *adj* : vigoroso

redcap [ˈrɛdˌkæp] → **porter**

redden [ˈrɛdən] *vt* : enrojecer — *vi* BLUSH : enrojecerse, ruborizarse

reddish [ˈrɛdɪʃ] *adj* : rojizo

redecorate [ˌriːˈdɛkəˌreɪt] *vt* **-rated; -rating** : renovar, pintar de nuevo

redeem [rɪˈdiːm] *vt* **1** RESCUE, SAVE : rescatar, salvar **2** : desempeñar ⟨she redeemed it from the pawnshop : lo desempeñó de la casa de empeños⟩ **3** : redimir (en religión) **4** : canjear, vender ⟨to redeem coupons : canjear cupones⟩

redeemer [rɪˈdiːmər] *n* : redentor *m*, -tora *f*

redefine [ˌriːdɪˈfaɪn] *vt* : redefinir

redemption [rɪˈdɛmpʃən] *n* : redención *f*

redesign [ˌriːdiˈzaɪn] *vt* : rediseñar

red–handed [ˈrɛdˈhændəd] *adj* : con las manos en la masa

redhead [ˈrɛdˌhɛd] *n* : pelirrojo *m*, -ja *f*

red–hot [ˈrɛdˈhɑt] *adj* **1** : al rojo vivo, candente **2** CURRENT : de candente actualidad **3** POPULAR : de gran popularidad

rediscover [ˌriːdiˈskʌvər] *vt* : redescubrir

redistribute [ˌriːdiˈstrɪˌbjuːt] *vt* **-uted; -uting** : redistribuir

red–letter [ˈrɛdˈlɛtər] *adj* **red–letter day** : día *m* memorable

redness [ˈrɛdnəs] *n* : rojez *f*

redo [ˌriːˈduː] *vt* **-did** [-dɪd]; **-done** [-ˈdʌn]; **-doing 1** : hacer de nuevo **2** → **redecorate**

redolence [ˈrɛdələnts] *n* : fragancia *f*

redolent [ˈrɛdələnt] *adj* **1** FRAGRANT : fragante, oloroso **2** SUGGESTIVE : evocador

redouble [riˈdʌbəl] *vt* **-bled; -bling** : redoblar, intensificar (esfuerzos, etc.)

redoubtable [rˈdaʊtəbəl] *adj* : temible

redress [rɪˈdrɛs] *vt* : reparar, remediar, enmendar

red snapper *n* : pargo *m*, huachinango *m Mex*

red tape *n* : papeleo *m*

reduce [rɪˈduːs, -ˈdjuːs] *v* **-duced; -ducing** *vt* **1** LESSEN : reducir, disminuir, rebajar (precios) **2** DEMOTE : bajar de categoría, degradar **3 to be reduced to** : verse rebajado a, verse forzado a **4 to reduce someone to tears** : hacer llorar a alguien — *vi* SLIM : adelgazar

reduction [rɪˈdʌkʃən] *n* : reducción *f*, rebaja *f*

redundancy [rɪˈdʌndəntsi] *n, pl* **-cies 1** : superfluidad *f* **2** REPETITION : redundancia *f*

redundant [rɪˈdʌndənt] *adj* : superfluo, redundante

redwood [ˈrɛdˌwʊd] *n* : secoya *f*

reed [ˈriːd] *n* **1** : caña *f*, carrizo *m*, junco *m* **2** : lengüeta *f* (para instrumentos de viento)

reef [ˈriːf] *n* : arrecife *m*, escollo *m*

reek[1] [ˈriːk] *vi* : apestar

reek[2] *n* : hedor *m*

reel[1] [ˈriːl] *vt* **1 to reel in** : enrollar, sacar (un pez) del agua **2 to reel off** : recitar de un tirón — *vi* **1** SPIN, WHIRL : girar, dar vueltas **2** STAGGER : tambalearse

reel[2] *n* **1** : carrete *m* (de pescar etc.), rollo *m* (de fotos) **2** : baile *m* escocés **3** STAGGER : tambaleo *m*

reelect [ˌriːɪˈlɛkt] *vt* : reelegir

reenact [ˌriːɪˈnækt] *vt* : representar de nuevo, reconstruir

reenter [ˌriːˈɛntər] *vt* : volver a entrar

reestablish [ˌriːɪˈstæblɪʃ] *vt* : restablecer

reevaluate [ˌriːɪˈvæljuˌeɪt] *vt* **-ated; -ating** : revaluar

reevaluation [ˌriːɪˌvæljuˈeɪʃən] *n* : revaluación *f*

reexamine [ˌriːɪgˈzæmən, -g-] *vt* **-ined; -ining** : volver a examinar, reexaminar
refer [rɪˈfər] *v* **-ferred; -ferring** *vt* DIRECT, SEND : remitir, enviar ⟨to refer a patient to a specialist : enviar a un paciente a un especialista⟩ — *vi* **to refer to** MENTION : referirse a, aludir a
referee[1] [ˌrɛfəˈriː] *v* **-eed; -eeing** : arbitrar
referee[2] *n* : árbitro *m*, -tra *f*; réferi *mf*
reference [ˈrɛfrənts, ˈrɛfə-] *n* **1** ALLUSION : referencia *f*, alusión *f* ⟨to make reference to : hacer referencia a⟩ **2** CONSULTATION : consulta *f* ⟨for future reference : para futuras consultas⟩ **3** *or* **reference book** : libro *m* de consulta **4** TESTIMONIAL : informe *m*, referencia *f*, recomendación *f*
referendum [ˌrɛfəˈrɛndəm] *n, pl* **-da** [-də] *or* **-dums** : referéndum *m*
refill[1] [ˌriːˈfɪl] *vt* : rellenar
refill[2] [ˈriːˌfɪl] *n* : recambio *m*
refinance [ˌriːˈfaɪˌnænts] *vt* **-nanced; -nancing** : refinanciar
refine [rɪˈfaɪn] *vt* **-fined; -fining 1** : refinar (azúcar, petróleo, etc.) **2** PERFECT : perfeccionar, pulir
refined [rɪˈfaɪnd] *adj* **1** : refinado (dícese del azúcar, etc.) **2** CULTURED : culto, educado, refinado
refinement [rɪˈfaɪnmənt] *n* : refinamiento *m*, fineza *f*, finura *f*
refinery [rɪˈfaɪnəri] *n, pl* **-eries** : refinería *f*
reflect [rɪˈflɛkt] *vt* **1** : reflejar ⟨to reflect light : reflejar la luz⟩ ⟨happiness is reflected in her face : la felicidad se refleja en su cara⟩ **2 to reflect that** : pensar que, considerar que — *vi* **1 to reflect on** : reflexionar sobre **2 to reflect badly on** : desacreditar, perjudicar
reflection [rɪˈflɛkʃən] *n* **1** : reflexión *f*, reflejo *m* (de la luz, de imágenes, etc.) **2** THOUGHT : reflexión *f*, meditación *f*
reflective [rɪˈflɛktɪv] *adj* **1** THOUGHTFUL : reflexivo, pensativo **2** : reflectante (en física)
reflector [rɪˈflɛktər] *n* : reflector *m*
reflex [ˈriːˌflɛks] *n* : reflejo *m*
reflexive [rɪˈflɛksɪv] *adj* : reflexivo ⟨a reflexive verb : un verbo reflexivo⟩
reform[1] [rɪˈfɔrm] *vt* : reformar — *vi* : reformarse
reform[2] *n* : reforma *f*
reformation [ˌrɛfərˈmeɪʃən] *n* : reforma *f* ⟨the Reformation : la Reforma⟩
reformatory [rɪˈfɔrməˌtori] *n, pl* **-ries** : reformatorio *m*
reformer [rɪˈfɔrmər] *n* : reformador *m*, -dora *f*
refract [rɪˈfrækt] *vt* : refractar — *vi* : refractarse
refraction [rɪˈfrækʃən] *n* : refracción *f*
refractory [rɪˈfræktəri] *adj* OBSTINATE : refractario, obstinado
refrain[1] [rɪˈfreɪn] *vi* **to refrain from** : abstenerse de

refrain[2] *n* : estribillo *m* (en música)
refresh [rɪˈfrɛʃ] *vt* : refrescar ⟨to refresh one's memory : refrescarle la memoria a uno⟩
refreshing [rɪˈfrɛʃɪŋ] *adj* : refrescante ⟨a refreshing sleep : un sueño reparador⟩
refreshment [rɪˈfrɛʃmənt] *n* **1** : refresco *m* **2 refreshments** *npl* : refrigerio *m*
refrigerate [rɪˈfrɪdʒəˌreɪt] *vt* **-ated; -ating** : refrigerar
refrigeration [rɪˌfrɪdʒəˈreɪʃən] *n* : refrigeración *f*
refrigerator [rɪˈfrɪdʒəˌreɪtər] *n* : refrigerador *m*, -dora *f*, nevera *f*
refuel [ˈriːˈfjuːəl] *v* **-eled** *or* **-elled; -eling** *or* **-elling** *vi* : repostar — *vt* : llenar de combustible
refuge [ˈrɛˌfjuːdʒ] *n* : refugio *m*
refugee [ˌrɛfjʊˈdʒiː] *n* : refugiado *m*, -da *f*
refund[1] [rɪˈfʌnd, ˈriːˌfʌnd] *vt* : reembolsar, devolver
refund[2] [ˈriːˌfʌnd] *n* : reembolso *m*, devolución *f*
refundable [rɪˈfʌndəbəl] *adj* : reembolsable
refurbish [rɪˈfərbɪʃ] *vt* : renovar, restaurar
refusal [rɪˈfjuːzəl] *n* : negativa *f*, rechazo *m*, denegación *f* (de una petición)
refuse[1] [rɪˈfjuːz] *vt* **-fused; -fusing 1** REJECT : rechazar, rehusar **2** DENY : negar, rehusar, denegar ⟨to refuse permission : negar el permiso⟩ **3 to refuse to** : negarse a
refuse[2] [ˈrɛˌfjuːs, -ˌfjuːz] *n* : basura *f*, desechos *mpl*, desperdicios *mpl*
refutation [ˌrɛfjʊˈteɪʃən] *n* : refutación *f*
refute [rɪˈfjuːt] *vt* **-futed; -futing 1** DENY : desmentir, negar **2** DISPROVE : refutar, rebatir
regain [riːˈgeɪn] *vt* **1** RECOVER : recuperar, recobrar **2** REACH : alcanzar ⟨to regain the shore : llegar a la tierra⟩
regal [ˈriːgəl] *adj* : real, regio
regale [rɪˈgeɪl] *vt* **-galed; -galing 1** ENTERTAIN : agasajar, entretener **2** AMUSE, DELIGHT : deleitar, divertir
regalia [rɪˈgeɪljə] *npl* : ropaje *m*, vestiduras *fpl*, adornos *mpl*
regard[1] [rɪˈgɑrd] *vt* **1** OBSERVE : observar, mirar **2** HEED : tener en cuenta, hacer caso de **3** CONSIDER : considerar **4** RESPECT : respetar ⟨highly regarded : muy estimado⟩ **5 as regards** : en cuanto a, en lo que se refiere a
regard[2] *n* **1** CONSIDERATION : consideración *f* **2** ESTEEM : respeto *m*, estima *f* **3** PARTICULAR : aspecto *m*, sentido *m* ⟨in this regard : en este sentido⟩ **4 regards** *npl* : saludos *mpl*, recuerdos *mpl* **5 with regard to** : con relación a, con respecto a
regarding [rɪˈgɑrdɪŋ] *prep* : con respecto a, en cuanto a
regardless [rɪˈgɑrdləs] *adv* : a pesar de todo

regardless of *prep* : a pesar de, sin tener en cuenta ⟨regardless of our mistakes : a pesar de nuestros errores⟩ ⟨regardless of age : sin tener en cuenta la edad⟩

regenerate [ri'dʒɛnə,reɪt] *v* **-ated; -ating** *vt* : regenerar — *vi* : regenerarse

regeneration [ri,dʒɛnə'reɪʃən] *n* : regeneración *f*

regent ['ri:dʒənt] *n* **1** RULER : regente *mf* **2** : miembro *m* de la junta directiva (de una universidad, etc.)

regime [reɪ'ʒi:m, rɪ-] *n* : régimen *m*

regimen ['rɛdʒəmən] *n* : régimen *m*

regiment¹ ['rɛdʒə,mɛnt] *vt* : reglamentar

regiment² ['rɛdʒəmənt] *n* : regimiento *m*

region ['ri:dʒən] *n* **1** : región *f* **2 in the region of** : alrededor de

regional ['ri:dʒənəl] *adj* : regional — **regionally** *adv*

register¹ ['rɛdʒəstər] *vt* **1** RECORD : registrar, inscribir **2** INDICATE : marcar (temperatura, medidas, etc.) **3** REVEAL : manifestar, acusar ⟨to register surprise : acusar sorpresa⟩ **4** : certificar (correo) — *vi* ENROLL : inscribirse, matricularse

register² *n* : registro *m*

registrar ['rɛdʒə,strɑr] *n* : registrador *m*, -dora *f* oficial

registration [,rɛdʒə'streɪʃən] *n* **1** REGISTERING : inscripción *f*, matriculación *f*, registro *m* **2 or registration number** : matrícula *f*, número *m* de matrícula

registry ['rɛdʒəstri] *n, pl* **-tries** : registro *m*

regress [ri'grɛs] *vi* : retroceder

regression [ri'grɛʃən] *n* : retroceso *m*, regresión *f*

regressive [ri'grɛsɪv] *adj* : regresivo

regret¹ [ri'grɛt] *vt* **-gretted; -gretting** : arrepentirse de, lamentar ⟨he regrets nothing : no se arrepiente de nada⟩ ⟨I regret to tell you : lamento decirle⟩

regret² *n* **1** REMORSE : arrepentimiento *m*, remordimientos *mpl* **2** SADNESS : pesar *m*, dolor *m* **3 regrets** *npl* : excusas *fpl* ⟨to send one's regrets : excusarse⟩

regretful [ri'grɛtfəl] *adj* : arrepentido, pesaroso

regretfully [ri'grɛtfəli] *adv* : con pesar

regrettable [ri'grɛtəbəl] *adj* : lamentable — **regrettably** [-bli] *adv*

regular¹ ['rɛgjələr] *adj* **1** NORMAL : regular, normal, usual **2** STEADY : uniforme, regular ⟨a regular pace : un paso regular⟩ **3** CUSTOMARY, HABITUAL : habitual, de costumbre

regular² *n* : cliente *mf* habitual

regularity [,rɛgjə'lærəṭi] *n, pl* **-ties** : regularidad *f*

regularly ['rɛgjələrli] *adv* : regularmente, con regularidad

regulate ['rɛgjə,leɪt] *vt* **-lated; -lating** : regular

regulation [,rɛgjə'leɪʃən] *n* **1** REGULATING : regulación *f* **2** RULE : regla *f*,

reglamento *m*, norma *f* ⟨safety regulations : reglas de seguridad⟩

regulator ['rɛgjə,leɪtər] *n* **1** : regulador *m* (mecanismo) **2** : persona *f* que regula

regulatory ['rɛgjələ,tori] *adj* : regulador

regurgitate [ri'gərdʒə,teɪt] *v* **-tated; -tating** : regurgitar, vomitar

rehabilitate [,ri:hə'bɪlə,teɪt, ,ri:ə-] *vt* **-tated; -tating** : rehabilitar

rehabilitation [,ri:hə,bɪlə'teɪʃən, ,ri:ə-] *n* : rehabilitación *f*

rehearsal [ri'hərsəl] *n* : ensayo *m*

rehearse [ri'hərs] *v* **-hearsed; -hearsing** : ensayar

reheat [,ri:'hi:t] *vt* : recalentar

reign¹ ['reɪn] *vi* **1** RULE : reinar **2** PREVAIL : reinar, predominar ⟨the reigning champion : el actual campeón⟩

reign² *n* : reinado *m*

reimburse [,ri:əm'bərs] *vt* **-bursed; -bursing** : reembolsar

reimbursement [,ri:əm'bərsmənt] *n* : reembolso *m*

rein¹ ['reɪn] *vt* : refrenar (un caballo)

rein² *n* **1** : rienda *f* ⟨to give free rein to : dar rienda suelta a⟩ **2** CHECK : control *m* ⟨to keep a tight rein on : llevar un estricto control de⟩

reincarnation [,ri:ɪn,kɑr'neɪʃən] *n* : reencarnación *f*

reindeer ['reɪn,dɪr] *n* : reno *m*

reinforce [,ri:ən'fors] *vt* **-forced; -forcing** : reforzar

reinforcement [,ri:ən'forsmənt] *n* : refuerzo *m*

reinstate [,ri:ən'steɪt] *vt* **-stated; -stating** **1** : reintegrar, restituir (una persona) **2** RESTORE : restablecer (un servicio, etc.)

reinstatement [,ri:ən'steɪtmənt] *n* : reintegración *f*, restitución *f*, restablecimiento *m*

reiterate [ri'ɪṭə,reɪt] *vt* **-ated; -ating** : reiterar, repetir

reiteration [ri,ɪṭə'reɪʃən] *n* : reiteración *f*, repetición *f*

reject¹ [ri'dʒɛkt] *vt* : rechazar

reject² ['ri:,dʒɛkt] *n* : desecho *m* (cosa), persona *f* rechazada

rejection [ri'dʒɛkʃən] *n* : rechazo *m*

rejoice [ri'dʒɔɪs] *vi* **-joiced; -joicing** : alegrarse, regocijarse

rejoin [,ri:'dʒɔɪn] *vt* **1** : reincorporarse a, reintegrarse a ⟨he rejoined the firm : se reincorporó a la firma⟩ **2** [ri'-] REPLY, RETORT : replicar

rejoinder [ri'dʒɔɪndər] *n* : réplica *f*

rejuvenate [ri'dʒu:və,neɪt] *vt* **-nated; -nating** : rejuvenecer

rejuvenation [ri,dʒu:və'neɪʃən] *n* : rejuvenecimiento *m*

rekindle [,ri:'kɪndəl] *vt* **-dled; -dling** : reavivar

relapse¹ [ri'læps] *vi* **-lapsed; -lapsing** : recaer, volver a caer

relapse² ['ri:,læps, ri'læps] *n* : recaída *f*

relate [ri'leɪt] v **-lated; -lating** vt **1** TELL : relatar, contar **2** ASSOCIATE : relacionar, asociar ⟨to relate crime to poverty : relacionar la delincuencia a la pobreza⟩ — vi **1** CONNECT : conectar, estar relacionado (con) **2** INTERACT : relacionarse (con), llevarse bien (con) **3 to relate to** UNDERSTAND : identificarse con, simpatizar con

related [ri'leɪtəd] adj : emparentado ⟨to be related to : ser pariente de⟩

relation [ri'leɪʃən] n **1** NARRATION : relato m, narración f **2** RELATIVE : pariente mf, familiar mf **3** RELATIONSHIP : relación f ⟨in relation to : en relación con, con relación a⟩ **4 relations** npl : relaciones fpl ⟨public relations : relaciones públicas⟩

relationship [ri'leɪʃən,ʃɪp] n **1** CONNECTION : relación f **2** KINSHIP : parentesco m

relative¹ ['rɛlətɪv] adj : relativo — **relatively** adv

relative² n : pariente mf, familiar mf

relativism ['rɛlətɪ,vɪzəm] n : relativismo m

relativity [,rɛlə'tɪvəti] n, pl **-ties** : relatividad f

relax [ri'læks] vt : relajar, aflojar — vi : relajarse

relaxation [,riː,læk'seɪʃən] n **1** RELAXING : relajación f, aflojamiento m **2** DIVERSION : esparcimiento m, distracción f

relaxing [ri'læksɪŋ] adj : relajante

relay¹ ['riː,leɪ, ri'leɪ] vt **-layed; -laying** : transmitir

relay² ['riː,leɪ] n **1** : relevo m **2** or **relay race** : carrera de relevos

release¹ [ri'liːs] vt **-leased; -leasing 1** FREE : liberar, poner en libertad **2** LOOSEN : soltar, aflojar ⟨to release the brake : soltar el freno⟩ **3** RELINQUISH : renunciar a, ceder **4** ISSUE : publicar (un libro), estrenar (una película), sacar (un disco)

release² n **1** LIBERATION : liberación f, puesta f en libertad **2** RELINQUISHMENT : cesión f (de propiedad, etc.) **3** ISSUE : estreno m (de una película), puesta f en venta (de un disco), publicación f (de un libro) **4** ESCAPE : escape m, fuga f (de un gas)

relegate ['rɛlə,geɪt] vt **-gated; -gating** : relegar

relent [ri'lɛnt] vi : ablandarse, ceder

relentless [ri'lɛntləs] adj : implacable, sin tregua

relentlessly [ri'lɛntləsli] adv : implacablemente

relevance ['rɛləvənts] n : pertinencia f, relación f

relevant ['rɛləvənt] adj : pertinente — **relevantly** adv

reliability [ri,laɪə'bɪləti] n, pl **-ties 1** : fiabilidad f, seguridad f (de una cosa) **2** : formalidad f, seriedad f (de una persona)

reliable [ri'laɪəbəl] adj : confiable, fiable, fidedigno, seguro

reliably [ri'laɪəbli] adv : sin fallar ⟨to be reliably informed : saber (algo) de fuentes fidedignas⟩

reliance [ri'laɪənts] n **1** DEPENDENCE : dependencia f **2** CONFIDENCE : confianza f

reliant [ri'laɪənt] adj : dependiente

relic ['rɛlɪk] n **1** : reliquia f **2** VESTIGE : vestigio m

relief [ri'liːf] n **1** : alivio m, desahogo m ⟨relief from pain : alivio del dolor⟩ **2** AID, WELFARE : ayuda f (benéfica), asistencia f social **3** : relieve m (en la escultura) ⟨relief map : mapa en relieve⟩ **4** REPLACEMENT : relevo m

relieve [ri'liːv] vt **-lieved; -lieving 1** ALLEVIATE : aliviar, mitigar ⟨to feel relieved : sentirse aliviado⟩ **2** FREE : liberar, eximir ⟨to relieve someone of responsibility : eximir a alguien de la responsabilidad de⟩ **3** REPLACE : relevar (a un centinela, etc.) **4** BREAK : romper ⟨to relieve the monotony : romper la monotonía⟩

religion [ri'lɪdʒən] n : religión f

religious [ri'lɪdʒəs] adj : religioso — **religiously** adv

relinquish [ri'lɪŋkwɪʃ, -'lɪn-] vt **1** GIVE UP : renunciar a, abandonar **2** RELEASE : soltar

relish¹ ['rɛlɪʃ] vt : saborear (comida), disfrutar con (una idea, una perspectiva, etc.)

relish² n **1** ENJOYMENT : gusto m, deleite m **2** : salsa f (condimento)

relive [,riː'lɪv] vt **-lived; -living** : revivir

relocate [,riː'loː,keɪt, ,riː'loˈkeɪt] v **-cated; -cating** vt : reubicar, trasladar — vi : trasladarse

relocation [,riː'loˈkeɪʃən] n : reubicación f, traslado m

reluctance [ri'lʌktənts] n : renuencia f, reticencia f, desgana f

reluctant [ri'lʌktənt] adj : renuente, reacio, reticente

reluctantly [ri'lʌktəntli] adv : a regañadientes

rely [ri'laɪ] vi **-lied; -lying 1** DEPEND : depender (de), contar (con) **2** TRUST : confiar (en)

remain [ri'meɪn] vi **1** : quedar ⟨very little remains : queda muy poco⟩ ⟨the remaining 10 minutes : los 10 minutos que quedan⟩ **2** STAY : quedarse, permanecer **3** CONTINUE : continuar, seguir ⟨to remain the same : continuar siendo igual⟩ **4 to remain to** : quedar por ⟨to remain to be done : quedar por hacer⟩ ⟨it remains to be seen : está por ver⟩

remainder [ri'meɪndər] n : resto m, remanente m

remains [ri'meɪnz] npl : restos mpl ⟨mortal remains : restos mortales⟩

remake¹ [riː'meɪk] vt **-made; -making 1** TRANSFORM : rehacer **2** : hacer una nueva versión de (una película, etc.)

remake² ['ri:ˌmeɪk] *n* : nueva versión *f*
remark¹ [rɪ'mɑrk] *vt* **1** NOTICE : observar **2** SAY : comentar, observar — *vi* **to remark on** : hacer observaciones sobre
remark² *n* : comentario *m*, observación *f*
remarkable [rɪ'mɑrkəbəl] *adj* : extraordinario, notable — **remarkably** [-bli] *adv*
rematch ['ri:ˌmætʃ] *n* : revancha *f*
remedial [rɪ'mi:diəl] *adj* : correctivo ⟨remedial classes : clases para alumnos atrasados⟩
remedy¹ ['rɛmədi] *vt* **-died; -dying** : remediar
remedy² *n, pl* **-dies** : remedio *m*, medicamento *m*
remember [rɪ'mɛmbər] *vt* **1** RECOLLECT : acordarse de, recordar **2** : no olvidar ⟨remember my words : no olvides mis palabras⟩ ⟨to remember to : acordarse de⟩ **3** : dar saludos, dar recuerdos ⟨remember me to her : dale saludos de mi parte⟩ **4** COMMEMORATE : recordar, conmemorar
remembrance [rɪ'mɛmbrənts] *n* **1** RECOLLECTION : recuerdo *m* ⟨in remembrance of : en conmemoración de⟩ **2** MEMENTO : recuerdo *m*
remind [rɪ'maɪnd] *vt* : recordar ⟨remind me to do it : recuérdame que lo haga⟩ ⟨she reminds me of Clara : me recuerda de Clara⟩
reminder [rɪ'maɪndər] *n* : recuerdo *m*
reminisce [ˌrɛmə'nɪs] *vi* **-nisced; -niscing** : rememorar los viejos tiempos
reminiscence [ˌrɛmə'nɪsənts] *n* : recuerdo *m*, reminiscencia *f*
reminiscent [ˌrɛmə'nɪsənt] *adj* **1** NOSTALGIC : reminiscente, nostálgico **2** SUGGESTIVE : evocador, que recuerda — **reminiscently** *adv*
remiss [rɪ'mɪs] *adj* : negligente, descuidado, remiso
remission [rɪ'mɪʃən] *n* : remisión *f*
remit [rɪ'mɪt] *vt* **-mitted; -mitting** **1** PARDON : perdonar **2** SEND : remitir, enviar (dinero)
remittance [rɪ'mɪtənts] *n* : remesa *f*
remnant ['rɛmnənt] *n* : restos *mpl*, vestigio *m*
remodel [rɪ'mɑdəl] *vt* **-eled** *or* **-elled; -eling** *or* **-elling** : remodelar, reformar
remonstrate [rɪ'mɑnˌstreɪt] *vi* **-strated; -strating** : protestar ⟨to remonstrate with someone : quejarse a alguien⟩
remorse [rɪ'mɔrs] *n* : remordimiento *m*
remorseful [rɪ'mɔrsfəl] *adj* : arrepentido, lleno de remordimiento
remorseless [rɪ'mɔrsləs] *adj* **1** PITILESS : despiadado **2** RELENTLESS : implacable
remote [rɪ'mo:t] *adj* **-moter; -est** **1** FAR-OFF : lejano, remoto ⟨remote countries : países remotos⟩ ⟨in the remote past : en el pasado lejano⟩ **2** SECLUDED : recóndito **3** : a distancia, remoto ⟨re-

mote control : control remoto⟩ **4** SLIGHT : remoto **5** ALOOF : distante
remotely [rɪ'mo:tli] *adv* **1** SLIGHTLY : remotamente **2** DISTANTLY : en un lugar remoto, muy lejos
remoteness [rɪ'mo:tnəs] *n* : lejanía *f*
removable [rɪ'mu:vəbəl] *adj* : removible
removal [rɪ'mu:vəl] *n* : separación *f*, extracción *f*, supresión *f* (en algo escrito), eliminación *f* (de problemas, etc.)
remove [rɪ'mu:v] *vt* **-moved; -moving** **1** : quitar, quitarse ⟨remove the lid : quite la tapa⟩ ⟨to remove one's hat : quitarse el sombrero⟩ **2** EXTRACT : sacar, extraer ⟨to remove the contents of : sacar el contenido de⟩ **3** ELIMINATE : eliminar, disipar
remunerate [rɪ'mju:nəˌreɪt] *vt* **-ated; -ating** : remunerar
remuneration [rɪˌmju:nə'reɪʃən] *n* : remuneración *f*
remunerative [rɪ'mju:nərəṭɪv, -ˌreɪ-] *adj* : remunerativo
renaissance [ˌrɛnə'sɑnts, -'zɑnts; 'rɛnəˌ-] *n* : renacimiento *m* ⟨the Renaissance : el Renacimiento⟩
renal ['ri:nəl] *adj* : renal
rename [ˌri:'neɪm] *vt* **-named; -naming** : ponerle un nombre nuevo a
rend ['rɛnd] *vt* **rent** ['rɛnt]; **rending** : desgarrar
render ['rɛndər] *vt* **1** : derretir ⟨to render lard : derretir la manteca⟩ **2** GIVE : prestar, dar ⟨to render aid : prestar ayuda⟩ **3** MAKE : hacer, volver, dejar ⟨it rendered him helpless : lo dejó incapacitado⟩ **4** TRANSLATE : traducir, verter ⟨to render into English : traducir al inglés⟩
rendezvous ['rɑndɪˌvu:, -deɪ-] *ns & pl* : encuentro *m*, cita *f*
rendition [rɛn'dɪʃən] *n* : interpretación *f*
renegade ['rɛnɪˌgeɪd] *n* : renegado *m*, -da *f*
renege [rɪ'nɪg, -'nɛg] *vi* **-neged; -neging** : no cumplir con (una promesa, etc.)
renew [rɪ'nu:, -'nju:] *vt* **1** REVIVE : renovar, reavivar ⟨to renew the sentiments of youth : renovar los sentimientos de la juventud⟩ **2** RESUME : reanudar **3** EXTEND : renovar ⟨to renew a subscription : renovar una suscripción⟩
renewable [rɪ'nu:əbəl, -'nju:-] *adj* : renovable
renewal [rɪ'nu:əl, -'nju:-] *n* : renovación *f*
renounce [rɪ'naʊnts] *vt* **-nounced; -nouncing** : renunciar a
renovate ['rɛnəˌveɪt] *vt* **-vated; -vating** : restaurar, renovar
renovation [ˌrɛnə'veɪʃən] *n* : restauración *f*, renovación *f*
renown [rɪ'naʊn] *n* : renombre *m*, fama *f*, celebridad *f*
renowned [rɪ'naʊnd] *adj* : renombrado, célebre, famoso
rent¹ ['rɛnt] *vt* : rentar, alquilar

rent² n **1** : renta f, alquiler m ⟨for rent : se alquila⟩ **2** RIP : rasgadura f
rental¹ ['rɛntəl] adj RENT : de alquiler
rental² n : alquiler m
renter ['rɛntər] n : arrendatario m, -ria f
renunciation [rɪˌnʌn tsiˈeɪʃən] n : renuncia f
reopen [ˌriːˈoːpən] vt : volver a abrir
reorganization [ˌriːˌɔrgənəˈzeɪʃən] n : reorganización f
reorganize [ˌriːˈɔrgənˌaɪz] vt -nized; -nizing : reorganizar
repair¹ [rɪˈpær] vt : reparar, arreglar, refaccionar
repair² n **1** : reparación f, arreglo m **2** CONDITION : estado m ⟨in bad repair : en mal estado⟩
reparation [ˌrɛpəˈreɪʃən] n **1** AMENDS : reparación f **2 reparations** npl COMPENSATION : indemnización f
repartee [ˌrɛpərˈtiː, -ˌpɑr-, -ˈteɪ] n : intercambio m de réplicas ingeniosas
repast [rɪˈpæst, ˈriːˌpæst] n : comida f
repatriate [rɪˈpeɪtriˌeɪt] vt -ated; -ating : repatriar
repay [rɪˈpeɪ] vt -paid; -paying : pagar, devolver, reembolsar
repeal¹ [rɪˈpiːl] vt : abrogar, revocar
repeal² n : abrogación f, revocación f
repeat¹ [rɪˈpiːt] vt : repetir
repeat² n : repetición f
repeatedly [rɪˈpiːtədli] adv : repetidamente, repetidas veces
repel [rɪˈpɛl] vt -pelled; -pelling **1** REPULSE : repeler (un enemigo, etc.) **2** RESIST : repeler **3** REJECT : rechazar, repeler **4** DISGUST : repugnar, darle asco (a alguien)
repellent or **repellant** [rɪˈpɛlənt] n : repelente m
repent [rɪˈpɛnt] vi : arrepentirse
repentance [rɪˈpɛntənts] n : arrepentimiento m
repentant [rɪˈpɛntənt] adj : arrepentido
repercussion [ˌriːpərˈkʌʃən, ˌrɛpər-] n : repercusión f
repertoire ['rɛpərˌtwɑr] n : repertorio m
repertory ['rɛpərˌtori] n, pl -ries : repertorio m
repetition [ˌrɛpəˈtɪʃən] n : repetición f
repetitious [ˌrɛpəˈtɪʃəs] adj : repetitivo, reiterativo — **repetitiously** adv
repetitive [rɪˈpɛtətɪv] adj : repetitivo, reiterativo
replace [rɪˈpleɪs] vt -placed; -placing **1** : volver a poner ⟨replace it in the drawer : vuelve a ponerlo en el cajón⟩ **2** SUBSTITUTE : reemplazar, sustituir **3** : reponer ⟨to replace the worn carpet : reponer la alfombra raída⟩
replaceable [rɪˈpleɪsəbəl] adj : reemplazable
replacement [rɪˈpleɪsmənt] n **1** SUBSTITUTION : reemplazo m, sustitución f **2** SUBSTITUTE : sustituto m, -ta f; suplente mf (persona) **3 replacement part** : repuesto m, pieza f de recambio
replenish [rɪˈplɛnɪʃ] vt : rellenar, llenar de nuevo

replenishment [rɪˈplɛnɪʃmənt] n : reabastecimiento m
replete [rɪˈpliːt] adj : repleto, lleno
replica ['rɛplɪkə] n : réplica f, reproducción f
replicate ['rɛpləˌkeɪt] v -cated; -cating vt : duplicar, repetir — vi : duplicarse
replication [ˌrɛpləˈkeɪʃən] n **1** REPRODUCTION : reproducción f **2** REPETITION : repetición f **3** : replicación f (celular)
reply¹ [rɪˈplaɪ] vi -plied; -plying : contestar, responder
reply² n, pl -plies : respuesta f, contestación f
report¹ [rɪˈport] vt **1** ANNOUNCE : relatar, anunciar **2** : dar parte de, informar de, reportar ⟨he reported an accident : dio parte de un accidente⟩ ⟨to report a crime : denunciar un delito⟩ **3** : informar acerca de (en un periódico, la televisión, etc.) — vi **1** : hacer un informe, informar **2 to report for duty** : presentarse, reportarse
report² n **1** RUMOR : rumor m **2** REPUTATION : reputación f ⟨people of evil report : personas de mala fama⟩ **3** ACCOUNT : informe m, reportaje m (en un periódico, etc.) **4** BANG : estallido m (de un arma de fuego)
report card n : boletín m de calificaciones, boletín m de notas
reportedly [rɪˈportədli] adv : según se dice, según se informa
reporter [rɪˈportər] n : periodista mf; reportero m, -ra f
repose¹ [rɪˈpoːz] vi -posed; -posing : reposar, descansar
repose² n **1** : reposo m, descanso m **2** CALM : calma f, tranquilidad f
repository [rɪˈpɑzəˌtori] n, pl -ries : depósito m
repossess [ˌriːpəˈzɛs] vt : recuperar, recobrar la posesión de
reprehensible [ˌrɛprɪˈhɛntsəbəl] adj : reprensible — **reprehensibly** adv
represent [ˌrɛprɪˈzɛnt] vt **1** SYMBOLIZE : representar ⟨the flag represents our country : la bandera representa a nuestro país⟩ **2** : representar, ser un representante de ⟨an attorney who represents his client : un abogado que representa su cliente⟩ **3** PORTRAY : presentar ⟨he represents himself as a friend : se presenta como amigo⟩
representation [ˌrɛprɪˌzɛnˈteɪʃən, -zən-] n : representación f
representative¹ [ˌrɛprɪˈzɛntətɪv] adj : representativo
representative² n **1** : representante mf **2** : diputado m, -da f (en la política)
repress [rɪˈprɛs] vt : reprimir
repression [rɪˈprɛʃən] n : represión f
repressive [rɪˈprɛsɪv] adj : represivo
reprieve¹ [rɪˈpriːv] vt -prieved; -prieving : indultar
reprieve² n : indulto m
reprimand¹ ['rɛprəˌmænd] vt : reprender

reprimand² *n* : reprimenda *f*
reprint¹ [ri'prɪnt] *vt* : reimprimir
reprint² ['ri:ˌprɪnt, ri'prɪnt] *n* : reedición
f
reprisal [ri'praɪzəl] *n* : represalia *f*
reproach¹ [ri'pro:ʧ] *vt* : reprochar
reproach² *n* **1** DISGRACE : deshonra *f* **2**
REBUKE : reproche *m*, recriminación *f*
reproachful [ri'pro:ʧfəl] *adj* : de reproche
reproduce [ˌri:prə'du:s, -'dju:s] *v*
-duced; -ducing *vt* : reproducir — *vi*
BREED : reproducirse
reproduction [ˌri:prə'dʌkʃən] *n* : reproducción *f*
reproductive [ˌri:prə'dʌktɪv] *adj* : reproductor
reproof [ri'pru:f] *n* : reprobación *f*, reprimenda *f*, reproche *m*
reprove [ri'pru:v] *vt* **-proved; -proving**
: reprender, censurar
reptile ['rɛpˌtaɪl] *n* : reptil *m*
republic [ri'pʌblɪk] *n* : república *f*
republican¹ [ri'pʌblɪkən] *adj* : republicano
republican² *n* : republicano *m*, -na *f*
repudiate [ri'pju:di,eɪt] *vt* **-ated; -ating**
1 REJECT : rechazar **2** DISOWN : repudiar, renegar de
repudiation [riˌpju:di'eɪʃən] *n* : rechazo
m, repudio *m*
repugnance [ri'pʌgnənts] *n* : repugnancia *f*
repugnant [ri'pʌgnənt] *adj* : repugnante, asqueroso
repulse¹ [ri'pʌls] *vt* **-pulsed; -pulsing 1**
REPEL : repeler **2** REBUFF : desairar,
rechazar
repulse² *n* : rechazo *m*
repulsive [ri'pʌlsɪv] *adj* : repulsivo, repugnante, asqueroso — **repulsively**
adv
reputable ['rɛpjətəbəl] *adj* : acreditado,
de buena reputación
reputation [ˌrɛpjə'teɪʃən] *n* : reputación
f, fama *f*
repute [ri'pju:t] *n* : reputación *f*, fama *f*
reputed [ri'pju: təd] *adj* : reputado,
supuesto ⟨she's reputed to be the best
: tiene fama de ser la mejor⟩
reputedly [ri'pju:tədli] *adv* : supuestamente, según se dice
request¹ [ri'kwɛst] *vt* : pedir, solicitar,
rogar ⟨to request assistance : solicitar
asistencia, pedir ayuda⟩ ⟨I requested
him to do it : le pedí que lo hiciera⟩
request² *n* : petición *f*, solicitud *f*, pedido *m*
requiem ['rɛkwiəm, 'reɪ-] *n* : réquiem *m*
require [ri'kwaɪr] *vt* **-quired; -quiring 1**
CALL FOR, DEMAND : requerir, exigir
⟨if required : si se requiere⟩ ⟨to require
that something be done : exigir que
algo se haga⟩ **2** NEED : necesitar, requerir
requirement [ri'kwaɪrmənt] *n* **1** NECES-
SITY : necesidad *f* **2** DEMAND : requisito *m*, demanda *f*

requisite¹ ['rɛkwəzɪt] *adj* : esencial,
necesario
requisite² *n* : requisito *m*, necesidad *f*
requisition¹ [ˌrɛkwə'zɪʃən] *vt* : requisar
requisition² *n* : requisición *f*, requisa *f*
reread [ˌri:'ri:d] *vt* **-read; -reading**
: releer
reroute [ˌri:'ru:t, -'raʊt] *vt* **-routed;**
-routing : desviar
rerun¹ [ri:'rʌn] *vt* **-ran; -run; -running**
: reponer (un programa televisivo)
rerun² ['ri:ˌrʌn] *n* **1** : reposición *f* (de un
programa televisivo) **2** REPEAT
: repetición *f*
resale ['ri:ˌseɪl, ˌri:'seɪl] *n* : reventa *f* ⟨re-
sale price : precio de venta⟩
rescind [ri'sɪnd] *vt* **1** CANCEL : rescindir,
cancelar **2** REPEAL : abrogar, revocar
rescue¹ ['rɛsˌkju:] *vt* **-cued; -cuing**
: rescatar, salvar
rescue² *n* : rescate *m*
rescuer ['rɛskjuər] *n* : salvador *m*, -dora
f
research¹ [ri'sərʧ, 'ri:ˌsərʧ] *v* : investigar
research² *n* : investigación *f*
researcher [ri'sərʧər, 'ri:ˌ-] *n* : investigador *m*, -dora *f*
resemblance [ri'zɛmblənts] *n* : semejanza *f*, parecido *m*
resemble [ri'zɛmbəl] *vt* **-sembled;**
-sembling : parecerse a, asemejarse a
resent [ri'zɛnt] *vt* : resentirse de, ofenderse por
resentful [ri'zɛntfəl] *adj* : resentido, rencoroso — **resentfully** *adv*
resentment [ri'zɛntmənt] *n* : resentimiento *m*
reservation [ˌrɛzər'veɪʃən] *n* **1** : reservación *f*, reserva *f* ⟨to make a reservation : hacer una reservación⟩ **2** DOUBT,
MISGIVING : reserva *f*, duda *f* ⟨without
reservations : sin reservas⟩ **3** : reserva
f (de indios americanos)
reserve¹ [ri'zərv] *vt* **-served; -serving**
: reservar
reserve² *n* **1** STOCK : reserva *f* ⟨to keep
in reserve : guardar en reserva⟩ **2** RE-
STRAINT : reserva *f*, moderación *f* **3 re-**
serves *npl* : reservas *fpl* (militares)
reserved [ri'zərvd] *adj* : reservado
reservoir ['rɛzərˌvwɑr, -ˌvwɔr, -ˌvɔr] *n*
: embalse *m*
reset [ˌri:'sɛt] *vt* **-set; -setting** : reajustar, poner en hora (un reloj), reiniciar
(una computadora)
reside [ri'zaɪd] *vi* **-sided; -siding 1**
DWELL : residir **2** LIE : radicar, residir
⟨the power resides in the presidency : el
poder radica en la presidencia⟩
residence ['rɛzədənts] *n* : residencia *f*
resident¹ ['rɛzədənt] *adj* : residente
resident² *n* : residente *mf*
residential [ˌrɛzə'dɛntʃəl] *adj* : residencial
residual [ri'zɪʤuəl] *adj* : residual
residue ['rɛzəˌdu:, -ˌdju:] *n* : residuo *m*,
resto *m*

resign [ri'zaın] *vt* **1** QUIT : dimitir, renunciar **2 to resign oneself** : aguantarse, resignarse

resignation [‚rɛzıg'neıʃən] *n* : resignación *f*

resignedly [ri'zaınədli] *adv* : con resignación

resilience [ri'zıljən*t*s] *n* **1** : capacidad *f* de recuperación, adaptabilidad *f* **2** ELASTICITY : elasticidad *f*

resiliency [ri'zıljən*t*si] → **resilience**

resilient [ri'zıljənt] *adj* **1** STRONG : resistente, fuerte **2** ELASTIC : elástico

resin ['rɛzən] *n* : resina *f*

resist [ri'zıst] *vt* **1** WITHSTAND : resistir ⟨to resist heat : resistir el calor⟩ **2** OPPOSE : oponerse a

resistance [ri'zıstən*t*s] *n* : resistencia *f*

resistant [ri'zıstənt] *adj* : resistente

resolute ['rɛzə‚lu:t] *adj* : firme, resuelto, decidido

resolutely ['rɛzə‚lu:tli, ‚rzə'-] *adv* : resueltamente, firmemente

resolution [‚rɛzə'lu:ʃən] *n* **1** SOLUTION : solución *f* **2** RESOLVE : resolución *f*, determinación *f* **3** DECISION : propósito *m*, decisión *f* ⟨New Year's resolutions : propósitos para el Año Nuevo⟩ **4** MOTION, PROPOSAL : moción *f*, resolución *f* (legislativa)

resolve[1] [ri'zalv] *vt* **-solved; -solving 1** SOLVE : resolver, solucionar **2** DECIDE : resolver ⟨she resolved to get more sleep : resolvió dormir más⟩

resolve[2] *n* : resolución *f*, determinación *f*

resonance ['rɛzənən*t*s] *n* : resonancia *f*

resonant ['rɛzənənt] *adj* : resonante, retumbante

resort[1] [ri'zɔrt] *vi* **to resort to** : recurrir ⟨to resort to force : recurrir a la fuerza⟩

resort[2] *n* **1** RECOURSE : recurso *m* ⟨as a last resort : como último recurso⟩ **2** HANGOUT : lugar *m* popular, lugar *m* muy frecuentado **3** : lugar *m* de vacaciones ⟨tourist resort : centro turístico⟩

resound [ri'zaʊnd] *vi* : retumbar, resonar

resounding [ri'zaʊndıŋ] *adj* **1** RESONANT : retumbante, resonante **2** ABSOLUTE, CATEGORICAL : rotundo, tremendo ⟨a resounding success : un éxito rotundo⟩

resource ['ri:‚sors, ri'sors] *n* **1** RESOURCEFULNESS : ingenio *m*, recursos *mpl* **2 resources** *npl* : recursos *mpl* ⟨natural resources : recursos naturales⟩ **3 resources** *npl* MEANS : recursos *mpl*, medios *mpl*, fondos *mpl*

resourceful [ri'sorsfəl, -'zors-] *adj* : ingenioso

resourcefulness [ri'sorsfəlnəs, -'zors-] *n* : ingenio *m*, recursos *mpl*, inventiva *f*

respect[1] [ri'spɛkt] *vt* : respetar, estimar

respect[2] *n* **1** REFERENCE : relación *f*, respeto *m* ⟨with respect to : en lo que respecta a⟩ **2** ESTEEM : respeto *m*, es-

tima *f* **3** DETAIL, PARTICULAR : detalle *m*, sentido *m*, respeto *m* ⟨in some respects : en algunos sentidos⟩ **4 respects** *npl* : respetos *mpl* ⟨to pay one's respects : presentar uno susrespetos⟩

respectability [ri‚spɛktə'bıləti] *n* : respetabilidad *f*

respectable [ri'spɛktəbəl] *adj* **1** PROPER : respetable, decente **2** CONSIDERABLE : considerable, respetable ⟨a respectable amount : una cantidad respetable⟩ — **respectably** [-bli] *adv*

respectful [ri'spɛktfəl] *adj* : respetuoso — **respectfully** *adv*

respectfulness [ri'spɛktfəlnəs] *n* : respetuosidad *f*

respective [ri'spɛktıv] *adj* : respectivo ⟨their respective homes : sus casas respectivas⟩ — **respectively** *adv*

respiration [‚rɛspə'reıʃən] *n* : respiración *f*

respirator ['rɛspə‚reıtər] *n* : respirador *m*

respiratory ['rɛspərə‚tori, rı'spaırə-] *adj* : respiratorio

respite ['rɛspıt, rı'spaıt] *n* : respiro *m*, tregua *f*

resplendent [ri'splɛndənt] *adj* : resplandeciente — **resplendently** *adv*

respond [ri'spand] *vi* **1** ANSWER : contestar, responder **2** REACT : responder, reaccionar ⟨to respond to treatment : responder al tratamiento⟩

response [ri'span*t*s] *n* : respuesta *f*

responsibility [ri‚span*t*sə'bıləti] *n, pl* **-ties** : responsabilidad *f*

responsible [ri'span*t*səbəl] *adj* : responsable — **responsibly** [-bli] *adv*

responsive [ri'span*t*sıv] *adj* **1** ANSWERING : que responde **2** SENSITIVE : sensible, receptivo

responsiveness [ri'span*t*sıvnəs] *n* : receptividad *f*, sensibilidad *f*

rest[1] ['rɛst] *vi* **1** REPOSE : reposar, descansar **2** RELAX : quedarse tranquilo **3** STOP : pararse, detenerse **4** DEPEND : basarse (en), descansar (sobre), depender (de) ⟨the decision rests with her : la decisión pesa sobre ella⟩ **5 to rest on** : apoyarse en, descansar sobre ⟨to rest on one's arm : apoyarse en el brazo⟩ — *vt* **1** RELAX : descansar **2** SUPPORT : apoyar **3 to rest one's eyes on** : fijar la mirada en

rest[2] *n* **1** RELAXATION, REPOSE : reposo *m*, descanso *m* **2** SUPPORT : soporte *m*, apoyo *m* **3** : silencio *m* (en música) **4** REMAINDER : resto *m* **5 to come to rest** : pararse

restart [ri'start] *vt* **1** : volver a empezar **2** RESUME : reanudar **3** : volver a arrancar (un motor), reiniciar (una computadora) — *vi* **1** : reanudarse **2** : volver a arrancar

restatement [‚ri:'steıtmənt] *n* : repetición *f*

restaurant ['rɛstə‚rant, -rənt] *n* : restaurante *m*

restful ['rɛstfəl] *adj* **1** RELAXING : relajante **2** PEACEFUL : tranquilo, sosegado

restitution [ˌrɛstə'tu:ʃən, -'tju:-] *n* : restitución *f*

restive ['rɛstɪv] *adj* : inquieto, nervioso

restless ['rɛstləs] *adj* **1** FIDGETY : inquieto, agitado **2** IMPATIENT : impaciente **3** SLEEPLESS : desvelado ⟨a restless night : una noche en blanco⟩

restlessly ['rɛstləsli] *adv* : nerviosamente

restlessness ['rɛstləsnəs] *n* : inquietud *f*, agitación *f*

restoration [ˌrɛstə'reɪʃən] *n* : restauración *f*, restablecimiento *m*

restore [rɪ'stor] *vt* **-stored; -storing 1** RETURN : volver **2** REESTABLISH : restablecer **3** REPAIR : restaurar

restrain [rɪ'streɪn] *vt* **1** : refrenar, contener **2 to restrain oneself** : contenerse

restrained [rɪ'streɪnd] *adj* : comedido, templado, contenido

restraint [rɪ'streɪnt] *n* **1** RESTRICTION : restricción *f*, limitación *f*, control *m* **2** CONFINEMENT : encierro *m* **3** RESERVE : reserva *f*, control *m* de sí mismo

restrict [rɪ'strɪkt] *vt* : restringir, limitar, constreñir

restricted [rɪ'strɪktəd] *adj* **1** LIMITED : limitado, restringido **2** CLASSIFIED : secreto, confidencial

restriction [rɪ'strɪkʃən] *n* : restricción *f*

restrictive [rɪ'strɪktɪv] *adj* : restrictivo — **restrictively** *adv*

rest room *n* : servicios *mpl*, baño *m*

restructure [rɪ'strʌkʃər] *vt* **-tured; -turing** : reestructurar

result¹ [rɪ'zʌlt] *vi* : resultar ⟨to result in : resultar en, tener por resultado⟩

result² *n* : resultado *m*, consecuencia *f* ⟨as a result of : como consecuencia de⟩

resultant [rɪ'zʌltənt] *adj* : resultante

resume [rɪ'zu:m] *v* **-sumed; -suming** *vt* : reanudar — *vi* : reanudarse

résumé *or* **resume** *or* **resumé** ['rɛzəˌmeɪ, ˌrɛzə'-] *n* **1** SUMMARY : resumen *m* **2** CURRICULUM VITAE : currículum *m*, currículo *m*

resumption [rɪ'zʌmpʃən] *n* : reanudación *f*

resurface [ˌri:'sərfəs] *v* **-faced; -facing** *vt* : pavimentar (una carretera) de nuevo — *vi* : volver a salir en la superficie

resurgence [rɪ'sərdʒənts] *n* : resurgimiento *m*

resurrect [ˌrɛzə'rɛkt] *vt* : resucitar, desempolvar

resurrection [ˌrɛzə'rɛkʃən] *n* : resurrección *f*

resuscitate [rɪ'sʌsəˌteɪt] *vt* **-tated; -tating** : resucitar, revivir

resuscitation [rɪˌsʌsə'teɪʃən] *n* : reanimación *f*, resucitación *f*

retail¹ ['ri:ˌteɪl] *vt* : vender al por menor, vender al detalle

retail² *adv* : al por menor, al detalle

retail³ *adj* : detallista, minorista

retail⁴ *n* : venta *f* al detalle, venta *f* al por menor

retailer ['ri:ˌteɪlər] *n* : detallista *mf*, minorista *mf*

retain [rɪ'teɪn] *vt* : retener, conservar, guardar

retainer [rɪ'teɪnər] *n* **1** SERVANT : criado *m*, -da *f* **2** ADVANCE : anticipo *m*

retaliate [rɪ'tæliˌeɪt] *vi* **-ated; -ating** : responder, contraatacar, tomar represalias

retaliation [rɪˌtæli'eɪʃən] *n* : represalia *f*, retaliación *f*

retard [rɪ'tɑrd] *vt* : retardar, retrasar

retardation [ˌri:ˌtɑr'deɪʃən] *n* **1** : retardación *f* **2** *or* **mental retardation** : retraso *m* mental

retarded [rɪ'tɑrdəd] *adj* : retrasado

retch ['rɛtʃ] *vi* : hacer arcadas

retention [rɪ'tɛntʃən] *n* : retención *f*

retentive [rɪ'tɛntɪv] *adj* : retentivo

rethink [ri:'θɪŋk] *vt* **-thought; -thinking** : reconsiderar, repensar

reticence ['rɛtəsənts] *n* : reticencia *f*

reticent ['rɛtəsənt] *adj* : reticente

retina ['rɛtənə] *n, pl* **-nas** *or* **-nae** [-əni, -ənˌaɪ] : retina *f*

retinue ['rɛtənˌu:, -ˌju:] *n* : séquito *m*, comitiva *f*, cortejo *m*

retire [rɪ'taɪr] *vi* **-tired; -tiring 1** RETREAT, WITHDRAW : retirarse, retraerse **2** : retirarse, jubilarse (de su trabajo) **3** : acostarse, irse a dormir

retiree [rɪˌtaɪ'ri:] *n* : jubilado *m*, -da *f*

retirement [rɪ'taɪrmənt] *n* : jubilación *f*

retiring [rɪ'taɪrɪŋ] *adj* SHY : retraído

retort¹ [rɪ'tort] *vt* : replicar

retort² *n* : réplica *f*

retrace [ˌri:'treɪs] *vt* **-traced; -tracing** : volver sobre, desandar ⟨to retrace one's steps : volver uno sobre sus pasos⟩

retract [rɪ'trækt] *vt* **1** TAKE BACK, WITHDRAW : retirar, retractarse de **2** : retraer (las garras) — *vi* : retractarse

retractable [rɪ'træktəbəl] *adj* : retractable

retrain [ˌri:'treɪn] *vt* : reciclar, reconvertir

retreat¹ [rɪ'tri:t] *vi* : retirarse

retreat² *n* **1** WITHDRAWAL : retirada *f*, repliegue *m*, retiro *m* ⟨to beat a retreat : batirse en retirada⟩ **2** REFUGE : retiro *m*, refugio *m*

retrench [rɪ'trɛntʃ] *vt* : reducir (gastos) — *vi* : economizar

retribution [ˌrɛtrə'bju:ʃən] *n* PUNISHMENT : castigo *m*, pena *f* merecida

retrieval [rɪ'tri:vəl] *n* : recuperación *f* ⟨beyond retrieval : irrecuperable⟩ ⟨data retrieval : recuperación de datos⟩

retrieve [rɪ'tri:v] *vt* **-trieved; -trieving 1** : cobrar ⟨to retrieve game : cobrar la caza⟩ **2** RECOVER : recuperar

retriever [rɪ'tri:vər] *n* : perro *m* cobrador

retroactive [ˌrɛtroˈæktɪv] *adj* : retroactivo — **retroactively** *adv*

retrograde [ˈrɛtrəˌgreɪd] *adj* : retrógrado

retrospect [ˈrɛtrəˌspɛkt] *n* **in retrospect** : mirando hacia atrás, retrospectivamente

retrospective [ˌrɛtrəˈspɛktɪv] *adj* : retrospectivo

return¹ [rɪˈtərn] *vi* **1** : volver, regresar ⟨to return home : regresar a casa⟩ **2** REAPPEAR : reaparecer, resurgir **3** ANSWER : responder — *vt* **1** REPLACE, RESTORE : devolver, volver (a poner), restituir ⟨to return something to its place : volver a poner algo en su lugar⟩ **2** YIELD : producir, redituar, rendir **3** REPAY : pagar, devolver ⟨to return a compliment : devolver un cumplido⟩

return² *adj* : de vuelta

return³ *n* **1** RETURNING : regreso *m*, vuelta *f*, retorno *m* **2** *or* **tax return** : declaración *f* de impuestos **3** YIELD : rédito *m*, rendimiento *m*, ganancia *f* **4 returns** *npl* DATA, RESULTS : resultados *mpl*, datos *mpl*

reunion [riˈjuːnjən] *n* : reunión *f*, reencuentro *m*

reunite [ˌriːjʊˈnaɪt] *v* **-nited; -niting** *vt* : (volver a) reunir — *vi* : (volver a) reunirse

reusable [riˈjuːzəbəl] *adj* : reutilizable

reuse [riˈjuːz] *vt* **-used; -using** : reutilizar, usar de nuevo

revamp [ˌriˈvæmp] *vt* : renovar

reveal [rɪˈviːl] *vt* **1** DIVULGE : revelar, divulgar ⟨to reveal a secret : revelar un secreto⟩ **2** SHOW : manifestar, mostrar, dejar ver

revealing [rɪˈviːlɪŋ] *adj* : revelador

reveille [ˈrɛvəli] *n* : toque *m* de diana

revel¹ [ˈrɛvəl] *vi* **-eled** *or* **-elled; -eling** *or* **-elling** **1** CAROUSE : ir de juerga **2 to revel in** : deleitarse en

revel² *n* : juerga *f*, parranda *f fam*

revelation [ˌrɛvəˈleɪʃən] *n* : revelación *f*

reveler *or* **reveller** [ˈrɛvələr] *n* : juerguista *mf*

revelry [ˈrɛvəlri] *n*, *pl* **-ries** : juerga *f*, parranda *f fam*, jarana *f fam*

revenge¹ [rɪˈvɛndʒ] *vt* **-venged; -venging** : vengar ⟨to revenge oneself on : vengarse de⟩

revenge² *n* : venganza *f*

revenue [ˈrɛvəˌnuː, -ˌnjuː] *n* : ingresos *mpl*, rentas *fpl*

reverberate [rɪˈvərbəˌreɪt] *vi* **-ated; -ating** : reverberar

reverberation [rɪˌvərbəˈreɪʃən] *n* : reverberación *f*

revere [rɪˈvɪr] *vt* **-vered; -vering** : reverenciar, venerar

reverence [ˈrɛvərənts] *n* : reverencia *f*, veneración *f*

reverend [ˈrɛvərənd] *adj* : reverendo ⟨the Reverend John Chapin : el reverendo John Chapin⟩

reverent [ˈrɛvərənt] *adj* : reverente — **reverently** *adv*

reverie [ˈrɛvəri] *n*, *pl* **-eries** : ensueño *m*

reversal [rɪˈvərsəl] *n* **1** INVERSION : inversión *f* (del orden normal) **2** CHANGE : cambio *m* total **3** SETBACK : revés *m*, contratiempo *m*

reverse¹ [rɪˈvərs] *v* **-versed; -versing** *vt* **1** INVERT : invertir **2** CHANGE : cambiar totalmente **3** ANNUL : anular, revocar — *vi* : dar marcha atrás

reverse² *adj* **1** : inverso ⟨in reverse order : en orden inverso⟩ ⟨the reverse side : el reverso⟩ **2** OPPOSITE : contrario, opuesto

reverse³ *n* **1** OPPOSITE : lo contrario, lo opuesto **2** SETBACK : revés *m*, contratiempo *m* **3** BACK : reverso *m*, dorso *m*, revés *m* **4** *or* **reverse gear** : marcha *f* atrás, reversa *f Col, Mex*

reversible [rɪˈvərsəbəl] *adj* : reversible

reversion [rɪˈvərʒən] *n* : reversión *f*, vuelta *f*

revert [rɪˈvərt] *vi* : revertir

review¹ [rɪˈvjuː] *vt* **1** REEXAMINE : volver a examinar, repasar (una lección) **2** CRITICIZE : reseñar, hacer una crítica de **3** EXAMINE : examinar, analizar ⟨to review one's life : examinar su vida⟩ **4 to review the troops** : pasar revista a las tropas

review² *n* **1** INSPECTION : revista *f* (de tropas) **2** ANALYSIS, OVERVIEW : resumen *m*, análisis *m* ⟨a review of current affairs : un análisis de las actualidades⟩ **3** CRITICISM : reseña *f*, crítica *f* (de un libro, etc.) **4** : repaso *m* (para un examen) **5** REVUE : revista *f* (musical)

reviewer [rɪˈvjuːər] *n* : crítico *m*, -ca *f*

revile [rɪˈvaɪl] *vt* **-viled; -viling** : injuriar, denostar

revise [rɪˈvaɪz] *vt* **-vised; -vising** : revisar, corregir, refundir ⟨to revise a dictionary : corregir un diccionario⟩

revision [rɪˈvɪʒən] *n* : revisión *f*

revival [rɪˈvaɪvəl] *n* **1** : renacimiento *m* (de ideas, etc.), restablecimiento *m* (de costumbres, etc.), reactivación *f* (de la economía) **2** : reanimación *f*, resucitación *f* (en medicina) **3** *or* **revival meeting** : asamblea *f* evangelista

revive [rɪˈvaɪv] *v* **-vived; -viving** *vt* **1** REAWAKEN : reavivar, reanimar, reactivar (la economía), resucitar (a un paciente) **2** REESTABLISH : restablecer — *vi* **1** : renacer, reanimarse, reactivarse **2** COME TO : recobrar el sentido, volver en sí

revoke [rɪˈvoːk] *vt* **-voked; -voking** : revocar

revolt¹ [rɪˈvoːlt] *vi* **1** REBEL : rebelarse, sublevarse **2 to revolt at** : sentir repugnancia por — *vt* DISGUST : darle asco (a alguien), repugnar

revolt² *n* REBELLION : rebelión *f*, revuelta *f*, sublevación *f*

revolting [rɪˈvoːltɪŋ] *adj* : asqueroso, repugnante

revolution [ˌrɛvəˈluːʃən] *n* : revolución *f*
revolutionary¹ [ˌrɛvəˈluːʃənɛˌri] *adj* : revolucionario
revolutionary² *n, pl* **-aries** : revolucionario *m*, -ria *f*
revolutionize [ˌrɛvəˈluːʃənˌaɪz] *vt* **-ized; -izing** : cambiar radicalmente, revolucionar
revolve [riˈvɑlv] *v* **-volved; -volving** *vt* ROTATE : hacer girar — *vi* **1** ROTATE : girar ⟨to revolve around : girar alrededor de⟩ **2 to revolve in one's mind** : darle vueltas en la cabeza a alguien
revolver [riˈvɑlvər] *n* : revólver *m*
revue [riˈvjuː] *n* : revista *f* (musical)
revulsion [riˈvʌlʃən] *n* : repugnancia *f*
reward¹ [riˈwɔrd] *vt* : recompensar, premiar
reward² *n* : recompensa *f*
rewrite [ˌriːˈraɪt] *vt* **-wrote; -written; -writing** : escribir de nuevo, volver a escribir
rhapsody [ˈræpsədi] *n, pl* **-dies 1** : elogio *m* excesivo ⟨to go into rhapsodies over : extasiarse por⟩ **2** : rapsodia *f* (en música)
rhetoric [ˈrɛtərɪk] *n* : retórica *f*
rhetorical [riˈtɔrɪkəl] *adj* : retórico
rheumatic [ruˈmætɪk] *adj* : reumático
rheumatism [ˈruːməˌtɪzəm, ˈrʊ-] *n* : reumatismo *m*
rhinestone [ˈraɪnˌstoːn] *n* : diamante *m* de imitación
rhino [ˈraɪˌnoː] *n, pl* **rhino** *or* **rhinos** → **rhinoceros**
rhinoceros [raɪˈnɑsərəs] *n, pl* **-eroses** *or* **-eros** *or* **-eri** [-ˌraɪ] : rinoceronte *m*
rhododendron [ˌroːdəˈdɛndrən] *n* : rododendro *m*
rhombus [ˈrɑmbəs] *n, pl* **-buses** *or* **-bi** [-ˌbaɪ, -bi] : rombo *m*
rhubarb [ˈruːˌbɑrb] *n* : ruibarbo *m*
rhyme¹ [ˈraɪm] *vi* **rhymed; rhyming** : rimar
rhyme² *n* **1** : rima *f* **2** VERSE : verso *m* (en rima)
rhythm [ˈrɪðəm] *n* : ritmo *m*
rhythmic [ˈrɪðmɪk] *or* **rhythmical** [-mɪkəl] *adj* : rítmico — **rhythmically** [-mɪkli] *adv*
rib¹ [ˈrɪb] *vt* **ribbed; ribbing 1** : hacer en canalé ⟨a ribbed sweater : un suéter en canalé⟩ **2** TEASE : tomarle el pelo (a alguien)
rib² *n* **1** : costilla *f* (de una persona o un animal) **2** : nervio *m* (de una bóveda o una hoja), varilla *f* (de un paraguas), canalé *m* (de una prenda tejida)
ribald [ˈrɪbəld] *adj* : escabroso, procaz
ribbon [ˈrɪbən] *n* **1** : cinta *f* **2 to tear to ribbons** : hacer jirones
rice [ˈraɪs] *n* : arroz *m*
rich [ˈrɪtʃ] *adj* **1** WEALTHY : rico **2** SUMPTUOUS : suntuoso, lujoso **3** : pesado ⟨rich foods : comida pesada⟩ **4** ABUNDANT : abundante **5** : vivo, intenso ⟨rich colors : colores vivos⟩ **6** FERTILE : fértil, rico

riches [ˈrɪtʃəz] *npl* : riquezas *fpl*
richly [ˈrɪtʃli] *adv* **1** SUMPTUOUSLY : suntuosamente, ricamente **2** ABUNDANTLY : abundantemente **3 richly deserved** : bien merecido
richness [ˈrɪtʃnəs] *n* : riqueza *f*
rickets [ˈrɪkəts] *n* : raquitismo *m*
rickety [ˈrɪkəti] *adj* : desvencijado, destartalado
ricksha *or* **rickshaw** [ˈrɪkˌʃɔ] *n* : cochecillo *m* tirado por un hombre
ricochet¹ [ˈrɪkəˌʃeɪ] *vi* **-cheted** [-ˌʃeɪd] *or* **-chetted** [-ˌʃɛtəd]; **-cheting** [-ˌʃeɪɪŋ] *or* **-chetting** [-ˌʃɛtɪŋ] : rebotar
ricochet² *n* : rebote *m*
rid [ˈrɪd] *vt* **rid; ridding 1** FREE : librar ⟨to rid the city of thieves : librar la ciudad de ladrones⟩ **2 to rid oneself of** : desembarazarse de
riddance [ˈrɪdənts] *n* : libramiento *m* ⟨good riddance! : ¡adiós y buen viaje!, ¡vete con viento fresco!⟩
riddle¹ [ˈrɪdəl] *vt* **-dled; -dling** : acribillar ⟨riddled with bullets : acribillado a balazos⟩ ⟨riddled with errors : lleno de errores⟩
riddle² *n* : acertijo *m*, adivinanza *f*
ride¹ [ˈraɪd] *v* **rode** [ˈroːd]; **ridden** [ˈrɪdən]; **riding** *vt* **1** : montar, ir, andar ⟨to ride a horse : montar a caballo⟩ ⟨to ride a bicycle : montar en bicicleta, andar en bicicleta⟩ ⟨to ride the bus : ir en autobús⟩ **2** TRAVERSE : recorrer ⟨he rode 5 miles : recorrió 5 millas⟩ **3** TEASE : burlarse de, ridiculizar **4** CARRY : llevar **5** WEATHER : capear ⟨they rode out the storm : capearon el temporal⟩ **6 to ride the waves** : surcar los mares — *vi* **1** : montar a caballo, cabalgar **2** TRAVEL : ir, viajar (en coche, en bicicleta, etc.) **3** RUN : andar, marchar ⟨the car rides well : el coche anda bien⟩ **4 to ride at anchor** : estar fondeado **5 to let things ride** : dejar pasar las cosas
ride² *n* **1** : paseo *m*, vuelta *f* (en coche, en bicicleta, a caballo) ⟨to go for a ride : dar una vuelta⟩ ⟨to give someone a ride : llevar en coche a alguien⟩ **2** : aparato *m* (en un parque de diversiones)
rider [ˈraɪdər] *n* **1** : jinete *mf* ⟨the rider fell off his horse : el jinete se cayó de su caballo⟩ **2** CYCLIST : ciclista *mf* **3** MOTORCYCLIST : motociclista *mf* **4** CLAUSE : cláusula *f* añadida
ridge [ˈrɪdʒ] *n* **1** CHAIN : cadena *f* (de montañas o cerros) **2** : caballete *m* (de un techo), cresta *f* (de una ola o una montaña), cordoncillo *m* (de telas)
ridicule¹ [ˈrɪdəˌkjuːl] *vt* **-culed; -culing** : burlarse de, mofarse de, ridiculizar
ridicule² *n* : burlas *fpl*
ridiculous [rəˈdɪkjələs] *adj* : ridículo, absurdo
ridiculously [rəˈdɪkjələsli] *adv* : de forma ridícula
rife [ˈraɪf] *adj* : abundante, común ⟨to be rife with : estar plagado de⟩

riffraff ['rɪf₁ræf] *n* : chusma *f*, gentuza *f*
rifle¹ ['raɪfəl] *v* **-fled; -fling** *vt* RANSACK : desvalijar, saquear — *vi* **to rifle through** : revolver
rifle² *n* : rifle *m*, fusil *m*
rift ['rɪft] *n* **1** FISSURE : grieta *f*, fisura *f* **2** BREAK : ruptura *f* (entre personas), división *f* (dentro de un grupo)
rig¹ ['rɪg] *vt* **rigged; rigging 1** : aparejar (un barco) **2** EQUIP : equipar **3** FIX : amañar (una elección, etc.) **4 to rig up** CONSTRUCT : construir, erigir **5 to rig oneself out as** : vestirse de
rig² *n* **1** : aparejo *m* (de un barco) **2** *or* **oil rig** : torre *f* de perforación, plataforma *f* petrolífera
rigging ['rɪgɪŋ, -gən] *n* : jarcia *f*, aparejo *m*
right¹ ['raɪt] *vt* **1** FIX, RESTORE : reparar ⟨to right the economy : reparar la economía⟩ **2** STRAIGHTEN : enderezar
right² *adv* **1** : bien ⟨to live right : vivir bien⟩ **2** PRECISELY : precisamente, justo ⟨right in the middle : justo en medio⟩ **3** DIRECTLY, STRAIGHT : derecho, directamente ⟨he went right home : fue derecho a casa⟩ **4** IMMEDIATELY : inmediatamente ⟨right after lunch : inmediatamente después del almuerzo⟩ **5** COMPLETELY : completamente ⟨he felt right at home : se sintió completamente cómodo⟩ **6** : a la derecha ⟨to look left and right : mirar a la izquierda y a la derecha⟩
right³ *adj* **1** UPRIGHT : bueno, honrado ⟨right conduct : conducta honrada⟩ **2** CORRECT : correcto ⟨the right answer : la respuesta correcta⟩ **3** APPROPRIATE : apropiado, adecuado, debido ⟨the right man for the job : el hombre perfecto para el trabajo⟩ **4** STRAIGHT : recto ⟨a right line : una línea recta⟩ **5** : derecho ⟨the right hand : la mano derecha⟩ **6** SOUND : bien ⟨he's not in his right mind : no está bien de la cabeza⟩
right⁴ *n* **1** GOOD : bien *m* ⟨to do right : hacer el bien⟩ **2** : derecha *f* ⟨on the right : a la derecha⟩ **3** *or* **right hand** : mano *f* derecha **4** ENTITLEMENT : derecho *m* ⟨the right to vote : el derecho a votar⟩ ⟨women's rights : los derechos de la mujer⟩ **5 the Right** : la derecha (en la política)
right angle *n* : ángulo *m* recto
right–angled ['raɪt₁æŋgəld] *or* **right–angle** [-gəl] *adj* **1** : en ángulo recto **2** **right–angled triangle** : triángulo *m* rectángulo
righteous ['raɪtʃəs] *adj* : recto, honrado — **righteously** *adv*
righteousness ['raɪtʃəsnəs] *n* : rectitud *f*, honradez *f*
rightful ['raɪtfəl] *adj* **1** JUST : justo **2** LAWFUL : legítimo — **rightfully** *adv*
right–hand ['raɪt₁hænd] *adj* **1** : situado a la derecha **2** RIGHT-HANDED : para

la mano derecha, con la mano derecha **3 right–hand man** : brazo *m* derecho
right–handed ['raɪt'hændəd] *adj* **1** : diestro ⟨a right-handed pitcher : un lanzador diestro⟩ **2** : para la mano derecha, con la mano derecha **3** CLOCKWISE : en la dirección de las manecillas del reloj
rightly ['raɪtli] *adv* **1** JUSTLY : justamente, con razón **2** PROPERLY : debidamente, apropiadamente **3** CORRECTLY : correctamente
right–of–way ['raɪtə'weɪ, -əv-] *n, pl* **rights–of–way 1** : preferencia (del tráfico) **2** ACCESS : derecho *m* de paso
rightward ['raɪtwərd] *adj* : a la derecha, hacia la derecha
right–wing ['raɪt'wɪŋ] *adj* : derechista
right wing *n* **the right wing** : la derecha
right–winger ['raɪt'wɪŋər] *n* : derechista *mf*
rigid ['rɪʤɪd] *adj* : rígido — **rigidly** *adv*
rigidity [rɪ'ʤɪdəti] *n, pl* **-ties** : rigidez *f*
rigmarole ['rɪgmə₁roːl, 'rɪgə-] *n* **1** NONSENSE : galimatías *m*, disparates *mpl* **2** PROCEDURES : trámites *mpl*
rigor ['rɪgər] *n* : rigor *m*
rigor mortis [₁rɪgər'mɔrtəs] *n* : rigidez *f* cadavérica
rigorous ['rɪgərəs] *adj* : riguroso — **rigorously** *adv*
rile ['raɪl] *vt* **riled; riling** : irritar
rill ['rɪl] *n* : riachuelo *m*
rim ['rɪm] *n* **1** EDGE : borde *m* **2** : llanta *f*, rin *m* Col, Mex (de una rueda) **3** FRAME : montura *f* (de anteojos)
rime ['raɪm] *n* : escarcha *f*
rind ['raɪnd] *n* : corteza *f*
ring¹ ['rɪŋ] *v* **rang** ['ræŋ]; **rung** ['rʌŋ]; **ringing** *vi* **1** : sonar ⟨the doorbell rang : el timbre sonó⟩ ⟨to ring for : llamar⟩ **2** RESOUND : resonar **3** SEEM : parecer ⟨to ring true : parecer cierto⟩ — *vt* **1** : tocar, hacer sonar (un timbre, una alarma, etc.) **2** SURROUND : cercar, rodear
ring² *n* **1** : anillo *m*, sortija *f* ⟨wedding ring : anillo de matrimonio⟩ **2** BAND : aro *m*, anillo *m* ⟨piston ring : aro de émbolo⟩ **3** CIRCLE : círculo *m* **4** ARENA : arena *f*, ruedo *m* ⟨a boxing ring : un cuadrilátero, un ring⟩ **5** GANG : banda *f* (de ladrones, etc.) **6** SOUND : timbre *m*, sonido *m* **7** CALL : llamada *f* (por teléfono)
ringer ['rɪŋər] *n* **to be a dead ringer for** : ser un vivo retrato de
ringleader ['rɪŋ₁liːdər] *n* : cabecilla *mf*
ringlet ['rɪŋlət] *n* : sortija *f*, rizo *m*
ringworm ['rɪŋ₁wɔrm] *n* : tiña *f*
rink ['rɪŋk] *n* : pista *f* ⟨skating rink : pista de patinaje⟩
rinse¹ ['rɪnts] *vt* **rinsed; rinsing** : enjuagar ⟨to rinse out one's mouth : enjuagarse la boca⟩
rinse² *n* : enjuague *m*
riot¹ ['raɪət] *vi* : amotinarse
riot² *n* : motín *m*, tumulto *m*, alboroto *m*

rioter ['raɪətər] *n* : alborotador *m*, -dora *f*

riotous ['raɪətəs] *adj* **1** UNRULY, WILD : desenfrenado, alborotado **2** ABUNDANT : abundante

rip¹ ['rɪp] *v* **ripped; ripping** *vt* : rasgar, arrancar, desgarrar — *vi* : rasgarse, desgarrarse

rip² *n* : rasgón *m*, desgarrón *m*

ripe ['raɪp] *adj* **riper; ripest 1** MATURE : maduro ⟨ripe fruit : fruta madura⟩ **2** READY : listo, preparado

ripen ['raɪpən] *v* : madurar

ripeness ['raɪpnəs] *n* : madurez *f*

rip–off ['rɪp,ɔf] *n* **1** THEFT : robo *m* **2** SWINDLE : estafa *f*, timo *m fam*

rip off *vt* **1** : rasgar, arrancar, desgarrar **2** SWINDLE *fam* : estafar, tifar

ripple¹ ['rɪpəl] *v* **-pled; -pling** *vi* : rizarse, ondear, ondular — *vt* : rizar

ripple² *n* : onda *f*, ondulación *f*

rise¹ ['raɪz] *vi* **rose** ['ro:z]; **risen** ['rɪz-ən]; **rising 1** GET UP : levantarse ⟨to rise to one's feet : ponerse de pie⟩ **2** : elevarse, alzarse ⟨the mountains rose to the west : las montañas se elevaron al oeste⟩ **3** : salir (dícese del sol y de la luna) **4** : subir (dícese de las aguas, del humo, etc.) ⟨the river rose : las aguas subieron de nivel⟩ **5** INCREASE : aumentar, subir **6** ORIGINATE : nacer, proceder **7 to rise in rank** : ascender **8 to rise up** REBEL : sublevarse, rebelarse

rise² *n* **1** ASCENT : ascensión *f*, subida *f* **2** ORIGIN : origen *m* **3** ELEVATION : elevación *f* **4** INCREASE : subida *f*, aumento *m*, alzamiento *m* **5** SLOPE : pendiente *f*, cuesta *f*

riser ['raɪzər] *n* **1** : contrahuella *f* (de una escalera) **2 early riser** : madrugador *m*, -dora *f* **3 late riser** : dormilón *m*, -lona *f*

risk¹ ['rɪsk] *vt* : arriesgar

risk² *n* : riesgo *m*, peligro *m* ⟨at risk : en peligro⟩ ⟨at your own risk : por su cuenta y riesgo⟩

risky ['rɪski] *adj* **riskier; -est** : arriesgado, peligroso, riesgoso

risqué [rɪ'skeɪ] *adj* : escabroso, picante, subido de tono

rite ['raɪt] *n* : rito *m*

ritual¹ ['rɪtʃuəl] *adj* : ritual — **ritually** *adv*

ritual² *n* : ritual *m*

rival¹ ['raɪvəl] *vt* **-valed** *or* **-valled; -valing** *or* **-valling** : rivalizar con, competir con

rival² *adj* : competidor, rival

rival³ *n* : rival *mf*; competidor *m*, -dora *f*

rivalry ['raɪvəlri] *n, pl* **-ries** : rivalidad *f*, competencia *f*

river ['rɪvər] *n* : río *m*

riverbank ['rɪvər,bæŋk] *n* : ribera *f*, orilla *f*

riverbed ['rɪvər,bɛd] *n* : cauce *m*, lecho *m*

riverside ['rɪvər,saɪd] *n* : ribera *f*, orilla *f*

rivet¹ ['rɪvət] *vt* **1** : remachar **2** FIX : fijar (los ojos, etc.) **3** FASCINATE : fascinar, cautivar

rivet² *n* : remache *m*

rivulet ['rɪvjələt] *n* : arroyo *m*, riachuelo *m* ⟨rivulets of sweat : gotas de sudor⟩

roach ['ro:tʃ] → **cockroach**

road ['ro:d] *n* **1** : carretera *f*, calle *f*, camino *m* **2** PATH : camino *m*, sendero *m*, vía *f* ⟨on the road to a solution : en vías de una solución⟩

roadblock ['ro:d,blɑk] *n* : control *m*

roadrunner ['ro:d,rʌnər] *n* : correcaminos *m*

roadside ['ro:d,saɪd] *n* : borde *m* de la carretera

roadway ['ro:d,weɪ] *n* : carretera *f*, calzada *f*

roam ['ro:m] *vi* : vagar, deambular, errar — *vt* : vagar por

roan¹ ['ro:n] *adj* : ruano

roan² *n* : caballo *m* ruano

roar¹ ['ror] *vi* : rugir, bramar ⟨to roar with laughter : reírse a carcajadas⟩ — *vt* : decir a gritos

roar² *n* **1** : rugido *m*, bramido *m* (de un animal) **2** DIN : clamor *m* (de gente), fragor *m* (del trueno), estruendo *m* (del tráfico, etc.)

roast¹ ['ro:st] *vt* : asar (carne, papas), tostar (café, nueces) — *vi* : asarse

roast² *adj* **1** : asado ⟨roast chicken : pollo asado⟩ **2 roast beef** : rosbif *m*

roast³ *n* : asado *m*

rob ['rɑb] *v* **robbed; robbing** *vt* **1** STEAL : robar **2** DEPRIVE : privar, quitar — *vi* : robar

robber ['rɑbər] *n* : ladrón *m*, -drona *f*

robbery ['rɑbəri] *n, pl* **-beries** : robo *m*

robe¹ ['ro:b] *vt* **robed; robing** : vestirse

robe² *n* **1** : toga *f* (de magistrados, etc.), sotana *f* (de eclesiásticos) ⟨robe of office : traje de ceremonias⟩ **2** BATHROBE : bata *f*

robin ['rɑbən] *n* : petirrojo *m*

robot ['ro:,bɑt, -bət] *n* : robot *m*

robotic [ro'bɑtɪk] *adj* : robótico, robotizado

robotics [ro'bɑtɪks] *ns & pl* : robótica *f*

robust [ro'bʌst, 'ro:,bʌst] *adj* : robusto, fuerte — **robustly** *adv*

rock¹ ['rɑk] *vt* **1** : acunar (a un niño), mecer (una cuna) **2** SHAKE : sacudir — *vi* SWAY : mecerse, balancearse

rock² *adj* : de rock

rock³ *n* **1** ROCKING : balanceo *m* **2** *or* **rock music** : rock *m*, música *f* rock **3** : roca *f* (substancia) **4** STONE : piedra *f*

rock and roll *n* : rock and roll *m*

rocker ['rɑkər] *n* **1** : balancín *m* **2** *or* **rocking chair** : mecedora *f*, balancín *m* **3 to be off one's rocker** : estar chiflado, estar loco

rocket¹ ['rɑkət] *vi* : dispararse, subir rápidamente

rocket² *n* : cohete *m*

rocking horse *n* : caballito *m* (de balancín)

rock salt *n* : sal *f* gema

rocky ['rɑki] *adj* **rockier; -est 1** : rocoso, pedregoso **2** UNSTEADY : inestable

rod ['rɑd] *n* **1** BAR : barra *f*, varilla *f*, vara *f* (de madera) ⟨a fishing rod : una caña (de pescar)⟩ **2** : medida *f* de longitud equivalente a 5.03 metros (5 yardas)

rode → **ride¹**

rodent ['ro:dənt] *n* : roedor *m*

rodeo ['ro:di,o:, ro'dei,o:] *n, pl* **-deos** : rodeo *m*

roe ['ro:] *n* : hueva *f*

rogue ['ro:g] *n* SCOUNDREL : pícaro *m*, -ra *f*; pillo *m*, -lla *f*

roguish ['ro:gɪʃ] *adj* : pícaro, travieso

role ['ro:l] *n* : papel *m*, función *f*, rol *m*

roll¹ ['ro:l] *vt* **1** : hacer rodar ⟨to roll the ball : hacer rodar la pelota⟩ ⟨to roll one's eyes : poner los ojos en blanco⟩ **2** : liar (un cigarrillo) **3** *or* **to roll up** : enrollar ⟨to roll (oneself) up into a ball : hacerse una bola⟩ **4** FLATTEN : estirar (masa), laminar (metales), pasar el rodillo por (el césped) **5 to roll up one's sleeves** : arremangarse — *vi* **1** : rodar ⟨the ball kept on rolling : la pelota siguió rodando⟩ **2** SWAY : balancearse ⟨the ship rolled in the waves : el barco se balanceó en las olas⟩ **3** REVERBERATE, SOUND : tronar (dícese del trueno), redoblar (dícese de un tambor) **4 to roll along** PROCEED : ponerse en marcha **5 to roll around** : revolcarse **6 to roll by** : pasar **7 to roll over** : dar una vuelta

roll² *n* **1** LIST : lista *f* ⟨to call the roll : pasar lista⟩ ⟨to have on the roll : tener inscrito⟩ **2** *or* **bread roll** : panecito *m*, bolillo *m* Mex **3** : rollo *m* (de papel, de tela, etc.) ⟨a roll of film : un carrete⟩ ⟨a roll of bills : un fajo⟩ **4** : redoble *m* (de tambores), retumbo *m* (del trueno, etc.) **5** ROLLING, SWAYING : balanceo *m*

roller ['ro:lər] *n* **1** : rodillo *m* **2** CURLER : rulo *m*

roller coaster ['ro:lər,ko:stər] *n* : montaña *f* rusa

roller–skate ['ro:lər,skeɪt] *vi* **-skated; -skating** : patinar (sobre ruedas)

roller skate *n* : patín *m* (de ruedas)

rollicking ['rɑlɪkɪŋ] *adj* : animado, alegre

rolling pin *n* : rodillo *m*

Roman¹ ['ro:mən] *adj* : romano

Roman² *n* : romano *m*, -na *f*

Roman Catholic *n* : católico *m*, -ca *f* — **Roman Catholic** *adj*

Roman Catholicism *n* : catolicismo *m*

romance¹ [ro'mænts, 'ro:,mænts] *vi* **-manced; -mancing** FANTASIZE : fantasear

romance² *n* **1** : romance *m*, novela *f* de caballerías **2** : novela *f* de amor, novela *f* romántica **3** AFFAIR : romance *m*, amorío *m*

Romanian [rʊ'meɪniən, ro-] *n* **1** : rumano *m*, -na *f* **2** : rumano *m* (idioma) — **Romanian** *adj*

Roman numeral *n* : número *m* romano

romantic [ro'mæntɪk] *adj* : romántico — **romantically** [-tɪkli] *adv*

romp¹ ['rɑmp] *vi* FROLIC : retozar, juguetear

romp² *n* : retozo *m*

roof¹ ['ru:f, 'rʊf] *vt* : techar

roof² *n, pl* **roofs** ['ru:fs, 'rʊfs; 'ru:vz, 'rʊvz] **1** : techo *m*, tejado *m*, techado *m* **2 roof of the mouth** : paladar *m*

roofing ['ru:fɪŋ, 'rʊfɪŋ] *n* : techumbre *f*

rooftop ['ru:f,tɑp, 'rʊf-] *n* ROOF : tejado *m*

rook¹ ['rʊk] *vt* CHEAT : defraudar, estafar, timar

rook² *n* **1** : grajo *m* (ave) **2** : torre *f* (en ajedrez)

rookie ['rʊki] *n* : novato *m*, -ta *f*

room¹ ['ru:m, 'rʊm] *vi* LODGE : alojarse, hospedarse

room² *n* **1** SPACE : espacio *m*, sitio *m*, lugar *m* ⟨to make room for : hacer lugar para⟩ **2** : cuarto *m*, habitación *f* (en una casa), sala *f* (para reuniones, etc.) **3** BEDROOM : dormitorio *m*, habitación *f* **4** (*indicating possibility or opportunity*) ⟨room for improvement : posibilidad de mejorar⟩ ⟨there's no room for error : no hay lugar para errores⟩

roomer ['ru:mər, 'rʊmər] *n* : inquilino *m*, -na *f*

rooming house *n* : pensión *f*

roommate ['ru:m,meɪt, 'rʊm-] *n* : compañero *m*, -ra *f* de cuarto

roomy ['ru:mi, 'rʊmi] *adj* **roomier; -est 1** SPACIOUS : espacioso, amplio **2** LOOSE : suelto, holgado ⟨a roomy blouse : una blusa holgada⟩

roost¹ ['ru:st] *vi* : posarse, dormir (en una percha)

roost² *n* : percha *f*

rooster ['ru:stər, 'rʊs-] *n* : gallo *m*

root¹ ['ru:t, 'rʊt] *vi* **1** : arraigar ⟨the plant rooted easily : la planta arraigó con facilidad⟩ ⟨deeply rooted traditions : tradiciones profundamente arraigadas⟩ **2** : hozar (dícese de los cerdos) ⟨to root around in : hurgar en⟩ **3 to root for** : apoyar a, alentar — *vt* **to root out** *or* **to root up** : desarraigar (plantas), extirpar (problemas, etc.)

root² *n* **1** : raíz *f* (de una planta) **2** ORIGIN : origen *m*, raíz *f* **3** CORE : centro *m*, núcleo *m* ⟨to get to the root of the matter : ir al centro del asunto⟩

rootless ['ru:tləs, 'rʊt-] *adj* : desarraigado

rope¹ ['ro:p] *vt* **roped; roping 1** TIE : amarrar, atar **2** LASSO : lazar **3 to rope off** : acordonar

rope² *n* : soga *f*, cuerda *f*

rosary ['ro:zəri] *n, pl* **-ries** : rosario *m*

rose¹ → **rise¹**

rose² ['ro:z] *adj* : rosa, color de rosa

rose³ *n* **1** : rosal *m* (planta), rosa *f* (flor) **2** : rosa *m* (color)

rosebush [ˈroːzˌbʊʃ] *n* : rosal *m*

rosemary [ˈroːzˌmɛri] *n*, *pl* **-maries** : romero *m*

rosette [roˈzɛt] *n* : escarapela *f* (hecho de cintas), roseta *f* (en arquitectura)

Rosh Hashanah [ˌraʃhaˈʃanə, ˌroːʃ-] *n* : el Año Nuevo judío

rosin [ˈrazən] *n* : colofonia *f*

roster [ˈrɑstər] *n* : lista *f*

rostrum [ˈrɑstrəm] *n*, *pl* **-trums** *or* **-tra** [-trə] : tribuna *f*, estrado *m*

rosy [ˈroːzi] *adj* **rosier; -est** **1** : sonrosado, de color rosa **2** PROMISING : prometedor, halagüeño

rot¹ [ˈrɑt] *v* **rotted; rotting** *vi* : pudrirse, descomponerse — *vt* : pudrir, descomponer

rot² *n* : putrefacción *f*, descomposición *f*, podredumbre *f*

rotary¹ [ˈroːt̬əri] *adj* : rotativo, rotatorio

rotary² *n*, *pl* **-ries** **1** : máquina *f* rotativa **2** TRAFFIC CIRCLE : rotonda *f*, glorieta *f*

rotate [ˈroːˌteɪt] *v* **-tated; -tating** *vi* REVOLVE : girar, rotar — *vt* **1** TURN : hacer girar, darle vueltas a **2** ALTERNATE : alternar

rotation [roˈteɪʃən] *n* : rotación *f*

rote [ˈroːt] *n* **to learn by rote** : aprender de memoria

rotor [ˈroːt̬ər] *n* : rotor *m*

rotten [ˈrɑtən] *adj* **1** PUTRID : podrido, putrefacto **2** CORRUPT : corrompido **3** BAD : malo ⟨a rotten day : un día malísimo⟩

rottenness [ˈrɑtənnəs] *n* : podredumbre *f*

rotund [roˈtʌnd] *adj* **1** ROUNDED : redondeado **2** PLUMP : regordete *fam*, llenito *fam*

rouge [ˈruːʒ, ˈruːdʒ] *n* : colorete *m*

rough¹ [ˈrʌf] *vt* **1** ROUGHEN : poner áspero **2 to rough out** SKETCH : esbozar, bosquejar **3 to rough up** BEAT : darle una paliza (a alguien) **4 to rough it** : vivir sin comodidades

rough² *adj* **1** COARSE : áspero, basto **2** UNEVEN : desigual, escabroso, accidentado (dícese del terreno) **3** : agitado (dícese del mar), tempestuoso (dícese del tiempo), violento (dícese del viento) **4** VIOLENT : violento, brutal ⟨a rough neighborhood : un barrio peligroso⟩ **5** DIFFICULT : duro, difícil **6** CRUDE : rudo, tosco, burdo ⟨a rough cottage : una casita tosca⟩ ⟨a rough draft : un borrador⟩ ⟨a rough sketch : un bosquejo⟩ **7** APPROXIMATE : aproximado ⟨a rough idea : una idea aproximada⟩

rough³ *n* **1 the rough** : el rough (en golf) **2 in the rough** : en borrador

roughage [ˈrʌfɪdʒ] *n* : fibra *f*

roughen [ˈrʌfən] *vt* : poner áspero — *vi* : ponerse áspero

roughly [ˈrʌfli] *adv* **1** : bruscamente ⟨to treat roughly : maltratar⟩ **2** CRUDELY : burdamente **3** APPROXIMATELY : aproximadamente, más o menos

roughneck [ˈrʌfˌnɛk] *n* : matón *m*

roughness [ˈrʌfnəs] *n* : rudeza *f*, aspereza *f*

roulette [ruːˈlɛt] *n* : ruleta *f*

round¹ [ˈraʊnd] *vt* **1** : redondear ⟨she rounded the edges : redondeó los bordes⟩ **2** TURN : doblar ⟨to round the corner : dar la vuelta a la esquina⟩ **3 to round off** : redondear (un número) **4 to round off** *or* **to round out** COMPLETE : rematar, terminar **5 to round up** GATHER : reunir

round² *adv* → **around**¹

round³ *adj* **1** : redondo ⟨a round table : una mesa redonda⟩ ⟨in round numbers : en números redondos⟩ ⟨round shoulders : espaldas cargadas⟩ **2 round trip** : viaje *m* de ida y vuelta

round⁴ *n* **1** CIRCLE : círculo *m* **2** SERIES : serie *f*, sucesión *f* ⟨a round of talks : una ronda de negociaciones⟩ ⟨the daily round : la rutina cotidiana⟩ **3** : asalto *m* (en boxeo), recorrido *m* (en golf), vuelta *f* (en varios juegos) **4** : salva *f* (de aplausos) **5 round of drinks** : ronda *f* **6 round of ammunition** : disparo *m*, cartucho *m* **7 rounds** *npl* : recorridos *mpl* (de un cartero), rondas *fpl* (de un vigilante), visitas *fpl* (de un médico) ⟨to make the rounds : hacer visitas⟩

round⁵ *prep* → **around**²

roundabout [ˈraʊndəˌbaʊt] *adj* : indirecto ⟨to speak in a roundabout way : hablar con rodeos⟩

roundly [ˈraʊndli] *adv* **1** THOROUGHLY : completamente **2** BLUNTLY : francamente, rotundamente **3** VIGOROUSLY : con vigor

roundness [ˈraʊndnəs] *n* : redondez *f*

roundup [ˈraʊndˌʌp] *n* **1** : rodeo *m* (de animales), redada *f* (de delincuentes, etc.) **2** SUMMARY : resumen *m*

round up *vt* **1** : rodear (ganado), reunir (personas) **2** SUMMARIZE : hacer un resumen de

roundworm [ˈraʊndˌwərm] *n* : lombriz *f* intestinal

rouse [ˈraʊz] *vt* **roused; rousing** **1** AWAKE : despertar **2** EXCITE : excitar ⟨it roused him to fury : lo enfureció⟩

rout¹ [ˈraʊt] *vt* **1** DEFEAT : derrotar, aplastar **2 to rout out** : hacer salir

rout² *n* **1** DISPERSAL : desbandada *f*, dispersión *f* **2** DEFEAT : derrota *f* aplastante

route¹ [ˈruːt, ˈraʊt] *vt* **routed; routing** : dirigir, enviar, encaminar

route² *n* : camino *m*, ruta *f*, recorrido *m*

routine¹ [ruːˈtiːn] *adj* : rutinario — **routinely** *adv*

routine² *n* : rutina *f*

rove [ˈroːv] *v* **roved; roving** *vi* : vagar, errar — *vt* : errar por

rover [ˈroːvər] *n* : vagabundo *m*, -da *f*

row¹ ['ro:] *vt* **1** : avanzar a remo ⟨to row a boat : remar⟩ **2** : llevar a remo ⟨he rowed me to shore : me llevó hasta la orilla⟩ — *vi* : remar

row² ['rau] *n* **1** : paseo *m* en barca ⟨to go for a row : salir a remar⟩ **2** LINE, RANK : fila *f*, hilera *f* **3** SERIES : serie *f* ⟨three days in a row : tres días seguidos⟩ **4** RACKET : estruendo *m*, bulla *f* **5** QUARREL : pelea *f*, riña *f*

rowboat ['ro:,bo:t] *n* : bote *m* de remos

rowdiness ['raudinəs] *n* : bulla *f*

rowdy¹ ['raudi] *adj* **-dier; -est** : escandaloso, alborotador

rowdy² *n, pl* **-dies** : alborotador *m*, -dora *f*

rower ['ro:ər] *n* : remero *m*, -ra *f*

royal¹ ['rɔɪəl] *adj* : real — **royally** *adv*

royal² *n* : persona de linaje real, miembro de la familia real

royalty ['rɔɪəlti] *n, pl* **-ties** **1** : realeza *f* (posición) **2** : miembros *mpl* de la familia real **3** **royalties** *npl* : derechos *mpl* de autor

rub¹ ['rʌb] *v* **rubbed; rubbing** *vt* **1** : frotar, restregar ⟨to rub one's hands together : frotarse las manos⟩ **2** MASSAGE : friccionar, masajear **3** CHAFE : rozar **4** POLISH : frotar, pulir **5** SCRUB : fregar **6 to rub elbows with** : codearse con **7 to rub someone the wrong way** : sacar de quicio a alguien, caerle mal a alguien — *vi* **to rub against** : rozar

rub² *n* **1** RUBBING : frotamiento *m*, fricción *f* **2** DIFFICULTY : problema *m*

rubber ['rʌbər] *n* **1** : goma *f*, caucho *m*, hule *m Mex* **2 rubbers** *npl* OVERSHOES : chanclos *mpl*

rubber band *n* : goma *f* (elástica), gomita *f*

rubber–stamp ['rʌbər'stæmp] *vt* **1** APPROVE : aprobar, autorizar **2** STAMP : sellar

rubber stamp *n* : sello *m* (de goma)

rubbery ['rʌbəri] *adj* : gomoso

rubbish ['rʌbɪʃ] *n* : basura *f*, desechos *mpl*, desperdicios *mpl*

rubble ['rʌbəl] *n* : escombros *mpl*, ripio *m*

ruble ['ru:bəl] *n* : rublo *m*

ruby ['ru:bi] *n, pl* **-bies** **1** : rubí *m* (gema) **2** : color *m* de rubí

rudder ['rʌdər] *n* : timón *m*

ruddy ['rʌdi] *adj* **-dier; -est** : rubicundo (dícese de la cara, etc.), rojizo (dícese del cielo)

rude ['ru:d] *adj* **ruder; rudest** **1** CRUDE : tosco, rústico **2** IMPOLITE : grosero, descortés, maleducado **3** ABRUPT : brusco ⟨a rude awakening : una sorpresa desagradable⟩

rudely ['ru:dli] *adv* : groseramente

rudeness ['ru:dnəs] *n* **1** IMPOLITENESS : grosería *f*, descortesía *f*, falta *f* de educación **2** ROUGHNESS : tosquedad *f* **3** SUDDENNESS : brusquedad *f*

rudiment ['ru:dəmənt] *n* : rudimento *m*, noción *f* básica ⟨the rudiments of Spanish : los rudimentos del español⟩

rudimentary [,ru:də'mɛntəri] *adj* : rudimentario, básico

rue ['ru:] *vt* **rued; ruing** : lamentar, arrepentirse de

rueful ['ru:fəl] *adj* **1** PITIFUL : lastimoso **2** REGRETFUL : arrepentido, pesaroso

ruffian ['rʌfiən] *n* : matón *m*

ruffle¹ ['rʌfəl] *vt* **-fled; -fling** **1** AGITATE : agitar, rizar (agua) **2** RUMPLE : arrugar (ropa), despeinar (pelo) **3** ERECT : erizar (plumas) **4** VEX : alterar, irritar, perturbar **5** : fruncir volantes en (tela)

ruffle² *n* FLOUNCE : volante *m*

ruffly ['rʌfəli] *adj* : con volantes

rug ['rʌg] *n* : alfombra *f*, tapete *m*

rugged ['rʌgəd] *adj* **1** ROUGH, UNEVEN : accidentado, escabroso ⟨rugged mountains : montañas accidentadas⟩ **2** HARSH : duro, severo **3** ROBUST, STURDY : robusto, fuerte

ruin¹ ['ru:ən] *vt* **1** DESTROY : destruir, arruinar **2** BANKRUPT : arruinar, hacer quebrar

ruin² *n* **1** : ruina *f* ⟨to fall into ruin : caer en ruinas⟩ **2** : ruina *f*, perdición *f* ⟨to be the ruin of : ser la perdición de⟩ **3 ruins** *npl* : ruinas *fpl*, restos *mpl* ⟨the ruins of the ancient temple : las ruinas del templo antiguo⟩

ruinous ['ru:ənəs] *adj* : ruinoso

rule¹ ['ru:l] *v* **ruled; ruling** *vt* **1** CONTROL, GOVERN : gobernar (un país), controlar (las emociones) **2** DECIDE : decidir, fallar ⟨the judge ruled that . . . : el juez falló que . . . ⟩ **3** DRAW : trazar con una regla — *vi* **1** GOVERN : gobernar, reinar **2** PREVAIL : prevalecer, imperar **3 to rule against** : fallar en contra de

rule² *n* **1** REGULATION : regla *f*, norma *f* **2** CUSTOM, HABIT : regla *f* general ⟨as a rule : por lo general⟩ **3** GOVERNMENT : gobierno *m*, dominio *m* **4** RULER : regla *f* (para medir)

ruler ['ru:lər] *n* **1** LEADER, SOVEREIGN : gobernante *mf*; soberano *m*, -na *f* **2** : regla *f* (para medir)

ruling ['ru:lɪŋ] *n* : resolución *f*, fallo *m*

rum ['rʌm] *n* : ron *m*

Rumanian [ru'meɪniən] → **Romanian**

rumble¹ ['rʌmbəl] *vi* **-bled; -bling** : retumbar, hacer ruidos (dícese del estómago)

rumble² *n* : estruendo *m*, ruido *m* sordo, retumbo *m*

ruminant¹ ['ru:mənənt] *adj* : rumiante

ruminant² *n* : rumiante *m*

ruminate ['ru:mə,neɪt] *vi* **-nated; -nating** **1** : rumiar (en zoología) **2** REFLECT : reflexionar, rumiar

rummage ['rʌmɪʤ] *v* **-maged; -maging** *vi* : hurgar — *vt* RANSACK : revolver ⟨they rummaged the attic : revolvieron el ático⟩

rummy ['rʌmi] *n* : rummy *m* (juego de naipes)

rumor[1] ['ru:mər] *vt* : rumorear ⟨it is rumored that . . . : se rumorea que . . ., se dice que . . . ⟩

rumor[2] *n* : rumor *m*

rump ['rʌmp] *n* 1 : ancas *fpl*, grupa *f* (de un animal) 2 : cadera *f* ⟨rump steak : filete de cadera⟩

rumple ['rʌmpəl] *vt* **-pled; -pling** : arrugar (ropa, etc.), despeinar (pelo)

rumpus ['rʌmpəs] *n* : lío *m*, jaleo *m fam*

run[1] ['rʌn] *v* **ran** ['ræn]; **run; running** *vi* 1 : correr ⟨she ran to catch the bus : corrió para alcanzar el autobús⟩ ⟨run and fetch the doctor : corre a buscar al médico⟩ 2 : circular, correr ⟨the train runs between Detroit and Chicago : el tren circula entre Detroit y Chicago⟩ ⟨to run on time : ser puntual⟩ 3 FUNCTION : funcionar, ir ⟨the engine runs on gasoline : el motor funciona con gasolina⟩ ⟨to run smoothly : ir bien⟩ 4 FLOW : correr, ir 5 LAST : durar ⟨the movie runs for two hours : la película dura dos horas⟩ ⟨the contract runs for three years : el contrato es válido por tres años⟩ 6 : desteñir, despintar (dícese de los colores) 7 EXTEND : correr, extenderse 8 **to run for office** : postularse, presentarse — *vt* 1 : correr ⟨to run 10 miles : correr 10 millas⟩ ⟨to run errands : hacer los mandados⟩ ⟨to run out of town : hacer salir del pueblo⟩ 2 PASS : pasar 3 DRIVE : llevar en coche 4 OPERATE : hacer funcionar (un motor, etc.) 5 : echar ⟨to run water : echar agua⟩ 6 MANAGE : dirigir, llevar (un negocio, etc.) 7 EXTEND : tender (un cable, etc.) 8 **to run a risk** : correr un riesgo

run[2] *n* 1 : carrera *f* ⟨at a run : a la carrera, corriendo⟩ 2 TRIP : vuelta *f*, paseo *m* (en coche), viaje *m* (en avión) 3 SERIES : serie *f* ⟨a run of disappointments : una serie de desilusiones⟩ ⟨in the long run : a la larga⟩ ⟨in the short run : a corto plazo⟩ 4 DEMAND : gran demanda *f* ⟨a run on the banks : una corrida bancaria⟩ 5 (*used for theatrical productions and films*) ⟨to have a long run : mantenerse mucho tiempo en la cartelera⟩ 6 TYPE : tipo *m* ⟨the average run of students : el tipo más común de estudiante⟩ 7 : carrera *f* (en béisbol) 8 : carrera *f* (en una media) 9 **to have the run of** : tener libre acceso de (una casa, etc.) 10 **ski run** : pista *f* (de esquí)

runaway[1] ['rʌnə,weɪ] *adj* 1 FUGITIVE : fugitivo 2 UNCONTROLLABLE : incontrolable, fuera de control ⟨runaway inflation : inflación desenfrenada⟩ ⟨a runaway success : un éxito aplastante⟩

runaway[2] *n* : fugitivo *m*, -va *f*

rundown ['rʌn,daʊn] *n* SUMMARY : resumen *m*

run–down ['rʌn'daʊn] *adj* 1 DILAPIDATED : ruinoso, destartalado 2 SICKLY, TIRED : cansado, débil

rung[1] *pp* → **ring**[1]

rung[2] ['rʌŋ] *n* : peldaño *m*, escalón *m*

run–in ['rʌn,ɪn] *n* : disputa *f*, altercado *m*

runner ['rʌnər] *n* 1 RACER : corredor *m*, -dora *f* 2 MESSENGER : mensajero *m*, -ra *f* 3 TRACK : riel *m* (de un cajón, etc.) 4 : patín *m* (de un trineo), cuchilla *f* (de un patín) 5 : estolón *m* (planta)

runner–up [,rʌnər'ʌp] *n, pl* **runners–up** : subcampeón *m*, -peona *f*

running ['rʌnɪŋ] *adj* 1 FLOWING : corriente ⟨running water : agua corriente⟩ 2 CONTINUOUS : continuo ⟨a running battle : una lucha continua⟩ 3 CONSECUTIVE : seguido ⟨six days running : por seis días seguidos⟩

runny ['rʌni] *adj* **-nier; -est** 1 WATERY : caldoso 2 **to have a runny nose** : moquear

run over *vt* : atropellar — *vi* OVERFLOW : rebosar

runt ['rʌnt] *n* : animal *m* pequeño ⟨the runt of the litter : el más pequeño de la camada⟩

runway ['rʌn,weɪ] *n* : pista *f* de aterrizaje

rupee [ru:'pi:, 'ru:,-] *n* : rupia *f*

rupture[1] ['rʌptʃər] *v* **-tured; -turing** *vt* 1 BREAK, BURST : romper, reventar 2 : causar una hernia en — *vi* : reventarse

rupture[2] *n* 1 BREAK : ruptura *f* 2 HERNIA : hernia *f*

rural ['rʊrəl] *adj* : rural, campestre

ruse ['ru:s, 'ru:z] *n* : treta *f*, ardid *m*, estratagema *f*

rush[1] ['rʌʃ] *vi* : correr, ir de prisa ⟨to rush around : correr de un lado a otro⟩ ⟨to rush off : irse corriendo⟩ — *vt* 1 HURRY : apresurar, apurar 2 ATTACK : abalanzarse sobre, asaltar

rush[2] *adj* : urgente

rush[3] *n* 1 HASTE : prisa *f*, apuro *m* 2 SURGE : ráfaga *f* (de aire), torrente *m* (de aguas), avalancha *f* (de gente) 3 DEMAND : demanda *f* ⟨a rush on sugar : una gran demanda para el azúcar⟩ 4 : carga *f* (en futbol americano) 5 : junco *m* (planta)

russet ['rʌsət] *n* : color *m* rojizo

Russian ['rʌʃən] *n* 1 : ruso *m*, -sa *f* 2 : ruso *m* (idioma) — **Russian** *adj*

rust[1] ['rʌst] *vi* : oxidarse — *vt* : oxidar

rust[2] *n* 1 : herrumbre *f*, orín *m*, óxido *m* (en los metales) 2 : roya *f* (en las plantas)

rustic[1] ['rʌstɪk] *adj* : rústico, campestre — **rustically** [-tɪkli] *adv*

rustic[2] *n* : rústico *m*, -ca *f*; campesino *m*, -na *f*

rustle[1] ['rʌsəl] *v* **-tled; -tling** *vt* 1 : hacer susurrar, hacer crujir ⟨to rustle a newspaper : hacer crujir un periódico⟩ 2 STEAL : robar (ganado) — *vi* : susurrar, crujir

rustle² *n* : murmullo *m*, susurro *m*, crujido *m*

rustler ['rʌsələr] *n* : ladrón *m*, -drona *f* de ganado

rusty ['rʌsti] *adj* **rustier; -est** : oxidado, herrumbroso

rut ['rʌt] *n* **1** GROOVE, TRACK : rodada *f*, surco *m* **2 to be in a rut** : ser esclavo de la rutina

ruthless ['ru:θləs] *adj* : despiadado, cruel — **ruthlessly** *adv*

ruthlessness ['ru:θləsnəs] *n* : crueldad *f*, falta *f* de piedad

Rwandan [rʊˈɑndən] *n* : ruandés *m*, -desa *f* — **Rwandan** *adj*

rye ['raɪ] *n* **1** : centeno *m* **2** *or* **rye whiskey** : whisky *m* de centeno

S

s ['ɛs] *n*, *pl* **s's** *or* **ss** ['ɛsəz] : decimonovena letra del alfabeto inglés

Sabbath ['sæbəθ] *n* **1** : sábado *m* (en el judaísmo) **2** : domingo *m* (en el cristianismo)

saber ['seɪbər] *n* : sable *m*

sable ['seɪbəl] *n* **1** BLACK : negro *m* **2** : marta *f* cebellina (animal)

sabotage¹ ['sæbəˌtɑʒ] *vt* **-taged; -taging** : sabotear

sabotage² *n* : sabotaje *m*

sac ['sæk] *n* : saco *m* (anatómico)

saccharin ['sækərən] *n* : sacarina *f*

saccharine ['sækərən, -ˌriːn, -ˌraɪn] *adj* : meloso, empalagoso

sachet [sæˈʃeɪ] *n* : bolsita *f* (perfumada)

sack¹ ['sæk] *vt* **1** FIRE : echar (del trabajo), despedir **2** PLUNDER : saquear

sack² *n* BAG : saco *m*

sacrament ['sækrəmənt] *n* : sacramento *m*

sacramental [ˌsækrəˈmɛntəl] *adj* : sacramental

sacred ['seɪkrəd] *adj* **1** RELIGIOUS : sagrado, sacro ⟨sacred texts : textos sagrados⟩ **2** HOLY : sagrado **3 sacred to** : consagrado a

sacrifice¹ ['sækrəˌfaɪs] *vt* **-ficed; -ficing 1** : sacrificar **2 to sacrifice oneself** : sacrificarse

sacrifice² *n* : sacrificio *m*

sacrilege ['sækrəlɪdʒ] *n* : sacrilegio *m*

sacrilegious [ˌsækrəˈlɪdʒəs, -ˈliː-] *adj* : sacrílego

sacrosanct ['sækroˌsæŋkt] *adj* : sacrosanto

sad ['sæd] *adj* **sadder; saddest** : triste — **sadly** *adv*

sadden ['sædən] *vt* : entristecer

saddle¹ ['sædəl] *vt* **-dled; -dling** : ensillar

saddle² *n* : silla *f* (de montar)

sadism ['seɪˌdɪzəm, 'sæ-] *n* : sadismo *m*

sadist ['seɪdɪst, 'sæ-] *n* : sádico *m*, -ca *f*

sadistic [səˈdɪstɪk] *adj* : sádico — **sadistically** [-tɪkli] *adv*

sadness ['sædnəs] *n* : tristeza *f*

safari [səˈfɑri, -ˈfær-] *n* : safari *m*

safe¹ ['seɪf] *adj* **safer; safest 1** UNHARMED : ileso ⟨safe and sound : sano y salvo⟩ **2** SECURE : seguro **3 to be on the safe side** : para mayor seguridad **4 to play it safe** : ir a la segura

safe² *n* : caja *f* fuerte

safeguard¹ ['seɪfˌgɑrd] *vt* : salvaguardar, proteger

safeguard² *n* : salvaguarda *f*, protección *f*

safekeeping ['seɪfˈkiːpɪŋ] *n* : custodia *f*, protección *f* ⟨to put into safekeeping : poner en buen recaudo⟩

safely ['seɪfli] *adv* **1** UNHARMED : sin incidentes, sin novedades ⟨they landed safely : aterrizaron sin novedades⟩ **2** SECURELY : con toda seguridad, sin peligro

safety ['seɪfti] *n*, *pl* **-ties** : seguridad *f*

safety belt *n* : cinturón *m* de seguridad

safety pin *n* : alfiler *m* de gancho, alfiler *m* de seguridad, imperdible *m* *Spain*

saffron ['sæfrən] *n* : azafrán *m*

sag¹ ['sæg] *vi* **sagged; sagging 1** DROOP, SINK : combarse, hundirse, inclinarse **2** : colgar, caer ⟨his jowls sagged : le colgaban las mejillas⟩ **3** FLAG : flaquear, decaer ⟨his spirits sagged : se le flaqueó el ánimo⟩

sag² *n* : combadura *f*

saga ['sɑgə, 'sæ-] *n* : saga *f*

sagacious [səˈgeɪʃəs] *adj* : sagaz

sage¹ ['seɪdʒ] *adj* **sager; -est** : sabio — **sagely** *adv*

sage² *n* **1** : sabio *m*, -bia *f* **2** : salvia *f* (planta)

sagebrush ['seɪdʒˌbrʌʃ] *n* : artemisa *f*

Sagittarius [ˌsædʒəˈtɛriəs] *n* : Sagitario *mf*

said → **say**

sail¹ ['seɪl] *vi* **1** : navegar (en un barco) **2** : ir fácilmente ⟨we sailed right in : entramos sin ningún problema⟩ — *vt* **1** : gobernar (un barco) **2 to sail the seas** : cruzar los mares

sail² *n* **1** : vela *f* (de un barco) **2** : viaje *m* en velero ⟨to go for a sail : salir a navegar⟩

sailboat ['seɪlˌboːt] *n* : velero *m*, barco *m* de vela

sailfish ['seɪlˌfɪʃ] *n* : pez *m* vela

sailor ['seɪlər] *n* : marinero *m*

saint ['seɪnt, *before a name* ˌseɪnt *or* sənt] *n* : santo *m*, -ta *f* ⟨Saint Francis : San Francisco⟩ ⟨Saint Rose : Santa Rosa⟩

saintliness ['seɪntlinəs] *n* : santidad *f*

saintly ['seɪntli] *adj* **saintlier; -est** : santo

sake ['seɪk] *n* **1** BENEFIT : bien *m* ⟨for the children's sake : por el bien de los niños⟩ **2** (*indicating an end or a purpose*) ⟨art for art's sake : el arte por el arte⟩ ⟨let's say, for argument's sake, that he's wrong : pongamos que está equivocado⟩ **3 for goodness' sake!** : ¡por (el amor de) Dios!

salable *or* **saleable** ['seɪləbəl] *adj* : vendible

salacious [sə'leɪʃəs] *adj* : salaz — **salaciously** *adv*

salad ['sæləd] *n* : ensalada *f*

salamander ['sælə,mændər] *n* : salamandra *f*

salami [sə'lɑmi] *n* : salami *m*

salary ['sæləri] *n, pl* **-ries** : sueldo *m*

sale ['seɪl] *n* **1** SELLING : venta *f* **2** : liquidación *f*, rebajas *fpl* ⟨on sale : de rebaja⟩ **3 sales** *npl* : ventas *fpl* ⟨to work in sales : trabajar en ventas⟩

salesman ['seɪlzmən] *n, pl* **-men** [-mən, -,mɛn] **1** : vendedor *m*, dependiente *m* (en una tienda) **2 traveling salesman** : viajante *m*

salesperson ['seɪlz,pərsən] *n* : vendedor *m*, -dora *f*; dependiente *m*, -ta *f* (en una tienda)

saleswoman ['seɪlz,wumən] *n, pl* **-women** [-,wɪmən] **1** : vendedora *f*, dependienta *f* (en una tienda) **2 traveling saleswoman** : viajante *f*, representante *f*

salient ['seɪljənt] *adj* : saliente, sobresaliente

saline ['seɪ,li:n, -,laɪn] *adj* : salino

saliva [sə'laɪvə] *n* : saliva *f*

salivary ['sælə,vɛri] *adj* : salival ⟨salivary gland : glándula salival⟩

salivate ['sælə,veɪt] *vi* **-vated; -vating** : salivar

sallow ['sælo:] *adj* : amarillento, cetrino

sally¹ ['sæli] *vi* **-lied; -lying** SET OUT : salir, hacer una salida

sally² *n, pl* **-lies 1** : salida *f* (militar), misión *f* **2** QUIP : salida *f*, ocurrencia *f*

salmon ['sæmən] *ns & pl* **1** : salmón *m* (pez) **2** : color *m* salmón

salon [sə'lɑn, 'sæ,lɑn, sæ'lɔ̃] *n* : salón *m* ⟨beauty salon : salón de belleza⟩

saloon [sə'lu:n] *n* **1** HALL : salón *m* (en un barco) **2** BARROOM : bar *m*

salsa ['sɑlsə, 'sɑl-] *n* : salsa *f* mexicana, salsa *f* picante

salt¹ ['sɔlt] *vt* : salar, echarle sal a

salt² *adj* : salado

salt³ *n* : sal *f*

saltwater ['sɔlt,wɔtər, -,wɑ-] *adj* : de agua salada

salty ['sɔlti] *adj* **saltier; -est** : salado

salubrious [sə'lu:briəs] *adj* : salubre

salutary ['sæljə,tɛri] *adj* : saludable, salubre

salutation [,sæljə'teɪʃən] *n* : saludo *m*, salutación *f*

salute¹ [sə'lu:t] *v* **-luted; -luting** *vt* **1** : saludar (con gestos o ceremonias) **2** ACCLAIM : reconocer, aclamar — *vi* : hacer un saludo

salute² *n* **1** : saludo *m* (gesto), salva *f* (de cañonazos) **2** TRIBUTE : reconocimiento *m*, homenaje *m*

Salvadoran [,sælvə'dorən] → **El Salvadoran**

salvage¹ ['sælvɪʤ] *vt* **-vaged; -vaging** : salvar, rescatar

salvage² *n* **1** SALVAGING : salvamento *m*, rescate *m* **2** : objetos *mpl* salvados

salvation [sæl'veɪʃən] *n* : salvación *f*

salve¹ ['sæv, 'sav] *vt* **salved; salving** : calmar, apaciguar ⟨to salve one's conscience : aliviarse la conciencia⟩

salve² *n* : ungüento *m*

salvo ['sæl,vo:] *n, pl* **-vos** *or* **-voes** : salva *f*

same¹ ['seɪm] *adj* : mismo, igual ⟨the results are the same : los resultados son iguales⟩ ⟨he said the same thing as you : dijo lo mismo que tú⟩

same² *pron* : mismo ⟨it's all the same to me : me da lo mismo⟩ ⟨the same to you! : ¡igualmente!⟩

sameness ['seɪmnəs] *n* **1** SIMILARITY : identidad *f*, semejanza *f* **2** MONOTONY : monotonía *f*

sample¹ ['sæmpəl] *vt* **-pled; -pling** : probar

sample² *n* : muestra *f*, prueba *f*

sampler ['sæmplər] *n* **1** : dechado *m* (de bordado) **2** COLLECTION : colección *f* **3** ASSORTMENT : surtido *m*

sanatorium [,sænə'toriəm] *n, pl* **-riums** *or* **-ria** [-iə] : sanatorio *m*

sanctify ['sæŋktə,faɪ] *vt* **-fied; -fying** : santificar

sanctimonious [,sæŋktə'mo:niəs] *adj* : beato, santurrón

sanction¹ ['sæŋkʃən] *vt* : sancionar, aprobar

sanction² *n* **1** AUTHORIZATION : sanción *f*, autorización *f* **2 sanctions** *npl* : sanciones *fpl* ⟨to impose sanctions on : imponer sanciones a⟩

sanctity ['sæŋktəti] *n, pl* **-ties** : santidad *f*

sanctuary ['sæŋktʃu,ɛri] *n, pl* **-aries 1** : presbiterio *m* (en una iglesia) **2** REFUGE : refugio *m*, asilo *m*

sand¹ ['sænd] *vt* : lijar (madera)

sand² *n* : arena *f*

sandal ['sændəl] *n* : sandalia *f*

sandbank ['sænd,bæŋk] *n* : banco *m* de arena

sandpaper *n* : papel *m* de lija

sandpiper ['sænd,paɪpər] *n* : andarríos *m*

sandstone ['sænd,sto:n] *n* : arenisca *f*

sandstorm ['sænd,stɔrm] *n* : tormenta *f* de arena

sandwich¹ ['sænd,wɪtʃ] *vt* : intercalar, encajonar, meter (entre dos cosas)

sandwich² *n* : sandwich *m*, emparedado *m*, bocadillo *m* Spain

sandy ['sændi] *adj* **sandier; -est** : arenoso

sane ['seɪn] *adj* **saner; sanest 1** : cuerdo **2** SENSIBLE : sensato, razonable

sang → **sing**

sanguine [ˈsæŋgwən] *adj* **1** RUDDY : sanguíneo, rubicundo **2** HOPEFUL : optimista

sanitarium [ˌsænəˈtɛriəm] *n, pl* **-iums** *or* **-ia** [-iə] → **sanatorium**

sanitary [ˈsænəteri] *adj* **1** : sanitario ⟨sanitary measures : medidas sanitarias⟩ **2** HYGIENIC : higiénico **3 sanitary napkin** : compresa *f*, paño *m* higiénico

sanitation [ˌsænəˈteɪʃən] *n* : sanidad *f*

sanitize [ˈsænəˌtaɪz] *vt* **-tized; -tizing 1** : desinfectar **2** EXPURGATE : expurgar

sanity [ˈsænəti] *n* : cordura *f*, razón *f* ⟨to lose one's sanity : perder el juicio⟩

sank → **sink**

Santa Claus [ˈsæntəˌklɔz] *n* : Papá Noel, San Nicolás

sap[1] [ˈsæp] *vt* **sapped; sapping 1** UNDERMINE : socavar **2** WEAKEN : minar, debilitar

sap[2] *n* **1** : savia *f* (de una planta) **2** SUCKER : inocentón *m*, -tona *f*

sapling [ˈsæplɪŋ] *n* : árbol *m* joven

sapphire [ˈsæˌfaɪr] *n* : zafiro *m*

sarcasm [ˈsɑrˌkæzəm] *n* : sarcasmo *m*

sarcastic [sɑrˈkæstɪk] *adj* : sarcástico — **sarcastically** [-tɪkli] *adv*

sarcophagus [sɑrˈkɑfəgəs] *n, pl* **-gi** [-ˌgaɪ, -ˌdʒaɪ] : sarcófago *m*

sardine [sɑrˈdiːn] *n* : sardina *f*

sardonic [sɑrˈdɑnɪk] *adj* : sardónico — **sardonically** [-nɪkli] *adv*

sarsaparilla [ˌsæspəˈrɪlə, ˌsɑrs-] *n* : zarzaparrilla *f*

sash [ˈsæʃ] *n* **1** : faja *f* (de un vestido), fajín *m* (de un uniforme) **2** *pl* **sash** : marco *m* (de una ventana)

sassafras [ˈsæsəˌfræs] *n* : sasafrás *m*

sassy [ˈsæsi] *adj* **sassier; -est** → **saucy**

sat → **sit**

Satan [ˈseɪtən] *n* : Satanás *m*, Satán *m*

satanic [səˈtænɪk, seɪ-] *adj* : satánico — **satanically** [-nɪkli] *adv*

satchel [ˈsætʃəl] *n* : cartera *f*, saco *m*

sate [ˈseɪt] *vt* **sated; sating** : saciar

satellite [ˈsætəˌlaɪt] *n* : satélite *m* ⟨spy satellite : satélite espía⟩

satiate [ˈseɪʃiˌeɪt] *vt* **-ated; -ating** : saciar, hartar

satin [ˈsætən] *n* : raso *m*, satín *m*, satén *m*

satire [ˈsæˌtaɪr] *n* : sátira *f*

satiric [səˈtɪrɪk] *or* **satirical** [-ɪkəl] *adj* : satírico

satirize [ˈsætəˌraɪz] *vt* **-rized; -rizing** : satirizar

satisfaction [ˌsætəsˈfækʃən] *n* : satisfacción *f*

satisfactory [ˌsætəsˈfæktəri] *adj* : satisfactorio, bueno — **satisfactorily** [-rəli] *adv*

satisfy [ˈsætəsˌfaɪ] *v* **-fied; -fying** *vt* **1** PLEASE : satisfacer, contentar **2** CONVINCE : convencer **3** FULFILL : satisfacer, cumplir con, llenar **4** SETTLE : pagar, saldar (una cuenta) — *vi* SUFFICE : bastar

saturate [ˈsætʃəˌreɪt] *vt* **-rated; -rating 1** SOAK : empapar **2** FILL : saturar

saturation [ˌsætʃəˈreɪʃən] *n* : saturación *f*

Saturday [ˈsætərˌdeɪ, -di] *n* : sábado *m*

Saturn [ˈsætərn] *n* : Saturno *m*

satyr [ˈseɪtər, ˈsæ-] *n* : sátiro *m*

sauce [ˈsɔs] *n* : salsa *f*

saucepan [ˈsɔsˌpæn] *n* : cacerola *f*, cazo *m*, cazuela *f*

saucer [ˈsɔsər] *n* : platillo *m*

sauciness [ˈsɔsinəs] *n* : descaro *m*, frescura *f*

saucy [ˈsɔsi] *adj* **saucier; -est** IMPUDENT : descarado, fresco *fam* — **saucily** *adv*

Saudi [ˈsaudi, ˈsɔ-] → **Saudi Arabian**

Saudi Arabian *n* : saudita *mf*, saudí *mf* — **Saudi Arabian** *adj*

sauna [ˈsɔnə, ˈsaunə] *n* : sauna *mf*

saunter [ˈsɔntər, ˈsɑn-] *vi* : pasear, parsearse

sausage [ˈsɔsɪdʒ] *n* : salchicha *f*, embutido *m*

sauté [soˈteɪ, sɔ-] *vt* **-téed** *or* **-téd; -téing** : saltear, sofreír

savage[1] [ˈsævɪdʒ] *adj* : salvaje, feroz — **savagely** *adv*

savage[2] *n* : salvaje *mf*

savagery [ˈsævɪdʒri, -dʒəri] *n, pl* **-ries 1** FEROCITY : ferocidad *f* **2** WILDNESS : salvajismo *m*

savanna [səˈvænə] *n* : sabana *f*

save[1] [ˈseɪv] *vt* **saved; saving 1** RESCUE : salvar, rescatar **2** PRESERVE : preservar, conservar **3** KEEP : guardar, ahorrar (dinero), almacenar (alimentos) **4** : guardar (en informática)

save[2] *prep* EXCEPT : salvo, excepto, menos

savior [ˈseɪvjər] *n* **1** : salvador *m*, -dora *f* **2 the Savior** : el Salvador *m*

savor[1] [ˈseɪvər] *vt* : saborear

savor[2] *n* : sabor *m*

savory [ˈseɪvəri] *adj* : sabroso

saw[1] → **see**

saw[2] [ˈsɔ] *vt* **sawed; sawed** *or* **sawn** [ˈsɔn]; **sawing** : serrar, cortar (con sierra)

saw[3] *n* : sierra *f*

sawdust [ˈsɔˌdʌst] *n* : aserrín *m*, serrín *m*

sawhorse [ˈsɔˌhɔrs] *n* : caballete *m*, burro *m* (en carpintería)

sawmill [ˈsɔˌmɪl] *n* : aserradero *m*

saxophone [ˈsæksəˌfoːn] *n* : saxofón *m*

say[1] [ˈseɪ] *v* **said** [ˈsɛd]; **saying; says** [ˈsɛz] *vt* **1** EXPRESS, UTTER : decir, expresar ⟨to say no : decir que no⟩ ⟨that goes without saying : ni que decir tiene⟩ ⟨no sooner said than done : dicho y hecho⟩ ⟨to say again : repetir⟩ ⟨to say one's prayers : rezar⟩ **2** INDICATE : marcar, poner ⟨my watch says three o'clock : mi reloj marca las tres⟩ ⟨what does the sign say? : ¿qué pone el letrero?⟩ **3** ALLEGE : decir ⟨it's said that she's pretty : se dice que es bonita⟩ — *vi* : decir

say² *n, pl* **says** [ˈseɪz] : voz *f*, opinión *f* ⟨to have no say : no tener ni voz ni voto⟩ ⟨to have one's say : dar uno su opinión⟩

saying [ˈseɪɪŋ] *n* : dicho *m*, refrán *m*

scab [ˈskæb] *n* **1** : costra *f*, postilla *f* (en una herida) **2** STRIKEBREAKER : rompehuelgas *mf*, esquirol *mf*

scabbard [ˈskæbərd] *n* : vaina *f* (de una espada), funda *f* (de un puñal, etc.)

scabby [ˈskæbi] *adj* **scabbier; -est** : lleno de costras

scaffold [ˈskæfəld, -ˌfoːld] *n* **1** *or* **scaffolding** : andamio *m* (para obreros, etc.) **2** : patíbulo *m*, cadalso *m* (para ejecuciones)

scald [ˈskɔld] *vt* **1** BURN : escaldar **2** HEAT : calentar (hasta el punto de ebullición)

scale¹ [ˈskeɪl] *v* **scaled; scaling** *vt* **1** : escamar (un pescado) **2** CLIMB : escalar (un muro, etc.) **3 to scale down** : reducir — *vi* WEIGH : pesar ⟨he scaled in at 200 pounds : pesó 200 libras⟩

scale² *n* **1** *or* **scales** : balanza *f*, báscula *f* (para pesar) **2** : escama *f* (de un pez, etc.) **3** EXTENT : escala *f*, proporción *f* ⟨wage scale : escala salarial⟩ **4** : escala *f* (en música, en cartografía, etc.) ⟨to draw to scale : dibujar a escala⟩

scallion [ˈskæljən] *n* : cebollino *m*, cebolleta *f*

scallop [ˈskɑləp, ˈskæ-] *n* **1** : vieira *f* (molusco) **2** : festón *m* (decoración)

scalp¹ [ˈskælp] *vt* : arrancar la cabellera a

scalp² *n* : cuero *m* cabelludo

scalpel [ˈskælpəl] *n* : bisturí *m*, escalpelo *m*

scaly [ˈskeɪli] *adj* **scalier; -est** : escamoso

scam [ˈskæm] *n* : estafa *f*, timo *m fam*, chanchullo *m fam*

scamp [ˈskæmp] *n* : bribón *m*, -bona *f*; granuja *mf*; travieso *m*, -sa *f*

scamper [ˈskæmpər] *vi* : corretear

scan¹ [ˈskæn] *vt* **scanned; scanning 1** : escandir (versos) **2** SCRUTINIZE : escudriñar, escrutar ⟨to scan the horizon : escudriñar el horizonte⟩ **3** PERUSE : echarle un vistazo a (un periódico, etc.) **4** EXPLORE : explorar (con radar), hacer un escáner de (en ecografía) **5** : escanear (una imagen)

scan² *n* **1** : ecografía *f*, examen *m* ultrasónico (en medicina) **2** : imagen *f* escaneada (en una computadora)

scandal [ˈskændəl] *n* **1** DISGRACE, OUTRAGE : escándalo *m* **2** GOSSIP : habladurías *fpl*, chismes *mpl*

scandalize [ˈskændəlˌaɪz] *vt* **-ized; -izing** : escandalizar

scandalous [ˈskændələs] *adj* : de escándalo

Scandinavian¹ [ˌskændəˈneɪviən] *adj* : escandinavo

Scandinavian² *n* : escandinavo *m*, -va *f*

scanner [ˈskænər] *n* : escáner *m*, scanner *m*

scant [ˈskænt] *adj* : escaso

scanty [ˈskænti] *adj* **scantier; -est** : exiguo, escaso ⟨a scanty meal : una comida insuficiente⟩ — **scantily** [-təli] *adv*

scapegoat [ˈskeɪpˌgoːt] *n* : chivo *m* expiatorio, cabeza *f* de turco

scapula [ˈskæpjələ] *n, pl* **-lae** [-ˌliː, -ˌlaɪ] *or* **-las** → **shoulder blade**

scar¹ [ˈskɑr] *v* **scarred; scarring** *vt* : dejar una cicatriz en — *vi* : cicatrizar

scar² *n* : cicatriz *f*, marca *f*

scarab [ˈskærəb] *n* : escarabajo *m*

scarce [ˈskɛrs] *adj* **scarcer; -est** : escaso

scarcely [ˈskɛrsli] *adv* **1** BARELY : apenas **2** : ni mucho menos, ni nada que se le parezca ⟨he's scarcely an expert : ciertamente no es experto⟩

scarcity [ˈskɛrsəti] *n, pl* **-ties** : escasez *f*

scare¹ [ˈskɛr] *vt* **scared; scaring** : asustar, espantar

scare² *n* **1** FRIGHT : susto *m*, sobresalto *m* **2** ALARM : pánico *m*

scarecrow [ˈskɛrˌkroː] *n* : espantapájaros *m*, espantajo *m*

scarf [ˈskɑrf] *n, pl* **scarves** [ˈskɑrvz] *or* **scarfs 1** MUFFLER : bufanda *f* **2** KERCHIEF : pañuelo *m*

scarlet [ˈskɑrlət] *n* : escarlata *f* — **scarlet** *adj*

scarlet fever *n* : escarlatina *f*

scary [ˈskɛri] *adj* **scarier; -est** : espantoso, pavoroso

scathing [ˈskeɪðɪŋ] *adj* : mordaz, cáustico

scatter [ˈskætər] *vt* : esparcir, desparramar — *vi* DISPERSE : dispersarse

scavenge [ˈskævəndʒ] *v* **-venged; -venging** *vt* : rescatar (de la basura), pepenar *CA, Mex* — *vi* : rebuscar, hurgar en la basura ⟨to scavenge for food : andar buscando comida⟩

scavenger [ˈskævəndʒər] *n* **1** : persona *f* que rebusca en las basuras; pepenador *m*, -dora *f CA, Mex* **2** : carroñero *m*, -ra *f* (animal)

scenario [səˈnæriˌoː, -ˈnɑr-] *n, pl* **-ios 1** PLOT : argumento *m* (en teatro), guión *m* (en cine) **2** SITUATION : situación *f* hipotética ⟨in the worst-case scenario : en el peor de los casos⟩

scene [ˈsiːn] *n* **1** : escena *f* (en una obra de teatro) **2** SCENERY : decorado *m* (en el teatro) **3** VIEW : escena *f* **4** LOCALE : escenario *m* **5** COMMOTION, FUSS : escándalo *m*, escena *f* ⟨to make a scene : armar un escándalo⟩

scenery [ˈsiːnəri] *n, pl* **-eries 1** : decorado *m* (en el teatro) **2** LANDSCAPE : paisaje *m*

scenic [ˈsiːnɪk] *adj* : pintoresco

scent¹ [ˈsɛnt] *vt* **1** SMELL : oler, olfatear **2** PERFUME : perfumar **3** SENSE : sentir, percibir

scent² *n* **1** ODOR : olor *m*, aroma *m* **2** : olfato *m* ⟨a dog with a keen scent : un

perro con un buen olfato⟩ **3** PERFUME
: perfume *m*
scented [ˈsɛntəd] *adj* : perfumado
scepter [ˈsɛptər] *n* : cetro *m*
sceptic [ˈskɛptɪk] → **skeptic**
schedule[1] [ˈskɛˌdʒuːl, -dʒəl, *esp Brit*
ˈʃɛdˌjuːl] *vt* **-uled; -uling** : planear, programar
schedule[2] *n* **1** PLAN : programa *m*, plan
m ⟨on schedule : según lo previsto⟩
⟨behind schedule : atrasado, con re-
traso⟩ **2** TIMETABLE : horario *m*
scheme[1] [ˈskiːm] *vi* **schemed; schem-
ing** : intrigar, conspirar
scheme[2] *n* **1** PLAN : plan *m*, proyecto
m **2** PLOT, TRICK : intriga *f*, ardid *m* **3**
FRAMEWORK : esquema *f* ⟨a color
scheme : una combinación de colores⟩
schemer [ˈskiːmər] *n* : intrigante *mf*
schism [ˈsɪzəm, ˈskɪ-] *n* : cisma *m*
schizophrenia [ˌskɪtsəˈfriːniə, ˌskɪzə-,
-ˈfrɛ-] *n* : esquizofrenia *f*
schizophrenic [ˌskɪtsəˈfrɛnɪk, ˌskɪzə-] *n*
: esquizofrénico *m*, -ca *f* — **schizophrenic** *adj*
scholar [ˈskɑlər] *n* **1** STUDENT : escolar
mf; alumno *m*, -na *f* **2** EXPERT : especialista *mf*
scholarly [ˈskɑlərli] *adj* : erudito
scholarship [ˈskɑlərˌʃɪp] *n* **1** LEARNING
: erudición *f* **2** GRANT : beca *f*
scholastic [skəˈlæstɪk] *adj* : académico
school[1] [ˈskuːl] *vt* : instruir, enseñar
school[2] *n* **1** : escuela *f*, colegio *m* (institución) **2** : estudiantes *mfpl* y pro-
fesores *mpl* (de una escuela) **3** : escuela
f (en pintura, etc.) ⟨the Flemish school
: la escuela flamenca⟩ **4 school of fish**
: banco *m*, cardumen *m*
schoolboy [ˈskuːlˌbɔɪ] *n* : escolar *m*,
colegial *m*
schoolgirl [ˈskuːlˌɡərl] *n* : escolar *f*, cole-
giala *f*
schoolhouse [ˈskuːlˌhaʊs] *n* : escuela *f*
schoolmate [ˈskuːlˌmeɪt] *n* : compañero
m, -ra *f* de escuela
schoolroom [ˈskuːlˌruːm, -ˌrʊm] →
classroom
schoolteacher [ˈskuːlˌtiːtʃər] *n* : maestro
m, -tra *f*; profesor *m*, -sora *f*
schoolwork [ˈskuːlˌwərk] *n* : trabajo *m*
escolar
schooner [ˈskuːnər] *n* : goleta *f*
science [ˈsaɪənts] *n* : ciencia *f*
science fiction *n* : ciencia ficción *f*
scientific [ˌsaɪənˈtɪfɪk] *adj* : científico —
scientifically [-fɪkli] *adv*
scientist [ˈsaɪəntɪst] *n* : científico *m*, -ca
f
scintillating [ˈsɪntəˌleɪtɪŋ] *adj* : chispeante, brillante
scissors [ˈsɪzərz] *npl* : tijeras *fpl*
sclerosis [skləˈroːsəs] *n, pl* **-roses** : esclerosis *f*
scoff [ˈskɑf] *vi* **to scoff at** : burlarse de,
mofarse de
scold ⟨ˈskoːld⟩ *vt* : regañar, reprender,
reñir

scoop[1] [ˈskuːp] *vt* **1** : sacar (con pala o
cucharón) **2 to scoop out** HOLLOW
: vaciar, ahuecar
scoop[2] *n* : pala *f* (para harina, etc.),
cucharón *m* (para helado, etc.)
scoot [ˈskuːt] *vi* : ir rápidamente ⟨she
scooted around the corner : volvió la
esquina a toda prisa⟩
scooter [ˈskuːtər] *n* : patineta *f*,
monopatín *m*, patinete *m*
scope [ˈskoːp] *n* **1** RANGE : alcance *m*,
ámbito *m*, extensión *f* **2** OPPORTUNI-
TY : posibilidades *fpl*, libertad *f*
scorch [ˈskɔrtʃ] *vt* : chamuscar, quemar
score[1] [ˈskor] *v* **scored; scoring** *vt* **1**
RECORD : anotar **2** MARK, SCRATCH
: marcar, rayar **3** : marcar, meter (en
deportes) **4** GAIN : ganar, apuntarse **5**
GRADE : calificar (exámenes, etc.) **6**
: instrumentar, orquestar (música) —
vi **1** : marcar (en deportes) **2** : obtener una puntuación (en un examen)
score[2] *n, pl* **scores** **1** *or pl* **score** TWEN-
TY : veintena *f* **2** LINE, SCRATCH : línea
f, marca *f* **3** : resultado *m* (en deportes)
⟨what's the score? : ¿cómo va el marcador?⟩ **4** GRADE, POINTS : calificación *f* (en un examen), puntuación *f*
(en un concurso) **5** ACCOUNT : cuenta *f* ⟨to settle a score : ajustar una cuen-
ta⟩ ⟨on that score : a ese respecto⟩ **6**
: partitura *f* (musical)
scorn[1] [ˈskɔrn] *vt* : despreciar, menospreciar, desdeñar
scorn[2] *n* : desprecio *m*, menosprecio *m*,
desdén *m*
scornful [ˈskɔrnfəl] *adj* : desdeñoso, despreciativo — **scornfully** *adv*
Scorpio [ˈskɔrpiˌoː] *n* : Escorpio *mf*, Escorpión *mf*
scorpion [ˈskɔrpiən] *n* : alacrán *m*, escorpión *m*
Scot [ˈskɑt] *n* : escocés *m*, -cesa *f*
Scotch[1] [ˈskɑtʃ] *adj* → **Scottish**[1]
Scotch[2] *npl* **the Scotch** : los escoceses
scot–free [ˈskɑtˈfriː] *adj* **to get off
scot–free** : salir impune, quedar sin
castigo
Scots [ˈskɑts] *n* : escocés *m* (idioma)
Scottish[1] [ˈskɑtɪʃ] *adj* : escocés
Scottish[2] *n* → **Scots**
scoundrel [ˈskaʊndrəl] *n* : sinvergüenza
mf; bellaco *m*, -ca *f*
scour [ˈskaʊər] *vt* **1** EXAMINE, SEARCH
: registrar (un área), revisar (documentos, etc.) **2** SCRUB : fregar, restregar
scourge[1] [ˈskərdʒ] *vt* **scourged; scourg-
ing** : azotar
scourge[2] *n* : azote *m*
scout[1] [ˈskaʊt] *vt* **1** RECONNOITER : reconocer **2 to scout around for** : explorar en busca de
scout[2] *n* **1** : explorador *m*, -dora *f* **2** *or*
talent scout : cazatalentos *mf*
scow [ˈskaʊ] *n* : barcaza *f*, gabarra *f*
scowl[1] [ˈskaʊl] *vi* : fruncir el ceño
scowl[2] *n* : ceño *m* fruncido

scram ['skræm] *vi* **scrammed; scramming** : largarse

scramble[1] ['skræmbəl] *v* **-bled; -bling** *vi* **1** : trepar, gatear (con torpeza) ⟨he scrambled over the fence : se trepó a la cerca con dificultad⟩ **2** STRUGGLE : pelearse (por) ⟨they scrambled for seats : se pelearon por los asientos⟩ — *vt* **1** JUMBLE : mezclar **2 to scramble eggs** : hacer huevos revueltos

scramble[2] *n* : rebatiña *f*, pelea *f*

scrap[1] ['skræp] *v* **scrapped; scrapping** *vt* DISCARD : desechar — *vi* FIGHT : pelearse

scrap[2] *n* **1** FRAGMENT : pedazo *m*, trozo *m* **2** FIGHT : pelea *f* **3** *or* **scrap metal** : chatarra *f* **4 scraps** *npl* LEFTOVERS : restos *mpl*, sobras *fpl*

scrapbook ['skræp,bʊk] *n* : álbum *m* de recortes

scrape[1] ['skreɪp] *v* **scraped; scraping** *vt* **1** GRAZE, SCRATCH : rozar, rascar ⟨to scrape one's knee : rasparse la rodilla⟩ **2** CLEAN : raspar ⟨to scrape carrots : raspar zanahorias⟩ **3 to scrape off** : raspar (pintura, etc.) **4 to scrape up** *or* **to scrape together** : juntar, reunir poco a poco — *vi* **1** RUB : rozar **2 to scrape by** : arreglárselas, ir tirando

scrape[2] *n* **1** SCRAPING : raspadura *f* **2** SCRATCH : rasguño *m* **3** PREDICAMENT : apuro *m*, aprieto *m*

scratch[1] ['skrætʃ] *vt* **1** : arañar, rasguñar ⟨to scratch an itch : rascarse⟩ **2** MARK : rayar, marcar **3 to scratch out** : tachar

scratch[2] *n* **1** : rasguño *m*, arañazo *m* (en la piel), rayón *m* (en un mueble, etc.) **2** : sonido *m* rasposo ⟨I heard a scratch at the door : oí como que raspaban a la puerta⟩

scratchy ['skrætʃi] *adj* **scratchier; -est** : áspero, que pica ⟨a scratchy sweater : un suéter que pica⟩

scrawl[1] ['skrɔl] *v* : garabatear

scrawl[2] *n* : garabato *m*

scrawny ['skrɔni] *adj* **scrawnier; -est** : flaco, escuálido

scream[1] ['skri:m] *vi* : chillar, gritar

scream[2] *n* : chillido *m*, grito *m*

screech[1] ['skri:tʃ] *vi* : chillar (dícese de las personas o de los animales), chirriar (dícese de los frenos, etc.)

screech[2] *n* **1** : chillido *m*, grito *m* (de una persona o un animal) **2** : chirrido *m* (de frenos, etc.)

screen[1] ['skri:n] *vt* **1** SHIELD : proteger **2** CONCEAL : tapar, ocultar **3** EXAMINE : someter a una revisión, hacerle un chequeo (a un paciente) **4** SIEVE : cribar

screen[2] *n* **1** PARTITION : biombo *m*, pantalla *f* **2** SIEVE : criba *f* **3** : pantalla *f* (de un televisor, una computadora, etc.) **4** MOVIES : cine *m* **5** *or* **window screen** : ventana *f* de tela metálica

screenplay ['skri:n,pleɪ] *n* SCRIPT : guión *m*

screw[1] ['skru:] *vt* : atornillar — *vi* **1 to screw in** : atornillarse **2 to screw up** *fam* : meter la pata

screw[2] *n* **1** : tornillo *m* (para fijar algo) **2** TWIST : vuelta *f* **3** PROPELLER : hélice *f*

screwdriver ['skru:,draɪvər] *n* : destornillador *m*, desarmador *m Mex*

scribble[1] ['skrɪbəl] *v* **-bled; -bling** : garabatear

scribble[2] *n* : garabato *m*

scribe ['skraɪb] *n* : escriba *m*

scrimmage ['skrɪmɪdʒ] *n* : escaramuza *f*

scrimp ['skrɪmp] *vi* **1 to scrimp on** : escatimar **2 to scrimp and save** : hacer economías

script ['skrɪpt] *n* **1** HANDWRITING : letra *f*, escritura *f* **2** : guión *m* (de una película, etc.)

scriptural ['skrɪptʃərəl] *adj* : bíblico

scripture ['skrɪptʃər] *n* **1** : escritos *mpl* sagrados (de una religión) **2 the Scriptures** *npl* : las Sagradas Escrituras

scriptwriter ['skrɪpt,raɪtər] *n* : guionista *mf*, libretista *mf*

scroll ['skro:l] *n* **1** : rollo *m* (de pergamino, etc.) **2** : voluta *f* (adorno en arquitectura)

scrotum ['skro:təm] *n*, *pl* **scrota** [-tə] *or* **scrotums** : escroto *m*

scrounge ['skraʊndʒ] *v* **scrounged; scrounging** *vt* **1** BUM : gorrear *fam*, sablear *fam* (dinero) **2 to scrounge around for** : buscar, andar a la busca de — *vi* **to scrounge off someone** : vivir a costa de alguien

scrub[1] ['skrʌb] *vt* **scrubbed; scrubbing** : restregar, fregar

scrub[2] *n* **1** THICKET, UNDERBRUSH : maleza *f*, matorral *m*, matorrales *mpl* **2** SCRUBBING : fregado *m*, restregadura *f*

scrubby ['skrʌbi] *adj* **-bier; -est 1** STUNTED : achaparrado **2** : cubierto de maleza

scruff ['skrʌf] *n* **by the scruff of the neck** : por el cogote, por el pescuezo

scrumptious ['skrʌmpʃəs] *adj* : delicioso, muy rico

scruple ['skru:pəl] *n* : escrúpulo *m*

scrupulous ['skru:pjələs] *adj* : escrupuloso — **scrupulously** *adv*

scrutinize ['skru:tən,aɪz] *vt* **-nized; -nizing** : escrutar, escudriñar

scrutiny ['skru:təni] *n*, *pl* **-nies** : escrutinio *m*, inspección *f*

scuba ['sku:bə] *n* **1** *or* **scuba gear** : equipo *m* de submarinismo **2 scuba diver** : submarinista *mf* **3 scuba diving** : submarinismo *m*

scuff ['skʌf] *vt* : rayar, raspar ⟨to scuff one's feet : arrastrar los pies⟩

scuffle[1] ['skʌfəl] *vi* **-fled; -fling 1** TUSSLE : pelearse **2** SHUFFLE : caminar arrastrando los pies

scuffle[2] *n* **1** TUSSLE : refriega *f*, pelea *f* **2** SHUFFLE : arrastre *m* de los pies

scull[1] ['skʌl] *vi* : remar (con espadilla)

scull² *n* OAR : espadilla *f*

sculpt ['skʌlpt] *v* : esculpir

sculptor ['skʌlptər] *n* : escultor *m*, -tora *f*

scuptural ['skʌltʃərəl] *adj* : escultórico

sculpture¹ ['skʌlptʃər] *vt* **-tured; -turing** : esculpir

sculpture² *n* : escultura *f*

scum ['skʌm] *n* **1** FROTH : espuma *f*, nata *f* **2** : verdín *m* (encima de un líquido)

scurrilous ['skərələs] *adj* : difamatorio, calumnioso, injurioso

scurry ['skəri] *vi* **-ried; -rying** : corretear

scurvy ['skərvi] *n* : escorbuto *m*

scuttle¹ ['skʌtəl] *v* **-tled; -tling** *vt* : hundir (un barco) — *vi* SCAMPER : corretear

scuttle² *n* : cubo *m* (para carbón)

scythe ['saɪð] *n* : guadaña *f*

sea¹ ['si:] *adj* : del mar

sea² *n* **1** : mar *mf* ⟨the Black Sea : el Mar Negro⟩ ⟨on the high seas : en alta mar⟩ ⟨heavy seas : mar gruesa, mar agitada⟩ **2** MASS : mar *m*, multitud *f* ⟨a sea of faces : un mar de rostros⟩

seabird ['si:ˌbərd] *n* : ave *f* marina

seaboard ['si:ˌbord] *n* : litoral *m*

seacoast ['si:ˌko:st] *n* : costa *f*, litoral *m*

seafarer ['si:ˌfærər] *n* : marinero *m*

seafaring¹ ['si:ˌfærɪŋ] *adj* : marinero

seafaring² *n* : navegación *f*

seafood ['si:ˌfu:d] *n* : mariscos *mpl*

seagull ['si:ˌgʌl] *n* : gaviota *f*

sea horse ['si:ˌhɔrs] *n* : hipocampo *m*, caballito *m* de mar

seal¹ ['si:l] *vt* **1** CLOSE : sellar, cerrar ⟨to seal a letter : cerrar una carta⟩ ⟨to seal an agreement : sellar un acuerdo⟩ **2 to seal up** : tapar, rellenar (una grieta, etc.)

seal² *n* **1** : foca *f* (animal) **2** : sello *m* ⟨seal of approval : sello de aprobación⟩ **3** CLOSURE : cierre *m*, precinto *m*

sea level *n* : nivel *m* del mar

sea lion *n* : león *m* marino

sealskin ['si:lˌskɪn] *n* : piel *f* de foca

seam¹ ['si:m] *vt* **1** STITCH : unir con costuras **2** MARK : marcar

seam² *n* **1** STITCHING : costura *f* **2** LODE, VEIN : veta *f*, filón *m*

seaman ['si:mən] *n, pl* **-men** [-mən, -ˌmɛn] **1** SAILOR : marinero *m* **2** : marino *m* (en la armada)

seamless ['si:mləs] *adj* **1** : sin costuras, de una pieza **2** : perfecto ⟨a seamless transition : una transición fluida⟩

seamstress ['si:mpstrəs] *n* : costurera *f*

seamy ['si:mi] *adj* **seamier; -est** : sórdido

séance ['seɪˌɑnts] *n* : sesión *f* de espiritismo

seaplane ['si:ˌpleɪn] *n* : hidroavión *m*

seaport ['si:ˌport] *n* : puerto *m* marítimo

sear ['sɪr] *vt* **1** PARCH, WITHER : secar, resecar **2** SCORCH : chamuscar, quemar

search¹ ['sərtʃ] *vt* : registrar (un edificio, un área), cachear (a una persona), buscar en — *vi* **to search for** : buscar

search² *n* : búsqueda *f*, registro *m* (de un edificio, etc.), cacheo *m* (de una persona)

searchlight ['sərtʃˌlaɪt] *n* : reflector *m*

seashell ['si:ˌʃɛl] *n* : concha *f* (marina)

seashore ['si:ˌʃor] *n* : orilla *f* del mar

seasick ['si:ˌsɪk] *adj* : mareado ⟨to get seasick : marearse⟩

seasickness ['si:ˌsɪknəs] *n* : mareo *m*

seaside → seacoast

season¹ ['si:zən] *vt* **1** FLAVOR, SPICE : sazonar, condimentar **2** CURE : curar, secar ⟨seasoned wood : madera seca⟩ ⟨a seasoned veteran : un veterano avezado⟩

season² *n* **1** : estación *f* (del año) **2** : temporada *f* (en deportes, etc.) ⟨baseball season : temporada de beisbol⟩

seasonable ['si:zənəbəl] *adj* **1** : propio de la estación (dícese del tiempo, de las temperaturas, etc.) **2** TIMELY : oportuno

seasonal ['si:zənəl] *adj* : estacional — **seasonally** *adv*

seasoning ['si:zənɪŋ] *n* : condimento *m*, aderezo *m*

seat¹ ['si:t] *vt* **1** SIT : sentar ⟨please be seated : siéntense, por favor⟩ **2** HOLD : tener cabida para ⟨the stadium seats 40,000 : el estadio tiene 40,000 asientos⟩

seat² *n* **1** : asiento *m*, plaza *f* (en un vehículo) ⟨take a seat : tome asiento⟩ **2** BOTTOM : fondillos *mpl* (de la ropa), trasero *m* (del cuerpo) **3** : sede *f* (de un gobierno, etc.)

seat belt *n* : cinturón *m* de seguridad

sea urchin *n* : erizo *m* de mar

seawall ['si:ˌwɑl] *n* : rompeolas *m*, dique *m* marítimo

seawater ['si:ˌwɔtər, -ˌwɑ-] *n* : agua *f* de mar

seaweed ['si:ˌwi:d] *n* : alga *f* marina

seaworthy ['si:ˌwərði] *adj* : en condiciones de navegar

secede [sɪ'si:d] *vi* **-ceded; -ceding** : separarse (de una nación, etc.)

seclude [sɪ'klu:d] *vt* **-cluded; -cluding** : aislar

seclusion [sɪ'klu:ʒən] *n* : aislamiento *m*

second¹ ['sɛkənd] *vt* : secundar, apoyar (una moción)

second² *or* **secondly** ['sɛkəndli] *adv* : en segundo lugar

second³ *adj* : segundo

second⁴ *n* **1** : segundo *m*, -da *f* (en una serie) **2** : segundo *m*, ayudante *m* (en deportes) **3** MOMENT : segundo *m*, momento *m*

secondary ['sɛkənˌdri] *adj* : secundario

secondhand ['sɛkəndˈhænd] *adj* : de segunda mano

second lieutenant *n* : alférez *mf*, subteniente *mf*

second–rate ['sɛkəndˈreɪt] *adj* : mediocre, de segunda categoría

secrecy ['si:krəsi] *n, pl* **-cies** : secreto *m*
secret¹ ['si:krət] *adj* : secreto — **secretly** *adv*
secret² *n* : secreto *m*
secretarial [ˌsɛkrə'triəl] *adj* : de secretario, de oficina
secretariat [ˌsɛkrə'triət] *n* : secretaría *f*, secretariado *m*
secretary ['sɛkrəˌtri] *n, pl* **-taries** **1** : secretario *m*, -ria *f* (en una oficina, etc.) **2** : ministro *m*, -tra *f*; secretario *m*, -ria *f* ⟨Secretary of State : Secretario de Estado⟩
secrete [sɪ'kri:t] *vt* **-creted; -creting** **1** : secretar, segregar (en fisiología) **2** HIDE : ocultar
secretion [sɪ'kri:ʃən] *n* : secreción *f*
secretive ['si:krətɪv, sɪ'kri:ṭɪv] *adj* : reservado, callado, secreto
sect ['sɛkt] *n* : secta *f*
sectarian [sɛk'triən] *adj* : sectario
section ['sɛkʃən] *n* : sección *f*, parte *f* (de un mueble, etc.), sector *m* (de la población), barrio *m* (de una ciudad)
sectional ['sɛkʃənəl] *adj* **1** : en sección, en corte ⟨a sectional diagram : un gráfico en corte⟩ **2** FACTIONAL : de grupo, entre facciones **3** : modular ⟨sectional furniture : muebles modulares⟩
sector ['sɛktər] *n* : sector *m*
secular ['sɛkjələr] *adj* **1** : secular, laico ⟨secular life : la vida secular⟩ **2** : seglar (dícese de los sacerdotes, etc.)
secure¹ [sɪ'kjur] *vt* **-cured; -curing** **1** FASTEN : asegurar (una puerta, etc.), sujetar **2** GET : conseguir
secure² *adj* **-curer; -est** : seguro — **securely** *adv*
security [sɪ'kjurəṭi] *n, pl* **-ties** **1** SAFETY : seguridad *f* **2** GUARANTEE : garantía *f* **3 securities** *npl* : valores *mpl*
sedan [sɪ'dæn] *n* **1** *or* **sedan chair** : silla *f* de manos **2** : sedán *m* (automóvil)
sedate¹ [sɪ'deɪt] *vt* **-dated; -dating** : sedar
sedate² *adj* : sosegado — **sedately** *adv*
sedation [sɪ'deɪʃən] *n* : sedación *f*
sedative¹ ['sɛdəṭɪv] *adj* : sedante
sedative² *n* : sedante *m*, calmante *m*
sedentary ['sɛdənˌteri] *adj* : sedentario
sedge ['sɛdʒ] *n* : juncia *f*
sediment ['sɛdəmənt] *n* : sedimento *m* (geológico), poso *m* (en un líquido)
sedimentary [ˌsɛdə'mɛntəri] *adj* : sedimentario
sedition [sɪ'dɪʃən] *n* : sedición *f*
seditious [sɪ'dɪʃəs] *adj* : sedicioso
seduce [sɪ'du:s, -'dju:s] *vt* **-duced; -ducing** : seducir
seduction [sɪ'dʌkʃən] *n* : seducción *f*
seductive [sɪ'dʌktɪv] *adj* : seductor, seductivo
see¹ ['si:] *v* **saw** ['sɔ]; **seen** ['si:n]; **seeing** *vt* **1** : ver ⟨I saw a dog : vi un perro⟩ ⟨see you later! : ¡hasta luego!⟩ **2** EXPERIENCE : ver, conocer **3** UNDERSTAND : ver, entender **4** ENSURE : asegurarse ⟨see that it's correct : asegúrese

de que sea correcto⟩ **5** ACCOMPANY : acompañar **6 to see off** : despedir, despedirse de — *vi* **1** : ver ⟨seeing is believing : ver para creer⟩ **2** UNDERSTAND : entender, ver ⟨now I see! : ¡ya entiendo!⟩ **3** CONSIDER : ver ⟨let's see : vamos a ver⟩ **4 to see to** : ocuparse de
see² *n* : sede *f* ⟨the Holy See : la Santa Sede⟩
seed¹ ['si:d] *vt* **1** SOW : sembrar **2** : despepitar, quitarle las semillas a
seed² *n, pl* **seed** *or* **seeds** **1** : semilla *f*, pepita *f* (de una fruta) **2** SOURCE : germen *m*, semilla *f*
seedless ['si:dləs] *adj* : sin semillas
seedling ['si:dlɪŋ] *n* : plantón *m*
seedpod ['si:dˌpɑd] → **pod**
seedy ['si:di] *adj* **seedier; -est** **1** : lleno de semillas **2** SHABBY : raído (dícese de la ropa) **3** RUN-DOWN : ruinoso (dícese de los edificios, etc.), sórdido
seek ['si:k] *v* **sought** ['sɔt]; **seeking** *vt* **1** : buscar ⟨to seek an answer : buscar una solución⟩ **2** REQUEST : solicitar, pedir **3 to seek to** : tratar de, intentar de — *vi* SEARCH : buscar
seem ['si:m] *vi* : parecer
seeming ['si:mɪŋ] *adj* : aparente, ostensible
seemingly ['si:mɪŋli] *adv* : aparentemente, según parece
seemly ['si:mli] *adj* **seemlier; -est** : apropiado, decoroso
seep ['si:p] *vi* : filtrarse
seer ['si:ər] *n* : vidente *mf*, clarividente *mf*
seesaw¹ ['si:ˌsɔ] *vi* **1** : jugar en un subibaja **2** VACILLATE : vacilar, oscilar
seesaw² *n* : balancín *m*, subibaja *m*
seethe ['si:ð] *vi* **seethed; seething** **1** : bullir, hervir **2 to seethe with anger** : rabiar, estar furioso
segment ['sɛgmənt] *n* : segmento *m*
segmented ['sɛgˌmɛntəd, sɛg'mɛn-] *adj* : segmentado
segregate ['sɛgrɪˌgeɪt] *vt* **-gated; -gating** : segregar
segregation [ˌsɛgrɪ'geɪʃən] *n* : segregación *f*
seismic ['saɪzmɪk, 'saɪs-] *adj* : sísmico
seize ['si:z] *v* **seized; seizing** *vt* **1** CAPTURE : capturar, tomar, apoderarse de **2** ARREST : detener **3** CLUTCH, GRAB : agarrar, coger, aprovechar (una oportunidad) **4 to be seized with** : estar sobrecogido por — *vi or* **to seize up** : agarrotarse
seizure ['si:ʒər] *n* **1** CAPTURE : toma *f*, captura *f* **2** ARREST : detención *f* **3** : ataque *m* ⟨an epileptic seizure : un ataque epiléptico⟩
seldom ['sɛldəm] *adv* : pocas veces, rara vez, casi nunca
select¹ [sə'lɛkt] *vt* : escoger, elegir, seleccionar (a un candidato, etc.)
select² *adj* : selecto
selection [sə'lɛkʃən] *n* : selección *f*, elección *f*

selective [sə'lɛktɪv] *adj* : selectivo
selenium [sə'li:niəm] *n* : selenio *m*
self ['sɛlf] *n, pl* **selves** ['sɛlvz] **1** : ser *m*, persona *f* ⟨the self : el yo⟩ ⟨with his whole self : con todo su ser⟩ ⟨her own self : su propia persona⟩ **2** SIDE : lado (de la personalidad) ⟨his better self : su lado bueno⟩
self–addressed [ˌsɛlfə'drst] *adj* : con la dirección del remitente ⟨include a self-addressed envelope : incluya un sobre con su nombre y dirección⟩
self–appointed [ˌsɛlfə'pɔɪntəd] *adj* : autoproclamado, autonombrado
self–assurance [ˌsɛlfə'ʃʊrəns] *n* : seguridad *f* en sí mismo
self–assured [ˌsɛlfə'ʃʊrd] *adj* : seguro de sí mismo
self–centered [ˌsɛlf'sɛntərd] *adj* : egocéntrico
self–confidence [ˌsɛlf'kɑnfədənts] *n* : confianza *f* en sí mismo
self–confident [ˌsɛlf'kɑnfədənt] *adj* : seguro de sí mismo
self–conscious [ˌsɛlf'kɑntʃəs] *adj* : cohibido, tímido
self–consciously [ˌsɛlf'kɑntʃəsli] *adv* : de manera cohibida
self–consciousness [ˌsɛlf'kɑntʃəsnəs] *n* : vergüenza *f*, timidez *f*
self–contained [ˌsɛlfkən'teɪnd] *adj* **1** INDEPENDENT : independiente **2** RESERVED : reservado
self–control [ˌsɛlfkən'tro:l] *n* : autocontrol *m*, control *m* de sí mismo
self–defense [ˌsɛlfdɪ'fɛnts] *n* : defensa *f* propia, defensa *f* personal ⟨to act in self-defense : actuar en defensa propia⟩ ⟨self-defense class : clase de defensa personal⟩
self–denial [ˌsɛlfdɪ'naɪəl] *n* : abnegación *f*
self–destructive [ˌsɛlfdɪ'strʌktɪv] *adj* : autodestructivo
self–determination [ˌsɛlfdɪˌtərmə'neɪʃən] *n* : autodeterminación *f*
self–discipline [ˌsɛlf'dɪsəplən] *n* : autodisciplina *f*
self–employed [ˌsɛlfɪm'plɔɪd] *adj* : que trabaja por cuenta propia, autónomo
self–esteem [ˌsɛlfɪ'sti:m] *n* : autoestima *f*, amor *m* propio
self–evident [ˌsɛlf'ɛvədənt] *adj* : evidente, manifiesto
self–explanatory [ˌsɛlfɪk'splænəˌtori] *adj* : fácil de entender, evidente
self–expression [ˌsɛlfɪk'sprʃən] *n* : expresión *f* personal
self–government [ˌsɛlf'gʌvərmənt, -vərn-] *n* : autogobierno *m*
self–help [ˌsɛlf'hɛlp] *n* : autoayuda *f*
self–important [ˌsɛlfɪm'pɔrtənt] *adj* **1** VAIN : vanidoso, presumido **2** ARROGANT : arrogante
self–indulgent [ˌsɛlfɪn'dʌldʒənt] *adj* : que se permite excesos
self–inflicted [ˌsɛlfɪn'flɪktəd] *adj* : autoinfligido

self–interest [ˌsɛlf'ɪntrəst, -təˌrst] *n* : interés *m* personal
selfish ['sɛlfɪʃ] *adj* : egoísta
selfishly ['sɛlfɪʃli] *adv* : de manera egoísta
selfishness ['sɛlfɪʃnəs] *n* : egoísmo *m*
selfless ['sɛlfləs] *adj* UNSELFISH : desinteresado
self–made [ˌsɛlf'meɪd] *adj* : próspero gracias a sus propios esfuerzos
self–pity [ˌsɛlf'pɪti] *n, pl* **-ties** : autocompasión *f*
self–portrait [ˌsɛlf'pɔrtrət] *n* : autorretrato *m*
self–propelled [ˌsɛlfpro'pɛld] *adj* : autopropulsado
self–reliance [ˌsɛlfri'laɪənts] *n* : independencia *f*, autosuficiencia *f*
self–respect [ˌsɛlfri'spɛkt] *n* : autoestima *f*, amor *m* propio
self–restraint [ˌsɛlfri'streɪnt] *n* : autocontrol *m*, moderación *f*
self–righteous [ˌsɛlf'raɪtʃəs] *adj* : santurrón, moralista
self–sacrifice [ˌsɛlf'sækrəˌfaɪs] *n* : abnegación *f*
selfsame ['sɛlfˌseɪm] *adj* : mismo
self–service [ˌsɛlf'sərvɪs] *adj* **1** : de autoservicio **2 self-service restaurant** : autoservicio *m*
self–sufficiency [ˌsɛlfsə'fɪʃəntsi] *n* : autosuficiencia *f*
self–sufficient [ˌsɛlfsə'fɪʃənt] *adj* : autosuficiente
self–taught [ˌsɛlf'tɔt] *adj* : autodidacta
sell ['sɛl] *v* **sold** ['so:ld]; **selling** *vt* : vender — *vi* : venderse
seller ['sɛlər] *n* : vendedor *m*, -dora *f*
selves → **self**
semantic [sɪ'mæntɪk] *adj* : semántico
semantics [sɪ'mæntɪks] *ns & pl* : semántica *f*
semaphore ['sɛməˌfor] *n* : semáforo *m*
semblance ['sɛmbləns] *n* : apariencia *f*
semen ['si:mən] *n* : semen *m*
semester [sə'mɛstər] *n* : semestre *m*
semicolon ['sɛmiˌko:lən, 'sɛˌmaɪ-] *n* : punto y coma *m*
semiconductor ['sɛmikənˌdʌktər, 'sɛˌmaɪ-] *n* : semiconductor *m*
semifinal ['sɛmiˌfaɪnəl, 'sɛˌmaɪ-] *n* : semifinal *f*
seminar ['sɛməˌnɑr] *n* : seminario *m*
seminary ['sɛməˌnɛri] *n, pl* **-naries** : seminario *m*
Semitic [sə'mɪtɪk] *adj* : semita
senate ['sɛnət] *n* : senado *m*
senator ['sɛnətər] *n* : senador *m*, -dora *f*
send ['sɛnd] *vt* **sent** ['sɛnt]; **sending 1** : mandar, enviar ⟨to send a letter : mandar una carta⟩ ⟨to send word : avisar, mandar decir⟩ **2** PROPEL : mandar, lanzar ⟨he sent it into left field : lo mandó al jardín izquierdo⟩ ⟨to send up dust : alzar polvo⟩ **3 to send into a rage** : poner furioso
sender ['sɛndər] *n* : remitente *mf* (de una carta, etc.)

Senegalese [ˌsɛnəgəˈliːz, -ˈliːs] *n* : senegalés *m*, -lesa *f* — **Senegalese** *adj*
senile [ˈsiːˌnaɪl] *adj* : senil
senility [sɪˈnɪləti] *n* : senilidad *f*
senior¹ [ˈsiːnjər] *adj* **1** ELDER : mayor ⟨John Doe, Senior : John Doe, padre⟩ **2** : superior (en rango), más antiguo (en años de servicio) ⟨a senior official : un alto oficial⟩
senior² *n* **1** : superior *m* (en rango) **2 to be someone's senior** : ser mayor que alguien ⟨she's two years my senior : me lleva dos años⟩
senior citizen *n* : persona *f* de la tercera edad
seniority [ˌsiːˈnjɔrəti] *n* : antigüedad *f* (en años de servicio)
sensation [sɛnˈseɪʃən] *n* : sensación *f*
sensational [sɛnˈseɪʃənəl] *adj* : que causa sensación ⟨sensational stories : historias sensacionalistas⟩
sense¹ [ˈsɛnts] *vt* **sensed; sensing** : sentir ⟨he sensed danger : se dio cuenta del peligro⟩
sense² *n* **1** MEANING : sentido *m*, significado *m* **2** : sentido *m* ⟨the sense of smell : el sentido del olfato⟩ **3 to make sense** : tener sentido
senseless [ˈsɛntsləs] *adj* **1** MEANINGLESS : sin sentido, sin razón **2** UNCONSCIOUS : inconsciente
senselessly [ˈsɛntsləsli] *adv* : sin sentido
sensibility [ˌsɛntsəˈbɪləti] *n, pl* **-ties** : sensibilidad *f*
sensible [ˈsɛntsəbəl] *adj* **1** PERCEPTIBLE : sensible, perceptible **2** AWARE : consciente **3** REASONABLE : sensato ⟨a sensible man : un hombre sensato⟩ ⟨sensible shoes : zapatos prácticos⟩ — **sensibly** [-bli] *adv*
sensibleness [ˈsɛntsəbəlnəs] *n* : sensatez *f*, solidez *f*
sensitive [ˈsɛntsətɪv] *adj* **1** : sensible, delicado ⟨sensitive skin : piel sensible⟩ **2** IMPRESSIONABLE : sensible, impresionable **3** TOUCHY : susceptible
sensitiveness [ˈsɛntsətɪvnəs] → **sensitivity**
sensitivity [ˌsɛntsəˈtɪvəti] *n, pl* **-ties** : sensibilidad *f*
sensitize [ˈsɛntsəˌtaɪz] *vt* **-tized; -tizing** : sensibilizar
sensor [ˈsɛnˌsɔr, ˈsɛntsər] *n* : sensor *m*
sensory [ˈsɛntsəri] *adj* : sensorial
sensual [ˈsɛntʃʊəl] *adj* : sensual — **sensually** *adv*
sensuality [ˌsɛntʃəˈwæləti] *n, pl* **-ties** : sensualidad *f*
sensuous [ˈsɛntʃʊəs] *adj* : sensual
sent → **send**
sentence¹ [ˈsɛntənts, -ənz] *vt* **-tenced; -tencing** : sentenciar
sentence² *n* **1** JUDGMENT : sentencia *f* **2** : oración *f*, frase *f* (en gramática)
sentiment [ˈsɛntəmənt] *n* **1** BELIEF : opinión *f* **2** FEELING : sentimiento *m* **3** → **sentimentality**

sentimental [ˌsɛntəˈmɛntəl] *adj* : sentimental
sentimentality [ˌsɛntəˌmɛnˈtæləti] *n, pl* **-ties** : sentimentalismo *m*, sensiblería *f*
sentinel [ˈsɛntənəl] *n* : centinela *mf*, guardia *mf*
sentry [ˈsɛntri] *n, pl* **-tries** : centinela *mf*
sepal [ˈsiːpəl, ˈsɛ-] *n* : sépalo *m*
separable [ˈsɛpərəbəl] *adj* : separable
separate¹ [ˈsɛpəˌreɪt] *v* **-rated; -rating** *vt* **1** DETACH, SEVER : separar **2** DISTINGUISH : diferenciar, distinguir — *vi* PART : separarse
separate² [ˈsɛprət, ˈsɛpə-] *adj* **1** INDIVIDUAL : separado, aparte ⟨a separate state : un estado separado⟩ ⟨in a separate envelope : en un sobre aparte⟩ **2** DISTINCT : distinto
separately [ˈsɛprətli, ˈsɛpə-] *adv* : por separado, separadamente, aparte
separation [ˌsɛpəˈreɪʃən] *n* : separación *f*
sepia [ˈsiːpiə] *n* : color *m* sepia
September [sɛpˈtɛmbər] *n* : septiembre *m*, setiembre *m*
septic [ˈsɛptɪk] *adj* : séptico ⟨septic tank : fosa séptica⟩
sepulchre [ˈsɛpəlkər] *n* : sepulcro *m*
sequel [ˈsiːkwəl] *n* **1** CONSEQUENCE : secuela *f*, consecuencia *f* **2** : continuación *f* (de una película, etc.)
sequence [ˈsiːkwənts] *n* **1** SERIES : serie *f*, sucesión *f*, secuencia *f* (matemática o musical) **2** ORDER : orden *m*
sequester [sɪˈkwɛstər] *vt* : aislar
sequin [ˈsiːˌkwən] *n* : lentejuela *f*
sequoia [sɪˈkwɔɪə] *n* : secoya *f*, secuoya *f*
sera → **serum**
Serb [ˈsərb] *or* **Serbian** [ˈsərbiən] *n* **1** : serbio *m*, -bia *f* **2** : serbio *m* (idioma) — **Serb** *or* **Serbian** *adj*
Serbo–Croatian [ˌsərbokroˈeɪʃən] *n* : serbocroata *m* (idioma) — **Serbo–Croatian** *adj*
serenade¹ [ˌsɛrəˈneɪd] *vt* **-naded; -nading** : darle una serenata (a alguien)
serenade² *n* : serenata *f*
serene [səˈriːn] *adj* : sereno — **serenely** *adv*
serenity [səˈrɛnəti] *n* : serenidad *f*
serf [ˈsərf] *n* : siervo *m*, -va *f*
serge [ˈsərdʒ] *n* : sarga *f*
sergeant [ˈsɑrdʒənt] *n* : sargento *mf*
serial¹ [ˈsɪriəl] *adj* : seriado
serial² *n* : serie *f*, serial *m* (de radio o televisión), publicación *f* por entregas
serially [ˈsɪriəli] *adv* : en serie
series [ˈsɪrˌiːz] *n, pl* **series** : serie *f*, sucesión *f*
serious [ˈsɪriəs] *adj* **1** SOBER : serio **2** DEDICATED, EARNEST : serio, dedicado ⟨to be serious about something : tomar algo en serio⟩ **3** GRAVE : serio, grave ⟨serious problems : problemas graves⟩
seriously [ˈsɪriəsli] *adv* **1** EARNESTLY : seriamente, con seriedad, en serio **2** SEVERELY : gravemente

seriousness ['sɪriəsnəs] *n* : seriedad *f*, gravedad *f*

sermon ['sərmən] *n* : sermón *m*

serpent ['sərpənt] *n* : serpiente *f*

serrated [sə'reɪţəd, 'sɛr̩eɪţəd] *adj* : dentado, serrado

serum ['sɪrəm] *n, pl* **serums** *or* **sera** ['sɪrə] : suero *m*

servant ['sərvənt] *n* : criado *m*, -da *f*; sirviente *m*, -ta *f*

serve ['sərv] *v* **served; serving** *vi* 1 : servir ⟨to serve in the navy : servir en la armada⟩ ⟨to serve on a jury : ser miembro de un jurado⟩ 2 DO, FUNCTION : servir ⟨to serve as : servir de, servir como⟩ 3 : sacar (en deportes) — *vt* 1 : servir ⟨to serve God : servir a Dios⟩ 2 HELP : servir ⟨it serves no purpose : no sirve para nada⟩ 3 : servir (comida o bebida) ⟨dinner is served : la cena está servida⟩ 4 SUPPLY : abastecer 5 CARRY OUT : cumplir, hacer ⟨to serve time : servir una pena⟩ 6 **to serve a summons** : entregar una citación

server ['sərvər] *n* 1 : camarero *m*, -ra *f*; mesero *m*, -ra *f* (en un restaurante) 2 *or* **serving dish** : fuente *f* (para servir comida) 3 : servidor *m* (en informática)

service¹ ['sərvəs] *vt* **-viced; -vicing** 1 MAINTAIN : darle mantenimiento a (una máquina), revisar 2 REPAIR : arreglar, reparar

service² *n* 1 HELP, USE : servicio *m* ⟨to do someone a service : hacerle un servicio a alguien⟩ ⟨at your service : a sus órdenes⟩ ⟨to be out of service : no funcionar⟩ 2 CEREMONY : oficio *m* (religioso) 3 DEPARTMENT, SYSTEM : servicio *m* ⟨social services : servicios sociales⟩ ⟨train service : servicio de trenes⟩ 4 SET : juego *m*, servicio *m* ⟨tea service : juego de té⟩ 5 MAINTENANCE : mantenimiento *m*, revisión *f*, servicio *m* 6 : saque *m* (en deportes) 7 **armed services** : fuerzas *fpl* armadas

serviceable ['sərvəsəbəl] *adj* 1 USEFUL : útil 2 DURABLE : duradero

serviceman ['sərvəs,mæn, -mən] *n, pl* **-men** [-mən, -,mɛn] : militar *m*

service station → gas station

servicewoman ['sərvəs,wumən] *n, pl* **-women** [-,wɪmən] : militar *f*

servile ['sərvəl, -,vaɪl] *adj* : servil

serving ['sərvɪŋ] *n* HELPING : porción *f*, ración *f*

servitude ['sərvə,tu:d, -,tju:d] *n* : servidumbre *f*

sesame ['sɛsəmi] *n* : ajonjolí *m*, sésamo *m*

session ['sɛʃən] *n* : sesión *f*

set¹ ['sɛt] *v* **set; setting** *vt* 1 SEAT : sentar 2 *or* **set down** PLACE : poner, colocar 3 ARRANGE : fijar, establecer ⟨to set the date : poner la fecha⟩ ⟨he set the agenda : estableció la agenda⟩ 4 ADJUST : poner (un reloj, etc.) 5 (*indicating the causing of a certain condition*) ⟨to set fire to : prenderle fuego a⟩ ⟨she

set it free : lo soltó⟩ 6 MAKE, START : poner, hacer ⟨I set them working : los puse a trabajar⟩ — *vi* 1 SOLIDIFY : fraguar (dícese del cemento, etc.), cuajar (dícese de la gelatina, etc.) 2 : ponerse (dícese del sol o de la luna)

set² *adj* 1 ESTABLISHED, FIXED : fijo, establecido 2 RIGID : inflexible ⟨to be set in one's ways : tener costumbres muy arraigadas⟩ 3 READY : listo, preparado

set³ *n* 1 COLLECTION : juego *m* ⟨a set of dishes : un juego de platos, una vajilla⟩ ⟨a tool set : una caja de herramientas⟩ 2 *or* **stage set** : decorado *m* (en el teatro), plató *m* (en el cine) 3 APPARATUS : aparato *m* ⟨a television set : un televisor⟩ 4 : conjunto *m* (en matemáticas)

setback ['sɛt,bæk] *n* : revés *m*, contratiempo *m*

set in *vi* BEGIN : comenzar, empezar

set off *vt* 1 PROVOKE : provocar 2 EXPLODE : hacer estallar (una bomba, etc.) — *vi or* **to set forth** : salir

set out *vi* : salir (de viaje) — *vt* INTEND : proponerse

settee [sɛ'ti:] *n* : sofá *m*

setter ['sɛţər] *n* : setter *mf* ⟨Irish setter : setter irlandés⟩

setting ['sɛţɪŋ] *n* 1 : posición *f*, ajuste *m* (de un control) 2 : engaste *m*, montura *f* (de una gema) 3 SCENE : escenario *m* (de una novela, etc.) 4 SURROUNDINGS : ambiente *m*, entorno *m*, marco *m*

settle ['sɛţəl] *v* **settled; settling** *vi* 1 ALIGHT, LAND : posarse (dícese de las aves), depositarse (dícese del polvo) 2 SINK : asentarse (dícese de los edificios) ⟨he settled into the chair : se arrellanó en la silla⟩ 3 : instalarse (en una casa), establecerse (en una ciudad o región) 4 **to settle down** : calmarse, tranquilizarse ⟨settle down! : ¡tranquilízate!, ¡cálmate!⟩ 5 **to settle down** : sentar cabeza, hacerse sensato ⟨to marry and settle down : casarse y sentar cabeza⟩ — *vt* 1 ARRANGE, DECIDE : fijar, decidir, acordar (planes, etc.) 2 RESOLVE : resolver, solucionar ⟨to settle an argument : resolver una discusión⟩ 3 PAY : pagar ⟨to settle an account : saldar una cuenta⟩ 4 CALM : calmar (los nervios), asentar (el estómago) 5 COLONIZE : colonizar 6 **to settle oneself** : acomodarse, hacerse cómodo

settlement ['sɛţəlmənt] *n* 1 PAYMENT : pago *m*, liquidación *f* 2 COLONY : asentamiento *m* 3 RESOLUTION : acuerdo *m*

settler ['sɛţələr] *n* : poblador *m*, -dora *f*; colono *m*, -na *f*

setup ['sɛt,ʌp] *n* 1 ASSEMBLY : montaje *m*, ensamblaje *m* 2 ARRANGEMENT : disposición *f* 3 PREPARATION : preparación *f* 4 TRAP, TRICK : encerrona *f*

set up *vt* **1** ASSEMBLE : montar, armar **2** ERECT : levantar, erigir **3** ESTABLISH : establecer, fundar, montar (un negocio) **4** CAUSE : armar ⟨they set up a clamor : armaron un alboroto⟩
seven¹ ['sɛvən] *adj* : siete
seven² *n* : siete *m*
seven hundred¹ *adj* : setecientos
seven hundred² *n* : setecientos *m*
seventeen¹ [ˌsɛvən'tiːn] *adj* : diecisiete
seventeen² *n* : diecisiete *m*
seventeenth¹ [ˌsɛvən'tiːnθ] *adj* : decimoséptimo
seventeenth² *n* **1** : decimoséptimo *m*, -ma *f* (en una serie) **2** : diecisieteavo *m*, diecisieteava parte *f*
seventh¹ ['sɛvənθ] *adj* : séptimo
seventh² *n* **1** : séptimo *m*, -ma *f* (en una serie) **2** : séptimo *m*, séptima parte *f*
seventieth¹ ['sɛvəntiəθ] *adj* : septuagésimo
seventieth² *n* **1** : septuagésimo *m*, -ma *f* (en una serie) **2** : setentavo *m*, setentava parte *f*, septuagésima parte *f*
seventy¹ ['sɛvənti] *adj* : setenta
seventy² *n*, *pl* **-ties** : setenta *m*
sever ['sɛvər] *vt* **-ered; -ering** : cortar, romper
several¹ ['sɛvrəl, 'sɛvə-] *adj* **1** DISTINCT : distinto **2** SOME : varios ⟨several weeks : varias semanas⟩
several² *pron* : varios, varias
severance ['sɛvrənts, sɛvə-] *n* **1** : ruptura *f* (de relaciones, etc.) **2 severance pay** : indemnización *f* (por despido)
severe [sə'vɪr] *adj* **severer; -est 1** STRICT : severo **2** AUSTERE : sobrio, austero **3** SERIOUS : grave ⟨a severe wound : una herida grave⟩ ⟨severe aches : dolores fuertes⟩ **4** DIFFICULT : duro, difícil — **severely** *adv*
severity [sə'vrəti] *n* **1** HARSHNESS : severidad *f* **2** AUSTERITY : sobriedad *f*, austeridad *f* **3** SERIOUSNESS : gravedad *f* (de una herida, etc.)
sew ['soː] *v* **sewed; sewn** ['soːn] *or* **sewed; sewing** : coser
sewage ['suːɪdʒ] *n* : aguas *fpl* negras, aguas *fpl* residuales
sewer¹ ['soːər] *n* : uno que cose
sewer² ['suːər] *n* : alcantarilla *f*, cloaca *f*
sewing ['soːɪŋ] *n* : costura *f*
sex ['sɛks] *n* **1** : sexo *m* ⟨the opposite sex : el sexo opuesto⟩ **2** COPULATION : relaciones *fpl* sexuales
sexism ['sɛkˌsɪzəm] *n* : sexismo *m*
sexist¹ ['sɛksɪst] *adj* : sexista
sexist² *n* : sexista *mf*
sextant ['sɛkstənt] *n* : sextante *m*
sextet [sɛk'stɛt] *n* : sexteto *m*
sexton ['sɛkstən] *n* : sacristán *m*
sexual ['sɛkʃʊəl] *adj* : sexual — **sexually** *adv*
sexuality [ˌsɛkʃʊ'æləti] *n* : sexualidad *f*
sexy ['sɛksi] *adj* **sexier; -est** : sexy
shabbily ['ʃæbəli] *adv* **1** : pobremente ⟨shabbily dressed : pobremente vestido⟩ **2** UNFAIRLY : mal, injustamente

shabbiness ['ʃæbinəs] *n* **1** : lo gastado (de ropa, etc.) **2** : lo mal vestido (de personas) **3** UNFAIRNESS : injusticia *f*
shabby ['ʃæbi] *adj* **shabbier; -est 1** : gastado (dícese de la ropa, etc.) **2** : mal vestido (dícese de las personas) **3** UNFAIR : malo, injusto ⟨shabby treatment : mal trato⟩
shack ['ʃæk] *n* : choza *f*, rancho *m*
shackle¹ ['ʃækəl] *vt* **-led; -ling** : ponerle grilletes (a alguien)
shackle² *n* : grillete *m*
shad ['ʃæd] *n* : sábalo *m*
shade¹ ['ʃeɪd] *v* **shaded; shading** *vt* **1** SHELTER : proteger (del sol o de la luz) **2** *or* **to shade in** : matizar los colores de — *vi* : convertirse gradualmente ⟨his irritation shaded into rage : su irritación iba convirtiéndose en furia⟩
shade² *n* **1** : sombra *f* ⟨to give shade : dar sombra⟩ **2** : tono *m* (de un color) **3** NUANCE : matiz *m* **4** : pantalla *f* (de una lámpara), persiana *f* (de una ventana)
shadow¹ ['ʃædoː] *vt* **1** DARKEN : ensombrecer **2** TRAIL : seguir de cerca, seguirle la pista (a alguien)
shadow² *n* **1** : sombra *f* **2** DARKNESS : oscuridad *f* **3** TRACE : sombra *f*, atisbo *m*, indicio *m* ⟨without a shadow of a doubt : sin sombra de duda, sin lugar a dudas⟩ **4 to cast a shadow over** : ensombrecer
shadowy ['ʃædowi] *adj* **1** INDISTINCT : vago, indistinto **2** DARK : oscuro
shady ['ʃeɪdi] *adj* **shadier; -est 1** : sombreado (dícese de un lugar), que da sombra (dícese de un árbol) **2** DISREPUTABLE : sospechoso (dícese de una persona), turbio (dícese de un negocio, etc.)
shaft ['ʃæft] *n* **1** : asta *f* (de una lanza), astil *m* (de una flecha), mango *m* (de una herramienta) **2** *or* **mine shaft** : pozo *m*
shaggy ['ʃægi] *adj* **shaggier; -est 1** HAIRY : peludo ⟨a shaggy dog : un perro peludo⟩ **2** UNKEMPT : enmarañado, despeinado (dícese del pelo, de las barbas, etc.)
shake¹ ['ʃeɪk] *v* **shook** ['ʃʊk]; **shaken** ['ʃeɪkən]; **shaking** *vt* **1** : sacudir, agitar, hacer temblar ⟨he shook his head : negó con la cabeza⟩ **2** WEAKEN : debilitar, hacer flaquear ⟨it shook her faith : debilitó su confianza⟩ **3** UPSET : afectar, alterar **4 to shake hands with someone** : darle la mano a alguien, estrecharle la mano a alguien — *vi* : temblar, sacudirse
shake² *n* : sacudida *f*, apretón *m* (de manos)
shaker ['ʃeɪkər] *n* **1 salt shaker** : salero *m* **2 pepper shaker** : pimentero *m* **3 cocktail shaker** : coctelera *f*
shake–up ['ʃeɪkˌʌp] *n* : reorganización *f*
shakily ['ʃeɪkəli] *adv* : temblorosamente

shaky [ˈʃeɪki] *adj* **shakier; -est 1** SHAK-
ING : tembloroso **2** UNSTABLE : poco
firme, inestable **3** PRECARIOUS : precario, incierto **4** QUESTIONABLE : dudoso, cuestionable ⟨shaky arguments
: argumentos discutibles⟩

shale [ˈʃeɪl] *n* : esquisto *m*

shall [ˈʃæl] *v aux, past* **should** [ˈʃʊd] *present s & pl* **shall 1** (*used to express a
command*) ⟨you shall do as I say : harás
lo que te digo⟩ **2** (*used to express futu-
rity*) ⟨we shall see : ya veremos⟩ ⟨when
shall we expect you? : ¿cuándo te
podemos esperar?⟩ **3** (*used to express
determination*) ⟨you shall have the
money : tendrás el dinero⟩ **4** (*used to
express a condition*) ⟨if he should die
: si muriera⟩ ⟨if they should call, tell
me : si llaman, dímelo⟩ **5** (*used to express obligation*) ⟨he should have said
it : debería haberlo dicho⟩ **6** (*used to
express probability*) ⟨they should arrive
soon : deben (de) llegar pronto⟩ ⟨why
should he lie? : ¿porqué ha de mentir?⟩

shallow [ˈʃæloː] *adj* **1** : poco profundo
(dícese del agua, etc.) **2** SUPERFICIAL
: superficial

shallows [ˈʃæloːz] *npl* : bajío *m*, bajos
mpl

sham¹ [ˈʃæm] *v* **shammed; shamming**
: fingir

sham² *adj* : falso, fingido

sham³ *n* **1** FAKE, PRETENSE : farsa *f*,
simulación *f*, imitación *f* **2** FAKER : impostor *m*, -tora *f*; farsante *mf*

shamble [ˈʃæmbəl] *vi* **-bled; -bling**
: caminar arrastrando los pies

shambles [ˈʃæmbəlz] *ns & pl* : caos *m*,
desorden *m*, confusión *f*

shame¹ [ˈʃeɪm] *vt* **shamed; shaming 1**
: avergonzar ⟨he was shamed by their
words : sus palabras le dieron vergüen-
za⟩ **2** DISGRACE : deshonrar

shame² *n* **1** : vergüenza *f* ⟨to have no
shame : no tener vergüenza⟩ **2** DIS-
GRACE : vergüenza *f*, deshonra *f* **3** PITY
: lástima *f*, pena *f* ⟨what a shame! : ¡qué
pena!⟩

shamefaced [ˈʃeɪmˌfeɪst] *adj* : avergonzado

shameful [ˈʃeɪmfəl] *adj* : vergonzoso —
shamefully *adv*

shameless [ˈʃeɪmləs] *adj* : descarado,
desvergonzado — **shamelessly** *adv*

shampoo¹ [ʃæmˈpuː] *vt* : lavar (el pelo)

shampoo² *n, pl* **-poos** : champú *m*

shamrock [ˈʃæmˌrɑk] *n* : trébol *m*

shank [ˈʃæŋk] *n* : parte *f* baja de la pierna

shan't [ˈʃænt] (*contraction of* **shall not**)
→ **shall**

shanty [ˈʃænti] *n, pl* **-ties** : choza *f*, rancho *m*

shape¹ [ˈʃeɪp] *v* **shaped; shaping** *vt* **1**
: dar forma a, modelar (arcilla, etc.),
tallar (madera, piedra), formar (carácter) ⟨to be shaped like : tener forma
de⟩ **2** DETERMINE : decidir, determi-

nar — *vi or* **to shape up** : tomar forma

shape² *n* **1** : forma *f*, figura *f* ⟨in the
shape of a circle : en forma de círcu-
lo⟩ **2** CONDITION : estado *m*, condiciones *fpl*, forma *f* (física) ⟨to get in
shape : ponerse en forma⟩

shapeless [ˈʃeɪpləs] *adj* : informe

shapely [ˈʃeɪpli] *adj* **shapelier; -est**
: curvilíneo, bien proporcionado

shard [ˈʃɑrd] *n* : fragmento *m*, casco *m*
(de cerámica, etc.)

share¹ [ˈʃɛr] *v* **shared; sharing** *vt* **1** AP-
PORTION : dividir, repartir **2** : compartir ⟨they share a room : comparten
una habitación⟩ — *vi* : compartir

share² *n* **1** PORTION : parte *f*, porción *f*
⟨one's fair share : lo que le corresponde
a uno⟩ **2** : acción *f* (en una compañía)
⟨to hold shares : tener acciones⟩

sharecropper [ˈʃɛrˌkrɑpər] *n* : aparcero
m, -ra *f*

shareholder [ˈʃɛrˌhoːldər] *n* : accionista
mf

shark [ˈʃɑrk] *n* : tiburón *m*

sharp¹ [ˈʃɑrp] *adv* : en punto ⟨at two
o'clock sharp : a las dos en punto⟩

sharp² *adj* **1** : afilado, filoso ⟨a sharp
knife : un cuchillo afilado⟩ **2** PENE-
TRATING : cortante, fuerte **3** CLEVER
: agudo, listo, perspicaz **4** ACUTE : agudo ⟨sharp eyesight : vista aguda⟩ **5**
HARSH, SEVERE : duro, severo, agudo
⟨a sharp rebuke : una reprimenda mor-
daz⟩ **6** STRONG : fuerte ⟨sharp cheese
: queso fuerte⟩ **7** ABRUPT : brusco, repentino **8** DISTINCT : nítido, definido
⟨a sharp image : una imagen bien
definida⟩ **9** ANGULAR : anguloso
(dícese de la cara) **10** : sostenido (en
música)

sharp³ *n* : sostenido *m* (en música)

sharpen [ˈʃɑrpən] *vt* : afilar, aguzar ⟨to
sharpen a pencil : sacarle punta a un
lápiz⟩ ⟨to sharpen one's wits : aguzar
el ingenio⟩

sharpener [ˈʃɑrpənər] *n* : afilador *m*
(para cuchillos, etc.), sacapuntas *m*
(para lápices)

sharply [ˈʃɑrpli] *adv* **1** ABRUPTLY : bruscamente **2** DISTINCTLY : claramente,
marcadamente

sharpness [ˈʃɑrpnəs] *n* **1** : lo afilado (de
un cuchillo, etc.) **2** ACUTENESS
: agudeza *f* (de los sentidos o de la
mente) **3** INTENSITY : intensidad *f*,
agudeza *f* (de dolores, etc.) **4** HARSH-
NESS : dureza *f*, severidad *f* **5** ABRUPT-
NESS : brusquedad *f* **6** CLARITY : nitidez *f*

sharpshooter [ˈʃɑrpˌʃuːtər] *n* : tirador
m, -dora *f* de primera

shatter [ˈʃætər] *vt* **1** : hacer añicos ⟨to
shatter the silence : romper el silencio⟩
2 to be shattered by : quedar destrozado por — *vi* : hacerse añicos,
romperse en pedazos

shave¹ ['ʃeɪv] v **shaved; shaved** or **shaven** ['ʃeɪvən]; **shaving** vt **1** : afeitar, rasurar ⟨she shaved her legs : se rasuró las piernas⟩ ⟨they shaved (off) his beard : le afeitaron la barba⟩ **2** SLICE : cortar (en pedazos finos) — vi : afeitarse, rasurarse

shave² n : afeitada f, rasurada f

shaver ['ʃeɪvər] n : afeitadora f, máquina f de afeitar, rasuradora f

shawl ['ʃɔl] n : chal m, mantón m, rebozo m

she ['ʃiː] pron : ella

sheaf ['ʃiːf] n, pl **sheaves** ['ʃiːvz] : gavilla f (de cereales), haz m (de flechas), fajo m (de papeles)

shear ['ʃɪr] vt **sheared; sheared** or **shorn** ['ʃɔrn]; **shearing 1** : esquilar, trasquilar ⟨to shear sheep : trasquilar ovejas⟩ **2** CUT : cortar (el pelo, etc.)

shears ['ʃɪrz] npl : tijeras fpl (grandes)

sheath ['ʃiːθ] n, pl **sheaths** ['ʃiːðz, 'ʃiːθs] : funda f, vaina f

sheathe ['ʃiːð] vt **sheathed; sheathing** : envainar, enfundar

shed¹ ['ʃd] vt **shed; shedding 1** : derramar (sangre o lágrimas) **2** EMIT : emitir (luz) ⟨to shed light on : aclarar⟩ **3** DISCARD : mudar (la piel, etc.) ⟨to shed one's clothes : quitarse uno la ropa⟩

shed² n : cobertizo m

she'd ['ʃiːd] (contraction of **she had** or **she would**) → **have, would**

sheen ['ʃiːn] n : brillo m, lustre m

sheep ['ʃiːp] ns & pl : oveja f

sheepfold ['ʃiːp,foːld] n : redil m

sheepish ['ʃiːpɪʃ] adj : avergonzado

sheepskin ['ʃiːp,skɪn] n : piel f de oveja, piel f de borrego

sheer¹ ['ʃɪr] adv **1** COMPLETELY : completamente, totalmente **2** VERTICALLY : verticalmente

sheer² adj **1** TRANSPARENT : vaporoso, transparente **2** ABSOLUTE, UTTER : puro ⟨by sheer luck : por pura suerte⟩ **3** STEEP : escarpado, vertical

sheet ['ʃiːt] n **1** or **bedsheet** ['bɛd-,ʃiːt] : sábana f **2** : hoja f (de papel) **3** : capa f (de hielo, etc.) **4** : lámina f, placa f (de vidrio, metal, etc.), plancha f (de metal, madera, etc.) ⟨baking sheet : placa de horno⟩

sheikh or **sheik** ['ʃiːk, 'ʃeɪk] n : jeque m

shelf ['ʃɛlf] n, pl **shelves** ['ʃɛlvz] **1** : estante m, anaquel m (en una pared) **2** : banco m, arrecife m (en geología) ⟨continental shelf : plataforma continental⟩

shell¹ ['ʃɛl] vt **1** : desvainar (chícharos), pelar (nueces, etc.) **2** BOMBARD : bombardear

shell² n **1** SEASHELL : concha f **2** : cáscara f (de huevos, nueces, etc.), vaina f (de chícharos, etc.), caparazón m (de crustáceos, tortugas, etc.) **3** : cartucho m, casquillo m ⟨a .45 caliber shell : un cartucho calibre .45⟩ **4** or **racing shell** : bote m (para hacer regatas de remos)

she'll ['ʃiːl, 'ʃɪl] (contraction of **she shall** or **she will**) → **shall, will**

shellac¹ [ʃəˈlæk] vt **-lacked; -lacking 1** : laquear (madera, etc.) **2** DEFEAT : darle una paliza (a alguien), derrotar

shellac² n : laca f

shellfish ['ʃɛl,fɪʃ] n : marisco m

shelter¹ ['ʃɛltər] vt **1** PROTECT : proteger, abrigar **2** HARBOR : dar refugio a, albergar

shelter² n : refugio m, abrigo m ⟨to take shelter : refugiarse⟩

shelve ['ʃɛlv] vt **shelved; shelving 1** : poner en estantes **2** DEFER : dar carpetazo a

shenanigans [ʃəˈnænɪɡənz] npl **1** TRICKERY : artimañas fpl **2** MISCHIEF : travesuras fpl

shepherd¹ ['ʃɛpərd] vt **1** : cuidar (ovejas, etc.) **2** GUIDE : conducir, guiar

shepherd² n : pastor m

shepherdess ['ʃɛpərdəs] n : pastora f

sherbet ['ʃərbət] or **sherbert** [-bərt] n : sorbete m, nieve f Cuba, Mex, PRi

sheriff ['ʃɛrɪf] n : sheriff mf

sherry ['ʃɛri] n, pl **-ries** : jerez m

she's ['ʃiːz] (contraction of **she is** or **she has**) → **be, have**

shield¹ ['ʃiːld] vt **1** PROTECT : proteger **2** CONCEAL : ocultar ⟨to shield one's eyes : taparse los ojos⟩

shield² n **1** : escudo m (armadura) **2** PROTECTION : protección f, blindaje m (de un cable)

shier, shiest → **shy**

shift¹ ['ʃɪft] vt **1** CHANGE : cambiar ⟨to shift gears : cambiar de velocidad⟩ **2** MOVE : mover **3** TRANSFER : transferir ⟨to shift the blame : echarle la culpa (a otro)⟩ — vi **1** CHANGE : cambiar **2** MOVE : moverse **3 to shift for oneself** : arreglárselas solo

shift² n **1** CHANGE, TRANSFER : cambio m ⟨a shift in priorities : un cambio de prioridades⟩ **2** : turno m ⟨night shift : turno de noche⟩ **3** DRESS : vestido m (suelto) **4** → **gearshift**

shiftless ['ʃɪftləs] adj : perezoso, vago, holgazán

shifty ['ʃɪfti] adj **shiftier; -est** : taimado, artero ⟨a shifty look : una mirada huidiza⟩

shilling ['ʃɪlɪŋ] n : chelín m

shimmer ['ʃɪmər] vi GLIMMER : brillar con luz trémula

shin¹ ['ʃɪn] vi **shinned; shinning** : trepar, subir ⟨she shinned up the pole : subió al poste⟩

shin² n : espinilla f, canilla f

shine¹ ['ʃaɪn] v **shone** ['ʃoːn] or **shined; shining** vi **1** : brillar, relucir ⟨the stars were shining : las estrellas brillaban⟩ **2** EXCEL : brillar, lucirse — vt **1** : alumbrar ⟨he shined the flashlight at it : lo alumbró con la linterna⟩ **2** POLISH : sacarle brillo a, lustrar

shine² n : brillo m, lustre m

shingle¹ ['ʃɪŋɡəl] vt **-gled; -gling** : techar

shingle² *n* : tablilla *f* (para techar)
shingles ['ʃɪŋgəlz] *npl* : herpes *m*
shinny ['ʃɪni] *vi* **-nied; -nying** → **shin¹**
shiny ['ʃaɪni] *adj* **shinier; -est** : brillante
ship¹ ['ʃɪp] *vt* **shipped; shipping 1**
LOAD : embarcar (en un barco) **2** SEND
: transportar (en barco), enviar ⟨to ship
by air : enviar por avión⟩
ship² *n* **1** : barco *m*, buque *m* **2** →
spaceship
shipboard ['ʃɪp,bord] *n* **on ~** : a bordo
shipbuilder ['ʃɪp,bɪldər] *n* : constructor
m, -tora *f* naval
shipment ['ʃɪpmənt] *n* **1** SHIPPING
: transporte *m*, embarque *m* **2** : envío
m, remesa *f* ⟨a shipment of medicine
: un envío de medicina⟩
shipping ['ʃɪpɪŋ] *n* **1** SHIPS : barcos *mpl*,
embarcaciones *fpl* **2** TRANSPORTA-
TION : transporte *m* (de mercancías)
shipshape ['ʃɪp,ʃeɪp] *adj* : ordenado
shipwreck¹ ['ʃɪp,rɛk] *vt* **to be shipwrecked** : naufragar
shipwreck² *n* : naufragio *m*
shipyard ['ʃɪp,jard] *n* : astillero *m*
shirk ['ʃərk] *vt* : eludir, rehuir ⟨to shirk
one's responsibilities : esquivar uno sus
responsabilidades⟩
shirt ['ʃərt] *n* : camisa *f*
shiver¹ ['ʃɪvər] *vi* **1** : tiritar (de frío) **2**
TREMBLE : estremecerse, temblar
shiver² *n* : escalofrío *m*, estremecimiento *m*
shoal ['ʃoːl] *n* : banco *m*, bajío *m*
shock¹ ['ʃak] *vt* **1** UPSET : conmover,
conmocionar **2** STARTLE : asustar, sobresaltar **3** SCANDALIZE : escandalizar
4 : darle una descarga eléctrica a
shock² *n* **1** COLLISION, JOLT : choque
m, sacudida *f* **2** UPSET : conmoción *f*,
golpe *m* emocional **3** : shock *m* (en
medicina) **4** *or* **electric shock** : descarga *f* eléctrica **5** SHEAVES : gavillas *fpl*
6 shock of hair : mata *f* de pelo
shock absorber *n* : amortiguador *m*
shocking ['ʃakɪŋ] *adj* **1** : chocante **2
shocking pink** : rosa *m* estridente
shoddy ['ʃadi] *adj* **shoddier; -est** : de
mala calidad ⟨a shoddy piece of work
: un trabajo chapucero⟩
shoe¹ ['ʃuː] *vt* **shod** ['ʃad]; **shoeing**
: herrar (un caballo)
shoe² *n* **1** : zapato *m* ⟨the shoe industry : la industria del calzado⟩ **2** HORSE-
SHOE : herradura *f* **3 brake shoe** : zapata *f*
shoelace ['ʃuː,leɪs] *n* : cordón *m* (de zapatos)
shoemaker ['ʃuː,meɪkər] *n* : zapatero *m*,
-ra *f*
shone → **shine**
shook → **shake**
shoot¹ ['ʃuːt] *v* **shot** ['ʃat]; **shooting** *vt*
1 : disparar, tirar ⟨to shoot a bullet
: tirar una bala⟩ **2** : pegarle un tiro a,
darle un balazo a ⟨he shot her : le pegó
un tiro⟩ ⟨they shot and killed him : lo
mataron a balazos⟩ **3** THROW : lanzar

(una pelota, etc.), echar (una mirada)
4 PHOTOGRAPH : fotografiar **5** FILM
: filmar — *vi* **1** : disparar (con un arma
de fuego) **2** DART : ir rápidamente ⟨it
shot past : pasó como una bala⟩
shoot² *n* : brote *m*, retoño *m*, vástago *m*
shooting star *n* : estrella *f* fugaz
shop¹ ['ʃap] *vi* **shopped; shopping**
: hacer compras ⟨to go shopping : ir de
compras⟩
shop² *n* **1** WORKSHOP : taller *m* **2** STORE
: tienda *f*
shopkeeper ['ʃap,kiːpər] *n* : tendero *m*,
-ra *f*
shoplift ['ʃap,lɪft] *vi* : hurtar mercancía
(de una tienda) — *vt* : hurtar (de una
tienda)
shoplifter ['ʃap,lɪftər] *n* : ladrón *m*,
-drona *f* (que roba en una tienda)
shopper ['ʃapər] *n* : comprador *m*, -dora
f
shore¹ ['ʃor] *vt* **shored; shoring** : apuntalar ⟨they shored up the wall : apun-
talaron la pared⟩
shore² *n* **1** : orilla *f* (del mar, etc.) **2**
PROP : puntal *m*
shoreline ['ʃor,laɪn] *n* : orilla *f*
shorn → **shear**
short¹ ['ʃort] *adv* **1** ABRUPTLY : repentinamente, súbitamente ⟨the car
stopped short : el carro se paró en seco⟩
2 to fall short : no alcanzar, quedarse
corto
short² *adj* **1** : corto (de medida), bajo
(de estatura) **2** BRIEF : corto ⟨short
and sweet : corto y bueno⟩ ⟨a short
time ago : hace poco⟩ **3** CURT : brusco, cortante, seco **4** : corto (de tiempo, de dinero) ⟨I'm one dollar short
: me falta un dólar⟩
short³ *n* **1 shorts** *npl* : shorts *mpl*, pantalones *mpl* cortos **2** → **short circuit**
shortage ['ʃortɪdʒ] *n* : falta *f*, escasez *f*,
carencia *f*
shortcake ['ʃort,keɪk] *n* : tarta *f* de fruta
shortchange ['ʃort'tʃeɪndʒ] *vt* **-changed;
-changing** : darle mal el cambio (a alguien)
short circuit *n* : cortocircuito *m*, corto
m (eléctrico)
shortcoming ['ʃort,kʌmɪŋ] *n* : defecto *m*
shortcut ['ʃort,kʌt] *n* **1** : atajo *m* ⟨to take
a shortcut : cortar camino⟩ **2** : alternativa *f* fácil, método *m* rápido
shorten ['ʃortən] *vt* : acortar — *vi* : acortarse
shorthand ['ʃort,hænd] *n* : taquigrafía *f*
short–lived ['ʃort'lɪvd, -'laɪvd] *adj*
: efímero
shortly ['ʃortli] *adv* **1** BRIEFLY : brevemente ⟨to put it shortly : para decirlo
en pocas palabras⟩ **2** SOON : dentro de
poco
shortness ['ʃortnəs] *n* **1** : lo corto
⟨shortness of stature : estatura baja⟩ **2**
BREVITY : brevedad *f* **3** CURTNESS
: brusquedad *f* **4** SHORTAGE : falta *f*,
escasez *f*, carencia *f*

shortsighted [ˈʃɔrtˌsaɪtəd] → **near-sighted**

shot [ˈʃɑt] n **1** : disparo m, tiro m ⟨to fire a shot : disparar⟩ **2** PELLETS : perdigones mpl **3** : tiro m (en deportes) **4** ATTEMPT : intento m, tentativa f ⟨to have a shot at : hacer un intento por⟩ **5** RANGE : alcance m ⟨a long shot : una posibilidad remota⟩ **6** PHOTOGRAPH : foto f **7** INJECTION : inyección f **8** : trago m (de licor)

shotgun [ˈʃɑtˌgʌn] n : escopeta f

should → **shall**

shoulder¹ [ˈʃoːldər] vt **1** JOSTLE : empujar (con el hombro) **2** : ponerse al hombro (una mochila, etc.) **3** : cargar con (la responsabilidad, etc.)

shoulder² n **1** : hombro m ⟨to shrug one's shoulders : encogerse los hombros⟩ **2** : arcén m (de una carretera)

shoulder blade n : omóplato m, omoplato m, escápula f

shouldn't [ˈʃʊdənt] (contraction of should not) → **shall**

shout¹ [ˈʃaʊt] v : gritar, vocear

shout² n : grito m

shove¹ [ˈʃʌv] v **shoved; shoving** : empujar bruscamente

shove² n : empujón m, empellón m

shovel¹ [ˈʃʌvəl] vt **-veled** or **-velled; -veling** or **-velling 1** : mover con (una) pala ⟨they shoveled the dirt out : sacaron la tierra con palas⟩ **2** DIG : cavar (con una pala)

shovel² n : pala f

show¹ [ˈʃoː] v **showed; shown** [ˈʃoːn] or **showed; showing** vt **1** DISPLAY : mostrar, enseñar **2** REVEAL : demostrar, manifestar, revelar ⟨he showed himself to be a coward : se reveló como cobarde⟩ **3** TEACH : enseñar **4** PROVE : demostrar, probar **5** CONDUCT, DIRECT : llevar, acompañar ⟨to show someone the way : indicarle el camino a alguien⟩ **6** : proyectar (una película), dar (un programa de televisión) — vi **1** : notarse, verse ⟨the stain doesn't show : la mancha no se ve⟩ **2** APPEAR : aparecer, dejarse ver

show² n **1** : demostración f ⟨a show of force : una demostración de fuerza⟩ **2** EXHIBITION : exposición f, exhibición f ⟨flower show : exposición de flores⟩ ⟨to be on show : estar expuesto⟩ **3** : espectáculo m (teatral), programa m (de televisión, etc.) ⟨to go to a show : ir al teatro⟩

showcase [ˈʃoːˌkeɪs] n : vitrina f

showdown [ˈʃoːˌdaʊn] n : confrontación f (decisiva)

shower¹ [ˈʃaʊər] vt **1** SPRAY : regar, mojar **2** HEAP : colmar ⟨they showered him with gifts : lo colmaron de regalos, le llovieron los regalos⟩ — vi **1** BATHE : ducharse, darse una ducha **2** RAIN : llover

shower² n **1** : chaparrón m, chubasco m ⟨a chance of showers : una posibil-idad de chaparrones⟩ **2** : ducha f ⟨to take a shower : ducharse⟩ **3** PARTY : fiesta f ⟨a bridal shower : una despedida de soltera⟩

show off vt : hacer alarde de, ostentar — vi : lucirse

show up vi APPEAR : aparecer — vt EXPOSE : revelar

showy [ˈʃoːi] adj **showier; -est** : llamativo, ostentoso — **showily** adv

shrank → **shrink**

shrapnel [ˈʃræpnəl] ns & pl : metralla f

shred¹ [ˈʃred] vt **shredded; shredding** : hacer trizas, desmenuzar (con las manos), triturar (con una máquina) ⟨to shred vegetables : cortar verduras en tiras⟩

shred² n **1** STRIP : tira f, jirón m (de tela) **2** BIT : pizca f ⟨not a shred of evidence : ni la mínima prueba⟩

shrew [ˈʃruː] n **1** : musaraña f (animal) **2** : mujer f regañona, arpía f

shrewd [ˈʃruːd] adj : astuto, inteligente, sagaz — **shrewdly** adv

shrewdness [ˈʃruːdnəs] n : astucia f

shriek¹ [ˈʃriːk] vi : chillar, gritar

shriek² n : chillido m, alarido m, grito m

shrill [ˈʃrɪl] adj : agudo, estridente

shrilly [ˈʃrɪli] adv : agudamente

shrimp [ˈʃrɪmp] n : camarón m, langostino m

shrine [ˈʃraɪn] n **1** TOMB : sepulcro m (de un santo) **2** SANCTUARY : lugar m sagrado, santuario m

shrink [ˈʃrɪŋk] vi **shrank** [ˈʃræŋk] or **shrunk** [ˈʃrʌŋk]; **shrunk** or **shrunken** [ˈʃrʌŋkən]; **shrinking 1** RECOIL : retroceder ⟨he shrank back : se echó para atrás⟩ **2** : encogerse (dícese de la ropa)

shrinkage [ˈʃrɪŋkɪdʒ] n : encogimiento m (de ropa, etc.), contracción f, reducción f

shrivel [ˈʃrɪvəl] vi **-veled** or **-velled; -veling** or **-velling** : arrugarse, marchitarse

shroud¹ [ˈʃraʊd] vt : envolver

shroud² n **1** : sudario m, mortaja f **2** VEIL : velo m ⟨wrapped in a shroud of mystery : envuelto en un aura de misterio⟩

shrub [ˈʃrʌb] n : arbusto m, mata f

shrubbery [ˈʃrʌbəri] n, pl **-beries** : arbustos mpl, matas fpl

shrug [ˈʃrʌg] vi **shrugged; shrugging** : encogerse de hombros

shrunk → **shrink**

shuck¹ [ˈʃʌk] vt : pelar (mazorcas, etc.), abrir (almejas, etc.)

shuck² n **1** HUSK : cascarilla f, cáscara f (de una nuez, etc.), hojas fpl (de una mazorca) **2** SHELL : concha f (de una almeja, etc.)

shudder¹ [ˈʃʌdər] vi : estremecerse

shudder² n : estremecimiento m, escalofrío m

shuffle¹ [ˈʃʌfəl] v **-fled; -fling** vt MIX : mezclar, revolver, barajar (naipes) — vi : caminar arrastrando los pies

shuffle² n **1** : acto m de revolver ⟨each player gets a shuffle : a cada jugador le toca barajar⟩ **2** JUMBLE : revoltijo m **3** : arrastramiento m de los pies

shun [ˈʃʌn] vi **shunned; shunning** : evitar, esquivar, eludir

shunt [ˈʃʌnt] vt : desviar, cambiar de vía (un tren)

shut [ˈʃʌt] v **shut; shutting** vt **1** CLOSE : cerrar ⟨shut the lid : tápalo⟩ **2 to shut out** EXCLUDE : excluir, dejar fuera a (personas), no dejar que entre (luz, ruido, etc.) **3 to shut up** CONFINE : encerrar — vi : cerrarse ⟨the factory shut down : la fábrica cerró suspuertas⟩

shut–in [ˈʃʌtˌɪn] n : inválido m, -da f (que no puede salir de casa)

shutter [ˈʃʌtər] n **1** : contraventana f, postigo m (de una ventana o puerta) **2** : obturador m (de una cámara)

shuttle¹ [ˈʃʌtəl] v **-tled; -tling** vt : transportar ⟨she shuttled him back and forth : lo llevaba de acá para allá⟩ — vi : ir y venir

shuttle² n **1** : lanzadera f (para tejer) **2** : vehículo m que hace recorridos cortos **3** → **space shuttle**

shuttlecock [ˈʃʌtəlˌkɑk] n : volante m

shut up vi : callarse ⟨shut up! : ¡cállate (la boca)!⟩

shy¹ [ˈʃaɪ] vi **shied; shying** : retroceder, asustarse

shy² adj **shier** or **shyer** [ˈʃaɪər]; **shiest** or **shyest** [ˈʃaɪəst] **1** TIMID : tímido **2** WARY : cauteloso ⟨he's not shy about asking : no vacila en preguntar⟩ **3** SHORT : corto (de dinero, etc.) ⟨I'm two dollars shy : me faltan dos dólares⟩

shyly [ˈʃaɪli] adv : tímidamente

shyness [ˈʃaɪnəs] n : timidez f

Siamese¹ [ˌsaɪəˈmiːz, -ˈmiːs-] adj : siamés ⟨Siamese twins : hermanos siameses⟩

Siamese² n **1** : siamés m, -mesa f **2** : siamés m (idioma) **3** or **Siamese cat** : gato m siamés

sibling [ˈsɪblɪŋ] n : hermano m, hermana f

Sicilian [səˈsɪljən] n : siciliano m, -na f — **Sicilian** adj

sick [ˈsɪk] adj **1** : enfermo **2** NAUSEOUS : mareado, con náuseas ⟨to get sick : vomitar⟩ **3** : para uso de enfermos ⟨sick day : día de permiso (por enfermedad)⟩

sickbed [ˈsɪkˌbɛd] n : lecho m de enfermo

sicken [ˈsɪkən] vt **1** : poner enfermo **2** REVOLT : darle asco (a alguien) — vi : enfermar(se), caer enfermo

sickening [ˈsɪkənɪŋ] adj : asqueroso, repugnante, nauseabundo

sickle [ˈsɪkəl] n : hoz f

sickly [ˈsɪkli] adj **sicklier; -est 1** : enfermizo **2** → **sickening**

sickness [ˈsɪknəs] n **1** : enfermedad f **2** NAUSEA : náuseas fpl

side [ˈsaɪd] n **1** : lado m, costado m (de una persona), ijada f (de un animal) **2** : lado m, cara f (de una moneda, etc.) **3** : lado m, parte f ⟨he's on my side : está de mi parte⟩ ⟨to take sides : tomar partido⟩

sideboard [ˈsaɪdˌbord] n : aparador m

sideburns [ˈsaɪdˌbərnz] npl : patillas fpl

sided [ˈsaɪdəd] adj : que tiene lados ⟨one-sided : de un lado⟩

side effect n : efecto m secundario

sideline [ˈsaɪdˌlaɪn] n **1** : línea f de banda (en deportes) **2** : actividad f suplementaria (en negocios) **3 to be on the sidelines** : estar al margen

sidelong [ˈsaɪdˌlɔŋ] adj : de reojo, de soslayo

sideshow [ˈsaɪdˌʃoː] n : espectáculo m secundario, atracción f secundaria

sidestep [ˈsaɪdˌstɛp] v **-stepped; -stepping** vi : dar un paso hacia un lado — vt AVOID : esquivar, eludir

sidetrack [ˈsaɪdˌtræk] vt : desviar (una conversación, etc.), distraer (a una persona)

sidewalk [ˈsaɪdˌwɔk] n : acera f, vereda f, andén m CA, Col, banqueta f Mex

sideways¹ [ˈsaɪdˌweɪz] adv **1** : hacia un lado ⟨it leaned sideways : se inclinaba hacia un lado⟩ **2** : de lado, de costado ⟨lie sideways : acuéstese de costado⟩

sideways² adj : hacia un lado ⟨a sideways glance : una mirada de reojo⟩

siding [ˈsaɪdɪŋ] n **1** : apartadero m (para trenes) **2** : revestimiento m exterior (de un edificio)

sidle [ˈsaɪdəl] vi **-dled; -dling** : moverse furtivamente

siege [ˈsiːdʒ, ˈsiːʒ] n : sitio m ⟨to be under siege : estar sitiado⟩

siesta [siˈɛstə] n : siesta f

sieve [ˈsɪv] n : tamiz m, cedazo m, criba f (en mineralogía)

sift [ˈsɪft] vt **1** : tamizar, cerner ⟨sift the flour : tamice la harina⟩ **2** or **to sift through** : examinar cuidadosamente, pasar por el tamiz

sifter [ˈsɪftər] n : tamiz m, cedazo m

sigh¹ [ˈsaɪ] vi : suspirar

sigh² n : suspiro m

sight¹ [ˈsaɪt] vt : ver (a una persona), divisar (la tierra, un barco)

sight² n **1** : vista f (facultad) ⟨out of sight : fuera de vista⟩ **2** : algo visto ⟨it's a familiar sight : se ve con frecuencia⟩ ⟨she's a sight for sore eyes : da gusto verla⟩ **3** : lugar m de interés (para turistas, etc.) **4** : mira f (de un rifle, etc.) **5** GLIMPSE : mirada f breve ⟨I caught sight of her : la divisé, alcancé a verla⟩

sighting [ˈsaɪtɪŋ] n : avistamiento m

sightless [ˈsaɪtləs] adj : invidente, ciego

sightseer [ˈsaɪtˌsiːər] n : turista mf

sign¹ [ˈsaɪn] vt **1** : firmar ⟨to sign a check : firmar un cheque⟩ **2** or **to sign on** HIRE : contratar (a un empleado), fichar (a un jugador) — vi **1** : hacer una seña ⟨she signed for him to stop : le hizo una seña para que se parara⟩ **2** : comunicarse por señas

sign² *n* **1** SYMBOL : símbolo *m*, signo *m* ⟨minus sign : signo de menos⟩ **2** GESTURE : seña *f*, señal *f*, gesto *m* **3** : letrero *m*, cartel *m* ⟨neon sign : letrero de neón⟩ **4** TRACE : señal *f*, indicio *m*

signal¹ [ˈsɪɡnəl] *vt* **-naled** *or* **-nalled; -naling** *or* **-nalling 1** : hacerle señas (a alguien) ⟨she signaled me to leave : me hizo señas para que saliera⟩ **2** INDICATE : señalar, indicar — *vi* : hacer señas, comunicar por señas

signal² *adj* NOTABLE : señalado, notable

signal³ *n* : señal *f*

signature [ˈsɪɡnəˌtʃʊr] *n* : firma *f*

signet [ˈsɪɡnət] *n* : sello *m*

significance [sɪɡˈnɪfɪkənts] *n* **1** MEANING : significado *m* **2** IMPORTANCE : importancia *f*

significant [sɪɡˈnɪfɪkənt] *adj* **1** IMPORTANT : importante **2** MEANINGFUL : significativo — **significantly** *adv*

signify [ˈsɪɡnəˌfaɪ] *vt* **-fied; -fying 1** : indicar ⟨he signified his desire for more : haciendo señas indicó que quería más⟩ **2** MEAN : significar

sign language *n* : lenguaje *m* por señas

signpost [ˈsaɪnˌpoːst] *n* : poste *m* indicador

silence¹ [ˈsaɪlənts] *vt* **-lenced; -lencing** : silenciar, acallar

silence² *n* : silencio *m*

silent [ˈsaɪlənt] *adj* **1** : callado ⟨to remain silent : quedarse callado, guardar silencio⟩ **2** QUIET, STILL : silencioso **3** MUTE : mudo ⟨a silent letter : una letra muda⟩

silently [ˈsaɪləntli] *adv* : silenciosamente, calladamente

silhouette¹ [ˌsɪləˈwɛt] *vt* **-etted; -etting** : destacar la silueta de ⟨it was silhouetted against the sky : se perfilaba contra el cielo⟩

silhouette² *n* : silueta *f*

silica [ˈsɪlɪkə] *n* : sílice *f*

silicon [ˈsɪlɪkən, -ˌkɑn] *n* : silicio *m*

silk [ˈsɪlk] *n* : seda *f*

silken [ˈsɪlkən] *adj* **1** : de seda ⟨a silken veil : un velo de seda⟩ **2** SILKY : sedoso ⟨silken hair : cabellos sedosos⟩

silkworm [ˈsɪlkˌwərm] *n* : gusano *m* de seda

silky [ˈsɪlki] *adj* **silkier; -est** : sedoso

sill [ˈsɪl] *n* : alféizar *m* (de una ventana), umbral *m* (de una puerta)

silliness [ˈsɪlinəs] *n* : tontería *f*, estupidez *f*

silly [ˈsɪli] *adj* **sillier; -est** : tonto, estúpido, ridículo

silo [ˈsaɪˌloː] *n, pl* **silos** : silo *m*

silt [ˈsɪlt] *n* : cieno *m*

silver¹ [ˈsɪlvər] *adj* **1** : de plata ⟨a silver spoon : una cuchara de plata⟩ **2** → **silvery**

silver² *n* **1** : plata *f* **2** COINS : monedas *fpl* **3** → **silverware 4** : color *m* plata

silverware [ˈsɪlvərˌwær] *n* **1** : artículos *mpl* de plata, platería *f* **2** FLATWARE : cubertería *f*

silvery [ˈsɪlvəri] *adj* : plateado

similar [ˈsɪmələr] *adj* : similar, parecido, semejante

similarity [ˌsɪməˈlærəti] *n, pl* **-ties** : semejanza *f*, parecido *m*

similarly [ˈsɪmələrli] *adv* : de manera similar

simile [ˈsɪməˌliː] *n* : símil *m*

simmer [ˈsɪmər] *v* : hervir a fuego lento

simper¹ [ˈsɪmpər] *vi* : sonreír como un tonto

simper² *n* : sonrisa *f* tonta

simple [ˈsɪmpəl] *adj* **simpler; -plest 1** INNOCENT : inocente **2** PLAIN : sencillo, simple **3** EASY : simple, sencillo, fácil **4** STRAIGHTFORWARD : puro, simple ⟨the simple truth : la pura verdad⟩ **5** NAIVE : ingenuo, simple

simpleton [ˈsɪmpəltən] *n* : bobo *m*, -ba *f*; tonto *m*, -ta *f*

simplicity [sɪmˈplɪsəti] *n* : simplicidad *f*, sencillez *f*

simplification [ˌsɪmpləfəˈkeɪʃən] *n* : simplificación *f*

simplify [ˈsɪmpləˌfaɪ] *vt* **-fied; -fying** : simplificar

simply [ˈsɪmpli] *adv* **1** PLAINLY : sencillamente **2** SOLELY : simplemente, sólo **3** REALLY : absolutamente

simulate [ˈsɪmjəˌleɪt] *vt* **-lated; -lating** : simular

simulation [ˌsɪmjəˈleɪʃən] *n* : simulación *f*

simultaneous [ˌsaɪməlˈteɪniəs] *adj* : simultáneo — **simultaneously** *adv*

sin¹ [ˈsɪn] *vi* **sinned; sinning** : pecar

sin² *n* : pecado *m*

since¹ [ˈsɪnts] *adv* **1** : desde entonces ⟨they've been friends ever since : desde entonces han sido amigos⟩ ⟨she's since become mayor : más tarde se hizo alcalde⟩ **2** AGO : hace ⟨he's long since dead : murió hace mucho⟩

since² *conj* **1** : desde que ⟨since he was born : desde que nació⟩ **2** INASMUCH AS : ya que, puesto que, dado que

since³ *prep* : desde

sincere [sɪnˈsɪr] *adj* **-cerer; -est** : sincero — **sincerely** *adv*

sincerity [sɪnˈsɛrəti] *n* : sinceridad *f*

sinew [ˈsɪnˌjuː, ˈsɪˌnuː] *n* **1** TENDON : tendón *m*, nervio *m* (en la carne) **2** POWER : fuerza *f*

sinewy [ˈsɪnjui, ˈsɪnui] *adj* **1** STRINGY : fibroso **2** STRONG, WIRY : fuerte, nervudo

sinful [ˈsɪnfəl] *adj* : pecador (dícese de las personas), pecaminoso

sing [ˈsɪŋ] *v* **sang** [ˈsæŋ] *or* **sung** [ˈsʌŋ]; **sung; singing** : cantar

singe [ˈsɪndʒ] *vt* **singed; singeing** : chamuscar, quemar

singer [ˈsɪŋər] *n* : cantante *mf*

single¹ [ˈsɪŋɡəl] *vt* **-gled; -gling** *or* **to single out 1** SELECT : escoger **2** DISTINGUISH : señalar

single² *adj* **1** UNMARRIED : soltero **2** SOLE : solo ⟨a single survivor : un solo sobreviviente⟩ ⟨every single one : cada uno, todos⟩

single³ *n* **1** : soltero *m*, -ra *f* ⟨for married couples and singles : para los matrimonios y los solteros⟩ **2** *or* **single room** : habitación *f* individual **3** DOLLAR : billete *m* de un dólar

single–handed ['sɪŋɡəl'hændəd] *adj* : sin ayuda, solo

singly ['sɪŋɡli] *adv* : individualmente, uno por uno

singular¹ ['sɪŋɡjələr] *adj* **1** : singular (en gramática) **2** OUTSTANDING : singular, sobresaliente **3** STRANGE : singular, extraño

singular² *n* : singular *m*

singularity [,sɪŋɡjə'lærəti] *n, pl* **-ties** : singularidad *f*

singularly ['sɪŋɡjələrli] *adv* : singularmente

sinister ['sɪnəstər] *adj* : siniestro

sink¹ ['sɪŋk] *v* **sank** ['sæŋk] *or* **sunk** ['sʌŋk]; **sunk**; **sinking** *vi* **1** : hundirse (dícese de un barco) **2** DROP, FALL : descender, caer ⟨to sink into a chair : dejarse caer en una silla⟩ ⟨her heart sank : se le cayó el alma a los pies⟩ **3** DECREASE : bajar — *vt* **1** : hundir (un barco, etc.) **2** EXCAVATE : excavar (un pozo para minar), perforar (un pozo de agua) **3** PLUNGE, STICK : clavar, hincar **4** INVEST : invertir (fondos)

sink² *n* **1** kitchen sink : fregadero *m*, lavaplatos *m Chile, Col, Mex* **2** bathroom sink : lavabo *m*, lavamanos *m*

sinner ['sɪnər] *n* : pecador *m*, -dora *f*

sinuous ['sɪnjuəs] *adj* : sinuoso — **sinuously** *adv*

sinus ['saɪnəs] *n* : seno *m*

sip¹ ['sɪp] *v* **sipped**; **sipping** *vt* : sorber — *vi* : beber a sorbos

sip² *n* : sorbo *m*

siphon¹ ['saɪfən] *vt* : sacar con sifón

siphon² *n* : sifón *m*

sir ['sər] *n* **1** (*in titles*) : sir *m* **2** (*as a form of address*) : señor *m* ⟨Dear Sir : Muy señor mío⟩ ⟨yes sir! : ¡sí, señor!⟩

sire¹ ['saɪr] *vt* **sired**; **siring** : engendrar, ser el padre de

sire² *n* : padre *m*

siren ['saɪrən] *n* : sirena *f*

sirloin ['sər,lɔɪn] *n* : solomillo *m*

sirup → syrup

sisal ['saɪsəl, -zəl] *n* : sisal *m*

sissy ['sɪsi] *n, pl* **-sies** : mariquita *f fam*

sister ['sɪstər] *n* **1** : hermana *f* **2** Sister : hermana *f*, Sor *f* ⟨Sister Mary : Sor María⟩

sisterhood ['sɪstər,hʊd] *n* **1** : condición *f* de ser hermana **2** : sociedad *f* de mujeres

sister–in–law ['sɪstərɪn,lɔ] *n, pl* **sisters–in–law** : cuñada *f*

sisterly ['sɪstərli] *adj* : de hermana

sit ['sɪt] *v* **sat** ['sæt]; **sitting** *vi* **1** : sentarse, estar sentado ⟨he sat down : se sentó⟩ **2** ROOST : posarse **3** : sesionar ⟨the legislature is sitting : la legislatu-

ra está en sesión⟩ **4** POSE : posar (para un retrato) **5** LIE, REST : estar (ubicado) ⟨the house sits on a hill : la casa está en una colina⟩ — *vt* SEAT : sentar, colocar ⟨I sat him on the sofa : lo senté en el sofá⟩

sitcom ['sɪt,kɑm] → **situation comedy**

site ['saɪt] *n* **1** PLACE : sitio *m*, lugar *m* **2** LOCATION : emplazamiento *m*, ubicación *f*

sitter ['sɪtər] → **baby–sitter**

sitting room → living room

situated ['sɪtʃu,eɪtəd] *adj* LOCATED : ubicado, situado

situation [,sɪtʃu'eɪʃən] *n* **1** LOCATION : situación *f*, ubicación *f*, emplazamiento *m* **2** CIRCUMSTANCES : situación *f* **3** JOB : empleo *m*

situation comedy *n* : comedia *f* de situación

six¹ ['sɪks] *adj* : seis

six² *n* : seis *m*

six–gun ['sɪks,ɡʌn] *n* : revólver *m* (con seis cámaras)

six hundred¹ *adj* : seiscientos

six hundred² *n* : seiscientos *m*

six–shooter ['sɪks,ʃuːtər] → **six–gun**

sixteen¹ [sɪks'tiːn] *adj* : dieciséis

sixteen² *n* : dieciséis *m*

sixteenth¹ [sɪks'tiːnθ] *adj* : decimosexto

sixteenth² *n* **1** : decimosexto *m*, -ta *f* (en una serie) **2** : dieciseisavo *m*, dieciseisava parte *f*

sixth¹ ['sɪksθ, 'sɪkst] *adj* : sexto

sixth² *n* **1** : sexto *m*, -ta *f* (en una serie) **2** : sexto *m*, sexta parte *f*

sixtieth¹ ['sɪkstiəθ] *adj* : sexagésimo

sixtieth² *n* **1** : sexagésimo *m*, -ma *f* (en una serie) **2** : sesentavo *m*, sesentava parte *f*

sixty¹ ['sɪksti] *adj* : sesenta

sixty² *n, pl* **-ties** : sesenta *m*

sizable *or* **sizeable** ['saɪzəbəl] *adj* : considerable

size¹ ['saɪz] *vt* **sized**; **sizing 1** : clasificar según el tamaño **2 to size up** : evaluar, apreciar

size² *n* **1** DIMENSIONS : tamaño *m*, talla *f* (de ropa), número *m* (de zapatos) **2** MAGNITUDE : magnitud *f*

sizzle ['sɪzəl] *vi* **-zled**; **-zling** : chisporrotear

skate¹ ['skeɪt] *vi* **skated**; **skating** : patinar

skate² *n* **1** : patín *m* ⟨roller skate : patín de ruedas⟩ **2** : raya *f* (pez)

skateboard ['skeɪt,bord] *n* : monopatín *m*

skater ['skeɪtər] *n* : patinador *m*, -dora *f*

skein ['skeɪn] *n* : madeja *f*

skeletal ['skɛlətəl] *adj* **1** : óseo (en anatomía) **2** EMACIATED : esquelético

skeleton ['skɛlətən] *n* **1** : esqueleto *m* (anatómico) **2** FRAMEWORK : armazón *mf*

skeptic ['skɛptɪk] *n* : escéptico *m*, -ca *f*

skeptical ['skɛptɪkəl] *adj* : escéptico

skepticism ['skɛptə,sɪzəm] *n* : escepticismo *m*

sketch¹ ['skɛtʃ] *vt* : bosquejar — *vi* : hacer bosquejos
sketch² *n* **1** DRAWING, OUTLINE : esbozo *m*, bosquejo *m* **2** ESSAY : ensayo *m*
sketchy ['skɛtʃi] *adj* **sketchier; -est** : incompleto, poco detallado
skewer¹ ['skju:ər] *vt* : ensartar (carne, etc.)
skewer² *n* : brocheta *f*, broqueta *f*
ski¹ ['ski:] *vi* **skied; skiing** : esquiar
ski² *n, pl* **skis** : esquí *m*
skid¹ ['skɪd] *vi* **skidded; skidding** : derrapar, patinar
skid² *n* : derrape *m*, patinazo *m*
skier ['ski:ər] *n* : esquiador *m*, -dora *f*
skiff ['skɪf] *n* : esquife *m*
skill ['skɪl] *n* **1** DEXTERITY : habilidad *f*, destreza *f* **2** CAPABILITY : capacidad *f*, arte *m*, técnica *f* ⟨organizational skills : la capacidad para organizar⟩
skilled ['skɪld] *adj* : hábil, experto
skillet ['skɪlət] *n* : sartén *mf*
skillful ['skɪlfəl] *adj* : hábil, diestro
skillfully ['skɪlfəli] *adv* : con habilidad, con destreza
skim¹ ['skɪm] *vt* **skimmed; skimming 1** *or* **to skim off** : espumar, descremar (leche) **2** : echarle un vistazo a (un libro, etc.), pasar rozando (una superficie)
skim² *adj* : descremado ⟨skim milk : leche descremada⟩
skimp ['skɪmp] *vi* **to skimp on** : escatimar
skimpy ['skɪmpi] *adj* **skimpier; -est** : exiguo, escaso, raquítico
skin¹ ['skɪn] *vt* **skinned; skinning** : despellejar, desollar
skin² *n* **1** : piel *f*, cutis *m* (de la cara) ⟨dark skin : piel morena⟩ **2** RIND : piel *f*
skin diving *n* : buceo *m*, submarinismo *m*
skinflint ['skɪn,flɪnt] *n* : tacaño *m*, -ña *f*
skinned ['skɪnd] *adj* : de piel ⟨toughskinned : de piel dura⟩
skinny ['skɪni] *adj* **skinnier; -est** : flaco
skip¹ ['skɪp] *v* **skipped; skipping** *vi* : ir dando brincos — *vt* : saltarse
skip² *n* : brinco *m*, salto *m*
skipper ['skɪpər] *n* : capitán *m*, -tana *f*
skirmish¹ ['skərmɪʃ] *vi* : escaramuzar
skirmish² *n* : escaramuza *f*, refriega *f*
skirt¹ ['skərt] *vt* **1** BORDER : bordear **2** EVADE : evadir, esquivar
skirt² *n* : falda *f*, pollera *f*
skit ['skɪt] *n* : sketch *m* (teatral)
skittish ['skɪtɪʃ] *adj* : asustadizo, nervioso
skulk ['skʌlk] *vi* : merodear
skull ['skʌl] *n* **1** : cráneo *m*, calavera *f* **2 skull and crossbones** : calavera *f* (bandera pirata)
skunk ['skʌŋk] *n* : zorrillo *m*, mofeta *f*
sky ['skaɪ] *n, pl* **skies** : cielo *m*
skylark ['skaɪ,lɑrk] *n* : alondra *f*
skylight ['skaɪ,laɪt] *n* : claraboya *f*, tragaluz *m*

skyline ['skaɪ,laɪn] *n* : horizonte *m*
skyrocket ['skaɪ,rɑkət] *vi* : dispararse
skyscraper ['skaɪ,skreɪpər] *n* : rascacielos *m*
slab ['slæb] *n* : losa *f* (de piedra), tabla *f* (de madera), pedazo *m* grueso (de pan, etc.)
slack¹ ['slæk] *adj* **1** CARELESS : descuidado, negligente **2** LOOSE : flojo **3** SLOW : de poco movimiento
slack² *n* **1** : parte *f* floja ⟨to take up the slack : tensar (una cuerda, etc.)⟩ **2 slacks** *npl* : pantalones *mpl*
slacken ['slækən] *vt* : aflojar — *vi* : aflojarse
slacker ['slækər] *n* : vago *m*, -ga *f*; holgazán *m*, -zana *f*
slag ['slæg] *n* : escoria *f*
slain → **slay**
slake ['sleɪk] *vt* **slaked; slaking** : saciar (la sed), satisfacer (la curiosidad)
slam¹ ['slæm] *v* **slammed; slamming** *vt* **1** : cerrar de golpe ⟨he slammed the door : dio un portazo⟩ **2** : tirar o dejar caer de golpe ⟨he slammed down the book : dejó caer el libro de un golpe⟩ — *vi* **1** : cerrarse de golpe **2 to slam into** : chocar contra
slam² *n* : golpe *m*, portazo *m* (de una puerta)
slander¹ ['slændər] *vt* : calumniar, difamar
slander² *n* : calumnia *f*, difamación *f*
slanderous ['slændərəs] *adj* : difamatorio, calumnioso
slang ['slæŋ] *n* : argot *m*, jerga *f*
slant¹ ['slænt] *vi* : inclinarse, ladearse — *vt* **1** SLOPE : inclinar **2** ANGLE : sesgar, orientar, dirigir ⟨a story slanted towards youth : un artículo dirigido a los jóvenes⟩
slant² *n* **1** INCLINE : inclinación *f* **2** PERSPECTIVE : perspectiva *f*, enfoque *m*
slap¹ ['slæp] *vt* **slapped; slapping** : bofetear, cachetear, dar una palmada (en la espalda, etc.)
slap² *n* : bofetada *f*, cachetada *f*, palmada *f*
slash¹ ['slæʃ] *vt* **1** GASH : cortar, hacer un tajo en **2** REDUCE : reducir, rebajar (precios)
slash² *n* : tajo *m*, corte *m*
slat ['slæt] *n* : tablilla *f*, listón *m*
slate ['sleɪt] *n* **1** : pizarra *f* ⟨a slate roof : un techo de pizarra⟩ **2** : lista *f* de candidatos (políticos)
slaughter¹ ['slɔtər] *vt* **1** BUTCHER : matar (animales) **2** MASSACRE : masacrar (personas)
slaughter² *n* **1** : matanza *f* (de animales) **2** MASSACRE : masacre *f*, carnicería *f*
slaughterhouse ['slɔtər,haʊs] *n* : matadero *m*
Slav ['slɑv, 'slæv] *n* : eslavo *m*, -va *f*
slave¹ ['sleɪv] *vi* **slaved; slaving** : trabajar como un burro
slave² *n* : esclavo *m*, -va *f*
slaver ['slævər, 'sleɪ-] *vi* : babear

slavery ['sleɪvəri] *n* : esclavitud *f*
Slavic ['slɑvɪk, 'slæ-] *adj* : eslavo
slavish ['sleɪvɪʃ] *adj* **1** SERVILE : servil **2** IMITATIVE : poco original
slay ['sleɪ] *vt* **slew** ['slu:]; **slain** ['sleɪn]; **slaying** : asesinar, matar
slayer ['sleɪər] *n* : asesino *m*, -na *f*
sleazy ['sli:zi] *adj* **sleazier; -est 1** SHODDY : chapucero, de mala calidad **2** DILAPIDATED : ruinoso **3** DISREPUTABLE : de mala fama
sled[1] ['slɛd] *v* **sledded; sledding** *vi* : ir en trineo — *vt* : transportar en trineo
sled[2] *n* : trineo *m*
sledge ['slɛdʒ] *n* **1** : trineo *m* (grande) **2 → sledgehammer**
sledgehammer ['slɛdʒ,hæmər] *n* : almádena *f*, combo *m Chile, Peru*
sleek[1] ['sli:k] *vt* SLICK : alisar
sleek[2] *adj* : liso y brillante
sleep[1] ['sli:p] *vi* **slept** ['slɛpt]; **sleeping** : dormir
sleep[2] *n* **1** : sueño *m* **2 to go to sleep** : dormirse
sleeper ['sli:pər] *n* **1** : durmiente *mf* ⟨to be a light sleeper : tener el sueño ligero⟩ **2** *or* **sleeping car** : coche *m* cama, coche *m* dormitorio
sleepily ['sli:pəli] *adv* : de manera somnolienta
sleepiness ['sli:pinəs] *n* : somnolencia *f*
sleepless ['sli:pləs] *adj* : sin dormir, desvelado ⟨to have a sleepless night : pasar la noche en blanco⟩
sleepwalker ['sli:p,wɔkər] *n* : sonámbulo *m*, -la *f*
sleepy ['sli:pi] *adj* **sleepier; -est 1** DROWSY : somnoliento, soñoliento ⟨to be sleepy : tener sueño⟩ **2** LETHARGIC : aletargado, letárgico
sleet[1] ['sli:t] *vi* **to be sleeting** : caer aguanieve
sleet[2] *n* : aguanieve *f*
sleeve ['sli:v] *n* : manga *f* (de una camisa, etc.)
sleeveless ['sli:vləs] *adj* : sin mangas
sleigh[1] ['sleɪ] *vi* : ir en trineo
sleigh[2] *n* : trineo *m* (tirado por caballos)
sleight of hand [,slaɪtəv'hænd] : prestidigitación *f*, juegos *mpl* de manos
slender ['slɛndər] *adj* **1** SLIM : esbelto, delgado **2** SCANTY : exiguo, escaso ⟨a slender hope : una esperanza lejana⟩
sleuth ['slu:θ] *n* : detective *mf*; sabueso *m*, -sa *f*
slew → slay
slice[1] ['slaɪs] *vt* **sliced; slicing** : cortar
slice[2] *n* : rebanada *f*, tajada *f*, lonja *f* (de carne, etc.), rodaja *f* (de una verdura, fruta, etc.), trozo *m* (de pastel, etc.)
slick[1] ['slɪk] *vt* : alisar
slick[2] *adj* **1** SLIPPERY : resbaladizo, resbaloso **2** CRAFTY : astuto, taimado
slicker ['slɪkər] *n* : impermeable *m*
slide[1] ['slaɪd] *v* **slid** ['slɪd]; **sliding** ['slaɪdɪŋ] *vi* **1** SLIP : resbalar **2** GLIDE : deslizarse **3** DECLINE : bajar ⟨to let

things slide : dejar pasar las cosas⟩ — *vt* : correr, deslizar
slide[2] *n* **1** SLIDING : deslizamiento *m* **2** SLIP : resbalón *m* **3** : tobogán *m* (para niños) **4** TRANSPARENCY : diapositiva *f* (fotográfica) **5** DECLINE : descenso *m*
slier, sliest → sly
slight[1] ['slaɪt] *vt* : desairar, despreciar
slight[2] *adj* **1** SLENDER : esbelto, delgado **2** FLIMSY : endeble **3** TRIFLING : leve, insignificante ⟨a slight pain : un leve dolor⟩ **4** SMALL : pequeño, ligero ⟨not in the slightest : en absoluto⟩
slight[3] *n* SNUB : desaire *m*
slightly ['slaɪtli] *adv* : ligeramente, un poco
slim[1] ['slɪm] *v* **slimmed; slimming** : adelgazar
slim[2] *adj* **slimmer; slimmest 1** SLENDER : esbelto, delgado **2** SCANTY : exiguo, escaso
slime ['slaɪm] *n* **1** : baba *f* (secretada por un animal) **2** MUD, SILT : fango *m*, cieno *m*
slimy ['slaɪmi] *adj* **slimier; -est** : viscoso
sling[1] ['slɪŋ] *vt* **slung** ['slʌŋ]; **slinging 1** THROW : lanzar, tirar **2** HANG : colgar
sling[2] *n* **1** : honda *f* (arma) **2** : cabestrillo *m* ⟨my arm is in a sling : llevo el brazo en cabestrillo⟩
slingshot ['slɪŋ,ʃɑt] *n* : tiragomas *m*, resortera *f Mex*
slink ['slɪŋk] *vi* **slunk** ['slʌŋk]; **slinking** : caminar furtivamente
slip[1] ['slɪp] *v* **slipped; slipping** *vi* **1** STEAL : ir sigilosamente ⟨to slip away : escabullirse⟩ ⟨to slip out the door : escaparse por la puerta⟩ **2** SLIDE : resbalarse, deslizarse **3** LAPSE : caer ⟨to slip into error : equivocarse⟩ **4 to let slip** : dejar escapar **5 to slip into** PUT ON : ponerse — *vt* **1** PUT : meter, poner **2** PASS : pasar ⟨she slipped me a note : me pasó una nota⟩ **3 to slip one's mind** : olvidársele a uno
slip[2] *n* **1** PIER : atracadero *m* **2** MISHAP : percance *m*, contratiempo *m* **3** MISTAKE : error *m*, desliz *m* ⟨a slip of the tongue : un lapsus⟩ **4** PETTICOAT : enagua *f* **5** : injerto *m*, esqueje *m* (de una planta) **6 slip of paper** : papelito *m*
slipper ['slɪpər] *n* : zapatilla *f*, pantufla *f*
slipperiness ['slɪpərinəs] *n* **1** : lo resbaloso, lo resbaladizo **2** TRICKINESS : astucia *f*
slippery ['slɪpəri] *adj* **slipperier; -est 1** : resbaloso, resbaladizo ⟨a slippery road : un camino resbaloso⟩ **2** TRICKY : artero, astuto, taimado **3** ELUSIVE : huidizo, escurridizo
slipshod ['slɪp,ʃɑd] *adj* : descuidado, chapucero
slip up *vi* : equivocarse
slit[1] ['slɪt] *vt* **slit; slitting** : cortar, abrir por lo largo

slit² *n* **1** OPENING : abertura *f*, rendija *f* **2** CUT : corte *m*, raja *f*, tajo *m*

slither ['slɪðər] *vi* : deslizarse

sliver ['slɪvər] *n* : astilla *f*

slob ['slɑb] *n* : persona *f* desaliñada ⟨what a slob! : ¡qué cerdo!⟩

slobber¹ ['slɑbər] *vi* : babear

slobber² *n* : baba *f*

slogan ['slo:gən] *n* : lema *m*, eslogan *m*

sloop ['slu:p] *n* : balandra *f*

slop¹ ['slɑp] *v* **slopped; slopping** *vt* : derramar — *vi* : derramarse

slop² *n* : bazofia *f*

slope¹ ['slo:p] *vi* **sloped; sloping** : inclinarse ⟨the road slopes upward : el camino sube (en pendiente)⟩

slope² *n* : inclinación *f*, pendiente *f*, declive *m*

sloppy ['slɑpi] *adj* **sloppier; -est 1** MUDDY, SLUSHY : lodoso, fangoso **2** UNTIDY : descuidado (en el trabajo, etc.), desaliñado (de aspecto)

slot ['slɑt] *n* : ranura *f*

sloth ['slɔθ, 'slo:θ] *n* **1** LAZINESS : pereza *f* **2** : perezoso *m* (animal)

slouch¹ ['slautʃ] *vi* : andar con los hombros caídos, repantigarse (en un sillón)

slouch² *n* **1** SLUMPING : mala postura *f* **2** BUNGLER, IDLER : haragán *m*, -gana *f*; inepto *m*, -ta *f* ⟨to be no slouch : no quedarse atrás⟩

slough¹ ['slʌf] *vt* : mudar de (piel)

slough² ['slu:, 'slau] *n* SWAMP : ciénaga *f*

Slovak ['slo:,vɑk, -,væk] *or* **Slovakian** [slo:'vɑkiən, -'væ-] *n* : eslovaco *m*, -ca *f* — **Slovak** *or* **Slovakian** *adj*

Slovene ['slo:,vi:n] *or* **Slovenian** [slo:-'vi:niən] *n* : esloveno *m*, -na *f* — **Slovene** *or* **Slovenian** *adj*

slovenly ['slʌvənli, 'slʌv-] *adj* : descuidado (en el trabajo, etc.), desaliñado (de aspecto)

slow¹ [slo:] *vt* : retrasar, reducir la marcha de — *vi* : ir más despacio

slow² *adv* : despacio, lentamente

slow³ *adj* **1** : lento ⟨a slow process : un proceso lento⟩ **2** : atrasado ⟨my watch is slow : mi reloj está atrasado, mi reloj se atrasa⟩ **3** SLUGGISH : lento, poco activo **4** STUPID : lento, torpe, corto de alcances

slowly [slo:li] *adv* : lentamente, despacio

slowness [slo:nəs] *n* : lentitud *f*, torpeza *f*

sludge ['slʌdʒ] *n* : aguas *fpl* negras, aguas *fpl* residuales

slug¹ ['slʌg] *vt* **slugged; slugging** : pegarle un porrazo (a alguien)

slug² *n* **1** : babosa *f* (molusco) **2** BULLET : bala *f* **3** TOKEN : ficha *f* **4** BLOW : porrazo *m*, puñetazo *m*

sluggish ['slʌgɪʃ] *adj* : aletargado, lento

sluice¹ ['slu:s] *vt* **sluiced; sluicing** : lavar en agua corriente

sluice² *n* : canal *m*

slum ['slʌm] *n* : barriada *f*, barrio *m* bajo

slumber¹ ['slʌmbər] *vi* : dormir

slumber² *n* : sueño *m*

slump¹ ['slʌmp] *vi* **1** DECLINE, DROP : disminuir, bajar **2** SLOUCH : encorvarse, dejarse caer (en una silla, etc.)

slump² *n* : bajón *m*, declive *m* (económico)

slung → sling

slunk → slink

slur¹ ['slər] *vt* **slurred; slurring** : ligar (notas musicales), tragarse (las palabras)

slur² *n* **1** : ligado *m* (en música), mala pronunciación *f* (de las palabras) **2** ASPERSION : calumnia *f*, difamación *f*

slurp¹ ['slərp] *vi* : beber o comer haciendo ruido — *vt* : sorber ruidosamente

slurp² *n* : sorbo *m* (ruidoso)

slush ['slʌʃ] *n* : nieve *f* medio derretida

slut ['slʌt] *n* PROSTITUTE : ramera *f*, fulana *f*

sly ['slaɪ] *adj* **slier** ['slaɪər]; **sliest** ['slaɪəst] **1** CUNNING : astuto, taimado **2** UNDERHANDED : soplado — **slyly** *adv*

slyness ['slaɪnəs] *n* : astucia *f*

smack¹ ['smæk] *vi* **to smack of** : oler a, saber a — *vt* **1** KISS : besar, plantarle un beso (a alguien) **2** SLAP : pegarle una bofetada (a alguien) **3** **to smack one's lips** : relamerse

smack² *adv* : justo, exactamente ⟨smack in the face : en plena cara⟩

smack³ *n* **1** TASTE, TRACE : sabor *m*, indicio *m* **2** : chasquido *m* (de los labios) **3** SLAP : bofetada *f* **4** KISS : beso *m*

small ['smɔl] *adj* **1** : pequeño, chico ⟨a small house : una casa pequeña⟩ ⟨small change : monedas de poco valor⟩ **2** TRIVIAL : pequeño, insignificante

smallness ['smɔlnəs] *n* : pequeñez *f*

smallpox ['smɔl,pɑks] *n* : viruela *f*

smart¹ ['smɑrt] *vi* **1** STING : escocer, picar, arder **2** HURT : dolerse, resentirse ⟨to smart under a rejection : dolerse ante un rechazo⟩

smart² *adj* **1** BRIGHT : listo, vivo, inteligente **2** STYLISH : elegante — **smartly** *adv*

smart³ *n* **1** PAIN : escozor *m*, dolor *m* **2** **smarts** *npl* : inteligencia *f*

smartness ['smɑrtnəs] *n* **1** INTELLIGENCE : inteligencia *f* **2** ELEGANCE : elegancia *f*

smash¹ ['smæʃ] *vt* **1** BREAK : romper, quebrar, hacer pedazos **2** WRECK : destrozar, arruinar **3** CRASH : estrellar, chocar — *vi* **1** SHATTER : hacerse pedazos, hacerse añicos **2** COLLIDE, CRASH : estrellarse, chocar

smash² *n* **1** BLOW : golpe *m* **2** COLLISION : choque *m* **3** BANG, CRASH : estrépito *m*

smattering ['smæt̬ərɪŋ] *n* **1** : nociones *fpl* ⟨she has a smattering of programming : tiene nociones de programación⟩ **2** : un poco, unos cuantos ⟨a smattering of spectators : unos cuantos espectadores⟩

smear¹ ['smɪr] *vt* **1** DAUB : embadurnar, untar (mantequilla, etc.) **2** SMUDGE : emborronar **3** SLANDER : calumniar, difamar

smear² *n* **1** SMUDGE : mancha *f* **2** SLANDER : calumnia *f*

smell¹ ['smɛl] *v* **smelled** *or* **smelt** ['smɛlt]; **smelling** *vt* : oler, olfatear ⟨to smell danger : olfatear el peligro⟩ — *vi* : oler ⟨to smell good : oler bien⟩

smell² *n* **1** : olfato *m*, sentido *m* del olfato **2** ODOR : olor *m*

smelly ['smɛli] *adj* **smellier; -est** : maloliente

smelt¹ ['smɛlt] *vt* : fundir

smelt² *n, pl* **smelts** *or* **smelt** : eperlano *m* (pez)

smile¹ ['smaɪl] *vi* **smiled; smiling** : sonreír

smile² *n* : sonrisa *f*

smirk¹ ['smərk] *vi* : sonreír con suficiencia

smirk² *n* : sonrisa *f* satisfecha

smite ['smaɪt] *vt* **smote** ['smo:t]; **smitten** ['smɪtən] *or* **smote; smiting 1** STRIKE : golpear **2** AFFLICT : afligir

smith ['smɪθ] *n* : herrero *m*, -ra *f*

smithy ['smɪθi] *n, pl* **smithies** : herrería *f*

smock ['smɑk] *n* : bata *f*, blusón *m*

smog ['smɑg, 'smɔg] *n* : smog *m*

smoke¹ ['smo:k] *v* **smoked; smoking** *vi* **1** : echar humo, humear ⟨a smoking chimney : una chimenea que echa humo⟩ **2** : fumar ⟨I don't smoke : no fumo⟩ — *vt* : ahumar (carne, etc.)

smoke² *n* : humo *m*

smoke detector [dɪ'tɛktər] *n* : detector *m* de humo

smoker ['smo:kər] *n* : fumador *m*, -dora *f*

smokestack ['smo:k,stæk] *n* : chimenea *f*

smoky ['smo:ki] *adj* **smokier; -est 1** SMOKING : humeante **2** : a humo ⟨a smoky flavor : un sabor a humo⟩ **3** : lleno de humo ⟨a smoky room : un cuarto lleno de humo⟩

smolder ['smo:ldər] *vi* **1** : arder sin llama **2** : arder (en el corazón) ⟨his anger smoldered : su rabia ardía⟩

smooth¹ ['smu:ð] *vt* : alisar

smooth² *adj* **1** : liso (dícese de una superficie) ⟨smooth skin : piel lisa⟩ **2** : suave (dícese de un movimiento) ⟨a smooth landing : un aterrizaje suave⟩ **3** : sin grumos ⟨a smooth sauce : una salsa sin grumos⟩ **4** : fluido ⟨smooth writing : escritura fluida⟩

smoothly ['smu:ðli] *adv* **1** GENTLY, SOFTLY : suavemente **2** EASILY : con facilidad, sin problemas

smoothness ['smu:ðnəs] *n* : suavidad *f*

smother ['smʌðər] *vt* **1** SUFFOCATE : ahogar, sofocar **2** COVER : cubrir **3** SUPPRESS : contener — *vi* : asfixiarse

smudge¹ ['smʌdʒ] *v* **smudged; smudging** *vt* : emborronar — *vi* : correrse

smudge² *n* : mancha *f*, borrón *m*

smug ['smʌg] *adj* **smugger; smuggest** : suficiente, pagado de sí mismo

smuggle ['smʌgəl] *vt* **-gled; -gling** : contrabandear, pasar de contrabando

smuggler ['smʌgələr] *n* : contrabandista *mf*

smugly ['smʌgli] *adv* : con suficiencia

smut ['smʌt] *n* **1** SOOT : tizne *m*, hollín *m* **2** FUNGUS : tizón *m* **3** OBSCENITY : obscenidad *f*, inmundicia *f*

smutty ['smʌti] *adj* **smuttier; -est 1** SOOTY : tiznado **2** OBSCENE : obsceno, indecente

snack ['snæk] *n* : refrigerio *m*, bocado *m*, tentempié *m fam* ⟨an afternoon snack : una merienda⟩

snag¹ ['snæg] *v* **snagged; snagging** *vt* : enganchar — *vi* : engancharse

snag² *n* : problema *m*, inconveniente *m*

snail ['sneɪl] *n* : caracol *m*

snake ['sneɪk] *n* : culebra *f*, serpiente *f*

snakebite ['sneɪk,baɪt] *n* : mordedura *f* de serpiente

snap¹ ['snæp] *v* **snapped; snapping** *vi* **1** : intentar morder (dícese de un perro, etc.), picar (dícese de un pez) **2** : hablar con severidad ⟨he snapped at me! : ¡me gritó!⟩ **3** BREAK : romperse, quebrarse (haciendo un chasquido) — *vt* **1** BREAK : partir (en dos), quebrar **2** : hacer (algo) de un golpe ⟨to snap open : abrir de golpe⟩ **3** RETORT : decir bruscamente **4** CLICK : chasquear ⟨to snap one's fingers : chasquear los dedos⟩

snap² *n* **1** CLICK, CRACK : chasquido *m* **2** FASTENER : broche *m* **3** CINCH : cosa *f* fácil ⟨it's a snap : es facilísimo⟩

snapdragon ['snæp,drægən] *n* : dragón *m* (flor)

snapper ['snæpər] → red snapper

snappy ['snæpi] *adj* **snappier; -est 1** FAST : rápido ⟨make it snappy! : ¡date prisa!⟩ **2** LIVELY : vivaz **3** CHILLY : frío **4** STYLISH : elegante

snapshot ['snæp,ʃat] *n* : instantánea *f*

snare¹ ['snær] *vt* **snared; snaring** : atrapar

snare² *n* : trampa *f*, red *f*

snare drum *n* : tambor *m* con bordón

snarl¹ ['snarl] *vi* **1** TANGLE : enmarañar, enredar **2** GROWL : gruñir

snarl² *n* **1** TANGLE : enredo *m*, maraña *f* **2** GROWL : gruñido *m*

snatch¹ ['snætʃ] *vt* : arrebatar

snatch² *n* : fragmento *m*

sneak¹ ['sni:k] *vi* : ir a hurtadillas — *vt* : hacer furtivamente ⟨to sneak a look : mirar con disimulo⟩ ⟨he sneaked a smoke : fumó un cigarrillo a escondidas⟩

sneak² *n* : soplón *m*, -plona *f*

sneakers ['sni:kərz] *npl* : tenis *mpl*, zapatillas *fpl*

sneaky ['sni:ki] *adj* **sneakier; -est** : solapado

sneer[1] ['snɪr] *vi* : sonreír con desprecio

sneer[2] *n* : sonrisa *f* de desprecio

sneeze[1] ['sni:z] *vi* **sneezed; sneezing** : estornudar

sneeze[2] *n* : estornudo *m*

snicker[1] ['snɪkər] *vi* : reírse disimuladamente

snicker[2] *n* : risita *f*

snide ['snaɪd] *adj* : sarcástico

sniff[1] ['snɪf] *vi* **1** SMELL : oler, husmear (dícese de los animales) **2 to sniff at** : despreciar, desdeñar — *vt* **1** SMELL : oler **2 to sniff out** : olerse, husmear

sniff[2] *n* **1** SNIFFING : aspiración *f* por la nariz **2** SMELL : olor *m*

sniffle ['snɪfəl] *vi* **-fled; -fling** : respirar con la nariz congestionada

sniffles ['snɪfəlz] *npl* : resfriado *m*

snip[1] ['snɪp] *vt* **snipped; snipping** : cortar (con tijeras)

snip[2] *n* : tijeretada *f*, recorte *m*

snipe[1] ['snaɪp] *vi* **sniped; sniping** : disparar

snipe[2] *n, pl* **snipes** *or* **snipe** : agachadiza *f*

sniper ['snaɪpər] *n* : francotirador *m*, -dora *f*

snippet ['snɪpət] *n* : fragmento *m* (de un texto, etc.)

snivel ['snɪvəl] *vi* **-veled** *or* **-velled; -veling** *or* **-velling 1** → **snuffle 2** WHINE : lloriquear

snob ['snɑb] *n* : esnob *mf*, snob *mf*

snobbery ['snɑbəri] *n, pl* **-beries** : esnobismo *m*

snobbish ['snɑbɪʃ] *adj* : esnob, snob

snobbishness ['snɑbɪʃnəs] *n* : esnobismo *m*

snoop[1] ['snu:p] *vi* : husmear, curiosear

snoop[2] *n* : fisgón *m*, -gona *f*

snooze[1] ['snu:z] *vi* **snoozed; snoozing** : dormitar

snooze[2] *n* : siestecita *f*, siestita *f*

snore[1] ['snor] *vi* **snored; snoring** : roncar

snore[2] *n* : ronquido *m*

snort[1] ['snɔrt] *vi* : bufar, resoplar

snort[2] *n* : bufido *m*, resoplo *m*

snout ['snaʊt] *n* : hocico *m*, morro *m*

snow[1] ['sno:] *vi* **1** : nevar ⟨I'm snowed in : estoy aislado por la nieve⟩ **2 to be snowed under** : estar inundado

snow[2] *n* : nieve *f*

snowball ['sno:ˌbɔl] *n* : bola *f* de nieve

snowdrift ['sno:ˌdrɪft] *n* : ventisquero *m*

snowfall ['sno:ˌfɔl] *n* : nevada *f*

snowplow ['sno:ˌplaʊ] *n* : quitanieves *m*

snowshoe ['sno:ˌʃu:] *n* : raqueta *f* (para nieve)

snowstorm ['sno:ˌstɔrm] *n* : tormenta *f* de nieve, ventisca *f*

snowy ['sno:i] *adj* **snowier; -est** : nevoso ⟨a snowy road : un camino nevado⟩

snub[1] ['snʌb] *vt* **snubbed; snubbing** : desairar

snub[2] *n* : desaire *m*

snub–nosed ['snʌbˌno:zd] *adj* : de nariz respingada

snuff[1] ['snʌf] *vt* **1** : apagar (una vela) **2** : sorber (algo) por la nariz

snuff[2] *n* : rapé *m*

snuffle ['snʌfəl] *vi* **-fled; -fling** : respirar con la nariz congestionada

snug ['snʌg] *adj* **snugger; snuggest 1** COMFORTABLE : cómodo **2** TIGHT : ajustado, ceñido ⟨snug pants : pantalones ajustados⟩

snuggle ['snʌgəl] *vi* **-gled; -gling** : acurrucarse ⟨to snuggle up to someone : arrimársele a alguien⟩

snugly ['snʌgli] *adv* **1** COMFORTABLY : cómodamente **2** : de manera ajustada ⟨the shirt fits snugly : la camisa queda ajustada⟩

so[1] ['so:] *adv* **1** (*referring to something indicated or suggested*) ⟨do you think so? : ¿tú crees?⟩ ⟨so it would seem : eso parece⟩ ⟨I told her so : se lo dije⟩ ⟨he's ready, or so he says : según dice, está listo⟩ ⟨it so happened that . . . : resultó que . . .⟩ ⟨do it like so : hazlo así⟩ ⟨so be it : así sea⟩ **2** ALSO : también ⟨so do I : yo también⟩ **3** THUS : así, de esta manera **4** : tan ⟨he'd never been so happy : nunca había estado tan contento⟩ **5** CONSEQUENTLY : por lo tanto

so[2] *conj* **1** THEREFORE : así que **2** *or* **so that** : para que, así que, de manera que **3 so what?** : ¿y qué?

soak[1] ['so:k] *vi* : estar en remojo — *vt* **1** : poner en remojo **2 to soak up** ABSORB : absorber

soak[2] *n* : remojo *m*

soap[1] ['so:p] *vt* : enjabonar

soap[2] *n* : jabón *m*

soapsuds ['so:pˌsʌdz] → **suds**

soapy ['so:pi] *adj* **soapier; -est** : jabonoso ⟨a soapy taste : un gusto a jabón⟩ ⟨a soapy texture : una textura de jabón⟩

soar ['sor] *vi* **1** FLY : volar **2** RISE : remontar el vuelo (dícese de las aves) ⟨her hopes soared : su esperanza renació⟩ ⟨prices are soaring : los precios están subiendo vertiginosamente⟩

sob[1] ['sɑb] *vi* **sobbed; sobbing** : sollozar

sob[2] *n* : sollozo *m*

sober ['so:bər] *adj* **1** : sobrio ⟨he's not sober enough to drive : está demasiado borracho para manejar⟩ **2** SERIOUS : serio

soberly ['so:bərli] *adv* **1** : sobriamente **2** SERIOUSLY : seriamente

sobriety [sə'braɪəti, so-] *n* **1** : sobriedad *f* ⟨sobriety test : prueba de alcoholemia⟩ **2** SERIOUSNESS : seriedad *f*

so–called ['so:'kɔld] *adj* : supuesto, presunto ⟨the so-called experts : los expertos, así llamados⟩

soccer ['sɑkər] *n* : futbol *m*, fútbol *m*

sociable ['so:ʃəbəl] *adj* : sociable

social[1] ['so:ʃəl] *adj* : social — **socially** *adv*

social[2] *n* : reunión *f* social

socialism ['soːʃə,lızəm] *n* : socialismo *m*
socialist[1] ['soːʃəlıst] *adj* : socialista
socialist[2] *n* : socialista *mf*
socialize ['soːʃə,laız] *v* **-ized; -izing** *vt* **1** NATIONALIZE : nacionalizar **2** : socializar (en psicología) — *vi* : alternar, circular ⟨to socialize with friends : alternar con amigos⟩
social work *n* : asistencia *f* social
society [sə'saıəti] *n, pl* **-eties 1** COMPANIONSHIP : compañía *f* **2** : sociedad *f* ⟨a democratic society : una sociedad democrática⟩ ⟨high society : alta sociedad⟩ **3** ASSOCIATION : sociedad *f*, asociación *f*
socioeconomic [,soːsio,iːkə'nɑmık, -,ɛkə-] *adj* : socioeconómico
sociology [,soːsi'ɑlədʒi] *n* : sociología *f*
sociological [,soːsiə'lɑdʒıkəl] *adj* : sociológico
sociologist [,soːsi'ɑlədʒıst] *n* : sociólogo *m*, -ga *f*
sock[1] ['sɑk] *vt* : pegar, golpear, darle un puñetazo a
sock[2] *n* **1** *pl* **socks** *or* **sox** ['sɑks] : calcetín *m*, media *f* ⟨shoes and socks : zapatos y calcetines⟩ **2** *pl* **socks** ['sɑks] PUNCH : puñetazo *m*
socket ['sɑkət] *n* **1** *or* **electric socket** : enchufe *m*, toma *f* de corriente **2** : glena *f* (de una articulación) ⟨shoulder socket : glena del hombro⟩ **3 eye socket** : órbita *f*, cuenca *f*
sod[1] ['sɑd] *vt* **sodded; sodding** : cubrir de césped
sod[2] *n* TURF : césped *m*, tepe *m*
soda ['soːdə] *n* **1** *or* **soda water** : soda *f* **2** *or* **soda pop** : gaseosa *f*, refresco *m* **3** *or* **ice–cream soda** : refresco *m* con helado
sodden ['sɑdən] *adj* SOGGY : empapado
sodium ['soːdiəm] *n* : sodio *m*
sodium bicarbonate *n* : bicarbonato *m* de soda
sodium chloride → **salt**
sofa ['soːfə] *n* : sofá *m*
soft ['sɔft] *adj* **1** : blando ⟨a soft pillow : una almohada blanda⟩ **2** SMOOTH : suave (dícese de las texturas, de los sonidos, etc.) **3** NONALCOHOLIC : no alcohólico ⟨a soft drink : un refresco⟩
softball ['sɔft,bɔl] *n* : softbol *m*
soften ['sɔfən] *vt* : ablandar (algo sólido), suavizar (la piel, un golpe, etc.), amortiguar (un impacto) — *vi* : ablandarse, suavizarse
softly ['sɔftli] *adv* : suavemente ⟨she spoke softly : habló en voz baja⟩
softness ['sɔftnəs] *n* **1** : blandura *f*, lo blando (de una almohada, de la mantequilla, etc.) **2** SMOOTHNESS : suavidad *f*
software ['sɔft,wær] *n* : software *m*
soggy ['sɑgi] *adj* **soggier; -est** : empapado
soil[1] ['sɔıl] *vt* : ensuciar — *vi* : ensuciarse

soil[2] *n* **1** DIRTINESS : suciedad *f* **2** DIRT, EARTH : suelo *m*, tierra *f* **3** COUNTRY : patria *f* ⟨her native soil : su tierra natal⟩
sojourn[1] ['soː,dʒərn, soː'dʒərn] *vi* : pasar una temporada
sojourn[2] *n* : estadía *f*, estancia *f*, permanencia *f*
solace ['sɑləs] *n* : consuelo *m*
solar ['soːlər] *adj* : solar ⟨the solar system : el sistema solar⟩
sold → **sell**
solder[1] ['sɑdər, 'sɔ-] *vt* : soldar
solder[2] *n* : soldadura *f*
soldier[1] ['soːldʒər] *vi* : servir como soldado
soldier[2] *n* : soldado *mf*
sole[1] ['soːl] *adj* : único
sole[2] *n* **1** : suela *f* (de un zapato) **2** : lenguado *m* (pez)
solely ['soːli] *adv* : únicamente, sólo
solemn ['sɑləm] *adj* : solemne, serio — **solemnly** *adv*
solemnity [sə'lɛmnəti] *n, pl* **-ties** : solemnidad *f*
solicit [sə'lısət] *vt* : solicitar
solicitous [sə'lısətəs] *adj* : solícito
solicitude [sə'lısə,tuːd, -,tjuːd] *n* : solicitud *f*
solid[1] ['sɑləd] *adj* **1** : macizo ⟨a solid rubber ball : una bola maciza de caucho⟩ **2** CUBIC : tridimensional **3** COMPACT : compacto, denso **4** STURDY : sólido **5** CONTINUOUS : seguido, continuo ⟨two solid hours : dos horas seguidas⟩ ⟨a solid line : una línea continua⟩ **6** UNANIMOUS : unánime **7** DEPENDABLE : serio, fiable **8** PURE : macizo, puro ⟨solid gold : oro macizo⟩
solid[2] *n* : sólido *m*
solidarity [,sɑlə'dærəti] *n* : solidaridad *f*
solidify [sə'lıdə,faı] *v* **-fied; -fying** *vt* : solidificar — *vi* : solidificarse
solidity [sə'lıdəti] *n, pl* **-ties** : solidez *f*
solidly ['sɑlədli] *adv* **1** : sólidamente **2** UNANIMOUSLY : unánimemente
soliloquy [sə'lıləkwi] *n, pl* **-quies** : soliloquio *m*
solitaire ['sɑlə,tɛr] *n* : solitario *m*
solitary ['sɑlə,tɛri] *adj* **1** ALONE : solitario **2** SECLUDED : apartado, retirado **3** SINGLE : solo
solitude ['sɑlə,tuːd, -,tjuːd] *n* : soledad *f*
solo[1] ['soː,loː] *vi* : volar en solitario (dícese de un piloto)
solo[2] *adv & adj* : en solitario, a solas
solo[3] *n, pl* **solos** : solo *m*
soloist ['soːloıst] *n* : solista *mf*
solstice ['sɑlstıs] *n* : solsticio *m*
soluble ['sɑljəbəl] *adj* : soluble
solution [sə'luːʃən] *n* : solución *f*
solve ['sɑlv] *vt* **solved; solving** : resolver, solucionar
solvency ['sɑlvəntsi] *n* : solvencia *f*
solvent ['sɑlvənt] *n* : solvente *m*
Somali [soː'mɑli, sə-] *n* : somalí *mf* — **Somali** *adj*
somber ['sɑmbər] *adj* **1** DARK : sombrío, oscuro ⟨somber colors : colores

oscuros⟩ **2** GRAVE : sombrío, serio **3** MELANCHOLY : sombrío, lúgubre

sombrero [sɑm'brɛr,o:] *n, pl* **-ros** : sombrero *m* (mexicano)

some¹ ['sʌm] *adj* **1** : un, algún ⟨some lady stopped me : una mujer me detuvo⟩ ⟨some distant galaxy : alguna galaxia lejana⟩ **2** : algo de, un poco de ⟨he drank some water : tomó (un poco de) agua⟩ **3** : unos ⟨do you want some apples? : ¿quieres unas manzanas?⟩ ⟨some years ago : hace varios años⟩

some² *pron* **1** : algunos ⟨some went, others stayed : algunos se fueron, otros se quedaron⟩ **2** : un poco, algo ⟨there's some left : queda un poco⟩ ⟨I have gum; do you want some? : tengo chicle, ¿quieres?⟩

somebody ['sʌmbədi, -,bɑdi] *pron* : alguien

someday ['sʌm,deɪ] *adv* : algún día

somehow ['sʌm,haʊ] *adv* **1** : de alguna manera, de algún modo ⟨I'll do it somehow : lo haré de alguna manera⟩ **2** : por alguna razón ⟨somehow I don't trust her : por alguna razón no me fío de ella⟩

someone ['sʌm,wʌn] *pron* : alguien

someplace ['sʌm,pleɪs] → **somewhere**

somersault¹ ['sʌmər,sɔlt] *vi* : dar volteretas, dar un salto mortal

somersault² *n* : voltereta *f*, salto *m* mortal

something ['sʌmθɪŋ] *pron* : algo ⟨I want something else : quiero otra cosa⟩ ⟨she's writing a novel or something : está escribiendo una novela o no sé qué⟩

sometime ['sʌm,taɪm] *adv* : algún día, en algún momento ⟨sometime next month : durante el mes que viene⟩

sometimes ['sʌm,taɪmz] *adv* : a veces, algunas veces, de vez en cuando

somewhat ['sʌm,hwʌt, -,hwɑt] *adv* : algo, un tanto

somewhere ['sʌm,hwɛr] *adv* **1** (*indicating location*) : en algún lugar ⟨it must be somewhere else : estará en otra parte⟩ **2** (*indicating destination*) : a algún lugar

son ['sʌn] *n* : hijo *m*

sonar ['so:,nɑr] *n* : sonar *m*

sonata [sə'nɑtə] *n* : sonata *f*

song ['sɔŋ] *n* : canción *f*, canto *m* (de un pájaro)

songbird ['sɔŋ,bərd] *n* : pájaro *m* cantor

songwriter ['sɔŋ,raɪt̬ər] *n* : compositor *m*, -tora *f*

sonic ['sɑnɪk] *adj* **1** : sónico **2 sonic boom** : estampido *m* sónico

son–in–law ['sʌnɪn,lɔ] *n, pl* **sons–in–law** : yerno *m*, hijo *m* político

sonnet ['sɑnət] *n* : soneto *m*

sonorous ['sɑnərəs, sə'norəs] *adj* : sonoro

soon ['su:n] *adv* **1** : pronto, dentro de poco ⟨he'll arrive soon : llegará pron-

to⟩ **2** QUICKLY : pronto ⟨as soon as possible : lo más pronto posible⟩ ⟨the sooner the better : cuanto antes mejor⟩ **3** : de buena gana ⟨I'd sooner walk : prefiero caminar⟩

soot ['sʊt, 'su:t, 'sʌt] *n* : hollín *m*, tizne *m*

soothe ['su:ð] *vt* **soothed; soothing 1** CALM : calmar, tranquilizar **2** RELIEVE : aliviar

soothsayer ['su:θ,seɪər] *n* : adivino *m*, -na *f*

sooty ['sʊt̬i, 'su:-, 'sʌ-] *adj* **sootier; -est** : cubierto de hollín, tiznado

sop¹ ['sɑp] *vt* **sopped; sopping 1** DIP : mojar **2** SOAK : empapar **3 to sop up** : rebañar, absorber

sop² *n* **1** CONCESSION : concesión *f* **2** BRIBE : soborno *m*

sophisticated [sə'fɪstə,keɪt̬əd] *adj* **1** COMPLEX : complejo **2** WORLDLY-WISE : sofisticado

sophistication [sə,fɪstə'keɪʃən] *n* **1** COMPLEXITY : complejidad *f* **2** URBANITY : sofisticación *f*

sophomore ['sɑf,mor, 'sɑfə,mor] *n* : estudiante *mf* de segundo año

soporific [,sɑpə'rɪfɪk, ,so:-] *adj* : soporífero

soprano [sə'præ,no:] *n, pl* **-nos** : soprano *mf*

sorcerer ['sɔrsərər] *n* : hechicero *m*, brujo *m*, mago *m*

sorceress ['sɔrsərəs] *n* : hechicera *f*, bruja *f*, maga *f*

sorcery ['sɔrsəri] *n* : hechicería *f*, brujería *f*

sordid ['sɔrdɪd] *adj* : sórdido

sore¹ ['sor] *adj* **sorer; sorest 1** PAINFUL : dolorido, doloroso ⟨I have a sore throat : me duele la garganta⟩ **2** ACUTE, SEVERE : extremo, grande ⟨in sore straits : en grandes apuros⟩ **3** ANGRY : enojado, enfadado

sore² *n* : llaga *f*

sorely ['sorli] *adv* : muchísimo ⟨it was sorely needed : se necesitaba urgentemente⟩ ⟨she was sorely missed : la echaban mucho de menos⟩

soreness ['sornəs] *n* : dolor *m*

sorghum ['sɔrgəm] *n* : sorgo *m*

sorority [sə'rɔrəṭi] *n, pl* **-ties** : hermandad *f* (de estudiantes femeninas)

sorrel ['sɔrəl] *n* **1** : alazán *m* (color o animal) **2** : acedera *f* (hierba)

sorrow ['sɑr,o:] *n* : pesar *m*, dolor *m*, pena *f*

sorrowful ['sɑrofəl] *adj* : triste, afligido, apenado

sorrowfully ['sɑrofəli] *adv* : con tristeza

sorry ['sɑri] *adj* **sorrier; -est 1** PITIFUL : lastimero, lastimoso **2 to be sorry** : sentir, lamentar ⟨I'm sorry : lo siento⟩ **3 to feel sorry for** : compadecer ⟨I feel sorry for him : me da pena⟩

sort¹ ['sɔrt] *vt* **1** : dividir en grupos **2** CLASSIFY : clasificar **3 to sort out** ORGANIZE : poner en orden **4 to sort out** RESOLVE : resolver

sort² *n* **1** KIND : tipo *m*, clase *f* ⟨a sort of writer : una especie de escritor⟩ **2** NATURE : índole *f* **3 out of sorts** : de mal humor

sortie ['sɔrṭi, sɔr'ti:] *n* : salida *f*

SOS [ˌɛsˌo:'ɛs] *n* : SOS *m*

so–so ['so:'so:] *adj & adv* : así así, de modo regular

soufflé [su:'fleɪ] *n* : suflé *m*

sought → seek

soul ['so:l] *n* **1** SPIRIT : alma *f* **2** ESSENCE : esencia *f* **3** PERSON : persona *f*, alma *f*

soulful ['so:lfəl] *adj* : conmovedor, lleno de emoción

sound¹ ['saʊnd] *vt* **1** : sondar (en navegación) **2** *or* **to sound out** PROBE : sondear **3** : hacer sonar, tocar (una trompeta, etc.) — *vi* **1** : sonar ⟨the alarm sounded : la alarma sonó⟩ **2** SEEM : parecer

sound² *adj* **1** HEALTHY : sano ⟨safe and sound : sano y salvo⟩ ⟨of sound mind and body : en pleno uso de sus facultades⟩ **2** FIRM, SOLID : sólido **3** SENSIBLE : lógico, sensato **4** DEEP : profundo ⟨a sound sleep : un sueño profundo⟩

sound³ *n* **1** : sonido *m* ⟨the speed of sound : la velocidad del sonido⟩ **2** NOISE : sonido *m*, ruido *m* ⟨I heard a sound : oí un sonido⟩ **3** CHANNEL : brazo *m* de mar, canal *m* (ancho)

soundless ['saʊndləs] *adj* : sordo

soundlessly ['saʊndləsli] *adv* : silenciosamente

soundly ['saʊndli] *adv* **1** SOLIDLY : sólidamente **2** SENSIBLY : lógicamente, sensatamente **3** DEEPLY : profundamente ⟨sleeping soundly : durmiendo profundamente⟩

soundness ['saʊndnəs] *n* **1** SOLIDITY : solidez *f* **2** SENSIBLENESS : sensatez *f*, solidez *f*

soundproof ['saʊndˌpru:f] *adj* : insonorizado

soundtrack ['saʊndˌtræk] *n* : banda *f* sonora

sound wave *n* : onda *f* sonora

soup ['su:p] *n* : sopa *f*

sour¹ ['saʊər] *vi* : agriarse, cortarse (dícese de la leche) — *vt* : agriar, cortar (leche)

sour² *adj* **1** ACID : agrio, ácido (dícese de la fruta, etc.), cortado (dícese de la leche) **2** DISAGREEABLE : desagradable, agrio

source ['sors] *n* : fuente *f*, origen *m*, nacimiento *m* (de un río)

sourness ['saʊrnəs] *n* : acidez *f*

south¹ ['saʊθ] *adv* : al sur, hacia el sur ⟨the window looks south : la ventana mira al sur⟩ ⟨she continued south : continuó hacia el sur⟩

south² *adj* : sur, del sur ⟨the south entrance : la entrada sur⟩ ⟨South America : Sudamérica, América del Sur⟩

south³ *n* : sur *m*

South African *n* : sudafricano *m*, -na *f* — **South African** *adj*

South American¹ *adj* : sudamericano, suramericano

South American² *n* : sudamericano *m*, -na *f*; suramericano *m*, -na *f*

southbound ['saʊθˌbaʊnd] *adj* : con rumbo al sur

southeast¹ [saʊ'θi:st] *adj* : sureste, sudeste, del sureste

southeast² *n* : sureste *m*, sudeste *m*

southeasterly [saʊ'θi:stərli] *adv & adj* **1** : del sureste (dícese del viento) **2** : hacia el sureste

southeastern [saʊ'θi:stərn] *adj →* **southeast¹**

southerly ['sʌðərli] *adv & adj* : del sur

southern ['sʌðərn] *adj* : sur, sureño, meridional, austral ⟨a southern city : una ciudad del sur del país, una ciudad meridional⟩ ⟨the southern side : el lado sur⟩

Southerner ['sʌðərnər] *n* : sureño *m*, -ña *f*

South Pole : Polo *m* Sur

southward ['saʊθwərd] *or* **southwards** [-wərdz] *adv & adj* : hacia el sur

southwest¹ [saʊθ'wɛst, *as a nautical term often* saʊ'wɛst] *adj* : suroeste, sudoeste, del suroeste

southwest² *n* : suroeste *m*, sudoeste *m*

southwesterly [saʊθ'wɛstərli] *adv & adj* **1** : del suroeste (dícese del viento) **2** : hacia el suroeste

southwestern [saʊθ'wɛstərn] *adj →* **southwest¹**

souvenir [ˌsu:və'nɪr, 'su:vəˌ-] *n* : recuerdo *m*, souvenir *m*

sovereign¹ ['sɑvərən] *adj* : soberano

sovereign² *n* **1** : soberano *m*, -na *f* (monarca) **2** : soberano *m* (moneda)

sovereignty ['sɑvərənti] *n*, *pl* **-ties** : soberanía *f*

Soviet ['so:viˌɛt, 'sɑ-, -viət] *adj* : soviético

sow¹ ['so:] *vt* **sowed; sown** ['so:n] *or* **sowed; sowing 1** PLANT : sembrar **2** SCATTER : esparcir

sow² ['saʊ] *n* : cerda *f*

sox → sock

soy ['sɔɪ] *n* : soya *f*, soja *f*

soybean ['sɔɪˌbi:n] *n* : soya *f*, soja *f*

spa ['spɑ] *n* : balneario *m*

space¹ ['speɪs] *vt* **spaced; spacing** : espaciar

space² *n* **1** PERIOD : espacio *m*, lapso *m*, período *m* **2** ROOM : espacio *m*, sitio *m*, lugar *m* ⟨is there space for me? : ¿hay sitio para mí?⟩ **3** : espacio *m* ⟨blank space : espacio en blanco⟩ **4** : espacio *m* (en física) **5** PLACE : plaza *f*, sitio *m* ⟨to reserve space : reservar plazas⟩ ⟨parking space : sitio para estacionarse⟩

spacecraft ['speɪsˌkræft] *n* : nave *f* espacial

spaceflight ['speɪsˌflaɪt] *n* : vuelo *m* espacial

spaceman ['speɪsmən, -ˌmæn] *n, pl* **-men** [-mən, -ˌmɛn] : astronauta *m*, cosmonauta *m*

spaceship ['speɪsˌʃɪp] *n* : nave *f* espacial

space shuttle *n* : transbordador *m* espacial

space suit *n* : traje *m* espacial

spacious ['speɪʃəs] *adj* : espacioso, amplio

spade[1] ['speɪd] *v* **spaded; spading** *vt* : palear — *vi* : usar una pala

spade[2] *n* **1** SHOVEL : pala *f* **2** : pica *f* (naipe)

spaghetti [spə'gɛti] *n* : espagueti *m*, espaguetis *mpl*, spaghetti *mpl*

spam ['spæm] *n* : spam *m*, correo *m* electrónico no solicitado

span[1] ['spæn] *vt* **spanned; spanning** : abarcar (un período de tiempo), extenderse sobre (un espacio)

span[2] *n* **1** : lapso *m*, espacio *m* (de tiempo) ⟨life span : duración de la vida⟩ **2** : luz *f* (entre dos soportes)

spangle ['spæŋgəl] *n* : lentejuela *f*

Spaniard ['spænjərd] *n* : español *m*, -ñola *f*

spaniel ['spænjəl] *n* : spaniel *m*

Spanish[1] ['spænɪʃ] *adj* : español

Spanish[2] *n* **1** : español *m* (idioma) **2 the Spanish** *npl* : los españoles

spank ['spæŋk] *vt* : darle nalgadas (a alguien)

spar[1] ['spɑr] *vi* **sparred; sparring** : entrenarse (en boxeo)

spar[2] *n* : palo *m*, verga *f* (de un barco)

spare[1] ['spær] *vt* **spared; sparing 1** : perdonar ⟨to spare someone's life : perdonarle la vida a alguien⟩ **2** SAVE : ahorrar, evitar ⟨I'll spare you the trouble : le evitaré la molestia⟩ **3** : prescindir de ⟨I can't spare her : no puedo prescindir de ella⟩ ⟨can you spare a dollar? : ¿me das un dólar?⟩ **4** STINT : escatimar ⟨they spared no expense : no repararon en gastos⟩ **5 to spare** : de sobra

spare[2] *adj* **1** : de repuesto, de recambio ⟨spare tire : llanta de repuesto⟩ **2** EXCESS : de más, de sobra ⟨spare time : tiempo libre⟩ **3** LEAN : delgado

spare[3] *n or* **spare part** : repuesto *m*, recambio *m*

sparing ['spærɪŋ] *adj* : parco, económico — **sparingly** *adv*

spark[1] ['spɑrk] *vi* : chispear, echar chispas — *vt* PROVOKE : despertar, provocar ⟨to spark interest : despertar interés⟩

spark[2] *n* **1** : chispa *f* ⟨to throw off sparks : echar chispas⟩ **2** GLIMMER, TRACE : destello *m*, pizca *f*

sparkle[1] ['spɑrkəl] *vi* **-kled; -kling 1** FLASH, SHINE : destellar, centellear, brillar **2** : estar muy animado (dícese de una conversación, etc.)

sparkle[2] *n* : destello *m*, centelleo *m*

sparkler ['spɑrklər] *n* : luz *f* de bengala

spark plug *n* : bujía *f*

sparrow ['spæro:] *n* : gorrión *m*

sparse ['spɑrs] *adj* **sparser; -est** : escaso — **sparsely** *adv*

spasm ['spæzəm] *n* **1** : espasmo *m* (muscular) **2** BURST, FIT : arrebato *m*

spasmodic [spæz'mɑdɪk] *adj* **1** : espasmódico **2** SPORADIC : irregular, esporádico — **spasmodically** [-dɪkli] *adv*

spastic ['spæstɪk] *adj* : espástico

spat[1] → **spit**[1]

spat[2] ['spæt] *n* : discusión *f*, disputa *f*, pelea *f*

spatial ['speɪʃəl] *adj* : espacial

spatter[1] ['spætər] *v* : salpicar

spatter[2] *n* : salpicadura *f*

spatula ['spætʃələ] *n* : espátula *f*, paleta *f* (para servir)

spawn[1] ['spɔn] *vi* : desovar, frezar — *vt* GENERATE : generar, producir

spawn[2] *n* : hueva *f*, freza *f*

spay ['speɪ] *vt* : esterilizar (una perra, etc.)

speak ['spi:k] *v* **spoke** ['spo:k]; **spoken** ['spo:kən]; **speaking** *vi* **1** TALK : hablar ⟨to speak to someone : hablar con alguien⟩ ⟨who's speaking? : ¿de parte de quien?⟩ ⟨so to speak : por así decirlo⟩ **2 to speak out** : hablar claramente **3 to speak out against** : denunciar **4 to speak up** : hablar en voz alta **5 to speak up for** : defender — *vt* **1** SAY : decir ⟨she spoke her mind : habló con franqueza⟩ **2** : hablar (un idioma)

speaker ['spi:kər] *n* **1** : hablante *mf* ⟨a native speaker : un hablante nativo⟩ **2** : orador *m*, -dora *f* ⟨the keynote speaker : el orador principal⟩ **3** LOUDSPEAKER : altavoz *m*, altoparlante *m*

spear[1] ['spɪr] *vt* : atravesar con una lanza

spear[2] *n* : lanza *f*

spearhead[1] ['spɪrˌhɛd] *vt* : encabezar

spearhead[2] *n* : punta *f* de lanza

spearmint ['spɪrmɪnt] *n* : menta *f* verde

special ['spɛʃəl] *adj* : especial ⟨nothing special : nada en especial, nada en particular⟩ — **specially** *adv*

specialist ['spɛʃəlɪst] *n* : especialista *mf*

specialization [ˌspɛʃələ'zeɪʃən] *n* : especialización *f*

specialize ['spɛʃəˌlaɪz] *vi* **-ized; -izing** : especializarse

specialty ['spɛʃəlti] *n, pl* **-ties** : especialidad *f*

species ['spi:ˌʃi:z, -ˌsi:z] *ns & pl* : especie *f*

specific [spɪ'sɪfɪk] *adj* : específico, determinado — **specifically** [-fɪkli] *adv*

specification [ˌspɛsəfə'keɪʃən] *n* : especificación *f*

specify ['spɛsəˌfaɪ] *vt* **-fied; -fying** : especificar

specimen ['spɛsəmən] *n* **1** SAMPLE : espécimen *m*, muestra *f* **2** EXAMPLE : espécimen *m*, ejemplar *m*

speck ['spɛk] *n* **1** SPOT : manchita *f* **2** BIT, TRACE : mota *f*, pizca *f*, ápice *m*

speckled ['spɛkəld] *adj* : moteado

spectacle ['spɛktɪkəl] n 1 : espectáculo m 2 **spectacles** npl GLASSES : lentes fpl, gafas fpl, anteojos mpl, espejuelos mpl

spectacular [spɛk'tækjələr] adj : espectacular

spectator ['spɛk.teɪţər] n : espectador m, -dora f

specter or **spectre** ['spɛktər] n : espectro m, fantasma m

spectrum ['spɛktrəm] n, pl **spectra** [-trə] or **spectrums** 1 : espectro m (de colores, etc.) 2 RANGE : gama f, abanico m

speculate ['spɛkjə.leɪt] vi -lated; -lating 1 : especular (en finanzas) 2 WONDER : preguntarse, hacer conjeturas

speculation [ˌspɛkjə'leɪʃən] n : especulación f

speculative ['spɛkjə.leɪţɪv] adj : especulativo

speculator ['spɛkjə.leɪţər] n : especulador m, -dora f

speech ['spi:tʃ] n 1 : habla f, modo m de hablar, expresión f 2 ADDRESS : discurso m

speechless ['spi:tʃləs] adj : enmudecido, estupefacto

speed¹ ['spi:d] v **sped** ['spɛd] or **speeded; speeding** vi 1 : ir a toda velocidad, correr a toda prisa ⟨he sped off : se fue a toda velocidad⟩ 2 : conducir a exceso de velocidad ⟨a ticket for speeding : una multa por exceso de velocidad⟩ — vt **to speed up** : acelerar

speed² n 1 SWIFTNESS : rapidez f 2 VELOCITY : velocidad f

speedboat ['spi:d.bo:t] n : lancha f motora

speed bump n : badén m

speed limit n : velocidad f máxima, límite m de velocidad

speedometer [spɪ'dɑməţər] n : velocímetro m

speedup ['spi:d.ʌp] n : aceleración f

speedy ['spi:di] adj **speedier; -est** : rápido — **speedily** [-dəli] adv

spell¹ ['spɛl] vt 1 : escribir, deletrear (verbalmente) ⟨how do you spell it? : ¿cómo se escribe?, ¿cómo se deletrea?⟩ 2 MEAN : significar ⟨that could spell trouble : eso puede significar problemas⟩ 3 RELIEVE : relevar

spell² n 1 TURN : turno m 2 PERIOD, TIME : período m (de tiempo) 3 ENCHANTMENT : encanto m, hechizo m, maleficio m

spellbound ['spɛl.baʊnd] adj : embelesado

speller ['spɛlər] n : persona f que escribe ⟨she's a good speller : tiene buena ortografía⟩

spelling ['spɛlɪŋ] n : ortografía f

spend ['spɛnd] vt **spent** ['spɛnt]; **spending** 1 : gastar (dinero, etc.) 2 PASS : pasar (el tiempo) ⟨to spend time on : dedicar tiempo a⟩

spendthrift ['spɛnd.θrɪft] n : derrochador m, -dora f; despilfarrador m, -dora f

sperm ['spərm] n, pl **sperm** or **sperms** : esperma mf

spew ['spju:] vi : salir a chorros — vt : vomitar, arrojar (lava, etc.)

sphere ['sfɪr] n : esfera f

spherical ['sfɪrɪkəl, 'sfɛr-] adj : esférico

spice¹ ['spaɪs] vt **spiced; spicing** 1 SEASON : condimentar, sazonar 2 or **to spice up** : salpimentar, hacer más interesante

spice² n 1 : especia f 2 FLAVOR, INTEREST : sabor m ⟨the spice of life : la sal de la vida⟩

spick–and–span ['spɪkənd'spæn] adj : limpio y ordenado

spicy ['spaɪsi] adj **spicier; -est** 1 SPICED : condimentado, sazonado 2 HOT : picante 3 RACY : picante

spider ['spaɪdər] n : araña f

spigot ['spɪgət, -kət] n : llave f, grifo m, canilla Arg, Uru

spike¹ ['spaɪk] vt **spiked; spiking** 1 FASTEN : clavar (con clavos grandes) 2 PIERCE : atravesar 3 : añadir alcohol a ⟨he spiked her drink with rum : le puso ron a la bebida⟩

spike² n 1 : clavo m grande 2 CLEAT : clavo m 3 : remache m (en voleibol) 4 PEAK : pico m

spill¹ ['spɪl] vt 1 SHED : derramar, verter ⟨to spill blood : derrame sangre⟩ 2 DIVULGE : revelar, divulgar — vi : derramarse

spill² n 1 SPILLING : derrame m, vertido m ⟨oil spill : derrame de petróleo⟩ 2 FALL : caída f

spin¹ ['spɪn] v **spun** ['spʌn]; **spinning** vi 1 : hilar 2 TURN : girar 3 REEL : dar vueltas ⟨my head is spinning : la cabeza me está dando vueltas⟩ — vt 1 : hilar (hilo, etc.) 2 : tejer ⟨to spin a web : tejer una telaraña⟩ 3 TWIRL : hacer girar

spin² n : vuelta f, giro m ⟨to go for a spin : dar una vuelta (en coche)⟩

spinach ['spɪnɪtʃ] n : espinacas fpl, espinaca f

spinal column ['spaɪnəl] n BACKBONE : columna f vertebral

spinal cord n : médula f espinal

spindle ['spɪndəl] n 1 : huso m (para hilar) 2 : eje m (de un mecanismo)

spindly ['spɪndli] adj : larguirucho fam, largo y débil (dícese de una planta)

spine ['spaɪn] n 1 BACKBONE : columna f vertebral, espina f dorsal 2 QUILL : púa f (de un animal) 3 THORN : espina f 4 : lomo m (de un libro)

spineless ['spaɪnləs] adj 1 : sin púas, sin espinas 2 INVERTEBRATE : invertebrado 3 WEAK : débil (de carácter)

spinet ['spɪnət] n : espineta f

spinster ['spɪnstər] n : soltera f

spiny ['spaɪni] adj **spinier; -est** : con púas (dícese de los animales), espinoso (dícese de las plantas)

spiral[1] ['spaɪrəl] *vi* **-raled** *or* **-ralled; -raling** *or* **-ralling** : ir en espiral

spiral[2] *adj* : espiral, en espiral ⟨a spiral staircase : una escalera de caracol⟩

spiral[3] *n* : espiral *f*

spire ['spaɪr] *n* : aguja *f*

spirit[1] ['spɪrət] *vt* **to spirit away** : hacer desaparecer

spirit[2] *n* **1** : espíritu *m* ⟨body and spirit : cuerpo y espíritu⟩ **2** GHOST : espíritu *m*, fantasma *m* **3** MOOD : espíritu *m*, humor *m* ⟨in the spirit of friendship : en el espíritu de amistad⟩ ⟨to be in good spirits : estar de buen humor⟩ **4** ENTHUSIASM, VIVACITY : espíritu *m*, ánimo *m*, brío *m* **5 spirits** *npl* : licores *mpl*

spirited ['spɪrətəd] *adj* : animado, enérgético

spiritless ['spɪrətləs] *adj* : desanimado

spiritual[1] ['spɪrɪtʃuəl, -tʃəl] *adj* : espiritual — **spiritually** *adv*

spiritual[2] *n* : espiritual *m* (canción)

spiritualism ['spɪrɪtʃuə,lɪzəm, -tʃə-] *n* : espiritismo *m*

spirituality [,spɪrɪtʃʊ'æləti] *n, pl* **-ties** : espiritualidad *f*

spit[1] ['spɪt] *v* **spit** *or* **spat** ['spæt]; **spitting** : escupir

spit[2] *n* **1** SALIVA : saliva *f* **2** ROTISSERIE : asador *m* **3** POINT : lengua *f* (de tierra)

spite[1] ['spaɪt] *vt* **spited; spiting** : fastidiar, molestar

spite[2] *n* **1** : despecho *m*, rencor *m* **2 in spite of** : a pesar de (que), pese a (que)

spiteful ['spaɪtfəl] *adj* : malicioso, rencoroso

spitting image *n* **to be the spitting image of** : ser el vivo retrato de

spittle ['spɪtəl] *n* : saliva *f*

splash[1] ['splæʃ] *vt* : salpicar — *vi* **1** : salpicar **2 to splash around** : chapotear

splash[2] *n* **1** SPLASHING : salpicadura *f* **2** SQUIRT : chorrito *m* **3** SPOT : mancha *f*

splatter ['splætər] → **spatter**

splay ['spleɪ] *vt* : extender (hacia afuera) ⟨to splay one's fingers : abrir los dedos⟩ — *vi* : extenderse (hacia afuera)

spleen ['spli:n] *n* **1** : bazo *m* (órgano) **2** ANGER, SPITE : ira *f*, rencor *m*

splendid ['splɛndəd] *adj* : espléndido — **splendidly** *adv*

splendor ['splɛndər] *n* : esplendor *m*

splice[1] ['splaɪs] *vt* **spliced; splicing** : empalmar, unir

splice[2] *n* : empalme *m*, unión *f*

splint ['splɪnt] *n* : tablilla *f*

splinter[1] ['splɪntər] *vt* : astillar — *vi* : astillarse

splinter[2] *n* : astilla *f*

split[1] ['splɪt] *v* **split; splitting** *vt* **1** CLEAVE : partir, hender ⟨to split wood : partir madera⟩ **2** BURST : romper, rajar ⟨to split open : abrir⟩ **3** DIVIDE, SHARE : dividir, repartir — *vi* **1** : par-

tirse (dícese de la madera, etc.) **2** BURST, CRACK : romperse, rajarse **3** *or* **to split up** : dividirse

split[2] *n* **1** CRACK : rajadura *f* **2** TEAR : rotura *f* **3** DIVISION : división *f*, escisión *f*

splurge[1] ['splərdʒ] *v* **splurged; splurging** *vt* : derrochar — *vi* : derrochar dinero

splurge[2] *n* : derroche *m*

spoil[1] ['spɔɪl] *vt* **1** PILLAGE : saquear **2** RUIN : estropear, arruinar **3** PAMPER : consentir, mimar — *vi* : estropearse, echarse a perder

spoil[2] *n* PLUNDER : botín *m*

spoke[1] → **speak**

spoke[2] ['spo:k] *n* : rayo *m* (de una rueda)

spoken → **speak**

spokesman ['spo:ksmən] *n, pl* **-men** [-mən, -ˌmɛn] : portavoz *mf*; vocero *m*, -ra *f*

spokeswoman ['spo:ks,wumən] *n, pl* **-women** [-ˌwɪmən] : portavoz *f*, vocera *f*

sponge[1] ['spʌndʒ] *vt* **sponged; sponging** : limpiar con una esponja

sponge[2] *n* : esponja *f*

spongy ['spʌndʒi] *adj* **spongier; -est** : esponjoso

sponsor[1] ['spɑntsər] *vt* : patrocinar, auspiciar, apadrinar (a una persona)

sponsor[2] *n* : patrocinador *m*, -dora *f*; padrino *m*, madrina *f*

sponsorship ['spɑntsər,ʃɪp] *n* : patrocinio *m*, apadrinamiento *m*

spontaneity [,spɑntə'ni:əti, -'neɪ-] *n* : espontaneidad *f*

spontaneous [spɑn'teɪniəs] *adj* : espontáneo — **spontaneously** *adv*

spoof ['spu:f] *n* : burla *f*, parodia *f*

spook[1] ['spu:k] *vt* : asustar

spook[2] *n* : fantasma *m*, espíritu *m*, espectro *m*

spooky ['spu:ki] *adj* **spookier; -est** : que da miedo, espeluznante

spool ['spu:l] *n* : carrete *m*

spoon[1] ['spu:n] *vt* : comer, servir, o echar con cuchara

spoon[2] *n* : cuchara *f*

spoonful ['spu:n,fʊl] *n* : cucharada *f* ⟨by the spoonful : a cucharadas⟩

spoor ['spʊr, 'spor] *n* : rastro *m*, pista *f*

sporadic [spə'rædɪk] *adj* : esporádico — **sporadically** [-dɪkli] *adv*

spore ['spor] *n* : espora *f*

sport[1] ['sport] *vi* FROLIC : retozar, juguetear — *vt* SHOW OFF : lucir, ostentar

sport[2] *n* **1** : deporte *m* ⟨outdoor sports : deportes al aire libre⟩ **2** JEST : broma *f* **3 to be a good sport** : tener espíritu deportivo

sporting ['sportɪŋ] *adj* : deportivo ⟨a sporting chance : buenas posibilidades⟩

sportsman ['sportsmən] *n, pl* **-men** [-mən, -ˌmɛn] : deportista *m*

sportsmanship ['sportsmən‚ʃɪp] *n* : espíritu *m* deportivo, deportividad *f Spain*

sportswoman ['sports‚wʊmən] *n, pl* **-women** [-‚wɪmən] : deportista *f*

sporty ['sporṭi] *adj* **sportier; -est** : deportivo

spot¹ ['spɑt] *v* **spotted; spotting** *vt* **1** STAIN : manchar **2** RECOGNIZE, SEE : ver, reconocer ⟨to spot an error : descubrir un error⟩ — *vi* : mancharse

spot² *adj* : hecho al azar ⟨a spot check : un vistazo, un control aleatorio⟩

spot³ *n* **1** STAIN : mancha *f* **2** DOT : punto *m* **3** PIMPLE : grano *m* ⟨to break out in spots : salirle granos a alguien⟩ **4** PREDICAMENT : apuro *m*, aprieto *m*, lío *m* ⟨in a tight spot : en apuros⟩ **5** PLACE : lugar *m*, sitio *m* ⟨to be on the spot : estar en el lugar⟩

spotless ['spɑtləs] *adj* : impecable, inmaculado — **spotlessly** *adv*

spotlight¹ ['spɑt‚laɪt] *vt* **-lighted** *or* **-lit** [-‚lɪt]; **-lighting 1** LIGHT : iluminar (con un reflector) **2** HIGHLIGHT : destacar, poner en relieve

spotlight² *n* **1** : reflector *m*, foco *m* **2 to be in the spotlight** : ser el centro de atención

spotty ['spɑṭi] *adj* **spottier; -est** : irregular, desigual

spouse ['spaʊs] *n* : cónyuge *mf*

spout¹ ['spaʊt] *vt* **1** : lanzar chorros de **2** DECLAIM : declamar — *vi* : salir a chorros

spout² *n* **1** : pico *m* (de una jarra, etc.) **2** STREAM : chorro *m*

sprain¹ ['spreɪn] *vt* : sufrir un esguince en

sprain² *n* : esguince *m*, torcedura *f*

sprawl¹ ['sprɔl] *vi* **1** LIE : tumbarse, echarse, despatarrarse **2** EXTEND : extenderse

sprawl² *n* **1** : postura *f* despatarrada **2** SPREAD : extensión *f*, expansión *f*

spray¹ ['spreɪ] *vt* : rociar (una superficie), pulverizar (un líquido)

spray² *n* **1** BOUQUET : ramillete *m* **2** MIST : rocío *m* **3** ATOMIZER : atomizador *m*, pulverizador *m*

spray gun *n* : pistola *f*

spread¹ ['sprɛd] *v* **spread; spreading** *vt* **1** *or* **to spread out** : desplegar, extender **2** SCATTER, STREW : esparcir **3** SMEAR : untar (mantequilla, etc.) **4** DISSEMINATE : difundir, sembrar, propagar — *vi* **1** : difundirse, correr, propagarse **2** EXTEND : extenderse

spread² *n* **1** EXTENSION : extensión *f*, difusión *f* (de noticias, etc.), propagación *f* (de enfermedades, etc.) **2** : colcha *f* (para una cama), mantel *m* (para una mesa) **3** PASTE : pasta *f* ⟨cheese spread : pasta de queso⟩

spreadsheet ['sprɛd‚ʃiːt] *n* : hoja *f* de cálculo

spree ['spri] *n* **1** : acción *f* desenfrenada ⟨to go on a shopping spree : comprar como loco⟩ **2** BINGE : parranda *f*, juerga *f* ⟨on a spree : de parranda, de juerga⟩

sprig ['sprɪg] *n* : ramita *f*, ramito *m*

sprightly ['spraɪtli] *adj* **sprightlier; -est** : vivo, animado ⟨with a sprightly step : con paso ligero⟩

spring¹ ['sprɪŋ] *v* **sprang** ['spræŋ] *or* **sprung** ['sprʌŋ]; **sprung; springing** *vi* **1** LEAP : saltar **2** : mover rápidamente ⟨the lid sprang shut : la tapa se cerró de un golpe⟩ ⟨he sprang to his feet : se paró de un salto⟩ **3 to spring up** : brotar (dícese de las plantas), surgir **4 to spring from** : surgir de — *vt* **1** RELEASE : soltar (de repente) ⟨to spring the news on someone : sorprender a alguien con las noticias⟩ ⟨to spring a trap : hacer saltar una trampa⟩ **2** ACTIVATE : accionar (un mecanismo) **3 to spring a leak** : hacer agua

spring² *n* **1** SOURCE : fuente *f*, origen *m* **2** : manantial *m*, fuente *f* ⟨hot spring : fuente termal⟩ **3** : primavera *f* ⟨spring and summer : la primavera y el verano⟩ **4** : resorte *m*, muelle *m* (de metal, etc.) **5** LEAP : salto *m*, brinco *m* **6** RESILIENCE : elasticidad *f*

springboard ['sprɪŋ‚bord] *n* : trampolín *m*

springtime ['sprɪŋ‚taɪm] *n* : primavera *f*

springy ['sprɪŋi] *adj* **springier; -est 1** RESILIENT : elástico **2** LIVELY : enérgico

sprinkle¹ ['sprɪŋkəl] *vt* **-kled; -kling** : rociar (con agua), espolvorear (con azúcar, etc.), salpicar

sprinkle² *n* : llovizna *f*

sprinkler ['sprɪŋkələr] *n* : rociador *m*, aspersor *m*

sprint¹ ['sprɪnt] *vi* : echar la carrera, esprintar (en deportes)

sprint² *n* : esprint *m* (en deportes)

sprinter ['sprɪntər] *n* : esprínter *mf*

sprite ['spraɪt] *n* : hada *f*, elfo *m*

sprocket ['sprɑkət] *n* : diente *m* (de una rueda dentada)

sprout¹ ['spraʊt] *vi* : brotar

sprout² *n* : brote *m*, retoño *m*, vástago *m*

spruce¹ ['spruːs] *v* **spruced; sprucing** *vt* : arreglar — *vi or* **to spruce up** : arreglarse, acicalarse

spruce² *adj* **sprucer; sprucest** : pulcro, arreglado

spruce³ *n* : picea *f* (árbol)

spry ['spraɪ] *adj* **sprier** *or* **spryer** ['spraɪər]; **spriest** *or* **spryest** ['spraɪəst] : ágil, activo

spun → spin

spunk ['spʌŋk] *n* : valor *m*, coraje *m*, agallas *fpl fam*

spunky ['spʌŋki] *adj* **spunkier; -est** : animoso, corajudo

spur¹ ['spər] *vt* **spurred; spurring** *or* **to spur on** : espolear (un caballo), motivar (a una persona, etc.)

spur² *n* **1** : espuela *f*, acicate *m* **2** STIM-
ULUS : acicate *m* **3** : espolón *m* (de aves
gallináceas)

spurious ['spjurɪəs] *adj* : espurio

spurn ['spərn] *vt* : desdeñar, rechazar

spurt¹ ['spərt] *vt* SQUIRT : lanzar un chorro de — *vi* SPOUT : salir a chorros

spurt² *n* **1** : actividad *f* repentina ⟨a
spurt of energy : una explosión de en-
ergía⟩ ⟨to do in spurts : hacer por
rachas⟩ **2** JET : chorro *m* (de agua, etc.)

sputter¹ ['spʌtər] *vi* **1** JABBER : farfullar
2 : chisporrotear (dícese de la grasa,
etc.), petardear (dícese de un motor)

sputter² *n* **1** JABBER : farfulla *f* **2** : chisporroteo *m* (de grasa, etc.), petardeo *m*
(de un motor)

spy¹ ['spaɪ] *v* **spied; spying** *vt* SEE : ver,
divisar — *vi* : espiar ⟨to spy on some-
one : espiar a alguien⟩

spy² *n* : espía *mf*

squab ['skwab] *n, pl* **squabs** *or* **squab**
: pichón *m*

squabble¹ ['skwabəl] *vi* **-bled; -bling**
: reñir, pelearse, discutir

squabble² *n* : riña *f*, pelea *f*, discusión *f*

squad ['skwad] *n* : pelotón *m* (militar),
brigada *f* (de policías), cuadrilla *f* (de
obreros, etc.)

squadron ['skwadrən] *n* : escuadrón *m*
(de militares), escuadrilla *f* (de
aviones), escuadra *f* (de naves)

squalid ['skwalɪd] *adj* : miserable

squall ['skwɔl] *n* **1** : aguacero *m* tormentoso, chubasco *m* tormentoso **2**
snow squall : tormenta *f* de nieve

squalor ['skwalər] *n* : miseria *f*

squander ['skwandər] *vt* : derrochar
(dinero, etc.), desaprovechar (una
oportunidad, etc.), desperdiciar (talen-
tos, energías, etc.)

square¹ ['skwær] *vt* **squared; squaring**
1 : cuadrar **2** : elevar al cuadrado (en
matemáticas) **3** CONFORM : conciliar
(con), ajustar (con) **4** SETTLE : saldar
(una cuenta) ⟨I squared it with him : lo
arreglé con él⟩

square² *adj* **squarer; -est 1** : cuadrado
⟨a square house : una casa cuadrada⟩
2 RIGHT-ANGLED : a escuadra, en ángulo recto **3** : cuadrado (en matemáticas) ⟨a square mile : una milla cuadra-
da⟩ **4** HONEST : justo ⟨a square deal
: un buen acuerdo⟩ ⟨fair and square
: en buena ley⟩

square³ *n* **1** : escuadra *f* (instrumento)
2 : cuadrado *m*, cuadro *m* ⟨to fold into
squares : plegar en cuadrados⟩ **3**
: plaza *f* (de una ciudad) **4** : cuadrado
m (en matemáticas)

squarely ['skwærli] *adv* **1** EXACTLY : exactamente, directamente, justo **2** HON-
ESTLY : honradamente, justamente

square root *n* : raíz *f* cuadrada

squash¹ ['skwaʃ, 'skwɔʃ] *vt* **1** CRUSH
: aplastar **2** SUPPRESS : acallar (protestas), sofocar (una rebelión)

squash² *n* **1** *pl* **squashes** *or* **squash**
: calabaza *f* (vegetal) **2** *or* **squash rac-
quets** : squash *m* (deporte)

squat¹ ['skwat] *vi* **squatted; squatting**
1 CROUCH : agacharse, ponerse en cuclillas **2** : ocupar un lugar sin derecho

squat² *adj* **squatter; squattest** : bajo y
ancho, rechoncho *fam* (dícese de una
persona)

squat³ *n* **1** : posición *f* en cuclillas **2**
: ocupación *f* ilegal (de un lugar)

squaw ['skwɔ] *n* : india *f* (norteameri-
cana)

squawk¹ ['skwɔk] *vi* : graznar (dícese de
las aves), chillar

squawk² *n* : graznido *m* (de un ave),
chillido *m*

squeak¹ ['skwi:k] *vi* : chillar (dícese de
un animal), chirriar (dícese de un objeto)

squeak² *n* : chillido *m*, chirrido *m*

squeaky ['skwi:ki] *adj* **squeakier; -est**
: chirriante ⟨a squeaky voice : una voz
chillona⟩

squeal¹ ['skwi:l] *vi* **1** : chillar (dícese de
las personas o los animales), chirriar
(dícese de los frenos, etc.) **2** PROTEST
: quejarse

squeal² *n* **1** : chillido *m* (de una persona
o un animal) **2** SCREECH : chirrido *m*
(de frenos, etc.)

squeamish ['skwi:mɪʃ] *adj* : impresionable, sensible ⟨he's squeamish about
cockroaches : las cucarachas le dan
asco⟩

squeeze¹ ['skwi:z] *vt* **squeezed;
squeezing 1** PRESS : apretar, exprimir (naranjas, etc.) **2** EXTRACT : extraer
(jugo, etc.)

squeeze² *n* : apretón *m*

squelch ['skwɛltʃ] *vt* : aplastar (una rebelión, etc.)

squid ['skwɪd] *n, pl* **squid** *or* **squids**
: calamar *m*

squint¹ ['skwɪnt] *vi* : mirar con los ojos
entornados

squint² *adj or* **squint–eyed** ['skwɪnt,aɪd]
: bizco

squint³ *n* : ojos *mpl* bizcos, bizquera *f*

squire ['skwaɪr] *n* : hacendado *m*, -da *f*;
terrateniente *mf*

squirm ['skwərm] *vi* : retorcerse

squirrel ['skwərəl] *n* : ardilla *f*

squirt¹ ['skwərt] *vt* : lanzar un chorro de
— *vi* SPURT : salir a chorros

squirt² *n* : chorrito *m*

stab¹ [stæb] *vt* **stabbed; stabbing 1**
KNIFE : acuchillar, apuñalar **2** STICK
: clavar (con una aguja, etc.), golpear
(con el dedo, etc.)

stab² *n* **1** : puñalada *f*, cuchillada *f* **2**
JAB : pinchazo *m* (con una aguja, etc.),
golpe *m* (con un dedo, etc.) **3 to take
a stab at** : intentar

stability [stə'bɪləti] *n, pl* **-ties** : estabilidad *f*

stabilize ['steɪbə,laɪz] *v* **-lized; -lizing** *vt*
: estabilizar — *vi* : estabilizarse

stable[1] ['steɪbəl] *vt* **-bled; -bling** : poner (ganado) en un establo, poner (caballos) en una caballeriza

stable[2] *adj* **-bler; -blest** **1** FIXED, STEADY : fijo, sólido, estable **2** LASTING : estable, perdurable ⟨a stable government : un gobierno estable⟩ **3** : estacionario (en medicina), equilibrado (en psicología)

stable[3] *n* : establo *m* (para ganado), caballeriza *f* o cuadra *f* (para caballos)

staccato [stə'kɑːto:] *adj* : staccato

stack[1] ['stæk] *vt* **1** PILE : amontonar, apilar **2** COVER : cubrir, llenar ⟨he stacked the table with books : cubrió la mesa de libros⟩

stack[2] *n* **1** PILE : montón *m*, pila *f* **2** SMOKESTACK : chimenea *f*

stadium ['steɪdiəm] *n, pl* **-dia** [-diə] *or* **-diums** : estadio *m*

staff[1] ['stæf] *vt* : proveer de personal

staff[2] *n, pl* **staffs** ['stæfs, stævz] *or* **staves** ['stævz, 'steɪvz] **1** : bastón *m* (de mando), báculo *m* (de obispo) **2** *pl* **staffs** PERSONNEL : personal *m* **3** *or* **stave** : pentagrama *m* (en música)

stag[1] ['stæg] *adv* : solo, sin pareja ⟨to go stag : ir solo⟩

stag[2] *adj* : sólo para hombres

stag[3] *n, pl* **stags** *or* **stag** : ciervo *m*, venado *m*

stage[1] ['steɪdʒ] *vt* **staged; staging** : poner en escena (una obra de teatro)

stage[2] *n* **1** PLATFORM : estrado *m*, tablado *m*, escenario *m* (de un teatro) **2** PHASE, STEP : fase *f*, etapa *f* ⟨stage of development : fase de desarrollo⟩ ⟨in stages : por etapas⟩ **3 the stage** : el teatro *m*

stagecoach ['steɪdʒ,ko:tʃ] *n* : diligencia *f*

stagger[1] ['stægər] *vi* TOTTER : tambalearse — *vt* **1** ALTERNATE : alternar, escalonar (turnos de trabajo) **2** : hacer tambalear ⟨to be staggered by : quedarse estupefacto por⟩

stagger[2] *n* : tambaleo *m*

staggering ['stægərɪŋ] *adj* : asombroso

stagnant ['stægnənt] *adj* : estancado

stagnate ['stæg,neɪt] *vi* **-nated; -nating** : estancarse

staid ['steɪd] *adj* : serio, sobrio

stain[1] ['steɪn] *vt* **1** DISCOLOR : manchar **2** DYE : teñir (madera, etc.) **3** SULLY : manchar, empañar

stain[2] *n* **1** SPOT : mancha *f* **2** DYE : tinte *m*, tintura *f* **3** BLEMISH : mancha *f*, mácula *f*

stainless ['steɪnləs] *adj* : sin mancha ⟨stainless steel : acero inoxidable⟩

stair ['stær] *n* **1** STEP : escalón *m*, peldaño *m* **2 stairs** *npl* : escalera *f*, escaleras *fpl*

staircase ['stær,keɪs] *n* : escalera *f*, escaleras *fpl*

stairway ['stær,weɪ] *n* : escalera *f*, escaleras *fpl*

stake[1] ['steɪk] *vt* **staked; staking** **1** : estacar, marcar con estacas (una

propiedad) **2** BET : jugarse, apostar **3 to stake a claim to** : reclamar, reivindicar

stake[2] *n* **1** POST : estaca *f* **2** BET : apuesta *f* ⟨to be at stake : estar en juego⟩ **3** INTEREST, SHARE : interés *m*, participación *f*

stalactite [stə'læk,taɪt] *n* : estalactita *f*

stalagmite [stə'læg,maɪt] *n* : estalagmita *f*

stale ['steɪl] *adj* **staler; stalest** : viejo ⟨stale bread : pan duro⟩ ⟨stale news : viejas noticias⟩

stalemate ['steɪl,meɪt] *n* : punto *m* muerto, impasse *m*

stalk[1] ['stɔk] *vt* : acechar — *vi* : caminar rígidamente (por orgullo, ira, etc.)

stalk[2] *n* : tallo *m* (de una planta)

stall[1] ['stɔl] *vt* **1** : parar (un motor) **2** DELAY : entretener (a una persona), demorar — *vi* **1** : pararse (dícese de un motor) **2** DELAY : demorar, andar con rodeos

stall[2] *n* **1** : compartimiento *m* (de un establo) **2** : puesto *m* (en un mercado, etc.)

stallion ['stæljən] *n* : caballo *m* semental

stalwart ['stɔlwərt] *adj* **1** STRONG : fuerte ⟨a stalwart supporter : un firme partidario⟩ **2** BRAVE : valiente, valeroso

stamen ['steɪmən] *n* : estambre *m*

stamina ['stæmənə] *n* : resistencia *f*

stammer[1] ['stæmər] *vi* : tartamudear, titubear

stammer[2] *n* : tartamudeo *m*, titubeo *m*

stamp[1] ['stæmp] *vt* **1** : pisotear (con los pies) ⟨to stamp one's feet : patear, dar una patada⟩ **2** IMPRESS, IMPRINT : sellar (una factura, etc.), acuñar (monedas) **3** : franquear, ponerle estampillas a (correo)

stamp[2] *n* **1** : sello *m* (para documentos, etc.) **2** DIE : cuño *m* (para monedas) **3** *or* **postage stamp** : sello *m*, estampilla *f*, timbre *m* CA, Mex

stampede[1] [stæm'pi:d] *vi* **-peded; -peding** : salir en estampida

stampede[2] *n* : estampida *f*

stance ['stænts] *n* : postura *f*

stanch ['stɔntʃ, 'stɑntʃ] *vt* : detener, estancar (un líquido)

stand[1] ['stænd] *v* **stood** ['stʊd]; **standing** *vi* **1** : estar de pie, estar parado ⟨I was standing on the corner : estaba parada en la esquina⟩ **2** *or* **to stand up** : levantarse, pararse, ponerse de pie **3** (*indicating a specified position or location*) ⟨they stand third in the country : ocupan el tercer lugar en el país⟩ ⟨the machines are standing idle : las máquinas están paradas⟩ **4** (*referring to an opinion*) ⟨how does he stand on the matter? : ¿cuál es su postura respecto al asunto?⟩ **5** BE : estar ⟨the house stands on a hill : la casa está en una colina⟩ **6** CONTINUE : seguir ⟨the order still stands : el mandato sigue vigente〉 — *vt* **1** PLACE, SET : poner, colocar 〈he stood them in a row : los colocó en hilera〉 **2** TOLERATE : aguantar, soportar 〈he can't stand her : no la puede tragar〉 **3 to stand firm** : mantenerse firme **4 to stand guard** : hacer la guardia

stand[2] *n* **1** RESISTANCE : resistencia *f* 〈to make a stand against : resistir a〉 **2** BOOTH, STALL : stand *m*, puesto *m*, kiosko *m* (para vender periódicos, etc) **3** BASE : pie *m*, base *f* **4** : grupo *m* (de árboles, etc.) **5** POSITION : posición *f*, postura *f* **6 stands** *npl* GRANDSTAND : tribuna *f*

standard[1] ['stændərd] *adj* **1** ESTABLISHED : estándar, oficial 〈standard measures : medidas oficiales〉 〈standard English : el inglés estándar〉 **2** NORMAL : normal, estándar, común **3** CLASSIC : estándar, clásico 〈a standard work : una obra clásica〉

standard[2] *n* **1** BANNER : estandarte *m* **2** CRITERION : criterio *m* **3** RULE : estándar *m*, norma *f*, regla *f* **4** LEVEL : nivel *m* 〈standard of living : nivel de vida〉 **5** SUPPORT : poste *m*, soporte *m*

standardization [ˌstændərdəˈzeɪʃən] *n* : estandarización *f*

standardize ['stændərˌdaɪz] *vt* **-ized; -izing** : estandarizar

standard time *n* : hora *f* oficial

stand by *vt* : atenerse a, cumplir con (una promesa, etc.) — *vi* **1** : mantenerse aparte 〈to stand by and do nothing : mirar sin hacer nada〉 **2** : estar preparado, estar listo (para un anuncio, un ataque, etc.)

stand for *vt* **1** REPRESENT : significar **2** PERMIT, TOLERATE : permitir, tolerar

standing ['stændɪŋ] *n* **1** POSITION, RANK : posición *f* **2** DURATION : duración *f*

stand out *vi* **1** : destacar(se) 〈she stands out from the rest : se destaca entre los otros〉 **2 to stand out against** RESIST : oponerse a

standpoint ['stændˌpɔɪnt] *n* : punto *m* de vista

standstill ['stændˌstɪl] *n* **1** STOP : detención *f*, paro *m* 〈to come to a standstill : pararse〉 **2** DEADLOCK : punto *m* muerto, impasse *m*

stand up *vt* : dejar plantado 〈he stood me up again : otra vez me dejó plantado〉 — *vi* **1** ENDURE : durar, resistir **2 to stand up for** : defender **3 to stand up to** : hacerle frente (a alguien)

stank → **stink**

stanza ['stænzə] *n* : estrofa *f*

staple[1] ['steɪpəl] *vt* **-pled; -pling** : engrapar, grapar

staple[2] *adj* : principal, básico 〈a staple food : un alimento básico〉

staple[3] *n* **1** : producto *m* principal **2** : grapa *f* (para engrapar papeles)

stapler ['steɪplər] *n* : engrapadora *f*, grapadora *f*

star[1] ['stɑr] *v* **starred; starring** *vt* **1** : marcar con una estrella o un aster-

isco **2** FEATURE : estar protagonizado por — *vi* : tener el papel principal 〈to star in : protagonizar〉

star[2] *n* : estrella *f*

starboard ['stɑrbərd] *n* : estribor *m*

starch[1] ['stɑrtʃ] *vt* : almidonar

starch[2] *n* : almidón *m*, fécula *f* (comida)

starchy ['stɑrtʃi] *adj* **starchier; -est** : lleno de almidón 〈a starchy diet : una dieta feculenta〉

stardom ['stɑrdəm] *n* : estrellato *m*

stare[1] ['stær] *vi* **stared; staring** : mirar fijamente

stare[2] *n* : mirada *f* fija

starfish ['stɑrˌfɪʃ] *n* : estrella *f* de mar

stark[1] ['stɑrk] *adv* : completamente 〈stark raving mad : loco de remate〉 〈stark naked : completamente desnudo〉

stark[2] *adj* **1** ABSOLUTE : absoluto **2** BARREN, DESOLATE : desolado, desierto **3** BARE : desnudo **4** HARSH : severo, duro

starlight ['stɑrˌlaɪt] *n* : luz *f* de las estrellas

starling ['stɑrlɪŋ] *n* : estornino *m*

starry ['stɑri] *adj* **starrier; -est** : estrellado

start[1] ['stɑrt] *vi* **1** JUMP : levantarse de un salto, sobresaltarse, dar un respingo **2** BEGIN : empezar, comenzar **3** SET OUT : salir (de viaje, etc.) **4** : arrancar (dícese de un motor) — *vt* **1** BEGIN : empezar, comenzar, iniciar **2** CAUSE : provocar, causar **3** ESTABLISH : fundar, montar, establecer 〈to start a business : montar un negocio〉 **4** : arrancar, poner en marcha, encender 〈to start the car : arrancar el motor〉

start[2] *n* **1** JUMP : sobresalto *m*, respingo *m* **2** BEGINNING : principio *m*, comienzo *m* 〈to get an early start : salir temprano〉

starter ['stɑrtər] *n* **1** : participante *mf* (en una carrera, etc.); jugador *m* titular, jugadora *f* titular (en beisbol, etc.) **2** APPETIZER : entremés *m*, aperitivo *m* **3** *or* **starter motor** : motor *m* de arranque

startle ['stɑrtəl] *vt* **-tled; -tling** : asustar, sobresaltar

start–up ['stɑrtˌʌp] *adj* : de puesta en marcha

starvation [stɑrˈveɪʃən] *n* : inanición *f*, hambre *f*

starve ['stɑrv] *v* **starved; starving** *vi* : morirse de hambre — *vt* : privar de comida

stash ['stæʃ] *vt* : esconder, guardar (en un lugar secreto)

stat ['stæt] → **statistic**

state[1] ['steɪt] *vt* **stated; stating** **1** REPORT : puntualizar, exponer (los hechos, etc.) 〈state your name : diga su nombre〉 **2** ESTABLISH, FIX : establecer, fijar

state[2] *n* **1** CONDITION : estado *m*, condición *f* 〈a liquid state : un estado líquido〉 〈state of mind : estado de ánimo〉

⟨in a bad state : en malas condiciones⟩ **2** NATION : estado *m*, nación *f* **3** : estado *m* (dentro de un país) ⟨the States : los Estados Unidos⟩

stateliness ['steɪtlinəs] *n* : majestuosidad *f*

stately ['steɪtli] *adj* **statelier; -est** : majestuoso

statement ['steɪtmənt] *n* **1** DECLARATION : declaración *f*, afirmación *f* **2** or **bank statement** : estado *m* de cuenta

stateroom ['steɪt,ru:m, -,rʊm] *n* : camarote *m*

statesman ['steɪtsmən] *n*, *pl* **-men** [-mən, -,mɛn] : estadista *mf*

static[1] ['stætɪk] *adj* : estático

static[2] *n* : estática *f*, interferencia *f*

station[1] ['steɪʃən] *vt* : apostar, estacionar

station[2] *n* **1** : estación *f* (de trenes, etc.) **2** RANK, STANDING : condición *f* (social) **3** : canal *m* (de televisión), estación *f* o emisora *f* (de radio) **4 police station** : comisaría *f* **5 fire station** : estación *f* de bomberos, cuartel *m* de bomberos

stationary ['steɪʃə,nɛri] *adj* **1** IMMOBILE : estacionario, inmovible **2** UNCHANGING : inmutable, inalterable

stationery ['steɪʃə,nɛri] *n* : papel *m* y sobres *mpl* (para correspondencia)

station wagon *n* : camioneta *f* ranchera, camioneta *f* guayín *Mex*

statistic [stə'tɪstɪk] *n* : estadística *f* ⟨according to statistics : según las estadísticas⟩

statistical [stə'tɪstɪkəl] *adj* : estadístico

statistician [,stætə'stɪʃən] *n* : estadístico *m*, -ca *f*

statue ['stæ,tʃu:] *n* : estatua *f*

statuesque [,stætʃʊ'ɛsk] *adj* : escultural

statuette [,stætʃʊ'ɛt] *n* : estatuilla *f*

stature ['stætʃər] *n* **1** HEIGHT : estatura *f*, talla *f* **2** PRESTIGE : talla *f*, prestigio *m*

status ['steɪtəs, 'stæ-] *n* : condición *f*, situación *f*, estatus *m* (social) ⟨marital status : estado civil⟩

statute ['stæ,tʃu:t] *n* : ley *f*, estatuto *m*

staunch ['stɔntʃ] *adj* : acérrimo, incondicional, leal ⟨a staunch supporter : un partidario incondicional⟩ — **staunchly** *adv*

stave[1] ['steɪv] *vt* **staved** *or* **stove** ['sto:v]; **staving 1 to stave in** : romper **2 to stave off** : evitar (un ataque), prevenir (un problema)

stave[2] *n* : duela *f* (de un barril)

staves → **staff**

stay[1] ['steɪ] *vi* **1** REMAIN : quedarse, permanecer ⟨to stay in : quedarse en casa⟩ ⟨he stayed in the city : permaneció en la ciudad⟩ **2** CONTINUE : seguir, quedarse ⟨it stayed cloudy : siguió nublado⟩ ⟨to stay awake : mantenerse despierto⟩ **3** LODGE : hospedarse, alojarse (en un hotel, etc.) — *vt* **1** HALT : detener, suspender (una ejecución, etc.) **2 to stay the course** : aguantar hasta el final

stay[2] *n* **1** SOJOURN : estadía *f*, estancia *f*, permanencia *f* **2** SUSPENSION : suspensión *f* (de una sentencia) **3** SUPPORT : soporte *m*

stead ['stɛd] *n* **1** : lugar *m* ⟨she went in his stead : fue en su lugar⟩ **2 to stand (someone) in good stead** : ser muy útil a, servir de mucho a

steadfast ['stɛd,fæst] *adj* : firme, resuelto ⟨a steadfast friend : un fiel amigo⟩ ⟨a steadfast refusal : una negativa categórica⟩

steadily ['stɛdəli] *adv* **1** CONSTANTLY : continuamente, sin parar **2** FIRMLY : con firmeza **3** FIXEDLY : fijamente

steady[1] ['stɛdi] *v* **steadied; steadying** *vt* : sujetar ⟨she steadied herself : recobró el equilibrio⟩ — *vi* : estabilizarse

steady[2] *adj* **steadier; -est 1** FIRM, SURE : seguro, firme ⟨to have a steady hand : tener buen pulso⟩ **2** FIXED, REGULAR : fijo ⟨a steady income : ingresos fijos⟩ **3** CALM : tranquilo, ecuánime ⟨she has steady nerves : es imperturbable⟩ **4** DEPENDABLE : responsable, fiable **5** CONSTANT : constante

steak ['steɪk] *n* : bistec *m*, filete *m*, churrasco *m*, bife *m Arg, Chile, Uru*

steal ['sti:l] *v* **stole** ['sto:l]; **stolen** ['sto:lən]; **stealing** *vt* : robar, hurtar — *vi* **1** : robar, hurtar **2** : ir sigilosamente ⟨to steal away : escabullirse⟩

stealth ['stɛlθ] *n* : sigilo *m*

stealthily ['stɛlθəli] *adv* : furtivamente

stealthy ['stɛlθi] *adj* **stealthier; -est** : furtivo, sigiloso

steam[1] ['sti:m] *vi* : echar vapor ⟨to steam away : moverse echando vapor⟩ — *vt* **1** : cocer al vapor (en cocina) **2 to steam open** : abrir con vapor

steam[2] *n* **1** : vapor *m* **2 to let off steam** : desahogarse

steamboat ['sti:m,bo:t] → **steamship**

steam engine *n* : motor *m* de vapor

steamroller ['sti:m,ro:lər] *n* : apisonadora *f*

steamship ['sti:m,ʃɪp] *n* : vapor *m*, barco *m* de vapor

steamy ['sti:mi] *adj* **steamier; -est 1** : lleno de vapor **2** EROTIC : erótico ⟨a steamy romance : un tórrido romance⟩

steed ['sti:d] *n* : corcel *m*

steel[1] ['sti:l] *vt* **to steel oneself** : armarse de valor

steel[2] *adj* : de acero

steel[3] *n* : acero *m*

steely ['sti:li] *adj* **steelier; -est** : como acero ⟨a steely gaze : una mirada fría⟩ ⟨steely determination : determinación férrea⟩

steep[1] ['sti:p] *vt* : remojar, dejar (té, etc.) en infusión

steep[2] *adj* **1** : empinado, escarpado ⟨a steep cliff : un precipicio escarpado⟩ **2** CONSIDERABLE : considerable, marcado **3** EXCESSIVE : excesivo ⟨steep prices : precios muy altos⟩

steeple ['sti:pəl] *n* : aguja *f*, campanario *m*

steeplechase ['sti:pəlˌtʃeɪs] *n* : carrera *f* de obstáculos

steeply ['sti:pli] *adv* : abruptamente

steer¹ ['stɪr] *vt* **1** : conducir (un coche), gobernar (un barco) **2** GUIDE : dirigir, guiar

steer² *n* : buey *m*

steering wheel *n* : volante *m*

stein ['staɪn] *n* : jarra *f* (para cerveza)

stellar ['stɛlər] *adj* : estelar

stem¹ ['stɛm] *v* **stemmed; stemming** *vt* : detener, contener, parar ⟨to stem the tide : detener el curso⟩ — *vi* **to stem from** : provenir de, ser el resultado de

stem² *n* : tallo *m* (de una planta)

stench ['stɛntʃ] *n* : hedor *m*, mal olor *m*

stencil¹ ['stɛntsəl] *vt* **-ciled** *or* **-cilled; -ciling** *or* **-cilling** : marcar utilizando una plantilla

stencil² *n* : plantilla *f* (para marcar)

stenographer [stə'nɑgrəfər] *n* : taquígrafo *m*, -fa *f*

stenographic [ˌstɛnə'græfɪk] *adj* : taquigráfico

stenography [stə'nɑgrəfi] *n* : taquigrafía *f*

step¹ ['stɛp] *vi* **stepped; stepping 1** : dar un paso ⟨step this way, please : pase por aquí, por favor⟩ ⟨he stepped outside : salió⟩ **2 to step on** : pisar

step² *n* **1** : paso *m* ⟨step by step : paso por paso⟩ **2** STAIR : escalón *m*, peldaño *m* **3** RUNG : escalón *m*, travesaño *m* **4** MEASURE, MOVE : medida *f*, paso *m* ⟨to take steps : tomar medidas⟩ **5** STRIDE : paso *m* ⟨with a quick step : con paso rápido⟩

stepbrother ['stɛpˌbrʌðər] *n* : hermanastro *m*

stepdaughter ['stɛpˌdɔtər] *n* : hijastra *f*

stepfather ['stɛpˌfɑðər, -ˌfa-] *n* : padrastro *m*

stepladder ['stɛpˌlædər] *n* : escalera *f* de tijera

stepmother ['stɛpˌmʌðər] *n* : madrastra *f*

steppe ['stɛp] *n* : estepa *f*

stepping–stone ['stɛpɪŋˌstoːn] *n* : pasadera *f* (en un río, etc.), trampolín *m* (al éxito)

stepsister ['stɛpˌsɪstər] *n* : hermanastra *f*

stepson ['stɛpˌsʌn] *n* : hijastro *m*

step up *vt* INCREASE : aumentar

stereo¹ ['stɛriˌoː, 'stɪr-] *adj* : estéreo

stereo² *n, pl* **stereos** : estéreo *m*

stereophonic [ˌstɛrio'fɑnɪk, ˌstɪr-] *adj* : estereofónico

stereotype¹ ['stɛrioˌtaɪp, 'stɪr-] *vt* **-typed; -typing** : estereotipar

stereotype² *n* : estereotipo *m*

sterile ['stɛrəl] *adj* : estéril

sterility [stə'rɪləti] *n* : esterilidad *f*

sterilization [ˌstɛrələ'zeɪʃən] *n* : esterilización *f*

sterilize ['stɛrəˌlaɪz] *vt* **-ized; -izing** : esterilizar

sterling ['stərlɪŋ] *adj* **1** : de ley ⟨sterling silver : plata de ley⟩ **2** EXCELLENT : excelente

stern¹ ['stərn] *adj* : severo, adusto — **sternly** *adv*

stern² *n* : popa *f*

sternness ['stərnnəs] *n* : severidad *f*

sternum ['stərnəm] *n, pl* **sternums** *or* **sterna** [-nə] : esternón *m*

stethoscope ['stɛθəˌskoːp] *n* : estetoscopio *m*

stevedore ['sti:vəˌdor] *n* : estibador *m*, -dora *f*

stew¹ ['stu:, 'stju:] *vt* : estofar, guisar — *vi* **1** : cocer (dícese de la carne, etc.) **2** FRET : preocuparse

stew² *n* **1** : estofado *m*, guiso *m* **2 to be in a stew** : estar agitado

steward ['stu:ərd, 'stju:-] *n* **1** MANAGER : administrador *m* **2** : auxiliar *m* de vuelo (en un avión), camarero *m* (en un barco)

stewardess ['stu:ərdəs, 'stju:-] *n* **1** MANAGER : administradora *f* **2** : camarera *f* (en un barco) **3** : auxiliar *f* de vuelo, azafata *f*, aeromoza *f* (en un avión)

stick¹ ['stɪk] *v* **stuck** ['stʌk]; **sticking** *vt* **1** STAB : clavar **2** ATTACH : pegar **3** PUT : poner **4 to stick out** : sacar (la lengua, etc.), extender (la mano) — *vi* **1** ADHERE : pegarse, adherirse **2** JAM : atascarse **3 to stick around** : quedarse **4 to stick out** PROJECT : sobresalir (de una superficie), asomar (por detrás o debajo de algo) **5 to stick to** : no abandonar ⟨stick to your guns : manténgase firme⟩ **6 to stick up** : estar parado (dícese del pelo, etc.), sobresalir (de una superficie) **7 to stick with** : serle fiel a (una persona), seguir con (una cosa) ⟨I'll stick with what I know : prefiero lo conocido⟩

stick² *n* **1** BRANCH, TWIG : ramita *f* **2** : palo *m*, vara *f* ⟨a walking stick : un bastón⟩

sticker ['stɪkər] *n* : etiqueta *f* adhesiva

stickler ['stɪklər] *n* : persona *f* exigente ⟨to be a stickler for : insistir mucho en⟩

sticky ['stɪki] *adj* **stickier; -est 1** ADHESIVE : pegajoso, adhesivo **2** MUGGY : bochornoso **3** DIFFICULT : difícil

stiff ['stɪf] *adj* **1** RIGID : rígido, tieso ⟨a stiff dough : una masa firme⟩ **2** : agarrotado, entumecido ⟨stiff muscles : músculos entumecidos⟩ **3** STILTED : acartonado, poco natural **4** STRONG : fuerte (dícese del viento, etc.) **5** DIFFICULT, SEVERE : severo, difícil, duro

stiffen ['stɪfən] *vt* **1** STRENGTHEN : fortalecer, reforzar (tela, etc.) **2** : hacer más duro (un castigo, etc.) — *vi* **1** HARDEN : endurecerse **2** : entumecerse (dícese de los músculos)

stiffly ['stɪfli] *adv* **1** RIGIDLY : rígidamente **2** COLDLY : con frialdad

stiffness ['stɪfnəs] *n* **1** RIGIDITY : rigidez *f* **2** COLDNESS : frialdad *f* **3** SEVERITY : severidad *f* stifle ['staɪfəl] vt -fled; -fling SMOTHER, SUPPRESS : sofocar, reprimir, contener ⟨to stifle a yawn : reprimir un bostezo⟩

stigma ['stɪgmə] n, pl stigmata [stɪg-'matə, 'stɪgmətə] or stigmas : estigma m

stigmatize ['stɪgmə,taɪz] vt -tized; -tizing : estigmatizar

stile ['staɪl] n : escalones mpl para cruzar un cerco

stiletto [stə'lɛ,to:] n, pl -tos or -toes : estilete m

still¹ ['stɪl] vt CALM : pacificar, apaciguar — vi : pacificarse, apaciguarse

still² adv 1 QUIETLY : quieto ⟨sit still! : ¡quédate quieto!⟩ 2 : de todos modos, aún, todavía ⟨she still lives there : aún vive allí⟩ ⟨it's still the same : sigue siendo lo mismo⟩ 3 IN ANY CASE : de todos modos, aún así ⟨he still has doubts : aún así le quedan dudas⟩ ⟨I still prefer that you stay : de todos modos prefiero que te quedes⟩

still³ adj 1 MOTIONLESS : quieto, inmóvil 2 SILENT : callado

still⁴ n 1 SILENCE : quietud f, calma f 2 : alambique m (para destilar alcohol)

stillborn ['stɪl,bɔrn] adj : nacido muerto

stillness ['stɪlnəs] n : calma f, silencio m

stilt ['stɪlt] n : zanco m

stilted ['stɪltəd] adj : afectado, poco natural

stimulant ['stɪmjələnt] n : estimulante m — stimulant adj

stimulate ['stɪmjə,leɪt] vt -lated; -lating : estimular

stimulation [,stɪmjə'leɪʃən] n 1 STIMULATING : estimulación f 2 STIMULUS : estímulo m

stimulus ['stɪmjələs] n, pl -li [-,laɪ] 1 : estímulo m 2 INCENTIVE : acicate m

sting¹ ['stɪŋ] v stung ['stʌŋ]; stinging vt 1 : picar ⟨a bee stung him : le picó una abeja⟩ 2 HURT : hacer escocer (físicamente), herir (emocionalmente) — vi 1 : picar (dícese de las abejas, etc.) 2 SMART : escocer, arder

sting² n : picadura f (herida), escozor m (sensación)

stinger ['stɪŋər] n : aguijón m (de una abeja, etc.)

stinginess ['stɪndʒinəs] n : tacañería f

stingy ['stɪndʒi] adj stingier; -est 1 MISERLY : tacaño, avaro 2 PALTRY : mezquino, mísero

stink¹ ['stɪŋk] vi stank ['stæŋk] or stunk ['stʌŋk]; stunk; stinking : apestar, oler mal

stink² n : hedor m, mal olor m, peste f

stint¹ ['stɪnt] vt : escatimar ⟨to stint oneself of : privarse de⟩ — vi to stint on : escatimar

stint² n : período m

stipend ['staɪ,pɛnd, -pənd] n : estipendio m

stipulate ['stɪpjə,leɪt] vt -lated; -lating : estipular

stipulation [,stɪpjə'leɪʃən] n : estipulación f

stir¹ ['stər] v stirred; stirring vt 1 AGITATE : mover, agitar 2 MIX : revolver, remover 3 INCITE : incitar, impulsar, motivar 4 or to stir up AROUSE : despertar (memorias, etc.), provocar (ira, etc.) — vi : moverse, agitarse

stir² n 1 MOTION : movimiento m 2 COMMOTION : revuelo m

stirrup ['stərəp, 'stɪr-] n : estribo m

stitch¹ ['stɪtʃ] vt : coser, bordar (para decorar) — vi : coser

stitch² n 1 : puntada f 2 TWINGE : punzada f, puntada f

stock¹ ['stɑk] vt : surtir, abastecer, vender — vi to stock up : abastecerse

stock² n 1 SUPPLY : reserva f, existencias fpl (en comercio) ⟨to be out of stock : estar agotadas las existencias⟩ 2 SECURITIES : acciones fpl, valores mpl 3 LIVESTOCK : ganado m 4 ANCESTRY : linaje m, estirpe f 5 BROTH : caldo m 6 to take stock : evaluar

stockade [stɑ'keɪd] n : estacada f

stockbroker ['stɑk,bro:kər] n : corredor m, -dora f de bolsa

stockholder ['stɑk,ho:ldər] n : accionista mf

stocking ['stɑkɪŋ] n : media f ⟨a pair of stockings : unas medias⟩

stock market n : bolsa f

stockpile¹ ['stɑk,paɪl] vt -piled; -piling : acumular, almacenar

stockpile² n : reservas fpl

stocky ['stɑki] adj stockier; -est : robusto, fornido

stockyard ['stɑk,jɑrd] n : corral m

stodgy ['stɑdʒi] adj stodgier; -est 1 DULL : aburrido, pesado 2 OLD-FASHIONED : anticuado

stoic¹ ['sto:ɪk] or stoical [-ɪkəl] adj : estoico — stoically [-ɪkli] adv

stoic² n : estoico m, -ca f

stoicism ['sto:ə,sɪzəm] n : estoicismo m

stoke ['sto:k] vt stoked; stoking : atizar (un fuego), echarle carbón a (un horno)

stole¹ → steal

stole² ['sto:l] n : estola f

stolen → steal

stolid ['stɑlɪd] adj : impasible, imperturbable — stolidly adv

stomach¹ ['stʌmɪk] vt : aguantar, soportar

stomach² n 1 : estómago m 2 BELLY : vientre m, barriga f, panza f 3 DESIRE : ganas fpl ⟨he had no stomach for a fight : no quería pelea⟩

stomachache ['stʌmɪk,eɪk] n : dolor m de estómago

stomp ['stamp, 'stɔmp] vt : pisotear — vi : pisar fuerte

stone¹ ['sto:n] vt stoned; stoning : apedrear, lapidar

stone² n 1 : piedra f 2 PIT : hueso m, pepa f (de una fruta)

Stone Age n : Edad f de Piedra

stony ['sto:ni] *adj* **stonier; -est 1** ROCKY : pedregoso **2** UNFEELING : insensible, frío ⟨a stony stare : una mirada glacial⟩

stood → **stand**

stool ['stu:l] *n* **1** SEAT : taburete *m*, banco *m* **2** FOOTSTOOL : escabel *m* **3** FECES : deposición *f* de heces

stoop[1] ['stu:p] *vi* **1** CROUCH : agacharse **2 to stoop to** : rebajarse a

stoop[2] *n* **1** : espaldas *fpl* encorvadas ⟨to have a stoop : ser encorvado⟩ **2** : entrada *f* (de una casa)

stop[1] ['stɑp] *v* **stopped; stopping** *vt* **1** PLUG : tapar **2** PREVENT : impedir, evitar ⟨she stopped me from leaving : me impidió que saliera⟩ **3** HALT : parar, detener **4** CEASE : dejar de ⟨he stopped talking : dejó de hablar⟩ — *vi* **1** HALT : detenerse, parar **2** CEASE : cesar, terminar ⟨the rain won't stop : no deja de llover⟩ **3** STAY : quedarse ⟨she stopped with friends : se quedó en casa de unos amigos⟩ **4 to stop by** : visitar

stop[2] *n* **1** STOPPER : tapón *m* **2** HALT : parada *f*, alto *m* ⟨to come to a stop : pararse, detenerse⟩ ⟨to put a stop to : poner fin a⟩ **3** : parada *f* ⟨bus stop : parada de autobús⟩

stopgap ['stɑp,gæp] *n* : arreglo *m* provisorio

stoplight ['stɑp,laɪt] *n* : semáforo *m*

stoppage ['stɑpɪʤ] *n* : acto *m* de parar ⟨a work stoppage : un paro⟩

stopper ['stɑpər] *n* : tapón *m*

storage ['storɪʤ] *n* : almacenamiento *m*, almacenaje *m*

storage battery *n* : acumulador *m*

store[1] ['stor] *vt* **stored; storing** : guardar, almacenar

store[2] *n* **1** RESERVE, SUPPLY : reserva *f* **2** SHOP : tienda *f* ⟨grocery store : tienda de comestibles⟩

storehouse ['stor,haʊs] *n* : almacén *m*, depósito *m*

storekeeper ['stor,ki:pər] *n* : tendero *m*, -ra *f*

storeroom ['stor,ru:m, -,rʊm] *n* : almacén *m*, depósito *m*

stork ['stork] *n* : cigüeña *f*

storm[1] ['storm] *vi* **1** : llover o nevar tormentosamente **2** RAGE : ponerse furioso, vociferar **3 to storm out** : salir echando pestes — *vt* ATTACK : asaltar

storm[2] *n* **1** : tormenta *f*, tempestad *f* **2** UPROAR : alboroto *m*, revuelo *m*, escándalo *m* ⟨a storm of abuse : un torrente de abusos⟩

stormy ['stormi] *adj* **stormier; -est** : tormentoso

story ['stori] *n, pl* **stories 1** NARRATIVE : cuento *m*, relato *m* **2** ACCOUNT : historia *f*, relato *m* **3** : piso *m*, planta *f* (de un edificio) ⟨first story : planta baja⟩

stout ['staʊt] *adj* **1** FIRM, RESOLUTE : firme, resuelto **2** STURDY : fuerte, robusto, sólido **3** FAT : corpulento, gordo

stove[1] ['sto:v] *n* : cocina *f* (para cocinar), estufa *f* (para calentar)

stove[2] → **stave**[1]

stow ['sto:] *vt* **1** STORE : poner, meter, guardar **2** LOAD : cargar — *vi* **to stow away** : viajar de polizón

stowaway ['sto:ə,weɪ] *n* : polizón *m*

straddle ['strædəl] *vt* **-dled; -dling** : sentarse a horcajadas sobre

straggle ['strægəl] *vi* **-gled; -gling** : rezagarse, quedarse atrás

straggler ['strægələr] *n* : rezagado *m*, -da *f*

straight[1] ['streɪt] *adv* **1** : derecho, directamente ⟨go straight, then turn right : sigue derecho, luego gira a la derecha⟩ **2** HONESTLY : honestamente ⟨to go straight : enmendarse⟩ **3** CLEARLY : con claridad **4** FRANKLY : francamente, con franqueza

straight[2] *adj* **1** : recto (dícese de las líneas, etc.), derecho (dícese de algo vertical), lacio (dícese del pelo) **2** HONEST, JUST : honesto, justo **3** NEAT, ORDERLY : arreglado, ordenado

straighten ['streɪtən] *vt* **1** : enderezar, poner derecho **2 to straighten up** : arreglar, ordenar ⟨he straightened up the house : arregló la casa⟩

straightforward [streɪt'forwərd] *adj* **1** FRANK : franco, sincero **2** CLEAR, PRECISE : puro, simple, claro

straightway ['streɪt'weɪ, -,weɪ] *adv* : inmediatamente

strain[1] ['streɪn] *vt* **1** EXERT : forzar (la vista, la voz) ⟨to strain oneself : hacer un gran esfuerzo⟩ **2** FILTER : colar, filtrar **3** INJURE : lastimarse, hacerse daño en ⟨to strain a muscle : sufrir un esguince⟩

strain[2] *n* **1** LINEAGE : linaje *m*, abolengo *m* **2** STREAK, TRACE : veta *f* **3** VARIETY : tipo *m*, variedad *f* **4** STRESS : tensión *f*, presión *f* **5** SPRAIN : esguince *m*, torcedura *f* (del tobillo, etc.) **6 strains** *npl* TUNE : melodía *f*, acordes *mpl*, compases *fpl*

strainer ['streɪnər] *n* : colador *m*

strait ['streɪt] *n* **1** : estrecho *m* **2 straits** *npl* DISTRESS : aprietos *mpl*, apuros *mpl* ⟨in dire straits : en serios aprietos⟩

straitened ['streɪtənd] *adj* **in straitened circumstances** : en apuros económicos

strand[1] ['strænd] *vt* **1** : varar **2 to be left stranded** : quedar(se) varado, quedar colgado ⟨they left me stranded : me dejaron abandonado⟩

strand[2] *n* **1** : hebra *f* (de hilo, etc.) ⟨a strand of hair : un pelo⟩ **2** BEACH : playa *f*

strange ['streɪnʤ] *adj* **stranger; -est 1** QUEER, UNUSUAL : extraño, raro **2** UNFAMILIAR : desconocido, nuevo

strangely ['streɪnʤli] *adv* ODDLY : de manera extraña ⟨to behave strangely : portarse de una manera rara⟩ ⟨strangely, he didn't call : curiosamente, no llamó⟩

strangeness ['streɪndʒnəs] *n* **1** ODD-NESS : rareza *f* **2** UNFAMILIARITY : lo desconocido

stranger ['streɪndʒər] *n* : desconocido *m*, -da *f*; extraño *m*, -ña *f*

strangle ['stræŋgəl] *vt* **-gled; -gling** : estrangular

strangler ['stræŋglər] *n* : estrangulador *m*, -dora *f*

strap¹ ['stræp] *vt* **strapped; strapping 1** FASTEN : sujetar con una correa **2** FLOG : azotar (con una correa)

strap² *n* **1** : correa *f* **2 shoulder strap** : tirante *m*

strapless ['stræpləs] *n* : sin tirantes

strapping ['stræpɪŋ] *adj* : robusto, fornido

stratagem ['strætədʒəm, -ˌdʒɛm] *n* : estratagema *f*, artimaña *f*

strategic [strə'tiːdʒɪk] *adj* : estratégico

strategist ['strætədʒɪst] *n* : estratega *mf*

strategy ['strætədʒi] *n, pl* **-gies** : estrategia *f*

stratified ['strætəˌfaɪd] *adj* : estratificado

stratosphere ['strætəˌsfɪr] *n* : estratosfera *f*

stratospheric [ˌstrætə'sfɪrɪk, -'sfɛr-] *adj* : estratosférico

stratum ['streɪtəm, 'stræ-] *n, pl* **strata** [-tə] : estrato *m*, capa *f*

straw *n* **1** : paja *f* ⟨the last straw : el colmo⟩ **2** *or* **drinking straw** : pajita *f*, popote *m Mex*

strawberry ['strɔˌbɛri] *n, pl* **-ries** : fresa *f*

stray¹ ['streɪ] *vi* **1** WANDER : alejarse, extraviarse ⟨the cattle strayed away : el ganado se descarrió⟩ **2** DIGRESS : desviarse, divagar

stray² *adj* : perdido, callejero (dícese de un perro o un gato), descarriado (dícese del ganado)

stray³ *n* : animal *m* perdido, animal *m* callejero

streak¹ ['striːk] *vt* : hacer rayas en ⟨blue streaked with grey : azul veteado con gris⟩ — *vi* : ir como una flecha

streak² *n* **1** : raya *f*, veta *f* (en mármol, queso, etc.), mechón *m* (en el pelo) **2** : rayo *m* (de luz) **3** TRACE : veta *f* **4** : racha *f* ⟨a streak of luck : una racha de suerte⟩

stream¹ ['striːm] *vi* : correr, salir a chorros ⟨tears streamed from his eyes : las lágrimas brotaban de sus ojos⟩ — *vt* : derramar, dejar correr ⟨to stream blood : derramar sangre⟩

stream² *n* **1** BROOK : arroyo *m*, riachuelo *m* **2** RIVER : río *m* **3** FLOW : corriente *f*, chorro *m*

streamer ['striːmər] *n* **1** PENNANT : banderín *m* **2** RIBBON : serpentina *f* (de papel), cinta *f* (de tela)

streamlined ['striːmˌlaɪnd] *adj* **1** : aerodinámico (dícese de los automóviles, etc.) **2** EFFICIENT : eficiente, racionalizado

street ['striːt] *n* : calle *f*

streetcar ['striːtˌkɑr] *n* : tranvía *m*

strength ['strɛŋkθ] *n* **1** POWER : fuerza *f* **2** SOLIDITY, TOUGHNESS : solidez *f*, resistencia *f*, dureza *f* **3** INTENSITY : intensidad *f* (de emociones, etc.), lo fuerte (de un sabor, etc.) **4** : punto *m* fuerte ⟨strengths and weaknesses : virtudes y defectos⟩ **5** NUMBER : número *m*, complemento *m* ⟨in full strength : en gran número⟩

strengthen ['strɛŋkθən] *vt* **1** : fortalecer (los músculos, el espíritu, etc.) **2** REINFORCE : reforzar **3** INTENSIFY : intensificar, redoblar (esfuerzos, etc.) — *vi* **1** : fortalecerse, hacerse más fuerte **2** INTENSIFY : intensificarse

strenuous ['strɛnjuəs] *adj* **1** VIGOROUS : vigoroso, enérgico **2** ARDUOUS : duro, riguroso

strenuously ['strɛnjuəsli] *adv* : vigorosamente, duro

stress¹ ['strɛs] *vt* **1** : someter a tensión (física) **2** EMPHASIZE : enfatizar, recalcar **3 to stress out** : estresar

stress² *n* **1** : tensión *f* (en un material) **2** EMPHASIS : énfasis *m*, acento *m* (en lingüística) **3** TENSION : tensión *f* (nerviosa), estrés *m*

stressful ['strɛsfəl] *adj* : estresante

stretch¹ ['strɛtʃ] *vt* **1** EXTEND : estirar, extender, desplegar (alas) **2 to stretch the truth** : forzar la verdad, exagerar — *vi* : estirarse

stretch² *n* **1** STRETCHING : extensión *f*, estiramiento *m* (de músculos) **2** ELASTICITY : elasticidad *f* **3** EXPANSE : tramo *m*, trecho *m* ⟨the home stretch : la recta final⟩ **4** PERIOD : período *m* (de tiempo)

stretcher ['strɛtʃər] *n* : camilla *f*

strew ['struː] *vt* **strewed; strewed** *or* **strewn** ['struːn]; **strewing 1** SCATTER : esparcir (semillas, etc.), desparramar (papeles, etc.) **2 to strew with** : cubrir de

stricken ['strɪkən] *adj* **stricken with** : aquejado de (una enfermedad), afligido por (tristeza, etc.)

strict ['strɪkt] *adj* : estricto — **strictly** *adv*

strictness ['strɪktnəs] *n* : severidad *f*, lo estricto

stricture ['strɪktʃər] *n* : crítica *f*, censura *f*

stride¹ ['straɪd] *vi* **strode** ['stroːd]; **stridden** ['strɪdən]; **striding** : ir dando trancos, ir dando zancadas

stride² *n* : tranco *m*, zancada *f*

strident ['straɪdənt] *adj* : estridente

strife ['straɪf] *n* : conflictos *mpl*, disensión *f*

strike¹ ['straɪk] *v* **struck** ['strʌk]; **striking** *vt* **1** HIT : golpear (a una persona) ⟨to strike a blow : pegar un golpe⟩ **2** DELETE : suprimir, tachar **3** COIN, MINT : acuñar (monedas) **4** : dar (la hora) **5** AFFLICT : sobrevenir ⟨he was stricken with a fever : le sobrevino una fiebre⟩ **6** IMPRESS : impresionar, parecer ⟨her voice struck me : su voz me impresionó⟩ ⟨it struck him as funny : le pareció chistoso⟩ **7** : encender (un fósforo) **8** FIND : descubrir (oro, petróleo) **9** ADOPT : adoptar (una pose, etc.) — *vi* **1** HIT : golpear ⟨to strike against : chocar contra⟩ **2** ATTACK : atacar **3** : declararse en huelga

strike² *n* **1** BLOW : golpe *m* **2** : huelga *f*, paro *m* ⟨to be on strike : estar en huelga⟩ **3** ATTACK : ataque *m*

strikebreaker ['straɪkˌbreɪkər] *n* : rompehuelgas *mf*, esquirol *mf*

strike out *vi* **1** HEAD : salir (para) **2** : ser ponchado (en béisbol) ⟨the batter struck out : poncharon al bateador⟩

striker ['straɪkər] *n* : huelguista *mf*

strike up *vt* START : entablar, empezar

striking ['straɪkɪŋ] *adj* : notable, sorprendente, llamativo ⟨a striking beauty : una belleza imponente⟩ — **strikingly** *adv*

string¹ ['strɪŋ] *vt* **strung** ['strʌŋ]; **stringing 1** THREAD : ensartar ⟨to string beads : ensartar cuentas⟩ **2** HANG : colgar (con un cordel)

string² *n* **1** : cordel *m*, cuerda *f* **2** SERIES : serie *f*, sarta *f* (de insultos, etc.) **3 strings** *npl* : cuerdas *fpl* (en música)

string bean *n* : judía *f*, ejote *m Mex*

stringent ['strɪndʒənt] *adj* : estricto, severo

stringy ['strɪŋi] *adj* **stringier; -est** : fibroso

strip¹ ['strɪp] *v* **stripped; stripping** *vt* : quitar (ropa, pintura, etc.), desnudar, despojar — *vi* UNDRESS : desnudarse

strip² *n* : tira *f* ⟨a strip of land : una faja⟩

stripe¹ ['straɪp] *vt* **striped** ['straɪpt]; **striping** : marcar con rayas o listas

stripe² *n* **1** : raya *f*, lista *f* **2** BAND : franja *f*

striped ['straɪpt, 'straɪpəd] *adj* : a rayas, de rayas, rayado, listado

strive ['straɪv] *vi* **strove** ['stro:v]; **striven** ['strɪvən] *or* **strived; striving 1 to strive for** : luchar por lograr **2 to strive to** : esforzarse por

strobe ['stro:b] *or* **strobe light** *n* : luz *f* estroboscópica

strode → **stride**

stroke¹ ['stro:k] *vt* **stroked; stroking** : acariciar

stroke² *n* : golpe *m* ⟨a stroke of luck : un golpe de suerte⟩

stroll¹ ['stro:l] *vi* : pasear, pasearse, dar un paseo

stroll² *n* : paseo *m*

stroller ['stro:lər] *n* : cochecito *m* (para niños)

strong ['strɔŋ] *adj* **1** : fuerte **2** HEALTHY : sano **3** ZEALOUS : ferviente

stronghold ['strɔŋˌho:ld] *n* : fortaleza *f*, fuerte *m*, bastión *m* ⟨a cultural stronghold : un baluarte de la cultura⟩

strongly ['strɔŋli] *adv* **1** POWERFULLY : fuerte, con fuerza **2** STURDILY

: fuertemente, sólidamente **3** INTENSELY : intensamente, profundamente **4** WHOLEHEARTEDLY : totalmente

struck → **strike¹**

structural ['strʌkʧərəl] *adj* : estructural

structure¹ ['strʌkʧər] *vt* **-tured; -turing** : estructurar

structure² *n* **1** BUILDING : construcción *f* **2** ARRANGEMENT, FRAMEWORK : estructura *f*

struggle¹ ['strʌgəl] *vi* **-gled; -gling 1** CONTEND : forcejear (físicamente), luchar, contender **2** : hacer con dificultad ⟨she struggled forward : avanzó con dificultad⟩

struggle² *n* : lucha *f*, pelea *f* (física)

strum ['strʌm] *vt* **strummed; strumming** : rasguear

strung → **string¹**

strut¹ ['strʌt] *vi* **strutted; strutting** : pavonearse

strut² *n* **1** : pavoneo *m* ⟨he walked with a strut : se pavoneaba⟩ **2** : puntal *m* (en construcción, etc.)

strychnine ['strɪkˌnaɪn, -nən, -ˌni:n] *n* : estricnina *f*

stub¹ ['stʌb] *vt* **stubbed; stubbing 1 to stub one's toe** : darse en el dedo (del pie) **2 to stub out** : apagarse

stub² *n* : colilla *f* (de un cigarrillo), cabo *m* (de un lápiz, etc.), talón *m* (de un cheque)

stubble ['stʌbəl] *n* **1** : rastrojo *m* (de plantas) **2** BEARD : barba *f*

stubborn ['stʌbərn] *adj* **1** OBSTINATE : terco, obstinado, empecinado **2** PERSISTENT : pertinaz, persistente — **stubbornly** *adv*

stubbornness ['stʌbərnnəs] *n* **1** OBSTINACY : terquedad *f*, obstinación *f* **2** PERSISTENCE : persistencia *f*

stubby ['stʌbi] *adj* **stubbier; -est** : corto y grueso ⟨stubby fingers : dedos regordetes⟩

stucco ['stʌko:] *n, pl* **stuccos** *or* **stuccoes** : estuco *m*

stuck → **stick¹**

stuck–up ['stʌk'ʌp] *adj* : engreído, creído *fam*

stud¹ ['stʌd] *vt* **studded; studding** : tachonar, salpicar

stud² *n* **1** *or* **stud horse** : semental *m* **2** : montante *m* (en construcción) **3** HOBNAIL : tachuela *f*, tachón *m*

student ['stu:dənt, 'stju:-] *n* : estudiante *mf*; alumno *m*, -na *f* (de un colegio)

studied ['stʌdid] *adj* : intencionado, premeditado

studio ['stu:diˌo:, 'stju:-] *n, pl* **studios** : estudio *m*

studious ['stu:diəs, 'stju:-] *adj* : estudioso — **studiously** *adv*

study¹ ['stʌdi] *v* **studied; studying 1** : estudiar **2** EXAMINE : examinar, estudiar

study² *n, pl* **studies 1** STUDYING : estudio *m* **2** OFFICE : estudio *m*, gabi-

stuff · subjugate 658

nete *m* (en una casa) **3** RESEARCH : investigación *f*, estudio *m*

stuff¹ [ˈstʌf] *vt* : rellenar, llenar, atiborrar ⟨a stuffed toy : un juguete de peluche⟩

stuff² *n* **1** POSSESSIONS : cosas *fpl* **2** ESSENCE : esencia *f* **3** SUBSTANCE : cosa *f*, cosas *fpl* ⟨some sticky stuff : una cosa pegajosa⟩ ⟨she knows her stuff : es experta⟩

stuffing [ˈstʌfɪŋ] *n* : relleno *m*

stuffy [ˈstʌfi] *adj* **stuffier; -est 1** CLOSE : viciado, cargado ⟨a stuffy room : una sala mal ventilada⟩ ⟨stuffy weather : tiempo bochornoso⟩ **2** : tapado (dícese de la nariz) **3** STODGY : pesado, aburrido

stumble¹ [ˈstʌmbəl] *vi* **-bled; -bling 1** TRIP : tropezar, dar un traspié **2** FLOUNDER : quedarse sin saber qué hacer o decir **3 to stumble across** *or* **to stumble upon** : dar con, tropezar con

stumble² *n* : tropezón *m*, traspié *m*

stump¹ [ˈstʌmp] *vt* : dejar perplejo ⟨to be stumped : no tener respuesta⟩

stump² *n* **1** : muñón *m* (de un brazo o una pierna) **2** *or* **tree stump** : cepa *f*, tocón *m* **3** STUB : cabo *m*

stun [ˈstʌn] *vt* **stunned; stunning 1** : aturdir (con un golpe) **2** ASTONISH, SHOCK : dejar estupefacto, dejar atónito, aturdir

stung → **sting¹**

stunk → **stink¹**

stunning [ˈstʌnɪŋ] *adj* **1** ASTONISHING : asombroso, pasmoso, increíble **2** STRIKING : imponente, impresionante (dícese de la belleza)

stunt¹ [ˈstʌnt] *vt* : atrofiar

stunt² *n* : proeza *f* (acrobática)

stupefy [ˈstuːpəˌfaɪ, ˈstjuː-] *vt* **-fied; -fying 1** : aturdir, atontar (con drogas, etc.) **2** AMAZE : dejar estupefacto, dejar atónito

stupendous [stʊˈpɛndəs, stjuː-] *adj* **1** MARVELOUS : estupendo, maravilloso **2** TREMENDOUS : tremendo — **stupendously** *adv*

stupid [ˈstuːpəd, ˈstjuː-] *adj* **1** IDIOTIC, SILLY : tonto, bobo, estúpido **2** DULL, OBTUSE : lento, torpe, lerdo

stupidity [stʊˈpɪdəti, stjuː-] *n* : tontería *f*, estupidez *f*

stupidly [ˈstuːpədli, ˈstjuː-] *adv* **1** IDIOTICALLY : estúpidamente, tontamente **2** DENSELY : torpemente

stupor [ˈstuːpər, ˈstjuː-] *n* : estupor *m*

sturdily [ˈstərdəli] *adv* : sólidamente

sturdiness [ˈstərdinəs] *n* : solidez *f* (de muebles, etc.), robustez *f* (de una persona)

sturdy [ˈstərdi] *adj* **sturdier; -est** : fuerte, robusto, sólido

sturgeon [ˈstərdʒən] *n* : esturión *m*

stutter¹ [ˈstʌtər] *vi* : tartamudear

stutter² *n* STAMMER : tartamudeo *m*

sty [ˈstaɪ] *n* **1** *pl* **sties** PIGPEN : chiquero *m*, pocilga *f* **2** *pl* **sties** *or* **styes** : orzuelo *m* (en el ojo)

style¹ [ˈstaɪl] *vt* **styled; styling 1** NAME : llamar **2** : peinar (pelo), diseñar (vestidos, etc.) ⟨carefully styled prose : prosa escrita con gran esmero⟩

style² *n* **1** : estilo *m* ⟨that's just his style : él es así⟩ ⟨to live in style : vivir a lo grande⟩ **2** FASHION : moda *f*

stylish [ˈstaɪlɪʃ] *adj* : de moda, elegante, chic

stylishly [ˈstaɪlɪʃli] *adv* : con estilo

stylishness [ˈstaɪlɪʃnəs] *n* : estilo *m*

stylist [ˈstaɪlɪst] *n* : estilista *mf*

stylize [ˈstaɪˌlaɪz, ˈstaɪə-] *vt* : estilizar

stylus [ˈstaɪləs] *n, pl* **styli** [ˈstaɪˌlaɪ] **1** PEN : estilo *m* **2** NEEDLE : aguja *f* (de un tocadiscos)

stymie [ˈstaɪmi] *vt* **-mied; -mieing** : obstaculizar

suave [ˈswɑv] *adj* : fino, urbano

sub¹ [ˈsʌb] *vi* **subbed; subbing** → **substitute¹**

sub² *n* **1** → **substitute²** **2** → **submarine**

subcommittee [ˈsʌbkəˌmɪti] *n* : subcomité *m*

subconscious¹ [səbˈkɑntʃəs] *adj* : subconsciente — **subconsciously** *adv*

subconscious² *n* : subconsciente *m*

subcontract [ˌsʌbˈkɑnˌtrækt] *vt* : subcontratar

subculture [ˈsʌbˌkʌltʃər] *n* : subcultura *f*

subdivide [ˌsʌbdəˈvaɪd, ˈsʌbdəˌvaɪd] *vt* **-vided; -viding** : subdividir

subdivision [ˈsʌbdəˌvɪʒən] *n* : subdivisión *f*

subdue [səbˈduː, -ˈdjuː] *vt* **-dued; -duing 1** OVERCOME : sojuzgar (a un enemigo), vencer, superar **2** CONTROL : dominar **3** SOFTEN : suavizar, atenuar (luz, etc.), moderar (lenguaje)

subgroup [ˈsʌbˌgruːp] *n* : subgrupo *m*

subhead [ˈsʌbˌhɛd] *or* **subheading** [-ˌhɛdɪŋ] *n* : subtítulo *m*

subject¹ [səbˈdʒɛkt] *vt* **1** CONTROL, DOMINATE : controlar, dominar **2** : someter ⟨they subjected him to pressure : lo sometieron a presiones⟩

subject² [ˈsʌbˌdʒɪkt] *adj* **1** : subyugado, sometido ⟨a subject nation : una nación subyugada⟩ **2** PRONE : sujeto, propenso ⟨subject to colds : sujeto a resfriarse⟩ **3 subject to** : sujeto a ⟨subject to congressional approval : sujeto a la aprobación del congreso⟩

subject³ [ˈsʌbˌdʒɪkt] *n* **1** : súbdito *m*, -ta *f* (de un gobierno) **2** TOPIC : tema *m* **3** : sujeto *m* (en gramática)

subjection [səbˈdʒɛkʃən] *n* : sometimiento *m*

subjective [səbˈdʒɛktɪv] *adj* : subjetivo — **subjectively** *adv*

subjectivity [ˌsʌbˌdʒɛkˈtɪvəti] *n* : subjetividad *f*

subjugate [ˈsʌbdʒɪˌgeɪt] *vt* **-gated; -gating** : subyugar, someter, sojuzgar

subjunctive [səb'dʒʌŋktɪv] *n* : subjunti- vo *m* — **subjunctive** *adj*

sublet ['sʌb,lɛt] *vt* -let; -letting : suba- rrendar

sublime [sə'blaɪm] *adj* : sublime

sublimely [sə'blaɪmli] *adv* 1 : de man- era sublime 2 UTTERLY : absoluta- mente, completamente

submarine[1] ['sʌbmə,ri:n, ,sʌbmə'-] *adj* : submarino

submarine[2] *n* : submarino *m*

submerge [səb'mərdʒ] *v* -merged; -merging *vt* : sumergir — *vi* : sumer- girse

submission [səb'mɪʃən] *n* 1 YIELDING : sumisión *f* 2 PRESENTATION : pre- sentación *f*

submissive [səb'mɪsɪv] *adj* : sumiso, dó- cil

submit [səb'mɪt] *v* -mitted; -mitting *vi* YIELD : rendirse ⟨to submit to : some- terse a⟩ — *vt* PRESENT : presentar

subnormal [,sʌb'nɔrməl] *adj* : por de- bajo de lo normal

subordinate[1] [sə'bɔrdən,eɪt] *vt* -nated; -nating : subordinar

subordinate[2] [sə'bɔrdənət] *adj* : subor- dinado ⟨a subordinate clause : una oración subordinada⟩

subordinate[3] *n* : subordinado *m*, -da *f*; subalterno *m*, -na *f*

subordination [sə,bɔrdən'eɪʃən] *n* : sub- ordinación *f*

subpoena[1] [sə'pi:nə] *vt* -naed; -naing : citar

subpoena[2] *n* : citación *f*, citatorio *m*

subscribe [səb'skraɪb] *vi* -scribed; -scribing 1 : suscribirse (a una revista, etc.) 2 **to subscribe to** : suscribir (una opinión, etc.), estar de acuerdo con

subscriber [səb'skraɪbər] *n* : suscriptor *m*, -tora *f* (de una revista, etc.); abona- do *m*, -da *f* (de un servicio)

subscription [səb'skrɪpʃən] *n* : suscrip- ción *f*

subsequent ['sʌbsɪkwənt, -sə,kwɛnt] *adj* : subsiguiente ⟨subsequent to : pos- terior a⟩

subsequently ['sʌb,sɪkwɛntli, -kwənt] *adv* : posteriormente

subservient [səb'sərviənt] *adj* : servil

subside [səb'saɪd] *vi* -sided; -siding 1 SINK : hundirse, descender 2 ABATE : calmarse (dícese de las emociones), amainar (dícese del viento, etc.)

subsidiary[1] [səb'sɪdi,ɛri] *adj* : secun- dario

subsidiary[2] *n, pl* -ries : filial *f*, sub- sidiaria *f*

subsidize ['sʌbsə,daɪz] *vt* -dized; -dizing : subvencionar, subsidiar

subsidy ['sʌbsədi] *n, pl* -dies : subven- ción *f*, subsidio *m*

subsist [səb'sɪst] *vi* : subsistir, manten- erse, vivir

subsistence [səb'sɪstənts] *n* : subsisten- cia *f*

substance ['sʌbstənts] *n* 1 ESSENCE : sustancia *f*, esencia *f* 2 : sustancia *f* ⟨a toxic substance : una sustancia tóx- ica⟩ 3 WEALTH : riqueza *f* ⟨a woman of substance : una mujer acaudalada⟩

substandard [,sʌb'stændərd] *adj* : infe- rior, deficiente

substantial [səb'stæntʃəl] *adj* 1 ABUN- DANT : sustancioso ⟨a substantial meal : una comida sustanciosa⟩ 2 CONSID- ERABLE : considerable, apreciable 3 SOLID, STURDY : sólido

substantially [səb'stæntʃəli] *adv* : con- siderablemente

substantiate [səb'stæntʃi,eɪt] *vt* -ated; -ating : confirmar, probar, justificar

substitute[1] ['sʌbstə,tu:t, -,tju:t] *v* -tuted; -tuting *vt* : sustituir — *vi* **to substitute for** : sustituir

substitute[2] *n* 1 : sustituto *m*, -ta *f*; su- plente *mf* (persona) 2 : sucedáneo *m* ⟨sugar substitute : sucedáneo de azú- car⟩

substitute teacher *n* : profesor *m*, -sora *f* suplente

substitution [,sʌbstə'tu:ʃən, -'tju:-] *n* : sustitución *f*

subterfuge ['sʌbtər,fju:dʒ] *n* : subterfu- gio *m*

subterranean [,sʌbtə'reɪniən] *adj* : sub- terráneo

subtitle ['sʌb,taɪtəl] *n* : subtítulo *m*

subtle ['sʌtəl] *adj* -tler; -tlest 1 DELI- CATE, ELUSIVE : sutil, delicado 2 CLEVER : sutil, ingenioso

subtlety ['sʌtəlti] *n, pl* -ties : sutileza *f*

subtly ['sʌtəli] *adv* : sutilmente

subtotal ['sʌb,to:təl] *n* : subtotal *m*

subtract [səb'trækt] *vt* : restar, sustraer

subtraction [səb'trækʃən] *n* : resta *f*, sus- tracción *f*

suburb ['sʌ,bərb] *n* : municipio *m* per- iférico, suburbio *m*

suburban [sə'bərbən] *adj* : de las afueras (de una ciudad), suburbano

subversion [səb'vərʒən] *n* : subversión *f*

subversive [səb'vərsɪv] *adj* : subversivo

subway ['sʌb,weɪ] *n* : metro *m*, subte- rráneo *m Arg, Uru*

succeed [sək'si:d] *vt* FOLLOW : suceder a — *vi* : tener éxito (dícese de las per- sonas), dar resultado (dícese de los planes, etc.) ⟨she succeeded in finish- ing : logró terminar⟩

success [sək'sɛs] *n* : éxito *m*

successful [sək'sɛsfəl] *adj* : exitoso, lo- grado — **successfully** *adv*

succession [sək'sɛʃən] *n* : sucesión *f* ⟨in succesion : sucesivamente⟩

successive [sək'sɛsɪv] *adj* : sucesivo, consecutivo — **successively** *adv*

successor [sək'sɛsər] *n* : sucesor *m*, -sora *f*

succinct [sək'sɪŋkt, sə'sɪŋkt] *adj* : sucin- to — **succinctly** *adv*

succor[1] ['sʌkər] *vt* : socorrer

succor[2] *n* : socorro *m*

succotash ['sʌkə,tæʃ] *n* : guiso *m* de maíz y frijoles

succulent¹ ['sʌkjələnt] *adj* : suculento, jugoso

succulent² *n* : suculenta *f* (planta)

succumb [sə'kʌm] *vi* : sucumbir

such¹ ['sʌtʃ] *adv* **1** SO : tan ⟨such tall buildings : edificios tan grandes⟩ **2** VERY : muy ⟨he's not in such good shape : anda un poco mal⟩ **3 such that** : de tal manera que

such² *adj* : tal ⟨there's no such thing : no existe tal cosa⟩ ⟨in such cases : en tales casos⟩ ⟨animals such as cows and sheep : animales como vacas y ovejas⟩

such³ *pron* **1** : tal ⟨such was the result : tal fue el resultado⟩ ⟨he's a child, and acts as such : es un niño, y se porta como tal⟩ **2** : algo o alguien semejante ⟨books, papers and such : libros, papeles y cosas por el estilo⟩

suck ['sʌk] *vi* **1** : chupar (por la boca), aspirar (dícese de las máquinas) **2** SUCKLE : mamar — *vt* : sorber (bebidas), chupar (dulces, etc.)

sucker ['sʌkər] *n* **1** : ventosa *f* (de un insecto, etc.) **2** : chupón *m* (de una planta) **3** → **lollipop 4** FOOL : tonto *m*, -ta *f*; idiota *mf*

suckle ['sʌkəl] *v* **-led; -ling** *vt* : amamantar — *vi* : mamar

suckling ['sʌklɪŋ] *n* : lactante *mf*

sucrose ['su:,kro:s, -,kro:z] *n* : sacarosa *f*

suction ['sʌkʃən] *n* : succión *f*

Sudanese [,su:dən'i:z, -'i:s] *n* : sudanés *m*, -nesa *f* — **Sudanese** *adj*

sudden ['sʌdən] *adj* **1** : repentino, súbito ⟨all of a sudden : de pronto, de repente⟩ **2** UNEXPECTED : inesperado, improviso **3** ABRUPT, HASTY : precipitado, brusco

suddenly ['sʌdənli] *adv* **1** : de repente, de pronto **2** ABRUPTLY : bruscamente

suddenness ['sʌdənnəs] *n* **1** : lo repentino **2** ABRUPTNESS : brusquedad *f* **3** HASTINESS : lo precipitado

suds ['sʌdz] *npl* : espuma *f* (de jabón)

sue ['su:] *v* **sued; suing** *vt* : demandar — *vi* **to sue for** : demandar por (daños, etc.)

suede ['sweɪd] *n* : ante *m*, gamuza *f*

suet ['su:ət] *n* : sebo *m*

suffer ['sʌfər] *vi* : sufrir — *vt* **1** : sufrir, padecer (dolores, etc.) **2** PERMIT : permitir, dejar

sufferer ['sʌfərər] *n* : persona que padece (una enfermedad, etc.)

suffering ['sʌfərɪŋ] *n* : sufrimiento *m*

suffice [sə'faɪs] *vi* **-ficed; -ficing** : ser suficiente, bastar

sufficient [sə'fɪʃənt] *adj* : suficiente

sufficiently [sə'fɪʃəntli] *adv* : (lo) suficientemente, bastante

suffix ['sʌ,fɪks] *n* : sufijo *m*

suffocate ['sʌfə,keɪt] *v* **-cated; -cating** *vt* : asfixiar, ahogar — *vi* : asfixiarse, ahogarse

suffocation [,sʌfə'keɪʃən] *n* : asfixia *f*, ahogo *m*

suffrage ['sʌfrɪdʒ] *n* : sufragio *m*, derecho *m* al voto

suffuse [sə'fju:z] *vt* **-fused; -fusing** : impregnar (de olores, etc.), bañar (de luz), teñir (de colores), llenar (de emociones)

sugar¹ ['ʃʊgər] *vt* : azucarar

sugar² *n* : azúcar *mf*

sugarcane ['ʃʊgər,keɪn] *n* : caña *f* de azúcar

sugary ['ʃʊgəri] *adj* **1** : azucarado ⟨sugary desserts : postres azucarados⟩ **2** SACCHARINE : empalagoso

suggest [səg'dʒɛst, sə-] *vt* **1** PROPOSE : sugerir **2** IMPLY : indicar, dar a entender

suggestible [səg'dʒɛstəbəl, sə-] *adj* : influenciable

suggestion [səg'dʒɛstʃən, sə-] *n* **1** PROPOSAL : sugerencia *f* **2** INDICATION : indicio *m* **3** INSINUATION : insinuación *f*

suggestive [səg'dʒɛstɪv, sə-] *adj* : insinuante — **suggestively** *adv*

suicidal [,su:ə'saɪdəl] *adj* : suicida

suicide ['su:ə,saɪd] *n* **1** : suicidio *m* (acto) **2** : suicida *mf* (persona)

suit¹ ['su:t] *vt* **1** ADAPT : adaptar **2** BEFIT : convenir a, ser apropiado a **3** BECOME : favorecer, quedarle bien (a alguien) ⟨the dress suits you : el vestido te queda bien⟩ **4** PLEASE : agradecer, satisfacer, convenirle bien (a alguien) ⟨does Friday suit you? : ¿le conviene el viernes?⟩ ⟨suit yourself! : ¡como quieras!⟩

suit² *n* **1** LAWSUIT : pleito *m*, litigio *m* **2** : traje *m* (ropa) **3** : palo *m* (de naipes)

suitability [,su:tə'bɪləti] *n* : idoneidad *f*, lo apropiado

suitable ['su:təbəl] *adj* : apropiado, idóneo — **suitably** [-bli] *adv*

suitcase ['su:t,keɪs] *n* : maleta *f*, valija *f*, petaca *f* Mex

suite ['swi:t, *for 2 also* 'su:t] *n* **1** : suite *f* (de habitaciones) **2** SET : juego *m* (de muebles)

suitor ['su:tər] *n* : pretendiente *m*

sulfur ['sʌlfər] *n* : azufre *m*

sulfuric acid [,sʌl'fjʊrɪk] *adj* : ácido *m* sulfúrico

sulfurous [,sʌl'fjʊrəs, 'sʌlfərəs, 'sʌlfjə-] *adj* : sulfuroso

sulk¹ ['sʌlk] *vi* : estar de mal humor, enfurruñarse *fam*

sulk² *n* : mal humor *m*

sulky ['sʌlki] *adj* **sulkier; -est** : malhumorado, taimado *Chile*

sullen ['sʌlən] *adj* **1** MOROSE : hosco, taciturno **2** DREARY : sombrío, deprimente

sullenly ['sʌlənli] *adv* **1** MOROSELY : hoscamente **2** GLOOMILY : sombríamente

sully ['sʌli] *vt* **sullied; sullying** : manchar, empañar

sultan ['sʌltən] *n* : sultán *m*
sultry ['sʌltri] *adj* **sultrier; -est 1** : bochornoso ⟨sultry weather : tiempo sofocante, tiempo bochornoso⟩ **2** SENSUAL : sensual, seductor
sum¹ ['sʌm] *vt* **summed; summing 1** : sumar (números) **2** → **sum up**
sum² *n* **1** AMOUNT : suma *f*, cantidad *f* **2** TOTAL : suma *f*, total *f* **3** : suma *f*, adición *f* (en matemáticas)
sumac ['ʃu:ˌmæk, 'su:-] *n* : zumaque *m*
summarize ['sʌmǝˌraɪz] *v* **-rized; -rizing** : resumir, compendiar
summary¹ ['sʌmǝri] *adj* **1** CONCISE : breve, conciso **2** IMMEDIATE : inmediato ⟨a summary dismissal : un despido inmediato⟩
summary² *n, pl* **-ries** : resumen *m*, compendio *m*
summer ['sʌmǝr] *n* : verano *m*
summery ['sʌmǝri] *adj* : veraniego
summit ['sʌmǝt] *n* **1** : cumbre *f*, cima *f* (de una montaña) **2** *or* **summit conference** : cumbre *f*
summon ['sʌmǝn] *vt* **1** CALL : convocar (una reunión, etc.), llamar (a una persona) **2** : citar (en derecho) **3 to summon up** : armarse de (valor, etc.) ⟨to summon up one's strength : reunir fuerzas⟩
summons ['sʌmǝnz] *n, pl* **summonses 1** SUBPOENA : citación *f*, citatorio *m Mex* **2** CALL : llamada *f*, llamamiento *m*
sumptuous ['sʌmptʃuǝs] *adj* : suntuoso
sum up *vt* **1** SUMMARIZE : resumir **2** EVALUATE : evaluar — *vi* : recapitular
sun¹ ['sʌn] *vt* **sunned; sunning 1** : poner al sol **2 to sun oneself** : asolearse, tomar el sol
sun² *n* **1** : sol *m* **2** SUNSHINE : luz *f* del sol
sunbeam ['sʌnˌbi:m] *n* : rayo *m* de sol
sunblock ['sʌnˌblɑk] *n* : filtro *m* solar
sunburn¹ ['sʌnˌbǝrn] *vi* **-burned [-ˌbǝrnd]** *or* **-burnt [-ˌbǝrnt]; -burning** : quemarse por el sol
sunburn² ['sʌnˌbǝrn] *n* : quemadura *f* de sol
sundae ['sʌndi] *n* : sundae *m*
Sunday ['sʌnˌdeɪ, -di] *n* : domingo *m*
sundial ['sʌnˌdaɪl] *n* : reloj *m* de sol
sundown ['sʌnˌdaʊn] → **sunset**
sundries ['sʌndriz] *npl* : artículos *mpl* diversos
sundry ['sʌndri] *adj* : varios, diversos
sunflower ['sʌnˌflaʊǝr] *n* : girasol *m*, mirasol *m*
sung → **sing**
sunglasses ['sʌnˌglæsǝz] *npl* : gafas *fpl* de sol, lentes *mpl* de sol
sunk → **sink¹**
sunken ['sʌŋkǝn] *adj* : hundido
sunlight ['sʌnˌlaɪt] *n* : sol *m*, luz *f* del sol
sunny ['sʌni] *adj* **sunnier; -est** : soleado
sunrise ['sʌnˌraɪz] *n* : salida *f* del sol
sunscreen ['sʌnˌskri:n] *n* : filtro *m* solar

sunset ['sʌnˌsɛt] *n* : puesta *f* del sol
sunshine ['sʌnˌʃaɪn] *n* : sol *m*, luz *f* del sol
sunspot ['sʌnˌspɑt] *n* : mancha *f* solar
sunstroke ['sʌnˌstro:k] *n* : insolación *f*
suntan ['sʌnˌtæn] *n* : bronceado *m*
sup ['sʌp] *vi* **supped; supping** : cenar
super ['su:pǝr] *adj* : súper ⟨super! : ¡fantástico!⟩
superabundance [ˌsu:pǝrǝ'bʌndǝnts] *n* : superabundancia *f*
superb [su'pǝrb] *adj* : magnífico, espléndido — **superbly** *adv*
supercilious [ˌsu:pǝr'sɪliǝs] *adj* : altivo, altanero, desdeñoso
supercomputer ['su:pǝrkǝmˌpju:tǝr] *n* : supercomputadora *f*
superficial [ˌsu:pǝr'fɪʃǝl] *adj* : superficial — **superficially** *adv*
superfluous [su'pǝrfluǝs] *adj* : superfluo
superhighway ['su:pǝrˌhaɪˌweɪ, ˌsu:pǝr'-] *n* : autopista *f*
superhuman [ˌsu:pǝr'hju:mǝn] *adj* **1** SUPERNATURAL : sobrenatural **2** HERCULEAN : sobrehumano
superimpose [ˌsu:pǝrɪm'po:z] *vt* **-posed; -posing** : superponer, sobreponer
superintend [ˌsu:pǝrɪn'tɛnd] *vt* : supervisar
superintendent [ˌsu:pǝrɪn'tɛndǝnt] *n* : portero *m*, -ra *f* (de un edificio); director *m*, -tora *f* (de una escuela, etc.); superintendente *mf* (de policía)
superior¹ [su'pɪriǝr] *adj* **1** BETTER : superior **2** HAUGHTY : altivo, altanero
superior² *n* : superior *m*
superiority [suˌpɪri'ɔrǝti] *n, pl* **-ties** : superioridad *f*
superlative¹ [su'pǝrlǝtɪv] *adj* **1** : superlativo (en gramática) **2** SUPREME : supremo **3** EXCELLENT : excelente, excepcional
superlative² *n* : superlativo *m*
supermarket ['su:pǝrˌmɑrkǝt] *n* : supermercado *m*
supernatural [ˌsu:pǝr'nætʃǝrǝl] *adj* : sobrenatural
supernaturally [ˌsu:pǝr'nætʃǝrǝli] *adv* : de manera sobrenatural
superpower ['su:pǝrˌpaʊǝr] *n* : superpotencia *f*
supersede [ˌsu:pǝr'si:d] *vt* **-seded; -seding** : suplantar, reemplazar, sustituir
supersonic [ˌsu:pǝr'sɑnɪk] *adj* : supersónico
superstar ['su:pǝrˌstɑr] *n* : superestrella *f*
superstition [ˌsu:pǝr'stɪʃǝn] *n* : superstición *f*
superstitious [ˌsu:pǝr'stɪʃǝs] *adj* : supersticioso
superstructure ['su:pǝrˌstrʌktʃǝr] *n* : superestructura *f*
supervise ['su:pǝrˌvaɪz] *vt* **-vised; -vising** : supervisar, dirigir
supervision [ˌsu:pǝr'vɪʒǝn] *n* : supervisión *f*, dirección *f*

supervisor [ˈsuːpərˌvaɪzər] n : supervisor m, -sora f

supervisory [ˌsuːpərˈvaɪzəri] adj : de supervisor

supine [suːˈpaɪn] adj 1 : en decúbito supino, en decúbito dorsal 2 ABJECT, INDIFFERENT : indiferente, apático

supper [ˈsʌpər] n : cena f, comida f

supplant [səˈplænt] vt : suplantar

supple [ˈsʌpəl] adj -pler; -plest : flexible

supplement¹ [ˈsʌpləˌmɛnt] vt : complementar, completar

supplement² [ˈsʌpləmənt] n 1 : complemento m ⟨dietary supplement : complemento alimenticio⟩ 2 : suplemento m (de un libro o periódico)

supplementary [ˌsʌpləˈmɛntəri] adj : suplementario

supplicate [ˈsʌpləˌkeɪt] v -cated; -cating vi : rezar — vt : suplicar

supplier [səˈplaɪər] n : proveedor m, -dora f; abastecedor m, -dora f

supply¹ [səˈplaɪ] vt -plied; -plying : suministrar, proveer de, proporcionar

supply² n, pl -plies 1 PROVISION : provisión f, suministro m ⟨supply and demand : la oferta y la demanda⟩ 2 STOCK : reserva f, existencias fpl (de un negocio) 3 **supplies** npl PROVISIONS : provisiones fpl, víveres mpl, despensa f

support¹ [səˈport] vt 1 BACK : apoyar, respaldar 2 MAINTAIN : mantener, sostener, sustentar 3 PROP UP : sostener, apoyar, apuntalar, soportar

support² n 1 : apoyo m (moral), ayuda f (económica) 2 PROP : soporte m, apoyo m

supporter [səˈportər] n : partidario m, -ria f

supportive [səˈportɪv] adj : que apoya ⟨his family is very supportive : su familia lo apoya mucho⟩

suppose [səˈpoːz] vt -posed; -posing 1 ASSUME : suponer, imaginarse 2 BELIEVE : suponer, creer 3 **to be supposed to** : tener que, deber

supposed [səˈpoːzd, -ˈpoːzəd] adj : supuesto — **supposedly** [səˈpoːzədli] adv

supposition [ˌsʌpəˈzɪʃən] n : suposición f

suppository [səˈpɑːzəˌtori] n, pl -ries : supositorio m

suppress [səˈprɛs] vt 1 SUBDUE : sofocar, suprimir, reprimir (una rebelión, etc.) 2 : suprimir, ocultar (información) 3 REPRESS : reprimir, contener ⟨to suppress a yawn : reprimir un bostezo⟩

suppression [səˈprɛʃən] n 1 SUBDUING : represión f 2 : supresión f (de información) 3 REPRESSION : represión f, inhibición f

supremacy [suˈprɛməsi] n, pl -cies : supremacía f

supreme [suˈpriːm] adj : supremo

Supreme Being n : Ser m Supremo

supremely [suˈpriːmli] adv : totalmente, sumamente

surcharge [ˈsərˌtʃɑrdʒ] n : recargo m

sure¹ [ˈʃur] adv 1 ALL RIGHT : por supuesto, claro 2 (used as an intensifier) ⟨it sure is hot! : ¡hace tanto calor!⟩ ⟨she sure is pretty! : ¡qué linda es!⟩

sure² adj **surer; -est** : seguro ⟨to be sure about something : estar seguro de algo⟩ ⟨a sure sign : una clara señal⟩ ⟨for sure : seguro, con seguridad⟩

surely [ˈʃurli] adv 1 CERTAINLY : seguramente 2 (used as an intensifier) ⟨you surely don't mean that! : ¡no me digas que estás hablando en serio!⟩

sureness [ˈʃurnəs] n : certeza f, seguridad f

surety [ˈʃurəti] n, pl -ties : fianza f, garantía f

surf [ˈsərf] n 1 WAVES : oleaje m 2 FOAM : espuma f

surface¹ [ˈsərfəs] v -faced; -facing vi : salir a la superficie — vt : revestir (una carretera)

surface² n 1 : superficie f 2 **on the surface** : en apariencia

surfboard [ˈsərfˌbord] n : tabla f de surf, tabla f de surfing

surfeit [ˈsərfət] n : exceso m

surfer [ˈsərfər] n : surfista mf

surfing [ˈsərfɪŋ] n : surf m, surfing m

surge¹ [ˈsərdʒ] vi **surged; surging** 1 : hincharse (dícese del mar), levantarse (dícese de las olas) 2 SWARM : salir en tropel (dícese de la gente, etc.)

surge² n 1 : oleaje m (del mar), oleada f (de gente) 2 FLUSH : arranque m, arrebato m (de ira, etc.) 3 INCREASE : aumento m (súbito)

surgeon [ˈsərdʒən] n : cirujano m, -na f

surgery [ˈsərdʒəri] n, pl -geries : cirugía f

surgical [ˈsərdʒɪkəl] adj : quirúrgico — **surgically** [-kli] adv

surly [ˈsərli] adj **surlier; -est** : hosco, arisco

surmise¹ [sərˈmaɪz] vt -mised; -mising : conjeturar, suponer, concluir

surmise² n : conjetura f

surmount [sərˈmaunt] vt 1 OVERCOME : superar, vencer, salvar 2 CLIMB : escalar 3 CAP, TOP : coronar

surname [ˈsərˌneɪm] n : apellido m

surpass [sərˈpæs] vt : superar, exceder, rebasar, sobrepasar

surplus [ˈsərˌplʌs] n : excedente m, sobrante m, superávit m (de dinero)

surprise¹ [səˈpraɪz, sər-] vt -prised; -prising : sorprender

surprise² n : sorpresa f ⟨to take by surprise : sorprender⟩

surprising [səˈpraɪzɪŋ, sər-] adj : sorprendente — **surprisingly** adv

surrender¹ [səˈrɛndər] vt 1 : entregar, rendir 2 **to surrender oneself** : entregarse — vi : rendirse

surrender² n : rendición m (de una ciudad, etc.), entrega f (de posesiones)

surreptitious [ˌsərəpˈtɪʃəs] *adj* : subrepticio — **surreptitiously** *adv*

surrogate [ˈsərəgət, -ˌgeɪt] *n* : sustituto *m*

surround [səˈraʊnd] *vt* : rodear

surroundings [səˈraʊndɪŋz] *npl* : ambiente *m*, entorno *m*

surveillance [sərˈveɪlənts, -ˈveɪljənts, -ˈveɪnts] *n* : vigilancia *f*

survey¹ [sərˈveɪ] *vt* **-veyed; -veying 1** : medir (un terreno) **2** EXAMINE : inspeccionar, examinar, revisar **3** POLL : hacer una encuesta de, sondear

survey² [ˈsərˌveɪ] *n, pl* **-veys 1** INSPECTION : inspección *f*, revisión *f* **2** : medición *f* (de un terreno) **3** POLL : encuesta *f*, sondeo *m*

surveyor [sərˈveɪər] *n* : agrimensor *m*, -sora *f*

survival [sərˈvaɪvəl] *n* : supervivencia *f*, sobrevivencia *f*

survive [sərˈvaɪv] *v* **-vived; -viving** *vi* : sobrevivir — *vt* OUTLIVE : sobrevivir a

survivor [sərˈvaɪvər] *n* : superviviente *mf*, sobreviviente *mf*

susceptibility [səˌsɛptəˈbɪləti] *n, pl* **-ties** : vulnerabilidad *f*, propensión *f* (a enfermedades, etc.)

susceptible [səˈsɛptəbəl] *adj* **1** VULNERABLE : vulnerable, sensible ⟨susceptible to flattery : sensible a halagos⟩ **2** PRONE : propenso ⟨susceptible to colds : propenso a resfriarse⟩

suspect¹ [səˈspɛkt] *vt* **1** DISTRUST : dudar de **2** : sospechar (algo), sospechar de (una persona) **3** IMAGINE, THINK : imaginarse, creer

suspect² [ˈsʌsˌpɛkt, səˈspɛkt] *adj* : sospechoso, dudoso, cuestionable

suspect³ [ˈsʌsˌpɛkt] *n* : sospechoso *m*, -sa *f*

suspend [səˈspɛnd] *vt* : suspender

suspenders [səˈspɛndərz] *npl* : tirantes *mpl*

suspense [səˈspɛnts] *n* : incertidumbre *f*, suspenso *m* (en una película, etc.)

suspenseful [səˈspɛntsfəl] *adj* : de suspenso

suspension [səˈspɛntʃən] *n* : suspensión *f*

suspicion [səˈspɪʃən] *n* **1** : sospecha *f* **2** TRACE : pizca *f*, atisbo *m*

suspicious [səˈspɪʃəs] *adj* **1** QUESTIONABLE : sospechoso, dudoso **2** DISTRUSTFUL : suspicaz, desconfiado

suspiciously [səˈspɪʃəsli] *adv* : de modo sospechoso, con recelo

sustain [səˈsteɪn] *vt* **1** NOURISH : sustentar **2** PROLONG : sostener **3** SUFFER : sufrir **4** SUPPORT, UPHOLD : apoyar, respaldar, sostener

sustainable [səˈsteɪnəbəl] *adj* : sostenible

sustenance [ˈsʌstənənts] *n* **1** NOURISHMENT : sustento *m* **2** SUPPORT : sostén *m*

svelte [ˈsfɛlt] *adj* : esbelto

swab¹ [ˈswɑb] *vt* **swabbed; swabbing 1** CLEAN : lavar, limpiar **2** : aplicar a (con hisopo)

swab² *n or* **cotton swab** : hisopo *m* (para aplicar medicinas, etc.)

swaddle [ˈswɑdəl] *vt* **-dled; -dling** [ˈswɑdəlɪŋ] : envolver (en pañales)

swagger¹ [ˈswægər] *vi* : pavonearse

swagger² *n* : pavoneo *m*

swallow¹ [ˈswɑlo:] *vt* **1** : tragar (comida, etc.) **2** ENGULF : tragarse, envolver **3** REPRESS : tragarse (insultos, etc.) — *vi* : tragar

swallow² *n* **1** : golondrina *f* (pájaro) **2** GULP : trago *m*

swam → **swim¹**

swamp¹ [ˈswɑmp] *vt* : inundar

swamp² *n* : pantano *m*, ciénaga *f*

swampy [ˈswɑmpi] *adj* **swampier; -est** : pantanoso, cenagoso

swan [ˈswɑn] *n* : cisne *f*

swap¹ [ˈswɑp] *vt* **swapped; swapping** : cambiar, intercambiar ⟨to swap places : cambiarse de sitio⟩

swap² *n* : cambio *m*, intercambio *m*

swarm¹ [ˈswɔrm] *vi* : enjambrar

swarm² *n* : enjambre *m*

swarthy [ˈswɔrði, -θi] *adj* **swarthier; -est** : moreno

swashbuckling [ˈswɑʃˌbʌklɪŋ] *adj* : de aventurero

swat¹ [ˈswɑt] *vt* **swatted; swatting** : aplastar (un insecto), darle una palmada (a alguien)

swat² *n* : palmada *f* (con la mano), golpe *m* (con un objeto)

swatch [ˈswɑtʃ] *n* : muestra *f*

swath [ˈswɑθ, ˈswɔθ] *or* **swathe** [ˈswɑð, ˈswɔð, ˈsweɪð] *n* : franja *f* (de grano segado)

swathe [ˈswɑð, ˈswɔð, ˈsweɪð] *vt* **swathed; swathing** : envolver

swatter [ˈswɑtər] → **flyswatter**

sway¹ [ˈsweɪ] *vi* : balancearse, mecerse — *vt* INFLUENCE : influir en, convencer

sway² *n* **1** SWINGING : balanceo *m* **2** INFLUENCE : influjo *m*

swear [ˈswær] *v* **swore** [ˈswor]; **sworn** [ˈsworn]; **swearing** *vi* **1** VOW : jurar **2** CURSE : decir palabrotas — *vt* : jurar

swearword [ˈswærˌwərd] *n* : mala palabra *f*, palabrota *f*

sweat¹ [ˈswɛt] *vi* **sweat** *or* **sweated; sweating 1** PERSPIRE : sudar, transpirar **2** OOZE : rezumar **3 to sweat over** : sudar la gota gorda por

sweat² *n* : sudor *m*, transpiración *f*

sweater [ˈswɛtər] *n* : suéter *m*

sweatshirt [ˈswɛtˌʃərt] *n* : sudadera *f*

sweaty [ˈswɛti] *adj* **sweatier; -est** : sudoroso, sudado, transpirado

Swede [ˈswiːd] *n* : sueco *m*, -ca *f*

Swedish¹ [ˈswiːdɪʃ] *adj* : sueco

Swedish² *n* **1** : sueco *m* (idioma) **2 the Swedish** *npl* : los suecos

sweep¹ [ˈswiːp] *v* **swept** [ˈswɛpt]; **sweeping** *vt* **1** : barrer (el suelo, etc.), limpiar (suciedad, etc.) ⟨he swept the books aside : apartó los libros de un manotazo⟩ **2** *or* **to sweep through** : extenderse por (dícese del fuego, etc.), azotar (dícese de una tormenta) — *vi* **1** : barrer, limpiar **2** : extenderse (en una curva), describir una curva ⟨the sun swept across the sky : el sol describía una curva en el cielo⟩

sweep² *n* **1** : barrido *m*, barrida *f* (con una escoba) **2** : movimiento *m* circular **3** SCOPE : alcance *m*

sweeper ['swi:pər] *n* : barrendero *m*, -ra *f*

sweeping ['swi:pɪŋ] *adj* **1** WIDE : amplio (dícese de un movimiento) **2** EXTENSIVE : extenso, radical **3** INDISCRIMINATE : indiscriminado, demasiado general **4** OVERWHELMING : arrollador, aplastante

sweepstakes ['swi:p,steɪks] *ns & pl* **1** : carrera *f* (en que el ganador se lleva el premio entero) **2** LOTTERY : lotería *f*

sweet¹ ['swi:t] *adj* **1** : dulce ⟨sweet desserts : postres dulces⟩ **2** FRESH : fresco **3** : sin sal (dícese de la mantequilla, etc.) **4** PLEASANT : dulce, agradable **5** DEAR : querido

sweet² *n* : dulce *m*

sweeten ['swi:tən] *vt* : endulzar

sweetener ['swi:tənər] *n* : endulzante *m*

sweetheart ['swi:t,hɑrt] *n* : novio *m*, -via *f* ⟨thanks, sweetheart : gracias, cariño⟩

sweetly ['swi:tli] *adv* : dulcemente

sweetness ['swi:tnəs] *n* : dulzura *f*

sweet potato *n* : batata *f*, boniato *m*

swell¹ ['swel] *vi* **swelled; swelled** *or* **swollen** ['swo:lən, 'swʌl-]; **swelling 1** *or* **to swell up** : hincharse ⟨her ankle swelled : se le hinchó el tobillo⟩ **2** *or* **to swell out** : inflarse, hincharse (dícese de las velas, etc.) **3** INCREASE : aumentar, crecer

swell² *n* **1** : oleaje *m* (del mar) **2** → **swelling**

swelling ['swelɪŋ] *n* : hinchazón *f*

swelter ['sweltər] *vi* : sofocarse de calor

swept → **sweep¹**

swerve¹ ['swərv] *vi* **swerved; swerving** : virar bruscamente

swerve² *n* : viraje *m* brusco

swift¹ ['swɪft] *adj* **1** FAST : rápido, veloz **2** SUDDEN : repentino, súbito — **swiftly** *adv*

swift² *n* : vencejo *m* (pájaro)

swiftness ['swɪftnəs] *n* : rapidez *f*, velocidad *f*

swig¹ ['swɪg] *vi* **swigged; swigging** : tomar a tragos, beber a tragos

swig² *n* : trago *m*

swill¹ ['swɪl] *vt* : chupar, beber a tragos grandes

swill² *n* **1** SLOP : bazofia *f* **2** GARBAGE : basura *f*

swim¹ ['swɪm] *vi* **swam** ['swæm]; **swum** ['swʌm]; **swimming 1** : nadar **2** FLOAT : flotar **3** REEL : dar vueltas ⟨his head was swimming : la cabeza le daba vueltas⟩

swim² *n* : baño *m*, chapuzón *m* ⟨to go for a swim : ir a nadar⟩

swimmer ['swɪmər] *n* : nadador *m*, -dora *f*

swindle¹ ['swɪndəl] *vt* **-dled; -dling** : estafar, timar

swindle² *n* : estafa *f*, timo *m fam*

swindler ['swɪndələr] *n* : estafador *m*, -dora *f*; timador *m*, -dora *f*

swine ['swaɪn] *ns & pl* : cerdo *m*, -da *f*

swing¹ ['swɪŋ] *v* **swung** ['swʌŋ]; **swinging** *vt* **1** : describir una curva con ⟨he swung the ax at the tree : le dio al arbol con el hacha⟩ **2** : balancear (los brazos, etc.), hacer oscilar **3** SUSPEND : colgar — *vi* **1** SWAY : balancearse (dícese de los brazos, etc.), oscilar (dícese de un objeto), columpiarse, mecerse (en un columpio) **2** SWIVEL : girar (en un pivote) ⟨the door swung shut : la puerta se cerró⟩ **3** CHANGE : virar, cambiar (dícese de las opiniones, etc.)

swing² *n* **1** SWINGING : vaivén *m*, balanceo *m* **2** CHANGE, SHIFT : viraje *m*, movimiento *m* **3** : columpio *m* (para niños) **4 to take a swing at someone** : intentar pegarle a alguien

swipe¹ ['swaɪp] *vt* **swiped; swiping 1** STRIKE : dar, pegar (con un movimiento amplio) **2** WIPE : limpiar **3** STEAL : birlar *fam*, robar

swipe² *n* BLOW : golpe *m*

swirl¹ ['swərl] *vi* : arremolinarse

swirl² *n* **1** EDDY : remolino *m* **2** SPIRAL : espiral *f*

swish¹ ['swɪʃ] *vt* : mover (produciendo un sonido) ⟨she swished her skirt : movía la falda⟩ — *vi* : moverse (produciendo un sonido) ⟨the cars swished by : se oían pasar los coches⟩

swish² *n* : silbido *m* (de un látigo, etc.), susurro *m* (de agua), crujido *m* (de ropa, etc.)

Swiss ['swɪs] *n* : suizo *m*, -za *f* — **Swiss** *adj*

swiss chard *n* : acelga *f*

switch¹ ['swɪtʃ] *vt* **1** LASH, WHIP : azotar **2** CHANGE : cambiar de **3** EXCHANGE : intercambiar **4 to switch on** : encender, prender **5 to switch off** : apagar — *vi* **1** : moverse de un lado al otro **2** CHANGE : cambiar **3** SWAP : intercambiarse

switch² *n* **1** WHIP : vara *f* **2** CHANGE, SHIFT : cambio *m* **3** : interruptor *m*, llave *f* (de la luz, etc.)

switchboard ['swɪtʃ,bord] *n* : conmutador *m*, centralita *f*

swivel¹ ['swɪvəl] *vi* **-veled** *or* **-velled; -veling** *or* **-velling** : girar (sobre un pivote)

swivel² *n* : base *f* giratoria

swollen *pp* → **swell¹**

swoon¹ ['swu:n] *vi* : desvanecerse, desmayarse

swoon² *n* : desvanecimiento *m*, desmayo *m*

swoop¹ ['swu:p] *vi* : abatirse (dícese de las aves), descender en picada (dícese de un avión)
swoop² *n* : descenso *m* en picada
sword ['sɔrd] *n* : espada *f*
swordfish ['sɔrd,fɪʃ] *n* : pez *m* espada
swore, sworn → **swear**
swum *pp* → **swim¹**
swung → **swing¹**
sycamore ['sɪkə,mor] *n* : sicomoro *m*
sycophant ['sɪkəfənt, -,fænt] *n* : adulador *m*, -dora *f*
syllabic [sə'læbɪk] *adj* : silábico
syllable ['sɪləbəl] *n* : sílaba *f*
syllabus ['sɪləbəs] *n*, *pl* **-bi** [-,baɪ] *or* **-buses** : programa *m* (de estudios)
symbol ['sɪmbəl] *n* : símbolo *m*
symbolic [sɪm'balɪk] *adj* : simbólico — **symbolically** [-kli] *adv*
symbolism ['sɪmbə,lɪzəm] *n* : simbolismo *m*
symbolize ['sɪmbə,laɪz] *vt* **-ized; -izing** : simbolizar
symmetrical [sə'mɛtrɪkəl] *or* **symmetric** [-trɪk] *adj* : simétrico — **symmetrically** [-trɪkli] *adv*
symmetry ['sɪmətri] *n*, *pl* **-tries** : simetría *f*
sympathetic [,sɪmpə'θɛtɪk] *adj* **1** PLEASING : agradable **2** RECEPTIVE : receptivo, favorable **3** COMPASSIONATE, UNDERSTANDING : comprensivo, compasivo
sympathetically [,sɪmpə'θɛtɪkli] *adv* : con compasión, con comprensión
sympathize ['sɪmpə,θaɪz] *vi* **-thized; -thizing** : compadecer ⟨I sympathize with you : te compadezco⟩
sympathy ['sɪmpəθi] *n*, *pl* **-thies 1** COMPASSION : compasión *f* **2** UNDERSTANDING : comprensión *f* **3** AGREEMENT : solidaridad *f* ⟨in sympathy with : de acuerdo con⟩ **4** CONDOLENCES : pésame *m*, condolencias *fpl*
symphonic [sɪm'fanɪk] *adj* : sinfónico
symphony ['sɪmpfəni] *n*, *pl* **-nies** : sinfonía *f*
symposium [sɪm'po:ziəm] *n*, *pl* **-sia** [-ziə] *or* **-siums** : simposio *m*
symptom ['sɪmptəm] *n* : síntoma *m*
symptomatic [,sɪmptə'mætɪk] *adj* : sintomático

synagogue ['sɪnə,gɑg, -,gɔg] *n* : sinagoga *f*
sync ['sɪŋk] *n* : sincronización *f* ⟨in sync : sincronizado⟩
synchronize ['sɪŋkrə,naɪz, 'sɪn-] *v* **-nized; -nizing** *vi* : estar sincronizado — *vt* : sincronizar
syncopate ['sɪŋkə,peɪt, 'sɪn-] *vt* **-pated; -pating** : sincopar
syncopation [,sɪŋkə'peɪʃən, ,sɪn-] *n* : síncopa *f*
syndicate¹ ['sɪndə,keɪt] *vi* **-cated; -cating** : formar una asociación
syndicate² ['sɪndɪkət] *n* : asociación *f*, agrupación *f*
syndrome ['sɪn,dro:m] *n* : síndrome *m*
synonym ['sɪnə,nɪm] *n* : sinónimo *m*
synonymous [sə'nɑnəməs] *adj* : sinónimo
synopsis [sə'nɑpsɪs] *n*, *pl* **-opses** [-,si:z] : sinopsis *f*
syntactic [sɪn'tæktɪk] *adj* : sintáctico
syntax ['sɪn,tæks] *n* : sintaxis *f*
synthesis ['sɪnθəsɪs] *n*, *pl* **-theses** [-,si:z] : síntesis *f*
synthesize ['sɪnθə,saɪz] *vt* **-sized; -sizing** : sintetizar
synthetic¹ [sɪn'θɛtɪk] *adj* : sintético, artificial — **synthetically** [-tɪkli] *adv*
synthetic² *n* : producto *m* sintético
syphilis ['sɪfələs] *n* : sífilis *f*
Syrian ['sɪriən] *n* : sirio *m*, -ria *f* — **Syrian** *adj*
syringe [sə'rɪnʤ, 'sɪrɪnʤ] *n* : jeringa *f*, jeringuilla *f*
syrup ['sərəp, 'sɪrəp] *n* : jarabe *m*, almíbar *m* (de azúcar y agua)
system ['sɪstəm] *n* **1** METHOD : sistema *m*, método *m* **2** APPARATUS : sistema *m*, instalación *f*, aparato *m* ⟨electrical system : instalación eléctrica⟩ ⟨digestive system : aparato digestivo⟩ **3** BODY : organismo *m*, cuerpo *m* ⟨diseases that affect the whole system : enfermedades que afectan el organismo entero⟩ **4** NETWORK : red *f*
systematic [,sɪstə'mætɪk] *adj* : sistemático — **systematically** [-tɪkli] *adv*
systematize ['sɪstəmə,taɪz] *vt* **-tized; -tizing** : sistematizar
systemic [sɪs'tɛmɪk] *adj* : sistémico

T

t ['ti:] *n*, *pl* **t's** *or* **ts** ['ti:z] : vigésima letra del alfabeto inglés
tab ['tæb] *n* **1** FLAP, TAG : lengüeta *f* (de un sobre, una caja, etc.), etiqueta *f* (de ropa) **2** → **tabulator 3** BILL, CHECK : cuenta *f* **4 to keep tabs on** : tener bajo vigilancia
tabby ['tæbi] *n*, *pl* **-bies 1** *or* **tabby cat** : gato *m* atigrado **2** : gata *f*
tabernacle ['tæbər,nækəl] *n* : tabernáculo *m*

table ['teɪbəl] *n* **1** : mesa *f* ⟨a table for two : una mesa para dos⟩ **2** LIST : tabla *f* ⟨multiplication table : tabla de multiplicar⟩ **3 table of contents** : índice *m* de materias
tableau [tæ'blo:, 'tæ,-] *n*, *pl* **-leaux** [-'blo:z, -,blo:z] : retablo *m*, cuadro *m* vivo (en teatro)
tablecloth ['teɪbəl,klɔθ] *n* : mantel *m*
tablespoon ['teɪbəl,spu:n] *n* **1** : cuchara *f* (de mesa) **2** → **tablespoonful**

tablespoonful [ˈteɪbəlˌspuːnˌfʊl] *n*
: cucharada *f*

tablet [ˈtæblət] *n* **1** PLAQUE : placa *f* **2**
PAD : bloc *m* (de papel) **3** PILL : tableta *f*, pastilla *f*, píldora *f* ⟨an aspirin
tablet : una tableta de aspirina⟩

table tennis *n* : tenis *m* de mesa

tableware [ˈteɪbəlˌwær] *n* : vajillas *fpl*,
cubiertos *mpl* (de mesa)

tabloid [ˈtæˌblɔɪd] *n* : tabloide *m*

taboo¹ [təˈbuː, tæ-] *adj* : tabú

taboo² *n* : tabú *m*

tabular [ˈtæbjələr] *adj* : tabular

tabulate [ˈtæbjəˌleɪt] *vt* **-lated; -lating**
: tabular

tabulator [ˈtæbjəˌleɪtər] *n* : tabulador *m*

tacit [ˈtæsɪt] *adj* : tácito, implícito — **tac-
itly** *adv*

taciturn [ˈtæsɪˌtərn] *adj* : taciturno

tack¹ [ˈtæk] *vt* **1** : sujetar con tachuelas
2 to tack on ADD : añadir, agregar

tack² *n* **1** : tachuela *f* **2** COURSE : rumbo *m* ⟨to change tack : cambiar de rum-
bo⟩

tackle¹ [ˈtækəl] *vt* **-led; -ling 1** : taclear
(en futbol americano) **2** CONFRONT
: abordar, enfrentar, emprender (un
problema, un trabajo, etc.)

tackle² *n* **1** EQUIPMENT, GEAR : equipo
m, aparejo *m* **2** : aparejo *m* (de un
buque) **3** : tacleada *f* (en futbol americano)

tacky [ˈtæki] *adj* **tackier; -est 1** STICKY
: pegajoso **2** CHEAP, GAUDY : de mal
gusto, naco *Mex*

tact [ˈtækt] *n* : tacto *m*, delicadeza *f*, discreción *f*

tactful [ˈtæktfəl] *adj* : discreto, diplomático, de mucho tacto

tactfully [ˈtæktfəli] *adv* : discretamente,
con mucho tacto

tactic [ˈtæktɪk] *n* : táctica *f*

tactical [ˈtæktɪkəl] *adj* : táctico, estratégico

tactics [ˈtæktɪks] *ns & pl* : táctica *f*, estrategia *f*

tactile [ˈtæktəl, -ˌtaɪl] *adj* : táctil

tactless [ˈtæktləs] *adj* : indiscreto, poco
delicado

tactlessly [ˈtæktləsli] *adv* : rudamente,
sin tacto

tadpole [ˈtædˌpoːl] *n* : renacuajo *m*

taffeta [ˈtæfətə] *n* : tafetán *m*, tafeta *f*
Arg, Mex, Uru

taffy [ˈtæfi] *n, pl* **-fies** : caramelo *m* de
melaza, chicloso *m Mex*

tag¹ [ˈtæg] *v* **tagged; tagging** *vt* **1** LA-
BEL : etiquetar **2** TAIL : seguir de cerca **3** TOUCH : tocar (en varios juegos)
— *vi* **to tag along** : pegarse, acompañar

tag² *n* **1** LABEL : etiqueta *f* **2** SAYING
: dicho *m*, refrán *m*

tail¹ [ˈteɪl] *vt* FOLLOW : seguir de cerca,
pegarse

tail² *n* **1** : cola *f*, rabo *m* (de un animal)
2 : cola *f*, parte *f* posterior ⟨a comet's
tail : la cola de un cometa⟩ **3 tails** *npl*
: cruz *f* (de una moneda) ⟨heads or tails
: cara o cruz⟩

tailed [ˈteɪld] *adj* : que tiene cola

tailgate¹ [ˈteɪlˌgeɪt] *vi* **-gated; -gating**
: seguir a un vehículo demasiado de
cerca

tailgate² *n* : puerta *f* trasera (de un vehículo)

taillight [ˈteɪlˌlaɪt] *n* : luz *f* trasera (de un
vehículo), calavera *f Mex*

tailor¹ [ˈteɪlər] *vt* **1** : confeccionar o alterar (ropa) **2** ADAPT : adaptar, ajustar

tailor² *n* : sastre *m*, -tra *f*

tailpipe [ˈteɪlˌpaɪp] *n* : tubo *m* de escape

tailspin [ˈteɪlˌspɪn] *n* : barrena *f*

taint¹ [ˈteɪnt] *vt* : contaminar, corromper

taint² *n* : corrupción *f*, impureza *f*

take¹ [ˈteɪk] *v* **took** [ˈtʊk]; **taken** [ˈteɪkən];
taking *vt* **1** CAPTURE : capturar, apresar **2** GRASP : tomar, agarrar ⟨to take
the bull by the horns : tomar al toro
por los cuernos⟩ **3** CATCH : tomar,
agarrar ⟨taken by surprise : tomado
por sorpresa⟩ **4** CAPTIVATE : encantar,
fascinar **5** INGEST : tomar, ingerir
⟨take two pills : tome dos píldoras⟩ **6**
REMOVE : sacar, extraer ⟨take an orange : saca una naranja⟩ **7** : tomar,
coger (un tren, un autobús, etc.) **8**
NEED, REQUIRE : tomar, requerir
⟨these things take time : estas cosas
toman tiempo⟩ **9** BRING, CARRY : llevar, sacar, cargar ⟨take them with you
: llévalos contigo⟩ ⟨take the trash out
: saca la basura⟩ **10** BEAR, ENDURE
: soportar, aguantar (dolores, etc.) **11**
ACCEPT : aceptar (un cheque, etc.),
seguir (consejos), asumir (la responsabilidad) **12** SUPPOSE : suponer ⟨I take
it that . . . : supongo que . . . ⟩ **13** (*indicating an action or an undertaking*)
⟨to take a walk : dar un paseo⟩ ⟨to take
a class : tomar una clase⟩ **14 to take
place** HAPPEN : tener lugar, suceder,
ocurrir — *vi* : agarrar (dícese de un
tinte), prender (dícese de una vacuna)

take² *n* **1** PROCEEDS : recaudación *f*, ingresos *mpl*, ganancias *fpl* **2** : toma *f* (de
un rodaje o una grabación)

take back *vt* : retirar (palabras, etc.)

take in *vt* **1** : tomarle a, achicar (un vestido, etc.) **2** INCLUDE : incluir, abarcar
3 ATTEND : ir a ⟨to take in a movie : ir
al cine⟩ **4** GRASP, UNDERSTAND : captar, entender **5** DECEIVE : engañar

takeoff [ˈteɪkˌɔf] *n* **1** PARODY : parodia
f **2** : despegue *m* (de un avión o cohete)

take off *vt* REMOVE : quitar ⟨take off
your hat : quítate el sombrero⟩ — *vi* **1**
: despegar (dícese de un avión o un cohete) **2** LEAVE : irse, partir

take on *vt* **1** TACKLE : abordar, emprender (problemas, etc.) **2** ACCEPT
: aceptar, encargarse de, asumir (una
responsabilidad) **3** CONTRACT : contratar (trabajadores) **4** ASSUME : adoptar, asumir, adquirir ⟨the neighborhood took on a dingy look : el barrio
asumió una apariencia deprimente⟩

takeover ['teɪk,oːvər] *n* : toma *f* (de poder o de control), adquisición *f* (de una empresa por otra)

take over *vt* : tomar el poder de, tomar las riendas de — *vi* : asumir el mando

taker ['teɪkər] *n* : persona *f* interesada ⟨available to all takers : disponible a cuantos estén interesados⟩

take up *vt* 1 LIFT : levantar 2 SHORTEN : acortar (una falda, etc.) 3 BEGIN : empezar, dedicarse a (un pasatiempo, etc.) 4 OCCUPY : ocupar, llevar (tiempo, espacio) 5 PURSUE : volver a (una cuestión, un asunto) 6 CONTINUE : seguir con

talc ['tælk] *n* : talco *m*

talcum powder ['tælkəm] *n* : talco *m*, polvos *mpl* de talco

tale ['teɪl] *n* 1 ANECDOTE, STORY : cuento *m*, relato *m*, anécdota *f* 2 FALSEHOOD : cuento *m*, mentira *f*

talent ['tælənt] *n* : talento *m*, don *m*

talented ['tæləntəd] *adj* : talentoso

talisman ['tælɪsmən, -lɪz-] *n, pl* **-mans** : talismán *m*

talk¹ ['tɔk] *vi* 1 : hablar ⟨he talks for hours : se pasa horas hablando⟩ 2 CHAT : charlar, platicar — *vt* 1 SPEAK : hablar ⟨to talk French : hablar francés⟩ ⟨to talk business : hablar de negocios⟩ 2 PERSUADE : influenciar, convencer ⟨she talked me out of it : me convenció que no lo hiciera⟩ 3 **to talk over** DISCUSS : hablar de, discutir

talk² *n* 1 CONVERSATION : charla *f*, plática *f*, conversación *f* 2 GOSSIP, RUMOR : chisme *m*, rumores *mpl*

talkative ['tɔkətɪv] *adj* : locuaz, parlanchín, charlatán

talker ['tɔkər] *n* : conversador *m*, -dora *f*; hablador *m*, -dora *f*

talk show *n* : programa *m* de entrevistas

tall ['tɔl] *adj* : alto ⟨how tall is he? : ¿cuánto mide?⟩

tallness ['tɔlnəs] *n* HEIGHT : estatura *f* (de una persona), altura *f* (de un objeto)

tallow ['tælo:] *n* : sebo *m*

tally¹ ['tæli] *v* **-lied; -lying** *vt* RECKON : contar, hacer una cuenta de — *vi* MATCH : concordar, corresponder, cuadrar

tally² *n, pl* **-lies** : cuenta *f* ⟨to keep a tally : llevar la cuenta⟩

talon ['tælən] *n* : garra *f* (de un ave de rapiña)

tambourine [,tæmbə'riːn] *n* : pandero *m*, pandereta *f*

tame¹ ['teɪm] *vt* **tamed; taming** : domar, amansar, domesticar

tame² *adj* **tamer; -est** 1 DOMESTICATED : domesticado, manso 2 DOCILE : manso, dócil 3 DULL : aburrido, soso

tamely ['teɪmli] *adv* : mansamente, dócilmente

tamer ['teɪmər] *n* : domador *m*, -dora *f*

tamp ['tæmp] *vt* : apisonar

tamper ['tæmpər] *vi* **to tamper with** : adulterar (una sustancia), forzar (un sello, una cerradura), falsear (documentos), manipular (una máquina)

tampon ['tæm,pɑn] *n* : tampón *m*

tan¹ ['tæn] *v* **tanned; tanning** *vt* 1 : curtir (pieles) 2 : broncear — *vi* : broncearse

tan² *n* 1 SUNTAN : bronceado *m* ⟨to get a tan : broncearse⟩ 2 : color *m* canela, color *m* café con leche

tandem¹ ['tændəm] *adv or* **in tandem** : en tándem

tandem² *n* : tándem *m* (bicicleta)

tang ['tæŋ] *n* : sabor *m* fuerte

tangent ['tændʒənt] *n* : tangente *f* ⟨to go off on a tangent : irse por la tangente⟩

tangerine ['tændʒə,riːn, ,tændʒə'-] *n* : mandarina *f*

tangible ['tændʒəbəl] *adj* : tangible, palpable — **tangibly** [-bli] *adv*

tangle¹ ['tæŋgəl] *v* **-gled; -gling** *vt* : enredar, enmarañar — *vi* : enredarse

tangle² *n* : enredo *m*, maraña *f*

tango¹ ['tæŋ,goː] *vi* : bailar el tango

tango² *n, pl* **-gos** : tango *m*

tangy ['tæŋi] *adj* **tangier; -est** : que tiene un sabor fuerte

tank ['tæŋk] *n* : tanque *m*, depósito *m* ⟨fuel tank : depósito de combustibles⟩

tankard ['tæŋkərd] *n* : jarra *f*

tanker ['tæŋkər] *n* : buque *m* cisterna, camión *m* cisterna, avión *m* cisterna ⟨an oil tanker : un petrolero⟩

tanner ['tænər] *n* : curtidor *m*, -dora *f*

tannery ['tænəri] *n, pl* **-neries** : curtiduría *f*, tenería *f*

tannin ['tænən] *n* : tanino *m*

tantalize ['tæntə,laɪz] *vt* **-lized; -lizing** : tentar, atormentar (con algo inasequible)

tantalizing ['tæntə,laɪzɪŋ] *adj* : tentador, seductor

tantamount ['tæntə,maʊnt] *adj* : equivalente

tantrum ['tæntrəm] *n* : rabieta *f*, berrinche *m* ⟨to throw a tantrum : hacer un berrinche⟩

tap¹ ['tæp] *vt* **tapped; tapping** 1 : ponerle una espita a, sacar líquido de (un barril, un tanque, etc.) 2 : intervenir (una línea telefónica) 3 PAT, TOUCH : tocar, golpear ligeramente ⟨he tapped me on the shoulder : me tocó en el hombro⟩

tap² *n* 1 FAUCET : llave *f*, grifo *m* ⟨beer on tap : cerveza de barril⟩ 2 : extracción *f* (de líquido) ⟨a spinal tap : una punción lumbar⟩ 3 PAT, TOUCH : golpecito *m*, toque *m*

tape¹ ['teɪp] *vt* **taped; taping** 1 : sujetar o arreglar con cinta adhesiva 2 RECORD : grabar

tape² *n* 1 : cinta *f* (adhesiva, magnética, etc.) 2 → **tape measure**

tape measure *n* : cinta *f* métrica

taper¹ ['teɪpər] *vi* 1 : estrecharse gradualmente ⟨its tail tapers towards the tip : su cola va estrechándose hacia la punta⟩ **2** *or* **to taper off** : disminuir gradualmente

taper² *n* **1** CANDLE : vela *f* larga y delgada **2** TAPERING : estrechamiento *m* gradual

tapestry ['tæpəstri] *n, pl* **-tries** : tapiz *m*

tapeworm ['teɪp,wərm] *n* : solitaria *f*, tenia *f*

tapioca [,tæpi'o:kə] *n* : tapioca *f*

tar¹ ['tar] *vt* **tarred; tarring** : alquitranar

tar² *n* : alquitrán *m*, brea *f*, chapopote *m* *Mex*

tarantula [tə'ræntʃələ, -'ræntələ] *n* : tarántula *f*

tardiness ['tardinəs] *n* : tardanza *f*, retraso *m*

tardy ['tardi] *adj* **-dier; -est** LATE : tardío, de retraso

target¹ ['targət] *vt* : fijar como objetivo, dirigir, destinar

target² *n* **1** : blanco *m* ⟨target practice : tiro al blanco⟩ **2** GOAL, OBJECTIVE : meta *f*, objetivo *m*

tariff ['tærɪf] *n* DUTY : tarifa *f*, arancel *m*

tarnish¹ ['tarnɪʃ] *vt* **1** DULL : deslustrar **2** SULLY : empañar, manchar (una reputación, etc.) — *vi* : deslustrarse

tarnish² *n* : deslustre *m*

tarpaulin [tar'pɔlən, 'tarpə-] *n* : lona *f* (impermeable)

tarragon ['tærə,gan, -gən] *n* : estragón *m*

tarry¹ ['tæri] *vi* **-ried; -rying** : demorarse, entretenerse

tarry² ['tari] *adj* **1** : parecido al alquitrán **2** : cubierto de alquitrán

tart¹ ['tart] *adj* **1** SOUR : ácido, agrio **2** CAUSTIC : mordaz, acrimonioso — **tartly** *adv*

tart² *n* : tartaleta *f*

tartan ['tartən] *n* : tartán *m*

tartar ['tartər] *n* **1** : tártaro *m* ⟨tartar sauce : salsa tártara⟩ **2** : sarro *m* (dental)

tartness ['tartnəs] *n* **1** SOURNESS : acidez *f* **2** ACRIMONY, SHARPNESS : mordacidad *f*, acrimonia *f*, acritud *f*

task ['tæsk] *n* : tarea *f*, trabajo *m*

taskmaster ['tæsk,mæstər] *n* **to be a hard taskmaster** : ser exigente, ser muy estricto

tassel ['tæsəl] *n* : borla *f*

taste¹ ['teɪst] *v* **tasted; tasting** *vt* : probar (alimentos), degustar, catar (vinos) ⟨taste this soup : prueba esta sopa⟩ — *vi* : saber ⟨this tastes good : esto sabe bueno⟩

taste² *n* **1** SAMPLE : prueba *f*, bocado *m* (de comida), trago *m* (de bebidas) **2** FLAVOR : gusto *m*, sabor *m* **3** : gusto *m* ⟨she has good taste : tiene buen gusto⟩ ⟨in bad taste : de mal gusto⟩

taste bud *n* : papila *f* gustativa

tasteful ['teɪstfəl] *adj* : de buen gusto

tastefully ['teɪstfəli] *adv* : con buen gusto

tasteless ['teɪstləs] *adj* **1** FLAVORLESS : sin sabor, soso, insípido **2** : de mal

gusto ⟨a tasteless joke : un chiste de mal gusto⟩

taster ['teɪstər] *n* : degustador *m*, -dora *f*; catador *m*, -dora *f* (de vinos)

tastiness ['teɪstinəs] *n* : lo sabroso

tasty ['teɪsti] *adj* **tastier; -est** : sabroso, gustoso

tatter ['tætər] *n* **1** SHRED : tira *f*, jirón *m* (de tela) **2 tatters** *npl* : andrajos *mpl*, harapos *mpl* ⟨to be in tatters : estar por los suelos⟩

tattered ['tætərd] *adj* : andrajoso, en jirones

tattle ['tætəl] *vi* **-tled; -tling 1** CHATTER : parlotear *fam*, cotorrear *fam* **2 to tattle on someone** : acusar a alguien

tattletale ['tætəl,teɪl] *n* : soplón *m*, -plona *f fam*

tattoo¹ [tæ'tu:] *vt* : tatuar

tattoo² *n* : tatuaje *m* ⟨to get a tattoo : tatuarse⟩

taught → **teach**

taunt¹ ['tɔnt] *vt* MOCK : mofarse de, burlarse de

taunt² *n* : mofa *f*, burla *f*

Taurus ['tɔrəs] *n* : Tauro *mf*

taut ['tɔt] *adj* : tirante, tenso — **tautly** *adv*

tautness ['tɔtnəs] *n* : tirantez *f*, tensión *f*

tavern ['tævərn] *n* : taberna *f*

tawdry ['tɔdri] *adj* **-drier; -est** : chabacano, vulgar

tawny ['tɔni] *adj* **-nier; -est** : leonado

tax¹ ['tæks] *vt* **1** : gravar, cobrar un impuesto sobre **2** CHARGE : acusar ⟨they taxed him with neglect : fue acusado de incumplimiento⟩ **3 to tax someone's strength** : ponerle a prueba las fuerzas (a alguien)

tax² *n* **1** : impuesto *m*, tributo *m* **2** BURDEN : carga *f*

taxable ['tæksəbəl] *adj* : sujeto a un impuesto

taxation [tæk'seɪʃən] *n* : impuestos *mpl*

tax–exempt ['tæksɪg'zɛmpt, -ɛg-] *adj* : libre de impuestos

taxi¹ ['tæksi] *vi* **taxied; taxiing** *or* **taxying; taxis** *or* **taxies 1** : ir en taxi **2** : rodar sobre la pista de aterrizaje (dícese de un avión)

taxi² *n, pl* **taxis** : taxi *m*, libre *m Mex*

taxicab ['tæksi,kæb] *n* → **taxi²**

taxidermist ['tæksə,dərmɪst] *n* : taxidermista *mf*

taxidermy ['tæksə,dərmi] *n* : taxidermia *f*

taxpayer ['tæks,peɪər] *n* : contribuyente *mf*, causante *mf Mex*

TB [,ti:'bi:] → **tuberculosis**

tea ['ti:] *n* **1** : té *m* (planta y bebida) **2** : merienda *f*, té *m* (comida)

teach ['ti:tʃ] *v* **taught** ['tɔt]; **teaching** *vt* : enseñar, dar clases de ⟨she teaches math : da clases de matemáticas⟩ ⟨she taught me everything I know : me enseñó todo lo que sé⟩ — *vi* : enseñar, dar clases

teacher ['tiːtʃər] *n* : maestro *m*, -tra *f* (de enseñanza primaria); profesor *m*, -sora *f* (de enseñanza secundaria)

teaching ['tiːtʃɪŋ] *n* : enseñanza *f*

teacup ['tiːˌkʌp] *n* : taza *f* para té

teak ['tiːk] *n* : teca *f*

teakettle ['tiːˌkɛtəl] *n* : tetera *f*

teal ['tiːl] *n, pl* **teal** *or* **teals** : cerceta *f* (pato)

team¹ ['tiːm] *vi or* **to team up** 1 : formar un equipo (en deportes) 2 COLLABORATE : asociarse, juntarse, unirse

team² *adj* : de equipo

team³ *n* 1 : tiro *m* (de caballos), yunta *f* (de bueyes o mulas) 2 : equipo *m* (en deportes, etc.)

teammate ['tiːmˌmeɪt] *n* : compañero *m*, -ra *f* de equipo

teamster ['tiːmstər] *n* : camionero *m*, -ra *f*

teamwork ['tiːmˌwərk] *n* : trabajo *m* en equipo, cooperación *f*

teapot ['tiːˌpɑt] *n* : tetera *f*

tear¹ ['tær] *v* **tore** ['tor]; **torn** ['torn]; **tearing** *vt* 1 RIP : desgarrar, romper, rasgar (tela) ⟨to tear to pieces : hacer pedazos⟩ 2 *or* **to tear apart** DIVIDE : dividir 3 REMOVE : arrancar ⟨torn from his family : arrancado de su familia⟩ 4 **to tear down** : derribar — *vi* 1 RIP : desgarrarse, romperse 2 RUSH : ir a gran velocidad ⟨she went tearing down the street : se fue como rayo por la calle⟩

tear² *n* : desgarradura *f*, rotura *f*, desgarro *m* (muscular)

tear³ ['tɪr] *n* : lágrima *f*

teardrop ['tɪrˌdrɑp] *n* → **tear³**

tearful ['tɪrfəl] *adj* : lloroso, triste — **tearfully** *adv*

tease¹ ['tiːz] *vt* **teased**; **teasing** 1 MOCK : burlarse de, mofarse de 2 ANNOY : irritar, fastidiar

tease² *n* 1 TEASING : burla *f*, mofa *f* 2 : bromista *mf*; guasón *m*, -sona *f*

teaspoon ['tiːˌspuːn] *n* 1 : cucharita *f* 2 → **teaspoonful**

teaspoonful ['tiːˌspuːnˌfʊl] *n, pl* **-spoonfuls** [-ˌfʊlz] *or* **-spoonsful** [-ˌspuːnzˌfʊl] : cucharadita *f*

teat ['tiːt] *n* : tetilla *f*

technical ['tɛknɪkəl] *adj* : técnico — **technically** [-kli] *adv*

technicality [ˌtɛknə'kæləti] *n, pl* **-ties** : detalle *m* técnico

technician [tɛk'nɪʃən] *n* : técnico *m*, -ca *f*

technique [tɛk'niːk] *n* : técnica *f*

technological [ˌtɛknə'lɑdʒɪkəl] *adj* : tecnológico

technology [tɛk'nɑlədʒi] *n, pl* **-gies** : tecnología *f*

teddy bear ['tɛdi] *n* : oso *m* de peluche

tedious ['tiːdiəs] *adj* : aburrido, pesado, monótono — **tediously** *adv*

tediousness ['tiːdiəsnəs] *n* : lo aburrido, lo pesado

tedium ['tiːdiəm] *n* : tedio *m*, pesadez *f*

tee ['tiː] *n* : tee *mf*

teem ['tiːm] *vi* **to teem with** : estar repleto de, estar lleno de

teenage ['tiːnˌeɪdʒ] *or* **teenaged** [-eɪdʒd] *adj* : adolescente, de adolescencia

teenager ['tiːnˌeɪdʒər] *n* : adolescente *mf*

teens ['tiːnz] *npl* : adolescencia *f*

teepee → **tepee**

teeter¹ ['tiːtər] *vi* : balancearse, tambalearse

teeter² *n or* **teeter-totter** ['tiːtərˌtɑtər] → **seesaw**

teeth → **tooth**

teethe ['tiːð] *vi* **teethed**; **teething** : formársele a uno los dientes ⟨the baby's teething : le están saliendo los dientes al niño⟩

telecast¹ ['tɛləˌkæst] *vt* **-cast**; **-casting** : televisar, transmitir por televisión

telecast² *n* : transmisión *f* por televisión

telecommunication [ˌtɛləkəˌmjuːnə'keɪʃən] *n* : telecomunicación *f*

telegram ['tɛləˌgræm] *n* : telegrama *m*

telegraph¹ ['tɛləˌgræf] *v* : telegrafiar

telegraph² *n* : telégrafo *m*

telepathic [ˌtɛlə'pæθɪk] *adj* : telepático — **telepathically** [-θɪkli] *adv*

telepathy [tə'lɛpəθi] *n* : telepatía *f*

telephone¹ ['tɛləˌfoːn] *v* **-phoned**; **-phoning** *vt* : llamar por teléfono a, telefonear — *vi* : telefonear

telephone² *n* : teléfono *m*

telescope¹ ['tɛləˌskoːp] *vi* **-scoped**; **-scoping** : plegarse (como un telescopio)

telescope² *n* : telescopio *m*

telescopic [ˌtɛlə'skɑpɪk] *adj* : telescópico

televise ['tɛləˌvaɪz] *vt* **-vised**; **-vising** : televisar

television ['tɛləˌvɪʒən] *n* : televisión *f*

tell ['tɛl] *v* **told** ['toːld]; **telling** *vt* 1 COUNT : contar, enumerar ⟨all told : en total⟩ 2 INSTRUCT : decir ⟨he told me how to fix it : me dijo cómo arreglarlo⟩ ⟨they told her to wait : le dijeron que esperara⟩ 3 RELATE : contar, relatar, narrar ⟨to tell a story : contar una historia⟩ 4 DIVULGE, REVEAL : revelar, divulgar ⟨he told me everything about her : me contó todo acerca de ella⟩ 5 DISCERN : discernir, notar ⟨I can't tell the difference : no noto la diferencia⟩ — *vi* 1 SAY : decir ⟨I won't tell : no voy a decírselo a nadie⟩ 2 KNOW : saber ⟨you never can tell : nunca se sabe⟩ 3 SHOW : notarse, hacerse sentir ⟨the strain is beginning to tell : la tensión se empieza a notar⟩

teller ['tɛlər] *n* 1 NARRATOR : narrador *m*, -dora *f* 2 *or* **bank teller** : cajero *m*, -ra *f*

temerity [tə'mɛrəti] *n, pl* **-ties** : temeridad *f*

temp ['tɛmp] *n* : empleado *m*, -da *f* temporal

temper¹ ['tɛmpər] *vt* 1 MODERATE : moderar, temperar 2 ANNEAL : templar (acero, etc.)

temper² *n* **1** DISPOSITION : carácter *m*, genio *m* **2** HARDNESS : temple *m*, dureza *f* (de un metal) **3** COMPOSURE : calma *f*, serenidad *f* ⟨to lose one's temper : perder los estribos⟩ **4** RAGE : furia *f* ⟨to fly into a temper : ponerse furioso⟩

temperament ['tɛmpərmənt, -prə-, -pərə-] *n* : temperamento *m*

temperamental [ˌtɛmpər'mɛntəl, -prə-, -pərə-] *adj* : temperamental

temperance ['tɛmprənts] *n* : templanza *f*, temperancia *f*

temperate ['tɛmpərət] *adj* : templado (dícese del clima, etc.), moderado

temperature ['tɛmpər͵tʃur, -prə-, -pərə-, -tʃər] *n* **1** : temperatura *f* **2** FEVER : calentura *f*, fiebre *f*

tempest ['tɛmpəst] *n* : tempestad *f*

tempestuous [tɛm'pɛstʃuəs] *adj* : tempestuoso

temple ['tɛmpəl] *n* **1** : templo *m* (en religión) **2** : sien *f* (en anatomía)

tempo ['tɛm͵po:] *n, pl* **-pi** [-͵pi:] *or* **-pos** : ritmo *m*, tempo *m* (en música)

temporal ['tɛmpərəl] *adj* : temporal

temporarily [ˌtɛmpə'rɛrəli] *adv* : temporalmente, provisionalmente

temporary ['tɛmpə͵rɛri] *adj* : temporal, provisional, provisorio

tempt ['tɛmpt] *vt* : tentar

temptation [tɛmp'teɪʃən] *n* : tentación *f*

tempter ['tɛmptər] *n* : tentador *m*

temptress ['tɛmptrəs] *n* : tentadora *f*

ten¹ ['tɛn] *adj* : diez

ten² *n* **1** : diez *m* (número) **2** : decena *f* ⟨tens of thousands : decenas de millares⟩

tenable ['tɛnəbəl] *adj* : sostenible, defendible

tenacious [tə'neɪʃəs] *adj* : tenaz

tenacity [tə'næsəti] *n* : tenacidad *f*

tenancy ['tɛnəntsi] *n, pl* **-cies** : tenencia *f*, inquilinato *m* (de un inmueble)

tenant ['tɛnənt] *n* : inquilino *m*, -na *f*; arrendatario *m*, -ria *f*

tend ['tɛnd] *vt* : atender, cuidar (de), ocuparse de — *vi* : tender ⟨it tends to benefit the consumer : tiende a beneficiar al consumidor⟩

tendency ['tɛndəntsi] *n, pl* **-cies** : tendencia *f*, proclividad *f*, inclinación *f*

tender¹ ['tɛndər] *vt* : entregar, presentar ⟨I tendered my resignation : presenté mi renuncia⟩

tender² *adj* **1** : tierno, blando ⟨tender steak : bistec tierno⟩ **2** AFFECTIONATE, LOVING : tierno, cariñoso, afectuoso **3** DELICATE : tierno, sensible, delicado

tender³ *n* **1** OFFER : propuesta *f*, oferta *f* (en negocios) **2** **legal tender** : moneda *f* de curso legal

tenderize ['tɛndə͵raɪz] *vt* **-ized; -izing** : ablandar (carnes)

tenderloin ['tɛndr͵lɔɪn] *n* : lomo *f* (de res o de puerco)

tenderly ['tɛndərli] *adv* : tiernamente, con ternura

tenderness ['tɛndərnəs] *n* : ternura *f*

tendon ['tɛndən] *n* : tendón *m*

tendril ['tɛndrɪl] *n* : zarcillo *m*

tenement ['tɛnəmənt] *n* : casa *f* de vecindad

tenet ['tɛnət] *n* : principio *m*

tennis ['tɛnəs] *n* : tenis *m*

tenor ['tɛnər] *n* **1** PURPORT : tenor *m*, significado *m* **2** : tenor *m* (en música)

tenpins ['tɛn͵pɪnz] *npl* : bolos *mpl*, boliche *m*

tense¹ ['tɛnts] *v* **tensed; tensing** *vt* : tensar — *vi* : tensarse, ponerse tenso

tense² *adj* **tenser; tensest** **1** TAUT : tenso, tirante **2** NERVOUS : tenso, nervioso

tense³ *n* : tiempo *m* (de un verbo)

tensely ['tɛntsli] *adv* : tensamente

tenseness ['tɛntsnəs] → **tension**

tension ['tɛntʃən] *n* **1** TAUTNESS : tensión *f*, tirantez *f* **2** STRESS : tensión *f*, nerviosismo *m*, estrés *m*

tent ['tɛnt] *n* : tienda *f* de campaña

tentacle ['tɛntɪkəl] *n* : tentáculo *m*

tentative ['tɛntətɪv] *adj* **1** HESITANT : indeciso, vacilante **2** PROVISIONAL : sujeto a cambios, provisional

tentatively ['tɛntətɪvli] *adv* : provisionalmente

tenth¹ ['tɛnθ] *adj* : décimo

tenth² *n* **1** : décimo *m*, -ma *f* (en una serie) **2** : décimo *m*, décima parte *f*

tenuous ['tɛnjuəs] *adj* : tenue, débil ⟨tenuous reasons : razones poco convincentes⟩

tenuously ['tɛnjuəsli] *adv* : tenuemente, ligeramente

tenure ['tɛnjər] *n* : tenencia *f* (de un cargo o una propiedad), titularidad *f* (de un puesto académico)

tepee ['ti:͵pi:] *n* : tipi *m*

tepid ['tɛpɪd] *adj* : tibio

tequila [tə'ki:lə] *n* : tequila *m*

term¹ ['tərm] *vt* : calificar de, llamar, nombrar

term² *n* **1** PERIOD : término *m*, plazo *m*, período *m* **2** : término *m* (en matemáticas) **3** WORD : término *m*, vocablo *m* ⟨legal terms : términos legales⟩ **4** **terms** *npl* CONDITIONS : términos *mpl*, condiciones *fpl* **5** **terms** *npl* RELATIONS : relaciones *fpl* ⟨to be on good terms with : tener buenas relaciones con⟩ **6** **in terms of** : con respecto a, en cuanto a

terminal¹ ['tərmənəl] *adj* : terminal

terminal² *n* **1** : terminal *m*, polo *m* (en electricidad) **2** : terminal *m* (de una computadora) **3** STATION : terminal *f*, estación *f* (de transporte público)

terminate ['tərmə͵neɪt] *v* **-nated; -nating** *vi* : terminar(se), concluirse — *vt* : terminar, poner fin a

termination [ˌtərmə'neɪʃən] *n* : cese *m*, terminación *f*

terminology [ˌtərmə'nɑlədʒi] *n, pl* **-gies** : terminología *f*

terminus ['tərmənəs] *n, pl* **-ni** [-͵naɪ] *or* **-nuses** **1** END : término *m*, fin *m* **2** : terminal *f* (de transporte público)

termite ['tər,maɪt] *n* : termita *f*
tern ['tərn] *n* : golondrina *f* de mar
terrace[1] ['tɛrəs] *vt* **-raced; -racing** : formar en terrazas, disponer en bancales
terrace[2] *n* **1** PATIO : terraza *f*, patio *m* **2** : terraplén *m*, terraza *f*, bancal *m* (en agricultura)
terra–cotta [,tɛrə'kɑtə] *n* : terracota *f*
terrain [tə'reɪn] *n* : terreno *m*
terrapin ['tɛrəpɪn] *n* : galápago *m* norteamericano
terrarium [tə'ræriəm] *n, pl* **-ia** [-iə] *or* **-iums** : terrario *m*
terrestrial [tə'rɛstriəl] *adj* : terrestre
terrible ['tɛrəbəl] *adj* : atroz, horrible, terrible
terribly ['tɛrəbli] *adv* **1** BADLY : muy mal **2** EXTREMELY : terriblemente, extremadamente
terrier ['tɛriər] *n* : terrier *mf*
terrific [tə'rɪfɪk] *adj* **1** FRIGHTFUL : aterrador **2** EXTRAORDINARY : extraordinario, excepcional **3** EXCELLENT : excelente, estupendo
terrify ['tɛrə,faɪ] *vt* **-fied; -fying** : aterrorizar, aterrar, espantar
terrifying ['tɛrə,faɪɪŋ] *adj* : espantoso, aterrador
territory ['tɛrə,tori] *n, pl* **-ries** : territorio *m* — **territorial** [,tɛrə'toriəl] *adj*
terror ['tɛrər] *n* : terror *m*
terrorism ['tɛrər,ɪzəm] *n* : terrorismo *m*
terrorist[1] ['tɛrərɪst] *adj* : terrorista
terrorist[2] *n* : terrorista *mf*
terrorize ['tɛrər,aɪz] *vt* **-ized; -izing** : aterrorizar
terry ['tɛri] *n, pl* **-ries** *or* **terry cloth** : (tela de) toalla *f*
terse ['tərs] *adj* **terser; tersest** : lacónico, conciso, seco — **tersely** *adv*
tertiary ['tər,ʃi,ɛri] *adj* : terciario
test[1] ['tɛst] *vt* : examinar, evaluar — *vi* : hacer pruebas
test[2] *n* : prueba *f*, examen *m*, test *m* ⟨to put to the test : poner a prueba⟩
testament ['tɛstəmənt] *n* **1** WILL : testamento *m* **2** : Testamento *m* (en la Biblia) ⟨the Old Testament : el Antiguo Testamento⟩
testicle ['tɛstɪkəl] *n* : testículo *m*
testify ['tɛstə,faɪ] *v* **-fied; -fying** *vi* : testificar, atestar, testimoniar — *vt* : testificar
testimonial [,tɛstə'moːniəl] *n* **1** REFERENCE : recomendación *f* **2** TRIBUTE : homenaje *m*, tributo *m*
testimony ['tɛstə,moːni] *n, pl* **-nies** : testimonio *m*, declaración *f*
test tube *n* : probeta *f*, tubo *m* de ensayo
testy ['tɛsti] *adj* **-tier; -est** : irritable
tetanus ['tɛtənəs] *n* : tétano *m*, tétanos *m*
tête–à–tête [,tɛtə'tɛt, ,teɪtə'teɪt] *n* : conversación *f* en privado
tether[1] ['tɛðər] *vt* : atar (con una cuerda), amarrar
tether[2] *n* : atadura *f*, cadena *f*, correa *f*

text ['tɛkst] *n* **1** : texto *m* **2** TOPIC : tema *m* **3** → **textbook**
textbook ['tɛkst,bʊk] *n* : libro *m* de texto
textile ['tɛk,staɪl, 'tɛkstəl] *n* : textil *m*, tela *f* ⟨the textile industry : la industria textil⟩
textual ['tɛkstʃʊəl] *adj* : textual
texture ['tɛkstʃər] *n* : textura *f*
Thai ['taɪ] *n* **1** : tailandés *m*, -desa *f* **2** : tailandés *m* (idioma) — **Thai** *adj*
than[1] ['ðæn] *conj* : que, de ⟨it's worth more than that : vale más que eso⟩ ⟨more than you think : más de lo que piensas⟩
than[2] *prep* : que, de ⟨you're better than he is : eres mejor que él⟩ ⟨more than once : más de una vez⟩
thank ['θæŋk] *vt* : agradecer, darle (las) gracias (a alguien) ⟨thank you! : ¡gracias!⟩ ⟨I thanked her for the present : le di las gracias por el regalo⟩ ⟨I thank you for your help : le agradezco su ayuda⟩
thankful ['θæŋkfəl] *adj* : agradecido
thankfully ['θæŋkfəli] *adv* **1** GRATEFULLY : con agradecimiento **2** FORTUNATELY : afortunadamente, por suerte ⟨thankfully, it's over : se acabó, gracias a Dios⟩
thankfulness ['θæŋkfəlnəs] *n* : agradecimiento *m*, gratitud *f*
thankless ['θæŋkləs] *adj* : ingrato ⟨a thankless task : un trabajo ingrato⟩
thanks ['θæŋks] *npl* **1** : agradecimiento *m* **2 thanks!** : ¡gracias!
Thanksgiving [θæŋks'gɪvɪŋ, 'θæŋks,-] *n* : el día de Acción de Gracias (fiesta estadounidense)
that[1] ['ðæt] *adv* (*in negative constructions*) : tan ⟨it's not that expensive : no es tan caro⟩ ⟨not that much : no tanto⟩
that[2] *adj, pl* **those** : ese, esa, aquel, aquella ⟨do you see those children? : ¿ves a aquellos niños?⟩
that[3] *conj & pron* : que ⟨he said that he was afraid : dijo que tenía miedo⟩ ⟨the book that he wrote : el libro que escribió⟩
that[4] *pron, pl* **those** ['ðoːz] **1** : ése, ésa, eso ⟨that's my father : ése es mi padre⟩ ⟨those are the ones he likes : ésos son los que le gustan⟩ ⟨what's that? : ¿qué es eso?⟩ **2** (*referring to more distant objects or time*) : aquél, aquélla, aquello ⟨those are maples and these are elms : aquéllos son arces y éstos son olmos⟩ ⟨that came to an end : aquello se acabó⟩
thatch[1] ['θætʃ] *vt* : cubrir o techar con paja
thatch[2] *n* : paja *f* (usada para techos)
thaw[1] ['θɔ] *vt* : descongelar — *vi* : derretirse (dícese de la nieve), descongelarse (dícese de los alimentos)
thaw[2] *n* : deshielo *m*

the¹ [ðə, *before vowel sounds usu* ði:] *adv* **1** (*used to indicate comparison*) ⟨the sooner the better : cuanto más pronto, mejor⟩ ⟨she likes this one the best : éste es el que más le gusta⟩ **2** (*used as a conjunction*) : cuanto ⟨the more I learn, the less I understand : cuanto más aprendo, menos entiendo⟩

the² *art* : el, la, los, las ⟨the gloves : los guantes⟩ ⟨the suitcase : la maleta⟩ ⟨forty cookies to the box : cuarenta galletas por caja⟩

theater *or* **theatre** ['θi:ətər] *n* **1** : teatro *m* (edificio) **2** DRAMA : teatro *m*, drama *m*

theatrical [θi'ætrɪkəl] *adj* : teatral, dramático

thee ['ði:] *pron* : te, ti

theft ['θɛft] *n* : robo *m*, hurto *m*

their ['ðɛr] *adj* : su ⟨their friends : sus amigos⟩

theirs ['ðɛrz] *pron* : (el) suyo, (la) suya, (los) suyos, (las) suyas ⟨they came for theirs : vinieron por el suyo⟩ ⟨theirs is bigger : la suya es más grande, la de ellos es más grande⟩ ⟨a brother of theirs : un hermano suyo, un hermano de ellos⟩

them ['ðɛm] *pron* **1** (*as a direct object*) : los (*Spain sometimes* les), las ⟨I know them : los conozco⟩ **2** (*as indirect object*) : les, se ⟨I sent them a letter : les mandé una carta⟩ ⟨give it to them : dáselo (a ellos)⟩ **3** (*as object of a preposition*) : ellos, ellas ⟨go with them : ve con ellos⟩ **4** (*for emphasis*) : ellos, ellas ⟨I wasn't expecting them : no los esperaba a ellos⟩

thematic [θi'mætɪk] *adj* : temático

theme ['θi:m] *n* **1** SUBJECT, TOPIC : tema *m* **2** COMPOSITION : composición *f*, trabajo *m* (escrito) **3** : tema *m* (en música)

themselves [ðəm'sɛlvz, ðɛm-] *pron* **1** (*as a reflexive*) : se, sí ⟨they enjoyed themselves : se divirtieron⟩ ⟨they divided it among themselves : lo repartieron entre sí, se lo repartieron⟩ **2** (*for emphasis*) : ellos mismos, ellas mismas ⟨they built it themselves : ellas mismas lo construyeron⟩

then¹ ['ðɛn] *adv* **1** : entonces, en ese tiempo ⟨I was sixteen then : tenía entonces dieciséis años⟩ ⟨since then : desde entonces⟩ **2** NEXT : después, luego ⟨we'll go to Toronto, then to Winnipeg : iremos a Toronto, y luego a Winnipeg⟩ **3** BESIDES : además, aparte ⟨then there's the tax : y aparte está el impuesto⟩ **4** : entonces, en ese caso ⟨if you like music, then you should attend : si te gusta la música, entonces deberías asistir⟩

then² *adj* : entonces ⟨the then governor of Georgia : el entonces gobernador de Georgia⟩

thence ['ðɛnts, 'θɛnts] *adv* : de ahí, de ahí en adelante

theologian [ˌθi:ə'lo:dʒən] *n* : teólogo *m*, -ga *f*

theological [ˌθi:ə'lɑdʒɪkəl] *adj* : teológico

theology [θi'ɑlədʒi] *n, pl* **-gies** : teología *f*

theorem ['θi:ərəm, 'θirəm] *n* : teorema *m*

theoretical [ˌθi:ə'rɛtɪkəl] *adj* : teórico — **theoretically** *adv*

theorist ['θi:ərɪst] *n* : teórico *m*, -ca *f*

theorize ['θi:ə,raɪz] *vi* **-rized; -rizing** : teorizar

theory ['θi:əri, 'θiri] *n, pl* **-ries** : teoría *f*

therapeutic [ˌθɛrə'pju:ţɪk] *adj* : terapéutico — **therapeutically** *adv*

therapist ['θɛrəpɪst] *n* : terapeuta *mf*

therapy ['θɛrəpi] *n, pl* **-pies** : terapia *f*

there¹ ['ðær] *adv* **1** : ahí, allí, allá ⟨stand over there : párate ahí⟩ ⟨over there : por allí, por allá⟩ ⟨who's there? : ¿quién es?⟩ **2** : ahí, en esto, en eso ⟨there is where we disagree : en eso es donde no estamos de acuerdo⟩

there² *pron* **1** (*introducing a sentence or clause*) ⟨there comes a time to decide : llega un momento en que tiene uno que decidir⟩ **2 there is, there are** : hay ⟨there are many children here : aquí hay muchos niños⟩ ⟨there's a good hotel downtown : hay un buen hotel en el centro⟩

thereabouts [ˌðærə'baʊts, 'ðærə,-] *or* **thereabout** [-'baʊt, -,baʊt] *adv or* **thereabouts** : por ahí, más o menos ⟨at five o'clock or thereabouts : por ahí de las cinco⟩

thereafter [ðær'æftər] *adv* : después ⟨shortly thereafter : poco después⟩

thereby [ðær'baɪ, 'ðær,baɪ] *adv* : de tal modo, de ese manera, así

therefore ['ðær,for] *adv* : por lo tanto, por consiguiente

therein [ðær'ɪn] *adv* **1** : allí adentro, ahí adentro ⟨the contents therein : lo que allí se contiene⟩ **2** : allí, en ese aspecto ⟨therein lies the problem : allí está el problema⟩

thereof [ðær'ʌv, -'ɑv] *adv* : de eso, de esto

thereupon ['ðærə,pɑn, -,pɔn; ˌðærə'pɑn, -'pɔn] *adv* : acto seguido, inmediatamente (después)

therewith [ðær'wɪð, -'wɪθ] *adv* : con eso, con ello

thermal ['θərməl] *adj* **1** : térmico (en física) **2** HOT : termal

thermodynamics [ˌθərmodaɪ'næmɪks] *ns & pl* : termodinámica *f*

thermometer [θər'mɑməţər] *n* : termómetro *m*

thermos ['θərməs] *n* : termo *m*

thermostat ['θərmə,stæt] *n* : termostato *m*

thesaurus [θɪ'sɔrəs] *n, pl* **-sauri** [-'sɔr,aɪ] *or* **-sauruses** [-'sɔrəsəz] : diccionario *m* de sinónimos

these → this

thesis ['θi:sɪs] *n, pl* **theses** ['θi:ˌsi:z] : tesis *f*

they ['ðeɪ] *pron* : ellos, ellas ⟨they are here : están aquí⟩ ⟨they don't know : ellos no saben⟩

they'd ['ðeɪd] (*contraction of* **they had** *or* **they would**) → **have, would**

they'll ['ðeɪl] (*contraction of* **they shall** *or* **they will**) → **shall, will**

they're ['ðɛr] (*contraction of* **they are**) → **be**

they've ['ðeɪv] (*contraction of* **they have**) → **have**

thiamine ['θaɪəmɪn, -ˌmi:n] *n* : tiamina *f*

thick[1] ['θɪk] *adj* **1** : grueso ⟨a thick plank : una tabla gruesa⟩ **2** : espeso, denso ⟨thick syrup : jarabe espeso⟩ — **thickly** *adv*

thick[2] *n* **1 in the thick of** : en medio de ⟨in the thick of the battle : en lo más reñido de la batalla⟩ **2 through thick and thin** : a las duras y a las maduras

thicken ['θɪkən] *vt* : espesar (un líquido) — *vi* : espesarse

thickener ['θɪkənər] *n* : espesante *m*

thicket ['θɪkət] *n* : matorral *m*, maleza *f*, espesura *f*

thickness ['θɪknəs] *n* : grosor *m*, grueso *m*, espesor *m*

thickset ['θɪkˈsɛt] *adj* STOCKY : robusto, fornido

thick–skinned ['θɪkˈskɪnd] *adj* : poco sensible, que no se ofende fácilmente

thief ['θi:f] *n, pl* **thieves** ['θi:vz] : ladrón *m*, -drona *f*

thieve ['θi:v] *v* **thieved; thieving** : hurtar, robar

thievery ['θi:vəri] *n* : hurto *m*, robo *m*, latrocinio *m*

thigh ['θaɪ] *n* : muslo *m*

thighbone ['θaɪˌbo:n] *n* : fémur *m*

thimble ['θɪmbəl] *n* : dedal *m*

thin[1] ['θɪn] *v* **thinned; thinning** *vt* : hacer menos denso, diluir, aguar (un líquido), enrarecer (un gas) — *vi* : diluirse, aguarse (dícese de un líquido), enrarecerse (dícese de un gas)

thin[2] *adj* **thinner; -est 1** LEAN, SLIM : delgado, esbelto, flaco **2** SPARSE : ralo, escaso ⟨a thin beard : una barba rala⟩ **3** WATERY : claro, aguado, diluido **4** FINE : delgado, fino ⟨thin slices : rebanadas finas⟩

thing ['θɪŋ] *n* **1** AFFAIR, MATTER : cosa *f*, asunto *m* ⟨don't talk about those things : no hables de esas cosas⟩ ⟨how are things? : ¿cómo van las cosas?⟩ **2** ACT, EVENT : cosa *f*, suceso *m*, evento *m* ⟨the flood was a terrible thing : la inundación fue una cosa terrible⟩ **3** OBJECT : cosa *f*, objeto *m* ⟨don't forget your things : no olvides tus cosas⟩

think ['θɪŋk] *v* **thought** ['θɔt]; **thinking** *vt* **1** : pensar ⟨I thought to return early : pensaba regresar temprano⟩ **2** BELIEVE : pensar, creer, opinar **3** PONDER : pensar, reflexionar **4** CONCEIVE : ocurrirse, concebir ⟨we've thought up a plan : se nos ha ocurrido un plan⟩ —

vi **1** REASON : pensar, razonar **2** CONSIDER : pensar, considerar ⟨think of your family first : primero piensa en tu familia⟩

thinker ['θɪŋkər] *n* : pensador *m*, -dora *f*

thinly ['θɪnli] *adv* **1** LIGHTLY : ligeramente **2** SPARSELY : escasamente ⟨thinly populated : poco populado⟩ **3** BARELY : apenas

thinness ['θɪnnəs] *n* : delgadez *f*

thin–skinned ['θɪnˈskɪnd] *adj* : susceptible, muy sensible

third[1] ['θərd] *or* **thirdly** [-li] *adv* : en tercer lugar ⟨she came in third : llegó en tercer lugar⟩

third[2] *adj* : tercero ⟨the third day : el tercer día⟩

third[3] *n* **1** : tercero *m*, -ra *f* (en una serie) **2** : tercero *m*, tercera parte *f*

third world *n* **the Third World** : el Tercer Mundo *m*

thirst[1] ['θərst] *vi* **1** : tener sed **2 to thirst for** DESIRE : tener sed de, estar sediento de

thirst[2] *n* : sed *f*

thirsty ['θərsti] *adj* **thirstier; -est** : sediento, que tiene sed ⟨I'm thirsty : tengo sed⟩

thirteen[1] [ˌθərˈti:n] *adj* : trece

thirteen[2] *n* : trece *m*

thirteenth[1] [ˌθərˈti:nθ] *adj* : décimo tercero

thirteenth[2] *n* **1** : decimotercero *m*, -ra *f* (en una serie) **2** : treceavo *m*, treceava parte *f*

thirtieth[1] ['θərtiəθ] *adj* : trigésimo

thirtieth[2] *n* **1** : trigésimo *m*, -ma *f* (en una serie) **2** : treintavo *m*, treintava parte *f*

thirty[1] ['θərti] *adj* : treinta

thirty[2] *n, pl* **thirties** : treinta *m*

this[1] ['ðɪs] *adv* : así, a tal punto ⟨this big : así de grande⟩

this[2] *adj, pl* **these** ['ði:z] : este ⟨these things : estas cosas⟩ ⟨read this book : lee este libro⟩

this[3] *pron, pl* **these** : esto ⟨what's this? : ¿qué es esto?⟩ ⟨this wasn't here yesterday : esto no estaba aquí ayer⟩

thistle ['θɪsəl] *n* : cardo *m*

thong ['θɔŋ] *n* **1** STRAP : correa *f*, tira *f* **2** FLIP-FLOP : chancla *f*, chancleta *f*

thorax ['θor̩æks] *n, pl* **-raxes** *or* **-races** ['θorəˌsi:z] : tórax *m*

thorn ['θɔrn] *n* : espina *f*

thorny ['θɔrni] *adj* **thornier; -est** : espinoso

thorough ['θəro:] *adj* **1** CONSCIENTIOUS : concienzudo, meticuloso **2** COMPLETE : absoluto, completo — **thoroughly** *adv*

thoroughbred ['θəroˌbrɛd] *adj* : de pura sangre (dícese de un caballo)

Thoroughbred *n* *or* **Thoroughbred horse** : pura sangre *mf*

thoroughfare ['θəroˌfær] *n* : vía *f* pública, carretera *f*

thoroughness ['θəronəs] *n* : esmero *m*, meticulosidad *f*

those → **that**
thou ['ðaʊ] *pron* : tú
though[1] ['ðo:] *adv* **1** HOWEVER, NEVERTHELESS : sin embargo, no obstante **2 as** ~ : como si ⟨as though nothing had happened : como si nada hubiera pasado⟩
though[2] *conj* : aunque, a pesar de ⟨though it was raining, we went out : salimos a pesar de la lluvia⟩
thought[1] → **think**
thought[2] ['θɔt] *n* **1** THINKING : pensamiento *m*, ideas *fpl* ⟨Western thought : el pensamiento occidental⟩ **2** COGITATION : pensamiento *m*, reflexión *f*, raciocinio *m* **3** IDEA : idea *f*, ocurrencia *f* ⟨it was just a thought : fue sólo una idea⟩
thoughtful ['θɔtfəl] *adj* **1** PENSIVE : pensativo, meditabundo **2** CONSIDERATE : considerado, atento, cortés — **thoughtfully** *adv*
thoughtfulness ['θɔtfəlnəs] *n* : consideración *f*, atención *f*, cortesía *f*
thoughtless ['θɔtləs] *adj* **1** CARELESS : descuidado, negligente **2** INCONSIDERATE : desconsiderado — **thoughtlessly** *adv*
thousand[1] ['θaʊzənd] *adj* : mil
thousand[2] *n, pl* **-sands** *or* **-sand** : mil *m*
thousandth[1] ['θaʊzəntθ] *adj* : milésimo
thousandth[2] *n* **1** : milésimo *m*, -ma *f* (en una serie) **2** : milésimo *m*, milésima parte *f*
thrash ['θræʃ] *vt* **1** → **thresh 2** BEAT : golpear, azotar, darle una paliza (a alguien) **3** FLAIL : sacudir, agitar bruscamente
thread[1] ['θrɛd] *vt* **1** : enhilar, enhebrar (una aguja) **2** STRING : ensartar (cuentas en un hilo) **3 to thread one's way** : abrirse paso
thread[2] *n* **1** : hilo *m*, hebra *f* ⟨needle and thread : aguja e hilo⟩ ⟨the thread of an argument : el hilo de un debate⟩ **2** : rosca *f*, filete *m* (de un tornillo)
threadbare ['θrɛd,bær] *adj* **1** SHABBY, WORN : raído, gastado **2** TRITE : trillado, tópico, manido
threat ['θrɛt] *n* : amenaza *f*
threaten ['θrɛtən] *v* : amenazar
threatening ['θrɛtənɪŋ] *adj* : amenazador — **threateningly** *adv*
three[1] ['θri:] *adj* : tres
three[2] *n* : tres *m*
3–D ['θri:'di:] *adj* → **three–dimensional**
three–dimensional ['θri:də'mɛntʃənəl] *adj* : tridimensional
threefold ['θri:,fo:ld] *adj* TRIPLE : triple
three hundred[1] *adj* : trescientos
three hundred[2] *n* : trescientos *m*
threescore ['θri:'skor] *adj* SIXTY : sesenta
thresh ['θrɛʃ] *vt* : trillar (grano)
thresher ['θrɛʃər] *n* : trilladora *f*
threshold ['θrɛʃ,ho:ld, -,o:ld] *n* : umbral *m*
threw → **throw**[1]

thrice ['θraɪs] *adv* : tres veces
thrift ['θrɪft] *n* : economía *f*, frugalidad *f*
thriftless ['θrɪftləs] *adj* : despilfarrador, manirroto
thrifty ['θrɪfti] *adj* **thriftier; -est** : económico, frugal — **thriftily** ['θrɪftəli] *adv*
thrill[1] ['θrɪl] *vt* : emocionar — *vi* **to thrill to** : dejarse conmover por, estremecerse con
thrill[2] *n* : emoción *f*
thriller ['θrɪlər] *n* **1** : evento *m* emocionante **2** : obra *f* de suspenso
thrilling ['θrɪlɪŋ] *adj* : emocionante, excitante
thrive ['θraɪv] *vi* **throve** ['θro:v] *or* **thrived; thriven** ['θrɪvən] **1** FLOURISH : florecer, crecer abundantemente **2** PROSPER : prosperar
throat ['θro:t] *n* : garganta *f*
throaty ['θro:ți] *adj* **throatier; -est** : ronco (dícese de la voz)
throb[1] ['θrɑb] *vi* **throbbed; throbbing** : palpitar, latir (dícese del corazón), vibrar (dícese de un motor, etc.)
throb[2] *n* : palpitación *f*, latido *m*, vibración *f*
throe ['θro:] *n* **1** PAIN, SPASM : espasmo *m*, dolor *m* ⟨the throes of childbirth : los dolores de parto⟩ **2 throes** *npl* : lucha *f* larga y ardua ⟨in the throes of : en el medio de⟩
throne ['θro:n] *n* : trono *m*
throng[1] ['θrɔŋ] *vt* CROWD : atestar, atiborrar, llenar — *vi* : aglomerarse, amontonarse
throng[2] *n* : muchedumbre *f*, gentío *m*, multitud *f*
throttle[1] ['θrɑtəl] *vt* **-tled; -tling 1** STRANGLE : estrangular, ahogar **2 to throttle down** : desacelerar (un motor)
throttle[2] *n* **1** : válvula *f* reguladora **2 at full throttle** : a toda máquina
through[1] ['θru:] *adv* **1** : a través, de un lado a otro ⟨let them through : déjenlos pasar⟩ **2** : de principio a fin ⟨she read the book through : leyó el libro de principio a fin⟩ **3** COMPLETELY : completamente ⟨soaked through : completamente empapado⟩
through[2] *adj* **1** DIRECT : directo ⟨a through train : un tren directo⟩ **2** FINISHED : terminado, acabado ⟨we're through : hemos terminado⟩
through[3] *prep* **1** : a través de, por ⟨through the door : por la puerta⟩ ⟨a road through the woods : un camino que atraviesa el bosque⟩ **2** BETWEEN : entre ⟨a path through the trees : un sendero entre los árboles⟩ **3** BECAUSE OF : a causa de, como consecuencia de **4** (*in expressions of time*) ⟨through the night : durante la noche⟩ ⟨to go through an experience : pasar por una experiencia⟩ **5** : a, hasta ⟨from Monday through Friday : de lunes a viernes⟩

throughout¹ [θru:'aʊt] *adv* **1** EVERY-WHERE : por todas partes **2** THROUGH : desde el principio hasta el fin de (algo)
throughout² *prep* **1** : en todas partes de, a través de ⟨throughout the United States : en todo Estados Unidos⟩ **2** : de principio a fin de, durante ⟨throughout the winter : durante todo el invierno⟩
throve → **thrive**
throw¹ [θro:] *vt* **threw** [θru:]; **thrown** [θro:n]; **throwing** **1** TOSS : tirar, lanzar, echar, arrojar, aventar *Col, Mex* ⟨to throw a ball : tirar una pelota⟩ **2** UNSEAT : desmontar (a un jinete) **3** CAST : proyectar ⟨it threw a long shadow : proyectó una sombra larga⟩ **4 to throw a party** : dar una fiesta **5 to throw into confusion** : desconcertar **6 to throw out** DISCARD : botar, tirar (en la basura)
throw² *n* TOSS : tiro *m*, tirada *f*, lanzamiento *m*, lance *m* (de dados)
thrower [θro:ər] *n* : lanzador *m*, -dora *f*
throw up *v* VOMIT : vomitar, devolver
thrush [θrʌʃ] *n* : tordo *m*, zorzal *m*
thrust¹ [θrʌst] *vt* **thrust; thrusting** **1** SHOVE : empujar bruscamente **2** PLUNGE, STAB : apuñalar, clavar ⟨he thrust a dagger into her heart : la apuñaló en el corazón⟩ **3 to thrust one's way** : abrirse paso **4 to thrust upon** : imponer a
thrust² *n* **1** PUSH, SHOVE : empujón *m*, empellón *m* **2** LUNGE : estocada *f* (en esgrima) **3** IMPETUS : ímpetu *m*, impulso *m*, propulsión *f* (de un motor)
thud¹ [θʌd] *vi* **thudded; thudding** : producir un ruido sordo
thud² *n* : ruido *m* sordo (que produce un objeto al caer)
thug [θʌg] *n* : matón *m*
thumb¹ [θʌm] *vt* : hojear (con el pulgar)
thumb² *n* : pulgar *m*, dedo *m* pulgar
thumbnail [θʌm,neɪl] *n* : uña *f* del pulgar
thumbtack [θʌm,tæk] *n* : tachuela *f*, chinche *f*
thump¹ [θʌmp] *vt* POUND : golpear, aporrear — *vi* : latir con vehemencia (dícese del corazón)
thump² *n* THUD : ruido *m* sordo
thunder¹ [θʌndər] *vi* **1** : tronar ⟨it rained and thundered all night : llovió y tronó durante la noche⟩ **2** BOOM : retumbar, bramar, resonar — *vt* ROAR, SHOUT : decir a gritos, vociferar
thunder² *n* : truenos *mpl*
thunderbolt [θʌndər,bo:lt] *n* : rayo *m*
thunderclap [θʌndər,klæp] *n* : trueno *m*
thunderous [θʌndərəs] *adj* : atronador, ensordecedor, estruendoso
thundershower [θʌndər,ʃaʊər] *n* : lluvia *f* con truenos y relámpagos
thunderstorm [θʌndər,stɔrm] *n* : tormenta *f* con truenos y relámpagos
thunderstruck [θʌndər,strʌk] *adj* : atónito

Thursday [θərz,deɪ, -di] *n* : jueves *m*
thus [ðʌs] *adv* **1** : así, de esta manera **2** SO : hasta (cierto punto) ⟨the weather's been nice thus far : hasta ahora ha hecho buen tiempo⟩ **3** HENCE : por consiguiente, por lo tanto
thwart [θwɔrt] *vt* : frustrar
thy [ðaɪ] *adj* : tu
thyme [taɪm, θaɪm] *n* : tomillo *m*
thyroid [θaɪ,rɔɪd] *n or* **thyroid gland** : tiroides *mf*, glándula *f* tiroidea
thyself [ðaɪ'sɛlf] *pron* : ti, ti mismo
tiara [ti'ærə, -'ɑr-] *n* : diadema *f*
Tibetan [tə'bɛtən] *n* **1** : tibetano *m*, -na *f* **2** : tibetano *m* (idioma) — **Tibetan** *adj*
tibia [tɪbiə] *n, pl* **-iae** [-bi,i:] : tibia *f*
tic [tɪk] *n* : tic *m*
tick¹ [tɪk] *vi* **1** : hacer tictac **2** OPERATE, RUN : operar, andar (dícese de un mecanismo) ⟨what makes him tick? : ¿qué es lo que lo mueve?⟩ — *vt or* **to tick off** CHECK : marcar
tick² *n* **1** : tictac *m* (de un reloj) **2** CHECK : marca *f* **3** : garrapata *f* (insecto)
ticket¹ [tɪkət] *vt* LABEL : etiquetar
ticket² *n* **1** : boleto *m*, entrada *f* (de un espectáculo), pasaje *m* (de avión, tren, etc.) **2** SLATE : lista *f* de candidatos
tickle¹ [tɪkəl] *v* **-led; -ling** *vt* **1** AMUSE : divertir, hacerle gracia (a alguien) **2** : hacerle cosquillas (a alguien) ⟨don't tickle me! : ¡no me hagas cosquillas!⟩ — *vi* : picar
tickle² *n* : cosquilleo *m*, cosquillas *fpl*, picor *m* (en la garganta)
ticklish [tɪkəlɪʃ] *adj* **1** : cosquilloso (dícese de una persona) **2** DELICATE, TRICKY : delicado, peliagudo
tidal [taɪdəl] *adj* : de marea, relativo a la marea
tidal wave *n* : maremoto *m*
tidbit [tɪd,bɪt] *n* **1** BITE, SNACK : bocado *m*, golosina *f* **2** : dato *m* o noticia *f* interesante ⟨useful tidbits of information : informaciones útiles⟩
tide¹ [taɪd] *vt* **tided; tiding** *or* **to tide over** : proveer lo necesario para aguantar una dificultad ⟨this money will tide you over until you find work : este dinero te mantendrá hasta que encuentres empleo⟩
tide² *n* **1** : marea *f* **2** CURRENT : corriente *f* (de eventos, opiniones, etc.)
tidily [taɪdəli] *adv* : ordenadamente
tidiness [taɪdinəs] *n* : aseo *m*, limpieza *f*, orden *m*
tidings [taɪdɪŋz] *npl* : nuevas *fpl*
tidy¹ [taɪdi] *vt* **-died; -dying** : asear, limpiar, poner en orden
tidy² *adj* **-dier; -est** **1** CLEAN, NEAT : limpio, aseado, en orden **2** SUBSTANTIAL : grande, considerable ⟨a tidy sum : una suma considerable⟩
tie¹ [taɪ] *v* **tied; tying** *or* **tieing** *vt* **1** : atar, amarrar ⟨to tie a knot : atar un nudo⟩ ⟨to tie one's shoelaces : atarse los cordones⟩ **2** BIND, UNITE : ligar, atar **3** : empatar ⟨they tied the score : em-

pataron el marcador⟩ — *vi* : empatar ⟨the two teams were tied : los dos equipos empataron⟩

tie² *n* **1** : ligadura *f*, cuerda *f*, cordón *m* (para atar algo) **2** BOND, LINK : atadura *f*, ligadura *f*, vínculo *m*, lazo *m* ⟨family ties : lazos familiares⟩ **3** *or* **railroad tie** : traviesa *f* **4** DRAW : empate *m* (en deportes) **5** NECKTIE : corbata *f*

tier ['tɪr] *n* : hilera *f*, escalón *m*

tiff ['tɪf] *n* : disgusto *m*, disputa *f*

tiger ['taɪgər] *n* : tigre *m*

tight¹ ['taɪt] *adv* TIGHTLY : bien, fuerte ⟨shut it tight : ciérralo bien⟩

tight² *adj* **1** : bien cerrado, hermético ⟨a tight seal : un cierre hermético⟩ **2** STRICT : estricto, severo **3** TAUT : tirante, tenso **4** SNUG : apretado, ajustado, ceñido ⟨a tight dress : un vestido ceñido⟩ **5** DIFFICULT : difícil ⟨to be in a tight spot : estar en un aprieto⟩ **6** STINGY : apretado, avaro, agarrado *fam* **7** CLOSE : reñido ⟨a tight game : un juego reñido⟩ **8** SCARCE : escaso ⟨money is tight : escasea el dinero⟩

tighten ['taɪtən] *vt* : tensar (una cuerda, etc.), apretar (un nudo, un tornillo, etc.), apretarse (el cinturón), reforzar (las reglas)

tightly ['taɪtli] *adv* : bien, fuerte

tightness ['taɪtnəs] *n* : lo apretado, lo tenso, tensión *f*

tightrope ['taɪt,ro:p] *n* : cuerda *f* floja

tights ['taɪts] *npl* : leotardo *m*, malla *f*

tightwad ['taɪt,wɑd] *n* : avaro *m*, -ra *f*; tacaño *m*, -ña *f*

tigress ['taɪgrəs] *n* : tigresa *f*

tile¹ ['taɪl] *vt* **tiled; tiling** : embaldosar (un piso), revestir de azulejos (una pared), tejar (un techo)

tile² *n* **1** *or* **floor tile** : losa *f*, baldosa *f*, mosaico *m Mex* (de un piso) **2** : azulejo *m* (de una pared) **3** : teja *f* (de un techo)

till¹ ['tɪl] *vt* : cultivar, labrar

till² *n* : caja *f*, caja *f* registradora

till³ *prep & conj* → **until**

tiller ['tɪlər] *n* **1** : cultivador *m*, -dora *f* (de la tierra) **2** : caña *f* del timón (de un barco)

tilt¹ ['tɪlt] *vt* : ladear, inclinar — *vi* : ladearse, inclinarse

tilt² *n* **1** SLANT : inclinación *f* **2** **at full tilt** : a toda velocidad

timber ['tɪmbər] *n* **1** : madera *f* (para construcción) **2** BEAM : viga *f*

timberland ['tɪmbər,lænd] *n* : bosque *m* maderero

timbre ['tæmbər, 'tɪm-] *n* : timbre *m*

time¹ ['taɪm] *vt* **timed; timing 1** SCHEDULE : fijar la hora de, calcular el momento oportuno para **2** CLOCK : cronometrar, medir el tiempo de (una competencia, etc.)

time² *n* **1** : tiempo *m* ⟨the passing of time : el paso del tiempo⟩ ⟨she doesn't have time : no tiene tiempo⟩ **2** MOMENT : tiempo *m*, momento *m* ⟨this is not the time to bring it up : no es el momento de sacar el tema⟩ **3** : vez *f* ⟨she called you three times : te llamó tres veces⟩ ⟨three times greater : tres veces mayor⟩ **4** AGE : tiempo *m*, era *f* ⟨in your grandparents' time : en el tiempo de tus abuelos⟩ **5** TEMPO : tiempo *m*, ritmo *m* (en música) **6** : hora *f* ⟨what time is it? : ¿qué hora es?⟩ ⟨it's time for dinner : es hora de comer⟩ ⟨at the usual time : a la hora acostumbrada⟩ ⟨to keep time : ir a la hora⟩ ⟨to lose time : atrasar⟩ **7** EXPERIENCE : rato *m*, experiencia *f* ⟨we had a nice time together : pasamos juntos un rato agradable⟩ ⟨to have a rough time : pasarlo mal⟩ ⟨have a good time! : ¡que se diviertan!⟩ **8** **at times** SOMETIMES : a veces **9** **for the time being** : por el momento, momento **10** **from time to time** OCCASIONALLY : de vez en cuando **11** **in time** PUNCTUALLY : a tiempo **12** **in time** EVENTUALLY : con el tiempo **13** **time after time** : una y otra vez

timekeeper ['taɪm,ki:pər] *n* : cronometrador *m*, -dora *f*

timeless ['taɪmləs] *adj* : eterno

timely ['taɪmli] *adj* **-lier; -est** : oportuno

timepiece ['taɪm,pi:s] *n* : reloj *m*

timer ['taɪmər] *n* : temporizador *m*, cronómetro *m*

times ['taɪmz] *prep* : por ⟨3 times 4 is 12 : 3 por 4 son 12⟩

timetable ['taɪm,teɪbəl] *n* : horario *m*

timid ['tɪmɪd] *adj* : tímido — **timidly** *adv*

timidity [tə'mɪdəti] *n* : timidez *f*

timorous ['tɪmərəs] *adj* : timorato, miedoso

timpani ['tɪmpəni] *npl* : timbales *mpl*

tin ['tɪn] *n* **1** : estaño *m*, hojalata *f* (metal) **2** CAN : lata *f*, bote *m*, envase *m*

tincture ['tɪŋktʃər] *n* : tintura *f*

tinder ['tɪndər] *n* : yesca *f*

tine ['taɪn] *n* : diente *m* (de un tenedor, etc.)

tinfoil ['tɪn,fɔɪl] *n* : papel *m* (de) aluminio

tinge¹ ['tɪndʒ] *vt* **tinged; tingeing** *or* **tinging** ['tɪndʒɪŋ] TINT : matizar, teñir ligeramente

tinge² *n* **1** TINT : matiz *m*, tinte *m* sutil **2** TOUCH : dejo *m*, sensación *f* ligera

tingle¹ ['tɪŋgəl] *vi* **-gled; -gling** : sentir (un) hormigueo, sentir (un) cosquilleo

tingle² *n* : hormigueo *m*, cosquilleo *m*

tinker ['tɪŋkər] *vi* **to tinker with** : arreglar con pequeños ajustes, toquetear (con intento de arreglar)

tinkle¹ ['tɪŋkəl] *vi* **-kled; -kling** : tintinear

tinkle² *n* : tintineo *m*

tinsel ['tɪntsəl] *n* : oropel *m*

tint¹ ['tɪnt] *vt* : teñir, colorear

tint² *n* : tinte *m*

tiny ['taɪni] *adj* **-nier; -est** : diminuto, minúsculo

tip¹ ['tɪp] *v* **tipped; tipping** *vt* **1** *or* **to tip over** : volcar, voltear, hacer caer **2** TILT : ladear, inclinar ⟨to tip one's hat : saludar con el sombrero⟩ **3** TAP : tocar, golpear ligeramente **4** : darle una propina (a un mesero, etc.) ⟨I tipped him $5 : le di $5 de propina⟩ **5** : adornar o cubrir la punta de ⟨wings tipped in red : alas que tienen las puntas rojas⟩ **6 to tip off** : dar información a — *vi* TILT : ladearse, inclinarse

tip² *n* **1** END, POINT : punta *f*, extremo *m* ⟨on the tip of one's tongue : en la punta de la lengua⟩ **2** GRATUITY : propina *f* **3** ADVICE, INFORMATION : consejo *m*, información *f* (confidencial)

tip–off ['tɪp,ɔf] *n* **1** SIGN : indicación *f*, señal *f* **2** TIP : información *f* (confidencial)

tipple ['tɪpəl] *vi* **-pled; -pling** : tomarse unas copas

tipsy ['tɪpsi] *adj* **-sier; -est** : achispado

tiptoe¹ ['tɪp,to:] *vi* **-toed; -toeing** : caminar de puntillas

tiptoe² *adv* : de puntillas

tiptoe³ *n* : punta *f* del pie

tip–top¹ ['tɪp'tɑp, -,tɑp] *adj* EXCELLENT : excelente

tip–top² *n* SUMMIT : cumbre *f*, cima *f*

tirade ['taɪ,reɪd] *n* : diatriba *f*

tire¹ ['taɪr] *v* **tired; tiring** *vt* : cansar, agotar, fatigar — *vi* : cansarse

tire² *n* : llanta *f*, neumático *m*, goma *f*

tired ['taɪrd] *adj* : cansado, agotado, fatigado ⟨to get tired : cansarse⟩

tireless ['taɪrləs] *adj* : incansable, infatigable — **tirelessly** *adv*

tiresome ['taɪrsəm] *adj* : fastidioso, pesado, tedioso — **tiresomely** *adv*

tissue ['tɪ,ʃu:] *n* **1** : pañuelo *m* de papel **2** : tejido *m* ⟨lung tissue : tejido pulmonar⟩

titanic [taɪ'tænɪk, tə-] *adj* GIGANTIC : titánico, gigantesco

titanium [taɪ'teɪniəm, tə-] *n* : titanio *m*

titillate ['tɪtəl,eɪt] *vt* **-lated; -lating** : excitar, estimular placenteramente

title¹ ['taɪtəl] *vt* **-tled; -tling** : titular, intitular

title² *n* : título *m*

titter¹ ['tɪtər] *vi* GIGGLE : reírse tontamente

titter² *n* : risita *f*, risa *f* tonta

tizzy ['tɪzi] *n, pl* **tizzies** : estado *m* agitado o nervioso ⟨I'm all in a tizzy : estoy todo alterado⟩

TNT [,ti:,ɛn'ti:] *n* : TNT *m*

to¹ ['tu:] *adv* **1** : a un estado consciente ⟨to come to : volver en sí⟩ **2 to and fro** : de aquí para allá, de un lado para otro

to² *prep* **1** (*indicating a place*) : a ⟨to go to the doctor : ir al médico⟩ ⟨I'm going to John's : voy a la casa de John⟩ **2** TOWARD : a, hacia ⟨two miles to the south : dos millas hacia el sur⟩ **3** ON : en, sobre ⟨apply salve to the wound : póngale ungüento a la herida⟩ **4** UP TO : hasta ⟨to a degree : hasta cierto grado⟩ ⟨from head to toe : de pies a cabeza⟩ **5** (*in expressions of time*) ⟨it's quarter to seven : son las siete menos

cuarto⟩ **6** UNTIL : a, hasta ⟨from May to December : de mayo a diciembre⟩ **7** (*indicating belonging or possession*) : de, a ⟨the key to the lock : la llave del candado⟩ **8** (*indicating response*) : a ⟨dancing to the rhythm : bailando al compás⟩ **9** (*indicating comparison or proportion*) : a ⟨it's similar to mine : es parecido al mío⟩ ⟨they won 4 to 2 : ganaron 4 a 2⟩ **10** (*indicating agreement or conformity*) : a, de acuerdo con ⟨made to order : hecho a la orden⟩ ⟨to my knowledge : a mi saber⟩ **11** (*indicating inclusion*) : en cada, por ⟨twenty to the box : veinte por caja⟩ **12** (*used to form the infinitive*) ⟨to understand : entender⟩ ⟨to go away : irse⟩

toad ['to:d] *n* : sapo *m*

toadstool ['to:d,stu:l] *n* : hongo *m* (no comestible)

toady ['to:di] *n, pl* **toadies** : adulador *m*, -dora *f*

toast¹ ['to:st] *vt* **1** : tostar (pan) **2** : brindar por ⟨to toast the victors : brindar por los vencedores⟩ **3** WARM : calentar ⟨to toast oneself : calentarse⟩

toast² *n* **1** : pan *m* tostado, tostadas *fpl* **2** : brindis *m* ⟨to propose a toast : proponer un brindis⟩

toaster ['to:stər] *n* : tostador *m*

tobacco [tə'bæko:] *n, pl* **-cos** : tabaco *m*

toboggan¹ [tə'bagən] *vi* : deslizarse en tobogán

toboggan² *n* : tobogán *m*

today¹ [tə'deɪ] *adv* **1** : hoy ⟨she arrives today : hoy llega⟩ **2** NOWADAYS : hoy en día

today² *n* : hoy *m* ⟨today is a holiday : hoy es día de fiesta⟩

toddle ['tadəl] *vi* **-dled; -dling** : hacer pininos, hacer pinitos

toddler ['tadələr] *n* : niño *m* pequeño, niña *f* pequeña (que comienza a caminar)

to–do [tə'du:] *n, pl* **to–dos** [-'du:z] FUSS : lío *m*, alboroto *m*

toe ['to:] *n* : dedo *m* del pie

toenail ['to:,neɪl] *n* : uña *f* del pie

toffee *or* **toffy** ['tɔfi, 'ta-] *n, pl* **toffees** *or* **toffies** : caramelo *m* elaborado con azúcar y mantequilla

toga ['to:gə] *n* : toga *f*

together [tə'gɛðər] *adv* **1** : juntamente, juntos (el uno con el otro) ⟨Susan and Sarah work together : Susan y Sarah trabajan juntas⟩ **2 ~ with** : junto con

togetherness [tə'gɛðərnəs] *n* : unión *f*, compañerismo *m*

togs ['tagz, 'tɔgz] *npl* : ropa *f*

toil¹ ['tɔɪl] *vi* : trabajar arduamente

toil² *n* : trabajo *m* arduo

toilet ['tɔɪlət] *n* **1** : arreglo *m* personal **2** BATHROOM : (cuarto de) baño *m*, servicios *mpl* (públicos), sanitario *m* Col, Mex, Ven **3** : inodoro *m* ⟨to flush the toilet : jalar la cadena⟩

toilet paper *n* : papel *m* higiénico

toiletries ['tɔɪlətriz] *npl* : artículos *mpl* de tocador

token ['to:kən] *n* **1** PROOF, SIGN : prueba *f*, muestra *f*, señal *m* **2** SYMBOL : símbolo *m* **3** SOUVENIR : recuerdo *m* **4** : ficha *f* (para transporte público, etc.)

told → **tell**

tolerable ['talərəbəl] *adj* : tolerable — **tolerably** [-bli] *adv*

tolerance ['talərənts] *n* : tolerancia *f*

tolerant ['talərənt] *adj* : tolerante — **tolerantly** *adv*

tolerate ['talə,reɪt] *vt* **-ated; -ating 1** ACCEPT : tolerar, aceptar **2** BEAR, ENDURE : tolerar, aguantar, soportar

toleration [,talə'reɪʃən] *n* : tolerancia *f*

toll¹ ['to:l] *vt* : tañer, sonar (una campana) — *vi* : sonar, doblar (dícese de las campanas)

toll² *n* **1** : peaje *m* (de una carretera, un puente, etc.) **2** CASUALTIES : pérdida *f*, número *m* de víctimas **3** TOLLING : tañido *m* (de campanas)

tollbooth ['to:l,bu:θ] *n* : caseta *f* de peaje

tollgate ['to:l,geɪt] *n* : barrera *f* de peaje

tomahawk ['tamə,hɔk] *n* : hacha *f* de guerra (de los indígenas norteamericanos)

tomato [tə'meɪto, -'ma-] *n, pl* **-toes** : tomate *m*

tomb ['tu:m] *n* : sepulcro *m*, tumba *f*

tomboy ['tam,bɔɪ] *n* : marimacho *mf*; niña *f* que se porta como muchacho

tombstone ['tu:m,sto:n] *n* : lápida *f*

tomcat ['tam,kæt] *n* : gato *m* (macho)

tome ['to:m] *n* : tomo *m*

tomorrow¹ [tə'maro] *adv* : mañana

tomorrow² *n* : mañana *m*

tom–tom ['tam,tam] *n* : tam-tam *m*

ton ['tən] *n* : tonelada *f*

tone¹ ['to:n] *vt* **toned; toning 1** *or* **to tone down** : atenuar, suavizar, moderar **2** *or* **to tone up** STRENGTHEN : tonificar, vigorizar

tone² *n* : tono *m* ⟨in a friendly tone : en tono amistoso⟩ ⟨a greyish tone : un tono grisáceo⟩

tongs ['taŋz, 'tɔŋz] *npl* : tenazas *fpl*

tongue ['tʌŋ] *n* **1** : lengua *f* **2** LANGUAGE : lengua *f*, idioma *m*

tongue–tied ['tʌŋ,taɪd] *adj* **to get tongue–tied** : trabársele la lengua a uno

tonic¹ ['tanɪk] *adj* : tónico

tonic² *n* **1** : tónico *m* **2** *or* **tonic water** : tónica *f*

tonight¹ [tə'naɪt] *adv* : esta noche

tonight² *n* : esta noche *f*

tonsil ['tantsəl] *n* : amígdala *f*, angina *f* *Mex*

tonsillitis [,tantsə'laɪtəs] *n* : amigdalitis *f*, anginas *fpl Mex*

too ['tu:] *adv* **1** ALSO : también **2** EXCESSIVELY : demasiado ⟨it's too hot in here : aquí hace demasiado calor⟩

took → **take¹**

tool¹ ['tu:l] *vt* **1** : fabricar, confeccionar (con herramientas) **2** EQUIP : instalar maquinaria en (una fábrica)

tool² *n* : herramienta *f*

toolbox ['tu:l,baks] *n* : caja *f* de herramientas

toot¹ ['tu:t] *vt* : sonar (un claxon o un pito)

toot² *n* : pitido *m*, bocinazo *m* (de un claxon)

tooth ['tu:θ] *n, pl* **teeth** ['ti:θ] : diente *m*

toothache ['tu:θ,eɪk] *n* : dolor *m* de muelas

toothbrush ['tu:θ,brʌʃ] *n* : cepillo *m* de dientes

toothless ['tu:θləs] *adj* : desdentado

toothpaste ['tu:θ,peɪst] *n* : pasta *f* de dientes, crema *f* dental, dentífrico *m*

toothpick ['tu:θ,pɪk] *n* : palillo *m* (de dientes), mondadientes *m*

top¹ ['tap] *vt* **topped; topping 1** COVER : cubrir, coronar **2** SURPASS : sobrepasar, superar **3** CLEAR : pasar por encima de

top² *adj* : superior ⟨the top shelf : la repisa superior⟩ ⟨one of the top lawyers : uno de los mejores abogados⟩

top³ *n* **1** : parte *f* superior, cumbre *f*, cima *f* (de un monte, etc.) ⟨to climb to the top : subir a la cumbre⟩ **2** COVER : tapa *f*, cubierta *f* **3** : trompo *m* (juguete) **4 on top of** : encima de

topaz ['to:,pæz] *n* : topacio *m*

topcoat ['tap,ko:t] *n* : sobretodo *m*, abrigo *m*

topic ['tapɪk] *n* : tema *m*, tópico *m*

topical ['tapɪkəl] *adj* : de interés actual

topmost ['tap,mo:st] *adj* : más alto

top–notch ['tap'natʃ] *adj* : de lo mejor, de primera categoría

topographic [,tapə'græfɪk] *or* **topographical** [-fɪkəl] *adj* : topográfico

topography [tə'pagrəfi] *n, pl* **-phies** : topografía *f*

topple ['tapəl] *v* **-pled; -pling** *vi* : caerse, venirse abajo — *vt* : volcar, derrocar (un gobierno, etc.)

topsoil ['tap,sɔɪl] *n* : capa *f* superior del suelo

topsy–turvy [,tapsi'tərvi] *adv & adj* : patas arriba, al revés

torch ['tɔrtʃ] *n* : antorcha *f*

tore → **tear¹**

torment¹ [tɔr'mɛnt, 'tɔr,-] *vt* : atormentar, torturar, martirizar

torment² ['tɔr,mɛnt] *n* : tormento *m*, suplicio *m*, martirio *m*

tormentor [tɔr'mɛntər] *n* : atormentador *m*, -dora *f*

torn *pp* → **tear¹**

tornado [tɔr'neɪdo] *n, pl* **-does** *or* **-dos** : tornado *m*

torpedo¹ [tɔr'pi:do] *vt* : torpedear

torpedo² *n, pl* **-does** : torpedo *m*

torpid ['tɔrpɪd] *adj* **1** SLUGGISH : aletargado **2** APATHETIC : apático

torpor ['tɔrpər] *n* : letargo *m*, apatía *f*

torrent ['tɔrənt] *n* : torrente *m*

torrential [tə'rɛntʃəl, tə-] *adj* : torrencial

torrid ['tɔrɪd] *adj* : tórrido

torso ['tɔr,so:] *n, pl* **-sos** *or* **-si** [-,si:] : torso *m*

tortilla [tɔr'tiːjə] *n* : tortilla *f* (de maíz)
tortoise ['tɔrtəs] *n* : tortuga *f* (terrestre)
tortoiseshell ['tɔrtəs,ʃɛl] *n* : carey *m*, concha *f*
tortuous ['tɔrtʃuəs] *adj* : tortuoso
torture[1] ['tɔrtʃər] *vt* **-tured; -turing** : torturar, atormentar
torture[2] *n* : tortura *f*, tormento *m* ⟨it was sheer torture! : ¡fue un verdadero suplicio!⟩
torturer ['tɔrtʃərər] *n* : torturador *m*, -dora *f*
toss[1] ['tɔs, 'tɑs] *vt* **1** AGITATE, SHAKE : sacudir, agitar, mezclar (una ensalada) **2** THROW : tirar, echar, lanzar — *vi* : sacudirse, moverse agitadamente ⟨to toss and turn : dar vueltas⟩
toss[2] *n* THROW : lanzamiento *m*, tiro *m*, tirada *f*, lance *m* (de dados, etc.)
toss–up ['tɔs,ʌp] *n* : posibilidad *f* igual ⟨it's a toss-up : quizá sí, quizá no⟩
tot ['tɑt] *n* : pequeño *m*, -ña *f*
total[1] ['toːtəl] *vt* **-taled** *or* **-talled; -taling** *or* **-talling 1** *or* **to total up** ADD : sumar, totalizar **2** AMOUNT TO : ascender a, llegar a
total[2] *adj* : total, completo, absoluto — **totally** *adv*
total[3] *n* : total *m*
totalitarian [toː,tælə'tɛriən] *adj* : totalitario
totalitarianism [toː,tælə'tɛriə,nɪzəm] *n* : totalitarismo *m*
totality [toː'tæləti] *n, pl* **-ties** : totalidad *f*
tote ['toːt] *vt* **toted; toting** : cargar, llevar
totem ['toːtəm] *n* : tótem *m*
totter ['tɑtər] *vi* : tambalearse
touch[1] ['tʌtʃ] *vt* **1** FEEL, HANDLE : tocar, tentar **2** AFFECT, MOVE : conmover, afectar, tocar ⟨his gesture touched our hearts : su gesto nos tocó el corazón⟩ — *vi* : tocarse
touch[2] *n* **1** : tacto *m* (sentido) **2** DETAIL : toque *m*, detalle *m* ⟨a touch of color : un toque de color⟩ **3** BIT : pizca *f*, gota *f*, poco *m* **4** ABILITY : habilidad *f* ⟨to lose one's touch : perder la habilidad⟩ **5** CONTACT : contacto *m*, comunicación *f* ⟨to keep in touch : mantenerse en contacto⟩
touchdown ['tʌtʃ,daʊn] *n* : touchdown *m* (en futbol americano)
touching ['tʌtʃɪŋ] *adj* MOVING : conmovedor
touchstone ['tʌtʃ,stoːn] *n* : piedra *f* de toque
touch up *vt* : retocar
touchy ['tʌtʃi] *adj* **touchier; -est 1** : sensible, susceptible (dícese de una persona) **2** : delicado ⟨a touchy subject : un tema delicado⟩
tough[1] ['tʌf] *adj* **1** STRONG : fuerte, resistente (dícese de materiales) **2** LEATHERY : correoso ⟨a tough steak : un bistec duro⟩ **3** HARDY : fuerte, robusto (dícese de una persona) **4** STRICT : severo, exigente **5** DIFFICULT : difícil **6** STUBBORN : terco, obstinado
tough[2] *n* : matón *m*, persona *f* ruda y brusca
toughen ['tʌfən] *vt* : fortalecer, endurecer — *vi* : endurecerse, hacerse más fuerte
toughness ['tʌfnəs] *n* : dureza *f*
toupee [tuː'peɪ] *n* : peluquín *m*, bisoñé *m*
tour[1] ['tʊr] *vi* : tomar una excursión, viajar — *vt* : recorrer, hacer una gira por
tour[2] *n* **1** : gira *f*, tour *m*, excursión *f* **2** **tour of duty** : período *m* de servicio
tourism ['tʊr,ɪzəm] *n* : turismo *m*
tourist ['tʊrɪst, 'tʊr-] *n* : turista *mf*
tournament ['tʊrnəmənt, 'tʊr-] *n* : torneo *m*
tourniquet ['tʊrnɪkət, 'tʊr-] *n* : torniquete *m*
tousle ['taʊzəl] *vt* **-sled; -sling** : desarreglar, despeinar (el cabello)
tout ['taʊt] *vt* : promocionar, elogiar (con exageración)
tow[1] ['toː] *vt* : remolcar
tow[2] *n* : remolque *m*
toward ['tɔrd, tə'wɔrd] *or* **towards** ['tɔrdz, tə'wɔrdz] *prep* **1** (*indicating direction*) : hacia, rumbo a ⟨heading toward town : dirigiéndose rumbo al pueblo⟩ ⟨efforts towards peace : esfuerzos hacia la paz⟩ **2** (*indicating time*) : alrededor de ⟨toward midnight : alrededor de la medianoche⟩ **3** REGARDING : hacia, con respecto a ⟨his attitude toward life : su actitud hacia la vida⟩ **4** FOR : para, como pago parcial de (una compra o deuda)
towel ['taʊəl] *n* : toalla *f*
tower[1] ['taʊər] *vi* **to tower over** : descollar sobre, elevarse sobre, dominar
tower[2] *n* : torre *f*
towering ['taʊərɪŋ] *adj* : altísimo, imponente
town ['taʊn] *n* : pueblo *m*, ciudad *f* (pequeña)
township ['taʊn,ʃɪp] *n* : municipio *m*
tow truck ['toː,trʌk] *n* : grúa *f*
toxic ['tɑksɪk] *adj* : tóxico
toxicity [tɑk'sɪsəti] *n, pl* **-ties** : toxicidad *f*
toxin ['tɑksɪn] *n* : toxina *f*
toy[1] ['tɔɪ] *vi* : juguetear, jugar
toy[2] *adj* : de juguete ⟨a toy rifle : un rifle de juguete⟩
toy[3] *n* : juguete *m*
trace[1] ['treɪs] *vt* **traced; tracing 1** : calcar (un dibujo, etc.) **2** OUTLINE : delinear, trazar (planes, etc.) **3** TRACK : describir (un curso, una historia) **4** FIND : localizar, ubicar
trace[2] *n* **1** SIGN, TRACK : huella *f*, rastro *m*, indicio *m*, vestigio *m* ⟨he disappeared without a trace : desapareció sin dejar rastro⟩ **2** BIT, HINT : pizca *f*, ápice *m*, dejo *m*
trachea ['treɪkiə] *n, pl* **-cheae** [-ki,iː] : tráquea *f*

tracing paper *n* : papel *m* de calcar

track¹ ['træk] *vt* **1** TRAIL : seguir la pista de, rastrear **2** : dejar huellas de ⟨he tracked mud all over : dejó huellas de lodo por todas partes⟩

track² *n* **1** : rastro *m*, huella *f* (de animales), pista *f* (de personas) **2** PATH : pista *f*, sendero *m*, camino *m* **3** *or* **railroad track** : vía *f* (férrea) **4** → **racetrack** **5** : oruga *f* (de un tanque, etc.) **6** : pista *f* (deporte) **7 to keep track of** : llevar la cuenta de

track–and–field ['trækənd'fi:ld] *adj* : de pista y campo

tract ['trækt] *n* **1** AREA : terreno *m*, extensión *f*, área *f* **2** : tracto *m* ⟨digestive tract : tracto digestivo⟩ **3** PAMPHLET : panfleto *m*, folleto *m*

traction ['trækʃən] *n* : tracción *f*

tractor ['træktər] *n* **1** : tractor *m* (vehículo agrícola) **2** TRUCK : camión *m* (con remolque)

trade¹ ['treɪd] *v* **traded; trading** *vi* : comerciar, negociar — *vt* EXCHANGE : intercambiar, canjear

trade² *n* **1** OCCUPATION : oficio *m*, profesión *f*, ocupación *f* ⟨a carpenter by trade : carpintero de oficio⟩ **2** COMMERCE : comercio *m*, industria *f* ⟨free trade : libre comercio⟩ ⟨the book trade : la industria del libro⟩ **3** EXCHANGE : intercambio *m*, canje *m*

trade–in ['treɪd,ɪn] *n* : artículo *m* que se canjea por otro

trademark ['treɪd,mɑrk] *n* **1** : marca *f* registrada **2** CHARACTERISTIC : sello *m* característico (de un grupo, una persona, etc.)

trader ['treɪdər] *n* : negociante *mf*, tratante *mf*, comerciante *mf*

tradesman ['treɪdzmən] *n, pl* **-men** [-mən, -,mɛn] **1** CRAFTSMAN : artesano *m*, -na *f* **2** SHOPKEEPER : tendero *m*, -ra *f*; comerciante *mf*

trade wind *n* : viento *m* alisio

tradition [trə'dɪʃən] *n* : tradición *f*

traditional [trə'dɪʃənəl] *adj* : tradicional — **traditionally** *adv*

traffic¹ ['træfɪk] *vi* **trafficked; trafficking** : traficar (con)

traffic² *n* **1** COMMERCE : tráfico *m*, comercio *m* ⟨the drug traffic : el narcotráfico⟩ **2** : tráfico *m*, tránsito *m*, circulación *f* (de vehículos, etc.)

traffic circle *n* : rotonda *f*, glorieta *f*

trafficker ['træfɪkər] *n* : traficante *mf*

traffic light *n* : semáforo *m*, luz *f* (de tránsito)

tragedy ['trædʒədi] *n, pl* **-dies** : tragedia *f*

tragic ['trædʒɪk] *adj* : trágico — **tragically** *adv*

trail¹ ['treɪl] *vi* **1** DRAG : arrastrarse **2** LAG : quedarse atrás, retrasarse **3 to trail away** *or* **to trail off** : disminuir, menguar, desvanecerse — *vt* **1** DRAG : arrastrar **2** PURSUE : perseguir, seguir la pista de

trail² *n* **1** TRACK : rastro *m*, huella *f*, pista *f* ⟨a trail of blood : un rastro de sangre⟩ **2** : cola *f*, estela *f* (de un meteoro) **3** PATH : sendero *m*, camino *m*, vereda *f*

trailer ['treɪlər] *n* **1** : remolque *m*, tráiler *m* (de un camión) **2** : caravana *f* (vivienda ambulante)

train¹ ['treɪn] *vt* **1** : adiestrar, entrenar (atletas), capacitar (trabajadores), amaestrar (animales) **2** POINT : apuntar (un arma, etc.) — *vi* : entrenar(se) (físicamente), prepararse (profesionalmente) ⟨she's training at the gym : se está entrenando en el gimnasio⟩

train² *n* **1** : cola *f* (de un vestido) **2** RETINUE : cortejo *m*, séquito *m* **3** SERIES : serie *f* (de eventos) **4** : tren *m* ⟨passenger train : tren de pasajeros⟩

trainee [treɪ'ni:] *n* : aprendiz *m*, -diza *f*

trainer ['treɪnər] *n* : entrenador *m*, -dora *f*

training ['treɪnɪŋ] *n* : adiestramiento *m*, entrenamiento *m* (físico), capacitación *f* (de trabajadores)

traipse ['treɪps] *vi* **traipsed; traipsing** : andar de un lado para otro, vagar

trait ['treɪt] *n* : rasgo *m*, característica *f*

traitor ['treɪtər] *n* : traidor *m*, -dora *f*

traitorous ['treɪtərəs] *adj* : traidor

trajectory [trə'dʒɛktəri] *n, pl* **-ries** : trayectoria *f*

tramp¹ ['træmp] *vi* : caminar (a paso pesado) — *vt* : deambular por, vagar por ⟨to tramp the streets : vagar por las calles⟩

tramp² *n* **1** VAGRANT : vagabundo *m*, -da *f* **2** HIKE : caminata *f*

trample ['træmpəl] *vt* **-pled; -pling** : pisotear, hollar

trampoline [,træmpə'li:n, 'træmpə,-] *n* : trampolín *m*, cama *f* elástica

trance ['trænts] *n* : trance *m*

tranquil ['træŋkwəl] *adj* : calmo, tranquilo, sereno — **tranquilly** *adv*

tranquilize ['træŋkwə,laɪz] *vt* **-ized; -izing** : tranquilizar

tranquilizer ['træŋkwə,laɪzər] *n* : tranquilizante *m*

tranquillity *or* **tranquility** [træŋ'kwɪləti] *n* : sosiego *m*, tranquilidad *f*

transact [træn'zækt] *vt* : negociar, gestionar, hacer (negocios)

transaction [træn'zækʃən] *n* **1** : transacción *f*, negocio *m*, operación *f* **2 transactions** *npl* RECORDS : actas *fpl*

transatlantic [,træntsət'læntɪk, ,trænz-] *adj* : transatlántico

transcend [træn'sɛnd] *vt* : trascender, sobrepasar

transcendent [træn'sɛndənt] *adj* : trascendente — **transcendence** [træn'sɛndənts] *n*

transcendental [,træntsɛn'dɛntəl, -sən-] *adj* : trascendental ⟨transcendental meditation : meditación trascendental⟩

transcribe [træn'skraɪb] *vt* **-scribed; -scribing** : transcribir

transcript ['træn‚skrɪpt] *n* : copia *f* oficial

transcription [træn'skrɪpʃən] *n* : transcripción *f*

transfer¹ [trænts'fər, 'trænts‚fər] *v* **-ferred; -ferring** *vt* **1** : trasladar (a una persona), transferir (fondos) **2** : transferir, traspasar, ceder (propiedad) **3** PRINT : imprimir (un diseño) — *vi* **1** MOVE : trasladarse, cambiarse **2** CHANGE : transbordar, cambiar (de un transporte a otro) ⟨he transfers at E Street : hace un transborde a la calle E⟩

transfer² ['trænts‚fər] *n* **1** TRANSFERRING : transferencia *f* (de fondos, de propiedad, etc.), traslado *m* (de una persona) **2** DECAL : calcomanía *f* **3** : boleto *m* (para cambiar de un avión, etc., a otro)

transferable [trænts'fərəbəl] *adj* : transferible

transference [trænts'fərənts] *n* : transferencia *f*

transfigure [trænts'fɪgjər] *vt* **-ured; -uring** : transfigurar, transformar

transfix [trænts'fɪks] *vt* **1** PIERCE : traspasar, atravesar **2** IMMOBILIZE : paralizar

transform [trænts'fɔrm] *vt* : transformar

transformation [‚træntsfər'meɪʃən] *n* : transformación *f*

transformer [trænts'fɔrmər] *n* : transformador *m*

transfusion [trænts'fju:ʒən] *n* : transfusión *f*

transgress [trænts'grɛs, trænz-] *vt* : transgredir, infringir

transgression [trænts'grɛʃən, trænz-] *n* : transgresión *f*

transient¹ ['trænʃənt, 'trænsiənt] *adj* : pasajero, transitorio — **transiently** *adv*

transient² *n* : transeúnte *mf*

transistor [træn'zɪstər, -'sɪs-] *n* : transistor *m*

transit ['træntsɪt, 'trænzɪt] *n* **1** PASSAGE : pasaje *m*, tránsito *m* ⟨in transit : en tránsito⟩ **2** TRANSPORTATION : transporte *m* (público) **3** : teodolito *m* (instrumento topográfico)

transition [træn'sɪʃən, -'zɪʃ-] *n* : transición *f*

transitional [træn'sɪʃənəl, -'zɪʃ-] *adj* : de transición

transitive ['træntsəṭɪv, 'trænzə-] *adj* : transitivo

transitory ['træntsə‚tori, 'trænzə-] *adj* : transitorio

translate [trænts'leɪt, trænz-; 'trænts‚-, 'trænz‚-] *vt* **-lated; -lating** : traducir

translation [trænts'leɪʃən, trænz-] *n* : traducción *f*

translator [trænts'leɪţər, trænz-; 'trænts‚-, 'trænz‚-] *n* : traductor *m*, -tora *f*

translucent [trænts'lu:sənt, trænz-] *adj* : translúcido

transmission [trænts'mɪʃən, trænz-] *n* : transmisión *f*

transmit [trænts'mɪt, trænz-] *vt* **-mitted; -mitting** : transmitir

transmitter [trænts'mɪţər, trænz-; 'trænts‚-, 'trænz‚-] *n* : transmisor *m*, emisor *m*

transom ['træntsəm] *n* : montante *m* (de una puerta), travesaño *m* (de una ventana)

transparency [trænts'pærəntsi] *n, pl* **-cies** : transparencia *f*

transparent [trænts'pærənt] *adj* **1** : transparente, traslúcido ⟨a transparent fabric : una tela transparente⟩ **2** OBVIOUS : transparente, obvio, claro — **transparently** *adv*

transpiration [‚træntspə'reɪʃən] *n* : transpiración *f*

transpire [trænts'paɪr] *vi* **-spired; -spiring 1** : transpirar (en biología y botánica) **2** TURN OUT : resultar **3** HAPPEN : suceder, ocurrir, tener lugar

transplant¹ [trænts'plænt] *vt* : trasplantar

transplant² ['trænts‚plænt] *n* : trasplante *m*

transport¹ [trænts'port, 'trænts‚-] *vt* **1** CARRY : transportar, acarrear **2** ENRAPTURE : transportar, extasiar

transport² ['trænts‚port] *n* **1** TRANSPORTATION : transporte *m*, transportación *f* **2** RAPTURE : éxtasis *m* **3** *or* **transport ship** : buque *m* de transporte (de personal militar)

transportation [‚træntspər'teɪʃən] *n* : transporte *m*, transportación *f*

transpose [trænts'po:z] *vt* **-posed; -posing** : trasponer, trasladar, transportar (una composición musical)

transverse [trænts'vərs, trænz-] *adj* : transversal, transverso, oblicuo — **transversely** *adv*

trap¹ ['træp] *vt* **trapped; trapping** : atrapar, apresar (en una trampa)

trap² *n* : trampa *f* ⟨to set a trap : tender una trampa⟩

trapdoor ['træp'dor] *n* : trampilla *f*, escotillón *m*

trapeze [træ'pi:z] *n* : trapecio *m*

trapezoid ['træpə‚zɔɪd] *n* : trapezoide *m*, trapecio *m*

trapper ['træpər] *n* : trampero *m*, -ra *f*; cazador *m*, -dora *f* (que usa trampas)

trappings ['træpɪŋz] *npl* **1** : arreos *mpl*, jaeces *mpl* (de un caballo) **2** ADORNMENTS : adornos *mpl*, pompa *f*

trash ['træʃ] *n* : basura *f*

trashy ['træʃi] *adj* : de pacotilla

trauma ['trɔmə, 'trau-] *n* : trauma *m*

traumatic [trə'mætɪk, trɔ-, trau-] *adj* : traumático

travel¹ ['trævəl] *vi* **-eled** *or* **-elled; -eling** *or* **-elling 1** JOURNEY : viajar **2** GO, MOVE : desplazarse, moverse, ir ⟨the waves travel at uniform speed : las ondas se desplazan a una velocidad uniforme⟩

travel² *n or* **travels** *npl* : viajes *mpl*

traveler *or* **traveller** ['trævələr] *n* : viajero *m*, -ra *f*

traverse [trə'vərs, træ'vərs, 'trævərs] *vt* **-versed; -versing** CROSS : atravesar, extenderse a través de, cruzar

travesty ['trævəsti] *n, pl* **-ties** : parodia *f*

trawl¹ ['trɔl] *vi* : pescar con red de arrastre, rastrear

trawl² *n or* **trawl net** : red *f* de arrastre

trawler ['trɔlər] *n* : barco *m* de pesca (utilizado para rastrear)

tray ['treɪ] *n* : bandeja *f*, charola *f Bol, Mex, Peru*

treacherous ['trɛtʃərəs] *adj* **1** TRAITOROUS : traicionero, traidor **2** DANGEROUS : peligroso

treacherously ['trɛtʃərəsli] *adv* : a traición

treachery ['trɛtʃəri] *n, pl* **-eries** : traición *f*

tread¹ ['trɛd] *v* **trod** ['trɑd]; **trodden** ['trɑdən] *or* **trod; treading** *vt* TRAMPLE : pisotear, hollar — *vi* **1** WALK : caminar, andar **2 to tread on** : pisar

tread² *n* **1** STEP : paso *m*, andar *m* **2** : banda *f* de rodadura (de un neumático, etc.) **3** : escalón *m* (de una escalera)

treadle ['trɛdəl] *n* : pedal *m* (de una máquina)

treadmill ['trɛd,mɪl] *n* **1** : rueda *f* de andar **2** ROUTINE : rutina *f*

treason ['tri:zən] *n* : traición *f* (a la patria, etc.)

treasure¹ ['trɛʒər, 'treɪ-] *vt* **-sured; -suring** : apreciar, valorar

treasure² *n* : tesoro *m*

treasurer ['trɛʒərər, 'treɪ-] *n* : tesorero *m*, -ra *f*

treasury ['trɛʒəri, 'treɪ-] *n, pl* **-suries** : tesorería *f*, tesoro *m*

treat¹ ['tri:t] *vt* **1** DEAL WITH : tratar (un asunto) ⟨the article treats of poverty : el artículo trata de la pobreza⟩ **2** HANDLE : tratar (a una persona), manejar (un objeto) ⟨to treat something as a joke : tomar(se) algo a broma⟩ **3** INVITE : invitar, convidar ⟨he treated me to a meal : me invitó a comer⟩ **4** : tratar, atender (en medicina) **5** PROCESS : tratar ⟨to treat sewage : tratar las aguas negras⟩

treat² *n* : gusto *m*, placer *m* ⟨it was a treat to see you : fue un placer verte⟩ ⟨it's my treat : yo invito⟩

treatise ['tri:tɪs] *n* : tratado *m*, estudio *m*

treatment ['tri:tmənt] *n* : trato *m*, tratamiento *m* (médico)

treaty ['tri:ti] *n, pl* **-ties** : tratado *m*, convenio *m*

treble¹ ['trɛbəl] *vt* **-bled; -bling** : triplicar

treble² *adj* **1** → **triple 2** : de tiple, soprano (en música) **3 treble clef** : clave *f* de sol

treble³ *n* : tiple *m*, parte *f* de soprano

tree ['tri:] *n* : árbol *m*

treeless ['tri:ləs] *adj* : carente de árboles

trek¹ ['trɛk] *vi* **trekked; trekking** : hacer un viaje largo y difícil

trek² *n* : viaje *m* largo y difícil

trellis ['trɛlɪs] *n* : enrejado *m*, espaldera *f*, celosía *f*

tremble ['trɛmbəl] *vi* **-bled; -bling** : temblar

tremendous [trɪ'mɛndəs] *adj* : tremendo — **tremendously** *adv*

tremor ['trɛmər] *n* : temblor *m*

tremulous ['trɛmjələs] *adj* : trémulo, tembloroso

trench ['trɛntʃ] *n* **1** DITCH : zanja *f* **2** : trinchera *f* (militar)

trenchant ['trɛntʃənt] *adj* : cortante, mordaz

trend¹ ['trɛnd] *vi* : tender, inclinarse

trend² *n* **1** TENDENCY : tendencia *f* **2** FASHION : moda *f*

trendy ['trɛndi] *adj* **trendier; -est** : de moda

trepidation [,trɛpə'deɪʃən] *n* : inquietud *f*, ansiedad *f*

trespass¹ ['trɛspəs, -,pæs] *vi* **1** SIN : pecar, transgredir **2** : entrar ilegalmente (en propiedad ajena)

trespass² *n* **1** SIN : pecado *m*, transgresión *f* ⟨forgive us our trespasses : perdónanos nuestras deudas⟩ **2** : entrada *f* ilegal (en propiedad ajena)

tress ['trɛs] *n* : mechón *m*

trestle ['trɛsəl] *n* **1** : caballete *m* (armazón) **2** *or* **trestle bridge** : puente *m* de caballete

triad ['traɪ,æd] *n* : tríada *f*

trial¹ ['traɪəl] *adj* : de prueba ⟨trial period : período de prueba⟩

trial² *n* **1** : juicio *m*, proceso *m* ⟨to stand trial : ser sometido a juicio⟩ **2** AFFLICTION : aflicción *f*, tribulación *f* **3** TEST : prueba *f*, ensayo *m*

triangle ['traɪ,æŋgəl] *n* : triángulo *m*

triangular [traɪ'æŋgjələr] *adj* : triangular

tribal ['traɪbəl] *adj* : tribal

tribe ['traɪb] *n* : tribu *f*

tribesman ['traɪbzmən] *n, pl* **-men** [-mən, -,mɛn] : miembro *m* de una tribu

tribulation [,trɪbjə'leɪʃən] *n* : tribulación *f*

tribunal [traɪ'bju:nəl, trɪ-] *n* : tribunal *m*, corte *f*

tributary ['trɪbjə,tɛri] *n, pl* **-taries** : afluente *m*

tribute ['trɪb,ju:t] *n* : tributo *m*

trick¹ ['trɪk] *vt* : engañar, embaucar

trick² *n* **1** RUSE : trampa *f*, treta *f*, artimaña *f* **2** PRANK : broma *f* ⟨we played a trick on her : le gastamos una broma⟩ **3** : truco *m* ⟨magic tricks : trucos de magia⟩ ⟨the trick is to wait five minutes : el truco está en esperar cinco minutos⟩ **4** MANNERISM : peculiaridad *f*, manía *f* **5** : baza *f* (en juegos de naipes)

trickery ['trɪkəri] *n* : engaños *mpl*, trampas *fpl*

trickle¹ ['trɪkəl] *vi* **-led; -ling** : gotear, chorrear

trickle² *n* : goteo *m*, hilo *m*

trickster ['trɪkstər] *n* : estafador *m*, -dora *f*; embaucador *m*, -dora *f*

tricky ['trɪki] *adj* **trickier; -est 1** SLY : astuto, taimado **2** DIFFICULT : delicado, peliagudo, difícil

tricycle ['traɪsəkəl, -ˌsɪkəl] *n* : triciclo *m*

trident ['traɪdənt] *n* : tridente *m*

triennial ['traɪ'ɛniəl] *adj* : trienal

trifle¹ ['traɪfəl] *vi* **-fled; -fling** : jugar, juguetear

trifle² *n* : nimiedad *f*, insignificancia *f*

trifling ['traɪflɪŋ] *adj* : trivial, insignificante

trigger¹ ['trɪgər] *vt* : causar, provocar

trigger² *n* : gatillo *m*

trigonometry [ˌtrɪgə'namətri] *n* : trigonometría *f*

trill¹ ['trɪl] *vi* QUAVER : trinar, gorjear — *vt* : vibrar ⟨to trill the *r* : vibrar la *r*⟩

trill² *n* **1** QUAVER : trino *m*, gorjeo *m* **2** : vibración *f* (en fonética)

trillion ['trɪljən] *n* : billón *m*

trilogy ['trɪlədʒi] *n, pl* **-gies** : trilogía *f*

trim¹ ['trɪm] *vt* **trimmed; trimming 1** DECORATE : adornar, decorar **2** CUT : recortar **3** REDUCE : recortar, reducir ⟨to trim the excess : recortar el exceso⟩

trim² *adj* **trimmer; trimmest 1** SLIM : esbelto **2** NEAT : limpio y arreglado, bien cuidado

trim³ *n* **1** CONDITION : condición *f*, estado *m* ⟨to keep in trim : mantenerse en buena forma⟩ **2** CUT : recorte *m* **3** TRIMMING : adornos *mpl*

trimming ['trɪmɪŋ] *n* : adornos *mpl*, accesorios *mpl*

Trinity ['trɪnəti] *n* : Trinidad *f*

trinket ['trɪŋkət] *n* : chuchería *f*, baratija *f*

trio ['tri:ˌo:] *n, pl* **trios** : trío *m*

trip¹ ['trɪp] *v* **tripped; tripping** *vi* **1** : caminar (a paso ligero) **2** STUMBLE : tropezar **3 to trip up** ERR : equivocarse, cometer un error — *vt* **1** : hacerle una zancadilla (a alguien) ⟨you tripped me on purpose! : ¡me hiciste la zancadilla a propósito!⟩ **2** ACTIVATE : activar (un mecanismo) **3 to trip up** : hacer equivocar (a alguien)

trip² *n* **1** JOURNEY : viaje *m* ⟨to take a trip : hacer un viaje⟩ **2** STUMBLE : tropiezo *m*, traspié *m*

tripartite [traɪ'parˌtaɪt] *adj* : tripartito

tripe ['traɪp] *n* **1** : mondongo *m*, callos *mpl*, pancita *f Mex* **2** TRASH : porquería *f*

triple¹ ['trɪpəl] *vt* **-pled; -pling** : triplicar

triple² *adj* : triple

triple³ *n* : triple *m*

triplet ['trɪplət] *n* **1** : terceto *m* (en poesía, música, etc.) **2** : trillizo *m*, -za *f* (persona)

triplicate ['trɪplɪkət] *n* : triplicado *m*

tripod ['traɪˌpad] *n* : trípode *m*

trite ['traɪt] *adj* **triter; tritest** : trillado, tópico, manido

triumph¹ ['traɪəmˌpf] *vi* : triunfar

triumph² *n* : triunfo *m*

triumphal [traɪ'ʌmfəl] *adj* : triunfal

triumphant [traɪ'ʌmfənt] *adj* : triunfante, triunfal — **triumphantly** *adv*

trivia ['trɪviə] *ns & pl* : trivialidades *fpl*, nimiedades *fpl*

trivial ['trɪviəl] *adj* : trivial, intrascendente, insignificante

triviality [ˌtrɪvi'æləti] *n, pl* **-ties** : trivialidad *f*

trod, trodden → **tread¹**

troll ['tro:l] *n* : duende *m* o gigante *m* de cuentos folklóricos

trolley ['trali] *n, pl* **-leys** : tranvía *m*

trombone [tram'bo:n] *n* : trombón *m*

trombonist [tram'bo:nɪst] *n* : trombón *m*

troop¹ ['tru:p] *vi* : desfilar, ir en tropel

troop² *n* **1** : escuadrón *m* (de caballería) **2** GROUP : grupo *m*, banda *f* (de personas) **3 troops** *npl* SOLDIERS : tropas *fpl*, soldados *mpl*

trooper ['tru:pər] *n* **1** : soldado *m* (de caballería) **2** : policía *m* montado **3** : policía *m* (estatal)

trophy ['tro:fi] *n, pl* **-phies** : trofeo *m*

tropic¹ ['trapɪk] *or* **tropical** [-pɪkəl] *adj* : tropical

tropic² *n* **1** : trópico *m* ⟨tropic of Cancer : trópico de Cáncer⟩ **2 the tropics** : el trópico

trot¹ ['trat] *vi* **trotted; trotting** : trotar

trot² *n* : trote *m*

trouble¹ ['trʌbəl] *v* **-bled; -bling** *vt* **1** DISTURB, WORRY : molestar, perturbar, inquietar **2** AFFLICT : afligir, afectar — *vi* : molestarse, hacer un esfuerzo ⟨they didn't trouble to come : no se molestaron en venir⟩

trouble² *n* **1** PROBLEMS : problemas *mpl*, dificultades *fpl* ⟨to be in trouble : estar en un aprieto⟩ ⟨heart trouble : problemas de corazón⟩ **2** EFFORT : molestia *f*, esfuerzo *m* ⟨to take the trouble : tomarse la molestia⟩ ⟨it's not worth the trouble : no vale la pena⟩

troublemaker ['trʌbəlˌmeɪkər] *n* : agitador *m*, -dora *f*; alborotador *m*, -dora *f*

troublesome ['trʌbəlsəm] *adj* : problemático, dificultoso — **troublesomely** *adv*

trough ['trɔf] *n, pl* **troughs** ['trɔfs, 'trɔvz] **1** : comedero *m*, bebedero *m* (de animales) **2** CHANNEL, HOLLOW : depresión *f* (en el suelo), seno *m* (de olas)

trounce ['traʊnts] *vt* **trounced; trouncing 1** THRASH : apalear, darle una paliza (a alguien) **2** DEFEAT : derrotar contundentemente

troupe ['tru:p] *n* : troupe *f*

trousers ['traʊzərz] *npl* : pantalón *m*, pantalones *mpl*

trout ['traʊt] *n, pl* **trout** : trucha *f*

trowel ['traʊəl] *n* **1** : llana *f*, paleta *f* (de albañil) **2** : desplantador *m* (de jardinero)

truant ['tru:ənt] *n* : alumno *m*, -na *f* que falta a clase sin permiso

truce ['tru:s] *n* : tregua *f*, armisticio *m*

truck[1] ['trʌk] *vt* : transportar en camión

truck[2] *n* **1** : camión *m* (vehículo automóvil), carro *m* (manual) **2** DEALINGS : tratos *mpl* ⟨to have no truck with : no tener nada que ver con⟩

trucker ['trʌkər] *n* : camionero *m*, -ra *f*

truculent ['trʌkjələnt] *adj* : agresivo, beligerante

trudge ['trʌdʒ] *vi* **trudged; trudging** : caminar a paso pesado

true[1] ['tru:] *vt* **trued; trueing** : aplomar (algo vertical), nivelar (algo horizontal), centrar (una rueda)

true[2] *adv* **1** TRUTHFULLY : lealmente, sinceramente **2** ACCURATELY : exactamente, certeramente

true[3] *adj* **truer; truest 1** LOYAL : fiel, leal **2** : cierto, verdadero, verídico ⟨it's true : es cierto, es la verdad⟩ ⟨a true story : una historia verídica⟩ **3** GENUINE : auténtico, genuino — **truly** *adv*

true–blue ['tru:'blu:] *adj* LOYAL : leal, fiel

truffle ['trʌfəl] *n* : trufa *f*

truism ['tru:ˌɪzəm] *n* : perogrullada *f*, verdad *f* obvia

trump[1] ['trʌmp] *vt* : matar (en juegos de naipes)

trump[2] *n* : triunfo *m* (en juegos de naipes)

trumped–up ['trʌmpt'ʌp] *adj* : inventado, fabricado ⟨trumped-up charges : falsas acusaciones⟩

trumpet[1] ['trʌmpət] *vi* **1** : sonar una trompeta **2** : berrear, bramar (dícese de un animal) — *vt* : proclamar a los cuatro vientos

trumpet[2] *n* : trompeta *f*

trumpeter ['trʌmpətər] *n* : trompetista *mf*

truncate ['trʌŋˌkeɪt, 'trʌn-] *vt* **-cated; -cating** : truncar

trundle ['trʌndəl] *v* **-dled; -dling** *vi* : rodar lentamente — *vt* : hacer rodar, empujar lentamente

trunk ['trʌŋk] *n* **1** : tronco *m* (de un árbol o del cuerpo) **2** : trompa *f* (de un elefante) **3** CHEST : baúl *m* **4** : maletero *m*, cajuela *f Mex* (de un auto) **5 trunks** *npl* : traje *m* de baño (de caballero)

truss[1] ['trʌs] *vt* : atar (con fuerza)

truss[2] *n* **1** FRAMEWORK : armazón *m* (de una estructura) **2** : braguero *m* (en medicina)

trust[1] ['trʌst] *vi* : confiar, esperar ⟨to trust in God : confiar en Dios⟩ — *vt* **1** ENTRUST : confiar, encomendar **2** : confiar en, tenerle confianza a ⟨I trust you : te tengo confianza⟩

trust[2] *n* **1** CONFIDENCE : confianza *f* **2** HOPE : esperanza *f*, fe *f* **3** CREDIT : crédito *m* ⟨to sell on trust : fiar⟩ **4** : fideicomiso *m* ⟨to hold in trust : guardar en fideicomiso⟩ **5** : trust *m* (consorcio empresarial) **6** CUSTODY : responsabilidad *f*, custodia *f*

trustee [ˌtrʌs'ti:] *n* : fideicomisario *m*, -ria *f*; fiduciario *m*, -ria *f*

trustful ['trʌstfəl] *adj* : confiado — **trustfully** *adv*

trustworthiness ['trəstˌwərðinəs] *n* : integridad *f*, honradez *f*

trustworthy ['trəstˌwərði] *adj* : digno de confianza, confiable

trusty ['trəsti] *adj* **trustier; -est** : fiel, confiable

truth ['tru:θ] *n, pl* **truths** ['tru:ðz, 'tru:θs] : verdad *f*

truthful ['tru:θfəl] *adj* : sincero, veraz — **truthfully** *adv*

truthfulness ['tru:θfəlnəs] *n* : sinceridad *f*, veracidad *f*

try[1] ['traɪ] *v* **tried; trying** *vt* **1** : enjuiciar, juzgar, procesar ⟨he was tried for murder : fue procesado por homicidio⟩ **2** : probar ⟨did you try the salad? : ¿probaste la ensalada?⟩ **3** TEST : tentar, poner a prueba ⟨to try one's patience : tentarle la paciencia a uno⟩ **4** ATTEMPT : tratar (de), intentar **5** *or* **to try on** : probarse (ropa) — *vi* : tratar, intentar

try[2] *n, pl* **tries** : intento *m*, tentativa *f*

tryout ['traɪˌaʊt] *n* : prueba *f*

tsar ['zar, 'tsar, 'sar] → **czar**

T–shirt ['ti:ˌʃərt] *n* : camiseta *f*

tub ['tʌb] *n* **1** CASK : cuba *f*, barril *m*, tonel *m* **2** CONTAINER : envase *m* (de plástico, etc.) ⟨a tub of margarine : un envase de margarina⟩ **3** BATHTUB : tina *f* (de baño), bañera *f*

tuba ['tu:bə, 'tju:-] *n* : tuba *f*

tube ['tu:b, 'tju:b] *n* **1** PIPE : tubo *m* **2** : tubo *m* (de dentífrico, etc.) **3** *or* **inner tube** : cámara *f* **4** : tubo *m* (de un aparato electrónico) **5** : trompa *f* (en anatomía)

tubeless ['tu:bləs, 'tju:b-] *adj* : sin cámara (dícese de una llanta)

tuber ['tu:bər, 'tju:-] *n* : tubérculo *m*

tubercular [tʊ'bərkjələr, tju-] → **tuberculous**

tuberculosis [tʊˌbərkjə'lo:sɪs, tju-] *n, pl* **-loses** [-ˌsi:z] : tuberculosis *f*

tuberculous [tʊ'bərkjələs, tju-] *adj* : tuberculoso

tuberous ['tu:bərəs, 'tju:-] *adj* : tuberoso

tubing ['tu:bɪŋ, 'tju:-] *n* : tubería *f*

tubular ['tu:bjələr, 'tju:-] *adj* : tubular

tuck[1] ['tʌk] *vt* **1** PLACE, PUT : meter, colocar ⟨tuck in your shirt : métete la camisa⟩ **2** : guardar, esconder ⟨to tuck away one's money : guardar uno bien su dinero⟩ **3** COVER : arropar (a un niño en la cama)

tuck[2] *n* : pliegue *m*, alforza *f*

Tuesday ['tu:zˌdeɪ, 'tju:z-, -di] *n* : martes *m*

tuft ['tʌft] *n* : penacho *m* (de plumas), copete *m* (de pelo)

tug[1] ['tʌɡ] *v* **tugged; tugging** *vi* : tirar, jalar, dar un tirón — *vt* : jalar, arrastrar, remolcar (con un barco)

tug[2] *n* **1** : tirón *m*, jalón *m* **2** → **tugboat**

tugboat ['tʌɡˌbo:t] *n* : remolcador *m*

tug–of–war [ˌtʌgəˈwɔr] *n*, *pl* **tugs–of–war** : tira y afloja *m*

tuition [tuˈɪʃən] *n or* **tuition fees** : tasas *fpl* de matrícula, colegiatura *f Mex*

tulip [ˈtuːlɪp, ˈtjuː-] *n* : tulipán *m*

tumble[1] [ˈtʌmbəl] *v* **-bled; -bling** *vi* 1 : dar volteretas (en acrobacia) 2 FALL : caerse, venirse abajo — *vt* 1 TOPPLE : volcar 2 TOSS : hacer girar

tumble[2] *n* : voltereta *f*, caída *f*

tumbler [ˈtʌmblər] *n* 1 ACROBAT : acróbata *mf*, saltimbanqui *mf* 2 GLASS : vaso *m* (de mesa) 3 : clavija *f* (de una cerradura)

tummy [ˈtʌmi] *n*, *pl* **-mies** BELLY : panza *f*, vientre *m*

tumor [ˈtuːmər, ˈtjuː-] *n* : tumor *m*

tumult [ˈtuːˌmʌlt, ˈtjuː-] *n* : tumulto *m*, alboroto *m*

tumultuous [tʊˈmʌltʃʊəs, tjuː-] *adj* : tumultuoso

tuna [ˈtuːnə, ˈtjuː-] *n*, *pl* **-na** *or* **-nas** : atún *m*

tundra [ˈtʌndrə] *n* : tundra *f*

tune[1] [ˈtuːn, ˈtjuːn] *v* **tuned; tuning** *vt* 1 ADJUST : ajustar, hacer más preciso, afinar (un motor) 2 : afinar (un instrumento musical) 3 : sintonizar (un radio o televisor) — *vi* **to tune in** : sintonizar (con una emisora)

tune[2] *n* 1 MELODY : tonada *f*, canción *f*, melodía *f* 2 **in tune** : afinado (dícese de un instrumento o de la voz), sintonizado, en sintonía

tuneful [ˈtuːnfəl, ˈtjuːn-] *adj* : armonioso, melódico

tuner [ˈtuːnər, ˈtjuː-] *n* : afinador *m*, -dora *f* (de instrumentos); sintonizador *m* (de un radio o un televisor)

tungsten [ˈtʌŋkstən] *n* : tungsteno *m*

tunic [ˈtuːnɪk, ˈtjuː-] *n* : túnica *f*

tuning fork *n* : diapasón *m*

Tunisian [tuːˈniːʒən, tjuːˈnɪziən] *n* : tunecino *m*, -na *f* — **Tunisian** *adj*

tunnel[1] [ˈtʌnəl] *vi* **-neled** *or* **-nelled; -neling** *or* **-nelling** : hacer un túnel

tunnel[2] *n* : túnel *m*

turban [ˈtʌrbən] *n* : turbante *m*

turbid [ˈtʌrbɪd] *adj* : turbio

turbine [ˈtʌrbən, -ˌbaɪn] *n* : turbina *f*

turboprop [ˈtʌrboˌprɑp] *n* : turbopropulsor *m* (motor), avión *m* turbopropulsado

turbulence [ˈtʌrbjələnts] *n* : turbulencia *f*

turbulent [ˈtʌrbjələnt] *adj* : turbulento — **turbulently** *adv*

tureen [təˈriːn, tjʊ-] *n* : sopera *f*

turf [ˈtʌrf] *n* SOD : tepe *m*

turgid [ˈtʌrdʒɪd] *adj* 1 SWOLLEN : turgente 2 : ampuloso, hinchado ⟨turgid style : estilo ampuloso⟩

Turk [ˈtʌrk] *n* : turco *m*, -ca *f*

turkey [ˈtʌrki] *n*, *pl* **-keys** : pavo *m*

Turkish[1] [ˈtʌrkɪʃ] *adj* : turco

Turkish[2] *n* : turco *m* (idioma)

turmoil [ˈtʌrˌmɔɪl] *n* : agitación *f*, desorden *m*, confusión *f*

turn[1] [ˈtʌrn] *vt* 1 : girar, voltear, volver ⟨to turn one's head : voltear la cabeza⟩ ⟨she turned her chair toward the fire : giró su asiento hacia la hoguera⟩ 2 ROTATE : darle vuelta a, hacer girar ⟨turn the handle : dale vuelta a la manivela⟩ 3 SPRAIN, WRENCH : dislocar, torcer 4 UPSET : revolver (el estómago) 5 TRANSFORM : convertir ⟨to turn water into wine : convertir el agua en vino⟩ 6 SHAPE : tornear (en carpintería) — *vi* 1 ROTATE : girar, dar vueltas 2 : girar, doblar, dar una vuelta ⟨turn left : doble a la izquierda⟩ ⟨to turn around : dar la media vuelta⟩ 3 BECOME : hacerse, volverse, ponerse 4 SOUR : agriarse, cortarse (dícese de la leche) 5 **to turn to** : recurrir a ⟨they have no one to turn to : no tienen quien les ayude⟩

turn[2] *n* 1 : vuelta *f*, giro *m* ⟨a sudden turn : una vuelta repentina⟩ 2 CHANGE : cambio *m* 3 CURVE : curva *f* (en un camino) 4 : turno *m* ⟨they're awaiting their turn : están esperando su turno⟩ ⟨whose turn is it? : ¿a quién le toca?⟩

turnaround [ˈtʌrnəˌraʊnd] *n* PROCESSING : procesamiento *m*

turncoat [ˈtʌrnˌkoːt] *n* : traidor *m*, -dora *f*

turn down *vt* 1 REFUSE : rehusar, rechazar ⟨they turned down our invitation : rehusaron nuestra invitación⟩ 2 LOWER : bajar (el volumen)

turn in *vt* : entregar ⟨to turn in one's work : entregar uno su trabajo⟩ ⟨they turned in the suspect : entregaron al sospechoso⟩ — *vi* : acostarse, irse a la cama

turnip [ˈtʌrnəp] *n* : nabo *m*

turn off *vt* : apagar (la luz, la radio, etc.)

turn on *vt* : prender (la luz, etc.), encender (un motor, etc.)

turnout [ˈtʌrnˌaʊt] *n* : concurrencia *f*

turn out *vt* 1 EVICT, EXPEL : expulsar, echar, desalojar 2 PRODUCE : producir 3 → **turn off** — *vi* 1 : concurrir, presentarse ⟨many turned out to vote : muchos concurrieron a votar⟩ 2 PROVE, RESULT : resultar

turnover [ˈtʌrnˌoːvər] *n* 1 : empanada *f* (salada o dulce) 2 : volumen *m* (de ventas) 3 : rotación *f* (de personal) ⟨a high turnover : un alto nivel de rotación⟩

turn over *vt* 1 TRANSFER : entregar, transferir (un cargo o una responsabilidad) 2 : voltear, darle la vuelta a ⟨turn the cassette over : voltea el cassette⟩

turnpike [ˈtʌrnˌpaɪk] *n* : carretera *f* de peaje

turnstile [ˈtʌrnˌstaɪl] *n* : torniquete *m* (de acceso)

turntable [ˈtʌrnˌteɪbəl] *n* : tornamesa *mf*

turn up *vi* 1 APPEAR : aparecer, presentarse 2 HAPPEN : ocurrir, suceder (inesperadamente) — *vt* : subir (el volumen)

turpentine [ˈtʌrpənˌtaɪn] *n* : aguarrás *m*, trementina *f*

turquoise ['tər‚kɔɪz, -‚kwɔɪz] *n* : turquesa *f*

turret ['tərət] *n* **1** TOWER : torre *f* pequeña **2** : torreta *f* (de un tanque, un avión, etc.)

turtle ['tərţəl] *n* : tortuga *f* (marina)

turtledove ['tərţəl‚dʌv] *n* : tórtola *f*

turtleneck ['tərţəl‚nɛk] *n* : cuello *m* de tortuga, cuello *m* alto

tusk ['tʌsk] *n* : colmillo *m*

tussle[1] ['tʌsəl] *vi* **-sled; -sling** SCUFFLE : pelearse, reñir

tussle[2] *n* : riña *f*, pelea *f*

tutor[1] ['tu:ţər, 'tju:-] *vt* : darle clases particulares (a alguien)

tutor[2] *n* : tutor *m*, -tora *f*; maestro *m*, -tra *f* (particular)

tuxedo [‚tək'si:‚do:] *n, pl* **-dos** *or* **-does** : esmoquin *m*, smoking *m*

TV [‚ti:'vi:, 'ti:‚vi:] → **television**

twain ['tweɪn] *n* : dos *m*

twang[1] ['twæŋ] *vt* : pulsar la cuerda de (una guitarra) — *vi* : hablar en tono nasal

twang[2] *n* **1** : tañido *m* (de una cuerda de guitarra) **2** : tono *m* nasal (de voz)

tweak[1] ['twi:k] *vt* : pellizcar

tweak[2] *n* : pellizco *m*

tweed ['twi:d] *n* : tweed *m*

tweet[1] ['twi:t] *vi* : piar

tweet[2] *n* : gorjeo *m*, pío *m*

tweezers ['twi:zərz] *npl* : pinzas *fpl*

twelfth[1] ['twɛlfθ] *adj* : duodécimo

twelfth[2] *n* **1** : duodécimo *m*, -ma *f* (en una serie) **2** : doceavo *m*, doceava parte *f*

twelve[1] ['twɛlv] *adj* : doce

twelve[2] *n* : doce *m*

twentieth[1] ['twʌntiəθ, 'twɛn-] *adj* : vigésimo

twentieth[2] *n* **1** : vigésimo *m*, -ma *f* (en una serie) **2** : veinteavo *m*, veinteava parte *f*

twenty[1] ['twʌnti, 'twɛn-] *adj* : veinte

twenty[2] *n, pl* **-ties** : veinte *m*

twice ['twaɪs] *adv* : dos veces ⟨twice a day : dos veces al día⟩ ⟨it costs twice as much : cuesta el doble⟩

twig ['twɪg] *n* : ramita *f*

twilight ['twaɪ‚laɪt] *n* : crepúsculo *m*

twill ['twɪl] *n* : sarga *f*, tela *f* cruzada

twin[1] ['twɪn] *adj* : gemelo, mellizo

twin[2] *n* : gemelo *m*, -la *f*; mellizo *m*, -za *f*

twine[1] ['twaɪn] *v* **twined; twining** *vt* : entrelazar, entrecruzar — *vi* : enroscarse (alrededor de algo)

twine[2] *n* : cordel *m*, cuerda *f*, mecate *m CA, Mex, Ven*

twinge[1] ['twɪndʒ] *vi* **twinged; twinging** *or* **twingeing** : sentir punzadas

twinge[2] *n* : punzada *f*, dolor *m* agudo

twinkle[1] ['twɪŋkəl] *vi* **-kled; -kling** **1** : centellear, titilar (dícese de las estrellas o de la luz) **2** : chispear, brillar (dícese de los ojos)

twinkle[2] *n* : centelleo *m* (de las estrellas), brillo *m* (de los ojos)

twirl[1] ['twərl] *vt* : girar, darle vueltas a — *vi* : girar, dar vueltas (rápidamente)

twirl[2] *n* : giro *m*, vuelta *f*

twist[1] ['twɪst] *vt* : torcer, retorcer ⟨he twisted my arm : me torció el brazo⟩ — *vi* : retorcerse, enroscarse, serpentear (dícese de un río, un camino, etc.)

twist[2] *n* **1** BEND : vuelta *f*, recodo *m* (en el camino, el río, etc.) **2** TURN : giro *m* ⟨give it a twist : hazlo girar⟩ **3** SPIRAL : espiral *f* ⟨a twist of lemon : una rodajita de limón⟩ **4** : giro *m* inesperado (de eventos, etc.)

twisted ['twɪstəd] *adj* : retorcido ⟨a twisted mind : una mente retorcida⟩

twister ['twɪstər] **1** → **tornado** **2** → **waterspout**

twitch[1] ['twɪtʃ] *vi* : moverse nerviosamente, contraerse espasmódicamente (dícese de un músculo)

twitch[2] *n* : espasmo *m*, sacudida *f* ⟨a nervous twitch : un tic nervioso⟩

twitter[1] ['twɪţər] *vi* CHIRP : gorjear, cantar (dícese de los pájaros)

twitter[2] *n* : gorjeo *m*

two[1] ['tu:] *adj* : dos

two[2] *n, pl* **twos** : dos *m*

twofold[1] ['tu:'fo:ld] *adv* : al doble

twofold[2] ['tu:‚fo:ld] *adj* : doble

two hundred[1] *adj* : doscientos

two hundred[2] *n* : doscientos *m*

twosome ['tu:səm] *n* COUPLE : pareja *f*

tycoon [taɪ'ku:n] *n* : magnate *mf*

tying → **tie**[1]

type[1] ['taɪp] *v* **typed; typing** *vt* **1** TYPEWRITE : escribir a máquina, pasar (un texto) a máquina **2** CATEGORIZE : categorizar, identificar — *vi* : escribir a máquina

type[2] *n* **1** KIND : tipo *m*, clase *f*, categoría *f* **2** *or* **printing type** : tipo *m*

typeface ['taɪp‚feɪs] *n* : tipo *m* de imprenta

typewrite ['taɪp‚raɪt] *v* **-wrote; -written** : escribir a máquina

typewriter ['taɪp‚raɪţər] *n* : máquina *f* de escribir

typhoid[1] ['taɪ‚fɔɪd, taɪ'-] *adj* : relativo al tifus o a la tifoidea

typhoid[2] *n or* **typhoid fever** : tifoidea *f*

typhoon [taɪ'fu:n] *n* : tifón *m*

typhus ['taɪfəs] *n* : tifus *m*, tifo *m*

typical ['tɪpɪkəl] *adj* : típico, característico — **typically** *adv*

typify ['tɪpə‚faɪ] *vt* **-fied; -fying** : ser típico o representativo de (un grupo, una clase, etc.)

typist ['taɪpɪst] *n* : mecanógrafo *m*, -fa *f*

typographic [‚taɪpə'græfɪk] *or* **typographical** [-fɪkəl] *adj* : tipográfico — **typographically** [-fɪkli] *adv*

typography [taɪ'pɑgrəfi] *n* : tipografía *f*

tyrannical [tə'rænɪkəl, taɪ-] *adj* : tiránico — **tyrannically** [-nɪkli] *adv*

tyrannize ['tɪrə‚naɪz] *vt* **-nized; -nizing** : tiranizar

tyranny ['tɪrəni] *n, pl* **-nies** : tiranía *f*

tyrant ['taɪrənt] *n* : tirano *m*, -na *f*

tzar ['zɑr, 'tsɑr, 'sɑr] → **czar**

U

u ['ju:] *n, pl* **u's** *or* **us** ['ju:z] : vigésima primera letra del alfabeto inglés

ubiquitous [ju:'bɪkwəṭəs] *adj* : ubicuo, omnipresente

udder ['ʌdər] *n* : ubre *f*

UFO [,ju:,ɛf'o:, 'ju:,fo:] *n, pl* **UFO's** *or* **UFOs** (*unidentified flying object*) : ovni *m*, OVNI *m*

Ugandan [ju:'gændən, -'gɑn-; u:'gɑn-] *n* : ugandés *m*, -desa *f* — **Ugandan** *adj*

ugliness ['ʌglinəs] *n* : fealdad *f*

ugly ['ʌgli] *adj* **uglier; -est 1** UNATTRACTIVE : feo **2** DISAGREEABLE : desagradable, feo ⟨ugly weather : tiempo feo⟩ ⟨to have an ugly temper : tener mal genio⟩

Ukrainian [ju:'kreɪniən, -'kraɪ-] *n* **1** : ucraniano *m*, -na *f* **2** : ucraniano *m* (idioma) — **Ukrainian** *adj*

ukulele [,ju:kə'leɪli] *n* : ukelele *m*

ulcer ['ʌlsər] *n* : úlcera *f* (interna), llaga *f* (externa)

ulcerate ['ʌlsə,reɪt] *vi* **-ated; -ating** : ulcerarse

ulceration [,ʌlsə'reɪʃən] *n* **1** : ulceración *f* **2** ULCER : úlcera *f*, llaga *f*

ulcerous ['ʌlsərəs] *adj* : ulceroso

ulna ['ʌlnə] *n* : cúbito *m*

ulterior [,ʌl'tɪriər] *adj* : oculto ⟨ulterior motive : motivo oculto, segunda intención⟩

ultimate ['ʌltəmət] *adj* **1** FINAL : último, final **2** SUPREME : supremo, máximo **3** FUNDAMENTAL : fundamental, esencial

ultimately ['ʌltəmətli] *adv* **1** FINALLY : por último, finalmente **2** EVENTUALLY : a la larga, con el tiempo

ultimatum [,ʌltə'meɪṭəm, -'mɑ-] *n, pl* **-tums** *or* **-ta** [-ṭə] : ultimátum *m*

ultrasound ['ʌltrə,saʊnd] *n* **1** : ultrasonido *m* **2** : ecografía *f* (técnica o imagen)

ultraviolet [,ʌltrə'vaɪələt] *adj* : ultravioleta

umbilical cord [,ʌm'bɪlɪkəl] *n* : cordón *m* umbilical

umbrage ['ʌmbrɪdʒ] *n* **to take umbrage at** : ofenderse por

umbrella [,ʌm'brɛlə] *n* **1** : paraguas *m* **2 beach umbrella** : sombrilla *f*

umpire[1] ['ʌm,paɪr] *v* **-pired; -piring** : arbitrar

umpire[2] *n* : árbitro *m*, -tra *f*

umpteenth [,ʌmp'ti:nθ] *adj* : enésimo

unable [,ʌn'eɪbəl] *adj* : incapaz ⟨to be unable to : no poder⟩

unabridged [,ʌnə'brɪdʒd] *adj* : íntegro

unacceptable [,ʌnɪk'sɛptəbəl] *adj* : inaceptable

unaccompanied [,ʌnə'kʌmpənid] *adj* : solo, sin acompañamiento (en música)

unaccountable [,ʌnə'kaʊntəbəl] *adj* : inexplicable, incomprensible — **unaccountably** [-bli] *adv*

unaccustomed [,ʌnə'kʌstəmd] *adj* **1** UNUSUAL : desacostumbrado, inusual **2** UNUSED : inhabituado ⟨unaccustomed to noise : inhabituado al ruido⟩

unacquainted [,ʌnə'kweɪnṭəd] *adj* **to be unacquainted with** : desconocer, ignorar

unadorned [,ʌnə'dɔrnd] *adj* : sin adornos, puro y simple

unadulterated [,ʌnə'dʌltə,reɪṭəd] *adj* **1** PURE : puro ⟨unadulterated food : comida pura⟩ **2** ABSOLUTE : completo, absoluto

unaffected [,ʌnə'fɛktəd] *adj* **1** : no afectado, indiferente **2** NATURAL : sin afectación, natural

unaffectedly [,ʌnə'fɛktədli] *adv* : de manera natural

unafraid [,ʌnə'freɪd] *adj* : sin miedo

unaided [,ʌn'eɪdəd] *adj* : sin ayuda, solo

unambiguous [,ʌnæm'bɪgjʊəs] *adj* : inequívoco

unanimity [,ju:nə'nɪməṭi] *n* : unanimidad *f*

unanimous [jʊ'nænəməs] *adj* : unánime — **unanimously** *adv*

unannounced [,ʌnə'naʊnst] *adj* : sin dar aviso

unanswered [,ʌn'ænṭsərd] *adj* : sin contestar

unappealing [,ʌnə'pi:lɪŋ] *adj* : desagradable

unappetizing [,ʌn'æpə,taɪzɪŋ] *adj* : poco apetitoso, poco apetecible

unarmed [,ʌn'ɑrmd] *adj* : sin armas, desarmado

unassisted [,ʌnə'sɪstəd] *adj* : sin ayuda

unassuming [,ʌnə'su:mɪŋ] *adj* : modesto, sin pretensiones

unattached [,ʌnə'tætʃt] *adj* **1** LOOSE : suelto **2** INDEPENDENT : independiente **3** : solo (ni casado ni prometido)

unattractive [,ʌnə'træktɪv] *adj* : poco atractivo

unauthorized [,ʌn'ɔθə,raɪzd] *adj* : sin autorización, no autorizado

unavailable [,ʌnə'veɪləbəl] *adj* : no disponible

unavoidable [,ʌnə'vɔɪdəbəl] *adj* : inevitable, ineludible

unaware[1] [,ʌnə'wær] *adv* → **unawares**

unaware[2] *adj* : inconsciente

unawares [,ʌnə'wærz] *adv* **1** : por sorpresa ⟨to catch someone unawares : agarrar a alguien desprevenido⟩ **2** UNINTENTIONALLY : inconscientemente, inadvertidamente

unbalanced [,ʌn'bælənst] *adj* : desequilibrado

unbearable [,ʌn'bærəbəl] *adj* : insoportable, inaguantable — **unbearably** [-bli] *adv*

unbecoming [,ʌnbɪ'kʌmɪŋ] *adj* **1** UNSEEMLY : impropio, indecoroso **2** UNFLATTERING : poco favorecedor

unbelievable [ˌʌnbə'liːvəbəl] *adj* : increíble — **unbelievably** [-bli] *adv*

unbend [ˌʌn'bɛnd] *vi* **-bent** [-'bɛnt]; **-bending** RELAX : relajarse

unbending [ˌʌn'bɛndɪŋ] *adj* : inflexible

unbiased [ˌʌn'baɪəst] *adj* : imparcial, objetivo

unbind [ˌʌn'baɪnd] *vt* **-bound** [-'baʊnd]; **-binding** 1 UNFASTEN, UNTIE : desatar, desamarrar 2 RELEASE : liberar

unbolt [ˌʌn'boːlt] *vt* : abrir el cerrojo de, descorrer el pestillo de

unborn [ˌʌn'bɔrn] *adj* : aún no nacido, que va a nacer

unbosom [ˌʌn'buzəm, -'buː-] *vt* : revelar, divulgar

unbreakable [ˌʌn'breɪkəbəl] *adj* : irrompible

unbridled [ˌʌn'braɪdəld] *adj* : desenfrenado

unbroken [ˌʌn'broːkən] *adj* 1 INTACT : intacto, sano 2 CONTINUOUS : continuo, ininterrumpido

unbuckle [ˌʌn'bʌkəl] *vt* **-led; -ling** : desabrochar

unburden [ˌʌn'bərdən] *vt* 1 UNLOAD : descargar 2 to unburden oneself : desahogarse

unbutton [ˌʌn'bʌtən] *vt* : desabrochar, desabotonar

uncalled–for [ˌʌn'kɔld,fɔr] *adj* : inapropiado, innecesario

uncanny [ən'kæni] *adj* **-nier; -est** 1 STRANGE : extraño 2 EXTRAORDINARY : raro, extraordinario — **uncannily** [-'kænəli] *adv*

unceasing [ˌʌn'siːsɪŋ] *adj* : incesante, continuo — **unceasingly** *adv*

unceremonious [ˌʌnˌsɛrə'moːniəs] *adj* 1 INFORMAL : sin ceremonia, sin pompa 2 ABRUPT : abrupto, brusco — **unceremoniously** *adv*

uncertain [ˌʌn'sərtən] *adj* 1 INDEFINITE : indeterminado 2 UNSURE : incierto, dudoso 3 CHANGEABLE : inestable, variable ⟨uncertain weather : tiempo inestable⟩ 4 HESITANT : indeciso 5 VAGUE : poco claro

uncertainly [ˌʌn'sərtənli] *adv* : dudosamente, con desconfianza

uncertainty [ˌʌn'sərtənti] *n, pl* **-ties** : duda *f*, incertidumbre *f*

unchangeable [ˌʌn'tʃeɪndʒəbəl] *adj* : inalterable, inmutable

unchanged [ˌʌn'tʃeɪndʒd] *adj* : sin cambiar

unchanging [ˌʌn'tʃeɪndʒɪŋ] *adj* : inalterable, inmutable, firme

uncharacteristic [ˌʌnˌkærɪktə'rɪstɪk] *adj* : inusual, desacostumbrado

uncharged [ˌʌn'tʃɑrdʒd] *adj* : sin carga (eléctrica)

uncivilized [ˌʌn'sɪvəˌlaɪzd] *adj* 1 BARBAROUS : incivilizado, bárbaro 2 WILD : salvaje

uncle ['ʌŋkəl] *n* : tío *m*

unclean [ˌʌn'kliːn] *adj* 1 IMPURE : impuro 2 DIRTY : sucio

unclear [ˌʌn'klɪr] *adj* : confuso, borroso, poco claro

Uncle Sam ['sæm] *n* : el Tío Sam

unclog [ˌʌn'klɑg] *vt* **-clogged; -clogging** : desatascar, destapar

unclothed [ˌʌn'kloːð] *adj* : desnudo

uncomfortable [ˌʌn'kʌmpfərtəbəl] *adj* 1 : incómodo (dícese de una silla, etc.) 2 UNEASY : inquieto, incómodo

uncommitted [ˌʌnkə'mɪtəd] *adj* : sin compromisos

uncommon [ˌʌn'kɑmən] *adj* 1 UNUSUAL : raro, poco común 2 REMARKABLE : excepcional, extraordinario

uncommonly [ˌʌn'kɑmənli] *adv* : extraordinariamente

uncompromising [ˌʌn'kɑmprəˌmaɪzɪŋ] *adj* : inflexible, intransigente

unconcerned [ˌʌnkən'sərnd] *adj* : indiferente — **unconcernedly** [-'sərnədli] *adv*

unconditional [ˌʌnkən'dɪʃənəl] *adj* : incondicional — **unconditionally** *adv*

unconscious[1] [ˌʌn'kɑntʃəs] *adj* : inconsciente — **unconsciously** *adv*

unconscious[2] *n* : inconsciente *m*

unconsciousness [ˌʌn'kɑntʃəsnəs] *n* : inconsciencia *f*

unconstitutional [ˌʌnˌkɑntstə'tuːʃənəl, -'tjuː-] *adj* : inconstitucional

uncontrollable [ˌʌnkən'troːləbəl] *adj* : incontrolable, incontenible — **uncontrollably** [-bli] *adv*

uncontrolled [ˌʌnkən'troːld] *adj* : incontrolado

unconventional [ˌʌnkən'vɛntʃənəl] *adj* : poco convencional

unconvincing [ˌʌnkən'vɪntsɪŋ] *adj* : poco convincente

uncouth [ˌʌn'kuːθ] *adj* CRUDE, ROUGH : grosero, rudo

uncover [ˌʌn'kʌvər] *vt* 1 : destapar (un objeto), dejar al descubierto 2 EXPOSE, REVEAL : descubrir, revelar, exponer

uncultivated [ˌʌn'kʌltəˌveɪtəd] *adj* : inculto

uncurl [ˌʌn'kərl] *vt* UNROLL : desenrollar — *vi* : desenrollarse, desrizarse (dícese del pelo)

uncut [ˌʌn'kʌt] *adj* 1 : sin cortar ⟨uncut grass : hierba sin cortar⟩ 2 : sin tallar, en bruto ⟨an uncut diamond : un diamante en bruto⟩ 3 UNABRIDGED : completo, íntegro

undaunted [ˌʌn'dɔntəd] *adj* : impávido

undecided [ˌʌndi'saɪdəd] *adj* 1 IRRESOLUTE : indeciso, irresoluto 2 UNRESOLVED : pendiente, no resuelto

undefeated [ˌʌndi'fiːtəd] *adj* : invicto

undeniable [ˌʌndi'naɪəbəl] *adj* : innegable — **undeniably** [-bli] *adv*

under[1] ['ʌndər] *adv* 1 LESS : menos ⟨$10 or under : $10 o menos⟩ 2 UNDERWATER : debajo del agua 3 : bajo los efectos de la anestesia

under[2] *adj* 1 LOWER : (más) bajo, inferior 2 SUBORDINATE : inferior 3 : insuficiente ⟨an under dose of medicine : una dosis insuficiente de medicina⟩

under³ *prep* **1** BELOW, BENEATH : debajo de, abajo de ⟨under the table : abajo de la mesa⟩ ⟨we walked under the arch : pasamos por debajo del arco⟩ ⟨under the sun : bajo el sol⟩ **2** : menos de ⟨in under 20 minutes : en menos de 20 minutos⟩ **3** (*indicating rank or authority*) : bajo ⟨under the command of : bajo las órdenes de⟩ **4** SUBJECT TO : bajo ⟨under suspicion : bajo sospecha⟩ ⟨under the circumstances : dadas las circunstancias⟩ **5** ACCORDING TO : según, de acuerdo con, conforme a ⟨under the present laws : según las leyes actuales⟩

underage [ˌʌndərˈeɪʤ] *adj* : menor de edad

underbrush [ˈʌndərˌbrəʃ] *n* : maleza *f*

underclothes [ˈʌndərˌkloːz, -ˌkloːðz] → **underwear**

underclothing [ˈʌndərˌkloːðɪŋ] → **underwear**

undercover [ˌʌndərˈkʌvər] *adj* : secreto, clandestino

undercurrent [ˈʌndərˌkərənt] *n* **1** : corriente *f* submarina **2** UNDERTONE : corriente *f* oculta, trasfondo *m*

undercut [ˌʌndərˈkʌt] *vt* **-cut; -cutting** : vender más barato que

underdeveloped [ˌʌndərdɪˈvɛləpt] *adj* : subdesarrollado, atrasado

underdog [ˈʌndərˌdɔg] *n* : persona *f* que tiene menos posibilidades

underdone [ˌʌndərˈdʌn] *adj* RARE : poco cocido

underestimate [ˌʌndərˈɛstəˌmeɪt] *vt* **-mated; -mating** : subestimar, menospreciar

underexposed [ˌʌndərɪkˈspoːzd] *adj* : subexpuesto (en fotografía)

underfoot [ˌʌndərˈfʊt] *adv* **1** : bajo los pies ⟨to trample underfoot : pisotear⟩ **2 to be underfoot** : estorbar ⟨they're always underfoot : están siempre estorbando⟩

undergarment [ˈʌndərˌgɑrmənt] *n* : prenda *f* íntima

undergo [ˌʌndərˈgoː] *vt* **-went** [-ˈwɛnt]; **-gone** [-ˈgɔn]; **-going** : sufrir, experimentar ⟨to undergo an operation : someterse a una intervención quirúrgica⟩

undergraduate [ˌʌndərˈgræʤuət] *n* : estudiante *m* universitario, estudiante *f* universitaria

underground¹ [ˌʌndərˈgraʊnd] *adv* **1** : bajo tierra **2** SECRETLY : clandestinamente, en secreto ⟨to go underground : pasar a la clandestinidad⟩

underground² [ˈʌndərˌgraʊnd] *adj* **1** SUBTERRANEAN : subterráneo **2** SECRET : secreto, clandestino

underground³ [ˈʌndərˌgraʊnd] *n* : movimiento *m* o grupo *m* clandestino

undergrowth [ˈʌndərˌgroːθ] *n* : maleza *f*, broza *f*

underhand¹ [ˈʌndərˌhænd] *adv* **1** SECRETLY : de manera clandestina **2** *or*

underhanded : sin levantar el brazo por encima del hombro (en deportes)

underhand² *adj* **1** SLY : solapado **2** : por debajo del hombro (en deportes)

underhanded [ˌʌndərˈhændəd] *adj* **1** SLY : solapado **2** SHADY : turbio, poco limpio

underline [ˈʌndərˌlaɪn] *vt* **-lined; -lining** **1** : subrayar **2** EMPHASIZE : subrayar, acentuar, hacer hincapié en

underlying [ˌʌndərˈlaɪɪŋ] *adj* **1** : subyacente ⟨the underlying rock : la roca subyacente⟩ **2** FUNDAMENTAL : fundamental, esencial

undermine [ˌʌndərˈmaɪn] *vt* **-mined; -mining** **1** : socavar (una estructura, etc.) **2** SAP, WEAKEN : minar, debilitar

underneath¹ [ˌʌndərˈniːθ] *adv* : debajo, abajo ⟨the part underneath : la parte de abajo⟩

underneath² *prep* : debajo de, abajo de

undernourished [ˌʌndərˈnərɪʃt] *adj* : desnutrido

underpants [ˈʌndərˌpænts] *npl* : calzoncillos *mpl*, calzones *mpl*

underpass [ˈʌndərˌpæs] *n* : paso *m* a desnivel

underprivileged [ˌʌndərˈprɪvlɪʤd] *adj* : desfavorecido

underrate [ˌʌndərˈreɪt] *vt* **-rated; -rating** : subestimar, menospreciar

underscore [ˈʌndərˌskor] *vt* **-scored; -scoring** → **underline**

undersea¹ [ˌʌndərˈsiː] *or* **underseas** [-ˈsiːz] *adv* : bajo la superficie del mar

undersea² *adj* : submarino

undersecretary [ˌʌndərˈsɛkrəˌtɛri] *n, pl* **-ries** : subsecretario *m*, -ria *f*

undersell [ˌʌndərˈsɛl] *vt* **-sold; -selling** : vender más barato que

undershirt [ˈʌndərˌʃərt] *n* : camiseta *f*

undershorts [ˈʌndərˌʃɔrts] *npl* : calzoncillos *mpl*

underside [ˈʌndərˌsaɪd, ˌʌndərˈsaɪd] *n* : parte *f* de abajo

undersized [ˌʌndərˈsaɪzd] *adj* : más pequeño de lo normal

understand [ˌʌndərˈstænd] *v* **-stood** [-ˈstʊd]; **-standing** *vt* **1** COMPREHEND : comprender, entender ⟨I don't understand it : no lo entiendo⟩ ⟨that's understood : eso se comprende⟩ ⟨to make oneself understood : hacerse entender⟩ **2** BELIEVE : entender ⟨to give someone to understand : dar a alguien a entender⟩ **3** INFER : tener entendido ⟨I understand that she's leaving : tengo entendido que se va⟩ — *vi* : comprender, entender

understandable [ˌʌndərˈstændəbəl] *adj* : comprensible

understanding¹ [ˌʌndərˈstændɪŋ] *adj* : comprensivo, compasivo

understanding² *n* **1** GRASP : comprensión *f*, entendimiento *m* **2** SYMPATHY : comprensión *f* (mutua) **3** INTERPRETATION : interpretación *f* ⟨it's my understanding that ... : tengo la impresión de que ..., tengo entendido que ... ⟩ **4** AGREEMENT : acuerdo *m*, arreglo *m*

understate [ˌʌndərˈsteɪt] *vt* **-stated; -stating** : minimizar, subestimar

understatement [ˌʌndərˈsteɪtmənt] *n* : atenuación *f* ⟨that's an understatement : decir sólo eso es quedarse corto⟩

understudy [ˈʌndərˌstʌdi] *n, pl* **-dies** : sobresaliente *mf*, suplente *mf* (en el teatro)

undertake [ˌʌndərˈteɪk] *vt* **-took** [-ˈtʊk]; **-taken** [-ˈteɪkən]; **-taking 1** : emprender (una tarea), asumir (una responsabilidad) **2** PROMISE : comprometerse (a hacer algo)

undertaker [ˈʌndərˌteɪkər] *n* : director *m*, -tora *f* de funeraria

undertaking [ˈʌndərˌteɪkɪŋ, ˌʌndərˈ-] *n* **1** ENTERPRISE, TASK : empresa *f*, tarea *f* **2** PLEDGE : promesa *f*, garantía *f*

undertone [ˈʌndərˌtoːn] *n* **1** : voz *f* baja ⟨to speak in an undertone : hablar en voz baja⟩ **2** HINT, UNDERCURRENT : trasfondo *m*, matiz *m*

undertow [ˈʌndərˌtoː] *n* : resaca *f*

undervalue [ˌʌndərˈvælˌjuː] *vt* **-ued; -uing** : menospreciar, subestimar

underwater[1] [ˌʌndərˈwɔtər, -ˈwɑ-] *adv* : debajo (del agua)

underwater[2] *adj* : submarino

under way [ˌʌndərˈweɪ] *adv* : en marcha, en camino ⟨to get under way : ponerse en marcha⟩

underwear [ˈʌndərˌwær] *n* : ropa *f* interior, ropa *f* íntima

underworld [ˈʌndərˌwərld] *n* **1** HELL : infierno *m* **2 the underworld** CRIMINALS : la hampa, los bajos fondos

underwrite [ˈʌndərˌraɪt, ˌʌndərˈ-] *vt* **-wrote** [-ˌroːt, -ˈroːt]; **-written** [-ˌrɪtən, -ˈrɪtən]; **-writing 1** INSURE : asegurar **2** FINANCE : financiar **3** BACK, ENDORSE : suscribir, respaldar

underwriter [ˈʌndərˌraɪtər, ˌʌndərˈ-] *n* INSURER : asegurador *m*, -dora *f*

undeserving [ˌʌndɪˈzərvɪŋ] *adj* : indigno

undesirable[1] [ˌʌndɪˈzaɪrəbəl] *adj* : indeseable

undesirable[2] *n* : indeseable *mf*

undeveloped [ˌʌndɪˈvɛləpt] *adj* : sin desarrollar, sin revelar (dícese de una película)

undies [ˈʌndiːz] → **underwear**

undignified [ˌʌnˈdɪgnəfaɪd] *adj* : indecoroso

undiluted [ˌʌndaɪˈluːtəd, -də-] *adj* : sin diluir, concentrado

undiscovered [ˌʌndɪˈskʌvərd] *adj* : no descubierto

undisputed [ˌʌndɪˈspjuːtəd] *adj* : indiscutible

undisturbed [ˌʌndɪˈstərbd] *adj* : tranquilo (dícese de una persona), sin tocar (dícese de un objeto)

undivided [ˌʌndɪˈvaɪdəd] *adj* : íntegro, completo

undo [ˌʌnˈduː] *vt* **-did** [-ˈdɪd]; **-done** [-ˈdʌn]; **-doing 1** UNFASTEN : desabrochar, desatar, abrir **2** ANNUL : anular **3** REVERSE : deshacer, reparar (daños, etc.) **4** RUIN : arruinar, destruir

undoing [ˌʌnˈduːɪŋ] *n* : ruina *f*, perdición *f*

undoubted [ˌʌnˈdaʊtəd] *adj* : cierto, indudable — **undoubtedly** *adv*

undress [ˌʌnˈdrɛs] *vt* : desvestir, desabrigar, desnudar — *vi* : desvestirse, desnudarse

undrinkable [ˌʌnˈdrɪŋkəbəl] *adj* : no potable

undue [ˌʌnˈduː, -ˈdjuː] *adj* : excesivo, indebido — **unduly** *adv*

undulate [ˈʌndʒəˌleɪt] *vi* **-lated; -lating** : ondular

undulation [ˌʌndʒəˈleɪʃən] *n* : ondulación *f*

undying [ˌʌnˈdaɪɪŋ] *adj* : perpetuo, imperecedero

unearth [ˌʌnˈərθ] *vt* **1** EXHUME : desenterrar, exhumar **2** DISCOVER : descubrir

unearthly [ˌʌnˈərθli] *adj* **-lier; -est** : sobrenatural, de otro mundo

uneasily [ˌʌnˈiːzəli] *adv* : inquietamente, con inquietud

uneasiness [ˌʌnˈiːzinəs] *n* : inquietud *f*

uneasy [ˌʌnˈiːzi] *adj* **-easier; -est 1** AWKWARD : incómodo **2** WORRIED : preocupado, inquieto **3** RESTLESS : inquieto, agitado

uneducated [ˌʌnˈɛdʒəˌkeɪtəd] *adj* : inculto, sin educación

unemployed [ˌʌnɪmˈplɔɪd] *adj* : desempleado

unemployment [ˌʌnɪmˈplɔɪmənt] *n* : desempleo *m*

unending [ˌʌnˈɛndɪŋ] *adj* : sin fin, interminable

unendurable [ˌʌnɪnˈdʊrəbəl, -ɛn-, -ˈdjʊr-] *adj* : insoportable, intolerable

unequal [ˌʌnˈiːkwəl] *adj* **1** : desigual **2** INADEQUATE : incapaz, incompetente ⟨to be unequal to a task : no estar a la altura de una tarea⟩

unequaled *or* **unequalled** [ˌʌnˈiːkwəld] *adj* : sin igual

unequivocal [ˌʌnɪˈkwɪvəkəl] *adj* : inequívoco, claro — **unequivocally** *adv*

unerring [ˌʌnˈɛrɪŋ, -ˈər-] *adj* : infalible

unethical [ˌʌnˈɛθɪkəl] *adj* : poco ético

uneven [ˌʌnˈiːvən] *adj* **1** ODD : impar (dícese de un número) **2** : desigual, desnivelado (dícese de una superficie) ⟨uneven terrain : terreno accidentado⟩ **3** IRREGULAR : irregular, poco uniforme **4** UNEQUAL : desigual

unevenly [ˌʌnˈiːvənli] *adv* : desigualmente, irregularmente

uneventful [ˌʌnɪˈvɛntfəl] *adj* : sin incidentes, tranquilo

unexpected [ˌʌnɪkˈspɛktəd] *adj* : imprevisto, inesperado — **unexpectedly** *adv*

unfailing [ˌʌnˈfeɪlɪŋ] *adj* **1** CONSTANT : constante **2** INEXHAUSTIBLE : in-

agotable **3** SURE : a toda prueba, indefectible
unfair [ˌʌnˈfær] *adj* : injusto — **unfairly** *adv*
unfairness [ˌʌnˈfærnəs] *n* : injusticia *f*
unfaithful [ˌʌnˈfeɪθfəl] *adj* : desleal, infiel — **unfaithfully** *adv*
unfaithfulness [ˌʌnˈfeɪθfəlnəs] *n* : infidelidad *f*, deslealtad *f*
unfamiliar [ˌʌnfəˈmɪljər] *adj* **1** STRANGE : desconocido, extraño ⟨an unfamiliar place : un lugar nuevo⟩ **2 to be unfamiliar with** : no estar familiarizado con, desconocer
unfamiliarity [ˌʌnfəˌmɪliˈærəti] *n* : falta *f* de familiaridad
unfashionable [ˌʌnˈfæʃənəbəl] *adj* : fuera de moda
unfasten [ˌʌnˈfæsən] *vt* : desabrochar, desatar (una cuerda, etc.), abrir (una puerta)
unfavorable [ˌʌnˈfeɪvərəbəl] *adj* : desfavorable, mal — **unfavorably** [-bli] *adv*
unfeeling [ˌʌnˈfiːlɪŋ] *adj* : insensible — **unfeelingly** *adv*
unfinished [ˌʌnˈfɪnɪʃd] *adj* : inacabado, incompleto
unfit [ˌʌnˈfɪt] *adj* **1** UNSUITABLE : inadecuado, impropio **2** UNSUITED : no apto, incapaz **3** : incapacitado (físicamente) ⟨to be unfit : no estar en forma⟩
unflappable [ˌʌnˈflæpəbəl] *adj* : imperturbable
unflattering [ˌʌnˈflætərɪŋ] *adj* : poco favorecedor
unfold [ˌʌnˈfoːld] *vt* **1** EXPAND : desplegar, desdoblar, extender ⟨to unfold a map : desplegar un mapa⟩ **2** DISCLOSE, REVEAL : revelar, exponer (un plan, etc.) — *vi* **1** DEVELOP : desarrollarse, desenvolverse ⟨the story unfolded : el cuento se desarrollaba⟩ **2** EXPAND : extenderse, desplegarse
unforeseeable [ˌʌnforˈsiːəbəl] *adj* : imprevisible
unforeseen [ˌʌnforˈsiːn] *adj* : imprevisto
unforgettable [ˌʌnforˈgɛtəbəl] *adj* : inolvidable, memorable — **unforgettably** [-bli] *adv*
unforgivable [ˌʌnfərˈgɪvəbəl] *adj* : imperdonable
unfortunate¹ [ˌʌnˈfortʃənət] *adj* **1** UNLUCKY : desgraciado, infortunado, desafortunado ⟨how unfortunate! : ¡qué mala suerte!⟩ **2** INAPPROPRIATE : inoportuno ⟨an unfortunate comment : un comentario poco feliz⟩
unfortunate² *n* : desgraciado *m*, -da *f*
unfortunately [ˌʌnˈfortʃənətli] *adv* : desafortunadamente
unfounded [ˌʌnˈfaʊndəd] *adj* : infundado
unfreeze [ˌʌnˈfriːz] *v* **-froze** [-ˈfroːz]; **-frozen** [-ˈfroːzən]; **-freezing** *vt* : descongelar — *vi* : descongelarse
unfriendliness [ˌʌnˈfrɛndlinəs] *n* : hostilidad *f*, antipatía *f*

unfriendly [ˌʌnˈfrɛndli] *adj* **-lier; -est** : poco amistoso, hostil
unfurl [ˌʌnˈfərl] *vt* : desplegar, desdoblar — *vi* : desplegarse
unfurnished [ˌʌnˈfərnɪʃt] *adj* : desamueblado
ungainly [ˌʌnˈgeɪnli] *adj* : desgarbado
ungodly [ˌʌnˈgɔdli, -ˈgɑd-] *adj* **1** IMPIOUS : impío **2** OUTRAGEOUS : atroz, terrible ⟨at an ungodly hour : a una hora intempestiva⟩
ungrateful [ˌʌnˈgreɪtfəl] *adj* : desagradecido, ingrato — **ungratefully** *adv*
ungratefulness [ˌʌnˈgreɪtfəlnəs] *n* : ingratitud *f*
unhappily [ˌʌnˈhæpəli] *adv* **1** SADLY : tristemente **2** UNFORTUNATELY : desafortunadamente, lamentablemente
unhappiness [ˌʌnˈhæpinəs] *n* : infelicidad *f*, tristeza *f*, desdicha *f*
unhappy [ˌʌnˈhæpi] *adj* **-pier; -est** **1** UNFORTUNATE : desafortunado, desventurado **2** MISERABLE, SAD : infeliz, triste, desdichado **3** INOPPORTUNE : inoportuno, poco feliz
unharmed [ˌʌnˈhɑrmd] *adj* : salvo, ileso
unhealthy [ˌʌnˈhɛlθi] *adj* **-thier; -est** **1** UNWHOLESOME : insalubre, malsano, nocivo a la salud ⟨an unhealthy climate : un clima insalubre⟩ **2** SICKLY : de mala salud, enfermizo
unheard–of [ˌʌnˈhərdəv] *adj* : sin precedente, inaudito, insólito
unhinge [ˌʌnˈhɪndʒ] *vt* **-hinged; -hinging** **1** : desquiciar (una puerta, etc.) **2** DISRUPT, UNSETTLE : trastornar, perturbar
unholy [ˌʌnˈhoːli] *adj* **-lier; -est** **1** : profano, impío **2** UNGODLY : atroz, terrible
unhook [ˌʌnˈhʊk] *vt* **1** : desenganchar, descolgar (de algo) **2** UNDO : desabrochar
unhurt [ˌʌnˈhərt] *adj* : ileso
unicorn [ˈjuːnəˌkɔrn] *n* : unicornio *m*
unidentified [ˌʌnaɪˈdɛntəˌfaɪd] *adj* : no identificado ⟨unidentified flying object : objeto volador no identificado⟩
unification [ˌjuːnəfəˈkeɪʃən] *n* : unificación *f*
uniform¹ [ˈjuːnəˌfɔrm] *adj* : uniforme, homogéneo, constante
uniform² *n* : uniforme *m*
uniformed [ˈjuːnəˌfɔrmd] *adj* : uniformado
uniformity [ˌjuːnəˈfɔrməti] *n, pl* **-ties** : uniformidad *f*
unify [ˈjuːnəˌfaɪ] *vt* **-fied; -fying** : unificar, unir
unilateral [ˌjuːnəˈlætərəl] *adj* : unilateral — **unilaterally** *adv*
unimaginable [ˌʌnɪˈmædʒənəbəl] *adj* : inimaginable, inconcebible
unimportant [ˌʌnɪmˈpɔrtənt] *adj* : intrascendente, insignificante, sin importancia
uninhabited [ˌʌnɪnˈhæbətəd] *adj* : deshabitado, desierto, despoblado

uninhibited [ˌʌnɪnˈhɪbətəd] *adj* : desenfadado, desinhibido, sin reservas

uninjured [ˌʌnˈɪndʒərd] *adj* : ileso

unintelligent [ˌʌnɪnˈtɛlədʒənt] *adj* : poco inteligente

unintelligible [ˌʌnɪnˈtɛlədʒəbəl] *adj* : ininteligible, incomprensible

unintentional [ˌʌnɪnˈtɛntʃənəl] *adj* : no deliberado, involuntario

unintentionally [ˌʌnɪnˈtɛntʃənəli] *adv* : involuntariamente, sin querer

uninterested [ˌʌnˈɪntəˌrɛstəd, -trəstəd] *adj* : indiferente

uninteresting [ˌʌnˈɪntəˌrɛstɪŋ, -trəstɪŋ] *adj* : poco interesante, sin interés

uninterrupted [ˌʌnˌɪntəˈrʌptəd] *adj* : ininterrumpido, continuo

union [ˈjuːnjən] *n* **1** : unión *f* **2** *or* **labor union** : sindicato *m*, gremio *m*

unionize [ˈjuːnjəˌnaɪz] *v* **-ized; -izing** *vt* : sindicalizar, sindicar — *vi* : sindicalizarse

unique [juˈniːk] *adj* **1** SOLE : único, solo **2** UNUSUAL : extraordinario

uniquely [juˈniːkli] *adv* **1** EXCLUSIVELY : exclusivamente **2** EXCEPTIONALLY : excepcionalmente

unison [ˈjuːnəsən, -zən] *n* **1** : unísono *m* (en música) **2** CONCORD : acuerdo *m*, armonía *f*, concordia *f* **3 in ~** SIMULTANEOUSLY : simultáneamente, al unísono

unit [ˈjuːnɪt] *n* **1** : unidad *f* **2** : módulo *m* (de un mobiliario)

unitary [ˈjuːnəˌtɛri] *adj* : unitario

unite [juˈnaɪt] *v* **united; uniting** *vt* : unir, juntar, combinar — *vi* : unirse, juntarse

unity [ˈjuːnəti] *n, pl* **-ties 1** UNION : unidad *f*, unión *f* **2** HARMONY : armonía *f*, acuerdo *m*

universal [ˌjuːnəˈvərsəl] *adj* **1** GENERAL : general, universal ⟨a universal rule : una regla universal⟩ **2** WORLDWIDE : universal, mundial — **universally** *adv*

universe [ˈjuːnəˌvərs] *n* : universo *m*

university [ˌjuːnəˈvərsəti] *n, pl* **-ties** : universidad *f*

unjust [ˌʌnˈdʒʌst] *adj* : injusto — **unjustly** *adv*

unjustifiable [ˌʌnˌdʒʌstəˈfaɪəbəl] *adj* : injustificable

unjustified [ˌʌnˈdʒʌstəˌfaɪd] *adj* : injustificado

unkempt [ˌʌnˈkɛmpt] *adj* : descuidado, desaliñado, despeinado (dícese del pelo)

unkind [ˌʌnˈkaɪnd] *adj* : poco amable, cruel — **unkindly** *adv*

unkindness [ˌʌnˈkaɪndnəs] *n* : crueldad *f*, falta *f* de amabilidad

unknowing [ˌʌnˈnoːɪŋ] *adj* : inconsciente, ignorante — **unknowingly** *adv*

unknown [ˌʌnˈnoːn] *adj* : desconocido

unlawful [ˌʌnˈlɔfəl] *adj* : ilícito, ilegal — **unlawfully** *adv*

unleash [ˌʌnˈliːʃ] *vt* : soltar, desatar

unless [ənˈlɛs] *conj* : a menos que, salvo que, a no ser que

unlike¹ [ˌʌnˈlaɪk] *adj* **1** DIFFERENT : diferente, distinto **2** UNEQUAL : desigual

unlike² *prep* **1** : diferente de, distinto de ⟨unlike the others : distinto a los demás⟩ **2** : a diferencia de ⟨unlike her sister, she is shy : a diferencia de su hermana, es tímida⟩

unlikelihood [ˌʌnˈlaɪkliˌhʊd] *n* : improbabilidad *f*

unlikely [ˌʌnˈlaɪkli] *adj* **-lier; -est 1** IMPROBABLE : improbable, poco probable **2** UNPROMISING : poco prometedor

unlimited [ˌʌnˈlɪmətəd] *adj* : ilimitado

unload [ˌʌnˈloːd] *vt* **1** REMOVE : descargar, desembarcar (mercancías o pasajeros) **2** : descargar (un avión, un camión, etc.) **3** DUMP : deshacerse de — *vi* : descargar (dícese de un avión, un camión, etc.)

unlock [ˌʌnˈlɑk] *vt* **1** : abrir (con llave) **2** DISCLOSE, REVEAL : revelar

unluckily [ˌʌnˈlʌkəli] *adv* : desgraciadamente

unlucky [ˌʌnˈlʌki] *adj* **-luckier; -est 1** : de mala suerte, desgraciado, desafortunado ⟨an unlucky year : un año de mala suerte⟩ **2** INAUSPICIOUS : desfavorable, poco propicio **3** REGRETTABLE : lamentable

unmanageable [ˌʌnˈmænɪdʒəbəl] *adj* : difícil de controlar, poco manejable, ingobernable

unmarried [ˌʌnˈmærid] *adj* : soltero

unmask [ˌʌnˈmæsk] *vt* EXPOSE : desenmascarar

unmerciful [ˌʌnˈmərsɪfəl] *adj* MERCILESS : despiadado — **unmercifully** *adv*

unmistakable [ˌʌnmɪˈsteɪkəbəl] *adj* : evidente, inconfundible, obvio — **unmistakably** [-bli] *adv*

unmoved [ˌʌnˈmuːvd] *adj* : impasible ⟨to be unmoved by : permanecer impasible ante⟩

unnatural [ˌʌnˈnætʃərəl] *adj* **1** ABNORMAL, UNUSUAL : anormal, poco natural, poco normal **2** AFFECTED : afectado, forzado ⟨an unnatural smile : una sonrisa forzada⟩ **3** PERVERSE : perverso, antinatural

unnecessary [ˌʌnˈnɛsəˌsɛri] *adj* : innecesario — **unnecessarily** [-ˌnɛsəˈsɛrəli] *adv*

unnerve [ˌʌnˈnərv] *vt* **-nerved; -nerving** : turbar, desconcertar, poner nervioso

unnoticed [ˌʌnˈnoːtəst] *adj* : inadvertido ⟨to go unnoticed : pasar inadvertido⟩

unobstructed [ˌʌnəbˈstrʌktəd] *adj* : libre, despejado

unobtainable [ˌʌnəbˈteɪnəbəl] *adj* : inasequible

unobtrusive [ˌʌnəbˈstruːsɪv] *adj* : discreto

unoccupied [ˌʌnˈɑkjəˌpaɪd] *adj* **1** IDLE : desempleado, desocupado **2** EMPTY : desocupado, libre, deshabitado

unofficial [ˌʌnəˈfɪʃəl] *adj* : extraoficial, oficioso, no oficial

unorganized [ˌʌnˈɔrgəˌnaɪzd] *adj* : desorganizado

unorthodox [ˌʌnˈɔrθəˌdɑks] *adj* : poco ortodoxo, poco convencional

unpack [ˌʌnˈpæk] *vt* : desempacar — *vi* : desempacar, deshacer las maletas

unpaid [ˌʌnˈpeɪd] *adj* : no remunerado, no retribuido ⟨an unpaid bill : una cuenta pendiente⟩

unparalleled [ˌʌnˈpærəˌlɛld] *adj* : sin igual

unpatriotic [ˌʌnˌpeɪtriˈɑṭɪk] *adj* : antipatriótico

unpleasant [ˌʌnˈplɛzənt] *adj* : desagradable — **unpleasantly** *adv*

unplug [ˌʌnˈplʌg] *vt* **-plugged; -plugging 1** UNCLOG : destapar, desatascar **2** DISCONNECT : desconectar, desenchufar

unpopular [ˌʌnˈpɑpjələr] *adj* : impopular, poco popular

unpopularity [ˌʌnˌpɑpjəˈlærəṭi] *n* : impopularidad *f*

unprecedented [ˌʌnˈprɛsəˌdɛntəd] *adj* : sin precedentes, inaudito, nuevo

unpredictable [ˌʌnpriˈdɪktəbəl] *adj* : impredecible

unprejudiced [ˌʌnˈprɛdʒədəst] *adj* : imparcial, objetivo

unprepared [ˌʌnpriˈpærd] *adj* : no preparado ⟨an unprepared speech : un discurso improvisado⟩

unpretentious [ˌʌnpriˈtɛntʃəs] *adj* : modesto, sin pretensiones

unprincipled [ˌʌnˈprɪnʃsəpəld] *adj* : sin principios, carente de escrúpulos

unproductive [ˌʌnprəˈdʌktɪv] *adj* : improductivo

unprofitable [ˌʌnˈprɑfəṭəbəl] *adj* : no rentable, poco provechoso

unpromising [ˌʌnˈprɑməsɪŋ] *adj* : poco prometedor

unprotected [ˌʌnprəˈtɛktəd] *adj* : sin protección, desprotegido

unprovoked [ˌʌnprəˈvoːkt] *adj* : no provocado

unpublished [ˌʌnˈpʌblɪʃt] *adj* : inédito

unpunished [ˌʌnˈpʌnɪʃt] *adj* : impune ⟨to go unpunished : escapar sin castigo⟩

unqualified [ˌʌnˈkwɑləˌfaɪd] *adj* **1** : no calificado, sin título **2** COMPLETE : completo, absoluto ⟨an unqualified denial : una negación incondicional⟩

unquestionable [ˌʌnˈkwɛstʃənəbəl] *adj* : incuestionable, indudable, indiscutible — **unquestionably** [-bli] *adv*

unquestioning [ˌʌnˈkwɛstʃənɪŋ] *adj* : incondicional, absoluto, ciego

unravel [ˌʌnˈrævəl] *v* **-eled** *or* **-elled; -eling** *or* **-elling** *vt* **1** DISENTANGLE : desenmarañar, desenredar **2** SOLVE : aclarar, desenmarañar, desentrañar — *vi* : deshacerse

unreal [ˌʌnˈriːl] *adj* : irreal

unrealistic [ˌʌnˌriːəˈlɪstɪk] *adj* : poco realista

unreasonable [ˌʌnˈriːzənəbəl] *adj* **1** IRRATIONAL : poco razonable, irrazon-

able, irracional **2** EXCESSIVE : excesivo ⟨unreasonable prices : precios excesivos⟩

unreasonably [ˌʌnˈriːzənəbli] *adv* **1** IRRATIONALLY : irracionalmente, de manera irrazonable **2** EXCESSIVELY : excesivamente

unrefined [ˌʌnriˈfaɪnd] *adj* **1** : no refinado, sin refinar (dícese del azúcar, de la harina, etc.) **2** : poco refinado, inculto (dícese de una persona)

unrelated [ˌʌnriˈleɪṭəd] *adj* : no relacionado, inconexo

unrelenting [ˌʌnriˈlɛntɪŋ] *adj* **1** STERN : severo, inexorable **2** CONSTANT, RELENTLESS : constante, implacable

unreliable [ˌʌnriˈlaɪəbəl] *adj* : que no es de fiar, de poca confianza, inestable (dícese del tiempo)

unrepentant [ˌʌnriˈpɛntənt] *adj* : impenitente

unresolved [ˌʌnriˈzɑlvd] *adj* : pendiente, no resuelto

unrest [ˌʌnˈrɛst] *n* : inquietud *f*, malestar *m* ⟨political unrest : disturbios políticos⟩

unrestrained [ˌʌnriˈstreɪnd] *adj* : desenfrenado, incontrolado

unrestricted [ˌʌnriˈstrɪktəd] *adj* : sin restricción ⟨unrestricted access : libre acceso⟩

unrewarding [ˌʌnriˈwɔrdɪŋ] *adj* THANKLESS : ingrato

unripe [ˌʌnˈraɪp] *adj* : inmaduro, verde

unrivaled *or* **unrivalled** [ˌʌnˈraɪvəld] *adj* : incomparable

unroll [ˌʌnˈroːl] *vt* : desenrollar — *vi* : desenrollarse

unruffled [ˌʌnˈrʌfəld] *adj* **1** SERENE : sereno, tranquilo **2** SMOOTH : tranquilo, liso ⟨unruffled waters : aguas tranquilas⟩

unruliness [ˌʌnˈruːlinəs] *n* : indisciplina *f*

unruly [ˌʌnˈruːli] *adj* : indisciplinado, díscolo, rebelde

unsafe [ˌʌnˈseɪf] *adj* : inseguro

unsaid [ˌʌnˈsɛd] *adj* : sin decir ⟨to leave unsaid : quedar por decir⟩

unsanitary [ˌʌnˈsænəˌteri] *adj* : antihigiénico

unsatisfactory [ˌʌnˌsæṭəsˈfæktəri] *adj* : insatisfactorio

unsatisfied [ˌʌnˈsæṭəsˌfaɪd] *adj* : insatisfecho

unscathed [ˌʌnˈskeɪðd] *adj* UNHARMED : ileso

unscheduled [ˌʌnˈskɛˌdʒuːld] *adj* : no programado, imprevisto

unscientific [ˌʌnˌsaɪənˈtɪfɪk] *adj* : poco científico

unscrupulous [ˌʌnˈskruːpjələs] *adj* : inescrupuloso, sin escrúpulos — **unscrupulously** *adv*

unseal [ˌʌnˈsiːl] *vt* : abrir, quitarle el sello a

unseasonable [ˌʌnˈsiːzənəbəl] *adj* **1** : extemporáneo ⟨unseasonable rain

: lluvia extemporánea⟩ 2 UNTIMELY : extemporáneo, inoportuno

unseemly [ˌʌn'siːmli] *adj* -lier; -est 1 INDECOROUS : indecoroso 2 INAPPROPRIATE : impropio, inapropiado

unseen [ˌʌn'siːn] *adj* 1 UNNOTICED : inadvertido 2 INVISIBLE : oculto, invisible

unselfish [ˌʌn'sɛlfɪʃ] *adj* : generoso, desinteresado — **unselfishly** *adv*

unselfishness [ˌʌn'sɛlfɪʃnəs] *n* : generosidad *f*, desinterés *m*

unsettle [ˌʌn'sɛtəl] *vt* -tled; -tling DISTURB : trastornar, alterar, perturbar

unsettled [ˌʌn'sɛtəld] *adj* 1 CHANGEABLE : inestable, variable ⟨unsettled weather : tiempo inestable⟩ 2 DISTURBED : agitado, inquieto ⟨unsettled waters : aguas agitadas⟩ 3 UNDECIDED : pendiente (dícese de un asunto), indeciso (dícese de una persona) 4 UNPAID : sin saldar, pendiente 5 UNINHABITED : despoblado, no colonizado

unshaped [ˌʌn'ʃeɪpt] *adj* : sin forma, informe

unsightly [ˌʌn'saɪtli] *adj* UGLY : feo, de aspecto malo

unskilled [ˌʌn'skɪld] *adj* : no calificado

unskillful [ˌʌn'skɪlfəl] *adj* : inexperto, poco hábil

unsnap [ˌʌn'snæp] *vt* -snapped; -snapping : desabrochar

unsociable *adj* : poco sociable

unsolved [ˌʌn'sɑlvd] *adj* : no resuelto, sin resolver

unsophisticated [ˌʌnsə'fɪstəˌkeɪtəd] *adj* 1 NAIVE, UNWORLDLY : ingenuo, de poco mundo 2 SIMPLE : simple, poco sofisticado, rudimentario

unsound [ˌʌn'saʊnd] *adj* 1 UNHEALTHY : enfermizo, de mala salud 2 : poco sólido, defectuoso (dícese de una estructura, etc.) 3 INVALID : inválido, erróneo 4 of unsound mind : mentalmente incapacitado

unspeakable [ˌʌn'spiːkəbəl] *adj* 1 INDESCRIBABLE : indecible, inexpresable, incalificable 2 HEINOUS : atroz, nefando, abominable — **unspeakably** [-bli] *adv*

unspecified [ˌʌn'spɛsəˌfaɪd] *adj* : indeterminado, sin especificar

unspoiled [ˌʌn'spɔɪld] *adj* 1 : conservado, sin estropear (dícese de un lugar) 2 : que no está mimado (dícese de un niño)

unstable [ˌʌn'steɪbəl] *adj* 1 CHANGEABLE : variable, inestable, cambiable ⟨an unstable pulse : un pulso irregular⟩ 2 UNSTEADY : inestable, poco sólido (dícese de una estructura)

unsteadily [ˌʌn'stɛdəli] *adv* : de modo inestable

unsteadiness [ˌʌn'stɛdinəs] *n* : inestabilidad *f*, inseguridad *f*

unsteady [ˌʌn'stɛdi] *adj* 1 UNSTABLE : inestable, variable 2 SHAKY : tembloroso

unstoppable [ˌʌn'stɑpəbəl] *adj* : irrefrenable, incontenible

unsubstantiated [ˌʌnsəb'stænʧiˌeɪtəd] *adj* : no corroborado, no demostrado

unsuccessful [ˌʌnsək'sɛsfəl] *adj* : fracasado, infructuoso

unsuitable [ˌʌn'suːtəbəl] *adj* : inadecuado, impropio, inapropiado ⟨an unsuitable time : una hora inconveniente⟩

unsuited [ˌʌn'suːtəd] *adj* : inadecuado, inepto

unsung [ˌʌn'sʌŋ] *adj* : olvidado

unsure [ˌʌn'ʃʊr] *adj* : incierto, dudoso

unsurpassed [ˌʌnsər'pæst] *adj* : sin par, sin igual

unsuspecting [ˌʌnsə'spɛktɪŋ] *adj* : desprevenido, desapercibido, confiado

unsympathetic [ˌʌnˌsɪmpə'θɛtɪk] *adj* : poco comprensivo, indiferente

untangle [ˌʌn'teɪŋɡəl] *vt* -gled; -gling : desenmarañar, desenredar

unthinkable [ˌʌn'θɪŋkəbəl] *adj* : inconcebible, impensable

unthinking [ˌʌn'θɪŋkɪŋ] *adj* : irreflexivo, inconsciente — **unthinkingly** *adv*

untidy [ˌʌn'taɪdi] *adj* 1 SLOVENLY : desaliñado 2 DISORDERLY : desordenado, desarreglado

untie [ˌʌn'taɪ] *vt* -tied; -tying *or* -tieing : desatar, deshacer

until¹ [ˌʌn'tɪl] *prep* : hasta ⟨until now : hasta ahora⟩

until² *conj* : hasta que ⟨until they left : hasta que salieron⟩ ⟨don't answer until you're sure : no contestes hasta que (no) estés seguro⟩

untimely [ˌʌn'taɪmli] *adj* 1 PREMATURE : prematuro ⟨an untimely death : una muerte prematura⟩ 2 INOPPORTUNE : inoportuno, intempestivo

untold [ˌʌn'toːld] *adj* 1 : nunca dicho ⟨the untold secret : el secreto sin contar⟩ 2 INCALCULABLE : incalculable, indecible

untouched [ˌʌn'tʌʧt] *adj* 1 INTACT : intacto, sin tocar, sin probar (dícese de la comida) 2 UNAFFECTED : insensible, indiferente

untoward [ˌʌn'tɔrd, -'toːərd, -tə-'wɔrd] *adj* 1 : indecoroso, impropio (dícese del comportamiento) 2 ADVERSE, UNFORTUNATE : desafortunado, adverso ⟨untoward effects : efectos perjudiciales⟩ 3 UNSEEMLY : indecoroso

untrained [ˌʌn'treɪnd] *adj* : inexperto, no capacitado

untreated [ˌʌn'triːtəd] *adj* : no tratado (dícese de una enfermedad, etc.), sin tratar (dícese de un material)

untroubled [ˌʌn'trʌbəld] *adj* : tranquilo ⟨to be untroubled by : no estar afectado por⟩

untrue [ˌʌn'truː] *adj* 1 UNFAITHFUL : infiel 2 FALSE : falso

untrustworthy [ˌʌn'trʌstˌwərði] *adj* : de poca confianza (dícese de una persona), no fidedigno (dícese de la información)

untruth [ˌʌn'truːθ, 'ʌnˌ-] *n* : mentira *f*, falsedad *f*

untruthful [ˌʌn'truːθfəl] *adj* : mentiroso, falso

unusable [ˌʌn'juːzəbəl] *adj* : inútil, inservible

unused [ˌʌn'juːzd, *in sense 1 usually* -'juːst] *adj* **1** UNACCUSTOMED : inhabituado **2** NEW : nuevo **3** IDLE : no utilizado (dícese de la tierra) **4** REMAINING : restante ⟨the unused portion : la porción restante⟩

unusual [ˌʌn'juːʒʊəl] *adj* : inusual, poco común, raro

unusually [ˌʌn'juːʒʊəli, -'juːʒəli] *adv* : excepcionalmente, extraordinariamente, fuera de lo común

unwanted [ˌʌn'wɑntəd] *adj* : superfluo, de sobre

unwarranted [ˌʌn'wɔrəntəd] *adj* : injustificado

unwary [ˌʌn'wæri] *adj* : incauto

unwavering [ˌʌn'weɪvərɪŋ] *adj* : firme, inquebrantable ⟨an unwavering gaze : una mirada fija⟩

unwelcome [ˌʌn'wɛlkəm] *adj* : importuno, molesto

unwell [ˌʌn'wɛl] *adj* : enfermo, mal

unwholesome [ˌʌn'hoːlsəm] *adj* **1** UNHEALTHY : malsano, insalubre **2** PERNICIOUS : pernicioso **3** LOATHSOME : repugnante, muy desagradable

unwieldy [ˌʌn'wiːldi] *adj* CUMBERSOME : difícil de manejar, torpe y pesado

unwilling [ˌʌn'wɪlɪŋ] *adj* : poco dispuesto ⟨to be unwilling to : no estar dispuesto a⟩

unwillingly [ˌʌn'wɪlɪŋli] *adv* : a regañadientes, de mala gana

unwind [ˌʌn'waɪnd] *v* **-wound** [-'waʊnd]; **-winding** *vt* UNROLL : desenrollar — *vi* **1** : desenrollarse **2** RELAX : relajar

unwise [ˌʌn'waɪz] *adj* : imprudente, desacertado, poco aconsejable

unwisely [ˌʌn'waɪzli] *adv* : imprudentemente

unwitting [ˌʌn'wɪtɪŋ] *adj* **1** UNAWARE : inconsciente **2** INADVERTENT : involuntario, inadvertido ⟨an unwitting mistake : un error inadvertido⟩ — **unwittingly** *adv*

unworthiness [ˌʌn'wərðinəs] *n* : falta *f* de valía

unworthy [ˌʌn'wərði] *adj* **1** UNDESERVING : indigno ⟨to be unworthy of : no ser digno de⟩ **2** UNMERITED : inmerecido

unwrap [ˌʌn'ræp] *vt* **-wrapped; -wrapping** : desenvolver, deshacer

unwritten [ˌʌn'rɪtən] *adj* : no escrito

unyielding [ˌʌn'jiːldɪŋ] *adj* : firme, inflexible, rígido

unzip [ˌʌn'zɪp] *vt* **-zipped; -zipping** : abrir el cierre de

up¹ ['ʌp] *v* **upped** ['ʌpt]; **upping; ups** *vt* INCREASE : aumentar, subir ⟨they upped the prices : aumentaron los precios⟩ — *vi* **to up and** : agarrar y *fam* ⟨she up and left : agarró y se fue⟩

up² *adv* **1** ABOVE : arriba, en lo alto ⟨up in the mountains : arriba en las montañas⟩ **2** UPWARDS : hacia arriba ⟨push it up : empújalo hacia arriba⟩ ⟨the sun came up : el sol salió⟩ ⟨prices went up : los precios subieron⟩ **3** (*indicating an upright position or waking state*) ⟨to sit up : ponerse derecho⟩ ⟨they got up late : se levantaron tarde⟩ ⟨I stayed up all night : pasé toda la noche sin dormir⟩ **4** (*indicating volume or intensity*) ⟨to speak up : hablar más fuerte⟩ **5** (*indicating a northerly direction*) ⟨the climate up north : el clima del norte⟩ ⟨I'm going up to Canada : voy para Canadá⟩ **6** (*indicating the appearance or existence of something*) ⟨the book turned up : el libro apareció⟩ **7** (*indicating consideration*) ⟨she brought the matter up : mencionó el asunto⟩ **8** COMPLETELY : completamente ⟨eat it up : cómetelo todo⟩ **9** : en pedazos ⟨he tore it up : lo rompió en pedazos⟩ **10** (*indicating a stopping*) ⟨the car pulled up to the curb : el carro paró al borde de la acera⟩ **11** (*indicating an even score*) ⟨the game was 10 up : empataron a 10⟩

up³ *adj* **1** (*risen above the horizon*) ⟨the sun is up : ha salido el sol⟩ **2** (*being above a normal or former level*) ⟨prices are up : los precios han aumentado⟩ ⟨the river is up : las aguas están altas⟩ **3** : despierto, levantado ⟨up all night : despierto toda la noche⟩ **4** BUILT : construido ⟨the house is up : la casa está construida⟩ **5** OPEN : abierto ⟨the windows are up : las ventanas están abiertas⟩ **6** (*moving or going upward*) ⟨the up staircase : la escalera para subir⟩ **7** ABREAST : enterado, al día, al corriente ⟨to be up on the news : estar al corriente de las noticias⟩ **8** PREPARED : preparado ⟨we were up for the test : estuvimos preparados para el examen⟩ **9** FINISHED : terminado, acabado ⟨time is up : se ha terminado el tiempo permitido⟩ **10 to be up** : pasar ⟨what's up? : ¿qué pasa?⟩

up⁴ *prep* **1** (*to, toward, or at a higher point of*) ⟨he went up the stairs : subió la escalera⟩ **2** (*to or toward the source of*) ⟨to go up the river : ir río arriba⟩ **3** ALONG : a lo largo, por ⟨up the coast : a lo largo de la costa⟩ ⟨just up the way : un poco más adelante⟩ ⟨up and down the city : por toda la ciudad⟩

upbraid [ˌʌp'breɪd] *vt* : reprender, regañar

upbringing ['ʌpˌbrɪŋɪŋ] *n* : crianza *f*, educación *f*

upcoming [ˌʌp'kʌmɪŋ] *adj* : próximo

update¹ [ˌʌp'deɪt] *vt* **-dated; -dating** : poner al día, poner al corriente, actualizar

update² ['ʌpˌdeɪt] *n* : actualización *f*, puesta *f* al día

upend [ˌʌp'ɛnd] *vt* **1** : poner vertical **2** OVERTURN : volcar

upgrade¹ [ˈʌpˌgreɪd, ˌʌpˈ-] *vt* **-graded;
-grading 1** PROMOTE : ascender **2** IM-
PROVE : mejorar
upgrade² [ˈʌpˌgreɪd] *n* **1** SLOPE : cuesta *f*, pendiente *f* **2** RISE : aumento *m*
de categoría (de un puesto), ascenso *m*
(de un empleado) **3** IMPROVEMENT
: mejoramiento *m*
upheaval [ˌʌpˈhiːvəl] *n* **1** : levantamiento *m* (en geología) **2** DISTURBANCE,
UPSET : trastorno *m*, agitación *f*, conmoción *f*
uphill¹ [ˌʌpˈhɪl] *adv* : cuesta arriba
uphill² [ˈʌpˌhɪl] *adj* **1** ASCENDING : en
subida **2** DIFFICULT : difícil, arduo
uphold [ˌʌpˈhoːld] *vt* **-held; -holding 1**
SUPPORT : sostener, apoyar, mantener
2 RAISE : levantar **3** CONFIRM : confirmar (una decisión judicial)
upholster [ˌʌpˈhoːlstər] *vt* : tapizar
upholsterer [ˌʌpˈhoːlstərər] *n* : tapicero
m, -ra *f*
upholstery [ˌʌpˈhoːlstəri] *n, pl* **-steries**
: tapicería *f*
upkeep [ˈʌpˌkiːp] *n* : mantenimiento *m*
upland [ˈʌplənd, -ˌlænd] *n* : altiplanicie
f, altiplano *m*
uplift¹ [ˌʌpˈlɪft] *vt* **1** RAISE : elevar, levantar **2** ELEVATE : elevar, animar (el
espíritu, la mente, etc.)
uplift² [ˈʌpˌlɪft] *n* : elevación *f*
upon [əˈpɔn, əˈpɑn] *prep* : en, sobre
⟨upon the desk : sobre el escritorio⟩
⟨upon leaving : al salir⟩ ⟨questions
upon questions : pregunta tras pre-
gunta⟩
upper¹ [ˈʌpər] *adj* **1** HIGHER : superior
⟨the upper classes : las clases altas⟩ **2**
: alto (en geografía) ⟨the upper Missis-
sippi : el alto Mississippi⟩
upper² *n* : parte *f* superior (del calzado,
etc.)
uppercase [ˌʌpərˈkeɪs] *adj* : mayúsculo
upper hand *n* : ventaja *f*, dominio *m*
uppermost [ˈʌpərˌmoːst] *adj* : más alto
⟨it was uppermost in his mind : era lo
que más le preocupaba⟩
upright¹ [ˈʌpˌraɪt] *adj* **1** VERTICAL : vertical **2** ERECT : erguido, derecho **3**
JUST : recto, honesto, justo
upright² *n* : montante *m*, poste *m*, soporte *m*
uprising [ˈʌpˌraɪzɪŋ] *n* : insurrección *f*,
revuelta *f*, alzamiento *m*
uproar [ˈʌpˌror] *n* COMMOTION : alboroto *m*, jaleo *m*, escándalo *m*
uproarious [ˌʌpˈroriəs] *adj* **1** CLAM-
OROUS : estrepitoso, clamoroso **2** HI-
LARIOUS : muy divertido, hilarante —
uproariously *adv*
uproot [ˌʌpˈruːt, -ˈrʊt] *vt* : desarraigar
upset¹ [ˌʌpˈsɛt] *vt* **-set; -setting 1** OVER-
TURN : volcar **2** SPILL : derramar **3**
DISTURB : perturbar, disgustar, inquietar, alterar **4** SICKEN : sentar mal a
⟨it upsets my stomach : me sienta mal
al estómago⟩ **5** DISRUPT : trastornar,
desbaratar (planes, etc.) **6** DEFEAT
: derrotar (en deportes)

upset² *adj* **1** DISPLEASED, DISTRESSED
: disgustado, alterado **2 to have an upset stomach** : estar mal del estómago,
estar descompuesto (de estómago)
upset³ [ˈʌpˌsɛt] *n* **1** OVERTURNING
: vuelco *m* **2** DISRUPTION : trastorno
m (de planes, etc.) **3** DEFEAT : derrota *f* (en deportes)
upshot [ˈʌpˌʃat] *n* : resultado *m* final
upside–down [ˌʌpˌsaɪdˈdaʊn] *adj* : al
revés
upside down [ˌʌpˌsaɪdˈdaʊn] *adv* **1** : al
revés **2** : en confusión, en desorden
upstairs¹ [ˌʌpˈstærz] *adv* : arriba, en el
piso superior
upstairs² [ˈʌpˌstærz, ˌʌpˈ-] *adj* : de arriba
upstairs³ [ˈʌpˌstærz, ˌʌpˈ-] *ns & pl* : piso
m de arriba, planta *f* de arriba
upstanding [ˌʌpˈstændɪŋ, ˈʌpˌ-] *adj* HON-
EST, UPRIGHT : honesto, íntegro, recto
upstart [ˈʌpˌstart] *n* : advenedizo *m*, -za
f
upswing [ˈʌpˌswɪŋ] *n* : alza *f*, mejora *f*
notable ⟨to be on the upswing : estar
mejorándose⟩
uptight [ˌʌpˈtaɪt] *adj* : tenso, nervioso
up to *prep* **1** : hasta ⟨up to a year : hasta un año⟩ ⟨in mud up to my ankles
: en barro hasta los tobillos⟩ **2 to be
up to** : estar a la altura de ⟨I'm not up
to going : no estoy en condiciones de
ir⟩ **3 to be up to** : depender de ⟨it's up
to the director : depende del director⟩
up–to–date [ˌʌptəˈdeɪt] *adj* **1** CURRENT
: corriente, al día ⟨to keep up-to-date
: mantenerse al corriente⟩ **2** MODERN
: moderno
uptown [ˈʌpˌtaʊn] *adv* : hacia la parte
alta de la ciudad, hacia el distrito residencial
upturn [ˈʌpˌtərn] *n* : mejora *f*, auge *m*
(económico)
upward¹ [ˈʌpwərd] *or* **upwards** [-wərdz]
adv **1** : hacia arriba **2 ~ of** : más de
upward² *adj* : ascendente, hacia arriba
upwind [ˌʌpˈwɪnd] *adv & adj* : contra el
viento
uranium [jʊˈreɪniəm] *n* : uranio *m*
Uranus [jʊˈreɪnəs, ˈjʊrənəs] *n* : Urano *m*
urban [ˈərbən] *adj* : urbano
urbane [ˌərˈbeɪn] *adj* : urbano, cortés
urchin [ˈərtʃən] *n* **1** SCAMP : granuja *mf*;
pillo *m*, -lla *f* **2 sea urchin** : erizo *m* de
mar
Urdu [ˈʊrduː, ˈər-] *n* : urdu *m*
urethra [jʊˈriːθrə] *n, pl* **-thras** *or* **-thrae**
[-ˌθriː] : uretra *f*
urge¹ [ˈərdʒ] *vt* **urged; urging 1** PRESS
: instar, apremiar, insistir ⟨we urged
him to come : insistimos en que
viniera⟩ **2** ADVOCATE : recomendar,
abogar por **3 to urge on** : animar, alentar
urge² *n* : impulso *m*, ganas *fpl*, compulsión *f*
urgency [ˈərdʒəntsi] *n, pl* **-cies** : urgencia *f*

urgent ['ərdʒənt] *adj* **1** PRESSING : urgente, apremiante **2** INSISTENT : insistente **3 to be urgent** : urgir

urgently ['ərdʒəntli] *adv* : urgentemente

urinal ['jʊrənəl, *esp Brit* jʊ'raɪnəl] *n* : orinal *m* (recipiente), urinario *m* (lugar)

urinary ['jʊrə,nɛri] *adj* : urinario

urinate ['jʊrə,neɪt] *vi* **-nated; -nating** : orinar

urination [,jʊrə'neɪʃən] *n* : orinación *f*

urine ['jʊrən] *n* : orina *f*

urn ['ərn] *n* **1** VASE : urna *f* **2** : recipiente *m* (para servir café, etc.)

Uruguayan [,ʊrə'gwaɪən, ,jʊr-, -'gweɪ-] *n* : uruguayo *m*, -ya *f* — **Uruguayan** *adj*

us ['ʌs] *pron* **1** (*as direct object*) : nos ⟨they were visiting us : nos visitaban⟩ **2** (*as indirect object*) : nos ⟨he gave us a present : nos dio un regalo⟩ **3** (*as object of preposition*) : nosotros, nosotras ⟨stay with us : quédese con nosotros⟩ ⟨both of us : nosotros dos⟩ **4** (*for emphasis*) : nosotros ⟨it's us! : ¡somos nosotros!⟩

usable ['ju:zəbəl] *adj* : utilizable

usage ['ju:sɪdʒ, -zɪdʒ] *n* **1** HABIT : costumbre *f*, hábito *m* **2** USE : uso *m*

use¹ ['ju:z] *v* **used** ['ju:zd, *in phrase "used to" usually* 'ju:stu:]; **using** *vt* **1** EMPLOY : emplear, usar **2** CONSUME : consumir, tomar (drogas, etc.) **3** UTILIZE : usar, utilizar ⟨to use tact : usar tacto⟩ ⟨he used his friends to get ahead : usó a sus amigos para mejorar su posición⟩ **4** TREAT : tratar ⟨they used the horse cruelly : maltrataron al caballo⟩ **5 to use up** : agotar, consumir, gastar — *vi* (*used in the past with* **to** *to indicate a former fact or state*) : soler, acostumbrar ⟨winters used to be colder : los inviernos solían ser más fríos, los inviernos eran más fríos⟩ ⟨she used to dance : acostumbraba bailar⟩

use² ['ju:s] *n* **1** APPLICATION, EMPLOYMENT : uso *m*, empleo *m*, utilización *f* ⟨out of use : en desuso⟩ ⟨ready for use : listo para usar⟩ ⟨to be in use : usarse, estar funcionando⟩ ⟨to make use of : servirse de, aprovechar⟩ **2** USEFULNESS : utilidad *f* ⟨to be of no use : no servir (para nada)⟩ ⟨it's no use! : ¡es inútil!⟩ **3 to have the use of** : poder usar, tener acceso a **4 to have no use for** : no necesitar ⟨she has no use for po-

etry : a ella no le gusta la poesía⟩

used ['ju:zd] *adj* **1** SECONDHAND : usado, de segunda mano ⟨used cars : coches usados⟩ **2** ACCUSTOMED : acostumbrado ⟨used to the heat : acostumbrado al calor⟩

useful ['ju:sfəl] *adj* : útil, práctico — **usefully** *adv*

usefulness ['ju:sfəlnəs] *n* : utilidad *f*

useless ['ju:sləs] *adj* : inútil — **uselessly** *adv*

uselessness ['ju:sləsnəs] *n* : inutilidad *f*

user ['ju:zər] *n* : usuario *m*, -ria *f*

usher¹ ['ʌʃər] *vt* **1** ESCORT : acompañar, conducir **2 to usher in** : hacer pasar (a alguien) ⟨to usher in a new era : anunciar una nueva época⟩

usher² *n* : acomodador *m*, -dora *f*

usherette [,ʌʃə'rɛt] *n* : acomodadora *f*

usual ['ju:ʒəl] *adj* **1** NORMAL : usual, normal **2** CUSTOMARY : acostumbrado, habitual, de costumbre **3** ORDINARY : ordinario, típico

usually ['ju:ʒəli, 'ju:ʒəli] *adv* : usualmente, normalmente

usurp [jʊ'sərp, -'zərp] *vt* : usurpar

usurper [jʊ'sərpər, -'zər-] *n* : usurpador *m*, -dora *f*

utensil [jʊ'tɛntsəl] *n* **1** : utensilio *m* (de cocina) **2** IMPLEMENT : implemento *m*, útil *m* (de labranza, etc.)

uterine ['ju:tə,raɪn, -rən] *adj* : uterino

uterus ['ju:tərəs] *n*, *pl* **uteri** [-,raɪ] : útero *m*, matriz *f*

utilitarian [ju:,tɪlə'tɛriən] *adj* : utilitario

utility [ju:'tɪləti] *n*, *pl* **-ties 1** USEFULNESS : utilidad *f* **2 public utility** : empresa *f* de servicio público

utilization [,ju:tələ'zeɪʃən] *n* : utilización *f*

utilize ['ju:tə,laɪz] *vt* **-lized; -lizing** : utilizar, hacer uso de

utmost¹ ['ʌt,mo:st] *adj* **1** FARTHEST : extremo, más lejano **2** GREATEST : sumo, mayor ⟨of the utmost importance : de suma importancia⟩

utmost² *n* : lo más posible ⟨to the utmost : al máximo⟩

utopia [jʊ'to:piə] *n* : utopía *f*

utopian [jʊ'to:piən] *adj* : utópico

utter¹ ['ʌtər] *vt* : decir, articular, pronunciar (palabras)

utter² *adj* : absoluto — **utterly** *adv*

utterance ['ʌtərənts] *n* : declaración *f*, articulación *f*

V

v ['vi:] *n*, *pl* **v's** *or* **vs** ['vi:z] : vigésima segunda letra del alfabeto inglés

vacancy ['veɪkəntsi] *n*, *pl* **-cies 1** EMPTINESS : vacío *m*, vacuidad *f* **2** : vacante *f*, puesto *m* vacante ⟨to fill a vacancy

: ocupar un puesto⟩ **3** : habitación *f* libre (en un hotel) ⟨no vacancies : completo⟩

vacant ['veɪkənt] *adj* **1** EMPTY : libre, desocupado (dícese de los edificios, etc.) **2** : vacante (dícese de los puestos) **3** BLANK : vacío, ausente ⟨a vacant stare : una mirada ausente⟩

vacate ['veɪˌkeɪt] *vt* **-cated; -cating** : desalojar, desocupar

vacation[1] [veɪ'keɪʃən, və-] *vi* : pasar las vacaciones, vacacionar *Mex*

vacation[2] *n* : vacaciones *fpl* ⟨to be on vacation : estar de vacaciones⟩

vacationer [veɪ'keɪʃənər, və-] *n* : turista *mf*, veraneante *mf*, vacacionista *mf CA, Mex*

vaccinate ['væksəˌneɪt] *vt* **-nated; -nating** : vacunar

vaccination [ˌvæksə'neɪʃən] *n* : vacunación *f*

vaccine [væk'si:n, 'væk-] *n* : vacuna *f*

vacillate ['væsəˌleɪt] *vi* **-lated; -lating** **1** HESITATE : vacilar **2** SWAY : oscilar

vacillation [ˌvæsə'leɪʃən] *n* : indecisión *f*, vacilación *f*

vacuous ['vækjuəs] *adj* **1** EMPTY : vacío **2** INANE : vacuo, necio, estúpido

vacuum[1] ['væˌkju:m, -kjəm] *vt* : limpiar con aspiradora, pasar la aspiradora por

vacuum[2] *n, pl* **vacuums** *or* **vacua** ['vækjuə] : vacío *m*

vacuum cleaner *n* : aspiradora *f*

vagabond[1] ['vægəˌbɑnd] *adj* : vagabundo

vagabond[2] *n* : vagabundo *m*, -da *f*

vagary ['veɪɡəri, və'ɡɛri] *n, pl* **-ries** : capricho *m*

vagina [və'dʒaɪnə] *n, pl* **-nae** [-ˌni:, -ˌnaɪ] *or* **-nas** : vagina *f*

vagrancy ['veɪɡrəntsi] *n, pl* **-cies** : vagancia *f*

vagrant[1] ['veɪɡrənt] *adj* : vagabundo

vagrant[2] *n* : vagabundo *m*, -da *f*

vague ['veɪɡ] *adj* **vaguer; -est** **1** IMPRECISE : vago, impreciso ⟨a vague feeling : una sensación indefinida⟩ ⟨I haven't the vaguest idea : no tengo la más remota idea⟩ **2** UNCLEAR : borroso, poco claro ⟨a vague outline : un perfil indistinto⟩ **3** ABSENTMINDED : distraído

vaguely ['veɪɡli] *adv* : vagamente, de manera imprecisa

vagueness ['veɪɡnəs] *n* : vaguedad *f*, imprecisión *f*

vain ['veɪn] *adj* **1** WORTHLESS : vano **2** FUTILE : vano, inútil ⟨in vain : en vano⟩ **3** CONCEITED : vanidoso, presumido

vainly ['veɪnli] *adv* : en vano, vanamente, inútilmente

valance ['vælənts, 'veɪ-] *n* **1** FLOUNCE : volante *m* (de una cama, etc.) **2** : galería *f* de cortina (sobre una ventana)

vale ['veɪl] *n* : valle *m*

valedictorian [ˌvælədɪk'toriən] *n* : estudiante *mf* que pronuncia el discurso de despedida en ceremonia de graduación

valedictory [ˌvælə'dɪktəri] *adj* : de despedida

valentine ['vælənˌtaɪn] *n* : tarjeta *f* que se manda el Día de los Enamorados (el 14 de febrero)

Valentine's Day *n* : Día *m* de los Enamorados

valet ['væˌleɪ, væ'leɪ, 'vælət] *n* : ayuda *m* de cámara

valiant ['væljənt] *adj* : valiente, valeroso

valiantly ['væljəntli] *adv* : con valor, valientemente

valid ['væləd] *adj* : válido

validate ['væləˌdeɪt] *vt* **-dated; -dating** : validar, dar validez a

validity [və'lɪdəti, væ-] *n* : validez *f*

valise [və'li:s] *n* : maleta *f* (de mano)

valley ['væli] *n, pl* **-leys** : valle *m*

valor ['vælər] *n* : valor *m*, valentía *f*

valorous ['vælərəs] *adj* : valeroso, valiente

valuable[1] ['væljuəbəl, 'væljəbəl] *adj* **1** EXPENSIVE : valioso, de valor **2** WORTHWHILE : valioso, apreciable

valuable[2] *n* : objeto *m* de valor

valuation [ˌvælju'eɪʃən] *n* **1** APPRAISAL : valoración *f*, tasación *f* **2** VALUE : valuación *f*

value[1] ['væljuː] *vt* **-ued; -uing** **1** APPRAISE : valorar, avaluar, tasar **2** APPRECIATE : valorar, apreciar

value[2] *n* **1** : valor *m* ⟨of little value : de poco valor⟩ ⟨to be a good value : estar bien de precio, tener buen precio⟩ ⟨at face value : en su sentido literal⟩ **2 values** *npl* : valores *mpl* (morales), principios *mpl*

valueless ['væljuːləs] *adj* : sin valor

valve ['vælv] *n* : válvula *f*

vampire ['væmˌpaɪr] *n* **1** : vampiro *m* **2** *or* **vampire bat** : vampiro *m*

van[1] ['væn] → **vanguard**

van[2] *n* : furgoneta *f*, camioneta *f*

vanadium [və'neɪdiəm] *n* : vanadio *m*

vandal ['vændəl] *n* : vándalo *m*

vandalism ['vændəlˌɪzəm] *n* : vandalismo *m*

vandalize ['vændəlˌaɪz] *vt* : destrozar, destruir, estropear

vane ['veɪn] *n or* **weather vane** : veleta *f*

vanguard ['vænˌɡɑrd] *n* : vanguardia *f*

vanilla [və'nɪlə, -'nɛ-] *n* : vainilla *f*

vanish ['vænɪʃ] *vi* : desaparecer, disiparse, desvanecerse

vanity ['vænəti] *n, pl* **-ties** **1** : vanidad *f* **2** *or* **vanity table** : tocador *m*

vanquish ['væŋkwɪʃ, 'væn-] *vt* : vencer, conquistar

vantage point ['væntɪdʒ] *n* : posición *f* ventajosa

vapid ['væpəd, 'veɪ-] *adj* : insípido, insulso

vapor ['veɪpər] *n* : vapor *m*

vaporize ['veɪpəˌraɪz] *v* **-rized; -rizing** *vt* : vaporizar — *vi* : vaporizarse, evaporarse

vaporizer ['veɪpəˌraɪzər] *n* : vaporizador *m*

variability [ˌvɛriə'bɪləti] *n, pl* **-ties** : variabilidad *f*

variable[1] ['vɛriəbəl] *adj* : variable ⟨variable cloudiness : nubosidad variable⟩

variable² *n* : variable *f*, factor *m*

variance ['vɛriənts] *n* **1** DISCREPANCY : varianza *f*, discrepancia *f* **2** DISAGREEMENT : desacuerdo *m* ⟨at variance with : en desacuerdo con⟩

variant¹ ['vɛriənt] *adj* : variante, divergente

variant² *n* : variante *f*

variation [ˌvɛri'eɪʃən] *n* : variación *f*, diferencias *fpl*

varicose ['værə,ko:s] *adj* : varicoso

varicose veins *npl* : varices *fpl*, várices *fpl*

varied ['vɛrid] *adj* : variado, dispar, diferente

variegated ['vɛriə,geɪtd] *adj* : abigarrado, multicolor

variety [və'raɪəti] *n, pl* **-ties 1** DIVERSITY : diversidad *f*, variedad *f* **2** ASSORTMENT : surtido *m* ⟨for a variety of reasons : por diversas razones⟩ **3** SORT : clase *f* **4** BREED : variedad *f* (de plantas)

various ['vɛriəs] *adj* : varios, diversos

varnish¹ ['vɑrnɪʃ] *vt* : barnizar

varnish² *n* : barniz *f*

varsity ['vɑrsəti] *n, pl* **-ties** : equipo *m* universitario

vary ['vɛri] *v* **varied; varying** *vt* : variar, diversificar — *vi* **1** CHANGE : variar, cambiar **2** DEVIATE : desviarse

vascular ['væskjələr] *adj* : vascular

vase ['veɪs, 'veɪz, 'vɑz] *n* : jarrón *m*, florero *m*

vassal ['væsəl] *n* : vasallo *m*, -lla *f*

vast ['væst] *adj* : inmenso, enorme, vasto

vastly ['væstli] *adv* : enormemente

vastness ['væstnəs] *n* : vastedad *f*, inmensidad *f*

vat ['væt] *n* : cuba *f*, tina *f*

vaudeville ['vɔdvəl, -ˌvɪl; 'vɔdə,vɪl] *n* : vodevil *m*

vault¹ ['vɔlt] *vi* LEAP : saltar

vault² *n* **1** JUMP : salto *m* ⟨pole vault : salto de pértiga, salto con garrocha⟩ **2** DOME : bóveda *f* **3** : bodega *f* (para vino), bóveda *f* de seguridad (de un banco) **4** CRYPT : cripta *f*

vaulted ['vɔltəd] *adj* : abovedado

vaunted ['vɔntəd] *adj* : cacareado, alardeado ⟨a much vaunted wine : un vino muy alardeado⟩

VCR [ˌviːˌsiːˈɑr] *n* : video *m*, videocasetera *f*

veal ['viːl] *n* : ternera *f*, carne *f* de ternera

veer ['vɪr] *vi* : virar (dícese de un barco), girar (dícese de un coche), torcer (dícese de un camino)

vegetable¹ ['vɛʤtəbəl, 'vɛʤətə-] *adj* : vegetal

vegetable² *n* **1** : vegetal *m* ⟨the vegetable kingdom : el reino vegetal⟩ **2** : verdura *f*, hortaliza *f* (para comer)

vegetarian [ˌvɛʤə'tɛriən] *n* : vegetariano *mf*

vegetarianism [ˌvɛʤə'tɛriəˌnɪzəm] *n* : vegetarianismo *m*

vegetate ['vɛʤə,teɪt] *vi* **-tated; -tating** : vegetar

vegetation [ˌvɛʤə'teɪʃən] *n* : vegetación *f*

vegetative ['vɛʤə,teɪtɪv] *adj* : vegetativo

vehemence ['viːəmənts] *n* : intensidad *f*, vehemencia *f*

vehement ['viːəmənt] *adj* : intenso, vehemente

vehemently ['viːəməntli] *adv* : vehementemente, con vehemencia

vehicle ['viːəkəl, 'viːˌhɪkəl] *n* **1** *or motor* **vehicle** : vehículo *m* **2** MEDIUM : vehículo *m*, medio *m*

vehicular [viˈhɪkjələr, və-] *adj* : vehicular ⟨vehicular homicide : muerte por atropello⟩

veil¹ ['veɪl] *vt* **1** CONCEAL : velar, disimular **2** : cubrir con un velo ⟨to veil one's face : cubrirse con un velo⟩

veil² *n* : velo *m* ⟨bridal veil : velo de novia⟩

vein ['veɪn] *n* **1** : vena *f* (en anatomía, botánica, etc.) **2** LODE : veta *f*, vena *f*, filón *m* **3** STYLE : vena *f* ⟨in a humorous vein : en vena humorística⟩

veined ['veɪnd] *adj* : veteado (dícese del queso, de los minerales, etc.)

velocity [və'lɑsəti] *n, pl* **-ties** : velocidad *f*

velour [və'lʊr] *or* **velours** [-'lʊrz] *n* : velour *m*

velvet¹ ['vɛlvət] *adj* **1** : de terciopelo **2** → **velvety**

velvet² *n* : terciopelo *m*

velvety ['vɛlvəti] *adj* : aterciopelado

venal ['viːnəl] *adj* : venal, sobornable

vend ['vɛnd] *vt* : vender

vendetta [vɛn'dɛtə] *n* : vendetta *f*

vendor ['vɛndər] *n* : vendedor *m*, -dora *f*; puestero *m*, -ra *f*

veneer¹ [və'nɪr] *vt* : enchapar, chapar

veneer² *n* **1** : enchapado *m*, chapa *f* **2** APPEARANCE : apariencia *f*, barniz *m* ⟨a veneer of culture : un barniz de cultura⟩

venerable ['vɛnərəbəl] *adj* : venerable

venerate ['vɛnə,reɪt] *vt* **-ated; -ating** : venerar

veneration [ˌvɛnə'reɪʃən] *n* : veneración *f*

venereal disease [və'nɪriəl] *n* : enfermedad *f* venérea

venetian blind [və'niːʃən] *n* : persiana *f* veneciana

Venezuelan [ˌvɛnə'zweɪlən, -zʊ'eɪ-] *n* : venezolano *m*, -na *f* — **Venezuelan** *adj*

vengeance ['vɛnʤənts] *n* : venganza *f* ⟨to take vengeance on : vengarse de⟩

vengeful ['vɛnʤfəl] *adj* : vengativo

venial ['viːniəl] *adj* : venial ⟨a venial sin : un pecado venial⟩

venison ['vɛnəsən, -zən] *n* : venado *m*, carne *f* de venado

venom ['vɛnəm] *n* **1** : veneno *m* **2** MALICE : veneno *m*, malevolencia *f*

venomous ['vɛnəməs] *adj* : venenoso
vent¹ ['vɛnt] *vt* : desahogar, dar salida a
⟨to vent one's feelings : desahogarse⟩
vent² *n* **1** OPENING : abertura *f* (de escape), orificio *m* **2** *or* **air vent** : respiradero *m*, rejilla *f* de ventilación **3** OUTLET : desahogo *m* ⟨to give vent to one's anger : desahogar la ira⟩
ventilate ['vɛntəl,eɪt] *vt* **-lated; -lating**
: ventilar
ventilation [,vɛntəl'eɪʃən] *n* : ventilación *f*
ventilator ['vɛntəl,eɪtər] *n* : ventilador *m*
ventricle ['vɛntrɪkəl] *n* : ventrículo *m*
ventriloquism [vɛn'trɪlə,kwɪzəm] *n* : ventriloquia *f*
ventriloquist [vɛn'trɪlə,kwɪst] *n* : ventrílocuo *m*, -cua *f*
venture¹ ['vɛntʃər] *v* **-tured; -turing** *vt* **1** RISK : arriesgar **2** OFFER : aventurar ⟨to venture an opinion : aventurar una opinión⟩ — *vi* : arriesgarse, atreverse, aventurarse
venture² *n* **1** UNDERTAKING : empresa *f* **2** GAMBLE, RISK : aventura *f*, riesgo *m*
venturesome ['vɛntʃərsəm] *adj* **1** ADVENTUROUS : audaz, atrevido **2** RISKY : arriesgado
venue ['vɛn,ju:] *n* **1** PLACE : lugar *m* **2** : jurisdicción *f* (en derecho)
Venus ['vi:nəs] *n* : Venus *m*
veracity [və'ræsəti] *n*, *pl* **-ties** : veracidad *f*
veranda *or* **verandah** [və'rændə] *n* : terraza *f*, veranda *f*
verb ['vərb] *n* : verbo *m*
verbal ['vərbəl] *adj* : verbal
verbalize ['vərbə,laɪz] *vt* **-ized; -izing** : expresar con palabras, verbalizar
verbally ['vərbəli] *adv* : verbalmente, de palabra
verbatim¹ [vər'beɪtəm] *adv* : palabra por palabra, textualmente
verbatim² *adj* : literal, textual
verbose [vər'bo:s] *adj* : verboso, prolijo
verdant ['vərdənt] *adj* : verde, verdeante
verdict ['vərdɪkt] *n* **1** : veredicto *m* (de un jurado) **2** JUDGMENT, OPINION : juicio *m*, opinión *f*
verge¹ ['vərdʒ] *vi* **verged; verging** : estar al borde, rayar ⟨it verges on madness : raya en la locura⟩
verge² *n* **1** EDGE : borde *m* **2** **to be on the verge of** : estar a pique de, estar al borde de, estar a punto de
verification [,vɛrəfə'keɪʃən] *n* : verificación *f*
verify ['vɛrə,faɪ] *vt* **-fied; -fying** : verificar, comprobar, confirmar
veritable ['vɛrətəbəl] *adj* : verdadero — **veritably** *adv*
vermicelli [,vərmə'tʃɛli, -'sɛli] *n* : fideos *mpl* finos
vermin ['vərmən] *ns & pl* : alimañas *fpl*, bichos *mpl*, sabandijas *fpl*
vermouth [vər'mu:th] *n* : vermut *m*
vernacular¹ [vər'nækjələr] *adj* : vernáculo

vernacular² *n* : lengua *f* vernácula
versatile ['vərsətəl] *adj* : versátil
versatility [,vərsə'tɪləti] *n* : versatilidad *f*
verse ['vərs] *n* **1** LINE, STANZA : verso *m*, estrofa *f* **2** POETRY : poesía *f* **3** : versículo *m* (en la Biblia)
versed ['vərst] *adj* : versado ⟨to be well versed in : ser muy versado en⟩
version ['vərʒən] *n* : versión *f*
versus ['vərsəs] *prep* : versus
vertebra ['vərtəbrə] *n*, *pl* **-brae** [-,breɪ, -,bri:] *or* **-bras** : vértebra *f*
vertebrate¹ ['vərtəbrət, -,breɪt] *adj* : vertebrado
vertebrate² *n* : vertebrado *m*
vertex ['vər,tɛks] *n*, *pl* **vertices** ['vərtə,si:z] **1** : vértice *m* (en matemáticas y anatomía) **2** SUMMIT, TOP : ápice *m*, cumbre *f*, cima *f*
vertical¹ ['vərtɪkəl] *adj* : vertical — **vertically** *adv*
vertical² *n* : vertical *f*
vertigo ['vərtɪ,go:] *n*, *pl* **-goes** *or* **-gos** : vértigo *m*
verve ['vərv] *n* : brío *m*
very¹ ['vɛri] *adv* **1** EXTREMELY : muy, sumamente ⟨very few : muy pocos⟩ ⟨I am very sorry : lo siento mucho⟩ **2** (*used for emphasis*) ⟨at the very least : por lo menos, como mínimo⟩ ⟨the very same dress : el mismo vestido⟩
very² *adj* **verier; -est 1** EXACT, PRECISE : mismo, exacto ⟨at that very moment : en ese mismo momento⟩ ⟨it's the very thing : es justo lo que hacía falta⟩ **2** BARE, MERE : solo, mero ⟨the very thought of it : sólo pensarlo⟩ **3** EXTREME : extremo, de todo ⟨at the very top : arriba de todo⟩
vesicle ['vɛsɪkəl] *n* : vesícula *f*
vespers ['vɛspərz] *npl* : vísperas *fpl*
vessel ['vɛsəl] *n* **1** CONTAINER : vasija *f*, recipiente *m* **2** BOAT, CRAFT : nave *f*, barco *m*, buque *m* **3** : vaso *m* ⟨blood vessel : vaso sanguíneo⟩
vest¹ ['vɛst] *vt* **1** CONFER : conferir ⟨to vest authority in : conferirle la autoridad a⟩ **2** CLOTHE : vestir
vest² *n* **1** : chaleco *m* **2** UNDERSHIRT : camiseta *f*
vestibule ['vɛstə,bju:l] *n* : vestíbulo *m*
vestige ['vɛstɪdʒ] *n* : vestigio *m*, rastro *m*
vestment ['vɛstmənt] *n* : vestidura *f*
vestry ['vɛstri] *n*, *pl* **-tries** : sacristía *f*
vet ['vɛt] *n* **1** → **veterinarian 2** → **veteran²**
veteran¹ ['vɛtərən, 'vɛtrən] *adj* : veterano
veteran² *n* : veterano *m*, -na *f*
Veterans Day *n* : día *m* del Armisticio (celebrado el 11 de noviembre en los Estados Unidos)
veterinarian [,vɛtərə'nɛriən, ,vɛtə'nɛr-] *n* : veterinario *m*, -ria *f*
veterinary ['vɛtərə,nɛri] *adj* : veterinario
veto¹ ['vi:to:] *vt* **1** FORBID : prohibir **2** : vetar ⟨to veto a bill : vetar un proyecto de ley⟩

veto[2] *n, pl* **-toes 1** : veto *m* ⟨the power of veto : el derecho de veto⟩ **2** BAN : veto *m*, prohibición *f*

vex ['vɛks] *vt* : contrariar, molestar, irritar

vexation [vɛk'seɪʃən] *n* : contrariedad *f*, irritación *f*

via ['vaɪə, 'viːə] *prep* : por, vía

viability [,vaɪə'bɪləti] *n* : viabilidad *f*

viable ['vaɪəbəl] *adj* : viable

viaduct ['vaɪə,dʌkt] *n* : viaducto *m*

vial ['vaɪəl] *n* : frasco *m*

vibrant ['vaɪbrənt] *adj* **1** LIVELY : vibrante, animado, dinámico **2** BRIGHT : fuerte, vivo ⟨dícese de los colores⟩

vibrate ['vaɪ,breɪt] *vi* **-brated; -brating 1** OSCILLATE : vibrar, oscilar **2** THRILL : bullir ⟨to vibrate with excitement : bullir de emoción⟩

vibration [vaɪ'breɪʃən] *n* : vibración *f*

vicar ['vɪkər] *n* : vicario *m*, -ria *f*

vicarious [vaɪ'kæriːəs, vɪ-] *adj* : indirecto — **vicariously** *adv*

vice ['vaɪs] *n* : vicio *m*

vice admiral *n* : vicealmirante *mf*

vice president *n* : vicepresidente *m*, -ta *f*

viceroy ['vaɪs,rɔɪ] *n* : virrey *m*, -rreina *f*

vice versa [,vaɪsi'vərsə, ,vaɪs'vər-] *adv* : viceversa

vicinity [və'sɪnəti] *n, pl* **-ties 1** NEIGHBORHOOD : vecindad *f*, inmediaciones *fpl* **2** NEARNESS : proximidad *f*

vicious ['vɪʃəs] *adj* **1** DEPRAVED : depravado, malo **2** SAVAGE : malo, fiero, salvaje ⟨a vicious dog : un perro feroz⟩ **3** MALICIOUS : malicioso

viciously ['vɪʃəsli] *adv* : con saña, brutalmente

viciousness ['vɪʃəsnəs] *n* : brutalidad *f*, ferocidad *f* (de un animal), malevolencia *f* (de un comentario, etc.)

vicissitudes [və'sɪsə,tuːdz, vaɪ-, -,tjuːdz] *npl* : vicisitudes *fpl*

victim ['vɪktəm] *n* : víctima *f*

victimize ['vɪktə,maɪz] *vt* **-mized; -mizing** : tomar como víctima, perseguir, victimizar *Arg, Mex*

victor ['vɪktər] *n* : vencedor *m*, -dora *f*

Victorian [vɪk'toːriən] *adj* : victoriano

victorious [vɪk'toːriəs] *adj* : victorioso — **victoriously** *adv*

victory ['vɪktəri] *n, pl* **-ries** : victoria *f*, triunfo *m*

victuals ['vɪtəlz] *npl* : víveres *mpl*, provisiones *fpl*

video[1] ['vɪdi,oː] *adj* : de video ⟨video recording : grabación de video⟩

video[2] *n* **1** : video *m* (medio o grabación) **2** → **videotape**[2]

video camera *n* : videocámara *f*

videocassette [,vɪdiokə'sɛt] *n* : videocasete *m*, videocassette *m*

videocassette recorder → **VCR**

video game *n* : videojuego *m*, juego *m* de video

videotape[1] ['vɪdio,teɪp] *vt* **-taped; -taping** : grabar en video, videograbar

videotape[2] *n* : videocinta *f*

vie ['vaɪ] *vi* **vied; vying** ['vaɪɪŋ] : competir, rivalizar

Vietnamese [vi,ɛtnə'miːz, -'miːs] *n* **1** : vietnamita *mf* **2** : vietnamita *m* (idioma) — **Vietnamese** *adj*

view[1] ['vjuː] *vt* **1** OBSERVE : mirar, ver, observar **2** CONSIDER : considerar, contemplar

view[2] *n* **1** SIGHT : vista *f* ⟨to come into view : aparecer⟩ **2** ATTITUDE, OPINION : opinión *f*, parecer *m*, actitud *f* ⟨in my view : en mi opinión⟩ **3** SCENE : vista *f*, panorama *f* **4** INTENTION : idea *f*, vista *f* ⟨with a view to : con vistas a, con la idea de⟩ **5 in view of** : dado que, en vista de (que)

viewer ['vjuːər] *n or* **television viewer** : telespectador *m*, -dora *f*; televidente *mf*

viewpoint ['vjuː,pɔɪnt] *n* : punto *m* de vista

vigil ['vɪdʒəl] *n* **1** : vigilia *f*, vela *f* **2 to keep vigil** : velar

vigilance ['vɪdʒələnts] *n* : vigilancia *f*

vigilant ['vɪdʒələnt] *adj* : vigilante

vigilante [,vɪdʒə'læn,tiː] *n* : integrante *mf* de un comité de vigilancia (que actúa como policía)

vigilantly ['vɪdʒələntli] *adv* : con vigilancia

vigor ['vɪgər] *n* : vigor *m*, energía *f*, fuerza *f*

vigorous ['vɪgərəs] *adj* : vigoroso, enérgico — **vigorously** *adv*

Viking ['vaɪkɪŋ] *n* : vikingo *m*, -ga *f*

vile ['vaɪl] *adj* **viler; vilest 1** WICKED : vil, infame **2** REVOLTING : asqueroso, repugnante **3** TERRIBLE : horrible, atroz ⟨vile weather : tiempo horrible⟩ ⟨to be in a vile mood : estar de un humor de perros⟩

vilify ['vɪlə,faɪ] *vt* **-fied; -fying** : vilipendiar, denigrar, difamar

villa ['vɪlə] *n* : casa *f* de campo, quinta *f*

village ['vɪlɪdʒ] *n* : pueblo *m* (grande), aldea *f* (pequeña)

villager ['vɪlɪdʒər] *n* : vecino *m*, -na *f* (de un pueblo); aldeano *m*, -na *f* (de una aldea)

villain ['vɪlən] *n* : villano *m*, -na *f*; malo *m*, -la *f* (en ficción, películas, etc.)

villainess ['vɪlənɪs, -nəs] *n* : villana *f*

villainous ['vɪlənəs] *adj* : infame, malvado

villainy ['vɪləni] *n, pl* **-lainies** : vileza *f*, maldad *f*

vim ['vɪm] *n* : brío *m*, vigor *m*, energía *f*

vindicate ['vɪndə,keɪt] *vt* **-cated; -cating 1** EXONERATE : vindicar, disculpar **2** JUSTIFY : justificar

vindication [,vɪndə'keɪʃən] *n* : vindicación *f*, justificación *f*

vindictive [vɪn'dɪktɪv] *adj* : vengativo

vine ['vaɪn] *n* **1** GRAPEVINE : vid *f*, parra *f* **2** : planta *f* trepadora, enredadera *f*

vinegar ['vɪnɪgər] *n* : vinagre *m*

vinegary ['vɪnɪɡəri] *adj* : avinagrado
vineyard ['vɪnjərd] *n* : viña *f*, viñedo *m*
vintage¹ ['vɪntɪʤ] *adj* **1** : añejo (dícese de un vino) **2** CLASSIC : clásico, de época
vintage² *n* **1** : cosecha *f* ⟨the 1947 vintage : la cosecha de 1947⟩ **2** ERA : época *f*, era *f* ⟨slang of recent vintage : argot de la época reciente⟩
vinyl ['vaɪnəl] *n* : vinilo
viola [vi:'o:lə] *n* : viola *f*
violate ['vaɪə,leɪt] *vt* **-lated; -lating 1** BREAK : infringir, violar, quebrantar ⟨to violate the rules : violar las reglas⟩ **2** RAPE : violar **3** DESECRATE : profanar
violation [,vaɪə'leɪʃən] *n* **1** : violación *f*, infracción *f* (de una ley) **2** DESECRATION : profanación *f*
violence ['vaɪlənts, 'vaɪə-] *n* : violencia *f*
violent ['vaɪlənt, 'vaɪə-] *adj* : violento
violently ['vaɪləntli, 'vaɪə-] *adv* : violentamente, con violencia
violet ['vaɪlət, 'vaɪə-] *n* : violeta *f*
violin [,vaɪə'lɪn] *n* : violín *m*
violinist [,vaɪə'lɪnɪst] *n* : violinista *mf*
violoncello [,vaɪələn'ʧelo:, ,vi:-] → **cello**
VIP [,vi:,aɪ'pi:] *n, pl* **VIPs** [-'pi:z] : VIP *mf*, persona *f* de categoría
viper ['vaɪpər] *n* : víbora *f*
viral ['vaɪrəl] *adj* : viral, vírico ⟨viral pneumonia : pulmonía viral⟩
virgin¹ ['vərʤən] *adj* **1** CHASTE : virginal ⟨the virgin birth : el alumbramiento virginal⟩ **2** : virgen, intacto ⟨a virgin forest : una selva virgen⟩ ⟨virgin wool : lana virgen⟩
virgin² *n* : virgen *mf*
virginity [vər'ʤɪnəti] *n* : virginidad *f*
Virgo ['vər,go:, 'vɪr-] *n* : Virgo *mf*
virile ['vɪrəl, -,aɪl] *adj* : viril, varonil
virility [və'rɪləti] *n* : virilidad *f*
virtual ['vərʧuəl] *adj* : virtual ⟨a virtual dictator : un virtual dictador⟩ ⟨virtual reality : realidad virtual⟩
virtually ['vərʧuəli, 'vərʧəli] *adv* : en realidad, de hecho, casi
virtue ['vər,ʧu:] *n* **1** : virtud *f* **2 by virtue of** : en virtud de, debido a
virtuosity [,vərʧu'asəti] *n, pl* **-ties** : virtuosismo *m*
virtuoso [,vərʧu'o:so:, -zo:] *n, pl* **-sos** *or* **-si** [-,si:, -,zi:] : virtuoso *m*, -sa *f*
virtuous ['vərʧuəs] *adj* : virtuoso, bueno — **virtuously** *adv*
virulence ['vɪrələnts, 'vɪrjə-] *n* : virulencia *f*
virulent ['vɪrələnt, 'vɪrjə-] *adj* : virulento
virus ['vaɪrəs] *n* : virus *m*
visa ['vi:zə, -sə] *n* : visa *f*
vis-à-vis [,vi:zə'vi:, -sə-] *prep* : con relación a, con respecto a
viscera ['vɪsərə] *npl* : vísceras *fpl*
visceral ['vɪsərəl] *adj* : visceral
viscosity [vɪs'kasəti] *n, pl* **-ties** : viscosidad *f*
viscount ['vaɪ,kæunt] *n* : vizconde *m*

viscountess ['vaɪ,kæuntɪs] *n* : vizcondesa *f*
viscous ['vɪskəs] *adj* : viscoso
vise ['vaɪs] *n* : torno *m* de banco, tornillo *m* de banco
visibility [,vɪzə'bɪləti] *n, pl* **-ties** : visibilidad *f*
visible ['vɪzəbəl] *adj* **1** : visible ⟨the visible stars : las estrellas visibles⟩ **2** OBVIOUS : evidente, patente
visibly ['vɪzəbli] *adv* : visiblemente
vision ['vɪʒən] *n* **1** EYESIGHT : vista *f*, visión *f* **2** APPARITION : visión *f*, aparición *f* **3** FORESIGHT : visión *f* (del futuro), previsión *f* **4** IMAGE : imagen *f* ⟨she had visions of a disaster : se imaginaba un desastre⟩
visionary¹ ['vɪʒə,neri] *adj* **1** FARSIGHTED : visionario, con visión de futuro **2** UTOPIAN : utópico, poco realista
visionary² *n, pl* **-ries** : visionario *m*, -ria *f*
visit¹ ['vɪzət] *vt* **1** : visitar, ir a ver **2** AFFLICT : azotar, afligir ⟨visited by troubles : afligido con problemas⟩ — *vi* : hacer (una) visita
visit² *n* : visita *f*
visitor ['vɪzətər] *n* : visitante *mf* (a una ciudad, etc.), visita *f* (a una casa)
visor ['vaɪzər] *n* : visera *f*
vista ['vɪstə] *n* : vista *f*
visual ['vɪʒʊəl] *adj* : visual ⟨the visual arts : las artes visuales⟩ — **visually** *adv*
visualize ['vɪʒʊə,laɪz] *vt* **-ized; -izing** : visualizar, imaginarse, hacerse una idea de — **visualization** [,vɪʒəwələ-'zeɪʃən] *n*
vital ['vaɪtəl] *adj* **1** : vital ⟨vital organs : órganos vitales⟩ **2** CRUCIAL : esencial, crucial, decisivo ⟨of vital importance : de suma importancia⟩ **3** LIVELY : enérgico, lleno de vida, vital
vitality [vaɪ'tæləti] *n, pl* **-ties** : vitalidad *f*, energía *f*
vitally ['vaɪtəli] *adv* : sumamente
vital statistics *npl* : estadísticas *fpl* demográficas
vitamin ['vaɪtəmən] *n* : vitamina *f* ⟨vitamin deficiency : carencia vitamínica⟩
vitreous ['vɪtriəs] *adj* : vítreo
vitriolic [,vɪtri'alɪk] *adj* : mordaz, virulento
vituperation [vaɪ,tu:pə'reɪʃən, -,tju:-] *n* : vituperio *m*
vivacious [və'veɪʃəs, vaɪ-] *adj* : vivaz, animado, lleno de vida
vivaciously [və'veɪʃəsli, vaɪ-] *adv* : con vivacidad, animadamente
vivacity [və'væsəti, vaɪ-] *n* : vivacidad *f*
vivid ['vɪvəd] *adj* **1** LIVELY : lleno de vitalidad **2** BRILLIANT : vivo, intenso ⟨vivid colors : colores vivos⟩ **3** INTENSE, SHARP : vívido, gráfico ⟨a vivid dream : un sueño vívido⟩
vividly ['vɪvədli] *adv* **1** BRIGHTLY : con colores vivos **2** SHARPLY : vívidamente
vividness ['vɪvədnəs] *n* **1** BRIGHTNESS : intensidad *f*, viveza *f* **2** SHARPNESS : lo gráfico, nitidez *f*

vivisection [ˌvɪvəˈsɛkʃən, ˈvɪvəˌ-] *n*
: vivisección *f*
vixen [ˈvɪksən] *n* : zorra *f*, raposa *f*
vocabulary [voˈkæbjəˌlɛri] *n, pl* **-laries**
1 : vocabulario *m* 2 LEXICON : léxico
m
vocal [ˈvoːkəl] *adj* 1 : vocal 2 LOUD,
OUTSPOKEN : ruidoso, muy franco
vocal cords *npl* : cuerdas *fpl* vocales
vocalist [ˈvoːkəlɪst] *n* : cantante *mf*, vocalista *mf*
vocalize [ˈvoːkəlˌaɪz] *vt* **-ized; -izing** : vocalizar
vocation [voˈkeɪʃən] *n* : vocación *f* ⟨to
have a vocation for : tener vocación
de⟩
vocational [voˈkeɪʃənəl] *adj* : profesional ⟨vocational guidance : orientación
profesional⟩
vociferous [voˈsɪfərəs] *adj* : ruidoso, vociferante
vodka [ˈvɑdkə] *n* : vodka *m*
vogue [ˈvoːg] *n* : moda *f*, boga *f* ⟨to
be in vogue : estar de moda, estar en
boga⟩
voice[1] [ˈvɔɪs] *vt* **voiced; voicing** : expresar
voice[2] *n* 1 : voz *f* ⟨in a low voice : en
voz baja⟩ ⟨to lose one's voice
: quedarse sin voz⟩ ⟨the voice of the
people : la voz del pueblo⟩ 2 **to make
one's voice heard** : hacerse oír
voice box → larynx
voiced [ˈvɔɪst] *adj* : sonoro
voice mail *n* : correo *m* de voz
void[1] [ˈvɔɪd] *vt* : anular, invalidar ⟨to
void a contract : anular un contrato⟩
void[2] *adj* 1 EMPTY : vacío, desprovisto
⟨void of content : desprovisto de con-
tenido⟩ 2 INVALID : inválido, nulo
void[3] *n* : vacío *m*
volatile [ˈvɑlətəl] *adj* : volátil, inestable
volatility [ˌvɑləˈtɪləti] *n* : volatilidad *f*, inestabilidad *f*
volcanic [vɑlˈkænɪk] *adj* : volcánico
volcano [vɑlˈkeɪˌnoː] *n, pl* **-noes** *or* **-nos**
: volcán *m*
vole [ˈvoːl] *n* : campañol *m*
volition [voˈlɪʃən] *n* : volición *f*, voluntad *f* ⟨of one's own volition : por voluntad propia⟩
volley [ˈvɑli] *n, pl* **-leys** 1 : descarga *f*
(de tiros) 2 : torrente *m*, lluvia *f* (de insultos, etc.) 3 : salva *f* (de aplausos) 4
: volea *f* (en deportes)
volleyball [ˈvɑliˌbɔl] *n* : voleibol *m*
volt [ˈvoːlt] *n* : voltio *m*
voltage [ˈvoːltɪdʒ] *n* : voltaje *m*
volubility [ˌvɑljəˈbɪləti] *n* : locuacidad *f*
voluble [ˈvɑljəbəl] *adj* : locuaz
volume [ˈvɑljəm, -ˌjuːm] *n* 1 BOOK : volumen *m*, tomo *m* 2 SPACE : capacidad
f, volumen *m* (en física) 3 AMOUNT

: cantidad *f*, volumen *m* 4 LOUDNESS
: volumen *m*
voluminous [vəˈluːmənəs] *adj* : voluminoso
voluntary [ˈvɑlənˌtɛri] *adj* : voluntario
— **voluntarily** [ˌvɑlənˈtɛrəli] *adv*
volunteer[1] [ˌvɑlənˈtɪr] *vt* : ofrecer, dar
⟨to volunteer one's assistance : ofrecer
la ayuda⟩ — *vi* : ofrecerse, alistarse
como voluntario
volunteer[2] *n* : voluntario *m*, -ria *f*
voluptuous [vəˈlʌptʃuəs] *adj* : voluptuoso
vomit[1] [ˈvɑmət] *v* : vomitar
vomit[2] *n* : vómito *m*
voodoo [ˈvuːˌduː] *n, pl* **voodoos** : vudú
m
voracious [vɔˈreɪʃəs, və-] *adj* : voraz
voraciously [vɔˈreɪʃəsli, və-] *adv* : vorazmente, con voracidad
vortex [ˈvɔrˌtɛks] *n, pl* **vortices** [ˈvɔrtə-
ˌsiːz] : vórtice *m*
vote[1] [ˈvoːt] *vi* **voted; voting** : votar ⟨to
vote Democratic : votar por los
demócratas⟩
vote[2] *n* 1 : voto *m* 2 SUFFRAGE : sufragio *m*, derecho *m* al voto
voter [ˈvoːtər] *n* : votante *mf*
voting [ˈvoːtɪŋ] *n* : votación *f*
vouch [ˈvæutʃ] *vi* **to vouch for** : garantizar (algo), responder de (algo), responder por (alguien)
voucher [ˈvæutʃər] *n* 1 RECEIPT : comprobante *m* 2 : vale *m* ⟨travel voucher : vale de viajar⟩
vow[1] [væu] *vt* : jurar, prometer, hacer
voto de
vow[2] *n* : promesa *f*, voto *m* (en la religión) ⟨a vow of poverty : un voto de
pobreza⟩
vowel [ˈvæuəl] *n* : vocal *m*
voyage[1] [ˈvɔɪɪdʒ] *vi* **-aged; -aging** : viajar
voyage[2] *n* : viaje *m*
voyager [ˈvɔɪɪdʒər] *n* : viajero *m*, -ra *f*
vulcanize [ˈvʌlkəˌnaɪz] *vt* **-nized; -nizing**
: vulcanizar
vulgar [ˈvʌlgər] *adj* 1 COMMON, PLE-
BIAN : ordinario, populachero, del vulgo 2 COARSE, CRUDE : grosero, de mal
gusto, majadero *Mex* 3 INDECENT : indecente, colorado (dícese de un chiste,
etc.)
vulgarity [ˌvʌlˈgærəti] *n, pl* **-ties**
: grosería *f*, vulgaridad *f*
vulgarly [ˈvʌlgərli] *adv* : vulgarmente,
groseramente
vulnerability [ˌvʌlnərəˈbɪləti] *n, pl* **-ties**
: vulnerabilidad *f*
vulnerable [ˈvʌlnərəbəl] *adj* : vulnerable
vulture [ˈvʌltʃər] *n* : buitre *m*, zopilote *m*
CA, Mex
vying → vie

W

w ['dʌbəl,ju:] *n, pl* **w's** *or* **ws** [-ju:z] : vigésima tercera letra del alfabeto inglés

wad¹ ['wɑd] *vt* **wadded; wadding 1** : hacer un taco con, formar en una masa **2** STUFF : rellenar

wad² *n* : taco *m* (de papel), bola *f* (de algodón, etc.), fajo *m* (de billetes)

waddle¹ ['wɑdəl] *vi* **-dled; -dling** : andar como un pato

waddle² *n* : andar *m* de pato

wade ['weɪd] *v* **waded; wading** *vi* **1** : caminar por el agua **2 to wade through** : leer (algo) con dificultad — *vt or* **to wade across** : vadear

wading bird *n* : zancuda *f*, ave *f* zancuda

wafer ['weɪfər] *n* : barquillo *m*, galleta *f* de barquillo

waffle ['wɑfəl] *n* **1** : wafle *m* **2 waffle iron** : waflera *f*

waft ['wɑft, 'wæft] *vt* : llevar por el aire — *vi* : flotar

wag¹ ['wæg] *v* **wagged; wagging** *vt* : menear — *vi* : menearse, moverse

wag² *n* **1** : meneo *m* (de la cola) **2** JOKER, WIT : bromista *mf*

wage¹ ['weɪʤ] *vt* **waged; waging** : hacer, librar ⟨to wage war : hacer la guerra⟩

wage² *n or* **wages** *npl* : sueldo *m*, salario *m* ⟨minimum wage : salario mínimo⟩

wager¹ ['weɪʤər] *v* : apostar

wager² *n* : apuesta *f*

waggish ['wægɪʃ] *adj* : burlón, bromista (dícese de una persona), chistoso (dícese de un comentario)

waggle ['wægəl] *vt* **-gled; -gling** : menear, mover (de un lado a otro)

wagon ['wægən] *n* **1** : carro *m* (tirado por caballos) **2** CART : carrito *m* **3** → **station wagon**

waif ['weɪf] *n* : niño *m* abandonado, animal *m* sin hogar

wail¹ ['weɪl] *vi* : gemir, lamentarse

wail² *n* : gemido *m*, lamento *m*

wainscot ['weɪnskət, -,skɑt, -,skɔːt] *or* **wainscoting** [-skəṭɪn, -,skɑ-, -,skɔː-] *n* : boiserie *f*, revestimiento *m* de paneles de madera

waist ['weɪst] *n* : cintura *f* (del cuerpo humano), talle *m* (de ropa)

waistline ['weɪst,laɪn] → **waist**

wait¹ ['weɪt] *vi* : esperar ⟨to wait for something : esperar algo⟩ ⟨wait and see! : ¡espera y verás!⟩ ⟨I can't wait : me muero de ganas⟩ — *vt* **1** AWAIT : esperar **2** DELAY : retrasar ⟨don't wait lunch : no retrase el almuerzo⟩ **3** SERVE : servir, atender ⟨to wait tables : servir (a la mesa)⟩

wait² *n* **1** : espera *f* **2 to lie in wait** : estar al acecho

waiter ['weɪṭər] *n* : mesero *m*, camarero *m*, mozo *m* *Arg, Chile, Col, Peru*

waiting room *n* : sala *f* de espera

waitress ['weɪtrəs] *n* : mesera *f*, camarera *f*, moza *f* *Arg, Chile, Col, Peru*

waive ['weɪv] *vt* **waived; waiving** : renunciar a ⟨to waive one's rights : renunciar a sus derechos⟩ ⟨to waive the rules : no aplicar las reglas⟩

waiver ['weɪvər] *n* : renuncia *f*

wake¹ ['weɪk] *v* **woke** ['woːk]; **woken** ['woːkən] *or* **waked; waking** *vi or* **to wake up** : despertar(se) ⟨he woke at noon : se despertó al mediodía⟩ ⟨wake up! : ¡despiértate!⟩ — *vt* : despertar

wake² *n* **1** VIGIL : velatorio *m*, velorio *m* (de un difunto) **2** TRAIL : estela *f* (de un barco, un huracán, etc.) **3** AFTERMATH : consecuencias *fpl* ⟨in the wake of : tras, como consecuencia de⟩

wakeful ['weɪkfəl] *adj* **1** SLEEPLESS : desvelado **2** VIGILANT : alerta, vigilante

waken ['weɪkən] → **awake**

walk¹ ['wɔk] *vi* **1** : caminar, andar, pasear ⟨you're walking too fast : estás caminando demasiado rápido⟩ ⟨to walk around the city : pasearse por la ciudad⟩ **2** : ir andando, ir a pie ⟨we had to walk home : tuvimos que ir a casa a pie⟩ **3** : darle base por bolas (a un bateador) — *vt* **1** : recorrer, caminar ⟨she walked two miles : caminó dos millas⟩ **2** ACCOMPANY : acompañar **3** : sacar a pasear (a un perro)

walk² *n* **1** : paseo *m*, caminata *f* ⟨to go for a walk : ir a caminar, dar un paseo⟩ **2** PATH : camino *m* **3** GAIT : andar *m* **4** : marcha *f* (en beisbol) **5 walk of life** : esfera *f*, condición *f*

walker ['wɔkər] *n* **1** : paseante *mf* **2** HIKER : excursionista *mf* **3** : andador *m* (aparato)

walking stick *n* : bastón *m*

walkout ['wɔk,aʊt] *n* STRIKE : huelga *f*

walk out *vi* **1** STRIKE : declararse en huelga **2** LEAVE : salir, irse **3 to walk out on** : abandonar, dejar

walkway ['wɔk,weɪ] *n* **1** SIDEWALK : acera *f* **2** PATH : sendero *m* **3** PASSAGEWAY : pasadizo *m*

wall¹ ['wɔl] *vt* **1 to wall in** : cercar con una pared o un muro, tapiar, amurallar **2 to wall off** : separar con una pared o un muro **3 to wall up** : tapiar, condenar (una ventana, etc.)

wall² *n* **1** : muro *m* (exterior) ⟨the walls of the city : las murallas de la ciudad⟩ **2** : pared *f* (interior) **3** BARRIER : barrera *f* ⟨a wall of mountains : una barrera de montañas⟩ **4** : pared *f* (en anatomía)

wallaby ['wɑləbi] *n, pl* **-bies** : ualabí *m*

walled ['wɔld] *adj* : amurallado

wallet ['wɑlət] *n* : billetera *f*, cartera *f*

wallflower ['wɔl,flaʊər] *n* **1** : alhelí *m* (flor) **2 to be a wallflower** : comer pavo

wallop¹ ['wɑləp] *vt* **1** TROUNCE : darle una paliza (a alguien) **2** SOCK : pegar fuerte

wallop² *n* : golpe *m* fuerte, golpazo *m*

wallow¹ ['wɑˌloː] *vi* **1** : revolcarse ⟨to wallow in the mud : revolcarse en el lodo⟩ **2** DELIGHT : deleitarse ⟨to wallow in luxury : nadar en lujos⟩

wallow² *n* : revolcadero *m* (para animales)

wallpaper¹ ['wɔlˌpeɪpər] *vt* : empapelar

wallpaper² *n* : papel *m* pintado

walnut ['wɔlˌnʌt] *n* **1** : nuez *f* (fruta) **2** : nogal *m* (árbol y madera)

walrus ['wɔlrəs, 'wɑl-] *n*, *pl* **-rus** *or* **-ruses** : morsa *f*

waltz¹ ['wɔlts] *vi* **1** : valsar, bailar el vals **2** BREEZE : pasar con ligereza ⟨to waltz in : entrar tan campante⟩

waltz² *n* : vals *m*

wan ['wɑn] *adj* **wanner; -est 1** PALLID : pálido **2** DIM : tenue ⟨wan light : luz tenue⟩ **3** LANGUID : lánguido ⟨a wan smile : una sonrisa lánguida⟩ — **wanly** *adv*

wand ['wɑnd] *n* : varita *f* (mágica)

wander ['wɑndər] *vi* **1** RAMBLE : deambular, vagar, vagabundear **2** STRAY : alejarse, desviarse, divagar ⟨she let her mind wander : dejó vagar la imaginación⟩ — *vt* : recorrer ⟨to wander the streets : vagar por las calles⟩

wanderer ['wɑndərər] *n* : vagabundo *m*, -da *f*; viajero *m*, -ra *f*

wanderlust ['wɑndərˌlʌst] *n* : pasión *f* por viajar

wane¹ ['weɪn] *vi* **waned; waning 1** : menguar (dícese de la luna) **2** DECLINE : disminuir, decaer, menguar

wane² *n* **on the wane** : decayendo, en decadencia

wangle ['wæŋɡəl] *vt* **-gled; -gling** FINAGLE : arreglárselas para conseguir

wannabe ['wɑnəˌbiː] *n* : aspirante *mf* (a algo); imitador *m*, -dora *f* (de alguien)

want¹ ['wɑnt, 'wɔnt] *vt* **1** LACK : faltar **2** REQUIRE : requerir, necesitar **3** DESIRE : querer, desear

want² *n* **1** LACK : falta *f* **2** DESTITUTION : indigencia *f*, miseria *f* **3** DESIRE, NEED : deseo *m*, necesidad *f*

wanting ['wɑntɪŋ, 'wɔn-] *adj* **1** ABSENT : ausente **2** DEFICIENT : deficiente ⟨he's wanting in common sense : le falta sentido común⟩

wanton ['wɑntən, 'wɔn-] *adj* **1** LEWD, LUSTFUL : lascivo, lujurioso, licencioso **2** INHUMANE, MERCILESS : despiadado ⟨wanton cruelty : crueldad despiadada⟩

wapiti ['wɑpəti] *n*, *pl* **-ti** *or* **-tis** : uapití *m*

war¹ ['wɔr] *vi* **warred; warring** : combatir, batallar, hacer la guerra

war² *n* : guerra *f* ⟨to go to war : entrar en guerra⟩

warble¹ ['wɔrbəl] *vi* **-bled; -bling** : gorjear, trinar

warble² *n* : trino *m*, gorjeo *m*

warbler ['wɔrblər] *n* : pájaro *m* gorjeador, curruca *f*

ward¹ ['wɔrd] *vt* **to ward off** : desviar, protegerse contra

ward² *n* **1** : sala *f* (de un hospital, etc.) ⟨maternity ward : sala de maternidad⟩ **2** : distrito *m* electoral o administrativo (de una ciudad) **3** : pupilo *m*, -la *f* (de un tutor, etc.)

warden ['wɔrdən] *n* **1** KEEPER : guarda *mf*; guardián *m*, -diana *f* ⟨game warden : guardabosque⟩ **2** *or* **prison warden** : alcaide *m*

wardrobe ['wɔrdˌroːb] *n* **1** CLOSET : armario *m* **2** CLOTHES : vestuario *m*, guardarropa *m*

ware ['wær] *n* **1** POTTERY : cerámica *f* **2 wares** *npl* GOODS : mercancía *f*, mercadería *f*

warehouse ['wærˌhaʊs] *n* : depósito *m*, almacén *m*, bodega *f* *Chile, Col, Mex*

warfare ['wɔrˌfær] *n* **1** WAR : guerra *f* **2** STRUGGLE : lucha *f* ⟨the warfare against drugs : la lucha contra las drogas⟩

warhead ['wɔrˌhɛd] *n* : ojiva *f*, cabeza *f* (de un misil)

warily ['wærəli] *adv* : cautelosamente, con cautela

wariness ['wærinəs] *n* : cautela *f*

warlike ['wærˌlaɪk] *adj* : belicoso, guerrero

warm¹ ['wɔrm] *vt* **1** HEAT : calentar, recalentar **2 to warm one's heart** : reconfortar a uno, alegrar el corazón **3 to warm up** : calentar (los músculos, un automóvil, etc.) — *vi* **1** : calentarse **2 to warm to** : tomarle simpatía (a alguien), entusiasmarse con (algo)

warm² *adj* **1** LUKEWARM : tibio, templado **2** : caliente, cálido, caluroso ⟨a warm wind : un viento cálido⟩ ⟨a warm day : un día caluroso, un día de calor⟩ ⟨warm hands : manos calientes⟩ **3** : caliente, que abriga ⟨warm clothes : ropa de abrigo⟩ ⟨I feel warm : tengo calor⟩ **4** CARING, CORDIAL : cariñoso, cordial **5** : cálido (dícese de colores) **6** FRESH : fresco, reciente ⟨a warm trail : un rastro reciente⟩ **7** (*used for riddles*) : caliente

warm–blooded ['wɔrm'blʌdəd] *adj* : de sangre caliente

warmhearted ['wɔrm'hɑrtəd] *adj* : cariñoso

warmly ['wɔrmli] *adv* **1** AFFECTIONATELY : calurosamente, afectuosamente **2 to dress warmly** : abrigarse

warmonger ['wɔrˌmɑŋɡər, -ˌmʌŋ-] *n* : belicista *mf*

warmth ['wɔrmpθ] *n* **1** : calor *m* **2** AFFECTION : cariño *m*, afecto *m* **3** ENTHUSIASM : ardor *m*, entusiasmo *m*

warm–up ['wɔrmˌʌp] *n* : calentamiento *m*

warn ['wɔrn] *vt* **1** CAUTION : advertir, alertar **2** INFORM : avisar, informar

warning ['wɔrnɪŋ] *n* **1** ADVICE : advertencia *f*, aviso *m* **2** ALERT : alerta *f*, alarma *f*

warp¹ ['wɔrp] *vt* **1** : alabear, combar **2** PERVERT : pervertir, deformar — *vi* : pandearse, alabearse, combarse

warp[2] *n* **1** : urdimbre *f* ⟨the warp and the weft : la urdimbre y la trama⟩ **2** : alabeo *m* (en la madera, etc.)

warrant[1] ['wɔrənt] *vt* **1** ASSURE : asegurar, garantizar **2** GUARANTEE : garantizar **3** JUSTIFY, MERIT : justificar, merecer

warrant[2] *n* **1** AUTHORIZATION : autorización *f*, permiso *m* ⟨an arrest warrant : una orden de detención⟩ **2** JUSTIFICATION : justificación *f*

warranty ['wɔrənti, ˌwɔrən'ti:] *n, pl* **-ties** : garantía *f*

warren ['wɔrən] *n* : madriguera *f* (de conejos)

warrior ['wɔriər] *n* : guerrero *m*, -ra *f*

warship ['wɔrˌʃip] *n* : buque *m* de guerra

wart ['wɔrt] *n* : verruga *f*

wartime ['wɔrˌtaim] *n* : tiempo *m* de guerra

wary ['wæri] *adj* **warier; -est** : cauteloso, receloso ⟨to be wary of : desconfiar de⟩

was → **be**

wash[1] ['wɔʃ, 'wɑʃ] *vt* **1** CLEAN : lavar(se), limpiar, fregar ⟨to wash the dishes : lavar los platos⟩ ⟨to wash one's hands : lavarse las manos⟩ **2** DRENCH : mojar **3** LAP : bañar ⟨waves were washing the shore : las olas bañaban la orilla⟩ **4** CARRY, DRAG : arrastrar **5 to wash away** : llevarse (un puente, etc.) — *vi* **1** : lavarse (dícese de una persona o la ropa) ⟨the dress washes well : el vestido se lava bien⟩ **2 to wash against** *or* **to wash over** : bañar

wash[2] *n* **1** : lavado *m* ⟨to give something a wash : lavar algo⟩ **2** LAUNDRY : artículos *mpl* para lavar, ropa *f* sucia **3** : estela *f* (de un barco)

washable ['wɔʃəbəl, 'wɑ-] *adj* : lavable

washboard ['wɔʃˌbord, 'wɑʃ-] *n* : tabla *f* de lavar

washbowl ['wɔʃˌbo:l, 'wɑʃ-] *n* : lavabo *m*, lavamanos *m*

washcloth ['wɔʃˌklɔθ, 'wɑʃ-] *n* : toallita *f* (para lavarse)

washed–out ['wɔʃt'aut, 'wɑʃt-] *adj* **1** : desvaído (dícese de colores) **2** EXHAUSTED : agotado, desanimado

washed–up ['wɔʃt'ʌp, 'wɑʃt-] *adj* : acabado (dícese de una persona), fracasado (dícese de un negocio, etc.)

washer ['wɔʃər, 'wɑ-] *n* **1** → **washing machine 2** : arandela *f* (de una llave, etc.)

washing ['wɔʃiŋ, 'wɑ-] *n* WASH : ropa *f* para lavar

washing machine *n* : máquina *f* de lavar, lavadora *f*

washout ['wɔʃˌaut, 'wɑʃ-] *n* **1** : erosión *f* (de la tierra) **2** FAILURE : fracaso *m* ⟨she's a washout : es un desastre⟩

washroom ['wɔʃˌru:m, 'wɑʃ-, -ˌrʊm] *n* : servicios *mpl* (públicos), baño *m*, sanitario *m* Col, Mex, Ven

wasn't ['wʌzənt] (*contraction of* **was not**) → **be**

wasp ['wɑsp] *n* : avispa *f*

waspish ['wɑspiʃ] *adj* **1** IRRITABLE : irritable, irascible **2** CAUSTIC : cáustico, mordaz

waste[1] ['weist] *v* **wasted; wasting** *vt* **1** DEVASTATE : arrasar, arruinar, devastar **2** SQUANDER : desperdiciar, despilfarrar, malgastar ⟨to waste time : perder tiempo⟩ — *vi or* **to waste away** : consumirse, chuparse

waste[2] *adj* **1** BARREN : yermo, baldío **2** DISCARDED : de desecho **3** EXCESS : sobrante

waste[3] *n* **1** → **wasteland 2** MISUSE : derroche *m*, desperdicio *m*, despilfarro *m* ⟨a waste of time : una pérdida de tiempo⟩ **3** RUBBISH : basura *f*, desechos *mpl*, desperdicios *mpl* **4** EXCREMENT : excremento *m*

wastebasket ['weistˌbæskət] *n* : cesto *m* (de basura), papelera *f*, zafacón *m* Car

wasteful ['weistfəl] *adj* : despilfarrador, derrochador, pródigo

wastefulness ['weistfəlnəs] *n* : derroche *m*, despilfarro *m*

wasteland ['weistˌlænd, -lənd] *n* : baldío *m*, yermo *m*, desierto *m*

watch[1] ['wɑtʃ] *vi* **1** *or* **to keep watch** : velar **2** OBSERVE : mirar, ver, observar **3 to watch for** AWAIT : esperar, quedar a la espera de **4 to watch out** : tener cuidado ⟨watch out! : ¡ten cuidado!, ¡ojo!⟩ — *vt* **1** OBSERVE : mirar, observar **2** *or* **to watch over** : vigilar, cuidar **3** : tener cuidado de ⟨watch what you do : ten cuidado con lo que haces⟩

watch[2] *n* **1** : guardia *f* ⟨to be on watch : estar de guardia⟩ **2** SURVEILLANCE : vigilancia *f* **3** LOOKOUT : guardia *mf*, centinela *f*, vigía *mf* **4** TIMEPIECE : reloj *m*

watchdog ['wɑtʃˌdɔg] *n* : perro *m* guardián

watcher ['wɑtʃər] *n* : observador *m*, -dora *f*

watchful ['wɑtʃfəl] *adj* : alerta, vigilante, atento

watchfulness ['wɑtʃfəlnəs] *n* : vigilancia *f*

watchman ['wɑtʃmən] *n, pl* **-men** [-mən, -ˌmɛn] : vigilante *m*, guarda *m*

watchword ['wɑtʃˌwərd] *n* **1** PASSWORD : contraseña *f* **2** SLOGAN : lema *m*, eslogan *m*

water[1] ['wɔtər, 'wɑ-] *vt* **1** : regar (el jardín, etc.) **2 to water down** DILUTE : diluir, aguar — *vi* **1** : lagrimear (dícese de los ojos), hacérsele agua la boca a uno ⟨my mouth is watering : se me hace agua la boca⟩

water[2] *n* : agua *f*

water buffalo *n* : búfalo *m* de agua

watercolor ['wɔtərˌkʌlər, 'wɑ-] *n* : acuarela *f*

watercourse ['wɔtərˌkors, 'wɑ-] *n* : curso *m* de agua

watercress ['wɔtərˌkrɛs, 'wɑ-] *n* : berro *m*

waterfall ['wɔtər₁fɔl, 'wɑ-] n : cascada f, salto m de agua, catarata f

waterfowl ['wɔtər₁faʊl, 'wɑ-] n : ave f acuática

waterfront ['wɔtər₁frʌnt, 'wɑ-] n 1 : tierra f que bordea un río, un lago, o un mar 2 WHARF : muelle m

water lily n : nenúfar m

waterlogged ['wɔtər₁lɔgd, 'wɔtər-₁lɑgd] adj : lleno de agua, empapado, inundado (dícese del suelo)

watermark ['wɔtər₁mɑrk, 'wɑ-] n 1 : marca f del nivel de agua 2 : filigrana f (en el papel)

watermelon ['wɔtər₁mɛlən, 'wɑ-] n : sandía f

water moccasin → moccasin

waterpower ['wɔtər₁paʊər, 'wɑ-] n : energía f hidráulica

waterproof¹ ['wɔtər₁pruːf, 'wɑ-] vt : hacer impermeable, impermeabilizar

waterproof² adj : impermeable, a prueba de agua

watershed ['wɔtər₁ʃɛd, 'wɑ-] n 1 : línea f divisoria de aguas 2 BASIN : cuenca f (de un río)

waterskiing ['wɔtər₁skiːɪŋ, 'wɑ-] n : esquí m acuático

waterspout ['wɔtər₁spaʊt, 'wɑ-] n WHIRLWIND : tromba f marina

watertight ['wɔtər₁taɪt, 'wɑ-] adj 1 : hermético 2 IRREFUTABLE : irrebatible, irrefutable ⟨a watertight contract : un contrato sin lagunas⟩

waterway ['wɔtər₁weɪ, 'wɑ-] n : vía f navegable

waterworks ['wɔtər₁wərks, 'wɑ-] npl : central f de abastecimiento de agua

watery ['wɔtəri, 'wɑ-] adj 1 : acuoso, como agua 2 : aguado, diluido ⟨watery soup : sopa aguada⟩ 3 : lloroso ⟨watery eyes : ojos llorosos⟩ 4 WASHED-OUT : desvaído (dícese de colores)

watt ['wɑt] n : vatio m

wattage ['wɑtɪʤ] n : vataje m

wattle ['wɑtəl] n : carúncula f (de un ave, etc.)

wave¹ ['weɪv] v **waved; waving** vi 1 : saludar con la mano, hacer señas con la mano ⟨she waved at him : lo saludó con la mano⟩ 2 FLUTTER, SHAKE : ondear, agitarse 3 UNDULATE : ondular — vt 1 SHAKE : agitar 2 BRANDISH : blandir 3 CURL : ondular, marcar (el pelo) 4 SIGNAL : hacerle señas a (con la mano) ⟨he waved farewell : se despidió con la mano⟩

wave² n 1 : ola f (de agua) 2 CURL : onda f (en el pelo) 3 : onda f (en física) 4 SURGE : oleada f ⟨a wave of enthusiasm : una oleada de entusiasmo⟩ 5 GESTURE : señal f con la mano, saludo m con la mano

wavelength ['weɪv₁lɛŋkθ] n : longitud f de onda

waver ['weɪvər] vi 1 VACILLATE : vacilar, fluctuar 2 FLICKER : parpadear, titilar, oscilar 3 FALTER : flaquear, tambalearse

wavy ['weɪvi] adj **wavier; -est** : ondulado

wax¹ ['wæks] vi 1 : crecer (dícese de la luna) 2 BECOME : volverse, ponerse ⟨to wax indignant : indignarse⟩ — vt : encerar

wax² n 1 BEESWAX : cera f de abejas 2 : cera f ⟨floor wax : cera para el piso⟩ 3 or **earwax** ['ɪr₁wæks] : cerilla f, cerumen m

waxen ['wæksən] adj : de cera

waxy ['wæksi] adj **waxier; -est** : ceroso

way ['weɪ] n 1 PATH, ROAD : camino m, vía f 2 ROUTE : camino m, ruta f ⟨to go the wrong way : equivocarse de camino⟩ ⟨I'm on my way : estoy de camino⟩ 3 : línea f de conducta, camino m ⟨he chose the easy way : optó por el camino fácil⟩ 4 MANNER, MEANS : manera f, modo m, forma f ⟨in the same way : del mismo modo, igualmente⟩ ⟨there are no two ways about it : no cabe la menor duda⟩ ⟨no way! : ¡de ninguna manera!⟩ 5 (indicating a wish) ⟨have it your way : como tú quieras⟩ ⟨to get one's own way : salirse uno con la suya⟩ 6 STATE : estado m ⟨things are in a bad way : las cosas marchan mal⟩ 7 RESPECT : aspecto m, sentido m 8 CUSTOM : costumbre f ⟨to mend one's ways : dejar las malas costumbres⟩ 9 PASSAGE : camino m ⟨to get in the way : meterse en el camino⟩ 10 DISTANCE : distancia f ⟨to come a long way : hacer grandes progresos⟩ 11 DIRECTION : dirección f ⟨come this way : venga por aquí⟩ ⟨which way did he go? : ¿por dónde fue?⟩ 12 **by the way** : a propósito, por cierto 13 **by way of** VIA : vía, pasando por 14 **out of the way** REMOTE : remoto, recóndito 15 → **under way**

wayfarer ['weɪ₁færər] n : caminante mf

waylay ['weɪ₁leɪ] vt **-laid** [-₁leɪd]; **-laying** ACCOST : abordar

wayside ['weɪ₁saɪd] n : borde m del camino

wayward ['weɪwərd] adj 1 UNRULY : díscolo, rebelde 2 UNTOWARD : adverso

we ['wiː] pron : nosotros, nosotras

weak ['wiːk] adj 1 FEEBLE : débil, endeble 2 : flojo, pobre ⟨a weak excuse : una excusa poco convincente⟩ 3 DILUTED : aguado, diluido ⟨weak tea : té poco cargado⟩ 4 FAINT : tenue (dícese de los colores, las luces, los sonidos, etc.)

weaken ['wiːkən] vt : debilitar — vi : debilitarse, flaquear

weakling ['wiːklɪŋ] n : alfeñique m fam; debilucho m, -cha f

weakly¹ ['wiːkli] adv : débilmente

weakly² adj **weaklier; -est** : débil, enclenque

weakness ['wiːknəs] n 1 FEEBLENESS : debilidad f 2 FAULT, FLAW : flaqueza f, punto m débil

wealth ['wɛlθ] *n* **1** RICHES : riqueza *f* **2** PROFUSION : abundancia *f*, profusión *f*

wealthy ['wɛlθi] *adj* **wealthier; -est** : rico, acaudalado, adinerado

wean ['wi:n] *vt* **1** : destetar (a los niños o las crías) **2 to wean someone away from** : quitarle a alguien la costumbre de

weapon ['wɛpən] *n* : arma *f*

weaponless ['wɛpənləs] *adj* : desarmado

weaponry ['wɛpənri] *n* : armamento *m*

wear¹ ['wær] *v* **wore** ['wor]; **worn** ['worn]; **wearing** *vt* **1** : llevar (ropa, un reloj, etc.), calzar (zapatos) ⟨to wear a happy smile : sonreír alegremente⟩ **2** *or* **to wear away** : desgastar, erosionar (rocas, etc.) **3 to wear out** : gastar ⟨he wore out his shoes : gastó sus zapatos⟩ **4 to wear out** EXHAUST : agotar, fatigar ⟨to wear oneself out : agotarse⟩ — *vi* **1** LAST : durar **2 to wear off** DIMINISH : disminuir **3 to wear out** : gastarse

wear² *n* **1** USE : uso *m* ⟨for everyday wear : para todos los días⟩ **2** CLOTHING : ropa *f* ⟨children's wear : ropa de niños⟩ **3** DETERIORATION : desgaste *m* ⟨to be the worse for wear : estar deteriorado⟩

wearable ['wærəbəl] *adj* : que puede ponerse (dícese de una prenda)

wear and tear *n* : desgaste *m*

weariness ['wɪrinəs] *n* : fatiga *f*, cansancio *m*

wearisome ['wɪrisəm] *adj* : aburrido, pesado, cansado

weary¹ ['wɪri] *v* **-ried; -rying** *vt* **1** TIRE : cansar, fatigar **2** BORE : hastiar, aburrir — *vi* : cansarse

weary² *adj* **-rier; -est 1** TIRED : cansado **2** FED UP : harto **3** BORED : aburrido

weasel ['wi:zəl] *n* : comadreja *f*

weather¹ ['wɛðər] *vt* **1** WEAR : erosionar, desgastar **2** ENDURE : aguantar, sobrellevar, capear ⟨to weather the storm : capear el temporal⟩

weather² *n* : tiempo *m*

weather–beaten ['wɛðər,bi:tən] *adj* : curtido

weatherman ['wɛðər,mæn] *n, pl* **-men** [-mən, -,mɛn] METEOROLOGIST : meteorólogo *m*, -ga *f*

weatherproof ['wɛðər,pru:f] *adj* : que resiste a la intemperie, impermeable

weather vane → **vane**

weave¹ ['wi:v] *v* **wove** ['wo:v] *or* **weaved**; **woven** ['wo:vən] *or* **weaved**; **weaving** *vt* **1** : tejer (tela) **2** INTERLACE : entretejer, entrelazar **3 to weave one's way through** : abrirse camino por — *vi* **1** : tejer **2** WIND : serpentear, zigzaguear

weave² *n* : tejido *m*, trama *f*

weaver ['wi:vər] *n* : tejedor *m*, -dora *f*

web¹ ['wɛb] *vt* **webbed; webbing** : cubrir o proveer con una red

web² *n* **1** COBWEB, SPIDERWEB : telaraña *f*, tela *f* de araña **2** ENTANGLEMENT, SNARE : red *f*, enredo *m* ⟨a web of intrigue : una red de intriga⟩ **3** : membrana *f* interdigital (de aves) **4** NETWORK : red *f* ⟨a web of highways : una red de carreteras⟩ **5 the Web** : la web

webbed ['wɛbd] *adj* : palmeado ⟨webbed feet : patas palmeadas⟩

Web site *n* : sitio *m* web

wed ['wɛd] *vt* **wedded; wedding 1** MARRY : casarse con **2** UNITE : ligar, unir

we'd ['wi:d] (*contraction of* **we had, we should,** *or* **we would**) → **have, should, would**

wedding ['wɛdɪŋ] *n* : boda *f*, casamiento *m*

wedge¹ ['wɛdʒ] *vt* **wedged; wedging 1** : apretar (con una cuña) ⟨to wedge open : mantener abierto con una cuña⟩ **2** CRAM : meter, embutir

wedge² *n* **1** : cuña *f* **2** PIECE : porción *f*, trozo *m*

wedlock ['wɛd,lɑk] → **marriage**

Wednesday ['wɛnz,dei, -di] *n* : miércoles *m*

wee ['wi:] *adj* : pequeño, minúsculo ⟨in the wee hours : a las altas horas⟩

weed¹ ['wi:d] *vt* **1** : desherbar, desyerbar **2 to weed out** : eliminar, quitar

weed² *n* : mala hierba *f*

weedy ['wi:di] *adj* **weedier; -est 1** : cubierto de malas hierbas **2** LANKY, SKINNY : flaco, larguirucho *fam*

week ['wi:k] *n* : semana *f*

weekday ['wi:k,dei] *n* : día *m* laborable

weekend ['wi:k,ɛnd] *n* : fin *m* de semana

weekly¹ ['wi:kli] *adv* : semanalmente

weekly² *adj* : semanal

weekly³ *n, pl* **-lies** : semanario *m*

weep ['wi:p] *v* **wept** ['wɛpt]; **weeping** : llorar

weeping willow *n* : sauce *m* llorón

weepy ['wi:pi] *adj* **weepier; -est** : lloroso, triste

weevil ['wi:vəl] *n* : gorgojo *m*

weft ['wɛft] *n* : trama *f*

weigh ['wei] *vt* **1** : pesar **2** CONSIDER : considerar, sopesar **3 to weigh anchor** : levar anclas **4 to weigh down** : sobrecargar (con una carga), abrumar (con preocupaciones, etc.) — *vi* **1** : pesar ⟨it weighs 10 pounds : pesa 10 libras⟩ **2** COUNT : tener importancia, contar **3 to weigh on one's mind** : preocuparle a uno

weight¹ ['weit] *vt* **1** : poner peso en, sujetar con un peso **2** BURDEN : cargar, oprimir

weight² *n* **1** HEAVINESS : peso *m* ⟨to lose weight : bajar de peso, adelgazar⟩ **2** : peso *m* ⟨weights and measures : pesos y medidas⟩ **3** : pesa *f* ⟨to lift weights : levantar pesas⟩ **4** BURDEN : peso *m*, carga *f* ⟨to take a weight off one's mind : quitarle un peso de encima a uno⟩ **5**

IMPORTANCE : peso *m* **6** INFLUENCE : influencia *f*, autoridad *f* ⟨to throw one's weight around : hacer sentir su influencia⟩

weighty ['weɪt̬i] *adj* **weightier; -est 1** HEAVY : pesado **2** IMPORTANT : importante, de peso

weird ['wɪrd] *adj* **1** MYSTERIOUS : misterioso **2** STRANGE : extraño, raro — **weirdly** *adv*

welcome¹ ['wɛlkəm] *vt* **-comed; -coming** : darle la bienvenida a, recibir

welcome² *adj* : bienvenido ⟨to make someone welcome : acoger bien a alguien⟩ ⟨you're welcome! : ¡de nada!, ¡no hay de qué!⟩

welcome³ *n* : bienvenida *f*, recibimiento *m*, acogida *f*

weld¹ ['wɛld] *v* : soldar

weld² *n* : soldadura *f*

welder ['wɛldər] *n* : soldador *m*, -dora *f*

welfare ['wɛl,fær] *n* **1** WELL-BEING : bienestar *m* **2** : asistencia *f* social

well¹ ['wɛl] *vi or* **to well up** : brotar, manar

well² *adv* **better** ['bɛt̬ər]; **best** ['bɛst] **1** RIGHTLY : bien, correctamente **2** SATISFACTORILY : bien ⟨to turn out well : resultar bien, salir bien⟩ **3** COMPLETELY : completamente ⟨well-hidden : completamente escondido⟩ **4** INTIMATELY : bien ⟨I knew him well : lo conocía bien⟩ **5** CONSIDERABLY, FAR : muy, bastante ⟨well ahead : muy adelante⟩ ⟨well before the deadline : bastante antes de la fecha⟩ **6 as well** ALSO : también **7** → **as well as**

well³ *adj* **1** SATISFACTORY : bien ⟨all is well : todo está bien⟩ **2** DESIRABLE : conveniente ⟨it would be well if you left : sería conveniente que te fueras⟩ **3** HEALTHY : bien, sano

well⁴ *n* **1** : pozo *m* (de agua, petróleo, gas, etc.), aljibe *m* (de agua) **2** SOURCE : fuente *f* ⟨a well of information : una fuente de información⟩ **3** *or* **stairwell** : caja *f*, hueco *m* (de la escalera)

well⁵ *interj* **1** (*used to introduce a remark*) : bueno **2** (*used to express surprise*) : ¡vaya!

we'll ['wiːl, wɪl] (*contraction of* **we shall** *or* **we will**) → **shall, will**

well-balanced ['wɛl'bælənst] *adj* : equilibrado

well-being ['wɛl'biːɪŋ] *n* : bienestar *m*

well-bred ['wɛl'brɛd] *adj* : fino, bien educado

well-defined [,wɛldi'faɪnd] *adj* : bien definido

well-done ['wɛl'dʌn] *adj* **1** : bien hecho ⟨well-done! : ¡bravo!⟩ **2** : bien cocido

well-known ['wɛl'noːn] *adj* : famoso, bien conocido

well-meaning ['wɛl'miːnɪŋ] *adj* : bien-intencionado, que tiene buenas intenciones

well-nigh ['wɛl'naɪ] *adv* : casi ⟨well-nigh impossible : casi imposible⟩

well-off ['wɛl'ɔf] → **well-to-do**

well-rounded ['wɛl'raʊndəd] *adj* : completo, equilibrado

well-to-do [,wɛltə'duː] *adj* : próspero, adinerado, rico

Welsh ['wɛlʃ] *n* **1** : galés *m*, galesa *f* **2** : galés *m* (idioma) — **Welsh** *adj*

welt ['wɛlt] *n* **1** : vira *f* (de un zapato) **2** WHEAL : verdugón *m*

welter ['wɛltər] *n* : fárrago *m*, revoltijo *m* ⟨a welter of data : un fárrago de datos⟩

wend ['wɛnd] *vi* **to wend one's way** : ponerse en camino, encaminar sus pasos

went → **go¹**

wept → **weep**

were → **be**

we're ['wɪr, 'wər, 'wiːər] (*contraction of* **we are**) → **be**

werewolf ['wɪr,wʊlf, 'wɛr-, 'wər-, -,wʌlf] *n, pl* **-wolves** [-,wʊlvz, -,wʌlvz] : hombre *m* lobo

west¹ ['wɛst] *adv* : al oeste

west² *adj* : oeste, del oeste, occidental ⟨west winds : vientos del oeste⟩

west³ *n* **1** : oeste *m* **2 the West** : el Oeste, el Occidente

westerly ['wɛstərli] *adv & adj* : del oeste

western ['wɛstərn] *adj* **1** : Occidental, del Oeste **2** : occidental, oeste

Westerner ['wɛstərnər] *n* : habitante *mf* del oeste

West Indian *n* : antillano *m*, -na *f* — **West Indian** *adj*

westward ['wɛstwərd] *adv & adj* : hacia el oeste

wet¹ ['wɛt] *vt* **wet** *or* **wetted; wetting** : mojar, humedecer

wet² *adj* **wetter; wettest 1** : mojado, húmedo ⟨wet clothes : ropa mojada⟩ **2** RAINY : lluvioso **3 wet paint** : pintura *f* fresca

wet³ *n* **1** MOISTURE : humedad *f* **2** RAIN : lluvia *f*

we've ['wiːv] (*contraction of* **we have**) → **have**

whack¹ ['hwæk] *vt* : golpear (fuertemente), aporrear

whack² *n* **1** : golpe *m* fuerte, porrazo *m* **2** ATTEMPT : intento *m*, tentativa *f*

whale¹ ['hweɪl] *vi* **whaled; whaling** : cazar ballenas

whale² *n, pl* **whales** *or* **whale** : ballena *f*

whaleboat ['hweɪl,boːt] *n* : ballenero *m*

whalebone ['hweɪl,boːn] *n* : barba *f* de ballena

whaler ['hweɪlər] *n* **1** : ballenero *m*, -ra *f* **2** → **whaleboat**

wharf ['hwɔrf] *n, pl* **wharves** ['hwɔrvz] : muelle *m*, embarcadero *m*

what¹ ['hwɑt, 'hwʌt] *adv* **1** HOW : cómo, cuánto ⟨what he suffered! : ¡cómo sufría!⟩ **2 what with** : entre ⟨what with one thing and another : entre una cosa y otra⟩

what² *adj* **1** (*used in questions*) : qué ⟨what more do you want? : ¿qué más quieres?⟩ ⟨what color is it? : ¿de qué

color es?⟩ **2** (*used in exclamations*)
: qué ⟨what an idea! : ¡qué idea!⟩ **3**
ANY, WHATEVER : cualquier ⟨give what
help you can : da cualquier contribución que puedas⟩

what³ *pron* **1** (*used in direct questions*)
: qué ⟨what happened? : ¿qué pasó?⟩
⟨what does it cost? : ¿cuánto cuesta?⟩
2 (*used in indirect statements*) : lo que,
que ⟨I don't know what to do : no sé
que hacer⟩ ⟨do what I tell you : haz lo
que te digo⟩ **3 what for** WHY : porqué
4 what if : y si ⟨what if he knows? : ¿y
si lo sabe?⟩

whatever¹ [*h*wɑt'ɛvər, ˌ*h*wʌt-] *adj* **1** ANY
: cualquier, cualquier ... que ⟨what-
ever way you prefer : de cualquier
manera que prefiera, como prefiera⟩ **2**
(*in negative constructions*) ⟨there's no
chance whatever : no hay ninguna posibi-
lidad⟩ ⟨nothing whatever : nada en
absoluto⟩

whatever² *pron* **1** ANYTHING : (todo) lo
que ⟨I'll do whatever I want : haré lo
que quiera⟩ **2** (*no matter what*) : whatever it may be : sea lo que sea⟩ **3** WHAT
: qué ⟨whatever do you mean? : ¿qué
quieres decir?⟩

whatsoever¹ [ˌ*h*wɑtso'ɛvər, ˌ*h*wʌt-] *adj*
→ **whatever¹**

whatsoever² *pron* → **whatever²**

wheal [*h*wi:l] *n* : verdugón *m*

wheat [*h*wi:t] *n* : trigo *m*

wheaten [*h*wi:tən] *adj* : de trigo

wheedle [*h*wi:dəl] *vt* **-dled; -dling** CA-
JOLE : engatusar ⟨to wheedle some-
thing out of someone : sonsacarle algo
a alguien⟩

wheel¹ [*h*wi:l] *vt* : empujar (una bicicleta, etc.), mover (algo sobre ruedas)
— *vi* **1** ROTATE : girar, rotar **2 to wheel
around** TURN : darse la vuelta

wheel² *n* **1** : rueda *f* **2** *or* **steering wheel**
: volante *m* (de automóviles, etc.),
timón *m* (de barcos o aviones) **3
wheels** *npl* : maquinaria *f*, fuerza *f* im-
pulsora ⟨the wheels of government : la
maquinaria del gobierno⟩

wheelbarrow [*h*wi:lˌbærˌo:] *n* : carretilla *f*

wheelchair [*h*wi:lˌtʃær] *n* : silla *f* de
ruedas

wheeze¹ [*h*wi:z] *vi* **wheezed; wheezing**
: resollar, respirar con dificultad

wheeze² *n* : resuello *m*

whelk [*h*wɛlk] *n* : buccino *m*

whelp¹ [*h*wɛlp] *vi* : parir

whelp² *n* : cachorro *m*, -rra *f*

when¹ [*h*wɛn] *adv* : cuándo ⟨when will
you return? : ¿cuándo volverás?⟩ ⟨he
asked me when I would be home : me
preguntó cuándo estaría en casa⟩

when² *conj* **1** (*referring to a particular
time*) : cuando, en que ⟨when you are
ready : cuando estés listo⟩ ⟨the days
when I clean the house : los días en que
limpio la casa⟩ **2** IF : cuando, si ⟨how
can I go when I have no money?

: ¿cómo voy a ir si no tengo dinero?⟩
3 ALTHOUGH : cuando ⟨you said it was
big when actually it's small : dijiste que
era grande cuando en realidad es pe-
queño⟩

when³ *pron* : cuándo ⟨since when are
you the boss? : ¿desde cuándo eres el
jefe?⟩

whence [*h*wɛnts] *adv* : de donde

whenever¹ [*h*wɛn'vər] *adv* **1** : cuando
sea ⟨tomorrow or whenever : mañana
o cuando sea⟩ **2** (*in questions*) : cuándo

whenever² *conj* **1** : siempre que, cada
vez que ⟨whenever I go, I'm disappointed : siempre que voy, quedo de-
silusionado⟩ **2** WHEN : cuando ⟨when-
ever you like : cuando quieras⟩

where¹ [*h*wɛr] *adv* : dónde, adónde
⟨where is he? : ¿dónde está?⟩ ⟨where
did they go? : ¿adónde fueron?⟩

where² *conj* : donde, adonde ⟨she knows
where the house is : sabe donde está la
casa⟩ ⟨she goes where she likes : va
adonde quiera⟩

where³ *pron* : donde ⟨Chicago is where
I live : Chicago es donde vivo⟩

whereabouts¹ [*h*wɛrəˌbaʊts] *adv*
: dónde, por dónde ⟨whereabouts is the
house? : ¿dónde está la casa?⟩

whereabouts² *ns & pl* : paradero *m*

whereas [*h*wɛr'æz] *conj* **1** : consideran-
do que (usado en documentos legales)
2 : mientras que ⟨I like the white one
whereas she prefers the black : me gusta el blanco mientras que ella prefiere
el negro⟩

whereby [*h*wɛr'baɪ] *adv* : por lo cual

wherefore [*h*wɛrˌfor] *adv* : por qué

wherein [*h*wɛr'ɪn] *adv* : en el cual, en el
que

whereof [*h*wɛr'ʌv, -'av] *conj* : de lo cual

whereupon [*h*wɛrəˌpan, -ˌpɔn] *conj*
: con lo cual, después de lo cual

wherever¹ [*h*wɛr'ɛvər] *adv* **1** WHERE
: dónde, adónde **2** : en cualquier parte
⟨or wherever : o donde sea⟩

wherever² *conj* : dondequiera que,
donde sea ⟨wherever you go : dondequiera que vayas⟩

wherewithal [*h*wɛrwɪˌðɔl, -ˌθɔl] *n*
: medios *mpl*, recursos *mpl*

whet [*h*wɛt] *vt* **whetted; whetting 1**
SHARPEN : afilar **2** STIMULATE : estimular ⟨to whet the appetite : estimular el apetito⟩

whether [*h*wɛðər] *conj* **1** : si ⟨I don't
know whether it is finished : no sé si
está acabado⟩ ⟨we doubt whether he'll
show up : dudamos que aparezca⟩ **2**
(*used in comparisons*) ⟨whether I like
it or not : tanto si quiero como si no⟩
⟨whether he comes or he doesn't : venga o no⟩

whetstone [*h*wɛtˌsto:n] *n* : piedra *f* de
afilar

whey [*h*weɪ] *n* : suero *m* (de la leche)

which¹ [*h*wɪtʃ] *adj* : qué, cuál ⟨which tie
do you prefer? : ¿cuál corbata pre-

fieres?⟩ ⟨which ones? : ¿cuáles?⟩ ⟨tell me which house is yours : dime qué casa es la tuya⟩

which² *pron* **1** : cuál ⟨which is the right answer? : ¿cuál es la respuesta correcta?⟩ **2** : que, el (la) cual ⟨the cup which broke : la taza que se quebró⟩ ⟨the house, which is made of brick : la casa, la cual es de ladrillo⟩

whichever¹ [*h*wɪtʃ'ɛvər] *adj* : el (la) que, cualquiera que ⟨whichever book you like : cualquier libro que te guste⟩

whichever² *pron* : el (la) que, cualquiera que ⟨take whichever you want : toma el que quieras⟩ ⟨whichever I choose : cualquiera que elija⟩

whiff¹ [*h*wɪf] *v* PUFF : soplar

whiff² *n* **1** PUFF : soplo *m*, ráfaga *f* **2** SNIFF : olor *m* **3** HINT : dejo *m*, pizca *f*

while¹ [*'h*waɪl] *vt* **whiled; whiling** : pasar ⟨to while away the time : matar el tiempo⟩

while² *n* **1** TIME : rato *m*, tiempo *m* ⟨after a while : después de un rato⟩ ⟨in a while : dentro de poco⟩ **2 to be worth one's while** : valer la pena

while³ *conj* **1** : mientras ⟨whistle while you work : silba mientras trabajas⟩ **2** WHEREAS : mientras que **3** ALTHOUGH : aunque ⟨while it's very good, it's not perfect : aunque es muy bueno, no es perfecto⟩

whim [*h*wɪm] *n* : capricho *m*, antojo *m*

whimper¹ [*h*wɪmpər] *vi* : lloriquear, gimotear

whimper² *n* : quejido *m*

whimsical [*h*wɪmzɪkəl] *adj* **1** CAPRICIOUS : caprichoso, fantasioso **2** ERRATIC : errático — **whimsically** *adv*

whine¹ [*'h*waɪn] *vi* **whined; whining 1** : lloriquear, gimotear, gemir **2** COMPLAIN : quejarse

whine² *n* : quejido *m*, gemido *m*

whinny¹ [*'h*wɪni] *vi* **-nied; -nying** : relinchar

whinny² *n, pl* **-nies** : relincho *m*

whip¹ [*'h*wɪp] *v* **whipped; whipping** *vt* **1** SNATCH : sacar (rápidamente), arrebatar ⟨she whipped the cloth off the table : arrebató el mantel de la mesa⟩ **2** LASH : azotar **3** DEFEAT : vencer, derrotar **4** INCITE : incitar, despertar ⟨to whip up enthusiasm : despertar el entusiasmo⟩ **5** BEAT : batir (huevos, crema, etc.) — *vi* FLAP : agitarse

whip² *n* **1** : látigo *m*, azote *m*, fusta *f* (de jinete) **2** : miembro *m* de un cuerpo legislativo encargado de disciplina

whiplash [*'h*wɪp,læʃ] *n or* **whiplash injury** : traumatismo *m* cervical

whippet [*h*wɪpət] *n* : galgo *m* pequeño, galgo *m* inglés

whir¹ [*'h*wər] *vi* **whirred; whirring** : zumbar

whir² *n* : zumbido *m*

whirl¹ [*'h*wərl] *vi* **1** SPIN : dar vueltas, girar ⟨my head is whirling : la cabeza me

está dando vueltas⟩ **2 to whirl about** : arremolinarse, moverse rápidamente

whirl² *n* **1** SPIN : giro *m*, vuelta *f*, remolino *m* (dícese del polvo, etc.) **2** BUSTLE : bullicio *m*, torbellino *m* (de actividad, etc.) **3 to give it a whirl** : intentar hacer, probar

whirlpool [*'h*wərl,pu:l] *n* : vorágine *f*, remolino *m*

whirlwind [*'h*wərl,wɪnd] *n* : remolino *m*, torbellino *m*, tromba *f*

whisk¹ [*'h*wɪsk] *vt* **1** : llevar ⟨she whisked the children off to bed : llevó a los niños a la cama⟩ **2** : batir ⟨to whisk eggs : batir huevos⟩ **3 to whisk away** *or* **to whisk off** : sacudir

whisk² *n* **1** WHISKING : sacudida *f* (movimiento) **2** : batidor *m* (para batir huevos, etc.)

whisk broom *n* : escobilla *f*

whisker [*'h*wɪskər] *n* **1** : pelo *m* (de la barba o el bigote) **2 whiskers** *npl* : bigotes *mpl* (de animales)

whiskey *or* **whisky** [*'h*wɪski] *n, pl* **-keys** *or* **-kies** : whisky *m*

whisper¹ [*'h*wɪspər] *vi* : cuchichear, susurrar — *vt* : decir en voz baja, susurrar

whisper² *n* **1** WHISPERING : susurro *m*, cuchicheo *m* **2** RUMOR : rumor *m* **3** TRACE : dejo *m*, pizca *f*

whistle¹ [*'h*wɪsəl] *v* **-tled; -tling** *vi* : silbar, chiflar, pitar (dícese de un tren, etc.) — *vt* : silbar ⟨to whistle a tune : silbar una melodía⟩

whistle² *n* **1** WHISTLING : chiflido *m*, silbido *m* **2** : silbato *m*, pito *m* (instrumento)

whit [*'h*wɪt] *n* BIT : ápice *m*, pizca *f*

white¹ [*'h*waɪt] *adj* **whiter; -est** : blanco

white² *n* **1** : blanco *m* (color) **2** : clara *f* (de huevos) **3** *or* **white person** : blanco *m*, -ca *f*

white blood cell *n* : glóbulo *m* blanco

whitecaps [*'h*waɪt,kæps] *npl* : cabrillas *fpl*

white–collar [*'h*waɪt'kɑlər] *adj* **1** : de oficina **2 white–collar worker** : oficinista *mf*

whitefish [*'h*waɪt,fɪʃ] *n* : pescado *m* blanco

whiten [*'h*waɪtən] *vt* : blanquear — *vi* : ponerse blanco

whiteness [*'h*waɪtnəs] *n* : blancura *f*

white–tailed deer [*'h*waɪt'teɪld] *n* : ciervo *f* de Virginia

whitewash¹ [*'h*waɪt,wɔʃ] *vt* **1** : enjalbegar, blanquear ⟨to whitewash a fence : enjalbegar una valla⟩ **2** CONCEAL : encubrir (un escándalo, etc.)

whitewash² *n* **1** : jalbegue *m*, lechada *f* **2** COVER-UP : encubrimiento *m*

whither [*'h*wɪðər] *adv* : adónde

whiting [*'h*waɪtɪŋ] *n* : merluza *f*, pescadilla *f* (pez)

whitish [*'h*waɪtɪʃ] *adj* : blancuzco

whittle [*'h*wɪtəl] *vt* **-tled; -tling 1** : tallar (madera) **2 to whittle down** : reducir, recortar ⟨to whittle down expenses : reducir los gastos⟩

whiz¹ or **whizz** [ˈʰwɪz] vi **whizzed; whizzing 1** BUZZ : zumbar **2 to whiz by** : pasar muy rápido, pasar volando

whiz² or **whizz** n, pl **whizzes 1** BUZZ : zumbido m **2 to be a whiz** : ser un prodigio, ser muy hábil

who [ˈhuː] pron **1** (used in direct and indirect questions) : quién ⟨who is that? : ¿quién es ése?⟩ ⟨who did it? : ¿quién lo hizo?⟩ ⟨we know who they are : sabemos quiénes son⟩ **2** (used in relative clauses) : que, quien ⟨the lady who lives there : la señora que vive allí⟩ ⟨for those who wait : para los que esperan, para quienes esperan⟩

whodunit [huːˈdʌnɪt] n : novela f policíaca

whoever [huːˈɛvər] pron **1** : quienquiera que, quien ⟨whoever did it : quienquiera que lo hizo⟩ ⟨give it to whoever you want : dalo a quien quieras⟩ **2** (used in questions) : quién ⟨whoever could that be? : ¿quién podría ser?⟩

whole¹ [ˈhoːl] adj **1** UNHURT : ileso **2** INTACT : intacto, sano **3** ENTIRE : entero, íntegro ⟨the whole island : toda la isla⟩ ⟨whole milk : leche entera⟩ **4 a whole lot** : muchísimo

whole² n **1** : todo m **2 as a whole** : en conjunto **3 on the whole** : en general

wholehearted [ˈhoːlˈhɑrtəd] adj : sin reservas, incondicional

whole number n : entero m

wholesale¹ [ˈhoːlˌseɪl] v **-saled; -saling** vt : vender al por mayor — vi : venderse al por mayor

wholesale² adv : al por mayor

wholesale³ adj **1** : al por mayor ⟨wholesale grocer : tendero al por mayor⟩ **2** TOTAL : total, absoluto ⟨wholesale slaughter : matanza sistemática⟩

wholesale⁴ n : mayoreo m

wholesaler [ˈhoːlˌseɪlər] n : mayorista mf

wholesome [ˈhoːlsəm] adj **1** : sano ⟨wholesome advice : consejo sano⟩ **2** HEALTHY : sano, saludable

whole wheat adj : de trigo integral

wholly [ˈhoːli] adv **1** COMPLETELY : completamente **2** SOLELY : exclusivamente, únicamente

whom [ˈhuːm] pron **1** (used in direct questions) : a quién ⟨whom did you choose? : ¿a quién elegiste?⟩ **2** (used in indirect questions) : de quién, con quién, en quién ⟨I don't know whom to consult : no sé con quién consultar⟩ **3** (used in relative clauses) : que, a quien ⟨the lawyer whom I recommended to you : el abogado que te recomendé⟩

whomever [huːmˈɛvər] pron WHOEVER : quienquiera, quien ⟨marry whomever you please : cásate con quien quieras⟩

whoop¹ [ˈʰwuːp, ˈʰwʊp] vi : gritar, chillar

whoop² n : grito m

whooping cough n : tos f ferina

whopper [ˈʰwɑpər] n **1** : cosa f enorme **2** LIE : mentira f colosal

whopping [ˈʰwɑpɪŋ] adj : enorme

whore [ˈhor] n : puta f, ramera f

whorl [ˈʰworl, ˈʰwərl] n : espiral f, espira f (de una concha), línea f (de una huella digital)

whose¹ [ˈhuːz] adj **1** (used in questions) : de quién ⟨whose truck is that? : ¿de quién es ese camión?⟩ **2** (used in relative clauses) : cuyo ⟨the person whose work is finished : la persona cuyo trabajo está terminado⟩

whose² pron : de quién ⟨tell me whose it was : dime de quién era⟩

why¹ [ˈʰwaɪ] adv : por qué ⟨why did you do it? : ¿por qué lo hizo?⟩

why² n, pl **whys** REASON : porqué m, razón f

why³ conj : por qué ⟨I know why he left : yo sé por qué salió⟩ ⟨there's no reason why it should exist : no hay razón para que exista⟩

why⁴ interj (used to express surprise) : ¡vaya!, ¡mira!

wick [ˈwɪk] n : mecha f

wicked [ˈwɪkəd] adj **1** EVIL : malo, malvado **2** MISCHIEVOUS : travieso, pícaro ⟨a wicked grin : una sonrisa traviesa⟩ **3** TERRIBLE : terrible, horrible ⟨a wicked storm : una tormenta horrible⟩

wickedly [ˈwɪkədli] adv : con maldad

wickedness [ˈwɪkədnəs] n : maldad f

wicker [ˈwɪkər] n : de mimbre

wicker² n **1** : mimbre m **2** → **wickerwork**

wickerwork [ˈwɪkərˌwərk] n : artículos mpl de mimbre

wicket [ˈwɪkət] n **1** WINDOW : ventanilla f **2** or **wicket gate** : postigo m **3** : aro m (en croquet), palos mpl (en críquet)

wide¹ [ˈwaɪd] adv **wider; widest 1** WIDELY : por todas partes ⟨to travel far and wide : viajar por todas partes⟩ **2** COMPLETELY : completamente, totalmente ⟨wide open : abierto de par en par⟩ **3 wide apart** : muy separados

wide² adj **wider; widest 1** VAST : vasto, extensivo ⟨a wide area : una área extensiva⟩ **2** : ancho ⟨three meters wide : tres metros de ancho⟩ **3** BROAD : ancho, amplio **4** or **wide–open** : muy abierto **5 wide of the mark** : desviado, lejos del blanco

wide–awake [ˈwaɪdəˈweɪk] adj : (completamente) despierto

wide–eyed [ˈwaɪdˈaɪd] adj **1** : con los ojos muy abiertos **2** NAIVE : inocente, ingenuo

widely [ˈwaɪdli] adv : extensivamente, por todas partes

widen [ˈwaɪdən] vt : ampliar, ensanchar — vi : ampliarse, ensancharse

widespread [ˈwaɪdˈsprɛd] adj : extendido, extenso, difuso

widow¹ [ˈwɪˌdoː] vt : dejar viuda ⟨to be widowed : enviudar⟩

widow² n : viuda f

widower ['wɪdowər] *n* : viudo *m*
width ['wɪdθ] *n* : ancho *m*, anchura *f*
wield ['wi:ld] *vt* **1** USE : usar, manejar ⟨to wield a broom : usar una escoba⟩ **2** EXERCISE : ejercer ⟨to wield influence : influir⟩
wiener ['wi:nər] → **frankfurter**
wife ['waɪf] *n*, *pl* **wives** ['waɪvz] : esposa *f*, mujer *f*
wifely ['waɪfli] *adj* : de esposa, conyugal
wig ['wɪg] *n* : peluca *f*
wiggle[1] ['wɪgəl] *v* **-gled; -gling** *vt* : menear, contonear ⟨to wiggle one's hips : contonearse⟩ — *vi* : menearse
wiggle[2] *n* : meneo *m*, contoneo *m*
wiggly ['wɪgəli] *adj* **-glier; -est 1** : que se menea **2** WAVY : ondulado
wigwag ['wɪg,wæg] *vi* **-wagged; -wagging** : comunicar por señales
wigwam ['wɪg,wɑm] *n* : wigwam *m*
wild[1] ['waɪld] *adv* **1** → **wildly 2 to run wild** : descontrolarse
wild[2] *adj* **1** : salvaje, silvestre, cimarrón ⟨wild horses : caballos salvajes⟩ ⟨wild rice : arroz silvestre⟩ **2** DESOLATE : yermo, agreste **3** UNRULY : desenfrenado **4** CRAZY : loco, fantástico ⟨wild ideas : ideas locas⟩ **5** BARBAROUS : salvaje, bárbaro **6** ERRATIC : errático ⟨a wild throw : un tiro errático⟩
wild[3] *n* → **wilderness**
wild card *n* **1** : factor *m* desconocido **2** : comodín *m* (carta o símbolo)
wildcat ['waɪld,kæt] *n* **1** : gato *m* montés **2** BOBCAT : lince *m* rojo
wilderness ['wɪldərnəs] *n* : yermo *m*, desierto *m*
wildfire ['waɪld,faɪr] *n* **1** : fuego *m* descontrolado **2 to spread like wildfire** : propagarse como un reguero de pólvora
wildflower ['waɪld,flaʊər] *n* : flor *f* silvestre
wildfowl ['waɪld,faʊl] *n* : ave *f* de caza
wildlife ['waɪld,laɪf] *n* : fauna *f*
wildly ['waɪldli] *adv* **1** FRANTICALLY : frenéticamente, como un loco **2** EXTREMELY : extremadamente ⟨wildly happy : loco de felicidad⟩
wile[1] ['waɪl] *vt* **wiled; wiling** LURE : atraer
wile[2] *n* : ardid *m*, artimaña *f*
will[1] ['wɪl] *v*, *past* **would** ['wʊd]; *pres sing & pl* **will** *vb* WISH : querer ⟨do what you will : haz lo que quieras⟩ — *v aux* **1** (*expressing willingness*) ⟨no one would take the car : nadie aceptaría el trabajo⟩ ⟨I won't do it : no lo haré⟩ **2** (*expressing habitual action*) ⟨he will get angry over nothing : se pone furioso por cualquier cosa⟩ **3** (*forming the future tense*) ⟨tomorrow we will go shopping : mañana iremos de compras⟩ **4** (*expressing capacity*) ⟨the couch will hold three people : en el sofá cabrán tres personas⟩ **5** (*expressing determination*) ⟨I will go despite them : iré a pesar de

ellos⟩ **6** (*expressing probability*) ⟨that will be the mailman : eso ha de ser el cartero⟩ **7** (*expressing inevitability*) ⟨accidents will happen : los accidentes ocurrirán⟩ **8** (*expressing a command*) ⟨you will do as I say : harás lo que digo⟩
will[2] *vt* **1** ORDAIN : disponer, decretar ⟨if God wills it : si Dios lo dispone, si Dios quiere⟩ **2** : lograr a fuerza de voluntad ⟨they were willing him to succeed : estaban deseando que tuviera éxito⟩ **3** BEQUEATH : legar
will[3] *n* **1** DESIRE : deseo *m*, voluntad *f* **2** VOLITION : voluntad *f* ⟨free will : libre albedrío⟩ **3** WILLPOWER : voluntad *f*, fuerza *f* de voluntad ⟨a will of iron : una voluntad férrea⟩ **4** : testamento *m* ⟨to make a will : hacer testamento⟩
willful *or* **wilful** ['wɪlfəl] *adj* **1** OBSTINATE : obstinado, terco **2** INTENTIONAL : intencionado, deliberado — **willfully** *adv*
willing ['wɪlɪŋ] *adj* **1** INCLINED, READY : listo, dispuesto **2** OBLIGING : servicial, complaciente
willingly ['wɪlɪŋli] *adv* : con gusto
willingness ['wɪlɪŋnəs] *n* : buena voluntad *f*
willow ['wɪ,lo:] *n* : sauce *m*
willowy ['wɪlowi] *adj* : esbelto
willpower ['wɪl,paʊər] *n* : voluntad *f*, fuerza *f* de voluntad
wilt ['wɪlt] *vi* **1** : marchitarse (dícese de las flores) **2** LANGUISH : debilitarse, languidecer
wily ['waɪli] *adj* **wilier; -est** : artero, astuto
wimp ['wɪmp] *n* **1** COWARD : gallina *f*, cobarde *mf* **2** WEAKLING : debilucho *m*, -cha *f*, alfeñique *m*
win[1] ['wɪn] *v* **won** ['wʌn]; **winning** *vi* : ganar — *vt* **1** : ganar, conseguir **2 to win over** : ganarse a **3 to win someone's heart** : conquistar a alguien
win[2] *n* : triunfo *m*, victoria *f*
wince[1] ['wɪnts] *vi* **winced; wincing** : estremecerse, hacer una mueca de dolor
wince[2] *n* : mueca *f* de dolor
winch ['wɪntʃ] *n* : torno *m*
wind[1] ['wɪnd] *vt* : dejar sin aliento ⟨to be winded : quedarse sin aliento⟩
wind[2] ['waɪnd] *v* **wound** ['waʊnd]; **winding** *vi* MEANDER : serpentear — *vt* **1** COIL, ROLL : envolver, enrollar **2** TURN : hacer girar ⟨to wind a clock : darle cuerda a un reloj⟩
wind[3] ['wɪnd] *n* **1** : viento *m* ⟨against the wind : contra el viento⟩ **2** BREATH : aliento *m* **3** FLATULENCE : flatulencia *f*, ventosidad *f* **4 to get wind of** : enterarse de
wind[4] ['waɪnd] *n* **1** TURN : vuelta *f* **2** BEND : recodo *m*, curva *f*
windbreak ['wɪnd,breɪk] *n* : barrera *f* contra el viento, abrigadero *m*
windfall ['wɪnd,fɔl] *n* **1** : fruta *f* caída **2** : beneficio *m* imprevisto
wind instrument *n* : instrumento *m* de viento

windlass ['wɪndləs] *n* : cabrestante *m*
windmill ['wɪnd,mɪl] *n* : molino *m* de viento
window ['wɪn,do:] *n* 1 : ventana *f* (de un edificio o una computadora), ventanilla *f* (de un vehículo o avión), vitrina *f* (de una tienda) 2 → **windowpane**
windowpane ['wɪn,do:,peɪn] *n* : vidrio *m*
window–shop ['wɪndo,ʃap] *vi* **-shopped; -shopping** : mirar las vitrinas
windpipe ['wɪnd,paɪp] *n* : tráquea *f*
windshield ['wɪnd,ʃi:ld] *n* 1 : parabrisas *m* 2 **windshield wiper** : limpiaparabrisas *m*
windup ['waɪnd,ʌp] *n* : conclusión *f*
wind up *vt* END : terminar, concluir — *vi* : terminar, acabar
windward[1] ['wɪndwərd] *adj* : de barlovento
windward[2] *n* : barlovento *m*
windy ['wɪndi] *adj* **windier; -est** 1 : ventoso ⟨it's windy : hace viento⟩ 2 VERBOSE : verboso, prolijo
wine[1] ['waɪn] *v* **wined; wining** *vi* : beber vino — *vt* **to wine and dine** : agasajar *m*
wine[2] *n* : vino *m*
wing[1] ['wɪŋ] *vi* FLY : volar
wing[2] *n* 1 : ala *f* (de un ave, un avión, o un edificio) 2 FACTION : ala *f* ⟨the right wing of the party : el ala derecha del partido⟩ 3 **wings** *npl* : bastidores *mpl* (de un teatro) 4 **on the wing** : al vuelo, volando 5 **under one's wing** : bajo el cargo de uno
winged ['wɪŋd, 'wɪŋəd] *adj* : alado
wink[1] ['wɪŋk] *vi* 1 : guiñar el ojo 2 BLINK : pestañear, parpadear 3 FLICKER : parpadear, titilar
wink[2] *n* 1 : guiño *m* (del ojo) 2 NAP : siesta *f* ⟨not to sleep a wink : no pegar el ojo⟩
winner ['wɪnər] *n* : ganador *m*, -dora *f*
winning ['wɪnɪŋ] *adj* 1 VICTORIOUS : ganador 2 CHARMING : encantador
winnings ['wɪnɪŋz] *npl* : ganancias *fpl*
winnow ['wɪ,no:] *vt* : aventar (el grano, etc.)
winsome ['wɪnsəm] *adj* CHARMING : encantador
winter[1] ['wɪntər] *adj* : invernal, de invierno
winter[2] *n* : invierno *m*
wintergreen ['wɪntər,gri:n] *n* : gaulteria *f*
wintertime ['wɪntər,taɪm] *n* : invierno *m*
wintry ['wɪntri] *adj* **wintrier; -est** 1 WINTER : invernal, de invierno 2 COLD : frío ⟨she gave us a wintry greeting : nos saludó fríamente⟩
wipe[1] ['waɪp] *vt* **wiped; wiping** 1 : limpiar, pasarle un trapo a ⟨to wipe one's feet : limpiarse los pies⟩ 2 **to wipe away** : enjugar (lágrimas), borrar (una memoria) 3 **to wipe out** ANNIHILATE : aniquilar, destruir
wipe[2] *n* : pasada *f* (con un trapo, etc.)

wire[1] ['waɪr] *vt* **wired; wiring** 1 : instalar el cableado en (una casa, etc.) 2 BIND : atar con alambre 3 TELEGRAPH : telegrafiar, mandarle un telegrama (a alguien)
wire[2] *n* 1 : alambre *m* ⟨barbed wire : alambre de púas⟩ 2 : cable *m* (eléctrico o telefónico) 3 CABLEGRAM, TELEGRAM : telegrama *m*, cable *m*
wireless ['waɪrləs] *adj* : inalámbrico
wiretapping ['waɪr,tæpɪŋ] *n* : intervención *f* electrónica
wiring ['waɪrɪŋ] *n* : cableado *m*
wiry ['waɪri] *adj* **wirier; -est** 1 : hirsuto, tieso (dícese del pelo) 2 : esbelto y musculoso (dícese del cuerpo)
wisdom ['wɪzdəm] *n* 1 KNOWLEDGE : sabiduría *f* 2 JUDGMENT, SENSE : sensatez *f*
wisdom tooth *n* : muela *f* de juicio
wise[1] ['waɪz] *adj* **wiser; wisest** 1 LEARNED : sabio 2 SENSIBLE : sabio, sensato, prudente 3 KNOWLEDGEABLE : entendido, enterado ⟨they're wise to his tricks : conocen muy bien sus mañas⟩
wise[2] *n* : manera *f*, modo *m* ⟨in no wise : de ninguna manera⟩
wisecrack ['waɪz,kræk] *n* : broma *f*, chiste *m*
wisely ['waɪzli] *adv* : sabiamente, sensatamente
wish[1] ['wɪʃ] *vt* 1 WANT : desear, querer 2 **to wish (something) for** : desear ⟨they wished me well : me desearon lo mejor⟩ — *vi* 1 : pedir (como deseo) 2 : querer ⟨as you wish : como quieras⟩
wish[2] *n* 1 : deseo *m* ⟨to grant a wish : conceder un deseo⟩ 2 **wishes** *npl* : saludos *mpl*, recuerdos *mpl* ⟨to send best wishes : mandar muchos recuerdos⟩
wishbone ['wɪʃ,bo:n] *n* : espoleta *f*
wishful ['wɪʃfəl] *adj* 1 HOPEFUL : deseoso, lleno de esperanza 2 **wishful thinking** : ilusiones *fpl*
wishy–washy ['wɪʃi,wɔʃi, -,wɑʃi] *adj* : insípido, soso
wisp ['wɪsp] *n* 1 BUNCH : manojo *m* (de paja) 2 STRAND : mechón *m* (de pelo) 3 : voluta *f* (de humo)
wispy ['wɪspi] *adj* **wispier; -est** : tenue, ralo (dícese del pelo)
wisteria [wɪs'tɪriə] *n* : glicinia *f*
wistful ['wɪstfəl] *adj* : añorante, anhelante, melancólico — **wistfully** *adv*
wistfulness ['wɪstfəlnəs] *n* : añoranza *f*, melancolía *f*
wit ['wɪt] *n* 1 INTELLIGENCE : inteligencia *f* 2 CLEVERNESS : ingenio *m*, gracia *f*, agudeza *f* 3 HUMOR : humorismo *m* 4 JOKER : chistoso *m*, -sa *f* 5 **wits** *npl* : razón *f*, buen juicio *m* ⟨scared out of one's wits : muerto de miedo⟩ ⟨to be at one's wits' end : estar desesperado⟩
witch ['wɪtʃ] *n* : bruja *f*
witchcraft ['wɪtʃ,kræft] *n* : brujería *f*, hechicería *f*

witch doctor *n* : hechicero *m*, -ra *f*

witchery ['wɪtʃəri] *n, pl* **-eries 1** → **witch-craft 2** CHARM : encanto *m*

witch–hunt ['wɪtʃ,hʌnt] *n* : caza *f* de brujas

with ['wɪð, 'wɪθ] *prep* **1** : con ⟨I'm going with you : voy contigo⟩ ⟨coffee with milk : café con leche⟩ **2** AGAINST : con ⟨to argue with someone : discutir con alguien⟩ **3** (*used in descriptions*) : con, de ⟨the girl with red hair : la muchacha de pelo rojo⟩ **4** (*indicating manner, means, or cause*) : con ⟨to cut with a knife : cortar con un cuchillo⟩ ⟨fix it with tape : arréglalo con cinta⟩ ⟨with luck : consuerte⟩ **5** DESPITE : a pesar de, aún con ⟨with all his work, the business failed : a pesar de su trabajo, el negocio fracasó⟩ **6** REGARDING : con respecto a, con ⟨the trouble with your plan : el problema con su plan⟩ **7** ACCORDING TO : según ⟨it varies with the season : varía según la estación⟩ **8** (*indicating support or understanding*) : con ⟨I'm with you all the way : estoy contigo hasta el fin⟩

withdraw [wɪð'drɔ, wɪθ-] *v* **-drew** [-'dru:]; **-drawn** [-'drɔn]; **-drawing** *vt* **1** REMOVE : retirar, apartar, sacar (dinero) **2** RETRACT : retractarse — *vi* : retirarse, recluirse (de la sociedad)

withdrawal [wɪð'drɔəl, wɪθ-] *n* **1** : retirada *f*, retiro *m* (de fondos, etc.), retraimiento *m* (social) **2** RETRACTION : retractación *f* **3 withdrawal symptoms** : síndrome *m* de abstinencia

withdrawn [wɪð'drɔn, wɪθ-] *adj* : retraído, reservado, introvertido

wither ['wɪðər] *vi* : marchitar, agostar — *vi* **1** WILT : marchitarse **2** WEAKEN : decaer, debilitarse

withhold [wɪθ'ho:ld, wɪð-] *vt* **-held** [-'hld]; **-holding** : retener (fondos), aplazar (una decisión), negar (permiso, etc.)

within¹ [wɪð'ɪn, wɪθ-] *adv* : dentro

within² *prep* **1** : dentro de ⟨within the limits : dentro de los límites⟩ **2** (*in expressions of distance*) : a menos de ⟨within 10 miles of the ocean : a menos de 10 millas del mar⟩ **3** (*in expressions of time*) : dentro de ⟨within an hour : dentro de una hora⟩ ⟨within a month of her birthday : a poco menos de un mes de su cumpleaños⟩

without¹ [wɪð'aʊt, wɪθ-] *adv* **1** OUTSIDE : fuera **2 to do without** : pasar sin algo

without² *prep* **1** OUTSIDE : fuera de **2** : sin ⟨without fear : sin temor⟩ ⟨he left without his briefcase : se fue sin su portafolios⟩

withstand [wɪθ'stænd, wɪð-] *vt* **-stood** [-'stʊd]; **-standing 1** BEAR : aguantar, soportar **2** RESIST : resistir, resistirse a

witless ['wɪtləs] *adj* : estúpido, tonto

witness¹ ['wɪtnəs] *vt* **1** SEE : presenciar, ver, ser testigo de **2** : atestiguar (una firma, etc.) — *vi* TESTIFY : atestiguar, testimoniar

witness² *n* **1** TESTIMONY : testimonio *m* ⟨to bear witness : atestiguar, testimoniar⟩ **2** : testigo *mf* ⟨witness for the prosecution : testigo de cargo⟩

witticism ['wɪtə,sɪzəm] *n* : agudeza *f*, ocurrencia *f*

witty ['wɪti] *adj* **-tier; -est** : ingenioso, ocurrente, gracioso

wives → **wife**

wizard ['wɪzərd] *n* **1** SORCERER : mago *m*, brujo *m*, hechicero *m* **2** : genio *m* ⟨a math wizard : un genio en matemáticas⟩

wizened ['wɪzənd, 'wi:-] *adj* : arrugado, marchito

wobble¹ ['wabəl] *vi* **-bled; -bling** : bambolearse, tambalearse, temblar (dícese de la voz)

wobble² *n* : tambaleo *m*, bamboleo *m*

wobbly ['wabəli] *adj* : bamboleante, tambaleante, inestable

woe ['wo:] *n* **1** GRIEF, MISFORTUNE : desgracia *f*, infortunio *m*, aflicción *f* **2 woes** *npl* TROUBLES : penas *fpl*, males *mpl*

woeful ['wo:fəl] *adj* **1** SORROWFUL : afligido, apenado, triste **2** UNFORTUNATE : desgraciado, infortunado **3** DEPLORABLE : lamentable

woke, woken → **wake¹**

wolf¹ ['wʊlf] *vt or* **to wolf down** : engullir

wolf² *n, pl* **wolves** ['wʊlvz] : lobo *m*, -ba *f*

wolfram ['wʊlfrəm] → **tungsten**

wolverine [,wʊlvə'ri:n] *n* : glotón *m* (animal)

woman ['wʊmən] *n, pl* **women** ['wɪmən] : mujer *f*

womanhood ['wʊmən,hʊd] *n* **1** : condición *f* de mujer **2** WOMEN : mujeres *fpl*

womanly ['wʊmənli] *adj* : femenino

womb ['wu:m] *n* : útero *m*, matriz *f*

won → **win**

wonder¹ ['wʌndər] *vi* **1** SPECULATE : preguntarse, pensar ⟨to wonder about : preguntarse por⟩ **2** MARVEL : asombrarse, maravillarse — *vt* : preguntarse ⟨I wonder if they're coming : me pregunto si vendrán⟩

wonder² *n* **1** MARVEL : maravilla *f*, milagro *m* ⟨to work wonders : hacer maravillas⟩ **2** AMAZEMENT : asombro *m*

wonderful ['wʌndərfəl] *adj* : maravilloso, estupendo

wonderfully ['wʌndərfəli] *adv* : maravillosamente, de maravilla

wonderland ['wʌndər,lænd, -lənd] *n* : país *m* de las maravillas

wonderment ['wʌndərmənt] *n* : asombro *m*

wondrous ['wʌndrəs] → **wonderful**

wont¹ ['wɔnt, 'wo:nt, 'want] *adj* : acostumbrado, habituado

wont² *n* : hábito *m*, costumbre *f*

won't ['wo:nt] (*contraction of* **will not**) → **will¹**

woo ['wu:] *vt* **1** COURT : cortejar **2** : buscar el apoyo de (clientes, votantes, etc.)

wood¹ ['wʊd] *adj* : de madera

wood² *n* **1** *or* **woods** *npl* FOREST : bosque *m* **2** : madera *f* (materia) **3** FIREWOOD : leña *f*

woodchuck ['wʊd,tʃʌk] *n* : marmota *f* de América

woodcut ['wʊd,kʌt] *n* **1** : plancha *f* de madera (para imprimir imágenes) **2** : grabado *m* en madera

woodcutter ['wʊd,kʌtər] *n* : leñador *m*, -dora *f*

wooded ['wʊdəd] *adj* : arbolado, boscoso

wooden ['wʊdən] *adj* **1** : de madera ⟨a wooden cross : una cruz de madera⟩ **2** STIFF : rígido, inexpresivo (dícese del estilo, de la cara, etc.)

woodland ['wʊdlənd, -,lænd] *n* : bosque *m*

woodpecker ['wʊd,pɛkər] *n* : pájaro *m* carpintero

woodshed ['wʊd,ʃɛd] *n* : leñera *f*

woodsman ['wʊdzmən] → **woodcutter**

woodwind ['wʊd,wɪnd] *n* : instrumento *m* de viento de madera

woodworking ['wʊd,wərkɪŋ] *n* : carpintería *f*

woody ['wʊdi] *adj* **woodier; -est 1** → **wooded 2** : leñoso ⟨woody plants : plantas leñosas⟩ **3** : leñoso (dícese de la textura), a madera (dícese del aroma, etc.)

woof ['wʊf] → **weft**

wool ['wʊl] *n* : lana *f*

woolen¹ *or* **woollen** ['wʊlən] *adj* : de lana

woolen² *or* **woollen** *n* **1** : lana *f* (tela) **2 woolens** *npl* : prendas *fpl* de lana

woolly ['wʊli] *adj* **-lier; -est 1** : lanudo **2** CONFUSED : confuso, vago

woozy ['wu:zi] *adj* **-zier; -est** : mareado

word¹ ['wərd] *vt* : expresar, formular, redactar

word² *n* **1** : palabra *f*, vocablo *m*, voz *f* ⟨word for word : palabra por palabra⟩ ⟨in one's own words : en sus propias palabras⟩ ⟨words fail me : me quedo sin habla⟩ **2** REMARK : palabra *f* ⟨by word of mouth : de palabra⟩ ⟨to have a word with : hablar (dos palabras) con⟩ **3** COMMAND : orden *f* ⟨to give the word : dar la orden⟩ ⟨just say the word : no tienes que decirlo⟩ **4** MESSAGE, NEWS : noticias *fpl* ⟨is there any word from her? : ¿hay noticias de ella?⟩ ⟨to send word : mandar un recado⟩ **5** PROMISE : palabra *f* ⟨to keep one's word : cumplir uno su palabra⟩ **6 words** *npl* QUARREL : palabra *f*, riña *f* ⟨to have words with : tener unas palabras con, reñir con⟩ **7 words** *npl* TEXT : letra *f* (de una canción, etc.)

wordiness ['wərdinəs] *n* : verbosidad *f*

wording ['wərdɪŋ] *n* : redacción *f*, lenguaje *m* (de un documento)

word processing *n* : procesamiento *m* de textos

word processor *n* : procesador *m* de textos

wordy ['wərdi] *adj* **wordier; -est** : verboso, prolijo

wore → **wear¹**

work¹ ['wərk] *v* **worked** ['wərkt] *or* **wrought** ['rɔt]; **working** *vt* **1** OPERATE : trabajar, operar ⟨to work a machine : operar una máquina⟩ **2** : lograr, conseguir (algo) con esfuerzo ⟨to work one's way up : lograr subir por sus propios esfuerzos⟩ **3** EFFECT : efectuar, llevar a cabo, obrar (milagros) **4** MAKE, SHAPE : elaborar, fabricar, formar ⟨a beautifully wrought vase : un florero bellamente elaborado⟩ **5 to work up** : estimular, excitar ⟨don't get worked up : no te agites⟩ — *vi* **1** LABOR : trabajar ⟨to work full-time : trabajar a tiempo completo⟩ **2** FUNCTION : funcionar, servir

work² *adj* : laboral

work³ *n* **1** LABOR : trabajo *m*, labor *f* **2** EMPLOYMENT : trabajo *m*, empleo *m* **3** TASK : tarea *f*, faena *f* **4** DEED : obra *f*, labor *f* ⟨works of charity : obras de caridad⟩ **5** : obra *f* (de arte o literatura) **6** → **workmanship 7 works** *npl* FACTORY : fábrica *f* **8 works** *npl* MECHANISM : mecanismo *m*

workable ['wərkəbəl] *adj* **1** : explotable (dícese de una mina, etc.) **2** FEASIBLE : factible, realizable

workaday ['wərkə,deɪ] *adj* : ordinario, banal

workbench ['wərk,bɛntʃ] *n* : mesa *f* de trabajo

workday ['wərk,deɪ] *n* **1** : jornada *f* laboral **2** WEEKDAY : día *m* hábil, día *m* laborable

worker ['wərkər] *n* : trabajador *m*, -dora *f*; obrero *m*, -ra *f*

working ['wərkɪŋ] *adj* **1** : que trabaja ⟨working mothers : madres que trabajan⟩ ⟨the working class : la clase obrera⟩ **2** : de trabajo ⟨working hours : horas de trabajo⟩ **3** FUNCTIONING : que funciona, operativo **4** SUFFICIENT : suficiente ⟨a working majority : una mayoría suficiente⟩ ⟨working knowledge : conocimientos básicos⟩

workingman ['wərkɪŋ,mæn] *n, pl* **-men** [-mən, -,mɛn] : obrero *m*

workman ['wərkmən] *n, pl* **-men** [-mən, -,mɛn] **1** → **workingman 2** ARTISAN : artesano *m*

workmanlike ['wərkmən,laɪk] *adj* : bien hecho, competente

workmanship ['wərkmən,ʃɪp] *n* **1** WORK : ejecución *f*, trabajo *m* **2** CRAFTSMANSHIP : artesanía *f*, destreza *f*

workout ['wərk,aʊt] *n* : ejercicios *mpl* físicos, entrenamiento *m*

work out *vt* **1** DEVELOP, PLAN : idear, planear, desarrollar **2** RESOLVE : solucionar, resolver ⟨to work out the answer : calcular la solución⟩ — *vi* **1** TURN OUT : resultar **2** SUCCEED : lograr, dar resultado, salir bien **3** EXERCISE : hacer ejercicio

workroom ['wərk,ruːm, -,rʊm] *n* : taller *m*

workshop ['wərk,ʃap] *n* : taller *m* ⟨ceramics workshop : taller de cerámica⟩

workstation ['wərk,steɪʃən] *n* : estación *f* de trabajo (en informática)

world¹ ['wərld] *adj* : mundial, del mundo ⟨world championship : campeonato mundial⟩

world² *n* : mundo *m* ⟨around the world : alrededor del mundo⟩ ⟨a world of possibilities : un mundo de posibilidades⟩ ⟨to think the world of someone : tener a alguien en alta estima⟩ ⟨to be worlds apart : no tener nada que ver (uno con otro)⟩

worldly ['wərldli] *adj* **1** : mundano ⟨wordly goods : bienes materiales⟩ **2** SOPHISTICATED : sofisticado, de mundo

worldwide¹ ['wərld'waɪd] *adv* : mundialmente, en todo el mundo

worldwide² *adj* : global, mundial

World Wide Web *n* : World Wide Web *f*

worm¹ ['wərm] *vi* CRAWL : arrastrarse, deslizarse (como gusano) — *vt* **1** : desparasitar (un animal) **2 to worm one's way into** : introducirse en ⟨he wormed his way into her confidence : se ganó su confianza⟩ **3 to worm something out of someone** : sonsacarle algo a alguien

worm² *n* **1** : gusano *m*, lombriz *f* **2 worms** *npl* : lombrices *fpl* (parásitos)

wormy ['wərmi] *adj* **wormier; -est** : infestado de gusanos

worn *pp* → **wear**

worn–out ['worn'aʊt] *adj* **1** USED : gastado, desgastado **2** TIRED : agotado

worried ['wərid] *adj* : inquieto, preocupado

worrier ['wəriər] *n* : persona *f* que se preocupa mucho

worrisome ['wərisəm] *adj* **1** DISTURBING : preocupante, inquietante **2** : que se preocupa mucho (dícese de una persona)

worry¹ ['wəri] *v* **-ried; -rying** *vt* : preocupar, inquietar — *vi* : preocuparse, inquietarse, angustiarse

worry² *n, pl* **-ries** : preocupación *f*, inquietud *f*, angustia *f*

worse¹ ['wərs] *adv* (*comparative of* **bad** *or of* **ill**) : peor

worse² *adj* (*comparative of* **bad** *or of* **ill**) : peor ⟨from bad to worse : de mal en peor⟩ ⟨to get worse : empeorar⟩ ⟨to feel worse : sentirse peor⟩

worse³ *n* : estado *m* peor ⟨to take a turn for the worse : ponerse peor⟩ ⟨so much the worse : tanto peor⟩

worsen ['wərsən] *vt* : empeorar — *vi* : empeorar(se)

worship¹ ['wərʃəp] *v* **-shiped** *or* **-shipped; -shiping** *or* **-shipping** *vt* : adorar, venerar ⟨to worship God : adorar a Dios⟩ — *vi* : practicar una religión

worship² *n* : adoración *f*, culto *m*

worshiper *or* **worshipper** ['wərʃəpər] *n* : devoto *m*, -ta *f*; adorador *m*, -dora *f*

worst¹ ['wərst] *vt* DEFEAT : derrotar

worst² *adv* (*superlative of* **ill** *or of* **bad** *or* **badly**) : peor ⟨the worst dressed of all : el peor vestido de todos⟩

worst³ *adj* (*superlative of* **bad** *or of* **ill**) : peor ⟨the worst movie : la peor película⟩

worst⁴ *n* **the worst** : lo peor, el (la) peor ⟨the worst is over : ya ha pasado lo peor⟩

worsted ['wʊstəd, 'wərstəd] *n* : estambre *m*

worth¹ ['wərθ] *n* **1** : valor *m* (monetario) ⟨ten dollars' worth of gas : diez dólares de gasolina⟩ **2** MERIT : valor *m*, mérito *m*, valía *f* ⟨an employee of great worth : un empleado de gran valía⟩

worth² *prep* **to be worth** : valer ⟨her holdings are worth a fortune : sus propiedades valen una fortuna⟩ ⟨it's not worth it : no vale la pena⟩

worthiness ['wərðinəs] *n* : mérito *m*

worthless ['wərθləs] *adj* **1** : sin valor ⟨worthless trinkets : chucherías sin valor⟩ **2** USELESS : inútil

worthwhile [wərθ'hwaɪl] *adj* : que vale la pena

worthy ['wərði] *adj* **-thier; -est 1** : digno ⟨worthy of promotion : digno de un ascenso⟩ **2** COMMENDABLE : meritorio, encomiable

would ['wʊd] *past of* **will 1** (*expressing preference*) ⟨I would rather go alone than with her : preferiría ir sola que con ella⟩ **2** (*expressing intent*) ⟨those who would ban certain books : aquellos que prohibirían ciertos libros⟩ **3** (*expressing habitual action*) ⟨he would often take his kids to the park : solía llevar a sus hijos al parque⟩ **4** (*expressing contingency*) ⟨I would go if I had the money : iría yo si tuviera el dinero⟩ **5** (*expressing probability*) ⟨she would have won if she hadn't tripped : habría ganado si no hubiera tropezado⟩ **6** (*expressing a request*) ⟨would you kindly help me with this? : ¿tendría la bondad de ayudarme con esto?⟩

would–be ['wʊd'biː] *adj* : potencial ⟨a would-be celebrity : un aspirante a celebridad⟩

wouldn't ['wʊdənt] (*contraction of* **would not**) → **would**

wound¹ ['wuːnd] *vt* : herir

wound² *n* : herida *f*

wound³ ['waʊnd] → **wind²**

wove, woven → **weave¹**

wow ['waʊ] *interj* : ¡guau!, ¡híjole! *Mex*, ¡hala! *Spain*

wrangle¹ ['ræŋgəl] *vi* **-gled; -gling** : discutir, reñir ⟨to wrangle over : discutir por⟩

wrangle² *n* : riña *f*, disputa *f*

wrap¹ ['ræp] *v* **wrapped; wrapping** *vt* **1** COVER : envolver, cubrir ⟨to wrap a package : envolver un paquete⟩

⟨wrapped in mystery : envuelto en misterio⟩ **2** ENCIRCLE : rodear, ceñir ⟨to wrap one's arms around someone : estrechar a alguien⟩ **3 to wrap up** FINISH : darle fin a (algo) — *vi* **1** COIL : envolverse, enroscarse **2 to wrap up** DRESS : abrigarse ⟨wrap up warmly : abrígate bien⟩

wrap² *n* **1** WRAPPER : envoltura *f* **2** : prenda *f* que envuelve (como un chal, una bata, etc.)

wrapper ['ræpər] *n* : envoltura *f*, envoltorio *m*

wrapping ['ræpɪŋ] *n* : envoltura *f*, envoltorio *m*

wrath ['ræθ] *n* : ira *f*, cólera *f*

wrathful ['ræθfəl] *adj* : iracundo

wreak ['riːk] *vt* : infligir, causar ⟨to wreak havoc : crear caos, causar estragos⟩

wreath ['riːθ] *n*, *pl* **wreaths** ['riːðz, 'riːθs] : corona *f* (de flores, etc.)

wreathe ['riːð] *vt* **wreathed; wreathing 1** ADORN : coronar (de flores, etc.) **2** ENVELOP : envolver ⟨wreathed in mist : envuelto en niebla⟩

wreck¹ ['rɛk] *vt* : destruir, arruinar, estrellar (un automóvil), naufragar (un barco)

wreck² *n* **1** WRECKAGE : restos *mpl* (de un buque naufragado, un avión siniestrado, etc.) **2** RUIN : ruina *f*, desastre *m* ⟨this place is a wreck! : ¡este lugar está hecho un desastre!⟩ ⟨to be a nervous wreck : tener los nervios destrozados⟩

wreckage ['rɛkɪdʒ] *n* : restos *mpl* (de un buque naufragado, un avión siniestrado, etc.), ruinas *fpl* (de un edificio)

wrecker ['rɛkər] *n* **1** TOW TRUCK : grúa *f* **2** : desguazador *m* (de autos, barcos, etc.), demoledor *m* (de edificios)

wren ['rɛn] *n* : chochín *m*

wrench¹ ['rɛntʃ] *vt* **1** PULL : arrancar (de un tirón) **2** SPRAIN, TWIST : torcerse (un tobillo, un músculo, etc.)

wrench² *n* **1** TUG : tirón *m*, jalón *m* **2** SPRAIN : torcedura *f* **3** *or* **monkey wrench** : llave *f* inglesa

wrest ['rɛst] *vt* : arrancar

wrestle¹ ['rɛsəl] *v* **-tled; -tling** *vi* **1** : luchar, practicar la lucha (en deportes) **2** STRUGGLE : luchar ⟨to wrestle with a dilemma : lidiar con un dilema⟩ — *vt* : luchar contra

wrestle² *n* STRUGGLE : lucha *f*

wrestler ['rɛsələr] *n* : luchador *m*, -dora *f*

wrestling ['rɛsəlɪŋ] *n* : lucha *f*

wretch ['rɛtʃ] *n* : infeliz *mf*; desgraciado *m*, -da *f*

wretched ['rɛtʃəd] *adj* **1** MISERABLE, UNHAPPY : desdichado, afligido ⟨I feel wretched : me siento muy mal⟩ **2** UNFORTUNATE : miserable, desgraciado, lastimoso ⟨wretched weather : tiempo espantoso⟩ **3** INFERIOR : inferior, malo

wretchedly ['rɛtʃədli] *adv* : miserablemente, lamentablemente

wriggle ['rɪɡəl] *vi* **-gled; -gling** : retorcerse, menearse

wring ['rɪŋ] *vt* **wrung** ['rʌŋ]; **wringing 1** *or* **to wring out** : escurrir, exprimir (el lavado) **2** EXTRACT : arrancar, sacar (por la fuerza) **3** TWIST : torcer, retorcer **4 to wring someone's heart** : partirle el corazón a alguien

wringer ['rɪŋər] *n* : escurridor *m*

wrinkle¹ ['rɪŋkəl] *v* **-kled; -kling** *vt* : arrugar — *vi* : arrugarse

wrinkle² *n* : arruga *f*

wrinkly ['rɪŋkəli] *adj* **wrinklier; -est** : arrugado

wrist ['rɪst] *n* **1** : muñeca *f* (en anatomía) **2** *or* **wristband** ['rɪst-,bænd] CUFF : puño *m*

writ ['rɪt] *n* : orden *f* (judicial)

write ['raɪt] *v* **wrote** ['roːt]; **written** ['rɪtən]; **writing** : escribir

write down *vt* : apuntar, anotar

write off *vt* CANCEL : cancelar

writer ['raɪtər] *n* : escritor *m*, -tora *f*

writhe ['raɪð] *vi* **writhed; writhing** : retorcerse

writing ['raɪtɪŋ] *n* **1** : escritura *f* **2** HANDWRITING : letra *f* **3 writings** *npl* WORKS : escritos *mpl*, obra *f*

wrong¹ ['rɔŋ] *vt* **wronged; wronging** : ofender, ser injusto con

wrong² *adv* : mal, incorrectamente

wrong³ *adj* **wronger** ['rɔŋər]; **wrongest** ['rɔŋəst] **1** EVIL, SINFUL : malo, injusto, inmoral **2** IMPROPER, UNSUITABLE : inadecuado, inapropiado, malo **3** INCORRECT : incorrecto, erróneo, malo ⟨a wrong answer : una mala respuesta⟩ **4 to be wrong** : equivocarse, estar equivocado

wrong⁴ *n* **1** INJUSTICE : injusticia *f*, mal *m* **2** OFFENSE : ofensa *f*, agravio *m* (en derecho) **3 to be in the wrong** : haber hecho mal, estar equivocado

wrongdoer ['rɔŋ,duːər] *n* : malhechor *m*, -chora *f*

wrongdoing ['rɔŋ,duːɪŋ] *n* : fechoría *f*, maldad *f*

wrongful ['rɔŋfəl] *adj* **1** UNJUST : injusto **2** UNLAWFUL : ilegal

wrongly ['rɔŋli] *adv* **1** : injustamente **2** INCORRECTLY : erróneamente, incorrectamente

wrote → write

wrought ['rɔt] *adj* **1** SHAPED : formado, forjado ⟨wrought iron : hierro forjado⟩ **2** *or* **wrought up** : agitado, excitado

wrung → wring

wry ['raɪ] *adj* **wrier** ['raɪər]; **wriest** ['raɪəst] **1** TWISTED : torcido ⟨a wry neck : un cuello torcido⟩ **2** : irónico, sardónico (dícese del humor)

X

x¹ *n, pl* **x's** *or* **xs** [ˈɛksəz] **1** : vigésima cuarta letra del alfabeto inglés **2** : incógnita *f* (en matemáticas)

x² [ˈks] *vt* **x-ed** [ˈɛkst]; **x-ing** *or* **x'ing** [ˈɛksiŋ] DELETE : tachar

xenon [ˈziː,nɑn, ˈzɛ-] *n* : xenón *m*

xenophobia [ˌzɛnəˈfoːbiə, ˌziː-] *n* : xenofobia *f*

Xmas [ˈkrɪsməs] *n* : Navidad *f*

x-ray [ˈɛks,reɪ] *vt* : radiografiar

X ray [ˈɛks,reɪ] *n* **1** : rayo *m* X **2** *or* **X-ray photograph** : radiografía *f*

xylophone [ˈzaɪlə,foːn] *n* : xilófono *m*

Y

y [ˈwaɪ] *n, pl* **y's** *or* **ys** [ˈwaɪz] : vigésima quinta letra del alfabeto inglés

yacht¹ [ˈjɑt] *vi* : navegar (a vela), ir en yate ⟨to go yachting : irse a navegar⟩

yacht² *n* : yate *m*

yak [ˈjæk] *n* : yac *m*

yam [ˈjæm] *n* **1** : ñame *m* **2** SWEET POTATO : batata *f*, boniato *m*

yank¹ [ˈjæŋk] *vt* : tirar de, jalar, darle un tirón a

yank² *n* : tirón *m*

Yankee [ˈjæŋki] *n* : yanqui *mf*

yap¹ [ˈjæp] *vi* **yapped**; **yapping 1** BARK, YELP : ladrar, gañir **2** CHATTER : cotorrear *fam*, parlotear *fam*

yap² *n* : ladrido *m*, gañido *m*

yard [ˈjɑrd] *n* **1** : yarda *f* (medida) **2** SPAR : verga *f* (de un barco) **3** COURTYARD : patio *m* **4** : jardín *m* (de una casa) **5** : depósito *m* (de mercancías, etc.)

yardage [ˈjɑrdɪʤ] *n* : medida *f* en yardas

yardarm [ˈjɑrd,ɑrm] *n* : penol *m*

yardstick [ˈjɑrd,stɪk] *n* **1** : vara *f* **2** CRITERION : criterio *m*, norma *f*

yarn [ˈjɑrn] *n* **1** : hilado *m* **2** TALE : historia *f*, cuento *m* ⟨to spin a yarn : inventar una historia⟩

yawl [ˈjɔl] *n* : yola *f*

yawn¹ [ˈjɔn] *vi* **1** : bostezar **2** OPEN : abrirse

yawn² *n* : bostezo *m*

ye [ˈjiː] *pron* : vosotros, vosotras

yea¹ [ˈjeɪ] *adv* YES : sí

yea² *n* : voto *m* a favor

year [ˈjɪr] *n* **1** : año *m* ⟨last year : el año pasado⟩ ⟨he's ten years old : tiene diez años⟩ **2** : curso *m*, año *m* (escolar) **3 years** *npl* AGES : siglos *mpl*, años *mpl* ⟨I haven't seen them in years : hace siglos que no los veo⟩

yearbook [ˈjɪr,bʊk] *n* : anuario *m*

yearling [ˈjɪrlɪŋ, ˈjərlən] *n* : animal *m* menor de dos año

yearly¹ [ˈjɪrli] *adv* : cada año, anualmente

yearly² *adj* : anual

yearn [ˈjərn] *vi* : anhelar, ansiar

yearning [ˈjərnɪŋ] *n* : anhelo *m*

yeast [ˈjiːst] *n* : levadura *f*

yell¹ [ˈjɛl] *vi* : gritar, chillar — *vt* : gritar

yell² *n* : grito *m*, alarido *m* ⟨to let out a yell : dar un grito⟩

yellow¹ [ˈjɛlo] *vi* : ponerse amarillo, volverse amarillo

yellow² *adj* **1** : amarillo **2** COWARDLY : cobarde

yellow³ *n* : amarillo *m*

yellow fever *n* : fiebre *f* amarilla

yellowish [ˈjɛloɪʃ] *adj* : amarillento

yellow jacket *n* : avispa *f* (con rayas amarillas)

yelp¹ [ˈjɛlp] *vi* : dar un gañido (dícese de un animal), dar un grito (dícese de una persona)

yelp² *n* : gañido *m* (de un animal), grito *m* (de una persona)

yen [ˈjɛn] *n* **1** DESIRE : deseo *m*, ganas *fpl* **2** : yen *m* (moneda japonesa)

yeoman [ˈjoːmən] *n, pl* **-men** [-mən, -mɛn] : suboficial *mf* de marina

yes¹ [ˈjɛs] *adv* : sí ⟨to say yes : decir que sí⟩

yes² *n* : sí *m*

yesterday¹ [ˈjɛstər,deɪ, -di] *adv* : ayer

yesterday² *n* **1** : ayer *m* **2 the day before yesterday** : anteayer

yet¹ [ˈjɛt] *adv* **1** BESIDES, EVEN : aún ⟨yet more problems : más problemas aún⟩ ⟨yet again : otra vez⟩ **2** SO FAR : aún, todavía ⟨not yet : todavía no⟩ ⟨as yet : hasta ahora, todavía⟩ **3** : ya ⟨has he come yet? : ¿ya ha venido?⟩ **4** EVENTUALLY : todavía, algún día **5** NEVERTHELESS : sin embargo

yet² *conj* : pero

yew [ˈjuː] *n* : tejo *m*

yield¹ [ˈjiːld] *vt* **1** SURRENDER : ceder ⟨to yield the right of way : ceder el paso⟩ **2** PRODUCE : producir, dar, rendir (en finanzas) — *vi* **1** GIVE : ceder ⟨to yield under pressure : ceder por la presión⟩ **2** GIVE IN, SURRENDER : ceder, rendirse, entregarse

yield² *n* : rendimiento *m*, rédito *m* (en finanzas)

yin and yang [ˈjɪnænd'jæŋ, -ˈjɑŋ] *n* : yin *m* y yang *f*

yodel¹ [ˈjoːdəl] *vi* **-deled** *or* **-delled**; **-deling** *or* **-delling** : cantar al estilo tirolés

yodel² *n* : canción *f* al estilo tirolés

yoga [ˈjoːgə] *n* : yoga *m*

yogurt [ˈjoːgərt] *n* : yogur *m*, yogurt *m*

yoke¹ [ˈjoːk] *vt* **yoked**; **yoking** : uncir (animales)

yoke² *n* **1** : yugo *m* (para uncir animales)

⟨the yoke of oppression : el yugo de la opresión⟩ **2** TEAM : yunta *f* (de bueyes) **3** : canesú *m* (de ropa)

yokel ['jo:kəl] *n* : palurdo *m*, -da *f*

yolk ['jo:k] *n* : yema *f* (de un huevo)

Yom Kippur [jo:mkɪ'pʊr, ˌjɑm-, -'kɪpər] *n* : el Día *m* del Perdón, Yom Kippur

yon ['jɑn] → **yonder**

yonder[1] ['jɑndər] *adv* : allá ⟨over yonder : allá lejos⟩

yonder[2] *adj* : aquel ⟨yonder hill : aquella colina⟩

yore ['jo:r] *n* **in days of yore** : antaño

you ['ju:] *pron* **1** (*used as subject — familiar*) : tú; vos (*in some Latin American countries*); ustedes *pl*; vosotros, vosotras *pl Spain* **2** (*used as subject — formal*) : usted, ustedes *pl* **3** (*used as indirect object — familiar*) : te, les *pl* (se *before lo, la, los, las*), os *pl Spain* ⟨he told it to you : te lo contó⟩ ⟨I gave them to (all of, both of) you : se los di⟩ **4** (*used as indirect object — formal*) : lo (*Spain sometimes* le), la; los (*Spain sometimes* les), las *pl* **5** (*used after a preposition — familiar*) : ti; vos (*in some Latin American countries*); ustedes *pl*; vosotros, vosotras *pl Spain* **6** (*used after a preposition — formal*) : usted, ustedes *pl* **7** (*used as an impersonal subject*) ⟨you never know : nunca se sabe⟩ ⟨you have to be aware : hay que ser consciente⟩ ⟨you mustn't do that : eso no se hace⟩ **8 with you** (*familiar*) : contigo; con ustedes *pl*; con vosotros, con vosotras *pl Spain* **9 with you** (*formal*) : con usted, con ustedes *pl*

you'd ['ju:d, 'jʊd] (*contraction of* **you had** *or* **you would**) → **have, would**

you'll ['ju:l, 'jʊl] (*contraction of* **you shall** *or* **you will**) → **shall, will**

young[1] ['jʌŋ] *adj* **younger** ['jʌŋgər]; **youngest** [-gəst] **1** : joven, pequeño, menor ⟨young people : los jóvenes⟩ ⟨my younger brother : mi hermano menor⟩ ⟨she is the youngest : es la más pequeña⟩ **2** FRESH, NEW : tierno (dícese de las verduras), joven (dícese del vino) **3** YOUTHFUL : joven, juvenil

young[2] *npl* : jóvenes *mfpl* (de los humanos), crías *fpl* (de los animales)

youngster ['jʌŋkstər] *n* **1** YOUTH : joven *mf* **2** CHILD : chico *m*, -ca *f*; niño *m*, -ña *f*

your ['jʊr, 'jo:r, jər] *adj* **1** (*familiar singular*) : tu ⟨your cat : tu gato⟩ ⟨your

books : tus libros⟩ ⟨wash your hands : lávate las manos⟩ **2** (*familiar plural*) : su, vuestro *Spain* ⟨your car : su coche, el coche de ustedes⟩ **3** (*formal*) : su ⟨your houses : sus casas⟩ **4** (*impersonal*) : el, la, los, las ⟨on your left : a la izquierda⟩

you're ['jʊr, 'jo:r, 'jər, 'ju:ər] (*contraction of* **you are**) → **be**

yours ['jʊrz, 'jo:rz] *pron* **1** (*belonging to one person — familiar*) : (el) tuyo, (la) tuya, (los) tuyos, (las) tuyas ⟨those are mine; yours are there : ésas son mías; las tuyas están allí⟩ ⟨is this one yours? : ¿éste es tuyo?⟩ **2** (*belonging to more than one person — familiar*) : (el) suyo, (la) suya, (los) suyos, (las) suyas; (el) vuestro, (la) vuestra, (los) vuestros, (las) vuestras *Spain* ⟨our house and yours : nuestra casa y la suya⟩ **3** (*formal*) : (el) suyo, (la) suya, (los) suyos, (las) suyas

yourself [jər'sɛlf] *pron, pl* **yourselves** [-'slvz] **1** (*used reflexively — familiar*) : te, se *pl*, os *pl Spain* ⟨wash yourself : lávate⟩ ⟨you dressed yourselves : se vistieron, os vestisteis⟩ **2** (*used reflexively — formal*) : se ⟨did you hurt yourself? : ¿se hizo daño?⟩ ⟨you've gotten yourselves dirty : se ensuciaron⟩ **3** (*used for emphasis*) : tú mismo, tú misma; usted mismo, usted misma; ustedes mismos, ustedes mismas *pl*; vosotros mismos, vosotras mismas *pl Spain* ⟨you did it yourselves? : ¿lo hicieron ustedes mismos?, ¿lo hicieron por sí solos?⟩

youth ['ju:θ] *n, pl* **youths** ['ju:ðz, 'ju:θs] **1** : juventud *f* ⟨in her youth : en su juventud⟩ **2** BOY : joven *m* **3** : jóvenes *mfpl*, juventud *f* ⟨the youth of our city : los jóvenes de nuestra ciudad⟩

youthful ['ju:θfəl] *adj* **1** : de juventud **2** YOUNG : joven **3** JUVENILE : juvenil

youthfulness ['ju:θfəlnəs] *n* : juventud *f*

you've ['ju:v] (*contraction of* **you have**) → **have**

yowl[1] ['jæʊl] *vi* : aullar

yowl[2] *n* : aullido *m*

yo–yo ['jo:ˌjo:] *n, pl* **-yos** : yoyo *m*, yoyó *m*

yucca ['jʌkə] *n* : yuca *f*

Yugoslavian [ˌju:go'slaviən] *n* : yugoslavo *m*, -va *f* — **Yugoslavian** *adj*

yule ['ju:l] *n* CHRISTMAS : Navidad *f*

yuletide ['ju:lˌtaɪd] *n* : Navidades *fpl*

yuppie ['jʌpi] *n* : yuppy *mf*

Z

z ['zi:] *n, pl* **z's** *or* **zs** : vigésima sexta letra del alfabeto inglés

Zambian ['zæmbiən] *n* : zambiano *m*, -na *f* — **Zambian** *adj*

zany[1] ['zeɪni] *adj* **-nier; -est** : alocado, disparatado

zany[2] *n, pl* **-nies** : bufón *m*, -fona *f*

zap[1] ['zæp] *vt* **zapped; zapping 1** ELIM-INATE : eliminar **2** : enviar o transportar rápidamente — *vi* : ir rápidamente

zap[2] *n* **1** ZEST : sabor *m*, sazón *f* **2** BLAST : golpe *m* fuerte

zap[3] *interj* : ¡zas!

zeal ['zi:l] *n* : fervor *m*, celo *m*, entusiasmo *m*

zealot ['zɛlət] *n* : fanático *m*, -ca *f*

zealous ['zɛləs] *adj* : celoso — **zealously** *adv*

zebra ['zi:brə] *n* : cebra *f*

zenith ['zi:nəθ] *n* **1** : cenit *m* (en astronomía) **2** PEAK : apogeo *m*, cenit *m* ⟨at the zenith of his career : en el apogeo de su carrera⟩

zephyr ['zɛfər] *n* : céfiro *m*

zeppelin ['zɛplən, -pəlɪn] *n* : zepelín *m*

zero[1] ['zi:ro, 'zɪro] *vi* **to zero in on** : apuntar hacia, centrarse en (un problema, etc.)

zero[2] *adj* : cero, nulo ⟨zero degrees : cero grados⟩ ⟨zero opportunities : oportunidades nulas⟩

zero[3] *n, pl* **-ros** : cero *m* ⟨below zero : bajo cero⟩

zest ['zɛst] *n* **1** GUSTO : entusiasmo *m*, brío *m* **2** FLAVOR : sabor *m*, sazón *f*

zestful ['zɛstfəl] *adj* : brioso

zigzag[1] ['zɪg,zæg] *vi* **-zagged; -zagging** : zigzaguear

zigzag[2] *adv & adj* : en zigzag

zigzag[3] *n* : zigzag *m*

Zimbabwean [zɪm'bɑbwiən, -bweɪ-] *n* : zimbabuense *mf* — **Zimbabwean** *adj*

zinc ['zɪŋk] *n* : cinc *m*, zinc *m*

zing ['zɪŋ] *n* **1** HISS, HUM : zumbido *m*, silbido *m* **2** ENERGY : brío *m*

zinnia ['zɪniə, 'zi:-, -njə] *n* : zinnia *f*

Zionism ['zaɪə,nɪzəm] *n* : sionismo *m*

Zionist ['zaɪənɪst] *n* : sionista *mf*

zip[1] ['zɪp] *v* **zipped; zipping** *vt* *or* **to zip up** : cerrar el cierre de — *vi* **1** SPEED : pasarse volando ⟨the day zipped by : el día se pasó volando⟩ **2** HISS, HUM : silbar, zumbar

zip[2] *n* **1** ZING : zumbido *m*, silbido *m* **2** ENERGY : brío *m*

zip code *n* : código *m* postal

zipper ['zɪpər] *n* : cierre *m*, cremallera *f*, zíper *m CA, Mex*

zippy ['zɪpi] *adj* **-pier; -est** : brioso

zircon ['zər,kɑn] *n* : circón *m*, zircón *m*

zirconium [,zər'ko:niəm] *n* : circonio *m*

zither ['zɪðər, -θər] *n* : cítara *f*

zodiac ['zo:di,æk] *n* : zodíaco *m*

zombie ['zɑmbi] *n* : zombi *mf*, zombie *mf*

zone[1] ['zo:n] *vt* **zoned; zoning 1** : dividir en zonas **2** DESIGNATE : declarar ⟨to zone for business : declarar como zona comercial⟩

zone[2] *n* : zona *f*

zoo ['zu:] *n, pl* **zoos** : zoológico *m*, zoo *m*

zoological [,zo:ə'lɑʤɪkəl, ,zu:ə-] *adj* : zoológico

zoologist [zo'ɑləʤɪst, zu:-] *n* : zoólogo *m*, -ga *f*

zoology [zo'ɑləʤi, zu:-] *n* : zoología *f*

zoom[1] ['zu:m] *vi* **1** : zumbar, ir volando ⟨to zoom past : pasar volando⟩ **2** CLIMB : elevarse ⟨the plane zoomed up : el avión se elevó⟩

zoom[2] *n* **1** : zumbido *m* ⟨the zoom of an engine : el zumbido de un motor⟩ **2** : subida *f* vertical (de un avión, etc.) **3** *or* **zoom lens** : zoom *m*

zucchini [zʊ'ki:ni] *n, pl* **-ni** *or* **-nis** : calabacín *m*, calabacita *f Mex*

Zulu ['zu:lu:] *n* **1** : zulú *mf* **2** : zulú *m* (idioma) — **Zulu** *adj*

zygote ['zaɪ,go:t] *n* : zigoto *m*, cigoto *m*

Common Spanish Abbreviations

SPANISH ABBREVIATION AND EXPANSION		ENGLISH EQUIVALENT	
abr.	abril	Apr.	April
A.C., a.C.	antes de Cristo	BC	before Christ
a. de J.C.	antes de Jesucristo	BC	before Christ
admon., admón.	administración	—	administration
a/f	a favor	—	in favor
ago.	agosto	Aug.	August
Apdo.	apartado (de correos)	—	P.O. box
aprox.	aproximadamente	approx.	approximately
Aptdo.	apartado (de correos)	—	P.O. box
Arq.	arquitecto	arch.	architect
A.T.	Antiguo Testamento	O.T.	Old Testament
atte.	atentamente	—	sincerely
atto., atta.	atento, atenta	—	kind, courteous
av., avda.	avenida	ave.	avenue
a/v.	a vista	—	on receipt
BID	Banco Interamericano de Desarrollo	IDB	Interamerican Development Bank
Bo	banco	—	bank
BM	Banco Mundial	—	World Bank
c/, C/	calle	st.	street
C	centígrado, Celsius	C	centigrade, Celsius
C.	compañía	Co.	company
CA	corriente alterna	AC	alternating current
cap.	capítulo	ch., chap.	chapter
c/c	cuenta corriente	—	current account, checking account
c.c.	centímetros cúbicos	cu. cm	cubic centimeters
CC	corriente continua	DC	direct current
c/d	con descuento	—	with discount
Cd.	ciudad	—	city
CE	Comunidad Europea	EC	European Community
CEE	Comunidad Económica Europea	EEC	European Economic Community
cf.	confróntese	cf.	compare
cg.	centígramo	cg	centigram
CGT	Confederación General de Trabajadores *or* del Trabajo	—	confederation of workers, workers' union
CI	coeficiente intelectual *or* de inteligencia	IQ	intelligence quotient
Cía.	compañía	Co.	company
cm.	centímetro	cm	centimeter
Cnel.	coronel	Col.	colonel
col.	columna	col.	column
Col. *Mex*	colonia	—	residential area
Com.	comandante	Cmdr.	commander
comp.	compárese	comp.	compare
Cor.	coronel	Col.	colonel

SPANISH ABBREVIATION AND EXPANSION		ENGLISH EQUIVALENT	
C.P.	código postal	—	zip code
CSF, c.s.f.	coste, seguro y flete	c.i.f.	cost, insurance, and freight
cta.	cuenta	ac., acct.	account
cte.	corriente	cur.	current
c/u	cada uno, cada una	ea.	each
CV	caballo de vapor	hp	horsepower
D.	Don	—	—
Da., D.ª	Doña	—	—
d.C.	después de Cristo	AD	anno Domini (in the year of Our Lord)
dcha.	derecha	—	right
d. de J.C.	después de Jesucristo	AD	anno Domini (in the year of Our Lord)
dep.	departamento	dept.	department
DF, D.F.	Distrito Federal	—	Federal District
dic.	diciembre	Dec.	December
dir.	director, directora	dir.	director
dir.	dirección	—	address
Dña.	Doña	—	—
do.	domingo	Sun.	Sunday
dpto.	departamento	dept.	department
Dr.	doctor	Dr.	doctor
Dra.	doctora	Dr.	doctor
dto.	descuento	—	discount
E, E.	Este, este	E	East, east
Ed.	editorial	—	publishing house
Ed., ed.	edición	ed.	edition
edif.	edificio	bldg.	building
edo.	estado	st.	state
EEUU, EE.UU.	Estados Unidos	US, U.S.	United States
ej.	por ejemplo	e.g.	for example
E.M.	esclerosis multiple	MS	multiple sclerosis
ene.	enero	Jan.	January
etc.	etcétera	etc.	et cetera
ext.	extensión	ext.	extension
F	Fahrenheit	F	Fahrenheit
f.a.b.	franco a bordo	f.o.b.	free on board
FC	ferrocarril	RR	railroad
feb.	febrero	Feb.	February
FF AA, FF.AA.	Fuerzas Armadas	—	armed forces
FMI	Fondo Monetario Internacional	IMF	International Monetary Fund
g.	gramo	g., gm, gr.	gram
G.P.	giro postal	M.O.	money order
gr.	gramo	g., gm, gr.	gram
Gral.	general	Gen.	general
h.	hora	hr.	hour
Hnos.	hermanos	Bros.	brothers
I + D, I & D, I y D	investigación y desarrollo	R & D	research and development
i.e.	esto es, es decir	i.e.	that is
incl.	inclusive	incl.	inclusive, inclusively
Ing.	ingeniero, ingeniera	eng.	engineer

SPANISH ABBREVIATION AND EXPANSION		ENGLISH EQUIVALENT	
IPC	índice de precios al consumo	CPI	consumer price index
IVA	impuesto al valor agregado	VAT	value-added tax
izq.	izquierda	l.	left
juev.	jueves	Thurs.	Thursday
jul.	julio	Jul.	July
jun.	junio	Jun.	June
kg.	kilogramo	kg	kilogram
km.	kilómetro	km	kilometer
km/h	kilómetros por hora	kph	kilometers per hour
kv, kV	kilovatio	kw, kW	kilowatt
l.	litro	l, lit.	liter
Lic.	licenciado, licenciada	—	—
Ltda.	limitada	Ltd.	limited
lun.	lunes	Mon.	Monday
m	masculino	m	masculine
m	metro	m	meter
m	minuto	m	minute
mar.	marzo	Mar.	March
mart.	martes	Tues.	Tuesday
mg.	miligramo	mg	milligram
miérc.	miércoles	Wednes.	Wednesday
min	minuto	min.	minute
mm.	milímetro	mm	millimeter
M-N, m/n	moneda nacional	—	national currency
Mons.	monseñor	Msgr.	monsignor
Mtra.	maestra	—	teacher
Mtro.	maestro	—	teacher
N, N.	Norte, norte	N, no.	North, north
n/o	nuestro	—	our
n.º	número	no.	number
N. de (la) R.	nota de (la) redacción	—	editor's note
NE	nordeste	NE	northeast
NN.UU.	Naciones Unidas	UN	United Nations
NO	noroeste	NW	northwest
nov.	noviembre	Nov.	November
N.T.	Nuevo Testamento	N.T.	New Testament
ntra., ntro.	nuestra, nuestro	—	our
NU	Naciones Unidas	UN	United Nations
núm.	número	num.	number
O, O.	Oeste, oeste	W	West, west
oct.	octubre	Oct.	October
OEA, O.E.A.	Organización de Estados Americanos	OAS	Organization of American States
OMS	Organización Mundial de la Salud	WHO	World Health Organization
ONG	organización no gubernamental	NGO	non-governmental organization
ONU	Organización de las Naciones Unidas	UN	United Nations
OTAN	Organización del Tratado del Atlántico Norte	NATO	North Atlantic Treaty Organization
p.	página	p.	page
P, P.	padre	Fr.	father

SPANISH ABBREVIATION AND EXPANSION		ENGLISH EQUIVALENT	
pág.	página	**pg.**	page
pat.	patente	**pat.**	patent
PCL	pantalla de cristal líquido	**LCD**	liquid crystal display
P.D.	post data	**P.S.**	postscript
p. ej.	por ejemplo	**e.g.**	for example
PNB	Producto Nacional Bruto	**GNP**	gross national product
p^o	paseo	**Ave.**	avenue
p.p.	porte pagado	**ppd.**	postpaid
PP, p.p.	por poder, por poderes	**p.p.**	by proxy
prom.	promedio	**av., avg.**	average
ptas., pts.	pesetas	—	
q.e.p.d.	que en paz descanse	**R.I.P.**	may he/she rest in peace
R, R/	remite	—	sender
RAE	Real Academia Española	—	—
ref., ref.^{a}	referencia	**ref.**	reference
rep.	república	**rep.**	republic
r.p.m.	revoluciones por minuto	**rpm.**	revolutions per minute
rte.	remite, remitente	—	sender
s.	siglo	**c., cent.**	century
s/	su, sus	—	his, her, your, their
S, S.	Sur, sur	**S, so.**	South, south
S.	san, santo	**St.**	saint
S.A.	sociedad anónima	**Inc.**	incorporated (company)
sáb.	sábado	**Sat.**	Saturday
s/c	su cuenta	—	your account
SE	sudeste, sureste	**SE**	southeast
seg.	segundo, segundos	**sec.**	second, seconds
sep., sept.	septiembre	**Sept.**	September
s.e.u.o.	salvo error u omisión	—	errors and omissions excepted
Sgto.	sargento	**Sgt.**	sergeant
S.L.	sociedad limitada	**Ltd.**	limited (corporation)
S.M.	Su Majestad	**HM**	His Majesty, Her Majesty
s/n	sin número	—	no (street) number
s.n.m.	sobre el nivel de mar	**a.s.l.**	above sea level
SO	sudoeste/suroeste	**SW**	southwest
S.R.C.	se ruega contestación	**R.S.V.P.**	please reply
ss.	siguientes	—	the following ones
SS, S.S.	Su Santidad	**H.H.**	His Holiness
Sta.	santa	**St.**	Saint
Sto.	santo	**St.**	saint
t, t.	tonelada	**t., tn.**	ton
TAE	tasa anual efectiva	**APR**	annual percentage rate
tb.	también	—	also
tel., Tel.	teléfono	**tel.**	telephone
Tm.	tonelada métrica	**MT**	metric ton
Tn.	tonelada	**t., tn.**	ton
trad.	traducido	**tr., trans., transl.**	translated

SPANISH ABBREVIATION AND EXPANSION		ENGLISH EQUIVALENT	
UE	Unión Europea	**EU**	European Union
Univ.	universidad	**Univ., U.**	university
UPC	unidad procesadora central	**CPU**	central processing unit
Urb.	urbanización	—	residential area
v	versus	**v., vs.**	versus
v	verso	**v., ver., vs.**	verse
v.	véase	**vid.**	see
Vda.	viuda	—	widow
v.g., v.gr.	verbigracia	**e.g.**	for example
vier., viern.	viernes	**Fri.**	Friday
V.M.	Vuestra Majestad	—	Your Majesty
V°B°, V.°B.°	visto bueno	—	OK, approved
vol, vol.	volumen	**vol.**	volume
vra., vro.	vuestra, vuestro	—	your

Common English Abbreviations

ENGLISH ABBREVIATION AND EXPANSION		SPANISH EQUIVALENT	
AAA	American Automobile Association	—	—
AD	anno Domini (in the year of Our Lord)	**d.C., d. de J.C.**	después de Cristo, después de Jesucristo
AK	Alaska	—	Alaska
AL, Ala.	Alabama	—	Alabama
Alas.	Alaska	—	Alaska
a.m., AM	ante meridiem	**a.m.**	ante meridiem (de la mañana)
Am., Amer.	America, American	—	América, americano
amt.	amount	—	cantidad
anon.	anonymous	—	anónimo
ans.	answer	—	respuesta
Apr.	April	**abr.**	abril
AR	Arkansas	—	Arkansas
Ariz.	Arizona	—	Arizona
Ark.	Arkansas	—	Arkansas
asst.	assistant	**ayte.**	ayudante
atty.	attorney	—	abogado, -da
Aug.	August	**ago.**	agosto
ave.	avenue	**av., avda.**	avenida
AZ	Arizona	—	Arizona
BA	Bachelor of Arts	**Lic.**	Licenciado, -da en Filosofía y Letras
BA	Bachelor of Arts (degree)	—	Licenciatura en Filosofía y Letras
BC	before Christ	**a.c., A.C., a. de J.C.**	antes de Cristo, antes de Jesucristo
BCE	before the Christian Era, before the Common Era	—	antes de la era cristiana, antes de la era común
bet.	between	—	entre
bldg.	building	**edif.**	edificio
blvd.	boulevard	**blvar., br.**	bulevar
Br., Brit.	Britain, British	—	Gran Bretaña, británico
Bro(s).	brother(s)	**Hno(s).**	hermano(s)
BS	Bachelor of Science	**Lic.**	Licenciado, -da en Ciencias
BS	Bachelor of Science (degree)	—	Licenciatura en Ciencias
c	carat	—	quilate
c	cent	—	centavo
c	centimeter	**cm.**	centímetro
c	century	**s.**	siglo
c	cup	—	taza
C	Celsius, centigrade	**C**	Celsius, centígrado
CA, Cal., Calif.	California	—	California
Can., Canad.	Canada, Canadian	—	Canadá, canadiense
cap.	capital	—	capital
cap.	capital	—	mayúscula
Capt.	captain	—	capitán

cent.	century	s.	siglo
CEO	chief executive officer	—	presidente, -ta (de una corporación)
ch., chap.	chapter	cap.	capítulo
CIA	Central Intelligence Agency	—	—
cm	centimeter	cm.	centímetro
Co.	company	C., Cía.	compañía
co.	county	—	condado
CO	Colorado	—	Colorado
c/o	care of	a/c	a cargo de
COD	cash on delivery, collect on delivery	—	(pago) contra reembolso
col.	column	col.	columna
Col., Colo.	Colorado	—	Colorado
Conn.	Connecticut	—	Connecticut
corp.	corporation	—	corporación
CPR	cardiopulmonary resuscitation	RCP	reanimación cardiopulmonar, resucitación cardiopulmonar
ct.	cent	—	centavo
CT	Connecticut	—	Connecticut
D.A.	district attorney	—	fiscal (del distrito)
DC	District of Columbia	—	—
DDS	Doctor of Dental Surgery	—	doctor de cirugía dental
DE	Delaware	—	Delaware
Dec.	December	dic.	diciembre
Del.	Delaware	—	Delaware
DJ	disc jockey	—	disc-jockey
dept.	department	dep., dpto.	departamento
DMD	Doctor of Dental Medicine	—	doctor de medicina dental
doz.	dozen	—	docena
Dr.	doctor	Dr., Dra.	doctor, doctora
DST	daylight saving time	—	—
DVM	Doctor of Veterinary Medicine	—	doctor de medicina veterinaria
E	East, east	E, E.	Este, este
ea.	each	c/u	cada uno, cada una
e.g.	for example (exempli gratia)	v.g., v.gr.	verbigracia
EMT	emergency medical technician	—	técnico, -ca en urgencias médicas
Eng.	England, English	—	Inglaterra, inglés
esp.	especially	—	especialmente
EST	eastern standard time	—	—
etc.	et cetera	etc.	etcétera
f	false	—	falso
f	female	f	femenino
F	Fahrenheit	F	Fahrenheit
FBI	Federal Bureau of Investigation	—	—
Feb.	February	feb.	febrero
fem.	feminine	—	femenino
FL, Fla.	Florida	—	Florida

ENGLISH ABBREVIATION AND EXPANSION		SPANISH EQUIVALENT	
Fri.	Friday	**vier., viern.**	viernes
ft.	feet, foot	—	pie(s)
g	gram	**g., gr.**	gramo
Ga., GA	Georgia	—	Georgia
gal.	gallon	—	galón
Gen.	general	**Gral.**	general
gm	gram	**g., gr.**	gramo
gov.	governor	—	gobernador, -dora
govt.	government	—	gobierno
gr.	gram	**g., gr.**	gramo
HI	Hawaii	—	Hawai, Hawaii
hr.	hour	**h.**	hora
HS	high school	—	colegio secundario
ht.	height	—	altura
Ia., IA	Iowa	—	Iowa
ID	Idaho	—	Idaho
i.e.	that is (id est)	**i.e.**	id est (esto es, es decir)
IL, Ill.	Illinois	—	Illinois
in.	inch	—	pulgada
IN	Indiana	—	Indiana
Inc.	incorporated	**S.A.**	sociedad anónima
Ind.	Indian, Indiana	—	Indiana
Jan.	January	**ene.**	enero
Jul.	July	**jul.**	julio
Jun.	June	**jun.**	junio
Jr., Jun.	Junior	**Jr.**	Júnior
Kan., Kans.	Kansas	—	Kansas
kg	kilogram	**kg.**	kilogramo
km	kilometer	**km.**	kilómetro
KS	Kansas	—	Kansas
Ky., KY	Kentucky	—	Kentucky
l	liter	**l.**	litro
l.	left	**izq.**	izquierda
L	large	**G**	(talla) grande
La., LA	Louisiana	—	Luisiana, Louisiana
lb.	pound	—	libra
Ltd.	limited	**S.L.**	sociedad limitada
m	male	**m**	masculino
m	meter	**m**	metro
m	mile	—	milla
M	medium	**M**	(talla) mediana
MA	Massachusetts	—	Massachusetts
Maj.	major	—	mayor
Mar.	March	**mar.**	marzo
masc.	masculine	—	masculino
Mass.	Massachusetts	—	Massachusetts
Md., MD	Maryland	—	Maryland
M.D.	Doctor of Medicine	—	doctor de medicina
Me., ME	Maine	—	Maine
Mex.	Mexican, Mexico	**Méx.**	mexicano, México
mg	milligram	**mg.**	miligramo
mi.	mile	—	milla
MI, Mich.	Michigan	—	Michigan
min.	minute	**min**	minuto
Minn.	Minnesota	—	Minnesota
Miss.	Mississippi	—	Mississippi, Misisipí
ml	milliliter	**ml.**	mililitro

ENGLISH ABBREVIATION AND EXPANSION		SPANISH EQUIVALENT	
mm	millimeter	**mm.**	milímetro
MN	Minnesota	—	Minnesota
mo.	month	—	mes
Mo., MO	Missouri	—	Missouri
Mon.	Monday	**lun.**	lunes
Mont.	Montana	—	Montana
mpg	miles per gallon	—	millas por galón
mph	miles per hour	—	millas por hora
MS	Mississippi	—	Mississippi, Misisipí
mt.	mount, mountain	—	monte, montaña
MT	Montana	—	Montana
mtn.	mountain	—	montaña
N	North, north	**N**	Norte, norte
NASA	National Aeronautics and Space Administration	—	—
NC	North Carolina	—	Carolina del Norte, North Carolina
ND, N. Dak.	North Dakota	—	Dakota del Norte, North Dakota
NE	northeast	**NE**	nordeste
NE, Neb., Nebr.	Nebraska	—	Nebraska
Nev.	Nevada	—	Nevada
NH	New Hampshire	—	New Hampshire
NJ	New Jersey	—	Nueva Jersey, New Jersey
NM, N. Mex.	New Mexico	—	Nuevo México, New Mexico
no.	north	**N**	norte
no.	number	**n.⁰**	número
Nov.	November	**nov.**	noviembre
N.T.	New Testament	**N.T.**	Nuevo Testamento
NV	Nevada	—	Nevada
NW	northwest	**NO**	noroeste
NY	New York	**NY**	Nueva York, New York
O	Ohio	—	Ohio
Oct.	October	**oct.**	octubre
OH	Ohio	—	Ohio
OK, Okla.	Oklahoma	—	Oklahoma
OR, Ore., Oreg.	Oregon	—	Oregon
O.T.	Old Testament	**A.T.**	Antiguo Testamento
oz.	ounce, ounces	—	onza, onzas
p.	page	**p.**	página
Pa., PA	Pennsylvania	—	Pennsylvania, Pensilvania
pat.	patent	**pat.**	patente
PD	police department	—	departamento de policía
PE	physical education	—	educación física
Penn., Penna.	Pennsylvania	—	Pennsylvania, Pensilvania
pg.	page	**pág.**	página
PhD	Doctor of Philosophy	—	doctor, -tora (en filosofía)

ENGLISH ABBREVIATION AND EXPANSION		SPANISH EQUIVALENT	
pkg.	package	—	paquete
p.m., PM	post meridiem	**p.m.**	post meridiem (de la tarde)
P.O.	post office	—	oficina de correos, correo
pp.	pages	**págs.**	páginas
PR	Puerto Rico	**PR**	Puerto Rico
pres.	present	—	presente
pres.	president	—	presidente, -ta
prof.	professor	—	profesor, -sora
P.S.	postscript	**P.D.**	postdata
P.S.	public school	—	escuela pública
pt.	pint	—	pinta
pt.	point	**pto.**	punto
PTA	Parent-Teacher Association	—	—
PTO	Parent-Teacher Organization	—	—
q, qt.	quart	—	cuarto de galón
r.	right	**dcha.**	derecha
rd.	road	**c/, C/**	calle
RDA	recommended daily allowance	—	consumo diario recomendado
recd.	received	—	recibido
Rev.	reverend	**Rdo.**	reverendo
RI	Rhode Island	—	Rhode Island
rpm	revolutions per minute	**r.p.m.**	revoluciones por minuto
RR	railroad	**FC**	ferrocarril
R.S.V.P.	please reply (répondez s'il vous plaît)	**S.R.C.**	se ruega contestación
rt.	right	**dcha.**	derecha
rte.	route	—	ruta
S	small	**P**	(talla) pequeña
S	South, south	**S**	Sur, sur
S.A.	South America	—	Sudamérica, América del Sur
Sat.	Saturday	**sáb.**	sábado
SC	South Carolina	—	Carolina del Sur, South Carolina
SD, S. Dak.	South Dakota	—	Dakota del Sur, South Dakota
SE	southeast	**SE**	sudeste, sureste
Sept.	September	**sep., sept.**	septiembre
so.	south	**S**	sur
sq.	square	—	cuadrado
Sr.	Senior	**Sr.**	Sénior
Sr.	sister	—	sor
st.	state	—	estado
st.	street	**c/, C/**	calle
St.	saint	**S., Sto., Sta.**	santo, santa
Sun.	Sunday	**dom.**	domingo
SW	southwest	**SO**	sudoeste, suroeste
t.	teaspoon	—	cucharadita
T, tb., tbsp.	tablespoon	—	cucharada (grande)
Tenn.	Tennessee	—	Tennessee

ENGLISH ABBREVIATION AND EXPANSION		SPANISH EQUIVALENT	
Tex.	Texas	—	Texas
Thu., Thur., Thurs.	Thursday	juev.	jueves
TM	trademark	—	marca (de un producto)
TN	Tennessee	—	Tennessee
tsp.	teaspoon	—	cucharadita
Tue., Tues.	Tuesday	mart.	martes
TX	Texas	—	Texas
UN	United Nations	NU, NN.UU.	Naciones Unidas
US	United States	EEUU, EE.UU.	Estados Unidos
USA	United States of America	EEUU, EE.UU.	Estados Unidos de América
usu.	usually	—	usualmente
UT	Utah	—	Utah
v.	versus	v	versus
Va., VA	Virginia	—	Virginia
vol.	volume	vol.	volumen
VP	vice president	—	vicepresidente, -ta
vs.	versus	v	versus
Vt., VT	Vermont	—	Vermont
W	West, west	O	Oeste, oeste
WA, Wash.	Washington (estado)	—	Washington
Wed.	Wednesday	miérc.	miércoles
WI, Wis., Wisc.	Wisconsin	—	Wisconsin
wt.	weight	—	peso
WV, W. Va.	West Virginia	—	Virginia del Oeste, West Virginia
WY, Wyo.	Wyoming	—	Wyoming
yd.	yard	—	yarda
yr.	year	—	año

Spanish Numbers

Cardinal Numbers

1	uno	28	veintiocho
2	dos	29	veintinueve
3	tres	30	treinta
4	cuatro	31	treinta y uno
5	cinco	40	cuarenta
6	seis	50	cincuenta
7	siete	60	sesenta
8	ocho	70	setenta
9	nueve	80	ochenta
10	diez	90	noventa
11	once	100	cien
12	doce	101	ciento uno
13	trece	200	doscientos
14	catorce	300	trescientos
15	quince	400	cuatrocientos
16	dieciséis	500	quinientos
17	diecisiete	600	seiscientos
18	dieciocho	700	setecientos
19	diecinueve	800	ochocientos
20	veinte	900	novecientos
21	veintiuno	1,000	mil
22	veintidós	1,001	mil uno
23	veintitrés	2,000	dos mil
24	veinticuatro	100,000	cien mil
25	veinticinco	1,000,000	un millón
26	veintiséis	1,000,000,000	mil millones
27	veintisiete	1,000,000,000,000	un billón

Ordinal Numbers

1st	primero, -ra	18th	decimoctavo, -va
2nd	segundo, -da	19th	decimonoveno, -na;
3rd	tercero, -ra		*or* decimonono, -na
4th	cuarto, -ta	20th	vigésimo, -ma
5th	quinto, -ta	21st	vigésimoprimero,
6th	sexto, -ta		vigésimaprimera
7th	séptimo, -ta	22nd	vigésimosegundo,
8th	octavo, -ta		vigésimasegunda
9th	noveno, -na	30th	trigésimo, -ma
10th	décimo, -ma	40th	cuadragésimo, -ma
11th	undécimo, -ca	50th	quincuagésimo, -ma
12th	duodécimo, -ma	60th	sexagésimo, -ma
13th	decimotercero, -ra	70th	septuagésimo, -ma
14th	decimocuarto, -ta	80th	octogésimo, -ma
15th	decimoquinto, -ta	90th	nonagésimo, -ma
16th	decimosexto, -ta	100th	centésimo, -ma
17th	decimoséptimo, -ma	1,000th	milésimo, -ma

English Numbers

Cardinal Numbers

1	one	50	fifty
2	two	60	sixty
3	three	70	seventy
4	four	80	eighty
5	five	90	ninety
6	six	100	one hundred
7	seven	101	one hundred and one
8	eight	200	two hundred
9	nine	300	three hundred
10	ten	400	four hundred
11	eleven	500	five hundred
12	twelve	600	six hundred
13	thirteen	700	seven hundred
14	fourteen	800	eight hundred
15	fifteen	900	nine hundred
16	sixteen	1,000	one thousand
17	seventeen	1,001	one thousand and one
18	eighteen	2,000	two thousand
19	nineteen	10,000	ten thousand
20	twenty	100,000	one hundred thousand
21	twenty-one	1,000,000	one million
30	thirty	1,000,000,000	one billion
40	forty	1,000,000,000,000	one trillion

Ordinal Numbers

1st	first	17th	seventeenth
2nd	second	18th	eighteenth
3rd	third	19th	nineteenth
4th	fourth	20th	twentieth
5th	fifth	21st	twenty-first
6th	sixth	30th	thirtieth
7th	seventh	40th	fortieth
8th	eighth	50th	fiftieth
9th	ninth	60th	sixtieth
10th	tenth	70th	seventieth
11th	eleventh	80th	eightieth
12th	twelfth	90th	ninetieth
13th	thirteenth	100th	hundredth
14th	fourteenth	1,000th	thousandth
15th	fifteenth	1,000,000th	millionth
16th	sixteenth	1,000,000,000th	billionth

Nations of the World

Africa/África

ENGLISH	SPANISH
Algeria	Argelia
Angola	Angola
Benin	Benin
Botswana	Botswana, Botsuana
Burkina Faso	Burkina Faso
Burundi	Burundi
Cameroon	Camerún
Cape Verde	Cabo Verde
Central African Republic	República Centroafricana
Chad	Chad
Comoro Islands	Islas Comores, Comoras
Congo	Congo
Democratic Republic of Congo	Congo, República Democrática del
Djibouti	Djibouti, Djibuti
Egypt	Egipto
Equatorial Guinea	Guinea Ecuatorial
Eritrea	Eritrea
Ethiopia	Etiopía
Gabon	Gabón
Gambia	Gambia
Ghana	Ghana
Guinea	Guinea
Guinea-Bissau	Guinea-Bissau
Ivory Coast	Costa de Marfil
Kenya	Kenya, Kenia
Lesotho	Lesotho, Lesoto
Liberia	Liberia
Libya	Libia
Madagascar	Madagascar
Malawi	Malawi, Malaui
Mali	Malí
Mauritania	Mauritania
Mauritius	Mauricio
Morocco	Marruecos
Mozambique	Mozambique
Namibia	Namibia
Niger	Níger
Nigeria	Nigeria
Rwanda	Ruanda, Rwanda
São Tomé and Principe	Santo Tomé y Príncipe
Senegal	Senegal
Seychelles	Seychelles
Sierra Leone	Sierra Leona
Somalia	Somalia
South Africa, Republic of	Sudáfrica, República de
Sudan	Sudán
Swaziland	Suazilandia, Swazilandia
Tanzania	Tanzanía, Tanzania
Togo	Togo

ENGLISH	SPANISH
Tunisia	Túnez
Uganda	Uganda
Zambia	Zambia
Zimbabwe	Zimbabwe, Zimbábue

Antarctica/Antártida

No independent countries

Asia/Asia

Afghanistan	Afganistán
Armenia	Armenia
Azerbaijan	Azerbaiyán, Azerbaiján
Bahrain	Bahrein
Bangladesh	Bangladesh
Bhutan	Bhután, Bután
Brunei	Brunei
Cambodia	Camboya
China	China
Cyprus	Chipre
Georgia, Republic of	Georgia
India	India
Indonesia	Indonesia
Iran	Irán
Iraq	Iraq, Irak
Israel	Israel
Japan	Japón
Jordan	Jordania
Kazakhstan	Kazajstán
Korea, North	Corea del Norte
Korea, South	Corea del Sur
Kuwait	Kuwait
Kyrgyzstan	Kirguistán, Kirguizistán
Laos	Laos
Lebanon	Líbano
Malaysia	Malasia
Maldive Islands	Maldivas
Mongolia	Mongolia
Myanmar	Myanmar
Nepal	Nepal
Oman	Omán
Pakistan	Pakistán
Philippines	Filipinas
Qatar	Qatar
Saudi Arabia	Arabia Saudita, Arabia Saudí
Singapore	Singapur
Sri Lanka	Sri Lanka
Syria	Siria
Taiwan	Taiwán
Tajikistan	Tayikistán
Thailand	Tailandia
Turkey	Turquía
Turkmenistan	Turkmenistán

ENGLISH	SPANISH
United Arab Emirates	Emiratos Árabes Unidos
Uzbekistan	Uzbekistán
Vietnam	Vietnam
Yemen	Yemen

Europe/Europa

Albania	Albania
Andorra	Andorra
Austria	Austria
Belarus	Belarús
Belgium	Bélgica
Bosnia and Herzegovina	Bosnia y Hercegovina, Bosnia y Herzegovina
Bulgaria	Bulgaria
Croatia	Croacia
Czech Republic	República Checa
Denmark	Dinamarca
Estonia	Estonia
Finland	Finlandia
France	Francia
Germany	Alemania
Greece	Grecia
Hungary	Hungría
Iceland	Islandia
Ireland	Irlanda
Italy	Italia
Latvia	Letonia
Liechtenstein	Liechtenstein
Lithuania	Lituania
Luxembourg	Luxemburgo
Macedonia	Macedonia
Malta	Malta
Moldavia	Moldavia
Monaco	Mónaco
Netherlands	Países Bajos
Norway	Noruega
Poland	Polonia
Portugal	Portugal
Romania	Rumania, Rumanía
Russian Federation	Rusia, Federación de
San Marino	San Marino
Serbia and Montenegro	Serbia y Montenegro
Slovakia	Eslovaquia
Slovenia	Eslovenia
Spain	España
Sweden	Suecia
Switzerland	Suiza
Ukraine	Ucrania
United Kingdom	Reino Unido
Vatican City	Ciudad del Vaticano

North America/Norteamérica

ENGLISH	SPANISH
Antigua and Barbuda	Antigua y Barbuda
Bahamas	Bahamas
Barbados	Barbados
Belize	Belice
Bermuda	Bermudas
Canada	Canadá
Costa Rica	Costa Rica
Cuba	Cuba
Dominica	Dominica
Dominican Republic	República Dominicana
El Salvador	El Salvador
Grenada	Granada
Guatemala	Guatemala
Haiti	Haití
Honduras	Honduras
Jamaica	Jamaica
Mexico	México, Méjico
Nicaragua	Nicaragua
Panama	Panamá
Saint Kitts-Nevis	Saint Kitts y Nevis
Saint Lucia	Santa Lucía
Saint Vincent and the Grenadines	San Vicente y las Granadinas
Trinidad and Tobago	Trinidad y Tobago
United States of America	Estados Unidos de América

Oceania/Oceanía

ENGLISH	SPANISH
Australia	Australia
Fiji	Fiji
Kiribati	Kiribati
Marshall Islands	Islas Marshall
Nauru	Nauru
New Zealand	Nueva Zelanda, Nueva Zelandia
Papua New Guinea	Papua Nueva Guinea
Solomon Islands	Islas Salomón
Tonga	Tonga
Tuvalu	Tuvalu
Vanuatu	Vanuatu
Western Samoa	Samoa del Oeste

South America/Sudamérica

ENGLISH	SPANISH
Argentina	Argentina
Bolivia	Bolivia
Brazil	Brasil
Chile	Chile
Colombia	Colombia
Ecuador	Ecuador
Guyana	Guyana
Paraguay	Paraguay
Peru	Perú
Suriname	Surinam
Uruguay	Uruguay
Venezuela	Venezuela

Metric System: Conversions

Length

unit	number of meters	approximate U.S. equivalents	
millimeter	0.001	0.039	inch
centimeter	0.01	0.39	inch
meter	1	39.37	inches
kilometer	1,000	0.62	mile

Longitud

unidad	número de metros	equivalentes aproximados de los EE.UU.	
milímetro	0.001	0.039	pulgada
centímetro	0.01	0.39	pulgada
metro	1	39.37	pulgadas
kilómetro	1,000	0.62	milla

Area

unit	number of square meters	approximate U.S. equivalents	
square centimeter	0.0001	0.155	square inch
square meter	1	10.764	square feet
hectare	10,000	2.47	acres
square kilometer	1,000,000	0.3861	square mile

Superficie

unidad	número de metros cuadrados	equivalentes aproximados de los EE.UU.	
centímetro cuadrado	0.0001	0.155	pulgada cuadrada
metro cuadrado	1	10.764	pies cuadrados
hectárea	10,000	2.47	acres
kilómetro cuadrado	1,000,000	0.3861	milla cuadrada

Volume

unit	number of cubic meters	approximate U.S. equivalents	
cubic centimeter	0.000001	0.061	cubic inch
cubic meter	1	1.307	cubic yards

Volumen

unidad	número de metros cúbicos	equivalentes aproximados de los EE.UU	
centímetro cúbico	0.000001	0.061	pulgada cúbica
metro cúbico	1	1.307	yardas cúbicas

Capacity

unit	number of liters	approximate U.S. equivalents		
		CUBIC	DRY	LIQUID
liter	1	61.02 cubic inches	0.908 quart	1.057 quarts

Capacidad

unidad	número de litros	equivalentes aproximados de los EE.UU.		
		CÚBICO	SECO	LÍQUIDO
litro	1	61.02 pulgadas cúbicas	0.908 cuarto	1.057 cuartos

Mass and Weight

unit	number of grams	approximate U.S. equivalents	
milligram	0.001	0.015	grain
centigram	0.01	0.154	grain
gram	1	0.035	ounce
kilogram	1,000	2.2046	pounds
metric ton	1,000,000	1.102	short tons

Masa y peso

unidad	número de gramos	equivalentes aproximados de los EE.UU.	
miligramo	0.001	0.015	grano
centigramo	0.01	0.154	grano
gramo	1	0.035	onza
kilogramo	1.000	2.2046	libras
tonelada métrica	1,000,000	1.102	toneladas cortas